South America
on a shoestring

Wayne Bernhardson
Andrew Draffen
Krzysztof Dydyński
Rob Rachowiecki
Robert Strauss
Deanna Swaney

W9-CCP-359

South America on a shoestring

5th edition

Published by
Lonely Planet Publications
Head Office: PO Box 617, Hawthorn, Vic 3122, Australia
Branches: 155 Filbert St, Suite 251, Oakland, CA 94607, USA
10 Barley Mow Passage, Chiswick, London W4 4PH, UK
'1 bis rue du Cardinal Lemoine, 75005 Paris, France

Printed by
Colorcraft Ltd, Hong Kong

Photographs by
Wayne Bernhardson (WB), Krzysztof Dydynski (KD), Ward Hulbert (WH),
Richard I'Anson (RI), John Maier (JM), Meagan Ward (
Front cover: Girl eating ice-cream, Cuzco, Peru (RI)
Back cover: (left) Witches' market, La Paz, Bolivia (RI)
(right) Fabrics, La Paz, Bolivia (RI)

Facing page 16
top: Stone buildings, Colombia (KD); Rio Negro, Brazil (JM); Kaieteur Falls, Guyana (WB)
middle: Inti Raymi, 'Festival of the Sun', Cuzco, Peru (RI); Moai, Easter Island, Chile (MW);
Aymara woman, La Paz, Bolivia (WH)
bottom: Volcano, Atacama region, Chile, (MW); La Boca, Buenos Aires, Argentina (MW);
Casa Pueblo, Punta Ballena, Uruguay (WB)

First Published
January 1980

This Edition
January 1994

**Although the authors and publisher have tried to make the information as
accurate as possible, they accept no responsibility for any loss, injury or
inconvenience sustained by any person using this book.**

National Library of Australia Cataloguing in Publication Data

South America on a shoestring.

5th ed.
Includes index.
ISBN 0 86442 199 0.

1. South America – Guidebooks. I Bernhardson, Wayne.
II. Crowther, Geoff, 1944- . South America on a shoestring.

918.0439

Wayne Bernhardson

Wayne was born in North Dakota, grew up in Tacoma, Washington, and spent most of the 1980s shuttling between North and South America en route to a PhD in geography from the University of California, Berkeley. He is co-author, with his wife María Massolo, of LP's *Argentina, Uruguay & Paraguay – a travel survival kit*, and sole author of the 2nd edition of *Chile & Easter Island – a travel survival kit*. Wayne lives with María, their daughter Clío, and Gardel, their Alaskan malamute, in Oakland, California.

Andrew Draffen

Australian-born Andrew has travelled and worked his way around Australia, Asia, North America and the Caribbean, settling just long enough in Melbourne to complete an Arts degree, majoring in history. During his first trip to South America, Andrew fell in love with both Brazil and his future wife, Stella. They have since toured extensively in Brazil, Europe and Asia, and today travel with their young daughter, Gabriela, whose great-great-grandfather introduced football to Brazil.

Krzysztof Dydyński

Krzysztof was born and raised in Warsaw, Poland, where he graduated in electronic engineering and became an assistant professor in the subject. He soon realised that there's more to life than microchips, and in the mid-1970s he took off to Afghanistan and India. In the 1980s a new passion for Latin America took him to Colombia, where he lived for over four years, and to travels throughout the continent. He has contributed to previous editions of *South America on a shoestring*, written LP guides to Colombia and Poland, and is now working on Venezuela. Between travels Krzysztof lives in Australia, where he has joined the LP gang as an artist and designer.

Rob Rachowiecki

Rob was born near London and became an avid traveller while still a teenager. In 1974, he left the UK to travel around the world. He spent several years in Latin America, travelling, mountaineering and teaching English, and he now works there part time for an adventure tour company. He has written many travel articles and guidebooks, including LP travel survival kits for *Ecuador, Peru* and *Costa Rica*. When not travelling, Rob lives in the US Southwest with his wife, Cathy, and children, Julia, Alison and David.

Robert Strauss

Robert was born in England. In the early 1970s he took the overland route to Nepal and then studied, taught and edited in England, Germany, Portugal and Hong Kong. For Lonely Planet he has worked on travel survival kits to *China, Tibet, Japan, Brazil*, and *Bolivia* and has contributed to LP's shoestring guides to South America, North-East Asia and Europe. He has also written the *Trans-Siberian Rail Guide* (Compass Publications, UK).

Deanna Swaney

An incurable travel addict, Deanna Swaney escaped encroaching yuppiedom in Anchorage, Alaska, and made a break for South America to write Lonely Planet's *Bolivia – a travel survival kit*. Subsequent wanders, on an erratic circuit of wildlife encounters and island paradises (both Arctic and tropical), resulted in more travel survival kits, to *Tonga*; *Iceland, Greenland & the Faroe Islands*; *Samoa*; and *Zimbabwe, Botswana & Namibia*. She has co-authored new editions of LP's *Brazil* and *Mauritius, Réunion & Seychelles* guides, and contributed to books on Africa, South America and Scandinavia. She was last seen somewhere in the Arctic in search of the perfect holiday.

From the Authors

From Wayne Thanks to all those who assisted on recent update trips to the Guianas, Brazil, Bolivia, Argentina, Paraguay and Uruguay, epecially Bob and Pat Raburn, who joined us in Buenos Aires, accompanied us to Uruguay, and undertook an unpaid research assistantship in Puerto Madryn and Ushuaia.

Others deserving special mention include Tony Thorne of the Guyana Tourism Association in Georgetown; Malcolm and Margaret Chan-a-Sue of Georgetown; Henk Reichardt of Stinasu in Suriname; Donato Calderón of La Paz, Bolivia; Fernando Moreira de Castro Junior of Paratur in Belém, Brazil; Susanne von Davidson of Rio de Janeiro; and Claire Sorensen and Sandy Girkin, both of Asunción, Paraguay.

From Rob I'm especially grateful to Petra Schepens, manager of the South American Explorers Club in Lima, for detailed information on Lima, Huancayo and Huaraz; to Greg Simmons of Arizona who provided a thorough report of his trip through Trujillo, Chiclayo, Cajamarca and Chachapoyas; and to José (Pepe) Correa C of Cuzco, for updates in Aguas Calientes and the Urubamba Valley.

This Book

The first editions of *South America on a shoestring* were written by Geoff Crowther, but later editions drew increasingly on the expertise of authors of Lonely Planet's guides to individual South American countries. This fifth edition has been completely revised and updated by a team of writers:

Wayne Bernhardson condensed the chapters on Argentina, Chile, Paraguay and Uruguay from his travel survival kits to those countries, and did additional field research to bring them up to date. He also researched and wrote the Guinas chapter for this book, and did field updates of the information on Bolivia and northern Brazil.

Andrew Draffen returned to Brazil to update the information on the southern part of the country

Krzysztof Dydyński researched and updated the chapters on Colombia and Venezuela, for which he is now preparing new travel survival kits.

Rob Rachowiecki condensed the chapters on Ecuador and Peru from his travel survival kits to those countries, and updated the information on his frequent return visits and through his numerous contacts in the region.

Robert Strauss condensed the Brazil chapter from *Brazil – a travel survival kit* by Andrew Draffen, Deanna Swaney & Robert Strauss; the information in the chapter was then updated by Andrew and Wayne.

Deanna Swaney condensed the Bolivia chapter from her book *Bolivia – a travel survival kit*, and Wayne covered the country again to update the information.

Thanks are also due to the many readers who wrote in with comments and useful suggestions; they are listed at the end of the book.

From The Publisher

This book was edited by James Lyon and Alison White, with help from Simone Calderwood and Jeff Williams. It was proofread by James and Alison, with help and guidance from Sue Mitra. Sharon Wertheim prepared the index, and the maps were drawn or updated by Vicki Beale, Rachel Black, Greg Herriman, Graham Imeson, Louise Keppie, Valerie Tellini and Sally Woodward. Book design and layout was by Greg and Vicki, with cover design by Margaret Jung.

Warning & Request

Things change – prices go up, hotels go out of business and new ones open up, even government policies on visas can suddenly change. This is especially true in a huge and fast-changing continent like South America.

If you find information which is outdated, please write and let us know. Your letters will help make future editions better and, where possible, important changes will be included as a Stop Press in reprints. The best letters are rewarded with a free copy of the next edition, or another Lonely Planet guide if you prefer, but unfortunately not every letter or postcard receives one.

Contents

Map Legend

BOUNDARIES

▬ ▪ ▬ ▪ ▬ ▪ ▬	.......International Boundary
▬▬ ▪▪ ▬▬ ▪▪ ▬▬	................Internal Boundary
+++++++++++++	....National Park or Reserve
- - - - - - - - -	.........................The Equator
....	..........................The Tropics

SYMBOLS

◉	NATIONAL	.........................National Capital
●	PROVINCIAL	........Provincial or State Capital
●	Major	...............................Major Town
●	Minor	...............................Minor Town
■		.........................Places to Stay
▼		..........................Places to Eat
⊠		..............................Post Office
✈		....Airport
i		....................Tourist Information
⊖		............Bus Station or Terminal
66		............Highway Route Number
☪ ✝ 🕌 ✝		...... Mosque, Church, Cathedral
∴		..........................Temple or Ruin
✚		.....................................Hospital
✳		.....................................Lookout
⊼		..........................Camping Area
⊓		...............................Picnic Area
⌂		...............................Hut or Chalet
▲		.........................Mountain or Hill
⊢⊣		.........................Railway Station
═		...............................Road Bridge
⊢⊣⊣		..........................Railway Bridge
⇒ ⇐		..............................Road Tunnel
→→ ←←		...........................Railway Tunnel
⌒⌒⌒		...................Escarpment or Cliff
⌣		....Pass
⊓⊔⊓⊔		............Ancient or Historic Wall

ROUTES

▬▬▬▬	.......Major Road or Highway
- - - - - - - - -	.........Unsealed Major Road
▬▬▬▬	........................Sealed Road
- - - - - - -	.....Unsealed Road or Track
═══════	..........................City Street
+++++++++++++	..................................Railway
●━◉━●━	...................................Subway
....	.............................Walking Track
- - - - - - - - -	...............................Ferry Route
++H+H++H+H+++	.... Cable Car or Chair Lift

HYDROGRAPHIC FEATURES

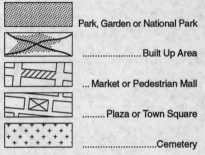

	.........................River or Creek
	.............Intermittent Stream
	........Lake, Intermittent Lake
	..........................Coast Line
	...................................Spring
	...............................Waterfall
	...............................Swamp
	.... Salt Lake or Reef
	..................................Glacier

OTHER FEATURES

	Park, Garden or National Park
	.......................Built Up Area
	... Market or Pedestrian Mall
	.........Plaza or Town Square
	...............................Cemetery

Note: not all symbols displayed above appear in this book

BOUNDARIES

International Boundary
Internal Boundary
National Park or Reserve
The Equator
The Tropics

ROUTES

Major Road or Highway
Unsealed Major Road
Sealed Road
Unsealed Road or Track
City Street
Railway
Walking Track
Ferry Route
Cable Car or Chair Lift

SYMBOLS

NATIONAL .... National Capital
PROVINCIAL .... Provincial State Capital
Major .... Major Town
Minor .... Minor Town
Places to Stay
Places to Eat
Post Office
Airport
Tourist Information
Bus Station or Terminal
Highway Route Number
Mosque, Church, Gurudwara
Temple or Ruin
Hospital
Lookout
Camping Area
Picnic Area
Hut or Chalet

Introduction

Generalising about a continent as large and diverse as South America is a risky business. The continent extends thousands of miles, from the equatorial tropics to the sub-Antarctic, and includes 13 countries and territories with diverse Indian cultures and a rich colonial legacy. Spain and Portugal have left a huge imprint on South America, and there is a rich cultural mix of indigenous peoples and immigrants, including Europeans, Africans, Caribbeans and Asians. This diversity makes South America a winner for budget travellers of many interests.

Your interest is mountains? The towering Andes are a trekker's and climber's paradise. Beaches? Loll on untouched tropical islands or soak up Rio's famed Copacabana. Cities? Try roaring cosmopolitan megacities like São Paulo or quiet colonial backwaters like

Colonia. History? There's mysterious Machu Picchu, or massive Spanish forts built to repel buccaneers like Francis Drake. Jungles? Despite deforestation, vast tracts of tropical rainforest still exist. Rivers? The Amazon is the biggest anywhere. Waterfalls? Both the highest and the most voluminous waterfalls are here.

None of these sights, adventures and experiences need cost you an arm and a leg. While prices have risen over the last few years, the Andean countries are still a bargain, and careful budget travellers can enjoy even relatively expensive countries like Argentina. In most Latin American countries, it's possible to find a roof over your head for around US$2 to US$5 per night, or a bit more in the southern part of the continent. Bus transport is always cheap, and there are also some bargain airfares.

There are continuing problems with the drug trade in some areas, and particularly fierce guerrilla movements in Peru. Nevertheless, the demise of several military regimes in favour of reasonably stable democratic governments, as well as recent economic improvements, have made the continent more attractive for many travellers.

It's obviously a good idea to avoid the main coca and cocaine-producing areas of Peru and Colombia, but many parts of those countries do offer fascinating and secure travel. Parts of Rio de Janeiro have well-founded reputations for theft, but so have the Paris Metro and the piazze of Rome, not to mention the downtown areas of many American cities. The Southern Cone countries of Chile, Argentina and Uruguay, inhabited largely by descendents of European immigrants, are among the safest areas in the world for travellers, but still different enough for a rewarding travel experience. Other countries, like Bolivia, Ecuador, Venezuela and the Guianas, continue to offer challenging experiences, even for the most intrepid traveller.

Facts about South America

HISTORY

Pre-Columbian South America

Prehistory Well over 12,000 years ago, when the accumulated ice of the great polar glaciers of the Pleistocene epoch lowered sea levels throughout the world, the ancestors of American Indians crossed from Siberia to Alaska via a land bridge over the Bering Strait. Over millennia, subsequent migrations distributed the population southward through North and Central America and down to the southern tip of South America.

The first inhabitants of South America were nomadic hunter-gatherers who lived in small bands, and this type of society existed on the continent even into very recent times. There is disagreement as to the earliest appearance of agriculture. It was probably a gradual development which began in the continent's tropical lowlands around 5000 BC or earlier, with the planting of wild tubers like manioc (cassava) and the sweet potato, under systems of shifting cultivation. One of the continent's greatest contributions to the world is the humble potato, a root crop domesticated in the Andean highlands.

About the same time, seed crops like beans began to appear in the highland areas, and large groups of animal bones are the first evidence of domesticated animals like the llama. About 4000 BC, seed agriculture appears in Peru's coastal lowlands, where irrigation later made intensive cultivation possible. The cultivation of maize, probably imported from Mexico before 2500 BC but perhaps much earlier, is closely correlated with the development of settled agriculture communities.

Coastal & Highland Civilisations The arid coast of Peru is one of the world's great hearths of civilisation. According to some anthropologists, complex societies developed in these valleys because populations grew to occupy all the available cultivable land and, in order to provide for their contin-ued subsistence, they turned to conquest of neighbouring valleys. Conquerors became rulers, and the conquered became their subjects, thus developing the social and economic hierarchies of these early states.

These embryonic states ultimately developed into major civilisations like the Wari Empire of the Peruvian central highlands, the Tiwanaku (Tiahuanaco) culture of highland Bolivia, the Chimú of northern coastal Peru and, ultimately, the Inca Empire of Cuzco, known more properly as Tawantinsuyu (or Tahuantinsuyo). Most of these cultures are known through archaeological remains, particularly ceramics (see the Peru chapter for more details).

Tropical Rainforest Peoples The inhabitants of tropical rainforest regions like the Amazon Basin did not develop the same sort of complex civilisations as those of the Andean peoples. Some anthropologists believe that this is because rainforest areas, despite their exuberant vegetation, have impoverished soils which can support only limited populations under basic technologies like hunting and gathering, or shifting (slash-and-burn) agriculture. Other anthropologists argue that the potential of the tropical forest is really unknown because the European invasions have truncated the processes of indigenous cultural evolution. According to this perspective, tropical rainforest peoples failed to develop complex civilisations not because of environmental limitations, but rather because of the nearly unlimited quantity of cultivable land. Unlike in the Andes, the consequences of conflict in the rainforest were not conquest, but retreat deeper into the forest, where the defeated peoples could retain their autonomy and an egalitarian culture.

Recent evidence indicates that the populations of tropical rainforest areas at the time of European contact were larger than once believed, with substantial villages of up to

5000 people, or even more. Unfortunately, except in a few sites (like the island of Marajó, at the mouth of the Amazon), archaeological remains are few because tools and other artefacts were made of largely perishable materials such as wood and bone.

Southern South America Inca rule barely touched the area of present-day central and southern Chile or northern Argentina, and never saw the lowlands of Paraguay or the Argentine Pampas. Patagonia and Tierra del Fuego were even further beyond their range.

The Araucanian (Picunche and Mapuche) Indians of Chile and Argentina fiercely resisted incursions from the north. The Picunche lived in permanent agricultural settlements, while the Mapuche, who practised shifting cultivation, were more mobile. Several groups closely related to the Mapuche (Pehuenches, Huilliches, and Puelches) lived in the southern lake district,

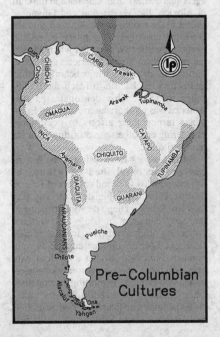

Pre-Columbian Cultures

while Cunco Indians fished and farmed on the island of Chiloé and along the shores of the gulfs of Reloncaví and Ancud. Not until the late 19th century did the descendents of Europeans establish a permanent presence south of the Río Biobío.

In the forested delta of the upper Río Paraná, Guaraní shifting cultivators relied on maize, and tuber crops like manioc and sweet potatoes. In the Pampas to the south and well into Patagonia, highly mobile people hunted the guanaco (a wild relative of the Andean llama) and the rhea (a flightless bird resembling the ostrich) with bow and arrow or *boleadoras* (heavily weighted thongs).

South of the mainland, on the islands of Tierra del Fuego, numerous small populations of Indians subsisted on hunting and fishing – the Chonos, Qawashqar (Alacalufes), Tehuelches, Yamaná (Yahgans), and Onas (Selknam). These isolated archipelagic peoples long avoided contact with Europeans, but are now extinct or nearly so.

The Inca Empire The Inca developed the most sophisticated of South America's pre-Columbian highland civilisations. At its peak, at the time of the Spanish invasion, the Inca Empire governed at least 12 million people from northern Ecuador to central Chile, traversing the Andes with over 8000 km of highways, but it was never able to penetrate deep into the Amazon lowlands. This overextended empire, wrought by dissension and civil war, proved vulnerable to invasion by a very small force of Spaniards, whose hold on Tawantinsuyu was tenuous even after the fall of Cuzco. Much modern knowledge of the Inca comes from archaeological evidence, which is described in the Peru chapter.

European Contact
Christopher Columbus (known throughout Latin America as Cristóbal Colón) led the first European 'discovery' of the Americas, though in fact he was seeking a new route to Asia's spice islands. Bankrolled by Queen Isabella of Spain, and given an exceedingly

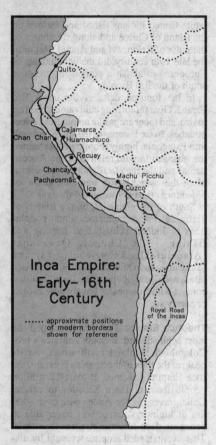

Inca Empire: Early–16th Century

..... approximate positions of modern borders shown for reference

Quito

Cajamarca
Chan Chan · Huamachuco
· Recuay
Chancay
Pachacamác · Machu Picchu
Ica · Cuzco

Royal Road of the Incas

Spanish monarchs asked the Pope to resolve the dispute. In 1494, representatives of the two countries met in the northern Spanish town of Tordesillas, where they established a line of demarcation at about 48° west of Greenwich, giving Africa and Asia to Portugal and all of the New World to Spain. Significantly, however, this line placed the coast of Brazil (not discovered until six years later) on the Portuguese side of the line, giving Portugal unanticipated access to the new continent. No other European maritime power, and certainly none of the indigenous people of the Americas, formally acknowledged this arrangement.

The Colonial Period

The island of Hispaniola (which now comprises Haiti and the Dominican Republic) was the first European settlement and Columbus' base for further exploration. Between 1496 and 1518, he and other voyagers charted the Caribbean Sea and the Gulf of Mexico, the Venezuelan and Guyanese shores to the mouth of the Amazon, and the Brazilian coastline. This phase of coastal exploration effectively ended when Magellan sailed down South America's east coast, through the strait which now bears his name, and across the Pacific to reach the Philippines in 1521. This demonstrated that America was no short cut to Asia, and Europeans turned their efforts to occupying, plundering and otherwise profiting from the new territories.

Spain's successful invasion of the Americas was accomplished by groups of adventurers, lowlifes and soldiers of fortune against whom the colonists of Botany Bay look like saints – Diego de Almagro, one of the early explorers of Chile and northern Argentina, originally arrived in Panamá after fleeing a Spanish murder charge. Few in number (Francisco Pizarro took Peru with only 180 men), the conquerors were determined and ruthless, exploiting factionalism among Indian groups and frightening indigenous peoples with their horses, vicious dogs and firearms, but their greatest ally was

broad grant of authority over any territory he might discover, this dubiously qualified Genoese mariner sailed westward, making landfalls on several Caribbean islands which he believed to be part of Asia. In granting Columbus a share in any profits which might result from his expedition, neither Isabella nor her court anticipated such momentous discoveries.

The Treaty of Tordesillas

When Portugal protested that the Spanish voyages had encroached on its Atlantic sphere of influence, in violation of earlier agreements, the

South America

0   500   1000 km

SURINAME
PARAMARIBO
CAYENNE
FRENCH GUIANA

Macapá
Ilha Marajó
Belém
São Luis
Fortaleza
Teresina
Natal
João Pessoa
Recife
Maceió
Aracaju
São Francisco
Tocantins
Araguaia
Xingu
Iriri
Salvador
Ilheus

BRAZIL

Cuiabá
Goiânia
BRASÍLIA
Campo Grande
Bauru
Belo Horizonte
Vitória
Campos
Rio de Janeiro
São Paulo
Santos
Curitiba
Paranaguá
Joinville
Florianópolis
Posadas
oz do Iguaçu

ATLANTIC OCEAN

Equator
Tropic of Capricorn

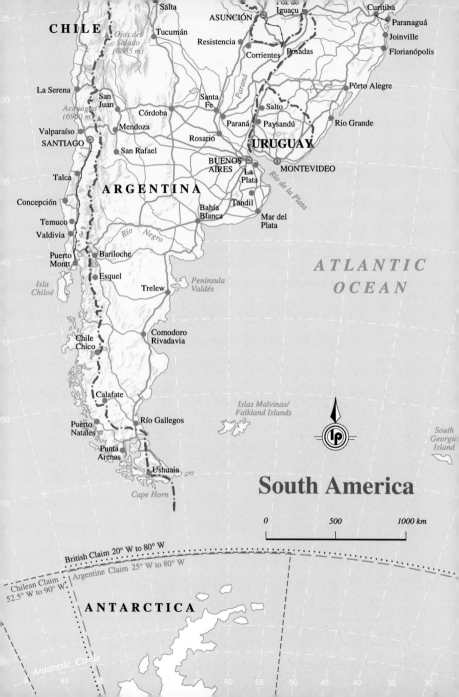

infectious disease to which indigenous American peoples lacked immunity.

Jamaica, Cuba and Puerto Rico followed Hispaniola as early Spanish settlements. Cortés' conquest of Mexico led to further land expeditions, one of which returned with rumours of a golden kingdom, Birú (Peru), to the south of Panama. After Francisco Pizarro's preliminary expeditions down South America's Pacific coast (1524 and 1526) confirmed some of these rumours, he went to Spain, where he convinced authorities to finance an expedition of 200 men and grant him authority over the lands he would survey.

The Advance of Pizarro Pizarro's advance into Peru was rapid and dramatic. His armoured, mounted and well-armed soldiers terrorised the Indians, but they also had invisible allies in the micro-organisms which preceded them. (Huayna Capac, the Inca ruler at the time of the first Spanish contacts,

died from an illness which was probably smallpox, contracted indirectly through messengers who had come into contact with the Spaniards.) In succeeding decades, these infectious agents changed the face of the Americas, as the decline of indigenous populations resulted in *mestizaje*, the creation of a mixed-race population of European and Indian descent.

In late 1532, Pizarro and Atahualpa (the new Inca ruler, son of Huayna Capac) met at a summit at Cajamarca, in northern Peru. Atahualpa was prepared to negotiate, but Pizarro ambushed him, massacred most of his guards and took him prisoner. Held for ransom, Atahualpa was put through a sham trial for crimes such as incest (marrying one's sister was traditional among Inca rulers), polygamy, worship of false gods and crimes against the (Spanish) king.

Despite Atahualpa's execution, resistance to the Spaniards continued for decades, with deadly intrigues amongst the conquistadores

---

Pizarro & Atahualpa

Huayna Capac was the 11th Inca, and the last to rule over a united empire, which extended from Quito (Ecuador) to south of Santiago (Chile). By the time his son Atahualpa was born, of a Quiteña mother, the Europeans had arrived in the New World, and epidemics of diseases such as smallpox and the common cold swept down from Central America and the Caribbean faster than the conquerors.

About 1525, Huayna Capac died in one such epidemic. Before his death, he divided the empire, giving the northern part to Atahualpa and the southern Cuzco area to another son, Huáscar. Civil war followed. In 1532, after several years of fighting, Atahualpa's troops defeated and captured Huáscar outside Cuzco.

Meanwhile, Francisco Pizarro had landed in northern Ecuador and marched south in the wake of Atahualpa's conquests. On 16 November 1532, a fateful meeting between Atahualpa and Pizarro took place in Cajamarca. Atahualpa was ambushed and captured by the Spaniards, who killed thousands of unarmed Indians. The conquest of the Incas had begun.

In an attempt to regain his freedom, Atahualpa offered a ransom – a roomful of gold and two of silver. Pizarro sent three of his soldiers to Cuzco in early 1533, and they proceeded to strip Coricancha, the Gold Courtyard, of its splendid ornamentation.

Pizarro exploited the Inca civil war in his conquest of South America. When he marched into Cuzco on 8 November 1533, after imprisoning and murdering Atahualpa, Pizarro was permitted into the heart of the Inca Empire by a people whose sympathy lay more with the defeated Huáscar than with Atahualpa. Pizarro then appointed Manco Inca, a half-brother of Huáscar, as a puppet Inca ruler.

In 1536, Manco Inca fled from the Spanish and raised a huge army, estimated at well over 100,000, and laid siege to Cuzco. They almost succeeded in annihilating the Spaniards. Only a desperate breakout from Cuzco, and violent battle at Sacsayhuamán, saved the Spaniards from defeat, and Manco Inca retreated into the jungle at Vilcabamba.

Rob Rachowiecki

themselves working in the Incas' favour. Manco Inca, Pizarro's hand-picked successor to Atahualpa, retreated into the mountains north of Cuzco to wage a guerrilla campaign. Atahualpa's nephew Tupac Amaru fought valiantly, until his beheading in the Plaza of Cuzco in 1572.

Further Exploration & Colonisation Lima, founded in 1535 as the capital of the new Viceroyalty of Peru, was the base for the further exploration and conquest of the continent. Sebastián Benalcázar travelled from Lima via Quito to the highlands of Colombia in 1538, and by 1540, Pedro de Valdivia had penetrated as far as Chile's Río Biobío. Expeditions south, along and over the Andes, founded Tucumán and Mendoza.

One exception to this pattern was Pedro de Mendoza's settlement at the mouth of the Río de la Plata (River Plate) in 1535, which later moved upriver to Asunción, Paraguay. Another exception was the coast of Venezuela, which was settled from Hispaniola and later became part of the Viceroyalty of Nueva Granada, the forerunner of Bolívar's short-lived Gran Colombia.

The Spanish Empire in South America
Administration Under Spain's highly centralised administration, the Viceroyalty of Peru was the seat of all power in Spanish America. As the monarch's representative in Lima, the viceroy headed a hierarchy of lesser officials. The main functionaries were: the presidents of *audiencias*, who held civil power in areas where no viceroy was resident; and the *corregidors*, who governed a provincial city and its surrounding area. The corregidor was usually associated with the *cabildo* (town council), which was probably the most representative institution in the region. Often, the same individual held more than one position in the hierarchy.

Only *peninsulares* (those born in Spain) could hold senior positions. *Criollos* (creoles), born in the New World of Spanish parents, could hold a commission in a colonial army or serve on a cabildo. As the peninsulares generally spent a term in the colonies before returning to Spain, the criollos became the main landholders, merchants and entrepreneurs. People of mixed parentage, usually of a Spanish father and an Indian mother, were known as *mestizos* and were

Colonial South America: Mid–17th Century

—— Boundaries of the Viceroyalty of Peru

1 Audiencia of Panamá, 1538 & 1567
2 Audiencia of Sante Fé, 1549
3 Audiencia of Quito, 1563
4 Audiencia of Lima, 1542
5 Audiencia of Charcas, 1559
6 Audiencia of Chile, 1565 & 1609
7 Captaincy of Grão-Pará
8 Captaincy of Maranhão
9 Captaincy of Ceará
10 Captaincy of Rio Grande do Norte
11 Captaincy of Paraíba
12 Captaincy of Pernambuco
13 Captaincy of Sergipe
14 Captaincy of Bahia
15 Captaincy of Espíritu Santo
16 Captaincy of Rio de Janeiro
17 Captaincy of São Vicente

generally excluded from higher positions, while *indígenas* (native Americans) comprised the bottom stratum of society.

Despite this highly centralised administrative structure, there were enormous practical difficulties in imposing imperial control. These limitations led to considerable local autonomy in government and commerce, as well as to abuse, corruption and a flourishing contraband trade, which further undermined peninsular authority.

Spaniards & Indians Ironically, the structure of pre-Columbian Indian societies determined, in many ways, the economic and political structure of early colonial society. The primary goal of the first Spaniards was the acquisition of gold and silver, and they ruthlessly appropriated precious metals, through outright robbery when possible and by other, no less brutal means when they thought it necessary. El Dorado, the legendary city of gold, proved elusive, but the Spaniards soon realised that the true wealth of the New World consisted of the surprisingly large Indian populations of Mexico, Peru, and other lands.

Disdaining physical labour, the Spaniards exploited indigenous populations through mechanisms like the *encomienda* (best translated as 'entrustment'), by which the Crown granted an individual Spaniard rights to Indian labour and tribute in a particular village or area. Institutions like the Catholic Church also held encomiendas. In theory, Spanish legislation required the holder of the encomienda to reciprocate with instruction in the Spanish language and the Catholic religion, but in practice, imperial administration could not ensure compliance or avoid serious abuses. Spanish overseers worked Indians mercilessly in the mines and extracted the maximum in agricultural produce.

An Inca Voice

Conventional history usually tells the victor's story, but in his *El Primer Nueva Corónica y Buen Gobierno*, the 16th-century indigenous chieftan Felipe Guamán Poma de Ayala presents the viewpoint of the vanquished.

Strictly speaking, Guamán Poma was not an Inca, since he came from the Huamanga (present-day Ayacucho) region of the Central Highlands, but he spent his entire life in Peru. In *Nueva Corónica*, Guamán chronicled the customs of the Incas and their predecessors, the arrival of the Spanish and the changes wrought by Spanish rule. Interpreting the *quipus* (coloured, knotted strings which were the basis of Inca record- keeping), speaking with survivors of the contact era, and travelling the countryside like an investigative journalist, he wrote his story in the form of a letter to the Spanish King Philip III.

Guamán Poma did not merely describe his subjects – he illustrated them, in a remarkable series of drawings depicting everything from Andean agriculture to the beheading of Atahualpa. Despite occasional inaccuracies – Atahualpa was strangled rather than beheaded, for instance – the illustrations provide unique ethnographic detail of a key period.

Much of the *Nueva Corónica* is a valuable record of Andean customs and history, though it is often awkwardly written and occasionally obscure. What made it a potential bombshell, despite its superficially respectful and humble tone, was a thinly disguised condemnation of colonial rule, often couched in irony. The indignant writer reproached the Spaniards for corruption and bribery, widespread violence against Indians, working conditions in the mines, assaults by priests on native women, and many other abuses.

Had King Philip ever received the letter, he would probably have ordered the detention and perhaps even execution of the writer. Perhaps fortunately, however, the *Nueva Corónica* never had the impact its author might have anticipated. Somewhere en route to Spain, it went astray, and ended up in the Royal Library of Copenhagen, where it lay in obscurity until a German scholar unearthed it in 1908. Since then, it has become a widely acknowledged classic, and its illustrations are familiar additions to many books on colonial Peru. ∎

In the most densely populated parts of the Americas, some encomenderos became extraordinarily wealthy, but the encomienda system itself failed when Indian populations declined rapidly. This decline was caused more by Old World diseases, such as smallpox, influenza and typhus, than by overwork or physical punishment. In some parts of the New World, these diseases reduced the indigenous population by more than 95%.

This demographic collapse had a lasting impact on South American societies and economies. As encomiendas became worthless, encomenderos and others assembled *latifundios* (large properties) from the holdings of the depleted Indian communities; these became a bone of contention as Indian populations recovered in the following centuries. After the countries of South America became independent, Indians were often restricted to *minifundios* (small peasant holdings) on generally inferior lands.

The Colonial Economy After the initial period of plunder, the mines were the principal source of royal revenue; one-fifth of all precious metals, the *quinto real*, went to the crown. To discourage piracy and simplify taxation, all colonial exports had to go to Spain via the ports of Veracruz (Mexico), Cartagena (Colombia) and Portobelo (Panama).

Under a crown monopoly, a merchant guild based in Spain controlled all trade with the colonies. With their related guilds in Lima and Mexico, Spanish merchants fixed high prices for European goods sold in the colonies, and taxes were also levied on these imports. In many cases, through an institution known as the *repartimiento de mercancias*, the Spanish Crown also forced the purchase of superfluous goods, like European clothing, upon the Indian populations. These taxes and restrictions on trade caused great discontent in the colonies, particularly amongst criollos, whose prosperity depended more on local development than on generating wealth for Spanish merchants and the crown.

Commerce was equally centralised, as all trade with the mother country had to pass through Lima; this meant that exports from Buenos Aires, for instance, went overland to Lima, by sea to Panama and overland across the isthmus before being loaded onto ships across the Atlantic, rather than by sea from the Río de la Plata.

Colonial South America: Late–18th Century

1 Viceroyalty of New Granada 1717 & 1739
2 Captaincy General of Venezuela 1777
3 Viceroyalty of Peru 1542
4 Captaincy General of Grão Pará
5 Captaincy General of Maranhão
6 Captaincy General of Mato Grosso
7 Captaincy General of Goiás
8 Captaincy General of Pernambuco
9 Captaincy General of Bahia
10 Captaincy General of Minas Gerais
11 Captaincy General of São Paulo
12 Viceroyalty of Río de la Plata 1777

Other European Colonies

Portugal's colonisation of Brazil was far less systematic than Spain's practices in the rest of South America. Whereas Spain set up a colonial bureaucracy accountable to the crown (though at a distance), Portugal divided the country into parallel strips extending to the Line of Tordesillas, and established 'donatary captaincies' (or 'hereditary captaincies'), which gave individuals almost unlimited powers within their domain. When this proved unsatisfactory, the crown assumed direct control. For details, see the Brazil chapter.

Other European powers to claim territory in South America were Britain, Holland and France, who sought to extend their influence from the Caribbean to the mainland. Though the Spanish and Portuguese always regarded the presence of these countries as an incursion, the territories on the north-east coast of the continent were, relatively, so unattractive that neither peninsular power could spare the resources to eject the rivals. See the chapter on the Guianas for details.

Revolution & Independence

The Spanish Colonies Pressure for independence came mainly from criollos, who resented the political and social dominance of the peninsulares, and the colonial administration's restrictive trade policies. Educated criollos' knowledge of the Enlightenment, and their sympathy with the US War of Independence and the French Revolution, may also have contributed to a pro-independence attitude, but it was events in Europe which really precipitated the movement.

The Paths of the Liberators

In liberating South America, the independence struggle's two major figures, Simón Bolívar and José de San Martín, converged on the centre from opposite ends of the continent. Bolívar began in the north, while San Martín led the charge from the south.

In retrospect, it is no surprise that the leaders should have come from the backwaters of the Spanish Empire, since peninsular control was strongest in Peru. In the far-flung viceroyalties of Nueva Granada and the Río de la Plata, both Bolívar and San Martín developed a criollo sense of identity which a privileged education in Spain did nothing to eradicate.

Still, the two differed greatly in background and temperament. Bolívar was born wealthy, in Caracas. By all accounts, he was a passionate person who, when his young Spanish wife died, sublimated his energy in grandiose plans for Spanish American independence. Despite early setbacks, his intensity and populist ability to inspire the masses proved a greater strength than his limited military skills. By sheer persistence and force of will, he turned former adversaries into supporters, and his movement gained strength.

San Martín, from the former Jesuit reduccion of Yapeyú on the Río Uruguay, had more humble origins than Bolívar, and was more methodical and conservative. On hearing of the events of the Revolution of May 1810, he immediately left for London to prepare for his return to Buenos Aires. His actions were those of a professional soldier who had spent 20 years in the ranks – rather than leap straight into battle, he first trained and organised his forces.

At their famous meeting at Guayaquil in 1822, the apolitical San Martín found himself in conflict with Bolívar, who had strong political ambitions; San Martín saw the installation of a powerful leader, even a monarch, as essential to avoid the disintegration of Peru, while Bolívar insisted on a constitutional republic. In a complicated exchange, which aroused ill-feeling among supporters of both leaders, the Venezuelan won the day and San Martín returned to the south.

In the long run, though, both were disappointed. The proliferation of *caudillos* (local warlords) appalled the two great soldier-statesmen, and set an often deplorable pattern for most of the 19th century. San Martín returned to an Argentina racked by internal dissension, and he left almost immediately for self-imposed exile in France, never to return. Bolívar's dream of a strong republic of Gran Colombia was shattered by difficulties which led to the secession of Ecuador and the separation of Colombia and Venezuela. He died of pulmonary tuberculosis in the Colombian town of Santa Marta. ■

In 1796, Spain formed an alliance with France, making Spanish vessels a legitimate target for the British navy (in addition to the privateers who had been attacking Spanish ships for years). This disrupted communication and trade with the Americas, forcing the colonies into practical, if not official, independence. The defeat of a British invasion of Buenos Aires in 1806 added to the colonists' growing sense of self-confidence and self-sufficiency.

The following year, Napoleon forced the abdication of Spanish monarch Charles IV, replacing him with Napoleon's own brother Joseph. Criollo leaders forced royal officials to hand over power to local juntas, supposedly until the restoration of a legitimate monarch. The criollos were reluctant to relinquish power when, after Napoleon's defeat in 1814, Ferdinand VII became King of Spain. The end of the European wars enabled more troops to be deployed in the Americas, but the burden was on the Spanish to reassert control, particularly in Venezuela and Argentina, which had effectively declared independence.

The two main currents of the independence movement converged on Peru from these two areas. Argentina overcame Spain's attempted reconquest, and its forces, under José de San Martín, crossed the Andes to liberate Chile (1817-18) and finally sailed up the coast to take Lima (1821). From 1819 to 1821, Simón Bolívar and his followers advanced overland to Peru from Venezuela via Colombia and Ecuador.

Brazil Brazil became autonomous in 1807, when the Portuguese prince regent, exiled after Napoleon's occupation of Portugal, established himself in Brazil. He later returned to Europe, leaving his son Pedro as prince regent, but when the Portuguese parliament tried to reclaim the colony, Dom Pedro proclaimed himself emperor of an independent Brazil.

After Independence

South America's modern political map reflects, to a great degree, the viceroyalties,

audiencias and presidencias of the Spanish Empire. After independence, the former colonies became separate countries whose borders generally followed colonial administrative divisions, modified by the ambitions of the independence leaders. The consolidations, secessions and territorial disputes which followed, and in some cases still persist, are outlined in the geography section and in individual country chapters.

The social structure of the new countries changed slowly. Criollos replaced peninsulares at the apex of the hierarchy, but mestizos and Indians continued to be their social and economic inferiors. Within the criollo elite, there emerged divisions between educated, urban liberals and conservative, rural landholders with traditional Spanish Catholic values. The former group favoured a centralised government which looked to Enlightenment Europe for inspiration, while the latter group sought to retain the privileges it had attained under colonial rule.

Rural landowners (*hacendados* or *gamonales)* prevailed in the short run. Rural *caudillos* (strongmen commanding private armies) exerted considerable influence on national politics by employing force or the threat of it, filling the vacuum left by the departed colonial regime. Because this strong leadership was based on personality and personal following rather than on ideology or collective interest, it did not offer any continuity beyond that individual leader. The instability and violence which have characterised the South American republics have many roots in this period.

While each country has developed separately since independence, there have been a number of common elements, particularly the alternation between dictatorship and instability, and the contrast between the powerful elite and the powerless masses. Indian populations have fared badly in almost every country, though some have begun to reassert their identity and exercise political power. Foreign economic and political intervention has also been a factor in the development of most countries in South America, though direct military involvement has been a rarity, and many of the republics have very independent foreign policies.

GEOGRAPHY

Apart from the main physical and political divisions of the continent, travellers will often hear references to the 'Andean countries' (usually meaning Colombia, Ecuador, Peru and Bolivia) and the 'Southern Cone' countries (Argentina, Uruguay, Paraguay, Chile, and some parts of Brazil).

Physical Features

The great mountain system of the Andes is one of the continent's most prominent features, snaking nearly 8000 km down the western margin of the continent from Venezuela to southern Patagonia. From its northern extremity in Venezuela, the *cordillera* (range) extends south-west to form the eastern segment of several Colombian

ranges, which rejoin into a single range. In Ecuador, it divides again into two major volcanic chains, separated by a broad plateau. In the Central Andes of Peru, three south-east trending ranges meet the *altiplano* (high plateau) on the Bolivian border. South of Bolivia, the mountains mark the border between Chile and Argentina, becoming lower towards the southern tip of the continent.

The other dominant feature, the Amazon Basin, drains an area of about seven million sq km, extending 3000 km from the eastern slopes of the Andes to the Atlantic, between the Guayana Highlands to the north and the Brazilian highlands to the south.

The smaller Orinoco Basin drains the Llanos (plains) of Venezuela, while to the south, the Paraná/Paraguay river system extends from the Pantanal marshes of the southern Brazilian highlands and the Chaco of southern Bolivia, to the Pampas of Argentina and Uruguay. Further south again, the Río Negro forms the boundary between the fertile Pampas and arid Patagonia.

Political Geography & Borders

South America's colonial political boundaries were indistinct, and the creation of new states resulted in many territorial disputes, some of which were immediate causes of contention, while others still smolder below the surface of international relations. In most cases, European countries divided territory as if the indigenous nations of pre-Columbian America did not even exist – a situation which has continued into the present.

Of the disputes which have survived into the present day, the most conspicuous has been that between Britain and Argentina over the Falklands Islands/Islas Malvinas, which led to open warfare in 1982. A long-standing dispute between Chile and Argentina over three small islands in the Beagle Channel barely escaped the same result only three years earlier.

One of the most serious conflicts on the continent was the War of the Pacific (1879-1883), a struggle between Chile on the one hand and Peru and Bolivia on the other, over the nitrate-rich Atacama Desert. Chile won the war, eventually returning territory to Peru and making other concessions to Bolivia, but neither Peru nor Bolivia has definitively accepted the loss.

Other potentially serious disputes involve the ill-defined Amazonian borders of many different countries – the Peru-Ecuador border is especially contentious. Venezuela maintains a claim to lands bordering the Río Essequibo, which would reduce the area of Guyana by two-thirds.

Geopolitics

One of the mainstays of military ideology and influence, especially in the Southern

Habitats

South America has a huge variety of habitats, each with particular associations of plants and animals. Some of the most important or interesting habitats are described here.

The coastal lowlands have many habitats, one of the most fascinating of which is mangrove swamp. Mangroves are trees with the remarkable ability to grow in salt water. They have a broadly spreading system of intertwining stilt roots to support the tree in unstable sandy or silty soils. Mangrove forests trap sediments and build up a rich organic soil, which in turn supports other plants. In between the roots, a protected habitat is provided for many types of fish, mollusc and crustacean as well as other animals, while the branches provide nesting areas for sea birds.

Tropical dry forest is a fast-disappearing habitat found in hot areas where there are well-defined wet and dry seasons, as on the coast. The trees lose their leaves during the dry season and are more widely spaced than in the rainforest, creating a more open habitat. Only about 1% of tropical dry forest remains undisturbed.

In remote valleys at higher elevations, tropical cloud forests are found. They are so named because they trap (and help create) clouds, which drench the forest in a fine mist, allowing some particularly delicate forms of plant life to survive. Cloud forest trees are adapted to steep rocky soils and a harsh climate. They have a characteristic low gnarled growth, dense small-leaved canopy, and moss-covered branches supporting orchids, ferns, bromeliads and a host of other epiphytes (aerial plants which gather moisture and nutrients without ground roots). The dense vegetation at all levels gives a tropical cloud forest a mysterious, delicate fairy-tale appearance. It is the home of such rare species as the woolly tapir, the Andean spectacled bear and the puma. This habitat is particularly important as a source of fresh water and to control erosion.

Above the cloud forest lies the *páramo*, or high-altitude grassland and shrubland. This is the natural 'sponge' of the Andes – it catches and gradually releases much of the water that is eventually used by city dwellers. The páramo is characterised by a harsh climate, high levels of ultraviolet light and wet, peaty soils. It is a highly specialised highland habitat unique to tropical America, and found only from the highlands of Costa Rica (at 10°N) to the highlands of northern Peru (at 10°S). Páramo flora is dominated by hard grasses, cushion plants and small herbaceous plants, which have adapted well to the harsh environment. The páramo also features dense thickets of small trees. These are often *Polylepis* species (*queñua* in Spanish), members of the rose family. With the Himalayan pines, they share the world altitude record for trees. Once considerably more extensive, they have been pushed back into small pockets by fire and grazing. Grasses are more common. A spiky, resistant tussock grass, locally called *ichu*, is often encountered. It grows in large clumps and makes walking uncomfortable.

Tropical rainforest is the habitat that attracts the most attention from visitors. A tropical forest, unlike a temperate forest, has great variety. If you stand in one spot and look around, you see scores of different species of trees, but you often have to walk several hundred metres to find another example of any particular species.

The incredible variety of plants is correlated with the high biodiversity of the animals which live within the forests. Terry Erwin, of the Smithsonian Institution, found 3000 species of beetle in five different areas of rainforest – each area was only about 12 sq metres! He estimated that each species of tree in the rainforest supports over 400 unique species of animal – given the thousands of known tree species, this means millions of species of animals, many of them insects and most unknown to science. These complex inter-relationships, and the great biodiversity, are among the reasons why many people are calling for a halt to the destruction of tropical rainforest.

Rob Rachowiecki

Cone countries, is the 19th-century European notion of geopolitics. According to this world view, first elaborated by German geographer Friedrich Ratzel and later exaggerated in National Socialist (Nazi) ideology in the 1930s, the state is akin to a biological organism which must grow (expand) or die. This means a state must effectively occupy the territories which it claims as its own, in which process it comes into conflict with other states. Such thinking was clearly a major factor in Argentine General Galtieri's decision to invade the Falklands/Malvinas in 1982.

Other South American countries share this perspective – Chile's former dictator, General Augusto Pinochet, has even written a textbook entitled *Geopolítica*. His Argentine and Brazilian counterparts expound on topics like the 'Fifth Column' of Chilean immigrants (largely illiterate sheep shearers) in Patagonia, or the justification of territorial claims in the Antarctic. In one instance, an Argentine military government transported a pregnant woman to give birth in Antarctica in order to strengthen its case for 'effective settlement'.

The tenets of geopolitics are most strongly held among the military, who publish detailed articles in journals like *Estrategia* (Strategy). Some of these analyses are much more sophisticated than others, but it would be a mistake to dismiss any of them too quickly. An Argentine naval officer observed to one of the authors that, 'For us, the Malvinas are a pact sealed in blood'.

CLIMATE

Because of South America's wide range of latitudes and altitudes, it has a great variety of climates. Warm and cold ocean currents, trade winds and topography also have an influence on the climate. Over two-thirds of the continent lies within the tropics. Some are wet, humid tropical areas, including the Amazon Basin, northern Brazil and the Guianas, and the west coast of Colombia and Ecuador. These are areas of *selva* (natural tropical rainforest), with average daily maximum temperatures of about 30°C all year round and over 2500 mm of rain per annum. There are also drier tropical areas, such as the Brazilian highlands and the Orinoco Basin, which are still hot but enjoy cool nights and a distinct dry season.

The Wealth of the Andes

More important than gold, the humble potato has been South America's greatest gift to the rest of the world. Few Europeans can imagine the spectrum of colours and forms taken by *Solanum tuberosum* in its region of origin, the Central Andean highlands.

The potato is cultivated mostly by Quechua and Aymará Indians in a six-year rotation on intensively tended mountain plots. The first year is devoted to potatoes, the second to *oca* and other Andean tubers, the third to *quinoa* and other grains, and the fourth to *habas* (broad beans, a Spanish introduction). In the fifth and six years the fields lie fallow as pasture.

The Andean environment, with its varied elevations and exposures, offers considerable climatic variation. An individual farmer may cultivate up to 40 scattered plots, each in a different stage of production. Such dispersal is a form of crop insurance, as no one plot is likely to be wiped out by pests or adverse weather.

Scientists have documented 6000 different varieties of potatoes raised by Andean peasants, some of the most successful plant breeders the world has ever known. In some areas, the average household cultivates 50 varieties, and a given village more than twice that many, reducing the crop's vulnerability to pests like nematodes.

Traditional highland agricultural systems are a source of innovation and genetic material for improved potato varieties. Scientists are making efforts to preserve the Andean heritage, by collecting plant germplasm in institutions like Lima's Centro Internacional de la Papa (International Potato Centre). Other varieties of potato are being preserved in botanical gardens. Commercial varieties degenerate within a few years and, without the genetic material to renew them, eventually fail. For this reason, everyone has a stake in the genetic future of the potato, the true wealth of the Andes. ■

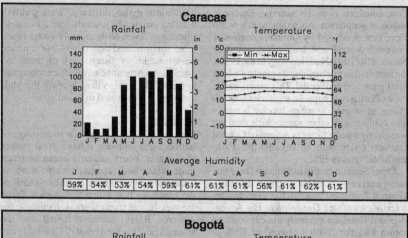

Caracas

Rainfall

Temperature

Min — Max

Average Humidity

J	F	M	A	M	J	J	A	S	O	N	D
59%	54%	53%	54%	59%	61%	61%	61%	56%	61%	62%	61%

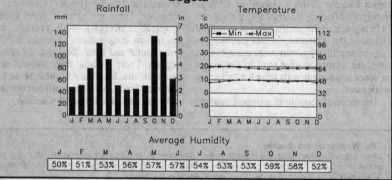

Bogotá

Rainfall

Temperature

Min — Max

Average Humidity

J	F	M	A	M	J	J	A	S	O	N	D
50%	51%	53%	56%	57%	57%	54%	53%	53%	59%	58%	52%

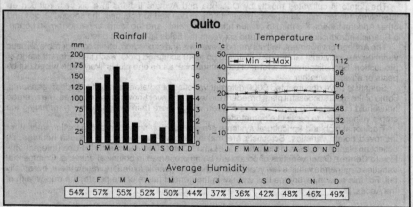

Quito

Rainfall

Temperature

Min — Max

Average Humidity

J	F	M	A	M	J	J	A	S	O	N	D
54%	57%	55%	52%	50%	44%	37%	36%	42%	48%	46%	49%

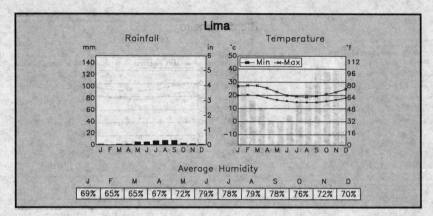

Lima

Rainfall

Temperature

Average Humidity

J	F	M	A	M	J	J	A	S	O	N	D
69%	65%	65%	67%	72%	79%	78%	79%	78%	76%	72%	70%

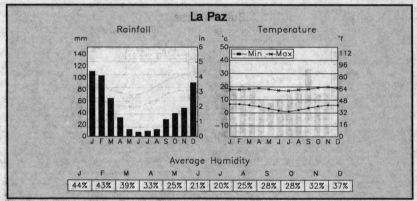

La Paz

Rainfall

Temperature

Average Humidity

J	F	M	A	M	J	J	A	S	O	N	D
44%	43%	39%	33%	25%	21%	20%	25%	28%	28%	32%	37%

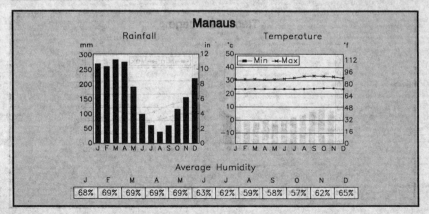

Manaus

Rainfall

Temperature

Average Humidity

J	F	M	A	M	J	J	A	S	O	N	D
68%	69%	69%	69%	69%	63%	62%	59%	58%	57%	62%	65%

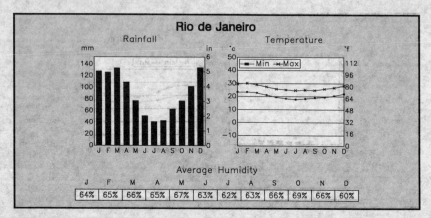

Rio de Janeiro

Rainfall

Temperature

Average Humidity

J	F	M	A	M	J	J	A	S	O	N	D
64%	65%	66%	65%	67%	63%	62%	63%	66%	69%	66%	60%

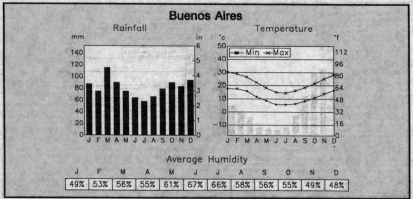

Buenos Aires

Rainfall

Temperature

Average Humidity

J	F	M	A	M	J	J	A	S	O	N	D
49%	53%	56%	55%	61%	67%	66%	58%	56%	55%	49%	48%

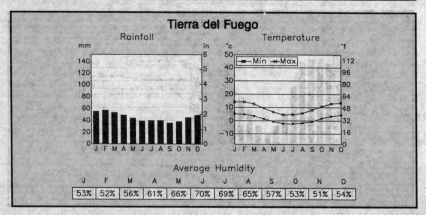

Tierra del Fuego

Rainfall

Temperature

Average Humidity

J	F	M	A	M	J	J	A	S	O	N	D
53%	52%	56%	61%	66%	70%	69%	65%	57%	53%	51%	54%

South of the Tropic of Capricorn, Paraguay and southern Brazil are humid sub-tropical zones, while most of Argentina and Chile have temperate mid-latitude climates, with mild winters and warm summers ranging from 12°C in July to 25°C in January, depending on landforms and latitude. Rainfall, occurring mostly in winter, varies from 200 mm to 2000 mm per annum, depending on winds and the rain shadow effect of the Andes.

The main arid regions are Patagonia, in the rain shadow east of the Andes, and northern Chile and Peru, between the Andes and the Pacific coast, where the cold Humboldt current creates a cloudy but dry climate. About every seven years, however, the El Niño effect, associated with changes in Pacific Ocean circulation patterns and rising sea surface temperatures, brings heavy rain and floods in these desert areas. There are two smaller arid zones – one along the north coast of Colombia and Venezuela, the other in the north-eastern Brazilian *sertão*, where severe droughts wreak great hardships on peasant peoples.

The high Andes, above 3500 metres, and far southern Chile and Argentina are cool climate zones, where average daily temperatures fall below 10°C.

ECOLOGY & ENVIRONMENT
Rainforests & the Amazon Basin

Over the past two decades, there has been a huge amount of publicity given to environmental problems in South America's tropical rainforests, particularly the Amazon Basin – among other catastrophes, there has been deforestation due to mining and agriculture, massive hydroelectric projects which have destroyed major rivers and inundated pristine forest, and the relocation and even destruction of indigenous peoples. Within the region, however, there is great variation, and dramatically different conditions which need more explanation than lament or a condemnation.

Bolivia, Brazil, Colombia, Ecuador, Guyana, French Guiana, Peru, Suriname and Venezuela all occupy parts of the world's greatest river basin. The Amazon itself, born inconspicuously in the Peruvian highlands, has a number of enormous tributaries and some truly imposing statistics: the distance from its source to its mouth is over 6200 km, its flow is 12 times that of the Mississippi, it carries one-fifth of the world's fresh water, and its discharge into the Atlantic every 24 hours equals that of the Thames in a full year. Atlantic tides can be felt at Óbidos, 500 km above its mouth, but early mariners collected fresh water from its discharge over 250 km out to sea; its sediments are indentifiable for hundreds of km more.

The Amazon drains two main areas, the Brazilian Shield, an eroded Precambrian upland south of the Solimões (the main channel of the Amazon) and the Guiana Shield, an equally eroded area to its north. Over 98% of this area consists of naturally forested *terra firme* uplands of low fertility. The remainder, only 2%, consists of *várzea*, a fertile alluvial floodplain, which is the only suitable area for intensive agriculture.

Tributaries north of the Solimões are mostly 'black water' rivers, whose dissolved organic matter consumes oxygen and renders the streams acidic and relatively lifeless. Those to the south are 'clear water' rivers with higher, more stable banks, and they support a greater amount of aquatic life. The most biologically productive channels are the upper 'white water' tributaries like the Marañon and Ucayali, which carry suspended sediments from the eastern slopes of the Peruvian Andes to the várzeas of the Solimões. Just west of Manaus, at the so-called Encontro das Aguas (Meeting of the Waters), these white waters flow alongside the black waters of the Rio Negro for some distance without mixing.

The tropics are far richer in species than the mid-latitudes, and tropical rainforest is the earth's most complex ecosystem. The Amazonian forest may contain as many as 50,000 species of higher plants, one-fifth of the world's total. In some two-hectare plots in the Amazon, one can find more than 500 tree species; a comparable plot in a mid-latitude forest might have no more than three or four.

The physical structure of the tropical rainforest also differs from that of mid-latitude forests. It consists of a overstorey of large trees buttressed by vines, and a lower storey of smaller trees – the canopy is so dense that almost no sunlight penetrates to the forest floor. So little grows in this shade that, except near watercourses, the forest floor itself is surprisingly open, and not at all like the dense 'jungle' which many people imagine.

The forest's exuberant vegetation gives a deceptive appearance of fertility. The heavy rainfall leaches almost all important chemical nutrients from the soil and, because of high temperatures and bacterial activity, there is almost no accummulation of humus – nutrients from the decayed material are

Farming, Fire & the Rainforest

The widespread practice of slash-and-burn agriculture has popularly been seen as a culprit in the deforestation of the Amazon and other rainforest regions. However, many agronomists, anthropologists, geographers and other scientists have come to view slash and burn agriculture, which they prefer to call *swidden* or 'shifting agriculture', as a indigenous technique well suited to the rainforest ecosystem. Sedentary indigenous peoples like the Kuikuru, of the upper Rio Xingú of Brazil, have farmed nearby forest for as long as 90 years at a stretch without exhausting its resources or reducing forest cover, and major civilisations like the Maya depended at least in part on swidden cultivation.

Shifting agriculture certainly appears disruptive. A swidden farmer hacks the forest understorey with a knife or machete and fells large trees by axe, then leaves the piled debris, perhaps for months, before burning. After this, unburnt material may be heaped up for a second burn. A variety of crops is then planted in anticipation of the rainy season. In tropical forests, heavy rainfall leaches nutrients from the poor soils, but burning liberates plant nutrients for growing crops. The energy cycle in the ecosystem depends on decomposition and reabsorption of plant materials, so burning represents an accelerated form of decomposition for agricultural purposes.

Like the rainforest itself, the swidden system is characterised by great diversity – in a single Yanomami Indian plot in Venezuela, one researcher found five varieties of bananas, three types of plantains, several tubers (including yams, sweet potatoes and cassava), tree crops (like peach palm, avocado and papaya), sugar cane, tobacco and cotton, and annuals like chilis, maize, beans, tomatoes and squash. Productivity can be very high – the caloric yield of a hectare of manioc is more than triple that of a hectare of maize in the Andean highlands.

The composition of the swidden plot mimics the structure of the rainforest, with an upper storey of fruit trees, an intermediate level of plants like maize and sugar cane, and a surface layer of tubers and groundcover plants which protect the soil surface from erosion. The plot has a disorderly appearance, with crops planted in close proximity, frequently overlapping each other. The variety of plants discourages natural pests (which thrive in large stands of a single crop), thus helping to ensure a steady harvest.

Fertility on these small plots drops rapidly after two or three years but, under this 'agroforestry' system, the field produces tree crops for several more years. A long fallow period, up to 30 years, then allows recovery of the forest, minimising environmental damage.

Vulnerable to disruption, the cycle is not sustainable under all circumstances. If increased population or market pressures reduce fallow periods, the forest may not have sufficient time to recover. The introduction of technological innovations such as chainsaws can upset the delicate balance on which the system depends. When the system is extended into drier environments, it may fail, and when inexperienced immigrants attempt to farm the forest, results can be disastrous. In Brazil, for example, landless peasants from the arid Nordeste have deforested substantial areas, under government incentives which have rewarded forest clearance in the Amazon Basin. In these cases, yields fall rapidly, and the depleted area is abandoned for newer colonisation sites, leaving the cleared land for cattle ranchers.

Nevertheless, swidden cultivators have much to teach the modern world. Travellers who see a smouldering plot in the rainforest should not always assume the worst – there is a strong correlation between the presence of indigenous peoples and the preservation of the selva. ∎

almost immediately reabsorbed into the living trees. This is why the forest is rarely able to regenerate itself after large areas are cleared.

Presently, it is the tributaries of the Amazon which have suffered the worst depredations. Brazilian projects like the Tucuruí dam on the Rio Tocantins, the Transamazon Highway, the tree plantations on the Rio Jarí, and the Roraima gold fields near the Venezuelan border have brought deforestation, siltation, mercury contamination of rivers and epidemic diseases to indigenous people.

The total deforestation may be less than some alarmist estimates have suggested. According to the respected World Resources Institute, only about 7% of Brazil's forested Amazon has been lost – but it is the *rate* of deforestation (at least 1.7 million hectares per annum) which is so startling that many scientists fear the trends are irreversible.

For a list of organisations concerned with rainforest preservation, see the Useful Organisations entry in the Facts for the Visitor chapter.

The Central Andean Region

The ecology of the Central Andean region, between the coast and the cordillera from northern Chile to northern Peru, is also unique. The coastal Atacama desert, the world's driest, is almost utterly barren in the rain shadow of the high Andes – the mountains prevent the intrusion of tropical storms from the Amazon Basin to the east. The cold Peru (Humboldt) current moderates the temperature one would expect at this tropical latitude, but produces convective fogs known as *garúa* or *camanchaca*, which support the hillside vegetation known as *lomas* in the coastal ranges. The only other vegetation occurs in the valleys of the several transverse rivers which descend from the Andes.

Precipitation and vegetation increase with altitude and distance from the coast, as well as from south to north. Traditionally, Andean peoples produced different, complementary products in different agro-pastoral 'niches', which they exchanged with their kin in other zones. Coastal products included cotton, fish, guano (for fertiliser) and coca, while the higher sierra (mountain range) yielded maize and tubers, such as potatoes, on impressive agricultural terraces. On the heights of the altiplano, where cultivation was impossible, salt, wool and meat were the bases of subsistence.

This integrated economic system, disrupted by the Spanish invasions and colonisation, nevertheless survives in many parts of the Andean world, and many modern agronomists have come to appreciate the durability of these farming practices. In coastal areas, modern cash crops like sugar have largely superseded traditional practices, and commercial fishing has depleted stocks of anchovies and other fish, but the Andes are still a repository for a plant genetic diversity which, in many ways, parallels that of the Amazon.

ECONOMY

Despite recent signs of improvement, South America is widely perceived as an economic disaster zone of low living standards, hyper-inflation and unsustainable levels of foreign debt. Some of these problems stem in part from a long history of foreign domination, political instability, social inequality and the failure to develop a sound domestic infrastructure. Other economic problems, like the debt crisis, are of more recent origin. The past few years have seen encouraging developments, but there are now dramatic differences among the republics with respect to problems like debt and inflation. There is a widespread trend towards reduction of the state's traditional economic role, as many countries have privatised former state services like telecommunications, railways and even highways.

Post-Independence Economies

From about 1850 to the start of WW I, several South American countries enjoyed a period of growth and relative prosperity based on commodity exports like coffee and sugar (Brazil), guano and copper (Peru), nitrates (Chile), and grain, beef and wool

(Argentina and Uruguay). Much of this development was supported by foreign capital and foreign expertise. Countries like Colombia, Bolivia and Ecuador lagged behind because of internal instability or lack of exploitable resources.

Wild fluctuations in the available foreign capital and in demand for exports during WW I and the Great Depression of the 1930s brought greater government intervention in South American economies. Initially, this took the form of regulations and controls aimed at protecting foreign investment, though there was direct government involvement in mining and transport. WW II was a time of strong demand for South America's food and raw materials, but imported manufactured goods from Europe and North America were in short supply. Industrialisation, often identified with nationalism, became a key economic goal after the war.

Industrialisation required more capital than foreign private investment could readily provide, especially given postwar Europe's ruinous economic situation. Moreover, in projects involving natural resources and infrastructure (roads, telecommunications, electricity), locals worried that overseas capital might compromise economic auton-

Conservation

Deforestation threatens local indigenous peoples living in tropical rainforests, relying on the forest to maintain a culture and a way of life that have lasted for centuries. Deforestation devastates tribal groups, who are as unable to survive in the Western world as New Yorkers would be if forced to live in the jungle. But the loss of tropical forests has important consequences for us all, no matter where we live.

Most people are aware that rainforests are important on a global scale because they moderate worldwide climatic patterns – scientists have recently determined that destruction of the rainforests is a major factor contributing to global warming. Perhaps less well known is the rainforest's role in maintaining biodiversity.

Roughly half of the planet's 1½ million known species live in tropical rainforests, and scientists predict that millions more rainforest species are still to be discovered. This incredible array of plants and animals cannot exist unless rainforest habitat is protected – deforestation is resulting in countless extinctions.

When a species dies out, what do we actually lose? One of the problems is that we really don't know. Numerous medicines have been extracted from forest trees, shrubs and flowers. These range from anaesthetics to antibiotics, from contraceptives to cures for heart disease, malaria and other illnesses. Countless medicinal uses of plants are known only to the indigenous inhabitants of the forest. Much of this knowledge is being lost as indigenous cultures are assimilated into the Western way of life, or when tribal groups are destroyed by disease or genocide. The secrets of other pharmaceutical treasures remain locked in the forests themselves, and may never be discovered if those forests are destroyed.

The rainforests are also important to modern commercial agriculture. Many tropical crops are almost identical monocultures, bred to produce strains which are high-yielding, easy to harvest, slow-ripening, etc. Should such a crop be eliminated by disease or pests, perhaps because its resistant characteristics have been bred out of the population, scientists could look to the forests for disease-resistant wild strains to breed into the commercially raised crops. Deforestation means losing these wild strains, and that means losing the genetic diversity which may help a species adapt to a changing world.

Efforts are now underway to show that the economic value of the standing rainforest is greater than the mineral, timber and grazing wealth to be realised by deforestation. One important way of making tropical rainforest economically productive, without cutting it down, is to protect it in national parks and reserves and make it accessible to travellers from all over the world. This type of ecotourism is becoming increasingly important to South American countries rich in such natural resources.

Rob Rachowiecki

omy and foreign investors feared nationalisation of their assets. The solution was for governments to borrow from overseas and become direct participants in economic enterprises. Argentina set up the YPF (Yacimientos Petrolíferos Fiscales) to develop oil reserves. Brazil's government entered the petroleum and steel industries, Bolivia's invested in tin, Chile's in copper, Colombia's in iron and steel, Uruguay's in meat packing, and so on.

In the 1970s and 1980s, as dictatorships provided an appearance of stability and Western banks were awash with petrodollars from the OPEC countries, South American governments accelerated their borrowing. Much of the money went to grandiose but unproductive developments such as the Amazonian capital of Brasilia, massive hydroelectric projects like Itaipú and Yacyretá, and the Swiss bank accounts of corrupt officials.

This infusion of foreign capital, supplemented by deficit spending without a corresponding increase in productivity, triggered serious inflation in most countries; the current leader is Brazil, where rates in mid-1993 consistently topped 30% per month. This and other economic problems decreased the ability to service foreign debt, and governments borrowed more just to pay the interest. With annual interest bills totalling more than 20% of export earnings, several countries had negotiated debt rescheduling agreements or were attempting to do so.

Brazil, Argentina and Chile have been most successful in achieving industrialisation, while the Andean countries of Bolivia, Colombia, Ecuador and Peru have lagged behind. Industry, however, has been largely geared to protected local markets, rather than to international trade; the traditional primary products of the mines, ranches, plantations and grain farms continue to dominate the export sector. Many rural people still survive on small subsistence plots, but lack of opportunity in the countryside has driven many to the shantytowns surrounding modern capitals and other large cities.

Gross National Products

The figures below show the estimated total and per capita GNP of South American countries for 1991:

	GNP (US$ billions)	GNP Per Capita (US$)
Argentina	129.60	2370
Bolivia	4.80	620
Brazil	404.10	2680
Chile	29.50	1940
Colombia	39.90	1240
Ecuador	10.90	960
French Guiana	unavailable*	
Guyana	0.17	370
Paraguay	6.19	1110
Peru	48.40	1160
Suriname	1.20	3050 **
Uruguay	9.20	2560
Venezuela	52.60	2560
Falkland Islands	0.02	9000

*Because French Guiana is legally part of metropolitan France, separate figures for GNP are unavailable, but it is probably safe to say that it has the highest per capita GNP on the continent.
**Because of an unrealistic official exchange rate for local currency, the per capita GNP figure for Suriname is exaggerated, probably by a factor of 10.

Foreign Debt

The following table gives the estimated total and per capita foreign debt at the end of 1991:

	Total Foreign Debt (US$ billion)	Debt per Capita (US$)
Argentina	63.707	1925
Bolivia	4.075	522
Brazil	116.514	772
Chile	17.902	1316
Colombia	17.369	506
Ecuador	12.469	1247
Guyana	1.898	2376
Paraguay	2.177	483
Peru	20.708	920
Uruguay	4.189	1351
Venezuela	34.372	1818

POPULATION & PEOPLE

While South America's population is growing at a fairly modest rate of 1.9% per annum, that growth rate varies widely both among and within countries. The Southern Cone states of Argentina, Chile and Uruguay have relatively stable populations, while the Andean and tropical countries have rapidly rising rates. Infant mortality rates are shockingly high in some countries, most notably Bolivia, Brazil and Peru.

Nearly three-quarters of all South Americans live in cities – this is the earth's most urbanised continent, yet large areas like the Amazon Basin and Atacama desert are almost uninhabited. Megalopolises like São Paulo and Buenos Aires have extraordinarily high population densities. A few areas, like south-central Chile, eastern Paraguay and the Brazilian Nordeste, have dense populations of peasants.

One major cause for concern is the very youthful population structure of countries like Bolivia, Ecuador, Peru, Colombia, Brazil and Venezuela, where nearly 40% of the people are younger than 15 years. Not only does this mean that the population will continue to grow rapidly as these individuals reach child-bearing age, but it is doubtful whether local economies can provide employment for so many in such a short time.

Population Estimates

	Population (mid-1992)	Persons per sq km
Argentina	33,100,000	12.0
Bolivia	7,800,000	6.9
Brazil	150,800,000	17.8
Chile	13,600,000	18.1
Colombia	34,300,000	30.1
Ecuador	10,000,000	35.1
French Guiana	100,000	1.0
Guyana	800,000	3.9
Paraguay	4,500,000	11.2
Peru	22,500,000	17.4
Suriname	400,000	2.7
Uruguay	3,100,000	17.8
Venezuela	18,900,000	20.8
Falkland Islands	2,050	0.2

ARTS
Music

Especially in recent years, South American music has had worldwide impact. The haunting melodies of the Andes, the Chilean New Song movement, the Argentine tango and the Brazilian samba and bossa nova are among the forms exported from the continent. Much of this music has become available on cassettes and compact discs in Europe, North America and elsewhere.

Andean Music The distinctive sound of traditional Andean music, characterised by wind instruments like the *quena* (flute) and *zampoña* (pan pipes) and the *charango* (a stringed instrument which uses an armadillo's carapace as its sound box), has passed into Western popular culture through adaptations like Paul Simon's version of *El Condor Pasa*. For more details on Andean music, see the music entry in the Bolivia chapter.

New Chilean Song Movement In the 1960s and later, Chilean musicians like Violeta Parra, her children Angel and Isabel, and others welded indigenous folk traditions with contemporary political consciousness in the 'Nueva Canción Chilena' (New Chilean Song Movement). It gained significant popularity in Europe and North America, especially as many musicians went into exile after the military coup of 1973. For more details, see the chapter on Chile.

The Tango Argentina's export of the tango to European salons in the 1920s and 1930s was perhaps South America's first significant contribution to European popular culture. Tango singer Carlos Gardel, a legendary figure whose cultural impact among Latin Americans was at least as great as Elvis Presley's among English-speaking people, is an icon in the Southern Cone. For more details, see the Argentina chapter.

Brazilian Music Brazilian popular music has been shaped by the mixing of a variety of musical influences from three different continents, and Brazil is still creating new and original forms.

Samba, tropicalismo and bossa nova are all national musical forms, but the Nordeste has the most regional musical styles and accompanying dances. The most important is *forró*, which sounds a bit like Mexican music. *Frevo* is a music specific to Recife;

trio elétrico, also called *frevo baiano*, began much more recently and is more of a change in technology than music. The Bahian *Afoxê*, the most African-sounding music in Brazil, is religious in origin and closely tied to Candomblé.

Lambada is a rhythm with a sensual dance that has become another international success story. The latest rage is *sertanejo*, a kind of Brazilian country and western music that's a favourite with truckdrivers and cowboys.

Cinema
Despite financial hardships, several South American countries have developed noteworthy film industries, especially Brazil, Argentina and, to a lesser degree, Chile. For more information, see the respective country chapters.

CULTURE
Traditional Cultures
It is important to avoid stereotypes when speaking of 'traditional' cultures. The peasant populations of the Andean highlands are widely considered to have the most 'traditional' way of life; they still raise potatoes on small plots and herd llamas and alpacas on the pastures of the altiplano. But over centuries, they have adopted many European customs, sold their surpluses in local markets and shipped wool to European mills. The notion that the Quechua and Aymara peoples of the Andes have a lifestyle unchanged since before the arrival of Europeans is clearly wrong, though many pre-Columbian customs survived the colonial period. Likewise, the belief that the indigenous peoples of the Amazon have lived in unspoilt isolation overlooks the fact that many of them obtained, indirectly, European goods like metal axes which they used to fell trees for slash-and-burn plots.

Avoiding Offence
In general, South Americans are friendly, gregarious and not easily offended, but will always expect to exchange pleasantries before getting to the point of a conversation; not to do so will seem the mark of an ill-bred person. Public behavior can be very formal, especially among government officials, who expect respect and deference.

In dealing with indigenous peoples and some others, travellers should take care to act inconspicuously and, especially, to refrain from photographing individuals without their permission. If someone is giving a public performance, such as a street musician or a dancer at Carnaval, or is incidental to a photograph, for example in a broad cityscape, it is not usually necessary to request permission – but if in doubt, ask or refrain.

Sport
In South America, sport means soccer. Argentina, Brazil and Uruguay have all won the World Cup, though many of the best athletes have abandoned their own countries to play for higher salaries in Europe. Other sports which enjoy widespread popularity are motor racing, basketball, cycling, tennis and volleyball (especially in Brazil). Travellers proficient in any of these sports will find them good ways to meet South Americans – but confine motor racing to the track!

RELIGION
About 90% of South Americans are at least nominally Roman Catholic. Virtually every town and city has a central church or cathedral, and a calendar loaded with Catholic holidays and celebrations. Spreading the faith was a major objective of colonisation.

Among Indian peoples, allegiance to Catholicism was often just a veneer, disguising precolonial beliefs which the Church ostensibly forbade. Similarly, Black slaves in Brazil gave Christian names and forms to their African gods, whose worship was discouraged or forbidden. Cults and sects have proliferated to this day, but they do not exclude Christianity – there is no conflict between attending mass on Sunday and seeking guidance from a *brujo* (witch) the next day.

A Different Sort of Liberator

The Spanish invaders of the New World acquired, and in many cases earned, a reputation for brutality toward the peoples of the Americas and often amongst themselves. Such cruelty contributed to the notorious 'Black Legend' of the invaders' 'deliberate sadism'.

While the Black Legend allowed northern European powers like Britain to claim a moral high ground to which they probably had no right, there is no lack of evidence for the legend. For instance, the Spaniards imported vicious mastiffs for combat, intimidation, punishment, torture, blood sport, guard duty and tracking Indian fugitives. In the invaders' footsteps followed representatives of the Catholic Church, enforcing 'Christian principles' among peoples they regarded as pagans. The official Church has often been identified with brutal authority since those early days, but a strong counter-current of thought began in early colonial times and has survived to the present.

Of several figures, the outstanding one was Father Bartolomé de las Casas – though he was at first glance an unlikely figure to protest maltreatment of the Indians. Born in Seville (Spain) in 1474, he first reached the Americas in 1502 as part of an expedition against the Indians of Higuey, on the island of Hispaniola. He soon held encomiendas there and in Cuba, but experienced a conversion which convinced him of the evils of the system, and devoted the rest of his life to the cause of justice for the indigenous peoples of Spanish America.

Renouncing his encomiendas, Las Casas returned to Spain to argue for reform of the abuses he had observed in the Indies. His impassioned advocacy of indigenous causes led to a failed attempt at peaceful evangelisation on the Venezuelan coast (Las Casas detested the idea of forced conversion), but his polemical *Very Brief Account of the Destruction of the Indies* persuaded King Carlos V to enact the New Laws of 1542, which included a major reform of the encomienda system. Though the New Laws proved difficult to enforce, Las Casas continued to speak out against corrupt officials and encomenderos from his position as bishop of Chiapas (Mexico) and then as Protector of the Indians at the Spanish court in Madrid until his death in 1566.

Before the court, the audacious Dominican reported one cacique's statement that, if Spaniards went to heaven, the Indians would prefer hell, and went so far as to defend cannibalism, to advocate restitution for all the wealth that Spain had plundered from the Americas, and even to imply the return of the lands themselves to the Indians in the interests of good government:

When we entered there...would we have found such great unions of peoples in their towns and cities if they had lacked the order of a good way of life, peace, concord and justice?

While Las Casas never achieved such utopian goals, his advocacy undoubtedly mitigated some of the worst abuses against the Indians. In this sense, he was a role model for the Latin American activist clergy of recent decades which, inspired by 'Liberation Theology', has worked to alleviate poverty and human rights abuses despite great personal risk. Las Casas was the original liberation theologist.

Las Casas also left valuable and accurate observations of Indian customs and history. His estimates of the dense population of Hispaniola, which he counted at about four million, have been confirmed and even increased by modern researchers. ■

Over recent decades, in part because of a complacent Church and rapid economic change, evangelical Protestantism has made inroads among traditionally Catholic peoples. At the same time, activist elements within the Catholic Church have promoted social justice in the name of 'Liberation Theology' – despite serious threats from reactionary elements in several South American countries.

LANGUAGE
Latin American Spanish

Spanish is the first language of the vast majority of South Americans; Brazilians speak Portuguese but often understand Spanish. Without a basic knowledge of Spanish, travel in South America can be difficult. Besides its practical value in helping you find your way around, order in restaurants and get yourself out of trouble, speaking the language enables you to communicate with locals and make friends.

Before going, try to attend an evening course in Spanish or borrow a record/cassette course from the library. Buy a book on grammar and a phrasebook (such as Lonely Planet's *Latin American Spanish Phrasebook*) and try to find a Latin American to practise with. Learning the basics of Spanish is not difficult for an English speaker, there are many cognate words, and Latin Americans are very tolerant of grammatical mistakes.

Remember that there are significant differences between European and American Spanish. Even within the Americas, accents, pronunciation and vocabulary vary considerably from one country to the next. Chilean Spanish, in particular, can be awkward for inexperienced speakers. Some words which are totally innocuous in one country can be grievous insults in another – avoid slang unless you are certain of its every meaning.

Pronunciation

Most sounds in Spanish have English equivalents, and written Spanish is largely phonetic. Once you've learnt to pronounce all the letters, and certain groups of letters, and know which syllable to stress, you can read any word or sentence and pronounce it more or less correctly.

Vowels Spanish vowels are very consistent and have easy English equivalents.

a	is like 'a' in 'father'
e	is like 'a' in 'sail' or the 'e' in 'met'
i	is like 'ee' in 'feet'
o	is like 'o' in 'for'
u	is like 'oo' in 'food'. After consonants other than 'q', it is more like the English 'w'. When modified by an umlaut, as in 'Güemes', it is also pronounced 'w'.
y	is a consonant, except when it stands alone or appears at the end of a word, in which case its pronunciation is identical to the Spanish 'i'

Diphthongs Diphthongs are combinations of two vowels which form a single syllable. In Spanish, the formation of a diphthong depends on combinations of 'weak' vowels ('i' and 'u') or strong ones ('a', 'e' and 'o'). Two weak vowels or a strong and a weak vowel make a diphthong, but two strong ones are separate syllables.

A good example of two weak vowels forming a diphthong is the word *diurno* ('during the day'). The final syllable of *obligatorio* ('obligatory') is a combination of weak and strong vowels.

Consonants Spanish consonants generally resemble their English equivalents, but there are some major exceptions:

b	resembles its English equivalent, but is undistinguished from 'v'. For clarification, refer to the former as 'b larga', the latter as 'b corta' (the word for the letter itself is pronounced like English 'bay')
c	is like the 's' in 'see' before 'e' and 'i', otherwise like the English 'k'
d	in an initial position, as the 'd' in 'dog'; otherwise, it closely resembles 'th' in 'feather'
g	is like a guttural English 'h' before Spanish 'e' and 'i', otherwise like 'g' in 'go'
h	is invariably silent. If your name begins with this letter, listen carefully when immigration officials summon you to pick up your passport
j	most closely resembles the English 'h', but is slightly more guttural
ll	as the 'y' in 'yellow', except in Argentina, where it is as the 'z' in 'azure'
ñ	is like 'ni' in 'onion'
r	is nearly identical to English, except at the beginning of a word, when it is often rolled
rr	is very strongly rolled
v	resembles English, but see 'b', above
x	is like 'x' in 'taxi', except for a very few words for which it follows Spanish or Mexican usage as 'j'
z	is like 's' in 'sun'

Stress Stress, often indicated by visible accents, is very important, since it can change the meaning of words. In general, words ending in vowels or the letters 'n' or 's' have stress on the next-to-last syllable, while those with other endings have stress on the last syllable. Thus *vaca* ('cow') and *caballos* ('horses'), both have accents on their next-to-last syllables.

Visible accents, which can occur anywhere in a word, dictate stress over these general rules. Thus *sótano* (basement), *América* and *porción* (portion) all have stress on different syllables. When words appear in all capitals, the written accent is generally omitted, but is still pronounced.

Grammar

This section, though brief, explains basic grammatical rules and should enable you to construct your own sentences.

Word Order Spanish word order resembles that of English, ie subject-verb-object. When the subject of the sentence is a pronoun, it is usually omitted.

The girl works in a restaurant.
La chica trabaja en un restaurante.
She works in a restaurant.
Trabaja en un restaurante.
Argentines eat a lot of meat.
Los Argentinos comen mucha carne.
We eat vegetables.
Comemos verduras.

Verbs There are three types of verbs in Spanish, with infinitives ending in *-ar*, *-er* and *-ir*. Each has a standard set of endings for first, second and third person, singular and plural, and if you follow those, you will manage very well. The verb *hablar*, 'to speak', is a regular *-ar* verb:

I speak	*(yo) hablo*
you speak (formal)	*(usted) habla*
you speak (familiar)	*(tú) hablas/(vos) hablás*
he/she/it speaks	*(él/ella) habla*
we speak	*(nosotros) hablamos*
you speak (plural)	*(ustedes) hablan*
they speak	*(ellos/ellas) hablan*

Some of the most common verbs, such as *ser* (to be) and *ir* (to go), are irregular, and must be learned by heart, but there is even some consistency among these verbs.

Tú, the familiar form of 'you' (singular), and its associated verb forms, are used with family and friends, particularly amongst young people. The more formal *usted* should be used to address officials and to show respect to older or more senior people.

Vos, another familiar form of 'you' with its own set of verb endings, is used in Argentina, Uruguay and Paraguay, but the people of the River Plate region readily understand *tú* forms.

Nouns Nouns are either masculine or feminine. Nouns ending in 'o', 'e' or 'ma' are usually masculine. Nouns ending in 'a', 'ión' or 'dad' are usually feminine.

masculine

book	*libro*
glass	*vaso*
bridge	*puente*
problem	*problema*
traveller	*viajero*

feminine

house	*casa*
song	*canción*
city	*ciudad*
reality	*realidad*
traveller	*viajera*

Plurals Plurals are generally formed by adding 's' to the noun, or adding 'es' if the noun ends in a consonant. Accents are usually dropped in the plural.

house, houses	*casa, casas*
election, elections	*elección, elecciones*

Articles The definite article (the) and the indefinite article (a, some) must agree with the noun in gender and number, so there are four forms of each.

the boy	*el chico*
the boys	*los chicos*
the bed	*la cama*
the beds	*las camas*
a boy	*un chico*
some boys	*unos chicos*
a bed	*una cama*
some beds	*unas camas*

Adjectives An adjective usually follows the noun it describes and, like the definite or indefinite article, must agree with it in gender and number.

the pretty house
  la casa bonita
some pretty rooms
  unos cuartos bonitos
a good boy
  un chico bueno
the good girls
  las chicas buenas

Greetings & Civilities

In their public behaviour, South Americans are very conscious of civilities, sometimes to the point of ceremoniousness. Never, for example, approach a stranger for information without extending a greeting like *buenos días* or *buenas tardes*.

Yes.	*Sí.*
No.	*No.*
Thank you.	*Gracias.*
You're welcome.	*De nada.*
Hello.	*¡Hola!*
Good morning.	*Buenos días.*
Good afternoon.	*Buenas tardes.*
Good evening.	*Buenas noches.*
Good night.	*Buenas noches.*
Goodbye.	*Adiós* or *Chau.*
I don't speak much Spanish.	*Hablo poco castellano.*
I understand.	*Entiendo.*
I don't understand.	*No entiendo.*
Mr, Sir	*Señor* (formal)
Madam, Mrs	*Señora* (formal)
unmarried woman	*Señorita*
pal, friend	*compadre*

Please.	*Por favor.*
Thank you.	*Gracias.*
Many thanks.	*Muchas gracias.*
You're welcome.	*De nada.*
Excuse me.	*Permiso.*
Sorry.	*Perdón.*
Excuse me.	*Disculpe.*
Good luck!	*¡Buena suerte!*

How are you?
  ¿Cómo está? (formal)
  or *¿Cómo estás?* (familiar)
How are things going?
  ¿Qué tal?
fine, thanks
  bien, gracias
very well
  muy bien
very badly
  muy mal
bye, see you soon
  hasta luego
I hope things go well for you.
  Qué le vaya bien (used when parting)

Small Talk

I'd like to introduce you to...
  Le presento a...
a pleasure (to meet you)
  mucho gusto
What is your name?
  ¿Cómo se llama? (formal)
  ¿Cómo te llamas? (familiar)
My name is...
  Me llamo...
Where are you from?
  ¿De dónde es? (formal)
  ¿De dónde eres? (familiar)

I am from...	*Soy de...*
Australia	*Australia*
Canada	*Canadá*
England	*Inglaterra*
Germany	*Alemania*
Israel	*Israel*
Italy	*Italia*
Japan	*Japón*
New Zealand	*Nueva Zelanda*
Norway	*Noruega*

Scotland	*Escocia*
Sweden	*Suecia*
the USA	*los Estados Unidos*

Feelings Spanish often uses the irregular verb *tener* (to have) to express feelings.

I am...	*Tengo...*
cold	*frío*
hot	*calor*
We are...	*Tenemos...*
sleepy	*sueño*
thirsty	*sed*
hungry	*hambre*

Work & Profession

Curious South Americans, from officials to casual acquaintances, will often want to know what travellers do for a living. If it's something that seems unusual (many would find it difficult to believe, for example, that a gardener could earn enough money to travel the world), it may be easiest to claim to be a student or teacher.

What do you do?
  ¿Qué hace?
What's your profession?
  ¿Cuál es su profesión?

I am a...	*So...*
student	*estudiante*
teacher	*profesor/a*
nurse	*enfermero/a*
lawyer	*abogado/a*
engineer	*ingeniero/a*
mechanic	*mecánico/a*

Can I take a photo?
  ¿Puedo sacar una foto?
of course/why not/sure
  por supuesto/cómo no/claro
How old are you?
  ¿Cuántos años tiene?
Do you speak English?
  ¿Habla inglés?
Could you repeat that?
  ¿Puede repetirlo?

Could you speak more slowly please?
  ¿Puede hablar más despacio por favor?
How does one say...?
  ¿Cómo se dice...?
What does... mean?
  ¿Que quiere decir...?

Family Matters

Families are very important in South America and people will generally ask you all about yours.

Are you married?
  ¿Es casado/a?
I am single.
  Soy soltero/a.
I am married.
  Soy casado/a.
Is your husband/wife here?
  ¿Está su esposo/a aquí?

If the conversation is more personal, the 'familiar' form is used:

How many children do you have?
  ¿Cuántos niños tienes?
How many brothers/sisters do you have?
  ¿Cuántos hermanos/hermanas tienes?
Do you have a boyfriend/girlfriend?
  ¿Tienes novio/a?

Accommodation

hotel	*hotel, pensión, residencial*
Is there...?	*¿Hay...?*
Are there...?	
single room	*habitación para una persona*
double room	*habitación doble*
What does it cost ?	*¿Cuanto cuesta?*
per night	*por noche*
full board	*pensión completa*
shared bath	*baño compartido*
private bath	*baño privado*
too expensive	*demasiado caro*
discount	*descuento*
cheaper	*más económico*
May I see it?	*¿Puedo verla?*
I don't like it.	*No me gusta.*
the bill	*la cuenta*

Toilets

The most common word for 'toilet' is *baño*, but *servicios sanitarios* ('services') is a frequent alternative. Men's toilets will usually bear a descriptive term such as *hombres*, *caballeros* or *varones*. Women's will be marked *señoras* or *damas*.

Transport

aeroplane	*avión*
train	*tren*
bus	*colectivo, micro, camión, omnibus, flota*
ship	*barco, buque*
car	*auto, carro, coche*
taxi	*taxi*
truck	*camión*
pick-up (truck)	*camioneta*
bicycle	*bicicleta*
motorcycle	*motocicleta* or *moto*
hitchhike	*hacer dedo*

I would like a ticket to...
  Quiero un boleto/pasaje a...
What's the fare to...?
  ¿Cuanto cuesta hasta...?
When does the next plane leave for...?
  ¿Cuando sale el próximo avión para...?
Is there a student/university discount?
  ¿Hay descuento estudiantil/universitario?

first/last	*primero/último*
1st/2nd class	*primera/segunda clase*
single (one-way)	*ida*
return (round trip)	*ida y vuelta*
sleeper	*camarote*
left luggage	*guardería, equipaje*

Around Town

tourist information	*oficina de turismo*
airport	*aeropuerto*
train station	*estación de ferrocarril*
bus terminal	*terminal de buses*
bathing resort	*balneario*

Post & Telecommunications

post office	*correo*
letter	*carta*
parcel	*paquete*
postcard	*postal*
airmail	*correo aéreo*
registered mail	*certificado*
stamps	*estampillas*
person to person	*persona a persona*
collect call	*cobro revertido*

Money

I want to change some money.
  Quiero cambiar dinero.
I want to change travellers' cheques.
  Quiero cambiar cheques de viajero.
What is the exchange rate?
  ¿Cuál es el tipo de cambio?
How many pesos/soles/sucres per dollar?
  ¿Cuántos pesos/soles/sucres por dólar?

cashier	*caja*
credit card	*tarjeta de crédito*
black market	*mercado negro* or *mecado paralelo*
banknote	*billete*
exchange houses	*casas de cambio*

Emergencies

Danger/Careful!	*¡Cuidado!*
Help!	*¡Socorro!*
Fire!	*¡Incendio!*
Thief!	*¡Ladrón!*
I've been robbed.	*Me robaron.*
They took...	*Se llevaron...*
my money	*mi dinero*
my passport	*mi pasaporte*
my bag	*mi bolso*
Where is...?	*¿Dónde hay...?*
a policeman	*un policía*
a doctor	*un médico*
a hospital	*un hospital*
Don't bother me!	*¡No me moleste!*
Go away!	*¡Déjeme!*
Go away! (stronger)	*¡Qué se vaya!*
Get lost!	*¡Váyase!*

Days

Monday	*lunes*
Tuesday	*martes*
Wednesday	*miércoles*
Thursday	*jueves*

Friday	*viernes*		10	*diez*
Saturday	*sábado*		11	*once*
Sunday	*domingo*		12	*doce*
			13	*trece*
Months			14	*catorce*
January	*enero*		15	*quince*
February	*febrero*		16	*dieciseis*
March	*marzo*		17	*diecisiete*
April	*abril*		18	*dieciocho*
May	*mayo*		19	*diecinueve*
June	*junio*		20	*veinte*
July	*julio*		21	*veintiuno*
August	*agosto*		22	*veintidós*
September	*septiembre/setiembre*		23	*veintitrés*
October	*octubre*		24	*veinticuatro*
November	*noviembre*		30	*treinta*
December	*diciembre*		31	*treinta y uno*
			32	*treinta y dos*
today	*hoy*		33	*treinta y tres*
this morning	*esta mañana*		40	*cuarenta*
this afternoon	*esta tarde*		41	*cuarenta y uno*
tonight	*esta noche*		42	*cuarenta y dos*
yesterday	*ayer*		50	*cincuenta*
tomorrow	*mañana*		60	*sesenta*
week/month/year	*semana/mes/año*		70	*setenta*
last week	*la semana pasada*		80	*ochenta*
next month	*el mes que viene*		90	*noventa*
always	*siempre*		100	*cien*
it's early/late	*es temprano/tarde*		101	*ciento uno*
now	*ahora*		102	*ciento dos*
before/after	*antes/después*		110	*ciento diez*
			120	*ciento veinte*
What time is it?			130	*ciento treinta*
¿Qué hora es?			200	*doscientos*
It is 1 o'clock.			300	*trescientos*
Es la una.			400	*cuatrocientos*
It is 7 o'clock.			500	*quinientos*
Son las siete.			600	*seiscientos*
			700	*setecientos*
			800	*ochocientos*
Cardinal Numbers			900	*novecientos*
1	*uno, una*		1000	*mil*
2	*dos*		1100	*mil cien*
3	*tres*		1200	*mil doscientos*
4	*cuatro*		2000	*dos mil*
5	*cinco*		5000	*cinco mil*
6	*seis*		10,000	*diez mil*
7	*siete*		50,000	*cincuenta mil*
8	*ocho*		100,000	*cien mil*
9	*nueve*		1,000,000	*un millón*

Ordinal Numbers

first	*primero*
second	*segundo*
third	*tercero*
fourth	*cuarto*
fifth	*quinto*
sixth	*sexto*
seventh	*séptimo*
eighth	*octavo*
ninth	*noveno, nono*
tenth	*décimo*
eleventh	*undécimo*
twelfth	*duodécimo*

Other Languages

Portuguese For information on Brazil's official language, see the Language entry in the Facts about the Country section of that chapter.

Indian Languages There are hundreds of different South American Indian languages, some of them spoken by very few people. In the Andean countries and parts of Chile and Argentina, however, millions of people speak Quechua and Aymara, and travellers may well come into contact with monolinguals in those languages.

Native English speakers may find grammar and pronunciation of these languages quite difficult. If you're serious about learning them, or will be spending a lot of time in remote areas, look around La Paz or Cuzco for a good course. Dictionaries and phrasebooks are available through Los Amigos del Libro and larger bookstores in La Paz, but the translations are in Spanish. Lonely Planet's *Quechua Phrasebook* is primarily for travellers to Peru, with grammar and vocabulary in the Cuzco dialect, but will also be useful for visitors to the Bolivian highlands.

The following list of words and phrases is obviously minimal, but it should be useful in areas where these languages are spoken. Pronounce them as you would a Spanish word. An apostrophe represents a glottal stop (the 'sound' in the middle of 'oh- oh!').

English	Aymara	Quechua
Where is...?	*Kaukasa...?*	*Maypi...?*
to the left	*chchekaru*	*lokeman*
to the right	*cupiru*	*pañaman*
How do you say...?	*Cun sañasauca'ha...?*	*Imainata nincha chaita...?*
It is called...	*Ucan sutipa'h...*	*Chaipa'g sutin'ha...*
Please repeat.	*Uastata sita.*	*Ua'manta niway.*
It's a pleasure.	*Take chuima'hampi.*	*Tucuy sokoywan.*
What does that mean?	*Cuna sañasa muniucha'ha?*	*Imata'nita munanchai'ja?*
I don't know.	*Janiwa yatkti.*	*Mana yachanichu.*
I am hungry.	*Mankatawa hiu'ta.*	*Yarkaimanta wañusianiña.*
How much?	*K'gauka?*	*Maik'ata'g?*
cheap	*pisitaqui*	*pisillapa'g*
condor	*malku*	*cóndor*
distant	*haya*	*caru*
downhill	*aynacha*	*uray*
father	*auqui*	*tata*
food	*manka*	*mikíuy*
friend	*kgochu*	*kgochu*
hello!	*laphi!*	*raphi!*
house	*uta*	*huasi*
I	*haya*	*ñoka*
llama	*yama-karhua*	*karhua*
lodging	*korpa*	*pascana*
man	*chacha*	*k'gari*

English	Aymara	Quechua
miner	koyiri	koya'g
moon	pha'gsi	kiya
mother	taica	mama
near	maka	kailla
no	janiwa	mana
river	jawira	mayu
ruins	champir	champir
snowy peak	kollu	riti-orko
sun	yinti	inti
teacher	yatichiri	yachachi'g
thirst	phara	chchaqui
trail	tapu	chakiñan
very near	hakítaqui	kaillitalla
water	uma	yacu
when?	cunapacha?	haiká'g?
woman	warmi	warmi
yes	jisa	ari
you	huma	khan
young	wuayna	huayna

English	Aymara	Quechua
1	maya	u'
2	paya	iskai
3	quimsa	quinsa
4	pusi	tahua
5	pesca	phiska
6	zo'hta	so'gta
7	pakalko	khanchis
8	quimsakalko	pusa'g
9	yatunca	iskon
10	tunca	chunca
11	tuncamayani	chunca u'niyo'g
12	tuncapayani	chuncaiskai'niyo'g
13	tuncaquimsani	chunca quinsa'niyo'g
14	tuncapusini	chunca tahua'yo'g
15	tuncapescani	chunca phiska'nio'g
16	tunca zo'htani	chunca so'gta'nio'g
17	tuncapakalkoni	chunca khanchisniyo'g
18	tunca quimsalalkoni	chunca pusa'gniyo'g
19	tunca yatuncani	chunca iskoniyo'g
20	pa tunka	iskai chunca

Facts for the Visitor

PLANNING
When to Go
When you go depends on what you want to do. Hikers and trekkers, for instance, will generally avoid the rainy season, which varies from country to country – in most of Peru, the winter months of June, July and August are the driest, while in Chile, the summer months of December, January and February are best. Visitors to the Southern Cone also find that longer summer days (around December) permit great flexibility in outdoor activities. Visitors from the northern hemisphere flock to Brazilian beaches in the northern winter, and many of them head to the country's famous Carnaval. Skiers will prefer the winter months, and those whose main interest is cities may find the season irrelevant. For more information, see the Climate section in the Facts about South America chapter, and the individual country chapters.

How Long?
For most travellers, South America is a remote destination which requires substantial expenditure just to get there, so budget travellers usually expect to stay for some time. Some can have a rewarding experience in only two weeks (generally staying in a single country or a relatively small area), but many stay for six months or longer. If you're using this book, you're probably a longer stayer, but good planning can make even a short trip worthwhile.

What to Bring
Travel light – overweight baggage soon becomes a nightmare, especially in hot weather. Official prejudice against backpacks has dissipated in recent years, so most budget travellers prefer them; internal frame packs are more suitable than those with external frames. If you travel very light, a bag with a shoulder strap is still easy to carry,

and perhaps more secure – a backpack is vulnerable to a thief with a razor.

Convertible backpacks, with straps which can be zipped away for convenience, are a good compromise, if they are robust. For long, dusty bus trips, carry a large, strong plastic bag or even a lockable duffel for the luggage compartment or roof.

Unless you're staying exclusively in the lowland tropics, bring a sleeping bag. Above 3000 metres, and at high latitudes in winter, nights get very cold; not all budget hotels provide enough blankets, and buses, trains and especially trucks are often unheated. If necessary, you can buy additional warm clothing at very reasonable prices in the Andean countries. A sheet sleeping bag can help keep you cool and discourage mosquitos in the tropics.

Some people take a small tent and portable stove, which give you greater independence in out-of-the-way places and expand your budget alternatives in the costlier Southern Cone. Hired equipment is available in popular trekking areas like Peru's Inca Trail, but if you want to camp regularly, you should bring your equipment with you.

Don't forget small essentials: a combination pocketknife or Swiss Army knife; needle, cotton and a small pair of scissors; a padlock; antimalarials; and one or two good long novels (English-language books are usually expensive). Most toiletries (toilet paper, toothpaste, shampoo, etc) are easily found in large cities and even small towns. Condoms (*presevativos*) are available in pharmacies. Virtually every small shop sells packets of washing powder just large enough for a pile of laundry.

Appearance & Conduct
Like the prejudice against backpacks, official discrimination against individuals of casual appearance has diminished in recent years, but foreign travellers should still try to be inconspicuous and not offend the local

standards of grooming and behavior. It is usually enough to be clean and neat but not formally dressed.

By local standards, even travellers of modest means may seem extraordinarily wealthy. Officials like the police and military, often poorly paid, may resent this casual affluence. Treat such individuals with a proper respect even in difficult situations, and avoid flaunting goods like cameras, watches, jewellery, etc – which can also attract thieves and robbers.

Highlights

The following list includes some of South America's best-known tourist attractions and some lesser, but still deserving, ones. The list starts in the north and works south.

Cartagena
This Colombian port on the Caribbean is one of the continent's great colonial treasures.

Angel Falls (Salto Angel)
Nearly 1000 metres in height, Venezuela's greatest tourist attraction is difficult to reach but worth the effort.

Kaieteur Falls
In the midst of nearly pristine rain forest in the interior of Guyana, Kaieteur falls a precipitous 250 metres in a single cascade.

St Laurent du Maroni
Before being sent to Devil's Island, Dreyfus and Papillon were processed as prisoners in this colonial town in French Guiana.

Galápagos Islands
Charles Darwin's biological laboratory, which inspired *The Origin of Species*, is 1000 km off the coast of Ecuador.

Machu Picchu
Everyone visits it, and it's less significant in archaeological terms than many other Peruvian sites, but it's still one of the continent's most spectacular sights. The three-day trek from the railroad to the ruins is a great attraction for budget travellers.

Salvador da Bahia
Brazil's first capital has a wealth of stunning colonial architecture and one of the country's liveliest Carnavals.

Gran Pantanal
For accessibility and wildlife, this subtropical marshland in southern Brazil is far superior to the Amazon.

Iguazú Falls
Despite the increasing commercialisation of the surrounding area, this is still one of the continent's most breathtaking sights.

Esteros del Iberá
Some travellers find this marshland in Argentina's Corrientes province even more appealing than the Pantanal.

Colonia
This small Uruguayan port, on the Río de La Plata, has the finest colonial remains in southern South America.

Juan Fernández Archipelago
Some 600 km west of Valparaíso, the Juan Fernández Islands were home to castaway Alexander Selkirk (the model for Daniel Defoe's Robinson Crusoe); they are also a storehouse of biological diversity.

Easter Island (Rapa Nui)
The enigmatic monuments of this remote island have long excited the Western imagination.

Chilean Fjords
Despite the difficulties of getting a passage, and rough conditions on the voyage, the boat trip from Puerto Montt to Puerto Natales (or viceversa) is the most spectacular on the continent.

Moreno Glacier
In southern Argentina, one of the world's few advancing glaciers is even more awesome when the lake behind it causes it to burst, at regular intervals (about every four years).

Torres del Paine
South America's finest national park is a miniature Alaska.

Falkland Islands (Islas Malvinas)
Despite bad publicity for its fickle climate and the 1982 war, this is the best place in the world to see Antarctic wildlife without actually going to Antarctica.

Tourist Traps

South America has its share of gaudy and costly tourist traps, or places that are simply distasteful or overrated. Like the previous list, this one starts in the north and works south.

Barranquilla
This dirty, dangerous port on Colombia's Caribbean coast has at least taken some of the development pressures off Cartagena.

Manaus
Uncontrolled growth has obliterated the shabby tropical charm of Brazil's great Amazonian port, which merits only a brief visit in its own right.

Oruro

    This Bolivian altiplano mining town is one of the coldest places on the continent – in terms of both its climate and its welcome to visitors.

Punta del Este

    Uruguay's Atlantic coastline is a treasure, but this overbuilt enclave for wealthy Argentines is no place to stay – try nearby Maldonado instead.

Mar del Plata

    Wealthy Argentines (see Punta del Este, above) have abandoned this summer madhouse, where hundred of thousands of middle-class tourists jam the beaches in January and February. If you must come, wait until March.

Calafate

    By all means visit Argentina's Moreno Glacier, but get in and out of this overpriced, but unavoidable, encampment of rapacious merchants as quickly as possible.

DOCUMENTS

Visas

A visa is a passport endorsement, usually a stamp, permitting you to enter a country and remain for a specified time. It is obtained from a foreign embassy or consulate of that country. If it's convenient, get them in your home country, but it's often possible to get them en route, especially if your itinerary is not fixed. Ask other travellers about the best places to get them, since two consulates of the same country may enforce different requirements: the fee (if any) might vary, one might want to see your money or an onward ticket while another might not ask, or one might issue them on the spot while another might take days to do so.

Visa requirements are given in the Facts for the Visitor section of individual country chapters. If you know you need a visa for a certain country and arrive without one, you may have to return to the nearest consulate for a visa before being admitted. Authorities sometimes issue visas at the border, but take nothing for granted.

Nationals of most European countries and Japan require few visas, but travellers from the USA need some and those from Australia and New Zealand need quite a few. You might carry a handful of photographs for visa applications, but even small border towns usually have a photographer who can shoot and develop them in a few minutes.

'Sufficient Funds' Getting visas is generally routine, but officials may ask, either verbally or on the application form, about your financial resources. If you lack 'sufficient funds' for your proposed length of stay (either at the consulate or at the border), officials may limit your stay, but once in the country, you can usually renew or extend your visa by showing a wad of travellers' cheques.

Onward/Return Tickets Several countries require you to have a ticket out of the country before granting you a visa, or admitting you at the border. This onward (or return) ticket requirement is a major nuisance for budget travellers, especially overlanders. Peru, Colombia, Venezuela, Brazil, Suriname, Guyana and French Guiana presently demand this, though enforcement is sometimes sporadic. This creates no problems if you plan to leave the country from your point of arrival, but if you want to enter at one point and leave at another, you may need an onward ticket.

It is no longer easy to evade this requirement by purchasing an MCO (Miscellaneous Charges Order), a document which looks like an airline ticket but can be refunded in cash or credited towards a specific flight with any IATA carrier. Most consular and immigration officials no longer accept an MCO as an onward ticket, so you may have to buy a refundable onward or return ticket; look for the cheapest available and be sure you can get a refund without waiting months. Don't forget to ask specifically where you can get a refund, as some airlines will only refund tickets at the office of purchase or at their head office.

Travellers from Costa Rica or Panama to Colombia or Venezuela cannot even buy a one-way ticket without also buying an onward ticket, and so must work out where to go after leaving Colombia or Venezuela.

You may be able to circumvent the onward ticket requirement by showing enough money for a ticket home, as well as sufficient funds for your stay. Having a recognised, international credit card might help.

Other Documents

The essential documents are a passport and an International Health Certificate. If you already have a passport, make sure it's valid for a reasonably long period of time (at least six months beyond the projected end of your trip) and has plenty of blank pages for stamp-happy officials. A government health department, your physician or the doctor who gives you your vaccinations can provide the Health Certificate.

If you're planning to drive anywhere, obtain an International Driving Permit or Inter-American Driving Permit (Uruguay theoretically recognises only the latter). For about US$10, any motoring organisation will issue one on presentation of a current state or national driving licence.

An International Student Identity Card (ISIC) is useful in some places for reductions on admission charges to archaeological sites and museums. At times, it will also entitle you to reductions on bus, train and air tickets, though it's less useful in Latin America than in Africa, the Middle East or Asia. In some countries, such as Argentina, almost any form of university identification will suffice. It's sometimes possible to obtain an ISIC card if you book a flight with one of the 'bucket shop' ticket agencies that have proliferated in certain cities in Europe and North America. Another possibility is to buy a fake card (average price around US$10), but examine them carefully if you decide to buy one, as they vary in quality.

A Youth Hostels Association (YHA) membership card can be useful in Chile, Argentina and Uruguay, where accommodation costs tend to be higher, though not all hostels require membership.

MONEY

It is preferable to bring money in US dollars, though banks and *casas de cambio* (exchange houses) in capital cities will change pounds sterling, German marks, Japanese yen and other major currencies. Changing these currencies in smaller towns and on the street can be next to impossible.

Travellers' Cheques

Travellers' cheques are the safest way to carry money. American Express, Thomas Cook, Citibank and Visa are among the best-known brands and, in most cases, offer instant replacement in case of loss or theft. Cheques issued by smaller banks with limited international affiliations may be difficult to cash, especially in more remote areas. To facilitate replacement in case of theft, keep a record of cheque numbers and the original bill of sale in a safe place. Even with proper records, replacement can take time – too many travellers have been selling cheques on the black market, or simply pretending to lose them and then demanding replacement.

Have plenty of small denomination travellers' cheques – US$20 and US$50. If you carry only large denominations, you might find yourself stuck with a large amount of local currency on leaving a country, which can only be reconverted at a poor rate of exchange.

In some countries, notably Argentina, travellers' cheques are increasingly difficult to cash and banks and cambios charge commissions as high as 10%. For this reason, travellers to Argentina and rural areas of some other countries may wish to consider cash dollars.

Cash

Carry some cash, because it's easier to change in small places or when banks are closed. It's also more convenient to change some small dollar bills just before leaving a country than a US$20 or US$50 travellers' cheque. Cash is also convenient when there's a black market, parallel market or unofficial exchange rate. On the other hand, it is riskier to carry cash than travellers' cheques – nobody will give you a refund for lost or stolen cash.

In some countries, like Chile and Uruguay, you can exchange US dollar travellers' cheques for cash dollars at banks and cambios, in order to top up on cash from time to time. In Argentina, cash is particularly preferable, as travellers' cheques are difficult to negotiate and carry very high commissions, while the hazards of carrying cash are relatively minor, because Argentina is one of the safest countries on the continent.

Credit Cards

Credit cards can be very useful in a pinch. As automatic teller machines become more widespread, some travellers are carrying fewer travellers' cheques and withdrawing cash from machines as they need it. Some banks will also issue cash advances on major credit cards. The most widely accepted are Visa and Mastercard (those with UK Access should insist on their affiliation to Mastercard). American Express, Diner's Club and others are also valid in many places.

Credit cards can also be used to pay shop, hotel and restaurant bills, but users should note two points. Firstly, in some countries (notably Argentina), businesses may add a surcharge (*recargo*) of 10% or more to credit card purchases, so ask first. Alternatively, merchants may give a discount of 10% or more for cash purchases. Secondly, the amount you have to pay depends on the exchange rate at the time of posting the overseas charge to your account at home, which can be weeks later. If the overseas currency is depreciating, the amount on your credit card account will be less than the dollar cost you calculated at the time of purchase; a strengthening currency in the country of the purchase will mean the cost in dollars (or other foreign currency) will be greater than you expected.

Exchange Rates

The unofficial exchange rate for the US dollar can be much higher than the bank rate, because official rates do not always reflect the market value of local currency. Official rates may be artificially high for political reasons, or may not be adjusted sufficiently for inflation, which sometimes reaches 50% per month.

The unofficial rate is often known as the *mercado negro* (black market) or *mercado paralelo* (parallel market). In some coun-

tries, like Brazil, you can obtain the current street rate at cambios or travel agencies. In other countries, you can change money at hotels or in shops which sell imported goods (electronics dealers are an obvious choice).

If you change money on the street, observe a few precautions. Be discreet, as it's often illegal, though it may be tolerated. Have the exact amount handy, to avoid pulling out large wads of notes. Beware of sleight-of-hand tricks – insist on personally counting out the notes you are handed one by one, and don't hand over your dollars until satisfied you have the exact amount agreed upon. One common trick is to hand you the agreed amount, less a few pesos, so that, on counting it, you will complain that it's short. They take it back, recount it, discover the 'mistake', top it up and hand it back, in the process spiriting away all but one of the largest bills. For certainty, recount it yourself and don't be distracted by supposed alarms like 'police' or 'danger'.

In recent years, inflation in the region has subsided from previously astronomical levels (except in Brazil), but prices can still be unpredictable. A currency devaluation means that local prices drop in relation to hard currencies like the US dollar, but normally local prices soon rise, so dollar costs soon return to previous levels (or higher). These factors make it difficult to quote prices in local currencies, but one thing is certain: if a hotel or restaurant was cheap before price increases, it's still going to be cheap afterwards, relative to other hotels and restaurants. Prices tend to be more stable in terms of US dollars, so prices have been quoted in dollars throughout most of this book.

Money Transfers

If you're out of money, ask your bank at home to send a draft, specifying the city, the bank and the branch of destination. Cable transfers should arrive in a few days, but you can run into complications, even with supposedly reliable banks. Mail drafts will take at least two weeks and often longer. Some banks delay releasing transferred money because they earn interest on hard currency deposits.

Some countries will let you have your money in US dollars, while others will only release it in local currency. Be certain before you arrange the transfer – otherwise, you could lose a fair amount of money if there's a major gap between official and unofficial exchange rates. Bolivia, Ecuador, Chile and Uruguay will let you have all your money in dollars, but regulations change frequently, so ask for the latest information.

If you find yourself penniless, you'll have to find a job or go to your nearest embassy for repatriation. If you are repatriated, many embassies will confiscate your passport and hold it until you repay the debt – and they'll fly you back in full-fare tourist class. French embassies don't usually repatriate their citizens and US embassies rarely do so.

Carrying Money

Everyone has a preferred way to carry money. Some use money belts, others have hidden pockets inside their trousers, or leg pouches with elastic bands, and others hang a pouch round their neck. Leather money belts, which appear from the outside to be ordinary belts, seem to be effective but their capacity is limited.

If you use a neck pouch, incorporate a length of guitar string into the strap so that it can't be cut without alerting you. All the same, there's no substitute for keeping your wits about you.

Bargaining

Probably the only things you'll have to haggle over are long-term accommodation and purchases from markets, especially craft goods whose prices are normally very negotiable. Haggling is the norm in the Andean countries, but in the Southern Cone, it's much less common. Patience, humour and an ability to speak the local language will make the process more enjoyable and productive.

POST & TELECOMMUNICATIONS
Sending Mail
Sending parcels home can be awkward, as often a customs officer must inspect the contents before a postal clerk can accept them. In Peru and Bolivia, the parcel must also be finally stitched up in linen before the clerk can accept it. In some countries, the place for posting overseas parcels is different from the main post office.

Receiving Mail
The simplest way of receiving mail is to have letters sent to you c/o 'Lista de Correos', followed by the name of the city and country where you plan to be. Mail addressed in this way will always be sent to that city's main post office. In most places, the service is free, but in Argentina, it's very expensive; try to use a hotel or private address if possible. American Express operates a mail service for clients, including those who use American Express travellers' cheques.

Some embassies will hold mail for their citizens, among them Australia, Canada, Germany, Israel and Switzerland. British and US embassies are very poor in this regard; letters addressed to a British embassy will be sent to the main post office.

To collect mail from a post office, American Express office or embassy, you need to produce identification, preferably a passport. Most post offices hold mail for a month or two, then return it to the country of origin or toss it into the incinerator.

If expected correspondence does not arrive, ask the clerk to check under every possible combination of your initials, even 'M' (for Mr, Ms, etc). There may be particular confusion if correspondents use your middle name, since Spanish Americans use both paternal and maternal surnames for identification, with the former listed first. Thus a letter to Chilean 'Augusto Pinochet Ugarte' will be filed under 'P' rather than 'U', while a letter to North American 'Ronald Wilson Reagan' may be found under 'W' even though 'Reagan' is the proper surname. Note that in Brazil, the maternal surname is listed first.

Telephone
Traditionally, governments have operated

systems and, traditionally, services have been wretched. Several countries have recently privatised their phone systems, choosing high rates over poor service (sometimes getting both), but direct overseas lines have made international calls, at least, much simpler. More often than not, it is cheaper to make a collect (reverse-charge) or credit card call to Europe or North America than to pay for the call at the source. For more detail, see individual country chapters.

Fax, Telex & Telegraph
These telecommunications services are sometimes private, sometimes still state-run. For more detail, see individual country chapters.

HEALTH
Travel health depends on predeparture preparations, your day-to-day health care while travelling, and how you handle any medical problem or emergency that does develop. While the list of potential dangers can seem quite frightening, with a little luck, basic precautions and adequate information, few travellers experience more than upset stomachs.

Travel Health Guide Books
Probably the best all-round guide is *Staying Healthy in Asia, Africa & Latin America* (Volunteers in Asia). It's compact but very detailed and well organised. Dr Richard Dawood's *Travellers' Health* (Oxford, 1989) is comprehensive, easy to read, authoritative and highly recommended, but rather large to lug around. David Werner's *Where There is No Doctor* (Hesperian Foundation) is a very detailed guide, more suited to those working in undeveloped countries than to travellers.

Travel with Children, by Maureen Wheeler (Lonely Planet), offers basic advice on travel health for younger children.

Pre-Departure Preparations
Health Insurance A travel insurance policy covering theft, loss and medical problems is a wise idea. There is a wide variety of policies and your travel agent will have

recommendations. The international student travel policies handled by STA or student travel organisations are usually good value. Some offer lower and higher medical expenses options, but the higher one is mostly for countries with extremely high medical costs, like the USA. Check the small print:

1 Some policies specifically exclude 'dangerous activities' like scuba diving, motorcycling, and even trekking. If these activities are on your agenda avoid this sort of policy.
2 You may prefer a policy which pays doctors or hospitals direct, rather than you having to pay first and claim later. If you have to claim later, keep all documentation. Some policies ask you to call back (reverse charges) to a centre in your home country for an immediate assessment of your problem.
3 Check whether the policy covers ambulance fees or an emergency flight home. If you have to stretch out, you will need two seats, and somebody has to pay for it!

Medical Kit It's useful to carry a small, straightforward medical kit. This should include:

1 Aspirin or panadol, for pain or fever;
2 Antihistamine (such as Benadryl), which is useful as a decongestant for colds, and to ease the itch from allergies, insect bites or stings, or to help prevent motion sickness;
3 Antibiotics, which are useful for travelling off the beaten track, but they must be prescribed and you should carry the prescription with you;
4 Kaolin preparation (Pepto-Bismol), Imodium or Lomotil, for stomach upsets;
5 Rehydration mixture, to treat severe diarrhoea, which is particularly important if travelling with children;
6 Antiseptic, mercurochrome and antibiotic powder or similar 'dry' spray, for cuts and grazes;
7 Calamine lotion, to ease irritation from bites or stings;
8 Bandages, for minor injuries;
9 Scissors, tweezers and a thermometer (airlines prohibit mercury thermometers);
10 Insect repellent, sunscreen lotion, chapstick and water purification tablets.

Ideally, antibiotics should be administered only under medical supervision and should never be taken indiscriminately, as they are quite specific to the infections they can treat. Overuse of antibiotics can weaken your body's ability to deal with infections naturally and can reduce the drug's efficacy. Take only the recommended dose at the prescribed intervals, and continue taking it for the prescribed period, even if the illness seems to be cured earlier. Stop taking antibiotics immediately if you have any serious reactions, and don't use them at all if you are not sure that you have the correct one.

In many countries, if a medicine is available at all, it will generally be available over the counter and the price will be much cheaper than in Europe or North America. However, check expiry dates and try to determine whether storage conditions have been adequate. In some cases, drugs which are no longer recommended, or have even been banned elsewhere, are still being dispensed in Third World countries.

Immunisations For some countries, no immunisations are necessary, but more precautions are necessary off the beaten track. Vaccination as an entry requirement is usually only enforced for arrivals from an infected area – yellow fever and cholera are the two most likely requirements. All vaccinations should be recorded on an International Health Certificate.

Plan ahead for vaccinations; some require an initial shot followed by a booster, while others should not be given together. Most travellers from Europe or North America will have had immunisations against various diseases during childhood, but doctors may still recommend boosters against measles or polio, which are still prevalent in some countries. Smallpox has now been wiped out worldwide, so immunisation is no longer necessary. The period of protection offered by vaccinations differs widely, and some are contraindicated for pregnant women.

In some countries, immunisations are available from airport or government health centres. Travel agents or airline offices will also tell you where you can get immunisations. The possible list of vaccinations includes:

Yellow Fever Protection lasts 10 years and is recommended for South America, where the disease is endemic. Now more widely available, this vaccination is contraindicated during pregnancy but probably advisable if you must travel to a high-risk area.

Tetanus Protection is highly recommended. Initial protection requires two doses, four to six weeks apart, followed by another dose after six to 12 months. Boosters are necessary every 10 years.

Diphtheria Protection is recommended, especially for children. The vaccine is usually given in conjunction with tetanus vaccine.

Typhoid Protection lasts for three years and is recommended if you are travelling for more than two or three weeks in rural, tropical areas. Initial protection requires two doses about four weeks apart. You may get some side effects, such as pain where you received the injection, fever, headache and general malaise.

Infectious Hepatitis Gamma globulin is not a vaccination but a ready-made antibody which has proved very successful in reducing the chances of hepatitis infection. Because it may interfere with the development of immunity, it should not be given until at least 10 days after administration of the last vaccine needed; it should also be given as close as possible to departure because its effectiveness lasts only about six months.

Cholera Cholera vaccination is not obligatory for South America, is not very effective, and lasts only six months, but some travellers may want to consider it because of recent outbreaks of the disease. Pregnant women should definitely avoid cholera vaccination.

Malaria Prophylaxis Chloroquine is the usual prophylactic; take a tablet once a week for two weeks before arriving in the infected area and for six weeks after leaving it. If you are travelling in an area infected with Chloroquine-resistant strains, which have been reported in the upper Amazon Basin and coastal Ecuador, supplement Chloroquine with a weekly dose of Maloprim or a daily dose of Proguanil. Chloroquine should be a satisfactory preventative in the other risk areas: the three Guianas; rural areas of Paraguay, Venezuela, Peru and northern Argentina; and lowland Bolivia, Colombia and Ecuador. For more information about malaria, see Insect-Borne Diseases on page 59.

Other Preparations Make sure you're healthy before travelling. If embarking on a

long trip, make sure your teeth are OK; there are lots of places where a visit to the dentist would be the last thing you'd want to do. If you wear glasses, take a extra pair and your prescription. Losing your glasses can be a real problem, though in many places, you can get new spectacles made up quickly, cheaply and competently.

If you require special medication which may not be available locally, carry an adequate supply. Take the prescription, with the generic rather than the brand name, as it will make getting replacements easier. It's a wise idea to have the prescription with you to show that you use the medication legally, as over-the-counter drugs from one place may be illegal without a prescription, or even banned, in another.

Basic Rules
A normal body temperature is 37°C or 98.6°F; more than 2°C higher is a 'high' fever. A normal adult pulse rate is 60 to 80 per minute (children 80 to 100, babies 100 to 140). You should know how to take a temperature and a pulse rate. As a general rule, the pulse increases about 20 beats per minute for each 1°C rise in fever.

Your respiration rate can also be an indicator of illness. Count the number of breaths per minute: from 12 to 20 is normal for adults and older children, up to 30 for younger children, and 40 for babies. People with high fever or serious respiratory illnesses like pneumonia (acute lung infection) breathe more quickly than normal. Over 40 shallow breaths a minute usually means pneumonia.

Many health problems can be avoided by basic hygiene. Wash your hands frequently, as it's quite easy to contaminate your own food. Clean your teeth with purified water rather than tap water. Avoid climatic extremes: avoid the sun when it's hot, dress warmly when it's cold. It is also important to dress sensibly. You can get worm infections from walking barefoot and dangerous coral cuts from walking over coral barefoot. Avoid insect bites by covering bare skin when insects are around, by screening windows or beds and by using insect repellents. Seek local advice: if you're told the water is unsafe because of jellyfish, crocodiles or bilharzia, don't go in. In situations where there is no information, play it safe.

Nutrition Take care in what you eat and drink, and make sure your diet is balanced. As your stomach becomes accustomed to South American microbes, you will have fewer problems and can explore the culinary possibilities with more daring. If your diet is poor or limited, if you're travelling hard and fast and therefore missing meals, or if you simply lose your appetite, you can soon start to lose weight and place your health at risk.

Eggs, beans and nuts are all safe ways to get protein. Fruit you can peel (bananas, oranges or mandarins, for example) is always safe and a good source of vitamins. Try to eat plenty of grains, like rice and bread. Remember that though well-cooked food is generally safer, overcooked food loses much of its nutritional value. If your diet isn't well balanced or if your food intake is insufficient, it's a good idea to take vitamin and iron pills. Drink lots of water if you take iron pills, as they can cause constipation.

In hot climates, make sure you drink enough – always carry a water bottle on long trips and don't depend on thirst to indicate when you should drink. Not needing to urinate or dark yellow urine is a danger sign. Excessive sweating can lead to loss of salt and therefore muscle cramping. Salt tablets are not a good idea as a preventative but, in places where salt is not used much, adding salt to food can help.

Drink Most cities have adequately treated tap water, but outside these areas, avoid unboiled water or ice, especially during the rainy season in tropical areas. Rivers can be contaminated by communities living upstream, so if you're walking in the mountains, drink only from springs or small streams. Unboiled water is a major source of diarrhoea and hepatitis.

Take care with fruit juice, particularly if water may have been added. Milk should also be treated with suspicion, as it is often unpasteurised. Where possible, stick to tea, *mate* (Paraguayan tea), coffee, mineral water and other soft drinks, or beer.

The best way to purify water is to boil it, about five minutes at sea level or longer at higher altitudes. Purification tablets like Halazone or Sterotab are effective against most micro-organisms but not against amoebic dysentery, for which you need an iodine-based steriliser like Potable Aqua. Alternatively, shake two or three drops of tincture of iodine (2%) in a litre of water, letting it stand for about 20 minutes. Iodised water has a strong and often unpleasant taste.

Food Salads and fruit should be washed with purified water or peeled where possible. Ice cream is usually OK if it is a reputable brand name, but beware of street vendors and of ice cream that has melted and been refrozen. Thoroughly cooked food is safest, but not if it has been left to cool or has been reheated. Take great care with shellfish or fish, which can be sources of cholera, and avoid undercooked meat. See individual country chapters for additional information.

Medical Problems & Treatment

Potential medical problems can be broken down into several areas: extremes of temperature, altitude or motion; insanitation; insect bites or stings; animal or human contact; and simple cuts, bites or scratches. South America has such a range of climates and conditions that travellers will encounter a wide variety of health problems, from heat exhaustion to hypothermia, coral cuts to altitude sickness. Don't be alarmed, but be aware.

Self-diagnosis and treatment can be risky, so seek qualified help if possible. Treatment dosages indicated in this section are for emergency use only. Seek medical advice before administering any drugs.

Embassies and consulates can usually recommend a good place to go for such advice. So can five-star hotels, which often recommend doctors with five-star prices (this is when medical insurance is really useful!).

Heat Exhaustion & Sunburn In the tropics, the sun's nearly direct rays can be devastating, especially at high altitude, and dehydration can be a very serious problem. Drink plenty of liquids and cover exposed body parts with light cotton clothing. Use salt tablets, quality sunglasses, and a broad-brimmed hat or baseball cap. Damage to the ozone layer may have increased the level of ultraviolet radiation in southern South America, so protection from the sun is especially important.

Heat Stroke Long, continuous periods of exposure to high temperatures can leave you vulnerable to this serious, sometimes fatal, condition, which occurs when the body's heat-regulating mechanism breaks down and body temperature rises to dangerous levels. Avoid excessive alcohol intake or strenuous activity when you first arrive in a hot climate.

Symptoms include feeling unwell, lack of perspiration and a high body temperature (39°C to 41°C). When sweating ceases, the skin becomes flushed and red. Severe, throbbing headaches and lack of coordination will also occur, and victims may become confused or aggressive. Eventually, they become delirious or go into convulsions. Hospitalisation is essential, but meanwhile, get them out of the sun, remove their clothing, cover them with a wet sheet or towel, and fan them continually.

Prickly Heat Prickly heat, an itchy rash caused by excessive perspiration trapped under the skin, usually strikes people who have just arrived in a hot climate and whose pores have not yet opened sufficiently to cope with greater sweating. Keeping cool, bathing often, using a mild talcum powder or even resorting to air-conditioning may help until you acclimatise.

Fungal Infections Hot weather fungal infections are most likely to occur on the scalp, between the toes or fingers (athlete's foot), in the groin (jock itch or crotch rot) and on the body (ringworm). You get ringworm (a fungal infection, not literally a worm) from infected animals or by walking on damp areas, like shower floors.

To prevent fungal infections, wear loose, comfortable clothes, avoid artificial fibres, wash frequently and dry carefully. If infected, wash the area daily with a disinfectant or medicated soap and water, and rinse and dry well. Apply an antifungal powder like the widely available Tinaderm. Try to expose the infected area to air or sunlight as much as possible. Wash all towels and underwear in hot water and change them often.

Hypothermia At high altitudes in the mountains or high latitudes in Patagonia, cold and wet can kill. Changeable weather can leave you vulnerable to exposure: after dark, temperatures can drop from balmy to below freezing, while a sudden soaking and high winds can lower your own body temperature so rapidly that you may not survive. Disorientation, physical exhaustion, hunger, shivering and related symptoms are warnings that you should seek warmth, shelter and food. If possible, avoid travelling alone; partners are more likely to avoid hypothermia successfully. If you must travel alone, especially when hiking, be sure someone knows your route and when you expect to return.

Seek shelter when bad weather is unavoidable. Woollen clothing and synthetics, which retain warmth even when wet, are superior to cottons. A quality sleeping bag is a worthwhile investment, though goose down loses much of its insulating quality when wet. Carry high-energy, easily digestible snacks such as chocolate or dried fruit.

Altitude Sickness At elevations above 3000 metres and sometimes even lower, altitude sickness (*apunamiento* or *soroche*) represents a potential health hazard. In the thinner atmosphere, lack of oxygen causes many individuals to suffer headaches, nausea, shortness of breath, physical weakness and other symptoms which can lead to very serious consequences, especially if combined with heat exhaustion, sunburn or hypothermia.

Most people recover within a few hours or days as their bodies produce more red blood cells to absorb oxygen, but if symptoms persist, it is imperative to descend to lower elevations. Avoid smoking, drinking alcohol, eating heavily or exercising strenuously.

For mild cases, everyday painkillers such as aspirin, or *chachacoma*, a herbal tea made from a common Andean shrub, will relieve symptoms until your body adapts.

Another excellent remedy is *mate de coca* (tea made from coca leaves), which you can get in most cafés in Peru and Bolivia. You can also buy leaves legally for US$4 to US$5 per kilo in *tiendas* (small general stores) throughout Peru and Bolivia, or from the herbal stalls found in every market. The practice of chewing coca leaves goes back centuries and is still common among the Indians of the Andean altiplano to dull the pangs of hunger, thirst, cold and fatigue. They chew the leaves with a little ash or bicarbonate of soda, as the alkalinity releases the mild stimulant.

Motion Sickness Eating lightly before and during a trip will reduce the chances of motion sickness. If you are prone to motion sickness, try to find a place that minimises disturbance, for example, near the wing on aircraft, close to midships on boats, near the centre on buses. Fresh air usually helps, while reading or cigarette smoke don't. Commercial antimotion sickness preparations, which can cause drowsiness, have to be taken before the trip commences; when you're feeling sick, it's too late. Ginger, a natural preventative, is available in capsule form.

Diseases of Insanitation

Diarrhoea Stomach problems can arise from dietary changes – they doesn't necessarily mean you've caught something. Introduce yourself gradually to exotic and/or highly spiced foods.

Avoid rushing to the pharmacy and gulping antibiotics at the first signs. The best thing to do is to avoid eating and to rest, drink plenty of liquids (tea or herbal solutions, without sugar or milk). Many cafés serve excellent camomile tea *(agua de manzanilla)*; otherwise, try mineral water *(agua mineral)*. About 24 to 48 hours should do the trick, but if symptoms persist, see a doctor. If you must eat, keep to bland foods like yoghurt, lemon juice and boiled vegetables.

After a severe bout of diarrhoea or dysentery (see below), you will probably be dehydrated, with painful cramps. Relieve these with fruit juices or tea, with a tiny bit of dissolved salt. Lomotil or Imodium can relieve the symptoms, but not actually cure them. For children, Imodium is preferable, but do not use such drugs in cases of high fever or severe dehydration.

Antibiotics can help treat severe diarrhoea, especially if accompanied by nausea, vomiting, stomach cramps or mild fever. Ordinary 'traveller's diarrhoea' rarely lasts more than a few days; if it lasts over a week, you must get treatment, start taking antibiotics or see a doctor.

Giardia This intestinal parasite is present in contaminated water. The symptoms are stomach cramps, nausea, a bloated stomach, watery, foul-smelling diarrhoea and frequent gas. Giardia can appear several weeks after exposure to the parasite. Symptoms may disappear for a few days and then return; this can go on for several weeks. Metronidazole, also known as Flagyl, is the recommended drug, but should only be taken under medical supervision. Antibiotics are of no use.

Dysentery This serious illness, caused by contaminated food or water, is characterised by severe diarrhoea, often with blood or mucus in the stool.

There are two kinds of dysentery. Bacillary dysentery is characterised by a high fever and rapid development; headache, vomiting and stomach pains are also symptoms. It generally lasts no longer than a week, but is highly contagious. Amoebic dysentery develops more gradually and causes no fever or vomiting, but will persist until treated and can recur and cause long-term damage.

A stool test is necessary to diagnose which kind of dysentery you have, so seek medical help urgently. In case of emergency, note that tetracycline is the prescribed treatment for bacillary dysentery and metronidazole for amoebic dysentery.

With tetracycline, the recommended adult dosage is one 250 mg capsule four times daily. Children aged between eight and 12 years should have half the adult dose; younger children should have a third of the adult dose. Remember that tetracycline should not be given to young children unless absolutely necessary, and only for a short period; pregnant women should not take it after the fourth month of pregnancy.

With metronidazole, the recommended adult dosage is one 750 mg to 800 mg capsule three times daily for five days. Children aged eight to 12 years should have half the adult dose; younger children should have a third of the adult dose.

Viral Gastroenteritis Caused, as the name suggests, by a virus, this is characterised by stomach cramps, diarrhoea and, sometimes, vomiting and a slight fever. All you can do is rest and drink lots of fluids.

Hepatitis Hepatitis A, the more common form of this disease, is spread by contaminated food or water. The first symptoms are fever, chills, headache, fatigue, feelings of weakness and aches and pains. This is followed by loss of appetite, nausea, vomiting, abdominal pain, dark urine, light-coloured faeces and jaundiced skin; the whites of the eyes may also turn yellow. In some cases, there may just be a feeling of being unwell or tired, accompanied by loss of appetite, aches and pains and jaundice. Seek medical advice, but in general, there is not much you can do apart from resting, drinking lots of

fluids, eating lightly and avoiding fatty foods. Gamma globulin as a prophylactic is effective against this form of hepatitis. People who have had hepatitis must forego alcohol for six months after the illness, as hepatitis attacks the liver, which needs that time to recover.

Hepatitis B, formerly called serum hepatitis, is spread through sexual contact or skin penetration – it can be transmitted through dirty needles or blood transfusions, for instance. Avoid having injections, ear piercing or tattoos if you have doubts about the sanitary conditions. Symptoms and treatment of type B are much the same as for type A, but gamma globulin is ineffective against type B.

Typhoid Typhoid fever is another intestinal infection that travels the fecal-oral route. Contaminated water and food are responsible. Vaccination is not totally effective, and since typhoid is one of the most dangerous infections, medical help must be sought.

In its early stages, typhoid resembles many other illnesses: sufferers may feel like they have a bad cold or flu, as early symptoms are a headache, a sore throat and a fever which rises a little each day until it is around 40°C or more. The victim's pulse is often slow relative to the degree of fever and gets slower as the fever rises, unlike a normal fever where the pulse increases. There may also be vomiting, diarrhoea or constipation.

In the second week, the high fever and slow pulse continue and a few pink spots may appear on the body; trembling, delirium, weakness, weight loss and dehydration are other symptoms. If there are no further complications, the fever and other symptoms will slowly go during the third week. However, you must get medical help before this, because typhoid is very infectious and because pneumonia or peritonitis are common complications.

The fever should be treated by keeping the victim cool; also beware dehydration. Chloramphenicol is the recommended antibiotic, but there are fewer side effects with ampicillin. The adult dosage is two 250 mg capsules, four times a day. Children from eight to 12 years should take half the adult dose; younger children should have a third of the adult dose.

Worms These parasites are common in the rural humid tropics. They can be present on unwashed vegetables or in undercooked meat and you can pick them up through your skin by walking in bare feet. Infestations may not show up for some time, and although they are generally not serious, they can cause severe health problems if left untreated. A stool test is necessary to pinpoint the problem and medication is often available over the counter.

Diseases Spread by People & Animals

Tetanus Difficult to treat but preventable with immunisation, this potentially fatal disease is found in the rural tropics. Tetanus occurs when a wound becomes infected by a germ which lives in the faeces of animals or people, so clean all cuts or animal bites. Tetanus is known as lockjaw, and the first symptom may be discomfort in swallowing, or stiffening of the jaw and neck; this is followed by painful convulsions of the jaw and entire body.

Rabies Dogs are noted carriers of rabies, which is caused by a bite or scratch from an infected animal. Any bite, scratch or even lick from a mammal should be cleaned immediately and thoroughly. Scrub with soap and running water, and then clean with an alcohol solution. If there is any possibility that the animal is infected, seek medical help immediately. Even if the animal is not rabid, treat all bites seriously, as they can become infected or result in tetanus. A rabies vaccination is now available and should be considered if you are in a high-risk category, eg, if you intend to explore caves (bat bites could be dangerous) or work with animals.

Meningococcal Meningitis This very serious disease attacks the brain and can be fatal. A scattered, blotchy rash, fever, severe headache, sensitivity to light and neck stiffness which prevents forward bending of the head are the first symptoms. Death can occur within a few hours, so immediate treatment is important.

Outbreaks of meningitis do occur in South America; 13,000 cases occurred in an epidemic in São Paulo in 1974. Check for reports of current epidemics and consider a vaccination, which offers protection for one year, if you plan to spend some time in a high-risk area. Treatment is large doses of penicillin.

Tuberculosis Although this disease is widespread in many developing countries, it is not a major risk to travellers. Young children are more susceptible than adults, and vaccination is a sensible precaution for children under 12 travelling in areas where it's endemic. TB is commonly spread by coughing or by unpasteurised dairy products from infected cows. Milk that has been boiled is safe to drink; the souring of milk to make yoghurt or cheese also kills the bacilli.

Bilharzia Bilharzia, also known as schistosomiasis, is carried in water by minute worms. The larvae infect certain varieties of freshwater snails, found in rivers, streams, lakes and particularly behind dams. The worms multiply and are eventually discharged into the water surrounding the snails.

They attach themselves to the intestines or bladder, where they produce large numbers of eggs. The worm enters through the skin, and the first symptom may be a tingling sensation and sometimes a light rash around the area where it entered. Weeks later, when the worm is busy producing eggs, a high fever may develop. A general feeling of poor health may be the first symptom; once the disease is established, abdominal pain and blood in the urine are other signs.

The main method of preventing the disease is to avoid swimming or bathing in fresh water where bilharzia is present. Even deep water can be infected. If you do get wet, dry off quickly and dry your clothes as well. Seek medical attention if you think you have been exposed to the disease and tell the doctor, as bilharzia in the early stages can be confused with malaria or typhoid. If you cannot get medical help immediately, Niridazole is the recommended treatment. The recommended adult dosage is 750 mg (1½ tablets) taken twice daily for a week. Children aged between 8 and 12 years should be given 500 mg (one tablet) twice daily for a week.

Bilharzia is less prevalent in the American tropics than in Africa or Asia, but visitors to Brazil's tropical lowlands in particular should take precautions.

Diphtheria Diphtheria, spread by contaminated dust contacting the skin or by the inhalation of infected cough or sneeze droplets, can be a skin infection or a more dangerous throat infection. Frequent washing and keeping the skin dry will help prevent skin infection. A vaccination is available to prevent the throat infection.

Sexually Transmitted Diseases
Sexual contact with an infected partner spreads these diseases, and while abstinence is the only certain preventative, condoms are also effective. Gonorrhoea and syphilis are the most common of these diseases; sores, blisters or rashes around the genitals, and discharges or pain when urinating are common symptoms. Symptoms may be less obvious or even absent in women. The symptoms of syphilis eventually disappear completely, but the disease can cause severe problems in later years. Antibiotics can treat both gonorrhoea and syphilis effectively. There is no cure for herpes nor for HIV/ AIDS.

HIV/AIDS AIDS (SIDA in Spanish) is becoming more common in South America, and is probably most widespread in Brazil. It can be transmitted sexually, for which the best preventatives are abstinence, monogamy or the use of condoms. Condoms (*preservativos*) are available in pharmacies. It can also be spread by transfusion of infected blood (many developing countries

cannot afford to screen blood) and by dirty needles.

Vaccinations, acupuncture and tattooing can potentially be as dangerous as intravenous drug use, if the equipment is not clean. If you do need an injection, buy a new syringe from a pharmacy and bring it to the doctor's surgery.

Insect-Borne Diseases
Malaria Spread by mosquito bites, this serious disease is endemic in the humid tropics. Symptoms include headaches, fever, chills and sweating, which may subside and recur. It is extremely important to take malarial prophylactics; without treatment, malaria can develop more serious and potentially fatal effects.

Mosquitos appear after dusk; avoid bites by covering bare skin and using an insect repellent. Insect screens on windows and mosquito nets on beds offer protection, as does burning a mosquito coil. Mosquitoes may be attracted by perfume, aftershave or certain colours. The risk of malarial infection is higher in rural areas and during the rainy season.

Antimalarial drugs do not prevent the disease, but suppress its symptoms. Prophylactic drugs must be taken for two weeks before arriving in the infected area and for six weeks after leaving it. Much of South America is a malaria risk area; see Pre-Departure Preparations on page 52 for more detailed information.

Chloroquine is quite safe for general use, side effects are minimal and pregnant women can take it. Maloprim can have rare but serious side effects if the weekly dose is exceeded, and some doctors recommend a check-up after six months' continuous use. Neither Maloprim nor Proguanil is available in the USA.

Fansidar is no longer recommended as a prophylactic, because of dangerous side effects, but may still be recommended as a treatment. Chloroquine is also used as a treatment, but in larger doses than for prophylaxis. Doxycycline can be used as another antimalarial if there is resistance to Chloroquine; it causes hypersensitivity to sunlight, so sunburn can be a problem.

Dengue Fever There is no prophylactic available for this mosquito-spread disease; the main preventative measure is to avoid mosquito bites. A sudden onset of fever, headaches and severe joint and muscle pains are the first signs. A rash then appears on the trunk of the body and spreads to the limbs and face. After a few more days, the fever will subside and recovery will begin. Serious complications are not common.

Yellow Fever This disease is present in Bolivia, Brazil, Colombia, Ecuador, the Guianas, Venezuela and Peru. It is transmitted to humans by mosquitos; the initial symptoms are fever, headaches, abdominal pain and vomiting. There may appear to be a brief recovery before the disease progresses to more severe complications, including liver failure. There is no medical treatment apart from keeping the fever down and avoiding dehydration, but yellow fever vaccination gives good protection for 10 years. Vaccination is an entry requirement for many countries.

Chagas' Disease In remote rural areas of South America, this parasitic disease is transmitted by the *vinchuca* (assassin bug or Reduvid bug), which infests crevices and palm fronds, often lives in thatched roofs, and comes out to feed at night. In about a week, a hard, violet swelling appears on the spot of the bite. The disease causes fever and inflammation of the heart muscles. Treatable in its early stages, it's eventually fatal if untreated. It is best to avoid thatched-roof huts; sleep under a mosquito net, use insecticides and insect repellents and check for hidden insects.

Typhus Typhus, spread by ticks, mites or lice, begins as a bad cold, followed by a fever, chills, headache, muscle pains and a body rash. There is often a large painful sore where the bite has occurred and nearby lymph nodes are swollen and painful.

Ticks spread tick typhus. Seek local advice in areas where ticks pose a danger and always check yourself carefully after walking in a danger area. A strong insect repellent can help, and serious walkers in tick areas should consider having their boots and trousers impregnated with benzyl benzoate and dibutylphthalate.

Cuts, Bites & Stings

Cuts & Scratches Cuts easily become infected in hot climates and may heal slowly. Treat any cut with an antiseptic solution and mercurochrome. Where possible, avoid bandages and band-aids, which can keep wounds wet. Coral cuts are notoriously slow to heal, as the coral injects a weak venom into the wound; avoid such cuts by wearing shoes when walking on reefs, and clean any cut thoroughly.

Bites & Stings Bee and wasp stings are more painful than dangerous. Use calamine lotion for relief and ice packs to reduce the swelling. There are some spiders with dangerous bites but antivenom is usually available. Scorpions often shelter in shoes or clothing and their stings are notoriously painful – check your clothing in the morning. Various sea creatures can sting or bite dangerously or be dangerous to eat – seek local advice.

Snakes To minimise the chances of being bitten, always wear boots, socks and long trousers when walking through undergrowth where snakes may be present. Don't put your hands into holes and crevices, and be careful when collecting firewood.

Snake bites do not cause instantaneous death and antivenom is usually available. Keep the victim calm and still, wrap the bitten limb tightly, as you would for a sprained ankle, and then attach a splint to immobilise it. Seek medical help and, if possible, take the dead snake for identification. Don't attempt to catch the snake if there is even a remote possibility of being bitten again. Tourniquets and sucking out the poison are now completely discredited.

Bedbugs & Lice Bedbugs live in various places, but particularly in dirty mattresses and bedding. Spots of blood on bedclothes or on the wall around the bed can serve as a suggestion to find another hotel. Bedbugs leave itchy bites in neat rows. Calamine lotion may help.

All lice cause itching and discomfort. They make themselves at home in your hair (head lice), your clothing (body lice) or in your pubic hair (crab lice). You catch lice through direct contact with infected people or by sharing combs, clothing and the like. Powder or shampoo treatment will kill the lice, and infected clothing should then be washed in very hot water.

Leeches & Ticks Leeches may be present in damp rainforest conditions; they attach themselves to your skin to suck your blood. Trekkers often get them on their legs or in their boots. Salt or a lighted cigarette end will make them fall off. Pulling them off increases the likelihood of infection. An insect repellent may keep them away. Check your body for ticks too (see under Typhus). Vaseline, alcohol or oil will induce ticks to let go.

Women's Health
Gynaecological Problems Poor diet, lowered resistance due to the use of antibiotics for stomach upsets, and even contraceptive pills can lead to vaginal infections when travelling in hot climates. Keeping the genital area clean; wearing cotton underwear and skirts or loose-fitting trousers will help prevent infections.

Yeast infections, characterised by rash, itch and discharge, can be treated with a vinegar or even lemon juice douche or with yoghurt. Nystatin suppositories are the usual medical prescription. Trichomonas is a more serious infection, with a discharge and a burning sensation when urinating. Male sexual partners must also be treated; if a vinegar-water douche is not effective, seek medical attention. Flagyl is the prescribed drug.

Pregnancy Most miscarriages occur during the first three months of pregnancy, so this is the riskiest time to travel. The last three months should also be spent within reasonable distance of good medical care. Pregnant women should avoid all unnecessary medication, but vaccinations and malarial prophylactics should still be taken where possible. Take additional care to prevent illness and pay particular attention to diet and nutrition.

DANGERS & ANNOYANCES
Theft
Theft is a big problem in some countries, especially Colombia, Peru and parts of Brazil. Rob Rachowiecki, author of the Peru chapter and several other LP guides, makes the following recommendations which are appropriate wherever there is a high risk of theft:

As well as pickpockets and bag-snatchers, there are the razor-blade artists, who slit open your luggage when you're not looking. This includes a pack on your back, or even your trouser pocket. To avoid this, many travellers carry their day packs on their chests during trips to markets, etc. When walking with my large pack, I move fast and avoid stopping, which makes it difficult for anyone intent on cutting the bag. If I have to stop, at a street crossing for example, I tend to swing gently from side to side so I can feel if anyone is touching my pack, and I look around a lot. I don't feel paranoid – walking fast and looking around on my way from bus station to hotel has become second nature to me, and I never place a bag on the ground unless I have my foot on it.

One of the best solutions to the rip-off problem is to travel with a friend and to watch one another. An extra pair of eyes makes a lot of difference. I often see shifty-looking types eyeing luggage at bus stations, but they notice if you are alert and are less likely to bother you. They'd much rather steal something from the tired and unalert traveller who has put a bag on a chair whilst buying a coffee. Ten seconds later, the traveller has the coffee – but the thief has the bag!

Thieves look for easy targets. Leave your wallet at home; it's an easy mark for a pickpocket. Carrying a small roll of bills loosely wadded under a handkerchief in your front pocket is as safe a way as any of carrying your daily spending money. The rest should be hidden. Always use at least a closeable inside pocket or preferably a body pouch, money belt or leg pouch to protect your money and passport. Carry some of your money in travellers' cheques.

Pickpockets are not the only problem. Snatch theft is also common so don't wear gold necklaces and expensive wristwatches or you're liable to have them snatched from your body. Snatch theft can also occur if you carry a camera loosely over your shoulder or place a bag down on the ground for just a second!

Thieves often work in pairs or groups. Whilst your attention is being distracted by one, another is robbing you. Distractions I have seen used include a bunch of kids fighting in front of you, an old lady 'accidentally' bumping into you, someone dropping something in your path or spilling something on your clothes – the possibilities go on and on. The only thing you can do is to try, as much as possible, to avoid being in very tight crowds and to stay alert, especially when something out of the ordinary occurs.

Definitely avoid any conversation with someone who offers you drugs. Travellers have talked to people on the street, only to be stopped a minute later by 'plain clothes policemen' and accused of talking to a drug dealer. In such a situation, *never* get into a vehicle with the 'police'. Insist on going to a bona fide police station on foot, if the police appear to be the real thing.

On buses and trains, keep an eye on your baggage at all times, but especially at night. Don't fall asleep in a railway compartment unless a friend is watching you and your gear, or you'll wake up with everything gone. When a bus stops, if you can't see what's happening to your gear, get off and have a look.

Trouble Spots

Peru and Colombia are probably the most hazardous countries for travellers at the moment. Peruvian authorities have improved policing of tourist areas over the last couple years, especially on trains, but be vigilant. There have been robberies, some of them armed, on the Inca Trail from km 88 to Machu Picchu. It's advisable not to go alone, but even groups have been robbed.

In Brazil, the main trouble spots are the beaches of Rio, where muggings are common even at midday and gangs of youths and even children roam the beaches watching for unattended articles. Other countries in which travellers should take special precautions are Venezuela and Guyana, where muggings are common; see individual country chapters for details.

Ecuador, Bolivia and Suriname are considerably safer, but travellers should not be complacent. Argentina, Chile, Uruguay, Paraguay and French Guiana are probably the safest places on the continent.

Baggage Insurance & Theft Reports

Given these circumstances, baggage insurance is worth its price in peace of mind. Make sure that if any clauses in the policy limit the amount you can claim on any article, the amount is sufficient to cover replacement. If you have anything stolen, you must usually inform the insurance company by airmail and report the loss or theft to local police within 24 hours. At the police station, you complete a *denuncia* (statement), a copy of which is given to you for your claim on the insurer. The denuncia usually has to be made on *papel sellado* (stamped paper), which you can buy for a few cents at any stationer.

In city police stations, you might find an English-speaking interpreter, but in most cases, you'll either have to speak Spanish or provide an interpreter. Prepare a list of stolen items and their value. When you make a claim, especially for a valuable item, the insurance company often demands a receipt to prove that you bought it in the first place.

It can be expensive and time-consuming to replace a lost or stolen passport. Apart from the cost of backtracking to the nearest embassy or consulate, there will be telex charges to your home country to check the details of your previous passport, plus the cost of a new passport.

Police & Military

Corruption is a very serious problem among Latin American police, who are generally poorly paid, poorly educated and poorly supervised. In many countries, they are not reluctant to plant drugs on unsuspecting travellers or enforce minor regulations to the letter in hopes of extracting *coimas* (bribes).

The military retain considerable influence even under civilian government. Avoid approaching military installations, which may display warnings like 'No stopping or photographs – the sentry will shoot'. In the event of a coup or other emergency, state-of-siege regulations suspend civil rights; always carry identification and be sure someone knows your whereabouts. Contact your embassy or consulate for advice.

Natural Hazards

On the Pacific coast of South America, part of the 'ring of fire' which stretches from Asia to Alaska and Tierra del Fuego, volcanic eruptions are not rare – in 1991, for example, the eruption of Volcán Hudson in Chile's Aisén Region buried parts of southern Patagonia knee-deep in ash. Earthquakes are common and can be very serious.

Vulcanism is unlikely to pose any immediate threat to travellers, since volcanos usually give some notice before blowing. Earthquakes, however, strike without warning and Andean construction rarely meets seismic safety standards – adobe buildings are particularly vulnerable. Travellers in budget accommodation should make contingency plans for safety and even evacuation before going to sleep at night.

WOMEN TRAVELLERS

Women in South America rarely travel alone, and single women travellers may find themselves the object of curiosity – sometimes well-intentioned, sometimes not. In the Andean region, dress and conduct should be modest, but in Brazil and the more liberal Southern Cone countries, standards are more relaxed, especially in beach areas. A good rule is to follow local standards. For more detail, see individual country chapters.

ACTIVITIES
Surfing

South America's best surfing areas are the coasts of Peru (despite the cool waters of the Humboldt current) and north-eastern Brazil. Surfers around São Luís and Recife should be aware of recent shark attacks in those areas.

Skiing

South America's most important ski areas are in the lake districts of Chile and Argentina, with lesser possibilities in Bolivia, Peru, Ecuador, Colombia and Venezuela. For more detail, see individual country chapters and Chris Lizza's *South America Ski Guide* (Bradt Publications, UK, or Hunter Publications, USA, 1992).

Trekking

South America is an increasingly attractive destination for trekkers. In the Andean countries, many of the old Inca roads are readymade for scenic excursions, but lesser-known mountain ranges like Colombia's Sierra de Santa Marta also have great potential. The national parks of southern South America, such as Chile's Torres del Paine and Argentina's Nahuel Huapi, are most like those of Europe and North America in their trail infrastructure and accessibility.

Mountaineering

On a continent with one of the world's great mountain ranges, climbing opportunities are almost unlimited. Ecuador's volcanos, the high peaks of Peru's Cordillera Blanca, and Argentina's Aconcagua (the continent's highest verified peak) are all suitable for mountaineering, but perhaps the most challenging technical climbs are in the Fitz Roy range of Argentina's Parque Nacional Los Glaciares.

River Rafting

Chile's Río Biobío features some of the world's finest Class-5 white water, though it's presently menaced by a proposed hydro-electric project. River running is also possible in Peru on the Urubamba and other rivers near Cuzco, and in the very difficult Río Colca canyon near Arequipa.

Sea Kayaking

Southern Chile, particularly the island of Chiloé and the Canal Moraleda south to Laguna San Rafael, are increasingly popular with sea kayakers.

Language Courses

In most South American capitals, other major cities, and a few smaller provincial towns, there are language courses in Spanish, Portuguese and Indian languages like Quechua and Aymara. For details, see individual country chapters.

WORK

Except for tutors of English, opportunities

for employment are few, poorly paid and often illegal. Even tutoring, despite good hourly rates, is rarely remunerative because it takes time to build up a clientele. The best places are probably Buenos Aires and Santiago, where living expenses are also high, but see individual country chapters for details.

USEFUL ORGANISATIONS
South American Explorers Club
This very informative, nonprofit organisation has offices in Lima (Peru), and Quito (Ecuador); for addresses, see the entries for those cities. There are plans to open a Bolivian office in La Paz in late 1993 – check with the club about this. There is also a US office (☎ (607) 277-0488) at 126 Indian Creek Rd, Ithaca, NY 14850. This is where their magazine is published; if you're interested in joining, send US$4 for a sample copy and further information.

The SAEC was founded in 1977 and functions as an information centre for travellers, adventurers, scientific expeditions, etc. The club's Lima office has an extensive library of books, maps and trip reports left by other travellers. Many maps and books are for sale. Useful current advice can be obtained about travel conditions, currency regulations, weather conditions and so on.

The club is an entirely member-supported, nonprofit organisation. Membership costs US$30 per individual per year (US$40 for a couple) and includes four quarterly issues of their excellent and informative *South American Explorer* magazine. In addition, members receive full use of the club facilities, which include: an information service and library; introductions to other travellers and notification of expedition opportunities; storage of excess luggage (anything ranging from small valuables to a kayak); storage or forwarding of mail addressed to you at the club; a relaxing place in which to read and research, or just to have a cup of tea and a chat with the friendly staff; a book exchange; buying and selling of used equipment; discounts on the books, maps and gear sold at the club; and hotel reservations, flight confirmations and other services. Nonmembers are welcome to visit the club but are asked to limit their visit to about half an hour, and they are not eligible for membership privileges until they cough up their US$30. Paid-up members can hang out all day – a welcome relief from the madhouse bustle of a large city like Lima. The club is highly recommended.

Environmental Organisations
Many organisations, both in South America and overseas, are promoting preservation of the rainforest and other endangered environments. For more details, contact any of the following groups; see also individual country chapters:

Australia
   Friends of the Earth, 222 Brunswick St, Fitzroy, 3065 (☎ (03) 419-8700)
   Greenpeace Australia Ltd, 3/389 Lonsdale St, Melbourne, 3000 (☎ (03) 670-1633)
Bolivia
   Fundación Amigos de la Naturaleza (FAN), Casilla 1615, Avenida Irala 421, Santa Cruz, Bolivia (☎ 33-3806)
   Conservación Internacional, Señor Guillermo Rioja Ballivián, Casilla 5633, Avenida Villazón 1958-10A, La Paz, Bolivia (☎ 341230)
   Instituto de Ecología, Casilla 10077, Calle 27, Cotacota, La Paz, Bolivia (☎ 792582, international fax: (591/2) 391176)
UK
   Friends of the Earth, 26/28 Underwood St, London N17JU
   Survival International, 310 Edgeware Rd, London W2 1DY (☎ (071) 723-5535)
USA
   The Rainforest Action Network (RAN), 301 Broadway, Suite A, San Francisco, CA 94133, (☎ (415) 398-4404)
   Conservation International, 1015 18th St, NW, Suite 1000, Washington, DC 20036 (☎ (202) 429-5660)
   Cultural Survival, 215 First St, Cambridge, MA 02142 (☎ (617) 621-3818)
   The Nature Conservancy, 1815 N Lynn St, Arlington, VA 22209 (☎ (703) 841-5300)
   The Chico Mendes Fund, Environmental Defense Fund, 257 Park Ave South, New York, NY 10010
   Rainforest Alliance, 270 Lafayette St, Suite 512, New York, NY 10012
   The Rainforest Foundation Inc, 1776 Broadway, 14th floor, New York, NY 10019

BOOKS
Many very fine books are readily available in general interest bookshops or, in the case of specialised items, in university libraries. See also recommendations in individual country chapters.

General

George Pendle's *A History Of Latin America* (Penguin) is a readable but very general account of the region since the European invasions.

Eduardo Galeano's *Open Veins of Latin America: Five Centuries of the Pillage of a Continent* (Monthly Review Press, New York & London, 1973) is an eloquent polemic on the continent's cultural, social and political struggles from a leftist perspective by a famous Uruguayan writer. John A Crow's *The Epic of Latin America*, 3rd edition (University of California Press, 1980) is an imposing but readable volume which covers nearly the whole of the region from Mexico to Tierra del Fuego, from prehistory to the present.

Prehistory & the Incas

One key book on early South America is Edward P Lanning's *Peru Before the Incas* (Prentice-Hall, 1967), but for an innovative approach to Amazonian prehistory, see Donald Lathrap's *The Upper Amazon* (Praeger, New York, 1970), which argues for the tropical lowlands as a hearth of South American cultural development.

Several indigenous and Spanish chroniclers left accounts of their times. Garcilaso de la Vega, son of an Inca princess, wrote *Royal Commentaries of the Incas*, available in many editions, but much criticised for exaggerations and misrepresentations of detail. Father Bernabé Cobo's 17th-century *History of the Inca Empire* (University of Texas, 1979) draws on Garcilaso but also includes much original material from his own observations. Huamán Poma de Ayala's 17th-century *Letter to a King* (Dutton, New York, 1978) is an eloquent letter of protest against Spanish abuses of indigenous peoples.

Conquest of the Incas (Harcourt Brace Jovanovich, 1970), by John Hemming, is a fine interpretation of the clash between the Spaniards and the lords of Cuzco.

European Invasion & the Colonial Era

Carl O Sauer's *The Early Spanish Main* (University of California, 1969) portrays Columbus as an audacious bumbler whose greed coloured his every perception of the New World. On the achievements of other early European explorers, see J H Parry's *The Discovery of South America* (Paul Elek, London, 1979). To learn who the conquistadores really were, read James Lockhart's fascinating *The Men of Cajamarca* (University of Texas, 1972), a series of biographical studies of the first Europeans in Peru, from Pizarro to his lowliest soldier.

James Lockhart & Stuart Schwartz's *Early Latin America* (Cambridge, 1983) makes an unusual but persuasive argument that the structures of indigenous societies were more important than Spanish domination in the cultural transitions of the colonial period. Magnus Mörner's *The Andean Past: Land, Societies and Conflicts* (Columbia University Press, New York, 1985) deals with the struggles of the Quechua and Aymara peoples in a cultural and ecological context. Charles Gibson's standard *Spain in America* (Harper Colophon, New York, 1962) focuses on the institutions of Spanish rule.

Alfred Crosby's *Ecological Imperialism: the Biological Expansion of Europe, 900-1900* (Cambridge, 1986) chronicles the environmental transformation of southern South America under colonial rule. His earlier book *The Columbian Exchange* (Greenwood Press, Westport, Connecticut, 1972) details the microbial invasion which changed South American demography, and evaluates the impact of European plants and animals in the Americas, and American plants and animals in Europe and worldwide. For a regional approach to the demographic collapse, see William Denevan's edited collection *The Native Population of the Americas in 1492* (University of Wisconsin, 1992).

Independence & the Republican Era

For the South American wars of independence, a standard work is John Lynch's *The Spanish-American Revolutions 1808-1826* (W W Norton, New York, 1973). For an overview of social problems in Latin America, see Eric Wolf & Edward Hansen's *The Human Condition in Latina America* (Oxford University Press, 1972). For other titles, see individual country chapters.

Amazonia

A classic 19th-century account is Henry Walter Bates's *The Naturalist on the River Amazons* (University of California Press, 1962). Roughly contemporaneous is A R Wallace's *Travels on the Amazon and Rio Negro*. Anthony Smith's *Explorers of the Amazon* (Viking, London & New York, 1990) is a series of essays on explorers of various kinds, from conquerors to scientists to plant collectors to rubber barons.

Despite shortcomings, Betty J Meggers' *Amazonia: Man and Culture in a Counterfeit Paradise* (Aldine Publishing, Chicago, 1971) is essential reading for its description of traditional rainforest cultures and the environment. Perhaps the best overall account of the plight of the global rainforests is journalist Catherine Caufield's *In the Rainforest* (University of Chicago, 1984), which contains substantial material on Amazonia but also covers other imperilled areas. More recent is *The Fate of the Forest: Developers, Destroyers, and Defenders of the Amazon*, Susanna Hecht & Alexander Cockburn (Verso, 1989).

On the situation of indigenous peoples, see Shelton Davis's *Victims of the Miracle: Development and the Indians of Brazil* (Cambridge, 1977). Julie Sloan Denslow & Christine Padoch's *People of the Tropical Rainforest* (University of California Press & Smithsonian Institution, 1988) is an edited and well-illustrated collection of articles on tropical ecology and development, which deals with rainforest immigrants as well as indigenous peoples. For an assessment of the impact of mining, see David Cleary's *Anatomy of the Amazon Gold Rush* (University of Iowa, 1990).

Travel Literature

US writer Peter Matthiessen describes a journey from the rivers of Peru to the mountains of Tierra del Fuego in *The Cloud Forest* (Penguin 1987, first published in 1961); his experiences led to his novel *At Play in the Fields of the Lord* (see below). Alex Shoumatoff's *In Southern Light* (Vintage, New York, 1990) explores first-hand some of the fantastic legends of the Amazon.

Many readers may feel ambivalent about anyone who drives from Tierra del Fuego to the North Slope of Alaska in 23½ days (verified in *The Guinness Book of Records)*, but Tim Cahill's hilarious encounters with customs officials and other bureaucrats alone make *Road Fever* (Vintage, 1992) worth reading. Eric Lawlor's *In Bolivia* (Vintage, 1989) moves at a slower pace, but with equally good humour and a greater appreciation of Andean culture. *Driving to Heaven*, by Derek Stansfield, describes a 10-month campervan trip in South and Central America; order from the author at Ropley, Broad Oak, Sturminster Newton, Dorset, UK.

Fiction

Mathiessen's *At Play in the Fields of the Lord*, set in Peru's Amazon rainforests, is a tale of conflict between the forces of 'development' and indigenous peoples. Another superb novel on similar themes is Raymond Sokolov's *Native Intelligence* (Dutton, New York, 1975).

Nobel Prize winner Gabriel García Márquez has been the leader of Latin America's fiction boom; his *One Hundred Years of Solitude* (Avon, New York, 1970) is perhaps South America's most famous fictional work. Another major writer is Peru's Mario Vargas Llosa, whose *The Real Life of Alejandro Mayta* (Vintage, New York, 1986) offers insights into his country's current political dilemmas; also try *Aunt Julia and the Scriptwriter* (Avon, New York, 1982).

Many books by the late Brazilian novelist Jorge Amado, most notably *Dona Flor and Her Two Husbands* and *Gabriela, Clove and Cinnamon*, are easy to find in English. Contemporary satirist Márcio Souza has written *Emperor of the Amazon* (Avon, 1980) and

Mad Maria (Avon, 1985), both of which deal with attempts to conquer the rainforest.

Flora & Fauna Guides

Neotropical Rainforest Mammals: A Field Guide, by Louise Emmons & François Feer, provides colour illustrations for identification. Birders in the Amazon region might try *South American Birds: A Photographic Aid to Identification* (1987), by John S Dunning, *A Guide to the Birds of Colombia*, by Stephen L Hilty & William L Brown, or *A Guide to the Birds of Venezuela*, by Rodolphe Meyer de Schauensee & William Phelps.

More inclusive is Meyer de Schauensee's *A Guide to the Birds of South America* (Academy of Natural Science, Philadelphia). The high-priced, multivolume reference work *The Birds of South America* (University of Texas Press, 1989), by R S Ridgley & G Tudor, is extremely detailed and often technical.

Piet van Ipenburg & Rob Boschhuizen's *Ecology of Tropical Rainforests: An introduction for Eco-tourists* (Free University Amsterdam, 1990) is a booklet packed with intriguing minutiae about sloths, bats, strangler figs and other rainforest biota. It's available in the UK from J Forrest, 64 Belsize Park, London NW3 4EH, or in the USA from M Doolittle, 32 Amy Rd, Falls Village, CT 06031; all proceeds go to the Tambopata Reserve Society, which is funding research in the south-eastern Peruvian rainforests.

William Leitch's beautifully written *South America's National Parks* (Seattle, 1990) is essential background for trekkers, superb on environment and natural history but weaker on practical matters.

Other Guide Books

It's impossible to cover every detail of travel in South America in this book, so if you have a particular interest to pursue or need greater detail on specific places, you may want to supplement it with other books.

Lonely Planet produces regularly updated Travel Survival Kits for individual South American countries, with a wealth of information, numerous maps, illustrations and colour photos. Titles to look for are:

Argentina, Uruguay & Paraguay, by Wayne Bernhardson & María Massolo

Bolivia, by Deanna Swaney

Brazil, by Andrew Draffen, Robert Strauss & Deanna Swaney

Chile & Easter Island, by Wayne Bernhardson

Colombia, by Krzysztof Dydynski

Ecuador & the Galapagos Islands, by Rob Rachowiecki

Peru, by Rob Rachowiecki

Venezuela, by Krzysztof Dydynski (due mid-1994)

If you're planning to visit Central America as well, get a copy of Lonely Planet's *Central America on a Shoestring*, by Nancy Keller, Tom Brosnahan & Rob Rachowiecki, which covers the region from Belize to Panama.

Since the 1920s, *The South American Handbook* (Trade and Travel Publications, Bath), edited by Ben Box, has been a standard travel guide to the continent, and many South American travellers still swear by it.

For trekking, look for Lonely Planet's *Trekking in the Patagonian Andes*, by Clem Lindenmayer. William Leitch's *South America's National Parks* (Seattle, 1990) is good background reading for trekkers, but is weaker on practical matters.

Bradt Publications guides also deserve consideration for anyone planning walks in the mountains or off-the-beaten-track excursions. Some of them may be hard to find, but the series includes the following:

Climbing & Hiking in Ecuador, by Hilary Bradt

No Frills Guide to Venezuela, by Hilary Dunsterville Branch

Backpacking and Trekking in Peru & Bolivia, by Hilary Bradt

Backpacking in Chile & Argentina, edited by Clare Hargreaves

Backcountry Brazil, by Alex Bradbury

South American River Trips, by Tanis & Martin Jordan

Backpacking in Mexico & Central America, by Hilary Bradt & Rob Rachowiecki, covers the trek through the Darién gap; it is out of print, but you may find a copy in a library.

Another useful title is *Trails of the Cordilleras Blanca & Huayhuash of Peru*, by Jim Bartle, which contains excellent trail descriptions with maps and colour photographs, but may be out of print.

If you're planning on taking your own vehicle, Theresa & Jonathan Hewat's *Overland and Beyond* is packed with practical information. The authors took their own Volkswagen Kombi round the world for 3½ years.

Lynn Meisch's *A Traveller's Guide to El Dorado & the Inca Empire* (Headlands Press & Penguin) has an excellent coverage of Andean crafts, especially weaving (a subject which takes up nearly half the book), but it's thin on practical details.

Periodicals

The best regular source of South American news is the *Miami Herald*, which publishes an overseas edition available in capital cities, and a few other centres, throughout South America. *The Economist* also has good coverage of the region.

MAPS

ITM (International Travel Map) Productions distribute an excellent, informative three-sheet map of the continent, at a scale of 1:4,000,000. ITM is at Box 2290, Vancouver, BC, V6B 3W5, Canada. In Europe, ITM maps are distributed by Bradt Publications, 41 Nortoft Road, Chalfont St Peter, Bucks, England SL9 0LA. The maps are drawn by Kevin Healey, an independent Melbourne cartographer. They might be a bit big for field use, but are helpful for planning a trip.

Bartholomew's *America, South* is a reasonable alternative, despite lack of detail and occasional inaccuracies.

FILM & PHOTOGRAPHY

The latest in consumer electronics is available throughout South America, but import duties make cameras and film very expensive, up to three times their cost in North America or Western Europe. Developing is also expensive. Bring as much film as you can; you can always sell anything you don't

need to other travellers. Locally manufactured film is reasonably good, but no cheaper than imported.

Colour slide film can now be purchased at reasonable prices in many parts of Bolivia, in Asunción, Paraguay, and in the duty free zones at Iquique and Punta Arenas, Chile. Paraguay and Chilean free zones are also good places to replace lost or stolen camera equipment, as prices are only slightly higher than in North America, even if the selection is not so great.

Some photographers who shoot slides in the humid tropics prefer Fujichrome, which renders greens exceptionally well and is readily available in the cities mentioned above. Kodachrome, which is better at portraying reds and nearby colours of the spectrum, is often more suitable for deserts and urban areas, but is only available at relatively slow speeds, up to 200 ASA. For the low light conditions of the Amazonian rainforests, it's a good idea to carry a few rolls of high-speed (ASA 400) film.

Always protect camera lenses with an ultraviolet (UV) filter. In high-altitude tropical light conditions in the Andes, the UV may not be sufficient to prevent washed-out photos; a polarising filter can correct this problem and, incidentally, dramatically emphasises cloud formations, often improving results on mountain and shoreline landscapes.

ACCOMMODATION

In most countries, one can find a room for around US$2 to US$10 per night, depending on the region. The Andean countries are the cheapest, while the Southern Cone is the most expensive (except for French Guiana, a special case, as it is officially part of metropolitan France).

Obviously, a great deal depends on your standards of comfort and cleanliness, – how much searching you care to do, and the size of the town. In general, however, budget accommodation is good value for money.

The cheapest places are *hospedajes, casas de huéspedes, pensiones, dormitorios* or *albergues* (hostels, including official 'youth hostels') – terminology varies in each country. These usually basic places provide a bed with clean sheets and a blanket or two, table and chair, sometimes a fan for cooling, but rarely heat in cold climates. Showers and toilets are communal, but cheap places may or may not have hot water. Cleanliness varies widely, but some places are remarkably good.

Hotels proper are generally dearer, but distinctions can be unclear. In some countries, especially southern Chile and Argentina, the cheapest places may be *casas familiares*, family houses whose hospitality makes them excellent value.

Many of the cheapest places have partitioned larger rooms to accommodate more guests. These hardboard (or cardboard!) partitions often fail to reach the ceiling, so though you can't see other occupants (unless someone has put a fist through the wall), you can certainly hear them, and vice versa. If the place doubles as a brothel, you may experience several hours of sighs, cries and giggles, banging doors, flushing toilets and testy customers. If you're really tired, this may not disturb you, but light sleepers can find it trying. Since South Americans are generally gregarious and tolerant of extraneous noise, complaining rarely helps. One solution is to choose a room well away from the foyer or TV lounge, perhaps at the end of the hall, where you'll only have neighbours on one side.

Some cheap hotels specialise in renting rooms by the hour. These 'love hotels' can be an acceptable budget accommodation alternative, though they may be reluctant to take travellers who want to use a room for the whole night. This applies especially on weekends, when the hotel can make more money from a larger number of shorter stays.

In Brazil and some other places, the room price includes breakfast, which may be just a cup of coffee and a piece of bread, with butter, jam or marmalade, but sometimes it's a buffet of cold cuts, fruit juice, fruit slices, bread, butter and jelly, biscuits and a pot of coffee. It's worth paying a little extra for a place which offers a quality breakfast,

because it's usually far cheaper than its restaurant counterpart.

Toilet facilities are rarely what you would expect at home. Hot water supplies are often erratic, or may only be available at certain hours of the day – ask, if you have something planned. Some hotels charge extra for hot showers, and a few have no showers at all – but you can always use public hot baths.

Beware the electric shower, a single cold-water shower head hooked up to an electric heating element which is switched on for a hot (more likely tepid) shower. Don't touch anything metal while in the shower or you may get a real shock – never strong enough to throw you across the room, but unpleasant nevertheless.

Flushing a toilet creates another hazard – overflow. Low-grade toilet paper clogs the system, so hotels usually provide a waste receptacle for the paper, which is more sanitary than clogged bowls and water on the floor. A well-run hotel, however cheap, will empty the receptacle and clean the toilet every day.

Camping

Camping is an obvious choice in parks and reserves, but also an important budget option in the more expensive countries of southern South America.

In the Andean countries and most of Brazil, there are few organised campgrounds, and accommodation is so cheap that camping is probably not worth the trouble or risk, but in Argentina, Chile, Uruguay and parts of Brazil, camping holidays have long been popular with local people. By camping, shoestring travellers can keep accommodation costs close to what they would be in the Andean countries. It's better to bring your own equipment from overseas than to buy locally. See individual country chapters, particularly Argentina, for details.

FOOD

Over the last few years, the variety of food has improved, especially at places which cater to travellers. *Pollo a las brasas* (grilled chicken) can be found almost anywhere (though it varies in quality and greasiness), while there's always good seafood in coastal towns. Restaurants in larger cities offer everything from Korean *kimchee* to Middle Eastern *shishkebab*, though exotic restaurants are usually more expensive.

At street stalls and small cafés frequented by local people, you can often eat a reasonable meal for US$1 or even less. Most cafés in South America offer a cheap *comida corrida* (set meal) for *almuerzo* (lunch), less often for *cena* (dinner). *Desayuno* (breakfast) is rarely a set meal, though many South Americans eat stuffed pasties *(empanadas* or *salteñas)* in the morning.

Lunch is the largest meal of the day, but the comida corrida can become monotonous, often consisting of potato or maize soup with a bit of meat, a main course of rice with chicken or a slice of grilled beef, and a dessert.

Brazil

Brazil's midday *lanche*, the main meal for budget travellers, usually consists of soup, plus a main course of rice, boiled black beans *(feijão)*, grilled or barbecued beef, lamb or chicken and manioc flour, perhaps vegetables and a dessert. Dinner is more varied and more expensive.

At Saturday lunch, most restaurants offer the traditional *feijoada completa*, a near-banquet with the same ingredients as lanche, but a greater variety of meats and vegetables.

Hotels often include breakfast in the room price, though in the cheaper places, it is very modest.

Vegetarian Food

Even in carnivorous countries like Argentina, vegetarianism is no longer the mark of an eccentric; even many nonvegetarian restaurants will prepare dishes without meat. If they seem doubtful, plead allergies *(alergia)*.

Every town has a market where fruits and vegetables are usually cheap and plentiful. Depending on the season and locale, these include bananas, coconuts, melons, guavas, pepino, mangos, oranges, mandarins, grapefruit, avocados, peaches, pomegranates, prickly pears, apples and many novelties – be adventurous.

DRINK

South Americans drink prodigious amounts of sugary soft drinks, including the ubiquitous Coca Cola and Seven-Up; Peru has the indigenous Inca Cola, which tastes like boiled lollipops and has a colour not found in nature. Mineral water *(agua mineral)*, both carbonated *(con gas)* and plain *(sin gas)*, is widely available.

Most cafés sell bottled lager-type beers, which vary in quality and cost about twice as much as a soft drink. *Chopp* (draught beer, pronounced 'shop') is cheaper and often better. Spirits include rum (in Venezuela, Colombia, Ecuador and Peru) and *aguardiente* (in Peru and Bolivia).

Chile, Peru, Bolivia, Argentina and Brazil are significant wine producers. Some of the Chilean and Argentine wines are among the world's best, while Bolivian wines from the Tarija region are excellent. Chilean wines are very reasonably priced, and Argentine wines remain inexplicably affordable, even in times of raging inflation. The grape brandy *pisco* is popular in Peru and Chile.

Getting There & Away

AIR

Flying directly to South America cheaply requires planning. The cost depends on many factors, among them your country of residence, the available travel agencies, your destination in South America, and the possibility of advance purchase and flexibility in arrangements. Patience and flexibility will get you the best deal.

Ticket Options

There are several types of discount tickets. The main ones are:

Advance Purchase
Usually only available on a return basis, with a 14 or 21-day advance purchase requirement, these have minimum and maximum stay requirements (usually 14 and 180 days, respectively), allow no stopovers and stipulate cancellation charges.

Courier Flights
This relatively new system, which businesses use to ensure the arrival of urgent freight without excessive customs hassles, can mean phenomenal bargains for travellers who can tolerate fairly strict requirements, eg short turnaround time (some tickets are valid for only a week or so, others for a month, but rarely any longer). In effect, the courier company ships business freight as your baggage, so that you can usually take only carry-on luggage, but you may pay as little as US$200 for Miami-Caracas-Miami or US$480 for New York-Buenos Aires-New York. For the latest information on courier and other budget fares, send US$5 for the latest newsletter from Travel Unlimited, PO Box 1058, Allston, MA 02134.

Excursion Fares
Priced midway between Advance Purchase and full economy fare, these have no advance booking requirements but may require a minimum stay. Their advantage over Advance Purchase is that you can change bookings and/or stopovers without surcharge.

Point to Point
This discount ticket can be bought on some routes in return for waiving stopover rights, though many flights no longer permit stopovers anyway.

RTW
Some excellent bargains are possible on 'Round-the-World' tickets, sometimes for less than the cost of a return excursion fare. You must travel round the world in one direction and cannot backtrack; you are usually allowed five to seven stopovers.

Economy Class
Symbolised by 'Y' on the airline ticket, this is the full economy fare, valid for 12 months.

MCO
The Miscellaneous Charges Order, a voucher for a given dollar amount, resembles a plane ticket and can be applied toward a specific flight with any IATA airline. MCOs, which are more flexible than a regular ticket, may satisfy the irritating onward ticket requirement, but some countries are now reluctant to accept them; for details, see individual country chapters for Brazil, Colombia and Guyana.

Bucket Shop Tickets

Outside the official ticket structure, certain travel agencies, known in the UK as 'bucket shops', offer unofficially discounted tickets; their US counterparts are 'consolidators'.

Bucket shop tickets generally cost less than Advance Purchase, without advance purchase or cancellation penalties, though some agents have their own penalties. Most bucket shops are well-established and honourable, but unscrupulous agents might accept your money and disappear before issuing a ticket, or even issue an invalid or unusable ticket. Check carefully before handing over the money.

Air Passes

Several South American carriers have domestic air passes, which usually must be bought outside the country and sometimes can only be bought in conjunction with an international ticket. Air passes are convenient for visiting widely separated parts of a country or, sometimes, several countries. For more detail, see the Getting Around chapter.

To/From the UK & Europe

Fares from London are cheaper than those

from other European cities. The cheapest destinations in South America are generally Caracas (Venezuela) and Bogotá (Colombia). Journey Latin America (JLA), 14-16 Devonshire Rd, Chiswick, London W4 2HD (☎ (081) 747-3108, fax (081) 742-1312), specialises in flights to Latin America and will make arrangements over the phone. Ask for *Papagaio*, their useful free magazine. They are very well informed on South American destinations, have a good range of South American air passes, and can issue tickets from South America to London and deliver them to any of the main South American cities, which is cheaper than buying the same ticket in South America.

Another reputable agency is Trailfinders, 42-50 Earls Court Rd, London W8 6EJ (☎ (071) 938-3366). Their useful travel newspaper, *Trailfinder*, is free. They have cheap flights to a wide variety of destinations; ask about RTW tickets.

One of the best sources of information about cheap fares around the world is the monthly *Business Traveller*, available at newsstands in many countries, or direct from 60/61 Fleet St, London EC4. See also the London weekly entertainment guide *Time Out*, available from newsstands in London, and *LAM*, a free London weekly magazine for entertainment, travel and jobs, available at underground stations. Other free weeklies with advertisements for cheap airfares include *City Limits* and *News & Travel Magazine (TNT*, formerly *Australasian Express)*.

Some current low-season fares advertised from London are:

To	One-Way	Return
Bogotá	£235-260	£404-475
Buenos Aires	£338-354	£561-600
Caracas	£194-230	£384-405
La Paz	£400-447	£615-722
Lima	£276-284	£487-492
Quito	£276-297	£497-503
Recife	£290-360	£466-603
Rio de Janeiro	£292-306	£468-540
Santiago	£337-351	£603-634

There are countless bucket shops, with well-advertised services and prices. Be sure to use a travel agent which is 'bonded' (eg by ATOL, ABTA or AITO), or you will have no protection if the company goes broke.

Flights are available from other European cities, but may be dearer than those from London. Possible options are: Air France from Paris to Cayenne; Air Portugal from Lisbon or Oporto to Rio, São Paulo, Santo Domingo or Caracas; or VASP from Brussels to Brazil. Another alternative might be LAP (Air Paraguay) flights from Frankfurt or Brussels to Asunción.

There are many charters from Europe to South America, with maximum-stay requirements the main restriction. LAN-Chile, for example, has flights from several European capitals with a maximum stay of 60 days. Some require fixed dates for both outward and return flights. It costs more to fly during high season, usually July, August, September and December.

The only courier flights seem to be London to Rio; Courier Travel Service (☎ (71) 351-0300), 346 Fulham Rd, London SW10 9UH charges £425 for 28 days return.

To/From North America

The major gateways of Miami, New York and Los Angeles all have similar fare structures. Inexpensive tickets from North America usually have restrictions – the fares must often be purchased two weeks in advance and usually you must stay at least a week and no more than three months (prices often double for longer periods). For an idea of what's available, peruse the Sunday travel sections of papers like *The New York Times*, *Los Angeles Times* and *San Francisco Examiner*. Details change frequently. Most cities in the USA also have free weekly 'alternative' newspapers which are good places to browse for travel bargains. It pays to shop around.

Travel agencies known as 'consolidators' generally have the best deals. They buy tickets in bulk, then discount them to their customers, or sell 'fill-up fares', which can be even cheaper (with additional restrictions). Look for agencies specialising in South America.

Offices of Council Travel and Student Travel Association (STA), neither of which requires student status, sell cheap tickets in most major cities, including New York, Boston, Dallas, Los Angeles, San Diego, San Francisco, Seattle and Honolulu. Travel CUTS, Canada's national student travel agency, has offices in Vancouver, Victoria, Edmonton, Saskatoon, Toronto, Ottawa, Montreal and Halifax. Again, you needn't be a student to use their services.

STA
    7202 Melrose Ave, Los Angeles, CA 90046
    (☎ (800) 777-0112, (213) 934-8722)
Council Travel
    205 East 42nd St, New York, NY 10017 (☎ (212) 661-1450, fax (212) 972-3231)
Travel CUTS
    171 College St, Toronto, Ontario M5T 1P7 (☎ (416) 977-3703, fax (416) 977-4796)

New York and Miami are the only places to look for courier flights to South America. For the widest selection of destinations, try Now Voyager (☎ (212) 431-1616), Air Facility (☎ (718) 712-0630) or Travel Courier (☎ (718) 738-9000) in New York, and Linehaul Services (☎ (305) 477-0651) or Discount Travel International (☎ (305) 538-1616) in Miami.

Sample Fares The best fares to a country are often with its national airline, eg:

Avianca (☎ 1 (800) 284-2622 toll free)
    The Colombian airline flies to Bogotá from Miami for as little as US$349 return, and from Los Angeles for US$769.
Sahsa (☎ 1 (800) 327-1225)
    The Honduran carrier flies from New Orleans to Colombia's Caribbean island of San Andrés (US$430 return), with connections to the mainland.
AeroPerú (☎ 1 (800) 777-7717)
    Typical low-season Advance Purchase return fares to Lima are US$569 from Miami, US$671 from New York and US$802 from Los Angeles.
Viasa (☎ 1 (800) 468-4272)
    A one-way ticket from Miami to Caracas costs US$294, but return fares are available as cheaply as US$310.

LAP (Líneas Aéreas Paraguayas) (☎ 1 (800) 677-7771)
    Air Paraguay is a traditional budget carrier, which has a six-month ticket from Miami to its Asunción hub for US$770, with connections to Bolivia, Peru, Chile, Argentina, Uruguay and Brazil. LAP also has a Visit South America pass which, as an extension of the international ticket, costs only US$789 in low season, US$989 in high season; valid for 30 days, it includes four coupons allowing flights to any of the above destinations.
LAB (Lloyd Aéreo Boliviano) (☎ 1 (800) 327-7407)
    LAB flies from Miami to La Paz for $425 one-way or $744 return for a two-month ticket, but also has a six-month fare to Santiago, Chile, for US$880.
LAN-Chile (☎ 1 (800) 735-5526)
    Has several flights weekly from New York, Miami, Los Angeles and Montreal. The normal one-way economy fare from Miami to Santiago is US$800, from New York US$954 and from Los Angeles US$1262, but there are return fares starting at US$1115 for up to 90 days, with restrictions. Flights from Montreal start at C$1499 for 30 days, but a special six-month ticket is available for C$1654.

Air Passes AeroPerú's Visit South America fare includes a return flight from the USA to Lima, and six coupons for flights within the continent to any of Guayaquil, La Paz, Santiago, São Paulo, Rio and Buenos Aires. Valid for 45 days and available only in the USA, low-season tickets cost US$999 from Miami, US$1314 from New York, and US$1396 from Los Angeles. Additional international coupons cost US$100 apiece, while internal coupons for Peruvian flights cost US$40 apiece. High-season tickets cost about US$100 more. AeroPerú's toll-free number in the USA and Canada is 1 (800) 777-7717.

LAP also sells passes valid for travel to other South American countries in conjunction with international flights to its Asunción hub. Its toll-free number for the USA and Canada is 1 (800) 677-7771.

To/From Australia & New Zealand
In terms of airfares only, the cheapest option may be to get a cheap fare to the USA, and find a cheap fare to South America from there – look for a connection via Los Angeles or Miami. For

example, Sydney-Los Angeles costs from about A$1200 return, valid for six months. A second connection from Los Angeles to say, Lima, could cost another A$922 return; a total of about A$2122. In practice, even a couple of days in the USA would eat up all the savings in airfares, so it's only good value if you want to visit the USA anyway. Qantas and Varig offer good combination fares to the USA and the northern half of South America.

For a more direct connection to South America from Australia or New Zealand, there are two main options. The most direct route is with Aerolíneas Argentinas from Sydney via Aucklandmand Ushuaia to Buenos Aires, with connections to Rio de Janiero, Lima or Santiago at little or no extra cost. From Melbourne you could fly to Auckland (eg with Air New Zealand) and join the Aerolíneas Argentinas flight there at about the same fare. From other Australian cities you will have to add the cost of getting to Sydney. As an excursion fare, the cost of this route depends on the length of stay: A$2125 return with a maximum stay of 21 days; A$2275 for 45 days; and A$2399 for six months. Up to six stopovers are permitted.

The other South American route is with Qantas or Air France/UTA to Tahiti, connecting with a LAN-Chile flight via Easter Island to Santiago, with free onward flight to either Rio or Buenos Aires. Again the cost depends on the length of stay: A$2090 return for 21 days; A$2299 for 45 days; and A$2399 for six months.

The best RTW options are probably those with Aerolíneas Argentinas combined with other airlines (including British Airways, Iberia, Singapore Airlines, Thai or KLM). A one-year RTW ticket with numerous stopovers will cost from A$2900 to A$3200, depending on the routing and how good a deal you can get.

For more information, contact:

Aerolíneas Argentinas
Level 2, 580 George St, Sydney 200 (☎ (02) 283-3660)
Level 6, Nauru House, 80 Collins St, Melbourne 3000 (☎ (03) 650-7111)

Air France/UTA
33 Bligh St, Sydney 2000 (☎ (02) 233-3277)
459 Collins St, Melbourne 3000 (☎ (03) 61-2041)
331 Queen St, Brisbane 7000 (☎ (07) 221-5655).
LAN-Chile
Level 4, 30 Clarence St, Sydney 2000 (☎ (02) 299-5599)
Varig
8-12 Bridge St, Sydney 2000 (☎ (02) 247-1821)

A number of agents offer cheap air tickets out of Australia. STA Travel has offices in all capital cities and on many university campuses. Flight Centres International also specialise in cheap airfares and have offices in most capital cities, and many suburban branches. Destination Holidays (☎ (03) 725-4655, (008) 33-7050) specialise in travel to Latin America. Also check out advertisements in Saturday editions of newspapers like the *Age* or the *Sydney Morning Herald*.

To/From Asia

There are few direct flights from Asia to South America. Varig flies from Tokyo to Rio (US$3249 one-way, US$3491 return) and Buenos Aires (US$3536 return), with a stopover or transit stop in Los Angeles, and Japan Airlines also flies from Tokyo to Rio, but your cheapest Asian options are via Europe or the USA.

The cheapest Asian cities in which to buy tickets are Hong Kong, Bangkok and Penang, with Singapore trailing behind those. The best connection is probably through Los Angeles. If you're heading to Colombia or Venezuela, try going to London for cheap flights to Caracas and Bogotá.

For information about cheap fares, the monthly *Business Traveller* is available at newsstands, or from 13th floor, 200 Lockhart Rd, Hong Kong.

To/From Central America

Flights from Central American countries are usually subject to high tax, and bucket shop deals are almost unobtainable. Nevertheless, most travellers fly from Central to South America, as it's still cheaper than going overland.

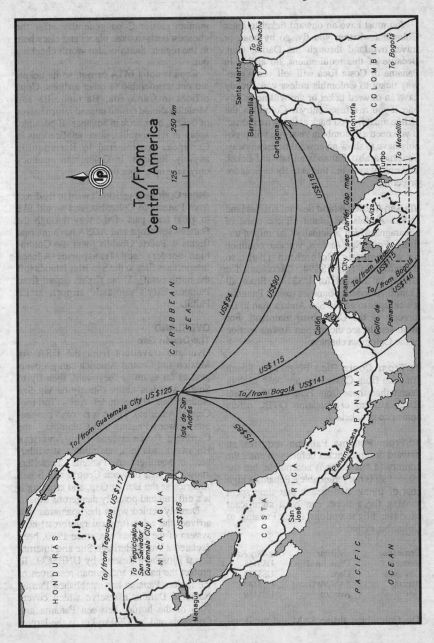

To/From Central America

0   125   250 km

CARIBBEAN SEA

To/from Guatemala City US$125
To/from Tegucigalpa US$117
To/from Tegucigalpa,
San Salvador &
Guatemala City

Isla de San Andrés

US$85

US$115

To/from Bogotá US$141

US$90

US$94

US$118

US$168

HONDURAS

NICARAGUA

Managua

COSTA RICA

San José

PACIFIC OCEAN

PANAMA

Panamericana

Gulfo de Panamá

Panama City — see Darién Gap map

Colón

To/from Medellín US$175
To/from Bogotá US$146

COLOMBIA

Turbo

To Medellín

Montería

Yaviza

Santa Marta

Barranquilla

Cartagena

To Riohacha

To Bogotá

You must have an onward ticket to enter Colombia whether you fly, go by boat, or travel overland through the Darién Gap. Because of this requirement, no airline in Panama or Costa Rica will sell you a one-way ticket to Colombia unless you already have an onward ticket or are willing to buy one; if you're refused entry to Colombia, the airline must fly you back at its own expense. If you need a Colombian visa, you will probably have to show an onward ticket anyway. Venezuela also demands an onward ticket. The only way avoid this is to fly to Ecuador or Peru.

Via San Andrés Island Several airlines land at San Andrés, an island off the coast of Nicaragua which is actually Colombian territory. From San Andrés, you can continue on a domestic Colombian flight to Barranquilla for US$94, Cartagena for US$90 or Bogotá for US$141. From all Central American countries except Panama, it's cheaper to go via San Andrés than to fly directly to the Colombian mainland. For more details, see the the San Andrés section of the Colombia chapter.

To/From Costa Rica Flights to South America from Costa Rica are only slightly dearer than those from Panama. The Costa Rican student organisation OTEC offers some cheap tickets.

To/From Panama Panama requires an onward or return ticket before you enter the country (a bus ticket is acceptable, but the return half is not refundable). Panama's high cost of living also means that time spent looking for a ticket can be a significant expense. Flight options from Panama to Colombia include:

Destination	Airline	One-Way Fare
Medellín	Copa, SAM	US$115
Cartagena	Copa	US$118
Bogotá	SAM, Avianca	US$146
Cali	Avianca	US$159

The Colombian airline SAM and the Pana-

manian carrier Copa generally offer the cheapest deals to these places and elsewhere in the region. Sahsa is also worth checking out.

Copa is not a IATA carrier, so its tickets are not transferable to other airlines. Copa offices in Cartagena, Barranquilla and Medellín should refund unused return halves of tickets, but check in advance. If possible, apply in Barranquilla, since applications in Cartagena are referred to Barranquilla anyway. Refunds, in Colombian currency only, take up to four days.

Other Options If you don't want to fly direct from Panama to Colombia, and would like to go at least part of the way through the Darién Gap, Copa and ADSA have internal flights to Puerto Obaldía (near the Colombian border), and Transportes Aéreos Interioranos flies to the San Blas Islands (off the north coast). These flights depart from Panama City's domestic airport, at La Paitilla.

OVERLAND
The Darién Gap
Overland travellers from the USA via Mexico and Central America can go overland as far south as they want, then fly to South America, either directly or via San Andrés (see above under Air – To/From Central America). There is no road connection between Panama and Colombia – the Carretera Panamericana (Pan-American Highway) ends in a vast rainforest wilderness in south-eastern Panama. Travellers know this area between Central and South America as the Darién Gap, and crossing it is a difficult and possibly dangerous trip.

Densely settled when the Spaniards first arrived, the *selva* (tropical rainforest) ecosystem of the Darién has, since 1980, been declared a World Heritage Site and International Biosphere Reserve by UNESCO. To protect the natural and human resources of the region, Panama has established Parque Nacional Darién, a reserve which covers 90% of the border between Panama and Colombia and, at 5790 sq km, is the largest national park in Central America. Across the border, the Colombian government has also established an equivalent reserve, Parque Natural Nacional Los Katíos.

Scientists have described this region, inhabited by the riverine Emberá and Wounaan peoples (often known together as Chocó Indians), as one of the most biologically diverse in tropical America. The better-known Cuna Indians live along the north coast of the Darién, and in the San Blas archipelago.

There are two main ways through the Gap. The first skirts the northern coast via the San Blas archipelago and Puerto Obaldía, using boat services and involving a minimum of walking. The second, through the rainforest from Yaviza (Panama) to the Río Atrato, in Colombia's Los Katíos national park, means walking most of the way. Either route is possible in as little as a week, but allow twice this time, especially for the rainforest route.

Remember that both Panama and Colombia demand onward tickets, so get one, and your visa if you need one, before setting out from either north or south. Many travellers have been turned back for lack of an onward ticket, especially coming from Colombia to Panama. Rumour has it that you *might* enter Colombia at Turbo without an onward ticket, so long as you have an impressive collection of travellers' cheques. Don't count on it – it's a long trip back to buy a ticket that you could have easily bought in the first place.

Take dried food with you, especially on the rainforest route, as there are few places to buy food. Carry drinking water and purification tablets or equipment.

Along the North Coast

This route starts at Colón (Panama) and goes via the San Blas archipelago to Puerto Obaldía, then to Capurganá (Colombia), Acandí, Titumate and on to Turbo. Thanks to Carlton Lee (USA), Krzysztof Dydynski, Juan Amado Iglesias (Panama), and various Colombian and Panamanian travellers for providing the information.

The first leg of the journey, from Colón to Puerto Obaldía via El Porvenir and the San

Blas archipelago, usually involves finding a cargo boat. This is not difficult, as merchant ships carrying passengers and supplies to the San Blas Islands ply the route regularly. Guardia Nacional cargo ships also sometimes take a few passengers on this route. Boats usually depart around midnight from Colón's Coco Solo pier, arriving in El Porvenir the next morning. You could also fly to El Porvenir from Panama City (there are several flights daily) and catch the boat from there.

A boat from Colón to Puerto Obaldía costs around US$25, meals included. It takes about five days, depending on how many of the 48 possible island stops are made en route. Make sleeping arrangements on deck – a hammock is very useful, but you might also spend a night or two on islands.

You could also fly directly from Panama City to Puerto Obaldía (US$21 one-way with Ansa, twice that with Aerotaxi).

Puerto Obaldía is a small tropical waystation between Colombia and Panama, with good beaches, palms and clear blue sea. If you're on a tight budget, you can sleep on the beach south of the town, though there are a few hotels if you'd prefer. If you're heading south, check with the immigration officer here for an exit stamp. If you're heading north, get an entry stamp here. Make sure you have all necessary papers, visas and onward tickets, as well as sufficient funds.

From Puerto Obaldía to the Colombian settlements of Capurganá and Acandí, there are infrequent launches and boats, but it's better to walk. The boats cost about US$17 for the one-hour trip. There's a well-defined, easily followed but often muddy trail to Acandí; if in doubt, ask directions at one of the many farmhouses along the way.

The first segment of the trail from Puerto Obaldía goes to La Miel, the last Panamanian village, a two-hour walk. From there, you climb a small hill, pass a border marker on the summit and descend to Sapzurro (Colombia), a beautifully set bayside fishing village, in another half-hour. Sapzurro has a couple of hospedajes, several restaurants and a Panamanian consulate – your last chance for a Panamanian visa if northbound. From Sapzurro, the footpath climbs again, then drops to the next coastal village, Capurganá, an easy 1½-hour walk.

Capurganá, the most touristy place in the whole area, gets pretty crowded from mid-December to late January (the Colombian holiday season), but at other times, it's a pleasant place to hang around for a day or two. It has a choice of budget hotels and restaurants, but if you want to get out quickly, you can fly to Medellín for about US$50.

From Capurganá, you can take a boat to Acandí (US$6, one hour) and continue on another to Turbo, but if you're not in a hurry, continue to Acandí on foot, allowing yourself the best part of a day for a beautiful walk. Start along the beach and follow the path, which sometimes goes a bit inland, climbing the hills to avoid the headlands.

An hour's walk brings you to Aguacate, a cluster of huts with a simple hospedaje. Follow the footpath another hour or so to Rufino, another cluster of houses (one used to be painted a conspicuous yellow), where the path continues inland, climbing the coastal ridge, passing it and dropping into the valley of the Río Acandí (another hour to this point). Follow the river downstream for a leisurely three-hour walk to Acandí. The path does not always follow the river and includes several fords, so be prepared to wet your shoes. This part of the track is often muddy.

Acandí is a fair-sized village with a church, two or three hotels, a few cafés, and several small shops selling mostly bottled and canned goods of limited variety and quantity. Some shops will change dollars into Colombian pesos, and will probably give a better rate than in Capurganá, or even in Turbo, the next stop.

Every morning, a launch goes from Acandí to Turbo via Titumate. The three to four-hour journey costs around US$10, but is only reliable during the first half of the year, when the sea is not too rough; at other times, it leaves in good weather only, but it's never a very smooth journey. Be

prepared to get soaked unless you have waterproof clothing, wrap anything you want to keep dry in plastic, and try to sit in the rear of the boat.

Turbo, a drab and dangerous port on the Golfo de Urabá, has a variety of fresh and canned foods, so northbound travellers should stock up here. Whether north or southbound, you need to obtain an exit or entry stamp at the Policía Distrito Especial, two blocks down from the harbour. It's very informal and quick as long as your papers are in order, but travellers who have arrived without an entry stamp, intending to get one in Cartagena, have been fined.

Turbo has no bank, but many shops and the more expensive hotels will exchange cash dollars – usually at a poor rate. Change just enough to get to Medellín or Cartagena. For accommodation and other details, see the Turbo section in the Colombia chapter.

Turbo has no Panamanian consulate, so northbound travellers should get a visa beforehand. It may be possible to get one in Sapzurro, but if the consulate there is closed for some reason, you will have to backtrack to Medellín or Barranquilla. To enter Panama, be sure you have an onward ticket as well; many travellers have been forced to backtrack to Medellín to get one.

The journey from Colón and Turbo is possible in as little as a week, but could easily take double that or longer, especially if you have to wait around for boats between Colón and Puerto Obaldía, or if you stay somewhere on the way. The San Blas archipelago, Sapzurro and Capurganá are the most pleasant places to break the journey.

Through the Rainforest
The original information about this journey comes from Lilian Wordell (Ireland), updated with more recent advice from both locals and travellers, particularly Peter Herlihy (USA).

Warning Though the Darién is still a wilderness area, it is not unpopulated; there are a fair number of people crossing the region by

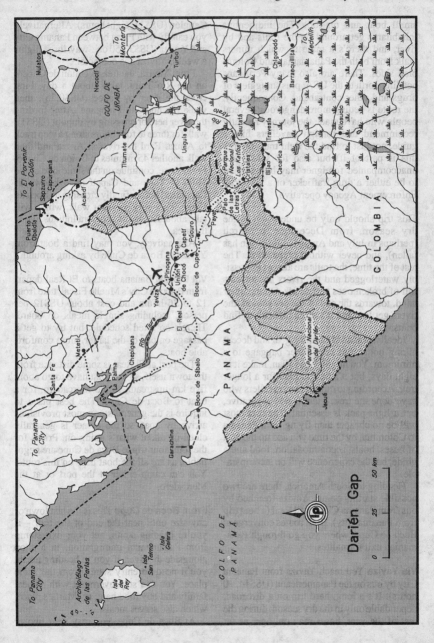

Darién Gap

small boat and on foot. The indigenous inhabitants get around on the trails and by river, and there's a mine to which miners walk from both the Panamanian and Colombian sides. There are also many Peruvians heading north to the USA, plus smugglers of drugs and other contraband. Consequently, the route is getting more dangerous; several people who have made the journey recently recommend that foreign travellers hire a guide, not just to find the right trail (though this is part of it) but also for safety. An unaccompanied foreigner may be assumed to be either a drug trafficker or a US Drug Enforcement Agency operative.

This trip should only be undertaken in the dry season, from December to March (perhaps in July and August, if little rain has fallen), and never without preparation. The rest of the time, the trails are almost impossibly waterlogged and the rivers are torrents full of broken trees and debris. On the other hand, towards the end of the dry season, the rivers get low and it's often difficult to find boats.

Ideally, you need camping gear and decent hiking boots, but keep other baggage to a minimum. You might, like Lilian, make it in eight days, but it's best to plan for a longer trek. According to quite a few travellers who have done the trek, a tent is not imperative, but a light pack *is* essential. The total cost will be no cheaper than flying from Panama to Colombia, by the time you add up the cost of buses, boats, accommodation, food and a guide, but the experience will be incomparable.

Heading to South America, there are two possible starting points: Yaviza (reached by bus from Panama City) or El Real (a boat trip from Panama City). Both routes converge at Boca de Cupe, where you go through Panamanian exit formalites.

Via Yaviza You reach Yaviza from Panama City by bus on the Panamericana (US$14, 10 hours). It's a long, hard trip on a dirt road, dependable only in the dry season; during the rest of the year, buses may only get as far

Canglón (US$11, eight hours). Alternatively you can fly with Parsa between Panama City and Yaviza (US$33.50 one-way, three flights a week). Yaviza has one hotel.

From Yaviza, the trek to Unión de Chocó, on the Río Tuira, takes about a day. First cross the river by canoe (US$0.25), then walk 1½ hours to Pinogana. After fording the river here or crossing by dugout (US$1), walk for three to four hours along a jeep track to Aruza. Ford the river at Aruza and then walk another 45 minutes to Unión de Chocó. From there, continue on the same side of the Tuira to Yape and Capetí (also known as Capetuira) before finally crossing to Boca de Cupe. It's a very pleasant walk, which will take about five hours. Emberá Indians live in the area.

Alternatively, you may find a boat from Yaviza to Boca de Cupe by asking around.

Via El Real Banana boats to El Real depart from Panama City's Muelle Fiscal, take from 12 to 36 hours and cost about US$12 per person, including simple meals on board. There's no fixed schedule, but try to get a passage on one of the larger, more comfortable boats.

The port at El Real is some distance from the town itself, so you first have to go about five km upstream, to the Mercadero, for a boat to Boca de Cupe. The best place to inquire is the general store; most provisions arrive by boat, so the owner is generally clued-up about what's going on. Prices for the four-hour trip to Boca de Cupe are negotiable, as are all the boat trips on this route. You can camp either at the port or at the Mercadero.

From Boca de Cupe This is the last town of any size until near the end of the trail – if you're heading south, get your exit stamp from Panamanian immigration, in a shop alongside the river. If you're heading north, you'll need an entry stamp from the same place. You can stay overnight with a local family and buy food here; try María's place, which also serves meals.

At Boca de Cupe, you may wait two or

three days for a boat to the Indian village of Púcuro, a five or six-hour trip (US$30). When the river is high, you land right at the village, but otherwise, it's a half-hour walk. Ask someone where you can stay for the night; the village chief may let you sleep in the meeting hall for a fee (but don't expect any privacy), but there are other possibilities. If you want to keep moving, ask where the trail to Paya starts.

Paya The 18-km walk to Paya, the next village, can be done in a day and involves four river crossings (all rivers are fordable); after the third crossing, the trail is faint. There are good camp sites just before the third crossing and just after the last. Guides can be hired in Púcuro for this section of the trail for about US$20, but don't pay in advance. The walk should take about six hours.

At Paya, you will probably meet the chief's son, who will have you taken either to the barracks (about two km away, where you can stay for the night and buy cheap meals) or to the house of any gringo who is staying there on a study programme.

Paya was once a centre of traditional learning, with a historic mountain where Cuna *sahilas* (shamans) came to study traditional arts like magic, medicine and history. The area fell on hard times about a century ago as the Emberá pushed the Cuna out. It's still an interesting place, but be discreet with your camera, and ask permission before taking photographs. There's a foot-and-mouth disease control station where arrivals from Colombia will have their baggage inspected and anything made of leather, or vaguely resembling leather, will be dipped in a mild antiseptic to kill any pathogens.

Paya to Cristales The next part of the trail, from Paya to Cristales via Palo de Letras (the border marker between Panama and Colombia), is the most difficult stage. It usually takes one or two days, though you can do it in 10 hours under ideal conditions. It's also the part where you're most likely to get lost, so you'll appreciate a guide.

The first part of the trail to Palo de Letras is uphill and well marked; a 1972 British Army expedition cut the trail, which is still about three metres wide and used constantly by local Indians. From the border, it's downhill about 30 km (seven hours) to Cristales, but there are several river crossings where the trail becomes indistinct or confusing. After the last crossing, you enter cultivated areas and must keep left whenever the trail forks. Quite a few travellers have had adventures (some would call them freak-outs) near the end of this leg of the journey, when they got lost at night and had to wade down the river for an hour to Cristales.

Cristales is the next stop, but only half an hour downstream is the headquarters of Parque Natural Nacional Los Katíos, where bed and board are available at very reasonable rates. The park is across the river and the staff at the park headquarters is very friendly and helpful. They may let you sleep on the porch free of charge.

Cristales to Turbo The last part of the trip is by a combination of motorised dugouts and banana boats, which shouldn't cost more than about US$25 in total. If park staff members are going for supplies in Turbo, it can be done in one haul, but if not, you'll first have to find a motorised dugout to Bijao (US$5, two hours) and then, possibly, another to Travesía on the Río Atrato (three hours). The best person to ask about boats in Bijao is the store owner, but you may have to wait a few days before a boat turns up. There is a shop in Travesía with expensive food, soft drinks and beer.

Fast passenger motorboats come through from the town of Riosucio every morning, stop at Travesía and continue to Turbo (US$9, two hours). If you decide to take one of the cargo boats on the Atrato, allow an entire day; your boat may stop en route several times to load, unload, fish, rest, fix the engine, visit the family or for a hundred other unexpected reasons. For information about Turbo, see the previous section, Along the North Coast.

If you take this rainforest route through the Darién Gap, take a copy of *Backpacking in Mexico & Central America* (see Guide Books in the Facts for the Visitor chapter).

SEA
To/From North America

The best chance for a passenger berth on a cargo ship is from US ports on the Gulf of Mexico. The cheapest option is Venezuelan Lines (CAVN) (☎ (713) 461-2286), 820 Gessner, Houston, TX 77024, which has monthly sailings to several Venezuelan ports – passengers must disembark at the first stop,

which is usually Maracaibo. They can take seven to 12 passengers for US$190 one-way, but usually need a month's notice; berths are almost unobtainable in July, August and September. Remember that, for most travellers, Venezuela requires a visa and a return or onward ticket.

Lykes Lines (☎ (504) 523-6611), 300 Poydras St, New Orleans, LA 70130, sails from Pensacola, New Orleans and Houston to the Peruvian ports of Callao, Matarani and Salaverry. Fares for the 10-day trip to Callao are about US$1000. For an account of one of their voyages on the Pacific coast of South America, read John McPhee's *Looking for a Ship* (Farrar Strauss Giroux, New York, 1990).

Getting Around

AIR

Because of vast distances between population centres and geographical barriers to overland travel, South America was one of the first regions to develop internal air services. There is an extensive pattern of domestic flights, with surprisingly low prices, especially in the Andean countries. After several 18-hour-plus bus journeys across mountains on atrocious roads, you may decide, as many travellers do, to take an occasional flight.

There are drawbacks, however, especially in Peru and Bolivia. Planes rarely depart on time, and AeroPerú and LAB are notorious for last-minute cancellations, so a backlog of passengers builds up, all intent on getting on the next flight, with resultant bedlam at the

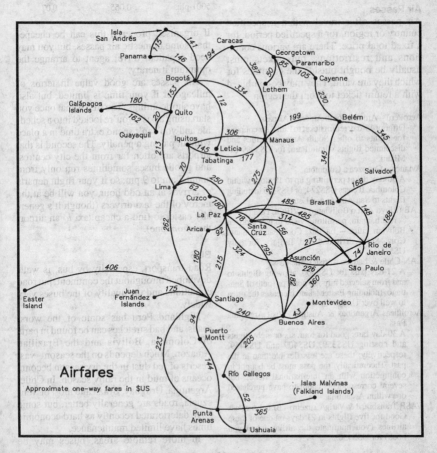

Airfares

Approximate one-way fares in $US

check-in counter. The most notorious spot for this is Ayacucho (Peru); fortunately, this is a pleasant place to stay for a few days, but it's still disastrous if you have to catch a connecting international flight in Lima. In Peru, reconfirm all flights 48 hours before departure, regardless of what anyone tells you, to be certain of a seat.

Internal flights in Chile, Argentina, Brazil and Venezuela tend to be considerably more expensive. You may hear stories about free flights on military aircraft from time to time, but you should never count on catching one.

Air Passes

Air passes offer travel within a specified country or region, for a specified period, for a fixed total price. There are various conditions and restrictions, but tickets must usually be bought outside the countries for which they are valid. They may be combined with a return ticket to/from the region.

AeroPerú – Around South America Airpass
Offers a 45-day return ticket to Lima, six coupons for flights to other South American cities and discounted flights within Peru, for US$999 ex-Miami.

Avianca – Conozca a Colombia
A 30-day ticket permitting up to 10 stops within Colombia. It costs US$224, or US$325 including flights to San Andrés and Leticia.

LAB (Lloyd Aéreo Boliviano) – VIBOL Pass
A real bargain, permitting visits to half a dozen Bolivian cities – La Paz, Cochabamba, Santa Cruz, Sucre, Trinidad and Tarija – for only US$150.

LAN-Chile & Ladeco – Visit Chile Pass
A 21-day pass for US$300, allowing flights to and from selected airports north or south of Santiago. Including Easter Island increases the price to well over US$1000.

Aerolíneas Argentinas & Austral – Visit Argentina Pass
A 30-day fare, good for four, six or eight flights and costing US$359, US$409 and US$459, respectively; these are less flexible than in the past. Theoretically, the pass must be bought in conjunction with an international ticket, but several correspondents claim to have purchased one within Argentina.

VASP, Transbrasil & Varig/Cruzeiro – Brazil Air Pass
Good for five flights in 21 days on one of these airlines (you nominate the airline when you book) for US$450.

Mercosur Pass This interesting new option is a mileage-based pass, which allows travellers to visit widespread areas in Brazil, Paraguay, Argentina and Uruguay on virtually any major carrier in those countries. Details are somewhat complicated, but the fare structure is roughly thus:

Distance (km)	Visiting 3-4 countries (US$ per km)	Visiting 2 countries (US$ per km)
2000-3000	0.085	0.09
3001-4000	0.075	0.08
4001-5000	0.07	0.075
5001-plus	0.065	0.07

If organised properly, this can be cheaper than some domestic air passes, but you may need a patient travel agent to arrange the optimum itinerary.

Air passes are good value in terms of mileage or if your time is limited, but also have shortcomings. The first is that once you start using a pass, you're locked into a schedule and you can't spend extra time in a place without paying a penalty. The second is that airports are often far from the city centres, and public buses sometimes run only from about 7 am to 9 pm, so if your flight departs or arrives at an odd hour, you will be at the mercy of the taxi drivers (though it's generally easier to find a cheap taxi *to* an airport than *from* one).

BUS

Road transport, especially by bus, is well-developed throughout the continent, but road conditions and the quality of the buses vary widely.

Highland Peru has some of the worst roads, and bad stretches can be found in parts of Colombia, Bolivia and the Brazilian Amazon. Much depends on the season – vast deserts of red dust in the dry season become oceans of mud in the rainy season. In Chile, Argentina, Uruguay, Brazil and most of Venezuela, roads are generally better, but some have deteriorated recently as hard economic times have limited maintenance.

In more remote areas, buses may be

stripped to their bare essentials; tyres often haven't seen tread for years and they all seem to be held together by a double set of springs at the back, which makes the suspension rock-hard and ensures that each and every bump is transmitted directly to your backside. Seats are numbered, after a fashion, and can be booked in advance. When all the seats are taken, the corridor is then packed to capacity and beyond, and the roof is loaded with cargo to at least half the height of the bus, and topped by the occasional goat. You may have serious doubts about ever arriving, and nearly panic when the bus hits a pothole or a section of road with the wrong camber and lurches to one side. But the buses usually make it, and after a shower and a sleep, you wake up and start laughing about the trip, remembering the beauty of the scenery, and you're ready for the next leg of your journey – almost!

At the other extreme, you'll find very comfortable coaches in Venezuela, Argentina, Brazil, Chile, Colombia and Uruguay. In the last four countries, there are even sleepers on long hauls, but the ordinary buses are comfy enough in comparison with those in the Andean countries.

Most major cities and towns have a *terminal de autobuses* (central bus terminal); in Brazil, it's called a *rodoviária*. Most companies maintain ticket offices at these terminals and have information boards showing routes, departure times, fares and whether the bus is direct or otherwise. The biggest and best terminals also have restaurants, shops, showers and other services, and the surrounding area is often a good place to look for cheap accommodation and food. In some smaller towns, particularly in Colombia, Ecuador and Peru, there may not be a central terminal; each company will have its own, which may be nothing more than a parking area and a ticket seller. Seats are numbered and booked in advance, but except on major routes between large cities, it's unlikely that all seats will be booked more than an hour before departure.

TRAIN

South American railways, covering some of the most spectacular routes on earth, are invariably cheaper than buses (even in 1st class) but they're also slower. Railway enthusiasts should note the following routes:

Santa Marta-Bogotá (Colombia)
> A slow rise from sea level to the capital, at 2640 metres.

Lima-Huancayo (Peru)
> One of the world's highest railways rises from sea level to the 4600-metre Oroya Pass, before dropping to about 3200 metres.

Puno/Juliaca-Arequipa (Peru)
> Climbing from the shores of Lake Titicaca (3812 metres), it crosses a 4600-metre pass.

La Paz-Arica (Bolivia-Chile)
> It descends from 4000 metres to sea level.

Oruro-Calama (Bolivia-Chile)
> The drop from 4000 metres to sea level takes you through spectacular lunar-type landscapes and extinct volcanos.

Salta-San Antonio de los Cobres (Argentina)
> The Tren a los Nubes (Train to the Clouds) runs through the arid foothills on the eastern slope of the Andes, with spectacular bridges and tunnels. It's difficult, but possible, to continue by freight train over the Andes to Chile.

There are several types of passenger trains in South America. The *ferrobus* is a relatively fast, diesel-powered single or double car, which caters for passengers going from A to B but not to intermediate stations. Meals are often available on board. You must book your ticket in advance (well in advance on popular routes like La Paz-Arica). These are the most expensive trains and the preferred means of transport in Bolivia; they're excellent value.

The *tren rápido* is more like an ordinary train, pulled by either a diesel or steam engine. It is relatively fast, makes only a few stops and is generally cheaper than a ferrobus. Ordinary passenger trains, sometimes called *expresos* ('express' is a relative term), are slower, cheaper and stop at most stations en route. There are generally two classes, with 2nd class being very crowded. Lastly, there are *mixtos*, mixed passenger and freight trains, which take everything and everyone, stop at every station and a lot of other places besides, take forever to reach their destination and are dirt cheap.

In several countries, most notably Argentina and Uruguay, passenger trains have nearly disappeared because the large operating deficits of these state enterprises were unsustainable. Brazil is also curtailing its passenger rail services.

DRIVING

In parts of South America like Patagonia, where distances are great and buses can be infrequent, driving yourself is worth considering, despite the expense. You must have an International or Inter-American Driving Permit to supplement your home driving licence.

Driving has both advantages and disadvantages. Advantages include freedom from timetables, the ability to stay wherever you like (particularly if you have camping equipment), the opportunity to get off the beaten track and the flexibility to stop whenever you see something interesting. Disadvantages include security problems, most notably in the Andean countries and Brazil; reinforce your security system before arriving in South America, avoid leaving valuables in the vehicle whenever possible and always lock it securely. Also, remember that many Argentines and Brazilians are very reckless and sometimes wilfully dangerous drivers.

Rental

Major international rental agencies such as Hertz, Avis and A1 have offices in South American capitals and other major cities, but there are also local agencies. To rent a car, you must have a valid driver's licence and be at least 25 years of age. It may also be necessary to present a credit card such as MasterCard or Visa, or pay a large cash deposit.

Even at smaller agencies, rental charges are very high, but if several people share expenses, it's feasible. If the vehicle enables you to camp out, the saving in accommodation may offset much of the car rental cost, especially in the Southern Cone countries.

Purchase

If you're spending several months in South America, purchasing a car is worth consideration. It's likely to be cheaper than renting, especially if you can resell it at the end of your stay. On the other hand, any used car can be a risk, especially on rugged back roads.

The best countries in which to purchase cars are Argentina, Chile and Brazil, but you must often deal with exasperating bureaucracies. Be certain of the title; as a foreigner, you may find it very useful to get a notarised document authorising your use of the car, since the bureaucracy may take some time to change the title. In some instances, you may find obstacles to taking a vehicle purchased in South America across international borders.

Shipping a Vehicle

A surprising number of people take their own transport. Jonathon Hewat, who drove a Volkswagen Kombi around the world, wrote a book called *Overland and Beyond* (Roger Lascelles, 47 York Rd, Brentford, Middlesex TW8 0QP, UK), which is worthwhile for anyone contemplating such a trip.

Documents You must submit three notarised copies of the car's title to the shipper, plus a letter of permission from the lienholder if the car is not completely paid for. Most countries have dispensed with the bothersome *carnet de passage en douane*, but check (well before shipping) with the consulate of the country where your vehicle will arrive. On arrival, make it clear to customs officials that the vehicle is only in transit; in the case of Chile, for example, the maximum stay is 90 days. Once you have entered South America, border crossings should be routine in a vehicle from your home country.

Some travellers have had horrendous experiences taking vehicles, especially motorcycles, from Panama to South America without proper documentation. Before heading south, check with the consulates of the countries you will be visiting.

To/From North America Shipping a car to South America is not cheap, but the bureaucracy is less demanding than in the recent past. Prices are variable, so call several places before committing yourself; look in the Yellow Pages under 'Automobile Transporters' for toll-free 800 numbers.

It is generally cheapest to ship from US Atlantic ports than from Pacific ports. As a destination, Valparaíso is one of the better choices, since Chile's bureaucracy is amongst the most reasonable; Barranquilla (Colombia) and Guayaquil (Ecuador) are other possibilities. You must usually give one or two weeks' notice to the shipper, and expect it to take a month or more from the date of sailing. Approximate costs from eastern US ports start at around US$1500 to Barranquilla or Valparaíso.

To/From Central America Another alternative is to drive through Central America and ship your vehicle from Panama to Colombia, which is neither cheap nor easy, but people do it. There is a lot of cargo traffic between the two countries, but shipping the vehicle will involve a lot of paperwork on both sides, and will require investigation, time, money and patience.

Shipping may be by boat or by air. Air cargo planes do have size limits, but a normal car, or even a Land Rover, can fit. For motorcyclists, air is probably the easiest option; you may be able to get a special rate for air cargo if you are also flying with the same airline. Start by asking the cargo departments of the airlines that fly there (like Copa), or at the cargo terminal at Tocumen international airport in Panama City. Travel agents can sometimes help.

To mainland Colombia, the options are the Pacific port of Buenaventura or the Caribbean ports Cartagena or Barranquilla; most people find the Caribbean easier. To find a cargo boat heading that way, go to the docks in Colón and ask what ships are going. You'll come up with many options, some better than others.

Smaller cargo vessels depart from Coco Solo pier in Colón. They may offer you the best price but may not be able to help you with Colombian paperwork. These smaller vessels are sometimes contraband boats, and their service is probably the most risky and uncomfortable, but also the cheapest. Prices are very negotiable; they might start out asking US$1500 and come down to half that, but you might prefer a more established shipper. As a general rule, you might expect to pay a minimum of about US$700 to ship a vehicle from Colón to Cartagena or Barranquilla, but it could easily cost US$1000 or more.

Via San Andrés Another option is to go first to the Colombian island of San Andrés, and then to the mainland. Various companies ship regularly between Colón and San Andrés; one with a good reputation is Mitchell Express, run by Mario Mitchell, but there are others. The rate to San Andrés will probably be around US$500 or US$600.

On San Andrés, you'll have to find another boat to the mainland, which will probably cost a further US$500 or US$600. Cargo ships run a semiregular schedule between San Andrés and Cartagena or Barranquilla, but only every week or two. Fortunately, San Andrés is a pleasant place to hang around in the meantime.

Domestic cargo flights run several times a week between San Andrés and mainland Colombia. These flights also take passengers, and may work out cheaper than boats. For information about cargo flights, ask Señor Turconi – he runs a minimarket in San Andrés, Carnicería Turconi, at Avenida 20 de Julio, No 3-79.

Security
If you cannot stay with your vehicle every minute, you can expect that something will be stolen from it. Stealing from vehicles being shipped is big business. If you ship the vehicle with all your possessions in it, take every precaution, and even then, don't be surprised if thieves get your stuff. Remove everything removable (hubcaps, wipers, mirrors, etc) and take everything visible out of the interior. Camper vans are a special

target – seal off the living area from the driving compartment, double-lock the living area, cover the windows so no one can see inside, and double-lock your possessions *again* inside the cabinets.

BICYCLE

Bicycling is an interesting and inexpensive alternative, especially in the Southern Cone countries, where roads are better and transport costs tend to be higher. Racing bicycles are suitable for paved roads, but on the mostly gravelled or dirt roads of the Andes, a mountain bike *(todo terreno)* is a better choice. Bring your own bicycle, since locally manufactured ones are less sturdy and dependable.

There are many good cycling routes, especially in the lake districts of Chile and Argentina. Travellers have even cycled the length of Brazil's Trans-Amazon Highway. Cycling's pace lets you cover a fair amount of ground without going too fast to enjoy the scenery, enables you to stop for anything interesting, keeps you in excellent physical condition and encourages contact with local people, who are often curious about cyclists.

Bicycle mechanics are common even in small South American towns but will almost certainly lack the parts you need.Before coming to South America, make an effort to become a competent bicycle mechanic, and purchase spares for the pieces most likely to fail.

There are several other drawbacks to cycling. One is the weather; rain in Brazil or wind in Patagonia can slow your progress to a crawl. High altitude and poor roads are factors in the Andean countries. Brazilian and Argentine motorists, with a total disregard of anyone but themselves, are a serious hazard to cyclists.

HITCHING

It's possible to hitchhike all over South America, but free lifts are the rule only in Argentina (where it's difficult in parts of Patagonia), Chile (difficult beyond Puerto Montt, where roads are few), Uruguay and parts of Brazil.

Elsewhere, drivers expect payment for lifts, and hitching is virtually a form of public transport, especially among poor people, and in the highlands, where buses can be infrequent. There are more or less fixed fares over certain routes – just ask the other passengers what they're paying. It's usually less than the bus fare, but can be the same in some places. You get a better view from the top of a lorry and people tend to be friendlier, but if you're hitching on the Andean altiplano, take warm clothing. Once the sun goes down or is obscured by clouds, it gets *very* cold.

There's no need to wait at the roadside for a lift, unless it happens to be convenient. Almost every town has its central lorry park, often in or near the market. Ask around for a lorry going in your direction and how much it will cost; be there about half an hour before the driver says he's going. If the driver has a full load of passengers, you'll leave more or less on time, but if not, he may spend some time driving around town hunting for more. It is often worth soliciting a ride at *servicentros* on the outskirts of large cities, where truck drivers refuel their vehicles. Private cars are often stuffed with families and children.

Although many travellers hitchhike, it is not a totally safe way to get around. Just because we explain how hitching works doesn't mean we recommend it. Women can and do hitchhike alone, but should exercise caution, and especially avoid getting into a car with more than one man.

BOAT

Many travellers dream about cruising down big rivers like the Orinoco or Amazon, but you'll have a more idyllic time on one of the smaller rivers like the Mamoré or Beni, where boats hug the shore and you can see and hear the wildlife.

The Amazon, by contrast, is densely settled, especially in its lower reaches, while economic imperatives have reduced opportunies for passenger travel in its upper reaches. An alternative is the Río Paraguay, upstream from Asunción (Paraguay) to Brazil.

For a comfortable trip, take a hammock, mosquito net, some food and a container for drinking water. Expect delays on longer trips and remember that local services move at local pace, which can be very slow.

There are outstanding lake excursions in southern Chile and Argentina. The best sea trip in South America is down the Chilean coast from Puerto Montt to Puerto Natales. An ocean trip from Valparaíso to the Juan Fernández Islands is also a possibility. See the Chile chapter for details.

Argentina

The cultural dominance of immigrants in Argentina led historian Alfred Crosby to call the River Plate (Río de la Plata) region a 'neo-Europe', in which trans-Atlantic plants and animals transformed the natural environment and ensured the demise of pre-Columbian cultures. Argentina's immigrant society fed its European parent with grains and beef, made a mark in literature and exported the tango to continental salons. Such links make it a society in which foreigners feel at ease and inconspicuous, but persistent regionalisms resist a uniform nationality and contribute to an unexpectedly great cultural diversity.

Argentina has a string of alpine parks among the glaciers and blue-green lakes of its southern cordillera. The central Andes contain some of the continent's highest peaks, the colourful northern deserts are no less impressive, and the Iguazú Falls, shared with Brazil, are legendary. Desolate southern Patagonia, with its massive concentrations of sub-Antarctic wildlife, forms a striking contrast to the cosmopolitan frenzy of Buenos Aires.

Facts about the Country

HISTORY

In pre-Columbian times, sedentary Diaguita Indians cultivated maize in the Andean North-West; to the east, in the forested Paraná delta, the Guaraní grew maize and tubers like manioc (cassava). Mostly, though, nomadic peoples hunted the guanaco (a relative of the llama) and the rhea (an ostrich-like bird) on the Pampas and in Patagonia, and Fuegian Indians gathered shellfish and birds' eggs.

Indian resistance forced early Spaniards out of Buenos Aires. Spanish forces re-established the city by 1580, but it languished compared to Tucumán, Córdoba and Salta, which provided mules, cloth and foodstuffs for the mines of Alto Peru (Bolivia). Spaniards from Chile settled the trans-Andean Cuyo region, which produced wine and grain.

The North-West's declining Indian population, and the Indians' relatively small numbers in the rest of the country, produced a peculiarly Argentine maldistribution of land. The hacienda was never so important as in Peru or Mexico; instead, the livestock *estancia* dominated development.

Spaniards returning to the Pampas in the late 16th century found that cattle and horses had become the agents of 'ecological imperialism' – with commerce shackled by Spanish mercantile interests, colonial Buenos Aires lived on livestock, though

Argentina

0   200   400 km

Islas Malvinas/Falkland Islands

ironically, the taming of feral horses aided the Indian resistance. Without horses and cattle, the legendary gaucho could never have existed, but their growing commercial importance brought about the gaucho's demise.

Growth & Independence

Buenos Aires' designation as capital of the new Viceroyalty of Río de la Plata, in 1776, demonstrated that it had outgrown Spanish domination. After expelling British invaders from Buenos Aires in 1806 and 1807, confident *criollos* revolted against Spain in 1810 and declared independence in 1816.

Despite this unity, provincial *caudillos* (local strongmen) resisted Buenos Aires' authority. President D F Sarmiento castigated demagogic caudillos in his classic *Life in the Argentine Republic in the Days of the Tyrants*, yet they commanded great loyalty – Darwin observed that Juan Manuel Rosas 'by conforming to the dress and habits of the Gauchos...obtained an unbounded popularity in the country'.

Provincial Federalists, allied to conservative landowners, opposed the Unitarists of Buenos Aires, who looked to Europe for capital, immigrants and ideas. For decades, their bloody, vindictive conflicts nearly exhausted the country.

The Reign of Rosas

Rosas represented *estancieros*, but also helped centralise power in Buenos Aires, building a large army, creating the ruthless *mazorca* (political police), institutionalising torture and forcing overseas trade through the port city. Sarmiento wrote that Rosas 'applied the knife of the gaucho to the culture of Buenos Ayres, and destroyed the work of centuries – of civilisation, law and liberty'. The Unitarists, and former allies, forced him from power in 1852.

The Roots of Modern Argentina

The Unitarist constitution of 1853 even allowed the President to dissolve provincial administrations. Its Liberal economic ideology opened the Pampas, Mesopotamia and Córdoba to foreign investment, trade and immigration, but barely affected interior provinces.

European immigrants filled key roles in crafts and commerce. Basque and Irish refugees tended the sheep which displaced semi-wild cattle on many estancias. After 1880, Argentina became a major producer of cereals for export, as immigrant Swiss, Germans and Italians proved successful farmers in Santa Fe and Entre Ríos; however, bargain sales of public lands encouraged speculation and reduced such opportunities. Many immigrants, faced with rural alternatives of sharecropping or seasonal labour, remained in Buenos Aires.

British capital went to infrastructure, such as the highly developed rail network that soon fanned out in all directions from Buenos Aires, but vulnerability to global economic fluctuations stimulated debate over foreign investment and encouraged protectionism. The only sectors to benefit from protection were agricultural commodities like wheat, wine and sugar, which encouraged land speculation, a boom in land prices and paper money loans, whose depreciation nearly bankrupted the country.

By reducing rural opportunities, speculation also encouraged urban growth. In the 1880s, immigration nearly doubled the population of Buenos Aires. Urban services like transport, power and water improved, but industry could not absorb all the immigrants, and at the onset of the 1929 depression, the military took power from ineffectual civilians. An obscure colonel, Juan Domingo Perón, was the first leader to really confront the crisis.

Perón & His Legacy

As Juan Perón (born 1895) grew to maturity, Argentina was one of the world's most prosperous countries, but many resented the *oligarquía terrateniente* (landed elite) and British interests which had built the railways and flooded local markets with cheap manufactures.

From a minor post in the labour ministry, Perón won the presidency in 1946, and again in 1952. His economic programme, stressing domestic industrialisation and economic independence, appealed to conservative nationalists and to working-class elements who mistrusted foreign capital and benefitted from improved wages, pensions, job security and working conditions. Remarkably, Perón avoided alienating either sector, despite a virtual civil war between them.

Perón's second presidency was undermined by economic difficulties, especially a shortage of investment funds as capital was unavailable from war-torn Europe. In 1955, a coup against him began nearly three decades of disastrous military rule.

Exile & Return
His party banned and factionalised, Perón wandered to several countries before landing in Spain, where he plotted his return with a bizarre retinue of advisors, including spiritualist José López Rega. Their opportunity came when, in 1973, the military permitted elections, in which Peronist Hector Cámpora won the presidency. Cámpora's early resignation brought new elections, won handily by Perón, but Perón's death, in mid-1974, left a country in chaos. Manipulated by López Rega, his ill-qualified wife, María Estela Martínez (Isabelita), inherited the presidency. The left-wing Montoneros went underground, kidnapping and executing their enemies, robbing banks and bombing foreign companies, while the ERP (Ejército Revolucionario Popular; Popular Revolutionary Army) battled in Tucumán's mountainous forests. López Rega's AAA (Alianza Argentina Anti-Comunista; Argentine Anti-Communist Alliance) assassinated labour leaders, academics and other 'subversives'.

The Dirty War (1976-83)
In March 1976, the military overthrew an inept Isabel Perón, who went to Spain and challenged Imelda Marcos and Nancy Reagan for the world's most extravagant wardrobe. The coup was bloodless, but the regime of General Jorge Videla instituted an unparalleled reign of terror, the so-called Proceso de Reorganización Nacional. In theory and rhetoric, the Proceso was meant to stabilise the economy by eliminating corruption, creating a basis for enduring democracy. In practice, it was an orgy of corruption in the name of development, accompanied by uncontrolled state-sponsored violence and anarchy.

The army quickly eliminated the naive ERP, but thousands of innocents died in the infamous 'Guerra Sucia' (Dirty War) against the more intricately organised Montoneros. Paramilitary death squads like the AAA claimed many more victims.

The 'Disappeared'
The dictatorship barely distinguished between guerrillas, those who assisted guerrillas, those who sympathised with the guerrillas without assisting them, and those who expressed reservations about the dictatorship's indiscriminate brutality in the war against the guerrillas. For at least 9000 people, to 'disappear' meant to be detained, tortured and probably killed, without legal process.

The government rarely acknowledged detentions, though it sometimes reported deaths of individuals in 'battles with security forces'. A few courageous individuals and groups, like Nobel Peace Prize winner Adolfo Pérez Esquivel and the Madres de la Plaza de Mayo (the women who kept a vigil for their disappeared sons in Buenos Aires' Plaza de Mayo), kept the story in public view, but the Dirty War ended only when the forces attempted a real military objective – the Falklands Islands.

The Falklands War
During military rule, economic decline continued, with triple-digit inflation, increased unemployment, and cheap imports which undermined local industry. Lip service to austerity attracted billions of loan dollars, which went to grandiose public works, Swiss bank accounts, and the latest weapons. Almost overnight, the import splurge and debt burden brought economic collapse, devaluation gutted the peso, inflation

returned to astronomical levels and the Proceso came undone.

In early 1981, General Roberto Viola replaced Videla as de facto president, but General Leopoldo Galtieri soon replaced the ineffectual Viola. When continuing economic deterioration and popular discontent brought mass demonstrations, a desperate Galtieri invaded the British-controlled Falkland (Malvinas) Islands, in April 1982.

Occupation of the Malvinas, claimed by Argentina for 150 years, unleashed a wave of nationalist euphoria, but Argentina's ill-trained and poorly motivated forces soon surrendered. The military meekly withdrew from government and, in 1983, Argentines elected Raúl Alfonsín, of the Radical Civic Union, to the presidency.

For more information on the war, see the Falkland Islands chapter.

Aftermath

Alfonsín's pledge to try military officers for human rights violations brought convictions of Videla, Viola and others for kidnap, torture and murder, but attempts to extend trials to junior officers led to uprisings which might have toppled Alfonsín but which, had they been more forcefully resisted, might have permanently subjugated the military. Instead, a 'Law of Due Obedience' almost eliminated prosecutions of those who had been 'following orders'.

Current President, Carlos Menem, himself a prisoner during the Dirty War, inexplicably pardoned Videla, other military officers, and Montonero Mario Firmenich (who, some speculated, still had access to funds which might benefit the Peronist party). As of mid-1993, no one anticipates military domination, but the spectre of intervention has not disappeared.

GEOGRAPHY & CLIMATE

Argentina's land area of about 2.8 million square km, excluding South Atlantic islands and Antarctic claims, makes it the world's eighth largest country, slightly smaller than India. The major geographic regions are:

Cuyo & the Andean North-West

The Andes are a formidable barrier in that area which was colonised from Peru. Perennial streams provide irrigation water, but only a few inhabitants live in scattered mining settlements or herd llamas on the high *puna*. South of Tucumán, Argentina's smallest province, rainfall is inadequate for crops, but irrigation has boosted the wine-producing Cuyo region (Mendoza, San Juan and San Luis provinces). La Rioja and Catamarca provinces are less well-to-do. In western Jujuy and Salta provinces, soaring volcanic peaks punctuate the puna and *salares* (salt lakes), while to the east, a range of foothills gives way to dissected river valleys and the lowlands of the Gran Chaco. Santiago del Estero is a hot subtropical lowland which is transitional between the Gran Chaco and the Andes.

Mesopotamia & the North-East

East of the Andes, northern Argentina is mostly a subtropical lowland with very hot summers. The provinces of Entre Ríos and Corrientes comprise most of the area known as Mesopotomia, the area between the Paraná and Uruguay rivers. Here, heavy rainfall supports swampy lowland forests and upland savannas. The province of Misiones, surrounded on three sides by Brazil and Paraguay, is even more densely forested and contains part of the awesome Iguazú Falls.

The Chaco

The arid western area, known as the Argentine Chaco, includes the provinces of Chaco and Formosa, eastern areas of Salta and Santiago del Estero, and the northern edges of Santa Fe and Córdoba. The Argentine Chaco is part of the much larger Gran Chaco region, which extends into Bolivia, Paraguay and Brazil. Open savanna alternates with thorn forest, and the erratic precipitation makes rain-fed cultivation risky. Summers are brutally hot.

The Pampas

Argentina's agricultural heartland is a nearly

level plain of wind-borne loess and river-deposited sediments, once covered by native grasses and now occupied by grain farms and estancias. More properly subdivided into the Humid Pampas, along the littoral, and the Dry Pampas of the west and south, the region comprises the provinces of Buenos Aires, La Pampa and the major parts of Santa Fe and Córdoba. The Atlantic coast features attractive sandy beaches.

Patagonia & the Lake District
Patagonia is the thinly populated region south of the Río Colorado, consisting of the provinces of Neuquén, Río Negro, Chubut and Santa Cruz. It is mostly arid, but the far southern Andes have the largest southern hemisphere glaciers outside Antarctica. East of the Andes, cool arid steppes pasture huge flocks of sheep, while the Río Negro and Río Chubut valleys support crop and fruit farming. Patagonia is also an energy storehouse, with oil and coal deposits. The climate throughout the region is generally temperate, but winter temperatures can drop well below freezing.

Tierra del Fuego
The 'Land of Fire' consists of one large island (Isla Grande de Tierra del Fuego), unequally divided between Chile and Argentina, and many smaller ones. Isla Grande's northern half resembles the Patagonian steppe, while its mountainous southern half is partly covered by forests and glaciers. The maritime climate is surprisingly mild, even in winter, but changeable.

GOVERNMENT
The constitution of 1853 established a federal system, with equal executive, legislative and judicial branches. The President and the 254-member Chamber of Deputies are popularly elected, but provincial legislatures choose the 46-member Senate. In practice, the President often governs by decree and intervenes in provincial matters.

Administratively, the country consists of the federal district of Buenos Aires, and 23 provinces. Argentina also claims some

islands in the South Atlantic (including the Falklands Islands/Islas Malvinas), which are under British control, and a slice of Antarctica, where claims are on hold by international agreement.

Political Parties
Of 18 parties in Congress, the most important are the Peronists (Justicialists) of current President Carlos Menem and the Radicals of ex-President Raúl Alfonsín. Until the 1940s, when Perónism absorbed labour unions and other under-represented sectors, the middle-class Radicals opposed parties tied to conservative landowners.

Within the Peronist party are implacable factions which, in the mid-1970s, conducted open warfare against each other. There is still friction between the economic 'neo-liberals' of Menem, and the leftists who see his policies as capitulation to institutions like the World Bank. Ultra-nationalists are no happier, despite their loathing of the left.

Menem's Economy Minister, Domingo Cavallo, who has tried to stabilise the currency and reduce budget deficits by eliminating unprofitable state enterprises, is a possible presidential candidate, but Menem is promoting a consitutional amendment to permit his own immediate re-election.

The Military
Since overthrowing Radical President Hipólito Yrigoyen in 1930, the military has often felt 'obliged' to intervene in government because of civilian incompetence and corruption, but they often undermine the civil order. Second in size only to Brazil's among Latin American powers, the privileged military sector numbers about 150,000, two-thirds of them in the army. Often used to control the civilian populace, they failed to achieve military goals during the Falklands War, but rearmed quickly, despite an economic crisis made worse by foolish belligerence.

ECONOMY
Since colonial times, the economy has relied

on export commodities – hides, wool, beef and grains – from the Pampas. Self-sufficient in energy resources, the country has failed to capitalise on its advantages, despite superficial prosperity. Its borrowing binge of the 1970s and 1980s funded capital-intensive projects which encouraged graft and fuelled inflation.

In the rural sector, control of the richest agricultural lands by a handful of individuals relegated many people to marginal lands or to roles as dependent labourers. Perón demonstrated that Argentina needed to develop its industrial base, and that workers needed to share in that development, but government intervention in industry outlived its usefulness. Corrupt, inefficient enterprises contributed to inflation, which often exceeded 50% per month.

The usual response to this was wage and price indexing, which in turn reinforced the inflationary spiral. The Menem administration has tried to break the spiral by reducing the deficit, selling state enterprises and restricting unionism, but side-effects have included recession and unemployment. Inflation has subsided, but it is premature to call the experiment a success, as several privatisation projects have gone awry.

Corruption is a continuing problem. Menem himself accepted a valuable sports car from potential foreign investors, and a millionaire labour leader has boasted that 'Nobody in Argentina ever got rich by working'. One study found that only 40% of workers laboured in the 'official' economy – the rest were paid in cash, and avoided taxes entirely.

POPULATION & PEOPLE

Over one-third of Argentina's 32 million people reside in Gran Buenos Aires (the federal capital and its suburbs), in the Capital Federal de Buenos Aires. Nearly 90% live in cities; other major urban centres are Rosario, Córdoba, Tucumán, Mendoza and Bahía Blanca. Patagonia's population is small and dispersed.

Following Juan Bautista Alberdi's dictum that 'to govern is to populate', early Uni-

tarists promoted European immigration. From the mid-19th century, Italians, Basques, Welsh, English, Ukrainians and others streamed into Buenos Aires. Some groups have maintained a distinctive cultural identity, like Buenos Aires' Jewish community and Anglo-Argentines across the country.

Middle Easterners, though few, have been influential; President Menem is of Syrian ancestry. Escobar, a Buenos Aires suburb, has a Japanese community, but non-Europeans have generally been unwelcome. Some groups are marginalised, like Chileans on sheep estancias in Patagonia, and Bolivian labourers (peones golondrinas, or 'swallow labourers') in the North-West's sugar harvests, but many Paraguayans and Uruguayans are permanent residents.

The major indigenous nations are the Quechua of the North-West and the Mapuche of northern Patagonia, but Matacos, Tobas and others inhabit the Chaco and north-eastern cities like Resistencia and Santa Fe.

EDUCATION

Argentina's 94% literacy rate is one of Latin America's highest. Primary education is compulsory to age 12, but attendance is low in some rural areas. Universities are traditionally free and open, but once students have chosen a career, the course of study is very rigid. Traditional education has glutted Buenos Aires with doctors and lawyers reluctant to relocate to the provinces.

ARTS

Though in many ways derivative of European precedents, Argentine arts have been influential beyond the country's borders. In the 19th and early 20th centuries Buenos Aires self-consciously emulated French cultural trends in art, music and architecture. There are many important museums and galleries, especially in Buenos Aires.

Literature

Writers of international stature include Jorge Luis Borges, Julio Cortázar, Ernesto Sábato,

Manuel Puig, Osvaldo Soriano and Adolfo Bioy Casares. For suggested reading, see the Facts for the Visitor section later in this chapter.

Classical Music & Theatre

Buenos Aires has a vigorous theatre tradition, and even in the provinces, live performances are well attended.

Cinema

Argentine cinema has achieved international stature, despite limited funds. Many films are available on video.

La Patagonia Rebelde chronicles the turn-of-the-century Anarchist rebellion in Santa Cruz province. *A Funny Dirty Little War* is a comic depiction of a possible military coup in a provincial town.

Several films address Dirty War themes, including *Apartment Zero*, *The Official Story*, and *Man Facing South-East*. *Kiss of the Spider Woman*, based on Manuel Puig's novel and directed by Argentine Héctor Babenco, reveals the abuse of political prisoners and exploitation of informers by police and military.

Tango & Folk Music

Legendary figures like Carlos Gardel, Julio Sosa and Astor Piazzola popularised the tango as music and dance, while contemporaries like Susana Rinaldi, Eladia Blásquez and Osvaldo Pugliese carry on the tradition. Folk musicians like Mercedes Sosa, Tarragó Ross, Leon Gieco and Conjunto Pro Música de Rosario are popular performers.

Simon Collier's *The Life, Music, & Times of Carlos Gardel* (University of Pittsburgh Press, 1986) is a serious biography of the tango master which avoids the exaggerations of Gardel's fanatical devotees.

Popular Music

Rock musician Charly García's version of the national anthem does what Jimi Hendrix did for *The Star-Spangled Banner*. After a judge dismissed a lawsuit alleging that García lacked 'respect for national symbols', the *Buenos Aires Herald* editorialised that García's defence was a victory over 'extremist nationalist sectors' which had too long 'imposed their warped and often authoritarian views on the rest of society'.

Les Luthiers, an Argentine Bonzo Dog Band, satirises the nationalist sectors. Other performers are more derivative – before reporting an Elvis sighting, be sure it isn't Sandro, a living local clone of The King.

CULTURE

Foreign travellers are less incongruous in Argentina than in countries with large indigenous populations, and gregarious Argentines often include them in daily activities. One such activity is to 'tomar un mate', a social ritual throughout the region; *mate*, 'Paraguayan tea', is drunk bitter in the south, or with added sugar and *yuyos* (herbs) in the north.

Sport

Rugby, polo, golf, skiing and fishing are popular participant sports, but soccer is an obsession – with teams like River Plate and Boca Juniors (based in Buenos Aires' immigrant Italian neighbourhood of La Boca) all over the country. The national team has twice won the World Cup.

RELIGION

Roman Catholicism is the state religion, but popular beliefs diverge from official doctrine. Spiritualism and veneration of the dead, for instance, are widespread – visitors to Recoleta and Chacarita cemeteries will see endless processions of pilgrims communicating with cultural icons like Juan and Evita Perón, Carlos Gardel and psychic Madre María. Cult beliefs like the Difunta Correa of San Juan province attract hundred of thousands of adherents, while evangelical Protestantism is also growing.

During the Dirty War, the Church generally supported the dictatorship despite the persecution, kidnapping, torture and murder of religious workers among the poor and dispossessed. Social activism by the Church has resumed in today's more permissive climate.

LANGUAGE

Spanish is universal, but some immigrants retain their language as a badge of identity. Italian is widely understood, while Anglo-Argentines speak a precise, clipped English. In Chubut, Welsh has nearly disappeared, despite persistent cultural traditions. Most of the 17 Indian languages are spoken by few individuals. Most Quechua speakers, numerous in the North-West, are bilingual in Spanish. At least 40,000 Mapuche speakers live in the southern Andes, while north-eastern Argentina has about 15,000 Guaraní speakers, as many Tobas and about 10,000 Matacos.

Argentine Spanish

Local characteristics readily identify an Argentine elsewhere in Latin America, or overseas. The most prominent are the *voseo* (usage of the pronoun *vos* in place of *tu)* and pronunciation of 'll' and 'y' as 'zh' (as in 'azure') rather than 'y' (as in English 'you').

Argentine Spanish is distinctive, but there are regional differences – Mesopotamians, for example, use words from Guaraní, while the speech of Buenos Aires abounds with *lunfardo*, the city's colourful slang.

Facts for the Visitor

VISAS & EMBASSIES

Most foreigners, including UK citizens, do not need advance visas, but Australians and New Zealanders must pay US$15 for one. At major border crossings, officials issue a free, renewable 90-day tourist card, but at minor crossings, they often ignore this formality.

Argentine Embassies & Consulates

For embassies and consulates in neighbouring countries, see those country chapters, under the entries for main cities and border towns.

Australia
   58 Mugga Way, Red Hill, ACT (☎ (06) 295-1570)

Canada
   Suite 620, 90 Sparks St, Ottawa, Ontario (☎ (613) 236-2351)
France
   6 Rue Cimarosa, Paris 75016 (☎ 45531469)
Germany
   Adenauerallee 50-52, Bonn ☎ 222011)
UK
   53 Hans Place, London SW1 X0LA ☎ (071) 584-6494, Consulate: 589-3104)
USA
   1600 New Hampshire Avenue NW, Washington DC (☎ 939-6400)

Foreign Embassies in Argentina

For details of foreign embassies in Argentina, see the Buenos Aires city section.

Visa Extensions

For a tourist card extension, go to the immigration office in Buenos Aires (Avenida Antártida Argentina 1365) or in provincial capitals, or to provincial delegations of the Policía Federal. For visits over six months, it's easier to leave the country and then return.

DOCUMENTS

Passports are obligatory, except for visitors from bordering countries. The police can demand identification at any time, so carry your passport, which is also essential for cashing travellers' cheques, checking into hotels and other routine matters.

Motorists need an International Driving Permit as well as their home licence, but police may not recognise it or, worse, may claim it is invalid and solicit a bribe. Politely refer them to the Spanish translation.

CUSTOMS

Officials usually defer to foreign visitors, but arrivals at Buenos Aires' Ezeiza airport may be asked about electronic equipment, which is much cheaper overseas. Arrivals from the central Andean countries may undergo drug searches, and officials will confiscate fruits and vegetables from Chile or Brazil. Even after passing customs, you may encounter police inspections at provincial borders and highway junctions.

MONEY

The *peso* ($) comes in denominations of one, two, five, 10, 20, 50 and 100. It is subdivided into 100 *centavos*, with coins of one, five, 10, 25 and 50 centavos. The few austral banknotes still in circulation as of early 1993 should disappear shortly.

Exchange Rates

Despite hyperinflation in the recent past, the Argentine currency has remained quite stable since early 1991. The new peso was introduced in January 1992, and set at a level equal to the US dollar. Currently, the peso is still holding its value against the dollar. Prices in this chapter are given in US dollars, and will be the same in pesos unless the currency devalues. For the latest trends, see *Ambito Financiero* or the *Buenos Aires Herald*.

Approximate official rates at August 1993 were as follows:

A$1	=	$1.48
DM1	=	$1.71
FF1	=	$6.05
UK£1	=	$1.48
US$1	=	$1

Changing Money

Cash dollars can be exchanged at banks, *casas de cambio* (exchange houses), hotels, travel agencies, in shops or on the street. Travellers' cheques are increasingly difficult to exchange, and attract large commissions. Dollars are widely accepted in lieu of pesos.

Credit Cards

Credit cards can be very useful in a pinch. Most widely accepted are MasterCard (Access) and Visa, but American Express and others are also valid in many places.

Many businesses add a *recargo* (surcharge) of 10% or more, because of delays between purchase and receipt of payment. Conversely, some give cash discounts of 10% or more. Be aware of exchange rate fluctuations, which can bring unpleasant (or pleasant) surprises when a transaction is finally posted to your overseas account.

Costs

A fixed exchange rate has driven some prices to European levels, but budget travel is not impossible. Modest lodging, food and transport are still reasonable; after the initial shock, arrivals from Brazil or Bolivia should adapt to local conditions, but allow around US$25 per day for food and lodging. Prices are subject to wild fluctuations.

Tipping

Waiters and waitresses are poorly paid, so if you can afford to eat out, you can afford the customary 10% *propina*.

Bargaining

Bargaining is customary in the North-West, and in artisan's markets country-wide. Even in Buenos Aires, downtown leather shops may listen to offers. Late in the evening, hotels may give a break on room prices; if you stay several days, they almost certainly will. Ask for cash discounts at better hotels.

WHEN TO GO & WHAT TO BRING

Buenos Aires' urban attractions transcend the seasons, but Patagonian destinations, such as the Moreno Glacier, are best in summer. Iguazú Falls are best visited in the southern winter or spring, when heat and humidity are less oppressive. Skiers will want to visit the Andes during winter or early spring (June to September).

The climate of mid-latitude Argentina resembles that of the south-eastern USA, warm and humid. For the subtropical north, bring lightweight cottons, but at higher elevations in the North-West and the high latitudes of Patagonia, take warm clothing, even in summer.

TOURIST OFFICES

Almost every province and municipality has a tourist office, often on the main plaza or at the bus terminal. Each province has a tourist office in Buenos Aires. A few municipalities have separate offices.

Overseas Representatives

Larger Argentine diplomatic missions, such

as those in New York and Los Angeles, usually have a tourist representative in their delegation.

USEFUL ORGANISATIONS

The student travel agency ASATEJ (☎ 312-8476), 1st floor Florida 833, Buenos Aires, is eager to encourage budget travellers. Parques Nacionales (☎ 311-1943), at Santa Fe 690, Buenos Aires, has information on national parks and reserves. Another useful contact for conservationists is the Fundación Vida Silvestre Argentina (☎ 331-4864), 6th floor, Defensa 245, Buenos Aires.

BUSINESS HOURS & HOLIDAYS

Traditionally, businesses open by 8 am, break several hours for lunch and a brief *siesta*, then reopen until 8 or 9 pm. This schedule is still common in the provinces, but government offices and many businesses in Buenos Aires have adopted an 8 am to 5 pm schedule for 'greater efficiency' and, especially in government, reduced corruption.

Government offices and businesses close on national holidays. The following list does not include provincial holidays.

1 January
    Año Nuevo (New Year's Day)
March/April (dates vary)
    Viernes Santo/Pascua (Good Friday/Easter)
1 May
    Día del Trabajador (Labour Day)
25 May
    Revolución de Mayo (May Revolution of 1810)
10 June
    Día de las Malvinas (Malvinas Day)
20 June
    Día de la Bandera (Flag Day)
9 July
    Día de la Independencia (Independence Day)
17 August
    Día de San Martín (Anniversary of San Martín's death)
12 October
    Día de la Raza (Columbus Day)
25 December
    Navidad (Christmas Day)

POST & TELECOMMUNICATIONS

Post

ENCOTEL, the postal service, is also responsible for telegraph, fax and telex. It is so frequently paralysed by strikes and corruption that many items never arrive and may be opened if they appear valuable; send essential mail *certificado* (registered).

Overseas rates, especially for airmail packages, are expensive; surface mail is cheaper but less dependable. International express mail is very expensive, but dependable.

ENCOTEL now imposes charges on *poste restante* or *lista de correos* services. Arrange for delivery to a private address, such as a friend or a hotel, to avoid this costly and bureaucratic annoyance.

Telephones

French and Spanish interests now control most telephone services, but improvements have been slow. Collect (reverse charge) calls to North America or Europe are possible from most (but not all) long-distance offices – be certain, or you may have to pay costs out of pocket. Offices in major cities have direct lines to overseas operators.

Most public telephones use tokens (*fichas* or *cospeles*), available from kiosks and telephone offices. Some hotels in Buenos Aires do not bill international calls accurately, so it may be better to call from a telephone office.

TIME

Most of the year, Argentina is three hours behind GMT. The city and province of Buenos Aires observe daylight savings time (summer time), but most provinces do not. Changeover dates vary from year to year.

LAUNDRY

Self-service laundromats are now common in cities but are costlier than their equivalent in North America or Europe. Budget hotels usually have laundry facilities or maid service (agree on charges in advance).

WEIGHTS & MEASURES

The metric system is used, but country folk may use the Spanish *legua* (league, about 5 km) for distance. Hands are used to measure horses, and carpenters often use Imperial measures.

BOOKS

Literature & Fiction

Jorge Luis Borges, known for short stories and poetry, is a world literary figure whose erudite language and references sometimes make him inaccessible to readers without knowledge of the classics. Ernesto Sábato's *On Heroes and Tombs*, a favourite among Argentine youth in the 1960s, is a psychological novel exploring people and places in Buenos Aires.

Parisian resident Julio Cortázar emphasised Argentine characters in novels like *Hopscotch* and *62: A Model Kit*; one of his short stories inspired the 1960s film *Blow-Up*. Manuel Puig's novels, like *Kiss of the Spider Woman* and *Betrayed by Rita Hayworth*, focus on popular culture's ambiguous role in Argentina. Adolfo Bioy Casares' *The Invention of Morel* also deals with inability or unwillingness to distinguish between fantasy and reality. Osvaldo Soriano, perhaps the most popular contemporary novelist, wrote *A Funny Dirty Little War* and the recently translated *Winter Quarters*.

History

For the colonial era, see the book section in the introductory Facts About the Region chapter. Do not miss Alfred Crosby's chronicle of the Pampas in *Ecological Imperialism: the Biological Expansion of Europe, 900-1900* (Cambridge, 1986).

D F Sarmiento's *Life in the Argentine Republic in the Days of the Tyrants* is an eloquent, but often condescending, contemporary critique of Federalist caudillos and their followers. José Luis Romero analyses Unitarism and Federalism in *A History of Argentine Political Thought* (Stanford, 1968).

James Scobie's *Argentina: A City & a Nation* (Oxford) is a standard history. David Rock's *Argentina 1516-1987: from Spanish Colonization to the Falklands War & Alfonsín* (University of California Press, 1987) is more comprehensive.

Several books have compared Argentina, Australia and Canada as commodity exporters, like Tim Duncan & John Fogarty's *Australia & Argentina – on Parallel Paths* (Melbourne, 1984) and Carl Solberg's *The Prairies & the Pampas: Agrarian Policy in Canada & Argentina, 1880-1930* (Stanford, 1987). On the gaucho, see Richard W Slatta's *Gauchos & the Vanishing Frontier* (University of Nebraska, 1983).

Perón & His Legacy

Among many books on Perón are Joseph Page's *Perón: a Biography* (Random House, New York, 1983) and Robert Crassweller's *Perón & the Enigma of Argentina* (Norton, New York, 1987). Tomas Eloy Martínez's *The Perón Novel* (Pantheon Books, New York, 1988) is a fascinating fictionalised effort. In his grim essay *The Return of Eva Perón* (Knopf, New York, 1980), V S Naipaul argues that state violence has long permeated Argentine politics.

Politics & the Military

Robert Potash has published two books on military interference in politics: *The Army & Politics in Argentina, 1928-1945: Yrigoyen to Perón* (Stanford 1969) and *The Army & Politics in Argentina, 1945-1962: Perón to Frondizi* (Stanford, 1980). A more general account, also dealing with Chile, Brazil and Paraguay, is Cesar Caviedes' *The Southern Cone: Realities of the Authoritarian State* (Totowa, N J, Rowman & Allenheld, 1984).

On the democratic transition, see Monica Peralta-Ramos & Carlos Waisman's *From Military Rule to Liberal Democracy in Argentina* (Westview Press, Boulder, Colorado, 1987).

The Dirty War

The classic account of state terrorism is Jacobo Timmerman's *Prisoner Without a Name, Cell Without a Number* (Knopf, New

York, 1981). *Nunca Más*, official report of the National Commission on the Disappeared, details military abuses from 1976 to 1983. In English, see John Simpson & Jana Bennett's *The Disappeared: Voices from a Secret War* (Robson Books, London, 1985).

Travel
Bruce Chatwin's *In Patagonia* (Summit Books, New York, 1977) is one of the most informed syntheses of life and landscape for any part of the world. American scientist George Gaylord Simpson's *Attending Marvels: a Patagonian Journal* (many editions) starts with a lively account of the coup against President Hipólito Yrigoyen in 1930.

In *The Voyage of the Beagle*, Darwin's account of the gauchos evokes a way of life to which Argentines still pay symbolic homage. Make a special effort to find Lucas Bridges' *The Uttermost Part of the Earth*, about his life among the Indians of Tierra del Fuego.

MAPS
The Automóvil Club Argentino (ACA) publishes up-to-date provincial maps, which are indispensable for motorists and an excellent investment for others (members pay less). Its headquarters is at Avenida del Libertador 1850, Buenos Aires, but it has offices in all major cities.

Tourist office maps vary in quality but are usually free.

MEDIA
Newspapers & Magazines
Buenos Aires' most important dailies are *La Prensa*, *La Nación* and the middle-of-the-road tabloid *Clarín*, which has an excellent Sunday cultural section. *Página 12* provides a refreshing leftist perspective and often breaks important stories which mainstream newspapers are slow to cover. *Ambito Financiero* is the morning voice of the business sector, *El Cronista Comercial* its afternoon rival.

The daily *Buenos Aires Herald* covers the world from an Anglo-Argentine perspective of business and commerce, but its perceptive weekend summaries of Argentine politics and economics are essential. It also has a well-deserved reputation for editorial boldness, having condemned military and police abuses during the Dirty War.

Radio & TV
On the AM band, nationwide Radio Rivadavia is a hybrid of top 40 and talk radio. At least a dozen FM stations in Buenos Aires specialise in styles from classical to pop to tango.

Cable TV and the legalisation of nonstate TV broadcasting have brought a wider variety of programming. There are Spanish and Chilean stations, as well as CNN for news and ESPN for sports.

HEALTH
Health hazards are few, but cholera is a concern in the subtropical north, especially Salta, Jujuy and the Chaco. For the latest details, contact your country's embassy in Buenos Aires.

Argentina requires no vaccinations, but visitors to nearby tropical countries should consider prophylaxis against typhoid, malaria and other diseases. Many common prescription drugs are available over the counter.

Meat-eaters should enjoy Argentine food, and for vegetarians, salad greens and fresh vegetables are safe in most of the country. Urban water supplies are usually potable.

WOMEN TRAVELLERS
For women travelling alone, Argentina is generally safer than most other Latin American countries, but avoid complacency. Single women in Buenos Aires may encounter unwelcome physical contact, particularly on crowded buses or trains. Other nuisances include vulgar language and *piropos* (sexist comments which can be complementary but are seldom appropriate).

Single women may encounter suspicion at budget hotels frequented by prostitutes, but this usually evaporates quickly. Since Argentine women rarely travel alone, single women arouse curiosity in the provinces.

Exercise judgment if you hitchhike, and avoid getting into a vehicle with more than one man. Argentine men rarely demonstrate their machismo except in the company of other males.

DANGERS & ANNOYANCES

Security is a minor concern compared with other South American countries. Both men and women can travel safely in most of Buenos Aires at any hour, but take precautions against petty theft.

Police often harass motorists for minor equipment violations which carry very high fines, but usually settle for cheaper *coimas* (bribes), which require discretion. A hint that you may phone your consulate can eliminate such problems.

Avoid military installations, which often display the warning 'No stopping or photographs – the sentry will shoot'. In event of a coup or other emergency, carry identification and make sure someone knows your whereabouts. Contact your embassy or consulate for advice.

WORK

Travellers do work as English-language instructors in Buenos Aires, but wages are low. Check the classified section of the *Buenos Aires Herald.* Travellers can work the fruit harvests in the Río Negro valley and El Bolsón, but may only break even.

ACTIVITIES

Professional soccer is world-class, but many Argentine footballers play for higher salaries in Europe. Other popular sports include tennis, basketball, motor racing, cycling and field hockey. Skiing, though expensive, is gaining popularity, as are canoeing, climbing, trekking, windsurfing and hang-gliding.

ACCOMMODATION
Camping & Refugios

Budget travellers *must* consider camping to control expenses. Almost every major city and many smaller towns have woodsy sites where you can pitch a tent for less than US$5, with hot showers, toilets, laundry, firepits and other facilities. Most Argentines arrive by car, but campgrounds are often central and backpackers are welcome.

Before coming to South America, invest in a good, dome-style tent with rainfly (fly sheet), a three-season sleeping bag and a multifuel stove. Avoid popular tourist areas in January and February, when sites can be crowded and noisy. Personal possessions are usually secure, but do not tempt anyone by leaving around cameras or cash. Bring or buy mosquito repellent for sites near rivers or lakes.

Organised sites in national parks resemble those in cities and towns, and more isolated, rustic alternatives exist. Some parks have *refugios*, basic high-country shelters for trekkers and climbers.

Hostels

The Asociación Argentina de Albergues de la Juventud (☎ 45-1001), at Talcahuano 214, 2nd floor, Buenos Aires, is open on weekdays from 11 am to 7 pm. Hostels, usually open in summer only, can be found in Buenos Aires, the Atlantic Coast, Sierra de la Ventana, the Lake District, Córdoba province, Puerto Iguazú, Mendoza and Humahuaca.

Casas de Familia

Tourist offices in small towns, and in some larger cities like Salta and Mendoza, keep lists of inexpensive *casas de familia* (family houses), which usually offer access to cooking and laundry facilities, hot showers and local hospitality.

Hospedajes, Pensiones & Residenciales

Differences among these types of permanent accommodation are unclear, but all may be called hotels. An *hospedaje* is usually a large family home with extra bedrooms (the bath is shared). A *pensión* offers short-term accommodation in a family home, but may have permanent lodgers and serve meals. *Residenciales* are permanent businesses in buildings designed for short-stay accommodation. Rooms and furnishings are modest; a few have private bath, but toilet and shower facilities are usually shared with other guests.

Hotels

Hotels proper vary from basic one-star accommodation to five-star luxury, but many one-stars are better value than three or four-star places. Rooms generally have private bath, often telephone, sometimes *música funcional* (elevator Muzak) or TV. Most hotels have a *confitería* or a restaurant; breakfast may be included. Those in higher categories have room and laundry service, swimming pools, bars, shops and other luxuries.

FOOD

No meal is complete without *carne* (meat), which means beef – lamb, venison and poultry are all something else. Carnivores will devour the *parrillada*, a mixed grill of steak, other beef cuts, and offal.

Italian influence is obvious in dishes like spaghetti, lasagna and ravioli, but don't overlook *ñoquis* ('gnocchi' in Italian), an inexpensive staple. Since the early 1980s, vegetarian fare has acquired a niche in Buenos Aires and a few other cities. Chinese food is not outstanding, but some restaurants offer *tenedor libre* (all you can eat).

The Andean North-West is notable for spicy dishes like those of Bolivia or Peru, while fish from Mesopotamian rivers are delectable. From Mendoza northward, Middle Eastern food is common. In Patagonia, game like trout, boar and venison are regional specialities, while in the south, lamb often replaces beef in the parrillada.

Places to Eat

Budget travellers in the north should frequent markets, where meals are often very cheap; *rotiserías* (delis) have quality chicken, empanadas, pies and *fiambres* (processed meats) for a fraction of restaurant prices.

For fast food, try bus terminals, train stations or the *comedor*, which usually has a limited menu with simple but filling fixed-price meals. Comedores also serve *minutas*

(short orders) like steak, eggs, *milanesa* (breaded steak), salad and chips.

Confiterías usually serve sandwiches like *lomito* (steak), *panchos* (hot dogs) and hamburgers. *Restaurantes* have larger menus, professional waiters and more elaborate decor.

Cafés & Bars

Cafés are important gathering places, the site for everything from marriage proposals to business deals to revolutions. Many Argentines dawdle for hours over a single cup of coffee, but simple meals are also available. Cafés also serve alcohol.

Bars are establishments for drinking alcohol. In small towns, they're a male domain and women usually avoid them.

Breakfast

Argentines eat little breakfast. Most common is coffee, tea or *mate* with *tostadas* (toast), *manteca* (butter) and *mermelada* (jam). In cafés, *medialunas* (croissants), either sweet or *saladas* (plain) accompany *café con leche* (coffee with milk). A *tostado* is a thin-crust toasted sandwich with ham and cheese.

Snacks

The *empanada* is a turnover of vegetables, hard-boiled egg, olive, beef, chicken, ham and cheese or other filling. Empanadas *al horno* (baked) are lighter than *fritas* (fried).

Pizzerías often sell cheap slices at the counter, but there are more options when seated for an entire pizza. Common slices include *fugazza*, a very cheap and delicious cheeseless variety with sweet onions, or *fugazzeta* (mozzarella added), sometimes eaten with *fainá*, a baked chickpea (garbanzo) dough.

Main Dishes

Argentines compensate for skimpy breakfasts with enormous lunches and dinners (never before 9 pm, often much later). An important custom is the *sobremesa*, dallying at the table to discuss family matters or other events of the day.

An *asado* or parrillada is the standard main course, prepared over hot coals and accompanied by *chimichurri* (a marinade), with chips or salad on the side. Carnivores will savour the tender, juicy *bife de chorizo*, but try also *bife de lomo* (short loin), *bife de costilla* or *chuleta* (T-bone steak), *asado de tira* (roast rib) or *vacío* (sirloin). *Matambre relleno* is stuffed and rolled flank steak, baked or eaten cold as an appetiser. Offal dishes include *chinchulines* (small intestines), *tripa gorda* (large intestine) and *morcilla* (blood sausage).

Most Argentines prefer beef *cocido* (well done), but restaurants serve it *jugoso* (rare) or *a punto* (medium) on request. *Bife a caballo* comes with two eggs and chips.

Carbonada is a beef stew of rice, potatoes, sweet potatoes, maize, squash, and chopped apples and peaches. *Puchero* is a casserole with beef, chicken, bacon, sausage, blood sausage, maize, peppers, tomatoes, onions, cabbage, sweet potatoes and squash. The cook may add garbanzos or other beans, accompanied by rice cooked in the broth.

Pollo (chicken) sometimes accompanies the parrillada, but usually comes separately, with chips or salad. The most common fish is *merluza* (hake), usually fried in batter and served with mashed potatoes.

Desserts
Fresh fruit is the usual *postre* at home. Common restaurant choices are *ensalada de fruta* (fruit salad), *flan* (egg custard) or *queso y dulce* (cheese with preserved fruit, also known as *postre vigilante*). Flan is topped with *crema* (whipped cream) or *dulce de leche* (caramelised milk).

Ice Cream
Italian-derived *helados* are South America's best. Smaller *heladerías* make their own in small batches on the premises or nearby – look for the words *elaboración propia* or *elaboración artesanal*.

DRINKS
Soft Drinks
Argentines drink prodigious amounts of the usual sugary soft drinks. If carbonated *(con gas)* mineral water is unavailable, *soda* in large bottles with siphons is usually the cheapest thirst-quencher.

Fruit Juices & Licuados
For fresh orange juice, ask for *jugo de naranja exprimido*; otherwise, you may get tinned juice. *Pomelo* (grapefruit), *limón* (lemon) and *ananá* (pineapple) are also common. *Jugo de manzana* (apple juice) is a speciality of Patagonia's Río Negro valley.

Licuados are milk-blended fruit drinks. Common flavours are banana, *durazno* (peach) and *pera* (pear).

Coffee, Tea & Chocolate
Foreigners should not decline an invitation for *mate* ('Paraguayan tea'). Caffeine addicts may overdose; even in the smallest town, coffee will be espresso. *Café chico* is thick, dark coffee in a very small cup. *Cortado* is a small coffee with a touch of milk, usually served in a glass – *cortado doble* is a larger portion. *Café con leche* (a *latte*) is served for breakfast only – after lunch or dinner in a restaurant, request a cortado.

Tea usually comes with lemon slices. If you want milk, avoid *té con leche*, a tea bag immersed in tepid milk; rather, ask for *un poquito de leche*. For breakfast, try a *submarino*, a semisweet chocolate bar dissolved in steamed milk. *Chocolate*, made of powdered cocoa, is very good.

Alcohol
Beer, wine, whiskey and gin should satisfy most drinkers, but *ginebra bols* and *caña* (cane alcohol) are national specialities. Quilmes and Bieckert are popular beers; in bars or cafés, ask for *chopp* (draught or lager).

Local wines are less famous than Chilean wines, but both reds *(tintos)* and whites *(blancos)* are excellent. When prices on everything else skyrocket, wines miraculously remain reasonable. The major wine-producing areas are near Mendoza, San Juan, La Rioja and Salta. Among the best-known brands are Orfila, Suter, San

Felipe, Santa Ana and Etchart. Avoid cheap boxed wines.

ENTERTAINMENT
Cinemas
Widespread use of video tapes has undercut many cinemas, but the latest films from Europe, the USA and Latin America still appear in the capital and in larger cities. Repertory houses, cultural centres and universities often show classics or less commercial films.

Most cinemas offer discounts midweek. On weekends, there are midnight showings (*trasnoches*).

Theatre
Both in the capital and in the provinces, live theatre is well-attended. Avenida Corrientes is Buenos Aires' Broadway or West End.

Clubs & Discos
Clubs open late – even on weeknights, nobody would go before midnight and things don't really jump before 2 am. After sunrise, when discos close, party-goers head to a confitería or home for breakfast, before collapsing into their beds.

Spectator Sports
Soccer is wildly popular but unfortunately, as in Britain, matches are prone to violence between supporters of opposing teams.

Other popular spectacles include motor racing, horse racing, boxing, tennis and basketball.

THINGS TO BUY
In Buenos Aires, many downtown shops cater to the tourist trade in leather jackets, handbags and shoes. Shopkeepers are aggressive, but sometimes receptive to bargaining; shop around.

There are good artisans' *ferias* in Buenos Aires (Plaza Francia), Mendoza, Bariloche and El Bolsón. In summer, the Atlantic coast has many others. *Mate* paraphernalia, like gourds and *bombillas* (straws) make good souvenirs. In Salta province, the distinctive *ponchos de Güemes* are a memorable choice.

Getting There & Away

AIR
To/From Chile
Many airlines fly between Aeropuerto Internacional Ezeiza (Buenos Aires) and Santiago (Chile), but major airlines also fly to the Argentine towns of Mendoza and Córdoba. Regional carriers connect Bariloche (Argentina) to Puerto Montt and Temuco (Chile).

To/From Bolivia
La Paz is the main Bolivian destination, but Santa Cruz de la Sierra is growing in importance, with direct flights from Salta (Argentina).

To/From Paraguay
Asunción is the only Paraguayan city connected by air with Argentina.

To/From Brazil
From Ezeiza airport, Rio de Janeiro and São Paulo are the main Brazilian destinations, but there are also flights from Bariloche, Córdoba, Mar del Plata, Puerto Iguazú and Rosario. Some go to the Brazilian towns of Florianópolis and Porto Alegre.

To/From Uruguay
Many flights go from Aeroparque Jorge Newbery (Buenos Aires) to Montevideo (Uruguay), others to the Uruguayan towns of Colonia and Punta del Este; a few international flights continue from Ezeiza airport (Buenos Aires) to Montevideo.

LAND
To/From Chile
There is a very long border between Argentina and Chile, with many places to cross. For details, see the Getting There & Away section of the Chile chapter, where there is a map showing many of the routes through the Lake District. Except in Patagonia, every land border involves crossing the Andes. The only train, from Baquedano (Chile) to Salta

(Argentina), is not a regular passenger service.

To/From Bolivia
La Quiaca to Villazón Many buses go from the Argentine towns of Jujuy and Salta to La Quiaca (on the border with Bolivia). You must walk or take a cab across the Bolivian border.

Aguas Blancas to Bermejo From Orán, reached by bus from Salta or Jujuy, take a bus to Aguas Blancas and then Bermejo, where you can catch a bus to Tarija.

Pocitos to Yacuiba Buses from Jujuy or Salta go to Tartagal and on to the Bolivian border at Pocitos/Yacuiba, where there are trains to Santa Cruz de la Sierra.

To/From Paraguay
Clorinda to Asunción Frequent buses cross the Puente Internacional Ignacio de Loyola to the Paraguayan capital, Asunción.

Posadas to Encarnación Buses use the new international bridge, but launches still connect the Paraná river docks.

Puerto Iguazú to Ciudad del Este Frequent buses connect Puerto Iguazú (in Misiones province) to Ciudad del Este (Paraguay) via the Brazilian city of Foz do Iguaçu. Occasional launches cross to the Paraguayan town of Puerto Presidente Franco without passing through Brazil.

To/From Brazil
The most common crossing is from Puerto Iguazú (Argentina) to Foz do Iguaçu (Brazil), but you can also go from Paso de Los Libres (in Corrientes province) to Uruguaiana (Brazil).

To/From Uruguay
Gualeguaychú to Fray Bentos Three buses daily cross the Puente Internacional Libertador General San Martín.

Colón to Paysandú The Puente Internacio-

nal General José Gervasio Artigas links these two cities.

Concordia to Salto The bridge across the Salto Grande hydroelectric complex, north of Concordia, unites these two cities.

RIVER
To/From Uruguay
Buenos Aires to Colonia Morning and evening ferries sail from Buenos Aires to Colonia (US$20, 2½ hours). Hydrofoils (US$25) take only an hour. For details, see the Buenos Aires section.

Tigre to Carmelo Launches cross the estuary of the Río de la Plata daily from Tigre, a Buenos Aires suburb reached from Retiro Station or via the No 60 bus ('Tigre') from Avenida Callao.

LEAVING ARGENTINA
Departure Tax
International passengers from Ezeiza airport pay a US$13 departure tax in either US dollars or local currency. On flights to Uruguay, the tax is US$5.

Getting Around

AIR
The Spanish carrier Iberia now owns Aerolíneas Argentinas (domestic and international routes) and Austral (domestic routes only). Líneas Aéreas del Estado (LADE) serves mostly Patagonian destinations. Smaller regional airlines like Transportes Aéreos Neuquén (TAN) operate in Patagonia. Fares are lower on state-owned LADE and TAN, but discounts have almost disappeared on all carriers.

LADE or TAN flights can be cheaper than buses. They use smaller, slower aircraft on fewer routes, and summer demand is heavy so flights are often overbooked. In desperation, go to the airport, where you may find a plane with tens of empty seats.

In recent years, fares have risen and air

passes, unfortunately, have become dearer and more restrictive. Aerolíneas and Austral offer comparable prices and services, and now often operate out of the same offices.

Air Passes
A combined 'Visit Argentina' fare with Aerolíneas and Austral is no longer a real bargain, but still lets short-term visitors fly anywhere, so long as they make no more than one stop in any city (except for an immediate connection). Airlines issue a minimum of four coupons, but intermediate stops now require a coupon; this means, for instance, that most return flights from Buenos Aires to Ushuaia require four coupons, rather than two, because of a stopover in Río Gallegos.

Four flight coupons, valid for 30 days, cost US$450; additional coupons cost US$120 each. Theoretically, the pass must be purchased overseas, but some readers claim to have done so in Buenos Aires. Visitors to neighbouring countries should consider the mileage-based Mercosur pass (see the introductory Facts for the Visitor chaper).

Timetables
Aerolíneas and Austral publish timetables, but Aerolíneas has recently been undependable. LADE may leave early if a flight is full or nearly full, so don't get to the airport late. For central airline offices, see the Buenos Aires section; for regional offices, see city entries.

Departure Tax
The domestic departure tax of US$3 is not included in ticket prices.

BUS
Most cities have central terminals, but in some, bus companies are clustered near the city centre. Fares and schedules are usually posted prominently. Long-distance buses are generally fast and comfortable, have toilets and serve coffee or snacks. A few provide meals, but most stop at roadside restaurants.

Some buses have reclining seats at premium prices, but ordinary buses on main routes are fine, even on very long rides. Local or provincial *común* services are more crowded, make frequent stops and take longer than *expreso* buses.

Reservations
During holiday periods or on routes with limited seats, buy tickets in advance. The winter holidays around Independence Day (9 July), and international services from Salta to Calama (Chile) and from Comodoro Rivadavia (in Chubut province) to Coyhaique (Chile) are often fully booked.

Costs
Bus fares are about US$0.06 per kilometre. Services are private and fares respond quickly to inflation, but university students and teachers may receive 20% discounts.

TRAIN
Most passenger rail services have been suspended. Buenos Aires province has taken over services to Mar del Plata and the beach resorts, but services are in a state of flux and no one should count on interprovincial passenger trains.

TAXI
In areas like Patagonia, where public transport can be scarce, try hiring a cab with driver to visit remote places. If you bargain, this can be cheaper than a rental car.

DRIVING
Especially in Patagonia, where distances are great and buses infrequent, even budget travellers may want to splurge on an occasional rental. The price of *nafta* (petrol) has risen to about US$0.75 per litre, though *gas-oil* (diesel fuel) is less than half that.

You must carry an International or Inter-American Driving Permit in addition to your national or state driver's licence. Police rarely examine these documents closely, but they do not ignore registration and tax documents, which must be up to date.

Road Rules
Police rarely patrol the highways, where

reckless drivers often cause high-speed, head-on crashes, but they do conduct meticulous document and equipment checks at major highway junctions and checkpoints.

Minor equipment violations, like a defective turn signal, carry fines of up to US$200 but are usually opportunities for graft. If uncertain of your rights, calmly state your intention to contact your consulate. Offer a coima only if confident that it is appropriate and unavoidable.

If driving your own car, consider joining the Automóvil Club Argentino (ACA), which has service stations throughout the country, free road service near major cities, excellent maps at reasonable prices, and insurance services. Membership (about US$35 per month) brings discounts on some accommodation and other tourist services.

Rental

Major international agencies have offices in Buenos Aires, major cities and other tourist areas. To rent a car, you must have a valid driver's licence, be 25 years of age, and leave a deposit or present a credit card.

Rental charges start at about US$20 per day plus US$0.20 per km. Adding insurance and petrol, operating a vehicle is very pricey indeed, unless you're sharing expenses with others. Camping rather than staying in hotels may offset some of these costs.

Purchase

For extended visits, buying a car is worth considering, though any used car is a risk, especially on rugged back roads. It may be cheaper than renting, especially if you can resell the car for a good price at the end of your stay.

Car owners must deal with an exasperating bureaucracy. Be sure of the title (tarjeta verde, or 'green card') and that licence tax payments are up to date. Obtain a notarised document authorising use of the vehicle, since the bureaucracy moves slowly in changing vehicle titles.

Some customs officials may refuse foreigners permission to take a car out of the country, even with a notarised authorisation,

but certain frontier posts (like Puerto Iguazú and Bariloche/Osorno) appear to be flexible. Contact your consulate for assistance and advice.

Argentina's automobile industry has left a reserve of decent used cars, mostly Peugeots and Ford Falcons. A usable car will cost at least US$2000, but prices will be higher for a gasolero, which uses cheaper diesel fuel.

BICYCLE

Racing bicycles are suitable for paved roads, but on gravelled roads in the North-West or Patagonia, a mountain bike (todo terreno) is essential. Recreational cycling is increasingly popular among Argentines, but locally made bikes are not as good as those from Europe or the USA.

The best routes are around Bariloche and in the Andean North-West – the highway from Tucumán to Tafí del Valle, the direct road from Salta to Jujuy, and the Quebrada de Cafayate are exceptionally beautiful rides on generally good surfaces. Drawbacks include the wind (a nuisance which can slow your progress to a crawl in Patagonia) and reckless motorists.

HITCHING

Argentine vehicles are often stuffed with families and children, but truck drivers may help. At servicentros on the outskirts of large cities, where they refuel their vehicles, it's worth soliciting a ride. In Patagonia, distances are great and vehicles few, so expect long waits and carry snack foods and warm, windproof clothing. Especially in the desert north, carry extra water as well.

BOAT

Opportunities for internal river travel are few. There is a passenger ferry from Rosario (in Santa Fe province) across the Río Paraná to Victoria (in Entre Ríos province). There are also launches around the River Plate delta from Tigre, a Buenos Aires suburb.

LOCAL TRANSPORT
To/From the Airport

Most cities have airport minibuses, operated

by the airline or a private carrier, but regular public transport often stops at the airport. See individual city entries for details.

Bus

Even small towns have good bus systems. Clearly numbered buses usually carry placards indicating their ultimate destination; pay attention to these placards, since many identically numbered buses cover slightly different routes. On boarding, indicate your destination and the driver will tell you the fare and give you a ticket, which may be inspected en route. A few cities use tokens in lieu of cash.

Train

Private operators have assumed control of commuter trains from Constitución, Retiro, Once and Lacroze stations to suburbs of Buenos Aires. There are also trains from Rosario to its suburbs.

Underground

Buenos Aires' Subte has seen better days, but is still an excellent way of getting around the city centre.

Taxi

Buenos Aires taxis are reasonably priced and have digital read-out meters. It is customary to leave small change as a tip. Outside Buenos Aires, where meters are less common, agree upon a fare in advance.

Buenos Aires

Argentina's capital and largest city is not actually in the province of Buenos Aires – it is a separate federal district, the Capital Federal. Most places of interest in Buenos Aires province are covered in later sections on the Atlantic Coast and the Pampas.

BUENOS AIRES

In 1536, Pedro de Mendoza's 1600 men camped on a bluff above the Río de La Plata, but within five years, Querandí resistance

forced them out, not to return for nearly half a century.

Mercantile restrictions slowed Buenos Aires' growth, but frustrated criollo merchants traded contraband with the Portuguese and British. Independence, in 1816, did not resolve conflicts between conservative provincial landowners and residents of Buenos Aires, who maintained an international orientation, both commercially and intellectually. European immigration swelled the population from 90,000 at the overthrow of caudillo Juan Manuel de Rosas (in 1851) to over a million by the turn of the century, when Buenos Aires was Latin America's largest city.

As families crowded into substandard housing, industry kept wages low, and labour became increasingly militant. In 1919, the Army's suppression of a metalworkers' strike in 'La Semana Trágica' (The Tragic Week) set an unfortunate precedent for coming decades. In the 1930s, a massive modernisation programme obliterated narrow colonial streets to create major avenues like Santa Fe, Córdoba and Corrientes.

After WW II, Gran (Greater) Buenos Aires absorbed many once-distant suburbs, and now faces massive pollution, noise, decaying infrastructure and declining public services, unemployment and underemployment, and spreading shantytowns. However, not all signs are negative. Since restoration of democracy in 1984, Buenos Aires has enjoyed a freewheeling political dialogue, the publishing industry has rebounded, and arts and music flourish, within economic limits. Fewer foolish public works projects are being undertaken. Buenos Aires may have seen its best days, but survives to offer a rich urban experience.

Orientation

Buenos Aires' size is intimidating, but a brief orientation suffices for its compact centre and more accessible neighbourhoods. On Plaza de Mayo, site of massive political rallies, at the east end of Avenida de Mayo, are the Casa Rosada (presidential palace),

Catedral and the original Cabildo. At the west end is the stately Congress building, opposite Plaza del Congreso.

Most Porteños (citizens of Buenos Aires) 'belong' to neighbourhoods which tourists rarely see, but five central *barrios* contain many of the capital's attractions: Plaza de Mayo and Central Buenos Aires, San Telmo, La Boca, Recoleta and Palermo. Broad Avenida 9 de Julio runs from Plaza Constitución to Avenida del Libertador and exclusive northern suburbs. One popular tourist zone is north of Avenida de Mayo and east of 9 de Julio, an area including the Florida and Lavalle pedestrian malls, Plaza San Martín and the commercial and entertainment areas of Corrientes, Córdoba and Santa Fe. Beyond Santa Fe are chic Recoleta and Palermo, while south of Plaza de Mayo are working-class San Telmo and La Boca.

Information
Tourist Offices The Dirección Nacional de Turismo (☎ 312-2232), at Avenida Santa Fe 883, is open on weekdays from 9 am to 5 pm. Municipal kiosks, on Florida between Córdoba and Paraguay, and at the intersection of Florida and Roque Sáenz Peña, are more helpful and have excellent maps; they're open on weekdays from 8.30 am to 8.30 pm, and on Saturdays from 9 am to 7 pm. The city's Dirección General de Turismo (☎ 45-3612), is in the Centro Cultural San Martín, Sarmiento 1551, 5th floor.

Money South of Avenida Corrientes, dozens of exchange houses line Calle San Martín. Hours are generally 9 am to 6 pm on weekdays, but a few are open on Saturday mornings. American Express, Arenales 707, will cash its own travellers' cheques, without additional commission. Visa and MasterCard holders can get cash advances at downtown banks.

Post The Correo Central, Sarmiento 189, is open on weekdays from 9 am to 7.30 pm. For international parcels weighing over one kg, go to the Correo Postal Internacional, on Antártida Argentina, near Retiro station.

Telephone For local calls, carry a pocketful of cospeles, available from almost any kiosk – each one is only good for about two minutes. There are many new phones on the street. The most convenient long-distance office, at Corrientes 701, is open 24 hours.

Telegram, Telex & Fax International telegrams, telexes and faxes can be sent from ENCOTEL, Corrientes 711.

Foreign Embassies Many countries maintain embassies in Buenos Aires.

Australia
   Santa Fe 846 (☎ 312-6841)
Bolivia
   25 de Mayo 611 (☎ 311-7365)
Brazil
   5th floor, Pelligrini 1363 (☎ 394-5260)
Canada
   Suipacha 1111 (☎ 312-9081)
Chile
   San Martín 439 (☎ 394-6582)
France
   Santa Fe 1391 (☎ 311-8240)
Germany
   Villanueva 1055 (☎ 771-5054)
Paraguay
   Maipú 464 (☎ 322-6536)
Peru
   Tucumán 637 (☎ 392-1344)
UK
   Dr Luis Agote 2412 (☎ 803-7070)
Uruguay
   Las Heras 1907 (☎ 803-6030)
USA
   Colombia 4300 (☎ 774-2282)

Cultural Centres One of the city's best resources, the Centro Cultural General San Martín offers galleries, plays, lectures and inexpensive films. Officially, the address is Sarmiento 1551 (where a shaded alcove hosts free concerts on summer weekends), but most people enter from Avenida Corrientes.

At Junín 1930, the Centro Cultural Recoleta offers art exhibits and free outdoor films on summer evenings. The US Information Agency's Lincoln Center, Florida 935, has an excellent library, which receives US

ARGENTINA

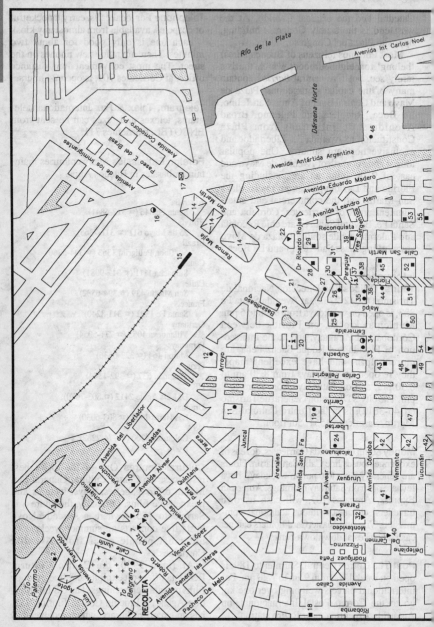

Río de la Plata

Avenida Int Carlos Noel

Dársena Norte

• 46

Avenida Antártida Argentina

Avenida Comodoro Py

Paseo E del Brasil

Avenida de los Immigrantes

⊠ 17

Avenida Eduardo Madero

San Martín

14

14

14

Ramos Mejía

⬤ 16

15

22

Avenida Leandro Alem

Reconquista

Calle San Martín

53

55

Dr Ricardo Rojas

29

39

Tres Sargentos

31

28

30

27

Paraguay

37

38

45

52

21

26

35

36

44

51

Desamparados

13

4

25

Florida

Maipú

50

Esmeralda

i 20

33 34

Suipacha

43

48 54

49

12

Arroyo

Carlos Pellegrini

Cerrito

11

19

Libertad

24

47

Juncal

Talcahuano

42

42

42

Avenida del Libertador

Posadas

Parera

Arenales

Avenida Santa Fe

Uruguay

Viamonte

Tucumán

Avenida Córdoba

Quintana

Ayacucho

Avenida Alvear

10

Avenida Callao

7

Guido

M T De Alvear

41

5

8

6

Paraná

23

32

Montevideo

3

2

Callao

Del Carmen

40

Dellepiane

Pizzurno

Ortiz

Rodríguez Peña

Vicente López

Roberto

Calle Junín

Avenida Callao

Luis Agote

Avenida Pueyrredón

To Belgrano

9

RECOLETA

Avenida General las Heras

18

Pacheco De Melo

Riobamba

To Palermo

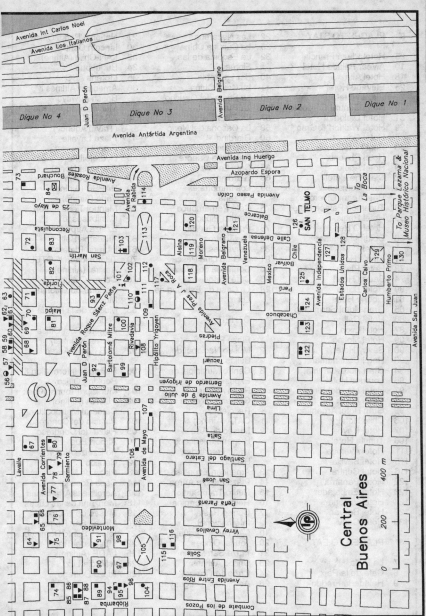

Central Buenos Aires

■ PLACES TO STAY

5 Hotel Plaza Francia
10 Alvear Palace Hotel
18 Hotel Alfa
25 Elevage Hotel
28 Plaza Hotel
29 Hotel Central Córdoba
31 Hotel Diplomat
39 Hotel Waldorf & Gran
   Hotel Orly
43 Petit Hotel Goya
45 Hotel Phoenix
49 Hotel Apolo
52 Claridge Hotel
53 Italia Romanelli/
   Restaurant Cicerón
55 Tucumán Palace Hotel
59 Hotel Regis
61 Hotel O'Rei
66 Columbia Palace
   Hotel
71 King's Hotel
73 Hotel Plaza
74 Bauen Hotel
80 Hotel Bahía
81 Liberty Hotel
85 Gran Hotel Sarmiento
86 Hotel Callao
87 Hotel Lyon
89 Hotel Molino
90 Savoy Hotel
93 Hotel Continental
94 Gran Hotel Oriental
95 Lourdes Hotel
97 Hotel Mar del Plata
98 Hotel Plaza
99 Gran Hotel Argentino
106 Chile Hotel
107 Hotel Reyna
109 Turista Hotel
111 Hotel Avenida
115 Hotel Sevilla
116 Hotel Central
122 Hotel Panamá
123 Hotel Embajador
124 Hotel Victoria
127 Hotel Bolívar
130 Hotel Carly

▼ PLACES TO EAT

7 La Biela
8 Café de la Paix
9 Heladería Freddo

22 Las Nazarenas
25 La Cantina China
32 La Esquina de las
   Flores
40 Bar La Robla
41 La Casa China
48 La Posta del Gaucho
54 La Rural
57 La Estancia
58 La Casona del Nono
60 Giardino
62 Restaurant Oriente
64 Heladería Cadore
65 Café La Paz
68 Giardino
69 Los Immortales
   Pizzería
75 Café Pernambuco
77 Parrilla Pippo
78 Pizzería Güerrín
79 Los Teatros
88 Cervantes II
91 El Gato Que Pesca
96 Confitería del Molino
108 Café Tortoni
128 La Casa de Esteban de
   Luca

OTHER

1 Plaza Francia
2 Museo Nacional de
   Bellas Artes
3 Centro Municipal de
   Exposiciones
4 Plaza Alvear
6 Cementerio de la
   Recoleta
11 CATA (Airline)
12 Museo de Arte
   Hispanoamericano
   Isaac Fernández
   Blanco
13 American Express
14 Plaza Fuerza Aérea
15 Retiro Train Station
16 Retiro Bus Terminal
17 Correo Postal
   Internacional
19 LAP (Air Paraguay)
20 Tourist Office
21 Plaza San Martín
23 United Airlines
24 Caño 14 (Tango)
26 Aerolíneas Uruguayas

27 National Parks Office
30 Lincoln Center
33 LAN-Chile (Airline)
34 Buquebus
35 Librería ABC
36 American Airlines &
   British Airways
37 Municipal Tourist Kiosk
38 ASATEJ
   (Travel Agency)
42 Plaza Lavalle
44 Ferrylíneas
46 Hydrofoil Port
   (Dársena Norte)
47 Teatro Colón
50 SAPSE (Airline)
51 Varig (Airline)
56 Manuel Tienda León
   (Minibuses to
   Ezeiza Airport)
63 Alíseafos Belt
67 Librería Platero
70 Telefónica/ENCOTEL
72 Austral (Airline)
76 Centro Cultural
   General San Martín
82 Museo Mitre
83 Museo de la Policia
   Federal
84 General Post Office
   (Correo Central)
92 LAB (Lloyd Aéreo
   Boliviano)
100 Railways Information &
   Booking Office
101 Municipal Tourist Kiosk
102 PLUNA (Airline)
103 Catedral Metropolitana
104 Palacio del Congreso
105 Plaza del Congreso
110 Airport Bus
   (to Ezeiza Airport)
112 Cabildo
113 Plaza de Mayo
114 Casa Rosada
117 Aerolíneas Argentinas
118 Manzana de las Luces
119 Museo de la Ciudad
120 Museo San Roque
121 Iglesia Santo Domingo
122 Museo del Traje
125 LADE (Airline)
126 A Media Luz
129 Plaza Dorrego

newspapers and magazines, has satellite TV and often shows free films.

Travel Agencies ACA's central office (☎ 802-6061), at Avenida del Libertador 1850, has all member services and a complete selection of provincial road maps. ASATEJ (☎ 312-8476), the student travel agency, at Florida 835, oficina 104, is open on weekdays from 11 am to 7 pm.

Bookshops El Ateneo, Florida 340, has an excellent selection of travel books, including Lonely Planet guides. Librería ABC, Córdoba 685, probably has the best selection of English-language books in town. Visiting academics and curiosity seekers should explore the basement stacks at Librería Platero, Talcahuano 485.

Maps ACA's *Carta Vial de Buenos Aires y Alrededores* is useful beyond the city centre. The *Guia Peuser*, available at downtown newsstands, has a good Subte diagram, and lists bus routes street by street.

Emergency The Hospital Municipal Juan Fernández (☎ 801-5555) is at Avenida Cerviño 3356; try also Hospital Güemes (☎ 89-1675), at Córdoba 3933, or the British Hospital (☎ 23-1081), at Perdriel 74.

Things to See

In 1580, Juan de Garay laid out the square, which became **Plaza de Mayo** after 1810. Most public buildings date from the 19th century, when Avenida de Mayo first connected Plaza de Mayo to **Plaza del Congreso**. Avenida Santa Fe is the most fashionable shopping area, and Florida and Lavalle are pedestrian malls. Demolition of older buildings created the avenues of Corrientes (the theatre district), Córdoba and Santa Fe. Even wider Avenida 9 de Julio, with its famous **Obelisco** at the intersection of Corrientes, is a pedestrian's nightmare, but has a tunnel beneath it.

At the north end of the city centre, beyond **Plaza San Martín** and its magnificent ombú tree, is the **Torre de los Ingleses**, a replica

of the tower of Big Ben. Since the Falklands War, it stands in the renamed **Plaza Fuerza Aérea Argentina** (Air Force Plaza).

Museo del Cabildo Modern construction truncated some of this building's colonial arches, which ran the width of Plaza de Mayo. Exhibits include early photographs of the plaza. At Bolívar 65, it's open Thursday to Sunday from 2 to 6 pm. Admission is US$1.50.

Catedral Metropolitana This religious landmark also contains the tomb of José de San Martín, Argentina's most revered historical figure.

Casa Rosada Off limits during the Proceso, the presidential palace is no longer a place to avoid. The basement museum, at Yrigoyen 218, displays the personal effects of Argentine presidents; it's open Tuesday to Friday from 9 am to 6 pm, and on Sunday from 3 to 6 pm.

Palacio del Congreso Completed in 1906 after costing twice its allotted budget, this building set a standard for Argentine public works projects. It faces Plaza del Congreso and its **Monumento a los Dos Congresos** (Buenos Aires in 1810 and Tucumán in 1816), which commemorates the events that led to independence. Its granite steps symbolise the Andes, while the fountain represents the Atlantic Ocean.

Teatro Colón This world-class facility for opera, ballet and classical music opened in 1908. Bounded by Libertad, Tucumán, Viamonte and Cerrito (Avenida 9 de Julio), the seven-storey building seats 2500 and has standing room for another 1000. Its museum is open on weekdays from noon to 6 pm.

Other Downtown Museums At San Martín 366, the **Museo Mitre** (admission US$1.50) was the residence of former President Bartolomé Mitre. Hours are Tuesday to Friday from 1 to 6 pm, and Sunday from 2 to 6 pm.

In the Centro Cultural San Martín, at Corrientes 1530, the **Museo de Arte Moderno** has works by Dalí, Picasso, and others. It's open daily, except Monday, from noon to 8 pm. At Sarmiento 2573, the **Museo del Cine** (film museum) is open on weekdays from 9 am to 4 pm.

San Telmo South of Plaza de Mayo, parts of San Telmo are still an artists' quarter with low rents. The barrio saw rugged street fighting in 1806 and 1807, when a creole militia drove British troops back to their ships. It was then fashionable until yellow fever drove the Porteño elite to higher ground, in the 19th century. Many houses became *conventillos*, sheltering immigrants in cramped quarters with poor sanitary facilities – conditions which have not totally disappeared.

The **Manzana de las Luces** (Block of Lights), bounded by calles Alsina, Bolívar, Perú and Moreno, includes the Jesuit **Iglesia San Ignacio**, Buenos Aires' oldest church. At Defensa and Humberto Primo, **Plaza Dorrego** hosts the Feria de San Telmo, a Sunday flea market. At Defensa and Brasil, **Parque Lezama** is believed to be the site of Pedro de Mendoza's first encampment.

The **Museo Histórico Nacional**, in Parque Lezama, is a panorama of the Argentine experience. Paintings in the Sala de la Conquista depict Spanish domination of wealthy Peru, a contrast with the struggle to survive on the Pampas. The Sala de la Independencia has portraits of historical figures like Simón Bolívar, his ally and rival San Martín, in youth and in disillusioned old age, and Rosas and his bitter enemy Sarmiento.

Reached by bus No 86 from Plaza del Congreso, the museum is open on Wednesday, Thursday, Friday and Sunday from 2 to 6 pm.

La Boca Literally Buenos Aires' most colourful neighbourhood, La Boca was built up by Italian immigrants along the **Riachuelo**, a narrow waterway lined by meat-packers and warehouses. Part of its colour comes from the brightly painted houses of the

Caminito, a pedestrian walk named for a popular tango. The rest comes from the petroleum sludge and toxics which tint the waters of the Riachuelo.

Immigrants could find a foothold here, but British diplomat James Bryce described Boca houses as 'dirty and squalid...their wooden boards gaping like rents in tattered clothes'. Boca's status as an artists' colony is the legacy of painter Benito Quinquela Martín, but it's also a solidly working-class neighbourhood, whose symbol is the Boca Juniors soccer team. The No 86 bus from Plaza del Congreso is the easiest way to get there.

Once the home and studio of Quinquela Martín, the **Museo de Bellas Artes de La Boca**, at Pedro de Mendoza 1835, is a fine-arts museum, open daily from 9 am to noon and 3 to 6 pm.

Recoleta Fashionable Recoleta, north-west of the city centre, is best known for the **Cementerio de la Recoleta**, a necropolis where, in death as in life, generations of Argentina's elite rest in splendour. The colonial **Iglesia de Nuestra Señora de Pilar** (1732) is an historical monument. Nearby are the **Centro Cultural Recoleta**, and the **Centro Municipal de Exposiciones**, which hosts many cultural events.

Upper-class Porteños relocated here after the San Telmo yellow fever epidemic of the 1870s. Attractive gardens and open spaces include **Plaza Alvear**, **Plaza Francia** (Sunday's crafts fair is Buenos Aires' largest) and other parks toward Palermo.

The **Museo Nacional de Bellas Artes**, Argentina's major art museum, houses works by Renoir, Rodin, Monet, Van Gogh, Picasso and Argentine artists. At Avenida del Libertador 1473, it's open daily, except Monday, from 9 am to 1 pm.

Palermo Rosas' most positive legacy is the open spaces of Palermo, which became parkland after his overthrow by Entre Ríos caudillo and former ally Justo José de Urquiza (who sits astride his horse in a massive monument at Sarmiento and Figueroa Alcorta).

Palermo contains the **Jardín Botánico Carlos Thays** (botanical gardens), **Jardín Zoológico** (zoo), **Rosedal** (rose garden), **Campo de Polo** (polo grounds), **Hipódromo** (racetrack) and **Planetarium**. Some of these uses were obviously not for the masses, but the elite no longer monopolises the area.

Language Courses

The Sunday classified section of the *Buenos Aires Herald* lists possibilities for language instruction and opportunities for teaching English. The Instituto de Lengua Española para Extranjeros (☎ 49-8208), oficina E, 3rd floor, Lavalle 1619, can also arrange accommodation with Porteño families.

Places to Stay

Youth Hostels The main hostel (☎ 362-9133) is at Brasil 675, near Constitución station. A newer hostel (☎ 582-8542), at Nicasio Oroño 1593, near Chacarita cemetery (Subte Federico Lacroze), charges US$5 per night, including kitchen and laundry privileges.

Hotels The best-located budget hotel is *Hotel O'Rei* (☎ 393-7186), Lavalle 733. Quiet, clean and very friendly, it has singles/doubles with shared bath for US$15/22. Almost as cheap is *Petit Hotel Goya* (☎ 392-9269), Suipacha 748. Another recommended place is *Hotel Bahía* (☎ 35-1780), Corrientes 1212, (US$20 single or double).

Close to San Telmo's Plaza Dorrego is *Hotel Carly* (☎ 361-7710), Humberto Primo 464 (US$10 a double). Try also *Hotel Zavalia* (☎ 362-4845) at Juan de Garay 474, or *Hotel Washington* (☎ 361-4738) at Juan de Garay 340, both near Parque Lezama.

Some accommodation near Constitución rents on an hourly basis, but possibilities for about US$20 a double include *Hotel La Casita* (☎ 27-0250) at Constitución 1549, *Hotel Atlas* (☎ 27-9587) at Perú 1681, *Hotel Miramar* (☎ 23-9069) at Salta 1429, or *Hotel Carlos I* (☎ 26-3700) at Carlos Calvo 1463.

Near Congreso, a good budget area, is *Hotel Alfa* (☎ 812-2889), Riobamba 1064 (US$15/20 with private bath). *Hotel Plaza* (☎ 40-9747), Rivadavia 1689, has doubles with shared bath for US$18. At friendly *Gran Hotel Sarmiento* (☎ 45-2764), on a quiet block at Sarmiento 1892, rates are US$20/30 with private bath. Greatly improved *Gran Hotel Oriental* (☎ 951-6427), Mitre 1840, has rooms with shared bath (US$16/18) or with private bath (US$20/22).

Travellers able to spend a bit more can find good value. Corner rooms at *Chile Hotel* (☎ 34-5664), Avenida de Mayo 1297, have huge balconies with views of the Congreso and the Casa Rosada (US$30/45 with private bath). The spacious air-conditioned rooms at newly remodelled *Hotel Avenida* (☎ 331-4341), Avenida de Mayo 623, are outstanding value (US$30/40 with private bath). *Hotel Central Córdoba* (☎ 311-1175), modest but friendly and pleasant, is also very central, at San Martín 1021 (US$27/34). One reader praised four-star *Hotel Regidor*, Tucumán 451 (US$44/55, about half the price of others in its category).

Few places can match the old-world charm of *Hotel Plaza Francia* (☎ 804-9631), Eduardo Schiaffino 2189 in Recoleta (about US$70 a double). The venerable *Claridge Hotel* (☎ 322-7700), Tucumán 535, has very comfortable rooms with cable TV and other amenities (from US$126/144). At the revered, elegant *Alvear Palace Hotel* (☎ 804-4031), Alvear 1891 in Recoleta, doubles can cost US$200 or more.

Places to Eat

In ordinary restaurants, standard fare is pasta, minutas like milanesa, and cheaper cuts of beef, plus chips, salads and desserts. For a little more, you can eat similar food of better quality, but meals at top restaurants can be very costly.

Parrillas Charles Darwin, crossing the Pampas in the 1830s, was astonished at the gauchos' meat diet, which 'would only have agreed with me with hard exercise'. Still, while in Argentina, you can probably indulge yourself on this succulent grilled meat.

If you visit only one parrilla, overlook the hired tourist gauchos for the experience of excellent, moderately priced food at *La Estancia*, Lavalle 941. One reader called *Dora*, on Reconquista near Paraguay, 'the best restaurant we found in Argentina'. It has reportedly moved to L N Alen 1016, and a new restaurant, *El Salmon*, has taken its place. A bit distant from the centre, but worth the trip on bus Nos 37 or 60, is *El Ceibal*, Las Heras 2265. San Telmo's *La Casa de Esteban de Luca* has very fine food at moderate prices, in a restored colonial house at Defensa 1000.

Bar La Robla, Viamonte 1613, has superb seafood and standard Argentine dishes, in a pleasant environment at moderate prices; try also the branch at Montevideo 194. *Cervantes II*, Perón 1883, serves enormous portions of standard Argentine fare at modest prices, but is often very crowded. One of the most popular, economical parrillas is *Pippo*, Paraná 356.

Cafés & Confiterías Porteños spend hours solving their own problems, the country's and the world's over a chessboard and a cortado at places like century-old *Café Tortoni*, Avenida de Mayo 829. The almost rococo interior at *Confitería del Molino*, Callao 20, also merits a visit.

Famous for Bohemian atmosphere is the spartan *Café La Paz*, Corrientes 1599. *Café Pernambuco*, Corrientes 1680, has good atmosphere for a cup of coffee or a glass of wine. *Florida Garden*, Florida 899, is popular among politicians, journalists and other influential people.

Some upper-class Porteños dawdle for hours over caffeine from *La Biela*, Quintana 598 in Recoleta. The rest exercise their pure-bred dogs nearby; watch your step crossing the street to *Café de la Paix*, Quintana 595.

Italian Genuinely Italian food tends to be pricey, but try *La Casona del Nono*, at Lavalle 827. Definitely up-market are *Cicerón*, at Reconquista 647, *Tommaso*, at Junín 1735, and *La Zí Teresa di Napoli*, Las Heras 2939.

Pizzerías Unsung *Pizzería Güerrín*, Corrientes 1372, has outstanding fugazza, fugazzeta and other specialities. Traditionally excellent *Pizzería Serafín*, at Corrientes 1328, is also worth a visit. *Los Inmortales* has branches at Lavalle 746, Callao 1165 and Alvear 1234.

Spanish *Los Teatros*, Talcahuano 360, has superb seafood, chicken and pasta. *El Pulpo*, Tucumán 400, is considered the city's best for seafood. *Taberna Baska*, Chile 980, serves Basque food.

French One of Buenos Aires' best restaurants, *Au Bec Fin*, Vicente López 1825 in Recoleta, has prices to match. *Hippopotamus*, Junín 1787, is in the same category. Others include *Chez Moi*, at San Juan 1223 and *El Gato Que Pesca*, at Rodríguez Peña 159.

Asian Most Asian food is standard Cantonese, but all-you-can-eat restaurants are a good budget option for about US$4; most also have salad bars with excellent ingredients. Try *Macau*, Suipacha 477, *La Fronda*, Paraná 342, or *Han Kung*, Rodríguez Peña 384.

For better quality, try *La Cantina China*, at Maipú 976, *La Casa China*, at Viamonte 1476, or *Oriente*, at Maipú 512.

European/International If price is irrelevant, check out Recoleta institutions like *Estilo Munich*, at Roberto Ortiz 1878, nearby *Gato Dumas*, at Ortiz 1813, or *Clark's*, at Ortiz 1777. *La Mosca Blanca*, Avenida Libertador 901, has a good reputation and more reasonable prices.

Vegetarian Since the mid-1980s, Buenos Aires has enjoyed a vegetarian boom. One of the city's most enduring places, *La Esquina* *de las Flores*, Córdoba 1599, also has a health-food store. One reader endorses *Giardino*, at Suipacha 429 and at Lavalle 835.

Ice Cream A favourite is the unpretentious *Heladería Cadore*, at Corrientes and Rodríguez Peña – chocoholics should not miss their exquisite chocolate amargo (semisweet chocolate) and chocolate blanco (white chocolate). In Recoleta, try *Freddo*, at Ayacucho and Quintana. Many ice-creameries close in winter.

Entertainment
Cinemas The main cinema zones, along Lavalle west of Florida, and on Avenidas Corrientes and Santa Fe, feature first-run films from around the world, but there's also an audience for unconventional and classic films. Many offer half-price tickets midweek, but agencies along Corrientes sell discount tickets at other times.

Two repertory houses change programmes almost daily: the Cinemateca Hebraica, Sarmiento 2255, and the Teatro General San Martín, Corrientes 1530, offer thematic foreign film cycles and reprises of outstanding commercial films.

Translations of English-language titles can be misleading, so check the *Buenos Aires Herald* to be sure what's playing. Foreign films usually have Spanish subtitles.

Theatre Avenida Corrientes is the capital's Broadway or West End. The Teatro General San Martín, Corrientes 1530, has several auditoriums and frequent free events. For complete listings, see the *Buenos Aires Herald* or *Clarín*.

Clubs & Discos Discos tend to be exclusive and expensive, such as Trump's, at Bulnes 2772, Hippopotamus, at Junín 1787, and Africa, at Alvear 1885 in the Alvear Palace Hotel.

Tango Spontaneous tango is not easy to find, but plenty of places in San Telmo and La Boca portray Argentina's most famous cultural export, for up to US$40 per show. Try La Casa Blanca, at Balcarce 868, or Taconeando, at Balcarce 725. Less formal are A Media Luz, at Chile 316, and Los Dos Pianitos, at Giuffra and Balcarce.

La Casa de Carlos Gardel (once Gardel's home) is at Jean Jaurés 735, in the Abasto neighbourhood. Downtown tango spots include Caño 14, at Talcahuano 975, and Tanguería Corrientes Angosta, at Lavalle 750.

Things To Buy
The main shopping zones are along Florida and Santa Fe, though Recoleta is also worthwhile. The Feria de San Telmo flea market takes place every Sunday from 10 am to about 5 pm, on Plaza Dorrego. Good antique shops and restaurants are nearby, with spontaneous live entertainment from buskers and mimes. Best buys are jewellery, leather, shoes and *mate* paraphernalia.

Getting There & Away
Air Nearly all domestic flights and some to bordering countries leave from Aeroparque Jorge Newbery (☎ 771-2071), just north of the city centre. Aeropuerto Internacional Ezeiza (☎ 620-0271) is 35 km south.

Many major international airlines have Buenos Aires offices.

Aerolíneas Argentinas
　　Perú 2 (☎ 362-5008)
American Airlines
　　Córdoba 657 (☎ 392-8849)
British Airways
　　Córdoba 657 (☎ 393-9090)
LAN-Chile
　　Córdoba 879 (☎ 311-5334)
LAP (Líneas Aéreas Paraguayas)
　　Cerrito 1026 (☎ 393-1000)
LAB (Lloyd Aéreo Boliviano)
　　Pellegrini 141 (☎ 35-3505)
PLUNA
　　Florida 1 (☎ 34-7000)
United Airlines
　　Alvear 590 (☎ 312-0664)
Varig
　　Florida 630 (☎ 35-3014)

The major domestic carriers are Aerolíneas Argentinas (☎ 30-8551) and Austral. Both serve nearly every major city from Bolivia to the Beagle Channel.

Austral
    Corrientes 485 (☎ 325-0777)
LADE (Líneas Aéreas del Estado)
    Perú 710, serves only Patagonian destinations (☎ 361-0583).
SAPSE
    Esmeralda 629, 10th floor; a new Patagonian carrier, with cheap fares (☎ 393-5268)
CATA
    Cerrito 1320, 3rd floor; another new, cheap Patagonian carrier (☎ 812-3390)
Aerolíneas Uruguayas
    Paraguay 617; charges US$29 one-way to Colonia, US$80 return to Montevideo, and US$130 return to Punta del Este (☎ 313-3331)
LAPA (Líneas Aéreas Privadas Argentinas)
    Santa Fe 1970, 2nd floor; has comparable fares to Colonia and Montevideo (☎ 812-3322).

To Uruguay, Aeroparque Jorge Newbery is cheaper and more convenient than Aeropuerto Internacional Ezeiza.

Bus At Retiro terminal, at Antártida Argentina and Ramos Mejía near the train station, each company has a desk like an airline ticket counter.

Buses de la Carrera and General Urquiza (☎ 313-2771) go daily to Montevideo, Uruguay (US$25). La Internacional (☎ 313-3164) has buses to Asunción, Paraguay (US$56 regular, US$76 for Servicio Diferencial). Nuestra Señora de la Asunción and Chevallier Paraguaya (☎ 313-2349) are comparable. Pluma (☎ 311-4871) goes to Brazilian cities like Foz do Iguaçu (US$55), Porto Alegre (US$71), São Paulo (US$101) and Río de Janeiro (US$112).

Cocorba goes to Córdoba (US$39) and Catamarca (US$58). ABLO (☎ 313-2835) goes to Rosario (US$16), Córdoba and its Sierras, and La Rioja. Chevallier has extensive routes to Rosario, Córdoba and the North-West, the Cuyo region, and Santiago, Chile (US$60). Fénix Pullman Norte (☎ 313-0134) and Ahumada also go to Santiago. TAC has buses to Mendoza (US$52) and Santiago, while Autotransportes San Juan has buses to San Juan (US$54).

La Estrella and El Trébol go to Santiago del Estero and Tucumán (US$65). La Veloz del Norte has buses to Salta (US$75) and to the Bolivian border at Pocitos. La Internacional also goes to Salta and Jujuy.

El Rápido serves the littoral cities of Santa Fe, Paraná (US$20) and Corrientes. El Turista and El Norte go to Resistencia and Reconquista. Expreso Río Paraná and La Encarnación follow similar routes. TATA (☎ 313-3836) has buses to Gualeguaychú, Colón and points north, passing Parque Nacional El Palmar. Expreso Singer (☎ 313-2355) goes to Posadas (US$40) and Puerto Iguazú (US$54).

Empresa Pehuenche goes to Santa Rosa and Neuquén. El Cóndor and La Estrella have buses to Neuquén and Bariloche (US$85). El Valle goes to Bariloche and San Martín de los Andes.

La Estrella serves destinations in the province of Buenos Aires. Empresa Argentina goes to Mar del Plata (US$25) and other beach resorts. Micro Mar (☎ 313-3128) also does the Atlantic coast.

Costera Criolla/Don Otto (☎ 313-2503), the major Patagonian carrier, has routes to Mar del Plata, Necochea, Bahía Blanca (US$39), Puerto Madryn (US$79), Comodoro Rivadavia (US$91) and Río Gallegos (US$107). La Estrella runs the same routes as far as Comodoro.

Train Passenger services have ceased on all intercity passenger lines, except the Roca line within Buenos Aires province, which departs from Constitución station.

Boat Alíscafos Belt (☎ 326-2747), at Lavalle and Florida, has fast hydrofoils to Colonia (Uruguay), from the new port at Dársena Norte, at the foot of Córdoba. Fares are US$26 to Colonia, US$32 to Montevideo, plus a US$5 departure tax (from this port only).

Ferrylíneas (☎ 394-8412), Florida 780, has hydrofoils (USUS$30) and ferries (USUS$21) from Dársena Sur, at the foot of Calle Brasil; ask for day-trip discounts. Ferry-bus combination Buquebus (☎ 313-

9861), Córdoba 867, has three sailings daily to Colonia (US$21, 2½ hours) and Montevideo (US$25, six hours), from Dársena Sur.

Getting Around
To/From the Airport
To Aeroparque Jorge Newbery, take bus No 33 from opposite Retiro station or bus No 12 from Avenida Callao. To Ezeiza (US$0.80, US$4 for Servicio Diferencial, 1½ hours), bus No 86 (be sure it says 'Ezeiza') starts in La Boca and comes up Avenida de Mayo past Plaza del Congreso.

Manuel Tienda León (☎ 396-2078), Carlos Pellegrini 509, runs minibuses to Ezeiza airport (US$13, 45 minutes), every half-hour from 5.30 to 10 am, every 20 minutes until 5 pm and every half-hour from 5.30 to 10 pm. At about US$40, taxis are expensive for individuals but reasonable for a group.

Bus Sold at nearly all kiosks and bookshops, the *Guia Peuser* details nearly 200 different bus routes, accompanied by a fold-out map. Many Porteños have memorised the system and can instantly tell you which bus to take and where to get off, but always check the window placard for the final destination. Fares depend on distance – tell the driver your destination.

Train Commuter trains serve most of Gran Buenos Aires from Retiro, Constitución, Lacroze and Once, but services and fares are in flux because of privatisation.

Underground Buenos Aires' antique Subte (1913) is fast and efficient, but reaches only certain parts of a city much larger than when the system opened. Four of the five lines (Líneas A, B, D, and E) run from the city centre to the capital's western and northern outskirts, while Línea C links Retiro and Constitución. A map of the system is available at tourist kiosks. Buy a pocketful of fichas (US$0.45) to avoid standing in lines.

Trains operate from 5.30 am to 1.30 am; they are frequent on weekdays, less so on weekends. From a few stations, you can only go in one direction, so you may have to backtrack to reach your destination.

Taxi Black and yellow cabs are numerous and reasonably priced, with new digital readout meters. Drivers customarily receive small change as a tip.

Tours Unless time is very limited, try to get around on your own. The municipal tourist office in the Centro Cultural San Martín may still offer free guided tours of inner barrios.

One destination which justifies a guided tour is the island of Martín García, site of a key naval battle during the wars of independence and, later, a penal colony. Cacciola (☎ 322-0026), at Florida 520, 1st floor, or in the suburb of Tigre (☎ 749-2369), at Lavalle 520, runs weekend excursions.

Atlantic Coast

In summer, millions of Porteños take a holiday from friends, families and co-workers, only to meet them on the beaches of Buenos Aires province. Beach access is open, but *balnearios* (resorts) are private – only those renting tents may use showers and toilets. Besides lifeguards and medical services, balnearios usually have confiterías, shops and paddle-ball courts (a current fad). Prices rise fortnightly from mid-December to mid-February, then decline until late March, when most hotels and residenciales close.

North of Mar del Plata, gentle dunes rise behind generally narrow beaches, while south-west toward Miramar, steep bluffs highlight a changing coastline. Beyond Miramar, broad sandy beaches delight bathers, fishing enthusiasts and windsurfers.

MAR DEL PLATA
In the mid-19th century, Portuguese investors established El Puerto de Laguna de los Padres here. In 1874, after buying the land, developer Patricio Peralta Ramos founded Mar del Plata proper, about 400 km from

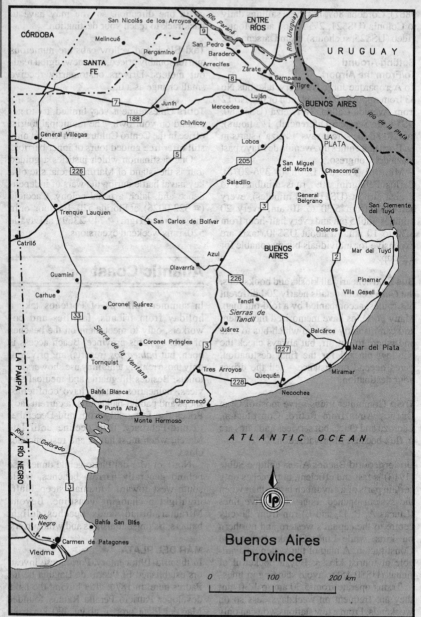

Buenos Aires Province

Buenos Aires. Since then, it has been a commercial and industrial centre, then a beach resort. Upper-class Porteño families built villas here, but 'Mardel' has become the main summer resort for middle-class holiday-makers. Some travellers may prefer spring or autumn, when prices are lower and the atmosphere more relaxed.

Information
Tourist Office The municipal tourist office (☎ 21777), Boulevard Marítimo 2267, has an efficient information system, good maps and useful brochures. There's a provincial office (☎ 25340) at the Rambla Hotel Provincial, Boulevard Marítimo 2500, Local 60.

Money Try Jonestur, San Martín 2574, or La Moneda, Rivadavia 2625.

Post & Telecommunications The Correo Central is at Luro 2460. Telefónica is at Luro 2554, Olavarría 2495, the train station and the bus terminal.

Emergency Hospital Mar del Plata (☎ 22021) is at Castelli 2460.

Things to See
Walking Tour A stroll past the old mansions reveals Mardel's upper-class origins. At Colón and Viamonte, the French-style **Villa Normandy** (1919) barely survived a 1950s renovation craze. At Brown and Viamonte is the hilltop **Iglesia Stella Maris** – its Virgin is the patron of the local fishing industry. The 88-metre **Torre Tanque**, at Falucho and Mendoza, has fine views.

After descending Viamonte to Rodríguez Peña, walk toward the ocean to Urquiza, whose **Chalet Los Troncos** gave its name to the neighbourhood; note the gate and fence of quebracho and lapacho hardwoods from Salta province. Return to the centre by the longer route, along Avenida Peralta Ramos and **Cabo Corrientes**.

Aficionados of art and architecture should visit the **Museo Municipal de Arte Juan Carlos Castagnino**, at Colón 1189, open daily (except Monday) from 6 to 11 pm. The

museum is housed in the Villa Ortiz Basualdo (1902), which resembles a Loire castle. Historic photographs in the **Museo Archivo Histórico Municipal** recall Mardel's past. The museum, in Villa Mitre, an elite summer residence at Lamadrid 3870, is open daily from 3 to 7 pm; take bus No 523.

Banquina de Pescadores At the picturesque wharf, sea lions monitor the fishing and stevedoring. Besides photographic opportunities, there's fine dining at a complex of restaurants or, more cheaply, at stand-up cafeterias. Take any of several southbound buses from the centre.

Villa Victoria Victoria Ocampo, founder of the literary journal *Sur*, hosted literary salons in the 1920s and 1930s at this pre-fab Norwegian home at Matheu 1851, open daily from 6 pm to midnight.

Places to Stay
It's worth reiterating that prices climb steadily in summer and fall in the off season. Prices below are from early high season.

Camping Mardel's several campgrounds, on Ruta 11 south of town (served by Bus Rápido del Sud), are crowded in summer. *Los Horneros* has large plots, clean showers and washing facilities. *Acuario* is also on Ruta 11, 7½ km south of the lighthouse.

Hostels, Hospedajes & Hosterías Rooms with shared bath are US$6 per person at the *Albergue de la Juventud* (☎ 27927), in a wing of *Hotel Pergamino*, at Tucumán 2728, a few blocks from the bus terminal.

At Sarmiento 2268, an anonymous hospedaje has four-bed rooms for US$7 per person, with a huge, clean shared bath. *Hostería La Madrileña*, Sarmiento 2955, has modest doubles with private bath (US$8 per person).

Also near the terminal are *Hospedaje Lamadrid* (☎ 25456), at Lamadrid 2518, *Hospedaje Colonial* (☎ 51-1039), at Olavarría 2663, and *Hospedaje Star*

(☎ 25044), at Falucho 1949. *Gran Hotel Pelayo*, Sarmiento 2899 (☎ 51-3579), is good value (US$20 per person, with breakfast). The landmark *Gran Hotel Provincial* (☎ 24081), Boulevard Marítimo 2500, is beyond budget travellers, but worth a look for its casino, restaurant and commercial gallery.

Places to Eat

Restaurants, pizzerías and snack bars find it hard to keep up with impatient summer crowds, but food is generally good; seafood at the Nuevo Complejo Comercial Puerto is excellent. For cheap minutas or sandwiches, look around the bus terminal.

Tía Pepina, at H Yrigoyen 2645, *La Biblioteca*, at Santa Fe 2633, and *Ambos Mundos*, at Rivadavia 2644, serve filling minutas at moderate prices. *La Cantina de Armando*, at San Lorenzo and Catamarca, and *Don Pepito*, across from the Casino, serve large portions at reasonable prices.

Vegetarian restaurants are good value, and include *Comedor Naturista*, Salta 1571, and *El Jardín*, on Plaza San Martín. *Joe*, at Lamadrid and Rawson, serves superb pizza and calzone, while *Manolo*, Rivadavia 2371, has varied, tasty pizza. *Il Vero Napoli*, Belgrano 3408, has superb lasagna.

Trenque Lauquen, Mitre 2807, and *La Marca*, Almafuerte 253, are good but pricey parrillas. *El Rey del Bife*, Colón 2863, and *Rincón de los Amigos*, Córdoba 2588, are more economical.

Entertainment

When Buenos Aires shuts down in January, many shows come here, and there are also several cinemas. The casino at Hotel Provincial, a black-tie venue at night, is more informal in the daytime.

Argentines dance all night at clubs on Avenida Constitución, nicknamed 'Avenida del Ruido' (Avenue of Noise), where bus No 551 runs all night.

Things to Buy

Avenida J B Justo ('Avenida del Pullover') is known for sweaters and jackets at near-wholesale prices. The fashion-conscious will find a multitude of boutiques along San Martín and Rivadavia. *Alfajores*, biscuit sandwiches filled with chocolate, dulce de leche or fruit, are delicious for afternoon tea or *mate*; try the popular brand Havanna.

Getting There & Away

Air Aerolíneas Argentinas (☎ 45626) and Austral (☎ 23085), both at the Hotel Provincial, fly often to Buenos Aires (US$77) from Aeropuerto Camet, 10 km north of town.

Bus From the busy terminal (☎ 51-5406), at Alberdi 1602, many buses go to Buenos Aires (US$25) in summer. El Rápido Argentino travels to La Plata (US$15) twice daily. Expreso Córdoba-Mar del Plata serves Córdoba, while Empresa Pampa goes to Bahía Blanca (US$29), with Patagonian connections. TAC and TIRSA travel to Mendoza.

Train Since the province of Buenos Aires assumed control of the Roca line, passenger services are unsettled; the station (☎ 72-9553) is at Luro 4599.

VILLA GESELL

This relatively new and sedate resort, 130 km north of Mar del Plata, attracts many summer visitors. Some people consider it exclusive and stay away. At Avenida Buenos Aires and Circunvalación, the tourist office (☎ 68596) has good maps, while several kiosks have data on accommodation, restaurants and buses. Avenida 3 is the shopping and entertainment centre.

Things to See & Do

Events like the 'Encuentros Corales' (a competition of choirs from around the country) take place at the **Anfiteatro** (amphitheatre). The **Muelle de Pesca**, at Playa and Paseo 129, offers year-round fishing. You can rent horses at the **Escuela de Equitación San Jorge**.

Places to Stay

Camping Only groups find camping cheap,

since campgrounds have minimum rates around US$20. At the north end of town, *Camping Africa*, at Avenida Buenos Aires and Circunvalación, and *Camping Caravan*, at Paseo 101 and Circunvalación, both have swimming pools. At the south end of Avenida 3 are *Camping Casablanca*, *Camping Mar Dorado* and *Camping Monte Bubi*. Nearly all close by late March.

The youth hostel/campground *El Coyote* is at Alameda 212 and Calle 304 bis.

Hospedajes Most accommodation includes private bath and even telephone. Figure about US$18/27 a single/double for *Hospedaje Aguas Verdes*, on Avenida 5 between paseos 104 and 105, or *Hospedaje Sarimar*, on Avenida 3 between paseos 117 and 118. *Hospedaje Antonio*, on Avenida 4 between paseos 104 and 106, has some rooms with shared bath.

Places to Eat
La Jirafa Azul, on Avenida 3 between Avenida Buenos Aires and Paseo 102, has a good, cheap standard menu. *Cantina Arturito*, on Avenida 3 between paseos 126 and 127, serves large portions of home-made pasta, plus shellfish and home-cured ham, at medium-plus prices. For tasty seafood, try *Marisquería El Gallego*, on Avenida 3 between paseos 108 and 109.

For sandwiches and friendly service, try *Sangucheto*, on Paseo 104 between avenidas 3 and 4, or *La Martona*, on Paseo 107 between avenidas 2 and 3. *El Faro*, a rotisería at Avenida 3 and Paseo 119, has moderately priced takeaway food.

Getting There & Away
Air Aerolíneas Argentinas (☎ 68228), at Avenida Buenos Aires and Avenida 10, flies to Buenos Aires daily in summer (US$77).

Bus The terminal (☎ 66058) is on the south side, at Avenida 3 and Paseo 140. Some long-distance buses stop at the Mini Terminal (☎ 62340), on Avenida 4 between paseos 104 and 105.

Empresa Río de la Plata, a block from the Mini Terminal, has several direct buses daily to Buenos Aires, as does Antón, on Paseo 108 between avenidas 3 and 4.

PINAMAR
Architect Jorge Bunge planned Pinamar around an axis formed by Avenida Libertador, parallel to the beach, and the perpendicular thoroughfare Avenida Bunge. Pinamar is an elegant resort for Argentines who needn't work for a living, but nearby Ostende and Valeria del Mar, 120 km from Mar del Plata, offer more moderate prices.

On each side of Bunge, the streets form large fans, making orientation tricky. The tourist office (☎ 82749), at Bunge and Libertador, has a good map with useful descriptions of Pinamar, Valeria, Ostende and Cariló (an even more exclusive country-club environment). Visitors enjoying the usual outdoor activities must dodge dune buggies on the beach and even along nature trails.

Places to Stay
Several campgrounds line the coast between Ostende and Pinamar. At Quintana and Nuestras Malvinas in Ostende, the youth hostel has dormitories and kitchen facilities in an interesting beachfront building.

Prices at Pinamar's few hospedajes are around US$18/27 for singles/doubles; try *Hospedaje Acacia*, at Del Cangrejo 1358, *Hospedaje Rose Marie*, at De las Medusas 1381, and *Hospedaje Valle Fértil*, at Del Cangrejo 1110. One-star hotels include *Hotel Berlín*, at Rivadavia and Artes, and *Hotel Sardegna*, at Bunge and Marco Polo.

Places to Eat
Parrilla Las Marías, at Bunge and Marco Polo, serves fine pork and chivito a la parrilla (grilled kid goat). For good paella, cazuela and empanadas tucumanas, try *El Negro B*, at Jason and Robinson Crusoe.

Paxapoga, at Bunge and Libertador, serves parrillada and pasta. *El Vivero*, also at Bunge and Libertador, has fine vegetarian meals. *Pizzería La Reja*, at Jason and Robinson Crusoe, offers varied pizza and great empanadas. For German desserts and baked goods, visit *Tante*, at De las Artes 35, or *Zur Tanne*, at Rivadavia and Artes.

Reservations are advisable for *Matarazzo Party*, at Bunge and Júpiter, whose spaghetti Matarazzo features nine different sauces – take your pick. *Mamma Liberata*, at Bunge and Simbad el Marino, and *Club Italiano*, at Eneas and Cazón, also offer pasta.

Getting There & Away
Empresas Antón (☎ 82378) and Río de la Plata (☎ 82247) serve Buenos Aires from the bus terminal on the corner of Avenida Shaw and Del Pejerrey. Costamar (☎ 82885) connects the beaches.

MIRAMAR
From Cabo Corrientes, car-clogged Ruta 11 follows spectacular cliffs past the presidential retreat at Chapadmalal, and trade union holiday complexes, before arriving at Miramar, 45 km south-west of Mar del Plata.

Miramar's tranquillity, safety and friendliness attract families with young children. Like La Plata, its conventional grid is sliced by diagonals off the main and secondary plazas. The Dirección Municipal de Turismo (☎ 20190), Calle 28 and Calle 21, has good brochures and a useful map.

Places to Stay & Eat
Camping El Durazno, two km toward Mar del Plata on Ruta 11, has clean plots with electricity and sanitary facilities (US$3.50 per person). Hospedajes (about US$11 per person) include *Hospedaje Familia*, at Calle 23, No 1701, *Hospedaje Dorimar*, at Calle 24, No 839, and *Hospedaje España*, at Calle 14, No 1046. One-star hotels charge about US$15 per person with private bath; try *Hotel Santa Eulalia II*, at calles 15 and 20, *Hotel Miramar*, at Calle 21, No 974, and *Hotel Ideal*, at Calle 21, No 632.

Círculo Italiano, on Avenida 9 between calles 30 and 28, serves abundant Italian dishes. *Restaurant El Aguila*, at Calle 19, No 1461, has a standard menu. *El Estribo*, on Calle 30 between calles 19 and 21, has good parrillada. For seafood, try *El Muelle*, at

Costanera and Calle 37, or *Mesón Español*, at Avenida 26, No 1351. Rotiserías include *Katty*, at Calle 21, No 780, *Popeye*, at Avenida 26 between calles 19 and 21, and *Valeria*, at Calle 25, No 620.

Getting There & Away
Bus Miramar has good bus connections but no central terminal. Several companies have offices (☎ 23359), at Avenida Mitre 1701, including El Rápido del Sur to Mar del Plata, CAT to Gran Buenos Aires and Micromar to Buenos Aires (US$28). Costera Criolla (☎ 20747), at calles 32 and 19, travels to Necochea; El Pampa, at the same office, goes to Bahía Blanca.

Train Inquire about services to Buenos Aires on the Roca line (☎ 20657), on Avenida 40 between calles 13 and 15.

NECOCHEA
Necochea is a tranquil, family-oriented resort 125 km south-west of Mar del Plata. Its most attractive feature is **Parque Miguel Lillo**, a huge green space along the beach whose dense pine woods are popular for cycling, riding or picnicking. The Río Quequén, rich in trout and mackerel, also allows for adventurous canoeing.

Places to Stay & Eat
The *Camping Municipal* is in Parque Lillo, but most accommodation is in the city centre. The most reasonable, at around US$12 per person, are places like *Hospedaje Bayo*, at Calle 87, No 338, *Hospedaje Colón*, at Calle 62, No 3034, and *Hospedaje Necomar*, at calles 20 and 79 bis. One-star hotels (about US$15 to US$25) include *Hotel Lido*, at Calle 81, No 328, and *Hotel Flamingo*, at Calle 83, No 333.

Parrilla El Palenque, at Avenida 79 and Calle 6, has reasonable prices.

Getting There & Away
Bus El Cóndor and Costera Criolla go to Buenos Aires several times daily from the terminal, at Avenida 47 and Calle 582.

The Pampas

Apart from their coastline and a few other features, the Pampas are unrelentingly flat, but this agricultural heartland contains a surprising number of tourist attractions in the provinces of Buenos Aires, La Pampa, and parts of Santa Fe and Córdoba. An integrated network of railroads and highways connects the towns of the Pampas to the city of Buenos Aires, a de facto secession from the province in the late 19th century.

Buenos Aires is Argentina's largest, richest, most populous and most important province. La Plata, the provincial capital, and the port of Bahía Blanca are key cities, while colonial Luján is a major religious centre.

Santa Fe city is the capital of Santa Fe province. Rosario, exporting agricultural produce, challenges Córdoba's status as the republic's 'second city'.

Settled later than Buenos Aires province because of Indian resistance and erratic rainfall, La Pampa did not attain provincial status until 1951. Its varied environments include rolling hills of native *caldén* forests, extensive grasslands, and salares (salt lakes) with flamingos. Parque Nacional Lihué Calel certainly justifies a detour from the usual routes to Patagonia.

History

In pre-Columbian times, the aboriginal Querandí hunted guanaco and rhea on the Pampas, but feral European livestock transformed the region. One 18th-century visitor estimated 48 million cattle between modern Paraguay and the Río Negro.

Having tamed wild horses, mobile Indians were formidable opponents, but the Pampas eventually fell to cattle ranchers and farmers. Feral livestock left two enduring legacies: the culture of the gaucho, who persisted for decades as a neohunter-gatherer and then as a symbol of *argentinidad* (a romantic nationalism) and environmental impoverishment, as grazing and European weeds altered the native pastures.

Only the relatively few estancieros with the luck to inherit or the foresight to grab large tracts of land benefitted from hides, tallow and salt beef, which had limited overseas markets. British-built railroads made it feasible to export wool and then beef, but improved cattle breeds required succulent feeds like alfalfa, which needed preparatory cultivation. Landowners therefore rented to *medieros* (sharecroppers who raised wheat for four or five years before moving on) and thus profitted both from their share of the wheat harvest and from new alfalfa fields. Maize, wheat and linseed soon exceeded the value of animal products.

The Pampas are still famous for beef, but there are now many smaller landholdings, and Argentina is now also a major grain exporter. Intensive cultivation of fruit and vegetables, as well as dairying, takes place near Buenos Aires and other large cities.

LA PLATA

After Buenos Aires became the federal capital, Governor Dardo Rocha founded La Plata, 56 km south-east, as the new capital of Buenos Aires province. An important administrative, commercial and cultural centre, it has one of the country's best universities.

The superposition of diagonals on a conventional grid forms a distinctive diamond pattern linking several plazas. Most public buildings are on or near Plaza Moreno, but the commercial centre is near Plaza San Martín. The Subsecretaría de Turismo (☎ 21-6894), on the 13th floor of the municipal tower, at calles 12 and 53, has excellent brochures and a good map.

Things to See

Paseo del Bosque Forest plantations cover this 60-hectare park at the north-east edge of town, whose **Anfiteatro Martín Fierro** hosts summer drama festivals. The architecturally eclectic **Museo de Ciencias Naturales de La Plata,** in Paseo del Bosque, houses the archaeological and anthropological collections of Patagonian explorer F P Moreno, and a recently opened botany display. The museum (admission US$2) is open daily (except for 1 January, 1 May and 25 December) from noon to 6 pm on weekdays, 10 am to 6 pm on weekends and holidays. Paseo del Bosque also features the **Observatorio Astronómico** and several university departments.

La República de los Niños A steam train circles this scale reproduction of a city for children, sponsored by Eva Perón and completed shortly before her death in 1952. The captivating **Museo Internacional del Muñeco**, a doll and puppet museum, is open daily from 10 am to 6 pm. From downtown La Plata, take bus Nos 518 or 273 to Camino General Belgrano Km 7, in the suburb of Gonnet.

Places to Stay & Eat

Friendly but run-down *Hotel Roca*, on Avenida 1 at Calle 42, has singles/doubles with private bath (US$18/25) and doubles with shared bath (US$20).

Among the cheaper restaurants are *Everton*, at Calle 14 between calles 63 and 64, and *Club Matheu*, on Calle 63 between Avenida 1 and Calle 2. A local recommendation is the *Colegio de Escribanos*, on Avenida 13 between calles 47 and 48.

On warm summer nights, you can dawdle at the 85-year-old *Cervecería Modelo*, at the corner of calles 54 and 5, with cerveza tirada (lager beer), snacks and complimentary peanuts.

Getting There & Away

Bus The bus terminal (☎ 21-2182) is at calles 4 and 42. Río de la Plata has buses every half-hour to Buenos Aires (US$3), plus beach service to Pinamar and Villa Gesell. Long-distance companies include Costera Criolla (to the Atlantic Coast) and El Cóndor (to Bahía Blanca via Sierra de la Ventana). Liniers goes daily to Santa Rosa, while Pampa goes to Tandil and Necochea.

Train Hourly trains to Buenos Aires' Constitución station leave from the turn-of-

the-century station (☎ 21-9377), at Avenida 1 and Calle 43.

LUJÁN

Legend says that, in 1630, a wagon would not budge on a rutted cart road until gauchos removed from it an image of the Virgin brought from Brazil. The devoted owner built a chapel on the spot. Argentina's patron saint, La Virgen de Luján, now occupies a neo-Gothic basilica here, 65 km west of Buenos Aires.

There is an Oficina de Turismo (☎ 20032) at the bus terminal, but the office (☎ 20453), at Edificio La Cúpula, at the west end of Lavalle, has more knowledgeable staff and is better stocked with brochures.

Things to See

Basílica Nuestra Señora de Luján At this huge basilica, four million pilgrims a year ask favours of the Virgencita. She stands in a *camarín* (chamber) behind the main altar, whose steps devotees have covered with appreciatory plaques. Her day is 8 May. Near the basilica, the **Museo Devocional** houses ex-votos (gifts) from around the world.

Museum Complex Between the bus terminal and the basilica, the Complejo Museográfico Enrique Udaondo includes the **Museo Colonial e Histórico**, housed in beautiful colonial buildings like the **Cabildo**, and the so-called **Casa del Virrey** (no viceroy ever lived there). The **Museo de Transporte** has four showrooms, plus a patio with colonial wagons, a windmill and a horse-powered mill. The complex is open on Wednesday from 12.30 to 4.30 pm, on Thursday and Friday from 11.30 am to 4.30 pm, and on weekends from 10.45 am to 6 pm.

Places to Stay & Eat

Basic *Camping 7*, on Ruta 7 across the Río Luján, costs US$3 per person. Near the Dirección Municipal de Turismo is another, more expensive site, but pilgrims camp just about anywhere they feel like it.

On the north side of the basilica, friendly *Hospedaje Carena*, Lavalle 114, has singles/doubles at US$9/16 with private bath. Slightly dearer is *Hotel Santa Rita*, on Lezica y Torrezuri, with small, musty but clean rooms with private bath for US$12/18.

At the many cheap restaurants along Avenida Nuestra Señora de Luján, aggressive waiters drag tourists off the sidewalk. Quieter *Restaurant Don Diego*, Colón 964, has excellent but pricier food.

Getting There & Away

Bus The bus terminal is on Avenida de Nuestra Señora del Rosario, four blocks north of the basilica. Transporte Luján (Línea 52) and TALSA go to Buenos Aires for US$3, while Transportes Atlántida (Línea 57) goes to Palermo.

Long-distance Empresa Argentina has three buses daily to Mar del Plata (US$26). La Estrella goes to San Juan (US$52) and to San Rafael, with connections to Mendoza (US$51). General Urquiza serves Rosario (US$15) and Córdoba (US$35).

Train The Sarmiento line has daily trains from Once (Plaza Miserere Subte), in Buenos Aires.

BAHÍA BLANCA

Bahía Blanca, 650 km south of Buenos Aires, is South America's largest naval base, and a key port for grain from Buenos Aires province and produce from the Río Negro valley. The coastal gateway to Patagonia, it is more a crossroads than a tourist city.

The tourist office is in the Municipalidad (☎ 20114), Alsina 65. Most cambios close by 4 pm, but try Cambio Pullman, at San Martín 171, or Iberotur, at Soler 144. ENCOTEL is at Moreno 34, while Telefónica is at O'Higgins 203.

Places to Stay & Eat

The municipal campground at *Balneario Maldonado*, four km south-west of the centre, is open all year, but has hot water and electricity in summer only. It charges US$1.50 per person.

Across from the train station, several run-down hospedajes charge around US$7 per

person. Try *Hospedaje Molinari*, at Cerri 719, *Hospedaje Los Vascos*, at Cerri 747, or *Hospedaje Roma*, at Cerri 759. Nearer the plaza, better accommodation costs about US$9 to US$12 per person at *Hospedaje Los Angeles*, Chiclana 367, *Hotel Argentino*, Chiclana 466, or *Hotel Bayón*, Chiclana 487.

Taberna Baska, Lavalle 284, and *La Española*, Zelarrayán 51, serve appetising Spanish food at reasonable prices. *El Aljibe*, at Donado and Thompson, offers conventional Argentine fare but is pricier. For breakfast, try *Bar Lácteo La Barra*, Chiclana 155.

Getting There & Away

Air Aerolíneas Argentinas (☎ 21033), San Martín 298, flies to Buenos Aires directly daily (US$101), with other flights via Santa Rosa, in La Pampa province.

Austral (☎ 21383), Colón 59, flies twice daily to Buenos Aires, except Sunday (one flight only). Daily, except Sunday, it flies to Comodoro Rivadavia, Río Gallegos (US$164), Río Grande and Ushuaia (US$207).

Bus At Estados Unidos and Brown, the terminal (☎ 29616) is about two km from the plaza, with frequent buses to Buenos Aires (US$39). Pampa goes to Mar del Plata (US$29) and Necochea, while El Valle serves Neuquén (US$35) and Zapala via the Río Negro valley. Don Otto has buses to coastal Patagonia, as far as Río Gallegos (US$75).

Train Since the province has recently assumed control of the railways, inquire about services from the railway station (☎ 21168), Cerri 750.

Hitching Hitching from Bahía Blanca to Buenos Aires or Neuquén is fairly easy, as many trucks pass through the port all year. Southbound, speak with truckers at El Cholo truck stop, on Ruta 3 Sur, at Km 696. For Buenos Aires, try either Ruta 3 Norte or provincial Ruta 51.

Getting Around

To/From the Airport Bus No 10 goes to Aeropuerto Bahía Blanca (☎ 21665), 15 km east of the city.

Bus Bus Nos 505, 512, 514, 516 and 517 go from the city centre to the bus terminal.

SIERRAS OF BUENOS AIRES PROVINCE

Granitic bedrock emerges from the deep Pampas sediments only in the ranges of Tandilia and Ventania, trending north-west to south-east. The easterly Sierras de Tandil are rounded hills of around 500 metres, while the westerly Sierra de la Ventana attracts hikers and climbers to scenic jagged peaks above 1300 metres.

Tandil

Tandil (population 81,000) is 380 km south of Buenos Aires and serves an important agricultural and livestock zone. Masses of Holy Week tourists come here to visit **Calvario**, a hill resembling the site of Christ's crucifixion. The Subsecretaría de Turismo (☎ 25661), at Avenida 9 de Julio 555, has a city map and useful brochures.

Parque Independencia offers good views of the city, particularly at night. For many years, a 300-tonne boulder atop **Cerro La Movediza** balanced precariously, before falling. In the early 1870s, a group of renegade gauchos, followers of an eccentric healer, distributed weapons here before going on a murderous rampage against European immigrants.

Places to Stay & Eat The clean, shady *Camping Municipal*, on the way to the Dique del Fuerte (balneario), charges US$3 per tent (up to four people), and has a grocery and hot showers. Some but not all No 500 (yellow) buses go there – ask the driver.

Friendly, modest and tidy *Hotel Kaiku*, Mitre 902, is good value at US$6/10 a single/double with breakfast. *Hotel Cristal*, Rodríguez 871, is very basic but also cheap (US$7 per person). At old-fashioned *Hospedaje Savoy*, at Alem and Mitre, the congenial owner charges US$11/18 for rooms with private bath.

For cheap eats, it's the *Comedor Universitario*, at the corner of Maipú and Fuerte Independencia. *Restaurant El Nuevo Don José*, Avenida Monseñor De Andrea 269, has great pollo a la piedra, while *El Estribo*, San Martín 759, has tasty pork. At *La Farola*, Pinto 681, order pejerrey (mackerel); for parrillada, visit *Parada 4*, on Rodríguez at Constitución.

Getting There & Away From the bus terminal (☎ 25585), at Avenida Buzón and Portugal, La Estrella and Río Paraná buses go to Buenos Aires three times daily. TAC goes to Córdoba and San Juan, while El Rápido serves Mar del Plata every two hours.

Until recently, Ferrocarril Roca (☎ 23002) had one daily train to Buenos Aires from the station at Avenida Machado and Colón.

Getting Around Bus No 500 (yellow) goes to Dique del Fuerte and the municipal campground. Bus No 501 (red) goes to the bus terminal and train station, while bus No 503 (blue) goes to La Movediza and the bus terminal.

Sierra de la Ventana

This charming town 125 km north of Bahía Blanca has conventional facilities like a casino, golf links and swimming pools, and also offers hiking, climbing, riding, cycling, kayaking and fishing.

Avenida San Martín is the main street, with most services near the train station. The tourist office (☎ 91-5032), at Roca and San Martín, has useful maps and pamphlets.

Parque Provincial Ernesto Tornquist This 6700-hectare park, popular for ranger-guided walks and independent hiking, has an informative visitors' centre, and a designated campground (US$2 per person) with toilets but no showers.

The best hike is 1136-metre Cerro de la Ventana, taking about two hours to reach the treeline and two to three more to the summit, with views of surrounding hills and the distant Pampas.

Places to Stay & Eat There are free camp sites along the river, but organised sites like *Autocamping*, on Diego Meyer, have good facilities (US$4 per adult, US$2 per child). *Camping Yamila*, at the balneario, charges half that. *Hotel Argentino*, on Roca, and *Hospedaje La Perlita*, at Malvinas and Pasaje 3, charge US$9 per person.

Besides hotel restaurants, try *Restaurant Irupé*, on Avenida San Martín, *Restaurant Espadaña*, on Ruta 76, one km from town, *Las Sierras* (great desserts), at Drago and Alberdi, or *Rali-Hue*, a parrilla on San Martín.

Getting There & Away La Estrella has daily buses to Buenos Aires (US$35) and to Bahía Blanca. Check on revised train services.

ROSARIO
After independence Rosario, 320 km upstream from Buenos Aires on the west bank of the Río Paraná, quickly superseded Santa Fe as an economic powerhouse, as the railroad brought agricultural exports from Córdoba, Mendoza and Tucumán. Curving bluffs and open space above the river channel modify Rosario's regular grid pattern, whose centre is Plaza 25 de Mayo. The pedestrian streets of San Martín and Córdoba are the focus of commerce.

Information
The municipal Dirección de Turismo (☎ 24-8382), in a cubicle in the Centro Cultural Rivadavia, at San Martín 1080, has a good city map, but little other information.

The main cambios are Bonsignore, at San Martín 998, and Exprinter, at Córdoba 960. ENCOTEL is at Córdoba 721, Telecom at San Luis 936.

Things to See
Monumento Nacional a la Bandera The biggest attraction in Rosario (literally) is the colossal, boat-shaped Monument to the Flag, whose bow holds the crypt of flag designer

General Manuel Belgrano. Its museum is open daily from 7 am to 7 pm (except Mondays, when hours are 1 to 7 pm). Every June, Rosario celebrates **La Semana de la Bandera** (Flag Week).

Historical Museums Focussed on the republican era, the **Museo Histórico Provincial**, in Parque Independencia, is open Tuesday to Friday from 9 am to 12.30 pm and 3 to 6.30 pm, and on weekends from 3 to 6.30 pm. The **Museo de la Ciudad**, Oroño 1540, is open Wednesday to Sunday from 9 am to noon and 3 to 7 pm.

Art Museums The **Museo Municipal de Bellas Artes**, at Pellegrini and Oroño, is open Wednesday to Sunday from 11 am to 7 pm. The **Museo Barnes de Arte Sacro**, with sculptures by the man responsible for parts of the Monument to the Flag, is open on Thursdays from 4 to 6 pm.

Science Museums Visitors interested in environment and wildlife should visit the **Museo Provincial de Ciencias Naturales**, Moreno 758, Tuesday to Friday 9 am to 12.30 pm and Tuesday, Friday and Sunday from 3 to 6 pm.

The planetarium, at the **Complejo Municipal Astronómico Educativo Rosario** in Parque Urquiza, has weekend shows from 5 to 6 pm. On Tuesdays and Thursdays from 9 to 10 pm, visitors can view the austral skies through the planetarium's telescopes.

Museo del Paraná y Las Islas River life – flora, fauna and people – permeates this museum in the waterfront Estación Fluvial. It's only open on Wednesday from 2.30 to 4 pm and on Sunday from 4 to 6.30 pm, but go at any hour to see the murals.

Places to Stay & Eat
Friendly *Hotel Normandie*, Mitre 1030, charges US$10/14 for rooms with shared bath, US$12/16 with private bath. *Hotel Bahía*, Maipú 1254, is comparable. Many of the rooms at the *Nuevo Hotel Linton*, Entre Ríos 1043, have attractive balconies, while

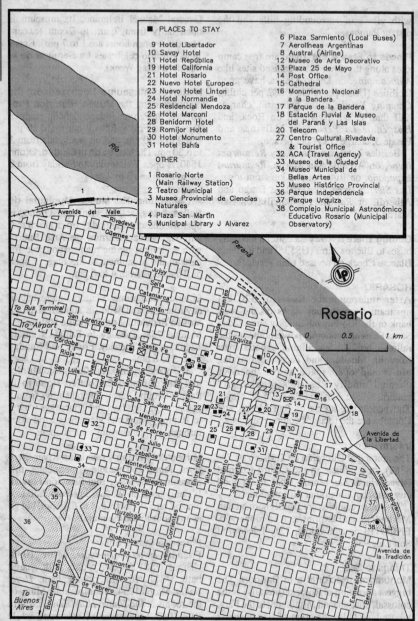

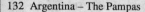

■ PLACES TO STAY

- 9 Hotel Libertador
- 10 Savoy Hotel
- 11 Hotel República
- 19 Hotel California
- 21 Hotel Rosario
- 22 Nuevo Hotel Europeo
- 23 Nuevo Hotel Linton
- 24 Hotel Normandie
- 25 Residencial Mendoza
- 26 Hotel Marconi
- 28 Benidorm Hotel
- 29 Romijor Hotel
- 30 Hotel Monumento
- 31 Hotel Bahía

OTHER

- 1 Rosario Norte (Main Railway Station)
- 2 Teatro Municipal
- 3 Museo Provincial de Ciencias Naturales
- 4 Plaza San Martín
- 5 Municipal Library J Alvarez
- 6 Plaza Sarmiento (Local Buses)
- 7 Aerolíneas Argentinas
- 8 Austral (Airline)
- 12 Museo de Arte Decorativo
- 13 Plaza 25 de Mayo
- 14 Post Office
- 15 Cathedral
- 16 Monumento Nacional a la Bandera
- 17 Parque de la Bandera
- 18 Estación Fluvial & Museo del Paraná y Las Islas
- 20 Telecom
- 27 Centro Cultural Rivadavia & Tourist Office
- 32 ACA (Travel Agency)
- 33 Museo de la Ciudad
- 34 Museo Municipal de Bellas Artes
- 35 Museo Histórico Provincial
- 36 Parque Independencia
- 37 Parque Urquiza
- 38 Complejo Municipal Astronómico Educativo Rosario (Municipal Observatory)

Rosario

Romijor Hotel, Laprida 1050, has quiet patio rooms for US$15/22.

One of the best and cheapest eateries is the Italian rotisería alongside *Restaurant Rich*, San Juan 1031. *Café de La Paz*, a confitería at Sarmiento and San Lorenzo, draws big crowds. The *Centro Gallego*, Buenos Aires 1127, serves all-you-can-eat meals.

Casablanca, Córdoba 1471, serves Italo-Argentine food and lager beer at reasonable prices. *Il Nuovo Pavarotti*, at Laprida 988, is a medium-priced parrilla. *Restaurant Il Gatto*, San Martín 533, has more strictly Italian specialities, and a good fixed-price lunch.

Getting There & Away
Air Aeropuerto Fisherton is eight km west of town. Aerolíneas Argentinas (☎ 24-9332), Santa Fe 1410, flies to Buenos Aires (US$57) twice on weekdays, but only once on Saturday and Sunday. Austral (☎ 64041), Paraguay 731, flies twice to Buenos Aires on weekdays, and to Bariloche on Sundays.

Bus City bus No 101 from Calle San Juan goes to the terminal (☎ 39-6011), at Cafferata 702, near Santa Fe. Buses go frequently to Buenos Aires (US$16, four hours), Córdoba and Santa Fe, less often to Tucumán and Mendoza. International destinations include Asunción (Paraguay), and Porto Alegre and Rio de Janeiro (Brazil).

Getting Around
To/From the Airport Both Austral and Aerolíneas run minibuses to Aeropuerto Fisherton.

Bus The local bus system is centred on the terminal at Plaza Sarmiento.

SANTA ROSA
Santa Rosa de Toay, 600 km from Buenos Aires, is a tidy, pleasant city of 75,000, with highway connections to the capital, Córdoba and Bahía Blanca. Plaza San Martín is the commercial centre of the city's standard grid, north of Avenida España. The modern

Centro Cívico is on Avenida Pedro Luro, seven blocks east.

Information
Open on weekdays from 7 am to 8 pm, and on weekends from 9 am to 1 pm and 6 to 10 pm, the Dirección Provincial de Turismo (☎ 25060), at Luro and San Martín, has maps, brochures and local crafts. Banco Nación, Avenida Roca 1, and others on Avenida Pellegrini change cash but not travellers' cheques. ENCOTEL is at Hilario Lagos 258, with Telefónica next door.

Museo Provincial
At Pellegrini 190, this museum holds natural science, archaeological, historical, artisanal and fine-arts collections. Summer hours are 7 am to 1.30 pm and 4 to 9 pm; it keeps shorter winter hours, but does not close at midday.

Places to Stay & Eat
One of Argentina's last free campgrounds is at Laguna Don Tomás, at the west end of Avenida Uruguay. From Plaza San Martín, take bus Nos 25 or 26, and mosquito repellent. At *Hospedaje Mitre*, Emilio Mitre 74, singles/doubles are US$10/15 with shared bath, US$13/19 with private bath. *Hostería Santa Rosa*, Hipólito Yrigoyen 696, charges a little more.

The *Club Español*, Lagos 237, has excellent Argentine and Spanish food at reasonable prices. For regional specialities, try *Rancho de Pampa Cuatro*, opposite the bus terminal. There are many parrillas along Luro and many confiterías around Plaza San Martín.

Getting There & Away
Air Aerolíneas Argentinas (☎ 33076), on Rivadavia near Yrigoyen, flies daily (except Saturday) to Buenos Aires (US$94), and occasionally to Bahía Blanca (US$63).

Bus The bus terminal (☎ 22592) is at the Centro Cívico, at Luro and San Martín. Chevallier has four buses daily to Buenos Aires (US$30, nine hours) and one to San

Martín de los Andes and Bariloche (US$60, 21 hours). Others go to the Mesopotamian littoral, Comodoro Rivadavia and Caleta Olivia, and Mendoza.

Getting Around
To rent a car for visits to Parque Nacional Lihué Calel, try Alquilauto (☎ 26513), at Avenida 9 de Julio 227.

PARQUE NACIONAL LIHUE CALEL
Lihué Calel's small, remote mountain ranges, 226 km south-west of Santa Rosa, were a stronghold of Araucanian resistance during General Roca's 'Conquista del Desierto' (Conquest of the Desert). Its salmon-coloured exfoliating granites, reaching 600 metres, offer a variety of subtle environments, which change with the season and even with the day.

In this 10,000-hectare desert, sudden storms can bring flash floods and create spectacular, temporary waterfalls. Even when there's no rain, subterranean streams nourish the *monte*, a scrub forest of surprising botanical variety.

Rangers have seen puma, but the most common mammals are guanaco, mara (Patagonian hare) and vizcacha, a wild relative of the chinchilla. Bird species include the rhea or ñandú and birds of prey like the carancho (crested caracara).

Things to See & Do
From the park campground, a signed trail leads through a dense thorn forest of caldén (*Prosopis caldenia*, a local species of a common genus) and similar trees, to a site with petroglyphs, unfortunately vandalised.

From the petroglyphs, another trail leads to the summit of 589-metre **Cerro de la Sociedad Científica Argentina**, with outstanding views of the entire sierra and surrounding marshes and *salares* (salt lakes). The boulders are slippery when wet; notice the flowering cacti between them.

With time or a vehicle, hike or drive to the **Viejo Casco**, house of the former Estancia Santa María. Continue to undamaged petro-glyphs at **Valle de las Pinturas**, before looping back to the highway.

Places to Stay
The free campground near the visitors' centre has shade, picnic tables, firepits, cold showers and many birds. Bring food – the nearest supplies are at the town of Puelches, 35 km south. The *ACA Hostería*, on the highway, has rooms and a restaurant.

Getting There & Away
Leaving Neuquén at 9.15 pm on Tuesdays, Thursdays and Saturdays, Cooperativa Alto Valle will drop you at the ACA station shortly after midnight (US$10). Express buses from Rosario to Neuquén will also drop you there, but charge full fare from Santa Rosa to Villa Regina.

SANTA FE
The capital of Santa Fe province, the city of Santa Fe is a leading agro-industrial centre. Tributaries of the Río Paraná surround Santa Fe, but the main channel flows about 10 km east; in 1983, the powerful rising river deformed the twisted Puente Colgante (Hanging Bridge) to the city of Paraná, 25 km east, forcing the province to build a replacement.

Relocated in the mid-17th century because of Indians, floods and isolation, the city duplicates the original plan of Santa Fe La Vieja, but a 19th-century neo-Parisian building boom and more recent construction have left only isolated colonial buildings, mostly within a short walk of Plaza 25 de Mayo. Avenida San Martín, north of the plaza, is the main commercial street.

Information
At the bus terminal, Belgrano 2910, the Dirección Municipal de Turismo (☎ 30982) has maps, brochures, and detailed information in looseleaf binders.

Try Cambio Bica, San Martín 2453, for moneychanging. ENCOTEL is at Avenida 27 de Febrero 2331. Telecom is here, and upstairs at the bus terminal. The Hospital

Provincial (☎ 21001) is at Lisandro de la Torre and Freyre, west of the city centre.

Things to See
Historic Buildings Some colonial buildings are museums, but the churches still serve ecclesiastical functions, like the mid-17th century **Templo de Santo Domingo**, at the corner of avenidas 3 de Febrero and 9 de Julio. The exterior simplicity of the Jesuit **Iglesia de la Compañía** (1696), on Plaza 25 de Mayo, masks an ornate interior. The **Casa de los Aldao**, Buenos Aires 2861, is a restored two-storey house from the early 18th century.

Museums are usually open from 8 am to noon and 3 to 7 pm, but are closed on Sunday mornings and Mondays.

Convento de San Francisco Built in 1680, this church at Amenábar 2257, south of Plaza 25 de Mayo, is Santa Fe's most important landmark. Its metre-thick walls support a roof of Paraguayan cedar and hardwood beams, fastened with fittings and wooden spikes rather than nails. The doors are hand-worked originals, while the baroque pulpit is laminated in gold. The patio is open to the public, but refrain from entering the cloisters. The adjacent **Museo Histórico** covers secular and religious topics from the colonial and republican eras.

Museo Histórico Provincial In a damp 17th-century building at San Martín 1490, this museum has permanent exhibits on the 19th-century civil wars, provincial governors (and caudillos), period furnishings and religious art, plus a room with displays on more contemporary themes.

Museo Etnográfico Colonial The most interesting display here is a scale model of Santa Fe La Vieja on the Río San Javier, but there are also colonial artefacts, Indian basketry, Spanish ceramics, and coins and money. It's at Avenida 25 de Mayo 1470.

Museo del Indígena This hybrid institution is really an informational-cultural centre for

Indians and others interested in indigenous issues, but the staff is eager to speak with foreign visitors. In the Galería Via Macarena, at San Martín 2945, it's open on weekdays from 9.30 am to 1 pm and 3.30 to 7.30 pm.

Places to Stay
Santa Fe tolerates free camping in Parque General Belgrano, at the south end of San Martín.

At *Hotel Gran Terminal*, Belgrano 2837, rooms with shared bath cost US$8 per person; those with private bath are US$12/18 a single/double. Comparably priced *Hotel Apolo*, at Belgrano 2821, is clean but dark. *Hotel Bristol*, Belgrano 2859, has air-conditioned rooms for US$12/18 with shared bath, US$20/28 with private bath.

More central, the very friendly but undistinguished *Hotel California*, at Avenida 25 de Mayo 2190, has rooms for US$15/22 with private bath. Dearer, but excellent value, is remodelled *Hotel Emperatriz*, at Irigoyen Freire, which once belonged to an elite local family. Rates are US$25/33 with private bath.

Places to Eat
On Belgrano, across from the bus terminal, many places serve basics like empanadas, pizza and parrilla. For a downtown treat, try *Restaurant España*, San Martín 2642. Tourists and locals flock to *El Quincho de Chiquito*, reached by bus No 16 on Avenida Gálvez to Almirante Brown and Obispo Vieytes. Service is impersonal and the place is not cheap, but it's earned its reputation for grilled river fish like boga and sábalo.

Getting There & Away
Air Aerolíneas Argentinas (☎ 20713), Lisandro de la Torre 2633, flies to Buenos Aires (US$65) on weekday mornings and every evening.

Bus Services from the terminal (☎ 40698), at Belgrano 2940, are almost identical to those from Paraná, though Chevallier has more extensive routes, with connections to

ARGENTINA

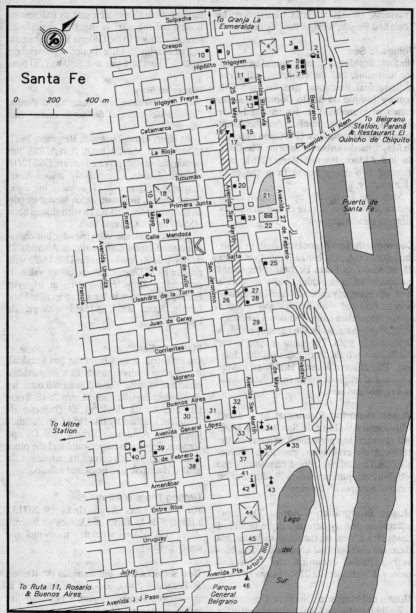

Santa Fe

0   200   400 m

To Granja La Esmeralda

Sulpacha

Crespo

Hipólito Yrigoyen

Irigoyen Freyre

Catamarca

La Rioja

Tucumán

Primera Junta

Calle Mendoza

Lisandro de la Torre

Juan de Garay

Corrientes

Moreno

Buenos Aires

Avenida General López

3 de Febrero

Amenábar

Entre Ríos

Uruguay

Jujuy

Avenida Pte Arturo Illia

To Mitre Station

To Ruta 11, Rosario & Buenos Aires

Avenida J J Paso

Parque General Belgrano

Lago del Sur

Puerto de Santa Fe

To Belgrano Station, Paraná & Restaurant El Quincho de Chiquito

Avenida Rivadavia

Belgrano

San Luis

Avenida L N Alem

25 de Mayo

Avenida San Martín

Avenida 27 de Febrero

Rivadavia

25 de Mayo

Avenida San Martín

4 de Enero

10 de Mayo

9 de Julio

San Jerónimo

Salta

Francia

Avenida Urquiza

■ PLACES TO STAY

3   Luka's Hotel
5   Hotel Bristol
6   Hotel Gran Terminal
7   Hotel Apolo
8   Hotel Colón
9   Hostal Santa Fe de la Vera Cruz
11 Hotel Emperatriz
12 Hotel Niza
13 Mini Hotel Uruguay
15 Conquistador Hotel
17 Gran Hotel España
23 Hotel Castelar
25 Hotel California
29 Hotel Corrientes
46 Camp Sites

▼ PLACES TO EAT

16 Restaurant España

    OTHER

1   Centro de Artes y Exposiciones
2   Bus Terminal/Tourist Office
4   Plaza España
10 Museo del Indígena

14 Austral
18 Plaza San Martín
19 Museo de Ciencias Naturales
20 Cambio Bica
21 Parque Alberdi
22 Post Office/Telecom
24 Municipalidad
26 Aerolíneas Argentinas
27 Museo de Artes Visuales
28 Teatro Municipal Primero de Mayo
30 Casa de los Aldao
31 Casa de Estanislao López (Provincial History Archive)
32 Catedral
33 Plaza 25 de Mayo
34 Iglesia de la Compañia
35 Museo Etnográfico Colonial
36 Museo Histórico Provincial
37 Casa de Gobierno (Provincial)
38 Templo de Santo Domingo
39 Museo de Bellas Artes
40 Provincial Legislature
41 Provincial Tourist Office
42 Asociación de Artesanos Santafesinos
43 Convento y Museo Histórico de San Francisco
44 Plaza Ciudad de Rosario
45 Municipal Ampitheatre

Buenos Aires, Puerto Iguazú and Córdoba. The information kiosk posts all fares.

AROUND SANTA FE
Alto Verde
Shaded by huge willows, Alto Verde is a picturesque fishing village on Isla Sirgadero. In flood years, families abandon the island for Santa Fe, returning to rebuild their houses when the waters recede. To reach the village, catch a canoe from Puerto del Piojo, at the east end of Calle Mendoza.

San José del Rincón
San José's shady earthen roads still offer a few colonial buildings and the excellent **Museo de la Costa** (Museum of the Coast). Many Santafesinos maintain weekend homes here, where camping and fishing are popular pastimes. Bus No 19 from Santa Fe goes directly to Rincón.

Mesopotamia, Misiones & the North-East

Mesopotamia is the area between the Paraná and Uruguay rivers. The rivers and parks of Entre Ríos and Corrientes provinces offer a variety of recreational opportunities, including camping and fishing. Subtropical Misiones province, nearly surrounded by Paraguay and Brazil, features ruined Jesuit missions and the spectacular Iguazú Falls.

History
After the Spaniards reached the upper Paraná, where they obtained provisions from the Guaraní, settlement proceeded southward from Asunción (Paraguay). Corrientes was founded in 1588, and Santa Fe at about the same time. For more information on early

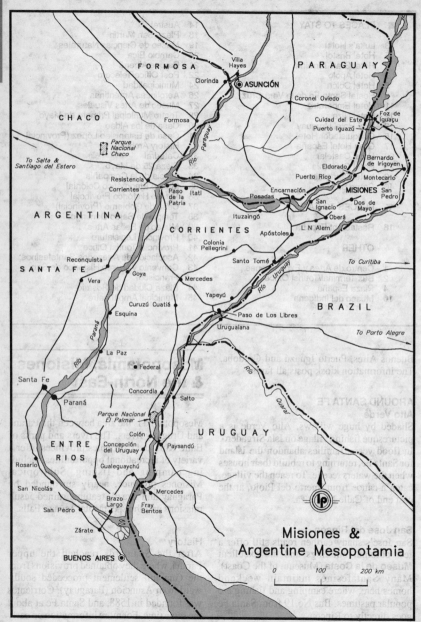

Misiones &
Argentine Mesopotamia

0   100   200 km

Spanish activities in this area, see the Paraguay chapter.

Jesuits established 30 Guaraní *reducciones* in the upper Paraná. These settlements resembled other Spanish municipalities, but non-Jesuits envied the political and economic autonomy they enjoyed – mostly because the Jesuits monopolised Indian labour in an area where the encomienda was weak. Concerned that Jesuits were creating a state within a state, Spain expelled them from the Americas in 1767. Argentina took definitive control of the territory, contested by Brazil and Paraguay, after the War of the Triple Alliance (1865-70).

Entre Ríos province also has an interesting history. Once an independent republic, it became a Unitarist stronghold after Rosas took power. Local caudillo Justo José Urquiza brought about Rosas' defeat and the adoption of Argentina's modern constitution.

In the dense thorn forests of Chaco and Formosa provinces, oppressive heat and hostile Indians discouraged early exploration. After 1850, woodcutters from Corrientes province, exploiting the *quebracho* (axe-breaker) tree for tannin, literally cleared the way for cotton and cattle.

PARANÁ

Paraná, capital of the Argentine Confederation from 1853 to 1861, is now capital of Entre Ríos province. It takes pride in having cooperated with Santa Fe to build the Hernandárias tunnel under the main channel of the Río Paraná, despite active opposition from the federal government.

On the east bank of the Río Paraná, the city's rather irregular plan has several diagonals, curving boulevards and complex intersections. From Plaza Primero de Mayo (1 de Mayo), the town centre, Calle San Martín is a peatonal for six blocks. At the west end of San Martín, Parque Urquiza extends over a km along the riverfront.

Information

The municipal tourist office (☎ 22-1632), at Avenida 25 de Mayo 44, also has a branch at the bus terminal. Hours are 8 am to 8 pm on weekdays, 8 am to 1 pm and 3 to 8 pm on Saturdays, and 9 am to 1 pm and 4 to 8 pm on Sundays.

Tourfe, the local cambio, is on the San Martín peatonal. ENCOTEL is at the corner of Avenida 25 de Mayo and Monte Caseros. Telecom is at San Martín 735. The public hospital (☎ 21-3459) is at Presidente Perón 450.

Things to See

Walking Tour The **Iglesia Catedral** has been on Plaza Primero de Mayo since 1730, but the current building dates from 1885; its museum is open from 5 to 7 pm daily. When Paraná was capital of the Confederation, the Senate deliberated at the **Colegio del Huerto**, at avenidas 9 de Julio and 25 de Mayo.

A block west, at Corrientes and Urquiza, are the **Palacio Municipal** (1889) and the **Escuela Normal Paraná**, a school founded by noted educator and President D F Sarmiento. Across San Martín, at Avenida 25 de Mayo 60, is the **Teatro Municipal Tres de Febrero** (1908). At the west end of the San Martín peatonal, **Plaza Alvear** has several notable museums.

Museums On Plaza Alvear, the **Museo Histórico de Entre Ríos Martín Leguizamón** flaunts provincial pride, as knowledgeable but patronising guides go to rhetorical extremes describing the role of local caudillos in Argentine history. Hours are Tuesday to Friday from 8 am to 1 pm and 4 to 8 pm, Saturday from 8 am to noon and 4 to 6 pm, and Sunday from 9 am to noon.

The adjacent **Museo de Bellas Artes Pedro E Martínez** shows works by provincial artists. Morning hours are 9 am to noon Tuesday to Sunday. Winter afternoon hours are 3 to 6 pm Tuesday to Saturday; in summer, afternoon hours are 5 to 8 pm.

Túnel Subfluvial Hernandárias Buenos Aires' refusal to allow the provinces to build a bridge over the Río Paraná forced them into the costlier and more difficult alternative of building this 2.4 km tunnel, completed in 1969. Any bus to Santa Fe will drop you at the tunnel entrance for guided tours, available from 8 am to noon daily; afternoon hours are 2 to 6 pm in winter, 3 to 9 pm in summer.

Activities

For river excursions, contact Turismo Fluvial (☎ 22-1632), at San Martín and Avenida Laurencena. Obtain fishing licences at the Dirección Provincial de Recursos Naturales, Monte Caseros 195; for equipment, visit El Ciervo (☎ 21-3991), Alem 886. Boating, water-skiing, windsurfing and swimming are also popular. For equipment, try Los Deportes (☎ 21-3991), Avenida 9 de Julio 178 or San Martín 732.

Places to Stay & Eat

Bus Nos 1 and 6 ('Thompson') link *Camping Balneario Thompson*, the most convenient campground, to the centre. Sites cost US$6.

Hotel City, at Racedo 231, opposite the train station, has cool rooms with high ceilings (US$10/15 a single/double with shared bath, US$15/24 with private bath). Rates are similar at *Hotel 9 de Julio*, half a block away, at Avenida 9 de Julio 674. *Hotel Bristol*, near the bus terminal, at Alsina 221, is slightly dearer but very clean and attractive. The crumbling but intriguing *Plaza Hotel*, San Martín 916, has many rooms with balconies (US$19/28 with shared bath, US$24/30 with private bath).

Restaurant Florentino, Gualeguaychú 186, serves local fish specialities. *Comedor Centro Comercial*, upstairs on Avenida 25 de Mayo, across from the plaza, serves an inexpensive parrillada and other Argentine dishes. For ice cream, try *Costa Azul*, San Martín 1059.

Entertainment

Since the 1960s, North American softball has been an obsession in Paraná, where youth and adult leagues play both slow and fast-pitch versions. Admission is free almost every night (except for special events like tournaments) at the Estadio Ingeniero Nafaldo Cargnel, near the entrance to the Hernandárias tunnel.

Getting There & Away

Air Aerolíneas Argentinas has offices on San Martín, across from Plaza Alvear, but flights leave from Santa Fe's Sauce Viejo airport.

Bus From the terminal (☎ 21-5053), at Echagüe and Ramírez, buses leave about every half-hour for Santa Fe (US$3), which has better long-distance services.

Empresa Tata goes to northern littoral destinations between Paraná and Corrientes. Chevallier also goes to Corrientes and to Patagonian destinations. El Rápido has seven buses daily to Rosario (US$10, three hours) and five to Buenos Aires (US$26, eight hours).

Empresa Kurtz goes to Puerto Iguazú (US$45) on Monday, Tuesday and Friday afternoons. El Litoral also goes via Posadas (US$25) to Puerto Iguazú. El Serrano travels to Córdoba (US$25), and TAC to Mendoza (US$50). International buses go to Montevideo (Uruguay) and Porto Alegre (Brazil).

GUALEGUAYCHÚ

National Ruta 14 passes west of Gualeguaychú, the first sizeable city north of Buenos Aires, on a tributary of the Río Uruguay. National Ruta 136, a lateral, bypasses the centre en route to Fray Bentos, Uruguay. Gualeguaychú's Carnaval has an international reputation, so stop here if you can't make Rio or Bahía.

Plaza San Martín marks the city centre. The municipal tourist office (☎ 3668) keeps long hours on the Avenida Costanera. Casa Goyo, on Ayacucho near San Martín, changes cash dollars but not travellers' cheques. Uruguay has a consulate (☎ 6168) at Rivadavia 510.

There is a good selection of handicrafts at the Centro Artesanal San José. It's housed in the colonial **Casa de Andrade**, at Andrade and Borques, once owned by poet-journalist Olegario Andrade. José Álvarez, founder of the satirical turn-of-the-century magazine *Caras y Caretas*, was born in the **Casa de**

Fray Mocho, Fray Mocho 135 (Fray Mocho was his pen name).

Places to Stay & Eat

Camping La Delfina, across the Río Gualeguaychú in Parque Unzué, has good facilities (US$6 for two people, US$8 for four). Clean, friendly *Pensión Gualeguaychú*, Avenida 25 de Mayo 456, has rooms for US$7 a single with shared bath. At *Hospedaje Mayo*, Bolívar 550, singles/doubles with private bath cost US$14/18.

Many restaurants line Avenida 25 de Mayo; try also the *Círculo Italiano*, at San Martín and Pellegrini.

Getting There & Away

From the bus terminal, at Bolívar and Chile, several companies go to Buenos Aires (US$13, three hours). Ciudad de Gualeguay has five buses daily to Paraná (US$16, six hours). Ciudad de Gualeguaychú goes daily to Corrientes.

ETA has three buses daily (except Sunday) to Fray Bentos, Uruguay (US$4), two of which continue to Mercedes, with connections to Montevideo.

COLÓN

Colón attracts Argentine tourists to a beautiful riverine landscape on the west bank of the Río Uruguay, opposite the Uruguayan city of Paysandú. The tourist office (☎ 21233) is at Emilio Gouchon and the Costanera. *Residencial Paysandú*, at Paysandú and Maipú, has singles/doubles for US$15/25.

PARQUE NACIONAL EL PALMAR

The yatay palm *(Syagrus yatay)* covered much of the littoral until 19th-century agriculture, ranching and forestry destroyed palm savannas and inhibited their reproduction. On the west bank of the Río Uruguay, 360 km north-west of Buenos Aires, the relict yatays of 8500-hectare El Palmar have again begun to thrive, under protection from fire and grazing. Reaching 18 metres in height, the larger specimens accentuate a soothing subtropical landscape.

To see wildlife, walk along the watercourses or through the palm savannas early in the morning or just before sunset. The most conspicuous bird is the ñandú, or rhea *(Rhea americana)*, but look for parakeets, cormorants, egrets, herons, storks, caracaras, woodpeckers and kingfishers. The *carpincho* (capybara), a semiaquatic rodent weighing up to 60 kg, and the vizcacha, a relative of the chinchilla, are the most conspicuous mammals.

At night, squeaking vizcachas infest the campground at Arroyo Los Loros and gigantic toads invade the showers and toilets, but both are harmless. The yarará, a highly poisonous pit viper, is not; bites are uncommon, but watch your step and wear high boots and long trousers when hiking.

Things to See & Do

Across from the campground, the **Centro de Interpretación** offers evening slide shows and contains a small herpetarium (reptile house). At Los Loros campground, rental canoes are available for boating on the **Río Uruguay**. A short hike from the campground, **Arroyo Los Loros** is a good place to observe wildlife.

Five km from the campground, **Arroyo El Palmar** is a pleasant stream with a beautiful swimming hole, and a good place for birds. Crossing the ruined bridge, you can walk several km along a palm-lined road being reclaimed by savanna grasses.

Places to Stay & Eat

Los Loros campground has good sites (US$4 per person), with hot showers, a store and a confitería.

Getting There & Away

Any northbound bus from Buenos Aires to Concordia can drop you at the entrance (admission US$2.50). No public transport serves the visitors' centre and camping area, but hitching should not be difficult.

CONCORDIA

This agricultural and livestock centre is the most northerly border crossing to Uruguay from the province of Entre Ríos, to the Uruguayan city of Salto. In December, there is a national citrus festival.

The tourist office (☎ 21-2137) is at Mitre 64. *Residencial Colonial*, Pellegrini 433, has singles/doubles for US$13/24.

CORRIENTES

Just below the confluence of the Paraná and Paraguay rivers, Corrientes city, the capital of Corrientes province, is 850 km from Buenos Aires by good roads, but the train system is antiquated and indirect. Across the Río Paraná is Resistencia, capital of Chaco province.

Plaza 25 de Mayo is the centre of Corrientes' extremely regular grid plan, but public buildings are more dispersed than in most Argentine cities. The commercial centre is the Calle Junín peatonal, between Salta and Catamarca.

Information

At La Rioja 475, the friendly, disorganised tourist office (☎ 23054) is open on weekdays from 7 am to 1 pm and 3 to 9 pm. Banco de la Provincia, at San Juan and Avenida 9 de Julio, and Banco del Iberá, at Avenida 9 de Julio 1002, are the only places to change money. ENCOTEL is at San Juan and San Martín. Telecom is at Pellegrini 1175.

Things to See

Walking Tour Avoid the heat by seeing the city early in the morning or late in the afternoon. Start at the colonial **Convento de San Francisco**, at Mendoza 450, whose museum is open on weekdays from 8 am to noon and 5 to 9.30 pm. From there, you can stroll to Parque Mitre and then back along the tree-lined Costanera, past the modest **Jardín Zoológico**. Returning by Edison and Bolívar, visit the **Santuario de la Cruz del Milagro**, whose 16th-century cross, according to legend, defied Indian efforts to burn it. Continue along Bolívar and up San Lorenzo to the **Catedral**, on Plaza Cabral, then return along Junín to Salta and back toward the river, past Plaza 25 de Mayo.

■	PLACES TO STAY
5	Hotel Guaraní
9	Hotel San Martín
11	Gran Hotel Corrientes
14	Orly Hotel
21	Residencial Aialay
23	Hotel Hostal del Pinar
24	Hotel Colón
31	Gran Hotel Turismo

▼	PLACES TO EAT
13	Las Espuelas

	OTHER
1	Iglesia de la Cruz
2	Plaza La Cruz
3	Museo de Ciencas Naturales Amado Bonpland
4	Edificio Correo Central
6	Plaza Torrent
7	Catedral
8	Plaza Cabral
10	Austral (Airline)
12	Aerolíneas Argentinas
15	Mercado Central
16	Museo Histórico de Corrientes
17	Telecom
18	Teatro Oficial Juan de Vera
19	ACA (Travel Agency)
20	Convento San Francisco & Franciscan Museum
22	Tourist Office
25	Museo de Bellas Artes Dr Juan Ramón Vidal
26	Local Bus Station
27	Estación Terminal de Colectivos Urbano
28	Casa de Gobierno
29	Plaza 25 de Mayo
30	Iglesia de la Merced
32	Hospital Escuela San Martín

Museums The **Museo Histórico de Corrientes**, Avenida 9 de Julio 1044, has exhibits of weapons, coins and antique furniture, as well as religious and civil history. The **Museo de Bellas Artes Dr Juan Ramón Vidal**, San Juan 634, emphasises sculpture. Hours are Tuesday to Saturday from 9 am to noon and 6 to 9 pm.

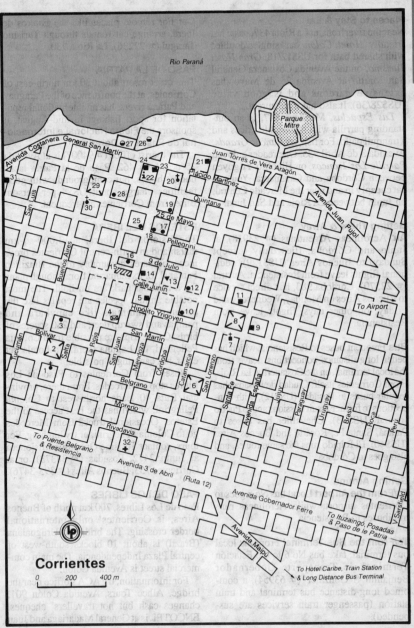

Río Paraná

Parque Mitre

Avenida Costanera General San Martín

Juan Torres de Vera Aragón

Avenida Juan Pujol

Plácido Martínez

Quintana

25 de Mayo

Pellegrini

9 de Julio

Calle Junín

Hipólito Yrigoyen

San Martín

To Airport

San Luis

Buenos Aires

La Rioja

San Juan

Mendoza

Córdoba

Catamarca

San Lorenzo

Santa Fe

Avenida España

Jujuy

Paraguay

Uruguay

Brasil

Roca

Perú

Tucumán

Bolívar

Salta

Belgrano

Moreno

Rivadavia

To Puente Belgrano
& Resistencia

Avenida 3 de Abril

(Ruta 12)

Avenida Gobernador Ferre

To Ituzaingó, Posadas
& Paso de le Patria

Avenida Maipú

To Hotel Caribe, Train Station
& Long Distance Bus Terminal

V Sarsfield

Corrientes

0   200   400 m

Places to Stay & Eat

Near the riverfront, at La Rioja 437, basic but friendly *Hotel Colón* has singles/doubles with shared bath for US$12/18. *Gran Hotel Turismo*, on the Avenida Costanera General San Martín at Avenida 25 de Mayo, has extensive gardens and is good value (US$28/36). It also has a restaurant.

Las Espuelas, Mendoza 847, is an outstanding parrilla with reasonable prices and a tranquil patio. For fish, try *Rancho Grande*, Avenida 3 de Abril 935. One reader enjoyed *Parrilla Los Troncos*, on Hipólito Yrigoyen between Córdoba and Catamarca. You can eat cheaply in and near the Mercado Central, on Junín between La Rioja and San Juan.

Getting There & Away

Air Aerolíneas Argentinas (☎ 23918), at Junín and Córdoba, flies daily (except Sunday) to Buenos Aires (US$129); additional flights leave from Resistencia. Austral (☎ 22570), Córdoba 983, has direct service to Buenos Aires on Monday, Wednesday and Friday; on other days, flights leave from Resistencia.

Bus Frequent buses to Resistencia, which has better long-distance connections, leave from the local terminal, on the Costanera at La Rioja. From Corrientes itself, Ciudad de Posadas has regular buses to Posadas (US$12), with connections to former Jesuit missions and to Puerto Iguazú (US$33). Chevallier has buses to Paraná, Santa Fe, Rosario and Buenos Aires (US$40). El Rápido runs the same routes, and also goes to Córdoba.

Getting Around

To/From the Airport Local bus No 8 goes to Corrientes airport, while Aerolíneas runs minibuses to Resistencia.

To/From the Bus Terminal From the local bus terminal, take bus No 6 to the Estación Terminal de Transporte Gobernador Benjamín S González (☎ 63954), a combined long-distance bus terminal and train station (passenger train services are suspended).

Car For remote places like the Esteros de Iberá, arrange car rentals through Turismo Taragui (☎ 22236), La Rioja 730.

PASO DE LA PATRIA

This quiet resort about 30 km north-east of Corrientes, at the confluence of the Paraguay and Paraná rivers, has an international reputation for sport fishing; in mid-August, it sponsors the **Fiesta Nacional e Internacional de Pesca de Dorados**.

The tourist office (☎ 94007) is at Avenida 25 de Mayo 462. Paso de la Patria lacks budget hotels, but campgrounds with good facilities charge about US$4 per person. Buses from Corrientes are frequent.

ESTEROS DEL IBERÁ

The Esteros del Iberá, a 13,000-sq-km marshland in north-central Corrientes province, compares favourably to the Brazilian Pantanal for its fauna and flora, though plans for a national park are on hold. The most notable animal species are reptiles like the cayman, mammals like capybara and pampas and swamp deer, and 280 species of birds. Canoe trips are possible from Colonia Pellegrini, on Laguna Iberá. No hotels yet exist, but camping is possible.

Buses from Corrientes to Paso de Los Libres stop at Mercedes. From there, provincial Ruta 40 leads north-west to Colonia Pellegrini, which has the best access to the Esteros. Occasional trucks from Mercedes go to Colonia Pellegrini, or try hitching. For tours, contact Turismo Operativo Misionero at Junín 2472, Posadas (☎ 38373), or at Corrientes 753, Buenos Aires (☎ 393-3476).

PASO DE LOS LIBRES

Paso de Los Libres, 700 km north of Buenos Aires, is Corrientes' only international border crossing. The bridge to Uruguaiana (Brazil) is about 10 blocks south-west of central Plaza Independencia. The main commercial street is Avenida Colón.

For information, try ACA's office near the bridge. Alhec Tours, Avenida Colón 901, changes cash but not travellers' cheques. ENCOTEL is at General Madariaga and Juan

Sitja Min, while Telecom is at General Madariaga 854.

The **Cementerio de la Santa Cruz**, just beyond the bus station, holds the tomb of Amado (Aimé) Bonpland, a naturalist and travel companion of Alexander von Humboldt. Ask for directions to 'El sabio Bonpland'. Paso de los Libres has a lively **Carnaval**.

Places to Stay

Residencial Colón, Avenida Colón 1065, has singles with private bath for US$9. Shabby but comfortable *Hotel Buen Comfort*, Coronel López 1091, has rooms with bath and air-conditioning for US$15/20.

Getting There & Away

Air Aerolíneas Argentinas (☎ 21017), Juan Sitja Min 1118, flies thrice weekly to Buenos Aires (US$81).

Bus Expreso Singer and Cruzero del Norte stop at the terminal (☎ 21608), San Martín and Santiago del Estero, three times daily en route between Buenos Aires and Posadas. There is daily service to Paraná and Santa Fe, and to Rosario (except Thursdays). Buses from Córdoba to Puerto Iguazú also stop daily, except Thursday. Provincial buses run three times daily to Corrientes.

YAPEYÚ

Birthplace of General José de San Martín, Yapeyú is a charming village, 55 km north of Paso de Los Libres. Founded in 1626, it once had a population of 8000 Guaraní Indians, who tended up to 80,000 cattle; after expulsion of the Jesuits, the Indians dispersed and the mission fell into ruins, but villagers built many houses of salvaged red sandstone blocks. The tourist office, at the entrance to town, is helpful but has almost no printed matter.

Things to See

The **Museo de Cultura Jesuítica**, consisting of several modern kiosks on the foundations of mission buildings, has a sundial, a few other mission relics and an interesting photographic display.

Among tributary plaques in the pretentious temple sheltering the **Casa de San Martín**, the modest birthplace of Argentina's greatest hero, is one from pardoned Dirty War lifer General Videla, asserting his 'most profound faith' in San Martín's ideals of liberty. Next door is the **Museo Sanmartiniano**.

Places to Stay & Eat

Sites at the riverside municipal campground cost US$4, with hot showers. At the entrance to town, *El Parador Yapeyú* has bungalows for US$20/30 a single/double.

Restaurant Bicentenario has well-prepared food, reasonable prices and friendly, attentive service. There's another adequate restaurant on the plaza.

Getting There & Away

Services from the bus station, two blocks south of the plaza, are like those from Paso de Los Libres.

POSADAS

Posadas (population 200,000), on the south bank of the upper Río Paraná, became capital of the new territory of Misiones in the 1880s. Travellers who stop here en route to Iguazú should not miss the restored missions at San Ignacio Miní, about 50 km east, or at Trinidad (Paraguay), reached by a new international bridge.

Orientation

Plaza 9 de Julio is the centre of Posadas' standard grid. Streets have recently been renumbered, but local preference for the old system has created confusion. Wherever possible, information below refers to locations instead of street numbers (which, if given, list the new number first and the old number in parentheses).

Information

The tourist office (☎ 30504), on Colón between Córdoba and La Rioja, is open on weekdays from 6.30 am to 12.30 pm and 2

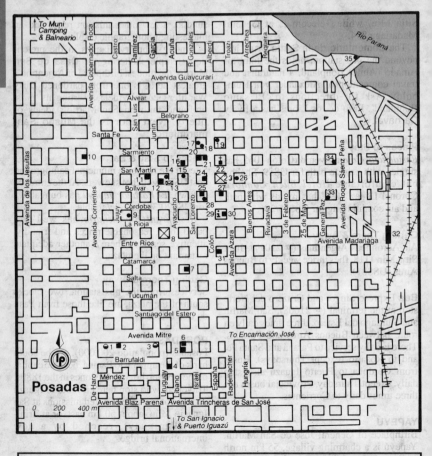

Posadas

To Muni Camping & Balneario

Río Paraná

Avenida Guaycurarí

To Encarnación José

To San Ignacio & Puerto Iguazú

0   200   400 m

PLACES TO STAY		25	Posadas Hotel	14	Austral (Airline)
		27	Hotel Continental	15	Aerolíneas Argentinas
2	Hotel Familiar	30	Residencial Misiones	17	Paraguayan Consulate
4	Residencial Nagel	31	Residencial Colón	18	Teatro El Desván
5	Gran Hotel Misiones			19	Telecom
6	Hotel Horianski		OTHER	22	Catedral
7	Hotel Libertador			23	Plaza 9 de Julio
10	Residencial Marlis	1	Expreso Singer Termi-	26	Casa de Gobierno
11	Hotel Canciller		nal (Buses)	28	ACA (Travel Agency)
12	Hotel de Turismo	3	Main Bus Station	29	Tourist Office
	Posadas	8	Plaza San Martín	32	Train Station
16	Plaza Hotel	9	Museo de Ciencias	33	Museo Argueológico
20	Pension Argentina		Naturales e	34	Municipal Market
21	Savoy Hotel		Históricas	35	Launches to Paraguay
24	City Hotel	13	Post Office		

to 8 pm. Holiday and weekend hours are 8 am to noon and 4 to 8 pm.

Money Turismo Posadas, on Colón south of the plaza, and Cambio Mazza, on Bolívar between San Lorenzo and Colón, will change cash and travellers' cheques.

Post & Telecommunications ENCOTEL is at Bolívar and Ayacucho. Telecom is at Colón and Santa Fe, but other long-distance phones on Junín, between Bolívar and Córdoba, are open from 7 am to midnight.

Consulates Open on weekdays from 8 am to noon, Paraguay's consulate (☎ 27421) is on San Lorenzo, between Santa Fe and Sarmiento. Near the international bridge, Brazil's consulate (☎ 2601), at Mitre 1242 (631), offers same-day visa service and does not insist on a photograph. Hours are 9 am to 1 pm and 4 to 6.30 pm on weekdays.

Museo de Ciencias Naturales e Históricas
On San Luis between Córdoba and La Rioja, this museum's natural history section focuses on invertebrates, vertebrates, and provincial geology and mineralogy; its historical section stresses prehistory, Jesuit missions and recent colonisation. It also has an excellent serpentarium, an aviary and an aquarium. Hours are long, but it's closed on Mondays.

Places to Stay & Eat
Budget travellers should consider Encarnación (Paraguay), for lower prices and better value. One popular place in Posadas is *Residencial Misiones*, on Avenida Azara between La Rioja and Córdoba, where singles/doubles with private bath are US$15/20. Other budget choices include *Residencial Nagel*, at Méndez and Uruguay (US$17/24), and *Hotel Horianski*, at Avenida Mitre and Líbano (US$20/31).

Look for inexpensive eateries along San Lorenzo west of the plaza. *La Gran Alegría*, a pizzería on Colón just north of the plaza, is worth a visit. The spiffiest of many parrillas

is *La Querencia*, on Bolívar, across from the plaza.

Getting There & Away
Air Aerolíneas Argentinas (☎ 22036), on San Martín between Ayacucho and San Lorenzo, flies daily to Buenos Aires (US$137). Austral (☎ 32889), at Ayacucho and San Martín, flies daily (except Sunday) from Posadas to Buenos Aires, and on weekdays to Puerto Iguazú and back.

Bus The main terminal is at Avenida Mitre and Uruguay, but Tigre and Expreso Singer have a separate terminal, three blocks west.

Singer has daily service to Buenos Aires (US$35) and intermediate destinations, and to Córdoba and Asunción. Martignoni, COTAL and Tigre have express buses to Puerto Iguazú (US$21, 5½ hours). Ciudad de Posadas has buses to Corrientes and Resistencia, with connections across the Chaco to the North-West.

Tigre's earliest reasonable bus to San Ignacio Miní leaves at 6.10 am, with hourly buses thereafter. Buses to Encarnación leave every 15 minutes (US$1.50, one hour with border formalities).

Boat Launches to Encarnación still leave from the dock at the east end of Avenida Guaycurarí, but will probably cease when the reservoir behind Yacyretá dam floods low-lying parts of the two cities.

Getting Around
To/From the Airport Both Aerolíneas and Austral run airport minibuses, but bus No 8 from Plaza San Martín also goes there.

AROUND POSADAS
Jesuit Missions
Buses from Posadas drop you at a clearly marked junction about one km from the Jesuit ruins at **Santa Ana** (founded 1637), which are mostly covered by forest and strangler figs. At **Loreto** (1632), the distance from the highway to the ruins is greater.

ARGENTINA

Yacyretá Dam

A vivid lesson in foreign debt, this gigantic hydroelectric project will submerge the Paraná over 200 km upstream and require the relocation of nearly 40,000 people. Presidential candidate Carlos Menem called it 'a monument to corruption' which may cost eight times the original estimate of US$1.5 billion, but his administration has not halted construction.

At Ituzaingó (Corrientes province), 1½ hours from Posadas by bus, the Entidad Binacional Yacyretá's public relations office offers four free tours daily to present this boondoggle in the best possible light.

SAN IGNACIO & SAN IGNACIO MINÍ

San Ignacio Miní is an easy day trip from Posadas, but staying overnight allows more time to explore the mission ruins. San Ignacio is 56 km east of Posadas via national Ruta 12.

Italian Jesuit Juan Brasanelli designed the enormous red sandstone church, embellished with bas-relief sculptures in a style known as 'Guaraní baroque'. Adjacent to the tile-roofed church were the cemetery and cloisters. In the same complex were classrooms, a kitchen, a dining room and workshops. On all sides of the Plaza de Armas were the living quarters – at its peak, in 1733, San Ignacio Miní had an Indian population of nearly 4000.

Places to Stay A short walk from the bus terminal, *Hospedaje Los Salpeterer*, at Sarmiento and Centenario, has singles for US$7 with shared bath, but you can pitch a tent for less. *Hospedaje El Descanso* is a bit farther from the ruins, at Pellegrini 270. *Hotel San Ignacio*, Sarmiento 823, has singles/doubles with bath for about US$15/25.

Getting There & Away

From the bus terminal, on Sarmiento, Empresa Tigre and others have 26 daily buses to Posadas. Tigre has buses to Puerto Iguazú (US$17) at 6.10 am and 2.10 and 8.10

pm, but you can also flag down buses on the highway.

PUERTO IGUAZÚ

Puerto Iguazú hosts most visitors to the Argentine side of Iguazú Falls. (For details

■	PLACES TO STAY
1	Hotel Esturión
3	La Cabaña
5	Hotel Turismo Iguazú
6	Hostel
7	Residencial Cataratas
9	Residencial Gloria
10	Hotel Tierra Colorada
11	Hotel Misiones
12	Hotel Paraná
14	Hotel Libertador
15	Residencial Iguazú
16	Hotel Alexander
17	Hostería San Fernándo
19	Residencial Paquita
24	Residencial Bonpland
26	Hotel Saint George/Restaurant Saint George
27	Hostería Los Helechos
32	Residencial Arco Iris
33	Residencial El Descanso
35	Hotel King

▼	PLACES TO EAT
13	Fechoría Bar
23	Confitería La Plaza
28	Charo
30	La Rueda

	OTHER
2	Buses to Iguazú Falls
4	National Parks Office
8	Post Office
18	Bus Terminal
20	Tourist Office
21	Aerolíneas/Argentinas/Austral (Airlines)
22	Argencam (Money Exchange)
25	Cabina Hola (Telephones)
29	Hospital
31	Brazilian Consulate
34	Telecom
36	Argencam (Money Exchange)
37	Cambio Dick

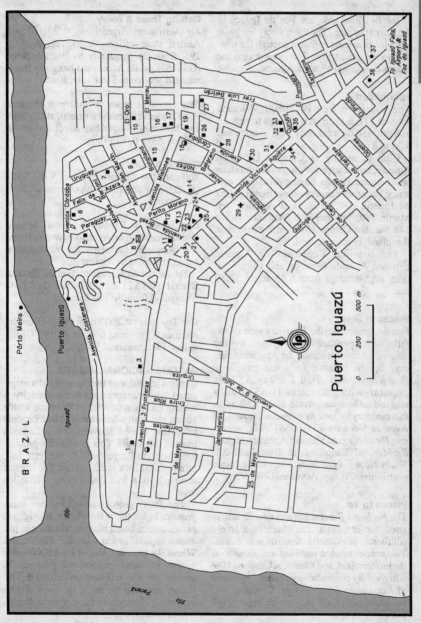

Puerto Iguazú

0   250   500 m

of the Brazilian side, see Foz do Iguaçu in the Brazil chapter.) The town's very irregular city plan is at least compact enough for relatively easy orientation. The main drag is the diagonal Avenida Victoria Aguirre.

Information
The tourist office (☎ 20800), Victoria Aguirre 311, is open on weekdays from 8 am to 8 pm, and on weekends 8 am to noon and 4.30 to 8 pm.

Change money at Cambio Dick, on Aguirre, but beware very high commissions on cheques. Before buying Brazilian currency, ask other travellers about trends in Foz do Iguaçu. ENCOTEL is at Avenida San Martín 780. Telecom is at Victoria Aguirre 146 Sur, but Cabina Hola, on Aguirre near Bonpland, is more central.

The Brazilian Consulate, on Aguirre between Avenida Córdoba and Curupy, is open on weekdays from 8.45 am to 12.30 pm.

Places to Stay
Foz do Iguaçu, on the Brazilian side of the falls, is cheaper than Puerto Iguazú, but the absence of street crime on the Argentine side may tip the balance for some travellers. *Residencial Arco Iris*, Curupy 152, is popular with travellers (US$15/20 a single/double with private bath). Others in this category include *Residencial Paquita*, at Avenida Córdoba 731 (US$15/22), attractive *Hotel King*, at Victoria Aguirre 916, and *Residencial Bonpland*, at Bonpland 33. Shady *Hostería Los Helechos*, on Almirante near Beltrán, is superb value (US$15/20).

Places to Eat
The *Fechoría Bar*, on Eppens near Brasil, is good for breakfast. *La Plaza* is a lively confitería, on Victoria Aguirre near Brasil. Two recommended parrillas are *Toma's*, at the bus terminal, and *Charo*, at Córdoba 106. After wildly contradictory readers' opinions of *Restaurant Saint George*, Córdoba 148, we found both food and service superb, but pricey.

Getting There & Away
Air Aerolíneas Argentinas (☎ 20168) and Austral share offices, at Victoria Aguirre 295. Both fly frequently to Buenos Aires (US$163), while Aerolíneas has daily international service to São Paulo, Brazil.

Bus Frequent buses to and from Posadas (US$21) leave from the terminal, at Córdoba and Misiones. Singer has direct service to Buenos Aires (US$55).

Getting Around
To/From the Airport Expreso A del Valle (☎ 20348), Entre Ríos 239, charges US$3 to the airport.

Bus Buses to Parque Nacional Iguazú (US$2) leave from Aguirre between Brasil and Bonpland, then pass the bus terminal before returning to Aguirre.

Frequent buses cross to Foz do Iguaçu, Brazil (US$2) and Ciudad del Este (Paraguay) from the bus terminal.

Car Try Avis (☎ 20020), at Hotel Esturión, Avenida 3 Fronteras 650, or A1 (☎ 20748), at Hotel Internacional Iguazú.

PARQUE NACIONAL IGUAZÚ
Guaraní legend says that Iguazú Falls originated when a forest god, enraged by a warrior escaping downriver by canoe with a young girl with whom the god had become infatuated, caused the riverbed to collapse in front of the lovers. This produced a precipitous waterfall over which the girl fell, turning into a rock at the bottom. The warrior survived, as a tree overlooking his fallen lover.

The falls' geological origins are more prosaic. In southern Brazil, the Río Iguazú passes over a basalt plateau which ends just above its confluence with the Río Paraná. Where the lava stopped, at least 5000 cubic metres of water per second plunges 70 metres into the sedimentary terrain below. Before reaching the edge, the river divides into many channels to form several distinctive *cataratas*.

The most awesome is the semicircular Garganta del Diablo (Devil's Throat), a deafening and dampening part of the experience, approached via a system of *pasarelas* (catwalks). Above the falls, the river is suitable for canoeing, kayaking and other water sports.

Despite pressures for development, the 55,000-hectare park is a nearly pristine area of subtropical rainforest, with over 2000 identified plant species, countless insects, 400 bird species, and many mammals and reptiles.

Iguazú Falls
Before seeing the falls themselves, look around the museum, and climb the nearby tower for a good overall view, but plan hikes before the midmorning influx of tour buses. Descending from the visitors' centre, you can cross by launch to **Isla Grande San Martín** (US$5 return), which offers unique views and a refuge from the masses on the mainland.

Flood damage has isolated the catwalks to **Garganta del Diablo**, but you can still reach the overlook by a road to Ñandú and a launch (US$5). Of all sights on earth, this must come closest to the experience of sailing off the edge of the earth imagined by early European sailors, as the deafening cascade plunges to a murky destination, blurred by the rising vapour which soaks the viewer.

Hiking, Bicycling & Rafting
Best in the early morning, the **Macuco Nature Trail** leads through dense forest, where a steep lateral goes to the base of a hidden waterfall. Another trail goes to the *bañado*, a marsh abounding in bird life.

To get elsewhere in the forest, explored by few visitors, hitch or hire a car to go out on Ruta 101 toward Bernardo de Irigoyen. Floating Iguazú, at the visitors' centre, arranges 4WD trips to the Yacaratía forest trail, organises rafting excursions and rents mountain bikes.

Getting There & Away
Buses leave Avenida Victoria Aguirre in Puerto Iguazú for the park visitors' centre (US$2, 20 km) regularly between 7 am and 5 pm. Park entry costs US$3 per person.

RESISTENCIA
Resistencia, across the Río Paraná from Corrientes, is capital of Chaco province and a major crossroads for Paraguay, Santa Fe, and trans-Chaco routes to the North-West. Despite a frontier past, it prides itself on a reputation as the 'city of sculptures', for the statues in almost every public space.

Plaza 25 de Mayo occupies four square blocks in the city centre. The tourist office (☎ 23547), upstairs at J B Justo 135, is open on weekdays from 6.30 am to 7.30 pm. Banco de la Provincia, at Güemes and Yrigoyen, changes cash readily but takes huge commissions on travellers' cheques. ENCOTEL faces the plaza, at Sarmiento and Yrigoyen, while Telecom is at the corner of J M Paz and J B Justo.

Things to See
Sculpture The tourist office map, pinpointing 75 outdoor sculptures, is a good introduction to the city. The **Museo Provincial de Bellas Artes**, which concentrates on sculpture, is at Avenida 9 de Julio 254.

El Fogón de los Arrieros This private museum (☎ 26418), at Brown 350, is famous for its eclectic assemblage of art objects from around the Chaco, Argentina and the world. It's open from 8 am to noon Monday to Saturday, with a bar open in the evenings. Admission is US$2.

Museo Policial This unexpectedly good museum features exhibits on *cuatrerismo* (cattle rustling, still common in the province today) and social banditry – some remarkably sympathetic to outlaws. At Roca 223, it's open from 9 am to noon and 6 to 8 pm Tuesday to Friday, and from 6 to 9 pm on Sundays and holidays.

Barrio Toba Toba Indians inhabit this modern *reducción*, which seems cohesive and well-maintained, if impersonal in its construction. At its Cooperativa de Artesanos, the traditional *yisca* (string bag) and other goods show local skills. Take bus No 2 from Plaza 25 de Mayo.

Places to Stay & Eat

Camping Parque 2 de Febrero, Avenida Avalos 1100, has excellent facilities for US$3 per person. Rather depressing *Hospedaje Anita*, Santiago del Estero 45, has singles with shared bath for US$9, but *Residencial Alberdi*, Alberdi 317, has decent rooms with shared bath for US$11 per person, though it's often full. *Residencial San José*, Rawson 304, is comparable.

El Círculo, Güemes 350, has fixed-price meals with huge portions. Most restaurants are parrillas, like *La Estaca*, at Güemes 202, but for variety try *Por la Vuelta*, at Obligado 33, or *Trattoria Italiana*, at Yrigoyen 236. For ice cream, try *Helados San José*, at Pellegrini and Saavedra.

Getting There & Away

Air Aerolíneas Argentinas (☎ 22854), J B Justo 136, flies four times weekly to Buenos Aires (US$129). Austral (☎ 25921), Rawson 99, has similar schedules. See also schedules for Corrientes.

Bus The bus terminal, at Santa María de Oro and Santiago del Estero, three blocks south of the plaza, is a key transport hub. La Internacional goes south to Buenos Aires, west to Roque Sáenz Peña and north to Formosa and Asunción, Paraguay. El Norte Bis serves the same southern routes, Mar del Plata, and Posadas. La Estrella connects with Roque Sáenz Peña and the village of Capitán Solari, for Parque Nacional Chaco. La Estrella and Cacorba alternate daily services to Córdoba.

Godoy SRL heads north to Formosa and Asunción. Central Sáenz Peña has four daily buses to Roque Sáenz Peña and alternates daily service to Salta with La Velóz del Norte; El Rayo goes to Santiago del Estero and Tucumán. Cotal serves Mendoza and San Juan twice weekly via Catamarca and La Rioja. Ciudad de Posadas goes to Posadas (thrice daily) and Puerto Iguazú (daily).

Getting Around

Take bus No 2 from the post office to Resistencia airport. Godoy Resistencia buses cross the Río Paraná to Corrientes.

PARQUE NACIONAL CHACO

This little-visited park, 115 km north-west of Resistencia, preserves 15,000 hectares of marshes, grasslands, palm savannas, scrub forest and denser gallery forests in the humid eastern Chaco. Mammals are few, but birds include rheas, jabirú storks, roseate spoonbills, cormorants, caracaras and many others. The most abundant species is the mosquito, so visit in the relatively dry, cool winter and bring insect repellent.

Hiking and birdwatching are best in the early morning or around sunset; park personnel will accompany visitors, if their duties permit. Some inundated areas are accessible only on horseback – inquire in Capitán Solari for horses and guides.

Places to Stay & Eat

Camping is the only accommodation option at the park. There are shaded free sites with clean showers (cold water only) and toilets, but a tent is essential. Sometimes on weekends, a snack bar sells meals, but bring supplies from Resistencia.

Getting There & Away

Capitán Solari is 2½ hours from Resistencia with La Estrella, which has buses daily at 6.30 am and 12.30, 5.30 and 8 pm. From Capitán Solari, you must walk or catch a lift to the park entrance.

ROQUE SÁENZ PEÑA

The cotton town of Roque Sáez Peña (population 75,000), 168 km west of Resistencia, features a major thermal baths complex, a good zoo and several immigrant communities, including Italians, Yugoslavs and Bulgarians.

The tourist office (☎ 22135) is at avenidas San Martín (the main commercial street) and 9 de Julio. ENCOTEL is at Belgrano 602, while Telecom is at Rivadavia 435.

Places to Stay & Eat

Residencial El Colono, San Martín 755, has singles with shared bath (US$7), and a good restaurant with sidewalk seating. There are numerous restaurants and confiterías along San Martín. Appealing *Pizzería Roma* is at Avenida Mitre and Mariano Moreno.

Getting There & Away

Bus Take bus No 1 from Avenida Mitre to the terminal (☎ 20280), where services resemble those from Resistencia.

FORMOSA

From Formosa city, capital of Formosa province, it's possible to cross the northern Chaco to Bolivia, or continue to Paraguay. There are also buses to the Argentine provinces of Jujuy and Salta. Aerolíneas Argentinas (☎ 29314) flies to Buenos Aires (US$145) daily, except Saturday.

Clean, comfortable *Residencial Rivas*, at Belgrano and Ayacucho, near the bus terminal, has doubles for US$18.

CLORINDA

Clorinda, the border crossing to Asunción (Paraguay), is known for ferocious customs checks. *Hotel Rosario*, at San Martín and 12 de Octubre, has singles with bath for US$9.

PARQUE NACIONAL RÍO PILCOMAYO

The marshlands of this 60,000-hectare park hug the Paraguay border. From Clorinda, there are buses on Ruta 86 beyond Laguna Naick-Neck, where a well-marked turn-off leads to the ranger station at Laguna Blanca.

From this turn-off, walk or hitch five km to Laguna Blanca, which has camping facilities, and pasarelas for viewing wildlife. At Laguna Blanca, 11 km beyond the turn-off, there is lodging at *Hotel Guaraní*.

Córdoba Province

Córdoba province is bounded by the Andean provinces to the north-west, Cuyo to the south-west, the Chaco to the north-east and the Pampas to the south-east. Popular with Argentine tourists, its key attractions are the city of Córdoba and its scenic mountain hinterland, the Sierras de Córdoba.

History

Comechingones Indians briefly resisted the Spaniards, but by 1573, Jerónimo Luis de Cabrera founded the city of Córdoba. In colonial times, Córdoba's ecclesiastical importance made it a centre for education, arts and architecture, but after independence, the city had to reorient itself to the political and economic whims of Buenos Aires as immigrants flooded the province, thanks to the railroad.

From 1882 to 1896, the number of agricultural colonies increased from just five to 176, but because of phenomenal growth on the Pampas, Córdoba's national role actually declined.

Eventually, the local establishment's exaggerated conservatism aroused an aggressive reform movement that had a lasting impact locally and nationally. In the late 1960s, a coalition of students and auto workers nearly unseated a de facto military government in an uprising known as the *cordobazo*. Today, after the chaos of the 1970s and early 1980s, the economy has declined, as the automobile industry has suffered from obsolete plant and general national economic stagnation.

CÓRDOBA

Sited on the south bank of the Río Primero (or Suquía), 400 metres above sea level at the foot of the Sierra Chica, the city of Córdoba has sprawled north of the river and into the countryside, but its compact centre is easily explored on foot.

Plaza San Martín is the nucleus for Córdoba's one million inhabitants, but the commercial centre is north-west of the plaza, where the Avenida 25 de Mayo and Indarte pedestrian malls cross. Calle Obispo Trejos, south of the plaza, has the finest concentration of colonial buildings.

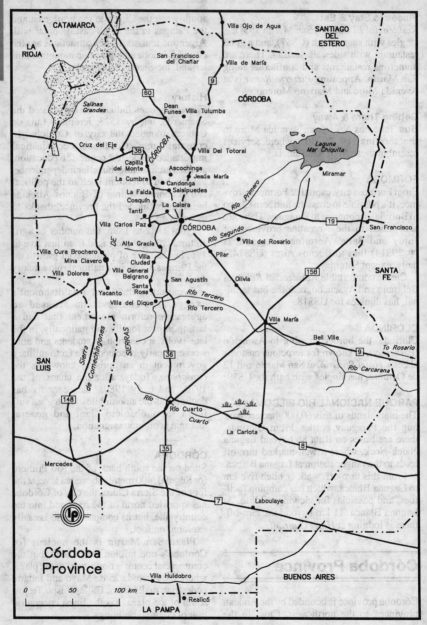

CATAMARCA

Villa Ojo de Agua

SANTIAGO DEL ESTERO

LA RIOJA

San Francisco del Chañar

Villa de María

Salinas Grandes

CÓRDOBA

Dean Funes   Villa Tulumba

Cruz del Eje

Laguna Mar Chiquita

Villa Del Totoral

Miramar

Capilla del Monte

Ascochinga

La Cumbre   Candonga   Jesús María
Salsipuedes

La Falda
Cosquín

La Calera

Río Primero

Tanti

Villa Carlos Paz

CÓRDOBA

San Francisco

Alta Gracia

Río Segundo

Villa del Rosario

Villa Cura Brochero

Pilar

Mina Clavero

Villa Ciudad

Villa Dolores

Villa General Belgrano

San Agustín

Olivia

SANTA FE

Santa Rosa

Yacanto

Villa del Dique

Río Tercero

Río Tercero

Villa María

Bell Ville

To Rosario

SAN LUIS

Río Carcaraña

Río Cuarto

Río Cuarto

La Carlota

Mercedes

Laboulaye

Córdoba Province

Villa Huidobro

BUENOS AIRES

Realicó

0   50   100 km

LA PAMPA

Information

The provincial Subsecretaría de Turismo (☎ 44027), open on weekdays from 7 am to 2 pm at Tucumán 25, also has a branch (☎ 34169) at the bus terminal, Avenida Perón 380, which keeps longer and weekend hours. The municipal tourist office (☎ 35031), downstairs at Rosario de Santa Fe 39, is open on weekdays from 8 am to 9 pm, and on weekends from 9 am to noon and 5 to 8 pm.

Try Exprinter, at Rivadavia 39, or Barujel, at San Martín 37, for cash or travellers' cheques (beware commissions). ENCOTEL is at Avenida General Paz 201, Telecom at Avenida General Paz 36. The Hospital de Urgencias (☎ 40243) is at Catamarca and Boulevard Guzmán.

Things to See

To see Córdoba's colonial buildings and monuments, start at the **Cabildo**, on Plaza San Martín, and the **Casa del Obispo Mercadillo**, at Rosario de Santa Fe 39. At the plaza's south-west corner, the **Iglesia Catedral** (begun in 1577) shows a mixture of styles, and is crowned by a Romanesque dome.

The **Iglesia de La Compañía** (1645), at Obispo Trejos and Caseros, has a modest exterior, but its unique interior features a timber roof shaped like an inverted ship's hull. The **Universidad Nacional de Córdoba** (1613) is at Obispo Trejos 242, but see also the nearby **Colegio Nacional de Monserrat** (1782). At Rosario de Santa Fe 218, the **Museo Histórico Provincial Marqués de Sobremonte** is open Tuesday to Friday from 8.30 am to 1.30 pm.

Places to Stay

Parque General San Martín, 13 km from the city centre, has a spacious but basic campground (US$3 per site). Bus No 31 from Plaza San Martín goes to the Complejo Ferial, an exhibition and entertainment complex within about one km of the park.

Very basic *Residencial La Soledad*, San Jerónimo 479, has singles for just US$4 per person with shared bath. Spotlessly clean *Hospedaje Suzy*, Entre Ríos 528, has doubles only at US$8 with shared bath.

For US$12/17 a single/double with private bath, dark and dingy *Hospedaje Dory's*, San Jerónimo 327, is quiet. *Residencial Central*, Perón 150, near the train station, is also dingy, but very clean. Other alternatives, for around US$16/24, include *Residencial Mallorca*, at Balcarce 73, and *Residencial San Francisco*, at Buenos Aires 272. *Hotel Claridge*, Avenida 25 de Mayo 218, has rooms with balcony and air-conditioning, on a quiet pedestrian street (US$14/24).

Places to Eat

The Mercado Norte, at Rivadavia and Oncativo, has excellent pizza, empanadas and lager beer. There are other cheapies on Perón, near the train and bus terminals, and on streets like San Jerónimo, where videos overshadow the food. *Pizzería Italiana*, San Jerónimo 610, is good, despite an unimpressive appearance.

University students hang out at *Bar Montserrat*, a confitería at Duarte Quiros and Obispo Trejos, which has superb croissants. For lunch, *Parrilla Acapulco*, at Obispo Trejos 169, has fine fixed-price meals as well as more elegant dishes.

Getting There & Away

Air Aeropuerto Pajas Blancas is 15 km north of town. Aerolíneas Argentinas (☎ 46041), Avenida Colón 520, has many flights to Buenos Aires (US$121). Its early Wednesday flight from the capital continues to Mendoza (US$69) and Santiago, Chile; its Sunday flight reverses that itinerary. The Sunday flight to Mendoza continues to Bariloche (US$214).

Austral (☎ 34883), Buenos Aires 59, also flies frequently to Buenos Aires, daily to Mendoza and twice weekly to Tucumán (US$74).

Bus More than just a bus station, NETOC, the Nueva Estación Terminal de Omnibus de Córdoba (☎ 34169) is at Perón 380. Its facilities include two banks, an automatic teller,

ARGENTINA

Córdoba

0   100   200 m

To Airport
Avenida Las Heras
Parque Las Heras
Río
To Santiago del Estero
Esquiú
Primero
To Belgrano Railway Station
12 de Octubre
Plaza General Paz
Igualdad
Rincón
Humberto Primo (1°)
La Tabiada
Libertad
Boulevard
Guzmán
1
2
Oncativo
Sarmiento
La Rioja
Jujuy
Sucre
Santa Rosa
Tucumán
Catamarca
San Martín
Avenida F Alcorta
Avenida Colón
3
4
Indarte
Lima
Avenida Maipú
5
Avenida General Paz
Ayacucho
9 de Julio
Avenida Olmos
Bolívar
Dean Funes
6
7
8
25
Calle Rivadavia
9
10
Belgrano
27 de Abril
12
11
Calle San Jerónimo
Plaza San Martín
14
Alvear
Calle Rosario de Santa Fe
18
Caseros
13
15
16
17
20 21
19
Salta
22
23
Duarte Quiros
36
35
34
33
32
Calle Independencia
Calle Buenos Aires
Chacabuco
25
24
26
27
28
29
30
Entre Ríos
31
Calle Obispo Trejo
Boulevard San Juan
Avenida
Corrientes
37
Avenida
To Villa Carlos Paz
Serafield
Avenida
Ituzaingó
Calle Colón
Salguero
Boulevard A Illia
38
39
40
San Luis
Vélez
H
Montevideo
Calle Paraná
Calle Balcarce
Allende
Dorrego
Avenida Yrigoyen
Rondeau
San Lorenzo
Lugones
To Buenos Aires
Calle Obispo Oro
Leopoldo
Avenida
Parque Sarmiento
42
41

■ PLACES TO STAY

8	Hotel Garden
9	Hotel Claridge
10	Hotel Crillon
15	Hotel Sussex
16	Hotel Nogaró
18	Hotel Florida
19	Hospedaje Dory's
22	Residencial La Soledad
23	Hotel Riviera
24	Residencial Mallorca
25	Residencial Crishsol
26	Residencial Central
27	Hotel Viña de Italia
28	Hotel Entre Ríos
29	Hotel Termini
31	Hospedaje Suzy
32	Residencial San Francisco
37	Hotel de la Cañada
38	Hotel Lady
39	Residencial Gran Bristol

▼ PLACES TO EAT

20	Parrilla Acapulco

OTHER

1	ACA (Auto Club; Travel Agency)
2	Mercado Norte
3	Aerolíneas Argentinas
4	Post Office
5	Hospital
6	Provincial Tourist Office
7	Telecom
11	Municipal Tourist Office
12	Cabildo
13	Iglesia Catedral
14	Austral (Airline)
17	Museo Histórico Provincial Marqués Sobremonte
21	Iglesia Santa Teresa
30	Mitre Railway Station
33	Museo de la Ciudad
34	Bar Monserrat
35	Colegio Nacional de Monserrat
36	Iglesia de la Compañía
40	Bus Terminal (NETOC)
41	Museum of Fine Arts
42	Plaza España

---

a pharmacy, a travel agency, telephones, a post office, a day care centre, first aid, a photo lab, and 40 shops and restaurants. By the way, 42 bus companies serve local, provincial, national and international destinations.

Many companies go to Buenos Aires (US$39, 10 hours). COTIL and Chevallier have buses to Catamarca (US$25). SOCASA goes to San Juan twice weekly, while Uspallata and TAC serve Mendoza (US$35).

Veloz del Norte goes to Salta, Balut to Salta and Jujuy, and Panamericano to Tucumán. La Estrella crosses the Chaco to Roque Sáenz Peña and Resistencia thrice weekly. El Serrano has buses to Santa Fe and Corrientes. Singer offers direct buses to Puerto Iguazú (US$69). CORA serves Montevideo four times weekly (US$70).

Getting Around
To/From the Airport From the bus terminal, take Empresa Ciudad de Córdoba's 'Salsipuedes' bus.

Bus The introduction of a computerised pass system for Córdoba's extensive bus network was planned.

Car For circuits in the Sierras de Córdoba, a car would be extremely useful. Try Avis (☎ 22483), Corrientes 452.

AROUND CÓRDOBA
West of the city, the Sierras de Córdoba contain many pleasant resorts.

Villa Carlos Paz
Only 36 km from Córdoba, on Lago San Roque reservoir, Carlos Paz is a minor-league, freshwater Mar del Plata. There's a tourist office (☎ 21624) at the bus terminal.

ACA's lakeshore Centro Turístico (☎ 22132), at Avenida San Martín and Nahuel Huapi, has its own campground, in addition to the municipal site, at Alfonsina Storni and A Magno. COTIL and COTAP have frequent buses from Córdoba, and some long-distance companies start and end their Córdoba routes here.

Cosquín

Cerro Pan de Azúcar, east of Cosquín, offers fine views of the Sierras and, on a clear day, Córdoba city. Hitch or walk five km to a saddle where an *aerosilla* (chairlift) goes to the 1260-metre summit (a steep 25-minute walk saves you US$5). At the saddle is a confitería, decorated with Gardel memorabilia.

Cosquín's annual January folklore festival has recently added classical music and ballet. In summer, the *Grand Sierras Hotel*, San Martín 733, has hostel facilities. Friendly, quiet, owner-operated *Petit Hotel*, Sabattini 739, charges about US$32 a double (but barely half that out of season). Santa María de la Punilla, just south of Cosquín, has a good campground. La Capillense and La Capilla run buses from Córdoba.

La Falda

This pleasant woodsy resort 78 km from Córdoba, at the western base of the Sierra Chica, has an interesting **Museo de Trenes en Miniatura** (Miniature Train Museum) and the **Museo Arqueológico Ambato**. The scenic zigzag road over the Sierra Chica to Salsipuedes, Río Ceballos and back to Córdoba climbs to 1500 metres, but there are no buses; try hitching in high season.

Wella Viajes, Avenida Edén 412, No 12, arranges hiking and trekking in the Sierras.

Places to Stay & Eat At US$15 per person with private bath, *Hotel El Piccolo*, at Uruguay 51, does much repeat business. *Old Garden Residencial*, Capital Federal 28, has a pool and beautiful gardens but is dearer. Nearby Villa Hermosa has a municipal campground, plus an historical museum in the old train station.

Among several decent restaurants on Avenida Edén is *Confitería Kattak*, Edén 444.

Getting There & Away La Capillense and El Cóndor have buses from Córdoba.

Candonga

Candonga's 18th-century chapel was once part of the Jesuit Estancia Santa Gertrudis, whose overgrown ruins are still visible in this placid canyon. In the absence of direct public transport, try hitching from El Manzano, 40 km north of Córdoba (reached by Empresa Ciudad de Córdoba or Sierras de Córdoba).

A day trip from Córdoba is possible, but *Hostería Candonga* (☎ 71-1092 in Córdoba) has good accommodation for US$30 per person, including all meals.

Alta Gracia

Only 35 km south-west of Córdoba, Alta Gracia's estancia supplied food and other provisions for Jesuits in the city until 1767. The house of Santiago Liniers, one of the last Spanish viceroys and a hero in the British invasion of 1806, is now a museum; Liniers was executed for resisting Argentine independence, and is buried in his native France. The late Spanish composer Manuel de Falla's house is also a museum.

SATAG has regular bus services to Alta Gracia from Córdoba.

MINA CLAVERO

Mina Clavero's clear streams, rocky waterfalls and verdant mountain landscapes, 170 km south-west of Córdoba, have attracted holiday-makers since the late 19th century.

The Dirección de Turismo (☎ 70171) is on Avenida San Martín 1464, near the bridge over the Río Mina Clavero. ENCOTEL is at San Martín and Pampa de Achala, while Telecom is at San Martín and Intendente Vila.

Museo Rocsen

This eclectic private museum displays apparently incompatible materials like European furniture and Peruvian mummies, but exhibits like the Rincón del Oligarca de Campo (Rural Landowner's Corner) and the Rincón del Oligarca de Ciudad (Urban Elite Corner) are exceptionally well-arranged.

Open from 10 am to 6 pm daily, the museum is in the village of Nono, nine km south of Mina Clavero; its shop sells ceramic reproductions of artefacts.

Places to Stay & Eat

Autocamping El Faro, three km south of town, has shady riverside sites with impeccable bathrooms, hot showers, laundry facilities and electricity (US$7 per group of four).

Hospedajes charge around US$10 per person, but many close by mid- March. Try *Hospedaje Italia* at Avenida San Martín 1176, *Hospedaje Las Moras* at Urquiza 1353, *Hospedaje Franchino* at Mitre 1544, or *Residencial El Parral* at Intendente Vila 1430. One-star hotels like *Hotel Agüero*, Avenida 12 de Octubre 1166, include breakfast and private bath for around US$18 a single.

Parrilla La Costanera, on riverside Avenida Costanera, has a good 'diente libre' (all you can eat) deal. *Restaurant Lo de Jorge*, on Poeta Lugones, serves good, abundant dishes at reasonable prices. *Restaurant La Nona*, Mitre 1600, has tasty pasta.

Getting There & Away

From the bus terminal, at Mitre 1191, El Petizo and Pampa de Achala have several daily buses to Córdoba. TAC has a daily bus to Merlo, San Luis and Buenos Aires. Chevallier goes to Buenos Aires (US$48) daily.

VILLA LAS ROSAS

South of Mina Clavero, Villa Las Rosas provides the most direct route to the summit of 2887-metre Cerro Champaquí, the province's highest peak. The tourist office (☎ 94407), in the Municipalidad, has a map listing local guides.

For accommodation, try *Hostería Las Rejas*, *Hotel Sierras Grandes* or the campground. *Restaurant Los Horcones* serves typical regional food.

The Cuyo

The Cuyo region consists of the Andean provinces of Mendoza and San Juan, and adjacent San Luis. Once part of Chile, Cuyo retains a strong regional identity. Despite the rain-shadow effect of Aconcagua (6960 metres) and other formidable peaks, enough snow accumulates to sustain rivers which irrigate extensive vineyards.

With its variety of terrain and climate, Cuyo offers outdoor activities all year round. Summer activities include climbing, trekking, riding, hang-gliding, canoeing, fishing, water-skiing, windsurfing and sailing. Skiing is increasingly popular in winter. Many travellers visit Mendoza, but the other provinces, especially San Juan, provide off-the-beaten-track experiences.

History

Spaniards from Chile crossed 3850-metre Uspallata pass to establish encomiendas among the indigenous Huarpe, but Mendoza's winter isolation stimulated economic independence and political initiative. Still, for a long time, links to the viceregal capital in Lima were via Santiago and the Pacific, rather than overland via Tucumán and Bolivia.

Colonial vineyards were important, but independence eliminated traditional outlets for their produce. Arrival of the railroad, in 1884, and improved irrigation brought expansion of grapes and olives, plus alfalfa for livestock. Today, Cuyo is one of Argentina's most important agricultural regions.

MENDOZA

Founded in 1561, at an altitude of 761 metres, the capital of Mendoza province is a lively city of 500,000, with an important university and, thanks to nearby oilfields, a growing industrial base. Modern quake-proof construction has replaced fallen historic buildings, but Mendoza's *acequias*

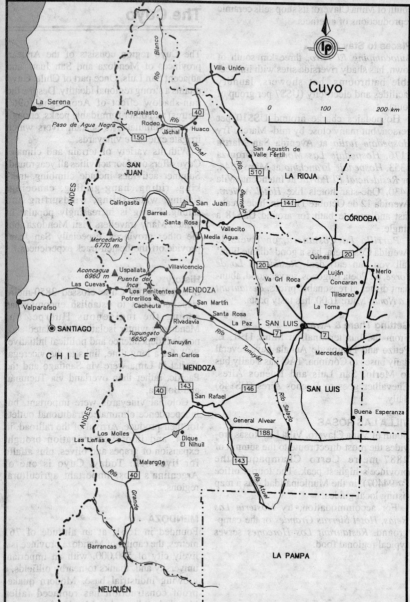

Cuyo

0   100   200 km

La Serena

Paso de Agua Negra

Angualasto

Rodeo

Jáchal

Huaco

Villa Unión

San Agustín de Valle Fértil

LA RIOJA

CÓRDOBA

SAN JUAN

Calingasta

Barreal

Santa Rosa

San Juan

Vallecito

Media Agua

Mercedario 6770 m

Aconcagua 6960 m

Uspallata

Puente del Inca

Las Cuevas

Los Penitentes

Potrerillos

Cacheuta

Villavicencio

MENDOZA

San Martín

Santa Rosa

La Paz

Quines

Va Grl Roca

Luján

Concarán

Tilisarao

La Toma

Merlo

SAN LUIS

ANDES

Valparaíso

SANTIAGO

CHILE

Tupungato 6650 m

Rivadavia

Tunuyán

San Carlos

MENDOZA

San Rafael

Los Molles

Las Leñas

Dique El Nihuil

Malargüe

General Alvear

Mercedes

Buena Esperanza

Barrancas

NEUQUÉN

LA PAMPA

Río Blanco

Río Jáchal

Río Bermejo

Río Tunuyán

Río Salado

Río Atuel

Río Grande

(irrigation canals) and tree-lined streets create a pleasing environment.

Orientation

Plaza Independencia fills four square blocks in the centre of town; two blocks from each of its corners are smaller satellite plazas. Plaza España deserves special attention for its Saturday artisans' market.

The sidewalk cafes on Avenida San Martín, which crosses the city from north to south, are good places to meet locals. The poplar-lined Alameda, beginning at the 1700 block of San Martín, was a traditional site for 19th-century promenades.

Information

Open on weekdays from 7 am to 9 pm, the provincial tourist office (☎ 24-2800), at San Martín 1143, has good maps and an excellent computerised information system. There's also a booth (☎ 25-9709) at the bus terminal.

Cambio Santiago, San Martín 1177, stays open on Saturdays until 8 pm. A cambio at the bus terminal opens early in the morning. ENCOTEL is at Avenida San Martín and Avenida Colón. Telecom is at Chile 1574. Chile's consulate (☎ 25-5024) is at Emilio Civit 296. American Express is at Rivadavia 80.

Things to See

A good starting point for orientation is the rooftop **Terraza Mirador**, at the Municipalidad, Avenida 9 de Julio 500, offering panoramic views of the city and surroundings. It's open on Monday and Friday from 8 am to 12 noon, and on Tuesday, Thursday and Saturday from 4 to 7 pm.

Those lacking time to visit wineries near Mendoza should see the **Enoteca Giol** wine museum, at Peltier 611, open daily (except Sunday) from 9 am to 7 pm. At the corner of Ituzaingó and Fray Luis Beltrán, the misnamed **Ruinas de San Francisco** (1638) were part of a Jesuit-built church/school later taken over by Franciscans.

The Virgin of Cuyo in the **Iglesia, Convento y Basílica de San Francisco** was the patron of San Martín's Army of the Andes. Public hours are 10 am to noon Monday to Saturday. The historical **Museo Sanmartiniano**, at Remedios Escalada de San Martín 1843, is open on weekdays from 9 am to noon and 5 to 8 pm.

Bus No 11 ('Favorita') from Plaza Independencia goes to the forested 420-hectare **Parque San Martín**, where a monument on the summit of **Cerro de la Gloria** honours the Army of the Andes for liberating Argentina, Chile and Peru.

The **Mercado Artesanal**, at San Martín 1133, has a fine display of Huarpe verticalloom weavings from the north-west of Mendoza province, and Araucanian horizontal looms from the south. You'll also see baskets woven in Lagunas del Rosario, and braided, untanned leather horse gear. Prices are reasonable at this must-see market, open on weekdays from 8 am to 1 pm.

Festivals

Mendoza's biggest annual event is the late-February **Fiesta Nacional de la Vendimia**, the wine harvest festival, with many concerts and folkloric events. A parade along San Martín features floats from each department of the province.

Places to Stay

Bus No 11 goes to campgrounds *El Challao*, six km from town, and *Parque Suizo*, nine km away, in Las Heras. Both have clean showers, laundry facilities, electricity, and a grocery store, and charge US$2 per person and US$2 per tent per day.

Cheap hotels near the train station are central, but the suspension of rail services makes those by the bus terminal more convenient. The tourist office keeps a list of *casas de familia*, charging about US$8 to US$12 a single.

Basic *Hotel Center*, at Alem 547, near the bus terminal, costs only US$8/13. On Güemes are several comparable places, like *Residencial Betty*, at No 456, nearby *Residencial San Fernando*, *Residencial 402*, at No 402, and *Residencial Evelyn*, at No 294.

ARGENTINA

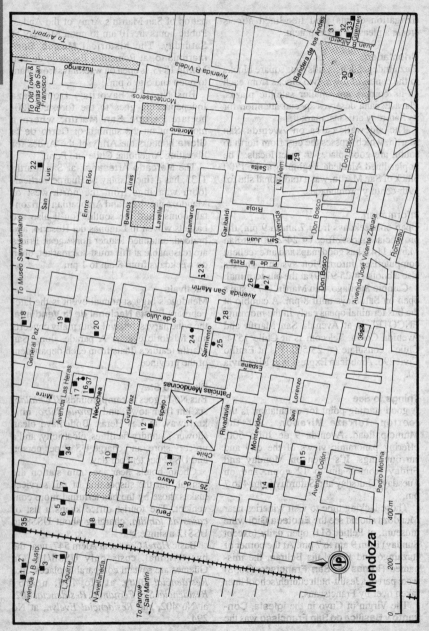

Mendoza

■ PLACES TO STAY		22	Hotel Escorial
1	Hotel Margal	29	Hotel Center
2	Hotel Penitentes	31	Hotel Terminal
3	Hotel Marconi	32	Residencial Evelyn
4	Hotel Laerte	33	Residenciales 402, San Fernando &
5	Hotel Presidente		Betty
6	Hotel Vigo	34	Hotel Rincón Vasco
7	Hotel Petit		
8	Hotel Savoy		OTHER
9	Hotel Provincial	21	Plaza Independencia
10	Hotel Horizonte	23	Provincial Tourist Office
11	Hotel Castelar	24	LAN-Chile (Airline)
12	Hotel Argentino	25	Ladeco (Airline)
13	Plaza Hotel	26	ACA (Travel Agency)
14	Hotel Aconcagua	27	Austral (Airline)
15	Hotel Lucense	28	Aerolíneas Argentinas
16	Hotel Necochea	30	Bus Terminal
17	Hotel Balbi	35	Railway Station
18	Hotel Vecchia Roma	36	Main Post Office
19	Hotel Royal	37	Iglesia de San Francisco
20	Hotel El Nevado		

Modest, friendly *Hotel Lucense*, Chile 759, has rooms with shared bath (US$12). *Hotel Vigo*, Necochea 749, has a nice garden and good restaurant (US$9/14). *Hotel Penitentes*, J B Justo 67, near the train station, has good rooms with bath (US$10/14). Friendly *Hotel Dardex*, Perú 1735, charges US$8/11.

Enthusiastically recommended *Hotel Laerte*, Leonidas Aguirre 19, is modern but homey (US$30/38).

Places to Eat

Montecatini, General Paz 370, near the train station, has good pasta at reasonable prices. *Trevi*, Las Heras 68, has superb lasagna. *Il Tuco*, at both Emilio Civit 556 and Sarmiento 68, has fine food and low prices. *Vecchia Roma*, Avenida España 1619, has superb Italian cuisine for medium to high prices. Despite their names, *Boccadoro*, Mitre 1976, and *Trattoria Aveni*, Avenida 25 de Mayo 1163, are parrillas, though the latter has good fish.

Vieja Recova, San Martín 924, emphasises seafood, while the *Centro Andaluz*, at L Aguirre 35, has tasty paella. *Club Español*, España 948, has moderately priced Spanish meals.

Al Arab, at Perú and Rivadavia, serves both Middle Eastern and Argentine dishes; try also the *Sociedad Libanesa*, at Necochea 538. For vegetarians, *Covindas*, at San Juan 840, and *Línea Verde*, at Montecaseros 1177, are good, wholesome and reasonable.

Getting There & Away

Air Aeropuerto Plumerillo is eight km from the city centre. Aerolíneas Argentinas (☎ 34-0170), Sarmiento 82, flies frequently to Buenos Aires (US$158), sometimes via Córdoba. There are twice-weekly services to Bariloche (US$150) and to Santiago, Chile (US$88).

Austral (☎ 24-9101), San Martín 921, flies twice every afternoon to Buenos Aires, except Saturdays (one flight). Early afternoon flights stop in Córdoba (US$69).

Ladeco, the Chilean airline, is at Sarmiento 144 (☎ 24-2778), while LAN-Chile is at Avenida 9 de Julio 1126 (☎ 23-0404). LAN-Chile also flies to Santiago on Tuesday and Sunday.

Bus From the terminal, on Avenida Videla, TAC has daily buses to Buenos Aires (US$68), Rosario (US$53), Bariloche

(US\$71), Córdoba (US\$39), La Rioja, Mar del Plata (US\$77), and across the Andes to Chile (Santiago and Valparaíso/Viña del Mar).

La Estrella and Libertador have daily buses to San Juan, La Rioja, Catamarca and Tucumán. Empresa del Sur y Media Agua has six buses daily to San Juan (US\$9, two hours), while La Veloz del Norte goes daily to Salta via San Juan.

Central Argentino serves northern beach resorts in Buenos Aires province en route to Villa Gesell, three times weekly in summer, and goes daily to Rosario. Colta has daily service to Córdoba via the Altas Cumbres route, as does Turismo Uspallata. COTAL goes to Posadas and Puerto Iguazú three times weekly.

Andesmar's daily service to Caleta Olivia, via Neuquén and Puerto Madryn, continues on Tuesday and Thursday to Río Gallegos. Andesmar also goes to Salta via Tucumán, four times weekly, and in summer has buses to the southern beach resorts of Buenos Aires province. Empresa Alto Valle has daily buses to Neuquén.

Getting Around
To/From the Airport Bus No 6 (Aeropuerto) from San Juan and Avenida Alem goes to the airport.

Bus Take local trolley 'Villa Nueva' from Lavalle, between San Martín and San Juan, to the large modern bus terminal, just beyond the city limits, at Avenida Gobernador Ricardo Videla and Alberdi.

AROUND MENDOZA
Wineries
Most wineries near Mendoza offer tours and tasting. Take Bus Nos 15 or 16 to **Bodega Giol**, at Ozamis 1040 in Maipú, open on weekdays from 9 am to noon and 3 to 8 pm, and on Saturdays from 9 am to noon.

Coquimbito, in Maipú, has two wineries: **Bodega Peñaflor**, on Mayorga, open on weekdays from 9 am to 4 pm, and **Bodega La Rural** on Montecaseros, whose museum

is open on weekdays from 10 am to noon and 3 to 6.30 pm. Take bus Nos 17A, 17B or 17C.

Bodega Toso, at Alberdi 808, San José, Guaymallén, opens weekdays 7 am to 6 pm; take bus No 2 or trolley 'Dorrego'. **Bodega Santa Ana**, at Roca and Urquiza, Villa Nueva, Guaymallén, opens on weekdays from 8.30 to 11 am and 2.30 to 3.30 pm; take bus No 2 ('Buena Nueva via Godoy Cruz').

USPALLATA
This village, 105 km north-west of Mendoza, 1751 metres above sea level, lies in an exceptionally beautiful valley surrounded by polychrome mountains. The relatively simple *Hostería Los Cóndores* is reasonably priced, while the local campground charges US\$4 per site.

VILLAVICENCIO
Panoramic views make the *caracoles* (winding road) to Villavicencio (at 1800 metres), 51 km from Mendoza, an attraction in itself. Local mineral water is sold countrywide, while the *Gran Hotel de Villavicencio* has thermal baths.

PARQUE PROVINCIAL ACONCAGUA
At 6960 metres, Cerro Aconcagua is the 'roof of the Americas'. Guides from the Asociación de Guías de Montaña lead two-week Aconcagua treks along the north route to the summit; the Club Andino Mendoza, on Lemus between Rioja and Salta, helps independent climbers with paperwork. Sol Andino (☎ 29-1544), Martínez de Rosas 489 in Mendoza, offers treks from the village of Los Penitentes, as well as rafting on the Río Mendoza.

Operadores Mendoza (☎ 25-3334, 23-1883), Las Heras 420 in Mendoza, organises three to six-day trips from Puente del Inca, partly by horse or mule, on the approach to the south face of Aconcagua.

For an eight-day pack trip across a route taken by part of San Martín's army, contact Turismo Masnú Barros (☎ 22444), at Sarmiento and Echeverría in Tunuyán.

PUENTE DEL INCA
This natural stone bridge over the Río Mendoza, 177 km from Mendoza, is a starting point for hikes to the base of Aconcagua, the pinnacles of Los Penitentes or the impressive snowcapped volcano of Tupungato (6650 metres). The pleasant *Hostería Puente del Inca* is cheaper in the off season.

CRISTO REDENTOR
Nearly 4000 metres above sea level on the Chile-Argentina border, battered by chilly winds, the high Andes are a fit setting for this monument, erected after settlement of a territorial dispute in 1902. The view is a must, either by tour or private car (Cristo Redentor is no longer a border crossing into Chile), but the first autumn snowfall closes the hairpin road. At Las Cuevas, 10 km before the border, you can stay at *Hostería Las Cuevas*.

VALLECITOS
At 2900 metres, in the Cordón del Plata, 80 km west of Mendoza, Vallecitos has six downhill ski runs. Open from early July to early October, it's the area's cheapest resort; for details, contact Valles del Plata (☎ 25-0972), España 1340, 10th floor, Mendoza.

LOS PENITENTES
At 2580 metres, 165 km from Mendoza, Penitentes has 21 runs for downhill and nordic skiing. Scenery and snow cover are excellent, lifts and accommodation very modern, but it's pricier than Vallecitos. For details, contact its Mendoza office (☎ 24-1770), at Rufino Ortega 644.

SAN RAFAEL
San Rafael (population 80,000) is a modern commercial and industrial centre whose nearby vineyards have earned an international reputation. The best-known wineries are Suter, Bianchi and Lávaque.

The tourist office (☎ 24217), at Avenida Yrigoyen and Avenida Balloffet, open from 7 am to 8.30 pm (11 pm in summer), has maps and brochures. ENCOTEL is at San Lorenzo and Barcala, Telecom at San Lorenzo 131.

Places to Stay & Eat
Hospedaje Ideal, San Martín 184, is the cheapest in town (US$12/20 a single/double). Other budget places are *Hospedaje La Esperanza*, at Avellaneda 263, and *Hospedaje Cerro Nevado*, at Yrigoyen 376.

For lunch or dinner, try *Restaurant ACA*, at H Yrigoyen 3522, *Club Español*, at the corner of Salas and Day, or *Jockey Club*, at Belgrano 338. Avenida Yrigoyen has several parrillas.

Getting There & Away
From the bus terminal, on Coronel Suárez, TAC has frequent buses to Mendoza and Malargüe, and three weekly to Las Leñas. Expreso Uspallata goes to Las Leñas on weekends and holidays.

Empresa Del Sur y Media Agua serves San Juan. Alto Valle has daily buses to Neuquén, and Andesmar goes to Comodoro Rivadavia via Puerto Madryn, and to Río Gallegos. La Estrella and TAC go nightly to Buenos Aires.

MALARGÜE
Petroleum and uranium are the main industries of Malargüe, but there are two nearby wildlife reserves, Payén and Laguna Llancanelo, and great skiing at Las Leñas. The tourist office is at F Inalicán and N Uriburu, and three of Malargüe's four hotels are on Avenida San Martín.

Transportes Diego Berbel, at Emilio Civit and Salas, has buses to Las Leñas and other destinations.

LAS LEÑAS
Las Leñas, 400 km south-west of Mendoza but only 70 km from Malargüe, is Argentina's most self-consciously prestigious ski centre, but despite the glitter, it's not impossible for budget travellers.

Open from June to October, at a base altitude of 2200 metres, it has four luxury hotels, self-catering 'apart-hotels', dorms with five to eight beds and shared bathrooms, a restaurant and a supermarket; you can stay more cheaply at Malargüe. For details, contact the Skileñas office (☎ 23-1628) in Mendoza, at Galería Caracol, Local 70, Avenida San Martín 1233.

LOS MOLLES
This small, quiet resort 55 km north-west of Malargüe, on the same road as Las Leñas, has several ski lifts up the relatively gentle slopes. The thermal baths are a local attraction. Los Molles has one hotel and a couple of guesthouses, which offer much cheaper accommodation than Las Leñas (stay here and ski at Las Leñas).

SAN JUAN
Though a provincial capital, San Juan de la Frontera, 170 km north of Mendoza, has kept the rhythm and cordiality of a small town. Juan Perón's relief efforts after San Juan's massive 1944 earthquake first made him a public figure; since then, modern construction, wide tree-lined streets and exceptional tidiness characterise the city centre.

Orientation & Information
San Juan's regular grid makes orientation easy, but the addition of cardinal points to street addresses helps even more. East-west Avenida San Martín and north-south Calle Mendoza divide the city into quadrants; the functional centre is south of San Martín.

The Direccion de Turismo (☎ 22-7219), at Sarmiento 24 Sur, open from 8 am to noon and 4 to 8 pm, has a good city map and useful brochures on the rest of the province. Change money at Cambio Cash (Tucumán 210 Sur), Cambio Santiago (General Acha 52 Sur) or at travel agencies. ENCOTEL is at Avenida José Ignacio de la Roza 259 Este. Telecom is at Ignacio de la Roza 123 Oeste.

Things to See
At Avenida San Martín and Entre Ríos, the only surviving part of the earthquake-ravaged 17th-century Convento de Santo Domingo is the cell occupied by San Martín in 1815, with a small museum at Laprida 96

■	PLACES TO STAY
1	Residencial El Mendocino
2	Hotel Jardín Petit
4	Residencial Jessy Mar
11	Residencial Embajador
12	Residencial San Francisco
13	Residencial Lara
14	Hotel Nogaró
17	Hotel Alhambra
18	Hotel Selby
23	Residencial Sussex
24	Hotel Plaza
25	Hotel Bristol
26	Hotel Capayán
27	Pensión Central
29	Residencial Hispano Argentino
30	Pensión España
34	Hotel América

	OTHER
3	Museo de Ciencias Naturales
5	Casino Provincial
6	Casa de Sarmiento
7	Tourist Office
8	San Martín's Cell
9	Austral Airlines
10	Cambio Santiago
15	Banco de San Juan
16	Iglesia Catedral
19	Telecom
20	Bolsa de Comercio
21	ENCOTEL
22	Train Station
28	Aerolíneas Argentinas
31	Museums
32	Bus Terminal
33	ACA (Travel Agency)

Oeste. The Italian-designed Iglesia Catedral, at Mendoza and Rivadavia, on the plaza, was inaugurated in 1979.

At San Martín and Catamarca, the Museo de Ciencias Naturales has a fine collection of provincial plants, animals and minerals, plus fossils from Ischigualasto and Ullum. In the Parque de Mayo, at Avenida 25 de Mayo and Urquiza, the Mercado Artesanal Tradicional has brightly coloured mantas (shawls) from Jáchal, pottery, horse gear, basketry, traditional silver knife handles and mate gourds.

San Juan

0   100   200 m

To Mercado
Artesanal
Tradicional

To Dique Ullum
& Parque
Rivadavia

Parque
de Mayo

To Aeropuerto
Las Chacritas

Domingo Faustino Sarmiento, an important educator, provincial governor and President of Argentina (1868-74), was born in the **Casa de Sarmiento**, a colonial house at Sarmiento 21 Sur. Exiled in Chile during the time of Rosas, he wrote the polemic *Life in the Argentine Republic in the Days of the Tyrants*, which argued that Unitarism embodied 'civilisation' on the European model, while Federalism represented unprincipled 'barbarism'. *Recuerdos de Provincia* recounted his childhood in this house, open daily except Monday.

At the **Bragagnolo winery** (☎ 21-1305), on Ruta 40 and Avenida Benavídez, in the suburb of Chimbas, sample *blanco sanjuanino* (white wine) and other specialities like *mistela* (a dessert wine), *moscato dulce* (muscatel), plus juices, raisins, and *arrope de uva*, a grape jam.

Places to Stay
Take Empresa de la Marina buses to *Camping El Pinar*, the municipal site on Avenida Benavídez Oeste, six km from the centre. Charges are US$1.50 per person and US$1.50 per tent.

Near the train station, *Residencial San Francisco*, Avenida España 248 Sur, has modest but clean singles/doubles for US$10/17. Similar in price and standard are *Residencial El Mendocino*, at España 234 Norte, and *Residencial Sussex*, at España 402 Sur.

Near the bus terminal, *Residencial Hispano Argentino*, Estados Unidos 381 Sur, has small rooms with shared bath for US$10 a single. Clean, quiet *Pensión Central*, Mitre 131 Este, is excellent value for US$18 a single, with firm beds and private bath.

Places to Eat
Attractive *Club Sirio Libanés*, Entre Ríos 33 Sur, serves Middle Eastern food at moderate prices. *La Nona María*, San Martín and P Moreno, has excellent pasta. *El Rincón Cuyano*, Sarmiento 394 Norte, has a good standard menu, with fine service and reasonable prices. Vegetarians can try *Xe Lu Cher*, at San Martín 1653 Oeste, or *Soychu*, at Ignacio de la Roza 223 Oeste.

Of several parrillas on Avenida Circunvalación, *La Bodega del 800*, at Tucumán, is recommended. *Bigotes*, Las Heras and Ignacio de la Roza, has 'tenedor libre' beef, chicken and salads at reasonable prices.

For sandwiches, try *Lomos al Tiro*, at Calle Mendoza and Avenida San Martín. Pizzería *Un Rincón de Napoli*, Rivadavia 175 Sur, has a wide selection of toppings, and good beer.

Getting There & Away
Air Aerolíneas Argentinas (☎ 22-0205), Mendoza 468 Sur, flies daily to Buenos Aires (US$158) from Aeropuerto Las Chacritas (☎ 25-0486), on national Ruta 20, 13 km south-east of town.

Bus From the terminal (☎ 22-1604), at Estados Unidos 492 Sur, Empresa Del Sur y Media Agua has four daily buses to Mendoza and daily service to Rosario and Neuquén. Autotransportes San Juan has three afternoon buses to Buenos Aires (US$54), and also goes to Mar del Plata (US$67).

SOCASA has two buses daily to Córdoba (US$32), one direct and another via La Rioja; 20 de Junio takes the scenic Altas Cumbres route. La Estrella serves Tucumán, Catamarca and La Rioja.

TICSA goes daily to Bahía Blanca and three times weekly to Neuquén (US$62) and Zapala. There is a Wednesday bus to San Martín de los Andes, Friday and Sunday buses to Bariloche (US$78), and Tuesday and Friday buses to Santiago de Chile (US$25).

TAC goes daily to Chile (Santiago and Valparaíso/Viña del Mar), and five times daily to Mendoza. It also serves northern San Juan (Jáchal and Pismanta) and Bariloche, and goes to San Luis, Merlo and Paraná.

Empresa Vallecito has a daily bus to the Difunta Correa shrine (US$2.50) and San Agustín del Valle Fértil.

AROUND SAN JUAN
Museo Arqueológico La Laja
Emphasising regional prehistory, this

museum 25 km north of San Juan displays mummies, artefacts, petroglyphs and plant remains in seven separate showrooms. Outdoors are reproductions of natural environments, farming systems, petroglyphs and house types, all built to scale.

The Moorish-style building was once a hotel, whose thermal baths are still in use. From Avenida Córdoba in San Juan, take bus No 20 ('Albardón') at 8 am or 1 or 4 pm. At other times, take any No 20 'Albardón' bus to Las Piedritas and hitch or walk the last five km.

Vallecito

According to legend, Deolinda Correa trailed her conscript husband on foot through the desert during the civil wars of the 1840s. She died of thirst, hunger and exhaustion, but passing muleteers found her infant son alive at her breast. Vallecito, 60 km south-east of San Juan, is widely believed to be the site of her death.

Since the 1940s, the once simple **Difunta Correa shrine** has become a small town, with its own petrol station, school, post office, police station and church, plus 17 chapels or exhibit rooms where devotees leave elaborate ex-votos in exchange for supernatural favours. Her cult may be the strongest popular belief system in a country with a variety of unusual religious practices tenuously related to Roman Catholicism, the official state religion.

Truckers are especially devoted believers. From La Quiaca to Ushuaia, roadside shrines display her image, surrounded by candles, small banknotes, and bottles of water left to quench her thirst. Despite the antagonism of the official Church, the shrine has grown rapidly; at Easter, 1 May and Christmas, up to 200,000 pilgrims visit the site.

Places to Stay & Eat Vallecito has one inexpensive hostería and a decent restaurant, but accommodation is better in San Juan. Like the pilgrims, you can camp almost anywhere. There is good street food – visit the kiosk of lively and personable Doña María, at the foot of the shrine.

Getting There & Away Empresa Vallecito goes daily from San Juan, but any other eastbound bus will drop you at the site. Another alternative is a bus to Caucete, between San Juan and Vallecito, and a lift with the water trucks of the Fundación Cementerio Vallecito.

PARQUE PROVINCIAL ISCHIGUALASTO

At every meander in the canyon of Parque Provincial Ischigualasto, a desert valley between sedimentary mountain ranges, the intermittent waters of the Río Ischigualasto have exposed a wealth of Triassic fossils, up to 180 million years old, and carved distinctive shapes in the monochrome clays, red sandstones and volcanic ash. The desert flora of algarrobo trees, shrubs and cacti complement the eerie landforms.

Camping and hiking are possible, but there are no clear rules. With persistence, if you can prove you are an experienced hiker, the rangers will let you pitch a tent by the visitors' centre and will supply water. There is a small confitería.

Getting There & Away

Ischigualasto is 75 km north of San Agustín del Valle Fértil. Given its isolation, a vehicle is imperative, and a ranger accompanies every party; if you can't afford to rent a vehicle, ask the tourist office at San Agustín about people making the trip. Alternatively, arrange a guided trip with an off-duty ranger, who will pick you up at the police checkpoint at Los Baldecitos, on provincial Ruta 510, reached by the COTIL bus to La Rioja. Write to Señor Pereira or Señor Villafañe, Parque Provincial Ischigualasto (5449), San Agustín del Valle Fértil, San Juan.

SAN LUIS

Capital of its province, San Luis (population 80,000) is 260 km east of Mendoza. Its commercial centre is along the parallel streets of San Martín and Rivadavia, between Plaza Pringles on the north and Plaza Independencia to the south.

The Dirección Provincial de Turismo, at San Martín 555, has flashy brochures with little information, but does keep a list of budget hotels. Alituris, Junín 868, changes dollars and Chilean pesos. ENCOTEL is at Arturo Illia and San Martín, Telecom at Colón and Lavalle.

Things to See

The 1930s **Iglesia de Santo Domingo**, on Plaza Independencia, replaced a 17th-century predecessor but kept its Moorish style. Part of the old church can be seen next door – note the algarrobo doors.

Next to the Santo Domingo church, on Avenida 25 de Mayo, the **Mercado Artesanal** sells fine handmade wool rugs, as well as ceramics, onyx carvings, and weavings from elsewhere in the province. It's open on weekdays from 7 am to 1 pm.

Places to Stay & Eat

Residencial María Eugenia, Avenida 25 de Mayo 741, has large, clean rooms with shared bath (US$8/11 a single/double). *Residencial Royal*, Colón 878, is slightly dearer. *Residencial 17*, at Estado de Israel 1475, and *Residencial Rivadavia*, across the street, at No 1470, are near the bus terminal.

The confitería at the bus terminal serves terrific café con leche and croissants. *La Taberna Vasca*, at Colón and Bolívar, has mostly Spanish cuisine – try the seafood. *El Triángulo*, at Illia and Caseros, has a varied menu and reasonable prices. *Restaurant Argentino*, Illia 352, serves large portions of pasta. *El Abuelo*, at Roca and General Paz, has good lunches at moderate prices.

Getting There & Away

Air Aerolíneas Argentinas (☎ 23407) flies twice weekly to Buenos Aires (US$120).

Bus From the terminal, on España between San Martín and Rivadavia, TAC has hourly buses to Mendoza, three per day to Córdoba and one to Rosario. Jocolí goes to Mendoza, Buenos Aires (US$48), Mar del Plata (US$55) and provincial destinations. Colta has buses to Córdoba, Mendoza and Santiago, Chile (US$30).

Autotransportes San Juan goes daily to San Juan, four times daily to Buenos Aires, and to Mar del Plata. Chevallier has three buses nightly to Buenos Aires. Empresa del Sur y Media Agua goes to Rosario and San Juan, while TICSA travels to Bariloche four times weekly. Dasso serves small provincial towns.

MERLO

In the Sierras de Comechingones, 180 km from San Luis and 900 metres above sea level, Merlo's gentle climate makes it a popular resort, though less frequented than the Sierras de Córdoba. The town's church and other buildings impart a colonial atmosphere amongst modern vacation homes, restaurants and hotels.

The tourist office, on the plaza, has complete data on hotels and campgrounds. Banco Provincia, also on the plaza, will change cash at better rates than most hotels. *Residencial Oviedo*, at Coronel Mercau 799, has singles with private bath for US$5.50, while *Residencial El Castaño*, on elegant Avenida del Sol, charges US$8/12 a single/double. Try the good, very inexpensive *Restaurant Plaza*, near the Casa del Poeta and the ACA station.

Empresa Jocolí runs buses to Merlo from San Luis.

The Andean North-West

The Andean North-West comprises the provinces of Jujuy, Salta, Tucumán, La Rioja, Catamarca and Santiago del Estero. Its pre-Columbian and colonial past make the trip to the Argentine heartland a journey through time as well as space.

History

In pre-Columbian times, the North-West was the most densely populated part of what is now Argentina, containing some two-thirds of the population. The widespread Diaguita, the Lule south and west of modern Salta, the Tonocote of Santiago del Estero, and the Omahuaca of Jujuy were all, in some ways, cultural outliers of the agricultural civilisations of the Central Andean highlands.

Diego de Almagro's expedition from Cuzco to Chile passed through Jujuy and Salta, but the earliest city was Santiago del Estero (1553). Indians destroyed several others before the founding of San Miguel de Tucumán (1565), Córdoba (1573), Salta (1582), La Rioja (1591) and San Salvador de Jujuy (1593). Catamarca was founded more than a century later. Unimpressive in their infancy, these settlements still established the basic elements of colonial rule: the *cabildo*, or town council, the church, and the rectangular plaza with its clustered public buildings.

As Indians fell to disease and exploitation, encomiendas lost their economic value, but colonial Tucumán provided mules, cotton and textiles for the mines of Potosí. Opening the Atlantic to legal shipping in late colonial times relegated Jujuy and Salta to marginality, but the sugar industry increased Tucumán's economic importance.

Even today, Argentina's northern provinces resemble the Andean countries and Quechua Indian communities reach as far south as Santiago del Estero.

JUJUY

San Salvador de Jujuy was a key stopover for colonial mule traders en route to Potosí, but sugar cane became a major commodity at Jesuit missions and, later, British plantations. During the wars of independence, General Manuel Belgrano directed the evacuation of the city to avoid its capture by royalists; Jujuy's biggest event, held every August, is the week-long **Semana de Jujuy**, which celebrates the 'éxodo jujeño' (Jujuy exodus).

At the mouth of the Quebrada de Humahuaca, the centre of the old city of Jujuy (population 170,000) is Plaza Belgrano. Between Necochea and Lavalle, the 700 block of Belgrano (the main commercial street) is a pedestrian mall. National Ruta 9 leads north up the quebrada, while national Ruta 66 leads south-east to national Ruta 34, the main route to Salta.

Information

The tourist office (☎ 28153), Belgrano 690, is open on weekdays from 7 am to 9 pm, and on weekends from 8 am to 8 pm. A branch at the bus terminal is open from 8 am to noon and 3 to 8 pm.

Try Cambio Dinar, at Belgrano 731, or Noroeste Cambio, at Belgrano 711, for moneychanging. ENCOTEL is at Lamadrid and Independencia, Telecom at Senador Pérez 141. There is a Bolivian consulate (☎ 22010) at Arenales 641, open on weekdays from 8 am to 1 pm.

Things to See

On Plaza Belgrano, Jujuy's **Iglesia Catedral** (1763) features a Spanish Baroque pulpit, built and laminated in gold, probably by local artisans under a European master. The colonnade along the Belgrano side has an artisans' market.

Also on the plaza, the colonial **Cabildo** deserves more attention than the **Museo Policial** within. The **Museo Histórico Provincial**, at Lavalle 256, has rooms dedicated to distinct themes in provincial history. The **Iglesia Santa Barbara**, at Lamadrid and San Martín, contains several paintings from the Cuzco school.

Jujuy's **Mercado del Sur**, opposite the bus terminal, is an Indian market where Quechua men and women swig *mazamorra* (a cold maize soup) and surreptitiously peddle coca leaves (illegal but unofficially tolerated for indigenous people).

Places to Stay

Take bus No 4 to the clean, friendly *Camping Municipal*, three km north of Parque San Martín on Avenida Bolivia. Charges are US$4 for vehicle, tent and up to four persons, and occasional hot water.

Residencial Río de Janeiro, west of the bus terminal, at José de la Iglesia 1356, has singles with shared bath for US$6. *Residencial Los Andes*, a few blocks east, at

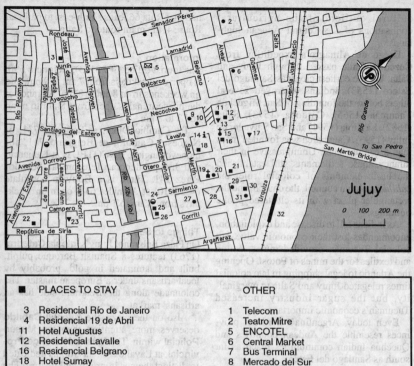

■ PLACES TO STAY

3 Residencial Río de Janeiro
4 Residencial 19 de Abril
11 Hotel Augustus
12 Residencial Lavalle
16 Residencial Belgrano
18 Hotel Sumay
21 Hotel Internacional
22 Residencial Los Andes
25 Hotel Avenida
26 Hotel Fenicia
30 Residencial Norte

▼ PLACES TO EAT

13 La Rueda
17 Chung King Restaurant
23 La Sucreña

OTHER

1 Telecom
2 Teatro Mitre
5 ENCOTEL
6 Central Market
7 Bus Terminal
8 Mercado del Sur
9 Aerolíneas Argentinas/Austral
10 Museo Histórico Provincial
14 Tourist Office
15 Iglesia San Francisco
19 Iglesia Catedral
20 Artisans' Market
24 Tea Turismo (Airport Minibuses)
27 Casa de Gobierno
28 Plaza Belgrano
29 Cabildo (Museo Policial)
31 Dirección General de Fauna y Parques
32 Railway Station

República de Siria 456, charges US$9/13 a single/double with shared bath, US$11/16 with private bath.

Residencial Norte, at Alvear 444, opposite the train station, has US$12 doubles and a decent restaurant. Comparably priced is *Residencial 19 de Abril*, Avenida 19 de Abril 943 (rooms with private bath are dearer). *Residencial Belgrano*, Belgrano 627, charges US$10/13 for rooms with shared bath.

Places to Eat

Upstairs restaurants at the central market, at

Alvear and Balcárce, serve regional specialities, generally spicier than those elsewhere in Argentina – try chicharrón con mote (stir-fried pork with boiled maize). Another local favourite is modest *La Sucreña*, on Leandro Alem, east of the bus terminal.

For standard Argentine fare, try *La Rueda*, Lavalle 329. The misleadingly named *Chung King*, Alvear 627, has an extensive Argentine menu and fine service. On the Belgrano peatonal are several confiterías and excellent ice-creameries.

Getting There & Away
Air Aeropuerto El Cadillal is 32 km south-east of town. Aerolíneas Argentinas and Austral (☎ 22384) have consolidated operations, at San Martín 735; each flies daily to Buenos Aires (US$204).

Bus From the terminal, at Dorrego and Iguazú, Panamericano goes south to Tucumán (US$15) and Córdoba, up the Quebrada de Humahuaca to La Quiaca (US$19), and to isolated puna settlements like Susques and Olaroz Chico. COTA Norte also goes to Humahuaca (US$7). Atahualpa's Salta-La Quiaca service also stops in Jujuy. Empresa Balut goes to Orán and the other Bolivian border crossing at Pocitos, while Empresa Itatí crosses the Chaco weekly to Corrientes and Iguazú.

Chile-bound buses from Salta stop in Jujuy before crossing the Paso de Jama to Calama and Iquique (US$55), but make reservations well in advance.

Getting Around
To/From the Airport Tea Turismo, 19 de Abril 485, runs minibuses (US$4.50) to the airport.

Car A1 (☎ 29697), Senador Pérez 398, rents Fiat 147s and other vehicles from about US$30 per day, plus petrol, insurance and mileage.

AROUND JUJUY
Termas de Reyes
Don't leave Jujuy without wallowing in the thermal baths (US$5) at *Hostería Termas de Reyes*, which overlooks the scenic canyon of the Río Reyes, easily reached from Jujuy. Bring food, since the hostería's restaurant is expensive.

QUEBRADA DE HUMAHUACA
North of Jujuy, the Quebrada de Humahuaca is a painter's palette of colour on barren hillsides, dwarfing hamlets where Quechua peasants scratch a living from maize and scrawny livestock. On this colonial post-route to Potosí, the architecture and other cultural features recall Peru and Bolivia.

Earthquakes levelled many adobe churches, but they were often rebuilt in the 17th and 18th centuries with thick walls, simple bell towers, and striking doors and wood panelling from the *cardón* cactus. Points of interest are so numerous that a car would be very useful, but buses are frequent enough that you should be able to flag one down when you need it.

Purmamarca
A few km off the main highway, polychrome Cerro Colorado is a backdrop for this tiny village's 17th-century church.

La Posta de Hornillos
This restored way station, part of a chain which ran from Lima to Buenos Aires, is 11 km north of the Purmamarca turn-off. Informal but informative guided tours make La Posta de Hornillos an obligatory stop; camping is possible (US$3 per site).

Maimará
Only a few km south of Tilcara, the hillside cemetery of this quaint valley settlement is a can't-miss photo opportunity.

Uquía
Artists of the Cuzco school painted the *Angeles harquebuseros* (angels with Spanish weapons), displayed in the restored collection of the 17th-century **Iglesia de San Francisco de Paula**.

TILCARA

Tilcara, 2461 metres above sea level, features a classic *pucará*, a fortress with unobstructed views in several directions. The village's museums and its artists' colony reputation make it a highly desirable stop-over. Tilcara is irregular beyond the centre, and people ignore street names and numbers. El Antigal, a hotel and restaurant, distributes a small, useful brochure. The telephone cooperative is on the ground floor of the Hotel de Turismo, Belgrano 590.

Things to See

Rising up through the sediments of the Río Grande valley, an isolated hill is the site of **El Pucará**, a pre-Columbian fortification (admission US$2), one km south of Tilcara's centre.

In a beautiful colonial house, open daily from 9 am to 9 pm, the **Museo Arqueológico Dr Eduardo Casanova** has a well-organised collection of regional artefacts. Admission is US$2 (free on Tuesdays).

The **Museo Ernesto Soto Avendaño** shows the work of a sculptor who spent most of his life here. It's open Tuesday to Saturday from 9 am to noon and 3 to 6 pm. The **Museo José Antonio Terry** honours a Buenos Aires-born painter whose themes were largely rural and indigenous. Hours are daily, except Monday, from 9 am to 5 pm. Admission is US$2 (free on Thursdays).

Places to Stay & Eat

Residencial El Edén, on Rivadavia 1½ blocks from Plaza Prado, charges US$5/8 a single/double for rooms with sagging beds and shared bath (cold showers only), but it's clean and friendly. Juan Brambati and family offer lodging for US$7 per person, with meals additional.

Residencial El Antigal, also on Rivadavia, half a block from the plaza, is a good choice at US$12/22 with private bath, hot water and a fine restaurant. *Restaurant Pucará*, on the plaza, is also popular.

Congenial *Camping El Jardín* has hot showers and attractive vegetable and flower gardens, all for US$2.50 per person. The free

site near the YPF petrol station has picnic tables, but lacks potable water and sanitary facilities.

Getting There & Away

Of nine daily buses to Jujuy, four continue to Salta. Northbound services to Humahuaca and La Quiaca also stop here.

HUMAHUACA

Straddling the Río Grande, nearly 3000 metres above sea level, Humahuaca is a mostly Quechua village of cobbled streets lined with adobe houses. The tourist office, in the Cabildo at Tucumán and Jujuy, is open on weekdays only. ENCOTEL is across from the plaza, while the telephone office, on the main floor of the Hotel de Turismo, on Buenos Aires, is open from 7 am to 8 pm daily.

Things to See

From the clocktower in the **Cabildo**, a life-size figure of San Francisco Solano emerges daily at noon to deliver a benediction. Arrive early, since the clock is erratic and the figure appears only very briefly.

Humahuaca's patron saint resides in the **Iglesia de la Candelaria** (1641), which also contains 18th-century oils by Cuzco painter Marcos Sapaca. Overlooking the town, Tilcara sculptor Ernesto Soto Avendaño's **Monumento a la Independencia** is a text-book example of *indigenismo*, a distorted nationalist tendency in Latin American art and literature which romanticises native cultures obliterated by European expansion.

The **Museo Folklórico Regional**, in the Humahuaca youth hostel at Buenos Aires 435/447, is open from 8 am to 8 pm daily, but for formal tours (US$5) only when a group of three or four justifies the effort, placing the artefacts in a living cultural context. Local writer Sixto Vázquez Zuleta, who prefers his Quechua name, Toqo, is a mine of information on local history and culture.

Ten km from Humahuaca by a dirt road leading north from the east side of the bridge over the Río Grande, north-western

Argentina's most extensive pre-Columbian ruins cover about 40 hectares at **Coctaca**. Many appear to be broad agricultural terraces on an alluvial fan, but there are also obvious outlines of clusters of buildings.

In the wet summer, the road may be impassable; if walking, carry water and leave before the heat of the day.

Places to Stay & Eat

The municipal camp site across the bridge is still closed, but it's possible to park or pitch a tent and use the showers at the youth hostel, at Buenos Aires 435, which is open all year and does not require an international hostel card. For US$6 a single, it offers hot showers, cooking facilities and the opportunity to meet both Argentine and international travellers. *Residencial Humahuaca*, at Córdoba 401 near Corrientes, charges US$12/15 a single/double for rooms with shared bath, slightly more with private bath. *Residencial Colonial*, Entre Ríos 110, is comparable in price and quality.

It doesn't look like much, but *Restaurant El Rancho*, near the bus terminal, has fine spicy empanadas and humitas (corn tamales). The bus terminal has an acceptable confitería, while restaurants like *La Cacharpaya* and *El Fortín* are near the plaza.

Getting There & Away

Bus From the terminal, at Belgrano and Entre Ríos, frequent buses go to Jujuy (US$7) and La Quiaca (US$12). Transportes Mendoza offers Saturday service to the Andean village of Iruya; ask at Almacén Mendoza for details. There are also buses to the altiplano village of Susques, which has an interesting Andean church and access to important wildlife reserves.

LA QUIACA

North of Humahuaca, gravelled Ruta 9 climbs steeply to the altiplano, where agriculture is precarious and peasants subsist on llamas, sheep, goats and a few cattle which can graze the sparse *ichu* grass. At the end of the road are La Quiaca and its Bolivian twin, Villazón. For more details on the border crossing, and a map of Villazon/La Quiaca, see under Villazon in the Bolivia chapter.

La Quiaca has no tourist office, but for maps or motorist services, try the ACA station on Ruta 9, at Avenida 9 de Julio. If Banco Nación will not cash travellers' cheques, try Universo Tours in Villazón. La Quiaca's Bolivian Consulate is open on weekdays from 8.30 to 11 am and 2 to 5 pm, and on Saturdays from 9 am to noon.

Places to Stay

Accommodation is cheaper on the Bolivian side of the border, but in La Quiaca, correspondents have recommended *Hotel Cristal*, Sarmiento 539 (about US$17/28 a single/double with private bath). Other possibilities are *Hotel Grand*, opposite the train station, and *Residencial Victoria*, on the plaza. In Yavi, accommodation is available at the *Hostería de Yavi*.

Getting There & Away

Panamericano and Atahualpa have frequent buses from La Quiaca to Jujuy and Salta.

Yavi

Take Flota La Quiaqueña or a shared cab to the village of Yavi, 16 km from La Quiaca, where the 17th-century **Iglesia de San Francisco** is renowned for its altar, paintings, and carved statues. A nearby **colonial house** belonged to the Marqués Campero, whose marriage to the holder of the original encomienda created a family which dominated the region's economy in the 18th century.

Short hikes around Yavi include one to rock paintings at **Las Cuevas** and another to springs at **Agua de Castilla**.

SALTA

Salta, 1200 metres above sea level, is in a basin surrounded by verdant peaks. Its agreeable climate attracted Spaniards, who could pasture animals nearby and raise crops which could not grow in the frigid Bolivian highlands. When the railway made it feasible to haul sugar to the Pampas, the city partly recovered from its 19th-century decline.

Salta

0   100 200 m

South-west of the central Plaza 9 de Julio is Salta's commercial centre. Alberdi and Florida are pedestrian malls between Caseros and Avenida San Martín.

Information

Open from 8 am to 9 pm, the tourist office (☎ 31-0950) at Buenos Aires 93 has maps and brochures, and will help arrange accommodation in private houses. The branch at the bus terminal closes for siesta. Cambio Dinar, Mitre 101, changes cash and travellers' cheques. ENCOTEL is at Dean Funes 140. Telecom is at Vicente López 146 (international calls) and at Belgrano 824.

Bolivia's consulate (☎ 21-1927) is at Santiago del Estero 179. The Chilean Consulate (☎ 21-0827) is at Ejército del Norte 312, behind the Güemes monument.

Things to See

Museums The 18th-century **Cabildo**, at Caseros 549, houses the **Museo Histórico del Norte** (admission US$1), with religious and modern art, period furniture, historic coins, paper money, and horse-drawn vehicles. Hours are Tuesday to Saturday from 10

■ PLACES TO STAY		5	Plaza Güemes
		8	Bolivian Consulate
2	Residencial Güemes	9	Museo Antropológico Juan M
3	Residencial Astur		Leguizamón
6	Residencial Balcarce	10	Telecom (International)
22	Residencial España	12	Telecom
24	Hotel California	13	Cambio Dinar
32	Residencial Florida	14	Iglesia Catedral
33	Residencial Royal	17	ENCOTEL
35	Hotel Italia	19	Casa de Gobierno
36	Residencial Elena	20	Plaza 9 de Julio
38	Hotel Petit	21	Museo de Arte Popular
39	Hotel Continental	23	Museo de Bellas Artes (Casa Arias Rengel)
▼ PLACES TO EAT		25	Cabildo/Museo Histórico del Norte
		26	Aerolíneas Argentinas/Austral
7	Sociedad Italiana	27	Movitren (Tren a las Nubes)
11	Snack Bar Whympy	28	Casa Uriburu
15	Heladería Gianni	29	Tourist Office
16	La Posta	30	Iglesia San Francisco
18	Café del Consejo	31	Convento de San Bernardo
37	Restaurant Alvarez	34	Central Market
		40	Géminis (Buses to Chile)
OTHER		41	Bus Station
1	Train Station		
4	ACA (Travel Agency)		

am to 2 pm and 3.30 to 7.30 pm, and Sunday from 10 am to 2 pm.

In Casa Arias Rengel, a colonial mansion with thick adobe walls at Florida 18, the **Museo de Bellas Artes** (admission US$1) displays modern painting and sculpture. It's open daily, except Monday, from 9 am to 1 pm and 3 to 9 pm.

Churches The 19th-century **Iglesia Catedral**, España 596, guards the ashes of General Martín Miguel de Güemes, a hero of the wars of independence; provincial gauchos still flaunt their red-striped *ponchos de Güemes*.

Ornate almost to gaudiness, the **Iglesia San Francisco**, at Caseros and Córdoba, is a local landmark. Only Carmelite nuns can enter the 16th-century **Convento de San Bernardo**, at Caseros and Santa Fe, but anyone can approach the dazzlingly white adobe building to admire its carved algarrobo door.

Museo de Arte Popular This private institution at Caseros 476 shows and sells crafts

from throughout the Americas. Admission is US$1; hours are 9.30 am to 12.30 pm and 5.30 to 9.30 pm Monday to Saturday (closed on Wednesday mornings).

Cerro San Bernardo For views of Salta and the Lerma valley, take the *teleférico* (gondola) from Parque San Martín to the top and back (US$6), or climb the trail from the top of Avenida General Güemes.

Places to Stay
Camping Municipal Carlos Xamena, one of Argentina's best campgrounds, features a gigantic swimming pool. Fees are US$2 per car, US$2.50 per tent and US$1.50 per adult. From the centre, take bus No 13 ('Balneario'). Salta's *youth hostel* is at Buenos Aires 936.

One of the best *private houses* is at Mendoza 915, run by one of three sisters (the other two let rooms at Nos 917 and 919). All have pleasant patios, cooking facilities and spotless bathrooms, for about US$8 per person.

Near the bus terminal, reasonably quiet *Residencial Royal*, Alvarado 107, has singles/doubles with shared bath for US$10/14. *Residencial España*, España 319, charges US$16/22.

On Ameghino, across from the train station, several residenciales have rock-bottom accommodation at around US$10/12. For US$15/22, try *Residencial Balcarce*, Balcárce 460 near the train station. *Residencial Elena*, Buenos Aires 256, a colonial building with an attractive patio, has drawn enthusiastic reports (US$15/22).

Places to Eat

One of the best and cheapest eateries is the main market at Florida and San Martín, where you can supplement cheap pizza, empanadas and humitas with fresh fruit and vegetables.

Despite its unappealing moniker, *Snack Bar Whympy*, at Zuviría 223, is good and inexpensive. The *Sociedad Italiana*, Zuviría and Santiago del Estero, has quality lunches for about US$3. *Restaurant Alvarez*, at San Martín and Buenos Aires, serves large portions of good, cheap food. Pricey *La Posta*, España 476, is a highly recommended parrilla. *Heladería Gianni*, España 486, has superb ice cream.

Getting There & Away

Air Aerolíneas Argentinas (☎ 21-4757) and Austral have consolidated operations, at Caseros 475. Both fly daily to Buenos Aires (US$199), while Aerolíneas flies on Mondays to Córdoba (US$115), and to Santa Cruz de la Sierra (Bolivia).

Bus Most companies are inside the bus terminal on Avenida Hipólito Yrigoyen, but a few are nearby.

Chevallier goes daily to Buenos Aires (US$75). Veloz del Norte serves Mar del Plata (US$90, 29 hours), Buenos Aires, Santa Fe (US$60), Mendoza (US$61), San Juan (US$50), Córdoba (US$45), Resistencia (US$42), La Rioja (US$35), Catamarca (US$26) and Santiago del Estero (US$20).

Panamericano goes frequently to Tucumán (US$17), Santiago del Estero and Córdoba, plus Mar del Plata. Atalhualpa goes to Jujuy, and up the Quebrada de Humahuaca to Formosa (US$40), and to Calama, Chile (US$45, on Wednesdays in summer only). Géminis, at Dionísio Puch 117 opposite the terminal, also has summer crossings on Saturdays to Antofagasta (US$50), Iquique (US$55) and Arica (US$60). Make early reservations for buses to Chile, which now use the Paso de Jama and may be boarded in Jujuy.

El Indio goes three times daily to Cafayate (US$10). There are daily buses up the Quebrada de Toro to San Antonio de los Cobres (US$11). Marcos Rueda, Islas Malvinas 393, serves the altiplano village of Cachi (US$13).

Train One of Salta's top attractions is the scenic ride to San Antonio de los Cobres on the Tren a las Nubes (Train to the Clouds), but this has become expensive – see the San Antonio entry for details. An alternative is the 10.15 am Wednesday freight train to the Chilean border at Socompa (US$18.50, 29 hours). Passenger services on the Belgrano line have been suspended.

Getting Around

Bus Local bus No 7 connects the train station and the city centre with the bus terminal.

Car Car rental agencies include López Fleming (☎ 21-1381), at Güemes 92, and Ruiz Moreno (☎ 21-2069), Buenos Aires 1.

Tours Visitors with little time, but genuine interest in sights off the beaten track, might contact Turismo Mallorca (☎ 22-2075), at Caseros 527, which operates treks, horseback and fishing trips, ornithological and archaeological tours, and visits to indigenous reserves. Parque Nacional Baritú and Parque Nacional El Rey are both difficult to reach by public transport.

PARQUE NACIONAL CALILEGUA

On Jujuy's eastern border, the arid altiplano surrenders to dense subtropical cloud forest in the Serranía de Calilegua, where 3600-metre Cerro Hermoso offers limitless views of the Gran Chaco. Bird life is abundant, and there is a wide variety of flora, changing with the increasing altitude.

Park headquarters (☎ 22046) is in the village of Calilegua, just north of Libertador General San Martín. Donated by the Ledesma sugar mill, the visitors' centre will soon have exhibits on all the region's national parks.

Things to Do

Calilegua's 230 species of birds include condor, brown eagle, torrent duck and toucan. Mammals (rarely seen in the dense forest) include tapir, puma, jaguar, collared peccary and otter. The best wildlife sites are near watercourses; from the ranger station at Mesada de las Colmenas, a steep, overgrown trail drops to a beautiful creek, where animal tracks are numerous. The descent takes an hour, the ascent twice that.

There are excellent views from Cerro Hermoso, but ask rangers for directions. From Valle Grande, west of the park, it is possible to hike to Humahuaca along the Sierra de Zenta.

Places to Stay

Beware mosquitos at the developed camp site at Aguas Negras, on a short lateral road near the entrance station. Camping is also possible on a level area near Mesada de las Colmenas.

Getting There & Away

Buses Veloz del Norte's Salta-Orán service stops at the excellent restaurant of the Club Social San Lorenzo, next door to park headquarters. From the bus terminal at Libertador General San Martín, a 4WD pick-up climbs to Parque Calilegua and Valle Grande (US$13) on Tuesdays and Saturdays at 7.30 am; return trips are on Sundays and Thursdays at 9 am. Also try hitching with logging trucks to Valle Grande.

QUEBRADA DE CAFAYATE

Beyond the village of Alemania, 100 km south of Salta, verdant forest becomes barren sandstone in the Quebrada de Cafayate. The eastern Sierra de Carahuasi is the backdrop for distinctive landforms like Garganta del Diablo (Devil's Throat), El Anfiteatro (The Amphitheatre), El Sapo (The Toad), El Fraile (The Friar), El Obelisco (The Obelisk) and Los Castillos (The Castles). Nearer Cafayate is an extensive dunefield at Los Médanos.

Getting There & Away

Other than car rental or brief, regimented tours, the only ways to see the Quebrada are by bus, thumb or foot. Disembark from any El Indio bus and catch a later one. The most interesting portion is too far to walk in a single day, but you can double back from Cafayate.

Walking lets you see the canyon at your own pace (carry food and water). A good starting point is the impressive box canyon of Garganta del Diablo.

CAFAYATE

Many tourists and several major vineyards enjoy the warm, dry and sunny climate of Cafayate (1600 metres), at the mouth of the Valle Calchaquí. It's not overrun with visitors, but there are many young artists and artisans. National Ruta 40 (Avenida Güemes) goes north-west to Molinos and Cachi, while provincial Ruta 68 goes to Salta.

The information kiosk on Güemes, opposite the plaza, keeps erratic hours. Change money in Salta, if possible, but in Cafayate, try Banco de la Nación or larger shops and hotels. Long-distance calls are an agonising experience at the cooperative on the west side of the plaza.

Things to See

Drop by Rodolfo Bravo's house, on Calle Colón, at any reasonable hour to see his personal **Museo Arqueológico** of Calchaquí (Diaguita) ceramics; admission is US$1 per person. Colonial and other artefacts include elaborate horse gear and wine casks.

On Güemes near Colón, the **Museo de Vitivinicultura** details the history of local wines. Ask at the bodegas for tours and tasting; try the sweet white *torrontés*.

Places to Stay & Eat
The municipal *Camping Lorahuasi* (US$1.50 per car, person and tent) has hot showers, a swimming pool and a small grocery. *Hotel Santa Barbara*, on Quintana de Niño, has singles for US$10; try also nearby *Hospedaje Arroyo*. *Residencial Colonial*, Diego de Almagro 124, has doubles for US$20, but sometimes lacks hot water.

Local cuisine emphasises parrillada, as at *La López Pereyra*. Try also *La Carreta de Don Olegario*, on Güemes at the plaza, but there are several cheaper places.

Getting There & Away
El Indio has three buses daily to Salta (US$10, four hours), except Thursday (four buses). Another four go to San Carlos, up the Valle Calchaquí, and one to Angastaco (US$6).

To visit Quilmes, in Tucumán province, use the daily buses to Santa María. Three buses a week go to Tucumán city via the scenic Tafí del Valle route.

AROUND CAFAYATE
Valles Calchaquíes
In this valley north and south of Cafayate, once a principal route across the Andes, Calchaquí Indians resisted Spanish attempts to impose forced labour obligations. Tired of having to protect their pack trains, the Spaniards relocated many Indians to Buenos Aires, and the land fell to Spaniards, who formed large rural estates.

Cachi
North-west of Cafayate, Cachi's scenic surroundings, 18th-century church and archaeological museum make it the most worthwhile stopover in the Valles Calchaquíes. For accommodation, try the municipal campground and hostel, or *Hotel Nevado de Cachi* (US$8 per person).

You can reach Cachi either from Cafayate or, more easily, by the Marcos Rueda bus from Salta (US$13). The latter route uses the scenic Cuesta del Obispo route past Parque Nacional Los Cardones (see below).

Quilmes
This pre-Hispanic pucará, in Tucumán province only 50 km south of Cafayate, is probably Argentina's most extensive preserved ruins. Dating from about 1000 AD, Quilmes was a complex urban settlement covering about 30 hectares, which housed perhaps 5000 people. The Quilmes Indians abided contact with the Incas, but could not outlast the Spaniards who, in 1667, deported the last 2000 to Buenos Aires.

Quilmes' thick walls underscore its defensive functions, but evidence of dense occupation sprawls north and south of the nucleus. Allow at least half a day to climb the slopes (for revealing views of the form, density and extent of the ruins) and explore the surrounding area.

Camping is possible near the small museum, where a payment of US$1.50 admits you to the ruins. Buses from Cafayate to Santa María pass the junction, but from there, it's five km to the ruins by foot or thumb.

SAN ANTONIO DE LOS COBRES
In colonial times, pack trains to Peru usually took the Quebrada de Humahuaca, but an alternative crossed the Puna de Atacama to the Pacific and thence to Lima. For travellers on this route, bleak San Antonio (altitude 3700 metres) must have seemed an oasis. Well into this century, it was a stopover for drovers moving stock to Chile's nitrate mines, but railways and roads have supplanted mules.

San Antonio, a largely Indian town with posters and political graffiti that tell you it's still part of Argentina, has neither luxury accommodation nor up-market food. What you see is what you get, which is basic lodging at *Hospedaje Belgrano* or *Hospedaje Los Andes* (about US$6 per person with shared bath). Hospedaje Los Andes has a restaurant.

Getting There & Away
There are five weekly buses from Salta (US$12, four hours) with El Quebradeño. See the El Tren a las Nubes entry for details of the train from Salta to San Antonio and beyond.

Tren a las Nubes
From Salta's Lerma valley, the Tren a las Nubes (Train to the Clouds) makes countless switchbacks and spirals to ascend the Quebrada del Toro and reach the heights of the puna. Its highlight is the La Polvorilla viaduct across a broad desert canyon, a magnificent engineering achievement unjustified on any economic grounds.

Movitren (☎ 21-6394, fax 31-1264), Caseros 441 in Salta, operates the newly privatised Tren a las Nubes. Except in the wet summer, it leaves every Saturday at 7 am and returns late in the evening. The US$100 fare does not include meals, which cost around US$10.

Freight Trains A cheaper way to experience this railway journey is to take one of the weekly freight trains that go as far as the Chilean border station at Socompa (3900 metres). From Socompa, a Chilean freight train goes to Baquedano (Chile), about 100 km from Antofagasta on the Ruta Panamericana. This segment is not for the squeamish – the Chilean crew is unfriendly and the train truly filthy. Purchase Chilean pesos before leaving Salta to pay for the ticket, which is not guaranteed.

At Socompa, clear Argentine and Chilean immigration before asking permission to ride the train – and expect to wait several days. It descends through vast deserts to the abandoned station of Augusta Victoria, where you may disembark to try hitching to Antofagasta – mining trucks are almost certain to stop. Otherwise, sleep in the abandoned station until the train returns.

PARQUE NACIONAL LOS CARDONES
Only 100 km from Salta, 70,000-hectare Los Cardones is named for the cardón cactus (*Trichocereus pasacana*), a key source of timber for native construction and colonial churches. Pending finalisation of park status, it has no visitor services, but buses on the winding highway over the Cuesta del Obispo from Salta to Cachi pass through it. It is the most easily accessible of Salta's three national parks.

PARQUE NACIONAL FINCA EL REY
Parque Nacional Finca El Rey, almost directly east of Salta, is the most southerly park protecting Argentina's subtropical humid forests. Its emblem is the giant toucan. Most of the mammals found in Calilegua are also found here. The staff maintains a vehicular nature trail along the Río Popayán, and a foot trail is planned. For up-to-date information and reservations, contact the Calilegua visitors' centre (☎ 22046).

Access is difficult, and in the wet summer, only 4WD vehicles can pass. Turismo Mallorca in Salta arranges excursions.

TUCUMÁN
In 1816, San Miguel de Tucumán hosted the congress which declared Argentine independence. Unlike Salta and Jujuy, it successfully reoriented its post-independence economy, as it was just close enough to Buenos Aires to take advantage of the federal capital's growing market for sugar, thanks in part to the railway.

Tucumán still preserves notable colonial remnants near Plaza de la Independencia. In the suburb of Yerba Buena, the Sierra de Aconquija offers good hiking on gaucho stock trails. Tucumán's Independence Day (9 July) celebrations are especially vigorous.

Information
The tourist office (☎ 21-8591), Avenida 24 de Setiembre 484, keeps long hours but lacks maps and brochures. Maguitur, San Martín 765, cashes travellers' cheques for a 2% commission. ENCOTEL is at Avenida 25 de

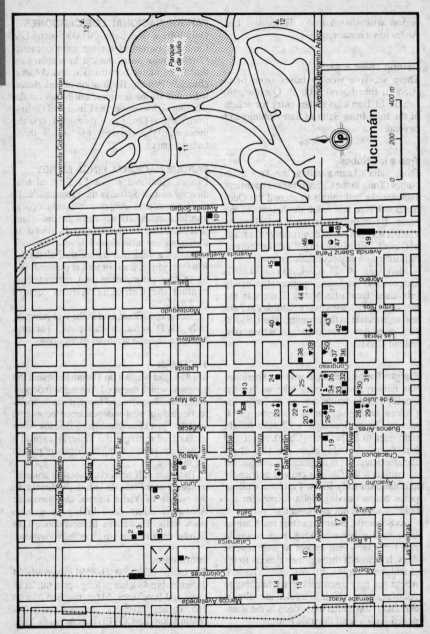

Parque 9 de Julio

Tucumán

0   200   400 m

Avenida Gobernador del Campo

Avenida Benjamin Aráoz

Avenida Soldati

Avenida Avellaneda

Avenida Sáenz Peña

Balcarce

Moreno

Monteagudo

Entre Ríos

Rivadavia

Las Heras

Lamadrid

Congreso

25 de Mayo

9 de Julio

Muñecas

Buenos Aires

España

Avenida Sarmiento

Santa Fe

Marcos Paz

Corrientes

Santiago del Estero

Maipú

San Juan

Córdoba

Mendoza

San Martín

Avenida 24 de Setiembre

Crisóstomo Alvarez

Chacabuco

Ayacucho

Junín

Salta

Jujuy

La Rioja

San Lorenzo

Las Piedras

Catamarca

Colombres

Alberdi

Marcos Avellaneda

Bernabé Aráoz

■ PLACES TO STAY

2	Hotel Norte
3	Hotel California
5	Hotel Tucumán
6	Hotel Miami
7	Residencial Viena
10	Gran Hotel de Tucumán
12	Municipal Camp Sites
14	Residencial Roni
15	Residencial Royal
19	Residencial Florida
24	Hotel Plaza
27	Hotel Metropol
28	Hotel Premier
32	Hotel Francia
36	Hotel Congreso/Hotel Astoria
38	Hotel del Sol
42	Hotel Impala
44	Residencial Independencia
45	Hotel Colonial
46	Hospedaje la Estrella
48	Residencial El Parque

▼ PLACES TO EAT

16	Sociedad Italiana
39	Feria de Artesanos Tucumanos
50	Adela

OTHER

1	Mitre Station
4	Plaza Alberdi
8	Telecom
9	Post Office
11	Casa de Obispo Colombres
13	Centro Cultural de la Universidad Nacional de Tucumán
17	ACA (Auto Club; Travel Agency)
18	Maguitur (Casa de Cambio)
20	Museo Folklórico Manuel Belgrano
21	Casa Padilla
22	Casa de Gobierno
23	Iglesia San Francisco
25	Plaza Independencia
26	Austral (Airline)
29	Iglesia Santo Domingo
30	Aerolíneas Argentinas
31	Casa Histórica
33	Museo de Bellas Artes
34	Tourist Office
35	Catedral
37	Museo Histórico de la Provincia
40	Casa de la Cultura Lola Mora
41	Iglesia la Merced
43	Museo Iramain
47	Bus Terminal
49	Belgrano Station

Mayo and Córdoba. Telecom is at Maipú 480.

Things to See
Museums There are collections of Argentine sculpture and painting at **Museo Iramain**, Entre Ríos 27, open on weekdays from 9 am to 1 pm. Other art museums include the **Museo de Bellas Artes**, Avenida 9 de Julio 44, open daily (except Monday) from 9 am to noon and 5.30 to 8.30 pm, and the **Museo de Arte Sacro**, at the Catedral, open Monday to Saturday from 10 am to noon.

President Nicolás Avellaneda once lived in the **Museo Histórico de la Provincia**, at Congreso 56, open on weekday mornings from 9 am to 12.30 pm, and every afternoon from 5 to 8 pm. For regional prehistory, the **Museo Arqueológico**, at Avenida 25 de Mayo 265, is open on weekdays from 8 am

to noon and 4 to 8 pm. The **Museo Folklórico Manuel Belgrano**, Avenida 24 de Septiembre 565, features horse gear, indigenous musical instruments and weavings, plus samples of *randa* lace. It's open Tuesday to Friday from 9 am to 12 noon, on other days 5.30 to 8.30 pm. Admission is US$1.

Casa de la Independencia On 9 July 1816, Unitarist lawyers and clerics declared independence in this whitewashed colonial house at Congreso 151. Portraits of the delegates line the walls of the room where the signing took place. The house is open Tuesday to Friday from 8.30 am to 1.30 pm, and on weekends from 9 am to 1 pm. Admission is US$1.

Casa de Obispo Colombres In Parque 9 de Julio, this 18th-century house contains

Tucumán's primitive first *trapiche* (sugar mill). Hours are 9 am to 12.30 pm and 3 to 6.30 pm on weekdays, 9 am to 6 pm on weekends. Admission is US$1. Guided tours are available.

Mercado de Abasto Photographers especially should not miss this wholesale/retail market, where brightly painted horsecarts unload produce from the countryside. Liveliest in the mid to late afternoon, it's about one km west of the centre, at San Lorenzo and Miguel Lillo. Market cafés have cheap meals.

Places to Stay

For *Camping Las Lomitas*, in Parque 9 de Julio, take bus No 1 from Crisóstomo Alvarez down Avenida Benjamín Aráoz, past the university. Fees are roughly US$2 per person plus US$1 per tent.

Near the Mitre station, try shabby but passable *Hotel Tucumán*, at Catamarca 563 (US$8/12 a single/double with shared bath). Near the bus terminal, check out friendly *Hospedaje La Estrella*, Avenida Benjamín Aráoz 36, where doubles are US$15. *Residencial Viena*, Santiago del Estero 1050, charges US$12/20 with private bath.

Residencial Petit, Crisóstomo Alvarez 765, has rooms with shared bath for US$11/18. For about US$24/32, *Hotel Colonial*, San Martín 35, comes very highly recommended.

Places to Eat

Best for cheap eats is the Mercado de Abasto (see above), but try also the Mercado del Norte, at Mendoza and Maipú. At the Feria de Artesanos Tucumanos, on Avenida 24 de Setiembre, half a block from Plaza Independencia, a variety of small stands prepare tasty regional specialities.

For pasta, try the *Sociedad Italiana*, Avenida 24 de Setiembre 1021. *Adela*, across from the Feria de Artesanos, has Middle Eastern food. One reader has praised *El Duque*, San Lorenzo 440.

Getting There & Away

Air Aerolíneas Argentinas (☎ 31-1747), Avenida 9 de Julio 112, flies to Buenos Aires (US$183) daily except Saturday. Austral (☎ 22-4920), Avenida 24 de Setiembre 546, also flies daily to Buenos Aires, stopping in Córdoba (US$74) on weekends.

Bus From the bus terminal, at the corner of avenidas Sáenz Peña and Benjamín Aráoz, a short walk from Plaza Independencia, Panamericano heads north to Salta and Jujuy (US$18), and south to Córdoba. La Estrella goes daily to Mendoza via Catamarca and La Rioja.

El Rayo crosses the Chaco to Roque Sáenz Peña, Resistencia and Corrientes. Empresa Itatí goes to Posadas, Puerto Iguazú (US$61) and Buenos Aires (US$55, 20 hours). Chevallier serves Rosario, Córdoba and Buenos Aires.

Aconquija has morning and afternoon buses to Tafí del Valle (US$7). La Unión and El Ranchilleño have several buses daily to Termas de Río Hondo (US$5) and Santiago del Estero (US$8).

Getting Around

The airport bus leaves from the Austral office. City buses do not accept cash, so buy cospeles at downtown kiosks.

TAFÍ DEL VALLE

South-west of Tucumán, Ruta 307 snakes up a narrow gorge; in places, a single vehicle can barely pass. About 100 km from Tucumán, it opens onto a misty valley where, in summer, Tucumanos seek relief in the cool heights around Tafí del Valle. Beyond Tafí, the road zigzags over the 3050-metre Abra del Infiernillo, an alternative route to Cafayate and Salta.

At 2000 metres, a temperate island in a subtropical sea, Tafí produces seed potatoes and fruits (apples, pears and peaches) for Tucumán, and pastures cattle, sheep and, at higher altitudes, llamas. There's a helpful tourist office at the Centro Cívico.

A short distance from town, the restored 18th-century Jesuit **Capilla La Banda** contains a museum and an artisans' market. At **Parque Los Menhires**, at the south end of La Angostura reservoir, over 80 aboriginal granite monuments, collected from various archaeological sites, resemble the standing stones of the Scottish Hebrides.

Residencial El Cumbre, Diego de Roca 120, charges US$11 per person for rooms with shared bath. If the municipal campground has not reopened, there is a free site, with picnic tables, just outside its entrance. Aconquija has two buses daily from Tucumán, but hitching is difficult.

SANTIAGO DEL ESTERO

Founded in 1553, 170 km south-east of Tucumán, Argentina's oldest city (population 150,000) was a stopover between the Pampas and the mines of Bolivia. Both city and province rely on cotton, and irrigation supplements undependable rainfall.

Avenida Libertad bisects the city from south-west to north-east. On either side of Plaza Libertad, the peatonal Avenida Tucumán and Avenida Independencia are important commercial areas. Avenida Belgrano is the main thoroughfare.

Information

The Dirección Provincial de Turismo (☎ 21-4243), Avenida Libertad 417, is open on weekdays from 7 am to 1 pm and 4 to 9 pm. Noroeste Cambio, on Avenida 24 de Setiembre between Avenida 9 de Julio and Urquiza, changes cash but not travellers' cheques. ENCOTEL is at Buenos Aires and Urquiza. Telecom is on Mendoza between Independencia and Buenos Aires.

Things to See

A friendly staff offer free guided tours of the **Museo Wagner's** well-presented collection of fossils, funerary urns and Chaco ethnography. At Avellaneda 355, it's open on weekdays from 7 am to 1 pm. Exhibits at the **Museo Histórico Provincial**, Urquiza 354, emphasise postcolonial history. It's open on weekdays from 8 am to noon.

Places to Stay & Eat

At shady *Campamento Las Casuarinas*, in Parque Aguirre, less than one km from Plaza Libertad, fees are US$2 per vehicle, plus US$1.50 per person and per tent.

Residencial Santa Rita, Santa Fe 273, has singles/doubles with shared bath for US$9/13. Tiny *Residencial Emaus*, Moreno Sur 673, is friendly and spotlessly clean (US$15/19).

The *Comedor Universitario*, Avellaneda 364, has cheap if uninspiring food, but offers a chance to meet local students. Meals at the *Comedor Centro de Viajantes*, Buenos Aires 37, are better and reasonably priced. For other restaurants and confiterías, look around Plaza Libertad.

Getting There & Away

Air Aerolíneas Argentinas (☎ 22-4088), Buenos Aires 60, flies to Buenos Aires (US$156) daily, except Tuesday and Thursday.

Bus From the bus terminal, at Pedro Gallo and Saavedra eight blocks south of Plaza Libertad, La Unión has 14 buses daily to Río Hondo (US$4, one hour), continuing to Tucumán (US$8). Panamericano goes north to Salta (US$26) and Jujuy (US$29, seven hours).

Cacorba has five buses daily to Córdoba (US$21, five hours) and one daily to Buenos Aires (US$47, 16 hours). Chevallier, slightly cheaper to Buenos Aires, has two daily buses to Rosario (US$28). La Estrella serves Santa Fe (US$33), Paraná (US$36) and Mar del Plata (US$58). El Rayo crosses the Chaco to Roque Sáenz Peña (US$20), Resistencia (US$24), Corrientes (US$26, nine hours) and Puerto Iguazú (US$54).

Libertador goes three times weekly to La Rioja (US$19), San Juan (US$36) and Mendoza (US$42). Bosio goes daily to Catamarca (US$16).

Getting Around

Walking suffices for almost everything, except connections to the airport (reached by bus No 19).

LA RIOJA

La Rioja, the capital of the province of the same name, is the home of historical figures including caudillo Facundo Quiroga and intellectual Joaquín V González, founder of La Plata university. Though not thriving economically, the region is politically influential – President Carlos Menem, something of a modern-day caudillo, is a Riojano.

The city was founded by Juan Ramírez de Velasco in 1591, 154 km south of Catamarca at the base of the Sierra del Velasco. It was originally called Todos los Santos de la Nueva Rioja. An 1894 earthquake destroyed many buildings, but the restored commercial centre, near Plaza 25 de Mayo, replicates colonial style.

Information

The Dirección General de Turismo (☎ 28834), open from 6.30 am to 9.30 pm at Avenida Perón and Urquiza, has a good city map and brochures. Most travel agencies will change cash dollars. ENCOTEL is at Avenida Perón 764. Telecom is at Pelagio Luna and Joaquín V González.

Things to See

The **Museo Folklórico**, which is in a re-created 19th-century house, displays ceramic reproductions of mythological figures from local folklore. At Pelagio Luna 811, it's open Tuesday to Sunday from 8 am to noon and 4 to 8 pm.

Over 12,000 pieces, from tools and artefacts to Diaguita ceramics and weavings, fill the **Museo Inca Huasi**, at Alberdi 650. The **Museo Histórico**, Adolfo Dávila 79, contains memorabilia of Facundo Quiroga.

Built by the Diaguita under Dominican overseers, the **Convento de Santo Domingo** (1623), at Pelagio Luna and Lamadrid, is the country's oldest. Indian artists also carved the algarrobo door frame.

The **Convento de San Francisco**, at Avenida 25 de Mayo and Bazán y Bustos, houses the Niño Alcalde, an important religious icon. The **Iglesia Catedral**, at San Nicolás and Avenida 25 de Mayo, contains the image of patron saint Nicolás de Bari, another devotional object.

Festivals

The 31 December ceremony **El Tinkunako** re-enacts San Francisco Solano's mediation between the Diaguitas and the Spaniards in 1593. For accepting peace, the Diaguitas imposed two conditions: resignation of the Spanish mayor and his replacement by the Niño Alcalde (see previous section).

Places to Stay & Eat

Parque Yacampis, at Avenida Ramírez de Velasco Km 3, has a shady, well-kept *camp-ground* with clean bathrooms and showers.

Residencial Sumaj Kanki, at Avenida Castro Barros and Coronel Lagos, has modest accommodation for US$6 a single, but can get noisy. Around the corner is *Residencial Petit*, Lagos 427, whose singles with bath (US$10) include kitchen and laundry privileges. *Residencial Margarita*, Perón 407, has small, dark but clean singles for US$7.50 with private bath.

For unique regional cuisine or standard Argentine dishes, try *Cavadini*, Avenida Quiroga 1135, *La Cantina de Juan*, Hipólito Yrigoyen 190, or *La Vieja Casona*, Rivadavia 427. *La Fragata*, Copiapó 235, serves basic dishes at reasonable prices. *Comedor de la Sociedad Española*, Avenida 9 de Julio 237, has tasty Spanish food, while *La Taverna de Don Carlos*, Rivadavia 459, serves Arab dishes.

Things to Buy

Typical mantas (bedspreads) feature floral patterns over a solid background. Also worthwhile are silverwork, religious objects and horse gear. The distinctive indigenous pottery uses local clay.

Getting There & Away

Air Aerolíneas Argentinas (☎ 24450), Belgrano 63, flies to Catamarca (US$28) and Buenos Aires (US$152) daily except Sunday. Aeropuerto Vicente Almonacíd is seven km east of La Rioja on Ruta 5.

Bus From the bus terminal (☎ 25453), at Artigas and España, El Cóndor serves provincial destinations, as well as Córdoba (US$19), Catamarca (US$8) and San Luis (US$22). COTIL serves Córdoba three times daily, plus local destinations like Chilecito and Chepes.

Expreso Nacate goes to San Juan three times weekly, while Transportes Libertador goes daily to Mendoza, San Juan, Catamarca and Tucumán (US$18), and three times weekly to Santiago del Estero (US$26).

ABLO goes to Córdoba, Santa Fe, San Luis, Buenos Aires and Mar del Plata. La Estrella goes to San Juan, Mendoza and Tucumán. Empresa General Urquiza has buses to Santa Fe and Buenos Aires.

CHILECITO
At one time, the provincial government relocated to Chilecito (population 20,000), 192 km north-west of La Rioja, to escape intimidation by Facundo Quiroga. Wine, walnuts and olives have superseded mining in the local economy.

The tourist office (☎ 2688), at Libertad and Independencia, has enthusiastic staff and good material. ENCOTEL is at González and Mitre, while Telecom is at Castro y Bazán 27.

Things to See
The **Museo Molino de San Francisco**, a colonial flour mill at Ocampo 63, is an eclectic assemblage of antique weapons, colonial documents, pre-Columbian tools, minerals, wood and leather crafts, and weavings and paintings. Hours are Tuesday to Sunday from 8 am to noon and 3 to 7 pm.

Samay Huasi, Joaquín V González's country home, has a natural sciences museum and a collection of Argentine painting. Three km from Chilecito past La Puntilla, it's open daily (except Monday) from 8 am to noon and 3 to 7 pm.

The Cooperativa La Riojana, La Plata 246, is open on weekdays for tours and **wine-tasting**.

Places to Stay & Eat
The tourist office keeps a list of casas de familia, which start around US$6 per person. At Libertad 68, *Residencial Americano* has singles/doubles with shared bath for US$8/14. Very central *Residencial Wamatinac*, Avenida 25 de Mayo 19, and *Residencial Riviera*, Castro Barros 133, are a bit dearer.

Restaurant Club Arabe, at Avenida 25 de Mayo and Santa Rosa, is top quality, despite its limited menu. *Listo El Pollo*, at Pelagio Luna 30, and *El Quincho*, J V González 50, serve parrillada. *El Gallo*, at Libertad and Illia, and *Toscanini*, at San Martín and Santa Rosa, offer standard menus.

Getting There & Away
COTIL goes daily to Villa Unión and La Rioja, while ABLO travels to Rosario and Buenos Aires.

PARQUE PROVINCIAL TALAMPAYA
Locals compare scenic Talampaya, a 270,000-hectare reserve, to Arizona's Grand Canyon. It is also an important paleontological and archaeological site, but only authorised guides may offer two-hour 4WD tours (US$20 for up to six persons) from the visitors' centre. With prior arrangements at the tourist office in Chilecito, it's possible to take a longer excursion that traverses the entire canyon, and also to trek and hike.

CATAMARCA
San Fernando del Valle de Catamarca, settled only in 1683, has remained an economic backwater, but major holidays attract many visitors. Flanked by the Sierra del Colorado in the west and the Sierra Graciana in the east, it is 156 km north-east of La Rioja. The shady Plaza 25 de Mayo offers refuge from summer heat in an otherwise treeless city.

Information
The municipal tourist office (☎ 24721), open 7 am to 1 pm and 2 to 8 pm at Urquiza 951, has knowledgeable staff but few materials. Around the corner on General Roca, the Dirección Provincial de Turismo is also

helpful. Banks, travel agencies and some hotels will change cash. ENCOTEL is at San Martín 753. Telecom, Rivadavia 758, is painfully slow arranging international calls.

Things to See

The neocolonial **Iglesia y Convento de San Francisco**, at Esquiú and Rivadavia, contains the cell of Fray Mamerto Esquiú, famous for vocal defence of the constitution. Some years ago, thieves stole a crystal box containing his heart and left it on the church's roof; it's now kept in a locked room.

Tedious presentation undermines outstanding materials in the three collections of the **Museo Arqueológico Adán Quiroga**, on Sarmiento 1½ blocks north of the plaza. Hours are 8 am to 1 pm and 2.30 to 8 pm on weekdays, 8 am to noon on weekends. Opposite the plaza, the **Catedral** contains the Virgen del Valle, one of northern Argentina's most venerated images.

Festivals

On the Sunday after Easter, thousands of pilgrims arrive to honor the Virgen del Valle in the **Fiesta de Nuestra Señora del Valle**. At the end of the *novena* (nine days of prayer), the Virgin is taken in procession around the plaza.

Places to Stay & Eat

By the Río El Tala, about four km from the centre, *Autocamping Municipal* is a pleasant spot, despite noisy weekend crowds and ferocious mosquitos. Rates are US$5 per tent per day. Take bus No 10 from Convento de San Francisco, on Esquiú, or from the bus terminal, on Vicario Segura.

The tourist office has a list of casas de familia. A nameless *pensión* at Tucumán 1294, near the bus terminal, has clean singles with shared bath (no hot water) for US$5. *Residencial Yunka Suma*, Vicario Segura 1255, is good value, at US$7 per person with bath. Modest *Pensión Molina*, Vicente Saadi 721, charges US$9 per person.

In the gallery behind the Catedral, *Comedor El Peregrino* serves cheap empanadas and pasta. *Restaurante y Parrilla La*

Abuela, on Sarmiento near Hotel Ancasti, is also inexpensive. *Rancho Chirot*, Vicente Saadi 750, has a plentiful parrillada for two with salad and wine for US$10; at night, it has folk music. *La Tinaja*, Sarmiento 533, also has music and low prices.

Things to Buy

For hand-tied rugs, visit the Mercado Artesanal Permanente y Fábrica de Alfombras, at Urquiza 945; see the rugmakers at work on weekdays from 7 am to noon. The market also sells ponchos, blankets, jewellery, onyx sculptures, musical instruments, hand-spun wool, and baskets.

Getting There & Away

Air Aeropuerto Felipe Varela is 22 km east of town on Ruta 33. Aerolíneas Argentinas (☎ 24450), at Sarmiento and Esquiú, flies to La Rioja and Buenos Aires (US$152) daily, except Sunday.

Bus From the terminal, Avenida Güemes 856, Chevallier has two evening buses to Buenos Aires (US$62) via Córdoba (US$23) and Rosario. Cacorba serves the same routes.

COTIL has buses to the Sierras de Córdoba via La Rioja and Chilecito. Bosio serves Tucumán (six buses daily), Salta, La Rioja, San Juan, Mendoza and Santiago del Estero.

Patagonia

Patagonia is the enormous region beyond Buenos Aires province, south of the Río Colorado to the Straits of Magellan. Beyond the Straits, Argentina and Chile share the archipelago of Tierra del Fuego. Glaciers dot the mountainous interior of Río Negro and Neuquén provinces, which stretch all the way to the Atlantic. Colonial Carmen de Patagones is a worthwhile stopover for southbound coastal travellers. Santa Cruz province features the Moreno Glacier and the pinnacles of the Fitz Roy range. Near the Andean divide, forests of southern beech,

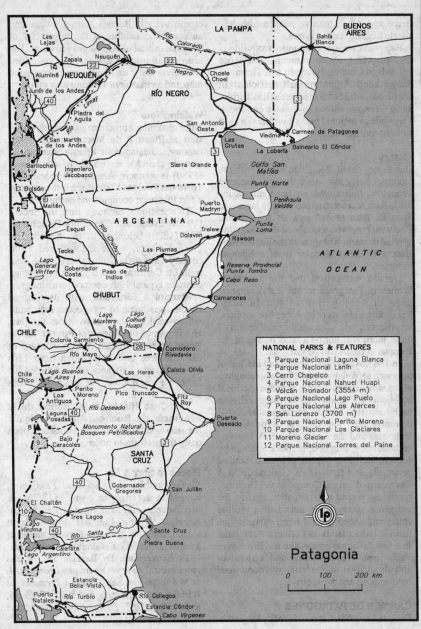

NATIONAL PARKS & FEATURES

1 Parque Nacional Laguna Blanca
2 Parque Nacional Lanín
3 Cerro Chapelco
4 Parque Nacional Nahuel Huapi
5 Volcán Tronador (3554 m)
6 Parque Nacional Lago Puelo
7 Parque Nacional Los Alerces
8 San Lorenzo (3700 m)
9 Parque Nacional Perito Moreno
10 Parque Nacional Los Glaciares
11 Moreno Glacier
12 Parque Nacional Torres del Paine

Patagonia

0   100   200 km

alerce and the distinctive pehuén (monkey puzzle tree) cover the slopes.

Patagonia's major economic institution is the sprawling sheep estancia, but large oilfields in Chubut, Neuquén and Tierra del Fuego keep Argentina self-sufficient in petroleum, while coal reserves at Río Turbio, Santa Cruz, are among few on the continent. The Andean national parks have encouraged a major tourism industry.

History

One theory credits Magellan's crew with the toponym Patagonia, after they encountered Tehuelche Indians whose large moccasins made their feet seem exceptionally large – in Spanish, *pata* means paw or foot. Bruce Chatwin, however, speculated that Magellan applied the term 'Patagon' to the Tehuelches, after a fictional monster from a Spanish romance.

Darwin recognised that the arrival of Whites in Patagonia meant the disappearance or subjugation of the Indians. Recording a massacre by Argentine soldiers, he observed that '... in another half century I think there will not be a wild Indian in the Pampas north of Río Negro'.

In 1863, Argentina offered land in Chubut province to Welsh nationalists who sought a place where they could exercise political autonomy and retain their language, religion and identity. Welsh surnames are still common here, and cultural traditions like teahouses and the *Eisteddfod* (folk festival) endure, but young people speak Spanish by preference. The Welsh colonists settled peaceably, but from 1879, General Julio A Roca carried out the Conquista del Desierto, a ruthless war of extermination against the indigenes. Soon, more than half a million cattle and sheep grazed large estancias on former Indian lands in northern Patagonia. In a few favoured zones, like the Río Negro valley near Neuquén, irrigated agriculture and the arrival of the railway encouraged colonisation and prosperity.

CARMEN DE PATAGONES

Founded in 1799, Carmen is really the south-ernmost city in Buenos Aires province and an economic satellite of the larger city of Viedma, capital of Río Negro province. The municipal tourist office, at Comodoro Rivadavia and 7 de Marzo, provides a good map and an excellent walking tour guide.

Walking Tour

After obtaining a brochure (in Spanish only), start at **Plaza 7 de Marzo**. In the 19th-century, Salesian-built **Iglesia Parroquial** (parish church), an image of the Virgin (1780) is southern Argentina's oldest. The **Torre del Fuerte** (1780) is the last vestige of a fort that once occupied the entire block.

Two antique cannons line the recent (1960s) **Escalinata**. The adobe **Rancho de Rial** (1820) belonged to the town's first elected mayor, while the restored 19th-century **Casa de la Cultura** was once a flour mill. **La Carlota**, named for its last owner, contains typical 19th-century furnishings.

Mazzini & Giraudini, with its restored façade, was home to prosperous merchants who owned the shop across from the pier, and is part of the **Zona del Puerto**. At the **Solar Natal de Piedra Buena** is a bust of naval officer and Patagonian hero Luis Piedra Buena. This area once included his father's general store, bar and naval stores supply.

The **Casa Histórica del Banco de la Provincia de Buenos Aires**, originally housing naval stores, is now a museum, open daily from 10 am to noon.

Places to Stay & Eat

Singles/doubles at *Residencial Patagones*, Rivadavia and Irigoyen, cost US$18/26; ask for cheaper multibed rooms. *Residencial Reggiani*, Bynon 422, has doubles with shared bath for US$19. Tiny *Residencial Strauss*, Italia 393, has doubles for US$24.

El Entrerriano, Dr Barajas 368, is the most central eatery. Others are *Leonardo I*, at M Crespo and San Juan, *La Terminal*, at Barbieri and Bertorello, and *Koki's Pizzería*, at Rivadavia 367. *La Confitería*, Rivadavia 218, is a pleasant café.

Getting There & Away

The bus terminal (☎ 62666) is at Barbieri and Méjico. Two bridges and a launch cross the river to Viedma, where connections are better.

VIEDMA

In 1779, Francisco de Viedma founded this city (population 40,000) on the Río Curru Leuvu (Río Negro), 30 km from the Atlantic; a century later, it became the administrative centre of Argentina's southern territories. Controversial plans to move the federal capital here in the 1980s never materialised.

Information

Open from 7 am to 1 pm, and 5 pm to midnight in summer, the municipal tourist office is on Plaza Alsina. The provincial tourist office (☎ 22150), at Costanera Avenida Francisco de Viedma 57, has a wider range of information.

Banco Hipotecario is on Sarmiento at Avenida 25 de Mayo. Banco Provincia is at the Centro Cívico. Travel agencies may also change money. ENCOTEL is at Rivadavia 151, Telefónica at Mitre 531.

Places to See

The **Museo Cardenal Cagliero**, Rivadavia 34, chronicles the Salesian catechisation of Patagonian Indians. At the **Museo del Río Negro**, on the Costanera Avenida Villarino, the Fundación Ameghino has organised an interesting display on the river's natural history. The **Museo Gobernador Eugenio Tello**, San Martín 263, is also a research centre in architecture, archaeology, physical and cultural anthropology and geography.

Places to Stay & Eat

Beware mosquitos at the riverside *Camping Municipal* (US$1.50 per person and US$2 per tent). *Hospedaje Buenos Aires*, Buenos Aires 153, is cheap but basic. Clean, friendly *Hostería Roma*, Avenida 25 de Mayo 174, charges US$15/20 for singles/doubles, and has good, inexpensive food. *Hostería Roca*, Roca 347, is worth trying (US$18/26).

Getting There & Away

Air Aerolíneas Argentinas (☎ 22018), on San Martín between Saavedra and Colón, flies directly from Buenos Aires (US$134) on Monday, Wednesday and Friday. LADE (☎ 24420), Saavedra 403, flies to Trelew (US$26), Neuquén (US$38), Esquel (US$56) and Comodoro Rivadavia (US$52).

Bus From the terminal (☎ 22748), at Zatti 350, La Puntual goes daily to Buenos Aires (US$41) and south along Ruta 3. La Estrella/El Cóndor has buses to Buenos Aires and to Bariloche.

LA LOBERÍA

Commercial slaughter once threatened this colony of southern sea lions *(Otaria flavescens)*, 60 km from Viedma on the Golfo San Matías, but a reserve has encouraged conservation, education and research. In the spring mating season, males establish harems of up to 10 females, who give birth from December on. Numerous coastal birds frequent the area, while dunes offer habitat for guanacos and other mammals. Camping is possible at a nearby beach, with sanitary facilities and a store.

BARILOCHE

In San Carlos de Bariloche, 460 km southwest of Neuquén, architect Ezequiel Bustillo adapted Middle European styles into an attractive urban plan, but commercial development and apartment blocks have obliterated quaint neighbourhoods and crowded Lago Nahuel Huapi's shoreline. Crowds and traffic are intolerable in the winter ski season and in summer, but the city is a good base for exploring Parque Nacional Nahuel Huapi.

At an altitude of 770 metres, the city has a fairly standard grid between the Río Ñireco and Bustillo's Centro Cívico; north-south streets rise steeply from the lake. The major commercial zone is Avenida Bartolomé Mitre.

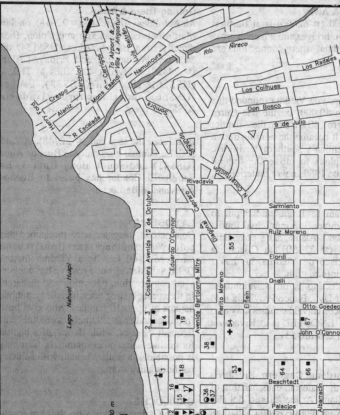

Bariloche

Lago Nahuel Huapi

500 m
250
0

To La Selva Negra
Campground &
Llao Llao

■ PLACES TO STAY	▼ PLACES TO EAT	20 Buses Cooperativa El
2 Hotel Pilmayquén	8 Confitería El Viejo	Valle, Don Otto, TAC
4 Hostería El Nire	Munich	& Bus Norte
12 Hotel Interlaken	10 Caffe Status	22 Telefónica
16 Residencial Sur	11 Pizzería Pin 9	23 ENCOTEL
18 Hostería Piuké	13 Restaurant Familia	24 Municipal Tourist Office
19 Residencial Tito	Weiss	27 Buses TIRSA
29 Hotel Internacional	14 Confitería Copos	28 Casa Piano
38 Hospedaje El Mirador	15 Restaurant Mangiare	30 Aerolíneas Argentinas
39 Hotel Aconcagua	17 El Mundo de la Pizza	& LADE
40 Residencial Elisabeth	21 Helados Bari	31 Buses Charter
41 Hotel Edelweiss	25 Confitería Cocodrilo's	32 Paseo de los Artesa-
47 Residencial Nogaré	26 Pizzería La Andinita	nos, Provincial
56 Residencial Campana	33 Restaurant Jauja	Tourist Office &
57 Hotel Carlos V	42 Restaurant Oriente	Spanish Consulate
58 Residencial Nikola	Jabalí	34 Airport Mini
59 El Ciervo Rojo	46 Restaurant La Alpina	Buses/Turismo
61 La Casa Nogueira	49 Restaurant Villegas	Catedral
(Residencial)	51 Restaurant La Vizca-	35 Local Bus Station
62 Residencial Wickter	cha	36 Buses La Estrella
63 Residencial Martín	55 Restaurant Chile	37 CATA
64 Hostería Ivalú/El Viejo	60 Parrilla 1810	43 Parques Nacionales
Aljibe		Office
65 Casa Familiar Arko	OTHER	44 Club Andino Bariloche
66 Casa Familiar		45 German Consulate
67 Residencial Torres	1 Catedral	48 Buses Chevallier &
68 Hospedaje Monte	3 ACA (Travel Agency)	Ko-Ko
Grande	5 Train Station	50 Salón Cultural de
	6 Museo de la Patagonia	USOS Múltiples
	7 TAN (Airline)	52 Chilean Consulate
	9 Austral (Airline)	53 Telefónica
		54 Hospital Zonal

Information

Tourist Office The municipal tourist office (☎ 23022) at the Centro Cívico, open from 8.30 am to 8 pm Monday to Saturday, has many giveaways, including the blatantly commercial but still useful *Guía Busch*. The Paseo de los Artesanos, at Perito Moreno and Villegas, has a smaller provincial office. The national parks office is at San Martín 24. Another good source of information on national parks is the Club Andino Bariloche (☎ 22266), Avenida 20 de Febrero 30.

Money Change cash or travellers' cheques at Casa Piano, Mitre 131.

Post & Telecommunications ENCOTEL is at the Centro Cívico. The best phone office is at Bariloche Center, San Martín and Pagano.

Chilean Consulate Open on weekdays from 9 am to 2 pm, the Chilean Consulate (☎ 23050) is at Rolando 310, 7th floor.

Centro Cívico

Recent construction has erased much of Bariloche's charm, but Bustillo's log-and-stone public buildings still merit a visit. Try morning or midday, before shadows from the tawdry casino block the sun.

On the Centro Cívico, the **Museo de la Patagonia** has lifelike natural history displays and well-prepared archaeological and ethnographic materials. Historical exhibits acknowledge Mapuche resistance to the Conquista del Desierto, and have included a valuable photo display on Bariloche's urban development. The museum is open Tuesday to Saturday from 10 am to 12.30 pm and 2 to 7 pm, and on Sundays from 2 to 7 pm. Admission is US$2.

Skiing
In winter at least, most people come to Bariloche for skiing. Since the Cerro Catedral and Lado Bueno areas have been amalgamated, you can buy one ticket for both lifts.

Places to Stay
The municipal tourist office's computer has the current prices of everything from campgrounds and private houses to five-star hotels. Reasonable lodging is available even in high season, but the ambience is more pleasant outside town.

Camping Motorists can camp for nothing across from the ACA station, at Goedecke and Costanera 12 de Octubre, but signs prohibit tent camping (a rule rarely enforced). There are recent negative reports on *La Selva Negra*, three km west of town on the Llao Llao road, but the site has good facilities in an orchard setting for US$5 per person. There are three other sites toward Llao Llao. *Hostels*, at Belgrano 660 and on the Llao Llao road five km from town, are open only for summer and winter holidays.

A homey place at Emilio Frey 635 charges US$6 per person, with hot showers and cooking facilities. Similar possibilities include Señora Carlotta Baumann at Los Pioneros 860, Señora Arko at Güemes 671, and Señora Heydée at Martín Fierro 1525.

Friendly but often full, *Residencial Tito* at Eduardo O'Connor 745, charges US$10 a single. *Hospedaje El Mirador*, Moreno 658, costs US$8 per person with shared bath, US$10 with private bath. Appealing *Residencial Wickter*, Güemes 566, charges US$12.

Residencial Sur, at Beschtedt 101, has very large beds and very small rooms; US$12 per person includes a generous breakfast and private bath. *Hostería Ivalú* at

Frey 535, and *El Viejo Aljibe* at Frey 571, are attractive hillside hotels for US$15/23 single/double with breakfast.

Hostería El Ñire, Eduardo O'Connor 702, is equally attractive and more central, a block from the Catedral. Comparably priced *Hotel Pilmayquén*, Costanera 12 de Octubre 705, has lakeview rooms for US$25 per person.

Places to Eat
Despite its faults, Bariloche has fine dining. Check discount coupons in the *Guía Gastronómico Datos*, available free from the municipal tourist office.

Familia Weiss, Palacios 167, specialises in smoked game and fish; *Restaurant Villegas*, Villegas 363, emphasises trout. *Restaurant Oriente Jabalí*, San Martín 130, serves all the above, plus a Chinese buffet. *La Vizcacha*, a very reasonable parrilla at Rolando 279, has pleasant atmosphere and excellent service. *Restaurant La Alpina*, Moreno 98, has been recommended for good food, large portions and moderate prices.

Pizzas, ñoquis and ravioli are superb at *Restaurant Mangiare*, Palacios 150; try also the unusual orange and onion salad with cream. *Pin 9*, Rolando 118, has good pizza but small portions. Also try *La Andinita* at Mitre 56, *El Mundo de la Pizza* at Mitre 370, or *Pizzaiola* at Pagano 275. *Helados Bari*, a block from the Centro Cívico, at España 7, has outstanding ice cream.

Copos, open 24 hours at Mitre 392, has caffeine and fresh croissants at reasonable prices. *El Viejo Munich*, Mitre 102, serves complimentary peanuts with excellent draught beer.

Things to Buy
Del Turista and Fenoglio, facing each other on Mitre, are chocolate supermarkets and good places for a stand-up cup of coffee, hot chocolate or dessert. Local artisans display their wares in wool, wood, leather and other media at the Paseo de los Artesanos, at Villegas and Perito Moreno.

Getting There & Away
Air Aerolíneas Argentinas (☎ 22425) and

LADE (☎ 22355) are both at Mitre 199. Aerolíneas flies 10 times weekly to Buenos Aires (US$227) and twice weekly to Mendoza (US$150). LADE flies to Patagonian destinations like Esquel (US$20), Comodoro Rivadavia (US$45) and Río Gallegos (US$100).

Austral (☎ 23123), Rolando 157, flies daily to Buenos Aires. TAN (☎ 24869), Mitre 26, flies to San Martín de los Andes and Esquel, and to Puerto Montt (Chile). Two new airlines, CATA (☎ 20251) at Palacios 266, and SAPSE at the new Puerto San Carlos development, fly to Buenos Aires for around US$135.

Bus Most buses leave from downtown offices, some shared between several companies. Chevallier (☎ 23090), Perito Moreno 107, goes daily to Buenos Aires (US$85, 22 hours) via Santa Rosa. La Estrella (☎ 22140), Palacios 246, and El Valle (☎ 20188), San Martín 283, also go to Buenos Aires. El Valle's Friday service to Mar del Plata takes 24 hours (US$55).

TUS (☎ 24565), at Elflein and Rolando, goes twice weekly to Córdoba (24 hours). Don Otto, at San Martín 283, goes twice weekly to Río Gallegos via Esquel and Comodoro Rivadavia (US$74 for an 'agonising' 28-hour trip, says one reader).

Charter (☎ 21689), Perito Moreno 126, goes twice daily to El Bolsón (US$10, 3½ hours). Mercedes (☎ 26000), Mitre 161, does the same route daily, twice on Tuesday, continuing to Esquel via El Maitén (US$28, nine hours). Mercedes also goes twice daily to Neuquén (US$28) and thrice weekly to Mar del Plata (US$52).

TAC, also at San Martín 283, runs three buses weekly to Mendoza (US$71, 22 hours) via Zapala, San Rafael and Malargüe. Chevallier has a twice-weekly service to Rosario (US$66, 24 hours) via Santa Rosa; TIRSA (☎ 26076), Quaglia 197, is similar. La Puntual (☎ 22231), San Martín 283, goes to Viedma (US$28) on Monday and Friday.

Turismo Algarrobal (☎ 22774), at San Martín 459, and Mercedes both serve Villa La Angostura (US$6, two hours) at least

twice daily. They are also agents for TICSA's three weekly buses to San Luis and San Juan (US$74, 27 hours). Ko-Ko (☎ 23090), at Perito Moreno 107, and El Valle both have buses to San Martín de los Andes (US$17), some travelling via La Rinconada rather than on the scenic Siete Lagos route.

Fares to Puerto Montt (Chile) are about US$30 with Mercedes and Bus Norte (☎ 20188) at San Martín 283, TAS Choapa (☎ 22774) at San Martín 459, or Cruz del Sur (☎ 24163) at San Martín 453.

Getting Around

To/From the Airport Turismo Catedral, Mitre 399, runs minibuses to Bariloche airport.

Bus Starting at 11 am, Transporte Mercedes at Mitre 161 runs six buses daily to Cerro Catedral (US$3). Bus No 20 from Moreno and Rolando goes every 20 minutes to the resort of Llao Llao, while bus No 50 goes to Lago Gutiérrez. Bus No 10 also goes to Llao Llao via Colonia Suiza seven times daily, facilitating the Circuito Chico on public transport (see below under Parque Nacional Nahuel Huapi).

Car The usual car rental agencies include Avis (☎ 25371) at Libertad 124, A1 (☎ 22582) at San Martín 235, and Budget (☎ 22482) at Perito Moreno 46.

Bicycle For bicycles, try Baratta e Hijos (☎ 22930) at Belgrano 50, Pochi (☎ 26693) at Moreno 1035, or Ramírez (☎ 25229) at Avenida 9 de Julio 961.

PARQUE NACIONAL NAHUEL HUAPI

Lago Nahuel Huapi, a glacial relic over 100 km long, attracts so many people that its natural attributes are at risk, though native and introduced fish species still offer excellent sport. To the west, 3554-metre Tronador marks the Andean crest and the Chilean border. Valdivian forest covers the lower slopes, while in summer, wildflowers blanket alpine meadows.

Things to See & Do

Travel agencies offer tours of the **Circuito Chico** between Bariloche and Llao Llao, but you can do it easily on public transport. **Cerro Campanario's** chairlift offers a panoramic view of the lake, while Llao Llao's **Puerto Pañuelo** is the point of departure for the boat-bus excursion to Chile; some of the best hiking country is most accessible by this route.

From Llao Llao, continue to **Colonia Suiza**, whose modest confitería has excellent pastries. The road passes the trailhead to 2075-metre **Cerro López** (a four-hour climb), before returning to Bariloche. **Cerro Otto** (1405 metres) is an eight-km walk on a gravel road west from Bariloche, but a gondola also goes to the summit.

At **Cerro Catedral** (2400 metres), a ski centre 20 km west of Bariloche, chairlifts and a large cable car climb to a restaurant/confitería with excellent panoramas (US$15). Several trails begin here, including one to the Club Andino's Refugio Frey.

Volcán Tronador is a full-day trip up a one-way dirt road from Lago Mascardi (traffic goes up in the morning and down in the afternoon). You can approach the Club Andino's Refugio Meiling on foot from Laguna Frías, or camp at Pampa Linda.

Boats to **Isla Victoria** and **Parque Nacional Los Arrayanes** leave from Puerto Pañuelo, but you can visit Los Arrayanes more easily and cheaply from Villa La Angostura (see the entry below).

Activities

Fishing Fishing in Argentina's Andean-Patagonian parks, from Lago Puelo and Los Alerces in the south to Lanín in the north, attracts many visitors from mid-November to mid-April. Licences are available at the parks administration centre in Bariloche, where it is also possible to rent equipment. For details, contact the Club de Caza y Pesca (☎ 22403), at Costanera 12 de Octubre and Onelli, Bariloche.

Water Sports Sailboating, windsurfing, canoeing and kayaking are popular on Nahuel Huapi and other lakes and streams. For equipment, try Baruzzi (☎ 24922), at Urquiza 250, Bariloche.

Places to Stay

Beyond Bariloche, there are *campgrounds* at Lago Mascardi, Lago Los Moscos, Lago Roca, Lago Guillelmo and Pampa Linda. Ask permission from rangers to camp for free in some areas.

Alpine *refugios* charge US$8 per night, US$2 for day use and US$2 for kitchen privileges.

EL BOLSÓN

In south-east Río Negro, 130 km from Bariloche and 300 metres above sea level, rows of poplars shelter chacras devoted to hops, soft fruits like raspberries, and orchard crops like cherries and apples. El Bolsón's self-proclaimed status as a 'nonnuclear zone' and 'ecological municipality' is a pleasant relief from Bariloche's commercialism; instead of upper-class Porteños, El Bolsón invites backpackers.

Most services are on Avenida San Martín, which runs along the landmark, semi-oval Plaza Pagano, but major attractions are outside town.

Information

At the north end of Plaza Pagano, the tourist office (☎ 92204) has good maps and brochures, plus thorough information on accommodation, food, tours and services.

Banco Nación is across from Plaza Pagano, while Banco de la Provincia is just north of the tourist office. ENCOTEL is at Avenida San Martín 2608. The telephone cooperative is at the south end of Plaza Pagano.

Markets

On Thursdays and Saturdays in summer (Saturdays only for the rest of the year), local artisans sell their wares at the Feria Artesanal, at the south end of Plaza Pagano, from 10 am to 2 pm.

For fresh fruit and home-made jams and preserves, visit Cabaña Micó, a few blocks from the east end of General Roca. Other places for local sweets are Dulces del Dr Miklos, on Balcarce near Sarmiento, and La Soja, on Dorrego just off San Martín. Heladería Jauja, San Martín 2867, and Regionales Lida, San Martín 3440, sell chocolates.

Taller del Arte Sano, Sarmiento 2350, sells paintings, sculptures, wood carvings and unique furniture from 3 to 8 pm daily. Centro Artesanal Cumey Antu, San Martín 2020, sells Mapuche clothing and weavings. At the Cooperativa de Ceramistas, upstairs at General Roca and Saavedra, you can buy local ceramics and chat with potters from 2 to 9 pm.

Places to Stay & Eat
Riverside *Camping del Sol*, at the west end of Avenida Castelli, has hot showers and a small confitería (US$2.50 per person). The *youth hostel*, at Avenida San Martín 1360, is a reasonable alternative, and the tourist office keeps a long list of private houses.

Hospedaje Los Amigos, on Islas Malvinas, at the east end of Balcarce, charges US$5 per person, less for a tent in the garden. At *Residencial Edelweiss*, Angel del Agua 360, rates are US$6/9 a single/double with shared bath. *Residencial Lostra*, Sarmiento 3212, is slightly dearer.

Achachay is a reasonable parrilla, at San Martín and Bolívar. *Cerro Lindo*, San Martín 2526, has large, tasty pizzas, good music and friendly service. *Café Plaza*, San Martín 2557, is a first-class confitería. Gorge yourself on astoundingly good ice cream at *Heladería Jauja*, San Martín 2867.

Getting There & Away
Air LADE (☎ 92206), at Castello 3259, stops here on twice-weekly flights between Bariloche and Comodoro Rivadavia (US$40).

Bus Charter SRL, at San Martín 2536, and Mercedes and Don Otto, both at Perito Moreno 2377, go to Bariloche. Mercedes and Don Otto go to Esquel, sometimes via Parque Nacional Los Alerces. Mercedes also serves El Maitén, Neuquén, Mar del Plata and Buenos Aires.

AROUND EL BOLSÓN
Cabeza del Indio
On a ridge eight km west of town, this metamorphic formation resembles a profile of the 'noble savage'. Part of the trail traverses a narrow ledge with the best views of the formation, but an earlier junction gives better views of the Río Azul and Lago Puelo.

Cascada Mallín Ahogado
This waterfall on the Arroyo del Medio, a tributary of the Río Quemquemtreu, is 10 km north of town. At **Cerro Perito Moreno**, reached by a trail beyond the falls, a refugio offers lodging for US$4 (meals extra), and winter skiing.

Cerro Piltriquitrón
This granitic ridge dominates the landscape east of Bolsón. From the 1000-metre level, reached by road, an hour's walk leads to a refugio (US$4 per person, meals extra). Bring a sleeping bag.

Parque Nacional Lago Puelo
Only 15 km south of El Bolsón, this windy azure lake is suitable for water sports and camping (some sites are free). There are regular buses, but reduced Sunday services.

NEUQUÉN
At the confluence of the Limay and Neuquén rivers, 265 metres above sea level, this provincial capital (population 300,000) is an agricultural service centre for the Río Negro valley. East-west national Ruta 22 is the main highway through town, while the main north-south thoroughfare is Avenida Argentina (Avenida Olascoaga beyond the train station).

Information
At Félix San Martín 182, the tourist office is open on weekdays from 7 am to 9 pm, and on weekends from 7.30 am to 9.30 pm. Neuquén province has one of Argentina's

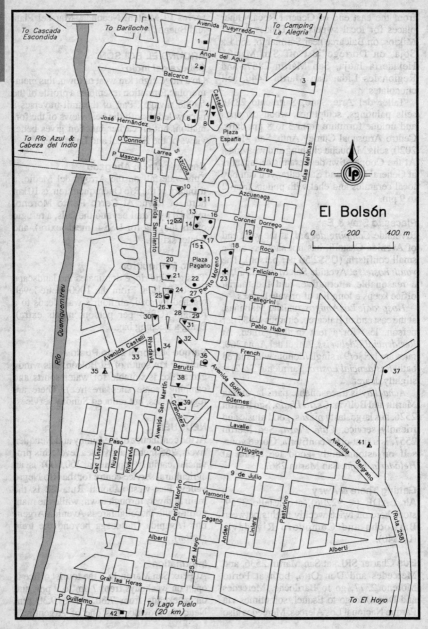

To Cascada Escondida

To Bariloche

Avenida Pueyrredón

To Camping La Alegria

Angel del Agua

Balcarce

José Hernández

To Río Azul & Cabeza del Indio

O'Connor

P Mascardi

Larrea

Castello

Plaza España

Islas Malvinas

Larrea

Azcuenaga

Coronel Dorrego

Roca

P Feliciano

Pellegrini

Pablo Hube

French

Güemes

Lavalle

O'Higgins

9 de Julio

Viamonte

Pagano

Anden

Liniers

Pastorino

Alberti

Alberti

Gral las Heras

P Guillelmo

To Lago Puelo (20 km)

To El Hoyo

(Ruta 258)

Avenida Belgrano

Avenida Bolivar

Berutti

Graciolls

Avenida San Martín

Perito Moreno

25 de Mayo

Cac Linares

Paso

Nuevo

Rivadavia

Avenida Castelli

Rivadavia

Avenida Sarmiento

Plaza Pagano

Perito Moreno

El Bolsón

0   200   400 m

■ PLACES TO STAY

1   Residencial Edelweiss
3   Hospedaje Los Amigos
6   Hotel Cordillera
8   Hotel Amancay
9   Residencial Lostra
35 Camping del Sol
39 La Posada de Hamelin
41 Camping La Chacra
42 Youth Hostel

▼ PLACES TO EAT

5   Restaurant Luigi
7   Restaurant Don Diego
10 Heladería Moni
13 Heladería Jauja
17 Confitería Ricar-Dos
20 Restaurant Viejo Maitén
21 Confitería Rivendel
26 Pizzería Cerro Lindo
28 Café Plaza
30 Restaurant El Candil
31 Restaurant Achachay
33 Restaurant Portal del Río
38 Restaurant El Rancho de Fernando

OTHER

2   Regionales Lida (Chocolates)
4   LADE (Airline)
11 Pulmari Turismo
12 Post Office
14 Banco de la Provincia del Río Negro
15 Tourist Office
16 La Soja
18 Municipalidad de El Bolsón
19 Cooperativa de Ceramistas
22 Feria Artesanal
23 Hospital
24 Banco de la Nación
25 Buses Charter SRL
27 Cooperativa Telefónica (Telephones)
29 Patagonia Adventure
32 ACA (Travel Agency)
34 Taller de Arte Sano
36 Buses Mercedes/Don Otto
37 Cabaña Micó
40 Centro Artesanal Cumey Antu

best tourist information services, with free, up-to-date maps and useful brochures.

Try Olano, at J B Justo 45, or Pullman, at Ministro Alcorta 163, for moneychanging.

ENCOTEL is at Rivadavia and Santa Fe. Telefónica is on Alberdi, between Santa Fe and Córdoba.

Provincial medical services are often free, so do not hesitate to consult the regional hospital (☎ 31474), at Buenos Aires 421.

Places to Stay & Eat

Residencial Ruca Puel, some distance from the centre at Coronel Suárez 1518, has singles/doubles for US$11/15. Comparably priced but more central is dingy *Hotel Imperio*, Yrigoyen 65. *Hotel Premier*, at Perito Moreno and Corrientes, has rooms with bath for US$14/20. *Hotel Charbel*, San Luis 268, charges about US$16/24.

Las Tres Marías, Alberdi 126, deserves special mention for its varied menu, reasonable prices, pleasant atmosphere and attentive service. *El Plato*, Alberdi 158, also has a good reputation. Confiterías along Avenida Argentina are fine for morning coffee.

Getting There & Away

Air Aerolíneas Argentinas (☎ 25087), at Avenida Argentina 16, flies daily to Buenos Aires (US$158). Austral (☎ 22409), Avenida Argentina 363, flies to Buenos Aires in the afternoons (except Sunday) and evenings.

LADE (☎ 22453), Almirante Brown 163, and TAN (☎ 23076), Avenida Argentina 383, serve Patagonian destinations like Bariloche, Esquel and Comodoro Rivadavia.

Bus From the terminal (☎ 24903), at Mitre 147, El Petróleo has regular services to Zapala (three hours), Junín de los Andes (six hours) and San Martín de los Andes (seven hours). El Valle runs the same routes, and to Bariloche, Mar del Plata and Buenos Aires. Andesmar connects Mendoza with Río Gallegos; Don Otto also goes to southern Patagonia. Alto Valle's Mendoza service costs about US$35. TUS goes to Córdoba.

Empresa Pehuenche goes to Buenos Aires via Santa Rosa; La Estrella also reaches Buenos Aires. La Unión del Sud and Empresa San Martín go to Villarrica and Temuco (Chile), via the Tromen pass.

Getting Around

Neuquén is a good province to explore by car, but some of Argentina's most dangerous drivers frequent Ruta 22, east along the Río Negro valley and west towards Zapala. Rental agencies include A1 (☎ 30362), at Avenida San Martín 1269, Avis (☎ 30216), at Avenida Argentina 363, Hertz (☎ 28872), at Leloir 639, and Rent Movil (☎ 20875), at La Pampa 462.

ZAPALA

Windy, dusty Zapala is an ordinary mining town, but a major crossroads east to Neuquén and north to Las Lajas, south-west to Junín and San Martín de los Andes, north to Chos Malal and west to Primeros Pinos.

The tourist office is a kiosk on the grassy median of Avenida San Martín, at Almirante Brown. Change money at Banco de la Provincia, Cháneton 460, open from 7 am to 1.30 pm. ENCOTEL is at Avenida San Martín and Cháneton, while Telefónica is at Italia 248.

Museo Olsacher

This private mineralogical museum at Olascoaga 421, south of the train station, contains over 3500 exhibits, including fossils, from 80 different countries. It's open from 4 pm on weekdays.

Places to Stay & Eat

Residencial Odetto, Ejército Argentino 455, has singles for about US$8 per person. *Residencial Coliqueo*, Etcheluz 165, and *Residencial Huincúl*, Avenida Roca 311, both have singles/doubles for about US$14/20.

Most residenciales and hotels have restaurants. *El Chancho Rengo*, at San Martín and Etcheluz, is good for a light lunch.

Getting There & Away

Air The airport is south of town, at the junction of rutas 40 and 46. LADE (☎ 21967), at Uriburu and Etcheluz, and TAN (☎ 21281), at San Martín and Cháneton, have infrequent flights.

Bus From the terminal (☎ 21370), at Etcheluz and Uriburu, El Petróleo goes direct to Buenos Aires (US$68) on Sundays; otherwise, change at Neuquén. It also goes twice daily to San Martín de los Andes and daily to Copahue, on the Chilean border. Chevallier goes daily to Buenos Aires.

In summer, Mutisia Viajes runs buses to Necochea and Mar del Plata (US$51). TICSA serves San Juan three times weekly, while TAC stops here three times weekly between Mendoza (US$45) and Bariloche (US$19). Four times weekly in summer, La Unión del Sud crosses the Andes to Temuco, Chile (US$40).

PARQUE NACIONAL LAGUNA BLANCA

Only 30 km from Zapala, in a striking volcanic desert, the attractive black-necked swan breeds at Laguna Blanca, a shallow interior drainage lake formed when lava flows dammed two small streams. Other bird species include coots, grebes, upland geese, gulls and even flamingos.

Departing at midnight on Mondays, Wednesdays and Fridays, the Zapala-Aluminé bus will drop passengers at the ranger station's basic, unsheltered campground. If this schedule does not serve you, try hitching. Ask the ranger for hiking information, but bring food.

JUNÍN DE LOS ANDES

Neuquén's 'trout capital' is a modest livestock centre (population 8000) on the Río Chimehuín, 41 km north of San Martín de los Andes. Much cheaper than fashionable San Martín, it has better access to many parts of Parque Nacional Lanín.

Junín's tourist office, at Padre Milanesio and Coronel Suárez, is open from 8 am to 9 pm. For detailed information on fishing and hunting, contact the Club de Caza y Pesca Chimehuín, San Martín 555. Banco de la Provincia is on Avenida San Martín, but change cash in the shop on Padre Milanesio, across the plaza, which is also the de facto telephone office. ENCOTEL is at Coronel Suárez and Don Bosco.

Places to Stay & Eat

The riverside campground, three blocks from the plaza, has all facilities for US$3 per person, plus a one-time charge of US$3 per tent. *Residencial El Cedro*, Lamadrid 409, and *Residencial Marisa*, Boulevard Rosas 360, both charge about US$10/15 a single/double, while *Hostería Rosters*, Lamadrid 66, is slightly dearer.

Fairly standard eateries include *Restaurant Ruca Hueney*, Padre Milanesio 641, and *Parrilla Nicolás*, Coronel Suárez 559. The rotisería at Coronel Suárez 431 has outstanding empanadas.

Getting There & Away

Air Aeropuerto Chapelco is midway between Junín and San Martín de los Andes; for details, see the San Martín entry.

Bus Bus services from the terminal, at Olavarría and Félix San Martín, closely resemble those from San Martín de los Andes (see below).

SAN MARTÍN DE LOS ANDES

San Martín (altitude 642 metres), on Lago Lácar, still has much of the charm that once attracted people to Bariloche. The tourist office (☎ 27347), at San Martín and Rosas, has hotel and restaurant details, good brochures and a superb provincial road map (US$3). The only exchange house is Andina Internacional, Avenida San Martín 876, but travel agencies will buy cash dollars. ENCOTEL is at the civic centre, Roca and Coronel Pérez; there's a telephone cooperative at Capitán Drury 761.

Skiing

Rental equipment is available on site at **Cerro Chapelco**, 1920 metres above sea level and 20 km south-east of San Martín. Provincial ski championships take place every August, along with the Fiesta Nacional del Montañes, the annual ski festival.

Places to Stay & Eat

Camping Los Andes, across the bridge over Arroyo Poca Hullo, charges US$4 per person, but conventional accommodation is fairly expensive in all categories – try *Residencial Villalago*, Villegas 717, for US$12 per person. Others start at around US$20/32 a single/double, like *Residencial Casa Alta* at Obeid 659, *Residencial Italia* at Coronel Pérez 977, and *Residencial Los Pinos* at Almirante Brown 420.

Piscis, at Villegas and Mariano Moreno, is a mid-price parrilla which is mobbed at night. *Sayhueque*, at Rivadavia 825, also draws big crowds. *Café de la Plaza*, at Avenida San Martín and Coronel Pérez, is a pleasant sidewalk confitería, but not cheap.

Getting There & Away

Air From Aeropuerto Chapelco, Aerolíneas Argentinas (☎ 27003), at San Martín and Belgrano, flies thrice weekly to Buenos Aires (US$227). LADE (☎ 27672) and TAN (☎ 27872), with adjacent offices at San Martín 915, fly to other Patagonian destinations; TAN also flies to Puerto Montt, Chile.

Bus From the terminal (☎ 27044), at Villegas and Coronel Díaz, El Petróleo serves northern destinations (Aluminé, Junín, Zapala), the Río Negro valley to the east, and Pirehueico (Chile). El Valle has four buses weekly to Buenos Aires (US$70); La Estrella and Chevallier also go to Buenos Aires.

TUS goes to Córdoba on Mondays; otherwise, make connections in Bariloche. JAC and Igi Llaima both go to Temuco (US$30) and other Chilean destinations.

Getting Around

Car rental agencies include A1 (☎ 27997), at San Martín 1142, Avis (☎ 27704), at San Martín 998, and National (☎ 27218), at San Martín 943.

PARQUE NACIONAL LANÍN

Tranquil Lanín, extending about 150 km north from Nahuel Huapi to Lago Ñorquinco, has escaped the frantic commercialism which has blemished the Bariloche area. Its centrepiece is the imposing snow-capped cone of 3776-metre Volcán Lanín.

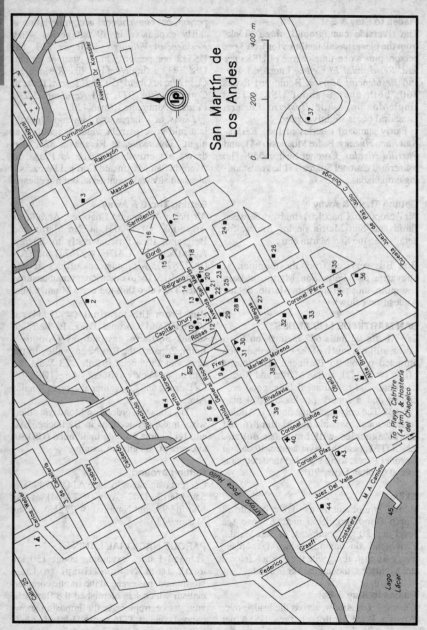

San Martín de
Los Andes

■ PLACES TO STAY	▼ PLACES TO EAT
1 Camping Los Andes	30 Café de la Plaza
2 Hotel Crismalu	38 Restaurant Piscis
3 Residencial Laura	39 Restaurant Sayhueque
4 Hostería Nevada	
5 Hotel Curruhuinca	OTHER
6 Hostería La Chemineé	
8 Hostería Las Lucarnas	7 Post Office
21 Hostería Peumayén	9 National Parks Office
22 Hotel Nevegal	10 Artesanías Mapuches
23 Hotel Chapelco Ski	11 Telephone Cooperative
24 Hostería Cumelén	12 Tourist Office/Artesanías Neuquinas
26 Hostería La Masia	13 Fenoglio (Chocolates)
27 Residencial Villalago	14 Cambio Andina Internacional
28 Hostería Anay	15 Astete Viajes (Airport Bus)
29 Hostería Tisú	16 Plaza Sarmiento
32 Residencial Italia	17 La Oveja Negra
33 Residencial Casa Alta	18 LADE/TAN (Airlines)
34 Hotel Berna	19 Aerolíneas Argentinas
35 Hostería La Raclette	20 Banco de La Provincia
36 Hostería Las Lengas	25 Kosem Artesanías
41 Residencial Los Pinos	31 Banco de la Nación
42 Hostal del Esquiador	37 Casino
44 Hostería La Posta del Cazador	40 Hospital
	43 Bus Terminal
	45 Pier

Extensive stands of the broadleaf deciduous southern beech *raulí* and the curious pehuén (monkey puzzle tree) flourish here, in addition to *lenga*, *ñire*, and *coihue* which characterise more southerly Patagonian forests. Pleistocene glaciers left behind numerous finger-shaped lakes with excellent camp sites.

For detailed information, contact the Intendencia of Parque Nacional Lanín, at Emilio Frey 749, San Martín de los Andes.

Things to See & Do
The towns of San Martín, Junín and Aluminé are the best starting points for exploring Lanín and its backcountry. This entry begins at San Martín and works north.

Lago Lácar From San Martín, you can sail west to Paso Hua Hum and cross by road to Pirihueico, Chile, but there is also bus service. Hua Hum has both free and organised camping, plus hiking trails.

Lago Lolog Fifteen km north of San Martín, this almost undeveloped area has good camping and fishing.

Lago Huechulafquen Source of the Río Chimehuín, this very central area is easily accessible from Junín, despite limited public transport. There are outstanding views of Volcán Lanín, and several excellent hikes.

If you camp at the free sites in the narrow area between the lakes and the road, dig a latrine and remove your rubbish. Consider organised sites which, while not luxurious, are at least maintained. Fees at Raquithue and Puerto Canoas, operated by Mapuche concessionaires, are US$4 per person, while Bahía Cañicul costs US$7. Bring supplies from Junín.

Lago Tromen This forested area, the northern approach to Volcán Lanín, should open for hikers and climbers earlier in the season than the route from Huechulafquen.

Getting There & Away

Public transport is limited, but hitching is feasible in high season. Buses to Chile over the Hua Hum and Tromen passes will drop passengers at intermediate points. Pick-up trucks from Junín will carry six or seven backpackers to Huechulafquen for US$5 each.

VILLA LA ANGOSTURA

On Nahuel Huapi's north shore, this placid resort is near the junction of routes from Bariloche to Osorno (Chile) and from San Martín de los Andes. It takes its name from the 91-metre isthmus which connects it to the Quetrihué peninsula ('angostura' means a 'narrowness' or a 'narrow pass'). The commercial centre of El Cruce straddles the highway, while residential La Villa (which still has hotels, shops and services) is closer to the lake.

El Cruce tourist office (☎ 94124) has a good selection of maps and brochures. Try exchanging cash dollars in almost any shop. ENCOTEL and the national parks office are in La Villa, while Telefónica is at El Cruce, near the tourist office.

Things to See & Do

Parque Nacional Los Arrayanes On the Quetrihué peninsula, this overlooked park protects the cinnamon-barked arrayán. At the south end of the peninsula, park headquarters is an easy three-hour hike from La Villa on an interpretive nature trail, but start early in the morning – hikers must leave the park by 4 pm (ask the El Cruce tourist office for brochures). An alternative is to rent mountain bikes (US$3 per hour) at El Cruce.

At the La Villa entrance, a very steep, 20-minute hike goes to two panoramic overlooks of Nahuel Huapi.

Siete Lagos Provincial Ruta 234 follows this exceptionally scenic route to San Martín de los Andes. For transport details, see the Getting There & Away section for La Villa (below).

Places to Stay & Eat

For US$2 per person, *Camping El Cruce*, 500 metres west of the tourist office, has hot showers, but toilets may be dirty. *Residencial La Granja*, on Nahuel Huapi in La Villa, charges US$20/30 a single/double. *Residencial Don Pedro*, on Belvedere in El Cruce, has rooms for US$22/34, but everything else costs at least twice that.

There are several restaurants and confiterías along Los Arrayanes and its cross streets in El Cruce.

Getting There & Away

Buses in all directions must pass El Cruce. Buy tickets for Transporte Algarrobal's two daily buses to Bariloche (US$7) at Village SA, on Los Arrayanes. Unión del Sud goes to Neuquén (US$27) via San Martín de los Andes (US$10) and Junín de los Andes (US$12) three times weekly; get information and tickets from Cantina Los Amigos, on Los Taiques.

International services to Osorno and Puerto Montt stop in El Cruce but are often very crowded. Inquire at Cantina Los Amigos.

PUERTO MADRYN

Street names are all that remain of the Welsh past of this desert port on the Golfo Nuevo, 1371 km south of Buenos Aires. The closest town to Península Valdés, Madryn is a common starting point for visits to coastal wildlife reserves. Its broad beach and shoreline Avenida Roca are the main areas of interest.

Information

The tourist office (☎ 73029), Roca 444, is open seven days a week, but hours vary. In summer, they offer a series of videos and lectures (9 pm daily).

Cambios include La Moneda and Golfo Nuevo, both at Avenida 28 de Julio 21, Coyun-Co at Roca 161, and Turismo Pu-ma at Avenida 28 de Julio 48. ENCOTEL is at Belgrano and Gobernador Maíz. Telefónica is on Roca near Belgrano and at 28 de Julio 334. Sur Turismo (☎ 73585), Roca 612, organises tours with English-speaking guides.

Beaches

Playa Acuario is the most central, developed and crowded beach – a pleasant place for cold beer, snacks and mixing with locals. More southerly beaches are less protected, but more suitable for windsurfing or diving.

Places to Stay

Toward Punta Cuevas, *Camping Municipal Sud* has comfy 'A' and 'B' areas (US$12.50 daily for four), but perfectly acceptable 'C' and 'D' areas cost less than half that.

Clean, friendly *Hotel Tandil*, J B Justo 770, has rooms with shared bath for US$10 per person. *Residencial Jo's*, at Bolívar 75, has singles/doubles for US$15/24. Friendly *Hotel París*, at Roque Sáenz Peña and Avenida 25 de Mayo, has very basic rooms at US$15/22.

Residencial Petit, at M T de Alvear 845, has rooms with bath at US$15/24. Slightly cheaper are residenciales *El Dorado*, at San Martín 545, and *Vaskonia*, at Avenida 25 de Mayo 43 (perhaps the best budget choice).

Places to Eat

Among several good parrillas are the highly praised *Estela* at Roque Sáenz Peña 28, *Parrilla de Matías* at Roque Sáenz Peña 214, and *Baldomero* at Roque Sáenz Peña 390. Family-run *La Cheminée*, Moreno 60, has up-market prices but is good value, especially the fondue.

Cheaper alternatives include the restaurant at *Hotel París* (despite complaints of poor service and mediocre food, it has a good local reputation), and *El Aguila*, at M A Zar 75. For fine Italian food, try *La Tua Pasta*, at Belgrano 138.

Pizzerías include *Almacén del 900*, at Avenida 9 de Julio 245, and especially *Cabil-Dos*, Yrigoyen and Roca, which also serves great baked empanadas and offers takeaway service.

Getting There & Away

Air Puerto Madryn has its own airport, but most flights arrive at Trelew, 65 km south.

Bus From the terminal, on Yrigoyen between M A Zar and San Martín, Empresa Andesmar has daily buses to Mendoza and Caleta Olivia. Empresa Don Otto has one direct bus daily to Buenos Aires (US$79), one to Comodoro Rivadavia (US$28) and one to Río Gallegos (US$50) and intermediates. It also goes to Neuquén five times weekly (US$31), and to Esquel (US$34) four times weekly. El Cóndor/La Puntual goes daily to Buenos Aires, four times weekly to Bahía Blanca and four times weekly to Comodoro Rivadavia.

Transportadora Patagónica has two buses weekly to Mar del Plata. TUP goes three times weekly to Córdoba, and to Camarones and Comodoro Rivadavia. Mar y Valle has three buses a week to Esquel.

Getting Around

To/From the Airport From the Trelew airport, Madryn-bound passengers must walk to the airport entrance on Ruta 3 and wait for the hourly intercity bus, which does not enter the airport.

Car Cars are useful on Península Valdés, but can cost upwards of US$100 per day. Rent-A-Car is at Roca 117, Fiorassi at Belgrano 196 and Cuyun-Co at Roca 171.

PENÍNSULA VALDÉS

On Ruta 3 about 18 km north of Puerto Madryn, provincial Ruta 2 branches off to Península Valdés, where large numbers of sea lions, elephant seals, guanacos, rheas, Magellanic penguins and many other sea birds frequent the beaches and headlands. August is the best month to see whales, but there are sightings as late as December. For an account of the isolated sheep estancias which occupy most of the interior, read Sara Mansfield Taber's *Dusk on the Campo* (Henry Holt, New York, 1991).

Provincial officials collect US$3.50 per person at the entrance on the Istmo Carlos

Ameghino. In the Golfo San José, just to the north, gulls, cormorants, flamingos, oystercatchers and egrets nest on **Isla de los Pájaros**, a sanctuary visible through a powerful telescope.

From July to December at Puerto Pirámide, the only village, launches can approach right whales in the harbour on the Golfo Nuevo, whose warm, clear waters lap at the sandy beach. Visitors without cars can walk four km to a sea-lion colony, with good views (and sunsets) across the gulf.

For other sites, rent a car or take an organised tour. Despite occasional soft sand, the gravelled roads are no obstacle to prudent drivers. Just north of Punta Delgada, a large sea-lion colony is visible from the cliffs, but better sites are farther north. It is foolish to try a descent of the unconsolidated cliffs to get close to the animals – and male sea lions are quick, aggressive and dangerous. *Faro Punta Delgada* has lodging for US$31 per person, with meals an additional US$12.

Farther north, Caleta Valdés is a sheltered bay with a long gravel spit, where elephant seals (easily photographed, but do not approach too closely) come ashore in spring, and guanaco stroll the beach. Between Caleta Valdés and Punta Norte is a substantial colony of burrowing Magellanic penguins. At Punta Norte proper, there is a huge mixed colony of sea lions and elephant seals; clearly marked trails and fences discourage visitors (and sea lions) from too close an encounter.

Places to Stay & Eat
Sites at the Puerto Pirámide's municipal campground, sheltered from the wind by dunes and trees, now cost US$13. It has clean toilets, hot showers (carefully timed because of water shortages) and a store with basic provisions. Outside Puerto Pirámide, camping is prohibited.

At *Hospedaje Paraíso*, basic accommodation means clean rooms, shared toilets and hot showers, for US$10 a single. *Hospedaje Torino* has doubles for US$20. *El Libanés* has modest rooms for US$30 to US$35 a double with bath, and a small confitería

serving a reasonable breakfast. *The Paradise*, a very casual place whose owner speaks fluent English, serves sandwiches and pizza. *Hostería ACA* has rooms (US$36/44) and a pricey restaurant.

Getting There & Away
A bus from Madryn goes to Puerto Pirámide (US$6) daily, except Monday, at 8.55 am, returning at 7 pm. If taking a tour from Puerto Madryn, you can stay at Pirámide and return on another day for no additional charge.

Getting Around
For sites any distance from Pirámide, the alternatives are renting a car or taking an organised tour. Several agencies in Madryn organise day trips for about US$25, but stay only briefly at each site.

TRELEW
Lewis Jones, who worked to bring the railway here, gave his name to Trelew, 65 km south of Puerto Madryn, in the Chubut valley. The centre of town is Plaza Independencia. Most of the main sights are on calles 25 de Mayo and San Martín, and along Avenida Fontana.

Information
The tourist office (☎ 33112) at the bus terminal has good maps and brochures. There are branches at the airport, and at Salón San David (at San Martín and Belgrano). Sur Turismo, Belgrano 326, changes cash and travellers' cheques. ENCOTEL is at Avenida 25 de Mayo and Mitre. Telefónica is at the corner of Julio Roca and Fontana.

Local travel agencies which organise tours to Península Valdés (US$35) and Punta Tombo (US$45) include Sur Turismo at Belgrano 326, Península Valdés Turismo at Belgrano 291, and Punta Tombo Turismo at San Martín 150.

Things to See
Walking Tour For a nominal charge, register at the tourist office or museum for a guided historical walk which includes: the Museo

Regional; Banco de la Nación (the first bank); Salón San David (a community centre where the Eisteddfod takes place); the Capilla Tabernacle (from 1889, the oldest building in town); the Teatro Verdi (1914); the Municipalidad; Plaza Independencia (with its Victorian kiosk); the Distrito Militar (which housed Trelew's first school); and the Teatro Español.

Museums In the former train station, at Avenida Fontana and 9 de Julio, the **Museo Regional** is open daily from 8.30 am to 12.30 pm and 4 to 8 pm. Displays include Welsh and indigenous history, as well as local flora and fauna.

Fossils and geological samples are superb at the new **Museo Paleontológico**, at Avenida 9 de Julio 631, open daily from 4 to 11 pm. Admission is US$2.50 for adults, US$1 for children under 12.

Places to Stay & Eat
Residencial San Carlos, Sarmiento 758, has small but clean rooms at US$7/12 a single/double with private bath. Quiet, friendly *Hostal Avenida*, near the bus terminal at Lewis Jones 49, has rooms for US$11/16 with shared bath, and a reasonable breakfast. *Hotel Touring Club*, Fontana 240, seems a classic hotel from the silent film era, with rooms at US$25/40 and a confitería which is a must for midmorning coffee.

The cheapest restaurants are *El Reloj*, at San Martín 60, and *La Ley*, at Avenida 25 de Mayo 128. The *Comedor Universitario*, at Fontana and Avenida 9 de Julio, offers cheap, wholesome meals. *Eulogia Fuentes*, Don Bosco 23, has good food at moderate prices. *La Cantina*, Avenida 25 de Mayo and A P Bell, has good pasta and parrillada. *Restaurant Valentino*, A P Bell 434, offers wild game as well as Italian cuisine.

Trelew's only Welsh teahouse is *Roger's Shop*, Moreno 463.

Getting There & Away
Air Trelew's modern airport (☎ 33746) is five km north of town on Ruta 3. Aerolíneas Argentinas (☎ 35297), Avenida 25 de Mayo

33, flies daily from Buenos Aires (US$171) to Ushuaia, with stops here and at Comodoro Rivadavia.

Austral (☎ 35603), Avenida 25 de Mayo 259, flies to Buenos Aires daily, and to Comodoro Rivadavia daily (except Sunday). LADE (☎ 35244), Fontana 227, flies daily to Río Gallegos and twice weekly to Esquel and Bariloche.

Bus From the bus terminal (☎ 31765), at Urquiza and Lewis Jones, Empresa 28 de Julio has buses to Puerto Madryn hourly, slightly less often on Sundays and holidays. It also goes to Gaiman and Dolavon.

On Wednesdays, Fridays, Saturdays and Sundays, Mar y Valle has buses to Puerto Pirámide (US$16 return) at 8.15 am, returning at 6.30 pm. Andesmar goes daily to Mendoza and to Caleta Olivia, and to Río Gallegos on Tuesday evenings. TUP travels to Córdoba three afternoons a week, and to Camarones and Comodoro Rivadavia three mornings a week.

El Cóndor/La Puntual has two daily buses to Buenos Aires (US$81) and four weekly to Bahía Blanca. Transportadora Patagónica has two weekly buses to Mar del Plata.

Don Otto has a daily direct bus to Buenos Aires, two to Comodoro Rivadavia (US$26, four hours) and one to Río Gallegos (US$40, nine hours). There are also three weekly to Puerto Deseado, two to Esquel and five to Neuquén.

Getting Around
Car rental agencies include Fiorassi, at España 344, VIP Car, at A P Bell 250, and Rent a Car, at Calle San Martín 90.

GAIMAN
Chubut's oldest municipality and one of few demonstrably Welsh towns remaining in Patagonia, Gaiman is 17 km west of Trelew. Later creole, German and Anglo immigrants also cultivated fruit, vegetables and fodder in the lower Chubut valley.

Welshness is palpable along Avenida Eugenio Tello, where teahouses offer homemade cakes and sweets. **Camwy** secondary school dates from 1899, while Welsh inscriptions grace many headstones at the **cemetery**, on the outskirts of town. The **Museo Histórico Regional**, attended by Welsh and English-speaking volunteers, is at the old railway station, at Sarmiento and 28 de Julio; it houses a collection of pioneer photographs and household items.

One of Patagonia's oddest sights is eclectic **Parque El Desafío**, built by local political protestor and conservationist Joaquín Alonso. Admission is US$5 for 'functionaries of the state, lawmakers, and politicians', US$0.50 for anyone else.

Places to Stay & Eat
Gaiman's only *residencial* is rarely open, while the small municipal *campground*, on Yrigoyen between Libertad and Independencia, is inaccessible when it rains.

Don't leave without tasting the abundant home-baked sweets at local teahouses. Most open around 3 pm, so eat only a light lunch.

Venerable *Plas y Coed*, Miguel D Jones 123, is run by Marta Rees, a charming and wonderful cook who speaks English. Try also *Ty Gwyn* at Avenida 9 de Julio 147, *Casa de Té Gaiman* on Yrigoyen between Sarmiento and San Martín, or *Elma* at Tello 571. Tourist buses stop at *Ty Nain*, Yrigoyen 283.

Getting There & Away
Empresa 28 de Julio has several buses a day from Trelew via Gaiman to Dolavon. The return fare to Gaiman is US$2.50.

DOLAVON
Provincial Ruta 7 leads 35 km west from Trelew to this historic town, whose old flour mill, now a museum, still has a functioning water wheel. There's a good camp site, one hotel and a teahouse. Empresa 28 de Julio runs 10 buses daily from Trelew.

RESERVA PROVINCIAL PUNTA TOMBO
From September to April, half a million Magellanic penguins breed at Punta Tombo, 110 km south of Trelew. Other sea birds and shore birds include cormorants, giant petrels,

kelp gulls, flightless steamer ducks and oystercatchers. There is a US$3.50 entry fee to the reserve.

Early morning visits beat tourist buses from Trelew, but camping is forbidden. Most of the nesting area is fenced off; this does not prevent approaching the birds for photos, but remember that penguin bites can require stitches.

To get there, arrange a tour in Trelew (about US$45), hire a taxi, or rent a car. The gravel road from Trelew via Rawson is in good condition.

CAMARONES
From Ruta 3, about 180 km south of Trelew, paved Ruta 30 leads 72 km to this quiet, dilapidated fishing port which figures, perhaps apocryphally, in Tomás Eloy Martínez's *The Perón Novel*.

Open all year, the municipal *campground* charges US$1 per person and per tent. *Hotel Kau-i-keukenk* serves outstanding grilled salmon, exquisite escabeche de mariscos (marinated shellfish) and home-made flan.

On Mondays and Fridays at 8 am, Empresa Don Otto leaves Trelew for Camarones (US$10, 3½ hours), returning at 4 pm.

COMODORO RIVADAVIA
Founded in 1901, Comodoro Rivadavia boomed a few years later, when well-diggers made a fortuitous petroleum strike. The state soon dominated the sector through Yacimientos Petrolíferos Fiscales (YPF), whose new petroleum museum is one of the best of its kind in the world. Argentina is self-sufficient in petroleum, about one-third of it coming from this area.

While not a major tourist destination, Comodoro is a frequent stopover for southbound travellers. The main commercial street is Avenida San Martín, which trends east-west below Cerro Chenque. With Avenida Alsina and the Atlantic shoreline, San Martín forms a triangle which defines the city centre.

For information, try ACA (☎ 24036), at Dorrego and Alvear, which has excellent maps. Banks and travel agencies along San Martín will change cash. ENCOTEL is at San Martín and Moreno, while Telefónica is at the corner of Urquiza and Rawson.

Museo del Petróleo

This exceptional museum, on Lavalle between Viedma and Carlos Calvo in the suburb of General Mosconi, has vivid exhibits on natural and cultural history, early and modern oil technology, and social and historical aspects of petroleum development. Historical photographs are remarkable, but there are also detailed models of tankers, refineries and the entire zone of exploitation. The grounds include the site of Comodoro's original gusher, with antique drilling equipment and vehicles. A bombastic taped narration mars an impressive slide show.

From April to November, the museum is open Tuesday to Friday from 9 am to noon and 2 to 6 pm, and on weekends from 3 to 9 pm. From December to March, hours are Tuesday to Sunday from 5 to 9 pm. Admission is free. To get there, take bus Nos 7 or 8 northbound from downtown Comodoro.

Places to Stay & Eat

Hotel Comercio, Rivadavia 341, merits a visit for its vintage bar and restaurant; singles/doubles cost US$9/13 with shared bath; slightly more with private bath. *Hotel Italiano*, opposite the bus terminal, at Rivadavia 481, has singles with shared bath for US$9. Others in this category are *Residencial Chubut*, Belgrano 738, *Hotel Sevilla* and *Residencial Paena*, both around the corner on Ameghino, and *Hotel Español*, on Avenida 9 de Julio near Sarmiento.

Jammed with locals at lunchtime, *La Cabaña*, at Rivadavia and Güemes, serves superb bife de chorizo and lasagna. *La Rastra*, Rivadavia 348, is another parrilla. *La Fonte D'Oro*, at San Martín and Avenida 25 de Mayo, is a good but expensive confitería. At Rivadavia and Alvear, a fine rotisería prepares exquisite takeaway empanadas.

Getting There & Away

Air Aerolíneas Argentinas (☎ 22294), San Martín 421, flies once or twice daily to Buenos Aires (US$181). Austral (☎ 22191), San Martín 291, flies twice daily to Buenos Aires, except Sunday (one flight). Southbound Austral flights continue to Río Gallegos, Río Grande and Ushuaia.

Comodoro is a good place to catch frequently overbooked LADE flights to destinations like Río Gallegos (US$43) and Bariloche (US$45). If you can't get a ticket at the office, on Rivadavia near Pellegrini, try getting one at the airport itself.

Bus From the terminal, at Pellegrini and Avenida 25 de Mayo, La Puntual has daily buses to Buenos Aires (US$108, 24 hours). Empresa Don Otto has identical service to Buenos Aires, but also goes to Río Gallegos (US$24), and on Tuesday and Sunday evenings to Bariloche (US$39).

Departing at 1 am on Mondays, Wednesdays and Fridays, Angel Giobbi buses to Coyhaique, Chile are often very full.

Getting Around

Bus No 9 goes directly to the airport from central Comodoro.

RÍO MAYO

Only gauchos and conscripts are likely to spend more than a night at this dusty western crossroads, 274 km from Comodoro Rivadavia, where highways head south to Perito Moreno and Los Antiguos, north to Esquel and west to Coyhaique, Chile.

Charging US$6 per person with shared bath, *Hotel San Martín*, Perito Moreno 693, also has a decent restaurant. *Hotel Covadonga*, San Martín 573, has singles with bath (US$10).

Three buses a week from Comodoro continue to Coyhaique but are usually full. On Mondays and Thursdays at 6 am, Angel Giobbi SA goes to Esquel (US$28), but no public transport goes south toward Perito Moreno and Los Antiguos; patience may get you a lift.

ESQUEL

North of sunny Esquel (population 23,000),

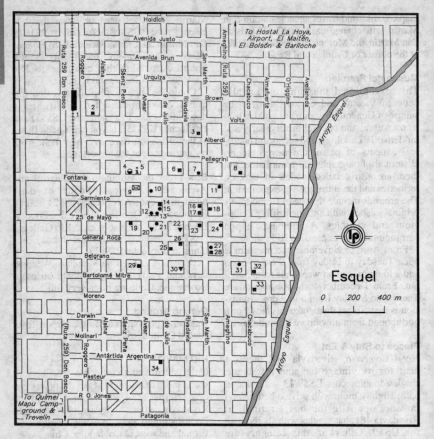

To Hostal La Hoya,
Airport, El Maitén,
El Bolsón & Bariloche

Esquel

0   200   400 m

Ruta 40 heads north to El Bolsón and
Bariloche, and south-east towards Comodoro Rivadavia. Southbound Ruta 259
leads to Welsh Trevelin, Parque Nacional
Los Alerces and other Andean attractions.

Information

At the bus terminal, at Fontana and Alvear,
the tourist office (☎ 2369) lists accommodation and prices in all categories, plus data on
travel agencies and tours, and transport and
recreation. Banco Nación, at Alvear and
Roca, changes American Express travellers'
cheques; others change only cash. Outside

bank hours, travel agencies may change
money. ENCOTEL is at Alvear 1192,
Telefónica at San Martín 850. Chile has a
consulate at Avenida 25 de Mayo 726.

Things to See

The **Museo Indigenista y de Ciencias
Naturales** is at Belgrano 330. The **Mercado
Comunitario**, at San Martín and Fontana,
has varied local crafts at reasonable prices.

Do visit the station to see **El Trencito**, the
narrow-gauge steam train which featured in
Paul Theroux's travel classic *The Old
Patagonian Express*. Passenger services on

■ PLACES TO STAY		▼ PLACES TO EAT	
2	Casa de Familia Barutta	20	Restaurant Jockey Club
3	Casa de Familia Alemán de	22	Restaurant Don Pipo
	Abraham	30	Parrilla Yauquén
6	Casa de Familia Gingins		
8	Hotel Los Tulipanes		OTHER
14	Hotel Sol del Sur		
16	Hotel Esquel	1	Train Station
17	Hotel Maika	4	Bus Terminal
18	Hostería La Tour D'Argent	5	Tourist Office
19	Hospedaje Argentino	7	Mercado Comunitario
23	Hotel Ski	9	Post Office
25	Hotel Tehuelche	10	Banco de la Provincia del Chubut
26	Hospedaje Zacarías	11	Aerolíneas Argentinas
28	Hotel Huenú	12	LADE (Airline)
29	Hostería Angelina	13	Chilean Consulate
32	Casa de Familia Al Sol	15	TAN (Airline)
33	Hostería Huentru-Niyeu	21	Banco del Sud
34	Hostería Arrayán	24	ACA (Travel Agency)
		27	Telefónica
		31	Museo Indigenista y de Ciencias Naturales

the route were suspended, but there are recent reports that they have resumed, with the support of some local enthusiasts.

Fishing
Season licences, valid from early November to mid-April in Chubut, Santa Cruz, Río Negro and Neuquén provinces, and in national parks, cost US$65; weekly and monthly licences are cheaper. Contact the tourist office or neighbouring municipalities.

Places to Stay & Eat
Family homes charge US$7 to US$10 per person, some with private bath. Try María Pasquini at Belgrano 844, Juana Gingins at Rivadavia 1243, Raquel Alemán de Abraham at Alberdi 529, or *Al Sol* at Chacabuco 762. English-speaking Isabel Barutta runs highly recommended *Alojamento Familiar Lago Verde*, Volta 1081.

Hospedaje Argentino, Avenida 25 de Mayo 862, charges US$22 a double. *Hospedaje Zacarías*, General Roca 634, has singles/doubles for US$18/25. Comparable

are *Hostería Huentru-Niyeu*, Chacabuco 606 (US$17/28), and *Hostería Angelina*, Alvear 758 (US$20/30).

Despite erratic service, *Parrilla Yauquén*, Rivadavia 740, is reasonable and pleasant. *Restaurant Jockey Club*, Alvear 949, is good, and comparably priced. *La Vascongada*, Avenida 9 de Julio and Mitre, has good food in generous portions, with attentive service.

Don Pipo, Rivadavia 924, has decent pizza. *Confitería Atelier*, open 24 hours at Avenida 25 de Mayo and San Martín, has excellent coffee and cocoa. There's a fine ice-creamery on Rivadavia, near Fontana.

Getting There & Away
Air The airport is 20 km east of town on Ruta 40. Aerolíneas Argentinas (☎ 3749), at Fontana and Ameghino, flies on Mondays, Thursdays and Saturdays to Buenos Aires (US$227), and on Tuesdays to Trelew (US$83).

LADE (☎ 2227), Avenida 25 de Mayo 777, flies to Patagonian destinations like El Maitén, El Bolsón, Bariloche (US$20),

Comodoro Rivadavia (US$39), Chapelco/San Martín de los Andes (US$24), Neuquén, Trelew (US$37), Viedma (US$56) and Zapala (US$34). TAN (☎ 2427), Avenida 9 de Julio 1086, flies twice weekly to Comodoro and three times weekly to Bariloche and Neuquén. Fares are higher than LADE's.

Bus To Bariloche (US$22), TAM has four buses weekly via El Maitén, two via Cholila and seven via Los Alerces; Don Otto's twice-weekly service via Epuyén is a bit cheaper. Transportes Esquel has daily buses to Los Alerces.

Don Otto also goes twice weekly to Comodoro (US$23), connecting to Río Gallegos (US$45), four times weekly to Buenos Aires (US$112), and to provincial destinations like Trevelin and Carrenleufú.

Empresa Chubut has five weekly buses to Trelew (US$19). Mar y Valle's three buses are slightly dearer.

Train Services on the narrow-gauge railway to Ingeniero Jacobacci have been suspended, but have a look around the station.

Getting Around

To/From the Airport Esquel Tours, Fontana 754, runs minibuses to the airport.

Tours Buying a ticket in Esquel assures a place on the crowded Circuito Lacustre boat trip in Parque Nacional Los Alerces. Try Esquel Tours, Fontana 754.

TREVELIN

Only 24 km south of Esquel, Trevelin (population 5500) is interior Chubut's only notable Welsh community. From Plaza Coronel Fontana, eight streets radiate like spokes of a wheel; one of these, Avenida San Martín, leads south to Corcovado.

Open daily from 8.30 am to 10.30 pm, the tourist office (☎ 8120) on the plaza, occasionally has discount coupons for local teahouses. Change money before noon at Banco de la Provincia, at San Martín and Brown. The **Museo Regional**, a restored

flour mill, is open Tuesday to Sunday from 3 to 7 pm. The landmark **Capilla Bethel** (1910) is a Welsh chapel.

Places to Stay & Eat

Auto Camping Trevelin, the former municipal site, a block from the plaza, has hot showers, running water and spotless toilet facilities for US$3 per person, plus a one-time charge of US$2 per tent.

Residencial Trevelin, San Martín 327, has rooms with shared bath for US$10 per person, with breakfast. *Hotel Estefania*, at Perito Moreno and 13 de Diciembre, charges US$12/20 a single/double.

Nain Maggie, Perito Moreno 179, is Trevelin's oldest teahouse, offering sweets of dulce de leche, chocolate, cream, rhubarb, cheese, traditional black cake, and oven-hot scones. Service is attentive but unobtrusive. Other teahouses, all worthwhile, are *El Adobe*, on Avenida Patagonia, and *Las Mutisias* and *Te Cymreig Yng Nghwm Hyfryd*, on San Martín.

Cheese-lovers should try local varieties – ask the owner of the clothing store at San Martín 302. For more than tea, sweets or cheese, try *El Quincho*, the local parrilla.

Getting There & Away

There are six buses on weekdays from Esquel (US$1.50), four on weekends, and three weekly to Carrenleufú, the main Chilean border crossing. Northbound travellers must first go to Esquel.

PARQUE NACIONAL LOS ALERCES

West of Esquel, this spacious Andean park protects extensive stands of alerce *(Fitzroya cupressoides)*, a large (up to 60 metres tall and four metres in diameter) and long-lived (400 years or more) conifer of the humid Valdivian forests. Other common trees include cypress, incense cedar, three species of southern beech, and the arrayán. The undergrowth of *chusquea*, a solid bamboo, is almost impenetrable.

The receding glaciers of Los Alerces' peaks, which barely reach 2300 metres, have left nearly pristine lakes and streams, with charming vistas and excellent fishing. Westerly storms drop nearly three metres of rain annually, but summers are mild and the eastern part of the park is much drier.

Things to See & Do

Villa Futalaufquen's **museum** has a good natural-history display (including an aquarium), plus historical exhibits on the park's creation.

Traditionally, the most popular excursion sails from Puerto Limonao on Lago Futalaufquen up the Río Arrayanes to Lago Verde, but dry years and low water have eliminated this segment. Launches from Puerto Chucao, on Lago Menéndez, cover the second segment of the trip to **El Alerzal**, an accessible stand of alerces which, except in parks, are under logging pressure. Buy advance tickets for the voyage (US$22, about two hours) in Esquel.

A one-hour layover permits a hike around a loop trail which passes Lago Cisne and an attractive waterfall to end up at **El Abuelo** (The Grandfather), the finest single alerce in the area. Guides are knowledgeable, but the group can be uncomfortably large. Camping is prohibited at El Alerzal or other parts of the 'zona intangible'.

Places to Stay

At organised campgrounds at Los Maitenes, Lago Futalaufquen, Bahía Rosales, Lago Verde and Lago Rivadavia, charges are US$4 to US$ per person per day, plus a one-time charge of US$2 to US$3 per car or tent. There are free sites near some of these locations. Lago Kruger, reached by foot from Futalaufquén, has a campground, and a refugio with beds for US$10 per night.

Cabañas Los Tepues, on Lago Futalaufquen, rents five-person cabins for US$70 per day. *Motel Pucón Pai* has singles/doubles with private bath and breakfast for US$60/64.

Getting There & Away

For details, see the Esquel entry above.

EL MAITÉN

This small, dusty town 70 km south-east of El Bolsón is the service centre for the narrow-gauge railway from Ingeniero Jacobacci to Esquel. A graveyard for antique locomotives and other hardware, it's a train buff's dream, but suspension of rail services may affect the February **Fiesta Provincial del Trencito**.

The municipal campground charges US$3 per person. *Hostería La Vasconia*, across from the train station, has rooms for US$10 per person. There are regular buses from Esquel and El Bolsón.

RÍO GALLEGOS

In addition to servicing the wool industry, this port (population 100,000) ships coal and refines oil. Many travellers only pass through en route to Calafate and the Moreno Glacier, Punta Arenas or Tierra del Fuego, but a day here need not be a wasted one.

Río Gallegos' two main streets, Avenida Julio Roca and Avenida San Martín, run at right angles to each other. Most areas frequented by tourists are in the south-west quadrant formed by these avenues.

Information

Open on weekdays from 8 am to 7 pm, the energetic tourist office, Roca 1551, has maps and a helpful list of accommodation and services. A branch at the bus terminal is open on weekends.

Cambio El Pingüino, Zapiola 469, will change US dollars, travellers' cheques (with commission) and Chilean pesos, but try also Cambio Sur, on San Martín near Roca. ENCOTEL is at Roca and San Martín, Telefónica at the intersection of Roca and Chile. The Chilean Consulate, Mariano Moreno 136, is open on weekdays from 9 am to 2 pm.

Things to See

At Perito Moreno 45, the **Museo Provincial Mario Echeverría Baleta** has good exhibits on geology, ethnology (superb photographs) and local history. It's open on weekdays from 8 am to 7 pm, and on weekends from 3 to 8

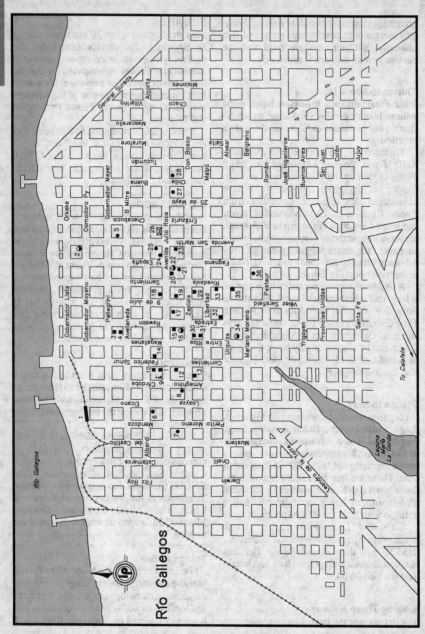

Río Gallegos

■ PLACES TO STAY		OTHER	
3	Hotel Mariano	1	Railway Station
4	Hotel Piscis	2	Transporte Mansilla & Transporte Vera
10	Residencial Internacional	5	Artesanías Keokén
11	Hotel Ampuero	6	Museo de los Pioneros
12	Hotel Alonso	7	Museo Provincial M E Baleta
13	Pensión Esmeralda	8	Police Station
14	Hotel Punta Arenas	9	Tourist Office
15	Hotel Comercio	16	Buses El Pingüino/Cambio Pingüino
17	Hotel Covadonga	21	LADE (Airline)
18	Hotel Central	22	Interlagos Turismo
19	Hotel Viejo La Fuente	24	Austral (Airline)
20	Hotel París	25	Aerolíneas Argentinas/Cambio Sur
23	Hotel Costa Río	26	ENCOTEL
29	Hotel Puerto Santa Cruz	27	Artesanías Santacruceñas
30	Hotel Río Turbio	28	Telefónica
31	Hotel Entre Ríos	34	Transporte Ruta 3 & A1 Car Rental
32	Hotel Laguna Azul	36	Chilean Consulate
33	Hotel Cabo Virgenes		
35	Hotel Colonial		

pm. In a typical metal-clad house at Elcano and Alberdi, the **Museo de los Pioneros** documents early immigrant life. It's open daily from 3 to 8 pm.

For local woollens, leatherwork, fruit preserves, sweets and other items, visit Artesanías Keokén, at Avenida San Martín 336.

Places to Stay & Eat
A private house at Rivadavia 1036 charges only US$10 a single, with breakfast. Basic *Hotel Viejo La Fuente*, Vélez Sarsfield 64, has warm, clean, spacious singles for US$10, with shared bath. Other acceptable places include *Hotel Colonial*, at Rivadavia and Urquiza, where singles/doubles with shared bath are US$10/13, and *Hotel Puerto Santa Cruz*, Zapiola 238 (US$12/18 with private bath).

Spotless, quiet, comfortable and central, *Hotel Covadonga*, Roca 1244, is excellent value; rooms with private bath are US$26/38, but those with washbasin and mirror (shared bath) cost only half that.

Restaurant Montecarlo, Zapiola 558, has informal decor and good seafood. *Snack Bar Jardín*, Avenida Julio Roca 1311, serves cheap, filling minutas. *Le Croissant*, at Zapiola and Estrada, has a wide variety of baked goods, prepared on the premises. Nearby *Heladería Tito* has very good and imaginative ice-cream flavours.

Getting There & Away
Air Aerolíneas Argentinas (☎ 22342), San Martín 545, flies daily to Buenos Aires (US$205) and Ushuaia (US$52). Austral (☎ 20038), Roca 917, flies daily to Río Grande, Ushuaia, Comodoro Rivadavia and Buenos Aires.

LADE (☎ 22249), Fagnano 53, is generally cheaper (and slower) than Aerolíneas and Austral, but reaches smaller or more remote destinations like Perito Moreno (US$45), Gobernador Gregores (US$25) and Río Turbio (US$15). Flights to Comodoro Rivadavia (US$43) have connections to Bariloche (US$100).

Aeroposta, a small private airline, flies daily to Ushuaia (US$37) and Calafate (US$31).

Bus El Pingüino, Zapiola 445, goes twice daily to Río Turbio (US$15), and daily to Punta Arenas (US$15) and Calafate

(US$17). Buenos Aires, a 32-hour nightly marathon, costs US$120. There are also daily services to Caleta Olivia (US$21) and intermediates, with connections to the Andean oasis of Los Antiguos (US$33). Empresa Don Otto also goes to Buenos Aires, connecting at Comodoro Rivadavia for Bariloche (US$53), Neuquén and Mar del Plata.

Transporte Ruta 3, Entre Ríos 354, covers the same northern routes, with services to Córdoba (US$123) on Tuesdays and Thursdays. Transporte Mansilla and Transporte Vera, both at San Martín 565, do the six-hour trip to Punta Arenas.

Interlagos Turismo, Fagnano 35, goes to Calafate and the Moreno Glacier. On Tuesday at 8 am and Friday at 2 pm, Transporte Trevisan has a new service from Río Gallegos to Chaltén (Fitz Roy sector of Parque Nacional Los Glaciares) via Piedra Buena and Tres Lagos, avoiding overpriced Calafate. The trip takes nine hours.

Getting Around

To/From the Airport Only taxis go to Río Gallegos airport, charging about US$7 from the centre. To save money, share a cab.

Bus Most long-distance bus companies have central offices, but the new terminal is at Avenida Evita Perón and Ruta 3, reached by bus Nos 1 or 12 (the placard must say 'Terminal') from Avenida Roca.

Car For car rental, A1 (☎ 22453) is at Entre Ríos 350.

RÍO TURBIO

Coal deposits, worked by Chileans who commute 30 km from Puerto Natales, sustain this desolate border town. Mine visits are possible, and there's a ski area nearby. *Albergue Municipal*, at Paraje Mina 1, has four-to-a-room dormitory beds (US$5 per person); try also *Hotel Gato Negro*, on Laprida (singles/doubles at US$12/16 with shared bath, US$20/24 with private bath), or the slightly cheaper *Hotel Azteca*, Jorge Newbery 98.

LADE, Mineros 375, has three flights weekly to Río Gallegos. Buses to Puerto Natales (1½ hours) leave from the west end of Newbery. El Pingüino, on Newbery near Mineros, has daily service to Río Gallegos (six hours); Buses San Ceferino, on Castillo, does the same trip thrice weekly. Patient inquiries might yield a seat on the steam train which carries coal to Río Gallegos.

CALAFATE

On Lago Argentino's south shore, overpriced Calafate swarms with Porteños who come to spend a few hours at the Moreno Glacier – try to avoid the January-February peak season. From May to September, prices are more reasonable but the main attractions are less accessible.

Open on weekdays from 8 am to 8 pm, the tourist office, near Arroyo Calafate, has maps, brochures and a list of hotels and prices. The national parks office, at San Martín and Ezequiel Bustillo, is open on weekday mornings. It has brochures with an adequate map of Parque Nacional Los Glaciares.

Change money before you arrive – Banco de la Provincia de Santa Cruz changes cash (but not travellers' cheques) at reasonable rates, but closes by 1 pm and is shut on weekends, when shops pay very poor rates. ENCOTEL is on Avenida del Libertador San Martín, between Avenida 9 de Julio and Espora. Collect calls are impossible from the phone cooperative on Espora, between Moyano and Gregores.

Things to See

The **Museo Regional El Calafate**, two blocks east of the tourist office, should have reopened following reorganisation. Rock paintings at **Cuevas de Gualicho**, seven km east of town, have recently been vandalised.

West and north of Calafate, **Parque Nacional Los Glaciares** offers spectacular natural features like the Moreno and Upsala glaciers, and the Fitz Roy Range. For details, see below. Beware of Audiovisual Tío Cacho's atrocious video presentation.

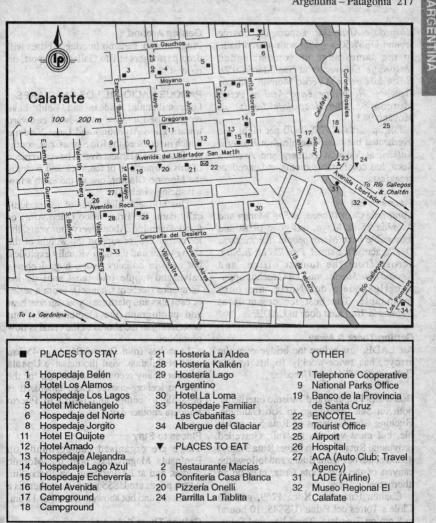

Calafate

0   100   200 m

To La Gerónima

■ PLACES TO STAY		21 Hostería La Aldea	OTHER
1	Hospedaje Belén	28 Hostería Kalkén	
3	Hotel Los Alamos	29 Hostería Lago	7 Telephone Cooperative
4	Hospedaje Los Lagos	Argentino	9 National Parks Office
5	Hotel Michelangelo	30 Hotel La Loma	19 Banco de la Provincia
6	Hospedaje del Norte	33 Hospedaje Familiar	de Santa Cruz
8	Hospedaje Jorgito	Las Cabañitas	22 ENCOTEL
11	Hotel El Quijote	34 Albergue del Glaciar	23 Tourist Office
12	Hotel Amado		25 Airport
13	Hospedaje Alejandra	▼ PLACES TO EAT	26 Hospital
14	Hospedaje Lago Azul	2 Restaurante Macías	27 ACA (Auto Club; Travel
15	Hospedaje Echeverría	10 Confitería Casa Blanca	Agency)
16	Hotel Avenida	20 Pizzería Onelli	31 LADE (Airline)
17	Campground	24 Parrilla La Tablita	32 Museo Regional El
18	Campground		Calafate

Places to Stay

After renovation and privatisation, the woodsy *municipal camp site* will no longer be a bargain, but it has good facilities and is within easy walking distance of any place in town.

The hostel *Albergue del Glaciar*, on Los

Pioneros, is sometimes monopolised by groups, so make reservations in Buenos Aires (☎ 71-9344, 312-8486); beds cost US$10, with kitchen and laundry facilities. *Hotel La Loma*, on Avenida Roca, has some hostel accommodation.

Prices vary seasonally, but family inns like

Hospedaje Alejandra, Espora 60, charge around US$7.50 a single with shared bath. In the same range are recommended *Hospedaje Echeverría* at San Martín 959, *Hospedaje Belén* at Perito Moreno and Los Gauchos, *Hospedaje Lago Azul* at Perito Moreno 83, and *Hospedaje Jorgito* at Moyano 943.

For upwards of US$50/70 per night, the overheated but otherwise pleasant *Hostería Kalkén*, at Valentín Feilberg and Avenida Roca, has comfortable rooms and excellent breakfasts.

Places to Eat
Confitería Casa Blanca, at San Martín and Avenida 25 de Mayo, has good pizza and reasonable beer. Many people like *Pizzería Onelli*, across the street. *Parrilla La Tablita*, across from the tourist office, and *Restaurante Macías*, on Los Gauchos opposite Hospedaje del Norte, are both reasonable. The best ice cream is at *Heladería Tito*, next door to LADE.

Getting There & Away
Air LADE, just before the bridge over the arroyo, has twice-weekly flights to Río Gallegos (US$21) and Ushuaia.

Bus Buses Pingüino and Turismo Interlagos, both on San Martín, go to Río Gallegos. Hitching from Gallegos on Ruta 5 is possible, but most vehicles are full. Gravelled provincial Ruta 9, which leaves Ruta 3 about 45 km south of Piedra Buena and follows the canyon of the Río Santa Cruz, may be an alternative.

Chaltén Patagonia, Roca 1269, goes to Chile's Torres del Paine (US$45, 10 hours) at 8 am on Tuesdays, Thursdays and Saturdays in summer. Daily at 6 am in summer, Buses Los Glaciares goes to El Chaltén (US$45 return), but may collect a surcharge on Mondays, Wednesdays and Fridays. Return service leaves Chaltén at 6 pm. Hitching to El Chaltén is difficult, and clearly inadvisable on northbound Ruta 40, which carries almost no traffic toward Perito Moreno and Los Antiguos.

Getting Around
Pingüino and Turismo Interlagos buses will drop passengers at Río Gallegos airport, on request.

PARQUE NACIONAL LOS GLACIARES
Over millennia, Andean snowfields have recrystallised into ice and flowed eastward toward Lago Argentino and Lago Viedma, which in turn feed the Río Santa Cruz, southern Patagonia's largest river. The centrepiece of this conjunction of ice, rock and water is the **Moreno Glacier**, one of the earth's few advancing glaciers.

This 60-metre-high river of ice periodically dams the Brazo Rico (Rico Arm) of Lago Argentino. About every four years, the ice can no longer support the weight of the rising water and the dam virtually explodes, but even in ordinary years, huge icebergs calve and topple into the Canal de los Témpanos (Iceberg Channel). From a series of catwalks and platforms, you can see, hear and photograph the glacier safely, but descending to the shores of the canal is now prohibited.

Launches from Puerto Bandera, 45 km west of Calafate, visit the massive **Upsala Glacier**; many recommend this trip for the hike to iceberg-choked Lago Onelli. It is possible to camp, and return to Puerto Bandera another day.

Places to Stay
There are organised campgrounds on Península Magallanes, near the Moreno glacier, and at La Jerónima, on Brazo Sur, where prices are US$5 per person; there is a confitería, and hot showers from 7 to 11 pm.

Getting There & Away
Calafate operators visit the Moreno (US$25) and Upsala (US$62) glaciers, but brief tours can be unsatisfactory if inclement weather limits visibility. Interlagos has English-speaking guides.

CERRO FITZ ROY
At tiny El Chaltén, north of Lago Viedma on an exposed floodplain pummelled by nearly

incessant winds, virtually everyone is a government employee, thanks to a lingering border dispute with Chile. However, it's also a mecca for hikers, climbers and campers, and a more agreeable place to stay than Calafate.

One popular hike goes to Laguna Torre and the base camp for climbing the spire of Cerro Torre (3128 metres). Another climbs steeply from the park campground to a signed junction, from which a lateral leads to backcountry camp sites at Laguna Capri. The main trail continues gently to Río Blanco, base camp for climbing Cerro Fitz Roy, and then very steeply to Laguna de los Tres, a tarn named for three Frenchmen who were the first to climb it.

Places to Stay & Eat
The free *campsite* in El Chaltén has running water and abundant firewood, but no toilets – dig a latrine. Shower at *Confitería La Senyera* for about US$1; after drying off, enjoy a light meal or a slice of chocolate cake.

Posada Lago del Desierto has basic four-bed cabins (no hot water) for US$10 per person, and very comfortable six-bed apartments with all facilities (US$15 per person). Meals are expensive, but for cheap eats, try Juan Borrego's converted bus, which is also a hang-out for climbers. Prices at the only grocery are higher than in Calafate.

Getting There & Away
Avoiding Calafate, Transporte Trevisan goes directly to Río Gallegos (nine hours) via Tres Lagos and Piedra Buena, leaving Chaltén on Wednesdays at 8 am and Sundays at 2 pm. See the Calafate entry for other transport details.

CALETA OLIVIA
Caleta Olivia (population 35,000) is the first stop in Santa Cruz for southbound travellers on Ruta 3, and a road junction for the Andean oasis of Los Antiguos. The enthusiastic tourist office (☎ 61085) is a cubbyhole on San Martín, near the 10-metre monument to El Gorosito, the oil worker.

Places to Stay & Eat
The municipal campground charges US$1.50 per car, per tent and per person. *Hotel Alvear*, Güemes 1676, has singles/doubles for US$15/20 with shared bath; *Hotel Grand*, at Avenida Jorge Newbery and Mosconi, is slightly more expensive.

Pizzería Romanela, José Hernández 1300, has Italo-Argentine food. *El Hueso Perdido*, a parrilla, is downstairs at Hotel Grand. *Restaurante Royal* and *El Abuelo*, the best in town, are both on Avenida Independencia, near El Gorosito.

Getting There & Away
From the bus terminal near the monument, Transporte La Unión goes often to Comodoro Rivadavia (US$4, one hour). El Pingüino goes to Río Gallegos (US$19). Don Otto goes directly to Buenos Aires twice weekly, but through buses from Río Gallegos also take northbound passengers.

Twice weekly, Transporte Co-mi goes to the town of Perito Moreno (not to be confused with Moreno Glacier or with Parque Nacional Perito Moreno) and Los Antiguos.

MONUMENTO NATURAL BOSQUES PETRIFICADOS
In Jurassic times, 150 million years ago, vulcanism levelled this area's extensive *Proaraucaria* forests and buried them in ash; later erosion exposed mineralised trees three metres in diameter and 35 metres long. Until legal protection, souvenir hunters regularly plundered the area; do not perpetuate this tradition for even the smallest specimen.

From Ruta 3, 157 km south of Caleta Olivia, a gravel road leads 50 km west to the park's modest headquarters. Camping is free at the dry creek nearby, but bring water if you have a vehicle; otherwise, the ranger *may* be able to spare some. Buses from Caleta Olivia will drop you at the junction, but you may wait several hours or more for a lift.

SAN JULIÁN
San Julián (population 4500) is 341 km south of Caleta Olivia. Magellan wintered here in

1520, but only the 19th-century wool boom brought permanent settlement. Seafood processing is a secondary industry.

Avenida San Martín, the main drag, is an eastward extension of the junction at Ruta 3. The waterfront **Museo Regional y de Arte Marino** features archaeological artefacts and historical exhibits on local estancias, as well as painting and sculpture. Launches can be hired to visit harbour rookeries of penguins, cormorants and other sea birds.

Places to Stay & Eat

The municipal campground charges only US$1 per person, plus US$1.50 per car, for excellent facilities. *Hotel Colón*, San Martín 301, is the cheapest regular accommodation.

Restaurant Sportsman, Mitre 301, has excellent parrillada and pasta at reasonable prices. For seafood, try *Dos Anclas*, Berutti 1080.

Getting There & Away

Transportadora Patagónica's Río Gallegos-Buenos Aires buses stop here, but passengers can flag down any bus at the junction on Ruta 3. Transportes Staller and El Cordillerano's weekly buses to Laguna Posadas (on the Chilean border) via Gobernador Gregores and Bajo Caracoles are the only public transport anywhere close to Parque Nacional Perito Moreno (see below).

GOBERNADOR GREGORES

Gobernador Gregores is more than 200 km from Parque Nacional Perito Moreno, but try arranging car and driver here rather than at the town of Perito Moreno. LADE's weekly flights between Comodoro Rivadavia and Río Gallegos stop here, and there is twice-weekly bus service from San Julián.

Hostería Adelino, Avenida San Martín 1043, charges US$20/32 a single/double; *Residencial Alvarez*, Pueyrredón 367, is a bit cheaper.

COMANDANTE LUIS PIEDRA BUENA

Southbound hitchhikers often wait in line near the ACA petrol station at Piedra Buena, 235 km north of Río Gallegos, while decid-

ing whether to take a passing bus. Forty-five km south, a decent gravel road passes numerous estancias, with panoramic views of the Río Santa Cruz canyon, en route to Calafate.

Hotel Iris, Ibáñez 13, has singles/doubles for US$12/20 with bath, less with shared bath. *Hotel Internacional*, Ibáñez 99, charges US$20/28 with shared bath.

PERITO MORENO

Visitors should not confuse this crossroads farm town with the Moreno Glacier (Parque Nacional Los Glaciares) or with Parque Nacional Perito Moreno. Avenida San Martín, the main street, leads north to paved Ruta 43, which leads west to Los Antiguos and east to Caleta Olivia. South of town it becomes Ruta 40, a *very* rough road to Bajo Caracoles and Parque Nacional Perito Moreno.

The tourist office is at the campground, which is the cheapest place to stay (US$2 per person for tentsites, US$8 per person for small cabins). Banco de la Provincia, Banco de la Nación and Hotel Belgrano will change cash dollars.

Hotel Argentino, at Buenos Aires and Belgrano, and nearby *Hotel Santa Cruz* both charge US$8. *Hotel Belgrano*, at San Martín 1001, costs US$20/28 a single/double with bath, and also has a restaurant.

Getting There & Away

Air LADE is at Mariano Moreno and San Martín. Thursday morning flights from Comodoro Rivadavia (US$22) stop here en route to Gobernador Gregores and Río Gallegos (US$37), returning by the same route in the afternoon.

Bus Transporte Co-mi, near Hotel Argentino, goes to Los Antiguos and Caleta Olivia. A group may find a car and driver to Parque Nacional Perito Moreno via Ruta 40, whose archaeological sites include the famous Cueva de las Manos (Cave of Hands), near the Río Pinturas.

BAJO CARACOLES

This bleak oasis south of Perito Moreno has

the only petrol for nearly 500 km. *Hotel Bajo Caracoles* has surprisingly good accommodation (US$10 per person) and food, though the restaurant is not cheap.

PARQUE NACIONAL PERITO MORENO

In this seldom-visited gem (officially Parque Nacional Perito Francisco P Moreno), 310 km by road from Perito Moreno, glacier-covered summits tower over aquamarine lakes, where migratory birds tarry and herds of guanacos graze peacefully. As the Patagonian steppe becomes a sub-Antarctic forest of southern beech above 900 metres, weather can be severe, and warm equipment is imperative even in summer. Bring all food and supplies, and be careful with fire in the frequent high winds.

As of early 1991, the park service intended to install a ranger at the Estancia Belgrano entrance. One good camp site is just beyond the isthmus separating the two arms of Lago Belgrano, about 10 km from the estancia. Several ponds on the peninsula harbour waterfowl and offer sheltered camp sites. You can also camp near Estancia La Oriental, on Lago Belgrano's north shore, to hike up nearby Cerro Léon.

LOS ANTIGUOS

Aged Tehuelche Indians frequented this 'banana belt' on the south shore of Lago Buenos Aires. Rows of poplars now shelter irrigated chacras whose abundant fruit, for lack of markets, is absurdly cheap. Los Antiguos has a three-day **Fiesta de la Cereza** (cherry festival) in mid-January. The nearby countryside has good fishing and hiking.

The August 1991 eruption of Volcán Hudson covered the area in ash and forced the town's evacuation, so inquire before you visit.

Both the tourist office and bank are on Avenida 11 de Julio, the main street, which runs the length of town. Local fruits (cherries, raspberries, strawberries, apples, apricots, pears, peaches, plums and prunes) are delectable. Purchase these, and home-made preserves, directly from producers –

Chacra El Porvenir is within easy walking distance of Avenida 11 de Julio.

Places to Stay & Eat

The cypress-sheltered municipal campground, at the east end of Avenida 11 de Julio, charges US$1 per person, plus US$0.25 per tent and per vehicle. Hot showers are available from 5.30 to 10 pm. *Restaurant-Confitería Pablo* also offers lodging (US$10 per person with shared bath). *Hotel Argentino* (US$16/28 a single/double with private bath) has excellent dinners and superb breakfasts. *Restaurant El Triunfo* is also inviting.

Getting There & Away

LADE serves Perito Moreno, 64 km to the east. Buses El Pingüino and Transportes Comi go to Caleta Olivia (US$13). Transportes VH crosses the border to Chile Chico (US$4 return) three times daily from Monday to Thursday, once on Fridays and Saturdays.

Tierra del Fuego

Over half of the Isla Grande de Tierra del Fuego, and much of the archipelago, is Chilean territory. Most travellers Argentine Tierra del Fuego will pass through Chile; details of Chilean towns are given in the Chile chapter.

History

Early European navigators feared and detested the stiff westerlies, hazardous currents and violent seas which impeded their progress toward Asia. None had any serious interest in this remote area, whose indigenous peoples were mobile hunter-gatherers.

The Ona (Selknam) and Haush subsisted on terrestrial animals like the guanaco, while Yahgans and Alacalufes ('Canoe Indians') lived on fish, shellfish and marine mammals. Despite inclement weather, they used little or no clothing, but constant fires, which gave the region its name, kept them warm.

Spain's withdrawal from the continent

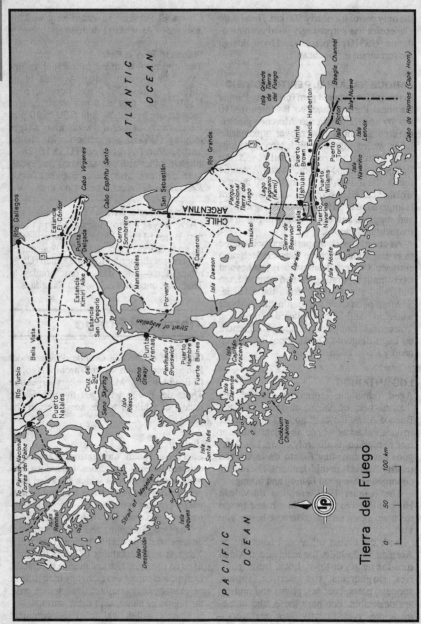

Tierra del Fuego

opened the area to European settlement, and the demise of the indigenous Fuegians began. Thomas Bridges, a young missionary from Keppel Island in the Falklands, learned to speak Yahgan and settled at Ushuaia, in what is now Argentine Tierra del Fuego. Despite honest motives, the Bridges family and others exposed the Fuegians to diseases to which they had little resistance. The estancieros made things worse by persecuting Indians who preyed on domestic flocks as the guanaco declined.

Despite minor gold and lumber booms, Ushuaia was at first a penal colony for political prisoners and common criminals. Wool is the island's economic backbone, but the area near San Sebastián has oil and natural gas. Since the 1960s, tourism has become so important that flights and hotels are heavily booked in summer.

Geography & Climate
Surrounded by the South Atlantic Ocean, the Strait of Magellan and the easternmost part of the Pacific Ocean, Tierra del Fuego is an archipelago of 76,000 sq km. Though most of the main island belongs to Chile, the Argentine cities of Ushuaia and Río Grande have the bulk of the population.

Northern Isla Grande is a steppe of unrelenting wind, oil derricks and enormous flocks of Corriedale sheep, while the wetter, mountainous south offers scenic glaciers, forests, lakes, rivers and sea coasts. The maritime climate is surprisingly mild, but changeable enough that warm, dry clothing is essential even in summer.

Getting There & Away
Since no public transport goes to the ferry at Punta Delgada, the simplest overland route to Argentine Tierra del Fuego is via Porvenir (Chile) across the Strait of Magellan from Punta Arenas. The main border crossing is San Sebastián, midway between Porvenir and Río Grande.

RÍO GRANDE
Río Grande is a bleak, windswept petroleum and agricultural service centre. Most visitors

pass through quickly en route to Ushuaia, but it's not completely without interest. Most services are near the plaza, including the tourist office (☎ 21701), at Rosales and Fagnano. For money exchange try Banco Nación, on San Martín at Avenida 9 de Julio. ENCOTEL is at Ameghino 712, between Piedrabuena and Estrada, while Telefónica is at Piedrabuena 787.

Places to Stay & Eat
Hospedaje Irmary, Estrada 743, has singles for US$8, as does *Hotel Anexo Villa*, Piedrabuena 641. *Hospedaje Miramar*, Mackinlay 595, has clean, well-heated rooms (US$15 per person with shared bath, US$18 with private bath).

Hospedaje Villa, at San Martín 277, *Hotel Ibarra*, on Rosales near Fagnano, and *Hotel Los Yaganes*, at Belgrano 319, all have restaurants, but try also *El Porteñito*, Lasserre 566, near Belgrano. Confiterías in and around the centre have minutas and sandwiches.

Getting There & Away
Air Aerolíneas Argentinas (☎ 22410) and LADE (☎ 21151) are both at San Martín 607. Aerolíneas flies daily to Buenos Aires (US$223). LADE flies daily to Calafate, Ushuaia (US$19) and Río Gallegos (US$22), with connections to Buenos Aires and northern Patagonia. Private Líneas Aéreas Kaikén serves the same destinations as LADE.

Austral (☎ 21388) is at Perito Moreno 352. Its daily flights from Ushuaia continue to Río Gallegos, Comodoro Rivadavia, Bahía Blanca and Buenos Aires.

Bus Transportes Los Carlos, Estrada 568, goes to Ushuaia (US$21, four hours) daily at 8 am in summer, less often in winter. Transporte Senkovic, San Martín 959, goes twice weekly to Porvenir, Chile (US$12, seven hours), with connections to Punta Arenas.

Getting Around
Given limited public transport, excursions

outside town are simpler with a rental car from A1, at Belgrano and Ameghino.

AROUND RÍO GRANDE
Things to See & Do
The missionary order which proselytised local Indians established the **Salesian Museum**, 11 km north of town on Ruta 3, which has exhibits on geology, natural history and ethnography. **Lago Fagnano**, the huge glacial trough on Ruta 3 between Río Grande and Ushuaia, merits a visit; stay at *Hostería Kaikén* (US$15 a single).

USHUAIA
In 1870 the British-based South American Missionary Society based itself at Ushuaia, but only artefacts, middens and memories remain of its Yahgan neophytes. Argentina incarcerated notorious criminals and many political prisoners here and on Isla de Los Estados (Staten Island) until 1947. A key naval base since 1950, Ushuaia has become a major tourist destination. Forestry and fishing are also significant, and efforts to attract electronics assembly have had some success. Ushuaia is a free port, but Punta Arenas has better bargains.

Shoreline Avenida Maipú leads west to Parque Nacional Tierra del Fuego. One block north is Avenida San Martín, the main commercial street and a pedestrian mall between avenidas 9 de Julio and 25 de Mayo. Above the steeply rising streets north of San Martín, jagged glacial peaks reach nearly 1500 metres. The surrounding area offers trekking, fishing and skiing, and the chance to go as far south as roads go: Ruta 3 ends at Lapataia Bay, 3242 km from Buenos Aires.

Information
Tourist Office At San Martín 660, the tourist office (☎ 24550) keeps a list of accommodation and current prices, including rooms with private families. English is spoken here, but the province has also instituted a programme in which local speakers of certain languages wear flag badges: red for English, blue for

■	PLACES TO STAY
1	Hostería América
2	Hotel Antártida
3	Hotel Las Lengas
6	Hostería Monte Cervantes
7	Hostería Mustapic
8	Pensión Rosita
9	Casa Familiar Ernesto Campos
10	Hospedaje Velásquez
11	Hospedaje Malvinas
14	Hotel Cabo de Hornos
15	Hospedaje César
20	Hotel Mafalda
22	Hospedaje Ona
23	Residencial Capri
27	Hotel Canal Beagle
28	Hotel Albatros
33	Hotel Maitén
34	Hospedaje Fernández

▼	PLACES TO EAT
17	Cafetería Pizzería Ideal
29	Moustacchio

	OTHER
4	Supermarket
5	Administración del Parque Nacional Tierra del Fuego
12	Telephones
13	Laundrette
16	Aerolíneas Argentinas/Austral
18	ENCOTEL
19	Telephones
21	Transporte Los Carlos
24	Buses to Parque Nacional Tierra del Fuego (Transporte Pasarela)
25	Tourist Office
26	LADE (Airline)
30	Líneas Aéreas Kaikén/Aventura Austral (Travel Agency)
31	Banco de la Nación
32	Museo Territorial Fin del Mundo
35	Chilean Consulate
36	Airport

French, white for German, green for Italian and yellow for Portuguese. Ask any wearer for information.

Money Most banks open from 10 am to 3 pm on weekdays, but Banco del Territorio, San Martín 936, is open from 5 to 9 pm.

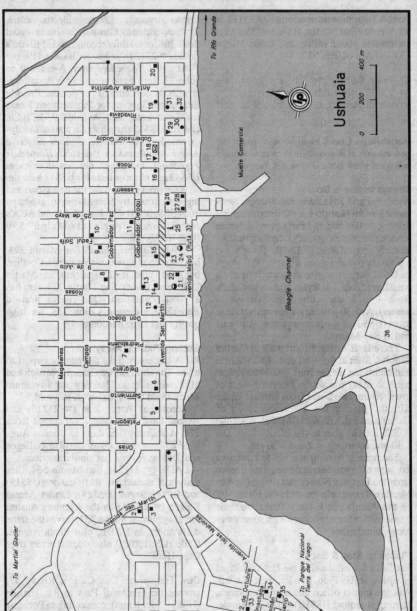

Ushuaia

To Río Grande

Muelle Comercial

Beagle Channel

To Martial Glacier

To Parque Nacional
Tierra del Fuego

0   200   400 m

Antártida Argentina

Rivadavia

Gobernador Godoy

Roca

Lasserre

25 de Mayo

Gobernador Paz

Gobernador Deloqui

Fadul Solís

9 de Julio

Rosas

Don Bosco

Piedrabuena

Belgrano

Campos

Magallanes

Sarmiento

Patagonia

Onas

Avenida San Martín

Avenida Malpú (Ruta 3)

Avenida San Martín

Avenida Islas Malvinas

12 de Octubre

Onachaga

Jainén

Kuanip

20
19
31
32
30
29
17 18
16
26
27 28
11
1
25
10
9
15
8
23
24
13
22
14
21
12
7
6
5
4
1
2
3
33
34
35
36

Post & Telecommunications ENCOTEL is on Avenida San Martín, at Godoy. The most convenient phone offices are at San Martín 133 and San Martín 957.

Chilean Consulate Chile's consulate (☎ 22177), Avenida Islas Malvinas 236 (corner of Jainén), is open from 9 am to 1 pm.

Bookshops Check local bookshops for the new edition of Rae Natalie Prosser Goodall's bilingual guidebook *Tierra del Fuego*.

Things to See & Do
At Maipú and Rivadavia, the **Museo Territorial Fin del Mundo** has exhibits on natural history, Indian life and early penal colonies (check the rogues' gallery), and replicas of an early general store and bank. There's also a bookshop and a good library. Well worth its US$2 admission, the museum is open on weekdays from 3 to 8 pm, and on weekends from 4 to 8 pm (closed on Sundays in winter). At 5.30 pm daily, museum staff lead tours (US$2) of the former prison, at the east end of San Martín.

There is is a magnificent walk to **Martial Glacier**. Start at the west end of San Martín and climb the zigzag road (with hiker short cuts) to a ski run seven km north-west of town. About two hours from the base of the lift, the glacier has awesome views of Ushuaia and the Beagle Channel. A shuttle (US$5 return) goes to the lift at 10 am and 1.30 pm, returning at 2 and 5.30 pm.

The nearest **fishing** site is Río Pipo, five km west of town; obtain the required licence from the Parques Nacionales office (on San Martín), Transporte Pasarela (at Fadul 40), or the Asociación Caza y Pesca. Ask the tourist office for a brochure with some other recommendations.

Places to Stay & Eat
Facilities are minimal at the free municipal *campsite* at Río Pipo, five km west of town. Ask the tourist office about private homes, starting at around US$10 to US$12 a single. One which has been highly praised is at

Primer Argentino 176, outside the centre. Try also Ernesto Campos, at Juana Fadul Solís 368, or warmly recommended Elvira's house (☎ 23123), at Fuegia Basket 419.

At noisy *Hospedaje Ona*, Avenida 9 de Julio 27, very basic rooms with dormitory-style beds cost US$10 per person. *Pensión Rosita*, on Gobernador Paz between Rosas (ex-Triunvirato) and Avenida 9 de Julio, charges US$15 per person in a more family-oriented environment, as does *Hostería América*, Gobernador Paz 1659. *Hospedaje Fernández*, Onachaga 68, has doubles at US$42 and cheaper beds for US$12 a single.

Waterfront hotels have the best views and highest prices – try *Hotel Albatros*, at Maipú 505 (US$90/110 with breakfast), and ACA's *Hotel Canal Beagle* at Maipú 599 (US$70/80).

Lively *Cafetería Ideal*, San Martín 393, has good food at reasonable prices. Costlier, but good value, is *Moustacchio*, San Martín 298. *Tante Elvira*, San Martín 234, also has a good reputation. One reader praised *Parrilla Tío Carlos*, Colón 758, for high quality and large portions.

Getting There & Away
Air A causeway links the nearby airport to town. The short runway, steep approach and high winds make landing an adventure which timid flyers may wish to avoid.

Aerolíneas Argentinas (☎ 21218) and Austral have consolidated offices, at Roca 126. Aerolíneas flies daily to Buenos Aires (US$239), with stopovers at Río Gallegos and Trelew. Austral has similar services.

LADE (☎ 21123), San Martín 564, flies daily to Calafate via Río Grande (US$19) and Río Gallegos (US$24). Líneas Aéreas Kaikén (☎ 21004), in the Aventura Austral travel agency, at Maipú 237, serves the same destinations as LADE, plus Punta Arenas, Chile (US$130). It also does charters over Cape Horn.

Bus Transporte Los Carlos, Rosas 57, crosses the Garibaldi Pass to Río Grande (US$21, four hours), connecting to Porvenir and Punta Arenas. For transport to Parque

Nacional Tierra del Fuego, see the separate entry for the park, below.

Boat At 9 am on Saturdays, a catamaran sails to Puerto Williams, Chile (US$65, three hours). There may be additional sailings in summer.

Getting Around
Only Tagle Rent A Car (22744), San Martín and Belgrano, presently rents cars.

PARQUE NACIONAL TIERRA DEL FUEGO
Argentina's only coastal national park, 18 km west of Ushuaia, extends north from the Beagle Channel to comprise rivers, lakes, forests and glaciers beyond Lago Fagnano. Southern beeches like the evergreen coihue and deciduous lenga thrive on heavy coastal rainfall, and the deciduous ñire tints the hillsides in autumn. *Sphagnum* peat bogs on the self-guided nature trail at Laguna Negra support ferns, wildflowers, and insectivorous plants. Marine mammals are most common on offshore islands.

Inland, there are guanacos and foxes, but visitors are most likely to see two unfortunate introductions: the European rabbit and the North American beaver. The Andean condor and the maritime black-browed albatross overlap ranges on the coast, but neither is common. Shore birds like cormorants, gulls, terns, oystercatchers, grebes, steamer ducks and kelp geese are common. The large,

striking upland goose *(cauquén)* is common inland. Claudio Venegas Canelo's *Aves de Patagonia y Tierra del Fuego Chileno-Argentina* (Punta Arenas, 1986) is an outstanding guide to the area's bird life.

Trekking
With permission from the Chilean Consulate and Argentine authorities in Ushuaia, it's possible to hike from Lapataia along the north shore of Lago Roca into Chile. An extended trek leads up the Río Pipo, across the Martial mountains to Lago Fagnano and back to Ushuaia; for details, consult Lonely Planet's *Trekking in the Patagonian Andes*.

Places to Stay
For US$8 per person, Lago Roca's organised camp site has hot showers and a confitería, but bring groceries from Ushuaia. There are free basic sites at Lapataia, Ensenada and Río Pipo.

Getting There & Away
In summer, Transporte Pasarela leaves daily for Lago Roca from Fadul Solís 40 in Ushuaia at 10 am, noon, and 3 and 7 pm, returning at 11 am and 1, 4 and 8 pm. The round-trip fare is US$8; you need not return the same day. Hitching is possible, though most vehicles are full. Park admission, payable at the Ruta 3 ranger station, is US$3.50 per person. There are also ranger stations at Lago Roca and Lapataia.

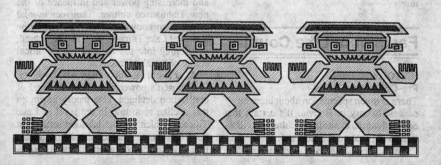

Bolivia

Bolivia is the Tibet of the Americas – the highest and most isolated of the Latin American republics. A landlocked country lying astride the widest stretch of the Andean Cordillera, Bolivia spills through a maze of tortured hills and valleys into the vast forests and savannas of the Amazon and Paraná basins, its geographical and climatic zones ranging from snowcapped Andean peaks to vast, unexplored, low-lying savannas and jungles. With two major Indian groups and several lesser ones, Bolivia is also the most Indian country on the South American continent. Over 50% of the population are of pure American Indian blood and maintain traditional cultural values and belief systems.

Bolivian history has certainly been turbulent and explosive; today, its political and social affairs attract mainly bad press, and will probably evoke images of coups d'état and drug barons. However, Bolivia offers much more than this stereotype might suggest, combining mind-blowing landscapes, colonial treasures, colourful indigenous cultures and remnants of mysterious ancient civilisations. Despite its former political strife and ongoing drug trade, it remains one of South America's most peaceful, secure and inviting countries. This, together with natural beauty and great diversity of cultures, makes Bolivia ideal for independent travel, discovery and adventure.

Facts about the Country

HISTORY
Pre-Columbian Times

There is much speculation about humanity's earliest history in Bolivia. It's certain that early advances towards agricultural civilisation took place on the altiplano.

From about 1500 BC, Aymara-speaking Indians, possibly from the mountains of what is now central Peru, swept across into the Bolivian Andes and occupied the altiplano. The years between about 500 and 900 AD were marked by the imperial expansion and increasing power and influence of the new Tiahuanaco culture. Their ceremonial centre (also known as Tiahuanaco), on the shores of Lake Titicaca, grew and prospered, developing into the religious and political centre of the altiplano.

After about the 9th century AD, however, Tiahuanaco's power waned and its level of civilisation declined. One theory attributes this decline to a drop in the level of Lake Titicaca, which left the lakeside settlement far from shore. Another theory postulates that Tiahuanaco was attacked and its popu-

BOLIVIA

lation massacred by the warlike Kollas (sometimes spelt Collas), also known as Aymara, from the west. The relics of Tiahuanaco culture can be seen in museums around the country, and they reflect a high level of technical precision.

Before the Spanish conquest, the Bolivian altiplano had been incorporated into the Inca Empire as the southern province of Kollasuyo. The Quechua-speaking Indians who now live around Lake Titicaca first immigrated under the Inca policies of resettling groups of their tribes in the newly conquered colonies and imposing

Quechua as the lingua franca of the Central Andes.

The Spanish Conquest

By the late 1520s internal rivalries had begun to take their toll on the Inca Empire, but it was the arrival of the Spaniards, first thought to be emissaries of the Inca Sun God, that dealt the final blow. The Inca emperor Atahualpa was captured in 1532, and by 1537, the Spanish had consolidated their forces in Peru and held Cuzco (the seat of Inca power) securely.

Alto Perú, as the Spaniards then called

Bolivia, fell briefly into the possession of Diego de Almagro. Then Francisco Pizarro dispatched his brother Gonzalo, at the head of an expedition, to subdue the southern province of Kollasuyo. He was, no doubt, attracted by the prospect of silver mines which had been worked in Inca times. Gonzalo Pizarro organised an administrative unit called Charcas in what is now central Bolivia. In 1538, Pedro de Anzures founded the township of La Plata there. La Plata later changed its name to Chuquisaca, and then changed again to Sucre, as it is called today. This town became the administrative, religious and educational centre of the eastern Spanish territories.

In 1545, the famous silver deposits of Potosí were discovered, and quickly gained prominence due to their abundant, high-quality ores. The settlement soon became one of the largest cities on the continent. Atrocious conditions in the Potosí mines led to the deaths of innumerable Indians and African slaves.

In 1548, the city of La Paz was founded by Alonso de Mendoza as an administrative and strategic staging post on the main silver route from Potosí to the Pacific coast. In 1574, the Spaniards founded Cochabamba, which soon became the granary of Bolivia, and Tarija, which served to contain the fierce Chiriguano Indians. Thus, at the close of the 16th century, the pattern of Bolivia's urban structure had been established, within the realm of the Spain's South American empire.

Independence

In 1781, a futile attempt was made to expel the Spaniards and re-establish the Inca Empire. Some 30 years later, in May 1809, Chuquisaca (now Sucre) became the scene of strong overt action for independence, and a local government was established. From Chuquisaca, one of the most fertile centres of liberal thinking on the continent, advanced political doctrines radiated throughout Spanish America.

In 1824, after 15 years of war, the libera-tion of Peru from Spanish domination was finally won in the battles of Junín and Ayacucho. However, in Alto Perú (Bolivia), the royalist General Pedro Antonio de Olañeta still opposed the liberating forces. In 1825, when offers of negotiation failed, Simón Bolívar dispatched an expeditionary force to Alto Perú under General Antonio José de Sucre. With the defeat of Olañeta at the battle of Tumusla, resistance came to an end. On 6 August 1825, independence was proclaimed and Alto Perú became the Republic of Bolivia. Bolívar and Sucre, incidentally, became the first and second presidents of the new republic.

In 1828, Andrés de Santa Cruz (who had a Spanish father and an Indian mother) took power and, influenced by romantic attachments to Inca ideals, formed a confederacy with Peru, constituted in 1836. This triggered a protest by Chile, whose army defeated Santa Cruz in 1839, breaking the confederation and submerging Bolivia in political chaos. The confusion peaked in 1841, at which time three governments claimed power simultaneously.

The pattern of spontaneous and unsanctioned changes of government took root at this time, and continued through the 1980s in a series of coups and military interventions. One military junta after another usurped power from its predecessor; in its 167 years as a republic, Bolivia has endured 188 changes of government. With such internal strife, it is not surprising that external affairs haven't always run smoothly either.

Loss of Territory

By the mid-19th century, the discovery of rich deposits of guano and nitrates in the Atacama region changed what had been a barren and sparsely desert into an economically strategic area. As Bolivia lacked population and resources to settle, develop and exploit the coastal area, it contracted with Chilean companies to carry out development projects. In 1879 the Bolivian government proposed a tax on the minerals, so Chile occupied Bolivia's Litoral Department, and Bolivia and Peru then declared war on Chile.

Between 1879 and 1883, in the War of the Pacific, Chile took 350 km of coastline, leaving Bolivia with no outlet to the sea. Though Chile tried to compensate Bolivia with a railway from Antofagasta to Oruro, and duty-free facilities for the export of Bolivian commodities, Bolivians refused to accept their *enclaustromiento* (landlocked status) and have taken every opportunity to voice their demand for access to the sea. Even now, the government uses the issue as a rallying cry whenever it wants to unite the people in a common cause.

Bolivia's next loss was in 1903, when Brazil annexed some 100,000 sq km of the Acre region, which stretched from Bolivia's present Amazonian border to about halfway up Peru's eastern border. The reason this time was rubber. Centred in Manaus (Brazil), the rubber boom took off in the second half of the 19th century and by 1890 accounted for one-tenth of Brazil's export earnings. Bolivia participated in the boom by plundering the forests of the Acre, until Brazil eventually engineered a dispute over sovereignty, and the Brazilian army was sent in.

Between 1932 and 1935, Bolivia fought a third devastating war, this time against Paraguay for control of the Chaco region. This area had previously been of little interest to either country, as it had very limited agricultural potential and was inhabited only by a few tribes of Indians.

The trouble started when various North American and European oil companies began to speculate about potential oil deposits in the area. In a bid to secure favourable franchises, a quarrel was engineered, with Standard Oil supporting Bolivia and Shell siding with Paraguay. Although Bolivia had more soldiers, fighting conditions in the Chaco favoured the Paraguayans. The climate took a heavy toll on the highland Indian troops of Bolivia, and Bolivia was gradually repulsed. By the terms of the peace settlement, negotiated in 1938, the greater part of the disputed areas of the Chaco went to Paraguay, costing Bolivia another 225,000

sq km of its territory. The anticipated oil reserves were never actually found in the Chaco.

The conflict with Paraguay disrupted the economy, discredited the army, spread new ideas among the urban workers and miners and sowed discontent among intellectuals, resulting in a process of social ferment.

Modern Times

After the Chaco war, friction between poor miners and their absentee bosses began to escalate. Radicals, especially in Oruro, gathered beneath the banner of the Movimiento Nacional Revolucionario (MNR), led by Victor Paz Estenssoro. The presidential elections of 1951 took place in an atmosphere of general unrest and finally brought victory to Paz Estenssoro, but a military coup that prevented him from taking power provoked an armed revolt by the miners. After heavy fighting in the April Revolution of 1952, military forces were dispersed and forced to capitulate, and Paz Estenssoro and the MNR took the helm for the first time.

The new government announced social and economic reforms aimed at ensuring the participation of all social sectors. The mining properties were nationalised and the sole right to export mineral products was vested in the state; universal suffrage and an unprecedented policy of agrarian and educational reform, including the redistribution of estates among the peasants and the restructuring of the educational system to provide schooling for everyone, were introduced.

For the first time since the invasion of the Spaniards, Indians felt that they had a voice in the Bolivian nation. The MNR government lasted 12 years under various presidents; Paz Estenssoro himself returned to power in 1960 for another four-year term, and was elected again in 1964.

The party, however, was unable to raise the standard of living substantially or increase food production, and Paz Estenssoro was forced to become more and more autocratic as dissension in his own ranks began to increase. Shortly after Paz Estenssoro's re-election in 1964, he was overthrown by General René Barrientos, thereby initiating another period of dictatorship and plunging Bolivia into renewed chaotic political instability.

A series of military regimes ensued until 1982, when the civilian left-wing leader of the MIR (Movimiento de Izquierda Revolucionaria), Hernán Siles Zuazo, came to power. His term was fraught with labour disputes, high levels of government spending, monetary devaluation and a staggering inflation rate.

When Siles Zuazo gave up after three years and called general elections, Victor Paz Estenssoro returned to politics to become president for the third time. During his four-year term (1985-89), the shattered economy was revived but social problems remained unsolved.

According to the Bolivian constitution, 50% of the popular vote is required for a candidate to become president in direct elections – otherwise, the Congress must make the decision. In the 1989 elections, none of the candidates obtained the necessary majority. Subsequently, the right-wing ADN (Acción Democrática Nacionalista) made a deal with the MIR, and the MIR leader, Jaime Paz Zamora, was elected president in exchange for leaving the most important ministries to the opposition.

Bolivia's new president, Gonzalo Sánchez de Losada, defeated former military dictator Huga Banzer Suárez in elections on 6 June 1993. Sánchez de Losada appealed to Indian peoples, and has indicated his intention of continuing free-market economic policies.

Coca, Cocaine & the Drug War

From time immemorial, coca has played a role in Bolivian culture and history. The Inca Love Goddess was represented with coca leaves in her hands. Legend has it that Manco Kapac, the son of the Sun God, who mystically appeared on Isla del Sol in Lake Titicaca, also brought the divine coca leaf, which alleviates hunger and strengthens the feeble.

By the time of the Spanish conquest, the use of coca, which had previously been restricted to privileged families and religious ceremonies, was widespread among Indians, sustaining them through prolonged periods of exhausting labour under severe conditions.

Coca leaves are still chewed. When combined with ashes of other plants, mainly *quinua*, they yield their alkaloid drug, the basis of cocaine. The juices extracted produce a feeling of wellbeing, giving a high degree of insensitivity to hunger, cold, fatigue and pain, and indifference toward hardship and anxiety. The Spaniards rapidly learnt that coca was a perfect stimulant to increase the efficiency of Indian labour, and promoted its use. Consequently, they introduced commercial plantations, first in the Yungas, still the country's leading producer of coca leaves. The success of La Paz as a city was partially due to the traffic of coca from the Yungas to the Potosí mines. Today, much of this leaf is refined into cocaine or taken to other Latin American countries to be processed. At least 60,000 hectares of coca are currently under cultivation.

In 1989, one-third of the Bolivian work force was dependent on the illicit production and trafficking of cocaine. Far and away the most lucrative of Bolivia's economic products, it was generating an annual income of US$1.5 billion, of which just under half remained in the country. Most of the miners laid off during Paz Estenssoro's austerity measures turned to cocaine as a source of income. Ensuing corruption, acts of terrorism and social problems threatened government control over the country, which in the international perspective became synonymous with cocaine production.

US threats to cease foreign aid unless efforts were made to stop cocaine production forced Paz Estenssoro to comply with their proposed coca eradication programme. Instead of eliminating the trade, however, the US eradication directive brought about the organisation of increasingly powerful and vociferous peasant unions and interest groups. This, combined with lax enforcement, corruption and skyrocketing profit potential, actually resulted in an increase in cocaine production.

Peasants were offered US$2000 each by the government to destroy their coca plantations and plant alternative crops, such as coffee, bananas and cacao. In early 1990, a drop in the price of coca paste brought about a temporary lull in production, and some coca farmers sold out to the government's proposed crop substitution programme. Many, however, simply collected the money and moved further north to replant.

As early as 1987, the USA had been sending Drug Enforcement Agency (DEA) squadrons into the Beni and Chapare regions of northern Bolivia to assist in the programme. In May 1990, Paz Zamora appealed for increased US aid to support the weakened Bolivian economy. In response, US President George Bush sent US$78 million in aid and stepped up US 'Operation Support Justice' activities. In June 1991, Bolivian police and DEA agents staged a daylight helicopter raid on Santa Ana del Yacuma, north of Trinidad, and seized 15 cocaine laboratories, nine estates, numerous private aircraft and 110 kg of cocaine base; however, no traffickers were captured, having been given sufficient warning to escape.

Several later surrendered under Bolivia's lenient 'repentance law'. In mid- 1992, Bolivia's Senate voted to expel US troops participating in antinarcotic activities.

GEOGRAPHY
Despite the loss of huge chunks of territory in wars and cessions, Bolivia remains South America's fifth largest country. It encompasses 1,098,000 sq km (the area of France and Spain combined) and is bounded by Peru, Brazil, Paraguay, Argentina and Chile.

There are five geographical regions:

The Altiplano
Through the western region of Bolivia run two chains of the Andes which extend from the Peruvian border to Chile and Argentina, with many peaks rising above 6000 metres. The western chain, the Cordillera Occidental, stands as a barrier between Bolivia and the Pacific Coast. The eastern chain, the Cordillera Real, runs first in a south-eastern direction, then turns south across central Bolivia, and becomes the Cordillera Central.

The altiplano (high plain), whose altitude ranges from from 3500 to 4000 metres, is bounded by these two great cordilleras. The altiplano itself is a haunting place – an immense, nearly treeless plain stretching to the horizon, punctuated by mountain barriers and solitary volcanic peaks. Near the northern end of the Bolivian altiplano, along the Peruvian border, lies Lake Titicaca, which is generally considered the world's highest navigable lake.

At its southern end, the land becomes drier and less populated. Here one finds the remnants of two other great lakes, the Salar de Uyuni and the Salar de Coipasa. These two salt deserts and the surrounding salty plains form an eerie expanse as empty as one can imagine.

Highland Valleys
East of the Cordillera Central are the Highland Valleys, a region of scrambled hills and valleys and fertile basins with a Mediterranean climate, where olives, nuts, wheat, maize and grapes are cultivated.

The Yungas
North of the Cordillera Real, where the Andes fall away into the Amazon Basin, the Yungas are a transition zone between dry, arid highlands and humid lowlands.

Gran Chaco
In the south-east corner of Bolivia lies the flat, nearly impenetrable scrubland of the Gran Chaco. The level terrain is covered by a tangled thicket of small thorny trees and cactus. As the region is almost completely uninhabited, native flora and fauna thrive undisturbed.

Amazon Basin
In the north and east of the country, this area is a flat and sparsely populated lowland composed largely of swamps, savannas, scrub and rainforest. It encompasses about half of Bolivia's total area.

CLIMATE
Because of its topography, Bolivia has a wide range of altitude-affected climatic patterns. Within its frontiers, every climatic zone can be found, from steaming rainforest heat to Arctic cold.

The rainy period lasts from November to March (the southern summer) in most of the country. Of the major cities, only Potosí consistently receives some snow between March and August (the southern winter), but in Oruro and La Paz snow is not uncommon near the end of the rainy season. On the altiplano and in the highlands, subzero temperatures are frequent, especially at night. Winter in Cochabamba, Sucre and Tarija is a time of clear skies and optimum temperatures. The Amazon Basin is always hot and wet, with the drier period falling between May and October. The Yungas region is cooler but fairly wet all year round.

FLORA & FAUNA
There are a number of national parks and reserves in Bolivia. They are home to a myriad of animal and bird species (see the Flora & Fauna section in the introductory Facts About South America chapter). Some of these parks have only recently become accessible to visitors, including:

BOLIVIA

Parque Nacional Amboró
Amboró, near Santa Cruz, was expanded and classified as a national park in 1990. It is home to the rare spectacled bear, jaguars, capybaras, peccaries and an astonishing variety of bird life. Access is via Buena Vista or Samaipata. Further information is available from FAN (Fundación Amigos de la Naturaleza) (☎ 33-3806, Santa Cruz), Casilla 4200, Avenida Irala 421, Santa Cruz.

Reserva Biosférica del Beni
The 334,200-hectare Beni Biosphere Reserve, near San Borja in the Amazon Basin, exists in conjunction with the adjacent Reserva Forestal Chimane. It is home to at least 500 species of tropical birds and more than 100 species of mammals. The entry station, at Porvenir, is on the main La Paz-Trinidad road.

Parque Nacional Isiboro-Sécure
Unfortunately, due to a 1905 policy to colonise this area of the Chapare (northern Cochabamba Department), the Indian population has been either displaced or exterminated, and most of the wildlife has vanished, except in the more remote areas. Access is difficult, and because this park lies along a major cocaine-producing route, extreme caution is required if you plan to visit the area. Tours are conducted by Fremen Tours (☎ 47126, Cochabamba), Casilla 1040, Calle Tumusla O-245, Cochabamba.

Parque Nacional Noel Kempff Mercado
This remote park near the Brazilian border is named in honour of the distinguished Bolivian biologist who was murdered by renegades in 1986. It contains a variety of Amazon wildlife and some of the most inspiring natural scenery in Bolivia. Overland access is possible but difficult; most visitors fly from Santa Cruz. The information address is the same as that for Parque Nacional Amboró.

Reserva de Vida Salvaje Ríos Blanco y Negro
This extremely remote 1.4 million-hectare wildlife reserve contains vast tracts of undisturbed rainforest. Wildlife includes giant anteaters, peccaries and tapirs, and there are over 300 bird species. Accommodation and access are quite expensive, but a visit is highly worthwhile. For information, contact Amazonas Adventure Tours (☎ 32-4099, Santa Cruz), Casilla 2527, Calle Andrés Manso 342, Santa Cruz.

Parque Nacional Sajama
This national park, which abuts the Chilean border and adjoins Chile's magnificent Parque Nacional Lauca, contains Volcán Sajama (6542 metres), Bolivia's highest peak. The park lies along the main route between La Paz and Arica, Chile, but no tourist facilities are available on the Bolivian side.

Parque Nacional Torotoro
Palaeontologists will be interested in the biped and quadruped dinosaur tracks from the Cretaceous period, which can be found in the enormous rock formations near the village of Torotoro. The Asociación Experimental Torotoro (☎ 25843, Cochabamba), Calle 25 de Mayo 482, Cochabamba, will supply information about visits.

Parque Nacional Tunari
This park, right in Cochabamba's back yard, features Lagunas de Huarahuara (small lakes containing trout) and pleasant mountain scenery. Picnic areas and camp sites are available. The park entrance lies practically within walking distance of the city centre.

Parque Nacional Ulla-Ulla
Excellent hiking is possible in this remote park abutting the Peruvian border beneath the Cordillera Apolobamba. It was established in 1972 as a vicuña reserve and presently contains 2500 vicuñas and a large population of condors. Information is available through INFOL (Instituto de Fomento Lanero) (☎ 37-9048, La Paz), Casilla 732, Calle Bueno 444, La Paz.

GOVERNMENT

In theory, Bolivia is a republic with legislative, executive and judicial branches of government. The first two convene in La Paz, the de facto capital, and the Supreme Court sits in Sucre, the legal capital.

The president is elected for a four-year term by popular vote, and cannot hold more than one consecutive term. Once elected, the president appoints a cabinet of 15 members and also selects departmental and local government officers.

The legislature consists of a Senate and a Chamber of Deputies. Each of the nine departments sends three elected senators for terms of six years, with one-third elected every two years. The Chamber of Deputies has 102 members, who are elected for four-year terms.

Despite its history of instability, the late 1980s and early 1990s have seen peaceful and democratic transitions of government. Politically, the country is currently one of the most stable in Latin America.

ECONOMY

Tin, tungsten, antimony, sulphur, copper, silver and gold are some of the major Bolivian mineral resources. In the first half of the 19th century, a French explorer described Bolivia as 'the beggar sitting on a chair of gold'. Or, as one Bolivian put it: 'Bolivia is like a donkey loaded with silver – all this potential wealth is nothing but a liability'. Despite its unquestionable wealth of natural resources, Bolivia remains among the poorest Latin American nations.

Due to the inaccessibility of the mines and the distances over which raw metals must be freighted, Bolivia is a high-cost mineral producer. This, together with lack of skill and capital, corruption, disorganisation, and internal strife between the miners' union, cooperatives and the state, makes the mining industry chaotic. The government is currently looking towards the eastern lowlands, where significant deposits of natural gas, iron, manganese and petroleum have been discovered.

In agriculture, Bolivia scarcely satisfies its own minimal requirements, and exports only small amounts of coffee and sugar. Exports of coca products, however, greatly exceed all legal agricultural exports combined.

POPULATION & PEOPLE

Bolivia, with 7.8 million people, is thinly populated. Despite its cold, arid climate, the altiplano has for centuries been the country's most densely populated region, with 70% of the people.

Between 50% and 60% of the total population is of pure Indian stock, and most people speak either Quechua or Aymara as a first language. They are traditional and strongly resist cultural change. About 35% of the population is made up of *mestizos* (of Spanish and Indian blood); nearly 1% is of African heritage, mostly descended from the slaves conscripted to work the Potosí mines. The remainder of the population is primarily of European descent, with a small Asian minority. The sparsely populated northern and eastern lowlands are currently in the relatively early stages of settlement. Mennonite farmers have established dairy industries, and Santa Cruz has become a cosmopolitan city, with immigrants from Japan, Germany and the USA.

The standard of living of most Bolivians is low – housing, nutrition, education, sanitation and hygiene are appalling. About 15% of infants die before their first birthday and the average life expectancy is only 51 years.

ARTS & CULTURE
Dance

The pre-Hispanic dances of the altiplano were celebrations of war, fertility, hunting prowess, marriage or work. After the Spanish arrived, traditional European dances and those of the African slaves brought to work in the mines were introduced; they developed into the hybrid dances that characterise Bolivian festivities today.

If Bolivia has a national dance, it is the *cueca*, danced by handkerchief-waving couples to 3/4 time. It is derived from the Chilean cueca, which in turn is a Creole adaptation of the Spanish fandango. Its liberally interpreted choreography is danced primarily during fiestas by whirling couples, called *pandillas*. The dance is intended to convey a story of courtship, love, loss of love and reconciliation. A favourite part of the dance comes at the shouting of 'Aro, aro, aro', which indicates that it's time for the couple to stop dancing for a moment and celebrate with a glass of spirits each. Another very popular dance is the *huayno*, which originated on the altiplano.

The *auqui-auqui* (old man dance) parodies high-born colonial gentlemen by portraying them ludicrously with a top hat, gnarled cane and exaggerated elderly posture.

Another tradition is the *tinku*; although it resembles a kind of disorganised dance, it is actually a ritual fight which takes place primarily in northern Potosí Department during festivals. Tinkus normally begin innocently enough but, near the end of the celebrations, often erupt into drunken mayhem.

In the south, around Tarija, where musical traditions depart dramatically from those of the rest of Bolivia, the festival dance is known as the *chapaqueada*. It is normally associated with religious celebrations, especially San Roque, and is performed to the strains of Tarija's host of unusual musical instruments. Also popular in Tarija is *la rueda* (the wheel), which is danced at all fiestas throughout the year.

In San Ignacio de Moxos and around the Beni lowlands, festivities are highlighted by the dancing of the *machetero*, a commemorative folkloric dance accompanied by drums, violins and bajones. Dancers carry wooden machetes and wear elaborate crowns of brilliant macaw feathers, wooden masks, and costumes made of cotton, bark and feathers.

Other popular dances in the northern lowlands

include the *carnaval* and the *taquirari Beniano*, both adapted from the altiplano, and the *chovena*, indigenous to north-eastern Bolivia.

Some of the most unusual and colourful dances are those performed at festivals on the high altiplano, particularly during Carnaval; *La Diablada* (The Dance of the Devils) fiesta at Oruro draws a large number of both foreign and Bolivian visitors. The most famous and recognisable of the Diablada dances is *la morenada*, which is a re-enactment of the dance of the Black slaves brought to the courts of Viceroy Felipe III. The costumes consist of hooped skirts and shoulder mantles, and dark-faced masks adorned with plumes. Another dance with African origins is *los negritos*. Performers beat on drums, the rhythm reminiscent of the music of the Caribbean.

The *los llameros* dancers represent Andean llama herders, the *waca takoris* satirise Spanish bullfighters and the *waca tintis* represent the *picadores*, also of bullfighting fame. The *los Incas* dance commemorates the original contact between the Incan and Southern European cultures, while the *las tobas* is performed in honour of those Indian groups of the tropical lowlands which were conquered by the Inca and forcefully absorbed into the empire.

Music

Although the musical traditions of the Andes have evolved from a series of pre-Inca, Inca, Spanish, Amazonian and even African influences, each region of Bolivia has developed distinctive musical traditions, dances and instruments. The strains of Andean music from the cold and bleak altiplano are suitably haunting and mournful, while those of warmer Tarija, with its complement of bizarre musical instruments, take on more vibrant and colourful tones.

Although the original Andean music was exclusively instrumental, recent trends toward popularisation of the magnificent melodies have inspired the addition of appropriately tragic, bittersweet or morose lyrics.

In the far eastern and northern lowland regions of Bolivia, Jesuit influences upon Chiquitano, Moxos and Guaraní musical talent left a unique legacy which is still in evidence and which remains particularly strong in the musical traditions of neighbouring Paraguay. In addition to economic ventures, the Jesuits encouraged education and European culture among the tribes.

Extremely able artists and musicians, the Indians handcrafted musical instruments – the renowned violins and harps featured in Chaco music today – and learned and performed Italian baroque music, including opera! In the remotest of settings, they gave concerts, dances and theatre performances which could have competed on a European scale.

In Bolivia, folk music shows are called *peñas* and operate, for locals and tourists, in most larger cities.

Musical Instruments Although the martial honking of tinny and poorly practised brass bands seems an integral part of most South American celebrations, the Andean musical traditions employ a variety of instruments which date back to precolonial days.

Only the popular ukelele-like *charango* (based on the Spanish *vihuela* and *bandurria*, early forms of the guitar and mandolin) has European roots. By the early 17th century, Andean Indians had blended and adapted the Spanish designs into one which would better reproduce their pentatonic scale: a 10-stringed instrument with llama-gut strings (arranged in five pairs) and a *quirquincho* (armadillo carapace) soundbox. Modern charangos are scarcely different from the earliest models, but due to the scarcity and fragility of quirquinchos, and to efforts to improve sound quality, wood is now the material of choice for charango soundboxes. Another stringed instrument, the *violín chapaco* originated in Tarija and is a variation on the European violin. Between Easter and the Fiesta de San Roque (held in early September), it is the favoured instrument.

Prior to the advent of the charango, melody lines were carried exclusively by woodwind instruments. Best recognised are the *quena* and the *zampoña* (pan flute), which feature in the majority of traditional musical performances. Quenas are simple reed flutes played by blowing into a notch at one end. The more complex zampoñas are played by forcing air across the open ends of reeds lashed together in order of their size, often in double rows. Both quenas and zampoñas come in a variety of sizes and tonal ranges. Although the quena was originally intended for solo interpretation of musical pieces known as *yaravies*, the two flutes are now played as part of a musical ensemble. The *bajón*, an enormous pan flute with separate mouthpieces in each reed, accompanies festivities in the Moxos communities of the Beni lowlands. While being played, it must be rested on the ground or carried by two people.

Other prominent wind instruments include the *tarka* and the *sikuri*, lead instruments in the breathy *tarkeadas* and *sikureadas* of the rural altiplano, and the *pinquillo*, a Carnaval flute which comes in various pitches.

Woodwinds unique to the Tarija area are the *erke*, the *caña* and the *camacheña*. The erke, also known as the *phututu*, is made from a cow's horn and is played exclusively between New Year and Carnaval. From San Roque (in early September) to the end of the year, the camacheña, a type of flute, is used. The caña, a three-metre cane pole with a cow's horn on the end, is similar in appearance and tone to an alphorn. It's featured all year round in Tarija.

Percussion also figures in most festivals and other folk musical performances as a backdrop for the typically lilting strains of the woodwind melodies. In highland areas, the most popular drum is the largish *huankara*. The *caja*, a tambourine-like drum played with one hand, is used exclusively in Tarija.

Artists & Recordings Although there is a wealth of yet-to-be-discovered musical talent in Bolivia, key players are influencing musical trends and tastes worldwide with their recordings and occasional performances abroad.

Many visitors, especially those who've attended peñas or fiestas, are captivated by the music and set out in search of recordings to take home. Compact discs haven't yet made their debut in Bolivia, so unless you have space to carry bulky and fragile record albums in your luggage, you'll have to resort to cassette tapes. Unfortunately, original recordings are hard to come by and those sold in music shops and markets are typically low-quality bootlegged copies which are prone to rapid self-destruction, so copy them onto a better tape before giving them much play time. They are cheap, however – around US$3 each.

Major artists you may want to look for include charango masters Ernesto Cavour, Celestino Campos and Mauro Núñez. Look out for the recording *Charangos Famosos*, a selection of well-known charango pieces.

The Bolivian group that's been the most successful abroad is Los Kjarkas. They've recorded at least a dozen albums, including the superb *Canto a la Mujer de Mi Pueblo*. The track entitled *Llorando se Fue*, by the late Bolivian composer Ulíses Hermosa and his brother Gonzalo, was recorded by the French group Kaoma in 1989 and became a worldwide hit as *The Lambada*. In June 1990, the Hermosa brothers finally received official recognition for their authorship of the song.

Other groups worth noting are Savia Andina (known for their protest songs), Chullpa Ñan, Rumillajta, Los Quipus, Grupo Cultural Wara, Los Masis and Yanapakuna.

In the USA, tapes of Bolivian music are available through the South American Explorers Club.

Weaving

Spinning and weaving methods have changed little in Bolivia for centuries. In rural areas, girls learn to weave before they reach puberty and women spend nearly all their spare time spinning with a drop spindle or weaving on heddle looms. Prior to Spanish colonisation, llama and alpaca wool were the materials of choice, but sheep's wool has now emerged as the most readily available and least expensive medium.

Bolivian textiles come in diverse patterns, and the majority display a degree of skill that results from millennia of experience. The beautiful and practical creations are true works of art, and motivated visitors who avoid such overtouristed haunts as Tarabuco and Calle Sagárnaga in La Paz may find real quality at good prices.

Regional differences are manifest in weaving style, motif and use. Weavings from Tarabuco, near Sucre, are made into the colourful costumes (men wear a *chuspa*, or coca pouch, and a trademark red poncho) and zoomorphic patterns seen around the popular and touristy Sunday market in Tarabuco.

Most famous and celebrated of Bolivian weavings are the red-and-black zoomorphic designs from Potolo, north-west of Sucre. Patterns range from faithful representations of animals to creative and mythical combinations of animal forms: horses figure prominently, as do avian aberrations. The patterns are not necessarily symmetrical, and the relative size of figures represented often does not conform to reality – it is not unusual for a gigantic horse to be depicted alongside a tiny house. Potolo pieces are prized by weavings buffs and command relatively high prices.

BOLIVIA

Zoomorphic patterns are also prominent in the wild Charazani country north of Lake Titicaca and in several areas in the vicinity of La Paz, including Lique and Calamarka. Some extremely fine weavings originate in Sica Sica, one of the many dusty and nondescript villages between La Paz and Oruro, while in Calcha, south-east of Potosí near the boundary of Chuquisaca, expert spinning and extremely tight weave – over 150 threads per inch – combine into some of Bolivia's best clothing textiles.

Those interested in Bolivian textiles may want to look at the books *A Travellers' Guide to Eldorado and the Inca Empire*, by weavings expert Lynn Meisch, or the hard-to-find *Weaving Traditions of Highland Bolivia*, by Laurie Adelson and Bruce Takami, published by the Los Angeles Craft & Folk Art Museum. Another excellent booklet on Bolivian textile arts is *Bolivian Indian Textiles*, by Tamara E Wasserman & Jonathon S Hill, available through the South American Explorers Club.

Chola Dress

The distinctive Aymara and Quechua women's dress, both colourful and utilitarian, has become a representative image of Bolivia. The most noticeable characteristic of the traditional Aymara dress is the ubiquitous dark green, black or brown bowler hat that would seem more at home on a London street than in the former Spanish colonies. You'd be hard-pressed to find a chola or campesina without one.

The women normally braid their hair into two long plaits, which are joined by a tuft of black wool known as a *pocacha*. The short *pollera* skirts they wear are constructed of several horizontal bands tucked under each other. This garment tends to make most of the women appear overweight, especially when several are combined with multiple layers of petticoats.

On top, the outfit consists of a factory-made blouse, a woollen *chompa* (pullover/ jumper), a short vest-like jacket and a cotton apron, or some combination of these. Usually, the women will add a woollen shawl known as a *llijlla* or *phullu*.

Slung across the back and tied around the neck is the *ahuayo*, a rectangle of manufactured or handwoven cloth decorated with brilliantly coloured horizontal bands. It is used as a carry-all and is filled with anything from coca or groceries to babies.

The Quechua of the highland valleys wear equally colourful but not so universally recognised attire. The hat, called a *montera*, is a flat-topped affair made of straw or finely woven white wool. It's often taller and broader than the bowlers worn by the Aymara. The most striking is the felt montera of Tarabuco, patterned after the Spanish conquistadores' helmets.

Architecture

The pre-Columbian architecture of Bolivia is seen in the largely ruined walls and structures of Tiahuanaco, and the numerous Inca remains scattered about the country. Restoration of these sites has been based on architectural interpretation by archaeologists, without revealing much about their artistic values. The classic polygonal cut stones which dominate many Peruvian Inca sites are, in Bolivia, found only on Isla del Sol and Isla de la Luna, in Lake Titicaca.

Surviving colonial architecture, the vast majority of which is religious, is divided into four major overlapping periods: renaissance (1550-1650); baroque (1630-1770); mestizo (1690-1790), which was actually a variation on baroque; and the modern period (post-1790). Around 1790, the beginnings of the modern period were marked by a brief experimentation with the neoclassical style, which was then followed by a return to the neo-Gothic.

Renaissance churches are simple in design. They were constructed primarily of adobe, with courtyards, massive buttresses and naves without aisles. One of the best examples may be seen at the village of Tiahuanaco. Some Andean renaissance churches indicate Moorish *mudéjar* influences. The three classic examples of mudéjar renaissance design are found at San Miguel and San Francisco (in Sucre) and at Copacabana, on the shores of Lake Titicaca.

Baroque churches were constructed in the form of a cross, with an elaborate dome and walls made of either stone or reinforced adobe. The best examples of pure baroque are the churches of the Compañía in Oruro, San Agustín in Potosí and Santa Bárbara in Sucre.

Mestizo elements in the form of whimsical decorative carvings were introduced late in the baroque period, and applied with what appears to be wild abandon. Prominent themes included densely packed tropical flora and fauna, Inca deities and designs, and bizarre masks, sirens and gargoyles. The interesting results are best seen at the churches of San Francisco (in La Paz), San Lorenzo, Santa Teresa and the Compañía (in Potosí) and the rural churches of Sica Sica and Guaqui (in La Paz Department).

Neoclassical design, which dominated between 1790 and the early 20th century, is observed in the church of San Felipe Neri in Sucre, and the cathedrals in Potosí and La Paz.

Paralleling the mainstream church construction in the mid-18th century, the Jesuits in the Beni and Santa Cruz lowlands were designing churches showing evidence of Bavarian rococo and Gothic influences. Their most unusual effort, however, was the bizarre mission church at San José de Chiquitos, the design of which is unique in Latin America. Its European origins aren't clear, but it bears superficial resemblance to churches in Poland and Belgium.

RELIGION

Bolivia enjoys complete religious freedom. Due to their Spanish past, 95% of Bolivians profess Roman Catholicism, but there is a blending of the traditions and beliefs of ancient cults with the Christian faith, which has resulted in a peculiar syncretism which remains very evident among Indian communities.

Facts for the Visitor

VISAS

Visa requirements for Bolivia change with astonishing frequency. Currently, citizens of Argentina, Austria, Ecuador, Israel, Switzerland, Uruguay, Scandinavian countries (including Finland and Iceland), the UK and most other European Community countries do not require visas for stays of up to 90 days. Citizens of the USA, France, Belgium, Netherlands, Luxembourg, Portugal and most other non-Communist and non-Middle Eastern countries are granted stays of 30 days without a visa. Canadians, Australians, New Zealanders, South Africans, Brazilians,

and Chileans require visas, issued by Bolivian representatives in their home countries or in neighbouring South American countries.

Officially, everyone entering Bolivia requires proof of onward transport and sufficient funds for their intended stay; in practice officials rarely scrutinise these items. Passports must be valid for one year beyond the date of entering the country. Most border officials will give only a 30-day entrance stamp, but the stay may be extended at immigration offices in major cities. The fee at the time of writing was B70, but travellers have reported that the fee is flexible – in Sucre, free extensions have been granted.

Personal documents – passports, visas, *cédulas* (identification cards), etc – must be carried at all times to avoid fines during police checks and several lost hours while paperwork is shuffled at the police station. This is strictly enforced in lowland regions where drug trafficking is rife – especially Santa Cruz.

Bolivian Embassies & Consulates
Australia
> Consulate: Suite 517, 210 Queen St, Brisbane, 4000 (PO Box 53; (☎ (07) 221-1606)

France
> 12 Avenue Presidente Kennedy, Paris (☎ 642249344)

Germany
> Konstantinstrasse 16, Bonn (☎ 362038)

UK
> 106 Eaton Square, SW12W London (☎ (071) 235-4248)

USA
> 3014 Massachusetts Ave, Washington DC (☎ 483-4410)

MONEY
Currency
Bolivia's unit of currency is the *boliviano* (B$), which is divided into 100 centavos. Bolivianos come in two, five, 10, 20, 50, 100 and 200 denomination notes, with coins worth two, five, 10, 20 and 50 centavos, and one boliviano. Bolivian currency is practically worthless outside Bolivia, so don't change more than you'll need.

After a catastrophic decline in the Bolivian currency in the first half of the 1980s and austerity measures undertaken in 1985, the boliviano remains one of the most stable currencies on the continent, with an average annual inflation not exceeding 15%. The official rate represents the currency's actual value, so there's no need for a black market in currency.

Exchange Rates

Approximate official rates at July 1993 were as follows:

A$1	=	B$2.92
DM1	=	B$2.52
FF1	=	B$0.71
UK£1	=	B$6.41
US$1	=	B$4.32

As a rule, visitors should carry US dollars, the only foreign currency accepted throughout Bolivia. Currencies of neighbouring countries may be exchanged in border areas. If you're carrying travellers' cheques, American Express seems to be the most widely accepted, though you won't have major problems with other brands.

As a rule, money is exchanged not at banks but in *casas de cambio*. You'll find them in larger cities, and they all change cash dollars. Some also change travellers' cheques. Apart from the casas de cambio, you can change money in some travel agencies, jewellery or appliance stores, pharmacies, etc. These establishments deal mainly with cash, though some also accept travellers' cheques. Street moneychangers operate virtually around the clock in most major towns and cities. They only change cash dollars, paying roughly the same as the casas de cambio and other establishments.

The rate for cash is similar all over the country, except in border areas, where it's slightly lower. The rate for travellers' cheques is best in La Paz, where nearly equals the cash rate; in other large cities it's 3% to 5% lower, and in smaller towns it may be impossible to change travellers' cheques at all. In La Paz, several casas de cambio exchange travellers' cheques for cash dollars for a 1% to 3% commission. It's a good idea to have some cash dollars if you are heading into the interior, especially off the La Paz-Cochabamba-Santa Cruz axis.

When you exchange money, ask for the cash in small denominations, as there are permanent problems with change – nobody has it. Another problem concerns mangled notes; bills with tiny pieces missing, repaired with tape, sewed with thread or even in separate halves are common – don't accept them as change.

Credit Cards

Major cards, such as Visa, MasterCard and American Express, may be used in larger cities at first-rate hotels, restaurants and tour agencies.

With travellers' cheques expensive and sometimes difficult to change, there's a good case for carrying a Visa card. Visa cash withdrawals of up to US$300 per day are available in 20 minutes, with no commission and a minimum of hassle, from the Banco de Santa Cruz in La Paz, Sucre, Cochabamba and Santa Cruz. Banco Mercantil offers similar services without commission, as does Banco Nacional de Bolivia. Banco de La Paz charges 1.75% commission on cash withdrawals.

TOURIST OFFICES

Tourist information is run by Dinatur (Dirección Nacional de Turismo), with offices in major cities. There is still little printed tourist information, but the typically young and enthusiastic staff members are usually friendly and will do their best to help.

BOOKS

There is a general reading list in the introductory Facts for the Visitor chapter. If you want more travel information on Bolivia, look for Lonely Planet's *Bolivia – a travel survival kit*, which gives a complete rundown on the country. If you intend to do a bit of walking, get a copy of *Backpacking and Trekking in Peru and Bolivia*, by Hilary Bradt (4th edition, Bradt Publications, UK, 1987), which includes descriptions of interesting hikes, mainly in the Cordillera Real and the Yungas.

A Traveller's Guide to El Dorado and the Inca Empire, by Lynn Meisch (3rd edition, Penguin Books, 1980) is an excellent book providing timeless information about Colombia, Ecuador, Peru and Bolivia, especially their weaving and textiles.

Le Guide du Routard – Pérou, Bolivie, Equateur – 1992 (Hachette, Mendon) is the best French-language guidebook, with good, updated information and a light, pleasantly quirky style.

English, German as well as some French-language books are available from Los Amigos del Libro, which has outlets in La Paz and Cochabamba. They tend to be quite pricey, but have a good selection of popular paperbacks, guidebooks, dictionaries and histories, as well as glossy coffee-table books dealing with the anthropology, archaeology and scenery of Bolivia.

The bookshop at El Alto Airport in La Paz also sells guides and souvenir books, but at staggering prices which are not negotiable. Some bookshops have a shelf or a box of used English-language paperbacks stashed away in a corner. Even if you don't find them displayed, it's worth asking. *Newsweek* and *Time* are available at kiosks and bookshops in La Paz and other large cities like Santa Cruz and Cochabamba.

Spanish-language books, including classic literature and popular novels, are also available at Los Amigos del Libro and similar shops. The majority of *librerías* (bookshops) and street sellers, however, mainly sell pulpy local publications, comics and school texts.

MAPS
General government mapping is available from the Instituto Geográfico Militar (IGM), Avenida 16 de Julio 1471 in La Paz, where you'll find good city maps, country maps and topographic sheets on a scale of 1:50,000 covering some 60% of Bolivia, including all the mountain ranges, which are excellent for trekking. You select the map you want, pay the bill and they'll have it ready for collection the following day.

HEALTH
Bolivia is not a particularly unhealthy country, but sanitation and hygiene are poor, and you should pay attention to what you eat. Unboiled water should not be drunk, but bottled water, available commercially in larger cities, is free of contaminants and is safe to drink.

Most people live between 3000 and 4000 metres, and altitude sickness can occur. Read carefully the information on altitude-related health problems in the Health section of the Facts for the Visitor chapter.

A yellow fever vaccination is legally required for travel in Santa Cruz Department, though you'll probably never be asked for one. If you're heading from Bolivia to Brazil, however, Brazilian authorities may not grant you entry without one.

WORK
There are a vast number of volunteer organisations at work in Bolivia and quite a few international companies with offices in the country, but those looking for paid work on the spot probably won't have much luck. Qualified English teachers interested in working in La Paz and several other cities may want to try the professionally run Centro Boliviano Americano (☎ 35-1627), Avenida Aniceto Arce at Parque Zenón Iturralde, La Paz. Alternatively, phone Señor Alandia or Señora Miranda at the Pan American English Language Centre (☎ 34-0796), 2308 Avenida Aniceto Arce, to arrange an interview.

If you are interested in voluntary work in Bolivia with an emphasis on environmental protection, contact Earthwatch (☎ (617) 926-8200), 680 Mt Auburn St, Box 403, Watertown, MA 02272, USA.

ACCOMMODATION
The Bolivian hotel rating system divides accommodation into categories which, from bottom to top, include *posadas, alojamientos, residenciales, casas de huéspedes, hostales* and *hoteles*. This rating system reflects the price scale and, to some extent, the quality. The Camara Boliviana de

Hotelería (☎ 37-2618), on the 3rd floor of the Shopping Miraflores, on Calle Panamá at the corner of Plaza Uyuni in La Paz, publishes an annual *Oferta Hotelera*, which details accommodation in all categories, with approximate prices.

Posadas are the bottom end – the cheapest basic roof and bed you'll be able to find. They cost between US$1 and US$2.50 per person and vary in quality, normally from bad to worse. Hot water is unknown, and some don't even have showers.

Alojamientos are also basic budget accommodation, but they're better than posadas and cost a bit more. Though they generally don't have private baths, some have hot water in communal showers. The value varies widely – some are clean and tidy, while others are disgustingly seedy. Prices range from US$1 per person in Copacabana to US$6 in the Amazon Basin.

Residenciales, casas de huéspedes and hostales all serve as finer budget hotels. Their quality also varies a great deal. Although not all are spotlessly clean and airy, most are acceptable. You will often have the option of shared or private baths, often with hot water. These places cost between US$9 and US$17 for a double with private bath, about 30% less without.

Going up-market, you have a whole constellation of hotels, which also vary in standard but are more expensive than the rest. Throughout Bolivia, the prices and value of accommodation are not uniform. The cheapest places you are likely to come across are in Copacabana, while the most expensive are in the Amazon region.

The vast majority of hotel owners are friendly, honest people who demand the same standards of their staff. Competition is such that a hotel can't afford to get a bad reputation, so your belongings should be safe left in the room. However, use your common sense, as not all hotel guests are necessarily honest.

Just about all hotels, if you stay for one or two days, will watch your luggage free of charge if you plan to be away for a few days.

Room availability should be no problem at all, except during major fiestas, when prices double and rooms are quickly occupied by visiting nationals.

Bolivia is a good country for camping. That doesn't mean that there are organised camping sites, but if you have camping gear, you can pitch your tent nearly anywhere outside population centres. Remember that highland nights can be freezing!

FOOD

Due to the various climatic zones, Bolivian cuisine is quite diverse. The fare of the altiplano tends to be starchy and loaded with carbohydrates. Potatoes come in dozens of varieties, mostly small and colourful. Freeze-dried potatoes, called *chuño* or *tunta*, often accompany the meals. In the lowlands, the potato and its relatives are replaced by *yuca* (cassava), and other vegetables figure more prominently.

The predominant meats are beef, chicken and fish. The poorer *campesinos* (peasants) eat *cordero* (mutton), *cabrito* (goat) and llama. The most popular fish on the altiplano is *trucha* (trout) from Lake Titicaca. The lowlands have a great variety of freshwater fish, of which *surubí* is the most delicious.

The most popular typical Bolivian dishes include *chairo* (a kind of lamb or mutton broth with potatoes, chuños and vegetables), *sajta* (chicken served in hot pepper sauce), *saice* (a spicy meat broth), *pacumutu* (beef fillet), *silpancho* (pounded beef with egg on top) and *pique a lo macho* (chopped beef served with onions and other vegetables).

Snack-wise, the most delicious Bolivian speciality is the *salteña*, a rugby ball-shaped meat and vegetable pie. It is stuffed with beef or chicken, olives, egg, potato, onion, peas, carrots and whatever else is on hand.

Standard meals are *desayuno* (breakfast), *almuerzo* (lunch) and *cena* (dinner). For the latter two, many restaurants, ranging from backstreet cubbyholes to classy establishments, offer bargain set meals consisting of soup, main course and tea or coffee. In better places, a salad starter and a dessert are included.

The set meals for almuerzo and cena are cheap, roughly half the price of any dish from the regular menu, somewhere between US$1 and US$3, depending on the class of restaurant. If you're on a strict budget, set meals are the best way to fill yourself up. Your bargain-basement alternative is the market; these exist in every city and town and have food stalls where filling and usually tasty meals are served.

DRINKS
Beyond the usual black tea, coffee and chocolate, typical local hot drinks include *mate de coca* (coca leaf tea) and *api*. Api, a sweet drink made of maize, lemon and cinnamon, is served mainly in markets.

Coke, Sprite, Pepsi, Fanta etc are available. Bolivia also produces locally invented soft drinks.

Grapes are grown around Tarija, and some acceptable wines are produced. The same companies also make *singani*, a spirit obtained by distilling poor-quality grape wine. There are several very good Bolivian beers. The favourite alcoholic drink of the Bolivian masses is *chicha cochabambina*, obtained by fermenting maize. It is made all over Bolivia, especially in the Cochabamba region. Other versions of chicha, normally nonalcoholic, are made from such items as maize, sweet potato, peanuts and yuca.

Getting There & Away

Only a limited number of airlines offer services directly to Bolivia; fares are high, those from Peru and Chile being the most economical. On the whole, it works out cheaper to fly into a neighbouring country (such as Peru, Chile, Brazil or Argentina), and then travel overland to Bolivia from any of those countries. If you decide to leave Bolivia by air, it's next to impossible to buy a discounted ticket out of the country.

AIR
The national airline is Lloyd Aéreo Bolivi-ano (LAB), and the only Bolivian airline offering international flights. Airports charge a US$20 tax on international flights for those who have spent less than 90 days in Bolivia. It's payable to the aviation authority, AASANA, when you check in for a flight.

To/From Argentina
LAB has a service from Buenos Aires to La Paz via Santa Cruz on Tuesday, Friday and Sunday. Fares are US$295 to La Paz and US$244 to Santa Cruz. Once a week, this flight also serves Salta, Argentina.

To/From Brazil
LAB has flights from Rio de Janeiro and São Paulo to La Paz on Monday, Wednesday, Friday and Sunday, stopping in Santa Cruz en route. One-way fares from Rio are US$341 to La Paz and US$273 to Santa Cruz. Varig/Cruzeiro flies the same route on Tuesday, Thursday, Friday and Saturday. On Friday, AeroPerú flies between La Paz, Santa Cruz, Rio de Janeiro and São Paulo. In addition, LAB does a Thursday run between Manaus and Santa Cruz for US$207 one-way.

To/From Chile
On Monday, Wednesday, Friday and Sunday, LAN Chile flies to La Paz from Santiago, stopping in Arica and Iquique. LAB flies to and from Arica and Santiago on Tuesday, Thursday and Saturday. The fare is US$90 from Arica, US$180 from Santiago.

To/From Paraguay
LAB and LAP (Air Paraguay) fly between Asunción, Santa Cruz and La Paz on Tuesday and Friday. One-way fares to Asunción are US$156 from Santa Cruz, US$211 from La Paz.

To/From Peru
LAB, AeroPerú, American Airlines and Lufthansa fly between Lima and La Paz. LAB has a service on Tuesday, Thursday, Saturday and Sunday (US$162 one-way). AeroPerú flies on Wednesday and Friday.

BOLIVIA

American Airlines and Lufthansa both fly on Thursday. In Peru there is a ticket tax of 21% for Peruvian residents, 7% for nonresident tourists.

LAND
To/From Argentina
From Salta or Jujuy in north-western Argentina, buses leave every couple of hours during the day for La Quiaca, opposite the Bolivian town of Villazón. It takes about half an hour to walk between the Argentine and Bolivian bus terminals, or take a taxi.

From Villazón, there are buses to Tupiza and Potosí and trains to Uyuni, Oruro and La Paz. There was a direct rail service between La Paz and Buenos Aires but all rural passenger rail services in Argentina have been suspended, and are unlikely to resume. If they do, you'll still have to walk or take a taxi between the Villazón and La Quiaca railway stations – about 40 minutes with luggage.

The border crossing at tiny Pocitos is just a short distance south of Yacuiba, Bolivia and north of Tartagal, Argentina. The walk across the border between Pocitos, Argentina and Pocitos, Bolivia takes about 10 minutes. There are taxis between Pocitos and Yacuiba and buses to and from Tartagal.

From Tucumán in north-central Argentina, take a bus to Embarcación and Tartagal, and from there to Pocitos on the frontier. Between Yacuiba and Santa Cruz, there are trains and *ferrobuses*, as well as buses to and from Tarija.

There's also a border crossing at Bermejo/Aguas Blancas, which is sometimes used by travellers.

To/From Brazil
Corumbá, opposite the Bolivian border town of Quijarro, has both rail and bus connections from São Paulo, Rio de Janeiro, Cuiabá and southern Brazil. It is the busiest port of entry between Bolivia and Brazil.

From Corumbá, take a bus to the frontier, and from there a taxi to the railhead at Quijarro. From Quijarro, a train leaves daily

during the dry season for Santa Cruz. During the wet, there may be waits of several days.

From Cáceres, south-west of Cuiabá, you can cross to San Matías in Bolivia, and from there either take a bus to San Ignacio de Velasco or fly to Santa Cruz (via Roboré) to connect with terrestrial transport.

From Brasiléia, in the state of Acre, you can cross into Cobija, Bolivia. Previously, it was necessary to fly from there to other Bolivian cities, but by the time this book is published, the new Cobija-Riberalta road should be open. From Riberalta, there is now a dry-weather road all the way to La Paz.

A more popular crossing is by ferry from Guajará-Mirim in Brazil across the Río Mamoré to Guayaramerín, Bolivia. From there, a road goes to Riberalta, where you can take the dusty route south toward Rurrenabaque and La Paz.

To/From Chile
There are trains and ferrobuses between La Paz and Arica, with immigration formalities at the border crossing between Visviri and Charaña. This trip can be a very cold proposition, though some trains are more comfortable than others.

By bus, Flota Litoral covers the very rough route between Arica and La Paz, via the Chungará/Tambo Quemado border crossing, twice-weekly, leaving from Calle Chacabuco in Arica.

Agencia Martínez, in Arica, runs a bus service from Arica to connect with Bolivian trains, going only as far as the frontier. Since Bolivian trains don't operate to a reliable schedule, the Martínez bus does a run whenever a train is expected to arrive at Charaña.

Going to Bolivia from Antofagasta, you must take a bus to Calama (US$3, two hours), from where there's one train a week to Ollagüe, eight hours *uphill* from Calama, on the Bolivian border. In Ollagüe, you have to walk across the border to Abaroa in Bolivia, and connect with the Bolivian train to Uyuni and Oruro.

At the Tramaca bus station in Antofagasta, you can buy a combination bus and train ticket all the way to La Paz. As on all routes between Chile and Bolivia, warm clothes are essential!

To/From Paraguay

The route overland into Bolivia from Paraguay is very rough and probably not worth considering, unless you don't mind long waits. Another option is to catch the boat along the Río Paraguay from Asunción to Corumbá on the Brazil/Bolivia frontier (see Getting There & Away for Corumbá, in the Brazil chapter).

To/From Peru

There are basically two routes from Puno, the main access point from Peru into Bolivia. The quickest but least interesting is by *micro* from Puno to the frontier at Desaguadero, where you can connect with a Bolivian bus to La Paz.

The more scenic and interesting route is via Copacabana and the Estrecho de Tiquina (Straits of Tiquina). Micros leave from Puno and enter Bolivia at Yunguyo, 11 km from Copacabana. There you connect with another micro, or with a bus company, for the four to five-hour trip to La Paz, including the boat across the lake. The entire run from Puno to La Paz can be done in a day, but it's worth stopping off at Copacabana for a couple of days to explore the area.

There are other very obscure border crossings, such as the one from Puerto Acosta north of Lake Titicaca and a couple of ports of entry along the rivers of the north, but they require some effort and there's no public transport available.

Getting Around

AIR

Domestic air services are provided by LAB, TAM (Transportes Aéreos Militares) and AeroXpress. LAB, the national airline, has the widest network and most frequent flights, and goes pretty much everywhere you might wish to go. However, it's not 100% reliable

and is notorious for delays and cancellations, especially in the Amazon lowlands.

The military airline, TAM, is equally unreliable. With a fairly developed network, it fills some gaps in LAB's schedule. Fares are cheaper than LAB's (on some routes considerably so), but you can't book a seat unless you buy a ticket. The following are sample one-way fares from La Paz with LAB:

Cochabamba	US$36
Puerto Suárez	US$150
Riberalta	US$97
Santa Cruz	US$78
Sucre	US$49
Tarija	US$67
Trinidad	US$37

AeroXpress is of limited interest for travellers, but it is the only airline which provides air services to Potosí (about US$57 from La Paz).

LAB offers a special deal called a Vibol Pass. This air pass costs US$160 and must be purchased outside Bolivia through a travel agent or LAB office. It allows you to fly to all cities served by LAB, beginning and ending in the same city of your choice. You can visit each city only once.

Airport tax is US$2.50 tax on domestic flights.

BUS & CAMIÓN

The road network in Bolivia isn't good, with only a handful of paved roads; the rest are unsurfaced, ranging from fairly good to the more widespread rough and potholed gravel tracks. Modern coaches use the best roads, while older vehicles cover minor secondary routes.

Long-distance bus lines are called *flotas*. Large buses are called *buses* and small ones are called *micros*. A bus terminal is a *terminal terrestre*.

Most buses depart in the evening and arrive in the morning; on the major routes, however, there are also a few daytime departures. It seems that no matter how many companies service a particular run, they all leave at the same time of day.

If you don't want to travel at night, opt for

a *camión* (truck). This is a very popular mode of transport among campesinos, as the *camiones* usually charge around half the bus fare. Camión rides can be rough, depending on the cargo you're riding on and the number of other passengers, but they certainly offer the best views.

To be on the safe side, reserve bus tickets at least several hours in advance. It's also essential on any bus or camión trip, day or night, to take plenty of warm clothing. At night, even in the lowland areas, it gets surprisingly cold, and on the altiplano, it is freezing.

TRAIN

With 4300 km of lines, the Bolivian railroad has two networks: the western one, with its nerve centre in Oruro and connections to La Paz, Cochabamba, Sucre, Potosí, Villazón (Argentine border), Abaroa and Charaña (both on the Chilean border); and the eastern one, with its focus in Santa Cruz and lines to Quijarro, near Puerto Suárez (Brazilian border), and Yacuiba (Argentine border).

The western section is a bit better organised and more reliable (if the word 'reliable' can be applied to Bolivian railways at all), while the eastern one is the epitome of disorganisation and chaos.

There are four sorts of trains. The best is the *ferrobus*, which is fairly quick and comfortable and usually runs on time. The others are the *tren bala* (laughably, 'bullet train') and *tren expreso* (or *tren especial*), both slower and less expensive than the ferrobus.

Next comes the *tren rápido* (literally 'fast train', though it is actually very, very slow) and, finally, the *tren mixto*, an excruciatingly slow mixed goods and passengers train. It's considerably cheaper than a ferrobus and carries both passenger coaches and *bodegas* (boxcars). Travel in the boxcars is normally more comfortable than in the coaches. The last two types never run to a real schedule and probably hold the slow speed record for the continent. Because of their low fares, these trains are the principal means of transport for the campesinos, their children, their

luggage, their animals... Needless to say, you'll have lots of company.

Most railway stations don't have printed train schedules; instead, departure times are scrawled on a chalkboard – I don't think the system needs further explanation.

You can buy tickets a day in advance for the ferrobus, but for other trains, tickets are available only on the day of departure. However, procuring a ticket is usually a battle and will mean at least several hours in a queue. Overall, train travel in Bolivia (especially on the mixto or rápido) requires some determination, a strong constitution and vast reserves of patience.

BOAT

Half of Bolivia's territory lies in the Amazon Basin, where rivers are the main transport arteries and transport is by cargo boats, which carry passengers, vehicles and livestock. The main highways of the region are the Ichilo, Mamoré, Beni, Madre de Dios and Guaporé rivers – all Amazon tributaries. For more information about boats, refer to the Amazon Basin section.

TOURS

Organised tours, based mainly in La Paz, are rapidly becoming more popular. Shorter tours are normally arranged through hotels, agencies and tourist offices, and if you're in a hurry, they're a convenient way to quickly visit an attraction you'd otherwise miss. They're also relatively inexpensive, averaging US$20 for a day trip and less for a half-day trip.

This is an excellent way to visit Tiahuanaco, for instance. An English-speaking guide is normally included, and the ruins can become something more than an impressive 'heap of rocks'. A short tour is also useful if you want to visit the Chacaltaya ski slopes or the Zongo ice caves, which are difficult to reach on your own. Similarly, longer excursions to such remote attractions as Laguna Colorada or the Cordillera

Apolobamba are most conveniently done through tour agencies.

For the more adventurous, who nevertheless don't want to strike out into the wilderness alone, there are a number of outfits which offer trekking, mountain climbing, river running and rainforest exploration packages. Recommended companies include: Abotours, Colibri, Guarachi Andes Expeditions, Paititi and TAWA Tours in La Paz; Amazonas Adventure Tours in Santa Cruz; and Fremen Tours in Cochabamba.

La Paz

The home of more than a million Bolivians, over half of Indian heritage, La Paz is the country's largest city and its centre of commerce, finance and industry. Although Sucre remains the judiciary capital, La Paz has usurped most government power and is now the de facto capital. La Paz was founded by Alonso de Mendoza in 1548, following the discovery of gold in the Río Choqueyapu. Although gold fever didn't last long, the town's location on one of the main silver routes from Potosí to the Pacific assured stable progress. It wasn't until the middle of the present century that peasant migration from the countryside caused the city to expand rapidly.

A visitor's first view of La Paz will never be forgotten; its spectacular setting rivals those of such cities as Rio, Capetown, San Francisco and Hong Kong. Poor and littered upper suburbs flank the city's bleak approaches from the altiplano. The muddy roads, which appear to have avoided much attention since Inca times, are lined with automobile repair shops and junk yards; unkempt children play in muddy potholes, and nearby, Indian women pound laundry in a sewage-choked river. Then, suddenly, La Paz appears. The earth drops away as if all the poverty and ugliness had been obliterated, and there, 400 metres below, is the city, filling the bowl and climbing the walls of a gaping canyon nearly five km from rim to rim. On a clear day, the snow-capped triple peak of Illimani (6402 metres) towers the city.

Since La Paz is nearly four km above sea level, warm clothing is essential throughout the year. During the summer, the climate can be harsh, rain falls daily in the afternoon and the canyon fills with clouds. Frequent hailstorms pelt the city with icy golfballs, and the steep streets become torrents of run-off. Daytime temperatures hover around 18°C, though the dampness makes it seem much colder. In the winter, days are slightly cooler, but the crisp, clear air is invigorating. While the sun shines, the temperature may keep to the mid-teens, while at night, it often dips below freezing. In a city where central heating systems are practically unknown, the cold can seem oppressive and debilitating. Occasionally, rain and even snow fall during the winter.

La Paz is the best place in Bolivia to sit back and watch urban Bolivians circulating through their daily tasks and routines. You can spend hours gazing at the passing crowds: the cholas with their obligatory bowler hats and voluminous skirts, the white-shirted businessmen and politicians, the beggars and the machine-gun toting military. La Paz has a wide range of hotels, restaurants, entertainment and activities for the visitor, and the longer you stay, the more you'll realise just how much there is to see and do.

Orientation

It's almost impossible to get lost in La Paz. There's only one major thoroughfare, the Prado, which follows the canyon of the Río Choqueyapu (which flows mostly underground these days). This main street changes names several times from top to bottom they are avenidas Ismael Montes, Mariscal Santa Cruz, 16 de Julio and Villazón. At the lower end, it splits into Avenida 6 de Agosto and Avenida Aniceto Arce. Away from the Prado everything is narrow and goes steeply uphill, and many streets are cobbled or unpaved. Above the downtown skyscrapers, the adobe

BOLIVIA

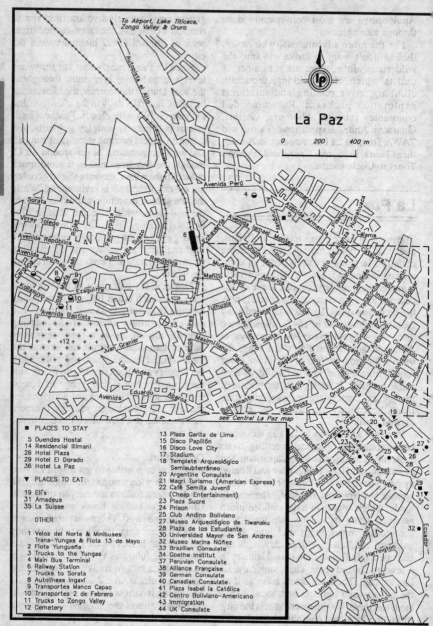

La Paz

0   200   400 m

PLACES TO STAY

5 Duendes Hostal
14 Residencial Illimani
26 Hotel Plaza
29 Hotel El Dorado
36 Hotel La Paz

▼ PLACES TO EAT

19 Eli's
31 Amadeus
35 La Suisse

OTHER

1 Veloz del Norte & Minibuses
   Trans-Yungas & Flota 13 de Mayo
2 Flota Yungueña
3 Trucks to the Yungas
4 Main Bus Terminal
6 Railway Station
7 Trucks to Sorata
8 Autolíneas Ingaví
9 Transportes Manco Capac
10 Transportes 2 de Febrero
11 Trucks to Zongo Valley
12 Cemetery

13 Plaza Garita de Lima
15 Disco Papillón
16 Disco Love City
17 Stadium
18 Templete Arqueológico
   Semisubterráneo
20 Argentine Consulate
21 Magri Turismo (American Express)
22 Café Semilla Juvenil
   (Cheap Entertainment)
23 Plaza Sucre
24 Prison
25 Club Andino Boliviano
27 Museo Arqueológico de Tiwanaku
28 Plaza de los Estudiante
30 Universidad Mayor de San Andres
32 Museo Marina Núñez
33 Brazilian Consulate
34 Goethe Institut
37 Peruvian Consulate
38 Alliance Française
39 German Consulate
40 Canadian Consulate
41 Plaza Isabel la Católica
42 Centro Boliviano-Americano
43 Immigration
44 UK Consulate

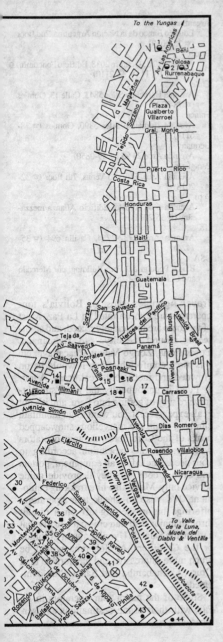

neighbourhoods and the informal commercial areas climb toward the canyon's rim. If you've become lost and want to return to the Prado, just head downhill.

Information

Tourist Office Dinatur (☎ 35-8213) has its La Paz office on the 18th floor of Edificio Ballivián, at Calle Mercado 1328. It's open Monday to Friday from 8.30 am to noon and 2.30 to 6.30 pm. They have a message box and a book of visitor recommendations, and distribute a host of other brochures dealing with La Paz and the entire country, some in English, French and German. The original Spanish versions, however, may make more sense than the mildly amusing translations. You'll get superb views of the city through the windows.

There is a new departmental tourist office at Comercio 1230, near Plaza Murillo, open weekdays from 9 am to 12.30 pm and 2.30 to 6.30 pm. It's very friendly and helpful, with a decent selection of brochures. El Lobo restaurant, at the corner of Calle Illampú and Avenida Mariscal Santa Cruz, has books of travellers' recommendations in both English and Hebrew.

Money Several casas de cambio are found on calles Ayacucho and Colón on the block just above Avenida Camacho. Casa de Cambio Sudamer, on Calle Colón, changes travellers' cheques and is open from 9 am to noon and 2 to 5 pm on weekdays. They also sell Peruvian and Chilean currency (when it's available), often at better rates than you can get in those countries. Casa de Cambio Silves, at Calle Mercado 979, and Cambio d'Argent, at Calle Mercado 1328, have also been recommended; they'll change travellers' cheques to cash US dollars for just 1% commission – others charge up to 3%.

One of the most popular places to change money is the Shampoo Shop, at Yanacocha 319, which gives the best rate for both cash and cheques. For 1.5% commission, they also change travellers' cheques into cash, which is worth considering, as outside La

BOLIVIA

Paz you will get significantly less for cheques than for cash.

On Saturdays, you can change cash or travellers' cheques either at the Hotel Gloria or at the Unitours travel agency, near the corner of calles Loayza and Mercado; rates are low. Along Avenida Camacho, *cambistas* (street changers) will change cash for about the same rate given by the casas de cambio.

Visa cash withdrawals of up to US$300 daily are available in 20 minutes, with no commission and a minimum of hassle, from the Banco de Santa Cruz, at Calle Mercado 1077. Banco Mercantil, on the corner of calles Mercado and Ayacucho, offers similar services without commission, as does Banco Nacional de Bolivia, at the corner of Calle Colón and Avenida Camacho. Banco de La Paz charges 1.75% commission on cash withdrawals.

The American Express representative is Magri Turismo (see under Travel Agencies).

Post & Telecommunications The main post office, at the corner of Avenida Mariscal Santa Cruz and Calle Rodríguez Oruro, is open Monday to Friday from 8.30 am to 8 pm and on Saturday from 9 am to 7 pm. This is the place to pick up poste restante. If you're having anything shipped to you in La Paz, it should be addressed as follows: your name (with surname underlined and capitalised), Poste Restante, Correo Central, La Paz, Bolivia. They hold mail for three months. The service is free, but you must present your passport when collecting letters.

The ENTEL office, at Calle Ayacucho 267, is open daily from 7.30 am to 10.30 pm. You can make national and international calls and send telegrams there. ENTEL also has telegram and telex services, and has recently opened a new but laboriously inefficient fax office. The public fax numbers in La Paz are 39-1784 and 36-7625.

Embassies & Consulates The following countries are among those with representation in La Paz:

Argentina
    Edificio Banco de la Nación Argentina, 2nd floor
    (☎ 35-3089)
Brazil
    Avenida 20 de Octubre 2038, Edificio Foncomin, Pisos 9, 10, 11 (☎ 32-2110)
Chile
    Avenida Hernando Siles 5843, Calle 13, Obrajes (☎ 78-5275)
France
    Avenida Hernando Siles 5390, Obrajes (☎ 78-6114)
Germany
    Avenida Arce 23 95 (☎ 39-0850)
Paraguay
    Avenida Arce, Edificio Venus, 7th floor (☎ 32-2018)
Peru
    Avenida 6 de Agosto, Edificio Alianza mezzanine (☎ 35-2031)
UK
    Avenida Arce 2732-2754, Casilla 694 (☎ 35-7424)
USA
    Banco Popular del Peru Building, cnr Mercado and Colón (☎ 35-0251)

Travel Agencies Most of Bolivia's tour operators are concentrated in La Paz. Most of the tours are moderately priced, and sightseeing around the city – to Tiahuanaco, Copacabana, Zongo Valley, Chacaltaya, etc – is more comfortable than it would be on crowded and inefficient local buses. A tour to Puno is undoubtedly the most straightforward way of getting into Peru, and it's not at all expensive. If you want to go mountain climbing up to the marvellous snowcapped peaks of the Cordilleras, the tour operators will organise the expedition according to your needs, including all equipment, porters and even a cook, or they'll provide guide service only. Many also hire trekking equipment. It's wise to check tour operators' offerings before setting off on a circuit through major Bolivian cities; it's likely that a trip to the Salar de Uyuni, Laguna Colorada or the Cordillera Apolobamba would be much more impressive and memorable than Oruro, Cochabamba and Santa Cruz combined!

Some of the major tour operators in La Paz, with their prime destinations and services, are:

Balsa Tours
Avenida 16 de Julio 1650, Edificio Alameda, Casilla 5889 (☎ 35-6566, fax (591-2) 39-1310). Among other things, Balsa Tours runs cruise excursions around the Islas Huyñaymarkas, Isla del Sol, Isla de la Luna and Copacabana.

Diana Tours
Calle Sagárnaga 328, in the Hotel Sagárnaga (☎ 35-8757). This company has city tours, and tours to Tiahuanaco, Valle de la Luna, Chacaltaya and the Yungas. Its tours to Copacabana and Puno are also among the cheapest.

Magri Turismo Limitada
Avenida 16 de Julio 1490, Edificio Avenida, 5th floor (☎ 34-1201, fax (591-2) 36-6309). Magri Turismo is the American Express representative in Bolivia, and although they sell sightseeing tours, they're primarily concerned with airline bookings and overseas reservations.

Transturin
Avenida Mariscal Santa Cruz 1295, 3rd floor, Casilla 5311, La Paz (☎ 32-0445, fax (591-2) 39-1162). This company, a bit more up-market than most, offers catamaran trips to the Lake Titicaca highlights, including Copacabana, Isla del Sol and Puno, Peru.

Other Tour Companies
Similar services to those of Diana Tours are offered by:
Vicuña Tours (☎ 32-3504), in Hotel Viena, Calle Loayza 420
Combitours (☎ 37-5378), in Residencial Copacabana, Calle Illampú 734
Nuevo Continente (☎ 37-3423), in Residencial Los Andes, Avenida Manco Capac 366
Turisbus (☎ 32-5348), in Residencial Rosário, Calle Illampú 704 (also has recommended tours to the Salar de Uyuni, Laguna Colorada and Laguna Verde)

Maps The best tourist map of the city is *La Paz Información*, sold by Dinatur. General government mapping is available from the Instituto Geográfico Militar (IGM), at Avenida 16 de Julio 1471.

Film & Photography Fujichrome colour slide film is widely available at about US$7 per roll; be cautious about purchasing film at street markets, where it is exposed to strong sun all day. Fujicolour is the most widely available print film.

For processing of both slides and print film, only two laboratories are reliable: Casa Kavlin, at Calle Potosí 1130, and Foto Linares, in the Edificio Alborada, on the corner of Calle Loayza and Juan de la Riva. The latter also sells a selection of Agfa film.

If you have camera problems, the person to see is Rolando Calla. You'll find him in Idem-Fuji Color (☎ 32-7391), at Calle Potosí 1316, between 10.30 am and noon, and at his home (☎ 37-3621), at Avenida Sánchez Lima 2178, from 3 to 7 pm.

Emergency The Unidad Sanitario Centro Piloto, near the brewery just off upper Avenida Ismael Montes, is open from 8.30 am to noon and 2.30 to 6.30 pm. Those heading for the lowlands may pick up yellow fever vaccinations, and free chloroquine to be used as a malaria prophylaxis. Don't take chloroquine, however, if you've previously been taking Lariam (mefloquine); they make a potentially dangerous combination.

Rabies vaccinations are available for US$1. Anyone bitten or scratched by a suspect animal must take daily vaccinations for seven subsequent days, and three more over the next two months.

If you're in need of an English-speaking doctor, try Clínica Americana (☎ 78-3371), at 5409 Avenida 14 de Septiembre, Calle 9, in the Obrajes district. The German clinic, Clínica Alemana (☎ 32-9155), is at Avenida 6 de Agosto 2216.

Immigration For visa extensions, go to the immigration office (☎ 37-0475), in the Edificio Ministerio del Interior, at Calle Gonsalves between avenidas Aniceto Arce and 6 de Agosto. Extensions can cost as much as B70 for up to 90 days.

Things to See
La Paz has conventional tourist attractions such as churches, museums, etc. For those seeking something different, it's a city that invites leisurely exploration, to appreciate the architectural mishmash, colourful street scenes, busy market life, and the strong flavour of Indian culture, which is more evident here than in other Latin American capitals.

The most unusual market is the **Mercado de Hechicería** (Witches' Market), near the corner of Calle Santa Cruz and Linares. Here, merchants sell a variety of herbs, seeds, magical ingredients and other strange things, supposed to be remedies for any combination of ills you may be experiencing and protection from the bad spirits which populate the Aymara world. In the same area, mainly along Sagárnaga and Linares, are plenty of handicrafts shops and street stalls selling beautiful Indian weavings (ponchos, *mantas*, coca pouches), musical instruments, silver antiques, 'original' Tiahuanaco rocks and a wealth of other artefacts.

Construction of the **Iglesia de San Francisco**, on the plaza of the same name, started in 1549 but was not finished until the mid-18th century. It stands out as La Paz' most imposing church, the architecture reflecting the mestizo style, with emphasis on nature and natural forms. If you pass by on Saturday mornings, you may see colourful Indian weddings. Other churches are of limited interest, though you might enjoy the impressive façade of **Iglesia de Santo Domingo**, at the corner of Yanacocha and Ingaví.

Museums La Paz has several worthwhile museums, some housed in beautiful old colonial mansions. The **Museo de Etnografía y Folklore** is in the former Casa del Marquez de Villaverde, on the corner of Ingaví and Sanjines. It has a fine collection of weavings and other crafts from several ethnic groups throughout the country. Of particular interest are artefacts and photos of the Chipayas, a group that inhabits the northern shores of the Salar de Coipasa, whose language, rites and customs differ greatly from those of other altiplano dwellers. The museum is open Monday to Friday from 8.30 am to noon and 2.30 to 6.30 pm. Admission is US$0.25.

The **Museo Nacional del Arte** is in the Palacio de los Condes de Arana, an impressive 18th-century mansion at the corner of Comercio and Socabaya. It displays colonial and contemporary painting and is open Tuesday to Friday from 9.30 am to 12.30 pm

and 3 and 7 pm and on Saturday from 9.30 am to 1.30 pm. Admission costs US$0.50.

The **Museo Arqueológico de Tiwanaku**, at the corner of Calle Federico Suazo and Tiwanaku, holds a collection of pottery, small stone sculptures, textiles and other artefacts, and utensils from different stages of the Tiahuanaco (Tiwanaku) culture. It's open Tuesday to Friday from 9 am to noon and 2.30 to 7 pm, and on Saturday from 10 am to 12.30 pm and 2.30 to 6.30 pm. Admission is US$0.25.

If you're interested in the city's past traditions, visit the **Museo Tambo Quirquincho**, a former *tambo* (wayside market and inn) on Calle Evaristo Valle, just off the Plaza Alonso de Mendoza. It displays old-time dresses, silverware, photos, artwork and a collection of Carnaval masks. It's open Tuesday to Friday from 9.30 am to 12.30 pm and 3.30 to 7 pm, and on weekends from 10 am to 12.30 pm. Admission is free.

Four interesting museums – **Museo de Metales Preciosos Precolombinos**, the **Museo del Litoral Boliviano**, the **Museo Casa Murillo** and the **Museo Costumbrista Juan de Vargas** – are clustered together along Calle Jaén, a beautifully restored colonial street, and can easily be visited in one shot; nonresidents pay US$0.75 for a combination ticket which covers admission to all four. They're open Tuesday to Friday from 9.30 am to noon and 2.30 to 6.30 pm, and on weekends from 10 am to 12.30 pm.

Festivals
La Paz enjoys several local festivals and holidays during the year, but El Gran Poder (late May/early June) and Alasitas, the festival of abundance (24 January), will be of particular interest to visitors.

Places to Stay
Look for acceptable budget accommodation in two main areas. The first is in the market area, particularly on Manco Capac and Illampú, relatively close to the railway station; the other is in the heart of the city, around Plaza Murillo. Midnight is lock-up time for most bottom-end hotels. All hotels

listed here have hot water, but it's wise to ask anyway, especially with the cheapies.

A new entry in La Paz is the *Duendes Hostal* (☎ 35-1125), at Avenida Uruguay 470, between Avenida Ismael Montes and the bus terminal. It's affiliated with Club Andino Boliviano and has applied to join the Youth Hostel Association. Single rooms with private bath cost US$8, while larger dormitory rooms are considerably less. Hot showers and laundry services are available.

If being central is your primary consideration, the *Hotel Torino* (☎ 34-1487), at Calle Socabaya 457, near Plaza Murillo, is still a good bet, although it has become a bit surly – an unfortunate by-product of its reputation as *the* budget travellers' haunt. It's still a clean place to crash, and has nice electric showers from 6 am to 1 pm. There's also a book exchange (open in the morning), a locked baggage room and a free left-luggage service for guests. Single/double/triple rooms cost US$4/6/7.50, with low-season prices about 15% less.

Another popular and centrally located place is *Hostal Austria* (☎ 35-1140), at 531 Yanacocha, also near Plaza Murillo. It has electric showers and one to four-bed rooms with shared bath for US$5 per person.

Alojamiento Universo, at Inca 175, has been recommended as a bargain-basement option, at US$4.50 a double. It's clean, friendly and secure, and has electric hot showers and a left-luggage service. Rooms on the ground floor are nicer than those upstairs.

From the outside, *Hotel Italia* (☎ 32-5101), at Calle Manco Capac 303, looks more expensive than it is, but it can be noisy. Single/double rooms with shared bath cost US$5/7.50, while rooms with private bath are US$8/10.

Just up the street, at Calle Manco Capac 364, the *Hotel Andes* (☎ 32-3461) has lots of rooms, and although the lifts rarely function, it's an increasingly popular digs for budget travellers. Single/double rooms cost US$7/12 with bath, US$5/9 without. Practically next door is the basic *Residencial Central* (☎ 35-6304), at Calle Manco Capac

384. It sometimes has hot water; rooms cost US$3 per person.

A good huff and puff from the centre is *Hotel Panamericano* (☎ 37-8370), at Calle Manco Capac 454, near the railway station. It's clean, and good value for money, catering to organised groups that don't want to pay for the Sheraton. Clean single/double rooms with private bath and hot water cost US$6/10. For a dollar more, you'll get a continental breakfast of juice, coffee, rolls and condiments.

Another pleasant inexpensive place is the *Residencial Illimani* (☎ 32-5948), at Avenida Illimani 1817, not far from the stadium. It's a bit further from the centre of things but is quiet, friendly and popular with more laid-back travellers. Single/double rooms without bath cost US$4/6. There's also a nice view of Illimani from the roof.

At Calle Sagárnaga 334, in the heart of artesanía alley, is the very pleasant *Hotel Alem* (☎ 36-7400). Singles/doubles cost US$6/8 without bath, US$10/13 with bath. Rooms with private bath also include breakfast.

It seems the much lauded (and equally scorned!) *Residencial Rosario* (☎ 32-5348), at Calle Illampú 704, has let success go to its top floor. The staff have become a bit blasé, prices have been raised, and all available space has been turned into a rabbit warren of stairways and passages to accommodate its enormous popularity. Even so, it remains ultraclean and pleasantly quiet: a sort of travellers' capsule with Bolivia just outside the door. Single/double rooms without bath cost US$9/12. Rooms with private bath are reserved primarily for tour groups and are priced accordingly: a budget-boggling US$20 for a double room.

Near the Residencial Rosario, at Calle Illampú 734, is *Residencial Copacabana* (☎ 36-7896). Singles/doubles cost US$7/10 with private bath, US$5/7.50 with shared bath. It's not bad but could be better.

An exceptional place to stay, with the entire city of La Paz at its feet, is the friendly *Hostería Florida* (☎ 36-3298), at Calle Viacha 489. As yet, it's almost unknown to

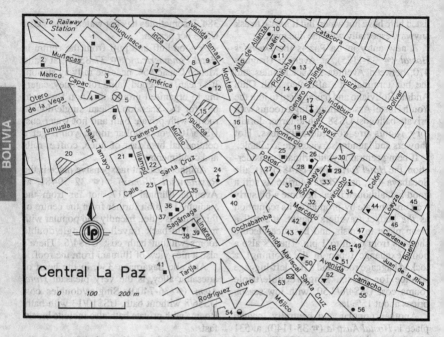

Central La Paz

0   100   200 m

travellers, probably due to its location amid shabby cheapies and because, from the outside, it appears to be quite expensive. It's a 10-storey modern building with comfortable rooms, all of which have private bath and hot water, for US$6 per person. Ask for a room on one of the upper floors with views over the city, and near the spacious common lounge, where you can rest or watch TV.

Down the street, at Calle Illampú 626, near Plaza Vicenta Juariste Eguino, is the two-star *Hotel Continental* (☎ 37-8226). Prices aren't bad: US$7/10 for single/double rooms without bath, US$10/15 with bath. Another recommended option is the *Hotel Milton* (☎ 36-8003), at Calle Illampú 1224. It's clean, has good hot showers and costs US$13/18 for single/double rooms with bath.

Hotel Sagárnaga (☎ 35-0252), at Calle Sagárnaga 326, is a pleasant, central option on a bustling street. Rooms cost US$13/16 for a single/double with bath, US$8/11

without. A continental breakfast is included in the room price.

The clean *Hostal República* (☎ 35-7966), at Calle Comercio 1455, near Calle Bueno, is in a magnificent historic building. Single/double rooms cost US$10/16 with private bath, US$6/9 without. Triple rooms are also available.

An interesting mid-range hotel is *Hotel Viena* (☎ 32-6090), at Calle Loayza 420, a baroque-style building with immense high-ceilinged rooms. If you're interested in unique accommodation, check out the suites; one reader recommends room 113. Double rooms with shared bath cost US$13.

Places to Eat

La Paz has a wealth of restaurants, and the quality is good, especially in more expensive places. Most budget places offer set meals (mainly almuerzo but sometimes also cena) and a short list of the most common dishes such as lomo, churrasco, milanesa and

■ PLACES TO STAY		OTHER		27	Shampoo Shop
				29	Catedral
1	Hostería Florida	5	Plaza Vicenta Juariste	30	Plaza Murillo
2	Hotel Panamericano		Eguino	33	Museo de la Catedral
3	Hotel Italia	8	Plaza Alonzo de	34	Departmental Tourist
4	Hotel Andes		Mendoza		Office
6	Hotel Continental	9	TAM	35	Mercado de Hechicería
19	Hostal Austria	10	Museos de Metales	39	Museo del Charango
21	Residencial Rosario		Preciosos Pre-Col-		(Museo de
25	Hotel Gloria		umbinos, Litoral,		Instrumentos
28	Hotel Torino		Costumbrista Juan		Nativos)
36	Hotel Sagárnaga		de Vargas & Casa	40	Peña Naira
37	Hotel Alem		de Don Pedro	42	ENTEL (Telephone
41	Hotel Milton		Domingo Murillo		Office)
45	Hostal República	11	Peña Marka Tambo	47	Los Amigos del Libro
46	Hotel Viena	12	Museo Tambo	48	US Consulate
			Quirquincho	49	DINATUR Tourist
▼ PLACES TO EAT		13	Cinemateca Boliviana		Office & Policía
		14	Teatro Municipal		Turística
7	El Palacio de Pescado	15	Mercado Lanza	51	Casa de Cambio
22	La Hacienda	16	Plaza Pérez Velasco		Sudamer
23	El Lobo	17	Iglesia de Santo	53	Main Post Office
31	Super Salteñas		Domingo	54	Plaza Belzú (Bus to
32	Confitería Marilín	18	Museo de Etnografía y		Ventilla)
38	Snack El Montañés		Folklore	55	LAB
43	Clap	20	Mercado Negro	56	Instituto Geográfico
44	Manjari	24	Iglesia de San Fran-		Militar
50	Confitería Club de La		cisco		
	Paz	26	Museo Nacional del		
52	Café Verona		Arte		

silpancho (all meat dishes). Some also include a couple of regional specialities like sajta, chairo and ranga.

Snacks If you don't mind a hectic setting, the cheapest end of the scale is the markets; the city has a host of them. Unfortunately, the most central, *Mercado Lanza*, just off the Plaza Pèrez Velasco, has a rather dirty, unpleasant comedor. Better is the *Mercado Camacho*, on the corner of Camacho and Bueno. There you'll find takeaway snack stands selling empanadas and chicken sandwiches, and comedors with covered sitting areas, where a filling meal of soup, a meat dish, rice, lettuce and oca or potato costs less than US$1. Furthermore, because most restaurants don't open until 9 or 9.30 am, early risers desperate for a caffeine jolt will find bread rolls and riveting coffee concentrate here for about US$0.40.

A good place for salteñas is *Super Salteñas*, on Calle Socabaya. They're billed as the world's best, but they're pricey, and some available in the markets at a third the price are just as good. Alternatively, try the salteñas at the *Tokio* (not to be confused with the New Tokyo), on the Prado, or at the *San Luis*, beside the main post office.

A favourite for snacks is *Kuchen Stube*, in the Edificio Guadalquivir, at Calle Rosendo Gutiérrez 461. You can stuff yourself with decadent European coffee, pastries, biscuits and other sweets, then work it off climbing back up the Prado to the city centre. Another friendly coffee shop is the *Pierrot*, on the ground floor of Hotel Gloria.

Breakfast For a hefty breakfast, nothing beats the *Residencial Rosario's* restaurant, which serves ham, eggs, breads, cheese, pancakes, orange juice and excellent cocoa and cappuccino. For doughnuts, try *California Donuts*, on Avenida Camacho, and wash them down with rich hot cocoa.

For healthy vegetarian breakfasts of porridge, yoghurt, juice, granola and crêpes, go to *El Vegetariano*, on Calle Loayza between calles Potosí and Comercio. They begin serving at 9.15 am.

At *Eli's*, on the Prado, you can get a continental breakfast, including juice, toast, marmalade and coffee, for US$1, or a heftier morning meal for US$1.50 to US$2 (don't be deterred by the prominently displayed poster for the Heimlich manoeuvre). If you just want to grab a quick coffee and a roll or salteña, try the *Confitería Club de La Paz*, a literary café and haunt of politicians and other interesting people, at the sharp corner of avenidas Camacho and Mariscal Santa Cruz. *Confitería Marilín*, at the corner of calles Potosí and Socabaya, is repeatedly recommended, but avoid the coffee.

Lunch Options for lunch are practically unlimited, and depend on what you're prepared to pay. If you are travelling on very limited funds, there are, apart from the markets, plenty of cubbyhole restaurants which display chalkboards with a menu at their doors. You can take it for granted that these places are really cheap. As a general rule, the higher you climb off the main central boulevard, the cheaper the meals get. A number of budget restaurants can be found on Evaristo Valle, where almuerzo or cena can cost less than US$1. Try the *Pensión Yungueña*, at Evaristo Valle 155, the recommended *Snack El Diamante*, at Calle Manco Capac 315, or *La Hacienda*, diagonally opposite the Residencial Rosario on Calle Illampú, which is known for its home-made chicken soup.

Bolivian specialities such as charque kan, chorizos, anticuchos and chicharrón are available as executive lunches at *Típicos*, which is on the 6th level of the Shopping Norte arcade, at the corner of calles Potosí and Socabaya.

A favourite lunchtime venue is the previously mentioned *Eli's*, which also has a

good pizzería on the other side of the cinema. Their lunch specials are superb, but they must vie for stomach space with a selection of tempting European pastries.

Café Verona, on Calle Colón near Avenida Mariscal Santa Cruz, is frequently recommended for its sandwiches, which will set you back about US$1.50. Pizza costs US$3; set lunches are US$3.50. *Amadeus*, opposite the university, on Avenida 16 de Julio below the Plaza de los Estudiantes, serves light meals and specialises in real Mexican tacos. *Snack El Montañés*, directly across from Hotel Sagárnaga, has good light meals and desserts, plus mate de coca made with fresh coca leaves rather than a tea bag.

For a reasonable burger, *California Burgers* (in the same building as California Donuts), on Avenida Camacho, is a possibility. You may also want to try those at the unfortunately named *Clap*, with three locations – Avenida Aniceto Arce, Calle Ayacucho and Belisario Salinas. For quick chicken, try *Pollo Copacabana*, where you'll get a quarter roast chicken, chips and fried plantain smothered in ketchup, mustard and ají for US$2. There are two locations, one on Calle Potosí and one on Calle Comercio. Beside the former is a wonderful *sweets shop* selling Bolivia's own Breick chocolate, some of the best!

El Vegetariano does vegetarian lunches for US$1. Another excellent vegetarian restaurant has recently opened in the *Hotel Gloria*, at Calle Potosí 909. They serve set lunches for US$1.50, but it's very popular, so arrive before 12.30 pm or risk missing out.

Dinner Many of the places suggested for lunch also serve dinner. Again, *Residencial Rosario* is recommended, especially their cream of asparagus and french onion soup, crumbed chicken (unheard of elsewhere in Bolivia) and pasta dishes. An excellent option for Italian food is the small, relaxed and cosy *Pronto Ristorante*, on Calle Jáuregui, half a block from Avenida 6 de Agosto. Their pasta is home-made, and the reasonable prices make it accessible to nearly everyone.

The *Manjari Restaurant*, at Calle Potosí 1315, near Calle Colón, has hearty vegetarian lunch and dinner specials. For just US$1.25 you get soup, salad, segundo, dessert and tea, served in what some travellers have described as 'prison trays'. Manjari no longer bakes its own bread, but the food is still worthwhile. Another restaurant with vegetarian specialties is *Nutricentro*, on Calle Comercio between Calle Socabaya and Yanacocha.

For fish, go to *El Palácio de Pescado*, on Avenida América. You'll pay an average of US$2 for surubí, pacu, trucha, pejerrey, sábalo, etc.

Inexpensive lunches or dinners are also available at the popular *El Lobo*, at the corner of calles Santa Cruz and Illampú. It specialises in chicken, and the curry is particularly nice.

The majority of La Paz's nicer and higher-priced restaurants are concentrated at the lower end of town, around avenidas 20 de Octubre, 6 de Agosto and 16 de Julio (it must be easy to remember historical dates in La Paz!) One of the best is *La Suisse* (☎ 35-3150), and if you don't mind paying for atmosphere and a view, try the *Utama Restaurant*, on the top floor of the Hotel Plaza.

Another pleasant place is *La Casa de los Paceños*, at Calle Sucre 856, near the corner of Pichincha. Besides offering lunches (US$1.50), this exceptional small restaurant, run by a very hospitable family, serves a number of typical La Paz dishes, including saice, sajta, fricasé and chairo paceño, and their fritanga (fried pork) is second to none. It's highly recommended (closed on Monday, open only till 3 pm on Saturday and Sunday).

Entertainment

Typical of La Paz (and all Bolivia) are folk music venues called peñas. They play predominantly pure Andean music (zampoñas, quenas, charangos), though sometimes guitar shows, singing recitals, etc slip in. The most famous is the Peña Naira, at Sagárnaga 161, just above the Plaza San Francisco. Geared toward foreign tourists, it's not the best one, but the four-course lunch special (US$1.50) makes it well worth a visit. The Casa del Corregidor (a very nice place in itself), at Murillo 1040, and Marka Tambo, at Jaén 710, are better. The Naira is open nightly, except Sunday; other peñas have shows only on Friday and Saturday nights. They all start at about 10 pm and go on till 1 or 2 am, with several groups on the programme. Admission is around US$5 to US$6 and normally includes one drink.

The very informal Café Semilla Juvenîl, Almirante Grau 443, has weekend talks and music events at which locals share their coca leaves with visitors.

One of the few good cinemas is the Cinemateca Boliviana, on the corner of Pichincha and Indaburo, which occasionally shows quality films. The Cine Teatro Monje Campero, next to Eli's on the Prado, shows first-run films. The Teatro Municipal, on the corner of Sanjinés and Indaburo, has an ambitious programme, and you can sometimes see folklore shows, folk music concerts or interesting foreign theatre groups.

Getting There & Away

Air El Alto airport sits on the altiplano at 4018 metres, 10 km from the centre of La Paz. Micro 212 runs between the centre and the airport and costs US$0.75; by taxi, it will cost around US$5. If you're headed into town from the airport, catch the micro outside the terminal; it will drop you anywhere along the Prado.

Baggage handlers at El Alto expect a small tip, and without one, you may wait some time for your luggage to be retrieved.

The following is a list of some of the airlines with offices in La Paz:

Aerolíneas Argentinas
  Avenida 16 de Julio 1486, Edificio Alameda, ground floor (☎ 39-1059)
AeroPerú
  Avenida 16 de Julio 1490, Edificio Avenida, (☎ 37-0002)
AeroXpress
  Plaza de los Estudiantes 1920 (☎ 34-3154)

American Airlines
Plaza Venezuela 1440, Edificio Herrmann (☎ 35-1360)
British Airways
Plaza de los Estudiantes 1920 (☎ 35-5541)
KLM
Avenida Aniceto Arce, Edificio Cobija 104 (☎ 36-6887, 39-0710)
LAN Chile
Avenida 16 de Julio, Edificio Mariscal de Ayacucho, ground floor (☎ 36-6563)
LAP (Líneas Aéreas Paraguayas)
Edificio Colón, 4 (☎ 32-0020, 37-7595)
LAB (Lloyd Aéreo Boliviano)
Avenida Camacho 1460 (☎ 35-3606, 35-3054)
TAM (Transportes Aéreos Militares)
Avenida Ismael Montes 728 (☎ 37-9285)
Varig/Cruzeiro
Edificio Cámara de Comercio, Avenida Mariscal Santa Cruz 1392 (☎ 36-7200)

Bus The main bus terminal (☎ 36-7275) is at Plaza Antofagasta, a 15-minute walk from the city centre. The recent lifting of price controls has caused fares to yo-yo, so check more than one company.

Buses to Oruro run every half-hour (US$2.50, three hours). Plenty of buses go to Cochabamba, leaving between 8 and 9 pm, though some also depart in the morning (from US$5, eight to 10 hours). Many continue on to Santa Cruz, but the evening buses stay all day in Cochabamba and leave only in the evening of the next day (so you also have to stay all day). Only morning buses have direct connections in Cochabamba. You can negotiate the fare from Cochabamba to Santa Cruz (US$10, 10 to 12 hours).

To Sucre (US$12), all buses go through Cochabamba, leaving in the evening; again, you have to wait the whole day there.

Nine flotas run daily to Potosí (Expreso Cochabamba is the best), and all depart between 6 and 6.30 pm for a 12-hour journey, costing US$5. Be sure to have warm clothes handy.

To Arica, in Chile, Flota Litoral officially leaves on Tuesday and Friday (US$22). Again, plenty of warm clothes are essential. Its Saturday service to Iquique costs US$25. Géminis, which goes to Iquique on Tuesday and Saturday, is more expensive.

Buses to Copacabana (US$3, four hours, four buses daily, two with Manco Capac and another two with Transtur 2 de Febrero) depart from Calle José María Aliaga, near the cemetery, quite a long way uphill from the centre. You can also go to Copacabana on any of the numerous tourist microbuses (see the Tours section). This trip, costing US$6, is more comfortable, and you'll be collected from your hotel.

Autolíneas Ingaví has four buses daily to Desaguadero via Tiahuanaco, leaving from Calle José María Asín, also near the cemetery. Nearby is Transportes Larecaja, at Calle Angel Babia, which operates daily buses to Sorata between 6.30 and 7 am; purchase your ticket at 2 pm on the afternoon prior to departure. Plenty of urban micros from the city centre go to the cemetery.

Flota Yungueña, on Avenida de las Américas in Barrio Villa Fátima, has four buses weekly to Coroico, in the Yungas, on Tuesday, Thursday, Friday and Saturday at 8.30 am (US$3.50, 3½ hours). Camiones to the Yungas leave from the same area, and several competing flotas, some running minibuses, have sprung up less than a block away.

During the dry season (March to October), Flota Yungueña has a service to Rurrenabaque on Monday and Saturday at around 1 pm (US$11, 18 hours). To Riberalta and Guayaramerín, buses depart on Wednesday and Friday. There's a Saturday service to San Borja and Trinidad.

Train The Estación Central (☎ 37-3068) is on upper Manco Capac. It is near to, but steeply uphill from, the city centre.

There are ferrobuses to Cochabamba on Monday and Wednesday at 8 am and Friday at 9 pm (US$8.50/7 pullman/especial, eight hours). The ferrobus to Potosí and Sucre leaves on Monday and Saturday at 6 pm and on Wednesday at 4.10 pm. Pullman/especial fares are US$10/7.50 to Potosí, US$19/15 to Sucre.

The ferrobus to Arica, Chile, departs on Monday and Friday at 7 am and costs US$51, while the regular El Dorado de los Andes train (US$45 turista, US$55 pullman) leaves on Tuesday at 9 am and Friday at 9 pm; buy tickets two weeks in advance. In summer, there may be only one train per week.

To Villazón (Argentine border), trains run on Monday and Thursday at 4.10 pm (US$12/9 1st/2nd class, 20 hours). Other trains run to Uyuni, Tupiza and Villazón from Oruro. The Expreso del Sur to Villazón on Friday at 7 pm (US$23 pullman only, 18 hours) formerly continued to Buenos Aires, but passenger services within Argentina are suspended and are unlikely to resume.

If you plan on taking any of these train trips, check the current schedule when you arrive in La Paz. Arranging a passage normally isn't easy, and you may waste time in the queue; in most cases, you're better off taking a bus to Oruro and arranging onward rail transport there.

AROUND LA PAZ
Valle de la Luna
The Valle de la Luna (Valley of the Moon) is a pleasant and quiet half-day break from urban La Paz. It isn't a valley at all but a bizarre eroded hillside maze of miniature canyons and pinnacles. It's about 10 km from the city centre down the canyon of the Río Choqueyapu. To get there, catch Micro 11 from Avenida 16 de Julio in the town centre. Go to its final stop at Barrio Aranjuez, then cross the bridge to your right and walk up the hill, following either the trail across a ditch (10 minutes) or the road (15 minutes) until you reach the cactus garden, a slightly artificial-looking stand of cactus. Continue walking uphill, again either by road or by trail (another 15 minutes or so), to the most striking section.

Chacaltaya
The world's highest developed ski area lies on the slopes of Chacaltaya, just below its summit, at an altitude of between 5200 and 5400 metres. It's accessible by a rough 35-km road from La Paz, but there's no public transport to the top. A walk to the top of the ski tow and on to the summit (5600 metres) will afford superb views of the surrounding snowcapped peaks.

The Club Andino Boliviano, Calle México 1638, takes groups (in their own minibuses) to Chacaltaya for skiing on weekends. They have a ski lodge, where you can buy snacks and hot drinks, hire skiing gear and sometimes you can arrange an overnight stay. There is a primitive cable tow installed on the slopes. Many tour operators offer trips to Chacaltaya during the week, at roughly the same price.

Tiahuanaco
Tiahuanaco, also spelled Tiwanaku, is Bolivia's most important archaeological site, 72 km from La Paz on the road toward Desaguadero, on the Peruvian border.

Little is known about the Tiahuanaco people who constructed the great ceremonial centre on the southern shore of Lake Titicaca over 1000 years ago. Archaeologists generally agree that the civilisation that spawned Tiahuanaco rose about 600 BC. The ceremonial site was under construction around 700 AD, but after about 1200 AD the group had melted into obscurity. Evidence of its influence, particularly in the area of religion, has been found throughout the vast area that later became the Inca Empire.

There are a number of large stone slabs (up to 175 tonnes) strewn around the site, a ruined pyramid, the remains of a ritual platform and a number of other ruins and piles of rubble. Across the rail line near the Tiahuanaco site is the excavation of Puma Punku, (Gateway of the Puma), and a site museum which is open only sporadically.

Guides, who will offer a greater appreciation of the history, are available outside the fence for around US$3, but you'll have to bargain them down to that price. Admission to the site is US$1.50 for foreigners, including entrance to the tiny visitor centre at the ticket office.

Getting There & Away One way to see Tiahuanaco is en route from La Paz to Puno, Peru. From La Paz, Autolíneas Ingaví has four buses daily to Tiahuanaco (US$1, 2½ hours). These buses continue to Desaguadero, so it's possible to catch onward transport after visiting Tiahuanaco. There are also micros to Desaguadero from the plaza in Tiahuanaco village, one km from the ruins.

To return to La Paz after a day trip to Tiahuanaco, flag down a bus, almost always a crowded option, or walk into the village and catch one along the main street.

A dozen or more tour agencies in La Paz offer guided tours to Tiahuanaco for about US$12.

The Yungas

The Yungas are a beautiful region north-east of La Paz, across the Cordillera Real. Here, steep jungle-covered cliffs loom above humid, cloud-filled gorges, forming a distinct natural division between the cold and barren altiplano and the level Amazon rainforest which covers most of northern Bolivia. The short (distance-wise, anyway!) trip from the 4600-metre La Cumbre pass into the Alto Beni entails a loss of 4343 metres elevation. Tropical fruits, coffee, sugar cane, cacao and coca all grow with minimal tending. The climate is humid and rainy throughout most of the year.

COROICO
Most popular among travellers is the small village of Coroico, perched on the shoulder of Cerro Uchumachi at an altitude of 1500 metres. It is a perfect place to relax and do short hiking trips into the surrounding countryside. If you enjoy riding, horses can be hired from Dany and Patricio at Rancho Beni for US$4 per hour.

Places to Stay
There are several hotels in the village. *Hostal Kory* is the best bet; it's clean, with a cheap restaurant and a swimming pool, and costs US$4 per person for rooms with marvellous views to the peaks of the Cordillera Real. The new *Residencial La Casa* is exceptionally clean and offers rooms with shared bath for US$3 per person. Another favourite is

German-run *Hostal Sol y Luna*, a half-hour walk from town. Double cabañas cost US$10, plus US$3 for each additional person. Dormitory rooms with sheet cost US$2 per person, and camp sites are US$1.50 per person. Reservations are recommended; book through Dolly Travel (☎ 37-3435) in La Paz. A recommended low-budget option is known simply as *Alojamiento*, beside the Veloz del Norte bus terminal. It costs only US$2 per person.

Places to Eat
One of the best restaurants in town is at the Hostal Kory, where travellers meet to swap tales and partake of spaghetti alla carbonara and banana pancakes. Excellent meals are available at the German-run *La Casa* (closed Monday), and at *El Rodeo*, 100 metres out of town along the road to Caranavi.

Getting There & Away
Buses to Coroico (Flota Yungeña services this route) depart from Barrio Villa Fátima in La Paz on Tuesday, Thursday, Friday and Saturday at 8.30 am (US$3.50, 3½ hours). Trucks leave regularly from behind the Flota Yungeña office. The frightening road, dropping over 3000 metres in 80 km, offers stunning vertical scenery. Buses from Coroico to La Paz run on Monday, Wednesday and Friday at 7 am, and on Sunday at 1 pm. Coroico is also a good jumping-off point for trips to Guanay, Rurrenabaque and further into the Bolivian Amazon Basin.

Other routes into the Yungas from La Paz include the following hikes.

TREKS FROM LA CUMBRE
There are several interesting treks between the altiplano and the Yungas, all of which cross the Cordillera Real on relatively low passes. La Cumbre to Coroico, La Cumbre to Taquesi, and La Cumbre to Yunga Cruz are the most popular. These are two to four-day walks, beginning near La Paz and ending in the Yungas. Each begins with a brief ascent, then trends downhill, offering spectacular scenery, varying from the high-mountain landscapes to the exuberant

vegetation of the Yungas. Hikers should carry food and camping equipment, including a tent, sleeping bag, rainproof gear, torch, etc. Security is a concern, especially on the Cumbre to Coroico trek, where there have been several nasty incidents.

For serious hikers, Lonely Planet's *Bolivia – a travel survival kit* (2nd edition, 1993) and *Backpacking and Trekking in Peru and Bolivia*, by Hilary Bradt (4th edition, Bradt Publications, UK, 1987) are recommended. They include maps and detailed descriptions of these treks, as well as other routes in the Cordillera Real.

SORATA

Sorata is often described as having the most beautiful setting in Bolivia, and this is no exaggeration. It sits at an elevation of 2695 metres in a valley beneath the towering snowcapped peaks of Illampú (6362 metres) and Ancohuma (6427 metres) and is popular with mountaineers.

Most visitors make a day trip of the 10-km hike to the Gruta de San Pedro (San Pedro Cave), near the village of San Pedro, a walk of two to 2½-hours from Sorata. More ambitious visitors set off on the six or seven-day trek along El Camino de Oro toward Guanay, an Inca road that has been used for nearly 1000 years as a commerce and trade link between the altiplano and the lowland goldfields along the Río Tipuani.

Information

Club Sorata, at the Hotel Copacabana, is the local branch of Club Andino Boliviano. The Swiss and Norwegian guides at the club lead walking and trekking expeditions for US$10 per person per day, including food. They've done a lot of research and have come up with a variety of three to seven-day trekking options from Sorata. The club sells maps and hires camping and climbing equipment, including mountain bikes. If you prefer to strike out on your own, they're happy to provide directions and other information about the most popular trips.

Places to Stay

Sorata's most popular travellers' digs is the German-run *Hotel Copacabana*, downhill from the plaza on the route to San Pedro. It boasts hot showers, excellent food and a swimming pool nearby. The clean rooms are a bargain at US$3 per person. Owners Edward and Diana are video fiends, and their growing collection is available to guests.

Another option is the *Hotel Paraíso*, near the plaza, which offers comfortable rooms with private bath for US$5 per person. The *Hotel San Cristóbal* (US$2 per person) has good food and cold water. *Hotel Central*, on the plaza, is even cheaper (US$1.50 per person), but the showers are dodgy.

The *Residencial Sorata*, in a rotting old mansion just off the main plaza, is a bit grimy around the edges. Rooms cost US$2.50 per person, with communal bath only.

Places to Eat

If you're after quality, shell out for the restaurant at the Hotel Copacabana. If your budget doesn't stretch that far, go for the small, inexpensive restaurants around the plaza; a filling set meal will cost only US$1. The Hotel Paraíso restaurant has also been recommended. Alternatively, try the new *Ristorante Italiano*, run by a gentleman from Bologna, which offers Italian cuisine and even a good espresso in a garden setting.

Getting There & Away

Sorata is a long way from the other Yungas towns. There's no road connecting it directly with Coroico or Chulumani, so access from La Paz is a 4½-hour trip via Huarina and Achacachi, near Lake Titicaca. From La Paz, Transportes Larecaja leaves for Sorata from Calle Angel Babia 1556, near the cemetery, at 6.30 and 7 am daily and returns to La Paz from Sorata's main plaza, departing at 12.30 pm. Tickets (US$3.50) go on sale at 2 pm the previous day. Alternatively, go to Huarina (near Lake Titicaca) on the Huatajata or Copacabana bus and catch a camión from there.

BOLIVIA

GUANAY

Guanay serves as a base for interesting excursions into some of the gold-mining operations along the Río Mapiri and Río Tipuani. The miners and panners along the way are generally relaxed and courteous, and if you can excuse the utter rape of the landscape they've perpetrated for the sake of gold, a visit will prove an interesting experience. Access to the gold-mining areas is by jeep up the road toward Llipi, on the Río Tipuani, or by motorised dugout canoes, which can be hired in Guanay for travel up the Río Mapiri.

Guanay and points upriver are certainly frontier settlements, and few visitors fail to be reminded of the Old West of film and legend. Gold is legal tender, and saloons, gambling, prostitutes and large hunks of beef seem to form the foundations of local culture.

Places to Stay & Eat

The *Hotel Estrella Azul*, which has clean, inexpensive rooms, is probably the nicest place in town. *Hotel Los Pinos* and *Hotel Santos* are also fine, but avoid *Hotel México*; it's a real dump.

For large steaks and fresh juices, try *Las Parrilladas*, on the road which leads down to the port. *Lila's*, between the Hotel México and the port, is also recommended.

Getting There & Away

Flota Veloz del Norte, in the La Paz suburb of Villa Fátima, has buses to Caranavi and Guanay twice daily, at 8.30 am and 2.30 pm, but camión traffic is plentiful and less expensive. The trip from La Paz to Caranavi takes seven hours, then it's four more hours to Guanay. A road now links Caranavi with Rurrenabaque, Riberalta and Guayaramerín.

From Guanay, it's possible to travel by outboard canoe down the Río Beni to Rurrenabaque; make arrangements through Agencia Fluvial in Guanay. These canoes will accommodate up to 10 people and their luggage, and you'll have to hire the entire canoe; they're getting used to tourists, so plan on an extortionate US$200 for up to 10 passengers. It's best to insist on paying half the fare in advance and half once you've arrived, or they'll continuously pick up and crowd in more passengers.

Lake Titicaca

Lake Titicaca, over 170 km long and 97 km wide, is the world's highest navigable lake. Straddling the Peru-Bolivia border, it lies in a depression of the altiplano at an elevation of 3820 metres, covering an area of over 8000 sq km. Titicaca is the last surviving stretch of the ancient inland sea known as Lago Ballivián, which once covered a good part of the altiplano, before its waters dropped to their present level, most probably due both to geological faults and evaporation.

The lake has an irregular shoreline, 36 islands and exceptionally clear, sapphire-blue water. Its serene beauty in the midst of the parched dreariness of the altiplano may account for some of its mystical significance. In ancient cosmological myths, the lake was the birthplace of the sun, and from it the Sun God created the human race. The lake is still revered by the Indians who live on its shores.

COPACABANA

Copacabana is a sunny town on the southern shore of Lake Titicaca, on the border with Peru. In the 16th century, miracles began happening after the town was presented with a statue of the Virgin of Candelaria, and since that time Copacabana has become the destination for pilgrims from all over the country. Today, the Virgin is the patron saint of Bolivia.

Copacabana has a couple of fiestas during which it springs to life. For the rest of the year it is a sleepy little town, a pleasant stopover between La Paz and Puno, Peru and a convenient starting point for visits to Isla del Sol (Island of the Sun – see the following section). The climate is generally pleasant

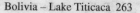

BOLIVIA

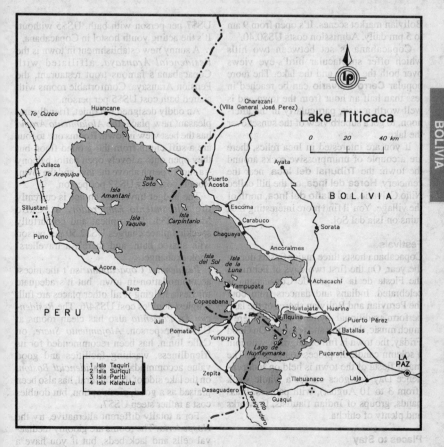

and sunny, but at this altitude, nights can be bitterly cold. Most of the annual rainfall occurs in December and January,

Information
Money The Banco del Estado, beside the Playa Azul Hotel on Calle 6 de Agosto, is reportedly open Wednesday to Sunday until 5 pm, and will apparently change travellers' cheques. To be sure, you may wish to carry some cash from either La Paz or Peru.

The Hotel Playa Azul changes Peruvian *soles* and cash US dollars, as does the dispensary beside the cathedral. Slightly better

rates are available around the plaza in Yunguyo, just beyond the Peruvian frontier.

Things to See
The huge, sparkling white, Moorish-style **Catedral**, built between 1605 and 1820, dominates the town. The famous statue of the Virgen de Copacabana, carved in wood by the Indian artist Francisco Tito Yupanqui, is housed in the Camarín de la Virgen, upstairs in the Catedral.

On the main plaza is the small **Museo en Miniatura**, a large collection of miniatures – bottles, dolls, furniture and even ceramic

Bolivian market scenes. It's open from 9 am to 5 pm daily. Admission costs US$0.40.

Copacabana is set between two hills which offer spectacular bird's-eye views over both the town and the lake. The more popular **Cerro Calvario** can be reached in less than half an hour from the town and is well worth a visit, particularly in the afternoon, to get a superb view of the sunset over the lake.

If you are interested in Inca relics, there are a couple of unimpressive rocks around the town: the **Tribunal del Inca**, near the cemetery, **Horca del Inca**, on the hill called Niño Calvario, and **Baño del Inca**, north of the village. You'll find more interesting Inca ruins on Isla del Sol.

Festivals

Copacabana hosts three major fiestas during the year. On the first two days of February, the Fiesta de la Virgen de Copacabana is celebrated. Indians and dancers from both the Peruvian and Bolivian shores of the lake perform traditional Aymara dances; there's much music, drinking and feasting. On Good Friday, the town is full of pilgrims, who join a solemn candle-lit procession at dusk. The major fiesta of the town is held on Independence Day but goes on for a whole week (from 3 to 10 August), with parades, brass bands, groups of Indian flautists, fireworks and plenty of chicha.

Places to Stay

For a town of its size, Copacabana is well-endowed with hotels, residenciales and alojamientos and is the least expensive town in Bolivia for accommodation. Unless you arrive at the height of a fiesta, when rooms fill up and rates double, you should have no trouble finding acceptable, inexpensive accommodation.

The *Alojamiento Urinsaya*, at 390 Calle Destacamento 211, looks shabby from the outside but is good, friendly value and highly recommended. Rooms cost US$2.50 per person. The *Hotel Ambassador*, around the corner on Calle General Gonzalo Jáuregui, is a bit grotty but offers reasonable value, at US$7 per person with bath, US$5 without. It's the acting youth hostel in Copacabana.

A sunny new establishment in town is the *Residencial Aransaya*, affiliated with Copacabana's famous trout restaurant, the Pensión Aransaya. Comfortable rooms with shared bath cost US$5 per person.

An oddly designed but quiet, friendly and pleasant new place, the *Alojamiento Aroma* has the best view in town. Rooms one to four are a stiff climb from the ground floor, but they open onto a lovely open patio/ balcony – a superb perch above the lake and the town. Rooms cost only US$2 per person.

The budget travellers' choice is currently the *Alojamiento Emperador*, at Calle Murillo 235. This upbeat and colourfully speckled place charges US$2.50 per person with shared bath, and there's a travellers' book exchange.

Residencial Copacabana isn't the nicest accommodation in town, but it's adequate for fiesta lodging if all other places are full. Singles/ doubles cost US$4/6. The *Residencial La Porteñita* also has clean rooms at US$4 per person. *Alojamiento Sucre*, on Calle Junín, has been recommended for its friendliness, washing facilities and good value accommodation. *Residencial Boston*, on the lake side of the Catedral, has also been praised as a good, clean option, but doubles cost a rather steep US$7.

For a totally different alternative, try the *Hospedería*. The rooms are gloomy mediaeval cells and lack beds, but if you have a sleeping bag and some sort of ground protection, you can stay for as little as US$1 per person. The building itself, an old mansion with plenty of rooms overlooking a marvellous flowery courtyard, makes up for any discomfort.

Nearly all tour groups wind up at the overpriced *Hotel Playa Azul* (☎ 227 in town, (☎ 32-0068 in La Paz). Rooms cost US$16 per person with private bath and a three-meal plan. The *Hotel Prefectural* (☎ 256), near the beach, affords a lovely view of the lake and surrounding mountains. It's utterly dead during the week but springs to life on weekends. Clean but stark rooms cost US$16 per person with the three-meal plan, US$8 without.

Places to Eat

There is, unfortunately, little originality in food preparation in Copacabana; all main courses are served with dry rice, fried potatoes and lettuce. The real highlight is Lake Titicaca trout, among the world's largest.

The best restaurant is *Pensión Aransaya*, on Calle 6 de Agosto, which is surprisingly accessible to those on tight budgets. *Snack 6 de Agosto*, just up the street, is also very good value, with huge portions of trout for a remarkable US$2.50. *Snack Cristal*, on Calle Murillo, also specialises in trout, and is recommended for inexpensive meals. The *Puerta del Sol*, at the corner of the plaza and Calle 6 de Agosto, serves good trout and pejerrey. Restaurant *Tito Yupanqui*, at Calle General Gonzalo Jáuregui 119, is known for its vegetable soup.

The overpriced *Restaurant Colonial*, on the plaza, is heated, so it's a viable option on those evenings when you just can't warm up. They serve trout and pejerrey but always seem to be out of everything else on their impressive menu.

The Tourist Palace, on Calle 6 de Agosto, has a menu with a table of contents. They serve continental and English breakfasts, as well as three local trout dishes, delicious pejerrey and all the other standards.

On sunny days, *El Rey* and several other beach restaurants have tables outside, where you can have a drink and observe Bolivian beach life, such as it is.

As usual, the bargain-basement food scene is the market food hall. If you need a sugar rush in the morning, treat yourself to a breakfast of hot api morado and syrupy buñuelos.

Getting There & Away

There are several daily buses to La Paz on Transportes Manco Capac and Transtur 2 de Febrero (which has better buses), and extra departures on Sunday. The spectacular trip costs US$3 and takes four hours.

The cheapest way to reach Puno (Peru) is to take a bus from Plaza Sucre across the border to Yunguyo (US$0.40), where you'll find transport to Puno.

You can also catch any of the numerous tourist minibuses going to/from Puno or La Paz. They gather in front of the Pensión Aransaya between noon and 2 pm, and charge US$7 to either destination. They're faster and more comfortable than other options, and will usually drop you at the hotel of your choice in La Paz or Puno. Although there are plenty of them, many arrive full, so if you want to be sure of a seat, book in advance at Pensión Aransaya or at Hotel Playa Azul.

The tours from Puno to La Paz (or vice versa) are very popular with travellers. Since they all pass through Copacabana, you can arrange with the agent to break the journey in Copacabana for a couple of days, and then continue on by minibus with the same agency.

Getting Around

Bicycles are available for rent at Calle 6 de Agosto 125 or on the beach, but foreigners are expected to pay several times the local rate: US$1.25 per hour, US$5 for six hours and US$8 for 12 hours (6 am to 6 pm). Negotiate!

ISLA DEL SOL & ISLA DE LA LUNA

These two islands on Lake Titicaca are the legendary site of the Incas' creation. Isla del Sol has been credited as the birthplace of all sorts of important entities, including the sun itself. It was there that the bearded white god Viracocha and the first Incas, Manco Kapac and his sister/wife Mama Huaca (also known as Mama Ocllo), all made their mystical appearances. The Aymara and Quechua people still accept these legends as history, and Isla del Sol remains sacred.

Isla del Sol is the larger and arguably more interesting of the two islands. There are a couple of tiny villages, of which Chal'la is the largest. Scattered about the island are ancient Inca ruins, including the Pilko Kaima and the sacred rock where the Inca creation legend began. Lots of walking tracks make exploration easy, although the altitude may take a toll.

Isla de la Luna (the Island of the Moon) is smaller and less visited by tourists. There are ruins of an Inca temple dedicated to the Virgins of the Sun.

Places to Stay & Eat

There aren't any hotels on Isla del Sol, but several very basic alojamientos have sprung up in response to tourist demand for a longer visit than day trips allow. The most popular is *Alojamiento Juan Mamani*, on the lakeshore near the school in Chal'lapampa. Beds cost US$2. Near the upper end of Yumani village is *Alojamiento Francisco*, with one double room and a dormitory for five guests. Beds cost US$1. Basic cooked food, such as potatoes, eggs and so on, may be found near Fuente del Inca, towards the island's southern tip. Both alojamientos serve basic meals and soft drinks for around US$1. It's also possible to camp outside of villages.

Getting There & Away

Boat Boats (sailboats and launches) and pilots may be hired at the lakeshore in Copacabana. A launch to Isla del Sol and Isla de la Luna costs US$50 per day for up to 12 passengers, although you may pay a bit more to visit the northern end of Isla del Sol. The journey itself takes about 1½ hours in either direction. A sailboat carrying up to four people costs only US$25 to Isla del Sol and around US$38 if you add Isla de la Luna. The journey can take up to four hours each way, depending on the wind, and you may even end up rowing.

Boats land on Isla del Sol at the foot of the Inca steps, and the two-hour stop only allows you a visit to the surrounding part of the island. A two-day trip can also be arranged; the price won't be much higher than for the one-day tour on a similar route.

Via Yampuputa If you want to visit at your own pace, walk from Copacabana to Yampupata, where the locals can take you across the strait to Isla del Sol for as little as

US$2.50 each way. This walk is highly recommended for its scenery and, combined with a couple of days on the island, makes a fabulous trip.

From Copacabana, head north-east along the road which runs across the flat plain. Continue along the coastal track for nearly an hour to the isolated Hinchaca fish hatchery and reforestation project on your left. Just beyond the hatchery, leave the track and cross the stream on your left, following the obvious Inca road up the steep hill. This stretch shows some good Inca paving and makes a short cut, rejoining the track at the crest of the hill.

Continue along the track to a fork in the road; take the left turning, which descends back to the shore and leads on through the village of Titicachi. Keep going through Sicuani, resisting offers of transport to Isla del Sol for US$20 or more.

Approximately four hours from Copacabana, you'll arrive at the village of Yampupata, a tiny collection of mud houses. Here, you can hire a rowboat to the Escalera del Inca (Inca Steps) on Isla del Sol for US$2.50. Arrange for the boat owner to wait or, better, to collect you at a later date.

To return from Yampupata to Copacabana, there are three possibilities: hop on one of the boats that leave for Copacabana between 8 and 9 am every Thursday, Saturday and Sunday (US$1.50 per person), take the Saturday camión, which costs US$0.75 per person and leaves in the early to mid-afternoon (the trip may be slow, since it stops to sell produce), or walk back to Copacabana.

Oruro

Oruro, the only city of the southern altiplano, lies at an altitude of 3702 metres immediately north of the lakes Uru Uru and Poopó, three hours by bus south of La Paz. It sits at the intersection of the rail lines between Cochabamba, La Paz and Chile/Argentina, crowded against a colourful range of low, mineral-rich hills. The aproximately 160,000 inhabitants of Oruro, of whom 90% are of pure Indian heritage, are for some reason known as quirquinchos (armadillos).

Visitors are rarely indifferent to Oruro – they either love it or hate it. Although it's one of Bolivia's most culturally colourful cities (it's known as the Folkloric Capital of Bolivia), for tourists it is neither a friendly nor welcoming place, and recent mining difficulties seem to have made matters worse. Don't arrive expecting the worst, however; if you can demonstrate that you pose no threat, people may open up. If you manage to attend La Diablada, a wild annual fiesta which takes place on the Saturday before Ash Wednesday, during Carnaval, you certainly won't regret it. La Diablada's main attraction is a spectacular parade of devils, performed by dancers in very elaborate masks and costumes. During the fiesta it can be extremely difficult to find anywhere to stay.

Oruro is a very cold and windy place. Although it lies at roughly the same altitude as La Paz, the nights are normally colder, and chilly winds blow all year round.

Information

Tourist Office The poor old tourist office is open weekdays from 9 am to noon and 2 to 6 pm, and on Saturday and Sunday from 9 am to noon. The staff try to be helpful, but without materials, it's difficult to impress.

Money Only a couple of places change travellers' cheques, and the rate is lower than for cash. Try the Farmacia Santa Marta, on Calle Bolívar, opposite the ENTEL office, or the Ferretería Findel, on the corner of Adolfo Mier and Pagador, facing the market. The same places exchange cash dollars, as will several other shops which display 'Compro Dólares' signs. You can find them in the centre, mostly on Calle Adolfo Mier.

Things to See

Several mines in the hills behind the city are open to tourists. The most popular is **Mina San José**, high on the mountain behind the city, which claims to have been in operation for more than 450 years. To get there take Micro 'D' (yellow) marked 'San José', which leaves from the north-west corner of Plaza 10 de Febrero, near the tourist office. Arrive at 7 am and visit the Superintendencia de Minas for a permit to enter.

The **Museo Etnográfico Minero** (Mining Museum), adjacent to the Santuario de la Virgen del Socavón, is an actual mine tunnel. It's open daily from 9 am to noon and 3 to 5.30 pm. Admission is US$0.65. The **Museo Nacional Antropológico Eduardo López Rivas**, at the south end of town, focuses on the Oruro area, with artefacts and information on the early Chipayas and Uru tribes. Take Micro 'C' (orange) marked 'Sud' from the north-west corner of the main plaza or from opposite the railway station, and get off just beyond the tin-foundry compound. Museum hours are 10 am to noon and 3 to 6 pm Tuesday to Sunday. Admission is US$0.65.

The **Museo Mineralógico**, on the university campus, south of the city centre, has a worthwhile exhibition of minerals, precious stones, fossils and crystals. Micro 'A', marked 'Sud', from the centre will drop you there. If you have more time, visit the **Museo Arqueológico** and the moth-eaten and sorry-looking collection of animals in a small **zoo** next to the museum. Take Micro C, marked 'Sud', from the main plaza.

Places to Stay

Cheap alojamientos in Oruro really deserve the description 'basic'. They are generally poor value, and usually have small, dark rooms and shared baths with cold water only. They charge somewhere around US$2 per person and are often 'full' to foreigners. The cheapies are concentrated in two areas: near the railway station and on Calle Ayacucho near Pagador. There is not much to choose between them, though the best of the bunch are supposedly the *Alojamiento San Juan de Diós*, at Velasco Galvarro 6344, and the *Alojamiento Porvenir*, at Aldana 317, the only two of this group that have hot water in their communal baths (US$0.75 extra). Slightly better is the *Residencial Ideal* (far from ideal), at Calle

BOLIVIA

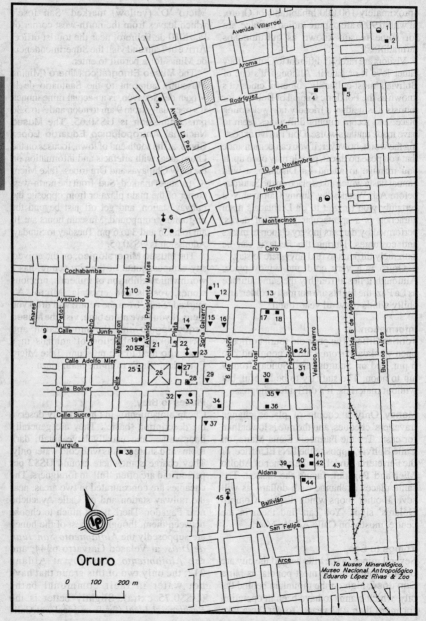

Oruro

0   100   200 m

To Museo Mineralógico,
Museo Nacional Antropológico
Eduardo López Rivas & Zoo

BOLIVIA

■ PLACES TO STAY		OTHER	
2	Hotel Terminal	1	Bus Terminal
4	Residencial Bolivia	3	Diablada Masks & Costumes
5	Hotel Lipton	6	Iglesia de Conchupata
13	Alojamiento Scala	7	Parque Abaroa & Teatro al Aire Libre
17	Alojamiento Ayacucho	8	Stop for Micro to Hot Springs
18	Alojamiento Pagador	9	Museo Etnográfico Minero & Santuario
30	Residencial Ideal		del Socavón
34	Hotel Sucre	10	Mercado Fermín López & Iglesia de
36	Hotel Repostero		Santo Domingo
38	Alojamiento Porvenir	11	Museo Patiño (Casa de la Cultura)
41	Alojamiento San Juan de Diós	19	LAB
42	Alojamiento Copacabana	20	Post Office
44	Hotel Prefectural	22	Iglesia San Francisco
		24	Ferretería Findel
▼ PLACES TO EAT		25	Tourist Office
		26	Plaza 10 de Febrero
12	Rabitos	27	Librería Elier
14	El Chef 312	28	ENTEL
15	Super Salteñas	31	Mercado Campero
16	Coral	33	Farmacia Santa Marta
21	La Casona	40	Lavandería Alemana
23	Confitería Paris	43	Railway Station
29	Heladería Alemana	45	Church
32	Le Grill		
35	El Huerto		
37	Burger Queen & Indianapolis Driving School		
39	Nayjama		

Bolívar 386, which has hot water and charges US$4/6 a single/double.

The *Hotel Repostero* (☎ 50505), at Calle Sucre 370, is Oruro's friendliest and most relaxed hotel. Singles/doubles cost US$10/14 with bath and hot shower, US$6/10 with shared bath.

A popular place with travellers is *Hotel Lipton* (☎ 41583), at the corner of Avenida 6 de Agosto and Rodríguez. It's a good option if you want to stay near the bus terminal but would rather avoid the rip-off Hotel Terminal. Spartan rooms without bath cost US$5 per person; loos are appalling.

Near Hotel Lipton is the *Residencial Bolivia*, on Rodríguez between Velasco Galvarro and Avenida 6 de Agosto. Singles/doubles without bath cost US$6.50/10. Alternatively, try the relatively friendly *Hotel Sucre* (☎ 53838), at Calle Sucre 510. Rooms are US$9/16 with bath and hot shower, US$6/10 without bath.

If you are looking for something upmarket near the transport terminals, check the *Hotel Prefectural*, opposite the railway station, where rooms with bath and hot water cost US$10/16, or the *Hotel Terminal*, inside the bus terminal, the most expensive in the city (nonresidents pay nearly twice as much as Bolivians).

Places to Eat

If you're hoping for anything but a market breakfast, you'll probably be out of luck. Most places don't open until 11 am or later, and the few that open earlier don't seem to have anything worthwhile. *Heladería Alemana*, which opens at 9 am, serves only salteñas and Pepsi until lunchtime. The best salteñas are found at *La Casona*, on Avenida Presidente Montes, just off the main plaza, and at *Super Salteñas*, on Soria Galvarro. Both these places serve pizza in the evening.

For bargain lunch specials, check out such

eateries as *Beirut*, *El Turista* and *San Juan de Diós*, opposite the railway station. Even better are *Coral* (on Calle 6 de Octubre), *Rabitos* (on Ayacucho) and *Le Grill* (on Calle Bolívar). *Nayjama*, on the corner of Pagador and Aldana, has good lunches and a variety of typical dishes for under US$4. The railway station has a passable bar and, although it's not saying much, the bus terminal confitería serves the best coffee in town.

About the only recommended Oruro restaurant is *El Chef 312*, at Calle Junín 676 between La Plata and Soria Galvarro. Daily lunch specials may include such exotics as pizzas and pasta. Vegetarian dishes are available at *El Huerto*, on Calle Bolívar.

Market food stalls in both the *Mercado Campero*, near the railway station, and *Mercado Fermín López*, on Calle Washington, are the cheapest options, featuring noodles in all forms, falso conejo, mutton soup, beef dishes and thimpu de cordero (boiled potatoes, oca, rice and carrots over mutton, smothered with hot llajhua sauce).

Things to Buy

The design, creation and production of Diablada costumes and masks has become an art and a small industry. On Avenida La Paz, between León and Villarroel, you can find shops selling these devilish things.

Getting There & Away

Bus All buses leave from and arrive at the new bus terminal, Terminal de Omnibuses Hernando Siles, outside the city centre. Buses to La Paz run every half-hour or so (US$2.50, three hours). There are several buses daily to Cochabamba (US$4.50, six hours). If you plan on continuing to Santa Cruz, remember that all buses from Cochabamba leave for Santa Cruz around 8 am and 6 pm.

There are two buses daily to Potosí (US$7, 10 hours), plus several more coming through from La Paz, but they're usually full. To Sucre, you can go via either Cochabamba or Potosí; travel time and fare work out roughly the same.

Train Thanks to its mines, Oruro is a railroad centre and has one of the most organised and efficient stations in Bolivia. In fact, the schedules for Bolivia's western rail network are devised here, and the proud planners have produced an impressive printed time-table – the only one found anywhere in the country – with schedules showing precision to the minute (though comparison with chalkboard announcements at the station will reveal its degree of reliability). Because rail service between La Paz and Oruro is slow and difficult to arrange, most people travel by bus from La Paz to Oruro and begin their rail journey there.

From Oruro, you can travel to Uyuni, where the rail line splits; one line goes to Tupiza and Villazón (Argentine border) and the other to Chile. Going east, there are lines to Cochabamba, and to Potosí and Sucre via Río Mulatos.

Some updated schedules and fares from Oruro are to:

Cochabamba
Ferrobus – Wednesday, Friday and Sunday at 8.15 am, also Monday and Wednesday at 12.10 pm coming through from La Paz (US$5/4 pullman/especial, five hours)

Villazón
Express Train – Tuesday and Friday at 7 pm (US$24/18 pullman 1st/2nd class, 15 hours)
Slow Train – Monday and Thursday at 9 pm, and Wednesday and Sunday 7.25 pm (US$10/8 1st/2nd class, 17 hours)

Tupiza
Ferrobus – Tuesday and Saturday at 11.30 am (US$15/12 pullman/especial, nine hours); trains to Villazón also pass through Tupiza

Potosí
Ferrobus – Tuesday and Saturday at 10 pm (US$9/7 pullman/especial, seven hours)
Slow Train – Wednesday at 9 pm (US$6.50/4.50 1st/2nd class, 10 hours); both the train and ferrobus continue to Sucre.

Abaroa
Slow Train – Wednesday at 7.25 pm (at least 12 hours), changing at Abaroa/Ollagüe (the border) from the Bolivian to Chilean train; take plenty of warm clothing and a sleeping bag or woollen blanket; a ticket to Antofagasta (bought in Oruro) costs US$18, 1st class only

Cochabamba

Founded in 1574 in a fertile valley with a mild climate, Cochabamba soon developed into one of the country's important granaries. It long held the status of Bolivia's second largest city, but due to recent development in Santa Cruz, that city has usurped the title. Nonetheless, Cochabamba continues as a progressive and economically active city, with a steadily growing population of over 400,000. In contrast to the altiplano, only a small percentage of inhabitants are of pure Indian extraction.

The city has a warm, dry and sunny climate, offering pleasant relief after the chilly altiplano. However, apart from its favourable climate and a good museum, Cochabamba doesn't have much for tourists. Though the centre retains some colonial flavour, the nicest attractions are in the city's hinterlands. Don't forget to sample the *chicha cochabambina*, an alcoholic maize brew typical of the region.

Radio Latina, at the upper end of the FM band, plays a fine mix of music, mostly Andean folk but also a variety of salsa and local rock, among other styles.

Information

Tourist Office The Dinatur kiosk is on Calle General Achá, in front of the ENTEL building. It's open from 9 am to noon and 2 to 6 pm, Monday to Friday. The staff is quite helpful with specific questions, and you can buy photocopied maps of the city for US$0.10.

Money Librería La Juventud and American Exchange, on Plaza 14 de Septiembre, change travellers' cheques at reasonable rates. Cambios Universo, on Calle España (just off the plaza), also exchange travellers' cheques, but American Exchange is a more professional operation and gives better rates. Street changers gather around the ENTEL office and near the Casa de la Cultura.

Health Cochabamba's serious cholera outbreak now appears to be under control, but visitors should still be careful with raw produce, animal products and drinking water. For further information, refer to the Health section in the Facts for the Visitor chapter.

Things to See

The **Museo Arqueológico**, on 25 de Mayo between Avenida de las Heroínas and Colombia, is one of Bolivia's finest. Exhibits include thousands of artefacts, dating from as early as 15,000 BC and as late as the colonial period. Admission is US$1.25, and the guided tour takes about 1½ hours. It's open Monday to Friday from 9 am to noon and 3 to 7 pm. On Saturday, it's open from 9 am to 1 pm.

The **Palacio de Portales** is evidence of the extravagance of the tin baron Simón Patiño. It was built between 1915 and 1925, and except perhaps for the brick, everything was brought from Europe – wood for the floors, fireplaces, furniture, tapestry, etc. It's open Monday to Friday from 5 to 6 pm, Saturday from 10 to 11.30 am and Sunday from 10 am to noon, and offers free guided tours. The palace is in the barrio of Queru-Queru; take Micro 'G' from near the corner of avenidas San Martín and Heroínas.

If you're fortunate enough to be in the area from 15 to 18 August, you can catch the **Fiesta de la Virgen de Urcupiña** at Quillacollo, 13 km from Cochabamba, the biggest annual celebration in Cochabamba Department.

Two to three hours' walk from the village of Sipe-Sipe, which is 27 km from Cochabamba and easily accessible by micro, are the worthwhile ruins of **Inca-Rakay**.

Places to Stay

The cheapest acceptable accommodation is *Alojamiento Cochabamba* (☎ 25067), at Calle Nataniel Aguirre S-591. Although basically a flophouse, it's popular with ultra-low-budget travellers. Rooms with common bath cost US$2 per person, without breakfast.

BOLIVIA

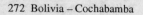

BOLIVIA

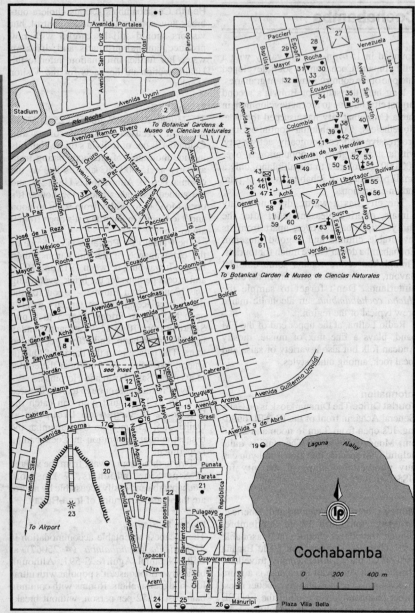

Cochabamba

0   200   400 m

BOLIVIA

■ PLACES TO STAY		
8	Hostal Central	
10	Residencial Familiar	
11	Residencial Florida	
12	Alojamiento Cochabamba	
13	Alojamiento Escobar	
14	Residencial Escobar	
18	Residencial Elisa	
32	Gran Hotel Ambassador	
35	Residencial Familiar Anexo	
36	Hotel Capitol	
38	Hotel Boston	
49	Uni Hotel	
55	Caesar's Plaza	
62	Residencial Imperial	
64	Gran Hotel Las Vegas	

▼ PLACES TO EAT		
3	Jamaica	
4	Bibossy	
9	Fonda Michoacán (Mexican Food)	
28	El Rincón Salón de Te	
29	La Cantonata	
31	Café Bistro El Carajillo	
33	Snack La Mejicana	
34	Gopal's Restaurante Vegetariano	
37	Confitería Bambi	
40	Tea Room Zürich	
50	Heladería Dumbo	
52	California Burgers & Donuts	
53	Confitería Cecy	

OTHER		
1	Palacio de Portales	
2	Parque Arqueológico	

5	Fremen Tours	
6	TAM	
7	The 'Big Screw'	
15	Mercado Cancha Calatayud	
16	Old Long-distance Bus Terminals	
17	Micros to Quillacollo, Payrumani, Sipe-Sipe, etc	
19	Micros to Chapare	
20	New Central Bus Terminal	
21	Mercado de Ferias Central	
22	Railway Station	
23	Colina San Sebastián	
24	Micros to Tarata	
25	Micros to Cliza	
26	Micros To Punata & Arani	
27	Plaza Colón	
30	Caminante Equipo de Camping	
39	Museo Arqueológico	
41	Los Amigos del Libro II	
42	Casa de la Cultura	
43	Post Office	
44	LAB	
45	Librería Cervantes	
46	ENTEL	
47	Tourist Office (DINATUR)	
48	Iglesia de la Compañía de Jesús	
51	Coincoca (Health Food Store)	
54	Iglesia & Convento de San Francisco	
56	Banco de Santa Cruz	
57	Plaza 14 de Septiembre	
58	Los Amigos del Libro	
59	American Exchange, Exprinter & Exprintbol (Casas de Cambio)	
60	Librería La Juventud	
61	Iglesia de Santo Domingo	
63	Catedral	
65	Mercado 25 de Mayo	

One of Bolivia's finest inexpensive digs is *Residencial Elisa* (☎ 27846), at Calle Agustín Lopez 0834 (just off Avenida Aroma). Although this part of town is aromatic, just inside the door of the Elisa is a different world, with a grassy courtyard and clean, sunny garden tables. The owner is friendly and knowledgeable about Cochabamba, and can help you with tourist information. Rooms with private baths and electric hot showers cost US$6, those with shared bath US$4.50, including breakfast.

Another pleasant and friendly place is *Residencial Florida* (☎ 27787), at Calle 25 de Mayo S-0583. Hot water is available until 1 pm, and the owner, a very nice lady, cooks a mean breakfast for her guests. You'll pay US$4 for rooms with communal bath, US$6 with private bath.

Centrally located *Residencial Imperial* costs US$3 per person, with common baths and hot showers. The *Residencial Familiar* (☎ 27988), at Calle Sucre E-554, and the *Residencial Familiar Anexo* (☎ 27986), at Calle 25 de Mayo N-0234, are popular with both Bolivian and foreign travellers. Clean rooms without private bath cost US$4 per person. Hot showers are available, but door locks aren't always secure. *Hostal Central*, three blocks west of the plaza on Calle General Achá, is good value, at US$6 for a single with private bath.

Near the old bus terminals but well off nerve-wracking Avenida Aroma are the *Residencial Escobar* (☎ 29275), at Uruguay E-0213, which charges US$3 per person with common bath, and *Alojamiento Escobar*, at Calle Aguirre S-0749, which charges only US$2 per person. They're nothing to write home about, but they are cheap.

Places to Eat

For breakfast or lunch, the market is the cheapest place, and the meals are varied and tasty. Actually, Cochabamba has three markets – the most central is the *Mercado 25 de Mayo*, just a block from the main plaza, along Calle 25 de Mayo, between Sucre and Jordán. Two other markets, much larger than the 25 de Mayo, are the *Mercado de Ferias*, near the train station, and *La Cancha Calatayud*, along Avenida Aroma between San Martín and Lanza. Though the food there is simpler, it's worth a walk just to savour some of the local colour. Due to the mild climate, the region produces a great variety of fruits, which you can find in the market. If you want something more traditional, try arroz con leche (rice pudding), a local breakfast speciality.

For breakfast, *Confitería Cecy*, at Avenida de las Heroínas E-452, serves great orange juice, eggs, toast and chocolate, as well as Irish coffee and award-winning cheese, chicken and beef salteñas. *California Burgers & Donuts* does pretty much the same for breakfast as the Cecy, but it doesn't quite measure up. Perhaps the best place for a blowout gringo breakfast is *Kivón Helados*, at Avenida de las Heroínas 352, where they pile on the pancakes, french toast, eggs, ham and so on for a predictably elevated price. If you want an early breakfast, *Heladería Dumbo*, in the same area, opens before 8 am.

For lunch, there is a wide range of places to choose from. One of the most economical is *Bar Pensión Familiar*, at Avenida Aroma O-176. For US$1.50 you get a complete meal of salad, soup, a main course and a dessert, and beer is inexpensive. Other good bets for quick traditional lunches are *Anexo El Negro* (at Calle Esteban Arce between Jordán and Calama), *Rellenos Calama* (on Calama between 16 de Julio and Antezana) and *El Caminante* (on Calle Esteban Arce near Cabrera). *Cafe Express Bolívar*, at Avenida Libertador Bolívar 485, has been recommended as having the best espresso and cappuccino in Cochabamba.

Avenida de las Heroínas is fast-food row, and the aforementioned Confitería Cecy is good for light lunches of burgers, chips, chicken, pizza and the like. The friendly owner produces delicious award-winning salteñas. Other fast-food places in the immediate vicinity include California Burgers & Donuts, with good strong Irish coffee, Kivón Helados, which serves snack meals, pastries, flan, and a variety of ice-cream concoctions (our nominee for the world's most superfluous public employee is the military policeman who spends the entire day guarding a nearby parking spot for Bolivia's nearly invisible navy), and the bizarrely decorated *Unicornio*. Heladería Dumbo, with its landmark flying elephant, and *Confitería Bambi*, at Colombia and 25 de Mayo, may infringe Disney copyrights, but both have good meals and ice cream.

El Rincón Salón de Te, at Mayor Rocha 355, offers coffee, cheesecake and lemon meringue pie – highly recommended for afternoon tea. Alternatively, try the coffee, doughnuts and eclairs at the *Tea Room Zürich*, at Avenida San Martín 143, open daily, except Tuesday, from 9.30 to 11.30 am and 2 to 7.30 pm.

Moving up the price scale, you'll find a string of sidewalk cafés along Avenida Ballivián which offer European, Bolivian and North American fare in a very pleasant environment. If you're really hungry, we recommend *Bibossy*, at Avenida Ballivián N-539, near Plaza Colón. Their lunch portions bury the plate!

Bolivia's most authentic Mexican food

(with fine margaritas) is available at *Snack La Mejicana*, at Ecuador and España. *Fonda Michoacán*, at Las Heroínas and Oquendo, also serves Mexican food.

Gopal's Restaurante Vegetariano, at Calle España 250, has a very fine Sunday buffet in a pleasant atmosphere for about US$1.50. Just half a block away, concealed behind rose-coloured stucco, is one of the city's best restaurants, *La Cantonata*, at España and Mayor Rocha, an exceptionally good splurge. Diagonally across the street is *Café Bistro El Carajillo*, a lively place for a drink.

Things to Buy
Coincoca, at 25 de Mayo and Las Heroinas, is a health food shop whose products are based on the coca leaf. There is no guarantee, however, that grape-flavoured coca chewing gum (an appetite suppressant for dieters) will deceive drug-sniffing dogs at airports.

Getting There & Away
Air Cochabamba is served by LAB, TAM and AeroXpress. LAB charges US$36 to La Paz, US$42 to Santa Cruz and US$25 to Sucre. TAM has only one or two flights weekly, at about 30% savings over LAB.

The airport (☎ 26548) is accessible by local transport – Micro 'B' from the main plaza will drop you there. Taxis cost about US$1.50 per person.

Bus Cochabamba's new central bus terminal is on Avenida Ayacucho, near the intersection with Punata. Most buses to La Paz (there are at least 20 buses per day) leave between 7 and 9 pm, though there are also a few morning departures (US$6 to US$8, eight to 10 hours). Similarly, most buses to Santa Cruz leave in the evening, between 4 and 6 pm (US$9 to US$10 negotiable, 10 to 12 hours). All Santa Cruz buses now follow the new road via Chapare rather then the former, more scenic, route through Samaipata.

Five buses leave for Sucre daily between 4.30 and 6.30 pm (US$8, 11 hours). Some then continue to Potosí (at least US$2 extra). To Puerto Villarroel in the lowlands, buses leave in the morning (US$3, five to six

hours) from the terminus at the corner of 9 de Abril and Oquendo.

Train The station (☎ 22402) is at Tarata and Angostura. Ferrobuses to La Paz run on Tuesday and Thursday at 8 am, and on Sunday at 8.20 pm (US$7.50/6 pullman/especial, eight hours). There are also ferrobuses to Oruro (US$4.50/3.50 pullman/especial, five hours) on Tuesday and Thursday at 8 am, Wednesday, Friday and Sunday at 2.15 pm, and another on Sunday at 8.30 pm.

Camión Camiones to Sucre and Santa Cruz leave from the junction of República and Barrientos, about 1½ km south of the railway station along Calle San Martín (which becomes Avenida Barrientos further on). Expect to pay roughly half the bus fare.

Potosí

The history of Potosí – its fame and splendour but also its tragedy and horror – is linked to silver. The city was founded in 1545, following the discovery of ore in silver-rich Cerro Rico, a hill overlooking the town. The veins proved to be so rich that the mines quickly became the world's most prolific. Silver from Potosí underwrote the Spanish economy, particularly its monarchy's extravagance, for over two centuries. Millions of conscripted labourers were put to work in the mines, where conditions were so appalling and dangerous that miners died in considerable numbers, either in accidents or from diseases like silicosis pneumonia.

Despite its setting at an altitude of 4070 metres, Potosí blossomed, becoming, towards the end of the 18th century, the largest city in Latin America and among the most glittering. The boom, however, was not to last. At the turn of the 19th century, when silver production waned, decline set in. During the 20th century, demand for tin rescued Potosí from obscurity and brought a slow but steady recovery, and Potosí was

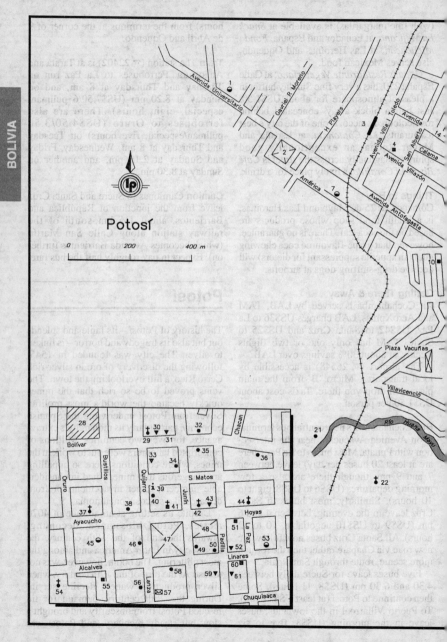

Potosí

0   200   400 m

BOLIVIA

POTOSÍ KEY

■ PLACES TO STAY

4　Alojamiento Ferrocarril
9　Residencial Copacabana
10　Residencial Sumaj
11　Hotel IV Centenario
13　Alojamiento La Paz
14　Posada Oruro
24　Hotel El Turista

▼ PLACES TO EAT

16　Chaplin's

OTHER

1　Bus Terminal
2　Plaza Chuquimia
3　Railway Station
5　Plaza Uyuni
6　Iglesia de San Roque
7　Transportes Quijarro & Camiones to Uyuni
8　Iglesia de Jerusalén
12　Iglesia de San Bernardo
15　Iglesia de San Lorenzo
17　Iglesia de Santa Mónica
18　ENTEL
19　Convento & Museo de Santa Teresa
20　Arcos de Cobija
21　Ribera de los Ingenios
22　Iglesia de San Benito
23　Ingenio Dolores
25　Convento & Museo de San Francisco
26　Iglesia de San Juan de Diós
27　Iglesia de San Martín

POTOSÍ INSET KEY

■ PLACES TO STAY

51　Hotel Colonial
55　Hotel Central
60　Hostal Carlos V

▼ PLACES TO EAT

30　Restaurante Marisel
31　Don Lucho
33　Sumac Orko
43　Heladería Alemana
52　El Aldabón & Heladería Tokyo
59　Cherry's Salón de Te & Maxim's
61　Las Vegas

OTHER

28　Market
29　Iglesia de San Agustín
32　Museo Universitario
34　Portón Mestizo
35　Distribuidora Cultural Sud
36　Casa de las Tres Portadas
37　Iglesia de la Compañía de Jesús
38　Casa Real de la Moneda
39　Tourist Office
40　Trans-Amazonas
41　Catedral
42　Former Iglesia de Belén
44　Iglesia de la Merced
45　Andesbus
46　El Cabildo (La Prefectura)
47　Plaza 10 de Noviembre
48　Plaza 6 de Agosto
49　Banco de La Paz
50　Balsa Tours & Top Wisquería
53　Transtin
54　Iglesia de Santo Domingo
56　Casa de Antonio López de Quiroga
57　Post Office
58　Edificio de Cajas Reales (Alcaldía)

revived as a mining centre. Silver extraction continues, but on a very small scale. Reminders of the grand colonial city are still evident in the narrow streets, formal balconied mansions and ornate churches.

Potosí is one of the highest cities in the world, which you'll soon realise while climbing some of the steeper streets or shivering with cold at night. Plenty of warm clothes are essential.

Information

Tourist Office The IBT tourist office, upstairs at the corner of Matos and Calle Quijarro, is open from 9 am to noon and 2 to 6 pm, Monday to Friday, but it's an unmitigated waste of time in a city where there are a number of better things to do.

Money With cash US dollars, changing money in Potosí is no problem; many businesses along Calle Bolívar and Calle Sucre change at a reasonable rate – look for the 'Compro Dólares' signs. Travellers' cheques may be changed at the Distribuidora Cultural Sud bookshop. If they are short of cash, try the Trans-Amazonas tour agency. Visa cash advances are available within 20 minutes at Banco de La Paz, on the plaza. There's a US$1.50 charge for the telex to determine the card's validity, and you can receive the cash in bolivianos or US dollars.

Post & Telecommunications The central post office is on Calle Lanza, a block south of the main plaza. The new ENTEL office is near the corner of Frias and Avenida Camacho.

Things to See
You'll find many of Potosí's finest colonial mansions on or around the main Plaza 10 de Noviembre. Allow yourself a couple of hours for a pleasant stroll around the centre. Unfortunately, most of the worthwhile churches are closed to the public or open only rarely. The **Catedral** (which is open regularly) has the nicest interior, while the **Iglesia de San Lorenzo** is famous for its classically wild mestizo façade.

The **Casa Real de la Moneda**, the Royal Mint, is the city's star attraction and one of Bolivia's best museums. The current building, which occupies an entire block near the Catedral, was built between 1753 and 1773 to control the minting of colonial coins right where the metal was mined. It's now a museum housing wooden minting machines dating from colonial times (still in working order but unused since the 1950s), a religious art gallery, a gold-covered altar from the Iglesia de San Francisco, war relics from many Bolivian wars and skirmishes, Tiahuanaco artefacts and even the first loco-motive used in the country – all definitely worth seeing. The building itself, which has been carefully restored, is of exceptional beauty. Guided tours are conducted twice daily, at 9 am and 2 pm, Monday to Saturday (US$1, three hours).

The city has two museums of religious art, one in the **Convento de San Francisco**

(open Monday to Saturday from 2.30 to 4.30 pm) and the other in the **Convento de Santa Teresa** (open Monday to Saturday from 9 am to noon and 2 to 5 pm); both are worth-while. Admission to either, including a one-hour guided tour, is US$1.

The **Museo Universitario**, on Calle Bolívar between Junín and Sucre, has a rather haphazard and mostly unlabelled col-lection of paintings, pottery, antique objects, stuffed birds, etc. It is open Monday to Friday from 9 am to noon and 2 to 6 pm; admission costs US$0.40.

Outside Potosí are several hot spring resorts, the most popular one at **Tarapaya**, 25 km from the city. To get there, find a camión from Plaza Chuquimia, near the bus terminal.

Potosí Mines
Visiting the mines is the most striking expe-rience you'll have in Potosí, and you'll probably be left in a state of shock. Basically, you have two options – cooperative or state-owned mines. A visit to the former is far more breathtaking, though a look around the state-owned mine will give you an idea of the contrast between the two types.

Working conditions in **cooperative mines,** unchanged from colonial times, are outrageous, and all work is done by hand with primitive tools. The temperature varies from freezing – the altitude is nearly 4500 metres – to stifling heat in the mountain's depths. Miners, exposed to all sorts of noxious chemicals and gases, normally die of silicosis pneumonia within 10 years of entering the mines.

Quite a few young men in the town provide guided tours through the mines. Eduardo Garnica Fajardo, the guide who is almost universally recommended, has expe-rience and a background which well qualify him for the job. He was a miner himself, and is closely acquainted with the traditions of the mines and with the men who work them. Contact him by telephone (☎ 23138 at home, 24708 at Koala Tours); his four-hour tours will be conducted in English if you wish. Alternatively, try Raúl Braulio Mamani

(☎ 25304 at home, ☎ 25786 at Potosí Tours), who makes a show of detonating a stick of dynamite as a finale. Tours cost US$4 per person.

Take the worst clothes you have; walking in the mine is difficult, ceilings are low and passageways are steep and muddy. You can speak with the miners, and it's nice to take some cigarettes, coca leaves, etc for them. Bring a flash attachment for your camera if you wish to take photos – photography is permitted.

The state-owned mine, **Pailaviri**, contrasts sharply with those of the cooperatives. Here, the government provides electric lamps, jackhammers, lifts, higher wages and superior medical and pension benefits. If you visit only the state mine, you will get a largely artificial picture of mining in Bolivia.

To reach Pailaviri, catch bus No 100 from the main plaza between 7 and 8 am to reach the mine entrance before 9 am. The tour lasts about three hours and costs US$9 per person.

Places to Stay

It gets very cold at night in Potosí and only some of the top-end hotels have heating. Check how many blankets you have; at least four per person should be about right. Alternatively, bring a down sleeping bag.

Potosí hotel prices are regulated, so if you feel that a price is too high or that you're being cheated, ask for *la tarifa oficial*, the official price list. Many cheapie hotels charge extra for hot showers.

There are several popular budget hotels, but the favourite seems to be the *Residencial Sumaj* (☎ 23336), near the Plaza del Estudiante, convenient to both the bus terminal and the railway station. Although its appeal escapes most people, it somehow keeps plugging along. Small, dark rooms without private bath cost US$4 per person, and for an additional US$1, you'll get a basic breakfast. The hot water situation is hit or miss. Beware of thieves posing as mine guides.

A budding favourite is the friendly *Hostal Carlos V* (☎ 25121). It's in a cosy old colonial building with a covered patio. Rooms cost US$5 per person.

Basically just a flophouse (with the emphasis on basic), the seedy *Posada Oruro* offers budget rooms for US$2 per person. Showers are available at the public baths just up the street. The *Residencial Copacabana* (☎ 22712), at Avenida Serrudo 319, costs US$3.50 per person without private bath. A reader has highly recommended *Residencial Felcar*, at Serrudo 345, with singles/doubles for US$2.50/4.50. *Residencial San Antonio* (☎ 23566), at Calle Oruro 136, costs US$3 per person with barely warmish showers.

An up-and-coming favourite is the *Alojamiento La Paz* (☎ 22632), at Calle Oruro 262, but it seems everyone has a shocking tale to tell about the showers! Rooms cost US$2.50 per person; the dodgy showers are US$0.40 extra. The *Hotel IV Centenario* (☎ 22791) is an odd and imposing structure attached to the cinema/church on the Plaza del Estudiante. Singles/doubles cost US$7/12.

Moving slightly up-market, the *Hotel El Turista* (☎ 22492), at Calle Lanza 19, is our favourite in Potosí, and worth the splurge. It's exceptionally friendly and clean, and offers some of Bolivia's finest hot showers from 6.30 and 11 am. The owner, Señor Luksic, who also runs the LAB desk in the lobby, provides the most reliable tourist information in town. Rooms cost US$7/11. For a room with a view, request something on the top floor, particularly room 32.

The friendly *Hotel Central* (☎ 22207), in a quiet old area of town, has a traditional Potosino overhanging balcony. Rooms cost US$3.50 per person. If you prefer to avoid lugging a heavy pack uphill from the bus terminal or railway station, try the basic *Alojamiento Ferrocarril* (☎ 24294), on Avenida Villazón. Rooms cost US$2.50 per person.

Places to Eat

The market *comedor* (dining area) has the best inexpensive breakfasts in town; nearly everything else is locked up tight until well into the morning. There are a few *panaderías* (bakeries) which open at 8 am, but there's not a lot to recommend them, except three-day-old pastries and coffee from the same era. *Heladería Alemana*, on the corner beside the Catedral, is one quick breakfast option, with snacks and ice-cream concoctions available the rest of the day.

The best and most innovative meals in town are found at *Don Lucho*, which serves a pretty good lunch for US$3, including soup, salad, a main course and dessert. Dinners are even better, ranging from killer pasta to filet mignon with béchamel sauce.

Almost as good, but a bit expensive, the *Las Vegas* is near the corner of calles Padilla and Linares. Its exhaustive four-course lunch specials run at about US$4; the house specialty is pique a lo macho.

The *Sumac Orko*, at Calle Quijarro 46, offers filling lunch specials of soup, potatoes, rice and a meat dish for just US$1.50, as well as more interesting dishes such as trucha al limón (lemon trout) and picante de perdíz (spicy partridge).

Another friendly option is *Chaplin's*, on Calle Sucre, where you can get a vegetarian lunch of vegetable noodle soup, spicy lentils, potatoes, rice, fruit juice and papaya for US$1.

If you're after decadent apfelstrudel, chocolate cake or other cakes and pastries, or just good coffee or tea, try *Cherry's Salón de Te*, on Calle Padilla near Calle Linares.

For great salteñas, go to *Café Imma Sumac*, at Calle Bustillos 987. In the morning, meatless salteñas Potosinas are available on the street near Iglesia de San Lorenzo for US$0.20 each. Meat empanadas are sold around the market until early afternoon, and in the evening, street vendors sell cornmeal humintas.

Entertainment

Don't miss the Friday night peña at *Don Lucho*, the best in Bolivia. If you're lucky, you'll have the opportunity to hear the lively and driving music of the local group, Arpegio Cinco, as well as some whiny and nasal accompaniment to Potosí Department's own tinku fights.

Getting There & Away

Air Only AeroXpress flies to/from Potosí, which makes air travel pretty expensive. Flights to La Paz cost around US$60. There are also flights to Sucre and Cochabamba.

Bus The bus terminal is a long way from the centre, but frequent micros run from the main plaza. There are nine buses daily to La Paz, and according to the inexplicable Bolivian custom, all leave together between 6 and 6.30 pm (US$8, 10 to 12 hours).

Heading south to Argentina through Villazón, there are basically two routes, via Tupiza or via Tarija. The former is shorter and cheaper. Four direct buses go daily to Tupiza (US$6.50, 11 hours) and Villazón (US$8, 13 hours). Buses to Tarija run at 7.30 am on Monday and Saturday with Veloz del Sud (US$9.50, 12 hours). There you must change buses for Villazón.

Buses to Sucre (four hours) depart from their respective offices, near the plaza. Andesbus, on Calle Bustillos near Ayacucho, leaves daily at 7 am and 5 pm. Lunch is included in the US$6 fare. Transtin, at Calle Linares 93, and Géminis, beside Andesbus, leave at 7.30 am and 5 pm; either costs US$5. The cheapest way between Potosí and Sucre is by camión or micro. They leave from Plaza Uyuni when full, normally every few minutes.

Transportes Quijarro has a daily bus to Uyuni, leaving at noon from Calle América (US$6, eight hours). Camiones to Uyuni leave from the same place.

Train The slow train to Oruro and La Paz leaves on Thursday at 10 pm (US$7/5 1st/2nd class, 15 hours). The ferrobus departs on Sunday at 8.15 am (US$10/11 pullman/especial, 11 hours). To Sucre, there's a ferrobus on Wednesday and Sunday at 5 am and Monday and Friday at 7.30 am (US$6/5 pullman/especial). The train to Sucre departs on Thursday at 7.10 am (US$4/3 1st/2nd class).

Sucre

Set in a valley surrounded by low mountains, Sucre remains Bolivia's official capital. Although La Paz has usurped most of the governmental power, the Supreme Court still convenes in Sucre and with some kind of twisted pride, the inhabitants of Sucre maintain that their city is still the real centre of Bolivian government.

The city was founded in 1538 (under the name of La Plata) as the Spanish capital of the Charcas, a vast region stretching from southern Peru to Río de la Plata in present-day Argentina. In 1776, when the new territorial division was created by the Spaniards, the city's name was changed to Chuquisaca.

During the long colonial period, La Plata/Chuquisaca was the most important centre in the eastern Spanish territories, and influenced much of Bolivia's history. It was here that independence was declared on 6 August 1825 and the new republic, named after its liberator, Simón Bolívar, was created. The name of the city was changed again, to Sucre, in honour of the general who promoted the independence movement.

Today, it's a pleasant, quiet city of 100,000 people which retains the colonial flavour of its heritage, in its numerous churches, museums and ancient mansions and in its atmosphere.

Information

Tourist Office The once efficient IBT tourist office (☎ 35994), in the Caserón de la Capellanía, is a shadow of its former self; it's now hardly worth a visit. It's open from 8 am to noon and 2 to 6 pm from November to April, from 8.30 am to noon and 2.30 to 6.30 pm from May to October. The Dinatur office at the airport is considerably more helpful, but it's a long way to carry casual queries. In addition to the government tourist offices, there's a most helpful university tourist information centre (☎ 23763) at Calle Nicolás Ortiz 182.

Money There are a couple of casas de cambio around the main market. Ambar, at Calle San Alberto 7, changes travellers' cheques at acceptable rates. Alternatively, try Almacén del Sol, at Calle Ravelo 74. Street moneychangers operate along Avenida Hernando Siles, at the back entrance to the main market. There are also quite a few businesses around town displaying 'Compro Dólares' signs, but they'll only accept cash. Visa cash advances take 10 minutes at the Banco de Santa Cruz, at the corner of calles San Alberto and España.

Post & Telecommunications The modern new ENTEL office is on Calle España, three blocks from the main plaza. The central post office is at Argentina 50, half a block from the plaza.

Things to See

Of many colonial churches in Sucre, the most interesting are the Catedral, La Merced, San Francisco and San Miguel. The **Catedral**, on the main plaza, dates from the 16th century, though there were major additions at the beginning of the 17th century. It is open in the morning. Be sure to visit the Catedral museum, the **Museo de la Iglesia**, Calle Ortiz 61, next door to the Capilla de la Virgen de Guadalupe. The museum contains a remarkable collection of religious relics, and is one of the best church museums in Bolivia. It's open Monday to Friday from 10 am to noon and 3 to 5 pm, and on Saturday from 10 am to noon.

The **Iglesia de la Merced** has Sucre's most beautiful interior, but it's rarely open. Both the **Iglesia de San Miguel** and the **Iglesia de San Francisco** reflect mudéjar influences, particularly in their ceiling designs.

It's worth trekking up the hillside to the **Iglesia de la Recoleta**, where you find superb views over the city from the plaza facing the church. The **Museo de la Recoleta**, in the church, contains quite a few anonymous paintings and sculptures, and is open Monday to Friday from 9 to 11 am and 3 to 5 pm. Admission and guided tour cost

US$1. If you're interested in sacred art, there's the **Museo de Santa Clara**, at Calvo 212, open Monday to Friday from 9 to 11 am and 5 to 7 pm, and on Saturday from 10 am to noon. Admission is US$1.

If you're interested in Bolivian history, visit the **Casa de la Libertad**, the house on the main plaza where the Bolivian declaration of independence was signed on 6 August 1825. It's now a museum displaying numerous mementos of the era. It is open Monday to Friday from 9 am to noon and 4.30 to 6 pm. Admission costs US$1; photography is an additional US$1.50.

The most interesting exhibits are in the **Museos Universitarios**, at Calle Bolívar 698, with separate museums for colonial relics, anthropology and modern art. They're open Monday to Friday from 9 am to noon and 2 to 6 pm, and on Saturday from 9 am to noon. Charges are the same as for Casa de la Libertad.

If you have extra time, you can also visit **La Glorieta**, an imposing castle-like structure built in a hotch-potch of European architectural styles, on the outskirts of the city. Micro 'G' from the centre will get you there. It's open Monday to Friday from 9 am to noon and 2 to 6 pm, and on Saturday from 9 am to noon. Admission is free, but you must leave your passport at the entrance.

Places to Stay

Sucre is quite popular with visitors, so there's a choice of inexpensive accommodation and hotel prices are negotiable. Most of the budget hotels are located around the market and on several blocks along Ravelo and San Alberto.

For good value accommodation, try *Residencial Oriental* (☎ 21644), which costs US$4 per person. There are no private baths, but rooms are cleaned daily and there's a popular TV set in the reception area. Another good backpackers' haunt is the *Residencial Bustillo* (☎ 21560), at Calle Ravelo 158, just a block from the market. They charge US$4.50/7 for singles/ doubles without bath. Breakfast is an additional US$0.65.

Alojamiento El Turista (☎ 23172), in the same area, at Calle Ravelo 118, is mediocre but friendly. At US$3/5 for a single/double, it's also good value for those on strict budgets. In the middle of nowhere, opposite the bus terminal, the misnamed *Alojamiento Central* (☎ 23935), Avenida Ostria Gutiérrez 456, has rooms without bath for US$3 per person.

For rock-bottom accommodation, try *Alojamiento Anexo San José* (☎ 25572), on Calle Ravelo beside the El Turista. It's cheap and basic, at US$2.50 per person with communal bath. If you prefer to be a bit further from the heart of things, try the quiet *Residencial Avenida* (☎ 21245), opposite the Gran Hotel Londres, for US$4 per person with bath.

The friendly *Residencial Charcas* (☎ 23972), at Calle Ravelo 62, is a real winner – the best value for money in Sucre. Showers are combined solar and electric, so hot water is available around the clock. Sparkling clean single/double rooms cost US$7/11 with bath, US$5/8 without.

Quirky *Residencial Bolivia* (☎ 24346), at Calle San Alberto 42, looks like someone has run amok with remaindered paint. Singles/doubles cost US$8/12 with bath, US$6/10 without.

Hostal Sucre (☎ 21411), at Calle Bustillos 113, easily gets the vote for Sucre's nicest hotel. It has a lovely antique dining room and a sunny, flowery courtyard where you can relax and read or catch up on letters. At US$16/20 a single/double, it's a rewarding splurge.

Places to Eat

Sucre has a pleasant variety of quality restaurants and is a good place to spend time lolling around coffee shops, and witnessing university life Bolivian-style.

For breakfast, try *Agencias Todo Fresco*, at Calle Ravelo 74 (the sign outside says 'Dillmann'). It's a bakery offering great fresh bread, pastries, coffee, tea, etc. In the market just opposite, you can have a typical breakfast of pastel (pastry) and api, or go for salteñas, for as little as US$0.25. The best

BOLIVIA

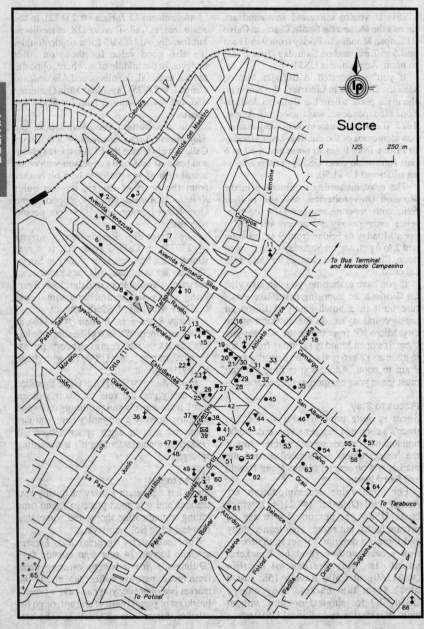

Sucre

0   125   250 m

To Bus Terminal
and Mercado Campesino

To Tarabuco

To Potosí

■ PLACES TO STAY

5	Hotel Municipal Simón Bolívar
7	Gran Hotel Londres
13	Residencial Bustillo
14	Alojamiento Anexo San José
15	Alojamiento El Turista
19	Residencial Charcas
20	Hotel La Plata & Saico del Sur
27	Hostal Colonial
28	Grand Hotel
30	Hostal Libertad & El China Restaurant
32	Residencial Oriental
33	Residencial Bolivia
47	Hostal Sucre

▼ PLACES TO EAT

2	Piso Cero
4	La Rotonda
21	El China
24	Arco Iris
25	Helados Cri Cri
37	Pecos Bill Pizzería
43	Pizza Napolitana
44	Las Vegas & Plaza
46	Piccolissimo
50	Bibliocafé
51	Snack Paulista
61	El Solar

OTHER

1	Railway Station
3	Discoteca Up-down
6	Parque Bolívar
8	Museo de Anatomía Humana

9	Teatro Gran Mariscal de Ayacucho
10	Iglesia Santa Rita
11	Iglesia San Sebastián
12	Transtin (Buses)
16	Market
17	Iglesia de San Francisco
18	ENTEL
22	Iglesia de Santa Monica
23	Iglesia de San Miguel
26	Casa de la Libertad
29	Alliance Française
31	Casa de Cambio Ambar
34	Banco de Santa Cruz
35	Museo de Historia Natural
36	Iglesia de San Agustín
38	Immigration
39	Post Office
40	Museo de la Iglesia
41	Catedral
42	Plaza 25 de Mayo
45	Andy Capp's Wisquería
48	LAB
49	Convento de San Felipe Neri
52	Andesbus & Laverap (Buses)
53	Iglesia de Santo Domingo
54	Museo de Santa Clara
55	IBT Tourist Office
56	Caserón de la Capellanía
57	Iglesia de Santa Teresa
58	Iglesia de la Merced
59	University Tourist Office
60	TAM
62	Museos Universitarios
63	Goethe Institut
64	Iglesia San Lázaro
65	Cemetery
66	La Recoleta

places for salteñas are *El Patio*, at Calle San Alberto 18, and *Don Sancho*, at Calle España 150.

Pizza Napolitana, on the plaza, seems to do well as a hang-out for the under-21 university crowd, with ice cream and pizzas leading the menu options. Alternatively, try *Pecos Bill Pizzería*, on Avenida Argentina, which thrills pizza freaks by opening at 10 am and serving the coldest Sureña beer in town. For roast chicken, choose from the selection of snack restaurants along Avenida Hernando Siles between Tarapaca and Calle Junín.

The frequently recommended *El China*, operated by fun-loving Shanghai Chinese, is upstairs on the corner of Avenida Aniceto Arce and Calle San Alberto. Another chifa, *Restaurant Shanghai*, on Ravelo, is particularly good at egg flower soup.

The long-running *Las Vegas*, on the main plaza, is good if you want to hang out in the centre of things, but it's a legend only in its own mind. Plusher restaurants with good fare are *El Solar*, at the corner of calles Bolívar and Azurduy, and better still, *Piso Cero*, at Avenida Venezuela 1241. For excellent up-market Italian food, including lasagna, ravioli and canneloni, there's *Piccolissimo*, at Calle San Alberto 237. It's about as elegant as Sucre gets. Plan on spending about US$5 to US$7 per person, more if you splurge on a bottle of Chilean wine. After the meal, try a cup of coffee – so good one could wax poetic about it!

For a real treat, go to *La Taverne*, belonging to Alliance Française, on Avenida Aniceto Arce just below the plaza. It serves a mean ratatouille for US$1.50, as well as coq au vin, quiche lorraine and other continental favourites. And then there are the desserts...

There's also a trio of German-run options. The best is *Bibliocafé*, with a dark but cosy atmosphere, good music and stacks of *Geo* and *Der Spiegel* on the shelves. The US$2.50 plate of spaghetti bolognaise is recommended, as is the banana, chocolate and cream crêpe for US$1.50. It's only open in the evening and gets very crowded, so come early. Another German option is *Kultur Café Berlin*, at Calle Abaroa 326, a German coffee shop and restaurant, which is open for lunch from 12.30 to 3 pm. For variety, try the *Arco Iris*, with its weird and starkly modern décor. There's a foreign atmosphere, and the menu is great, including such delights as roeschti, fondue bourguignonne, mousse au chocolat and head-buzzing cappuccino. Vegetarian food is also available, and they show videos and occasionally arrange peñas featuring local bands.

The fruit salads and other fruit concoctions available in the market are Bolivian highlights. For something different (unless you're coming from Brazil or the lowlands), try jugo de tumbo (the juice of maracuyá) or yellow passion fruit. Alternatively, they'll mix up any combination of melon, guava, pomelo, strawberry, papaya, banana, orange, lime and so on, throw it in a blender and come up with something indescribably delicious.

Getting There & Away

Air Three airlines operate flights to/from Sucre: LAB, at Calle Bustillos 127; TAM, at Calle Ortiz 110; and the newly created AeroXpress, at Calle España 66. LAB flies to La Paz, Cochabamba, Santa Cruz, Tarija, Camiri and other, smaller towns. TAM only has flights to Santa Cruz (once weekly). AeroXpress flies to Potosí. Airport access is on Micro 'F', or by taxi for US$1.50.

Bus The bus terminal is accessed by Micro 'A' from the centre, but the trip would be a nightmare with luggage. There are five buses daily to Cochabamba (US$7, 12 hours); all leave around 6 pm. Direct buses go to Santa Cruz three times weekly (US$10, at least 18 hours). Three companies, Transtin, Géminis and Andesbus, leave daily for Potosí (US$7 to US$8, 4½ hours) between 7 and 7.30 am and at 5 pm, from their respective offices. These services are good, reliable and comfortable, and go directly to the Potosí city centre.

Train To Potosí and Tupiza, there's a train leaving on Saturday at 5.30 pm. To Oruro, there's a train service on Thursday at 3.30 pm (US$7/5 1st/2nd class) and a ferrobus on Wednesday and Sunday at 6.50 pm (US$13/10 pullman/especial). To nearby Tarabuco, the *autocarril*, a very odd ferrobus, leaves on Sunday morning at 7 am and returns the same day at 2 pm (US$2, 2½ hours).

AROUND SUCRE
Tarabuco

This small, predominantly Indian town, some 65 km south-east of Sucre, should not be missed. It's widely known for its beautiful handmade weavings and for the colourful Sunday market which spreads over the length and breadth of the town. You can buy amazing ponchos and mantas, as well as charangos (please have mercy on endangered armadillos and purchase only wooden ones), but prices are high and the scene is extremely touristy.

Camiones leave from the parking area one km from the top of Calle Calvo in Sucre between 6.30 and 9.30 am on Sundays. They charge US$0.60 to ride *atrás* (in the bed of the camión), US$1.25 in the cab. The trip takes at least two hours, with beautiful scenery en route. Camiones returning to Sucre park at the top of the main plaza in Tarabuco. They're meant to leave between 2 and 3.30 pm on Sundays but will wait until they are 'full' (by local definition), so you may not get away until late afternoon.

The best option is to go by *autocarril*, a bizarrely concocted hybrid train and bus, which departs from the Sucre railway station at 7 am on Sunday and returns at 2 pm. The fare is US$2.50 per person, but arrive early at the station because there aren't many seats. The Tarabuco railway station lies 500 metres from the village.

Santa Cruz

Santa Cruz de la Sierra was founded in 1561 by Ñuflo de Chaves, a Spaniard who hailed from what is now Paraguay. The town originally lay 220 km east of its current location, but around the end of the 16th century, it proved too vulnerable to Indian attacks and was moved to its present position, 50 km east of the Cordillera Oriental foothills.

Since 1950, Santa Cruz has mushroomed from a backwater cow town of 30,000 to its present position as Bolivia's second largest city, with over 800,000 people. Despite continuing to grow at a phenomenal rate, this cosmopolitan city retains traces of its dusty past, evident in its wide streets, frontier architecture and small-town atmosphere.

Santa Cruz today is a big city at the edge of the wilderness. Once an isolated agricultural outpost, it has developed into a hub of transport and trade. It is connected by rail with Argentina and Brazil and by road with Cochabamba, the Chaco and Trinidad. It has an international airport with direct flights to Miami, but forest-dwelling sloths hang in the trees of the main plaza. The area serves as a centre of cocaine-smuggling, but is also Bolivia's primary source of rice, cotton, soybeans and other warm-weather crops.

In Santa Cruz, you'll find people from all corners of the earth and many walks of life – Japanese businessmen, Plattdeutsch-speaking Canadian Mennonites, Sikh agriculturalists, Arabs, foreign oil workers, drug traffickers, campesinos from highland Bolivia and environmental activists.

The climate is tropical, but Santa Cruz enjoys more sun and less- stifling temperatures than the humid, rainy Bolivian Amazon further north-west. At times during the winter, cold winds called *surazos* blow in from the Argentine pampas, bringing surprisingly chilly temperatures.

Information

Tourist Office The new tourist office (☎ 34-8644) is upstairs in the immigration building, at Avenida Irala 563; you'll have to present your documents to enter the building. The staff is quite helpful with specific queries, and there is a small assortment of informative brochures. The office is open from 8.30 am to 1.30 pm, Monday to Friday.

Money Currency exchange is possible at cambios Sudamer, Alemán and Mendicambio (the most straightforward), all around the main plaza. All exchange houses charge 3% commission on travellers' cheques. We've had reports of less-than-scrupulous dealings by Cambios Alemán. Be on your guard!

If you're changing American Express travellers' cheques, you must have them certified at the American Express office before presenting them to the casas de cambio. Quick and convenient Visa cash advances are available at the Banco de Santa Cruz, Calle Junín 154, near the main plaza.

Post & Telecommunications The post office is half a block from the main plaza, on Calle Junín. The ENTEL office is on Calle Warnes between René Moreno and Chuquisaca.

Foreign Consulates The Argentine Consulate (☎ 32-4153) is in the Edificio del Banco de la Nación Argentina, on the northern side of the main plaza. The Brazilian Consulate (☎ 34-4400) is on Avenida Busch 330, quite a long way from the centre.

Santa Cruz

To Zoo & Viru-Viru Airport

Primer Anillo

Avenida Uruguay

0   200   400 m

To University
(500 m)

To Río Piray &
Jardín Botánico

To Train
Station

To Cochabamba-bound camiones

To TAM Office &
El Trompillo Airport

Dangers & Annoyances

When walking around Santa Cruz, carry your passport at all times. If you're caught in the street without documents, you'll be required to pay the usual 'fine' of about US$50 and will waste several hours at the police station while paperwork is shuffled.

Things to See

There is not much to see in Santa Cruz. The most outstanding attraction is the **zoo**, one of the few on the continent worth the time and money. The collection is limited to South American animals (including tapirs, pumas,

jaguars, monkeys, spectacled bears, llamas, alpacas and vicuñas), many birds (such as Andean condors, pink flamingos, parrots, macaws, toucans and a variety of amazing owls) and quite a lot of snakes (including anacondas and boas). All appear to be humanely treated and well fed, but the llamas are a bit overdressed for the climate. The zoo is open daily from 9 am to 7.30 pm; admission costs US$1. To get there, take Micro 8, 11 or 17 from the centre or from El Arenal, or catch a taxi (US$1.50).

Locals relax at **Parque El Arenal**, a park with a lagoon. On an island in the centre of

BOLIVIA

■ PLACES TO STAY		OTHER	
6	Alojamiento Santa Bárbara	1	Museo del Carnaval
7	Alojamiento Oriente	2	Parque El Arenal
8	Hotel Bibosi	3	Mercado Los Pozos
9	Hotel Amazonas	4	Buses to Cotoca & Puerto Pailas
14	Hotel Copacabana	10	LAP (Air Paraguay)
19	Residencial Bolívar	11	Banco de Santa Cruz
27	Hotel Italia	12	Post Office
34	Residencial Monte Carlos	16	Plaza 24 de Septiembre
35	Alojamiento Lemoine	17	Cambios Alemán & Mendicambio
38	Alojamiento 15 de Octubre	20	Bus Stop for Zoo
40	Residencial Grigotá	21	Lavandería
		22	Basílica Menor de San Lorenzo &
▼ PLACES TO EAT			Museo de la Catedral
		23	US Consulate
5	Crêperie El Boliche	24	Museo de Arte/Casa de la Cultura
13	El Jacuú 85	25	Mercado Siete Calles
15	El Sirari & Bonanza	26	Magri Turismo (American Express)
18	El Gaucho	29	Uimpex Travel
28	Bar El Tapekua	30	LAB
32	California Donuts	31	ENTEL
33	The Jungle Restaurant	37	Bus Terminal
36	La Bella Napoli	39	Mercado La Ramada
		41	Aerosur
		42	Tourist Office & Immigration
		43	Amazonas Adventure Tours

the lake, a large bas-relief mural with a collage depicts historical and modern-day aspects of the city. The park is within walking distance of the centre.

The Casa de la Cultura Raúl Otero Reiche has recently opened a **Museo de Arte**, on Calle Sucre near the corner of Quijarro. Highlights include the works of such contemporary Bolivian artists as Lorgio Vaca, Herminio Pedraza and Tito Kurasotto. Originality runs high, and the place is a breath of fresh air for anyone overdosed on the blood and flagellation evident in most other Bolivian museums. It's open daily from 8.30 to noon and 2.30 to 6 pm; admission is free. The museum sponsors frequent live music performances for an admission charge of US$1.

Places to Stay

If you don't feel like walking too far on arrival at the bus terminal, or you're just passing through the city, you can select from several cheap places near the bus terminal.

The best among them seems to be the *Residencial Grigotá*, at the corner of Avenida Grigotá and Calle Muchurí, two blocks from the terminal. It has fairly clean rooms (US$4 per person), and hot water in one of the communal baths. The proprietors are friendly.

Another nearby option is *Alojamiento 15 de Octubre*, at Calle Guaraní 33. It costs the same as the Grigotá but is more basic and lacks hot water. Another place in the bus terminal area is the *Alojamiento Lemoine* (☎ 34-6670), at Calle Lemoine 469. It's in the same class and price range as the Grigotá, and sometimes has hot water.

There are lots of similarly inexpensive residenciales, alojamientos and posadas near the bus terminal. Some are gloomy and grotty, so look at several rooms before deciding.

The current favourite travellers' hotel seems to be the *Residencial Bolívar* (☎ 34-2500), at Calle Sucre 131. It's a little bit overpriced for what you get, but it's clean, bright and offers good hot showers. Singles/doubles without bath cost US$6/7.

Alojamiento Santa Bárbara (☎ 32-1817), at Calle Santa Bárbara 151, is simple but clean. Rooms without bath cost US$4/5. The similarly priced *Alojamiento 24 de Septiembre* (☎ 32-1992), at Calle Santa Bárbara 79, is a bit dirty and not particularly friendly, but it seems popular with young Bolivians. *Alojamiento Oriente* (☎ 32-1976), at Calle Junín 364, is marginally clean, with rooms surrounding a green courtyard. Rooms without bath cost US$3 per person.

The *Hotel Copacabana* (☎ 32-1845), at Junín 217, is very good value. It's ultraclean and costs only US$9/13 with private bath, US$5/9 without.

A bit more up-market is *Hotel Italia* (☎ 32-3119), at Calle René Moreno 167. It is both clean and central, offering fans, private phones, air-conditioning and hot showers for US$13/20. The very centrally located *Hotel Bibosi* (☎ 34-8548, fax (591-3) 34-8887), at Calle Junín 218, is extremely friendly, with clean, spacious rooms and a great view from the roof. Rooms with fan, telephone and private bath cost US$10/15, including breakfast.

Places to Eat

For an inexpensive breakfast, go to the mercados La Ramada, Siete Calles or Los Pozos for jugo de papaya, guineo or naranja con leche – papaya, banana or orange juice with milk, whipped in a blender and served cold for US$0.50. The markets also serve meals during the day, but you may be put off by the heat. Mercado Los Pozos is good for a variety of unusual tropical fruits.

If you're interested in roast chicken, churrasco, chips and fried bananas, take a stroll down Pollo Alley (also called Avenida Cañoto), where there are dozens of nearly identical grill restaurants. *Restaurante 30 de Marzo* is recommended.

At Calle Junín 85 is *El Jacuú 85* (☎ 32-3512). It serves good lunches, and the staff

will prepare Mexican food for dinner if you ring in the afternoon and order it.

Vegetarian meals are available at *Su Salud*, Quijarro 375, near the market. It's open Sunday to Friday for breakfast, lunch and dinner. There's also a whole-food shop, *La Alternativa*, at Cuéllar 175.

Popular *El Gaucho* (also known as *La Pascana*), at 24 de Septiembre and Sucre, on the main plaza, serves huge four-course dinners (platos fuertes) for US$4. Try the refreshing lemonade. The equally popular *El Dorado*, at the opposite corner of the plaza, offers good lunch specials for only US$1.25. Yet another plaza lunch option is the quiet *Restaurante Plaza*, at Calle Libertad 116, which is especially good for soup and set lunches (US$1.50).

La Bella Napoli, in a rustic old barn at Calle Independencia 635, six blocks south of the main plaza, offers excellent pasta dishes served on chunky hardwood tables. Prices have risen, however (perhaps because meals are now accompanied by *Strangers in the Night* and *Moon River*), and it's a dark walk back to the centre at night. A great splurge choice is *Crêperie El Boliche*, at Calle Beni 222. You can choose from crêpe dishes, salads, ice-cream confections, cakes and cocktails for around US$11 per person.

The cosy Swiss/Bolivian-owned *Bar El Tapekua* (☎ 34-3390), at the corner of calles Ballivián and La Paz, serves pub meals. The musician owner appreciates good music, and on Thursday, Friday and Saturday nights, there are live performances for a US$1 cover charge. Phone in advance to find out what's on.

For ice cream and sundaes, locals recommend *Helados Casimba*, at the corner of Figueroa and Calle René Moreno, and *Kivon*, at Ayacucho 267.

Entertainment

There are quite a few discos in Santa Cruz which are popular with the more affluent younger folk. The best are outside the central area, so you're going to need a taxi to get there. Entry generally costs around US$2. If you want to conserve your funds after that, stay away from the bar. Beers are rarely less than US$1, and spirits cost much more. Discos usually open around 9 pm but don't start warming up until 11 pm, then continue until 3 am. Among the best known are the Champagne (on Avenida Ejército Nacional near de Garay), Swing (five km away on the highway to Cochabamba) and Fizz (near the zoo).

Getting There & Away

Air Viru Viru international airport (☎ 44411), about 15 km from the centre, is the most modern in the country. It handles all domestic and international flights (Miami, Buenos Aires, Asunción, São Paulo, Rio de Janeiro, Manaus). Minibus service between the airport and the bus terminal is frequent (US$0.75, half an hour).

LAB (on the corner of Warnes and Chuquisaca) has three daily flights to Cochabamba, La Paz and Sucre, and serves most other Bolivian cities, including Trinidad, Riberalta and Puerto Suárez, at least several times weekly. Flights to Puerto Suárez (US$77) are usually heavily booked in advance. TAM (at El Trompillo airport, near the centre) is cheaper but has fewer seats available. AeroSur is building new offices, at Irala and Colón.

Bus Most of the flotas represented in the long-distance bus terminal (☎ 38391), at the junction of avenidas Cañoto and Irala, use the new Chapare road to Cochabamba (US$9, 10 to 12 hours), from where they connect with La Paz, Oruro, Sucre, Potosí and Tarija services. Nearly all depart between 5 and 7 pm. A couple of flotas have now begun a morning service to Cochabamba – worthwhile for the scenery.

Flota Unificado offers direct service to Sucre (ie avoiding Cochabamba) at 5 pm on Monday, Wednesday and Saturday (US$15). From Sucre, the bus continues to Potosí. Flota Trans-Copacabana goes directly to Sucre on Wednesday, Friday and Saturday at 5 pm.

There are several evening departures to Trinidad, a journey of about 12 hours under optimum conditions. Although the road is theoretically open all year round, it can become problematic in the rainy season. Flota Trans-Copacabana departs at 6.30 pm.

For a camión to Cochabamba (US$4 to US$6, about 16 hours), go to Avenida Grigotá near the third *anillo* (ring road); most cargo traffic still uses the old road. Carry warm clothing!

Train The new train station (☎ 46-3388), on Avenida Brasil, is beyond easy walking distance from the centre, but bus No 12 takes only 10 minutes or so to get there. There are two rail lines: one to Quijarro (near Puerto Suárez, on the Brazilian border) and one to Yacuiba (on the Argentine border). The schedule is 'flexible' and getting tickets can be a nightmare.

During times of high demand, tickets probably aren't worth the hassle required to secure them. Carriages become so crowded with people and luggage that there's no room to sit, anyway. As an alternative, you may want to stake out a place in the bodegas (boxcars) and purchase a 2nd-class ticket from the acrobatic conductor (for 20% above the ticket window price) when he comes by.

There are plenty of plain-clothes police at the station, so keep your passport handy. For the Quijarro run, they sometimes employ the dirty tactic of checking your documents the moment before the train is set to leave. Hoping for a bribe, they'll prevent you from boarding if you don't have an exit stamp from the immigration office in town. This is not necessary; the stamp is picked up at Quijarro. React politely but firmly. If you're worried, get the stamp at immigration beforehand or perhaps explain to the officer that you're only visiting Quijarro and have no intention of crossing into Brazil.

To/From Argentina Tickets for the Yacuiba train are a bit easier to come by. From Santa Cruz, the bodegas are just about empty, but on the return journey they're brimming with Argentine contraband and are not as comfortable.

There's a ferrobus to Yacuiba at 8 am on

Tuesdays and Fridays, returning to Santa Cruz at 9 pm the same night (US$19/15 pullman/especial). The tren expreso leaves on Wednesday at 7 pm, the tren rápido at 5 pm on Monday, Thursday and Saturday, and the tren mixto at 9.30 am on Tuesday and Sunday.

The casas de cambio in Yacuiba change dollars, bolivianos and Argentine pesos, but none exchanges travellers' cheques. From Yacuiba, take a shared taxi to Pocitos, on the border (US$0.50 per person, five km) and then walk through Bolivian and Argentine immigration (thorough luggage and body searches). The bus terminal on the Argentine side is a two-minute walk from the immigration posts, with buses every two hours or so to nearby Tartagal and frequent departures to elsewhere in Argentina. Bus tickets may be reserved in Yacuiba at TVO Expreso Café; remember that Bolivian time is one hour behind Argentine time.

To/From Brazil The rail line between Santa Cruz and Quijarro passes through lush jungle, Chaco scrub and oddly shaped mountains to the steamy, sticky Pantanal area near the frontier. Be sure to have plenty of mosquito repellent on hand; there are often long and unexplained stops in low-lying, swampy areas. A particularly pleasant place to break the journey is San Jose de Chiquitos, a former Jesuit mission with a unique and beautiful church. *Hotel Raquelita* is recommended (US$5.50/7.50 single/double).

Four classes of service are available – bracha, pullman, first and second. Although the boxcars have their drawbacks, if you can't afford bracha or pullman, they're still more comfortable than the overcrowded 1st-class and 2nd-class coaches! If you do ride inside in any class, chain your luggage to the racks, especially at night.

Timetables are theoretical at best, more often than not pure fantasy and fabrication, so don't rely on the following descriptions for more than a rough idea.

On Wednesday and Sunday, the ferrobus leaves at 6 pm and arrives in Quijarro at 6 am the following day (US$21/16 pullman/especial). It returns to Santa Cruz from Quijarro at 9 am on Wednesday, Friday and Sunday.

On Monday and Friday at 2 pm eastbound, Tuesday and Saturday at 3.30 pm westbound, there's the optimistically named tren expreso (US$15 pullman). It also carries the bracha carriage, a locked, air-conditioned car with videos and marginal food service. The fare is US$36 and seats may be booked through Santa Cruz travel agencies. The tren rápido runs on Tuesday, Thursday and Saturday at 1.50 pm, and the tren mixto, which has no delusions about its velocity, departs at 9.10 am on Monday and Friday. It pulls only 2nd-class carriages.

When you arrive at Quijarro, take a taxi (they wait for arriving trains) to the border, two km from the station. The fare shouldn't be more than US$1.50 per person. Change bolivianos into cruzeiros on the Bolivian side or, better still, come to Quijarro with a minimum of Bolivian currency, as the rate is poor. Cash dollars can be easily exchanged for cruzeiros – ask travellers coming from Brazil for the latest rates (they change daily).

If you need a Brazilian visa, get it beforehand, as there is no Brazilian consulate in Quijarro. Yellow fever certificates are officially required to enter Brazil at Corumbá.

The South-West

Geographically, south-western Bolivia consists of the southern altiplano and Highlands, one of the most marvellous regions of the country. The southern altiplano is a harsh, sparsely populated wilderness of scrubby windswept basins, lonely volcanic peaks and glaring salt deserts – a land of lonely mirages and indeterminable distances. Further to the east, the altiplano drops into spectacular red rock country and then, lower still, into dry, eroded badlands, vineyards and orchards.

SALAR DE UYUNI & SALAR DE COIPASA

The Salar de Uyuni, an immense saltpan at an altitude of 3653 metres, stretches over an area of about 12,000 sq km. It was part of a

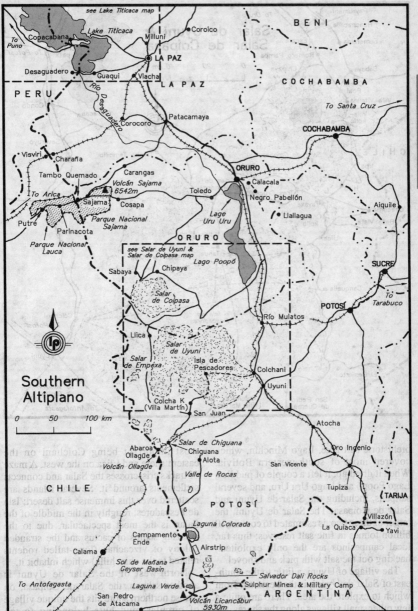

BOLIVIA

Southern
Altiplano

0   50   100 km

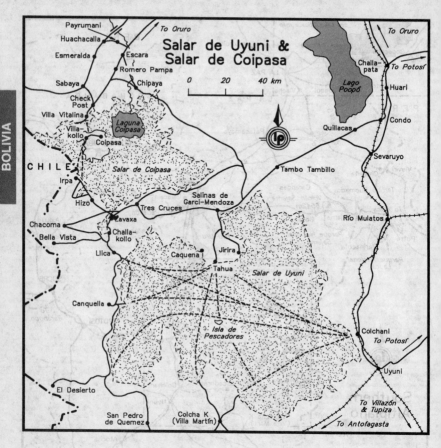

Salar de Uyuni & Salar de Coipasa

prehistoric salt lake, Lago Minchín, which covered most of south-western Bolivia. When it dried up, it left a couple of puddles, Lago Poopó and Lago Uru Uru, and several saltpans, including the Salar de Uyuni and Salar de Coipasa. The Salar de Uyuni, the larger of these two, is estimated to contain 10 billion tonnes in fine salt reserves; thus far, local campesinos are the only exploiters, hacking out the salt with pick and shovel.

The village of Uyuni, a little to the south-east of Salar de Uyuni, is the best base from which to explore the area. There are quite a few other small villages along the shores, the most important being Colchani on the eastern shore and Llica on the west. A maze of tracks crisscrosses the Salar and connects settlements around it. Several islands are scattered over this immense salt desert; Isla de Pescadores, roughly in the middle of the Salar, is the most spectacular, due to the amazing stands of cactus and the stranded colony of vizcachas (long-tailed rodents related to the chinchilla) which inhabit it.

North-west of the Salar de Uyuni is another saltpan, the Salar de Coipasa, on whose northern shore sits the unique village of circular mud huts belonging to the

Chipaya Indians, who may be descendants of the lost Tiahuanaco civilisation. If you do travel this far off the beaten path, please be sensitive to local culture; photography of people in this region is discouraged.

Tours

Three tour agencies in Uyuni arrange tours of the Salar de Uyuni (as well as Laguna Colorada, Sol de Mañana and Laguna Verde), but they're not low-budget options:

Tours Uyuni
  Hotel Avenida, Avenida Ferroviario. For a five-day tour to the Salar de Uyuni, Laguna Colorada and Laguna Verde, they charge US$450 for four people, excluding food and lodging.
Voyage Tours
  Calle Camacho, Ferroviario 2, Uyuni (☎ 838), attention Arlina Valdivia T). Tours to the Salar de Uyuni, Laguna Colorada, Laguna Verde and Sol de Mañana for up to six people cost US$400, excluding food and lodging.
Andes Tours
  Calle Camacho 92, Casilla 18, Uyuni (☎ 32-0901 La Paz, fax (591-2) 32-0901, attention Celina Ignacio). Andes Tours offers several different itineraries, including four or five-day trips from Uyuni. To the Salar de Uyuni and Laguna Colorada only, including food, they charge US$400 for up to six people; if you add Laguna Verde, the price goes up to US$500.

If you have plenty of time, you can try to see the Salar on your own – it's difficult but not impossible. There are infrequent unscheduled trucks which cross the Salar from Colchani to Llica. Expect to wait a couple of days before someone passes through to take you back to Uyuni. However, it's much more intriguing to head north, cross the Salar de Coipasa, visit the Chipaya Indians (if possible) and continue on to Oruro. Occasionally, private cars and motorbikes take this route, but come equipped for long, cold waits.

Uyuni

The largest and the most important village near the Salar is Uyuni, a cold, windy and unattractive desert community; bring your winter woollies, because there's no escaping the elements.

Places to Stay & Eat There are a couple of cheap hotels in Uyuni, but only the *Hotel Avenida*, opposite the railway station, is acceptable. Single/double rooms cost US$7/13 with bath, US$2.50/5 without.

Uyuni's favourite food haunt is *El Rosedal*, on the plaza; check out the unique kerosene drip heater in the middle of the room! Also on the plaza is the *Restaurante 16 de Julio*, with bland but warming high-carbohydrate fare. For a dose of charque kan (mashed hominy with strips of dried llama meat, an Uyuni speciality) or chicken and chips, try the *Snack Ducal*.

Getting There & Away The railway links Uyuni with Oruro (to the north) and Tupiza (to the south). See the respective sections for more details about trains. There are daily buses to Potosí at 12.30 pm with Transportes Quijarro (US$6, eight hours).

Llica

On the north-west shore of the Salar de Uyuni, at Llica, there's a basic alojamiento. Alternatively, you can stay at the *alcaldía* (town hall) for US$1. Basic food is available in the village.

LAGUNA COLORADA, SOL DE MAÑANA & LAGUNA VERDE

These spectacular attractions lie in the far south-west, the most remote highland area of Bolivia, in a surreal and nearly treeless landscape interrupted by gentle hills that resemble spilt chocolate sundaes and by high volcanos that rise abruptly near the Chilean border.

Laguna Colorada, a fiery red lake about 25 km from the Chilean border, is inhabited by rare James' flamingos. On its western shore is Campamento Ende, and beside it, there's a squalid meteorological station, where visitors without tents will find a place to crash. For a very marginal bed in a drafty, unheated room, they charge US$2 per person. If you're relegated to the adobe floor, you'll pay only US$1.

The clear air is bitterly cold, and at night the temperature drops below -20°C. The air is perfumed with the scent of the yareta – a dense-growing shrub which is almost as hard as rock and must be broken apart to be burned for fuel.

Most transport to and around Laguna Colorada will be supplying or servicing mining and military camps or the developing geothermal project 50 km south at Sol de Mañana. The real interest here is the 4800-metre high geyser basin, with its bubbling mud pots, hellish fumaroles and thick aroma of sulphur fumes. Be extremely careful when approaching the site; any damp or cracked earth is potentially dangerous, and cave-ins do occur, sometimes causing serious injury.

Laguna Verde, a stunning blue-green lake at 5000 metres, is tucked into the south-western corner of Bolivia, 92 km from Sol de Mañana. Behind the lake rises the cone of 5930-metre Volcán Licancábur, whose summit shelters an ancient Inca crypt.

Getting There & Around

The easiest but most expensive way to visit far south-western Bolivia is with an organised tour. See above, under Tours from Uyuni. It's also possible to arrange tours in La Paz and Potosí.

Alternatively, you can attempt a trip on your own, but this is not to be taken lightly. Transport is basically by cargo or fuel trucks that serve the mines; be prepared for lengthy waits, as days often pass without a sign of activity. The best time to explore the region is between April and September, when the days are cold but dry. During the rest of the year, the roads can turn into quagmires and transportation is scarce.

Sparsely populated, this region is even more remote than the salares. However, as a result of mining activity, there are several camps; locals, miners and military people will often provide a place to crash, but you must nevertheless be self-sufficient; bring camping gear, warm clothing, food, water, compass, maps and so on.

TUPIZA

Tupiza, a tranquil and friendly town with around 20,000 inhabitants, is set in the valley of the Rió Tupiza, surrounded by the rugged Cordillera de Chichas. There is nothing special or extraordinary here, apart from the fact that it is the smallest town on the continent to have traffic lights, though traffic is virtually nonexistent.

The charm of Tupiza lies in the surrounding countryside – an amazing land of rainbow-coloured rocks, hills and mountains. A reddish colour predominates, but brown, sepia, cream, green, blue, yellow and violet can all be found in the landscape. Hiking opportunities are numerous, and whichever route you take, you'll be amazed by a variety of strange rock formations, deep gorges and canyons, chasms of rugged spires and pinnacles, dry washes and cactus forests.

The region is easily accessible on foot, and this seems to be the best way to appreciate the countryside. There are several roads, so you can also hitch a ride in the fairly frequent trucks. Day trips from Tupiza are the most convenient way to explore; if you wish to do longer excursions, camping gear is necessary. Some recommended destinations include El Sillar (16 km each way), Quebrada Seca (five to 10 km each way) and Quebrada de Palala (five km each way). You'll find topographic maps of the area at the Instituto Geográfico Militar in La Paz.

Money

You'll see lots of 'Compro Dólares' signs around town. Try the Cooperativa El Chorolque, on Plaza Independencia, or the two hardware stores, Ferretería Cruz (on Avenida Santa Cruz) and Ferretería Marco Hermanos (on the corner of Avenida Santa Cruz and Florida). There's no place to change travellers' cheques, but in an emergency, ask around for Señor Umberto Bernal, who may be able to help out.

Places to Stay

The *Residencial Centro*, on Avenida Santa Cruz, costs US$3/5 for a single/double with private bath. Another popular option is the cosy-sounding *Residencial My Home*, at

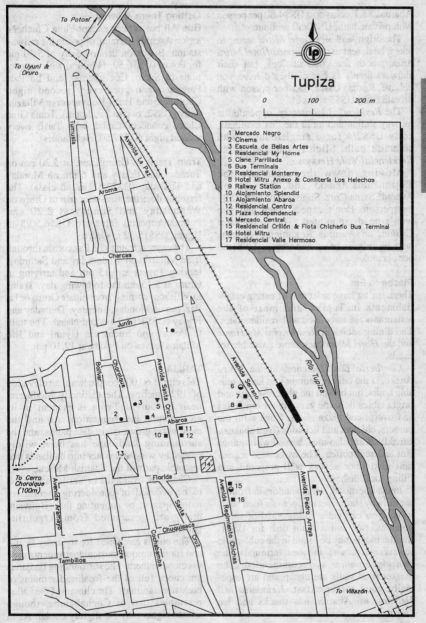

Abaroa 288. Rooms cost US$4.50 per person with private bath, US$2.50 without.

The bright and airy *Hotel Mitru* seems to take a back seat to the affiliated *Hotel Mitru Anexo*; both are good choices, but their showers aren't as hot as they'd have you believe. Rooms cost US$5 per person with private bath, US$3 without.

The *Residencial Monterrey*, opposite the railway station and amid the bus terminals, costs US$2/4 for a single/double with common bath. Slightly cheaper is the *Residencial Valle Hermoso*.

Moving down the scale are the alojamientos *Abaroa* and *Splendid*, on Avenida Santa Cruz. Simple beds cost US$1 per person. Don't expect much and you won't be disappointed. The *Residencial Crillón*, on Avenida Regimiento Chichas near Florida, is basic and cheap (US$1.50 per person).

Places to Eat

There isn't a large selection of eating establishments in Tupiza, and most of the restaurants are associated with residenciales. The dining rooms at *Residencial My Home* and the *Hotel Mitru* each serve palatable set meals.

Confitería Los Helechos, at the Mitru Anexo, is the only restaurant that keeps reliable hours, but behind the glittering sign and bright tables lie some very greasy omelettes and overpriced pizza slices. Stick with the burgers, chicken and licuados (fruit shakes). Breakfasts are also nice, served with quince jam and real coffee. The associated restaurant next door serves well-prepared and filling local dishes.

In the afternoon, street vendors in front of the railway station set up open-air food stalls where you can get a filling meal of salad, potatoes, rice and a main dish for US$1. Similar meals may be found in the cubbyhole restaurants around the bus terminals; the *Pensión Familiar* is recommended. The market food stalls are cheap and are especially good for breakfast. *Heladería Mil Delicias*, on Abaroa, has snacks and ice cream.

Getting There & Away

Bus All bus offices except Flota Chicheño are on Avenida Serrano, opposite the railway station. Boquerón departs daily at 5.30 pm for Potosí (US$6.50, 11 hours) with connections to Sucre, Cochabamba and La Paz; Panamericano goes every second night. Chorolque and Trans-Bolívar serve Villazón daily (US$2, two to 2½ hours). Trans Gran Chaco connects Tupiza with Tarija every second night (US$7.50, eight hours).

Train Trains to Oruro leave at 5.20 pm on Tuesday and Friday and 6 pm on Monday and Thursday (US$7/5 1st/2nd class). The ferrobus does the nine-hour trip to Oruro on Wednesday and Sunday at 8.20 am. Pullman/especial fares are US$6.50/5 to Uguni, US$15/12 to Oruro.

The express train to La Paz comes through from Villazón on Wednesday and Saturday, leaving Tupiza at 6.15 pm and arriving in Oruro at 5.15 am the following day. Trains to Villazón, coming from either Oruro or La Paz, run on Monday, Tuesday, Thursday and Friday (US$2/1.50 1st/2nd class). The train to Potosí and Sucre via Uyuni and Río Mulatos leaves on Friday at 12.10 pm.

TARIJA

This city of 60,000 people lies at an elevation of 1924 metres. The distinctly Mediterranean flavour of Tarija is evident in its architecture and vegetation. Around the main plaza grow stately date palms, and the surrounding landscape has been wildly eroded by wind and water into badlands that resemble parts of the Spanish Meseta.

Chapacos (residents of Tarija) are proud to be accused of considering themselves more Spanish or Argentine than Bolivian; many are descended from Argentine gauchos.

The city is renowned for its many fiestas and for the unique musical instruments used to celebrate them. The surrounding badlands are chock full of the fossilised remains of prehistoric animals. The climate of the valley resembles that of Cochabamba, though winter nights may be slightly cooler. As in

BOLIVIA

Tarija

0   100   200 m

To Potosí
& Villazón

To La Tablada
(4 km)

To Airport, Fossil
Area, Bermejo &
Yacuiba

41

Río Guadalquivir

Avenida de las Américas

PLACES TO STAY

4   Residencial Zeballos
8   Hostal Miraflores
10 Hotel América
12 Hotel Libertador
15 Alojamiento Ocho Hermanos
17 Residencial Bolívar
31 Hotel Prefectura
31 Hostal Cristal Gringo Limón
40 Alojamiento El Hogar &
    Restaurant El Piter

PLACES TO EAT

27 Restaurant Carenahí
28 Club Social Tarija
29 Heladería La Fontana
30 Churrasquería Don Rato
33 Snack Pío-Pío
36 Villingos
37 El Solar

OTHER

1   Municipal Park & Zoo
2   Mirador Loma de San Juan
3   Iglesia de San Roque
6   Ferretería El Lorito
8   Iglesia de San Juan
9   Market
9   Casas de Cambio
11 Argentine Consulate
13 Casa Dorada
14 International Tarija Travel Agency
16 LAB
18 Castillo de Moisés Navajas
20 Cathedral
21 TAM
22 Tourist Office
23 Disco Foto Rodríguez
24 Basílica San Francisco & Museum
25 Film Foto Muñoz
26 Plaza Luis de Fuentes y Vargas
32 Museo Universitario
35 Plaza Sucre
38 Post Office
39 ENTEL
41 Bus Terminal

most of Bolivia, the dry season lasts from April to November.

Information

Tourist Office The tourist office (☎ 25948), at Calle General Bernardo Trigo 883, between La Madrid and Calle Ingaví, is helpful with queries regarding sites both within the city and out of town. They no longer distribute maps, but do offer a tourist booklet containing a small map.

Money The several casas de cambio on Calle Bolívar between Calle Sucre and Daniel Campos take only US dollars and Argentine pesos for bolivianos. For travellers' cheques, go to the Banco del Perú, or the travel agencies International Tarija (at Calle Sucre N-721) or Pulido (at Calle Bolívar O-226). In a pinch, the hardware shop Ferretería El Lorito will change travellers' cheques, but for an extortionate commission of 5% to 10%!

Post & Telecommunications The new central post office is at the corner of Calle Sucre and Virginio Lema. ENTEL is at the corner of Virginio Lema and Daniel Campos. It's open Monday to Saturday from 8 am to midnight and on Sunday from 8 am to 9 pm. Tarija's public fax number is (066) 23402.

Things to See

Tarija retains some of its colonial atmosphere; it's worth spending some time strolling around the centre. The **Museo Universitario**, on the corner of General Trigo and Virginio Lema, one block from the main plaza, provides a convenient overview of the prehistoric creatures and the early peoples that once inhabited the Tarija area. Other sections focus on history and geology. The museum is open from 8.30 am to 12.30 pm and 2.30 to 6 pm. Admission is free.

Tarija was the home of the wealthy merchant Moisés Navajas, who left behind two curious buildings. One is the **Casa Dorada**, now the Casa de la Cultura, at the corner of Ingaví and General Trigo. It could be considered imposing, but is really nothing but a large façade sloppily splashed with gold and silver paint and topped with a row of liberating angels! The other, **Castillo de Moisés Navajas**, is an obtrusive home at Calle Bolívar E-644.

There is a zoo on the western outskirts of the town but it is small and run-down. Nearby, the **Mirador Loma de San Juan**, above the tree-covered slopes of Loma de San Juan, provides a lovely view over the city and is a favourite with students.

The Tarija region is known for its wines. To visit the wineries and cellars or sample the product, inquire at the offices of the largest companies; the managements are friendly and you may be able to get a lift with the staff. Companies include Kohlberg (Calle 15 de Abril O-275), Aranjuez (Calle 15 de Abril O-241), Casa Real (Calle 15 de Abril O-246) and Rujero (on the corner of La Madrid and Suipacha). Only the Aranjuez vineyard is close to town; Kohlberg and Casa Real are in Santana, 15 km from Tarija, and Rujero is near Concepción, 27 km from town.

Kohlberg, Aranjuez and Casa Real have small shops attached, where they sell their wines at factory prices. Rujero has separate shops, at Calle Ingaví E-311 and at O'Connor N-642. Besides the wine, they also produce singani, a spirit distilled from wine.

Festivals

Tarija's best known festival, the Fiesta de San Roque, honours the patron saint of the city. The celebration begins on the first Sunday of September and continues for eight days. The intial procession is the *chunchus*, a parade of costumed dancers, musical groups and festively dressed canines (San Roque is also the patron saint of dogs).

Places to Stay

For recommended budget accommodation, try *Alojamiento Ocho Hermanos* (☎ 22111), at Calle Sucre N-782. Tidy and pleasant rooms cost US$4 per person with shared bath. *Alojamiento El Hogar*, opposite the bus terminal, offers similar accommodation and prices but is a good walk from the centre. More central is the *Alojamiento Familiar* (☎ 22024), at Calle Sucre 626. Dank and musty double rooms cost US$9/6 with/without private bath.

The *Hostal Miraflores* charges US$5 for dormitory-style rooms without bath. Individual rooms cost US$7. The *Residencial Zeballos* (☎ 22068), at Calle Sucre N-966, has bright, comfortable rooms with bath and hot water for US$8/12.

In quiet Barrio El Molino is *Hostal Carmen* (☎ 23372), Calle Ingaví O-0784, which bills itself as 'su segundo hogar' (your second home). Prices have risen, so that doubles with private bath, hot water and TV now cost US$18. The *Residencial Bolívar* (☎ 22741), at Calle Bolívar 256, is friendly and tidy, with hot showers, a TV room and a pleasant, sunny courtyard. Prices are high – US$10/12 for singles/doubles with bath.

More expensive is the central *Hostal Cristal* (☎ 25534), at Calle 15 de Abril 363, on the Plaza Luis de Fuentes y Vargas. Singles/doubles cost US$16/22, including breakfast. All rooms have private bath.

Places to Eat

North-east of the market, at the corner of Calle Sucre and Domingo Paz, *street vendors* sell local pastries and snacks not available in other parts of Bolivia, including some delicious and very cheap crêpe-like concoctions known as panqueques.

For lunch, you'll enjoy *El Solar*, a vegetarian restaurant at the corner of Campero and Virginio Lema. The food is superb, but this now restaurant attracts Tarija's New Age fringe. It experiments with such nontraditional practices as serving the dessert before the meal; you'd think it was southern California! Lunch (US$1.50) is served from noon to 2 pm, but get there early to beat the herd.

For more conservative lunches, try the *Club Social Tarija*, at calles 15 de Abril and Sucre, on the corner of Plaza Luis de Fuentes y Vargas. *Snack Pio-Pio* and *Chingos*, near the corner of calles Sucre and 15 de Abril, are local youth hang-outs serving chicken

and chips. Beneath the Hostal Cristal, on the plaza, is *Gringo Limón*, an upbeat fast-food café. *Heladería La Fontana* is a good choice for ice-cream confections.

Cheap regional dishes are served at the *Villamontes*, at Belgrano E-1054, a rustic place popular with locals. For meat dishes, try *Churrasquería Don Ñato*, at Calle 15 de Abril 842; beware of grease in indigestible doses.

Much better is the friendly *Restaurant Carenahi*, on the plaza. There's no sign; it's beside the Club Social Tarija. Set lunches cost US$2, and they have an interesting menu that includes lots of pasta, fish, port and other nonstandard items. Meals include salads, and prices are reasonable. It's also a good place to sample local wines.

Getting There & Away

Air The Oriel Lea Plaza airport is three km east of town, past the bus terminal along Avenida de las Américas. LAB (Calle Ingaví O-236) flies to/from La Paz, Santa Cruz, Cochabamba, Yacuiba and Sucre. TAM (La Madrid O-472) flies to/from La Paz, Yacuiba, Santa Cruz and Villamontes.

Bus The bus terminal is at the east end of town, on Avenida de las Américas, a 20-minute walk from the city centre.

Buses to Potosí, with connections to Oruro, Cochabamba and Sucre, run daily at 4.30 pm (US$10, 12 hours). To Villazón, Expreso Yacuiba departs daily at 8 pm (US$6.50). For Tupiza, Trans Cristal leaves on Monday, Wednesday and Friday at 7.30 pm (US$7.50, eight hours) and Flota Trans Gran Chaco (US$6, seven hours) leaves at 7.30 am daily.

To Yacuiba, the Bolivian border town opposite Pocitos, Argentina, Trans Gran Chaco has a service leaving at 6 pm; Expreso Yacuiba departs at 7 pm (US$10, 12 hours). Unfortunately, this spectacular journey is done at night. To Villamontes, you'll have to hitch a ride in a petrol truck – wait at the *tranca* (police post) east of town. Or take the Yacuiba bus as far as Palos Blancos and wait

BOLIVIA

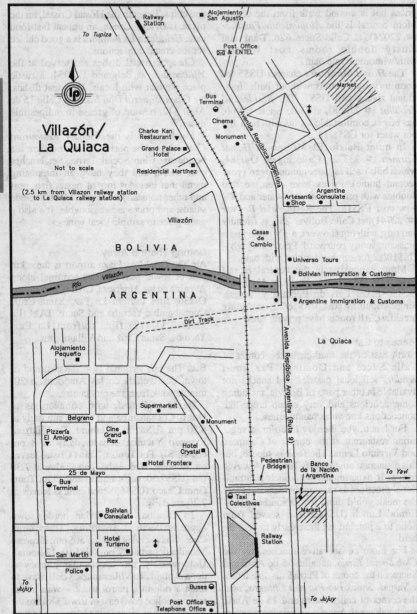

BOLIVIA

Villazón/ La Quiaca

Not to scale

(2.5 km from Villazon railway station to La Quiaca railway station)

Railway Station

To Tupiza

Alojamiento San Agustín

Post Office & ENTEL

Market

Bus Terminal

Cinema

Monument

Charke Kan Restaurant

Grand Palace Hotel

Residencial Martínez

Avenida República Argentina

Artesanía Shop

Argentine Consulate

Villazón

Casas de Cambio

B O L I V I A

Río Villazón

A R G E N T I N A

Universo Tours

Bolivian Immigration & Customs

Argentine Immigration & Customs

Dirt Track

La Quiaca

Alojamiento Pequeño

Avenida República Argentina (Ruta 9)

Supermarket

Belgrano

Pizzería El Amigo

Cine Grand Rex

Hotel Crystal

Hotel Frontera

Monument

25 de Mayo

Bus Terminal

Bolivian Consulate

Pedestrian Bridge

Banco de la Nación Argentina

To Yavi

Hotel de Turismo

San Martín

Police

To Jujuy

Taxi Colectivos

Railway Station

Market

Buses

Post Office Telephone Office

To Jujuy

To Yavi

there for a bus heading from Yacuiba to Villamontes.

VILLAZÓN

Villazón is the main border crossing between Bolivia and Argentina, just over the Río Villazón from La Quiaca, Argentina (see the Argentina chapter for details). Villazón is a dusty, haphazard settlement which contrasts sharply with tidy La Quiaca. In addition to being a point of entry, Villazón serves as a warehousing and marketing centre for contraband (food products, electronic goods and alcohol) which is smuggled into Bolivia via the *comercio de hormigas* (ant trade). Thousands of kg of goods are carried across the bridge daily on the backs of peasants, who form a continuous human cargo train across the frontier.

Information

Money If you're changing cash dollars or Argentine pesos into bolivianos, you can get reasonable rates at the numerous casas de cambio along Avenida República Argentina near the international bridge. Not all places offer the same rates, so shop around. Universo Tours, at República Argentina 387, beside the bridge, will change travellers' cheques if US dollars are currently in demand. Beware of counterfeit US dollar notes!

Time From October to April, there's a one-hour time difference between Bolivia and Argentina (noon in Villazón is 1 pm in La Quiaca). From May to September, the Argentine province of Jujuy, where La Quiaca is located, operates on Bolivian time (only a bit more efficiently).

Places to Stay & Eat

The nicest place to crash is the *Residencial Martínez* (☎ 562), near the bus terminal. Double rooms with/without bath cost US$10/6. The *Grand Palace Hotel* (☎ 333), also opposite the bus terminal, is fairly clean. Rooms cost US$5 per person with private bath, US$3 per person without. Near the railway station, at Antofagasta 860, is the marginal *Alojamiento San Agustín*, without private baths or hot water. It costs US$2 per person.

For meals, there isn't much choice. Try the *Charke Kan Restaurant*, opposite the bus terminal – good, but rather grimy. Alternatively, pop over to La Quiaca for an immense steak at the *Hotel de Turismo* or a pasta al pesto at the *Confitería La Frontera*.

Getting There & Away

Bus All northbound buses depart from the central terminal in Villazón. Several buses leave at 5 pm for Potosí via Tupiza (US$6, 13 hours). Several flotas leave for Tupiza, a beautiful trip, between 3 and 5 pm daily (US$2, 2½ hours). Buses to Tarija leave at 7 and 8 pm daily (US$6.50, seven hours).

Train Trains to Uyuni and Oruro depart on Wednesday and Saturday at 3.30 pm.

Crossing the Border Crossing the border should be no problem at all. Immigration offices and federal police are stationed on either side of the bridge, and immigration formalities are normally minimal and friendly, but prepare for thorough and exhaustive customs searches if you're entering Argentina. If you need an Argentine visa, pick it up at the consulate in Villazón or Tarija. Going in the other direction, there's a Bolivian consulate in La Quiaca.

The Amazon Basin

The Bolivian portion of the Amazon Basin, roughly half the country's total territory, is probably more interesting than the Amazon proper. While the accessible part of the Brazilian Amazon, along the large rivers, is eroded, heavily populated wasteland, the northern part of Bolivia remains little developed and has a much lower population density, so opportunities for viewing wildlife are much better. The rivers here are also narrower, so boats travel nearer the shore, allowing better observation.

BOLIVIA

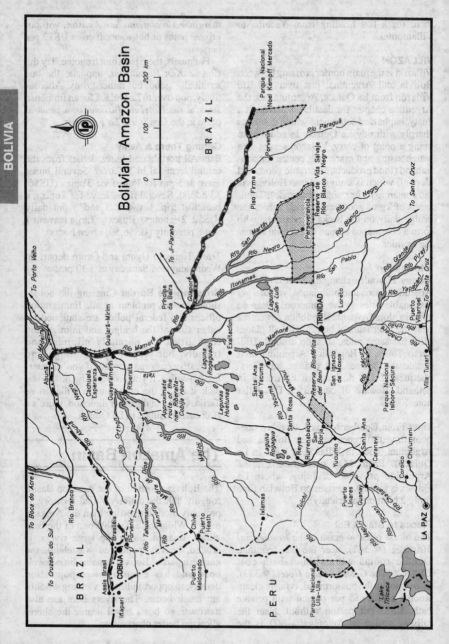

Bolivian Amazon Basin

There is no scheduled passenger service; boats that ply the northern rivers are primarily cargo vessels, and passenger comfort was the last thing the boat builders had in mind. Accommodation can be uncomfortable; cabins are reserved for the crew and rarely made available to passengers. Most passages include meals, but the food can become monotonous. Water comes directly from the river.

If you plan on doing a river trip, take along a hammock, a sleeping bag (nights can be surprisingly chilly, and you may have to crash out on deck), a water container and purifying tablets, antimalarials, mosquito protection and a supply of goodies to supplement your diet. Bring along enough cash dollars, or better still bolivianos, for the entire trip; travellers' cheques are difficult to change.

The most popular river routes in the Bolivian Amazon are Puerto Villarroel to Trinidad on the Río Ichilo, Trinidad to Guayaramerín on the Río Mamoré, and Rurrenabaque to Riberalta on the Río Beni.

Towns with air services include Cobija, Guayaramerín, Riberalta, Trinidad, Rurrenabaque, Reyes, San Borja, Santa Ana, San Joaquín and Magdalena. Remember that timetables are 'flexible': flights tend to be delayed, postponed or cancelled, especially during the rainy season.

PUERTO VILLARROEL

The river port of Puerto Villarroel lies at the southern edge of the Amazon Basin, northeast of Cochabamba. Perched on the banks of the Río Ichilo. it serves as a popular gateway to northern Bolivia.

Actually, Puerto Villarroel is a muddy jungle settlement with nothing of interest for the traveller, except its relatively busy port which serves as a departure point for Trinidad and points to the north. Puerto Villarroel is linked to Cochabamba by a 250-km road and lies only 18 km north of the new Cochabamba-Santa Cruz highway.

Places to Stay & Eat

There are only two places to stay. The *Hotel*
Hannover, near the port, is the better; it has a pleasant shady courtyard and costs US$2.50 per person. A loud disco enlivens the scene. Otherwise, there's the basic *Alojamiento Petrolero*, for US$2. Half a dozen shack restaurants along the main street offer sustenance, but little menu variety.

Getting There & Away

Bus Direct access is on the bus marked 'Chapare' which leaves from the corner of 9 de Abril and Oquendo in Cochabamba (US$3, five to six hours). The first bus departs around 6.30 am and returns to Cochabamba at 7 am daily. Subsequent buses leave when full. Cochabamba-Santa Cruz buses do not pass through Puerto Villarroel.

Boat Several kinds of boats run down the Río Ichilo. Small, family-run cargo boats normally travel only during the day and tie up for the night (a mosquito net is essential); they may take a week or more to reach Trinidad. Larger commercial craft travel through the night and arrive in about four days. The fare to Trinidad is roughly US$20 to US$30, including meals.

Ask for boats in the port area. Check also the port captain's office, which theoretically has departure information. If the river level is normal, you probably won't wait more than three days. During periods of low water, only small boats can get through.

The upper Ichilo doesn't pass through pristine rainforest; the countryside is partially cultivated, with banana plantations and cattle ranches. The wildlife is interesting but not as striking or abundant as it is further north.

RURRENABAQUE

Rurrenabaque, a bustling little frontier settlement on the Río Beni, is the loveliest village in the Bolivian lowlands. The original people of the area, the Tacana, were one of the few lowland tribes who resisted Christianity and Western-style civilisation. The main draw for tourists is the surrounding rainforest, which still supports Amazonian wildlife in relatively large numbers.

Most of Rurrenabaque's appeal is natural, and it's worth spending a day or two here. Beni's changing moods can be magical; the Amazonian sunsets are normally superb, and at night, a dense cloud of fog rolls down the river and creates a beautiful effect, especially at full moon.

Money

There's no bank in Rurrenabaque, but cash US dollars may be changed with Tico Tudela at Agencia Fluvial.

Jungle Trips

For those interested in the wilder side of Bolivia, jungle trips from Rurrenabaque could not be improved upon. They're tailored to travellers' interests, with no two trips alike. The guides, most of whom have been reared in the area, are knowledgeable about the fauna, flora and forest lore, including the forest's natural medicine cabinet.

A standard trip will include a motorised canoe trip, which begins by travelling up the Río Beni, winding through impressive hills. From there, you ascend the Río Tuichi, visiting various camps and taking shore walks along the way. For part of the return journey, you may ride a log raft. Groups that wish to do so can also visit a remote Chimane Indian village for the 'cultural enlightenment' of a game of football!

Arrangements can be made through the floating office of Agencia Fluvial, or through Eco-Tour, a company formed by local brothers Leo and Negro Janko, two of the friendliest and most knowledgeable guides in Bolivia. Normally, groups must form themselves, so if possible, organise four or five people before leaving La Paz or Coroico. For a four-day trip, you'll pay between US$80 and US$95 per person, including canoe transport, guides and food. Lots of good, strong mosquito repellent is essential. Accommodation is quite basic – you'll sleep on the river sand, beneath a tarpaulin tent surrounded by a mosquito net, at several of the 30-odd possible campsites along the Río Tuichi.

Places to Stay

The favourite travellers' haunt in Rurrenabaque is the *Hotel Santa Ana*. It has a nice courtyard with tables, for enjoying the sun whilst sipping a cup of Yungas coffee. Rooms with/without bath cost US$5/3 per person. *Hotel Berlin*, on the riverfront, offers reasonable but rather unkempt accommodation with private bath and cold showers for a negotiable US$5 per person.

Alojamiento Aurora, further from the river, doesn't offer the warmest reception around, but at US$2 per person, it's a cheap place to crash. *Hotel Porteño*, the standard accommodation for Bolivian travellers, costs US$5 per person without private bath.

Unbelievably, Rurrenabaque has a five-star option: the out-of-place *Hostal Taquara*, where relatively luxurious single/double rooms with carpet and private bath cost US$21/38.

Places to Eat

Everywhere in Rurrenabaque, you can get excellent freshly brewed Yungas coffee.

The nicest inexpensive food in town is found at Hotel Berlin's thatched restaurant, with great breakfasts, tropical specialties and Bolivian standards in a garden-like setting. The *Sede Social*, on the main street, serves drinks and set meals for US$1 per person. Another great place to eat is the unnamed, home-style *restaurant* in the post office building; vegetarian food is available on request.

On the river, the floating *Agencia Fluvial* offers fish and other dishes. Lunch is served daily, as are beer and refreshments. Dinner places must be reserved in the afternoon. Other fish restaurants occupy shelters along the riverfront. *La Chocita* and *La Playa* are sporadically good, depending on the prevailing temperament and the catch of the day. La Playa, however, is holding prisoner a very dejected spider monkey, the unfortunate victim of taunting; you may want to let them know what you think.

Getting There & Away
Air The flight to Rurrenabaque from La Paz is glorious on a clear day. LAB flies from La Paz at sunrise on Monday morning, and TAM has a flight on Thursday. For the return trip, LAB flies on Sunday and TAM on Thursday.

Bus When the roads are dry, Flota Yungueña runs Thursday and Saturday buses to Riberalta and Guayaramerín. Buses to La Paz depart on Monday, Wednesday, Thursday, Saturday and Sunday at 1 pm (US$13). The Wednesday and Sunday buses originate in Guayaramerín.

In theory, there's a daily Flota 16 de Noviembre bus to Yucumo, the turn-off for San Borja and Trinidad, at 12.30 pm (US$3, 2½ to three hours).

Boat Ferries between Rurrenabaque and San Buenaventura, on the opposite shore of the Río Beni, cost US$0.25.

Due to the opening of the Guayaramerín road, river-cargo transport down the Beni to Riberalta is limited, and there's no traffic at all during periods of low water. If you do find something, plan on five days at around US$7 per day for the 1000-km trip, including three meals daily. Make inquiries at the restaurant in the same building as the post office.

TRINIDAD
The city of La Santísima Trinidad (the Most Holy Trinity) was founded by Padre Cipriano Barace, on 13 June 1686, as the second Jesuit mission in the flatlands of the southern Beni. At an altitude of 237 metres, Trinidad is the capital of Beni Department and the nerve centre of the Bolivian Amazon. Trinidad looks like Santa Cruz did 20 years ago; the population has already passed 40,000 and is likely to continue increasing.

Information
Tourist Office Trinidad's tourist office is found on Calle José de Sucre, half a block from the main plaza. It's open Monday to Friday in the morning and afternoon, but don't expect miracles.

Money Street changers are found on Avenida 6 de Agosto between Calle Nicolás Suárez and Calle 18 de Noviembre, but they only deal in cash US dollars.

The only place that will even consider changing travellers' cheques is the Hotel Ganadero. It helps if you're staying there, of course, but if they're in need of foreign exchange, you may be able to persuade them with a hard-luck story.

Things to See
Trinidad's most interesting sights are outside town. In the **Llanos de Mojos**, well over 100 km of canals and causeways, and hundreds of *lomas* (artificial mounds), built to permit cultivation in a seasonally flooded area, are evidence of much larger aboriginal populations in pre-Columbian times. **Chuchini**, 17 km from Trinidad, is one of the few easily accessible sites. It has a small and interesting archaeological museum, a restaurant, a campground and some expensive bungalows (US$35 per person). To reach Chuchini, you might try hitching (best on Sunday), though you may have to walk the final five km from Loma Suárez. It's also a good motorbike destination; bikes can be rented on the plaza in Trinidad for around US$30 per 24-hour day.

Laguna Suárez (not to be confused with Loma Suárez) is a large, artificial lake five km from Trinidad. Probably constructed by the Paititis, it's a relaxing spot and, like Chuchini, is popular on Sundays, when local families turn out to picnic, drink in the bar and eat lunch at the lakeside Restaurante Tapacaré. There's no public transport, so you'll have to walk, take a taxi, hire a motorbike or hitch. Again, Sundays are best. Admission is US$0.30.

Even further afield is the lovely Ignaciano Indian village of **San Ignacio de Moxos**, 89 km west of Trinidad. The annual highlight is the huge Fiesta del Santo Patrono de Moxos, held on 31 July. There are frequent buses and camionetas (US$5, three hours, including Mamoré balsa crossing) to San Ignacio from the small terminals on Avenida Mariscal Santa Cruz.

BOLIVIA

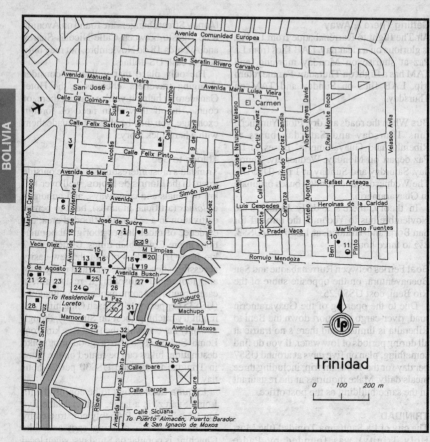

Trinidad

0   100   200 m

■ PLACES TO STAY	▼ PLACES TO EAT	9 Post Office
		10 Mercado Fátima
2 Hotel Bajío	3 El Pacumutu	11 Bus Terminal
4 Alojamiento Ortiz	5 El Moro	17 Motorbike Rentals
12 Hotel Monte Verde	15 Carlitos	21 Distrito Naval
13 Hotel Beni	18 La Casona	23 LAB
14 Residencial Brasilia &	19 Heladería Kivón	24 Bus to San Ignacio
Snack Brasilia	31 El Dragón Chino	26 Catedral
16 Residencial Paulista		27 Immigration
20 Mi Residencia	OTHER	29 Transportes Fluviales
22 Residencial Palermo		(River Transport
25 Hotel Ganadero	1 Airport	Office)
28 Hotel Yacuma	6 TAM	30 Mercado Central
	7 Tourist Office	32 Pompeya Bridge
	(Fegabeni)	33 Mercado Pompeya
	8 ENTEL	

Places to Stay

The best budget hotel is *Hotel Yacuma* (☎ 20690), at the corner of Calle La Paz and Avenida Santa Cruz. Singles/doubles without bath cost US$6 per person.

Trinidad also has a whole crop of medium to worse budget hotels strung mainly along Avenida 6 de Agosto. *Residencial Palermo* (☎ 20472), two blocks from the plaza, costs US$6 per person with bath. *Hotel Beni* (☎ 20522) charges US$8/12 for singles/doubles with private bath, US$5/8 without. The cheapest place in town is *Alojamiento Ortiz*, which charges US$3 per person. *Residencial Paulista* (☎ 20018) charges US$4 per person in singles or doubles.

A recommended mid-range hotel is *Hotel Monte Verde* (☎ 22750), at Avenida 6 de Agosto 76. With a bit of friendly bargaining, you can get singles/doubles with bath for US$12/16.

Places to Eat

Snacks, light meals and English breakfasts are served at the bright *Heladería Kivon*, on the plaza. Most importantly, it's open when everything else is closed, such as on Saturday afternoon. Another option for breakfast or snacks is the *Hotel Yacuma* patio.

Snack Brasilia, on Avenida 6 de Agosto, has a standard menu of good, inexpensive lunches. Also on the plaza are *La Casona* pizzeria and *Carlitos*, which specialises in parrillada.

Trinidad is cattle country, so beef is plentiful. Recommended for its food and atmosphere is the popular *El Pacumutu*. Pacumutus are chopped chunks of beef; get a *medio* (half) for two people. It'll still be too much, especially with all the trimmings.

For fish specialties, try *El Moro*, on the corner of avenidas Simón Bolívar and José Natusch Velasco. Also good is *El Dragón Chino*, on Calle Cipriano Barace opposite the Mercado Central.

If your budget is such that you're shocked by the prices at even the nondescript greasy spoon joints, there's always the *Mercado Municipal*. For a pittance, you can try the

local specialty: arroz con queso (rice with cheese), kebab, yuca, plantain and salad.

Getting There & Away

Air Both LAB and TAM operate flights to/from Trinidad. LAB flies three times weekly to La Paz, Cochabamba and Santa Cruz. TAM is cheaper but usually has only one flight a week. Both carriers also fly to Riberalta, Guayaramerín and Cobija.

The airport is on the outskirts of the town, a 15 to 20-minute walk from the centre. Don't take a taxi – the fare (US$10) is one of the biggest rip-offs in Bolivia!

Bus Numerous buses run nightly to Santa Cruz (US$15, 11 to 12 hours) from the central bus terminal, at the corner of Pinto and Romulo Mendoza. During the rainy season, the road can be impassable. Trans-Copacabana leaves for San Ignacio and San Borja daily at 9 am. Other transport west

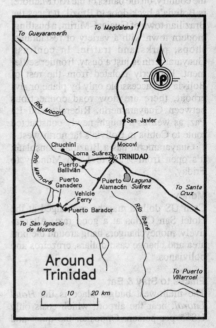

Around Trinidad

0   10   20 km

from Trinidad departs from the small terminals on Mariscal Santa Cruz.

Boat Trinidad isn't actually on the bank of a navigable river; Puerto Barador lies on the Río Mamoré, 13 km away, and Puerto Almacén is on the Ibaré, eight km from Trinidad. Trucks from town cost US$1 to Puerto Almacén, US$2 to Puerto Barador.

If you are looking for a boat north to Guayaramerín or south to Puerto Villarroel, inquire at the Transportes Fluviales office in Trinidad (on Calle Mamoré between Pedro de la Rocha and 18 de Noviembre) or check at the ports themselves. The trip to Guayaramerín won't take longer than a week (larger boats can do it in three days) and costs about US$40 to US$45, including food. To go to Puerto Villarroel, smaller boats may take up to 10 days.

GUAYARAMERÍN

Guayaramerín, in the northernmost corner of the country, on the banks of the Río Mamoré, is Bolivia's back door to Brazil. It faces the Brazilian town of Guajará-Mirim, a bustling, modern town with a variety of restaurants, shops, parks and traffic. In contrast, Guayaramerín is just a dusty, frontier settlement. Formerly isolated from the rest of Bolivia and accessible only by plane or riverboat, there are now road connections between Guayaramerín, Riberalta and La Paz, as well as a rough, newly constructed route to Cobija in Bolivia's far north-west.

Guayaramerín has a Brazilian consulate; it's open from 9 am to 1 pm Monday to Friday.

Money

Cash US dollars may be exchanged at the Hotel San Carlos at a good rate. Alternatively, moneychangers hang around the port area and change cash dollars, cruzeiros and bolivianos.

Places to Stay & Eat

The mellowest budget place is the *Hotel Litoral*, near the airport, which costs only US$5 per person. Opposite, the quiet and shady *Hotel Santa Ana* (☎ 2206), offers similar amenities for US$4 per person. The very basic *Hotel Central* (☎ 2042) costs US$3 per person. *Hotel Plaza* (☎ 2085) charges US$6.50/4.50 per person for rooms with/without private bath. Nicer is the *Hotel Plaza Anexo* (☎ 2086), with clean rooms, electric hot showers and a pleasant ambience, for US$6 per person.

Guayaramerín is fortunate enough to have the Beni's best restaurant, which is, in fact, called the *Only Restaurant* (☎ 2397)! With an extensive international menu and a pleasant outdoor garden, it's very popular. Out of town but also excellent is *Sujal*; motorbike taxis will get you there for US$0.30 each way.

On the corner of the plaza, *Pollo Pio Pio* isn't bad for cold drinks and snacks, but check your bill for spontaneous additions. *Los Bibosis*, also on the plaza, serves meals and snacks but is mostly a drinking joint.

Getting There & Away

Air LAB has flights from Trinidad daily, except Tuesday, from Cochabamba on Wednesday and Sunday, and from La Paz on Friday. TAM flies from La Paz on Monday and Wednesday and to La Paz on Tuesday and Thursday. You can fly to Cobija (US$50) with TAM on Tuesday and with LAB on Friday.

Bus Flota Yungueña has services to La Paz (via Rurrenabaque) only during the dry season, roughly May to October (US$45, 36 hours), on Tuesday and Sunday. The office is at the western end of town, beyond the market. To Riberalta, Flota Trans-Oriente departs at 8 am and 3 pm daily (US$3, three hours). There are also cars and camiones to Riberalta, leaving from near the Flota Yungueña terminal.

Boat Boats up the Río Mamoré to Trinidad leave almost daily (US$40 to US$45, including food, five to seven days). A notice board outside the port captain's office lists departures.

To Brazil There are no restrictions on the passage between Guayaramerín and Guajará Mirim, but if you go further into Brazil, or are entering Bolivia, you must pick up entry or exit stamps. The Bolivian immigration office is in the port area, beside the captain's office. On the Brazilian side, have your passport stamped at the Polícia Federal. A yellow fever vaccination certificate is technically required to enter Brazil.

Frequent ferries cross the river between the two ports (US$1 per person).

RIBERALTA
Located on the Río Beni in far northern Bolivia, Riberalta is the major town in the region. Originally, it was a thriving centre of rubber production, but when that industry declined due to international competition and the development of synthetics, the town resorted to its current mainstay industry: the growing, producing and exporting of oil from brazil nuts. Since the building of the road link with La Paz, Riberalta's importance as a river port has declined.

There isn't a lot to interest visitors, but this is one of the more pleasant towns of the Bolivian Amazon. Mostly, Riberalta is a place that invites you to sit back and relax. In the heat of the day, strenuous activity is suspended and the locals search out the nearest hammock; visitors would be advised to follow their example – the heat can be paralysing. On a clear night, however, the place comes to life with cruising motorbikes. Amid the buzz of activity, don't fail to notice the technicolour Amazonian sunsets; you can count on them for an impressive show.

Places to Stay & Eat
The nicest place is the spotless *Residencial Los Reyes* (☎ 615), near the airport. It costs US$6.50 per person for a room with fan and private bath. If the Los Reyes is full, you can stay at the *Hotel Noroeste* (☎ 597) which, for US$10 per person upstairs or US$7 downstairs, is nothing special. All rooms have baths.

A short motorbike taxi ride from the

centre, *Alojamiento Navarro* is a quiet, friendly, low-key place from where it is easy to catch lifts to Guayaramerín. Male or female dormitory accommodation, popular with itinerant workers, costs US$1.50 per person (don't leave your belongings in the rooms!). Double rooms are only US$3.

For meals, try the sandwich/snack shop *Cola*, on the main plaza. Also on the plaza is the *Club Social*, with inexpensive set lunches, superb filtered coffee, drinks and fine desserts. Determine prices in advance. The *Club Social Japonés*, near the market, is an option for Bolivian and Amazonian dishes.

At the *Heladería Eslaba*, you'll get good coffee, breakfast, ice cream, juices, milkshakes, flan and sandwiches, as well as Beni beef. What's more, the footpath seating provides a front-row seat for the nightly Kawasaki derby on the plaza. Two blocks away are rows of outdoor street restaurants (or rather, 'middle of the street' restaurants), which serve inexpensive dishes in a barbecue-style atmosphere.

Getting There & Away
Air Both LAB and TAM serve Riberalta, with several weekly flights to Trinidad, La Paz, Santa Cruz and Cobija. The airport is a 10-minute walk from the main plaza.

Bus Flota Trans-Oriente departs for Guayaramerín at noon and 6 pm daily (US$3.50, three hours). Alternatively, wait for a car or camión just out of town along the road to Guayaramerín.

Flota Yungueña leaves for Rurrenabaque (US$22, 15 hours) and La Paz (US$42, 33 hours) on Tuesday and Sunday at 6 pm.

Boat Boats up the Río Beni to Rurrenabaque are rare these days, thanks to the new road; those looking for river transport may have the most luck during the rainy season (October to May). If you find something, plan on spending US$40 to US$45 for the (at least) five-day trip. The port captain's office has a blackboard listing departure times.

Brazil

Facts about the Country

HISTORY
Pre-Columbian Times

The Brazilian Indians did not develop a bureaucratic, centralised civilisation like those of the Andes, and left little for archaeologists to discover, because the artefacts of their society were largely made of perishable materials. Some scholars believe that when the Portuguese arrived, at least seven million Indians were living in the territory that is now Brazil. Today, there are less than 200,000, most in the jungles of the interior.

Some Indians lived in small groups and were primarily hunter-gatherers, but most were shifting agriculturalists who lived in villages, some of which may have been as large as 5000 inhabitants. They lived in long communal huts, and music, dance and games played a very important role in their culture. Little surplus was produced and they had very few possessions. Every couple of years, the village would pack up and move on. This life was punctuated by frequent tribal warfare and ritual cannibalism.

The Colonial Period

In 1500, Pedro Cabral sailed from Lisbon down the coast of Africa, bound for India. Nobody knows quite why he wandered so far off course, but he veered west across the Atlantic and discovered Brazil, landing at present-day Porto Seguro. Cabral and his crew stayed only nine days in the land they dubbed Terra da Vera Cruz (Land of the True Cross), then sailed on.

Subsequent Portuguese expeditions were disappointed by what they found. The Indians' stone-age culture produced nothing for the European market, though a few Portuguese merchants sent ships to harvest the *pau do brasil* (brazil wood tree), which produced a red dye. Brazil wood remained the only exportable commodity for the first half of the 16th century – long enough for the colony to change its name from Terra de Vera Cruz to Brazil.

In 1531, King João III of Portugal sent the first settlers to Brazil, under the direction of Martin Afonso de Sousa. They founded São Vicente, near the modern-day port of Santos. In 1534, fearing the ambitions of other European countries, the king divided the coast into 12 hereditary captaincies, which were given to friends of the crown. Four captaincies were never settled and four were destroyed by Indians. Only Pernambuco and São Vicente were profitable. In 1549, the king sent Tomé de Sousa to be the first governor of Brazil, to centralise authority and to save the remaining captaincies. The new capital of Portuguese Brazil was established at Bahia.

The colonists soon discovered that the land and climate were ideal for growing sugar cane, but they needed labour, so they enslaved the Indians. The capture and sale of Indian slaves became Brazil's second commerce, dominated by the *bandeirantes*, men from São Paulo who were mostly sons of Portuguese fathers and Indian mothers. They hunted the Indians into the interior, and by the mid-1600s, they had reached the peaks of the Peruvian Andes. Their exploits, more than any treaty, secured the huge interior of South America for Portuguese Brazil.

The Jesuits, seeking to protect Indians fleeing from bandeirante attacks, built missions in the remote interior, near the present-day borders with Paraguay and Argentina. But these were not, as they had hoped, beyond the grasp of the bandeirantes. The Jesuits armed the Indians, and desperate battles took place. Eventually, with the collusion of the Portuguese and Spanish crowns, the missions fell, and the Jesuits were expelled from Brazil in 1759.

During the 17th century, African slaves largely replaced Indians on the plantations. They were better workers and less vulnerable to European diseases but they resisted slavery strongly. *Quilombos*, communities of runaway slaves, were common throughout the colonial period. They ranged from *mocambos*, small groups hidden in the forests, to the great republic of Palmares in northern Alagoas and southern Pernambuco states, which survived for much of the 17th century.

In the 1690s, gold was discovered in south-central Minas Gerais, and soon the rush was on. Brazilians and Portuguese immigrants flooded into this territory, and countless slaves were brought from Africa to dig and die in Minas. Wild boom towns arose in the mountain valleys: Sabara, Mariana, São João del Rei and the greatest, Vila Rica de Ouro Prêto (Rich Town of Black Gold). But the gold did little to develop Brazil's economy: most of the wealth went to Portuguese merchants and to the king.

By 1750, the mining regions were in decline and coastal Brazil was returning to prominence. Apart from some public works and many beautiful churches, the only important legacy of Brazil's gold rush was the shift in population from the north-east to the south-east regions.

Independence & the Brazilian Empire

In 1807, Napoleon's army marched on Lisbon. Two days before the invasion, the Portuguese Prince Regent (later known as Dom João VI) set sail for Brazil. When he arrived, he made Rio de Janeiro the capital of the United Kingdom of Portugal, Brazil and the Algarves. Brazil became the only New World colony to serve as the seat of a European monarch. In 1821, Dom João returned to Portugal, leaving his son Dom Pedro I in Brazil as regent.

In 1822, the Portuguese parliament attempted to return Brazil to colonial status. According to legend, Dom Pedro I responded by pulling out his sword and yelling 'Independência ou morte!' (independence or death). Portugal was too weak to fight its favourite son, so Brazil became an independent empire without spilling blood, and Dom Pedro I became its first emperor.

Dom Pedro I – from all accounts a bumbling incompetent – only ruled for nine years. He was forced to abdicate in favour of his five-year-old son. Until Dom Pedro II reached adolescence, Brazil went through a period of civil war under the rule of a weak triple regency. In 1840, the nation rallied round the emperor. During his 50-year reign, he nurtured an increasingly powerful parliamentary system, went to war with Paraguay, meddled in Argentine and Uruguayan affairs, encouraged mass immigration, abolished slavery and ultimately forged a state that would do away with the monarchy for ever.

During the 19th century, coffee replaced sugar as Brazil's major export, at one time supplying three-quarters of the world's demand. At first, production was labour-intensive and favoured large enterprises

BRAZIL

using slave labour. When slavery ended in 1888, the transition to a free labour force was made easier by the establishment of Brazil's first railroads and the introduction of machinery. Over the next decade, 800,000 European immigrants, mostly Italians, came to work on the coffee estates, called *fazendas*.

The Brazilian Republic & Military Rule

In 1889, a military coup, supported by the coffee aristocracy, toppled the Brazilian Empire. The emperor went into exile, and died a couple of years later. The new Brazilian republic adopted a constitution modelled on that of the USA, and for nearly 40 years, Brazil was governed by a series of military and civilian presidents supervised, in effect, by the armed forces.

The late 19th century was a period of messianic popular movements among Brazil's poor. During the 1880s, Antônio Conselheiro had wandered through the backlands of the north-east, prophesying the appearance of the Antichrist and the coming end of the world. He railed against the new republican government. Suspecting a plot to return Brazil to the Portuguese monarchy, the government set out to subdue the rebels who had gathered in the town of Canudos. Only on the fourth attempt were they successful, but in the end, the military killed every man, woman and child, and burned the town to the ground to erase it from the nation's memory. In spite of this, the struggle is remembered, even immortalised, in the masterpiece of Brazilian literature, *Os Sertões* (Rebellion in the Backlands), by Euclides de Cunha.

Coffee was king, until the market collapsed with the global economic crisis of 1929. This weakened the planters of São Paulo, who controlled the government, and an opposition Liberal Alliance was formed with the support of nationalist military officers. When their presidential candidate, Getúlio Vargas, lost the 1930 elections, the military seized power and installed him as provisional president.

Vargas proved to be a skilled strategist,

Brazil

0   250   500 km

BRAZIL

and was to dominate the political scene for the next 20 years. In 1937, on the eve of a new election, Vargas sent in the military to shut down Congress and took complete control of the country. His regime was inspired by Mussolini's and Salazar's fascist states, but during WW II, he sided with the Allies. At the end of the war, Vargas was forced by the military authorities to step down, but had another term as president, from 1951 to 1954, before finally being forced out of office.

Juscelino Kubitschek was elected president in 1956. The first of Brazil's big spenders, he built Brasília, the new capital, which was supposed to catalyse the development of the interior. By the early 1960s, the economy was battered by inflation, and fears of communism were fuelled by Castro's victory in Cuba. Again, Brazil's fragile democracy was crushed and the military overthrew the government.

Borrowing heavily from the international banks, the generals benefitted from the Brazilian 'economic miracle' of steady growth in the late 1960s and early 1970s. But in the 1980s, with the miracle petering out and popular opposition growing, the military announced the *abertura* (opening) and began a cautious return to civilian government. A presidential election was held in 1985, under an electoral college system designed to ensure the victory of the military's candidate. Surprisingly, the opposition candidate, Tancredo Neves, was elected, but he died before he could take office, and José Sarney, the vice president elect, took office as president.

In 1987, with Sarney at the helm, the politicians were working on a new constitution (Brazil has had several). The military remained powerfully in the background, and little had changed in the day-to-day lives of most Brazilians.

Modern Times

November 1989 saw the first presidential election by popular vote in nearly 30 years. Voters elected Fernando Collor de Mello over the socialist Luiz da Silva, by a narrow but secure majority.

Collor gained office promising to fight corruption and reduce inflation, but by the end of 1992, the man who once reminded George Bush of Indiana Jones had been removed from office and was being indicted by Federal Police on charges of corruption – accused of being the leader of a gang which used extortion and bribery to suck more than US$1 billion from the economy. Collor joined the long list (11 out of 24) of Brazilian presidents who have left office before the end of their mandate.

'Collorgate' had a positive side. It proved to the Brazilian people that the constitution of their fragile democracy is capable of removing a corrupt president from office without military interference.

Vice President Itamar Franco, a conservative (though less so than Collor de Mello) from Minas Gerais, became president in December 1992, on Collor's resignation.

As Brazil approaches the 21st century, it has many lingering problems – corruption, violence, urban overcrowding, lack of essential health and education facilities, environmental abuse and dramatic extremes of wealth and poverty. It has long been known as a land of the future, but the future never seems to arrive.

GEOGRAPHY

The world's fifth largest country, after Russia, Canada, China and the USA, Brazil borders every country in South America, except Chile and Ecuador. Its 8½ million sq km cover almost half the continent.

Geographic Regions

Brazil can be divided into several major geographic regions: the south-eastern coastal area of São Paulo and its hinterland; the Paraná Basin of the far south; the 'drought polygon' of the north-east; the central west of the Brazilian Shield; and the tropical north of the Amazon Basin and the southward-draining Guyana Shield.

The south-eastern coastal area is bordered

The States of Brazil

NUMBERED STATES
1 RIO GRANDE DO NORTE
2 PARAÍBA
3 PERNAMBUCO
4 ALAGOAS
5 SERGIPE

BRAZIL

by the mountain ranges that lie between it and the central plateau. From Rio Grande do Sul to Bahia, the mountains come right to the coast, but beyond Bahia, in the drought-prone north-east, the coastal lands are flatter.

South of the Amazon, the Brazilian Shield is an extensive area of weathered bedrock whose key feature is the Planalto, a plateau with an average elevation of only 500 metres. Several minor mountain ranges rise out of it, the highest of them in Minas Gerais. The western Planalto is a huge expanse of savanna grassland known as the Mato Grosso.

Many rivers drain into the Amazon Basin from the Brazilian Shield to the south, the Andes to the west and the Guyana Shield to the north. The 6275-km Rio Amazonas is the world's largest river, and with its tributaries carries about 20% of the world's fresh water. The basin contains some 30% of the world's remaining forest.

The Paraná Basin is characterised by open forest, low woods and scrub land. Its two principal rivers, the Paraná and the Paraguay, run south through Paraguay and Argentina. The swampy area of the basin, towards the Paraguayan border, is known as the Pantanal.

Administrative Regions

For political and administrative purposes, Brazil is generally divided into five regions: the South-East, the South, the Central West, the North-East and the North.

The South-east region (the Sudeste) is formed by the states of Rio de Janeiro, Espirito Santo, São Paulo and Minas Gerais.

The Southern region (Região Sul) includes the states of Paraná, Santa Catarina and Rio Grande do Sul.

The Central West (the Centro-Oeste) includes the states of Mato Grosso, Mato Grosso do Sul, Goiás and the Distrito Federal of Brasília.

The North-East region (the Nordeste) is divided into nine states: Bahia, Sergipe, Alagoas, Pernambuco, Paraíba, Rio Grande do Norte, Ceará, Piauí and Maranhão.

The North (Norde) is composed of seven states: Pará, Amapá, Tocantins, Amazonas, Roraima, Rondônia and Acre.

CLIMATE & WHEN TO GO

The Brazilian winter is from June to August, but it is cold only south of Rio de Janeiro, where the average temperature during the winter months is between 13°C and 18°C.

During summer (December to February), when many Brazilians are on vacation, travel is difficult and expensive. School holidays begin in mid-December and continue until Carnaval, which is usually in late February. The humidity south of Rio can be oppressive during this period.

In most of Brazil, short tropical rains are frequent all year round but rarely interfere with travel plans. The *sertão* (the dry interior of the North-east) is an exception – here, there are heavy rains for a few months of the year, and periodic droughts devastate the region.

The Amazon Basin receives the most rain in Brazil. It is not nearly as hot as most people presume – the average temperature is 27°C – but it *is* humid.

GOVERNMENT

Brazil slowly returned to democracy in the 1980s, with a new constitution in 1988. In 1989, Fernando Collor de Mello became the first president elected by popular vote in 28 years to take office. (Tancredo Neves was the first elected president, but he never took office.) The 1988 constitution allows the president to choose ministers of state, initiate pieces of legislation and maintain foreign relations, and gives the right of total veto. It also makes the president commander-in-chief of the armed forces.

These presidential powers are balanced by a bicameral legislature, which consists of a 72-seat Senate and a 487-seat Chamber of Deputies. Presidential elections are slated to be held every five years, with congressional elections every four years. State government elections are also held every four years, and municipal elections every three years.

Elections are colourful affairs, regarded by the democracy-starved Brazilians as yet another excuse for a party, but politics itself remains largely the preserve of the wealthy – cost forced several candidates to drop out of the 1990 elections.

In October 1993, a referendum will be held to decide the form of government – republic or constitutional monarchy (unlikely) and the system of government – a presidency or a parliamentary system. A parliamentary system, which divides the functions of chief of state and chief of government, would considerably reduce the power of the president.

ECONOMY

Boom and bust cycles have destabilised the Brazilian economy in recent years. Record-breaking industrial growth fuelled by foreign capital in the early 1970s was followed by recession and explosive inflation, about 1200% in 1992.

Brazil now has an estimated 64 million working people, one-third of them women; 17% work in agriculture and 12% work in industry. Most others are forced to sell their labour dirt cheap in jobs that are economically unproductive for society and a dead end for the individual.

The richest 10% of Brazilians control 54% of the nation's wealth; the poorest 10% have just 0.6% – and the gap is widening. Unemployment is rampant. In this developing country of 148 million people, 40 million people are malnourished, 25 million live in *favelas* (shantytowns), 12 million children are abandoned and more than seven million children between the ages of seven and 14 don't attend school. Sixty million people live in squalor, without proper sanitation, clean water or decent housing. Brazil, with its dreams of greatness, has misery that compares with the poorest countries in Africa and Asia.

Skyrocketing inflation and the world recession have battered the Brazilian economy in the last few years. When Collor took office, he pledged, amongst other things, to reduce inflation and cut back government spending, responsible for the majority of the country's US$118 billion foreign debt. At the end of 1992, Collor had been ousted from government and the annual inflation rate was almost 1200% – the highest in the world. The new president, Itamar Franco, has until December 1994 to try and perform the economic miracle the country needs, but the first few months of his presidency have not been encouraging.

POPULATION & PEOPLE

Brazil's population is around 148 million, making it the world's sixth most populous country. The population has doubled in the last 30 years. Still, Brazil is one of the least densely populated countries in the world, averaging only 15 people per sq km. The population is concentrated along the coastal strip and in the cities, where two out of every three Brazilians now live. Greater São Paulo has over 19 million residents, and greater Rio has over 10 million.

The Portuguese colonised Brazil largely through miscegenation with both the Indian population and with African slaves. The Blacks and the Indians also intermarried, and the three races became thoroughly mixed. This intermarriage continued, almost as a semiofficial colonial policy, for hundreds of years, and has led to a greater mixing of the races than in any other country on the continent. Most Brazilians have some combination of European, African, Amerindian, Asian and Middle Eastern ancestry.

FUNAI, the government Indian agency, has documented 174 different Indian languages and dialects in Brazil. Customs and belief systems vary equally widely. Growing international concern over the destruction of the Amazon rainforest has also highlighted the plight of Brazilian Indians, who are facing the loss of their lands and livelihood. At present, the number of Indians in Brazil is estimated at less than 200,000. Of the several hundred tribes already identified, most are concentrated in the Amazon region, and virtually all Brazilian Indians face a host of problems which threaten to destroy their environment and way of life.

ARTS & CULTURE

Brazilian culture has been shaped not only by the Portuguese, who gave the country its language and religion, but also by Amerindians, Black Africans and settlers from Europe, the Middle East and Asia.

Although often ignored, denigrated or feared by urban Brazilians, Indian culture has helped shape modern Brazil and its legends, dance and music. Many indigenous foods and beverages, such as tapioca, manioc, potatoes, *mate*, and *guaraná*, have become Brazilian staples. The Indians also gave the colonisers numerous objects and skills which are now in daily use in Brazil, such as hammocks, dugout canoes, thatched roofing, and weaving techniques.

The influence of African culture is also very powerful, especially in the North-east. The slaves imported by the Portuguese brought with them their religion, music and cuisine, all of which have profoundly influenced Brazilian identity. *Capoeira*, an African martial art developed by slaves to fight their oppressors, has become very popular in recent years, and throughout Brazil, you will see *rodas de capoeiras*, semicircles of spectator-musicians who sing the initial *chula* before the fight and provide the percussion during the fight.

RELIGION

It's usually said that Brazil is a Catholic country, and that it has the largest Catholic population of any country in the world. However, religion in Brazil is notable for its diversity and syncretism. There are dozens of sects and religions, though the differences are often ill-defined.

The religion of the African slaves was prohibited, for fear that it would serve to reinforce group identity. To avoid persecution, the slaves assimilated their African gods *(orixás)* with the Catholic saints, developing cults such as Macumba and Candomblé that also included aspects of Indian religions and European spiritualism. Today, these cults are thriving in Brazil, along with less orthodox ones, some involving animal sacrifice, black magic and hallucinogens. Much of Candomblé is still secret – it was prohibited in Bahia until 1970.

Candomblé is also a medium for cultivating African traditions (music, dance and language) into a system that aims to worship and enjoy life in peace and harmony.

In Candomblé, each person has a particular orixá to protect them and their spirit, and relies on Exú, a mediator between the material and spiritual worlds. To keep them strong, the orixás and Exú must be given food. Exú likes alcoholic drinks, cigarettes, cigars, strong perfumes and meats. The orixás, like the Greek gods, are often involved in struggles for power.

The Afro-Brazilian rituals are practised in a *casa de santo* or *terreiro*, directed by a *pai* or *mãe de santo* (literally father or mother of the saint – the Candomblé priest or priestess). In Bahia and Rio, millions of Brazilians go to the beach during the festivals at the year's end to pay homage to Iemanjá, the queen of the sea. Flowers, perfumes, fruits and even jewellery are tossed into the sea to please the mother of the waters and to gain her protection in the new year.

LANGUAGE

When they settled Brazil in the 16th century, the Portuguese encountered the diverse languages of the Indians. These, together with the various idioms and dialects spoken by the Africans brought in as slaves, extensively changed the Portuguese spoken by the early settlers. Along with Portuguese, Tupi-Guaraní, written down and simplified by the Jesuits, became a common language, understood by the majority of the population. It even became the main language spoken by the general public until the middle of the 18th century, but its usage diminished with the great number of Portuguese gold-rush immigrants and a royal proclamation in 1757 prohibiting its use. With the expulsion of the Jesuits in 1759, Portuguese was well and truly established as the national language.

Still, many words remain from the Indian and African languages. From Tupi-Guaraní come lots of place names (eg Guanabara, Carioca, Tijuca and Niterói), animal names (eg piranha, capivara and urubu) and plant names (eg mandioca, abacaxí, caju and jacarandá). Words from the African dialects, mainly those from Nigeria and Angola, are used in Afro-Brazilian religious ceremonies (eg Orixá, Exú and Iansã), cooking (eg vatapá, acarajé and abará) and general conversation (eg samba, moleque and moc-ambo).

Within Brazil, accents, dialects and slang *(gíria)* vary regionally. The Carioca inserts the 'sh' sound in place of 's'. The gaúcho speaks a Spanish-sounding Portuguese, the Baiano (from Bahia) speaks slowly and the accents of the Cearense are often incomprehensible to outsiders.

Portuguese is similar to Spanish on paper, but sounds completely different. You will do quite well if you speak Spanish in Brazil, although in general, Brazilians will understand you better than you understand them. Try to develop an ear for Portuguese – it's a beautiful-sounding language. Brazilians are easy to befriend, but the vast majority speak little or no English. This is changing, as practically all Brazilians in school are learning English.

Most phrasebooks are not very helpful; their vocabulary is often dated and contains the Portuguese spoken in Portugal, not Brazil. Notable exceptions are Lonely

Planet's *Brazilian Phrasebook*, and a Berlitz phrasebook for travel in Brazil. Make sure any English-Portuguese dictionary is a Brazilian Portuguese one. It's easy to arrange tutorial instruction through any of the Brazilian-American institutes where Brazilians go to learn English, or at the IBEU (Instituto Brazil Estados Unidos) in Rio.

Useful Words & Phrases

Yes.	*Sim.*
No.	*Não.*
Perhaps.	*Talvez.*
Please/Thank you.	*Por favor.*
Thank you.	*Obrigado.* (males)
	Obrigada. (females)
That's alright.	*Nada.*
Good morning.	*Bom dia.*
Good afternoon.	*Boa tarde.*
Good evening.	*Boa noite.*
Goodbye.	*Tchau.*
See you soon.	*Até logo.*
How are you?	*Como vai?* or
	Tudo bem?
good	*bom*
a pleasure	*muito prazer*
(meeting you)	
Speak more slowly.	*Fale mais devagar.*
I don't speak	*Não falo português.*
Portuguese.	
Do you speak	*Você fala inglês?*
English?	
Excuse me.	*Com licença.*
Pardon me.	*Desculpe.*
Sorry.	*Perdão.*
The bill please.	*A conta por favor*
How much?	*Quanto?*
How much time	*Quanto tempo*
does it take	*demora?*
where	*onde*
Where is...located?	*Onde fica...?*
left/right	*esquerda/direita*
when	*quando*
how	*como*
who	*quem*
what	*que*
why	*porque*
I want to buy...	*Eu quero comprar...*
expensive	*caro*

cheap	*barato*
more	*mais*
less	*menos*
yesterday	*ontem*
today	*hoje*
tomorrow	*amanhã*
morning	*(a) manhã*
afternoon	*(a) tarde*
night	*(a) noite*
What time is it?	*Que horas são?*

Numbers

0	*zero*
1	*um, uma*
2	*dois, duas*
3	*três*
4	*quatro*
5	*cinco*
6	*seis* (when quoting telephone or house numbers, Brazilians will often say *meia* instead of *seis*)
7	*sete*
8	*oito*
9	*nove*
10	*dez*
11	*onze*
12	*doze*
13	*treze*
14	*catorze*
15	*quinze*
16	*dezesseis*
17	*dezessete*
18	*dezoito*
19	*dezenove*
20	*vinte*
30	*trinta*
40	*quarenta*
50	*cinqüenta*
60	*sessenta*
70	*setenta*
80	*oitenta*
90	*noventa*
100	*cem*
first	*primeiro/a*
last	*último/a*

BRAZIL

Days of the Week

Sunday	*domingo*
Monday	*segunda-feira*
Tuesday	*terça-feira*
Wednesday	*quarta-feira*
Thursday	*quinta-feira*
Friday	*sexta-feira*
Saturday	*sábado*

Slang

Brazilians pepper their language with strange oaths and odd expressions (literal translation in parentheses):

curse word	*palavrão*
shooting the breeze	*batendo um papo*
Gosh!	*nossa!* (Our Lady!)
Great, cool, OK	*'ta lógico, 'ta ótimo, 'ta legal*
I'm mad at...	*Eu fiquei chatiado com...*
money	*grana*
Whoops!	*Opa!*
Wow!	*Oba!*
Hello.	*Oi.*
You said it!	*Falou!*
bum	*bum-bum/bunda*
bald	*careca*
a mess	*cambalacho*
the famous Brazilian bikini	*fio dental* (dental floss)
marijuana	*fumo* (smoke)
guy	*cara*
girl	*garota*
My god!	*¡Meu deus!*
It's crazy, You're crazy	*'ta louco*
Everything OK?	*Tudo bem?*
Everything's OK.	*Tudo bom.*
That's great, cool.	*Chocante.*
That's bad/Shit.	*Merda.*
a fix, a troublesome problem	*abacaxí*
Is there a way?	*Tem jeito?*
There's always a way	*Sempre tem jeito.*

Body Language

Brazilians accompany their oral communication with a rich body language, a sort of parallel dialogue. The thumbs up of *tudo bem* is used as a greeting, or to signify OK or thank you. The authoritative *não, não* finger-wagging is most intimidating when done right under a victim's nose, but it's not a threat. To indicate *rápido!* (speed and haste), thumb and middle finger touch loosely while rapidly shaking the wrist. If you don't want something (*não quero*), slap the back of your hands as if ridding yourself of the entire affair.

Facts for the Visitor

VISAS & EMBASSIES

At the time of writing, Brazilian visas are necessary for visitors who are citizens of countries which require visas for visitors from Brazil. American, Canadian, Australian and NZ citizens require visas, but UK citizens do not. Tourist visas are issued by Brazilian diplomatic offices. They are valid for arrival in Brazil within 90 days of issue and then for a 90-day stay in Brazil. Visas can be renewed in Brazil for an additional 90 days.

It should only take about three hours to issue a visa, though this can vary (we found it took 24 hours in San Francisco but was virtually on the spot in Posadas, Argentina); you will need a passport (valid for at least six months), a single passport photograph (either B&W or colour) and either a round-trip ticket or a statement from a travel agent, addressed to the Brazilian diplomatic office, stating that you have the required ticketing. If you only have a one-way ticket, they may accept a document from a bank or similar organisation proving that you have sufficient funds to stay and buy a return ticket.

Visitors under 18 years of age must submit a notarised letter of authorisation from their parents or legal guardian.

Tourist Card

When you enter Brazil, you will be asked to fill out a tourist card, which has two parts. Immigration officials will keep one part. The other part will be attached to your passport;

when you leave Brazil, this will be detached from your passport by immigration officials. Make sure you don't lose your part of the card whilst travelling around Brazil – otherwise, your departure could be delayed while officials check your story.

Visa Extensions

The Polícia Federal handles visa extensions, but you must go to them before your visa lapses, preferably 15 days in advance. They have offices in major cities. An extension costs about US$5, and in most cases, it is granted automatically. However, the police may require you to have a ticket out of the country and proof of sufficient funds. You are not obliged to extend your visa for the full 90 days, and you cannot re-enter Brazil until your current visa expires.

Brazilian Embassies & Consulates

Brazil has embassies and consulates in the neighbouring countries, and also in:

Australia
    19 Forster Crescent, Yarralumla, ACT 2600 (☎ (06) 273-2772)
Canada
    255 Albert St, Suite 900, Ottawa, Ontario K1P-6A9
France
    5 rue Am d'Estaing, Paris (☎ 47237266)
Germany
    Kurfürstendamm 11, 1 Stock, 1 Berlin 15 (☎ (30) 883-1208)
UK
    32 Green St, London W1Y 4AT (☎ (071) 499-0877)
USA
    3006 Massachusetts Ave, Washington DC (☎ 745-2700)

New Zealanders must apply to the Brazilian Embassy in Australia for their visas; this can be done easily through a travel agent.

For addresses of foreign representatives in Brazil, see under individual cities. Embassies are in Brasília, the national capital, but there are consulates many other cities, which are more convenient for most travellers.

MONEY

US cash dollars are easier to trade and are worth a bit more on the parallel market than travellers' cheques. Travellers' cheques, however, can be replaced if lost, and can be exchanged at the turismo rate, so it makes sense to use them. American Express is the most recognised brand, but Thomas Cook, Barclays and First National City Bank are also good. Get travellers' cheques in US dollars and carry some small denominations for convenience. Have some emergency US cash to use when the banks are closed.

Currency

Because of the high rate of inflation in Brazil, all prices in this chapter are quoted in US dollars. From early 1992 the Brazilian currency was in free fall. A new currency unit, the *cruzeiro real* (Crz$), equal to 1000 of the old cruzeiros, was introduced in August 1993.

Exchange Rates

There are currently three types of exchange rate in Brazil: official (also known as *comercial* or *câmbio livre*), *turismo* and *paralelo*. Exchange rates are written up every day on the top right-hand corner of the front page of *O Globo*, and in the 'Dinheiro' section of the *Folha de São Paulo*. They are also announced on the evening TV news.

Approximate official exchange rates in August 1993 were as follows:

A$1 = Crz$53.09
DM1 = Crz$45.77
FF1 = Crz$12.97
UK£1 = Crz$116.38
US$1 = Crz$79.82

Turismo and paralelo rates were approximately 10% higher than these figures.

Changing Money

Changing money in Brazil is easy in the large cities. Almost anyone can direct you to a *casa de câmbio* (money exchange house). Most large banks now have a foreign section where you can change money at the slightly lower turismo rate, but sometimes this may involve a bit of time-wasting bureaucracy. You can also exchange travellers' cheques at most casas de câmbio. Make sure you ask them before you sign the cheque.

Change, variously referred to as *troco* or *miúdo*, is often unobtainable. When you change money, ask for lots of small bills and take very few notes in denominations larger than the equivalent of US$10.

Credit Cards
International credit cards such as Visa and American Express are accepted by the more expensive hotels, restaurants and shops. At present, you get billed at the turismo rate in cruzeiros, and by the time the transaction is posted to your overseas account, you may actually pay less in dollar terms than you had figured. Bear in mind that hotels will be very reluctant to give you a room discount if you pay with a credit card.

Costs
Because of wild fluctuations in the economy, it's difficult to make solid predictions about costs. If you're travelling on buses every couple of days, staying in hotels for US$10 a night and eating in restaurants and/or drinking in bars, US$30 a day would be a rough estimate, perhaps a bit less if you travel with a partner. Two people can travel cheaper than one in Brazil – double rooms cost only a bit more than singles and meals are large enough to split. It's possible to spend even less, of course. If you plan to lie on a beach for a month, eating rice, beans and fish, US$10 to US$15 a day would be enough.

Bargaining
Bargaining for hotel rooms should become second nature. Before you agree to take a room, ask for a better price. 'Tem desconto?' (Is there a discount?) and 'Pode fazer um melhor preço?' (Can you make a better price?) are phrases to use. There's often a discount for paying 'á vista' (in cash), or for staying during the *época baixa* (low season), when hotels need guests to cover running

costs. It's also possible to reduce the price if you state that you don't want a TV, private bath or air-con. If you're staying longer than a couple of days, ask for a discount. When a discount is quoted, make sure it is noted on your bill at the time – this avoids 'misunderstandings' at a later date. Bargain also in markets and unmetered taxis.

TOURIST OFFICES
The headquarters of Embratur, the Brazilian Tourist Board (☎ 224-2872), is at Setor Comercial Norte, Quadra 2, Bloco G, Brasília, DF, CEP 70710. There is also an Embratur office in Rio de Janeiro, at Rua Mariz e Barros 13, 14th floor.

Tourist offices elsewhere in Brazil are generally sponsored by individual states and municipalities. In many places, these offices rely on shoestring budgets, which are chopped or maintained according to the whims (or feuds) of regional and local politicians. Keep your sense of humour, prepare for pot luck and don't expect too much!

USEFUL ORGANISATIONS
The Brazilian American Cultural Center (☎ (212) 730-1010, or toll-free (1-800) 222-2746), at 16 West 46th St, New York, NY 10036, is a tourism organisation which offers its members discounted flights and tours. Members can send money to South America using BACC's remittance service. The organisation can also secure tourist visas for members, through the Brazilian Consulate in New York.

For information about the network of Brazilian youth hostels, contact the Federação Brasileira dos Albergues de Juventude (telefax (021) 221-8753), Rua da Assembléia 10, sala 1211, Centro, Rio de Janeiro, CEP 20011, RJ. Include an envelope and postage.

BUSINESS HOURS
Most shops and government services are open Monday to Friday from 9 am to 6 pm, and on Saturday from 9 am to 1 pm. Some shops stay open later than 6 pm in the cities, and the huge shopping malls often stay open

until 10 pm. Banks, always in their own little world, are generally open from 10 am to 4.30 pm. Business hours vary by region, and are taken less seriously in remote locations.

HOLIDAYS

National holidays fall on the following dates:

1 January
New Year's Day
6 January
Epiphany
February or March (four days before Ash Wednesday)
Carnaval
March or April
Easter
21 April
Tiradentes Day
1 May
May Day
June
Corpus Christi
7 September
Independence Day
12 October
Our Lady of Aparecida Day
2 November
All Souls' Day
15 November
Proclamation Day
25 December
Christmas Day

FESTIVALS

Major festivals include:

1 January
New Year & *Festa de Iemanjá* (Rio de Janeiro)
Procissão do Senhor Bom Jesus dos Navegantes (Salvador, Bahia)
1 -20 January
Folia de Reis (Parati, Rio de Janeiro)
2nd Sunday in January
Bom Jesus dos Navegantes (Penedo, Alagoas)
2nd Thursday in January
Lavagem do Bonfim (Salvador, Bahia)
24 January to 2 February
NS de Nazaré (Nazaré, Bahia)
February
Grande Vaquejada do Nordeste (Natal, Rio Grande do Norte)
2 February
Festa de Iemanjá (Salvador, Bahia)
February or March
Lavagem da Igreja de Itapoã (Itapoã, Bahia)
Shrove Tuesday (and the preceding three days to two weeks, depending on the place)

Mid-April
Drama da Paixão de Cristo (Brejo da Madre de Deus, Pernambuco)
April or May (15 days after Easter)
Cavalhadas (Pirenópolis, Goiás)
Late May or early June
Festa do Divino Espírito Santo (Parati, Rio de Janeiro)
June
Festas Juninas & Bumba meu boi (celebrated throughout June in much of the country, particularly São Luis, Belém and throughout Pernambuco and Rio states)
Festival Folclórico do Amazonas (Manaus, Amazonas)
22 -24 June
São João (Cachoeira, Bahia & Campina Grande, Paraíba)
July
Festa do Divino (Diamantina, Minas Gerais)
Regata de Jangadas Dragão do Mar (Fortaleza, Ceará)
15 August
Festa de Iemanjá (Fortaleza, Ceará)
Mid-August
Festa da NS de Boa Morte (Cachoeira, Bahia)
September
Festival de Cirandas (Itamaracá, Pernambuco)
Cavalhada (Caeté, Minas Gerais)
12 October
Festa de Nossa Senhora Aparecida (Aparecida, São Paulo)
Starting 2nd Sunday in October
Círio de Nazaré (Belém, Pará)
October (2nd half)
NS do Rosário (Cachoeira, Bahia)
November
NS da Ajuda (Cachoeira, Bahia)
1-2 November
Festa do Padre Cícero (Juazeiro do Norte, Ceará)
8 December
Festa de Nossa Senhora da Conceição (Salvador, Bahia)
Festa de Iemanjá (Belém, Pará & João Pessoa, Paraíba)
31 December
Celebração de Fim de Ano & Festa do Iemanjá (Rio de Janeiro)

POST & TELECOMMUNICATIONS

Post

Postal services are pretty good in Brazil. Most mail seems to get through, and airmail letters to the USA and Europe usually arrive in a week or so. For Australia, allow two weeks. Rates for mail leaving Brazil are amongst the highest in the world – almost

US$1 for an international letter or postcard! Most *correios* (post offices) are open from 9 am to 6 pm Monday to Friday, and on Saturday morning.

The *posta restante* system seems to function reasonably well; they will hold mail for 30 days. A reliable alternative for American Express customers is to have mail sent to an American Express office.

Telephone

International Calls Phoning abroad from Brazil is very expensive. To the USA and Canada, figure approximately US$3 a minute. To the UK, the charge is US$3.50 a minute. Prices are 25% lower from 8 pm to 6 am daily and all day Sundays. To Australia and New Zealand, calls cost US$5 a minute (there are no cheaper times to these two countries).

Every town has a *posto telefônico* (phone company office) for long-distance calls, which require a large deposit. If you're calling direct from a private phone, dial 00, then the country code number, then the area code, then the phone number. For information on international calls, dial 00-0333.

International collect calls *(a cobrar)* can be made from any phone. To get the international operator, dial 00-0111 or 107 and ask for the *telefônista internacional*. Embratel, the Empresa do Sistema Telebrás, now offers Home Country Direct Services for Canada (☎ 000-8014), France (☎ 000-8033), Italy (☎ 000-8039), Japan (☎ 000-8081), the Netherlands (☎ 000-8031), the UK (☎ 000-8044) and the USA (☎ 000-8010 for AT&T, 000-8012 for MCI, 000-8016 for Sprint).

National Calls National long-distance calls can also be made at the local phone company office, unless you're calling collect. For calling collect within Brazil, dial 107.

Local Calls Brazilian public phones are nicknamed *orelhões* (big ears). They use *fichas*, coin-like tokens, which can be bought at many newsstands, pharmacies, etc for less than US$0.05. When your time is up, you will be disconnected without warning. To call the operator, dial 100; for information, call 102.

Fax, Telex & Telegraph

Post offices send and receive telegrams, and the larger branches also have fax services. Fax costs US$13 per page to the USA and Canada, US$23 to Australia and New Zealand, and US$15 to the UK.

TIME

Brazil has four official time zones, generally depicted on maps as a neat series of lines. The standard time zone for Brazil covers the eastern, north-eastern, southern, and south-eastern parts of Brazil, including Brasília, Amapá, Goiás, Tocantins and a portion of Pará. This zone is three hours behind GMT. So, when it is noon in Brazil it is 3 pm in London, 10 am in New York, 7 am in San Francisco, 1 am the next day in Sydney or Melbourne, and 3 am in New Zealand.

Moving westwards, the next time zone covers part of Pará, as well as Roraima, Rondônia, Mato Grosso, Mato Grosso do Sul and all but the far western fringe of Amazonas. This zone is one hour behind Brazilian standard time and four hours behind GMT.

The time zone for the far west covers Acre and the western fringe of Amazonas. This zone is two hours behind Brazilian standard time and five hours behind GMT.

The island of Fernando de Noronha, far to the east of the Brazilian mainland, has its own time zone, one hour ahead of Brazilian standard time and two hours behind GMT.

Finally, you'll surely be thrilled to know that these time zones may vary if Brazil continues to adopt daylight savings time, which requires clocks to be set one hour ahead in October and go back one hour in March or April.

BOOKS
History
John Hemming's *Red Gold: The Conquest of the Brazilian Indians* (Harvard University

Press, 1978) follows the colonists and Indians from 1500 to 1760, when the great majority of Indians were effectively either eliminated or pacified. Hemming, a founder of Survival International and an eloquent campaigner for Indian rights, has extended his analysis of Indian history in *Amazon Frontier: The Defeat of the Brazilian Indians* (Harvard, 1987).

Caio Prado Junior, Brazil's leading economic historian, presents probably the single best interpretation of the colonial period (in English) in *The Colonial Background of Modern Brazil*.

Charles R Boxer's *Golden Age of Brazil, 1695-1750* (University of California Press, 1962) has an excellent introductory chapter summarising life in 17th-century Brazil, and then focuses on the gold rush in Minas Gerais and its consequences in the rest of the colony.

The most famous book on Brazil's colonial period is Gilberto Freyre's *The Masters & the Slaves: A Study in the Development of Brazilian Civilization* (University of California Press, 1986).

Finally, the not-to-be-believed rebellion in Canudos by the followers of the mystic Antônio Conselheiro has been immortalised in *Rebellion in the Backlands* (University of Chicago Press, 1985), by Euclides da Cunha. Mixing history, geography and philosophy, *Os Sertões* (in Portuguese) is considered the masterpiece of Brazilian literature. An eloquent and engrossing fictionalised account of Canudos is given by Mario Vargas Llosa in his novel *The War of the End of the World* (Avon Bard, 1985) – entertaining reading for the traveller.

For readers who like their history with a dose of fiction, *Brazil* by Errol Lincoln Uys (Simon & Schuster, 1986) is an interesting novel that traces the history of two Brazilian families.

Travel

Highly recommended for its style and humour, Peter Fleming's *Brazilian Adventure* (Penguin, 1978) is about the young journalist's expedition into Mato Grosso in search of the missing Colonel Fawcett.

Moritz Thomsen's *The Saddest Pleasure: A Journey on Two Rivers* (Graywolf Press, 1990) is a highly recommended book (skip the sickly introduction) about the author's experiences in South America, including journeys through Brazil and along the Amazon.

The Amazon & Indians

Both of John Hemming's works, described in the Books section, detail the history of the Portuguese colonisation, subjugation and enslavement of the Indian.

Other interesting titles are *The Last Indians: South America's Cultural Heritage*, by Fritz Tupp, and *Aborigines of the Amazon Rain Forest: The Yanomami* by Robin Hanbury-Tenison (Time Life Books, 1982). *Amazonia* by Loren McIntyre (1991), the renowned explorer and photographer, records in magnificent photographs the gradual demise of the region and its original inhabitants. The Brazilian satirist, Márcio Souza, describes life in the Amazon in books such as *Mad Maria* and *Emperor of the Amazon*.

Alex Shoumatoff has written three excellent Amazon books, all of them entertaining combinations of history, myth and travelogue. His latest work, *The World is Burning* (Little Brown, 1990), recounts the Chico Mendes story.

The Fate of the Forest: Developers, Destroyers, and Defenders of the Amazon by Susanna Hecht & Alexander Cockburn (Verso, 1989) is one of the best analyses of the complex web of destruction, and provides ideas on ways to mend the damage.

Travel Guides

A Brazilian travel guide is published annually by Quatro Rodas. Called *Quatro Rodas: Guia Brasil*, it's readily available at most newsagents and contains a wealth of information (in Portuguese) about accommodation, restaurants, transport, sights, etc. If you buy it in Brazil, it also comes with an excellent fold-out map of the country. Unfortunately, it doesn't cover the real budget accomodation options.

MAPS

Within Brazil, the mapping used by most Brazilian and foreign travellers is produced by Quatro Rodas, which also publishes the *Quatro Rodas: Guia Brasil*. This guide is complemented by *Guia Rodoviário*, a compact book of maps in a handy plastic case, which covers individual states. The city maps provided in *Quatro Rodas: Guia Brasil* help with orientation.

MEDIA
Newspapers & Magazines
English By far the best newspaper in English is the Latin American edition of the *Miami Herald*, which costs about US$3. The *Brazil Post* is published Tuesday to Saturday in Brazil. It has advertisements for both São Paulo and Rio, including apartment rentals, and general news. *Time* and *Newsweek* are available throughout Brazil. In the big cities, you can find all sorts of imported newspapers and magazines at some newsstands, but they are very expensive.

Portuguese The *Folha de São Paulo* is Brazil's finest newspaper. It has excellent coverage of national and international events and is a good source for entertainment in São Paulo. The *Jornal do Brasil* and *O Globo* are Rio's main daily papers. Among weekly magazines, *Veja*, the Brazilian *Time* clone, is the country's best selling magazine.

The latest environmental and ecological issues (both national and international) are covered in the monthly magazine *Ecología e Desenvolvimento*, published by Editora Terceiro Mundo (☎ 252-7440) in Rio de Janeiro.

TV
English Cable TV is a recent addition to the media, with ESPN (the sports network), CNN (Cable News Network), RAI (Radio Televisione Italia) and, of course, MTV (music television) available to those few who can afford them.

Portuguese Many of the worst American movies and TV shows are dubbed into Por-

tuguese and shown on Brazilian TV. The most popular programmes on Brazilian TV are the *novelas* (soap operas), which go on the air at various times from 7 to 9 pm. The news is on several times a night, but broadcast times vary from place to place.

CINEMA
Foreigners planning a trip to Brazil can learn a great deal about the country through viewing some of the outstanding Brazilian films of the past several decades, many of which are available on video. One of the best known is *Black Orpheus*, an adaptation of the classical myth, set in Rio during Carnaval. More recent successes include *Dona Flor and Her Two Husbands* (an adaptation of Jorge Amado's novel starring Sonia Braga), *Pixote*, a naturalistic tale of street children in southern Brazil, made more disturbing by the fact that its 'star' died several years later in a robbery, and *Bye Bye Brasil*, an entertaining but poignant road movie showing recent changes in Brazilian society (including the development of the Amazon) through the eyes of a travelling circus.

FILM & PHOTOGRAPHY
Kodak and Fuji print film are sold and processed almost everywhere, but you can only get slide film developed (expensively) in the big cities. If you're shooting slides, it's best to bring film with you and have it processed back home.

If you must get your film processed in Brazil, have it done either at a large lab in São Paulo, or in Rio at Kronokroma Foto (☎ 285-1993), Rua Russel 344, Loja E, near Praia do Flamengo's Hotel Glória.

It's foolish to bring a camera to a beach unless it will be closely guarded. Some Candomblé temples do not permit photography. Respect the wishes of the locals and ask permission before taking a photo of them.

HEALTH
Your chances of contracting a serious illness in Brazil are slight. You will be exposed to environmental factors, foods and sanitation standards that are probably quite different

from what you're used to, but if you take the recommended jabs, faithfully pop your anti-malarials and use common sense, there shouldn't be any problems.

While there's no worry of any strange tropical diseases in Rio and points further south, remember that Amazonas, Pará, Mato Grosso, Amapá, Rondônia, Goiás, Espírito Santo and the North-east have some combination of the following: malaria, yellow fever, dengue fever, leprosy and leishmaniasis. Health officials periodically announce high rates of tuberculosis, polio, sexually transmitted diseases, hepatitis and other endemic diseases.

Bichos de pé are small parasites that live on Bahian beaches and in sandy soil. They burrow into the thick skin of the heel, toes and under toenails, appearing as dark boils. Bichos de pé must be incised and removed completely – if you do it yourself, use a sterilised needle and blade. Better still, avoid them by wearing footwear on beaches and dirt trails.

For more information on Health, see the Facts for the Visitor chapter at the beginning of the book.

WOMEN TRAVELLERS

In São Paulo, where there are many people of European ancestry, White women without travelling companions will scarcely be given a sideways glance, but in the more traditional rural areas of the North-east, where a large percentage of the population is of mixed European, African and Indian origin, blonde-haired and light-skinned women – especially those without male escorts – may arouse curiosity. It's best to dress conservatively. What works in Rio will not necessarily be appropriate in a North-eastern city or a Piauí backwater.

Flirtation (often exaggerated) is a prominent element in Brazilian male/female relations. It goes both ways, and is nearly always regarded as amusingly innocent banter. If unwelcome attention is forthcoming, you should be able to stop it by merely expressing distaste or displeasure.

It's a good idea to keep a low profile in the cities at night, and avoid going alone to bars and nightclubs if you'd rather not chance being misconstrued. Similarly, women should not hitch, either alone or in groups, and even men or couples should exercise discretion when hitching. Most importantly, the remote rough-and-ready areas of the north and west, where there are lots of men but few local women, should be considered off limits to lone female travellers.

DANGERS & ANNOYANCES

Robberies on buses, on city beaches and in heavily touristed areas are extremely common. Thieves tend to work in gangs, are armed with knives and guns, and are capable of killing those who resist them. Much of the petty street crime in Rio, São Paulo, Salvador and Manaus is directed against tourists – Rio's thieves refer to them as *filet mignon*. Be especially careful on the city beaches; take enough money for lunch and drinks, and nothing else. Don't hang out on the beaches at night. When reporting a theft, be wary of the police. They have been known to plant drugs and to sting gringos for bribes. For advice on security precautions, see the Dangers & Annoyances section in the Facts for the Visitor chapter.

WORK

Travellers on tourist visas aren't supposed to work in Brazil. The only viable paid work is teaching English in one of the big cities, but you need to speak a bit of Portuguese. Earnings range between US$5 and US$10 per hour. To find work, look in the classifieds under 'Professor de Ingles', or ask around at the English schools. Volunteer work with welfare organisations is quite easy to find if you're prepared to do some door-knocking.

ACCOMMODATION

Camping is becoming increasingly popular in Brazil, and is a viable alternative for travellers on limited budgets or those who want to explore some of the country's national or state parks. For detailed information on camping grounds, buy the *Guia Quatro Rodas Camping Guide* from any newsstand.

BRAZIL

You may also want to contact the Camping Club of Brazil, Rua Senador Dantas 75, 25th floor, Rio de Janeiro. The club has 52 sites in 14 states.

There are now more than 120 *albergues de juventude* (youth hostels) in Brazil, and more are planned. Most state capitals and popular tourist areas have at least one. A night in a hostel will cost around US$5 per person, if you're a member. It's not always necessary to be a member to stay in one, but it'll cost you more if you're not. International Youth Hostel cards are accepted, but if you arrive in Brazil without one, you can buy guest membership cards. For the address of the Brasilian Youth Hostel Federation, see the Useful Organisations section in this chapter.

The cheapest places to stay are *dormitórios*. These have dormitory-style sleeping, with several beds to a room, and may cost as little as US$2 to US$3 per night. Most budget travellers stay at a cheaper *pensão* (small hotel) or *hotel*, where a *quarto* (room without a bathroom) costs as little as US$4 to US$5. Rooms with a private bathroom are called *apartamentos*.

Most hotels in Brazil are regulated by Embratur, the Brazilian tourism authority, which rates the quality of hotels from one to five stars. Regulated hotels must have a price list with an Embratur label, a copy of which is usually posted on the wall in each room. Even so, it still pays to bargain.

If you're travelling where there are no hotels – the Amazon or the North-east – a hammock and a mosquito net are essential. With these basics, and help from friendly locals, you can get a good night's rest anywhere. Most fishing villages along the coast have seen an outsider or two and will put you up for the night. If they've seen a few more outsiders, they'll probably charge you a couple of dollars.

FOOD

The staples of the Brazilian diet are *arroz* (white rice), *feijão* (black beans) and *farofel* (manioc flour), also called *farinha*. These are usually combined with *carne* (steak), *galinha* (chicken) or *peixe* (fish) to make up the *prato feito* (set meal) or *prato do dia* (plate of the day). These set meals are typically enormous and cheap, but after a while, they can become monotonous. Lunch is the big meal of the day, and *lanchonetes* (snack bars) throughout the country will have a prato do dia on offer. In the cities, there is more variety.

Rodízios provide all the meat you can eat, and a variety of other goodies, for a fixed price (around US$5 in Rio). A *churrascaria* is a restaurant serving barbecued meat. Rodízios have a meat smorgasbord, and are especially good in the south.

Some Brazilian Dishes

Acarajé – this is what the Baianas, Bahian women in flowing white dresses, traditionally sell on street corners throughout Bahia. Acarajé is made from peeled brown beans, mashed in salt and onions and then fried in dendê oil. Inside these delicious fried balls is *vatapá* (see this list), dried shrimp, pepper and tomato sauce. Dendê oil is strong stuff. Many stomachs can't handle it.

Carne de sol – this tasty salted meat is grilled, then served with beans, rice and vegetables.

Caruru – one of the most popular Brazilian dishes brought from Africa, this is made with okra or other vegetables cooked in water. The water is then drained, and onions, salt, shrimps and malagueta peppers are added, mixed and grated together with the okra paste and dendê oil. Traditionally, a sea fish such as garoupa is then added.

Cozido – the term refers to any kind of stew, usually with more vegetables than other stew-like Brazilian dishes (eg potatoes, sweet potatoes, carrots and manioc).

Feijoada – the national dish of Brazil, feijoada is a meat stew served with rice and a bowl of beans. It's served throughout the country, and there are many variations, depending on what animal happens to be walking through the kitchen while the chefs are at work.

Moqueca – this is both a kind of sauce or stew and a style of cooking from Bahia. There are many kinds of moqueca: fish, shrimp, oyster, crab or a combination. The moqueca sauce is defined by its heavy use of dendê oil and coconut milk, often with peppers and onions. A moqueca must be cooked in a covered clay pot.

Pato no tucupi – roast duck, flavoured with garlic and cooked in the *tucupi* sauce made from the juice of the manioc plant and *jambu*, a local vegetable, is a very popular dish in Pará.

Peixe a delícia – this dish of broiled or grilled fish is usually made with bananas and coconut milk. It's delicious in Fortaleza.

Pirarucu ao forno – pirarucu is the most famous fish from the rivers of Amazônia. It's oven-cooked with lemon and other seasonings.

Tutu á mineira – this bean paste with toasted bacon and manioc flour, often served with cooked cabbage, is typical of Minas Gerais.

Vatapá – a seafood dish with a thick sauce made from manioc paste, coconut and dendê oil, vatapá is perhaps the most famous Brazilian dish of African origin.

Fruit

From the savoury nirvana of *graviola* to the confusingly clinical taste of *cupuaçú*, fruits and juices are a major Brazilian highlight. Many of the fruits of the North-East and Amazon have no English equivalent, so there's no sense in attempting to translate their names: you'll just have to try their exotic tastes.

DRINKS

Fruit juices, called *sucos*, are divine in Brazil. If you don't want sugar and ice, ask for them *sem açúcar e gelo* or *natural*. To avoid getting water mixed with them, ask for a *suco com leite*, also called a *vitamina*. Orange juice is rarely diluted. The Brazilian soft drink guaraná is made from the berry of an Amazonian plant, and has a delicious, distinctive taste.

A *cerveja* is a 600-ml bottled beer. Brazil-ians gesture for a tall one by horizontally making the Boy Scout sign (three fingers together) a foot above their drinking tables. A *cervejinha* is 300 ml of bottled or canned beer. *Chopp* (pronounced 'shoppee') is a pale blond Pilsner draft, lighter and far superior to canned or bottled beer.

Cachaça, *pinga* or *aguardente* is a high-proof, dirt-cheap, sugar-cane alcohol, produced and drunk throughout the country. Cachaça literally means booze. Pinga (which literally means drop) is considered more polite, but by any name, it's cheap and toxic. A cheap cachaça can cut a hole in the strongest stomach lining. Velho Barreiro, Ypioca, Pitú, Carangueijo and São Francisco are some of the better labels.

Caipirinha is the Brazilian national drink. The ingredients are simple (cachaça, lime, sugar and crushed ice), but a well-made caipirinha is a work of art. *Caipirosca* is a caipirinha made with vodka instead of cachaça. *Caipirissima* is still another variation, using Bacardi rum instead of cachaça. *Batidas* are wonderful mixes of cachaça, sugar and fruit juice.

SPORTS
Football

Soccer was introduced to Brazil after a young student from São Paulo, Charles Miller, returned from England and organised the first league. It quickly became the national passion, and the creative and artistic wizardry of Brazilian footballers has since won three World Cups. Matches (played on Sundays and Wednesdays) are intense and colourful events – well worth a visit.

Volleyball

This is a very popular sport in Brazil. The national team won the gold medal at the Barcelona Olympics. *Futvolei*, played using only the head and feet, is a spectacular variation seen on the beaches of Rio.

Motor Racing

Brazilians love speed. Taxi drivers may give you a hint of it, and since the early 1970s, Brazilians have won more Formula One

Grand Prix world championships than any other nationality. The Brazilian Grand Prix, held in Rio, traditionally kicks off the Formula One season, around March each year.

Getting There & Away

For information on getting to South America from the rest of the world, see the introductory Getting There & Away chapter at the start of this book.

AIR

To/From Argentina
There are several flights every day between Buenos Aires and Rio de Janeiro, and good air connections to other main Brazilian cities.

To/From Bolivia
There are five Varig flights per week between La Paz and Rio, all of which stop over at São Paulo.

To/From Colombia
Varig has two flights a week between Bogotá and Rio.

To/From French Guiana & Suriname
Cruzeiro and Suriname Airways (SLM) fly once or twice weekly between Belém (Brazil), Cayenne (French Guiana) and Paramaribo (Suriname).

To/From Guyana
Taba Airlines flies twice weekly between Manaus (Brazil) and Georgetown (Guyana), via Boa Vista.

To/From Paraguay
Varig has daily flights from Asunción to Rio, and other airlines also cover the route.

To/From Peru
AeroPerú and Varig fly between Lima (Peru) and Rio several times a week. Cruzeiro do

Sul flies twice a week from Iquitos (Peru) to Manaus (Brazil).

To/From Uruguay
There are flights every day between Montevideo and Rio.

To/From Venezuela
Varig has two flights per week between Caracas and Rio.

LAND

To/From Argentina
Coming from or going to Argentina, most travellers pass through Foz do Iguaçu (see the Foz do Iguaçu entry in the Paraná section for more information).

To/From Bolivia
Corumbá Corumbá, opposite the Bolivian border town of Quijarro, is the busiest port of entry along the Bolivia/Brazil border. It has both rail and bus connections from São Paulo, Rio de Janeiro, Cuiabá and southern Brazil. Between Quijarro and Santa Cruz, there's a daily train during the dry season, but during the wet, there may be waits of several days. For further information, see Corumbá in the Central West section.

Cáceres From Cáceres, west of Cuiabá, you can cross to San Matías in Bolivia. Daily buses do the 4½-hour trip for US$10. Bolivia's Transportes Aereos Militares (TAM) operates flights each way between San Matías and Santa Cruz, Bolivia (via Roboré) on Saturdays. During the dry season, there's also a daily bus between the border town of San Matías and San Ignacio de Velasco (in Bolivia's Jesuit Missions), where you'll find flights and bus connections to Santa Cruz.

Coming from Bolivia, there are daily *micros* (again, only during the dry season) from San Ignacio de Velasco to the border at San Matías, from where you'll find onward transport to Cáceres and Cuiabá.

Guajará-Mirim Another popular crossing is between Guajará-Mirim in Brazil and

Guayaramerín, Bolivia, via motorboat ferry across the Rio Mamoré. Guayaramerín is connected with Riberalta by a road, which should be extended to Cobija/Brasiléia in the near future – and another route runs south to Rurrenabaque and La Paz, with a spur to Trinidad. For further information see Guajará-Mirim and Guayaramerín in the Rondônia & Acre section.

Brasiléia In Acre state, there's a border crossing between Brasiléia and Cobija, Bolivia. For more details, see Brasiléia in the Acre section.

To/From Colombia
The Colombian border crossing is at Leticia/Tabatinga. For further information on the Triple Frontier region, refer to Benjamin Constant and Tabatinga in the Amazonas section.

To/From French Guiana (Guyane)
Travellers of all nationalities may now enter and leave French Guiana at Oiapoque by motorised dugout from St Georges (the French Guianese town opposite Oiapoque). Those who require a French visa should pick it up in Belém. For further information, see Macapá in the Amapá section.

To/From Guyana
The border crossing is at Bonfim, in Roraima state, and is reached via Boa Vista. You may want to save yourself the trouble of a difficult overland passage by flying directly to Georgetown. See Boa Vista in the Roraima section for more details.

To/From Paraguay
Foz do Iguaçu/Ciudad del Este and Ponta Porã/Pedro Juan Caballero are the two major border crossings. See Foz do Iguaçu in the Paraná section and Ponta Porã in the Mato Grosso section for details.

To/From Peru
There is a border crossing to Iñapari (Peru) at Assis Brasil. For more details, see Brasiléia and Assis Brasil in the Acre section.

To/From Uruguay
Coming from Uruguay, travellers usually pass through the border towns of Chuy/Chuí (Chuy, Uruguay and Chuí, Brazil); the international border is the main street. There are four other border crossings: at Aceguá; from Rivera to Santana do Livramento; from Artigas to Quaraí; and at Barra do Quaraí, near the border with Argentina.

If you're driving from Brazil, you'll need to stop at the Brazilian checkpoint to get an exit stamp, and at the Uruguayan checkpoint for the Uruguayans to check that you have a Brazilian exit stamp and a Uruguayan visa (if you need one). Buses will stop at the checkpoints.

To/From Venezuela
From Boa Vista (Roraima state), you can cross into Venezuela via the border town of Santa Elena. Further information is included under Boa Vista in the Roraima section.

RIVER
To/From Paraguay
There are boats sailing along the Río Paraguay between Asunción and Corumbá (Mato Grosso do Sul). For further information, see Getting There & Away for Corumbá.

To/From Peru
The main route between Brazil and Peru is along the Amazon between Iquitos and Islandia (the Peruvian port village on an island at the junction of the Rio Yauari and the Amazon, opposite Benjamin Constant). Some boats leave from Ramón Castilla, a few km further upstream in Peru. For further information on the Triple Frontier region, refer to Benjamin Constant and Tabatinga in the Amazonas section.

LEAVING BRAZIL
The airport tax for international flights, around US$17, is usually added to the price of your ticket.

BRAZIL

Getting Around

AIR

Flying in Brazil is not cheap, but as distances are enormous, the occasional flight may be worth it. Brazil has three major national carriers and several smaller regional airlines. The biggies are VASP, Transbrasil and Varig/Cruzeiro. Every major city can be reached by at least one of the airlines. It's usually not difficult to get on a flight, except between December and Carnaval time (late February) and in July. The smaller domestic airlines include Nordeste, Rio Sul, TABA, Votec and TAM. There are also many air-taxi companies, which mostly fly in the Amazon region.

FAB (Força Aerea Brasileira) has been known to give free flights, when they have extra space. Go to the desk marked 'CAN' in the airport and ask about the next military flight, then show up again two days before scheduled departure time and sign up. It helps to have a letter of introduction from a consulate.

Air Pass

The Brazil Air Pass is no longer the great deal that it once was. There are often delays flying in Brazil, and it's rare that you don't waste a day in transit. Unless you're intent on a whistle-stop tour of the country, it may not suit your purpose.

The air pass costs US$450 and buys you five flight coupons for five flights. For US$100 each, you can buy an additional four flight coupons. All travel must be completed within 21 days. The pass must be purchased outside Brazil – you'll get an MCO (Miscellaneous Charges Order; refundable if not used) in your name with Brazil Air Pass stamped on it; you exchange this for an air pass from one of the three airlines in Brazil. Alternatively, you can decide your itinerary in advance.

All three airlines offer the same deal, and all three fly to most major cities, though Varig/Cruzeiro flies to more cities than the other two. If you are buying an air pass and have specific plans to go to a smaller city, check with a travel agent to see which airline goes there.

The air pass cannot be used to fly on the Rio to São Paulo shuttle, which lands at the downtown airports of both cities, but it can be used to fly between the international airports of both cities. WARNING: Air-pass holders who get bumped from a flight for any reason should reconfirm *all* their other flight reservations.

Airport Tax

Passengers on domestic flights pay an airport tax. This tax varies, depending on the classification of the airport, but is usually about US$2 to US$3.

BUS

Except in the Amazon Basin, buses are the primary form of long-distance transportation for the vast majority of Brazilians. Bus services are generally excellent – departure times are usually strictly adhered to, and the buses are clean, comfortable, well-serviced Mercedes, Volvos and Scanias.

Bus travel throughout Brazil is very cheap (fares work out to less than US$2 per hour): for example, the six-hour trip from Rio to São Paulo costs US$8; the 22-hour trip from Rio to Foz do Iguaçu is US$27.

All major cities are linked by frequent buses, and there is a surprising number of scheduled long-distance buses. It's rare that you will have to change buses between two major cities, no matter what the distance. For tips on security and bus travel, see the Dangers & Annoyances section in the introductory Facts for the Visitor chapter.

There are two types, or classes, of long-distance buses. The ordinary (*comum*) is the most common. It's comfortable, usually with air-con and a toilet. The *leito* or *executivo* is Brazil's version of the couchette. Leitos, which often depart late at night, usually take as long to reach their destination as a comum and cost twice as much, but they are exceptionally comfortable. If you don't mind missing the scenery, a leito bus can get you there in comfort and save you the cost of a hotel room. Long-distance buses generally make pit-stops every three or four hours.

In every big city, and most small ones, there is a central bus terminal *(rodoviária)*. The rodoviárias are most frequently on the outskirts of the city. Some are modern, comfortable stations. All have restaurants, newsstands, toilets, etc, and some even have post offices and long-distance telephone facilities. Most importantly, all the long-distance bus companies operate out of the same place, making it easy to find your bus. A combined train and bus station is a *ferrorodoviária*.

In general, it's advisable to buy a ticket at least a few hours in advance, or if it's convenient, the day before departure. On weekends, holidays and from December to February, this is always a good idea.

You don't always have to go to the rodoviária to buy your bus ticket. Selected travel agents in major cities sell long-distance bus tickets. This incurs no extra charges and can save you a long trip out to an often chaotic rodoviária.

TRAIN
There are very few railway passenger services in Brazil, and the trend to scale down or cut more and more services continues.

Enthusiasts should not despair, however, as there are still some interesting train rides. The Curitiba- Paranaguá train offers some unforgettable views, and the 13-km run from São João del Rei to Tiradentes, in Minas Gerais, is great fun.

Probably the train service of most interest to travellers is the one between São Paulo and Corumbá, on the Bolivian border.

TAXI
Taxi rides are reasonably priced, if not cheap, but you should be aware of various tricks used by some drivers to increase the charges.

Taxis in the large cities usually have meters, with prices subject to frequent updates. A *tabela* (price sheet) is used to convert the price on the meter to a new price. This is OK, as long as the meter works and

the tabela is legal and current (don't accept photocopies). Unless you are certain about a standard price for a standard trip (and have verified this with the driver), or you have purchased a ticket from a taxi ticket office (described later in this section), you must *insist* that drivers turn on their meters (no excuses) at the beginning of the ride and show you a valid tabela at the end.

What you see is what you pay – no extras if you've only loaded a couple of pieces of baggage per person, even if the driver thinks the trip to the town centre has required 'extra' fuel. If the meter doesn't work or the driver won't engage it, for whatever reason, then negotiate a fare before getting on board or find another cab. If you want to get a rough idea about the 'going rate' prior to taking a taxi ride into town, ask a newsagent or an official at the rodoviária, train station, airport, etc.

As a general rule, Tarifa I (standard tariff) applies from approximately 6 am to 10 pm Monday to Saturday; Tarifa II (higher tariff) applies outside these hours, on holidays and outside city limits. Sometimes there is a standard charge, typically for the trip between the airport and the city centre. Many airports and rodoviárias now have a system that allows you to purchase a taxi ticket from a *bilheteria* (taxi ticket office). If taking an early morning taxi to the airport, ask drivers the day before about the going rate – you might even arrange your fare at that time.

The same general advice applies to taxis without meters. You *must* agree on the price beforehand, and make sure there is no doubt about it. Learn the numbers in Portuguese.

If the driver claims to have 'no change', hold firm and see if this is just a ploy to extract more from you. You can avoid this scenario by carrying change (see Money in the Facts for the Visitor section earlier in this chapter).

If possible, orient yourself before taking a taxi, and keep a map handy in case you find yourself being taken for a blatant detour. Never use taxi touts – an almost certain rip-off. The worst place to get a cab is wherever the tourists are, so don't hire a cab near one of the expensive hotels. In Rio, for example, walk a block away from the beach at Copacabana to flag down a cab. Many airports have special airport taxis, which are about 50% more expensive than the regular taxi probably waiting just around the corner. If you are carrying valuables, however, the special airport taxi or a radio-taxi can be a worthwhile investment. These are probably the safest taxis on the road.

For more tips on security, see the Dangers & Annoyances section in the introductory Facts for the Visitor chapter.

CAR & MOTORBIKE

Driving in Brazil is hazardous – because it is not policed, because of the national cult of speed and because of the poor quality of the roads in many areas.

Car Rental

Renting a car is expensive, with prices similar to those in the USA and Europe. Familiar multinationals dominate the car rental business. Hiring a car is safe and easy, if you have a driver's licence, a credit card and a passport.

Shop around, as companies often have promotional deals and, in times of high inflation, some are slower to put up their prices than others.

Fiat Unos are the cheapest cars to rent. If the rental companies claim to be out of these, shop around. Also, when you get prices quoted on the phone, make sure they include insurance, which is required.

The big companies have airport offices in most cities, and often in the city centre as well.

Motorbike

Hiring a bike is almost as expensive as hiring a car. If you want to buy a bike, Brazil manufactures its own, but they are also expensive.

Motorbikes are popular in Brazil, especially in and around the cities. Theft is a big problem; you can't even insure a bike because theft is so common. Most people keep their bike in a guarded place, at least

overnight. For the traveller, this can be difficult to organise, but if you can manoeuvre around the practical problems, Brazil is a great place to have a motorbike.

HITCHING

Hitching in Brazil, with the possible exception of the Amazon and Pantanal areas, is difficult. The word for hitching in Portuguese is *carona*, so 'pode dar carona' is 'can you give (me/us) a lift'. The best way to hitch is to wait at a petrol station or a truck stop and talk to the drivers, but even this can be difficult. A few years back, there were several assaults by hitch-hikers, and the government started making public announcements to discourage the giving of rides.

LOCAL TRANSPORT

Local bus services tend to be pretty good, with a comprehensive network of routes. Municipal buses are usually frequent, and are always cheap and crowded. In most city buses, you enter at the back and exit from the front. Crime can be a problem on buses – rrrfor tips about security and travel on local buses, see the Dangers & Annoyances section in the introductory Facts for the Visitor chapter.

TOURS

Tatu Tours (☎ (071) 237-3161), Rua Afonso Celso 447, sala 105, Barra, Salvador, CEP 40160, Bahia, specialises in natural and cultural history tours around Bahia. Tatu Tours is represented in the UK by Traveller's Tree (☎ (071) 935-2291), 116 Crawford St, London W1H 1AG.

Focus Tours (☎ (031) 223-0358), Rua Alagoas 1460, sala 503, 30130, Belo Horizonte, Minas Gerais, is rated highly for its dedication to conservation and its use of naturalists as guides. In the USA, contact Focus Tours (☎ (612) 892-7830), 14821 Hillside Lane, Burnsville, MN 55337.

Rio de Janeiro State

The west coast, or Costa Verde, of Rio de Janeiro State is lined with hundreds of islands, which shelter the coast and make for easy swimming and boating.

Due north of Rio city, in the Serra dos Órgãos, are the mountain resort cities of Petrópolis and Teresópolis, and superb hiking and climbing in the Parque Nacional da Serra dos Órgãos.

The quiet and clean beaches east of Rio are a welcome change from the famous beaches of Rio and Guanabara Bay, with their high-rise hotels and bars spilling out onto the sands.

RIO DE JANEIRO

The city of Rio de Janeiro is known as 'a cidade maravilhosa' (the marvellous city). Jammed between ocean and escarpment are nine million *cariocas*, as the inhabitants are called. This makes Rio one of the most densely populated places on earth. Despite the city's enormous problems, the cariocas pursue pleasure like no other people. Carnaval is the best known expression of their dionysian spirit, but there are many others.

History

A Portuguese navigator, Gaspar de Lemos, discovered Guanabara Bay in January 1502. He mistook the bay for a river, and named it Rio de Janeiro. The first settlement in the bay was established by the French under Nicolas de Villegagnon in 1555. 'Antarctic France', as it was called, was not a success, and despite the French alliance with the formidable Tamoio Indians, it fell to the Portuguese in 1560.

During the 17th century, Rio became an important sugar town and port. The city flourished with the gold rush in Minas Gerais at the beginning of the 18th century, and in 1763, it replaced Salvador as the colonial capital. Rio was the capital of independent Brazil until Brasília took over in 1960, but it has retained its capital attractions for tourism.

Orientation

Rio is divided into a zona norte (north zone) and a zona sul (south zone) by the Serra da Carioca, a steep mountain range in the Parque Nacional da Tijuca. Favelas cover steep hillsides on both sides of town.

Centro (the city centre) is all business during the day and absolutely deserted at night. The main airline offices are here, as are foreign consulates, Brazilian government agencies, money exchange houses, banks and travel agencies. The centre is also the site of the original settlement of Rio, and most of the city's important museums and colonial buildings are here.

Two wide avenues cross the centre: Avenida Rio Branco, where buses leave for the zona sul, and Avenida Presidente Vargas, which heads out to the *sambódromo* (stadium) and the zona norte. Rio's modern subway follows these two avenues as it burrows under the city.

Information

Tourist Offices Riotur (☎ 242-8000) has a tourist information hotline. Call them from 9 am to 5 pm on weekdays with any questions. Their main office is at Rua da Assembléia 10, Centro, with a special 'tourist room' on the 9th floor, *sala* (room) 924. It's open weekdays from 9 am to 6 pm; the metro stop is Carioca. The Riotur booths at the airport and rodoviária can save you time – staff will phone around town and make your hotel reservation.

Money At the international airport, there are three exchange houses. In the centre of the city, on Avenida Rio Branco, there are several travel agencies/casas de câmbio, (be cautious carrying money in the city centre). The Casa Piano office, Avenida Rio Branco 88, is one of the best places to change money. Most of the banks in the city have currency exchange facilities. There are also a few casas de câmbio in Copacabana and Ipanema.

BRAZIL

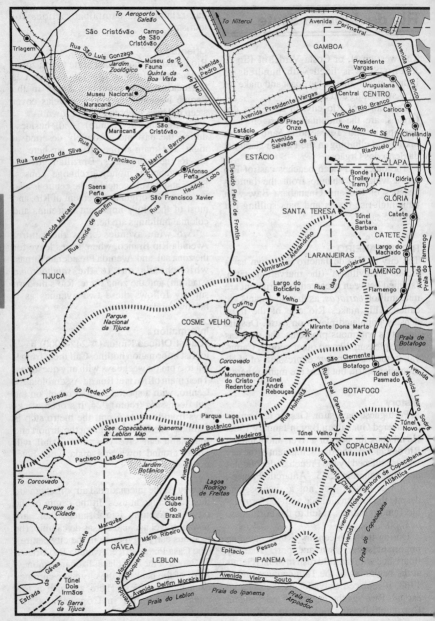

Rio de Janeiro

The American Express agent in Rio is Kontik-Franstur SA (☎ 235-1396). They have three offices:

Botafogo
Praia do Botafogo 228, Bloco A, sala 514, (☎ 552-7299)
Centro
Avenida Presidente Vargas 309/4 (☎ 296-3131)
Copacabana
Avenida Atlântica 2316-A, CEP 20040

Travellers should beware of robbers when leaving American Express offices.

Post & Telecommunications Mail addressed to Posta Restante, Rio de Janeiro, Brazil, ends up at the post office at Rua Primeiro de Março 64, in the city. They hold mail for 30 days and are reasonably efficient.

International phone calls can be made from your hotel, direct or with operator assistance (☎ 00011), or from the following locations in Rio:

Aeroporto Santos Dumont
6 am to 11 pm
Centro
Praça Tiradentes 41, open 24 hours
Copacabana
Avenida NS de Copacabana 462, open 24 hours
Ipanema
Rua Visconde de Pirajá 111, open from 6 am to 11 pm
Rodoviária Novo Rio
open 24 hours

Foreign Consulates The following countries have consulates in Rio:

Argentina
Praia de Botafogo 228, 2nd floor, Botafogo (☎ 551-5498); open from noon to 5 pm Monday to Friday
Australia
Rua Voluntários da Pátria 45, 5th floor, Botafogo (☎ 286-7922); open from 9 am to noon Monday to Friday. Note that this is only an office; for the Australian Embassy, call Brasília (☎ (061) 248-5569).
Bolivia
Avenida Rui Barbosa 664, No 101, Botafogo (☎ 551-1796); open from 8.30 am to 1 pm Monday to Friday

Canada

Rua Dom Gerardo 35, 3rd floor, Centro (☎ 233-9286); open from 9 am to 1 pm Monday to Friday

Chile

Praia do Flamengo 344, 7th floor, Flamengo (☎ 552-5349); open from 8.30 am to 12.30 pm Monday to Friday

Colombia

Praia do Flamengo 284, No 111, Flamengo (☎ 552-5048); open from 9 am to 1 pm Monday to Friday

Ecuador

Praia do Botafogo 528, No 1601, Botafogo (☎ 275-9491); open from 8.30 am to 1 pm Monday to Friday

France

Avenida Presidente Antonio Carlos 58 (☎ 210-1272)

Germany

Rua Presidente C de Campos 417 (☎ 285-2333)

Paraguay

Avenida NS de Copacabana 538, No 404, Copacabana (☎ 255-7572); open from 9 am to 1 pm Monday to Friday

Peru

Avenida Rui Barbosa 314, 2nd floor, Botafogo (☎ 551-6296); open from 9 am to 1 pm

UK

Praia do Flamengo 284, 2nd floor, Flamengo (☎ 552-1422); open from 8.30 am to 12.30 pm and 1.30 to 5 pm Monday to Friday

Uruguay

Rua Arthur Bernardes 30, Catete (☎ 225-0089); open from 8 am to 1 pm

USA

Avenida Presidente Wilson 147, Centro (☎ 292-7117); open from 8 am to 5 pm Monday to Friday

Visa Extensions You can obtain visa extensions at the Polícia Marítima building (☎ 203-2142, *ramal* (extension) 37), Avenida Venezuela 2, Centro (near the far end of Avenida Rio Branco) between 8 am and 4 pm.

Bookshops Nova Livraria Leonardo da Vinci is Rio's best bookshop; it's at Avenida Rio Branco 185 (one floor down, on the *sobreloja* level). A crowded bookstore, with knowledgeable staff and Rio's largest collection of foreign books, it's open from 9 am to 7 pm Monday to Friday, and from 10 am to 10 pm on weekends.

Emergency You don't need fichas to call the

following emergency services from public phones: police (☎ 190), ambulance (☎ 192) and fire (☎ 193). The Rio Health Collective (☎ 325-9300, extension 44) offers a free telephone referral service. The staff speaks English.

Dangers & Annoyances Rio has a reputation for crime. For hints on reducing risks, refer to Dangers & Annoyances in the Facts for the Visitor section earlier in this chapter.

Things to See

Walking Tour There's more to Rio than beaches. Take a bus or the metro to the Cinelândia area, to **Praça Floriano**, the main square along Avenida Rio Branco, and the heart of Rio today. Praça Floriano comes to life at lunch time and after work, when the outdoor cafés are filled with beer drinkers, samba musicians and political debate.

Behind Praça Mahatma Gandhi, in the direction of the bay, the large aeroplane hangar is the **Museu de Arte Moderna** (Modern Art Museum). It's open Tuesday to Sunday from 1 to 7 pm. The museum grounds were designed by Brazil's most famous landscape architect, Burle Marx (who landscaped Brasília).

The most impressive building on Praça Floriano is the **Teatro Municipal**, home of Rio's opera, orchestra and gargoyles. The theatre was built in 1905, and renovated in 1934 under the influence of the Paris Opéra. The front doors are rarely open, but you can visit the ostentatious Assyrian Room Restaurant & Bar downstairs (entrance on Avenida Rio Branco). Built in the 1930s, it's completely covered in tiles, with beautiful mosaics.

In Avenida Rio Branco, you'll also find the **Museu Nacional de Belas Artes**, housing some of Brazil's best paintings. The most important gallery is the Galeria de Arte Brasileira, with 20th-century classics such as Cândido Portinari's *Café*. The museum is open Tuesday to Friday from 10 am to 5.30 pm, and on weekends and holidays from 3 to 6 pm. Photography is prohibited.

Now do an about-face, head back to the

other side of the Teatro Municipal and walk down the pedestrian-only Avenida 13 de Maio (on your left are some of Rio's best suco bars). Cross a street and you're in the Largo da Carioca. Up on the hill is the recently restored **Convento de Santo Antônio**. The church's sacristy, which dates from 1745, has some beautiful jacaranda-wood carving and Portuguese blue tiles. The original church here was started in 1608, making it Rio's oldest.

If you have time for a side trip, consider heading over to the nearby *bondinho* (little tram) that goes up to **Santa Teresa**, a beautiful neighbourhood of cobblestone streets and old homes. The tram goes from the corner of Avenida República do Chile and Senador Dantas, over the old aqueduct, to Santa Teresa. The Museu Chácara do Céu, Rua Murtinho Nobre 93, has a good collection of art and antiques. Favelas down the hillsides have made this a high-crime area; don't take valuables.

Returning to the centre, find the shops along 19th-century **Rua da Carioca**. The old wine and cheese shop has some of Brazil's best cheese, and bargains in Portuguese and Spanish wines. Two shops sell fine Brazilian-made instruments, including all the Carnaval rhythm-makers, which make great gifts – try Casa Oliveira, at Rua da Carioca 70. There are several good jewellery stores off Rua da Carioca, on Rua Ramalho Ortigão.

Whenever I'm near Rua da Carioca 39, I stop at the **Bar Luis** for a draft beer and lunch or snack. Rio's longest running restaurant (opened in 1887), Bar Luis was called Bar Adolf until WW II. For decades, many of Rio's intellectuals have chewed the fat here while drinking the best chopp in the centro.

At the end of the block, you'll pass the **Cinema Iris**, once Rio's most elegant theatre, and emerge into the hustle of Praça Tiradentes. It's easy to see that this used to be a fabulous part of the city. On opposite sides of the square are the **Teatro João Caetano** and the **Teatro Carlos Gomez**, which present plays and dance performances. The narrow streets in this part of

town house many old, mostly dilapidated, small buildings. It's worth exploring along Rua Buenos Aires as far as **Campo de Santana**, then returning along Rua da Alfândega to Avenida Rio Branco. Campo de Santana is a pleasant park, once the scene – re-enacted in every Brazilian classroom – of Emperor Dom Pedro I, King of Portugal, proclaiming Brazil's independence from Portugal.

Pão de Açúcar (Sugar Loaf) Sugar Loaf, God's gift to the picture postcard industry, is dazzling. Two cable cars lift you 1300 metres above Rio and the Baía de Guanabara. Sunset on a clear day provides the most spectacular ascent. Avoid going between 10 and 11 am or between 2 and 3 pm, when most tourist buses arrive.

The two-stage cable cars (☎ 295-8244) leave about every half-hour from Praça General Tibúrcio, at Praia Vermelha in Urca. They operate daily from 8 am to 10 pm and cost US$5. On top of the lower hill, there's a restaurant/theatre. They have some excellent musicians; check the local papers for listings.

To get to Sugar Loaf, take a bus marked 'Urca' (No 107) from Centro and Flamengo; from the zona sul, take bus No 511 or 512. The open-air bus that runs along the Ipanema and Copacabana beaches also goes to Sugar Loaf.

Corcovado & Cristo Redentor Corcovado (Hunchback) is the mountain (709 metres), and Cristo Redentor (Christ the Redeemer) is the statue on the peak – the views from here are spectacular. The statue, with its welcoming outstretched arms, stands 30 metres high and weighs over 1000 tonnes (a popular song talks about how the Cristo should have its arms closed against its chest, because for most who come to Rio, the city is harsh and unwelcoming).

Corcovado lies within the Parque Nacional da Tijuca. You are strongly advised to resist the temptation to walk to the top, as there's a very good chance you will be robbed. You can get there by car or by taxi,

BRAZIL

BRAZIL

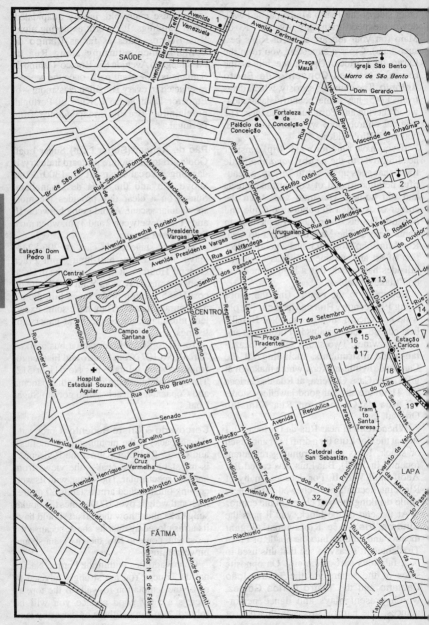

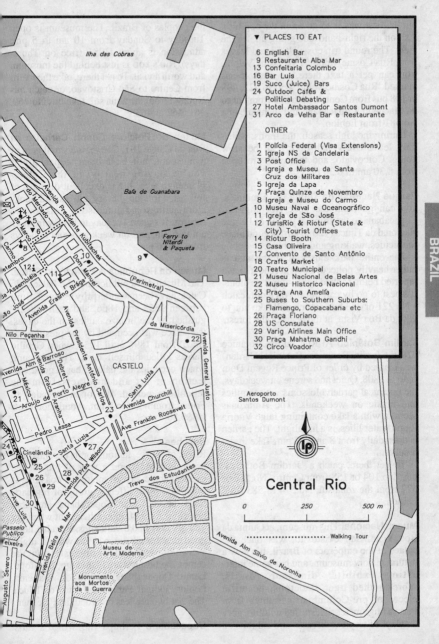

▼ PLACES TO EAT

6 English Bar
9 Restaurante Alba Mar
13 Confeitaria Colombo
16 Bar Luis
19 Suco (Juice) Bars
24 Outdoor Cafés &
   Political Debating
27 Hotel Ambassador Santos Dumont
31 Arco da Velha Bar e Restaurante

OTHER

1 Polícia Federal (Visa Extensions)
2 Igreja NS da Candelaria
3 Post Office
4 Igreja e Museu da Santa
   Cruz dos Militares
5 Igreja da Lapa
7 Praça Quinze de Novembro
8 Igreja e Museu do Carmo
10 Museu Naval e Oceanográfico
11 Igreja de São José
12 TurisRio & Riotur (State &
   City) Tourist Offices
14 Riotur Booth
15 Casa Oliveira
17 Convento de Santo Antônio
18 Crafts Market
20 Teatro Municipal
21 Museu Nacional de Belas Artes
22 Museu Historico Nacional
23 Praça Ana Amelía
25 Buses to Southern Suburbs:
   Flamengo, Copacabana etc
26 Praça Floriano
28 US Consulate
29 Varig Airlines Main Office
30 Praça Mahatma Gandhi
32 Circo Voador

Central Rio

0   250   500 m

·················· Walking Tour

but the best way is to go up in the cog train – sit on the right-hand side going up, for the view. The round trip costs US$7 and leaves from Rua Cosme Velho 513 (Cosme Velho). You can get a taxi there, or catch a bus marked 'Rua Cosme Velho' – a No 422, 498 or 108 bus from Centro, a No 583 from Largo do Machado, Copacabana and Ipanema, or a No 581 from Leblon.

During the high season, the trains, which only leave every half-hour, can be slow going. Corcovado, and the train, are open from 8.30 am to 6.30 pm.

Parque Nacional da Tijuca In 15 minutes, you can go from the concrete jungle of Copacabana to the tropical jungle of Parque Nacional da Tijuca (120 sq km), a good place for picnics, walking and climbing.

The entire park closes at sunset and is rather heavily policed. Several readers have reported being robbed here – don't go alone. It's best to go by car, but if you can't, catch a No 221 or 233 bus, which will take you to Alto da Boa Vista, at the heart of the forest.

Jardim Botânico At Rua Jardim Botânico 920, the Jardim Botânico (Botanical Garden) was planted by order of Prince Regent Dom João in 1808. Quiet and serene on weekdays, the botanical garden blossoms with families and music on weekends. The Amazonas section, with a lake containing huge Vitória Regia water lilies, is a highlight. The garden is open daily from 8 am to 5 pm. Take insect repellent.

To get there, catch a 'Jardim Botânico' bus: No 104 or 158 from Centro, No 512 or 572 from the zona sul, No 574 or 583 from Leblon.

Museu Nacional This museum, at Quinta da Boa Vista, São Cristóvão, was once the palace of the emperors of Brazil. It's now a natural history museum, and has some interesting exhibits: dinosaur fossils, sabre-toothed tiger skeletons, beautiful pieces of pre-Columbian ceramics from Peru, a huge meteorite, stuffed wildlife, gory displays of tropical diseases and exhibits on

the peoples of Brazil. The museum is open Tuesday to Sunday from 10 am to 5 pm; admission is about US$1 (free on Thursdays). Rio's **zoo** is just behind the museum, and worth a visit. To get there, take the metro from Centro to São Cristóvão, or catch bus No 284; from the zona sul, take bus No 460, 461, 462 or 463.

Museu do Folclore Edson Carneiro At Rua do Catete 181, Catete, is a small gem of a museum, not to be missed, especially if you're staying nearby, in the Catete/Flamengo area. It has excellent displays of folk art, a folklore library and a small bookstore with some interesting folk music records. It's open Tuesday to Friday from 11 am to 6 pm, and on weekends and holidays from 3 to 6 pm.

Museu da República & Palácio do Catete The Museu da República and the Palácio do Catete have been wonderfully restored. Built between 1858 and 1866, and easily distinguished by the bronze eagles on the eaves, the palace was occupied by the president of Brazil from 1896 until 1954, when Getúlio Vargas killed himself here. The museum, which occupies the palace, has a good collection of art and artefacts from the republican period. It's open Tuesday to Friday from noon to 5 pm. Admission costs US$0.30.

Beaches
Rio is, of course, famous for its beaches. The beach is a ritual and a way of life for the carioca, and every 20 metres of coastline is populated by a different group of regulars. Some beaches, like Copacabana, are more notorious for theft than others, but wherever you go, don't take valuables. It's also not a good idea to walk down by the water at night.

Sweeping round south-east from the centre, the beaches are Flamengo, Botafogo, Leme, Copacabana, Arpoador, Ipanema, Leblon, Vidigal, Pepino and Barra da Tijuca. The last two are less crowded, and cleaner.

Copacabana Perhaps the world's most

famous beach, it runs for 4½ km in front of one of the world's most densely populated residential areas. There's always something happening on the beach during the day and on the sidewalks at night: drinking, singing, eating and all kinds of people checking out the scene.

Ipanema This is Rio's richest and most chic beach. There isn't quite the frenzy of Copacabana. Ipanema is an Indian word for dangerous, bad waters – the waves can get big and the undertow is often strong, so be careful, and swim only where the locals are swimming.

Different parts of the beach attract different crowds. Posto Nine is Garota de Ipanema beach, right off Rua Vinícius de Morais. Today, it's also known as the Cemetério dos Elefantes, because of the old leftists, hippies and artists who hang out there. The Farme de Armoedo also called Land of Marlboro, at Rua Farme de Armoedo, is the gay section. In front of the Caesar Park Hotel, there's a very young crowd.

Carnaval

Rio's glitzy Carnaval has become a big tourist attraction. More than anywhere else in Brazil, it is a spectator event, but it's a fantastic spectacle nonetheless. Every year, wealthy and spaced-out foreigners descend on Rio en masse, get drunk, get high, bag some sunrays and exchange exotic diseases. Everyone gets a bit unstuck and there are lots of car accidents. Apartment rates and taxi fares triple and quadruple, and some thieves, in keeping with the spirit of the season, rob in costume.

A month before Carnaval starts, rehearsals at the *escolas de samba* (samba clubs) are open to visitors on Saturdays. These are usually in the favelas. They're fun to watch, but for your safety, go with a carioca.

The escolas de samba are, in fact, predated by *bandas* (nonprofessional equivalents of the escolas de samba), which are now returning to the Carnaval scene as part of the movement to bring Rio's Carnaval back to the streets. In 1992, there was a Banda da

Ipanema, a Banda do Leblon, a Banda da Boca Maldita and a Banda Carmen Miranda, among others. The bandas are great fun, a good place to loosen up your hip joints for samba, and excellent photo opportunities; transvestites always keep the festivities entertaining.

Riotur has information on the scheduled bandas, or you could just show up in Ipanema (most of them are in Ipanema), at Praça General Osório or at Praça Paz around 5 pm or so, a couple of weekends before official Carnaval. Other street festivities are held in Centro, on Avenida Rio Branco. Riotur has all the information in a special Carnaval guide.

Carnaval balls are surreal and erotic events. Tickets go on sale about two weeks before Carnaval starts, and the balls are held nightly for the week preceding Carnaval and through Carnaval. Scala (☎ 239-4448, US$40) and Monte Líbano (☎ 239-0032, US$20), in Leblon, host some of the cheaper, wilder balls. If you go, don't take more money than you're willing to lose.

The 16 top-level samba schools prepare all year for an hour of glory in the Sambódromo, a stadium on Rua Maquis Sapucai. The extravaganza starts around 7 pm and goes until 9 am the next day. Many tickets are sold a month in advance of the event. Getting tickets at the legitimate prices can be tough; people queue up for hours, and travel agents and scalpers snap up the best seats. But if you show up at the Sambódromo at about midnight, three or four hours into the show, you can get tickets at the grandstand for about US$15. If you can avoid it, don't take the bus to or from the Sambódromo – a taxi is safer.

The starting dates for Carnaval in coming years are: 14 February 1994, 26 February 1995, 17 February 1996, and 9 February 1997.

Places to Stay

Hostels The best place for budget travellers to stay in Copacabana is the *Copacabana Praia Youth Hostel* (☎ 235-3817), at Rua Tenente Marones de Gusmão 85. Although it's a few blocks from the beach, it's still excellent value. A relaxed and friendly place, they charge US$5 for members, US$7 for nonmembers, or US$20 for double apartments with a stove and a refrigerator. Another good hostel in Copacabana is the *Copacabana Chalé* (☎ 236-0047), at Rua Pompeu Loureira 99. It's closer to the beach.

In Glória, there's a youth hostel, *Hostel Bello* (☎ 222-8576), at Rua Santo Amaro 162. It's a reasonable place to stay but a bit of a hike from the metro.

Hotels The best area for budget hotels is the Glória, Catete and Flamengo district. Hotels here are often full from December to February, so reservations are not a bad idea.

From Glória to Lapa, on the edge of the business district, near the aqueduct, there are several more budget hotels. In general, these are more run-down but hardly any cheaper, and the area is less safe at night. If, however, everything else is booked up, you'll see several hotels if you walk along Rua Joaquim Silva (near the Passeio Público), then over to Avenida Mem de Sá, turn up Avenida Gomes Freire then right to Praça Tiradentes. The *Hotel Marajó*, at Avenida Joaquim Silva 99, is recommended.

Glória The *Hotel Turístico* (☎ 225-9388), Ladeira da Glória 30, is one of Rio's most popular budget hotels, and there are always plenty of gringos staying here. It's across from the Glória metro station, 30 metres up the street that emerges between two sidewalk restaurants. The rooms are clean and safe, with small balconies. The hotel is often full but does take reservations. Singles/doubles start at US$8/10 for quartos, US$11/13 for apartamentos.

Right near the Glória metro station, the *Hotel Benjamin Constant*, Rua Benjamin Constant 10, is one of the cheapest places around. The rooms are small and dingy, but the cost is only US$2 per person.

Catete & Flamengo The *Hotel Monte Blanco* (☎ 225-0121), at Rua do Catete 160, a few steps from the Catete metro stop, is

very clean, with air-con, and has singles/doubles for US$9/11. Ask for a quiet room towards the back.

The *Hotel Hispánico Brasileiro* (☎ 265-5990), at Rua Silveira Martins 135, has big, clean apartamentos (US$7/9).

Turn down the quiet Rua Arturo Bernardes for a couple more budget hotels: the *Monterrey* (☎ 265-9899) and *Hotel Rio Lisboa* (☎ 265-9599), at Nos 39 and 29, respectively. At both places, single quartos cost US$5 and apartamentos are US$8/10.

The recently renovated *Hotel Flórida* (☎ 245-8160), one of Rio's best budget hotels, is at Rua Ferreira Viana 81, near the Catete metro station. The Flórida has only two faults: it's not in Ipanema and it always seems to be booked up. Singles/doubles cost US$20/23 (air-con is available). There's a rooftop pool, a restaurant and a safe deposit for valuables. Make your reservations well in advance for stays during the high season.

Further into Flamengo, near the Largo do Machado metro station, the elegant, tree-lined Rua Paiçandú has two excellent mid-range hotels. The *Hotel Venezuela* (☎ 205-2098), at No 34, is clean and cosy. All rooms have double beds, air-con, TV and hot water; it costs US$16 a double. The *Hotel Paysandú* (☎ 225-7270), at No 23, is a two-star Embratur hotel with singles/doubles for US$18/21. Both are good value for money.

Copacabana Near the youth hostel, at Rua Décio Vilares 316, the delightful mid-range hotel *Santa Clara* (☎ 256-2650) has singles/doubles starting at US$20/23.

As far as budget hotels go, the *Hotel Angrense* (☎ 255-0594) is one of Copacabana's cheapest. Clean, dreary singles/doubles cost US$14/21 with bath, US$10/15 without. It's at Travessa Angrense 25. The road isn't on most maps, but it intersects Avenida NS de Copacabana just past Rua Santa Clara.

The *Grande Hotel Canada* (☎ 257-1864), Avenida NS de Copacabana 687, has singles/doubles for US$20/25 (there is no elevator for the cheapest rooms). The rooms are modern, with air-con and TV.

BRAZIL

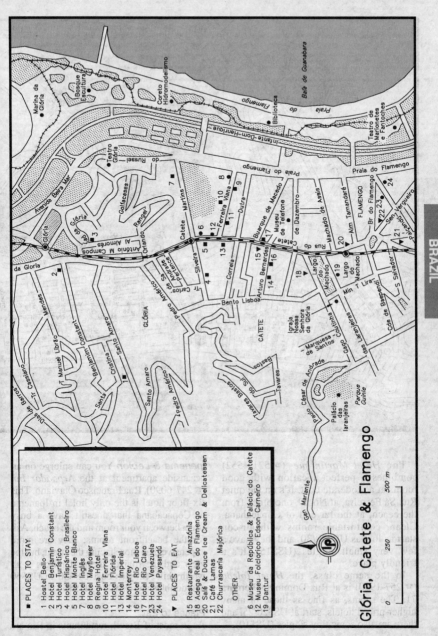

Glória, Catete & Flamengo

0   250   500 m

■ PLACES TO STAY

1   Hostel Bello
2   Hotel Benjamin Constant
3   Hotel Turístico
4   Hotel Hispânico Brasileiro
5   Hotel Monte Blanco
7   Hotel Inglês
8   Hotel Mayflower
9   Regina Hotel
10 Hotel Ferreira Viana
11 Hotel Flórida
13 Hotel Imperial
14 Monterrey
16 Hotel Rio Lisboa
17 Hotel Rio Claro
23 Hotel Venezuela
24 Hotel Paysandú

▼ PLACES TO EAT

15 Restaurante Amazônia
18 Adega Real do Flamengo
20 Salé & Douce Ice Cream & Delicatessen
21 Café Lamas
22 Churrascaria Majórica

OTHER

6   Museu da República & Palácio do Catete
12 Museu Folclórico Edson Carneiro
19 Dantur

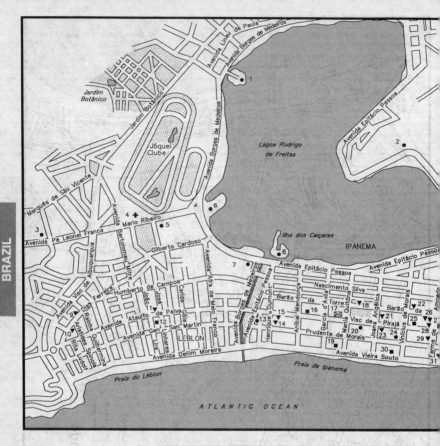

The *Hotel Martinique* (☎ 521-4552) combines a perfect location with good rooms at a moderate cost. It's on the quiet Rua Sá Ferreira, at No 30, one block from the beach, at the far end of Copacabana. Clean, comfortable rooms with air-con start as low as US$20/30, and they have a few very small singles (US$15). It's a friendly place.

In the same class, the *Hotel Toledo* (☎ 257-1990) is at Rua Domingos Ferreira 71. The rooms, as fine as those in many higher-priced hotels, start at US$20/25, and there are also some tiny singles (US$10).

Ipanema & Leblon You can splurge on an oceanside apartment at the *Arpoador Inn* (☎ 247-6090), Rua Francisco Otaviano. This six-floor hotel is the only hotel in Ipanema or Copacabana that doesn't have a busy street between your room and the beach. Ask for the beachfront rooms; they are more expensive than those facing the street, but the view and the roar of the surf makes it all worthwhile. Singles cost US$30 to US$60 and doubles are US$32 to US$63.

Places to Eat

As in most of Brazil, restaurants in Rio are

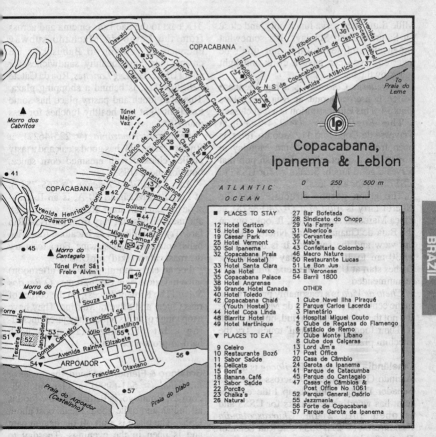

Copacabana, Ipanema & Leblon

ATLANTIC OCEAN

0   250   500 m

■ PLACES TO STAY
12 Hotel Carlton
16 Hotel São Marco
19 Caesar Park
25 Hotel Vermont
28 Sol Ipanema
32 Copacabana Praia
   (Youth Hostel)
33 Hotel Santa Clara
34 Apa Hotel
35 Copacabana Palace
38 Hotel Angrense
39 Grande Hotel Canada
40 Hotel Toledo
42 Copacabana Chalé
   (Youth Hostel)
44 Hotel Copa Linda
48 Biarritz Hotel
49 Hotel Martinique

▼ PLACES TO EAT
9 Celeiro
10 Restaurante Boz6
11 Sabor Saúde
14 Delicats
15 Boni's
18 Banana Café
21 Sabor Saúde
22 Porcão
23 Chalka's
26 Natural

27 Bar Bofetada
28 Sindicato do Chopp
29 Via Farme
31 Alberico's
36 Cervantes
37 Mab's
43 Confeitaria Colombo
46 Macro Nature
50 Restaurante Lucas
51 Le Bon Jus
53 Il Veronese
54 Barril 1800

OTHER
1 Clube Navel Ilha Piraqué
2 Parque Carlos Lacerda
3 Planetário
4 Hospital Miguel Couto
5 Clube de Regatas do Flamengo
6 Estácio de Remo
7 Clube Monte Líbano
8 Clube dos Calçaras
13 Lord Jim's
17 Post Office
20 Casa de Câmbio
24 Garota da Ipanema
41 Parque de Catacumba
45 Parque do Cantagalo
47 Casas de Câmbios &
   Post Office No 1061
52 Parque General Osório
55 Jazzmania
56 Forte de Copacabana
57 Parque Garota de Ipanema

abundant and cheap. The servings at the many lanchonetes are big enough to feed two and cost only US$1 to US$2. For something lighter, you can try a suco bar. Most have sandwiches and fruit salads. Rio also has a host of enticing vegetarian restaurants with low-priced menus. Make a habit of asking for an *embalagem* (doggie bag) when you don't finish your food. Wrap it and hand it to a street person.

City Centre *Bar Luis*, Rua da Carioca 39, is a Rio institution that opened in 1887. The city's oldest *cervejaria*, on Rio's oldest street, is a bar-less old dining room serving good German food and dark draft beer at moderate prices. It's open Monday to Saturday for lunch and dinner, until midnight.

Hotel Ambassador Santos Dumont, at Rua Santa Luzia 651, off Avenida Graça Aranha, has a business lunch buffet – a good way to fill your belly for US$4.

Café do Teatro (☎ 262-6164), at Avenida Epitácio Pessoa 1244, under the Teatro Municipal is a place to recall the good old days. Entering the dark, dramatic Assyrian Room, with its elaborate tilework and ornate columns, is like walking into a Cecil B De

Mille film. They serve lunch only, and close on Saturdays and Sundays. It's somewhat expensive and semiformal, but don't be deterred – you can have a drink and light snack by the bar.

Confeiteria Colombo is a big Viennese coffee house/restaurant at Rua Gonçalves Dias 34. This Rio institution is a real classic.

The *English Bar* (☎ 224-2539), at Travessa do Comércio 11, Arco do Teles, is open from 11.30 am to 4 pm Monday to Friday. It's a quiet, classy English pub that serves a good lunch. Steaks go for US$5 to US$7, fish for a bit less.

The green gazebo structure near the Niterói ferry is *Alba Mar* (☎ 240-8378), at Praça Marechal Âncora 184. It looks out on the Baía de Guanabara and Niterói. Go for the view and the seafood. It is open from 11.30 am to 10 pm Monday to Saturday. Dishes start at US$5 – the peixe brasileira is recommended.

Cheio de Vida is a reasonably priced place in the centre, at Avenida 13 de Maio 33, 403. It's not the easiest place to find, but it's worth it. Their food has a 'natural' touch. Try the zucchini pizza.

Cinelândia *Lanchonete Bariloche* is at Rua Alcindo Guanabara 24-D, across from Rua Senador Dantas. This cheap little counter joint has wood-grilled steaks for US$3 and is open until 2 am. *Churrascolândia Restaurante* (☎ 220-9534), at Rua Senador Dantas 31, is a steakhouse.

Vegetarian *Macrobiótica* (☎ 220-7585), on the 1st floor at Rua Embaixador Regis de Oliveira 7, is open Monday to Friday from 11 am to 3 pm. Try the soup and rice dishes.

Lapa & Santa Teresa *Arco da Velha Bar e Restaurante*, at Praça Cardeal Câmara 132, Lapa, is literally under the arch of the viaduct that the trolley crosses to head up to Santa Teresa. The Arco da Velha has great Bahian food, and there is live music upstairs.

Largo do Machado Area *Salé & Douce Ice Cream & Delicatessen* is at Rua do Catete 311, next to the São Luis cinema and across from the Largo do Machado subway entrance. In addition to Babushka's ice cream, they have healthy sandwiches for about US$2. *Leg Leg Lanches*, Rua da Catete 228, loja 111, is behind a shopping plaza. This little lunch and pastry place has some excellent light and healthy lunches for less than US$2.

Restaurant Amazónia (☎ 225-4622), at Rua do Catete 234, has good steak and a tasty broiled chicken with creamed corn sauce, both for about US$3.

Adega Real do Flamengo (☎ 265-7549), at Largo do Machado 30-A, is an Iberian-style bar and restaurant. It serves various fish and meat dishes that vary from the usual Rio fare. Try the bolinhos de bacalhau (cod-fish balls) with a Portuguese wine. For a feast, try the roast cabrito (kid) for US$5.

For an early morning (or late afternoon) juice in Catete, you can't go past *O Rei dos Sucos* (The King of Juices), on the corner of ruas Catete and Silveira Martins. They have a top range of fruits which they juice, including a lot of Amazonian ones with hard-to-pronounce names.

Botafogo & Flamengo David, the owner of *Rajmahal* (☎ 541-6999), at General Polidoro 29, Botafogo, is British, but the food is all Indian and quite good. Meals cost about US$7. The place is a bit off the beaten path and is open in the evenings, Tuesday to Sunday.

The popular *Churrascaria Majórica* (☎ 245-8947), Rua Senador Vergueiro 11/15, Flamengo, has good meat, reasonable prices and an interior done in gaucho kitsch. It's open for lunch and dinner.

Cafe Lamas (☎ 205-0799), at Rua Marques de Abrantes 18-A, Flamengo, has been operating since 1874 and is one of Rio's most renowned eateries. It's open for lunch and dinner.

Leme *Marius* (☎ 542-2393), at Avenida Atlântica 290, Leme, has an all-you-can-eat deal for US$6. Many people think this is

Rio's best churrascaria, and they may be right. Be prepared to wait during prime time, as they get a big tourist crowd. It's open from 11.30 to 1.30 am.

Restaurante Shirley, at Rua Gustavo Sampaio 610-A, has delicious seafood plates (US$5 to US$10). Try the mussel vinaigrette appetiser or the octopus and squid in ink (US$8).

Copacabana *Lope's Confeiteria*, at Avenida NS de Copacabana 1334, off Júlio de Castilhos, is an excellent lanchonete, with big portions, low prices and typical Brazilian food.

The *Americana Restaurant*, Avenida Rainha Elizabete, off Avenida NS de Copacabana, has lunches and dinners which are hearty and reasonably priced.

Confeitaria Colombo, at the intersection of Avenida NS de Copacabana and Barão de Ipanema, is a smaller version of the Colombo in the centre, and has the same colonial charm. For coffee, desserts and snacks, stay downstairs, but take a look upstairs at the elegant dining room. They now serve a great breakfast too.

Arataca, at Rua Domingues Ferreira 41 (near the American Express office), is one of several Arataca restaurants in Rio which feature the exotic cuisine of the Amazon. This place is actually a counter-lunch stand and deli. In addition to regional dishes, such as vatapá for US$4 and pato (duck) for US$5, they serve real guaraná juice (try it), and delicious sorbets made from Amazonas fruits.

Mab's, on Avenida Atlântica (the Copacabana side of Princesa Isabel, across from the Meridien), has excellent seafood soup in a crock (US$4).

Cervantes, on Avenida Prado Junior, is Rio's best sandwich joint, and a late night hang-out for a strange and colourful crowd.

Vegetarian *Macro Nature*, down the Travessa Cristiano Lacorte, is the best vegetarian restaurant/health-food store in Copacabana. The menu is brief and very organic; the soups are excellent. They have sucos, sandwiches, yoghurt and health foods to go, and everything is cheap. The 'ponto de encontro de pessoas saudáveis' (meeting point for healthy people), as it calls itself, is open from 9 am to 10.30 pm Monday to Friday, and from 9 am to 6 pm on weekends.

Ipanema If you can't afford to stay at the *Caesar Park* hotel, go down there one Wednesday or Saturday between noon and 4 pm to sample their famous Brazilian feijoada. The former president Collor considered it the best around, and it's excellent value at US$15.

Via Farme (☎ 227-0743), at Rua Farme de Amoedo 47, offers a good plate of pasta at a reasonable price. Portions are large enough for two to share. Most dishes cost less than US$5. It's open from noon to 2 am.

Barril, at both 1800 Avenida Vieira Souto and Avenida Rainha Elizabete, at the beach, is open late into the night. This trendy beach café, below Jazzmania (see Entertainment), is for people-meeting and watching.

Chaika's, Rua Visconde de Pirajá 321, is open from 8 am to 2 am; this is where the girl from Ipanema really eats. There's a stand-up fast-food bar, and a restaurant in the back with delicious hamburgers, pastries and good cappuccino (a rarity in Rio). Chaika's stays busy late into the night.

Il Veronese, Rua Visconde de Pirajá 29A, is off Gomes Carneiro. For an inexpensive meal, Veronese has takeaway Italian pastas (the best in Rio, according to local sources), pizzas and pastries.

Porcão (☎ 521-0999), Rua Barão da Torre 218, has steadily been moving up in the churrasco ratings game. Again, it's all you can eat for about US$6 a person. They open at 11 am and close at 2 am.

Bar Lagoa, on the lake, is Rio's oldest bar/restaurant. It doesn't open till 7 pm but stays open till 3 am and always has a good crowd. You can just drink beer, or have a meal for US$5 to US$6. The food is excellent, the menu typical and the atmosphere great.

Delicats, at Avenida Henrique Dumont near Rua Visconde de Pirajá, is Rio's only

BRAZIL

deli and has lots of home-made food. They make the best potato knish (dumplings) south of New York. They also have pastrami, herring, rye bread and other treasures, but sadly, no bagels.

Le Bon Jus, at the corner of Teixeira de Meio and Visconde de Pirajá, is one of the best juice and sandwich stands in the city.

Banana Café, at Rua Barão da Torre 368, is a trendy bar/restaurant. They have 19 different types of pizza and eight types of sandwich. If you're drinking, try a Black Velvet (dark chopp with champagne). They're open till 6 am.

Vegetarian *Natural* (☎ 267-7799), at Rua Barão da Torre 171, is a very natural health-food restaurant which has an inexpensive lunch special (soup, rice, vegetables and beans for less than US$3). *Sabor Saúde*, also in Leblon, has a restaurant on the corner of ruas Visconde de Pirajá and Joana Angelica.

Leblon Don't let the silly name put you off *Restaurante Bozó* (☎ 274-0147), Rua Dias Ferreira 50 – as these people are very serious about their food. Try the scrumptious and filling medallions of filet mignon wrapped in bacon and smothered in pepper sauce.

Plataforma (☎ 274-4052), at Rua Adalberto Ferreira 32, is one of the best churrascarias in Rio. It's always busy late at night and is a big hang-out for actors and musicians. The restaurant is open from 11 am to 2 am daily.

Café Leblon specialises in sandwiches. The turkey with plum chutney (US$2) is great. The decor is interesting too, with marble tables and photos of old Rio. It's at Avenida Bartolomeu Mitre 297 and stays open late.

Vegetarian *Sabor Saúde*, Avenida Ataulfo de Paiva 630, is Rio's best health-food emporium and is open daily from 8.30 am to 10.30 pm. They have two natural-food restaurants: downstairs has good meals for US$3, while upstairs is more expensive (they have great buffet feasts for US$4). There's also a small grocery store and takeaway food counter.

Celeiro, at Rua Dias Ferreira 199, has a fantastic salad bar. It's open from 11.30 am to 5 pm every day except Sunday.

Gávea *Guimas* (☎ 259-7996), Jose Roberto Macedo Soares 5, is a favourite. The food is terrific. Try the creative cooking: pernil de carneiro (lamb with onions) for US$6 or the Oriental shrimp curry (US$10) and a Rio salad. The small but comfortable open-air restaurant opens at 8 pm and becomes crowded later in the evening.

Entertainment
To find out what's going on at night, pick up the *Jornal do Brasil* at any newsstand and turn to the entertainment section. On Fridays they insert an entertainment magazine called *Programa*, which lists the week's events. The big shows and fancier clubs will have announcements in the *Brazil Post*.

Nightlife varies widely by the neighbourhood. Leblon and Ipanema have up-market trendy clubs with excellent jazz. Botafogo has cheaper, popular clubs with more dancing and samba. Cinelândia and Lapa, in the centre, have a lot of samba and pagode and are also the heart of gay Rio. Try some of the bars around Sala Cecília Mendez. Copacabana is a mixed bag – it has some good local hang-outs but also a strong tourist influence, with a lot of sex for sale.

Centro & Lapa The following clubs have popular Brazilian music like samba and *forró*, and Rio's popular dance classes. You're unlikely to find any tourists or middle-class Brazilians there. If you want to learn about Brazil and dance, or just watch Brazilians dancing, these are the places.

Pagode da Passarela has samba and *pagode* on Friday and Saturday nights. It's very crowded because it's affordable to almost everyone: US$0.50 for women and US$1 for men. It's in the centre, near Praça 11. Bola Preta (☎ 240-8049) is a big dance house with different types of popular music each night. They have *serestas*, *roda de samba* and pagode. The club's right in the centre, on Avenida 13 de Maio.

Another club for forró is Estudantina (☎ 232-1149), at Praça Tiradentes 79, Centro, open Thursday, Friday and Saturday nights until about 4 am. The cover charge is US$2.

These areas are a good change from the zona sul club scene, but don't bring too much money. Getting a taxi late at night in Lapa or Cinelândia isn't a problem; there is also a limited bus service all night long.

Botafogo O Viro da Ipiranga (☎ 225-4762), at Rua Ipiranga 54, is a warm bar with a relaxed scene and great local musicians, and it costs only a couple of dollars to get in. The music varies, but they have a couple of nights a week of *chorinho*, a bittersweet instrumental music from Rio. Beco Da Pimenta, Rua Real Grandeza 176, is a great little joint for samba, pagode and traditional Rio music, and it's very cheap. There's a lively, mixed crowd that knows how to dance and drink.

Cochrane, off Rua Voluntários da Pátria, is one of Rio's more popular gay bars.

Copacabana If you are homesick for punk culture, try Kitschnet, at Barata Ribeiro 543. It's frequented by 'gothicos' – Brazilian punks who wear black clothing and listen to Brazilian rock. Galeria Alaska, on Avenida NS de Copacabana, has a transvestite show and dancing and is a centre of gay Rio.

Ipanema & Leblon Jazzmania (☎ 287-0085), Avenida Rainha Elizabete, is Rio's most serious jazz venue. It has more international stars than any other club, as well as the best of Brazilian jazz. The club is expensive, at around US$10 cover on weekends and a little less on weekdays. The music starts about 11 pm and goes till late.

If you want to speak English and play darts, Lord Jim's British pub is the place. It's at Rua Paul Redfern 63, in Ipanema. The Garota de Ipanema, Rua Vinícius de Morais 49, has open-air dining. There are always a few foreigners checking out the place where Tom Jobim was sitting when he wrote *The Girl from Ipanema*.

My favourite bar is also Rio's oldest. In a town that's rapidly losing its traditions to modern Western schlock, Bar Lagoa is a comforting breeze. It's open from about 9 pm to 3 or 4 am, with food, drink and a loud Carioca crowd. Botanic, at Rua Pacheco Leão 70, in Jardim Botânico, gets crowded with cariocas wanting to dance to samba-reggae.

Samba Schools As early as October or November, the samba schools begin holding rehearsals and dances, typically on Saturday nights. These are generally open to the public for watching and joining in the samba. Almost all the escolas da samba are on the north side of town and, of course, things get going late, so you need a car or a taxi. Check with Riotur or the newspaper for schedules and locations. More details about samba are given earlier in this chapter, in the section on Carnaval.

Big Shows Circo Voador, under the Arcos da Lapa, is a big tent with reggae, samba and *trio elétrico* music. Many of the best bands from Bahia and São Paulo play here. The crowd is mostly from the north side. The cover charge is US$3.

Discos Interestingly, many of the discos have stiff dress codes and admission charges, designed in part to deter the many prostitutes who come to meet tourists. Help calls itself the biggest disco in Latin America, and no one seems to doubt it. It's at Avenida Atlântica 3432, in Copacabana. Lots of drunken gringos seem to get robbed just outside. The current favourite is Resumo da Ópera; it's in Lagoa, at Avenida Borges de Medeiros 1426.

Things to Buy
Most stores are open Monday to Friday from 9 am to 7 pm (some stay open even later). Saturday is a half-day for shopping, from 9 am to 1 pm. The malls usually open from 10 am to 10 pm Monday to Friday, and from 10 am to 8 pm on Saturdays. It's illegal for stores to open on Sundays.

BRAZIL

Pé de Boi Pé de Boi is in Botafogo, on Rua Ipiranga 53. It is open Monday to Friday until 7 pm, and on Saturdays from 10 am to 1 pm. This store sells the traditional artisan handicrafts of Brazil's North-east and Minas Gerais. Although the items are not cheap, it's all fine work.

FUNAI Craft Shop Brazil's Indian agency has a tiny craft shop at the Museu do Índio, Rua das Palmeiras 55, Botafogo. Open Monday to Friday from 8.30 am to 4.30 pm, the store has woven papoose slings, jewellery and musical instruments.

Casa Oliveira This beautiful music store is in Centro, at Rua da Carioca 70 – Rio's oldest street. It sells a wide variety of instruments, including all the noise makers that fuel the Carnaval *baterias* (rhythm sections).

Bum Bum This place is the trendsetter of the bikini world, and it knows it. It's not cheap, but you're paying for style not fabric. Bum Bum is in Ipanema, at Rua Vinicius de Morais 130.

Nordeste or São Cristóvão Fair The nordeste fair is held at the Pavilhão de São Cristóvão, on the north side of town, every Sunday, starting early and going until about 3 pm. The fair is very North-eastern in character. Besides food, stallholders sell cheap clothes, hammocks at bargain prices, and a few nordeste gifts like leather vaqueiro (cowboy) hats. It's great fun, as long as you're careful.

Getting There & Away
Air From Rio, flights go to all parts of Brazil and Latin America. Shuttle flights to São Paulo leave from the conveniently located Aeroporto Santos Dumont, in the city centre, along the bay. Almost all other flights – domestic and international – leave from Aeroporto Galeão.

Incoming visitors at Galeão pass through customs and then continue into a large lobby, where there's a tourist information counter run by a private company called RDE; they can arrange hotel and taxi reservations. Don't listen to nonsense from RDE staff trying to sell their sham 'travellers passport' – it's a junk package and a blatant rip-off.

All three major Brazilian airlines have their main offices in the centre (metro stop Cinelândia). You can also walk over to Aeroporto Santos Dumont, where they have ticket counters, and make reservations from there.

Varig/Cruzeiro (☎ 292-6600 for reservations, 282-1319 for information) has its main office in Centro, at Avenida Rio Branco 277. VASP (☎ 292-2122) has a city office at Rua Santa Luzia 735. Transbrasil (☎ 297-4422) is in the centre, at Rua Santa Luzia 651. Nordeste Linhas Aéreas (☎ 220-4366) is at Aeroporto Santos Dumont. It goes to Porto Seguro, Ilhéus and other smaller cities in the North-east. Rio Sul (☎ 262-6911) does the same for the south, and is also at Aeroporto Santos Dumont.

International airlines include:

Aerolíneas Argentinas
    Rua São José 40, Centro (☎ 221-4255)
    Avenida NS de Copacabana, Copacabana 312 (☎ 255-7144)
AeroPerú
    Praça Mahatma Gandhi 2, No 201, Centro (☎ 210-3124)
Air France
    Avenida Presidente Antônio Carlos 58, 9th floor, Centro (☎ 220-8661)
Alitalia
    Presidente Antônio Carlos 40, 6th floor, Centro (☎ 210-2192)
American Airlines
    Avenida Presidente Wilson 165, 5th floor, Centro (☎ 210-3126)
Avianca
    Avenida Presidente Wilson 165, No 807 (☎ 240-4413)
British Airways
    Avenida Rio Branco 108, 21st floor, Centro (☎ 221-0922)
Canadian Airlines
    Rua da Ajuda 35, 29th floor, Centro (☎ 220-5343)
Iberia
    Avenida Presidente Antônio Carlos 51, 8th floor, Centro (☎ 282-1336)

Japan Air Lines
  Avenida Rio Branco 156, No 2014, Centro
  (☎ 220-6414)
KLM
  Avenida Rio Branco 311, Centro (☎ 210-3242)
Lan Chile
  Avenida Nilo Peçanha 50, No 1305, Centro
  (☎ 220-9722)
LAP (Lineas Aereas Paraguayas)
  Avenida Rio Branco 245, 7th floor, Centro
  (☎ 220-4148)
LAB (Lloyd Aero Boliviano)
  Avenida Calógeras 30, Centro (☎ 220-9548)
Lufthansa
  Avenida Rio Branco 156, Centro (☎ 262-0273)
SAS
  Avenida Presidente Wilson 231, 6th floor, Centro
  (☎ 210-1222)
United Airlines
  Avenida Presidente Antônio Carlos 51, 5th floor,
  Centro (☎ 532-1212)
Viasa
  Rua do Carmo 7, 4th floor, Centro (☎ 224-5345)

Bus All long-distance buses leave from the
Novo Rio Rodoviária, Avenida Francisco
Bicalho in São Cristóvão, about 10 minutes
north of the centre. Many travel agents in the
city sell bus tickets – it's best to purchase
these a couple of days in advance.

Getting Around

To/From the Airport There are three
options: air-con buses, local buses and taxis.
If you have any valuables, an air-con bus or
a taxi is safer than a local bus.

Air-conditioned buses run on two routes
to and from Aeroporto Galeão. The buses
operate from 5.20 am to 11 pm, leave every
40 minutes to one hour and cost about US$3.
One route goes to the centre and to the Santos
Dumont airport; the other route goes to the
city centre and along the beaches of
Copacabana, Ipanema, Leblon, Vidigal and
São Conrado.

You can catch the bus on the 2nd floor
(arrivals) of the main terminal, at the Galeão
sign. If you ask the driver, the buses will stop
anywhere along the route. Both stop at the
rodoviária, if you want to catch a bus out of
Rio immediately.

If you're heading to the airport, you can

catch the Empresa Real bus in front of the
major hotels along the beach, but you have
to flag it down. 'Galeão' should be written
on the direction sign.

If you decide to travel by local bus, there
is a small terminal for city buses, on Rua
Ecuador (on the far corner, to your right as
you leave the main terminal at Galeão). Bus
numbers and routes are posted, so it's pretty
easy to work out which bus to catch.

For Copacabana, the best are bus Nos 126,
127 or 128. The best bus to Ipanema and
Leblon is No 128, but you can also take No
126 or 127 to Copacabana and then catch
another bus to Ipanema and Leblon. For the
budget hotels in Catete and Glória, take bus
No 170 ('Gávea – via Jóquei'), which goes
down Rua do Catete and then turns up Rua
Pedro Américo and along Rua Bento Lisboa.
If you want the Catete budget hotels, get off
at the stop near the corner of Bento Lisboa
and Rua Silveira Martins, then walk a block
down to Rua Catete.

An alternative is to take any bus that goes
to the centre on Avenida Rio Branco. Get off
near the end of Avenida Rio Branco and hop
on the metro. Get off the metro at Catete
station, which is in the heart of the budget
hotel area.

A taxi is a good option if you have valuables, though many taxis from the airport
will try to rip you off. The safest and most
expensive course is to take a radio-taxi,
where you pay a set fare at the airport. A
yellow-and-blue *comum* (common) taxi is
about 25% cheaper, if the meter is working
and if you pay what is on the fare schedule.
A trip from the airport to Copacabana costs
about US$15 in a yellow-and-blue taxi,
US$20 in a radio-dispatched taxi. If you're
entering Brazil for the first time, on a budget,
a good compromise is to take a bus to somewhere near your destination, then take a short
taxi ride to your hotel. Sharing a taxi from
the airport is a good idea. Taxis will take up
to four people. To ensure a bit of security,
before entering the taxi at the airport you can
usually get a receipt with the licence plate of
your taxi and a phone number to register
losses or complaints.

BRAZIL

Bus If you're staying in the Catete/Flamengo area and want to get to the beaches by bus, you can either walk to the main roadway along Parque Flamengo and take any bus marked 'Copacabana', or you can walk to Largo do Machado and take the No 570 bus.

Metro Rio's excellent subway system is limited to points north of Botafogo. It is open from 6 am to 11 pm daily, except Sunday. The two air-con lines are cleaner, faster and cheaper than the buses – discounts are offered on purchase of multiple tickets. The main stops for Centro are Cinelândia and Carioca.

Taxi Rio taxis are quite reasonably priced, if you're dividing the fare with a friend or two. Taxis are particularly useful late at night and when carrying valuables, but they are not a completely safe and hassle-free ride. First, there have been a few cases of people being assaulted and robbed by taxi drivers. Second, and much more common, the drivers have a marked tendency to exaggerate fares. For more hints on dealing with taxis, see the information on taxis in the Getting Around section near the beginning of this chapter. The white radio-taxis (☎ 260-2022) are 25% more expensive than the comums, but they will come to you and they are safer.

Car Car rental agencies can be found at the airport, or clustered together on Avenida Princesa Isabel in Copacabana. Rental is not cheap (about US$40 a day), but rates go down a bit in the off season. When agencies quote prices on the phone, they usually leave out the cost of insurance, which is mandatory. Most agencies will let you drop off their cars in another city without extra charge.

ANGRA DOS REIS

Angra dos Reis is a transit point for nearby islands and beaches, not a tourist attraction in itself. The closest beaches are at Praia Grande and Vila Velha. Take the 'Vila Velha' municipal bus.

Angra dos Reis is almost three hours (US$6) by bus from Rio de Janeiro's Novo Rio Rodoviária. To Parati, it's a two-hour trip (US$4).

ILHA GRANDE

Ilha Grande is all beach and tropical jungle, and because of a maximum-security prison and a limitation on new hotels, it is likely to remain this way. There are only three towns on the island: Freguesia de Santana (a small hamlet without accommodation), Parnaioca (a collection of homes beside a lovely strip of beach near the prison) and Abraão (which has plenty of pousadas, camping grounds and ferry connections to Mangaratiba and Angra dos Reis). If you really want to get away from it all, Ilha Grande may well be the place to go. You can rent a boat for US$6 per hour, and buzz around to Freguesia or Parnaioca.

There are trails through the jungle to Praia Lopes Mendes (said by some to be the most beautiful beach in Brazil) and the island's other 102 beaches.

Places to Stay & Eat

The cheapest option is to camp in Abraão. *Camping Renato*, up a small path beside Dona Penha's, has well-drained, secure sites and basic facilities, as well as a café/bar on site. They charge US$3 per person. Other campgrounds include *Gilson*, *Holandes* (which also has rooms) and *Das Palmas*, right on the beach at Praia Grande das Palmas. Off-site camping is forbidden, and not advised.

It may be possible to arrange a stay in a private home in Freguesia. One of the cheaper accommodation possibilities in Abraão is *Pousada Teté*, which has singles/doubles for US$15/25. The *Tropicana*, Rua da Praia 28, is run by a French/Brazilian couple and is similarly priced (US$13/24). The *Hotel Mar da Tranquilidade* restaurant is open to everyone – just give the cook several hours' advance notice. Around the corner is *Restaurante Janethe's*, which serves prato feitos with abundant portions of fresh fish for US$3.

Rua da Igreja becomes a dirt road and

continues over a little footbridge to the house of *Dona Penha*. Look for the yellow gate on the right-hand side. She has some rooms for US$18 a double.

Getting There & Away

Catch a Conerj ferry from either Mangaratiba or Angra dos Reis. If you take the 5.30 am bus from Rio to Mangaratiba, you can catch the daily 8.30 am ferry from Mangaratiba to Abraão. The boat returns from Abraão to Mangaratiba on Monday, Wednesday and Friday at 4.30 pm, on Tuesday and Thursday at 11 am, and on Saturday and Sunday at 4 pm. If you're stuck in Mangaratiba, you can stay at the *Hotel Rio Branco*, on the praça, which has doubles for US$5 (US$10 with bath).

The ferry (US$5, 1½ hours) from Angra dos Reis to Abraão sails on Monday, Wednesday and Friday at 3 pm, returning from Abraão at 10.15 am on the same days.

PARATI

Parati, one of Brazil's most enchanting colonial towns, is a good place from which to explore a dazzling section of the coast. It is now one of the most popular holiday spots between Rio and São Paulo, and prices are high.

Information

Tourist Offices The Centro de Informações Turísticas (☎ 71-1266), on Avenida Roberto Silveira, is open daily from 7 am to 7 pm. The Secretaria de Turismo e Cultura (☎ 71-1256), in the Antigo Quartel do Forte, near the port, is open daily from 8 am to 7 pm.

Things to See

Parati's 18th-century prosperity is reflected in its beautiful old homes and churches. In the 18th century, the population was divided amongst the three main churches: **NS do Rosário** (1725) for slaves, **Santa Rita dos Pardos Libertos** (1722) for freed mulattos and **NS das Dores** (1800) for the white elite.

The **Forte Defensor Perpétuo** was built in 1703 to protect the gold being exported from Minas Gerais, which was subject to attack by pirates. It's a 20-minute walk north from town. The fort houses the **Casa de Artista e Centro de Artes e Tradições Populares de Parati**.

To see the **beaches and islands**, many tourists take the schooner that leaves from the docks at noon and returns at 5 pm (on Sunday, it leaves at 9 am and returns at 3 pm). It costs US$15 per person. Lunch is served on board for an additional US$7. The boat makes three beach stops of about 45 minutes each. Because it's the least expensive cruise in the bay, the schooner is usually crowded and stifling.

A better alternative is to rent a small motorboat at the port. For US$10 per hour (somewhat more in summer), the skipper will take you where you want to go. Bargaining may be difficult.

The mainland beaches tend to be better than the ones on the islands. The closest fine beaches on the coast – Vermelha, Lula and Saco – are about an hour away by boat; camping is allowed. The most accessible beaches, just north of town, are Praia do Pontal, Praia do Forte and Praia do Jabaquara.

Places to Stay

From about October to February, hotels in Parati get booked up and room prices double, so reservations are a good idea. The prices quoted here are off-season rates.

There are several campgrounds on the edge of town, just over the bridge. Cheap accomodation is not hard to find in Parati. The *Pousada Familiar* (☎ 71-1475), at Rua José Vieira Ramos 262, is close to the bus station and charges US$7 per person, including a good breakfast. It's a friendly place, run by a Brazilian/Belgian couple. Also recommended is the *Pousada Marendaz* (☎ 71-1369), at Rua Dr Derly Ellena 9. Run by Rachel and her four sisters, it's more of a family home than a hotel. They charge US$9 per person.

Hotel Solar dos Gerânios (☎ 71-1550), on Praça da Matriz (also known as Praça Monsenhor Hélio Pires), is a beautiful old hotel. Singles/doubles start as low as US$13/23.

The *Hotel Coxixo* (☎ 71-1568), Rua do Comercio 362, is cosy and colonial, with beautiful gardens and a pool. Most doubles go for US$60, but if you make reservations early, they have some standard doubles, which are a fine deal at US$37.

Places to Eat

Parati has many pretty restaurants, which all seem to charge too much. To beat the inflated prices in the old part of town, try the sandwiches at the lanchonete on Praça Matriz. The best restaurants in the old town include the *Galeria do Engenho*, Rua da Lapa, which serves large and juicy steaks for US$6, and *Vagalume*, Rua da Ferraria. Another recommended restaurant is *Mare Alta*, Praça da Bandeira, which has tasty pizzas.

Getting There & Away

The rodoviária is on the main road into town, Rua Roberto Silveira, half a km up from the old town. There are six daily buses (US$8, four hours) from Parati to Rio.

Six daily buses (US$4, two hours) go from Parati to Angra dos Reis. There are also daily buses to Ubatuba, Cunha and São Paulo.

PETRÓPOLIS

Petrópolis is a lovely mountain retreat with a decidedly European flavour, only 60 km from Rio de Janeiro – an ideal day trip. The main attraction is the **Museu Imperial**, the perfectly preserved and impeccably appointed palace of Dom Pedro II.

Places to Stay

The *Hotel Comércio* (☎ 42-3500), at Rua Dr Porciúncula 56, is directly across from the rodoviária. Quartos are clean and cheap, at US$3.50/5 for singles/doubles. Apartamentos cost US$12/16. If you want to spend a bit more, both the *Hotel York* (☎ 43-2662), at Rua do Imperador 78, and the *Casablanca Palace* (☎ 42-0162), Rua 16 de Março 123, have singles/doubles for US$25/28.

Getting There & Away

From Rio, buses to Petrópolis leave every half-hour from 5 am onwards (US$2.50, 1½ hours).

TERESÓPOLIS

Teresópolis is the climbing and trekking centre of Brazil. The city itself is modern, prosperous and dull; the principal attraction is the surrounding landscape of the Serra dos Orgãos.

There are extensive hiking trails, and it's possible to trek to Petrópolis. The trails aren't marked, but guides are inexpensive. Guidebooks to Teresópolis (with trail maps) are sold at the Cupela Banco de Jornais, in the square in front of the Igreja Matriz de Santa Tereza.

The main entrance to the **Parque Nacional Serra dos Orgãos** is open daily from 8 am to 5 pm. There's a 3½-km walking trail, waterfalls, swimming pools, tended lawns and camp sites. It's a very pretty park for a picnic. There are also some camp sites and chalets for rent at the park substation, 12 km towards Rio.

Places to Stay

The *Várzea Palace Hotel* (☎ 742-0878), at Rua Prefeito Sebastião Teixeira 41/55, behind the Igreja Matriz, is a grand old white building with red trim which has been a Teresópolis institution since 1916. Can this be a budget hotel? Classy singles/doubles are US$10/13 without bath, US$13/16 with a bath. Other relatively cheap hotels are nearby, including the *Center Hotel* (☎ 742-5890), at Sebastião Teixeira 245, which costs US$17/23. The *Hotel Avenida* (☎ 742-2751) is in front of the Igreja Matriz, at Rua Delfim Moreira 439. Rooms here cost US$7/13.

Places to Eat

Bar Gota da Água, at Praça Baltazar da Silveira 16, is also known as *Bar do Ivam*. This comfy little place serves trout with a choice of sauces (US$6). For dessert, stroll a few doors down to *Lanches Mickey*. *Tudo em Cima*, Avenida Delfim Moreira 409, serves an admirable soufflé of bacalhau

(US$4). *O Tigre de Papel* is a good Chinese restaurant in the centre, at the end of Rua Francisco Sá.

Getting There & Away
The rodoviária is on Rua 1 do Maio, off Avenida Tenente Luiz. Buses to Rio (US$3, 1½ hours) leave every half-hour between 5 am and 10 pm. There are also buses to Petrópolis (every two hours from 9 am to 9 pm) and Nova Friburgo.

NOVA FRIBURGO
This mountain town was established by Swiss immigrants in 1818. The Cónego neighbourhood is interesting for its German-style architecture, and for its flowers, which seem to bloom perpetually.

You can survey the surrounding area from Morro da Cruz (1800 metres). The cable-car station is in the centre, at Praça do Suspiro, and gondolas run up to the top from 9 am to 5.30 pm. **Pico da Caledônia** (2310 metres) also offers fantastic views.

The more energetic can hike to Pedra do Cão Sentado or explore the Furnas do Catete rock formations. Interesting nearby villages include the mountain towns of Bom Jardim (23 km north on BR-492) and Lumiar (25 km from Mury, just before the entrance to Friburgo). Hippies, cheap pensions, water-falls, walking trails and white-water canoe trips abound in Lumiar.

Places to Stay
Fabris Hotel (☎ 22-2852), at Avenida Alberto Braune 148, asks US$10/12 for clean singles/doubles. *Hotel Montanus* (☎ 22-1235), at Rua Fernando Bizzotto 26, has simple singles/doubles for the same price, but you can bargain them down.

A good mid-range place in the centre is the *Sanjaya Hotel* (☎ 22-6052), at Avenida Alberto Braune 58. They charge US$25/30.

Places to Eat
To eat very well, try one of the two Swiss/German delis on Rua Fernando Bizzotto for a hefty cold-cut sandwich on black bread with dark mustard; *Oberland*, at No 12, doubles as a restaurant, with great food – try the weisswurst (veal sausage) with sauerkraut (US$2), and the chocolate cakes for dessert. The *Churrascaría Majórica*, in the centre at Praça Getúlio Vargas 74, serves good filet mignon for US$6. *Pizzaria Papillon*, on the other side of Praça Getúlio Vargas, makes excellent pizzas.

Getting There & Away
Nova Friburgo is a little over two hours (US$4.50) by bus from Rio, via Niterói, on 1001 Lines. To Teresópolis, there are four daily buses (US$4, two hours).

ITATIAIA REGION
The Itatiaia region, in the Serra da Mantiqueira, is a curious mix of old-world charm and new-world jungle. Food and lodging are expensive. Access to this region is via Resende.

Parque Nacional de Itatiaia
This 120-sq-km national park contains alpine meadows and Atlantic rainforests, lakes, rivers and waterfalls. It is the home of jaguars, monkeys and sloths.

The park headquarters, museum and Lago Azul (Blue Lake) are 10 km in from the Via Dutra highway. The museum, open Tuesday to Sunday from 8 am to 4 pm, has glass cases full of stuffed animals, pinned moths and snakes in jars.

Every two weeks, a group guided by Senhor Carlos Zikan scales the Agulhas Negras peak, at 2787 metres the highest in the area. For more information, call the Grupo Excursionista de Agulhas Negras (☎ 54-2639). Lúcia Teireira (☎ 58-2324) is another excellent guide.

It's a 26-km, eight-hour trek from the park entrance to the Abroucas refuge, at the base of Agulhas Negras. The refuge can sleep 24 people. Reservations are required. Call the IBAMA (National Parks Service) (☎ 52-1461) in Resende, and get maps and advice from the park IBAMA office before setting off.

Simpler hikes include the walk between

BRAZIL

Hotel Simon and Hotel Repouso, and the 20-minute walk from the Sítio Jangada to the Poronga waterfalls.

Places to Stay

Pousada do Elefante, close to the Hotel Simon, is the cheapest place in the park. Basic but well located, it charges US$20/40 for singles/doubles with board. Not far from the park entrance, *Hotel Aldéia da Serra* (☎ 52-1152) has reasonably priced chalets at US$35/50, all inclusive.

Getting There & Away

Buses from Resende to Itatiaia run every 20 minutes on weekdays, every 40 minutes on weekends, from 7 am to 11.20 pm. From the town, take a 'Circular' bus to the park entrance.

SAQUAREMA

Saquarema, 100 km from Rio de Janeiro, is a horse-breeding and fruit-growing centre. You can visit the orchards and pick fruit, or hire horses and take to the hills. The town shuns pollution and takes unusual pride in the natural beauty of its surroundings, so it's still possible to encounter wildlife in the jungles. The beaches are a major attraction; Bambui, Ponta Negra and Jaconé, south of town, are long and empty, except for a couple of fishing villages. The waves are big, particularly in Ponta Negra, and three km north of Saquarema in Praia Itaúna, where an annual surfing contest is held during the last two weeks of May.

Places to Stay

A great place to stay is *Pousada da Mansão*, at Avenida Oceanica 353. Rooms in the old mansion cost US$10/20, and you can also camp. For reservations, (☎ (021) 259-2100) in Rio. *Pousada da Titia* (☎ 51-2058), at Avenida Salgado Filho 774, is a good alternative, with quartos (US$14 a double) and apartamentos (US$20). *Pousada dos Socos* (☎ 51-1205), at Rua dos Socos 592, Itaúna, charges US$25 a double. There are stacks of places charging around US$40 a double. A popular one is *Maasai Hotel Club* (☎ 51-1092), near Itaúna beach.

Getting There & Away

Saquarema is serviced by frequent buses from Rio (US$4, two hours). To get to Cabo Frio, take a local bus to Bacaxá. From there, buses depart every half-hour to Cabo Frio.

ARRAIAL DO CABO

Arraial do Cabo, 10 km south of Cabo Frio, has beaches that compare with the finest in Búzios. Praia dos Anjos has beautiful turquoise water, but there's a little too much boat traffic for comfortable swimming.

Things to See

The **Oceanographic Museum**, on the beach, is open Tuesday to Sunday from 9 am to 4.30 pm.

To see the **Gruta Azul** (Blue Cavern), on the far side of Ilha de Cabo Frio, ask the fisherfolk at Praia dos Anjos for a tour, or inquire at the Pousada Restaurante dos Navegantes. The tour should cost around US$15. The favourite beaches in town are Praia do Forno, Praia Brava and Praia Grande.

Places to Stay & Eat

In the centre of town, the *Hotel Praia Grande* (☎ 22-1369), at Rua Dom Pedro 41, is a good cheapie (US$10/14). The *Pousada Restaurante dos Navegantes* (☎ 22-1611), on Praia Grande, is a very pretty resort hotel with a courtyard pool; singles/doubles cost US$20/27. *Camping Praia Grande* is a walled-in grassy area reasonably close to the beach.

Garrafa de Nansen Restaurante is a classy seafood place where you can eat very well for about US$8. For cheaper eats, try the *Hotel Churrascaria Gaucha*, Praça Lions Clube 35.

Getting There & Away

The municipal bus from Cabo Frio loops around Arraial and returns to Cabo Frio every 20 minutes.

BÚZIOS

Búzios is on a peninsula scalloped by 17 beaches. It was a simple fishing village until Brigitte Bardot and her Brazilian boyfriend discovered it. Now it is a highly developed, expensive resort.

Búzios is actually three settlements on the peninsula (Ossos, Manguinhos and Armação) and one further north, on the mainland (Rasa). Ossos (which means bones), at the northernmost tip of the peninsula, is the oldest and most attractive.

Information

The Ekoda Tourist Agency (☎ 23-1490) in Armação, at Avenida José Bento Ribeiro Dantas 222, is open every day from 10 am to 8 pm. The staff sells maps of Búzios, changes money, represents American Express, speaks English, French, German and Spanish, and arranges accommodation and tours.

Things to See

In general, the southern beaches are trickier to get to, but they're prettier and have better surf. The northern beaches are more sheltered and are closer to the settlements.

The schooner *Queen Lory* makes daily trips to Ilha Feia, Tartaruga and João Fernandinho. There is a 2½-hour trip (US$12) and a four-hour trip (US$20). These trips are excellent value, especially since caipirinhas, soft drinks, fruit salad and snorkelling gear are included in the price. To make a reservation, ask at your pousada or visit Queen Lory Tours, Rua Angela Diniz 35.

Places to Stay

Campers should try *Geribá*, at Praia de Geribá. They also have a few chalets for US$10 per person.

Accommodation is somewhat expensive, so consider staying in Saquarema or Cabo Frio. *Casa Márcia Vanicoru* (☎ 23-1542), Rua João Fernandes 60, is a private home with rooms to let. Márcia has doubles for US$28 in the off season, US$45 in the high season. She speaks English, is an excellent cook and will rent you a bike to get to the beaches. *Pousada la Chimere* (☎ 23-1460), Praça Eugênio Harold 36, is an excellent splurge: it has a lovely courtyard and large, well-appointed rooms with a view over the square. Doubles are US$45 in the low season, US$73 in the high season.

Places to Eat

For good, cheap food, have grilled fish right on the beaches. Brava, Ferradura and João Fernandes beaches have fish and beer restaurants. Try *Restaurante David* in Armação, on Rua Manoel Turibe de Farias. *Chez Michou Crêperie*, on Rua das Pedras, makes almost any kind of crêpe you want.

Getting There & Away

Buses to Rio depart daily from the bus stop on Rua Turibe de Faria in Armação (US$6, three hours). From Cabo Frio to Búzios (Ossos), it's a 50-minute trip on the municipal bus.

Espírito Santo

Espírito Santo is a small state which has little to interest the traveller. Some of the fishing villages and beaches on the southern coast are attractive, but they are no match for those in Rio or Bahia.

Minas Gerais State

The main attractions for visitors to this state are the national parks, and the historic gold cities nestled in the Serra Do Espinhaço, with their baroque churches and sacred art.

BELO HORIZONTE

Belo Horizonte has nothing of special interest to the traveller. Mostly, those who stop here are on their way to Ouro Prêto or Diamantina. Belotur (☎ 222-5500), the municipal tourist organisation, has booths at both airports, and in Praça 7 do Setembro (often abbreviated to Praça Sete) at the intersection with Rua Rio de Janeiro.

Places to Stay

There are two youth hostels in town: *Pousada Beagá* (☎ 275-3592), at Rua Timbiras 2330, and *Pousadinha Mineira* (☎ 446-2911), Rua Araxá 514. Each charges US$5 per head.

You'll see lots of hotels right next to the rodoviária, but they're pretty dingy and the area is sleazy after dark. However, there are lots of inexpensive hotels that are centrally located and not too far from the rodoviária. *Hotel Magalhães* (☎ 222-9233), at Rua Espírito Santo 237, has clean, comfortable singles/doubles without bath for US$4/7 and doubles with bath for US$10. Next door, *Hotel São Salvador* (☎ 222-7731) has singles/doubles for US$5/10 without bath and doubles with bath for US$12. The *Hotel Continental* (☎ 201-7944), at Avenida Paraná 241, in the centre, is clean, friendly and not too noisy, and some of its rooms have little balconies. Fifties-style apartamentos are a good deal at US$13/20.

Places to Eat

For lunch, *Vida Campestre Natural*, at Rua Afonso Pena 774, has good, cheap, natural food. The *Dragon Centre* is a reasonable Chinese restaurant close to Praça Sete, at Afonso Pena 549.

Getting There & Away

Air Belo Horizonte is connected to Rio and São Paulo by frequent VASP/Cruzeiro/Transbrasil *ponte aerea* (air bridge) flights. There are also daily flights to most other major cities in Brazil.

Bus Buses will take you to Rio (US$10, seven hours), São Paulo (US$12, 9½ hours), Brasília (US$18, 12 hours) and Salvador (US$32, about 22 hours). There are hourly departures for Ouro Prêto (US$4, 1¾ hours), and daily buses to Mariana (US$4.50, two hours), Diamantina (US$8, 5½ hours) and São João del Rei (US$5, 3½ hours).

CONGONHAS

Little is left of Congonhas' colonial past, except for Aleijadinho's extraordinary statues of the 12 prophets. For these alone, the town warrants a visit, but it's not worth staying here. With an early start, you can go by bus from São João del Rei to Congonhas, spend a few hours at the 12 Prophets, then go on to Conselheiro Lafaiete and Ouro Prêto (or vice versa), all in one day.

The 12 Prophets

Aleijadinho, the son of a Portuguese architect and a Black slave, lived from 1730 to 1814. He lost the use of his hands and legs at the age of 30, but with hammer and chisel strapped to his arms, he advanced Brazilian sculpture from the excesses of the baroque to a finer, more graceful rococo. The 12 Prophets, in front of the Basílica do Bom Jesus do Matosinhos, are his masterwork.

Getting There & Away

There are six buses daily from Belo Horizonte to Congonhas (US$4, 1¾ hours). The last return bus to Belo Horizonte leaves Congonhas at 8 pm. Buses leave every half-hour for Conselheiro Lafaiete. From there, you can catch the midnight bus to Rio. To get from Congonhas to Ouro Prêto, you can go to Belo Horizonte or make a connection in Conselheiro Lafaiete.

There are no direct buses from Congonhas to São João del Rei, so catch a local or a Conselheiro Lafaiete bus to the turn-off at Murtinho. From the Petrobras station there, known as Posto Queluz, catch a bus either direct to São João or to Lagoa Dourada, from where there are frequent buses to São João.

OURO PRÊTO

Vila Rica, the predecessor of Ouro Prêto, was founded in 1711, in the early days of the gold rush, and became the capital of Minas Gerais in 1721. At the height of the boom, in the mid-18th century, Ouro Prêto had a population of 110,000 and was the richest city in the New World.

As the boom declined, the miners found it more and more difficult to pay the ever-

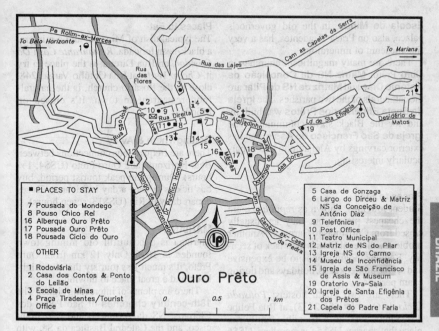

PLACES TO STAY

7 Pousada do Mondego
8 Pouso Chico Rei
16 Alberque Ouro Prêto
17 Pousada Ouro Prêto
18 Pousada Ciclo do Ouro

OTHER

1 Rodoviária
2 Casa dos Contos & Ponto do Leilão
3 Escola de Minas
4 Praça Tiradentes/Tourist Office
5 Casa de Gonzaga
6 Largo do Dirceu & Matriz NS da Conceição de António Diaz
9 Telefônica
10 Post Office
11 Teatro Municipal
12 Matriz de NS do Pilar
13 Igreja NS do Carmo
14 Museu da Inconfidência
15 Igreja de São Francisco de Assis & Museum
19 Oratorio Vira-Saia
20 Igreja de Santa Efigénia dos Prêtos
21 Capela do Padre Faria

Ouro Prêto

0   0.5   1 km

increasing gold taxes exacted by the Portuguese crown. In 1789, the Inconfidência Mineira, an attempt to overthrow the Portuguese, was crushed in its early stages.

By decree of Emperor Dom Pedro I, Vila Rica became the Imperial City of Ouro Prêto. In 1897, the state capital moved from Ouro Prêto to Belo Horizonte, thus preserving Ouro Prêto's colonial flavour. It's now a university town.

Orientation

Praça Tiradentes, a few blocks down from the rodoviária on the main road, is the town centre. The town is very hilly and the rain-slicked, cobblestone streets are steep – bring good walking shoes.

Information

The tourist office, Praça Tiradentes 41, is open from 8 am to 6 pm on weekdays, and from 8 am to 5 pm on weekends. The friendly staff speaks English, provides leaflets, sells maps and arranges guides.

To pack in a lot of sightseeing with little effort, hire an official guide (US$25 for a full-day tour) at the tourist office. Cássio is one who speaks excellent English and really knows his baroque. Beware of unofficial guides: there are some nasty characters hanging around.

If you plan to spend only one day in Ouro Prêto, make sure it's not a Monday, when virtually everything is closed!

Things to See

To see the town properly, you'll need a couple of days. Keep quirky opening times in mind when planning your itinerary.

The **Museu da Inconfidência**, on Praça Tiradentes, was formerly the municipal building and jail. It contains Tiradentes' tomb, documents of the Inconfidência Mineira, torture instruments and important works by Ataíde and Aleijadinho. The

Escola de Minas, in the old governor's palace, also on Praça Tiradentes, has a very fine museum of mineralogy.

There are many magnificent churches in Ouro Prêto. **Matriz NS da Conceição de António Dias** and **Matriz de NS do Pilar** are the cathedrals of the two parishes. The **Igreja de Santa Efigênia dos Prêtos** was built by and for the Black slave community. The **Igreja de São Francisco de Assis** also has exterior carvings by Aleijadinho and is particularly interesting.

Places to Stay

Student lodgings, known as *repúblicas*, are the cheapest places, but they are usually closed from Christmas to Carnaval. Another problem with repúblicas is their lack of security. Regular lodging tends to be expensive and scarce on weekends, holidays and during exam periods.

There are two youth hostels: *Pousada Ciclo do Ouro* (☎ 551-2433), at Rua Felipe dos Santos 241, is a friendly, family-run place that charges US$5 for members, US$6 for others. *Ouro Prêto* (☎ 551-3170), at Rua das Merces 136, is very close to Igreja NS das Mercês and Praça Tiradentes.

A good pousada is the *Pousada Ouro Prêto* (☎ 551-3081), Largo Musicista José das Anjos Costa 72. It's a friendly place, run by Gerson, who speaks English. It has a good view, and all the comforts that delight the traveller. They charge US$5 per person for quartos, a bit more for apartamentos. Gerson also runs another pousada nearby. The rooms are better but don't have the view.

For more comfort, try *Pouso Chico Rei* (☎ 551-1274), Rua Brigideiro Mosqueira 90, which has wonderful doubles completely furnished in antiques (US$44 with bath, US$30 without). If you're lucky, there's one single room (US$13). Reserve way in advance. For a splurge, try *Pousada do Mondego* (☎ 551-2040), Largo do Coimbra 38, close to Igreja São Francisco. It's in an 18th-century colonial mansion. Singles/doubles cost US$65/75, a bit more if you want the view.

Places to Eat

The typical dish of Minas is tutu a mineira, a black-bean feijoada. *Restaurante Casa Do Ouvidor*, on Rua Direita, is the place to try it. *Cheiro Verde*, at Rua Getúlio Vargas 248, close to the Rosário church, is the natural-food restaurant in town. It's closed on Mondays.

Getting There & Away

There are frequent bus connections between Belo Horizonte and Ouro Prêto (US$4, 1¾ hours). During the peak tourist period, buy bus tickets at least a day in advance. Buses depart daily to Rio (US$13, seven hours).

MARIANA

Mariana is a beautiful old mining town founded in 1696. Only 12 km from Ouro Prêto, it's much less touristy than its neighbour, and a great place to unwind.

There are plenty of interesting sights. The **18th-century churches** of São Pedro dos Clérigos, NS da Assunção and São Francisco, and the Catedral Basílica da Sé, with its fantastic German organ dating from 1701, are all worthwhile. The **museum** at Casa Capitular is also worth a look. Walking through the old part of town, you'll come across painters and wood sculptors at work in their studios.

Places to Stay & Eat

Hotel Providência (☎ 557-1444), Rua Dom Silveiro 233, is an interesting cheapie. Originally the living quarters for nuns, who still run a school next door, it also has an excellent swimming pool. Quartos are US$7 per person, apartamentos US$9. *Hotel Central* (☎ 557-1630), Rua Frei Durão 8, is a real budget hotel, with quartos for US$4/7 a single/double. The best hotel in town is the *Pouso da Typographia* (☎ 557-1577), at Praça Gomes Freire 220. Singles/doubles cost US$30/50, but discounts are available during the week.

Portão da Praça, on Praça Gomes Freire 108, serves excellent regional food and tasty Sirio/Lebanese sandwiches. *Papinna Della*

Nonna, at Rua Dom Viçoso 27, is Mariana's Italian restaurant.

Getting There & Away
A bus leaves Ouro Prêto for Mariana every half-hour from the far side of the School of Mineralogy. The trip takes 15 minutes. There are direct buses from Mariana to Belo Horizonte.

SÃO JOÃO DEL REI
Unlike many of the other historic cities in Minas Gerais, São João del Rei has not been frozen in time. The old central section, with its fine churches and colonial mansions, is surrounded by a small but thriving modern city.

The city is sandwiched between two hills, both of which provide excellent views, particularly at sunset. The tourist information office is in the Terminal Turistico, in Praça Antonio Vargas. It's open from 6 am to 6 pm.

Things to See
The exquisite baroque **Igreja de São Francisco de Assis** looks out on a lyre-shaped plaza lined with palm trees. This church was Aleijadinho's first complete project, though much of his plan was not realised. It is open from 8.30 am to noon and 1.30 to 9 pm. The **Igreja de NS do Carmo** was also designed by Aleijadinho. In the second sacristy is a famous unfinished Christ. The church is open from 4 to 7 pm. The **Catedral de NS do Pilar** has exuberant gold altars and fine Portuguese azulejos. It's open from 7 to 11 am and 2 to 4 pm. Make sure to take a walk at night, when floodlights illuminate the churches.

One of the best museums in Minas Gerais is the **Museu Regional do SPHAN**, a well-restored, 1859 colonial mansion which has good sacred art on the first two floors and an industrial section on the 3rd floor. It's open from noon to 5.30 pm daily, except Mondays.

A must for train freaks is the **Museu Ferroviário**, in the train station. This expertly renovated railway museum houses a wealth of artefacts and information about the old train days of the late 19th century. Don't forget to walk down the track to the large roundhouse; it houses the trains and is the best part of the museum. The museum is open Tuesday to Sunday from 8 am to 5 pm, though it's sometimes closed for lunch. Entry costs US$0.50. See also the discussion of the Maria Fumaça train under the Getting There & Away section below.

Festivals
The **Semana da Inconfidência**, from 15 to 21 April, celebrates Brazil's first independence movement and the local boys who led it. São João also has a very lively Carnaval.

Places to Stay & Eat
The *Hotel Brasil* (☎ 371-2804), at Avenida Presidente Tancredo Neves 395, is a former grand hotel, and a real bargain at US$3 a single.

The historic *Hotel Colonial* (☎ 371-1792) is clean, if a bit funky, and very colonial. Rooms without bath go for US$5 a person, and most have a view of the river.

For a splurge, try the *Pousada Casarão* (☎ 371-1224), at Rua Ribeiro Bastos 94. It's an elegant Minas mansion converted into an exquisite pousada, complete with swimming pool. Singles/doubles cost US$25/35.

Pizzeria Primus, at Rua Arthur Bernardes 97, has good pizza (try the primus special). It's open late. For regional cooking, try *Restaurante Rex*, at Rua Arthur Bernardes 137, or *Quinto do Ouro*, at Praça Severiano de Resende 4. For a vegetarian lunch and a good juice, *Opção Saudavel*, Avenida Tiradentes 792, has a set menu, but order at least an hour in advance, because they bring the food from home. On the same street, *Zoti* is a lively late-night place for beer and light meals.

Getting There & Away
Bus Buses leave Rio direct for São João three times daily (US$7, five hours). There are eight buses a day from São João to Belo Horizonte via Lagoa Dourada. For bus services to Belo Horizonte and Congonhas, see

the respective Getting There & Away sections.

Train Chugging along at 25 km/h on the steam-powered Maria Fumaça down a picturesque stretch of track from São João to Tiradentes makes a great half-hour train ride. The line has operated nonstop since 1881 with the same Baldwin locomotives and is in perfect condition, after being restored. The train runs only on Friday, Saturday, Sunday and holidays, leaving São João at 10 am and 2.15 pm and returning from Tiradentes at 1 and 5 pm. This schedule often changes, so it's best to double-check. Arrive early to buy your ticket (US$2.50). Going to Tiradentes, sit on the left-hand side for a better view.

Getting Around

From the small bus stop in front of the train station, catch the yellow local bus for the 10-minute ride to the rodoviária. You can also take a taxi for US$4. To catch a bus to the Terminal Turístico from the rodoviária, go to the bus stop on your left as you leave the rodoviária – don't go to the more obvious one directly in front of the exit.

TIRADENTES

This very pretty town, 10 km down the valley from São João del Rei, has changed little over the last two centuries. The Secretaria de Turismo, at Rua Resende Costa 71, provides maps and gives information about guides and walks in the mountains of Serra de São José.

Things to See & Do

Named after the town's patron saint, the **Igreja Matriz de Santo António** stands on top of the hill. There are two bell towers, and a frontispiece by Aleijadinho, who also made the sundial in front of the church. The church is open from 8 am to 6 pm but usually closes from noon to 1 pm for lunch.

The **Museu do Padre Toledo** is dedicated to another hero of the Inconfidência, Padre Toledo, who lived in this 18-room house where the *inconfidêntes* used to meet. The

museum features regional antiques and documents from the 18th century.

From Tiradentes, it's a three-km walk (25 minutes) to Mãe d'Agua, at the base of the **Serra de São José**, which are renowned for their untouched segments of Atlantic rainforest. Other walks include A Calçada (a stretch of the old road that linked Ouro Prêto with Rio de Janeiro), Cachoeiras do Mangue (the falls where you can see an old gold mine on the road made by slaves) and Cachoeira do Bom Despacho (a waterfall on the Tiradentes-Santa Cruz road). Each of these takes about four or five hours. A seven-hour walk will allow you to cross the range. For guides, and information about walks into the mountains, ask at the tourist office.

Places to Stay

Tiradentes has lots of good but expensive pousadas and only a few cheap places. If you can't find anything within your budget, ask around for homes to stay in, or commute from São João del Rei. Try to avoid staying here on the weekend, as it gets crowded and the prices quoted below double.

Pousada do Laurito is the best cheapie in town, with a good central location and singles/doubles for US$6/12. Next to the bus station, *Pousada Tiradentes* (☎ 355-1232) has charm and costs US$8/15. *Quatro Encantos*(☎ 355-1202), near the Santo Antônio church, has a great little garden and charges around US$10/20. The *Porão Colonial* (☎ 355-1251) and the *Pousada Maria Barbosa* (☎ 355-1227) are both near the train station, have pools and charge around US$14/28.

Getting There & Away

The best approach to Tiradentes is by train from São João del Rei (see the section on that city for details). Buses come and go between São João and Tiradentes every 40 minutes (slightly less frequently on weekend afternoons).

SÃO TOMÉ DAS LETRAS

São Tomé das Letras is a small village in a beautiful mountainous region in southern

Minas, 310 km from Belo Horizonte. The name refers to inscriptions in some of the local caverns. These have inspired strange stories of flying saucers, extraterrestrials, a subterranean passageway to Machu Picchu, and so on. This is also a beautiful mountain region, with great walks and several waterfalls.

Places to Stay & Eat
São Tomé has grown a lot in the last few years, so there are lots of pousadas. They all charge US$4 to US$8 per person, but not all provide breakfast. Spotlessly clean is *Pensão Dona Célia* (☎ 244), Rua Joaquim José Mendes Peixoto 11. *Pousada Arco Iris* (☎ 215), Rua João Batista Neves 19, is popular with travellers. Just up the road, *Pousada Serra Branca* is one that does provide breakfast. Near the bus stop in the main square is *Pousada Por do Sul*, very simple and one of the cheapest. There's a youth hostel 20 metres up behind the stone church to the right, and you can camp at Gruta do Leão, which supposedly has enchanted water.

Bar das Letras serves a good prato feito and *Bar do Gê* is a surprisingly good restaurant.

Getting There & Away
The town is best reached from Três Corações, 38 km to the west. Buses leave at 3.30 pm Monday to Saturday. São Tomé das Letras can also be reached from Caxambu, 60 km to the south, but not by local bus.

DIAMANTINA
Diamantina boomed when diamonds were discovered in the 1720s, after the gold finds in Minas. The diamonds are gone, but fine colonial mansions and excellent hiking in the surrounding mountains still draw visitors.

The house of Padre Rolim, one of the Inconfidêntes, is now the **Museu do Diamante** (Diamond Museum) and houses furniture, coins, instruments of torture and other relics of the diamond days. It's open from noon to 6 pm (closed on Mondays). The

Igreja NS do Carmo, built in 1758, is the most opulent church in the town.

Places to Stay & Eat
The *Hotel Nosson* (☎ 931-1565), opposite the bus terminal, is friendly and cheap (US$4 per person), but when returning from the centre, it's a long uphill walk back. For a bit extra, the *Hotel Dália* (☎ 931-1477), at Praça Juscelino Kubitschek 25, is much better. It's in a nice old building in a good location, almost next door to the diamond museum. Quartos cost US$8/16 for singles/doubles and apartamentos go for US$10/20.

Popular pick of Diamantina's eateries is the *Cantinha do Marinho*, in Beco do Motta, which has good mineiro dishes. Try their frango com quiabo. *Restaurante Grupiara*, at Rua Campos Carvalho 12, is also recommended.

Getting There & Away
There are five buses running daily between Diamantina and Belo Horizonte (US$8, five hours).

PARQUE NACIONAL DE CAPARAÓ
This park, containing the highest mountains in southern Brazil, is popular with climbers and hikers. The panoramic views are superb and the major peaks can all be reached via a good network of trails within the park. Climbing gear isn't necessary. The park retains a few lush remnants of mata atlântica and wildlife, such as opossums, spider monkeys and eagles. The best time to visit the park is between June and August. Although these are the coldest months, the days are clear. Bring warm clothes! The park is open daily from 7 am to 5 pm and costs US$0.50 to enter. Make sure you pick up a map.

Places to Stay
There are two official camp sites inside the park: Tronqueira, eight km from the park entrance, and Terreirão, a further 4½ km and halfway to the summit of Pico da Bandeira. Camping costs US$2 a night. It's a good idea to reserve a site about a week before you

arrive – ring IBAMA in Belo Horizonte (☎ 33-5661). If you don't have a tent, the nearest place to stay is the *Caraparó Park Hotel* (☎ 741-2559), one km from the park entrance. It's a pleasant, friendly place, but on the expensive side, with singles/doubles for US$35/55. For cheaper rooms try the *Dormitório da Dona Manita*, in Alto do Caparaó, the village closest to the park.

Getting There & Away

Caparaó can be reached via Belo Horizonte or Vitória, in Espírito Santo. You'll need to catch a bus to the town of Manhumirim and then another local bus to Alto do Caparaó, a further 25 km away.

Unfortunately, the bus timetables work against the budget traveller. There are two buses a day to Manhumirim from both Belo Horizonte and Vitória. The trip from either takes around five hours. To avoid staying in Manhumirim, catch one of the many buses going to Presidente Soares and ask to be dropped off at the Caparaó turn-off, then hitch the rest of the way. If you can afford a taxi from Manhumirim to Alto do Caparaó, expect to pay US$10 to US$20.

São Paulo State

São Paulo is the richest state in South America – the industrial engine that powers Brazil's economy: 30 of Brazil's 50 largest companies are in São Paulo, as is 50% of the nation's industry.

SÃO PAULO CITY

With over 19 million inhabitants, the city of São Paulo is South America's biggest. Its extraordinary growth over the past century has been boosted by migration from inside and outside Brazil, encouraged by the area's industrial development. Rapid growth has created massive problems, including traffic congestion, pollution and shortage of housing.

Orientation

São Paulo is a difficult city in which to orient yourself. The solution is to go underground – São Paulo's subway system (metro) is one of the best in the world (and it's cheap).

If you are staying for a while, buy the *Guia Caroplan*, a street guide with an extensive English section, or *Guia São Paulo*, by Quatro Rodas, which has street maps and hotel and restaurant listings.

Information

Tourist Offices The city's tourist information booths have excellent city and state maps, as well as *São Paulo This Month* – a monthly entertainment guide with an English section. They are also good for bus and metro information. The information booth on Praça da República (along Avenida Ipiranga) is very helpful; it's open daily from 9 am to 6 pm. The phone number for the main tourism office is ☎ 267-2122, ext 627 or 581.

Other tourist offices are found at Praça da Sé (in front of the Sé metro station entrance, open from 9 am to 6 pm), Praça da Liberdade (in front of Liberdade metro station entrance, open from 9 am to 6 pm), Teatro Municipal (open on weekends from 10 am to 4 pm) and Avenida São Luis (on the corner of Praça Dom José Gaspar, open from 9 am to 6 pm daily).

Money There are several travel agencies and casas de câmbio across from the airline offices on Avenida São Luis, close to Praça da República. Most banks in this area have foreign-exchange counters.

American Express/Kontik-Franstur (☎ 259-4211) is at Rua Marconi (1st floor). They close for mail pick-up from noon to 2 pm.

Post & Telecommunications The main post office is on Praça do Correio. The Posta Restante downstairs holds mail for 30 days. Fax services are available in the same building. The Telesp long-distance telephone office is close to Praça da República, on the Ipiranga side.

Visa Extensions For visa extensions, the Polícia Federal office is on the 1st floor at Avenida Prestes Maia 700. It's open from 10 am to 4 pm.

Bookshops For a good selection of English books, visit the Book Centre at Rua Gabus Mendes 29 (near Praça da República), or Livraria Cultura at Avenida Paulista 2073.

Emergency Deatur (☎ 231-0044), the English-speaking tourist police service, has two offices in the city: Avenida São Luis 115 and Rua 15 de Novembro. They're not open on weekends. For serious health problems, Einstein Hospital (☎ 845-1233) is one of the best in Latin America.

Dangers & Annoyances Pickpockets and bag-snatchers are common around Praça da Sé – don't carry valuables.

Things to See

The **Museu de Arte de São Paulo** (MASP) is at Avenida Paulista 1578. It has a good collection of European art and some great Brazilian paintings. The museum is open from 1 to 5 pm Tuesday to Friday, and from 2 to 6 pm on weekends. Go early, as the light can be very bad late in the day. To get there, take the metro to Paraiso station, then change for Trianon.

There's lots to do in the **Parque do Ibirapuera**. You can visit several museums, including Museu de Arte Contemporânea (Contemporary Art Museum) and Museu de Arte Modern (Modern Art Museum). There is also a planetarium and a Japanese pavilion. Take the metro to the Ana Rosa station, then catch Monções bus 675-C.

At the **Butantã Snake Farm & Museum**, you can watch the snakes being milked to make serum. Open Tuesday to Saturday from 9 am to 4.45 pm, the farm and museum are at Avenida Vital Brasil 1500. Take the No 702-U bus marked 'Butantã-USP' from in front of the tourist booth at Praça da República.

Places to Stay

Sampa City (☎ 288-1592), at Rua dos Franceses 100, is a well-located youth hostel, reasonably close to Avenida Paulista and Rua 13 de Maio. In a spacious old house, this is a good alternative to hotels in the centre. The cost is US$5 for members, and breakfast is available for US$2.

The budget hotel area is between the Luz metro station and the Praça da República. There are dozens of cheap hotels on Rua dos Andradas, Rua Santa Efigênia and the streets that intersect them from Avenida Ipiranga to Avenida Duque de Caxias. This area is seedy at night, and the cheapest hotels often double as brothels. Those listed here do not.

The *Pauliceía Hotel* (☎ 220-9733), Rua Timbiras 216 (at the corner of Santa Efigênia), is a very good deal, and is clean and safe. Single/double quartos go for US$4/8. Apartments cost US$7/9. The *Galeão Hotel* (☎ 220-8211), at Rua dos Gusmões 394, is excellent. It's really a mid-range hotel (apartments start at US$13), but it has cheap quartos (US$5 per person).

In the pedestrian part of Avenida São João, between the post office and Largo de Paissandu, are three relatively cheap places – the *Municipal Hotel* (☎ 228-7833), at No 354, the *Britannia Hotel* (☎ 222-9244), at No 300, and the *Hotel Central* (☎ 222-3044), at No 288. The Municipal has quartos from US$12 and apartamentos from US$15 a single. The Britannia has single/double quartos for US$8/10 and apartamentos for US$12/15. The Central is around the same price.

On the other side of Praça da República, in Avenida Vieira de Carvalho, are a couple of slightly more expensive favourites. *Hotel Itamarati* (☎ 222-4133), at No 150, is a well-kept old place, with clean rooms and helpful management. Single/double quartos are US$10/12, apartamentos a couple of dollars more. The *Hotel Amazonas* (☎ 220-4111) is in a great spot, at the corner where Avenida Vieira de Carvalho meets the Praça da República. With lots of wood panelling, this one is a fine mid-range choice. Singles/

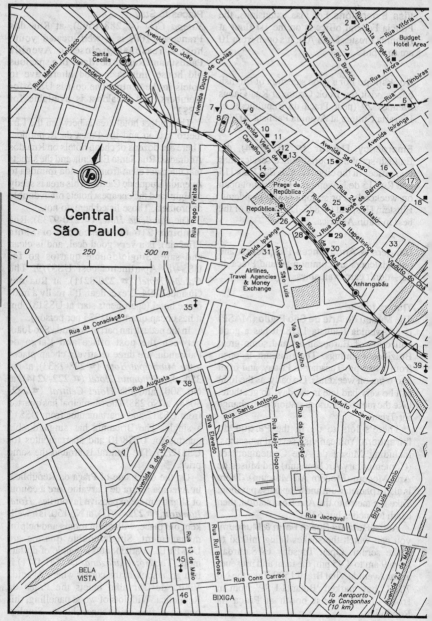

Central
São Paulo

Praça da
República

República

Airlines,
Travel Agencies
& Money
Exchange

Anhangabaú

Budget
Hotel Area

BELA
VISTA

BIXIGA

To Aeroporto
de Congonhas
(10 km)

0   250   500 m

BRAZIL

Rua Martim Francisco
Rua Frederico Abranches
Santa
Cecilia
Avenida São João
Avenida Duque de Caxias
Rua Santa Efigênia
Rua Vitória
Avenida Rio Branco
Rua Aurora
Rua Timbiras
Avenida Ipiranga
Avenida São João
Rua 24 de Barros
Rua Barão de Itapetininga
Rua José de Barros
Rua Dom José de Itapetininga
Viaduto do Chá
Rua 7 de Abril
Avenida Vieira de Carvalho
Rua Rego Freitas
Avenida Ipiranga
Avenida São Luis
Via 9 de Julho
Rua da Consolação
Rua Augusta
Silva Elevado
Avenida 9 de Julho
Rua Santo Antonio
Rua Major Diogo
Rua da Abolição
Viaduto Jacarei
Brig Luiz Antonio
Rua Jaceguai
Rua 13 de Maio
Rua Rui Barbosa
Rua Cons Carrao
Avenida 23 de Maio

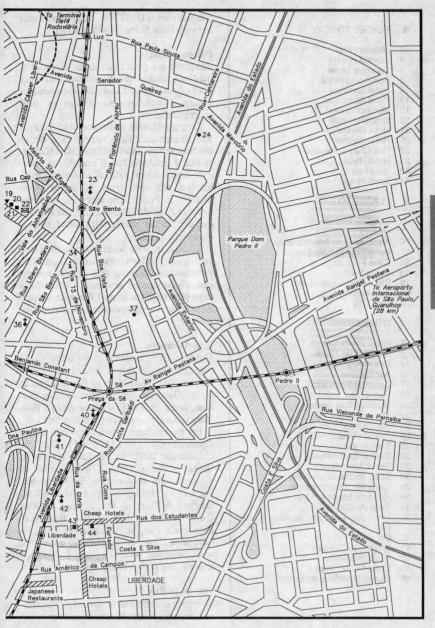

To Terminal
Tietê
Rodoviária

Luz

Rua Paula Souza

Avenida

Senador

Queiroz

Rua Cantareira

Avenida do Estado

Avenida Mercúrio

Avenida Cásper Líbero

Viaduto Sta Efigênia

Rua Florêncio de Abreu

● 24

Rua Cap

23
✞

19
20
22
27

São Bento

Vale do Anhangabaú

Rua Líbero Badaró

Rua São Bento

34
✞

Rua Boa Vista

Parque Dom
Pedro II

Rua 15 de Novembro

37 ●

Avenida do Estado

Avenida Exterior

36
✞

Avenida Rangel Pestana

To Aeroporto
Internacional
de São Paulo/
Guarulhos
(28 km)

Benjamin Constant

Sé

Av Rangel Pestana

Pedro II

Praça da Sé

40
✞

Rua Anita Garibaldi

Rua Visconde de Parnaíba

Dna Paulina

41
✞

Rua Liberdade

Rua da Glória

Rua Cons

Costa E Silva

42
✞

Cheap Hotels

Rua dos Estudantes

43
44

Furtado

Costa E Silva

Liberdade

Rua Américo

de Campos

Cheap
Hotels

LIBERDADE

Avenida do Estado

Japanese
Restaurants

BRAZIL

■ PLACES TO STAY

2   Galeão Hotel
4   Luanda Hotel
5   Pauliceía Hotel
6   San Remo Hotel
10 Hotel Itamarati
13 Hotel Amazonas
18 Municipal Hotel
20 Britannia Hotel
21 Hotel Central
25 Hotel Joamar
27 Hotel São Sebastião
29 Hotel Rivoli
43 Isei Hotel
44 Ikeda Hotel

▼ PLACES TO EAT

3   Lanches Aliados
7   Dinho's Place
9   Arroz de Ouro (macrobiotic)
11 Baby-Beef Rubaiyat
12 Casa Ricardo
16 Ponto Chic
19 Bar e Restaurante Leão
30 Viva Melhor
38 Ca'd'Oro

OTHER

1   Igreja Santa Cecília
8   Mercado de Flores
14 Bus to Airports
15 Bar Brahma
17 Largo de Paissandu
22 Post Office
23 Mosteiro São Bento
24 Mercado Municipal
26 Tourist Information Booth
28 Telesp (Telephone)
31 Edifício Italia
32 Deatur Tourist Police
33 Teatro Municipal
34 State Tourist Information
35 Igreja NS de Consolação
36 Igreja de Santo Antonio
37 Patío do Colégio
39 Igreja São Francisco de Assis & Law
    Faculty
40 Catedral
41 Igreja São Gonçalo
42 Igreja das Almas
45 Igreja NS Achiropita
46 Museu Memórias do Bixiga

doubles start at US$22/26. Both these hotels are very close to the airport bus stop.

Places to Eat

São Paulo is a great place to eat. Because of the city's ethnic diversity, you can find every kind of cuisine, and there are thousands of cheap lanchonetes, pizzerias and churrascarias.

Lanches Aliados, on the corner of Avenida Rio Branco and Rua Vitória, is a cheap lanchonete with excellent food. *Viva Melhor*, at Rua 7 de Abril 264 (Centro), has some excellent, cheap natural and vegetarian lunches. It's open from 11 am to 4 pm Monday to Friday. The *Bar e Restaurante Leão*, at Avenida São João 320, has all-you-can-eat Italian meals with salad bar, at reasonable prices.

Nearby, in Bela Vista district, there are two good Italian restaurants on Rua Avanhandava: *Gigetto* and *Famiglia Mancini*. The prices are moderate – US$4 for a large plate of pasta. In the Liberdade district, there are lots of inexpensive Oriental restaurants.

Entertainment

The best list of events is in the weekly *Veja* magazine, which has a special São Paulo edition. Rua 13 de Maio in Bixiga hums at night. There are several clubs and restaurants, and even a revival movie theatre. Bela Vista is another good area for nightlife.

For the best jazz in town, try Café Teatro Opus 2004 (☎ 256-9591), Rua da Consolação 2004. At the Luar do Sertão (Sertão Moonlight), you'll find the music of the sertão and the dances of the North-east. For a 1940s atmosphere, go to Riviera Restaurant & Bar, at the corner of Rua Consolacão and Avenida Paulista. Finnegan's Pub, at Alameda Itú 1541, in Cerqueira César, is the place to go if you want to speak some English. Paulistanos know it as a gringo bar, and it gets lively.

Things to Buy

Shopping is almost as important to Paulistanos as eating out. Much more interesting than the endless shopping malls are the many markets and fairs that take place around town, especially on weekends. One of the most popular is held in the Praça da República, on Sundays from 8 am to 2 pm. Liberdade, the Oriental district (only five minutes from the centre by metro), also has a big street fair all day on Sundays.

Getting There & Away

Air From São Paulo, there are flights to everywhere in Brazil and to many of the world's major cities. Before buying your ticket, be sure to check from which airport the flight departs – see the Getting Around section for details. The São Paulo to Rio shuttle flies at least every half-hour from Congonhas airport into Santos Dumont airport, in central Rio. The flight takes less than an hour, and you can usually go to the airport, buy a ticket and be on a plane within the hour.

Most of the major airlines have offices on Avenida São Luis, near the Praça da República. Varig/Cruzeiro (☎ 231-9244) is at Rua da Consolação 362, Transbrasil (☎ 259-7066) is at Avenida São Luis 250 and VASP (☎ 220-3622) is at Rua Libero Badaró 106.

Bus Terminal Tietê is easy to reach – it's connected to the Tietê metro station – but it can be hard to find your way around. There's an information desk in the middle of the main concourse on the 1st floor, but only Portuguese is spoken. Bus tickets are sold on the 1st floor, except for the Rio shuttle bus, which has its ticket offices on the ground floor, at the rear of the building.

Buses leave for destinations throughout Brazil, and there are also buses to major cities in Argentina, Paraguay, Chile and Uruguay.

All the following buses leave from the Terminal Tietê. Frequent buses traverse the Via Dutra highway to Rio (429 km, six hours). The cost is US$9 for the regular bus, US$16 for the leito. There are also buses to Brasília (US$22, 16 hours), Belo Horizonte (US$12, 9½ hours), Foz do Iguaçu (US$20,

15 hours), Cuiabá (US$28, 24 hours), Campo Grande (US$19, 15 hours), Salvador (US$40, 33½ hours), Curitiba (US$8, six hours) and Florianópolis (US$15, 12 hours).

Buses to Santos, Guarujá and São Vicente leave every five minutes from a separate bus station at the end of the southern metro line (Jabaquara station). Buses to southern Minas leave from Rodoviária Bresser – take the metro to Bresser.

Train Long-distance trains leave for Bauru (connections to Campo Grande and Corumbá) from Estação da Luz train station. To get there, take the metro to the Luz station. Cuts in long-distance routes continue, so check details at the information booth (☎ 991-3062) at Luz station. At present, to connect with the Bauru-Campo Grande train (departing Bauru every Tuesday and Friday at 11 am), you need to take the São Paulo-Bauru train which departs on Monday and Thursday at 11 pm. You'll arrive in Bauru at 6.30 am.

Getting Around

To/From the Airport Three airports serve São Paulo: Aeroporto de Congonhas (14 km south of the centre), Aeroporto Internacional de São Paulo/Guarulhos (30 km east of the centre) and Aeroporto Viracopos (100 km from the centre, near Campinas).

At Congonhas, avoid the radio-taxis at the front of the terminal and ask for the comuns (regular taxis); there's a small sign marking the place. The ride into town is about US$8. To catch a bus into the city, walk out of the terminal and to your right, where you'll see a busy street with a pedestrian overpass. Head to the overpass, but don't cross; you should see a crowd of people waiting for the buses along the street, or ask for the bus marked 'Banderas'. The trip takes about an hour, and the last bus leaves around 1 am.

From Aeroporto Internacional de São Paulo/Guarulhos, there's a bus that goes to Praça da República, Terminal Tietê rodoviária and Congonhas airport. It costs US$7. For the same price, another bus does a circuit of up-market hotels in the Jardims

BRAZIL

area and the centre. To the centre, a comum taxi will cost US$20, a radio-taxi US$30.

The Aeroporto Viracopos is near Campinas. Avoid this airport if possible. A taxi from here into town will cost about US$60.

Bus Buses are slow, crowded during rush hours and not too safe. When you can, use the metro.

Metro If you're on a limited budget, a combination of metro and foot is the best way to see the city. The metro, open from 5 am to midnight, is new, cheap, safe and fast. There are currently three lines. Two intersect at Praça da Sé; the other, newer line gives access to Avenida Paulista. Tickets cost US$0.40 for a single ride, or buy a *multiplo 10*, which gives you 10 rides for US$3.

Taxi Both the comum and radio-taxi services are metered. Radio-taxis (☎ 251-1733) cost 50% more than the comums but will pick you up anywhere in the city.

ILHABELA
Ilhabela is the biggest island along the Brazilian coast, and is known for its excellent jungle hiking and fine cachaça.

During the summer, Ilhabela is besieged by holiday-makers from São Paulo. Weekdays in the off season are the time to go. Once you arrive, try to get away from the west coast, either by catching a boat or hiking. Of the sheltered beaches on the island's north side, Praia Pedra do Sino and Praia Jabacuara are recommended. On the east side, where the surf is stronger, try Praia dos Castelhanos, Praia do Gato or Praia da Figueira.

Places to Stay
There are lots of campgrounds near Barra Velha, where the ferry stops, and just a bit further south, at Praia do Curral. Try the *Hotel São Paulo* (☎ 72-1158), on Rua Dr Carvalho, for relatively inexpensive lodging (US$30/35 a single/double), or the slightly cheaper *Pousada dos Hibiscos* (☎ 72-1375), at Avenida Pedro Paula de Morais 714, with doubles for US$30.

Getting There & Away
The ferry from São Sebastião runs frequently. The service operates from 5.30 am until midnight. The ride lasts 15 minutes and is free for pedestrians.

Paraná

CURITIBA
Curitiba, the capital of Paraná, is one of Brazil's urban success stories. There's not much for the traveller, but it's possible to spend a pleasant day there waiting for your bus or train to leave.

Information
The tourist information booths at the *rodoferroviária* (long-distance bus terminal) are useless. The travel agencies are the best bet for money exchange and information. Jade is at Rua 15 de Novembre 477, and Diplomatur is at Rua Presidente Faria 143.

Things to See
Close to Praça Tiradentes and the Catedral Metropolitana, take the pedestrian tunnel and you'll be in the cobblestoned historic quarter, **Largo da Ordem**, a good place for a drink and some music at night.

Train Ride to Paranaguá
The railroad journey from Curitiba to the port of Paranaguá, descending a steep mountainside to the coastal lowlands, is the most exciting and spectacular in Brazil. Due to government cutbacks, trains run daily only from November to February and during July. At other times, they run only on weekends.

There are two types of train: a regular train *(trem)* and a tourist train *(litorina)*. The trem leaves Curitiba at 7 am and does the return trip at 4.30 pm. The air-con litorina leaves at 8.30 am and starts back at 3.30 pm. Both trains take about three hours each way. For the best view on the way down to the coast, sit on the left-hand side.

Tickets for the trem (US$3.50) and the litorina (US$8) are sold at the train station

BRAZIL

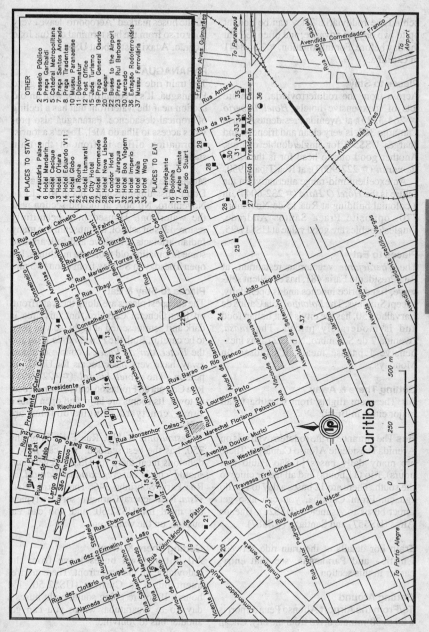

PLACES TO STAY
4 Araucária Palace
6 Hotel Mandarin
9 Hotel Cacique
11 Hotel O'Hara
14 Hotel Eduardo VII
21 Hotel Globo
25 La Rocha
26 Hotel Itamarati
27 City Hotel
28 Hotel Promenade
29 Hotel Nova Lisboa
30 Condor Hotel
31 Hotel Jaragua
32 Hotel Boa Viagem
33 Hotel Imperio
34 Hotel Mala
35 Hotel Wang

PLACES TO EAT
1 Vherdejante
16 Bolonha
17 Arabe Oriente
18 Bar do Stuart

OTHER
2 Passeio Público
3 Praça Garibaldi
5 Catedral Metropolitana
7 Praça Santos Andrade
8 Praça Tiradentes
10 Museu Paranaense
12 Diplomatur
13 Post Office
15 Jade Turismo
19 Praça General Osorio
20 Telepar
22 Buses to the Airport
23 Praça Rui Barbosa
24 Mercado
36 Estação Rodoferroviária
37 Museu Ferroviária

Curitiba

behind the rodoviária. They can be bought up to two days in advance, and often sell out the day before. For information, ☎ 234-8441 in Curitiba.

Places to Stay
Across from the rodoferroviária, there are lots of inexpensive hotels. *Hotel Imperio* (☎ 264-3373), at Avenida Presidente Afonso Camargo 367, is very clean and friendly, and charges US$5/9 for single/double quartos. Another good one to head for is the *Hotel Itamarati* (☎ 222-9063), at Rua Tibagi 950.

An excellent mid-range alternative in the centre is the *Hotel O'Hara* (☎ 232-6044), in a colonial building at Rua 15 de Novembro 770, opposite Praça Santos Andrade. Singles/doubles are good value at US$17/25.

Places to Eat
The *Vherdejante* vegetarian restaurant, at Rua Presidente Faria 481, has excellent self-serve, fixed-price lunches and is open daily, except Sundays. The *Bolonha*, Rua Carlos de Carvalho 150, has the city's best Italian food and is moderately priced. The *Yuasa*, Avenida 7 de Setembro, No 1927, has inexpensive Japanese meals; it's closed on Mondays.

Getting There & Away
Air There are flights from Curitiba to all major cities in Brazil.

Bus The entrance to the rodoferroviária is on Avenida Presidente Afonso Camargo. There are many daily buses to São Paulo (six hours), Rio (11 hours) and all major cities to the south. There are 12 buses a day to Foz do Iguaçu. From Curitiba, you can also get direct buses to Asunción (US$21), Buenos Aires (US$57) and Santiago (US$87).

Train For details of the train ride between Curitiba and Paranaguá, see that entry, earlier in this section.

Getting Around
To/From the Airport Alfonso Pena airport is a 20 to 30-minute drive from the city. Cheap

public buses marked 'Aeroporto' leave every hour or so from the bus terminal on Rua João Negrão. A taxi costs about US$13.

PARANAGUÁ
The train ride isn't the only reason to go to Paranaguá. It's a colourful city, with an old section near the waterfront that has a feeling of tropical decadence. Paranaguá also provides access to Ilha do Mel. There's a tourist information office in front of the train station.

Museu de Arquelogia e Artes Popular
Don't miss this museum, it's at Rua 15 de Novembro, No 567, in the old section near the waterfront. Housed in a beautifully restored Jesuit school, the museum has many Indian artefacts, primitive and folk art, and some fascinating old tools and machines. It's open Tuesday to Sunday from noon to 5 pm.

Places to Stay & Eat
The cheapest places are along the waterfront, on Rua General Carneiro, but this area is dark and semideserted at night, so you need to be careful. Both the *Pensão Bela Vista* and the *Hotel Mar de Roses* a couple of doors away, have very basic rooms for US$2 per person. The *Hotel Litoral* (☎ 422-0491), Rua Correia de Freitas 66, offers the best deal in town. Its rooms are large and open onto a sunny courtyard. Singles/doubles are US$4/6.

Restaurante Bobby, Rua Faria Sobrinho 750, has the best seafood. You can have a delicious meal there for US$4. Vegetarians should check out *Vegetariano Natural*, at Rua Faria Sobrinho 346. The *Pensão Bela Vista*, Rua General Carneiro, serves a typical big meal for US$2.50, and you can eat outside, on the waterfront.

Getting There & Away
All out-of-town buses leave from the rodoviária, on the waterfront. There are frequent buses to Curitiba (US$2.50, 1¾ hours). If you're going south, eight buses a day go to Guaratuba, where you can get another bus to Joinville.

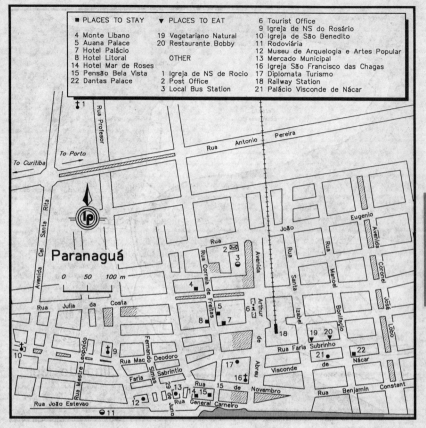

PLACES TO STAY
4 Monte Libano
5 Auana Palace
7 Hotel Palácio
8 Hotel Litoral
14 Hotel Mar de Roses
15 Pensão Bela Vista
22 Dantas Palace

PLACES TO EAT
19 Vegetariano Natural
20 Restaurante Bobby

OTHER
1 Igreja de NS de Rocio
2 Post Office
3 Local Bus Station
6 Tourist Office
9 Igreja de NS do Rosário
10 Igreja de São Benedito
11 Rodoviária
12 Museu de Arqueologia e Artes Popular
13 Mercado Municipal
16 Igreja São Francisco das Chagas
17 Diplomata Turismo
18 Railway Station
21 Palácio Visconde de Nácar

BRAZIL

For details of the train ride between Paranaguá and Curitiba, see the Curitiba section.

ILHA DO MEL

Ilha do Mel is an oddly shaped island at the mouth of the Baía de Paranaguá. It is popular in the summer because of its excellent beaches, scenic walks and relative isolation.

Ilha do Mel consists of two parts, connected by the beach at Nova Brasília. The bigger part is an ecological station, little visited except for Praia da Fortaleza. The main attractions of the island are close to Nova Brasília. Nearby, on the ocean side, are the best beaches – Praia Grande, Praia do Miguel and Praia de Fora. The best walks are along the ocean side (east), from the southern tip of the island up to Praia da Fortaleza. There are *bichos de pé*, so keep your shoes on when you're off the beach.

Places to Stay & Eat

If you arrive on the island on a holiday weekend or during peak season, rooms may be in short supply, but it's easy to rent some space to sling a hammock. There's also

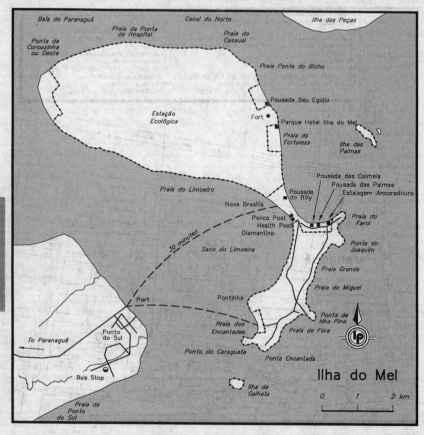

Ilha do Mel

plenty of room to camp. If you decide to sleep on the beach watch out for the tides.

There are about 10 pousadas on the island, all charging between US$5 and US$10 per night. The best one is *Estalagem Ancoradouro*, run by Arnaldo. It's out towards the lighthouse, about a 10-minute walk from the police post at the far right of Brasília, as you face the island. They also serve a good *prato feito*. About halfway between the lighthouse and the fort is *Pousada do Billy*. Although it looks like a prison camp, this is a good place to stay. It costs US$8 per person, including breakfast.

Just before you get to the fort is the island's only hotel, *Parque Hotel Ilha do Mel* (☎ 223-2585), with rooms for US$40 a night. They have a boat that will pick you up and take you directly to the hotel.

You will find *barracas* with food and drink at Encantadas, Brasília and Fortaleza. On Friday and Saturday nights, there is music and dancing. At Encantadas, Lucia is the most popular cook, and her *Bar Delirio* stays open late.

Getting There & Away
Take the 'Pontal do Sul' bus from Paranaguá.

The bus stops three km from the canal where the boats leave for Ilha do Mel. There's usually a taxi, which charges an extortionate US$3 for the five-minute ride, or you can walk.

If you decide to walk when you get off the bus, go back 20 metres to the paved main road and turn right. Follow this road for a little more than one km, until it veers right and approaches the sea. Then turn left on a sandy but well-travelled road and continue for about two km, until the end, where you'll find barracas and a couple of boats. That's it.

From December to March, boats (US$1, half an hour) make the trip to the island every hour or so between 8 am and 5 pm. The rest of the year, boats aren't as frequent, but you should have no problems finding one.

FOZ DO IGUAÇU

Obviously, people visit Foz do Iguaçu to see Iguaçu Falls. It's a frenzied, unfinished-looking town that can be dangerous, particularly at night. On the Paraguayan side of the river, Ciudad del Este is a bit better. Puerto Iguazú, in Argentina, is much more mellow. Nevertheless, most budget travellers stay in Foz because there are more places to stay and it's cheaper, so details are given here. For information about Puerto Iguazú and the falls, see the Argentina chapter.

Information

Tourist Office Teletur's downtown tourist office (☎ 139) has new quarters, on Rio Barão do Branco near Avenida Juscelino Kubitschek, open 24 hours a day. Staff members speak English and are very helpful. The telephone information service is attended from 6 am to 8 pm. There is also a helpful office at the new bus terminal.

Money Cambio Dick, at Avenida Brasil 1162, or Frontur, at Avenida Brasil 746, are recommended. These companies change both cash and travellers' cheques.

Visas Visitors who spend the day outside Brazil will not require visas, but those who intend to stay longer must go through all the formalities. In Foz do Iguaçu, the Argentine Consulate (☎ 74-2969) is at Travessa Eduardo Braneti 26 and the Paraguayan Consulate (☎ 72-1169) is at Rua Bartolomeu de Gusmão 480.

The Falls

Argentina has more of the falls than Brazil, but to see them properly, which takes at least two full days, you must visit both sides – the Brazilian park for the grand overview and the Argentine park for a closer look. The best season to see them is from August to November. From May to July, you may not be able to approach the falls on the catwalks, but the volume of water can make them even more impressive.

Places to Stay

There are three campgrounds on the Brazilian side. *Camping Club do Brasil* (☎ 74-1013) is the closest to the falls, at Rodovia das Cataratas (eight km from Foz). At Rua Rebouças 335 is the youth hostel *Vale Verde* (☎ 74-2925).

Near the old bus terminal are some cheap hotels. Two decent ones are the *Hotel NS de Aparecida* (☎ 74-5139) and *Hotel Senhor do Bonfim* (☎ 74-4540), next to each other in Travessa C, a short cul-de-sac just off Rua Almirante Barroso. They charge US$3 per person, and have fans in every room. The town's cheapest hotel with a pool is the *Ilha de Capri* (☎ 23-2300), at Rua Barão Rio do Branco 409. Singles/doubles go for US$20/24.

For a massive splurge, try *Hotel das Cataratas* (☎ 23-2266), right at the waterfalls. Singles/doubles cost US$60/70, but Brazil Air Pass holders can get a 15% discount.

Places to Eat

The best buffet deal in town is *Restaurante Calamares*, at Rua Rebouças 476. At US$3 for all you can eat, it's a good energy boost after a hard day at the falls. For Italian food, *4 Sorelle* is at Rua Almirante Barroso 650. For seafood, *Restaurante Du Cheff* is at Rua Almirante Barroso 683; it's expensive but

BRAZIL

PLACES TO STAY
- 2 Vale Verde Youth Hostel
- 4 Imperial Hotel
- 6 Minas Foz Hotel
- 7 Hotel Diplomata
- 8 Hotel NS de Aparecida & Hotel Senhor do Bonfim
- 10 Hotel Internacional Foz
- 16 Hotel Luz
- 18 Ilha do Capri

▼ PLACES TO EAT
- 5 Rafain Centro Gastronômico
- 7 Restaurante Calamares
- 11 4 Sorelle
- 12 Restaurante Du Cheff
- 13 Restaurante Pei-kin
- 15 Barbarela
- 16 Bebs

OTHER
- 1 Urban Bus Terminal to Iguaçu Falls, Argentina & Paraguay
- 3 Cambio Dick
- 9 Telefônica
- 14 Varig/Cruzeiro
- 17 Coert Artists Cooperative
- 19 Teletur Tourist Information
- 20 Local Bus to Itaipú Dam
- 21 Post Office

To Rodonária

Rua Rio de Janeiro
Rua Mato Grosso
Rua Minas Gerais
Avenida Paraná
Rua Patrulheiro Vernanto
Rua Pres. Castelo Branco

To Curitiba & São Paulo

To Paraguay & Itaipú Dam

Rua Duarte da Costa
Rua Mem de Sá
Avenida República
Rua Rebouças
Rua Xavier
Rua Najpi
Rua Tarobá
Rua da Silva
Rua Bartolomeu de Gusmão
Rua Rui
Rua Barroso
Rua Brasil
Rua Peixoto
Rua Floriano
Rua Marechal Deodoro da Fonseca
Rua Santos Dumont
Avenida Juscelino Kubitschek
Avenida Bocaiuva
Avenida Brasil
Rua Almirante Barroso
Rua Marechal
Rua Jorge Sanways
Rua Edmundo de Barros
Avenida Jorge Schimmelpfeng
Rua Barão do Rio Branco
Avenida Raposo
Rua Antônio

Av. das Cataratas

To Iguaçu Falls & Airport

To Argentina & Porto Meira

Rio Iguaçu

Foz do Iguaçu

0   250   500 m

excellent. A good churrascaria is *Búfalo Branco*, at Rua Rebouças 530.

Getting There & Away

Air There are frequent flights from Foz do Iguaçu to Asunción, Buenos Aires, Rio and São Paulo. VASP (☎ 23-2212) is at Avenida Brasil 845, Transbrasil (☎ 74-3886) is at Avenida Brasil 1225 and Varig/Cruzeiro (☎ 23-2111) is at Avenida Brasil 821.

Bus Foz's new bus terminal (☎ 22-2680) is on Avenida Costa e Silva, several km outside town, but buses from Argentina go directly there after stopping at the local bus terminal downtown. The 'Anel Viario' bus also goes there (US$0.25).

From Foz do Iguaçu, there are seven buses a day to Curitiba (US$13, 12 hours), eight to São Paulo (US$21, 15 hours) and six to Rio (US$25, 22 hours). There are several buses a day from Ciudad del Este to Asunción (US$8, seven hours).

There are three buses a day from Puerto Iguazú to Buenos Aires (US$55, 20 hours). There are 17 daily buses to Posadas (US$21, six hours).

Getting Around

To/From the Airport Catch a 'P Nacional' bus for the half-hour trip (US$0.40). The buses run every 35 minutes from 5.30 am to 7 pm, then every hour until 11.15 pm. A taxi costs US$15.

Bus All local buses leave from the urban bus terminal on Avenida Juscelino Kubitschek.

Brazilian Falls Catch a 'Cataratas' bus to get to the Brazilian side of the falls. At the park entrance, the bus waits while you get out and pay the US$1.50 entry fee. On weekdays, the first bus leaves the terminal at 8 am, and buses run every two hours until 6 pm. On weekends and public holidays, the first bus leaves the terminal at 8 am and the second at 10 am; thereafter, buses leave every hour until 6 pm. The last bus leaves the falls at 7 pm.

Argentine Falls In Foz, catch a bus to 'Puerto Iguazú' to get to the Argentine side of the falls. Buses start running at 7 am, and run every hour until 9 pm. The fare is US$1.50. In Puerto Iguazú, transfer to a 'Trans Cataratas' bus.

At the bus station in Puerto Iguazú, you can pay for everything in one go: the bus fares to and from the park, the bus to and from Puerto Canoas, entry to the park and the boat ride to Isla San Martín. The entrance fee for the park must be paid in Argentine pesos. If you only have cruzeiros, the ticket seller at the bus station will exchange the appropriate amount of cruzeiros required for the park entrance to the equivalent in pesos, which can then be paid on arrival at the park. This is the only time you'll need Argentine currency; everything else can be paid for with cruzeiros.

The 'Trans Cataratas' bus leaves every hour from 8 am to 6 pm – but not at 1 pm, which is siesta time.

Ciudad del Este From the urban terminal in Foz, buses for Ciudad del Este begin running at 7 am and leave every five minutes.

Santa Catarina

Santa Catarina is one of Brazil's most prosperous states. Most travellers come for the beaches, many of which have become 'in' vacation spots for well-to-do Brazilians and Argentines. Rapid growth is changing the coastline at an unbelievable pace, often with ugly results.

FLORIANÓPOLIS

Florianópolis, the state capital, is a modern city. The central section is on the island, facing the Baía Sul. The island side of the city is easy to get around on foot, and there are regular public buses to the island's beautiful beaches.

Information

The information desks at the rodoviária and

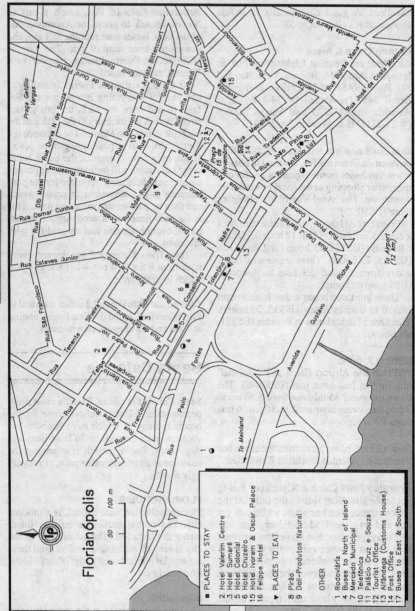

Florianópolis

0   50   100 m

PLACES TO STAY
2 Hotel Valerim Centre
3 Hotel Sumaré
5 Hotel Colonial
6 Hotel Cruzeiro
15 Hotel Ivoram & Oscar Palace
16 Felippe Hotel

PLACES TO EAT
8 Pirão
9 Doll-Produtos Natural

OTHER
1 Rodoviária
4 Buses to North of Island
7 Mercado Municipal
10 Telefônica
11 Palácio Cruz e Souza
12 Tourist Office
13 Alfândega (Customs House)
14 Post Office
17 Buses to East & South

at the airport are good for maps. The information post in Praça 15 de Novembre is also useful. Ask there for detailed maps of the walks you can do around Lagoa de Conceição.

Places to Stay

There's a good *youth hostel* (☎ 22-3781) at Rua Duarte Schutell. It's a 10-minute walk from the rodoviária.

Most of the cheap hotels are in the centre of town. The *Hotel Sumaré*, Rua Felipe Schmidt 53, is quite good but often full. It has singles/doubles for US$6/10. Also good is the *Felippe Hotel* (☎ 22-4122), a couple of blocks past Praça 15 de Novembro, at Rua João Pinto 26. They charge US$5 per person, with breakfast.

Places to Eat

There are plenty of cheap lanchonetes in town, many of which are health-food oriented; try *Doll-Produtos Natural*. *Pirão*, in the market, is popular and has live music. For a great splurge, *Macarronada Italiana*, at Avenida Rubens de Arruda Ramos 196, has some of Brazil's best pasta and formal service. It's open daily for lunch and dinner, and there's live music Monday to Wednesday at dinner.

Getting There & Away

Air There are daily direct flights to São Paulo and Porto Alegre, as well as connections to most other cities.

The airlines all have offices in the centre: Varig/Cruzeiro (☎ 24-2811) is at Rua Felipe Schmidt 34, Transbrasil (☎ 23-7177) is at Praça Pereira Oliveira 16 and VASP (☎ 22-1122) is at Rua Osmar Cunha 15.

Bus Long-distance buses travel to Porto Alegre (US$10, 7½ hours), Curitiba (US$8, five hours), São Paulo (US$15, 12 hours), Rio (US$25, 20 hours), Foz do Iguaçu (US$20, 16 hours), Buenos Aires, Argentina (US$50, 27 hours) and Montevideo, Uruguay (US$35, 21 hours).

Getting Around

To/From the Airport The airport is 12 km south of the city. A taxi costs US$8. Buses marked 'Aeroporto' shuttle regularly to the airport until 10 pm, departing from the first platform at the central rodoviária. It's a half-hour ride.

ILHA DE SANTA CATARINA

The east coast beaches are the prettiest and emptiest, and have the biggest waves. Most do not have hotels. The north coast beaches are calm, baylike and have resorts, while the west coast, facing the mainland, has great views and a quiet Mediterranean feel.

In the interior, the beautiful Lagoa da Conceição, surrounded by mountains and sand dunes, is a great place for walks or boat rides.

Getting Around

Local buses serve all of the island's beach towns, but they are infrequent and the schedule changes with the season, so it's best to get the times at the tourist office or the central rodoviária. During the tourist season, additional microbuses leave from the centre and go directly to the beaches. Unfortunately, surfboards aren't allowed on buses.

The buses for the east and south of the island leave from the local bus station, near the Felippe Hotel. Buses for the north leave from the local bus station opposite the central rodoviária.

The island is one of those places where a one-day car rental is a good idea, though fairly expensive. With a car, or on one of the bus tours offered by the travel agencies (Ponto Sul (☎ 23-0399) is a good one – US$12 for an eight-hour tour), you can see most of the island and pick a beach to settle on.

Another excursion is with Scuna-Sul (☎ 24-1806). They have a big sailboat that cruises Baía Norte for three hours for a reasonable US$10.

BRAZIL

BRAZIL

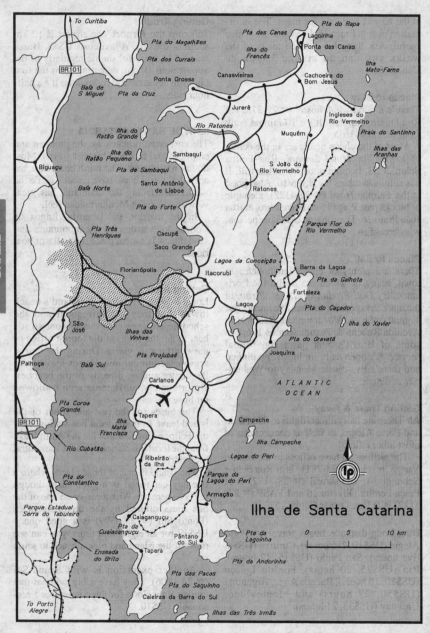

Ilha de Santa Catarina

To Curitiba

Pta do Rapa

Pta das Canas

Lagoinha

Ponta das Canas

Ilha do Francês

Pta do Magalhães

Pta dos Currais

Canasvieiras

Cachoeira do Bom Jesus

Ilha Mato-Fame

BR101

Ponta Grossa

Jurerê

Ingleses do Rio Vermelho

Baía de S Miguel

Pta da Cruz

Muquém

Praia do Santinho

Rio Ratones

Ilha do Ratão Grande

Ilhas das Aranhas

Ilha do Ratão Pequeno

Sambaqui

S João do Rio Vermelho

Biguaçu

Pta de Sambaqui

Ratones

Santo Antônio de Lisboa

Baía Norte

Pta do Forte

Parque Flor do Rio Vermelho

Pta Três Henriques

Cacupé

Saco Grande

Lagoa da Conceição

Barra da Lagoa

Florianópolis

Itacorubi

Pta da Galhota

Fortaleza

Lagoa

Pta do Caçador

São José

Ilhas das Vinhas

Ilha do Xavier

Pta do Gravatá

Palhoça

Baía Sul

Pta Pirajubaé

Joaquina

ATLANTIC OCEAN

Carianos

BR101

Pta Coroa Grande

Tapera

Ilha Maria Francisca

Campeche

Rio Cubatão

Ilha Campeche

Ribeirão da Ilha

Lagoa do Peri

Pta do Constantino

Parque da Lagoa do Peri

Parque Estadual Serra do Tabuleiro

Armação

Caiacanguçu

Pta da Cuaiacanguçu

Pântano do Sul

Pta da Lagoinha

0   5   10 km

Tapera

Pta da Andorinha

Enseada do Brito

Pta das Pacas

Pta do Saquinho

To Porto Alegre

Caieiras da Barra do Sul

Ilhas das Três Irmãs

Rio Grande do Sul

PORTO ALEGRE
Porto Alegre, capital of Rio Grande do Sul and Brazil's sixth biggest city, lies on the eastern bank of Rio Guaiba. Although most travellers just pass through Porto Alegre, it's a modern city and an easy place in which to spend a few days.

Information
Tourist Offices CRTur at Rua dos Andradas 736, on the ground floor of the Casa de Cultura Mario Quintana, is the state tourism authority. It also has branches at the airport and the bus station.

Foreign Consulates The following South American countries are represented by consulates in Port Alegre:

Argentina
    Rua Prof Annes Dias 112, 1st floor (☎ 224-6799)
Paraguay
    Quintino Bocaiuva 577, sala 805 (☎ 346-1314)
Uruguay
    Rua Siqueira Campos 1171, 6th floor (☎ 224-3499)

Things to See
A good place to see gauchos at play is the big, central **Parque Farroupilha**. On Sunday mornings, the **Brique da Redenção**, a market/fair, fills a corner of the park with antiques, leather goods and music.

Places to Stay
Youth hostel *Tchê*, at Rua Colonel Fernando Machado 681, costs US$4 per person and is a friendly place to stay, but it's a bit of a hike from the metro station.

The *Hotel Uruguai* (☎ 228-7864), Rua Dr Flores 371, is a clean, secure and cheap place to stay. They have single/double quartos for US$3/6 and apartamentos for US$4/8. Nearby, at Avenida Vigarió José Inácio 644, is the *Hotel Palácio* (☎ 225-3467), popular with travellers and very friendly. Quartos cost US$7/13 and apartamentos go for

US$10/15. An interesting place to stay is the *Hotel Praça Matriz* (☎ 225-5772), at Largo João Amorim de Albequerque 72. In an ornate old building, it costs US$12 a single and US$20 for a double with TV.

Rua Andrade Neves also has a good selection of hotels, and places to eat.

Places to Eat
Wherever you are, a juicy steak will be nearby. For sucos and sandwiches in the city, try *Fruta na Boca* in the subsolo Malcom. With an excellent US$3 buffet lunch, *Ilha Natural Restaurante Vegetariano*, Rua Andrade Neves 42, packs the locals in. For traditional gaucho cooking and a folkloric floorshow, try *Tio Flor*, Avenida Getúlio Vargas 1700. It's not too expensive and the show is well done. *Chalé da Praça XV*, on Praça 15 de Novembre, in front of the market, is the most traditional bar/restaurant in the city. *Banca 40*, at the Mercado Público, has excellent ice cream.

Getting There & Away
There are international buses to Montevideo, Uruguay (US$26, 13 hours), Buenos Aires, Argentina (US$40, 24 hours) and Asunción, Paraguay (US$36, 16 hours). Other buses run to Foz do Iguaçu (US$23, 18 hours), Florianópolis (US$10, 7½ hours), Curitiba (US$17, 11 hours), São Paulo (US$25, 18 hours) and Rio de Janeiro (US$35, 27 hours).

Getting Around
Porto Alegre has a one-line metro that goes from the city centre to the rodoviária and the airport. The central station, Estação Mercado Modelo, is by the port. The rodoviária is the next stop, and the airport is three stations further. The metro runs from 5 am to 11 pm.

CHUÍ
The small border town of Chuí is about 225 km south of Rio Grande on a good paved road. One side of Avenida Brasil, the main street, is Brazilian; the other side is the Uruguayan town of Chuy. The Uruguayan side is a good place to change some money, buy

BRAZIL

BRAZIL

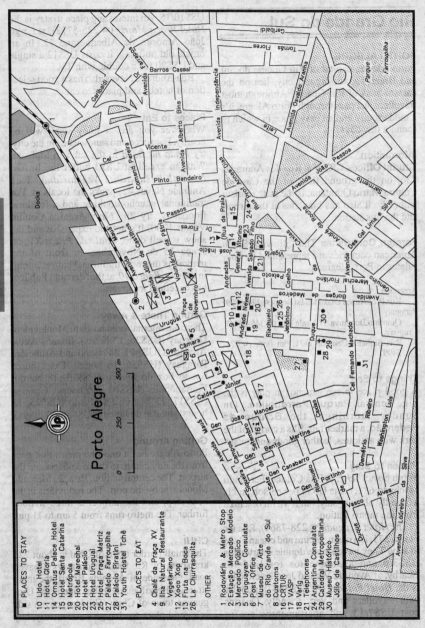

Porto Alegre

0   250   500 m

PLACES TO STAY
10 Lido Hotel
11 Hotel Glória
14 Ornatus Palace Hotel
15 Hotel Santa Catarina
19 Metrópole
20 Hotel Marechal
22 Hotel Palácio
23 Hotel Uruguai
25 Hotel Praça Matriz
27 Palácio Farroupilha
28 Palácio Piratini
31 Youth Hostel Tchê

PLACES TO EAT
4   Chalé da Praça XV
9   Ilha Natural Restaurante
    Vegetariano
12 Xoco Xop
13 Fruta na Boca
26 La Churrasquita

OTHER
1   Rodoviária & Metro Stop
2   Estação Mercado Modelo
3   Mercado Público
5   Uruguayan Consulate
6   Post Office
7   Museu de Arte
    do Rio Grande do Sul
8   Customs
16 CRTUR
17 VASP
18 Varig
21 Telephones
24 Argentine Consulate
29 Catedral Metropolitana
30 Museu Histórico
    Júlio de Castilhos

cheap, duty-free Scotch whisky and post letters.

Visas

It's much better to get your Uruguayan visa in Porto Alegre than at the border at Chuí, but it can be done here. You will have to wait overnight. The Uruguayan Consulate (☎ 65-1151) is at Rua Venezuela 311 and is open from 9 am to 3 pm. Visas cost US$20.

Places to Stay & Eat

If you have to stay overnight in Chuí, there are a few simple hotels. Try the *Hotel e Restaurante São Francisco* (☎ 65-1096), at Rua Columbia 741. It charges US$5 per person. Across the road, *Hospedagem Bianca* and *Hospedagem Roberto* are a bit cheaper. In Uruguay, the *Plaza Hotel*, Rua General Artigas 553, has singles/doubles for US$20/30. The restaurant in the São Francisco is as good as any around town.

Getting There & Away

The rodoviária is at Rua Venezuela 247, and buses leave frequently for most cities in southern Brazil. You can buy tickets to Montevideo on the Uruguayan side of Avenida Brasil. Seven buses leave daily for Punta del Este and Montevideo. The first leaves at 4 am and the last at midnight.

Crossing the Border All buses to Uruguay stop at the Polícia Federal on Avenida Argentina, a couple of km from town. You must get out to get your Brazilian exit stamp. In Uruguay, the bus will stop again for the Uruguayan officials to check that you have a Brazilian exit stamp and Uruguayan visa (if you need one).

SERRA GAÚCHA

North of Porto Alegre is the beautiful Serra Gaúcha, which is popular with hikers. The mountain towns of Gramado and Canela are popular resorts.

Canela

While not as up-market as Gramado, Canela is the best jumping-off point for some great hikes and bike rides in the area. Bikes can be hired in the park, just outside the tourist office. There are cheaper hotels here than in Gramado, so budget travellers should make this their base. The tourist office (☎ 282-1287), in Praça João Correa, is helpful, and hands out a brochure that has some entertaining English translations.

Places to Stay & Eat The youth hostel *Pousada do Viajante* (☎ 282-2017), at Rua Ernesto Urbani 132, is the best cheapie in Canela. It's clean, friendly and excellent value (US$5 per person, with breakfast). The *Hotel Bela Vista* (☎ 282-1327), at Rua Osvaldo Aranha 160, has rooms and separate cabanas for US$13/20 a single/double. Camping is available at *Camping Club do Brasil*, eight km from town on the park road.

Highly recommended is *Cantina de Nono*, Avenida Osvaldo Aranha 161. They have excellent pizza and reasonable Italian food. Big meat-eaters will enjoy *Bifão & Cia*, at Avenida Osvaldo Aranha 456.

Getting There & Away The rodoviária is in the centre of town. There are frequent buses to Porto Alegre, all travelling via Gramado.

Parque Estadual do Caracol

Eight km from Canela, the major attraction of this park is a spectacular waterfall, 130 metres high. You don't have to do any hiking to see it, as it's very close to the park entrance. The park is open daily from 7.30 am to 6 pm. Entry is US$0.40. A public bus to the park, marked 'Caracol Circular', leaves the rodoviária at 8.15 am, noon and 5.30 pm.

Parque Nacional de Aparados da Serra

This park, 70 km north of the town of São Francisco de Paula, is Rio Grande do Sul's most magnificent area and one of Brazil's great natural wonders. It preserves one of the country's last forests of *araucária* (a pine-like tree that stands up to 50 metres tall), and contains the Itaimbezinho, a fantastic narrow canyon, 120 metres deep.

Places to Stay The closest town to the park is Cambará do Sul, where you can find simple accomodation in the *Pousada Fortaleza* (☎ 251-1224) for US$6 per person. The best place to stay is in the park itself. Camping is the only alternative, but don't do any sleepwalking! There are good spots near the now-defunct Paradouro hotel and near the Fortaleza canyon.

Getting There & Away If you can't afford to take a US$45, four-hour taxi ride from Cambará do Sul, or to hire a car (or plane) for a day, put on your walking shoes if you expect to see both Itaimbézinho and Fortaleza. No public buses go to either, and the hitching is lousy. The closest you can get is three km from Itaimbézinho, by taking the bus to Praia Grande and asking to be dropped at the park entrance. From the other entrance, on the road between Cambará and Tainhas, it's a 15-km walk to the canyon. To get to Fortaleza, you'll either have to walk 23 km or make a deal with Borges, the taxi driver, to take you out there. There and back costs around US$25, but it's worth it.

There are various ways to get to the park itself. The best option is to come up from the coast via Praia Grande and get off the 'Cambará do Sul' bus at the park entrance. Another route is to come up from São Francisco de Paula and get off at the other entrance to the park.

There's also the possibility of hiking 20 km from Praia Grande into the canyon itself, but it's dangerous without a guide. People have been trapped in the canyon by flash flooding.

JESUIT MISSIONS
In 1608, Hernandarias, governor of the Spanish province of Paraguay, ordered the local leader of the Jesuits, Fray Diego de Torres, to send missionaries to convert the infidels. The first mission was founded in 1609.

Preferring indoctrination by the Jesuits to serfdom on Spanish estates or slavery at the hands of the Portuguese, the Indians were recruited into missions. The missions soon spread over a vast region encompassing much of the present-day Brazilian states of Paraná, Santa Catarina and Rio Grande do Sul, plus portions of Paraguay and northern Argentina.

The Jesuit territory was too large to defend; the northern missions were raided by Portuguese slave-traders and attacked by hostile Indian tribes, but a defensible group of 30 missions in the south survived.

Under an administration based in Candelaria, the missions grew into miniature centres of culture and intellect as well as religion. In effect, the Jesuit territory became a nation within the colonies, and at its height in the 1720s, there were 150,000 Guaraní Indians living in the missions. The Jesuit nation became an embarrassment to the Iberian kings, and finally, in 1767, Portuguese Prime Minister Marques de Pombal convinced Carlos III to expel the Jesuits from Spanish lands. During the wars of independence in the early 1800s, the mission villages were destroyed and then abandoned.

Orientation & Information
There are 30 ruined Jesuit missions: seven lie in Brazil, in the western part of Rio Grande do Sul, eight are in the southern region of Itapuá, Paraguay, and the remaining 15 are in Argentina.

Brazil
Use Santo Angelo as a base for the Brazilian missions. São Miguel das Missões (58 km from Santo Angelo) is the most interesting of these. Every evening at 8 pm, there's a sound and light show. Nearby are the missions of São João Batista, on the way to São Miguel, and São Lourenço das Missões, 10 km from São João Batista by dirt road.

Santo Angelo has several modest hotels, but it's great to stay out at São Miguel to see the sound and light show and enjoy the view. The *Hotel Barichello* is the only place to stay and eat. It's very clean, and run by a friendly family. Singles cost US$4 and doubles with a shower are US$9.

Paraguay

Encarnación should be your base to see the missions of Paraguay. The best mission to visit is Trinidad, 25 km from Encarnación. Posadas and San Ignacio are also convenient. (See the Encarnación section in the Paraguay chapter.)

Encarnación is a cheap place to stay, with a couple of cheap, modest hotels and Chinese restaurants.

Argentina

Use Posadas as your base. The most interesting mission is San Ignacio Miní, 60 km from Posadas. (See Posadas in the Corrientes section of the Argentina chapter.)

Posadas is across the Rio Paraná from Encarnación, and there are numerous buses over the bridge. Everything is more expensive in Posadas, but the food is better and the lodging (10 hotels to choose from) is fancier. Lodging is good, and much cheaper in Encarnación.

Getting Around

It is best to travel in this area by car, but unfortunately, car rental fees are high and driving a rented car over borders is difficult. It's possible to hire a taxi from any of the three base cities – Posadas, Encarnación and Santo Angelo.

You can cross over into Argentina from the Brazilian town of Uruguaiana. The Argentine Consulate in Uruguaiana (☎ 412-1925) is at Rua Santana 2496 (2nd floor), and the Uruguayan Consulate (☎ 412-1514) is at Rua Domingos de Almeida 1709.

Brasília

Brasília is in a federal district, Distrito Federal, and does not belong to any of the states. It must have looked good on paper and still looks good in photos, but the city was built for cars and air-conditioners, not people. It's a lousy place to visit and no- one wanted to live there. It's probably better to read about it instead: try Alex Shoumatoff's

The Capital of Hope (Vintage, New York, 1990).

Orientation

The city is divided into two halves: Asa Sul and Asa Norte. Avenida W3, the main commercial street, and Avenida L2 run the length of the city and are also divided into north and south.

Information

Tourist Office Detur is the government tourist information service. Its office is inconveniently located on the 3rd floor of the Centro de Convenções and is open Monday to Friday from 1 to 6 pm. The Detur tourist desk at the airport is open Monday to Friday from 8 am to 1 pm and 2 to 7 pm. The best map is in the phone book *Achei! (Found it!) O Guia de Brasília.*

Money Banks with moneychanging facilities are in SBS (the Setor Bancário Sul, Banking Sector South) and SBN (Setor Bancário Norte, Banking Sector North). Both are close to the rodoviária. Travel agencies will also change cash dollars.

Foreign Embassies In the following addresses, SES stands for Setor de Embaixadas Sul.

Australia
  SHIS, Q I-9, cj 16, casa 1 (☎ 248-5569)
Canada
  SES, Avenida das Nações Q 803, lote 16 sl 130 (☎ 321-2171)
France
  SES, Avenida das Nações, lote 4 (☎ 312-9100)
Germany
  SES, Avenida das Nações 25 (☎ 43-7466)
UK
  SES, Avenida das Nações, Q 801, cj K lote 8 (☎ 225-2710)
USA
  SES, Avenida das Nações, Q 801, lote 3 (☎ 321-7272)

Things to See

Start at the **Memorial JK**, open from 8 am to 6 pm, then head to the observation deck of the **TV tower**. It's open from 9 am to 8 pm.

BRAZIL

The **Catedral Metropolitana**, open from 8.30 to 11.30 am and 2 to 6 pm, is worth seeing too. The most interesting **government buildings** are the Palácio do Itamaraty (open Monday to Friday until 4 pm), the Palácio da Justiça (open Monday to Friday from noon to 6 pm) and the Palácio do Congresso (open Monday to Friday from 10 to noon and 2 to 5 pm).

The **Parque Nacional de Brasília**, an ecological reserve, is a good place to relax if you're stuck in the city. The Agua Mineral bus from the city rodoviária goes past the front gate.

Places to Stay

Camping is possible not far from the city in the Setor de Garagens Oficiais. There aren't any cheap hotels in Brasília, but there are a few cheap pensions, mostly located on W3 Sul. The best is *Cury's Solar* (☎ 243-6252). Prices vary with room size: singles cost from US$6 to US$10 and doubles from US$10 to US$22. The address is Quadra 707 south, Bloco I, casa 15. There's no sign but it's easy to find. A couple of other places close by are *Santos* (☎ 244-6672) in Quadra 705 south, Bloco M, casa 43, and *Jonas* (☎ 224-6775), at Quadra 704 south, Block M, casa 9. Each charges US$10 per person.

A good mid-range hotel is the *Mirage Hotel* (☎ 225-7150) in the Hotel Sector North (SHN Q 02 Bloco N). They charge US$20/25 for singles/doubles.

Places to Eat

Both of the shopping complexes near the rodoviária have lots of places to eat, and many of them have lunchtime specials. The one on the north side (Conjunto Nacional) has the best selection.

Places with a good selection of restaurants and bars are the commercial areas between Quadras 109 and 110 South, 405 and 406 South and between Quadras 303 and 304 North.

Getting There & Away

Air With so many domestic flights making a stopover in Brasília, it's easy to catch a plane

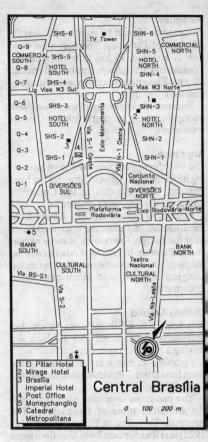

Central Brasília

1 El Pillar Hotel
2 Mirage Hotel
3 Brasília Imperial Hotel
4 Post Office
5 Moneychanging
6 Catedral Metropolitana

0   100   200 m

out of the city at almost any time. Airlines in Brasília include Transbrasil (☎ 243-6133), TAM (☎ 223-5168), Varig/Cruzeiro (☎ 226-2186) and VASP (☎ 321-3636).

Bus The giant rodoferroviária (☎ 233-7200) is due west of the centre. Buses go to Goiânia (US$5, three hours), Cuiabá (US$28, 20 hours, with connections to Porto Velho and Manaus), Anápolis (US$4, 2½ hours), Belém (US$52, 36 hours), Belo Horizonte (US$18, 12 hours), Rio (US$26, 18 hours), São Paulo (US$22, 16 hours) and Salvador (US$34, 25 hours).

Getting Around

You can rent a car, take a bus tour or combine a city bus with some long walks to see the bulk of Brasília's edifices. To get a bus tour, visit the Hotel Garvey-Park (full of travel agencies offering sightseeing tours) or book at the airport or rodoviária.

To/From the Airport The international airport (☎ 248-5588) is 12 km south of the centre. There are two buses marked 'Aeroporto' that do the 35-minute trip from the city rodoviária to the airport every 15 minutes. A taxi will cost US$15.

Bus To get from the city rodoviária to the rodoferroviária (for long-distance buses), take the No 131 bus (you can also flag it down along the main drag).

Car There are car rental agencies at the airport, the Hotel Nacional and the Hotel Garvey-Park.

Goiás

GOIÂNIA

The capital of the state of Goiás, Goiânia is 200 km south-west of Brasília. It's a fairly pleasant place, with lots of open spaces laid out around circular streets in the centre. The best source of tourist information is *Nova Guia Turístico de Goiânia*, a book available for US$2 at most newsstands. Turisplan Turismo (☎ 224-1941) at Rua 8, 388 is a central travel agency that sells plane and bus tickets.

Places to Stay & Eat

The *Hotel Del Rey* (☎ 225-6306) is centrally located in the Rua 8 pedestrian mall at No 321. Apartamentos cost US$9/15 a single/double. Another cheapie is the *Hotel Paissandú* (☎ 224-4925), at Avenida Goiás 1290. All rooms have fans. Quartos are US$6/9 and apartamentos are US$10/14. The *Principe Hotel* (☎ 224-0085) is a couple

of dollars more but is better value. It's at Avenida Anhanguera 2936.

For typical Goiânian dishes, go to the *Centro de Tradições Goiânas*, Rua 4, 515, above the Parthenon Centre, or *Dona Beija* on Avenida Tocantins between Rua 4 and Avenida Anhanguera. Natural food is available, naturally, at *Restaurante Naturalmente Natural* in the centre at Rua 15, 238.

Getting There & Away

Air For major airlines, call Varig/Cruzeiro (☎ 224-5049) or VASP (☎ 224-6144). If you're interested in an air taxi call Sete Taxi Aereo (☎ 207-1519) or União (☎ 207-1600).

Bus The rodoviária (☎ 224-8466) is at Rua 44, No 399. There are buses to Brasília (US$5, three hours), Goiás Velho (US$4, 2½ hours, every hour from 5 am to 8 pm), Cuiabá (US$20, 16 hours), Pirenópolis (US$4, two hours, 7 am and 5 pm) and Caldas Novas (US$5, three hours).

Getting Around

Aeroporto Santo Genoveva (☎ 207-1288) is six km from the city. A taxi there will cost US$10. To get from the rodoviária to the corner of Avenida Anhanguera and Avenida Goiás is a 15-minute walk. Local buses can be caught from the bus stop 50 metres from the main terminal as you walk towards town.

GOIÁS VELHO

The historic city of Goiás Velho, formerly known as Vila Boa, enjoyed a brief gold rush in the 18th century and was once the state capital.

Things to See

Walking through Goiás Velho, you quickly notice the main legacies of the gold rush: 18th-century architecture and a large mulatto and mestizo population. Of the seven churches, the most impressive is the oldest, the **Igreja de Paula** (1761), on Praça Zaqueu Alves de Castro. The **Museu das Bandeiras**, in the old town council building (1766) on Praça Brasil Caiado, is also worth a visit.

Festivals

The big occasion here is **Semana Santa** (Holy Week). The main streets of town are lit by hundreds of torches, carried by the townsfolk and dozens of hooded figures in a procession which re-enacts the removal of Christ from the cross and his burial.

Places to Stay

You can camp in town next to the river at the *Chafariz da Carioca*. The best low-budget place is the *Hotel Araguaiá* (☎ 371-1462), Avenida Dr Deusdete Ferreira de Moura. It's a 15-minute hike from the bus station, but has very comfortable apartamentos (US$5/10 a single/double). *Ypê* (☎ 371-2065) at Rua Boavista 32, in a colonial house, charges similar prices. They also arrange treks.

Getting There & Away

There are frequent buses to Goiânia, 144 km away.

PIRENÓPOLIS

Another historic gold city, Pirenópolis is 70 km from Anápolis and 128 km from Goiânia on the Rio das Almas.

Festivals

The city is famous for the **Festa do Divino Espírito Santo**, 45 days after Easter. If you're in the area, don't miss this curious spectacle, which is more folkloric than religious. There is a series of mediaeval tournaments, dances and festivities, including a mock battle between Moors and Christians in Iberia.

Places to Stay & Eat

There are a few simple pousadas in town. *Pensão Central*, at Praça Emanuel Jayme, and *Dormitório da Geny*, at Rua dos Pirineus 29 each charge around US$5 a head. The *Rex Hotel* (☎ 331-1121) is a step up but still pretty basic, with quartos for US$6/10 a single/double. The *Pousada das Cavalhadas* (☎ 331-1261), at Praça da Matriz 1, has apartamentos for US$20 a double.

All these places fill up during the festival,

so most visitors camp out near the Rio das Almas or rent a room from a local.

The *Restaurante As Flor*, in Avenida São Jayme, serves huge plates of good regional cuisine, including 18 different desserts, each one sweeter than the last. *Restaurante Aravinda* in Rua do Rosário is also recommended.

Getting There & Away

There are bus services from Anápolis and Goiânia as well as from Brasília.

PARQUE NACIONAL DA CHAPADA DOS VEADEIROS

Just over 200 km north of Brasília, this scenic park located in the highest area of the Central West has become a popular destination for Brazilian ecotourists. The best time to visit the park is between May and October. The entry fee is US$0.50. Camping is the best option here (about US$1 a night), but basic accommodation can be found in the small nearby town of São Jorge.

Getting There & Away

From Brasília, take a bus to Alto Paraiso de Goias, from where you can either catch a local bus to São Jorge, or walk to the park, a couple of hours away.

Mato Grosso

The Mato Grosso is home to many of Brazil's remaining Indians, whose lands are threatened by rapid agricultural development following construction of the roads from Belém to Brasília and from Cuiabá to Santarém.

CUIABÁ

Cuiabá is a lively place and a good base for excursions into the Pantanal and Chapada dos Guimarães.

Orientation & Information

The city is actually two sister-cities separated by the Rio Cuiabá: old Cuiabá, on the

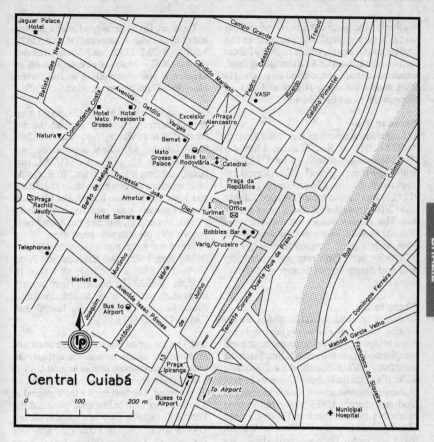

Central Cuiabá

0   100   200 m

Map labels:
Jaguar Palace Hotel
Campo Grande
Franco
Celestino
Cândido Mariano
Pedro
Ricardo
Caldino Pimentel
Balista das Neves
VASP
Avenida
Comandante Costa
Getúlio Vargas
Hotel Mato Grosso
Hotel Presidente
Excelsior
Praça Alencastro
Natura
Bernat
Barão de Melgaço
Mato Grosso Palace
Bus to Rodoviária
Catedral
Travessia
João
Praça da República
Coimbra
Praça Rachid Jaudy
Ametur
Diaz
Post Office
Turimat
Hotel Samara
Bobbies Bar
Manoel
Rua
Telephones
Varig/Cruzeiro
Tenente Coronel Duarte (Rua da Praia)
Domingos Ferreira
Murtinho
Market
Mária
Avenida Isaac Póvoas
Bus to Airport
Junho
Manoel Garcia Velho
Joaquim
Antônio
de
Francisco de Siqueira
13
Praça Ipiranga
To Airport
Buses to Airport
Municipal Hospital

BRAZIL

south-west where the airport is; and Várzea Grande, where the centre of the modern town is located. The Turimat office (☎ 322-5363) is in the centre on Praça da República, near the post office. It's open Monday to Friday from 8 am to 6 pm.

Things to See
The **Museu do Indio** (Rondon) has exhibits on the Xavantes, Bororos and Karajas tribes, and is worth a visit. It is at the university, on Avenida Fernando Correia da Costa, and opens Monday to Friday from 8 to 11.30 am and 1.30 to 5.30 pm. The **market** by the

bridge that crosses the Rio Cuiabá is a good one. Try the waterfront bars for a drink afterwards.

Tours
Travel agencies in town arrange reservations, guides and transport for photo-safaris into the Pantanal, weekend trips to Chapada dos Guimarães, and can help with the logistics of more ambitious trips to Emas. Ametur (☎ 321-4948), Rua Joaquim Murtinho 242, close to Turimat, has been recommended. Their tours are expensive (around US$75 a day) but well organised. An alternative and

relatively cheap excursion is with Joel Souza, a very enthusiastic guide (fluent in English and German), whose two-day Pantanal trips cost around US$120 including food, accommodation, transport and boat ride. He often meets incoming flights and has an office in the Hotel Presidente.

Places to Stay

A cheapie in the town centre is *Hotel Samara* (☎ 322-6001), at Rua Joaquim Murtinho 270. Their single quartos go for US$5 and double apartamentos cost US$9. A travellers' favourite is the *Hotel Mato Grosso* (☎ 321-9121), at Rua Comandante Costa 2522. It has US$12/16 apartamentos and a good breakfast. The *Jaguar Palace* (☎ 322-6698), at Avenida Getúlio Vargas 600, is a three-star hotel with a pool. Singles/doubles go for US$30/50, but if you take a Pantanal trip with Joel Souza he can arrange a 50% discount here.

Places to Eat

To splurge on exotic local fish dishes, try the floating restaurant *Flutuante*, next to Ponte Nova bridge. It's six km from the centre and complicated to get to by public bus. From the waterfront market though, it's a 20-minute walk. It's open daily from 11 am to 11 pm. *O Regionalissimo* serves excellent regional food and charges US$3.50 for buffet-style meals. It's open for lunch and dinner, closed Mondays, and is next to the Casa do Artesão, Rua 13 de Junho. For a vegetarian lunch, try *Naturama*, on Rua Comandante Costa near the Hotel Mato Grosso. *Bobbies Bar*, at Travessa João Dias 42, is a lanchonete run by Bob Lassam, an expatriate English/Australian. He enjoys a chat and a beer with travellers passing through.

Getting There & Away

Air The airport (☎ 381-2211) is in Várzea Grande, about seven km from the city. To catch the local bus to town, cross the road and walk to the left to Las Velas hotel. The bus stop is opposite the hotel entrance. Catch a Jardim Primavera, Cohabcanela or Costa Verde bus to the centre.

There are flights between Cuiabá and the rest of Brazil with Transbrasil (☎ 381-3347), VASP (☎ 381-3737) and Varig/Cruzeiro (☎ 381-2051). Make reservations well in advance if you're travelling in July, when many Brazilians are on vacation.

Bus Cuiabá's rodoviária (☎ 323-3008) is on Avenida Marechal Rondon. To reach the city from the rodoviária, take the No 202 Rodoviária bus to its final stop. Six buses a day make the trip to Poconé (US$4, two hours); the first leaves at 6 am. To Barão de Melgaço there are two buses daily at 7.30 am and 3 pm (US$5, three hours). For Chapada dos Guimarães there are six buses daily (US$3, 1½ hours), but take the 8 am bus if you've only got a day to spend there.

There are three buses daily to Cáceres (US$8, three hours); two buses daily to Porto Velho (US$30, 24 hours); and five to Goiânia (US$20, 16 hours). There are six buses daily on the route to Rondonópolis (three hours), Coxim (seven hours) and Campo Grande (10 hours).

Car The car rental places all have branches in the centre and in or near the airport. On average, a rental car will cost around US$40 a day. There are often promotional rates, so shop around. The best car for the Pantanal is a Volkswagen Golf or Fiat Uno. Note that the Porto Jofre station only has gas and diesel; Poconé and Pousada do Pixaim (55 km from Poconé, 85 km from Porto Jofre) have *álcool*.

CHAPADA DOS GUIMARÃES

After the Pantanal, Chapada dos Guimarães is the region's leading attraction. Surprisingly different from the typical Mato Grosso terrain, this place is not to be missed. The two exceptional sights in the Chapadas are the 60-metre Véu de Noiva (Bridal Veil) falls and the Mirante lookout, the geographic centre of South America.

If you don't have a car, your best bet is to take an excursion with Jorge Mattos, who runs Ecoturismo (☎ 791-1393), on Praça Dom Wunibaldo 486 in the town of

Chapada. He speaks English and meets the 8 am bus from Cuiabá every day (it arrives at 9.30 am).

An alternative is to hire a car and explore the area on your own, stopping at different rock formations, waterfalls and bathing pools at leisure. If you travel by car, visit the Secretaria de Turismo, on the left-hand side as you enter town, just before the square. It's open on weekdays from 8 to 11 am and 1 to 4 pm, and a useful map is available. You'll need it.

Places to Stay & Eat

There is good camping at Salgadeira, just before the climb into Chapada, but if you wanted to rough it, you could basically camp anywhere.

Accommodation in the area ranges from the very basic but friendly *Hotel São José* (☎ 791-1152), Rua Vereador José de Souza 50, which charges US$2.50 per person, to the *Hotel Pousada da Chapada* (☎ 791-1330), a couple of km from town on the road to Cuiabá. They charge US$35 a double.

In between are a couple of good alternatives. The very popular *Turismo Hotel* (☎ 791-1176), at Rua Fernando Correo Costa 1065, offers apartamentos at US$10 per person, and also has a restaurant. *Quinco* (☎ 791-1284), at Praça Dom Wunibaldo 464 (next to Ecoturismo), has simple, clean apartamentos for US$7/10 a single/double. On the main praça, *Nivios* has excellent regional food – all you can eat for US$4.

Getting There & Away

Buses leave for Chapada dos Guimarães from Cuiabá's rodoviária every 1½ hours from 8 am to 6 pm (US$3).

The Pantanal

The Amazon may have all the fame and glory, but the Pantanal is a far better place to see wildlife. This vast area of wetlands, about half the size of France, lies mostly within the states of Mato Grosso and Mato Grosso do Sul, but also extends into the border regions of Bolivia and Paraguay.

The Pantanal is a vast alluvial plain, much of which is flooded by the Rio Paraguai and its tributaries during the wet season (October to March). It is what remains of an ancient inland sea called the Xaraés, which began to dry out, along with the Amazon Sea, 65 million years ago.

Birds are the most frequently seen wildlife, but the Pantanal is also a sanctuary for giant river otters, anacondas, iguanas, jaguars, cougars, crocodiles, deer, anteaters, black howler monkeys and capybaras.

The area has few people and no towns. The only road that plunges deep into the Pantanal is the Transpantaneira, which ends 145 km south of Poconé, at Porto Jofre. Only a third of the intended route from Poconé to Corumbá has been completed, because of ecological concerns and lack of funds. The best way for the budget traveller to see the wildlife of the Pantanal is to drive or hitch down the Transpantaneira, preferably all the way to Porto Jofre.

The best time to visit the Pantanal is the dry season (April to September or October). The best time to see birds is July to September. Flooding, incessant rains and extreme heat make travel difficult from November to March.

The tourist office (☎ 322-5363) in Cuiabá has a list of local guides. If language or time is a problem and money isn't, you can write to Douglas Trent of Focus Tours (☎ 892-7830), 14821 Hillside Lane, Burnsville, MN 55337, USA; in Brazil, contact Focus (☎ 223-0358) at Rua Alagoas 1460/s503, Belo Horizonte, Minas Gerais. Focus specialises in nature tours and Doug is active in trying to preserve the Pantanal.

Places to Stay

Pantanal accommodation is divided into three general categories – *fazendas*, *pesqueiros* and *botels*. Fazendas are ranch-style hotels which usually have horses, and often boats, for hire. Pesqueiros are hangouts for anglers, and boats and fishing gear can usually be rented from them. A botel, a

The Pantanal

0   50   100 km

contraction of boat and hotel, is a floating lodge (usually very expensive). Reservations are needed for all accommodation, especially in July, when lots of Brazilian tourists spend their holidays there.

Unfortunately, nearly all accommodation is expensive. It usually includes good food, modest lodging and transport by plane, boat or 4WD from Corumbá or Cuiabá,. More often than not, reservations are handled through a travel agent, and you must pay in advance. It's also a good idea to call ahead for weather conditions.

Along the Transpantaneira At km 30 *Pousada do Araras* charges US$15 a single, US$25 a double and US$33 a triple. They have a pool and also show films about the Pantanal. At km 65 the *Pousada Pixaim* (☎ (065) 322-8961) has a friendly manager, clean rooms with electric showers, tasty meals (included in the room price) and the last álcool and gas pump until you return to Poconé. This is the budget travellers' favourite, at US$20 per person. Across the bridge, the *Fazenda-Hotel Beira Rio* (☎ (065) 321-9445) is more expensive, charging US$35 a single and US$50 a double. They rent boats for US$20 an hour and horses for US$12 an hour. Boats can also be rented at Pousada Pixaim for about the same price.

Porto Jofre is a one-hotel hamlet. Campers can stay at Senhor Jamil's, near the river, for US$5 per person. He provides clean bathrooms and cooking facilities, and also rents boats. Alternatively, take the turn-off and go a couple of km to the *Hotel Santa Rosa Pantanal* (☎ 322-0948), which charges US$70/80 for a single/double bungalow, including meals; boats, horses (expensive) and beer cost extra; reservations are a good idea.

Mato Grosso There are several fazendas in the northern Pantanal that are off the Transpantaneira. The *Hotel Porto Cercado* (☎ 682-1300 in Cuiabá) is easily reached by car; it costs US$56/66/84 a single/double/triple with meals included. It's along the Rio Cuiabá about 50 km from Poconé.

The expensive *Hotel Cabanas do Pantanal* (☎ 322-4142 in Cuiabá) is 42 km from Poconé. A three-day package costs US$300.

Pirigara Pantanal Hotel (☎ 322-8961 in Cuiabá) is on the banks of the Rio Cuiabá, 20 minutes by plane from Poconé and about six hours by boat from Porto Cercado. To stay in the hotel costs only US$20 per person all inclusive, but the plane ride costs US$200. Renting a boat in Porto Cercado is much cheaper.

Mato Grosso do Sul One of the cheapest places to stay in the Pantanal is the *Pesqueiro Clube do Pantanal* (☎ 242-1464 in Miranda), 168 km from Corumbá in the direction of Campo Grande. It charges about US$25 per person with full board, and fishing trips by boats can be arranged. Eight km from Miranda is the *Hotel Beira Rio* (☎ 242-1262 in Miranda). They charge US$30 per person (full board) for rooms with air-con and hot showers.

There are a few places deeper into the Pantanal, at Passo do Lontra, 120 km and two hours (dry season) from Corumbá; to get there, take the dirt road leading off the road to Campo Grande. Alternatively, you can take the train to Campo Grande and have the lodge pick you up at the Carandazal station.

Sixteen km from Passo da Lontra is *Fazenda Santa Clara* (☎ 231-5797 in Miranda). This one is popular because it's well-organised, caters for independent travellers and supplies transport. It charges US$75/90/115 for two/three/four days, full board included, and has boats, horses and fishing gear.

Around Aquidauana, there are a number of medium-priced to expensive hotel-fazendas. *Aguapé Pousada* is 57 km away and charges US$80 a day, but you can camp there for US$5 a day and buy meals at the restaurant. For more information about these places, see Panbratour in Aquidauana.

Getting There & Away

There are two main approach routes to the Pantanal: via Cuiabá in the north and via Corumbá in the south. From Cuiabá there are

BRAZIL

three gateways to the Pantanal; Cáceres, Barão de Melgaço and Poconé – all of which lead to Porto Jofre on the Transpantaneira. Corumbá is best accessed by bus from Campo Grande; the route runs via Aquidauana and Miranda. Coxim, a small town on the east of the Pantanal, is a third point of entry to the Pantanal, but has a very limited tourist infrastructure.

Getting Around
Since the lodges are the only places to sleep, drink and eat, and public transportation doesn't exist, independent travel is difficult in the Pantanal. Driving is an option, but not easy. Only a few roads reach the periphery of the Pantanal; they are frequently closed by rains and reconstructed yearly. Only the Transpantaneira highway goes deep into the region.

Transpantaneira If you're in it for the wildlife and your budget is limited, the best way to visit the Pantanal is driving down the Transpantaneira, preferably all the way to Porto Jofre. Wildlife is abundant along the length of the Transpantaneira, especially in the meadows about 10 to 20 km before Porto Jofre.

Renting a car in Cuiabá and driving down the Transpantaneira is less expensive than most Pantanal excursions, which require flying, boating or hiring a guide with a 4WD. If you're on a very tight budget, you can take a bus to Poconé and hitch from there (pretty easy); if you have to, return to Poconé for cheap accommodation.

If you are driving from Cuiabá, get going early. Leave at 4 am and you'll reach the Transpantaneira by sunrise, when the animals come to life, then have a full day's light in which to drive to Porto Jofre.

The approach road to the Transpantaneira begins in Poconé (two hours from Cuiabá), by the Texaco station. Follow the road in the direction of Hotel Aurora. The official Transpantaneira Highway Park starts 17 km south of Poconé. There's a sign and guard station (where you pay a small entry fee) at the entrance.

Hitching Hitching down the Transpantaneira is easy enough – it's hitching back that's difficult. There aren't a lot of cars or trucks, but many stop to give rides. The best time to hitch is on weekends, when the locals drive down the Transpantaneira for a day's fishing. Make sure you get on the road early.

Mato Grosso do Sul

CORUMBÁ
Corumbá, a port city on the Rio Paraguai (the Bolivian border), is the southern gateway to the Pantanal. The town has a reputation for drug traffic, gun-running and poaching, so be cautious.

Information
Tourist Office Corumbá has no tourist office, but try the many travel agencies in town. Good ones are Pantanal Safari (π 231-2112), at Rua Antônio Maria Coelho 330, and Pantur (π 231-4666), at Rua América 969.

Foreign Consulates The Bolivian Consulate (π 231-5605) is at Rua Antônio Maria Coelho 852, near the intersection of Rua América. It's open from 8.30 am to 1.30 pm on weekdays. Oddly, intending visitors to Bolivia may have to leave Brazil before applying for a visa here. The Paraguayan Consulate (π 231-2030) is on Rua Cuiabá.

Visas For a Brazilian entry/exit stamp, go to the Polícia Federal at the rodoviária.

Pantanal Tours
Corumbá's star attraction is the Pantanal, and you can get a preview of it from Morro Urucum (1100 metres). Daily boat tours of the Corumbá area are available from all travel agencies. An all-day trip on the boat *Pérola do Pantanal* will set you back US$25, including lunch.

Many budget travellers are choosing to go on cheap three to four- day tours into the Pantanal. These trips, generally costing around US$20 a day, can be very rough-and-ready affairs. Accommodation is in hammocks, under thatch or in somebody's shack. You'll see lots of birds and plenty of crocodiles, but the mammals are understandably a bit shy, especially when they get chased by a truck at 80 km/h.

If you want something well organised, and riding around in the back of a pick-up truck doesn't grab you, pay a bit more and stay at a hotel-fazenda for a few days. If you're prepared to take it as it comes, you might have a good time. Before signing on for one of these trips, and certainly before parting with any cash, find out how far into the Pantanal you go – it should be at least 200 km, preferably more. Your chances of enjoying the Pantanal and its wildlife are greatly increased if you go with a reputable guide who forsakes the 'mechanical chase' approach, accompanies small groups (preferably less than five people) on an extensive walking trip through the area for several days, camping out at night (away from drinking dens!) and taking you on walks at the optimum times to observe wildlife – before sunrise, at dusk and during the night. A trip along these lines will need at least four days (preferably five).

In Corumbá, disreputable guides, known as *guias piratas* (pirate guides), are plentiful; there is a lot of cachaça-drinking to convince tourists that they're having a good time. Tales of woe with pirate guides include abandonment in the marshes, assorted drunken mayhem and even attempted rape. The following guides are recommended: Clovis Carneiro (☎ 231-4473), an elderly guy with excellent local knowledge, Rodrigues (☎ 231-6746), Ico (☎ 231-2629), who is president of the Associação das Guias, and Johnny Indiano (☎ 231-6835). Several travellers have complained about Necolândia Tours, particularly two associated guides called Murilo and Nolasco.

A Welsh woman named Karen Williams is starting a company to do tours of the Pantanal, based on a nearby fazenda. Contact Tucantur (☎ 231-5323), 13 de Junho 744, Corumbá.

Places to Stay & Eat
The budget travellers' favourite is *Hotel Schabib* (☎ 231-1404), at Rua Frei Mariano 1153. At US$3 per person, it's good value. Close by is *Hotel Londres* (☎ 231-6717), with quartos for US$4 a head and singles/doubles with fan for US$5/9. At the *Condor*, in the town centre, quartos with fan are good value, at US$3 per person. A couple of doors along, the *Moderno* is also good value, with quartos for US$3.50 a head. There's a youth hostel (☎ 231-2305) at Rua Antônio Maria Coelho 677.

Moving up in price a bit, the *Grande Hotel* (☎ 231-1012), at Rua Frei Mariano 468, has good big quartos for US$9/12 and apartamentos for a bit more, but they don't include breakfast.

Bar El Pacu, on Rua Cabral, is a good, cheap restaurant. *Churrascaria Rodeio*, at 13 de Junho 760, has live music as well as tasty meat dishes.

Getting There & Away
Like Campo Grande, Corumbá is a transit point for travel to/from Bolivia and Paraguay. See the Crossing the Border section for more details.

Air The airport is three km from the town centre. VASP (☎ 231-4441, 31-1456 at the airport), at Rua 15 de Novembro 392, is the only large company flying into Corumbá.

For Bolivian air connections – LAB (Lloyd Aereo Boliviano) and TAM (Transportes Aereos Militares) – contact Pantur (see the Information section under The Pantanal heading earlier in this chapter).

Bus From the rodoviária, buses run to Campo Grande eight times a day (US$11, eight hours). The bus is much quicker than the train.

Train To Campo Grande, there are trains every Tuesday, Thursday and Sunday, leaving at 9 pm (US$7 in pullman class, US$18 for a double sleeping berth), and on Monday, Wednesday and Friday at 8 am (US$5/3 in 1st/2nd class).

Once across the Bolivian border, most people will be heading towards Santa Cruz. For more details, see the requisite section of the Bolivia chapter. In Corumbá, seats on the Expreso Especial Bracha, a special 'luxury' service between the Bolivian border town of Quijarro and Santa Cruz, should be reserved three or four days in advance through Receptivo Pantanal, at Rua Frei Mariano 502. Tickets cost US$36 per person.

Boat The Paraguayan government's Flota Mercantil del Estado runs boat services between Asunción (Paraguay) and Corumbá on the Río Paraguay. In theory, boats leave on alternate Fridays, but services are very erratic on this five-day voyage, which costs US$40 for a cabin, US$30 for a hammock. It's much cooler if you take the cheap class and sling your hammock on deck. Meals are not included in the ticket price, but acceptable food is available in the restaurant on board.

Crossing the Border Brazilian immigration is at the federal police post at the Corumbá rodoviária. Anyone entering or exiting Brazil must check in here and complete immigration formalities. For about US$0.20, a city bus will take you into Corumbá, five km from the border. Everyone entering Brazil from Bolivia is required to have a yellow fever vaccination certificate.

Getting Around
A taxi to the centre of Corumbá from either the bus or the train station costs US$1.50. For a taxi from the centre to the Bolivian border, expect to pay US$3.50. The city bus between the centre and the Brazilian border runs about twice an hour (US$0.60). The Brazilian border post is open daily from 8 to 11 am and 2 to 5 pm.

Bahia

Bahia is Brazil's most Africanised state. Its capital, Salvador da Bahia, is a fascinating city, loaded with historic buildings. If beaches are what you want, the only difficulty is choosing. The inland regions of Bahia are less well known, but are well worth a visit. Lençois provides a handy base for hiking trips inside the spectacular Parque Nacional da Chapada Diamantina.

Bahia has some of Brazil's best artisans, who usually have small shops or sell their folk art in the local market. You can buy this in Salvador, but the best place to see or purchase the real stuff is in the town of origin.

SALVADOR DA BAHIA
Salvador da Bahia, often abbreviated to Bahia by Brazilians but also commonly called Salvador, is the capital of Bahia state and is one of Brazil's cultural highlights.

On 1 November 1501, All Saints' Day, Amerigo Vespuccio sailed into the bay, which was accordingly named Baía de Todos os Santos. In 1549, on the shores of the bay, Tomé de Souza founded what was to be Brazil's most important city for 300 years.

Thriving on the sugar trade until the mid-18th century, Salvador was the Portuguese Empire's second city, after Lisbon. It was famous for gold-filled churches, beautiful mansions and many festivals. It was also famous for its sensuality and decadence. Growing industries are currently changing the urban landscape, though they have done little to reduce the great number of jobless, homeless and hungry Bahians.

Orientation
Salvador sits at the southern tip of a V-shaped peninsula at the mouth of Baía de Todos os Santos. A steep bluff divides central Salvador into two parts: Cidade Alta (Upper City), the historic section, and Cidade Baixa (Lower City), the commercial and financial centre. These are linked by the Plano Inclinado Gonçalves (funicular railway), the Lacerda Elevator and some very steep roads (ladeiras).

Information
Tourist Offices Emtursa, the state of Bahia's

tourism authority, has its main office (☎ 243-6911) at Largo do Pelourinho 12. For tourist information and maps, visit the nearby Emtursa information post (next to the Casa da Cultura Jorge Amado); it's open 8 am to noon and 2 to 5 pm on weekdays, and on Saturday from 8 am to noon.

The main tourist office of Bahiatursa (☎ 241-4333), in Palácio Rio Branco, Rua Chile 2, is open from 8 am to 6 pm on weekdays. There are also Bahiatursa offices at Mercado Modelo (☎ 241-0242, open from 8 am to noon and 2 to 6 pm Monday to Saturday), the rodoviária (☎ 231-2831, open from 9 am to 6 pm Monday to Saturday) and the airport (☎ 204-1244, open from 8 am to 10 pm Monday to Friday). Bahiatursa operates an alternative lodging service, locating rooms in private houses during Carnaval and summer holidays.

Money The main branch of Banco do Brasil is at Avenida Estados Unidos 561, in Cidade Baixa. In Cidade Alta, a convenient place with fair rates is Olimpia Tours e Viagens, on Praça Anchieta.

Whatever you do, don't change money on the street, particularly near the Lacerda Elevator or the Cantina da Lua. Men posing as moneychangers will lead you to some side alley and rip you off.

There's an American Express/Kontik-Franstur SA office (☎ 242-0433) in Cidade Baixa, at Praça da Inglaterra 2, which holds mail for travellers.

Post The central post office is in Cidade Baixa. There are also post offices at Avenida 7 de Setembro, Rua Ruy Barbosa 19 (in Cidade Alta), the airport and the rodoviária.

Emergency Useful emergency telephone numbers include ☎ 131 for Disque Turismo (Dial Tourism), ☎ 192 for Pronto Socorro (First Aid) and ☎ 197 for Polícia Civil (Police).

Dangers & Annoyances Salvador has a justifiable reputation for theft and muggings.

For more detail, see Dangers & Annoyances in the Facts for the Visitor section near the beginning of this chapter.

Things to See
Walking Tour Historic Salvador is easy to see on foot, and you should plan on spending a couple of mornings wandering through the old city. The most important sections of Salvador's colonial quarter extend from Praça Castro Alves along ruas Chile and da Misericórdia to Praça da Sé and Terreiro de Jesus, then down through Largo do Pelourinho and up the hill to Largo do Carmo.

Starting at the Praça da Sé, walk a block to the **Terreiro de Jesus**. The biggest church on the plaza is the **Catedral Basílica**, built between 1657 and 1672. It's open from 8 to 11 am and 3 to 6 pm Monday to Saturday, and from 5 to 6.30 pm on Sunday. Next door is the **Antiga Faculdade de Medicina** (Old Medical Faculty), which now houses our favourite museum in Bahia, the **Museu Afro-Brasileira** (Afro-Brazilian Museum), with its small collection of displays focusing primarily on orixás from Africa and Bahia. The museum is open Tuesday to Friday from 9 am to noon and 2 to 5 pm, and on Saturday from 9 am to noon.

In the basement of the same building, and with the same hours, is the **Museu de Arqueologia e Etnologia** (Museum of Archaeology & Ethnology). As you exit the museum, turn left, walk to the far end of the plaza, and continue one block to **Igreja São Francisco**. Defying the teachings and vows of poverty of its namesake, this baroque church is crammed with displays of wealth and splendour. Opening hours are 7.30 to 11.30 am and 2 to 6 pm Monday to Saturday, and 7 am to noon on Sunday.

To see the city's oldest architecture, turn down Rua Alfredo de Brito, the small street which descends into the **Pelourinho** district. *Pelourinho* means 'whipping post', and this is where the slaves were tortured and sold (whipping of slaves was legal in Brazil until 1835). The old slave auction site on Largo do Pelourinho has recently been renovated

BRAZIL

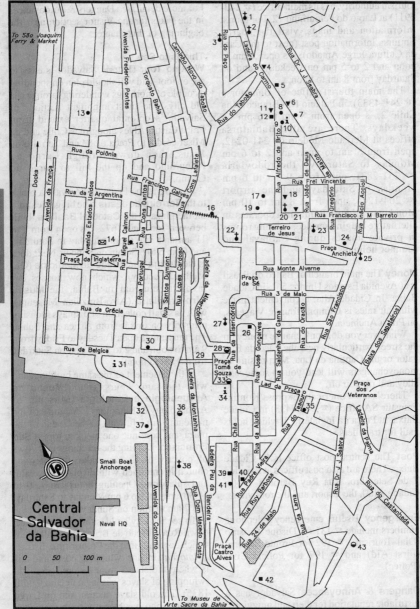

Central
Salvador
da Bahia

0   50   100 m

To São Joaquim
Ferry & Market

Docks

Avenida da França

Avenida Frederico Pontes

Torquato Bahia

Caminho Novo do Taboão

Rua da Polônia

Rua Francisco Galves

Rua da Argentina

Avenida Estados Unidos

Rua da Grécia

Rua Cons Dantas

Rua Miguel Calmon

Rua Cons Lafaiete

Rua Portugal

Rua Santos Dumont

Rua Lopes Cardoso

Rua da Bélgica

Rua do Paço

Ladeira do Carmo

Rua do Taboão

Rua Dr J J Seabra

Rua Alfredo de Brito

Rua João de Deus

Rua Frei Vincente

Rua Gregório

Rua Inácio Accioli

Rua Francisco M Barreto

Terreiro
de Jesus

Praça
Anchieta

Rua Monte Alverne

Praça
da Sé

Rua 3 de Maio

Rua São Francisco

Rua do Oração

Ladeira da Misericórdia

Rua da Misericórdia

Praça
Tomé de
Souza

Rua José Gonçalves

Rua Saldanha da Gama

Bahia dos Sapateiros

Praça
dos
Veteranos

Ladeira da Montanha

Ladeira da Palma

Lad da Praça

Rua do Tesouro

Rua Chile

Rua da Ajuda

Rua do Castanheda

Rua Dr J J Seabra

Small Boat
Anchorage

Naval HQ

Avenida do Contorno

Ladeira Pru da Bandeira

Rua Dom Macedo Costa

Rua Padre Vieira

Rua Ruy Barbosa

Rua da Lima

Rua 24 de Maio

Praça
Castro
Alves

To Museu de
Arte Sacre da Bahia

Praça da Inglaterra

■	**PLACES TO STAY**	16	Plano Inclinado Gonçalves (Funicular Railway)
5	Hotel Solara	17	Antiga Faculdade de Medicina (Old Medical Faculty)
12	Hotel Pelourinho	19	Museu Afro-Brasileiro/Museu de Arqueologia e Etnologia
26	Hotel Themis		
39	Hotel Chile	20	Igreja São Pedro dos Clérigos
40	Palace Hotel	22	Catedral Basílica
42	Hotel Maridina	23	Igreja da Ordem Terceira de São Domingos
▼	**PLACES TO EAT**	24	Olimpia Tours e Viagems (Money Exchange)
4	Casa do Benin Restaurant	25	Igreja São Francisco
6	Senac Restaurant	27	Igreja da Misericórdia
11	Banzo Restaurant	28	Police Post/Buses to Airport & Rodoviária
18	Meson Espanhol Restaurant		
21	Cantina da Lua	29	Lacerda Elevator
		30	Casa dos Azulejos
	OTHER	31	Mercado Modelo & Bahiatursa Tourist Office
1	Igreja e Convento de NS do Carmo/Museu do Carmo	32	Boat to Itaparica
		33	Buses to Rodoviária & to Barra
2	Igreja da Ordem Terceira do Carmo	34	Palácio Rio Branco & Bahiatursa Tourist Office
3	Igreja do Santíssimo Sacramento da Rua do Paço		
		35	Casa de Ruy Barbosa
7	Olodum	36	Buses to Mercado São Joaquim, São Joaquim Ferry & Igreja do Senhor do Bonfim
8	Largo do Pelourinho		
9	Museu da Cidade/Casa da Cultura Jorge Amado		
		37	Bunda Statue
10	Emtursa Tourist Office	38	Igreja NS da Conceição
13	Banco do Brasil	41	VASP
14	Central Post Office	43	Terminal da Barroquinha
15	VASP		

and converted into the **Casa da Cultura Jorge Amado** (Jorge Amado Museum). The museum is open Monday to Friday from 8 am to noon and 2 to 6 pm.

Igreja NS do Rosário dos Pretos, across the Largo do Pelourinho, was built by (and for) the slaves. The 18th-century church has some lovely azulejos. It's open from 8 am to 5.30 pm Monday to Friday, and from 8 am to 2 pm on Saturday and Sunday.

From Pelourinho, go down the hill, then continue uphill before climbing a set of steps to the left, leading up to **Igreja do Santíssimo Sacramento da Rua do Paço** – an approach which is reminiscent of the Spanish steps of Rome.

At the top of the hill is **Igreja da Ordem Terceira do Carmo**. Founded in 1636, it contains a baroque altar and an organ dating

from 1889. For a glimpse of unspoilt, old Salvador, walk a few blocks further, past very old, dilapidated buildings which teem with life.

To continue on a walking tour of the city, it's best to retrace your steps to Praça da Sé. Praça Tomé de Souza, just beyond, has several beautiful sites, including the **Palácio Rio Branco**. The **Lacerda Elevator**, inaugurated in 1868, was an iron structure with clanking steam elevators. Today, electric elevators truck up and down in less than 15 seconds. Watch out for petty crime here, particularly after dusk.

Further along the Itapagipe peninsula, past Mercado São Joaquim, is the **Igreja so Senhor do Bonfim**. Built in 1745, the shrine is famous for its miraculous power to effect cures. For Candomblistas, Bonfim is the most important church. In January, the Lavagem do Bonfim, one of Bahia's most important festivals, takes place here. The church is open from 6 am to noon and 2.30 to 6 pm Tuesday to Sunday.

Museu de Arte Sacra da Bahia From Praça Castro Alves, it's a short walk to the Museu de Arte Sacra da Bahia, at Rua do Sodré 276. The sacred art is displayed in a beautifully restored 17th-century convent. Opening hours are 9.30 to 11.30 am and 2 to 5.30 pm Monday to Friday.

Museu de Arte Moderna On the bay, further down from the centre toward Campo Grande, is the Solar do Unhão, an old sugar estate that now houses the small Museu de Arte Moderna, a restaurant (see Places to Eat) and a ceramic workshop. This area has a reputation for crime (especially mugging of tourists), so take a taxi to and from the Solar do Unhão; walking is not advisable. Opening hours are 1 to 5 pm Tuesday to Sunday.

Beaches Salvador has many beautiful beaches. If you want to swim, it's advisable to head for Placaford, Itapoã or further north. If you just want to wander through the city beach scene, Barra is the first Atlantic beach, and the liveliest, but heavy pollution makes swimming inadvisable. See the Getting Around section for details of transport to these beaches.

Candomblé Much of Bahian life revolves around the Afro-Brazilian cults known as Candomblé (see Religion in the Facts about the Country section near the beginning of this chapter). Before doing anything in Salvador, find out about the schedule for Candomblé ceremonies, so that you don't miss a night in a terreiro. Bahiatursa can provide a complete list of terreiros and advise you on the schedule for the month. The centre for Candomblé in Salvador is Casa Branca, on Avenida Vasco da Gama 463, in the Engenho Velho neighbourhood.

Capoeira School To visit a capoeira school, it's best to get the up-to-date schedule from Bahiatursa. The Associação de Capoeira Mestre Bimba is an excellent school. It's at Rua Francisco Muniz Barreto 1, 1st floor, Terreiro de Jesus, and operates Monday to Saturday from 9 to 11 am and 4 to 7 pm. Speak to Manuel or Ari.

Festivals
Although Carnaval in Salvador is justly world famous, it is by no means the only festival worth attending. Combining elements of the sacred and profane, Candomblé and Catholicism, many of Salvador's festivals are as wild as Carnaval, and possibly more colourful.

Carnaval Carnaval, usually held in February or March, starts on a Thursday night and continues until the following Monday. Everything, but everything, goes during these four days. In recent years, Carnaval has revolved around the trios elétricos.

Carnaval brings so many tourists and so much money to Salvador that there's been an inevitable tendency towards commercialisation, though this trend is still light years behind Rio.

Many clubs have balls just before and during Carnaval. If you're in the city before the festivities start, you can also see the *blocos* (musical street groups) practising. Just ask Emtursa or Bahiatursa.

Take a look at the newspaper or go to Emtursa or Bahiatursa for a list of events. Don't miss the *afoxés* (Afro blocos). The best place to see them is in Liberdade, Salvador's largest Black district.

Hotels do fill up during Carnaval, so reservations are a good idea. Stay near the centre or in Barra. Violence can be a problem during Carnaval, and some women travellers have reported violent approaches from locals. A common danger you may encounter at Carnaval is being sucked into the pack right behind a trio elétrico, then having to dodge all the dancers, and their flying elbows!

Places to Stay

Salvador has many hotels, but they can all fill up during the summer season, so reservations are a good idea. Readers have commented that they felt safer staying south of the city centre or near the beaches than in the historic centre.

Camping On the outskirts of Itapoã, there are several campgrounds, such as *Cabana da Praia* (☎ 248-8477), Alamedas da Praia, s/n (no number), which is open from December to March, and *Camping Clube do Brasil* (☎ 249-2101), also at Alamedas da Praia, s/n (no number).

Hostels Most of Salvador's youth hostels, a relatively recent addition to the range of accommodation options, have been established away from the city centre and close to the beaches.

The following beach hostels are listed in sequence, from Barra district along the Atlantic coast towards Itapoã: *Albergue de Juventude Casa de Pedra* (☎ 247-5678), Rua Florianópolis 134, Jardim Brasil, Barra; *Albergue de Juventude Solar* (☎ 248-0577), Rua Macapá 461, Ondina; *Albergue de Juventude Lagash* (☎ 248-7399), Rua Visconde de Itaboraí 514, Amaralina; *Albergue de Juventude Casa Grande* (☎ 248-0527), Rua Minas Gerais 122, Pituba; *Albergue de Juventude Boca do Rio* (☎ 230-8371), Avenida Dom Eugênio Sales 72, Lote 11, Boca do Rio; and *Albergue de Juventude CNEC* (☎ 249-4802), Rua Bicuíba, s/n (no number), Loteamento Patamares.

Hotels *Hotel Pelourinho* (☎ 321-9022), at Rua Alfredo de Brito 20, is right in the heart of the historic Pelourinho area. It's an older, converted mansion with character, and the management appears to be security conscious. Interior apartamentos are good value, at US$12 for a single, including a superb buffet breakfast, but you'll pay at least 50% more for a room with a view.

Hotel Themis (☎ 243-1668), at Praça da Sé 57, Edifício Themis (7th floor), offers good value in the centre of town. Apartamentos with a view cost US$14/21 a single/double; quartos are US$11/16.

Just a short walk from Bahiatursa is *Hotel Chile* (☎ 321-0246), at Rua Chile 7 (1st floor). It's a bit grubby, but a good deal. Quartos start at US$8/11, while apartamentos cost US$14/16 without air-con, slightly more with.

Close by is *Hotel Maridina* (☎ 242-7176), at Avenida 7 de Setembro, Ladeira de São Bento 6 (1st floor). This is a friendly hotel which offers good value for money. Quartos cost US$8/13 and apartamentos without TV start at US$10/16.

Hotel Anglo-Americano (☎ 247-7681), at Avenida 7 de Setembro 1838, is usually good value but was closed for repairs in early 1993. Ask at the hotel desk about guides for visits to Candomblé ceremonies. In the same area, very close to Museu de Arte da Bahia, is *Hotel Caramuru* (☎ 336-9951), at Avenida 7 de Setembro 2125. It has been highly recommended by readers. The hotel is a large colonial mansion with a leafy courtyard. Prices for single/double apartamentos start around US$10/13. Quartos are slightly cheaper.

In Barra district, readers have recommended *Hotel Bella Barra* (☎ 237-8401, 235-2313), at Rua Afonso Celso 439. It's a much quieter place to stay than the hotels on the seafront. Clean, bright apartamentos cost US$21/29.

If you plan to pass most of your days at the beach, going into the city only on occasion, consider staying in Itapoã, the nicest Atlantic beach suburb. It's also close to the airport, which can make it convenient if you're flying out the next day.

Along the beach, in the heart of Itapoã, *Hotel Europa* (☎ 249-9344) is a personal favourite. It has very clean apartamento doubles for around US$12.

A couple of more expensive hotels represent good value. In the city centre, *Palace Hotel* (☎ 243-1155), at Rua Chile 20, offers single/double apartamentos for US$28/33 without air-con or TV, US$34/40 with these amenities.

Opposite the beach in the Barra district, and within easy reach of the city centre, is *Hotel Porto da Barra* (☎ 247-4939), at Avenida 7 de Setembro 3783. Single/double apartamentos without air-con cost US$27/30; air-con doubles cost US$33.

Places to Eat

Bahian cuisine is an intriguing blend of African and Brazilian recipes based on characteristic ingredients such as coconut cream, ginger, hot peppers, coriander, shrimp and dendê oil. For names and short descriptions of typical Bahian dishes, see Food in the Facts for the Visitor section of this chapter.

With a large working population, Cidade Baixa has lots of cheap, lunch-only restaurants. Vegetarians will want to try *Restaurante Naturel*, three doors to your right as you leave the elevator (base station). The restaurant is on the 2nd floor. It offers an excellent self-service lunch but is closed in the evenings.

Inexpensive food is also easy to find in Cidade Alta. A popular hang-out with cheap victuals is *Cantina da Lua*, on Terreiro de Jesus, at the edge of the Pelourinho district.

At Rua Alfredo de Brito 11, there's an excellent restaurant called *Meson Espanhol* (☎ 321-3523). It's on the 1st floor, with a bird's-eye view of street life. Main dishes average US$6 – the moqueca de peixe (fish stew) is excellent. Opening hours are noon to 10 pm Monday to Saturday. To promote security for evening diners, this restaurant offers a free transport service (there and back) – just phone ahead for a reservation.

Banzo, the restaurant next door to the Hotel Pelourinho, is bright, animated and good value. There's a great selection of Bahian and European dishes, plus all sorts of exotic drinks; expect to pay around US$5 for a main dish plus a drink. The décor features works of art by local artists, and there's often live music in the evening. Opening hours are erratic.

Across the street is *Senac* (☎ 321-5502), a cooking school which offers a huge spread of 30 regional dishes in the form of a self-service buffet. It's not the best Bahian cooking, but for US$8 you can discover which Bahian dishes you like... and eat till you explode! Senac is open from 6.30 to 9.30 pm Monday to Saturday. Folklore shows are presented from 8 to 9 pm Thursday to Saturday – tickets cost US$2 per person.

At the crossroads downhill from Largo do Pelourinho is *Casa do Benin* (☎ 243-7629), a superb restaurant serving excellent African food in a small courtyard, complete with palm trees, pond and thatched hut. Main dishes start at around US$6 – the frango ao gengibre (ginger chicken) is close to culinary heaven! The restaurant has recently extended its hours, and is now open in the evenings.

Solar do Unhão (☎ 321-5551), which houses the Museu de Arte Moderna described previously, also has a restaurant, on the lower level in the old *senzala* (slave quarters). The view from the restaurant is as good a reason as any for a visit. The Bahian cooking is unexceptional. The restaurant is open Monday to Saturday from noon to midnight. Reservations are recommended. Dinner is usually accompanied by live music, and a folklore show at 10 pm – expect to pay an extra US$3 cover charge. As mentioned previously for the Museu de Arte Moderna, crime is a problem in this area – take a taxi to or from the Solar do Unhão.

Excellent Bahian dishes at moderate prices are served at *Restaurante Iemanjá* (☎ 231-5570), Avenida Otávio Mangabeira, s/n (no number), on Armação beach. It's open daily from noon to 5 pm and 7 pm to midnight.

Last, best and hardest to find is *Bargaço* (☎ 231-5141), at Rua P, Quadra 43, Jardim Armação; it's on a small residential street near the Centro de Convenções (Convention Centre). Main dishes start around US$12 – fame has set an upward trend for the prices. Bargaço is open daily from noon to midnight.

Entertainment

Salvador is justly renowned for its music. The security advice provided under Dangers

& Annoyances in the Facts for the Visitor section is especially relevant after dark.

The Pelourinho area often has blocos, such as Olodum, practising on Sunday nights and drawing crowds of dancers into the streets – definitely a musical highlight. Banzo, described under Places to Eat, is a great bar and restaurant in Pelourinho, with live reggae music.

Barra is full of nightlife. Some places are quite good, but it's more touristy and Westernised than other neighbourhoods. Habeas Copos (☎ 235-7274), at Avenida Marquês de Leão 172, is an old favourite with the bohemian crowd.

Danceterias Those in search of *danceterias* (dance halls) could try Holandés Voodor (☎ 247-7140), Rua João Gomes 88, in Rio Vermelho, or head towards Amaralina to visit New Fred's (☎ 247-4399), Rua Visconde de Itaboraí 125, which is a huge lambada mecca with room for 600 dancers.

Folklore Shows Usually consisting of displays of Candomblé, capoeira, samba, lambada, etc, these shows are presented in the evening at Senac, in Pelourinho, and at Solar do Unhão, south of city centre (see Places to Eat).

Getting There & Away

Air The big three domestic airlines all fly to Salvador, as does Nordeste, which goes to smaller cities in the region, like Ilhéus and Porto Seguro. There are regular international flights between Salvador and Miami, Frankfurt, Paris, Rome and Buenos Aires. Following is a list of Brazilian airlines represented in Salvador:

Nordeste
    Avenida D João VI 259, Brotas (☎ 244-7755, 204-2554)
Transbrasil
    Rua Carlos Gomes 616, Centro (☎ 242-3344)
    Airport (249-2467)
Varig/Cruzeiro
    Rua Carlos Gomes 6, Centro (☎ 243-1344)
    Airport (☎ 204-1030)

VASP
    Rua Pinto Martins, Comércio (☎ 243-7044)
    Rua Chile 27, Centro (☎ 243-7044)
    Airport (☎ 249-2495)

Bus There are numerous departures daily to Rio (US$43, US$85 for leito, 28 hours). Buses to São Paulo leave four times daily (US$50, US$98 for leito, 33 hours). There are four daily departures to Brasília (US$43, US$85 for leito, around 22 hours) and Belo Horizonte (US$34, US$67 for leito, around 22 hours).

There are six departures daily to Aracaju (US$9, US$16 for leito, 16 hours), five to Recife (US$21, US$40 for leito, 12 to 14 hours) and one to Belém (US$51, 36 hours). There are two daily departures to Fortaleza (US$34, 20 hours), and a thrice-weekly leito (US$65).

There are three daily departures to Lençóis (US$10, seven hours) and two for Ilhéus (US$11, seven hours). There are frequent departures daily to Valença (US$8, five hours) and two evening departures to Porto Seguro (US$16, US$32 for leito, 12 hours), as well as frequent departures, between 5.30 am and 7 pm, to Cachoeira (US$3.50, two hours) – take the bus marked 'São Felix'.

Getting Around

The Lacerda Elevator runs daily from 5 am to midnight, linking the lower and upper cities.

To/From the Airport Aeroporto Dois de Julho (☎ 204-1010) is over 30 km from the city centre, inland from Itapoã. At the airport, there's a bilheteria (ticket office) for taxi transport. A taxi ride to Praça da Sé costs US$20, but in the other direction, you can arrange it for about half that. The best way to go is to take the Executivo bus marked 'Praça da Sé/Aeroporto' (US$1). It starts at Praça da Sé (the stop is signposted), follows the coast, then runs inland to the airport. You can flag it down along the way. Allow 1½ hours for the ride. A municipal bus (US$0.20) marked 'Aeroporto' follows the same route, but it gets very crowded and is not recommended if you're carrying a bag.

Bus Buses from Praça da Sé go to Campo Grande, Vitória and Itapoã via Barra. Air-conditioned executive buses marked 'Praça da Sé/Aeroporto' also leave from here, and go along the beaches from Barra to Itapoã (US$1). This is one way to go to the Atlantic coast beaches. Another way is to take the 'Jardineira' service, which operates from 7.30 am to 7.30 pm daily between Campo Grande (bus stop outside Hotel da Bahia) and Itapoã (US$1.75, 40 minutes). The trip, on an open-deck bus, follows a scenic route along the coast.

The Avenida da França stop is in Cidade Baixa, beside the Lacerda Elevator (base station). From here, take either the 'Ribeira' or the 'Bonfim' bus to the Itaparica ferry (get off after a couple of km, when you see the Pirelli Pneus store on your left) or the Mercado São Joaquim market (get off at the stop after Pirelli Pneus), or continue to Igreja do Senhor do Bonfim.

To/From the Rodoviária The rodoviária (☎ 231-5711) is five km from the city centre, but it's a bit messy taking a bus there. For a quicker trip, take a taxi, which costs US$4 from Praça da Sé. At the rodoviária, there's a bilheteria which sells fixed-price taxi tickets.

Buses to the rodoviária leave from Terminal da Barroquinha, just south of the city centre. Take the bus marked 'Rodoviária R3', get off at Iguatemi shopping centre and use the pedestrian crossing which arcs above the highway.

CACHOEIRA

Cachoeira – the jewel of the recôncavo (a fertile region around the Baía de Todos os Santos) – is a small city in the centre of Brazil's best tobacco-growing region. It is full of beautiful colonial architecture, uncompromised by modern buildings.

Cachoeira is separated from São Felix by the Rio Paraguaçu, which flows into the Baía de Todos os Santos. It can be visited in a day from Salvador de Bahia (120 km away), if you get an early start, but it's better to stay overnight.

Information

The municipal tourist office, in a renovated building on Rua 13 de Maio, should be able to help with accommodation and with general details about the town's sights.

Things to See

Cachoeira is an important centre for **Candomblé**. The ceremonies are held in small homes and shacks up in the hills, usually at 8 pm on Friday and Saturday nights. Visitors are not as common here as in Salvador, and the tourist office is sometimes reluctant to give out information, but you may inspire confidence if you show an interest in Candomblé and respect for its traditions.

Cachoeira and São Felix are best seen on foot. The recently restored **Igreja da Ordem Terceira do Carmo** features a gallery of suffering polychrome Christs imported from the Portuguese colonies in Macau. Visiting hours are 2 to 5 pm Tuesday to Saturday, and 9 to 11.30 am on Sunday.

The **Hansen Bahia Museum** was set up in the home and birthplace of Brazilian heroine Ana Neri, who organised the nursing corps during the Paraguay War. Now, the work of German (naturalised Brazilian) artist Hansen Bahia is displayed here. The museum is open from 10 am to noon and 2 to 5 pm, closed on Tuesday and Sunday afternoons. Prints are also on sale here.

The tiny **NS d'Ajuda**, on Largo da Ajuda, is Cachoeira's oldest church. Phone ☎ 724-1396 to arrange a visit to the church and the **Museu da Boa Morte**, an interesting museum with displays of photos and ceremonial apparel of the exclusively female Boa Morte cult.

Festivals

One of Cachoeira's many festivals is the fascinating **Festa da NS de Boa Morte**, organised by the Irmandade da Boa Morte (Sisterhood of the Good Death), a secret,

Black, religious society. At this festival, descendants of slaves celebrate their liberation with dance and prayer. The festival falls on the Friday closest to 15 August and lasts three days. The **Festa de São João**, from 22 to 24 June, is the big popular festival of Bahia's interior.

Places to Stay

Pensão Tia Rosa (☎ 725-1792), opposite Museu Hansen Bahia, has pleasant quartos for US$10/11 a single/double, including a superb breakfast. *Massapé* (☎ 725-1392) charges US$9 per person for adequate quartos. *Pousada do Guerreiro* (☎ 725-1203), at Rua 13 de Maio 14, has ragged but cheap quartos (US$11/14).

Pousada do Convento de Cachoeira (☎ 725-1716, or 243-0741 in Salvador) is a lovely hotel with a courtyard and swimming pool. The dark wood rooms of the old convent cost US$26/30, including a major spread for breakfast. An extra bed costs US$7, or you can splurge on the suite (US$35).

Places to Eat

The *Gruta Azul* (☎ 725-1295), Praça Manoel Vitorino 2, is Cachoeira's best restaurant. If you're adventurous, ask for the boa morte (good death) drink. Opening hours are 11 am to 3 pm and 7 to 9 pm every day (except Sunday, when it's closed in the evening).

Rian restaurant – locals delight in inverting the name to Nair – provides excellent moqueca dishes and local specialties. There's more good food at *Cabana do Pai Thomáz* (the restaurant is part of the pousada), open daily from 11 am to midnight, and *Massapé*, open daily from 11 am to midnight.

Getting There & Away

There are frequent buses, between 5.30 am and 7 pm, to Salvador (US$3.50, two hours).

PRAIA DO FORTE

Praia do Forte is 80 km north of Salvador on the Rodovia do Coco (the Coconut Highway). Praia do Forte has fine beaches,

a beautiful castle fortress, a sea turtle reserve and, unfortunately, only expensive hotels. Until recently a fishing village, it is being developed as an ecologically minded – and decidedly up-market – beach resort.

TAMAR Turtle Reserve

The reserve is on the beach, right next to the lighthouse. TAMAR (Tartaruga Marinha) is a project started in 1982 to protect several species of marine turtles that are, or were, threatened.

Places to Stay & Eat

The only cheap place to stay is the campground, which is just 10 minutes on foot from the beach. One of the cheaper hotels is *João Sol* (☎ 876-1054), on Rua da Corvina, but prices for most hotels are spiralling upwards. If you have an urge to splurge, the recently revamped *Pousada Praia do Forte* (☎ 835-1410) has bungalows on the beach (US$75 for two, including full board).

Getting There & Away

The São Luís bus company runs a bus service from Iguatemi Shopping Centre (opposite the rodoviária in Salvador) to Praia do Forte. The trip takes two hours, and the service operates daily between 7.30 am and 6 pm.

MORRO SÃO PAULO

Morro São Paulo, at the northern tip of Ilha do Tinharé, is a tranquil, isolated fishing village with incredible beaches. Since its discovery by hip Brazilians and international travellers, it has rapidly acquired fame and a place on the best-beach lists of several Brazilian magazines. Beware: there are many bichos de pé (see Health in the Facts for the Visitor section of this chapter), so keep something on your feet when walking through town.

Places to Stay & Eat

The food and lodging scene is changing quickly, and accommodation can be scarce during the summer. Apart from a couple of campgrounds on the beaches, there are nearly 40 pousadas, or you could ask about renting a house from one of the local fishers. *Pousada da Praia*, on Rua da Graça, has inexpensive apartamentos.

The *Restaurante-Pousada Gaúcho* charges US$6 for rooms which can sleep three people. They also rent two-room houses for US$14 per day. *Pousada da Praia* has quartos starting at around US$13/16 for a single/double, and *Ilha da Saudade Pousada-Restaurant* (☎ 741-1702 in Valença for reservations) has attractive single/double apartamentos for US$30/35.

Naturalmente serves a prato feito for US$3.

Getting There & Away

Take the *Brisa Biônica* (Bionic Breeze) or *Brisa Triônica* between Morro de São Paulo and Valença for a relaxed boat ride (US$2, 1½-hours) which rivals the Caribbean and South Pacific in beauty.

During the summer, the schedule is as follows: Monday to Saturday, two boats per day leave from Valença at 8 am and noon for Morro de São Paulo, returning at 6 am and 12.20 pm. On Sundays, they leave Valença at 6 am and 12.20 pm and Morro de São Paulo at 8 am and noon. Check the times carefully; the increasing popularity of Morro de São Paulo will undoubtedly cause frequent schedule changes.

At other times of year, there is only one boat per day in either direction. It leaves Monday to Saturday at 6 am from Morro de São Paulo, returning from Valença at 12.30 pm. On Sundays, there is a 6 am boat from Valença to Morro de São Paulo; it returns at 12.30 pm. If you're coming from Salvador, you can confirm these times at Bahiatursa.

ILHÉUS

Ilhéus, the town where Jorge Amado lived and which he wrote about in *Gabriela, Clove & Cinnamon*, retains some of the charm and lunacy that Amado fans know well. The colonial centre is interesting and the beaches are superb, yet the area has remained largely unaffected by tourism.

Things to See

The best thing to do in Ilhéus is just wander. If you walk up the hill to the **Convento NS da Piedade**, there's a good view of the city and littoral. The **Igreja de São Jorge** (1534), the city's oldest church, houses a small sacred art museum. It's on Praça Rui Barbosa and is open Tuesday to Sunday from 8 to 11 am and 2 to 5.30 pm.

CEPLAC, the Centro de Pesquisa do Cacao (☎ 214-3014), is the government cacao agency. They run a **demonstration cacao plantation** and research station near Itabuna, about 30 km inland; it's open to the public from 8.30 to 11.30 am and 2.30 to 3.30 pm on weekdays. Arrange your tour at the CEPLAC office in Ilhéus first.

Places to Stay

There is a lack of accommodation in Ilhéus; consequently, hotels are generally overpriced and filled with guests. Most are within a 15-minute walk of the central bus station.

For campgrounds en route to Olivença, you can try *Camping Colónia da Stac* (☎ 231-7015), 13 km from Ilhéus, or *Camping Estância das Fontes* (☎ 212-2505), 18 km from Ilhéus.

Pousada Kazarão (☎ 231-5031), at Praça Coronel Pessoa 38, has the nicest quartos in town (US$9/12 a single/double, without breakfast). *Luka's* (☎ 231-4071), Rua 7 de Setembro 177, offers adequate apartamentos for around US$15/16, as does *Britânia Hotel* (☎ 231-1722), Rua 28 Junho 16, which is in a similar price range. *Pousada do Sol* (☎ 231-7000), just south of the airport, is very pleasant and is reasonably priced.

For a total splurge, there's *Transamérica Ilha de Comandatuba* (☎ 212-1122), which is on its own island (Ilha de Comandatuba) opposite the town of Una, 70 km south of Ilhéus. For US$155 per person per day (including meals), you have the run of immense grounds, private beach and every imaginable recreational facility.

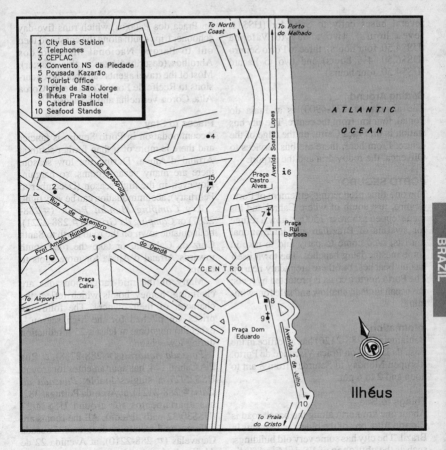

1 City Bus Station
2 Telephones
3 CEPLAC
4 Convento NS da Piedade
5 Pousada Kazarão
6 Tourist Office
7 Igreja de São Jorge
8 Ilhéus Praia Hotel
9 Catedral Basílica
10 Seafood Stands

To North Coast
To Porto do Malhado

ATLANTIC OCEAN

Avenida Soares Lopes

Praça Castro Alves

Ld Teresópolis

Rua 7 de Setembro

Praça Rui Barbosa

Prof. Amélia Nunes

do Dendê

CENTRO

Praça Cairu

To Airport

Praça Dom Eduardo

Avenida 2 de Julho

Ilhéus

To Praia do Cristo

Places to Eat

The tiny but mighty *Asa Branca*, with a wide array of natural juices and cheap sandwiches, is at Rua Pedro II, No 110. For good seafood, try *Os Velhos Marinheiros* (open daily from 11 am to midnight), at Avenida 2 de Julho, and *O Céu é o Límite* (open daily from 11 am to 11 pm), four km west of town, on Avenida Itabuna. *Bar Vezúvio*, on Praça Dom Eduardo, has been described in Amado's works and is consequently a tourist magnet. For Swiss and Bahian food, try *Ô-lá-lá*, at Avenida 2 de Julho 785; for Japanese food, try *Tokyo*, on the same street, at No 1039.

Getting There & Away

Air There's a small airport, which is serviced by Nordeste, VASP, Varig/Cruzeiro and air taxis.

Bus For most major destinations, buses leave more frequently from Itabuna than from Ilhéus, so it's usually quicker to go to Itabuna first, then shuttle down to Ilhéus. The rodoviária in Ilhéus is a 15-minute bus ride from the centre. Buses to Salvador go through the recôncavo via Cachoeira or via Nazaré and connect with the ferry from Itaparica Island to Salvador. Ilhéus has several buses daily to Salvador (US$11, seven hours), two a day to Valença (US$4.50, four hours), three to Porto Seguro (US$6.50, 4½ hours) and two to Itacaré (US$4.50, four hours).

Getting Around

The airport (☎ 231-4900) is at Praia do Pontal, four km from the centre. The city bus station is on Praça Cairu, on the edge of the centre. From here, there are bus services to Olivença, the rodoviária and the airport.

PORTO SEGURO

The one-time pioneering settlement of Porto Seguro, just south of where Cabral and his men stepped ashore in 1500, is now a refuge for swarms of Brazilian and international tourists, who come to party and to take in some mesmerising beaches. The town itself has no beaches, but there are plenty nearby. The Porto Seguro coast is protected by reefs; the ocean is clear, shallow and safe for swimming.

Information

Bahiatursa (☎ 288-2126) has an office in the Casa da Lenha, on Praça Visconde de Porto. It's open Monday to Saturday from 8 am to noon and 2 to 6 pm.

Things to See

About one km north along the beach road is **Cidade Alta**, one of the oldest settlements in Brazil. The city has some very old buildings, such as the **churches** of NS da Misericórdia (perhaps the oldest church in Brazil), NS da Pena (1535, rebuilt 1773) and NS do Rosário dos Jesuitas (1549). It also has the small Museu Antigo Paço Municipal (1772) and the old fort (1503).

The **Reserva Biológica do Pau Brasil**, a 10-sq-km reserve 15 km from town, was set aside principally to preserve the brazil wood tree. For details about visiting this reserve, ask Bahiatursa or one of the travel agencies.

Tours

Excursions can be arranged with Companhia do Mar Passeios de Escunas (☎ 288-2981),

on Praça dos Pataxos, which runs five-day schooner trips south along the coast and then out to Parque Nacional Marinho dos Abrolhos (described later in this chapter). Most of the travel agents can organise excursions to Recife de Fora (Coral Reef), Coroa Alta, Coroa Vermelha and Trancoso.

Places to Stay

Accommodation in Porto Seguro is fancier and there is more of it than further south at Arraial d'Ajuda. During the low season, there are many vacant rooms, so bargain. However, in the high season (December to February), accommodation can be very tight.

Try *Camping Mundaí Praia* (☎ 288-2287) or *Camping da Gringa* (☎ 288-2221), both outside town on the road north to Santa Cruz da Cabrália, or take the road south towards Arraial d'Ajuda for more spots to camp.

Many of the mid-range pousadas are charming, homey hotels which reflect the character of their owners. The following prices are pitched for the high season – expect to negotiate at least a 25% reduction during low season.

Pousada Aquarius (☎ 288-2738), at Rua P A Cabral 174, has apartamentos for around US$25/27 a singles/double. *Pousada do Cais* (☎ 288-2121), at Avenida Portugal 382, has apartamentos for around US$24/27 (US$30/32 with air-con). All the rooms are different and tastefully decorated. Pousada Caravelas (☎ 288-2210), at Avenida 22 de Abril, s/n (no number), near the sea, has pleasant apartamentos at US$23/24.

Places to Eat

The *Bar-Restaurant Tres Vintens*, Avenida Portugal 246, serves a delicious bobo de camarão (shrimp dish) for US$4. For good Japanese food (US$3 to US$6), take the ferry to Arraial d'Ajuda and visit *Restaurante do Japonês*, in the orange building.

La Tarrafa, at Avenida Portugal 360, is a rustic oyster bar. *Restaurant Primadonna*, Praça dos Pataxos 247, is run by Italians who know their pasta. Pastas start at US$3, seafood at US$4.50. It's open from noon to

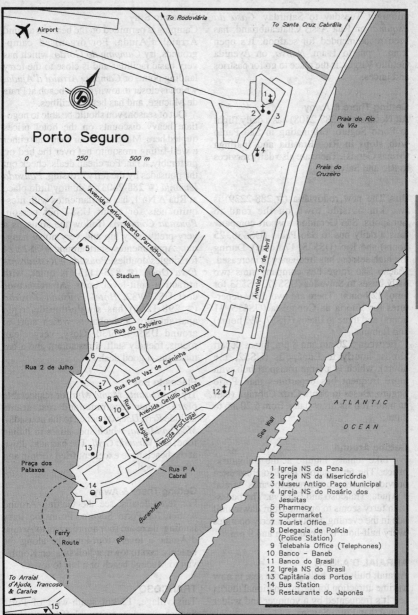

Porto Seguro

0   250   500 m

To Rodoviária

To Santa Cruz Cabrália

Airport

Praia do Rio da Vila

Praia do Cruzeiro

Avenida Carlos Alberto Parracho

Avenida 22 de Abril

Stadium

Rua do Cajueiro

Rua 2 de Julho

Rua Pero Vaz de Caminha

Avenida Getúlio Vargas

Rua Itaúba

Avenida Portugal

ATLANTIC OCEAN

Sea Wall

Rua P A Cabral

Praça dos Pataxos

Ferry Route

Buranhém

Rio

To Arraial d'Ajuda, Trancoso & Caraíva

1 Igreja NS da Pena
2 Igreja NS da Misericórdia
3 Museu Antigo Paço Municipal
4 Igreja NS do Rosário dos Jesuitas
5 Pharmacy
6 Supermarket
7 Tourist Office
8 Delegacia de Polícia (Police Station)
9 Telebahia Office (Telephones)
10 Banco – Baneb
11 Banco do Brasil
12 Igreja NS do Brasil
13 Capitânia dos Portos
14 Bus Station
15 Restaurante do Japonês

BRAZIL

midnight Tuesday to Saturday. *Casa da Esquina*, on Rua Assis Chateaubriand, has been recommended for seafood. It's open from 7 pm to 1 am. *Nativo*, on Avenida Getúlio Vargas, is the place to go for pastries and juices.

Getting There & Away

Air Nordeste (☎ 288-2108) has a daily flight to Porto Seguro, originating in São Paulo with stops in Rio, Brasília and Ipatinga (Minas Gerais). There are also daily services to Rio and Salvador.

Bus The new rodoviária (☎ 288-2239) is two km outside town on the road to Eunápolis. São Geraldo transport company runs a daily bus to São Paulo (US$36, 25 hours) and Rio (US$28, 17 hours). During the high season, bus frequency is increased. Viação São Jorge bus company runs two daily buses to Salvador (US$17, US$33 for leito, 12 hours). There are two daily departures for Vitória da Conquista (US$15, 11 hours) and three to Ilhéus (US$7, 4½ hours) and Itabuna.

Between 5.20 am and 8 pm, buses depart almost hourly to Eunápolis (US$2, 1½ hours), which is a large transport hub with more frequent bus departures than Porto Seguro. Buses to Santa Cruz Cabrália (half an hour) run six times daily, from 6.20 am to 7 pm.

Getting Around

For bike rentals, inquire at the Bahiatursa office. The ferry across the Rio Buranhém provides access to the road towards Arraial d'Ajuda, Trancoso and Caraíva. The pedestrian ferry seems to operate from dawn until late in the evening, but the car ferry operates every half-hour between 7 am and 9 pm.

ARRAIAL D'AJUDA

Arraial, built on a hilltop by the sea, is now a prime attraction for the international tourist set. It's frequented by a younger and wilder crowd than Porto Seguro.

Places to Stay

Camping is permitted on the beaches around Arraial d'Ajuda. For organised campgrounds, try *Camping do Gordo*, which has very basic facilities and is close to the ferry landing point, or *Camping Arraial d'Ajuda*, which is closer to town, on the beach at Praia de Mucugê, and has better facilities.

Out of season, you should be able to negotiate heavy discounts on the hotel prices quoted here. Make sure your room has either a well-fitting mosquito net over the bed or, preferably, a fan. For cheap deals, check out the pousadas by the ferry crossing. *Pousada Iemanjá* (☎ 288-2403), a dumpy little place at Rua A No 1, has apartamentos with mosquito nets for about US$7 per person. *Pousada Coqueiros* (follow the signs) is a very pretty, very hip and very noisy hangout. Apartamentos start around US$22/24 for singles/doubles. *Pousada e Restaurante Erva Doce* (☎ 875-1113) is quiet, with attractive split-level units. Apartamentos cost US$30/32. *Hotel Pousada Tororão* (☎ 298-1266) has single/double/triple apartamentos and chalets which start at around US$24/26/30. Cosy, very clean rooms, friendly staff, a restaurant and a bar make this a good deal.

Places to Eat

Try *Restaurante Mama Mia* for respectable pizza. Other recommended restaurants include *Erva Doce* (attached to the pousada), *Mão na Massa*, which specialises in Italian food, and *Varanda Grill*. The barracas down at the beach have excellent fried shrimp and other seafood.

Getting There & Away

For ferry details, see the Getting Around section for Porto Seguro. From the ferry landing, there are four approaches to Arraial d'Ajuda: a lovely four-km hike along the beach, a taxi to town, a Volkswagen Kombivan to Mucugê beach or a bus to town.

TRANCOSO

This village, 12 km south-west of Porto Seguro, is on a grassy bluff overlooking

fantastic beaches. At the Telebahia office
(☎ 867-1115), you can leave a telephone
message to reserve accommodation.

Places to Stay & Eat

Pousadas and restaurants are being
revamped and are going up-market, but
campgrounds are OK. If you are planning a
long stay, rent a house on the beach. Count
on paying US$20/25 for single/double
apartamentos (negotiate reductions during
low season) at pousadas such as *Le Refuge*,
Canto Verde and *Hibiscus*.

Caipim Santo, close to the central square,
is recommended for its health food. It's open
from 2.30 to 9.30 pm Monday to Saturday.

Getting There & Away

Buses to Trancoso leave Arraial d'Ajuda
three times a day, at 7 and 10 am and 2 pm,
from the ferry landing opposite Porto
Seguro, stopping on Broadway in Arraial
d'Ajuda. There are more buses during the
high season. The walk from Trancoso back
along the beach to Arraial d'Ajuda is beautiful.

CARAIVA

Without running water, electricity or throngs
of tourists, the hamlet of Caraiva is primitive
and beautiful. Boats to Caraiva (40 km south
of Trancoso) leave daily from Trancoso's
pier during high season, as soon as the boat
fills (US$5 per person), and irregularly
during the rest of the year. In high season,
there are also boat services operating to
Caraiva from Porto Seguro.

LENÇOIS

Lençois lies in a wooded, mountain region –
the Chapada Diamantina, an oasis in the
dusty sertão. Here you'll find old mining
towns and great hiking. If you have time for
only one excursion into Brazil's north-
eastern interior, this is the one. Note that the
Banco do Brasil in Lençois does not change
travellers' cheques.

Things to See & Do

The city is pretty and easily seen on foot,

though unfortunately, most of the buildings
are closed to the public. See the old **French
vice-consulate**, a blue 19th-century building where diamond commerce was
negotiated, and **Casa de Afrânio Peixoto**, a
house museum with the personal effects and
works of the writer Afrânio Peixoto. Also
worth a visit is the **Museu do Garimpo**
(Miners' Museum), which has various
mining relics and artefacts.

For details about hikes, see the following
section on the Parque Nacional da Chapada
Diamantina.

Places to Stay

Reserve accommodation in advance at
weekends, and throughout January and February.

Camping Lumiar, on Praça do Rosário,
has shady sites, passable bathrooms, a bar
and a restaurant. The cost is US$1.50 per
person. *Pousalegre* (☎ 334-1124) is a
favourite with travellers. Quartos cost
US$5/10 a single/double. *Pensão Alcino*
(☎ 334-1171) is a bright, clean place which
charges US$6 per person for quartos, includ-
ing a highly recommended breakfast.
Pensão Angela (☎ 334-1167) provides
similar quality at similar prices.

Pousada Canto das Águas (☎ 334-1154)
is recommended for its superb position, in a
landscaped garden beside the river. The
apartamentos, overlooking the cascades,
cost around US$22/26, including an enor-
mous breakfast. *Hotel Colonial* (☎ 334-
1114) has pleasant apartamentos at
US$13/18. At the top end of the price range
is the attractive *Pousada de Lençois* (☎ 334-
1102). Standard apartamentos with air-con
cost US$30/33/41 for singles/doubles/
triples. Deluxe versions of these rooms cost
around US$8 more.

Places to Eat

Pousalegre serves excellent, inexpensive
meals, with several natural foods on the
menu. *ResTAOrant* is a type of New Age
eatery run by a Berliner. The food is not
cheap, but there's a good selection of natural
foods. Other restaurants worth visiting

include *Ynave*, and those attached to *Pousada de Lençóis* and *Pousada Canto das Águas*.

The *Lajedo Bar & Restaurant*, *Amigo da Onça* (bar) and *Dançataria Restaurant Luar* are evening hang-outs.

Getting There & Away

Bus The rodoviária is on the edge of town, beside the river. Buses to Salvador (US$10, seven hours) leave daily at 9 am and 11 pm; on Sunday, there's an additional departure, at 9 pm. Buses from Salvador leave at 9.15 am and 8.15 pm. Buses to Palmeiras and Seabra leave at 3 am and 4 pm.

AROUND LENÇÓIS

For day trips around Lençóis, walk or hire a horse. For day trips further afield, you can walk, hire transport or use the bus. For horse rental, contact either Angela, at Pensão Angela (see Places to Stay in Lençóis), who will only rent out horses for trips in the immediate vicinity of Lençóis, or Senhor Dazim, who will go further afield. Sample prices per person are US$0.50 for one hour, US$15 a half-day, US$22 a day and US$45 for three days. Groups of three receive a 30% discount.

Parque Nacional da Chapada Diamantina

This park, 1520 sq km of the Sincora range of the Diamantina plateau, has several species of monkeys, beautiful views, clean waterfalls, rivers and streams, and an endless network of trails. Many of the foreigners and Brazilians living in Lençóis have joined a strong ecological movement which is in direct opposition to the extractive mentality of the *garimpeiros* (prospectors) and many of the locals. Riverbeds have been dug up, waters poisoned and game hunted for food and sport. The park is particularly interesting for rock hounds, who will appreciate the curious geomorphology of the region.

Information The park has little, if any, infrastructure for visitors. Knowledgeable guides, such as Roy Funch and Luís Krug, can greatly enhance enjoyment of any trip into the park. Roy Funch can be contacted at Funkart Artesanato, in Lençóis. Contact Luís at Pousada Canto das Águas, in Lençóis.

Short Hikes A pleasant 1½-hour hike can be taken upstream along the Rio Lençóis to Salão de Areias Coloridas (Room of Coloured Sands), where artisans gather their matéria prima for bottled sand paintings, then on to Cachoeira da Primavera waterfall.

Another relaxing hike (45 minutes) can be made to Ribeirão do Meio, a series of swimming holes with a natural waterslide (bring old clothes or borrow a burlap sack). It is *very* important not to walk up the slide: several bathers who have done so have met with nasty accidents. Instead, swim across to the far side of the pool and climb the dry rocks at the side of the slide before launching off.

Lapa Doce About 70 km north-west of Lençóis, then a 25-minute hike to the entrance, is a huge cave formed by a subterranean river which dried up. You will need a guide (Luís is an expert on the place) and you should bring a torch. Admission costs US$0.35. Lapa Doce is best visited by car.

Rio Mucugêzinho This river, 30 km from Lençóis, is a super day trip. Take the 8 am 'Palmeiras/Seabra' bus and ask the driver to let you off at Barraca do Pelé – the bus passes this place again around 4 pm on its return trip to Lençóis. From Barraca do Pelé, pick your way about two km downstream to Poço do Diabo (Devil's Well), a swimming hole with a 30-metre waterfall. Further upstream, you'll find Rita and Marco, who have set up in a cave and run a snack bar outside.

Morro do Pai Inácio At 1120 metres, this is the most prominent peak in the immediate area. It's 27 km from Lençóis and easily accessible from the highway. An easy but steep trail takes you to the summit (200 metres above the highway) for a beautiful view.

Hikers may want to take the trail along **Barro Branco** between Lençóis and Morro do Pai Inácio; allow four or five hours one-way for the hike.

Palmeiras This is a drowsy little town 56 km west of Lençóis, with a slow pace, a scenic riverside position and streets lined with colourful houses. There are several cheap pensões.

The hamlet of **Capão** is 20 km from Palmeiras by road (or use the hiking trail connecting Capão with Lençóis). From here, there's a six-km trail (two hours on foot) to the top of **Cachoeira da Fumaça**, also known as the Glass waterfall (after missionary George Glass), which plummets 420 metres – the longest waterfall in Brazil. Although marked on the map, the route to the bottom of the waterfall is very difficult and not recommended.

For a much longer trip, there's the **Grand Circuit Route**, a 100-km walk, best done on foot in a clockwise direction. It takes about five days, but allow eight days if you include highly recommended side trips such as **Igatú** and Cachoeira da Fumaça.

Sergipe

Sergipe, north of Bahia, is Brazil's smallest state. There are a couple of interesting historical towns, but beaches are not up to standard and the capital, Aracaju, is as memorable as last Monday's newspaper.

ARACAJU

Aracaju, 367 km north of Salvador and 307 km south of Maceió, has little to offer the visitor, but it's a base for trips to the colonial villages of Laranjeiras and São Cristóvão.

Places to Stay

Most of the hotels are in the centre or out at Praia Atalaia Velha on Avenida Atlântica. For a short stay, hotels in the centre are much more convenient and generally less expensive. Ask for low-season discounts between March and June, and during August and September.

For camping, try *Camping Clube do Brasil* (☎ 243-1413), on Atalaia Velha. Also on Atalaia Velha, *Pousada das Redes* (☎ 231-9165) is an agreeable youth hostel. For a rock-bottom choice, there's *Hotel Sergipe* (☎ 222-7898), in the centre. Quartos cost US$2.50 per person. For much better value, try *Hotel Oasis* (☎ 224-1181), which charges US$12/14 for single/double apartamentos. *Hotel Brasília* (☎ 222-5112) has apartamentos at US$13/20. A popular mid-range hotel is the *Jangadeiro* (☎ 222-5115), in the city centre. It provides clean apartamentos at US$24/26.

Places to Eat

Cacique Chá (closed on Sunday), a good garden restaurant, is on Praça Olímpio Campos. *Artnatus* serves plain vegetarian food; it's only open for lunch. Good seafood restaurants at Atalaia Velha include *Taberna do Tropeiro* (live music in the evening), at Avenida Oceânica 6, and the highly recommended *O Miguel* (closed on Monday), at Rua Antônio Alves 340.

Getting There & Away

Long-distance buses leave from the *rodoviária nova* (new bus terminal), which is about four km from the centre. There are six buses a day to Salvador (US$9, US$16 for leito, six hours), three to Maceió (US$7, five hours) and two to Recife (US$14, nine hours).

For transport details on São Cristóvão and Laranjeiras, see their respective Getting There & Away sections. Note that bus services for these two towns operate from the *rodoviária velha* (old bus terminal) – *not* from the rodoviária nova. There's a shuttle service between the bus terminals (US$0.30, 25 minutes). A taxi between the rodoviária nova and the centre costs around US$4.

SÃO CRISTÓVÃO

Founded in 1590, São Cristóvão was the capital of Sergipe until 1855. The old part of town, up a steep hill, has a surprising number of 17th and 18th-century buildings along its narrow stone roads. Of particular distinction

BRAZIL

are the **Igreja e Convento de São Francisco**, on Praça São Francisco, and the **Igreja de Senhor dos Passos**, on Praça Senhor dos Passos.

São Cristóvão is 25 km south of Aracaju and seven km off BR-101. The rodoviária is down the hill, below the historic district on Praça Dr Lauro de Freitas. There are frequent buses to Aracaju (from the Rodoviária Velha) and Estância.

LARANJEIRAS

Nestled between three lush, church-topped hills, Laranjeiras is the colonial gem of Sergipe. It has several churches and museums worth visiting, and the surrounding hills offer picturesque walks with good views.

There is a city tourism office inside the Trapiche building in the Centro de Tradições, on Praça Samuel de Oliveira, where you can obtain brochures, and information about guides for hire. The only pousada in town is *Pousada Vale dos Outeiros* (☎ 281-1019), at Rua José do Prado Franco 124. It's a friendly place with cheap quartos (around US$5.50 per person), and apartamentos (around US$11/13 a single/double).

Hourly buses (US$0.50, 35 minutes) run between Laranjeiras and Aracaju's rodoviária velha, with the first bus leaving for Laranjeiras at 5 am and the last returning at 9 pm.

Alagoas

The small state of Alagoas is one of the pleasant surprises of the North-East. Its beaches are enchanting, and inland there is a fabulous stretch of lush, sugar-cane country.

MACEIÓ

Maceió, the capital of Alagoas, is 292 km north of Aracaju and 259 km south of Recife.

Information

Ematur (☎ 221-9393), the state tourist agency, is on Avenida Siqueira Campos (Estádio Rei Pelé). There are also information booths at the airport and at the rodoviária.

Things to See & Do

For the best beaches, head north to Pajuçara (three km from the centre), Sete Coqueiros (four km), Ponta Verde (five km), Jatiúca (six km), Jacarecica (nine km), Guaxuma (12 km), Garça Torta (14 km), Riacho Doce (16 km) and Pratagi (17 km) – from town, there are frequent buses going as far as Riacho Doce. On shore, there are loads of barracas, *jangadas* (local sailboats) and beach enthusiasts.

The schooner *Lady Elvira* departs daily from Restaurante do Alípio in Pontal da Barra for a five-hour cruise to islands and beaches (US$16 per person, without lunch). For information and reservations, contact Restaurante do Alípio (☎ 225-2565), Avenida Alípio Barbosa 321, Pontal da Barra.

Places to Stay

Campers can try *Camping Pajuçara* (☎ 235-7561), on Praia de Pajuçara, or *Camping Jatiúca* (☎ 231-4183), on Praia Cruz das Almas, around six km from the centre.

There are also three youth hostels near Maceió: *Albergue de Juventude Pajuçara* (☎ 231-0631), at Rua Quintino Bocaiuva 63, Praia de Pajuçara, *Albergue de Juventude Nossa Casa* (☎ 231-2246), at Rua Prefeito Abdon Arroxelas 177, on Praia de Ponta Verde, and *Albergue de Juventude Stella Maris* (☎ 231-5217), at Avenida Engenheiro Paulo Brandão Nogueira 336, on Praia Jatiúca.

Hotel Florida (☎ 221-4485) has adequate apartamentos (US$10/17 for singles/doubles with fan, US$14/21 with air-con). *Hotel Ney* (☎ 221-6500) is midway between the city centre and Praia de Pajuçara. Attractive apartamentos cost US$16/19. It's a clean, safe hotel.

For a good mid-range choice, try the *Hotel Beiriz* (☎ 221-1080), at Rua João Pessoa 290. Room prices start around US$30/48.

Close to the beach, *Pousada da Praia* (☎ 232-2697) has friendly management and is a good low-budget option, with quartos at US$8/11. *Pousada Anço Marzio* (☎ 231-0034) has bright rooms. Quartos cost US$8/12 with fan, US$11/14 with air-con. *Pousada Saveiro* (☎ 231-9831) is friendly and offers apartamentos (with fan) at US$13/16. For an extra US$2, you can have an apartamento with air-con.

For a splurge, there's *Praia Hotel Sete Coqueiros* (☎ 231-8583), on Praia Pajuçara, a spiffy three-star hotel with swimming pool. Prices officially start around US$50/56.

Places to Eat
Restaivant Nativa is a good natural-food eatery, close to the Hotel Ney. If you feel like a seafood splurge, visit *Lagostão* (☎ 221-6211), at Avenida Duque de Caxias 1384. A cheaper option is *Como Antigamente*.

Most of the beaches offer a wide choice of food in barracas and snack bars along the beachfront, but pestering from vendors and assorted sandpeople can become wearisome if you sit outside. On Praia de Pajuçara, two pleasant restaurants are *Anço Marzio*, an Italian restaurant with great home-made pasta, and *Gôgo da Ema* (seafood dishes around US$5), with tables on an open patio.

Getting There & Away
Air Maceió is connected by air with Rio, São Paulo, Brasília and all the major centres of the North-east. Varig/Cruzeiro (☎ 223-7334) is at Rua Dr Luiz Pontes de Miranda 42, VASP (☎ 221-2855) is at Rua do Comércio 56 and Transbrasil (☎ 221-8344) is at Rua Barão de Penedo 213.

Aeroporto Dos Palmares is 20 km from the centre. There is a circular bus route that stops at the rodoviária, the airport and the city centre, near the Hotel Beiriz, at Rua João Pessoa 290 (ask about the schedule in the hotel). A taxi to the airport costs around US$10.

Bus The rodoviária (☎ 223-4105) is about four km from the centre. To reach the centre, take the bus marked 'Ouro Preto'. A taxi to

the centre costs around US$3, and a dollar more to Pajuçara. There are frequent daily departures to Recife (US$6.50, four hours) and Aracaju (US$7, five hours). Services operate five times daily to Salvador (US$19, 10 hours).

PENEDO
Penedo, known as the capital of the lower São Francisco, is a fascinating colonial city almost untouched by tourism. There's a tourist information desk (open daily from 9 am to noon) and a small city museum in the Casa da Aposentadoria, just up from the fort, at Praça Barão de Penedo. The street market is held every day, but Saturday is the day that attracts countryfolk from near and far.

Saturday (major market day) is the easiest day to find a boat up or down the São Francisco. For a short excursion, take one of the motorboats crossing to Neópolis, a few km downriver. The 15-minute trip costs a few cents, and boats depart every half-hour between 5.30 am and 11.30 pm. Alternatively, take one of the frequent boats (operating between 6 am and 6 pm) to Carrapicho, a small town noted for its ceramics.

Places to Stay & Eat
The *Hotel Imperial* (☎ 551-2198), on Avenida Floriano Peixoto, is old but clean, with single/double quartos at US$4/6. Perhaps the best deal in town is *São Francisco* (☎ 551-2273), on Avenida Floriano Peixoto, which is clean, quiet and has spacious apartamentos around US$14/19. The *Pousada Colonial* (☎ 551-2677), at Praça 12 de Abril, is more romantic; it's a beautiful converted colonial home on the waterfront, with apartamentos at US$13/17.

For meals, we recommend *Forte da Rocheira*, a restaurant in an old fort overlooking the river.

Getting There & Away
The rodoviária is on Avenida Duque de Caxias. There are three buses a day to Maceió (US$6, three hours) and one bus a day to Aracaju (US$4, three hours).

Maceió

BRAZIL

To Riacho Doce

Avenida Alm Alvaro Calheiros

Shopping Centre

Avenida Dn Constança

Avenida Empr Carlos da Nogueira

Avenida Dr Antônio Gomes de Barros

Avenida Ernesto Gomes Maranhão

Rua Pio XII

Avenida Dr Julio Marques Luz

Rua Hamilton de Barros Coutinho

Rua Ângelo Martins

Rua Prof Abdon Arroxelas

Almeda Cel Adauto Gomes Barbosa

Rua Dep José Lages

Almeda Capitão Marinho Falcão

Rua Mário Pradines

Avenida Brasil

Avenida Prof Sandoval Arroxelas

Avenida Des Mário Guimarães

Avenida Prof Vital Barbosa

Rua Pedro Américo

Avenida Dr José Sampaio Luz

Rua Dr Ant Cansanção

Rua Lafayete Pacheco

Rua Durval Guimarães

Rua Eng Mário de Gusmão

Rua Humberto Guimarães

24

Avenida Pres Robert Kennedy

Praia de Jatiúca

Praia de ponte Verde

Praia dos Sete Coqueiros

ATLANTIC OCEAN

To Piscina Natural (400 m)

23

Praia de Pajuçara

■ PLACES TO STAY

4 Hotel Beiriz
6 Hotel Florida
9 Hotel Parque
17 Hotel Ney
18 Pousada da Praia
20 Pousada Anço Marzio & Restaurant
21 Pousada Saveiro
22 Hotel Praia Bonita
24 Praia Hotel Sete Coqueiros

▼ PLACES TO EAT

14 Restaurant Lagostão
15 Restaurant Como Antigamente

16 Restaurant Nativa
19 Restaurant Gôgo da Ema

OTHER

1 Rodoviária
2 Ematur Tourist Office
3 Instituto Histórico
5 Banco do Brasil
7 Post Office
8 Cathedral
10 Buses to Pajuçara & Ponte Verde (Beaches)
11 Buses to Marechal Deodoro
12 Minibuses to Marechal Deodoro & Praia do Francês
13 Museu Theo Brandão
23 Jangadas to Reef & Piscina Natural

Pernambuco

RECIFE
Recife, the capital of Pernambuco, is a sprawling, confusing, modern conurbation. Although it has lots of churches and museums, few are must-sees. Most visitors come for the marginal stretch of beach and jungle of hotels that define the suburb of Boa Viagem.

Information
Tourist Office The headquarters of Empetur (☎ 231-7941), the state tourism bureau, is at Avenida Conde da Boa Vista 700.

Post & Telecommunications The main post office is at Avenida Guararapes 250. There are also convenient post offices at the airport and TIP (Terminal Integrado de Passageiros – rodoviária). TELPE (the state telephone company) has 24-hour telephone stations with international service at TIP, at the airport and at Rua Diário de Pernambuco 38, in the centre.

Visa Extensions These can be organised at the Polícia Federal building, on Rua Cais do Apolo (Ilha do Recife). It's best to phone first; ask the tourist office for the appropriate information.

Travel Agencies Andratur (☎ 326-4388), at Avenida Conselheiro Aguiar 3150, Loja 6 (Boa Viagem), is a good option for package tours, albeit expensive, to the paradise isles of Fernando de Noronha.

Things to See
Olaria de Brennand This ceramics factory and exhibition hall is set in thickly forested surroundings, a rare landscape for suburban Recife and an even rarer chance for travellers in the North-east to see what the Mata Atlântica looked like several centuries ago. The buildings and exhibits in Olaria de

Brennand are perhaps the most bizarre highlight of the North-east, and are highly recommended.

The gallery/museum houses a permanent exhibition of around 2000 pieces, which are *not* for sale. It's open from 8 am to 5 pm Monday to Thursday, and from 8 am to 4 pm on Friday. Olaria Brennand produces superb ceramics, which are sold in its shop (☎ 325-0025), at Avenida Conselheiro Aguiar 2966, Loja 4, Galeria Vila Real, in Boa Viagem.

To get there from the centre, take the bus marked 'Caxangá' for the 11-km ride to

■ PLACES TO STAY
1 Hotel das Fronteiras
2 Hotel Central
4 Hotel Suiça
8 Hotel do Parque
9 Hotel América
16 Hotel 7 de Setembro
21 Hotel 4 de Outubro

▼ PLACES TO EAT
5 China Brasil Restaurant

OTHER
3 Empetur Tourist Office
5 Livro 7 Bookshop
6 Galeria de Arte Metropolitana
7 Museu Archeológico
10 Fortaleza de São João Batista do Brum
11 Polícia Federal
12 Palácio do Governo & Teatro Santa Isabel
13 Capela Dourada da Ordem Terceira de São Francisco
14 Post Office
15 Matriz de Santo Antônio
17 Praça da Independência
18 Praça 17
19 Mercado do São José
20 Pátio de São Pedro
22 Casa da Cultura de Recife
23 Recife Metro Station & Museu do Trem
24 Forte das 5 Pontas (Museu da Cidade)
25 Joana Bezerra Metro Station

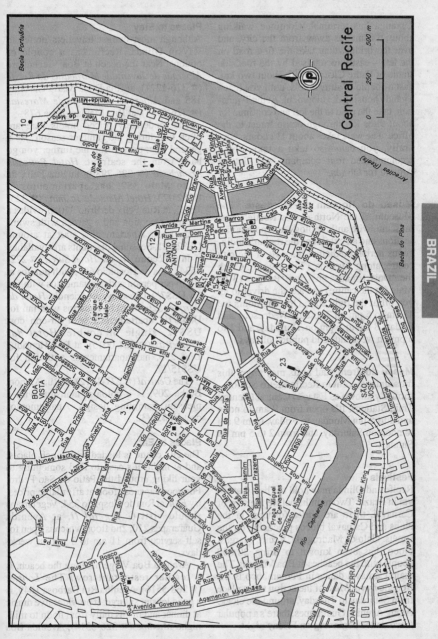

Central Recife

0   250   500 m

Caxangá bus terminal. Continue walking about 100 metres away from the city, and over the bridge, then take the first road on the left – easily recognised by the roadside statue of Padre Cicero. Walk about two km, past a couple of stray hotels, until you reach a gaudy housing development. At the T-junction, take the road to the left and continue for about three km through dense forest to the office. The walk takes about 1¼ hours. Naturally, you can also take a taxi. For a recommended tour company, see Getting Around for Olinda.

Museu do Homem do Nordeste The Museum of the North-east is Recife's best museum, with anthropology and popular art sections and an exhibit of the region's indigenous herbal medicine. It's east of the city centre, along Avenida 17 de Agosto. Catch the 'Dois Irmãos' bus from Parque 13 de Maio (in the centre) and ask the driver to let you off at the right spot. Opening hours are 11 am to 5 pm on Tuesday, Wednesday and Friday, 8 am to 5 pm on Thursday, and 1 to 5 pm on weekends and public holidays.

Museu do Trem Rail buffs may enjoy this museum, adjacent to Recife Metro Station – formerly known as Estação Central (Central Train Station). It's open from 9 am to noon and 2 to 5 pm Monday to Friday, from 9 am to noon on Saturday, and from 2 to 5 pm on Sunday.

Festivals
Recife and Olinda may hold the best **Carnaval** in Brazil. Two months before the start of Carnaval, there are *bailes* (dances) in the clubs and Carnaval blocos practising on the streets. Galo da Madrugada, Recife's largest bloco, has been known to bring 20,000 people onto the beaches at Boa Viagem. The main Carnaval dance in Pernambuco is the frenetic *frevo*. Most of the action takes place from Saturday to Tuesday, around the clock. Along Avenida Guararapes, there's a popular frevo dance beginning on Friday night.

Places to Stay
Although most budget travellers prefer to stay in Olinda, Recife has a couple of options. Near the beach at Boa Viagem are *Albergue de Juventude Maracatus do Recife* (☎ 326-1221), at Rua Dona Maria Carolina 185 and *Albergue de Juventude Maresias* (☎ 326-6284), at Rua Mamanguape 678.

The moderately priced hotels here are often full during the summer season. As a general rule, prices drop the further you go back from the seafront. *Hotel Pousada Aconchego* (☎ 326-2989), at Rua Felix de Brito Melo 382, has apartamentos at US$21/23. *Hotel Alameda Jasmins* (☎ 325-1591), at Rua Felix de Brito 370, provides a friendly reception and a garden with swimming pool. Apartamentos start at around US$20/21. Seasonal discounts are available.

In the centre, try the *Hotel Suiça* (☎ 222-3534), Rua do Hospício 687, with quartos at US$6 per person and apartamentos with fan for US$7/9. Close by, the friendly *Hotel do Parque* (326-4666) has quartos with fan for US$8/10; apartamentos with air-con cost US$12, single or double. *Hotel das Fronteiras* (☎ 221-0015), at Rua Henrique Dias 255, has apartamentos with fan for US$15/17.

The *Central* (☎ 221-1472), at Rua Manoel Borba 209, is a colonial mansion with a pleasant, rambling design. Apartamentos cost US$28/32.

Places to Eat
The city centre is loaded with lunch places, and at night, it's easy to find something to your liking around the Pátio de São Pedro. For good Japanese food at affordable prices, try *Fuji*, at Rua do Hospício 354. Vegetarians should visit *O Vegetal II*, at Avenida Guararapes 210, 2nd floor, which is open for self-service from 11 am to 3 pm on weekdays.

Avenida Boa Viagem, along the beach, is a regular restaurant row. The *Lobster* (☎ 268-5516), Avenida Rui Barbosa 1649, is a good lobster splurge. It provides live music at dinner and opens daily from noon to midnight. *Maxime* (☎ 326-5314), Avenida Boa

Viagem 21, serves traditional seafood dishes at moderate prices.

Entertainment

For reviews and listings of cultural events in Recife, pick up a copy of *Veja*, which includes them in its weekly supplement entitled '28 Graus'. There is usually live music in the centre, around the Pátio de São Pedro, on Thursday, Friday and Saturday evenings. The major nightlife centre for Recife is Graças district, which is packed with bars, clubs and general nightspots. It's a short taxi ride north-west of the city centre.

Getting There & Away

Air Aeroporto Guararapes is 10 km south of the city centre. From the airport, there are regular buses and *micro* buses (more expensive) to NS do Carmo (Olinda) and Dantas Barreto (central Recife). Both routes stop at Boa Viagem. To get to the airport, take a bus from NS do Carmo or Dantas Barreto. Taxis cost about US$10 to the centre.

There are flights to most major Brazilian cities, and also to Lisbon, London, Paris and Miami. Useful airline offices include:

Transbrasil
  Avenida Conde da Boa Vista 1546, Boa Vista (☎ 231-0522)
  Aeroporto Guararapes (☎ 326-2081)
Varig-Cruzeiro
  Avenida Guararapes 120, Santo Antônio (☎ 224-9066)
  Aeroporto Guararapes (☎ 341-4411)
VASP
  Avenida Guararapes 111, Santo Antônio (☎ 222-3611)
  Rua Manoel Borba 488, Boa Vista (☎ 421-3088)
  Aeroporto Guararapes (☎ 326-1699)

Bus The old rodoviária (rodoviária velha) has been superseded by TIP (☎ 251-4666), which is a combined Metro terminal and rodoviária, 14 km from the centre. TIP now handles all interstate departures and many connections for local destinations.

There are frequent departures to Maceió (US$6.50, four hours), at least five daily departures to Salvador (US$21, US$40 for leito, 12 to 14 hours) and daily departures to Rio (US$52, US$104 for leito, about 40 hours). Heading north, there are buses to João Pessoa (US$5, two hours), Natal (US$9, five hours), Fortaleza (US$23, 12 hours), São Luís (US$44, 23 hours) and Belém (US$53, 34 hours). There are frequent services to Caruaru (US$5, two hours), Garanhuns (US$8, 2½ hours) and Triunfo (US$17, 7½ hours).

Getting Around

Bus From the city centre to Olinda, catch any bus marked 'Rio Doce'. The main bus stop in Olinda is Praça do Carmo. Taxis from the centre of Recife to Olinda cost about US$5 and take 20 minutes.

From the centre to Boa Viagem, take any bus marked 'Cidade Universitária/Boa Viagem'. To return to the centre, take any bus marked 'Dantas Barreto'. A taxi from the centre to Boa Viagem costs around US$5.

Metro The metro system is very useful for the 25-minute trip (US$0.50) between TIP and the metro terminus at the Recife Metro Station, in the centre. Travellers who want to go straight to Boa Viagem from TIP should get off at metro stop 'Joana Bezerra' and catch a bus from there to Boa Viagem.

OLINDA

Olinda, Brazil's first capital, sits on a hill overlooking Recife and the Atlantic. After Ouro Prêto, it has Brazil's biggest and best-preserved collection of colonial buildings.

Information

The main tourist office (☎ 429-0397), at Rua 13 de Maio, No 322, is open from 8 am to 1 pm Monday to Friday.

Walking Tour

Starting at Praça do Carmo, visit **Igreja NS do Carmo** (currently under restoration). Then, follow Rua de São Francisco to **Convento São Francisco** (1585), which contains the convent, the **Capela de São Roque** (chapel) and the **Igreja de NS das Neves** (church) – approximate daily

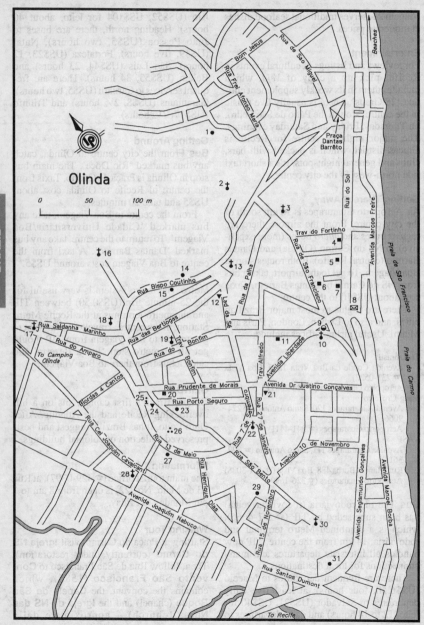

Olinda

0   50   100 m

■ PLACES TO STAY

4 Pousada do Fortim
5 Albergue de Olinda
6 Pousada Flor da Manhã
7 Hotel Pousada São Francisco
11 Albergue Pousada do Bonfim
20 Pousada dos Quatro Cantos

▼ PLACES TO EAT

12 Restaurant Cantinho da Sé
21 Mourisco Restaurant
24 Atelier Restaurant

OTHER

1 Farol de Olinda (Lighthouse)
2 Seminário de Olinda/Igreja NS da Graça
3 Convento São Francisco
8 Post Office
9 Praça do Carmo & Buses to Recife
10 Igreja NS do Carmo
13 Igreja da Sé
14 Museu de Arte Sacra de Pernambuco
15 Observatorio Astronômico
16 Recolhimento das Irmãs Dorotéias/Igreja NS da Conceição
17 Igreja NS do Amparo
18 Igreja da Misericórdia
19 Igreja NS do Bonfim
22 Igreja São Pedro
23 Mercado da Ribeira
25 Tourist Office
26 Senado Ruins
27 Museu de Arte Contemporânea
28 Igreja da Boa Hora
29 Palaçio dos Governadores
30 Mosteiro de São Bento
31 Mercado Popular (Market)

opening hours for this group are 8 to 11.30 am and 2 to 4.30 pm.

At the end of the street, turn left onto Rua Frei Afonso Maria and you'll see the **Seminário de Olinda** and **Igreja NS da Graça** (1549), on the hill above. Daily visiting hours are 8 to 11.30 am and 2 to 5 pm.

Continue up the street, then turn left at Rua Bispo Coutinho and climb up to **Alto da Sé**, (Cathedral Heights), which is a good spot to enjoy superb views of Olinda and Recife. There are outdoor restaurants and a small craft market. It's a big hang-out at night – good for meeting people, eating and drinking and, with a bit of luck, hearing some local music. The imposing **Igreja da Sé** (1537) is open from 7 am to 7 pm on Saturday and Sunday.

Continue a short distance along Rua Bispo Coutinho until you see the **Museu de Arte Sacra de Pernambuco** (MASPE), on your right. MASPE is housed in a beautiful building (1696) that was once Olinda's Episcopal Palace & Camara (Government Council). The museum contains a good collection of sacred art. It's open Tuesday to Friday from 8 am to noon and 2 to 6 pm. On Saturdays and Sundays, it's open from 2 to 5.30 pm.

About 75 metres further down the street, on your left, turn into a patio to visit **Igreja NS da Conceição** (1585).

Retrace your steps and continue down the street, now named Ladeira da Misericórdia, to **Igreja da Misericórdia** (1540), which has fine azulejos and gilded carvings inside. It's open from 9 to 11 am Monday to Friday, and from 2 to 5 pm on Saturday and Sunday.

Turn right onto Rua Saldanha Marinho to see **Igreja NS do Amparo** (1581), which is currently under renovation.

Descend Rua do Amparo to join Rua 13 de Maio, and walk about 100 metres until you see **Museu de Arte Contemporânea** (MAC), on your right. It's open Tuesday to Friday from 9 am to 5 pm, and on Saturdays and Sundays from 2 to 5 pm.

Rua 13 de Maio continues in a tight curve to a junction with Rua Bernardo de Melo and Rua São Bento. If you walk up Rua Bernardo de Melo, you'll come to **Mercado da Ribeira**, an 18th-century structure that is now home to art and artisan galleries.

If you walk down Rua São Bento, you'll reach the huge **Mosteiro de São Bento** (1582), which has some exceptional woodcarving in the chapel. Do some exploring in here by going up the stone stairs on your left as you enter. The monastery is open daily from 8 to 11 am and 1 to 5 pm.

Festivals

Olinda's **Carnaval**, which lasts a full 11

BRAZIL

days, has been very popular with Brazilians and travellers for years. Because so many residents know each other, it has an intimacy and security that you don't get in big city carnavals. Apart from Carnaval, there's the festival known as **Folclore Nordestino**, held at the end of August, which features dance, music and folklore from many parts of the North-east.

Places to Stay

Reserve accommodation several months in advance and be prepared for massive price hikes, if you want to stay in Olinda during Carnaval.

Within easy reach of the historical district is *Camping Olinda* (☎ 429-1365), Rua do Bom Sucesso 262. If you don't mind dormitory-style sleeping, the *Albergue Pousada do Bonfim* (☎ 429-1674), at Rua do Bonfim 115-B, is neat, clean and offers a bed in an eight-bed room for US$6. *Albergue de Olinda* (☎ 429-1592), at Rua do Sol 233, has collective quartos that sleep two to six people (US$7 a head). Apartamentos are also available (US$10/17 for singles/doubles). Similar hostel lodging is provided by *Albergue de Juventude Cheiro do Mar* (☎ 429-0101), at Avenida Marcos Freire 95, and *Hotel Albergue* (☎ 429-1409), at Avenida Marcos Freire 153.

Pousada Flor da Manhã (☎ 429-2266), at Rua de São Francisco 162, is an old villa, now revamped as a hotel under German/Brazilian management. Individual apartamentos are assigned names of countries, and decorated accordingly. Prices range from US$6 for 'India' (dormitory) to US$19/23 for 'Chile'.

Pousada do Fortim (☎ 439-1881), at Rua do Sol 311, has adequate apartamentos at US$13/14 – for apartamentos with air-con, you'll pay an additional US$3.

For a splurge, we'd recommend *Pousada dos Quatro Cantos* (☎ 429-0220), at Rua Prudente de Morais 441. It's a fine colonial building with a leafy courtyard. Quartos cost around US$16/32. Apartamentos start at US$38/42.

Places to Eat

Pousada Flor da Manhã has good seafood and salads at reasonable prices. Pousada dos Quatro Cantos is more expensive, but the moqueca de peixe is superb. In a similar price range is *Mourisco*, one of Olinda's best fish restaurants. It's open from 11 am to 3 pm and 7 to 11 pm (closed on Monday).

Getting There & Away

The main bus stop in Olinda is on Praça do Carmo. Buses marked 'Rio Doce/Conde da Boa Vista' go to the centre of Recife. Taxis cost about US$5.

Getting Around

Viagens Sob O Sol (☎ 429-3303), opposite Pousada dos Quatro Cantos, has a variety of vehicles for hire, with or without a driver/guide. This is an interesting option if you can form a group of three or more. Trips can be arranged, for example, to Porto de Galinhas, Caruaru, Fazenda Nova (Nova Jerusalém) and Olaria Brennand. A minibus (maximum eight passengers) trip to Nova Jerusalém costs about US$150, plus US$20 for transfer between Olinda and the airport or TIP.

CARUARU

On Wednesday and Saturday, Caruaru has an interesting folk-art fair, at which you can see the town's famous ceramic artwork and hear singers and poets perform the *literatura de cordel* (literally, string literature) – poetry by and for the people, sold in little brochures which hang from the stands by string (hence the name). Caruaru is an easy day trip from Recife on shuttle buses (US$5, two hours), which depart half-hourly.

FAZENDA NOVA & NOVA JERUSALÉM

The small town of Fazenda Nova, 50 km from Caruaru, is famous for its theatre-city reconstruction of Jerusalem, known as Nova Jerusalém. The time to visit is during Semana Santa (Holy Week, held in March or April – dates vary), when several hundred of the inhabitants of Fazenda Nova perform the Paixão de Cristo (Passion Play).

Places to Stay

There's a campground, *Camping Fazenda Nova*, or you can stay in the centre of town, at the *Grande Hotel* (☎ 732-1137), at Avenida Poeta Carlos Pena Filho, s/n (no number), which has apartamentos for US$20/22.

Getting There & Away

During Holy Week, there are frequent buses from Recife and special package tours are offered by travel agencies. At other times, there are daily buses between Fazenda Nova and Caruaru.

Paraíba

JOÃO PESSOA

João Pessoa, the capital of Paraíba, is a noisy, bustling place, worth a quick look before heading to the beaches.

Information

The office of PBTUR (☎ 226-7078) is at Avenida Almirante Tamandaré 100, in Tambaú. It provides maps and leaflets.

Igreja São Francisco

This is the town's principal tourist attraction and one of Brazil's finest churches. Its construction was interrupted by battles with the Dutch and the French, so the result is a beautiful but architecturally confused complex built over three centuries. Once renovation is completed, opening hours will probably be 8 to 11 am and 2 to 5 pm Wednesday to Sunday.

Beaches

The beaches are clean. Praia Tambaú, seven km directly west of the city centre, is rather built-up, but nice. South of Tambaú is Praia Cabo Branco. From there, it's a glorious 15-km walk along Praia da Penha to Ponta de Seixas, the easternmost tip of South America. There are good beaches north of Tambaú too.

Forty km south of João Pessoa, Praia

Jacumã is a long, thin strip of sand featuring coloured sand bars, natural pools, potable mineral water springs, a shady grove of palms and barracas (open for business on weekends). There are several camp sites, and a hotel with apartamentos for US$25/30, including meals.

About nine km south of Jacumã is Praia de Tambaba, rated among the 10 best beaches in Brazil. It's the only official nudist beach in the North-east. The Associação dos Amigos da Praia de Tambaba (Association of Friends of Tambaba, ☎ 290-1037 evenings only) can provide information. If you want to stay, there's an organised campground with facilities.

Places to Stay

At the easternmost tip of Brazil is *Camping-PB-01*, run by Camping Clube do Brasil at Praia de Seixas, 16 km from João Pessoa.

The central *Albergue de Juventude Cidade das Acácias* (☎ 222-2775), at Avenida das Trincheiras 554, Palácio dos Esportes, is accessible from the rodoviária; take the bus marked 'Cruz das Almas'. Get off at the 'Palácio dos Esportes' (Sports Palace) stop, opposite the hostel. There's another youth hostel at Tambaú beach, *Albergue de Juventude Tambaú* (☎ 226-5460), at Rua Bezerra Reis 82.

The best deal for a beach hotel in Tambaú – if you can get a room – is the *Hotel Gameleira* (☎ 226-1576), at Avenida João Maurício 157. Quartos cost US$11/14 and standard apartamentos (with fan) cost US$15/19.

In the centre, *Hotel Aurora* (☎ 241-3238), at Praça João Pessoa 51, charges US$9/13 for singles/doubles. Another option is *Hotel Guarany* (☎ 241-2161), at Rua Marechal Almeida Barreto 181. Apartamentos with fan start at around US$18/21. For a splurge, go to the rather palatial *Paraíba Palace Hotel* (☎ 221-3107), at Praça Vidal de Negreiros, s/n (no number). It's an impressive colonial palace. Standard apartamentos start at US$38/43 and luxury rooms cost US$50/55.

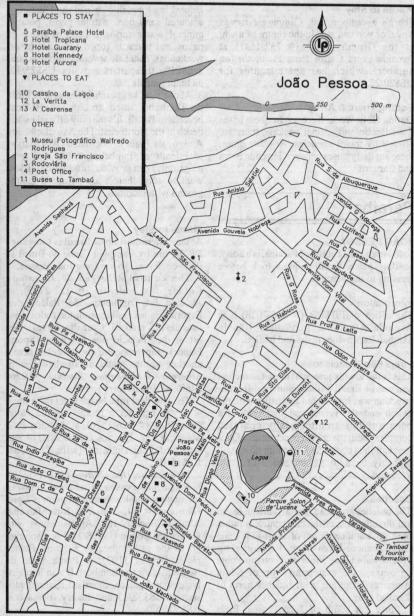

■ PLACES TO STAY

5 Paraíba Palace Hotel
6 Hotel Tropicana
7 Hotel Guarany
8 Hotel Kennedy
9 Hotel Aurora

▼ PLACES TO EAT

10 Cassino da Lagoa
12 La Veritta
13 A Cearense

OTHER

1 Museu Fotográfico Walfredo Rodrigues
2 Igreja São Francisco
3 Rodoviária
4 Post Office
11 Buses to Tambaú

João Pessoa

0   250   500 m

Places to Eat

Cassino da Lagoa has an open patio and a fine position beside the Lagoa, with live music on Friday nights. *La Veritta*, at Rua Desembargador Souto Maior 331, does good Italian food. *A Cearense*, at Rua Almeida Barreto 270, is a good bet for regional dishes. Vegetarians can head for *O Natural*, at Rua Rodrigues de Aquino 177, which serves lunch only.

In Tambaú, try *Adega do Alfredo*, at Rua Coração de Jesus 22, which specialises in Portuguese dishes. *Wan Li*, at Rua Coração de Jesus 100, is an inexpensive option for Chinese food. For a splurge on French cuisine, there's *Casier*, at Rua Coração de Jesus 144. It's closed on Monday. *Peixada do João*, at Rua Coração de Jesus 147, does excellent seafood.

Entertainment

Gulliver Pub, at Avenida Olinda 500, Tambaú, is run by an Anglophile Brazilian. For forró and lambada dancing in Tambaú, the Palladium, at Rua João Maurício 33, bops after 11 pm on Friday, Saturday and Sunday. Admission costs US$6.

Getting There & Away

Air Aeroporto Presidente Castro Pinto (☎ 229-3200) is 11 km from the city centre (about US$20 by taxi). Flights operate to Rio, São Paulo and the major cities in the North-east and the North.

Transbrasil (☎ 241-2822) is at Rua General Osório 177, sala 1, Varig/Cruzeiro (☎ 221-1133) is at Avenida Getúlio Vargas 183 and VASP (☎ 222-0715) is at Parque Solon de Lucena 530, Edifício Lago Center.

Bus The rodoviária (☎ 221-9611) is on the western edge of the city, on Avenida Francisco Londres. There are frequent buses to Recife (US$5, two hours), Natal (US$5.50, 2½ hours) and Fortaleza (US$19, 10 hours).

Getting Around

Local buses can be boarded at the rodoviária, at the bus stop next to the main post office and at the bus stops next to the Lagoa. Bus

No 510 runs frequently to Tambaú (US$0.30, 25 minutes). Bus No 507 runs to Cabo Branco.

Rio Grande do Norte

NATAL

Natal, the capital of Rio Grande do Norte, is a clean, bright city which is being developed at top speed into the beach capital of the North-East.

Information

The office of EMPROTUR (☎ 221-1452), the state tourism authority, is at Avenida Deodoro 249. It's open from 7 am to 1 pm Monday to Friday. SEMITUR (☎ 221-5729), the municipal tourism authority, is at Rua Trairi 563, Petrópolis.

Things to See & Do

The pentagonal **Forte dos Reis Magos** and the **Museu da Câmara Cascudo**, at Avenida Hermes da Fonseca 1398, are the principal sights of Natal. The museum features a collection of Amazon Indian artefacts. It's open from 8 to 11.30 am and 2 to 5 pm Tuesday to Friday, and from 8 to 11.30 am on Saturday.

Natal's **city beaches**, Praia do Meio, Praia dos Artistas, Praia da Areia Preta, Praia do Pinto and Praia Mãe Luiza, stretch well over nine km, from the fort to the lighthouse. Most have bars, nightlife and big surf.

Places to Stay

In Cidade Alta, one of the cheapest options is *Hotel Fenícia* (☎ 222-1366), at Avenida Rio Branco 586, which offers standard single/double apartamentos for US$9/11. *Hotel São Paulo* (☎ 222-4536), at Avenida Rio Branco 697, has apartamentos at US$13/16. One block down the street is *Hotel Natal* (☎ 222-2792), with apartamentos at similar prices.

The three-star *Hotel Jaraguá* (☎ 221-2355), at Rua Santo Antônio 665, has a sauna, a swimming pool and a panoramic

BRAZIL

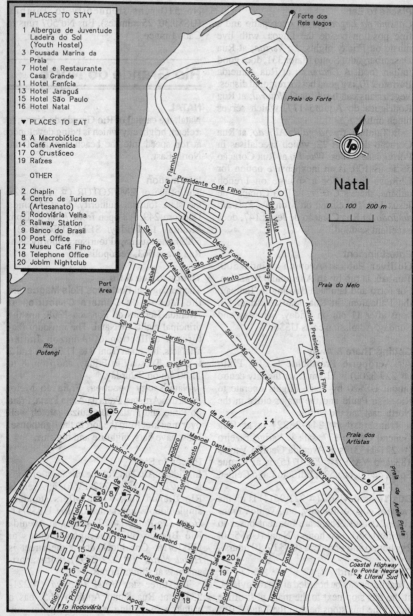

PLACES TO STAY

1 Albergue de Juventude
  Ladeira do Sol
  (Youth Hostel)
3 Pousada Marina da
  Praia
7 Hotel e Restaurante
  Casa Grande
11 Hotel Fenícia
13 Hotel Jaraguá
15 Hotel São Paulo
16 Hotel Natal

PLACES TO EAT

8 A Macrobiótica
14 Café Avenida
17 O Crustáceo
19 Raízes

OTHER

2 Chaplin
4 Centro de Turismo
  (Artesanato)
5 Rodoviária Velha
6 Railway Station
9 Banco do Brasil
10 Post Office
12 Museu Café Filho
18 Telephone Office
20 Jobim Nightclub

Forte dos
Reis Magos

Praia do Forte

Natal

0   100   200 m

Praia do Meio

Praia dos
Artistas

Rio
Potengi

Port
Area

Praia da Areia Prata

Coastal Highway
to Ponta Negra
& Litoral Sud

view from the 17th floor. Apartamentos cost US$40/55.

There's a nifty youth hostel, *Albergue de Juventude Ladeira do Sol* (☎ 221-5361), at Rua Valentim de Almeida, on Praia dos Artistas. *Pousada Marina da Praia* (☎ 222-0678), at Avenida Presidente Café Filho 860, has standard apartamentos (with fan) at US$14/16.

Places to Eat
Natural-food freaks will run to *A Macrobiótica*, on Rua Princesa Isabel. It's open from 11 am to 2 pm and 6 to 8 pm Monday to Friday, and from 11 am to 2 pm on Saturday.

Raízes, at Avenida Campos Sales 609, serves a rodízio dinner with a choice of 35 regional dishes for US$6 per person. *O Crustáceo*, at Rua Apodi 414, specialises in seafood – a large tree pokes through the roof in the centre of the restaurant.

Entertainment
Chaplin is a pricey and popular bar on Praia dos Artistas. Jobim, at Rua Mossoró 561, is a combination nightclub/bar with live music and dancing – US$3 cover charge. For folkloric shows and dancing, try Zás-Trás, at Rua Apodi 500, in the Tirol district.

Getting There & Away
Long-distance buses use the rodoviária nova (☎ 231-1170), about six km south of the city centre. A bus service connects the rodoviária nova with the rodoviária velha (old bus terminal), which is on Praça Augusto Severo, in the city centre. Taxis to the centre are around US$5.

There are two daily departures to Salvador (US$26, 21 hours), four to Recife (US$9, five hours) and frequent departures to João Pessoa (US$5.50, 2½ hours). To Fortaleza, there are three regular buses (US$20, eight hours) and one leito (US$32) daily. Buses depart twice a day for Rio (US$68, 46 hours). There are eight daily departures to Mossoró (US$11, five hours) and two (at 8 am and 7 pm) for Juazeiro do Norte (US$19, 10 hours).

Getting Around
The rodoviária velha is the hub for bus services to the airport, and the rodoviária nova is the terminal for the city beaches (such as Praia dos Artistas), southern beaches (such as Ponta Negra and Pirangi) and northern beaches (as far as Genipabu).

Ceará

Ceará's pride and glory is its coastline – nearly 600 km of magnificent beaches.

FORTALEZA
Fortaleza, the capital of Ceará, is now a major fishing port and commercial centre in the North-east.

Orientiation & Information
The city is laid out in a convenient grid pattern. The centre lies above the old historical section and includes the Mercado Central (Central Market), the *sé* (cathedral), and major shopping streets and government buildings.

East of the centre are the beaches of Praia de Iracema and Praia do Ideal. Continuing eastwards, Avenida Presidente John Kennedy links Praia do Diário and Praia do Meireles, which are lined with glitzy hotels and restaurants.

EMCETUR, the state tourism organisation, has its Centro de Turismo (☎ 231-3566), at Rua Senador Pompeu 350, inside a renovated prison.

Festivals
The **Regata de Jangadas**, a jangada regatta between Praia do Meireles and Praia Mucuripe, is held in the second half of July. The **Iemanjá** festival is held on 15 August at Praia do Futuro. The **Semana do Folclore**, the town's folklore week, takes place in the Centro do Turismo from 22 to 29 August.

Places to Stay
The *Albergue de Juventude da Fortaleza* (☎ 244-1850), at Rua Rocha Lima 1186

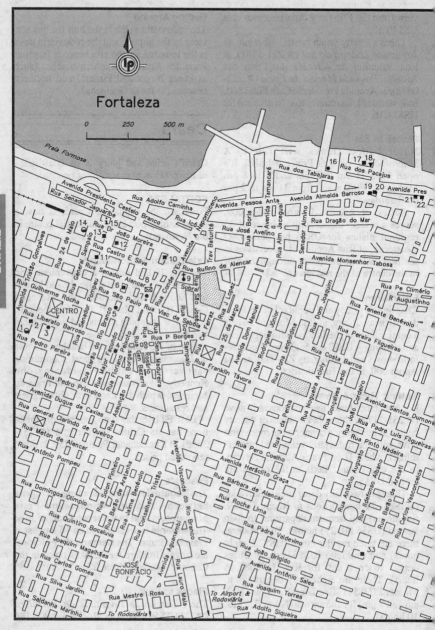

Fortaleza

0   250   500 m

Praia Formosa

Rua Senador Jaguaribe
Avenida Presidente Castelo Branco
Rua Adolfo Caminha
Rua Icó
Avenida A Nepomuceno
Avenida Pessoa Anta
Rua dos Tabajaras
16
17 18
Rua dos Pacajus
19 20 Avenida Pres
21 22
Avenida Almeida Barroso
Tamancaré

Rua Dr João Moreira
14
13
Rua Castro E Silva
12
11
Rua Senador Alencar
10
Trav Baturité
Rua José Avelino
Rua Boris
Avenida Jacegua
Rua Dragão do Mar
Rua Senador Almino
Rua Alm

Rua 24 de Maio
Rua General Sampaio
Rua Tristão Gonçalves
6
Rua Conde D'EU
Rua Rufino de Alencar
Rua São Gonçalo
Avenida Monsenhor Tabosa
Rua Pe Climério
R Augustinho

Avenida Guilherme Rocha
Rua São Paulo
8
7
9
Rua Sobral
Rua J Lopez
Rua Dom Joaquim
Rua Tenente Benévolo

CENTRO
Rua Liberato Barroso
1
2 3
5
4
Rua Visc de Saboia
Rua 25 de Março
Rua Dom Manuel
Rua Pereira Filgueiras
Rua Costa Barros

Rua Pedro Pereira
Rua Barão do Rio Branco
Rua Major Facundo
Rua Floriano Peixoto
R Borges
Rua Sena Madureira
Rua P Borges
Rua Cel Ferraz
Rua Franklin Távora
Avenida Dom Pedro
Rua Rodrigues Júnior
Rua Dona Leopoldina
Rua Gonçalves Ledo
Avenida Santos Dumont

Rua Pedro Primeiro
Rua Gen Bezerril
Rua Rosário
Rua Assunção
Avenida Santos Dumont
Rua João Cordeiro
Rua Padre Luís Filgueiras
Rua Pinto Madeira

Avenida Duque de Caxias
Rua General Clarindo de Queiroz
Rua Meton de Alencar
Rua Antônio Pompeu
Avenida Visconde do Rio Branco
Rua J da Penha
Rua Nogueira Acioly
Rua Pero Coelho
Avenida Heráclito Graça
Rua Bárbara de Alencar
Rua Rocha Lima
Rua Padre Valdevino

Rua Domingos Olímpio
Rua Solon Pinheiro
Rua Barão de Aratanha
Jaime Benévolo
Rua Conselheiro Tristão
Avenida Aguanambi
Rua Antônio Augusto
Rua Idelfonso Albano
Rua Barão de Aracati
Rua Carlos Vasconcelos

Rua Quintino Bocaluva
Rua Joaquim Magalhães
Rua Carlos Gomes
Rua Silva Jardim
Rua Saldanha Marinho
JOSÉ BONIFÁCIO
Rua Mestre Rosa
Rua Lauro Maia
Rua João Brigido
Avenida Antônio Sales
Rua Joaquim Torres
Rua Adolfo Siqueira
33

To Rodoviária
To Airport & Rodoviária

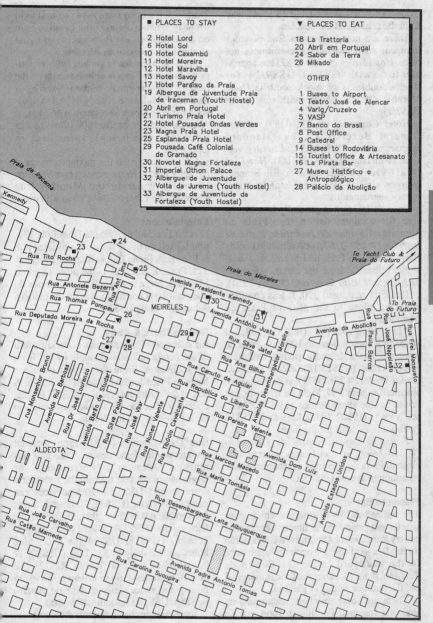

■ PLACES TO STAY

2 Hotel Lord
6 Hotel Sol
10 Hotel Caxambú
11 Hotel Moreira
12 Hotel Maravilha
13 Hotel Savoy
17 Hotel Paraíso da Praia
19 Albergue de Juventude Praia
de Iraceman (Youth Hostel)
20 Abril em Portugal
21 Turismo Praia Hotel
22 Hotel Pousada Ondas Verdes
23 Magna Praia Hotel
25 Esplanada Praia Hotel
29 Pousada Café Colonial
de Gramado
30 Novotel Magna Fortaleza
31 Imperial Othon Palace
32 Albergue de Juventude
Volta da Jurema (Youth Hostel)
33 Albergue de Juventude da
Fortaleza (Youth Hostel)

▼ PLACES TO EAT

18 La Trattoria
20 Abril em Portugal
24 Sabor da Terra
26 Mikado

OTHER

1 Buses to Airport
3 Teatro José de Alencar
4 Varig/Cruzeiro
5 VASP
7 Banco do Brasil
8 Post Office
9 Catedral
14 Buses to Rodoviária
15 Tourist Office & Artesanato
16 La Pirata Bar
27 Museu Histórico e
Antropológico
28 Palácio da Abolição

BRAZIL

(Aldeota district), is good, but it's a long way from the centre and the beaches.

There are many dives on Rua Senador Pompeu; shop around for cleanliness not price. *Hotel Savoy* (☎ 252-2582) has apartamentos (with fan) at US$9/14 for singles/doubles. One block south is *Hotel Moreira* (☎ 252-4665), with quartos at US$7/11.

Hotel Caxambú (☎ 231-0339), at Rua General Bezerril 22, has standard apartamentos at US$20/25 and luxury versions (with frigobar) at US$21/31. *Hotel Sol* (☎ 211-9166), at Rua Barão do Rio Branco, charges similar prices for standard and luxury apartamentos.

Praia de Iracema is generally less expensive for accommodation than Praia do Meireles. *Albergue de Juventude Praia de Iracema* (☎ 252-3267), at Avenida Almeida Barroso 998, on Praia de Iracema, is a convenient distance from the centre. *Albergue de Juventude Volta da Jurema* (☎ 244-1254), at Rua Frei Mansueto 370, is less comfortable, but close to the glitz of Praia do Meireles.

Abril em Portugal (☎ 231-9508), at Avenida Almeida Barroso 1006, on Praia de Iracema, has a friendly owner and new apartamentos (US$13/18). *Hotel Pousada Ondas Verdes* (☎ 226-0871), at Avenida Presidente Kennedy 934, Praia de Iracema, has bright double apartamentos at US$27 (with sea view), US$22 (with fan) and US$18 (without fan – wait for the breeze).

Pousada Café Colonial de Gramado (☎ 224-1499), at Rua Nunes Valente 275, close to Praia do Meireles, is recommended. Apartamentos cost US$15/17.

Places to Eat

The centre has lots of eateries which offer snacks and prato feito at lunch. Vegetarians can try *Restaurante Alivita*, at Avenida Barão do Rio Branco 1486; it's open for lunch only. In the courtyard inside the Centro de Turismo, there's *Xadrez*; the food is marginal but the outdoor setting is pleasant.

There are some excellent restaurants on Praia de Iracema. For Italian food, try *La Trattoria*. It's open from 6 pm to midnight Monday to Saturday, and from 11 am to 3 pm on Sunday. *Abril em Portugal* is run by an affable Portuguese from Alentejo.

Praia do Meireles is packed with restaurants. *Sabor da Terra* is a churrascaria on the beach. The curiously named *Smell's*, at Avenida Presidente Kennedy 4456, is a sandwich bar. The Japanese restaurant *Mikado*, at Avenida Barão de Studart 600 (three blocks back from the beach), specialises in teppanyaki.

For a treat, try the the moqueca mixta at the aptly named *Restaurante Água Na Boca* (literally Water in the Mouth), Rua República do Líbano 1084 (Varjota district).

Entertainment

London London, at Avenida Dom Luis 131, prides itself on being the most animated pub in Fortaleza. Pirata Bar, at Rua dos Tabajaras 325, Praia de Iracema, is the place to go on Mondays, for 'a segunda feira mais louca do planeta' (the craziest Monday on the planet). Admission costs US$2.

Getting There & Away

Air Aeroporto Pinto Martins is six km south of the centre and just a couple of km from the rodoviária. From the airport there are buses to Praça José Alencar, in the centre. A taxi to the centre costs around US$6. Flights operate to Rio, São Paulo and major cities in the North-east and the North.

Bus The rodoviária (☎ 272-1566) is about six km south of the centre. Take any bus marked 'Alencar', 'Ferroviária' or 'Aguanambi'. A taxi to/from the rodoviária costs around US$3.50. Bus services run daily to Salvador (US$34, 20 hours), thrice daily to Natal (US$20, eight hours), plus one leito service (US$33), at least twice daily to Teresina (US$18, US$34 for leito, nine hours), thrice daily to São Luis (US$30, 17 hours), once daily to Recife (US$21, 12 hours), six times daily to Belém (US$40, 25 hours) and twice daily to Rio de Janeiro (US$80, US$160 for leito, 48 hours).

Ipu Brasileira bus company runs services

to Ubajara seven times a day (US$10, six hours). The daily bus to Gijoca (for Jericoacoara) leaves at 8 am and takes eight hours. There are four buses a day to Aracati (two hours), the small town which provides access to Canoa Quebrada.

Getting Around
To visit the city beaches, catch a bus marked 'Praia do Meireles' or 'Praia de Iracema', from Rua Castro e Silva (near the Centro de Turismo). From Praça Castro Carreiro (close to the Centro de Turismo), take any of the following buses for Praia do Futuro: 'Praia do Futuro', 'Serviluz' or 'Caça e Pesca'.

CANOA QUEBRADA
Once a tiny fishing village, Canoa Quebrada is south-east of Fortaleza, and cut off from the world by its huge pink sand dunes. It is still tiny and pretty, but the village has peaked. Other than the beach, the main attractions are watching the sunset from the dunes, riding horses bareback and dancing forró by the light of gas lanterns.

The cheapest accommodation is *Albergue Lua Estrela* (☎ 421-1401), on Rua Principal, which is a youth hostel with 32 bunks, a restaurant and a bar. Other options include *Pousada Maria Alice* (☎ 421-0401), on Rua Principal, and *Pousada Tenda do Cumbe*, on Avenida da Praia.

There are no direct buses to Canoa Quebrada. From Praça do Mercado Antigo in Aracati, there are infrequent buses and Volkswagen Kombis to Canoa Quebrada until 5.30 pm – after that, the only option is a taxi. Tour operators in Fortaleza offer day trips (transport only) to Canoa Quebrada for US$20 per person. The tour leaves at 8 am and returns at 6.30 pm.

JERICOACOARA
This latest remote and primitive 'in' beach, north-west of Fortaleza, has become popular among backpackers and hipper Brazilians, supplanting Canoa Quebrada. It's quite hard to get there, so you might as well stay a while.

You can boogie at the forró held every evening – just follow the music. Alternatively, hitch a ride on a jangada or walk to Pedra Furada, a rock three km east along the beach. You can also hire horses and ride 18 km west along the beach from Jericoacoara to the even smaller town of Mangue Seco. Trucks go to Mangue Seco on Monday and Thursday.

Places to Stay & Eat
Cheap accommodation options aren't necessarily clean, and don't count on electricity or running water. You can rent a house for about US$3 or hang your hammock for US$1. Bring a large cotton hammock or bed roll with sheet sleeping sack, as well as bottled water. A good inexpensive option is *Pousada Casa do Turismo* (☎ 261-2368 in Fortaleza for reservations).

The up-market lodgings include *Pousada Hippopotamus* (☎ 244-9191 in Fortaleza for reservations), *Pousada Papagaio* (☎ 224-1515 in Fortaleza for reservations) and *Pousada Matusa* (☎ 244-6500 in Fortaleza for reservations). Package deals for these pousadas typically include return transport from Fortaleza, two nights' accommodation and one breakfast. For this type of package, expect to pay US$40/48 per person for standard/luxury apartamentos.

There are plenty of restaurants in town, including *Acoara do Jérico*, *Pousada do Alemão*, *Freddyssimo* (Italian food) and *Da Isabel*. Most of the budget places to stay also serve food.

Getting There & Away
A daily bus leaves from Fortaleza's rodoviária at 8 am and arrives 24 km shy of Jericoacoara, in Gijoca, roughly by 4 pm – a gruelling eight-hour ride. From there an irregular jeep, pick-up truck and (sometimes) burro service runs to Jericoacoara. When the bus from Fortaleza arrives, the vehicles fill up and leave en masse. Collective bargaining should bring the fare to US$2.50 (or less) per person.

If you have come by car or even in a Volkswagen Fusca, take your vehicle no further. Leave it parked in Gijoca, where some of the pousada owners can keep an eye on it. Transport back to Gijoca usually leaves Jericoacoana after 5 pm.

Tour operators in Fortaleza and up-market pousadas in Jericoacoara offer tour packages for Jericoacoara. The tours usually leave Fortaleza twice a week, at 7 pm on Tuesday and Friday, and return from Jericoacoara on Thursday and Sunday at 3 pm.

PARQUE NACIONAL DE UBAJARA

The main attractions of the Parque Nacional de Ubajara, just a few km from the small town of Ubajara, are the caves and the cable-car ride down to them. The cable-car operates from noon to 4 pm Wednesday to Friday, and from 10 am to 4 pm on Saturday and Sunday. The ride costs US$2.50. Guides accompany you on the one-hour tour round the caves. Bring a torch. Visit IBAMA at the park entrance for information.

Just 100 metres from the park entrance, the *Pousada da Neblina* (☎ 634-1270), on the Estrada do Teleférico, has apartamentos (US$10/13 for singles/doubles), a camp-ground, a swimming pool and a restaurant. The *Hotel Ubajara* (☎ 634-1261), at Rua Juvêncio Luís Pereira 370, in Ubajara, has apartamentos for US$10/13; quartos are cheaper.

There are seven daily buses from Fortaleza to Ubajara (US$10, six hours). To reach the park entrance from the town of Ubajara, either walk or take a taxi – buses are very infrequent.

Piauí

Although Piauí is usually bypassed by travellers, it deserves more attention – for the superb beaches along its short coast, the friendly city of Teresina and interesting hikes in the Parque Nacional de Sete Cidades.

TERESINA

Teresina, the capital of Piauí and the hottest city in Brazil, is an interesting quirky place which seems addicted to giving a Middle Eastern slant to the names of its streets, hotels and sights.

Information

PIEMTUR (☎ 223-0775), the state tourism organisation, at Rua Alvaro Mendes 1988, has helpful staff members, who appear delighted to dole out literature and advice. It's open from 9 am to 6 pm Monday to Friday. The IBAMA office (☎ 232-1652), at Avenida Homero Castelo Branco 2240 (Jockey Club district), is efficient and has information on the Piauí national parks. It's open from 8 am to 5.45 pm on weekdays.

Things to See

The **Museu Histórico do Piauí** displays an eclectic assortment of historical objects, fauna, flora, antique radios and other ancient wonders. Admission costs US$0.40. The museum is open from 8 am to 5 pm Tuesday to Friday, and from 8 am to noon on Saturday and Sunday. A free guide is provided. For a complete cultural change, visit **Museu de Arte Didática**, which houses artworks from the ancient civilisations of Assyria, Babylon and Egypt. Opening hours are 7 to 11 am and 1 to 6 pm Tuesday to Friday.

The **Centro Artesanal** is a centre for *artesanato* from Piauí, a pleasant spot to browse among shops which sell leather articles, furniture made from fibres, extremely intricate lacework, colourful hammocks, opals and soapstone (from Pedro Segundo).

Places to Stay

PIEMTUR Camping (☎ 222-6202) is 12 km out of the city on Estrada da Socopo, the road running east towards União.

Rua São Pedro is the street for rock-bottom options. For more comfort, try *Hotel Fortaleza* (☎ 222-2984), on Praça Saraiva; single/double apartamentos are US$9/15 with fan, US$14/26 with air-con. *Hotel Central* (☎ 222-3222), on Rua 13 de Maio 85, provides apartamentos for US$13/16 with fan, US$18/22 with air-con.

The two-star *Hotel Sambaiba* (☎ 222-6711), at Rua Gabriel Ferreira 340, gives a good deal, with apartamentos at US$38/42.

Places to Eat

Restaurante Típico do Piauí, inside the Centro Artesanal, serves regional dishes. For seafood, try *Camarão do Elias*, at Avenida Pedro Almeida 457, or *O Pesqueirinho*, which is at Avenida Jorge Velho 6889, several km outside town, on the riverside. For a splurge, visit the *Forno e Fogão*, inside the Hotel Luxor, which charges US$8 per person for a gigantic buffet lunch. *Chez Matrinchan*, at Avenida NS de Fatima 671 (Jockey Club district), is divided into three sections: a restaurant serving French cuisine, a pizzeria and a nightclub. There's live music here on Friday and Saturday nights – US$2 cover charge.

Getting There & Away

Teresina has regular bus connections with Sobral (US$11, seven hours) and Fortaleza (US$18, US$35 for leito, nine hours). To São Luis (seven hours), there is a frequent daily service (US$11), and a midnight leito (US$21) which runs twice a week. There are four buses a day to Belém (US$27, 16 hours).

To Parnaíba, there are executivo (US$12, four hours) and standard (US$9, six hours) buses – both types run twice daily. There are bus connections thrice daily to São Raimundo Nonato (US$19, 10 hours). Buses depart hourly between 7 am and 6 pm for Piripiri (US$8, three hours).

Getting Around

From the rodoviária to the centre, the cheapest, slowest and hottest option is to take the bus from the stop outside the rodoviária. A taxi costs US$6 at the bilheteria, but much less if you flag it down outside the perimeter of the rodoviária.

LITORAL PIAUIENSE

Parnaíba, once a major port at the mouth of the Rio Parnaíba, is being developed as a beach resort, along with the town of Luís Correia, which is 18 km away. Porto das Barcas, the old warehouse section currently under restoration, contains a PIEMTUR information office, a youth hostel, a mari-time museum, an artesanato centre and several bars and restaurants.

Praia Pedra do Sal, 15 km north-east of the centre, on Ilha Grande Santa Isabel, is a good beach. Lagoa do Portinho, a lagoon surrounded by dunes, is about 14 km east of Parnaíba on the road to Luís Correia.

Places to Stay

There's a *youth hostel* in Porto das Barcas (Parnaíba) and a campground at Lagoa do Portinho, where the *Centro Recreativa Lagoa do Portinho* (☎ 322-2165) provides apartamentos and chalets. The *Hotel Cívico* (☎ 322-2470), at Avenida Governor Chagas Rodrigues 474, in the centre of town, has a swimming pool and apartamentos (US$16/20 for singles/doubles).

Getting There & Away

For bus services between Parnaíba and Teresina, see the Getting There & Away section for Teresina.

PARQUE NACIONAL DE SETE CIDADES

Sete Cidades is a small national park. Its interesting rock formations, estimated to be at least 190 million years old, resemble 'sete cidades' (seven cities). The appeal for visitors lies in the walking opportunities; the loop through the seven cities is a leisurely couple of hours' stroll. The park is 180 km from Teresina and 141 km from Ubajara (Ceará state) on a fine paved road. Take any bus between Fortaleza and Teresina and get off at Piripiri. From there, IBAMA courtesy bus transport for the 26-km trip to the park leaves from Piripiri at 7 am and returns from Abrigo do IBAMA at 4 pm. The park is open from 6 am to 6 pm.

Abrigo do IBAMA is the most popular place to stay, with an inexpensive hostel and designated camp sites at the park entrance. More up-market is *Hotel Fazenda Sete Cidades* (☎ 276-1664), a two-star resort hotel with attractive apartamentos (US$15/20). It's a cool and shady spot, six km from the park entrance, and there's a restaurant and pool.

Maranhão

Maranhão is the North-East's second largest state (after Bahia) but has a population of only five million.

SÃO LUÍS

São Luís, the capital of Maranhão, is a city with unpretentious colonial charm and a rich folkloric tradition – definitely a highlight for travellers in the North-east. Perched on a hill overlooking the Baía de São Marcos is the historic core of São Luís (now known as Projeto Reviver – Project Renovation – completed in the late 1980s), which offers the best restored colonial architecture in the North-East.

Information
Tourist Office Maratur, the state tourism organisation, has an information office on Rua da Estrêla, in the historic centre. Opening hours are 8 am to 6 pm weekdays.

Travel Agencies In the shopping gallery at Rua do Sol 141 are several travel agencies offering organised tours to Alcântara and other Maranhão destinations. An efficient agency in the shopping gallery is Taguatur (☎ 222-0100), at Loja 14. Babaçu Viagens (☎ 222-7028), at Loja 3 in the same gallery, is also reliable. For personalised tours, contact local guides such as Simon Ramos (☎ 236-4069) or Nelito (leave a message at the front desk of Hotel Vila Rica – ☎ 232-3535).

Things to See
The real highlight is Projecto Reviver, but there are a couple of worthwhile museums and buildings. The most interesting is the **Museu do Centro de Cultura Popular**. It's open Monday to Friday from 9 am to 6 pm. Also worth a visit is the **Museu de Artes Visuais**. It's open from 8 am to 1 pm and 4 to 6 pm Monday to Friday. The **Cafua das Mercês**, the old slave market, now houses the worthwhile **Museu do Negro**. It's open

from 1.30 to 6 pm Monday to Friday, and from 2.30 to 5.30 pm on Saturday. The **Palácio dos Leões**, a French fortress built in 1612, is now the state governor's residence and office. Visiting hours are 3 to 6 pm on Monday, Wednesday and Friday.

Festivals
Carnaval here is supposedly a real hit, with active samba clubs and distinctive local dances and music. The **Tambor de Mina** festivals, held in July, are important events for followers of the Afro-Brazilian religions, and São Luís' famous **Bumba Meu Boi** festival commences in the second half of June, continuing until the second week of August.

Places to Stay
The nearest campground, *Unicamping* (☎ 222-2552), is close to Calhau beach – eight km out of town. For long-term lets (houses or rooms), call 222-2425.

The youth hostel, *Albergue de Juventude O Cortiço* (☎ 222-6258), is at Rua 14 de Julho 93, in a refurbished colonial mansion. It is excellent value. *Hotel Estrêla* (☎ 222-1083), at Rua da Estrêla 370, is a good cheapie in the heart of the historic district. Quartos (with fan) cost US$6.50 per person. Don't leave valuables in your room.

Hotel Lord (☎ 222-5544), at Rua de Nazaré 258, is a large, time-worn hotel with clean, comfortable quartos (US$16/26 for singles/doubles) and apartamentos (US$26/32, including air-con).

The *Athenas Palace Hotel* (☎ 221-4163), at Rua Antônio Rayol 431, just east of the Mercado Central, also offers good value. Apartamentos cost US$16/23.

The *Pousada Colonial* (☎ 232-2834), at Rua Afonso Pena 112, is in a recently restored colonial mansion and offers excellent value. Clean and comfortable apartamentos cost US$40/48 – discounts can be negotiated for cash payment.

Places to Eat
The *Base da Lenoca*, on Praça Dom Pedro II, is a popular restaurant with a great position, overlooking the Rio Anil. Good

regional seafood is served at *Solar do Ribeirão* (☎ 222-3068), at Rua das Barrocas 141. Just down the street, at Rua das Barrocas 48, is *La Boheme*, an up-market restaurant with international cuisine, and live music on Friday and Saturday nights. *Restaurante Aliança*, at Rua de Nazaré 300, serves pizzas, chicken dishes and steaks. In the heart of the historic district, on Rua da Estrêla, there's *Restaurante Antigamente*. Live music is offered here in the evening on weekends.

Entertainment

São Luís is currently the top reggae centre of the North-east, and many of the nightspots cater to *reggeiros* (reggae fans). The Cooperativa de Reggae, just a few doors down from the tourist office, might be a good place to start.

Getting There & Away

Air Air services connect São Luís with Rio, São Paulo and the major cities in the North-east and the North.

Bus The rodoviária (☎ 223-0253) is about eight km south-east of the city centre, on Avenida dos Franceses. To Teresina, there are frequent daily buses (US$11, seven hours), and a midnight leito (US$21) which runs twice a week. There are two buses a day to Belém (US$22, 12 hours) and regular bus services to Fortaleza (US$25, 18 hours) and Recife (US$43, 24 hours).

Boat From the *hidroviária* (boat terminal) on the quayside, there are regular ferries to Alcântara; sailing times depend on the tides. Buy your ticket the day before departure. The boat leaves at around 8 am, but it's often crowded, so get there early for the 1½-hour journey. The sailboats used for this service are real beauties – the stuff of pirate tales. The boat normally leaves Alcântara around 2 pm for the return trip.

Getting Around

The Aeroporto do Tirirical (☎ 225-0044) is 15 km south-east of the city. The bus marked 'São Cristóvâo' runs from the bus stop beside Igreja de São João (on Rua da Paz) to the airport in 45 minutes.

To get to the rodoviária, catch the 'Rodoviária' bus from the bus stop at the junction of Avenida Magalhães de Almeida and Rua Regente Braulio.

ALCÂNTARA

Across the Baía de São Marcos from São Luís is the old colonial town of Alcântara. Founded in the early 1600s with extensive slave labour, the town was the hub of the region's sugar and cotton economy. The beneficiaries of this wealth, Maranhão's landowners, preferred living in Alcântara.

Things to See

The town is very poor and decaying, but don't miss the following: the beautiful row of two-storey houses on Rua Grande, the **Igreja de NS do Carmo** (1665), Rua Amargura, and the best preserved **pelourinho** (whipping post) in Brazil, on Praça da Matriz.

The Museu Histórico, on the Praça da Matriz, displays a collection of sacred art, festival regalia and furniture. Opening hours are 8 am to 2 pm Tuesday to Saturday, and 8 am to 1 pm on Sunday. The cost of admission (US$0.50) is not included in the price of tours from São Luís.

Festivals

On the first Sunday after Ascension~~ Day~~, Alcântara celebrates the **Festa do Divino**, one of the most colourful annual festivals in Maranhão.

Places to Stay & Eat

Alcântara has simple camp sites close to Praça da Matriz and near the *farol* (lighthouse). There are also several inexpensive hotels, such as *Pousada do Mordomo Régio* (☎ 101) – recommended – and *Pousada do Imperador*, both on Rua Grande, and *Pousada Senzala* and *Pousada Pelourinho*, beside Praça da Matriz. If you value relaxation, peace and quiet, stay a night or two.

Most of the hotels have restaurants, and

BRAZIL

BRAZIL

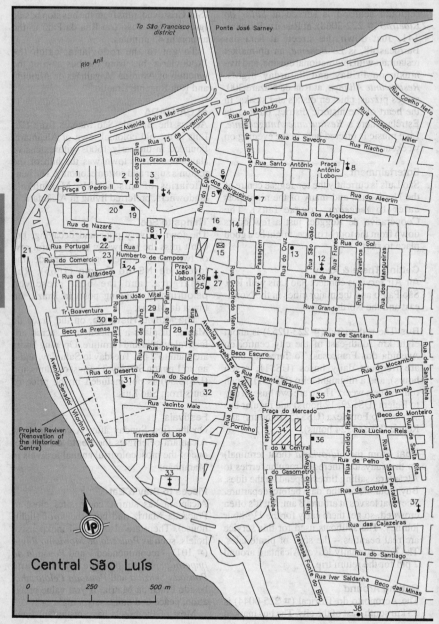

To São Francisco district
Ponte José Sarney

Rio Anil

Avenida Beira Mar

Rua 15 de Novembro

Rua do Machado

Rua da Ribeirão

Rua da Savedro

Rua Riacho

Rua Jonsem

Miller

Rua Coelho Neto

Rua Graca Aranha

Rua da Silva

1
Praça D Pedro II

2

3

†4

Beco

Rua do Egito

Rua dos Barqueiros

6

5

Rua Santo Antônio

Praça Antônio Lobo

†8

Rua do Alecrim

20
19

7

Rua de Nazaré

Rua dos Afogados

16

14

18 17

Rua Portugal

22

Rua

Humberto de Campos

i 24

Praça João Lisboa

Rua Godofredo Viana

15

Rua do Comercio

23

Rua da Alfândega

Trav da Passagem

Rua São João

Rua do Cruz

13

Rua São João

12

Rua Flores

Rua Craveiros

Rua do Sol

Rua dos Mangueiras

21

Rua João Vital

29

26
25

27

Rua da Palma

Rua da Paz

Rua dos

Tr Boaventura

30

Beco da Prensa

Rua da Estrela

Rua 28 de Julho

28

Rua Afonso Pena

Avenida Magalhães de Almeida

Rua Grande

Rua de Santana

Rua de Santaninha

Rua do Deserto

Rua Direita

Rua do Saúde

Beco Escuro

Rua Regente Braulio

Rua do Mocambo

Rua do Inveja

31

32

35

Beco do Monteiro

Rua de Santa Rita

Projeto Reviver (Renovation of the Historical Centre)

Avenida Senador Vitorino Feira

Rua Jacinto Maia

Rua Portinho

Praça do Mercado

34

T do M Central

36

Rua Candido Ribeiro

Rua Luciano Reis

Rua de Pelho

Rua de São Pantaleão

Travessa da Lapa

Rua da Manga

Avenida Guaxenduba

T do Gasometro

Rua Antônio Raiol

Rua da Cotovia

33
†

37

Rua das Cajazeiras

Rua do Santiago

Rua Ivar Saldanha

Beco das Minas

Rua do Bisp

38

Central São Luís

0   250   500 m

lp

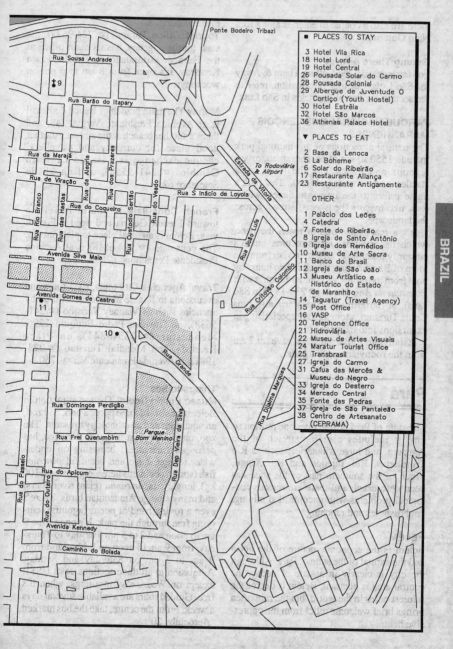

BRAZIL

Ponte Bodeiro Tribazi

Rua Sousa Andrade

Rua Barão do Itapary

Rua da Marajá

Rua de Viração

Rua da Alegria

Rua dos Prazeres

Rua Rio Branco

Rua das Hastes

Rua do Coqueiro

Rua Custodio Sertão

Rua do Veado

Rua S Inácio de Loyola

To Rodoviária & Airport

Estrada da Vitória

Rua João Luís

Avenida Silva Maia

Avenida Gomes de Castro

Rua Cristovão Colombo

Rua Grande

Rua Domingos Perdigão

Rua Frei Querumbim

Rua do Passeio

Rua do Apicum

Rua do Outeiro

Avenida Kennedy

Caminho do Boiada

Parque Bom Menino

Rua Dep Vieira da Silva

Rua Dijalma Marques

PLACES TO STAY

3 Hotel Vila Rica
18 Hotel Lord
19 Hotel Central
26 Pousada Solar do Carmo
28 Pousada Colonial
29 Albergue de Juventude O Cortiço (Youth Hostel)
30 Hotel Estrêla
32 Hotel São Marcos
36 Athenas Palace Hotel

PLACES TO EAT

2 Base da Lenoca
5 La Boheme
6 Solar do Ribeirão
17 Restaurante Aliança
23 Restaurante Antigamente

OTHER

1 Palácio dos Leões
4 Catedral
7 Fonte do Ribeirão
8 Igreja de Santo Antônio
9 Igreja dos Remédios
10 Museu de Arte Sacra
11 Banco do Brasil
12 Igreja de São João
13 Museu Artístico e Histórico do Estado de Maranhão
14 Taguatur (Travel Agency)
15 Post Office
16 VASP
20 Telephone Office
21 Hidroviária
22 Museu de Artes Visuais
24 Maratur Tourist Office
25 Transbrasil
27 Igreja do Carmo
31 Cafua das Mercês & Museu do Negro
33 Igreja do Desterro
34 Mercado Central
35 Fonte das Pedras
37 Igreja de São Pantaleão
38 Centro de Artesanato (CEPRAMA)

there are also a couple of eateries along Rua Neto Guterrez.

Getting There & Away
For ferry details, see Getting There & Away for São Luís. For tour information, refer to the section on Travel Agencies in São Luís.

PARQUE NACIONAL DOS LENÇOIS MARANHENSES
The natural attractions of this national park include 1550 sq km of beaches, mangroves, lagoons and dunes, and the local fauna (turtles and migratory birds). The park's name refers to the immense dunes, which look like *lençois* (bedsheets) strewn across the landscape.

It's a real expedition to reach the park, which has minimal infrastructure, but it's currently possible to arrange a visit from the town of Barreirinhas, which is two hours by boat from the dunes. Accommodation is with *Pousada da Ana Maria* (☎ 238-1334 in São Luís), in Barreirinhas. Ana Maria also runs Cafua Turismo, a tour agency specialising in excursions into the park.

A daily bus to Barreirinhas leaves at 7 am from the rodoviária in São Luís.

Pará

The state of Pará covers over one million sq km. It includes a major stretch of the Amazon, and huge tributaries, such as Rio Trombetas, Rio Tapajós and Rio Xingu. Much of the southern part of the state has been deforested, and there are serious ecological problems with uncontrolled mining, land disputes and ranching.

BELÉM
Belém is the economic centre of the north and the capital of the state of Pará. Although the city is clearly in a state of decay, the central area is pleasant. Belém is one of the rainiest cities in the world, but the rain often brings brief welcome relief from the oppressive heat.

Information
Tourist Office Paratur (☎ 224-9633), the state tourism agency, has its main office at the Feira de Artesanato do Estado, Praça Kennedy. It's open from 8 am to 6 pm on weekdays.

Money The main branch of Banco do Brasil is at Avenida Presidente Vargas 248, and there's another branch at the airport. Another good place for currency and travellers' cheque exchange is Casa do Cruzeiro Câmbio (☎ 241-5558), at Rua 28 de Setembro 62.

French Consulate If you're travelling toward French Guiana and need a French visa, Belém is an ideal place to pick one up. The consulate (☎ 224-6818) is at Avenida Presidente Pernambuco 269.

Travel Agencies City tours, river tours and excursions to Ilha de Marajó are offered by agencies such as Vianney Turismo (☎ 241-5638), at Travessa Padre Eutíquio 2296, Mendestur (☎ 235-0841), on Praça Kennedy, and Mundial Turismo (☎ 223-1981), at Avenida Presidente Vargas 780.

Things to See
Museo Emílio Goeldi The top attraction in Belém consists of three parts: a park and zoo, an aquarium and an ethnology museum. The zoo, one of the best in South America, has *peixe-boi* (manatees) browsing on underwater foliage, huge and beautiful *pirarucu* fish (some specimens here weigh at least 100 kg), jungle cats, *ariranha* (giant river otters) and many strange Amazonian birds. There's even a roving band of *pacas* (agoutis) scurrying free through the park. It's open from 9 am to noon and 2 to 5 pm Tuesday to Thursday, from 9 am to noon on Friday, and from 9 am to 5 pm on Saturday and Sunday. Admission to all three sections costs US$1, except on Wednesday mornings, when it's free. Guided tours are available several days a week. From the centre, take the bus marked 'Aeroclube 20'.

Basílica de NS de Nazaré Built in 1909, the Basílica de NS de Nazaré has fine marble and gold inside, and downstairs, there is a sacred art museum. It's on Praça Justo Chermont and is open daily from 6.30 to 11.30 am and 3 to 9 pm.

Mercado Ver-o-Peso Spanning several blocks along the waterfront, this big market goes all day, every day. There's not much for tourists to buy, but the display of fruits, vegetables, plants, animals and fish, not to mention the people, is fascinating. It's best to get there early, when the boats are unloading their catches at the far end of the market.

Festivals

Every year, on the morning of the second Sunday in October, the city explodes with the sound of hymns, bells and fireworks. The **Círio de Nazaré**, Brazil's biggest religious festival, is a tribute to the Virgin of Nazaré, a statue supposed to have been sculpted in Nazareth.

Places to Stay

Belém's budget hotels have remained reasonable, but its mid-range accommodation is no longer such a bargain. *Albergue de Juventude Ver-O-Verde* (☎ 229-2006) is at Travessa Francisco Caldera Castelo Branco 1128 (São Brás district), near the rodoviária.

At the very cheap places scattered along the waterfront on Rua Castilho França, prices are rock bottom, but you must compromise on security and cleanliness. Try the *Transamazônica*, *Grajaú*, *São Jorge* and *Miranda Nova*. Prices average US$5/6 for a single/double quarto. Much better is *Hotel Fortaleza* (☎ 222-2984), at Travessa Frutuoso Guimarães 276. It provides good-value quartos at (US$5/6 for singles/doubles). Filled with Surinamese tourists, the *Vitória Régia* (☎ 241-3475), at Travessa Frutuoso Guimarães 260, offers standard apartamentos at US$7.50/9 and special apartamentos (with air-con) at US$11/13. *Hotel Sete Sete*, at Primeiro de Março 677, is secure and good value, with air-con apartamentos for US$9/11.

Vidonho's Hotel (☎ 225-1444), at Rua Ó de Almeida 476, is spic and span, with all the amenities of an expensive hotel. Apartamentos start at US$15/23, but rooms at those rates are few. The *Cambará Hotel* (☎ 224-2422), in the Cidade Velho, at Avenida 16 de Novembro 300, is in the same league.

Places to Eat

The food in Belém is tasty and varied, with a bewildering variety of fish and fruit and, unlike much of Brazil, a distinct regional cuisine. Pato no tucupi is a lean duck cooked in fermented manioc extract. Endangered species, regularly served in restaurants in Belém, include tartaruga (turtle) and peixe-boi (manatee). Don't contribute to their extinction – choose something else.

Mercado Ver-o-Peso has a thousand and one food stands serving big lunches for small prices. It's also a good place to sample the local fish. Vegetarians can try the *Restaurante Vegetariano Mercado do Natural*, at Rua Alfredo Santo Antônio. For heavenly sucos made from Amazon fruits, go to *Casa do Suco*, at Avenida Presidente Vargas 794 (close to the Hilton Hotel). Close by is the *Bar do Parque*, an outside bar and popular meeting place where you can order a snack and a drink.

Belém has several excellent restaurants where you can do some fine dining for US$4 to US$7. *Lá Em Casa* and *O Outro* (☎ 241-4064), two restaurants on the same site at Avenida Governador José Malcher 247, have all the best regional dishes. The *O Círculo Militar*, at the old Forte do Castelo, on Praça Frei Caetano Brandão, has a great bay view and good regional cooking. The *Miako*, at Primeiro de Março 766, behind the Hilton Hotel, is one of Brazil's best Japanese restaurants north of São Paulo.

Entertainment

The region has some great traditional music and dance, such as *carimbó*. The best samba clubs are Rancho Não Posso me Amofiná (☎ 225-0918), at Travessa Honório José dos

BRAZIL

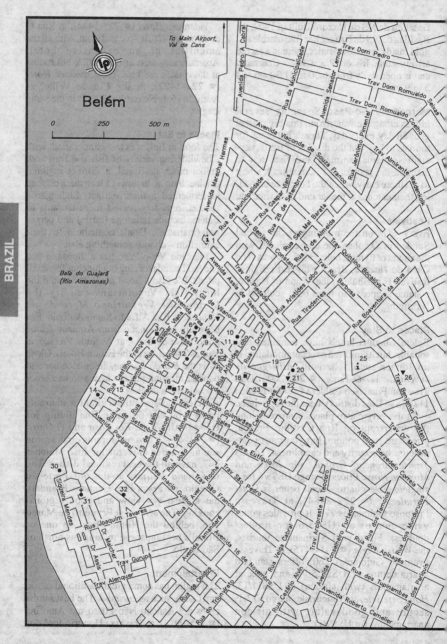

Belém

0   250   500 m

Baía do Guajará
(Rio Amazonas)

To Main Airport,
Val de Cans

BRAZIL

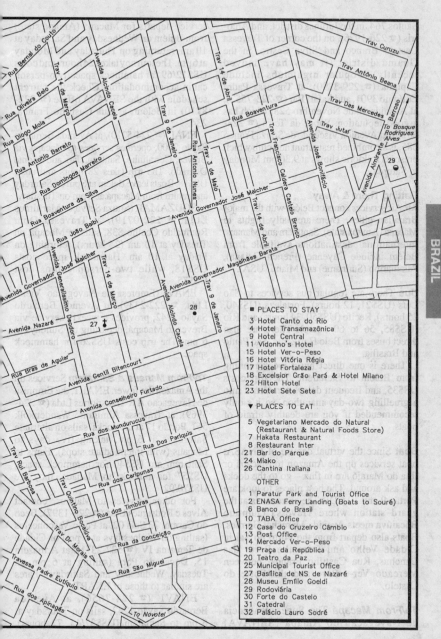

■ PLACES TO STAY
3 Hotel Canto do Rio
4 Hotel Transamazônica
9 Hotel Central
11 Vidonho's Hotel
15 Hotel Ver-o-Peso
16 Hotel Vitória Régia
17 Hotel Fortaleza
18 Excelsior Grão Pará & Hotel Milano
22 Hilton Hotel
23 Hotel Sete Sete

▼ PLACES TO EAT
5 Vegetariano Mercado do Natural
   (Restaurant & Natural Foods Store)
7 Hakata Restaurant
8 Restaurant Inter
21 Bar do Parque
24 Miako
26 Cantina Italiana

   OTHER
1 Paratur Park and Tourist Office
2 ENASA Ferry Landing (Boats to Souré)
6 Banco do Brasil
10 TABA Office
12 Casa do Cruzeiro Câmbio
13 Post Office
14 Mercado Ver-o-Peso
19 Praça da República
20 Teatro da Paz
25 Municipal Tourist Office
27 Basílica de NS de Nazaré
28 Museu Emílio Goeldi
29 Rodoviária
30 Forte do Castelo
31 Catedral
32 Palácio Lauro Sodré

Santos 764, in the Jurunas district, and Arco-Íris (☎ 226-1926), on the corner of Travessa Castelo Branco and Silva Castro, in the Guamá district (it may have moved recently). Popular nightclubs include Lapinha (☎ 229-3290), at Travessa Padre Eutíquio 3901, and Safari Bar (☎ 223-7553), at Avenida 16 de Novembro 528, which has a good reputation. Sabor da Terra (☎ 223-6820), at Avenida Visconde de Souza Franco 685, is a combined restaurant and club which presents folkloric shows at 9.30 pm Monday to Saturday.

Getting There & Away

Air Air services connect Belém with the major Brazilian cities. There are daily flights to Macapá (Amapá state), Santarém and Manaus. International destinations available from Belém include Cayenne (French Guiana), Paramaribo (Suriname) and Miami (USA).

Bus There are regular bus services to São Luís (US$21, 12 hours), Fortaleza (US$40, 25 hours), Recife (US$50, 34 hours) and Rio (US$85, 56 to 60 hours). There are also direct buses from Belo Horizonte, São Paulo and Brasília.

There is one direct bus a week running from Belém to Santarém. The trip costs US$35, and frequent delays can turn it into a gruelling two-day marathon, so it's only recommended if you are deathly afraid of boats.

Boat Since the virtual demise of ENASA, boat services up the Amazon to Macapá or Ilha do Marajó are in flux – go to the docks and ask around. The best places to look are Portão 9 and 10 CDP. The entrance is at the guard station where Travessa Quintino Bocaiúva meets Avenida Marechal Hermes. Boats also depart from the Porto do Sal in Cidade Velho and from the Porto das Lanchas, Rua Castilho França, between Mercado Ver-o-Peso and the Forte do Castelo.

To/From Macapá The Superintendência de Navegação do Amapá (SENAVA)

service departs for Macapá (Amapá state) from Belém on Wednesday and Saturday at 10 am, returning on Thursday and Monday at 6 pm. The journey takes 24 hours and costs US$12/69 for hammock space/two-person cabin accommodation. Check the current schedule with the SENAVA office (☎ 222-8710) in Belém, at Rua Castilho França, 234.

ENAL (☎ 224-5210), at Avenida Bernardo Sayão 2000, operates services to Macapá via Breves, Curralinho, Santana, Jari and Monte Dourado. The trip takes 28 hours and costs US$18. Boats leave Belém at 6 pm on Saturday and return from Macapá at 6 pm on Tuesday.

SOUZAMAR (Souza Serviços Marítimos Ltda, ☎ 222-0719), at Travessa Dom Romualdo Coelho 838, sails to Macapá on Tuesday at 10 am (24 hours), returning on Friday at 10 am. Hammock space costs US$18, while two-person cabins cost US$75.

ENAVI (Empresa de Navegacão Vieira Ltda, ☎ 222-2339), at Avenida Bernardo Sayão 1242, provides a weekly service via Breves to Macapá, departing on Sundays at 6 pm. The trip costs US$26 for hammock space.

To/From Manaus & Santarem Services up the Amazon are fewer. ENART, the Empresa de Navegaçao A R Transportes Ltda (☎ 224-3969), at Travessa Almirante Wandenkolk 561, Portão 17 at the docks, sails on alternate Saturdays at 6 pm, taking five days to Manaus (with intermediate stops). Fares to Santarém are US$40 for hammock space, US$57 for a bunk; to Manaus, they are US$70/92.

For other services to Manaus, contact Alves e Rodrigues Ltda (☎ 223-1397), Beco do Carmo, 73 Sala 02, at Porto Vasconcelos (sailing on Wednesdays at 6 pm) or Cidade de Terezina IV (☎ 522-2371), at Armazem 15, Docas do Pará (sailing at 6 pm on Tuesday, Wednesday and Saturday). Fares are similar to those of ENART.

ENAVI (☎ 224-7656), at Avenida Bernardo Sayão 1242, sails on Thursday at 6 pm to Santarém (US$37/43, 72 hours).

Porto Fé em Deus, at Avenida Bernardo Sayão 3590, operates a weekly service to Santarém, leaving at 6 pm on Fridays (US$37 for hammock space).

To/From Souré (Ilha de Marajó) ENASA (☎ 223-3011), at Avenida Presidente Vargas 41, still runs a ferry to Souré on Ilha de Marajó. It leaves on Friday at 8 pm, returning on Sunday at 3 pm. The five-hour trip costs US$20/29 economy/1st class (the only difference is a separate cabin with more comfortable chairs).

Getting Around
To/From the Airports Belém's main airport, Aeroporto Internacional Val de Cans (☎ 233-4122), is on Avenida Júlio César. Take the bus marked 'Perpétuo Socorro' from the centre – it's quick (half an hour) and, of course, cheap. Some air taxis leave from a different airport, Aeroporto Júlio César (☎ 233-3868), at Avenida Senador Lemos 4700.

At inconvenient hours, a cab from the city centre to Val de Cans will cost US$6 (from the airport, it will cost nearly twice that).

To/From the Rodoviária The rodoviária (☎ 228-0500) is at the corner of avenidas Almirante Barroso and Ceará – about a 15-minute bus ride from the city. To reach the city centre from the rodoviária, take any bus marked 'Aeroclube 20', 'Cidade Nova 6' or 'Universidade (Presidente Vargas)'. Buses marked 'Cidade Nova 5' or 'Souza' run via Mercado Ver-o-Peso.

PRAIA DO ALGODOAL & MARUDÁ
Algodoal, a remote fishing village on the Atlantic coast north-east of Belém, with dunes and beaches, attracts younger Belenenses and a handful of foreign travellers. For around US$9 to US$10 a quarto, *Pousada da Aldeia* (☎ 224-2096), *Hotel Bela Mar* (☎ 222-7582) and *Hotel Caldeirão* are all cheap places to stay on Praia do Algodoal.

Getting to Algodoal requires a three-hour bus ride from Belém to the town of Marudá,

and then a boat across the bay. When you get off the boat, you have to negotiate with a taxi driver to take you to the other side of the cape. Buses leave the rodoviária in Belém daily at 7 and 10 am, 1.30, 3.30 and 5.30 pm, and also at 8 pm on Friday. The last bus leaves Marudá for Belém at 5 pm.

ILHA DE MARAJÓ
Ilha de Marajó, one of the largest fluvial islands in the world (slightly larger than Switzerland!), lies at the mouths of the Amazon and Tocantins rivers.

Souré
The island's principal town, Souré, is on the Rio Paracauari, a few km from the Baía de Marajó. With regular boat services from Belém and easy access to several of the best beaches and fazendas, it's probably the best place to go on the island. Souré is primarily a fishing village, but it's also the commercial centre for the island's buffalo business; legend has it that the buffalo arrived when a ship sailing to French Guiana sank offshore. On the second Sunday of November, Souré celebrates its own Círio de Nazaré.

Praia Araruna is the most beautiful beach, and the closest to town (five km, a 10-minute taxi ride). At low tide, you can walk along the beach about five km in either direction. **Praia do Pesqueiro** is 13 km from town (a 25-minute drive).

Salvaterra is a short boat trip across the river from Souré. Shuttle boats go every 15 minutes during the day. Salvaterra has restaurants and an expensive hotel. A 10-minute walk from town, **Praia Grande de Salvaterra** is a long, pretty beach on the Baía de Marajó. It's a good place to see the beautiful fence corals, which use the falling tide to capture fish.

Places to Stay In Souré, there's *Pousada Marajoara* (☎ 741-1287 in Souré, 223-2128 in Belém for reservations), which does most of its business through package excursions. A one-day trip by plane costs US$65. A three-day boat trip costs US$105/170 for a single/double apartamento, and includes food. The pousada buses you around to a fazenda with buffalo and to the local beaches. Independent travellers may reserve rooms directly – apartamentos cost around US$25/30.

For the same price on the other side of town, the *Hotel Marajó* (☎ 741-1376) is less crowded on weekends. For cheaper lodging, try the *Souré Hotel* (☎ 741-1202), in the centre of town, which has apartamentos with ceiling fan for US$9/15 (US$12/18 with aircon). It's simple but a bit dowdy.

In Salvaterra, there is the expensive *Pousada dos Guarás* (☎ 241-0891 in Belém for reservations).

The fazendas where the buffalo roam are enormous estates which occupy most of the island's eastern half – rustic refuges filled with birds and monkeys. Most have dormitories with an extra bunk or a place to hitch a hammock, but not all welcome outsiders. The following fazendas have primitive dormitories for tourists.

Fazenda Bom Jardim (☎ 231-3681 in Souré, 222-1380 in Belém for reservations) is recommended. It's a three-hour boat ride or a slightly shorter taxi ride from Souré. Air taxis take half an hour from Belém. *Fazenda Jilva* (☎ 225-0432), 40 km from Souré, has accommodation for about 20 people and charges around US$60 per person per day. It's a 45-minute flight from Belém to the fazenda.

Getting There & Away

Air Air taxis fly regularly between Belém and Souré, and to other towns on the island. It's a beautiful 25-minute flight over thick forest. The standard price per passenger is US$50, but it's cheaper if you form a small group. A five-seater from Belém to Souré, for example, costs US$175. Split five ways, that's only US$35 per person. For details about air-taxi companies, see the Getting There & Away section for Belém.

Boat For details about boat services between Belém and Ilha de Marajó, see the Getting There & Away section for Belém.

From Macapá (Amapá state), there are boats to Afuá, on Ilha de Marajó. It's possible to use local fishing boats to get all the way around the island and to some of the fazendas.

Tours Excursions to Ilha de Marajó are offered by agencies in Belém, such as Gran-Pará Turismo (☎ 224-3233), at Avenida Presidente Vargas 676, Vianney Turismo (☎ 241-5638), at Travessa Padre Eutíquio 2296, and Mundial Turismo (☎ 223-1981), at Avenida Presidente Vargas 780. Excursions include transport (by either boat or plane) and full board at a hotel in Souré or at one of the remote fazendas. As a rough rule of thumb, most of these package deals cost around US$65 per person per day, if the trip is done by plane; two-day tours by boat cost about US$80.

SANTARÉM

Santarém, about halfway between Manaus and Belém, is the third largest city of the Amazon, but a sleepy backwater compared to its peers.

Orientation & Information

The city layout is simple: the Cuiabá-Santarém highway runs directly to the Docas do Pará, dividing the city into old (eastern) and new (western) halves.

There is no tourist office, but you may be able to get tourist information by phoning the municipal department of tourism (☎ 522-1185). Two additional sources of information in Santarém are Bill Dieter, an American bush pilot, and Mr Alexander, author of *Alexander's Guide to Santarém*.

Things to See

Walk along the waterfront on Avenida Tapajós from the Docas do Pará to Rua Adriano Pimentel, where the drifters, loners and fishers congregate. The **Casa da Cultura**, on the corner of Avenida Borges Leal and Travessa Barão do Rio Branco, has a small collection of pre-Columbian pottery.

Santarém's natural **river beaches** are magnificent. Like elsewhere in the Amazon, the seasonal rise and fall of the waters uncovers lovely white river beaches and sweeps them clean of debris at the end of the beach season.

Tours
Amazon Tours (☎ 522-2620), at Travessa Turiano Meira 1084, organises jungle tours. Gil Serique (☎ 522-5174), at the Quick & Easy English School, Rua 24 de Outubro 1111, also acts as a guide for trips around Santarém.

Places to Stay
Hotel São Luís (☎ 522-1043), Travessa Senador Lemos 118, is cheap but dumpy. Quartos cost US$4/7 for singles/doubles, and meals and laundry service are also available. *Restaurante e Hotel Ponte Certo*, on the corner of Avenida Cuiaba and Mendoza Fortado, is cleanish but a bit out of the way. Apartamentos cost US$9/12. *Hotel Camino* (☎ 522-2981), at Praça Rodrigues dos Santos 877, near the market, and *Hotel Central Plaza*, also by the market, have apartamentos at US$10/13 with fan, and air-conditioned versions for a couple of dollars more.

The two mid-range hotels are inferior in quality but still adequate. The *Santarém Palace Hotel* (☎ 522-5285), at Avenida Rui Barbosa 726, and the *Hotel Uirapuru* (☎ 522-1531), at Avenida Adriano Pimentel 140, provide apartamentos for about US$17/21.

The *Hotel Tropical* (☎ 522-1533), at Avenida Mendoça Furtado 4120, is the only luxury hotel in Santarém. Despite the amenities, it's a bit frayed around the architectural edges. Room rates start around US$26/31.

Places to Eat
Restaurante O Mascote, on Praça do Pescador 10 (just off Rua Senador Lameira Bittencourt), is Santarém's best restaurant and music hang-out. *Restaurant Tapaiu*, in the lobby of the Hotel Tropical, also has a pleasing menu. Ice-cream fans will stampede to *Sorveteria Go-Go*, at Rua Siquiera Campos 431.

Getting There & Away
Air TABA serves the small towns of the Amazon interior, while Varig/Cruzeiro and VASP provide connections to other major cities in Brazil, via Manaus and Belém. TABA (☎ 522-1939) is at Rua Floriano Peixoto 607, Varig/Cruzeiro (☎ 522-2084) is at Rua Siquiera Campos 277 and VASP (☎ 522-1680) is at Avenida Rui Barbosa 786.

Bus The rodoviária (☎ 522-3392) is five km from the Docas do Pará, on Avenida Cuiabá. During the dry season, there are buses to Cuiabá, Belém (1369 km) via Imperatriz, Itaituba (370 km) and Marabá (1087 km).

The Transamazônica highway (BR-230) and Santarém-Cuiabá highway (BR-163) intersect 190 km south of Santarém, at Rurópolis. Bus travel can be miserable/impossible during the rainy season because about 1800 km of BR-163 (between Itaituba and Sinop) is unpaved. Most travellers still rely on river transport.

Boat For details about boat services to Manaus, Santarém and Belém, see the Getting There & Away sections for Belém and Manaus. Boat schedules are erratic, but anticipate three days to Manaus, three days to Belém and 12 hours to Itaituba.

There are also boat services twice a week (US$20/16 in 1st/2nd class, two days) between Santarém and Porto Santana, the major port 20 km down the coast from Macapá (Amapá state); see the Getting There & Away section for Macapá.

Getting Around
The airport is 15 km from the centre, and a bus service to the centre operates from 6 am to 7 pm. Alternatively, you may be able to use the courtesy shuttle bus which runs between the Hotel Tropical and the airport. The taxi fare is US$10.

Amapá

There's not much to the state of Amapá, other than Macapá, where three-quarters of its inhabitants live.

MACAPÁ

Macapá, capital of the state of Amapá, was officially founded in 1815 in a strategic position on the Amazon estuary.

Information

The provisional tourist information office, DETUR (☎ 222-0733), is at Avenida FAB, Centro Cívico Administrativo. Some travellers planning to continue north into French Guiana will require a visa. There is no French consulate in Amapá; the closest ones are in Belém and Manaus.

Things to See

The **Forte São José de Macapá** was built in 1782 by the Portuguese for defence against French invasions. The African village of **Curiaú**, eight km from Macapá, was founded by escaped slaves. You can catch a bus at Praça São José which goes to **Marco Zero do Equador** (the equator) via Porto Santana and Fazendinha and then returns to Macapá. **Bonito** and the **Igarapé do Lago**, 72 km and 85 km from Macapá, are good places for swimming, fishing and jungle walks.

Places to Stay & Eat

The *Mara Hotel* (☎ 222-0859), on Rua São Jose, has single/double quartos for US$6/8. The *Hotel Tropical* (☎ 231-3739), at Avenida Antônio Coelho de Carvalho 1399, offers good-value apartamentos at around US$6/8.

The *Amapaense Palace* (☎ 222-3366), on Avenida Tiradentes, is a two-star hotel with standard apartamentos for US$27/33.

Eat your meals either at the *Peixaria* (☎ 222-0913), at Avenida Mãe Luzia 84, or at *Restaurante Boscão* (☎ 231-4097), Rua Hamilton Silva 997.

Getting There & Away

Air It's possible to fly with Air France from Paris to Cayenne, French Guiana, and then continue overland to Amapá; however, travellers who want to avoid overland hassles may prefer to take the more convenient Air France flight between Belém and Cayenne.

The Varig/Cruzeiro office (☎ 223-1743) is at Rua Candido Mendes 1039, VASP (☎ 223-2411) is at Avenida Júlio Maria Lombard 115 and TABA (☎ 222-2083) is on Avenida Independência. Check the latest schedules and prices for flights to Oiapoque, Cayenne or Belém with these airlines.

At the time of writing, TABA was operating daily flights (except Sundays) between Macapá and Oiapoque (US$60 one way, 1¼ hours).

Bus Macapá is linked by BR-156 to Oiapoque, the Brazilian border town beside the Rio Oiapoque, on the border with French Guiana. The 560-km road is paved as far as Calçoene and then degenerates into an 'unpaved track'. The road is frequently washed out, and you should be prepared to hire vehicles or hitch on an impromptu basis. Transport between Macapá and Oiapoque is erratic and best attempted in two stages: by bus from Macapá to Calçoene (US$14, nine hours) and from there to Oiapoque (US$11, at least seven hours) by occasional *colectivo* (collective taxi or minibus). For details about crossing the border, see Crossing the Border section.

Boat For information about boat schedules and fares, contact SENAVA (☎ 222-3648), at Avenida Engenheiro Azarias Neto 20, or Capitânia dos Portos (☎ 222-0415), at Avenida FAB 427.

There is at least one boat a month to Oiapoque, but there appears to be no set pattern for departures, so you'll have to ask at the docks.

For details about boat services to Belém and Santarém, see their respective Getting There & Away sections. Note: boats to Santarém and Belém depart from Porto Santana, the main port 20 km down the coast from Macapá. If you need to stay overnight in this archetypal Amazon port (the exotic wares in the market are reportedly worth a look), a reader has recommended *Hotel Muller* (☎ 632-6881), at Rua Filinto Muller 373, which charges US$5 per person for an apartamento with fan. There is a regular bus service between Porto Santana and Macapá.

Crossing the Border The Brazilian border town of Oiapoque, 560 km north of Macapá, is the main crossing point for overland travellers between Brazil and French Guiana. The transport options available from Macapá to the border are covered in the air, bus and boat descriptions above.

Unless you have a great deal of time and patience or absolutely *have* to do the trip overland, you may prefer to avoid all the hassles and hop on a plane. For more advice, see To/From French Guiana – Land, in the general Getting There & Away section earlier in this chapter.

There's a clean, state-owned hotel in Calçoene, which is excellent value, at US$5 for a double apartamento. The two hotels in Oiapoque charge US$5 for a double quarto and US$6 for a double apartamento.

Get your Brazilian exit stamp from the Polícia Federal in Oiapoque and your French Guianese entry stamp at the *gendarmerie* in St Georges (French Guiana), which is reached by motorboat (US$2.50, 20 minutes) from Oiapoque. There are also plans to construct a bridge over the river. If you need to change money, there's a casa de câmbio at the harbour in Oiapoque.

Tocantins

On 1 January 1989, a constitutional amendment creating the new state of Tocantins came into effect. This state now encompasses what was previously the northern half of the state of Goiás. After ferocious politicking with two or three rivals, the town of Palmas was officially declared the state capital. At this early stage in the life of the state, very little information is available.

RIO ARAGUAIA
The Rio Araguaia begins in the Serra dos Caiapós and flows 2600 km northwards,

forming the borders of Mato Grosso, Goiás and Pará before joining the Rio Tocantins near Marabá. The stretch of the river from Aruanã to Ilha do Bananal offers some of the world's best freshwater fishing. The best access to the river from Mato Grosso is via Barra do Garças, about 500 km from Cuiabá, which has camping facilities (open from May to October) and four simple hotels.

If you want to explore the river without a tour, catch a boat in Aruanã or Barra do Garças, but if you want to get as far north as Ilha do Bananal and don't have a lot of money, it's best to take a bus up to São Felix do Araguaia and hire a boat from there.

Ilha do Bananal
The Ilha do Bananal, where the Rio Araguaia divides, is the world's largest river island, covering 20,000 sq km. Much of the island is covered with forest, and a big chunk is an Indian reserve, the Parque Nacional do Araguaia, inhabited by Carajás and Javaés Indians.

Permission to visit the park can be obtained from IBAMA (the national parks service) in Brasília, or from the park director (☎ 224-2457, 224-4809), who lives in Goiânia (Goiás state). Of course, if you just show up, you may save a lot of time and hassle and get in just the same. The ranger responsible is Senhor Bonilho, who knows the park quite well. There is simple accommodation available on the island but no food, other than what you bring. Senhor Bonilho can provide 4WDs and boats.

Getting There & Away
To/From Aruanã It's probably easier to reach the Araguaia from the state of Goiás (Goiânia, in particular) than from Mato Grosso. For those without a 4WD at their disposal, the town of Aruanã, accessible by bus from both Goiânia (310 km) and Goiás Town, is the gateway to the Araguaia. There is a campground (open in July) at Aruanã. Hire a *voadeira* (a small aluminium motorboat) and guide for a river trip to Ilha do Bananal.

To/From Barra do Garças The long, dusty road to Ilha do Bananal begins 400 km west of Goiânia, at Barra do Garças in Mato Grosso. The bus from Barra do Garças to São Felix do Araguaia leaves daily at 5 am. If you don't want to take the bus, air taxis cover the distance in one hour.

Amazonas

Amazonas, covering an area of over 1.5 million sq km, is Brazil's largest state.

MANAUS

Manaus lies beside the Rio Negro, 10 km upstream from the confluence of the Solimões and Negro rivers, which join to form the Amazon. Although Manaus continues to be vaunted in countless glossy advertising brochures as an Amazon wonderland, the city itself has few attractions. In addition, it is dirty, ugly and increasingly crime-ridden. Many travellers now only use the city for the briefest of stopovers before making excursions far beyond Manaus, where it is still possible to experience the rainforest wonders that Manaus glibly promises but cannot deliver.

Orientation

The most interesting parts of Manaus, as far as the tourist is concerned, are close to the waterfront. Avenida Eduardo Ribeiro is lined with airline offices, banks and Manaus' fancier stores.

Information

Tourist Office Emamtur (☎ 243-5983), the state tourism organisation, has its headquarters at Avenida Tarumã 379, a bit out of the way. It's only open from 7 am to 1 pm Monday to Friday. The municipal tourist office (☎ 232-1646), at the Canto da Cultura (Culture Corner), opposite the Teatro Amazonas (Manaus Opera Theatre), is more convenient. It's open from 9 am to noon and

2 to 6 pm Monday to Friday, and from 9 am to noon on Saturday.

Money There is a new and dependable exchange house, Câmbio Cortéz, at the corner of avenidas 7 de Setembro and Getúlio Vargas.

Post & Telecommunications Manaus' post office is on Rua Marechal Deodoro. It's open Monday to Saturday from 8 am to 6 pm, and on Sunday from 8 am to 2 pm. The Amazon postal system has a poor reputation, and foreign residents in Manaus don't entrust their correspondence to Brazilian correios, preferring to wait for US or Europe-bound couriers and friends to take it.

There's a central office of TeleAmazon, the state telephone company, on Rua Guilherme Moreira. It's open daily from 8 am to 11 pm.

Foreign Consulates It's best to arrange visas to neighbouring countries well in advance through consulates in Manaus.

If you're going beyond Leticia to Colombia, tell the consul, who'll probably demand to see an onward ticket and proof of 'sufficient funds' before issuing a visa.

Foreign consulates in Manaus include:

Bolivia
   Avenida Tefé, Bloco B4A, Apartamento 202, Parque Solimões (☎ 237-8686)
Colombia
   Rua Dona Libânia 262 (☎ 234-6777)
Ecuador
   Rua 6, casa 6, Jardim Belo Horizonte (☎ 236-3698)
France
   Rua Monsenhor Coutinho 164 (☎ 233-6851)
Germany
   Rua Barroso 355, 1 Andar, sala A (☎ 232-5877)
Peru
   Conjunto Aristocrático, Rua A, casa 19, Chapada (☎ 236-3666)
UK
   Edifício Manaus Shopping Center, sala 1212 (☎ 234-1018)
USA
   Rua Recife 1010, Pq 10 (☎ 234-4546)
Venezuela
   Rua Recife 1620 (☎ 236-0406)

Maps Mundo dos Mapas, at Rua Saldanha Marinho 773, has good topographic maps of parts of the Amazon backcountry.

Things to See

The **Porto Escadaria dos Remédios** is a good place to watch the locals at work. Looming above the dock is the imposing cast-iron structure of the **Mercado Municipal**, designed in 1882 by Adolfo Lisboa after Les Halles in Paris. Inside and about the market, you can buy provisions for jungle trips. At the back end of the market, there's a grimy cafeteria, where you can have lunch and contemplate Manaus' complete disregard for sanitation.

The **Teatro Amazonas**, the famous opera house, was designed by Doménico de Angelis in Italian Renaissance style at the height of the rubber boom, in 1896. Renovated in 1990, it's now open from 10 am to 5 pm Tuesday to Sunday. Admission costs US$2 and includes a compulsory guided tour.

The **Museu do Homem do Norte**, at Avenida 7 de Setembro 1385, is an ethnology and anthropology museum dedicated to the river-dwelling *caboclos* (people of White and Indian mix). It's open Tuesday to Friday from 9 am to noon and 2 to 6 pm, and from 9 am to noon on Monday. To reach the museum from the city centre, take the bus marked 'Coroado'.

The **Museu do Indio**, near the intersection of avenidas Duque de Caxias and 7 de Setembro, has exhibits on tribes of the upper Rio Negro. It's open Monday to Friday from 8 am to noon and 2 to 5 pm, and from 8 am to noon on Saturday.

The **Encontro das Águas** (Meeting of the Waters), where the inky-black waters of the Rio Negro meet the lemon-yellow waters of the Rio Solimões, is well worth seeing, but it's not absolutely necessary to take a tour. It can be seen just as well from the ferry which shuttles between Careiro and the Porto Velho highway (BR-319). If you do include the meeting of the waters in your tour, you may lose time that could be spent exploring the more interesting sights further along the river.

Jungle Tours

The number one priority for most visitors to Manaus is a jungle tour to see the wildlife and experience the rainforest close at hand. Here, it's possible to arrange anything from standard day trips and overnight excursions to months of travel in the hinterland.

It is common for travellers to be greeted at the airport by groups of tour-agency representatives keen to sign them up for trips. These representatives are a useful source of information, and may even offer transport into the centre to a budget hotel, but you should hold off booking a tour until you've had time to shop around for the best deals. There are now dozens of agencies vying for your custom, with trendy names ('Eco' and 'Green' have quickly become standard prefixes) and glossy brochures often making wild promises.

What you get out of your trip depends on several factors: expectations, previous experience, competence and breadth of knowledge of tour operators and guides, and the ability to accept life in the the Amazon at face value.

What you *can* expect on day trips or on boat tours lasting three or four days is a close-up experience of the jungle flora, with abundant bird life and a few jacaré (more easily located at night by guides using powerful torches). It is also a chance to see what life is like for the caboclos in the vicinity of Manaus.

You *cannot* expect to meet remote Indian tribes or dozens of free-ranging beasts, because the former have sensibly fled from contact (after centuries of annihilation or forced assimilation) and the latter have been systematically hunted to the brink of extinction. In both cases, access has become synonymous with destruction.

This does not mean that the tours are not worthwhile, merely that prospective tour participants should ignore flowery propaganda and instead ask the tour operators for exact details. Does the tour include extended

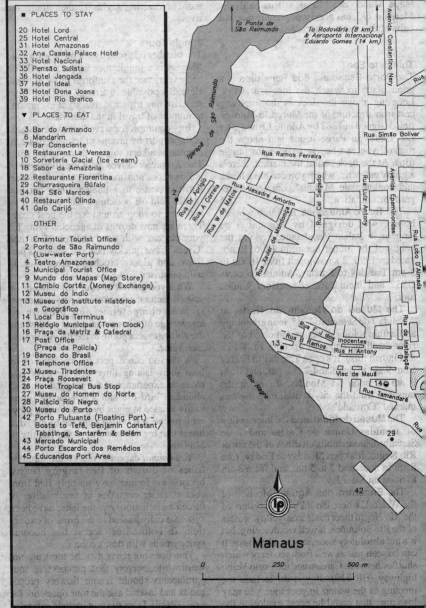

■ PLACES TO STAY

20 Hotel Lord
25 Hotel Central
31 Hotel Amazonas
32 Ana Cassia Palace Hotel
33 Hotel Nacional
35 Pensão Sulista
36 Hotel Jangada
37 Hotel Ideal
38 Hotel Dona Joana
39 Hotel Rio Branco

▼ PLACES TO EAT

3 Bar do Armando
6 Mandarim
7 Bar Consciente
8 Restaurant La Veneza
10 Sorveteria Glacial (Ice cream)
18 Sabor da Amazônia
22 Restaurante Fiorentina
29 Churrasqueira Búfalo
34 Bar São Marcos
40 Restaurant Olinda
41 Galo Carijó

OTHER

1 Emamtur Tourist Office
2 Porto de São Raimundo
  (Low-water Port)
4 Teatro Amazonas
5 Municipal Tourist Office
9 Mundo dos Mapas (Map Store)
11 Câmbio Cortéz (Money Exchange)
12 Museu do Índio
13 Museu do Instituto Histórico
   e Geográfico
14 Local Bus Terminus
15 Relógio Municipal (Town Clock)
16 Praça da Matriz & Catedral
17 Post Office
   (Praça da Polícia)
19 Banco do Brasil
21 Telephone Office
23 Museu Tiradentes
24 Praça Roosevelt
26 Hotel Tropical Bus Stop
27 Museu do Homem do Norte
28 Palácio Rio Negro
30 Museu do Porto
42 Porto Flutuante (Floating Port) –
   Boats to Tefé, Benjamin Constant/
   Tabatinga, Santarém & Belém
43 Mercado Municipal
44 Porto Escardio dos Remédios
45 Educandos Port Area

To Ponte de
São Raimundo

To Rodoviária (8 km)
& Aeroporto Internacional
Eduardo Gomes (14 km)

Avenida Constantino Nery

Rua Simão Bolivar

Rua Ramos Ferreira

Igarapé de São Raimundo

Rua Dr Aprígio

Rua A Corrêa

Rua W de Matos

Rua Alexadre Amorim

Rua Xavier de Mendonça

Rua Cel Salgado

Rua Luiz Antony

Avenida Epaminondas

Rua Lobo D'Almada

Rio Negro

Rua F J dos Inocentes

Rua B Ramos

Rua H Antony

Rua da Instalação

Visc de Maúa

Rua Tamandaré

Manaus

0   250   500 m

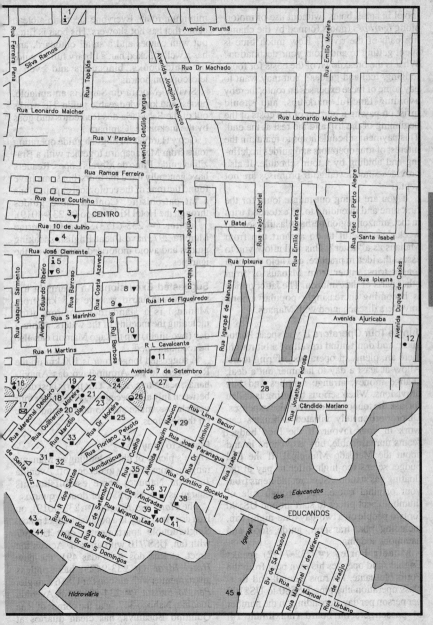

BRAZIL

travel in small boats (without use of motor) along *igarapés* (pools formed by the changing path of the river)? How much time is spent getting to and from your destination? What is the breakdown of the costs for food, lodging, fuel and guides? You may want to pay some of these expenses en route, thereby avoiding fanciful mark-ups, and should insist on paying a portion of the costs at the beginning of the trip and the rest at the end. This payment schedule helps to maintain the interest of tour operators and guides in defining and abiding by a tour schedule. It also provides some leverage if promises are not kept.

If you are trying out jungle tours for the first time and intending to do extended trips in the Amazon region perhaps lasting several weeks, it's useful to do a short trip from Manaus as a 'taster'. This will allow you to assess the idea in practice, and help you plan longer trips, either from Manaus or from other parts of the Amazon. The latter option is becoming increasingly popular among travellers disenchanted with Manaus.

Jungle Tour Operators If you speak Portuguese and don't mind travelling a bit rough, there are plenty of operators offering tours. Allow at least a day to hammer out a deal, change money, arrange supplies and buy provisions. When serious haggling is called for, ask the tour operator to itemise expenses. Disproportionately inflated estimates can work in your favour. If the food budget seems unreasonable, buy provisions in and about the Mercado Municipal. If the fuel budget seems too high, offer to pay at the floating gas stations. Subtract the items from your original quote. As a rough rule of thumb, expect prices to start around US$90 for two people on a two-day (one-night) trip, including boat transport, guide, food and hammock lodging.

Moaçir Fortes (☎ 232-7492) speaks English, and operates his own boat from the Porto Flutuante. He runs a small and first-class operation charging US$80 to US$100 per person per day, depending on the number of passengers on board (maximum 14,

minimum four). Everyone sleeps in a clean cabin that has hot showers. His boat is fitted out with canoes and a small outboard, and has a well-stocked bar, a library full of wildlife guidebooks, binoculars and even a telescope on board.

Sivilino Moeira do Santo is an amiable, honest and knowledgeable guide. He works out of the Escadaria dos Remédios and goes by the nickname 'Capibara'.

Gerry Hardy is an English guide operating tours from Manacapuru together with a Brazilian guide, Elmo de Morais Lopes. Readers have generally liked the tours, but some have found the tone of the ecological explanations a bit patronising. Contact these guides through the Hotel Rio Branco (☎ 233-4019).

Iaratur (☎ 233-6173), Rua Guilherme Moreira 297, have fluent English-speaking guides and avoid motorised transport on the igarapés.

Suggested Excursions An overnight trip to Lago Janauário reserve (15 km from Manaus) is a standard excursion often including the meeting of the waters. A three-day (two-night) trip to Lago Mamori can also be recommended.

A suggested longer tour is 100 km up the Rio Negro to the Arquipélago das Anavilhanas, near Nova Airão. This trip is best done between July and December. Whichever tour you choose, make sure to take a canoe ride on the igarapés.

Places to Stay
There's plenty of cheap lodging in Manaus, ranging from grungy to decent, off Avenida Joaquim Nabuco; some establishments charge as little as US$6 for double quartos.

The *Hotel Rio Branco* (☎ 233-4019), on Rua dos Andradas, is a popular budget place. Single/double apartamentos cost US$5/7 with fan, US$7/10 with air-con. Across the street, at Rua dos Andradas 491, the new *Hotel Ideal* (☎ 233-9423) has spotless apartamentos with air-con for US$6 a single. *Pensão Sulista* (☎ 234-5814), at Avenida Joaquim Nabuco 347, near the corner of Rua Quintino Bocaiúva, has clean quartos at

US$4/7. Readers have warned that the *Hotel Paraíso* is notorious for theft.

Hotel Dona Joana (☎ 233-7553), at Rua dos Andradas 553, has been one of the best budget hotels but has had some recent negative reports. Apartamentos (with air-con) start around US$8/12, and the suite costs US$18. Rooms at the top have good views across the river.

In the mid-range, there are a couple of options. *Hotel Aquarius* (☎ 232-5526), at Rua Dr Moreira 116, is a three-star hotel for US$35/45 a single/double. The *Ana Cassia Palace Hotel* (☎ 622-3637), at Rua dos Andradas 14, provides rather cranky service, but the apartamentos are passable, at US$45/55, and it gives 30% discounts for cash payment.

The full-tilt splurge option is the *Tropical Hotel* (☎ 238-5757), a self-contained resort 16 km out of Manaus, at Ponta Negra. Rooms start around US$120/140, and suites are available for a mere US$320. Even if you don't stay, you may want to visit this huge complex, which has a well-arranged small zoo and a giant swimming pool (with waves, beach, palm trees and even Vitória Regia lilies). The hotel also provides a shuttle service (US$2) to and from the centre of Manaus. Buses leave every couple of hours between 8.30 am and 7 pm. The bus stop is on Rua Dr Moreira, in the centre.

Places to Eat

There are two good seafood restaurants a bit out of the way, in the Adrianópolis neighbourhood: *Chapéu de Palha* (☎ 234-2133), at Rua Fortaleza 619, enjoys the better reputation, but excellent fish dishes can also be found at *Restaurante Panorama* (☎ 232-3177), Rua Recife 900.

For surprisingly good pizza and pasta dishes, try *Restaurante Fiorentina* (☎ 232-1295), at Praça Roosevelt 44. Vegetarians should head for *Chapaty Restaurante Vegetariano*, near the Opera House, at Rua Costa Azevedo 105. It's open from 11 am to 2.30 pm Sunday to Friday. *Mandarim*, at Avenida Eduardo Ribeiro 650, serves inexpensive Chinese food. *Sabor da Amazônia*, at the

corner of ruas Marechal Deodoro and Quintino Bocaiúva, specialises in regional cuisine and exotic ice cream. *Galo Carijó*, opposite Hotel Dona Joana, on Rua dos Andradas, is recommended for its fish and 'uma cerveja estupidamente gelada' (an idiotically cold beer). Very nearby, on Rua Pedro Botelho, *Restaurant Olinda* is very popular with travellers.

Sorveteria Glacial, at Getúlio Vargas and Henrique Martins, has very fine ice cream with imaginative flavours. Down the block, at Vargas 257, *Restaurant La Veneza* has good lunches for US$2, and more elaborate Italian meals.

Things to Buy

Indian crafts are sold at the Museu do Índio, where FUNAI has a shop selling articles produced by the Wai-wai and Tikuna peoples. The store is open Monday to Friday from 8 am to noon and 2 to 6 pm, and from 8 am to noon on Saturday. Casa das Redes, a couple of blocks inland from the Mercado Municipal, in front of the Hotel Amazonas, has a good selection of hammocks at reasonable prices.

Getting There & Away

Air The Aeroporto Internacional Eduardo Gomes (☎ 621-1431) is on Avenida Santos Dumont, 14 km from the city centre. There are international flights to Caracas (Venezuela), Iquitos (Peru), Bogotá (Colombia) and La Paz (Bolivia). US-bound flights from Manaus are in flux. In general, it's cheaper to purchase the ticket abroad and have it sent to Brazil by registered mail.

VASP, Transbrasil and Varig/Cruzeiro serve all major cities in Brazil; air taxis and TABA fly to smaller Amazonian settlements. Varig/Cruzeiro (☎ 234-1116) is at Rua Marcílio Dias 284, TABA (☎ 232-0224) is at Avenida Eduardo Ribeiro 664, VASP (☎ 234-1266) is at Rua Guilherme Moreira 179 and, nearby, Transbrasil (☎ 233-2288) is at Rua Guilherme Moreira 150.

Bus The rodoviária (☎ 236-2732) is six km from the town centre, at the junction of Rua

BRAZIL

Recife and Avenida Constantino Nery. Phone for information on road conditions. All roads from Manaus involve ferry transport.

Overland travel from Manaus southwards to Porto Velho on BR-319 has been impossible for some time (a really determined motorcyclist might get through). River travel along the Rio Madeira takes up the slack.

The 770-km road from Manaus north to Boa Vista (BR-174) has more unpaved sections, but is usually passable. The daily União Cascavel bus to Boa Vista (US$37) takes about 18 hours, but delays are common and the trip can take a lot longer.

Boat Three major ports in Manaus function according to high and low-water levels. Bairro Educandos is the port for sailings to Porto Velho. For sailings on the Rio Negro as far as Caracaraí, the requisite high-water port is Ponte de São Raimundo; the low-water port is Bairro de São Raimundo, about 2½ km away. The Porto Flutuante serves mainstream Amazon destinations – Belém, Santarém, Tefé and Benjamin Constant – and is the port used by ENASA.

For information, visit the Porto Flutuante, which now has a complex of counters arranged like those at a bus terminal, with fares and destinations prominently posted. A more time-consuming method of locating a boat is to go to Escadaria dos Remédios, the docks by the Mercado Municipal, and poke around.

Ports of call are marked on the boats, and fares are pretty much standardised according to distance. The boats usually pull out at 6 pm regardless of the destination.

Although food and drink are included in the fare, bring bottled water and snacks as a supplement. Unless you have cabin space, you'll need a hammock, as well as rope to string it up. It can get windy and cool at night, so a sleeping bag is also recommended. Spend a bit more money and hang your hammock on the cooler upper deck, preferably towards the bow. Beware of theft on boats – a very common complaint.

To/From Benjamin Constant & Tabatinga
From Manaus, it's a seven-day trip to Tabatinga on the *Almirante Monteiro*, if all goes well. On the *Avelino Leal* and *Cidade de Terezina*, it's at least a week's journey to Tabatinga, with stops at Fonte Boa, Foz do Jutai, Vila Nova, Santo Antônio do Iça, Amaturé, São Paulo de Olivença and Benjamin Constant. Average prices for passage are US$95/55 for cabin/hammock accommodation.

To/From Leticia (Colombia) & Iquitos (Peru) Travellers can cruise the river between Manaus and Iquitos, Peru. The return or outgoing leg can be flown with Varig/Cruzeiro (four flights a week) between Iquitos and Manaus, via Tefé and Tabatinga. From Tabatinga, it's three more days and 280 km to Iquitos via Leticia. *Oro Negro* is a recommended boat for this trip.

To/From Caracaraí On the Rio Branco, the *Rio Uaquiry* leaves every Friday from Manaus and arrives on Monday in Caracaraí. It leaves Caracaraí on Tuesday and arrives back in Manaus on Thursday. Passage costs US$50/30 for cabin/hammock accommodation. Food is included in the price. The high-water port in Manaus for this boat is Ponte de São Raimundo; the low-water port is Bairro de São Raimundo. There's a bus service between Boa Vista and Caracaraí (about four hours).

To/From Porto Velho Another long river trip can be taken from Manaus up the Rio Madeira to Porto Velho. The trip takes about a week and tickets cost US$53/45 for cabin/hammock accommodation. For more details, see the Getting There & Away section for Porto Velho.

To/From Santarém & Belém ENASA services to Santarém and Belém have been superseded by other companies; see the Getting There & Away section for Belém.

Getting Around
To/From the Airport Aeroporto Internacio-

nal Eduardo Gomes (☎ 621-1431) is 14 km from the city centre, on Avenida Santos Dumont. The bus marked 'Aeroporto Internacional' runs between the local bus terminus and the airport from 6 am to midnight (US$0.35, 40 minutes). There's a bilheteria system for taxis; the fare from the airport to the centre is US$13.

Bus The local bus terminus is on Praça da Matriz – near the cathedral and a few blocks from the Hotel Amazonas. From this terminus, you can catch buses to Ponta Negra. A more expensive but quicker way to reach Ponta Negra is on the Tropical Hotel shuttle bus (details provided in Places to Stay).

To/From the Rodoviária The rodoviária (☎ 236-2732) is six km from the centre of town. Buses marked 'Ileia', 'Santos Dumont' or 'Aeroporto Internacional' run from the centre via the rodoviária. A taxi to the centre costs around US$7.

TABATINGA & BENJAMIN CONSTANT
These two Brazilian ports are on the border between Brazil, Colombia and Peru, known as the Triple Frontier. Neither is particularly attractive, and most travellers view them as transit points. If you have to wait a few days for a boat, the Colombian border town of Leticia is a much more salubrious place to hang out.

Getting There & Away
Air From Tabatinga, there are four flights weekly to Manaus, Brazil (US$90) and two to Iquitos, Peru (US$75). Apart from these commercial passenger flights, cargo planes operate irregularly from Tabatinga to Manaus. There are military planes from Ramón Castilla to Iquitos (both in Peru).

Boat Boats down the Amazon to Manaus leave from Benjamin Constant. There are regular boats departing (theoretically) on Wednesday and Saturday nights, taking four days and costing US$35 in your own hammock, US$40 in a cabin. Many other irregular cargo boats take passengers on

deck, and some have cabins. Prices and journey times are similar. In the opposite direction, upstream from Manaus to Benjamin Constant, the trip takes between six and 10 days. Food is included but is of poor quality.

There are frequent colectivos between the Leticia and Tabatinga ports (US$0.35); otherwise, it's a 20-minute walk. In Tabatinga, you must get an entry stamp in your passport from Brazilian officials, who like prospective foreign visitors to dress neatly. There is a ferry service with two boats daily between Tabatinga and Benjamin Constant (US$2, 1½ hours).

Upstream to Iquitos (Peru), boats leave irregularly from Ramón Castilla, across the river from Tabatinga, and Islandia, on an island opposite Benjamin Constant. The journey takes about three days and costs about US$40, food included. Travelling in the opposite direction, downstream from Iquitos to Ramón Castilla, the trip takes around 36 hours. You can obtain your entry stamp from Peruvian officials in Puerto Alegría.

Roraima

This mountainous region straddling the Venezuelan border to the north of Roraima is perhaps the ultimate Amazon frontier. It is home to the Yanomami, who represent about one-third of the remaining tribal Indians of the Amazon. Although the Brazilian government has declared their lands a special Indian reserve, this declaration will be worthless unless the government is prepared to enforce it and eject trespassers.

BOA VISTA
Most travellers consider this city nothing more than a transit point between Brazil and Venezuela. The city is shaped like an archway, with the base of the arch on the Rio Branco and the arch itself formed by avenidas Major Williams and Terencio Lima. The scale of the place is totally

BRAZIL

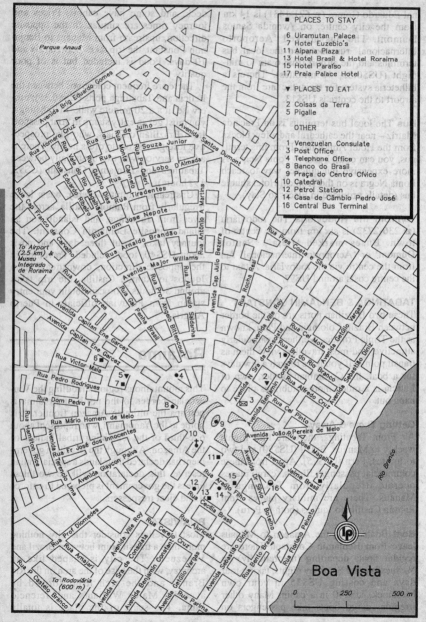

Boa Vista

0   250   500 m

unsuited to pedestrians, who could quite easily spend a whole day trying to do a couple of errands on foot.

Information
Money Banco do Brasil is in the centre. A useful moneychanger, with longer opening hours than the bank, is Casa de Câmbio Pedro José (☎ 224-4277), on Rua Araújo Filho. It's open from 8 am to 6 pm Monday to Friday.

Venezuelan Consulate The Venezuelan Consulate is on Avenida Benjamin Constant and is open from 8 am to noon Monday to Friday. If you arrive early in the morning, you may be able to pick up your visa at noon. You will require one photo, a completed application form and an outbound ticket from Venezuela. Current visa fees are US$10 for British applicants, US$2 for US nationals (cash dollars only). You'd be advised to get your visa beforehand and avoid the delay in Boa Vista.

Places to Stay & Eat
Cheaper hotels include the *Hotel Paraíso* (☎ 224-9335), at Rua Araújo Filho 228 (a real dive which charges US$5 per person), *Hotel Brasil* (☎ 224-9421), at Avenida Benjamin Constant 331 (a rock-bottom cheapie with quartos at US$3.50/7 for singles/doubles), and *Hotel Roraima* (☎ 224-9843), at Avenida Benjamin Constant 351 (with quartos at US$5/8). *Hotel Euzebio's* (☎ 224-0300), at Rua Cecília Brasil 1107, provides excellent value for money. It has a swimming pool, garden and restaurant, and offers comfortable apartamentos for around US$13/20.

There are lots of food stalls selling inexpensive food at the municipal bus terminal. *Coisas da Terra*, on Avenida Benjamin Constant, serves savoury snacks, cakes and sucos. *Pigalle*, on Avenida Capitan Ene Garcez, does great pizza, and hosts live music at weekends. Also worth trying are the various hotel restaurants, such as those at Euzebio's, Aipana Plaza and Uiramutan Palace.

Getting There & Away
Air Varig/Cruzeiro operates flights to and from Manaus twice weekly. The Varig/Cruzeiro (☎ 224-2226) office is at Avenida Getúlio Vargas 242.

Bus Boa Vista to Manaus is a US$37, 15-hour bus ride (road conditions and trip time are erratic) with two ferry crossings along the way. There's one departure daily, at 8 am. Hitching is very difficult, as most of the traffic (gravel trucks) is only local.

Another option is to take the bus between Boa Vista and Caracaraí (US$5, four hours), where there's a boat service to Manaus – for details, see Getting There & Away for Manaus.

Crossing the Borders From Boa Vista, there are overland routes to Venezuela and Guyana.

If the weather cooperates, it's a beautiful six-hour ride between Boa Vista and Santa Elena (Venezuela). The bus departs daily at 8 am from the rodoviária in Boa Vista. Tickets (US$13) should be bought a day in advance. For more details about the border crossing, see the Getting There & Away section for Santa Elena, in the Venezuela chapter.

A bus leaves Boa Vista for Bonfim on Monday, Thursday and Friday at 4 pm (US$8, 125 km, four hours). Once in Bonfim, pick up your exit stamp from the Polícia Federal, then slog the five km from there to the Guyanese border at the Rio Tacutu. Here, you can hire a canoe across to Lethem, in Guyana. Overland travel to Georgetown, Guyana is conceivable but very difficult, and travellers to whom time (and personal safety) are at all important generally prefer to go by air. Guyanese officials tend to scrutinise travellers carefully here.

Getting Around
Getting around on foot is difficult. The airport (☎ 224-3680) is four km from the city centre. Take a bus marked 'Aeroporto' from the municipal bus terminal.

The rodoviária (☎ 224-0606) is three km from the centre – about 40 minutes on foot! Take a bus marked '13 de Setembro' from the municipal bus terminal and get off at the bus stop beside a supermarket which is opposite the rodoviária.

Rondônia

The states of Rondônia and Acre, previously undeveloped frontier regions, have undergone rapid development, mainly as a result of the construction of BR-364. Many travellers will only be passing through these states en route to or from Peru or Bolivia – probably all will be impressed by the massive deforestation which has left vast tracts of land looking like the aftermath of a holocaust. You should be aware that both these states, especially Rondônia, are major distribu-tion centres for cocaine from neighbouring Peru and Bolivia. Travellers are generally left alone, providing they mind their own business.

PORTO VELHO

Porto Velho, capital of Rondônia, is on the south bank of the Rio Madeira, near the border with the state of Amazonas. There's not much of interest for visitors, but it is an access point to Rio Branco, further west, and to Guajará-Mirim and the Bolivian border.

Information

The office of the state tourist authority, DETUR (☎ 223-2276), is some distance from the centre, and keeps moving around. It's at Avenida Padre Chiquinho 670, Esplanada das Secretarias, and is open on weekdays from 8 am to noon.

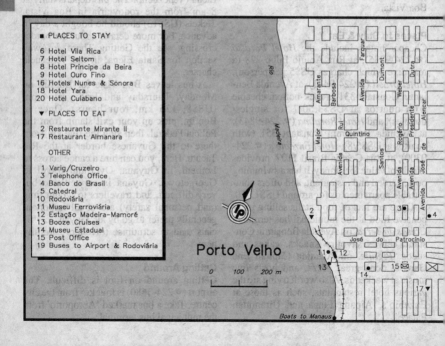

■ PLACES TO STAY

6 Hotel Vila Rica
7 Hotel Seltom
8 Hotel Príncipe da Beira
9 Hotel Ouro Fino
16 Hotels Nunes & Sonora
18 Hotel Yara
20 Hotel Cuiabano

▼ PLACES TO EAT

2 Restaurante Mirante II
17 Restaurant Almanara

OTHER

1 Varig/Cruzeiro
3 Telephone Office
4 Banco do Brasil
5 Catedral
10 Rodoviária
11 Museu Ferroviária
12 Estação Madeira–Mamoré
13 Booze Cruises
14 Museu Estadual
15 Post Office
19 Buses to Airport & Rodoviária

Porto Velho

0   100   200 m

Boats to Manaus

Estação Madeira-Mamoré & Museu Ferroviário

If you have some time to spare, visit this dilapidated remnant of the failed Madeira to Mamoré railway, on the waterfront. It is now being restored and developed as a cultural centre, though at present, the steam locomotive to and from Santo Antônio (seven km from Porto Velho) is not in service.

Places to Stay

Hotels The best of the budget hotels is *Hotel Nunes* (☎ 221-1389), which has quartos at US$4/5 a single/double and apartamentos at US$6/7. Just a few metres away are the slightly cheaper *Hotel Sonora* and *Hotel Cuiabano* (☎ 221-4084). *Hotel Yara*, on Avenida Osorio, has comfortable apartamentos (US$9/12). *Hotel Principe da Beira* (☎ 221-0086), on the edge of the centre, at Avenida Getúlio Vargas 2287, is a friendly place with an in-house travel agency, Princetur. Apartamentos cost US$22/29.

Jungle Lodge *Tapiri Selva Hotel* (☎ 221-4785 for reservations) is a jungle lodge complex with wooden huts in the midst of forest, close to Lago de Cujubim, 70 km from Porto Velho. Access to the lodge is provided by boat from the docks. On Friday, Saturday and Sunday, boats depart from Porto Velho at 8 am and return at 5 pm. A day trip costs US$20 per person. If you want to stay one or more nights, the price is around US$40 per person per night (transport included).

Places to Eat

The best place for fish is *Remanso do Tucunaré*, at Avenida Brasília 1506, which offers fabulous dourado á baiana and, according to a prominent sign, accepts all social classes, as long as they practise 'order

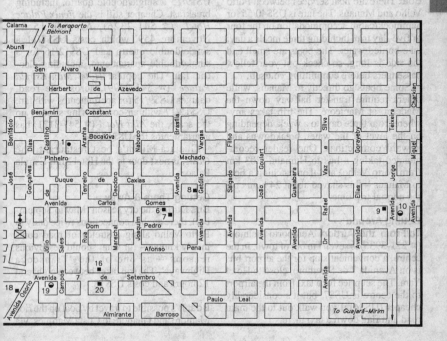

and respect'. *Restaurante Mirante II* serves fish dishes and has an outdoor patio with a great view of the river.

A good place for breakfast or lunch is the Lebanese-Brazilian *Restaurant Almanara*, on Avenida José de Alencar, just south of Avenida 7 de Setembro.

Getting There & Away

Air There are flights from Porto Velho to all major Brazilian cities. The airline offices are: VASP (☎ 223-3755), Rua Tenreiro Arenha 2326, Varig/Cruzeiro (☎ 221-8555), Rua Campos Sales 2666, and TABA (☎ 221-5172), Rua Prudente de Moraes 39.

Bus Porto Velho has bus connections to Rio Branco, Guajará-Mirim, Cuiabá, Humaitá and Costa Marques. Road conditions are generally poor (roads are often impassable during the wet season), so you should view schedules as optimistic approximations.

Boat There are boat services between Porto Velho and Manaus. The fare is US$40/55 for hammock/cabin accommodation on the four or five-day trip, including three meals a day; take bottled water. The boats are small and the ride is long, so check out your fellow passengers before committing yourself.

Some boats go directly to Manaus, while others require transfer halfway down the Madeira, at Manicoré. The trip takes anywhere from three days to a week, depending on the level of the water, breakdowns and onward connections. One reader recommended taking a bus to Humaitá (203 km from Porto Velho) and then catching a boat to Manaus – this shaved about 24 hours off the normal trip time.

Getting Around

To/From the Airport Aeroporto Belmont (☎ 221-3935) is seven km out of town. In the centre, a convenient stop for the airport bus is on Avenida 7 de Setembro, close to Hotel Yara. The set price for a taxi from the airport to the centre is US$7, but it's considerably cheaper (US$4) if you walk out to the main road and flag down a taxi there.

To/From the Rodoviária The rodoviária (☎ 221-2141) is about two km from the centre, on Avenida Jorge Teixeira. The bus to the rodoviária can be caught on Avenida 7 de Setembro, close to Hotel Yara.

GUAJARÁ-MIRIM

The contrast between Guajará-Mirim and Guayaramerín, the towns on either side of the Brazil/Bolivia border, is striking. While the Brazilian town is bustling, the Bolivian town is still a small, dusty, frontier settlement.

Bolivian Consulate

The Bolivian Consulate (☎ 541-2862), upstairs in the Alfa Hotel building, at Avenida Leopoldo dos Matos 239, is open only on weekday mornings.

Places to Stay & Eat

A favourite for travellers is *Hotel Guaporé*, on Avenida Benjamin Constant. It costs US$9/15 a single/double quarto, including breakfast. Cheaper still is the *Fenix Palace Hotel* (☎ 541-2326), Avenida 15 de Novembre 459, which costs US$7/11 a single/double quarto and US$12/16 for a single/double apartamento, including electric fan. The popular *Hotel Mini-Estrela Palace* (☎ 541-2399), across the road, charges US$9/15 for apartamentos with fan, US$12/17 with air-con. Moving slightly up the scale, the *Alfa Hotel* (☎ 541-3121) has apartamentos for US$18/28.

Guajará-Mirim's best restaurant, the *Oasis*, is next door to the Hotel Mini-Estrela Palace.

Getting There & Away

Bus During the dry season (May to September), there are bus connections twice daily to Porto Velho along a stretch of road commonly known – for what should be obvious reasons – as one of the 'Transcoca Highways'. The trip takes between eight and 12 hours and costs US$18.

Boat It's possible to travel by boat up the rios Mamoré and Guaporé to Costa Marques, via

Forte Príncipe da Beira. Inquire about schedules at the not-terribly-helpful Capitânia dos Portos (☎ 541-2208).

Crossing the Border Even if you're not planning to travel further into Bolivia, you can pop across the Rio Mamoré and visit Guayaramerín, a frontier settlement with more charm and cheaper accommodation than Guajará-Mirim. Between early morning and 6.30 pm, small motorised canoes and larger motor ferries cross the river from Guajará-Mirim every few minutes for US$1. After hours, there are only express motorboats, which cost US$4 to US$5.50 per boat. You may travel back and forth across the river at will, but those travelling beyond the frontier area will have to complete border formalities.

Leaving Brazil, get your exit stamp from the Polícia Federal (☎ 541-2437), Avenida Dr Antônio da Costa 842, five blocks from the port in Guajará-Mirim. Once across the Rio Mamoré, pick up an entrance stamp at Migración (Bolivian Immigration), at the ferry terminal.

If you're leaving Bolivia, visit first Migración in Guayaramerín and then the Polícia Federal in Guajará-Mirim, where you'll get a Brazilian entry stamp. Although officials don't always check, technically everyone needs a yellow fever vaccination certificate to enter Brazil here.

Acre

The state of Acre has become a favoured destination for developers and settlers, who have followed BR-364 through Rondônia and started claiming lands, clearing forest and setting up ranches. The resulting conflict over land ownership and sustainable use of the forest received massive national and international attention when Chico Mendes, a rubber-tapper and opponent of rainforest destruction, was assassinated in 1988, and even more notoriety when his prominent killers escaped from jail in early 1993.

RIO BRANCO
Rio Branco, capital of Acre state, was founded in 1882 on the banks of the Rio Acre.

Information
The Departamento de Turismo (☎ 224-3997), at Avenida Getúlio Vargas 659, is helpful. It's open from 8 am to 1 pm Monday to Friday.

Things to See
The **Casa do Seringueiro** is a museum which portrays the life of a typical *seringueiro* (rubber-tapper). Also on display are videos and pictures of Chico Mendes. The museum is open from 8 to 11 am and 3 to 8 pm Tuesday to Friday, and from 4 to 8 pm on Saturday and Sunday. Another museum worth a visit is **Museu da Borracha**, with interesting ethnological, archaeological and historical exhibits. The museum is open from 9 am to 6 pm Tuesday to Friday, and from 4 to 8 pm on Saturday and Sunday.

The **Colônia Cinco Mil** (literally Colony of the 5000) is a religious community which follows the doctrine of Santo Daime. Visits can be arranged either through a travel agency – Acretur for example – or by contacting the Daimistas at Kaxinawá, or the Daimista restaurant in Rio Branco. The best day to visit is Wednesday, when the main weekly festival is celebrated. If you stay overnight, no fee will be charged, but you will be expected to share the costs of transport and food.

In 1991, the **Parque Ecológico Plácido de Castro** was opened 94 km east of Rio Branco, on the Brazilian/Bolivian border. The park offers good swimming at river beaches, and walks through the forests along the paths originally used by rubber-tappers. There are two bus departures daily from Rio Branco to Plácido de Castro, where there's a hotel, Hotel Carioca (☎ 237-1064) on Rua Juvenal Antunes, and various inexpensive *pensões* and restaurants. Acretur runs Sunday excursions to the park, leaving Rio Branco at 8.30 am and returning from Plácido de Castro at 6 pm. The cost of the excursion is US$7 per person.

Places to Stay

Albergue de Juventude Fronteira Verde (☎ 225-7128), on Travessa Natanael de Albuquerque, is a cheap, friendly place to stay. From the city centre, the hostel is a short walk across the bridge at the southern end of Avenida Getúlio Vargas.

Albemar Hotel (☎ 224-1938), at Rua Franco Ribeiro 99, has comfortable apartamentos at US$10/13/22 for singles/doubles/ triples. There is a friendly bar and restaurant in the same building. *Loureiro Hotel* (☎ 224-3560), at Rua Marechal Deodoro 196, has apartamentos (without TV) at US$7/11. For good value, try *Hotel Rio Branco* (☎ 224-1785), at Rua Rui Barbosa 193. Apartamentos cost US$17 per person, including an excellent breakfast.

Places to Eat

Anexo Bar & Restaurant does a good buffet lunch for US$3 per person. *Pizzeria*, at the junction of ruas Rui Barbosa and Marechal Deodoro, and *Tutti Frutti Sorveteria & Pizzeria*, at Avenida Ceará 1132, both serve tasty Italian dishes. *Casarão Restaurant*, at Avenida Brasil 310, serves regional dishes, and has live music in the evening. Vegetarians will appreciate the health-food shop next to the Hotel Rio Branco. *Kaxinawá* is the Daimista restaurant in Rio Branco (see the section on Colônia Cinco Mil).

Getting There & Away

There are flights between Rio Branco and Cruzeiro do Sul, Manaus, Porto Velho, Cuiabá, Rio and São Paulo. VASP (☎ 224-6585) is at Avenida Epaminondas Jácome 611, and Varig/Cruzeiro (☎ 224-2226) is at Rua Marechal Deodoro 115. There are also various air-taxi companies at the airport, such as TACEZUL (☎ 224-3242), TAFETAL (☎ 224-2465) and TAVAJ (☎ 224-5981).

There are bus services between Rio Branco and Porto Velho (US$24, at least 15 hours, four departures daily), Brasiléia (US$10, six hours, four departures daily), Plácido de Castro and Boca do Acre.

To inquire about boats, either visit the tourist office or go direct to the port, which is at the eastern end of Avenida Epaminondas Jácome. It should be possible to find a ride at least as far as Boca do Acre (Amazonas state), where there is river traffic along the Rio Purus as far as the Amazon, and even Manaus.

Getting Around

The airport, Aeroporto Internacional Presidente Medici (☎ 224-6833), is about two km out of town, at AC-40, Km 1. The rodoviária (☎ 224-1182) is also a couple of km out of town, at AC-40, 1018 (Cidade Nova district).

From the airport, the bus marked 'Norte/Sul' runs via the rodoviária to the centre. A taxi from the centre to the airport costs US$3, and it's about the same price to the rodoviária.

XAPURI

Xapuri, 188 km south-west of Rio Branco, hit world headlines when Chico Mendes, a rubber-tapper and opponent of rainforest destruction, was assassinated here in 1988. There are several bus services daily between Rio Branco and Xapuri.

BRASILÉIA

The small town of Brasiléia lies on Brazil's border with Bolivia and is separated from Cobija, its Bolivian counterpart, by the Rio Acre. There are also connections to Assis Brasil, from where you can cross to Iñapari (Peru) and continue, by very rough roads, to Puerto Maldonado.

Brasiléia possesses nothing of interest to travellers, save an immigration stamp into or out of Brazil. The Polícia Federal is two km from the centre; dress nicely (no shorts allowed). If you're stuck for the night, try the *Carioca Charmé Hotel* (☎ 546-3045), near the church, which charges US$7/9 for single/double apartamentos.

From the rodoviária, there are four buses

daily to Rio Branco (US$10, six hours). If you're going to or coming from Bolivia, you'll have to get entry/exit stamps from migración (immigration) in Cobija, Bolivia and the Polícia Federal just outside Brasiléia. The easiest access to Cobija is the rowboat ferry (US$0.30 per person) across the Rio Acre to the landing in the centre of Brasiléia.

Chile

Chile stretches 4300 km from Peru to the Strait of Magellan. Its contrasts include the scenic but nearly sterile Atacama desert in the north, the metropolis of Santiago and its Mediterranean central valley, a verdant lake district, and the glacial landscapes of Patagonia in the south. Within just hours of each other are world-class Andean skiing and scores of Pacific beach resorts.

Most Chileans are of European descent, but indigenous traditions persist. In the north, Aymara Indians farm the Andean foothills and tend llamas and alpacas on the altiplano, and Mapuche Indians still inhabit areas in the south.

Adventurous visitors will appreciate insular possessions like Polynesian Easter Island (Rapu Nui), with its giant stylised statues, and the Juan Fernández Islands, a botanical wonderland best known for Scotsman Alexander Selkirk, who inspired the novel *Robinson Crusoe*.

Facts about the Country

HISTORY

Inca rule touched Chile but northern Aymara and Atacameño farmers and herders predated the Inca lords of Cuzco, while Changos had long fished the coastal areas and Diaguitas farmed the interior of Coquimbo. Beyond the central valley, Araucanian (Mapuche) Indians resisted Inca aggression. Cunco Indians fished and farmed on the island of Chiloé, while smaller groups long avoided European contact in the far south, but are now nearly extinct.

The Spanish Invasion & Colonial Society

A year after leaving Peru in 1540, Pedro de Valdivia reached the Mapocho valley to found the city of Santiago. Mapuche assaults threatened the fledgling capital, but the determined Spaniards held out and their situation improved. Valdivia also worked southward, founding Concepción, Valdivia, and Villarrica. Before his death in 1553 at the hands of the Mapuche, he had laid the foundation for a new society.

Failing to find much gold and silver, the Spanish invaders set up *encomiendas* (forced labour system) to exploit the north's relatively large, sedentary population. They also dominated central Chile, but Mapuche defenders made the area south of the Río Biobío unsafe for over three centuries.

As Spanish men formed families with Indian women, their descendants, or *mestizos*, soon outnumbered Indians as many natives died from epidemics, forced labour and warfare.

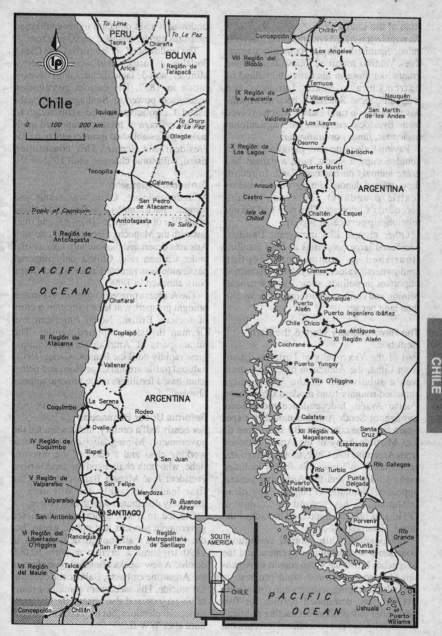

CHILE

Rise of the Latifundio

As population-based encomiendas lost their value, Spaniards sought economic alternatives. Valdivia rewarded followers with land grants like those in his native homeland of Extremadura in Spain. Landless and 'vagrant', these Spaniards became *inquilinos* (tenants) on rural estates which evolved from livestock *estancias* into agricultural haciendas, *fundos* or *latifundio*.

Paying little or no rent, inquilino families could occupy a shack, raise a garden and graze animals on hacienda land. In return, they offered labour during annual *rodeos* (cattle roundups) and defended the hacendado's interests. This man and master relationship permeated society.

Other groups, like immigrant Basques, purchased large properties as their families flourished in commerce. Adopting landowners' values, they have remained important in politics, society and business. Mining and commerce brought more wealth than land per se.

The Revolutionary Wars & the Early Republic

Part of the Viceroyalty of Peru but distant from Lima, the Audiencia of Chile (which was a subdivision of the Viceroyalty) stretched roughly from modern Chañaral to Puerto Aysén. Independence movements throughout South America united to expel Spain from the continent. By 1818, José de San Martín's Army of the Andes marched from Argentina into Chile, took Santiago and sailed north to Lima. His forces included many Chileans, and the Argentine general appointed Bernardo O'Higgins, son of an Irishman, as his second-in-command. O'Higgins became Supreme Director of the new Chilean republic.

Independent Chile shared ambiguous boundaries with Bolivia, Argentina and the Mapuche. It lost the Cuyo region to Argentina, but soon achieved rapid progress in agriculture, mining, industry and commerce.

O'Higgins dominated politics for five years after independence, enacting political, social, religious and educational reforms, but landowners soon objected to his egalitarian measures and he resigned under pressure.

The landowners' spokesperson was Diego Portales, a businessman who, as Interior Minister, was de facto dictator until his execution in 1837. His custom constitution centralised power in Santiago and established Catholicism as the state religion, limited suffrage to literate, propertied adult males, and established indirect elections for President and Senate. This constitution lasted, with some changes, until 1925.

Territorial Expansion

At independence, Chile was small and compact, but triumphs over Peru and Bolivia in the War of the Pacific (1879-83) and treaties with the Mapuche placed the nitrate-rich Atacama desert and the southern lake district under Chilean rule. Chile's only imperial possession was remote Easter Island (Rapa Nui), annexed in 1888.

The Atacama proved a bonanza, as nitrates brought prosperity, at least to certain sectors of society. British, North American and German investors supplied capital. The nitrate ports of Antofagasta and Iquique grew rapidly until the Panama Canal (1914) reduced traffic around Cape Horn and petroleum-based fertilisers made mineral nitrates obsolete.

Reforms Under Balmaceda

For nearly half a century, nitrates funded the government. Mining also created a new working class and a class of the nouveau riche, who both challenged the landowners. President José Manuel Balmaceda was the first leader to tackle the dilemma of unequally distributed wealth and power.

Elected in 1886, Balmaceda promoted government services and public works, but the Congress's attempt to depose him in 1890 triggered a civil war with 10,000 deaths. A few weeks after taking asylum in the Argentine embassy, Balmaceda committed suicide. His successors continued many of his projects and also opened the Congress to popular elections, but major reform lagged until after WW II.

The Postwar Period

Despite hard times due to declining nitrates, President Arturo Alessandri Palma instituted land and income taxes to fund health, education and welfare reforms, but conservative obstruction and army opposition forced his resignation in 1924. Dictatorial General Carlos Ibáñez del Campo held the presidency and other power positions, but opposition to his policies (exacerbated by global depression) forced him into exile.

Stalinists, Trotskyites and other radicals and reformists created a bewildering mix of new political entities, but the democratic left dominated the 1930s and 1940s. CORFO, the state development corporation, played a major economic role. The USA's economic role also grew as North American companies gained control of copper mines, now the cornerstone of the economy.

Rural Developments

In the 1920s, up to 75% of Chile's rural population still lived on latifundios holding 80% of prime agricultural land. Inquilinos' subsistence depended on haciendas and their votes belonged to landowners. As industry expanded and public works advanced, urban workers' welfare improved, but that of rural workers declined, forcing day labourers to the cities. Inquilinos suffered reduced privileges, while their labour obligations became more burdensome. Abundant labour gave haciendas little incentive to modernise, and production stagnated until the crisis of the 1960s.

The Christian Democratic Ascendancy

In 1952, Ibáñez del Campo again won the presidency, because of widespread disenchantment with predecessor Gabriel González Videla, but his surprising attempts to curtail landowners' power faltered. In the 1958 presidential elections, Arturo Alessandri's popular son, Jorge, won a close race, defeating Salvador Allende, who led the leftist Popular Action Front (FRAP), and Eduardo Frei, standing for the reformist Christian Democrats (DC). In 1961 congres-

sional races, opposition parties improved their showing, and forced Alessandri to accept a modest land reform which began a decade's battle with the fundos.

In the 1964 presidential election Frei, supported by both the DC and conservative groups, won a landslide over Allende, who was undermined by party factionalism. The DC's genuinely reformist policies threatened both the elite's privileges and the left's working-class base, but the government soon encountered serious problems as economic decline drove displaced rural workers to urban squatter settlements (callampas, or mushrooms, since they seemed to spring up overnight). One common response to these problems was to attack the US-dominated export sector; Frei advocated Chileanisation of copper, while Allende and his backers supported nationalisation.

The Christian Democrats also faced challenges from violent groups like MIR (the Leftist Revolutionary Movement), who worked among coal miners, textile workers and other urban labourers, and also agitated for land reform. Too slow for leftists, Frei's reforms were too rapid for obstructionist conservatives in the Congress – and there was even dissension among Christian Democrats in an increasingly polarised society.

Allende Comes to Power

In 1970, Allende's Unidad Popular (Popular Unity or UP) coalition, offered a radical programme advocating nationalisation of industry and expropriation of latifundios. After winning a small plurality and agreeing to constitutional guarantees, Allende took office with the Congress's approval, but the coalition quarrelled over the administration's objectives.

Allende's programme, evading rather than confronting the Congress, included state control of many private enterprises and massive income redistribution. Increased public spending briefly stimulated growth, but falling production brought shortages, soaring inflation and black marketeering.

Politics grew more confrontational as peasants, frustrated with agrarian reforms

CHILE

which favoured inquilinos over sharecroppers and *afuerinos* (day labourers), seized land, and harvests declined. Expropriation of copper mines and other enterprises, plus conspicuously friendly relations with Cuba, provoked hostility from the USA. Compromise was impossible between extreme leftists, who believed that only force could achieve socialism, and their rightist counterparts, who believed only force could prevent socialism.

Golpe de Estado

On 11 September 1973, General Augusto Pinochet led a brutal *golpe de estado* (coup d'etat) which resulted in the death of Allende (an apparent suicide) and thousands of his supporters. The military argued that force was necessary because Allende fomented chaos and was planning to overthrow the constitutional order.

Inept policies had brought about economic chaos, but reactionary sectors also undercut Allende's government by manipulating scarcities of commodities and food. Allende's pledges to the opposition were credible, but his inability or unwillingness to control groups to his left terrified the middle classes and outraged the oligarchy, underlining his failure.

The Military Dictatorship

Most politicians expected a quick return to civilian rule, but Pinochet took 16 years to remake Chile's political and economic culture, largely by terror. International assassinations were not unusual – the most notorious was the murder of ex-Foreign Minister Orlando Letelier by a car bomb in Washington DC in 1976. In 1980, Pinochet submitted a new constitution to the voters; about two-thirds approved it and ratified his presidency until 1989, despite many abstentions. For more information about recent political events, see the Government section in this chapter.

GEOGRAPHY & CLIMATE

In 800,000 sq km, Chile contains stony Andean peaks, snowcapped volcanos, broad river valleys and deep canyons, sterile deserts, icy fjords, deep blue glaciers, turquoise lakes, sandy beaches and rocky headlands. Continental Chile extends from tropical Arica to sub-Antarctic Punta Arenas; on average less than 200 km wide, Chile rises from sea level to above 6000 metres. Its Antarctic claims overlap those of Britain and Argentina.

Chile's 13 administrative regions are numbered ordinally from north to south, except for the Metropolitan Region of Santiago. The regions of Tarapacá and Antofagasta comprise the Norte Grande (Great North), dominated by the barren Atacama desert.

The regions of Atacama and Coquimbo form the mineral-rich Norte Chico (Little North), an area of scrub and occasional forest. Beyond the Río Aconcagua begins the fertile Mediterranean heartland of Middle Chile, where the Valle Central contains the capital, Santiago, the port of Valparaíso, and most of the country's industry and employment.

South of Concepción, the Río Biobío marks Chile's 19th-century frontier and the Mapuche Indian homeland. South of Temuco, the scenic Lake District has snowcapped volcanos, many still active, framing its numerous foothill lakes. South of Puerto Montt, Chiloé is the country's largest island, with a lengthy coastline, dense forests and many small farms.

Chilean Patagonia, comprising the regions of Aisén and Magallanes, experiences cool summers but relatively mild winters, as does the island of Tierra del Fuego, divided between Chile and Argentina.

The Andes run the length of the country. In the far north, volcanos reach above 6000 metres, creating imposing walls of sedimentary and volcanic peaks east of Santiago. South of the Biobío, the Andes are a less formidable barrier.

GOVERNMENT

The constitution allows a popularly elected President and the establishment of a Congress with a 46-member Senate and a

120-member Chamber of Deputies, but eight institutional Senators are Pinochet appointees. The President resides in Santiago but the Congress meets in Valparaíso. Despite regionalisation, administration is highly centralised.

Political Parties

In October 1988, voters rejected Pinochet's bid to extend his presidency until 1997. In 1989, 17 parties formed the coalition Concertación para la Democracia (Concertation for Democracy). Patricio Aylwin, who was chosen as a compromise presidential candidate, defeated both Pinochet's reluctant protégé, Hernán Büchi, standing for Renovación Nacional party, and a right-wing independent candidate, Francisco Errázuriz. Aylwin's four-year term expires in 1994, and new elections are scheduled for late 1993.

The Military

All the services enjoy autonomy, despite a proposed constitutional amendment to strengthen presidential authority. Of Chile's 100,000 uniformed personnel, more than half are in the army; nearly half of those are officers and noncommissioned officers. The services are highly disciplined, cohesive and more loyal to their commanders than to civilian authority. Thanks to provisions assuring them 10% of profits from state copper sales, Chile's military budget is larger than any of its neighbours.

ECONOMY

One Latin American economist has called Chile a fruit fly because every economic experiment happens so much faster there. Pinochet's government enlisted economists from the famous (or notorious) University of Chicago Economics Department to reduce expenditures and to encourage foreign investment through the adoption of laissez-faire practices.

For some years, inflation remained high, industrial production declined and some inefficient industries disappeared, but 'nontraditional' exports like off-season temperate fruits to Europe and North America helped compensate for falling copper prices.

The new policies had great social costs, as only soup kitchens prevented starvation in some callampas; the government's Minimum Employment Program (PEM) paid a token salary to individuals who swept streets or performed other minor public works. In recent years, the economy has improved on a macro scale, but growth has benefitted the poor only incidentally. Chile has repaid some of its foreign debt, and inflation has fallen to a modest 15%, but countless city dwellers still earn a precarious livelihood as street vendors.

The Aylwin government has been more sympathetic toward the poor, but macroeconomic policies represent continuity between the junta and civilian rule. At the same time, exports are more diverse and less vulnerable to international market fluctuations. Since 1987, Chile has enjoyed an increasing trade surplus, and in 1991, gross domestic product grew at 6%. Its most important trading partners are the USA, Japan, Germany, Brazil and Argentina.

POPULATION & PEOPLE

Over a third of Chile's 13.5 million people reside in Gran Santiago (the capital and suburbs). About 75% live in Middle Chile, only 20% of the country's total area. More than 80% live in cities, but south of the Biobío, the peasant population is still dense.

As most Chileans are mestizos, class is a greater issue than race – the working class resentfully call the elite *momios* (mummies). La Araucanía has a large Mapuche population. In the north, Aymara and Atacameño peoples farm terraces in the precordillera and pasture llamas and alpacas in the altiplano.

After 1848, many Germans settled in the Lake District. Other European immigrants were French, Italian, Yugoslav (especially in Magallanes and Tierra del Fuego), European Jews and Palestinians.

ARTS

Famous Chilean writers include Nobel Prize poets Gabriela Mistral and Pablo Neruda (also an important political activist). Much of their work is available in English translation – see the Facts for the Visitor section later in this chapter.

Until 1973, Chilean cinema was among Latin America's most experimental. Director Alejandro Jodorowsky's surrealistic *El Topo* (The Mole) was an underground success overseas, while exiled Miguel Littín's *Alsino and the Condor*, nominated for an Academy Award in 1983, is readily available on video.

'La Nueva Canción Chilena' (the New Chilean Song Movement) wedded Chile's folkloric heritage to the political passions of the late 1960s and early 1970s. Its most legendary figure is Violeta Parra, but her performing children, Isabel and Angel, established the first of many *peñas* (musical and cultural centres) in the mid-1960s. Individuals like Victor Jara (executed in 1973) and groups like Quilapayún and Inti-Illimani acquired international reputations.

CULTURE

Because of the European influence, English-speaking visitors will find Chile more accessible than some other Latin American countries. Chileans are exceptionally hospitable and frequently invite foreigners to their homes.

RELIGION

About 90% of Chileans are Roman Catholic; the Church has many factions, but its Vicaria de la Solidaridad staunchly defended human rights during the dictatorship. Evangelical Protestantism is growing but the proselytising of Mormons has made their churches targets of leftist bombings.

LANGUAGE

Spanish is the official language, but there is a handful of Indian languages. In the north, over 20,000 speak Aymara; in the south are perhaps half a million Mapuche speakers. About 2000 individuals speak Rapa Nui, the Polynesian language of Easter Island.

Chilean Spanish

Chileans relax terminal and even some internal consonants, making it difficult to distinguish plural from singular – 'las islas' (the islands) may sound more like 'la ila'. They also speak more rapidly than other South Americans, and rather less clearly – the conventional *¿quieres?* (Do you want ...?) sounds more like *¿querí?* on the tongue of a Chilean.

Facts for the Visitor

VISAS & EMBASSIES

A few nationalities (most notably New Zealanders) need advance visas. Arriving visitors receive a 90-day tourist card, renewable for another 90 days at the Departamento de Extranjería (☎ 672-5320), Moneda 1342 in Santiago. If staying more than six months, make a brief visit to a neighbouring country, then return.

Chilean authorities take the tourist card very seriously; for a replacement, go to the Policía Internacional (☎ 37-1292), General Borgoño 1052, Santiago.

Chilean Embassies & Consulates

Australia
  10 Culgoa Circuit, O'Malley ACT 2606 (☎ 286-2430)
Canada
  Suite 605, 151 Slater St, Ottawa, Ontario (☎ 235-4402)
  Consulate: Suite 1003, 330 Bay Street, Toronto, Ontario (☎ 366-9570)
Germany
  Kronprinzenstrasse 20, Bonn (☎ 363080)
UK
  12 Devonshire Rd, London (☎ 580-6393)
USA
  1736 Massachusetts Avenue NW, Washington, DC (☎ 785-3159)
  Consulates: 1732 Massachusetts Avenue NW, Washington, DC (☎ 785-1746)
  Room 302, 866 United Nations Plaza, New York, NY (☎ 980-3366)
  Suite 1204, 510 West Sixth St, Los Angeles, CA (☎ 624-6357)
  Suite 1062, 870 Market St, San Francisco, CA (☎ 982-7662)

Foreign Embassies & Consulates in Chile

For details of foreign representation in Chile, see the Santiago section.

Tourist Offices

Chilean consulates often have an overseas tourist representative. Try also LAN-Chile or Ladeco, the two major international airlines, for information.

DOCUMENTS

Passports are essential for cashing travellers' cheques, checking into hotels and other routine activities. Motorists need an International Driving Permit as well as a state or national licence. International Health Certificates are optional.

CUSTOMS

There are no currency restrictions. Duty-free allowances include 400 cigarettes or 50 cigars or 500 grams of tobacco, 2½ litres of alcoholic beverages, and perfume for personal use.

Inspections are usually routine, but some travellers have undergone more thorough examinations because of drug smuggling from Peru and Bolivia. Arrivals from free zones in the First Region (Tarapacá) and the Twelfth Region (Magallanes) are subject to internal customs inspections. The Servicio Agrícola-Ganadero (SAG) inspects luggage for fresh produce, at international borders and domestic checkpoints.

MONEY

The unit of currency is the *peso* (Ch$). Bank notes are for 500, 1000, 5000 and 10,000 pesos; coins are for one, five, 10, 50 and 100 pesos. Changing bills larger than Ch$1000 can be difficult in small villages.

US dollars are the preferred currency, but Argentine pesos can be readily exchanged in Santiago, at border crossings and in tourist areas like Viña del Mar and the Lake District.

Exchange Rates

Approximate official rates at August 1993 were as follows:

A$1	=	Ch$267
DM1	=	Ch$230
FF1	=	Ch$65
UK£1	=	Ch$586
US$1	=	Ch$395

As of June 1993, the official bank rate was about US$1 to the Ch$390, but cambios pay a parallel rate of about 5% more. Cash earns a slightly better rate than travellers' cheques and avoids commissions (usually modest). Hotels, travel agencies, street changers and some shops also change cash. For the latest information, see the financial newspaper *Estrategia*.

Costs

Chile is no longer a bargain, but modest lodgings, food and transport are still cheaper than in Europe, North America or Argentina. Allow at least US$15 per day for food and accommodation; by purchasing market food or eating at modest restaurants, you may get by for US$10.

Tipping

In restaurants, 10% tipping (*propina*) is customary.

Bargaining

Bargaining is customary only in markets. Hotel prices are generally fixed and prominently displayed, but try haggling in a slow summer or the off-season period.

Credit Cards

Fincard offices will provide cash advances for Visa or MasterCard. Usually, though, purchases and advances will be charged at the disadvantageous bank rate.

WHEN TO GO & WHAT TO BRING

Santiago and Middle Chile are best in spring or during the autumn harvest, but skiers will prefer the northern summer. Natural attractions like Torres del Paine and the Lake District are best in summer, but rain is always possible and a compact umbrella is useful. Even noncampers may consider a warm sleeping bag for budget hotels in Patagonia.

CHILE

At high altitudes, carry warm clothing even in summer. The altiplano's summer rainy season usually means only a brief afternoon thunderstorm.

Rapa Nui is cooler, slightly cheaper and far less crowded outside the summer. Likewise, March is an excellent time for the Juan Fernández Islands.

TOURIST OFFICES

Sernatur, the national tourist service, has offices in regional capitals and several other cities. Many cities have their own tourist offices, usually on the main plaza or at the bus terminal, sometimes only open in summer.

USEFUL ORGANISATIONS

Corporación Nacional Forestal, or CONAF (☎ 696-6749), administers national parks from Avenida Bulnes 285, Departamento 303, Santiago, but its regional offices are also very helpful.

Environmentally aware travellers may also contact Comité Pro Defensa de la Fauna y Flora, or CODEFF (☎ 37-7290, 277-0393), Santa Filomena 185, Santiago. Climbers should call the Federación de Andinismo (☎ 222-0888), Almirante Simpson 77, Santiago. The Sociedad Lonko Kilápan, Balmaceda 1533, Oficina 8, Temuco, promotes sustainable development among indigenous peoples.

BUSINESS HOURS & HOLIDAYS

Most businesses open by 8 am, but shops close at midday for three or four hours, then reopen until 8 or 9 pm. In Santiago, government offices and many businesses have adopted a 9 am to 6 pm schedule. Banks and some government offices open to the public only in the mornings. Government offices and businesses close on national holidays.

1 January
 Año Nuevo (New Year's Day)
March/April (dates vary)
 Semana Santa (Holy Week)
1 May
 Día del Trabajo (Labor Day)

21 May
 Glorias Navales (Naval Battle of Iquique)
30 May
 Corpus Christi
29 June
 San Pedro y San Pablo (St Peter's & St Paul's Day)
15 August
 Asunción de la Virgen (Assumption)
11 September
 Pronunciamiento Militar de 1973 (Military Coup of 1973)
18 September
 Día de la Independencia Nacional (Independence Day)
19 September
 Día del Ejército (Armed Forces Day)
12 October
 Día de la Raza (Columbus Day)
1 November
 Todo los Santos (All Saints' Day)
8 December
 Inmaculada Concepción (Immaculate Conception)
25 December
 Navidad (Christmas Day)

CULTURAL EVENTS

Throughout the year, Chileans celebrate a variety of local and national cultural festivals. Other than religious holidays, the most significant are the mid-September Fiestas Patrias.

POST & TELECOMMUNICATIONS

Postal services are sometimes slow but the telephone service has improved greatly over the past decade. Telegraph, telex and fax services are also good.

Postal Services

Post offices are open on weekdays from 9 am to 6 pm, and on Saturdays from 9 am to noon. Send essential overseas mail *certificado* to ensure its arrival. Parcel post is efficient, though a customs official may inspect your package before a clerk will accept it. Vendors near the post office wrap parcels, for a small charge.

Poste Restante and Lista de Correos are equivalent to general delivery. Lista de Correos charges a nominal fee (about US$0.10 per letter). Santiago's American Express office holds client mail, as do some embassies for their citizens. Instruct correspondents to address letters clearly and to indicate a date of arrival.

Telephone

ENTEL, the former state monopoly, and CTC (Compañía de Teléfonos de Chile) offer domestic and international long-distance services throughout the country. ENTEL is slightly cheaper. From the Tenth Region south, Telefónica del Sur is the main carrier.

Domestic long-distance calls from Santiago are generally less than US$1 for three minutes. Approximate charges to North America are US$3 per minute, to Europe and Australia US$3.50 per minute, and to other Latin American countries US$2.70 per minute. There are late-evening discounts but most offices close by 10 pm.

Calls from public phones cost Ch$50 (about US$0.15) for five minutes, but also take Ch$100 coins. When the liquid-crystal readout reaches zero, insert another coin. Phone boxes do not provide change, but if there is at least Ch$50 credit remaining, you may make another call by pressing a button.

Long-distance domestic and overseas calls are possible from CTC phone boxes; some accept coins, but others take only *fichas* (tokens). Collect overseas calls are simple but credit card calls appear possible in theory only. Dial 182 for an overseas operator.

TIME

Most of the year, Chile is four hours behind GMT, but from mid-December to mid-March (summer time), it observes daylight savings time. Easter Island is two hours behind the mainland.

LAUNDRY

In recent years, self-service laundromats have become more common, but it is only slightly dearer to leave your load and pick it up later. Most budget hotels have a place to wash clothes; maid service is usually reasonable, but agree on charges beforehand.

BOOKS

Literature & Fiction

Poets Pablo Neruda and Gabriela Mistral are major literary figures. Available in translation are Neruda's *The Heights of Macchu Picchu* (Jonathan Cape, London, 1966), *Canto General* (University of California, 1991), *Passions and Impressions* (Farrar, New York, Strauss & Giroux, 1983) and his rambling *Memoirs* (Farrar, Strauss & Giroux, 1977). US poet Langston Hughes translated *Selected Poems of Gabriela Mistral* (Indiana University, 1957); the Library of Congress and Johns Hopkins Press published a different book by the same title in 1971.

Isabel Allende's novels in the magical realism genre have made her popular overseas and in Chile; *House of Spirits*, *Of Love and Shadows* and *Eva Luna* are available in paperback. José Donoso's novel *Curfew* (Weidenfield & Nicholson, New York, 1988) offers a view of life under dictatorship through the eyes of a returned exile.

History

For general history, read Arnold Bauer's *Chilean Rural Society from the Spanish Conquest to 1930* (Cambridge, 1975).

A wide-ranging attempt to explain Allende's failure is Edy Kaufman's *Crisis in Allende's Chile: New Perspectives* (Praeger, New York & London, 1988).

On US subversion of the Unidad Popular, try James Petras & Morris Morley's *The United States & Chile: Imperialism & the Overthrow of the Allende Government* (Monthly Review Press, New York, 1975). For a more neutral perspective, read Robert J Alexander's *The Tragedy of Chile* (Greenwood Press, Westport, Connecticut, 1978).

Thomas Hauser's *The Execution of Charles Horman: An American Sacrifice* (Harcourt Brace Jovanovich, New York, 1978), which implicated US officials in the death of a US activist in the 1973 coup, was the basis of the 1982 film *Missing*.

Chile: The Pinochet Decade, by Phil O'Brien & Jackie Roddick (Latin America Bureau, London, 1983), covers the Pinochet

CHILE

government's early years and its radical economic measures. Genaro Arriagada's *Pinochet: the Politics of Power* (Unwin Hyman, Boston, 1988) details the regime's evolution from a collegial junta to a personalistic, but institutionalised dictatorship.

Pamela Constable & Arturo Valenzuela's *A Nation of Enemies* (Norton, New York, 1991) eschews partisan rhetoric to focus on the intricacies and implications of events since 1973.

Easter Island (Rapa Nui)

See the Easter Island section for details on the voluminous literature about this island.

Travel Guides

Illustrated with exceptional photographs, the *APA Insight Guides* volume on Chile is excellent (if selective) in cultural and historical analysis but weak on practical matters. The annually updated and reasonably priced Turistel series, published by the Compañía de Teléfonos, has separate volumes on northern, central and southern regions, plus an additional one on camping. A new English version combines the three main guides in a single volume. Oriented toward motorists, Turistel provides excellent maps and thorough background, but ignores budget alternatives.

MAPS

Turistel is great value, but several other maps are available from shops and street vendors. Esso's inexpensive *Planos* has indexed street maps of Santiago, Antofagasta, Valparaíso, Viña del Mar, Concepción and Talcahuano.

The Instituto Geográfico Militar's *Plano Guía del Gran Santiago* (1989) is the equivalent of *London A-Z*, while its *Guía Caminera* (1991) is an up-to-date highway map. Their 1:50,000 topographic series (about US$8 per sheet) is valuable for trekkers.

MEDIA

The press is still recovering from the dictatorship but the end of state monopoly in the electronic media has opened the airwaves to a greater variety of programming.

Newspapers & Magazines

Santiago's oldest daily, *El Mercurio*, follows a conservative editorial policy. *La Epoca*, born during the 'No' campaign against Pinochet's continuance in office, is a serious Christian Democratic tabloid, while *La Nación* is the official government daily. Sleazy tabloids like *La Segunda* sensationalise crime and radical political dissent (which they seem to consider synonymous).

Estrategia, voice of the financial sector, is the best source on exchange rate trends. The weekly *News Review* serves the English-speaking population.

Radio & TV

Broadcasting is less regulated than before, with many stations on both AM and FM bands. TV stations include state-owned TVN (Televisión Nacional), the Universidad Católica's Channel 13, and several private stations. International cable service is widely available.

HEALTH

After localised cholera outbreaks in 1992, the Ministry of Health prohibited restaurants from serving *raw* vegetables like lettuce, cabbage, celery, cauliflower, beets and carrots. *Ceviche* (raw seafood) is also suspect. Santiago's drinking water is adequately treated, and the author has drunk tap water in most areas without problems, but bottled mineral waters are good alternatives.

Basic Rules & Precautions

Food & Water Most Chilean food is relatively bland and shouldn't cause problems but be careful about eating some varieties of shellfish. Take precautions with rural drinking water, as latrines may be close to wells or local people may take untreated water from streams or ditches. Water in the Atacama has a high mineral content; Easter Island's water has a similar reputation, but the author found it both safe and tasty.

DANGERS & ANNOYANCES
Personal Security & Theft
Truly violent crime is rare in Santiago, but purse snatchings are not unusual; Valparaíso has a reputation for robberies in some neighbourhoods. Summer is the crime season in beach resorts – be alert for pickpockets and be careful with valuables.

Despite the return to democracy, armed opposition groups sometimes commandeer taxis or private cars and are pursued by the police, but the odds of being caught in the crossfire are small.

Unauthorised political demonstrations can be very contentious; the police may use tear gas or water cannons – known as *guanacos*, after the spitting wild camelids – to break them up. US institutions, like banks and churches, may be targets of protest – 53 Mormon chapels were bombed in 1990.

The Police & the Military
In routine circumstances, police behave professionally and politely; *never* attempt to bribe them. Avoid photographing military installations. In the event of a coup or other emergency, carry identification and contact your embassy or consulate for advice.

Natural Hazards
Volcanic eruptions are not rare – in 1991, Volcán Hudson, in the Aisén Region, buried Chile Chico and Los Antíguos, Argentina, knee-deep in ash. Earthquakes are very common and can be very serious.

Volcanos usually give notice before blowing big, but a few resorts are especially vulnerable, notably Pucón, at the base of Volcán Villarrica. Earthquakes strike without warning and local buildings, especially adobe, are often unsafe; travellers in budget hotels should make contingency plans for safety or evacuation before going to sleep.

Recreational Hazards
Many of the finest beach areas have dangerous offshore currents. Because of accidents, authorities no longer permit solo trekking in wilderness areas like Torres del Paine.

WORK
Many travellers work as English-language instructors in Santiago, but wages are fairly low and full-time employment is rare. Reputable employers insist on work or residence permits from the Departamento de Extranjería (☎ 672-5320), Moneda 1342 in Santiago, open from 9 am to 1.30 pm on weekdays.

ACTIVITIES
Of the many participant and spectator sports, soccer is the most widespread. Others include tennis, basketball, volleyball and cycling, while outdoor activities like canoeing, climbing, kayaking, trekking, windsurfing and hang-gliding are gaining popularity. Rivers like the Maipo, Claro and Biobío are popular for white-water rafting, but hydroelectric development threatens the Biobío.

In summer, most Chileans head to the beach. For winter skiing, consult Chris Lizza's *South America Ski Guide* (1992), published by Bradt Publications in the UK and by Hunter Publications in the USA.

ACCOMMODATION
Accommodation, ranging from hostels and campgrounds to five-star hotels, is usually reasonable by North American or European standards.

Camping & Refugios
Sernatur has a free brochure listing campgrounds nationwide. The usually woodsy sites ordinarily have hot showers, toilets and laundry, firepits, a restaurant or snack bar, and a grocery; some have swimming pools or lake access. The Turistel camping guide has more detail and superb maps.

Campgrounds discriminate against backpackers, with a five-person minimum, so for singles or couples are often dearer than basic hotels. (Remember, however, that camping is an important budget alternative in Argentina.) Free camping is possible in some remote areas, but often without any facilities.

Refugios are rustic shelters, either free or very cheap, in national parks. *Juventud,*

CHILE

Turismo y Naturaleza, available from Sernatur or CONAF, is a fine practical guidebook to the parks.

Youth Hostels
Inexpensive hostels occupy temporary sites at stadiums, campgrounds, schools or churches, and are generally open in January and February only. For the latest information, contact the Asociación Chilena de Albergues Turísticos Juveniles (☎ 233-3220), Avenida Providencia 2594, Oficina 420, Santiago.

Casas de Familia
In summer, especially in the Lake District, families offer inexpensive rooms with kitchen and laundry privileges, hot showers, and local hospitality. Ask at tourist offices.

Hospedajes, Pensiones, & Residenciales
Differences among these inexpensive permanent forms of accommodation are vague – all may be called hotels.

FOOD
The cool waters of the Humboldt current provide superb fish and shellfish, while the fields, orchards and pastures of Middle Chile fill the table with excellent produce and meat. The best Chilean cuisine however may be beyond the reach of budget travellers.

Places to Eat
Distinctions among 'restaurants', ranging from simple snack bars to sumptuous international venues, are ambiguous. The central market in most cities has many small, cheap restaurants of surprisingly high quality.

Bars serve snacks and drinks (alcoholic and nonalcoholic), while *fuentes de soda* do not offer alcohol. *Cafeterías* serve modest meals. A *salón de té* is not literally a teahouse, but a bit more up-market than a cafetería. Quality and service distinguish full-fledged *restaurantes*. Many places offer a cheap set meal (*comida corrida* or *colación*) for lunch and, less often, for dinner. Some common dishes are listed below.

Breakfast
Toast, marmalade, eggs, coffee and tea are usual breakfast fare. Sandwiches are common throughout the day; among the fillings are *churrasco* (steak), *jamón* (ham) and *queso* (cheese). Cold ham and cheese make an *aliado* which, heated to melt the cheese, is a *Barros Jarpa*, after a Chilean painter. Steak with melted cheese is a *Barros Luco*, after former President Ramón Barros Luco (1910-15). Beefsteak with tomato and other vegetables is a *chacarero*.

Snacks
The cheapest fast food is a *completo*, a hot dog with absolutely everything. Arrivals from Argentina will find the individual Chilean empanada much larger than its trans-Andean counterpart, so don't order a dozen for lunch or your bus trip. *Humitas* are corn tamales.

Main Meals
Lunch is the day's biggest meal. Set menus, almost identical at cheaper restaurants, usually consist of *cazuela* (a broth with potato or maize and beef or chicken), a main course of rice with beef or chicken, and a simple dessert. *Porotos* (beans) are a common budget entree. *Pastel de choclo*, a maize casserole filled with vegetables, chicken and beef, is delicious and filling.

The biggest standard meal is *lomo a lo pobre*, an enormous slab of beef topped with two fried eggs and buried in chips – monitor your cholesterol count. Beef, in a variety of cuts and styles of preparation, is the most popular main course at *parrillas* like those in Argentina. *Pollo con arroz* (chicken with rice) is another common offering.

Seafood
Chilean seafood is among the world's best. *Curanto*, a hearty stew of fish, shellfish, chicken, pork, lamb, beef and potato, is a specialty of Chiloé and Patagonia.

Popular soups are *sopa de mariscos*, a

delicious seafood soup, or *cazuela de mariscos*, more a stew. Fish soup is *sopa de pescado*, while *paila marina* is a fish chowder. Try *chupe de cóngrio* (conger eel stew) or, if available, *chupe de locos* (abalone stew), both cooked in a thick sauce of butter, breadcrumbs, cheese and spices. Abalone or locos may be in *veda* (quarantine) because of overexploitation. Some dishes, like *erizos* (sea urchins), are acquired tastes.

Do not miss market restaurants in cities like Iquique, Concepción, Temuco and Puerto Montt, but insist on thorough cooking of all shellfish. A few seafood terms worth knowing are:

shrimp	*camarones*
prawns	*camarones grandes*
crab	*cangrejo* or *jaiva*
king crab	*centolla*
mussels	*cholgas*
oysters	*ostras*
scallops	*ostiones*
shellfish	*mariscos*
squid	*calamares*

Desserts

Dessert is commonly fresh fruit or ice cream. Also try *arroz con leche* (rice pudding), *flan* (egg custard) and *tortas* (cakes). Lake District bakers of German descent prepare exquisite *kuchen* (pastries) filled with local fruit – especially raspberries.

Ethnic Food

Santiago's ethnic restaurants fill eight pages in the phone book. French, Italian, Spanish, German and Chinese are the most common, but Brazilian, Arab, Mexican and others are also available.

Northern Chilean cities have many *chifas* (Chinese restaurants), which offer a pleasant change of food.

Vegetarian Food

Most Chileans are large meat eaters, but vegetarianism is no longer the mark of an eccentric. Santiago has excellent vegetarian fare and every town has a market with fresh produce.

DRINKS
Nonalcholic Drinks

Chileans guzzle all the usual soft drinks and some local varieties, plus mineral water.

Mote con huesillo, sold by street vendors but closely monitored for hygiene, is a peach nectar with barley kernels. *Licuados* are milk-blended fruit drinks, sometimes made with water and often with too much sugar. Common flavours are banana, peach (*durazno*) and pear (*pera*).

Except in a few exclusive locations, semi-soluble Nescafé coffee is the norm. Normally, tea is served black, usually with lemon. Try herbal teas (*aguas*) like camomile (*manzanilla*) and *boldo*.

Alcohol

Chilean wines should satisfy most alcoholic thirsts, but don't miss the powerful grape brandy (*pisco*), often served in the form of a *pisco sour* (with lemon juice, egg white and powdered sugar). It may also be served with ginger ale (*chilcano*) or vermouth (*capitán*).

Escudo is the best bottled beer, but draught beer (*chopp*, pronounced 'shop') is cheaper and often better. A cherry-like fruit, (*guinda*) is the basis of *guindado*, a fermented alcoholic drink with brandy, cinnamon and cloves.

Wines & Wine Regions

Wine-growing districts stretch from the Copiapó valley of the Norte Chico as far as the Biobío. The variety of regions and the abrupt topography produce a great variety. Atacama wineries specialise in pisco, but also produce small quantities of white and sparkling wines. Middle Chile's *zona de regadío* produces mostly cabernets and other reds, but acreages planted for whites are increasing. Reds give way to whites in the transitional zone of the Maule, while the Biobío drainage is a pioneer area. Farther south, commercial production is precarious.

Wine lovers should see Harm de Blij's *Wine Regions of the Southern Hemisphere*

CHILE

(Rowman & Allenheld, Totora, New Jersey, 1985).

ENTERTAINMENT
Cinemas
In the capital and in larger cities like Valparaíso and Viña del Mar, theatres screen the latest from Europe, Hollywood and Latin America. Repertory houses, cultural centres and universities offer the classics or less commercial films. Prices have risen in recent years, but are still reasonable; midweek, many cinemas offer discounts.

Theatre
Throughout the country, live theatre is well attended and of a high quality, from the classics and serious drama to burlesque. In the Lake District, many towns offer summer stock at cultural festivals.

Peñas
Peñas are nightclubs where the performers offer unapologetically political, but folk-based material. The New Chilean Song Movement had its origins in the peñas of the 1960s.

Nightclubs
In cities like Santiago and Viña, nightclubs can be tacky affairs, where traditional music and dances are sanitised and presented in glitzy settings for foreigners. In port cities, they can be disreputable joints.

Spectator Sports
The most popular is soccer, and the British origins are obvious in team names like Santiago Morning and Everton. Other popular spectator sports include tennis, boxing and, increasingly, basketball.

THINGS TO BUY
Artisans' *ferias* (markets) display a variety of quality crafts, especially in the suburb of Bellavista in Santiago, Viña del Mar, Valdivia, the Puerto Montt suburb of Angelmó, and the village of Dalcahue (on the island of Chiloé). Copper and leather are typical choices, while northern woollens resemble those of Peru or Bolivia. Mapuche artisans produce varied ceramics, basketry, silverwork, weavings and carvings.

Getting There & Away

AIR
Paying for fares in local currency takes advantage of the parallel exchange rate, but the difference is relatively small. International departure tax is US$12.50.

To/From Peru
AeroPerú flies from Lima to Santiago (US$262) four days a week, and daily to Tacna (US$79), just 50 km from Arica.

To/From Bolivia
LAB flies twice weekly from Santiago to La Paz (US$215) and also connects La Paz to Arica (US$92). LAN-Chile also flies to La Paz.

To/From Argentina
Many airlines fly from Santiago to Buenos Aires (US$240), but some also serve Mendoza (US$88) and Córdoba. The Argentine carrier TAN links Puerto Montt to Bariloche (US$56).

LAND
To/From Peru
Tacna to Arica is the only land crossing from Peru; for details, see the Arica section.

To/From Bolivia
Road and rail connections between Bolivia and Chile are slow and rough. Buses from La Paz to Arica are cheaper and more frequent than the weekly passenger train, but there is a faster *ferrobus* (bus on rails). There are also buses from Colchane (Bolivia) to Iquique.

A weekly train and occasional buses link Calama to Ollagüe, connecting to Oruro and La Paz. For details, see the Calama section.

To/From Argentina
Except in far southern Patagonia and Tierra

del Fuego, travel to Argentina involves crossing the Andes; some passes close in winter. The Salta-Baquedano rail crossing is not a regular passenger service.

Lake District crossings, involving bus-boat shuttles, are very popular in summer, so make advance bookings. Since the opening of the Camino Austral south of Puerto Montt, it has become more common to cross the border there.

Calama to Salta Buses on this route now use the Paso de Jama via Jujuy, but bookings are heavy. A weekly Argentine freight train also carries passengers from Salta to Socompa, where a very uncomfortable Chilean freight goes to the abandoned station of Augusta Victoria (where it is possible to hitch to Antofagasta), or to Baquedano, on the Ruta or Carretera Panamericana.

La Serena to San Juan The 4779-metre Agua Negra pass has reopened for automobile traffic; ask about bus services.

Santiago to Mendoza & Buenos Aires Many buses and taxi colectivos serve this most popular crossing between the two countries.

Temuco to Zapala & Neuquén Occasional buses use the 1884-metre Pino Hachado pass along the upper Biobío in summer. An alternative is the 1298-metre Icaima pass.

Temuco to San Martín de los Andes On this popular route, regular summer buses use the Mamuil Malal pass (Paso Tromen to Argentines).

Valdivia to San Martín de los Andes This is a bus-ferry combination over Paso Hua Hum.

Osorno to Bariloche via Paso Puyehue Very frequent buses use this quick crossing in the Lake District.

Puerto Montt to Bariloche via Parque Nacional Vicente Pérez Rosales This bus-ferry combination crosses scenic Lago Todos los Santos.

Puerto Ramírez to Esquel There are two options here, via Futaleufú or Carrenleufú.

Coyhaique to Comodoro Rivadavia The three weekly bus services are usually heavily booked.

Chile Chico to Los Antiguos From Puerto Ibáñez, take the ferry to Chile Chico, on the south shore of Lago Carrera, and a bus over the border.

Puerto Natales & Parque Nacional Torres del Paine to Río Turbio & Calafate Frequent buses connect Puerto Natales to Río Turbio, with connections to Río Gallegos and Calafate. At least twice weekly in summer, buses go from Torres del Paine and Puerto Natales to Calafate, gateway to Argentina's Parque Nacional Los Glaciares.

Punta Arenas to Río Gallegos There are many buses daily on this route (six hours).

Punta Arenas to Tierra del Fuego From Punta Arenas, it's a three-hour ferry ride or a 10-minute flight to Porvenir, on Chilean Tierra del Fuego, with two buses going weekly to Río Grande (Argentina), connecting to Ushuaia.

Puerto Williams to Ushuaia On Saturdays, if demand is sufficient, a ferry sails from Isla Navarino to Ushuaia, but service is often interrupted.

Getting Around

AIR

LAN-Chile, Ladeco and a new cut-rate competitor, Pacific Air, offer domestic services. On most flights, a small number of half-price seats are available.

Regional airlines include DAP (from

Punta Arenas to Tierra del Fuego, the Falkland Islands and Antarctica), and Lassa and Líneas Aéreas Robinson Crusoe (to the Juan Fernández Islands). Air taxis connect settlements in the Aisén region.

Air Passes

For US$300, LAN-Chile's 21-day Visit Chile Pass allows flights to and from selected airports north or south of Santiago; for US$1080, this includes Easter Island. Available only to foreigners and nonresidents, passes must be purchased outside Chile. Ladeco's more flexible pass allows stopovers at Balmaceda/Coyhaique, but it does not fly to Easter Island.

Reservations & Timetables

Both Ladeco and LAN-Chile have computerised booking services, accept phone reservations and publish detailed timetables.

Departure Tax

The domestic airport departure tax, about US$5, is usually included in the fare.

BUS

Long-distance buses are comfortable (sometimes luxurious), fast and punctual. They usually have toilets and either serve meals or make regular stops. By European or North American standards, fares are a bargain, but they differ among companies. Promotions (*ofertas*) can reduce normal fares by half; ask for 25% student discounts.

Most cities have a central terminal, but in a few towns, companies have separate offices. Except near holidays, advance booking is unnecessary.

Types of Buses

Long-distance buses are either pullman or sleepers, with extra leg room and reclining seats (*salón cama*). The latter cost about twice as much as ordinary buses, but merit consideration on long hauls.

On back roads, transport is slower and less frequent and the buses (*micros*) older and more basic. They often lack reclining seats

and may be packed with the local people and their produce.

TRAIN

Southbound trains connect Santiago with Temuco, continuing to Puerto Montt in summer only. Classes of service are *economía*, *salón* and *cama* (sleeper). Hardbacked economy seats, though very cheap, are uncomfortable; most travellers will prefer salón. The cama class has upper and lower bunks; this class is costlier.

Schedules change, so check an official timetable. Major destinations (with salón fares) include Concepción (US$13, nine hours), Temuco (US$17, 13 hours) and Puerto Montt (US$24, 20-plus hours).

Commuter trains run from Rancagua to Santiago, and from Los Andes and San Felipe to Viña del Mar and Valparaíso.

DRIVING

Operating a car is cheaper than in Europe but dearer than in the USA; the price of petrol (*bencina*) is about US$0.45 per litre, that of diesel fuel (*gas-oil*) rather less. There is little price difference between 93-octane (*super*) and 81-octane (*común*). Foreign drivers will require an International or Inter-American Driving Permit.

The Automóvil Club Chileno, or ACCHI (☎ 212-5702), Avenida Vitacura 8620, Santiago, offers members of affiliated overseas clubs low-cost road service and towing, plus discounts on accommodation, camping, rental cars, tours and other services. ACCHI also has a tourist information service (☎ 274-9078), at Fidel Oteíza 1964.

Car Rental

To rent a car, you must have a valid driver's licence, be at least 25 years of age and present either a credit card or a large cash deposit.

The cheapest vehicles can be hired for about US$20 per day plus US$0.20 per km, plus insurance, petrol and tax. Unlimited mileage weekend rates (about US$100) or weekly rates (US$250) are better value.

BICYCLE

Racing bicycles are suitable for paved routes, but on gravelled roads, a mountain bike *(todo terreno)* is a better choice. Southwards from Temuco, be prepared for rain; north of Santiago, water is scarce. In some areas, the wind can slow your progress; north to south is generally easier than south to north. Motorists are usually courteous, but on narrow roads, they can be a hazard.

HITCHING

Chile is one of the best countries on the continent for hitching. Vehicles are often packed with families but truck drivers can be helpful – try asking for rides at *servicentros* on the Panamericana. In Patagonia, where distances are great and vehicles few, expect long waits and carry warm, windproof, waterproof clothing. Also carry snacks and water, especially in the desert.

Along the Panamericana, hitching is fairly easy as far as Puerto Montt, but summer competition is heavy. In the Atacama, you may wait for some time, but almost every lift will be a long one. Along the Camino Austral, vehicles are few, except from Coyhaique to Puerto Aisén.

Bear in mind, however, that although many travellers hitchhike, it is not a totally safe way of getting around. Just because hitching tips are included doesn't mean hitching is recommended.

BOAT

Although buses cover parts of the Camino Austral between Puerto Montt and Coyhaique, it's easier to take a ferry from Puerto Montt or Chiloé to Chaitén or Puerto Chacabuco. For detailed information, see the individual sections.

Puerto Montt to Puerto Chacabuco

Navimag and Transmarchilay boat services sail from Puerto Montt or nearby Pargua to Puerto Chacabuco (port of Coyhaique). Transmarchilay also runs the tourist ship *Skorpios* to Laguna San Rafael.

Puerto Montt to Puerto Natales

Navimag ferries cover this route about three times monthly in three or more days.

Chiloé to the Mainland

The most frequent connection is with Transmarchilay or Cruz del Sur ferries from Chacao, at the northern tip of the island, to Pargua, across the Canal de Chacao. Others are by Transmarchilay from Chonchi or Quellón (on Chiloé) to Chaitén or Puerto Chacabuco (on the mainland).

Punta Arenas to Tierra del Fuego

There are frequent ferries from Punta Arenas to Porvenir.

LOCAL TRANSPORT
To/From the Airport

LAN-Chile and Ladeco often provide an airport shuttle. In a few places, you will have to use public transport or a taxi.

Bus

Even small towns have extensive bus systems; buses are clearly numbered and usually carry a sign indicating their destination. Pay your fare and the driver will give you a ticket, which may be checked by an inspector.

Taxi

Most cabs are metered but fares vary. In some towns, like Viña del Mar, cabs may cost twice as much as in Santiago. In others, like Coquimbo, meters are infrequent, so agree upon the fare in advance. Tipping is unnecessary, but round off the fare for convenience.

Santiago & Middle Chile

Middle Chile comprises the Metropolitan Region, plus the regions of Valparaíso, O'Higgins, Maule and Biobío. Its fertile central valley, endowed with rich soils, a pleasant climate and snowmelt for irrigation, is ideal for cereals, fruit and vineyards.

CHILE

SANTIAGO

Since the 1970s, Santiago, the capital, has grown out and up. It continues to sprawl, and highrises have sprouted up in the downtown area and in Providencia, a suburb which may become the city's commercial and financial centre. With over four million inhabitants, Santiago is one of South America's largest cities.

History

Indians nearly obliterated Santiago six months after Pedro de Valdivia founded it in 1541. Even in the late 16th century, only 700 Spaniards and mestizos, plus Indian labourers and servants, inhabited its 200 adobe houses. Occasionally flooded by the Río Mapocho, it still lacked a safe water supply and communications between town and country were hazardous.

By the late 18th century, new dikes (*tajamares*) restrained the Mapocho and improved roads handled increased commerce. By the 19th century, a railway linked the capital, with more than 100,000 inhabitants, with the port of Valparaíso.

Poverty and paternalistic fundos drove farm labourers and tenants north to the nitrate mines and then into the cities – from 1865 to 1875, Santiago's population increased from 115,000 to more than 150,000, a trend which has continued.

Industrialisation created jobs, but never enough to satisfy demand. In the 1960s, continued rural turmoil resulted in squatter settlements around Santiago. Planned decentralisation has eased the pressure, and regularisation, including granting of titles, has transformed many callampas, but they still contrast with affluent eastern suburbs like El Golf, Vitacura, La Reina, Las Condes and Lo Curro.

Orientation

Santiago's core is in a compact, triangular area bounded by the Río Mapocho on the north, the Vía Norte Sur to the west, and Avenida General O'Higgins (the Alameda) on the south. Key public buildings line the Plaza de Armas, from which the pedestrian Paseo Ahumada leads south. Paseo Huérfanos is a block south of the plaza.

Attractive Cerro Santa Lucía overlooks the Alameda near Plaza Baquedano. The other main park is Cerro San Cristóbal, north of Avenida Providencia. Between the park and the Río Mapocho, on either side of Avenida Pío Nono, is the lively and fashionable area of Bellavista. Parque Forestal is a verdant buffer between the city centre and residential areas.

Information

Tourist Office Sernatur (☎ 698- 2151), at Avenida Providencia 1550 (Metro station Manuel Montt), is open on weekdays from 9 am to 5 pm, and on Saturdays from 9 am to 1 pm. English is spoken, and the office has maps and abundant leaflets on the entire country. There's another office at Pudahuel Airport.

The municipal tourist kiosk, at the intersection of paseos Ahumada and Huérfanos, is also very helpful, and distributes the monthly English-language publication *Santiago Tour* (US$1.50). The kiosk is open daily from 9 am to 9 pm. Another useful publication, often free despite a cover price of US$2, is the bilingual *Guiamérica*, which lists up-market hotels and travel agencies but also has articles on out-of-the-way places and unusual topics.

All offices provide a free pocket-size *Plano del Centro de Santiago*, a map of the city centre, Providencia and other inner suburbs, with a useful Metro diagram.

Money Many cambios, on Agustinas between Bandera and Ahumada, change cash and travellers' cheques. On Saturday, when most are closed, try Lacov Tour, at Ahumada 131, Local 13.

American Express (☎ 672-2156), Agustinas 1360, will exchange travellers' cheques for US cash. Visa (☎ 672-8518) and MasterCard (☎ 695- 2023) are both at Morandé 315.

Post & Telecommunications The Correo Central, on the Plaza de Armas, handles poste restante and also has a philatelic desk. For long-distance calls, go to ENTEL, at Paseo Huérfanos 1133, or CTC's central office, at Moneda 1151.

Foreign Embassies The following countries maintain embassies in Santiago:

Argentina
    Vicuña MacKenna 41 (☎ 222-8977)
Australia
    Gertrudis Echeñique 420 (☎ 228-5065)
Bolivia
    Avenida Santa María 2796 (☎ 232-8180)
Canada
    10th floor, Ahumada 11 (☎ 696-2256)
France
    Avenida Condell 65 (☎ 225-1030)
Germany
    Calle Agustinas 785 (☎ 33-5031)
New Zealand
    Isidora Goyenechea 3516 (☎ 231-4204)
Peru
    Providencia 2653 (☎ 232-6275)
UK
    3rd floor, Avenida El Bosque Norte 0125 (☎ 231-3737)
USA
    Embassy: Agustinas 1343
    Consulate (visas): Merced 230 (☎ 671-0133)

Cultural Centres The restored Estación Mapocho, on the south bank of the river, has art exhibits, a theatre and a café. The Centro de Extensión de la Universidad Católica, Alameda 390, regularly presents artistic and photographic exhibits.

The Instituto Chileno-Norteamericano de Cultura, Moneda 1467, also has frequent exhibits on various topics. Its library carries North American newspapers and magazines, and shows free films (usually in video format).

Travel Agencies For good prices on air tickets, try Miguel Gallegos at Latour (☎ 672-7918), Agustinas 1476, Oficina 602. Several agencies operate adventure or nature tourism excursions; probably the most comprehensive is Southern Summits (☎ 39-3712), Merced 102.

Bookshops & Newsstands The best-stocked shop is Feria Chilena del Libro, Huérfanos 623. Librería Albers, Merced 820, carries books and magazines in German and English, including Lonely Planet guides.

Luis Rivano, San Diego 119, Local 7, has a fine selection on Chilean history (not all displayed to the public). Chile Ilustrado (☎ 46-0683), Avenida Providencia 1652, Local 6, specialises in rare materials in history, anthropology and folklore and has a lot of general interest stock. In the same complex, a smaller shop, known simply as Books, sells used English paperbacks.

Two kiosks at the junction of paseos Ahumada and Huérfanos carry North American and European newspapers and magazines. If a paper is more than a few days old, haggle over the price.

Emergency For medical emergencies, contact the Posta Central (☎ 34-1650), at Portugal 125 (Metro station Universidad Católica).

Things to See
Walking Tour Santiago's central market, **Mercado Central**, is a wrought-iron structure built in 1872. At Balmaceda and Puente, it is a great place for lunch or an early dinner. The **Posada del Corregidor** (1780), Esmeralda 732, is a whitewashed adobe with an attractive wooden balcony; the **Casa Manso de Velasco**, Santo Domingo 899, is similar. To the west, at Santo Domingo 961, is the massive **Templo de Santo Domingo** (1808).

Santiago's historical centre is the Plaza de Armas, flanked by the Correo Central (GPO), the **Museo Histórico Nacional** and the colonial **Catedral**. At its south-west corner is Paseo Ahumada, where hawkers peddle everything from shampoo to seat belts. Buskers of diverse style and quality congregate in the evening.

At Morandé 441 stands the former **Congreso Nacional**, now the Foreign Ministry. The nearby **Palacio Edwards**, Catedral 1187, belonged to one of Chile's elite families. The **Museo Chileno de Arte Precolombino**, at Bandera 361, was the colonial customs house, built in 1805. This

CHILE

Santiago

0   250   500 m

To La Serena &
Mendoza (Arg)

Carretera Panamericana Norte

Río Mapocho

Avenida Balmaceda

Rivera

Maruri

Lastra

Avenida Mapocho

Avenida Mapocho

Vía Norte Sur

Riquelme

7

General Mackenna

8

9

10

Testinos

Rosas

24

San Martín

Martínez de Rozas

San Pablo

Matucana

Ricardo Cumming

Almirante Barroso

Anuátegui

42

Catedral

Cueto

General Bulnes

García Reyes

32

M

Paseo   Huérfanos

5

64

65

63

66

Chacabuco

Matucana

Huérfanos

Avenida Portales

Brasil

80
Pretot

Parque
Quinta
Normal

78

Erasmo Escala

Los
Héroes

M

79

M

San Ignacio

To Airport

M

Cifuentes

Vergara

Ejército Libertador

Vía Norte Sur

Dieciocho

100

101

102

Carrera

Avenida República

Latorre

98

99

Sazie

Molina

Avenida España

Gorbea

103

Toesca

Gay

Avenida Exposición

Avenida Grajales

M

To Parque
O'Higgins

CHILE

■ PLACES TO STAY

8 Hotel Souvenir
9 Hotel Caribe
10 Hotel Pudahuel
11 Hotels Retiro, Colonial, Florida & San Felipe
13 Nuevo Hotel
17 Residencial Santo Domingo
24 Hotel Indiana
25 Hotel Cervantes
26 Hotel España
32 Casa Familiar Señora Marta
33 Hotel Metropoli
37 Hotel Tupahue
40 Hostal del Parque
42 Hotel Panamericano
49 Hotel São Paulo
51 Hotel Monte Carlo
52 Holiday Inn Crowne Plaza
56 Hotel Principado
58 Hotel Gran Palace
59 Hotel Ritz
62 Hotel Santa Lucía
63 Hotel Japón
68 Hotel Carrera
77 Hotel Riviera
84 Hotel Conquistador
86 Hotel El Libertador
87 Hotel Galerías
93 Residencial Londres & Hotel Paris
101 Residencial Vicky
102 Residencial Eliana
103 Residencial Gloria

▼ PLACES TO EAT

14 Bar Central
15 Mercado Central
21 La Venezia
22 La Zingarella
23 Restaurant Arabe Karim
30 Kan-Thu
31 Da Carla
39 Bontón Oriental

47 Chez Henry
60 Le Due Torri
61 Pastelería Tout Paris
71 El Novillero
74 Pizza Napoli
85 El Naturista
104 Los Adobes de Argomedo

OTHER

1 Estación Cumbre
2 Santuario de la Inmaculada Concepción
3 Jardín Zoológico
4 La Chascona
5 Teatro La Feria
6 Estación Mapocho
7 Terminal de Buses Norte
12 Sala Agustín Sire
16 Posada del Corregidor
18 Casa Manso de Velasco
19 Goethe Institute
20 Palacio de Bellas Artes
27 CTC (Telephone)
28 Correo Central (Main Post Office)
29 Museo Histórico Nacional
34 Municipalidad
35 Catedral
36 Plaza de Armas
38 CTC (Telephone)
39 Teatro la Comedia
40 Instituto Chileno-Francés
41 US Consulate
43 Ladeco
44 ENTEL (Overseas Telephone Service)
45 Museo Chileno de Arte Precolombino
46 Municipal Tourist Kiosk
48 Museo de Santiago; Casa Colorada
50 Feria Chilena del Libro
53 Argentine Embassy
54 Plaza Baquedano

55 Teatro Universidad de Chile
57 US Embassy
64 Airport Buses
65 Latour
66 Instituto Chileno-Norteamericano de Cultura
67 American Express
69 Plaza de la Constitución
70 Telex Chile (Telegraph & Telex)
72 Post Office
73 Thomas Cook
75 Teatro Municipal
76 LAN-Chile
79 Museo Aeronautico
78 Museo Nacional de Historia Natural
80 Terminal de Buses Los Héroes
81 Palacio de la Moneda
82 Bolsa de Comercio (Stock Exchange)
83 Club de la Unión
88 Biblioteca Nacional
89 Universidad Católica
90 Parque Manuel Rodríguez
91 Universidad de Chile
92 Iglesia de San Francisco
94 Feria Artesanal Santa Lucía
95 Posta Central (Medical)
96 CONAF
97 Librería Rivano
98 Terminal de Buses Santiago (Terminal Sur)
99 Terminal de Buses Alameda
100 Estación Central (Central Railway Station)

◯ Low Budget Hotel Area

museum chronicles 4500 years of pre-Columbian civilisations. It's open Tuesday to Saturday from 10 am to 6 pm, and on Sundays from 10 am to 1 pm. Admission, usually US$0.85, is free on Sundays.

The late-colonial **Palacio de La Moneda**

fills a block between Plaza de la Constitución and Plaza de La Libertad. Construction of the neoclassical mint began in 1788 in a flood-prone site near the Mapocho, but was completed at its present location in 1805, and later became the presidential palace. After the coup of 1973, it required extensive restoration. Other notable buildings near the palace are the **Bolsa de Comercio** (stock exchange), at La Bolsa 64, and the **Club de la Unión**, at Alameda 1091.

Just across the Alameda are the **Universidad de Chile** and the colonial **Iglesia de San Francisco**. Further up the Alameda is the monolithic **Biblioteca Nacional**, at the corner of MacIver. Also of interest is the **Teatro Municipal**, Agustinas 794.

Museo de Santiago This intriguing museum in the historic Casa Colorada documents the capital's history with maps, paintings, dioramas and colonial dress. At Merced 860, it's open Tuesday to Saturday from 10 am to 4 pm, and on Sundays and holidays from 10 am to 3 pm. Admission is US$0.85.

Salvador Allende's Grave Many pilgrims visit the grave, at the Cementerio General.

Cerro Santa Lucía Covered with gardens, footpaths and fountains, Santa Lucía (Huelén to the Mapuche) is a hilltop sanctuary from a congested city centre. An easy walk from the city centre, it has a reputation for muggings at night, and is much safer during the day.

La Chascona (Museo Neruda) The Fundación Neruda (☎ 777-8741) maintains this eclectic Bellavista house on a shady cul-de-sac at Márques de La Plata 0195. Call for reservations for very thorough, hour-long tours (US$2) or drop by if you're in the neighbourhood. The Fundación also arranges tours of Neruda's houses at Isla Negra and Valparaíso.

Cerro San Cristóbal North of the Mapocho, 860-metre San Cristóbal towers above San-

tiago. Reached by funicular railway, *teleférico* (cable car), bus and foot, it's part of **Parque Metropolitano**, the capital's largest open space.

The funicular from Plaza Caupolicán, at the north end of Pío Nono, operates daily from 10 am to 8.30 pm. A short walk from the **Terraza Bellavista**, at the Estación Cumbre, the 2000-metre teleférico connects San Cristóbal to Avenida Pedro de Valdivia Norte (a short hike from Metro Pedro de Valdivia). For about US$4, the funicular-teleférico combination offers a good orientation to Santiago's complex geography.

Places to Stay
Youth Hostels Santiago's three hostels, all fairly central and south of the Alameda, offer summer accommodation for about US$5. Small and cosy *Residencial Eliana* (☎ 672-6100) is at Grajales 2013, *Residencial Gloria* (☎ 698-8315) at Avenida Latorre 449 and *Residencial Vicky* (☎ 672-2269) at Sazie 2107.

Hotels, Hospedajes & Residenciales Budget accommodation is abundant, but be selective – lodgings differ much more in quality than in price. A Santiago woman named Eliana Dockendorff (☎ 204-3778) is attempting to organise accommodation in family homes for budget travellers. She speaks English and German.

Around the Northern Bus Terminal In the main budget hotel zone, a seedy area near the Terminal de Buses Norte, accommodation ranges from squalid to acceptable. Single women may wish to avoid General Mackenna, a hang-out for prostitutes.

Labyrinthine *Hotel Caribe* (☎ 696-6681), San Martín 851, is good value at US$5 per person with shared bath and hot showers. Though popular, it's large and there's usually a room, though not always a single. Rivalling the Caribe is the recently remodelled, more central and slightly cheaper *Nuevo Hotel* (☎ 671-5698), on the corner of San Pablo and Morandé. One reader liked *Hotel*

Pudahuel, San Pablo 1417-19, an old, beautiful European-style building with large, bright rooms.

Around the Alameda A better area is the Barrio París Londres, south of the Alameda, near Iglesia San Francisco. *Residencial Londres* (☎ 382215), at Londres 54, is great value at US$5/10 a single/double with hot water; it has clean, secure rooms and pleasant staff, but it fills up quickly and singles are few.

At *Hotel París*, around the corner, at Calle Parfs 813, doubles cost US$15. Readers have recommended nearby *Hotel Opera*, claiming it's a little shabby but has spacious rooms and friendly management. It's about US$7 for a single with shared bath.

Near the Plaza Costlier, but very central, is *Residencial Santo Domingo*, Santo Domingo 735. Also convenient is *Hotel España* (☎ 698-5245), at Morandé 510, with clean but stark rooms at US$15/25 for a single/double. West of the plaza is the family-run *Residencial del Norte* (☎ 695-1876), Catedral 2207, charging US$10 per person.

Places to Stay – middle
Mid-range hotels are generally better value. Central *Hotel Cervantes* (☎ 696-5318), Morandé 631, has rooms with private bath at US$27/35 for a single/double. Some rooms are a bit cramped but others are spacious and bright. *Hotel Japón* (☎ 698-4500), at Almirante Barroso 160, good value at US$29/34, has pleasant gardens and an English-speaking owner who exchanges books.

One highly recommended place is the centrally located *Hotel Metropoli* (☎ 672-3987), Sótero del Río 465, for US$37/41 with private bath. At friendly *Hotel Monte Carlo* (☎ 38-1176), Victoria Subercaseaux 209, rooms are small but cheery, all with private baths, but beware of street noise. Rather quieter is *Hotel Principado* (☎ 222-8142), at Arturo Buhrle 015, just off Vicuña

Mackenna (Metro station Baquedano), at US$44/53.

One correspondent thought *Hotel Santa Lucía* (☎ 39-8201), at Huérfanos 779, 4th floor, far better value than the prestigious Hotel Carrera. At about US$50/60 with TV, telephone, fridge and private bath, rooms are attractive, but those rooms facing the street can be very noisy.

Places to Stay – top end
Hotel Aloha (☎ 233-2230), Francisco Noguera 146 in Providencia (Metro station Pedro de Valdivia), with doubles for US$90, has been praised. At venerable *Hotel Carrera* (☎ 698-2011), Teatinos 180, rates start at US$189/201. One correspondent complained of an erratic hot water supply, but affluent activists might relish the room in which, in 1985, deadly serious opponents of the dictatorship aimed a time-delay bazooka at General Pinochet's office. The recoil was too strong for the photo tripod and the shell destroyed the room's interior.

Places to Eat
Restaurants range from basic (around the bus terminals) to better and even elegant (around Huérfanos and Ahumada, the Plaza de Armas and the Alameda, and in Providencia). Turistel's Centro volume has a very comprehensive list.

There's a string of cheap stand-up places in the south arcade of the Plaza de Armas, where highly regarded *Chez Henry* is no longer cheap, but neither is it outrageous – for about US$3.50, their pastel de choclo is the only meal you'll need all day.

Don't miss croissants, pastries and coffee at *Pastelería Tout Paris*, Agustinas 847. The modest exterior at *Bontón Oriental*, Merced 345, camouflages delicacies like a very fine apple strudel. For good, cheap coffee and cocoa, go to stand-up bars like *Café Haití* and *Café Caribe*, on Paseo Ahumada.

Many readers have recommended *Bar Central*, San Pablo 1063, for seafood. *Queijo e Mel*, Huérfanos 749, offers moderately priced Brazilian food. Carnivores can try *El Novillero*, Moneda 1145, while vegetarians can munch at the moderately priced *El Naturista*, Moneda 846, or *El Vegetariano*, Huérfanos 872. There are fine lunch specials at *Silvestre*, Huérfanos 965. One reader raved about *Kan-Thu*, Santo Domingo 769.

For seafood, visit the historic Mercado Central, a few blocks north of the plaza. The tables among the fruit and vegetable stands have great atmosphere, but the smaller, cheaper places on the periphery are just as good.

Bellavista, north of the Mapocho, is a great dining area. Eateries in Pablo Neruda's old haunts include the pizzería, *La Zingarella*, at Pío Nono 185, *La Venezia*, at Pío Nono 200, and *Restaurant Arabe Karim*. South of the Mapocho, try *Pérgola de la Plaza*, at Lastarria 305-321, behind the Hostal del Parque, for wine and pastries.

For pasta, try *Da Carla*, at MacIver 577, or *San Marco*, at Huérfanos 618. More than one reader found *Le Due Torri*, San Antonio 258, among the best value in town. French cuisine is the rule at *Les Assassins*, Merced 297.

For ice cream, go to *Sebastián*, Andrés de Fuenzalida 26, in Providencia (Metro Pedro de Valdivia), or *Coppelic*, on Avenida Providencia.

Entertainment

The cinema district is along Paseo Huérfanos and nearby streets. Many cinemas have half-price discounts on Wednesdays. The Universidad Católica's Centro de Extensión, Alameda 390, has low-price international film cycles on a regular basis, as does Cine Arte Normandie, Tarapacá 1181.

Things to Buy

Crafts and gemstones include lapis lazuli, pottery and copperware, plus carved wooden moai (statues) from Easter Island. The Feria Artesanal La Merced, on the corner of Merced and MacIver, is a good place for an overview, but there are two well-stocked shops in the gallery at Moneda 1025. Try also Claustro del 900, in an old convent, at Portugal 351.

Several readers enjoyed the market at Los Graneros del Alba, Avenida Apoquindo 8600. Take the Metro to Escuela Militar and catch a bus out to Avenida Apoquindo.

Getting There & Away

Air Nearly every visitor arrives in Santiago or passes through the capital at some time. Aeropuerto Internacional Arturo Merino Benítez (☎ 601-9001) is 26 km from Santiago, at Pudahuel. Some domestic flights (including those to the Juan Fernández Islands) leave suburban (☎ 557-2640).

Major international airlines with offices in Santiago include:

Aerolíneas Argentinas
    Moneda 756 (☎ 39-4121)
AeroPerú
    Fidel Oteíza 1953, 5th floor (☎ 274-3434)
American Airlines
    Huérfanos 1199 (☎ 671-6266)
British Airways
    Huérfanos 669, 5th floor (☎ 33-8366)
Canadian Pacific
    Huérfanos 669, Local 9 (☎ 39-3058)
Ladeco
    Huérfanos 1157 (☎ 698-2778)
    Pedro de Valdivia 0210, Providencia (☎ 251-7204)
LAN-Chile
    Agustinas 640 (☎ 632-3442)
    Pedro de Valdivia 0139, Providencia (☎ 232-8712)
LASSA
    Avenida Larraín 7941, La Reina (☎ 273-4354)
LAP (Líneas Aéreas Paraguayas)
    Agustinas 1141, 2nd floor (☎ 671-4404)
LAB (Lloyd Aéreo Boliviano)
    Moneda 1170 (☎ 671-2334)
Transportes Aéreos Robinson Crusoe
    Monumento 2570, Maipú (☎ 531-3772)

LAN-Chile and Ladeco are the main domestic carriers, but a new budget airline, Pacific Air, has recently begun services.

Bus – domestic Northbound buses leave from the Terminal de Buses Norte (☎ 671-2141), at Amunátegui 920, three blocks west of Metro Cal y Canto. Most southbound buses depart from the Terminal de Buses Sur (☎ 779-1385), Alameda (O'Higgins) 3800, one block west of Metro station Universidad de Santiago, but some leave from the new

Terminal Los Héroes, on Pretot near the Alameda. The Alameda terminal, corner of Alameda and Jotabeche, primarily serves Valparaíso and Viña del Mar.

Sample fares (in US dollars) and journey times from Santiago are:

Antofagasta	$27	18 hours
Arica	$40	28 hours
Chillán	$8	6 hours
Concepción	$9	8 hours
Copiapó	$17	11 hours
La Serena	$12	7 hours
Puerto Montt	$19	16 hours
Punta Arenas	$51	60 hours
Temuco	$11	11 hours
Valparaíso	$2.50	2 hours

Bus – international Most international buses use the Terminal Sur. Argentina is the most frequent destination; Mendoza (US$20) is about seven hours by bus. Other typical fares include Bariloche (US$35), Córdoba (US$57) and Buenos Aires (US$64).

Taxi colectivos to Mendoza are much quicker and only slightly more expensive than buses – and drivers may stop on request for photo opportunities. Outside the peak season, try haggling for discount on tickets.

Train Southbound trains leave from the Estación Central (☎ 689-5199), Alameda 3322 (Metro Estación Central). Only in summer is there a service south of Temuco. The station is open daily from 7 am to 11 pm. If the Estación Central is inconvenient, book at the Venta de Pasajes (☎ 39-8247), in the Galería Libertador, Alameda 853, Local 21, open on weekdays from 8.30 am to 7 pm, and on Saturdays from 9 am to 1 pm. For fares to some destinations, see the Getting Around section.

If the rail service to Valparaíso is still operating, it costs barely half as much as the bus (about US$1.40) but takes longer.

Getting Around
To/From the Airport To Aeropuerto Internacional Arturo Merino Benítez, Tour Express (☎ 671-7380), Moneda 1523, has

about 30 buses daily (US$1.50, half an hour) from 6.30 am to 9 pm. Metropuerto provides a similar and slightly cheaper service from Los Héroes Metro station. Minibuses Shuttle (☎ 635-3030) offers door-to-door service between Pudahuel and any part of Santiago for US$7; call a day ahead. Negotiated cab fares are about US$10 (if your Spanish is good).

Aeropuerto Nacional Cerrillos is reached by bus or taxi colectivo from the Alameda.

Bus Buses go everywhere, but it takes a while to learn the system – check destination signs or ask waiting passengers. Fares are usually a flat rate of around US$0.25.

Metro The Metro operates Monday to Saturday from 6.30 am to 10.30 pm, and on Sundays and public holidays from 8 am to 10.30 pm. Platform signs indicate the direction. On the east-west (Pudahuel) line, Dirección Las Condes heads toward Escuela Militar in the eastern suburbs, while Dirección Pudahuel goes to San Pablo. (It does *not* reach the international airport.) On the newer north-south (Centro) line, Dirección Centro goes to Puente Cal y Canto near the Mapocho, while Dirección La Cisterna heads towards the southern suburb of Lo Ovalle. Los Héroes, on the Alameda, is the only transfer station.

Fares are a flat US$0.15 on the Centro line, a flat US$0.30 on the Pudahuel line. Carnets (10-ticket booklets), available at a small discount, save time during rush hour.

Taxi Colectivos Taxi colectivos carry up to five passengers on fixed routes and are quicker than buses. Fares are about US$0.70 within the city limits; to outlying suburbs, it is dearer.

Taxi Santiago has abundant metered taxis; fares vary but may soon be standardised. Most drivers are honest, courteous and helpful but a few take roundabout routes and a handful have 'funny' meters. It costs Ch$150 (about US$0.40) to lower the flag (*bajar la bandera*) plus either Ch$20, Ch$21 or Ch$30 per 100 metres. This irregular system may soon be standardised.

Car Rental For details of rates, see the Getting Around section. Lesser-known companies tend to be cheaper. Several well-known companies have offices outside the airport terminal at Pudahuel. City offices are:

Automóvil Club de Chile (ACCHI)
    Marchant Pereira 122, Providencia (☎ 274-4167)
Avis
    La Concepción 334 (☎ 49-5757)
    Hotel Sheraton, Santa María 1742 (☎ 274-7621)
Bert
    Bilbao 2032 (☎ 43736)
Budget
    Bilbao 3028 (☎ 204-9091)
Hertz
    Costanera 1469 (☎ 225- 9328)

AROUND SANTIAGO
Wineries
The nearest winery is **Viña Santa Carolina** (☎ 238-2855), Rodrigo de Araya 1341, in Ñuñoa. The sprawling capital has displaced the vineyards, but the historical *casco* and *bodegas* (warehouses) are open on weekends. Also within city limits is **Viña Cousiño Macul**; tours of the bodegas take place daily at 11 am. Take any bus or taxi colectivo out to Américo Vespucio Sur to Avenida Quilín.

At Pirque, south-east of Santiago, **Viña Concha y Toro** (☎ 850-3123) is Chile's largest winery. Tours take place daily at 10.30 am and at 1, 3 and 5.30 pm. From Plaza Italia, at Tarapacá and San Francisco, taxi colectivos cost about US$1.

Viña Undurraga (☎ 817-2308), 34 km south-west of Santiago on the old road to Melipilla, is open on weekdays from 9.30 am to noon and 2 to 4 pm. Take Buses Peñaflor

(☎ 776-1025) from the Terminal de Buses Borja, Alameda 3250.

Pomaire

In this small, dusty village near Melipilla, master potters produce fine and remarkably inexpensive ceramics. Take Buses Melipilla from the Terminal Borja, Alameda 3250.

Reserva Nacional Río Clarillo

Río Clarillo is a scenic tributary canyon of the Cajón del Maipo, south-east of Santiago. Take a taxi colectivo to Puente Alto's Plaza de Armas, where Buses LAC leave every hour to within about two km of the reserve.

Ski Resorts

Chilean ski resorts are open from June to October. Rates are lower in the early and late seasons. The closest sites are near **Farellones**, 45 km east of the capital. Centro de Ski El Colorado (☎ 246-3344, fax 220-7738), Avenida Apoquindo 4900, Local 47/48 in the Santiago suburb of Las Condes, offers day excursions with round-trip transport, rental equipment and lift tickets for US$55.

The site of several downhill speed records, **Portillo** (☎ 231-3411, fax 231-7164), Roger de Flor 2911, Santiago, is 152 km north-east of Santiago. *Hotel Portillo* is not cheap but the price includes all meals, eight days of lift tickets, and taxes. Cheaper alternatives, involving bunks and shared bath, run at $475 per person per week.

Backpackers and other would-be skiers on modest budgets could try the ski tour agency run by Anke Kessler (☎ 737- 1958), Arzobispo Casanova 25, Bellavista, Santiago. Skitotal (☎ 246-6881, 246-5847), Qpoquindo 4900, Local 32/33 has daily shuttle buses to Farellones (US$8) and also rents equipment.

Parque Nacional la Campana

Darwin's ascent of 1840-metre Cerro La Campana was one of his most memorable experiences. In the coast range, this park occupies 8000 hectares of jagged scrub land which shelters the rare Chilean palm (with edible fruit) and the northernmost remaining stands of southern beech.

Palmas de Ocoa is the northern entrance to the park. The saddle of the **Portezuelo de Granizo**, a two-hour climb through a palm-studded canyon, offers some of the views which impressed Darwin. Camping is possible but water is limited and fire is a hazard, especially in summer and fall.

Getting There & Away Sectors Granizo and Cajón Grande can be reached by Línea Ciferal from Valparaíso and Viña del Mar, every half-hour in summer. AGDABUS leaves every 20 minutes from Limache and Olmué. Both involve about a one-km walk to the entrance.

For Sector Ocoa, any northbound bus from Santiago will drop you at Hijuelas (watch for the poorly marked turn-off just before the bridge over the Río Aconcagua), but from there you must hitch or walk 12 km to the entrance.

Valparaíso & the Coast

North-west of Santiago, the port of Valparaíso is one of South America's most distinctive cities, while Viña del Mar and other coastal towns are favourite summer playgrounds. South of Santiago is a string of agricultural and industrial centres.

VALPARAÍSO

Mercantilism retarded colonial Valparaíso's growth, but after independence, foreign merchants so permeated the city that one visitor remarked that 'a stranger might almost fancy himself arrived at a British settlement'. After completion of the Santiago railroad in 1880, Valparaíso (or Valpo) became Chile's financial powerhouse, with over 100,000 residents, but in the 20th century, the opening of the Panama Canal clobbered the local economy, as shipping avoided the Cape Horn route. The calamitous Great Depression reduced demand for minerals until after WW II.

Viña del Mar
San Felipe
Portillo
Los Andes
Valparaíso
Algarrobo
El Quisco
Santiago
San Antonio
PACIFIC OCEAN
Volcan San José
San José de Malpó
Rancagua
Pichilemu
San Fernando
Volcan Tinguiririca
Curicó
ARGENTINA
Constitución
Talca
CHILE
Cauquenes
Chillán
Volcan Chillán
Talcahuano
Concepción
Río Biobío
Salto del Laja
Los Angeles
Parque Nacional Laguna del Laja
Angol
To Temuco

Middle Chile

0   35   70 km

Capital of the Fifth Region and site of the National Congress, Valparaíso is 120 km north-west of Santiago and the second biggest city in Chile. It has a population of 300,000 and is an administrative centre, whose key industries are food processing, and mining and fruit exports. It depends less on tourism than neighbouring Viña del Mar, but many vacationers arrive from nearby beach towns. The navy also plays an important economic role.

Orientation

Probably only a lifetime resident can fathom Valparaíso's complex geography. In its congested centre of sinuous cobbled streets and irregular intersections, most major streets parallel the shoreline, which curves north toward Viña del Mar. Avenida Errázuriz runs the length of the waterfront, alongside the railway. Behind and above the centre, the hills are a warren of steep footpaths, zigzag roads and blind alleys where even the best map often fails.

Information

Tourist Office The Municipalidad, Condell 1490, is open on weekdays from 8.30 am to 2 pm and 3 to 5 pm. The well-informed municipal kiosk on Muelle Prat has limited printed matter. It's open on Fridays from 4 to 8 pm, and on weekends from 10.30 am to 2.30 pm and 4 to 8 pm. Another office at the bus terminal (☎ 213246) is open in summer only.

Money Try Inter Cambio, on Plaza Sotomayor, or Exprinter, at Prat 895.

Post & Telecommunications Correos de Chile is on Prat at Plaza Sotomayor. CTC has offices at Esmeralda 1054, Pedro Montt 2023 and the bus terminal.

Consulates The Argentine Consulate (☎ 21-3691) is at Blanco 1215, Oficina 1102, and the British Consulate (☎ 25-6117) is at Blanco 725, Oficina 26.

Emergency Hospital Carlos van Buren (☎ 25-4074) is at Avenida Colón 2454.

Dangers & Annoyances The hill neighbourhoods have a reputation for thieves and robbers. Also watch for suspicious characters and diversions in the area west of Plaza Sotomayor and even in the city centre. Avoid poorly lighted areas at night, and if possible, walk with a companion.

Valparaíso has the highest rate of AIDS in Chile, associated with the sex industry of this major port.

Hills of Valparaíso

On a sunny Sunday, you can spend hours riding Valparaíso's 16 *ascensores* (funiculars) and strolling the back alleys of its picturesque hillside neighbourhoods. Some ascensores, built from 1883 to 1916, are remarkable engineering feats – **Ascensor Polanco**, on Avenida Argentina, is more like an elevator.

One of the best areas for urban explorers is Cerro Concepción, reached by **Ascensor Turri**, corner of Prat and Almirante Carreño,

CHILE

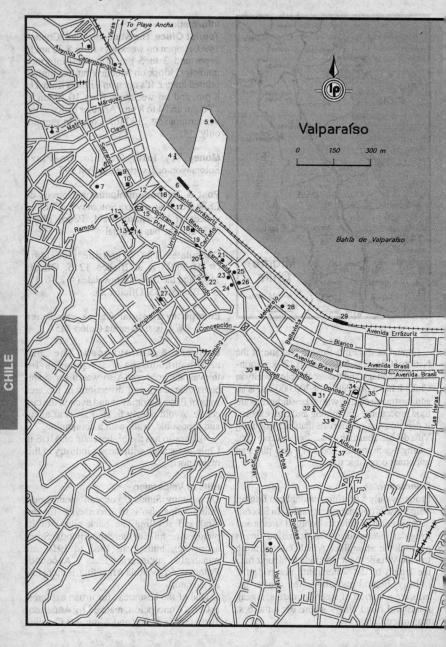

Valparaíso

0   150   300 m

Bahía de Valparaíso

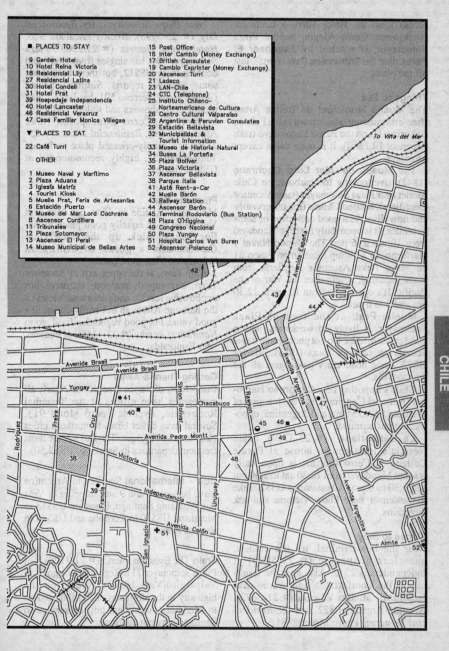

■ PLACES TO STAY

9 Garden Hotel
10 Hotel Reina Victoria
18 Residencial Lily
27 Residencial Latina
30 Hotel Condell
31 Hotel Prat
39 Hospedaje Independencia
40 Hotel Lancaster
46 Residencial Veracruz
47 Casa Familiar Monica Villegas

▼ PLACES TO EAT

22 Café Turri

OTHER

1 Museo Naval y Marítimo
2 Plaza Aduana
3 Iglesia Matríz
4 Tourist Kiosk
5 Muelle Prat, Feria de Artesanías
6 Estación Puerto
7 Museo del Mar Lord Cochrane
8 Ascensor Cordillera
11 Tribunales
12 Plaza Sotomayor
13 Ascensor El Peral
14 Museo Municipal de Bellas Artes

15 Post Office
16 Inter Cambio (Money Exchange)
17 British Consulate
19 Cambio Exprinter (Money Exchange)
20 Ascensor Turri
21 Ladeco
23 LAN-Chile
24 CTC (Telephone)
25 Instituto Chileno-
   Norteamericano de Cultura
26 Centro Cultural Valparaíso
28 Argentine & Peruvian Consulates
29 Estación Bellavista
32 Municipalidad &
   Tourist Information
33 Museo de Historia Natural
34 Buses La Porteña
35 Plaza Bolívar
36 Plaza Victoria
37 Ascensor Bellavista
38 Parque Italia
41 Asté Rent-a-Car
42 Muelle Barón
43 Railway Station
44 Ascensor Barón
45 Terminal Rodoviario (Bus Station)
48 Plaza O'Higgins
49 Congreso Nacional
50 Plaza Yungay
51 Hospital Carlos Van Buren
52 Ascensor Polanco

To Viña del Mar

Avenida España
Avenida Argentina

CHILE

Avenida Brasil
Avenida Brasil
Yungay
Simón Bolívar
Chacabuco
Rawson
Freire
Cruz
Rodríguez
Avenida Pedro Montt
Victoria
Francia
Independencia
Uruguay
Avenida Colón
San Ignacio
Almte

across from the **Reloj Turri**, a landmark clocktower. Cerro Alegre, behind Plaza Sotomayor, is reached by **Ascensor El Peral**, near the **Tribunales** (law courts), just off the plaza.

Things to See
The **Museo Municipal de Bellas Artes** (fine-arts museum, also known as the Palacio Baburizza) is on the Paseo Yugoeslavo (take Ascensor El Peral). It is open daily, except Mondays.

The **Museo del Mar Lord Cochrane** (1842), overlooking the harbour, on Calle Merlet near Plaza Sotomayor (take Ascensor Cordillera), housed Chile's first observatory and now displays a good collection of ships in bottles. It is open daily (except Mondays) from 10 am to 6 pm. The **Museo Naval y Marítimo**, in a hilltop location on Paseo 21 de Mayo (take Ascensor Artillería from Plaza Aduana), emphasises the War of the Pacific. It's open daily from 10 am to 12.30 pm and 3 to 6 pm.

Muelle Prat, at the foot of Plaza Sotomayor, is lively on weekends, with a good crafts market. Do not photograph naval vessels on harbour tours (US$1.50); for US$2, some boats carry passengers all the way to Viña.

Chile's imposing new **Congreso Nacional** (National Congress) is at the junction of avenidas Pedro Montt and Argentina, opposite the bus terminal.

La Sebastiana (☎ 23-3759), Pablo Neruda's least-known house at Pasaje Collado 1, Cerro Florida, is open daily (except Mondays) from 10.30 am to 2.30 pm and 3.30 to 6 pm. Admission is US$2. Take the ascensor near Plaza Victoria and ask directions.

Places to Stay
Near the bus terminal, try the modest, nameless hospedaje (☎ 23-5840) at Independencia 2312. Also near the terminal is the comfortable and warm *casa familiar* of Monica Villegas (☎ 21-5673), Avenida Argentina 322, and the *Residencial Veracruz*, Pedro Montt 2881.

Near Plaza Sotomayor, try *Residencial Lily* (☎ 25-5995), Blanco Encalada 866. *Hotel Reina Victoria* (☎ 21-2203), Plaza Sotomayor 190, has singles from US$6 and doubles from US$12, but there have been some negative reports. Similarly priced *Garden Hotel*, Serrano 501, has large, clean rooms, good showers and toilets, and a restaurant. On Cerro Concepción (take Ascensor Turri), *Residencial Latina* (☎ 25-2350) is a family-oriented place at Pasaje Templeman 51, highly recommended at US$7 a single.

Places to Eat
Most visitors dine in Viña del Mar, but Valparaíso is an equally good place to eat. For ideas, pick up the free *Guía Gastronómica*, a guide to dining in Valparaíso, Viña and Concón.

Café Turri, at the upper exit of Ascensor Turri, has superb seafood, attentive but unobtrusive service and panoramic views of the harbour. Although not really cheap, it's good value. For good vegetarian food, go to *Naturalista Bambu* (☎ 23-4216), at Puoleto, near Esmeralda.

Getting There & Away
Bus – long-distance & regional Nearly all companies have offices at the Terminal Rodoviario, Avenida Pedro Montt 913. Several have direct buses to northern cities like Arica and Iquique. Tur-Bus has the most frequent departures to Santiago (US$2.50).

Bus – international Services to Argentina leave between 8 and 9 am, stopping in Viña but bypassing Santiago. Fares are US$18 to Mendoza, US$50 to Córdoba and US$60 to Buenos Aires.

Train The Estación Puerto (☎ 21-7108) is at Plaza Sotomayor 711. Regular trains go from Valparaíso/Viña to Los Andes, on the highway to the ski resort of Portillo, and on to Mendoza, Argentina, but the service to Santiago may not continue.

Getting Around

Valpo and Viña are connected by local buses (US$0.25), commuter train, and boats (US$2) from Muelle Prat.

AROUND VALPARAÍSO

Isla Negra (Museo Neruda)

Neruda's outlandish oceanside house, on a rocky headland south of Valparaíso, houses the poet's collections of bowsprits, ships in bottles, nautical instruments and other memorabilia. Isla Negra is *not*, by the way, an island.

In summer, reservations (☎ (035) 21-2284) are imperative for half-hour weekday tours (US$2), between 10 am and 7.45 pm, but hang around the grounds as long as you like.

From Santiago's Alameda terminal, buses beyond Algarrobo leave pilgrims almost at the door. Buses also leave frequently from Valparaíso's Terminal Rodoviario.

VIÑA DEL MAR

Popularly known as the *Ciudad Jardín* (Garden City), Viña del Mar has Chile's premier beach resort, ever since the railroad linked Valparaíso to Santiago, even though the ocean south of La Serena is very cold for swimming. The *porteños* of Valparaíso flocked to Viña because of its easy access to beaches and broad green spaces, and soon built grand houses and mansions away from the congested port. Because of high costs and its perceived exclusivity, Viña has since lost ground to competing resorts like La Serena.

Information & Orientation

Ten km north of Valparaíso, Viña consists of an older area south of Estero Marga Marga and a newer residential grid to its north, where most streets are identified by number and direction, either Norte (north), Oriente (east), or Poniente (west). Avenida Libertad separates the Ponientes and the Orientes. Activity centres are south of the Marga Marga, on Plaza Vergara and Avenidas Arlegui and Valparaíso.

Tourist Office The Central de Turismo e Informaciones (☎ 88-3154), north of Plaza Vergara, is open on weekdays from 9 am to 7 pm, on Saturdays from 9 am to 2 pm and 3 to 7 pm, and on Sundays from 9 am to 2 pm. It provides an adequate map and a useful calendar of events.

Money Try Symatour (at Arlegui 684/686), Afex (at Arlegui 641) or Inter Cambio (at Uno Norte 655-B).

Post & Telecommunications Correos de Chile is at Valparaíso 846. CTC has offices at 14 Norte 1184 and Valparaíso 628.

Emergency Hospital Gustavo Fricke (☎ 68-0041) is east of the city centre, at Alvarez 1532.

Things to See

Specialising in Mapuche silver and on Easter Island, the **Museo Arqueológico Sociedad Fonck**, at 4 Norte 784, is open Tuesday to Friday from 10 am to 6 pm, and on weekends from 10 am to 2 pm. Two blocks east, at Quillota 214, the **Museo Palacio Rioja** is now a municipal museum, open daily, except Mondays.

The magnificently landscaped **Quinta Vergara** contains the Venetian-style **Palacio Vergara** (1908), which in turn contains the **Museo de Bellas Artes** (fine-arts museum, admission US$0.30)). It's open daily, except Mondays, from 10 am to 6 pm (7 pm in summer).

Frequent summer concerts complement the Song Festival (see the following section). Grounds are open daily, 7.30 am to 6 pm (8 pm in summer).

Song Festival

For a week every February in the Quinta Vergara, the ostentatious Festival Internacional de la Canción features the kitschiest artists from the Spanish-speaking world (for balance, there's usually at least one really insipid Anglo performer) and paralyses the country, as ticketless Chileans gaze at TV sets in homes, cafés, restaurants and bars.

CHILE

Patient, selective listeners may hear worthwhile folk performers.

Beaches
Northern suburbs like Reñaca and Concón have the best beaches – take Bus No 9 from Calle 2 Norte. For more details, see the Around Viña del Mar section.

Places to Stay
This is only a sample of the accommodation available. After Chileans finish their holi-

days in February, supply exceeds demand and prices drop but the weather is still ideal.

Youth Hostel In summer 1991-92, hostel accommodation was available at *Residencial La Montaña* (☎ 62-2230), Agua Santa 153, for about US$5.

Hospedajes, Residenciales & Hotels For budget alternatives, look on or near Agua Santa and Von Schroeders, or near the bus station. Off-season prices run about US$5 per person, in season twice that or more. One

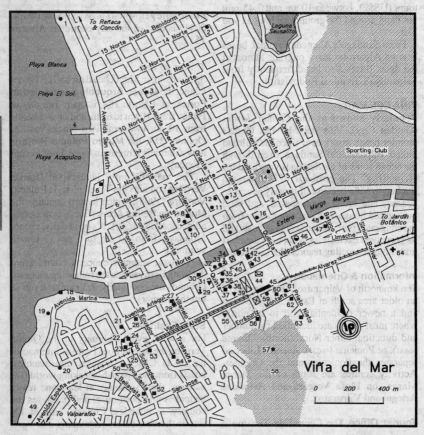

Viña del Mar

reader loved *Residencial Verónica*, Von Schroeders 150, for about US$6. *Residencial Agua Santa* (☎ 90-1351), Agua Santa 36, is an attractive blue Victorian building and charges US$7 in the off season, US$10 peak; almost next door, at Agua Santa 48, is *Residencial Patricia* (☎ 66-3825), where singles are US$8.

Recommended *Hospedaje Calderón* (☎ 97-0456), a block from the bus terminal, at Batuco 147 (there is no sign on the door), costs US$7 per person. For the same price, *Residencial France* (☎ 68-5976), on the 'wrong side of the tracks' (in Viña, at least – everything is relative), at Montaña 743, has small, box-like rooms, but pleasant common areas. Near the Quinta Vergara is *Residencial La Gaviota* (☎ 97-4439), Alcalde Prieto Nieto 0332, a bargain at US$8 with shared

bath, US$10 with private bath. Also recommended is *Residencial Oxarón* (☎ 88-2360) at Villanello 136, a quiet location between Arlegui and Valparaíso (US$11 for a single with breakfast).

One affluent reader was enthusiastic over *Hotel Rondó* (☎ 68-5073), Errázuriz 690, with an English-speaking owner (US$43/60 for a single/double with breakfast). If you have lots of cash, the best choice would be the venerable *Hotel O'Higgins* (☎ 88-2016), on Plaza Latorre. Rates start at US$71/103.

Places to Eat

Several readers have commended *Restaurant Puerto Montt*, on Valparaíso, for large portions of well-prepared seafood. For good, moderately priced Italian and Middle Eastern food, choose *Panzoni*, Pasaje

■	PLACES TO STAY		▼	PLACES TO EAT		20	Reloj de Flores del
							Mar (Clock of
6	Hotel San Martín		31	Cafetería Anayak			Flowers)
7	Residencial 555		36	Confitería Samoiedo		28	CTC (Telephone)
8	Residencial Helen		39	Restaurant Panzoni &		29	Sernatur (Tourist
	Misch			El Naturista			Office)
18	Hotel Cap Ducal		55	Centro Español		32	Cambios Afex (Money
21	Residencial Verónica						Exchange)
22	Residencial Marbella			OTHER		33	Sala Viña del Mar
23	Residencial Victoria					34	Central de Turismo e
24	Residencial Blanchait		1	Reloj de Sol (Sun Dial)			Informaciones,
25	Residencial Caribe		2	CTC (Telephone)			Municipalidad
26	Residencial Villarrica		3	Rent-a-Car Mach		35	Cambios Symatour
27	Residencial Oxarón		4	Muelle Vergara			(Money Exchange)
30	Residencial Magalla-		5	Instituto Chileno-		38	CTC (Telephone)
	nes			Británico		40	Plaza Vergara
37	Residencial Ona Berri		9	CONAF		42	Sala Municipal de
41	Hotel O'Higgins		10	Instituto Chileno-			Exposiciones
47	Hospedaje Calderón			Norteamericano		43	Teatro Municipal
50	Residencial Agua		11	Centro Cultural/Viña		44	Post Office
	Santa & Residen-			del Mar		45	Railway Station
	cial Patricia		12	Museo Arqueológico		46	Terminal Rodoviario
51	Residencial La			Sociedad Fonck		48	Mercado Municipal
	Montaña		13	Instituto Chileno-		49	Disco Scala
52	Residencial Lausanne			Británico		57	Palacio Vergara,
53	Residencial Casino		14	Museo Palacio Rioja			Museo de Bellas
54	Residencial Palace		15	Rentauto			Artes
56	Hotel Rondó		16	Automóvil Club de		58	Quinta Vergara
60	Residencial France			Chile		59	Bert Rent-a-Car
62	Residencial Edhison		17	Casino Municipal		61	Disco Spa
63	Residencial La		19	Museo de la Cultura		64	Hospital Gustavo
	Gaviota						Fricke

Cousiño 12-B, which is small and very popular for lunch (Cousiño is a small passage off Valparaíso, near Plaza Sucre).

On the same block is vegetarian *El Naturista*, where the bargain lunch costs US$2. For coffee and dessert, try *Cafetería Anayak*, at Quinta 134, or especially, *Confitería Samoiedo*, at Valparaíso 637.

Entertainment
Cinemas For first-run movies, try Cine Arte (at Plaza Vergara 42), Cine Olímpo (at Quinta 294), Cine Premier (at Quillota 898) or Cine Rex (at Valparaíso 758).

Discos For dancing, Viña has Scala (at Caleta Abarca), Scratch (at Bohn 970), Spa (at Montaña 879) and Arenna (at Bohn 770-A). Not really a disco, Hotel Alcázar, Alvarez 646, holds a *noche de tango* every Saturday from 9 pm.

Getting There & Away
The Terminal de Buses is on the corner of Valparaíso and Quilpué, two blocks from Plaza Vergara. Most buses from Valparaíso pick up passengers here, though a few lines start in Viña. There are frequent buses to San Felipe, Los Andes and Santiago.

Getting Around
Buses marked Puerto or Aduana go to Valparaíso from Avenida Arlegui; from Muelle Vergara, you can also catch a boat to Plaza Sotomayor for US$2.

Taxis are twice as expensive as those in Santiago.

Car For the cheapest rates, try Bert Rent A Car (☎ 68-5515), at Alvarez 750.

AROUND VIÑA DEL MAR
North of Viña are less celebrated but still attractive beach towns. **Reñaca** has its own tourist office (☎ 90-0499), at Avenida Borgoño 14100, plus the area's most extensive beach, but little budget accommodation. **Concón**, 15 km from Viña, is another popular and exclusive *balneario* (bathing resort).

Another 23 km beyond Concón is **Quintero**, a peninsula community once part of Lord Cochrane's hacienda. For reasonable accommodation, try *Residencial María Alejandra* (☎ 93-0266), Cochrane 157, where singles with shared bath cost about US$6. Farther north, the port of **Horcón** is an artists' colony with a bohemian flavour and outstanding seafood restaurants, reached by Sol del Pacífico bus from Avenida San Martín in Viña.

The Southern Heartland

RANCAGUA
Capital of the Sixth Region and 86 km south of Santiago, the agricultural service centre of Rancagua (population 160,000) also depends on the copper of El Teniente, the world's largest subsurface mine. In 1814, the *Desastre de Rancagua* (Disaster of Rancagua) was a temporary setback for Chilean self-determination, at the hands of the Spanish Royalist troops.

For information, visit Sernatur, Germán Riesco 277. To change money, try Fincard, at Astorga 485. CONAF (☎ 23-3769), Cuevas 480, has information on Reserva Nacional Río de los Cipreses.

Rancagua's late colonial buildings include the **Iglesia de La Merced** (O'Higgins' headquarters during the battle of Rancagua), the **Casa del Pilar de Piedra** and the **Museo Histórico Regional**.

Places to Stay & Eat
Several travellers have recommended *Hotel España* (☎ 23-0141), San Martín 367, which has singles/doubles for US$11/18 but may have cheaper rooms with shared bath. *Hotel Rancagua* (☎ 23-2663), San Martín 85, is slightly dearer. *Restaurant Casas Viejas*, Rubio 216, has been recommended.

Getting There & Away
Bus The terminal, on Ocarrol, has frequent buses to Santiago (US$2). Many southbound buses also stop in Rancagua.

Train Long-distance trains stop at the station on Viña del Mar between Ocarrol and Carrera Pinto, and there are also commuter services to Santiago.

AROUND RANCAGUA
Termas de Cauquenes
Only 28 km east of Rancagua, these hot springs have hosted both O'Higgins and Darwin (who called the facilities 'a square of miserable little hovels, each with a single table and bench' ... 'a quiet solitary spot with a good deal of quiet beauty'). Improvements have placed it beyond budget travellers, but you can still spend the afternoon here by taking a bus from Rancagua's Mercado Municipal.

Reserva Nacional de los Cipreses
Fifty km south-east of Rancagua, 37,000-hectare los Cipreses has varied volcanic landforms, hanging glacial valleys, and riverscapes. Its extensive forests shelter wildlife like guanaco, fox, vizcacha and condor. There are many petroglyphs to see and places to camp, hike and horse-ride.

No direct public transport exists, but you can take a bus to Termas de Cauquenes and walk 15 km to the entrance, or try to arrange transport with CONAF in Rancagua.

CURICÓ
An attractive city surrounded by orchards and vineyards, 195 km south of Santiago, Curicó is a good base for trips into the countryside, coastal areas and parts of the Andes. Its palm-lined Plaza de Armas, one of Chile's prettiest, has a wrought-iron bandstand and cool fountains with black-necked swans.

For information, visit the private Cámara de Turismo, in the Gobernación, on the east side of the plaza. Curi Cambio, Merced 255, changes money on weekdays only. Correos de Chile is at Carmen 556, while CTC has long-distance offices at Peña 650 and Camilo Henríquez 414. ENTEL, Prat 373, is open until midnight.

Vineyards
Bodega Miguel Torres (☎ 31-0455) is south of Curicó on the Panamericana. Phone ahead and take a taxi colectivo toward the village of Molina. On the same route, near the village of Lontué, is **Viña San Pedro** (☎ 49-1517).

Places to Stay
Friendly *Hotel Prat*, Peña 427, is a bargain at US$4 per person with shared bath and hot showers, but some rooms are dark and a bit drab. *Residencial Rahue*, across the street, is equally satisfactory.

Places to Eat
Restaurant Villota, Merced 487, has fine lunches in pleasant surroundings. For parrillada, try *El Fogón Chileno*, at Yungay 802. Pizzas, sandwiches and a variety of snacks are available at *Luzzi*, Yungay 720. Try also the *Centro Italiano*, Estado 531.

Getting There & Away
Bus The long-distance terminal is on Camilo Henríquez, three blocks north of the plaza. Buses to Santiago (US$4) leave every half-hour. For local and regional services, the Terminal de Buses Rurales is at the west end of Calle Prat.

Train Trains from Santiago and Temuco stop at the station, five blocks from the plaza, at the west end of Calle Prat.

AROUND CURICÓ
Radal Siete Tazas
East of Molina, Radal Siete Tazas' major attraction is a series of falls and pools in the upper Río Claro. There are scenic trails up Cerro El Fraile and at Valle del Indio, with camping at Radal and Parque Inglés sectors. CONAF's visitors' centre, 50 km from Molina, can be reached from Curicó and Molina by bus, daily in summer, less often in other seasons.

TALCA
Founded in 1690 but refounded in 1742 after shaky beginnings (a major earthquake), Talca is capital of the Seventh Region of Maule, 257 km south of Santiago. Long the

CHILE

residence of landowners, it's also an important commercial centre. For information, visit Sernatur, at 1 Poniente 1234. CONAF is at 2 Poniente 1180.

In 1818, Bernardo O'Higgins signed the declaration of independence in the late-colonial **Museo O'Higginiano y de Bellas Artes**.

Places to Stay & Eat

Near the train station, *Hotel Alcázar*, 2 Sur 1359, is clean for US$6 per person with shared bath. Across the street, *Residencial Cordillera* has singles with shared bath for US$8, with private bath for US$14. Restaurants include the *Centro Español*, at 3 Oriente 1109, *Ibiza* (with take-away service), at 1 Sur 1168, *El Gallo Marino*, at 1 Norte 1718, and *Mykonos*, at 1 Sur 942.

Getting There & Away

Bus Many north-south buses stop at the Rodoviario Municipal (☎ 24-3270) at 2 Sur 1920, behind the train station.

Train All trains from Santiago stop at the station (☎ 22-6116), 11 Oriente 1000, at the east end of 2 Sur.

AROUND TALCA
Vilches

Vilches is a CONAF preserve 65 km east of Talca. It's possible to camp in the upper Río Lircay basin and hike to Laguna El Alto, Laguna Tomate and up the canyon of the Valle del Venado. Buses Vilches go daily, except Sundays, at 1 and 5 pm, from Talca.

CHILLÁN

Birthplace of O'Higgins, Chillán is the approximate northern border of *La Frontera*, an area controlled by the Mapuche until the late 19th century. Of all the towns on the Panamericana from Santiago to Temuco, Chillán most deserves a stopover.

Orientation & Information

Chillán (population 125,000), 400 km south of Santiago, sits on an alluvial plain between the Río Ñuble and the Río Chillán. Sernatur (☎ 22-3272), in the Edificios Públicos 422, on the Plaza de Armas, is open on weekdays from 9 am to 1 pm and 3 to 7 pm, and on Saturdays from 9 am to 1 pm only.

Biotour, at Constitución 550, Local 9, should change US cash and travellers'

■	PLACES TO STAY	▼	PLACES TO EAT	16	Automóvil Club de Chile
1	Hospedaje Sonia Segui	5	Planka	18	Sernatur (Tourist Office) & Post Office
3	Hotel Floresta	9	Kuranepe		
4	Claris Hotel	12	Taipe	19	Catedral
10	Hotel Martín Ruiz de Gamboa	13	Jai Yang	21	Hospital
		20	Centro Español	22	Centrotur
11	Hotel Real	32	Cocinerías del Mercado	23	Biotour (Money Exchange)
14	Hotel Americano			26	CTC (Telephone)
17	Hotel Rucamanqui		OTHER	28	Hispanotur
24	Gran Hotel Isabel Riquelme			29	Feria
25	Hotel Cordillera	2	Escuela México (Murals)	30	Terminal de Buses Rurales
27	Hotel Quinchamalí	6	Museo Franciscano	34	Museo Naval Arturo Prat
31	Hospedaje Su Casa	7	Railway Station		
33	Hospedaje Tino Rodríguez Sepúlveda	8	Terminal de Buses Inter-regionales		
		15	ENTEL (Telephone)		

cheques. Correos de Chile is at Libertad 505, while CTC is at Arauco 625.

Things to See

Murales de la Escuela México After a 1939 earthquake, Mexican President Lázaro Cárdenas donated a new school to Chillán. At Pablo Neruda's urging, Mexican artist Davíd Alfaro Siqueiros decorated the library with murals honouring indigenous and post-Columbian figures in each country's history – the northern wall is devoted to Mexico and the southern wall to Chile. Siqueiros's countryman Xavier

Guerrero's simple but powerful mural, *Hermanos Mexicanos*, flanks the library stairs.

The school is at O'Higgins 250. It does still function as a school but the staff welcomes visitors.

Feria de Chillán Especially lively on Saturdays, this is one of Chile's most colourful markets, with a great selection of crafts (leather, basketry, horse gear and weavings) and mountains of fresh produce. The Feria occupies the entire Plaza de la Merced and spills over into adjacent streets.

Chillán

Places to Stay & Eat

Chillán has budget accommodation from about US$4, such as *Hospedaje Sonia Seguí*, Itata 288, which includes breakfast. *Su Casa*, at Cocharcas 555, is comparable. Try also *Hospedaje Tino Rodríguez Sepúlveda*, Purén 443, for US$6.

Hotel Americano, Carrera 481, has singles with shared bath for US$5, while the comparable *Claris Hotel*, 18 de Septiembre 357, is dearer with private bath. *Hotel Real*, Libertad 219, costs US$7/12 for a single/double with shared bath.

The *Cocinerías del Mercado*, at Prat 826, 2nd floor, has several simple but excellent restaurants, which may move as the central market is remodelled. The *Centro Español* is at Arauco 555; also worth a try are *Planka*, at Arauco 103, and *Kuranepe*, at O'Higgins 420.

Getting There & Away

The Terminal de Buses Inter-regionales (☎ 22-1014) is at Constitución 01, corner of Avenida Brasil. It has frequent north-south services, plus daily buses to Bariloche, Argentina (US$32), and to Neuquén via San Martín de Los Andes and Zapala.

For local buses, the terminal (☎ 22-3606) is at Maipón and Sargento Aldea.

The train station (☎ 22-2424) is on Avenida Brasil at Libertad.

AROUND CHILLAN
Termas de Chillán

Renowned for its hot springs and skiing, Termas de Chillán is 80 km east, at 1800 metres, on the slopes of Volcán Chillán. Accommodation is costly, but check travel agencies for day trips.

CONCEPCIÓN

Menaced by Indians and devastated by earthquakes, Concepción moved several times in the colonial era, but maintained seaborne

■	PLACES TO STAY	▼	PLACES TO EAT	27	Instituto Chileno-Francés
1	Hospedaje María Inés Jarpa	7	China Town	29	Plaza Independencia
6	Residencial	24	Pastelería Suiza & Salón Inglés	30	Pawulska Tour
14	Hotel Cruz del Sur	28	Centro Español	31	Teatro Concepción
15	Residencial Colo Colo	49	El Naturista	32	Instituto Chileno-Español
16	Residencial Antuco & Residencial San Sebastián	52	Chungwa	33	Mercado Central
17	Hotel Ritz		OTHER	34	Inter-Santiago (Money Exchange)
18	Hotel Tabancura	2	Hospital	35	ENTEL (Telephone)
23	Hotel Alonso de Ercilla	3	Casa del Arte	38	Instituto Chileno-Norteamericano
25	Hotel de la Cruz	4	Barrio Universitario	39	Automóvil Club de Chile
36	Hotel Araucano	5	Buses Varmontt	40	Parque Ecuador
37	Residencial Concepción	8	Tur Bus & Bus Chevalier	41	Cerro Caracol
42	Casa de Huéspedes	9	Buses Cruz del Sur	43	Ladeco
44	Hotel Alborada	10	Centro Italiano	44	LAN-Chile
45	Residencial Metro	11	Buses Tas Choapa	46	German Consulate
48	Casa Familiar González	12	Buses Igi Llaima	47	Argentine Consulate
50	Hotel El Dorado	13	Buses Biobío	49	Peruvian Consulate
53	Apart Hotel Concepción	19	CTC (Telephone)	51	Galería de Historia de Concepción
55	Hotel Cecil	20	Post Office	54	CONAF
		21	Sernatur (Tourist Office)	56	Buses Los Alces
		22	UK Consulate	57	Buses J Ewert
		26	Instituto Chileno-Alemán	58	Railway Station

Concepción

To Museo de Concepción

To Bus Terminal, Chillán & Santiago

0   150   300 m

Paicaví

Larenas

Ongolmo

Orompello

Tucapel

Castellón

Colo Colo

Aníbal Pinto

Rengo

Freire

Angol

Salas

Serrano

Avenida Arturo Prat

Río Biobío

Railway Bridge

Puente Viejo

To Coronel & Lota

Avenida Roosevelt

P A Cerda

O'Higgins

Los Carreras

Malpú

Las Heras

Cruz

M de Rozas

Bulnes

M Rodríguez

Cochrane

San Martín

Chacabuco

Avenida Lamas

Caupolicán

Lincoyán

Barros Arana

Esmeralda

San Pedro

CHILE

communications with Santiago. After independence, coal on the Península de Lebú encouraged an autonomous industrial tradition, and glass-blowing, lumbering and textiles industries emerged. The railroad arrived in 1872 and, when the Mapuche threat receded, bridging the Biobío gave the city a strategic role in further colonisation.

Since WW II, the major industrial project has been the steel plant at Huachipato, but wages and living standards are low. Coupled with activism at the Universidad de Concepción, these conditions fostered a highly politicised labour movement which strongly supported Salvador Allende.

Orientation & Information

On the north bank of the Biobío, Concepción is capital of the Eighth Region. Few old buildings have survived around the pleasantly landscaped Plaza Independencia – the utilitarian buildings are a response to earthquake risk. With the port of Talcahuano, the urban area has nearly half a million people.

Well-stocked Sernatur (☎ 22-7976), at Aníbal Pinto 460, is open daily from 8.30 am to 8 pm in summer; the rest of the year, it's weekdays only, from 8.30 am to 1 pm and 3 to 6.30 pm. For money exchange, try Inter-Santiago, at Caupolicán 521, Local 58.

Correos de Chile is at O'Higgins 799. CTC has offices at Colo Colo 487 and Barros Arana 673, Local 5, while ENTEL is at Caupolicán 567, Local A.

Things to See

On the grounds of the **Barrio Universitario**, on the corner of Chacabuco and Larenas, the highlight of the **Casa del Arte** (art museum) is *La Presencia de América Latina*, a mural by Mexican artist Jorge González Camarena.

On the edge of Parque Ecuador, the very fine **Galería de Historia de Concepción** features vivid dioramas of local and regional history. Subjects include Mapuche subsistence activities, battles with the Spaniards (note Mapuche tactics), literary figure Alonso de Ercilla, the 1939 earthquake and a finely detailed model of a local factory. It's

open daily, except Mondays, from 10 am to 1 pm and 2 to 7 pm; admission is free.

Places to Stay

North of the centre, *Hospedaje María Inés Jarpa* (☎ 22-6238), Maipú 1757, is a bargain at US$4 a single (US$9 with three meals), but call ahead because of its limited space and popularity with students. The basic *Casa de Huéspedes*, at Rengo 855, charges US$5, with hot water, laundry and kitchen.

Residencial Metro, Barros Arana 464, has rooms for US$7 per person; *Residencial O'Higgins*, O'Higgins 457, includes breakfast for the same price. *Residencial Colo Colo*, Colo Colo 743, is very fine and friendly at US$11 per person.

Places to Eat

Filling the entire block bounded by Caupolicán, Maipú, Rengo and Freire, the Mercado Central has many excellent eateries, though aggressive waiters literally try to drag customers into some venues. Try pastel de choclo, a meal in itself.

Pastelería Suiza, O'Higgins 780, has a fixed-price lunch for about US$2. The *Salón Inglés*, next door, is equally appealing. *El Naturista*, Barros Arana 342, serves vegetarian food; *El Novillo Loco*, Pasaje Portales 539, is for carnivores. The *Centro Español*, at Barros Arana 675, and the *Centro Italiano*, at Barros Arana 935, add European flavour. For a cheap cappuccino, try *Café Haití*, at Caupolicán 511, or *Café Caribe*, at Caupolicán 521.

Things to Buy

Look for woollens, basketry, ceramics, carvings and leather at the Mercado Central, La Gruta (Caupolicán 521, Local 64), Antumalal (Aníbal Pinto 450, Local 10) and Minga del Biobío (Barros Arana 1112).

Getting There & Away

Air Aeropuerto Carriel Sur is five km northwest of town. LAN-Chile (☎ 24-0025), Barros Arana 451, has at least two flights daily to Santiago (US$72), except on weekends (one flight daily). On Friday evenings, it also has a flight to Punta Arenas (US$191). Ladeco (☎ 24-3261), Barros Arana 401, flies to Santiago twice daily, except Sundays.

Bus Terminal Rodoviario (☎ 31-0896) is at Tegualda 860, on the outskirts of town. Many companies have downtown offices.

Tur Bus (☎ 22-2404), Tucapel 530, and Buses Lit (☎ 23-0722) have many buses to Santiago. Tas Choapa (☎ 23-0720), Barros Arana 1010, has excellent connections to northern Chile and to Argentina, along with Chevalier (☎ 31-0896), Tucapel 516. Sol del Pacífico also has frequent services to Santiago and Valparaíso.

Varmontt (☎ 23-0779), at Paicaví 427, Igi Llaima (☎ 31-2498), at Tucapel 432, and Cruz del Sur (☎ 31-4372), at Barros Arana 935, Local 9, as well as Tur Bus and Lit, go to Temuco and Puerto Montt. Biobío (☎ 24-2751), Aníbal Pinto 822, has frequent service to Temuco; Igi Llaima has buses to Los Angeles. For services to Coronel and the Costa del Carbón, try Los Alces (☎ 22-1712), at Prat 699, or Ewert (☎ 22-2586), at Prat 535.

Typical fares include Chillán or Los Angeles US$2, Angol US$3, Talca US$4, Temuco US$5, Santiago US$10, Valparaíso US$12 and Puerto Montt US$12.

Train The station (☎ 22-7777) is on Avenida Prat, at the foot of Barros Arana, but there's a ticket office (☎ 22-5286) at Pinto 450, Local 16. There are four trains daily to Santiago (US$11, nine hours).

Getting Around
LAN-Chile and Ladeco run airport vans (US$2.50) from Hotel El Araucano and Hotel Alborada.

AROUND CONCEPCIÓN
La Costa del Carbón
The Coast of Coal beyond the Biobío draws

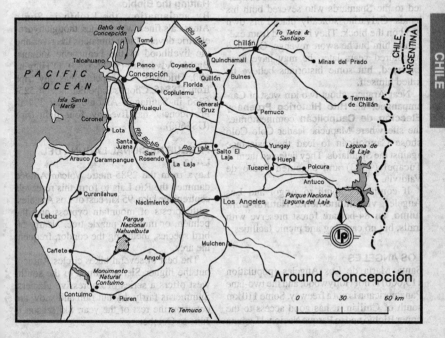

Around Concepción

crowds to beaches near Coronel (which reeks of fishmeal), Lota, Arauco and the Península de Lebú. The best day trip is to Lota's **Parque Isidora Cousiño**, designed by an English landscape architect.

At ENACAR's undersea mine, you can put on a hard hat, ride in a mine cart, and chip off a hunk of coal with a pneumatic drill. These tours (US$17) take place at 10.50 and 3 pm every day, all year. Contact the Parque Isidora Cousiño (☎ 24-9039), Carlos Cousiño 199 in Lota Alto, 8 am to 6 pm on weekdays.

Ruta de la Araucana

Local and regional authorities have begun to erect historical markers honouring soldier-poet Alonso de Ercilla y Zuñiga's epic tale *La Araucana*, which honoured the Mapuche resistance. At Escuadrón, 22 km south of Concepción, the **Hito Histórico Galvarino** marks the battle of Lagunillas (1557), where the Mapuche *toqui* (chief) Galvarino submitted to the Spaniards who severed both his hands. Galvarino stoically placed his own head on the block. They refrained from executing him but he swore revenge. On being recaptured years later, he may have been executed, but some historians believe he killed himself.

Near Arauco, about two km west of Carampangue, the **Hito Histórico Prueba y Elección de Caupolicán** commemorates the site where Mapuche leader Colo Colo chose Caupolicán to lead the resistance against the Spaniards. They defeated them at Tucapel (1553) and executed Pedro de Valdivia.

If continuing south to Angol and Los Angeles, visit **Monumento Natural Contulmo**, an 84-hectare forest preserve with trails, but no camping and picnic facilities.

LOS ANGELES

Santa María de Los Angeles (population 115,000) is not Hollywood, and the two-lane Panamericana is not a freeway. Some 110 km south of Chillán, it has good access to the upper Biobío and to Parque Nacional Laguna del Laja. the Plaza de Armas has an information kiosk.

True budget accommodation is scarce, but the very central *Hotel Mazzola* (☎ 32-1643), Lautaro 579, has singles/doubles for US$19/25. For parrilla, the best choice is *El Arriero*, Colo Colo 235, but the *Centro Español*, at Colón 482, has more varied fare. A Lonely Planet correspondent praised the Italian food at *Di Leone*, Colón 285.

Getting There & Away

Bus The terminal is at Caupolicán and Valdivia, but most north-south buses leave from the junction of Avenida Alemania and the Panamericana. There are many buses to Concepción and to Angol (US$1.50), gateway to Parque Nacional Nahuelbuta.

Train On Caupolicán, the station is three long blocks west of the plaza.

AROUND LOS ANGELES
Rafting the Biobío

By acclamation, the Biobío is South America's finest white water, though hydroelectric development threatens the river and the livelihood of the Pehuenche Indians. Biobío Adventure (☎ 22-5745), O'Higgins 680, Oficina 9, Concepción, has day trips from US$45. Chonos Expediciones (☎ 525-6256 in Santiago), Antonio Bellet 304 in Providencia, has five-day, four-night trips (US$600).

PARQUE NACIONAL LAGUNA DEL LAJA

Lava from the 2985-metre Volcán Antuco dammed the Río Laja to form this reserve's centrepiece lake, 95 km east of Los Angeles, with forests of mountain cypress and the pehuén, or monkey puzzle tree. Nearly 50 bird species, including the condor, frequent the area.

The best of several hikes circles Antuco, but the higher Sierra Velluda to the southwest offers a series of impressive glaciers. Summer is fairly dry but rain and snow are common the rest of the year. Ski season is June to October.

Places to Stay & Eat

Near the park entrance, at km 90, *Cabañas y Camping Lagunillas* (☎ 32-3606), Caupolicán 332 in Los Angeles, charges US$10 per site plus US$1 per person.

In winter, the Antuco lodge has bunks (US$9) for 50 skiers, a restaurant, and rents equipment on site. For reservations, contact DIGEDER (☎ 22-9054), at O'Higgins 740, Oficina 23, in Concepción. Try also Los Angeles' *Refugio Municipal* (☎ 32-2333 in Los Angeles).

Getting There & Away

From Los Angeles, Buses Antuco runs half a dozen buses per day to the village of Abanico (1½ hours), but walking the 11 km to CONAF's Chacay visitors' centre takes several hours more. Hitching is possible.

Norte Grande

The Norte Grande's main features are the Pacific Ocean, the desolate Atacama desert, and the Andean altiplano and high peaks. Many Indians remain, but earlier populations left huge stylised geoglyphs of humans and animals on the dry hillsides.

The Atacama is arid, but El Niño events (sea surface circulation changes in the western Pacific, occurring every seven years or so) can bring phenomenal downpours. Coastal *camanchaca* (fog) supports scattered *lomas* vegetation, and rainfall and vegetation increase with elevation and distance from the sea. In the precordillera (foothills), Aymara farmers cultivate potatoes up to 4000 metres, while herders pasture llamas and alpacas on the higher *puna*.

After the War of the Pacific, Chile annexed these copper and nitrate-rich lands from Peru and Bolivia; most Atacama cities owe their existence to minerals. Nitrate *oficinas* like Humberstone flourished in the early 20th century, then withered or died when petroleum-based fertilisers superseded mineral nitrates, and are now ghost towns. Copper continues to be mined at open-pit mines like Chuquicamata, the world's largest.

Militant trade unions first developed in this area, introducing a new force into Chilean politics.

ARICA

A 19th-century visitor called Arica 'one bleak, comfortless, miserable, sandy waste', but in colonial times it was an export point for silver from Potosí. Where Chile and Peru battled in the War of the Pacific, tourists now lounge on the beach, and Indians sell handicrafts, vegetables and trinkets. Industrialisation failed in the 1960s, but international trade and a duty-free zone (Zona Franca) caused a dramatic increase in the population. About half of Bolivia's exports pass through Arica's port.

Orientation

At the foot of El Morro, a dramatic headland, the city centre is a slightly irregular grid. The Peruvian border is 20 km north.

Information

Tourist Office Sernatur (☎ 23-2101), at Prat 305 (2nd floor), has city maps and abundant brochures on the entire country. It's open on weekdays from 8.30 am to 1 pm and 3 to 6.30 pm, and on Saturdays from 8.30 am to 1 pm. A municipal kiosk on 21 de Mayo near Colón is open late into the evening.

Money Cambios on 21 de Mayo change US cash and travellers' cheques plus Peruvian, Bolivian and Argentine currency. They close on Sundays, so try the street changers at 21 de Mayo and Colón. Get pesos here if proceeding to Calama, where exchange is difficult.

Post & Telecommunications Correos de Chile is at Prat 305. ENTEL is at Baquedano 388, CTC telephone offices are at Colón 476 (no international collect calls at the latter). The alcove outside Sernatur has overseas direct lines but it's accessible only during regular business hours.

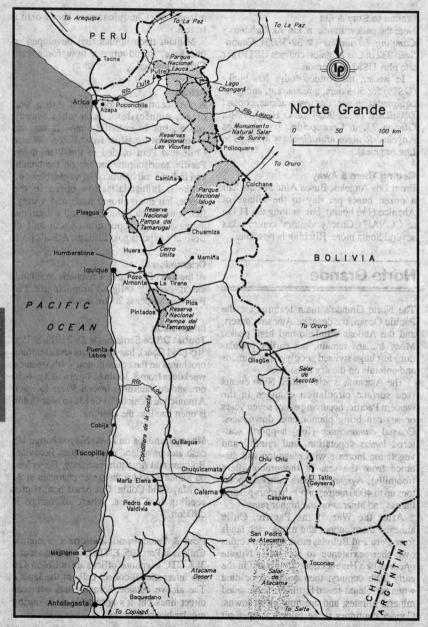

Norte Grande

0   50   100 km

Consulates Peru has a consulate (☎ 23-1020) at San Martín 220, open on weekdays from 9 am to 2 pm. The Bolivian Consulate (☎ 23-1030), 21 de Mayo 575, is open on weekdays from 9 am to 1 pm.

Visa Extensions For visa matters, see the Departamento de Extranjería (☎ 23-1397) at 7 de Junio 188, 3rd floor.

Emergency Hospital Dr Juan Noé (☎ 23-1331) is at 18 de Septiembre 1000.

Things to See

Take the footpath from the top of Calle Colón for exceptional views from **El Morro de Arica**, site of a crucial battle in the War of the Pacific. Alejandro Gustavo Eiffel designed the **Iglesia San Marcos de Arica** (1875), on Plaza Colón. **Pasaje Bolognesi**, a narrow passage between Sotomayor and 21 de Mayo, has a lively artisans' market in the evenings.

Beaches

The finest beaches are along Avenida Comandante San Martín, south of town, where the Pacific is warm enough for swimming.

Places to Stay

Youth Hostel In 1992, there was an inexpensive *Albergue Juvenil* (☎ 22-2943) at Las Acacias 2124.

Hotels & Residenciales Many lower-end places are cramped and some lack hot water. *Residencial Sur* (☎ 25-2457), Maipú 516, is basic and very drab but has hot water and clean sheets. It is US$4 per person. Comparable *Residencial Muñoz*, Patricio Lynch 565, is rundown but tolerable.

Residencial Madrid (☎ 23-1479), at Baquedano 685, has singles/doubles for US$5/9 but is sometimes noisy and the manager can be brusque. *Residencial Chungará* (☎ 23-1677), Patricio Lynch 675, is probably the pick of the category – bright, friendly and quiet (except for rooms nearest the TV), for US$7 per person.

Excellent value is *Hotel Lynch* (☎ 23-1581), Patricio Lynch 589, where the simple and clean rooms with shared bath start at US$11/17.

Places to Eat

Numerous eateries line 21 de Mayo, 18 de Septiembre, Maipú, Bolognesi and Colón. Foreign travellers congregate at *21*, 21 de Mayo 201, which serves snacks, coffee and excellent lager beer. For breakfast, try sandwiches and licuados at *Buen Gusto No 2*, Baquedano 559. *Restaurant Casino La Bomba*, inside the fire station at Colón 357, is an Arica institution for inexpensive midday meals and attentive service.

For seafood, there's *El Rey del Marisco*, at Colón and Maipú, 2nd floor. *El Arriero*, 21 de Mayo 385, is a fine parrilla with pleasant atmosphere and friendly service.

Getting There & Away

Air Aeropuerto Chacalluta (☎ 22- 2831) is 18 km north of Arica.

Ladeco (☎ 25-2021), 21 de Mayo 443, and LAN-Chile (☎ 224738), 7 de Junio 148, have daily flights to Santiago (US$180, ask about discounts) and intermediates. Sit on the left side southbound or the right side northbound for awesome views of the desert and the Andes. LAB (☎ 25-1919), Patricio Lynch 298, has three flights weekly to La Paz.

Bus & Colectivo – domestic All major companies have offices at the bus terminal (☎ 24-1390), Diego Portales 948. Frequent buses go to Iquique (US$5, four hours); taxi colectivos charge about US$8. Other typical southbound fares are Calama US$9, Antofagasta US$13, Viña del Mar or Valparaíso about US$30, and Santiago US$32.

For destinations on the altiplano, including Parinacota (US$6), Visviri (US$7.50) and Charaña, contact Buses Martínez (☎ 23-2265), Pedro Montt 620, or Transporte Humire (☎ 23-1891), Pedro Montt 662.

Buses La Paloma (☎ 22-2710), Germán Riesco 2071, goes to Socoroma (US$2), Putre (US$3) and Belén five times weekly.

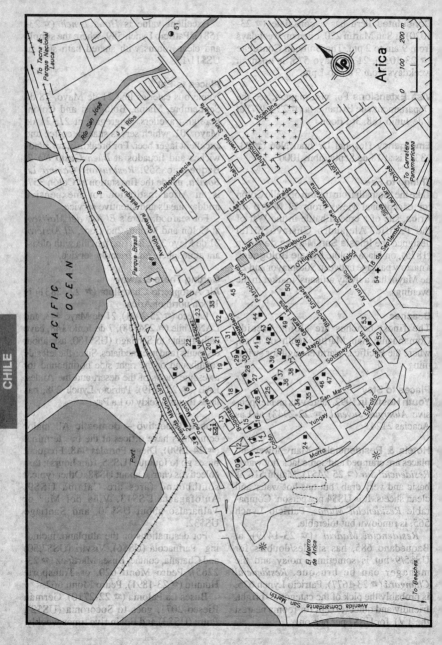

Arica

To Tacna &
Parque Nacional
Lauca

To Carretera
Panamericana

PACIFIC
OCEAN

Parque Brasil

Port

El Morro
de Arica

To Beaches

Avenida Comandante San Martín

To Beaches

CHILE

0   100   200 m

■	PLACES TO STAY	47	Hotel Tacora	4	Sernatur (Tourist
		49	Residencial Sur		Office), Post Office
5	Residencial Las	50	Residencial El Cobre		& Telex-Chile
	Parinas	53	Hostal Jardín del Sol	7	Casino
6	Residencial Durán			8	Hertz Rent-a-Car
8	Hotel El Paso	▼	PLACES TO EAT	9	University of Chile
16	Hotel Plaza Colón			10	LAN-Chile
20	Residencial Patricia	13	Restaurant Natura	11	Departamento de
22	Residencial Velásquez	17	Restaurant Casino La		Extranjería (Visas)
23	Residencial Chillán		Bomba	12	Plaza Colón
24	Hotel Savona	18	Restaurant El Arriero	14	Iglesia San Marcos de
25	Hotel San Marcos	19	El Rey del Marisco		Arica
26	King Hotel	21	Café Bavaria	15	CONAF
29	Hotel Aragón	27	Café 21	28	CTC (Telephone)
31	Residencial Madrid	30	Buen Gusto No 2	33	Colectivos to Tacna
32	Residencial Venecia	38	Chifa Chin Huang Tao	36	UK Consulate
34	Residencial Sotomayor			37	ENTEL (Telephone)
35	Hotel Diego de		OTHER	39	Ladeco
	Almagro			45	Automóvil Club de
40	Residencial 21	1	Railway Station (Arica-		Chile
41	Residencial La		Tacna)	46	Lloyd Aéreo Boliviano
	Blanquita	2	Railway Station (Arica-	48	Bolivian Consulate
42	Residencial Muñoz		La Paz)	51	Bus Terminal
43	Hotel Lynch	3	Plazoleta Estación	52	Peruvian Consulate
44	Residencial Chungará			54	Hospital

Bus Lluta serves Poconchile from the corner of Chacabuco and Vicuña Mackenna four times daily; if hitching to Lauca National Park, take this bus and proceed from the Carabineros checkpoint.

Bus & Colectivo – international
Adsubliata (☎ 24-1972) goes often to Tacna in Peru (US$2). Taxi colectivos to Tacna (US$3.50, one hour) leave from Chacabuco between Baquedano and Colón.

Buses Litoral (☎ 25-1267), Chacabuco 454, run buses from Arica to La Paz (US$20, 18 hours, weather permitting), on Tuesdays and Fridays at 1 am.

Tramaca (☎ 24-1198) makes connections in Calama with buses from Antofagasta to Salta, Argentina. Comfortable, heavily booked Géminis buses (☎ 24-1647) go to La Paz on Wednesdays (US$30) and to Salta, weekly (US$45, 28 hours), via Calama (summer only).

Train The Ferrocarril Arica-Tacna (☎ 23-

1115), Máximo Lira 889, departs around noon and 6 pm (1½ hours, US$1.75).

The Ferrocarril Arica-La Paz (☎ 23-1786) is opposite the Plazoleta Estación, at 21 de Mayo 51. The new *El Dorado de los Andes* service leaves on Mondays and Thursdays at 8 am. A *coche salón* (a reclining seat) is US$50 and a *coche dormitorio* (a sleeper) is US$60.

The Ferrobus Arica-La Paz (☎ 23-2844) operates weekly (US$49 in US currency only, 11 hours).

Getting Around
To/From the Airport Both LAN-Chile and Ladeco operate buses to Aeropuerto Chacalluta (☎ 222831), 18 km north of Arica.

Bus The bus terminal can be quickly reached by Boliviano taxi colectivo from 18 de Septiembre.Slow local buses and faster taxi colectivos connect the centre and the bus terminal. Only taxi colectivos serve the

CHILE

Azapa valley (US$1), 7 am to 10 pm daily, from the corner of Maipú and Patricio Lynch.

Car The main agencies are Hertz (☎ 23-1487), at General Velásquez 1109, American (☎ 25-2234), at General Lagos 559, and Viva (☎ 25-1121), at 21 de Mayo 821.

AROUND ARICA
Museo Arqueológico San Miguel de Azapa
Twelve km from Arica, this archaeological museum has elaborate displays on regional cultures from the 7th century BC to the Spanish invasion. Ask about nearby geoglyphs. The museum is open Tuesday to Friday from 10 am to 6 pm, and on Saturdays from 11 am to 6 pm. The museum can be reached by taxi colectivo.

The Lluta Geoglyphs
Ten km north of Arica, paved Ruta 11 leads up the Lluta valley to Poconchile. A short distance inland, a series of hillside geoglyphs depicting llamas recalls pre-Columbian pack trains to Tiahuanaco.

Poconchile
Poconchile's 17th-century **Iglesia de San Gerónimo**, restored earlier this century, is one of Chile's oldest churches.

Pukará de Copaquilla
As Ruta 11 zigzags up the desolate mountainside above the Lluta valley, it passes many 'candle-holder' cacti, which absorb moisture from the camanchaca. Tours to Parque Nacional Lauca stop briefly at the 12th-century **Pukará de Copaquilla**, built to protect farmlands in the canyon below – notice the abandoned terraces, evidence of a much larger pre-Columbian population.

PUTRE
Putre was a 16th-century *reducción* (a Spanish settlement established to control the Indians). It is 3500 metres high and 150 km from Arica. Many buildings retain colonial features, most notably the restored adobe **Iglesia de Putre** (1670). Local farmers raise alfalfa for llamas, sheep and cattle on ancient stone-faced terraces. In November 1994, Putre will experience a six-minute total solar eclipse.

Restaurant Oasis, at Cochrane and O'Higgins, offers basic lodgings for US$3, and good plain meals. Opposite the army camp, CONAF's comfortable refugio charges US$8. Buses La Paloma serves Putre five times weekly from Arica but buses to Lauca pass by the turn-off to Putre. Mining trucks from *Hostería Las Vicuñas* may take you to the park's Las Cuevas entrance.

PARQUE NACIONAL LAUCA
Parque Nacional Lauca is a 138,000-hectare altiplano biosphere reserve with vicuña, vizcacha and 150 species of birds, plus cultural and archaeological landmarks. The Pallachata volcanos behind sprawling Lago Chungará are dormant, but nearby Volcán Guallatire smokes ominously.

Lauca is 160 km north-east of Arica, between 3000 and 6300 metres above sea level; those who suffer from altitude sickness should try the herbal tea remedy *chachacoma*. Wear sunblock for the brutal tropical rays, but it can also snow during *invierno boliviano* (Bolivian winter, the summer rainy season).

Flocks of vicuña graze the verdant *bofedales* (boglands) and lower mountain slopes, along with domestic llamas and alpacas. Note the ground-hugging *llareta*, a bright green shrub with a deceptive cushion-like appearance – the Aymara need a pick or mattock to crack open dead plants for fuel.

Things to See & Do
The **Las Cuevas** entrance is an excellent place to photograph vicuñas, which have increased from barely 1000 in the early 1970s to over 27,000 today. Also have a soak in the rustic thermal baths.

Domestic stock graze the **Ciénegas de Parinacota** between the hamlets of Chucuyo and Parinacota, and wildlife and cultural relics are abundant – see Chucuyo's colonial chapel. *Guallatas* (Andean geese) and ducks drift on the Río Lauca and nest on shore, while the chinchilla-like vizcacha peeks out from rockeries. **Parinacota**, an Aymara village five km off the highway, has a fascinating 17th-century church, with strange interior murals. Alpaca woollens are available here.

Over 4500 metres above sea level and 28 km from Las Cuevas, shallow **Lago Chungará** was formed when lava from the 6350-metre Volcán Parinacota dammed the snowmelt stream. Birds include flamingos, giant coots and Andean gulls. Arica's demand for hydroelectricity and the Azapa valley's thirst have created an intricate system of pumps and canals which may compromise Chungará's ecological integrity.

Places to Stay & Eat

In a pinch, the refugio at Las Cuevas may offer a bed. In Chucuyo, Matilde and Máximo Morales usually have a spare bed at a very reasonable price, and Matilde will prepare alpaca steaks and other simple meals for about US$1; there are two other cheap restaurants. Buy most supplies in Arica.

In Parinacota, CONAF charges US$8 for beds in a large but sparsely furnished refugio with infrequent hot water; bring a sleeping bag. Tent sites cost US$4 here and at Chungará, which has picnic tables, some shelter and *very* cold nights.

Getting There & Away

The park straddles the Arica-La Paz highway, which will be paved to the Bolivian border by 1995. For buses, see the Arica section.

Many Arica travel agencies offer tours (about US$20), leaving around 7.30 am and returning about 8.30 pm. Among them are Turismo Payachatas (☎ 25-1514), at Prat 484, Vicuña Tour (☎ 22-2971), in the Galería El Morro, at 18 de Septiembre 399, Turismo Jurasi (☎ 25-1696), at Bolognesi 360, and Inti Tour (☎ 25-1354), at Prat 336.

Tours are a good introduction, but try to arrange a longer stay – a rental car lets you visit more remote areas like Guallatire, Caquena and Salar de Surire (only with a high-clearance vehicle, since it involves fording the river). Carry extra fuel.

IQUIQUE

Iquique was a collection of shanties until the 19th-century mining boom, when nitrate barons built mansions and authorities piped in water from the Andes. A Plaza de Armas with a Victorian clocktower and a theatre with corinthian columns was built.

Iquique's port now ships more fishmeal than any other in the world, while the modern duty-free shopping centre, *Zona Franca*, has added prosperity. The centre's ramshackle wooden houses, sailors' bars and street life preserve a 19th-century atmosphere.

Orientation

At the base of the coast range, Iquique (population 140,000) is 1853 km north of Santiago and 315 km from Arica. Avenida Baquedano, which runs north to south, is the main thoroughfare. Calle Tarapacá, which runs from Plaza Prat east to Plaza Condell, is the secondary centre of activity.

Information

Tourist Office Sernatur (☎ 411523) is at Aníbal Pinto 436, with a branch at the Zona Franca. Open weekdays 8 am to 1 pm and 2.30 to 6.15 pm, it provides a free leaflet with information about what's on in Iquique.

Money Fincard, Serrano 372, is the only downtown cambio, but there's another at the Zona Franca.

Post & Telecommunications Correos de Chile is at Bolívar 458. CTC offices are at Ramírez 587 and at the Zona Franca, Módulo 212, 2nd level. ENTEL is at Gorostiaga 287.

Consulates The Bolivian Consulate (☎ 42-1777) is at Latorre 399, Oficina 41-A. The Peruvian Consulate (☎ 43-1116) is at Los Rieles 131.

Emergency The Hospital Regional Doctor

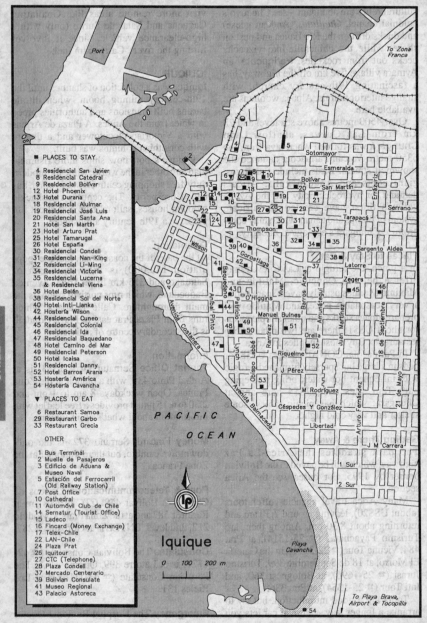

PLACES TO STAY

4 Residencial San Javier
8 Residencial Catedral
9 Residencial Bolívar
12 Hotel Phoenix
13 Hotel Durana
18 Residencial Alulmar
19 Residencial José Luis
20 Residencial Santa Ana
21 Hotel San Martín
23 Hotel Arturo Prat
25 Hotel Tamarugal
26 Hotel España
30 Residencial Condell
31 Residencial Nan-King
32 Residencial Li-Ming
34 Residencial Victoria
35 Residencial Lucerna
   & Residencial Viena
36 Hotel Belén
38 Residencial Sol del Norte
42 Hotel Inti-Llanka
44 Residencial Cuneo
45 Residencial Colonial
46 Residencial Ida
47 Residencial Baquedano
48 Hotel Camino del Mar
49 Residencial Peterson
50 Hotel Icaisa
51 Residencial Danny
52 Hotel Barros Arana
53 Hostería América
54 Hostería Cavancha

PLACES TO EAT

6 Restaurant Samoa
29 Restaurant Garbo
33 Restaurant Grecia

OTHER

1 Bus Terminal
2 Muelle de Pasajeros
3 Edificio de Aduana &
  Museo Naval
5 Estación del Ferrocarril
  (Old Railway Station)
7 Post Office
10 Cathedral
11 Automóvil Club de Chile
14 Sernatur (Tourist Office)
15 Ladeco
16 Fincard (Money Exchange)
17 Telex-Chile
22 LAN-Chile
24 Plaza Prat
26 Iquitour
27 CTC (Telephone)
28 Plaza Condell
37 Mercado Centerario
39 Bolivian Consulate
41 Museo Regional
43 Palacio Astoreca

PACIFIC OCEAN

Iquique

0   100   200 m

Port

To Zona Franca

Sotomayor
Esmeralda
Bolívar
San Martín
Tarapacá
Sargento Aldea
Latorre
Zegers
Thompson
Gorostiaga
O'Higgins
Manuel Bulnes
Orella
Riquelme
J J Pérez
M Rodríguez
Céspedes Y González
Libertad
J M Carrera
1 Sur
2 Sur

Wilson
Baquedano
Aníbal Pinto
Patricio Lynch
Ramírez
Vivar
Barros Arana
Arnúñategui
Juan Martínez
18 de Septiembre
Arturo Fernández
21 de Mayo

Avenida Costanera
Avenida Balmaceda

Serrano
Errázuriz

Playa Cavancha

To Playa Brava,
Airport & Tocopilla

Torres (☎ 42-2370) is on the corner of Serrano and Avenida Héroes de la Concepción.

Things to See
Architectural landmarks on or near Plaza Prat include the 1877 **Torre Reloj** (clocktower), the neoclassical **Teatro Municipal** and the Moorish **Centro Español** (1904). Calle Baquedano has several Georgian-style buildings.

The **Museo Naval** occupies the 1871 **Edificio de Aduana**, which is on Esmeralda between Aníbal Pinto and Baquedano. Just west of the Aduana, harbour tours leave from the **Muelle de Pasajeros** (passenger jetty), built in 1901. At Sotomayor and Vivar, the **Estación del Ferrocarril** (train station) once served the nitrate oficinas.

Once a courthouse, the **Museo Regional** features many Neolithic artefacts, a mock altiplano village, Aymara crafts, photos of Iquique's early days and a detailed model of Oficina Peña Chica, near Humberstone. At Baquedano 951, it's open on weekdays from 9 am to 1 pm and 3 to 7 pm, and on Saturdays from 10 am to 1 pm. Admission is US$0.45.

Zona Franca
Most Chileans visit Iquique, and many have moved here because of this sprawling shopping centre for imported goods. All of the Tarapacá region is a duty-free zone, and the *Zofri* (Zone Franca de Iquique) has given Iquique the country's lowest unemployment rate.

To see or join in the feeding frenzy, take any northbound taxi colectivo from the centre on weekdays from 9.30 am to 1 pm and 4.30 to 9 pm, or on Saturdays from 9.30 am to 1 pm only.

Beaches
Playa Cavancha, at Balmaceda and Amunátegui, is Iquique's most popular beach; farther south, along Avenida 11 de Septiembre, the Playa Brava is rough for swimming but fine for sunbathing. South of Iquique, public transport does not reach the many fine and less crowded beaches, despite

a superb paved highway, but renting a car is worth considering.

Places to Stay
There's a cluster of seedy residenciales on Amunátegui between Sargento Aldea and Thompson, all charging about US$4 per person. *Residencial Sol del Norte*, Juan Martínez 852, charges US$5 per person, but lacks hot water. One reader enjoyed a nameless hospedaje at Gorostiaga 451 (also without hot water). A step up is *Residencial José Luis*, San Martín 601, which gets short-stay trade. Singles are US$7, doubles US$10 with private bath; all rooms have large, comfortable double beds.

Probably the best value is *Residencial Catedral*, Obispo Labbé 233, with singles/doubles for US$9/17 with shared bath. For US$8 a single, rambling *Residencial Bolívar*, around the corner at Bolívar 478, is less obviously appealing but perhaps friendlier. One reader found *Residencial Condell*, Thompson 684, most hospitable.

Places to Eat
At the Mercado Centenario (Central Market), on Barros Arana between Sargento Aldea and Latorre, several upstairs restaurants have excellent seafood at fair prices. Another good choice is *Restaurant Grecia*, Thomson 865. A reader has praised *Restaurant Samoa*, Bolívar 396, for a fine fixed-price lunch.

The *Circolo Italiano*, Tarapacá 477, specialises in pasta. Iquique's trendiest snack bar is *Restaurant Garbo*, on Tarapacá between Barros Arana and Vivar. For a splurge, try the ornate *Club Español*, on Plaza Prat, with its Moorish interior and artwork.

Getting There & Away
Air Aeropuerto Diego Aracena is 30 km south of the city centre. Ladeco has daily flights to Antofagasta and Santiago. LAN-Chile has eight flights weekly to Santiago, four stop in Antofagasta. Ladeco (☎ 41-2956) is at Prat and Serrano, LAN (☎ 41-2540) at Pinto 444.

CHILE

Bus The terminal is at the north end of Patricio Lynch but most companies have offices near the Mercado Centenario.

Buses – long distance To Arica, try Buses Carmelita, at Barros Arana 841, Cuevas y González, at Sargento Aldea 850, or Fénix Pullman Norte, at Pinto 531.

Taxi colectivos (US$8) include Tamarugal, at Sargento Aldea 783, Turis Auto, at Serrano 724, or Turis Taxi, at Barros Arana 897-A.

To Calama and Antofagasta, try Tramaca, at Sargento Aldea 988, Kenny Bus, at Latorre 944, Flota Barrios, at Sargento Aldea 987, or Géminis, at Obispo Labbé 187.

For Santiago, companies include Carmelita, Flota Barrios, Fénix amd Buses Evans, at Vivar 955, and Chile Bus, at Latorre 773. Chile Bus and Buses Zambrano, Sargento Aldea 742, go to Viña del Mar and Valparaíso.

Buses – regional Buses San Andrés, Sargento Aldea 798, go daily to Pica, Arica and Santiago. Buses Lirima, at Baquedano 823, and Buses Julita Santa Rosa, at Latorre 973, go to Pica and Mamiña.

Other companies to Mamiña include Flonatur, at Sargento Aldea 790, Transportes Rojas, at Sargento Aldea 783, and Turismo Mamiña, at Latorre 779.

Taxitur, Sargento Aldea 791, has taxi colectivos to Mamiña and Pica.

Buses – international At 1 am on Saturdays, Géminis go to Oruro (US$26) and La Paz, Bolivia (US$29, 24 hours). On Tuesdays in summer, they go to Salta, Argentina, via Calama (US$46).

Kenny Bus serves the altiplano border town of Colchane (US$6) on Tuesdays and Fridays at 10 pm.

Getting Around

To/From the Airport Ladeco or LAN-Chile taxi colectivos or minibuses (US$4) go to Aeropuerto Diego Aracena.

Car Try Hertz (☎ 42-6316), at Souper 650, or Rent's Procar (☎ 42-4607), at Serrano 796.

AROUND IQUIQUE

Unfortunately, the scenic coast highway to Tocopilla lacks regular public transport, but the paved surface will soon reach the Río Loa. On the steeper sections south of the Loa, the road tends to resemble a washboard surface but is always passable. It is also vulnerable to slides.

Several readers have complained of poor service by Iquitour (☎ 42-2009), at Tarapacá 465-B in Iquique, which offers tours of the interior. Turismo Lirima (☎ 42-2049), Baquedano 823, may be more dependable.

Humberstone & Santa Laura

In this eerie nitrate ghost town, 45 km from Iquique, nearly all the original buildings, such as the market and the theatre, are still standing; some are being restored. For recreation, there were tennis and basketball courts, and an enormous swimming pool. At the west end are the power plant and the railway to the older Oficina Santa Laura.

Any bus from Iquique will drop you at the ruins, where it is easy to catch a lift or bus back. Take food, water and your camera.

El Gigante de Atacama

The 86-metre, pre-Columbian Giant of the Atacama, 14 km east of Huara on the slopes of Cerro Unita, is best seen from a distance on the desert pampa; avoid climbing the hill and damaging the figure. The best way to visit the site is to hire a car or taxi.

Pintados

Over 400 geoglyphs of humans, llamas and geometric shapes blanket this coast range hillside, seven km west of the Panamericana between Iquique and Antofagasta, nearly opposite the turn-off to Pica. It's actually a derelict railyard, a dry and dusty but easy walk from the highway – figure about 1½ hours each way, perhaps with a detour to avoid the junkyard dogs. Remember to take food and water.

La Tirana

In mid-July, up to 30,000 dancing pilgrims invade La Tirana (population 250), 72 km from Iquique, to worship the Virgin of Carmen. The **Santuario de La Tirana** is a broad plaza with one of Chile's oddest churches, but despite several restaurants, there are no hotels or residenciales – pilgrims camp in the open spaces to the east. The **Museo del Salitre** exhibits a haphazard assortment of artefacts from nitrate oficinas.

RESERVA NACIONAL PAMPA DEL TAMARUGAL

The dense groves lining the Panamericana south of Pozo Almonte are not a natural forest, but they are a native species – the tamarugo covered thousands of sq km until woodcutting for the mines nearly destroyed it.

CONAF's 108,000-hectare reserve has restored much of this forest, which flourishes in highly saline soils by reaching deep for groundwater. The visitors' centre, 24 km south of Pozo Almonte, has fine displays on local ecology. The guesthouse charges US$8 for a single; across the road is a campground (US$4 for shaded sites with tables and benches).

MAMIÑA

Mamiña, 73 km east of Pozo Almonte, has been a popular hot springs resort since the nitrate era, but is much older – the **Pukará del Cerro Inca** is a pre-Columbian fortress, while the **Iglesia de Nuestra Señora del Rosario** dates from 1632.

Residencial Sol de Ipla, on Calle Ipla, charges US$11 per person with shared bath, but there are several others – the historic nitrate-era *Hotel Refugio del Salitre* is worth a splurge. For transport, see the Iquique entry.

PICA

Diego de Almagro skirmished with Indians at Pica, another popular hot springs, 119 km south-east of Iquique on the road from La Tirana. In late colonial times, it was famous for wines and fruits, while in the 19th century, it supplied wheat, wine, figs, raisins and alfalfa to the oficinas.

Pica was so dependent on outside water that the Spaniards developed an elaborate delivery system of more than 15 km of tunnels. When Iquique boomed, the Tarapacá Water Company piped water to the coast, while Pica became a 'hill station' for the nitrate barons.

Places to Stay & Eat

Camping Miraflores, charging about US$3 per person, has been reported to be in disrepair. *Hostería O'Higgins* and *Hotel San Andrés* charge about US$6 per person. There are several cheap restaurants. For transport, see the previous Iquique section.

Antofagasta Region

Nitrates drew this region into the modern world but copper has supplanted them – Chuquicamata dominates the mining sector, but fishing and tourism are growing.

ANTOFAGASTA

Antofagasta (population 221,000), 1350 km north of Santiago and 700 km south of Arica, exports most of the Atacama's minerals, especially copper. Founded in 1870, it offered the easiest route to the interior and soon handled the highest tonnage of any South American Pacific port.

Freak floods in 1991 obliterated the southern access road to the Panamericana, but in general, the climate is always clear and dry, neither too hot nor too cold.

Orientation

The city centre's western boundary is the north-south Avenida Balmaceda, which eventually becomes Aníbal Pinto; to the south, it becomes Avenida Grecia. Within this central grid, bounded also by Bolívar and Ossa, streets run south-west to north-east. Plaza Colón is at the centre.

CHILE

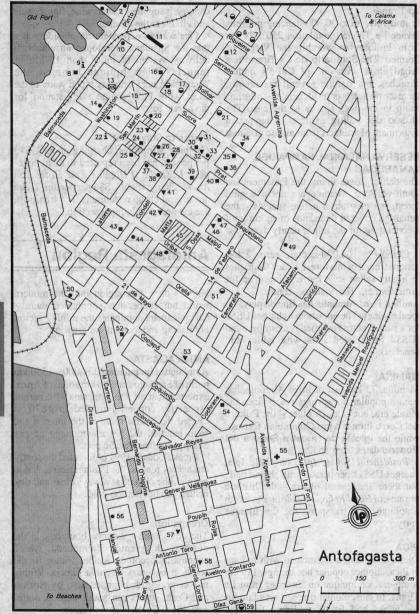

Antofagasta

0   150   300 m

To Calama
& Arica

To Beaches

■ PLACES TO STAY	32	Restaurant Apoquindo	18	Buses Fénix Pullman
	34	Casino de Bomberos		Norte
5 Residencial Libertad	41	Restaurant Shanghai	19	LAN-Chile
8 Hotel Antofagasta	42	Rincón Don Quijote	20	Fincard (Money
12 Hotel San Marcos	46	Restaurant Bavaria		Exchange)
16 Hotel San Martín	53	Restaurant Un Dragón	21	Buses Flota Barrios
24 Hotel Plaza	57	Chifa Chong Hua (1)	22	Sernatur (Tourist
25 Residencial Riojanita	58	Chifa Chong Hua (2)		Office)
30 Hotel Diego de			26	Cambio Inter-Santiago
Almagro		OTHER		(Money Exchange)
35 Hotel Rawaye			29	CTC (Telephone)
36 Residencial El Cobre	1	Muelle Salitrero	33	ENTEL (Telephone)
39 Hotel Astore	2	Terminal Pesquero	37	Banco del Estado
40 Residencial Paola		(Fish Market)	38	Teatro Pedro de la
43 Hotel San Antonio	3	SOQUIMICH		Barra
47 Hotel Rinconada	4	Buses Géminis	44	Automóvil Club
52 Hotel Brasil	6	Buses Rurales	45	Mercado Central
54 Hotel América	7	Buses Fichtur	48	CTC (Telephone)
	9	Tourist Kiosk	49	CONAF
▼ PLACES TO EAT	10	Museo Regional	50	Bolivian Consulate
	11	Railway Station	51	Buses Tramaca &
23 Café Caribe & Café	13	Post Office & Telex-		Buses Atalhualpa
Haití		Chile	55	Hospital Regional
27 Fiori di Gelatto	14	Ladeco	56	Argentine Consulate
28 Pizzería D'Alfredo	15	Plaza Colón	59	Bus Terminal
31 Restaurant El Arriero	17	Buses Flecha Dorada		

Information

Tourist Office Sernatur (☎ 26-4044), Baquedano 360, is open on weekdays from 8.30 am to 1 pm and 3 to 7.30 pm. An information kiosk near Hotel Antofagasta is open daily from 9.30 am to 1.30 pm and 4.30 to 7.30 pm. Sunday hours are 10.30 am to 2 pm.

Money Cambios include Fincard, Prat 427, (weekdays only) and Inter-Santiago, Latorre 2528, No 12.

Post & Telecommunications Correos de Chile is at Washington 2613. CTC offices are at Uribe 746 and Condell 2527, while ENTEL is at Prat 649.

Consulates The Argentine Consulate (☎ 22-2854), Manuel Verbal 1632, is open from 9 am to 2 pm on weekdays. The Bolivian Consulate (☎ 22-1403), Grecia 563, Oficina 23, keeps the same hours.

Emergency The Hospital Regional (☎ 26-9009) is at Avenida Argentina 1962.

Things to See

Like Iquique, Antofagasta is an architectural curiosity – the British community left a visible imprint through the **Torre Reloj** (clocktower) replica of Big Ben, on Plaza Colón, the **Barrio Histórico**, between the plaza and the old port, and the **Muelle Salitrero** (Nitrate Pier), at the foot of Bolívar.

On the corner of Balmaceda and Bolívar, the former **Gobernación Marítima** (Port Authority) houses the **Museo Regional** (Regional Museum). Across the street is the former **Aduana** (Customs House), moved from the town of Mejillones in 1888. Across Bolívar is the **Estación Ferrocarril** (1887), terminus of the La Paz railway.

Places to Stay

Residencial Paola, Prat 766, is friendly, clean and quiet for US$5 a single. Across the street, at Prat 749, *Residencial El Cobre* attracts budget travellers with clean but barren rooms for US$4. *Hotel Rawaye*, Sucre 762, is friendly, clean and excellent value at US$6/10 for a single/double with a common bath. Slightly dearer, at US$11/17 with shared bath, is the unusual *Hotel Tatio* (☎ 24-4761), Grecia 1000, built from reconditioned tour buses.

Places to Eat

The best value is the unpretentious *Terminal Pesquero*, at the old port, where simple stands peddle tasty fresh shellfish and masses of pelicans jam the pier waiting for scraps. Carnivores will enjoy *El Arriero*, at Condell 2644, a fine parrilla with excellent service. The *Casino de Bomberos*, Sucre 763, has good set lunches.

Popular *Apoquindo*, Prat 616, serves drinks, sweets and snacks. For snacks, coffee, superb ice cream and desserts, try *Fiori di Gelatto*, Latorre 250. *Café Caribe*, at Prat 486, and *Café Haiti*, at Prat 482, have quality caffeine.

Other recommended places include *Rincón Don Quijote*, at Maipú 642, *Casa Vecchia*, at O'Higgins 1456, and *La Papa Nostra*, at Medina 052. *Pizzería D'Alfredo*, Condell 2539, has many pizza varieties.

Getting There & Away

Air Aeropuerto Cerro Moreno is 25 km north of the Mejillones Peninsula.

Flight schedules resemble those to Iquique and Arica. LAN-Chile (☎ 26-5151) is at Washington 2552 and Ladeco (☎ 26-9170) is nearby at Washington 2589.

Bus The terminal is at Avenida Argentina 1155, at the south end of town, but most companies use more central offices.

Tramaca, Uribe 936, has frequent buses to Calama, plus daily service to Arica, Iquique, Santiago and intermediates; it also handles tickets for the Calama-Oruro (Bolivia) railway.

Atalhualpa, at the same address, crosses the Andes to Salta, Argentina on Saturdays

at 4 pm in summer (US$33). Géminis (☎ 26-3968), Latorre 3055, also goes to Salta.

Flota Barrios, Condell 2764, has daily buses going to most of the same destinations as Tramaca. Flecha Dorada, Latorre 2751, serves Calama, Santiago and Arica. Fénix Pullman Norte (☎ 22-5293), San Martín 2717, runs similar routes.

From the Buses Rurales terminal, at Riquelme 513, Fepstur and Chadday both go to Mejillones, while Chile Bus covers major stops between Arica and Santiago. Libac, at the main terminal, connects Antofagasta with Calama and Santiago. Three lines go to Tocopilla, including Buses Camus and Turis Norte, at the main terminal, and Incatur, at Maipú 554. Turis Norte sometimes takes the scenic coastal route to Iquique.

Typical fares are Calama US$4, Iquique US$10, Arica US$13 and Santiago US$24.

Getting Around

To/From the Airport Ladeco's airport bus goes to Aeropuerto Cerro Moreno, 25 km north of the Península de Mejillones, or you can share a taxi from the stand opposite LAN-Chile's city offices.

AROUND ANTOFAGASTA
La Portada

The Pacific has eroded a photogenic natural arch in La Portada, an offshore stack 16 km north of Antofagasta. Take colectivo No 20, which leaves from the corner of Latorre and Prat at 7.40, 9.40 and 11.40 am and at 1.40 and 3.40 pm.

Mejillones

Mejillones, a small beach resort 60 km north of Antofagasta, has reasonable accommodation at *Residencial Elizabeth*, Almirante Latorre 440. Fepstur and Chadday buses leave from the Buses Rurales terminal, at Riquelme 513, Antofagasta.

Cobija & Gatico

Only a few km apart, 130 km north of Antofagasta, Cobija and Gatico are ghost towns where a few families eke out a living by fishing and collecting seaweed. In the early 19th century, despite a precarious water supply, Cobija was a flourishing port which served Bolivia's altiplano mines. After an 1877 earthquake and tsunami, it declined rapidly; by 1907, it had only 35 inhabitants.

Fresh fish may be available, but everything else is scarce, except for camping among the atmospheric adobe walls.

Tocopilla

Tocopilla (population 22,000), 190 km north of Antofagasta, is an important port for the remaining nitrate oficinas of Pedro de Valdivia and María Elena, and the site of Codelco's thermoelectric plant for Chuquicamata. It is the last town before the coast highway to Iquique.

Cheap hotels include *Residencial Royal*, at 21 de Mayo 1988, and *Residencial Sonia*, at Washington 1329, each charging about US$4. The best restaurant is the *Club de la Unión*.

Turis Norte, 21 de Mayo 1348, runs buses to Antofagasta, and sometimes to Iquique. Hitching, if not utterly impossible, is difficult.

María Elena, Pedro de Valdivia & the Nitrate Ghost Towns

Near the junction of the Panamericana and the Tocopilla-Chuquicamata road, María Elena is one of the last functioning oficinas. Its street plan, patterned after the Union Jack, looks better on paper than in reality. For tours, contact the SOQUIMICH public relations office (☎ 63-2731).

Some Tramaca and Flota Barrios buses from Antofagasta to Calama stop here. There's no accommodation, but decent food is available at *Restaurante Yerco* and *Restaurante Club Social*.

Pedro de Valdivia, 40 km south, is also open to the public. Meals are available at the *Club Pedro de Valdivia*. Tramaca and Flota Barrios buses go to Antofagasta.

Dozens of ghost towns line both sides of the Baquedano-Calama road and the Panamericana north of the Tocopilla-Chuquicamata highway.

Baquedano

Between Antofagasta and Calama, Baquedano was a major rail junction where the *Longino* (Longitudinal Railway) met the Antofagasta-La Paz line. The **Museo Ferroviario** is an open-air rail museum, but an infrequent, agonisingly slow and indescribably filthy freight train still goes to the Argentine border at Socompa for truly intrepid and persistent travellers.

CALAMA

Calama (population 120,000), 220 km from Antofagasta and 2700 metres above sea level, is the gateway to Chuquicamata, the oases of San Pedro de Atacama and Toconao, and the eerie Tatio Geysers. It's also the terminus of the Calama-Oruro (Bolivia) railway.

Orientation

Plaza 23 de Marzo is the centre of Calama. On the north bank of the Río Loa, the town has sprawled, because labourers prefer it to higher, colder Chuquicamata, but its core is pedestrian-friendly.

Information

Tourist Office The municipal tourist office (☎ 21-2654, extension 60), Latorre 1689, is open on weekdays from 8.30 am to 1 pm and 3 to 6 pm.

Money It's a good idea to arrive with Chilean cash though recent reports praise a new cambio at Sotomayor 1818.

Post & Telecommunications Correos de Chile is at Vicuña Mackenna 2167. CTC has offices at Abaroa 1756, Abaroa 1987 and Vargas 1927, while ENTEL is at Hurtado de Mendoza 2139.

Bolivian Consulate The Bolivian Consulate (☎ 21-1976), Vicuña Mackenna 2020, is open on weekdays from 9.30 am to 12.30 pm and 4.30 to 6.30 pm.

Emergency Calama's hospital (☎ 21-2347)

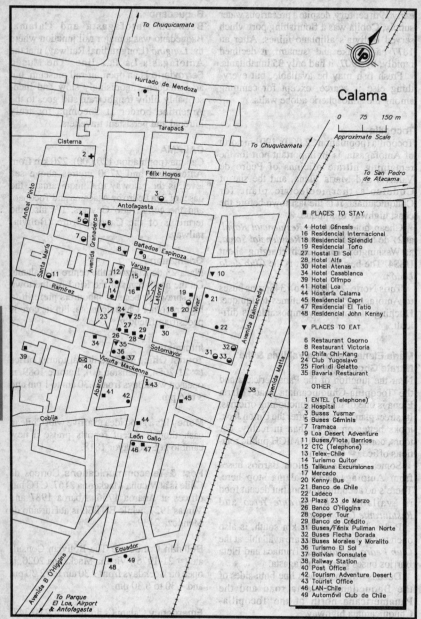

Calama

0   75   150 m

Approximate Scale

To Chuquicamata

To Chuquicamata

To San Pedro de Atacama

To Parque El Loa, Airport & Antofagasta

Avenida B O'Higgins

■ PLACES TO STAY

4   Hotel Génesis
16 Residencial Internacional
18 Residencial Splendid
19 Residencial Toño
27 Hostal El Sol
28 Hotel Alfa
30 Hotel Atenas
34 Hotel Casablanca
39 Hotel Olimpo
41 Hotel Loa
44 Hostería Calama
45 Residencial Capri
47 Residencial El Tatio
48 Residencial John Kenny

▼ PLACES TO EAT

6   Restaurant Osorno
8   Restaurant Victoria
10 Chifa Chi-Kang
24 Club Yugoslavo
25 Fiori di Gelatto
35 Bavaria Restaurant

OTHER

1   ENTEL (Telephone)
2   Hospital
3   Buses Yusmar
5   Buses Géminis
7   Tramaca
9   Loa Desert Adventure
11 Buses/Flota Barrios
12 CTC (Telephone)
13 Telex-Chile
14 Turismo Quitor
15 Talikuna Excursiones
17 Mercado
20 Kenny Bus
21 Banco de Chile
22 Ladeco
23 Plaza 23 de Marzo
26 Banco O'Higgins
28 Copper Tour
29 Banco de Crédito
31 Buses/Fénix Pullman Norte
32 Buses Flecha Dorada
33 Buses Morales y Moralito
36 Turismo El Sol
37 Bolivian Consulate
38 Railway Station
40 Post Office
42 Tourism Adventure Desert
43 Tourist Office
46 LAN-Chile
49 Automóvil Club de Chile

is on the corner of Avenida Granaderos and Cisterna, north of the plaza.

Places to Stay

Residencial Capri, Vivar 1639, is tolerable by budget standards at US$3 per person. *Residencial Toño*, Vivar 1970, is popular with foreign visitors. It charges US$4, has clean sheets, offers many blankets and is reasonably quiet. *Residencial El Tatio*, León Gallo 1987, has good rooms at US$7 a single.

The clean and recently renovated *Residencial Splendid*, Ramírez 1960, has singles/doubles with shared bath for US$7/10. Rates are similar at *Residencial Internacional*, General Velásquez 1976. *Hotel Atenas*, Ramírez 1961, has small, neat rooms for US$8/11.

Places to Eat

Restaurant Victoria, Vargas 2102, and *Restaurant Osorno*, upstairs at Granaderos 2013-B, are ordinary budget eateries. *Club Yugoslavo*, Abaroa 1869, is slightly up-market. *Bavaria Restaurant*, Sotomayor 2035, is part of an uninspiring chain. *Restaurant Sándolo*, Vivar 1982, is a parrilla which also offers fish and other seafood. For ice cream, other desserts, sandwiches and coffee, visit *Fiori di Gelatto*, Ramírez 2099.

Getting There & Away

Air Aeropuerto El Loa (☎ 212348) is a short distance south of town. Ladeco (☎ 31-2626), Ramírez 1937, has four flights weekly to Antofagasta and Santiago. LAN-Chile (☎ 21-1394), Latorre 1499, has a similar schedule.

Bus – domestic Calama has no central terminal, but most companies are near each other.

Tramaca, Granaderos 3048, has frequent buses to Antofagasta, Santiago, Arica and Iquique. Buses Flecha Dorada, Ramírez 1802, has daily buses to Santiago and Arica. Flota Barrios Buses, Ramírez 2298, also serves Panamericana destinations, as does Fénix Pullman Norte, Sotomayor 1808.

Kenny Bus, Vivar 1954, serves Iquique via María Elena and Pozo Almonte.

Géminis, Granaderos 2034, has daily buses to Santiago and Arica, and goes to San Pedro de Atacama on Sundays. Morales y Moralito, Sotomayor 1802, goes to San Pedro three times a week. Yusmar, Antofagasta 2041, goes intermittently to Toconao (US$4).

Typical fares are San Pedro US$2.50, Antofagasta US$4, Iquique US$7, Arica US$9 and Santiago US$24.

Bus – international Make reservations to cross the Andes to Salta, Argentina (US$40 to US$45), with Géminis or Tramaca on Wednesday afternoons.

Train On Fridays at 11 pm, the train goes to Ollagüe, on the Bolivian border, with connections to Uyuni (US$11) and Oruro (US$18). Obtain tickets at Tramaca or at Calama station (☎ 21-2004), Balmaceda 1777.

Getting Around

To/From the Airport The airport is just a short taxi ride south of town.

Car Calama has many car rental agencies; to visit El Tatio Geysers, rent a jeep or pick-up truck – ordinary passenger cars lack clearance for the rugged roads.

Organised Tours Limited public transport makes tours a reasonable alternative. Itineraries vary, but the most complete one (for about US$25) goes from Calama to the El Tatio Geysers and returns via villages with traditional Andean churches.

Others involve staying overnight in San Pedro de Atacama, stopping at Valle de La Luna (Valley of the Moon) before visiting El Tatio. Another visits the Salar de Atacama, including the village of Toconao (US$20 from San Pedro). In general, it's cheaper and more convenient to make arrangements for El Tatio in San Pedro, because it's cheaper, shorter and less tiring (tours to El Tatio leave by 4 am).

Calama tour agencies include Turismo El Sol (☎ 21- 0152), at Abaroa 1781, Talikuna Excursiones (☎ 21-2595), at General Velásquez 1948, Copper Tour (☎ 21-2414), at Sotomayor 2016, Tuyaj Tour (☎ 31-2864), at Latorre 1724, Loa Desert Adventure (☎ 21-2200), at Bañados Espinoza 2191, Tourism Adventure Desert (☎ 21-2242), at Latorre 1602, and Turismo Quitor (☎ 31-4159), Ramírez 2116, 2nd floor.

CHUQUICAMATA

Chuquicamata (population 30,000), a company town 16 km north of Calama, provides half of Chile's copper output and at least 25% of its total export income. Chuqui's 400-metre-deep pit is the world's largest.

Chuqui changed hands several times before the US Anaconda Copper Mining Company began excavations in 1915. Out of nothing, Anaconda created a city with housing, schools, cinemas, shops, a hospital and clinics – though many accused it of taking out more than it put back.

By the 1960s, Anaconda was a target for those who advocated nationalisation of copper. During the Frei administration, the state gained a majority shareholding and, in 1971, Congress enthusiastically approved nationalisation. After 1973, the junta compensated companies for loss of assets, but retained ownership through the Corporación del Cobre de Chile (Codelco).

Chuqui is a clean, orderly town whose landscape is a reminder of its history. The stadium is the **Estadio Anaconda**, while the **Auditorio Sindical** is a huge theatre with an interior mural which commemorates a contentious strike. A prominent statue honours workers who operated equipment like the behemoth power shovel nearby.

Places to Eat

For good meals, visit the *Club de Empleados* and the *Arco Iris Center*, both across from the plaza, on Avenida J M Carrera. Also recommended is the *Club de Obreros*, on Mariscal Alcázar two blocks south of the

stadium, and *Restaurant Carloncho*, on Avenida Comercial O'Higgins.

Getting There & Away

Taxi colectivos (US$0.75) leave Calama from Abaroa near Vicuña Mackenna. There are also buses from Granaderos and Ramírez.

Getting Around

Organised Tours For weekday three-hour tours, report to the Oficina Ayuda a la Infancia, at the top of Avenida J M Carrera, by 9.45 am. Bring your passport and make a modest donation (about US$0.50). Demand is high in January and February, so get there early; with enough demand, there are afternoon tours.

To enter the smelter building, you must wear sturdy footwear, long trousers and a long-sleeved jacket, but the mine provides jackets, helmets and eye protection.

SAN PEDRO DE ATACAMA

San Pedro de Atacama is an oasis village at the north end of the Salar de Atacama, a vast saline lake. It is 120 km south-east of Calama. To its east rise immense volcanos, both active and extinct. Nearby is the Valle de la Luna (Valley of the Moon).

At 2440 metres above sea level, San Pedro's adobe houses preserve a colonial feeling. In the early 20th century, it was a major stop on cattle drives from Argentina to the nitrate mines, but the Salta-Antofagasta railway ended this colourful era.

No longer on the cattle trail, San Pedro is now on the 'gringo trail', but many young Chileans also spend their holidays here. Despite increasing tourist trade, it is attractive and affordable. The municipal tourist office, on the north side of the plaza, keeps irregular weekday hours.

Things to See

Museo Gustavo Le Paige In 1955, Belgian priest/archaeologist Gustavo Le Paige, assisted by villagers and the Universidad del Norte, began to assemble artefacts on the area's cultural evolution for this exceptionally well-organised museum. It also includes exhibits on the Inca conquest, the Spanish invasion and modern cultural anthropology.

The museum is half a block from the plaza and charges US$0.85 admission, but show student ID for a discount.

Around the Plaza Over 450 years ago, Pedro de Valdivia's entourage passed through here with seeds, pigs and chickens, and farming tools. On the east side of the plaza stands the **Casa de Pedro de Valdivia**, a restored adobe reportedly built around 1540. On the west side, the modified 17th-century **Iglesia San Pedro** was built with local materials – adobe, wood from the *cardón* cactus, and leather straps in lieu of nails.

Places to Stay
Local accommodation is hard to find around holiday periods like Chile's mid-September independence days.

Camping Puri, at the west end of O'Higgins, charges US$2 per person. *Camping Takha Takha*, south of town on Tocopilla, charges about US$3.

Residencial Andacollo, Tocopilla 11, with very comfortable beds, is cheapest (US$4 per person). *Residencial La Florida*, on Tocopilla, a block west of the plaza, is spartan but very clean and friendly, with dependable hot showers (US$5); its restaurant serves good economical meals and is a good place to meet people. Adjacent *Residencial El Pukará* is similar in price and quality.

There are mixed opinions on *Hostería San Pedro*, operated by an Australian woman and her Chilean husband. Rooms start at US$23/29 for a single/double with private bath, swimming pool, solar-heated showers and restaurant.

Places to Eat
Besides hotel restaurants, try *Restaurant Juanita*, on the plaza, and the excellent *Tambo Cañaveral*, which doubles as San Pedro's hottest night spot.

Things to Buy
For handicrafts, including cardón carvings and llama and alpaca ponchos, try the craft shop on the plaza or Hostería San Pedro.

Getting There & Away
Géminis has buses from Calama on Sundays. Morales y Moralito has buses from Calama (US$3) daily and to Toconao three days a week. Yusmar goes twice daily to Calama and four days a week to Toconao.

AROUND SAN PEDRO DE ATACAMA
Local operators offer reasonably priced tours to most attractions, which are some distance from town. Among the best-established are Turismo Ochoa, on Calle Toconao, south of the plaza, Turismo Roberto Sánchez, on O'Higgins, Turismo Florida, in the Residencial La Florida, and Atacama Desert Expeditions, on the plaza. Turismo Nativa visits really out-of-the-way places like Salar de Uyuni in Bolivia.

Pukará de Quitor & Catarpe
Three km north-west of San Pedro, on a promontory above the Río San Pedro, are the ruins of a 12th-century *pucará* (fortress). Across the river, Catarpe was an Inca administrative centre.

Valle de la Luna
This area of oddly eroded landforms, 15 km west of San Pedro, is a popular excursion. If driving, don't get stuck in the sand; if hiking, carry water and food, and smear yourself with sunblock.

Termas de Puritama
Camping is possible at these volcanic hot springs, about 30 km north of San Pedro, toward El Tatio, but there's no fuel for a fire and it gets very cold. For a small charge, arrange transport with sulphur mine trucks, which leave San Pedro early every morning; the driver drops you off at a signed junction for a 20-minute walk on an obvious gravel track. Unless you intend to camp, return to the main road by 1 pm and flag down the first available truck.

El Tatio Geysers

At 4300 metres, 95 km north of San Pedro, El Tatio is the world's highest geyser field. In the azure clarity of the altiplano, the sight of the steaming fumaroles at sunrise is unforgettable, while the individual structures formed by evaporation of boiling water and mineral deposition are strikingly beautiful. Watch your step – people have suffered serious burns after falling through the thin crust into scalding water. Camping is possible but nights are freezing.

About 6 am is the best time; most tours leave by about 8.30. San Pedro has better access and its tours are a bit cheaper (about US$20 with lunch and a stop at Puritama). If driving, take a high-clearance vehicle; leave San Pedro by 4 am. The route is signed, but in the dark it's easier to follow tour agencies' minibuses. If you rent a car in Calama, you can return via the villages of Caspana, Toconce, Ayquina and Chiu Chiu, rather than San Pedro.

TOCONAO

Known for its finely hewn volcanic stone, Toconao is a fruit-growing oasis about 40 km south of San Pedro. The **Iglesia de San Lucas**, with a separate bell tower, dates from the mid-18th century.

The Quebrada de Jeria, with an intricate irrigation system, is a delightful place for a walk or even a swim. Affluent San Pedro families once despatched peons with mules here to fetch casks of drinking water.

Near the plaza, there are several inexpensive residenciales and restaurants. Buses from Calama and San Pedro arrive late at night. Hitching is possible, but leave San Pedro early and be prepared to return early or stay the night.

Norte Chico

A semi-arid transition zone from the Atacama to the Valle Central, the *Norte*

Chico (Little North) is also the region of 10,000 mines. Irrigated agriculture is significant.

Politically, the Norte Chico includes the Third Region of Atacama (capital Copiapó) and the Fourth Region of Coquimbo (capital La Serena), but its customary boundaries encompass a slightly greater area. The main attractions are a pleasant climate, fine beaches and the city of La Serena, but intriguing mountain villages lie off the beaten track. Near the Panamericana are the national parks Pan de Azúcar and Fray Jorge.

History

Decades before the Spaniards, the Incas subdued Diaguita farmers, but the area was always peripheral to the Central Andean civilisations. Europeans first arrived in 1535, when Diego de Almagro crossed the Andes from Salta.

A few years later, Pedro de Valdivia founded La Serena, but Copiapó lagged behind until an 18th-century gold boom. When gold failed, silver took its place and Copiapó really took off, tripling its population to 12,000 after a bonanza find at Chañarcillo in 1832.

When silver declined in the late 19th century, copper took its place in Potrerillos and, later, El Salvador. Recently, La Serena and Bahía Inglesa have enjoyed tourist booms, but mining continues to be significant. The area is also important culturally – Nobel Prize poet Gabriela Mistral was a native of Vicuña, in the Elqui valley. The Copiapó, Huasco and Elqui valleys have contributed to Chile's flourishing fruit exports in recent years.

COPIAPÓ

Discovery of silver at nearby Chañarcillo provided Copiapó with several firsts: South America's first railroad (completed in 1852 to the port of Caldera), Chile's first telegraph and telephone lines, and the first gas works. While not a major destination for travellers, its pleasant climate and historical interest make it a worthwhile stopover between La Serena and Antofagasta.

Copiapó (population 69,000) is 800 km north of Santiago and 565 km south of Antofagasta. Sernatur (☎ 21-2838) occupies a concrete bunker on Plaza Prat; once you find the entrance, the congenial staff has a helpful list of accommodation, an excellent free map and many brochures.

Things to See

Founded in 1857, the **Museo Mineralógico**, at Colipíand Rodríguez, is a literally dazzling tribute to the raw materials to which the city owes its existence. The **Museo de**

Ferrocarriles, on Juan Martínez, was the terminal for the Copiapó-Caldera line.

Notable buildings from the mining boom include the **Iglesia Catedral** and the **Municipalidad**, on the Plaza de Armas. At the foot of Batallón Atacama, directly south of the station, the **Palacete Viña de Cristo** was the town's most elegant mansion. A few blocks west, at the **Universidad de Atacama** (the former Escuela de Minas), is the Norris Brothers locomotive, first on the Caldera-Copiapó line.

Places to Stay

In summer, Copiapó has a hostel at Juan Antonio Ríos 371. *Residencial Chacabuco*, Chacabuco 271, is the cheapest at US$5 per person (twice that with private bath). *Residencial Chañarcillo*, Chañarcillo 741, has small but clean rooms for US$5/9 a single/double. *Anexo Residencial Chañarcillo*, at O'Higgins 804, is rundown but friendly at US$6/11, with hot water available from 7 to 11 am only.

Dearer, but excellent value, is *Hotel Palace*, Atacama 741, with very attractive rooms around a delightful garden patio for US$20/29 with private bath. Colonial-style *Hotel La Casona*, O'Higgins 150, offers rooms in a beautiful garden setting for US$39/53.

Places to Eat

El Pollo, Chacabuco 340, has a fine three-course lunch for about US$4. *Helados Diavoletto*, Henríquez 431-A, has excellent ice cream. For seafood, try *Restaurant Galería*, at Colipí 635, or *Il Pirón de Oro*, at Atacama 1. The *Club Social Libanés*, Los Carrera 350, has Middle Eastern food, while *Villa Rapallo*, Chañarcillo 705, offers Italian fare. *Hao Hwa*, Colipí 340, is one of northern Chile's better Chinese restaurants.

Getting There & Away

Air Aeropuerto Chamonate (☎ 21- 4360) is seven km west of town. LAN-Chile has flights to Calama and Antofagasta four times weekly, to Santiago three times.

CHILE

Bus All companies have offices (some shared) at the terminal (☎ 21-2577) at the foot of Chacabuco, three blocks south of Plaza Prat, but some have downtown offices. Virtually all north-south buses, and many to the interior destinations, stop here. Approximate fares are: Arica US$24, Iquique US$22, Tocopilla or Calama US$16, Antofagasta US$12, La Serena US$7, and Santiago or Viña del Mar US$14.

Pullman Bus (☎ 21-1039), Colipí 109, and Inca Bus cover southerly destinations off the Panamericana, including Illapel and Salamanca, and northern mining towns like Diego de Almagro, El Salvador and Potrerillos. Regional carriers run frequently to Caldera and Bahía Inglesa (US$1), and to the upper Copiapó valley.

Getting Around
LAN-Chile (☎ 21-3512), O'Higgins 640, operates its own minibus to Aeropuerto Chamonate.

CALDERA & BAHÍA INGLESA
Caldera, 75 km west of Copiapó, grew rapidly with the discovery of silver in the Andes and the arrival of the railroad – which gave people in Copiapó easy access to the beach. Bahía Inglesa, a refuge for privateers in colonial times, has better beaches, but Caldera is livelier and much cheaper.

Things to See
Caldera's **Cementerio Laico** was Chile's first non-Catholic cemetery, with interesting ironwork. Between the plaza and the **Muelle Pesquero** (the fishing jetty) are many distinctive 19th-century buildings, including the **Iglesia San Vicente**, with its gothic tower, the **Municipalidad**, the **Aduana** (old customs house), at Gana and Wheelwright, and the **Estación Ferrocarriles** (train station).

Activities
Besides swimming and sunbathing, windsurfing is a popular pastime at Bahía Inglesa; rental equipment is available.

Places to Stay
Camping Bahía Inglesa, on Playa Las Machas, has good facilities but costs nearly US$20 per site in the high season. Cabañas start at US$28 for up to five persons with shared bath.

The cheapest alternatives, about US$6 a single, are *Residencial Molina*, at Montt 346, and *Hotel Los Andes*, at Edwards 360. *Residencial Fenicia*, Gallo 370, has singles/doubles with shared bath for US$10/18.

Places to Eat
Seafood is about the only reasonable choice – try *Il Pirón de Oro*, at Cousiño 218, or *Nuevo Miramar*, at the foot of Gana. *Helados Diavoletto*, Cousiño 315, has excellent ice cream.

In Bahía Inglesa, *El Coral* offers superb seafood, especially locally cultivated scallops. It's expensive, but careful ordering may preserve your budget.

Getting There & Away
Frequent buses to Copiapó leave from near the plaza. To catch a north-south bus, wait at the turn-off at the east end of Avenida Diego de Almeyda.

Getting Around
Buses and taxi colectivos shuttle visitors from Caldera to Bahía Inglesa.

PARQUE NACIONAL PAN DE AZÚCAR
Just 30 km north of the dilapidated mining port of Chañaral, Pan de Azúcar is 44,000 hectares of coastal desert and precordillera, with beautiful coves among stony headlands, white sandy beaches, abundant wildlife and unique flora. The rich Humboldt current feeds otters, sea lions and many birds; pelicans, cormorants and penguins nest on Isla Pan de Azúcar, but access is restricted – bring binoculars. At higher altitudes, the camanchaca nurtures unique cacti and succulents, while further inland, guanacos and foxes are common.

Places to Stay

CONAF camp sites (US$3) have picnic tables with shade provided at Cerro Soldado, Playa Piqueros and Caleta Pan de Azúcar, but bring your own water. The nearest supplies are at Chañaral, but try buying fish at Caleta Pan de Azúcar.

Getting There & Away

Arrange a taxi from Chañaral for about US$20 – double that if you want to be picked up. On weekends, try hitching, but carrying provisions (ie water) might be a problem. CONAF collects an admission charge of US$1 at the south entrance.

LA SERENA

Founded in 1544, La Serena (population 107,000) maintains a colonial façade, thanks to President Gabriel González Videla's 'Plan Serena' of the late 1940s. Silver and copper were its economic backbone, along with irrigated agriculture. Capital of the Fourth Region of Coquimbo and 470 km north of Santiago, it's a very agreeable place which may supplant Viña del Mar as Chile's premier beach resort.

Orientation

Centred on the Plaza de Armas, the city plan is a regular grid. Most areas of interest fall within a rectangular area marked by Avenida Bohón and Parque Pedro de Valdivia on the west, the Río Elqui on the north, Calle Benavente on the east and Avenida Aguirre to the south.

Information

Tourist Office Sernatur (☎ 22- 5199) is on the 1st floor of the post office complex, on the corner of Prat and Matta, opposite the plaza. The municipal kiosk is much more helpful, at Prat and Balmaceda, and is open Monday to Saturday from 10 am to 10 pm, and on Sundays from 10 am to 2 pm. There's also an office at the bus terminal.

Money Exchange money at Gira Tour, at Prat 689, or the nameless cambio at Prat 515.

Post & Telecommunications Correos de Chile is on the corner of Matta and Prat, opposite the plaza. CTC offices are at Cordóvez 446 and in the Mercado La Recova. ENTEL is at Prat 571.

Emergency La Serena's hospital (☎ 22-5569) is at Balmaceda 916.

Things to See

Many key features are on or near the nicely landscaped Plaza de Armas. On the east side is the **Iglesia Catedral** (1844), while at the south-west corner, facing a smaller plaza, is the colonial **Iglesia Santo Domingo**.

In an annex of the colonial **Iglesia San Francisco**, at Balmaceda 640, the **Museo Colonial de Arte Religioso** features polychrome sculptures from Cuzco and paintings from 17th-century Quito.

La Serena's native son and the President from 1946 to 1952, González Videla was a controversial figure who drove Pablo Neruda out of the Senate and into exile. Exhibits on González Videla's life in the **Museo Histórico Gabriel González Videla**, at Matta 495, omit such episodes, but the museum also includes material about the region's history.

The **Museo Arqueológico** is on the corner of Cordóvez and Cienfuegos. Add this collection of Diaguita artefacts to the González Videla and you'd have one fine museum instead of two mediocre ones.

Admission, about US$0.70, is valid for both museums.

Check **Mercardo La Recova** for musical instruments, woollens and dried fruits.

Beaches

On a two-week vacation, you can visit a different beach every day, but watch out for the strong currents. Safe for swimming are Canto del Agua, Las Gaviotas, El Pescador, La Marina, La Barca, Playa Mansa, Los Fuertes, Playa Blanca, El Faro (Sur), and Peñuelas (Coquimbo).

Suitable only for sunbathing are Cuatro Esquinas, El Faro (Norte), Playa Changa

CHILE

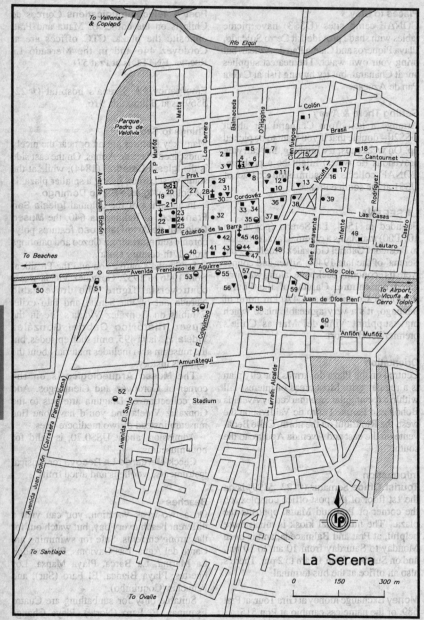

To Vallenar
& Copiapó

Río Elqui

Parque
Pedro de
Valdivia

To Beaches

To Santiago

To Ovalle

To Airport,
Vicuña &
Cerro Tololo

To Beaches

La Serena

0   150   300 m

	PLACES TO STAY	6	Restaurant Domingo Domingo	29	Municipalidad
				30	CTC (Telephone)
1	Pensión Matús	9	La Pizza Mía	32	CEMA-Chile Gallery
2	Hotel Pucará	13	Restaurant Mai Lan	35	Buses Tas Choapa
5	Residencial Brasilia		Fan	38	Museo Arqueológico
7	Residencial El Loa	31	La Crísis	39	Teatro Municipal
10	Gran Hotel La Serena	34	Restaurante Naturista	40	Buses Flecha Dorada
16	Hotel Casablanca		Maracuyá	42	Automóvil Club de
17	Pensión López	56	Yugoslav Club		Chile
18	El Hostal del Turismo			43	Línea Ruta 41
19	Hotel Francisco de Aguirre		OTHER	44	Buses Tal
				45	Iglesia San Francisco
24	Residencial Lido	4	Iglesia La Merced &		& Museo Colonial
25	Residencial Chile		Tourist Kiosk		de Arte Religioso
26	Hotel Pacífico	8	ENTEL (Telephone)	46	Buses Expreso Norte
33	Hotel Berlín	11	Gira Tour	47	Calle Domeyko, col-
36	Hotel Mediterráneo	12	LAN-Chile		ectivos to Tongoy,
37	Residencial Petit	14	Iglesia San Agustín		Andacollo & Ovalle
41	Hotel Alameda	15	Mercado La Recova	50	Hertz Rent-a-Car
48	Residencial Norte Verde	20	Sernatur (Tourist Office)/Post Office	51	Symatour (Money Exchange)
49	Turismo 2000	21	Museo Histórico	52	Bus Terminal
59	Hotel Los Balcones de Alcalá		Gabriel González Videla	53	Buses Tramaca
		22	Iglesia Santo Domingo	54	Buses Frontera Elqui
▼	PLACES TO EAT	23	CONAF	55	Buses Libac
		27	Plaza de Armas	57	Diaguita Tour
3	Boccaccio	28	Catedral	58	Hospital
				60	Museo Mineralógico

(Coquimbo), Punta de Teatinos, Los Choros, Caleta Hornos, San Pedro and Chungungo. All have regular bus and taxi colectivo service from the city centre.

Places to Stay

Many families house university students, and rent to tourists in summer only, but may have a spare bed at other times. *Pensión López*, Cantournet 815, has spacious singles with comfortable beds and excellent hot showers for about US$5.

Residencial El Loa, O'Higgins 362, charges US$7 per person with shared bath, as does *Residencial Lido*, Matta 547, at very good value. Recommended *Residencial Chile*, at Matta 561, charges US$11/20 for a single/double.

Several correspondents have recommended *Hotel Pacífico*, Eduardo de la Barra 252, with rooms for US$15/21 with breakfast. One reader raved about *Hotel Los Balcones de Alcalá*, Larraín Aguirre 781, where singles cost US$34.

Places to Eat

For seafood, any restaurant in the Mercado La Recova, on the corner of Cienfuegos and Cantournet, is a good choice, but try *Caleta Hornos*, Local 220. *Restaurante Naturista Maracuyá* is a vegetarian restaurant at Cordovéz 533. *Mai Lan Fan*, Cordovéz 740, has decent Chinese food. One reader has praised *Domingo Domingo*, Prat 568.

Coffee, ice cream and desserts are outstanding at *Boccaccio*, corner of Prat and Balmaceda. *La Crisis*, Balmaceda 487, is another popular ice-cream parlour and snack bar. For coffee, snacks and sandwiches, try *Café do Brasil*, at Balmaceda 465; for pizza, visit *La Pizza Mía*, O'Higgins 460.

Getting There & Away

Air Aeropuerto La Florida is a short distance

CHILE

east of the city centre. Ladeco (☎ 22-5753), Cordovéz 484, flies to Santiago daily, except Saturdays; the Saturday flight from Santiago continues to Calama and Iquique.

Bus The Terminal Rodoviario (☎ 22-4573), which also serves nearby Coquimbo, is on the outskirts of town, on the corner of Amunátegui and Avenida El Santo. Many companies also have offices in town.

Buses – long-distance Via Elqui and Frontera Elqui, corner of Juan de Dios Pení and Regimiento Coquimbo, serve upper Elqui valley destinations like Vicuña. Los Diamantes de Elqui goes to Vicuña and Ovalle, as does Expreso Norte, O'Higgins 675.

Tas Choapa, at O'Higgins 599, Buses Tal, at Balmaceda 594, and Buses Palacios, at Amunátegui 251, also serve Ovalle. Postal Bus and Buses Carlos Araya, at Frontera Elqui offices, both go to Andacollo. Fares to these destinations range from US$1 to US$3.

Buses – regional Companies serving Santiago (seven hours) include Inca Bus, Tramaca (at Aguirre 375), Buses Lit (at Balmaceda 1302), Flota Barrios (at Domeyko 550), Los Diamantes de Elqui, Tas-Choapa (at O'Higgins 599), Buses Palacios, Flecha Dorada (at Aguirre 344), Expreso Norte, Libac (at Aguirre 452) and Pullman Bus (at O'Higgins 663). Los Corsarios, Inca Bus and Pullman Bus all serve Valparaíso and Viña del Mar.

For Copiapó and other northern destinations, try Inca Bus, Flecha Dorada, Flota Barrios, Libac, Pullman, Tramaca, Chile Bus, Carmelita or Fénix Pullman Norte.

Typical fares include Santiago or Viña/Valparaíso US$9, Los Vilos US$6, Illapel/Salamanca or Copiapó US$7, Chañaral US$10, Antofagasta US$15, Calama US$19, Iquique US$23 and Arica US$25.

Bus – international Covalle Bus connects La Serena with Mendoza and San Juan,

Argentina (US$30, 16 hours), via the Libertadores pass, twice weekly in summer.

Taxi Colectivo Taxi colectivos serve many regional destinations frequently and rapidly. Anserco, which goes to Andacollo, and Nevada and Sol Elqui, both of which go to Vicuña, share offices at Domeyko 524, near the corner of Cienfuegos and Aguirre. Línea Ruta 41, Aguirre 460, goes to the upper Elqui. Secovalle, at the same address, goes to Ovalle.

AROUND LA SERENA
Observatorio Cerro Tololo
At 2200 metres above sea level, 88 km southeast of La Serena, this is one of the southern hemisphere's most important observatories. Make tour reservations by calling the La Serena office (☎ 22-5415), but there is no public transport; hitching is possible from the junction on the highway to Vicuña, but allow plenty of time.

VICUÑA
Vicuña (population 7000) is a quiet village of adobe houses in the upper Elqui valley, 62 km from La Serena, in an area which produces grapes, avocados, papayas and other fruit. Thanks to several groups convinced that UFOs frequent the area, the village and nearby countryside have acquired an oddball reputation. The tourist office is in the eccentric Torre Bauer, resembling a castle with wooden battlements, opposite the plaza.

Vicuña's **Museo Gabriela Mistral** is a tangible eulogy to the famous literary figure. Gabriela Mistral was born Lucila Godoy Alcayaga in 1889, in the village of Montegrande. The museum's exhibits include a photo biography, modest personal possessions like a desk and bookcase, and a replica of her adobe birthplace. Her genealogy indicates Spanish, Indian and even African ancestry.

Places to Stay & Eat
Residencial La Moderna, on Mistral near Baquedano, costs US$4 per person, as does *Hotel Yasna*, at Mistral 542 (one reader

reported plumbing problems). *Hotel Sol del Valle*, next to the museum, charges US$6 a single and also has a good restaurant. Several modest restaurants include *Yo y Soledad*, at Mistral 448, and the nearby *Restaurant Halley* – probably inspired by the local space cadets.

Getting There & Away
Frequent buses and taxi colectivos to La Serena leave from the Plaza de Armas.

OVALLE
Ovalle (population 75,000), half an hour off the Panamericana, is the tidy capital of the prosperous agricultural province of Limarí. The tourist office is a kiosk opposite the plaza, on Victoria, between Hotel Turismo and Banco de Chile.

The **Museo del Limarí**, Independencia 329, is a modest endeavour which stresses the trans-Andean links between the Diaguita people of coastal Chile and north-west Argentina. The **Feria Modelo**, a lively fruit and vegetable market with several restaurants, occupies the former repair facilities of the railroad.

Places to Stay & Eat
Hotel Roxy, Libertad 155, is great value at US$5 per person with shared bath, very friendly and clean, and has a huge, attractive patio. *Hotel Francia*, Libertad 261, is slightly cheaper but less appealing.

For a good fixed-price lunch, try the *Club Comercial*, at Aguirre 244. The *Club Social Arabe*, Arauco 255, offers Middle Eastern specialties.

Getting There & Away
Bus North-south bus services resemble those leaving from La Serena, though some companies bypass Ovalle. Those with local offices include Incabus, at Ariztia Oriente 398, Pullman, at Ariztia Poniente 159, Carmelita, at Ariztia Poniente 351, and Tramaca.

AROUND OVALLE
Monumento Arqueológico Valle del Encanto
Valle del Encanto, 19 km from Ovalle, is a rocky tributary canyon of the Río Limarí, with pre-Columbian petroglyphs, pictographs and mortars. Any westbound bus will drop you at the highway marker. It's an easy five-km walk on a clearly marked road to the canyon.

PARQUE NACIONAL FRAY JORGE
Moistened by the camanchaca, Fray Jorge is an ecological island of Valdivian cloud forest in a semi-arid region, 110 km south of La Serena. Its 10,000 hectares contain only 400 of this truly unique vegetation – still enough to make it a UNESCO International Biosphere Reserve. Some believe this area is evidence of dramatic climate change, but others argue that such forests were more extensive before their destruction by humans.

Fray Jorge is open to the public in summer (January to mid-March) Thursday to Sunday, plus holidays, from 8.30 am to 6 pm; at other seasons, it's open on weekends only. Admission is US$1.50 for Chileans, US$3 for foreigners. A visitors' centre is in preparation.

Places to Stay
El Arrayancito has 13 camp sites (US$4) with fireplaces, picnic tables, water and toilets.

Getting There & Away
Fray Jorge is reached by a westward lateral off the Panamericana, about 20 km north of the Ovalle junction. Several agencies offer tours from La Serena and Ovalle. You could ask about leaving the tour and returning on another day. North-south buses can drop you at the clearly marked turn-off, 22 km from the gate – walking is not easy, but try hitching.

LOS VILOS
Los Vilos is a crowded beach resort midway between Santiago and La Serena, with cheap

accommodation and fine seafood. On Sundays, the fish market offers live crab, dozens of kinds of fish, a roving hurdy-gurdy man and thousands of colourful balloons.

In summer, there's an information kiosk on Caupolicán, the main road. It's open from 9 am to 2 pm and 4 to 9 pm.

Places to Stay & Eat

Residencial Drake, on Caupolicán between Talcahuano and Rengo, is the cheapest central hotel, at US$4 per person. *Residencial El Taxista*, Tilama 247, is far from the beach but convenient to the highway, with comfortable singles with TV and shared bath for US$5.

Hotel Bellavista, popular and central, at Rengo 020, charges US$6 per person with breakfast and shared bath, and has a fine restaurant with large portions. There are good reports on *Residencial Turismo*, Caupolicán 437, for US$7 per person.

Restaurant El Faro, at Colipí 224, is also highly regarded. Beachfront cafés along the Costanera are cheap and good – try *El Refugio del Pescador*.

Getting There & Away

Few buses enter town, but it's easy to flag one near the Copec petrol station on the Panamericana. Companies which stop in town include Pullman Bus (Santiago), Inca Bus (La Serena) and Tas Choapa (Illapel and Salamanca).

La Araucanía & the Lake District

Beyond the Biobío, glaciated volcanos tower over deep blue lakes, ancient forests, and verdant farmland, while waterfalls spill into limpid pools. Temuco, capital of the Ninth

Region (La Araucanía), is the staging point for visiting Parque Nacional Conguillío, the upper Biobío, and lakeside resorts like Villarrica and Pucón. Farther south, near Osorno, is an easy land crossing to Argentina via Lago Puyehue, and a more scenic bus-boat combination.

Puerto Montt, on the Gulf of Reloncaví, is capital of the Tenth Region (Los Lagos) and gateway to Chiloé Island and Chilean Patagonia. Hikers in this area should acquire Clem Lindenmayer's *Trekking in the Patagonian Andes* (Lonely Planet, 1992), which also covers Argentina.

History

South of Concepción, the Spaniards found small gold mines, good farmland and a large potential workforce, but constantly suffered Mapuche attacks or natural disasters. By the mid-17th century, they abandoned most settlements, except for heavily fortified Valdivia. Early 19th-century travellers still referred to 'Arauco' as a separate country, which was not safe for European settlers until the 1880s.

Several hundred thousand Mapuche in *La Frontera*, the area between the Biobío and the Río Toltén, still earn a precarious livelihood from farming and crafts. Nineteenth-century German immigrants started industries and left a palpable architectural heritage, and Chilean-Germans have left their mark in food and the agricultural landscape.

TEMUCO

Fast-growing Temuco (population 220,000), 675 km south of Santiago, serves a large hinterland with a range of industries, including steel, textiles, food processing and wood products. The gateway to the Lake District, it's also a market town for Mapuche produce and crafts.

Information

Tourist Office Sernatur (☎ 21-1969), Bulnes 586, has city maps and the very useful brochure, *Datos Utiles Temuco*. It's open Monday to Saturday and on Sunday morning.

Money Change cash and travellers' cheques at Turismo (Bulnes 655, Local 1), Turcamb (Claro Solar 733) or Christopher Money Exchange (Prat 696, Oficina 419).

Post & Telecommunications Correos de Chile is on the corner of Diego Portales and Arturo Prat. CTC offices are at Prat 565, Manuel Bulnes 368, and at Caupolicán and Manuel Montt.

Emergency Temuco's Hospital (☎ 21-2525) is at Manuel Montt 115.

Things to See

The historical park **Monumento Natural Cerro Ñielol** is where Mapuche leaders ceded land for Temuco in 1881. It is popular for picnics, with a small lagoon, trails and an environmental information centre.

The **Mercado Municipal**, three blocks north of the plaza, combines community service (food and clothing) with tourist appeal (restaurants and crafts). It's open Monday to Saturday from 8 am to 7 pm, and on Sundays from 8.30 am to 2 pm.

Open daily from 9 am to 2 pm or whenever the last Mapuche vendors pack up, the **Feria Libre** (produce market) fills several blocks along Barros Arana near the train station.

At Alemania 084, reached by bus No 9 from the city centre, the **Museo Regional de la Araucanía** chronicles the Mapuche story since pre-Columbian times. It also has materials on European colonisation, historical maps, a gallery of regional art and a library.

It's open Tuesday to Saturday from 9 am to 1 pm and 3 to 7 pm, and on Sundays and holidays from 10 am to 1 pm.

Places to Stay

In summer, many families rent rooms for about US$6 a single – ask the tourist office or try side streets near the plaza. *Hospedaje Espejo*, Aldunate 124, has singles for US$5; nearby is the very attractive and friendly *Hospedaje Aldunate*, Aldunate 187, for

CHILE

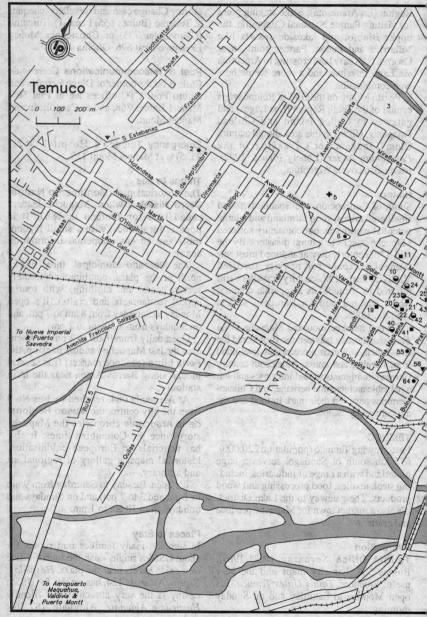

Temuco

0   100   200 m

To Nueva Imperial
& Puerto
Saavedra

To Aeropuerto
Maquehue,
Valdivia &
Puerto Montt

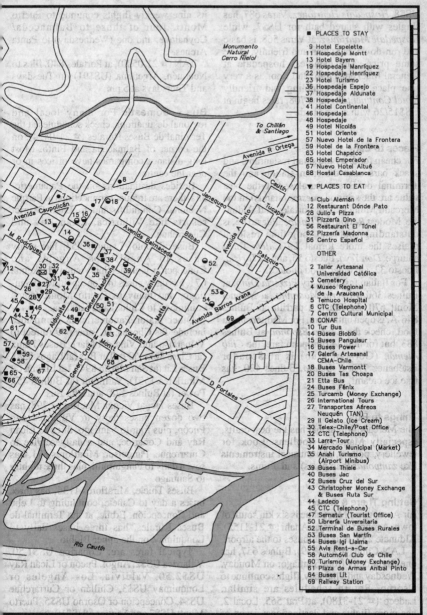

CHILE

■ PLACES TO STAY

9 Hotel Espelette
11 Hospedaje Montt
13 Hotel Bayern
19 Hospedaje Manríquez
22 Hospedaje Henríquez
23 Hotel Turismo
36 Hospedaje Espejo
37 Hospedaje Aldunate
38 Hospedaje
41 Hotel Continental
46 Hospedaje
48 Hospedaje
49 Hotel Nicolás
51 Hotel Oriente
57 Nuevo Hotel de la Frontera
59 Hotel de la Frontera
63 Hotel Chapelco
65 Hotel Emperador
67 Nuevo Hotel Aitué
68 Hostal Casablanca

▼ PLACES TO EAT

1 Club Alemán
12 Restaurant Dónde Pato
28 Julio's Pizza
31 Pizzería Dino
56 Restaurant El Túnel
62 Pizzería Madonna
66 Centro Español

OTHER

2 Taller Artesanal
   Universidad Católica
3 Cemetery
4 Museo Regional
   de la Araucanía
5 Temuco Hospital
6 CTC (Telephone)
7 Centro Cultural Municipal
8 CONAF
10 Tur Bus
14 Buses Biobío
15 Buses Panguisur
16 Buses Power
17 Galería Artesanal
   CEMA-Chile
18 Buses Varmontt
20 Buses Tas Choapa
21 Etta Bus
24 Buses Fénix
25 Turcamb (Money Exchange)
26 International Tours
27 Transportes Aéreos
   Neuquén (TAN)
29 Il Gelato (Ice Cream)
30 Telex-Chile/Post Office
32 CTC (Telephone)
33 Larra-Tour
34 Mercado Municipal (Market)
35 Anahi Turismo
   (Airport Minibus)
39 Buses Thiele
40 Buses Jac
42 Buses Cruz del Sur
43 Christopher Money Exchange
   & Buses Ruta Sur
44 Ladeco
45 CTC (Telephone)
47 Sernatur (Tourist Office)
50 Librería Unversitaria
52 Terminal de Buses Rurales
53 Buses San Martín
54 Buses Igi Llaima
55 Avis Rent-a-Car
58 Automóvil Club de Chile
60 Turismo (Money Exchange)
61 Plaza de Armas Aníbal Pinto
64 Buses Lit
69 Railway Station

US$8. *Hospedaje Henríquez*, Varas 687, has singles with shared bath for US$7, while *Hospedaje Manríquez*, at Varas 568, is basic and run-down, but clean and friendly, at the same price. The nameless hospedaje at General Mackenna 496, 2nd floor, is a very fine place. At the rambling and friendly *Hotel Continental*, Varas 708, rates begin at US$15/26 with shared bath.

Places to Eat
For cheap food, try the small restaurants and snack bars near the train station and the Terminal de Buses Rurales, but the best value are the seafood *puestos* (stands) in the Mercado Municipal, at Portales and Aldunate. Modest *Restaurant Caribe*, Puesto 45, is outstanding, but one long-time resident praises the more formal *La Caleta* for a splurge. *Don Yeyo*, Puesto 55, and *El Turista*, Puesto 32, are other good choices.

For Italian fast food, try *Pizzería Dino*, at Bulnes 360, *Pizzería Madonna*, at Manuel Montt 670. *El Túnel*, a parrilla at Bulnes 846-A, is open until 2 am. For Mediterranean food, check the *Centro Español*, at Bulnes 883, but for middle European fare, the *Club Alemán* (German club) is at Senador Estébanez 772. *Il Gelato*, Bulnes 420, has fine ice cream.

Things to Buy
The Mercado Municipal has the best crafts, especially Mapuche woollens. Look for jewellery, pottery, and musical instruments like *zampoñas* (pan pipes) and drums.

Getting There & Away
Air Aeropuerto Maquehue is six km south of town. Agencia de Viajes Anahi (☎ 21-1155), Aldunate 235, runs minibuses to the airport.

LAN-Chile (☎ 21-1339), Bulnes 657, has one flight daily from Santiago; on Monday, Wednesday and Thursday, flights continue to Osorno. Return schedules are similar. Ladeco (☎ 21-3180), at Prat 565, Local 2, has more flights and destinations; seven of

its nine weekly flights continue to Puerto Montt, four of those to Balmaceda/Coyhaique, and one (Wednesday) to Punta Arenas.

TAN (☎ 21-0500), at Portales 840, flies to Neuquén, Argentina (US$91) on Tuesdays and Thursdays at 5 pm.

Bus – domestic For many local and regional destinations, check schedules at the Terminal de Buses Rurales (☎ 21-0494), on the corner of Balmaceda and Pinto. Most long-distance companies have offices in or near the centre.

Besides destinations on the Panamericana, there are frequent connections to Parque Nacional Conguillío and to Lake District resorts like Villarrica, Licán Ray and Curarrehue.

Buses Biobío, Lautaro 853, has many buses to Angol, Los Angeles and Concepción. Cruz del Sur, Vicuña Mackenna 671, has daily buses to Concepción and Santiago, and many to Puerto Montt (some continuing to Chiloé) and Valdivia.

Other major Panamericana companies include Tas Choapa, at Varas 609 (direct to Valparaíso and Viña del Mar), Buses Fénix (at Claro Solar 609), Tur Bus (at Lagos 538), Buses Lit (at San Martín 894), Igi Llaima (at Miraflores 1551), Varmontt (at Bulnes 45), Power (at Bulnes 178) and Etta Bus.

Buses Jac, at Vicuña MacKenna 798, has two dozen buses daily to Villarrica and Pucón, plus four to Santiago, three to Licán Ray and Coñaripe, and a daily service to Curarrehue. Panguisur, Miraflores 871, has seven daily to Panguipulli, plus three nightly to Santiago.

Buses Thiele, Miraflores 1136, has three buses a day to Cañete, continuing to Lebú and Concepción. Erbuc, at the Terminal de Buses Rurales, has three buses daily to Lonquimay, on the upper Biobío.

Typical fares are: Coñaripe US$1.50, Villarrica US$2, Angol, Pucón or Licán Ray US$2.50, Valdivia, Los Angeles or Lonquimay US$3, Chillán or Curarrehue US$4, Concepción or Osorno US$5, Puerto Montt US$7 and Santiago US$10.

Bus – international Buses Fénix goes to Buenos Aires on Mondays and Wednesdays via Santiago (US$70). Both Fénix and Tas Choapa have nightly buses to Mendoza (US$30) via Santiago.

Jac, Igi Llaima and San Martín, at Balmaceda 1598, connect Temuco with Junín de los Andes, San Martín de los Andes and Neuquén, usually via Paso Mamuil Malal, east of Pucón. Ruta Sur, Claro Solar 692, and Igi Llaima both go to Neuquén via Zapala. Typical fares are Junín or San Martín US$15, Zapala US$23 and Neuquén US$29.

Tas Choapa and Cruz del Sur have daily service to Bariloche (US$27) via Osorno.

Train Trains go north to Santiago (all year) and south to Puerto Montt (summer only). Buy tickets at the station (☎ 23-3416), eight blocks west of the plaza on Barros Arana, or in the city centre (☎ 23-3522) at Bulnes 582.

Getting Around
To/From the Airport Taxis from the Banco Osorno, Prat 606, to the airport charge US$4.

Bus The station and bus terminal are some distance from the centre but taxi colectivos are quick. Bus No 1 goes to the train station.

Car Consider a rental car for easy access to national parks and Indian villages. Agencies include the Automóvil Club (☎ 21-5132), at Bulnes 763, Hertz (☎ 23-5385), at Bulnes 750, Avis (☎ 21-1515), at Prat 800, First (☎ 23-3890), at Varas 1036, and Budget (☎ 21-4911), on the corner of General Mackenna and Varas.

PARQUE NACIONAL CONGUILLÍO
Towering above 60,000 hectares of alpine lakes, canyons and forests, 3125-metre Volcán Llaima has recorded violent eruptions as recently as 1957. Conguillío's Los Paraguas sector protects the monkey puzzle tree (meaning 'the umbrella' in Spanish because of its unusual shape; pehuén to the Mapuche, who gather its edible nuts). Southern beeches blanket lower elevations, but the Sierra Nevada's glaciated peaks exceed 2000

metres. Three metres of snow can accumulate in winter.

Things to See & Do
From November to March, CONAF's Lago Conguillío visitors' centre offers slide shows, ecological talks, guided hikes and boat trips, but independent travellers can undertake many of the same activities.

Experienced climbers can tackle Llaima from Los Paraguas. For skiing, contact the Escuela de Ski (☎ 23-5193) in Temuco.

Places to Stay
From mid-December to early March, *Cabañas y Camping Conguillío* (☎ 22-0254 in Temuco) rents rustic but comfortable six-bed cabañas for US$50 per night. Camp sites are not cheap at US$17 (up to five persons) – the best alternative is the backcountry.

At Los Paraguas, the *Refugio Escuela Ski* has 40 beds and a restaurant.

Getting There & Away
For Los Paragua, take Erbuc or Nar Bus from Temuco's Terminal de Buses Rurales to Cherquenco (US$1), then walk or hitch 17 km to the ski lodge.

For the northern entrance to the Conguillío sector, take a bus to Curacautín, 42 km from park headquarters, via Victoria (US$1.75) or Lautaro (US$2). From Curacautín, it is necessary to hitch. A southern approach passes through Cunco and Melipeuco (US$2), where buses leave Hostería Hue-Telén for the headquarters. With a rental car, you can make a loop from Temuco.

ANGOL
Destroyed half a dozen times by the Mapuche, Angol finally survived after 1862. Some distance off the Panamericana, it offers the best access to Parque Nacional Nahuelbuta, which preserves the largest remaining stands of coastal Araucarias (monkey puzzle trees).

Angol's hard-working, well-informed tourist office is near the bridge, on the east side of the Río Vergara. CONAF, on the

CHILE

corner of Prat and Chorrillos, may offer transport to Nahuelbuta.

The **Escuela Agrícola El Vergel**, created in the 19th century as a plant nursery and gardens, has a national reputation for training gardeners and farmers. Its **Museo Bullock** has local natural history specimens and archaeological artefacts. Five km east of Angol, reached by taxi colectivo No 2 from the plaza, it's open from 9 am to 8 pm daily.

Places to Stay & Eat

Accommodation at the *Casa del Huésped*, Dieciocho 465, is US$4 per person; *Pensión Chorrillos*, Chorrillos 724, is slightly dearer but also serves good, cheap lunches. *Residencial Olímpia*, Caupolicán 625, charges US$7/12 a single/double, while *Hostería Las Araucarias*, Prat 499, has singles with breakfast for US$7.

Café Stop, Lautaro 176, offers sandwiches and parrillada, while *Pizzería Sparlatto*, at Lautaro 418, has the obvious. For wider selections, try *Las Totoras*, at Ilabaca and Covandonga, or the *Club Social*, Caupolicán 498.

Things to Buy

Angol is known for its ceramics from two small factories: Cerámica Serra, at Bunster 153, and Cerámica Lablé, at Purén 864.

Getting There & Away

The Terminal Rodoviario, at Caupolicán 200, north of the plaza, has buses to Santiago, Temuco, and Concepción. The Terminal Rural, on the corner of Ilabaca and Lautaro, has buses along the Costa del Carbón to Concepción. Buses J B has 14 buses daily to Los Angeles (US$1.50).

Buses Angol goes to Vegas Blancas (US$1.75), seven km from the entrance to Parque Nacional Nahuelbuta, on Mondays, Wednesdays and Fridays at 7 am and 4 pm. For tours, see the following section.

PARQUE NACIONAL NAHUELBUTA

Araucarias up to 50 metres in height and two metres in diameter cover the slopes of Nahuelbuta, one of the monkey puzzle's last non-Andean refuges. About 35 km west of Angol, most of the park is a slightly undulating plain, 950 metres above sea level, but permanent streams have cut deep canyons, and jagged granitic peaks reach to 1565 metres. Summers are warm and dry but snow touches the summits in winter.

Things to See & Do

Rangers offer audiovisual presentations at CONAF's Pehuenco visitors' centre. Nahuelbuta has 30 km of roads and 15 km of footpaths, so car-touring, camping and hiking are all possible. Admission is US$1.75.

Piedra del Aguila, a four-km hike from Pehuenco, is a 1400-metre overlook with views to the Andes and the Pacific. **Cerro Anay**, 1450 metres, is similar.

Places to Stay

Campgrounds at Pehuenco and at Coimallín cost US$5 per site.

Getting There & Away

Besides regular services to Vegas Blancas, Buses Angol offers Sunday tours for US$8, leaving the Terminal Rural at 7 am.

PUCÓN

Until Volcán Villarica's next major eruption obliterates it, the up-market resort of Pucón will offer fine accommodation and superb food. Villarrica is cheaper (and less vulnerable to lava flows), but a visit to Pucón is worthwhile.

Information

Tourist Office In summer, the tourist office (☎ 44-1916), Brasil 115, is open from 8 am to 10 pm Monday to Saturday, and from 10 am to 1 pm and 6 to 9 pm Sundays. Winter hours are shorter.

Money Turcamb, O'Higgins 472, will change cash and travellers' cheques.

Travel Agencies Pucón is Chile's adventure travel mecca, with climbing, rafting, mountain biking, horse-riding, fishing and other activities. Most agencies are on or near O'Higgins, but prices do not vary greatly – Volcán Villarrica, a day climb if the weather holds, costs about US$35 per person. It is normally obligatory to have a local guide for the climb to the summit.

National Parks CONAF (☎ 441261), Lincoyán 372, may help with transport to Villarrica and Huerquehue national parks.

Places to Stay
In summer, several hospedajes charge around US$6 to US$7 (some with breakfast or kitchen privileges), including *Hospedaje Sonia* (a good place to meet people), at Lincoyán and Brasil, *Hospedaje Lucía*, at Lincoyán 565, and *Hospedaje Juan Torres*, at Lincoyán 443. One reader reports a fine hospedaje (about US$7) in the back of the Holzapfel Bäckerei.

Clean, pleasant *Hostería Don Pepe*, at General Urrutia and Arauco, is open all year (US$11 for singles). *Residencial Lincoyán*, Lincoyán 323, and *Hostería Millarrahue* (where the restaurant has received a warm endorsement), O'Higgins 460, are similar in price and quality.

Places to Eat
Besides hotel restaurants, there are scores of other eateries. For empanadas, visit *Los Hornos de Pucón*, Caupolicán 710. Nearby *Marmonch*, Ecuador 175, has a different, inexpensive lunch daily. *El Fogón*, O'Higgins 480, is a parrilla, while *El Conquistador*, O'Higgins 323, has pizza, pancakes, meat and seafood.

For Italian food, go to *Trattoria Mangiare*, Caupolicán 243. *Club 77*, O'Higgins 635, offers traditional specialties like pastel de choclo, baked empanadas and smoked trout. For exquisite Germanic goodies, try *Holzapfel Bäckerei*, Clemente Holzapfel 524. The all-you-can-eat *Buffet Cordillera* is on Ansorena between Urrutia and O'Higgins.

Getting There & Away
The bus terminal is on Palguín between Urrutia and O'Higgins. Buses Jac has many departures to Villarrica (US$0.50, 25 km). Tur-Bus, Fénix and Power have service to Santiago.

Buses Cordillera go to Paillaco, on Lago Caburgua (Parque Nacional Huerquehue). Buses Regional Villarrica has several buses to Currarehue and Puesco, the last stop before Junín de los Andes, Argentina.

VILLARRICA
Founded in 1552, colonial Villarrica withered under repeated Mapuche attacks until treaties were signed in 1883. The present resort, 86 km south-west of Temuco, on Lago Villarrica, also shares its name with a smouldering, snowcapped volcano.

Information
Tourist Office The tourist office (☎ 41-1162), Pedro de Valdivia 1070, has a very useful *Datos Utiles Villarrica* and an updated list of accommodation and prices. In summer, it stays open from 8.30 am to 11 pm; at other seasons, hours are 8.30 am to 1 pm and 1.30 to 6.30 pm.

Money To change US and Argentine cash, and US travellers' cheques, go to Turcamb, Valentín Letelier 704.

Post & Telecommunications Correos de Chile is on General Urrutia near Anfión Muñoz. CTC is at Henríquez 430.

Emergency Villarrica's hospital (☎ 41-1169) is at San Martín 460.

Things to See
Next to the tourist office, a skeletal **museum** shows Mapuche jewellery, musical instruments and roughly hewn wooden masks. Nearby is an oblong Mapuche **ruca**, with thatched walls and roof.

Behind the tourist office, the **Feria Artesanal** has a selection of crafts and traditional Mapuche food.

Places to Stay
The most convenient and economical place

CHILE

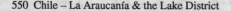

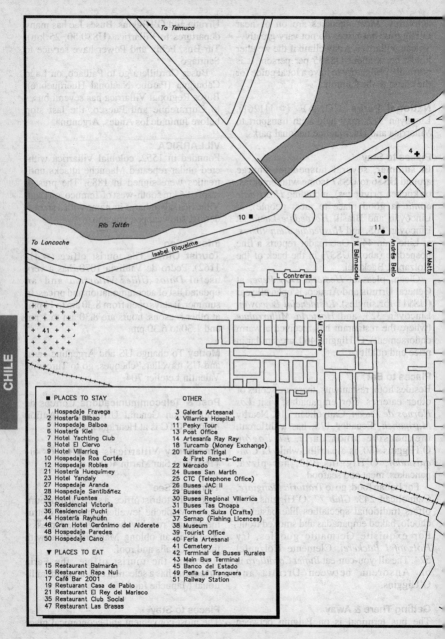

To Temuco

To Loncoche

Río Toltén

Isabel Riquelme

L Contreras

J. M. Balmaceda

Andrés Bello

M A Matta

J. M. Carrera

1

4

3

11

10

41

PLACES TO STAY

1 Hospedaje Fravega
2 Hostería Bilbao
5 Hospedaje Balboa
6 Hostería Kiel
7 Hotel Yachting Club
8 Hotel El Ciervo
9 Hotel Villarrica
10 Hospedaje Roa Cortés
12 Hospedaje Robles
21 Hostería Huequimey
23 Hotel Yandaly
27 Hospedaje Aranda
28 Hospedaje Santibáñez
32 Hotel Fuentes
33 Residencial Victoria
36 Residencial Puchi
44 Hostería Rayhuén
46 Gran Hotel Gerónimo del Alderete
48 Hospedaje Paredes
50 Hospedaje Cano

PLACES TO EAT

15 Restaurant Balmarán
16 Restaurant Rapa Nui
17 Café Bar 2001
19 Restaurant Casa de Pablo
21 Restaurant El Rey del Marisco
35 Restaurant Club Social
47 Restaurant Las Brasas

OTHER

3 Galería Artesanal
4 Villarrica Hospital
11 Pesky Tour
13 Post Office
14 Artesanía Ray Ray
18 Turcamb (Money Exchange)
20 Turismo Trigal
   & First Rent-a-Car
22 Mercado
24 Buses San Martín
25 CTC (Telephone Office)
26 Buses JAC II
29 Buses Lit
30 Buses Regional Villarrica
31 Buses Tas Choapa
34 Tornería Suiza (Crafts)
37 Sernap (Fishing Licences)
38 Museum
39 Tourist Office
40 Feria Artesanal
41 Cemetery
42 Terminal de Buses Rurales
43 Main Bus Terminal
45 Banco del Estado
49 Peña La Tranquera
51 Railway Station

CHILE

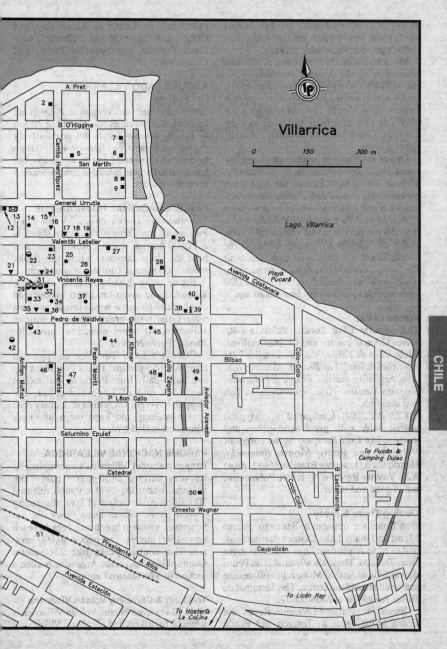

CHILE

to stay is *Camping Dulac*, two km east of town. It can be crowded, but the shady sites (US$7) provide reasonable privacy.

Many hotels operate in summer only, like *Hospedaje Cano*, Aviador Acevedo 1057, for US$4.50 a single without breakfast, US$6 with. One reader enjoyed *Hospedaje Balboa*, San Martín 734, with singles for US$7, despite describing its owner as nosy but nice. Check the tourist office for additional listings.

One of the cheapest permanent places, for about US$7 per person, is *Hotel Fuentes*, Vicente Reyes 665. Rooms are basic, but pleasant and comfortable, while the downstairs bar and restaurant are cosy in winter.

Residencial Victoria, Anfión Muñoz 530, is US$6 per person, and *Residencial Puchi*, Pedro de Valdivia 678, costs US$6/10 for singles/doubles with shared bath. *Hostería Rayhuén*, Pedro Montt 668, is a charming place with well-heated rooms (US$17/29 with breakfast) and a very fine restaurant.

Places to Eat
The popular *Club Social*, Valdivia 640, serves German cuisine and Chilean seafood, while *Casa de Pablo*, Valentín Letelier 726, has Spanish food. *Las Brasas*, Alderete 768, is an Argentine parrilla. *El Rey del Marisco*, Valentín Letelier 1030, specialises in fish and shellfish.

Café Bar 2001, Henríquez 379, is a typical tourist café, with good sandwiches and kuchen, like *Café Scorpio*, on the corner of Valdivia and Pedro Montt. *Baimarán*, Henríques 331, serves Brazilian food. *Rapa Nui*, Vicente Reyes 678, is not Polynesian, but is good and cheap.

Getting There & Away
Bus Buses are frequent to Santiago, Puerto Montt and many Lake District destinations, and even to Argentina; fares resemble those from Temuco. The main terminal is on Pedro de Valdivia at Anfión Muñoz, but offices are scattered around the centre. The Terminal de Buses Rurales is at Muñoz 657.

Buses Jac, corner of Vicente Reyes and Pedro Montt, goes to Temuco and Pucón

every half-hour, and to Licán Ray and Coñaripe. Buses Regional Villarrica, near Hotel Fuentes, has buses to Pucón and Curarrehue.

AROUND LAGO VILLARRICA
Hot Springs
Termas de Huife and Termas de Palguín are up-market hot springs resorts within 30 km of Pucón, but day use is not prohibitively expensive. Buses Cordillera (☎ 44-1903) go to Huife at 12.30 and 5 pm on weekdays, but transport to Palguín is hard to arrange, except for taxis or tours.

PARQUE NACIONAL HUERQUEHUE
Mountainous Huerquehue, 35 km from Pucón on Lago Caburgua's eastern shore, is a 12,500-hectare reserve. Rushing streams have cut deep canyons, where the flanks reach 2000 metres. Bird life is abundant.

From park headquarters at Lago Tinquilco, the seven-km **Lago Verde Trail** climbs through dense beech forests and past waterfalls, with great views of Volcán Villarrica. At upper elevations are solid stands of pehuén trees.

CONAF's Lago Tinquilco campground charges US$5 per site. Buses Cordillera has two buses daily from Pucón to Paillaco, at the south end of Lago Caburgua, but Tinquilco is eight km further on a dusty road – start walking and hope for a lift. Park admission is US$1.75.

PARQUE NACIONAL VILLARRICA
Parque Nacional Villarrica's centrepiece is its very active, 2850-metre namesake volcano, where the 1971 eruption released 30 million cubic metres of lava, displacing several rivers. Where these flows did not penetrate, southern beech and pehuén reach up to 1500 metres. The park's 60,000 hectares also contain peaks like 2360-metre Quetrupillán and, on the Argentine border, a section of 3746-metre Lanín.

Trekking & Climbing Volcán Villarrica
Only 12 km from Pucón, Volcán Villarrica is a mecca for hikers and climbers. Villarrica's

summit is not technically demanding but requires equipment and either experience or someone who knows the route. Turn back in bad weather. A reader has advised that a local guide is normally obligatory for the climb.

Many Pucón travel agencies rent equipment and lead one-day excursions (about US$35 per person). Several travellers have praised an English-speaking guide named Aldo, who lives at Uruguay 650 in Pucón.

The most convenient of several long treks circles the volcano's southern flank and exits the park at Palguín; from Palguín, another route goes to Puesco, near the Argentine border.

Skiing

The Refugio Villarrica accommodates skiers in winter; contact Pucón's Centro de Esqui (☎ 44-1176).

Getting There & Away

Though Villarrica is very near Pucón, there is no scheduled public transport to Sector Rucapillán, but a shared taxi should be reasonable. To Sector Puesco, there is regular transport with Buses Regional Villarrica.

LICÁN RAY

On Lago Calafquén, 30 km south of Villarrica, visitors pack fashionable Licán Ray's fine beaches, restaurants, hotels, and cafés, but out of season, it's very tranquil. The tourist office is on General Urrutia between Huenumán and Marichanquín.

There are two nightly crafts fairs: one, on Calle Esmeralda, behind the tourist office, focuses on products by local artisans; the other, on Urrutia, across from the tourist office, has goods from around the region and the country.

Places to Stay & Eat

For US$2 per person, *Camping Licán Ray*, at the junction of Urrutia with the Panguipulli road, is the best bargain; other campgrounds charge for a minimum of six persons.

One reader called *Chambres d'Hote*, Catriñi 140, the best hospedaje on her entire

trip, at US$8 a single. *Hotel Refugio Inaltulafquén*, Punulef 510, has singles with shared bath for US$14.

El Candíl, Urrutia 845, has good Spanish food and Chilean seafood. *Ñaños*, also on Urrutia, is a very popular eatery.

Getting There & Away

Bus Buses Jac goes often to Villarrica (45 minutes) from its own terminal, at Urrutia and Marichanquín, but most buses leave from the corner of Urrutia and Huenumán. Every morning at 7.45 am, a local bus goes to Panguipulli (two hours) via back roads. There is a direct service to Santiago.

COÑARIPE

At the east end of Lago Calafquén, 22 km from Licá Ray, Coñaripe's black-sand beaches sprout multicoloured tents in summer. Pleasant but basic *Hotel Antulafquén* has singles for US$4. The cafeteria across the street has fabulous humitas, and *Restaurant El Mirador* is an attractive place for an unhurried meal.

Buses Jac has several buses daily from Villarrica via Licán Ray (US$1).

VALDIVIA

Pedro de Valdivia himself founded Santa María La Blanca de Valdivia. After Mapuche raids, it became a military camp, but its architecture, surnames of the people and regional cuisine show the influence of 19th-century German immigrants. Valdivia (population 110,000), 'City of the Rivers', is 160 km south-west of Temuco, 45 km off the Panamericana. Across the Río Calle Calle is Isla Teja, a leafy suburb.

Information

Tourist Office Sernatur (☎ 21-3596), on the riverfront, at Avenida Prat 555, is open on weekdays from 9 am to 8.30 pm, on Saturdays from 10 am to 4 pm, and on Sundays from 10 am to 2 pm.

Money Try Turismo Money Exchange, at Arauco 331, Local 23, or Money Exchange El Libertador, at Carampangue 325.

CHILE

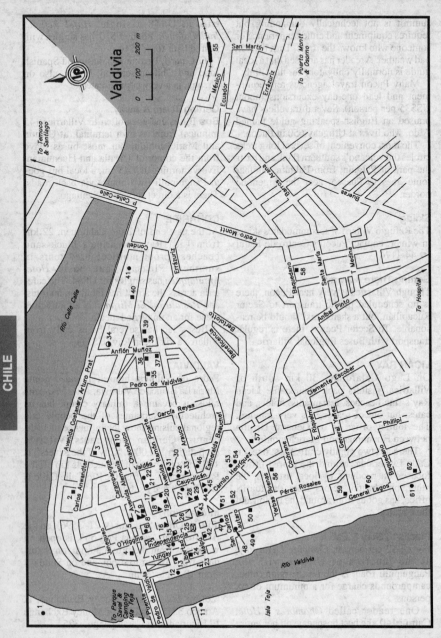

Valdivia

0   100   200 m

To Temuco & Santiago

To Puerto Montt & Osorno

San Martín

To Puerto Montt & Osorno

To Hospital

Río Calle Calle

P Calle-Calle

Pedro Montt

México

Ecuador

Errázuriz

Barros Arana

Bueras

Condell

Errázuriz

Santa María

Baquedano

Anfbal Pinto

T Medina

Bertolotto

Beneficencia

García Reyes

Clemente Escobar

E Riquelme

Cochrane

General Yáñez

Phillipi

Pérez Rosales

Baquedano

General Lagos

Yerbas Buenas

Camilo Henríquez

Esmeralda Beauchef

Arauco

Avenida Ramón Picarte

Caupolicán

Maipú

San Carlos

Lautaro

Independencia

Libertad

Yungay

O'Higgins

Janequeo

Carampangue

Avenida Alemania

Chacabuco

Avenida Costanera Arturo Prat

Carlos Anwandter

Valdés

Pedro de Valdivia

Anfbal Muñoz

Río Valdivia

Isla Teja

To Parque Saval & Camping Isla Teja

Pedro de Valdivia

J Puente Valdivia

Río Calle Calle

34

40

41

39

38

36

35   37

3

10

2

1

12

11

55

58

57

57

59

60

61   62

48   49

50

51   52

53   54

46

44   45

43

42

23   24

22

25

26

27   28   29

30   32   33

31

9

8   7

6

5

4

13

14   15   16   17   18   19   20   21

	PLACES TO STAY	15	Restaurant El Con-quistador	22	Music Pub Gay-Lussac
2	Hospedaje Anwandter 482	16	Café Hausmann	23	Sernatur (Tourist Office) &
3	Hospedaje Anwandter 601	17	Restaurant La Vie Claire & Pastelería La Baguette		Corporación Cultural de Valdivia
4	Hotel Pedro de Valdivia	18	Centro Español	25	Post Office
9	Hotel Palace	28	Club de la Unión	26	Plaza de la República
10	Hotel Melillanca	33	Restaurant La Bomba	27	Ladeco
24	Hotel Unión	43	Café Palace	29	Crafts Market
35	Hotel Montserrat	45	Restaurant El Patio	30	Chocolatería Camino de Luna
36	Residencial Aínlebu & Residencial Germa-nia	51	Gelatería Entrelagos (Ice Cream)	31	Telefónica del Sur
37	Residencial Calle Calle	60	Restaurant Yang Cheng	32	Turismo Cochrane
38	Hospedaje Picarte 953			34	Bus Terminal
39	Hotel Regional		OTHER	41	Torreón del Barro
40	Hostal Chalet Alemán			42	Turismo Cono Sur
50	Hostal Centro Torreón	1	Universidad Austral	44	Turismo (Money Exchange)
56	Hostal Villa Paulina	5	El Libertador (Money Exchange)	46	Discotheque Izma
57	Hostal 403	6	Telefónica del Sur	47	Turismo Paraty
58	Hospedaje Olivera	11	Museo Histórico y Arqueológico	48	Telefónica del Sur
59	Hospedaje Turiños	12	Feria Fluvial	49	Centro Cultural El Austral
62	Hotel Raitué	13	Mercado	52	First Rent-a-Car
		14	London Pub Disco-theque	53	Artesanía CEMA-Chile
▼	PLACES TO EAT	19	Bánco Concepción	54	Ruca Indiana
		20	Automóvil Club de Chile	55	Railway Station
7	Restaurant Shanghai	21	Libros Chiloé	61	Asset & Méndez Rent-a-Car
8	Establecimientos Delicias (Café)				

CHILE

Post & Telecommunications Correos de Chile is at O'Higgins 575. Telefónica del Sur has offices at at San Carlos 107, O'Higgins 386 and Picarte 461, Local 2.

Emergency The Hospital Regional (☎ 21-4066) is at Bueras 1003, near Aníbal Pinto.

Things to See
On Sundays, people jam the **Feria Fluvial**, a riverside market north of the tourist office, to buy fish and fruit for the week, float downstream to Niebla and Corral or just loll in the sun. On Isla Teja, shady **Parque Saval** has a riverside beach and a pleasant trail to lily-covered **Laguna de los Lotos**. Nearby, the **Universidad Austral** operates a first-rate dairy outlet, with ice cream, yoghurt and cheese at bargain prices.

In a riverfront mansion on Isla Teja, the **Museo Histórico y Arqueológico** has a well-labelled (Spanish only) collection containing fine displays of Mapuche artefacts and household items from early German colonists. Well-organised tours (Spanish only) are a bit rushed but the guides respond well to questions. Admission is about US$1.

Places to Stay
Most hospedajes take their name from the street on which they're located, so don't be surprised to find three or more with identical names – get the exact number. Sernatur provides a thorough list of seasonal accommodation, much of which is on avenidas Ramón Picarte and Carlos Anwandter.

For US$8 per site, *Camping Isla Teja*

(☎ 21-3584), at the end of Calle Los Robles, has a pleasant orchard setting, good facilities and a riverside beach. Cheaper but less comfortable sites at Parque Saval cost about US$4.

Residencial Calle Calle, Anfión Muñoz 597, has singles for US$4. *Hotel Regional*, Picarte 1005, is plain but clean, with hot water, friendly staff and a small restaurant (US$6). Highly regarded *Hostal 403*, Yerbas Buenas 403, charges US$8 with breakfast and has a good restaurant.

Hospedaje Picarte 953, Picarte 953, opposite the bus terminal, is very clean and attractive, at US$11/20 for a single/double with breakfast. *Residencial Germania*, at Picarte 873, has singles for US$11 with breakfast, hot showers, clean rooms and friendly German-speaking owners. *Hospedaje Anwandter 601*, at Anwandter 601, is comparable. Another popular place is *Hotel Montserrat*, a few doors from the Germania, at Picarte 849, for US$9/16 with breakfast.

Dearer, but excellent value, is *Hotel Isla Teja* (☎ 21-5014), across the bridge, at Las Encinas 220, for US$38/45. Costly but unique is *Hotel Pedro de Valdivia* (☎ 21-2931), a pink palace with elaborate gardens, at Carampangue 190. Expect to pay about US$67/80 with breakfast.

Places to Eat

Stroll Arauco between Caupolicán and Pérez Rosales for eateries like *El Patio*, Arauco 347. *Hostal 403* has a different dinner special nightly.

Restaurant El Conquistador, O'Higgins 477, has a simple downstairs café and a fancier upstairs restaurant. *Club de La Unión*, Camilo Henríquez 540, offers wellprepared three-course meals for about US$4. Try also the *Centro Español*, at Henríquez 436, or *La Bomba*, Caupolicán 594.

For coffee and snacks, check out *Café Palace*, Pérez Rosales 580. For fine pastries and desserts, try *Establecimientos Delicias*, at Henríquez 372, or *Café Hausmann*, at O'Higgins 394. For very fine kuchen, visit *La Baguette*, at Caupolicán 435-B; for ice cream, it's *Entrelagos*, Pérez Rosales 630.

Things to Buy

For chocolate specialties, go to Chocolatería Entrelagos, at Pérez Rosales 622, Confitería Sur, at Henríquez 374, or Camino de Luna, at Picarte 417. There's an interesting, informal evening crafts market at the north-east corner of Maipú and Henríquez.

Getting There & Away

Air Aeródromo Las Marías is north of the city via the Puente Calle Calle. Ladeco (☎ 21-3392), Caupolicán 579, flies to Santiago four times a week.

Bus From the Terminal de Buses (☎ 212212), Anfión Muñoz 360, there are frequent buses to destinations on or near the Panamericana, from Puerto Montt to Santiago. Typical fares are Temuco US$3.50, Puerto Montt US$5, Concepción US$8 and Santiago US$13.

Turibus and Buses Norte serve Bariloche, Argentina (US$22). There are three buses weekly to Punta Arenas (US$57) via Argentina.

Línea Verde, Pirehueico, Valdivia and Chile Nuevo go to Panguipulli (US$2.50), and Línea Verde to Futrono. Buses Jac has a regular service to Villarrica and Temuco.

Getting Around

From the bus terminal, any bus marked 'Plaza' goes to the central Plaza de la República. Buses from the plaza to the terminal go down Arauco before turning onto Picarte.

AROUND VALDIVIA

Corral

At Corral, Niebla and Isla Mancera, at the mouth of the Río Valdivia, is a series of 17th-century Spanish forts. Largest and most intact is the Fuerte de Corral (1645), site of a key naval encounter between Chilean patriots and Spanish loyalists in 1820.

Corral and nearby Armagos are most easily reached by boat, but buses from

Valdivia go directly to Niebla (launches across the river cost US$0.75). The best alternative is a morning cruise from Valdivia's Puerto Fluvial, returning by afternoon bus.

PANGUIPULLI

Quieter and slower-paced than other resorts, Panguipulli is 115 km east of Valdivia by paved highway via Lanco. It has sensational views across Lago Panguipulli to Volcán Choshuenco. In summer, the tourist office, on the plaza, is open daily from 10 am to 8.30 pm.

One reader has praised *Hospedaje Berrocal*, at Carrera 834, but a nameless hospedaje on Pedro de Valdivia, directly opposite the bus terminal, charges only US$4 per person. The family house of Nicolás Pozas in Calle Pedro de Valdivia, opposite the bus terminal, for US$6. *Hostal España*, corner of O'Higgins and Rodríguez, has singles for US$11 with breakfast.

Erwin Bittner, a German, rents rooms or camping space 18 km from Panguipulli but will offer free housing and meals in return for work on his organic farm. Contact him through Restaurant Girasol (which also has accommodation), on Calle Martínez de Rozas.

Try *Restaurant Chapulín*, at Rozas 639, for meat and seafood, or *Girasol*, on Rozas near Matta, which is recommended. The most intriguing choice is *Restaurant Didáctico El Gourmet*, a highly regarded cooking school, at Freire 0394.

Getting There & Away

Bus Panguipulli's main terminal, on Pedro de Valdivia near Gabriela Mistral, has regional and long-distance service, plus buses to Choshuenco, Neltume and Puerto Fuy (Lago Pirehueico). Several companies have daily buses to Valdivia (2½ hours); Tur-Bus has a separate terminal, at Valdivia and Rozas.

For the latest information on the ferry from Puerto Fuy to Puerto Pirehueico and the Argentine border, ask at Hostería Quetropillán.

Ruta Andes uses a smaller terminal, on Freire near Etchegaray, for daily service to Coñaripe (US$1.75), Licán Ray and Villarrica.

CHOSHUENCO

Tiny Choshuenco, at the east end of Lago Panguipulli, survives from farming, a sawmill and visitors who enjoy its attractive black-sand beach. *Hotel Rucapillán*, near the beach, is very clean, with heated rooms, a good restaurant, hot showers and friendly staff, for about US$10 per person. Basic but agreeable *Claris Hotel* charges US$6.

Getting There & Away

Buses from Panguipulli to Puerto Fuy pass through Choshuenco. From Puerto Fuy, there are daily ferries to Puerto Pirehueico, but times vary.

OSORNO

In the late 16th century, huge encomiendas supported over 1000 Spaniards and mestizos in San Mateo de Osorno, but rebellion in 1599 forced them to flee to Chiloé. Only in 1796 was resettlement successful, and well after independence, the Mapuche still made overland travel difficult and dangerous.

German immigrants have left a mark on Osorno in dairying and manufacturing. Tourism is increasing because Osorno (910 km south of Santiago, population 110,000) is a key road junction for Lagos Puyehue and Rupanco, Parque Nacional Puyehue, and the Argentine border.

Information

Tourist Office Sernatur's (☎ 23-4104) well-informed office, on the ground floor of the Edificio Gobernación Provincial, is well stocked with maps and brochures. *El Diario Austral*, the daily newspaper, publishes a free, monthly *Guía de Servicios*.

Money Try Turismo Frontera, in the Galería Catedral, Ramírez 949, Local 5, or Agencia de Viajes Mundial (just across the hall).

Post & Telecommunications Correos de

CHILE

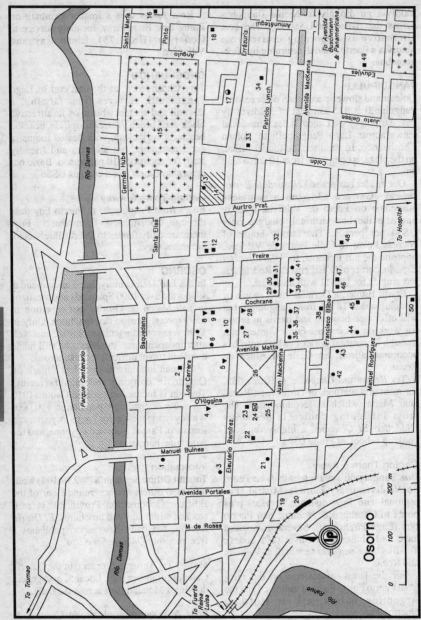

Osorno

To Avenida Buschmann & Panamericana

To Avenida Buschmann & Panamericana

To Hospital

To Trumao

To Fuerte Reina Luisa

Santa María

Pinto

Angulo

Errázuriz

Amunátegui

Avenida MackKenna

Justo Geisse

Patricio Lynch

Colón

Germán Hube

Santa Elisa

Aurtro Prat

Freire

Cochrane

Baquedano

Los Carrera

O'Higgins

Ramírez

Eleuterio

Manuel Bulnes

Avenida Portales

M de Rosas

Avenida Matta

Juan MacKenna

Francisco Bilbao

Manuel Rodríguez

Río Damas

Río Damas

Parque Centenario

Río Rahue

0   100   200   300   400 m

■ PLACES TO STAY	▼ PLACES TO EAT	15 German Cemetery
		17 Main Bus Terminal
2 Hospedaje	4 Deutscher Verein	19 Disco Mario's
9 Hotel Interlagos	5 Dino's Restaurant	20 Railway Station
11 Residencial Schulz	8 Pizzería Lucas	21 CONAF
12 Residencial Aitué	28 Pasterlería Rhenania	24 Post Office
16 Hospedaje	39 Restaurant Casa del	25 Sernatur (Tourist
Amunátegui	Altillo	Office)
18 Hospedaje de la	40 Pizzería Los Platos	26 Plaza de Armas
Fuente		27 Galería Cated-
22 Hotel Tirol	OTHER	ral/Turismo Frontera
23 Gran Hotel Osorno		29 Telefónica del Sur
31 Hotel García Hurtado	1 Automóvil Club de	30 Cambiotur (Money
de Mendoza	Chile	Exchange)
33 Residencial Ortega	3 Cine Lido	32 Los Detalles (Crafts)
34 Hotel Rayantú	6 Centro Cultural	35 Banco de Chile
38 Residencial La Posada	7 Ñiltur Rent-a-Car	36 First Rent-a-Car
45 Residencial Hein	10 Galería	37 German Consulate
46 Hotel Waeger	Rombocól/Osorno	41 Alta Artesanía
47 Residencial Bilbao	Tour	42 Hertz Rent-a-Car
48 Residencial Stop	13 Orlandina Regalos	43 Museo Histórico
49 Hotel Villa Eduvijes	14 Mercado Munici-	Municipal
50 Residencial Riga	pal/Terminal de	44 LAN-Chile & Budget
	Buses Rurales	Rent-a-Car

Chile is at O'Higgins 645. Telefónica del Sur is at Mackenna 1004.

Emergency The Hospital Base (☎ 23-5572) is on Avenida Bühler, the southern extension of Arturo Prat.

Things to See
Between the plaza and the railway station, the **Historic District** has numerous obsolete factories and weathered Victorian houses. West of the station, **Fuerte Reina Luisa** (1793) once guarded river access to Osorno. While unspectacular, the well-restored ruins are a pleasant site for a lunchtime breather.

Osorno's **Museo Histórico Municipal**, Matta 809, with its unusual collection, traces the region and the city from prehistory to the present.

Places to Stay
Camping Olegario Mohr, just off the Panamericana, has picnic tables and firepits, but no hot water and limited toilet facilities. However, it's free, and the attendants sell hot fresh bread for breakfast. Any taxi colectivo on Avenida Buschmann goes within a few minutes' walk of the site.

Clean but ramshackle *Residencial Stop*, Freire 810, has hostel accommodation (US$4 with kitchen privileges). *Hospedaje Amunátegui*, Amunátegui 372, has very clean singles for US$4. After amicable haggling, *Hospedaje de la Fuente*, Los Carrera 1587, charges about US$4 a single for spotless rooms with sagging beds. *Residencial Hein*, Cochrane 843, has small but well-kept rooms for US$10/17 with shared bath. *Hotel Villa Eduvijes*, Eduvijes 856, is good value at US$13/23.

Places to Eat
Pizzería Lucas, Cochrane 559, is bright, small and very popular – go early for lunch. *La Naranja*, Local 13, in the Mercado Municipal on the corner of Prat and Errázuriz, has very good, inexpensive food, while there are fine pastries and short orders at *Pastelería Rhenania*, Ramírez 977. The *Deutscher Verein*, O'Higgins 563, more Chilean than German, has very good food and fine service at moderate prices. For a

CHILE

splurge, try *Casa del Altillo*, Mackenna 1011.

Getting There & Away

Air Aeropuerto Carlos Hott Siebert (also called Cañal Bajo) is seven km east of the city centre. LAN-Chile (☎ 23-6688), Matta 862, Block C, now flies to and from Santiago via Temuco, three times weekly. Ladeco (☎ 23-4355) has offices at Cochrane 816, but flies from Puerto Montt.

Bus For long-distance services, the Terminal de Buses (☎ 23-4149) is at Avenida Errázuriz 1400. Some, but not all, buses to local and regional destinations leave from the Mercado Municipal, two blocks west, on the corner of Errázuriz and Prat.

Bus – long-distance Buses Puyehue has several buses daily to Termas de Puyehue en route to Aguas Calientes (US$2), and to the Chilean customs and immigration at Pajaritos (US$3). Transur, in the Igi Llaima office at the main terminal, goes to Las Cascadas, on the eastern shore of Lago Llanquihue. Buses Via Octay, also in the main terminal, serves Puerto Octay and Frutillar, on Lago Llanquihue.

Bus – regional Many companies go to Puerto Montt (US$2); most also cover northern destinations. Typical fares include Temuco US$4, Los Angeles or Concepción US$8, Santiago US$12 and Viña del Mar/Valparaíso US$14.

Bus – international Osorno has convenient services to Argentina via Puyehue, but there are also connections for Mendoza and Buenos Aires via Santiago. Buses to Chilean Patagonia (Coyhaique, Punta Arenas, Puerto Natales) also use Puyehue; most of these services originate in Puerto Montt.

Fares to Bariloche are about US$20, to Mendoza US$40.

Train The train station (☎ 23-2991) is at the west end of Mackenna, corner of Portales. Summer trains go to Temuco and Santiago.

AROUND OSORNO

Termas de Puyehue

Termas de Puyehue is a very expensive place to stay, but worth a visit for its old-world elegance. It's 76 km east of Osorno, where paved Ruta 215 forks; the north fork goes to Anticura and the Argentine border, while its southern lateral goes to Aguas Calientes and Antillanca, in Parque Nacional Puyehue.

PARQUE NACIONAL PUYEHUE

Puyehue's 107,000 hectares of verdant montane forest and starkly awesome volcanic scenery are about 75 km east of Osorno. In its lower Valdivian forest, the dominant tree is the multitrunked *ulmo*. The dense understorey includes the delicate, rust-barked *arrayán* (a myrtle), *quilla* (a solid bamboo which make some areas impenetrable), and wild fuchsia. At higher altitudes, southern beeches dominate.

Birds are the most visible fauna. On the peaks, you may spot the Andean condor, and look for the Chilean torrent duck in river rapids.

Altitudes range from 250 metres on the Río Golgol to 2236 metres on Volcán Puyehue. January and February are best for the high country, but winter skiing is also popular. Despite the moist climate, Volcán Puyehue's western slopes have been barren since 1960, when a major eruption left now extinct fumaroles and still active hot springs.

Aguas Calientes

At Aguas Calientes, CONAF's **Centro de Visitantes**, open daily from 9 am to 1 pm and 2.30 to 8.30 pm, has a simple but effective display on natural history and geomorphology, with slide shows daily at 5 pm.

Nearby **Sendero El Pionero** is a steep 1800-metre nature trail with splendid views of Lago Puyehue, the valley of the Golgol, and Volcán Puyehue. Watch for the *nalca*, resembling an enormous rhubarb with edible stalks and leaves the size of umbrellas, and the *ulmo*, which grows to 45 metres. For a longer excursion, take the 11-km trail to **Lago Bertín**.

CONAF rangers lead overnight trips to Lago Paraíso, Volcán Puyehue, Lago Constancia and Pampa Frutilla. For schedules and to reserve a spot (free of charge), contact CONAF here or in Osorno (☎ 23-4393), at Mackenna 674, 3rd floor. Bring your own tent, food and rain gear.

Skiing
For some of the finest views of Puyehue and its surroundings, visit the Antillanca ski lodge, at the foot of Volcán Casablanca. The season runs from early June to late October.

Anticura
Anticura is the best base for exploring Puyehue's wildest areas. The highway follows the Río Golgol, but the finest scenery is the desolate plateau at the base of Volcán Puyehue, reached by an overnight backpack from El Caulle, two km west of Anticura.

On Puyehue's western slope, a steep morning's walk from El Caulle, CONAF's well-kept refugio is a good place to lodge or camp. From the refugio, it's another four hours over a moonscape of lava flows and fumaroles to a spring with rustic thermal baths, and a fine and private camp site.

Places to Stay & Eat
CONAF charges US$4 for camp sites at Catrue, near Anticura, which has fresh water, picnic tables, firepits and basic toilets. At Aguas Calientes, concessionaires operate *Camping Chanleufú* (US$14 per site) and *Camping Los Derrumbes* (US$11), both for up to eight persons. Fees include use of the thermal baths, but these sites are crowded and noisy in summer.

Getting There & Away
From Osorno, Buses Puyehue has several buses daily to Termas de Puyehue and Aguas Calientes (US$2), and to Chilean immigration at Pajaritos (US$3). In winter, the Club Andino de Osorno (☎ 23-2297) offers direct services to Antillanca.

PUERTO OCTAY
In the early days of German settlement, Puerto Octay was an important port on Lago Llanquihue between Puerto Montt and Osorno. Its municipal tourist office is on Pedro Montt. The **Museo El Colono**, on Independencia near Esperanza, displays antique farm machinery and other turn-of-the-century artefacts.

Many readers have praised the clean, comfortable and friendly hospedaje upstairs at Wulf 712 (US$8 per person with breakfast). The same folks run *Restaurant Cabaña*, across the road. *Café Kali*, opposite the Plaza de Armas, is good for breakfast, drinks and desserts. For empanadas, try *La Naranja*, at Independencía and Pedro Montt.

Via Octay buses go to and from Osorno's main bus terminal several times daily. On weekdays, one late afternoon bus goes to Las Cascadas.

LAS CASCADAS
Las Cascadas, a village on the eastern shore of Lago Llanquihue, has an attractive black-sand beach. Highly recommended *Hostería Irma*, one km south of town on the Ensenada road, charges about US$12 per person. Diagonally opposite, along the lake, is a peaceful, quiet and free camp site with almost no facilities. *Camping Las Cañitas*, three km down the road, charges US$5 per site for basic services, including cold showers.

The bus from Puerto Octay arrives in the early evening, but there is no service on the poor 20-km road to Ensenada, the entry point to Parque Nacional Vicente Pérez Rosales – either walk, hitch or return to the Panamericana and take the bus from Puerto Varas.

FRUTILLAR
From Frutillar, 70 km south of Osorno, snowcapped Volcán Osorno seems to float on the horizon across Lago Llanquihue. Noted for its Germanic architecture, Frutillar consists of lakeside Frutillar Bajo and of Frutillar Alto, two km west, near the Panamericana.

Frutillar Bajo's helpful tourist kiosk, at the jetty on Avenida Philippi, is open from 9 am to 9 pm in January and February; the rest of the year, it's open from 10 am to 6 pm.

CHILE

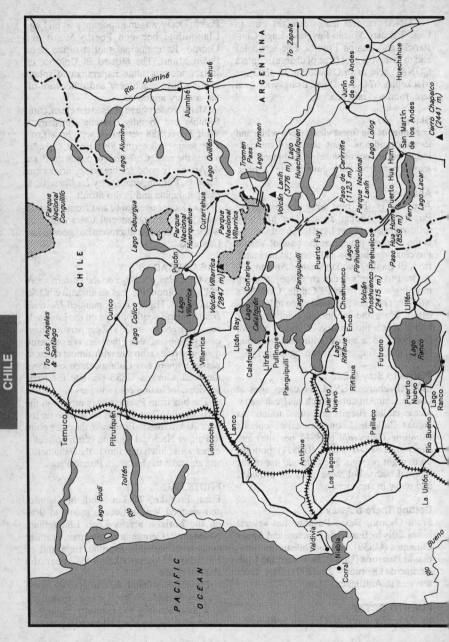

Museo de la Colonización Alemana

The Museum of German Colonisation displays immaculate 19th-century farm implements and household artefacts, perfectly reconstructed buildings, including a water mill and a functioning blacksmith's building, and a typical mansion (as typical as a mansion can be) among manicured gardens.

A short walk up from the lakeshore, it's open from 10 am to 2 pm and 5 to 9 pm in summer, 10 am to 6 pm at other seasons. Admission is US$1.

Places to Stay

Camping Los Ciruelillos, at the far south end of Frutillar Bajo, has shady sites with beach access for US$11. There are hot showers, and fresh home-made bread is available in the morning.

Hospedaje Winkler, Philippi 1155, has hostel accommodation for US$8, with regular rooms in the mid-range category. *Residencial Bruni*, at Las Piedras 60, on the escarpment above the lake, is just US$8.50 per person, but is open in summer only. *Hostería Trayén*, Philippi 1285, is open all year, with rooms with private bath for US$10 and a highly regarded restaurant. With a hearty breakfast, *Hospedaje Kaiserseehaus*, Philippi 1333, charging $US12 per person, has earned very enthusiastic recommendations.

Places to Eat

For kuchen and fruit preserves, try the mobile *Cinco Robles* stand on Avenida Philippi. The *Club Alemán*, on San Martín above Philippi, has fixed-price lunches for US$7. *Café del Sur*, Pérez Rosales 580, serves reasonable home-cooked lunches.

Things to Buy

Local specialties include fresh raspberries, jams and kuchen, and miniature wood carvings of the buildings at the museum.

Getting There & Away

Buses Varmontt and Cruz del Sur, on Alessandri in Frutillar Alto, have buses to Puerto Montt and Osorno every half-hour most of the day. Trains also stop at Frutillar Alto.

Getting Around

Taxi colectivos shuttle between Frutillar Alto and Frutillar Bajo.

PUERTO VARAS

Puerto Varas, a 19th-century lakeport 20 km north of Puerto Montt, is the gateway to Lago Todos los Santos and the popular boat-bus crossing to Bariloche, Argentina.

Information

Tourist Office The municipal tourist office (☎ 23-2437), Del Salvador 328, has free maps and brochures about the entire area. It's open daily from 9 am to 9 pm.

Money Change cash and travellers' cheques at Turismo Los Lagos, Del Salvador 257, Local 11.

Post & Telecommunications Correos de Chile is at San José 324. Telefónica del Sur, on the corner of Santa Rosa and Del Salvador, is open from 8 am to 11 pm.

Emergency Hospital San José (☎ 23-2336) is at Dr Bader 810.

Activities

Several agencies on Del Salvador organise adventure travel activities like trekking, climbing, bird-watching and rafting. The lake and its hinterland provide opportunities for swimming, windsurfing and cycling. Rent mountain bikes at the **Feria Artesanal** (about US$14 per day) and check the agencies for rental equipment for other sports.

Places to Stay

Hospedaje Novoa, San José 544, is a bit ramshackle and run-down, but has singles for US$5.50 without breakfast. *Hospedaje Hernández*, Del Salvador 1025, is comparably priced, but most others are in the

US$10-plus range. *Hospedaje Ceronni*, Estación 262, has been recommended.

Clean, with hot showers and a decent restaurant, the very basic *Residencial Unión*, San Francisco 669, has lousy beds and is chilly in winter. Rooms are US$8 per person with breakfast. *Residencial Hellwig*, San Pedro 210, is recommended, with reasonably spacious rooms at US$10 per person.

Places to Eat
Café Real, upstairs at Del Salvador 257, has cheap lunches, while *Café Central*, at San José 319, is good for coffee and desserts. *El Gordito* and *El Mercado*, both in the Mercado Municipal, at Del Salvador 582, have very fine seafood. The *Club Alemán*, San José 415, is another good choice, as is *Il Gato Renzo*, Del Salvador 314. *Country House*, Walker Martínez 584, has appealing if rather expensive meals.

Getting There & Away
Bus Puerto Varas has no central terminal, but most companies are near the centre. Many northbound buses from Puerto Montt pick up passengers here.

Varmontt, San Francisco 666, has daily buses to Santiago and many to Puerto Montt. Cruz del Sur, Del Salvador 237, has frequent buses daily to Osorno, Valdivia, Temuco and Chiloé. Other nearby companies include Lit, at Del Salvador 310, Igi Llaima, at Del Salvador 100, Tas Choapa, at San José 341, and ETC and Buses Norte (both at San Francisco 447). All go to Santiago and to Argentina.

At 11 am daily in summer (except Sundays), Buses Esmeralda, at San Pedro 210, goes to Ensenada (US$1) and Petrohué (US$2). The rest of the year, these run only on Tuesdays, Thursdays and Saturdays.

From September to March, Andina del Sud, Del Salvador 243, has daily buses to Ensenada and Petrohué, connecting to its own bus-boat crossing to Bariloche. These leave Puerto Montt at 8.30 am and return at 5 pm; the rest of the year, they run Wednesday to Sunday, leaving Puerto Montt at 10 am and returning at 5 pm. From November

to mid-March, Varastur, at San Francisco 242, runs buses to Petrohué, Wednesday to Sunday at 10 am, returning at 5 pm.

For fares, see the Puerto Montt section.

Train The station is up the hill on Klenner, across from the Casino.

ENSENADA
Ensenada, on the road to Petrohué and Lago Todos los Santos, is on the eastern shore of Lago Llanquihue, at the base of Volcán Osorno. To the south is the jagged crater of Calbuco, which blew its top during the Pleistocene.

For US$11/20 a single/double, *Hostería Ruedas Viejas* has cosy cabins with double beds, private bath and small wood stoves. Meals are cheap and helpings bountiful. The hostería also has very limited hostel accommodation (US$4).

Buses Bohle has four buses daily from Puerto Montt; for other services, see the Puerto Varas section.

PARQUE NACIONAL VICENTE PÉREZ ROSALES
Beneath Volcán Osorno's flawless cone, the scoured glacial basin of Lago Todos los Santos offers dramatic views and a scenic boat-bus route to Argentina. Volcán Puntiagudo's needle point lurks to the north, while Volcán Tronador marks the Argentine border.

Chile's first national park (established 1926), the 251,000-hectare Vicente Pérez Rosales is 50 km east of Puerto Varas via paved Ruta 225. Its forests and climate (more than 200 rainy days yearly) resemble those of Puyehue, but January and February are fairly dry.

Volcán Osorno
Many companies in Puerto Varas and Puerto Montt organise guided ascents of Osorno, which requires snow and ice gear, but experienced climbers can handle it solo. In winter, try skiing at the **Centro de Esqui La Burbuja**, 1250 metres above sea level; for reservations, contact Hotel Vicente Pérez

CHILE

Rosales (☎ 25-2571), Antonio Varas 447 in Puerto Montt.

The *Teski Ski Club* has a refugio just below the snow line, a nine-km uphill hike from the signpost on the Ensenada-Puerto Octay road. Beds are available for US$5.50 per night, all year.

Petrohué

In the shadow of Volcán Osorno, Petrohué is the departure point for the ferry to Peulla, which leaves early in the morning and returns after lunch.

CONAF's **Centro de Visitantes** has several interesting displays. From Hotel Petrohué, a dirt track leads to **Playa Larga**, a long black-sand beach. The **Sendero Rincón del Osorno** is a five-km trail on the western shore of Lago Todos los Santos.

Peulla

Approaching the tiny village of Peulla, which bustles in summer with tourists en route to Argentina, Lago Todos los Santos' deep blue becomes an emerald green. **Cascada de los Novios** is a waterfall just a few minutes' walk from Hotel Peulla by an easy footpath. For a longer excursion, take the eight-km **Sendero Laguna Margarita**, a rewarding climb.

Across the river at the Küscher house (reached by rowboat), you can camp or rent a room for US$7.50 a single. The army now occupies the lakeside campground, which may be available in a pinch. Bring food from Puerto Varas.

One km from the dock, *Hotel Peulla* (☎ 25-8041) charges US$60/85 with half-pension (satisfied correspondents say it's 'worth the splurge') and has a US$10 buffet in summer. Modest *Residencial Palomita* has rooms for US$12 per person with half-pension. There's a camp site opposite CONAF, and recommended lodgings with Elmo and Ana Hernández, on the right side as you leave the jetty, for US$6.

Getting There & Away

Bus For bus services, see Getting There & Away for Puerto Varas. Some buses from Varas arrive after the ferry, so plan to stay overnight at Petrohué.

Boat Andina del Sud's ferry departs Petrohué early for the three-hour voyage to Peulla, the first leg of the journey to Bariloche. Get tickets (US$7) at the kiosk near the jetty, or from Andina del Sud in Puerto Varas or Puerto Montt.

PUERTO MONTT

Puerto Montt (population 90,000), capital of the Tenth Region (Los Lagos), on the Golfo de Reloncaví, resembles Seattle or Vancouver in site, but its older architecture is middle European. It has excellent transport connections to Chiloé, Aysén and Patagonia.

Information

Tourist Office The municipal kiosk, on the Plaza de Armas, is open daily from 9 am to 2 pm and 3 to 9 pm. Sernatur's helpful but inconvenient office (☎ 25-2720), overlooking the city from the annex of the Edificio Intendencia Regional, at O'Higgins 480, has much more material. It's open on weekdays from 8.30 am to 1 pm and 1.30 to 5.48 pm (not a typo!).

English-run Traucomontt Tours (☎ or fax 25-8555), Egaña 82, is also an information centre for overseas travellers.

Money Cambios include Turismo Los Lagos (at Varas 595, Local 3) El Libertador (at Urmeneta 529) and La Moneda de Oro (at the bus terminal).

Post & Telecommunications Correos de Chile is at Rancagua 126. Telefónica del Sur has offices at Pedro Montt 114, Chillán 98, and at the bus terminal.

Argentine Consulate The Argentine Consulate (☎ 25-3996), at Cauquenes 94, 2nd floor, is open on weekdays from 8 am to 1 pm.

Emergency Puerto Montt's hospital (☎ 25-3991) is on Seminario, behind the hilltop Intendencia Regional.

Things to See

About three km west of the city centre, the fishing port of **Angelmó** has an outstanding crafts market, with handmade boots, curios, copperwork, ponchos, and woollen sweaters, hats and gloves. Don't leave Puerto Montt without trying a dish of curanto at one of the waterfront cafés. For a quieter perspective on the Gulf, launches from the docks go to **Isla Tenglo**.

Places to Stay

Youth Hostel Summer accommodation (US$1.40) is available at Escuela No 1, on the corner of Lillo and Lota, opposite the bus terminal. Cold showers, an 11.30 pm curfew and the need to supply your own sleeping bag may put off some travellers.

Hospedajes, Residenciales & Hotels The unnamed hospedaje at Gallardo 552 charges about US$4 with hot water and kitchen privileges. Rooms at Raúl Arroyo's popular *house*, Concepción 136, are about US$6, but recent visitors write that his standards have fallen. The hospedaje at Aníbal Pinto 328 has been recommended as warm, clean, friendly and good value. Another popular choice is *Hospedaje Uribe*, at Trigal 312 (up Pérez Rosales from the bus terminal), whose amusing owner speaks English and French.

Several readers have recommended *Hospedaje Steffen*, at Serrano 286, reached by colectivo No 3 from Egaña, and an unnamed hospedaje at Vial 754, near Balmaceda. East of the city centre, *Hospedaje Balneario Pelluco*, at Juan Soler 96, is a friendly, comfortable house with beach views and breakfast for US$9 a single with shared bath, US$12 with private bath. Taxi colectivos go almost to the front door.

Places to Eat

For drinks, snacks and Streuselkuchen (highly recommended by a German correspondent), try *Café Central*, Rancagua 117. There is a fine bakery, *Pastelería Lisel*, at Cauquenes 82. Another possibility is *Café Real*, at Rancagua 137. *Café Vicorella*, Varas 515, is a mecca for caffeine addicts.

Dino's, at Varas 550, has been recommended, as has the paila marina at *El Jabalí*, Andrés Bello 976. One reader praised the paella at the *Centro Español*, O'Higgins 233, as the best he ever ate.

Pelluco, east of the city centre via Avenida Juan Soler, is a good hunting ground for restaurants – try the parrillada at *El Fogón Criollo*. Don't leave without trying curanto or other seafood specialties at Angelmó's waterfront cafés – among recommended choices are *Marfino*, Angelmó 1856, and *Asturias*. Another fine choice is *Restaurant Embassy*, Ancud 104 in Puerto Montt.

Getting There & Away

Air Ladeco (☎ 25-3002), Benavente 350, flies twice daily to Santiago, except Saturdays (one flight only), to Punta Arenas daily, except Saturdays, and to Balmaceda/ Coyhaique four times weekly.

LAN-Chile (☎ 25-3141), San Martín 200, has 15 flights weekly to Santiago, eight to Punta Arenas and nine to Coyhaique.

Inquire about the new discount carrier Pacific Air, which flies thrice weekly between Santiago and Punta Arenas via Puerto Montt.

TAN (☎ 25-5146), Varas 445, flies to Argentine Patagonia, as does a new carrier, Spasa. Transportes Aéreos Don Carlos (☎ 25-3219), Quillota 139, and Aerosur (☎ 25-2523), Serena 149, fly air taxis to the Aisén region. Local buses go to Aeropuerto El Tepual, 16 km west of town.

Bus The Terminal de Buses (☎ 25-3143) is on the waterfront, at Avenida Portales and Lota, serving all Lake District destinations, Chiloé, Santiago, Coyhaique, Punta Arenas and Argentina.

Bus – long-distance As of writing, Buses Fierro had daily buses on the Camino Austral as far as Hornopirén. Transport information changes frequently, so check details in Puerto Montt.

Bus – regional Cruz del Sur and Trans Chiloé have frequent services to Ancud

CHILE

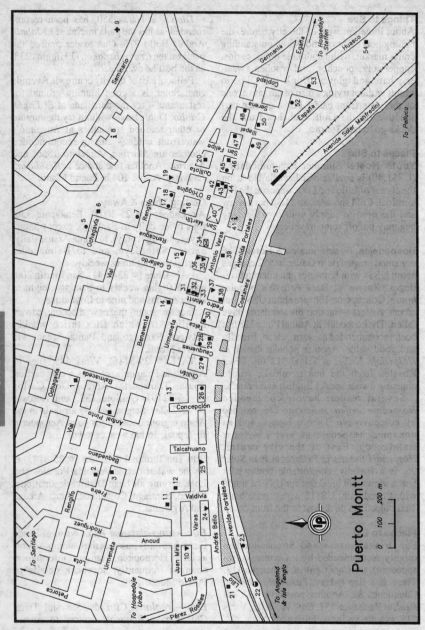

Puerto Montt

0   100   200 m

■	PLACES TO STAY	54	Hospedaje El Toqui	26	Telefónica del Sur (Telephones)
1	Hospedaje	▼	PLACES TO EAT	27	Automóvil Club de Chile
2	Hospedaje Benavente			28	Argentine Consulate
3	Hospedaje	10	Restaurant Embassy		& Pastelería Lisel
4	Hospedaje	19	Centro Español	29	Colina Rent-a-Car
6	Hotel Le Mirage	24	El Jabalí	30	Turismo Los Lagos
11	Hospedaje Polz	25	Restaurant El		(Money Exchange)
12	Residencial Embassy		Bodegón	32	Telefónica del Sur
13	Raúl Arroyo's House	33	Dino's Restaurant		(Telephones)
	(Hospedaje)	35	Café Real	34	Post Office
14	Hotel Gamboa	36	Café Central	39	Andina del Sud
20	Residencial Urmeneta	37	Café Vicorella	40	Plaza de Armas
21	Escuela No 1 (Youth			41	Tourist Office
	Hostel)		OTHER	43	Transportes Aéreos
29	Hotel Colina				Don Carlos
31	Hospedaje Pedro	5	CONAF	45	Casa del Arte Diego
	Montt	7	Turismo Odisea		Rivera
38	Hotel Burg & Restau-	8	Edificio Intendencia	48	Aerosur
	rant Amsel		Regional (Sernatur)	49	Transmarchilay
39	Hotel Vincent Pérez	9	Hospital	51	Railway Station
	Rosales	15	Banco de Chile	52	Traucomontt Tours
42	Gran Hotel Don Luis	16	Budget Rent-a-Car	53	Avis Rent-a-Car
44	Hotel Montt	17	LAN-Chile		
46	Residencial Sur	18	Ladeco		
47	Residencial Millantú	22	Bus Terminal		
50	Hotel El Candíl	23	Museo Juan Pablo II		

(US$4) and Castro (US$6). Varmontt, Igi Llaima, Lit and Etta Bus all go to Concepción (US$12) and Santiago (US$17). Other companies to Santiago include Turibus, Bus Norte, Tas Choapa, Tur Bus, Vía Tur and Inter Sur. Lit and Tur Bus have daily services to Valparaíso/Viña del Mar.

For Punta Arenas (US$57), via Argentina, contact Turibus, Bus Norte or Bus Sur. Turibus also goes to Coyhaique (US$40) on Thursdays and Saturdays via Argentina.

Bus – international Bus Norte and Río de La Plata have daily buses to Bariloche via Puyehue (US$20). Igi Llaima goes four times weekly to San Martín de los Andes (US$23) and Neuquén. Tas Choapa, Turismo Lanín and Cruz del Sur go less frequently.

Andina del Sud and Varastur, both at Varas 437, offer one-day bus-boat combinations to Bariloche via Lago Todos los Santos (US$33). With an overnight at Peulla, this costs about US$80.

Train The station (☎ 25-2922) is at the east end of Avenida Portales. Daily trains depart for Santiago at 8.15 am and 4.30 pm, taking 20 to 22 hours, in summer only. Fares start at US$19.

Boat The most appealing route south is by sea, but schedules change frequently and the information following should only be considered a general guide.

Ferry or bus-ferry combinations go to Chiloé and Chaitén, in the Tenth Region; those to Chiloé leave from Pargua, on the Canal de Chacao, as do other southbound ferries on occasion. Some continue to Puerto Chacabuco (port of Coyhaique), in the Eleventh Region (Aisén), or go to Puerto Natales, in the Twelfth Region (Magallanes). Travellers prone to motion sickness may consider medication before crossing the gut-wrenching Golfo de Penas.

Navimag (☎ 25-3754), at the port of Angelmó, sails to Puerto Chacabuco twice

CHILE

weekly on the ferry *Evangelistas*, and three times monthly to Puerto Natales, a memorable three days if space is available, but Navimag seems to discourage passengers.

Fares to Puerto Chacabuco start at US$43 without meals. These sailings continue to Laguna San Rafael; see the Aisén section for more details.

Fares to Puerto Natales range from US$100 to US$150. Try to book at Navimag's Santiago offices (☎ 696-3211), Miraflores 178, 12th floor, but Traucomontt Tours (see the previous Information section) has a good record for arranging passages.

Transmarchilay (☎ 25-4654), Varas 215, sails to Chaitén (10 hours, departures on Tuesdays, Fridays and Sundays) and to Puerto Chacabuco (26 hours, departures on Tuesdays and Fridays). Fares to Chaitén start at US$10 for deck space and US$20 for a reclining seat. Fares to Chacabuco are slightly less than double the fares to Chaitén.

Transmarchilay also runs automobile-passenger ferries from Pargua, 60 km south-west of Puerto Montt, to Chacao, on Chiloé Island. Fares are about US$2 for walk-ons, US$10 per car (no matter how many passengers).

Getting Around
Auto rental agencies include the Automóvil Club (☎ 25-2968) at Cauquenes 75, Budget (☎ 25-4888) at San Martín 200, First (☎ 25-2036) at Urmeneta 883, Hertz (☎ 25-2122) at Urmeneta 1036, and Avis (☎ 25-6575) at Copiapó 43.

PARQUE NACIONAL ALERCE ANDINO
Only 40 km south-east of Puerto Montt, this 40,000-hectare reserve of Andean peaks and glacial lakes shelters *Fitzroya cupressoides*, a conifer similar to California's giant sequoia in appearance and longevity. A 3000-year-old specimen can reach 40 metres in height and four metres in diameter, but its attractive wood has exposed it to commercial over-exploitation.

Exposed to Pacific storms, Alerce Andino gets up to 4500 mm of rain and snow annually, but hiking the backcountry is the best

reason for a visit. Lonely Planet's *Trekking in the Patagonian Andes* describes a good trail, with several refugios, between Río Chamiza and Río Chaica sectors. CONAF has a 10-site campground at Río Chamiza, at the park's north, and a three-site facility at Lago Chaiquenes, at the head of the Río Chaica valley.

From Puerto Montt, Buses Fierro goes daily to the village of Correntoso, three km from the Río Chamiza entrance. Fierro also has buses to the crossroads at Lenca, on the Camino Austral, where a lateral up the valley of the Río Chaica gives better access to a number of lakes and peaks – probably a better choice for the nontrekker.

CHAITÉN
Pioneer Chaitén is a tiny, quiet port and military base towards the north end of the Camino Austral. The tourist office in the Mercado Municipal has a handful of leaflets and a list of hospedajes, but change money elsewhere – Banco del Estado gives very poor rates.

Places to Stay & Eat
Look for handwritten signs on private houses, which may be open only from mid-December to late March. Most charge US$4 to US$6, including *Hospedaje Lo Watson*, at Ercilla 580, *Hospedaje Mary*, at Piloto Pardo 593, *Hospedaje Sebastián*, at Todesco 188, and *Hospedaje Gabriel*, at Todesco 141. *Residencial Astoria*, Corcovado 442, has rooms for US$7 a single.

For seafood restaurants, try the Mercado Municipal. Hotel El Triángulo's restaurant has also drawn praise.

Getting There & Away
Air Aerosur, on Corcovado, and Don Carlos, Todesco 42, have air taxis.

Bus Details change rapidly as the highway improves. Connections are best to the south: Transaustral (once weekly) and Artetur (twice weekly) go to Coyhaique (US$26, 12 hours). Chaitur and Bus Yelcho go to Palena and Futaleufú (US$10), on the Argentine border.

Boat Transmarchilay, Corcovado 266, has eight ferries monthly to Quellón or Chonchi, on the island of Chiloé, and another eight to Puerto Montt or Pargua. Confirm schedules at Transmarchilay; for fares, see the sections for Quellón, Chonchi and Puerto Montt.

FUTALEUFÚ

Futaleufú, at the confluence of the Río Espolón and the Río Futaleufú, is 155 km from Chaitén via an indirect route around Lago Yelcho. Only a few km from Argentina's Chubut province, it is renowned for fishing and white-water rafting.

Accommodation costs about US$4 to US$7 at *Residencial Carahue* at O'Higgins 332, *Hospedaje El Campesino* at Prat 107, *Hospedaje Cañete* at Gabriela Mistral 374, and *Hotel Continental* at Balmaceda 595. Chaitur has buses to Chaitén (US$10), while Transporte Samuel Flores has minibuses to Argentina.

PARQUE NACIONAL QUEULAT

Along the Camino Austral between Chaitén and Coyhaique, 154,000-hectare Queulat is a zone of steep sided fjords, rushing rivers, evergreen forests, creeping glaciers and high volcanic peaks. More accessible since completion of the highway, it's still an off-the-beaten-track destination. The Río Cisnes and the glacial fingers of Lago Rosselot, Lago Verde and Lago Risopatrón offer excellent fishing.

Queulat is popular with adventure travel agencies, but also attracts independent travellers – though heavy brush inhibits off-trail exploration. There is a good two-km trail to the **Ventisquero Colgante** (Hanging Glacier), 36 km south of Puyuhuapi, and another up the **Río Guillermo**. Consult rangers at Pudú, Ventisquero, Puyuhuapi, El Pangue or La Junta.

Places to Stay

Camping El Pangue, on Lago Risopatrón five km north of Puyuhuapi, charges US$5 per site. *Camping Río Queulat*, 34 km south of Puyuhuapi, is free.

Puyuhuapi's *Hostería Ludwig* has singles/doubles for US$11/14. At the village of La Junta, at the north end of the park, near the turn-off to Lago Rosselot and Lago Verde, *Hostería Copihue* and *Hostería Valdera* both charge about US$7 to US$8 a single.

Getting There & Away

Buses from Chaitén or Coyhaique will drop passengers at points along the park's western boundary. Renting a car in Coyhaique is more flexible, but expensive without several people to share the costs.

Chiloé

Isla Grande de Chiloé is a well-watered, forested island of undulating hills, 180 km long but just 50 km wide. Surrounded by many smaller islands, it has a temperate maritime climate. Distinctive shingled houses line the streets and punctuate the verdant countryside. When the sun finally breaks through the rain and mist, it reveals majestic panoramas of snowcapped mainland volcanos.

Huilliche Indians first raised potatoes and other crops in the fertile volcanic soil. Jesuits were among the earliest European settlers, but mainland refugees arrived after the Mapuche uprising of 1599. A Spanish Royalist stronghold, Chiloé resisted criollo attacks on Ancud until 1826.

Chiloé is part of the Tenth Region (Los Lagos). Ancud and Castro are the only large towns. Castro and some villages have picturesque *palafitos*, rows of houses on stilts over estuaries. In rural areas, there are more than 150 distinctive wooden churches up to two centuries old.

Nearly all the 115,000 *Chilotes* live within sight of the sea. More than half make a living from farming, but many also depend on fishing for food and money. The eastern littoral contributes wheat, oats, vegetables

CHILE

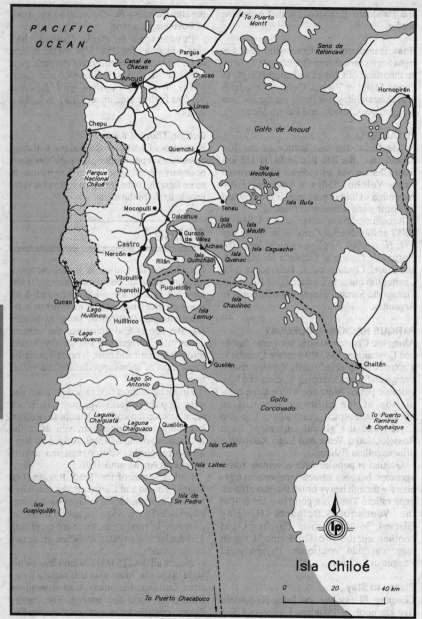

Isla Chiloé

PACIFIC OCEAN

To Puerto Montt

Seno de Reloncaví

Pargua

Canal de Chacao

Chacao

Ancud

Linao

Hornopirén

Chepu

Golfo de Ancud

Quemchi

Isla Mechuque

Parque Nacional Chiloé

Isla Buta

Mocopulli

Tenaún

Dalcahue

Isla Linlín

Isla Meulín

Curaco de Vélez

Achao

Castro

Isla Caguache

Nercón

Rilán

Isla Quinchao

Isla Quenac

Vilupulli

Chonchi

Puqueldón

Cucao

Isla Chaulinec

Lago Huillinco

Huillinco

Isla Lemuy

Lago Tepuhueco

Chaitén

Lago Sn Antonio

Queilén

Laguna Chaiguata

Laguna Chaiguaco

Quellón

Golfo Corcovado

To Puerto Ramírez & Coyhaique

Isla Caith

Isla Laitec

Isla Guapiquilán

Isla de Sn Pedro

LP

0   20   40 km

To Puerto Chacabuco

and livestock to a precarious economy, but the nearly roadless western shores and interior preserve extensive forests.

Despite its natural beauty, Chiloé is one of Chile's poorest areas, and perpetual hardship has forced many Chilotes to leave. The island's rich folkloric tradition has contributed to Chilean literature, but to some urbanites, 'Chilote' is synonymous with 'bumpkin'. In part, this reputation derives from insularity, but isolation has encouraged self-reliance, courtesy and a hospitality which has changed little since Darwin wrote, more than 150 years ago, 'I never saw anything more obliging and humble than the manners of these people'.

ANCUD

Founded in 1767 to defend the coastline, Chiloé's largest town (population 17,000) is an attractive fishing port on the Bahía de Ancud, at the north end of the island.

Information

Tourist Office At Libertad 665, the tourist office (☎ 2665) is open on weekdays from 8.30 am to 12.30 pm and 2.30 to 8 pm, and on weekends from 10 am to 2 pm. It has brochures, maps, and lists of accommodation.

Money Change money in Puerto Montt if possible; otherwise, try Banco de Crédito, at Ramírez 257.

Post & Telecommunications Correos de Chile is on the corner of Pudeto and Blanco Encalada. The Compañía Nacional de Teléfonos is at Chacabuco 745.

Emergency The hospital (☎ 2355) is at Latorre 405.

Things to See

Ancud's **Museo Regional Aurelio Bórquez Canobra** (or Museo Chilote) shows ethnographic and historical materials (including outstanding photographs), a fine natural history collection and a patio displaying figures from Chilote folklore. The traditional

kitchen in the patio's thatched Chilote house serves a fine curanto for US$4 on weekends.

Watercolours by local artist Francisco Vera Cárcamo depict Chilote landscapes. Note the varied *tejuelas* (shingles) on scale models of wooden churches, and a relief map indicating major settlements. The museum is on Libertad, just south of the Plaza de Armas. Admission is US$1 and it is open on weekdays from 9 am to 12.30 pm and 2.30 to 6.30 pm, on Saturdays from 10 am to 12.30 pm and 2.30 to 6 pm, and on Sundays from 11 am to 12.30 pm and 2.30 to 5 pm.

Places to Stay

Hostels In summer, the *Albergue Juvenil* (☎ 2065), Latorre 478, offers floor space for US$1.50, but travellers can pitch tents in the patio for less than US$1. The *Casa del Apostulado* (☎ 3256), on the corner of Chacabuco and Errázuriz, offers floor space for US$1.50, mattresses for US$2.50 and proper beds for US$3.50 per night.

Hospedajes, Residenciales & Hotels Many private houses offer seasonal accommodation for around US$4 to US$5, but year-round places include *Hospedaje Navarro*, at Pudeto 361, and *Hospedaje Miranda* (an especially good choice), at Mocopulli 753. *Hospedaje Bellavista*, at Bellavista 449, and *Residencial Madryn*, at Bellavista 491, both charge around US$7 a single (doubles are cheaper at the Madryn).

Residencial Wechsler, Cochrane 480, has a reputation for Germanic austerity but is very well kept. Comfortable singles with shared bath cost US$8.50, while those with private bath cost US$14, with breakfast. *Hotel Lydia*, Pudeto 256, has a highly regarded restaurant and clean, agreeable rooms from US$13/20 a single/double.

Places to Eat

For seafood, try *El Sacho*, in the Mercado Municipal, on Dieciocho between Libertad and Blanco Encalada. Other good seafood restaurants include *Polo Sur*, at Avenida Costanera 630, *La Pincoya*, at Prat 61, and *Restaurant Capri*, at Mocopulli 710.

CHILE

El Jardín, Pudeto 263, has relatively modest prices for enormous slabs of meat. For good dinners, desserts and coffee, try *Café Lydia*, Pudeto 256. The *Hamburgería*, at Prat 94, claims one reader, is better and more varied than its name suggests.

Things to Buy
Ancud has a plethora of outlets for woollens, carvings and pottery. Besides the museum, try Artesanía Moai, at Baquedano 429, or the Taller de Artesanía, at Blanco Encalada 730.

Getting There & Away
Bus Cruz del Sur, Chacabuco 672, has a dozen buses a day to Puerto Montt (US$4), Osorno and points north. Another dozen go to Castro (US$2) and several more to Chonchi (US$3) and Quellón. Varmontt, on the Costanera, has buses to Puerto Montt and southbound on Chiloé.

Trans Chiloé, Chacabuco 750, has several buses daily to Castro, Chonchi, Quellón and Puerto Montt. Turibus, on Dieciocho at Libertad, goes to Concepción and Santiago, Punta Arenas and Puerto Natales. Bus Norte, Pudeto 250, also goes to Punta Arenas and Puerto Natales.

CASTRO
Founded in 1567, Castro is the capital of the Chiloé province, 90 km south of Ancud. In 1834, Darwin found it 'a most forlorn and deserted place', but its most conspicuous landmark – the bright, incongruously painted catedral – dates from 1906. Waterfront palafitos, with their crafted *tejuelas* vernacular architectural distinction.

Information
Tourist Office Sernatur (☎ 5699) has recently opened an office at O'Higgins 549, 1½ blocks north of the plaza, open on weekdays from 8.30 am to 1.30 pm and 2.30 to 6.30 pm. Its very complete list of accommodation includes cheap hospedajes.

Money For cash, try Julio Barrientos (☎ 5079), Chacabuco 286, instead of banks.

Post & Telecommunications Correos de Chile is at O'Higgins 388. CNT telephone services are at Latorre 289.

Emergency The hospital (☎ 2445) is at Freire 852.

Things to See
At the north end of the Plaza de Armas, Castro's **Iglesia San Francisco de Castro** assaults the vision with its dazzling exterior – salmon with violet trimmings. On Esmeralda, half a block south of the plaza, the **Museo Regional de Castro** houses an idiosyncratic collection of Huilliche Indian relics, farm implements and exhibits on Chilote urbanism.

The waterfront **Feria Artesanal** has a selection of woollens and basketry. Note the bundles of dried seaweed and nalca, both eaten by Chilotes, and the chunks of peat fuel.

Palafitos
All around Castro, shingled houses on stilts stretch into the estuaries and lagoons, but from the street, the houses resemble any other. Look along the Costanera Pedro Montt, at the north end of town, at the Feria Artesanal (where some are restaurants), and at both ends of the bridge over the Río Gamboa.

Places to Stay
In summer, the *Albergue Juvenil*, in the Gimnasia Fiscal, at Freire 610, charges about US$2.

Hospedajes charge about US$5, but some are only seasonal – ask Sernatur, or look for handwritten signs on the 600 to 800 blocks of San Martín and O'Higgins, near the bus terminal.

Despite an unimpressive exterior, *Hotel La Bomba*, at Esmeralda 270, has simple but bright and airy rooms for US$6 a single with private bath. *Hospedaje O'Higgins*, O'Higgins 831, charges US$8.50 with shared bath, US$12 with private bath.

Places to Eat

Palafito restaurants at the waterfront market have the best food for the fewest pesos. *Brisas del Mar* and *Mariela* both have cheap fixed-price lunches as well as specialties. *Restaurant Octavia*, Lillo 67, has three-course dinners for about US$3. *Restaurant Maucari*, Lillo 93, has curanto for US$4.

Try *Chilos*, at San Martín 449, for meat and seafood, *El Fogón Chilote*, at Luis Espinoza 309, for a varied menu stressing parrillada, or *Sacho*, at Thompson 213, for curanto.

Getting There & Away

Bus The Terminal de Buses Rurales is on San Martín near Sargento Aldea. Buses Arroyo has two to three buses a day to Huillinco and Cucao (US$2), gateway to the Parque Nacional Chiloé, while Ocean Bus has two per day.

Dalcahue Expreso, Ramírez 233, has buses every half-hour to Dalcahue on week-days but fewer on weekends. Buses Lemuy serves Chonchi and Isla Lemuy, including Puqueldón, while Buses Queilén (also a tour operator) has regular service to Queilén and intermediates.

Most but not all long-distance companies have offices nearby. Cruz del Sur, on San Martín at Sotomayor, has a dozen buses daily to Ancud, Puerto Montt (US$6) and points north, as does Varmontt, at Balmaceda 289. Cruz del Sur also has several to Chonchi and Quellón (US$3), as does Regional Sur, at the terminal. Trans Chiloé, at the terminal, has several north-south buses daily.

Castro has a direct service to Punta Arenas (US$63 in summer, 36 hours) and Puerto Natales via Argentina, twice weekly with Buses Ghisoni and two to four times weekly with Bus Sur at the Terminal. Turibus, Esmeralda 252, goes to Puerto Montt, Concepción and Punta Arenas.

DALCAHUE

Dalcahue, 20 km north-east of Castro, takes its name from the seagoing *dalcas* (canoes) of Chiloé. A tsunami in 1960 washed away the palafitos, but it still has a 19th-century church and the island's best crafts market. Its tourist office, in the Municipalidad, is open daily (except Mondays) from 9.30 am to 1.30 pm and 3 to 7 pm.

Artisans from offshore islands travel to the casual **Feria Artesanal**, with a fine selection of woollens, wooden crafts and basketry, plus good cheap eateries. Sellers often drop their prices without even hearing a counter offer.

Places to Stay & Eat

For about US$3 per person, try the very friendly *Pensión Montana*, at Rodríguez 009, or if it's full, the less amiable *Pensión La Feria*, next door. For excellent cheap food and waterfront atmosphere, try *Restaurant Brisas Marinas*, on palafitos above the Feria Artesanal.

Getting There & Away

Buses also load and unload at the feria. Expreso Dalcahue has buses to Castro every half-hour on weekdays, fewer on weekends. Taxi colectivos charge US$1 for the half-hour trip. There are launches to Isla Quinchao, with bus connections to Achao and its landmark 18th-century church.

CHONCHI

Jesuits founded Chonchi in 1767, but the **Iglesia San Carlos de Chonchi**, with its three-storey tower and multiple arches, dates from the 19th century. Connected by launch and ferry to the island of Lemuy, the town is 23 km south of Castro. The tourist office is at Sargento Candelaria and Centenario.

Hospedaje Mirador, Alvarez 198, is the most economical in town at US$4.50 per person, US$6 with breakfast. *Hotel Huildín*, Centenario 102, has singles with breakfast and shared bath for US$10. For seafood dinners, try *El Trébol*, on the second floor of the Mercado Municipal, or *La Sirena*, at Irarrázaval 52.

Getting There & Away

Cruz del Sur and Trans Chiloé have several buses daily from Castro. Taxi colectivos from Chacabuco and Esmeralda in Castro cost US$1; in Chonchi, they leave from Pedro Montt, opposite Iglesia San Carlos.

Transmarchilay is at the foot of the pier; ferries to Chaitén and Puerto Chacabuco sometimes leave from here, but see the Quellón section for details.

There are launches to Ichuac, on Isla Lemuy, but the ferry leaves every two hours from 8 am to 8 pm from Puerto Huichas, five km south, with connections to Puqueldón.

PARQUE NACIONAL CHILOÉ

Nowhere in South America can a traveller follow Darwin's footsteps more closely than in Parque Nacional Chiloé. The great naturalist's vivid account of his passage to Cucao merits lengthy citation:

At Chonchi we struck across the island, following intricate winding paths, sometimes passing through magnificent forests, and sometimes through pretty cleared spots, abounding with corn and potato crops. This undulating woody country, partially cultivated, reminded me of the wilder parts of England, and therefore had to my eye a most fascinating aspect. At Vilinco (Huillinco), which is situated on the borders of the lake of Cucao, only a few fields were cleared...

The country on each side of the lake was one unbroken forest. In the same periagua (canoe) with us, a cow was embarked. To get so large an animal into a small boat appears at first a difficulty, but the Indians managed it in a minute. They brought the cow alongside the boat, which was heeled towards her; then placing two oars under her belly, with their ends resting on the gunwale, by the aid of these levers they fairly tumbled the poor beast, heels overhead into the bottom of the boat, and then lashed her down with ropes.

Chiloé's Pacific coast still harbours native coniferous and evergreen forests, plus an almost pristine coastline. The Chilote fox and pudú inhabit the shadowy forests of the contorted *tepú*, while the 110 bird species include the penguin. About 30 km west of Chonchi and 54 km south-west of Castro, the park is open all year, but fair weather is likelier in summer.

Bruce Chatwin, the late gifted travel writer, left a superlative essay on Cucao in his *What Am I Doing Here?* (Penguin, 1989). Huilliche communities resent CONAF'S park management plan, which has restricted access to traditional subsistence while allowing some commercial exploitation. Ironically, Darwin, 150 years ago, also wrote of the 'harsh and authoritative manner' of government officials toward Chilotes.

Sector Chanquín

CONAF's **Centro de Visitantes**, across the suspension bridge from Cucao, is open daily from 9 am to 7.30 pm, with good displays on flora and fauna, the Huilliche people, the early mining industry and local folklore. The **Museo Artesanal** is a typical Chilote house, with farm and household implements, reed-insulated walls, and a recessed fireplace in the floor – a feature which caused many such houses to burn to the ground.

The **Sendero Interpretivo El Tepual** is a winding nature trail through gloomy forest where you might meet the Trauco, a troll-like creature from Chilote folklore. The **Sendero Dunas de Cucao** leads to a series of dunes behind a long, white sandy beach, but the sea is too cold for swimming.

Three km north on the coastal trail, at **Lago Huelde**, is a Huilliche community. At Río Cole Cole, 12 km north of Chanquín, and at Río Anay, eight km beyond, are rustic refugios, but a tent is advisable in this changeable climate. Wear water-resistant footwear and wool socks since, in Darwin's words, 'everywhere in the shade the ground soon becomes a perfect quagmire'.

Places to Stay & Eat

Camping Chinquín, 200 metres beyond the visitors' centre, has secluded sites with running water, firewood and cold showers (US$1.40 per person).

Within easy walking distance of the park entrance, *Hospedaje El Paraíso* and *Hospedaje Pacífico* have bed and breakfast for US$4 per person, while *Posada Cucao* is slightly dearer.

Getting There & Away

From Castro, Buses Arroyo has two or three buses a day to Cucao (US$2). Ocean Bus has two per day.

QUELLÓN

From Quellón, 92 km south of Castro, ferries sail to Chaitén and Puerto Chacabuco. *Anexo Hotel Playa*, at Pedro Montt 245, is a decent place with single rooms for US$5 with hot water and a good cheap restaurant. Comparably priced *Pensión Vera*, Gómez García 18, is OK despite a shabby exterior. Quellón has fine seafood restaurants near the jetty. Also recommended is *Las Quilas*, at La Paz 053, *Quilineja*, at Pedro Montt 201, and *Estrella del Mar*, at Gómez García 18.

Getting There & Away

Bus Cruz del Sur, at Aguirre Cerda 52, around the corner from the jetty, goes to Castro (US$2, 1½ hours).

Boat Transmarchilay is at the foot of the jetty. You can reach the Aisén Region from Quellón via Chaitén or directly to Puerto Chacabuco (port of Coyhaique). Schedules change, so verify the following information. The car ferry *La Pincoya* sails to Puerto Chacabuco (18 hours) on Saturdays and alternate Mondays at 6 pm.

Camarotes (sleepers) are expensive, but *butaca proa* (US$34 to Puerto Chacabuco) and *butaca popa* (US$30) are comfortable. *Clase económica* (US$20) is an upright bench seat, while *pasaje general* (US$14) is an uncomfortable deck or corridor space.

La Pincoya and *El Colono* alternate sailings to Chaitén (six hours), Monday and Thursday afternoons. The cheapest *pasaje general* is about US$9.

Aisén

The islands, fjords and glaciers of Aisén resemble Alaska's Inside Passage or New Zealand's South Island. Air and sea access, and overland routes from Argentina, are much better than the Camino Austral which supposedly links the area to Puerto Montt.

For millennia, Chonos and Alacalufes Indians fished and hunted the intricate canals and islands. Several expeditions visited the area in the late 18th and early 19th centuries, and Chilean naval officer Enrique Simpson's survey, in the 1870s, mapped areas as far south as the Península de Taitao.

Chile later promoted colonisation with grazing and timber leases, allowing a single company to control nearly a million hectares near Coyhaique. The bleached trunks of downed trees still litter hillsides where, encouraged by a land law which rewarded clearance, the company and colonists burned nearly three million hectares of lenga forest in the 1940s.

COYHAIQUE

Founded in 1929, Coyhaique (sometimes spelt Coihaique) has outgrown its pioneer origins to become a modest but tidy regional capital with a population of 40,000. Most visitors arrive by air from Puerto Montt or by ferry at Puerto Chacabuco, 80 km west.

Information

Tourist Office Sernatur (☎ 23-1752), Lord Cochrane 320, is open from 9 am to 1 pm and 3 to 7 pm on weekdays.

Money Change cash or travellers' cheques at Cambio El Libertador, at Arturo Prat 340, Oficina 207, or at Turismo Prado, 21 de Mayo 417.

Post & Telecommunications Correos de Chile is at Cochrane 202. The CTC telephone is at Moraleda 495.

Emergency The Hospital Base (☎ 23-1286) is on Calle Hospital, at the west end of Carrera.

National Parks For transport to parks and reserves which have no bus transport, inquire at CONAF (☎ 23-1065), Avenida Ogana 1060.

Things to See & Do

On most lakes and rivers, fishing season runs from November to May. Sernatur's brochure *Pesca Deportiva in Aysén* details locations and restrictions.

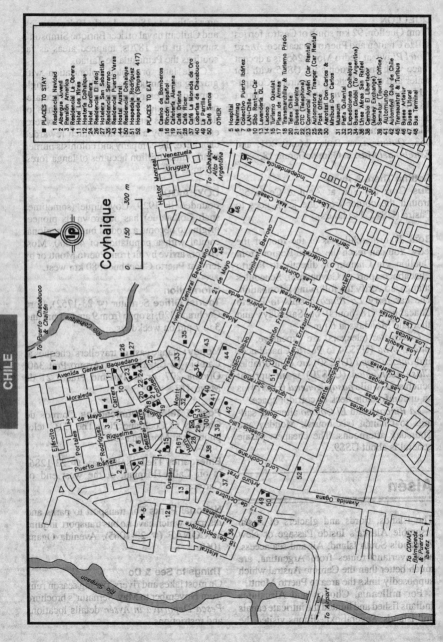

Coyhaique

0   150   300 m

From May to September, the **Centro de Ski El Fraile**, 29 km from Coyhaique, operates two lifts on five different runs.

Places to Stay

In summer, the cheapest accommodation (US$1.75) is the *Albergue Juvenil* (☎ 23-1961), in the Liceo BN-2, Carrera 485.

Pensión America, at 21 de Mayo 233, and *Residencial La Obrera*, at 21 de Mayo 264, both charge around US$4 per person. *Hospedaje Rodríguez*, a friendly family house at Colón 495, has singles for US$6. At *Residencial Serrano*, Serrano 91, the proprietor has small, bright and comfortable singles for US$8.50 with shared bath (breakfast extra).

Places to Eat

Café Samoa, Prat 653, is a cosy bar/restaurant with cheap meals and snacks. *Café Ricer*, Horn 48, has good lunches with large portions and fine service. Lively *Café Oriente*, Condell 201, has snacks and light meals, as does more sedate *Cafetería Alemana*, Condell 119.

Rincón Español, Prat 230, also has good lunches, and the *Casino de Bomberos*, General Parra 365, also has very fine meals at reasonable prices. For seafood, try *Loberías de Chacabuco*, Almirante Barroso 553. For meat, the choice is *La Parrilla*, Prat 601.

Getting There & Away

Air Aeropuerto Teniente Vidal, five km south of town, has a short runway and a steep approach.

Most flights originate or terminate in Santiago. LAN-Chile (☎ 23-1188), General Parra 215, has eight flights a week from Puerto Montt. Ladeco (☎ 23-1300), on the corner of Prat and Dussen, has fewer flights, but one continues to Punta Arenas; its larger planes land at Balmaceda, 30 km south.

Aerotaxi Don Carlos (☎ 23-2981), Subteniente Cruz 63, flies to Cochrane (US$43), to Villa O'Higgins (US$76), to Lago Verde and to Chile Chico (US$27), once or twice a week. Línea Aérea San Rafael (☎ 23-3408),

18 de Septiembre 469, flies daily to Chaitén (US$28).

Bus & Colectivo Only a few companies use the bus terminal on the corner of Lautaro and Magallanes. For frequent buses to Puerto Aisén (US$2), go to La Cascada, at the terminal, Transaustral, at Baquedano 1171, or Don Carlos, at Cruz 63. Buses del Norte runs eight buses weekly to Valle Simpson, Seis Lagunas, Lago Atravesado, Villa Frei and El Salto.

Buses Litoral, on Baquedano at Independencia, has Tuesday and Saturday buses to Puerto Cisnes, on a lateral off the Camino Austral, for US$13, but Colectivos Basoli, at Pasaje Puyuhuapi 47, is slightly cheaper, on Wednesdays and Sundays. Artetur, Baquedano 1347, goes to Puyuhuapi (US$13) and Las Juntas (US$15) on Tuesdays and Saturdays; Transaustral, on Wednesdays and Saturdays, is slightly dearer. To Chaitén (US$28, 12 hours), Transaustral and Artetur both have Saturday buses, Artetur an additional Tuesday service.

Colectivo Puerto Ibáñez, Presidente Ibáñez 30, sells a bus-ferry combination to Chile Chico (US$8.50); Aerobus has Monday, Wednesday and Friday buses to Puerto Ibáñez (US$6). Buses Pudú goes on Tuesdays and Saturdays to Villa Cerro Castillo (US$7), Bahía Murta (US$14), Puerto Tranquilo (US$15), Puerto Guadal (US$17) and Cochrane (US$22). Aerobus covers most of these same destinations on Mondays, Wednesdays and Fridays.

To Osorno and Puerto Montt (US$38), Buses Moreira, in the Galería Barrientos, on Condell, and Turibus, at Baquedano 1171, go on Tuesday and Friday afternoons via Argentina. Buses Giobbi, Bolívar 194, has three buses weekly to Comodoro Rivadavia, Argentina (US$29).

Boat Ferries to Chiloé, Chaitén and Puerto Montt leave from Puerto Chacabuco, two hours from Coyhaique by bus.

Transmarchilay (☎ 22-1971), upstairs at 21 de Mayo 417, sails to Chaitén and Puerto Montt on Mondays at noon, Wednesdays at

8 pm, and Saturdays at 4 pm; fares range from US$17 to US$43. To Quellón, times are Tuesdays at 4 pm and Sundays at 6 pm. Fares range from US$13 to US$35. Schedules are subject to change.

Navimag (☎ 22-3306), Presidente Ibáñez 347, Oficina 1, sails from Chacabuco to Puerto Montt on Tuesdays, Thursdays and Sundays at 4 pm (US$43).

Getting Around
To/From the Airport Shared cabs from the airport to the city centre cost only about US$3; cabs to the airport leave from the LAN-Chile office or will pick you up at an address of your choice.

Car Shoestring travellers might consider pooling resources to rent a car to explore the region. Shop around, since prices vary, but try Comercial Aisén, at Moraleda 420, or Sibb Rent-a-Car, at General Parra 95. The Automóvil Club, Bilbao 583, meets clients at the airport and picks up the car there as well.

AROUND COYHAIQUE
Reserva Nacional Coyhaique
Despite its proximity to Coyhaique, this 2150-hectare reserve is wild country, with exhilarating panoramas of the town and the enormous basalt columns of Cerro Macay. A popular retreat for town residents, it's spacious and forested enough never to feel crowded.

On the slopes of Cerro Cinchao, about 1000 metres above sea level, the reserve is only five km south of town via the paved highway and a steep dirt lateral. With a tent, you can stay at CONAF's rustic campgrounds (US$3) at Laguna Verde and El Brujo. Without a car, it's a casual hike of about 1½ hours to the park entrance (admission US$1), plus another hour to Laguna Verde.

Reserva Nacional Río Simpson
Río Simpson is an accessible, scenic combination of river, canyon and valley, 37 km west of Coyhaique. CONAF's **Centro de**

Visitantes consists of a small natural history museum and botanical garden. There's a beach for swimming, and many people fish in the river. It's a short walk to the **Cascada La Virgen**, a shimmering waterfall.

Camping Río Correntoso, 24 km west of Coyhaique, has spacious riverside sites for US$10. Buses from Coyhaique will drop you anywhere on the route.

PUERTO CHACABUCO
Connected to Coyhaique by an excellent paved highway, Chacabuco is the usual port of entry to the region. *Hotel Moraleda* (☎ 35-1155), on O'Higgins just outside the harbour compound, has singles/doubles for US$8/11 and is convenient for late arrivals on the ferries.

Navimag and Transmarchilay sail to Quellón or Chonchi, on the island of Chiloé, and to Puerto Montt; for details, see the Coyhaique section. Buses to Coyhaique meet arriving ferries.

PARQUE NACIONAL LAGUNA SAN RAFAEL
Glaciers brush the sea at the edge of the massive Campo de Hielo Norte (northern Patagonian ice sheet). Dense with floating icebergs from its namesake glacier, Laguna San Rafael is a memorable sight even beneath the sombre clouds which often hang over surrounding peaks.

Although it is almost an enclosed inlet of the sea, Laguna San Rafael is 225 km southwest of Puerto Chacabuco via a series of channels between the Chonos archipelago and the Patagonian mainland. At higher elevations, snow nourishes the 19 major glaciers which form a 300,000-hectare icefield, but the San Rafael glacier is receding because of the relatively mild maritime climate.

Things to See & Do
Sightseeing is the major attraction, but fishing, climbing and hiking are possible for well-equipped travellers in top physical condition. Darwin cautioned that:

Southern Patagonia

0   100   200 km

The coast is so very rugged that to attempt to walk in that direction requires continued scrambling up and down over the sharp rocks of mica-slate; and as for the woods, our faces, hands and shin-bones all bore witness to the maltreatment we received, in attempting to penetrate their forbidding recesses.

Those who overcome these obstacles may see flightless steamer ducks, albatrosses and Magellanic penguins. Otters, sea lions and elephant seals also frequent the icy waters, while pudú, pumas and foxes inhabit the surrounding forests.

Places to Stay
Laguna San Rafael has no permanent accommodation. Most visitors stay on board the ship, but CONAF may allow campers in the unheated basement of the abandoned hotel which serves as park headquarters. It has recently levied an entrance fee of about US$10 per visitor.

Getting There & Away
Air Charter flights from Coyhaique land at the gravel airstrip. Contact Línea Aérea Hein (☎ 23-2772), at Bilbao 968, or Línea Aérea San Rafael (☎ 23-3408), at 18 de Septiembre 469.

Boat Broom Austral's (☎ 35-1134 in Chacabuco) *Calbuco* sails on Fridays at 6 pm from Chacabuco and returns on Sundays at 7 am, with reclining seats for US$86 and berths for US$114. Navimag's (☎ 23-3306, Presidente Ibáñez 347 in Coyhaique) *Evangelistas* (from US$137 return) sails three times a month from Puerto Montt, taking five days and four nights.

Transmarchilay (☎ 23-1971), 21 de Mayo 417 in Coyhaique, runs the ferry *El Colono*, with fares from US$114 to US$171.

PUERTO INGENIERO IBÁÑEZ
Puerto Ingeniero Ibáñez, on Lago General Carrera, has recovered quickly from the 1991 eruption of Volcán Hudson, which nearly buried it in ash. Local *huasos*, counterpart to the Argentine gaucho, drive cattle and sheep along the roads, but orchard crops do well in the lakeside microclimate; rows of poplars separate the fields. Ferries cross the lake to Chile Chico.

Residencial Ibáñez, Dickson 31, has unheated singles with plenty of extra blankets for about US$5 with breakfast; other meals are available. *Hotel Monica*, next door, is slightly dearer.

Getting There & Away
For transport from Coyhaique, see the Coyhaique section.

Transmarchilay's car and passenger (US$3) ferry sails on Tuesday, Wednesday and Saturday mornings to Chile Chico. On alternate Tuesdays it calls at all the small ports along Lago Carrera.

RESERVA NACIONAL CERRO CASTILLO
This reserve, south of Coyhaique, consists of 180,000 hectares of southern beech forests. It is overshadowed by the 2700-metre basalt spires of Cerro Castillo, flanked by three major glaciers on its southern slopes. CONAF operates two modest campgrounds for US$3 per site, but camping is free and spectacular in the backcountry, after CONAF's US$1 admission fee.

There is an excellent four-day trek from km 75, at the north end of the reserve, to Villa Cerro Castillo, at the south end, detailed in Lonely Planet's *Trekking in the Patagonian Andes*. At Villa Cerro Castillo, *Pension El Viajero* has rooms (US$3 a single), a bar and a cheap restaurant.

CHILE CHICO
On the south shore of Lago Carrera, tiny Chile Chico derived its early prosperity from copper, but fruit cultivation in its unique microclimate has kept it alive – though not prosperous, since it's remote from markets. In summer only, there's a tourist office at the corner of O'Higgins and Blest Gana.

Residencial Nacional, at Freire 24, and *Residencial Aguas Azules*, at Manuel Rodríguez 252, both charge about US$7 per person with breakfast. For snacks and drinks, try *Café Elizabeth y Loly* on Gonzáles, opposite the plaza, or *Restaurant Rapanui*, on the corner of O'Higgins and Blest Gana.

Aerotaxi Don Carlos has three flights weekly from Coyhaique, but there are regular ferries from Puerto Ibáñez (see the previous section).

Transportes VH crosses the border to Los Antíguos, Argentina, just nine km east (US$3 return). There are three buses daily from Monday to Thursday, one each on Friday and Saturday and none on Sundays. Los Antíguos has connections to southern Argentine Patagonia.

Magallanes

Magallanes is a rugged, mountainous and stormy area accessible only by air or sea unless you pass through Argentina. Its original inhabitants were Ona, Yahgan, Haush, Alacaluf and Tehuelche Indians who lived by fishing, hunting and gathering. Early Spanish colonisation failed, and Chile assumed definite control only in 1843.

The California gold rush nurtured the port of Punta Arenas, which further developed with wool and mutton in the late 19th century, but maritime traffic declined when the Panama Canal opened. Still wool, commerce, petroleum, and fisheries have made this Chile's most prosperous region and its natural assets, particularly Parque Nacional Torres del Paine, have made it a favourite tourist destination.

PUNTA ARENAS
On the western shore of the Strait of Magellan, Punta Arenas has nearly 100,000 inhabitants. Its port attracts vessels from the South Atlantic fishery as well as Antarctic research and tourist ships, while a customs free zone (Zona Franca) has promoted commerce and encouraged immigration. Wool boom mansions preserve a turn-of-the-century atmosphere.

History
Punta Arenas' early economy relied on wild animal products like sealskins, guanaco hides, and feathers; mineral products like coal, gold and guano; and firewood and timber. Though well situated for the California gold rush, it really flourished after 300 pure bred sheep arrived from the Falkland Islands in the late 19th century; soon two million animals grazed the territory's pastures.

As the wool market boomed, Asturian entrepreneur José Menéndez became one of the wealthiest and most influential individuals in South America. First engaged solely in commerce, his Sociedad Explotadora de Tierra del Fuego soon controlled nearly a million hectares in Magallanes and other properties in Argentina.

Menéndez and his colleagues built their empires with immigrant labour from many European lands. In the municipal cemetery, modest markers on all sides of his opulent mausoleum remember those whose efforts made the great wool fortunes possible.

Information
Tourist Office Sernatur (☎ 22-4435), Waldo Seguel 689, is open on weekdays from 8.30 am to 6.45 pm. It publishes an annually updated list of transport and accommodation, and provides a message board for foreign visitors. There's also an information kiosk on Avenida Colón, between Bories and Magallanes.

Money Change cash and travellers' cheques at cambios and travel agencies along Lautaro Navarro, on weekdays and Saturday mornings.

Post & Telecommunications Correos de Chile is on Bories, near José Menéndez. CTC telephone is at Nogueira 1116.

Argentine Consulate The Argentine Consulate, 21 de Mayo 1878, is open on weekdays from 10 am to 2 pm.

Things to See
Start at the **Plaza de Armas**, around which are the **Club de la Unión** (the former Sara

Punta Arenas

STRAIT OF MAGELLAN

0   200   400 m

Braun mansion), the **Catedral** and other turn-of-the-century monuments. Half a block north, at Magallanes 949, the **Casa Braun-Menéndez** is now a cultural centre and museum. Three blocks west of the plaza, **Avenida España 959** belonged to Charly Milward, whose eccentric exploits inspired his distant relation Bruce Chatwin to write the extraordinary travelogue, *In Patagonia*.

Four blocks south of the plaza, at the foot of Avenida Independencia, the port is frequented by ships and sailors from many countries, as well as local fisher people, the Chilean navy and countless sea birds. Take your camera.

Six blocks north of the plaza, on the corner of Bories and Sarmiento, is the **Museo Salesiano** (Salesian Museum). Another four blocks north is the **Cementerio Municipal** (Municipal Cemetery), an open-air historical museum in its own right.

Instituto de la Patagonia This institute displays early European farm and industrial machinery, a typical pioneer house and shearing shed (both reconstructed), and a wooden-wheeled shelter for outside shepherds. Ask the caretaker at the library for admission to see the buildings.

Hours are weekdays from 8.30 am to 12.30 pm and 2.30 to 6.30 pm. Any taxi colectivo to the Zona Franca will drop you across the street.

Places to Stay

Colegio Pierre Faure, at Lautaro Navarro 842, a private school which serves as a hostel in summer, may accommodate visitors at other seasons. Singles are US$5 with breakfast and shared bath, but you can also pitch a tent in the rear garden for US$3. It's a good place to meet other travellers.

One reader enjoyed *Hospedaje Rivero*, Boliviana 366, at US$4 per person. Another correspondent exuberantly praised *Hospedaje Guisande*, Carrera 1270, at US$6 per person. *Residencial Rubio*, España 640, is good value at US$6.50 a single with breakfast. *Hotel Montecarlo*, a dilapidated but clean and spacious building at Colón 605,

has singles/doubles with shared bath at US$9/16.

Highly recommended *Hotel Ritz*, Pedro Montt 1102, costs about US$20/28. According to one Lonely Planet reader, it's a 'labyrinth of entrance halls and corridors with decor from an Edwardian seaside boarding house and the mystique of an abandoned casino', while the shared baths are 'large enough for minor social functions'.

Places to Eat

The *Centro Español*, above the Teatro Cervantes, on the Plaza de Armas, serves delicious conger eel and scallops, among other specialties. *Restaurante del Mercado*, upstairs on the corner of Mejicana and Chiloé, prepares a spicy ostiones al pil pil (scallops). If you're with a group, order curanto. Many restaurants (including all the ones mentioned) serve more conventional parrilla.

La Carioca, corner of Chiloé and Menéndez, has good sandwiches and lager beer, but small pizzas. *Café Garogha*, Bories 817, is good for breakfast and onces.

Readers' recommendations include *Venus*, on Pedro Montt half a block from Hotel Ritz, *Quijote*, on Navarro at Pedro Montt, and *Monaco*, on Nogueira near the post office. One reader praised *Golden Dragon*, Colón 529, for the finest Chinese food outside Asia.

Things to Buy

The Zona Franca (duty-free zone), open daily except Sundays, is a good for cameras, film and other luxuries. Taxi colectivos to the shopping centre are numerous.

Getting There & Away

Air Aeropuerto Presidente Carlos Ibáñez del Campo is 20 km north of town.

LAN-Chile (☎ 22-3338), Lautaro Navarro 999, flies to Puerto Montt (US$144) and Santiago (US$223) daily, except Thursdays. Ladeco (☎ 226100), Roca 924, flies the same routes daily, except Wednesdays. Cut-rate Pacific Air is hoping to provide cheaper competition.

CHILE

Aerovías DAP (☎ 22-3958), O'Higgins 891, flies to Porvenir twice daily, except Sundays (US$13.50 one-way). On Tuesdays, they fly to Puerto Williams, on Isla Navarino (US$62). In summer, there are weekly flights to the Falkland Islands (US$365); in winter, these flights depart on alternate weeks.

The Chilean Air Force (FACh) has cheap unscheduled flights to Puerto Montt. Inquire at the tourist office or airport.

Bus Each company has its own office, though most are on or near Lautaro Navarro. Courteous, responsible Buses Fernández, Sanhueza 745, goes to intriguing Puerto Natales at 7 am and at 2.30 and 6.30 pm. Bus Sur, José Menéndez 556, has buses to Puerto Natales (US$6), daily at 3 and 7 pm. Victoria Sur, Colón 793, also goes to Puerto Natales daily at 8 am and 7.30 pm and on Sundays at 10 am, and is slightly dearer.

Pacheco, Lautaro Navarro 601, goes on Mondays and Thursdays to Río Grande, Argentina (US$25). Of numerous services to Río Gallegos (US$15), the most frequent is Buses Pingüino, Roca 915. Buses Ghisoni, Navarro 975, and Agencia Taurus, 21 de Mayo 1502, also have several departures. Buses Mansilla, Menéndez 556, is less frequent.

Ghisoni, Bus Sur, Fernández and Bus Norte (on the Plaza de Armas), Turibus (at Menéndez 647) and Ettabus (at Roca 886, Local 7) all go to Osorno and Puerto Montt. Santiago fares range from US$66 (Bus Norte) to US$100 (Bus Sur).

Boat Navimag (☎ 22-2593), Avenida Independencia 830, sails from Puerto Natales to Puerto Montt. For details, see the Puerto Natales section.

Austral Broom (☎ 22-8204) sails to Porvenir (US$6); on Sundays and holidays, when it returns at 5 pm, it's possible to do this as a day trip without rushing.

Getting Around
To/From the Airport Aerovías DAP runs its own bus to the airport, while LAN-Chile and Ladeco use local companies.

Bus & Colectivo Taxi colectivos are much quicker, more comfortable and only slightly dearer than buses (about US$0.30, a bit more late at night and on Sundays).

Car A shared rental car can be a good deal for budget travellers. Avis (☎ 22-7050) is at the airport, and in the city centre, at Navarro 1065, while Hertz (☎ 22-2013) is across the street, at Navarro 1064. Budget (☎ 22-5696) and the Automóvil Club (☎ 22-1888) are at O'Higgins 964 and O'Higgins 931, respectively.

Organised Tours Several agencies organise tours of the Otway penguin colony, Fuerte Bulnes and Torres del Paine. These include Karú-Kinká (☎ 22-7868), at Arauco 1792, Turismo Pali Aike (☎ 22-3301), at José Menéndez 556, Arka Patagonia (☎ 22-6370), at Roca 886, Local 7, Traveltur (☎ 22-8159), at Roca 886, Local 25, and Buses Fernández (☎ 22- 2313), at Chiloé 930 (one correspondent especially recommends guide Antonio Busolich).

AROUND PUNTA ARENAS
Penguin Colonies
Near Punta Arenas are two colonies of Magellanic penguins (also gulls, cormorants and sea lions), at Otway Sound (north-west of the city) and at Parque Nacional Los Pingüinos (boat access only). There is no public transport to this area, so it's necessary to rent a car or take a tour.

Spheniscus magellanicus, also known as the Jackass penguin, for its characteristic braying, comes ashore in the spring to nest in burrows or under shrubs. The birds stay from October to March. Naturally curious, Jackasses will back into their burrows or toboggan into the water if approached too quickly. Their bills can inflict serious cuts – *never* stick your hand or face into a burrow, but sit nearby and wait for them to emerge.

Fuerte Bulnes

Several agencies make half-day excursions to Fort Bulnes, 55 km south of Punta Arenas, which was abandoned soon after its founding in 1843, because of its poor soil and pasture, lack of potable water and exposed site. Across the Strait are Dawson Island (a 19th-century Salesian mission to the Yahgans and a notorious prison camp after the 1973 coup) and the Cordillera Darwin.

PUERTO NATALES

On the shores of Seno Ultima Esperanza (Last Hope Sound), Puerto Natales (population 18,000) is 250 km north-west of Punta Arenas. Once dependent on wool, mutton and fishing, it's now an essential stopover for visitors to Parque Nacional Torres del Paine, has the best access to Parque Nacional Balmaceda and the famous Milodon Cave, and is the terminus for ferries from Puerto Montt.

Information

Tourist Office The tourist office, on the Costanera Pedro Montt, has maps and other

Puerto Natales

0   200   400 m

Seno Ultimo Esperanza

To Bories, Cueva del Milodón, Punta Arenas & Torres del Paine

PLACES TO STAY	OTHER
3 Residencial Grey	1 Harbour Master
4 Hotel Palace	2 Navimag Ferry
6 Hotel Eberhard	Company
7 Hotel Juan Ladrilleros	5 Cutter to Parque
9 Residencial Dickson	Nacional Bernado
11 Hotel Natalino	O'Higgins
12 Residencial Carahue	8 Tourist Office
13 Residencial Bulnes	14 Post Office
17 Residencial La Florida	15 Municipalidad
24 Residencial Temuco	16 Parish Church
25 Hotel Austral	19 Ladeco
	20 Buses Fernández
▼ PLACES TO STAY	21 CTC (Telephone)
	22 LAN–Chile
10 Café Midas	23 Bus Sur
18 Café Tranquera	26 Bus Sur

Señoret

Estero Natales

R Freire

Tucapel

Bories

Valdivia

Manuel Bulnes

Esmeralda

O'Higgins

Chorrillos

Yungay

Miraflores

CHILE

information. It's open from 9.30 am to 1 pm and 3 to 7 pm, daily except Sundays.

Money On Blanco Encalada near Eberhard, a block east of the plaza, Relojería Omega changes cash and travellers' cheques.

Post & Telecommunications Correos de Chile is at Eberhard 423. CTC telephone is at Blanco Encalada 23.

Places to Stay
Sergio Nitrigual's hostel at Bories 206 (US$3 with kitchen privileges) comes highly recommended.

Residencial La Florida, O'Higgins 431, and *Residencial Grey*, at Manuel Bulnes 90, both cost about US$3 a single. Readers' choices include *Hospedaje Elsa*, at Phillippi 427 (US$5 with breakfast), *Hospedaje Teresa*, at Esmeralda 463 (recommended for meals), and *Residencial Dickson*, at Bulnes 307 (US$4.50). English is spoken at *Hospedaje Knudsen*, Blanco Encalada 284, where cooking is possible.

Highly recommended is an unnamed hospedaje at Ignacio Carrera Pinto 442 (US$6 with fine breakfast, including home-made bread) – the owner even nursed our correspondent through typhoid!

A favourite mid-range place is *Hotel Austral*, at Valdivia 955, where rooms with shared bath are US$7.50/10; those with private bath are US$10/14.

Places to Eat
Restaurants specialise in seafood. Hotel Austral has a good restaurant (one correspondent tired of salmon, however), while the huge dining room at unpretentious *La Bahía*, Serrano 434, can accommodate large groups for a superb curanto.

Another popular, lively place is *Café Midas*, Tomás Rogers 169. *Café Tranquera*, Bulnes 579, has been recommended for snacks and sandwiches. Other readers' choices include *Restaurant Reymar*, on Baquedano, *Tierra del Fuego*, at Bulnes 29

(especially for lamb and seafood), and *La Burbuja*, at Bulnes 371.

Getting There & Away
Bus Buses Fernández is at Eberhard 555, Bus Sur at Baquedano 534. See the Punta Arenas section for details.

In summer, Bus Sur also goes daily to Torres del Paine (US$7) and twice weekly to Río Gallegos, Argentina (US$15). Some buses continue from Torres del Paine to Calafate, Argentina (US$45). Servitur, on Prat between Bulnes and Esmeralda, and Buses J B, Bulnes 370, both run minibuses to Paine.

Turisur and Cotra have many buses daily to the Argentine coal town of Río Turbio (US$1), for overland connections and infrequent flights to Río Gallegos and to Calafate.

Boat Navimag (☎ 41-1287), on the Costanera Pedro Montt, sails to Puerto Montt via the Chilean fjords three times a month in summer, but seems to discourage passengers. If you manage to secure a spot, the trip takes three days and four nights.

Passages, with meals, start at US$100, but it can be a rough trip not just because of the weather and the turbulent Golfo de Penas, but also because of hurried meals, inadequate toilets and the odour of livestock. The crew, however, make a serious effort to keep everyone happy.

Getting Around
Car Andes Patagónicos offers mid-size cars for US$20 per day, plus US$8 insurance and US$0.20 per km, but for US$60 plus insurance, you are allowed 350 km per day.

Organised Tours English-speaking Eduardo Scott, at Hotel Austral, can take eight to 10 passengers to Torres del Paine and elsewhere in his minibus. Andes Patagónicos, Blanco Encalada 226, and Stop Cambios, Baquedano 380, have similar services.

AROUND PUERTO NATALES
Cueva del Milodón

At this site, 24 km north-west of Puerto Natales, Captain Hermann Eberhard discovered the well-preserved remains of an enormous ground sloth, in the 1890s. Twice the height of a man, the herbivorous milodon ate the succulent leaves of small trees and branches, but became extinct in the late Pleistocene. The 30-metre-high cave contains a full-size replica of the animal.

CONAF charges US$1.50 admission; camping and picnicking are possible. Torres del Paine buses pass the entrance, which is several km from the cave proper. Alternatively, take a taxi or hitch.

Parque Nacional Balmaceda

A scenic four-hour cruise up Seno Ultima Esperanza ends at Puerto Toro and the Serrano glacier; on a clear day, the Torres del Paine are visible in the distance. En route are the **frigorífico** (meat freezer) at Bories, several estancias, glaciers and waterfalls, a large cormorant rookery and a smaller sealion colony, and the occasional condors.

Weather permitting, sailings occur daily in summer, at other times on demand, for US$28 per person. Decent meals on board cost about US$6. For reservations, contact the owners of the cutter *21 de Mayo* (☎ 41-1176), at Ladrilleros 171 in Puerto Natales.

PARQUE NACIONAL TORRES DEL PAINE

The Torres del Paine, granite pillars soaring almost vertically above the Patagonian steppe, are only one feature of perhaps South America's finest national park. There are also shimmering turquoise lakes, roaring creeks and rivers, cascading waterfalls, sprawling glaciers, dense forests and abundant wildlife. A Unesco Biosphere Reserve, the 180,000-hectare park has a well-developed trail network, but trekking requires a warm sleeping bag, good rain gear and a tent. Weather is changeable, but long summer days encourage outdoor activities late into the evening.

Paine's major conservation success has been the guanaco *(Lama guanicoe)*, which grazes the open steppes. The elusive huemul, or Chilean deer, is more difficult to spot.

Information

There is a new Spanish/English guidebook entitled *Conociendo Torres del Paine,* by Gladys Garay Nancul & Oscar Guineo Nenén (Instituto don Bosco, Punta Arenas, 1992). It costs US$15.

CONAF charges a US$8 entry fee at the Laguna Amarga entrance, where maps and brochures are available. Trekkers on the popular Paine circuit must register here or at Río Serrano. Because of trail mishaps, rangers collect passports and only return them when you finish the trek; if you leave your passport in Puerto Natales, you will be sent to the park headquarters for a lecture on personal safety.

Maps & Trekking

The Sociedad Turística Kaonikén publishes an excellent 1:100,000 topographic map (US$2) which includes details of the Paine circuit (closed at least temporarily by a fire near Lago Grey in early 1993) and other hikes. Do not, however, assume that everything on this map is correct.

Most trekkers start at Laguna Amarga and finish at Río Serrano, where you can get hot food and a shower, but a launch (US$5) from Guardería Pehoé now carries trekkers to Refugio Lago Pehoé, saving hours of tedious hiking from Río Serrano. Bring as much food as possible from Puerto Natales.

The Paine circuit requires a minimum of five days, with at least one layover day for unpredictable weather. The strenuous route has at least one potentially hazardous stream ford and a rickety log bridge. Despite a prohibition of solo trekking, it's easy to find a companion. Some veteran hikers recommend seeking out other, less frequented, sections of the park.

Places to Stay & Eat

Hostería Pehoé is beyond budget travellers, but its restaurant and bar are open to the public. More economical is *Posada Río Serrano* (☎ 41-1355 in Puerto Natales), a

CHILE

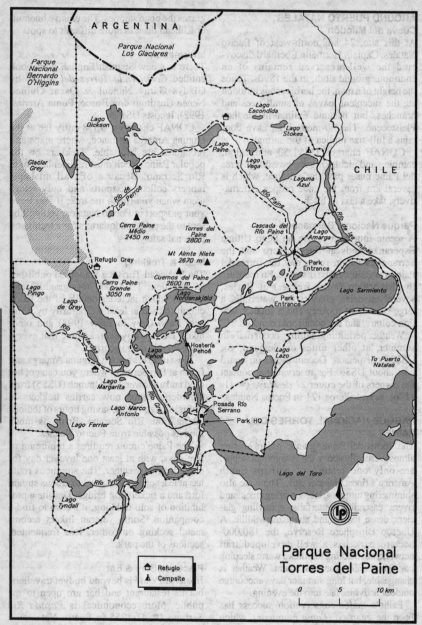

ARGENTINA

Parque Nacional
Los Glaciares

Parque
Nacional
Bernardo
O'Higgins

CHILE

Lago
Escondida

Lago
Dickson

Lago
Stokes

Lago
Paine

Glaciar
Grey

Lago
Vega

Laguna
Azul

Río
de
Los
Perros

Río Paine

Lago
Amarga

Río de las Chinas

Cascada del
Río Paine

Cerro Paine
Médio
2450 m

Torres del
Paine
2800 m

Refugio Grey

Mt Almte Niete
2670 m

Park
Entrance

Cerro Paine
Grande
3050 m

Cuernos del Paine
2600 m

Lago
Pingo

Lago
Nordenskjöld

Park
Entrance

Lago Sarmiento

Lago
de Grey

Río
Aviléerdos

Lago
Pehoé

Hostería
Pehoé

Lago
Lazo

To Puerto
Natales

Lago
Margarita

Lago Marco
Antonio

Posada Río
Serrano

Park HQ

Lago Ferrier

Río Grey

Lago del Toro

Río Tyndall

Lago
Tyndall

N

Refugio
Campsite

Parque Nacional
Torres del Paine

0   5   10 km

remodelled estancia building, where rooms with shared bath start at US$24/31.

Near Posada Río Serrano, a CONAF refugio offers floor space for US$4, but queue for the single hot shower. Free refugios, like that at Pudeto, on Lago Pehoé, are *very* rustic. Campsites at Lago Pehoé and at Río Serrano charge US$8 for up to six people, with firewood and hot showers (usually mornings only). The more remote Laguna Azul site (no showers) charges US$5.

Getting There & Away
For details, see the Puerto Natales section. Buses go as far as Río Serrano, though you can disembark at Laguna Amarga for the Paine circuit, or elsewhere upon request. Hitching competition is heavy.

Summer buses connect Torres del Paine and Calafate, Argentina.

PORVENIR
Porvenir (population 6400), the largest settlement on Chilean Tierra del Fuego, is a cluster of corroding, metal-clad Victorian buildings belying its optimistic name (the future). For most travellers, it's just a stopover en route to Ushuaia, Argentina. Many inhabitants descended from Yugoslav participants in a brief 1880s gold rush.

For information, visit the kiosk on the costanera, which also sells ferry tickets to Punta Arenas. The ferry terminal bus arrives and departs here.

Places to Stay & Eat
The cheapest accommodation is *Residencial Colón*, Damián Riobó 108, at US$5 a single with shared bath. Other reasonable choices are *Hotel Rosas*, Phillippi 296, or *Hotel Central*, Phillippi 298.

Hotel Rosas has a fine seafood restaurant. The former Yugoslav Club, on the costanera, is now the *Club Croata*.

Getting There & Away
Air Aerovías DAP flies to Punta Arenas (US$13.50, 10 minutes), twice daily, except Sundays.

Bus Transporte Senkovic, Bories 295, goes on Tuesdays and Saturdays to Río Grande, Argentina (US$11).

Boat Broom Austral's daily car/passenger ferry to Punta Arenas (2½ hours) costs US$6. The ferry terminal bus (US$0.75) leaves the tourist kiosk an hour before departure, providing a goodbye tour of Porvenir; taxis cost at least four times as much.

PUERTO WILLIAMS
Tiny Puerto Williams, on Isla Navarino in the Beagle Channel, directly opposite Argentine's Tierra del Fuego, is primarily a naval base. Nearby, Captain Fitzroy of the *Beagle* encountered the Yahgan Indians, some of whom he took back with him to England, but it was the 19th-century missionaries and gold-seekers who established a permanent European presence.

A cluster of public services on Presidente Ibáñez includes telephone, post, supermarket and tourist office. The **Museo Martín Gusinde** honours a German priest/ethnographer who worked among the Yahgans, whose few survivors live at **Ukika**, east of town. The surrounding countryside offers good hiking, but demands warm, water-resistant clothing.

Places to Stay & Eat
Basic *Residencial Onashaga* is clean and comfortable for US$9 a single. Camping is possible near up-market *Hostería Patagonia*, on the edge of town. Both hotels serve meals.

A reader strongly recommends *Pensión Temuco*, Piloto Pardo 224, which won the prize for the best pensión in Puerto Williams! It costs US$8 per day (US$15 with all meals) and has hot water at all times.

Getting There & Away
Air DAP flies to Punta Arenas (US$62) on Tuesdays. Seats are limited and reservations are essential.

Boat Unscheduled Chilean naval supply vessels sometimes take passengers to Punta

Arenas. On Saturdays, at least in summer, a passenger ferry goes to Ushuaia for US$50.

Juan Fernández Islands

In 1966, a tourist-motivated government renamed Isla Masatierra to Isla Robinson Crusoe, after literature's most renowned castaway. Scottish maroon Alexander Selkirk was the real-life model for Daniel Defoe's fictional character, but the tranquil Juan Fernández archipelago is also a national park and world biosphere reserve.

History

In 1574, Juan Fernández discovered the islands which still bear his name. For over two centuries, the islands sheltered pirates and sealers, but were most renowned for Alexander Selkirk's four-year exile on Masatierra after going ashore, at his own request, in 1704. Most castaways soon starved or shot themselves, but the adaptable Selkirk survived on feral goats (a Spanish introduction).

In 1708, Commander Woodes Rogers, of the privateers Duke and Duchess, rescued Selkirk. On returning to Scotland, Selkirk became a celebrity; Defoe's fictionalised account, set in the Caribbean, became a classic.

After Selkirk's departure, the presence of privateers and sealers compelled Spain to found the village of San Juan Bautista in 1750. There was no really permanent presence until 1877. During WW I, the British navy sank a German cruiser at Cumberland Bay.

Since then, the islands have played a less conspicuous but more significant role. In 1935, Chile declared them a national park for their unique flora and fauna, then undertook a programme to remove the feral goats. Mainland demand for the tasty local lobster provides substantial income for some Islanders.

Geography & Climate

Separated from Valparaíso by 670 km of the open Pacific, Juan Fernández consists of Isla Robinson Crusoe, Isla Alejandro Selkirk (ex-Masafuera) and Isla Santa Clara. The islands are really emergent peaks from a submarine mountain range. Robinson Crusoe's area is only 93 sq km, its length a maximum 22 km and its width a maximum 7.3 km. Cerro El Yunque (The Anvil) reaches 915 metres. The climate is Mediterranean, but rainfall varies greatly because of irregular topography.

Getting There & Away

Air Two companies fly air taxis almost daily in summer, less often in other seasons, from Santiago's Los Cerrillos airport. Travellers should allow for an extra two or three days' stay when poor weather makes landings risky at Robinson Crusoe's dirt airstrip.

LASSA (☎ 273-4309), in the Aeródromo Tobalaba, at Avenida Larraín 7941 in the

Santiago suburb of La Reina, flies six-passenger taxis, as does Transportes Aéreos Isla Robinson Crusoe (☎ 531-3772), at Monumento 2570 in the suburb of Maipú. Fares are about US$175 one-way, but check for discount packages with accommodation and all meals.

From the airstrip, it is about 1½ hours by a combination of 4WD (to the jetty at Bahía del Padre) and subsequent motor launch (sailing along the island's awesome volcanic escarpments) to San Juan. Both flight and voyage can be rough, so some travellers may consider medication.

Boat Sailing to Juan Fernández is not easy, but quarterly naval supply ships carry passengers very cheaply. Since even the most innocuous naval movements are top secret, it's hard to learn departure dates, but try calling the Comando de Transporte (☎ 25-8457), at the Primera Zona Naval, opposite Plaza Sotomayor in Valparaíso.

Fishing boats visit the islands irregularly, but will carry passengers for about US$85 from Valparaíso. Contact Empresa Pesquera Chris (☎ 681-1543) at Cueto 622 in Santiago, or in Valparaíso (☎ 21-6800), at Cochrane 445.

Getting Around

Getting around sometimes requires hiring a fishing boat (rates are fixed by the Municipalidad) or accompanying lobster catchers on their rounds. To arrange a launch, contact Polo González at LASSA's office on the plaza. CONAF rangers visiting outlying sites may take along passengers.

PARQUE NACIONAL JUAN FERNÁNDEZ

Juan Fernández is a storehouse of rare plants and animals, evolved in isolation and adapted to specific ecological niches. Its native flora have suffered from the introduction of non-native species, but much remains in terrain where even the agile goat could not penetrate or dominate.

Local flora have evolved into something very distinct from their continental and insular origins. Of the 87 plant genera, 16 are endemic, found nowhere else on earth; of 140 plant species, 101 are endemic.

The most notable animal species is the only native mammal, the Juan Fernández fur seal, nearly extinct a century ago; about 2500 individuals now breed here. Of 11 endemic bird species, the bright-red male Juan Fernández hummingbird is the most eye-catching; the female is a more subdued green, with a white tail. About 250 individuals survive, feeding off the endemic cabbage which grows in many parts of San Juan Bautista, but the species does best in native forest. Introduced rodents and feral cats have endangered nesting marine birds like Cook's petrel, by preying on their eggs or young.

Books

Defoe's classic is an obvious choice, but Rogers' *A Cruising Voyage Round the World* is available as a Dover Publications facsimile (New York, 1970). The most thorough history is Ralph Lee Woodward's *Robinson Crusoe's Island* (University of North Carolina Press, 1969).

Things to See & Do

Yielding great views, the **Mirador Alejandro Selkirk**, Selkirk's overlook, is at the end of a steep three-km walk from San Juan Bautista. Hikers can continue to the airstrip for the flight back to the mainland, but should confirm their reservations in San Juan.

Plazoleta El Yunque, half an hour from San Juan, is a tranquil forest clearing with picnic and camping areas. Only 15 minutes from San Juan by launch, **Puerto Inglés** has a reconstruction of Selkirk's shelter, ruins of a cowherd's shed and adequate water for camping, but no firewood. The boat is expensive without a group, but a steep trail from San Juan takes about two hours.

Robinson Crusoe's only breeding colony of fur seals is **Lobería Tierras Blancas**, a short distance from the airstrip. The trail to the airstrip from San Juan passes near the colony, which lacks drinking water. If you

CHILE

can't visit Tierras Blancas, you can still see fur seals at Bahía del Padre on arrival, or just north of San Juan's cemetery.

SAN JUAN BAUTISTA

San Juan Bautista (population 600) is one of the most tranquil places in Chile. Most visitors stay here or at nearby Pangal, and camping is possible.

The economy depends on fishing, mostly for lobster, which are flown to Santiago by air taxi, but many Islanders never visit the continent.

The Municipalidad, near the plaza, has Sernatur leaflets with decent maps and information, but bring money from the mainland, preferably in small bills. Hotels accept US dollars in payment for accommodation. CONAF offices are at the top of Vicente González, about 500 metres above the Costanera.

Things to See

Near the lighthouse, the polyglot European surnames in San Juan's **cemetery** provide a unique perspective on local history – the Germans were survivors of the WW I battleship *Dresden*.

Over 40 participants in Chile's independence movement spent years in the **Cuevas de Los Patriotas** after defeat at Rancagua in 1814. Directly above the caves, Spain built **Fuerte Santa Bárbara** in 1749, to discourage incursions by pirates.

Places to Stay & Eat

Camping is permitted just about anywhere except the *zona intangible*, but in some areas you'll need to carry water. At El Palillo, at the south end of San Juan, CONAF has a quiet, pleasant and free campground, with running water and a pit latrine. The nearest shower (cold water only) is a 15-minute walk to the jetty. There is another site at Plazoleta El Yunque.

Hotel accommodation starts at about US$50 per day, but usually includes all meals (with lobster every day). If not staying at a hotel, give restaurants several hours' notice for lunch or dinner.

Despite its modest appearance, *Restaurant La Bahía* is outstanding value, as owner Jorge Angulo prepares an extraordinary ceviche and succulent lobster for about US$11 per person, but requires a two-person minimum so the other half of the lobster doesn't go to waste. The tasty vidriola (a type of fish) is much cheaper, about US$5.

Hostería Daniel Defoe is dearer and no better, but will prepare lobster for one. *Restaurant Remo*, on the plaza, serves only sandwiches and drinks. Cholera warnings do not apply to the Juan Fernández Islands, so eating seafood should be fine.

Easter Island

Discovery of the earth's most remote inhabited island is an enigma as great as its hundreds of colossal *moai*, sculpted from hard basalt, transported from quarry to coast, and raised on stone *ahu* (platforms). Polynesians named the tiny volcanic land mass Rapa Nui, but Dutchman Jacob Roggeveen named it Easter Island, a legacy which survived among Europeans.

HISTORY

Easter Island raises issues disproportional to its size (117 sq km) and population (about 2000). The nearest populated land mass, 1900 km west, is even tinier Pitcairn; the next nearest neighbours are the Mangarévas (Gambier) Islands, 2500 km west. The South American coast is 3700 km east.

Among these very big questions are the initial Islander' origins, their arrival at this unlikely destination, the inspiration for such monuments, and their techniques. Larger questions deal with early trans-Pacific contacts and cultural exchanges.

Asiatic peoples first reached the Americas across the Bering Strait on a land bridge submerged by rising seas at the end of the Pleistocene, 12,000 years ago. Some of their descendants created the civilisations of Mexico and Peru, while others reached

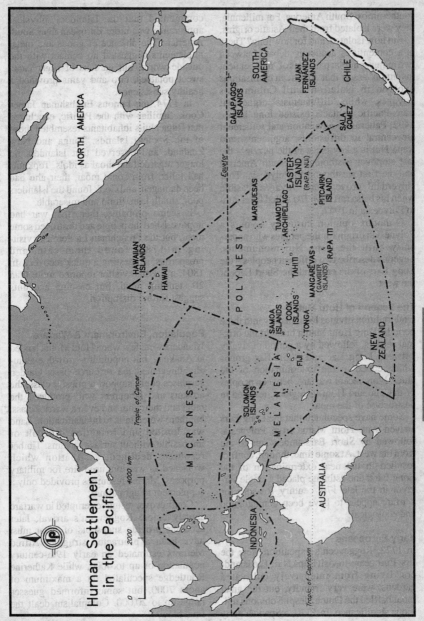

Human Settlement
in the Pacific

southernmost South America. For millennia, they were isolated from their Asiatic origins.

But how isolated, and for how long? There is a contentious academic debate between two major schools: partisans of 'independent invention' assert that American civilisations evolved in isolation until Columbus's voyages, while 'diffusionists' argue that trans-Pacific contacts existed long before 1492. Patterns of navigation and settlement are central to diffusionist arguments, and Rapa Nui is a key piece in the puzzle – the last stopover eastbound to South America and the first westbound to Polynesia. Thor Heyerdahl proved such voyages feasible when his balsa raft *Kon-Tiki* sailed from Peru to Polynesia in 1947.

Orthodox opinion currently favours a Polynesian origin for the peoples who apparently built the Rapa Nui monuments. Legends describe two different peoples – the Long Ears of the east and the Short Ears of the west.

The Legend of Hotu Matua

Oral tradition divides local history into three periods. King Hotu Matua brought the original settlers, followed by a period of rivalry between Long Ear and Short Ear groups which ended in the extermination of the latter. More recent warfare, between peoples of the Tuu and Hotu-iti regions, resulted in destruction of the moai.

Some have speculated that the Long Ears arrived with Hotu Matua from Polynesia, followed by Short Ears under Tuu-ko-ihu from the west. At some time, though, conflict resulted in the near extermination of the Long Ears; one estimate placed a single survivor in the late 17th century. Reasons for warfare appear to have been demographic and ecological.

Early Europeans

In 1722, Roggeveen's expedition were the first Europeans to visit Rapa Nui. The Islanders, living from intensively cultivated gardens, were very friendly, but the great moai baffled the Dutch, despite obvious religious significance. In 1770, a Spanish party commented that the Islanders' physical appearance was more European than South America. The absence of goods and metal implements suggested no contact with the outside world, but gardens of sugar cane, sweet potatoes, taro and yams provided a healthy subsistence.

In 1774, the famous Englishman James Cook, familiar with the Pacific, concluded that Rapa Nui's inhabitants resembled those of the Society Islands, Tonga and New Zealand, and observed that Islanders no longer regarded the moai as idols. Topknots had fallen from some moai, their ahu had been damaged, and Cook found the Islanders poor, small, lean, timid and miserable.

It seems probable, then, that war had impoverished the people and destroyed some moai, but the Frenchman La Perouse, visiting in 1786, found them calm and prosperous, suggesting a quick recovery. In 1804, a Russian visitor reported more than 20 standing moai, but ensuing accounts suggest further disruption.

Population, Environment & Warfare

Islanders were few when Hotu Motua landed at Anakena, but population growth eventually threatened the resource base. Garden surpluses could support a priestly class, the artisans and labourers who produced the moai and their ahu, and even a warrior class, but there were limits to intensification. Land was limited and irrigation difficult or impossible without surface streams. Timber resources declined, a situation which worsened as warriors used fire for military purposes. Marine resources provided only a supplement to agriculture.

Conflict over resources erupted in warfare shortly before Roggeveen's arrival; later accounts provide snapshots of what must have been a protracted struggle. Alfred Metraux estimated an early 19th-century population of up to 4000, while Katherine Routledge speculated on a maximum of about 7000, but some informed guesses range up to 20,000. Colonialism dealt the final blow.

CHILE

Colonialism in the Pacific

The Rapa Nui people may have inflicted havoc on themselves but outsiders nearly annihilated them. A Peruvian slave raid in 1862 led directly or indirectly to many deaths, followed by transportation to foreign mines and plantations, the arrival of previously unknown diseases, and forced emigration at the hands of missionaries.

Spain had always ignored Rapa Nui, but Chile annexed it in 1888 during a period of expansion. Chile valued the island as a naval station, to prevent its use by a hostile power, for its location on a potential trade route to East Asia, and for the prestige of having overseas possessions in an era of imperialism.

Williamson, Balfour & Company

By 1897, the island came under the control of a Valparaíso businessman who had bought or leased nearly all the land for wool, but it soon fell into the hands of Williamson, Balfour & Company, a British-Chilean enterprise which managed the island through their Compañía Explotadora de la Isla de Pascua (CEDIP). CEDIP was the island's de facto government until the 1950s.

Islanders' welfare under CEDIP is a controversial topic, but there were several uprisings against the company. In 1953, the government revoked CEDIP's lease and the navy took charge of the island, continuing imperial rule.

Chilean Colonialism

Rapa Nui was under military rule until the mid-1960s, when the Chilean presence became more benevolent, with advances in water supply, medical care, education and electrification. After 1967, external contacts increased after the establishment of a regular commercial air link between Santiago and Tahiti, with Easter Island as a refuelling stop. The coup of 1973 once again brought direct military control, but there is now local self-government. Cattle and sheep still graze on parts of the island, but nearly everyone now makes a living, directly or indirectly, from the tourist trade.

In 1990, Islanders protested about fare increases by LAN-Chile (the only air carrier) and occupied Mataveri airport, even preventing the landing of a jetload of Carabineros by blocking the runway with cars and rubble. The global impulse toward self-determination has clearly reached Rapa Nui, as some Islanders argue for return of native lands and speak of independence or at least autonomy – but tempered by realism. Asked if he would like to expel the Chileans, one Islander responded, 'We can't – but we'd like them to leave'.

GEOGRAPHY & CLIMATE

Just south of the Tropic of Capricorn, Rapa Nui was formed when lava flows from three separate cones coalesced in a single, triangular land mass. The coastal terrain is mostly gentle and grass-covered, except where wave erosion has created nearly vertical cliffs. Rugged lava fields cover much of the interior, but several areas have soil which can be cultivated. Vulcanism left many caves, some of which served as permanent shelters, wartime refuges, or storage or burial sites.

Rapa Nui rests on a submarine platform which drops precipitously just off the coast. There are no reefs and no natural sheltered harbour. Anakena, on the north coast, is the only broad sandy beach.

In the subtropical climate, the hottest months are January and February, the coolest July and August. May is the wettest month, but downpours can occur at any time. The volcanic soil is so porous that water quickly drains underground.

CULTURE

Rapa Nui Stonework

Easter Island's 245 or so ahu form an almost unbroken line along the coast; only a handful are inland. The density of ruins implies a much larger population than at present. Of the several types, the most impressive are the *ahu moai* which support the massive statues. The moai themselves reach up to 10 metres, but larger ones were under construction at Rano Raraku when work suddenly ceased.

Researchers have learned little about ceremonies connected with ahu complexes. One theory is that the moai represented clan ancestors. Ahu were also burial sites: originally, bodies were interred in stone-lined tombs, but after the moai had fallen, bodies were placed around them, then covered with stones.

Many structures were partially demolished or rebuilt by the original inhabitants, and the moai fell during intertribal wars, but CEDIP dismantled many ahu, burial cairns and house foundations for piers at Caleta Hanga Roa and Caleta Hanga Piko, and for walls for grazing areas. Windmills were built over the original stone-lined wells to provide water for livestock.

Collectors removed a few moai, but museums and private collections pillaged wooden *rongo-rongo* (a form of indigenous writing or hieroglyphics) tablets, Orongo wall tablets and other artefacts. Islanders themselves removed building materials from some sites.

On the other hand, archaeologists have restored many sites. It's possible to visit the major ones on three loops out of Hanga Roa – the South-West Route, the Northern Loop and the Island Circuit – with minimal backtracking.

BOOKS & MAPS
On geography and environment, the most thorough source is Juan Carlos Castilla's edited collection *Islas Oceánicas Chilenas* (Ediciones Universidad Católica de Chile, Santiago, 1987), which also covers the Juan Fernández Islands.

Thor Heyerdahl's *Kon-Tiki* (Rand McNally, Chicago, 1952) and *Aku-Aku: The Secret of Easter Island* (Allen & Unwin, 1958) are well known. Bavarian priest Sebastian Englert, a long-time resident, retells its history through oral tradition in *Island at the Center of the World* (Scribner's, New York, 1970).

In the debate over diffusion, independent invention and trans-Pacific contacts, Heyerdahl's *American Indians in the Pacific: The Theory Behind the Kon-Tiki Expedition* (Allen & Unwin, London, 1952) compares American Indian and Pacific cultures, legends, religion, stonework, watercraft, physical characteristics and cultivated plants. However, there is now consensus that the initial settlers were Polynesian. A valuable but diverse collection, dealing partly with pre-Columbian contacts across the Pacific, is *Man Across the Sea* (University of Texas Press, 1971), edited by Carroll L Riley.

The outstanding 1:30,000 scale *Isla de Pascua-Rapa Nui: Mapa Arqueológico-Turístico* (Ediciones del Pacífico Sur, Santiago) is available at the tourist office and in island shops for about US$10.

GETTING THERE & AWAY
LAN-Chile (☎ 78), the only airline, connects Santiago to Tahiti two or three times weekly. From Australia or New Zealand, you can take a Melbourne/Sydney-Tahiti flight with Qantas or an Auckland-Tahiti flight with Air New Zealand and then transfer to LAN for the onward flight. For fares, see the Getting There & Away section. Reconfirm flights at both ends, especially in summer. Service is excellent and attentive on the 5½ hour flight from Santiago. The return is at least an hour quicker because of the jet stream.

GETTING AROUND
With good locomotion, you can visit all major sites in about three days. Cars, motorbikes and horses are your main options. Walking is feasible, but the heat, lack of shade, and scattered water supply are good reasons not to do so.

On horseback or motorbike, carry a daypack with a long-sleeved shirt, sunglasses and headgear, plus a powerful sunblock. Also carry extra food and water.

Motorbikes & Cars
Formal hotels rent Suzuki jeeps for US$70 per day, but locals rent them for around US$40 per 12-hour day. Try Easter Island Rent A Car (☎ 328), on Policarpo Toro, Te Aiki (☎ 366), at the Residencial Tekena, or

look for signs in windows. Outside high season, prices are negotiable.

Motorbikes rent for about US$30 to US$35 a day. Given occasional tropical downpours, a jeep is more convenient, and even more economical for two or more people.

Horses

For sites near Hanga Roa, horses can be hired for about US$15 per day. Horse gear is very basic and potentially hazardous for inexperienced riders, but Hotel Hotu Matua or Hotel Hanga Roa may organise riding excursions and locate proper stirrups and reins.

HANGA ROA

Nearly all Islanders live in Hanga Roa, a sprawling village with an irregular street plan. Nearly everyone depends on the tourist trade, but there is some fishing, plus livestock (mostly cattle) and kitchen gardens. Government and small shops are the only other employers. In early 1993, an American movie was in production on the island, so prices of accomodation, food and car rental may have increased.

Information

Tourist Office Sernatur (☎ 55) is on Tuu Maheere at Apina, near Caleta Hanga Roa. The staffs speak Rapa Nui, Spanish, English and French. An airport office is open for arriving flights.

Money Banco del Estado, next to Sernatur, changes US dollars, but pays the disadvantageous official rate and charges high commissions on travellers' cheques, so bring Chilean currency from the mainland.

Post & Telecommunications Correos de Chile is on Te Pito o Te Henua, half a block above Caleta Hanga Roa. ENTEL, with its conspicuous satellite dish, is on a cul-de-sac opposite Sernatur.

Emergency The hospital is one long block above the church.

Museo Antropológico Sebastián Englert

Researchers and visitors often neglect the Rapa Nui people and their experience, but this museum partly redresses that shortcoming. It clearly shows, for instance, that they are a Polynesian people whose subsistence depended on crops like *kumara* (sweet potato), a staple which Islanders still prefer to wheat. Kumara and other crops grew in excavated garden enclosures *(manavai)*, as well as terraces on Rano Kau crater and the humid entrances to volcanic caves.

Historical photographs depict the encounter with European culture since the mid-19th century. Legal documents illustrate how, for instance, the Chilean civil register corrupted the surname Te Ave into Chávez. The musem also displays obsidian spearheads, *moai kavakava* (the strange statues of ribs) and replicas of rongo-rongo tablets.

The museum (admission US$1) is midway between Ahu Tahai and Ahu Akapu – see the map for directions. Opening hours are weekdays from 9 am to 12.30 pm and 2 to 7 pm and Sundays from 9 am to noon only. It's closed on Saturdays.

Places to Stay

The least expensive rooms will be about US$15/25 for a single/double, with breakfast. Other meals may cost up to US$10 each, but Hanga Roa has several reasonable restaurants. Neither streets nor residenciales are well signposted, and buildings rarely have numbers, so locate places by referring to the map.

Reservations are not essential, except in summer. Hosts often meet incoming flights with a discount offer, including transport to town; most charge around US$45/75 with full board, but this is inconvenient if you can't return to Hanga Roa for lunch.

Camping Some residenciales offer garden camp sites, but CONAF allows camping only at Anakena (ask about the water supply).

Residenciales Residenciales start around US$15/25 for a single/double with breakfast,

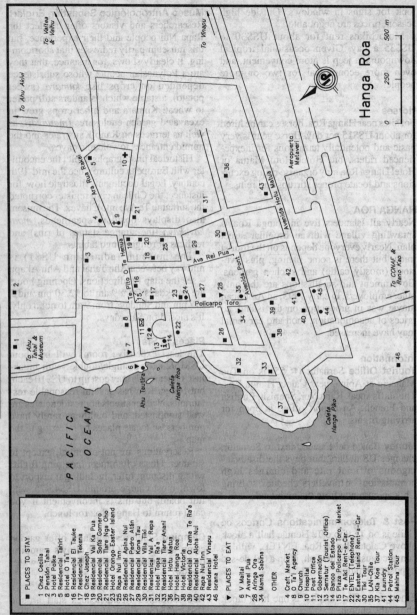

Hanga Roa

To Valtea & Vaihu

To Vinapu

To Ahu Akivi

To Ahu Tahai & Museum

PACIFIC OCEAN

Ahu Tautira

Caleta Hanga Roa

Caleta Hanga Piko

Aeropuerto Mataveri

To CONAF & Rano Kao

0   250   500 m

■	PLACES TO STAY
1	Chez Cecilia
2	Pensión Tahai
3	Hotel Poike
5	Residencial Tahiri
8	Hotel O Tai
16	Residencial El Tauke
17	Residencial Tekena
18	Chez Joseph
19	Residencial Vai ka Pua
20	Residencial Sofia Gomero
21	Residencial Tiare Nga Oho
23	Hotel Orongo Easter Island
25	Rapa Nui Inn
26	Residencial Apina Nui
27	Residencial Pedro Atán
29	Residencial Kona Tau
30	Residencial Villa Tiki
31	Residencial Vai A Repa
32	Hotel Topa Ra'a
33	Residencial Tiare Anani
36	Hotel Hotu Matua
38	Hotel Hanga Roa
39	Hotel Victoria
40	Residencial O Tama Te Ra'a
42	Residencial Aloha Nui
43	Rapa Nui Inn
46	Iorana Hotel

▼	PLACES TO EAT
6	V Maitai
7	Avarei Pua
28	Aringa Ora
34	Mamá Sabina

	OTHER
4	Craft Market
9	O Ta'i Agency
10	Church
11	Hospital
12	Post Office
13	Gobernación
14	Sernatur (Tourist Office)
15	Banco del Estado
17	Plaza Policarpo Toro, Market
22	Te Aliki Rent-a-Car
24	ENTEL (Telephone)
30	Easter Island Rent-a-Car
35	Tiki Tour
37	LAN-Chile
41	Kia Koe Tour
44	Laundry
45	Petrol Station
	Mahina Tour

including the popular and friendly *Residencial El Tauke* (☎ 253), *Residencial Tekena* (☎ 289), *Residencial Vai A Repa* (☎ 331), *Residencial Tiare Anani* (☎ 358) and *Residencial Tiare Nga Oho* (☎ 259).

A perennial favourite is María Hey's *Pensión Tahai* (☎ 395), for US$20/35 with breakfast in a very clean bungalow in a large, quiet and relaxing garden, on the Ahu Tahai road. Another good place is the *Rapa Nui Inn* (☎ 228), on the corner of Policarpo Toro and Avenida Hotu Motua. Rates are US$20/30 with breakfast, for a large, clean room with double bed and private bath. In the same range, *Residencial Vinapu* (☎ 393) has also been recommended.

Places to Eat
Restaurants offer fine seafood at reasonable prices (except for lobster, which is expensive). Try *V Maitai*, at Caleta Hanga Roa, *Avarei Pua*, across the street, *Mamá Sabina* (very well-prepared and appetising), across from LAN-Chile, or *Aringa Ora*.

If camping or cooking your own food, get provisions at general stores and bakeries on the main street. The open-air market on Policarpo Toro, across from the Gobernación, has fresh fish and vegetables.

Things to Buy
For crafts, the best selection and prices (open to haggling) are at the market across from the church. Look for stone or wooden replicas of standard moai, as well as moai kavakava, replica rongo-rongo tablets, and obsidian fragments from Orito (sometimes made into earrings).

PARQUE NACIONAL RAPA NUI
Since 1935, Easter Island's monuments have been part of this open-air museum administered by CONAF. Non-Chileans pay admission fees of about US$10 to Orongo ceremonial village and Ahu Tahai. These are valid for the length of your stay.

In cooperation with foreign and Chilean archaeologists as well as locals, the government has successfully restored monuments and attracted visitors, but some Islanders view the park as a land grab. A native rights organisation, the Consejo de Ancianos (Council of Elders) wants the park (a third of the island's surface) returned to its aboriginal owners, who control almost no land outside the town of Hanga Roa. However, many Islanders work for CONAF and other government agencies.

The South-West Route
From Hanga Roa, take the road to the top of Rano Kau crater and Orongo ceremonial village. After backtracking to Hanga Roa, take the road north of the airport to the old obsidian quarries at Orito, then south to Ahu Vinapu.

Orongo Ceremonial Village Perched 400 metres above the reedy crater lake of Rano Kau, Orongo is one of the island's most dramatic sites, a much later construction than the great moai and ahu.

Overlooking several small *motu* (islets), Orongo was the centre of an island-wide bird cult in the 18th and 19th centuries. The climax of its rituals was a competition for the first egg of the sooty tern *(Sterna fuscata)*, which bred on the motu just off Cabo Te Manga; whoever found the first egg won the god Makemake's favour and great status.

Built into the slope, Orongo's semisubterranean houses had walls of horizontally overlapping stone slabs, with an earthcovered arched roof. Since walls were thick to support the roof's weight, the doorway is a low, narrow tunnel. At the crater's edge is a cluster of boulders with birdman petroglyphs.

Orito Having overthrown the Long Ears, Short Ear tribes enjoyed peace until resource-centred conflicts resulted in bloody warfare, leading to the toppling of the moai. Their weapons were made from hard black obsidian, quarried at Orito.

Ahu Vinapu Follow the Mataveri road to the end of the runway, then head south between the airstrip and some large oil tanks to an

CHILE

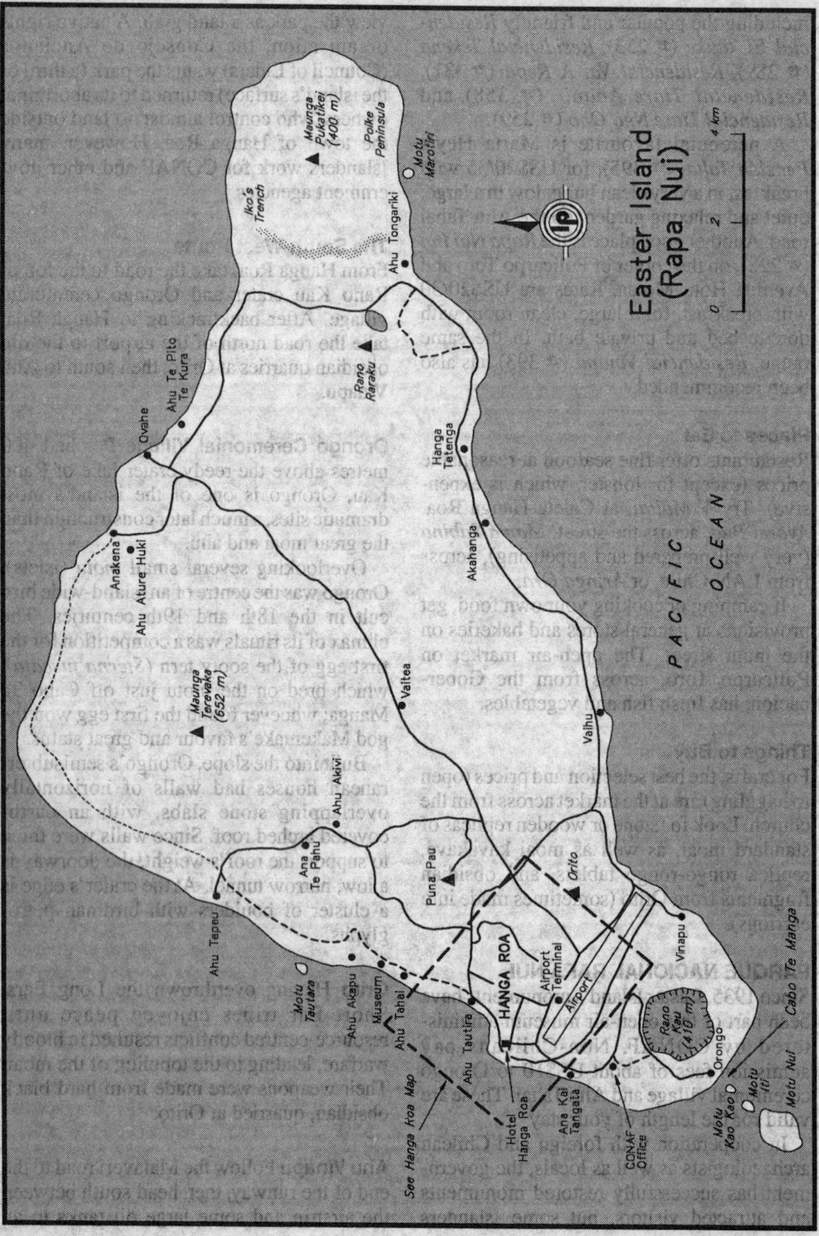

CHILE

Easter Island
(Rapa Nui)

PACIFIC OCEAN

0   2   4 km

Maunga Pukatikei
(400 m)

Poike Peninsula

Iko's Trench

Motu Marotiri

Ahu Tongariki

Maunga Pahu

Ahu Te Pito Te Kura

Rano Raraku

Ovahe

Ahu Ature Huki

Anakena

Hanga Tetenga

Akahanga

Maunga Terevaka
(652 m)

Ahu Akivi

Vaitea

Vaihu

Ahu Pahu

Ana Pahu

Ahu Tepeu

Motu Tautara

Ahu Akapu

Museum

Ahu Tahai

See Hanga Roa Map

Ahu Tautira

HANGA ROA

Hotel Hanga Roa

Ana Kai Tangata

Puna Pau

Orito

Airport Terminal

Airport

Vinapu

Cabo Te Manga

Rano Kau
(410 m)

Orongo

CONAF Office

Motu Nui

Motu Iti

Motu Kao Kao

opening in a stone wall, where a sign points to Ahu Vinapu.

Vinapu's tight-fitting stonework so resembles that of the Inca Cuzco and pre-Inca Tiahuanaco that some researchers have concluded South American origins. Others argued for independent invention.

The Northern Loop
Take the route from Hanga Roa to Puna Pau crater, source of the reddish volcanic scoria for moai topknots, and continue inland to Ahu Akivi, where the seven moai have been re-erected. From Ahu Akivi, follow the track to Ahu Tepeu, on the coast, then south to Hanga Roa past several restored ahu with their moai re-erected.

Puna Pau Quarried from soft, easily worked stone from Puna Pau, the reddish cylindrical topknots on some moai reflect a once common hairstyle for Rapa Nui males. Most *pukao* had a partly hollow underside which allowed them to be slotted onto the heads of the moai.

Ahu Akivi Unlike most others, the seven moai on this restored inland ahu look out to sea.

Ana Te Pahu Follow the faint, rough, but passable track to Ahu Tepeu, on the west coast, stopping at Ana Te Pahu, a former cave dwelling where the entry way is a garden planted with sweet potatoes, taro and other plants of the Polynesian horticultural complex.

Ahu Tepeu This large ahu is on the northwest coast between Ahu Akapu and Cabo Norte. Maunga Terevaka, to the north-east, is the island's highest point; to the south, a large grassy plain covers jagged lava sheet. To the west, the Pacific breaks against rugged cliffs.

Several moai here have fallen. Nearby is an extensive village site with foundations of several *hare paenga* (elliptical houses) and the walls of several round houses. South of

here, the road is very rough but always passable.

Ahu Akapu Ahu Akapu, with its solitary moai, stands on the coast between Ahu Tepeu and Ahu Tahai.

Ahu Tahai A short hike north of Hanga Roa, this site contains three restored ahu: Ahu Tahai proper is in the middle, supporting a large, solitary moai with no topknot. To one side is Ahu Ko Te Riku, which has a large, solitary moai with its topknot in place. On the other side is Ahu Vai Uri, supporting five moai of varying sizes.

Ahu Tautira Ahu Tautira overlooks Caleta Hanga Roa, the fishing port at the foot of Calle Te Pito o Te Henua. Torsos of two broken moai have been re-erected.

The Island Circuit
From Hanga Roa, follow the south coast to Vaihu and Akahanga, then continue west and detour inland to Rano Raraku, a quarry for the moai. Leaving Rano Raraku, follow the road west to Ahu Tongariki, where a 1960 tsunami hurled moai and masonry far inland.

From Tongariki, follow the north coast to Ahu Te Pito Te Kura, with the largest moai ever erected on an ahu, then continue east to the beach at Ovahe and to Anakena, the island's main beach and site of two more restored ahu. Return to Hanga Roa via Vaitea.

Ahu Vaihu This south coast ahu's eight large moai now lie face down, their topknots scattered nearby.

Ahu Akahanga This large ahu has many large fallen moai, while a second ahu across the estuary has several more. On the slopes opposite are the remains of several elliptical and rounded houses.

Ahu Hanga Tetenga Almost completely ruined, this coastal ahu's two large moai are both in fragments. Just beyond Hanga

Tetenga, a faint track off the main road branches inland toward Rano Raraku crater.

Rano Raraku Rano Raraku was the source for the hard basalt from which the moai were cut. Moai in all stages of progress litter its southern slopes and the crater, which contains a small lake. Most are upright but partly buried, so that only their heads gaze across the grassy slopes. A trail leads straight up the slope to a 21-metre giant – the largest moai ever built – but most moai range from 5½ to seven metres.

The total number of moai from Rano Raraku exceeds 600. Most were carved face up, horizontal or slightly reclined. Leaving each attached only along its back, workers excavated a channel large enough for carvers. Nearly all the carving with basalt *tokis*, including fine detail, occurred at this stage, after which the moai was detached and transported downslope for further details on the back. Rano Raraku's most unique discovery was the kneeling Moai Tukuturi, slightly less than four metres high, which now sits on the south-eastern slope of the mountain.

Transporting the moai must have been difficult and dangerous, but despite obvious difficulty, Islanders placed 300 moai on distant ahu or left them along the old roads.

Ahu Tongariki In 1960, a tsunami demolished several moai and scattered topknots far inland from the largest ahu ever built, which supported 15 massive moai. Nearby petroglyphs show a variety of designs.

The Poike Peninsula Rapa Nui's eastern end is a high plateau called the Poike Peninsula, crowned by the extinct volcano Maunga Pukatikei.

Legend says that Long Ears built the trench to defend themselves, filling it with branches and tree trunks to be fired should the Short Ears try to storm across. The ditch was once thought natural, but carbon dating of ash and charcoal suggested that a great fire occurred perhaps 350 years ago, while genealogical research placed the onset of conflict around 1680.

Ahu Te Pito Te Kura Overlooking a fishers' cove at La Perouse Bay is the largest moai ever moved from Rano Raraku and erected on an ahu. Nearly 10 metres high, in proportion and general appearance it resembles the moai still partly buried at Rano Raraku and, thus, was probably the last ever erected on an ahu.

Playa de Ovahe Between La Perouse and Anakena, this is an attractive beach with interesting caves. Beware of sharks.

Playa de Anakena Anakena is the legendary landing of Hotu Matua. One of several caves may have sheltered him as he waited for completion of his hare paenga – an unusual one, about 25 metres long, may have been that house.

The sheltered, white-sand beach is popular for swimming and sunbathing. It's a pleasant place to spend the afternoon. Overnight at CONAF'S campground, but bring food and water from Hanga Roa.

Ahu Ature Huki On the hillside above Anakena stands Ahu Ature Huki and its lone moai. Heyerdahl and a dozen Islanders took nine days to raise the moai on its ahu with wooden poles, supporting the giant with stones, and levering the logs with ropes when the men could no longer reach them.

Legend says that priests moved the moai by the power of *mana*, an ability to make it walk a short distance each day. After suggestions that Islanders could have moved the moai with a forked sledge, pulled with ropes made from tree bark, Heyerdahl organised 180 Islanders to pull a four-metre moai across the field at Anakena, and speculated that they could have moved a larger one with wooden runners and more labour. US archaeologist William Mulloy proposed a different method, which involved fitting a sledge to the moai and dragging it forward with ropes on a bipod. His complex theory, requiring large amounts of timber, may partly explain the island's deforestation.

Ahu Nau Nau In 1979, excavation and restoration of Ahu Nau Nau revealed that the moai were not 'blind' but had inlaid coral and rock eyes – 'eyes that look to the sky', in a Rapa Nui phrase.

Fundo Vaitea Midway between Anakena and Hanga Roa, Vaitea was the centre of food and livestock production under Williamson, Balfour & Company – the large building on the east side of the road is the former shearing shed. The property on the west side belongs to the state-controlled development agency CORFO, which raises fruit and vegetables.

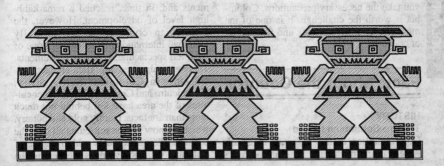

Colombia

For most travellers, Colombia is unknown territory – a land of myths, of cocaine, emeralds, orchids and the mysterious El Dorado. It is the land of Gabriel García Márquez and his famous *One Hundred Years of Solitude* – a tale as magical as the country itself. And it is the land which bears the name of Columbus, discoverer of the Americas, but where people have changed the order of the letters to make Locombia, the mad country.

In many ways, Colombia is a concentration of all that is to be found in Latin America. Its geography, flora and fauna are amazingly diverse. The inhabitants, too, form an intriguing ethnic mosaic, with over 50 different Indian tribes still living traditional lifestyles. In its people, climate, topography, culture, crafts and architecture, Colombia is representative of most other Latin American countries. In effect, it's several countries rolled into one.

In its stormy and turbulent history, Colombia has been soaked with blood in innumerable civil wars. The country has endured the largest and longest guerrilla insurgency on the continent. It is also the world's major producer of cocaine. With such a background, it's no wonder that violence is a constant problem, and Colombia is not as safe as neighbouring countries.

These comments might make you hesitate to go to Colombia, but don't be put off. If you take the necessary precautions, Colombia is worth the challenge. It is one of the most exotic, wild, complex and fascinating of countries.

Facts about the Country

HISTORY
The Pre-Columbian Period
Colombia lies at the gateway to South America, and must have been on the route for the first inhabitants who migrated from North and Central America. Some tribes headed further south, while others established their new homes in what is now Colombia. They formed permanent settlements and, in time, reached a remarkably high level of development. However, the Colombian civilisations are virtually unknown internationally, as almost none of them left spectacular, enduring monuments. There are only three important archaeological sites in Colombia: San Agustín, Tierradentro and Ciudad Perdida. Other cultures of the area have left behind not much more than artefacts, mainly gold and pottery, which are now held in museums all over the country. Their art reveals a high degree of skill, and their goldwork is the best in the

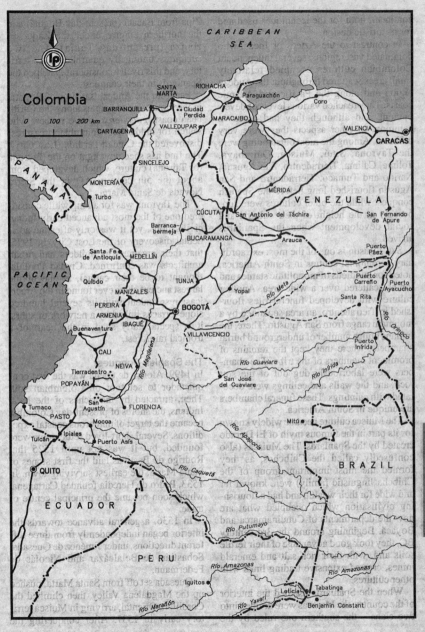

Colombia

continent, both for the techniques used and for its artistic design.

In contrast to the Aztecs or Incas, who dominated vast regions, several independent Colombian cultures occupied relatively small areas scattered throughout the Andean region and along the Pacific and Atlantic coasts. They reached various levels of development, and although they had much in common, in other aspects they were very different. Among the most outstanding were the Tayrona, Sinú, Muisca, Quimbaya, Tolima, Calima, Tierradentro, San Agustín, Nariño and Tumaco. Tierradentro and San Agustín flourished long before the Spanish conquest while the other cultures were supposedly at the height of their cultural and social development when the Spaniards arrived.

San Agustín is one of the most extraordinary ceremonial centres in South America, noted for hundreds of monolithic statues and tombs scattered over a wide area. Another culture with developed funeral rites flourished in Tierradentro, an area separated by a mountain range from San Agustín. There, the Indians built a number of underground burial chambers, where they kept the remains of prominent members of the tribe. The chambers were laboriously dug out of the soft rock, and the walls and ceilings were decorated with paintings. These funeral chambers are unique in South America.

The Muisca culture became widely known for its part in the famous myth of El Dorado created by the Spaniards. The Muiscas (also confusedly called the Chibchas, as they formed the most important group of the Chibcha linguistic family) were known far and wide for their wealth, and had a flourishing civilisation which occupied what are now the departments of Cundinamarca and Boyacá. Beginning around the 3rd century BC, they took good advantage of their fertile soils and, with their rich salt and emerald mines, created extensive trading links with other cultures.

When the Spaniards reached the interior of the country, the Muiscas were divided into two clans – the southern one ruled by the Zipa from Bacatá (present-day Bogotá) and the northern empire under the Zaque in Hunza (present-day Tunja). The two *caciques* continually quarrelled over territory, and this rivalry considerably helped the Spaniards in their conquest.

Far from the Andean savanna of Bogotá, in the mountainous jungles along the Caribbean coast, *guaqueros* (grave robbers who search for hidden pre-Columbian treasures) discovered the Ciudad Perdida (Lost City). The find has shed new light on the Tayrona (or Tairona) culture, which developed from about the 5th century AD in the Sierra Nevada de Santa Marta.

The Tayrona was for a long while considered one of the most advanced early Indian civilisations, yet it was only after the accidental discovery of the Lost City, in 1975, that their greatness as builders and urban architects was confirmed. Ciudad Perdida, thought to be their capital, is one of the largest ancient cities ever found in the Americas; resplendent with its several hundred stone terraces linked by a network of stairs, it is spectacularly sited in the heart of a tropical rainforest.

The Spanish Conquest

In 1499, Alonso de Ojeda was the first conquistador to set foot on Colombian soil. Then, attracted by the riches of the local Indians, the shores of present-day Colombia became the target of numerous coastal expeditions. Several short-lived settlements were founded, but it was not until 1525 that Rodrigo de Bastidas laid the first stones of Santa Marta, the earliest surviving town. In 1533, Pedro de Heredia founded Cartagena, which soon became the principal centre of trade.

In 1536, a general advance towards the interior began independently from three different directions, under Jiménez de Quesada, Sebastián de Belalcázar and Nicolás de Federmann.

Quesada set off from Santa Marta, pushed up the Magdalena Valley, then climbed the Cordillera Oriental, arriving in Muisca territory early in 1537. After conquering the

Muiscas without undue difficulty, he founded Santa Fe de Bogotá on the site of Bacatá, the former capital of the Zipa culture. Quesada actually didn't find gold, in spite of the elaborate rituals of the Indians, who threw gold offerings into the waters of their sacred lake, the Laguna de Guatavita (which gave birth to the mysterious legend of El Dorado).

Belalcázar deserted from Francisco Pizarro's army, which was conquering the Inca Empire, and mounted an expedition from Ecuador. He subdued the southern part of Colombia, founding Pasto, Popayán and Cali along the way, and reached Bogotá in 1539.

The third expedition was led by a German, Nicolás de Federmann. He started from the Venezuelan coast and, after successfully crossing Los Llanos, arrived in Bogotá shortly after Belalcázar.

The three groups fought tooth and nail for supremacy, and it was not until 1550 that King Charles V of Spain, in an effort to establish law and order, created the Real Audiencia del Nuevo Reino de Granada, a tribunal based in Bogotá. Administratively, the new colony was subject to the viceroyalty of Peru.

The Colonial Period

With the growth of the Spanish Empire in the New World, a new territorial division was created in 1717, and Santa Fe de Bogotá became the capital of its own viceroyalty, the Virreinato de la Nueva Granada. It comprised the territories of what are today Colombia, Panama, Venezuela and Ecuador.

Towards the end of the 18th century, the general disillusionment and discontent with Spanish domination gave rise to open protests and rebellions. This, together with external events such as the North American and French revolutions and, most importantly, the invasion of Spain by Napoleon Bonaparte, slowly paved the way to independence.

When, in 1808, Napoleon replaced Ferdinand VII with his own brother on the Spanish throne, the colonies refused to recognise the new monarch. One by one, Colombian towns started to declare their independence.

In 1812, Simón Bolívar, who was to become the hero of the independence struggle, arrived in Cartagena to take the offensive against the Spanish armies. In the brilliant campaign to seize Venezuela, he won six battles but was unable to hold Caracas, and had to withdraw to Cartagena.

By then, Napoleon was defeated at Waterloo, and Spain set about reconquering its colonies. Colonial rule was finally re-established in 1817.

Bolívar took up arms again. After assembling an army of horsemen from the Venezuelan Llanos, strengthened by a British legion, he freed Venezuela and marched across the Andes into Colombia. The last and most decisive battle took place at Boyacá on 7 August 1819. Independence was won.

After Independence

With Colombia free, a revolutionary congress was held in Angostura (modern-day Ciudad Bolívar, in Venezuela) in 1819. Still euphoric with victory, the delegates proclaimed the Gran Colombia, a new state uniting Venezuela, Colombia and Ecuador. This congress was followed by another, held in Villa del Rosario, near Cúcuta, in 1821. It was there that the two opposing tendencies, centralist and federalist, came to the fore. Bolívar supported a centralised unified republic, while Francisco de Paula Santander favoured a federal republic of sovereign states. Bolívar succeeded in imposing his will, and the Gran Colombia came into being. Bolívar was elected president and Santander became vice president.

The Gran Colombia didn't last long. From its inception, the young state started to disintegrate. It soon became apparent that a central regime was incapable of governing such a vast territory comprising three economically and socially different countries. Venezuela broke away in 1829, and Ecuador a year later. Bolívar's dream of a sacred union of the countries he had freed came to an end.

COLOMBIA

Thus begun a new, inglorious page of Colombian history. The two political currents, centralist and federalist, born in the struggles for independence, were formalised in 1849 when two political parties were established: the Conservatives (with centralist tendencies) and the Liberals (with federalist leanings). The country became the scene of fierce rivalries between the two forces, resulting in complete chaos, with insurrections and civil wars following each other with astonishing frequency. In the course of the 19th century, the country experienced no less than eight civil wars. Between 1863 and 1885, there were more than 50 antigovernment insurrections.

In 1899, the Liberal revolt turned into a full-blown civil war, the so-called War of a Thousand Days. That carnage resulted in a Conservative victory and left 100,000 dead. In 1903, the USA took advantage of the country's internal strife and fomented a secessionist movement in Panama, then a Colombian province. By creating a new and independent republic, the USA was able to build an interocean canal across the Central American isthmus under its control. Only in 1921 did Colombia finally recognise the sovereignty of Panama, and settle its dispute with the USA.

La Violencia

After a period of relative peace, the struggle between Liberals and Conservatives broke out again in 1948 with La Violencia, the most cruel and destructive of Colombia's many civil wars (some say it still hasn't finished). With a toll of some 300,000 dead, La Violencia was one of the bloodiest conflicts in the western hemisphere, comparable to the Mexican Revolution or the American Civil War.

The first urban riots broke out on 9 April 1948 in Bogotá with the assassination of Jorge Eliécer Gaitán, a charismatic populist Liberal leader. Liberals soon took up arms throughout the country.

In Colombia, even today, a person is born a Liberal or a Conservative and reared with a mistrust of the members of the other party.

In the 1940s and 1950s, these 'hereditary hatreds' prevailed over any rational difference of ideology or politics, and were the cause of countless atrocities, rapes and murders, particularly in rural areas. Hundreds of thousands of people took to the hills and shot each other for nothing more than the name of their party. The elite political leaders of both parties, safely entrenched in the cities, supported the actions of their followers, providing ideological justification, arms and supplies. By 1953, however, some of the peasant *comandantes* of the Liberal guerrillas had begun to demonstrate a dangerous degree of independence, in some cases making alliances with the small bands of communist guerrillas that also operated in certain zones during this period.

As it became evident that the partisan conflict was taking on revolutionary overtones, the leaders of both the Liberal and Conservative parties made the decision to support a military coup as the best means to retain power and pacify the countryside. In a country long dominated by one or other of the traditional parties, the 1953 coup of General Gustavo Rojas Pinilla was the only military intervention the country has experienced this century.

Frente Nacional

The dictatorship of General Rojas was not to last. In 1957, the political leaders of the two factions signed a pact to share power for the next 16 years. The agreement, later approved by a plebiscite (in which women were, for the first time, allowed to vote), became known as the Frente Nacional (National Front). During the life of the accord, the two parties alternated in the presidency every four years. The National Front formally came to an end in 1974, when Liberal president Alfonso López Michelsen was elected.

Recent Presidents

Colombian presidents are constitutionally limited to one four-year term. López was succeeded by another Liberal, Julio César Turbay Ayala (1978-82). The Conservatives regained the presidency in 1982, with the election of Belisario Betancur.

However, don't let the party labels confuse you. Turbay was one of the most conservative presidents in recent Colombian history, launching a major military campaign against the country's left-wing guerrillas and severely repressing labour strikes and popular mobilisations. In contrast, Conservative president Betancur presented himself as a populist, and opened direct negotiations with the guerrillas in an attempt to reincorporate the armed opposition into the nation's political life and restore peace to the country.

Guerrillas

Guerrillas are, unfortunately, quite an important part of Colombian political life, with roots that extend back to the violence of the 1940s and 1950s. That makes them the oldest insurgent forces in Latin America.

Colombia saw the birth of not just one but perhaps a dozen different guerrilla groups, each with its own ideology, its own programmes and its own political and military strategies. The movements which have had the biggest impact on local politics (and left the largest number of dead) include the FARC (Fuerzas Armadas Revolucionarias de Colombia), the ELN (Ejército de Liberación Nacional) and the M-19 (Movimiento 19 de Abril).

Following the failure of Betancur's peace process, the Liberal government of Virgilio Barco (1986-90), after long and complicated negotiations with the M-19, signed an agreement under which this group handed over its arms, ceased insurgent activity and transformed itself into a political party. However, the two other major guerrilla groups, the FARC and the ELN, remain under arms and are more violent than ever. Widely confused in their ideologies since the fall of communism, they are more and more dedicated to extorting money through kidnapping, blackmailing petrol companies (with threats to blow up their pipelines) and 'taxing' landowners for leaving them in peace, and other activities far distant from their initial ideals.

Furthermore, they are increasingly involved in the drug business.

Cocaine & the Mafia

The cocaine industry is another factor which has affected Colombia's politics and economy. Colombia is the world's biggest producer of cocaine, controlling some 80% of the world market. The mafia started in a small way in the early 1970s but, within a short time, developed the trade into a powerful industry, with their own plantations, laboratories, transport services and protection.

The boom years began in the early 1980s, and the bosses lived quietly in freedom and luxury. They even founded their own political party and two newspapers. It was not until 1983 that the government launched a campaign against the drug trade, which gradually turned into a real war. The mafia responded violently to every hostile act of the government, and managed to liquidate many of their adversaries.

The war became even bloodier in August 1989, when Luis Carlos Galán, the leading Liberal contender for the 1990 presidential election, was assassinated. Only a day after the murder, the government responded with the confiscation of 500 mafia-owned properties, and announced new laws on extradition – a nightmare for the drug barons.

The mafia resorted, for the first time in Colombia, to the use of terrorist tactics, principally car bombs. Although these were generally directed at specific targets, such as party headquarters or the police, thousands of innocent people have also been killed. Two more presidential candidates, Bernardo Jaramillo (of the left-wing Unión Patriótica) and Carlos Pizarro (the leader of the former M-19 guerrilla group), were assassinated. For its part, the army succeeded in killing one of the top bosses of the Cartel de Medellín, José Gonzalo Rodríguez Gacha, commonly known as El Mejicano.

Presidente Gaviria

The election campaign of 1990 was the bloodiest in the country's history. César

Gaviria, the candidate of the ruling Liberal Party following Galán's assassination, was elected. His election brought a brief period of hope: Pablo Escobar surrendered and the Coordinadora Guerrillera Simón Bolívar (the unified FARC and ELN front) declared a truce to negotiate with the government. However, Escobar escaped from his palace-like prison (commonly known as La Catedral) and, after the peace talks got bogged down early on, the guerrillas went back to the hills.

After three years in office, Gaviria has not yet produced any progress towards political stability nor solved the questions of the mafia and the guerrillas, and the future looks precarious. The front pages of the local press have almost daily reports of skirmishes between the guerrillas and the army, and of car-bomb attacks, attributed to the drug lords. The cat-and-mouse game between the government and Pablo Escobar periodically hits the headlines all over the world. Meanwhile, local TV advertises several times a day the latest government offer: US$6 million to anyone whose information leads to the capture of the godfather. But even if this happens, the cartels have become stronger than their bosses. There are lots of new adepts willing to share the billions. More importantly, they operate in a more modern, efficient and 'silent' way than the old boys. Furthermore, the flourishing poppy plantations indicate that cartels are switching to the even more profitable heroin business, yet another nightmare for the government.

In such an explosive and unstable socio-political climate, President Gaviria's manoeuvres focus on the emergency issues and on short-term solutions, without clear long-term directions. And, since there are no brighter candidates for the forthcoming election, there remains deep scepticism about the country's future.

GEOGRAPHY

Colombia covers approximately 1,140,000 sq km, roughly equal to the area of France, Spain and Portugal combined. It is the fourth largest country in South America, after Brazil, Argentina and Peru. Colombia occupies the north-western end of the continent and is the only country in South America with coasts on both the Pacific (1350 km long) and the Atlantic (over 1600 km). Colombia is bordered by Panama, Venezuela, Brazil, Peru and Ecuador.

The country is very varied in its geography. The western part, about 45% of the total territory, is mountainous, with three Andean chains – the Cordillera Occidental, Cordillera Central and Cordillera Oriental – running roughly parallel north-south across the whole country.

The Sierra Nevada de Santa Marta, an independent and relatively small formation, rises from the Caribbean coastline to permanent snows. It is the highest coastal mountain range in the world, and its peaks of Simón Bolívar (5775 metres) and Cristóbal Colón (5770 metres) are the highest in Colombia.

Over 50% of the territory east of the Andes is a vast lowland, which can be generally divided into two regions: Los Llanos in the north and the Amazon in the south.

Colombia has several small islands. The major ones are the archipelago of San Andrés and Providencia (in the Caribbean Sea, closer to Nicaragua than to mainland Colombia), the Islas del Rosario and San Bernardo (along the Caribbean coast) and Gorgona and Malpelo (in the Pacific Ocean).

CLIMATE

Because of its proximity to the equator, Colombia's temperature varies little throughout the year. However, the temperature does change with altitude, creating various climatic zones, from hot lowlands to permanent snows. Because of the varied topography, you can experience completely different climates within a couple of hours.

Colombia has two seasons: dry and wet. The dry season is called *verano* (literally summer) and the rainy months are known as *invierno* (winter).

The pattern of seasons varies in different parts of the country. In the Andean regions, there are two dry and two rainy seasons per year. The main dry season falls between December and March, with a shorter and less dry period between July and August. This general pattern has wide variations throughout the Andean zone, with the seasons being wetter or drier, shorter or longer and occurring at different times. In southern Colombia particularly, it is very complicated, with considerable differences between neighbouring regions.

The weather in Los Llanos has a more definite pattern. There is one dry season, between December and March, and the rest of the year is wet. The Amazon doesn't have a uniform climate but, in general, is quite wet all year round.

GOVERNMENT

A new constitution came into effect in July 1991. The executive president, currently Cesar Gaviria Trjillo, is directly elected for a four-year term, as are the 114 members of senate and the 199 members of the house of representatives. The cabinet is appointed by the president.

ECONOMY

Colombia is the world's second largest coffee producer, after Brazil. The other main agricultural products are sugar (with production concentrated in the Cali region), cotton and bananas. Thanks to the diversity of the climatic zones, there is a variety of other crops, such as rice, maize, potatoes, tobacco, barley, beans and cocoa.

Mineral resources are plentiful but underexploited, and the extent of deposits has still not been thoroughly explored. During the 1990s, coal mining could become one of the most dynamic sectors of the economy, as the country possesses the largest deposits of coal in Latin America.

With the discovery of new oil fields, principally in Arauca, the country has now joined the ranks of the world's oil-producing nations, a fact which might have significant repercussions on the overall economy, though so far, Colombia continues to import petrol. The country also has deposits of gold, silver, platinum, nickel, copper and iron, to list just a few.

Colombia produces half of the world's emeralds, and Colombian stones are considered to be the best.

Industry has grown notably in recent decades, mainly in the fields of petrochemicals, metallurgy, car assembly (Renault, Chevrolet, Mazda), textiles, domestic electrical appliances, and the food and agricultural industries.

And then, behind the official economic statistics, there is the unofficial export of cocaine. It generates astronomical amounts of money, called locally *dinero caliente* – hot money. How much of it comes back into Colombia can only be guessed at. According to rough estimates, about two tonnes of top-quality cocaine enters the USA every week, with net profit modestly estimated at US$5 billion a year. The head of the Medellín mafia, Pablo Escobar, is one of the richest men in the world, with a fortune rated at US$3 billion.

POPULATION & PEOPLE

In 1992, the population had reached 33 million, making Colombia the second most populous country in South America, after Brazil. The rate of population growth is about 2%, among the highest in Latin America.

Population density varies a great deal across the country. The western half, consisting of the Andean region and the coasts, has over 90% of the total population.

About 75% of the people are of mixed blood. About 50% are *mestizos* (of European-Indian blood) and about 20% are *mulatos* (of European-African blood). There are also some *zambos* (of African-Indian blood).

Whites, mainly descendants of the Spaniards, constitute about 20% of the population and live almost entirely in the urban centres. Blacks represent about 5% of the total population and are most numerous on the Caribbean and Pacific coasts.

Indians number between 300,000 and 400,000, or 1% to 1.5% of the total popula-

COLOMBIA

tion. This number includes over 50 Indian tribes, belonging to several linguistic families.

RELIGION

The great majority of Colombians are Roman Catholic. Other creeds are officially permitted but their numbers are small, even though there has been a significant proliferation of various Protestant congregations over the past few years.

Many Indian tribes adopted the Catholic faith, incorporating some of their traditional beliefs. Only a few indigenous communities, particularly those living in isolation, still practise their ancient native religions.

On the islands of San Andrés and Providencia, the Protestant faith is still practised – a sign of their English past.

LANGUAGE

The official language of Colombia is Spanish, and apart from several Indian tribes, almost all inhabitants speak it. On San Andrés and Providencia, English is still widely used.

The Spanish spoken in Colombia is generally clear and easy to understand, though there are regional variations which Colombians easily recognise. For the visitor, these differences won't be so noticeable, except for the *costeños* speech, which is faster and more difficult to understand.

Facts for the Visitor

VISAS

Only Chinese nationals need a visa to enter Colombia. Upon arrival at any international airport or land border crossing, you will get the entry stamp in your passport from DAS (the security police who are also responsible for immigration). The official will note on your passport the period you can stay in the country – usually 90 days, the maximum allowed.

Officially, an onward ticket is required, but this is no longer strictly enforced, espe-

cially at land crossings. Keep in mind a general rule: the better your appearance, the less hassle you are likely to have about tickets.

You are entitled to one extension, of 30 days. This can be obtained in the major cities, from DAS, and costs US$18. If you want to stay longer in Colombia, go to any of the surrounding countries and come back.

Colombian Embassies

Australia
    101 Northbourne Avenue, Canberra (☎ 2572027)
Canada
    1 Dundas Street West, Suite 2108, Toronto, Ontario M56 1Z3 (☎ 9770098)
France
    11 Rue Christophe Colomb, Paris 8 (☎ 47233605)
Germany
    Friedrich-Wilhelm Strasse 35, Bonn (☎ 234565)
UK
    Suite 10, 140 Park Lane, London W1Y 3DF (☎ 4954233)
USA
    2118 Leroy Place, Washington DC (☎ 3878338)

Foreign Embassies in Colombia

A number of countries have representation in Bogotá (see that section). If yours is not listed, ask at the tourist office or consult the telephone directory.

CUSTOMS

On arrival, the duty-free allowance is 200 cigarettes or 50 cigars or 500 grams of tobacco, and two bottles of wine or spirits. You are also allowed to bring in still, cine and video cameras plus accessories, a portable typewriter, hi-fi set, radio, calculator, record player, etc – in effect, one item of each class, 'with evident traces of use'.

You will rarely be asked to declare these things. Customs procedures are almost a formality, both on entering and on leaving the country, and your luggage is likely to pass through with only a cursory glance. However, thorough checks occasionally happen, more often at the airports than at the land borders, and then they can be very exhaustive – a body search included. They aren't looking for your extra Walkman, but for drugs. Smuggling dope through the border is the best way to see what a Colombian jail looks like, for quite a few years!

On departure, you will need receipts for any emeralds, antiques, and articles of gold and platinum purchased in Colombia.

MONEY

There is no black market in Colombia, and you will probably never get a better exchange rate than in the bank. Given this, and the country's hazards, it's advisable to carry American Express travellers' cheques, though some US dollars in small notes may be useful if you get stuck without pesos somewhere off the road.

There is a control on the amount of foreign currency a tourist can spend in Colombia. This is meant to make it harder to launder drug money as 'travel expenses'. When you enter Colombia, customs officials now stamp a seal in your passport, where every money exchange operation has to be recorded; the maximum a tourist can exchange during any one visit to the country is set at US$25,000.

Currency

The official Colombian currency is the *peso*, comprising 100 *centavos*. There are five, 10, 20, 50 and 100-peso coins, and paper notes of 100, 200, 500, 1000, 2000, 5000 and 10,000 pesos. Forged notes do exist, so watch exactly what you get – they are generally of poor quality and easy to recognise.

Exchange Rates

Exchange rates vary from bank to bank, but the rate for travellers' cheques will always be some 2% to 3% higher than for cash. Some banks charge commission on changing cheques, so the difference can be less; before signing your cheques, ask if there is any commission. The approximate exchange rates for traveller's cheques given by banks at August 1993 were as follows:

A$1 =	544	pesos
DM1 =	469	pesos
FF1 =	133	pesos
UK£1 =	1193	pesos
US$1 =	804	pesos
US$1 =	778	pesos (for cash)

The devaluation of the peso against hard currencies is roughly 25% per year.

Money Exchange

Some banks change cash and travellers' cheques, and pay peso advances to credit card holders. However, not all banks handle all these operations, and many change nothing. Some branches of a bank will change your money while other branches of the same bank will refuse. This seems to change constantly from bank to bank, city to city, day to day, and can be further complicated by a myriad of other factors – the bank may reach the daily limit of foreign exchange, or it may run out of money, or the cashier may be out of the office.

All banks in Colombia have the same opening hours: Monday to Thursday from 8 to 11.30 am and 2 to 4 pm, and on Friday from 8 to 11.30 am and 2 to 4.30 pm. (Bogotá is the exception – see that section for details.) However, they usually operate foreign exchange within limited hours, which may mean only one hour daily; each branch of every bank seems to have its own schedule (your best chances are in the morning).

Your passport is needed in any bank operation. Moreover, some banks will also want to have the photocopy of your passport (two pages are required, the one with your photo and personal details and the one with the entry stamp), while other banks won't change your travellers' cheques before sighting the receipt. Finally, as the banks are often crowded and there's much paperwork involved in changing money, the process may be time consuming.

The banks which are most likely to exchange your cash and/or travellers' cheques are Banco Anglo Colombiano, Banco Unión Colombiano, Banco Popular,

Banco Industrial Colombiano and Banco Sudameris Colombia.

Apart from the banks, you can change cash (but not travellers' cheques) in *casas de cambio* (authorised money exchange offices) which are in most of the major cities and the border towns. These are open till 5 or 6 pm, and usually till noon on Saturday. They deal mainly with US dollars and offer rates about 2% lower than the banks.

Credit Cards
Credit cards (Visa and Mastercard) are generally accepted in top-class hotels and restaurants, and when buying air tickets; elsewhere, their use is limited. The banks which will probably give advance payments on credit cards are Banco Industrial Colombiano (Mastercard), Banco de Occidente (Mastercard), Banco Colombo Americano (Visa) and Banco de Bogotá (Visa).

American Express
The Tierra Mar Aire (TMA) travel agency, which has offices in major cities, represents American Express. It doesn't change travellers' cheques, but is the place to go if your cheques are lost or stolen.

WHEN TO GO
The best time to visit Colombia is in dry season, but avoid the period from late December to mid-January, when Colombians leave for their vacations.

INFORMATION
Tourist Offices
The Corporación Nacional de Turismo (CNT), the national tourist information board, until recently had a score of offices throughout the country, and plenty of free publications, but is gradually disintegrating. At the time of writing, CNT still had offices in half a dozen cities, Bogotá included. Regional tourist information bureaux are attempting to fill the vacuum, with varying degrees of success. The best and most helpful tourist offices are in San Agustín and Popayán.

Inderena
Inderena is the government-run body which deals with national parks. The central office is in Bogotá, and there are subsidiary offices in the main towns of the areas where the parks are located. If you plan on visiting the parks, you must first go through the formality of getting a permit from Inderena. See the Bogotá section for details.

USEFUL ORGANISATIONS
The Youth Hostel Association (YHA) office (☎ 2803125, 2803202) is at Carrera 7 No 6-10 in Bogotá. Here you can get the youth hostel card (US$15) and information about YHA hostels throughout the country. The office is open Monday to Friday from 8.30 am to 12.30 pm and 2 to 5.30 pm.

BUSINESS HOURS & HOLIDAYS
The following days are observed as public holidays in Colombia:

1 January
   La Circuncisión (Circumcision)
6 January
   Los Reyes Magos (Epiphany)
19 March*
   San José (St Joseph)
March/April (dates vary)
   Jueves Santo (Maundy Thursday)
   Viernes Santo (Good Friday)
1 May
   Día del Trabajo (Labour Day)
May (date varies)
   La Ascensión del Señor (Ascension)
May/June (date varies)
   Corpus Cristi (Corpus Christi)
June (date varies)
   Sagrado Corazón de Jesús (Sacred Heart)
29 June*
   San Pedro y San Pablo (St Peter & St Paul)
20 July
   Día de la Independencia (Independence Day)
7 August
   Batalla de Boyacá (Battle of Boyacá)
15 August*
   La Asunción de Nuestra Señora (Assumption)
12 October*
   Diá de la Raza (Discovery of America)
1 November*
   Todos los Santos (All Saints' Day)
11 November*
   Independencia de Cartagena (Independence of Cartagena)

8 December
    Inmaculada Concepción
25 December
    Navidad (Christmas Day)

* When the dates marked do not fall on a Monday, the holiday is moved to the following Monday.

FESTIVALS

Colombians love fiestas. The official tourist guide lists over 200 of them, from small, local events to international festivals lasting several days. Most of the celebrations are regional, and the most interesting ones are listed in the sections on individual places.

POST & TELECOMMUNICATIONS
Post

The Colombian postal service seems to be quite efficient and reliable. There's an array of airmail post offices, for both domestic and international mail, controlled by Avianca. They are in most major cities, and they will hold poste restante mail.

Telephone

Telecom (Empresa Nacional de Telecomunicaciones) is the place to go for long-distance national and international calls. The Telecom offices are almost everywhere, even the most remote villages. In major cities, they tend to be open till late; in the countryside, they usually close around 3 pm.

The telephone system is largely automated for both domestic and international calls, and it usually doesn't take long to get a connection. On the other hand, international calls from Colombia are expensive, roughly twice the price of calling from, say, the USA or Australia. Collect calls *(pago revertido)* are possible to a number of countries, including the UK, Canada, the USA, New Zealand, France and Italy, but not to Germany, Denmark or Australia.

TIME

All of Colombia lies within the same time zone, five hours behind GMT.

ELECTRICITY

Electricity is 110 volts, 60 cycles AC all over the country, except for small areas in Bogotá where the old, 150-volt system still exists.

BOOKS

For more detailed travel information, look for Lonely Planet's *Colombia – a travel survival kit*, which covers in depth many more places than could be included here.

For reading about the pre-Columbian cultures, history, economy and people, try *Colombia*, by Françoise de Tailly (Delachaux & Niestlé, Neuchâtel, Switzerland).

A Traveller's Guide to El Dorado and the Inca Empire, by Lynn Meisch (Penguin Books, 3rd edition, 1984), provides comprehensive information about food, drugs, folk art, fiestas and music in Colombia, Ecuador, Peru and Bolivia.

The Search for El Dorado, by John Hemming, is a very readable insight into the Spanish conquest of Colombia.

The Politics of Colombia, by Robert H Dix (Praeger, New York & London, 1987), provides a concise analysis of Colombian politics.

The Fruit Palace, by Charles Nicholl (Picador, London, 1985), one of the most fascinating travel books ever published, is possibly the best introduction to Colombia's crazy reality. It's a journalist's account of his investigation of the cocaine trade in Colombia. He did not get to the heart of the cartels, but he provides a vivid picture of the country, from Indian mountain villages to shabby bars.

For a detailed insight into Colombia's drug cartels, get a copy of *Kings of Cocaine*, by Guy Gugliotta and Jeff Leen (Simon & Schuster, 1990). It reads like a thriller.

Colombia's most famous contemporary writer is Gabriel García Márquez, winner of the 1982 Nobel Prize for literature. You shouldn't set off for Colombia before reading at least his most famous achievement, *One Hundred Years of Solitude*. Mixing myths, dreams and reality, the novel helps enormously to understand Colombian

COLOMBIA

history, culture, mentality and philosophy of life.

MAPS

The Instituto Geográfico Agustín Codazzi (IGAC), at Carrera 30 No 48-51, is Colombia's main cartographic institute. It publishes and sells a large selection of maps (general, departmental, specialist, the 1:100,000 sheets and city maps). The office is open Monday to Friday from 8 am to 3.30 pm.

MEDIA

There are two main national daily papers, both Bogotá based, and most other cities have their own dailies. There are many commercial radio stations, both AM and FM, and a number of national and regional colour TV stations.

HEALTH

A yellow fever vaccination certificate is required if you arrive from an infected area; other than this, no vaccinations are necessary, though some are recommended. In particular, guard against malaria and hepatitis.

The pharmacy network is extensive, and there are *droguerías* even in small towns. In the cities, they are usually well stocked. Many drugs are available without prescription, but always check the expiry date.

In most of the larger cities, the water is OK and can be safely drunk from the tap, though it is best to avoid it if possible. Outside these areas, drink boiled water.

Travel in Colombia is almost always up and down, from humid tropical lowlands to cold, windy highlands. When travelling by bus, you can experience dramatic climate changes within a few hours, so have appropriate clothes handy to avoid getting frozen solid.

DANGERS & ANNOYANCES

It is not pleasant news, but Colombia definitely isn't the safest of countries, and you should be careful and on your guard at all times. Your biggest potential dangers are being ripped off or robbed. The problem is more serious in the major cities, Bogotá, Medellín and Cali being the worst.

Keep your passport and money next to your skin and your camera inside your bag, and don't wear jewellery or expensive watches. If you can, leave your money and valuables somewhere safe before walking around the city streets. Always carry your passport with you, as document checks on the streets are not uncommon. If stopped by a plain-clothes man who claims to be from the secret police, check his documents first. If still in doubt, call any uniformed police officer.

Robbery can be very dangerous. Armed hold-ups become more common every year, mainly in slum *barrios* of the large cities. Avoid dubious-looking areas, especially if you are alone and particularly at night. If you are accosted by robbers, it is best to give them what they are after.

Be exceptionally careful about drugs – never carry them. The police and army can be extremely thorough in searching, particularly travellers, often looking for a nice fat bribe. Don't buy dope on the street; the vendors may well be setting you up for the police. There have been reports of drugs being planted on travellers, so keep your eyes open.

Burundanga is more bad news. It is a drug, commonly called *borrachero* or *cacao sabanero*, obtained from a species of tree widespread in Colombia. Burundanga is used by thieves to render a victim unconscious. It can be put into sweets, cigarettes, chewing gum, spirits, beer – virtually any kind of food or drink – and it doesn't have any particular taste or smell. The main effects are loss of will and memory, and sleepiness which can last from a few hours to several days. An overdose can be fatal. Unfortunately, its use has recently been spreading into neighbouring countries. Think twice before accepting a cigarette from a stranger or a drink from a new 'friend'.

Finally, while travelling, keep an eye on the current guerrilla movements, so as not to get caught in the crossfire. The local press is your best source of information. Unfortunately, certain regions of Colombia (parts of the Amazon Basin, Los Llanos, Urabá and the Sierra Nevada de Santa Marta) are becoming off limits for secure travel.

ACCOMMODATION

There is a constellation of places to stay in Colombia, and they exist even in the smallest villages, appearing under a variety of names – *hotel, residencias, hospedaje, pensión, hostería, hospedería, estadero, apartamentos, amoblados* and *posada*. Residencias and hospedajes are budget places. A hotel is generally of a higher standard, or at least a higher price; though not always. The distinction is often academic.

Budget accommodation is usually clustered around the bus company offices, the bus terminal or the market. On the whole, residencias and hospedajes are unremarkable places without any style or atmosphere. This is particularly true in larger towns and cities, where the budget places are generally poor or overpriced, or both. At their most primitive, you get a bare room with a bed and sometimes a chair and/or a table. Hardboard partitions instead of walls are not unusual, making noise and security a problem.

Some budget hotel rooms have a toilet and shower attached. Note that cheap hotel plumbing can't cope with toilet paper, so throw it in the box or basket which is usually provided.

In hot places (ie the lowland areas), a ceiling fan or table fan is often provided. Always check the fan before you take a room. On the other hand, above 2500 metres, where the nights can be chilly, look to see how many blankets you have, and check the hot water if they claim to have it.

In general, residencias (even the cheapest) provide a sheet and some sort of cover (another sheet or blankets, depending on the temperature). Most also give you a towel, a small piece of soap and a roll of toilet paper. The cheapies cost around US$2 to US$4 for a single room, US$3 to US$6 for a double.

The mid-range hotels are mostly found in the centre of the town, close to the main square. Their main advantage is their better location, and you can often expect your own bathroom.

Some hospedajes have *matrimonios*, rooms with a double bed intended for married couples. A matrimonio is often cheaper than a double, and only slightly more expensive than a single (or even the same price). Travelling as a couple considerably reduces the cost of accommodation.

Most residencias offer a deposit facility, which usually means that they put your gear into their own room, as there are no other safe places. Better hotels usually have the reception desk open round the clock, with proper facilities to safeguard your things. Remember that a hotel (no matter what hotel it is) is almost always safer than the street of a big city at night.

There are almost no gringo hotels in Colombia. Except for a handful of places which have gained popularity among travellers, the rest are straight Colombian hotels where you are unlikely to meet foreigners. Whorehouses are not uncommon in Colombia, so check before booking (these places are usually easy to recognise by the hoards of *putas* at the entrance or on the closest street corner).

Another kind of accommodation, very common in Colombia, is the so-called 'love hotel'. These places accept couples for a few hours or for a full night. Most residencias have at least one or two rooms for this purpose. Intentionally or not, you are likely, from time to time, to find yourself in such a place. Actually, these places are usually clean, as safe as any other, and do not allow prostitutes.

Quite recently, Colombia became a member of the International Youth Hostel Federation. So far, it hasn't many youth hostels, but the network is growing. Inquire at their main office in Bogotá, where they also have an excellent hostel (see the Bogotá section for details).

Camping

Camping is not popular in Colombia, and

COLOMBIA

there are only a handful of genuine camp sites in the country. Camping wild is theoretically possible almost anywhere outside the urban centres, but given the country's dangers, you should be extremely careful with it. If you plan on camping, try to pitch your tent under someone's protection (next to a *campesino* house or in the grounds of a holiday centre), after getting permission from the owners, guards or management. Only far away from human settlement is camping relatively safe, such as in the mountains. Even there, you never should leave your tent or gear unattended.

FOOD

The Colombian cuisine is varied and regional. Among the most typical regional dishes are:

Ajiaco – this soup, the main ingredients of which are chicken and three varieties of potato, is served with corn and capers. It is a Bogotano speciality.

Bandeja paisa (also called *plato montañero*) – this typical Antioquian dish consists of ground beef, a sausage (*chorizo*), red beans (*frijoles*), rice, fried green banana (*plátano*), a fried egg, a piece of fried salt pork (*chicharrón*) and avocado. Today, it can be found almost everywhere.

Chocolate santafereño – a cup of hot chocolate accompanied by a piece of cheese and bread (traditionally, you put the cheese into the chocolate) is another Bogotano speciality.

Cuy or *curí* – grilled guinea pig is typical of Nariño.

Hormiga culona – this is probably the most sophisticated Colombian speciality, consisting of large fried ants. It is unique to Santander.

Lechona – a whole suckling pig is stuffed with pork and rice, and roasted on a spit – a speciality of Tolima.

Tamales – chopped pork with rice and vegetables is folded in a maize dough, wrapped in banana leaves and steamed; there are plenty of regional varieties.

Unfortunately, the cheapest meals are, despite some local additions, almost exactly the same across the length and breadth of the country.

The basic meal is the *comida corriente*. At lunchtime (from midday to 2 pm), it is called *almuerzo*. At dinner time (after 6 pm), it becomes *comida*, but it is in fact identical to lunch. It is a set two-course meal consisting of *sopa* (soup) and *bandeja* or *seco* (main course), and usually includes a *sobremesa* (a bottled fizzy drink or a juice).

The almuerzos and comidas are the staple, sometimes the only, offering of the budget restaurants. Some serve them continuously from noon until they close at night, but most only serve them for lunch. The comida corriente is the cheapest way to fill yourself up, costing between US$1 and US$2 – roughly half the price of any à la carte dish.

The barbecued chicken restaurants (there are plenty of them) are a good alternative to the comida. Half a chicken with potatoes will cost you around US$3. One more budget option, particularly in smaller towns and villages, is the market, where the food is usually fresh, tasty and cooked in front of you.

Western food is readily available in the up-market restaurants but is rather expensive.

Colombia has an amazing variety of fruits, some of which are to be found only in particular regions of the country. You should try *guanábana*, *lulo*, *curuba*, *zapote*, *mamoncillo*, *uchuva*, *fraijoa*, *granadilla*, *maracuyá*, *tomate de árbol*, *borojó*, *mamey* and *tamarindo*.

DRINKS

Coffee is undoubtedly the number one drink and almost a ritual. *Tinto* (a small cup of black coffee) is served everywhere. Other coffee drinks are *perico* or *pintado*, a small milk coffee, and *café con leche*, which is larger and uses more milk.

In contrast to coffee, tea is of poor quality and not very popular. On the other hand, the *aromáticas* – herb teas made with various plants like *cidrón* (citrus leaves), *yerbabuena* (mint) and *manzanilla* (camomile) – are very cheap and good. *Agua de panela* (unrefined sugar melted in hot water) is very tasty with lemon.

Beer is popular, cheap and generally not bad. This can't be said about Colombian wine, which is best avoided.

Aguardiente is the local alcoholic spirit, flavoured with anis and produced by several companies throughout the country under their own brand names. *Ron* (rum) is another popular local spirit, particularly on the Caribbean coast.

In some regions, mostly in rural areas, you will find *guarapo* and *chicha*, which are low (or not so low) in alcohol. They are made by the fermentation of fruit or maize in sugar or panela water.

THINGS TO BUY

Colombia is the world's largest producer of emeralds, and the local stones are most sought after for their quality. If you are interested and have extra pesos to spend, the right place to buy them is Bogotá, which has the best selection and the most reasonable prices.

For original antiques, particularly pre-Columbian pottery, the best place is again Bogotá, but prices are high, so don't expect to find a bargain.

The best filigree gold jewellery is found in Mompós. Another place for goldwork is Santa Fe de Antioquia.

Colombian handicrafts vary in kind and by region. Some regions or even particular towns are famous for their local crafts. Boyacá is the best department for handicrafts, and produces excellent handwoven items, basketry and pottery. The basketwork of the Pacific coast is also interesting, with the best selection supposedly found in Cali. Pasto is noted for its decorative items covered with the famous *barniz de Pasto*, a kind of vegetable resin. Pitalito has become famous for its ceramic miniatures of *chivas*. (A *chiva* is a sort of Disneyland bus which was, until the 1960s, the main means of transport. Chivas are still common on country roads.)

Ruanas, the Colombian woollen ponchos, are found all over the colder parts of the Andean zone. In many villages, they are still made by hand, with simple patterns and natural colours, but the best selection is in Bogotá.

The best and most fashionable *mochilas* (a kind of woven handbag) are those of the Arhuaco Indians from the Sierra Nevada de Santa Marta, but they are not cheap. Colourful hammocks are especially nice in San Jacinto, a small town near Cartagena.

Colombian leather goods are among the best in South America and are relatively cheap.

Getting There & Away

As the northernmost country on the continent, Colombia is something of a gateway to South America for many travellers.

AIR

If you buy an international air ticket in Colombia, you pay 19% tax (9.5% on a return ticket) on top of the fare. This makes air travel out of Colombia expensive. The airfares given in this section don't include tax.

Flying out of Colombia, there's an airport tax of US$17 if you have stayed in the country up to 60 days, US$30 for longer stays.

To/From Europe

From Europe, the cheapest flights to Colombia are from London – tickets to Bogotá start at around £220 one-way, £420 to £500 return.

To/From North America

From the USA, you can go by land through Central America, with a short flight to bypass Panama, but food and accommodation expenses will add considerably to the total cost of getting to Colombia.

Avianca offers discount return flights from the USA to Colombia. Currently, the most interesting include Miami-Cartagena-Miami (US$419) and Miami-Bogotá-Miami (US$449). A maximum stay of two months is allowed.

Zuliana de Aviación, an almost unknown Venezuelan carrier, flies from Miami to Medellín and Bogotá for US$205 to either (US$385 one-year return). It also has an attractive fare from Miami to San Antonio del Táchira, in Venezuela, on the Colombian border, across from Cúcuta (US$165 one-way, US$330 return).

To/From Central America

Colombia has regular flight connections with all Central American capitals. It usually works out cheaper to go via the Colombian island of San Andrés and then fly to the Colombian mainland by a domestic flight (see the San Andrés section). Airfares to San Andrés are as follows (discount fares for a 30-day return ticket are given in brackets):

From	Airline	Fare
Managua	Sahsa	US$168 (260)
San Salvador	Sahsa	US$150 (240)
Guatemala	Sam/Sahsa	US$125 (215)
Tegucigalpa	Sahsa	US$117 (200)
Panama	Sahsa	US$115
San José	Sam	US$85

To/From Panama

From Panama, there are direct flights to the Colombian cities of Medellín with Copa and Sam (US$115), to Cartagena with Copa (US$115), to Bogotá with Avianca, Sam and Air Panama (US$146), and to Cali with Avianca and Copa (US$158).

To/From Ecuador

There are over a dozen regular flights a week between Quito and Bogotá, operated by Avianca, Ecuatoriana, Viasa and Servivensa, (US$153 one-way, US$246 return, minimum five days, maximum two months).

To/From Venezuela

There are several flights daily between Caracas (Venezuela) and Bogotá, with Viasa, Avianca, Avensa and a few other carriers. The regular one-way fare is US$194; a discount return ticket, valid for one year, originating from either end, costs US$250. Zuliana de Aviación advertises the same route for US$79 (US$158 return).

Other connections between Venezuela and Colombia include Caracas- Cartagena with Viasa (US$172, US$199 one-year return), Caracas- Barranquilla with Lacsa (US$161, US$193 30-day return), Valencia-Bogotá

with Valenciana de Aviación (US$120, US$200 60-day return) and Maracaibo-Medellín or Bogotá with Zuliana de Aviación (US$50, US$100 one-year return).

LAND
To/From Central America

The Darién Gap very effectively separates Colombia and Panama, and Central America from South America. There are no roads, and it will be a long time before one is built to fill the missing part of the Pan-American Highway. There are basically two ways to pass the Darién Gap: along the northern coast or through the jungle. See the introductory Getting There chapter for details. In both cases, you get the Colombian exit/entry stamp in your passport in Turbo.

To/From Ecuador

Almost all travellers use the Pan-American Highway border point passing through Tulcán and Ipiales. There are no direct buses between these two towns, but frequent *colectivos* (shared taxis) run to/from the border. All passport formalities are done on the border. See the Ipiales section for more information.

Another, rather adventurous way to get to Colombia passes the fringe of the Amazon, through Lago Agrio and San Miguel. From Lago Agrio, several buses daily run to La Punta, on the Ecuadorian border (US$1, one hour). From there, take a canoe to San Miguel in Colombia (US$3, half an hour). There are about 10 buses or chivas daily from San Miguel to Puerto Asís (US$5, five hours). The region around Puerto Asís is partly controlled by the guerrillas and is unsafe, so unsafe that the DAS office closed down and moved to Mocoa, where you get the entry stamp in your passport (check to see whether the Puerto Asís office has reopened). From Puerto Asís, there are several buses daily to Mocoa (US$5, five hours), continuing to Pasto by the rough, dangerous, but extremely spectacular mountain roads across the cordillera.

One more way to get to Colombia is by

boat along the Pacific coast from Limones (Ecuador) to Tumaco (Colombia).

To/From Venezuela

There are four border crossings between Colombia and Venezuela. By far the most popular with travellers is the route via San Antonio del Táchira and Cúcuta, on the main Caracas-Bogotá road. See the Cúcuta section in this chapter and the San Antonio del Táchira section in the Venezuela chapter for details.

Another entry point to Colombia is Paraguachón, on the Maracaibo-Maicao road. This may be your route if you plan on heading directly to the Colombian Caribbean coast. There are buses and shared taxis between Maracaibo and Maicao. You get your passport stamped by both Venezuelan and Colombian officials in Paraguachón, on the border. You'll find further details on transport in the rrrMaracaibo section of the Venezuela chapter.

The third possible route to Colombia leads through the Orinoquia, from either Puerto Páez or Puerto Ayacucho (both in Venezuela) to Puerto Carreño (in Colombia). See the Puerto Ayacucho section of the Venezuela chapter for details.

Finally, you can reach Arauca, Colombia via El Amparo de Apure (Venezuela), then continue overland or by air further into Colombia. Note that the Arauca Department has serious guerrilla problems. This route is rarely used by travellers.

BOAT
To/From Brazil & Peru

The most popular routes are from Iquitos (Peru) and Manaus (Brazil), reached by either air or boat, and then along the Amazon to Leticia in Colombia. For details of options from Colombia, see the Leticia section.

Getting Around

AIR

Colombia has a well-developed airline system and a dense network of internal flights. There are six main passenger airlines: Avianca, Sam, Aces, Aires, Intercontinental de Aviación and Satena. Avianca, Sam and Aces also have international flights. There are also several small airlines, which operate over limited areas, mainly in the Amazon and Llanos. Airfares differ between the carriers: Avianca and Sam are the most expensive, while Satena and Intercontinental are the cheapest; the difference in fares over the same route may be up to 30%. In this chapter, the fares listed are those of the more expensive carriers.

Generally speaking, Colombian airfares are high compared to those of, say, Venezuela or Ecuador. There's a US$3.50 airport tax on domestic flights departing from about 30 main airports. This tax is included in the airfares listed here. Be sure to reconfirm your reservation a couple of days before departure. If you don't, you may find yourself bumped off your flight.

BUS

Buses are the main means of getting around the country. The bus transport system is well developed and extensive, reaching even the smallest villages, if there is a road.

There are three principal classes of buses: ordinary (called *corriente*, *sencillo* or *ordinario*), 1st class (which goes by a variety of names, such as *pullman*, *metropolitano*, *de lujo* or *directo*) and the air-conditioned buses (called *climatizado* or, more proudly, *thermoking*).

The corriente buses range from geriatric crates to fairly good modern models; the antiques usually ply the rough minor roads, while those of more recent technology run on the main routes. The pullman and climatizado buses are pretty good, reliable and comfortable, with plenty of leg room, reclining seats and large luggage compartments. They are predominantly long-distance buses covering the main routes, and many travel at night. The climatizado category is expanding these days, and new buses are equipped with bathrooms and seats that recline to almost horizontal position.

Apart from these, there is one more kind of bus – the chiva. This trolley-type vehicle was the principal means of transport a few decades ago. Its body is made almost entirely of wood, covered with colourful decorative patterns, with a main painting on the back. Today, the chivas have disappeared from the main roads, but they still play an important role on outback roads between small villages.

Colectivos are quite widespread in Colombia. These shared taxis (sometimes jeeps) cover fixed routes, mainly on short and medium distances. They leave when full, not according to a schedule, and are a good option if there is a long wait for the next bus or if you want more comfort and speed.

On the main roads, buses run every hour, or more frequently, so there is little point in booking a seat in advance. In some places off the main routes, where there are only a couple of buses daily, it's better to buy a ticket a few hours before departure. The only time you need to book is during the Christmas and Easter periods, when hordes of Colombians are on holiday.

Many cities already have, or are in the process of building, a central bus terminal. Where there isn't one, bus company terminals tend to be concentrated along one or two adjacent streets.

Bus travel is not as cheap as in neighbouring countries. As a rule of a thumb, the corriente bus costs between US$2 and US$2.50 for every 100 km. Pullmans cost about 20% more than corrientes and the air-conditioned buses 15% more than pullmans. Colectivos charge roughly 50% more than pullmans.

TRAIN
There are no longer rail routes you would be interested in using. Only a few local railway lines still operate passenger services.

BOAT
With some 3000 km of Pacific and Atlantic coastline, there is a considerable amount of shipping, consisting mostly of irregular cargo boats. These may also take passengers, which may interest you if you plan on exploring the Pacific coast. The main port on this coast is Buenaventura.

Rivers are also important transport routes, particularly in the Chocó and the Amazon, where there is no other way of getting around. Very few riverboats run on any regular schedule, and as most are primarily cargo boats, they are far from fast. Conditions are primitive and food (when provided) is poor. The fares are a matter of discussion with the captain, but are not cheap.

Bogotá

The capital of Colombia is a large metropolitan city – a chaotic mixture of everything from sparkling prosperity to oppressive poverty: the spontaneous architecture, from shabby shacks to modern skyscrapers, beyond all rules of urban planning, the wild and disorganised city traffic that includes every means of transport from mules to Masserattis, and the people – a racial and social mosaic ranging from beggars and *gamines* (street urchins) to traditionally dressed, aged *cachacos* (Bogotanos).

Bogotá is a bustling, noisy and aggressive city – amazing but awful, exciting but dangerous. You may love it or hate it, but it won't leave you indifferent.

The city was founded in 1538 and baptised Santa Fe de Bogotá, but after independence, the name was shortened to Bogotá. Though it always played an important political role as the capital, its rapid progress only came in the 1940s, with industrialisation and the consequent migrations from the countryside towards the city. In only 50 years, Bogotá has grown twentyfold to its present population of between six and seven million inhabitants. Recently, the city's official name was changed back to the traditional one, though no one can agree on how to spell it (you'll find Santa Fe, Santa Fé or Santafé de

Bogotá). Anyway, people are used to just Bogotá.

Bogotá lies at an altitude of about 2600 metres, and the temperature averages 14°C all year round, with cold nights and pretty warm days. The dry season is from December to March, and there is also a semidry period (with only light rainfall), from July to August.

Bogotá is not a safe city. Large parts of the city centre become quite dangerous after dark and are notorious for robbery. Keep nighttime strolls to a minimum and don't carry money or valuables. In practice, it's good to have a bundle of small notes, the equivalent of, say, US$5 to US$10, to hand over in case of an assault; if you really don't have a peso, robbers can get frustrated and unpredictable.

Orientation

The city, set in the Sabana de Bogotá, has grown along its north-south axis and is bordered to the east by a mountain range with the two remarkable peaks of Monserrate and Guadalupe. Having expanded up the mountain slopes as far as possible, Bogotá is now rapidly filling the savanna to the west and north.

The central city area divides the metropolis into two very different parts. The northern sector consists mainly of elegant residential districts, while the southern part is a vast spread of very undistinguished poor brick architecture. The western part, away from the mountains, is the most heterogeneous and is more industrial. This is where the airport and the bus terminal are located.

Information

Tourist Offices Bogotá has three tourist bureaux. The CNT office (☎ 2843761) is at Calle 28 No 13A-59, on the ground floor. You can easily find the place, as it's in Bogota's highest skyscraper, with the Banco Cafetero logo on the top. The office is open Monday to Friday from 9 am to 12.15 pm and 2 to 5 pm. They still have some publications, left over from their good times, available in English, French and German.

It's a good idea to stock up here with brochures, as they can be hard to find elsewhere around the country. If you come by air, there is a branch of the CNT office on the 1st floor of the El Dorado Airport (departure hall). It's open Monday to Friday from 7 am to 8 pm, and on Saturday and Sunday from 7 am to 2 pm.

The Instituto Distrital de Cultura y Turismo (☎ 3346010, 2865554), the city tourist board, focuses on Bogotá itself. The office is at the corner of Plaza de Bolívar and is open Monday to Friday from 8.30 am to 5 pm. There is another outlet, at the airport (ground floor), open from 7 am to 8 pm Monday to Saturday.

The Corporación de Turismo de Cundinamarca (☎ 2840600), at Calle 16 No 7-76, deals with Cundinamarca Department, the region surrounding Bogotá. The office is open Monday to Friday from 9 am to noon and 2 to 6 pm.

Inderena The government body which deals with national parks, Inderena (☎ 2830964), is at Carrera 10 No 20-30, oficina 805. This is the place to get permits for the parks, as well as information about them, including a good English-language parks guidebook (about US$4).

Colombia has 33 national parks and several smaller nature reserves. Only a few parks provide lodging and food; several others offer the possibility of camping, and the rest nothing at all in the way of tourist facilities.

In theory, you need a permit to enter each park, though in most of them, nobody will ask you for it. Some parks have established admission fees (usually about US$1), while the entry to others is free.

When you apply for the permit, you must state when you are going to visit the park, pay the entrance fee (if applicable) and the accommodation (if the park has these facilities, and you are going to use them). The office receives applications on Monday and Wednesday from 9 am to noon and 2 to 4 pm, and on Tuesday and Friday from 9 am to

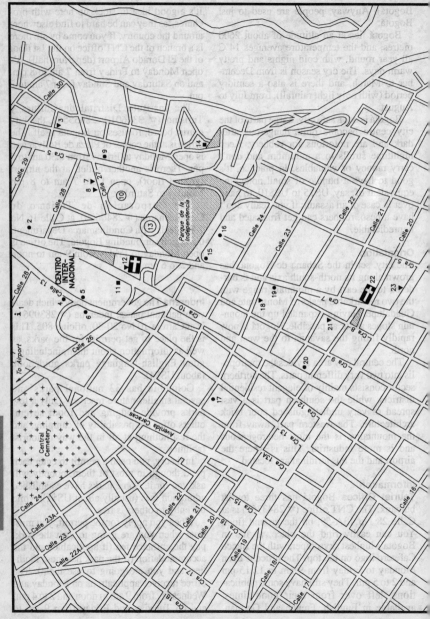

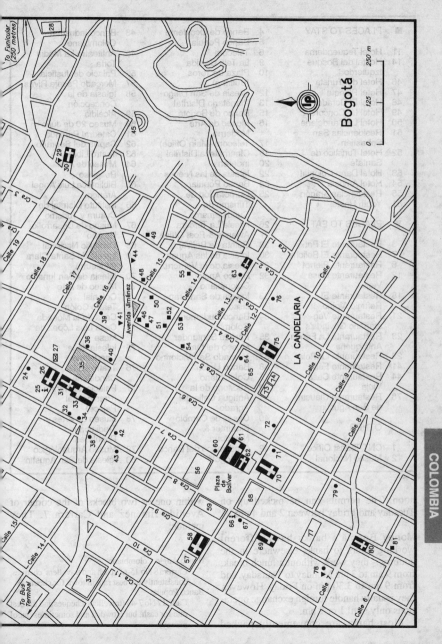

Bogotá

COLOMBIA

noon. The permits can be picked up on Tuesday and Friday between 2 and 4 pm.

Money Bogotá's banks have different working hours to banks elsewhere in the country – they work without a lunch break, from 9 am to 3 pm Monday to Thursday, and from 9 am to 3.30 pm on Friday. However, they usually handle foreign exchange operations only until 1 or 2 pm.

Most banks are conveniently packed within one or two blocks of the corner of Avenida Jiménez and Carrera 7. They include:

Banco Anglo Colombiano
　　Carrera 8 No 15-60 (cash and travellers' cheques, consistently the best rate in town for cheques)
Banco Popular
　　Calle 17 No 7-43 (travellers' cheques and the best rate for cash, but crowded and sometimes out of money)

Banco Sudameris Colombia
Carrera 8 No 15-42 (cash only, but at a good rate)
Banco Unión Colombiano
Carrera 8 No 14-45 (low rate for cash and relatively good for cheques)
Banco Industrial Colombiano
Carrera 8 No 13-55 (cash and Mastercard)
Banco Colombo Americano
Carrera 7 No 16-36, above the Avianca post office (Visa)
Credibanco of Banco de Bogotá
Calle 14 No 7-73 (Visa, in their extended business hours: Monday to Friday from 9 am to 5 pm, and Saturday from 10 am to 4 pm)

There's another concentration of useful banks in the area of the Centro Internacional, about one km north.

The many casas de cambio generally don't accept travellers' cheques but do change cash, paying roughly 1% to 2% less than the banks. They are open till 5 or 6 pm on weekdays and usually till noon on Saturday. In the central area, you have Exprinter and Novatours, next door to each other near the corner of Avenida Jiménez and Carrera 6.

Tierra Mar Aire (TMA) travel agency (☎ 2832955), which represents American Express, has its office in the Centro Internacional, Carrera 10 No 27-91.

Post & Telephone The Avianca main post office is at Carrera 7 No 16-36. They also have poste restante there. The office is open Monday to Friday from 7.30 am to 7 pm, and on Saturday from 8 am to 3 pm.

DHL Worldwide Express (☎ 2172200) has its main office at Carrera 13 No 75-74 and a branch in the city centre, opposite the Hotel Tequendama (San Diego Church).

The main office of Telecom is at Calle 23 No 13-49. You can also make long-distance calls and send telegrams from the branch Telecom offices scattered throughout the city.

Visa Extensions A 30-day visa extension can be obtained from the DAS office (☎ 6107315, extension 214, 2268220), Calle 100 No 11B-29. Only your passport is required (no photos, no onward ticket). The office is open Monday to Thursday from 7.30 am to 4 pm, and on Friday from 7.30 am to 3.30 pm, but be there earlier, as you have to pay the US$18 fee at the bank. You get the extension on the spot.

Foreign Consulates All Latin American countries except Cuba, have consulates in Bogotá.

Australia
There is no Australian embassy in Colombia.
Brazil
Calle 93 No 14-20, piso 8 (☎ 2180800)
Costa Rica
Carrera 15 No 80-87 (☎ 2361098)
Canada
Calle 76 No 11-52 (☎ 2175555)
Ecuador
Calle 100 No 14-63 (☎ 2579947)
France
Carrera 11 No 93-12 (☎ 6181863)
Germany
Carrera 4 No 72-35, Piso 6 (☎ 2120511)
Guatemala
Carrera 15 No 83-43, apto 301 (☎ 2361103)
Honduras
Carrera 13 No 63-51, oficina 202 (☎ 2353158)
Panama
Calle 87 No 11A-64 (☎ 2568280)
Peru
Carrera 7 bis No 94-43 (☎ 2360607)
UK
Calle 98, No 9-03 (☎ 2185111)
USA
Calle 38 No 8-61 (☎ 2851300)
Venezuela
Avenida 13 No 103-16 (☎ 2563015)

Things to See
Bogotá has enough tourist sights to keep you busy for several days. It also has a far more vibrant and diversified cultural and artistic life than any other city in the country. Almost all major tourist attractions are conveniently sited in the central city area, within easy walking distance of each other.

Old Town The **Plaza de Bolívar** is the heart of the original town, but what you can see around it is a real mishmash of architectural styles. The massive stone building in classical Greek style on the southern side is the **Capitolio Nacional**, the seat of the Congress. Opposite is the modern **Palacio de**

Justicia, which replaces an earlier building which was taken by the M-19 guerrillas in November 1985 and gutted by fire. The ruin was subsequently demolished, and the new palace, in a totally different style, is now being constructed. The whole of the western side of the plaza is taken up by the French-style **Alcaldía** (Mayor's office), dating from the early 20th century. Finally, **La Catedral Primada** and the **Capilla del Sagrario**, the only colonial buildings on the square, stand on its eastern side. Further east is the colonial *barrio* of **La Candelaria**, well worth a stroll. Some of the houses have been carefully restored, others continue in a dilapidated shape, but on the whole the sector preserves an agreeable old-time appearance, even though a number of modern edifices replaced original buildings. Possibly the best-preserved part of the barrio is between calles 9 and 13 and carreras 2 and 5.

Museums Bogotá has a number of good museums. The star attraction is, no doubt, the **Museo del Oro** (Gold Museum), at Calle 16 No 5-41, the most important of its kind in the world. It contains over 30,000 gold pieces from all the major pre-Hispanic cultures in Colombia. Most of the gold is displayed in a huge strong room on the top floor – a breath-taking sight. There are tours conducted in English once or twice a day. The museum is open Tuesday to Saturday from 9 am to 4.30 pm, and on Sunday from 10 am to 4.30 pm. Admission is US$1.20 (US$0.70 on Saturday and Sunday). The shop next to the ticket office has a large choice of coffee-table books on art and architecture.

To complement your knowledge of pre-Columbian cultures, go to the **Museo Arqueológico**, in the beautifully restored colonial house at Carrera 6 No 7-43. It has an extensive collection of pottery from Colombia's most outstanding pre-Hispanic groups. You can have an English-speaking guide at no additional cost. The museum is open Tuesday to Saturday from 9 am to 12.30 pm and 1.30 to 5 pm, and on Sunday from 10 am to 1 pm. The admission fee is US$1 (US$0.25 for students).

The **Museo de Artes y Tradiciones Populares**, housed in the old Augustinian monastery at Carrera 8 No 7-21, displays and sells a variety of handicrafts from all over the country. It's open Tuesday to Friday from 8.30 am to 5.30 pm, and on Saturday from 9.30 am to 5 pm. There's also a good restaurant here.

The **Museo de Desarrollo Urbano**, just off the Plaza de Bolívar, provides a good insight into the urban development of Bogotá, through old maps, photos, drawings, models, antiques and the like. It's in an old colonial house, dating from 1650. The museum is open Monday to Friday from 8.30 am to 4.30 pm.

There are several more museums in the same area, including the **Museo de Arte Colonial**, at Carrera 6 No 9-77, and **Museo de Arte Religioso**, at Calle 12 No 4-33.

In the northern part of the city centre, be sure to visit the **Museo Nacional**, housed in an old prison at Carrera 7 No 28-66. It is actually three museums (Anthropology & Ethnography, History and Fine Arts), and also puts on various temporary shows. It's open Tuesday to Saturday from 9 am to 5 pm, and on Sunday from 10 am to 4 pm.

For contemporary art, visit the **Museo de Arte Moderno**, at Calle 26 No 6-05 (enter from Calle 24), which runs frequently changing displays of national and sometimes foreign artists. It's open Tuesday to Sunday from 10 am to 7 pm.

The **Quinta de Bolívar**, Calle 20 No 2-23 Este, is an old country house donated to Bolívar in gratitude for his services. Today, it's a museum displaying the Libertador's possessions, documents, maps, etc. It's open Tuesday to Sunday from 10 am to 5 pm.

Churches As the capital since the early days of Spanish rule, and a centre of evangelism in the vast province, Bogotá boasts a good selection of colonial churches, most dating from the 17th and 18th centuries. They are usually austere on the outside, but internal decoration is often very rich.

One of the most interesting is **Santa Clara**, today open as a museum, Monday to

Saturday from 9 am to 1 pm and 2 to 5 pm, and on Sunday from 10 am to 4 pm.

Other churches worth a look include: **San Francisco**, noted for its extraordinary decoration of the presbytery; **La Concepción** with probably Bogotá's most beautiful Mudejar vault; **San Ignacio**, distinguished by both its size and its valuable works of art; **La Tercera**, remarkable for its walnut and cedar woodcarvings; and **San Diego**, a charming country church (it was well outside the town when built), now surrounded by a forest of high-rise buildings.

Cerro de Monserrate For a spectacular view of the city, go to the top of the Cerro de Monserrate, the mountain overlooking the city centre from the east. There is a church on the summit, with a statue of the Señor Caido (Fallen Christ), to which many miracles have been attributed.

There are three ways to get to the top: by cable car, funicular railway or along the footpath.

Both the cable car and the funiculâr operate Monday to Saturday from 9 am to midnight, and on Sunday from 6 am to 6 pm. The one-way ticket for either costs US$1.50; the return fare is US$3. If you want to do the trip on foot (one hour uphill), do it only on Sunday, when crowds of pilgrims go; on weekdays, take it for granted that you will be robbed. The lower stations of cable car and funicular are close to the city centre, but the access road leads through a shabby barrio, so it's better to take the bus marked 'Funicular', from Avenida Jiménez, or a taxi.

Other Sights The city has interesting botanical gardens, the **Jardín Botánico José Celestino Mutis**, at Carrera 66A No 56-84, with a variety of national flora from different climatic zones. On Sunday, don't miss the **Mercado de las Pulgas**, a colourful flea market, on Carrera 3 between calles 19 and 23.

Places to Stay

The best budget place to stay is the *youth hostel* (☎ 2803125), at Carrera 7 No 6-10,

four blocks south of Plaza de Bolívar. It has spotlessly clean six and eight-bed dormitories. There are only shared baths, but they are clean, and there is hot water in the morning. The hostel, set in an old house with a pleasant patio in the middle, also operates a good, cheap good restaurant. Holders of the youth hostel card pay US$3.50 per bed; nonmembers pay US$5 (or they can buy the youth hostel card here and sleep at members' rates). The hostel keeps the door open from 6 am to midnight.

Apart from this exceptional place, Bogotá has loads of hotels, but unfortunately, what is really cheap is pretty poor. At the bottom, for about US$3 to US$4 per person, you can choose between the *Residencias Aragón* (☎ 2848325), Carrera 3 No 14-13, which has fairly large rooms without bath or hot water, the *Residencias San Sebastián* (☎ 2548634), Calle 14 No 4-80, which sometimes has hot water, and the *Hotel La Concordia* (☎ 3429102), Carrera 3 No 15-64, which has claustrophobic cell-like rooms with private bath and hot water.

Appreciably better is the recently refurbished *Hotel El Dorado* (☎ 3343988), Calle 15 No 3-98, which has hot water and private baths (US$5 per person). For a dollar more, *Hotel La Candelaria* (☎ 2439857), Carrera 4 No 14-87, has rooms with bath and hot water, but they vary in size and value, so look around.

The *Hotel Turístico de Santafé* (☎ 3420560), Calle 14 No 4-48, has large, clean rooms with bath attached (US$10/13/18 a single/double/triple). You can eat in the hotel restaurant, which is cheap and has acceptable food. For the same price, there's also the small *Hotel del Turista* (☎ 3420649), at Avenida Jiménez No 4-95.

The *Hotel Ambalá* (☎ 3412376), Carrera 5 No 13-46, has small but comfortable rooms with bath, TV and phone (US$12/16 a single/double).

For something a little plusher, go to the *Hotel Planeta* (☎ 2842711), at Carrera 5 No 14-64 (US$16/22/28). Even better is the *Hotel Dann Colonial* (☎ 3411680), at Calle 14 No 4-21 (US$33/44/55). Don't be con-

COLOMBIA

fused by the name: the hotel is modern, not colonial.

All the hotels listed above are a stone's throw from each other, and there are several more around. The zone is not particularly safe at night, but neither is the whole city centre. There is also a choice of hotels in the northern part of the centre, though you won't find cheapies there.

A place with particular charm is the *Hostal del Bosque Izquierdo* (☎ 3411384), at Carrera 4A No 25B-12, in a beautiful old house. There are five rooms only, four of which have one double and one single bed, costing US$50 per room, breakfast included. Choose your room, as each is different. There's an atmospheric restaurant-cum-bar downstairs.

Places to Eat

Innumerable places have set meals for US$1 to US$2 – just drop into the first one, see what people are eating, and stay or move on to the next one. For cheap vegetarian food try *Govinda's*, Carrera 8 No 20-55.

Dominó, Carrera 3 No 18-55, is one of the best places for empanadas. *Pastelería Florida*, Carrera 7 No 20-82, is an ugly-looking but popular bakery, good for chocolate santafereño (hot chocolate with cheese, accompanied by pan de yuca or almojábanas). Bogotá has a number of barbecued-chicken restaurants, where a half chicken with potatoes or chips makes a really filling meal for, at most, US$3. For pizza, there's a row of pizzerias on Calle 19, between carreras 3 and 7.

The *Claustro de San Agustín* (open Monday to Friday till 5 pm), in the Museo de Artes y Tradiciones Populares, has delicious typical food (served until 3 pm only).

La Pola, Calle 19 No 1-85, has a list of fine regional dishes, including a puchero sabanero which is second to none. *Félix*, Avenida Jiménez No 4-80, is well-known for its paella valenciana.

La Fonda Antioqueña, at Calle 19 No 5-98, has good Antioquian food at reasonable prices. *El Patio*, a cosy Bohemian place with only a few tables, is at Carrera 4 No

27-86. It is becoming one of the trendiest places for lunch in the centre, serving excellent Italian food.

Casa Vieja is acclaimed for its regional food. It has two atmospheric outlets in the centre: at Avenida Jiménez No 3-73 and at Carrera 10 No 26-50 (San Diego Church). *El Refugio Alpino*, Calle 23 No 7-49, serves rich European food at up-market prices. *La Fragata*, in the Centro Internacional, is one of the best places in the city centre for seafood.

At night, go to *El Boliche*, Calle 27 No 5-64, for reasonably priced Italian food and a good atmosphere. Next door, *Pierrot* is plusher and more expensive, and often has live music.

Entertainment

Bogotá has lots of cinemas offering the usual commercial fare, mainly from the USA. Film clubs (*Cinematecas* and *cine clubes*) present more significant art movies. In the city centre, there are the Cinemateca Distrital (Carrera 7 No 22- 79), the Cine Club (in the Museo de Arte Moderno, Calle 26 No 6- 05) and the Cine Club de Colombia (screening films in the Auditorio de la Antigua Calle del Agrado, Calle 16 No 4-75).

Several groups have their own theatres, and many more put on productions here and there. For at least a decade, the Teatro de la Candelaria, Calle 12 No 2-59 has been one of the most interesting venues in town. The Taller de Investigación de la Imagen Dramática is a new experimental theatre which has already gained some international attention. Look for them in the Universidad Nacional to find out if and where they currently perform.

There are plenty of discos, offering a variety of music, from Western rock to old Cuban songs. Some places have live music, usually on weekends.

There are several music spots around the corner of Carrera 5 and Calle 27, the best-known of which is La Teja Corrida, Carrera 5 No 26A-54, which often has good *salsa* groups. The area is gradually losing its popularity in favour of the increasingly trendy

Zona Rosa, around Carrera 15, in the northern sector of the city. The Zona is particularly alive on weekend nights, a good time to pop into such nightspots as Café Libro, Carrera 15 No 82-87, or Salomé, a block away, the latter playing pure Cuban salsa music.

Getting There & Away

Air El Dorado Airport is 13 km north-west of the city centre. The terminal has snack bars, restaurants, handicrafts shops and two tourist offices (see the Tourist Office section for details), but no luggage lockers or left-luggage room. There's a branch of the Banco Popular on the ground floor, between the departure and arrival sectors, which is open daily from 7 am to 10 pm; it changes both cash and travellers' cheques at the same rate as branches in the city centre.

There's another terminal, Puente Aéreo, about one km before El Dorado. It handles international flights to the USA, and domestic ones to Cali, Medellín and a few other destinations. Make sure to check which terminal your flight departs from.

Most of the airline offices are in the Centro Internacional. Avianca is at Carrera 7 No 16-36, next to the main post office.

There are plenty of domestic flights to destinations all over the country, including Medellín (US$57), Cali (US$62), Cartagena (US$102), San Andrés (US$141) and Leticia (US$112). Aerosucre has cargo flights to Leticia (see the Leticia section for details).

Satena has noncommercial passenger flights to San Andrés, roughly one per month (about US$60). These flights are heavily booked in advance, but it's sometimes possible to get on one by calling the Satena office a day before, or by going directly to the airport on flight day.

Bus The well-organised bus terminal is a long way west of the city centre. To get there from the centre, take the bus or colectivo marked 'Terminal'. To get to the city centre from the terminal, take the 'Ruta 1/Centro' bus, or a colectivo. Taxis between the terminal and the city centre should cost about US$4.

On the main roads, buses run frequently round the clock to Cali (US$18, 12 hours), Medellín (US$16, nine hours) and Bucaramanga (US$15, 10 hours). There are direct buses to Cartagena (US$38), Santa Marta (US$33), Cúcuta (US$23), San Agustín (US$14), Popayán (US$22) and Ipiales (US$35). All prices (except for San Agustín) are for climatizados, the dominant class of bus on these routes.

Getting Around

To/From the Airport You can get to the airport by buseta (US$0.20), colectivo (US$0.30) or taxi (about US$5). You catch busetas and colectivos marked 'Aeropuerto' at Calle 19 or Carrera 10. At the airport, they stop in front of the terminal.

AROUND BOGOTÁ

Zipaquirá

Zipaquirá, 50 km north of Bogotá, is noted for its salt mines. Although the mines date back to the Muisca period and have been intensively exploited, they still contain vast reserves; it is virtually a huge mountain of rock salt. In the heart of the mountain, an underground salt cathedral has been carved out of the solid salt. It is some 25 metres high and is capable of holding 10,000 people. The cathedral is currently closed, and it's not clear when it might open. Check the tourist office for news.

Buses to Zipaquirá run from Bogotá every 10 minutes along Avenida Caracas (US$1, 1¼ hours). The mines are a 20-minute walk uphill from the centre of town.

Guatavita

Also called Guatavita Nueva, this town was built in the late 1960s when the old colonial Guatavita was flooded by the waters of a hydroelectric reservoir. The town is architecturally interesting, with modern forms added to the best of the colonial style to create a curious blend of old and new. Among the things to see are the museum of religious art, the bullring and the church – don't miss its lovely altar.

About 15 km from the town is the famous Laguna de Guatavita, the ritual centre and sacred lake of the Muisca Indians, and a cradle of the myth of El Dorado. The lagoon was an object of worship, where gold pieces, emeralds and food were offered by Indians. The myth of incalculable treasures at the bottom gave rise to numerous attempts to salvage the riches. However, in spite of enormous efforts undertaken by the Spanish, very little has actually been found. Legend claims that the lake retains its treasures.

To get to Guatavita Nueva, take a bus from Avenida Caracas in Bogotá (US$2, two hours). Buses run every hour on weekdays and every 15 minutes on Sunday. For the lake, get off 11 km before the town (drivers will let you off at the right place) and walk five km uphill along a dirt track.

Boyacá, Santander & Norte de Santander

The three departments of Boyacá, Santander and Norte de Santander cover the northern part of the Cordillera Oriental to the north of Bogotá. The region offers a variety of landscapes, from green fertile valleys like Valle de Tenza, in southern Boyacá, to the arid Cañon del Chicamocha (Santander) and the snowy peaks of the Sierra Nevada del Cocuy (northern Boyacá).

Once the territory of the Muiscas (Boyacá) and the Guane Indians (central Santander), the region was one of the first to be explored and inhabited by the Spaniards. Many small colonial towns founded by them are preserved to this day in remarkably good shape. Villa de Leyva, Barichara and Girón are among the best-known examples.

Of the three departments, Boyacá is perhaps the safest, easiest and most pleasant in which to travel. It is also the most traditional province, widely known for its handicrafts, particularly pottery, basketwork and weaving.

TUNJA

Tunja, the capital of Boyacá Department, is one of the oldest Colombian cities, founded in 1539 on the site of Hunza, the ancient Muisca seat. Though almost nothing is left of the Indian period, much colonial architecture remains. The central sector has been carefully restored for the town's 450-year anniversary, and many old public houses have recovered their original splendour. Unfortunately, the streets further off the main square are slowly losing their colonial character, as modern buildings and apartment blocks mushroom between fine old mansions. Tunja is a city of churches: several imposing examples from the 16th century are almost untouched by time.

The city, at an altitude of nearly 2800 metres, has a cool climate, and you'll need warm clothing, especially at night.

Information
Tourist Office The regional tourist office (☎ 422924) is in the Casa del Fundador, on the Plaza de Bolívar. It's open daily from 8 am to noon and 2 to 6 pm, and the management is helpful.

Money Only the Banco del Estado will change cash dollars. The Banco del Estado and Banco de Bogotá exchange travellers' cheques; the latter pays a better rate. Both these banks, and the Banco Popular, give cash advances on Visa card, while the Banco de Occidente and the Banco Industrial Colombiano will honour your Mastercard. Cash and travellers' cheques are changed only from 8 to 10 am. If you are stuck without pesos, the casa de cambio on the Plaza de Bolívar changes cash dollars (at a poor rate) till 6 pm, and on Saturday till noon.

Things to See
The **Casa del Fundador Suárez Rendón** (the house of the founder of Tunja) and the **Casa de Don Juan de Vargas** have both been converted into museums containing colonial artworks. The ceilings are covered with intriguing paintings featuring human figures, animals and plants, coats of arms and

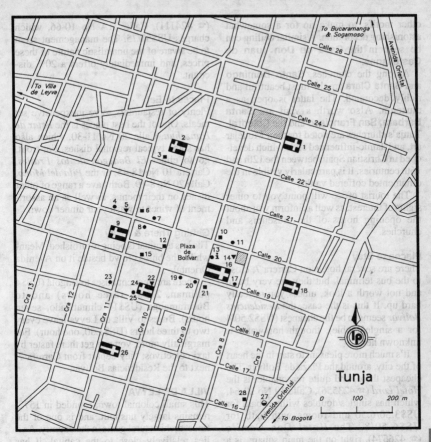

Tunja

To Bucaramanga & Sogamoso

To Villa de Leyva

To Bogotá

1	Iglesia de San Agustín	11	Casa de Don Juan de Vargas	19	Casa de Cambio
2	Iglesia de San Francisco	12	Hotel Don Camilo	20	Telecom
3	Hotel Hunza	13	Tourist Office & Casa del Fundador Suárez Rendón	21	Hotel San Francisco
4	Banco Popular			22	Restaurante El Bodegón de los Frailes
5	Restaurante Estar de Hunzahua	14	Restaurante Pila del Mono	23	Banco del Estado
6	Hostería San Carlos	15	Hotel Lord	24	Iglesia de San Ignacio
7	Banco de Bogotá	16	Catedral	25	Banco de Occidente
8	Banco Industrial Colombiano	17	Casa de Don Juan de Castellanos	26	Iglesia de Santa Bárbara
9	Iglesia de Santo Domingo	18	Iglesia de Santa Clara (Museum)	27	Bus Terminal
10	Hotel El Conquistador			28	Residencias Bolívar

other motifs, to make up for a somewhat astonishing decoration. A similar ceiling can be seen in the **Casa de Don Juan de Castellanos**.

Among the churches, **Santo Domingo** and **Santa Clara** are the most beautiful and richly decorated. The latter is open as a museum. Also worth a visit are **Santa Bárbara**, **San Francisco** and the **Catedral**. Tunja's churches are noted for their Mudejar art, an Islamic-influenced style which developed in Christian Spain between the 12th and 16th centuries. It is particularly visible in the ornamented coffered vaults.

The tourist office will point you to other sights of interest, as well as inform you about the opening hours of the museums and churches.

Places to Stay

There are several hotels on Carrera 7, close to the bus terminal, but they are very basic and not worth a look, unless you're really hard up. If this is the case, the *Residencias Bolívar* seems to be the cheapest (US$2.50/4 for a single/double), though hot water is unknown here.

It's much more pleasant to stay in the heart of the city, around the Plaza de Bolívar. The cheapest there, and quite reasonable, is the *Hotel Lord* (☎ 423556), Calle 19 No 10-64, which has singles/doubles without bath for US$3.50/6.50 and rooms with bath for US$6.50/8. The *Hotel Don Camilo* (☎ 426574), right on the main square, is a small, family-run place. It has rooms without bath for US$4.50/7.

The slightly unkempt *Hotel El Conquistador* (☎ 423534), Calle 20 No 8-92, has large rooms without bath for US$7/11, a bit too much for what it offers. For marginally more, the *Hotel San Francisco* (☎ 426645), Carrera 9 No 18-90, has smaller rooms but with bath attached. All the hotels listed have hot water in the morning only.

Going up the price scale, there's the pleasant (if perhaps overrated) *Hostería San Carlos* (☎ 423716), Carrera 11 No 20-12, for US$16/24. However, the town record in overpricing is held by the *Hotel Hunza*

(☎ 424111), Calle 21A No 10-66, which charges US$55/75. The management seem to be aware of the unrealistic nature of these prices, and immediately offers a 20% discount.

Places to Eat

Plenty of restaurants serve inexpensive set meals. One of the best places is the *Estar de Hunzahua*, Calle 20 No 11-30, which also has some typical regional dishes. For trout, go to either *El Bodegón de los Frailes*, Carrera 10 No 18-45, or the *Pila del Mono*, Calle 20 No 8-19. Both have a range of other dishes on their menus, as well as an assortment of wines to wash your dinner down.

Getting There & Away

The bus terminal is being refurbished. Meanwhile, the buses crowd beside it on Avenida Oriental.

There are frequent buses to Bogotá (US$4 pullman, 2½ to three hours) and to Bucaramanga (US$11 climatizado, seven hours). Buses to Villa de Leyva leave every two to three hours (US$1.50, one hour). For marginally more, you can get there faster by taxi colectivos; they depart from Carrera 7, next to the Residencias Bolívar.

VILLA DE LEYVA

This small colonial town, founded in 1572, remains largely unspoilt, and is one of the finest architectural gems in the country. As it lies relatively close to the capital, it has become a trendy weekend spot for Bogotanos. This has made the town somewhat artificial, with a noticeably split personality – on weekdays, it is a quiet, sleepy, old-style village, but on weekends and holidays, it comes alive, crammed with tourists and their cars. It's up to you to choose which of the town's faces you prefer, but don't miss it.

Information

Tourist Office The tourist office (☎ 411), at the corner of the main square, is open Tuesday to Sunday from 10 am to 1 pm and 2 to 6 pm. The staff is friendly and knowledgeable.

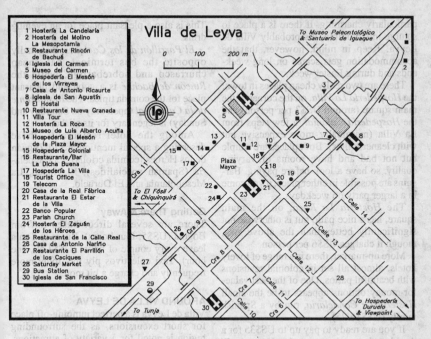

Villa de Leyva

1 Hostería La Candelaria
2 Hostería del Molino La Mesopotamia
3 Restaurante Rincón de Bachué
4 Iglesia del Carmen
5 Museo del Carmen
6 Hospedería El Mesón de los Virreyes
7 Casa de Antonio Ricaurte
8 Iglesia de San Agustín
9 El Hostal
10 Restaurante Nueva Granada
11 Villa Tour
12 Hostería La Roca
13 Museo de Luis Alberto Acuña
14 Hospedería El Mesón de la Plaza Mayor
15 Hospedería Colonial
16 Restaurante/Bar La Dicha Buena
17 Hospedería La Villa
18 Tourist Office
19 Telecom
20 Casa de la Real Fábrica
21 Restaurante El Estar de la Villa
22 Banco Popular
23 Parish Church
24 Hostería El Zaguán de los Héroes
25 Restaurante de la Calle Real
26 Casa de Antonio Nariño
27 Restaurante El Parrillón de los Caciques
28 Saturday Market
29 Bus Station
30 Iglesia de San Francisco

Money Come prepared, as you can't change cash or travellers' cheques in Villa de Leyva. The Banco Popular, on the main square, may accept your Visa card.

Things to See
The **Plaza Mayor** is an impressive central square, different from any other, paved with massive cobbed stones and lined with white-washed colonial houses. Drop in to the **parish church**, on the square, and to the **Iglesia del Carmen**, a block away; both have interesting interiors. Opposite the latter church is a good museum of religious art, the **Museo El Carmen**, open only on Saturdays and Sundays from 10 am to 1 pm and 2 to 6 pm.

Some of the historic mansions have been converted into museums and are open to the public. The **Museo de Luis Alberto Acuña**, on the main square, contains various works of this painter, sculptor, writer and historian. Other places worth visiting include the **Casa de Antonio Nariño**, in the house where this forefather of independence lived; the **Casa de Antonio Ricaurte**, the home of another national hero; and the **Museo Paleontológico**, one km out of town on the road to Arcabuco, displaying fossils collected in the region and dating from the period when the area was a seabed (some 100 to 150 million years ago). Most museums are open Wednesday to Sunday from 10 am to 1 pm and 3 to 6 pm.

Give yourself a couple of hours to wander about the charming cobbled streets, and climb the hill behind the Hospedería Duruelo for a marvellous bird's-eye view of the town. Inspect handicrafts shops noted for fine basketry and good-quality woven items, such as sweaters and ruanas. The market on Saturday is very colourful.

Places to Stay
The town has over a score of places to stay, and except for the bottom end, the hotels are

particularly charming. If there is a place to splurge in Colombia, it's probably Villa de Leyva. Keep in mind, however, that the accommodation gets scarce on long weekends and during Easter week.

There are two really cheap places in town: the *Hospedería La Villa*, on the corner of the main square (around US$3 per person) and the *Hospedería Colonial*, a few steps from La Villa (marginally more expensive but with cleaner toilets). Both places are simple but not bad and have rooms of varying quality, so have a look before paying. Bargains are possible in either place, if you come in a larger party on weekdays.

The *Hostería La Roca*, on the main square, has a nice patio but is otherwise not significantly better than the above two, though it charges US$6 per person.

More up-market, there is a range of lovely hotels, almost all set in colonial mansions with beautiful patios. One of the best value-for-money options appears to be the small *Hostería La Candelaria*, run by a Spanish family (US$16/25).

If you are ready to pay up to US$35 for a double, choose between the *Hostería El Zaguán de los Héroes* (☎ 476), the *Hospedería El Mesón de la Plaza Mayor* (☎ 425), *El Hostal* (☎ 668) and the *Hospedería El Mesón de los Virreyes* (☎ 497). All are atmospheric places with an old colonial flavour.

At the top of the range, you have the slightly unkempt *Hostería del Molino La Mesopotamia* (☎ 235), installed in an amazing 400-year-old flour mill; and the beautifully cared for, hacienda-style *Hospedería Duruelo* (☎ 222). They both charge about US$35/50, and both have excellent restaurants.

Places to Eat

A rash of restaurants has opened in Villa de Leyva over the past few years, so there's a lot to choose from. The cheapest set meals (US$1.50) are probably to be found in the *Nueva Granada*. For about US$2, you'll get better almuerzos and comidas at *El Estar de la Villa*. Tasty vegetarian dishes, though a bit expensive, are served at *La Dicha Buena*.

This is also a pleasant place for an evening drink.

El Parrillón de los Caciques, diagonally opposite the bus terminal, has cheap churrasco and sobrebarriga, while the *Rincón de Bachué* is a good and pleasant place for the comida típica. The *Restaurante de la Calle Real* (open only on Saturday and Sunday) is legendary for its ajiaco.

Among the hotel restaurants, those deserving a special mention are El Zaguán de los Héroes (comida criolla), La Candelaria (Spanish specialities), El Hostal, La Mesopotamia and El Duruelo.

Getting There & Away

There are several direct buses to/from Bogotá (US$5, four hours). Buses to Tunja leave every couple of hours (US$1.50, one hour). Taxi colectivos ply this route more frequently and charge a bit more.

AROUND VILLA DE LEYVA

Villa de Leyva is a perfect jumping-off place for short excursions, as the surrounding region is noted for a variety of attractions. Fossil hunters will also be happy, for the region abounds in fossils.

You can move around the area on foot, and use some local buses. The Villa Tour agency, on the main square in Villa de Leyva, operates chiva tours, providing an easy way of visiting some of the sights. The 3½-hour tours depart on Saturday and Sunday, and on request on weekdays if there are at least six people. If you want to visit the area's attractions on your own, the tourist office will give you details on sights and their opening hours, and public transport to get there.

El Fósil

This is a reasonably complete fossil of a kronosaurus, a prehistoric marine reptile vaguely resembling a crocodile, about 110 million years old. It is off the road to Chiquinquirá, six km from Villa de Leyva. You can walk there by a path in one hour, or the Chiquinquirá buses will drop you one km from El Fósil.

El Infiernito

About two km from El Fósil, this recently uncovered astronomic observatory of the Muiscas was also a ritual site of the Indians, notable for a number of large, phallic stone monoliths.

Convento del Santo Ecce Homo

This convent, founded in 1620, is a large stone and adobe construction with a lovely patio. Look out for fossils in the floor and in the base of a statue in the chapel. The convent is 13 km from Villa de Leyva. The morning bus to Santa Sofía will drop you a 15-minute walk from the convent.

Ráquira

A small village 25 km from Villa de Leyva, Ráquira is known for its pottery, which is some of the best in Colombia. You can see and buy a great variety of pottery, ranging from excellent kitchen utensils to fine copies of indigenous pots. There are several small workshops in the village where you can see the production process. There are a hotel and a restaurant on the main square, if you wish to stay longer. Two buses daily run between Villa de Leyva and Ráquira.

La Candelaria

This tiny hamlet, seven km beyond Ráquira, is famous for the Monasterio de la Candelaria, founded in 1597 by the Augustinians. Part of it is open to the public; the young monks will show you around. The *Parador La Candelaria*, close to the monastery, is a nice place to stay and eat. Only two buses a day call at La Candelaria. Otherwise, walk by a short cut from Ráquira (one hour).

Santuario de Iguaque

About 15 km north-east of Villa de Leyva, at an altitude of some 3600 metres, is a group of eight small lakes, including the Laguna de Iguaque, which was a sacred lake of the Muiscas. The area was declared a natural reserve and is run by Inderena. At the spacious visitors' centre, a couple of km off the Villa de Leyva-Arcabuco road, you can stay in a dormitory for US$6. From the centre, it's a leisurely three-hour walk uphill to the Iguaque Lake. You can get your permit and book accommodation at the Inderena office in Bogotá, or in the park.

SAN GIL

This 300-year-old town, on the main Bogotá-Bucaramanga road, is worth a stop to see El Gallineral, a riverside park where the trees are covered with *barbas de viejo* (long silvery fronds of tillandsia that form spectacular transparent curtains of foliage). San Gil also has a pleasant main square with huge old ceibas and an 18th-century cathedral.

If you stop here, make a short trip to Barichara, a fascinating small colonial town nearby (see below).

Places to Stay

There are several basic residencias. Try, for example, *Iskala*, Calle 10 No 10-41, or *San Gil*, Carrera 11 No 11-25, where you won't pay more than US$3 per person. If you need something better, *Alcantuz*, Carrera 11 No 10-15, has clean singles/doubles with bath (US$10/15). The best place is the *Hotel Bella Isla*, out of town, off the road to Bucaramanga.

Places to Eat

Plenty of budget restaurants around the cheap residencias serve basic meals. If you visit El Gallineral, there's an agreeable restaurant in the park, with typical food at reasonable prices.

Getting There & Away

All the bus companies are in the recently built bus terminal. Frequent buses run north and south along the main road. There are buses to Bucaramanga (US$3, 2½ hours) and to Bogotá (US$12, 7½ hours). Cotrasangil operates half-hourly minibuses to/from Bucaramanga (US$4, two hours). Buses to Barichara leave every hour or two.

BARICHARA

Barichara is a small 250-year-old town founded on Guane Indian territory. It's surprisingly well preserved and maintained.

COLOMBIA

The streets are paved with massive stone slabs and lined with fine single-storey houses. Although there are no particular sights to see, the town's charm lies in its beauty as a whole, and its lazy old-world atmosphere.

From Barichara, you might want to visit the tiny village of Guane, 10 km away. It has a fine rural church, and a museum with a collection of locally found fossils and Guane Indian artefacts. There's no reliable transport, except for a morning *lechero* (milk truck), so you may have to walk, by road (a good two hours) or by the path (which shortens a long bend of the road and takes half an hour less). Ask for directions, or tag on to a local.

Places to Stay & Eat
There are several hotels in Barichara, including the *Hotel Coratá*, Carrera 7 No 4-02, close to the main square, which also has a restaurant. There are a couple more cheap restaurants around the square.

The most comfortable accommodation in town is in the *Hostal Misión Santa Bárbara*, Calle 5 No 9-12. It's in a tastefully refurbished old colonial house, and meals are available for guests.

Getting There & Away
There are several buses daily between Barichara and San Gil (US$1, one hour).

BUCARAMANGA
Bucaramanga, the capital of Santander Department, is a fairly modern, busy commercial and industrial centre with a very agreeable climate. It is noted for its cigars and the famous hormiga culona, a large ant which is fried and eaten.

There is not much to do here, but it may be a stopover on the long route from Bogotá to Santa Marta or Cúcuta. If so, take a side trip to Girón, 10 km away (see below).

In the city itself, you can visit the **Casa de Bolívar**, which contains the Museums of Ethnography and History (open Tuesday to Friday from 8 am to noon and 2 to 6 pm, and on Saturday from 9 am to 1 pm), and have a

walk in the **Jardín Botánico Eloy Valenzuela**, in the Bucarica suburb, open daily from 8 to 11 am and 2 to 5 pm. To get there, take the Bucarica bus from Carrera 15, in the city centre.

Information
Tourist Office The office is in the Hotel Bucarica, at the corner of Carrera 19 and Calle 35.

Money Banks which might deal with your cash, travellers' cheques and credit cards (Visa or Mastercard) are marked on the Bucaramanga city map; they are packed within a small central area. Shop around, as the rate varies from one to another.

Venezuelan Consulate The Venezuelan Consulate (☎ 476872) is at Carrera 35 No 54-54.

1	Hotel Elena
2	Residencias Amparo
3	Residencias ABC
4	Hotel Tamaná
5	Parque Centenario
6	Banco Sudameris Colombia
7	Restaurante El Consulado Antioqueño
8	Market
9	Banco Unión Colombiano
10	Hotel Balmoral
11	Banco Popular
12	Hotel Morgan No 2
13	Hotel Morgan No 1
14	Banco Industrial Colombiano
15	Tourist Office & Hotel Bucarica
16	Parque Santander
17	Banco de Colombia
18	Banco de Bogotá
19	Colectivos to Airport
20	Telecom
21	Restaurante El Paisa
22	Catedral
23	Banco de Occidente
24	Banco Anglo Colombiano
25	Capilla de los Dolores
26	Parque García Rovira
27	Casa de Bolívar
28	Avianca & Post Office

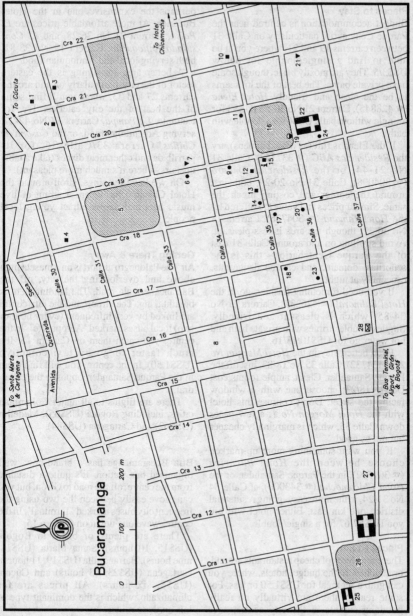

Bucaramanga

To Hotel Chicamocha

To Cúcuta

To Santa Marta & Cartagena

To Bus Terminal, Airport, Girón & Bogotá

Cra 22
Cra 21
Cra 20
Cra 19
Cra 18
Cra 17
Cra 16
Cra 15
Cra 14
Cra 13
Cra 12
Cra 11

Calle 30
Calle 31
Calle 33
Calle 34
Calle 35
Calle 36
Calle 37

Seca
Quebrada
Avenida

200 m
100
0

COLOMBIA

Places to Stay

Budget accommodation is centred near the Parque Centenario, particularly on Calle 31 between carreras 19 and 21, where you'll be able to find a single/double for below US$3/5. They are mostly basic, though some have private baths. The best of the lot seems to be the clean and friendly *Hotel Elena* (☎ 428845), Carrera 21 No 30-55 (US$3 for a single without bath, US$6 for a double with bath).

If the Elena is full (as often happens), try the *Residencias ABC* (☎ 337352), Calle 31 No 21-44, or the *Residencias Amparo* (☎ 304098), Calle 31 No 20-29, both just around the corner, and costing much the same. Similar prices and value are offered by the *Hotel Tamaná* (☎ 304726), Carrera 18 No 30-31, though the area is less pleasant. Avoid strolling on and around Calle 31 east of the Parque Centenario – this is the señoritas' domain, and can be dangerous, especially at night.

If you need something flashier, go to the *Hotel Balmoral* (☎ 426232), Carrera 21 No 34-85, which is pleasant and friendly. Singles/doubles/triples with private bath and hot water go for US$10/13/16.

Even better, stay in the *Hotel Morgan No 2* (☎ 424732), Calle 35 No 18-83, just off the Parque Santander. Clean, ample rooms cost US$13/18/23; choose one with a window facing the street. Don't confuse this hotel with the *Hotel Morgan No 1*, a few paces down Calle 35, which is marginally cheaper but not as good.

If you want something more up-market, choose between the *Hotel Bucarica* (☎ 301592), in the Parque Santander, and the *Hotel Chicamocha* (☎ 343000), at Calle 34 No 31-24, in the more easy-going residential district, one km east. Either hotel will bill you US$57/67 for a single/double.

Places to Eat

There are plenty of cheap restaurants around, or attached to, the budget hotels, where you can grab a set meal for US$1.50 or less. For some reason, there are virtually no really good restaurants in the city centre, save perhaps the expensive one in the Hotel Bucarica. At more affordable prices are *El Paisa*, Carrera 21 No 36-28, and *El Consulado Antioqueño*, Carrera 19 No 33-81, both serving local and Antioquian food.

A better area for dining is the eastern sector of the city, particularly on and around carreras 27 and 33, where you'll find some of the best of the city eateries. Try, for example, *La Pampa*, Carrera 27 No 42-27, serving Argentinian food, or the *Casona de Chiflas*, Carrera 33/Calle 36, for its parrillada and other meat dishes (take a table upstairs, where it's much more pleasant).

On weekend evenings, stroll around the Hotel Chicamocha, where a string of live music bars and discos attract young local people.

Getting There & Away

Air The Palonegro airport is on a meseta high above and overlooking the city, off the Barrancabermeja road. The landing here is breathtaking. The airport and the city centre are linked by very infrequent (every hour or two) local buses marked 'Aeropuerto'. In the centre, you catch them on Carrera 15. It's much faster to go by taxi colectivo (US$1.50). In the centre, you will find them in the Parque Santander, opposite the cathedral.

There are flights to all major Colombian cities, including Bogotá (US$65), Medellín (US$62) and Cartagena (US$84).

Bus Bucaramanga has a brand-new, well organised bus station. It's quite a distance from the centre, off the road to Girón, but you can move easily between the two using the frequent city buses marked 'Terminal'. In the centre, wave one down on Carrera 15.

There are plenty of buses to Bogotá (US$15, 10 hours), Santa Marta (US$18, nine hours), Barranquilla (US$19, 11 hours), Cartagena (US$23, 13 hours) and Cúcuta (US$8, six hours). All prices are for climatizado, which is the dominant type of bus on these routes.

GIRÓN

Girón, founded in 1631, is a small town whose colonial character has been preserved almost intact. It's a nice place to stroll around for a couple of hours, looking at the fine houses, charming patios, a few small bridges, the **Catedral** and the **Capilla de las Nieves**. Also drop into the **Mansión del Fraile**, on the main square, which has a museum displaying objects related to the town's history. It was closed recently but may reopen in the future.

The town has become a trendy place, and is the home of several artists. Due to its proximity to the city, Girón fills up with Bucaramangans at weekends.

Places to Stay

Girón is just a day trip from Bucaramanga, but if you wish to stay longer, there is the good and pleasant *Hotel Las Nieves* (☎ 468968), on the main square. It has large, comfortable rooms – most with three beds – apparently intended for well-off families and charging accordingly (US$30 to US$40 per room). If you travel in a large party, or on weekdays, when the hotel is half empty, they may charge you less.

A cheaper alternative is the *Hotel Río de Oro*, also on the main square. It's a poorly kept, slowly decaying old mansion with a certain old-world charm. The price seems to be negotiable; count on around US$10 per double and not much more if you are in a group of four or five.

Places to Eat

Antón García, Calle 29 No 24-47, and *El Carajo*, Carrera 25 No 28-08, are two places for cheap food. More up-market are *La Casona*, Calle 28 No 27-47, and *Mansión del Fraile*, on the main square, both pleasant and serving good, typical food.

Try the Santanderian speciality, the mute, a thick soup made from peeled maize with pork or beef, potatoes and other vegetables. It's served by most of the restaurants but, curiously, only on Sundays.

Getting There & Away

There are frequent city buses from Carrera 15 in Bucaramanga, which will deposit you on the main square of Girón in half an hour.

CÚCUTA

Unless you're travelling to or from Venezuela, there's little reason to come here, as the city doesn't have much to offer tourists.

If you do pass through Cúcuta and have a couple of hours to spare, visit the **Museo de Arte e Historia de Cúcuta**, Calle 14 No 1-03, which has an extensive private collection of objects relating to the town's history. It's open Tuesday to Saturday from 8 am to noon and 2 to 6 pm.

Outside the city, on the way to the border, about 10 km from Cúcuta, is **Villa del Rosario**. This is where the Gran Colombia was born, in 1821. The central park, on the main road, contains several historic buildings, including the Casa de Santander and the Templo del Congreso. The Casa de la Bagatela, across the road, houses a modest archaeological collection.

Information

Tourist Office The tourist office (☎ 713395) is at Calle 10 No 0-30.

Money At the time of writing, no banks in Cúcuta were interested in changing cash dollars, and only the Banco del Estado and Banco Industrial Colombiano changed travellers' cheques. Other banks marked on the Cúcuta city map may give advances on Visa or MasterCard.

Plenty of casas de cambio, at the bus terminal and in the city centre, change dollars, pesos and *bolívares* in any direction. There's also a rash of casas de cambio in San Antonio, paying much the same as in Cúcuta.

Venezuelan Consulate The Venezuelan Consulate is on the corner of Calle 8 and Avenida 0. The office is officially open Monday to Friday from 8 am to 3 pm but is closed for almuerzo. Regardless of your nationality, you do need a visa for an overland crossing to Venezuela.

COLOMBIA

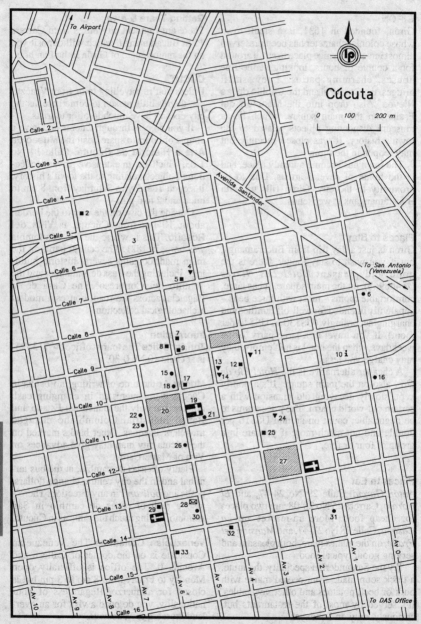

Cúcuta

0   100   200 m

1	Bus Terminal
2	Hotel Casa Real
3	Market
4	Restaurante Vegetariano Salud y Vida
5	Hotel Don Paco
6	Venezuelan Consulate
7	Hotel Daytona
8	Hotel Colonial
9	Hotel Central
10	Tourist Office
11	Restaurante Don Pancho
12	Hotel La Bastilla
13	Restaurante Doña Pepa
14	Restaurante La Mazorca
15	Banco del Estado
16	Telecom (Main Office)
17	Hotel Amaruc
18	Banco de Colombia
19	Catedral
20	Parque Santander
21	Banco de Occidente
22	Banco Industrial Colombiano
23	Banco de Bogotá
24	Restaurante Mi Cabaña
25	Hotel Su Familia
26	Banco Popular
27	Parque Colón
28	Avianca & Post Office
29	Hotel Louis
30	Telecom
31	Museo de Arte e Historia de Cúcuta
32	Hotel Internacional
33	Hotel Casa Blanca

This is apparently the only Venezuelan consulate in Colombia which issues visas for non-Colombians. You need your passport and one photo, and you have to fill a form. The visa costs US$30. You may be lucky enough to get it the same afternoon – start queuing early, because you pay the fee at the bank (not at the consulate), and this can only be done before 11 am.

The visa is supposedly given for a 30-day stay, but this seems to be up to the whim of the officials.

Immigration The DAS office in Cúcuta (where you have to get an exit/entry stamp in your passport) is at Avenida 1 No 28-57, on the opposite side of the city from the bus terminal. Take the city bus marked 'San Rafael', or a taxi. Taxi drivers wait at the bus terminal for incoming tourists, to take them to the DAS office and then straight to the DIEX office in San Antonio, across the border (for a fat fare, naturally). It works out much cheaper to take a taxi from the terminal to the DAS office, then go by colectivo or bus to San Antonio.

The DAS office is theoretically open daily from 8 am to noon and 2 to 8 pm. If you fly into Cúcuta and head straight to Venezuela, you can have your passport stamped at the airport. The DAS authorities were planning to open their check post on the border, so check for news.

The DIEX office in San Antonio is on Carrera 9, between calles 6 and 7, and is open daily from 6 am to 9 pm. This is where you have your passport stamped when leaving or entering Venezuela.

Places to Stay

There are plenty of residencias around the bus terminal, particularly along Avenida 7, but they range from basic to ultrabasic. Most double as love hotels, and some are genuine brothels. The area is far from attractive and gets dangerous at night. The only positive comment which can be made about these hotels is that they are cheap, and you can find a single/double for less than US$3/4. The *Hotel Casa Real* (☎ 728932), Avenida 7 No 4-45, is one of the few acceptable places. Doubles with bath and fan go for US$4.50.

It's safer and much more pleasant to stay in the city centre, though hotels there are not as cheap. All those listed below have rooms with fans and private bath. Among the cheapest, at US$4/6 for a single/double, are the *Hotel Central* (☎ 713673), on the corner of Avenida 5 and Calle 9, and the *Hotel Su Familia* (☎ 710354), Avenida 3 No 11-41. For a dollar more, you have a range of fairly decent places, including *Hotel La Bastilla* (☎ 712576), Avenida 3 No 9-42, *Hotel Daytona* (☎ 717927), Avenida 5 No 8-57, and perhaps the best for that price, *Hotel Colonial* (☎ 712661), Avenida 5 No 8-62.

If you are prepared to pay some US$7/13 for a single/double, there's possibly nothing

COLOMBIA

better in town than the *Hotel Internacional* (☎ 712718), Calle 14 No 4-13, which has spacious clean rooms, a fine patio and a swimming pool.

If you need somewhere with air-conditioning at a reasonable price, choose between the *Hotel Louis* (☎ 730598), at the corner of Avenida 6 and Calle 13, and *Hotel Don Paco* (☎ 731902), Calle 7 No 4-44. Both cost around US$10/14; the latter is more pleasant, though but the surrounding area isn't.

The *Hotel Amaruc* (☎ 717625), overlooking the main square from the corner of Avenida 5 and Calle 10, and the *Hotel Casa Blanca* (☎ 721455), Avenida 6 No 14-55, are options for those who don't need to count every peso. Both have good singles/doubles with air-conditioning for US$25/32. In both hotels, ask for a room on one of the upper floors.

Places to Eat

There are several cheap restaurants around the corner of Calle 9 and Avenida 6, but nothing terrific. Better set meals, and local specialities are served at *Doña Pepa*, Avenida 4 No 9-59, or next door, at *La Mazorca*. The *Don Pancho*, Avenida 3 No 9-21, does good parrillada and cabrito al vino at reasonable prices. For vegetarians, the *Salud y Vida*, on Avenida 4, is the budget place to go, while the pleasant restaurant on the top floor of the Hotel Amaruc has vegetarian food at more up-market prices. *Mi Cabaña*, Calle 11 No 2-53, is one of the best restaurants in town, noted particularly for its churrasco and róbalo (a kind of fish).

Getting There & Away

Air The airport is five km from the centre; city buses, which you catch on Avenida 3 in the centre, will drop you nearby. There are flights to all major Colombian cities, including Bogotá (US$82), Medellín (US$76), Cartagena (US$78) and San Andrés (US$141). There are no direct flights to Venezuela – you must go to San Antonio, the Venezuelan town on the border, 12 km from Cúcuta. (rrrSee under San Antonio del Táchira in the Venezuela chapter.)

Bus The bus terminal is on the corner of Avenida 7 and Calle 1. It's very dirty and very busy – one of the poorest in Colombia. Watch your belongings closely. If you come from Venezuela, you may be approached by well-dressed English-speaking gentlemen who will offer their help in buying the bus ticket for you. Ignore them – they are conmen. Buy your ticket directly from the bus office.

There are frequent buses to Bucaramanga (US$8, six hours). At least a dozen air-conditioned buses daily run to Bogotá (US$23, 16 hours).

Heading to Venezuela, there are no direct buses to Caracas, but plenty of buses and shared taxis run from Cúcuta's bus terminal to San Antonio (US$0.30 and US$0.50 respectively, paid in either pesos or bolivares).

Caribbean Coast

The Colombian Caribbean coast stretches over 1600 km from the dense jungles of the Darién Gap, on the border with Panama, to the desert of La Guajira in the east, near Venezuela. To the south, the region extends to the foot of the Andes. Administratively, the area falls into seven departments: Guajira, Cesar, Magdalena, Atlántico, Bolívar, Sucre and Córdoba.

The coast is steeped in sun, rum and tropical music. Its inhabitants, the costeños (predominantly mulatos), are an easy-going, fun-loving people who give the coast a touch of carnival atmosphere.

Special attractions include the Islas del Rosario, with their magnificent coral reefs. You can take it easy on the beach – the best are supposedly in the Parque Nacional Tayrona. Cartagena is one of the most beautiful colonial cities in Latin America, and the town of Mompós is a small architectural gem. There's also La Ciudad Perdida, the ancient lost city of the Tayronas, hidden deep in the lush tropical forest on the slopes of the Sierra Nevada de Santa Marta. Some travellers report both the site itself and the trek to get there as their most memorable experiences in Colombia.

SANTA MARTA

Founded in 1525, Santa Marta is the oldest surviving town in Colombia, though its colonial character has virtually disappeared. Today, it is the capital of Magdalena Department. The climate is hot, but the sea breeze, especially in the evening, cools the city, making it agreeable to wander about, or sit over a beer in any of the numerous open-air waterfront cafés. Santa Marta has become a popular tourist centre, not for the city itself but for its surroundings. Nearby El Rodadero is one of Colombia's most fashionable beach resorts, though its beach and water are getting dangerously polluted by the Santa Marta port.

Don't miss out on trips to Taganga and the Parque Nacional Tayrona. Santa Marta is also the place to arrange a tour to Ciudad Perdida.

Information

Tourist Office The departmental tourist office (☎ 212425) is in the former Convent of Santo Domingo, Carrera 2 No 16-44. It's open Monday to Friday from 8 am to noon and 2 to 6 pm.

The CNT tourist office is in El Rodadero, in a kiosk on the beach at the outlet of Calle 8. It's open daily from 7.30 am to 6 pm.

Money The Banco Popular and the Banco Industrial Colombiano will change your travellers' cheques and cash. Other banks marked on the map deal only with credit cards.

Things to See

There is a very good museum, the **Museo Arqueológico Tayrona**, in the Casa de la Aduana, at the corner of Calle 14 and Carrera 2, open Monday to Friday from 8 am to noon and 2 to 6 pm. It has an excellent collection of Tayrona objects, mainly in pottery and gold. Don't miss the model of Ciudad Perdida, especially if you plan on visiting the place.

The **Quinta de San Pedro Alejandrino** is in the far suburb of Mamatoco (take the Mamatoco bus from the waterfront to get there). This is the hacienda where Simón Bolívar spent his last days and died, and is today a national monument. The **Museo Bolivariano**, built on the grounds, features contemporary art donated by artists from Colombia, Venezuela, Panama, Ecuador, Peru and Bolivia, the countries liberated by Bolívar. The Quinta is open daily from 9.30 am to 4.30 pm (it may be closed on Tuesday in the off season); entry is US$1.50.

The **Catedral**, a large, whitewashed building on the corner of Carrera 4 and Calle 17, is supposedly the oldest church in Colombia, but the work was not actually completed until the end of the 18th century. It holds the ashes of the founder, Rodrigo de Bastidas (just to the left as you enter the church).

If you've read the *Fruit Palace*, by Charles Nicholl, you might like to know that the famous Palacio de las Frutas which gave the name to the book was at Calle 10C No 2-49. It no longer exists; now it's the Tienda El Progreso.

Places to Stay

The *Hotel Miramar* (☎ 214756), Calle 10C No 1C-59, is an exceptional place. Not only does it offer the cheapest accommodation in town, but it also has a better range of tourist facilities and information than you'll find in virtually any other budget hotel in Colombia. No wonder it has become the archetypal gringo hotel, where you're likely to meet the majority of foreign backpackers passing through the town. It's obviously not a Hilton, but has acceptable rooms with fan (some with private bath) for about US$1.50 per person. If the rooms are full, the manager can give you a hammock or a mattress (either for US$1), or find somewhere for you. If you have your own hammock, you can string it up for a nominal charge.

The manager organises treks to Ciudad Perdida and runs tours to the Parque Nacio-

Santa Marta

0   100   200 m

To El Rodadero, Airport & Barranquilla

To Bus Terminal

COLOMBIA

nal Tayrona in his own chiva (see the appropriate sections for details). He will store gear free of charge.

If you find the Miramar too noisy, too jovial or too freak-filled, go to the *Casa Familiar* (☎ 211697), Calle 10C No 2-14, a few steps from the Miramar. It's smaller, quieter and costs US$2 per person in rooms with bath. It's also popular with gringos.

If you need more comfort (but less atmosphere), there are several fairly good, modern places on the waterfront (Carrera 1C). In ascending order of price (and possibly value) they are: the *Sol Hotel Inn*

(☎ 211131), Carrera 1C No 20-23, at US$8/10, the *Park Hotel* (☎ 211215), Carrera 1C No 18-67, at US$9/12, the *Hostal Miramar* (☎ 214751), at US$12/16 (don't confuse it with the abovementioned Hotel Miramar), and the *Hotel Sompallón* (☎ 214195), on the corner of Carrera 1C and Calle 10C, at US$10/18.

For something with more individual style, go to the *Hotel Tayrona Mar* (☎ 212408), Carrera 1C No 11-41, in an old house with a fine wooden interior and beautiful decorative tiling. It costs US$8 per person in a room with bath. The *Hotel Yuldama* (☎ 210063),

■ PLACES TO STAY

1 Hotel Sompallón
2 Hotel Miramar
3 Casa Familiar
4 Hotel Tayrona Mar
6 Hotel Yuldama
20 Hostal Miramar
21 Park Hotel
22 Sol Hotel Inn

▼ PLACES TO EAT

5 Restaurante La Casa Vieja
7 Restaurante Rincón Paisa
19 Restaurante Panamerican

OTHER

8 Iglesia de San Francisco
9 Telecom
10 Museo Arqueológico Tayrona
11 Banco Industrial Colombiano
12 Banco de Bogotá
13 Banco de Colombia
14 Banco Popular
15 Banco de Occidente
16 Tourist Office
17 Catedral
18 Avianca & Post Office
23 Inderena

Carrera 1C No 12-19, is the top-end place in the area (US$22/30/35 a single/double/triple).

Places to Eat

There are a lot of cheap restaurants around the Hotel Miramar, particularly on calles 11 and 12 near the waterfront, where you can get an unsophisticated set meal for about US$1.25. The *Rincón Paisa*, next to the Hotel Yuldama, and *La Casa Vieja*, Calle 12 No 1C-58, perhaps have tastier food than their neighbours.

The waterfront (Carrera 1C) is packed with restaurants offering almost anything from snacks and pizzas to local cuisine and seafood. The *Panamerican*, on the corner of Calle 18, is one of the best places.

Several thatched restaurants between calles 26 and 28, close to the beach, are noted

for good fish. Choose between the *Terraza Marina* and *El Gran Manuel*.

Getting There & Away

Air The airport is 16 km out of the city on the road to Barranquilla. City buses marked 'El Rodadero Aeropuerto' will take you there from Carrera 1C (45 minutes).

There are flights to Bogotá (US$112), Medellín (US$87) and Cúcuta (US$79).

Bus The small, poor bus terminal is on the corner of Carrera 8 and Calle 24, a 10-minute walk from the seafront. Half a dozen air-conditioned buses daily run to Bogotá (US$33, 19 hours). Plenty of buses go to Barranquilla (US$2.50, two hours). Frequent buses depart for Riohacha; take any of these to get to the Parque Nacional Tayrona.

A new terminal is under construction on the south-eastern outskirts of the city.

AROUND SANTA MARTA
Taganga

Taganga is a small fishing village set in a beautiful bay, five km north of Santa Marta. The waterfront is packed with boats and is worth a stroll. Boat excursions along the coast can be arranged with locals, or you can walk around the surrounding hills, which offer splendid views. Don't miss the Playa Grande, a magnificent bay north-west of the village. Either walk there (20 minutes) or take a boat from Taganga (US$0.50). The beach is lined with palm-thatched restaurants serving good fish. You can walk further along the coast on a path which winds the slopes of the hilly coast up to the Playa Granate.

There's a choice of accommodation in Taganga. The best budget bet seems to be the *Hotel El Delfín* (US$4 per person). The *Hotel Playa Brava* offers more comfort (US$15 a double, US$20 with air-conditioning). The *Hotel La Ballena Azul* focuses on more affluent tourists (US$30 a double) and has a good (though not cheap) restaurant. All three hotels are on the waterfront.

Urban buses between Santa Marta and

COLOMBIA

Taganga run every 20 minutes; catch them on Carrera 1C in Santa Marta.

Parque Nacional Tayrona

This is supposedly the most popular national park in the country. It is set on the jungle-covered coast to the east of Santa Marta. The beaches in the park, set in deep bays and shaded with coconut palms, are probably the most lovely on the entire Colombian coast. Some are bordered by coral reefs, and snorkelling is good, but be careful of the treacherous offshore currents.

The region was once the territory of the Tayrona Indians, and some remains have been found in the park, the most important being the ruins of the ancient town of Pueblito.

The main entrance to the park is in El Zaíno, 35 km from Santa Marta on the coastal road to Riohacha. From El Zaíno, walk four km on a paved road to Cañaveral, on the shore. Here you'll find the administrative centre of the park, and Inderena's cabañas (US$30 for four people). Alternatively, pitch your tent in the camping ground. There is also a restaurant. For more spectacular beaches, walk 50 minutes along a well-marked trail to Arrecifes, where locals run cabañas, a camp site and restaurants, and also hire hammocks (about US$1.50).

From Arrecifes, you can walk to Pueblito in two hours along a path with splendid tropical forest scenery. There have been some cases of robbery on this route, so don't walk alone. Inderena organises free guided walks to Pueblito on Monday, Wednesday and Friday at 7.30 am. Inquire in the cabañas in Cañaveral.

Other spectacular sites in the park include Bahía Concha and Naguange, but they are difficult to get to, as there is no public transport. Tours from Santa Marta are organised by several travel agents. The Hotel Miramar runs the chiva to Bahía Concha and Cañaveral, and is the cheapest operator (US$6 return to either destination).

CIUDAD PERDIDA

La Ciudad Perdida, the Lost City, is one of the largest ancient towns discovered in the Americas. It was built by the Tayrona Indians between the 11th and 14th centuries, on the northern slopes of the Sierra Nevada de Santa Marta, and was most probably their biggest urban centre, supposedly a 'capital'. During the Conquest, the Spaniards burned the wooden dwellings of the Tayronas, leaving only the stone structures, which disappeared without trace under the lush tropical vegetation. So did Ciudad Perdida, until its discovery in 1975 by guaqueros (robbers of pre-Columbian tombs).

La Ciudad Perdida lies on the relatively steep slopes of the Buritaca Valley, at an altitude of between 1100 and 1300 metres. The central part of the city is set on a ridge, from which various paths lead down to other sectors on the slopes. There are about 150 stone terraces, which once served as foundations for the houses; most have been restored. Originally, the urban centre was completely cleared of trees, but it was reclaimed by the jungle. Today, the city has been cleared of forest, except for tall palms, which give a somewhat mysterious atmosphere to the ruins.

Getting There & Away

There are two ways of getting to Ciudad Perdida: a helicopter tour or a trek. Both begin from Santa Marta. The first takes less than three hours; the other takes five to seven days.

Helicopter Aviatur has irregular helicopter tours during the peak holiday seasons (Christmas and Easter), and sporadically at other times, if there's sufficient demand. It is a 20-minute flight from Santa Marta airport to Ciudad Perdida, followed by a two-hour guided visit and the return journey. In all, it takes about two hours and 40 minutes and costs US$225 per person. If you are captivated by this whirlwind speed, and are not deterred by the price, contact the Aviatur office in any of the major cities.

Trekking There are basically two trekking routes leading to the Lost City: through La

Tagua and Alto de Mira; and through El Mamey, up along the Río Buritaca. The sections between Santa Marta and La Tagua and between Santa Marta and El Mamey are done by jeep.

Both routes take about three days uphill to Ciudad Perdida, and two days back down, plus one day at the site. The La Tagua trail is more demanding, with up and downhill sections (the total walking time is about 18 hours), while the Río Buritaca route is shorter (about 13 hours altogether) but is mostly uphill.

Neither trail is very difficult, though much depends on the weather: if it's wet (as it is most of the year), the paths are pretty muddy. The only fairly dry period is from late December to February or early March. There are several creeks to cross on the way; be prepared to get you shoes wet.

There are about 15 official guides approved by Inderena in Santa Marta, and many unregistered guides without a licence. They all organise treks to Ciudad Perdida, either independently or under the auspices of travel agents, hotel owners or other sponsors. Most offer roughly the same conditions and facilities. They provide transport, food, accommodation (in hammocks), porters and guides, and arrange necessary permits. You carry your own personal belongings. Take a sleeping bag (the nights can be pretty cold), a torch, water container and insect repellent. Treks, in groups of up to 10 people, take five to seven days for the round trip. The route can be chosen by the group, though most guides prefer the Buritaca trail up and down, as it's easier, shorter and supposedly safer (there has been some occasional guerrilla activity on La Tagua trail). The total cost is somewhere between US$120 and US$180 per person, depending on the route, time, facilities, the number of people in the group, and the negotiating ability of both you and the guide.

Officially, visits to Ciudad Perdida are allowed in December and January, the Easter week and from June to August. At other times, Inderena doesn't give the permit; some independent guides have been known to run tours despite that, but there's always a risk that you won't be allowed into the site.

The major tour operator in Santa Marta is Jairo Portillo, the manager of the Hotel Miramar. He has the most frequent tours, using seven of the registered guides, and his tours are the cheapest.

Don't do this trip without a guide. Apart from the strictly practical reasons (you can easily get lost), the region is an important marijuana and coca-growing area. There are also guerrillas operating in the zone, though as yet they haven't shown much of a presence on the trails to Ciudad Perdida.

BARRANQUILLA

With a population of over a million, Barranquilla is Colombia's fourth largest city. It's the country's main seaport and an important industrial and commercial centre but doesn't have much to offer tourists. The biggest attraction is **El Carnaval de Barranquilla**, probably the most colourful and undoubtedly the maddest Colombian carnaval. During this four-day fiesta, which precedes Ash Wednesday (February or March), the whole city goes wild.

Other than that, there's little to look for here. Moreover, like every big city, Barranquilla can be unsafe. Its coastal neighbours, Santa Marta and Cartagena, are far more attractive places to hang around, and there's frequent transport to both of them.

If you happen to be in town and have some time to kill, go to the **Jardín Zoológico**, Calle 77 No 68-70, probably the best zoo in Colombia, though it is tightly packed into a small area. It's open daily.

The **Museo de Antropología**, at the corner of Calle 68 and Carrera 54, displays some fine pieces of pre-Columbian pottery from different regions.

Places to Stay

Most likely, you'll be in Barranquilla overnight on your way to somewhere else. In this case, stay close to the bus terminals, either in the centre (around Plaza de Bolívar) or near the corner of Calle 45 and Carrera 35, depending on where you are heading.

COLOMBIA

In the centre, the Paseo Bolívar and adjacent streets are the focus of budget accommodation. The whole sector is very noisy and busy during the day and not very safe at night.

The budget places here are mostly seedy, flash establishments that rent rooms by the hour, and some are really brothels. Try *El Famoso Hotel* (☎ 316513), Paseo Bolívar No 43-42, which is anything but famous and costs some US$3/4 for a single/double. One of the few places with style is the *Hotel Victoria* (☎ 410055), Calle 35 No 43-140. It is set in an old house with a fine façade, antique lift and spacious high corridors. Ample rooms with fan and bath cost US$6/9. Add US$3 if you want air-con.

The other area of bus offices, on Calle 45, is also circled by a range of budget residencias. The *Aparta Hotel Salerno* (☎ 516881), Calle 45 No 35-62, is perhaps the cheapest here (US$3 for a double bed). There are several other shabby joints around, for marginally more.

If this is not what you're after, there are two significantly better hotels in the area: the *Hotel Montecarlo* (☎ 413126), Calle 45 No 33-140 (US$8/11) and the *Hotel Canadiense* (☎ 415391), Calle 45 No 36-142 (US$12/18).

The best hotel in town is probably the *Hotel El Prado* (☎ 456533), Carrera 54 No 70-10, in a more elegant residential district north-west of the city centre. It has all you could possibly wish for, at around US$150/180.

Places to Eat

The central city area, along and off Paseo Bolívar, is full of cheap restaurants. You also can eat in the street or in the *market* – the centre is actually one huge market. Many stalls sell delicious arepas de huevo (a fried maize dough with an egg inside), the local speciality. You can get good fish in the market proper, towards the river; just point to the one you want and they will fry it in front of you.

The best restaurants, like the finest accommodation, are in the north-western sector of the city. The restaurant of the *Hotel El Prado* will not disappoint you, though it isn't cheap.

Two good and reasonably priced restaurants for typical food are *El Calderito*, Carrera 52 No 72-107, and *La Plaza*, Carrera 53 No 70-150 ; the latter also has a choice of Antioquian food.

Getting There & Away

Air The airport is about 10 km from the city and is connected to the centre by frequent urban buses. There are flights to all major Colombian cities: Bogotá (US$102), Medellín (US$86), Cali (US$118) and San Andrés (US$94).

Aerosucre (the cargo carrier) flies once or twice a week to the island of San Andrés. It occasionally takes passengers, for roughly half the commercial fare. The terminal is just before the main passenger terminal, on your right going towards the airport.

Copa, the Panamanian airline, has two flights a week to Panama (US$115 plus 19% Colombian tax). Lacsa, the carrier of Costa Rica, flies three times a week to Caracas (US$161 plus 19% tax).

Bus Barranquilla has no central bus terminal; bus companies have separate offices, which are grouped in two areas.

The companies which ply the coastal Cartagena-Barranquilla-Santa Marta route are all located on the Plaza de Bolívar, in the heart of the city. There's frequent transport to both Cartagena (US$3.50, three hours) and Santa Marta (US$2.50, two hours), but only till around 6 pm.

The companies which cover the long-distance inland routes are found on Calle 45, around Carrera 35. There are a dozen buses daily to Bogotá (US$34 climatizado, 20 hours) and more than 20 buses to Bucaramanga (US$19 climatizado, 10 hours). Buses to Medellín depart every hour or so (US$24 climatizado, 14 hours).

CARTAGENA

Cartagena de Indias is a legend, for both its history and its beauty. It is Colombia's most fascinating city, and an absolute must. Don't be in a hurry, as the charm of the city will keep you here for at least a few days.

Dating from 1533, Cartagena was one of the first cities founded by the Spanish in South America. Within a short time, the town blossomed into the main Spanish port on the Caribbean coast and the gateway to the north of the continent. It was the place where treasure plundered from the Indians was stored until the galleons could ship it to Spain. As such, it became a tempting target for pirates marauding the Caribbean, and in the 16th century alone, the town suffered five dreadful sieges, the best known of which was the one led by Francis Drake in 1586.

It was in response to pirate attacks that the Spaniards decided to make Cartagena an impregnable port, and constructed elaborate walls encircling the town and a chain of outer forts. These fortifications made the city unique in South America, helping to save Cartagena from subsequent sieges, particularly the fiercest and biggest attack of all, led by Edward Vernon in 1741.

In spite of the pirate attacks, Cartagena continued to flourish. During the long colonial period, the city was an important centre of the Spanish Empire, and influenced much of Colombia's history.

Today, Cartagena has expanded dramatically and is surrounded by vast suburbs. It is now Colombia's second port and an important industrial centre. Nevertheless, the old walled town has changed very little. It is a living museum of 16th and 17th-century Spanish architecture, with narrow winding streets, palaces, churches, monasteries, plazas and large mansions with overhanging balconies, shady patios and formal gardens.

Over the past couple of decades, Cartagena has become a fashionable seaside resort, though its beaches are actually not very good. An expensive modern tourist district has sprung up on Bocagrande and El Laguito, an L-shaped peninsula which fronts the Caribbean. This sector, packed with top-class hotels and expensive restaurants has become the main destination point for moneyed Colombians and international charter tours.

The climate is hot, but a fresh breeze blows in the evening, making it a pleasant time to stroll around the city. The driest period is from December to March.

Information

Tourist Offices The CNT office (☎ 647015) is in the Casa del Marqués de Valdehoyos, on Calle Santo Domingo. It's open daily from 8 am to noon and 2 to 6 pm.

The local tourist board has three offices: at the airport; at the Muelle de los Pegasos, outside the walls of inner town (☎ 651843); and in Bocagrande (☎ 654987), on the corner of Carrera 1 and Calle 4. All three are open Monday to Friday from 7 am to 7 pm, and on Saturday and Sunday from 7 am to noon.

Money Three banks currently change travellers' cheques and cash: Banco Sudameris Colombia (best rate for cheques), Banco Industrial Colombiano (best rate for cash) and Banco Unión Colombiano. Most major banks will accept your Visa card, while Mastercard may be honoured only by Banco Industrial Colombiano and Banco de Occidente.

There are plenty of casas de cambio, particularly around Plaza de los Coches. They are open till 6 or 7 pm, and change cash (at slightly lower rates than the banks) but usually not travellers' cheques.

Cartagena is probably the only Colombian city where you will have plenty of offers to change money in the street. Give the street changers a big miss – they are almost all con artists.

If your American Express travellers' cheques have been lost or stolen, contact the Tierra Mar Aire office (☎ 651062) in Bocagrande, Carrera 4 No 7-196.

Things to See

The old town is the principal attraction, particularly the inner walled town, consisting of the historical districts of El Centro and San Diego. Almost every street is worth strolling down. Getsemaní, the outer walled town, is

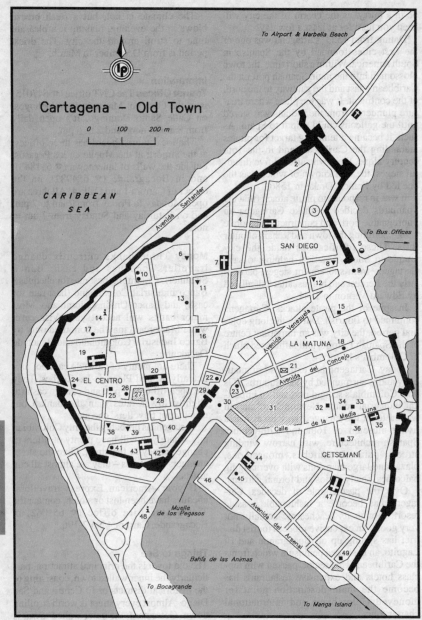

Cartagena – Old Town

0   100   200 m

CARIBBEAN SEA

To Airport & Marbella Beach

Avenida Santander

SAN DIEGO

To Bus Offices

LA MATUNA

Avenida Venezuela

EL CENTRO

Avenida del Concejo

Avenida de la

Calle

Media Luna

GETSEMANÍ

Muelle
de los Pegasos

Bahía de las Ánimas

Avenida del Arsenal

To Bocagrande

To Manga Island

COLOMBIA

■ PLACES TO STAY

15 Hotel del Lago
16 Hotel Bucarica
25 Hostal Santodomingo
32 Hotel Viena
33 Hotel El Refugio
34 Hostal Valle
36 Hotel Doral
37 Hotel Familiar
49 Aparta Hotel Portón del Baluarte

▼ PLACES TO EAT

6 Restaurante Novedades del Tejadillo
8 Restaurante Nautilius
11 Restaurante Jardines Turísticos
12 Restaurante Vegetariano Govinda's
38 Restaurante Classic de Andrei
39 Restaurante El Bodegón de la Candelaria

OTHER

1 Casa de Rafael Núñez (Museum)
2 Las Bóvedas
3 Old Bullring
4 Convento de Santa Clara
5 Buses to La Boquilla
7 Iglesia de Santo Toribio de Mangrovejo
9 Statue of India Catalina

10 Universidad Jorge Tadeo Lozano & Teatro Heredia
13 Universidad de Cartagena
14 CNT Tourist Office & Casa del Marqués de Valdehoyos
17 Copa Airlines
18 Telecom
19 Iglesia de Santo Domingo
20 Catedral
21 Avianca & Post Office
22 Banco Unión Colombiano
23 Banco Industrial Colombiano
24 Bar La Vitrola
26 Palacio de la Inquisición
27 Plaza de Bolívar
28 Museo del Oro y Arqueología
29 Plaza de los Coches & Puerta del Reloj
30 Statue of Pedro de Heredia
31 Parque del Centenario
35 Iglesia de San Roque
40 Plaza de la Aduana
41 Museo Naval
42 Museo de Arte Moderno
43 Iglesia y Convento de San Pedro Claver
44 Iglesia de la Santa Orden
45 Banco Sudameris Colombia
46 Centro de Convenciones
47 Iglesia de la Santísima Trinidad
48 City Tourist Office

less impressive and not so well preserved, but it is also worth exploring.

The inner town is surrounded by **Las Murallas**, the thick walls built to protect it. Construction was begun towards the end of the 16th century, after the attack by Francis Drake; until that time, Cartagena was almost completely unprotected. The project took two centuries to complete, due to repeated damage from storms and pirate attacks.

The main gateway to the inner town was what is now the **Puerta del Reloj** (the clock tower was added in the 19th century). Just behind it is the **Plaza de los Coches**, a square once used as a slave market. It is lined with fine old houses with colonial arches and balconies.

A few steps south is the **Plaza de la Aduana**, the largest and oldest square in the old town. It was used as a parade ground, and

all administrative buildings were gathered around it. In the centre stands the statue of Christopher Columbus.

Close by, to the west, is the **Iglesia y Convento de San Pedro Claver**, built by the Jesuits, originally under the name of San Ignacio de Loyola. The name was later changed in honour of the Spanish-born monk Pedro Claver, who lived and died in the convent. He spend all his life ministering to the slaves brought from Africa. The convent, built in the first half of the 17th century, is a monumental three-storey building surrounding the tree-filled courtyard, and a part of it is open to visitors. The cell where Pedro Claver lived and died can be seen. You can also climb a narrow staircase to the choir of the church and, at times, get to the roof of the church. The convent is open daily from 8 am to 6 pm. The church along-

COLOMBIA

side was built long after, and has an imposing façade. The remains of San Pedro Claver are kept in a glass coffin in the high altar.

Nearby, on Calle de las Damas, is a beautiful mansion, the **Casa de la Candelaria**, housing an excellent though expensive restaurant. You can visit the house without eating; go up to the bar in the tower for views of the town.

The **Plaza de Bolívar** is in a particularly beautiful area of the old town. On one side of it stands the **Palacio de la Inquisición** completed in 1776, a fine example of late colonial architecture, with its overhanging balconies and magnificent baroque stone gateway. It is now a museum displaying instruments of torture used by the Inquisitors, works of art from the colonial and independence periods, and some pre-Columbian pottery. It's open Monday to Friday from 8 to 11.30 am and 2 to 5.30 pm, and on Saturday and Sunday from 10 am to 5.30 pm.

Directly opposite, across the plaza, the **Museo del Oro y Arqueología** has a good collection of gold and pottery of the Sinú culture. It's open Monday to Friday from 8.30 am to noon and 2 to 6 pm. On the corner of the plaza is the **Catedral**, which was begun in 1575 but partially destroyed by the cannons of Francis Drake in 1586, and not completed until 1612. The dome on the tower was built early in this century. Apart from this, the church basically retains its original form; it is a massive structure with a fortlike exterior and a simply decorated interior.

One block west of the plaza is Calle Santo Domingo, a street which has hardly changed since the 16th century. On it stands the **Iglesia de Santo Domingo**, the oldest church in the city. It is a huge, heavy construction, and buttresses had to be added to the walls to support the naves of the church. The convent is right alongside, and you can see its fine courtyard.

Further north on the same street is the **Casa del Marqués de Valdehoyos**, a magnificent colonial mansion dating from the 18th century, now open as a museum (daily from 8 am to noon and 2 to 6 pm). The CNT tourist office is located here.

At the northern tip of the old city are **Las Bóvedas**, 23 dungeons built in the city walls at the end of the 18th century. This was the last construction done in colonial times, and was destined for military purposes. Today, they are tourist shops.

While you're wandering around, call at the **Muelle de los Pegasos**, a lovely old port full of fishing, cargo and tourist boats.

Several forts were built at key points outside the wall to protect the city from pirates. The greatest and strongest fortress is undoubtedly the **Castillo de San Felipe de Barajas**. This huge stone structure was begun in 1639 but not completed until some 150 years later. It is open daily from 8 am to 5 pm; the entrance fee for foreigners is US$2.50. Don't miss an impressive walk through the complex system of tunnels, built to facilitate the supply and evacuation of the fortress.

Another fortress, the **Fuerte de San Fernando**, is on the southern tip of Tierrabomba Island. It can only be reached by water. Boats leave from the Muelle de los Pegasos between 8 and 10 am and return in the afternoon. The tour costs US$8, including lunch and entrance to the fort, or pay US$6 for the journey only.

The **Convento de la Popa**, perched on top of a 150-metre hill beyond the San Felipe castle, was founded by the Augustinians in 1607. It has a nice chapel and a lovely flower-filled patio, and offers panoramic views over the city.

Places to Stay

Despite its touristy status, Cartagena is not a very expensive place for budget accommodation; the prices of the residencias are much the same as in other cities. The tourist peak goes from late December to late January but, even then, it's quite easy to find a room.

If you need something cheap, walk directly to the Getsemaní area. There are plenty of cheapies there, mostly on Calle de la Media Luna. Many are dives of suspicious reputation that double as love hotels or brothels, but you have several 'clean' and safe options to choose from.

The *Hotel Doral* (☎ 641706) has already got a reputation as a travellers' lodge. It has spacious, comfortable rooms surrounding a large pleasant courtyard with several umbrella-shaded tables, where travellers gather. The singles/doubles cost US$4/7 (US$1 more for a private bath).

The owner also runs two smaller hotels in the area: the *Hotel Familiar* (☎ 648374) and *Hotel El Refugio* (☎ 643507). The former has a nice patio and charges the same as the Doral; the latter is more basic and slightly cheaper.

Another place popular with foreign backpackers is the *Hostal Valle* (☎ 642533). It's small and fairly simple, but clean and with a familiar atmosphere. Singles/doubles cost about US$4/7. For a similar price, you can stay in the friendly *Hotel Viena* (☎ 646242), run by an Austrian guy.

In El Centro, the heart of the old town, all the cheapies have apparently ended up as love hotels. If you do insist on staying there, the only tolerably clean budget place is the *Hotel Bucarica* (☎ 641263), which costs US$7/10 with private bath.

If you don't mind staying outside the old town, try *Hotel Bellavista* (☎ 646411), at Marbella Beach, on Avenida Santander, a 10-minute walk from the walled city. It is a good place, and many tourists stay there. Clean rooms with bath and fan cost US$7 per person.

There are a few mid-range hotels in the old town area (and not a single top-class one) but they are nothing special. You can choose between the large, impersonal *Hotel del Lago* (☎ 653819), in La Matuna (US$15/20 a single/double), the more stylish but noisy *Aparta Hotel Portón del Baluarte* (☎ 647035), in the far southern corner of Getsemaní (US$10 per person), and the perfectly located but overrated *Hostal Santodomingo* (☎ 642268), in El Centro (US$18/24 a double/triple).

The city's best hotels are all in Bocagrande or El Laguito, including the pseudocolonial *Hotel Caribe* (☎ 650155) and the modern *Cartagena Hilton* (☎ 650666).

Cartagena has a camp site: *Camping La Boquilla* (☎ 654538) is three km north of the airport (six km off the walled city) on the road to La Boquilla. It costs US$4 per person in your own tent, US$6 in a tent provided by the management – it works out to be more expensive than staying in a budget hotel in the city.

Places to Eat

Cartagena is a good place to eat, particularly up-market, but cheap places are also plentiful. In the inner town, you can get good, filling set meals in the *Jardines Turísticos* or *Novedades del Tejadillo*. *Govinda's* serves cheap vegetarian meals.

Plenty of cafés all over the old town serve arepas de huevo, dedos de queso, empanadas and a large variety of other snacks. A dozen stalls on the Muelle de los Pegasos operate round the clock and have an unbelievable choice of delicious fruit juices.

Cartagena has a few local specialities worth trying. Huevos de iguana (iguana eggs), cooked and threaded together like rosaries, are sold from small carts throughout the centre (January to April only). Try them, but don't think too hard about the ecological havoc. *Butifarras* are a kind of small meatball, only sold on the street by *butifarreros*, who walk along with big pots and strike them with a knife to get your attention. Peto is a sort of milk soup made of maize, sweetened with panela and served hot. It, too, is only sold by street vendors.

If your wallet is full enough, there are plenty of truly excellent restaurants. Among the recommended places are: *El Bodegón de la Candelaria*, in the old town (ask for their lobster); *Classic de Andrei*, just a few steps from La Candelaria; *Nautilius* (there are two, one in the old town and one in Bocagrande), with good seafood; *La Pampa*, in Bocagrande (their churrasco is second to none); and *La Capilla del Mar*, also in Bocagrande (probably the best place for seafood).

Entertainment

A number of tabernas, discos and other venues stay open late at night. A particular concentration of bars is to be found on Avenida del Arsenal in Getsemaní, close to the Centro de Convenciones. On Fridays and Saturdays, the street is closed to traffic, and fills with tables and chairs and bands of different styles.

La Vitrola, in El Centro, facing Las Murallas, is a nice Bohemian bar with tables outside and good old salsa music on tape. Paco's, opposite the church of Santo Domingo, has a band that plays Caribbean music and some marvellous old Cuban songs (Wednesday to Saturday).

In Bocagrande the place to go is La Escollera (Carrera 1/Calle 5), a disco in a large thatched open hut, which goes nightly till 4 am. On the beach beside La Escollera, plenty of *vallenato* groups play music till dawn.

Getting There & Away

Air The airport is three km north-east of the old city and is serviced by frequent local buses from the centre. Avianca, Sam and Aces operate flights, and all have offices in La Matuna. There are flights to Bogotá (US$102), Medellín (US$83), Cali (US$115), Cúcuta (US$78), San Andrés (US$90) and other major cities. A young local carrier, Aerocorales, flies every morning (except weekends) to Mompós and returns in the afternoon (US$38 one-way).

Avianca flies to Miami and New York, while Copa, the Panamanian airline, has two flights weekly to Panama (US$115 plus 19% tax).

Bus Almost all the bus offices are clustered at the foot of San Felipe castle. Expreso Brasilia and Rápido Ochoa are about one km further east, on Avenida Pedro de Heredia.

There are a dozen buses daily to Bogotá (US$38 climatizado, 22 hours) and even more buses to Medellín (US$23 climatizado, 13 hours). Buses to Barranquilla run every 15 minutes or so (US$3.50, three hours).

Unitransco has one corriente bus to Mompós, at 5.30 am (US$8, eight hours).

Boat Cargo ships depart for the island of San Andrés from the Muelle de los Pegasos but don't take passengers. In the opposite direction, from San Andrés to Cartagena, you might get a lift (about US$35, two to three days). Irregular cargo boats go to Turbo (about US$15, one to two days), and it's relatively easy to get a ride. Take a hammock.

You may be approached by men offering you fabulous trips around the Caribbean in their boats for a little help on board; if you are interested, they will ask you to pay some money for a boarding permit or the like. Don't pay a cent – you'll never see the man or your money again.

AROUND CARTAGENA

La Boquilla

This is a small, poor fishing village seven km north of Cartagena. The entire population is Black and lives by fishing. You can see them in the afternoon with their famous *atarrayas*, a kind of fishing net. Plenty of palm-thatched shack restaurants on the beach attract people from Cartagena on Saturday and Sunday; mostly, they're closed at other times. The fish is good but not cheap. Frequent city buses run to La Boquilla from India Catalina in Cartagena, taking half an hour.

Islas del Rosario

This archipelago of small coral islands is about 35 km south-west of Cartagena. There are about 25 islands altogether, including tiny islets only big enough for a single house. The archipelago is surrounded by coral reefs, where the colour of the sea ranges from turquoise to purple. The whole area has been declared a national park.

The cruise through the islands is a well-established business. Tours operate daily all year round from the Muelle de los Pegasos in Cartagena, and in the tourist season, there are plenty of boats running to the islands. They all leave between 7 and 9 am and return about 4 to 5 pm. The tour costs roughly

US$12 to US$18 per person, including lunch, but bargaining is possible with smaller boats, especially at the last minute when some seats remain unoccupied.

MOMPÓS

Mompós is an exceptional town with its own particular identity. It was founded in 1537, on the eastern branch of the Río Magdalena, which in this part has two arms: Brazo Mompós and Brazo de Loba. The town soon became an important port, through which all the merchandise from Cartagena passed to the interior of the country. Several imposing churches and many luxurious mansions were built.

Towards the end of the 19th century, navigation on the Magdalena was diverted to the other branch of the river, bringing an end to the town's prosperity. Mompós has been left in isolation, and its colonial character is almost intact.

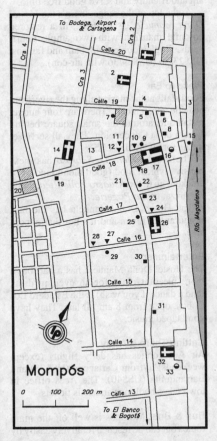

■ PLACES TO STAY

4 Residencias La Valerosa
5 Residencias Isleña
6 Residencias La Estrella
8 Residencias Solmar
19 Residencias Unión
21 Hostal Doña Manuela
23 La Posada del Virrey
30 Residencias Aurora
31 Residencias Villa de Mompox

▼ PLACES TO EAT

10 Restaurante Tebe's
11 Restaurante Robin Hood
12 Restaurante Frío Carlis
18 Restaurante Milena Paola
24 La Pizzería
27 Asadero Pollo Rico
28 Piqueteadero Lo Sabroso

OTHER

1 Iglesia de San Francisco
2 Iglesia de San Juan de Dios
3 Market
7 Alcaldía
9 Aces Airlines
13 Colegio Pinillos
14 Iglesia de Santo Domingo
15 Boats to El Banco & Magangué
16 Plaza Real de la Concepción & Jeeps to Bodega & El Banco
17 Iglesia de la Concepción
20 Cemetery
22 Museo Cultural
25 Casa de la Cultura
26 Iglesia de San Agustín
29 Estadero Los Cobos
32 Iglesia de Santa Bárbara
33 Unitransco Bus Office (Buses to Cartagena)

COLOMBIA

Mompós has a long tradition in hand-worked filigree gold jewellery, and it's really of outstanding quality. However, the gold is slowly being replaced by silver. Another speciality of the town is its furniture, particularly rocking chairs.

Things to See

Most of the central streets are lined with rows of fine whitewashed colonial houses with characteristic metal-grille windows, imposing doorways and lovely patios hidden behind. Six colonial churches complete the scenery; all are interesting, though rarely open. In particular, don't miss the **Iglesia de Santa Bárbara**, with its Moorish-style tower, unique in Colombian religious architecture. The **Casa de la Cultura**, a fine old *casona*, houses memorabilia relating to the town's history, and **Museo Cultural**, installed in the house where Simón Bolívar once stayed, displays some religious art.

There are two workshops near the museum where you can see and buy the local jewellery. The management of the Hostal Doña Manuela can give you the addresses of artisans who work at home.

It's fun to wander aimlessly about this clean and tranquil town, absorbing its old-time atmosphere. In the evening, people rest in front of their homes, sitting in – of course – the Mompós-made rocking chairs.

Festivals

Holy Week celebrations are very elaborate in Mompós. The solemn processions circle the streets for several hours on Maundy Thursday and Good Friday nights.

Places to Stay

Except for Holy Week, you won't have problems finding somewhere to stay. There are about 10 hotels in town, most of them pleasant and cheap.

The cheapest is the *Residencias La Estrella* (US$2 per bed – a single or a couple), but it's the most basic place. For a dollar more, you can stay in the *Residencias Solmar* or *Residencias La Valerosa*, both on the basic side, the latter undergoing a recon-

struction process which may improve its value and affect the price.

Appreciably better are the *Residencias Isleña* (☎ 855245), which costs US$3.50 per person in rooms with bath, and *Residencias Unión* (☎ 855723), which offers much the same, for US$4 per person.

There are three reasonably priced and good places to stay in town: *Residencias Villa de Mompox* (☎ 855208), at US$4.50 per person in rooms with bath, *Residencias Aurora*, at US$6 per person with bath, and *La Posada del Virrey* (☎ 855630), at US$6/7 per person without/with bath. All are pleasant and friendly and serve good free tinto.

At the top of the range, there's the *Hostal Doña Manuela* (☎ 855620), in a restored colonial mansion with two ample courtyards. Single/doubles with bath and fan cost US$23/30 (US$29/36 with air-con).

Place to Eat

Food stalls at the market along the riverfront provide cheap meals. There are four budget restaurants around the small square behind Iglesia de la Concepción. They all serve set meals for about US$1.75.

The *Piqueteadero Lo Sabroso* has inexpensive typical food (good mondongo). For chicken, go to the *Asadero Pollo Rico*, while for pizza, try *La Pizzería*.

The Hostel Doña Manuela has the best restaurant in town, and it's not that expensive.

Entertainment

The Hostel Doña Manuela has a bar, but a more pleasant place for an evening drink (and a dance if you wish) is the Estadero Los Cobos, open from 8 am till late. They have good taped music.

Getting There & Away

Air Aerocorales has daily flights (except weekends) to/from Cartagena (US$38) and Barranquilla (US$40). The Aces office in town takes bookings and sells tickets.

Bus & Boat Mompós is well off the main routes but can be reached relatively easily by dirt road and river. Most probably, you will come here from Cartagena. There is one direct bus daily, with Unitransco, leaving Cartagena at 5.30 am (US$8, eight hours). Otherwise, take a bus to Magangué (US$7, 5 hours, at least 10 per day with Unitransco or Brasilia), continue by boat to Bodega (US$1.50, 20 minutes, frequent departures till about 3 pm) and take a jeep to Mompós (US$2, one hour); the jeeps wait for the boats. There are also direct boats from Magangué to Mompós, but they're not so frequent.

If you head for Mompós from Bucaramanga, take a bus to El Banco (US$11, seven hours) and continue to Mompós by jeep or boat (either costs US$5 and takes two hours); jeep is a bit faster but the trip is less comfortable and can be pretty dusty.

From Santa Marta, there are two options. Either take a bus to El Banco (US$9, six hours) and continue as above, or catch any of the frequent buses to Bosconia (US$4.50, three hours), from where the morning Valledupar bus goes to Mompós on the backroad via La Gloria and Santa Ana (US$7, five hours).

San Andrés & Providencia

This archipelago of small coral islands in the Caribbean lies about 700 km north-west of the Colombian mainland and only 230 km east of Nicaragua. The archipelago is Colombian territory and is made up of two groups: the southern one (with San Andrés as the largest and most important island) and the northern group (with Providencia the main island).

For a long time, the islands were a British colony, and although the Spanish took possession after independence, the English influence on language, religion and architecture is still much in evidence. The native inhabitants are descendants of Jamaican

slaves, and speak a West Indian patois which is an English dialect. They are friendly and easy-going.

In the 1950s, when a regular domestic air service was established with the Colombian mainland and San Andrés was declared a duty-free zone, the situation started to change. A significant migration of Colombians to the islands, a tourist and commercial boom, and government policies have meant that some of the original character of San Andrés has been lost. Providencia will probably be in a similar position in the near future.

Nonetheless, the islands, especially Providencia, provide an ideal opportunity to experience the ambience of the Caribbean. The turquoise sea, extensive coral reefs and rich underwater life are a paradise for snorkellers and scuba divers.

San Andrés lies on the most convenient and cheapest route between Central America and Colombia, and is quite popular among travellers. All visitors to San Andrés are charged US$15 on arrival and handed the so-called Tarjeta de Turista. This is a local government regulation designed to improve the island's budget; in practical terms, it's the entry ticket to the islands.

The dry season on the archipelago goes from January to May, with another not-so-dry period from August to September.

SAN ANDRÉS
San Andrés, the main island of the southern archipelago, is about 13 km long and three km wide. It is relatively flat and almost entirely covered by coconut palms. A scenic paved road, 30 km long, circles the island, and a few more roads cross inland.

The urban centre and the capital of the whole archipelago is the town of San Andrés (known locally as El Centro), in the extreme north. It has more than two-thirds of the island's 45,000 inhabitants and is the principal tourist and commercial area, packed with hotels, restaurants and stores.

Information
Tourist Office The CNT office (☎ 4230) is

on Avenida Colombia, near the airport. It's open Monday to Friday from 9 am to 1 pm and 2.30 to 6.30 pm.

Money Travellers' cheques and cash can be changed at the Banco Popular (the best rate for both cash and cheques), the Banco Industrial Colombiano and the Banco del Estado. Plenty of shops and some hotels accept payments in cash dollars, and can change them for pesos (but at a lower rate than the banks).

Consulates Costa Rica, Guatemala, Honduras and Panama have consulates here (see the map), usually located in shops, so don't be confused. It's a good idea to get visas on the mainland, as consuls do not always stay on the island and you may be stuck for some days waiting for one to return.

Things to See
You will probably stay in El Centro, but you should take some time to look around the island. The small village of **La Loma**, in the centre, is perhaps the most traditional place on the island and is noted for its Baptist church, the first to be established on San Andrés.

El Cliff is a rocky hill, 50 metres high, a 20-minute walk from the airport. It offers good views over the town and the surrounding coral reefs. The **Cueva de Morgan** is an underwater cave where the Welsh pirate Henry Morgan is said to have buried some of his treasure. The **Hoyo Soplador**, at the southernmost tip of the island, is a sort of small geyser where the sea water spouts into the air through a natural hole in the coral rock. This phenomenon can be observed only during certain periods, when the winds and tide are right.

Buses run along the circular coastal road, as well as on the inner road to La Loma and El Cove, and can drop you near any of the sights. Otherwise, hire a bicycle in town (US$1.50 per hour or US$8 for a full day). Motorbikes, scooters, minimokes and cars can also be hired at various locations throughout the centre. Shop around, as prices and conditions vary.

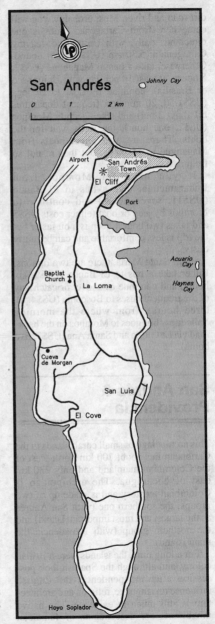

Yet another way of visiting the island is the Tren Blanco, a sort of road train pulled by a tractor dressed up like a locomotive. It leaves twice daily from the corner of avenidas Colombia and 20 de Julio to circle the island, stopping at sites of interest (US$4, three hours). The same route can be done by taxi for US$14 (up to five people fit). Taxi drivers will be happy to show you around other sights.

There are several small **cays** (coral islets) off the coast which are worth visiting, especially with snorkelling gear, which can be rented in the town (about US$5 per day). The most popular trip is to Johnny Cay, opposite the main town beach (US$3 return). Acuario Cay and Haynes Cay are off the eastern coast of the island; they are even better for snorkelling and are not so crowded (US$4 return). You can go by one boat and return by another, but make sure there will be another boat to take you back.

The best beach is right in town, overlooking Johnny Cay, but it may be crowded. There are no beaches along the western shore, and those along the east coast are nothing special, except for the good beach in San Luis.

Places to Stay

Accommodation in San Andrés is expensive. The cheapest place to stay is the *Hotel Restrepo* (☎ 26744), on the opposite side of the runway from the airport terminal. It has become a Mecca for foreign backpackers; Colombians are rare guests here. It is simple, pleasant and friendly, and costs US$3 per person, regardless of what room you get – some have their own bath, others don't, but all rooms have fans. There is a dining room, where you can get a good breakfast, lunch and dinner (US$1.50 per meal). If the rooms are full, and you don't mind mosquitos (they are only a problem during certain periods), ask for a hammock (US$2). Of course, you can string up your own, if you have one.

The only other low-budget hotel in San Andrés seems to be the *Apartamentos El Español* (☎ 3337), one block south of the airport terminal. This is essentially the Colombian budget hotel, with hardly a foreigner at sight. It is not an attractive place to stay, but all rooms have private bath, and the price, by San Andrés standards, is a bargain – US$7 for a dark double, US$8 for the one with a window facing the street (the latter are appreciably better).

If you can't get a room at either, or you need more comfort, be prepared to pay at least US$15/20 for a single/double. More expensive places include: the *Hotel Mediterráneo* (☎ 26722), which is simple but relatively inexpensive (US$20/25 a double/triple); *Hotel Coliseo* (☎ 23330), which is similar (US$15/20); *Hotel Mary May Inn* (☎ 25669), a very good small hotel (US$22 for the first person plus US$5 for each additional person); and *Hotel Hernando Henry* (☎ 23416), one of the best bets for a double (US$25, breakfast included). *Hotel Malibú* (☎ 24342) is another good choice for a double (US$30, without breakfast but with air-conditioning). *Hotel Los Delfines* (☎ 24083) is supposedly the cheapest hotel facing the sea (US$28/35).

All these places have private baths and fans, and some have air-conditioning. Most are crowded with Colombian shoppers busily packing and repacking the goods they have purchased.

If money is not a problem, San Andrés has a range of top-priced hotels, some of which are marked on the San Andrés map.

Places to Eat

Other than the Hotel Restrepo, there is not much in the way of budget restaurants. The comida corriente is the most economical bet (around US$2), but it is the same undistinguished meal which you have all over Colombia. It's better to pay a little more for something typical from the island.

Fisherman Place, on the beach near Restrepo, has crab soup for US$2 and fried fish for US$3. *Miss Bess*, in the Coral Palace Centre, is an ordinary-looking place but serves filling home-made meals, and good rondón (a local soup prepared with coconut milk, vegetables, fish and caracoles) for US$6, as well as other seafood dishes.

COLOMBIA

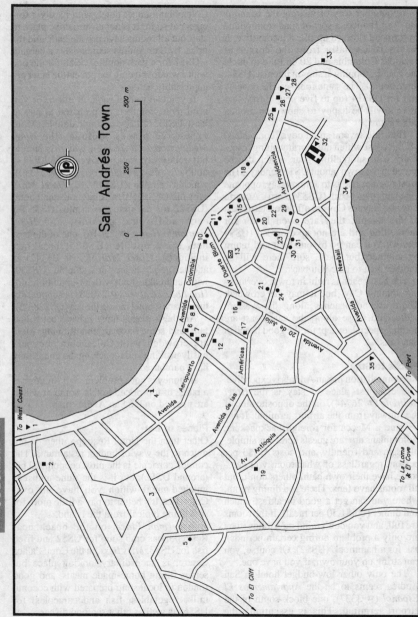

San Andrés Town

COLOMBIA

■ PLACES TO STAY		28	Hotel Tres Casitas	10	SAM Office
		33	Hotel Aquarium	11	Costa Rican Consulate
2	Hotel Restrepo			13	Avianca & Post Office
6	Hotel Cacique Toné	▼	PLACES TO EAT	15	Sahsa Office
7	Hotel Malibú			18	Boats to Johnny Cay,
8	Hotel Bahía Sardina	1	Fisherman Place		Acuario Cay &
9	Hotel Coliseo	27	Michael's Restaurant		Haynes Cay
10	Hotel Tiuna	32	Seafood House	20	Banco Industrial
11	Calypso Beach Hotel		Restaurant		Colombiano
12	Hotel Mediterráneo	34	Jairo Hansa	21	Guatemalan
14	Hotel Casablanca		Restaurant		Consulate
16	Hotel Mary May Inn	35	Miss Bess	23	Honduran Consulate
17	Hotel Hernando Henry			24	Panamanian
19	Apartamentos El		OTHER		Consulate
	Español			29	Banco del Estado
22	Gran Hotel Caribe	3	Airport Terminal	30	Banco Popular
25	Lord Pierre Hotel	4	CNT Tourist Office	31	Telecom
26	Hotel Los Delfines	5	Aerosucre Office		

The top-end restaurants are not cheap but serve delicious food, particularly comida de mar (seafood). Among the places deserving recommendation are *Jairo Hansa Restaurant*, *Michael's* (try their fiesta del mar) and *Seafood House Restaurant*.

Entertainment

San Andrés has a range of discos, including the Extasis (in the Gran Hotel Caribe) and Las Palmas (on the top floor of Hotel Tiuna). The best place, however, is the Atlántida, about 15 km out of town, near Morgan's Cave. It is an amazingly designed, huge two-storey open hut, thatched with palm leaf. They have good reggae/Caribbean/rock/salsa music. The place is open nightly, but Friday and Saturday after midnight are when things are hottest. The entrance fee is US$3. A free bus shuttles between the disco and the town (opposite Hotel Tiuna), taking guests there and back.

Getting There & Away

Air International Avianca and Sahsa (the Honduran airline) have regular connections between San Andrés and the USA: Miami (US$260), New Orleans (US$270) and Houston (US$310).

All Central American capitals are covered by Sam or Sahsa, with flights to San José (US$85), Panama (US$115), Tegucigalpa (US$117), Guatemala (US$125) and San Salvador (US$150). On some routes, there are discounts for a 30-day return ticket. For example, a round trip to Tegucigalpa costs US$200; to Guatemala, it's US$215.

If you buy a ticket in San Andrés for any international flight, you pay 5% Colombian tax on top of these prices (2.5% on round-trip tickets). Elsewhere in Colombia, you pay tax of 19% or 9.5%, respectively. The airport tax on international flights from San Andrés is US$17, if you have stayed in Colombia less than 60 days; otherwise, it is US$30.

If you plan on flying to San Andrés from Central America, you'll probably be obliged by the agent or airline to buy a return ticket, to fulfil Colombia's onward ticket requirement. In this case, it's better to fly with Sahsa than with Sam, for the Sahsa office in San Andrés may be able to refund you the difference between the return and one-way ticket. If not, try again at the Sahsa office in Bogotá.

Flights from Central America (especially from Tegucigalpa and Guatemala) to Colombia via San Andrés have become very popular with travellers as a cheap and convenient way to bypass the Darién Gap. Buy the ticket to San Andrés only, then another ticket on a domestic flight to the Colombian mainland (a ticket covering the whole route will be more expensive). The same rule applies if you're going in the opposite direction.

Air Domestic Avianca, Sam, Aces and Intercontinental have flights to all major Colombian cities: Bogotá (US$141), Cartagena (US$90), Barranquilla (US$94), Medellín (US$122), Cali (US$141) and Cúcuta (US$141).

There are two cheaper ways to get to the mainland, with Aerosucre or Satena. Aerosucre has one or two cargo flights weekly to Barranquilla and Bogotá. They usually take passengers and charge roughly half of the commercial fare. Inquire in the Aerosucre office, near the passenger terminal. It's in the green-roofed building next to the building with the Marlboro cowboy advertisement on top. The entrance is on the right side, not at the front.

Another option is to fly with Satena. They have irregular noncommercial passenger flights to Bogotá, roughly one per month (about US$60). The flights are heavily booked in advance, but there is always a chance; go to the airport before the flight and try your luck.

Sam and Satena have several flights daily to Providencia (US$31). In the high season, book in advance.

Boat There are no regular ferries to the Colombian mainland or elsewhere. Cargo ships run to Cartagena every few days and sometimes take passengers (about US$35, including food, two to three days). Occasional freighters go to Colón (in Panama), but they are hard to track down. Cargo boats for Providencia leave once a week (about US$14, eight hours).

PROVIDENCIA

Providencia, about 90 km north of San Andrés, is the second largest island of the archipelago, seven km long and four km wide. It is a mountainous island of volcanic origin, much older than San Andrés. The highest peak is El Pico, at 320 metres, and there are a few others slightly lower.

A 18-km road skirts the island, and virtually the entire population of 5000 lives along it, in scattered houses or in one of the several hamlets. Santa Isabel, a village at the northern tip of the island, is the administrative seat. Santa Catalina, a smaller island to the north, is separated from Providencia by the shallow Canal Aury, spanned by a pedestrian bridge.

Providencia is much less affected by tourism than San Andrés. English is widely spoken, and there's still much Caribbean English-style architecture to be seen. The locals are even friendlier than on San Andrés, and the duty-free business fever is unknown. However, the island is quite rapidly becoming a fashionable spot for Colombian tourists. Aguadulce, on the western coast, has already been converted into a tourist centre, with hotels and restaurants, and boat, motorcycle and snorkelling gear for hire. So far, the rest of the island is still largely unspoilt, though this situation is changing.

The coral reefs around Providencia are more extensive than those around San Andrés, and snorkelling and scuba diving are even better. The interior of the island provides for pleasant walks, with El Pico being the major goal. The trail to the peak begins from Casabaja, at the southern side of the island. It's a steady hour's walk to the top.

Getting around the island is pretty straightforward. Two chivas and several pick-ups run the circular road, charging US$0.50 for any distance. Providencia is an expensive island for food and accommodation, even more so than San Andrés.

Information
There's a tourist office at the airport, theoretically open from 8 am to noon and 2 to 6 pm. The Banco Central Hipotecario in Santa Isabel may change cash (but not cheques) at a very poor rate. Bring enough pesos with you from San Andrés.

Places to Stay

The only really cheap place to stay is the *Residencias Sofía* (☎ 48109), in Pueblo Viejo, two km south of Santa Isabel. Get off by the SENA centre and take the rough track that branches off the main road (next to a two-storey, green-painted shop) and leads towards the seaside; the residencias is only a couple of hundred metres away, on the shore. This very rustic place costs US$3.50 per person, and Miss Sofía can cook meals for you (around US$2.50 each).

The next cheapest, and far better, is the *Cabañas Santa Catalina* (☎ 48037), on the island of Santa Catalina, just opposite Santa Isabel, by the pedestrian bridge. It's a very pleasant place with a family atmosphere, and costs US$9 per person in rooms with private bath.

The overwhelming majority of places to stay are in Aguadulce, which is apparently an exclusively tourist village. A dozen cabañas line the main road, charging US$15 to US$20 per person. Supposedly the cheapest of them is the small *Cabañas Marcelo* (☎ 48190), at the southern end of the village.

Places to Eat

Food is expensive, though usually good, particularly the seafood. Most restaurants are in Aguadulce. One of the best for comida isleña, and reasonably priced, is the *Miss Elma*. In Santa Isabel, there are three restaurants, of which the *Junto al Mar* is the cheapest. Set meals go for around US$3, fried fish for a dollar more. You can buy good, fresh coconut bread in some of the shops.

Getting There & Away

Air Sam and Satena shuttle between San Andrés and Providencia several times per day (US$31). Buy your ticket in advance, and be sure to reconfirm return tickets at the Satena office at the airport, or the Sam office in Santa Isabel.

The North-West

In broad terms, the north-west is made up of two large regions, quite different in their geography, climate, people and culture. The first, the Chocó Department, along the Pacific coast, is essentially an extensive stretch of tropical forest with an average rainfall largely surpassing that of the Amazon. The region is sparsely populated, mainly by Blacks. As the roads are few and poor, transport is either by water or air, and is expensive. One of the loveliest areas, with facilities and relatively easy access, is Los Katíos national park, on the Panamanian border.

The other part of the north-west, the departments of Antioquia, Caldas, Risaralda and Quindío, cover the hilly portions of the Cordillera Occidental and the Cordillera Central. This is picturesque mountainous country, crisscrossed by an array of roads and sprinkled with little towns noted for their distinctive architecture. The region is interesting and relatively easy to explore. The population is predominantly White – this is actually Colombia's 'whitest' region. Medellín, the capital of Antioquia, is the main city of the whole of the north-west.

MEDELLÍN

Medellín was founded in 1616, but only at the beginning of the 20th century did it begin to expand rapidly, first as a result of the coffee boom and then as the centre of the textile industry. Today, it is a dynamic industrial and commercial city with a population of over two million; the country's largest urban centre after Bogotá. The city is spectacularly set in the Aburrá Valley, with the modern centre in the middle and vast slum barrios all over the surrounding slopes.

For tourists, it isn't an outstandingly interesting place, nor is it very safe. Medellín is the world capital of the cocaine business, home to the Cartel de Medellín and its boss, Pablo Escobar. A strong presence of fully armed military police on the streets makes

COLOMBIA

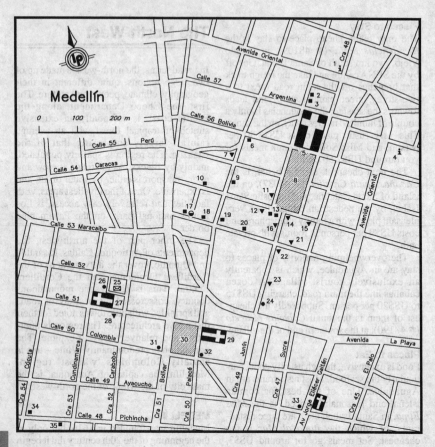

Medellín

the city centre appear safe and quiet during the daytime, but keep your nighttime strolls to a minimum.

Information

Tourist Offices The Oficina de Turismo y Fomento (☎ 2540800), at Calle 57 No 45-129, has information about the city. It's open Monday to Friday from 7.30 am to 12.30 pm and 2 to 6 pm. You can also try Turantioquia (☎ 2543335), at Carrera 48 No 58-11, especially if you are interested in tours.

Money The Banco Popular and Banco Anglo Colombiano change travellers' cheques and cash. The Banco Unión Colombiano will also exchange your cheques, but not cash. All three banks pay advances on Visa. The Banco Industrial Colombiano will honour your Mastercard, and will change cash but not cheques.

Tierra Mar Aire (☎ 2420820), Calle 52 No 43-124, is the place to go if your American Express cheques are lost or stolen.

Panamanian Consulate The Panamanian Consulate (☎ 2662390) is at Carrera 43A No 11-85, oficina 201.

■ PLACES TO STAY

2	Hotel El Capitolio
3	Aparta Hotel El Cristal
6	Hotel Tropical
9	Hotel Veracruz
10	Hotel Cumanday
13	Hotel Plaza & Hotel Americano
17	Aparta Hotel Santelmo
18	Hotel La Bella Villa
19	Hotel Eupacla
20	Hotel Europa Normandie
34	Hotel Comercial
35	Nuevo Hotel

▼ PLACES TO EAT

7	Restaurante Los Toldos No 3
11	Restaurante La Estancia
12	Restaurante Los Toldos No 1
14	Restaurante Aleros del Parque
15	Restaurante Los Toldos No 2

16	Café Versalles
21	Restaurante La Posada de la Montaña
22	Restaurante Hato Viejo
23	Boulevard de Junín
28	Restaurante Vegetariano Govinda's

OTHER

1	Turantioquia
4	Oficina de Turismo y Fomento
5	Basílica Metropolitana
8	Parque de Bolívar
17	Minibuses to Airport
24	Banco Industrial Colombiano
25	Avianca & Post Office
26	Museo de Antioquia
27	Ermita de la Veracruz
29	Basìllica de la Candelaria
30	Parque Berrío
31	Banco Anglo Colombiano
32	Banco Popular
33	Banco Unión Colombiano

Things to See & Do

Apart from a couple of old churches, the city's colonial architecture has virtually disappeared. The most interesting of the churches is the **Basílica de la Candelaria**, in Parque Berrío. You also might like to visit the **Basílica Metropolitana**, in the Parque de Bolívar, completed early in this century and considered to be the largest church on the continent.

The **Museo de Antioquia**, Carrera 52A No 51A-29 (open Monday to Friday from 10 am to 5.30 pm, and on Saturday from 9 am to 2 pm), features a collection of paintings and sculptures by Fernando Botero, the most internationally known Colombian contemporary artist. The city has a fine botanical garden, the **Jardín Botánico Joaquín Antonio Uribe**, open daily from 9 am to 5 pm. In April and May every year, they have an orchid exposition in their Orquideorama.

For panoramic views of the city, go to the **Cerro Nutibara**, a hill quite close to the centre. The **Pueblito Paisa**, a replica of a typical Antioquian village, has been built on the summit and is home to several handicrafts shops. The best place for handicrafts, however, is the **Mercado de San Alejo**, held

in the Parque de Bolívar on the first Saturday of every month.

On the last Friday of every month, the **Tangovía** springs to life, on Carrera 45 in the Manrique district. This is tango night, when you can hear and dance to the nostalgic rhythms. Medellín is Colombia's capital of tango; it was here that Carlos Gardel, the legendary King of Tango, died in an air accident in 1935.

Festivals

If you come in early August, you have a chance to see the biggest event in Antioquia, the **Feria de las Flores**. The highlight of the festival is the Desfile de Silleteros, when hundreds of campesinos come down from the mountains and parade along the streets carrying *silletas* full of flowers on their backs.

Places to Stay

Medellín doesn't shine in the area of budget lodging. What is really cheap is poor, or of suspect reputation. The cheapest hotels are located around the street market, between carreras 52 and 54 and calles 47 and 50, but the area is dirty, noisy and unpleasant. One

COLOMBIA

of the cheapest in this sector is the slowly disintegrating but still acceptable *Nuevo Hotel* (☎ 5122471), Calle 48 No 53-29. It costs US$3 for a single or a couple, US$4 for a double.

The best budget bet in the market area is the *Hotel Comercial* (☎ 5129349), Calle 48 No 53-102. This big, clean, well-run hotel has singles/doubles/triples without bath for US$4/6/8 (US$6/8/10 with bath).

In the city centre, around the Parque de Bolívar, genuinely cheap accommodation is only to be found in 'love hotels'. The *Hotel Americano*, Calle 54 No 49-15, is ideally located, on the square but may not accept you for the whole night until after about 7 pm (never on weekends), for US$6. They only have rooms with one double bed, bath and TV. Next door, at Calle 54 No 49-23, the *Hotel Plaza* has, apart from matrimonios, a few rooms with two beds, and is more tolerant of tourists, charging US$5/6 for a couple/double. Yet another love dive, the *Hotel Tropical*, Calle 56 No 49-105, is cheaper but shabbier. It's only one block from the Parque de Bolívar but is on the edge of the brothel area to the west, so take care.

The *Hotel Cumanday* (☎ 5124400), Calle 54 No 50-48, is the cheapest 'clean' accommodation in the area, and has fairly good singles/doubles with bath (US$6/9).

The *Aparta Hotel El Cristal* (☎ 5120001), Carrera 49 No 57-12, is one of the best value-for-money options and is therefore often full. This clean and pleasant place costs US$9/11/13 for a single/double/triple. All rooms have bath (with hot water), telephone, fan, colour TV and fridge. Some rooms are even equipped with a stove.

The *Aparta Hotel Santelmo* (☎ 2312728), Calle 53 No 50A-08, and the *Hotel La Bella Villa* (☎ 5110144), Calle 53 No 50-28, are two good, centrally located places, very convenient if you fly into Medellín, as the airport minibuses deposit you a few steps from either. Both have comfortable singles/doubles with bath for US$11/14. The latter is slightly better.

Further up the price scale, there are plenty of hotels in the city centre, including (in ascending order of price and standards): the *Hotel El Capitolio* (☎ 2310970), Carrera 49 No 57-24 (US$12/18 a single/double); the *Hotel Eupacla* (☎ 2311844), Carrera 50 No 53-16 (US$15/20); the *Hotel Europa Normandie* (☎ 5124025), Calle 53 No 49-100 (US$22/30); and the *Hotel Veracruz* (☎ 5115511), Carrera 50 No 54-18 (US$40/50).

Places to Eat

As usual, the cheapest places are clustered in the market area – there are plenty of restaurants on carreras 53 and 54 between calles 48 and 49.

In the heart of the city, in the Parque de Bolívar, *La Estancia*, Carrera 49A No 54-15, is by far the cheapest place to eat. It's not very clean or pleasant but does have filling set meals for only US$1.

There are many moderately priced restaurants and cafés on and around the pedestrian walkway Avenida Junín (Carrera 49), between the Parque de Bolívar and Calle 52. For example, *Versalles*, Avenida Junín No 53-39, has a tasty menú económico, good cakes, fruit juices and tinto. The area on the 1st floor is more pleasant.

The *Aleros del Parque*, on a terrace overlooking Avenida Junín and the Parque de Bolívar, is a popular rendezvous, where you can get typical food or just sit over a beer watching the world go by. If you just want to grab something quickly, go to the *Boulevard de Junín*, where several self-service joints serve pizza, chicken, pasteles, salpicón and ice cream.

Los Toldos has reasonably priced Antioquian dishes. There are several branches: No 1 is at Calle 54 No 49-53; No 2 is at Calle 54 No 47-11; and No 3 is at Carrera 50 No 55-23. *Hato Viejo*, on the 1st floor of the Centro Comercial Los Cámbulos on the corner of Avenida Junín and Calle 53, is pleasant, and a good place for regional dishes. *La Posada de la Montaña*, Calle 53 No 47-44, has even better typical food at affordable prices.

Getting There & Away

Air The new airport, 30 km from the city, was opened in 1985, and all domestic and international flights land there, except some regional flights on light planes (which still use the old airport right inside the city). There's no tourist office in the terminal, but a few travel agencies on the upper level (departure hall) will give you some information. There are branch offices of a few banks, though perhaps none of them will change your travellers' cheques. They will change cash, in their usual working hours (Monday to Friday from 8 to 11.30 am and 2 to 4 pm). Otherwise, ask the porters, who often change cash dollars (but give poor rates). In this case, change only enough to get to the city.

Frequent minibuses shuttle between the city centre and the airport from the corner of Carrera 50A and Calle 53 (US$1.50, one hour).

There are plenty of flights throughout the country – to Bogotá (US$57), Cali (US$62), Cartagena (US$83), Cúcuta (US$76) and San Andrés (US$122). There are also flights to Panama (US$115). Zuliana de Aviación (a Venezuelan carrier) has daily flights to Maracaibo (US$81) and Caracas (US$110). Add 19% tax to the cost of international flights, if you buy the ticket in Colombia.

Bus All buses arrive at and leave from the central bus terminal, on the corner of Autopista Norte and Calle 78, 15 minutes from the city centre by urban bus. Frequent buses depart to Bogotá (US$16, nine hours), Cartagena (US$23, 13 hours) and Cali (US$16, nine hours); all prices are for climatizados. Six buses daily travel the rough road to Turbo (US$12 corriente, about 13 hours).

AROUND MEDELLÍN

The hilly region surrounding Medellín is picturesque, and attractive to travel in. The temperate climate means that there is a variety of plants and flowers, including orchids. The region is sparkled with haciendas and *pueblos paisas*, lovely little towns noted for their particular style of architecture, known as Antioquia.

If you have a couple of days to spare, it is a good idea to do a trip around Medellín to see what Antioquia is really like. Among the most interesting places are the towns of La Ceja, El Retiro and Marinilla (all good examples of the regional architecture), Carmen de Viboral (well known for its hand-painted ceramics) and the spectacular, 200-metre-high granite rock of El Peñol.

There is accommodation in all of these places, as well as an array of restaurants. The buses are frequent. A number of travel agents in Medellín can put together a tour to suit your interests.

SANTA FE DE ANTIOQUIA

This is the oldest town in the entire region, and well worth a visit. Founded in 1541, it was the capital of the Department of Antioquia until 1826, and still retains its colonial architecture and atmosphere. The town is about 80 km north-west of Medellín, on the way to Turbo.

Things to See

Give yourself a couple of hours to wander through the streets, to see the decorated doorways of the houses, the windows with their carved wooden guards, and the patios in bloom. Of the town's four churches, the nicest is the **Iglesia de Santa Bárbara**. The **Museo Juan del Corral** (open Tuesday to Saturday from 9.30 am to noon and 2 to 6 pm, and on Sunday from 10 am to 5 pm) displays interesting antique objects collected in the region, while the **Museo de Arte Religioso** (open Saturdays and Sundays only, from 10 am to 5 pm) features sacral art.

There is a curious pedestrian bridge over the Río Cauca, the **Puente de Occidente**, six km out of town. When built in 1887, it was one of the first suspension bridges in the Americas. Walk there, or negotiate a round trip with taxi drivers in Santa Fe.

Places to Stay

The best budget place is the *Residencias Colonial*, Calle 11 No 11-72. Located in a nice old mansion, it's quiet and friendly. Rooms on the upper floor are more pleasant and have a balcony. Doubles cost US$9. The hotel serves cheap set meals.

El Mesón de la Abuela, Carrera 11 No 9-31, is in the same price range. It's quite simple, but clean and with a friendly atmosphere. It has its own restaurant, which offers good breakfast, lunch and dinner but is more expensive than the restaurant in the Colonial. There are several cheaper residencias in town, including the *Franco*, Carrera 10 No 8-67, and *Dally*, Calle 10 No 8-50.

At the top of the range, you have the *Hotel Mariscal Robledo*, Carrera 12 No 9-70, which costs US$15 per person. It has a swimming pool and a restaurant.

Places to Eat

The cheapest place to eat is the market on the main square, where you can get a tasty bandeja for a bit over US$1. Apart from the hotel restaurants, there are at least half a dozen other places to eat. One of the best is *Los Faroles*, next to El Mesón de la Abuela.

Don't miss trying pulpa de tamarindo, a local sweet made from tamarind, sold on the main square.

Getting There & Away

There are several buses daily from/to Medellín (US$2, three hours). There are also minibuses every 45 minutes until 7 pm (US$3, 2½ hours).

There are six buses a day to Turbo, on the Gulf of Urabá, (US$10, 11 hours). They all come through from Medellín, and might be full when they reach Santa Fe.

TURBO

Turbo is a port on the Gulf of Urabá, an obligatory stopover to get an entry or exit stamp in your passport if you are coming from or heading to the Darién Gap. See the introductory Getting There & Away chapter for details.

This is a poor town of no interest, and it's not safe, especially at night. There is nowhere to exchange travellers' cheques, and the rate for cash dollars is poor. If you

are going to Panama by the coastal route, your last chance to get a visa is in Sapzurro, near the border, but it's better to get it beforehand. For Los Katíos national park, you need a permit from Inderena. Their office is a 20-minute walk along the road to Medellín from the town centre.

Places to Stay

Try the *Marcela*, one block from the church (US$4 per person). If it is full, you have the *Turbo*, next door, or *El Viajero*, just round the corner, both about the same price as the Marcela. There are also several budget hotels near the port.

Getting There & Away

Air There are three flights daily to Medellín (US$55).

Bus Six buses daily run to Medellín (US$12, 13 hours). If you are heading for Cartagena, take a jeep to Montería (from the market), and make a connection there.

Boat To Los Katíos national park, take one of the boats which go up the Río Atrato to Riosucio; get off at Sautatá (US$11, 1½ hours). The boats leave early in the morning.

If you are heading for Panama along the north coast, take a boat to Capurganá (US$14, four hours), then walk 1½ hours to Sapzurro (the last village on the Colombian side), cross the border and keep walking for a couple of hours to Puerto Obaldía (Panama).

PARQUE NATURAL NACIONAL LOS KATÍOS

This is one of the most beautiful parks in Colombia. Set on the border with Panama, the park protects an extensive stretch of hilly land covered by thick tropical rainforest, and a marshy plain with a chain of lakes and mangroves. Several footpaths through the woods allow you to enjoy the rich vegetation and animal life, mainly birds and butterflies. Perhaps the major attractions of the park are the waterfalls, the most spectacular, the Salto de Tilupo, being some 100 metres high.

There are tourist facilities in the administrative centre, including accommodation (US$5 per person) camping, and food. The friendly rangers will give you lot of information or even take you around.

The permit for the park can be obtained in Bogotá or Turbo. See the Turbo section for information on how to get to the park. From the Sautatá wharf, it's a 20-minute walk to the administrative centre.

The best time to visit the park is from December to March, which is really the only relatively dry period. August may be OK, but in other months, it rains a lot and the paths are muddy (at times, impassable).

The South-West

Administratively, the south-west covers the departments of Nariño, Cauca, Valle del Cauca and Huila. The region is very diverse, both culturally and geographically, and offers virtually everything you could wish for. The biggest tourist attractions are the two outstanding archaeological sites of San Agustín and Tierradentro, and the colonial city of Popayán. Cali is the area's largest urban centre.

CALI

Cali is a young, prosperous and lively city with a fairly hot climate. Although founded in 1536, its growth came only in this century, primarily with the development of the sugar industry, followed by dynamic progress in other sectors. Today, Cali is Colombia's third largest city, with a population of almost 1½ million.

The city, apart from a few fine churches and museums, hasn't got many tourist attractions. Its charm lies in its atmosphere and its inhabitants, who are, in general, easy-going, open and friendly. Be careful of thieves, however, as in most of the big cities.

The women of Cali, *las caleñas*, are considered to be the most beautiful in the nation. Cali is also noted for its salsa music. These hot rhythms originated in Cuba in the 1940s

and spread like wildfire throughout the Caribbean, reaching Colombia in the 1960s. Today, salsa music is heard all over the country, but the Cali region and the Caribbean coast traditionally remain the major centres of salsa, due to their sizeable Black and Mulato populations.

Orientation

The city centre is split in two by the Río Cali. To the south is the original centre, laid out on a grid plan and centred around the Plaza de Caycedo. This is the area of tourist attractions, including old churches and museums.

To the north of the river is the new centre, whose main axis is Avenida Sexta (Avenida 6N). This sector is essentially modern, with trendy shops and good restaurants, and it comes alive in the evening, when a refreshing breeze cools down the city heat. Here, you can stroll and eat after a day of sightseeing on the opposite side of the river.

Information

Tourist Offices The main city tourist office is the Cortuvalle (☎ 675614), at Avenida 4N No 4N-20. It's open Monday to Friday from 8.30 am to 5 pm. They also have an outlet at the airport.

Money Most of the major banks are grouped around Plaza de Caycedo. At the time of writing, there is apparently only one bank, the Banco Popular, which changes cash (at a good rate), but it's always packed with people, so you'll probably spend a lot of time in the queue.

The Banco Popular and the Banco Industrial Colombiano seem to be the only two banks changing travellers' cheques. The former pays better rates, but has long queues, while the latter has no queues but is totally inefficient, so the paperwork will take half an hour.

With a Visa card, try the Banco Anglo Colombiano, Banco de Bogotá or Banco de Colombia. Mastercard is honoured in the Banco de Occidente and the Banco Industrial Colombiano.

The Tierra Mar Aire office (for lost or

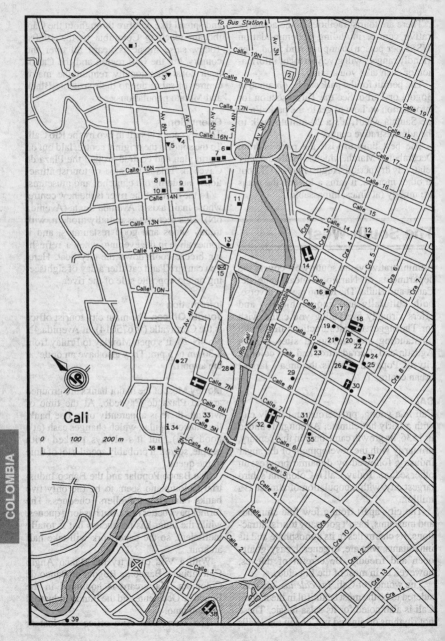

To Bus Station

Calle 19N
Calle 18N
Calle 17N
Calle 16N
Calle 15N
Calle 14N
Calle 13N
Calle 12N
Calle 10N

Av 3N
Av 8N
Av 6N
Av 5N
Av 4N
Av 2N

Cali

0   100   200 m

COLOMBIA

Río Cali

Avenida Colombia

Calle 19
Calle 18
Calle 17
Calle 16
Calle 15
Calle 14
Calle 13
Calle 12
Calle 11
Calle 10
Calle 9
Calle 8
Calle 7
Calle 6
Calle 5
Calle 4
Calle 3
Calle 2
Calle 1

Cra 2
Cra 3
Cra 4
Cra 5
Cra 6
Cra 7
Cra 8
Cra 9
Cra 10
Cra 12
Cra 13
Cra 14

■ PLACES TO STAY		14	Iglesia de la Ermita
1	Hostal Santor	15	Avianca Post Office
6	Residencial Chalet	17	Plaza de Caycedo
7	Casa del Viajero, Hotel California &	18	Catedral
	Hotel Granada	19	Banco Anglo Colombiano
8	Residencial JJ	21	Banco de Bogotá
9	Hotel La Familia	22	Banco de Colombia
10	Residencial 86	23	Banco Popular
11	Residencial Paseo Bolívar	24	Banco Industrial Colombiano
16	Hotel Royal Plaza	25	Telecom
20	Hotel Astoria	26	Iglesia de San Francisco
36	Pensión Stein	27	Sifonería Martyn's
		28	Avianca Office
▼ PLACES TO EAT		29	Club Bingo Social
		30	Torre Mudéjar
3	Restaurante Vegetariano Raices	31	Museo del Oro
4	Restaurante El Caballo Loco	32	Iglesia de la Merced, Museo de Arte
5	Restaurante El Fuerte del Norte		Colonial & Museo/Arqueológico
12	Restaurante Vegetariano Hare Krishna	33	Taberna Alexander
		34	Cortuvalle Tourist Office
OTHER		35	Teatro Municipal
		37	Teatro Experimental de Cali (TEC)
2	La Torre de Cali	38	Iglesia de San Antonio
13	Banco de Occidente	39	Museo de Arte Moderno La Tertulia

stolen American Express cheques) is at Calle 22N No 5BN-53.

Ecuadorian Consulate The Ecuadorian Consulate (☎ 801937) is at Carrera 3 No 11-32, oficina 409.

Things to See
There is a beautiful colonial church, the **Iglesia de la Merced**, on the corner of Carrera 4 and Calle 7. It is Cali's oldest church, begun soon after the city was founded. The monastery adjoining the church houses two good museums: the **Museo de Arte Colonial** (open Monday to Saturday from 9 am to noon), with mostly religious objects from the colonial period, and the **Museo Arqueológico** (open Monday to Saturday from 9 am to 12.45 pm and 1.45 to 6 pm), with pre-Columbian pottery of several cultures from southern Colombia.

The **Museo del Oro**, one block away, is open Monday to Friday from 10 am to 6 pm. It has a small collection of gold from the

Calima culture. Another interesting museum, the **Museo de Arte Moderno La Tertulia**, Avenida Colombia No 5 Oeste-105, presents temporary exhibitions of contemporary painting, sculpture, photography etc.

To get a view of the city centre, go to the **Iglesia de San Antonio**, set on top of a hill only a short walk from the centre. The church itself is also worth seeing. Alternatively, go to **La Torre de Cali**, the highest building in the city, on the corner of Avenida 3N and Calle 19N. It's an expensive hotel, but ask at reception on the ground floor for permission to go up to a viewpoint on the 43rd floor, or go to eat at their top-floor restaurant.

Festivals
The main city event is the Feria de Cali, which breaks out annually on 25 December and goes till the end of the year, with parades, masquerades, music, theatre, bullfights and much overall fun.

COLOMBIA

Places to Stay

There is a selection of budget accommodation right in the heart of the new (northern) city centre, which is a relatively secure and pleasant area. The dark side is that the residencias are pretty poor, and some double as love hotels.

Three hotels side by side on Calle 15N are used by budget travellers, despite their not-very-innocent status: *Hotel Granada* (☎ 612477), Calle 15N No 4N-44, *Hotel California* (☎ 612483), Calle 15N No 4N-52, and *Casa del Viajero* (☎ 610906), Calle 15N No 4N-60. All have rooms with private bath and charge US$5/7 for a single/double. The California seems to have the highest ratio of couples per day. Check all three and take your pick. Just around the corner, at Avenida 4N No 15N-43, is yet another love venue, the *Residencial Chalet* (☎ 612709). It's more primitive, but a dollar cheaper than the previous three.

If you prefer somewhere with a better reputation (though not a higher standard), there are three family-run hotels around the corner of Calle 14N and Avenida 8N: the *Residencial 86* (☎ 612054), Avenida 8N No 14N-01; the *Hotel La Familia* (☎ 612925), Calle 14N No 6N-42; and the *Residencial JJ* (☎ 613134), Avenida 8N No 14-47. The first has rooms with bath (US$5/7) and is the best of the lot. Another basic family hotel is the *Residencial Paseo Bolívar* (☎ 682863), at Avenida 3N No 13N-43. All four rent rooms by the week or the month, and may be often full.

One of the best places to stay in the area is the relatively cheap *Hostal Santor* (☎ 686482), Avenida 8N No 20N-50, which has rooms with bath for around US$10/15. There are also several cheaper rooms without bath, but they are rather poor.

On the southern side of the Río Cali, in the historic centre, there's not much budget accommodation, except for the maze of seedy hospedajes east of Calle 15. However, you shouldn't walk there – this is one of the most dangerous areas of central Cali. On the other hand, there's quite a choice of mid-range hotels located within a couple of blocks of the Plaza de Caycedo, a convenient area to stay.

Perhaps the best value for money is the *Hotel Astoria* (☎ 830140), on the corner of the plaza, Calle 11 No 5-16. Airy comfortable singles/doubles with TV and private bath cost US$20/26. Ask for a room on one of the top floors, for less noise and better views.

On the diagonally opposite corner of the square is the *Hotel Royal Plaza* (☎ 839243), Carrera 4N No 11-69. It's marginally better than the Astoria but more expensive: US$26/33/39 for a single/double/triple. Here, too, the rooms on the upper floors are more attractive. There's also a fine restaurant, on the top floor.

If you are looking for something up-market, there's one exceptional place, though it's a bit far from the centre: the *Pensión Stein* (☎ 614927), at Avenida 4N No 3N-33, in a large, beautiful house. Run by a Swiss couple, the hotel offers spotlessly clean rooms with bath and also has its own restaurant. Singles/doubles cost US$30/40, breakfast included.

Places to Eat

The best eating sector is on and around Avenida 6N, where loads of restaurants and cafés are grouped together; you can get nearly everything, from simple snacks, burgers and pizzas, through regional Colombian cuisine, to rich Chinese, Arab and German specialities. Cheap restaurants in the area, serve set meals for around US$1.50.

For vegetarian food, the best budget place in town is the attractive *Restaurante Vegetariano Raices*, Calle 18N No 6N-25, but it only serves meals between 11.30 am and 2.30 pm. Not as pleasant, but open from 6 am to 8 pm, is the *Restaurante Vegetariano Hare Krishna*, at Calle 14 No 4-49.

For a satisfying dinner, try *El Caballo Loco*, Calle 16N No 6N-31 (ask for their castellana – roasted beef or pork roll with cheese and ham, served in béchamel sauce), *El Fuerte del Norte*, Avenida 8N No 15AN-06 (good seafood), or *Los Girasoles*, on the corner of Avenida 6N and Calle 35N. There are plenty of other, equally good restaurants in the area.

Entertainment

Colombia's national theatre started with the foundation of the Teatro Experimental de Cali (TEC). If you understand Spanish well enough, go to the TEC theatre, at Calle 7 No 8-63, and see one of their plays.

There are several *salseaderos* (discos with salsa music) on Calle 5, but the best-known place is Juanchito, a popular suburb on the Río Cauca. Go there on Friday or Saturday night but don't take anything of value; better still, find some local company to take you there.

For a night drink, try the Sifonería Martyn's, at Avenida 4N No 7N-10, or Taberna Alexander, at Calle 5N No 1N-74. For opera buffs, there's the Video Taberna El Trovador, Avenida Circunvalación No 4 Oeste-42, open Tuesday to Saturday from 8 pm to 2 am. They serve drinks, and have 50 operas on video and twice that number on compact disc. The programme is up to the public.

Bingo is a feature of Cali. There are several bingo halls in the centre, one of the more popular being *Club Bingo Social*, Carrera 4 No 9-21 (open 24 hours).

Night tours in chivas depart from the Hotel Intercontinental, Avenida Colombia No 2-72, on Friday and Saturday at 8 pm. The five-hour tour includes a few nightspots. The excursion costs US$15, including half a bottle of aguardiente and a snack.

Getting There & Away

Air The airport is 16 km from the city. Minibuses between the airport and the bus terminal run every 10 minutes till about 8 pm (US$1, half an hour). There are plenty of flights to all major Colombian cities – Bogotá (US$62), Medellín (US$62), Cartagena (US$115) and San Andrés (US$141).

Bus The bus terminal is a 20-minute walk from the city centre, or less than 10 minutes by one of the frequent city buses. Buses to Bogotá run at least every half-hour (US$18

climatizado, 12 hours). Air-conditioned buses go regularly to Medellín (US$16, nine hours) and to Pasto (US$15, 10 hours). The Pasto buses will put you down in Popayán (US$4, three hours). There are also a number of cheaper pullman buses to both Popayán and Pasto.

AROUND CALI

There's a fine mountain national park, the **Parque Nacional Farallones de Cali**, to the west of the city, popular with the caleños. It's noted for its lush vegetation and diverse wildlife.

If you just want to do a day trip to the park, take a bus from the bus terminal to Pance, on the border of the park; from there, footpaths lead into the reserve. For overnight stays, contact the Fundación Farallones (☎ 568335), Carrera 24B No 2A-99, for the permit (US$1.50). They operate cabañas (US$12, including three meals) and offer other facilities, such as horse rental (US$6 per day) and guides. You can camp in the park free of charge.

There are plenty of old haciendas in the region of Cali. Most date from the 18th and 19th centuries, and some were engaged in the cultivation and processing of sugar cane. The **Hacienda Cañasgordas** is on the outskirts of the city, beyond the Universidad del Valle. It's currently closed for renovation, but may open by the time you read this.

The two best known are the **Hacienda El Paraíso** and **Hacienda Piedechinche**, close to each other, about 40 km north-east of Cali. Both are open as museums. There are frequent tours from Cali, or you can visit them on your own using public transport, though this is a bit time-consuming, as both places are off the main roads. The tourist office in Cali will give you information.

POPAYÁN

Popayán is one of the most beautiful colonial cities in Colombia. Founded in 1537 by Sebastián de Belalcázar, the town quickly became an important political, cultural and religious centre, and was an obligatory stopover on the route between Cartagena and

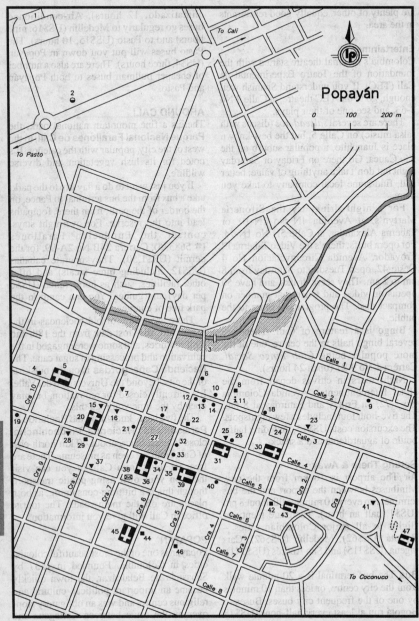

Popayán

0   100   200 m

To Cali

To Pasto

To Coconuco

Quito. Its mild climate attracted the wealthier Spanish families from the tropical sugar states of the Cali region. They came to live here, building mansions and founding schools. Several imposing churches and monasteries were built in the 17th and 18th centuries.

During the 20th century, while many other Colombian cities were caught up in the race to modernise and industrialise, Popayán somehow managed to retain its colonial character. In March 1983, a violent earthquake seriously damaged a lot of the historic buildings and most of the churches. The difficult restoration work has continued for a decade, and the result is admirable – little can be seen of the disaster and the city looks much better than it did before it had happened. Apart from its beauty, Popayán is a very inviting, tranquil and clean city, and truly worth a visit. Furthermore, it has an excellent tourist office and a range of good

places to stay and eat, and is not expensive by Colombian standards.

Information
Tourist Office The Caucatur tourist office (☎ 242251), Calle 3 No 4-70, is one of the best in the country – a recommended first stop in town. The staff are very helpful and friendly, with a lot of good information about the city and the region. They will also store your luggage free of charge. The office is open Monday to Friday from 8 am to noon and 2 to 6.30 pm, and on Saturday and Sunday from 10 am to 5 pm.

Money No bank in Popayán will change cash or travellers' cheques, so come prepared. If you happen to run out of money, the best place to go is the Almacén (store) Salvador Duque, on the main square, Calle 5 No 6-25. The owner changes both cash and cheques and consistently pays about the best rate in

COLOMBIA

town, though it's less than you could get in banks in Cali or Pasto, the two nearest places to change money. Note also that San Agustín and Tierradentro, two popular tourist destinations from Popayán, don't have banks, so bring along enough pesos to last you the whole trip.

Banco de Bogotá, Banco de Colombia and Banco de Occidente, all on the main square, might deal with your credit cards.

Things to See

Most of the churches have been carefully restored and are open for worship. They are only open for mass, usually early in the morning and late in the afternoon, so plan your sightseeing accordingly. Don't miss the **Iglesia de Santo Domingo**, for its rich original decoration, particularly the side altars, and the **Iglesia de San Agustín**, which has probably the most magnificent high and side altars. **Iglesia La Ermita** is Popayán's oldest church (from 1546), worth seeing for its fine high altar, and for the fragments of old frescos, which were only discovered after the earthquake of 1983.

The **Catedral** dates from the second half of the 19th century. It was almost completely destroyed by the earthquake (as was its internal decoration) and rebuilt, virtually from the ground up. It's now the most manicured church in town, though there's something strange about it: it has no soul.

The **Iglesia de San Francisco**, reputedly the best of all the city churches, is waiting for restoration. Its cracked façade gives you an idea of how destructive the earthquake was.

All of Popayán's renowned museums are open again, daily from 9 am to noon and 2 to 5 pm. The **Casa Museo Mosquera** contains a collection of colonial art, including some religious objects. More sacred art is to be found in the **Museo de Arte Religioso**. The **Casa Museo Negret** features abstract sculpture by this distinguished contemporary artist, while the **Museo Guillermo Valencia** is dedicated to the poet who once lived here.

The **Museo de Historia Natural** is possibly the best of its kind in the country, noted for its extensive collections of insects, butterflies and, particularly, stuffed birds. Part of the top floor is taken up by an archaeological display of pre-Columbian pottery of several cultures from southern Colombia.

Churches and museums are only a part of what Popayán has to offer. The best approach is to take a leisurely walk along the streets lined with whitewashed **colonial mansions**, savouring the architectural details and dropping inside to see marvellous patios (most are open to the public). Have a look at the Palacio Nacional, the Puente del Humilladero, the Casa de la Cultura and a curious house, different from the others, the Casa de Julio Arboleda.

For **city views**, go to the Capilla de Belén or, even better, to El Morro de Tulcán, a hill topped by an equestrian statue of the town's founder.

Festivals

If you are in the area during Holy Week, you'll have the chance to see the famous nighttime processions on Maundy Thursday and Good Friday. Popayan's Easter celebrations are the most elaborate in the country. Note that hotels are full around that time, so get there earlier or book in advance.

Places to Stay

Popayán has a good array of accommodation to suit every pocket. Many hotels are in old colonial houses, and have a style and atmosphere not common in Colombian accommodation.

If you are really hard up, there are half a dozen residencias on Carrera 5 between calles 7 and 8. They are basic but very cheap: about US$2.50/3.50 for a single/double. The best of the lot seems to be the *Hotel Bolívar*, on Carrera 5, near the corner of Calle 7.

The place which has recently become the most popular among foreign backpackers is the *Casa Familiar Turística* (☎ 240019), Carrera 5 No 2-41 (no sign on the door). The hotel register revealed that only two Colombians had stayed there over the preceding six months. It has a friendly, family atmosphere, and just five rooms (you pay US$3.50 per bed). You can have a filling breakfast for US$1, and leave gear free of charge if you go away. The Casa is the only budget hotel where you can make overseas calls, including collect calls. If reverse- charge calls are impossible to your country, they will let you have a one-minute call to ask your party to call you back.

Another place deserving warm recommendation is the friendly *La Casa del Virrey* (☎ 240836), Calle 4 No 5-78, just off the main square. This is a beautiful colonial house with a charming patio. Comfortable rooms with bath attached (choose one facing the street) cost US$8/13/18 a single/double/triple. The *Casa Grande* (☎ 240908), Carrera 6 No 7-11, has similar prices and standards but is less atmospheric.

The *Hotel La Ermita* (☎ 241936), near the church of the same name, Calle 5 No 2-77, combines the old and new, with airy modern rooms and a delightful old patio. It costs US$24/33/42.

There's a choice of colonial mansions turned into stylish hotels, including *Hotel La Plazuela* (☎ 241084), Calle 5 No 8-13, and the *Hotel Camino Real* (☎ 241254), Calle 5 No 5-59. They cost US$28/38 for a single/double; the latter is better (ask for a room with balcony facing the street).

Places to Eat

Popayán has plenty of good places to eat. The cheapest set meals are served at *La Brasa Roja*, Calle 6 No 5-91. The *Lonchería La Viña*, Calle 4 No 7-85, is open till late and is popular among locals for its cheap, filling set meals. *La Oficina*, Calle 4 No 8-01, just a few steps down the street from La Viña, has rich Antioquian food at reasonable prices, and also serves set meals at lunchtime. For tasty vegetarian food, go to *Restaurante Vegetariano El Museo*, Calle 4 No 4-62.

Los Kingos de Belén, Calle 4 No 0-55, has good regional food; try their bandeja típica and wash it down with champús. For delicious and very cheap empanadas de pipián and tamales de pipián (local specialities not to be found elsewhere), the place to go is *La Fresa*, a small cubbyhole (there's no sign) at Calle 5 No 8-83. You can also have tamales and a variety of other typical snacks in the *Cafetería Riquísimo*, at Carrera 8 No 3-61. The owner, Silvio, has plenty of information about the region.

Casa de Sebastián, Calle 3 No 2-54, is a delightful colonial pizzeria-cum-bar with a beautiful patio and friendly management. It's open from 7 pm to 1 am. An alternative place for a drink is *La Topatolondra*, a night bar at Calle 3 No 5-69 with good salsa music.

The restaurant of the Hotel Camino Real is commonly and justly acclaimed as the best in town you won't find such mouthwatering steaks and French specialities for miles.

Getting There & Away

Air The airport is just behind the bus terminal, a 15-minute walk from the city centre. There are daily flights to Bogotá (US$59) and to Ipiales (US$32).

Bus All buses arrive at and leave from the bus terminal, a short walk from the city centre. There are plenty of buses to Cali (US$4, three hours). The pullman buses run regularly throughout the day to Pasto (US$10, seven hours) and Ipiales (US$12, nine hours). The climatizado buses to Bogotá run every hour or two (US$22, 15 hours).

For Tierradentro, take a Sotracauca bus to Belalcázar (four daily) and get off in El Cruce de San Andrés (US$6, five hours), then walk two km to the museum.

Two buses daily (with Cootranshuila and Sotracauca) run to San Agustín on a short road via Coconuco and Isnos (US$9, six to seven hours). The road is very rough, but the trip through the lush rainforest of the cordillera is spectacular. If you prefer to walk to San Agustín, there's an attractive and popular trek via the Laguna de la Magdalena. The tourist office will give you all necessary information.

AROUND POPAYÁN
Silvia

A small town 60 km north-east of Popayán, Silvia is the centre of the Guambianos, one of the most traditional Indian communities in Colombia. Though the Indians no longer live in the town, they come to Silvia on Tuesday, market day, to sell fruits, vegetables and handicrafts. That's the best day to visit Silvia – a perfect day trip from Popayán. There are plenty of Indians in town on that day, almost all in their traditional dresses, the women in colourful garments and beaded necklaces, busily spinning wool.

There's a curious **Museo de Artesanías del Mundo** in the town, in the Casa Turística, Carrera 2 No 14-39. It displays an assortment of handicrafts from all over the world.

If you decide to stay longer in Silvia, there are at least half a dozen cheap residencias, though the *Casa Turística* is perhaps the most agreeable place (US$9/17 a single/double), as you actually stay in the museum.

Freddy Vargas, the local guide (you'll find him in the Casa Turística), can arrange tours around the region in a jeep, or you can rent horses next to the *Centro Vacacional Silvia*, a large, expensive hotel just off the main square.

Getting There & Away Coomotoristas has buses from Popayán to Silvia at 8, 9.30 and 11 am (US$1.50, 1½ hours). You can also take any of the frequent buses from Popayán to Cali, get off in Piendamó (US$0.80, 45 minutes), then take a colectivo to Silvia (US$0.80, another 45 minutes). On Tuesday, there are also direct colectivos between Popayán and Silvia. The tourist office was planning to provide their own transport for the Tuesday market, so ask them about this.

Parque Nacional Puracé

The park, about 60 km east of Popayán, is one of the most picturesque in Colombia, offering a wide variety of landscapes and sights, from volcanos and lagunas to waterfalls and sulphur springs. Only the northern part of the park can be easily reached, as the Popayán-La Plata road passes through. Don't miss the spectacular hot sulphur springs, the **Termales de San Juan**, set in beautiful surroundings. The hot waters

meeting the icy-cold mountain creeks create multicoloured moss, algae and lichens. The relatively regular Popayán-La Plata buses will put you down a 15-minute walk from the springs.

If you feel fit enough, make the climb to the top of the **Volcán Puracé** (4780 metres). It is about a five-hour steady ascent from Pilimbalá. You can do it easily in a day, but start early. The weather is precarious all year round, so take good rain gear. Generally, only the early mornings are sunny; later on, the volcano gets covered with clouds.

In the southern part of the park, the trek from Valencia to San Agustín (or vice versa) is becoming increasingly popular. You can do it in two days on foot or on horseback; horses can be hired at either end. Camping gear is not necessary. Tourist offices in San Agustín and Popayán know all the details of this trek. There's one bus daily in either direction between Popayán and Valencia.

Places to Stay Other than camping, the only place to stay in the park is Pilimbalá, where there are three cabins and a restaurant. The cabin with attached bath and hot water costs US$36 and can sleep up to seven people, or you can just pay US$6 for a bed. The Inderena office in Popayán is at Calle 3 No 5-73.

SAN AGUSTÍN

This is one of the most important archaeological sites on the continent. The region was inhabited by a mysterious civilisation which left behind several hundred freestanding monumental statues carved in stone, as well as a number of large underground tombs.

There is still little known about the culture which created the statues. Most probably, it flourished between about the 6th and 14th centuries AD, though its initial stages are thought to have been perhaps a millennium earlier. The best statuary was made only in the last phase of the civilisation's existence. The culture had presumably vanished before

San Agustín

the Spaniards came. Perhaps, like many other civilisations of the Andean region, it fell victim to the Incas – this area of Colombia was the northernmost point of the Inca Empire. All this is still open to discussion. What is certain is that the statues were not discovered until the middle of the 18th century.

So far, some 500 statues have been found and excavated. A great number of them are anthropomorphic figures – some of them realistic, some very stylised, resembling masked monsters. Others are zoomorphic, identifying sacred animals such as the eagle,

the jaguar and the frog. The statues vary in size, from some 20 cm up to seven metres, and in their degree of detail.

The site was no doubt a ceremonial centre where the Agustinians buried their dead, placing the statues next to the tombs. Pottery and gold objects were left in more important tombs.

The statues and tombs are scattered in groups over a wide area on both sides of the gorge formed by the upper Río Magdalena. The main town of the region is San Agustín, where you'll find most of the accommodation and restaurants. From there, you can explore the region; count on three days for leisurely visits to the most interesting places.

The weather is varied, with the driest period from December to February and the wettest from April to June.

Information

Tourist Office The tourist office (☎ 373019), Calle 5 No 14-75, is very friendly and helpful, probably the best in Colombia. Staff members speak English, French, Italian. They have comprehensive information about the region, and plenty of leaflets on the whole country – stock up here, as they can be difficult to find elsewhere. They sell a good booklet (Spanish/English edition) about San Agustín and Tierradentro cultures, which contains a description of the sights and is illustrated with maps. The tourist office offers jeep tours and horse rentals, and has a full list of routes, with prices, licensed guides etc. They also have a complete list of hotels in the area.

Money There are no banks changing money in San Agustín. The tourist office will help you to change cash dollars, but at a poor rate. Travellers' cheques are apparently unchangeable. The Caja Agraria may or may not give peso advances to Visa card holders.

Things to See

By far the most important and interesting place is the **Parque Arqueológico**, about 2½ km west of the town of San Agustín, where you can see a hundred statues, including some of the best in the region. The park covers several archaeological sites with statues, tombs and burial mounds. It also has a museum displaying smaller statues and pottery, and the Bosque de las Estatuas, where 35 statues of different origins are placed along a footpath that snakes through the forest.

The second important place in the region is the **Alto de los Ídolos**, another archaeological park, noted for burial mounds and large stone tombs. The largest statue, seven metres high, is to be found here. The park is a few km south-west of San José de Isnos, on the other side of the Río Magdalena.

Both parks are open daily from 8 am to 5 pm (the museum is closed on Monday). You buy one entrance ticket (US$3), which is valid for two days for entry to both parks.

Apart from these two places, there are some 15 other archaeological sites scattered over the area. The region is also noted for its natural beauty, with two lovely **waterfalls**, Salto de Bordones and Salto de Mortiño.

The tourist office offers a number of excursions, by jeep or on horseback, to practically all places of interest. Horses are hired out for a specific route, or by the hour (US$2) or the day (US$10). Jeeps, which take up to five people, cover sights accessible by road. The most popular jeep tour includes Alto de los Ídolos, Alto de las Piedras, Salto de Bordones and Salto de Mortiño. It takes six hours and costs US$36 per jeep.

Places to Stay

The accommodation in San Agustín is good and cheap. There are a dozen residencias in town, most of which are clean and friendly and have hot water; all cost much the same (about US$2 per person in rooms without bath, a dollar more in rooms with private bath).

If you don't feel like walking when you arrive, there are a few residencias right by the bus offices, including the *Colonial*, Calle 3 No 11-54, and the *Central*, Calle 3 No 10-54. Both are good, if a bit noisy from street traffic, and cost US$3.50 per person in rooms with bath.

If you prefer a quieter area, walk five blocks west along Calle 4, where you will find several residencias. *Mi Terruño*, Calle 4 No 15-85, is perhaps the most pleasant, with a long balcony overlooking the garden. It has some rooms with private bath. If it is full, try the two others just a few steps away (they don't have signs): *Luis Tello*, Calle 4 No 15-33, and *Eduardo Motta*, Calle 4 No 15-71. A block away, on the corner of Calle 5 and Carrera 16, is one more budget place, the *Ñáñez*.

You can also stay in a pleasant family

house, *Posada Campesina Silvina Patiño*, one km outside town towards El Tablón. You can also camp there.

The *Nelly*, run by a French lady, is a good new place popular with travellers. It's on the western outskirts of town.

There are two up-market hotels, the *Osoguaico* (US$18/24 a single/double) and *Yalconia* (US$22/30). Both are outside town, on the road leading to the Parque Arqueológico.

There are two simple camp sites, *Camping San Agustín* and *Camping El Ullumbe*, near the Hotel Yalconia.

Should you need somewhere to stay in Isnos, there's the cheap *El Balcón*, on the main square.

Places to Eat

Brahama, Calle 5 No 15-11, is recommended for cheap set meals, vegetarian food and fruit salads. *Los Ídolos*, Carrera 11 No 2-48, serves inexpensive, tasty meals.

La Martina, Carrera 12 No 3-40, known locally as Las Negras, serves good regional food. It's open only on Saturdays, Sundays and Mondays. Outside town, opposite the Hotel Yalconia, there is the reasonably priced *La Brasa*, good for churrasco, carne asada and the like.

Getting There & Away

There are three buses daily to Bogotá (US$14, 12 hours). To Popayán, two buses run early in the morning via a short rough road through Isnos (US$9, six hours if everything goes well).

There are frequent jeeps between San Agustín and Pitalito (US$1, 45 minutes). As there is not much room inside, luggage is put on the roof. Keep a constant eye on your backpack, especially if you board the jeep in Pitalito. There have been many reports of travellers whose packs were loaded in Pitalito but then disappeared somewhere along the way.

There are no direct buses to Tierradentro; you must first go to La Plata (US$7, four hours, one or two buses daily). The only bus from La Plata to Tierradentro leaves at 5 am

(US$3, three hours). Get off at El Cruce de San Andrés and walk for 20 minutes to the museum of Tierradentro. If you don't catch this bus and don't want to waste the day, take a chiva to Belalcázar and get off in Guadualejo. From there, you can catch the Belalcázar-Popayán bus passing about 11.30 am, or another (less reliable) one, around 2 pm. Otherwise, you have to stay overnight in La Plata – there are a number of cheap residencias. Don't count on the hotel staff to wake you up for the 5 am bus.

TIERRADENTRO

Tierradentro is an archaeological zone where a number of underground burial chambers have been found. They are circular tombs ranging from two to seven metres in diameter, scooped out of the soft rock. The dome-like ceilings of the larger tombs are supported by massive columns. The chambers were painted in geometric patterns, and some of the decoration is preserved very well. About a hundred tombs have been discovered to date. These funeral temples contained the cremated remains of tribal elders. The ashes were kept in ceramic urns, which are now displayed in the museum of Tierradentro.

A number of stone statues similar to those of San Agustín have also been found in the region, probably the product of a broad cultural influence.

Not much is known about the people who built the tombs and the statues. Most likely, they were of different cultures, and the people who constructed the tombs preceded those who carved the statues. Today, the region is inhabited by the Páez Indians, who have lived here since before the Spanish Conquest, but it is doubtful whether they are descendants of the statue builders.

Things to See

There are four sites with tombs and one with statues, as well as a museum and the village of San Andrés de Pisimbalá. Except for El Aguacate, all the sites are quite close to one another.

COLOMBIA

You start your visit from the museum, where you buy one combined ticket (US$3), valid for two days to all archaeological sights and the museum itself. It actually consists of two museums across the road one from each other. The **Museo Arqueológico** contains pottery urns which have been found in the tombs, while the **Museo Etnográfico** has utensils and artefacts of the Páez Indians. Both museums are open daily from 8 am to 5 pm.

A 10-minute walk up the hill from the museum is **Segovia**, the most important burial site. There are 28 tombs here, some with well-preserved decoration. Seven of them are lit; for the others, you need a torch – don't forget to bring one.

The village of Pisimbalá, a 25-minute walk from the museum, is noted for its beautiful thatched church. You can see its very simple interior through the gap in the entrance doors. There are about a dozen churches similar in style in the region; the

one in Santa Rosa (a two-hour walk) is perhaps the most amazing.

Places to Stay

As in San Agustín, the accommodation in Tierradentro is good and cheap – you will pay some US$2 per person for a simple but clean room. There are two areas where you can stay: close to the museum or in San Andrés de Pisimbalá.

The *Lucerna*, in a house several paces up the road from the museum, is clean, pleasant and friendly. Some 150 metres further on is *Pisimbalá*, one of the cheapest in the area. Another 150 metres further on is another small residencias, the *Ricabet*. Next to it is the only more expensive hotel, *El Refugio* (US$10/14 a single/double). It has a swimming pool and a restaurant, and you can camp on the grounds. The friendly people who run the hotel promote some ecological programmes in the area.

In San Andrés de Pisimbalá, there are

three residencias, *El Viajero*, *El Cauchito* and *Los Lagos de Tierradentro*. El Cauchito has a camping site (US$1 per person). Los Lagos is the cheapest and friendliest – recommended. It's 100 metres down the road past the church; if you can't find it, ask anybody for Edgar Bolaños Velasco, the owner.

Places to Eat

In the museum area, the *Pisimbalá* (see Places to Stay) is the cheapest place to eat, serving set meals for about US$1.50. Slightly more expensive, but better, is the *Restaurante 86*, just across the road. Possibly the best of all is the restaurant of *El Refugio*.

In San Andrés de Pisimbalá, *El Viajero* has cheap meals, or you can eat in *La Gaitana*, next to the church.

Getting There & Away

Only sporadic buses call at San Andrés de Pisimbalá. Most buses ply the Popayán-Belalcázar road, passing El Cruce de San Andrés, so you must walk there (20 minutes from the museum). In theory, there are three buses daily to Popayán, at about 7.30 am, 12.30 and 3 pm (US$6, five hours). It's a bumpy but very spectacular trip on a windy mountain road. Also theoretically, there are three buses to La Plata which pass by El Cruce at around 6 am, noon and 3 pm. If no bus passes by, try to hitch a ride to Guadualejo, where you can catch one of the relatively regular chivas coming through from Belalcázar.

PASTO

Founded in 1537 at the foot of the Galeras Volcano, Pasto was for centuries an important cultural and religious centre, and is today the capital of Nariño Department. Though it has lost much of its colonial character, the churches retain the splendour of its past.

The town is noted for its barniz de Pasto, a kind of processed vegetable resin used on wooden bowls, plates, boxes, etc to decorate them with colourful patterns. Pasto is also a good place to shop around for leatherware. Try Bomboná Handicraft Market and the shops around it for both barniz and leatherwork.

Pasto lies at an altitude of over 2500 metres, so it gets cold at night – have something warm handy.

Information

Tourist Office The Oficina Departamental de Turismo de Nariño (☎ 234962) is at Calle 18 No 25-25. The office is open Monday to Friday from 8 am to noon and 2 to 6 pm.

The Instituto Geográfico Agustín Codazzi (IGAC), Calle 18A No 21A-18, sells good departmental and city maps. The office is open Monday to Friday from 7.30 to 11 am and 2 to 5 pm.

Money Most major banks are located around the main square, Plaza de Nariño. It seems that only the Banco Industrial Colombiano changes cash. It also changes travellers' cheques, as does Banco de Bogotá. Other banks marked on the Pasto city map only handle credit card operations.

Óptica San Francisco, on the main square, changes cash till 7 pm on weekdays and is the best private moneychanger, though it pays less than the banks.

Things to See

Pasto is a town of churches. There are a dozen colonial churches in town, most of which are large constructions with richly decorated interiors. The **Iglesia Cristo Rey**, with its fine stained-glass windows, is supposedly the most beautiful. Also have a look at the elaborately decorated **Iglesia de San Juan Bautista**, the oldest city church. See the Pasto city map for the location of other churches.

There is a small but good **Museo del Oro** in the building of the Banco de la República, Calle 19 No 21-27, containing gold and pottery of the pre-Columbian cultures of Nariño. It's open Monday to Friday from 8 am to noon and 2 to 6 pm.

Another interesting museum, the **Casona de Taminango**, is at Calle 13 No 27-67.

COLOMBIA

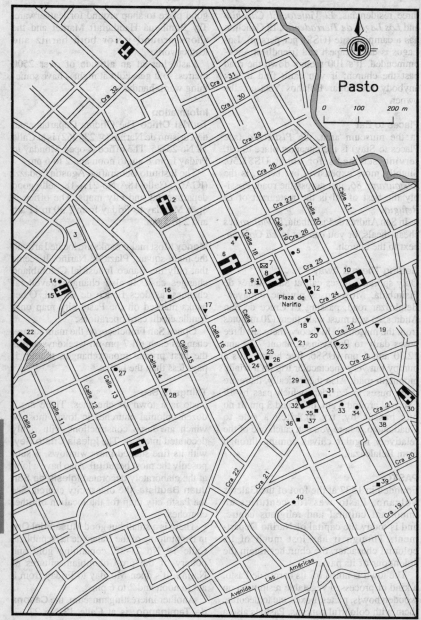

Pasto

0   100   200 m

■	PLACES TO STAY
13	Hotel Agualongo
16	Hotel El Paisa
25	Hotel Don Saul
29	Hotel Isa
31	Hotel Manhattan
35	Hotel Ri\'o Nilo
36	Hotel Canchalá
37	Hotel El Duque
38	Residencias Colonial
39	Residencias Viena

▼	PLACES TO EAT
4	Restaurante Don Pancho
17	Restaurante La Cabaña
18	Punto Rojo
19	Salsa Cazuela & Ceviche
20	Picantería Ipiales
28	Restaurante Vegetariano Govinda's

	OTHER
1	Museo Maridíaz
2	Iglesia de San Andrés
3	Plaza de Bomboná
5	Banco Industrial Colombiano
6	Catedral
7	Avianca & Post Office
8	Iglesia de San Juan Bautista
9	Oficina Departamental de Turismo de Nariño
10	Iglesia Cristo Rey
11	Óptica San Francisco (Money Exchange)
12	Banco de Bogotá & Banco de Colombia
14	Casona de Taminango (Museum & Restaurant)
15	Iglesia de Lourdes
21	Banco de Occidente
22	Iglesia de San Felipe
23	Banco del Estado
24	Iglesia de San Agustín
26	Telecom
27	Casa del Barniz
30	Iglesia del Rosario
32	Iglesia La Merced
33	Instituto Geográfico Agustín Codazzi
34	Museo del Oro
40	Museo María Goretti

Installed in a meticulously reconstructed 17th-century house, the museum displays artefacts and other antique objects from the region. It's open Monday to Friday from 9 am to noon and 2 to 6 pm, and on Saturday from 9 am to 1 pm.

The **Museo Maridíaz** and **Museo María Goretti** both have missionary collections and, as such, resemble antique shops crammed with anything from images of the saints to cannonballs. However, you may want to visit them for their modest archaeological collections.

Festivals

The city's major event is the **Carnaval de Blancos y Negros**, held on 5 and 6 January. Its origins go back to the time of Spanish rule, when slaves were allowed to celebrate on 5 January and the masters showed their approval by painting their faces black. Likewise, the following day, the slaves painted their faces white. The tradition is maintained quite well, and on these two days, the city goes wild, with everybody painting one another with anything available. It's a serious affair – wear the worst clothes you have and buy an *antifaz*, a sort of mask to protect the face, widely sold for this occasion.

Places to Stay

For something at the bottom end, go to the *Residencias Colonial*, Carrera 21 No 19-32 (US$1.50 per person). It is clean and quiet, and has hot water early in the morning. It's highly improbable that you will find something better at this price.

There are plenty of cheapies around the bus terminals but nothing to recommend except, perhaps, the *Residencias Viena* (☎ 231790), at Carrera 19B No 18-39. This small, family-run place has rooms with common bath and hot water (around US$2 per person).

For US$3 per person, you have the *Hotel Manhattan*, at Calle 18 No 21B-14. It is a lovely place to stay, with old-world style and atmosphere. It has large, clean rooms, some with private bath.

If the Manhattan is full, try the *Hotel Río Nilo* (☎ 237389), at Calle 18 No 21A-45, just across the street. With its central courtyard, it also has some style, but is not as well kept and has smaller rooms (without bath) than the Manhattan. It costs US$3 per person.

Alternatively, go to the *Hotel Canchalá*, Calle 17 No 20A-38, which is better but lacks style. It has ample rooms with bath (US$5/7/9 a single/double/triple).

Marginally better is the *Hotel Isa* (☎ 235343), Calle 18 No 22-23, at US$7/10/14. Rooms have bath attached, but as in most low-budget and many mid-range hotels in Pasto, hot water is only available in the morning.

Yet another reasonably priced place is the *Hotel El Duque* (☎ 237390), Carrera 20A 17-17, at US$12/15/18. Rooms have TV, bath and hot water round the clock.

For something up-market, try the *Hotel Agualongo* (☎ 235216), Carrera 25 No 17-83, possibly the best in town. It costs about US$40/50/60, with discounts available at times.

Places to Eat

There are several cheap restaurants and cafés around the bus park where you can get a meal for not much more than a dollar, but it obviously won't be anything special.

There are also some cheap eateries in the central sector of the city. For vegetarian food, go to *Govinda's*, Carrera 24 No 14-04. The self-service *Punto Rojo*, on the main square, is a good place to put together a reasonably priced meal. It's clean, and open 24 hours.

The *Picantería Ipiales*, Calle 19 No 23-37, has typical food; try their lapingacho. The restaurant in the *Casona de Taminango* (closed on Monday) is not atmospheric but has a choice of regional dishes at reasonable prices.

In the *Don Pancho*, Calle 18 No 26-93, you'll get a filling plate of comida criolla (such as sobrebarriga, chuleta or arroz con pollo) for less than US$3. The hotel restaurante *El Paisa*, Carrera 26 No 15-37,

serves good Antioquian food, including bandeja paisa. *La Cabaña*, Calle 16 No 25-20, has good churrasco and parrillada.

The *Salsa Cazuela & Ceviche*, Carrera 23 No 20-40, is the place to go for ceviche and cheap beer, with good taped salsa music.

The restaurant at the *Hotel Don Saul*, Calle 17 No 23-52, is one of the best places to eat in the city centre, with a long menu including some Arab specialities.

Getting There & Away

Air The airport is 35 km north of the city on the road to Cali. Shared taxis go there from the corner of Calle 18 and Carrera 25 (US$2.50), or if you want to save, take any bus to Cali which will drop you near the airport. There are daily flights to Cali (US$46) and to Bogotá (US$80).

Bus All bus companies are clustered around the square at the corner of Calle 18 and Carrera 20. Buses to Ipiales run every 15 minutes or so (US$2.50, two hours). Frequent buses depart for Cali (US$13 pullman, US$15 climatizado, 10 hours). It's a very spectacular road, so do it in the daytime. These buses will put you down in Popayán in seven hours. There are a dozen direct buses to Bogotá (US$32 climatizado, 22 hours).

AROUND PASTO

A trip to the top of the **Volcán Galeras** (4267 metres) van not be recommended for the time being. Its activity rose dangerously in mid-1989, putting Pasto and the surrounding region in a state of emergency. Since that time, it has had several eruptions and is still smoking. Check for news with the tourist office.

What you can do is go to the **Laguna de la Cocha,** one of the biggest and most beautiful lakes in Colombia, about 25 km east of Pasto. The small island of La Corota, covered by dense forest, was declared a national reserve, due to its various species of flora. It is accessible by boat from the lakeshore. You can stay at the lake, as there is accommodation and food (fairly expensive) available. Alternatively, you can make a day trip from Pasto. All buses heading to Putumayo (Sibundoy, Mocoa, Puerto Asís, etc) will drop you near the lake (US$1, one hour). You can also go there by jeep (US$1, 40 minutes), departing from the back of the Hospital Departamental, at the corner of Calle 22 and Carrera 7. Frequent city buses will take you to the hospital.

IPIALES

Ipiales, a couple of km from the Ecuadorian border, is an uninteresting, busy commercial centre driven by contraband trade across the frontier. There is little to see, except for the big, colourful Saturday market, where the campesinos from surrounding villages come to sell and buy goods. A short side trip to Las Lajas is a must (see below).

Information

Money No bank in Ipiales changes cash or travellers' cheques. The Banco de Bogotá and Banco de Colombia may give advances on Visa card, while the Banco de Occidente will do the same on Mastercard. Plenty of moneychangers on the main square and at the border will change dollars, pesos and Ecuadorian *sucres*.

Immigration All passport formalities are done at the border, not in Ipiales or Tulcán. On the Colombian side of the frontier, there's a newly constructed brick building which houses the DAS office, the Ecuadorian Consulate and the Telecom office. The DAS office claims to be open from 6 am till midnight, but it's better to arrive at a more reasonable hour.

Ecuadorian Consulate The consulate on the border is open Monday to Friday from 8.30 am to noon and 2.30 to 6 pm, and it's your last chance to get a visa, if you need one. There's no Ecuadorian consulate in Ipiales nor in Pasto; the nearest is in Cali.

Places to Stay

The hotels tend to fill up early (particularly on Saturdays), and you may have to look around a bit if you arrive late. The nights are quite chilly, so check the number of blankets before you book a room.

The cheapest acceptable is the *Residencias Nueva York*, at the corner of Carrera 4 and Calle 13, which has fairly good rooms but without bath or hot water. It costs US$1.50 per person. Next door is the *Hotel Bahamas* (☎ 2884), which has hot water in common baths and costs US$2 per head.

The *Hotel San Fernando 1* has rooms with private bath and hot water (US$3/5 for a single/double). The *Hotel San Fernando 2* has similar standards but common baths only, for the same price.

The *Hotel Belmonte* (☎ 2771), Carrera 4 No 12-111, is a small, friendly, family-run place, possibly the most popular with foreign backpackers. It has no private baths but does have hot water. It costs US$3 per person.

The *Hotel ABC* (☎ 2311), Carrera 5 No 14-43, is yet another place offering good value for money. Singles/doubles/triples with bath and hot water cost US$3.50/6.50/8. For something appreciably better, check the *Hotel Rumichaca Internacional* (☎ 2692), Calle 14 No 7-114 (about US$10/s15/18). The best in the region is the expensive *Hostería Mayasquer* (☎ 2643), on the road to Ecuador, a few hundred metres before the border.

Places to Eat

Several cheap restaurants on the main square serve set meals, and many more are scattered around the town. Better eating places include *Greenhouse*, *Mi Casita*, *El Gran Pajar* and *Los Tejados*. The last two are more expensive.

Getting There & Away

Air The airport is seven km from Ipiales on the road to Guachucal, accessible by colectivo (US$0.50) or taxi (US$4). There are daily flights to Cali (US$57) and to Bogotá (US$88).

Bus Expreso Bolivariano has a dozen buses daily to Bogotá (US$35 climatizado, 24 hours). Trans Ipiales and Cootranar run

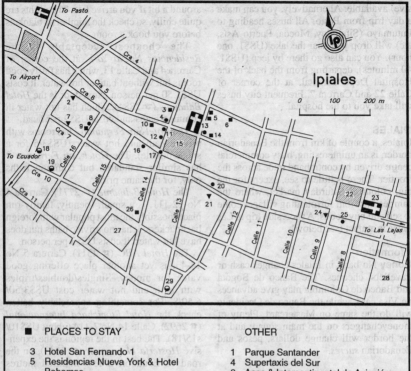

To Pasto

To Airport

To Ecuador

Ipiales

0   100   200 m

To Las Lajas

■ PLACES TO STAY

3 Hotel San Fernando 1
5 Residencias Nueva York & Hotel
   Bahamas
6 Hotel Belmonte
9 Hotel Angasmayo
10 Hotel ABC
14 Hotel San Fernando 2
26 Hotel Rumichaca Internacional

▼ PLACES TO EAT

2 Restaurante Greenhouse
7 Restaurante El Gran Pajar
21 Restaurante Los Tejados
24 Restaurante Mi Casita

OTHER

1 Parque Santander
4 Supertaxis del Sur
8 Aces & Intercontinental de Aviación
11 Cootranar
12 Banco de Colombia
13 Trans Ipiales
15 Plaza La Pola
16 Banco de Bogotá
17 Moneychangers
18 Trans Ipiales
19 Expreso Bolivariano
20 Banco de Occidente
22 Plaza de la Independencia
23 Catedral
25 Telecom
27 Market
28 Saturday Market
29 Taxi Colectivos to Ecuadorian Border

regular buses to Cali (US$16 pullman, 12 hours). All these buses will drop you in Popayán (US$12, nine hours).

Buses to Pasto leave every 15 minutes from the main square (US$2.50, two hours). Frequent taxi colectivos travel the 2½ km to the border, leaving from the corner of Calle 13 and Carrera 11 (US$0.30). After crossing the border, take another colectivo (US$0.40) or a minibus (US$0.30) to Tulcán (six km). On both routes, Colombian and Ecuadorian currency is accepted.

LAS LAJAS

A short detour to the **Santuario de Las Lajas**, seven km from Ipiales, is highly recommended. It is a neo-Gothic church built in the first half of this century on a bridge which spans a spectacular gorge. The church was constructed to commemorate the appearance of the Virgin, whose image, according to a legend, appeared on an enormous vertical rock about 45 metres above the river. The church is set up against the gorge cliff in such a way that the rock with the image is its main altar.

Pilgrims from all over Colombia and from abroad come here all year round. Many of them leave donations, marked by inscribed plaques along the alley heading to the church. Note the number of miracles which are said to have occurred.

You can stay in Las Lajas, in the *convent* which overlooks the gorge. Double rooms with bath attached cost US$2.50 per person.

Getting to Las Lajas is very easy. Frequent colectivos run from Ipiales, leaving from the corner of Carrera 6 and Calle 4 (US$0.40, 15 minutes). A taxi from Ipiales' main square to Las Lajas will cost about US$3.50. A return taxi trip for four people, including one hour of waiting in Las Lajas, shouldn't cost more than US$9.

Colombian Amazonia

The Amazon Basin covers the entire southeast portion of Colombia, comprising more than a third of its territory. Almost all the region is thick tropical forest, crisscrossed by rivers and sparsely inhabited by Indian tribes. There are no roads; transport is either by air (Satena is the major carrier) or by river. The most important rivers are the Putumayo (the main transport route) and the Caquetá (part of which is not navigable).

Road access to the Colombian Amazon is only from the west, the major starting points being the towns of Florencia and Puerto Asís. From Florencia, you can head into the jungle by the ríos Orteguaza and Caquetá as far as Araracuara. From Puerto Asís you can go by the Putumayo to Puerto Leguízamo, Leticia or further into Brazil. These trips can take weeks, as none of the boats runs on any regular schedule. Most are cargo boats, which leave when sufficient freight has been accumulated. The conditions on board are primitive – you sleep in a hammock or on the deck – and food is poor and monotonous. Water is taken straight from the river. There are plenty of mosquitos on the smaller rivers, though rarely any out on the middle of the larger rivers.

If you plan on doing any of these trips, you need plenty of time, huge doses of patience, a hammock, some of your own food, a water container, torch, insect repellent, antimalarials, water purifying tablets and quite a lot of money. Travel in the Amazon is not cheap, but it is, without doubt, a remarkable adventure.

LETICIA

On the Río Amazon where the borders of Colombia, Brazil and Peru meet, Leticia is the most popular place in Colombian Amazonia, principally due to its developed tourist facilities and its good flight connections with Bogotá and, through it, the rest of the country. Leticia has become the leading tourist centre for Colombians thirsty to see primitive tribes and buy their handicrafts, and to get a taste of the jungle. The influx has, to some degree, upset the natural balance, and today, the Indians work hard on their crafts to keep up with tourist demand.

As most products such as food, petrol, machinery and consumer goods have to be shipped or flown in from far away, Leticia is expensive for food and accommodation, and (especially) for the tours offered by travel agents and independent operators.

For travellers, Leticia is interesting

COLOMBIA

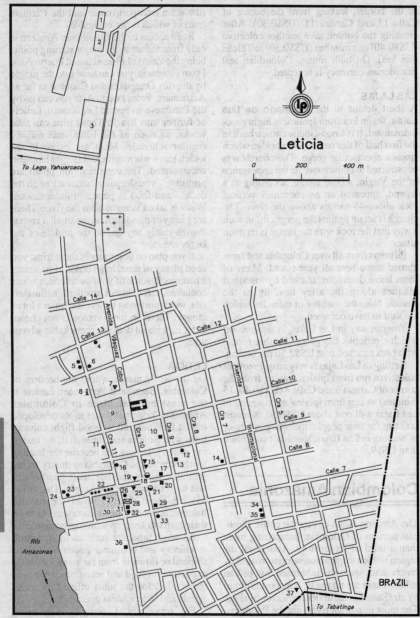

Leticia

0   200   400 m

To Lago Yahuarcaca

To Tabatinga

BRAZIL

COLOMBIA

■ PLACES TO STAY		19	Cafetería La Barra	16	Telecom
10	Residencias Marina	25	Restaurante El Viejo	18	Colectivos to Tabatinga
13	Residencias Fernando		Tolima	21	Taxi Stand
17	Residencias La	37	Restaurante Murallas	22	Casas de Cambio
	Manigua		de Cartagena	23	Market, Tres Fronteras
20	Residencias				& Expreso
	Primavera		OTHER		Amazonas
29	Hotel Colonial			24	Wharf
31	Hotel Anaconda	1	Aerosucre Warehouse	26	Banco Ganadero
35	Residencias	2	Airport Terminal	27	Expreso Aéreo
	Internacional	3	Jardín Botánico	28	Avianca & Post Office
36	Parador Ticuna		Zoológico	30	Parque Orellana
		4	Brazilian Consulate	32	Peruvian Consulate
▼ PLACES TO EAT		5	Inderena & Satena	33	Banco de Bogotá
		6	Police Station	34	Amazon Jungle Trips
7	La Casa del Pan	8	Tourist Office		
15	Restaurante Bucca-	9	Parque Santander		
	neer & Restaurante	11	Museo Etnográfico		
	Sancho Panza	12	DAS Office		
		14	Gallera		

because it is linked via the Amazon to Manaus and Iquitos and therefore offers reasonably easy travel between Brazil, Colombia and Peru. The best time to visit the region is in July or August, which are the only relatively dry months. The wettest period is from March to May.

Orientation

Leticia lies right on the Colombian-Brazilian border. Just across the frontier sits Tabatinga, the first Brazilian settlement, smaller and poorer than Leticia, but with its own airport. Leticia and Tabatinga are virtually merging together, and there are no border check posts between the two. Frequent colectivos link the two settlements, or you can just walk from one centre to the other in 20 minutes. Traffic of both locals and foreigners is allowed without visas, but if you plan on heading further into either country, you must get exit/entry stamps in your passport from DAS in Leticia and Polícia Federal in Tabatinga (not on the actual border).

On the opposite bank of the Amazon from Leticia/Tabatinga is Santa Rosa, a Peruvian village. A boat goes across the river and back from Tabatinga wharf, not from Leticia. The one-way fare is US$1.50.

About 20 km down the Amazon from Santa Rosa, on the same side of the river, is the Brazilian town of Benjamin Constant, the main port for boats downstream to Manaus. Tabatinga and Benjamin Constant are connected by one boat daily in each direction (US$2.50 either way).

Information

Tourist Office At the time of writing, the new regional tourist office (☎ 27505) was about to open at Carrera 11 No 11-35.

Money The Banco de Bogotá, at the corner of Carrera 10 and Calle 7, is the only bank which changes travellers' cheques for pesos (from 10.30 am to 1.30 pm). It also gives advances to Visa card holders, as does the Banco Ganadero, on Carrera 11. No bank in Leticia will exchange cash dollars.

There are plenty of casas de cambio on Calle 8, from Carrera 11 down towards the river. They change US dollars, Colombian pesos, Brazilian cruzeiros and Peruvian *nuevos soles* in any direction. They are open till 5 or 6 pm on weekdays and till around 2 pm on Saturday. Shop around, as the rates vary.

Many shops in the same area also change money, at rates similar to those in the casas de cambio. One which might be of interest is

COLOMBIA

the Importadora Miscelánea No 1, Calle 8 No 10-90. It pays slightly better rates for your dollars than its neighbours, and is one of the few places that change travellers' cheques, though at a poor rate.

There are also moneychanging facilities in Tabatinga and Benjamin Constant, but they are fewer and usually pay less than you can get in Leticia. If you have a Visa card and you are travelling from Colombia or Peru into Brazil, the Banco do Brasil in Tabatinga will pay you a cash advance in cruzeiros.

Immigration The DAS office in Leticia, on Calle 9, is open Monday to Saturday from 7 am to noon and 2 to 6 pm. This is where you get your passport stamped when leaving or entering Colombia.

Entry/exit stamps for Brazil must be obtained at the Policía Federal, on the main road in Tabatinga, near the hospital. The office is open daily from 8 am to noon and 2 to 6 pm. Dress neatly for a visit to either office.

If you arrive or depart by air you get your passport stamped at the Leticia or Tabatinga airport. If heading for/coming from Iquitos (Peru) by boat, you get your entry/exit stamp in Santa Rosa.

Consulates The Peruvian Consulate in Leticia, on Carrera 11, next to the Hotel Anaconda, is open Monday to Friday from 8.30 am to 2.30 pm. If you need a visa, it will be issued within a couple of hours (around US$12).

The Brazilian Consulate, on Calle 13, is open Monday to Friday from 8 am to 2 pm. A visa is given within a day and is valid for a stay of 90 days. rrrUS and French citizens won't be given Brazilian visas in Leticia, nor in Bogotá.

Inderena The Inderena office (☎ 27619), on Carrera 11, will give you information about the Parque Nacional Amacayacu, sell the entry permit (US$1) and book accommodation there.

Things to See

There's not much to see or do in the town itself. You can visit the small **Jardín Botánico Zoológico**, near the airport, which has almost nothing in the way of flora but does have some snakes and crocodiles. It's open daily from 7 am to 6 pm; the admission fee is US$1.

A modern library was built by the Banco de la República on Carrera 11. It's worth a visit for its **Museo Etnográfico**, open Monday to Friday from 8 am to noon and 2 to 6 pm, featuring artefacts and household implements of Indian tribes living in the region.

Have a look around the market near the river and stroll along the waterfront, crammed with boats and with stalls selling fish which has just arrived from the river.

On Sunday evening, there are cockfights at the local *gallera*. Cockfights are said to be an aspect of Colombian culture, but hopefully visitors will spurn such cruel 'entertainment'.

Leticia has become a tourist spot not for what the town itself offers but for the surrounding region. However, as all transport is by river and there are no regular passenger boats, it's difficult to get around cheaply on your own. All trips are monopolised by tourist agents and by locals with their own boats, and are expensive.

Among the places to visit, the **Isla de los Micos** (Monkey Island), some 40 km up the Amazon from Leticia, is the number one spot for the tour business. There are over 10,000 small, yellow-footed monkeys living on the island. A footpath has been traced through a part of the island to give you a taste of the lush jungle vegetation.

Parque Nacional Amacayacu

This natural reserve takes in a large area of jungle to the north-west of Leticia. A spacious visitors' centre with food and accommodation facilities has been built on the bank of the Amazon. Accommodation in bed/hammock costs US$6/4 per person, and three meals (breakfast, lunch and dinner) will run at about US$9. You have to book and pay for this at the Inderena office in Leticia or Bogotá.

Tres Fronteras and Expreso Amazonas, both near the waterfront in Leticia, operate fast passenger boats to Puerto Nariño, daily around noon. They will put you down in the park's visitors' centre, for US$8.

From the centre, you can explore the park, either by marked paths or by water. In the high-water period (March to June), much of the land turns into swamps and lagoons, greatly reducing walking options.

The main Indian tribes living in the region are the Ticunas and Yaguas. The major settlement of the Ticunas is Arara, but the village is on the route of almost every tour and has become something of a theatre with Indians as the actors. The Yaguas are more traditional and ethnically different; they are noted for their *achiote*, a red paint used on the face.

Other places popular with the tour operators are Puerto Nariño, the second largest town in the region, some 100 km upriver from Leticia, and Lago Tarapoto to the west of Puerto Nariño.

The wilderness begins well off the Amazon proper, on its small tributaries. The further you go, the more chance you have to observe wildlife and see Indians in relatively undamaged habitat.

Jungle Tours

Several travel agencies in Leticia run the tour business. The two best-known are Turamazonas (in the Hotel Parador Ticuna) and Anaconda Tours (in the Hotel Anaconda). These days they focus on standard one-day tours, rarely offering anything more adventurous. A seven to eight-hour trip to Monkey Island, Bellavista or Puerto Nariño, with a visit to an Indian village on the way, will cost roughly US$30, lunch included. These excursions are well organised, comfortable and trouble-free but can hardly give you a real picture of the jungle or the Indians. They are probably not worth the time and money, unless you have just a day

to spend or no time to look for something better.

To get in closer touch with the forest, its wildlife and the indigenous people, you must get further off the tourist track. This will obviously involve more time and money, but the experience will be much more rewarding. A tour of some three to five days is suggested.

A recommended agent for an adventurous trip is Antonio Cruz Pérez of Amazon Jungle Trips (☎ 27377), Avenida Internacional No 6-25, near the border. He speaks English and has a good guide and boatman/cook who will take you into wild areas of the region in Brazil, Peru and Colombia (no visas necessary). Tours of two to 10 days (or more) can be organised. You'll sleep in the huts of the locals or in camps arranged by your guides. Count on around US$35 per person per day in a group of six, all inclusive. Four people are usually a minimum for a trip, unless you are prepared to pay substantially more.

Contact the agent soon after arrival in Leticia, as it may take a couple of days to collect the party and arrange the trip. He usually waits at the airport for incoming flights from Bogotá. You might also want to check other agencies, such as Amazon Explorers and Amaturs, both next door to the Hotel Anaconda.

There are many independent operators who don't have offices; they will find you to offer their services, usually starting their show by presenting thick albums of photos from their trips. The prices they ask for at the beginning may be similar to or even higher than those offered by the agencies, but are open to negotiation. Always fix clearly the conditions, places to be visited, time and price. Make it clear who's going to pay the entrance fee (US$4) to Monkey Island, and to some Indian settlements for visiting their villages. If you don't insist on including it in the tour's price, you'll pay all these extras. Pay only a part of the cost of the trip before departure and the rest at the end. Avoid Joel Mendoza, known locally as Tatoo – there have been repeated complaints about his services.

Bring enough mosquito repellent from Bogotá because you can't get good stuff in Leticia. Take high-speed film – the jungle is always dark.

Places to Stay
Accommodation in Leticia is not plentiful but is generally sufficient to cope with the tourist traffic. There are a dozen places to stay, offering a fairly good standard. All have private bath and fan. However, they are not that cheap.

At the bottom end, expect to pay around US$5/7 for a single/double. At this price, among the best are the *Residencias La Manigua* (☎ 27121), *Apartamentos Jolamar* (☎ 27016) and *Residencias Marina*, all clean and friendly. *Residencias Primavera* (no sign on the door), across the street from La Manigua, is more basic and noisy for the same price, but you have a good chance of getting a room here if the other hotels are full.

Another place to check is *Residencias Internacional* (☎ 28066), on Avenida Internacional, near the border, which is better than Primavera and usually has vacancies.

Residencias Fernando (☎ 27362) is a pleasant place to stay, though a bit over-priced at US$8/12.

There are three up-market hotels, all with air-conditioning and swimming pools. The most pleasant is the *Parador Ticuna* (☎ 27241), with a spacious courtyard filled with tropical plants. Large rooms cost US$40/55, and there's a restaurant on the premises. The hotel runs the Monkey Island Lodge on the Isla de los Micos (US$36 per person, three meals included) and houses the office of the Turamazonas travel agency.

The *Hotel Colonial* costs the same as the Parador Ticuna but isn't as good, in either location or in the standard of the rooms. *Hotel Anaconda* (☎ 27119) is modern though rather styleless, and costs the same as the above two. It has good views over the Amazon (particularly at sunset), if you are lucky enough to get the room on the top floor facing the river. There have been some critical comments about the hotel's services.

You can also stay in Tabatinga, across the border. It is a less attractive place than Leticia but is cheaper. Both pesos and cruzeiros are accepted in most establishments.

Places to Eat
The food is not bad in Leticia, though it is fairly expensive. The local speciality is the fish; don't miss the delicious gamitana. Also try cupuasú juice, from a local fruit somewhat similar in taste to guanábana. Fizzy drinks and beer are expensive.

The *Sancho Panza*, on Carrera 10, is possibly the cheapest restaurant for set almuerzos and comidas (US$1.75), though the food is only OK. For marginally more, you can have tastier set meals at the *Buccaneer*, next door, or at *El Viejo Tolima*, on Calle 8, one block away. The latter looks pretty ordinary but has good fish and meat dishes and fruit juices. One more restaurant worth a mention is the *Murallas de Cartagena*, next to the border, which is open till late at night.

More up-market, you can eat in the restaurants of either the *Hotel Anaconda* or the *Parador Ticuna*.

Cafetería La Barra, on Calle 8, opposite El Viejo Tolima, is a place popular with locals for a good tinto and cheap fruit juices, while *La Casa del Pan*, in the Parque Santander, is a tiny café which always has fresh bread and pastries – a good place for breakfast.

Getting There & Away – Air
Domestic Avianca has three direct flights per week to/from Bogotá, on Monday, Wednesday and Friday (US$112). Satena flies to/from Bogotá on Sunday, and is cheaper (US$96). Satena's flights are usually in light planes and call at one or two small Amazon ports on the way. Consequently, the trip takes longer than with Avianca, but you'll see more. It may be difficult to get on these flights without advance booking. Satena also flies from Leticia to Mitú (US$55), Araracuara (US$55), La Pedrera and some other Colombian Amazon localities.

Before you book on a commercial flight to Bogotá, check the cargo flights. Aerosucre shuttles between Leticia and Bogotá almost daily and usually takes passengers. Avesca, another cargo carrier, comes to Leticia a few times per week and is also willing to generate some extra cash by carrying passengers. The price is about US$75. Both carriers use large jet planes. You must hunt for them at the airport, as there is no fixed schedule. The Aerosucre *bodega* (warehouse) is just behind the passenger terminal. In Bogotá, the Aerosucre departure point for the planes is the cargo building (Edificio de Carga No 1) just before the El Dorado passenger terminal, on your right going towards the airport from the city centre.

To/From Brazil There are no flights into Brazil from Leticia, but from Tabatinga, Varig/Cruzeiro has three flights per week to Manaus, on Monday, Wednesday and Saturday (US$140). The airline's office is just 300 metres past the frontier. The airport is some two km from Tabatinga, linked by frequent colectivos. Remember to get your exit/entry stamps in your passport. The yellow fever vaccination certificate is required by Brazilian officials.

To/From Peru Varig/Cruzeiro has a flight on Saturday at noon from Tabatinga to Iquitos (US$121 one-way, US$156 return, minimum five days, maximum two months). The Expreso Aéreo, a new and still unestablished local carrier, has flights from Leticia to Iquitos on Wednesday and Sunday in light Fokker planes (about US$102, 19% Colombian tax included).

Getting There & Away – Boat

Sitting on the border between Brazil, Colombia and Peru, Leticia is an attractive transit point for travellers looking for a somewhat adventurous, backwater route between these three countries. As there are no roads in the region, transport is by either air or water. Although boat fares have risen considerably over the past few years, they are still interesting, for the adventure they provide.

To/From Puerto Asís Irregular cargo boats depart from Leticia to Puerto Asís, on the upper reaches of the Putumayo. The trip can take up to 20 days, and the price varies substantially, from US$100 to US$150, food included. From Puerto Asís, you can continue on by road to Pasto or head to Ecuador via San Miguel. It's better to do this route in reverse (ie downstream), as it is faster and cheaper.

To/From Manaus (Brazil) Boats down the Amazon to Manaus leave from Benjamin Constant but usually come up to Tabatinga to unload/load. They anchor in Porto de Tabatinga, one km south of the town's fishing wharf.

Theoretically, there are two boats per week, leaving Tabatinga on Wednesday and Saturday mornings and Benjamin Constant the same evenings. The trip to Manaus takes four days and costs US$85 in your own hammock, US$250 for a double cabin. Food is included but is poor and monotonous. It's a good idea to buy some snacks as a supplement, and bottled water, easily available in Leticia.

The boats come to Tabatinga a couple of days before their scheduled departure back down the river. You can string up your hammock or occupy the cabin as soon as you've paid the fare, saving on hotels. Food, however, is only served after departure. Beware of theft on board. If the boat doesn't come up to Tabatinga but only to Benjamin Constant, you must go there by passenger boat, which departs daily from Tabatinga around 5 pm (US$2.50), or 'pagar expreso' (hire a boat) for 10 times as much.

In the opposite direction, upstream from Manaus to Benjamin Constant, the trip takes six to seven days.

You can buy a typical net-type Indian hammock made of the fibre of a species of palm known as *chambira*. They are sold in artefact shops in Leticia, and around the market near the riverfront. These hammocks are decorative, but not very comfortable if you are not used to them. It's better to buy an ordinary cloth hammock. The cheapest place to get one (for US$6 to US$8) is the Esplanada Tecidos shop, near the wharf in Tabatinga.

To/From Iquitos (Peru) Expreso Loreto in Tabatinga, near the wharf, initiated the *rápido* (fast boat) passenger service from Tabatinga to Iquitos. The boats are supposed to depart on Tuesday and Sunday at 5 am, to reach the destination 10 to 12 hours later (in reverse, the trip is about two hours shorter). The boats call at Santa Rosa's immigration posts. The journey costs US$50 in either direction.

There are irregular cargo boats to Iquitos once or twice a week, departing from Santa Rosa. The journey takes three days and costs US$25 to US$30, after some negotiations. In reverse, downstream from Iquitos to Santa Rosa, it takes around 36 hours.

Note that there are no roads out of Iquitos into Peru. You have to fly or continue by river to Pucallpa (five to seven days), from where you can go overland to Lima and elsewhere.

The cheapest place to stay in Tabatinga is the *Hotel Halley*. It's very basic, but rooms have their own bath and cost US$4 a double. Next door is the considerably better *Hotel Pajé*, also with private bath, charging US$4/5.

If you need a room with air-conditioning, try the *Hotel Miraflores*, 300 metres past the border from Leticia (US$7/11), or better, the *Hotel Belo Brasil*, on the road to the wharf (US$15 a double).

Like accommodation, food is cheaper in Tabatinga than in Leticia. The restaurants to try there are the *Bella Época* (diagonally opposite the church), the *Canto da Peixada* (near the Banco do Brasil) and the *Tres Fronteras* (which has recently moved from Leticia to Tabatinga).

Ecuador

Ecuador is the smallest of the Andean countries, and in many ways it is the easiest and most pleasant to travel in. From the well-preserved colonial capital of Quito, in the highlands, you can travel by frequent buses to Andean Indian markets, remote jungle towns and warm Pacific beaches. From Quito, you can get to most points in the country in less than a day by public transport.

The highlands have many colourful Indian markets, some world-famous and deservedly so, and others which are rarely visited by foreigners. Journeys in the highlands are dominated by magnificent volcanos such as Cotopaxi – at 5897 metres, the highest active volcano in the world.

Jungle travel in Ecuador is easier than in other countries because the distances involved are shorter, so you can be in the jungle after a day of bus travel from Quito. From the towns on the jungle fringe, you can hire local guides or strike out on your own from places such as Misahuallí, on the Río Napo, a tributary of the Amazon.

The coast, too, is interesting. Go to a fishing village and watch the fishers expertly return their traditional balsa-wood rafts through the ocean breakers to the sandy shore, or help them pull in their nets in return for some of the catch. Laze on the beach in the equatorial sun, swim in the warm seas, and in the evening, listen to salsa music in a local bar.

The Galápagos Islands (Islas Galápagos), 1000 km off Ecuador's Pacific coast, attract people interested in wildlife. Swim with penguins and sea lions, or walk along beaches while pelicans flap by and huge land and marine iguanas scurry around your feet. The animals are so unafraid of humans that, at times, it's difficult to avoid stepping on them.

Facts about the Country

HISTORY

Ecuadorian stone-age tools have been dated to 9000 BC, and the oldest signs of a more developed culture date back to 3400 BC. These are mainly ceramics of the Valdivia period, found on the central coastal area of Ecuador. The humid conditions of coastal Ecuador were not conducive to the preservation of artefacts, so these cultures may have been older and more complex than expected; in any event, they pre-date the earliest artifacts from Peru considerably.

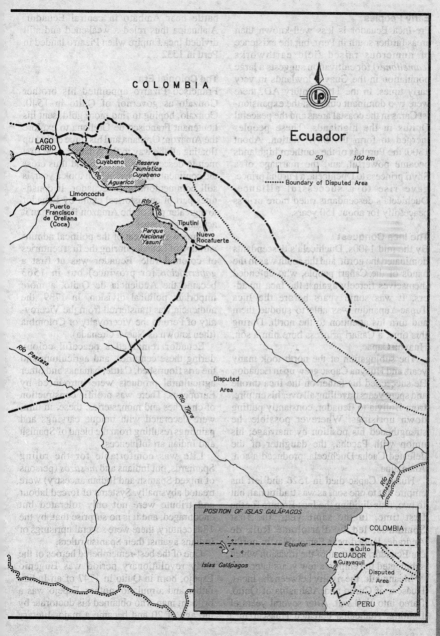

COLOMBIA

Ecuador

0   50   100 km

.... Boundary of Disputed Area

LAGO
AGRIO

Cuyabeno   Reserva
Faunística
Aguarico   Cuyabeno

Río

Limoncocha

Puerto
Francisco
de Orellana
(Coca)

Río Napo

Tiputini

Parque
Nacional
Yasuní   Nuevo
Rocafuerte

Río Pastaza

Disputed
Area

Río Tigre

Río Amazonas

POSITION OF ISLAS GALÁPAGOS

COLOMBIA

Equator

ECUADOR

Islas Galápagos   Quito

Guayaquil

Disputed
Area

PERU

ECUADOR

Early Peoples

Pre-Inca Ecuador is less well-known than areas farther south in Peru, but the existence of numerous raised field earthworks (*camellones*) for cultivation suggests a large population in the Guayas lowlands in very early times. In the 11th century AD, there were two dominant cultures: the expansionist Caras in the coastal areas and the peaceful Quitus in the highlands. These peoples merged to form the Shyri nation. About 1300, the Puruhás of the southern highlands became powerful, and the marriage of a Shyri princess to Duchicela, a Puruhá prince, gave rise to a successful alliance. Duchicela's descendants ruled more or less peacefully for about 150 years.

The Inca Conquest

By the mid 1400s, Duchicela's descendants dominated the north, and the south was in the hands of the Cañari people, who defended themselves fiercely against the Inca invaders. It was some years before the Inca Tupac-Yupanqui was able to subdue them and turn his attention to the north. During this time, a Cañari princess bore him a son, Huayna Capac.

The subjugation of the north took many years and Huayna Capac grew up in Ecuador. He succeeded his father on the Inca throne and spent years travelling all over his empire, from Bolivia to Ecuador, constantly putting down uprisings. Wherever possible, he strengthened his position by marriage; his union with Paccha, the daughter of the defeated Cacha Duchicela, produced a son, Atahualpa.

Huayna Capac died in 1526 and left his empire not to one son, as was traditional, but to two, thus dividing the Inca Empire for the first time. In the same year, the first Spaniards, led by Bartolomé Ruiz de Andrade, landed near Esmeraldas in northern Ecuador, a portent of the invasion which subjugated the empire a few years later.

Meanwhile, the rivalry between the Incas, Huáscar of Cuzco and Atahualpa of Quito, flared into civil war. After several years of fighting, Atahualpa defeated Huáscar in a battle near Ambato in central Ecuador. Atahualpa thus ruled a weakened and still divided Inca Empire when Pizarro landed in Peru in 1532.

The Colonial Era

Francisco Pizarro appointed his brother Gonzalo as governor of Quito in 1540. Gonzalo, hoping to find more gold, sent his lieutenant Francisco de Orellana to explore the Amazon; Orellana and his force ended up floating all the way to the Atlantic – the first men to descend the Amazon and thus cross the continent. This feat, which took a year, is still commemorated in Ecuador. It constitutes part of an historical claim by Ecuador to a greater part of the Amazon Basin than it actually possesses.

Lima was the seat of the political administration of Ecuador during the first centuries of colonial rule. Ecuador was at first a *gobernación* (or province) but in 1563 became the Audiencia de Quito, a more important political division. In 1739, the audiencia was transferred from the Viceroyalty of Peru to the Viceroyalty of Colombia (then known as Nueva Grenada).

Ecuador remained a peaceful colony during these centuries, and agriculture and the arts flourished. Cattle, bananas and other agricultural products were introduced by Europeans. There was prolific construction of churches and monasteries; these, in turn, were decorated with unique carvings and paintings resulting from the blend of Spanish and Indian art influences.

Life was comfortable for the ruling Spaniards, but Indians and *mestizos* (persons of mixed Spanish and Indian ancestry) were treated abysmally. Systems of forced labour and tribute were not only tolerated but encouraged, and it is no surprise that, by the 18th century, there were several uprisings of Indians against their Spanish rulers.

One of the best-remembered heroes of the early revolutionary period was Eugenio Espejo, born in Quito in 1747 of an Indian father and a mulatto mother. Espejo was a brilliant man who obtained his doctorate by the age of 20 and became a major literary voice for independence. He wrote political satire, founded a liberal newspaper and spoke out strongly against colonialism. He was imprisoned several times, and died in jail in 1795.

Independence

The first serious attempt at independence was by a partisan group led by Juan Pío Montúfar, on 10 August 1809. The group managed to take Quito and install a government, but this lasted only 24 days before royalist troops were able to regain control.

Independence was finally achieved when Simón Bolívar, the Venezuelan liberator, marching southward from Caracas, freed Colombia in 1819. Then Bolívar supported the people of Guayaquil when they claimed independence on 9 October 1820. It was almost two years before Ecuador was entirely liberated from Spanish rule. The decisive battle was fought on 24 May 1822, when Field Marshal Sucre, one of Bolívar's best generals, defeated the royalists at Pichincha and took Quito.

Bolívar's idealistic dream was to form a United South America, and he began by amalgamating Venezuela, Colombia and Ecuador into the independent state of Gran Colombia. This lasted eight years, and Ecuador became fully independent in 1830. In the same year, a treaty was signed with Peru, drawing up a boundary between the two nations. This boundary is marked on Ecuadorian maps, but after a war with Peru, the border was redrawn in the 1942 protocol of Rio de Janeiro, and it is this border that is found on all non-Ecuadorian maps.

Independent Ecuador's internal history has been a typically Latin American turmoil of political and open warfare between liberals and conservatives. Quito emerged as the main centre for the church-backed conservatives and Guayaquil has traditionally been considered liberal and socialist. This rivalry continues on a social level today; Quiteños have nicknamed Guayaquileños *monos* (monkeys) and the lively coastal people think of the highland inhabitants as very staid and dull.

The rivalry between the groups frequently escalated to extreme violence: conservative President García Moreno was shot and killed in 1875 and liberal President Eloy Alfaro was killed and burned by a mob in Quito in 1912. The military began to assume control, and the 20th century has seen more periods of military rule than of civilian.

Ecuador's most recent period of democracy began in 1979, when President Jaime Roldos Aguilera was elected. He died in an aeroplane crash in 1981 and his term of office was completed by his vice president, Osvaldo Hurtado Larrea.

In 1984, the conservative León Febres Cordero was elected. On 10 August 1988, following democratic elections, the Social Democrat Rodrigo Borja became president and the government leant to the left. The most recent elections, in 1992, saw the conservative Quiteño Sixto Duran, of the Republican Unity Party, pitted against Guayaquileño Jaime Nebot, leader of the Social Christian Party. Sixto Duran emerged the winner and has a mandate to lead the country until 1996.

GEOGRAPHY

Ecuador straddles the equator on the Pacific coast of South America and is bordered by only two countries: Colombia to the north and Peru to the south. Geographically, Ecuador is one of the world's most varied countries, despite its small size, which at 283,520 sq km is a little larger than the UK.

The country is divided into three regions. The backbone of Ecuador is the Andean range, which runs from north to south. Nestled in these mountains is the capital, Quito. At 2850 metres above sea level, it is the second highest capital in the world (after La Paz, Bolivia). The mountains split the country into the western coastal lowlands and the eastern jungles of the upper Amazon Basin, known in Ecuador as the Oriente. In only 200 km as the condor flies, you can climb from the coast to snowcaps at over six km above sea level, then descend back down to the steaming rainforest on the eastern side.

ECUADOR

FLORA & FAUNA

Ecuador, despite its small size, has many more plant and animal species than do much larger countries. In fact, acre for acre, Ecuador is one of the most species-rich countries on the globe. Scientists have long realised that the tropics harbour many more species (greater biodiversity) than do more temperate countries, but the reasons for this are still a matter of debate and research. The most commonly held belief is that the tropics acted as a refuge for plants and animals during the many ice ages affecting more temperate regions – the much longer and relatively stable climatic history of the tropics has enabled speciation to occur.

Another reason for Ecuador's biodiversity is simply that there are a great number of different habitats within the borders of this small country. Obviously, the Andes will support very different species from the low tropical rainforests, and when intermediate habitats are included and the coastal areas added, the result is a wealth of habitats, ecosystems and wildlife. Ecologists consider Ecuador to be one of the world's 'mega-diversity hot spots'. This has attracted increasing numbers of nature lovers from all over the world.

Plants

There are over 20,000 species of vascular plants in Ecuador and new species are being discovered every year. Compare this to the 17,000 species in the entire North American continent.

Birds

Bird-watchers come to Ecuador because of the great number of species recorded here – some 1500, or about twice the number found in any one of the continents of North America, Europe or Australia. New species are often added to the list.

Mammals

These, too, are well represented, with some 300 species recorded in the country. These vary from monkeys in the Amazonian lowlands to the rare Andean spectacled bear in the highlands. The most diverse mammals are the bats – there are well over 100 species in Ecuador alone.

National Parks

Ecuador's first *parque nacional* (national park) was the Islas Galápagos, formed in 1959. The first mainland park was Cotopaxi, established in 1975, followed by Machalilla, Yasuní, and Sangay in 1979, and Podocarpus in 1982.

As well as these six national parks, there are six *reservas* (reserves) of various kinds, most created in 1979; included are Mangalares-Churute, Cotocachi-Cayapas and Cuyabeno. The two national recreation areas include Cajas, near Cuenca. Additionally, local conservation organisations such as the Fundación Natura and others have begun to set aside private nature reserves.

Together, these areas cover about 10% of the national territory. All of Ecuador's major ecosystems are partly protected in one (or more) of these areas.

The national parks do not have the tourist infrastructure which one may be used to in other parts of the world. There are almost no hostels, drive-in campgrounds, restaurants, ranger stations, museums, scenic overlooks, or information centres. Some of the parks or reserves are remote, difficult to get to, and lacking all facilities. Many are inhabited by indigenous peoples who had been living in the area for generations before the area achieved park or reserve status.

All of these areas are susceptible to interests which are incompatible with full protection – oil drilling, logging, mining, ranching and colonisation. Despite this, the national parks do preserve large tracts of pristine habitat and many travellers visit at least one park or reserve during their stay in Ecuador.

The national park system is administered (perhaps not protected) by La División e Areas Naturales y Vida Silvestre (Division of Natural Areas and Wildlife), which is part of El Ministerio de Agricultura y Ganadería (Ministery of Agriculture and Ranching, or more commonly, MAG).

Conservation

Ecotourism is becoming increasingly important for the economy of Ecuador and other nations with similar natural resources. People are more likely to visit Ecuador to see monkeys in the forest than to see cows at pasture. Those visitors then spend money on hotels, transport, food, etc. Many people who spend time in the tropics become more understanding of the problems facing the forests and of the importance of preserving them. As a result, visitors return home and become goodwill ambassadors for tropical forests.

Other innovative projects for sustainable development of tropical forests are being researched and implemented. Conservation International has developed the sustainable harvesting of the tagua nut – as hard as ivory and used to carve ornaments (as souvenirs).

Other international agencies have developed programmes such as the 'debt for nature' swaps, whereby parts of Ecuador's national debt was paid off in return for local groups receiving Ecuadorian funds for preserving crucial habitats.

Local conservation groups have blossomed in the late 1980s and early 1990s. Some groups have been quite successful in providing legal protection for forests. Other groups have concentrated on improving environmental data collection and on training members in the disciplines needed to create a strong information base for national conservation research.

Small local groups protect specific natural areas. These groups involve nearby communities through environmental education, agroforestry and community development projects. Such community involvement at the grass roots level is essential for viable conservation in Ecuador.

CLIMATE

Instead of the four seasons, Ecuador has wet and dry seasons. The local weather patterns vary greatly, depending on which geographical region you are in.

The Galápagos and coastal areas have a hot and rainy season from January to April.

It doesn't rain all the time but you can expect torrential downpours which often disrupt communications. Daytime temperatures average about 31°C but are often much higher, and it is generally unpleasant to travel in the coastal regions during this time. From May to December, temperatures are a few degrees lower and it rarely rains.

If you want to travel in the Oriente, bring your rain gear, as it rains during most months. September to December are usually the driest months, and June to August are the wettest – with regional variations. It's usually almost as hot as the coast.

The dry season in the highlands is from June to September, and a short dry season also occurs during the month around Christmas. It doesn't rain daily in the wet season, however. April, the wettest month, averages one rainy day in two. Daytime temperatures in Quito average a high of 20°C to 22°C and a low of 7°C to 8°C all year round. One should remember, however, that the most predictable aspect of Ecuador's weather is its unpredictability.

GOVERNMENT

Ecuador is a republic with a democratic government headed by a president. The first constitution was written in 1830, but has had several changes since then, the most recent in 1978. Democratically elected governments have regularly been toppled by coups, often led by the military. Since 1979, however, all governments have been freely elected. All literate citizens over 18 have the vote, and the president must receive over 50% of the vote to be elected. With at least 13 different political parties, 50% of the vote is rarely achieved, in which case there is a second round between the top two contenders. A president governs for a maximum of five years and cannot be re-elected.

The president is also the head of the armed forces and appoints his or her own cabinet ministers. There are 12 ministries forming the executive branch of the government.

The legislative branch of government consists of a single Chamber of Representatives (or Congress) which has 77 members. The

ECUADOR

Congress appoints the justices of the Supreme Court.

There are 21 provinces (*provincias*), each with a governor appointed by the president and democratically elected prefects. The provinces are subdivided into smaller political units called *cantones*; each cantón has a democratically elected *alcalde*, or mayor.

ECONOMY

Until recently, Ecuador was the archetypal 'banana republic'. Bananas were the most important export until the early 1970s, and most other exports were agricultural. This changed with the discovery of oil. Petroleum exports rose to first place in 1973 and by the 1980s accounted for about half of the total export earnings. The 1986 drop in world oil prices combined with the 1987 earthquake (which damaged the pipelines and caused a temporary stop to oil exportation) exacerbated economic problems. Although the pipeline has been repaired, Ecuador's current output of about 350,000 barrels per day does not provide as much income as it did in the early to mid-1980s. Nevertheless, oil is Ecuador's economic mainstay – at least until oil reserves are depleted, which may happen by early in the next century. Bananas remain important (accounting for about 14% of the nation's exports), followed by shrimp (13%), manufactured goods (13%) and coffee (6%). Tourism is rapidly becoming an important part of the economy.

The new-found wealth produced by oil exportation has definitely improved the standards of living. Nevertheless, Ecuador remains a poor country. Distribution of wealth has been patchy, and much of the rural population continues to live at the same standards it did a decade ago. However, education and medical services have improved. Per capita Gross National Product (GNP) is a little over $1000 annually and inflation rates have been 50% to 100% in recent years. The foreign debt stands at about $12,000 million.

POPULATION & PEOPLE

In 1993, the population was well over 11 million. The population density of 39 people per sq km is the highest of any South American country. The birth rate is 31 per 1000 inhabitants, which means the population will double by about 2020 AD.

Over 40% of the population are Indians and almost as many are mestizos. The remainder are White, Black or Asian.

Most of the Indians are Quechua-speaking and live in the highlands. A few other small groups live in the lowlands. About 48% of the population live on the coast (and the Galápagos) and about 46% in the highlands. The remainder live in the jungle region of the Oriente, where colonisation is slowly increasing. The urban population is 55%. In recent years, the indigenous peoples have become more involved in national politics and have mobilised to protect their special interests.

EDUCATION

Elementary education (two grades of kindergarten and six grades of school) are mandatory, though about 50% of children drop out of school before sixth grade. In the highlands, the school year is from October to July. On the coast, however, the school year is from May to January. There are about 20 universities and technical colleges.

ARTS
Visual Arts

The Spanish conquistadors trained the local indigenous artists to produce the colonial religious art which is now seen in many churches and art museums. Thus arose the Quito School of Art – Spanish religious concepts executed and heavily influenced by Indian artists.

The Quito School died out with the coming of independence – the 19th century is referred to as the Republican period, and its art is characterised by formalism. Favourite subjects include heroes of the revolution, important members of the new republic's high society and rather florid landscapes.

The 20th century saw the rise of the indigenist school, whose unifying theme is the oppression and the burdens of Ecuador's indigenous inhabitants. Important artists include Eduardo Kingman, Endara Crow, Camilo Egas and Oswaldo Guayasamín. These and other artists have works in modern galleries and museums in Quito; Egas (died 1962) and Guayasamín (still alive) have museums in their homes.

Architecture
Many of Quito's churches were built during the colonial period, and the architects were influenced by the Quito School. In addition, churches often had Moorish (Arab) influences. The overall appearance of the architecture of colonial churches is overpoweringly ornamental, and almost cloyingly rich – in short, baroque.

Many colonial houses had two storeys, with the upper floors bearing ornate balconies. The walls were whitewashed and the roofs were of red tile. Quito's colonial architecture has been well preserved and led to UNESCO declaring the old part of Quito *Patrimonio de Humanidad* (Patrimony of Humanity) in 1978. Several other towns, notably Cuenca, have attractive colonial architecture.

Music
Traditional Andean music has a distinctive and haunting sound which has been popularised in Western culture by songs like Paul Simon's version of *El Condor Pasa* and the score of the excellent TV natural history series *The Flight of the Condor*.

Two main reasons contribute to the otherworldly quality of traditional music. The first is the scale: it is pentatonic, or consisting of five notes, compared to the eight-note octaves Westerners are used to. The second is the fact that string and brass instruments were imported by the Spanish – pre-Columbian instruments consisted of wind and percussion, which effectively portrayed the windswept quality of páramo life.

Most traditional music is a blend of pre-Columbian and Spanish influences. It is best heard in a *peña*, or folk music club. Traditional music can also be heard on the streets during fiestas, but increasingly often, fiesta ensembles are cacophonous brass bands.

Literature
Ecuadorian literature is not well known outside Latin America, but indigenist novelist Jorge Icaza's *Huasipungo*, a naturalistic tale of the miserable conditions on Andean haciendas in the early 20th century, is available in English (Southern Illinois University Press, Carbondale, Illinois, 1964, or D Dobson, London, 1962).

RELIGION
The predominant religion is Roman Catholicism, though a small minority of other churches are found. The indigenous peoples tend to blend Catholicism with their own traditional beliefs.

LANGUAGE
Spanish is the main language. Most Indians are bilingual, Quechua being their mother tongue and Spanish their second language. Also, some small lowland groups speak their own languages. English is understood in the best hotels, airline offices and tourist agencies.

Facts for the Visitor

VISAS & DOCUMENTS
Most tourists entering Ecuador require a passport (valid for six months or more) and a T-3 tourist card, which is obtainable on arrival in Ecuador. The T-3 is free, but don't lose it, as you will need it for stay extensions, passport checks and leaving the country. Lost cards can be replaced at the immigration office in Quito or Guayaquil, or at the exit point from the country.

On arrival, you are given an identical stamp on both your passport and T-3 which indicates how long you can stay. The maximum is 90 days, but usually, less is given. You can get an extension in Quito at the immigration office, at Avenida Amazonas 2639.

Tourists can't stay in the country for more than 90 days in any 12-month period. (If you leave Ecuador with, say, only 60 of your 90 days used, you will receive your balance of 30 days upon re-entry with no problem.) The only official way to stay longer is with business, work, student or residence visas, which are difficult to obtain in Ecuador.

If you want to stay longer than 90 days, simply leaving the country and returning a few days later doesn't work, because the border immigration officials check your passport for entry and exit dates. Should you leave Ecuador and get a new passport at your embassy because your previous one was lost, stolen or has expired, then returning to Ecuador is another story. With no Ecuadorian stamps in your new passport, you have no problem.

Officially, a ticket out of the country and evidence of sufficient funds for your stay (US$20 per day) are required, but rarely asked for. If you're flying in, it's safest to buy an onward ticket. It can be refunded if you don't use it. In Ecuador, this can take a couple of weeks, but they'll give you the money in US dollars.

Always carry your passport and your T-3 card, as there are occasional document checks on public transport. You can be arrested without identification. Failure to produce a visa or tourist card can result in deportation.

International vaccination certificates are not required by law, but some vaccinations are advisable.

Ecuadorian Embassies
Ecuador has embassies in the neighbouring countries of Colombia and Peru, and also in the following countries:

Canada
    50 O'Connor St, Suite 1311, Ottawa K1P 6L2
    (☎ 563-8206)
France
    34 avenue de Messine, 75008 Paris (☎ 45 61 10 21)
Germany
    Koblenzer Strasse 37, 5300 Bonn 2 (☎ 352544)

UK
    3 Hans Crescent, Knightsbridge, London SW1X 0L5 (☎ 235-4248)
USA
    2535 15th St NW, Washington DC 2009 (☎ 234-7200)

Foreign Embassies & Consulates
Most foreign embassies are in Quito, and there are a number of consulates in Guayaquil. There are Colombian consulates in Guayaquil, Quito and Tulcán.

MONEY
The currency in Ecuador is the *sucre*, written as S/. There are bills of 5000, 1000, 500, 100, 50, 20, 10 and five sucres – a S/10,000 bill is planned. There are coins of 50, 20, 10, five and one sucres.

There are two rates of exchange; the lower one is the official rate, used in international business transactions, and is of no concern to the traveller. The higher free market rate is available at all exchange houses. The sucre is frequently devalued, so it is impossible to give accurate exchange rates. The following table gives some idea:

1981 US$1 = S/30
1985 US$1 = S/120
1989 US$1 = S/530

Approximate official rates at August 1993 were as follows:

A$1 = S/1253
DM1 = S/1066
FF1 = S/306
UK£1 = S/2745
US$1 = S/1850

The US dollar is the easiest currency to exchange, and all prices in this chapter are given in US$. Other hard currencies can be exchanged in Quito, Guayaquil and Cuenca, but otherwise, carry sucres or US dollars. Exchange rates are lower in smaller towns. In some places, notably the Oriente, it is difficult to exchange money. Exchange houses, or *casas de cambio*, are normally the best places to change money, though banks also will. Normally, exchange rates are within 2% of one another in any given city. There is little difference between exchange rates for cash and travellers' cheques.

There is a black market on the streets of the major towns, near the big casas de cambio. Rates are slightly better, but street moneychanging is illegal and forged currency has been a recent problem. Moneychangers seen on the streets, at the international borders, are generally OK.

Credit cards are useful (particularly when buying dollars from a bank) and most major cards are widely accepted.

You can receive money from home by picking an Ecuadorian bank which will cooperate with your bank at home (eg Bank of America, Bank of London & South America) and telexing someone to deposit the money in your name at the bank of your choice. Allow at least three days. Ecuador allows you to receive the money in the currency of your choice (US dollars). Ecuador is one of the best Latin American countries to have money sent to.

Banks are open for business from 9 am to 1 pm Monday to Friday. In some cities, banks may stay open later or open on Saturday, especially if Saturday is market day. Casas de cambio are usually open from 9 am to 6 pm Monday to Friday, and until noon on Saturday. There is usually a lunch hour.

You can buy back dollars at international airports when leaving the country. You can also change money at the major land borders.

Costs

Costs in Ecuador are low. If you're on a very tight budget and attempting to be really economical, you could survive on under US$5 per day. This entails staying in the cheapest US$1 pensiones and eating the meal of the day in restaurants. For a little more, a simple room, with private hot shower and table and chair, can be had for as little as US$2.50 per person.

Save time and energy by flying back from a remote destination which took several days of land travel to reach. At present, the most expensive internal flight on the Ecuadorian mainland is about US$25, and many flights are much cheaper. A taxi, particularly when you're in a group, isn't expensive and usually costs less than US$1 for short but convenient rides.

The one major stumbling block for budget travellers is reaching the Galápagos Archipelago. Getting there is very expensive and staying there isn't particularly cheap; see the Galápagos Islands section in this chapter for more information.

Tipping

Better restaurants add 10% tax and 10% service charge to the bill. Cheaper restaurants don't include tax or service charge and tipping is not necessarily expected. If you want to tip your server, do so directly – don't just leave the money on the table.

Tip porters at the airport US$0.20 per bag. Taxi drivers are not normally tipped, though you can leave them the small change from a metered ride.

WHEN TO GO

Travellers can visit Ecuador at any time of the year. Certain areas are better at certain times of year, but there are no general cut-and-dried rules. The coast is hot and wet from January to May (when tropical rainstorms may make some of the poorer roads impassable) and drier and cooler during the rest of the year. The dry season in the highlands is normally June to August – but this coincides with the wettest months in the Oriente, when roads may be closed. So, there is no perfect time for a general tour of the country.

WHAT TO BRING

Clothes can be bought relatively cheaply in Ecuador if you need them, though shoes bigger than size 43 Ecuadorian (size 10 American, size nine British) are very hard to find. Use Quito as a base for storing unneeded luggage as you take short trips around the country.

The highlands are often cold, so bring a windproof jacket and a warm layer to wear

ECUADOR

beneath, or plan on buying a thick sweater. Cheap highland hotels often lack heat in their rooms – they often provide extra blankets on request, but a sleeping bag is useful.

Tampons are expensive and hard to find – sanitary pads are cheaper and more common. Also, tampons are available in regular sizes only in the major cities, so make sure you stock up before visiting smaller towns, the jungle or the Galápagos.

Condoms are widely sold, but spermicidal jelly for diaphragms is hard to find. The choice of oral contraceptives is limited, so bring your preferred brand from home. Good insect repellent and sunscreen are hard to find and expensive so, again, bring your own. Many toilets don't have any toilet paper.

TOURIST OFFICES
The government tourist information agency is called CETUR and they have offices in the major cities. CETUR seem mostly geared towards helping affluent tourists and are rarely of much help with information about budget hotels, etc. English is sometimes spoken. Usually, the officials are friendly and help as much as they can.

USEFUL ORGANISATIONS
South American Explorers Club
The Quito office (☎ 566 076) is at Toledo 1254 y Cordero, La Floresta; mail to Apartado 21-431, Quito, Ecuador. For more information about the club, see the Facts for the Visitor chapter.

BUSINESS HOURS
Banks are open from 9 am to 1 pm Monday to Friday. Most stores, businesses, exchange houses and government offices are open from about 9 am to 5.30 pm Monday to Friday; usually an hour is taken in this time for lunch. In smaller towns, however, lunch breaks of two or more hours are common. On Saturday, many stores and businesses are open from 9 am to noon.

Restaurants tend to remain open late in the big cities, where 10 pm is not an unusual time to eat the evening meal. In smaller towns, restaurants often close by 9 pm (much earlier in villages). Restaurants are often closed on Sunday.

HOLIDAYS & FESTIVALS
Many of the major festivals are oriented to the Roman Catholic liturgical calendar. These are often celebrated with great pageantry, especially in highland Indian villages, where a Catholic feast day is often the excuse for a traditional Indian fiesta with drinking, dancing, rituals and processions. Other holidays are of historical or political interest. On the major holidays, banks, offices and other services are closed and transportation is often very crowded; book ahead if possible.

The following list describes the major holidays; they may well be celebrated for several days around the actual date.

1 January
New Year's Day
6 January
Epiphany
March/April
Carnaval – the last few days before Lent, celebrated with water fights. Ambato has its fruit and flower festival
March/April (dates vary)
Easter – Palm Sunday, Holy Thursday, Good Friday, Holy Saturday and Easter Sunday, celebrated with religious processions
1 May
Labour Day – Workers' parades
24 May
Battle of Pichincha – National holiday commemorating the decisive battle in the struggle for independence from the Spanish in 1822
June
Corpus Christi – Religious feast day combined with the traditional harvest fiesta in many highland towns. Includes processions and street dancing
24 June
St John the Baptist – Fiestas in Otavalo area
29 June
St Peter & St Paul – Fiestas in Otavalo area and other northern highland towns
24 July
Simón Bolívar's Birthday – National holiday
25 July
Founding of Guayaquil – Major festival for Guayaquil
10 August
Quito's Independence Day

1-15 September
  Fiesta del Yamor – Held in Otavalo
9 October
  Guayaquil's Independence Day
12 October
  Columbus Day – National holiday
1-2 November
  All Saints' Day
  All Souls' Day – Celebrated by flower-laying ceremonies in the cemeteries. Especially colourful in rural areas, where entire Indian families show up at the cemeteries to eat, drink, and leave offerings in memory of their departed relatives
3 November
  Cuenca's Independence Day
6 December
  Founding of Quito – Celebrated throughout the first week of December with bullfights, parades and street dancing
24-25 December
  Christmas Eve/Christmas Day
28-31 December
  End-of-year celebrations – Parades and dances culminate in the burning of life-size effigies in the streets on New Year's Eve

POST & TELECOMMUNICATIONS

Most letters sent from Ecuador arrive at their destinations, sometimes in as little as a week to the USA or Europe. Incoming mail is another matter. Some letters take as long as two months to arrive, and a few never do.

Sending Mail

Aerograms are available at the post office, and because they contain no enclosure, they're more likely to arrive safely. For a few cents extra, you can send them *certificado* (certified). Sending parcels of two kg or more is best done from special post offices such as the one on Calle Ulloa near Calle Dávalos, in Quito – it is cheap and the parcels arrive at their destination.

Receiving Mail

Mail sent to the post office is filed alphabetically, so make sure that your last name is clear, eg John PAYSON, Lista de Correos, Correo Central, Quito (or town and province of your choice), Ecuador. American Express will hold mail for their clients (c/o American Express, Aptdo 2605, Quito, Ecuador; their street address is Avenida Amazonas 339).

The South American Explorers Club holds mail for members. You may have to recover your mail from customs if it weighs over two kg.

Telephones IETEL provides long-distance national and international telephone, telex and telegram services. The IETEL offices open from 6 am to 10 pm on a daily basis (except in small, remote towns or in hotels, where they keep shorter hours).

Even the most remote villages can often communicate with Quito and connect you into an international call. These cost about US$9 for three minutes to the USA, and about US$12 to Europe. Rates are cheaper on Sunday. Waiting time to make a connection can vary from 10 minutes to over an hour. Collect or reverse-charge phone calls are possible to a few countries. You can call an AT&T operator in the USA direct from a few places in Quito, and from many phones in Guayaquil, by dialling 119.

There are three area codes: Quito and the north are 2; Guayaquil and the south coast are 4; Cuenca and the inland south are 7. For a national operator, dial 105; for information, dial 104.

Local calls can be made from some stores or restaurants, for a small fee. Public phone booths are not found very frequently and require a special token (*ficha*) to operate them. The fichas are often sold by street newspaper vendors – ask around.

Fax services are available from private companies in the larger cities.

TIME

The Ecuadorian mainland is five hours behind GMT and the Islas Galápagos are six hours behind GMT.

LAUNDRY

There are no self-service laundries in Ecuador. There are *lavanderías* in major cities, where washing service takes 24 hours or more; many of these are limited to dry-cleaning.

Many hotels will do your laundry; this can cost very little in the cheaper hotels but usually takes a day or more. You can wash your own clothes – most cheaper hotels will show you a cement sink and scrubbing board. If the sink is full of water, use a bowl to scoop water out. Don't dunk your clothes in this water, as it is an emergency supply in the event of water failure.

BOOKS & MAPS
Ecuador – a fragile democracy by David Corkill & Davbid Cubitt (Latin American Bureau, London, 1988) is a recent look at the history and trends of Euadorian politics.

Tom Miller's *The Panama Hat Trail* (Vintage Departures, New York, 1988) is a good recent travel book on Ecuador which focuses on the hat industry. For an amusing description of the monument to the equator at La Mitad del Mundo, its history and Ecuadorian bureaucracy, see Thurston Clarke's *Equator* (Avon, New York, 1988).

Ecuador & the Galápagos Islands – a travel survival kit, 3rd edition, by Rob Rachowiecki (Lonely Planet, 1992), gives detailed travel information, along with dozens of maps and a comprehensine section on the wildlife found on the Galápagos.

Climbing & Hiking in Ecuador, 2nd edition, by Rob Rachowiecki & Betsy Wagenhauser (Bradt Publications, 1990), is a detailed guide to climbing Ecuador's mountains, and also describes many beautiful hikes, some of which are simple day hikes suitable for the beginner. Bradt Publications also sells maps of Ecuador (and other countries); their address is 41 Nortoft Rd, Chalfont St Peter, Bucks SL9 OLA, England.

Ecuadorian bookstores have a limited selection of Ecuadorian maps. The best selection is available from the Instituto Geográfico Militar (IGM) or the South American Explorers Club; both are in Quito. A new booklet, *The Pocket Guide to Ecuador* (Latin American Travel Consultants, Quito, 1993) has maps of the entire country plus major city maps.

MEDIA
The best newspapers are *El Comercio* and *Hoy* (published in Quito) and *El Telégrafo* and *El Universo* (published in Guayaquil).

Foreign newspapers and magazines are sold at good bookshops and at the international airports. Latin American editions (in English) of *Time* and *Newsweek* are available for about US$2.

FILM & PHOTOGRAPHY
Camera gear is very expensive in Ecuador and film choice is limited. Always check expiry dates. Slide film, especially Kodachrome, is hard to find, and slide developing tends to be shoddy. Print film is cheaper and better developing is available. Try the El Globo stores in major cities for film and Ecuacolor, at Amazonas 848 in Quito, for same-day printing.

DANGERS & ANNOYANCES
Although Ecuador is safer than Peru and Colombia, you should still be careful. Pickpocketing is definitely on the increase and is common in crowded places. Armed robbery is still unusual in most of Ecuador although parts of Guayaquil, some coastal areas, and the stairs up the Panecillo in Quito do have a reputation for being very dangerous.

Every year or so, a couple of long-distance night buses are held up and robbed in the Guayaquil area. Avoid taking night buses through Guayas Province unless you have to.

Take the normal precautions as outlined in the Dangers section at the beginning of the book. If you are robbed, get a police report *(denuncia)* within 48 hours – they won't process a report after that. In Quito, go to the Servicio de Investigaciones Criminales de Pichincha (SICP), at the intersection of Montúfar and Esmeraldas, in the old town. In other towns, go to the main police headquarters.

Talk to other travellers and to the folks at the South American Explorers Club for advice and up-to-date information.

WORK
Officially you need a work visa to be allowed to work in Ecuador. You might, however, get a job teaching English in language schools, usually in Quito. Pay is low but enough to live on if you're broke. Schools, such as the

American School in Quito, will often hire teachers with bona fide teaching credentials in mathematics, biology and other subjects, and may help you get a work visa if you want to stay on. They also pay much better than the language schools.

Another way of making money is by selling good-quality equipment such as camping or camera items. The South American Explorers Club in Quito can help you post notices about the equipment you wish to sell.

ACTIVITIES
Climbing & Hiking
Gear can be rented in Quito and some other towns. Adventures around Cotopaxi, the Baños area, Las Cajas (near Cuenca) and on Chimborazo (Ecuador's highest mountain) are all worthwhile.

Wildlife Watching
The Islas Galápagos, the Amazon and birds throughout the country are all big attractions for nature lovers. The Galápagos may be too expensive for most budget travellers (though a great number get there anyway), but the Amazon can be visited easily and relatively cheaply.

ACCOMMODATION
There is no shortage of places to stay in Ecuador, but during major fiestas or the night before market day, accommodation can be rather tight, so as many hotels as possible are shown on the town maps. If you are going to a town specifically for a market or fiesta, try to arrive a day early, or at least by early afternoon of the day before the market commences.

Sometimes, single rooms are hard to find, and you may get a room with two or three beds. Often, you are only charged for one bed and won't have to share, unless the hotel is full. Check that you won't be asked to share with a stranger, or to pay for all the beds – this is no problem 90% of the time. Note that youth hostels, of the type common to Europe and North America, are not found in Ecuador.

FOOD
For breakfast, the usual eggs and bread rolls or toast are available. A good local change from eggs are sweet corn tamales called *humitas*, often served for breakfast with coffee.

Lunch is the main meal of the day for many Ecuadorians. A cheap restaurant will serve a decent *almuerzo* (lunch of the day) for under US$1. An almuerzo consists of a sopa and a *segundo* or 'second dish,' which is usually a stew with plenty of rice. Sometimes, the *segundo* is *pescado* (fish) or a kind of lentil or pea stew (*lenteja, arveja*). Some places serve a salad (often cooked), juice and *postre* (dessert) as well as the two main courses.

The supper of the day is usually similar to lunch. Ask for the *merienda*. If you don't want the almuerzo or merienda, you can choose from the menu, but this is always more expensive.

A *churrasco* is a hearty plate with a slice of fried beef, one or two fried eggs, vegetables (usually boiled beet slices, carrots and beans), fried potatoes, a slice of avocado and tomato, and the inevitable rice. *Arroz con pollo* is a mountain of rice with little bits of chicken mixed in. *Pollo a la Brasa* restaurants serve roasted chicken, often with fried potatoes on the side. *Gallina* is usually boiled chicken as in soups, and *pollo* is more often spit-roasted or fried. Pollo tends to be underdone, but you can send it back to get it cooked longer.

Parrilladas are the product of steak houses or grills. Steaks, pork chops, chicken breasts, blood sausages, liver and tripe are all served on a table-top grill – a lot of food! If you don't want the whole thing, choose just a chop or a steak. Although parrilladas aren't cheap, they are reasonably priced and good value.

Seafood is good, even in the highlands, as it is brought fresh from the coast and iced. The most common types of fish are *corvina* (white sea bass) and *trucha* (trout). *Ceviche* is popular throughout Ecuador; this is seafood marinated in lemon and served with popcorn and sliced onions, and it's delicious.

ECUADOR

Ceviche can be *de pescado* (fish), *de camarones* (shrimp), *de concha* (shellfish, such as clams, mussels or oysters) or *mixto*. (Unfortunately, improperly prepared ceviche is a source of cholera – so avoid it if in any doubt.)

Chinese restaurants called *chifas* are generally inexpensive and good value. Apart from rice dishes, they serve *tallarines*, or noodles mixed with your choice of pork, chicken, beef or vegetables *(legumbres, verduras)*. Portions tend to be filling. Vegetarians will find that chifas offer the best choice for nonmeat dishes. Vegetarian restaurants are rare in Ecuador.

Restuarants usually have a wide range of dishes, including the following:

Caldo Soups and stews are very popular and are often served in markets for breakfasts. Soups are known as *caldos, sopas,* or *locros*. Chicken soup, or *caldo de gallina*, is the most popular. *Caldo de patas* is soup made by boiling cattle hooves and, to my taste, is as bad as it sounds

Cuy Whole roasted guinea pig is a traditional food dating back to Inca times. It tastes rather like a cross between rabbit and chicken. The sight of the little paws and teeth sticking out and eyes tightly closed is a little unnerving, but cuy is supposed to be a delicacy and some people love it

Lechón Suckling pig is often roasted whole and is are a common sight at Ecuadorian food markets. Pork is also called *chancho*

Llapingachos Fried mashed-potato-and-cheese pancakes are often served with *fritada* – scraps of fried or roast pork

Seco Literally 'dry' (as opposed to a 'wet') soup, this is stew, usually meat served with rice. It can be *seco de gallina* (chicken stew), *de res* (beef), *de chivo* (goat) or *de cordero* (lamb)

Tostadas de maíz These are tasty fried corn pancakes

Yaguarlocro This is potato soup with chunks of barely congealed blood sausage floating in it. Many people prefer straight *locro*, which usually has potatoes, corn and an avocado or cheese topping.

DRINKS
Water
Purify all tap water. Bottled mineral water, *agua mineral*, is carbonated – a 650-ml bottle costs US$0.25 in most restaurants, less in a store. *Güitig* (pronounced 'Weetig') is the most popular brand.

Soft Drinks
Bottled drinks are cheap, but the deposit on the bottle is usually worth more than the drink.

All the usual soft drinks are available, and some local ones have such endearing names as Bimbo or Lulu. Ask for your drink *helada* if you want it out of the refrigerator, *al clima* if you don't. Remember to say *sin hielo* (without ice) unless you really trust the water supply.

Fruit Juices
Juices *(jugos)* are available everywhere. Make sure you get *jugo puro* (pure) and not *con agua* (with water). The most common kinds are *mora* (blackberry), *naranja* (orange), *toronja* (grapefruit), *piña* (pineapple), *maracuya* (passion fruit), *sandía* (watermelon), *naranjilla* (a local fruit tasting like bitter orange) or *papaya*.

Coffee & Tea
Coffee is available almost everywhere but is often disappointing. A favourite Ecuadorian way of making coffee is to boil it for hours until only a thick syrup remains. This is then poured into cruets and diluted with milk or water. It doesn't taste that great and it looks very much like soy sauce, so always check before pouring it into your milk (or over your rice)! Espresso is available in the better restaurants.

Tea, or *té*, is served black with lemon and sugar. Hot chocolate is also popular.

Alcohol
Local beers *(cerveza)* are good and inexpensive. Pilsener usually comes in 650-ml bottles and Club comes in 330-ml bottles.

Local wines are terrible. Imported wines are expensive.

Rum *(ron)* is cheap and good. The local firewater, *aguardiente*, or sugar-cane alcohol, is an acquired taste but is also good. It's very cheap; you can get a half bottle of Cristal aguardiente for about US$0.75. Imported spirits are expensive.

THINGS TO BUY
Souvenirs are good, varied and cheap. For just one big shopping expedition, the Saturday market at Otavalo is both convenient and

full of variety. In markets and smaller stores, bargaining is expected, though don't expect to reduce the price by more than about 20%. In 'tourist stores' in Quito, prices are usually fixed. Some of the best stores are quite expensive; on the other hand, the quality of their products is often superior.

Clothing

Woollen goods are popular and are often made of a pleasantly coarse homespun wool. The price of a thick sweater will begin at under US$10, depending on size and quality. Wool is also spun into a much tighter textile used for making ponchos. Otavaleño Indian ponchos are among the best in Latin America. Hand-embroidered clothes are also attractive, but it's worth getting them from a reputable shop; otherwise, they may shrink or run.

Panama hats are worth buying. A really good panama is so finely made that it can be rolled up and passed through a man's ring. They are made from a palmlike bush which grows abundantly in the coastal province of Manabí; Montecristi is a major centre.

Other Things to Buy

Weavings are found all over the country, with Otavalo having a good selection. Two small weavings are often stitched together to make a shoulder bag. Agave fibre is used to make macramé bags or tough woven bags called *shigras*. Cotacachi and Ambato are centres for leatherwork. San Antonio de Ibarra, between Otavalo and Ibarra, is the major woodworking centre of Ecuador. Balsa-wood models, especially of brightly coloured birds, are popular – these are made in the jungles of the Oriente and sold in many of Quito's gift stores. Painted and varnished ornaments made of bread dough are unique to Ecuador and are best obtained in Calderón, north of Quito.

Getting There & Away

AIR

Guayaquil and Quito have international airports with flights to other Latin American countries, North America and Europe. An internal flight between Guayaquil and Quito costs about US$20.

OVERLAND

To/From Colombia

Buses go from Colombia to Ecuador via Tulcán (Ecuador). See Tulcán in this chapter for further details.

To/From Peru

Buses go from Peru to Ecuador via either Huaquillas or Macará (both in Ecuador). See Huaquillas and Macará in this chapter for further details.

Getting Around

You can usually get anywhere quickly and easily. The bus is the most common method of transportation; buses can take you from the Colombian to the Peruvian border in 18 hours if you wish to do so. Aeroplanes and boats (especially in the Oriente) are also frequently used, but trains less often.

Whichever form of transport you use, remember to have your passport with you, as you will need to show it to board most planes and boats. People without documents may be arrested. Buses go through a transit police checkpost upon entering many towns, and passports may be asked for. If your passport is in order, these procedures are cursory. If you're travelling anywhere near the borders or in the Oriente, you can expect more frequent passport checks.

AIR

With the exception of flying to the Galápagos, internal flights are cheap; the most expensive is currently only US$25. Most flights originate or terminate in Quito or Guayaquil.

Ecuador's major domestic airline is TAME, which flies to almost all internal destinations. There is also SAN-Saeta, which has flights between Quito, Guayaquil and Cuenca. Both companies have the same prices. A third airline is AECA, which flies small aircraft along the coast, and there are other small, local airlines.

TAME flies from Quito to and from Guayaquil, Cuenca, Loja, Macas, Coca, Tarapoa, Lago Agrio, Tulcán, Esmeraldas, Manta, Portoviejo and the Galápagos. TAME also flies from Guayaquil to and from Quito, Cuenca, Loja, Machala and the Galápagos. There are seasonal TAME flights to Salinas. There are about eight flights a day both ways between Quito and Guayaquil. Other flights usually operate several times a week but not on a daily basis.

There are no seat reservations on domestic flights, and no separate sections for smokers and nonsmokers. Flights are subject to frequent delays, changes and cancellations. Some flights give good views of the snowcapped Andes. When flying from Quito to Guayaquil, the mountain views are on the left-hand side.

Flights on the mainland cost the same for Ecuadorians and foreigners. Flights to the Galápagos cost about US$330 for the round trip from Guayaquil, but are much cheaper for Ecuadorians.

If you can't get a ticket for a particular flight (especially out of small towns), go to the airport early and get on the waiting list in the hopes of a cancellation. If you have a reservation, confirm it and reconfirm it or you may be bumped off the flight list. Find someone to reconfirm for you if you're unable to do so.

BUS
Long-Distance
Most towns have a central bus terminal (*Terminal Terrestre*). Some towns haven't completed their central terminals, so they have several smaller ones (where possible, these are indicated on the maps). Timetables change frequently and are not necessarily adhered to.

Busetas are fast, small buses which carry 22 passengers in rather cramped seats. Standing passengers are not normally allowed and service is direct. Larger coaches have more space, but they allow standing passengers and so can get rather crowded.

They are generally slower than the busetas, but can be more interesting, with passengers getting on and off, perhaps accompanied by chickens or 50-kg bags of potatoes.

Buy tickets in advance from the terminal to get your choice of seat – avoid those rows over the wheels, as there is less space, and remember that back seats are the bumpiest. Some companies don't sell tickets in advance because they have frequent departures. During long holiday weekends or special fiestas, buses can be booked up for several days in advance.

If you're travelling light, keep your luggage with you inside the bus. If your luggage is too big to fit under the seat, it will have to go on top or in a luggage compartment. Sometimes, the top is covered with a tarpaulin, but not always, so pack your gear in large plastic bags (garbage bags are good) to keep it dry. The luggage compartment is sometimes filthy, so place your luggage in a large protective sack. You can buy grain sacks cheaply in general stores or markets.

Every time a bus stops on the main routes, vendors selling fruit, rolls, ice cream or drinks suddenly appear. Long-distance buses usually stop for 20-minute meal breaks at the appropriate times. The food in the terminal restaurants is basic.

For immediate travel, go to the terminal and you'll often find the driver's assistant hustling up passengers for his bus. Make sure your bus goes to your destination if you don't want to change.

There are no toilets on buses, but long-distance buses have rest stops every few hours.

Local
These are usually slow, crowded but cheap. You can get around most towns for about US$0.05. Local buses often go out to nearby villages, and this is a good way to see an area.

To get off a local bus, yell *Baja!*, which means 'Down!', or *Esquina!*, which means 'Corner!' (they'll stop at the next one).

TRUCKS
In remote areas, trucks often double as buses. If the weather is OK, you get fabulous views;

otherwise, you have to crouch underneath a dark tarpaulin. Truck drivers charge standard fares, depending on distance, which are almost as much as bus fares.

TRAIN

Trains run from Quito to Riobamba, from Guayaquil to Alausí, and from Cuenca to Sibambe (just west of Alausí). In the north, trains run from Ibarra to San Lorenzo, on the coast, and from Ibarra to Otavalo. *Autoferros*, which are buses mounted on railway chassis, are often used.

BOAT

Motorised dugout canoes, which carry up to three dozen passengers, are the only way to get around many roadless areas. Regularly scheduled boats are quite affordable, though not as cheap as a bus for a similar distance. Hiring your own boat and boatman is possible but expensive. You are most likely to travel in dugouts in the Misahuallí and Coca regions of the Oriente, and on the north-west coast.

Seating is on hard, low wooden benches, so bring something padded to sit on. Luggage is stashed under a tarpaulin, so carry hand baggage containing essentials for the journey. Pelting rain or glaring sun are major hazards and an umbrella is excellent defence against both. Use a good sunscreen lotion, or wear long sleeves, long pants and a sun hat. A light jacket is worth having against chilling rain. Insect repellent is useful during stops along the river. A water bottle and food will complete your hand baggage. Keep your spare clothes in plastic bags or they'll get soaked by rain or spray.

TAXI

Taxis are cheap. Ask the fare beforehand, or you'll be overcharged more often than not. A long ride in a large city (Quito or Guayaquil) shouldn't go over US$3 and short hops can cost as little as US$0.50. Meters are obligatory in Quito and rarely seen elsewhere. At weekends and at night, fares are always about 25% to 50% higher.

A half-day taxi hire might cost about US$10 to US$15 if you bargain. If you hire a taxi to take you to another town, expect to pay about US$1 for every 10 km. Remember to include the km for the return trip. You can also hire pick-up trucks to take you to remote places, such as climbers' refuges.

CAR

Car rental is available in Quito, Guayaquil and Cuenca. It is not cheap. It's hard to find anything for much less than US$200 a week – and this will typically include only 1200 'free' km.

HITCHING

Private cars are not very common and trucks are used as public transport in remote areas, so trying to hitch a free ride is not easy. If the driver is stopping to drop off and pick up other passengers, then you can assume that he or she will expect payment. If you are the only passenger, the driver may have picked you up just to talk to a foreigner, and may waive payment.

Quito

Quito, at 2850 metres above sea level and only 22 km south of the equator, has a wonderful springlike climate. It is in a valley flanked by mountains, and on a clear day, several snowcapped volcanos are visible from the capital.

Quito was a major Inca city that was destroyed by Atahualpa's general, Rumiñahui, shortly before the arrival of the Spanish conquistadors; there are no Inca remains. The present capital was founded on top of the Inca ruins by Sebastián de Benalcázar on 6 December 1534, and many colonial buildings survive in the old town.

In 1978, UNESCO declared Quito one of the world's cultural heritage sites, and now, building and development in Quito's old town is strictly controlled. There are almost no modern buildings next to centuries-old architecture, and no flashing neon signs to disrupt the ambience of the past.

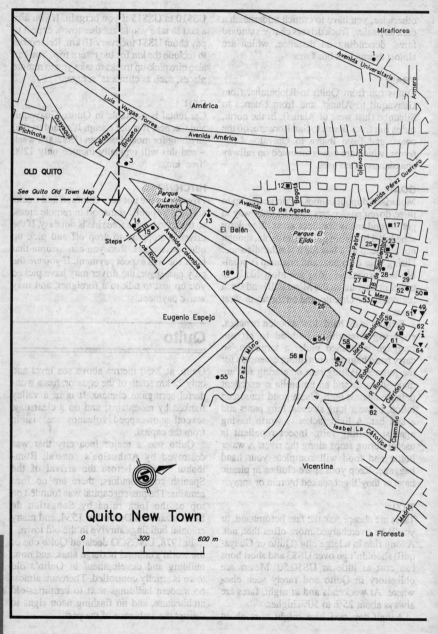

Quito New Town

Miraflores

Avenida Universitaria

Avenida Pérez Guerrero

Luis Vargas Torres

América

Avenida América

Pichincha

Guayaquil

Caldas

Briceño

OLD QUITO

See Quito Old Town Map

Parque La Alameda

Avenida Colombia

El Belén

Parque El Ejido

Steps

Los Ríos

Eugenio Espejo

Paz Y Miño

F Robles

R. Roca

Portoviejo

Bogotá

Avenida 10 de Agosto

Avenida Patria

18 de Septiembre

J L Mera

Jorge Washington

Isabel La Católica

M Caamaño

P. Carrión

Vicentina

La Floresta

Madrid

Armero

0   300   600 m

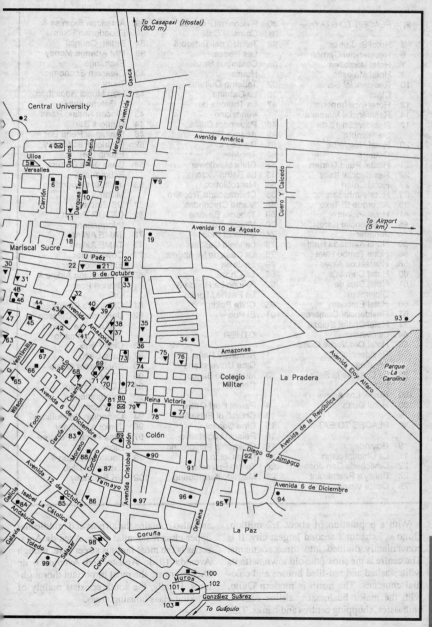

With a population of about 1.2 million, Quito is Ecuador's second largest city. It is conveniently divided into three segments. The centre is the site of the old town, with its whitewashed and red-tiled houses and colonial churches. The north is modern Quito, with the major businesses, airline offices, embassies, shopping centres and banks. This area also contains the airport and middle and upper-class residential areas. Avenida Amazonas is the most famous street here, though Avenida 10 de Agosto and Avenida 6 de Diciembre are the most important thoroughfares. Finally, the south consists mainly of working-class housing areas.

ECUADOR

Information

Tourist Offices The main CETUR tourist information office is at Calle Reina Victoria 514 (☎ 527 074, 527 002). There is also one at the airport (rarely open and not very good) and one in the Municipal Palace, on the Plaza de la Independencia, in the old town.

South American Explorers Club The club (☎ 566 076), is at Toledo 1254 in the La Floresta district. Mail should be sent to Apartado 21-431, Eloy Alfaro, Quito, Ecuador. See the introductory Facts for the Visitor chapter for a full description of the club and its services.

Money Many banks are on Avenida Amazonas and are open from 9 am to 1.30 pm. Casas de cambio are open from 9.30 am to 12.30 pm and 3 to 6 pm on weekdays, and also on Saturday morning. These are the usual place to exchange money. Rodrigo Paz is the best known casa de cambio with an old town office (☎ 511 222, 511 551), at Calle Venezuela 659, and a new town office (☎ 563 900, 564 500), at Avenida Amazonas 370. Jaramillo Arteaga (☎ 516 844), on Amazonas near Colón, is also good.

The Rodrigo Paz office at the airport is open on Sunday. Also, their office at the Hotel Colón is open on Sunday and often until 7 pm on weekdays.

You can receive cash with your credit card – commissions vary.

American Express
    Ecuadorian Tours, Avenida Amazonas 339 and Jorge Washington (☎ 560 488)
Diners Club
    Avenida República and Eloy Alfaro (☎ 553 211)
MasterCard
    Amazonas 720 and Veintimilla (☎ 542 566)
Visa
    Banco de Guayaquil, Avenida Colón and Reina Victoria (☎ 566 824)

Post & Telephone The main post office (☎ 519 875) is in the old town, at Calle Benalcázar, behind the Plaza de la Independencia. This is where you pick up Lista de Correos mail. There is a branch office (☎ 523 787), in the new town, near the corner of Colón and Reina Victoria. Hours are 9 am to 5 pm on weekdays. To mail a package of over two kg, use the office at Calle Ulloa 943, near Ramirez Dávalos (☎ 546 917).

The main IETEL office (☎ 553 350) for international calls is on Avenida 6 de Diciembre near Avenida Colón; hours are 6 am to 9.30 pm daily. There are smaller IETEL offices at the central bus station, the airport and on Calle Benalcázar, near Calle Mejía, in the old town.

Foreign Embassies Most embassies and consulates don't work all day – call ahead for hours. Also check the address – many embassies and consulates change addresses every year or two but often retain the same phone number.

Canada
    6 de Diciembre 2816 and J Orton, office 4N (☎ 543 214)
Colombia
    Colón 1133 and Amazonas, 7th floor (☎ 524 622) (an unconfirmed report is that they are now at Atahualpa 955 near República)
France
    General Plaza 107 and Patria (☎ 560 873)
Germany
    Edificio Eteco, Patria and 9 de Octubre, 6th floor (☎ 567 233)
Peru
    Edificio España, Colón 1222 and Amazonas, 2nd floor (☎ 520 134)
UK
    González Suárez 111 and 12 de Octubre (☎ 560 670)
USA
    Patria and 12 de Octubre (☎ 562 890)

Immigration For tourist card extensions, go to Migraciónes (☎ 454 122, 454 099), Avenida Amazonas 2639 (also numbered 3149) and Avenida de la República, open from 8 am to noon and 3 to 6 pm Monday to Friday. It takes anywhere from 10 minutes to two hours to get a tourist card extension. Onward tickets out of Ecuador and 'sufficient funds' are rarely asked for. It's still worth bringing any airline tickets or travellers' cheques you may have, just in

ECUADOR

case. For other visas, go to the Extranjería, at Calle Reina Victoria near Colón. They are open mornings only, Monday to Thursday.

Jungle Permits To travel to remote parts of the Oriente, close to the Peruvian border, a permit is required from the *Ministerio de Defensa* (Ministry of Defense). It's on Avenida Maldonado, about one km south of the Plaza Santo Domingo, in the old town. It is open from 8 am to 4 pm Monday to Friday.

To obtain a permit, you need a letter stating that you are a citizen of that country. The letter can be provided by your embassy, a government agency from your home, or authorised by a notary public. Also, you need two passport-sized photos of yourself, two photocopies of your passport (the page with the number), and a letter stating where, why and when you are going. The procedure may take a couple of days, and it is very helpful to speak Spanish.

Bookshops Libri Mundi (☎ 234 791), J L Mera 851, has a good selection of books in English, German and French. Another recommended bookshop is Libro Express, at Amazonas 816.

Maps The best maps are available at the Instituto Geográfico Militar, which is on top of a hill at the end of Calle Paz y Miño. It is open from 8 am to 3 pm Monday to Friday. You must leave your passport at the gate to be allowed in.

Emergency The Hospital Voz Andes (☎ 241 540), at Juan Villalengua 263, near the intersection of avenidas América and 10 de Agosto, is an American-run hospital with an outpatient department and emergency room. Fees are under US$10 for many basic services. The No 1 Iñaquito bus passes close by.

A newer hospital which has been recommended is the Metropolitano (☎ 431 457/520), Avenida Mariana de Jesús and Occidental. A private clinic specialising in women's medical problems is Clínica de la Mujer (☎ 454 058), Amazonas and Gaspar de Villarroel.

Recommended dental clinics include the Clínica de Especialides Odontológicas (☎ 521 383, 237 562), Orellana 1782 and 10 de Agosto, Clínica Dental Arias Salazar (☎ 524 582), Amazonas 239 and 18 de Septiembre, and Clínica Dental Dr Pedro Herrera (☎ 554 361), Amazonas 353 and Jorge Washington.

Emergency services include police (☎ 101), fire department (☎ 102) and ambulance (☎ 214 977, 214 966, 210 567).

Spanish Courses Quito is one of the better places for learning Spanish in South America. All levels, private or group, live-in with family or not are available – talk to several schools to see what is best for you. Most schools charge about US$2 to US$2.50 per hour, though cheaper and rather more expensive places exist. The South American Explorers Club and other travellers are good sources for recent recommendations.

Student Cards Ecuadorian Tours, Amazonas 339, issue student cards for a US$16 fee – they verify your student status.

Laundry At the following places, they wash, dry, and fold your clothes in 24 to 48 hours:

Lava Seco
Cordero 614 and Tamayo (☎ 529 009)
Junior's (they plan a name change soon)
San Javier 232 and Orellana, a block uphill from 6 de Diciembre (☎ 527 551)
Lavanderías Modernas
6 de Diciembre 2400 and Orellana

Dangers & Annoyances The 2850-metre elevation will make you somewhat breathless if you arrive from sea level. This is a mild symptom of altitude sickness and will disappear after a day or two. Take things easy on arrival. Don't overexert yourself. Eat lightly and cut back on cigarettes and alcohol to minimise altitude-sickness symptoms.

Unfortunately, crime has been on the increase over the last few years, especially in Quito's old town. Plaza San Francisco has had many thefts reported recently. Pickpockets work crowded areas such as public buses, markets and church plazas. Thieves often work in groups to distract your attention – see the Facts for the Visitor chapter at the beginning of this book for more details. If you are robbed, obtain a police report within 48 hours from Servicio de Investigaciones Criminales de Pichincha (SICP), Montúfar and Esmeraldas.

Definitely avoid the climb up El Panecillo hill. I have received repeated reports of armed muggers on this climb, and even one of an armed assault on travellers taking a taxi to the top. Generally, the new town is safer than the old town, but you should still stay alert, especially at night.

Watch your belongings when travelling – snatch theft of poorly attended luggage will occur at the bus terminal and at the airport. Watch your luggage like a hawk.

Despite the above warnings, I don't think that Quito is particularly dangerous. If you avoid attracting undue attention to yourself, it's unlikely that you'll have many problems.

Things to See

Opening hours of museums, churches, etc are haphazard and entrance fees are often changed, so this information is given only as a guideline. Monday is the worst day to visit museums, as many are closed. There are many museums and the collection in the Banco Central is considered the best. Seeing the old colonial centre is also well worth while – though some people complain that the narrow streets, bustling crowds and constant traffic jams make walking around the old city a noisy, grimy and uncomfortable experience. My advice is to go on Sunday if you can – there's much less traffic and fewer people.

Walking Tour The area bounded by calles Flores, Rocafuerte, Cuenca and Manabí has most of the colonial churches and plazas, including the **Plaza de la Independencia**, with the **Palacio Presidencial** and **Catedral**. If you are short on time, see at least the Plaza de la Independencia and continue south-west on Calle García Moreno for two blocks to the church of **La Compañía**. From

here, it is one block to the north-west (right) along Sucre to the **Plaza y Monasterio de San Francisco** – a wonderful area, but watch for pickpockets, bag slashers and camera snatchers. Two blocks to the southeast (left) of La Compañía brings you to Calle Guayaquil; turn south-west (right) for one block to see the **Plaza y Iglesia de Santo Domingo**.

From the old town, head north-west along Calle Guayaquil towards the new town. Turn left on Avenida 10 de Agosto and you will pass the Banco Central (with **museums**) on your left. Opposite the Banco Central is an impressive **monument** to Simón Bolívar – it's at the southernmost point of the triangular Parque La Alameda. Head north through the park, pass the astronomical observatory and continue northward on the important thoroughfare of Avenida 6 de Diciembre.

After three blocks, you pass the modern **Congreso Nacional** building on your right, on Calle Montalvo. If you continue on 6 de Diciembre you pass the popular **Parque El Ejido** on your left and the huge, circular, mirrored-wall **Casa de la Cultura Ecuatoriana** building on your right. Past the Casa de la Cultura, turn left for three blocks along Avenida Patria, with Parque El Ejido to your left, and you reach a small **stone arch**. Opposite this is the beginning of Quito's most famous modern street, **Avenida Amazonas**.

It is about three km from the old town centre to the beginning of Avenida Amazonas. Amazonas has banks, boutiques, souvenir stands and sidewalk cafés and is a great gringo meeting place. The parallel street of J L Mera has the best bookshops and handicraft stores.

Museums – new town The **Museo del Banco Central** (☎ 510 302), is located on the 5th floor of the bank. This is the best archaeological museum, housing ceramics, gold ornaments, skulls showing deformities, early surgical methods (trepanning), a mummy, and much else of interest. On the floor above is a display of colonial furniture and religious art and carving.

The bank is on Avenida 10 de Agosto at

the apex of the Parque La Alameda. The museum entrance is through the gate to the right of the bank and then through a side door (there is an elevator). It is open from 10.30 am to 6 pm, Tuesday to Friday, and 10.30 am to 3 pm on weekends. The entrance fee is US$0.30.

There are supposedly plans to move the Banco Central collection to the **Casa de la Cultura Ecuatoriana** (☎ 565 808). This large, circular glass building at the corner of avenidas Patria and 12 de Octubre houses several collections. There is an excellent 19th-century and contemporary art collection, a fascinating display of traditional musical instruments, and examples of traditional Ecuadorian regional dress. Hours are 10 am to 6 pm Tuesday to Friday, 9 am to 5 pm on Saturday, and 10 am to 2 pm on Sunday.

The **Museo de Jacinto Jijón y Caamaño** (☎ 521 834, 529 240) is in the Catholic University, on Avenida 12 de Octubre. It has an interesting private archaeology museum on the 3rd floor of the library. It is open from 9 am to 4 pm Monday to Friday; admission is US$0.20.

The **Museo Guayasamín** (☎ 242 779, 244 373) is the home of Oswaldo Guayasamín, the renowned Ecuadorian Indian painter. The museum is at Calle José Bosmediano 543 in the Bellavista district, to the north-east of Quito. It's an uphill walk, or the No 3 Colmena-Batan bus passes nearby. Its hours are 9 am to 12.30 pm and 3 to 6 pm Monday to Friday, and Saturday morning; admission is free.

The **Museo Amazonico** has a small collection of jungle Indian artefacts collected by the Salesians. It sells Indian cultural publications (in Spanish). The museum is at 12 de Octubre 1436. It is open from 8.30 am to noon and 2.30 to 6.30 pm Monday to Friday, and 9 am to noon on Saturday. Admission is US$0.50.

The **Instituto Geográfico Militar** (☎ 522 066) has a geographical museum and planetarium. The IGM is at the end of the steep climb up Calle Paz y Miño, to the south-east of the Parque El Ejido. Its hours are 8 am to

noon and 2 to 5 pm Tuesday to Friday, and 10 am to noon and 2 to 5 pm on the weekend. There are several half-hour shows daily in the planetarium; admission is about US$0.30. You have to leave your passport at the IGM entrance gate to be allowed in.

The new **Museo de Ciencias Naturales** (☎ 449 824) houses a natural history collection. It is at Parque La Carolina, on the Avenida Los Shyris side, opposite Avenida República de El Salvador. Hours are 9 am to 4.30 pm Monday to Friday, and 9 am to 1 pm on Saturday. Admission is about US$0.10.

The **Vivarium** (☎ 432 915) has a number of live animals, including the highly poisonous fer-de-lance snake, boa constrictors, turtles and tortoises, lizards and iguanas, etc. The address is Shyris 1130, opposite Calle Portugal, in the Parque La Carolina. Call ahead to arrange a tour. Admission is about US$0.50 – donations to support this research and educational institution are welcomed.

Museums – old town The **Museo de Arte y Historia** (☎ 214 018, 210 863), Espejo 1147, contains a wealth of 16th and 17th-century colonial art. It is open from 8.30 am to 6.30 pm Tuesday to Friday, and from 10 am to 3 pm on Saturday and Sunday. Admission is US$0.10.

The **Casa de Sucre** (☎ 512 860), where the hero of the revolution lived, is well restored and contains period (1820s) furniture and a small museum. It is at Calle Venezuela 573. It's open from 9 am to 3.30 pm, Tuesday to Friday, and mornings only on weekends. Admission is free.

Dating from 1534, the **Casa de Benalcázar** (☎ 218 102), at Calle Olmedo 962, was restored in 1967. There are sometimes classical piano recitals here; entrance is free.

The **Museo de Arte Colonial** (☎ 212 297), on Calle Cuenca near Mejía, houses what many consider to be Quito's best collection of colonial art. It is open from 8.30 am to 4.30 pm Tuesday to Friday, and from 10 am to 2.30 pm on the weekend.

The **Museo Camilo Egas** (☎ 514 511), Venezuela 1302, contains works by

Ecuadorian painter Camilo Egas (1889-1962) and others; admission is free.

Churches There is a wealth of churches, chapels, convents, monasteries, cathedrals and basilicas in Quito, particularly in the old town. Photography is not normally permitted because the intensity of the flash has a detrimental effect on the pigment in the many valuable religious paintings.

The **Monasterio de San Francisco** is on the plaza of the same name. Construction began only a few days after the founding of Quito in 1534, but it was not finished until 70 years later. It is the largest and oldest colonial structure in Quito. Much of the church has been rebuilt because of earthquake damage, but some is original. The chapel of Señor Jesus de Gran Poder, to the right of the main altar, has original tilework. The main altar itself is a spectacular example of baroque carving, and the roof and walls are also wonderfully carved and richly covered in gold leaf. Much of the roof shows Moorish influence. It is open from 7 to 11 am daily and 3 to 6 pm Monday to Thursday.

To the right of the main entrance is the **Museo Franciscano** (☎ 211 124) which contains some of the monastery's finest artwork. There are paintings, sculptures and furniture dating back to the 16th century. Admission is US$0.50 and it's open from 9 to 11 am and 3 to 6 pm Monday to Saturday.

It is claimed that seven tonnes of gold were used to decorate **La Compañía**, famous as the most ornate church in Ecuador. Note the Moorish influence in the intricate designs carved on the magnificent red-and-gold columns and ceilings. There is a beautiful cupola over the main altar. The remains of the Quiteño saint Mariana de Jesus, who died in 1645, are kept here. A sign just inside the door gives visiting hours as 9.30 to 11 am daily, 4 to 6 pm on weekdays and 4 to 5 pm on weekends – but don't rely on it. The church is on García Moreno near Sucre.

The **Catedral**, the oldest colonial church in South America (1562), though much

remodelled, is a stark structure which overlooks the Plaza de la Independencia. Plaques on the outside walls commemorate Quito's founders. General Sucre, the leading figure of Quito's independence struggle, is buried inside. To the left of the main altar is a statue of Juan José Flores, Ecuador's first president. Behind the main altar, there is a plaque marking where President Gabriel García Moreno died, on 6 August 1875; he was shot outside the presidential palace and was carried, dying, to the cathedral. Next door, the church of **El Sagrario** is being renovated, and it is interesting to see how the restoration work is carried out.

Two blocks away from the Plaza de la Independencia is the monastery and church of **San Agustín**, which is also the site of the signing of Ecuador's declaration of independence, on 10 August 1809. The church is another fine example of 17th-century architecture. A museum (☎ 515-525, 580-263), where you can see various independence mementoes and colonial art, is in the convent to the right of the church. It was recently being restored – telephone to find out opening hours.

In the evening, when the domes of **Santo Domingo** are floodlit, the church is especially attractive. It, too, dates back to early Quito. In the busy Plaza Santo Domingo, in front of the church, is a statue of General Sucre. He is pointing in the direction of Pichincha, where he won the decisive battle for independence in 1822.

Begun in 1700 and completed in 1742, **La Merced**, on Cuenca near Chile, is one of colonial Quito's most recent churches. Its tower is the highest (47 metres) in colonial Quito and contains the largest bell of Quito's churches. The church has a wealth of fascinating art. Paintings depict volcanos glowing and erupting over the church roofs of colonial Quito, the capital covered with ashes, General Sucre going into battle and many other scenes. The stained-glass windows also show various scenes of colonial life such as priests and conquistadors among the Indians of the Oriente.

The 17th-century monastery, museum and

cemetery of **San Diego** are to the east of the
Panecillo hill, between calles Calicuchima
and Farfán. The monastery and monks'
living areas can be visited. The colonial art
includes a pulpit by the notable Indian wood-
carver, Juan Bautista Menacho; it is
considered one of the country's finest
pulpits. The cemetery, with its numerous
tombs, mausoleums and other memorials, is
also worth a visit. Guided tours, costing
about US$0.80, are available daily (except
Monday) from 9 am to noon and 3 to 5 pm –
ring the doorbell.

The **Santuario of Guápulo**, in a precipitous valley on the east side of town, was built
between 1644 and 1688. You get the best
views of this delightful colonial church from
behind the Hotel Quito, at the end of Avenida
12 de Octubre. A steep footpath leads down
to Guápulo and it's a pleasant walk, though
somewhat strenuous coming back. The No
21 Santo Domingo-Guápulo bus goes there.

High on a hill, on Calle Venezuela, is the
unfinished **Basílica**. Construction was commenced in 1926, so the tradition of taking
decades to construct a church is obviously
still alive. At the north end of the Parque La
Alameda is the small church of **El Belén**,
built where the first Catholic mass was held
in Quito.

Other Sights The historic alley of **La
Ronda** (also called Juan de Dios Morales) is
just off Avenida 24 de Mayo, between calles
García Moreno and Venezuela, and on to
Maldonado. This street is perhaps the best-
preserved in colonial Quito and is full of old,
balconied houses. Just walk along the street
and you'll see which ones are open to visitors; they usually have handicrafts for sale.

You can sometimes visit the **Palacio de
Gobierno** (or **Palacio Presidencial**), the
low white building on the north-west side of
the Plaza de la Independencia. The entrance
is flanked by a pair of handsomely uniformed presidential guards. Inside you can
see a mural depicting Francisco de
Orellana's descent of the Amazon. Sightseeing is limited to the mural and lower
courtyard.

Places to Stay
Old Town Most cheap hotels are found in the
Plaza Santo Domingo area, especially on
Calle Rocafuerte, Avenida Maldonado and
Calle Flores running off the Plaza, and on La
Ronda south of the Plaza. Here you'll find a
score or more cheap hotels within a few
blocks of one another. The Terminal Terrestre de Cumandá is nearby. This is the area
where many budget travellers stay – but
watch your belongings on the streets outside
and ensure your room is always locked.
Some travellers (particularly single women)
do not feel comfortable staying in this area.

The *Hotel Grand* (☎ 210 192, 519 411),
Rocafuerte 1001, two blocks south-east of
the Plaza Santo Domingo, is currently very
popular with international budget travellers
and has been well recommended. Basic but
clean rooms are about US$2 per person, or
US$4 per person with private bath. (There
are few singles with private bath.) The hotel
is family-run and friendly, with hot water and
a laundry service, and an Italian restaurant
downstairs. A bar is being opened.

The legendary *Hotel Gran Casino* (☎ 516
368), Calle García Moreno 330, is nicknamed the 'Gran Gringo' and is a classic
backpackers' dive in a poor area of town.
There is a cheap restaurant, notice board,
laundry facilities, left-luggage room (ensure
luggage is clearly labelled and locked), and
a good view from the roof.

Extremely basic and old rooms cost about
US$1.60 for a single – these go fast. Rooms
with two to six beds are about US$1.40 per
person. Communal hot showers are available
from 7 am to 3 pm only. A few rooms with a
private shower are US$2 per person. Next
door to the hotel are Turkish baths and a
sauna, where you can soak away your travel
grime and tensions for about US$1.

Two blocks away is the *Gran Casino
Internacional* (☎ 514 905, 216 595), at 24 de
Mayo and Bahía de Caráquez. They have
much newer and nicer rooms with private
bath and hot water for about US$3 per person
(there are a few singles). Nearby, is the *Gran
Casino Colonial*, opened in 1992 – both
places attract international budget travellers.

Not far away, on Calle Loja near Venezuela, is a small red-light district with some very cheap hotels. Travellers occasionally stay here and the hotels are reportedly OK. The *Pensión Astoria*, at Loja 630, and the *Hotel Minerva*, at Loja 656, charge about US$1 per person.

On the Plaza Santo Domingo is the *Hotel Roma*, at Rocafuerte 1331, and the *Hotel Santo Domingo*, next door. At the corner of the Plaza is the *Caspicara Hotel*, at Rocafuerte 1415. All three charge about US$1.70 per person, are basic but clean, and have hot water. The attractive *Hotel Juana del Arco* (☎ 214 175, 511 417), Rocafuerte 1311, has hot water and pleasant but noisy rooms (good views of the Plaza) for US$2.40 per person, or US$4.50 per person with private bath. The quieter rooms at the back lack windows.

Just off the Plaza, at Guayaquil 431, is the *Hotel Félix*, which has pretty flowers on the balconies, though the rooms are still basic. There is reportedly only one hot shower for about 30 rooms but the place is secure – ring the bell to get in. The nearby *Hotel Venecia*, on Calle Rocafuerte near Venezuela, is basic but clean – the electric showers deliver lukewarm water. These hotels charge about US$1.50 per person and are often full.

There are several cheap and basic hotels on La Ronda. *Residencial Los Shyris*, La Ronda 691, charges US$1.40 or US$2 per person depending on whether you have a private bath; hot water is available. There are other cheaper but worse places on the same block.

There are many hotels down on Maldonado. In the first block (away from Santo Domingo), on the right, are the *Interamericano*, *Capitalino* and *Zulia*. The Interamericano (☎ 214 320), at Maldonado 3263, charges US$2 to US$4 for a single, depending on whether or not you have a bathroom, telephone, or TV in your room. The Capitalino is US$1.80 each and looks basic but clean; they have hot water all day long. The Zulia is a basic cold-water hotel charging US$1 per person.

On the left side are the basic but safe hotels *Guayaquil* (☎ 211 520) and *Ingatur*. The Guayaquil, at Maldonado 3248, charges US$1.50 or US$3 per person, depending on whether you have a bathroom or not. There is hot water and the rooms vary; some are good and spacious, others less so. The Ingatur, at Maldonado 3226, has hot water, is clean and charges US$1.50 per person but has few singles. Its simple restaurant serves cheap almuerzos and meriendas.

The *Hotel Colonial* (☎ 510 338), down an alley from Maldonado 3035, is quiet and has hot water. Basic but clean rooms are US$1.20 per person; if you want a private bath, the rooms are US$2.75/5 for a single/double.

On the other side of Maldonado are several more hotels which cost about US$1.40 per person but look grimy and have only cold water. These include the *Hotel Caribe* (☎ 212 966), at Maldonado 2852, and the nearby *Hotel Los Andes* and *Residencial Los Andes*. A little better is the cleaner *Hotel Indoamericano* (☎ 515 094), at Maldonado 3022, which charges US$1.50 per person and has hot water in the mornings.

Going in the opposite direction from Plaza Santo Domingo along Calle Flores, you'll find some more hotels to choose from. The friendly *Huasi Continental* (☎ 517 327), Flores 330, has spartan but clean rooms with private bathrooms and hot water for US$3.25/5.50 a single/double; rooms with shared bathrooms are US$3.50 a double. Opposite is the *Hotel Flores*, at Flores 335. They have a courtyard and nice rooms for about US$3.50 per person – they have been recommended. The nearby *Hotel Montúfar*, Sucre 160, is also recommended. It is quiet, clean, has hot water and is very good value for about US$2 per person. The *Residencial Quitumbe*, Espejo 815, is very clean and secure and has hot water but no private bathrooms. They charge US$3.50 per person in spacious rooms. The *Hotel Viena* (☎ 213 132), Flores 562, charges US$1.50 per person and has hot water – there has been a report of petty theft from the rooms. The nearby *Hotel Viena Internacional* is more expensive.

ECUADOR

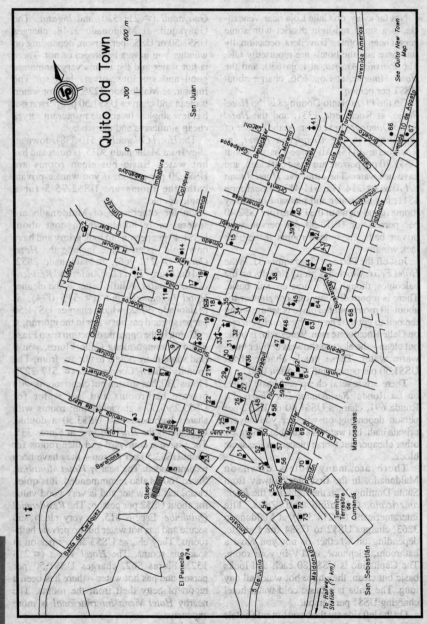

ECUADOR

■	PLACES TO STAY	71	Hotel Indoamericano & Residencial Los	19	Museo de Arte y Historia
4	Hotel Gran Casino Internacional		Andes	20	Church of La Compañía
5	Hotel Gran Casino	72	Hostal Cumandá	28	Cine Atahualpa
7	Hotel Sucre	73	Hotels Los Andes & Caribe	29	Casa de Sucre
8	Hotel Benalcázar			31	Rodrigo Paz Money
11	Ecuahotel	▼	PLACES TO EAT		Exchange & Cine
22	Hotel Venecia				Metro
23	Pensión Astoria & Hotel Minerva	6	Pollo Gus	32	Catedral
24	Hotel Felix	17	Las Cuevas de Luis Candela	33	Church of El Sagrario
25	Caspicara Hotel	21	Restaurant Royal	34	Plaza de la Independencia
27	Hotel Real Audiencia	25	Restaurant Los Olivos and others	35	Palacio de Gobierno
30	Auca Hotel	26	Chifa El Chino	37	Municipalidad & CETUR Tourist
42	Hotel Plaza del Teatro	36	Pollo Broaster		Office
47	Residencial Quitumbe	39	Govinda Vegetarian Restaurant	38	Jaramillo Arteaga Money Exchange
49	Hotels Roma & Santo Domingo	44	El Criollo	40	Museo Camilo Egas
50	Hotel Juana del Arco	46	Restaurant Oasis	41	Church of La Basílica
51	Residencial Los Shyris	47	Pizza Hut	43	Plaza del Teatro, Teatro Sucre &
52	Hotel Interamericano		OTHER		Pastelería El Torreón
53	Hotels Capitalino & Zulia	1	Monastery of San Diego	45	Monastery of San Agustín
54	Hotel Colonial	2	Mitad del Mundo Bus	47	Teatro Bolívar
56	Hotel Ingatur		Stop	48	Plaza Santo Domingo
57	Hotel Guayaquil	3	Indian Market Area	55	Cine Cumandá
59	Hotel Huasi Continental	9	Plaza San Francisco	58	Church of Santo Domingo
60	Hotel Montúfar	10	Monastery of San Francisco	66	Museo del Banco
61	Hostal Rumiñahui	12	Ipiales Market Area		Central
62	Hotel Italia	13	Church of La Merced	67	Simón Bolívar Monument
63	Hotel Viena	14	Museo de Arte Colonial	68	Plaza La Marín
64	Hotels Viena Internacional & San Agustín	15	Casa de Benalcázar	74	La Virgen de Quito
65	Hotel Los Canarios	16	IETEL		
69	Hotel Hogar	18	Central Post Office		
70	Hotel Grand				

Further down is the better *Hotel San Agustín* (☎ 216 051, 212 847), at Flores 626, and the *Hotel Los Canarios*, at Flores 856. Both charge about US$5/8 for clean singles/doubles with private bath and hot water. The San Agustín also has cheaper rooms with shared baths for US$3.50/5 for a single/double.

There are two cheap hotels on Calle Montúfar, which parallels Flores to the south-east. The *Hotel Hogar* (☎ 218 183), Montúfar 208, is US$2.25 per person in rooms with private baths; they have hot

water in the mornings. The *Hostal Rumiñahui* (☎ 211 407), Montúfar 449, charges US$3.50/6 for singles/doubles or US$4.50/7 for rooms with private bath. The hotel is clean, has hot water and is recommended. Nearby is the friendly *Hotel Italia*, on Junín between Montúfar and Flores. Clean but basic rooms are about US$1.50 per person and hot water is available.

Other budget hotels in the old town include the *Hotel Sucre*, on Calle Cuenca near Bolívar, close to the corner of Plaza San Francisco. The hotel is attractive from the

ECUADOR

outside but has only basic rooms inside, though some have good views. Warm water is available on request and rooms are only US$1.10 per person. Also on this plaza is the *Hotel Benalcázar* (☎ 518 302), Benalcázar 388. They charge about US$2.40 for a double with private bath and have been recommended by budget travellers.

The *Hotel Plaza del Teatro* (☎ 216 195, 514 293, 519 462), Guayaquil 1317, at the theatre plaza, charges about US$4 per person in good rooms with private bath. The *Ecuahotel* (☎ 515 984), Chile 1427, has a few rooms with good views and charges US$5 for a double room with a bath or US$3.50 for a double with communal bathrooms.

East of the old town is *Casa Patty* (☎ 510 407), Iquique 233 and Manosalvas, in the La Tola neighbourhood. It is run by the same family that has Pensión Patty in Baños. The large house has a few rooms for U$1.60 per person – kitchen facilities are available and the management is friendly.

Several hotels in the old town offer comfortable mid-priced rooms for travellers wishing to splurge. The best hotel near the Terminal Terrestre is the *Hostal Cumandá* (☎ 516 984, 513 592), Morales 449, behind the bus terminal. Clean, carpeted rooms with bathrooms and hot water are US$5.50/8.50 for singles/doubles. TV and telephone are available in some rooms. Avoid the rooms on the terminal side, as they can be noisy – otherwise, it's good value.

The *Hotel Viena Internacional* (☎ 213 605, 211 329), Flores 600, is popular with travellers wanting reasonably priced comfort in the old town. They have large carpeted rooms – some have balconies and all have telephones, bathrooms and hot water. There is a book exchange and restaurant. Rooms are US$8/15 for singles/doubles.

New Town Conventional wisdom has long dictated that budget travellers stay in the old town and only the rich stay in the new. This is no longer true, and there are several cheap places to stay in the new area.

A popular (and often full) budget hotel

closer to the new part of town is the *Residencial Marsella* (☎ 515 884), Los Ríos 2035, just east of the Parque La Alameda. Rates are about US$4 for a double room with bath. The hotel is clean, with hot water and a roof with a view, is family-run and is well recommended. The rooms vary quite widely in quality, from comfortable doubles to a few airless singles. If this is full, try the newer *Residencial Margarita*, around the corner, which has clean, safe rooms with private bath for about US$4.50 a double.

Near the main drag of Amazonas, you can stay at the small, family-run *Residencial Italia*, 9 de Octubre 237. They charge about US$2 for basic single rooms or US$5 for doubles with a bath, and are often full.

Around the corner is the very basic *Residencial 18 de Septiembre*, on the street of the same name – they charge only about US$1.50 per person but aren't up to much. A better choice for budget accommodation in the new town is the *Residencial Los Angeles* (☎ 238 290, 565 643), Cordero 779. They charge about US$2.50 per person and are often full – a recent unconfirmed report indicates that some singles with private bath are US$8.

The *Residencial Portoviejo* (☎ 235 399), on Avenida América near Portoviejo, is a recent recommendation. International budget travellers like it – the US$2 per person rooms fill fast.

Several small, family-run hostales have recently opened – they cater especially to backpackers and students. Hot showers, kitchen and laundry facilities, luggage storage, living room, notice board and information are available in a friendly and relaxed environment. They normally have a few small (single, double) rooms and a larger dormitory-style room. It is best to phone ahead for availability. *Casapaxi* (☎ 525 331), at Pasaje Navarro 326 near Avenida La Gasca, is about one km north and uphill of Avenida América; the No 19 bus passes by. It is run by a friendly Ecuadorian woman, Martha, who charges US$4 per person and includes a 'tropical' breakfast of fruit and juice. *La Casa de la Feliz Eliza* (☎ 233 602),

Isabel La Católica 1559, is run by (who else?) a happy woman named Eliza. She charges US$4 per person. Very close by is *La Casona* (☎ 230 129, 544 036), at Andalucia 213 – they charge US$5 per person, including breakfast. Nearer the business centre is *Albergue El Taxo* (☎ 232 593), at Foch 909. They charge about US$5 per person and have information about mountaineering and guides.

There are several good small hotels in the area between Avenida 10 de Agosto and the university. One of the cheapest is the *Hotel Versalles* (☎ 547 321), Versalles 1442. They charge US$6/9 for singles/doubles with a bathroom. It's OK but nothing fancy. The *Residencial Santa Clara* (☎ 541 472), Darquea Teran 1578, has recently enjoyed a great deal of popularity among travellers and is often full. The residencial is a pleasant-looking house and it's clean, comfortable and friendly. Rooms are available both with (US$5.60 per person) and without (US$4.70 per person) bathrooms; meals are also available. The clean *Hotel St James* (☎ 565 972, 567 972), Versalles 1075, is excellent value at US$8/9.50 for rooms which include a bath. Pleasant cheaper rooms with shared bath are also available. There is a cafeteria.

The *Hotel Pickett* (☎ 541 453, 551 205), Presidente Wilson 712, charges US$5.50/10 for rooms with telephone and a bath (with plenty of hot water). This is a centrally located and reasonable place to stay.

Places to Eat

If economising, stick to the standard almuerzos or meriendas. There are several cheap restaurants on the 1400 block of Rocafuerte, near the Plaza Santa Domingo. One is the *Restaurant Los Olivos* (☎ 514 150), at Rocafuerte 1421 – there are equally good places within a block.

There are many other simple and inexpensive restaurants in the old town but most of them are unremarkable. Some which have been recommended include the *Restaurant Royal*, at García Moreno 666, the *Restaurant Oasis*, at Espejo 812, and the more expensive

El Criollo (☎ 219 828), at Flores 825 – this last restaurant serves no beer.

Also in the old town, the *Govinda* is a cheap, Hare Krishna-run vegetarian restaurant at Esmeraldas 853. They are open only for lunch from Monday to Friday. A good Chinese restaurant is *Chifa El Chino*, on Bolívar near Guayaquil. *Pollo Broaster*, Sucre 258, serves chicken as well as desserts such as cakes and ice cream. Also good for desserts, snacks and juices is *Pastelería El Torreón*, on the Plaza del Teatro Sucre – a place for rest and refreshment during a busy sightseeing visit to the old town.

In the new town, I have eaten well at *Cevichería Don José*, Veintimilla 1254. The service is friendly, they open every day and you can get a decent meal for about US$1. *La Finca*, at the corner of 9 de Octubre and Cordero, is another good budget choice, particularly for set meals, which are well under US$1.

La Chiminea Inn, on Darquea Terán, just off 10 de Agosto, is a nice-looking restaurant that serves good meals for about US$1.25. Other inexpensive places can be found by wandering around and seeing where the local office workers eat.

For fast food, walk down Calle Carrión, east of Amazonas. This block has been nick-named 'Hamburger Alley' and has about a dozen places serving burgers and their usual accompaniments. It is very popular with students.

Mama Chlorindas (☎ 544 362), Reina Victoria 1144, is a good, cheap place to try local food, particularly at lunchtime – meals are only about US$1.

Avenida Amazonas is a good place to watch the world go by. *Manolo's* pavement café is a popular meeting-place and is not exorbitant. They serve a decent cup of coffee and don't hassle you if you sit there for hours. It's at Amazonas 420, and there are several similar places nearby.

The *Colón Coffee Shop*, at Amazonas and Jorge Washington, is reasonably priced considering that it is in one of the capital's most luxurious hotels. It is open 24 hours and serves meals as well as snacks. The café opposite the Libri Mundi bookstore on J L Mera is recommended for a light alfresco snack, with less of the hustle and bustle of Amazonas.

The American-run *Adam's Rib*, on J L Mera near Roca, serves ribs and a variety of other American-style dishes at medium prices. The place has a pool table and is popular with young travellers.

Entertainment

Quito is not the world's most exciting capital for nightlife. Entertainment reaches its height during the various fiestas, such as the founding of Quito, in the first week of December, when there are bullfights at the Plaza de Toros. There is also street dancing on the night of 6 December. On New Year's Eve, life-sized puppets (often of politicians) are burnt in the streets at midnight. Carnaval is celebrated with intense water fights – no one is spared. Colourful religious processions are held during Easter week.

There are some 20 cinemas – a few show good English-language films with Spanish subtitles. These include the Cine Colón, at the intersection of Avenida Colón and 10 de Agosto, and the Universitario, at the Indoamerican Plaza, on Avenida América near Perez Guerrero. Entrance is less than US$1.

Plays in Spanish are presented at the Teatro Sucre, on Guayaquil in the old town, or the Teatro Prometeo, on Avenida 6 de Diciembre, behind the Casa de la Cultura in the new town.

There are several 'pubs' which are not cheap by Ecuadorian standards. The La Reina Victoria (☎ 233 369), Reina Victoria 530, is managed by a friendly US/British couple, and has a fireplace, dart board, bumper pool and excellent pub ambience. Cheers! Also noteworthy are the little Rumors Bar, on J L Mera near Veintimilla, the Cowboy Bar, on the 1100 block of Almagro near La Pinta (which plays country and western tapes only), and the Latin Jazz Bar (locally known as *El Papillón*), on Almagro near Santa María. Recently, the Papillón was the 'in' place, and each night

sees crowds of gringo travellers and young Ecuadorians filling the place to overflowing and yelling over the sounds of The Doors – not a place for a quiet drink and a chat. Other popular drinking holes include the Arriba Bar, on Cordero near Colón, and the People's Bar, on Amazonas near Carrión. These places come and go – ask around about the latest 'in' place.

Getting There & Away

Air The airport (☎ 241-580) is 10 km north of the city centre and has a domestic and international terminal. Services include tourist information, money exchange, post office, cafeteria/bar, IETEL international telephone office and gift shops. The domestic terminal opens at 5 am, so don't arrive any earlier.

Flight schedules and prices change frequently. TAME and SAN-Saeta have flights to Guayaquil (about US$20) from six to 14 times a day, most frequently on weekdays. Flights to Cuenca (US$21) leave one to three times a day. TAME operates services to the following cities (flights are several times a week and sometimes daily): Tulcán, Esmeraldas, Portoviejo, Manta, Macas, Coca, Lago Agrio and Tarapoa.

TAME has several ticket offices – addresses change frequently, so check before you go. In the old town, TAME is at Manabí 635 (☎ 512 988). In the new town, TAME is at Avenida Colón 1001 (☎ 554 905) and 10 de Agosto 239 (☎ 512 910, 510 305). SAN-Saeta share an office at Guayaquil 1228 in the old town (☎ 211 431). SAN has an office at Avenida Colón 535 (☎ 561 995) and at Avenida Colombia 610 (☎ 527 555). Saeta has an office at 10 de Agosto 2356 (☎ 551 782). Most reputable travel agents sell air tickets at the same cost as if purchased direct from the airlines.

Bus The Terminal Terrestre de Cumandá is at Maldonado 3077 near Cumanda, a few hundred metres south of the Plaza Santo Domingo in the old town. The terminal is best reached from Maldonado on foot or by bus, or from the back by taxi.

Dozens of bus companies serve most destinations from Quito. There is an information window (☎ 571 163, 570 670). If travelling during holiday periods and just before the weekend, it's best to go to the terminal and book in advance. There are several snack bars, a post office, IETEL office, banking machines and small stores. Watch your luggage very carefully inside the terminal and watch for bag squirters setting you up for slashings.

With literally hundreds of departures each day, it is impossible to give accurate timetables. There are several buses a day to most destinations, and some places – such as Ambato or Otavalo – may have several departures an hour.

The major destinations served and the approximate cost and length of a journey are shown below. US$0.05 is added to each ticket as a terminal departure tax. These fares and times are subject to change.

To	Cost (US$)	Hours
Ambato	1.10	2½
Bahía de Caráquez	3.80	8
Baños	1.50	3½
Coca	3.30	13
Cuenca	3.00	10
Guaranda	1.70	5
Guayaquil	2.80	8
Ibarra	0.90	3
Lago Agrio	3.00	10
Latacunga	0.80	1½
Loja	4.90	18
Machala	3.70	11
Manta	3.90	8
Otavalo	0.75	2¼
Portoviejo	3.90	8
Puyo	2.00	8
Riobamba	1.60	4
Santo Domingo	1.10	2½
Tena	2.90	6
Tulcán	2.00	5½

There are companies (eg TEPSA) which will sell international bus tickets to Peru or Colombia. Avoid these – it's much cheaper and far more convenient to buy tickets as you go.

Train There is intermittent service from Quito to Riobamba. Trains are old and slow,

but cheap (US$0.60 to Riobamba, about five hours); service is unpredictable. Check with the train station (☎ 266 142/4), on Avenida Sincholagua near Vincente Maldonado, about two km south of the old town. The No 2 Colón-Camal bus from the Plaza Santo Domingo goes there.

Getting Around
To/From the Airport The easiest way to the airport using public transport is aboard the blue double-decker London buses or the new articulated buses which start from the south end of Parque El Ejido and run along Avenida Amazonas. The fare is US$0.10 but the buses do not run after dark.

Other buses to the airport are more crowded. They are usually marked 'Aeropuerto'. The No 1 Villa Flora-Iñaquito bus runs from Plaza Santo Domingo, in the old town, past the airport. A taxi costs about US$2 to US$3 (or about US$4 at night). From the airport, taxi drivers try to overcharge – bargain hard.

Bus The crowded local buses have a flat fare of US$0.05, which you pay as you board. Generally speaking, buses run north-south and have a fixed route. The drivers are usually helpful and will tell you which bus to take if they are not going to your destination. Traffic in the old town is very heavy, and you may often find it faster to walk than to take a bus, especially during the rush hours. Buses have both a name and a number, and although they usually have a fixed route, this may vary because of heavy traffic, road repair or the whim of the driver. There are about 40 different routes. A selection of the ones you might use follows:

1 Iñaquito-Villa Flora
   Airport-10 de Agosto-Guayaquil-Santo Domingo-Maldonado-Villa Flora
2 Colón-Camal
   Coruña-Colón-10 de Agosto-Guayaquil-Santo Domingo-Maldonado-Terminal Terrestre
3 La Colmena-Batán
   La Colmena-24 de Mayo-García Moreno-Vargas Torres-Manuel Larrea-Patria-J L Mera-Colón-6 de Diciembre-El Batán

7 Marín-Cotocollao
    Plaza La Marín-10 de Agosto-Airport-Cotocollao
9 Ermita-Las Casas
    Ermita-24 de Mayo-García Moreno-América-Universidad Central-La Gasca-Las Casas
10 San Bartolo-Miraflores
    San Bartolo-Maldonado-Santo Domingo-10 de Agosto-18 de Septiembre-Miraflores
11 El Tejar-El Inca
    El Tejar-Mejía-La Alameda-6 de Diciembre-El Inca (end of 6 de Diciembre)
15 Marín-Quito Norte
    Plaza La Marín-10 de Agosto-Airport-North Quito
19 Camal-La Gasca
    Patria-Pérez Guerrero-América-La Gasca
21 Dos Puentes-Guápulo
    Bahía de Caráquez (Dos Puentes)-Rocafuerte-Santo Domingo-Venezuela-Guayaquil- Colombia-12 de Octubre-Madrid-Guápulo
El Tejar-Mitad del Mundo
    El Tejar-América-10 de Agosto-La Prensa-Mitad del Mundo

Some main streets, especially 10 de Agosto, are serviced by minibuses – these cost a few cents extra, are a little faster and run later at night.

Taxi Taxi cabs are all yellow and have red taxi stickers in the window. Usually, there are plenty available, but rush hour can leave you waiting 10 or 15 minutes for an empty cab. Quito cabs have meters and most drivers use them, though occasionally, a fare is arranged beforehand to enable the driver to take a roundabout route to avoid traffic, thus saving both of you time. Short journeys downtown cost about US$0.50 to US$3 for a long trip. Cabs can be rented by the hour or day.

AROUND QUITO
The most famous excursion is to the equator at **La Mitad del Mundo**, 22 km north of Quito. Here, there is a large stone monument and an interesting ethnographical museum. It is open Tuesday to Friday from 9 am to 3 pm, and 10 am to 4 pm on weekends; admission is US$0.50. There is also a planetarium, a wonderful scale model of Quito's old town and other attractions.

Rumicucho is a small pre-Inca site under excavation about 3½ km north of Mitad del Mundo. About five km north of Mitad del Mundo, on the way to the village of Calacalí, is the ancient volcanic crater of **Pululahua**, which can be descended into on foot – an interesting walk.

From Quito, the No 22 Mitad del Mundo bus leaves frequently from the El Tejar bus stop. This is on the short street of J López, between Hermano Miguel and Mejía, near the Ipiales street market in the old town. It's not an obvious bus stop, so ask. The one-hour trip costs about US$0.15 – beware of overcharging.

Various companies offer tours – an inexpensive but recently recommended one is with Calimatours (☎ 565 877, 533 506), at U Páez 162 near 18 de Septiembre. Two-hour guided trips to the monument plus a look at the nearby Pululahua Crater are US$3 per person (four minimum). Longer tours cost up to US$20 per person with other companies.

The Indian market nearest the capital is the **Sangolquí** Sunday morning market. Local buses go there frequently from Plaza Marín, on Calle Chile near M de Solanda.

The **Reserva Forestal de Pasochoa** is operated by the Fundación Natura (☎ 447 341/2/3/4), Avenida América 5663. The reserve is 30 km south-east of Quito and has one of the last stands of undisturbed humid Andean forest left in the central Ecuadorian valley. Over 100 species of birds and many rare plants have been recorded – it is recommended to naturalists and bird-watchers. There are several trails ranging from short and easy to long and strenuous.

The daily fee is US$7 for foreign visitors. Overnight camping in designated areas is US$12 per person (including the daily fee). There are latrines, picnic areas and water. Check with the Fundación Natura to obtain directions, maps, information and permits.

Quito's closest volcano is **Pichincha**, looming over the western side of the city. There are two summits, the closer Rucu Pichincha (about 4700 metres) and the higher Guagua Pichincha (4794 metres). Both can be climbed from Quito in a very long day,

ECUADOR

but the hiking routes are plagued with thieves, muggers, rapists and rabid dogs. These warnings should not be taken lightly. Go in a large group and check for the latest information before you go. The South American Explorers Club is always an excellent source of up-to-date information.

North of Quito

The Andean highlands north of Quito are one of the most popular destinations in Ecuador. Few travellers spend any time in the country without visiting the famous Indian market at the small town of Otavalo, where you can buy a wide variety of weavings, clothing and handicrafts.

The dramatic mountain scenery of the region is dotted with shining white churches set in tiny villages, and includes views of Cayambe, the third highest peak in the country, as well as a beautiful lake district. Several small towns are noted for specialty handicrafts such as woodcarving or leatherwork.

Ibarra is a small, charmingly somnolent colonial city at the beginning of the Ibarra to San Lorenzo railway, which links the northern highlands with the coast. If you are travelling overland to or from Colombia, it's almost impossible to avoid this region.

OTAVALO

This town of 20,000 inhabitants is justly famous for its friendly people and their Saturday market. The market dates back to pre-Inca times, when jungle products were brought up from the eastern lowlands and traded for highland goods.

One of the most evident features of the Otavaleños' culture is their traditional dress. The men wear long single pigtails, calf-length white pants, rope sandals, reversible grey or blue ponchos and dark felt hats. The women are very striking, with beautifully embroidered blouses, long black skirts and shawls, and interesting folded head cloths. They also wear bright jewellery: many

strings of gold-coloured blown-glass beads around their necks, and bracelets consisting of long strands of red beads.

Of the 20,000 inhabitants of Otavalo, the majority are Whites or mestizos. There are about 40,000 Indians, most of whom live in the many nearby villages and come into Otavalo for market day. However, quite a few Indians own stores in Otavalo where you can buy most items if you are unable to visit on market day.

Money
Exchange rates are lower than in Quito – the Banco de Pichincha on the main plaza usually will change money.

Information
Zulaytour (☎ 921 176), east corner of Sucre and Colón, 2nd floor, is an excellent information and guide service run by the friendly and knowledgeable Señor Rodrigo Mora. A variety of guided tours enable you to visit local Indian homes, learn about the entire weaving process, buy products off the loom and take photographs. An emphasis on anthropological and sociological background information makes these tours very worthwhile. The most popular tour visits several local villages and takes all day. Transportation is included and the tour costs about US$7 per person. There are other companies nearby.

Things to See
The main market day is Saturday. There are three main plazas, with the overflow spilling out onto the streets linking them. **Poncho Plaza** is the main centre for crafts (a form of 'market' takes place here most days). Bargaining for every purchase is expected. The market gets under way soon after dawn and continues until about noon. It can get rather crowded mid-morning, when the big tour groups arrive. Thieves and bag-slashers are reported in the markets. There is an animal market beginning in the predawn hours (4 to 8 am) on the outskirts of town.

The **Fiesta del Yamor** is held in the first

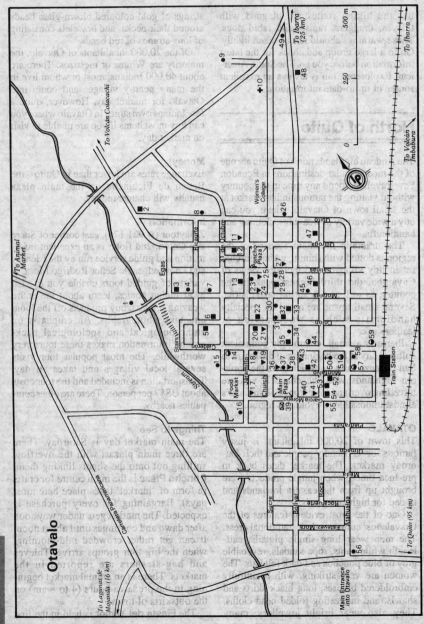

Otavalo

To Ibarra (25 km)

To Ibarra

To Volcán Imbabura

500 m

250

0

To Volcán Cotacachi

To Animal Market

To Volcán Cotacachi

Women's College

Quito

31 de Octubre

Poncho Plaza

Ricaurte

Egas

Sucre

Bolívar

Morales

Colón

Calderón

Stairs

Steam

Jaramillo

Church

Main Plaza

García Moreno

Piedrahita

Quiroga

Olmedo

Mejía

Roca

Atahualpa

Hospscene

Sucre

Bolívar

Flávez Mora

Train Station

Main Entrance into Otavalo

To Quito (95 km)

To Lagunas de Mojanda (16 km)

Carretera Panamericana

Food Market

ECUADOR

■ PLACES TO STAY		24	Parenthese Pizza	23	Amauta Peña
			Restaurant	24	Tucano Peña-Bar
2	Hotel Ali Shungu	25	Shenandoah Pie	26	Fire Station
3	Residencial El Rocío		Shop & La Galería	28	Public Toilet
5	Residencial Colón	27	Tabascos	30	Several Tourist
6	Residencial Santa	36	Royal Cafetería &		Agencies
	Martha		Chino's Fuente de	31	Rodrigo Mora &
12	Residencial		Soda		Zulaytour
	Centenario	38	Restaurant	34	Cine Bolívar
13	Residencial		Copacabana	35	Lasso Turismo
	Samar-Huasy	40	Chifa Tien An Men	37	Banco de Pichincha
20	Residencial El Indio	41	Chifa Casa de Korea	39	Municipalidad & Post
22	Pensión Imbabura	43	Camba Huasy		Office
29	Hotel El Indio		Chicken Restaurant	44	Transportes Otavalo
32	Pensión Los Angeles				(Buses)
33	Residencial La		OTHER	45	Inti Peña Salsateca
	Herradura	1	Stadium	49	Petrol (Gas) Station
35	Hotel Los Pendoneros	4	Bar La Choza	50	Santo Domingo
42	Pensión Otavalo	7	Peña Tuparina -		Church
46	Hotel San Sebastian		Centro de Difusion	51	Transportes Los
47	Residencial Isabelita		Andino		Lagos (Buses)
48	Hotel Yamor	8	Baha'i Institute	52	Museo Archaeológico
	Continental	9	Instituto Otavaleño de	55	Cine Apollo
52	Pensión Los Andes		Antropología	56	Petrol (Gas) Station
53	Hotel Otavalo	10	Hospital	57	Buses to San Pablo
54	Hotel Riviera-Sucre	14	Buses to Local	58	Plaza Copacabana &
			Villages		New Covered
▼ PLACES TO EAT		15	Cockfight Stadium,		Market (under
			Cine San Gabriel &		construction)
11	Ali Micui's		Public Toilet	59	Cooperativa
17	Café El Triunfo	16	Police Station		Imbaburapac
19	Mama Rosita's	18	IETEL		Churimi Canchic
21	El Mesón del Arrayan	21	Peña Oraibi		(Buses to Agato)

two weeks of September. There are processions, music and dancing, as well as firework displays, cockfights and the election of the Queen of the Fiesta.

Places to Stay

Otavalo gets crowded on Friday nights, so arrive early for the best choice. Cheaper rates can be negotiated for long stays. There have been reports of theft from hotel rooms in Otavalo. Keep doors locked, even if leaving for just a little while.

A popular cheapie is the friendly *Residencial Santa Martha* (☎ 920 568), Colón 7-04. It is small and tends to fill up quickly. Beds are about US$1.25 each in quads, and a few cents more in the singles and doubles – these go really fast. Most rooms are large and

there's a pretty courtyard, but the showers are only tepid. Also friendly and rather larger is the *Pensión Otavalo*, on Montalvo near Roca. There's hot water most of the time and small rooms are around US$1.50 per person, depending on the room and when you arrive.

The *Residencial Samar-Huasy*, at Jaramillo 6-11, by the Poncho Plaza, has clean, small rooms. Hot showers are available at certain times of day. Rooms are US$1.50 per person.

The *Residencial La Herradura*, on Bolívar near Morales, has been described by one reader as 'dirty' and by another as 'pretty good, with clean rooms' (one's trash is another's treasure). There are hot showers and a restaurant. They tend to lock up early, so let them know if you are going to a peña. Rates are about US$1.80 per person.

ECUADOR

The *Residencial Isabelita*, Roca 11-07, is clean, friendly and charges US$2 per person. Kitchen facilities are available. The *Residencial Centenario* (☎ 920 467), Quiroga 7-03, is another budget choice.

For a little more money, the clean and safe *Residencial El Rocío* (☎ 920 584), Morales 11-70, is well recommended by budget travellers. Rates are US$2 per person, or US$3 per person in rooms with private bath. There is hot water and a nice view from the roof. The owner is friendly and hires a van for local trips. The *Hotel Riviera-Sucre* (☎ 920 241), Moreno 3-14, is good, clean and popular with budget travellers. It is run by a friendly Belgian-Ecuadorian couple who charge about US$3/5 for single/double rooms. There are hot showers, a nice courtyard and a notice board, and a map and information are available.

The *Hostal San Sebastian*, Roca 9-05, is run by friendly people and has large singles/doubles with bath for US$4/6. The *Hostal Los Pendoneros*, on Calderón near Bolívar, is clean and recommended. They charge US$3 per person and there are plenty of bathrooms with hot water. The restaurant downstairs is popular.

The *Hotel El Indio* (☎ 920 004), Sucre 12-14, by the Poncho Plaza, is clean, and has hot water and a restaurant. It is very popular and always full of gringos on the weekend. Rooms vary in price – from about US$5 a double with shared bath to US$10 for a double with private bath, TV and balcony. The *Residencial El Indio*, on Colón near Sucre, charges about US$2 per person and is OK but not as good as the hotel.

Places to Eat
The *Shenandoah* pie shop, on the Poncho Plaza, has a wide selection of fruit pies and juices but the wares are not very cheap. There is a notice board and the place is very popular with travellers. Nearby, the Ecuadorian/Austrian-run *La Galería* has a wider range of meals and serves the best expresso in town. *Ali Micui's*, on the north corner of the Poncho Plaza, serves both vegetarian and non-vegetarian food at reasonable prices.

Half a block south-east of the Plaza, on Salinas, is *Tabascos*. The place is run by an Ecuadorian/US couple. They serve good Mexican food and decent breakfasts, have music some evenings and have a rack of magazines in English to read.

The US-run *Parenthese Pizza Restaurant* is on Morales and Sucre, one block from the Poncho Plaza. Apart from home-made vegetarian and meat pizzas, they serve snacks, sandwiches and salads. They are closed on Tuesday.

If you just want a snack, there's *Chino's Fuente de Soda*, on the main plaza, for ice cream. Next door is the *Royal Cafetería*, which is very clean and has good snacks and meals at reasonable prices. The *Café El Triunfo*, by the food market, on García Moreno near Jaramillo, has been recommended for cheap meals and good early breakfasts.

The best chifas are the *Tien An Men*, on García Moreno near Roca, and the *Casa de Korea*, on the same block. If you're after fried chicken, try the *Camba Huasy*, on Bolívar near Calderón, or the *Centro Latino*, on Sucre near Calderón. Inexpensive vegetarian food is sold at *Jatun Pacha*, at Morales 410.

The popular and friendly *Restaurant Tuparina Encuentro*, Bolívar 815, has been recommended for inexpensive meals and beer. For a splurge, try the excellent *Ali Shungu*, in the best hotel in town, on Quito near Quiroga.

Entertainment
Otavalo is quiet during the week but lively on the weekend. The popular Amauta Peña (☎ 920 967) is at Jaramillo 6-14. Music gets underway after 10 pm and there is a US$1 cover charge. The music and ambience can vary from abysmal to enjoyable – take your chances.

The newer Peña Tuparina, on Morales near 31 de Octubre, is similar and popular – the cover charge here is about US$0.50. A third place which has received recommendations is the Peña Oraibi (☎ 920 333), at Sucre 10-11. They have a restaurant as well.

The Tucano Peña-Bar, at Morales 5-10, has both folkloric and salsa music and may open midweek. The place can get rather wild – machos and drunks may spoil a single woman's evening.

Finally, there's the weekly cockfight, held at the west end of 31 de Octubre every Saturday afternoon. Vote against blood sports with your absence!

Getting There & Away

Bus The main bus terminal area is near the Plaza Copacabana, where you'll probably arrive from Quito. There is a taxi rank if you need it; US$0.50 will get you to most hotels. This is where you catch return buses to Quito and old local buses to some of the villages around Lago San Pablo.

A couple of blocks away, on Avenida Calderón, is Transportes Otavalo, which has frequent buses to Ibarra, where you change for buses further north. There are no buses direct to Tulcán at the moment. Transportes Otavalo also has many Quito-bound buses. Further down Calderón, at 31 de Octubre, there are decrepit old buses going to other local villages.

Train Autoferros run intermittently to Ibarra – ask.

AROUND OTAVALO

Many of the Indians live and work in the nearby villages of Peguche, Ilumán and Agato. These are loosely strung together on the north-east side of the Panamericana, a few km away from Otavalo. There are many other Otavaleño villages in the area, and a visit to Zulaytour in Otavalo will yield much more information. You can walk or take local buses to these villages. The *Cafetería Aya Huma*, near Peguche, serves cheap home-made snacks. Sunday is not a good day to visit the villages – many people prefer to get blind drunk than to deal with gringos.

Lago San Pablo can be reached on foot from Otavalo by heading roughly south-east on any of the paths heading over the hill behind the railway station. When you get to the lake, you'll find that a paved road goes all the way around it, with beautiful views of both the lake and Volcán Imbabura behind it.

COTACACHI

This small village, some 15 km north of Otavalo, is famous for its leatherwork, which is sold in stores all along the main street. From Otavalo, there are buses every hour. There are a couple of pricey hotels.

LAGUNA CUICOCHA

About 18 km east of Cotacachi is an extinct, eroded volcano, famous for the deep lake in its crater. There are half-hour boat rides around the islands on the lake (US$0.30). On sunny weekends, these are popular with locals. A walk around the lake takes about six hours. Don't eat the blue berries – they are poisonous. The lake is part of the Reserva Ecológica Cotacachi-Cayapas, established to protect a large area of western Andean forest which extends from Volcán Cotocachi (4939 metres) to the Río Cayapas in the coastal lowlands. The entrance fee is US$0.15. There are trucks, taxis and occasional buses from Cotacachi.

IBARRA

About 22 km north of Otavalo and 135 km north of Quito is the attractive colonial town of Ibarra, the provincial capital of Imbabura. One of the main reasons for coming here is to take the train from Ibarra to San Lorenzo, on the coast.

Horse-drawn carts clatter along cobbled streets flanked by 19th-century buildings, dark-suited old gentlemen sit in the shady parks discussing the day's events, and most people are in bed by 10 pm. It's a very quiet town, and some travellers prefer to stay here when visiting the Otavalo area.

Information

CETUR is at Colón 7-43. Change money at the Banco Continental, on Olmedo near Colón, or at the Polycambios casa de cambio, on Olmedo near Oviedo – rates are better in Quito.

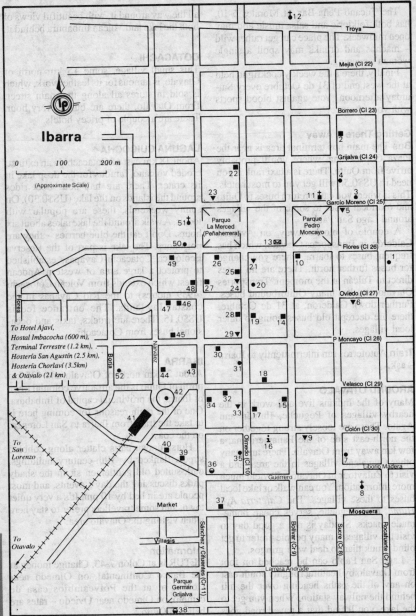

Ibarra

Troya

Mejía (Cl 22)

Borrero (Cl 23)

Grijalva (Cl 24)

García Moreno (Cl 25)

Flores (Cl 26)

Oviedo (Cl 27)

P Moncayo (Cl 28)

Velasco (Cl 29)

Colón (Cl 30)

Liborio Madera

Mosquera

Larrera Andrade

0   100   200 m
(Approximate Scale)

Flores

Borja

Narváez

Zaldumbide

Sánchez y Cifuentes

Olmedo (Cl 10)

Guerrero

Bolívar (Cr 9)

Sucre (Cr 8)

Rocafuerte (Cr 7)

Parque
La Merced
(Peñaherrera)

Parque
Pedro
Moncayo

Market

Villasís

Parque
German
Grijalva

To Hotel Ajaví,
Hostal Imbacocha (600 m),
Terminal Terrestre (1.2 km),
Hostería San Agustín (2.5 km),
Hostería Chorlaví (3.5km)
& Otavalo (21 km)

To
San
Lorenzo

To Otavalo

■ PLACES TO STAY		46	Hotel Imbabura	7	Public Hot Baths
		47	Residencial Los	8	Ruined Church of La
2	Residencial		Ceibos		Dolorosa
	Yahuarcocha	48	Residencial Primavera	11	Catedral
10	Residencial Imperial	49	Residencial Imbabura	12	Plazoleta Boyaca &
14	Residencial Vaca				Church of Santo
15	Hostal El Ejecutivo	▼ PLACES TO EAT			Domingo
17	Residencial San			13	Post Office
	Lorenzo	5	Luchino Pizza & Bar	16	CETUR Tourist
18	Residencial Los Alpes	6	Bar Restaurant El		Information
19	Residencial Imperio		Dorado	20	Polycambios
22	Hotel Nueva Colonia	9	Crema Juguetaría	23	Museo Archaeológico
25	Residencial Majestic	21	Restaurant La Chagra	31	El Encuentro Bar
26	Hotel Berlin	23	Restaurant La	35	Banco Continental
27	Residencial El		Estancia	36	Buses 28 de
	Principe	24	Café Pushkin		Septiembre & San
28	Residencial Madrid	29	Manolo's		Miguel de Ibarra
30	Residencial Madrid	32	Heladería La Nevada	38	Buses to La
32	Pensión Olmedo 1	33	Rincón Familiar		Esperanza
34	Residencial Atahualpa			41	Railway Station
37	Hotel Ibarra	OTHER		42	Obelisk
39	Residencial Tahuando			50	Taxis Lagos
40	Pensión Olmedo 2	1	Frederico Café	51	Church of La Merced
43	Pensión Varsovia		Musical	52	Cine Popular
44	Residencial Colón	3	Cine Grand Colombia		
45	Residencial Guayas	4	IETEL		

Places to Stay

The friendly *Hotel Imbabura*, Oviedo 9-33, has a pretty little courtyard with flowers. The best rooms are on the quiet street, at US$1.40 per person. The rather dark inside rooms are US$1 per person; there's hot water. The more basic *Residencial Imbabura*, Flores 9-53, is only US$0.90 per person and is reasonable for the price. The rather dark-looking *Residencial Los Ceibos*, Oviedo 9-53, charges US$1 and has only cold water. Another reasonably clean but basic cold-water cheapie is the *Residencial Imperial*, Bolívar 6-22. They charge about US$1.20 per person. Also, there are the similar *Residencial San Lorenzo*, Olmedo 10-56, and *Residencial El Principe* (☎ 952 786), Sánchez y Cifuentes 8-82. If you are really broke, the *Residencial Guayas*, P Moncayo 8-54, has tolerable rooms for US$0.90 per person. Hot showers are available at the public baths on Sucre and Guerrero, open from 6 am to 9 pm daily.

The *Hotel Berlin*, Flores 8-51, on the Parque La Merced, has spacious rooms and

tepid showers. Some front rooms have little balconies and views of the park. The *Residencial Majestic* (☎ 950 052), Olmedo 7-63, has good hot water, as does the *Residencial Vaca* (☎ 950 854), Bolívar 7-53. All three are basic but clean and charge US$1.75 to US$2 per person.

The popular (but often full by 3 pm) *Residencial Colón* (☎ 950 093), at Narváez 8-62, is clean, friendly, pleasant and has warm showers. Rooms with bath are US$2.80 per person, and a little less for communal bath. For the safety of your valuables, lock your doors. The *Residencial Los Alpes*, Velasco 7-32, is also in this price range and is OK.

The good *Residencial Imperio* (☎ 952 929), Olmedo 8-54, charges a reasonable US$3.50/5.50 for single/double rooms with private bath and sometimes a TV. The *Residencial Madrid* (☎ 951 760), Olmedo 8-57, charges US$6.50 for doubles with private bath. Many of the rooms are carpeted and have TV. The *Residencial Madrid* (☎ 952 177), at P Moncayo 7-41, is a little more expensive. The nice-looking *Hotel Nueva Colonia* (☎ 952 918, 955 543), Olmedo 5-19, charges US$4.50 per person in carpeted rooms with private bath and telephone; there is a restaurant.

Places to Eat

The *Café Pushkin*, Olmedo 7-75, has decent breakfasts and fresh home-made bread. *La Chagra*, Olmedo 7-48, has large helpings, reasonable prices and is popular with the locals. There are several good and cheap chifas on this street. *Luchino Pizza & Bar*, on the Parque Pedro Moncayo, has Italian food and snacks; *El Horno*, P Moncayo 6-30, also has pizza. *Rincón Familiar*, on Olmedo near Velasco, is cheap and clean.

El Encuentro, Olmedo 9-35, is a popular bar to hang out in.

Getting There & Away

Bus Buses from Quito leave once or twice an hour. The trip takes 2½ to four hours. The fastest is Transportes Andinos but the buses are small, uncomfortable and scary. They all charge about US$1. There are also frequent buses from Otavalo and Tulcán.

In Ibarra, the Terminal Terrestre is 1½ km south of the town centre. There are frequent departures for Quito, Tulcán (US$1.10, 2½ hours) and Otavalo (US$0.20, half an hour) and other towns (normally with a change in Quito).

Train The Ibarra-San Lorenzo railway links the highlands with the coast. There is supposedly one departure on most days (6.30 am, US$1) but this may be cancelled. Recently trains ran only on Saturday, Monday and Wednesday, and tickets were sold out the day before. Landslides cause frequent delays. A road is being built and passengers may be bussed part of the way, depending on the state of the road. Watch luggage very closely in the station.

The spectacular journey from Ibarra, at 2225 metres above sea level, to San Lorenzo, at sea level and 193 km away, gives a good cross-sectional view of Ecuador. You can ride on the roof – beware of overhanging branches. At several stops, food is sold, but

take a water bottle and some emergency food. There is a passport check in Lita, the halfway point.

Getting Around

Taxis from the Ibarra bus terminal to the centre are under US$1. Local buses charge US$0.05 and leave from outside the terminal for the centre.

SAN ANTONIO DE IBARRA

This village, almost a suburb of Ibarra, is famous for its woodcarving. It has a pleasant main square around which are a number of stores selling carvings.

The *Hostería Los Nogales* has rooms for US$2.50 per person, but it's easier to stay in Ibarra.

Buses from Guerrero and Sánchez y Cifuentes in Ibarra leave frequently. Otherwise, walk five km south on the Panamericana from Ibarra.

LA ESPERANZA

This pretty little village, seven km south of Ibarra, is the place for travellers to stay if they are looking for peace and quiet. There's nothing to do except talk to the locals and take walks in the surrounding countryside.

The basic but friendly *Casa Aida* costs US$1 per person. They serve good cheap meals here. You may be able to rent a basic room at the *Restaurant María*.

Buses from Parque Germán Grijalva in Ibarra serve the village frequently.

TULCÁN

This small city of 40,000 is the provincial capital of Carchi, the northernmost province of the Ecuadorian highlands and an important market town. For travellers, it is the gateway to Colombia, only seven km away.

Money

Exchange is better in Tulcán than at the border. The bus between Tulcán and the border accepts Colombian or Ecuadorian currency. Banco de los Andes sometimes does foreign exchange. There are several casas de cambio, which pay about 4% less

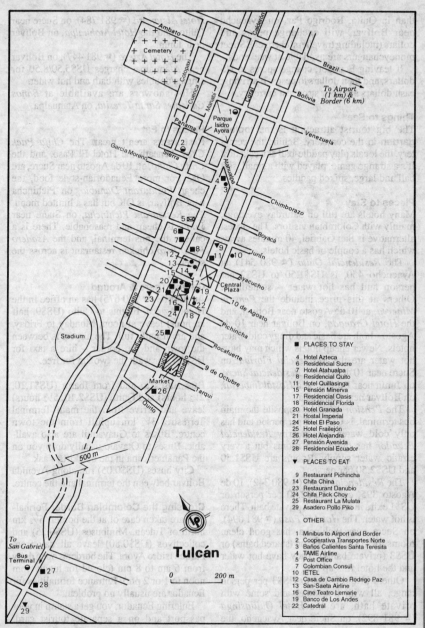

Tulcán

0   200 m

To
San Gabriel
Bus
Terminal

500 m

To Airport
(1 km) &
Border (6 km)

Stadium

Market

Central
Plaza

Parque Isidro
Ayora

Cemetery

■ PLACES TO STAY

4   Hotel Azteca
6   Residencial Sucre
7   Hotel Atahualpa
8   Residencial Quito
11 Hotel Quillasinga
15 Pensión Minerva
16 Residencial Oasis
18 Residencial Florida
20 Hotel Granada
21 Hostal Imperial
24 Hotel El Paso
25 Hotel Frailejón
26 Hotel Alejandra
27 Pensión Avenida
28 Residencial Ecuador

▼ PLACES TO EAT

9   Restaurant Pichincha
14 Chifa China
23 Restaurant Danubio
24 Chifa Pack Choy
25 Restaurant La Mulata
29 Asadero Pollo Piko

OTHER

1   Minibus to Airport and Border
2   Cooperativa Transportes Norte
3   Baños Calientes Santa Teresita
4   TAME Airline
5   Post Office
7   Colombian Consul
10 IETEL
12 Casa de Cambio Rodrigo Paz
13 San-Saeta Airline
17 Cine Teatro Lemarie
19 Banco de Los Andes
22 Catedral

ECUADOR

than in Quito. Rodrigo Paz, on Ayacucho near Bolívar, will exchange pesos and dollars (including travellers' cheques). Street moneychangers are available at weekends.

If leaving Ecuador, change sucres to US dollars, and then dollars to pesos. If arriving, cash dollars are your strongest currency.

Things to See
The big tourist attraction is the **topiary garden** in the cemetery. Behind the cemetery, the locals play paddle-ball at weekends. It's a strange game, played with a small, soft ball and large, spiked paddles.

Places to Stay
Many hotels are full on Saturday evenings, mainly with Colombian visitors. The closest alternative is San Gabriel, 40 minutes away, which has a couple of basic hotels.

The *Residencial Quito* (☎ 980 541), at Ayacucho 450, is US$1.50 to US$2 per person and has hot water – sometimes. Others at this price include the *Pensión Minerva*, at 10 de Agosto near Bolívar, and the *Hotel Granada*, on Bolívar near 10 de Agosto – both are basic and dingy cold-water hotels. Newer cheap hotels which may have hot water are the *Residencial Florida*, on Sucre near 10 de Agosto, *Residencial Sucre*, on Junín near Bolívar, and *Hostal Imperial*, on Bolívar near Pichincha.

The *Pensión Avenida*, opposite the main bus terminal, is US$1.20 per person and has only cold water. The nearby *Residencial Ecuador* has quite nice rooms but a very erratic water supply. Rooms are US$1.50 and US$2.50 per person.

The *Residencial Oasis* (☎ 980 342), 10 de Agosto 395, costs US$2.80 per person or US$1 extra in rooms with private bath. There is hot water. The *Hotel El Paso* (☎ 981 094), on Sucre near Pichincha, has good clean rooms for US$2 per person (shared baths) or US$3 (private baths). They have hot water and the hotel fills up fast.

Others in the US$2 to US$3 per person range, all with hot water and some with private bath, are the *Hotel Quillasinga* (☎ 981 892), on Sucre near Ayacucho, the

Hotel Alejandra (☎ 981 784), on Sucre near Quito, and the *Hotel Atahualpa*, on Bolívar near Junín.

The *Hotel Azteca* (☎ 981 447), on Bolívar near Atahualpa, charges US$5.50/8.50 for singles/doubles with bath and hot water.

Hot showers are available at *Baños Calientes Santa Teresita*, on Atahualpa.

Places to Eat
Restaurants aren't great. The *Chifa Pack Choy*, beneath the Hotel El Paso, and the *Chifa China*, on 10 de Agosto near Sucre, are OK. For more Ecuadorian-style food, the cheap *Restaurant Danubio*, on Pichincha near Bolívar, is OK but has a limited menu. The *Restaurant Pichincha*, on Sucre near Junín, is cheap and reasonable. There is a cafe in the bus terminal, and the *Asadero Pollo Piko* chicken restaurant is across the street.

Getting There & Around
Air TAME (☎ 980 675) has an office in the Hotel Azteca. Flights to Quito (US$9, half an hour) leave at noon, Monday to Friday, and are usually full. The airport is between the town and the border – hire a taxi for US$0.75 or walk the two km for free.

Bus Buses to and from Ibarra (US$1.10, 2½ hours) and Quito (US$2.10, 5½ hours) leave and arrive from the main Terminal Terrestre, 3½ km uphill from the town centre. Buses to Guayaquil are also available. Buses to Otavalo usually drop you on the Panamericana in the outskirts – ask.

City buses (US$0.05) run along Avenida Bolívar between the terminal and the centre.

Crossing the Colombian Border Formalities are taken care of at the border, 6½ km north of Tulcán. Minibuses (US$0.25) and collectivos (US$0.80) leave all day from Parque Isidro Ayora. The border is open daily from 6 am to 8 pm (closed for lunch from noon to 1 or 2 pm). Entrance formalities for Ecuador are usually no problem.

Entering Ecuador, you get a stamp in your passport and on a separate tourist card.

Leaving Ecuador, you get an exit stamp in your passport and hand in your tourist card. If you lose it, they should give you another one free – but it's best not to lose it. (See Visas & Documents in the Facts for the Visitor section of this chapter.)

Those needing a Colombian visa can try the Colombian Consulate (☎ 980 559), on Bolívar near Junín. They are subject to lengthy closures – at times, it is best to try in Quito.

South of Quito

The Panamericana heads almost directly south of Quito along a long valley flanked by two parallel ranges of mountains, many of which are volcanos. This central valley contains almost half of Ecuador's population. The relatively rich volcanic soils are good for agriculture and the central valley makes a good communication route between north and south. A string of towns stretches south from the capital to Ecuador's third largest city, Cuenca, some 300 km away. In between lies some of Ecuador's wildest scenery, with nine of the country's 10 highest peaks, and scores of tiny villages of Andean Indians whose lives have changed little over the centuries.

LATACUNGA

Latacunga (population 40,000) is the capital of Cotopaxi Province and a good base for several excellent excursions. The drive from Quito is magnificent. Cotopaxi is the cone-shaped mountain looming to the east of the Panamericana. At 5897 metres, it is the second highest peak in Ecuador and the highest active volcano in the world. The two Ilinizas (Sur and Norte), also snowcapped, are on your right, and several other peaks are visible during the 90-km drive.

Festivals

The major annual fiesta honours La Virgen de las Mercedes, and is held from 23 to 24 September. This is more popularly known as the **Fiesta de la Mama Negra**, and there are processions, costumes, street dancing, Andean music and fireworks. This is one of those festivals which, though superficially Christian, has much Indian influence, and is worth seeing.

Places to Stay

Both the *Hotel Costa Azul*, near where you get off the bus on the Panamericana, and the *Residencial La Estación*, by the railway station, are extremely basic and the cold showers work infrequently. Prices are US$1.20 per person. The *Hostal Residencial Jackeline* (☎ 801 033), across the river, is cleaner and friendlier, but also suffers from water problems. A better and more popular budget hotel (with clean rooms and hot communal showers) is the *Hotel Estambul* (☎ 800 354), on Quevedo near Salcedo, at US$2.20 per person. The *Hotel Cotopaxi* (☎ 801 310), on the attractive Parque Vicente León, charges US$4 per person in rooms with private bath and hot water. There are at least three more expensive hotels on the Panamericana.

Hotels fill fast on Wednesday afternoons for the Thursday morning Indian market at Saquisilí.

Places to Eat

Parrilladas Los Copihues and *Restaurant La Carreta*, both on Calle Quito in the town centre, are supposedly the best, though neither is worth getting too excited about. Near La Carreta (on Quito) is the *Pizzería Rodelu*, which has been recommended and is popular with travellers. Also on Quito, *Pingüino* is good for ice cream and *Gran Pan* bakery is good for bread for picnics. *Restaurant Los Alpes*, on Sánchez de Orellana, is open fairly early for breakfasts (and all day) and is inexpensive. *El Mashca*, on Valencia and Orellana, is a reasonable chicken restaurant.

Most restaurants close by 8.30 pm. Two which stay open later are the *Pollos Gus* and *Koko Riko*, on the Panamericana. They serve fast-food-style hamburgers and roast chicken.

ECUADOR

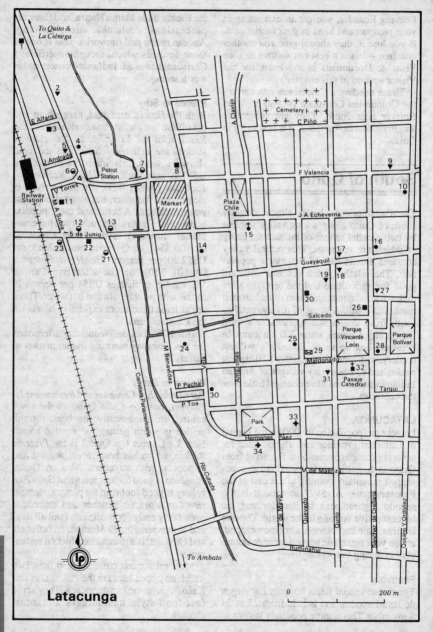

To Quito &
La Ciénega

To Quito &
La Ciénega

E Alfaro

J Andrade

V Torres

Railway
Station

M A Subia

5 de Junio

Petrol
Station

Market

A Clavijo

Cemetery

C Piño

F Valencia

Plaza
Chile

J A Echeverria

Guayaquil

Salcedo

Amazonas

Maldonado

Parque
Vincente
León

Parque
Bolívar

Tarqui

M Benavidez

P Pacha

P Toa

Río Cutuchi

Carretera Panamericana

Pasaje
Catedral

Park

Hermanas Paez

M de Maenza

Z de Mayo

Quevedo

Quito

Sanchez de Orellana

Oriente Y Ordoñez

Rumiñahui

To Ambato

0   100   200 m

Latacunga

ECUADOR

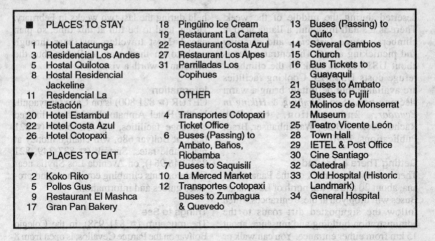

■ PLACES TO STAY		18	Pingüino Ice Cream	13	Buses (Passing) to
		19	Restaurant La Carreta		Quito
1	Hotel Latacunga	22	Restaurant Costa Azul	14	Several Cambios
3	Residencial Los Andes	27	Restaurant Los Alpes	15	Church
5	Hostal Quilotoa	31	Parrilladas Los	16	Bus Tickets to
8	Hostal Residencial		Copihues		Guayaquil
	Jackeline			21	Buses to Ambato
11	Residencial La		OTHER	23	Buses to Pujilí
	Estación	4	Transportes Cotopaxi	24	Molinos de Monserrat
20	Hotel Estambul		Ticket Office		Museum
22	Hotel Costa Azul	6	Buses (Passing) to	25	Teatro Vicente León
26	Hotel Cotopaxi		Ambato, Baños,	28	Town Hall
			Riobamba	29	IETEL & Post Office
▼ PLACES TO EAT		7	Buses to Saquisilí	30	Cine Santiago
		10	La Merced Market	32	Catedral
2	Koko Riko	12	Transportes Cotopaxi	33	Old Hospital (Historic
5	Pollos Gus		Buses to Zumbagua		Landmark)
9	Restaurant El Mashca		& Quevedo	34	General Hospital
17	Gran Pan Bakery				

Getting There & Away

Bus Buses usually drop and pick up passengers on the Panamericana, at the corner of Avenida 5 de Junio. Some go direct to and from Latacunga's Plaza Chile – these may be slower but a seat is usually guaranteed. Buses go to Quito (US$0.60, two hours), Ambato (US$40, one hour), Riobamba (US$1, 2¼ hours) and Baños (US$0.75, 1¾ hours).

The bus stop for Pujilí (US$0.10) and further west is on Avenida 5 de Junio, near the Panamericana. Beyond Pujilí (Sunday market), the road deteriorates but continues past the tiny village of Zumbagua, at 3500 metres (US$0.60, two hours), and down through the western slopes of the Andes to Quevedo (US$1.60, six hours). Zumbagua has a small but fascinating Saturday market, but it is not easy to find a place to stay in the town. From Zumbagua, a 12-km side road leads to the beautiful volcanic Laguna Quilotoa – there is very little transport, so be prepared to walk or hire a taxi in Latacunga. Carry water – the lake is alkaline; camping near the lake is possible.

The road to Quevedo is the roughest, least travelled and perhaps most spectacular bus route joining the highlands with the western

lowlands. Transportes Cotopaxi has departures every two hours; their office is on the Panamericana just north of the petrol (gas) station.

Buses for Saquisilí (US$0.15, half an hour) and other nearby villages (Sigchos, Chugchilán and Mulaló) leave from Plaza Chile (also known as El Salto), near the market. Departures are every few minutes on market-day mornings, but less frequently otherwise.

SAQUISILÍ

Saquisilí's Thursday morning market is for the inhabitants of remote Indian villages, most of whom are recognised by their little felt 'pork pie' hats and red ponchos. Ecuadorian economists consider this to be the most important Indian village market in the country and many travellers rate it as the most interesting in Ecuador. Be alert for pickpockets.

Buses leave from Quito's terminal terrestre on Thursday morning and go directly to Saquisilí. Many buses also leave from Latacunga.

PARQUE NACIONAL COTOPAXI

This is mainland Ecuador's most frequently visited national park, though it is almost deserted during the middle of the week. There is a small museum, a llama herd, a climbers' refuge (*refugio*), and camping and picnicking areas. The entrance fee is about US$0.25. A bunk in the climbers' refuge costs US$3.75. Cooking facilities are available, but definitely bring a warm sleeping bag. (See *Climbing & Hiking in Ecuador*, 2nd edition, by Rob Rachowiecki & Betsy Wagenhauser, Bradt Publications, 1990.)

Getting There & Around

There are two entrances on the Panamericana, about 20 and 26 km north of Latacunga. Buses will drop you at these entrances – then follow the signposted dirt roads to the administration building and museum, about 15 km from either entrance. You can walk or hitchhike into the park, but there is very little traffic, except on weekends. Pick-up trucks from Latacunga cost about US$20, but bargain. The owner of the Hotel Estambul provides a truck service to the park; clarify how far in you want to go.

The Limpiopungo lake area for camping (very cold) and picnicking is about four km beyond the museum, and the climbers' refuge is about 12 km further on. You can drive up a very rough road to a parking lot about one km before the refuge. The lake is at 3800 metres and the refuge is 1000 metres higher – it is very hard work walking at this altitude if you are not used to it. Altitude sickness is a very real danger, so acclimatise for several days in Quito before attempting to walk in.

Continuing beyond the climbers' refuge requires snow and ice-climbing gear and expertise – guides and gear are available in Quito and Ambato. Ask at the South American Explorers Club in Quito for advice.

AMBATO

About 40 km south of Latacunga is the important town of Ambato (population 140,000), the capital of Tungurahua Province. It was badly damaged in a 1949 earthquake but is now a modern and growing city. Ambato is famous for its flower festival,

held during the last two weeks in February. Hotels tend to be full at this time, so plan ahead. Most travellers just pass through Ambato on their way to Baños, but the museum is worth a visit.

Information

CETUR (☎ 821 800) is on Calle Guayaquil, by the Hotel Ambato. Banks have limited exchange facilities, but Cambiato (☎ 821 008), at Bolívar 686, will change money at reasonable rates. Surtrek (☎ 827 349, 821 353, 846 964), on Avenida Los Shyris near Cordero, rents climbing equipment and provides guides and information.

Things to See

The **museum** (☎ 821 958), in the Colegio Bolívar on the Parque Cevallos, is open from 8 am to 12.30 pm and 2 to 6 pm Monday to Friday; the entrance fee is US$0.25. There are hundreds of stuffed birds, mammals and reptiles, and there is a fine display of photographs taken around 1910 by Nicolás Martínez, the famous Ecuadorian mountaineer.

The main **market day** is Monday, and smaller markets are held on Wednesday and Friday.

The walk to the pleasant, modern suburb of **Miraflores** has been recommended.

Places to Stay

Residencial América (☎ 821 092), J B Vela 737, has tepid showers (maybe electric shocks!) but is one of the better cheapies. Rooms are US$1 per person. Next door is the similarly priced *Residencial Europa*, which claims to have hot water but often doesn't. *Residencial Europa 2*, at E Espejo and Sucre, is marginally better. The *Hotel Nacional* (☎ 823 820), on J B Vela near Lalama, charges US$1.25 and has hot water – sometimes.

For US$1.60, the *Residencial Laurita* (☎ 821 377), at J L Mera 333, is basic but friendly, and has hot water in one bathroom; so too does the similar *Hotel Guayaquil* (☎ 821 194, 823 886), at J L Mera 311. The *Residencial 9 de Octubre* (☎ 820 018), at J L Mera 325, is also US$1.60, but has only cold water. There are several other very basic, grungy-looking hotels in this area (which I enjoyed researching, ha!).

The noisy *Hotel Carrillo* (☎ 827 200), above the bus terminal, has hot showers and charges US$2 per person. A walk of several minutes brings you to the friendly *Residencial Pichincha*, at 12 de Noviembre 2323. Clean singles/doubles are US$1.60/2.80 but the showers are cold. The *Hotel Imperial* (☎ 824 837), at 12 de Noviembre 2494, charges US$3 per person in rooms with private bath and hot water, but the water supply is erratic, as it is in many cheaper hotels in Ambato. The *Hotel Ejecutivo* (☎ 820 370), at 12 de Noviembre 1230, has reasonable rooms with shared baths for US$1.80 per person, or dark, small rooms with private bath and hot water at US$4/6 for singles/doubles.

The *Gran Hotel* (☎ 824 235), on Lalama near Rocafuerte, has reasonable rooms with private bath and hot water for US$2.50 per person. The *Hotel Cumandá* (☎ 826 792), at M Egüez 837, is a clean, good hotel charging US$3.25/6 for singles/doubles with private bath and hot water (less with shared bath). Also good is the *Hotel Vivero* (☎ 820 088, 821 000), at J L Mera 504, for US$5/7 for singles/doubles with shared bathrooms and US$7/9 with private hot showers.

Places to Eat
Chifa Jao Fua (☎ 829 306), on Cevallos near J L Mera, has good meals for just over US$1. Cheaper and almost as good is the *Chifa Nueva Hong Kong*, at Bolívar 768. For breakfast pastries and coffee, try *Panadería Enripan* or *Pastelería Quito*, both on J L Mera.

El Coyote Inn Restaurant (☎ 822 424), at Bolívar 432, sells a variety of good meals for US$2 to US$3 – there may be dancing here on the weekend. Nearby, *El Coyote Cafetería* (☎ 827 886), at Bolívar 313, serves snacks, steaks and Mexican food – not cheap, but popular. The *Kangaroo Bar*, on Cevallos near J L Mera, serves Mexican snacks but is primarily a bar, which opens at 3 pm. *Mama Miche Restaurant* (☎ 822 913),

on 13 de Abril, behind the Centro Comercial Ambato, is quite good value considering it's open so late (supposedly 24 hours).

The good Swiss-run *Restaurant El Alamo* (☎ 821 710), at Sucre 660, is medium priced and *El Alamo Junior*, at Cevallos 612, is a self-service-style cafeteria. For good, medium-priced steak, try *Parrilladas El Gaucho* (☎ 828 969), on Bolívar near Quito. The *Pizzería La Cigarra* (☎ 828 411), at Bolívar 373, cooks a reasonable pizza.

Entertainment
The Peña Tungurahua Bar, on Martínez near 13 de Abril, has a peña at weekends; it doesn't get going until 11 pm. There is a disco opposite, in the Centro Comercial Ambato building. The Taberna Disco Bar is by the Cine Bolívar, on 12 de Noviembre near E Espejo. There are six cinemas in Ambato.

Getting There & Away
Bus The terminal terrestre is two km from the centre. There are frequent departures for Baños (US$0.30, 45 minutes), Riobamba (US$0.50, one hour), Quito (US$1.10, three hours) and Guayaquil (US$2.40, six hours). There are also buses to Guaranda (US$0.70, 2½ hours), Cuenca (US$4, seven hours) and Tena (US$2.25, six hours). There is an information office at the terminal.

Local buses marked 'Terminal' leave from Parque Cevallos in the centre. Outside the terminal, buses marked 'Centro' go to Parque Cevallos for US$0.05. There are also other local buses.

BAÑOS
This small town, famous for its hot springs, is popular with Ecuadorian and foreign tourists alike. Baños' elevation of 1800 metres gives it an agreeable climate. The surroundings are green and attractive and offer good walking and climbing opportunities. Baños is also the gateway to the jungle via Puyo and Misahuallí. East of Baños, the road descends, and spectacular views of the upper Amazon Basin stretch away before you. The

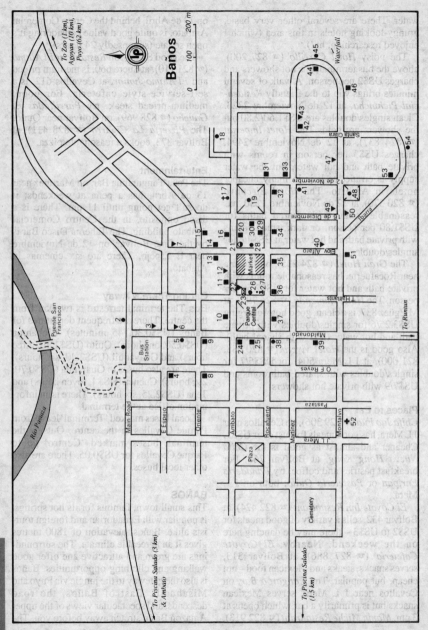

Baños

To Zoo (1 km),
Agoyan (10 km),
Puyo (62 km)

0   100   200 m

Puente San
Francisco

Rio Pastaza

Bus
Station

Main Road

E Espejo

Oriente

Ambato

Rocafuerte

Martinez

J L Mera

Montalvo

Plaza

Cemetery

To Piscina Salado (3 km)
& Ambato

To Piscina Salado
(1.5 km)

Santa Clara

12 de Noviembre

16 de Diciembre

Eloy Alfaro

T Halflants

Maldonado

O F Reyes

Pastaza

Ibarra

Waterfall

To Runtun

Market

Parque
Central

ECUADOR

■ PLACES TO STAY		
4	Residencial Julia	
8	Residencial El Rey	
9	Residencial Charvic	
10	Residencial La Delicia 1	
11	Hotel Humboldt/ Paraíso	
13	Pensión Angela	
14	Pensión Patty	
15	Residencial Magdalena	
16	Residencial Baños, Hostal Bolívar & others	
20	Residencial Cordillera & others	
24	Hostal Flor de Oriente	
25	Residencial La Delicia 2	
29	Residencial Lucy	
30	Hotels Alborada & Achupallas	
31	Residencial Teresita	
32	Hotel Guayaquil, Hostal Agoyán, Residencial Acapulco	
33	Hotel Americano	
34	Residencial Anita	
35	Hotel Danubio	

36	Hostal Los Helechos/Las Orquideas
37	Residenciales Olguita & Los Piños
39	Residencial Timara
42	Hostal El Castillo
44	Hotel Sangay
46	Hotel Palace
51	Villa Gertrudis
53	Residencial Villa Santa Clara

▼ PLACES TO EAT	
3	Cafeteria Chushi
6	El Eden
7	Restaurant Monica
10	Rico Pan
12	Chifa Central
16	Donde Marcelo
22	Chifa Oriental
29	Rincón de Suecia
30	Mi Pan
40	Le Petit
43	Restaurant El Paisano
47	Café Cultura
49	Regine Café Alemán
50	El Marqués & Restaurant Vegetariano y Carnes

OTHER	
1	Sugar-Cane Stalls
2	Peña
5	Backpackers' Store
10	Bus Stop for El Salado
13	Hard Rock Café & Video Cine
17	Basílica & Museum
18	La Burbuja Disco
19	Parque de la Basílica
21	Bus Stop for Zoo & Agoyán
23	Post Office
26	IETEL
27	Town Hall & Clocktower
28	Peña Nuestra America
37	Banco del Pacífico
38	Marco Bermeo Store & Book Exchange
41	Banco del Pacífico
45	Piscina de La Virgen (Hot Baths)
48	Children's Playground
52	Hospital
54	Santa Clara Swimming Pool

annual fiesta is held on 16 December and preceding days.

Information

There is no CETUR office, but many 'guides' provide travel information and other services – talk to other travellers for recommendations.

The Cafetería Chushi, by the bus terminal, has a library of guidebooks and provides information – one traveller claims that they overcharge gringos eating there. A couple of doors down is a tourist information office, with maps, information and rental gear. The backpackers' store, on Maldonado near E Espejo, has information and sells gear.

The Banco del Pacífico changes US dollars and travellers' cheques, at rates comparable to those in Quito.

Things to See

The **Santuario de Nuestra Señora de Agua Santa** and museum are worth seeing. Hours are 7.30 am to 4 pm; the entry is a mere US$0.10. An annual October celebration in the Virgin's honour sees Indian musicians flock to the streets.

There are two **baths** in Baños and a third out of town. All have a small fee and provide changing rooms and clothes storage. Towels and bathing costumes can be rented. The best-known bath is the Piscina de La Virgen, under the waterfall. The entrance fee is US$0.20; it opens by dawn. The Piscina El Salado is two km west of town and charges US$0.25 – there is a regular bus srvice.

Hiking & Climbing

Behind the sugar-cane stalls, by the bus station, is a short trail leading to the San

ECUADOR

Francisco bridge across the Río Pastaza. Continue up the other side as far as you want. South, on Calle Maldonado, is a footpath leading to a building with a white cross, high over Baños; it continues to the tiny settlement of Runtun, two hours away. There are great views along this path, but there have been muggings and thefts reported on it, too.

Walk east of town on the main road to the zoo, a couple of km away. Continue down to the river beyond the zoo, cross a suspension bridge and follow the trail back to Baños, crossing the Puente San Francisco; allow three hours.

Climbers with crampons can reach the summit of Tungurahua (5016 metres) in two days. It is an easy climb for those with gear and experience. The volcano is part of Parque Nacional Sangay – there is a US$1 entrance fee and a US$2 fee to overnight in the climbers' refuge. A road goes halfway up from Baños – a ride in a truck will cost US$1.50.

The jagged, extinct volcano El Altar (5319 metres) is hard to climb but the wild páramo surrounding it is a target for adventurous backpackers with gear – don't leave anything unattended or it will disappear.

Take a bus to Penipe, halfway between Baños and Riobamba. Occasional trucks go to Candelaria, 15 km away. From here, it is two km to the Parque Nacional Sangay station. A US$2 park fee is charged. It is a full-day hike to the crater. Guides and mules can be hired in Candelaria.

Places to Stay

Ask for long-stay discounts everywhere. *Pensión Patty* (☎ 740 202), at Eloy Alfaro 556, has basic but clean rooms for US$1.50 and is very popular with gringos. There is one hot and several cold showers, and a communal kitchen. Opposite is the *Pensión Angela*, which is also cheap and OK.

Other good cheap hotels include the basic but clean and friendly *Hotel Americano* (☎ 740 352), on 12 de Noviembre near Martínez, with a simple restaurant and large rooms for only US$1 per person. Nearby is *Residencial Teresita* (☎ 740 471), on 12 de

Noviembre near Rocafuerte, with clean rooms, some of which overlook the Parque de la Basílica. They have hot showers and charge between US$1.25 and US$2 per person. These hotels provide kitchen facilities on request.

The Parque de la Basílica is surrounded by hotels, some of which have rooms with views of the Parque and the basílica. The *Hostal Agoyán* is US$1.50 per person and has hot water. The similarly priced *Hotel Guayaquil* (☎ 740 434) has large rooms, hot showers and a restaurant. Nearby is the *Residencial Acapulco* (☎ 740 457). The modern *Hotel Alborada* (☎ 740 814) has good clean rooms with private bath and hot water for US$3/5 a single/double (less with shared bath). Next door is the *Hotel Achupallas* (☎ 740 422/389), which is also good and charges about US$3.50 per person in rooms with private bath and hot water.

West of the Parque, on Rocafuerte, is the friendly *Residencial Lucy* (☎ 740 466), where it is US$1.60 per person in rooms with private bath and hot water, or less in rooms with shared bath. The equally friendly *Residencial Anita* (☎ 740 319) has small, clean rooms with comfortable beds for US$2.50 per person with private bath and hot water (or US$1.25 with shared bath). You can use the kitchen.

The friendly *Residencial Timara* (☎ 740 599), on Maldonado near Martínez, is about US$1.25 per person and has hot water and kitchen facilities. The similarly priced *Residencial Villa Santa Clara* (☎ 740 349), on 12 de Noviembre near Ibarra, is popular and has kitchen facilities, hot showers and a garden.

On the Parque Central, the basic *Residencial Olguita* (☎ 740 271) has hot showers, and front rooms with views of the Parque for US$1.25 per person. Next door, the better *Residencial Los Piños* (☎ 740 252) has some rooms with parque views at US$2 per person. On the corner of the Parque, the *Hostal Las Orquideas* (☎ 740 387) is US$3/5 for clean singles/doubles with private hot showers.

The management of *Residencial La Delicia 1* (☎ 740 477) is friendly, but this place has only one hot shower for 22 rooms, some which overlook the Parque. The newer *Residencial La Delicia 2* (☎ 740 537) also has some rooms overlooking the Parque. In both places, rooms cost US$1.40 per person.

The pleasant *Hostal El Castillo* (☎ 740 285), at Martínez 255, is well recommended. Rates are US$5 per person in rooms with hot showers, and included are three home-cooked meals – a good deal. Rooms without meals are US$2.50 per person.

There are several cheap hotels on Ambato, east of the market. *Residencial Baños* (☎ 740 284) is a good, clean place which charges US$2 per person. They have hot water and some rooms with private bath. Also quite good are the *Hostal Bolívar* (☎ 740 497) and *Residencial Cordillera* (☎ 740 536).

Places to Eat

Several European-style restaurants are slightly pricey but popular with travellers. The *Rincón de Suecia* (☎ 740 365), on Rocafuerte near 6 de Diciembre, sells pizza, steaks and seafood. The meals are good but the restaurant is smoky. *Regine Café Alemán*, on Montalvo near 6 de Diciembre, is good for breakfast (from 8 am), light meals and drinks – it's German in style. *Le Petit*, Eloy Alfaro 246, has a French menu. The Danish-run *Café Cultura* (☎ 740 419), on Montalvo near Santa Clara, features home-made breads, quiches, fruit pies, fresh fish, etc.

Donde Marcelo, on Ambato near 6 de Diciembre, has Ecuadorian food and friendly service, and there's a very popular bar upstairs. A reader recommends *Mario's*, at Rocafuerte 275 near Eloy Alfaro, for seafood. The *Chifa Oriental* and *Chifa Central*, both on Ambato, by the market, are good for Chinese and local food. *Cafe Mercedes*, on Oriente near Maldonado, is good for breakfast. There are several other cheap restaurants and bakeries on Ambato and around the market.

Entertainment

The Hard Rock Café, on Eloy Alfaro near Ambato, has inexpensive drinks and plays old rock classics. The somewhat pricier bar above Donde Marcelo is popular, plays rock music and has a dance floor. Papagayo's, on Ambato near Pastaza, is a recent recommendation.

Peña América Nuestra, at Alfaro 420, and the Peña, a couple of blocks east of the bus terminal on the main road, have folklórico music late on weekend nights.

Getting There & Away

From many towns, it may be quicker to change buses in Ambato, where there are frequent buses to Baños (US$0.30, 45 minutes).

From the Baños Terminal Terrestre, many buses leave for Quito (US$1.40, 3½ hours) and Riobamba (US$0.50, one hour), and less frequently for Puyo (US$1, two hours) and Tena (US$2, five hours).

Getting Around

Tour Agencies & Guides Carlos and José, at the Pensión Patty, have information, gear and transportation and provide guides for Tungurahua. Also recommended is Andean Discovery on Maldonando near E Espejo. US$50 per person is the going rate for the two-day climb.

For Oriente trips, Tsantsa Tours, also based at the Pensión Patty, is recommended. Guides are Shuar Indians (Sebastian Moya is good) who are sensitive of the local people and environment. Marco Bermeo, based at the Residencial Timara, has also been recommended (though some of his guides are not as good). Bermeo speaks English and has a store, on Maldonado near Rocafuerte, with information and a book exchange. Fluvial Ayahuasca Tours and Turisamazonas have received poor reports.

Three to seven-day jungle tours are US$25 to US$40 per person (four minimum) per day, depending on where you go.

Various people rent horses for about $10 per half-day, with a guide. Christián, known in all the European restaurants, is frequently recommended for the care he takes of his horses. Local tourist offices recommend Julio Albán and Luis Sánchez.

GUARANDA

This small, quiet provincial capital is worth a visit for the spectacular views of Chimborazo on the wild, unpaved road from Riobamba or the paved road from Ambato. Saturday is market day.

Places to Stay & Eat

Basic cheapies include the *Pensión Tequendama*, on Rocafuerte near José García (US$1.50 per person), the *Residencial Acapulco* (☎ 981 953), on 10 de Agosto near 9 de Abril (about US$2 per person), and the *Residencial Santa Fé* (☎ 981 526), on 9 de Abril near 10 de Agosto (from US$1.50 to US$2 per person).

The *Hotel Matiaví*, at the bus terminal, has hot water and charges US$2 per person. The *Hotel Bolívar* (☎ 980 547), on Sucre near Olmedo, has clean rooms and hot showers. Rooms with private bath are US$3.50/4.50 for singles/doubles (or US$1 less with shared bath). The 'best' is the *Hotel Cochabamba* (☎ 819 583), on García Moreno near 7 de Mayo, charging US$6 for a single with bath and US$4 without – rooms vary widely in quality.

Most restaurants close by 7.30 pm. The *Restaurante Rumipamba*, on the Parque Bolívar, is nothing great, but is one of the better ones. The restaurant in the Hotel Cochabamba is the 'best', but overpriced.

Getting There & Away

The bus terminal is a km east of town. Buses leave for Ambato (US$0.70, 2½ hours), Quito (US$1.70, five hours), Babahoyo (US$1.40, four hours), Guayaquil (US$1.80, five hours) and Riobamba (US$0.70, three hours), and also go to remote towns and villages.

RIOBAMBA

'All roads lead to Riobamba' proclaims a road sign as you enter this city – Riobamba is at the heart of an extensive and scenic road network. Plan your journey for the daylight hours to enjoy the great views.

■ PLACES TO STAY

5	Hotel Whymper
11	Hotel Segovia
14	Hotel Humboldt
16	Hotel Ecuador
17	Hotel Americano
20	Residencial Venecia
21	Hotel Imperial
22	Residencial Ñuca Huasi
28	Hotel Metro
29	Residenciales Villa Ester & Guayas
31	Residencial Colonial
32	Hotel Bolívar
33	Hostal Los Shyris
40	Residencial Chimborazo

▼ PLACES TO EAT

7	Steak House
8	El Delirio
15	Restaurant Los Alamos
23	Restaurant León Rojo
24	Restaurant Kikirimiau
34	Restaurant Candilejas
35	Restaurant El Pailón
37	Chifa Pak Hao
38	La Cabaña Montecarlo
41	Chifa Joy Sing

OTHER

1	Museo de Arte Religioso
2	Andes Guides
3	Catedral
4	Basilica
6	Banco Central
9	Post Office
10	Colegio, Museo & Teatro Maldonado
12	Municipalidad (Town Hall)
13	IETEL
18	Cine Imperial
19	Cine Fenix
25	Teatro T León
26	Consejo Provincial (Government Buildings)
27	Bullring
30	Railway Station
36	Banco Internacional
39	CETUR Tourist Information

Information

CETUR was on Tarqui near Primera Constituyente, though as we go to press, we hear they moved to León Borja near España. The

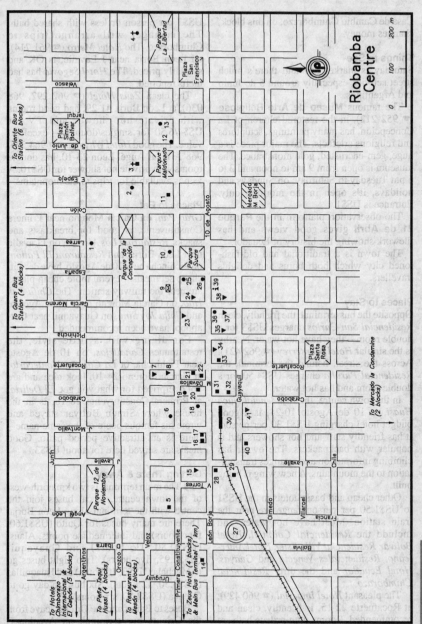

Riobamba Centre

To Oriente Bus Station (6 blocks)

To Guano Bus Station (4 blocks)

Parque La Libertad

Plaza San Francisco

Velasco

Plaza Simón Bolívar

Tarqui

5 de Junio

Parque Maldonado

E Espejo

Colón

Larrea

Parque de la Concepción

España

Parque Sucre

García Moreno

Pichincha

Rocafuerte

Mercado M Borja

10 de Agosto

Carabobo

J Montalvo

Junín

Parque 12 de Noviembre

Lavalle

Torres

Ángel León

Veloz

Orozco

Ibarra

Uruguay

Primera Constituyente

Olmedo

Villaroel

Chile

Guayaquil

Plaza Santa Rosa

To Oriente Bus Station (6 blocks)

To Mercado la Condamine (2 blocks)

To Zeus Hotel (4 blocks) & Main Bus Terminal (1 km)

To Restaurant El Mesón (4 blocks)

To Peña Taqui Huasi (4 blocks)

To Hotels Chimborazo Internacional & El Galpón (5 blocks)

ECUADOR

Casa de Cambio Chimborazo, on this block, changes money.

Things to See

Saturday is market day and there's much street activity, especially around 5 de Junio and Argentinos.

The famous **Museo de Arte Religioso** (☎ 952 212), in the restored church of La Concepción, has many paintings, sculptures and religious artefacts. The major piece is a huge, gem-encrusted, gold monstrance. The museum is open from 9 am to noon and 3 to 6 pm Tuesday to Saturday; on Sundays and holidays, it's open in the morning only. Entrance is US$1.

The observation platform in the **Parque 21 de Abril** gives good views and has tilework showing the history of Ecuador.

The town is a traditional and old-fashioned city which both bores and delights travellers.

Places to Stay

Opposite the bus terminal, the friendly, clean *Residencial San Carlos* charges US$3 for a double room – they have hot water. Nearby is the similar *Hotel Monterrey* (☎ 962 421). Across the street, behind the terminal, the *Residencial Puruha* charges US$4.50 for a double room and has hot water.

In the town centre, the *Residencial Ñuca Huasi*, at 10 de Agosto 10-24, is a good budget hotel charging US$1.30 per person. It has friendly staff and hot showers and is popular with backpackers. The owner has climbing information and arranges transportation to the mountains. A new wing is being built.

Other cheap and basic hotels in the US$1 to US$1.50 per person range are near the train station. Most have hot water, and include the *Residencial Colonial*, *Hotel Bolívar*, *Residencial Villa Ester*, *Hotel Americano*, *Residenciales Venecia* and *Guayas*, *Hotel Ecuador* and the dirty *Residencial Chimborazo*.

The pleasant *Hotel Imperial* (☎ 960 429), at Rocafuerte 22-15, is friendly, clean and recommended. Rooms with private bath are US$3 per person or less with shared bath. The manager will arrange trips to Chimborazo. The *Hotel Metro* (☎ 961 714), on León Borja near J Lavalle, is OK and similarly priced. The *Hotel Segovia* has had thefts reported.

The clean *Zeus Hotel* (☎ 962 292, 968 036), at León Borja 41-29, had good rooms with private hot shower and TV for US$4/6.50 for singles/doubles – excellent value. The good *Hotel Whymper* (☎ 964 575, 968 137), at Angél León 23-10, has double rooms with private hot shower for US$10. A jeep is available for trips to the mountains.

Places to Eat

Gran Pan, on García Moreno near Primera Constituyente, is good for breakfasts and snacks. *Restaurant Los Alamos*, on J Lavalle near León Borja, and *Restaurant El Pailón*, on Pichincha near 10 de Agosto, have decent, cheap set meals. Several more cheap places are near the railway station. The *Chifa Pak Hao*, on García Moreno near 10 de Agosto, and *Chifa Joy Sing*, on Guayaquil near Carabobo, have been recommended.

For dining with a little style, the restaurantes *Candilejas*, on 10 de Agosto near Pichincha, or *La Cabaña Montecarlo*, at García Moreno 24-10, look nice and are not overpriced for what you get. *El Delirio*, at Primera Constituyente 28-16, is in the house where Simón Bolívar stayed and wrote his famous poem of the same name – there is an attractive period patio. Good meals are served here for about US$3.

Getting There & Away

Bus The main terminal is two km north-west of the town centre. Local buses join the centre with the terminal along León Borja. There are many buses for Quito (US$1.60, four hours) and intermediate points, Alausí (US$0.80, 1½ hours) and Guayaquil (US$1.95, five hours). Two night buses go to Machala (US$3, 10 hours) and Huaquillas (US$3.50, 12 hours). Six buses a day go to Cuenca (US$2.50, six hours).

Buses to Baños and the Oriente leave from the Oriente bus terminal, on Avenida E

Espejo near Avenida Luz Elisa Borja, some two km north-east of town. No buses link the two terminals – a taxi is US$0.50.

Train There is intermittent service to Quito – ask at the train station in the town centre.

CHIMBORAZO

At 6310 metres, this is Ecuador's highest peak. There is a climbers' refugio at 5000 metres which can almost be reached by truck from Riobamba (you have to walk the last couple of hundred metres) – under US$20 with hard bargaining at the railway station or a few dollars more if arranged in one of the hotels. Trucks go to San Juan (US$0.30), where a truck to the refugio can be hired for about U$7 – very few will be available.

Beyond the refugio, technical gear and experience is needed to get much higher on Chimborazo. The following guides in Riobamba have been recommended: Marco Cruz (☎ 964 915, 962 845), at Expediciones Andinas, Argentinos 38-60, is very expensive but perhaps Ecuador's best climber, Silvio Pesantz (☎ 962 681), Argentinas 11-40, Casilla 327, is well recommended, Marcelo Puruncajas (☎ 966 344), Andes, E Espejo 24-43, guides and rents gear, and Enrique Veloz (☎ 960 916), Chile 33-21, is president of the Asociación de Andinismo de Chimborazo. Other, cheaper guides may be very inexperienced – check carefully, as a climb at this altitude is not to be taken lightly.

ALAUSÍ

Just below Alausí is the famous Nariz del Diablo, where a hair-raising series of railway switchbacks negotiate the steep descent towards the lowlands. This spectacular ride is the main reason to visit this small town.

Places to Stay & Eat

Hotels are along the one main street (Avenida 5 de Junio) and are often full on Saturday night. The clean and family-run *Hotel Tequendama* (☎ 930 123) has hot water and charges US$2 per person. Other possibilities are the similarly priced *Hotel*

Panamericano (☎ 930 156), which has electric showers and a basic restaurant below, or the *Hotel Europa*, which also has a restaurant. The *Hotel Gampala* (☎ 930 138) has erratic hot water and is US$3 per person in rooms with private bath, but is reportedly dirty.

Apart from the hotel restaurants, there are a couple of basic restaurants along the main street – little choice.

Getting There & Away

Bus There are hourly buses to and from Riobamba (US$0.90, 1½ hours). Buses for Cuenca (US$1.50, four hours) leave several times daily. Riobamba to Cuenca buses leave passengers on the Panamericana – a one-km walk into town. Pick-up trucks act as buses to various local destinations.

Train The train leaves Alausí daily at 9 am and tickets (US$0.30 to Bucay, US$0.60 to Durán, near Guayaquil) go on sale at 7.30 am. It is three to four hours to Bucay and about eight hours to Durán. Passengers may ride on the roof – wear old clothes because of steam, soot and cinders. It is possible to get off at Sibambe (no facilities) to connect for Cuenca.

BUCAY

The most spectacular part of the train ride to Durán is between Alausí and Bucay (General Elizalde on most maps). Many people get off the train here and continue by bus. It is two hours to Guayaquil. There are also buses to Riobamba. There are a couple of basic pensiones.

Cuenca & the Southern Highlands

CUENCA

Founded by the Spanish in 1557, Cuenca is Ecuador's third largest city and its prettiest. The old centre has churches dating from the

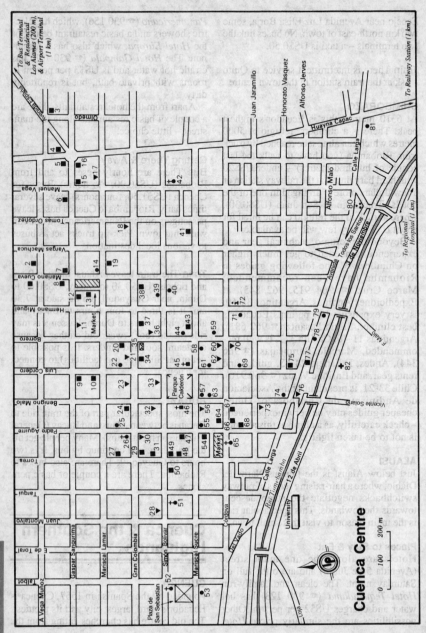

Cuenca Centre

0   100   200 m

■ **PLACES TO STAY**

1 Hotel Las Américas
2 Residencial Sánchez
3 Residencial La Alborada
4 Hotel Los Libertadores
5 Hostal Hurtado de Mendoza
6 Hostal El Galeon
7 Pensión Taiwan
8 Pensión Andaluz
9 Residencial Atenas
10 Hostal Paredes
12 Residencial La Ramada
13 Residenciales Norte & Colombia
15 Residencial Tito
16 Hotel España
19 Residencial Niza
20 Hotel Cuenca
24 Hotel Internacional
27 Residencial Paris
29 Hotel Emperador
31 Gran Hotel
34 Hotel El Dorado
37 Hotels El Conquistador & Presidente
38 Residencial Siberia
41 Hotel Atahualpa
43 Internacional Hotel Paris
47 Hotel Catedral
48 Hotel Inca Real
49 Hotel Pichincha
50 Tomebamba Hotel
54 Pensión Azuay
64 Hotel Alli Tiana
66 Hotel Milan
67 Hotel Cantabri
68 Hostal San Francisco
75 Hotel Crespo Annexe
77 Hotel Crespo

▼ **PLACES TO EAT**

11 El Balcón Quiteño
17 El Paraiso Vegetarian Restaurant
18 El Paraiso Vegetarian Restaurant
21 Los Pibes Pizzería
23 Pizzería La Tuna
28 Café Austria
30 El Pedregal Azteca
32 Heladería Holandesa

33 Pio Pio Chicken Restaurant
36 D'Bernardo's Restaurant
47 Govinda Vegetarian Restaurant
48 Restaurant El Túnel
56 Café El Carmen
60 La Cantina Bar & Restaurant
62 Chifa Pack How
70 Restaurant El Jardín
73 Panadería Centenario
76 La Napoletana Pizzería

OTHER

14 Cine 9 de Octubre
22 Metrotours & YAZ Casa de Cambio
25 Teatro Cuenca
26 Santo Domingo Church
35 Post Office
37 TAME Airline
38 Ecuatoriana Airline
39 MAG Office
40 SAN Airline
42 San Blas Church
43 Cambistral Casa de Cambio
44 Several Casas de Cambio
45 Old Cathedral (El Sagrario)
46 New Cathedral
51 San Cenáculo Church
52 San Sebastián Church
53 Museo de Arte Moderno
55 Plazoleta del Carmen & Flower Market
56 Casa de Cultura
57 Municipio
58 Teatro Sucre
59 Picadilly Bar
60 Excursiones Santa Ana
61 Teatro Casa de Cultura
63 IETEL
65 San Francisco Church
69 Mi Comisariato Supermercado
71 Museo de las Conceptas
72 CETUR Tourist Information
74 Yroo Tours
78 Museo Remigio Crespo Toral
79 Museo de Artes Populares
80 Inca Ruins
81 Museo del Banco Central
82 Museo de la Historia de la Medicina
   (Hospital Militar)

16th and 17th centuries, and many other old buildings and cobblestone streets. Nearby is the Inca fortress of Ingapirca, Ecuador's best-preserved precolonial ruin.

Information
CETUR (☎ 831 414) is at Hermano Miguel 6-86. The MAG office is on Remigio Crespo Toral, off Vicente Solano and behind the

stadium south of town. Money exchange rates are the best in Ecuador. Cambistral, on Mariscal Sucre near Borrero, changes various currencies.

Things to See

The **Rió Tomebamba** is attractively lined with colonial buildings, and people doing their washing place their clothes to dry on its grassy banks. There is a pleasant walk along Avenida 3 de Noviembre, following the north bank of the river.

The **Museo del Banco Central** (no sign) is off Calle Larga, near the river. Entrance is free and opening hours are 9 am to 4 pm, Tuesday to Friday. There are old B&W photographs of Cuenca, ancient musical instruments and temporary exhibitions.

There are **Inca ruins** near the river. Most of the stonework was destroyed to build colonial buildings but there are some fine niches and walls (though don't expect to compare them with those you'll see in Peru).

The **Museo de Artes Populares** (☎ 828 878), at Hermano Miguel 3-23, by the river, has a small but worthwhile collection of traditional instruments, clothing and crafts. Its hours are 8.30 am to 12.30 pm and 2.30 to 6.30 pm Monday to Friday – entry is free. The **Museo Remigio Crespo Toral**, Calle Larga 7-07, is under restoration – check with CETUR for current conditions. The **Museo de las Conceptas**, at Hermano Miguel 6-33, has a fine display of religious art and artefacts, and the collection is housed in a 17th-century convent. Its hours are 9 am to 4 pm Tuesday to Friday, and 10 am to 1 pm on Saturday. Admission is US$0.75.

The **Parque Calderón** (main plaza) is dominated by the rather stark new catedral, with its huge blue domes. Opposite is the squat **old catedral** (or El Sagrario). At the south-west corner is the **Casa de la Cultura**, with a good gallery of local art.

The **Plazoleta del Carmen**, at the corner of Sucre and Aguirre, has a colonial church and a colourful flower market.

Plaza San Sebastián is a quiet and pleasant park with the interesting old church of San Sebastián at the north end. The park has a mural of infant art on one wall, a couple of art galleries, and the **Museo de Arte Moderno** (☎ 830 499) at the south end. The museum's hours are 9 am to 1 pm and 3 to 6 pm Monday to Friday, and Saturday morning – entry is free.

Markets Market day is Thursday, with a smaller market on Saturday. The main market areas are around the Church of San Francisco and at the Plaza by the corner of avenidas Mariscal Lamar and Hermano Miguel. The colourful market is aimed more at locals than tourists. Watch out for pickpockets.

Festivals

Cuenca's independence is celebrated on 3 November – a major fiesta. Christmas Eve (24 December) parades are very colourful. Carnaval is celebrated with boisterous water fights.

Places to Stay

Hotels are often full (and prices rise) for the 1-3 November celebrations, so arrive early.

Opposite the bus terminal is the *Residencial Los Alamos*, with a simple restaurant. Clean rooms with shared and private baths are US$2 and US$4 per person. *Residencial La Alborada*, at Olmedo 13-82, charges US$2 per person and has shared baths. The *Hotel Los Libertadores*, on España near Gaspar Sangurima, has clean rooms with private bathroom and electric shower for US$3.75 per person. Nearby, the good *Hostal Hurtado de Mendoza* (☎ 831 909, 827 909) has a restaurant, and clean rooms with private bath, carpet and telephone for US$4.50 per person. Opposite is the friendly *Hotel España* (☎ 824 723), at Gaspar Sangurima 1-19, which is US$2 per person, or US$5.60 a double with private bath. Rooms vary in quality – some have TVs; there is a restaurant.

The *Residencial Tito* (☎ 829 734), at Gaspar Sangurima 1-49, is US$2.30 per person. The rooms are clean but mostly windowless; their restaurant is inexpensive and good. The modern, clean *Hostal El*

Galeon (☎ 831 827), at Gaspar Sangurima 2-36, has spacious rooms with private bathrooms for US$3.50/6.50 a single/double.

The basic but adequate *Residencial Norte*, at Mariano Cueva 11-63, near the market, charges US$1.50 per person, or US$2 for a single with private hot shower. The basic *Residencial Colombia* (☎ 827 851), at Mariano Cueva 11-61, is OK and charges US$1.60 per person in large rooms, some with balcony. The similar *La Ramada*, at Gaspar Sangurima 5-51, charges from US$1.50 per person. The *Residencial Sánchez* (☎ 831 519), at A Vega Muñoz 4-28, is OK for US$1.40 per person. Other poorer cheapies are nearby. The *Residencial Niza* (☎ 823 284), at Mariscal Lamar 4-51, is clean and friendly. Rooms are $2 per person, or US$3/5 for singles/doubles with private bath.

The *Residencial Siberia*, at Gran Colombia 5-31, is old and basic but has fairly reliable hot water. Rooms are about US$1.50 per person. The cheap *Pensión Azuay*, *Hotel Cantabri* and *Hostal San Francisco* are very basic indeed.

The friendly *Hotel Pichincha* (☎ 823 868), on Torres near Bolívar, has large, clean rooms for US$2.25 per person. The *Hotel Emperador* (☎ 825 469), at Gran Colombia 10-77, is not as good but charges US$2.75 per person.

The friendly *Hotel Milan* (☎ 835 351), at Córdova 9-89, is very popular and charges US$3/5 for singles/doubles with bath, less with shared bath. Some rooms have balconies and there is a simple restaurant. The friendly *Gran Hotel* (☎ 831 934, 835 154), at Torres 9-70, charges US$3.25 per person with bath and has also been recommended. There is a restaurant and an attractive courtyard. Also good at this price is the *Residencial Paris* (☎ 842 656, 827 257), at Torres 10-48, which has a helpful English-speaking manager. The clean, friendly *Residencial Atenas*, at Luis Cordero 11-89, charges US$3.50/6 for singles/doubles with bath and US$2.75/5 without – but their left-luggage facilities have been criticised.

For a little more comfort, try the *Hotel Las Américas* (☎ 831 160), at Mariano Cueva 13-59, where singles/doubles are US$7/11, or the *Hotel Crespo Annexe* (☎ 829 989), at Luis Cordero 4-22, for US$8.75/12.

Places to Eat

Many restaurants are closed on Sunday. The restaurants at the *Hotel España*, *Residencial Tito* and *Hotel Las Américas* are OK and inexpensive. The *El Balcón Quiteño* (☎ 824 281), at Gaspar Sangurima 6-49, is popular with locals, which is a good sign. *Chifa Pak How*, on Córdova near Cordero, is popular and has meals for around US$1.50. The Hare Krishna-run *Govinda*, at Aguirre 8-15, serves vegetarian fare. The *Restaurant El Paraiso* at Tomas Ordoñez 10-19, and a branch of it at Mariscal Lamar 1-82, are homely little places serving cheap vegetarian lunches.

The *Heladería Holandesa*, at Benigno Malo 9-45, has excellent ice cream, cakes, coffee, yoghurt and fruit salad – it is a very popular hang-out for international travellers. Also good is the small *Café Austria*, on Bolívar near Juan Montalvo, which has delicious Austrian-style cakes and coffee. The *Café El Carmen*, on the south-west corner of the Parque Calderón, has good snacks and inexpensive local dishes, many of which are not on the menu – ask.

The *Panadería Centenario*, on Benigno Malo near Juan Jaramillo, sells fresh bread from 7 am till 10 pm.

Two pizzerías on Gran Colombia, on either side of Luis Cordero, are the *Los Pibes* and *La Tuna*. Both have been recommended. Also good is the small and homely *La Napoletana Pizzería*, at Benigno Malo 4-104.

El Pedregal Azteca Restaurant & Bar (☎ 823 652), at Gran Colombia 10-33, is in an attractive old building and serves good Mexican food at medium prices. Also pleasant is *D'Bernardo's Restaurant*, at Borrero 9-68, serving good and reasonably priced local dishes and more expensive international food.

Getting There & Away

Air The airport is two km from the centre on Avenida España. Schedules and fares change frequently. There are daily flights to Guayaquil (US$14) and to Quito (US$22). There may be flights to Macas and Loja. TAME is at the airport (☎ 800 193), and in the city centre (☎ 827 809), on Gran Colombia between the hotels Presidente and El Conquistador (it may move to Cordero 10-15). SAN-Saeta is at the airport (☎ 804 033), and in the city centre (☎ 823 403, 828 557), at Bolívar 5-39.

Bus The terminal is also on Avenida España, 1½ km from the centre. The terminal has an information desk and 24-hour cafeteria.

Buses leave for Guayaquil (US$2.40, five hours) every few minutes. For Quito (US$3, nine hours), there are buses about every hour. Also, buses go to Machala (US$2, five hours) every hour – a few continue to Huaquillas. There are hourly buses for Azogues (US$0.25, 45 minutes), many continuing to Cañar (US$0.45, 1½ hours) and Alausí (US$1.50, four hours). Six buses a day leave for Saraguro (US$1.90, 4½ hours) continuing to Loja (US$2.30, six hours). There are a few buses each day to Macas (US$3.10, 10 hours) and a couple to Gualaquiza (US$2, seven hours).

Buses for Gualaceo leave from Calle España near Benalcázar, 100 metres southwest of the terminal.

Train The station on the south-eastern outskirts of town has daily autoferro service at 2 pm to Sibambe (US$0.80, five hours), with connections to Guayaquil and Alausí – but there are no facilities in Sibambe and an overnight is required. Half an hour before Sibambe is Chunchi, with a basic pensión and bus services to Alausí.

There are two steam trains to Azogues on Sunday.

Getting Around

To/From the Airport Local airport buses leave from the flower market on Calle Aguirre. A taxi to the airport is about US$0.70.

Bus Local buses leave from the flower market on Calle Aguirre.

AROUND CUENCA
Ingapirca

The Inca site of Ingapirca is 50 km north of Cuenca. The structures were built with the same mortarless, polished-stone technique as those in Peru. Excavation and reconstruction work is still going on. Admission to the ruins and museum is US$2. The museum is open from 9 am to 5 pm Tuesday to Saturday. Guides (both human and written) are available.

Ingapirca village has a craft shop/museum, by the church, a couple of basic restaurants but no accommodation. A shelter by the ruins may be available for overnighting. Friday is market day.

Getting There The Cuenca-Sibambe train stops at Ingapirca or San Pedro stations which are about four km from the ruins.

Alternatively, take a bus to El Tambo (seven km beyond Cañar). Pick-up trucks leave El Tambo every hour for the eight-km ride to Ingapirca. The fare is US$0.30 – but beware of gross overcharging. There is a basic hotel in El Tambo and two more in Cañar.

Area Nacional de Recreación Cajas

This high páramo 30 km west of Cuenca is famous for its many lakes (good fishing) and rugged camping and hiking. Buses leave Cuenca at 6.30 am (except Thursday) from San Sebastián church and return in the afternoon. The journey takes two hours. There is a refugio where you can sleep for a fee, but don't rely on it. Camping is allowed; a permit costs US$1 from the MAG offices in Cuenca, where further information, maps and permits are available.

GUALACEO, CHORDELEG & SÍGSIG

These villages are famous for their Sunday markets. If you start early from Cuenca, you can visit all three and be back in the afternoon. Gualacéo has the biggest market, with fruit and vegetables, animals and various household goods. Chordeleg's market, five km away, is smaller and more touristy but sells textiles and jewellery. Sígsig market is 25 km from Gualacéo and less visited by tourists.

There are a few cheap hotels in Gualacéo and a basic one in Sígsig. Chordeleg has a small but interesting museum, on the Plaza.

Getting There & Away

Buses from Cuenca to Gualaceo take 40 minutes and leave about every hour (more frequently on Sunday). Walk or take a local bus to Chordeleg. A 40-minute local bus ride goes to Sígsig. CITES buses return from Sígsig to Cuenca hourly for US$0.40.

LOJA

Loja is an attractive provincial city with beautiful surrounding countryside. It makes a convenient stopover on the route to Peru via Macará. The village of Vilcabamba and Parque Nacional Podocarpus are delightful attractions not far from Loja.

Information

CETUR (☎ 962 964) is on Bernardo Valdivieso near 10 de Agosto. The MAG office (☎ 961 534) is at Miguel Riofrío 13-54. Banks on the Parque Central change money at poor rates – it's better to change money in Cuenca or Macará.

The main market day is Sunday. The annual fiesta of the Virgen del Cisne is on 8 September – there are huge parades and a produce fair is held.

Hidaltur (☎ 963 378, 962 554), at 10 de Agosto 15-34, sells discounted AeroPerú tickets for domestic Peruvian flights.

A short walk east of town crosses the Río Zamora and climbs a hill to the statue of the Virgin of Loja; there are good views.

Places to Stay

The basic pensiones near the Transportes Loja Terminal are very noisy and poor value. The cheap, basic *Residencial San Andres*, on Miguel Riofrío near Lauro Guerrero, is better.

The basic, clean *Residencial Primavera*, at Colón 16-44, is secure but has only cold water. Rates are US$1.25 per person. The friendly *Hostal Carrión* (☎ 961 127), at Colón 16-30, is similar but offers hot showers and charges US$1.75 per person. Other basic cheapies at these prices include the *Hotel Americano*, at 10 de Agosto 16-62, and the *Hotel Mexico*, on 18 de Noviembre near Antonio Eguiguren, which has hot water. The friendly *Hostal Pasaje*, on Antonio Eguiguren near Bolívar, charges US$1.25 per person, or US$1.75 with private hot shower.

The *Hotel Londres* and *Hotel Cuxubamba*, on Sucre near 10 de Agosto, charge US$1.50 per person, are clean and have hot water. The Londres has had thefts from rooms reported. The Cuxubamba is friendly and has some rooms with bath for US$2.50 per person. The *Hotel Acapulco* (☎ 960 651), at Sucre 7-47, is clean, safe and has hot water at times. They charge US$1.75 per person, or US$2.25 in rooms with bath.

The friendly *Hotel Internacional*, at 10 de Agosto 15-28, has hot water and charges US$1.70 per person, or US$2.30 with private bath. The *Hotel Caribe* (☎ 962 102), at Rocafuerte 15-52, charges US$1.60 per person, is clean and has hot water. The *Hostal Crystal*, at Rocafuerte 15-39, charges US$1.70 per person and has large rooms and hot water.

The friendly *Hotel Miraflores*, at 10 de Agosto 16-65, is US$2/3 for singles/doubles or US$3/5 with private bath. Rooms are large and clean. The *Hotel Paris* (☎ 961 639), at 10 de Agosto 16-37, is US$2 for a single or $3.50 with private bath, hot water and TV.

The *Hotel Inca* (☎ 961 308, 962 478), on Universitaria near 10 de Agosto, is OK and charges US$3.50 per person in rooms with private hot shower. On the same block, the *Hotel Riviera* (☎ 962 863) charges US$4.50/6.50 for singles/doubles with hot shower, and the *Hostal Quinara* (☎ 960 785, 963 132) charges US$4 per person in clean carpeted rooms with bathroom and TV. The

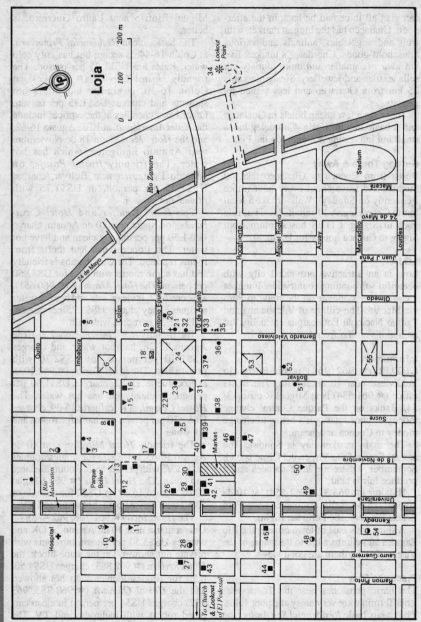

Loja

200 m

100

0

Lookout Point

Río Zamora

Stadium

Macará

24 de Mayo

Mercadillo

Lourdes

Azuay

Miguel Riofrío

Rocafuerte

Olmedo

Bernardo Valdivieso

Bolívar

Sucre

18 de Noviembre

Universitaria

Kennedy

Lauro Guerrero

Ramón Pinto

Juan J Peña

Antonio Eguiguren

Colón

Imbabura

Quito

24 de Mayo

Parque Bolívar

Río Malacatos

Hospital

Market

To Church
& Lookout
of El Pedestal

■ PLACES TO STAY

7	Hotel Ramses
13	Hostal Carrión & Residencial Primavera
14	Hotel Metropolitan
16	Hotel Libertador
17	Hotel Mexico
22	Hostal Pasaje
25	Hotels Acapulco, Londres & Cuxubamba
26	Hotel Saraguros Internacional
27	Hotel Hidalgo
28	Pensión (above Transportes Loja Bus Terminal)
29	Hotel Miraflores
30	Hotel Paris
38	Hotel Rocafuerte
39	Hotels Internacional & Paraiso
41	Hotel Americano
42	Hostal Quinara, Hotels Riviera & Inca
43	Residencial Macará
44	Residencial San Andres
45	Hotel Vilcabamba Internacional
46	Hostal Crystal & Hotel Loja
47	Hotel Caribe
49	Hotel Los Ejecutivos

▼ PLACES TO EAT

3	Restaurant La Tullpa
9	Pollos Gusy
11	Top Cream
15	Don Pepe's Restaurant
22	Casa China
30	Restaurant 85

31	Restaurant La Cordillera
45	Restaurant Kennedy
50	Pescadería Las Redes

OTHER

1	Las Ruedes Disco Club
2	Viajeros & Ejecutivo San Luis Buses
4	Peña Bar Don Pancho's
5	Latino's Discotheque
6	Plaza San Francisco
8	Branch Post Office
10	Transportes Saraguro Buses
12	Petrol (Gas) Station
18	Post Office & Government Buildings
19	TAME Airline
20	IETEL
21	Cathedral
23	Cine Velez & Unicornio Piano Bar
24	Parque Central
28	Transportes Loja Bus Terminal
32	Filanbanco
33	Banco de Azuay
34	Virgin of Loja Statue
35	CETUR Tourist Information
36	Cine El Dorado
37	Museo del Banco Central
40	Hidaltur
43	Transportes Yantzaza
44	Transportes Cariamanga Buses
48	Transportes Sur-Oriente Buses
51	Teatro Popular
52	MAG Office
53	Plaza Santo Domingo
54	Transportes Catamayo Buses
55	Plaza de la Independencia

Hotel Saraguros Internacional (☎ 960 552), at Universitaria 7-24, and the *Hotel Los Ejecutivos* (☎ 960 004), at Universitaria 10-76, have similar rooms for US$4/6 a single/double.

Places to Eat

Restaurantes *La Cordillera*, at 10 de Agosto 14-19, and *Don Pepe's*, on Colón near Sucre, are cheap and good. The *Restaurant La Tullpa*, at 18 de Noviembre 5-12, is good for inexpensive Chinese and other food.

Pollos Gusy, at Kennedy 5-55, is a chicken restaurant popular with local youngsters. Nearby, *Top Cream* is good for ice cream. Also good for ice cream, snacks and

coffee is *Heladería Sinai*, in Hotel Ramses, at Colón 14-3. *Restaurant Kennedy*, on Kennedy near Miguel Riofrio, is a fairly inexpensive all-purpose restaurant. Also reasonably priced are the *Chifa 85*, opposite the Parque Central, and the *Restaurant 85*, next to the Hotel Paris.

I like the *Pescadería Las Redes*, at 18 de Noviembre 10-41. They serve seafood and other dishes in pleasant surroundings – meals are under US$2.

Getting There & Away

Air Loja's airport is in Catamayo, 30 km west. TAME (☎ 963 030) has daily flights (except Sunday) to Guayaquil and Quito.

TAME is on the Parque Central in Loja. There are basic hotels in Catamayo.

Bus The main company is Transportes Loja, on Avenida 10 de Agosto near Lauro Guerrero. Book seats early. There are four buses a day to Quito (US$4.50, 18 hours), four to Macará (US$1.80, seven hours), five to Guayaquil (US$3.20, 11 hours), four to Machala (US$2.10, eight hours), eight to Zamora (US$0.80, three hours) and a number to other destinations.

Several smaller terminals around the Parque 18 de Noviembre serve Machala, Cuenca, Saraguro and other places. For Vilcabamba, Transportes Sur-Oriente, on Azuay near Kennedy, has several buses a day. For Catamayo, Transportes Catamayo leaves from Mercadillo, in an alley just behind Kennedy.

A new central terminal is planned for Loja.

PARQUE NACIONAL PODOCARPUS
This park protects a wide range of habitats in the southern Ecuadorian Andes at altitudes ranging from 3600 metres in the páramo near Loja to 1000 metres in the rainforests near Zamora. The topography is rugged and complex, and many different plant and animal species exist here, some of which are found nowhere else in the world. This is one of the biologically richest areas in a country known for its biodiversity.

The park's namesake, *Podocarpus*, is Ecuador's only native conifer. Also of interest is *Chinchona*, the tree from which the malarial preventative drug quinine is extracted. There are nature and walking trails which give good opportunities for birdwatching, plant study and maybe glimpses of various mammals.

Although the park is officially protected, poaching, illegal ranching and logging are threatening problems.

Admission to the park is US$2. Maps, information and permits are available at the Loja MAG office. Get to the park on a Vilcabamba bus – get off at the Cajanuma entrance, some 10 km south of Loja. From here, a track leads 8½ km up to Cajanuma

ranger station. A taxi costs about US$6 (one-way) from Loja. Camping is allowed, but carry everything you need.

VILCABAMBA
This village, 45 km south of Loja, is in the 'valley of longevity', whose inhabitants supposedly live to be 100 or more. Scientists have found no basis for this claim, but the area is attractive, healthy and enjoying some minor tourism because of its fame – a lovely place to relax in for a few days.

Places to Stay & Eat
The *Hotel Valle Sagrado*, on the main square, is US$1 per person. About one km from the square is the *Parador Turístico Vilcabamba*, with a restaurant, where rooms with private bath are US$4 per person. Just north of town, the *Hostería de Vilcabamba* is more expensive, but has a pool, sauna and the best restaurant in town (open to non-guests).

The current favourite of travellers is the tranquil *Hostal Madre Tierra*, two km north of town (reservations at PO Box 354, Loja). About 24 people can be accommodated in this rustic, laid-back hostal run by an Ecuadorian/Canadian couple. Lodging is US$8 per person including breakfast and dinner. Local hiking and riding information, a book exchange, a sauna, a video room and table games are available.

About five km south of town, the even more rustic and slightly cheaper *Cabañas Río Yambala* is run by a friendly guy named Charlie. Ask in Señora Carmita's store on the main plaza for directions.

Getting There & Away
Buses from Loja leave hourly. Two buses a day continue to Zumba, near Peru – in Zumba, there are a couple of basic pensiones but no border crossing.

MACARÁ
This small town on the Peruvian border offers a more scenic but less comfortable and less travelled route to Peru than via the conventional border crossing at Huaquillas.

The Peruvian Consulate is at 10 de Agosto 658. Visas are US$11.50.

Places to Stay & Eat

There are a few cheap, basic, cold-water hotels in the town centre charging US$1 to US$2 per person. The *Hotel Paraiso* and *Hotel Espiga de Oro* are better and charge about $3.75/5.50 for singles/doubles with private cold bath (less without).

There are a few basic restaurants, near the corner of Bolívar and M Rengel, open only at meal times.

Getting There & Away

Transportes Loja has five buses to Loja (US$1.80, seven hours), Guayaquil (departs at 6 pm, US$4, 12 hours), Quito (departs at 10 am, US$5.20, 22 hours). Transportes Cariamanga has three daily buses to Loja.

Crossing the Peruvian Border

Pick-up trucks leave the market often (US$0.15, or about US$1 for private hire) – the same applies for the border to Macará. Border hours are 8 am to 6 pm daily. Formalities are OK if your papers are in order. Macará has hotels, but Peru doesn't have much accommodation until Sullana, 150 km away. Cross in the morning for bus connections.

Moneychangers hang out around the market. Arrive with little Ecuadorian or Peruvian money and change into US dollars before crossing.

The Oriente

The Oriente is that part of Ecuador east of the Andes in the lowlands of the Amazon Basin. A 1942 treaty cedes a large portion of the Oriente to Peru. This treaty is internationally recognised, but Ecuador continues to claim the land as far as Iquitos and the Amazon. The dispute means that foreign travellers are unable to cross the border into the Peruvian jungle.

The Oriente can be conveniently divided into north and south by the Río Pastaza.

More travellers visit the northern region; the southern Oriente has a real sense of remoteness. Buses from Cuenca go through Limón (officially General Plaza Gutiérrez) to Macas. Buses from Loja go via Zamora to Limón and on to Macas. From Macas, a very rough road has recently been opened to Puyo and the northern Oriente. Buses from Quito frequently go to the northern Oriente towns of Puyo, Tena, Coca and Lago Agrio. This Oriente section is described from south to north.

ZAMORA

Three hours from Loja by bus, this town on the edge of the jungle has boomed since the recent discovery of gold in Nambija, a few km to the north. Food prices are relatively high. There are military checkposts near the town. There are a few cheap hotels. There is also an entrance to the Parque Nacional Podocarpus, described earlier.

Continuing by bus into the southern Oriente, you will find basic hotels in the small towns of Gualaquiza, Limón, Méndez and Sucúa.

MACAS

This small town is the capital of the province of Morona-Santiago and is the biggest in the southern Oriente.

The best hotel is the *Peñon del Oriente* at US$4.50 per person. There are several cheaper places.

TAME has two flights a week to Quito. TAO flies light aircraft to Shell-Mera (for Puyo) daily. The new bus terminal has several daily departures for Cuenca and Gualaquiza. Two or three buses a day leave for the Río Pastaza, which is crossed by passenger ferry. On the other side, buses wait to continue to Puyo. This trip can be problematical after heavy rain.

PUYO

North of the Río Pastaza are the provinces of Pastaza, Napo and Sucumbíos, which make up the northern Oriente. Two good roads, from which there are impressive views, go from Quito into the northern Oriente.

Puyo, on the edge of the jungle, is one of the most important towns in the Oriente and is used as a stopover for travellers. There may be good views of the volcanos to the west at sunrise. There is a passport check where you must get a stamp, near the Shell-Mera airstrip, a few km north of town (bus drivers will stop).

Places to Stay & Eat
Hotel Granada, by the market, charges US$1.20 per person and is OK. Other cheapies include the *Residencial Ecuador*, on 24 de Mayo, which is old but well looked after, and the *Residencial Carmita*, on 9 de Octubre near Atahualpa, which is basic but reasonably clean. Others include the very basic *Pensión Georginita*, *Residencial Santa*, *Pensiones Tungurahua*, *Guayaquil*, *Paris*, *Ambato* and the *Residencial El Alamo* – all pretty poor.

The *Hotel Europa* (☎ 885 220), 9 de Octubre and Atahualpa, and the *Hotel California*, next door, are better hotels charging US$2.40/3.60 for singles/doubles with a private bath or less with communal bath. The *Hotel Europa Internacional*, 9 de Octubre and Orellana, is better still and charges US$4.50 per person for rooms with a bath.

The *Restaurant El Ejecutivo*, on Marín near 27 de Febrero, is OK. The *Europa Internacional* hotel has a decent restaurant. The *Restaurant Su Casa*, on Atahualpa near Villamil, is OK for chicken. The *Pastelería Francesa*, 9 de Octubre and Marín, is good for pizza and snacks.

Getting There & Away
Air Busetas heading to the Shell airstrip (10 km away) leave from the market. There are flights to Macas and elsewhere sometimes.

Bus The terminal is on the south-west edge of town. There are buses to Ambato (US$1.20, three hours), Quito (US$2, six hours) and Riobamba. Direct buses to Tena (US$1, three hours) should be booked ahead – buses from Ambato often come through full. There are buses to Macas (with a change at the Río Pastaza).

TENA
Tena is the capital of Napo province and is a convenient stopover for travellers doing the Quito, Baños, Puyo, Tena, Baeza, Quito bus circuit through the jungle.

Amaroncachi (☎ 886 372), at Tarqui 321, does jungle tours for US$25 per person per day and has been recommended.

Places to Stay & Eat
The cheapest hotels suffer from water shortages. The basic *Hotel Tena*, on J Montalvo near J L Mera, charges US$1.20 per person. The *Hotel Amazonas*, across the street, is better and cleaner and charges US$1.50 per person. The *Residenciales Jumandy* and *Cumanda*, just north of the main plaza, are also US$1.50 and are OK. The Jumandy serves early breakfast.

The *Residenciales Alexander* and *Enmita*, at the north end of town, on Bolívar, are about US$2.50 per person in rooms with bath (less without). The *Enmita Restaurant* is simple but good.

The clean *Residencial Hilton*, across the bridge, at the north end of 15 de Noviembre, charges US$4 for a double room. Nearby, *Residencial Napoli* (☎ 886 194) is US$2 per person. The *Residencial Danubio* is cheaper. The clean and friendly *Residencial Alemán* (☎ 886 409) charges US$3/5 for singles/doubles with a private bath and fans, less without.

The *Hotel Baños* (☎ 886 477) and *Residencial El Dorado* are near the bus terminal, 1½ km from the city centre. Singles/doubles are about US$3/5. There are some pricier places.

Getting There & Away
The bus terminal is across the river and 1½ km from town. There are several buses a day for Quito (US$2, six hours), Lago Agrio (US$3.50, 10 hours), Coca (US$3, seven hours) and other places.

There are military flights to Shell and Coca – ask at the airstrip.

MISAHUALLÍ
This small village is popular for jungle tours.

However, this isn't virgin jungle: the area has been colonised and most of the animals have gone. What you can see is a variety of jungle birds, tropical flowers, army ants and dazzling butterflies. You can arrange an excursion deeper into the jungle. This requires patience and money but is still less expensive than most jungle expeditions.

Moneychanging facilities are limited, so bring plenty of sucres.

Jungle Tours

Guided tours of one to 18 days are available, but few guides speak English. Tours of one or two days go to places you can visit yourself, and longer tours are generally recommended if you want to see wildlife. Some tours visit 'primitive' Auca villages. These are degrading for the Indians and definitely not recommended.

Plan details carefully beforehand to avoid disappointment. Make sure that costs, food, equipment, itinerary and group numbers are discussed before the tour. It is essential to have a good guide, and you may have to wait if you want a specific one. Some outfitters try to switch guides at the last moment – this is not to your advantage. The South American Explorers Club in Quito makes good recommendations, or talk to other travellers in the restaurants of Misahuallí. Tours usually require a minimum of four people and are cheaper per person with larger groups – meet other travellers in Misahuallí's restaurants or organise a group in Quito or Baños. Most tours cost US$25 to US$35 per person per day.

Guides and outfitters which have been recommended include the following:

Douglas Clarke's Expediciones Dayuma They have a Quito office (☎ or fax 564 924), at 10 de Agosto 38-15, near Mariana de Jesús, Edificio Villacis Pasos, Office 301. In Tena (☎ 571 513), the address is Casilla 291, Tena, Provincia de Napo. In Misahuallí, they are a block from the Plaza. This outfit has been around for many years and their costs are a bit higher, but they'll arrange tours in advance.

Fluvial River Tours Héctor Fiallos (☎ 239 044 in Quito) run this company; it has also been here for years. There is an office on the Misahuallí plaza and at Residencial Sacha. I've had mixed reports – inferior guides are sometimes provided. This seems to be improving, but check guides carefully.

Caimán Safaris The guide, Adonis Muñoz, of Casilla 255, Puerto Misahuallí, Tena, speaks English and has been recommended.

Emerald Forest Expeditions The guide, Luis Alberto García, of Casilla 247, Puerto Misahuallí, Tena, also speaks English and is a good cook. He lacks environmental awareness, particularly regarding Indians. Talk to him about this!

Other Guides Some other places which have been recommended are Ñuca Shasha Tours (☎ 355 590 in Quito), particularly the guides Domingo and Enrique. Some other guides include Julio Angeles, Elias Arteaga and Socrates Nevarez. Luis Duarte is good but relies too heavily on hunting and fishing to feed his groups. Other guides usually have signs or booths up in the corner of the main square. Guides should be able to produce a Tourist Guide Card on request.

Cruceros Fluvial Guacamayo and *Cruceros Fluvial Primavera* have been criticised.

Places to Stay & Eat

Water and electricity failures are frequent. *Residencial El Balcón de Napo*, on the Plaza, has small rooms – ask for one with a window. It's clean, though the showers are a bit grungy. They charge just over a US$1, as does the rambling old *Residencial La Posada*, nearby. Others on the Plaza for US$1 to US$2 per person are the basic but adequate *Hotel Etsa*, *Hotel 55* and the *Hotel Jennifer*.

Half a block from the Plaza is the *Dayuma Lodge* and restaurant. Prices vary from US$1 to US$5 per person, depending on the room – some have a private shower and fan. *Residencial Sacha*, by the river, has very basic bamboo rooms for US$1.60 per person. Guests wade to the hotel after heavy rains (June to August).

El Paisano restaurant and hotel is popular with travellers. Clean, basic rooms are US$2 per person, or US$5.50 for a double with private bath. There is a garden with hammocks. The *Hotel Albergue Español* charges US$3.50 per person in rooms with private bath – water is heated by solar energy. There is jazz music in the dining room. The hotel is past the Dayuma Lodge.

ECUADOR

All the hotels have some kind of restaurant. The *Dayuma*, *Albergue Español* and *El Paisano* are all good.

Getting There & Away

Boat Motorised dugout canoes take all day to reach Coca; they leave every two days. Tickets are US$10. You must register your passport with the Capitanía (Port Captain). Be prepared for strong sun – bring sunscreen and a hat.

Daily canoes go to various villages along the river, and as far up as halfway to Coca.

Bus Buses to Tena leave frequently from the Plaza.

COCA

Located at the junction of the Coca and Napo rivers, this sprawling oil town is officially named Puerto Francisco de Orellana. River travellers must report to the Capitanía by the landing dock.

Tours

There is a burgeoning tourist industry – see the Misahuallí section for more background. Coca is closer to virgin jungle, though tourism is not yet as advanced as in Misahuallí. Trips down the Río Tiputini and into the **Parque Nacional Yasuní** are possible. This is the largest Ecuadorian national park, and contains a variety of rainforest habitats, wildlife and a few Waorani. Unfortunately, there is no money for staffing and protection, so poaching and, increasingly, oil exploration are damaging the park.

Recommended guides are Ernesto Juanka (of Pato Tours), Whymper Torres (at the Hotel Auca), Walter Vasco and Carlos Lastra. None of them speaks English.

Places to Stay & Eat

Water shortages are frequent. The *Hotel El Auca* (☎ 880 127) is popular (often full before nightfall) and isn't bad for US$2.50 per person, or US$3.75/5.50 for singles/doubles with private bath. Three basic residenciales are a block from the Auca and charge US$1.50 to US$2 per person. The

Pensión Rosita, by the port, is one of the cheapest – but not recommended. The *Hotel Oasis* (☎ 880 174), behind the TAME office on the river, is better for US$3 per person – some rooms have private bath and air-conditioning. The *Hotel Florida* (☎ 880 177) is similarly priced and OK, but out of town, near the airport.

The *Hotel Auca* has a halfway-decent restaurant, though the menu is limited. The *Parrilladas El Buho* serves big portions and is frequented by North American oil workers, among others. Around the corner, the *Cebichería El Delfín* is quite good. The *Restaurant El Cóndor* sells roast chicken.

Getting There & Around

Air TAME flies to Quito (US$12) once or twice daily, except Sunday. The airport is two km north of town; the TAME office is by the river, east of the bridge.

Boat It takes 14 hours to get to Misahuallí, but travel is much quicker in the opposite direction. Boats leave every few days.

Trips towards Nuevo Rocafuerte, on the Peruvian border, require a military permit. Boats leave on Monday, and there is a basic *pensión* there. Passenger boats for other destinations leave every few days.

Bus Transportes Baños and Transportes Jumandy are the two main companies. There are buses to Lago Agrio (US$1, three hours), Quito (US$4, 12 hours) and Tena (US$3, seven hours).

LAGO AGRIO

This town was built in virgin jungle after the discovery of oil in the 1970s. It is Ecuador's largest and most important oil town and is a convenient stopping place for travellers in the Oriente. It is also the capital of Ecuador's newest province, Sucumbíos, created in 1989.

Most places of importance are on Avenida Quito. The IETEL office, on 18 de Noviembre near Francisco de Orellana, is an exception. A tourist industry is beginning to develop to visit the nearby **Reserva**

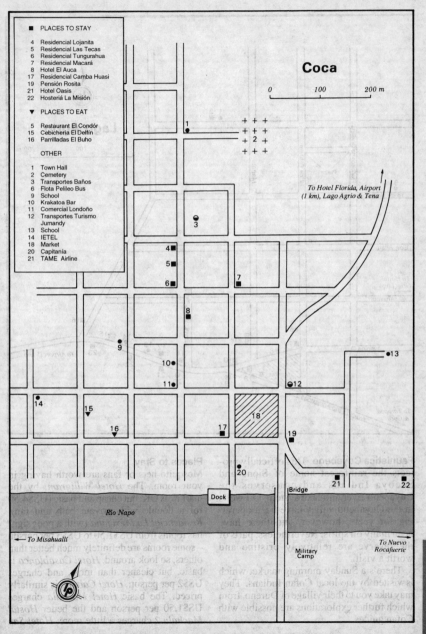

Coca

0   100   200 m

■ PLACES TO STAY

4 Residencial Lojanita
5 Residencial Las Tecas
6 Residencial Tungurahua
7 Residencial Macará
8 Hotel El Auca
17 Residencial Camba Huasi
19 Pensión Rosita
21 Hotel Oasis
22 Hostería La Misión

▼ PLACES TO EAT

5 Restaurant El Cóndor
15 Cebichería El Delfín
16 Parrilladas El Buho

  OTHER

1 Town Hall
2 Cemetery
3 Transportes Baños
4 Flota Pelileo Bus
9 School
10 Krakatoa Bar
11 Comercial Londoño
12 Transportes Turismo
   Jumandy
13 School
14 IETEL
18 Market
20 Capitanía
21 TAME Airline

To Hotel Florida, Airport
(1 km), Lago Agrio & Tena

Río Napo

Dock

← To Misahuallí

To Nuevo
Rocafuerte

Military
Camp

Bridge

ECUADOR

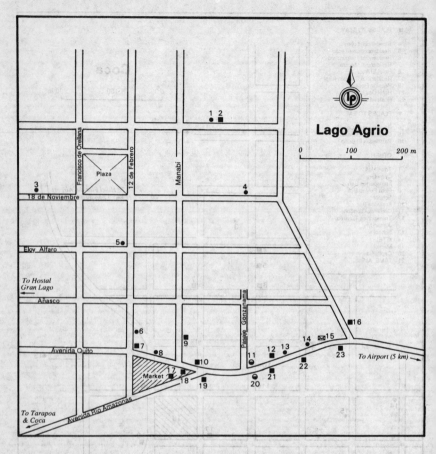

Lago Agrio

0   100   200 m

Faunistica Cuyabeno.
This officially protects the rainforest home of Siona and Secoya Indians and conserves the Cuyabeno river and lake system. Oil wells in the Cuyabeno valley have been operating for years, however, and there have been many oil spills. Nevertheless, parts of the reserve are relatively pristine and worth a visit.

There's a Sunday morning market which is visited by the local Cofan Indians. They may take you to their village of Dureno, from which further explorations are possible with Cofan guides.

Places to Stay
Mosquito nets or fans are worth having in your room. The *Hotel Willigram*, by the market, is OK, but cheap and basic (US$4.50 for a double with private bath and fan). *Residencial La Mexicana* (with a poor sign) has rooms from US$1.50 to US$3 per person – some rooms are definitely much better than others, so look around. *Hotel Casablanca* is basic, but cleaner than most, and charges US$2 per person. *Hotel Cabaña* is similarly priced. The basic *Hotel Machala* charges US$1.50 per person and the better *Hostal Machala 2* charges a little more. *Hotel San*

Carlos, by the TAME office and several blocks north of Avenida Quito, is OK for about US$6 a double – some rooms have air-conditioning. Basic places recommended for cheapness but nothing else are the *Residenciales Chimborazo*, *Ecuador*, *Acapulco*, *El Dorado* and *Lago Agrio* and the *Hotel Oriental*, all on or near Avenida Quito.

Getting There & Away
Air The airport is five km east of town. TAME has Monday to Saturday flights to Quito for US$12 – often booked up well in advance. The office is four blocks north of Avenida Quito, along Manabí.

Bus Most companies have offices on or near Avenida Quito. There are buses to Quito (US$4, 10 hours), Coca, Tena and other places. Transportes Putumayo has buses to the Río San Miguel, at the Colombian border (US$0.40, one hour).

Crossing the Colombian Border
Migración is at Avenida Quito 111, and there is a Colombian consulate nearby. Boats cross the Río San Miguel to Puerto Colón, Colombia. It's a six-hour bus ride to Puerto Asís, the main Colombian town in the area. This is a route rarely used by gringos; keep your wits about you and take care of your belongings!

Getting Around
A TAME pick-up truck may take people from the office to the airport for US$0.20; it leaves about an hour before the flight.

The Western Lowlands

West of the Andes lies a large coastal plain where you will see huge banana and palm plantations. The descent from the mountains is dramatic, particularly if you take the route from Quito to Santo Domingo.

SANTO DOMINGO DE LOS COLORADOS
Santo Domingo de los Colorados is an important road hub and a convenient place to break the journey from the highlands to the coast. The descent from the highlands is spectacular, and best done in the morning to avoid afternoon fog.

The town used to be famous for the Colorado Indians who painted their faces with black stripes and dyed their hair a brilliant red. You can buy postcards of them all over

ECUADOR

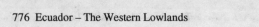

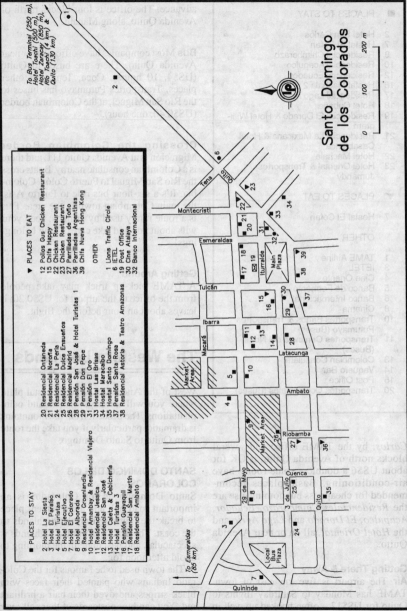

Ecuador, but the Indians are now fairly Westernised, and you are unlikely to see them in their traditional finery. Taxis go to **Chihuilpe**, seven km south of Santo Domingo, where there is a small tourist centre and a few Colorados will dress up for a fee – about US$4 for photographs. Most Indians prefer to be left alone.

Sunday is the main market day, so the town closes down on Mondays.

Places to Stay

The basic but clean and helpful *Residencial San Martín*, on 29 de Mayo, is US$1.75 per person and a good budget choice. The clean and friendly *Residencial Noroña*, also on 29 de Mayo, is US$1.60. Also OK are the *Hotel Ejecutivo* (☎ 751 943), 29 de Mayo, at US$1.50 per person, or US$2.50 with private bathroom, and the *Residencial La Perla*, 3 de Julio, at US$1.80 per person with private bath. The basic *Hotel Turistas 1, 2,* and *3* (at scattered locations) have hot water and charge US$1.80 per person. Other basic cheapies for about US$1.50 per person are the *Astoria, Guayaquil, San José, Ontaneda, El Paraíso, Amambay, Viajero, El Oro, Maracaibo, Don Pepe, Madrid, Santa Rosa, Groenlandia* and *Alborada.*

The *Hostal Las Brisas* (☎ 750 560), on Quito near Iturralde, is OK at US$2 per person, or US$3.50 with private bath. *Hostal Santo Domingo* (☎ 754 078), at Avenida Quito 715, is clean and charges US$2.50 per person with private bath. *Hotel Caleta* (☎ 750 277), at Ibarra 137, is clean and pleasant and charges US$3.50 per person with private bath. *Hotel El Colorado* (☎ 750 226, 754 299), on 29 de Mayo near Quinindé, is huge and has simple, clean rooms with private cold bath for US$3 per person. The new *Residencial Jessica*, 29 de Mayo, looks quite good for US$3.50/5.50 for singles/doubles with bath. The *Residencial Dulce Ensueños*, on 3 de Julio near Cuenca, has hot water in its private bathrooms and charges US$4 per person. The *Hotel La Siesta* (☎ 751 860/013, 750 013), at Quito 606, on the outskirts of town, has

nice gardens. They charge a reasonable US$3 per person with bath.

Places to Eat

Two inexpensive chifas are on the main square (*Happy* and *Nueva Hong Kong*). *Pollos Gus* is a clean fried chicken restaurant. There are a couple of other cheap chicken places. The *Hotel Caleta Cebichería* has tables on the street and serves good snacks and meals. *Parrilladas Argentinas*, on Quito near Riobamba, is an unpretentious and reasonably priced steak house.

Getting There & Away

Bus The new bus terminal is 1½ km northeast of the centre on Avenida Quito, by the Lions' traffic circle. Buses leave for Quito (US$1.10, 2½ hours), Guayaquil (US$1.90, five hours), Machala (US$2.60, eight hours), Esmeraldas (US$1.50, four hours) and other towns.

QUEVEDO

This is another convenient stopover between the highlands and the coast, particularly on the wild descent from Latacunga. The town is important commercially and is known for its Chinese community and chifas, but has no special attractions.

Places to Stay & Eat

The hotels are poor. The best budget choice is the *Hotel Imperial*, by the river, at Séptima – clean, safe rooms with cold showers for US$2.50 per person. The *Hotel Condado*, on Quinta, near the river, is OK for US$2.50 per person. Basic hotels around US$2 per person include the *Guayaquil, Vilmita, Hilton, Charito* and *Turistas*. Worse and cheaper are the *Patricia, Azuay, Florida, Familiar, San Marcos* and *Mayrita*. Most are on or near Avenida 7 de Octubre.

The *Hotel Ejecutivo Internacional*, at 7 de Octubre near Quarta, has good air-conditioned singles/doubles with private bath for US$5.50/9.50.

Most cheap restaurants are along 7 de Octubre.

ECUADOR

Getting There & Away

Many of the bus companies are near the second and third blocks of 7 de Octubre. There are many buses to Guayaquil (US$1.30, three hours) but only a few to Quito. Buses go to Santo Domingo, Babahoyo, Portoviejo and other places. Transportes Cotopaxi, on the south-west side of the market, has buses to Latacunga.

Travelling around the area is interesting because of the banana and other tropical fruit plantations. In the dry season, rice is spread out on huge concrete slabs to dry in the sun.

The Coast

The Ecuadorian mainland has 2800 km of coastline. Unlike Peru to the south, Ecuador has warm coastal waters, and swimming is pleasant all year round. The northern coastal rainy season is from December to June and the dry season is the rest of the year. The south coast, consisting of the provinces of Guayas and El Oro, is generally drier and more barren than the north, and has a January to April rainy season.

The rainy season is hot, humid and uncomfortable, and people flock to the beaches for relief. January to March are popular months. Mosquitos are a problem in the wet months, so bring repellent and consider the use of malaria pills.

The north coast is less developed and has some tropical rainforest. Further south, there are remnants of tropical dry forest protected in the interesting Parque Nacional Machalilla. Guayas and El Oro provinces use irrigation to enable huge plantations to produce bananas, rice, coffee, cacao and African palm. Shrimping is a fast-growing industry.

Apart from Guayaquil and the ports of Esmeraldas, Manta and Machala, there are fishing villages and popular beach resorts scattered along the coast, but none is outstanding. As a general rule, theft is a major problem on beaches – never leave anything unattended. This section describes the coast from north to south.

SAN LORENZO

There are no roads to San Lorenzo, so travellers arrive by train from Ibarra (a beautiful ride) and continue south by boat. San Lorenzo is small and not very attractive but is the best stopover between Ibarra and further south. Marimba music can sometimes be heard in town – ask around about joining in or listening. A road under construction from the highlands may reach San Lorenzo by the late 1990s.

Orientation & Information

The centre is a 15-minute walk from the station and about five minutes from the port.

There are no proper moneychanging facilities, so ask around for people who change small amounts of Colombian or US currency. There are boats to/from Tumaco, Colombia, but there is no immigration in San Lorenzo, so go to Esmeraldas migración for the necessary formalities. This route is used by locals but rarely and with difficulty by international travellers.

Places to Stay & Eat

Hotels are all basic. Get a room with a net or fan to guard against mosquitos. Water shortages or stoppages are frequent. Friendly but persistent kids badger travellers for tips if they show them to a hotel.

The basic *Hotel Vilma*, US$1.40 per person, is the closest to the station. The clean *Hotel Margaritas*, 10 minutes from the station, is US$1.80 per person.

On or near the central plaza is the basic but adequate *Hotel Ecuador* at US$1.30 per person. The friendly *Residencial Jhonny* has basic, clean rooms (with mosquito nets) for US$1.50. The *Residencial Ibarra* has basic, clean rooms (with a fan and net) for US$1.60. The friendly *Hotel Carondolet* has clean rooms (with nets) for US$2.30 per person, or US$3 with private bath. The *Yeaniny* is new and similar.

Meals are not cheap. Both the *Ecuador* and *Jhonny* hotels have decent restaurants.

The set meals are the cheapest. The nearby *El Fogón* is considered the 'best' but is more expensive.

Getting There & Away

Train The autoferro for Ibarra leaves at 7 am – sometimes daily or every two days. The fare is US$1, and people line up from 6 am for the tickets, which are sold from 6.30 am. The trip takes all day. The autoferro is always full but you can ride on the roof. Have your passport handy for the check at Lita, which is about halfway.

Boat The Capitanía on the waterfront has lists of departing and arriving boats. These are motorised dugouts – if travelling in them, be prepared for sun, wind and spray.

Two companies between them have hourly departures for **La Tola** (US$1.50, 2½ hours), from 5.30 am to 3.30 pm. The ride through coastal mangroves, with pelicans and frigatebirds flying around, is interesting. Early boats connect with a bus to Esmeraldas (US$1.50, four hours) so you can reach Atacames or Quito in one day from San Lorenzo. Accommodation in La Tola is almost nonexistent.

Boats for Borbón (US$1.80, 3½ hours) leave twice a day and boats for Tumaco (US$7) leave on most days. Boats for other destinations can be arranged.

BORBÓN

This small port with a predominantly Black population of 5000 is on the Río Cayapas. There are buses to Esmeraldas and boats up the Río Cayapas and San Miguel rivers to the **Reserva Ecológica Cotacachi-Cayapas** – an interesting trip to a remote area. Market day is Sunday. The US-run mission can help in an emergency.

Places to Stay & Eat

Angel Cerón, the school principal, runs the *Pampa de Oro Hotel* (US$2.50 per person) and is a good source of information. Other basic hotels are the clean *Panama City* (US$2.30), the *Residencial Capri*, with clean rooms but primitive toilet facilities (US$1.30), and the *Anny Christina*.

The waterfront *Restaurant Santiago* serves simple decent meals for US$1 during daylight hours. The 'centre', a block from the waterfront, has basic comedores. Most of these close by 7.30 pm.

Getting There & Away

Bus La Costeñita runs six buses a day to Esmeraldas (US$1.25, 4½ hours). The road may close temporarily in the wet months.

Boat Boats to San Lorenzo (US$1.80, three hours) leave at 7 and 11 am. A daily boat leaves at 11 am for San Miguel (US$3.75, five hours), passing the Catholic mission of **Santa María** and the Protestant mission of **Zapallo Grande** (both have basic accommodation).

SAN MIGUEL

This tiny village is the entry point for the Reserva Ecológica Cotacachi-Cayapas. A store sells sardines and soft drinks, and basic meals are served by the villagers. The inhabitants are Black; Cayapas Indians live across the river and can be visited. They sell basketware.

The ranger station has four beds (US$3 per person), or you may camp outside. Beware of ferocious chiggers – put insect repellent on ankles and legs upon arrival. Rangers will guide you into the reserve by dugout and on foot; camping is possible. Guides and boat rentals are inexpensive, but you should provide food and shelter for the guide. There are waterfalls, rainforest with poorly marked trails, great bird-watching, and the chance of seeing monkeys, sloths, armadillos and other wildlife.

The boat returning to Borbón leaves before dawn. The boatman lives downriver, not in San Miguel, so arrange in advance which day you want to return.

ESMERALDAS

The Spanish conquistadors made their first landfall in Ecuador near Esmeraldas, which has been a major port throughout Ecuador's

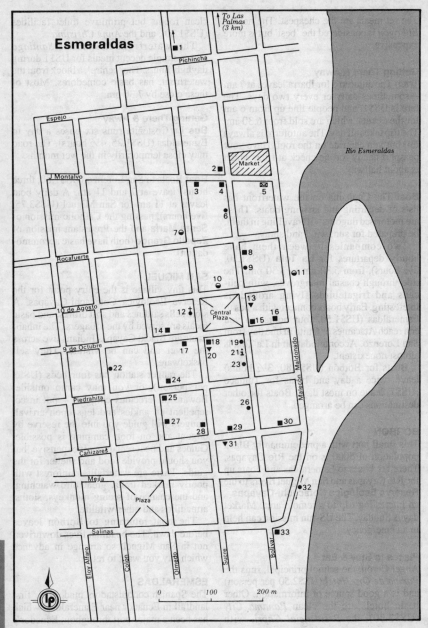

Esmeraldas

■ PLACES TO STAY

1 Two Blocks to Apart Hotel
   Esmeraldas
2 Hotel Chaberrin Internacional
3 Hotel Rita
4 Hotel Turismo
8 Hotel Royal
14 Pensión 9 de Octubre
15 Hostal Miraflores
16 Hotel Asia
17 Pensión Elsita
18 Nuevo Hotel
24 Hotel Galeon
25 Hotel Roma
27 Residencial Sulema
28 Hotel Americano
29 Hotels Beatriz & Diana
30 Hotel Korea
33 Hotel Suiza

▼ PLACES TO EAT

13 Fuente de Soda Estrecho de Bering
    & Las Redes Restaurant
20 Restaurant Bo Derek
31 Chifa Asiatica

OTHER

5 IETEL & Post Office
6 Banco Central
7 CITA (Buses)
9 Cinema
10 Aero Taxi Buses & Transportes
    Esmeraldas
11 Transportes La Costeñita (Buses)
12 Church
16 Reina del Camino (Buses)
17 Transportes Occidentales (Buses)
19 TAME
21 CETUR Tourist Office
22 Portón 26 Disco
23 Cine Bolívar
26 Filanbanco
32 Fish & Vegetable Market

history. The nearby oil refinery is a major source of income and employment.

The beaches are dirty and the city has theft and drug problems. Avoid poor or ill-lit areas. Most travellers just spend the night on their way to somewhere else.

Information

CETUR is on the 2nd floor of the Edificio de Alcadia, on Bolívar and half a block south of the main plaza.

The immigration office is by the Capitanía in the suburb of Las Palmas, five km from the centre. The Banco Popular, on the main plaza, changes money.

Places to Stay

The cheapest hotels close to bus terminals and main plaza are noisy and in poor condition. For under US$1.50 per person, try *Pensión Elsita, Pensión 9 de Octubre, Hostal Miraflores* and *Hotel Suiza* (☎ 710 243), or *Nuevo Hotel* at US$1.70. *Hotel Royal* (☎ 710 210), at Bolívar 724, is US$2 per person but unfriendly. None of these is recommended.

The *Hotel Asia*, on 9 de Octubre near the Malecón, and *Hotel Turismo* (☎ 714 416), on Montalvo near Bolívar, are US$2 per person and not too bad.

The friendly *Hotel Diana* (☎ 710 333), on Cañizares near Sucre, is US$3.50 per person with private shower, and is one of the best for this price. The similarly priced *Hotel Beatriz* (☎ 710 440), next door, looks OK. Other reasonable possibilities at this price are the *Residencial Sulema* (☎ 711 789), on Olmedo near Cañizares, and the *Hotel Americano* (☎ 713 798/978), at Sucre 709.

The *Hotel Korea*, on Cañizares near Bolívar, has good rooms with private bath and fan for US$4 per person. *Hotel Roma* (☎ 710 136), at Olmedo 718, has some good rooms with private bath and TV at US$6/10 for singles/doubles. *Hotel Galeon* (☎ 713 116/470), on Olmedo near Piedrahita, is well kept and is US$5.50 per person – some rooms have air-conditioning.

Places to Eat

The food in the small pavement cafés and comedores, along Olmedo between Mejía and Piedrahita, is cheap and good. On the central plaza, *Las Redes Restaurant* is good for seafood, and the nearby *Fuente de Soda Estrecho de Bering* is good for snacks, ice

ECUADOR

cream and people-watching. The *Chifa Asiática*, on Cañizares near Sucre, has good Chinese food.

Getting There & Away

Air The airport is 25 km away. TAME has Monday to Saturday service to Quito for US$15. The TAME office (☎ 712 663) is on Bolívar, by the main plaza.

AECA (☎ 288 110 in Guayaquil) has small aircraft to Guayaquil (US$20), stopping at Pedernales, Bahía or Manta if there is passenger demand; the baggage allowance is limited to 10 kg.

Bus There is no central bus terminal, though one is planned. Aerotaxi is frighteningly fast to Quito (US$2.50, five hours); Transportes Occidentales and Esmeraldas are slower. Occidentales has many buses to Guayaquil (US$3, eight hours), as well as Ambato, Machala and other cities. CITA has buses to Ambato. Reina del Camino has buses to Manta and Bahía de Caráquez.

For provincial buses, use Transportes La Costénita. There are frequent buses for Atacames and Súa (US$0.30) and Muisne (US$1, 2½ hours). Buses to La Tola leave several times a day, and the US$3 ticket includes the boat to San Lorenzo. Several daily buses go to Borbón (US$1.25, four hours).

Getting Around

To/From the Airport Airport taxis leave from here and five passengers would pay US$2 each – the same thing applies from the airport to the town centre. A taxi from the airport direct to Atacames is US$10. La Costeñita buses to La Tola can drop you at the airport entrance road for US$0.30 – allow plenty of time.

ATACAMES

This small resort town, 30 km west of Esmeraldas, is popular among young travellers looking for a beach vacation. It is cheaper and less developed than the beaches in the Guayaquil area, and accommodation can be found right on the ocean front. Weekends are busy with many visitors from Quito, Colombia and all over the world. The nightlife is often loud and boisterous.

Warning

There is a powerful undertow and no lifeguards. People drown every year, so keep within your limits.

Bring insect repellent or mosquito coils, especially in the wet season. The cheapest hotels may have rats, and water shortages are frequent. The freshwater in bathrooms is often brackish.

I have received frequent reports of assaults on late-night beach walkers and on single people or couples in quiet areas during the day. Stay in brightly lit and well-travelled areas, and go with friends. Don't leave anything unattended on the beach.

Places to Stay

Atacames gets full on holiday weekends, so arrive early. January to March is the high season and prices rise substantially. Bargain at other times, especially if you're staying a few days.

Most hotels are near the beach, which is reached by a footbridge. New hotels open and old ones change hands frequently. There's a wide choice of places to stay. Always check your room or cabin for security before you rent it.

For the cheapest accommodation, the best selection is to your right after you cross the footbridge. The *San Baye* is US$4 a double, or US$5 with private bathroom. A good choice is the *Hostal Jennifer* (☎ 710 482, 731 055), which has clean, spacious rooms for US$3 per person. The best of the budget places is the often-full *Hotel Galerias Atacames* (☎ 731 149). The owners speak excellent English and the rooms are good value for US$3/5 for singles/doubles with private bath.

The *Cabañas Los Bohíos* (☎ 731 089, 525 228) has small, clean cabins with showers for about US$4/7.50 for singles/doubles – prices rise in the busy season. Similarly priced is the *Hotel Rodelu* (☎ 731 033, 712 244), with basic clean rooms with private bath. The friendly *Hotel Chavalito* (☎ 731 113) has doubles with private bath for US$7.50.

For families or groups, the following can be recommended. *Villas Arco Iris* (☎ 731 069) have clean and comfortable cabins with private bath and kitchen facilities. Rates are US$16 for four beds. *Residencial Jorgé's* (☎ 731 064) has clean rooms sleeping six, for US$20. Each room has a balcony, refrigerator, and private bathroom. Other possibilities in this price range include the *Hotel Casa Blanca* (☎ 731 031), the *Cabañas Le'Castell* (☎ 731 289) and the *Casitas Familiares Marbella* (☎ 731 129).

Places to Eat
Many comedores are close to the beach, near the footbridge. They serve the same thing – that morning's catch. Ask the price before being served or you may be overcharged. Many of the comedores double as bars or dancing places in the evenings, and their popularity changes with the seasons. Keep your ears open and you'll soon hear where it's all happening.

Getting There & Away
Buses stop on the main road near the footbridge to the beach. There are many buses from Esmeraldas to Súa and back. Buses to Muisne are often full – ride on the roof or return to Esmeraldas for a seat.

SÚA
Súa is a little fishing port six km south of Atacames. You can get here by walking along the beach at low tide – but go with a large group to avoid being robbed. There are a few basic hotels. The fishing activity is interesting but the beach is dirtier than at Atacames.

MUISNE
Muisne is on an island, two hours away from Atacames by bus. Boat operators meet the bus and take you across to Muisne for a few cents. From the dock, the main road heads into the town 'centre' and deteriorates into a grassy track as it continues to the beach about 1½ km away. The beach is a quieter hang-out than Atacames, but nothing fancy. The usual beach precautions apply.

Places to Stay & Eat
There is a residencial on the mainland side of the river, and several more in Muisne. All are cheap and basic – the best is the *Pensión Sarita*, but avoid the *Narcisita*. About halfway to the beach, a block to the left, the *Hotel Galápagos* charges US$3 per person with private bath – this is the best hotel. Near the beach are several sets of cheap cabins – check that the rooms have locks, as thefts have occurred. *Cabinas Ipanema* are among the best.

There are basic comedores along the beach, and the *Bambu Bar*, on the Plaza.

Getting There & Away
Bus La Costeñita has hourly buses to Esmeraldas (US$1, 2½ hours) via Atacames. Buses go south to Bolívar.

Boat A couple of boats go to Cojimíes (US$3, two hours) daily.

SOUTH OF MUISNE
It's possible to walk along the beach at low tide to **Bolívar**, crossing several rivers along the way by dugouts, for a few hundred sucres – bring change. It takes a full day on foot.

Bolívar can be reached by bus. There are no hotels. Passenger boats go to **Cojimíes** for US$1.50 per person on demand. Cojimíes is more easily reached by direct boat from Muisne. There are a few cheap and very basic hotels.

From Cojimíes, buses go via **Pedernales** (several cheap and basic hotels) and **Jama** (a basic pensión) to San Vicente (US$4, five hours). These buses depend on low tides and favourable conditions – services are disrupted in the rainy season.

AECA (☎ 288 110 in Guayaquil) provides a Monday to Saturday service from Guayaquil to Pedernales in small aircraft. NICA has flights from San Vicente. Both airlines may continue to Cojimíes on demand. Travel light, as there are baggage restrictions.

SAN VICENTE

This resort village is a short ferry ride across the Río Chone from the more important town of Bahía de Caráquez. It has nearby beaches and the regional airport.

Places to Stay & Eat

A few blocks to the right of the pier are two basic places for US$1 per person: the *Residencial San Vicente* and *Lilita*. There are several fancier hotels with decent restaurants. Behind the market are some cheap and clean comedores, such as the *Yessenia*.

Getting There & Away

Air The airstrip is behind the market, about 10 minutes' walk from the pier (turn right). It serves Bahía de Caráquez, where further information is given.

Boat Passenger ferries to Bahía de Caráquez ($US0.10, 10 minutes) leave frequently. After 9 pm, boats charge US$1.25 (four passengers maximum). There is a car ferry.

Bus Costa del Norte has three or four buses (trucks, rancheros) a day to Pedernales, one or two to Cojimíes, and two inland to Chone. The office is near the boat pier.

BAHÍA DE CARÁQUEZ

This small port and holiday resort has beaches here and in San Vicente. The mouth of the Río Chone is quite busy, and you can laze around at a riverside café and watch the boats go by. It's a quiet and pleasant town.

Information

It's hard to get currency exchanged here. The best beaches are about 500 metres north on Avenida Montúfar. The locals call the town 'Bahía'.

Places to Stay & Eat

The cheapest places have singles/doubles for US$2/3.50, and most have water supply problems. The *Residencial Tamarindo* (☎ 690 513) is a friendly place at the west end of Ascazubi. Other friendly, basic places are the *Hotel Manabí* and *Pensión Victoria*. There are also the *Residencial San José,* on Ascazubi, and *Pensión Miriam,*on Montúfar.

The *Hotel Vera*, on Ante near Montúfar, is better and charges US$2.25 per person, or US$3.25 with private bath – there are a few single rooms. The clean and secure *Hotel Palma*, on Bolívar near Ríofrio, is similarly priced – but many rooms lack windows. Most other hotels are much more expensive.

The parrillada opposite the Coactur terminal is locally popular – there are several other riverfront places. The *Chifa China,* on Bolívar, is simple but serves decent Chinese food. The *Restaurant El Galpón,* on Montúfar, by the market, is cheap and good. *Paolo's* is popular for ice cream and snacks.

Getting There & Away

Air The regional airport is in San Vicente. AECA and NICA (☎ 690 377, 690 332) are both on Aguilera near the Malecón. They have TAME information (no TAME flights). Between them, they have daily (not Sunday) flights to Guayaquil, Pedernales and sometimes Cojimíes. They may also go to Esmeraldas and other places, depending on demand. Flights leave early in the morning – get to the airport before 7 am for standby. Boat ferries go direct to the airport on demand.

Bus The bus offices are at the south end of the malecón. Buses out of Bahía climb a hill with good views of the Río Chone estuary – the left side is best. Coactur serves Portoviejo (US$0.80, two hours) and Manta (US$1, 2½ hours) every hour. Reina del Camino has buses to Portoviejo, Quito (US$3.20, eight hours), Esmeraldas (US$2.90, eight hours), Santo Domingo de

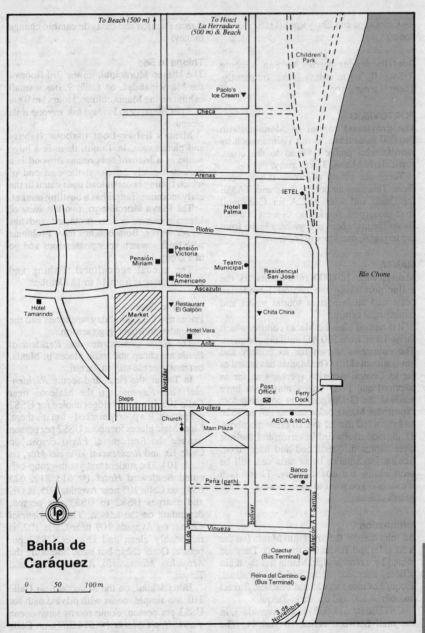

To Beach (500 m)

To Hotel
La Herradura
(500 m) & Beach

Children's
Park

Paolo's
Ice Cream ▼

Checa

Arenas

IETEL

Hotel
Palma ■

Ríofrio

Pensión
Victoria ■
Pensión
Miriam ■
Teatro
Municipal

Río Chone

Residencial
San José ■

Hotel
Americano ■

Ascazubi

Hotel
Tamarindo ■

▼ Restaurant
El Galpón

▼ Chifa China

Market

Hotel Vera ■

Ante

Post
Office
✉

Ferry
Dock

Montúfar

Steps

Aguilera

Church ♦

AECA & NICA

Main Plaza

Banco
Central

Peña (path)

M de Jesús

Bolívar

Malecón A F Santos

Bahía de
Caráquez

Vinueza

Coactur
(Bus Terminal) ⊙

Reina del Camino
(Bus Terminal) ⊙

0   50   100 m

3 de Noviembre

ECUADOR

los Colorados and Guayaquil (US$2.50, six hours).

Boat Passenger ferries to San Vicente (US$0.10, 10 minutes) leave frequently. There is a car ferry.

PORTOVIEJO

The provincial capital of Manabí, with 110,000 inhabitants, is not visited much by tourists who prefer to head to the coast, particularly Manta, 37 km away.

There are plenty of hotels if you need them. There are air connections with TAME for Quito and with AECA for Guayaquil from the airport, two km north-west of town. Buses for just about everywhere leave from the terminal, one km west of town.

MANTA

Manta, with 140,000 inhabitants, is the major port along the central Ecuadorian coast and an important tourist resort and commercial centre.

It is named after the Manta culture, which thrived here from 500 AD until the conquest. The culture is known for its pottery and navigational skills. The Mantas navigated as far as Central America (perhaps as far as Mexico) and Peru – they may even have reached the Galápagos. The conquistadors captured a Manta balsa sailing raft in 1526 and recorded that of the 20 crew members, 11 jumped overboard in terror and the rest were captured, questioned and later freed. Similar but smaller balsa rafts can still be seen along the coast today. There is a museum if you want to learn more about the Manta culture.

Information

An inlet divides the town into Manta (on the west side) and Tarqui (on the east). They are joined by a road bridge. Manta has the main offices, shopping areas and bus terminal. Tarqui has more hotels and beaches. Streets numbered 100 and up are in Tarqui.

CETUR (☎ 611 558) is on Avenida 3, in the mall between calles 10 and 11. The Banco Pacífico and casas de cambio change money.

Things to See

The **Museo Municipal**, on the 3rd floor of the Municipalidad, on Calle 9, has a small exhibit on the Manta culture. Hours are 9 am to 3 pm Monday to Friday; ask anyone if its closed.

Manta's **fishing-boat harbour** is busy and picturesque. In Tarqui, there is a huge statue of a Manabí fisherman. Beyond is a protected sandy beach, at the east end of which fishing boats unload their catch in the early morning. Tarqui has a bustling market.

The **Playa Murciélago**, two km west of Manta's centre, is less protected and has bigger waves. Both beaches have problems with theft – watch your possessions and go in a group.

The annual agricultural, fishing and tourism show is from 14 to 18 October.

Places to Stay

Prices rise during holiday weekends and the December to March high season.

The *Hotel Chimborazo* and *Residencial Paula* are cheap and basic places in Manta, but most people stay in Tarqui.

In Tarqui, the clean and secure *Residencial Villa Eugenia*, on the Malecón near Calle 105, is a good budget choice for US$2 per person. It's poorly marked – but it's there. More basic places for about US$2 per person include the *Residencial Playa Brava*, on Calle 10, and *Residencial Viña del Mar*, on Calle 104. The student and youth-group-oriented *Boulevard Hotel* (☎ 613 812, 625 633), on Calle 103 near Avenida 105, is OK and charges US$2 to US$3 per person, depending on the season. The *Residencial Chone*, on Avenida 109 near Calle 102, is reasonably clean and charges US$2 per person. Other cheap but basic hotels are the *Acapulco, Montecarlo, Astoria, Ideal* and *Tarqui*.

Hotel Miami, on the Malecón near Calle 110, has simple rooms with private bath for US$3 per person. Some rooms have ocean views. *Hotel Clarke* (☎ 614 367), on Calle

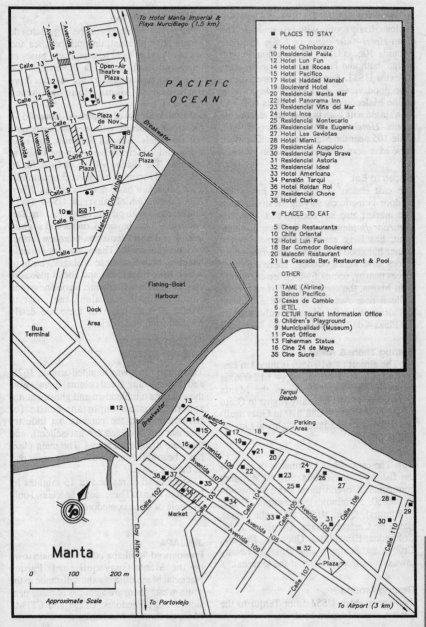

To Hotel Manta Imperial & Playa Murciélago (1.5 km)

PACIFIC OCEAN

Open-Air Theatre & Plaza

Plaza 4 de Nov

Plaza

Plaza

Civic Plaza

Breakwater

Malecón Eloy Alfaro

Fishing-Boat Harbour

Dock Area

Bus Terminal

Breakwater

Tarqui Beach

Parking Area

Malecón

Avenida 106

Avenida 107

Market

Eloy Alfaro

Calle 102

Calle 103

Calle 104

Calle 105

Calle 106

Calle 110

Calle 108

Calle 107

Avenida 108

Avenida 109

Avenida 105

Plaza

Manta

0   100   200 m

Approximate Scale

To Portoviejo

To Airport (3 km)

■ PLACES TO STAY

4 Hotel Chimborazo
10 Residencial Paula
12 Hotel Lun Fun
14 Hotel Las Rocas
15 Hotel Pacifico
17 Hotel Haddad Manabí
19 Boulevard Hotel
20 Residencial Manta Mar
22 Hotel Panorama Inn
23 Residencial Viña del Mar
24 Hotel Inca
25 Residencial Montecarlo
26 Residencial Villa Eugenia
27 Hotel Las Gaviotas
28 Hotel Miami
29 Residencial Acapulco
30 Residencial Playa Brava
31 Residencial Astoria
32 Residencial Ideal
33 Hotel Americana
34 Pensión Tarqui
36 Hotel Roldan Rol
37 Residencial Chone
38 Hotel Clarke

▼ PLACES TO EAT

5 Cheap Restaurants
10 Chifa Oriental
12 Hotel Lun Fun
18 Bar Comedor Boulevard
20 Malecón Restaurant
21 La Cascada Bar, Restaurant & Pool

OTHER

1 TAME (Airline)
2 Banco Pacifico
3 Casas de Cambio
6 IETEL
7 CETUR Tourist Information Office
8 Children's Playground
9 Municipalidad (Museum)
11 Post Office
13 Fisherman Statue
16 Cine 24 de Mayo
35 Cine Sucre

ECUADOR

102 near Avenida 108, is US$3.25 per person in clean, basic rooms with private bath. The clean *Hotel Americana*, on Calle 105 near Avenida 106, is US$7.50 for a double with private bath and fan; air-conditioning costs an extra US$1. Some of the upper rooms have good views. *Residencial Manta Mar*, on the Malecón near Calle 104, is US$5.50 for a single with bath in clean and reasonable rooms. *Hotel Inca* (☎ 620 440, 610 986), Calle 105 near the Malecón, is similar. Both these have some rooms with ocean views.

Places to Eat
The east end of Tarqui beach has cheap outdoor comedores serving fresh seafood. The market also has cheap food. The *Bar Comedor Boulevard*, on the Tarqui waterfront, has large servings. Opposite is the pricier but good *Malecón Restaurant* – both places have tables outside. There are other places nearby, some of which are cheaper.

In Manta, the cheap *Chifa Oriental* is on Calle 8 near Avenida 4. There are cheap restaurants near the Hotel Chimborazo, by the Plaza 4 de Noviembre.

Getting There & Away
Air The airport (☎ 610 450) is three km east of Tarqui. The TAME office (☎ 612 006) is on Malecón Eloy Alfaro, on the Manta waterfront. TAME has daily flights to Quito (US$22). AECA (☎ 288 810 in Guayaquil) has daily (except Sunday) flights to Guayaquil (US$18).

Bus The central bus terminal is in front of the fishing-boat harbour. Several different companies between them serve Portoviejo (US$0.50, 50 minutes), Guayaquil (US$2, 3½ hours), Quito (US$3.80, eight hours), Bahía de Caráquez, Santo Domingo de los Colorados, Esmeraldas, Quevedo, Jipijapa, Crucita and nearby towns. Buses to nearby towns leave from in front of the terminal.

Getting Around
Taxis cost about US$1 from Tarqui to the airport, if you bargain hard.

BAHÍA DE MANTA
Several coastal villages on the large Bahía de Manta have pleasant, unspoilt beaches and are favoured as local resorts. Local buses or rancheros reach them via Portoviejo (the long way), or during low tide, vehicles drive north-east of Manta along the beach (quicker).

Eight km east of Manta is **Jaramijó**, a picturesque fishing village with comedores but no hotels. Beyond Jaramijó, the road stops, and vehicles drive along the beach at low tide. The fishing village of **Crucita**, 16 km beyond Jaramijó, has several restaurants, a long beach, a basic pensión and the *Hotel Hipocampo*, which charges US$7 for a double room with private bath. Next are **San Jacinto**, 13 km beyond Crucita and slightly inland, and **San Clemente**, three km further and on the coast. There are good sandy beaches between these villages, both of which have restaurants and cheap places to stay. Beyond San Clemente, a good new road continues north-east along the coast to Bahía, 20 km away. All these are easily reached from Portoviejo.

MONTECRISTI
This small town was founded around 1628, and its many unrestored colonial houses give the village a tumbledown and ghostly atmosphere. It is an important centre for wickerwork and the panama hat industry (tourists are besieged by hat sellers), and there are many craft stores. The main plaza has a beautiful church built in the early part of the last century.

Montecristi is reached in 15 minutes by bus from Manta. There are no hotels and only a couple of basic comedores.

JIPIJAPA
Pronounced 'hipihapa', this is the main town on the Manta-Guayaquil road. Parque Nacional Machalilla is a short distance to the south-west. There are a couple of basic pensiones and comedores. CITM and CITMS buses go through Machalilla.

PARQUE NACIONAL MACHALILLA

Ecuador's only coastal national park preserves beaches, unusual tropical dry forest, coastal cloud forest, several archaeological sites, and 20,000 hectares of ocean containing Ecuador's only mainland coral formations and two offshore islands.

The tropical dry forest is characterised by weirdly bottle-shaped trees whose heavy spines provide protection against herbivores. As well, there are a variety of figs, cacti and the giant kapok tree. Parrots, parrotlets and parakeets are some of the forest's many inhabitants. Along the coastal edges, frigatebirds, pelicans and boobies are seen, some of which nest in colonies on the offshore islands. The tropical dry forest used to stretch along much of the Pacific coast of Central and South America but has now almost entirely disappeared. Machalilla is, therefore, a unique park.

The park headquarters and museum are in Puerto López (see below). It is open from 8 am to 4 pm daily and visitor information is available. The park entrance is six km north of Puerto López and, from here, a dirt road goes five km to **Agua Blanca**, a little village with an archaeological museum and a nearby Manta archaeological site. There are hiking and horse trails, and guides are available. Camping is permitted – check water availability. You can stay in people's houses.

Ask at the headquarters about boat hire to the **Isla de la Plata**, 40 km north-west of Puerto López, where there are nesting seabird colonies. A boat carrying 10 passengers will charge about US$60 – get a group together.

PUERTO LÓPEZ

This coastal fishing village has the national park headquarters, a few restaurants (*Carmita's*, on the shorefront, is the best), and three very basic pensiones.

Buses between La Libertad (2½ hours) and Jipijapa (1½ hours) stop in Puerto López every hour or so. These buses can drop you at the national park entrance, as well as at other points along the coast (see later in this chapter).

SOUTH OF PUERTO LÓPEZ

Salango, five km south of Puerto López, has a worthwhile archaeological museum (US$0.30) and a good seafood restaurant.

The **Alandaluz** Ecological Tourist Centre is five km south of Salango. This unusual Ecuadorian-run hotel, built from fast-growing (and easily replaced) local bamboos and palm leaves, is a popular rustic getaway for travellers. An undisturbed beach is nearby, horses can be rented, there is volleyball and the atmosphere is very relaxed.

Rooms are US$4 to US$7 per person, with communal solar showers outside. Camping can be arranged. Meals are US$1.80 for breakfast, and US$2.50 for lunch or dinner. Food is good and often features vegetables from the garden. Reservations can be made in Quito (☎ 450 992) by depositing half the fee in advance. Otherwise, show up early in the day.

About 12 km south of Alandaluz is the coastal village of **Olón**, where there is a nice beach. Rooms in the hotel are US$4.50 per person. A few km further south is the village of **Montañita**, with good surfing. Beach bums and travellers like the basic but friendly *El Rincón del Amigo*, where dormitory bunks are US$1 and private rooms start around US$2 per person. Food is available. Four km south is **Manglaralto**, with a few basic pensiones and comedores. Good waves are found around here, too. Ten km further on is **Valdivia**, where Ecuador's oldest archaeological site is found. The best artefacts are in museums in Quito and Guayaquil, but there is a small museum at the site. (Artefacts offered for sale are fakes.)

LA LIBERTAD

La Libertad, with 50,000 inhabitants, is the largest town and the hub of Península de Santa Elena. It is a fishing village and port of some importance, which makes it more interesting than the other nearby towns.

Places to Stay & Eat

Hotels in the US$1.50 to US$2 per person range include the *Libertad*, *Reina del Pacífico* and *Turis Palm*, which are basic but

OK. The *Lido* and *Zambano* are bad in comparison. The *Hotel Viña del Mar* (☎ 785 979), on Guayaquil near Avenida 3, has nice double rooms with bath for US$7.

Most restaurants are on either Avenida 9 de Octubre or Avenida Guayaquil.

Getting There & Away

Buses for Guayaquil (US$1.10, three hours) leave from several places along Avenida 9 de Octubre. Buses north along the coast leave from the market on Avenida Guayaquil. Various local destinations are also served.

SALINAS

Salinas, the so-called 'best' resort in Ecuador, has casinos, high-rise condominiums and expensive deep-sea fishing trips, making it the haunt of affluent Ecuadorians. The beaches are OK but nothing special. There are some decent hotels but none is very cheap.

PLAYAS

This, the nearest beach resort to Guayaquil, is busy during the wet season but almost deserted at other times. Playas is a fishing village, and you can still see a few traditional small balsa rafts with one sail, though most boats are motorised nowadays.

In the high season, hotel prices may rise; in other months, many of the hotels, especially the cheaper ones, close down.

Places to Stay

The cheapest places sometimes lack running water and are pretty basic. Get a room with mosquito netting or a fan. The best of the cheapies is the *Hotel Marianela*, at US$2.25 per person with private bath. Others for US$2 per person are the clean *Hostería Costa Verde* (☎ 760 645), the rundown-looking *Hotel Turismo* and the *Hotel Posada del Sol*. The basic *Residencial Caracol* charges US$2.75 per person.

The *Residencial El Galeon* (☎ 760 270), is clean, friendly and good value for US$3 per person in rooms with private showers and mosquito nets. The *Hotel San Andrés* is OK and charges US$5.50 for a double with

bath. *Hotel La Terraza* (☎ 760 430) is US$3 to US$4 per person, in clean rooms with private bath, but there are no mosquito nets. *Hotel Miraglia* is a sprawling old wooden building, but the rooms are adequate for US$3.25 per person – some have private bathrooms. There is a library of English books. The *Hotel Acapulco* and *Hostería La Sirena* are about US$4 per person.

Places to Eat

The restaurant in the *Residencial Galeon* is good and fairly cheap. The *Hotel Acapulco* and *Hostería La Sirena* also have reasonable restaurants. For Italian food, try *Pizzería Diana* – a friendly place run by a US-Ecuadorian couple. The *Restaurant Jalisco* has fairly good cheap meals.

Getting There & Away

Buses to Guayaquil (US$1.15, 1¾ hours) leave every half-hour with Transportes Villamil.

GUAYAQUIL

With 1.7 million inhabitants, this is Ecuador's largest city and major port. Travellers to Ecuador tend to avoid Guayaquil. It has a reputation as a hot and humid city with too many inhabitants and little of interest. But it has a bustling river front, shady plazas, colonial buildings, friendly people and interesting museums. It's worth a visit, particularly in the dry season. (Nevertheless, most readers of previous editions find little to recommend in Guayaquil.)

Information

Tourist Office CETUR (☎ 328 312), at Aguirre 104 near the Malecón, is open from 8.30 am to 4.30 pm Monday to Friday.

Money Casas de cambio are on the first few blocks of Avenida 9 de Octubre, by the waterfront, and the first few blocks of Avenida Pichincha. Few are open on Saturday. The one at the airport is open at weekends for incoming international flights. Some banks change money.

Immigration T-3 tourist card extensions are available from Migraciones (☎ 322 541, 514 925), in the Palacio de Gobierno, on the waterfront.

Consulates The Peruvian Consulate (☎ 322 538) is at 9 de Octubre 411, 6th floor. At least 30 countries have consulates in Guayaquil – ask CETUR or consult the phone book.

Bookstores The best store for English-language books is the Librería Científica (☎ 514 555), at Luque 223.

Emergency The best hospital is the Clínica Kennedy (☎ 286 963), in the Nueva Kennedy suburb.

Dangers & Annoyances Guayaquil has a growing reputation for thefts and muggings. Be alert everywhere and at all times.

Things to See
The **Museo Municipal** (☎ 516 391), P Carbo at Sucre, is small but varied; there are archaeology, colonial art, modern art and ethnography rooms The last houses the famous *tsantsas*, or shrunken heads; it is open from 9 am to noon and 3 to 6 pm Wednesday to Friday, from 10 am to 3 pm on Saturday, and from 10 am to 1 pm on Sunday. Admission is US$0.40, but it is free on Saturday. Nearby is the **Museo Nahim Isaías B**, Pichincha and Ballén, with religious art and some archaeological pieces.

The **Museo de Arqueología del Banco Central** (☎ 320 576, 327 402), 9 de Octubre and José de Antapara, is open from 10 am to 6 pm Monday to Friday, and 10 am to 1 pm on weekends. It is free, well laid out, and has a varied and changing display of ceramics, textiles, metallurgy (some gold) and ceremonial masks. The archaeology and gold museum in the **Casa de Cultura** (☎ 300 500), 9 de Octubre and Moncayo, was recently closed – call or ask CETUR for current hours.

There are several impressive monuments and government buildings along the waterfront, at the north end of which is the picturesque colonial district of **Las Peñas**. This area is unsafe, but is recommended by Ecuadorian guides as 'typical and historical', so ask at CETUR about visiting the area. The most interesting street is **Calle Numa Pompillo Llona**, at the end of the Malecón. Here, a short flight of stairs leads up to the small **Plaza Colón**, where there are two cannons pointing towards the river. The short, narrow and winding Calle Numa Pompillo Llona begins from the corner of the Plaza. Several past presidents had their residences here, and the colonial architecture is interesting. Several artists now live in the area and there are a few art galleries.

The **Parque Bolívar**, between Ballén and 10 de Agosto, has small, well-planned gardens, which are home to prehistoric-looking land iguanas of up to a metre in length. The modern catedral is on the west side and some of the best hotels are nearby.

The **Parque del Centenario** is the city's biggest plaza, covering four blocks. There are many monuments, the most important of which is the monument to patriotism – a huge work. Watch for thieves working in and around this park.

The most impressive church is **San Francisco**, which has been reconstructed and beautifully restored since a devastating fire in 1896. Also worth seeing is the dazzling white **City Cemetery**, near Coronel and Picincha, but beware of robbers midweek.

The **'Black Market'**, by the waterfront, between Colón and Olmedo, is a huge open-air affair selling almost anything. It's colourful, interesting and reasonably safe, but watch for pickpockets.

Festivals
The whole city parties in the last week of July, celebrating **Bolívar's birthday** (24 July), followed by **Guayaquil Foundation Day** (25 July), and hotels may be full. Banks and other services are also disrupted. **Guayaquil's Independence Day** (9 October), combined with America or **Columbus Day** (12 October), is an important local holiday period. **New Year's Eve** (31 December) is celebrated with bonfires.

To Airport, Bus Terminal,
Urdesa & Durán

Cemetery

Central
Guayaquil

0   200 m

To Manta

To Puerto
Nuevo

P Solano

Urdaneta

Quisquis

de Mayo

Quito

9 de Octubre

Hurtado

Vélez

Parque del
Centenario

Olympic
Pool

García Moreno

José de Antepara

Machala

Tulcán

Los Ríos

Esmeraldas

Masote

Ejercito

51

52   53 54

55 56

57   58   59

60   61

62

63

64

65

10 de Agosto

Parque
Victoria

Monçeyo

6 de Marzo

Garaycoa

Montúfar

Sucre

Colón

67   68

Alcedo

Market

66

1

2

3

4
5

6

7

9

10

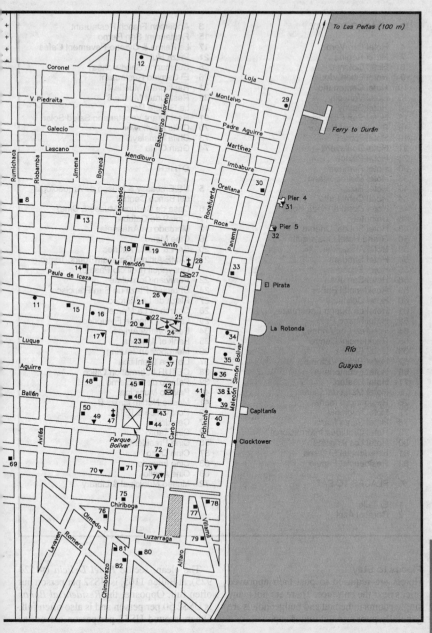

To Las Peñas (100 m)

Coronel

12

V Piedraita

Loja

J Montalvo

29

Galecio

Padre Aguirre

Ferry to Durán

Lascano

Martínez

Mendiburo

Imbabura

Baquerizo Moreno

Orellana

30

Escobedo

Rocafuerte

Roca

Pier 4

31

8

Pier 5

13

32

Junín

18   19

V M Rendón

28

33

14

27

Paula de Icaza

El Pirata

26

11   15   16

21

22

La Rotonda

20   25

Río

17   23   24

34

Luque

35

Guayas

Chile

37

36

Aguirre

Ballén

48

42

41

38

Simón Bolívar

45

39

50   49   46

43

40

Capitanía

47

44

Pichincha

Aviles

Parque
Bolívar

72

Clocktower

69

70   71   73
74

75

Chiriboga

78

76

Olmedo

77

Villamil

Luzárraga

79

Lavayen   Romero

81

80

Chimborazo

82

Malecón

P Carbo

Alfaro

Rumichaca   Riobamba   Jimena   Boyacá

ECUADOR

■ PLACES TO STAY		3	Anderson French Restaurant

■ PLACES TO STAY

4	Hotel Oro Verde
7	Hotel Regina
8	Hotel Colonial
9	Hotel Libertador
10	Hotel Centenario
13	Hotel Venecia
14	Hotel Savoy
15	Hotel San Francisco
18	Residencial Pauker
19	Hotel Tourist
21	Hotel Boulevard
23	Hotel Palace
30	Hotel Ramada
33	Hotel Metropolitana
43	Hotel Rizzo
44	Hotel Continental
45	Hotel Doral & Plaza Hotel
46	Unihotel
48	Hotel Sol del Oriente
50	Grand Hotel Guayaquil
53	Hotel Alexander
54	Hotel Sanders
55	Hotel Ecuador
58	Hotel San Juan
59	Residencial Baños
60	Hotel Delicia
61	Hotel La Buena Esperanza
62	Hotel Marco Polo
64	Hotel de Los Andes
65	Residencial Centro
66	Hotel El Inca
67	Hotel Reina Victoria
69	Hotel Ecuatoriana
71	Hotel Boston
75	Hotel María del Cisne
76	Residencial María
77	Hotel Nacional
78	Hotel Santa María
79	Hotel Orquidea Internacional
80	Hotel Los Angeles
81	Residencial El Cisne
82	Residencial Espejo

▼ PLACES TO EAT

1	El Taller
2	Caracol Azul
3	Anderson French Restaurant
15	Restaurant San Remo
17	La Palma & Cyrano Pavement Cafés
21	Pizza Hut
25	Submarine Sandwiches
26	El Camino Restaurant
31	Restaurant Muelle 4
32	Restaurant Muelle 5
49	La Galleta Pecosa
51	Restaurant Vegetariano Salud Solar
70	Chifa Mayflower
73	Chifa Himalaya
74	Gran Chifa

OTHER

5	US Embassy & Museo de Arqueología del Banco Central
6	Casa de Cultura (Museo & Cine)
11	Cine 9 de Octubre
12	Mercado de Artesanía
16	Cine Metro
20	SAN & Saeta Airlines
21	TAME Airline, Galasam Tours, Teatro Guayaquil (Edificio Pasaje)
22	Peruvian Consulate
24	Church & Plaza de San Francisco
27	Plaza de La Merced
28	Church of La Merced
29	La Peña Rincón Folklórico
34	Ecuatoriana Airline
35	Bank of America
36	Metropolitan Touring
37	Librería Científica
38	CETUR Information Office
39	Palacio de Gobierno
40	Palacio Municipal
41	Museo Nahim Isaías B
42	Post Office & IETEL
47	Catedral
52	Cine Tauro
56	Cine Presidente
57	Cine Quito
63	Cine Imperio
68	Cine Apollo
72	Museo Municipal & Library

Places to Stay

Hotels are required to post their approved prices near the entrance. There are not many single rooms to be had and budget hotels are generally poor and not that cheap.

The clean, secure *Hotel Delicia* (☎ 524 925), at Ballén 1105, is US$2 per person but often full. Opposite, the *Residencial Baños* is US$2.50 per person and is also often full. Others around US$2 per person are not as good and include the very basic *Residencial Espejo, Residencial María* and *Residencial El Cisne*, on Olmedo near Chimborazo – a poor area of town, particularly at night. *Hotel La Buena Esperanza*, on Ballén near 6 de Marzo, is similar. The *Hotel Los Angeles*, on Olmedo near Chile, is fairly basic, but has better rooms with bath and fans for US$3 per person.

The *Hotel San Juan*, on Quito near Ballén, has shabby rooms with private bath for US$3.50 (one or two people). The *Hotel Ecuatoriana* (☎ 518 105), at Rumichaca 1502, charges US$4 a double for the night, or US$2 'for a short while'. It is clean and fairly secure, despite the short-stay clients. Some of the cheap hotels near the market double as brothels, and lone females may be improperly treated or molested. *Hotel El Inca*, on 10 de Agosto, opposite the market, is reasonably well run and has many rooms, most with bathrooms, for US$2 per person. The *Hotel Ecuador*, Moncayo 1117, is decent and friendly. Rooms are US$6/10 for doubles/triples with private bath and fan. The *Hotel Marco Polo*, on 6 de Marzo, is not recommended for single women.

Hotel Santa María, at Villamil 102, is US$4/7 for shabby but clean singles/doubles with bath. Opposite, *Hotel Nacional* is similar, with cheaper rooms lacking baths or windows. Short-stay couples have brief liaisons here. *Hotel Boston*, Chimborazo 711, is US$3 per person in tiny wooden boxes with fans.

The *Residencial Pauker* (☎ 517 348), Barquerizo Moreno 902, is rundown and has basic rooms for US$3 per person. Opposite, the *Hotel Tourist* is a little better for US$4/7 in rooms with bath; air-conditioning costs more. *Hotel Libertador*, on Garaycoa near V M Rendón, has clean rooms with bath and fan for US$3.50 per person. The *Hotel Savoy*, on V M Rendón near Boyacá, is similarly priced. The *Hotel Reina Victoria*, on Colón near Moncayo, has clean rooms with bath and fan for US$4.50/6.50.

Clean air-conditioned rooms with private bath are US$4.50/6.50 in the *Hotel Regina* (☎ 312 754), at Garaycoa 421; thieves hang

around outside this hotel. The *Hotel Colonial*, on Rumichaca near Urdaneta, is a clean and friendly hotel. Rooms are US$4.50/7.50 with private bath and fan – some rooms have balconies. A block away, on Rumichaca near Junín, is the *Hotel USA* (☎ 307 804), which is similarly priced and looks OK.

The clean *Hotel Metropolitana* (☎ 305 250), at V M Rendón 120 (4th floor), is good at US$8.50 a double. *Hotel Venecia*, on Urdaneta near Jimena, is US$7/10 with private bath and air-conditioning (less with fans). *Hotel Centenario* (☎ 524 467), at Vélez 726, is US$8 a double with private baths and air-conditioning (less with fans); it's OK. The similarly priced *Hotel Sanders* (☎ 320 030, 510 030), on Moncayo near Luque, is quite good – rooms and prices vary.

Places to Eat

For breakfast, *La Palma* and *Cyrano* pavement cafés, next to one another on Escobedo, sell good coffee and croissants.

La Galleta Pecosa, on 10 de Agosto near Boyaca, sells good home-made cookies.

The *Gran Chifa* (☎ 510 794, 512 488), at P Carbo 1016, is elegant but reasonably priced. The cheaper *Chifa Himalaya* (☎ 529 593), at Sucre 308, is good and popular. Also popular is the *Chifa Mayflower*, on Colón near Chimborazo.

The *Restaurant Vegetariano Salud Solar*, on Luque near Moncayo, serves good, simple and cheap food. *El Camino*, on Paula de Icaza near Córdova, serves inexpensive lunches, including a few meatless ones.

There are several piers along the Malecón where restaurant boats are moored; these are OK for lunch, when you can watch the river traffic go by – they get pricier at dinner time. One is *El Pirata*, another is the pricier *Muelle 5*. Modern cafeterias, restaurants and fast-food places line Avenida 9 de Octubre, but they are not very cheap.

The suburb of Urdesa, six km north-west of the centre, has good and popular restaurants, some reasonably priced but none dirt cheap. There is some nightlife – this is a good area to hang. The main drag is V E Estrada,

ECUADOR

and most of the restaurants, bars and clubs are found along this street.

La Parrillada del Ñato (☎ 387 098), on V E Estrada near Laurales, serves good Ecuadorian-style steaks, grills and barbecues, as well as pizza. *Pizzería Ch'Enano* (☎ 388 333), at V E Estrada 1320, also serves good pizzas. *La Tablita* (☎ 388 162), at Ebanos 126 near V E Estrada, has good Ecuadorian-style grills and steaks. For Mexican dinners, try *Paco's* (☎ 442 112), at Acacias 725 near Guayacanes. They sometimes have mariachi bands playing.

Entertainment
El Telégrafo and *El Universo* publicise entertainment. There are some 18 cinemas; English-language movies with Spanish subtitles are often shown.

Friday newspapers advertise weekend peñas, which are rarely cheap and always start late. A good one is La Peña Rincón Folklórico, at Malecón 208. It opens at 10 pm for food and drinks, the show starts about midnight and continues until the early hours; the cover charge is US$3 and drinks aren't cheap.

Along V E Estrada in Urdesa, there are several clubs, bars and discos – ask around for the current 'in' place.

Getting There & Away
Air The main airport is on Avenida de las Américas, five km north of the centre. The international/domestic terminals are side by side. A casa de cambio is open for all incoming international flights. There is a cafeteria, car rental company, gift shop and IETEL.

Flights go to other parts of Latin America, North America and Europe. International flights out of Guayaquil are all subject to a US$25 departure tax. There are many flights to Quito (US$20) with TAME or SAN-Saeta. Other flights go to Cuenca, Loja, Machala, Salinas (seasonal), and Macará (irregular).

Flights to the Galápagos (US$330 for the round trip) go to Baltra with TAME, or to San Cristóbal with SAN-Saeta (most days).

One km south is the Avioneta (light aircraft) terminal, with flights to Machala, Manta, Esmeraldas and other coastal destinations. The baggage limit is 10 kg and passenger weight limit is 100 kg.

AECA
    Avioneta Terminal (☎ 286 640, 288 110)
AvioPacifico
    Avioneta Terminal (☎ 283 304/5)
CEDTA
    Avioneta Terminal (☎ 280 065)
    Escobedo 924 and V M Rendón (☎ 301 954, 301 165)
EDSAN
    Avioneta Terminal (☎ 915 138)
LANSA
    Avioneta Terminal (☎ 280 898, 280 665)
SAN & Saeta
    Vélez 206 and Chile (☎ 329 855, 326 466)
TAME
    9 de Octubre 424, Gran Pasaje (☎ 303 128, 302 277)

Bus The terminal terrestre is two km beyond the airport. There are dozens of bus offices, stores, restaurants, tourist information, a bank, hairdresser and so on. You can get buses to most towns; ask at the passenger information desk. For fares and hours, see under the town you wish to go to.

Train Daily trains for Alausí (US$0.60, all day) leave from the Durán railway station at 6.30 am – see under Alausí for further descriptions. On some days, the service is by autoferro. Durán is a suburb on the opposite side of the Río Guayas – the first ferry from Guayaquil enables you to connect with the train. Passengers arriving from Alausí will find the ferry just west of the station. Beware of thieves at the ferry terminals, especially in the dark. Durán has basic hotels, including *Hotel Buenos Aires*, at Loja 516 near Esmeraldas (US$1.50 per person). The train ride is spectacular.

Boat The Durán ferry across the Río Guayas (US$0.05, 15 minutes) leaves three or four times an hour from 5.30 am to 7.30 pm daily. This is a great sightseeing trip for the impecunious! The dock is on the Malecón near Montalvo.

ECUADOR

Getting Around

A taxi from the centre to the airport or bus terminal is about US$2, but at the airport, higher fares are given. For cheaper taxis, cross Avenida de las Américas in front of the airport and bargain. From this street, there are buses to the town centre or bus terminal.

From the centre, the '2 Especial' bus runs along the Malecón and goes to the airport (US$0.05, half an hour) – leave plenty of time if catching a flight. Buses to the Terminal Terrestre leave from Parque Victoria, near 10 de Agosto and Moncayo.

MACHALA

This is the capital of El Oro Province and the centre of an important banana-growing area. Most travellers to and from Peru pass through here, but few stay more than a night.

Machala is not totally devoid of interest, however, as **Puerto Bolívar**, the international port, seven km away, is worth visiting.

Information

CETUR (☎ 932 106), is by the Hotel Mosquera, on Guayaquil near Olmedo.

Casa de Cambio Illauri, at Paez 17-23, changes US cash and travellers' cheques. So does Banco del Pacífico, on Rocafuerte near Tarqui. Rates are a little lower than in Guayaquil.

The Peruvian Consulate (☎ 920 680), on Bolívar near Colón, is open from 8 am to 1 pm Monday to Friday.

The No 1 bus to Puerto Bolívar leaves from Machala's main plaza. Boats can be hired to visit the mangroves. There are several passenger boats daily to **Jambelí** (US$0.40, half an hour), where there is a beach and basic hotels. There are seafood restaurants on the waterfront.

Places to Stay

Most cheap hotels have only cold water and are neither very cheap nor very good. The basic but clean and friendly *Hotel La Delicia*, on Olmedo near Páez, is US$2.50 per person – but is often full.

Other very basic places (also US$2.50) are the dirty *Residencial Almache*, on Sucre near Montalvo, the rundown *Residencial El Oro*, 9 de Mayo, and the better-looking *Residencial Pichincha*, on Sucre near 9 de Mayo.

Residencial La Internacional, on Guayas near Olmedo, is friendly but has received mixed reports. Rooms are US$3/5.50 for singles/doubles. *Residencial Machala*, on Sucre near Guayas, is friendly and is US$2 per person, or US$3 with bath, though the toilets aren't too clean. The cleaner *Hotel La Cueva de los Tayos*, on Sucre near Buenavista, is US$3 per person.

Gran Hotel Machala (☎ 920 530), on Montalvo near Rocafuerte, is US$3.75 per person, or US$4.50 with private bath and fan. Some rooms have air-conditioning, but others are shabby. *Hotel Ecuatoriana Pullman* (☎ 921 164), at 9 de Octubre 912, is above a bus terminal, but some rooms are quiet and have air-conditioning, though bathrooms are grubby. It's US$4 per person.

The small, clean *Hostal Mercy*, at Junín 609, is US$4.50 per person in rooms with private bath and fan; it is often full. *Hotel Suites Guayaquil* (☎ 922 570), on Páez near 9 de Octubre, is US$5.50/9.50 for a single/double with bath (some have air-conditioning). *Hotel El Mosquero*, on Olmedo near Guayas, has singles with baths for US$5.50 and air-conditioned rooms for US$8. *Hotel Encalada* (☎ 920 247) has clean rooms with private bath and fans for US$8/12 a single/double.

Places to Eat

Restaurant Chifa Central, on Tarqui near 9 de Octubre, is good and reasonably priced, especially the filling chaulafan (fried rice with pork, chicken, egg etc). Other cheap places are along 9 de Octubre.

El Jeff Pizzería is on Junín near Sucre. *Bar Restaurant El Bosque* (☎ 924 344), on 9 de Mayo near Bolívar, has an outdoor dining area and simple but decent meals for US$2.

Puerto Bolívar has seafood restaurants.

Getting There & Away

Air The airport is one km south-west of town along Montalvo. At the airport, CEDTA and

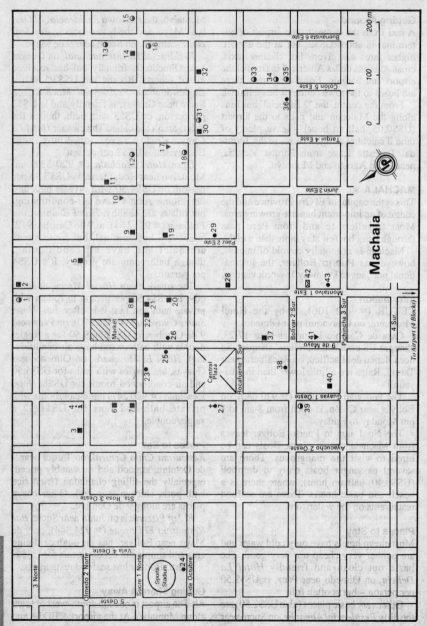

Machala

■ PLACES TO STAY		OTHER	
2	Hotel Ines	1	Transportes Azuay (Buses)
3	Hotel El Mosquero	4	CETUR Tourist Information
5	Hotel La Delicia	12	Transportes Pullman Sucre (Buses)
6	Residencial La Internacional	13	Transportes Occidentales (Buses)
7	Residencial Machala	15	Transportes Union Yantzaza (Buses)
8	Hotel Oro	16	Transportes Cooperativa Loja (Buses)
9	Hotel Perla de Pacifico	18	Rutas Orenses (Buses)
11	Hostal Mercy	23	Cinema
14	Hotel La Cueva de los Tayos	24	IETEL
19	Hotel Suites Guayaquil	25	Ecuatoriana Airline
20	Hotel Reina Paccha	26	Cinema Central
21	Residencial Almache	27	Church
22	Residencial Pichincha	29	Casa de Cambio Illauri
28	Gran Hotel Machala	31	CIFA Buses to Guayaquil
30	Hotel Encalada	32	Ecuatoriana (Buses)
32	Hotel Ecuatoriana Pullman	33	Cuidad de Piñas (Buses)
37	Residencial El Oro	34	Transportes TAC (Buses)
40	Rizzo Hotel	35	Panamericana (Buses)
▼ PLACES TO EAT		36	Peruvian Consulate
		38	Travel Agencies
10	El Jeff Pizzería	39	CIFA Buses to Huaquillas
17	Restaurant Chifa Central	42	Post Office
41	Bar Restaurant El Bosque	43	TAME Airline

LANSA have light aircraft for Guayaquil. TAME (☎ 920 130), on Montalvo near Pichincha, has weekday flights to Guayaquil (US$12).

Bus There is no central bus terminal. To the Peruvian border at Huaquillas (US$0.70, two hours), use CIFA, which operates frequent buses from the corner of Bolívar and Guayas. Be prepared for passport checks en route. You must leave the bus to register, but the driver will wait.

CIFA buses also go to Guayaquil (US$2, 3½ hours) from Avenida 9 de Octubre near Colón. Several other companies in the area also serve Guayaquil.

Panamericana has several coaches a day to Quito (US$3.50, 10 to 12 hours). Ciudad de Piñas has nine buses a day to Piñas, a few of which continue to Loja. They also have one or two buses to Cuenca (US$2.20, five hours). Transportes Cooperativa Loja also goes to Loja (US$2.20, eight hours).

Pullman Express has eight buses daily to Cuenca.

HUAQUILLAS
Huaquillas, 80 km from Machala, is the main border town with Peru. It is called Aguas Verdes on the Peruvian side. There is a busy street market on the Ecuadorian side of the border, which is full of Peruvians shopping on day passes. Almost everything happens on the long main street.

Information
Banks don't change money, but there are street moneychangers. They offer poor rates but soon become more reasonable if you know what the real rate is. Check with travellers going the opposite way for up-to-date exchange rates.

It is a better idea to use US dollars for exchange, so try to arrive at the border with as few sucres (or Peruvian *soles nuevos*) as possible.

ECUADOR

Places to Stay & Eat

There are several cheap hotels on the main street near the immigration office. None of them is particularly good. There are cheap restaurants nearby; again, none is very good. Most travellers stay in Machala or Tumbes, Peru, where there are better choices.

The *Parador Turístico Huaquillas* (☎ 907 374) is about 1½ km from the border, on the right-hand side of the main road out of town. Simple but clean singles/doubles with fans and private bathrooms are US$6/10 – this is the best hotel in town, and it also has the best restaurant.

Getting There & Away

CIFA buses run frequently to Machala (US$0.70, two hours). They leave from the main street, a block or two beyond the immigration office. Panamericana has four daily buses to Quito (US$4.20, 13 hours). Ecuatoriana Pullman has buses to Guayaquil (US$2.20, 5½ hours). A few buses go to Loja and Cuenca.

To/From Peru

The Ecuadorian immigration office is 200 metres from the international bridge and is identified by the yellow, blue and red striped Ecuadorian flag. All entrance and exit formalities are carried out here. The Ecuadorian office is open daily from 8 am to noon and 2 to 5 pm.

Those entering Ecuador need an exit stamp in their passport from the Peruvian authorities. Entrance formalities are usually straightforward. Travellers need a T-3 tourist card, which is available free at the immigration office. Usually, only 30 days are given, but it is easy to obtain a renewal in Quito or Guayaquil. Show of funds or onward tickets are very rarely asked for.

Those leaving Ecuador need an exit stamp from the Ecuadorian immigration office before entering Peru. If you have lost your T-3 card, you should be able to get a free replacement at the border, as long as the stamp in your passport has not expired.

After showing your passport to the international bridge guard, continue to the Peruvian immigration building, about 100 metres beyond the border, on the left.

The Galápagos Islands

The Galápagos archipelago is famous for its fearless and unique wildlife. Here, you can swim with sea lions, float eye-to-eye with a penguin, stand next to a blue-footed booby feeding its young, watch a giant 200-kg tortoise lumbering through a cactus forest, and try to avoid stepping on iguanas scurrying over the lava. The scenery is barren and volcanic and has its own haunting beauty, though some people find it bare and ugly. Compared to the rest of Ecuador, visiting the Galápagos is very expensive, so a visit to the islands is for the wilderness and wildlife enthusiast, not the average sun-seeker.

The islands were uninhabited when they were first discovered by the Spanish in 1535. They lie on the equator, about 1000 km west of Ecuador, and consist of 13 major islands and many small ones. Five islands are inhabited. The archipelago's most famous visitor was Charles Darwin, who came here in 1835. The Galápagos as a whole are one of Ecuador's 21 provinces.

FACTS FOR THE VISITOR
Orientation

The most important island, from a traveller's point of view, is Isla Santa Cruz, which is in the middle of the archipelago. On the south side of the island is Puerto Ayora, the largest town in the Galápagos and the place from which most tours are based. There is a good range of hotels and restaurants. North of Isla Santa Cruz, and separated from it by a narrow strait, is Isla Baltra, which has the islands' major airport. A public bus and a ferry connect the Baltra Airport with Puerto Ayora – a three-hour journey.

Isla San Cristóbal, at the south-eastern end of the Galápagos, is the seat of the provincial capital, Puerto Baquerizo Moreno. This town has a few hotels, and less frequent air connections with the mainland than Puerto

Ayora/Baltra. Although most travellers fly into Baltra, Puerto Baquerizo Moreno is slowly becoming more important for the traveller.

The other inhabited islands are Isla Isabela, with the small port of Puerto Villamil, and Isla Santa María (Floreana), with Puerto Velasco Ibarra – both have places to stay. Interisland transportation is exclusively by boat, but public ferries are infrequent.

Information

The islands are a national park. All foreign visitors must pay US$80 upon arrival; keep your ticket, as it is valid for your entire stay. The high seasons are from December to January, around Easter and from June to August; during these periods, prices rise and budget tours are more difficult to arrange. Note that most of the islands have two or even three names. Galápagos time is one hour behind the mainland.

Tourist Office CETUR has an office in Puerto Ayora near the main docks. Self-styled tourist information agencies mainly provide information about their own boat trips and charters. The South American Explorers Club in Quito can provide members with up-to-date information on the Galápagos.

Money Moneychanging facilities are poor; Puerto Ayora is the best bet, but try to change what you need on the mainland. The Banco Pacífico, near the Hotel Sol y Mar, changes money.

Post & Telecommunications Be aware that the mail is slow. Make sure your stamps are franked to avoid them being removed. IETEL connections are often out of service.

Electricity Electricity is turned off by 11 pm or earlier in many places – carry a flashlight.

Books & Maps

The best general guide to the plant and animal life, with much background informa-

tion on history and geology, is Michael H Jackson's *Galápagos: A Natural History Guide* (University of Calgary Press, 1985). Bird-watchers should consult *A Field Guide to the Birds of the Galápagos*, by Michael Harris (Collins, 1982). Amateur botanists are referred to the pocket-sized *Plants of the Galápagos Islands*, by Eileen K Schofield (New York, 1984). There is also *A Guide to the Fish of the Galápagos*, by Godfrey Merlen (Quito, 1988). Most of these are available at the Libri Mundi bookstore in Quito or the Librería Científica in Guayaquil.

Ecuador & the Galápagos Island – a travel survival kit, by Rob Rachowiecki (Lonely Planet), has plenty of Galápagos information, plus a wildlife guide for the nonspecialist.

Maps of the Galápagos are available from the IGM in Quito. A good map, full of useful information about wildlife, history and tourism, was republished in 1992 by Bradt Publications, 41 Nortoft Rd, Chalfont St Peter, Bucks SL9 OLA, England.

What to Bring

Many things are expensive or unavailable in the Galápagos. Stock up on sunscreen, insect repellent, film, toiletries and medication on the mainland.

GETTING THERE & AWAY

Flying to the Galápagos is recommended. If you go by boat, you will probably waste a lot of time in the port of Guayaquil getting one of the infrequent passages. With the extra food and accommodation costs, you are unlikely to save much money.

Air

Most visitors fly to Isla Baltra, from where public transport (buses and a ferry) goes to Puerto Ayora, on Isla Santa Cruz. (Tour groups, whose itineraries have been prearranged, are often picked up directly from Baltra by their boats.) It is also possible to fly to Puerto Baquerizo Moreno, on Isla San Cristóbal. Although this is officially the capital of the archipelago, there are more facilities in Puerto Ayora, and travellers wanting to arrange their own tours are advised to go there.

TAME operates morning flights from Monday to Saturday from both Quito (US$374 round trip) and Guayaquil (US$330 round trip, 1½ hours) to Baltra. SAN-Saeta flights to Puerto Baquerizo Moreno are similarly priced with departures daily except Thursday and Sunday. TAME and SAN-Saeta do not honour one another's tickets; it is possible to buy one-way tickets to arrive in one island and leave from the other. It is also possible to buy tickets with open return dates. Always reconfirm flights, especially in Puerto Ayora.

Ecuadorian nationals or foreigners on residence visas pay about US$80 for the round trip.

If you fly Miami-Ecuador-Galápagos with an Ecuadorian carrier, the Galápagos portion is almost US$100 cheaper. Ecuatoriana has connections with TAME only, Saeta with SAN-Saeta. These save money if you can plan ahead.

Military *logístico* (supply) flights leave on Saturday from Quito to Baltra (US$140 one-way). These are difficult to get seats on, Ecuadorians are given preference and departures are unreliable. Go to the military airport (just north of the civil airport) no earlier than the Monday before you want to fly, put your name on the list, then return on Friday morning to confirm and buy the ticket (have exact US dollars). If you have exceptional contacts, visiting Señor Comandante de la Fuerza Aerea Ecuatoriana, at the Ministry of Defense, on Avenida Maldonado in Quito, may get you a special authorisation for a logístico – this is rarely granted. Beware of people selling logístico tickets cheaply, as they may be invalid or nonrefundable.

Travellers with international student cards can try getting student discounts, variously reported as 20%, 25% and impossible to obtain!

Some tour agencies will give you discounts on air fares if you take their tours, especially during the off season (February to May, September to November). Sometimes,

an agency will sell you a discount ticket at the last moment because they can't sell the reserved tour space.

All scheduled flights may be booked up well in advance, but if you go to the airport, you may find that some people don't show up. Travel agencies book up blocks of seats for their all-inclusive Galápagos tours. They release the seats on the day of the flight (these are full-price tickets).

Boat

The navy-run *Calicuchima* leaves Guayaquil twice a month for an 11-day trip. Only half this time is available for visiting the islands, and some naval bases are visited en route. The accommodation, crew, guides and food have been criticised. The tour costs about US$330 and the office (☎ 308 400) is at Transnave, 9 de Octubre 416, Guayaquil. (A recent report indicates that this boat no longer takes tourists.)

Cargo ships leave irregularly and charge about US$100 for a one-way trip. Most passengers get round trips of 15 to 20 days. Conditions are tolerable but basic. The journey out takes 3½ days; bring a sleeping bag or hammock, though a bunk in one of five cabins may be available. These ships normally do round trips and are mainly for cargo purposes, not for wildlife viewing. A reader reports that she enjoyed her 20-day round trip from Guayaquil in the *Piquero* – she paid US$300 in 1991, and saw a fair amount of wildlife. She found the crew helpful and was given a cabin to sleep in. Similar excursions may be offered on the *Congal* and the *Iguana*.

The agent for *Piquero* is Acotramar (☎ 401 004, 401 711, 402 371), at Général Gómez 522 and Chimborazo, Guayaquil. Another contact is Señor Rafael Castro, at TRAMFSA, Office 602, Baquerizo Moreno 1119, Guayaquil. Also ask at the Capitanía in Guayaquil, or at the boats, which anchor near dock No 4. Be prepared to wait days or weeks for a departure – though you might get lucky.

GETTING AROUND

Arriving air passengers in Baltra are either met by a crew member (if they have a pre-arranged tour) or take a bus-ferry-bus combination to Puerto Ayora (US$3, three hours). Tickets are sold in the departure/arrival lounge – get one as soon as possible and don't miss the bus. It can get very crowded, with passengers on the roof.

From Puerto Ayora, buses leave at 8 am from the park for the return trip to Baltra.

Air passengers arriving in Puerto Baquerizo Moreno can walk into town or take a taxi.

Interisland transportation is with INGALA. They give priority to Ecuadorians, and it is not easy to get a ticket. You may have to wait several days or more. Departure dates change frequently, but there are normally two trips a week between Puerto Ayora and Puerto Baquerizo Moreno – recently, on Tuesday and Saturday, returning on Wednesday and Monday (US$20 one-way). There is also a weekly boat leaving Puerto Ayora on Monday for Isabela, continuing to Floreana on Tuesday and returning to Puerto Ayora on Wednesday. If you can't get on an INGALA boat, ask around for private trips, which are more expensive.

Travelling between the islands by public transport is unreliable and not designed for wildlife viewing. Most people take guided tours – for more information, see the Tours section at the end of this chapter.

PUERTO AYORA
Places to Stay

It may be possible to camp near the Charles Darwin Research Station – ask. Near TAME is *Residencial Los Amigos*, where rooms are US$2.50/4.50 for singles/doubles; this place has recently been very popular and recommended among budget travellers. A block inland is the good and clean *Residencial Flamingo*, which charges US$2.50 per person in rooms with private bath.

One km north of the town centre, on the way to the Charles Darwin Research Station, is *Pensión Gloria*, a small and very basic

hotel run by Señora Gloria, whose husband is a guide. They are friendly and will help organise a tour boat group. They charge US$2 per person. The basic but larger *Residencial Angermeyer* is run by members of the family who were among the earliest permanent residents. They provide useful information and help to put you in contact with boats. It is also popular with budget travellers, but I have received reports that the management is rather eccentric! Rooms are about US$3 per person.

The *Hotel Lobo del Mar* is popular with Ecuadorian tour groups and tends to be noisy. Most of their rooms are basic but reasonably clean, with private showers. They charge US$6/9 for singles/doubles, and have some triple and quadruples which are not much more. For about US$4 more per person, they include three meals a day. The hotel organises day trips to various islands for about US$35 to US$40 per passenger.

The *Hotel Las Palmeras* is quite good but often full. Prices are around US$5/7 for clean singles/doubles with private bath. Similarly priced and also clean and modern-looking is the *Hotel Salinas*, opposite. *Hotel Elizabeth* is about the same price, though is reportedly open to bargaining. They have improved since my negative comments in the last edition. In this price range are the *Hotel Darwin* and *Hotel Santa Cruz*, which are both on the road out of town.

Places to Eat, Drink & Dance

Restaurants and bars in Puerto Ayora are good places to meet people. Service is leisurely. Some places have changed owners and names quite often, as places frequented by seasonal influxes of people tend to do. Most of the following have been around for a few years.

Perla Oriental, by the dock, has been the standard meeting place during the day for years – it was formerly called Las Ninfas. Grab a beer, snack or meal here while waiting for your panga.

A short walk into town from the dock, along the main street, brings you to *Restaurant Asia*, which is the best chifa in town. A

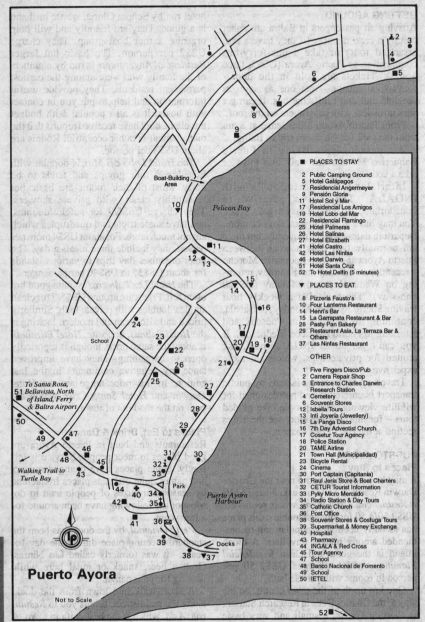

Puerto Ayora

Boat-Building Area

Pelican Bay

School

To Santa Rosa,
Bellavista, North
of Island, Ferry
& Baltra Airport

Walking Trail to
Turtle Bay

Puerto Ayora
Harbour

Park

Docks

Not to Scale

■ PLACES TO STAY
2   Public Camping Ground
5   Hotel Galápagos
7   Residencial Angermeyer
9   Pensión Gloria
11 Hotel Sol y Mar
17 Residencial Los Amigos
19 Hotel Lobo del Mar
22 Residencial Flamingo
25 Hotel Palmeras
26 Hotel Salinas
27 Hotel Elizabeth
41 Hotel Castro
42 Hotel Las Ninfas
46 Hotel Darwin
51 Hotel Santa Cruz
52 To Hotel Delfín (5 minutes)

▼ PLACES TO EAT
8   Pizzería Fausto's
10 Four Lanterns Restaurant
14 Henri's Bar
15 La Garrapata Restaurant & Bar
28 Pasty Pan Bakery
29 Restaurant Asia, La Terraza Bar &
    Others
37 Las Ninfas Restaurant

OTHER
1   Five Fingers Disco/Pub
2   Camera Repair Shop
3   Entrance to Charles Darwin
    Research Station
4   Cemetery
6   Souvenir Stores
12 Isbella Tours
13 Inti Joyería (Jewellery)
15 La Panga Disco
16 7th Day Adventist Church
17 Cosetur Tour Agency
18 Police Station
20 TAME Airline
21 Town Hall (Municipalidad)
23 Bicycle Rental
24 Cinema
30 Port Captain (Capitanía)
31 Raul Jería Store & Boat Charters
32 CETUR Tourist Information
33 Pyky Micro Mercado
34 Radio Station & Day Tours
35 Catholic Church
36 Post Office
38 Souvenir Stores & Costuga Tours
40 Supermarket & Money Exchange
43 Hospital
44 Pharmacy
44 INGALA & Red Cross
45 Tour Agency
47 School
48 Banco Nacional de Fomento
49 School
50 IETEL

ECUADOR

few doors away is the *Pasty Pan* bakery – good for baked goods and also for boat contacts. There are several other places on the same block, including the restaurant and upstairs bar at *La Terraza*, which gets pretty rowdy at nights.

Further along the main ocean-front street is *La Garrapata Bar/Restaurant*, which is popular and serves good, though not particularly cheap, meals. The bar often stays open until the early hours and is a favourite with locals and visitors alike. The Garrapata is often closed in the afternoons and all day pm Sunday. Next door is the *La Panga* disco, which was the place to dance in the early 1990s – local guides assure me that this is where 'the landings are always wet'.

Opposite is *Henri's Bar*, which is German-run (they speak English and Spanish) and has recently been a popular meeting place for gringo travellers. They sell good breakfasts and pricey beer, have a notice board and rent snorkelling equipment.

Further along you'll find *Four Lanterns Restaurant*, which has been recommended for good pizzas, sandwiches, other snacks and coffee. *Fausto's Pizzería* is also good for pizzas. They used to have a book exchange, and screen videos in the evenings for a fee. I don't know if they still do. A couple of blocks inland is the *Five Fingers Disco Pub*, which is an alternative to La Panga.

For the cheapest meals, ask around and eat where the locals go. There are a bunch of inexpensive comedores which come and go; *El Pescador*, *El Pirata* and *Las Peñas* have been recommended to me by travellers (but are not on the map).

Things to Buy

The famous Galápagos T-shirts are sold in several shops in Puerto Ayora, and at reasonable prices. Souvenirs made from black coral, turtle and tortoise shell are also sold. Don't buy these, as the animals which provide the material are protected species.

The Pyky Micro Mercado has basic food supplies for picnics and excursions. A couple of places sell drinking water (not fizzy Güitig), but you need to bring your own

container. Note that there are sometimes drinking water shortages on the smaller boats.

AROUND PUERTO AYORA

The **Charles Darwin Research Station** is about a 20-minute walk by road north-east of Puerto Ayora. It contains a national park information centre, a museum, a baby tortoise nursery, and a walk-in adult tortoise enclosure where you can meet these Galápagos giants face to face. In addition, there are paths through arid-zone vegetation such as prickly pear and other cacti, salt bush and mangroves. You can see a variety of land birds, including Darwin's finches.

A three-km trail takes you to **Bahía Tortuga (Turtle Bay)**, south-west of Puerto Ayora. Take the path which leaves from behind the IETEL office; carry insect repellent, sunscreen and water. There is a very fine white-sand beach and protected swimming behind a spit (there are strong currents on the exposed side of the spit). There are harmless sharks, marine iguanas, pelicans, occasional flamingos, and mangroves. This is one of the few visitor sites where you can go without a guide, and camping may be permitted. Ask at the Darwin Research Station for more information.

Buses leave in the mornings from the Puerto Ayora park to the villages of Bellavista or Santa Rosa, allowing you to get off to explore some of the interior. Neither of these villages has hotels, and sometimes the return bus is full with passengers from the airport. The most convenient way of seeing the interior and ensuring that you don't get stuck is to hire a bus or truck for the day with a group of other travellers. Ask at your hotel about this.

From the village of Bellavista, seven km north of Puerto Ayora, you can turn either west on the main road, or east and go about two km to the **Lava Tubes**. These are underground tunnels over one km in length. They are on private property and the owners charge a US$2 entrance fee; bring a torch (flashlight).

A footpath north from Bellavista leads

towards **The Highlands**, including Cerro Crocker and other hills and extinct volcanos. This is a good chance to see the vegetation of the area, and to look for the vermilion flycatcher, the elusive Galápagos rail or the paint-billed crake. It is about five km from Bellavista to the crescent-shaped hill of Media Luna, and a further three km to the base of Cerro Crocker.

The twin craters called **Los Gemelos** can be visited from the trans-island road, two km beyond Santa Rosa, which is about 12 km west of Bellavista. They are sink holes rather than volcanic craters and are surrounded by *Scalesia* forest. Vermilion flycatchers are often seen, and short-eared owls are spotted on occasion. Although less than 100 metres from the road, the craters are hidden by vegetation, so ask where they are.

Near Santa Rosa, there is a **Tortoise Reserve**, where there are giant tortoises in the wild. There is a trail from the village (ask for directions) which leads through private property to park land about three km away. The trail is downhill and often muddy. It forks at the park boundary, with the right fork going up to the small hill of Cerro Chato (three more km) and the left fork going to La Caseta (two km), where camping is permitted. Bring your own water. These sites can all be visited without an official guide. Horses can be hired in Santa Rosa.

Pirate Tunnel Tours, between Pensión Gloria and Residencial Angermeyer, has recently been recommended for half-day tours to see the highlands, lava tunnels, pit craters and tortoises. The guide is Spanish-speaking and the cost is US$10 per person.

PUERTO BAQUERIZO MORENO
Places to Stay & Eat

With the recent increase in tourism, more hotels are being opened. The cheapest hotels include the *Hotel San Francisco*, which is reportedly clean and good value (US$6 a double), the *Pension Monica* and the *Residencial Delfín* (about US$2 per person) the *Northia Hotel* and the *Cabañas Don Jorge*. Nearby is the similar *Pensión Laurita*. There are some expensive hotels.

The *Laurita* has reasonably priced meals, the *Cafetería Tagu* is popular, and the good *Rositas Restaurant* serves tasty bacalao (a local fish). The *Restaurante Iris* has also been recommended.

AROUND PUERTO BAQUERIZO MORENO

Frigatebird Hill is about 1½ km east of Puerto Baquerizo Moreno and can be reached on a foot trail without a guide. There is a national park information office en route. From the hill, there is a beautiful view of a bay below and the town behind. Frigatebirds nest here and lava lizards are seen.

There are a few buses a day from Barquerizo Moreno to the farming centre of El Progreso, about eight km to the east, and lying at the base of the Cerro San Joaquín (896 metres), the highest point on San Cristóbal. From here, there are occasional buses, or hire a jeep or walk 10 km to the visitor site of **El Junco Lagoon**, a freshwater lake at about 700 metres above sea level. The road continues beyond the lagoon, though is in poor shape. It may reach the north end of the island, at the **Los Galápagos** visitors' site, where giant tortoises can be seen in the wild. Inquire in town.

About an hour north of Puerto Baquerizo Moreno by boat is the tiny, rocky **Isla Lobos**, which is the main sea-lion and blue-footed booby colony for visitors to San Cristóbal. There is a 300-metre trail, and you can see lava lizards here.

ISABELA

Most hotels are in Puerto Villamil, from which an 18-km road leads up to the tiny village of Santo Tomás.

The *Hotel Ballena Azul*, in town, is recommended for budget travellers. It charges about US$3.50 per person. Down on the beach is the *Hotel Alexander*, which is roughly the same price, and *El Rincón del Bucanero*, which is more expensive. There is also the *Tero Real*, which has been recommended – I don't know the price, but it's bottom to mid-range. The *Hotel Loja*, on the road up to the highlands, is fairly cheap, friendly and has been recommended.

The *Hotel Loja* has a good restaurant. The *Costa Azul Restaurant*, near the Tero Real, has also been recommended. There are some cheap *comedores* in the port, but you need to ask them in advance to cook a meal for you – that gives you an idea of how few visitors there are.

FLOREANA

The approximately 100 inhabitants are centered around Puerto Velasco Ibarra. There is a small hotel and restaurant, run by the famous Margaret Wittmer and her family. They also have a small gift shop and post office. You can write for reservations (Señora Wittmer, Puerto Velasco Ibarra, Santa María, Galápagos – allow a couple of months) or just show up. They are rarely full. Rates are about US$20 per person per day, including meals. There is nowhere else.

VISITOR SITES

To protect the islands, the national park authorities limit access to about 50 visitor sites, in addition to the towns and public areas. These sites are where the most interesting wildlife and geology is seen. Apart from the ones mentioned above (near Puerto Ayora and Baquerizo Moreno), most are reached by boat. Normally, landings are made in a *panga*, the small dinghy that every boat carries for shore trips. Boat captains will not take groups to places other than designated visitor sites.

On a cruise of under a week, try to visit the following islands. South Plaza has land iguana, sea-lion and swallow-tailed gull colonies, an *Opuntia* cactus forest and good snorkelling. Seymour has nesting colonies of both blue-footed boobies and magnificent frigatebirds. Caleta Tortuga Negra (Black Turtle Cove), on the north shore of Santa Cruz, has marine turtles and white-tipped sharks.

Isla Bartolomé has a volcanic cone that is easy to climb and gives one of the best views of the islands. There are also penguins, sea lions and good snorkelling on Isla Bartolomé. On San Salvador, you can walk on a lava flow by Sullivan Bay, and see marine iguanas, sea lions, fur seals, Galápagos hawks and many kinds of sea birds near Puerto Egas. Rábida has a flamingo colony, as well as a colony of irascible bachelor sea lions. You'll see other species almost everywhere. Masked and blue-footed boobies, pelicans, mockingbirds, finches, Galápagos doves, frigatebirds, lava lizards and red sally lightfoot crabs are common.

If you have a full week or more, visit some outlying islands. The red-footed booby is found on Genovesa and the small islets surrounding Santa María. The waved albatross breeds only on Española, and the flightless Galápagos cormorant is found on the western islands of Isabela and Fernandina.

ACTIVITIES
Snorkelling

If you don a mask and snorkel, a new world will unfold for you. Baby sea lions stare at you, various species of rays come slowly undulating by, and penguins dart past in a stream of bubbles. The hundreds of species of fish are spectacularly colourful, and you can watch flapping sea turtles as they circle you. This won't, of course, happen immediately you enter the water, but you have a good chance of seeing most of these things if you spend, say, half an hour a day in the water during a week of cruising the islands.

A mask and snorkel also allow you to observe more sedentary forms of marine life. Sea urchins, starfish, sea anemones, algae and crustaceans combine colourfully in an exotic underwater display. Bring a snorkel and mask. You may be able to buy a snorkel and mask in sporting goods stores in Quito or Guayaquil. Consider bringing them from home to ensure a good fit.

The water temperature is generally around 21°C from January to April, and around 19°C during the rest of the year. If you plan to spend a lot of time in the water, you may want to bring a wet-suit top with you.

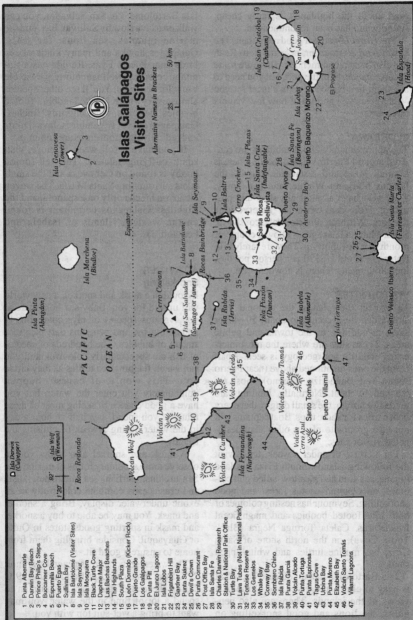

Islas Galápagos
Visitor Sites

Alternative Names in Brackets

0   25   50 km

1   Punta Albemarle
2   Darwin Bay Beach
3   Prince Philip's Steps
4   Buccaneer Cove
5   Espumilla Beach
6   Puerto Egas
7   Sullivan Bay
8   Isla Bartolomé (Visitor Sites)
9   Isla Seymour
10 Isla Mosquera
11 Black Turtle Cove
12 Daphne Major
13 Las Bachas Beaches
14 The Highlands
15 South Plaza
16 León Dormido (Kicker Rock)
17 Puerto Grande
18 Los Galápagos
19 Punta Pitt
20 El Junco Lagoon
21 Isla Lobos
22 Frigatebird Hill
23 Gardner Bay
24 Punta Suárez
25 Devil's Crown
26 Punta Cormorant
27 Post Office Bay
28 Isla Santa Fe
29 Charles Darwin Research
    Station & National Park Office
30 Turtle Bay
31 Lava Tubes (Not in National Park)
32 Tortoise Reserve
33 Los Gemelos
34 Whale Bay
35 Conway Bay
36 Sombrero Chino
37 Isla Rábida
38 Punta Garciá
39 Volcán Alcedo
40 Punta Tortuga
41 Punta Espinosa
42 Tagus Cove
43 Punta Moreno
44 Urbina Bay
45 Elizabeth Bay
46 Volcán Santo Tomás
47 Villamil Lagoons

Islas Galápagos:
- Isla Darwin (Culpepper)
- Isla Wolf (Wenman)
- Isla Pinta (Abingdon)
- Isla Marchena (Bindloe)
- Isla Genovesa (Tower)
- Isla San Salvador (Santiago or James)
- Isla Bartolomé
- Rocas Bainbridge
- Isla Seymour
- Isla Baltra
- Cerro Crocker
- Islas Plazas
- Isla Santa Cruz (Indefatigable)
- Isla Santa Fe (Barrington)
- Isla San Cristóbal (Chatham)
- Cerro San Joaquín
- Isla Lobos
- Isla Española (Hood)
- Isla Santa María (Floreana or Charles)
- Isla Rábida (Jervis)
- Isla Pinzón (Duncan)
- Isla Fernandina (Narborough)
- Isla Isabela (Albemarle)
- Isla Tortuga
- Volcán Wolf
- Volcán Darwin
- Volcán la Cumbre
- Volcán Alcedo
- Volcán Santo Tomás
- Volcán Cerro Azul
- Roca Redonda

PACIFIC OCEAN

Equator

Puerto Ayora
Santa Rosa
Bellavista
Academy Bay
Puerto Baquerizo Moreno
El Progreso
Puerto Velasco Ibarra
Santo Tomás
Puerto Villamil

Scuba Diving

You can go scuba diving in the Galápagos, but you must have all your own equipment and book a tour in advance, usually through a diving company. Tanks and compressed air are supplied on boats which run dive tours.

TOURS

There are three kinds of tours: day trips, returning to the same hotel each night, hotel-based trips, where you stay on different islands, and boat-based trips, with nights spent aboard. These can be arranged in advance from home, or in Quito and Guayaquil, or can be arranged when you get to the islands.

Day Trips

Most are based in Puerto Ayora, and a few in Puerto Baquerizo Moreno. Several hours are spent sailing to the visitor site(s), the island is visited during the middle of the day, and you'll probably be part of a large group. Only a few central islands are close enough to either Santa Cruz or San Cristóbal to be visited on day trips.

Because of the time spent going back and forth and because you don't visit the islands early or late in the day, I don't recommend day tours. The cheapest boats may be slow and overcrowded. The island visits may be too brief, the guides poorly informed and the crew lacking an adequate conservationist attitude.

Day-trip operators in Puerto Ayora charge around US$40 per person per day. Talk to other travellers about how good the guide and boat are, or ask at CETUR.

Better and more expensive day trips, using fast boats with knowledgeable guides and staying in good hotels, can be arranged at the mainland travel agencies. Prices range from US$600 to US$1000 per week, including guided trips, hotel and meals, but not airfare and park fee.

Hotel-Based Trips

These tours go from island to island and you sleep in hotels on three or four different islands (Santa Cruz, San Cristóbal, Floreana, Isabela). Tours typically last a week and cost US$600 to US$1000 per person, plus airfare and park fee. Few companies offer this kind of tour, and they are harder to arrange in Puerto Ayora.

Try Coltur (☎ 545 777), Paéz 370 (Box 2771) in Quito, Isbella (☎ 390 658, 396 393), Leonidas Plaza Dañin 802 (near Guayaquil Airport), or Playa de Oro (☎ 543 221), 6 de Diciembre 2396 and La Niña, 5th floor, Quito.

Boat-Based Trips

Most visitors (particularly non-Ecuadorians) go on boat tours, and sleep aboard overnight. Tours from four to eight days are the most common. I don't think you can do the Galápagos justice on a tour lasting less than five days, and a full week is preferable. If you want to visit the outlying islands of Isabela and Fernandina, a two-week cruise is recommended. On the first day of a pre-arranged tour, you arrive from the mainland by air at about lunchtime, and so this is only half a day in the Galápagos; on the last day, you have to be in the airport in the morning. Thus a five-day tour gives only three full days in the islands.

Boats used for tours range from small yachts to large cruise ships. The most common type of boat is the motor sailer which carries six to 12 passengers. Most people arrive in the islands with a pre-arranged tour; some people come hoping to hook up with a tour when they get there.

Arranging Tours – in the Galápagos

It is cheaper to arrange a tour for yourself in Puerto Ayora than to pay for a pre-arranged tour from the mainland. The cheapest boats are usually available in the Galápagos. The better boats are almost always full with pre-arranged tours bought on the mainland. Arranging a tour can take several days or more, though you may get lucky and find a boat leaving the next day. This is not an option, therefore, for people with a limited amount of time, nor is it for people wanting a comfortable boat.

The best place to organise an independent tour is Puerto Ayora. It is possible to do this in Puerto Baquerizo Moreno, but there are fewer boats available. Avoid the high season if possible – most boats have pre-arranged charters then.

If you are alone or with a friend, find some more people, as even the smallest boats take four passengers. Getting a group together and finding a boat involves checking the hotels and restaurants for other travellers and asking around for boats. If they have no business lined up, captains will be looking for passengers. Your hotel manager can often introduce you to someone. After all, almost everyone knows everybody else, so word will quickly get around.

The cheapest and most basic boats are available for about US$50 per day per person, and this should include everything. The cheaper the boat, the more rice and fish you can expect to eat, and the more crowded the accommodation.

Boats won't sail unless all passenger berths are taken – empty spots add to group space and comfort, but they must be paid for. Bargaining over the price is acceptable and sometimes necessary.

The most important thing is to find a boat whose crew you get along with and which has a good and enthusiastic naturalist guide who will be able to point out and explain the wildlife and other items of interest. It is worth paying a little more for a good guide. The cheapest boats may have Spanish-speaking 'aux-

ECUADOR

iliary guides' whose function is to fulfil the legal obligation that every boat has a certified guide aboard. Some of these auxiliary guides know very little about the wildlife and simply act as rangers, making sure that groups stay together on the trails and don't molest the wildlife. (You cannot land without a guide and you must always walk around in more or less of a group.)

Owners, captains, guides, cooks, etc change frequently and, in addition, many boats make changes and improvements from year to year. Generally speaking, a boat is only as good as its crew. You should be able to meet the naturalist guide and captain and inspect the boat before you leave, and you should have an itinerary agreed upon with the boat owner or captain. You can deal with a crew member or boat representative during your search, but don't hand over any money until you have an agreed itinerary, and then pay only the captain.

It is recommended that you have the itinerary in writing to avoid disagreements between you and other passengers and the crew during the cruise. Even with a written agreement, the itinerary may sometimes be changed, but at least it does give you some measure of bargaining power. The South American Explorers Club in Quito has a Galápagos information packet, which is updated every year and includes a detailed contract, in Spanish/English, which is suitable.

Conditions can be cramped and primitive. Washing facilities vary from a bucket of sea water on the very cheapest boats to freshwater deck hoses or showers on the better boats. If you don't want to stay salty for a week, ask about washing facilities. You should also inquire about drinking water. I'd recommend treating the water on most of the cheaper boats or, alternatively, bringing your own large containers of fresh water. Bottled drinks are carried but cost extra – agree on the price before you leave port, and make sure that enough beer and coke is loaded aboard if you don't want to run out of your favourite refreshments.

Because a boat is only as good as the crew running it, it is difficult to make foolproof recommendations. However, two or more travellers have sent me recommendations for the following boats, though there are many others which are also good: *Cormorant, Española, Golondrina, Elizabeth II* and *San Juan*.

I have also received single recommendations for *Daphne, Aida Maria, Angelito* and *San Antonio*. The *Fénix* has received several good reports and a couple of bad ones. The *Flamingo, Estrella del Mar* and *Lobo del Mar* have received good and bad reports. No boats received consistently poor reports.

This is just a small selection. If you have a particularly good or bad experience with a boat, please write.

Arranging Tours – in advance

If you don't have the time or patience, then you can arrange tours from your home country (expensive but efficient) or from Quito or Guayaquil (cheaper but you sometimes have to wait several days or weeks during the high season).

You might get a substantial discount by checking various agencies and seeing if they have any spaces to fill on departures leaving in the next day or two. This applies both to the cheaper and some of the more expensive tours. Particularly out of the high season, agencies may let you travel cheaply at the last minute rather than leave berths unfilled. This depends on luck and your skill at bargaining.

The cheapest prearranged tours that I know of are sold by César Gavela, at the Gran Casino Hotel in Quito. Departures are on limited dates and getting something suitable is largely a matter of luck – don't expect any luxury. The boats used are similar to those run by Galasam.

A little more expensive and with more frequent departure dates are the economy tours run by Galasam (Economic Galápagos Tours) in Quito (☎ 550 094), at Pinto 523, and in Guayaquil (☎ 306 289), at 9 de Octubre 424. Galasam have three levels of tours: economy, tourist and luxury.

Seven-day economy tours are aboard small boats with six to 12 bunks in double, triple and quadruple cabins. All bedding is provided and the accommodation is clean but spartan, with little privacy. Plenty of simple but fresh food and juice is served at all meals and an auxiliary guide accompanies the boat (few guides on the economy tours speak English).

There are toilets, and fresh water is available for washing of faces and drinking. Bathing facilities may be buckets of sea water, though showers are available on some boats. There are pre-set itineraries, which visit most of the central islands and give enough time to see the wildlife.

I have received many letters criticising both the Gran Casino trips and the economy-class Galasam tours. Things go wrong occasionally, and when they do, a refund is extremely difficult to obtain. Problems have included last-minute changes of boat, poor crew, lack of bottled drinks, not sticking to the agreed itinerary, mechanical breakdowns and overbooking. Generally speaking, the cheaper the tour the less comfortable the boat and the less knowledgeable the guide. On the other hand, for every letter I get saying a tour was poor, I get another letter saying that they had a great trip which was good value.

One-week (eight-day) economy tours cost about US$500 per person. There are weekly departures. Shorter and cheaper tours are available – four days for US$300 and five days for US$350. The US$80 park fee, airfare and bottled drinks are not included.

If you add up the cost of the cheapest one-week tour plus airfare and park fees, you get almost no change out of US$1000. Sorry, budget travellers, that's the way it is. My feeling is that if you're going to spend that much, the Galápagos are probably an important destination for you and you want to get as much out of it as possible. The economy-class boats are usually OK, but if something is going to go wrong, it's more likely to happen on the cheaper boats. If this is all you can afford and you really want to see the Galápagos, go! It'll probably be the adventure of a lifetime. But you might consider spending an extra few hundred dollars and go on a more comfortable, reliable boat and get a decent guide (though more expensive boats have their problems too).

For about US$800 for eight days, you can take a tourist-class tour with Galasam or several other companies – the usual extra costs apply. Other companies

with tours at about this price are Turgal (☎ 524 878, 553 658), at Robles 653, Quito, Soleil Turismo (☎ 524 805, 553 658), at Pinto 427, Quito, and Etnotur (☎ 230 552, 564 565), at Cordero 1313, Quito. Etnotur's cheapest cruises have been criticised.

More luxurious tours are also available with other agencies which advertise in Quito and Guayaquil. These typically cost US$1000 or more per person per week, plus the usual extras. The most expensive boats are reasonably comfortable, with superb food and excellent crews.

Guyana, Suriname & French Guiana

On the north coast of South America, the Guianas were leftovers in the age of European expansionism. British, Dutch and French colonisation bequeathed the area a complex heritage and a curious political geography comprising the independent republics of Guyana and Suriname and the colony of French Guiana (Guyane Français, officially a *département* of metropolitan France). Still, the peoples of the humid, densely forested region have much in common, and because Europeans never dominated the interior, some of the world's best-preserved tropical forests and other natural areas are here.

Given these similarities, this chapter details the region's many shared features, such as history and geography, in the Guyana section, while those entries on Suriname and French Guiana emphasise features which differ significantly from Guyana. Other entries, such as What to Bring, appear in the Guyana section only.

Guyana

FACTS ABOUT THE COUNTRY
History

In cultural terms, the Guianas are an outlier of the 'Euro-African rimland', a term applied to the Caribbean islands and continental tropical lowlands where, after virtual extinction of indigenous peoples, mostly through introduced diseases, there developed plantation economies which relied on coerced labour – first slaves and later indentured servants. This contrasts with the uplands of the 'Euro-Indian mainland', such as Mexico, where native peoples eventually recovered from demographic disaster.

The aboriginal inhabitants of the Guyanese coast were Carib Indians who, having driven the more peaceful Arawak north and westward into the Antilles, deterred early European settlement. Covered by mangroves, the thinly populated, muddy coastline failed to attract Spaniards in search of gold or *encomiendas*, though they made occasional slave raids. Interior tropical forest peoples like the Macushi and Tirió, speaking Carib-related languages, also survived in relative isolation.

Spaniards first saw the coast in 1499. Several 16th-century explorers, including Sir Walter Raleigh, placed the mythical city of El Dorado in the region, but Spain's European rivals displayed no sustained interest until the mid-17th century. These rivalries created a multiplicity of colonies with shifting territorial and commercial arrangements.

The Netherlands made the first move, placing a settlement on the lower Essequibo

Guyana, Suriname & French Guiana

| 0 | 125 | 250 km |
| 0 | 75 | 150 miles |

River in 1615. After forming the Dutch West India Company in 1621, they traded with Indian peoples of the interior, but also established riverside plantations of sugar, cocoa and other tropical commodities. Sugar quickly became the key product, and to expand their plantations, the Dutch imported West African slaves to construct dykes and polders. From the mid-18th century, escaped slaves formed Maroon (Bush Negro) settlements in the interior, and retained many African customs.

While the coast remained under Dutch control, England established sugar and tobacco plantations on the west bank of the Suriname River around 1650, followed by the founding of what is now Paramaribo. Within two decades, however, the Dutch took possession and, after a brief conflict, accepted Suriname in exchange for New Amsterdam (present-day New York). Continuing English presence among the planter class, and increasing French activity, engendered further conflicts in which parts of the region changed hands many times.

After dissolution of the West India Company in 1796, Britain became the dominant power, though Suriname remained under Dutch control. France retained a precarious hold on Cayenne, whose sugar production lagged far behind its Caribbean islands.

The abolition of slavery led to labour shortages in the early 19th century, and many plantations closed or consolidated. The British company Bookers resurrected the industry by importing indentured labour from India; from 1846 to 1917, nearly 250,000 labourers entered Guyana, drastically transforming its demographic balance and laying the basis for today's fractious racial politics. Smaller numbers of East Indians entered Suriname, while France's radically different immigration policies made Cayenne one of the world's most notorious penal colonies. All three, however, exploited cheap labour.

In the 20th century, each has developed a more distinctive identity. In reaction to its colonial heritage, Guyana nationalised its sugar industry and diversified its agricultural base through production of wet rice for export. Bauxite, still under state control but with resurgent foreign influence, is the major export commodity.

Colonial rule left an unfortunate legacy of

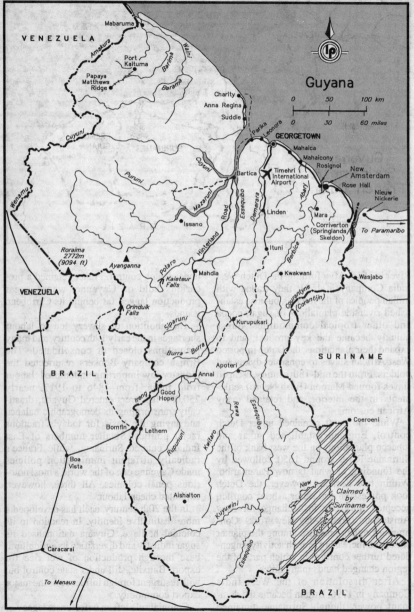

VENEZUELA

Mabaruma

Port Kaituma

Papaya Matthews Ridge

Amakura

Waini

Barima

Barama

Charity
Anna Regina
Suddie

Parika
Leonora

GEORGETOWN

Mahaica
Mahaicony
Rosignol

New Amsterdam
Rose Hall

Nieuw Nickerie

Cuyuni

Puruni

Cuyuni

Mazaruni

Bartica

Timehri International Airport

Linden

Mara

Corriverton
(Springlands
Skeldon)

To Paramaribo

Issano

Hinterland Road

Essequibo

Demerara

Ituni

Berbice

Kwakwani

Wasjabo

Roraima
2772m
(9094 ft)

Ayanganna

Potaro

Kaieteur Falls

Mahdia

Corantyne
(Corantijn)

VENEZUELA

Wenamu

Orinduik Falls

Siparuni

Kurupukari

SURINAME

Burra - Burra

Apoteri

BRAZIL

Annai

Ireng

Good Hope

Essequibo

Rewa

Kwitaro

Coeroeni

Bomfin

Lethem

Rupununi

New River

Claimed by Suriname

Boa Vista

Oronoque

Aishalton

Kuyuwini

Essequibo

Caracarai

To Manaus

BRAZIL

Guyana

0   50   100 km

0   30   60 miles

border disputes. Neighbouring Venezuela claims 130,000 sq km of Guyanese territory west of the Essequibo, while Suriname claims another 13,000 km along its border with Guyana and Brazil. Fortunately, Venezuela appears content to press its claims diplomatically, and Suriname has been too preoccupied with its own civil war to pursue any other territorial goals.

Geography
Beyond the arc of the Antilles which separates the Caribbean from the open Atlantic, Guyana occupies some 215,000 sq km (83,000 sq miles; Guyana uses the imperial system of measurement) of coastal plains and interior uplands, of tropical rainforest and savanna. Roughly the size of the UK or the US state of Idaho, the country takes its name from an Amerindian word meaning 'land of many waters', after the many north-flowing rivers.

Its most prominent geological feature is the Guiana Shield, an extensive, weathered crystalline upland north of the Rio Solimões, the main channel of the Amazon. Once part of the larger Brazilian Shield to the south, it became separated in Tertiary times when the rising Andes reversed the course of west-flowing rivers and created the Amazon Basin. Itself unaffected by tectonic uplift, the Shield falls away in steps from 2772 metre (9094 foot) Mount Roraima, on the Brazilian border, to the coast.

Dense tropical rainforest covers most of the interior, though south-western Guyana features an extensive savanna, between the Rupununi River and the Brazilian border. Most people live within 25 miles (40 km) of the coast, whose population density of 41 per sq mile (115 per sq km) is nearly 40 times that of the country as a whole. The Guianas generally lack sandy beaches, but the marshy coastal zone has proven suitable for agriculture when transformed into polders.

Climate
The equatorial climate features high temperatures with little seasonal variation, and heavy rainfall, though constant breezes moderate the heat. Guyana has two distinct rainy seasons: from April to mid-August and from mid-November to late January. Precipitation declines toward the interior, where temperatures are more variable.

Government
Since 1966, Guyana has been an independent republic within the British Commonwealth. Its 1980 constitution establishes an executive branch with an elected president (head of state) and a prime minister, appointed by the president; the 65-member National Assembly is also elected, mostly by proportional representation. The High Court is the supreme judicial authority.

The main political parties are the People's National Congress (PNC) and the Marxist-oriented People's Progressive Party (PPP). Politics are racially polarised between the East Indian majority (supporting the PPP) and the Afro-Guyanese minority (supporting the PNC) which occupied most of the important posts after independence and which dominates the Guyanese Defence Force and the police. In October 1992, in an election marred by violence, PPP candidate Cheddi Jagan easily defeated the re-election bid of the PNC's President Desmond Hoyte.

Economy
Guyana's economy relies on exports of primary commodities, especially bauxite, but also sugar, rice, timber and shrimp.

Multinational corporations, including US-based Reynolds Metals and Canada's Alcan, are major investors in the mineral sector. Petroleum exploration licences have been granted for the offshore Guyana Basin and the Rupununi savanna's Takutu Basin, but commercial exploitation has not yet commenced. Foreign investors have recently returned to the agricultural sector, whose Demerara sugar has a global reputation. Guysuco, the state-controlled sugar enterprise, employs more Guyanese than any other industry.

The domestic economy reflects ethnic divisions. East Indians and their families control most small business, while the Afro-Guyanese dominate the government sector. In recent years, the government has encouraged foreign investment, but the PPP has expressed scepticism about multinationals, and may exercise more control.

Population & People

Guyana's population is about 800,000, but emigration may have reduced that number by 10% or more. More than half are ethnically Indian (ie from the Indian subcontinent). About 43% are Afro-Guyanese; another 2% are of Chinese and European heritage. Amerindians, in scattered interior settlements, comprise about 4% of the population; the main groups are Arawak, Carib, Wapisiana and Warao. The Caribs comprise several subgroups, including Akawaio, Macushi, Patamona and Waiwai.

Public education is free of charge to university level, but physical facilities have deteriorated, books and supplies are limited, and qualified teachers are few. The literacy rate is about 90%, but many educated Guyanese live overseas, mostly in London or New York.

Arts & Culture

The visual arts, especially painting and sculpture, are very highly developed; look for special exhibitions at the Georgetown Museum.

Probably the best-known work of literature by a Guyanese is E R Braithwaite's novel *To Sir With Love*, which is actually set in London and became a popular film. British-based Guyanese actor Norman Beaton is a well-known stage, film and television presence.

In racially polarised Guyana, sport is one of few unifying factors, and sport mainly means cricket, though football and boxing are also popular and basketball is growing rapidly.

Religion

Most Afro-Guyanese are Christian, usually Anglican, but a handful are Black Muslim. The East Indian population is mostly Hindu, with a sizeable Muslim minority, but Hindu-Muslim friction is uncommon here.

Language

English is the official national language, but most Guyanese speak a creole which can challenge the skills of native English speakers from other regions. Some East Indians speak Hindi, while some Muslims speak Urdu. Amerindian languages include Arawak, Akawaio, Carib, Macushi, Patamona, Wapishana, Waiwai and Warao. Along the Brazilian border, many Guyanese are bilingual in Portuguese.

FACTS FOR THE VISITOR

Visas & Embassies

Guyana's traditional fussiness about foreign visitors, especially journalists and photographers, appears to have relaxed, though most travellers from outside the Commonwealth Caribbean still need visas. Guyana's embassy in the USA requires a visa application in triplicate, with three passport photos, and recommends beginning the process at least six weeks before departure. In practice, officials at Guyana's international airport will issue visas on the spot, but airlines often refuse to let passengers without visas board a plane to Guyana.

Guyanese Embassies Guyana's overseas diplomatic representation is limited, but the following are most likely to be useful to visitors:

Canada
  151 Slater St, Suite 309, Ottawa (☎ 235-7249)
  505 Consumers Rd, Suite 900, Willowdale, Toronto (☎ 494-6040)
Germany
  Av des Arts 21-22, Brussels (☎ 230-6065)
UK
  3 Palace Court, Bayswater Rd, London (☎ 229-7684)
USA
  866 United Nations Plaza, New York, NY (☎ 527-3215)
  2490 Tracy Place, Washington DC (☎ (202) 265-6900)

Documents

Passports are obligatory and nearly all visitors require visas. Carry an international yellow fever vaccination certificate, and keep other immunisations up to date as well.

Money

The currency is the Guyanese dollar (G$). As of late 1992, the official exchange rate of about US$1 to G$126 had been stable for some time. There are no coins, only notes, in denominations of G$5, G$20, G$100, G$500 and G$1000.

A$1   = G$85
DM1   = G$74
Ff1   = G$21
UK£1 = G$187
US$1 = G$126

Recent reforms have eliminated the black market, and money is relatively easy to change in Georgetown *cambios* (exchange houses); some hotels accept US dollars at a fair rate. Travellers' cheques are much safer than cash, and exchange rates are nearly equal. Banks are more bureaucratic and are generally open only in the mornings, while cambios keep long weekday hours. Credit cards are little used, except at some of Georgetown's better hotels and restaurants.

On the jetty at Springlands, street changers offer Surinamese *guilders* for US cash, at very good rates. This is reasonably safe, but do exercise caution.

When to Go & What to Bring

The best time to visit Guyana may be at the end of either rainy season, in late January or late August, when the discharge of water over Kaieteur Falls is greatest. Some locals recommend mid-October to mid-May.

The warm, humid climate encourages informal dress – coats and ties are exceptional, even among businessmen and state officials. Light cottons are most comfortable, though a sweater can be useful in the evenings or at higher elevations in the interior. Downpours can occur even in the 'dry' seasons, so an umbrella is worthwhile.

Tourist Offices

The government has no official tourist representative overseas, and only in Georgetown does it maintain a formal tourist office.

The private Tourism Association of Guyana (☎ 70267), PO Box 101147, Georgetown, is more active in promoting the country, and publishes *Guyana Tourist Guide*, a useful brochure. Try its US and UK contacts for the most current information.

UK
    FT Caribbean, 3A Sloane Avenue, London SW3 3JD (☎ (071) 581-8872)
USA
    Ms Mary Lou Schloss, Unique Destinations, 14 Alewives Rd, Norwalk, Connecticut (☎ (203) 838-6864)

Business Hours & Holidays

There are numerous national holidays, on which government offices and businesses are closed.

1 January
    New Year's Day
Early January (date varies)
    Youman Nabi
23 February
    Republic Day (Slave Rebellion of 1763)
Early March (date varies)
    Phagwah (Hindu New Year)
March/April (dates vary)
    Good Friday/Easter
1 May
    Labour Day
6 July
    Caricom Day
First Monday in August
    Freedom Day (Emancipation)
November (date varies)
    Divali
25 & 26 December
    Christmas Day/Boxing Day

Festivals

Republic Day celebrations in February are the most important national cultural event of the year, though Hindu and Muslim religious festivals are important to those communities.

Post & Telecommunications

Postal services are generally unreliable; use registered mail for essential correspondence.

Based in the US Virgin Islands, Atlantic Tele-Network Company operates the new Guyana Telecommunications Corporation, a joint venture with the government, and has promised major improvements in local and international telephone services.

At blue public telephones, scattered around Georgetown, you can make reverse charge overseas calls, but credit card calls have been suspended because of frequent fraud. For a USA Direct (AT&T) line, dial 165; to Canada, dial 161; and to the UK, dial 169. Hotels and restaurants generally allow use of their phones for local calls for a very small charge.

Time

Guyanese time is four hours behind GMT and one hour behind Suriname.

Weights & Measures

The metric system is official but is almost totally ignored in favour of imperial measures. This section gives some imperial measures as well as metrics; there is a conversion table at the back of the book.

Books & Maps

Covering all the Guianas, David Lowenthal's *West Indian Societies* (Oxford, 1972) is deep in history and geography. V S Naipaul's *The Middle Passage* (Vintage Books, New York, 1981) is a more literary and philosopical travelogue, originally published in 1962 but still a valuable introduction to the region. British author Evelyn Waugh described a rugged trip through the interior in *Ninety-Two Days* (out of print).

V S Naipaul's late brother Shiva wrote movingly of the Jonestown massacre at the People's Temple colony in *Journey to Nowhere: a New World Tragedy* (Penguin, New York, 1982). In the UK, its title was *Black and White*.

Media

Georgetown has two daily newspapers, *Stabroek News* and the *Guyana Chronicle*, plus the influential weekly *Catholic Standard*. Local television programming is limited, but international cable services are widely available.

Health

Adequate medical care is available in Georgetown, at least at private hospitals, but elsewhere, facilities are few and malaria is endemic – take medication. Typhoid inoculation is recommended, and dengue fever is also a danger. A yellow fever vaccination certificate is required for travellers arriving from infected areas. Drinking water is suspect – use only boiled water, even in Georgetown.

In late 1992, a cholera outbreak in the North-West District near the Venezuelan border caused several deaths and later spread to Georgetown. Only areas with very unsanitary conditions appear to have been affected, but take precautions.

Dangers & Annoyances

Guyana in general, and Georgetown in particular, are notorious for street crime and physical violence. Avoid potentially hazardous situations; if walking alone, be aware of others on the street, especially in front of and behind you. For further pointers, see the Georgetown entry.

Experienced travellers generally do not arrive at Georgetown's Timehri Airport at night, to avoid drunken cab drivers and 'choke and rob' assaults along the highway. It is better to fly into Port of Spain (Trinidad) or to Curaçao (Netherlands Antilles), spend the night there and continue to Georgetown the next morning.

Baggage security is another concern, though the situation has improved. All baggage should be locked and, preferably, enclosed in a duffel or other secure covering. Backpacks are particularly vulnerable.

Accommodation

Guyanese hotels range from very basic to

real luxury (you'll find up-market accommodation in Georgetown and in the growing number of rainforest lodges). Even modest hotels have firm, comfortable beds, ceiling fans, and often air-conditioning. Accommodation is available for about US$10 to US$12 a single in Georgetown, about half that elsewhere.

Food & Drink

Guyanese food is distinctive, especially seafood and creole dishes like pepperpot, a spicy stew. The East Indian element has added dishes like curry and *roti* to the everyday diet. Chinese food is also common.

Local rum is a favourite drink, as is Banks beer, but no visitor should fail to try fruit punch at Georgetown's better restaurants.

Entertainment

The Guyanese party at Georgetown discos until the early hours; a few venues have live reggae. Before visiting a place, inquire as to its suitability for foreigners.

Things to Buy

Gold and silver jewellery are popular acquisitions, but wood carvings and paintings are more distinctive and appealing. Amerindian pottery is worth a look.

GETTING THERE & AWAY
Air

Most travellers arrive from North America or the Caribbean, less frequently from neighbouring Venezuela (via Trinidad) and Suriname.

To/From Europe There are no direct flights from Europe. The most direct route is from the UK to Barbados, from where there are several flights weekly to Georgetown. TAP (Air Portugal) has inexpensive flights from mainland Europe to Trinidad & Tobago.

To/From North America BWIA International has the most extensive schedule, with direct flights daily from New York and Miami. ALM and Guyana Airways also have flights from Atlanta, Miami and

Toronto. Most stop over in Trinidad. Both ALM and BWIA include overnight hotel accommodation at Trinidad or Curaçao on flights from Miami.

To/From Brazil Taba Airways has flights from Manaus and Boa Vista to Georgetown.

To/From Suriname SLM (Surinam Airways) flies between Georgetown and Paramaribo two or three times weekly.

To/From Venezuela It is currently necessary to fly to Trinidad for connections to Venezuela.

Overland

The land border with Venezuela is closed.

To/From Brazil A road goes from Lethem, in Guyana's south-western Rupununi savanna, to Bomfim (Brazil), with connections to the larger Brazilian city of Boa Vista. The road from Georgetown to Lethem may be impassable.

To/From Suriname A rickety passenger ferry from Corriverton (Springlands) crosses the Courantyne River to the Surinamese border town of Nieuw Nickerie.

Leaving Guyana

Airport Tax Travellers from Timehri International Airport pay an exit tax of US$8.

GETTING AROUND
Air

Guyana Airways has scheduled flights to Lethem and a few other interior destinations, but there are also charter services.

Bus

Minibuses link Georgetown with secondary towns like Parika, Linden, New Amsterdam, and Corriverton. These have no fixed schedules, and leave when full from stops in or near Stabroek Market.

Taxi

In Georgetown, taxis are imperative for

foreign travellers, especially at night. Elsewhere, taxis are advisable at night.

Car & Motorbike
Guyana requires foreign visitors to carry the International Driving Permit. Traffic drives on the left. Paved two-lane roads connect Georgetown with Corriverton, on the border with Suriname, and Linden, on the upper Demerara River, but other roads are few and generally poor.

Bicycle
Guyana's modest road network also limits cycling, but truly dedicated mountain bikers might be able to follow the road to Lethem and Bomfim (Brazil). Beware of bandits on this road.

Hitching
Hitching is not advisable because of security problems.

Boat
Ferries cross most major rivers. There is regular service on the Essequibo between Charity and Bartica, stopping at Parika (reached by paved highway from Georgetown). More frequent, but relatively expensive, speedboats ('river taxis') carry passengers from Parika to Bartica.

Ferry docks are known as *stellings*, a term adapted from Dutch.

Tours
Recently, Guyanese companies have begun to promote 'adventure tourism' in rainforest and riverside lodges, which are beyond the means of most budget travellers. For details, contact the Tourism Association of Guyana, PO Box 101147, Georgetown.

GEORGETOWN
Originally designed by the Dutch on a regular grid pattern, Georgetown (population 200,000), is Guyana's capital and only large city. Georgetown's 19th-century colonial architecture distinguishes the central city, while well-maintained botanical and zoological gardens contrast with the dilapidation elsewhere.

Orientation
Low-lying Georgetown sits on the east bank of the Demerara River, where it empties into the Atlantic. A long sea wall prevents flooding, while the Dutch canal system drains the town. Tree-lined pedestrian paths pass between the traffic lanes of the town's broad avenues, and there are many open spaces, but the heavily polluted canals often carry unpleasant smells.

Street numbering is discontinuous in Georgetown's various boroughs, so that the same number may appear twice on the same street, say in Cummingsburg and Lacytown. Some streets change names west of Main St and Avenue of the Republic.

Information
Tourist Offices The Ministry of Trade, Tourism & Industry (☎ 63182), upstairs on the corner of Main and Urquhart streets, is open on weekdays from 8 am to 4.30 pm. The private Tourism Association of Guyana (☎ 70267), PO Box 101147, Georgetown, which publishes a useful *Guyana Tourist Guide*, has no permanent office as yet, but check the Wieting & Richter Travel Agency, on Church St.

Money Cambios offer better rates and less red tape than banks; a reliable one is the Trust Company (Guyana) Ltd, upstairs at Joe Chin's Travel Agency, 69 Main St. Another is Globe Trust and Investment, at 92 Middle St next to Rima Guest House.

Post & Telecommunications The GPO is on North Rd, just west of Avenue of the Republic. Guyana Telephone & Telegraph, in the Bank of Guyana Building (entrance on North St, near Avenue of the Republic), is open daily from 7 am to 10 pm.

Visa Extensions The Immigration Office (☎ 51744, 63011) is on Camp Rd, just north of Cowan St. It's open on weekdays from 8 am to 11.30 am and 1 to 3 pm.

Foreign Embassies Most foreign legations are in central Georgetown. The Surinamese Consulate provides same-day visa service but is only open on Monday, Wednesday and Friday from 8 to 11 am, and may charge up to US$20 for the privilege.

Brazil
    308-309 Church St (☎ 57970)
Canada
    High & Young streets (☎ 72081)
France
    Sherriff St & East Coast Highway
Suriname
    304 Church St (☎ 67844)
UK
    44 Main St (☎ 65881)
USA
    100 Young St (☎ 54900)
Venezuela
    Thomas St, between Murray and Church streets
    (☎ 61543)

Cultural Centres The National Cultural Centre (☎ 63845), on Mandela Avenue in D'Urban Park, offers frequent plays and concerts.

Travel Agencies For excursions to the interior, contact Malcolm and Margaret Chan-A-Sue, at Torong Guyana (☎ 65298), 56 Coralita Avenue, Bel Air Park East. While many of their trips are not cheap, they will advise budget travellers on alternatives, and their service on flights to Kaieteur Falls and Orinduik Falls (US$160) is excellent.

Wonderland Tours (☎ 72011), in the Hotel Tower, also runs trips to Kaieteur and Orinduik (US$155), Santa Mission (US$50), Essequibo and Mazaruni (US$100), and Georgetown (US$25). Eco-Tours (☎ 59430), in the Woodbine Hotel on New Market St, has similar offerings. Tropical Adventures, in the Forte Crest Hotel (☎ 52853), PO Box 101147, near the seafront, runs seven to 14-day tours starting at US$750.

Bookshops For a good selection of paperback novels, mostly by Caribbean writers, visit the National Book Store, on Church St.

Emergency Georgetown Public Hospital (☎ 56900), on New Market St, has inadequate and rundown facilities; travellers may prefer private clinics and hospitals like St Joseph's Mercy Hospital (☎ 72070), 130-132 Parade St (behind the US Embassy).

Dangers & Annoyances Street crime, often violent, is common in Georgetown. The city is vulnerable to frequent blackouts, and street lighting is poor even at the best of times. Avoid walking anywhere after dark, be alert even in daylight, and *never* enter the Tiger Bay area (north of Church St and west of Main St) under any circumstances. Hotels, restaurants and other businesses gladly ring cabs for visitors. It may seem extreme to hail a taxi to go a block or two, but defer to the judgment of local people.

Georgetown has many beggars, plus persuasive street people who follow foreign tourists in hopes of extracting meal money (or more). Most are harmless, but it can be tiresome.

Things to See
Georgetown has many architecturally distinguished buildings, even if poor maintenance has tarnished some. Most are on or near Main St and, especially, Avenue of the Republic, just east of the Demarara River.

On an oval at Church and Carmichael streets is the Gothic-style **St George's Cathedral**. Built mostly with indigenous materials, most notably the Guyanese hardwood 'greenheart', it's the world's tallest wooden cathedral. The nearby **Non-Aligned Monument**, at Company Path Garden, is a reminder of the outspoken Third World activism of the late President Forbes Burnham. It contains busts of former presidents Nasser of Egypt, Nkrumah of Ghana and Tito of Yugoslavia, and Prime Minister Nehru of India.

Farther south on Avenue of the Republic is the distinctive Gothic **Town Hall** (1889), and just beyond are the **Victoria Law Courts** (1887). At its south end is the well-kept **Parliament Building** (1833), while to its west is the landmark **Stabroek Market**, on Water St, a striking cast-iron building with

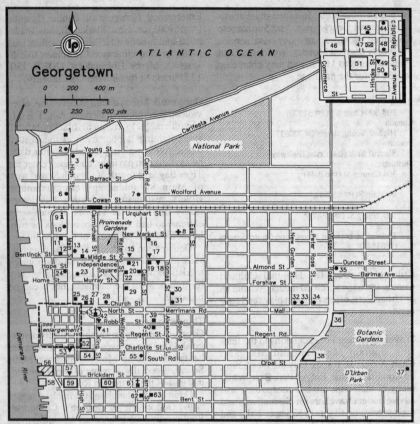

Georgetown

an impressive clocktower. Don't go in unless accompanied by Guyanese friends.

At the north end of the Avenue, at Church St, is the **National Library**. Three blocks farther north, at Main and New Market streets, is the 1852 **State House**, currently being refurbished as the presidential residence. The fenced **Promenade Gardens**, at Middle and Carmichael streets, are a welcome relief from midday heat but are dark and dangerous at night.

Near the Forte Crest Hotel, the conical **Umana Yana** is an Amerindian *benab* (communal dwelling) erected by the Wai Wai people of the interior for the 1972 Non-Aligned Foreign Ministers' Conference. It has recently deteriorated but is still a prominent landmark. Beyond the Forte Crest is Georgetown's **Seawall**, a popular site for late-afternoon walks.

Museum of Guyana Opposite the GPO, on North St, this curious institution seems frozen in time. Permanent exhibits still refer to 'the colony', and one even describes Blacks as the only race vigorous enough to be 'pork-knockers' (small-scale Guyanese miners). It's superannuated rather than dilap-

■ PLACES TO STAY	OTHER	33 Colombian Consulate
		34 Brazilian Consulate
1 Forte Crest Hotel	2 Umana Yana	35 Xanadu Disco
11 Woodbine Hotel	3 Canadian Consulate	36 Zoo
12 Park Hotel	4 US Embassy	37 National Cultural
14 Rima Guest House	5 St Joseph's Mercy	Centre
19 Belvedere Hotel	Hospital	38 President's Residence
20 Alpha Guest House	6 Cuban Consulate	43 St George's Cathedral
21 Hotel Ariantze	7 Immigration Office	44 Bank of Guyana
22 Hotel Tropicana	8 Public Hospital	Building
25 Hotel Tower	9 Ministry of Trade,	(Telephone Office &
29 Water Chris Hotel	Tourism & Industry	LIAT Airline)
39 German's Hotel	10 British High	45 Museum of Guyana
40 Friends Hotel	Commission	46 Barclay's Bank
62 Trio La Chalet Guest	13 Roth Museum of	47 GPO
House	Anthropology	48 BWIA (Airlines)
63 Campala International	16 Library Club & Disco	50 Houseproud
Hotel	23 Joe Chin's Travel	51 Royal Bank of Canada
	Agency (Money	52 Town Hall
▼ PLACES TO EAT	Exchange)	54 Victoria Law Courts
	24 Guyana Airways	55 ALM & SLM (Airlines)
15 Caribbean Rose	26 National Library	56 Stabroek Market
17 Orient	27 Wieting & Richter	58 Ferry Stelling
18 Del Casa	Travel Agency/	59 Parliament Building
41 Country Pride	Tourism Association	60 Brickdam Police
42 Rice Bowl	of Guyana	Station
49 Coal Pot	28 Trump Card Disco	61 Roman Catholic
53 Hack's Halaal	30 Venezuelan Consulate	Cathedral
57 Arawak Steak House	31 N&R Car Rental	
	32 Surinamese Consulate	

idated, a reminder of what museums once were, but occasional special exhibitions of Guyanese painting and sculpture are imaginative, unique and first-rate.

It's open on weekdays from 8.30 am to 5 pm, and on Saturdays from 9 am to noon. Admission is free.

Botanical Gardens & Zoo At the east end of Regent Rd, Georgetown's Botanical Gardens are attractive and well-maintained. The zoo within focuses on animals found in Guyana, with a very fine selection of birds (most notably the rare hyacinth macaw and the harpy eagle), a good aquarium and large ponds, where visitors can feed fresh grass to the herbivorous manatees. Admission is a token US$0.04.

Places to Stay
One of Georgetown's cheapest lodgings is

Hotel Tropicana (☎ 62108), 177 Waterloo St, with singles for US$5. *German's Hotel* (☎ 53972), 53 Robb St, is comparable. *Trio La Chalet Guest House* (☎ 56628), 5 Camp St, is slightly dearer, at US$7.50 single, as is *Alpha Guest House* (☎ 54324), 203 Camp St. The *Water Chris Hotel* (☎ 71980), 184 Waterloo St, has singles for US$8 with shared bath, US$12 with private bath. At *Friends Hotel* (☎ 72383), 82 Robb St, Lacytown, rates start around US$10 for a single with private bath and fan.

Highly recommended is the very friendly, central and secure *Rima Guest House* (☎ 57401), 92 Middle St, for US$12 a single with shared bath. Comparable in price and quality is *Hotel Ariantze* (☎ 65363), at 176 Middle St.

The rambling *Park Hotel* (☎ 54911), 37 Main St, has rooms ranging from US$22/24 a single/double to US$50/53, depending on amenities; its dining room is cheap, but there are many better restaurants. The *Campala International* (☎ 52951), 10 Camp St, Werken-Rust, charges US$45/55, about the same as the *Woodbine International* (☎ 59430), 41 New Market St.

For up-market comfort, *Hotel Tower* (☎ 72011), 74-75 Main St, has rooms from US$75. Try also the *Forte Crest Hotel* (☎ 52856), on Seawall Rd.

Places to Eat

Some of Georgetown's many quality restaurants have dress codes; they are not that restrictive – no faded jeans or sneakers – but check before you go.

Palm Court, 35 Main St, is lively and popular, with good seafood. *Caribbean Rose*, 175 Middle St, is a superb rooftop restaurant. It's also good value, though not cheap; at least US$10 for a meal. *Arawak Steak House*, on Brickdam, has better, more varied food than its name would suggest. The *Coal Pot*, 17 Hinck St, has a diverse lunch menu; it is often crowded, but its seafood is much cheaper than elsewhere in town; meals start at around US$2 to US$3. For East Indian food, try *Hack's Halaal*, on Commerce St near Avenue of the Republic. The *Rice Bowl*, 34 Robb St, is also worth a try.

Del Casa, 232 Middle St, is fairly expensive and formal, with a dress code and surprisingly indifferent service, but has good meat and seafood. *Country Pride*, 64 Robb St, is also very worthwhile, while the *Orient*, at Camp and Middle streets, is a fine Chinese place with good service.

Main Street Cafe, in the Hotel Tower, is good for breakfast (diners may or may not be reassured by its explicit notice that 'The firing of firecrackers in the confines of this hotel is prohibited'). The Tower's *Cazabon* is also highly regarded, while the Forte Crest has two good restaurants.

Entertainment

Georgetown's popular discos stay open very late. Try Mingles, at Albert and Third streets, or The Library Club & Disco, 226 Camp St, which is jammed with Guyanese and foreign gold miners; Wednesday is ladies night. Admission is less than US$1. Other possibilities include the Trump Card (on Church St, near Carmichael) and Xanadu (at Vliessengen Rd and Duncan St).

Things to Buy

Handicrafts are remarkably good and attractive, particularly pottery, paintings and wood sculptures. Try Houseproud at 6 Avenue of the Republic, Creation Craft at 7A Water St, or The Basket Shop at 72 Sixth St.

Getting There & Away

Air Timehri International Airport is 25 miles (41 km) south of Georgetown. For intercontinental connections, see the general Getting There & Away section earlier in this chapter.

Regional airlines link the capital to Caribbean islands and to Suriname but not directly to Venezuela. Taba Airways is now flying to Boa Vista, Brazil (about US$130 return for a 30-day excursion) and on to Manaus (about US$185), on Tuesdays and Thursdays.

ALM
    232 Camp St (☎ 67414)
BWIA
    4 Robb St (☎ 58900, 71250)
Guyana Airways
    32 Main St (☎ 57337, 64011)
LIAT
    Bank of Guyana Bldg, Church St & Avenue of the Republic (☎ 61260)
SLM (Surinam Airways)
    230 Camp St (☎ 54894, 53473)

SLM has two flights weekly, on Tuesday and Saturday, to Paramaribo and Cayenne. Barbados-based LIAT (☎ 64011) has daily flights with connections to other Caribbean islands, including Antigua, Dominica, Grenada, Martinique, Port of Spain (Trinidad), St Lucia and St Vincent.

Bus Minibuses to Parika (No 32, for ferries to Bartica and Charity), to Rosignol (No 44, for the ferry to New Amsterdam, connecting to Springlands and the ferry to Suriname) and Linden leave from Stabroek Market. If you're interested in overland travel to

Lethem, ask at Stabroek about trucks, but the route can be hazardous.

Getting Around

To/From the Airport Minibuses connect Timehri with Georgetown for about US$1; they are safe enough in the daytime, but at night, a taxi is a better choice, despite the US$16 price tag (taxis may be shared). For early morning flights from Timehri, make taxi arrangements the day before.

Bus Minibuses within the city limits cost about US$0.10.

Taxi Taxis within central Georgetown cost about US$1 per ride or US$5 per hour. Try Main Street Taxi Service (☎ 63866), in front of Hotel Tower, Khan's (☎ 54488) or Cyril's (☎ 54488).

AROUND GEORGETOWN
Linden

Linden, 66 miles (107 km) upriver from Georgetown by excellent paved road, is a mining centre of 60,000, with a lively riverside market on Sunday mornings. It is the headquarters of Guymine, the state bauxite enterprise. To arrange a visit, contact the Public Relations office (☎ 2839).

Modest accommodation is available at the friendly *Centurion Guest House* (☎ 3666), 47 Republic Ave, which has big, clean rooms with air-conditioning for US$8.

Getting There & Away Minibuses from Stabroek Market in Georgetown charge about US$1.60 a single. Returning from Linden, drivers are very competitive, and you are likely to upset one when you choose another.

THE COASTAL PLAIN
New Amsterdam

New Amsterdam is a sugar port on the east bank of the Berbice River, about 65 miles (100 km) east of Georgetown. It has no special attractions, but may be a convenient

stopover (or an unavoidable one, depending on ferry schedules).

Like Georgetown, New Amsterdam experiences a good deal of street crime, sometimes violent. It also suffers blackouts, during which the city is particularly unsafe. Avoid areas east of Main St, especially at night.

Places to Stay & Eat Reasonable accommodations include the *Aster Hotel*, near the ferry stelling, where basic singles with private bath cost US$6.50; with air-conditioning, the cost rises to US$11. *Hotel Penguin*, near the market at Liberty St, costs about the same but seems less secure. The *Church View Hotel*, at Main and King streets, has singles/doubles with fan for US$7/10 and doubles with air-conditioning for US$20.

The *Brown Derby Restaurant*, at Church and Main streets, has a nice upstairs verandah. Its mostly East Indian menu has some Chinese dishes.

Getting There & Away Minibuses (No 44) from Stabroek Market in Georgetown charge US$1.50 to the stelling at Rosignol, where there are eight ferries daily, from 4 am to 7.45 pm, across the Berbice to New Amsterdam (US$0.10 for passengers). Launches (US$0.20) also cross the river, from the sugar docks about one km north; minibuses will drop you there if no ferry is due to leave soon.

To continue to Corriverton, take the 'CWC' (Crabwood Creek) minibus (US$1) from the New Amsterdam stelling or market.

Corriverton

Together known as Corriverton, the towns of Springlands and Skeldon, on the west bank of the Courantyne River, are the present terminus of the highway from Georgetown. From Springlands, a rickety Surinamese passenger ferry crosses the river daily. A new ferry terminal is under construction at Crabwood Creek, a short distance up the river.

Main St is an elongated ribbon around whose market Brahmin (Zebu) cattle roam

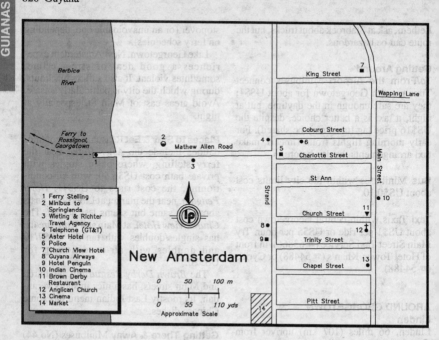

1 Ferry Stelling
2 Minibus to Springlands
3 Wieting & Richter Travel Agency
4 Telephone (GT&T)
5 Aster Hotel
6 Police
7 Church View Hotel
8 Guyana Airways
9 Hotel Penguin
10 Indian Cinema
11 Brown Derby Restaurant
12 Anglican Church
13 Cinema
14 Market

New Amsterdam

Berbice River

Ferry to Rossignol, Georgetown

Mathew Allen Road

King Street

Wapping Lane

Coburg Street

Charlotte Street

St Ann

Church Street

Trinity Street

Chapel Street

Pitt Street

Strand

Main Street

0   50   100 m
0   55   110 yds
Approximate Scale

like the sacred cows of India. There are Hindu temples, Islamic mosques and many denominations of Christian churches. The Skeldon Estate of the Guyana Sugar Company (Guysuco) is the largest employer.

Places to Stay & Eat *Hotel Par Park*, near the stelling, is clean, cheap and secure. It charges US$4 for a single with private bath, US$5 with private bath and verandah. Small windows make some rooms very dark, but at least it has its own generator for blackouts. Probably next best is the *Swiss Guest House*, at about the same price.

N B Campbell's, on Main St, is a good place for lunch if you can conform to posted requirements such as 'no fighting in here', 'do not spit on the floor', 'dancing not allowed' and 'payment for breaking bottles and glasses'. The Chinese restaurant next to the Par Park is truly awful.

Getting There & Away For travellers

heading to Suriname, the overloaded *Lily II* sails daily to Nieuw Nickerie (US$1, payable in Surinamese guilders only). (Those who are not strong swimmers may wish to avoid the trip by returning to Georgetown and flying to Paramaribo.) People queue on the stelling around 6 am, but it's usually 8 am before they open the sliding door for booking, after which you enter a separate line for immigration formalities. It may be 1.30 pm before the boat departs, depending on its arrival from Nieuw Nickerie.

Moneychangers on the stelling sell guilders at rates nearly as good as the black market in Paramaribo. It is fairly safe to change, but do be careful.

THE INTERIOR
Bartica
Bartica is a friendly mining town at the junction of the Essequibo and Mazaruni rivers, upstream from Parika. The best accommodation is the *Hotel Modern*, at the ferry stelling,

which has comfortable singles for about US$6. The hotel has a good restaurant and bar (request meals in advance).

Getting There & Away From Stabroek Market in Georgetown, take minibus No 32 to Parika (US$1, 45 minutes), then catch a river taxi to Bartica (about US$4, one hour); these 15-passenger speedboats leave when full and carry only one or two life jackets. There is a cheaper, slower ferry (US$1, four hours) on Monday, Thursday and Saturday at 9.30 am.

From Bartica, it is possible to travel to Kaieteur Falls on a combination of mining trucks and your own two feet, but expect to return the same way – planes to and from Kaieteur rarely have an empty seat.

Around Bartica

Fort Island In the Essequibo River, Fort Island was an early Dutch outpost; the ferry from Parika to Bartica makes a brief stop here, but it is also possible to arrange a speedboat from Parika or Bartica. There is a 17th-century graveyard.

Kyk-Over-Al This ruined Dutch fortress, at the junction of the Mazaruni and Cuyuni rivers, dates from 1616. Nearby Marshall Falls is a good place for riverine wildlife. Again, you can arrange boats from Bartica.

Kaieteur Falls

Guyana's best-known attraction, majestic Kaieteur Falls is the most impressive of a series of three falls on the upper Potaro River, a tributary of the Essequibo. An Amerindian legend tells that a Patamona chieftain sacrificed himself by canoeing over the falls, to save his people from destruction by an evil spirit.

In its own way, Kaieteur is no less impressive than the better-known Iguazú Falls of Argentina and Brazil. Its waters drop precipitously 822 feet (250 metres) from a sandstone tableland, much higher than Iguazú. Depending on the season, the falls range in width from 250 feet (76 metres) to 400 feet (122 metres). Swifts nest under the overhang of the falls and dart in and out of the waters.

There is presently no accommodation, but camping is possible nearby.

Getting There & Away Several operators offer day trips in small planes for about US$150 to US$160 per person; make early inquiries, since these leave only when a full load of eight passengers can be arranged. For details, see Travel Agencies in the Georgetown section.

Overland travel from Bartica (via the village of Mahdia) is possible, but it's rugged and very time-consuming, usually requiring a guide and several days' walking. It is difficult to catch a plane back to Georgetown, even if you have money – miners are often lined up waiting on the airstrip.

Orinduik Falls

Orinduik Falls, a miniature Niagara on the Ireng River, on the Guyanese-Brazilian frontier, is a secondary destination for most day trips to Kaieteur Falls. Patamona Indians live nearby. There is a minor border crossing, from which it is possible to get a bus to the Brazilian settlement of Bomfim and on to the cities of Boa Vista and Manaus.

Lethem

In the Rupununi savanna along the Brazilian border, Lethem itself has little of interest, but its scenic surroundings harbour lots of wildlife. At Easter, it has a worthwhile rodeo.

The Guyanese are suspicious about drug smuggling in this area, so seek permission before visiting – ask Colonel Fabian Liverpool of Home Affairs (☎ 62444), in Brickdam, Georgetown.

Getting There & Away Guyana Airways flies three times weekly from Georgetown (about US$50 one-way), but seats can be difficult to book. In the dry season, overland truck transport is feasible from Linden (via Kurupukari), but this is only for travellers with both time and stamina. The Hinterland Road to Lethem is even more difficult.

Suriname

Suriname is an unusual cultural enclave whose extraordinary ethnic variety derives from Dutch colonisation, the early importation of African slaves and, later, indentured labourers from India and Indonesia. Despite its rather incongruous appearance of Amsterdam in the tropics, Paramaribo, the capital, is a good introduction, though Suriname's greatest attraction is a well-managed system of nature parks and reserves.

FACTS ABOUT THE COUNTRY
History
Suriname was the last outpost of a once substantial Dutch presence in South America – the Netherlands controlled large parts of Brazil and most of the Guianas until territorial conflicts with Britain and France left them only Dutch Guiana and a few Caribbean islands.

Suriname's 19th-century influx of Hindustanis and Indonesians resulted in less overt racial tension than in Guyana, though manipulative Creole politicians limited representation of immigrants in the colonial Staten (parliament). Despite limited autonomy, Suriname remained a colony until 1954, when it became a self-governing state; another 20 years passed before it became independent.

Since independence, political developments have been discouraging. Two years after a military coup in 1980, the regime brutally executed more than a dozen prominent opponents, and also carried out a vicious campaign to suppress a rebellion of Bush Negros, whose interior villages suf-

fered systematic human rights violations. Many fled to neighbouring French Guiana.

Suriname's erratic Marxist junta briefly flirted with Cuba (to the displeasure of both the USA and Brazil), then with Libya (to the alarm of the French in French Guiana), before attempting reconciliation with its opponents. The political situation has improved recently but is still unstable.

Suriname's economy resembles that of Guyana, as its highly capitalised bauxite industry relies on foreign investment and technology. Despite leftist rhetoric, the government has been hesitant to challenge multinationals like Suralco (a subsidiary of Alcoa) and Billiton (a subsidiary of Royal Dutch Shell).

Geography & Climate
With an area of 164,000 sq km, Suriname is about the size of New Zealand's South Island. To the west, the Corantijn River (this is the Dutch spelling; it's Courantyne in Guyana) forms the border, disputed in its most southerly reaches, with Guyana; the Marowijn (Maroni) and Litani rivers form the border with French Guiana (also disputed in the south).

The majority of Surinamese inhabit the Atlantic coast, where most of the country's few roads are located. The major links to the interior are by air or north-south rivers, though there is a road to Brokopondo. The nearby Afobaka Dam created one of the world's largest reservoirs (1550 sq km), the W J van Blommestein Meer, on the upper Suriname River. Rapids limit the navigability of most rivers. Interior mountain ranges are not so high as Guyana's – 1280-metre Julianatop is the highest point in the country.

Temperatures and humidity are high. The major rainy season is from April to July, with a shorter one in December and January.

Government
Suriname gained formal independence in 1975 as a parliamentary democracy, but in 1980, a group of disgruntled noncommissioned officers overthrew the government

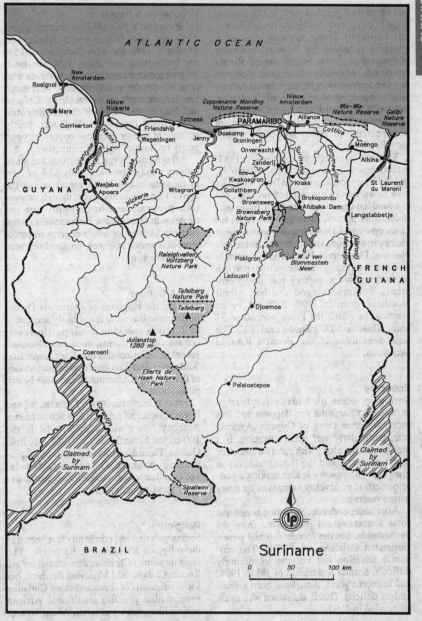

ATLANTIC OCEAN

GUYANA

BRAZIL

FRENCH GUIANA

New Amsterdam
Rosignol
Mara
Corriverton
Nieuw Nickerie
Totness
Friendship
Wageningen
Jenny
Boskamp
Groningen
Onverwacht
Coppename Monding Nature Reserve
Nieuw Amsterdam
Wia–Wia Nature Reserve
Galibi Nature Reserve
PARAMARIBO
Alliance
Moengo
Albina
St Laurent du Maroni
Langatabbetje
Cottica
Zanderij
Kwakoegron
Goliathberg
Brownsweg
Brownsberg Nature Park
Brokopondo
Afobaka Dam
Kraka
Wasjabo
Apoera
Witagron
Raleighvallen/ Voltzberg Nature Park
Tafelberg Nature Park
Tafelberg
Julianatop 1280 m
Coeroeni
Eilerts de Haan Nature Park
Pokigron
Ladouani
W J van Blommestein Meer
Djoemoe
Peleloetepoe
Claimed by Surinam
Claimed by Surinam
Sipaliwini Reserve

Courantyne
Corantijn
Nanni
Nickerie
Maratakka
Coppename
Saramacca
Suriname
Commewijne
Cottica
Maroni (Marowijne)
Litani
Corantijn

Suriname

0   50   100 km

and banned all political parties. The ensuing reign of terror under Sergeant (later Lieutenant Colonel) Desi Bouterse fuelled a guerrilla rebellion by Bouterse's former bodyguard, a Bush Negro named Ronny Brunswijk. Militarily challenged, Bouterse had to compromise with the political parties, which once again operated openly, and negotiate with Brunswijk's 'Jungle Commando' in Cayenne. Tensions have subsided but not disappeared, and certain parts of the interior are still off limits.

The new constitution, approved in 1987, establishes a 51-seat National Assembly, headed by a president chosen from within its own ranks. Parties run along ethnic lines, but a broad coalition of Hindu, Creole and Indonesian parties, known as the Front for Democracy and Development, won a major victory in elections later that year. Bouterse's National Democratic Party (NDP) won only a few seats, but the constitution institutionalises a military role in government. Bouterse staged another, albeit bloodless, coup in 1990, followed by an election, in which the Front won 30 of 51 seats, while the NDP gained a total of 12. The new president is the Front's Ronald Venetiaan.

Economy

Suriname relies on bauxite for foreign exchange, though its ore deposits are less accessible than those of Guyana. Agriculture, particularly wet rice cultivation, is a major industry, along with palm oil and other forest products, and the fishing industry is growing. The country is also making a conscious effort to develop tourism in its many nature reserves.

After independence, Suriname benefitted from a massive aid programme from the Netherlands, but the former colonial power suspended assistance after 1980. The economic situation has become increasingly difficult, despite restoration of aid in 1987, and in recent years, there have been serious budget deficits. Dutch assistance was again suspended in 1991.

Population & People

Of Suriname's 400,000-plus citizens, about 35% are East Indian (both Hindu and Muslim), 32% are Afro-Surinamese, 15% are Indonesian and about 10% are Bush Negros (descendants of escaped slaves who now inhabit the upland forests), with much smaller numbers of Amerindians, Chinese and Europeans. Many of the intelligentsia live abroad (mostly in Holland), partly because of greater economic opportunity and partly because of military repression.

A fragmented linguistic heritage has made literacy a major problem; only 83% of Surinamese males and 75% of females above the age of 15 can read and write, though innovative programmes have improved the situation in recent years. Paramaribo's Anton de Kom University offers degrees in medicine, law, social sciences, physical sciences and engineering.

Arts & Culture

Because the language of literacy is Dutch, Surinamese literature is not easily accessible to English-speaking visitors. However, certain cultural events, such as Indonesian *gamelan*, offer insights into Surinamese life. Sculptures and carvings express the values of the country's Amerindian and Bush Negro populations.

Sport is important to the Surinamese, and it was a source of great pride when swimmer Anthony Nesty won a gold medal in the 100-metre butterfly at the 1988 Olympic Games. There are national organisations promoting basketball, boxing, tennis, volleyball, cycling, weightlifting and many other sporting activities.

Religion

Suriname's unusual ethnic mix is reflected in the religious allegiance of its people. The most important Christian denominations are Roman Catholic and Moravian Brethren, but some adherents of these and other Christian groups also practise traditional African beliefs like *obeah* and *winti*. About 80% of

East Indians are Hindu; most of the remainder are Muslim, as is part of the Indonesian population. Small numbers of Buddhists, Jews and Amerindians follow distinct religious traditions.

Language
Dutch is the official national language, and standard English is widely understood, but Suriname is a linguistic potpourri whose vernacular language is Sranan (also known as Surinaams), an English-based creole.

Other languages are Hindi, Javanese, Chinese, and Djuka and Saramaccan (both also English-based creoles). Amerindian languages include Arawak, Carib, Tirió, Warao and Waiana.

FACTS FOR THE VISITOR
Visas & Embassies
Nearly all travellers need to get a visa in advance. For a multiple entry visa, the Surinamese Embassy in Washington, DC requires an application in duplicate, with two passport photos. Consulates in Georgetown (Guyana) and Cayenne (French Guiana) charge upwards of US$20 for a visa.

Suriname's overseas representation is very limited. The embassy in Washington provides a superb collection of tourist information, including a very fine publication on biological conservation, to correspondents who send a self-addressed envelope (8½ by 11 inches); include postage of US$2.50.

Surinamese Embassies & Consulates
There are representatives in Guyana, French Guiana, Brazil, Venezuela (for addresses, see the city entries in each of those countries), and also in:

Germany
   Adolf-Kolping-Strasse 16, Munich (☎ 55-3363)
Netherlands
   Alexander Gogelweg 2, The Hague (☎ (070) 65-0844)
   De Cuserstraat 11, Amsterdam (☎ (020) 42-6137)

USA
   4301 Connecticut Ave NW, Suite 108, Washington, DC (☎ 244-7488)
   7235 NW 19th St, Miami, FL (☎ 593-2163)

Foreign Embassies & Consulates
Several countries have representatives in Paramaribo; see that section for addresses.

Documents
Passports are obligatory and nearly all visitors need visas. In theory, all visitors staying over a week must register with the police and obtain an exit visa at the police station in Nieuwe Haven, Paramaribo (see the Paramaribo section for more details). There are so many baffling regulations in Suriname that even bureaucrats cannot comprehend or explain them, and enforcement is lax.

Customs
Surinamese regulations permit the importation of two cartons of cigarettes, 100 cigars or 200 cigarillos, or one-half kilo of tobacco; two litres of spirits or four litres of wine may also be imported. In theory, there is a limit of eight rolls of unexposed film and 60 metres of cine film, as well as 100 metres of recording tape, and officials may demand an 'export licence' for souvenirs, but these rules are rarely enforced.

Money
Despite links to the Netherlands, the US dollar is the key foreign currency in Suriname. Banks are open on weekdays from 7 am to 2 pm. Changing money can be time-consuming because of the paperwork involved, and many people opt to change on the black market. Rates are not much higher than in the bank, but the black market is useful to change money quickly and outside of bankers' hours. This is technically illegal and not without risk (shortchanging is the most frequent problem), but regulations are often ignored.

Currency The official currency is the Surinamese guilder (Sf), divided into 100 cents.

There are coins for 25 and 50 cents and one guilder, and banknotes for five, 10, 25, 50, 100 and 500 guilders. New banknotes are coming into circulation, so check on the validity of older notes.

Exchange Rates The guilder was artificially on a par with the Dutch guilder for some years – which in mid-1993 gave a wildly unrealistic exchange rate of US$1 = 1.78 Sf. As we go to press, the artificial rate has been relaxed and the official rate is now approximately US$1 = 50 Sf, and the black market rate is US$1 = 80 to 100 Sf, depending on current trading conditions

Arriving passengers at the international airport must change the equivalent of US$180 at the official rate. All arrivals, including those at land borders, must fill out a currency declaration to be surrendered upon departure; it may be politic to change a small amount at the official rate to satisfy customs and immigration officials. Some officials maintain that departing foreigners must have exchanged their money at the Centrale Bank van Suriname, but they are unlikely to delay departure for anyone who has changed elsewhere.

Costs At the official rate, Suriname is moderately priced; at the black market rate, it is cheap. Prices in this chapter reflect the black market rate. Some businesses, including airlines and travel agencies, are requiring total or partial payment for some transactions in US dollars at the official rate.

Good accommodation can be found for US$2 per night, while truly outstanding meals cost less than US$5. Budget travellers can get by on less than US$10 per day, and live very well by spending just a little more.

Credit Cards Credit cards are accepted at major hotels and at travel agencies, but charges are converted to foreign currency at the official rate, so it will usually be disadvantageous to use them, except for items like international air tickets, for which US dollar payment is obligatory.

When to Go
Suriname's dry seasons, from early February to late April and from mid-August to early December, are the best time for a visit. From March to July, several species of sea turtles come ashore to nest at Wia Wia and Galibi reserves.

Tourist Offices
The Suriname Tourist Department office (☎ 471163) is at Cornelius Jongbawstraat 2, Paramaribo; its postal address is PO Box 656, Paramaribo. Intending visitors should contact Surinamese consulates for tourist information.

Useful Organisations
Visitors interested in Suriname's exemplary system of national parks and reserves should contact Stinasu (Stichting Natuur Behoud Suriname; the Foundation for Nature Preservation in Suriname), which coordinates both research and tourist traffic to these areas. For further information, see the Paramaribo section.

Business Hours & Holidays
Most businesses and government offices open by 7 am and close by mid-afternoon, slightly earlier on Fridays. Banks are open on weekdays from 7 am to 2 pm. Shops mostly open from 8 am to 4 pm on weekdays but close by 1 pm on Saturdays. Government offices and businesses are closed on national holidays.

1 January
    New Year's Day
25 February
    Day of the Revolution
Early March (date varies)
    Phagwah (Hindu New Year)
March/April
    Good Friday/Easter Monday
1 May
    Labour Day
1 July
    National Union Day
25 November
    Independence Day

25 & 26 December
Christmas Day/Boxing Day

Festivals

The Hindu New Year's festival, Holi Phagwah, is held in March or April, while the Muslim holiday Id ul Fitr (Lebaran or Bodo in Indonesian) celebrates the end of fasting at Ramadan.

Post & Telecommunications

Postal services are probably only dependable in Paramaribo.

Telesur (Telecommunicatiebedrijf Suriname) is the national telephone company. Making an overseas call from a public office is an endurance test: first you must submit a written form, after which your call is scheduled (pay in advance), then you have to reappear for your call, perhaps the following day.

To call the USA from Paramaribo, it is simpler to use the AT&T USA Direct lines at the Hotel Torarica or Hotel Krasnapolsky (which may charge nonguests).

Time

Surinamese time is three hours behind GMT.

Books & Maps

A good introduction is Henk E Chin's and Hans Buddingh's *Surinam: Politics, Economics & Society* (Frances Pinter Publishers, London, 1987), complemented by Betty Sedoc-Dahlberg's edited collection *The Dutch Caribbean: Prospects for Democracy* (Gordon & Breach, New York, 1990).

William F Leitch's *South America's National Parks* (The Mountaineers, Seattle, 1990) is one of few easily available sources for readers interested in nature parks and reserves.

The locally published and printed *A Portrait of the Republic of Suriname*, available in local shops, is a large-format book with some useful text, and many colour photographs of varying quality. It is not worth the cover price of US$208.50 at the official exchange rate, but it is worth US$15 at the black market rate.

Media

After the coup of 1980 there was strict censorship, and many newspapers and radio stations were destroyed, but some have reopened. There are two daily newspapers, *De Ware Tijd* and *De West*. The *Suriname Weekly*, a fledgling paper in both English and Dutch, is a bit skeletal.

The Surinaams Nieuws Agentschaap (Suriname News Agency, or SNA) prints a daily bulletin in readable if imperfect English, copies of which can be found on the front desk of the Hotel Torarica.

There are two TV stations and seven commercial radio stations. TV broadcasts are in Dutch, but radio transmissions are also in Hindustani, Javanese and Sranan (Surinaams).

Health

A yellow fever vaccination certificate is required for travellers arriving from infected areas, while typhoid and malaria prophylaxis are recommended. For free malaria medication, visit the Public Health Office, 15 Rode Kruislaan, Paramaribo.

Tap water outside Paramaribo is generally unsafe.

Dangers & Annoyances

The civil war has ended, but there are still armed freelance bandits, or guerillas, in the countryside. The main coastal highway is usually safe, despite occasional incidents on the section between Moengo and Albina, but it is best to avoid interior roads at night, especially the one between Zanderij (site of the international airport) and Brokopondo, where armed groups have attacked the police station and robbed travellers.

Suriname in general, however, presents fewer security problems than Guyana. Paramaribo is mostly safe, even at night, though individuals may feel more secure in taxis at late hours.

Accommodation

Good, reasonably priced accommodation is available in guesthouses and hotels, though Paramaribo has far less budget accommodation than Georgetown. Expect to pay US$2 to US$8 a single for basic to fairly comfortable lodging.

Food & Drink

Suriname's food reflects its ethnic diversity and can be superb. The cheapest eateries are *warungs* (Javanese food stalls) serving *bami goreng* (fried noodles) and *nasi goreng* (fried rice), but some of the best up-market restaurants are also Javanese. Creole food uses tubers such as manioc (cassava), and sweet potatoes, plantains, chicken and fish (including shrimp, which is particularly choice). Chinese and Hindustani food are also common.

Parbo, the local beer, is acceptable and much cheaper than imported Heineken. Rum is the most common hard liquor.

Things to Buy

Bush Negro handicrafts, especially folding chairs and stools carved from single pieces of cedar, are very appealing. Amerindian and Javanese crafts are also attractive.

One of Suriname's quirkiest bureaucratic requirements is an export licence for any item costing over Sf50 (about US$1 at the black market rate). Even though, according to one customs agent, 'it takes only two days' to obtain one, enforcement appears even more lax than of exit visa and currency exchange requirements; still, you should be aware of it.

GETTING THERE & AWAY

Air

To/From Europe The most direct connection is with KLM, which flies from Amsterdam to Paramaribo twice weekly. SLM (Surinam Airways) also has a weekly flight on the same route. It is cheaper to fly Air France from Paris to Cayenne (French Guiana) and then go overland to Paramaribo.

To/From North America Miami and Atlanta are the main departure points, but most flights stop in Curaçao, Aruba or Bonaire. SLM flies directly to Paramaribo from Miami and New York weekly.

To/From the Caribbean From Paramaribo, there are connections to the islands of Curaçao, Bonaire and Aruba, in the Netherlands Antilles.

To/From Brazil Cruzeiro do Sul and SLM fly between Paramaribo and Belém, in the Brazilian state of Pará.

To/From French Guiana Air France, SLM and Cruzeiro do Sul connect Paramaribo with Cayenne (US$105 one-way).

To/From Guyana SLM flies to Georgetown two or three times weekly (US$85 one-way).

Overland

Overland routes to Guyana and French Guiana involve crossing rivers. Since the end of hostilities, the main crossings are open once again.

To/From French Guiana From Albina, there is a passenger ferry across the Marowijne (Maroni) River to St Laurent de Maroni, with road connections to Cayenne.

To/From Guyana A rickety passenger ferry from Nieuw Nickerie crosses the Corentijn (Courantyne) River to Springlands (Corriverton), Guyana, with connections to Georgetown. Crossings are daily, except Sundays and holidays.

Leaving Suriname

Airport Tax International departure tax is a hefty US$17.

GETTING AROUND

Air

Gum Air and Gonini operate services to the interior, usually on a charter basis.

Bus

Medium-sized buses on the coastal highway are frequent and exceptionally cheap, but crowded. Off these main routes, they are few.

Taxi

Shared taxis cover routes along the coast, from Paramaribo to Nieuw Nickerie in the west and to Albina in the east. Several times more expensive than buses, they are still very reasonable by European or North American standards, and are notably faster.

Car

Rental cars are available but expensive. If you are driving from Paramaribo to Albina, watch for demolished bridges (there are usually temporary replacements), and for 'potholes' (created by the Jungle Commando) which are big enough to swallow an unsuspecting car.

When passing through villages, slow for *drempels*, the huge speed bumps on the highway.

Bicycle

Bicycles are a popular means of transport, but good roads are relatively few, so a mountain bike would be the best choice.

Boat

To visit the interior or some coastal areas, such as the Galibi marine turtle reserve near Albina, river transport is the only option. There are few scheduled services, and prices are negotiable. Ferries and launches cross some major rivers, like the Suriname and the Coppename, and are very cheap.

Local Transport

Bus The tourist office in Paramaribo provides a list of bus lines and their routes. Fares are very low.

Taxi Taxis are reasonable but unmetered, so set a price before getting in a cab; rarely will a fare exceed US$2. Most Paramaribo taxi drivers speak English.

Tours

Operators have trips for many budgets, but even parsimonious travellers should take advantage of Stinasu's guided trips to Suriname's rainforest and coastal reserves, to which access can otherwise be difficult. The most popular excursion is to the montane rainforest of Brownsberg, only two hours from Paramaribo. Trips to Raleighvallen/Voltzberg National Park, on the upper Coppename River, have also recommenced. Other choices include Galibi Nature Reserve, at the mouth of the Marowijne River, and the Coppename Monding Nature Park.

As the country recovers from civil war, trips should be more frequent and comfortable. Contact Stinasu, in Paramaribo, for details.

PARAMARIBO

Suriname's capital city, Paramaribo (often abbreviated to 'Parbo' in speech and print), is a curious hybrid of northern Europe and tropical America, where imposing brick buildings overlook grassy squares and wooden houses crowd narrow streets, but towering palms shade some areas and mangroves still hug the riverside. Mosques and synagogues sit side by side, while Javanese vendors peddle bami and satay and Dutch-speaking Creoles guzzle Parbo beer at sidewalk cafés. It has a vigorous street life which, however, shuts down fairly early.

Unlike Georgetown, Parbo is relatively safe, though nighttime robberies are not unknown.

Orientation

Sprawling Parbo sits on the west bank of the meandering Suriname River. Its core is a compact triangular area whose boundaries are Gravenstraat on the north, Zwartenhovenbrugstraat on the west, and the river to the south-east. It is linked by ferry to Meerzorg, on the east bank of the river, with connections to Albina and French Guiana.

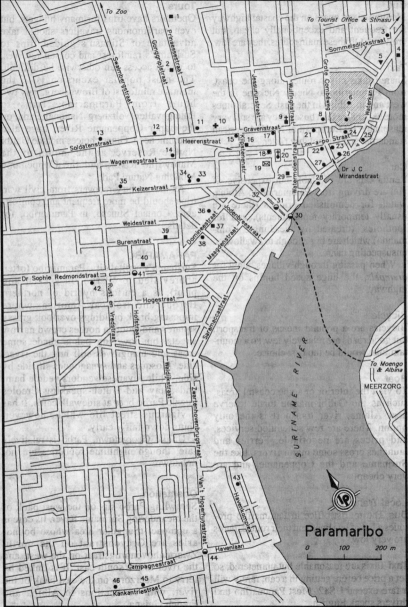

To Zoo

To Tourist Office & Stinasu

Sommelsdijckstraat

Swalmbergstraat
Prinsessestraat
Gongrijpstraat

Jessurunstraat
Wulfinghstraat
Grote Combeweg
Waterkant

Gravenstraat

Heerenstraat
Klipstenenstr

Lim-a-po Straat

Soldatenstraat

Wagenwegstraat

Dr J C
Mirandastraat

Keizerstraat

Watermolenstraat

Weidestraat

Dominéestraat
Jodenbreestraat
Maagdenstraat

Burenstraat

Saramaccastraat

Dr Sophie Redmondstraat

Rust en Vredestraat

Hogestraat

Holstraat

Waldijkstraat

Zwartenhovenbrugstraat

SURINAME RIVER

To Moengo
& Albina

MEERZORG

Van't Hogerhuysstraat

Havenkanpark

Havenlaan

Campagnestraat

Paramaribo

0   100   200 m

Kankantriestraat

	PLACES TO STAY	17	Venezuelan Embassy
		18	Algemene Bank Nederland
1	Blue Moon Hotel	19	Post Office
2	Fanna Guest House	20	Dutch Reformed Church
4	Hotel Suriname Torarica	21	French Consulate
16	YWCA Guest House	22	KLM
29	La Brise Guest House	23	Netherlands Embassy
37	Hotel Krasnapolsky	24	Onafhankelijksplein (Unity Square)
39	Lisa's Guest House	25	Fort Zeelandia
40	Hotel Ambassador	26	Air France
		27	Centrale Bank van Suriname
▼	PLACES TO EAT	28	Waterkant Market
		30	Ferry Terminal & Buses to Moengo & Albina
5	La Bastille	31	Local Bus Terminal
		32	Telesur (Telephone Office)
	OTHER	33	Synagogue
		34	Mosque
3	District Commissaris	35	National Car Rental
6	Palmentuin (Park)	36	Vaco Bookshop
7	Presidential Palace	38	Kersten's (Department Store)
8	National Assembly	41	Buses to Nieuw Nickerie & the West
9	Roman Catholic Cathedral	42	US Embassy
10	Hospital	43	Vreemdelingendienst (Immigration)
11	Guyanese Embassy	44	POZ minibus (to Zanderij Airport)
12	Centrum Cultureel Suriname	45	Torarica Car Rental
13	Hindu Temple	46	De Paarl Airport Service
14	SLM (Surinam Airways)		
15	Varig/Cruzeiro (Airlines)		

Information

Tourist Office The Suriname Tourist Department office (☎ 47-1163) has moved to Cornelius Jongbawstraat 2, a short distance east of Hotel Torarica. It's open Monday to Thursday from 7 am to 3 pm, but closes half an hour earlier on Fridays. The friendly staff speaks English and German, and there is an excellent city map and some useful brochures; the country maps are less useful.

Money Changing money legally is tiresome and financially disadvantageous, but token evidence on currency declarations may please immigration officials on departure. The Centrale Bank van Suriname is at Waterkant 20, while the Algemene Bank Nederland is at Kerkplein 1.

Changing money near Waterkant Market is not difficult and need not be hazardous, though it is better to conduct this activity with a discreet shopkeeper, or one of the banks, which pay almost the same rate. Carry only a modest amount, do not pull out your wallet and count your money carefully, twice.

Post & Telecommunications The main post office is at the corner of Korte Kerkstraat and Wagenwegstraat. Telesur's long-distance telephone office is a block south of the post office.

Visas In theory, visitors spending more than a week in Suriname require an exit visa (blue card) from the police at the Vreemdelingendienst (Immigration, ☎ 47-3101), Nieuwe Haven, though this irritating requirement is rarely enforced. Getting an exit visa involves completing a rather long form and submitting two passport photographs, then crossing town to the District Commissaris Paramaribo (☎ 47-1131), on

Wilhelminastraat, to pay a Sf10 (US$0.20) fee, and returning to Nieuwe Haven for the stamp (the police at Nieuwe Haven are an unpleasant exception to Surinamese courtesy). Some foreign visitors ignore the whole procedure.

Foreign Embassies Most delegations, except Brazil's, are in central Paramaribo:

Brazil
     Maratakastraat 2, Zorg-en-Hoop (☎ 49-1011)
Canada
     Waterkant 92-94 (☎ 47-1222)
France
     Gravenstraat 5-7 (☎ 47-6455)
Guyana
     Gravenstraat 82 (☎ 47-7895)
Netherlands
     Dr J C Mirandastraat 10 (☎ 47-7211)
UK
     VSH United Bldg, Van't Hogerhuysstraat (☎ 47-2870)
USA
     Dr Sophie Redmondstraat 129 (☎ 47-2900)
Venezuela
     Gravenstraat 23-25 (☎ 47-5401)

Cultural Centres The Centrum Cultureel Suriname (CCS, (☎ 47-3309) is at Gravenstraat 112-114.

Stinasu The Foundation for Nature Preservation in Suriname is at Cornelius Jongbawstraat 14 (☎ 47-5845) Their postal address is PO Box 436, Paramaribo.

Travel Agencies Besides Stinasu (see above), Suriname Safari Tours (☎ 45-5116), Dr Axwijkstraat 61, runs eight-day trips up the Tapanahony River. Palumeu Tours (☎ 46-5700), Coppenamestraat 136, operates similar excursions.

Bookshops Vaco, Domineestraat 26, has a good selection of books in Dutch and a handful in English, as does Kersten's, a department store at Domineestraat and Steenbakkerijstraat.

Emergency Paramaribo's main hospital is on Gravenstraat.

Things to See
Central Paramaribo's focus is the **Onafhankelijksplein** (Unity Square), fronting the **Presidential Palace**, on Gravenstraat, which is currently being restored. Immediately behind the palace is the **Palmentuin**, an attractive park with tall palms, picnic tables and benches, and a good sample of tropical birds. To the east is **Fort Zeelandia**, a 17th-century riverside fortification used for the detention and torture of political prisoners after the coup of 1980.

Paramaribo's commercial centre is around **Domineestraat** and nearby streets. **Waterkant Market** is at the foot of Jodenbreestraat; ferries to Meerzorg leave from nearby.

Other interesting features in this area are the city's numerous religious monuments, including the main **Mosque** and the **Dutch Israeli Synagogue**, side by side on Keizerstraat; there is another, Portuguese, synagogue on Gravenstraat. Also on Gravenstraat, near Wulfinghstraat, is the **Kathedraal** (1885), the Roman Catholic church, which is closed until its sagging superstructure is repaired. There is an interesting **Dutch Reformed Church** on the Kerkplein. The main **Hindu Temple** is further out along Gravenstraat, on Soldatenstraat near Rust en Vredestraat.

Surinaams Museum This suburban museum features good collections of Amerindian artefacts and worthwhile special exhibits; the lobby of the Hotel Torarica usually has a small display publicising the museum's current exhibits.

At Commewijnstraat 18, Zorg-en-Hoop, the museum is open on weekdays from 7.30 am to 2 pm, and on Friday, Saturday and Sunday from 5 to 8 pm. Admission is about US$0.10, while a cab from the city centre will cost about US$1. The museum also has a modest selection of souvenirs and very cheap books, including some in English.

Culturtuin Paramaribo's zoo is a pretty grim place – filthy, with small enclosures – despite some interesting animals, but the surrounding parkland (out Swalmbergstraat) is woodsy, and many Surinamese go jogging in the area. Admission is nominal.

Places to Stay

Paramaribo's most popular budget accommodation is the friendly *YWCA Guest House* (☎ 47-0289), Heerenstraat 14-16, which has clean, simple singles for US$2. It often fills up early; if you know when you'll be in Paramaribo, make reservations.

Lisa's Guest House (☎ 47-6927), Burenstraat 6, has singles for about US$6. *Fanna Guest House* (☎ 47-6709), Prinsessestraat 31, is cheaper but less attractive, with basic singles for about US$2; if you take a costlier room with air-conditioning, check to see that it works. A short distance up Prinsessestraat is the friendlier *Blue Moon Hotel* (☎ 47-3062), for about the same price.

Rundown *Hotel Krasnapolsky* (☎ 47-5050), Domineestraat 39, is one of Paramaribo's more expensive places, at US$30/36 a single/double, but has little in common with its prestigious Amsterdam namesake. *Hotel Ambassador* (☎ 477555), Dr Sophie Redmondstraat 66, is shabby and depressing but not cheap.

The *Hotel Suriname Torarica* (☎ 47-1500), Mr L J Rietbergplein 1, is Paramaribo's best; singles start at US$40 (black market rate). Budget travellers are unlikely to stay here, but the hotel coffee shop and restaurant both have very good food at reasonable prices.

Places to Eat

Hotel Torarica has a Friday evening all-you-can-eat poolside barbecue (US$3), and a Sunday breakfast buffet (US$2.40) in the *Plantation Room*; both great value. The cinnamon rolls (also available in the mornings, from the patisserie) are especially good. The hotel coffee shop also serves very fine meals.

La Bastille, at Kleine Waterstraat 3 near the Hotel Torarica, has superb Indonesian and creole food at very reasonable prices. Take a cab to *Sarinah*, a long way out of town at Verlengde Gemenelandsweg 187, for a spectacular Indonesian rijstaffel which is exceptional value.

Chinese restaurants are very common; they include *New China*, at Verlengde Gemenelandsweg 136b, and *Iwan's*, at Grote Hofstraat 6. For creole food, try *Sunshine*, Wilhelminastraat 23.

Things to Buy

Several shops along Domineestraat have attractive souvenirs, most notably wood carvings, but before buying any major item, ask about 'export licence' requirements.

Getting There & Away

Air Paramaribo has two airports, nearby Zorg-en-Hoop (for domestic flights and some flights to Georgetown, Guyana) and larger Zanderij (for all other international flights). Note that SLM's Paramaribo office will not reconfirm a reservation made at another travel agency.

Airlines with offices in Paramaribo include:

Air France
    Waterkant 12 (☎ 47-3838)
ALM
    Keizerstraat 85bv (☎ 47-6288)
Varig/Cruzeiro do Sul
    Klipstenenstraat, near Gravenstraat (☎ 47-6897)
Gonini Air Service
    Dookhieweg Oost 1 (☎ 49-9098)
Gum Air
    Kwattaweg 254 (☎ 49-8888)
KLM
    Mirandastraat, near Lim-a-Po Straat (☎ 47-2421)
SLM (Surinam Airways)
    Coppenamestraat 136 (☎ 46-5700)

Bus Minibuses to Nieuw Nickerie and other western destinations leave from the corner of Dr Sophie Redmondstraat and Hofstraat. Buses to Moengo, Albina and other eastern destinations leave from the ferry terminal at the foot of Heiligenweg.

Taxi Taxis, charging roughly four times the bus fare (still cheap at black market rates), leave from the same terminals as do minibuses.

Car Rental agencies include National (☎ 47-

1385) at Keizerstraat 230, and Torarica (☎ 47-9977), Kankantriestraat 44-48.

Getting Around

To/From the Airport Johan Adolf Pengel Airport, also known as Zanderij, is 45 km south of Paramaribo. A taxi will cost about US$10, but De Paarl Airport Service (☎ 47-9600), Kankantriestraat 42, is cheaper. The much cheaper POZ minibus goes to Zanderij from the corner of Campagnestraat and Van't Hogerhuysstraat, near Nieuwe Haven, in daytime hours only.

Zorg-en-Hoop airfield is about a US$1.50 taxi ride from central Paramaribo.

Bus The tourist office has photocopied routes of Paramaribo's extensive bus system; most buses leave from Heiligenweg, just above the Meerzorg ferry terminal.

Taxi Taxis are reasonably priced but unmetered, so agree on the fare in advance; most drivers speak passable English.

AROUND PARAMARIBO
Nieuw Amsterdam

At the confluence of the Commewijne and Suriname rivers, Nieuw Amsterdam is a ruined Dutch colonial fort, but the 18th-century armory is in good repair and the jail, used into this century, is being restored. There is no admission charge to the open-air museum, but an English-speaking attendant will probably accompany you and subtly hint for a small tip.

Take Bus No 4 from central Parbo to the end of the line, at Leonsberg (US$0.05), then catch a launch across the river (US$0.10). For a few guilders more, the boat will take you to the fort's jetty; otherwise, walk north along the river road about one km to the entrance.

Natuurpark Brownsberg

Stinasu operates occasional day trips to Brownsberg Nature Park, an area of montane tropical rainforest overlooking Brokopondo Stuwmeer (reservoir), about 1½ hours south of the capital via a good highway. The visit

starts with a short walk on the Mazaroni plateau, whose 500-metre elevation gives fine views of the reservoir to the east, then includes a longer hike which involves a steep descent into a canyon with small but attractive waterfalls.

The day trip to Brownsberg costs about US$11, including lunch and transport. Weekend trips cost US$18; it is possible to arrange an overnight stay at other times, but transport is problematical. Put some insect repellent around the ankles to discourage chiggers, whose irritating but otherwise harmless bites may not become apparent for some days. Spreading lime juice on the affected area may relieve itching.

Like the rest of the country, Stinasu was seriously affected by civil war, and its facilities and services are slowly recovering from war damage and unavoidable neglect. The Brownsberg trip leaves on Wednesdays at 8 am, if it has at least a dozen starters. Interestingly, many visitors are Surinamese resident in Holland.

NIEUW NICKERIE

Near the mouth of the Nickerie River, Nieuw Nickerie is Suriname's second port, exporting rice and bananas. It has a daily passenger ferry to Springlands (Corriverton), Guyana.

Places to Stay & Eat

Hotel Ameerali, Maynardstraat 32, has very fine accommodation for US$8/10 a single/double, and an equally fine, reasonably priced restaurant. *Hotel de Vesting*, Balatastraat 6, is also very good; doubles with private bath and air-conditioning cost US$9. Cheaper *pensions* include the *Luxor*, at St Jozefstraat 22, the *Dorien*, at Voorland Waldeck 19-21, and the *Nickerie*, at Voorland Waterloo 15-16.

Getting There & Away

Air SLM (☎ 03-1359), Gouverneurstraat 96, has occasional flights to Paramaribo.

Bus Buses to Paramaribo (US$1, four hours) leave from the market on Maynardstraat. In theory, Parbo-bound travellers need an

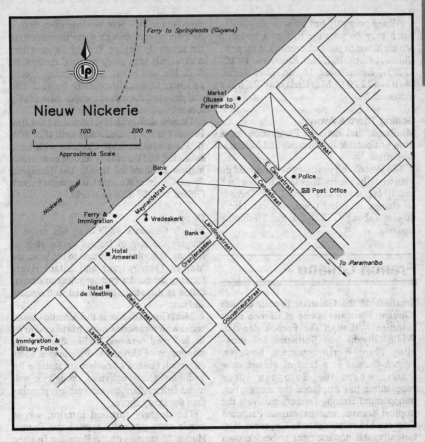

Nieuw Nickerie

Ferry to Springlands (Guyana)

Market
(Buses to Paramaribo)

Bank

Nickerie River

Ferry & Immigration

Maynardstraat

Vredeskerk

Bank

Hotel Ameerali

Hotel de Vesting

Immigration & Military Police

Balatastraat

Lashlystraat

Oranjenassau

Landingstraat

Gouverneurstraat

E. Canalstraat

W. Canalstraat

Emmenstraat

Police

Post Office

To Paramaribo

0   100   200 m
Approximate Scale

immigration stamp not just at the stelling but also at the immigration office, at the west end of Maynardstraat; however, this bothersome requirement appears to be enforced only against Guyanese citizens.

Taxi Taxis to Paramaribo, slightly faster but several times dearer than buses, also leave from the market.

Boat There is a ferry to Corriverton (Guyana) every morning, returning to Nieuw Nickerie in the afternoon. For details, see the Corriverton entry.

MOENGO
Moengo, a centre for bauxite mining and shipping on the Cottica river, 160 km east of Paramaribo. There is a reasonably priced *YWCA Guesthouse* at Lijneweg 18.

ALBINA
Recovering from the civil war, Albina is a small, rundown village on the Marowijne River, the border with French Guiana. With permission from Carib Indians (and a hired canoe), it is possible to visit the nearby **Galibi Nature Reserve**, where Ridley, green and leatherback turtles nest in June and July.

Albina presently has no accommodation, but it may be possible to find a bed in a private house or sling a hammock in the park. Check to see if *Hotel Riverview* (☎ 02-42283), Emmastraat 16, or *Hotel Rorico* (☎ 02-42270), Martinstraat 7, have reopened.

Getting There & Away

Minibuses and taxis to Paramaribo leave from just outside the customs and immigration office.

The French ferry crosses to St Laurent du Maroni daily, except Tuesday afternoon, at 8 and 10 am, noon, and 3 and 5 pm. There is no charge. At other times, you can hire a dugout (about US$2) for the 10-minute crossing.

French Guiana

Smallest of the Guianas, French Guiana (Guyane Français) is one of Europe's last colonies – though the French deny it. While Guyana and Suriname are struggling Third World countries, however, French Guiana is a land of bizarre contrasts, where the European space programme has displaced the mangroves, transplanted Hmong farmers cultivate the tropical forests, and expatriate Parisians dine at chic restaurants in Cayenne. Historically, the département is best known for the notorious offshore prison at Île du Diable (Devil's Island).

FACTS ABOUT FRENCH GUIANA
History

After the abolition of slavery, the French resorted to convict labour, but yellow fever, malaria, corruption and unmitigated brutality retarded long-term progress. Several celebrated cases attested to the notoriety of French Guiana, most notably the persecution of Captain Alfred Dreyfuss at the end of the 19th century, but countless lesser-known individuals suffered as much or more at the hands of French 'justice'. Many who sur-

vived the hellish boat voyages from France died soon after, though some flourished on the relatively benign Îles du Salut, where trade winds kept away malarial mosquitos. Still, life was brutal, as the French forced prisoners to watch executions by guillotine and punished attempted escapes with deadly torture.

Despite such brutality, France did not alter French Guiana's penal status until after WW II. Paris now supports Cayenne with large subsidies, and the colony has the continent's highest standard of living. The European Space Centre at Kourou has brought French Guiana into the modern world.

Geography

French Guiana's 98,000 sq km make it roughly the size of Ireland or the state of Indiana. It borders Suriname to the west, the Maroni (Marowijne) and Litani rivers forming the border (whose southern demarcation is disputed), and Brazil to the south and east.

Most Guyanais live in the Atlantic coastal zone, which contains most of the country's limited road network. Unlike the swampy mangroves of Guyana and Suriname, some of French Guiana's beaches are suitable for traditional tourist activities, though the sediment-laden Atlantic waters are less pleasing than the sandy shore.

The densely forested interior, whose terrain rises gradually toward the Tumac-Humac Mountains on the Brazilian frontier, is very thinly populated. The highest peaks barely exceed 900 metres.

Climate

French Guiana's rainy season runs from December to June, with the heaviest rains in May.

Government

As part of metropolitan France, French Guiana elects one representative to the French Senate and one to National Assembly. As an overseas region, it also elects, by proportional representation, a 34-member regional council. Executive authority resides

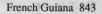

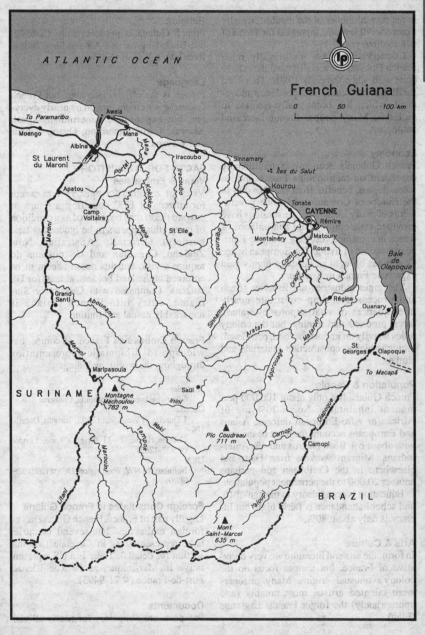

French Guiana

ATLANTIC OCEAN

0   50   100 km

To Paramaribo

Moengo

Awala
Mana
Albina
St Laurent
du Maroni   Iracoubo   Sinnamary
                                          Îles du Salut
Apatou   Kourou
Camp   Tonate
Voltaire   St Elie   CAYENNE
                                          Rémire
                        Montsinéry   Matoury
                                          Roura   Baie
Grand   de
Santi   Comté   Oiapoque
                        Approuague
                        Régina
                        Arataï   Ouanary

Maripasoula   Sinnamary   St   Oiapoque
                                         Georges
SURINAME   To Macapá
        Montagne
        Machoulou
        782 m   Saül
                       Inini

                       Pic Coudreau
                       711 m   Camopi
                                        Camopi

                                        BRAZIL

                       Mont
                       Saint-Marcel
                       635 m

in the commissioner of the republic, usually a career civil servant, appointed for a term of two to three years.

Conservatives have traditionally ruled French Guiana, but socialist candidates have done well since the early 1980s. There is a small but dedicated independence movement, which has occasionally resorted to violence. Many people favour increased autonomy.

Economy
French Guiana's economy is traditionally dependent on metropolitan France and, to some degree, benefits from membership in the European Community. French governments of many ideological persuasions have provided state employment and millions of francs in subsidies, resulting in a near-European standard of living. The European Space Centre has brought an influx of highly paid expatriate French to Kourou.

The main industries are fisheries (fresh and processed shrimp constitute nearly three-quarters of total exports by value), forest products and mining, but the colony relies heavily on imports of food, petroleum, motor vehicles, construction materials and clothes.

Population & People
French Guiana has only about 100,000 permanent inhabitants. Some 70% are of African or Afro-European descent; Asians and Europeans account for most of the rest, with about 6% Bush Negros and 4% Amerindians. Migrant workers from Haiti and elsewhere in the Caribbean add perhaps another 20,000 to the permanent population.

Education is compulsory to the age of 16, and school attendance is fairly high, but literacy is only about 80%.

Arts & Culture
In form, the arts and literature are very derivative of France, but themes focus on the colony's unusual origins. Many prisoners were talented artists, most notably (and appropriately) the forger Francis Lagrange (Flag).

Religion
French Guiana is predominantly Catholic, but Bush Negros and Amerindians follow their own religious traditions.

Language
French is the official language, but French Guianese is a creole spoken by nearly everyone but expatriates. Amerindians speak Arawak, Carib, Emerillon, Oyapi, Palicur and Wayana.

FACTS FOR THE VISITOR
Visas & Embassies
Visas are required for most visitors except for citizens of EEC countries; a return or onward ticket may be required as a condition of entry (this appears to be ignored at land borders). Officially, Australian, New Zealand, Canadian and US citizens do require a visa, but this doesn't seem to be enforced at the land borders, at least for US citizens. Compared with Guyana or Suriname, entry into French Guiana is remarkably casual and routine.

French Embassies France, of course, has widespread diplomatic representation throughout the world, including:

Australia
    6 Darwin Avenue, Yarralumla, Canberra
Canada
    1 Dundas St West, Suite 2405, Toronto, Ontario
UK
    College House, 29-31 Wright's Lane, London (☎ 937-1202)
USA
    Belmont Rd NW, Washington, DC (☎ (202) 328-2600)

Foreign Consulates in French Guiana
Legally part of France, French Guiana has no foreign embassies, but several countries have representatives in Cayenne (see that section for details). There is a US representative in Martinique, at 14 Rue Blenac, Fort-de-France (☎ 71-9493).

Documents
Passports are obligatory for nearly all visi-

tors, except those from France or its former African possessions.

Money

The French *franc* (FF) is the official currency, divided into 100 *centimes*. There are copper-coloured five, 10 and 20-centime coins, silver-coloured 50-centime, one-franc, two-franc and five-franc coins, and banknotes for 20, 50, 100 and 500 francs.

It is easy to change US cash or travellers' cheques in Cayenne. Credit cards are widely accepted, and it is easy to get Visa or MasterCard cash advances from automatic teller machines. Travellers arriving from neighbouring countries may wish to bring some francs from home. Exchange rates are usually slightly lower in French Guiana than in metropolitan France. In August 1993, echange rates were:

A$1   =   FF4.09
DM1   =   FF3.53
UK£1 =   FF8.97
US$1 =   FF6.04

Costs French Guiana is the most expensive territory on the continent, with prices comparable to metropolitan France. It is difficult to find accommodation for less than FF100 (in a few places, travellers can sling a hammock, or camp, for a fraction of the cost) or restaurant meals for less than FF50; public transport is far dearer than in neighbouring countries, and tourist services to the rainforest interior are very expensive. Even parsimonious travellers should allot at least FF250 per day, and congratulate themselves if they can get by on less.

When to Go

It is best to go after the long rainy season ends in July, but before it recommences in December.

Tourist Offices

French tourist offices in many countries can supply basic information about French Guiana.

Canada
    1 Dundas St West, Suite 2405, Toronto, Ontario
UK
    178 Piccadilly, London (☎ 491-7622)
USA
    610 Fifth Ave, New York, NY (☎ 757-1125)

Business Hours & Holidays

There are many holidays, both French and local, on which both government offices and businesses are closed.

January 1
    New Year's Day
Early March (dates vary)
    Ash Wednesday (Carnaval)
March/April (dates vary)
    Good Friday/Easter Monday
May 1
    Labour Day
July 14
    Bastille Day
August 15
    Assumption Day
November 1
    All Saints Day
November 2
    All Souls Day
November 11
    Veterans Day
December 25
    Christmas Day

Festivals

Throughout the French West Indies, Carnaval is celebrated on the first three days of Holy Week, including Ash Wednesday.

Post & Telecommunications

Postal services are good and efficient, especially to Europe.

French Guiana has no central telephone offices; to make an overseas call from a local telephone, dial 19, then the country code, then the area code, then the local number. For an operator, dial 19, then 594. Local coin telephones cost FF1.

Time

French Guiana is three hours behind GMT.

Laundry

Laundry service is available in Cayenne and other large towns, but is rather expensive.

Books & Maps

Many books have documented the history of French Guiana's penal colony on the Îles du Salut, the best known of which is Henri Charriére's novel *Papillon*, made into a Hollywood film. A very readable nonfiction account, based in part on interviews with former prisoners, is Alexander Miles's *Devil's Island: Colony of the Damned* (Ten Speed Press, Berkeley, 1988).

Thurston Clarke's seriously hilarious *Equator* (Avon, New York, 1988) devotes a chapter to his experiences in French Guiana on an imaginatively conceived trip around the midsection of the globe, a 20th-century counterpart to Mark Twain's *Following the Equator*.

France's Institut Géographique National publishes a superb 1:500,000 map of French Guiana which includes very fine city maps of Cayenne and Kourou; it sells for FF39 in Cayenne. More detailed maps (at 1:25,000 and 1:50,000) of some areas are also available.

Media

France Guyane is Cayenne's daily newspaper, with good local and international coverage. French newspapers and magazines are readily available. The *International Herald Tribune* arrives regularly at local newsstands.

Cayenne has two TV channels and several FM radio stations.

Health

During its years as a penal colony, French Guiana was a distinctly unsalubrious place from which few returned, and malaria is still a menace in the backcountry. Good medical care is available, but few doctors speak English. Officials require a yellow fever vaccination certificate from travellers arriving from infected areas. Typhoid and malaria prophylaxes are also recommended. Drinking water is questionable outside the towns.

Dangers & Annoyances

French Guiana is one of the safest places on the continent, but areas along the Suriname border were militarised during that country's recent civil war, and travellers should keep abreast of events in that area, especially if travelling upriver on the Maroni.

Work

High wages and labour shortages draw workers from neighbouring countries, especially in construction; despite official disapproval, it is not uncommon for travellers to find work, with payment in cash. A European Community passport simplifies matters, but there are frequent deportations of illegal workers when demand slackens.

Accommodation

Accommodation is excellent and, consequently, expensive; budget travellers will have trouble finding a single (or double) for less than FF100 (or even more) in the towns, but in rural areas, it is possible to hang a hammock for about FF20.

Food & Drink

Food is good, but restaurant meals are very expensive, rarely less than FF50 and frequently more than twice that. Exceptions to this rule are Indonesian and Hmong street and market vendors, who prepare excellent simple meals and large sandwiches for about FF20 to FF25. Food from markets is fairly reasonable.

Imported alcoholic drinks are particularly expensive in bars and restaurants.

Entertainment

Bars and restaurants in Cayenne often have excellent live entertainment, which budget travellers can sometimes enjoy from the sidewalk if they can't afford drinks.

Things to Buy

Souvenirs are far more expensive than those in Guyana and Suriname, which they resemble. Not found in those countries are elaborate Hmong tapestries; these are good value, though not cheap.

GETTING THERE & AWAY
Air
Connections with Europe, some via France's other Caribbean colonies, are much better than those with North America. There are also links with Suriname and Brazil.

To/From Europe The most direct route is Paris to Cayenne with Air France, but there are also connections via the islands of Guadeloupe and Martinique. AOM French Airlines has charters from Paris for about FF3700 return.

To/From North America There are regular flights from Miami and other US cities to Guadeloupe and Martinique, with connections to Cayenne.

To/From Brazil Cruzeiro do Sul flies from Cayenne to Belém, in the Brazilian state of Pará, twice weekly. SLM flies the same route.

To/From Suriname Air France, SLM and Cruzeiro do Sul connect Cayenne with Paramaribo, Suriname, as do regional carriers Gum Air and Gonini.

Overland
To/From Suriname From St Laurent de Maroni, on the east bank of the Maroni River, there is a passenger ferry to Albina, Suriname (where the river is known as the Marowijne), with road connections to Paramaribo. The border with Suriname was closed because of the guerrilla insurgency, but is once again open.

To/From Brazil From St Georges, on the Oiapoque River, there are launches to the Brazilian town of Oiapoque, in Amapá state.

Leaving French Guiana
Airport Tax Since French Guiana is legally part of France, passengers to Paris leaving from Cayenne's Rochambeau Airport pay the domestic tax of FF10. To Suriname and Brazil, the tax is FF15.

GETTING AROUND
Air
Air Guyane has scheduled flights to St Georges, Régina, Saül and Maripasoula.

Bus
There is daily service from Cayenne to St Laurent du Maroni via Kourou, Sinnamary and Iracoubo.

Taxi
Taxis colectifs (actually minibuses) are faster, much more comfortable and only very slightly more expensive than the bus to St Laurent. They also run frequently from Cayenne to Kourou.

Car & Motorbike
Both car and motorbike rentals are available in Cayenne and Kourou; elsewhere, vehicle availability may be limited, even where agencies exist, as in St Laurent.

Hitching
Because private cars are numerous and roads are fairly good, hitching is a realistic alternative for budget travellers, but competition is considerable in certain areas, such as on the outskirts of Cayenne on the highway to Kourou.

Boat
River transport into the interior is possible but requires patience and good timing, unless you are taking an expensive tour.

Local Transport
Bus In Cayenne, the local SNTC bus services the beach areas of Rémire-Montjoly, but in general, public transport is limited.

Taxi Taxis are unmetered, so agree on charges in advance. Fares average a bit over FF4 per km.

Bicycle Bicycle rentals are possible in Cayenne.

Tours
Because public transport is so limited, espe-

cially in the interior, tours are a good way to see the country, but they are not cheap. For example, a five-day ascent of the Maroni, starting and ending in Cayenne, costs about FF3500 per person, all-inclusive. See Cayenne and other individual city entries for more details.

Do not sign up with private agencies for tours of the European Space Centre, which are free of charge.

CAYENNE

Dating from 1664, French Guiana's capital (population 40,000) has only a handful of early colonial buildings. Still, it exudes an atmosphere of 'France in the tropics', even though the Guyanais seem less formal than the metropolitan French.

Orientation

Cayenne is at the west end of a small, somewhat hilly peninsula between the Cayenne and Mahury rivers. The shores of the Atlantic and the Cayenne River make the city's northern and western boundaries rather irregular, but the Avenue de la Liberté and the Boulevard Jubelin circumscribe a fairly regular

grid to the south and east. The liveliest area is the Place de Palmistes, in the north-west corner of town, where there are many cafés and outdoor food stalls. To its west, the Place Grenoble (also known as Place Léopold Héder) is one of the oldest parts of Cayenne.

Information

Tourist Office The Agence Regionale de Developement du Tourisme et des Loisirs de la Guyane (☎ 30-0900), at 12 Rue Lalouette, is open on weekdays from 8 am to noon and 3 to 6 pm (closing at 5 pm on Friday), and on Saturday from 8 am to 1 pm. It has good maps of Cayenne, many brochures, and some of the staff members speak English.

Money The Bureau de Change Caraïbes, at 64 Avenue du Général de Gaulle, is open daily (except Sunday) from 8 am to 1 pm, and from 3 to 6.30 pm on weekdays. Guyane Change, in an arcade on Avenue du Général de Gaulle near the Place des Palmistes, pays the same rates for cash but slightly more for travellers' cheques.

Post & Telecommunications The most

■ PLACES TO STAY	7	Havas Voyages
	8	Museum
21 Chez Matilde	9	Place des Palmistes
23 Hotel Central	10	Maison de la Presse
24 Hotel Phigarita	11	British Consulate
28 Hotel Neptima	12	Gare Routiére (Taxis Colectifs)
	13	Brazilian Consulate
▼ PLACES TO EAT	14	Air France
	15	Air Guyane & SLM (Surinam Airways)
19 Pakhap	16	Tourist Office
20 Fanny	17	Cathedral
26 Crêperie La Sarrasine	18	Jardin Brasilien Café/Bar;
27 Porto Verde		Guyane Change
	22	Surinamese Consulate
OTHER	25	Bureau de Change Caraïbes
	29	Vital (Car Rental)
1 Fort Cépérou	30	J L Voyages
2 Préfecture	31	Avis (Car Rental)
3 Hôpital Jean Martial	32	Varig/Cruzeiro (Airlines)
4 Post Office	33	Buses Ruffinel
5 Mairie (Town Hall)	34	Hôpital St Denis
6 Place Victor Schoelcher		

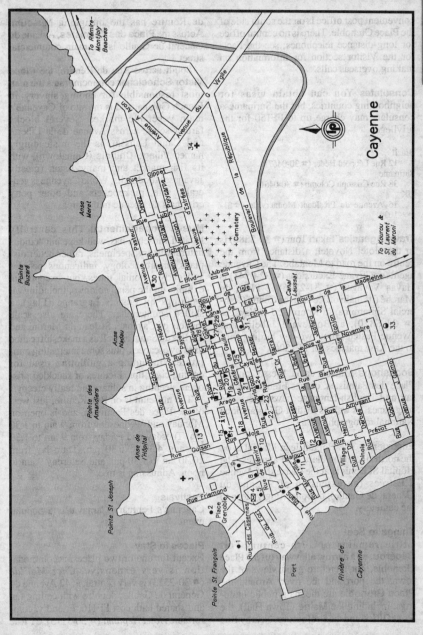

Cayenne

convenient post office is on the south side of the Place Grenoble. There is no central office for long-distance telephones; see the Facts for the Visitor section for information on making overseas calls.

Consulates You can obtain visas for neighbouring countries, but the Surinamese consulate may charge up to FF150 for the privilege.

Brazil
   12 Rue Léopold Héder (☎ 30-0467)
Suriname
   38 Rue Cristoph Colomb (☎ 30-0461)
UK
   16 Avenue du Prèsident Monnerville (☎ 31-1034)

Travel Agencies Takari Tour (☎ 30-3888) is in the Hotel Novotel, a distance from the centre on the road to Montabo. The Cayenne agent for Guyane-Excursions (☎ 32-0541) is Havas Voyages (☎ 31-2726), 2 Place du Marché (its main office is in the Centre Comercial Simarouba, in Kourou). J L Voyages (☎ 31-6820), at Boulevard Jubelin and Avenue Pasteur, runs two-day birding trips to the Kaw marshes for FF1300.

Bookshops Maison de la Presse, on the Place des Palmistes, carries French, Brazilian and English-language newspapers and magazines, as well as Institut Géographique National topographic maps.

Emergency The Hôpital Jean Martial is on the north side of the Place des Palmistes. The Hôpital St Denis is at the east end of Avenue d'Estrées (an extension of Avenue du Général de Gaulle), disconcertingly close to the cemetery.

Things to See
Little remains of 17th-century **Fort Cépérou**, up a narrow alleyway off the Place Grenoble, but there are good views of the town, the port and the river. Around the **Place Grenoble** are the main public buildings, including the **Mairie** (Town Hall), the **Post Office** and the **Préfecture**. Nearby Rue de Rémire has the intriguing **Museum**. Across the **Place des Palmistes**, Avenue du Général de Gaulle is the main commercial street.

South across Rue de Rémire, the **Place Victor Schoelcher** commemorates the man most responsible for ending slavery in French Guiana, and is the site of Cayenne's main vegetable market. Several blocks farther south, across Avenue de la Liberté and Canal Laussat, is the misleadingly named **Village Chinois** (Chinatown), with its fish market and many Asian (mostly Javanese) food stalls. While Cayenne is generally safe, pickpockets and other petty criminals do operate in this area.

Musée Departamental This centrally located museum has well-kept but tedious natural-history specimens, rather better displays on archaeology, indigenous peoples and early colonial times, but exceptional exhibits on the penal colonies, including oil paintings by Francis Lagrange (Flag), a skilled counterfeiter. There are also scale models of Cayenne, St Jean du Maroni and the Îles du Salut, as well as a makeshift canoe used by escapees, plus some interesting miniatures, including a guillotine used for cutting cigar tips. Pictures of shackled prisoners sleeping in solitary are really creepy.

The museum is on Rue Rémire, just west of the Place des Palmistes, and is open on Monday and Wednesday from 9 am to 1.30 pm, Tuesday and Friday from 9 am to 1.30 pm and 4.30 to 6.30 pm, Thursday from 10.30 am to 1.30 pm, and Saturday 9 am to noon. Admission is free.

Festivals
Cayenne's February Carnaval is a popular event.

Places to Stay
Except for one or two places, accommodation is very expensive. *Chez Matilde* (☎ 30-2513) is very central, at 42 Avenue du Général de Gaulle; doubles with ceiling fan and shared bath cost FF110. Friendly, comfortable *Hotel Neptima* (☎ 30-1115), 21 Rue

Félix Eboué, has singles with private bath and air-conditioning from FF150, but most rooms are more expensive. Other places are much dearer, like *Hotel Amazonia* (☎ 31-0000), 26 Avenue du Général de Gaulle, where singles/doubles start at FF350/400.

Places to Eat
Best quality for the lowest price are the mobile food stalls around the Place des Palmistes, mostly but not exclusively Javanese; one or two prepare very fine crêpes, at prices only a fraction of those at, say, *Crêperie La Sarrasine*, 55 Rue du Lt Goinet.

Porto Verde, 58 Rue du Lt Goinet, has good fixed-price Brazilian meals for about FF45, plus very cold imported beer. Reasonably priced Chinese food is available at *Fanny*, 42 Rue Justin Cayatée, and *Pakhap*, 29 Rue Arago. Beyond these and similar places, prices rise rapidly beyond the range of budget travellers. Plenty of first-class places charge more than FF150 per person, but the cheap places still offer very good food.

Entertainment
Jardin Brasilien, an open-air café/bar on Avenue du Général de Gaulle, at the southeast corner of the Place des Palmistes, is an expensive place to drink but has great live jazz, so many locals stand on the sidewalk and listen for free.

Several cinemas on and near Avenue du Général de Gaulle show good European and North American films.

Things to Buy
There are several souvenir shops along Avenue du Général de Gaulle; items are similar to those in Suriname, but prices are much higher.

Getting There & Away
Air Rochambeau Airport, about 15 km south-west of Cayenne, has flights to Suriname, Brazil, the French Caribbean and France. Air Guyane flights to St Georges de l'Oiapoque, on the Brazilian border, are often booked several days in advance.

Note that SLM offices in Cayenne will not reconfirm Saturday flights from Paramaribo to Georgetown, because those flights leave from Zorg-en-Hoop rather than Zanderij.

Airlines with offices in Cayenne include:

Air France
    Place Léon Gontran Damas (☎ 30-2740)
Air Guyane
    2 Rue Lalouette (☎ 31-7200)
Varig/Cruzeiro do Sul
    90 Rue René Jadfard (☎ 30-3967)
SLM (Surinam Airways)
    2 Rue Lalouette (☎ 31-7298)

Bus Buses Ruffinel (☎ 31-2666), Digue Galmot 8, has a scheduled service to St Laurent du Maroni (FF140, five hours) and intermediate destinations like Kourou (FF50) at 5.30 am, but that's really when they start warming up the diesel; they usually leave after 6 am.

Taxi Taxi colectifs to Kourou and St Laurent du Maroni leave when full from the Gare Routière on Avenue de la Liberté. Only FF10 dearer than the bus to St Laurent, they are much faster and more comfortable.

Car Because of limited public transport, car rental is worth considering, even though it's expensive. Vital (☎ 31-8030), 83 Avenue du Général de Gaulle, has good weekend rates (three days for FF900) with unlimited mileage but does not accept credit cards for deposit (FF2000) or payment. Avis (☎ 31-2527), 91 Rue du Lt Becker, has weekend rates of FF975. There are also Avis offices at Aéroport Rochambeau (☎ 35-6676), Kourou and St Laurent du Maroni.

Bicycle Try the shops along Avenue du Général de Gaulle to buy or rent a bike.

Hitching Hitching to Kourou and St Laurent is feasible, but competition is considerable at the junction of the Kourou and Régina highways.

Getting Around
To/From the Airport Taxis to Rochambeau

cost about FF100, but they may be shared. It is far cheaper to take a taxi colectif to Matoury, but that still leaves a five-km hitch or walk to Rochambeau.

Bus The bus network serves mostly the beach resort of Rémire-Montjoly, east of the capital.

Taxi Taxis are unmetered, so agree on fares in advance.

AROUND CAYENNE
Rémire-Montjoly
Rémire-Montjoly is Cayenne's main beach area, reached by SNTC buses or by taxi. A prime residential zone, it also features historical ruins at **Fort Diamant**, a hiking trail to the top of **Montagne du Mahury** and an early colonial sugar mill at **Vidal de Lingendes**.

Roura
In a scenic area on the highway to Kaw, this village on the east bank of the Mahury River has an interesting 19th-century church. It is the beginning of a series of hills, the Montagne de Kaw, covered by well-preserved tropical rainforest (despite occasional slash-and-burn clearings and commercial timber operations). An unsurfaced highway follows the ridge to the Kaw marshes.

Near Roura is the Laotian village of **Dacca**; canoe trips are possible on Gabrielle Creek, and there is a lateral road to Fourgassier Falls. *Le Relais de Patawa* (☎ 31-9395), on the Kaw highway, has hammock space (FF20), rents hammocks (FF40) and offers beds (FF60). Meals cost FF70 to FF90.

Kaw
Reached by paved and dirt highway to the Kaw river, then by launch across the river, this is one of French Guiana's most accessible wildlife areas. There are many birds, and the marshes are also home to caimans. Some tour agencies run expensive trips from Cayenne, but there is basic lodging available. It is also possible to catch a launch downstream from Régina.

Montsinéry
On the Rivière Montsinéry, some 45 km west of Cayenne, this town is known for its church and zoo (admission is a whopping FF50). The zoo is open daily from 9 am to 7 pm, but its big attraction is the feeding of the caimans, on Sunday at 6 pm.

Cacao
Cacao is about 75 km from Cayenne by a lateral off the paved highway to Régina. This village of Hmong refugees, transplanted from the Asian to the American tropics, has a fascinating Sunday market (weavings are a good purchase). It also offers very fine and inexpensive food – about FF20 for a huge noodle soup which is meal in itself.

From Cayenne, there are Monday morning and Friday afternoon minibuses to Cacao with Transport Collectif Bruno Le Vessier (☎ 30-5132), making it possible to spend the weekend. For lodging, try *Restaurant Lau Faineng* (☎ 30-2830).

Régina
On the Approuague river, about 100 km from Cayenne, Régina is literally the end of the road, in this case Route Nationale 2 (projected to continue to St Georges). Despite its otherwise neglected and even dilapidated appearance, Régina is the site of a new football stadium. Air Guyane flies daily from Cayenne to Régina.

ST GEORGES DE L'OIAPOQUE
This town on the Brazilian border is only accessible by heavily booked, twice-daily flights from Cayenne. Take your chances on food and accommodation at *Chez Modestine* where, wrote Thurston Clarke, a French companion complained that 'It is truly disgusting, this cuisine. It is almost raw, but cooking would be no help'.

From St Georges, you can take a launch (FF20) across the river to the Brazilian town of Oiapoque, where a scheduled daily bus ostensibly departs for Macapá at noon (in fact, it leaves when it's full).

There is much illegal immigration from Oiapoque to Cayenne, by precarious, ocean-

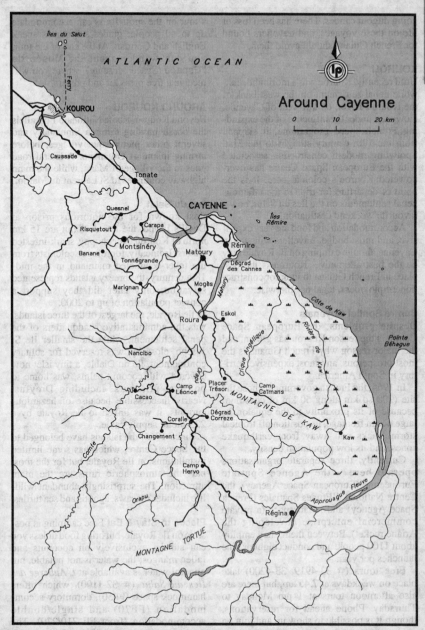

ATLANTIC OCEAN

Around Cayenne

0   10   20 km

Îles du Salut

Ferry

KOUROU

Caussade

Tonate

Quesnel

CAYENNE

Risquetout

Carapa

Montsinéry

Matoury

Rémire

Îles Rémire

Banane

Tonnégrande

Dégrad des Cannes

Marignan

Mogès

Roura

Eskol

Mahury

Côte de Kaw

Nancibo

Rivière de Kaw

Pointe Béhague

Placer Trésor

Camp Léonce

Camp Catmans

Cacao

MONTAGNE DE KAW

Coralie

Dégrad Correze

Kaw

Changement

Comté

Camp Hervo

Orapu

Approuague Fleuve

Régina

MONTAGNE TORTUE

going dugout canoes. There has been loss of life on these voyages, and travellers bound for French Guiana should avoid them.

KOUROU

Until recently, Kourou was a moribund, erstwhile penal settlement on the west bank of the Kourou River, 65 km west of Cayenne. However, under the influence of the expanding French space programme, it skipped from the 19th century straight to the 21st. Sprawling modern construction associated with the European Space Centre has overpowered Kourou's colonial core. It is the point of departure for trips to the infamous penal settlements on the Îles du Salut, now a favourite weekend destination.

Accommodation and food are very expensive, and most budget travellers will stay in Cayenne, though camping on Île Royale may be the best alternative. Kourou is the best place in French Guiana to look for construction employment, legal or otherwise.

Centre Spatial Guyanais

Despite problems, the European Space Centre is the reason Kourou has grown, and the major reason why French Guiana is the most prosperous, and most expensive, territory in South America.

In 1964, the French government chose the site (900 sq km along 50 km of coastline) because of its proximity to the equator, its large ocean frontage, its position off tropical storm tracks and away from earthquake zones, and its low population density.

Currently, three separate organisations operate here – the Agence Spatiale Européenne (European Space Agency), the Centre National d'Études Spatiales (French Space Agency) and Arianespace (a private commercial enterprise developing the Ariane rocket). Between them, they employ about 1100 people and conduct eight or nine launches per year.

Free tours (☎ 33-4919, 33-4200) take place on weekdays at 7.45 am, but there are also afternoon tours at 1 pm Monday to Thursday. Phone ahead for reservations, though it is possible to show up and join on a tour on the spot. Tours can accommodate up to 40 people; guides sometimes speak English and German. At the end of the tour, you can wander about the **Musée de l'Espace** (Space Museum), where you will receive a free press kit and posters.

AROUND KOUROU

Beyond Kourou, Route Nationale 1 parallels the coast, passing through Sinnamary and several other picturesque villages, before turning inland at Organabo. A lateral road goes to the village of Mana, while the main highway continues to St Laurent du Maroni.

Îles du Salut

Best known for the notorious prison at Devil's Island, the Îles du Salut are 15 km north of Kourou over choppy, shark-infested waters. Ironically, for refugee colonists from the fever-decimated mainland in the mid-18th century, the breezy islands represented salvation; only later did they support a convict population of up to 2000.

Île Royale, the largest of the three islands, was the administrative headquarters of the penal settlement, while the smaller Île St Joseph, close by, was reserved for solitary confinement. Île du Diable, a tiny islet now covered with coconut palms, was home to political prisoners, including Dreyfus. Nearly inaccessible because of hazardous currents, it was linked to Île Royale by a 225-metre supply cable.

Since 1965, the islands have belonged to the Space Centre, which has some limited installations on Île Royale, but for the most part the atmospheric ruins are the main attraction. The surprisingly abundant wildlife includes macaws, agoutis and sea turtles.

Places to Stay & Eat Free camping is possible on Île Royale, but bring food unless you can subsist exclusively on coconuts and fallen mangos; the water is not potable, but mineral water is available at *L'Auberge des Îles du Salut* (☎ 32-1100), which offers hammock space (FF50), dormitory accommodation (FF70) and single/double accommodation (from FF 210/270). The midday prix fixe meal is good (though probably not worth the FF130 charge); dining so well where prisoners survived on bread and water is a bizarre irony.

Getting There & Away
From Kourou's Marché de Poisson (Fish Market), a very comfortable launch crosses to Île Royale daily at 8 am (FF180 return, one hour). Make reservations with Carbet des Îles (☎ 32-0995), or through Takari Tours (☎ 31-1969) in Cayenne, though on most days it is possible to show up and buy a ticket on the spot. If not overnighting in Kourou, take the Ruffinel bus or an early taxi colectif (these don't leave until nearly full, and may cut it close). On the return trip, it's easy to catch a lift back to Cayenne by asking drivers in the parking lot.

Sinnamary
Sinnamary, a village of 3500 people, is 50 km west of Kourou. It has a substantial Indonesian community, producing excellent handicrafts including woodwork and jewellery. The cheapest accommodation is the *Sinnarive Motel* (☎ 34-5646), at FF260 a single or double.

Iracoubo
Iracoubo, 30 km west of Sinnamary, is best known for its parish church, whose nondescript exterior masks an interior elaborately painted by a convict who remained in the area after his release. Nearby is the Amerindian village of Bellevue, with attractive Galibi pottery.

Buses and taxi colectifs between Cayenne and St Laurent usually stop long enough for travellers to see the interior of the church.

ST LAURENT DU MARONI
St Laurent's architectural heritage of attractive colonial buildings derives from a past in which convicts arrived for processing. It is also the centre for excursions up the Maroni (Marowijne) River, the colony's most densely populated river. If encouraging political trends continue, it may be possible to organise these trips on the Surinamese side of the border at a price within the reach of budget travellers.

Information
Tourist Office St Laurent's helpful Office de Tourisme (☎ 34-2398), at the corner of Avenue de la Marne and Rue August Boudinot, is open daily (except Sunday) from 8 am to noon and 4 to 6 pm. Limited English is spoken, and the office has several maps and brochures.

Money The Banque Nationale de Paris is at the corner of Avenue Félix Eboué and Rue Montravel.

Post The Bureau de Poste is on Avenue du Général de Gaulle, near Avenue Malouet.

Travel Agencies For river excursions, contact Youkaliba Expeditions (☎ 34-1645), 3 Rue Simon, or Guyane Aventure (☎ 34-2128), 2 Avenue Carnot. A five-day trip up the Maroni River to Maripasoula costs FF3200 per person, but there are cheaper trips of shorter distance and duration.

Emergency The Hôpital André Bouron (☎ 34-1037) is on Avenue du Général de Gaulle.

Camp de la Transportation
At the Camp de la Transportation (1857), prisoners arrived for processing and transfer to the various prison camps throughout the territory. You can walk through the same gates as Dreyfus and Papillon – but you can leave more easily than they did.

In many places, exuberant tropical vegetation has obscured this grim reality, but it is still possible to 'appreciate' the long common cells, with shackles and open toilets, and the solitary confinement cells, with their hard bunks and tiny windows. Currently, several buildings are being restored, most notably the kitchen, while Surinamese refugees occupy what was once prison staff housing. The camp is open daily from 8.30 am to 12.30 pm and 2.30 to 6.30 pm.

St Laurent
du Maroni

0   100   200 m

Place de la
République

Malouet

Avenue Franklin Roosevelt

Avenue de la Gare

1

2

3

Rue du Lt Colonel Chandon

4

5

Camp de la
Transportation

Rue Montravel

8

La Roche
Bleue

6

7

9

Rue Schoelcher

Avenue Félix V Hugo

10

11

12

Allée des Bambous

To Kourou
& Cayenne

13

14

Rue Rousseau

15

16

Rue Marceau

17

18   19

Avenue du Lieutenant Colonel Tourtet

Rue Thiers

20

Cemetery

Rue Simon

21

22

23

Rue Guynemer

Fleuve Maroni

Rue Justin Cayece

Avenue du Général de Gaulle

Rue Marie Barret

Rue R Barret

Village
Chinois

Rue René Vadiard

Rue René Marran

Avenue René Roudinot

Rue Auguste
Roudinot

24

Rue Nouvelle No 8

Rue Nouvelle No 9

Rue Nouvelle No 7

25

To Aérodrome
& St Maurice

To St Jean

Ferry to
Albina (Suriname)

26   27

■ PLACES TO STAY		OTHER	
5	Hotel La Tentiaire	1	Post Office
7	Relais de Barcarel	2	Office Nationale de Forêts
10	Hotel Le Toucan	3	Guyane Aventure
23	Hotel Star	4	Mairie (Town Hall)
		6	Gendarmerie (Police)
▼ PLACES TO EAT		8	Banque Nationale de Paris
		9	Avis (Car Rental)
7	Le Saramacca	12	Market
11	Le Punch de Coco	13	Hôpital André Bouron
14	Chez Felicia	20	Youkaliba Expeditions
15	Loon Fa	23	Buses Ruffinel
16	Chez Bushie	24	Tourist Office
17	Restaurant Vietnam	25	Eldorado Voyages
18	Tai Loong	26	Customs & Immigration
19	Double Bonheur	27	Taxi Colectifs to Cayenne
21	Casablanca Marocain		
22	Mamies		

Places to Stay & Eat

At *Hotel Le Toucan* (☎ 34-1017), on Avenue du Général de Gaulle at the corner of Rue Schoelcher, the brusque management charges from FF100 (availability limited) to FF170 a single for rooms with peeling linoleum, private bath and air-conditioning. *Relais de Barcarel* (☎ 34-1023), on Avenue Félix Eboué at the corner of Rue Montravel, is a better choice for about the same price. *Hotel Star* (☎ 34-1084), at 109 Rue Thiers, is only slightly dearer, with one budget room at FF150 and others at FF180 or FF220. *Hotel La Tentiaire* (☎ 34-2600), 12 Avenue Franklin Roosevelt, is the best in town, starting at FF240 a single.

St Laurent has many good but mostly expensive restaurants; the cheapest alternative is the Javanese food stalls along Avenue Eboué, which offer a good and filling bami goreng with a side order of satay for about FF20. Other Asian eateries include the reasonably priced *Restaurant Vietnam*, 19 Avenue Félix Eboué, the nearby *Tai Loong*, and the *Double Bonheur*, on Rue Jean-Jacques Rousseau. For North African cuisine, try *Le Punch de Coco*, 17 Rue Rousseau, across Rue Eboué, or *Casablanca Marocain*, on Rue Guynemer. *Mamies*, on Rue Eboué near Rue Simon, is a reasonable snack bar.

Getting There & Away

Bus Service de Transport Ruffinel leaves Hotel Star for Cayenne daily, at 5 am (FF140).

Taxi Taxi colectifs leave from the pier when full, or nearly so. They are faster, more comfortable and more convenient than a bus, and only slightly dearer, at FF150 to Cayenne. One good driver is Jean-Marie Merlin (☎ 34-1883).

Boat Free ferries cross to Suriname daily at 7, 9 and 11 am, and 2 and 4 pm. There is no Tuesday afternoon service.

At other hours, motorised Saramacca and Boni *pirogues* cross the river on demand (US$2).

Getting Around

Avis (☎ 34-2456) has an office at 20 Rue Montravel, but there are often no rental vehicles available.

AROUND ST LAURENT DU MARONI

Mana

About 50 km north-west of St Laurent by a good road is the rustic village of Mana. There are Indian settlements at Aouara, 20 km west, while at nearby **Plage Les Hattes**, leatherback turtles come ashore to nest from April to July; eggs hatch from July to September. Between St Laurent and Mana is **Acarouany**, a Hmong refugee village. It has a popular Sunday market, and accommodation at the *Relais de l'Acarouany* (☎ 34-1720), once a leprosarium.

Maripasoula

Maripasoula is a popular destination for upstream travellers from St Laurent du Maroni, because it has an airfield with connections to Cayenne. Going beyond Maripasoula to the Amerindian villages in the area requires permission from the Préfecture in St Laurent or Maripasoula.

Paraguay

Despite its centrality on the continent, Paraguay has long been South America's isolated 'empty quarter'. Once a notorious police state, it now welcomes visitors to the riverside capital of Asunción, the Jesuit missions of the upper Río Paraná, and the vast, arid Chaco.

Facts about the Country

HISTORY
Pre-Hispanic Cultures
Before European contact, Guaraní cultivators occupied most of what is now eastern Paraguay, but several hunter-gatherer groups, known collectively as Guaycurú, inhabited the Chaco, west of the Río Paraguay. Other hunter-gatherers lived in forest enclaves near the modern Brazilian border. Though usually peaceful, the Guaraní sometimes ventured into Guaycurú territory and had even raided the Andean foothills.

Arrival of the Spanish
In 1524, Alejo García walked across southern Brazil, Paraguay and the Chaco with Guaraní guides, and his discoveries of silver led to the Río de Solís being renamed the Río de la Plata (River of Silver). Sebastián Cabot sailed up the Río Paraguay in 1527, but founded no permanent settlements.

Pedro de Mendoza's expedition, fleeing Buenos Aires, settled at Asunción, where Spanish-Indian relations took an unusual course: the Guaraní absorbed the Spaniards into their social system by providing them with women, and therefore food, since women were the farmers in Guaraní society. This informal arrangement was later ratified by the *encomienda*. The Spaniards adopted Guaraní food, language and other customs, but there gradually emerged a hybrid, Spanish-Guaraní society in which Spaniards

dominated politically, while *mestizo* children adopted many Spanish cultural values.

The Jesuit Missions
Colonial 'Paraguay' also encompassed parts of modern Brazil and Argentina, where Jesuit missionaries created highly organised settlements in which the Guaraní learned many aspects of European high culture, as well as new crafts, crops and methods of cultivation. Until their expulsion in 1767, the Jesuits deterred Portuguese intervention and protected Spanish interests. For more information on Jesuit missions, see the section on Argentine Mesopotamia.

The Jesuits were less successful among the Guaycurú, for whom, wrote one Austrian father, the Chaco was a refuge 'which the

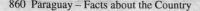

Paraguay

NATIONAL PARKS

1 Parque Nacional Defensores del Chaco
2 Parque Nacional Teniente Enciso
3 Parque Nacional Tinfunqué
4 Parque Nacional Cerro Corá
5 Parque Nacional Ybycuí
6 Parque Nacional Caaguazú

Spanish soldiers look upon as a theatre of misery, and the savages as their Palestine and Elysium'. There they had 'mountains for observatories, trackless woods for fortifications, rivers and marshes for ditches, and plantations of fruit trees for storehouses...' After secular Spaniards realised that the Chaco lacked precious metals, they ignored the area.

Independence & the Reign of 'El Supremo'

Spain failed to contest Paraguay's declaration of independence in 1811, and within a few years, José Gaspar Rodríguez de Francia emerged as the strongest member of a governing junta. Until 1840, the xenophobic Francia ruled as 'El Supremo', sealing the country's borders to promote national self-sufficiency/subsistence. To accomplish his aims, he expropriated the properties of landholders, merchants and even the Church, establishing the state as the dominant power and controlling the small agricultural surplus – mostly *yerba mate* and tobacco. He ruled by fear, imprisoning opponents in what a visiting Englishman called 'state dungeons'.

Francia himself was a victim of the

climate of terror. After escaping an attack in 1820, El Supremo so feared assassination that his food and drink were consistently checked for poison, no one could approach him closer than six paces, streets were cleared for his carriage and he slept in a different place every night. Perhaps thanks to these precautions, he died a natural death in 1840; in 1870, opponents who knew how to hold a grudge disinterred his remains and threw them into the river.

The López Dynasty & the War of the Triple Alliance

Francia's successor Carlos Antonio López ended Paraguay's isolation, building railways, telegraph, an iron foundry, a shipyard – and a standing army of 28,000, with another 40,000 reserves by the early 1860s (at the time Argentina had only 6000 men in uniform).

His megalomaniacal son, Francisco Solano López, led the country into a catastrophic war against the triple alliance of Argentina, Uruguay and Brazil. Paraguay lost 150,000 sq km of territory, and perhaps 20% of its population through combat, famine and disease – it was said that only women, children and burros remained.

Reconstruction & the Chaco War

After 1870, a trickle of European and Argentine immigrants resuscitated the agricultural sector, but political life did not stabilise for decades.

At the turn of the century, tension arose with Bolivia over the ill-defined borders of the Chaco, but full-scale hostilities did not erupt until 1932. A 1935 cease-fire left no clear victor, but a treaty awarded Paraguay three-quarters of the disputed territory. Speculation over oil fueled the hostilities, but none was ever found.

Modern Developments

After the Chaco War, Paraguay endured a decade of disorder before a brief civil war brought the Colorado party to power in 1949. A military coup in 1954 installed General Stroessner, who ruled the country harshly for 35 years, often employing torture and murder, until his overthrow in 1989. Since then political conditions have improved, but Stroessner supporters still dominate a faction of the Colorado party. For more information on the regime and its successor, see the Government section below.

GEOGRAPHY & CLIMATE

Surrounded by Brazil, Argentina and Bolivia, Paraguay appears small on the map, but at 407,000 sq km it is larger than Germany and almost exactly the size of California. About 40% of its territory and the great majority of the population are east of the Río Paraguay. This well-watered plateau of rolling grasslands, with patches of subtropical forest, extends all the way to the Río Paraná, which forms much of its borders with Brazil and Argentina.

Rainfall is distributed evenly throughout the year. Near the Brazilian border, it averages an abundant 2000 mm per annum, declining to about 1500 mm near Asunción. Summer highs average 35°C; winter temperatures average a pleasant 22°C in July, the coldest month. Spring and autumn cold fronts sometimes cause temperatures to drop 20°C within only a few hours.

West of the Río Paraguay is the Chaco, an extensive plain whose principal economic activity is cattle ranching; only about 4% of Paraguayans live here. Hotter than eastern Paraguay, its erratic rainfall and high rates of evaporation make rain-fed agriculture undependable, but Mennonite immigrants have raised cotton and other commercial crops successfully.

FLORA & FAUNA

Like the rainfall, vegetation diminishes from east to west. Humid subtropical forests are dense in the valleys of Eastern Paraguay and sparse on thinner upland soils. Toward the Río Paraguay, the dominant vegetation is savanna grass, with occasional gallery forests, while to its west, palm savanna gives way to scrub and thorn forest.

Wildlife is diverse, but the dense rural population has put great pressure on eastern

Paraguay's fauna. A notable success has been the protection of the Chacoan peccary (or Wagner's peccary), once thought extinct, by local and international conservationists.

Bird life is abundant, especially in the Chaco. Paraguay has 21 species of parrot and parakeet, including the stunning hyacinth macaw and the nearly extinct spix macaw in the eastern forests. In the Chaco, the most visible species are jabirú and wood storks. Many reptiles, including caiman, anaconda and boa constrictor, inhabit the riverine lowlands.

Paraguay has half a dozen national parks and several other reserves protecting a variety of habitats. The three largest are in the Chaco, with three smaller and more biologically diverse parks in eastern Paraguay. Because of corruption, economic pressure and traditionally weak political commitment, some have experienced serious disruption.

GOVERNMENT

Paraguay is a republic whose constitution establishes a strong president, popularly elected for a five-year term; Congress consists of a 60-member Chamber of Deputies and a 30-member Senate, elected concurrently with the president. The party with the most votes automatically gains two-thirds of the seats in Congress.

In practice, the country has experinced one of the continent's most corrupt, odious and durable dictatorships since 1947 Stroessner's Colorado party, aligned with the military, has been the dominant political organisation. Both the Liberales and the Febreristas Revolucionarios (Revolutionary Febreristas; a moderate labour-oriented party) operated within Stroessner's limits. Others, including Liberal and Colorado factions, have boycotted bogus elections. With the Liberales and Febreristas, the Democracia Cristiana (Christian Democrat) party and MOPOCO (a dissident Colorado faction) constitute the *Acuerdo Nacional* (National Accord).

After deposing Stroessner in 1989, General Andrés Rodríguez won the presidency, unopposed, in an election in which opposition parties gained more congressional representation than ever before.

In May 1993 elections, the winner was Colorado candidate Juan Carlos Wasmosy, a corrupt engineer from Stroessner's faction. The election took place in an atmosphere of intimidation, but were probably the fairest in Paraguayan history.

ECONOMY

Historically, the economy depends on agriculture and livestock. Principal exports have been beef, maize, sugar cane, soybeans, lumber and cotton, but many rural people cultivate subsistence crops on small holdings. By most measures, Paraguay has a low standard of living. Infant mortality is higher than in any other South American country except Colombia, Bolivia and Peru, and only Bolivians and Peruvians have a lower life expectancy than the average Paraguayan's 65 years.

Paraguay lacks mineral energy resources, but enormous multinational dam projects have developed its hydroelectric potential over the past 15 years. Brazil takes most of the power from Itaipú, while the corruption-plagued Yacyretá dam, on the border with the Argentine province of Corrientes, may never be finished. Paraguayan industry (mostly processing of agricultural products) benefits little from this hydroelectric capacity. Slowing of construction activity, due to the completion of Itaipú and stalling of the Yacyretá project, has nearly eliminated the economic growth experienced in the 1970s. Paraguay's major industry is now contraband, most of which passes through Ciudad del Este to or from Brazil. Besides smuggled soybeans and coffee, stolen cars and illegal drugs also pass into or through Paraguay.

POPULATION & PEOPLE

Paraguay's population is about 4.8 million, with about 43% living in the cities, of which Asunción (population 800,000) is the largest. Many Paraguayans have returned since the fall of Stroessner, but for economic reasons, many others still live in Brazil and Argentina.

More than 75% of Paraguayans are mestizos, speaking Guaraní by preference, though almost all speak Spanish as well. Another 20% are descendents of European immigrants, including German Mennonite farmers in the central Chaco. Japanese immigrants have settled parts of eastern Paraguay, along with Brazilian colonists who have moved across the border in recent years. Asunción has seen a substantial influx of Koreans, mostly involved in commerce.

Most of Paraguay's Indians, about 3% of the population, live in the Chaco. The largest groups are the Nivaclé and Lengua, each numbering around 10,000. Isolated peoples like the Ayoreo have lived almost untouched by European civilisation, but many Indians have become dependent labour for immigrant farmers.

EDUCATION

Education is compulsory to the age of 12. Literacy is 81%, lower than Argentina or Uruguay but higher than all the Andean countries except Ecuador. Higher education is provided by the Universidad Nacional and the Universidad Católica, both in Asunción.

ARTS

Paraguay's major literary figure is poet-novelist Augusto Roa Bastos, winner of the 1990 Cervantes Prize. Despite many years in exile, Roa Bastos has focused on Paraguayan themes and history in the context of politics and dictatorship. Little Paraguayan literature is available to English-speaking readers; for suggestions, see the Books & Maps entry in the Facts for the Visitor section.

Theatre is popular, with occasional offerings in Guaraní as well as Spanish. Numerous art galleries emphasise modern, sometimes very unconventional works. Both classical and folk music are performed in venues in Asunción.

CULTURE

English-speaking visitors may find Paraguay exotic because of its unique racial and cultural mix, but Paraguayans are eager to meet and speak with foreigners. An invitation to drink *mate*, often in the form of ice-cold *tereré*, can be a good introduction.

An ability to speak German may dissolve barriers in the culturally insular Mennonite communities, but it is more difficult to meet the region's indigenous people, and undiplomatic to probe too quickly into relations between the two. Many Chaco Indians speak German (rather than Spanish) as a second language.

Paraguayans in general are sports-minded; the most popular soccer team, Olímpia, has beaten the best Argentine sides. Tennis and basketball have become popular spectator sports.

RELIGION

Roman Catholicism is the official religion, but folk variants are important, and the Church is less influential than in other Latin American countries. Native peoples have retained their own religious beliefs, or modified them only slightly, despite nominal allegiance to Catholicism or evangelical Protestantism.

Protestant sects have made fewer inroads than in some other countries, although Mennonites have proselytised among Chaco Indians since the 1930s. Other evangelical groups, including the controversial New Tribes Mission, operated with the collusion, and some say the active support, of the Stroessner dictatorship.

LANGUAGE

Spanish is the language of government and commerce, though Paraguay is officially bilingual. The Guaraní language has been influenced by Spanish, but it has also modified Spanish in vocabulary and speech patterns. During the Chaco War against Argentina, Guaraní enjoyed resurgent popularity when, for security reasons, field commanders prohibited Spanish on the battlefield.

Several other Indian languages, including Lengua, Nivaclé and Aché, are spoken in the Chaco and isolated parts of eastern Paraguay.

Facts for the Visitor

VISAS & EMBASSIES

All foreigners need visas, except those from bordering countries (who need national identification cards), most Western European countries and the USA. Canadian, Australian and New Zealand applicants need a clean police record, a bank statement and a US$10 fee. Canadians should apply through the consulate in New York. In theory, visitors need a tourist card (US$3), valid for 90 days and obtained at the airport or border crossing, but recently there was no such requirement at Asunción's airport. At land crossings, officials may accept local currency only.

Paraguayan Embassies & Consulates

Paraguay has no diplomatic representation in Australia or New Zealand, but is represented in neighbouring countries, and also in:

UK
  Braemar Lodge, Cornwall Gardens SW7 4AQ, London (☎ (071) 937-1253)

USA
  2400 Massachusetts Ave NW, Washington, DC (☎ 483-6960)
  7205 NW 19th St, Miami, FL (☎ 477-4002)
  Suite 1947, 1 World Trade Center, New York, NY (☎ 432-0733)

Foreign Embassies & Consulates in Paraguay

South American countries, the USA and most Western European countries have representatives in Asunción. Argentina and Brazil have consulates in border towns. See under the relevant city or town for addresses.

DOCUMENTS

Passports are essential for cashing travellers' cheques, checking into hotels, and passing military and police checkpoints in the Chaco. Foreign motorists need an International Driving Permit, but checks are perfunctory.

CUSTOMS

Paraguayan customs admits 'reasonable quantities' of personal effects, alcohol and tobacco.

MONEY

The unit of currency is the *guaraní* (plural guaraníes), indicated by a capital letter 'G' with a forward slash. Banknote values are 100, 500, 1000, 5000 and 10,000 guaraníes; there are coins for one, five, 10, 20, 50 and 100 guaraníes.

Cambios in Asunción and at border towns change both cash and travellers' cheques (with a small commission); try banks in the interior. Street changers give slightly lower rates but can be helpful on weekends or in the evening. Many hotels, restaurants and shops in Asunción accept credit cards, but their use is uncommon elsewhere.

At the time of writing, Paraguay was cheaper for the traveller than Argentina or Uruguay but more expensive than Brazil or Bolivia.

Exchange Rates

Prices in this chapter are given in US dollars, the most popular foreign currency. No black market exists.

A$1	=	G/1250
FFr1	=	G/290
DM1	=	G/990
US$1	=	G/1640
UK£1	=	G/2820

WHEN TO GO & WHAT TO BRING

Visitors from the mid-latitudes may prefer to come during the cooler winter months, when days are normally warm, but nights can be quite cold.

Because of the heat, Paraguayans dress informally. Light cottons suffice, except in winter, but a sweater or jacket is useful in changeable spring weather. Bring a wide-brimmed hat or baseball cap, a lightweight long-sleeved shirt, sunblock and mosquito repellent.

TOURIST OFFICES

There are tourist offices in Asunción,

Encarnación, Ciudad del Este and a few other places.

Overseas Representatives
The larger Paraguayan consulates, such as those in New York and Miami (see above), usually have a tourist representative.

Líneas Aéreas Paraguayas (LAP) The
national airline also provides tourist information. Its excellent information package, free on request in the USA, includes a thick multicolour brochure on Paraguayan natural history, with intelligent text and fine photographs.

Germany
   Kaiserstrasse 33, Frankfurt (☎ 23-3751)
USA
   Suite 920, 510 W Sixth St, Los Angeles, CA (☎ 627-7681)
   Suite 875, 7270 NW 12th St, Miami, FL (☎ 591-1916)
   Suite 1919, 342 Madison Avenue, New York, NY (☎ 972-3830)
   toll free: ☎ 800 677-7771

USEFUL ORGANISATIONS
The Fundación Moisés Bertoni (☎ 44-0238), Rodríguez de Francia 770 in Asunción, sponsors projects which encourage biological diversity and restoration of degraded ecosystems, cooperates with the state in strengthening national parks, promotes environmental education and research, and tries to involve local citizens and private enterprise in conservation. It also organises moderately priced tours to reserves which are otherwise difficult to reach.

BUSINESS HOURS & HOLIDAYS
Most shops open on weekdays and Saturdays from 7 am to noon, close until mid-afternoon and reopen until 7 or 8 pm. Banks are usually open from 7.30 to 11 am weekdays, but casas de cambio keep longer hours. Because of summer heat, Paraguayans go to work very early – from mid-November to mid-March, govern-

ment offices open as early as 6.30 am and close before noon. Holidays include:

1 January
   Año Nuevo (New Year's Day)
3 February
   Día de San Blas (Patron Saint of Paraguay)
1 March
   Cerro Corá (Death of Marshal López)
March/April (dates vary)
   Viernes Santo/Pascua (Good Friday/Easter)
1 May
   Día de los Trabajadores (Labour Day)
15 May
   Independencia Patria (Independence Day)
12 June
   Paz del Chaco (End of Chaco War)
15 August
   Fundación de Asunción (Founding of Asunción)
29 September
   Victoria de Boquerón (Battle of Boquerón)
8 December
   Día de la Virgen (Immaculate Conception)
25 December
   Navidad (Christmas Day)

POST & TELECOMMUNICATIONS
Essential mail should be registered. Antelco, the state telephone monopoly, has central long-distance offices in Asunción with direct links to operators in the USA and Japan. Credit card or collect calls to the USA and other overseas destinations are cheaper than paying locally. Public phone boxes, which are few, take fichas.

TIME
Paraguay is three hours behind GMT except in summer, when daylight savings time adds an extra hour.

BOOKS
Roa Bastos' novel Son of Man (Monthly Review Press, New York, 1988), originally published in 1961, ties together several episodes in Paraguayan history, including the Francia dictatorship and the Chaco War. I the Supreme (Knopf, New York, 1986) is a historical novel about the paranoid dictator Francia.

History
Elman and Helen Service's Tobatí:

Paraguayan Town (University of Chicago, 1954) is a standard account of rural Paraguay, in historical context. Harris Gaylord Warren's *Rebirth of the Paraguayan Republic* (University of Pittsburgh, 1985) tells of Paraguay's incomplete recovery from the War of the Triple Alliance.

The Stroessner Period
Rule by Fear: Paraguay After Thirty Years Under Stroessner (Americas Watch, New York, 1985) is an account of human rights abuses. Carlos Miranda's *The Stroessner Era* (Westview Press, Boulder, Colorado, 1990) is a thoughtful, nonpolemical analysis with a short political obituary.

Guidebooks
Lonely Planet's *Argentina, Uruguay & Paraguay* has more detailed information about travel in Paraguay. *Conozca Paraguay* (about US$8) is a regularly updated guide in Spanish, Portuguese and fractured English. Loaded with advertisements, it is still a useful resource (despite some curious theories on prehistory).

MAPS
Good maps are hard to find, but try the Instituto Geográfico Militar on Avenida Artigas. The Touring y Automóvil Club sells an *Hoja de Rutas* booklet, in Spanish only, with useful information but very poor maps. Shops in Filadelfia sell a detailed map of the Mennonite colonies.

MEDIA
The Stroessner dictatorship severely repressed media criticism, but Asunción's daily *ABC Color* made its reputation opposing him; independent Radio Ñandutí also criticised the regime. The newspaper *Ultima Hora* is relatively independent, but *Hoy* and *Patria* (the official Colorado newspaper) are controlled by Stroessner cronies. *El Pueblo* is an independent with a small circulation.

Asunción's German community publishes a twice-monthly newspaper, *Neues für Alle*. The *Buenos Aires Herald* and other Argentine papers are available in Asunción.

HEALTH
Paraguay is not an exceptionally unhealthy destination, though the recent South American cholera epidemic may spread to the country. Ask for the latest information, and drink mineral water if you have any doubts.

Malaria is not a major threat, though Itaipú dam appears to have created mosquito vector habitat. Other causes for concern, but not hysteria, are tuberculosis, typhoid, hepatitis, and hookworm *(susto)* – avoid going barefoot. Cutaneous leishmaniasis *(ura)*, transmitted by biting sandflies and resulting in open sores, is unpleasant and dangerous if untreated.

DANGERS & ANNOYANCES
In the run-up to the 1993 election, Asunción experienced a crime wave, with carjackings of conspicuously valuable vehicles a particular problem. Nevertheless, personal safety concerns are generally far less serious than in Brazil.

Since the ousting of Stroessner, police operate with less impunity, but try not to aggravate them or the military; always carry your passport. At Chaco road checkpoints you may encounter teenage conscripts with disconcertingly large automatic rifles (reportedly unloaded); be calm and polite, show your papers, and you are unlikely to be seriously inconvenienced. Tension exists between the pacifist Mennonites and Paraguayan officials in the Chaco.

Watch for poisonous snakes, especially in the Chaco, but mosquitos are a more likely nuisance.

FOOD & DRINK
Parrillada is a restaurant standard, but meat consumption is lower than in Argentina or Uruguay. Tropical and subtropical foodstuffs play a greater role in the Paraguayan diet.

Grains, particularly maize, and tubers like manioc (cassava) are part of almost every meal. *Locro*, a maize stew, resembles its Argentine namesake, while *mazamorra* is a corn mush. *Sopa paraguaya* is a cornbread with cheese and onion; *chipa guazú* is a variant. *Mbaipy so-ó* is a hot maize pudding with meat chunks, and *bori-bori* is a chicken soup with cornmeal balls. *Sooyo sopy* is a thick soup of ground meat, accompanied by rice or noodles, while *mbaipy he-é* is a dessert of corn, milk and molasses.

Manioc nourishes the rural poor. In *chipa de almidón*, manioc flour replaces the corn meal of chipa guazú. *Mbeyú*, or *torta de almidón*, is a grilled manioc pancake resembling the Mexican tortilla. During Holy Week, the addition of eggs, cheese and spices transforms ordinary food into a holiday treat.

Paraguayans consume quantities of *mate*, most commonly as ice-cold tereré. Roadside stands offer *mosto* (sugar-cane juice), while *caña* (cane alcohol) is a popular alcoholic beverage.

THINGS TO BUY

The women of Itauguá, near Asunción, weave Paraguay's famous *ñandutí* lace, ranging in size from doilies to bedspreads. In the town of Luque, artisans produce stunningly beautiful handmade musical instruments, particularly guitars and harps.

Paraguayan leather offers better bargains than that of either Argentina or Uruguay. Chaco Indians produce fine carvings from the aromatic *palo santo*, replicas of spears and other weapons, and traditional string bags *(yiscas)*.

Getting There & Away

Asunción is a convenient hub for Southern Cone air transport, but overland travellers to destinations other than Iguazú and Posadas will find Paraguay a bit out of the way.

AIR
To/From South American Countries
To Brazil, LAP and Varig fly to Rio and São Paulo several times weekly. LAP also flies on Tuesday to Santa Cruz (Bolivia), continuing to Lima (Peru), and five times weekly to Buenos Aires (Argentina). LAP and American Airlines fly to Lima. LAB also

flies to Santa Cruz, and Aerolíneas Argentinas to Buenos Aires (Ezeiza airport). LAP and PLUNA fly to Montevideo (Uruguay) via Buenos Aires weekly, while LAP and Ladeco each have three flights a week to Santiago de Chile.

Departure Tax
Passengers departing Asunción's Aeropuerto Pettirossi on international flights pay two separate taxes, one of US$9 and another of US$6. Those who have spent less than 24 hours in Paraguay are exempt.

OVERLAND
To/From Argentina
Asunción to Clorinda There is a frequent bus service from Asunción to Clorinda, in Formosa province.

Encarnación to Posadas Buses use the new international bridge to Argentina, but it is still possible to take a launch across the Río Paraná.

Ciudad del Este to Puerto Iguazú Frequent buses link Ciudad del Este to the Brazilian city of Foz do Iguaçu (see below), with easy connections to Puerto Iguazú, Argentina. Alternatively, cross directly to Puerto Iguazú by unscheduled launch from Puerto Presidente Franco, a few km south of Ciudad del Este, without passing through Brazil.

To/From Bolivia
No public transportation exists between Colonia La Patria, on the Ruta Trans-Chaco 85 km from the border, and the Bolivian town of Boyuibe, another 135 km west. Beyond Filadelfia, the dirt road is subject to long rain delays. Before attempting the crossing, contact the Bolivian Consulate in Asunción.

At military checkpoints you can wait for days for a truck to Bolivia. Take the bus to Colonia La Patria and ask about trucks, although Mariscal Estigarribia, which has a petrol station, may be a more comfortable place to wait.

To/From Brazil

Ciudad del Este to Foz do Iguaçu Vehicles and pedestrians move freely across the Puente de la Amistad (Friendship Bridge) over the Río Paraná. If spending more than a day in either country, complete immigration formalities.

Pedro Juan Caballero to Ponta Porã a small town on the Brazilian border is reached by road from Asunción, Pedro Juan Caballero. Ponta Porã is its Brazilian counterpart.

BOAT

To/From Brazil

From Asunción, the Flota Mercantíl del Estado (and some private boats) carries passengers on its irregular trips on the Río Paraguay to and from the Brazilian city of Corumbá. For details, see the Asunción section.

Getting Around

Public transportation is cheap and efficient. Travellers spending more than a week or two might acquire Alberto Hoffman's *Horarios de Transportes del Paraguay*, an exhaustive listing of inter-city transport. Available at many bookshops for about US$3, it's an amazing bargain.

AIR

Líneas Aéreas de Transporte Nacional (LATN) and Transportes Aéreos Militares (TAM), the air force passenger service, fly to destinations in upper Paraguay like Concepción, Pedro Juan Caballero and parts of the Chaco. Fares are low. For further details, see appropriate text entries.

BUS

Bus quality varies. *Servicio removido* stops at every shady tree, while *servicio directo* adds passengers only at fixed locations. Larger towns have central terminals, but elsewhere companies are within easy walking distance of each other.

TRAIN

Paraguay's antique, wood-burning trains are interesting and absurdly cheap, but impractical except for the 28-km line from Asunción to Areguá, on Lago Ypacaraí. Avoid the slow, dusty train to Encarnación, which averages barely 20 km per hour and whose nighttime departure deprives you of the landscape.

DRIVING

High-wheeled wooden oxcarts and livestock are road hazards; carts usually stick to tracks which parallel the highway, but on occasion they must cross. Night driving is not advisable.

Paraguay officially requires the International Driving Permit, but cars with foreign number plates are rarely stopped, except at military checkpoints in the Chaco. Theft is common, so be certain your vehicle is secure. Conspicuously valuable vehicles have become the object of carjackings.

The Touring y Automóvil Club Paraguayo (☎ 24366), on the corner of Brasil and 25 de Mayo in Asunción, is friendly and helpful, but its maps are terrible.

LOCAL TRANSPORT

Asunción has an extensive bus system. There are also taxis, with meters; the minimum fare is about US$1.20.

Asunción

From its central location, Asunción is the pivot of Paraguay's political, economic and cultural life. Only about 20% of Paraguayans live in the capital, but most of the rest live within 150 km.

History

Early Spaniards found Asunción more attractive than Buenos Aires because of Guaraní food and hospitality, but the city lost favour when the arid Chaco, with its hostile Indians, proved an unsuitable route to Peru.

When the López dynasty opened the country to foreign influence in the mid 1800s, they nearly obliterated the city's colonial remains in the process of erecting major public buildings, which were described as 'extravagant luxuries' among modest surroundings. Well into the 20th century, much of central Asunción was unpaved, but the city's appearance gradually improved.

The Chaco War retarded progress, but the sprawling city has encompassed ever more distant suburbs like San Lorenzo. Despite a recent construction boom, the centre retains a 19th-century atmosphere, with low buildings lining narrow streets. The influx of people from the impoverished countryside has resulted in large shantytowns along the riverfront, the railway and elsewhere.

Orientation

Its riverside location and some modern developments have created irregularities in Asunción's conventional colonial grid, which is centred on Plaza de los Héroes. Names of east-west streets change at Independencia Nacional. Nearby Plaza Uruguay offers shade from the midday heat, but at night prostitutes frequent the area.

North, along the riverfront, Plaza Constitución contains the Congreso Nacional. Below the bluff, subject to flooding, lie *viviendas temporarias*, Asunción's shantytowns. El Paraguayo Independiente, a diagonal street, leads west to the Palacio de Gobierno (Presidential Palace).

Information

Tourist Office The Dirección General de Turismo, Palma 468, supplies a good city centre map, some brochures, a list of hotels with updated prices, and looseleaf notebooks full of other information. It's open on weekdays from 7 am to 7 pm, Saturday from 8 to 11.30 am.

Money Cambios along Palma and its side streets post exchange rates prominently.

Street changers hang out at the corner of Palma and Chile.

Post & Telecommunications The main post office is at Alberdi and El Paraguayo Independiente. Antelco, Presidente Franco 198, has direct lines to operators in the USA and Japan for collect or credit card calls. Another office is upstairs at the bus terminal.

Embassies & Consulates The nearest Australian and New Zealand embassies are in Buenos Aires.

Argentina
    cnr Avenida España & Perú (☎ 21-2320)
Bolivia
    Eligio Ayala 2002 (☎ 20-3654)
Brazil
    3rd floor, General Díaz 523 (☎ 44-8084); open weekdays from 8 am to 1 pm
Canada (Honorary Consul)
    Artigas 2006 (☎ 29-3301)
France
    Avenida España 676 (☎ 23111)
Germany
    Venezuela 241 (☎ 24006)
UK
    4th floor, Presidente Franco 706 (☎ 44-4472)
USA
    Avenida Mariscal López 1776 (☎ 21-3715)

Cultural Centres Asunción's several international cultural centres offer frequent films at little or no cost, plus artistic and photographic exhibitions. These include the Casa de la Cultura Paraguaya at the corner of 15 de Agosto and El Paraguayo Independiente, the Centro Juan de Salazar (☎ 44-9221) at Herrera 834, and the architecturally weird and inappropriate Centro Paraguayo Japonés, a neoclassical structure at Julio Correa and Portillo (take bus No 16), with a superb theatre and a modern gymnasium open to the public.

Bookshops Librería Comuneros, Cerro Corá 289, offers historical and contemporary books on Paraguay. Another good shop is Librería Internacional, Caballero 270. Plaza Uruguay has open-air bookstalls.

PARAGUAY

PARAGUAY

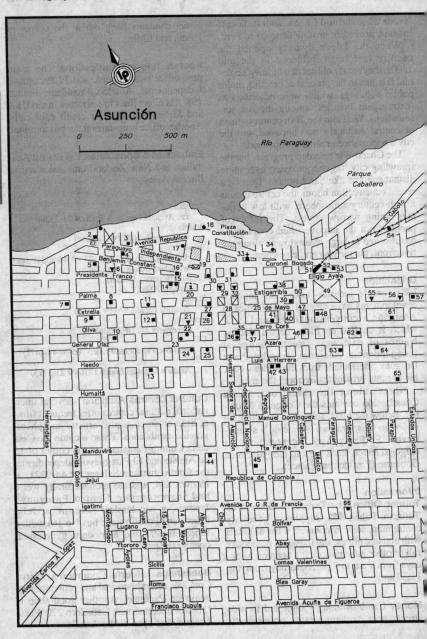

Asunción

0   250   500 m

Río Paraguay

Parque
Caballero

S. Caboto

54

1
2
El Paraguayo
3
Avenida Republica
Independiente
17
Benjamin Constant
24
5
6
Presidente Franco
16
Palma   8   15   14
11
Estrella   7   9
Oliva   10   12
General Díaz   23
Haedo   13
Humaitá
Manduvirá
Jejui
Igatimi
Ytororo

18 Plaza
Constitución

34

33

Coronel Bogado   52 53
51
Eligio Ayala
30 31
29 32   38   50   49
20   Estigarribia   39
27 28   25 de Mayo   47
21 26   41 40   48
22   35   Cerro Corá   46
36   37   Azara   63   64
24 25
Luis A Herrera   65
42 43
Moreno
Nuestra Señora de la Asunción
Yegros
Iturbe
Caballero
Manuel Dominguez
Tte Fariña
44   45   México
Republica de Colombia
Avenida Dr G R de Francia   66
Montevideo   Juan O'Leary   15 de Mayo   14 de Mayo   Alberdi   Chile   Bolívar
Lugano   Abay
Sicilia   Lomas Valentinas
Roma   Blas Garay
Francisco Dupuis   Avenida Acuña de Figueroa

Avenida Carlos A. López
Hernandarias
Avenida Colón

Independencia Nacional
Paraguay
Antequera
Tacuary
Parapiti
Estados Unidos

55 56 57
61
62

PARAGUAY

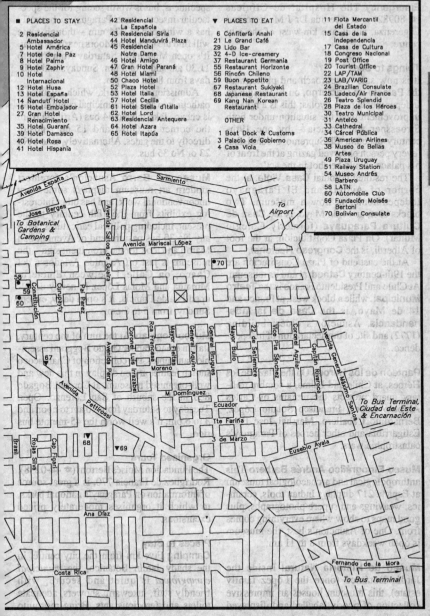

■ PLACES TO STAY

2 Residencial Ambassador
5 Hotel América
7 Hotel de la Paz
8 Hotel Palma
9 Hotel Zaphir
10 Hotel Internacional
12 Hotel Husa
13 Hotel España
14 Ñandutí Hotel
16 Hotel Embajador
27 Gran Hotel Renacimiento
35 Hotel Guaraní
39 Hotel Damasco
40 Hotel Rosa
41 Hotel Hispania
42 Residencial La Española
43 Residencial Siria
44 Hotel Manduvirá Plaza
45 Residencial Notre Dame
46 Hotel Amigo
47 Gran Hotel Paraná
48 Hotel Miami
50 Chaco Hotel
52 Plaza Hotel
53 Hotel Italia
57 Hotel Cecilia
61 Hotel Stella d'Italia
62 Hotel Lord
63 Residencial Antequera
64 Hotel Azara
65 Hotel Itapúa

▼ PLACES TO EAT

6 Confitería Anahí
21 Le Grand Café
29 Lido Bar
32 4-D Ice-creamery
37 Restaurant Germania
55 Restaurant Horizonte
56 Rincón Chileno
59 Buon Appetito
67 Restaurant Sukiyaki
68 Japanese Restaurant
69 Kang Nan Korean Restaurant

OTHER

1 Boat Dock & Customs
3 Palacio de Gobierno
4 Casa Viola
11 Flota Mercantil del Estado
15 Casa de la Independencia
17 Casa de Cultura
18 Congreso Nacional
19 Post Office
20 Tourist Office
22 LAP/TAM
23 LAB/VARIG
24 Brazilian Consulate
26 Teatro Splendid
30 Teatro Municipal
31 Antelco
33 Cathedral
34 Cárcel Pública
36 American Airlines
38 Museo de Bellas Artes
49 Telco Uruguay
51 Railway Station
54 Museo Andrés Barbero
58 LATN
60 Automobile Club
66 Fundación Moisés Bertoni
70 Bolivian Consulate

Emergency The Hospital de Clínicas (☎ 80982) is at Avenida Dr J Montero and Lagerenza, about one km west of the city centre.

Things to See

It is now safe to approach and photograph the **Palacio de Gobierno**, on El Paraguayo Independiente near Ayolas; this is a notable improvement over the situation under both Stroessner and Francia – by one 19th-century account, El Supremo ordered that 'every person observed gazing at the front of his palace should be shot in the act'.

The restored colonial **Casa Viola**, at the corner of Ayolas and El Paraguayo Independiente, is now a museum. Two blocks east, at 14 de Mayo, is the **Casa de Cultura Paraguaya** (formerly Colegio Militar). On Plaza Constitución, at the foot of Alberdi, is the **Congreso Nacional**.

At the east end of Plaza Constitución are the 19th-century **Cathedral** and its museum. At Chile and Presidente Franco is the **Teatro Municipal**, while a block west, at Franco and 14 de Mayo, is the **Casa de la Independencia**, Asunción's oldest building (1772) and site of the declaration of independence.

Panteón de los Héroes On the Plaza de los Héroes, at Chile and Palma, a sombre military guard protects the remains of Carlos Antonio López, Francisco Solano López, Bernardino Caballero, Marshal José Félix Estigarribia and other heroes of Paraguay's catastrophic wars.

Museo Etnográfico Andrés Barbero This anthropological and archaeological museum at España 217 displays Indian tools, ceramics, weavings and superb photographs, plus good maps to show where everything comes from. One of Asunción's best, the museum is open weekdays from 8 to 11 am.

Museo de Historia Natural Inside the Jardín Botánico (once the López family estate), this museum houses an impressive collection of poorly labelled and displayed specimens, but is worth seeing for the spectacular insects – one Paraguayan butterfly has a wingspan of 274 mm – though some will find the variety outdoors nearly as great. It's open Monday to Saturday from 7.30 to 11.30 am and 1 to 5 pm, Sundays and holidays from 8 am to 1 pm.

Admission to the park, which includes a pathetic zoo and the municipal campground, is cheap. Take the No 44 bus (Artigas) from the corner of Oliva and 15 de Agosto, directly to the gates. Alternatively, take a No 23 or No 35 bus.

Museo del Barro Asunción's foremost modern art museum displays some very unconventional work, and has other interesting exhibits from the 18th century to the present, including political caricatures. Take any No 30 bus past the end of Avenida San Martín and look for the prominent sign – the museum is just off Avenida Aviadores del Chaco, on Calle 1 between Emeterio Miranda and Molas López in newly developed Isla de Francia. It's open daily, except Sunday, from 5 to 8 pm.

Museo Boggiani At the turn of the century, Italian ethnographer Guido Boggiani assembled an impressive collection of Chamacoco Indian feather art, on display in this new and well-organised museum, at Coronel Bogado 888 in the suburb of San Lorenzo. Open Tuesday to Saturday from 10 am to noon and 3 to 6 pm, it's well worth the 45-minute bus ride.

Organised Tours

The Fundación Moisés Bertoni (☎ 44-0238), Rodríguez de Francia 770, is a great source of information on Paraguay's national parks, to which it organises moderately priced excursions.

Places to Stay

Camping Five km from the city centre, in the shady Jardín Botánico, the *municipal campground* is quiet and secure, with friendly staff, lukewarm showers, adequate toilets and ferocious ants. Bring mosquito repellent. Fees are negligible; when returning at night, tell the attendant at the entrance on Artigas that you are camping.

From the centre, take bus Nos 44 (Artigas), 23 or 35.

Residenciales & Hotels *Residencial Ambassador* (☎ 44-5901), Montevideo 110, is basic and a bit musty, but it's friendly, has ceiling fans and charges only US$3/5 single/double. *Hotel Hispania* (☎ 44-4108), Cerro Corá 265, has been a popular budget alternative for years, with clean but gloomy downstairs rooms for US$5/7 with shared bath, US$6.50/9 with private bath. *Hotel Itapúa* (☎ 44-5121), Moreno 943, costs about US$6 per person, as does *Residencial Siria* (☎ 44-7258), Herrera 166. *Hotel Azara* (☎ 44-9754), Azara 850, has rooms with private bath, fridge and air-conditioning for US$7.50/12.

Korean-run *Hotel Amigo* (☎ 49-1987), Caballero 521, charges US$8/13 for rooms with private bath and air-conditioning. *Hotel Stella d'Italia* (☎ 44-8731) at Cerro Corá 933, popular with US Peace Corps volunteers, has singles with shared bath for US $9, including breakfast, plus a quiet upstairs lounge with international cable TV. At *Hotel Miami* (☎ 44-4950), México 449, rates are US$9/15 for rooms with private bath, breakfast and air-conditioning. For excellent value try *Ñandutí Hotel*, (☎ 44-6780), Presidente Franco 551 – US$10/15 with shared bath, US$12/18 with private bath.

Travellers catching an early bus can stay near the terminal at quiet, friendly *Hotel Familiar Yasy* (☎ 55-1623), Fernando de la Mora 2390, for US$5.50 per person, with private bath. Nearby *Hotel 2000* (☎ 55-1628) charges US$12/18.

Places to Eat
Asunción's best dining areas are downtown and in neighbourhoods to the east, around avenidas Mariscal López and España. One of the best breakfast/lunch places is *Lido Bar*, at Chile and Palma, with tasty local specialities at reasonable prices. *Anahi*, at Presidente Franco and Ayolas, is a fine confitería with good meals and ice cream at moderate prices. A few doors away, toward Montevideo, is an outstanding *German bakery*.

Rincón Chileno, Estados Unidos 314, has good, moderately priced Chilean food. A block south, at Estados Unidos 422, is *Choppería Vieja Bavaria*, a German hangout with good beer and short orders. *Restaurant Germania*, Cerro Corá 180, comes highly recommended, as does *Restaurant Munich*, Eligio Ayala 163. *Gauchao*, Herrera 1568, serves Brazilian cuisine, as does *Do Gaúcho*, at Colón and Manduvirá. Along Avenida Brasil, north of Avenida España, are several *parrillas*.

Talleyrand, Mariscal Estigarribia 932, is one of Asunción's most highly regarded international restaurants, expensive but good for a special occasion. *La Maison des Alpes*, on Bruselas near Viena, and *La Preferida*, a German restaurant at 25 de Mayo 1005, are also worth a visit. Another attractive dinner place is *La Pergola Jardín*, Avenida Perú 240. For Spanish food, try *El Antojo*, Ayolas 631.

For Italian food in a pleasant outdoor setting, try *Buon Appetito*, 25 de Mayo 1199. *Il Capo*, Perú 291, and *Spaghettoteca*, San Martín 893 in Villa Morra, are also deserving. *Pizzometro*, Bruselas 1789 in the Luis Herrera neighbourhood, has all-you-can-eat pizza.

Asunción has fine and varied Asian food because of Korean immigration – try *Kang Nan*, Perú 1129. *Sukiyaki*, Constitución 763, attracts many Japanese, but Chinese cuisine is still more common, with places like *Formosa* at España 780, *Celestial* at Herrera 919, and *Taipei* at Brasil 976.

Asunción's popular ice-creamery *4-D* now has a downtown branch on Mariscal Estigarribia near Independencia Nacional, but the original at San Martín and Olegario Andrade (take bus Nos 12, 16 or 28) carries a wider selection of flavours.

Entertainment
Cinemas Downtown cinemas offer mostly cheap porno or kung fu movies, but many

cultural centres show quality films. Check *Fin de Semana* for listings.

Theatre Asunción compensates for poor cinemas with live theatre and music at venues like the Casa de Cultura Paraguaya (see Cultural Centres, above), Teatro Arlequín (☎ 60-5107), at De Gaulle and Quesada in Villa Morra, and others. The season runs from March to October.

Things to Buy
Artesanía Viva, José Berges 993, offers Chaco Indian crafts, including ponchos, hammocks and bags, plus books and information. Artesanía Hilda, at the corner of Presidente Franco and O'Leary, sells ñandutí and other handicrafts. Casa Over-all, Estigarribia 397, has a good selection of ñandutí and leather goods.

In the suburb of San Lorenzo, the Centro de Promoción de Artesanía Indígena, at Coronel Bogado and Mariscal López, has very fine Chaco Indian artefacts – baskets, wood carvings, spears, weavings – at very low prices. It's open Tuesday to Friday from 8.30 am to noon and 2 to 6 pm, Saturdays from 8.30 am to 6 pm.

Getting There & Away
Air Asunción's centrality on the continent makes it a good place for flights to neighbouring countries, Europe and the USA.

Aerolíneas Argentinas
    Independencia Nacional 1365 (☎ 49-1012)
American Airlines
    Independencia Nacional 557 (☎ 43-3330)
Iberia
    25 de Mayo 161 (☎ 49-3351)
LADECO (Líneas Aéreas del Cobre
    General Díaz 347 (☎ 44-7028)
LAB (Lloyd Aéreo Boliviano)
    14 de Mayo & Oliva (☎ 49-4715)
LAP (Líneas Aéreas Paraguayas)
    Oliva 467 (☎ 49-1046)
LATN
    on the corner of Brasil and Mariscal Estigarribia
    (☎ 21-2277)
Lufthansa
    Estrella & Chile, 3rd floor (☎ 44-7964)
PLUNA
    Alberdi 513 (☎ 49-0128)
Varig
    General Díaz & 14 de Mayo (☎ 49-7351)
TAM
    Olivia 471, next door to LAP, (☎ 44-5843)

Bus The new bus terminal (☎ 55-1732) is at Fernando de la Mora and República Argentina, reached from the centre by bus Nos 8, 10, 25, 31 or 38 from Calle Oliva, but some companies retain ticket offices on Plaza Uruguay.

Asunción has frequent international connections, but for Argentina or Brazil it is generally cheaper to take a local bus to the border and then purchase a long-distance ticket. From the corner of Presidente Franco and Avenida Colón, buses leave for Falcón, on the Argentine border, several times daily. For other Argentine destinations, direct buses leave the terminal for Clorinda (US$1.50), and there are frequent buses to Posadas (four hours) and Buenos Aires (US$50, 20 hours). Fewer buses run to Córdoba (18 hours).

There are buses to Montevideo, Uruguay and Santiago, Chile (30 hours, Monday and Thursday). Brazilian destinations include Foz do Iguaçu (five hours), São Paulo (18 hours), Rio (22 hours), Curitiba (14 hours) and Paranaguá (16 hours), and occasionally Brasilia.

Countless domestic buses link Asunción with other Paraguayan cities, including Ciudad del Este (US$7, six hours) and Encarnación (US$5, five hours). Services to north-eastern destinations such as Pedro Juan Caballero and Concepción are less frequent, but those to Filadelfia (US$10, eight hours) and other Chaco destinations are dependable. Towns near Asunción, like San Bernardino and Caacupé, have very frequent services.

Train The 1856 railway station is on Plaza Uruguay. Daily (except Sunday), the steam train to Lago Ypacaraí leaves at noon for Areguá (US$0.35) via the back yards of Asunción's shantytowns.

To Encarnación, the locomotive takes 16 hours but costs only US$4. Argentine rail services from Posadas to Buenos Aires are suspended.

Boat Launches from Puerto Itá Enramada, west of Asunción, to Puerto Pilcomayo (Argentina) leave every half hour from 7 am to 5 pm on weekdays, irregularly from 7 to 10 am on Saturday. It is possible to return by bus from Clorinda, Argentina.

The erratic Flota Mercantíl del Estado (☎ 44-8544), Estrella 672, ostensibly sails up the river to Concepción and Brazil, but getting hard information from them is like pulling wisdom teeth. Fares to Concepción are US$10 1st class, US$6 tourist; to Corumbá, US$35 tourist, US$25 deck space. Travellers have had better luck inquiring at the port at the foot of Calle Montevideo.

Getting Around

To/From the Airport Bus No 30A from Cerro Corá will take you to Aeropuerto Pettirossi (about 45 minutes, US$0.20). Taxis charge about US$12.

Bus City buses go almost everywhere for around US$0.20, but there are few after about 10 or 11 pm. Try to avoid travel at midday, when buses are jammed with people going home for an extended lunch.

Taxi Cabs are metered and reasonable. The minimum fare is about US$1.20.

AROUND ASUNCIÓN
Villa Hayes

Across the river from Asunción, Villa Hayes honours one of the USA's most undistinguished presidents, Rutherford B Hayes (1877-1881). Nearly forgotten even in his home town of Delaware, Ohio, he is here commemorated by a club and local soccer team, a school and a monument.

Why this homage to a man who never set foot in Paraguay? After the War of the Triple Alliance, Argentina claimed the entire Chaco, but the two countries eventually submitted claims over a smaller area

to arbitration; in 1878, Argentine and Paraguayan diplomats presented their cases to Hayes in Washington. After he decided in Paraguay's favour, the Paraguayan Congress immortalised him by renaming Villa Occidental, the territory's largest town.

To reach Villa Hayes, take bus No 46 from downtown Asunción. It leaves every half hour from 5.30 am to noon, then every 45 minutes from noon to 9 pm.

Eastern Paraguay

East of the Río Paraguay is the nucleus of historical Paraguay. About 90% of Paraguayans live within 100 km of Asunción, but the border towns of Encarnación (opposite Posadas, Argentina) and Ciudad del Este (opposite Foz do Iguaçu, Brazil) have grown rapidly because of multinational hydroelectric projects.

Attractions near Asunción include the weaving centre of Itaguá, the lakeside resorts of San Bernardino and Areguá, the shrine of Caacupé, colonial villages like Piribebuy and Yaguarón and, a bit farther, Parque Nacional Ybycuí. Between Asunción and Encarnación, Jesuit ruins match or surpass those of Argentina. Ciudad del Este is Paraguay's gateway to Iguazú Falls and the gigantic Itaipú hydroelectric project.

Eastern-most Paraguay, along the Brazilian frontier, is a boom zone. Brazilian colonists are moving across the border, deforesting the countryside for coffee and cotton, squeezing out Paraguayan peasants and the few remaining Aché Indians.

CIRCUITO CENTRAL

A 200-km round trip from Asunción, the Circuito Central is suitable for day trips, weekend excursions or longer outings.

Areguá

This resort on Lago Ypacaraí, 28 km from Asunción, is higher and cooler than the capital. *Hospedaje Ozli* has rooms with fan

PARAGUAY

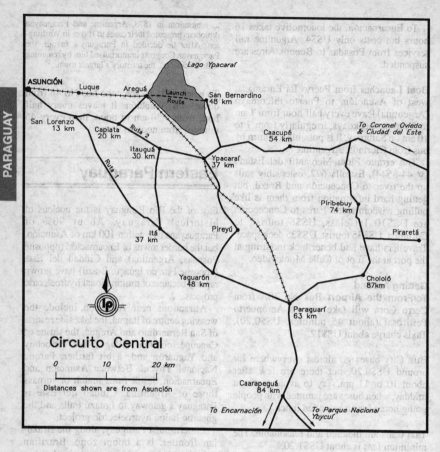

Lago Ypacaraí

ASUNCIÓN
Luque Areguá Launch Route San Bernardino 48 km
San Lorenzo 13 km Capiatá 20 km Ruta 2
Itauguá 30 km Caacupé 54 km To Coronel Oviedo & Ciudad del Este
Ypacaraí 37 km
Ruta 1
Itá 37 km Pireyú Piribebuy 74 km Piraretá
Yaguarón 48 km Choloó 87 km
Paraguarí 63 km

Circuito Central

0   10   20 km

Distances shown are from Asunción

Caarapeguá 84 km

To Encarnación To Parque Nacional Ybycuí

for US$5 per person, with pleasant gardens and good food.

Most visitors arrive by train and return by bus (about every half hour). A launch crosses the lake to San Bernardino, half-hourly from 10.15 am to 2.15 pm.

Itauguá

For the women of Itauguá, 30 km from Asunción, weaving multicoloured ñandutí is a cottage industry from childhood to old age. Pieces range in size from doilies to bedspreads; smaller ones cost only a few dollars but larger ones range upwards of US$50.

Two blocks south of Ruta 2, the dilapidated **Museo Parroquial San Rafael** displays Franciscan and secular relics, plus early samples of ñandutí. Hours are 7 to 11 am and 3 to 5 pm daily.

From Asunción, Transporte Ñandutí (Línea 165) buses leave for Itauguá every 15 minutes from 5 am to 11 pm.

San Bernardino

Up-market restaurants, cafés and hotels line the shady streets of San Bernardino, 48 km by road from Asunción on Lago Ypacaraí's eastern shore. Asunción's elite spend weekends here, but there are still reasonable budget alternatives.

Restaurant Las Palmeras and the *German bakery* on Calle Colonos Alemanes are good places to eat, while *Hotel Santa Rita* has good value accommodation for US$7.50 a single. From Asunción, Transporte Villa del Lago (Línea 210) and Transporte Cordillera de los Andes (Línea 103) have frequent buses.

Caacupé

On 8 December every year, pilgrims descend upon Caacupé, Paraguay's most important religious centre, for the Día de la Virgen (Immaculate Conception). The imposing **Basílica de Nuestra Señora de Los Milagros** dominates the townscape from its huge cobblestone plaza, which easily accommodates 300,000 faithful. Opposite the plaza is a block of cheap restaurants and tacky souvenir stands.

Hospedaje Uruguayo, midway between Ruta 2 and the Basílica, has comfortable garden singles for US$8 with private bath and fan, US$13 with air-conditioning. *Hospedaje San Blas I*, only 1½ blocks from the Basílica but north of the highway, has singles/doubles for US$5/8 with shared bath.

La Caacupeña (Línea 119) and Villa Serrana (Línea 110) leave Asunción every 10 minutes from 5 am to 10 pm.

Piribebuy

Founded in 1640, Piribebuy was briefly Paraguay's capital during the war of 1865-70; its mid-18th century church retains some original woodwork and sculpture. Only 74 km from Asunción, south of Ruta 2, it is a good place to glimpse rural Paraguay.

The **Museo Histórico** opposite the church, with interesting but deteriorating exhibits, opens on request – ask Don Alfredo Bernal at Maestro Fermín López 1048, a block off the plaza. *Restaurant Hotel Rincón Viejo*, across the street from Don Alfredo's, has doubles with private bath for US$12, but haggle for a lower price. Transporte Piribebuy (Línea 197) has buses from Asunción every half hour from 5 am to 9 pm.

South of Piribebuy, the scenic road leads to **Chololó**, less a village than a series of riverside *campgrounds*; a branch goes to a modest waterfall at **Piraretá**.

At **Paraguarí**, where *Hotel Chololó* offers singles for around US$20 in attractive hill country, the road connects with Ruta 1. Ciudad Paraguarí (Línea 193) has buses to Asunción every 15 minutes from 5 am to 8 pm.

Yaguarón

Yaguarón's 18th-century Franciscan church is a landmark of colonial architecture, while the nearby **Museo del Doctor Francia** has good period portraiture, including El Supremo at different ages. It's open Tuesday, Thursday and Saturday from 3 to 5 pm, Sundays and holidays from 9.30 to 11.30 am and 3 to 5 pm.

Across from the church is a nameless *restaurant* with mediocre food, except for excellent homemade ice cream. It also has basic accommodation for US$3 per person. Ciudad Paraguarí (Línea 193) has buses to Asunción (48 km) every 15 minutes from 5 am to 8.15 pm.

Itá

Founded in 1539, Itá is known for local *gallinita* pottery and, more recently and notoriously, for the apparent discovery of Nazi war criminal Martin Bormann's burial site. There are very frequent buses to Asunción (37 km) with 3 de Febrero (Línea 159) and Cotrisa (Línea 159).

PARQUE NACIONAL YBYCUÍ

Parque Nacional Ybycuí preserves one of eastern Paraguay's last stands of Brazilian rainforest. Its steep hills, dissected by creeks with attractive waterfalls and pools, reach 400 metres. The dense forest makes it difficult to see animals, which hide rather than run.

Things to See & Do

Ybycuí is tranquil and undeveloped, though weekenders can disrupt its peacefulness; in this event, take refuge on the extensive

PARAGUAY

hiking trails. For information, see the ranger on duty at park headquarters, or the two US Peace Corps volunteers assigned to park improvements.

The **Salto Guaraní** waterfall is near the campground. Below it, a bridge leads to a pleasant creekside trail where you will see a wealth of butterflies, including the metallic blue morpho. Watch for poisonous snakes. The trail continues to **La Rosada**, an iron foundry which was destroyed by Brazilian forces in the War of the Triple Alliance. Ybycuí's forest has recovered in the century since the foundry operated on charcoal. Note the waterwheel; engineers dammed Arroyo Mina to provide water and power for the bellows, while oxcarts brought ore from 25 km away.

At La Rosada is a **museum**, with irregular hours, at the park entrance two km west of the campground.

Places to Stay

The only option is *camping* at Arroyo Mina, which has adequate sanitary facilities, cold showers and a confitería serving weekend meals. Level sites are few and insects are a nuisance.

Getting There & Away

Parque Nacional Ybycuí is 151 km from Asunción. Ruta 1, to Encarnación, leads 84 km south to Carapeguá, where a turn-off continues another 67 km via the villages of Acahay and Ybycuí. Transporte Emilio Cabrera has eight buses daily to Acahay for local connections to Ybycuí village. A bus leaves daily at noon for the park entrance, returning to the village every morning at 7 am.

The Fundación Moisés Bertoni (see the Facts for the Visitor section) runs occasional full-day excursions, including transport, guides and picnic lunch, for US$20.

ENCARNACIÓN

Encarnación is in limbo because the lake created by the Yacyretá dam will inundate much of the city. As established businesses move onto high ground, the riverside area has become a tawdry bazaar of imported trinkets – digital watches, Walkmans and other electronic goodies – and decaying public buildings and housing.

Orientation

Encarnación sits on the north bank of the Río Paraná, directly opposite Posadas, Argentina. A new international bridge links the two cities. From the riverside, Avenida Mariscal J F Estigarribia leads from the old commercial centre to the new one around Plaza Artigas.

Information

Tourist Office The Sección de Cultura at the

■	PLACES TO STAY
2	Hotel Repka
3	Hotel City
4	Hotel Viera
5	Hotel Paraná
10	Hotel Cristal
14	Hotel Restaurant Itapúa
18	Hotel Viena
20	Hotel Suizo
21	Hotel Central
▼	PLACES TO EAT
9	Restaurant Rancho Grande
	OTHER
1	Train Station
6	Banco Continental
7	Plaza Artigas
8	Japanese Consulate
11	Touring y Automóvil Club Paraguayo
12	Tourist Office/Municipalidad
13	Argentine Consulate
15	Bus Terminal
16	Brazilian Vice-Consul
17	Hospital
19	Antelco
22	Feria Municipal
23	Cambios Guaraní
24	Post Office
25	Boats to Posadas

Encarnación

Municipalidad, at Estigarribia and Kreusser, is helpful but lacks printed matter. It's open weekdays from 7 am to 12.30 pm.

Money Cambios Guaraní is at Estigarribia 307 in the old city. On higher ground, try Banco Continental, Estigarribia 1418, or nearby Citibank. On weekends, the bus terminal is loaded with moneychangers.

Post & Telecommunications The post office is at Capellán Molas 337, in the old city. Antelco is at P J Caballero and López, next to Hotel Viena.

Consulates The Argentine Consulate, Mallorquín 788, is open weekdays from 7.30 am to 1.30 pm. The Brazilian Consulate, Memmel 452, is open weekdays from 8 am to noon.

Film & Photography Serpylcolor, at Estigarribia and Curupayty, has very cheap film; travellers may want to stock up here.

Feria Municipal
At the corner of López and Gamarra, petty merchants are milking every last peso out of visiting Argentines before the flood. The market's liveliness transcends its baubles and gadgets, and it's also a good, inexpensive place to eat.

Places to Stay
Visitors to Posadas will find accommodation relatively cheap here. Home-style *Hotel Repka*, Tomás Romero Pereira 44, charges US$3/4 for a single/double with shared bath; *Hotel City*, Antequera 1659, costs US$3/5.

Hotel Suizo, Estigarribia 566, charges US$6/11, as does *Hotel Central*, López 542. Clean, quiet *Hotel Viena*, Caballero 568, is excellent value at US$8/12 for rooms with private bath.

Places to Eat
Restaurant Cuarajhy, at Estigarribia and Pereira, is a popular, moderately priced parrilla. *Rancho Grande*, at Estigarribia and

Cerro Corá, is a larger place under a thatched roof, with Paraguayan folk music at night.

Getting There & Away
Air Posadas, across the river in Argentina, has air connections with Buenos Aires and Puerto Iguazú – see the Argentina chapter.

Bus There are 27 daily buses to Asunción (US$8, five to six hours), 30 to Ciudad del Este (US$6, four to five hours).

There is direct service to Buenos Aires (18 hours) but you can have a much greater selection of departures from Posadas. From 6 am to 11 pm, frequent local buses cross to Posadas.

Boat Launches (US$1) still cross the Río Paraná to Posadas at frequent intervals.

Train The station is on Pereira, six blocks west of Plaza Artigas. Trains to Asunción (US$4, 16 hours) leave on Sunday at 5 am and Wednesday at 3.30 pm.

TRINIDAD
Paraguay's best-preserved Jesuit *reducción*, Trinidad fills an imposing hilltop site 28 km from Encarnación. Founded in 1706, by 1728 it boasted a Guaraní population of more than 4000. Its centrepiece was the church, whose elaborate pulpit, frescos and statues are in excellent repair.

The fenced grounds and museum are open 7.30 to 11.30 am and 1.30 to 5.30 pm, but many people climb through and wander about after closing time, with no objections from the staff. Many buses pass through Trinidad en route to nearby Hohenau.

SAN IGNACIO GUAZÚ
About 100 km north of Encarnación, San Ignacio has few ruins, but its **Museo Jesuítico** holds valuable Guaraní carvings. Open daily from 8 to 11.30 am and 2 to 5 pm, it charges US$0.40 admission.

Budget accommodation is available at *Hotel del Puerto*, on the main highway at the plaza, for US$4/6 single/double with shared bath. There are many buses to Asunción

(3½ hours), Encarnación and the village of Santa María.

SANTA MARÍA

Twelve km east of San Ignacio, the former reducción of Santa María has a **Museo Jesuítico** with a superb collection of Jesuit statuary, open daily from 8.30 to 11.30 am and 1.30 to 5 pm. Admission is US$0.75.

Basic *Pensión San José* charges US$3 a single. There are five buses daily from San Ignacio Guazú.

CORONEL OVIEDO

Midway between Asunción and Ciudad del Este, Coronel Oviedo is a major crossroads, with routes north to Saltos del Guairá and Pedro Juan Caballero (with a branch to Concepción), and south to Villarrica.

Hotel Alemán, at the crossroads, has reasonable accommodation, while *Parador La Tranquera* has good food. Three km north of the crossroads, the highly recommended *Hotel Colonial* has US$10 singles. *Hotel del Rey*, Estigarribia 261, is cheaper, at US$5/7 single/double.

Between Coronel Oviedo and San José, a road leads to **Nueva Australia**, a socialist experiment founded by late-19th century Australian immigrants. Named Hugo Stroessner (for Alfredo's father) on some maps, the dissension-ridden colony splintered in 1896 after failing to live up to exaggerated claims of the area's potential.

ITAIPÚ DAM

Itaipú, the world's largest hydroelectric project, has benefited Paraguay because of the construction activity, and Brazil's purchase of surplus power. However, should the price of competing sources of electricity drop, reduced Brazilian demand could saddle Paraguay with unexpected costs.

Project propaganda omits the US$25 billion price tag and ignores environmental concerns. The 1350 sq km reservoir, 220 metres deep, drowned Sete Quedas, a more impressive set of waterfalls than Iguazú, while stagnant water has provided new habitat for anopheline mosquitos, increasing the risk of malaria.

Free tours leave from the Centro de Recepción de Visitas daily at 8.30, 9.30 and 10.30 pm, and Monday to Saturday at 2, 3 and 4 pm. Passports are required. There is a documentary film half an hour before the tour departs.

From the roundabout at Avenida San Blas and Alejo García, take Hernandarias Transtur or Tacurú Pucú buses, which leave every 10 to 15 minutes and pass the conspicuous project entrance north of Ciudad del Este.

CIUDAD DEL ESTE

Ciudad del Este (formerly called Puerto Stroessner) is an important border crossing where Brazilian and Argentine shoppers jam the streets in search of cheap electronic goods.

On the west bank of the Paraná, across from Foz do Iguaçu, Ciudad del Este has an irregular plan, but its centre is compact and easily managed on foot. Avenida San Blas, the westward extension of the bridge from Foz, becomes Ruta 2 to Asunción.

Information

Tourist Office The Municipalidad, on Avenida Alejo García, closes before midday. Many businesses distribute the *Guía Turística y Comercial Ciudad del Este*, which contains useful information and a map.

The Touring y Automóvil Club Paraguayo, on Avenida San Blas about one km west of Plaza Madame Lynch, is friendly and helpful, but its road atlas is atrocious.

Money Ubiquitous street changers give poorer rates than cambios. Guaraní Cambios is at Avenida Monseñor Rodríguez and Pampliega.

Telecommunications Antelco is at Alejo García and Pai Pérez.

Consulates The Brazilian Consulate, Coronel Pampliega 337, is open from 8 am to 6 pm weekdays.

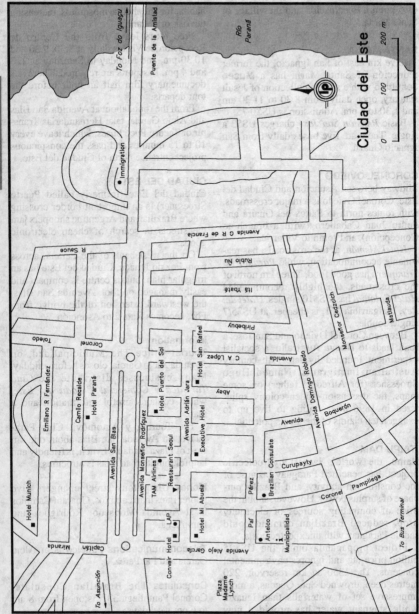

Ciudad del Este

0   100   200 m

Places to Stay & Eat

Accommodation here is dearer than elsewhere in Paraguay. The most reasonable is *Hotel El Cid*, Camilo Recalde 425, for US$6/7.50 single/double. *Hotel Paraná*, Camilo Recalde 128, costs US$11/15. Cozy, friendly *Hotel Mi Abuela*, with an attractive garden, has singles/doubles with private bath and fans for US$15/18; for air-conditioning, add about US$2. Also good value is *Hotel Munich*, at the corner of Emilio Fernández and Capitán Miranda, where singles/doubles with private bath, breakfast and air-conditioning cost US$12/17.

In spite of its name, open-air *Restaurant Seoul*, at Curupayty and Adrián Jara, is a parrillada, offering good meals for about US$4, with live folk music.

Getting There & Away

Air Foz do Iguaçu (Brazil) and Puerto Iguazú (Argentina) have major international airports; see the respective country chapters.

The military airline TAM (☎ 68352), in the Edificio SABA just off Monseñor Rodríguez, offers flights to Asunción from Itaipú's airstrip.

Bus Buses to Foz do Iguaçu leave from near the bridge every 10 minutes on weekdays and Saturdays, less frequently on Sundays and holidays. On the other side, disembark for Brazilian immigration (unless you are just crossing for the day); if you hold on to your ticket, any following bus will take you to Foz.

From Avenida Alejo García, take bus No 8 (red) to the bus terminal, south of town. To Asunción (US$8, six hours), there are 34 buses daily; nearly as many go to Encarnación.

Boat If you prefer to bypass Brazil, try to locate one of the (infrequent) launches from Puerto Presidente Franco to Puerto Iguazú, Argentina.

PEDRO JUAN CABALLERO

Capital of Amambay department, Pedro Juan Caballero is adjacent to Ponta Porã, Brazil.

Locals cross the border at will, but to continue any distance into either country, visit immigration at Calle General Bruguez 1247. There are reports of contraband drugs, so beware of unsavoury characters.

Cambios Amambay is at Estigarribia 22, and there are several others. The Brazilian Consulate (open weekdays, 8 am to noon and 2 to 6 pm) is in *Hotel La Siesta*, at Alberdi and Dr Francia, which has singles for US$7.50. Several hotels along Mariscal López offer accommodation for about US$5/8: *Hotel Cerro Corá* at López 1511, *Hotel Guavirá* at López 1325 and *Hotel Peralta* at López 1257.

Ten buses daily serve Asunción (532 km, eight to 12 hours depending on weather and road conditions). Another 10 go to Concepción, with downriver connections to Asunción, and one per day travels to Ciudad del Este. NASA goes daily to Campo Grande, Brazil.

TAM and LATN fly cheaply to Asunción 12 times weekly.

PARQUE NACIONAL CERRO CORÁ

Visitors to north-eastern Paraguay should not overlook Cerro Corá, 40 km west of Pedro Juan Caballero in an area of dry tropical forest and savanna, among steep, isolated hills. Cultural and historical features include pre-Columbian caves, petroglyphs and the site of Francisco Solano López's death at the end of the War of the Triple Alliance.

The park has self-guiding nature trails, a *camping area* and a few basic *cabañas*. There are rangers, but no formal visitors centre.

CONCEPCIÓN

On the east bank of the Paraguay, 310 km upstream from Asunción, Concepción has an interesting market and considerable river trade with Brazil. *Hotel Victoria*, Presidente Franco 902, and *Hotel Victoria*, Franco 693, both charge around US$9/14 for singles/doubles with shared bath.

Getting There & Away

For details of boat traffic to Corumbá, Brazil, see the Asunción Getting There & Away section.

TAM and LATN have 15 flights weekly to Asunción. Bus services, subject to cancellation over the bad roads, go via Pozo Colorado in the Chaco or via Coronel Oviedo (nine hours). There are daily buses to Pedro Juan Caballero (continuing to Campo Grande, Brazil) and to Ciudad del Este.

The Chaco

In Paraguay's Chaco frontier, great distances separate tiny settlements. Its only paved highway, the Ruta Trans-Chaco, leads 450 km to Filadelfia, colonised by Mennonites since the late 1920s. Here the pavement ends, but the highway continues 300 km to the Bolivian border.

The Chaco is an almost featureless plain of three rather distinct zones. Across the Río Paraguay, the low Chaco is a soothing palm savanna whose ponds and marshes shelter colourful birds; peasant cultivators build picturesque houses of palm logs, but the main industry is cattle ranching.

In the middle Chaco, farther west, thorny drought-tolerant scrub replaces the savanna, though Mennonites have farmed this area successfully. Only army bases and cattle *estancias* inhabit the denser thorn forests of the high Chaco beyond Mariscal Estigarribia, where rainfall is highly unpredictable.

Historically, the Chaco has been a refuge of Indian groups who subsisted independently by hunting, gathering and fishing. Later industries included cattle ranching and extraction of the tannin-rich *quebracho*. The first Mennonites arrived in 1927.

Place names beginning with the word *Fortín* indicate fortifications and trenches of the Chaco War (1932-35). During the war, Paraguay built a network of roads which are now mostly impassable without 4WD,

though Mennonites have maintained roads within their jurisdiction.

There is little accommodation outside the few towns, though one can camp almost anywhere. In a pinch, estancias or *campesinos* will give you a bed with a mosquito net if they have one.

THE MENNONITE COLONIES

There are about 10,000 Mennonites and a slightly larger number of Indians in the Chaco. Mennonites believe in adult baptism, separation of church and state, and pacifist opposition to military service. They speak Plattdeutsch (Low German), and also Hochdeutsch (High German), the language of school instruction. Most adults now speak Spanish and some speak passable English. Indians are as likely to speak German as Spanish.

The first Mennonites to arrive, in 1927, were *Sommerfelder* (Summerfield) Mennonites, from the Canadian prairies, who left after Canadian authorities reneged on guarantees against conscription. The Sommerfelder formed Menno Colony, centred around the town of Loma Plata. A few years later, refugees from the Soviet Union established Fernheim (Distant Home), with its capital at Filadelfia. Ukrainian Germans, many of whom served unwillingly in WW II, founded Neuland (New Land) in 1947. Its largest settlement is Neu-Halbstadt.

As more Paraguayans settle in the Chaco, Mennonites worry that the government may eliminate their privileges. Few are reinvesting in Paraguay, and some are openly looking elsewhere. Others are disgruntled with developments in Filadelfia, whose material prosperity has spawned a generation more interested in motorbikes and videos than traditional values. Beer and tobacco, once absolutely *verboten*, are now sold openly.

Filadelfia

Filadelfia is Fernheim's administrative and service centre. Dairy foods and cotton are the main products of the region.

Still a religious community, Filadelfia shuts down on Sundays. On weekday mornings, farmers drive to town in their pick-up trucks in search of Indians for day labour, returning them in the afternoon. At midday, the town is exceptionally quiet, as Mennonites have adopted the custom of the tropical siesta.

Orientation & Information Filadelfia is 480 km from Asunción via the Trans-Chaco and a 20-km lateral to its north. Its dusty streets form an orderly grid whose *Hauptstrasse* (main street) is north-south Hindenburg. Perpendicular Calle Trébol leads east to Loma Plata (Menno Colony) and west to the Trans-Chaco and Fortín Toledo.

For information, visit Reisebüro, a travel agency on Hindenburg between Trébol and Bender. For changing money, try here or at the cooperative supermarket (whose building also contains the post office), at Unruh and Hindenburg. Antelco is across the street.

Unger Museum On Hindenburg opposite the Hotel Florida, this museum chronicles Fernheim from 1930 to the present, and also displays materials on Chaco Indians. It has no regular hours, but Hartmut Wohlgemuth, manager of the Florida, provides guided tours in Spanish or German when his schedule permits. Admission is about US$1.

Places to Stay & Eat Shady Parque Trébol, five km east of Filadelfia, has free *camping*, but no water and only a single pit toilet. At Hindenburg and Unruh, *Hotel Florida* has a bargain annex – US$4 for a single with comfortable beds, fans and shared bath with refreshing cold showers.

The Florida has a decent restaurant, and several shops offer snacks and ice cream. Try also the parrillada at *La Estrella*, on Unruh around the corner from the Florida.

Getting There & Away Several bus companies have offices along Hindenburg near Industrie, with daily service to Asunción. Buses are less frequent to Mariscal Estigarribia and Colonia La Patria, farther west on the Trans-Chaco.

Getting Around Expreso CV connects Filadelfia with Loma Plata (25 km) daily at 8 am, returning at 9 am. Buses to Asunción also stop at Loma Plata and most continue to Neu-Halbstadt. Hitching, or asking for lifts, is worth a try at odd hours.

Around Filadelfia

Fortín Toledo About 40 km west of Filadelfia, Fortín Toledo hosts the **Proyecto Taguá**, a small reserve nurturing a population of Wagner's peccary (*Catagonus wagneri*), thought extinct for nearly half a century until its rediscovery in 1975. Managers Jakob and María Unger speak German, Spanish and English, and if their schedules permit, welcome visits. Contact Jakob and María through the Mennonite radio station in Filadelfia, and they may help with transport.

To get to Fortín Toledo, hitch or take a bus out along Calle Trébol to the Trans-Chaco. Cross the highway and continue three km to an enormous tyre with the painted words 'pasar prohibido'; continue another seven km on the main road, passing several squatter-occupied buildings, before taking a sharp right leading to a sign reading 'Proyecto Taguá'. You may be able to hitch along this segment.

Loma Plata This town is the administrative centre of Menno Colony, and the oldest and most traditional of the Mennonite settlements. Its excellent museum has an outdoor exhibit of early farming equipment, a typical pioneer house and an outstanding photographic history of the colony. Ask for keys at the nearby Secretariat.

Hotel Loma Plata has singles for about US$20 but no budget annex, so it's cheaper to make a day trip from Filadelfia.

Neu-Halbstadt Founded in 1947, Neu-Halbstadt is the centre of Neuland Colony, south of Filadelfia. *Hotel Boquerón* has singles/doubles for US$15/22, and a good restaurant. Nearby Fortín Boquerón preserves a sample of Chaco War trenches.

South of Neuland are Indian reserves, where many Lengua and Nivaclé have become settled farmers. Neu-Halbstadt is a good place for Indian handicrafts like bags, hammocks and woven goods. For information and a great selection, contact Walter and Verena Regehr, who sell goods on a non-profit basis here and at Artesanía Viva in Asunción.

Several buses from Asunción to Filadelfia continue to Neu-Halbstadt, while others come directly from Asunción.

PARQUE NACIONAL DEFENSORES DEL CHACO

Once the province of nomadic Ayoreo foragers, Defensores del Chaco is a wooded alluvial plain about 100 metres in elevation. Isolated 500-metre Cerro León is its greatest landmark. The dense thorn forest harbours important animal species, despite the pressures of illicit hunting. This is the likeliest place in Paraguay to view large cats like jaguar, puma, ocelot and Geoffroy's cat.

Defensores del Chaco is 830 km from Asunción over roads impassable to ordinary vehicles. The Fundación Bertoni in Asunción conducts four-day excursions in 4WD vehicles, usually in the dry and comfortable month of August. Alternatively, the Fundación may put you in contact with rangers, who sometimes take passengers when they return from trips to Asunción, if space is available.

MARISCAL ESTIGARRIBIA

Mariscal Estigarribia, 540 km from Asunción, is the last sizeable settlement before the Bolivian border. Stay at *Hotel Alemán* while you try begging a lift at the petrol station.

Every Friday at 8 am, a NASA bus goes to Colonia La Patria (three hours). To Asunción (US$12.50, 10 hours), buses leave daily except Sunday, when there are two.

COLONIA LA PATRIA

Only 85 km from the Bolivian border, Colonia La Patria is becoming a service centre for high Chaco estancias. Every Friday at 2 pm, a bus leaves for Mariscal Estigarribia (three hours), Filadelfia (five hours) and Asunción (14 hours).

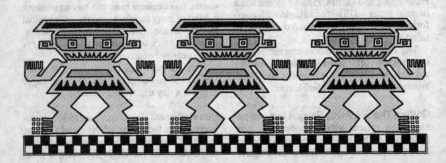

Peru

Travellers cannot fail to be impressed by the great variety of culture, geography and exciting travel possibilities that Peru offers.

Peru is renowned as the land of the Incas, but it is the overlay of many great civilisations that makes the country so fascinating. You can visit the ancient Inca capital of Cuzco or explore the lost city of Machu Picchu. There are the mysterious Nazca Lines or the vast adobe ruins of Chan Chan, as well as the opulent cities of the Spanish conquerors.

All of this is set in some of the most varied and spectacular scenery in South America – from the long coastal desert to the snow-capped Andes and down to the Amazon jungle.

Distinctive and exotic plants and animals inhabit these different regions. Llamas and condors, piranhas and toucans – it is a naturalist's paradise.

If you want to hike the Inca trail, explore the high valleys of the Andes, stroll through Indian markets, visit the islands in Lake Titicaca, go by boat down the Amazon or just sit in the shady plaza of an old colonial town, Peru is for you.

Warning

Governments of several countries, including Australia and the USA, have recently advised their citizens not to visit Peru because of terrorist activity there. Our author was in Peru in 1993, and reported that the main tourist areas of Lima, Cuzco, Machu Picchu, Lake Titicaca, Arequipa, Iquitos, Puerto Maldonado, Cajamarca, Chachapoyas, Huaraz, the Cordillera Blanca, and all the coastal towns were reasonably safe to visit, though theft was a real problem. (See the section on Dangers & Annoyances in the Introduction.)

Travellers should not take the Nazca-Abancay overland route from Lima to Cuzco. There have been several incidents of buses being held up and passengers being robbed or murdered – in July 1993, two young travellers were killed near the town of Puquio on this route. It is unclear whether the killers were terrorists, or bandits taking advantage of unrest in the area. Overland travellers from Lima to Cusco should take the Arequipa-Juliaca (Puno) route. Other areas which should definitely be avoided are buses to the Huancavelica-Ayacucho-Abancay area, and the Huallaga valley. For other destinations, travel by day where possible, because night buses in remote areas are occassionally held up by bandits.

Travellers are advised to seek up-to-date information before travelling around the country.

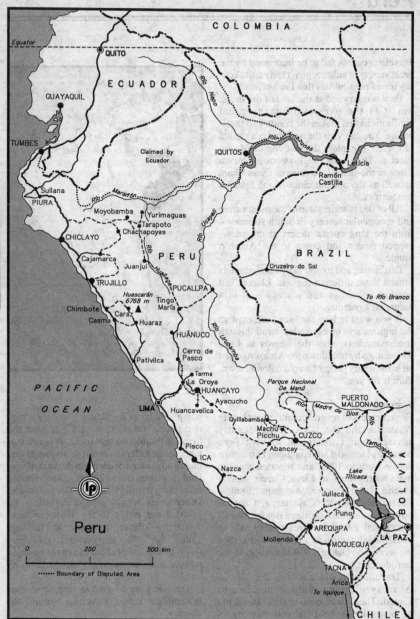

Peru

0   250   500 km

········· Boundary of Disputed Area

Facts about the Country

ARCHAEOLOGY & HISTORY

Peru is unequalled in South America for its archaeological wealth, thanks to excellent preservation conditions on the arid coast and in highland caves. For many travellers, visiting centuries-old ruins is one of the highlights of their journey, and even people with little interest in archaeology enjoy visiting a few major sites. Peru's pre-Columbian history is the subject of debate and disagreement amongst scholars, so if the outline given here is not consistent with other sources, feel free to do your own research and reach your own conclusions.

The famous Inca civilisation is merely the tip of the archaeological iceberg. Peru had many pre-Columbian cultures preceding the Incas, though it is difficult to put them into chronological order because none of them had a written language – knowledge of them is based almost entirely on archaeological research. Furthermore, as each culture succeeded the last, it imposed its own values, as the Spanish did when they conquered the Inca nation. The Spanish, however, left written records that give us an insight into the Incas.

One of the main sources of information for archaeologists has been the realistic decoration on the ceramics, textiles and other artefacts of Peru's pre-Columbian inhabitants. These relics often depict everyday life in some detail, so it is worth inspecting them in Peru's museums. Scholars have recently begun to decipher the knotted-cord *quipus* which the Incas used for detailed record-keeping.

The Preceramic Period

The first inhabitants of Peru were nomadic hunter-gatherers who lived in caves or along the coast and roamed the country in loose-knit bands. Pikimachay cave, near Ayacucho, is the oldest site in central Peru, dating from 12,000 BC or earlier.

Early cultural development included the improvement of stone implements for hunting. Hunting scenes recorded in cave paintings have been found near Huánuco at Lauricocha (which dates from 8000 BC), and at Toquepala near Tacna. People knew how to make fires, wore animal skins and made simple tools and weapons from stone and bone. Domestication of the llama and guinea pig began between 7000 and 5000 BC.

By about 4000 BC (some sources claim earlier), people began planting seeds and improving crops by simple methods such as weeding. In those days, the coastal strip was wetter than today, and a number of small settlements were established. Crops included cotton, chilli peppers, beans, squash and, later, corn. Cassava was important in the Amazonian region. The cotton was used to make clothing by the simple techniques of twining and, later, weaving. Cotton was also used for fishing nets. The people lived in primitive one-room stone-lined pit dwellings, or in branch or reed huts. Jewellery of bone, shell, etc was used, but metalwork and ceramics were unknown, which is why many archaeologists refer to this period as preceramic.

Lower Formative Period

Our knowledge of this period, which extends from about 2000 to 1000 BC, derives mainly from remains in the Virú valley and Guañape area, 50 km south of Trujillo on the north coast. Ceramics developed from rude undecorated pots to sculptured, incised and simply coloured pots of high quality. Weaving, fishing and horticulture also improved, and simple funerary offerings have been found.

Early Horizon

Lasting roughly from 1000 to 300 BC (archaeologists differ by several centuries as to the earlier date), this period has also been called the Chavín Horizon, after the site of Chavín de Huantar, 40 km east of Huaraz. Termed a 'horizon' because its artistic and religious influences can be seen in several contemporary cultures (including the Cupisnique ceramics of the Lambayeque region and the early pottery of Paracas Cavernas), the Chavín influenced an area covering most of northern Peru's highlands and coast. The salient feature of the Chavín is the repeated representation of a stylised jaguar, with clearly religious overtones. Most importantly, this period represents great cultural developments – weaving, pottery, agriculture, religion and architecture.

Intermediate Period
Around 300 BC, the Chavín style inexplicably disappeared, but over the next 500 years, several cultures became locally important. Well known are the Salinar culture of the Chicama valley near Trujillo, and the Paracas Necropolis south of Lima. The Salinar ceramics show advanced firing techniques, whilst the Paracas textiles are considered the finest pre-Columbian textiles in the Americas.

Between about 100 AD and 700 AD, pottery, metalwork and textiles reached a pinnacle of technological development throughout Peru, and so this period is often referred to as the 'Florescent' or 'Classic'. The Moche of the Trujillo area and the Nazca of the south coast depicted their ways of life on their ceramics, providing archaeologists with invaluable information. The Moche also built massive pyramids, such as the temples of the Sun and Moon near Trujillo, and the Nazca made the enigmatic giant petroglyphs known as the Nazca Lines in the coastal desert.

The Wari Empire
Wari (Huari) was the capital and the name of the first expansionist empire known in the Andes. Unlike the earlier Chavín Horizon, its expansion was not limited to the diffusion of artistic and religious influence. The Wari were vigorous military conquerors who built and maintained important outposts throughout much of Peru, including Piquillacta (near Cuzco), Cajamarquilla (near Lima) and Wilkawain (near Huaraz).

The Wari imposed their own cultural values on the peoples they subdued, and

from about 600 to 1000 AD, Wari influence is apparent in the art, technology and architecture of most of Peru. Archaeologists call this period the Middle Horizon, which culminated with the decline of the Wari.

The Regional States
The next three or four centuries are sometimes called the Late Intermediate Period, during which several separate regional states thrived. The best-known is the Chimú Kingdom, in the Trujillo area, whose capital was the huge adobe city of Chan Chan. Roughly contemporary with the Chimú was the Chachapoyas culture of the Río Utcubamba basin, in the modern-day Department of Amazonas. They left Kuelap, a mysterious highland ruin which is reasonably accessible to the traveller. Other contemporaries were the Chancay people, just north of Lima (their artefacts can be seen in Lima's Museo Amano), and the Ica-Chincha culture, further south, whose artefacts can be seen in Ica's Museo Regional.

Several small altiplano tribes lived near Lake Titicaca and frequently warred with one another. They left impressive, circular funerary towers dotting the bleak landscape – the best are to be seen at Sillustani. There were also the Chanka (of the Ayacucho/Apurímac area) and the Kingdom of Cuzco, predecessor of the Inca Empire.

The Inca Empire
For all its greatness, the Inca Empire existed for barely a century. Prior to 1430, the Incas ruled over only the valley of Cuzco, but victory over the Chankas in the 1430s marked the beginning of a rapid military expansion. The Incas conquered and incorporated most of the area from southern Colombia to central Chile. About 1525, a civil war broke out between followers of the Inca Huáscar, in Cuzco, and followers of his half-brother Atahualpa, in Quito. When the Spaniards arrived, they took advantage of the civil war to divide and conquer the Inca Empire.

The Spanish Conquest

In November 1526, Francisco Pizarro headed south from Panama, and by 1528 had explored as far as Peru's Río Santa. He noted coastal Inca settlements, became aware of the richness of the Inca Empire, and returned to Spain to raise money and recruit men for the conquest. On his next expedition he left Panama in late 1530, landed on the Ecuadorian coast and began to march overland towards Peru. In September 1532, Pizarro founded the first Spanish town in Peru – San Miguel de Piura. Then he marched into the heart of the Inca Empire, reached Cajamarca in November 1532, captured the Inca Atahualpa, and put an end to Inca rule.

Colonial Peru

In 1535, Pizarro founded the coastal city of Lima, which became the capital of the Viceroyalty of Peru. The next 30 years were a period of turmoil, with the Incas resisting their conquerors who, in turn, were fighting among themselves for control of the rich colony. Pizarro was assassinated in 1541. Manco Inca nearly regained control of the highlands in 1536, but by 1539, he had retreated to his rainforest hideout of Vilcabamba, where he was killed in 1544. Inca Tupac Amaru attempted to overthrow the Spaniards in 1572, but was defeated and executed.

The next 200 years were relatively peaceful. Lima became the major political, social and commercial centre of the Andean nations, while Cuzco became a backwater whose main colonial legacy was the Cuzqueño School of Art which resulted from a unique blend of Spanish and highland Indian influences. The Indians were exploited and treated as peóns or expendable labourers under the *encomienda* system. This led to an uprising in 1780 under the self-styled Inca Tupac Amaru II. The uprising was quelled and its leaders cruelly executed.

Independence

By the early 19th century, the colonists were dissatisfied with the lack of freedom and high taxation imposed upon them by Spain, and the area was ripe for revolt and independence. For Peru, the change came from two directions. José de San Martín liberated Argentina and Chile, and in 1821 entered Lima. Meanwhile, Simón Bolívar had freed Venezuela and Colombia. In 1822, San Martín and Bolívar met in Ecuador, and as a result of this meeting, San Martín left Latin America to live in France and Bolívar continued with the liberation of Peru. The two decisive battles for independence were at Junín on 6 August 1824 and Ayacucho on 9 December 1824.

Peru won a brief war with Spain in 1866, and lost a longer war with Chile (1879-83) over the nitrate-rich areas of the northern Atacama Desert. As a result, Chile annexed much of coastal southern Peru. The area around Tacna was returned in 1929. Peru went to war with Ecuador over a border dispute in 1941. The 1942 treaty of Rio de Janeiro gave Peru the area north of the Río Marañón, but Ecuador disputes this border and armed skirmishes occur every few years.

Modern Times

Government in modern Peru has, for the most part, been by military dictatorship and coups, with shorter periods of civilian rule. The most recent of these began in 1980. In the late 1980s, after some years of relative stability, the country began experiencing some of its worst economic and guerilla problems in decades.

The Maoist group Sendero Luminoso (Shining Path) has been waging a guerrilla campaign against the central government for over a decade, and the struggle has claimed some 23,000 lives. The group is now believed to be linked to drug cartels, and is active mainly in the central part of the country. Another, smaller, rebel group is the Movimiento Revolucionario Tupac Amaru (MRTA).

The elections of June 1990 saw Alberto Fujimori, the 52-year-old son of Japanese immigrants, elected as president. Fujimori lacked a majority, and had difficulty implementing his programmes to improve

PERU

the economy and combat terrorism, drug trafficking and corruption. In April 1992, Fujimori suspended Congress and the courts and seized dicatatorial powers, leading to the suspension of foreign aid.

Fujimori gained political strength during 1992, however, with the captures of MRTA leader Victor Polay in mid-1992 and the Sendero Luminoso leader, Abimael Guzmán, and several top aides in September 1992. After foiling a coup attempt in November, Fujimori won legislative elections – this may pave the way for the resumption of foreign aid in 1993.

In 1993, a government amnesty programme has been devised in an attempt to further break down the terrorist groups – reportedly, several high-ranking MRTA members have turned themselves in.

GEOGRAPHY

Peru covers 1,285,215 sq km (over five times the area of the UK) and is the third largest country in South America. It lies entirely within the tropics.

Geographically, Peru has three major regions – a narrow coastal belt, the wide Andean mountains and the Amazon rainforest. The coastal strip is mainly desert, but contains Peru's major cities and its best highway, the Carratera Panamericana. Rivers running down the western slopes of the Andes form about 40 oases, which are agricultural centres.

The Andes rise rapidly from the coast; heights of 6000 metres are reached just 100 km inland. Huascarán (6768 metres) is Peru's highest mountain. Most of Peru's Andes lie between 3000 and 4000 metres, with jagged ranges separated by deep, vertiginous canyons. Although the roads are often in terrible condition, the traveller is rewarded by spectacular scenery.

The eastern Andes receive much more rainfall than do the dry western slopes and so are covered in green cloud forest. As elevation is lost, the cloud forest becomes the rainforest of the Amazon Basin, a region of few roads. The traveller wishing to penetrate the Amazon Basin must do so by river or air.

FLORA & FAUNA

Peru's varied geography, with long coastal deserts, glaciated mountain ranges, vast tropical rainforests and almost every imaginable habitat in between, means that the country is host to one of the world's richest assemblages of plants and animals.

Although the desert coast has few plants, the marine and bird life is very abundant. This has had profound influence on Peru's economy – the fishing grounds are among the best in the world and the harvesting of guano (bird dung) for fertiliser has historically been extremely important (though overshadowed today by chemical fertilisers). Travellers come to places like the Islas Ballestas and the Península de Paracas to view sea-lion colonies and vast numbers of seabirds and shorebirds such as Humboldt penguin, guanay cormorant, Peruvian and brown booby, Chilean flamingo, seaside cinclodes, Peruvian pelican and the exquisitely pretty Inca tern.

The Andean condor is seen along the coast on occasion, but this, among the largest of flying birds, is normally a denizen of the highlands. Other interesting birds of the mountains are puna ibis, Andean geese and a variety of hummingbirds eking out a precarious existence in the forbidding elevations. The highlands, too, are the home of all four members of the South American cameloids: the llama, alpaca, guanaco and vicuña. In the high country are bleak páramo and puna habitats with hardy and unique plants adapted to withstand the rigours of high altitude: blazing tropical sun alternating with freezing winds and rains. Small, colourful patches of *Polylepis* woodland are found – this shrubby tree regularly grows at the highest elevation of any tree in the world.

The Amazon Basin begins in Peru – the most distant tributary rises in the southern mountains of the country. The eastern slopes of the Andes, as they tumble to the Amazon Basin, are among the least accessible and least known areas of the planet. These are the haunts of jaguars and Andean spectacled bears and tapirs – spectacular large mammals only rarely seen in the wild. Peru's Amazon

Peru – Facts about the Country 893

is home to most of the country's approximately 1700 bird species. Peru is considered the world's most diverse country for birds, as well as having the third greatest mammal diversity and the fifth greatest plant diversity. Areas such as the Zona Reservada Tambopata (5,500 hectares) have had over 540 bird and 1100 butterfly species recorded; Parque Nacional Manu (over 1.5 million hectares) has about 1000 bird species (compare with about 700 for the USA) and 13 different species of monkey.

This vast wealth of wildlife is being protected in a system of national parks and reserves with almost 30 areas covering nearly 5% of the country. For the most part, this national park system includes remote and inaccessible places which are rarely visited – but they are there, nonetheless. Protecting these areas is vitally important but difficult because of the lack of finance. Groups like the Worldwide Fund for Nature (formerly World Wildlife Fund), Conservation International and The Nature Conservancy are all active in Peruvian conservation and you can donate money to these organisations and specifically request that the funds are used in Peru. The Fundación Peruana para la Conservación de la Naturaleza (FPCN) is a local organisation which can help with information: Apartado 18-1393, Lima, Peru (fax 42-7853). They accept donations. US citizens can make tax-deductible donations to the FPCN at The Nature Conservancy Peru Program, Latin American Division, 1815 North Lynn Street, Arlington, VA 22209, USA (fax (703) 841 4880).

CLIMATE

Peru's climate can be divided into two seasons – wet and dry – though this varies, depending on the geographical region.

The coast and western Andean slopes are generally dry. During the coastal summer (late December to early April), the sky is often clear and the weather tends to be hot and sticky. This is when Peruvians go to the beach. During the rest of the year, the garúa (coastal fog) moves in, and the sun is rarely

seen. Nazca is some 60 km inland and 600 metres above sea level, high enough to avoid the garúa, and is thus hot and sunny for most of the year. Generally, the western slopes of the Andes have weather like this.

In the Andes proper, the dry season is from May to September. Although at that altitude it can be cold at night, with occasional freezing temperatures in Cuzco (3326 metres), the dry weather means beautiful sunshine during the day. The wet season in the mountains is from October to May, but it doesn't get really wet until late January.

On the eastern slopes of the Andes, the drier months are the same as in the highlands, but the wet season tends to be more pronounced. The wettest months are January to April, when roads are often closed by landslides or flooding. The Amazon lowlands have a similar weather pattern.

GOVERNMENT

Peru is a constitutional republic (temporarily suspended in 1992). The President heads the executive branch, with 12 cabinet members. Presidential terms are five years, and presidents are not allowed two terms in succession. The legislative branch, headed by a Prime Minister, consists of 60 senators and 180 deputies. The country is divided into 13 administrative regions. Voting is compulsory for citizens aged 18 to 60.

In 1993 President Fujimori was attempting to change the constitution to enable presidents to be elected to two successive terms. He intends to run for re-election in 1994.

ECONOMY

The main economic problems are inflation, which has been running at several thousand per cent in recent years, and foreign debt, which totals about US$23 billion. Major exports are copper, coffee, cotton and fishmeal. Fear of terrorism has led to a 90% decrease in the value of the tourism industry in recent years.

POPULATION & PEOPLE

Over half of Peru's 23 million inhabitants are

PERU

PERU

the second and third largest cities, Arequipa and Trujillo, are also in the coastal region, with populations of about 750,000 each.

Almost half of the population lives in the highlands, and these people are mainly *campesinos* – rural people who practise subsistence agriculture. There are few large cities in the highlands. The standard of living there is poor, and many campesinos have migrated to the coast, where population growth is a problem.

Over 60% of the geographic area of Peru is in the Amazon Basin, but only 5% of the population lives there. The region is slowly becoming colonised.

About half the population is Indian and one-third is *mestizo*. About 12% are White and 5% are Black. Most of the Blacks live on the coast, but some live in the Amazon region. There is a small Asian population, and *chifas* (Chinese restaurants) are found throughout Peru.

RELIGION

The main religion in Peru is Roman Catholicism, and some of the older towns have splendid colonial churches. The Indians, outwardly Catholic, often blend Catholicism with their traditional beliefs.

LANGUAGE

Spanish is the main language. In the highlands, most Indians are bilingual, with Quechua being their mother tongue (Aymara around Lake Titicaca) and Spanish their second language. Between one and two million inhabitants of remote areas speak no Spanish. In remote parts of the Peruvian Amazon there are about 70 ethnic groups speaking languages from 70 different ethnic families – they cannot understand one another, and very few speak Spanish. English is understood in the best hotels, airline offices, etc. Spanish courses are available in Lima.

Facts for the Visitor

VISAS

Most travellers do not need visas to enter Peru. Notable exceptions are Australians, New Zealanders and South Africans.

Your passport should be valid for six months or more. A tourist card is given to everybody on arrival. This card is free, but don't lose it, as you will need it for stay extensions, passport checks and leaving the country. If you lose it, you can get a replacement at one of the Migraciones (immigration offices) in the major cities.

On arrival, you can usually get a 90-day stay if you ask for it, though sometimes only 30 days are given. Extensions cost US$20 for 60 days. The easiest place for tourist card extensions is the Migraciones, where the process can take less than an hour. After one extension, you must leave the country, but you are allowed to return the next day and begin again.

In addition to your passport and tourist card, you officially need a ticket out of the country, but evidence of sufficient funds for your stay is not normally required. It's rare to be asked for an exit ticket, unless you are travelling on a visa, in which case you may be asked to show it.

You should carry your passport and tourist card at all times, as there are occasional document checks on public transport – you can be arrested if you don't have identification. If you're just walking around town, you can carry a photocopy and leave the original passport in a safe place, but don't travel without it.

Documents

International vaccination certificates are not required by law, but vaccinations are advisable. Student cards save you money at many archaeological sites, museums, etc.

Peruvian Embassies

Peruvian embassies are found in all neighbouring countries, and addresses are listed in those chapters. There are also Peruvian representatives in:

Australia
Qantas House, Suite 1, 9th floor, 97 London Circuit, Canberra, ACT 2601 (☎ (06) 257-2953, fax (06) 257-5198)
Postal address: PO Box 971, Civic Square, ACT 2608

Canada
170 Laurier Ave West, Suite 1007, Ottawa K1P 5V5 (☎ (613) 238-1777, fax (613) 232-3062)

France
50 Ave Kléber, 75007 Paris (☎ (1) 47 83 54 77)

Germany
5300 Bonn 1, Godesbergerallee 127 (☎ (0228) 37-3045)

Israel
52 Rehov Pinkas, Apt 31, 8th floor, Tel Aviv 62261 (☎ (03) 45-4065)

New Zealand
35-37 Victoria St, 3rd floor, PO Box 11- 510, Wellington (☎ (04) 72-5171)

Spain
Principe de Vergara 36, Madrid (☎ 431-4242)

UK
52 Sloane St, London SW1X 9SP (☎ (71) 235-1917)

USA
1700 Massachusetts Ave, NW, Washington DC 20036 (☎ (202) 833-9860, fax (202) 659- 3660)

MONEY

Currency

When the *inti* was introduced in 1986, there were 17 intis to a US dollar. By 1991, severe inflation had driven the exchange down to about one million intis to a US dollar. A new currency, the *sol nuevo*, was introduced, with each sol nuevo being worth one million intis. At the end of April 1993, the exchange rate was 1.86 soles nuevos to one US dollar. A sol nuevo is divided into 100 *centimos*.

The following bills are in circulation: 10, 20, 50, 100 soles nuevos. In addition, old inti bills are still being used but are slowly being phased out. (Check locally.) Inti bills are used by ignoring the last six zeros on the bill. Coins of one, five, 10 and 50 centimos and one sol nuevo are in use. In August 1993, exchange rares were:

A$1 = SN1.40
Can$1 = SN1.58
DM1 = SN1.21
FF1 = SN0.34
UK£ = SN3.08
US$1 = SN2.05

Changing Money

The easiest currency to change is the US dollar. Money can be changed in banks, *casas de cambio* (exchange houses) or with street moneychangers. First-class hotels and restaurants will also accept dollars, at lower rates. Most cities or towns of any size have, at least, street changers giving fairly reasonable rates.

Banking hours are erratic. In the summer (January to March), banks are open only from 8.30 to 11.30 am. During the rest of the year, they are open longer – sometimes into the afternoon, but you can't count on it. Expect long queues in banks and go early in the morning. Casas de cambio are often open from 9 am to 6 pm, or later in tourist areas such as Cuzco, but tend to close for a couple of hours at lunch time. Street changers are useful for exchange outside banking hours, or at borders where there are no banks. Rates are equivalent to bank rates, but you may be cheated, so beware. Fixed calculators and shortchanging are common – count the money carefully before handing over the dollars.

The exchange rates for cash dollars tend to be better than those for travellers' cheques. Recently, travellers' cheques were being changed at a loss of 1% to 5%. Street changers only take cash. Torn bills are not accepted.

Bank transfers from home are possible, but take at least three days, even if you use telex. Check with the bank to ensure that you can receive your money in US dollars. Only some banks will provide this service (for a small commission); the Banco de Crédito has been recommended. Money can be advanced on credit cards, at a commission – about 8%. Visa is the most easily accepted (at the Banco de Crédito).

You can buy back dollars, at a slight loss, when leaving the country. There are moneychangers working on the land borders, and the airport in Lima has a Banco de la Nación open for international departures. Don't get left with a lot of excess cash, because occasional strikes or currency freezes mean banks won't buy back intis.

The currency exchange rules can change at any time, so consult a traveller who has been in the country for a while.

Costs

Costs in Peru have increased dramatically (about threefold) in the last three years. If you were on a tight budget, you could get by at the time of writing on US$10 to US$15 per day, but that meant staying in the most basic hotels and travelling slowly. Big cities are more expensive than small towns. Most budget travellers spend over US$20 per day, because of the large distances that have to be covered to visit Peru properly. Prices can triple (even in dollar terms) within a couple of months, and they can fall equally rapidly. Please bear this in mind when reading this chapter.

Tipping

Fancy restaurants add 31% in service charges and tax to your bill, but cheap restaurants don't – check before you order if in any doubt. You don't have to tip the server in the cheapest restaurants, but they don't make much money, so leaving some change isn't a bad idea. Don't leave it on the table – make sure the money goes into the hands of the server.

WHEN TO GO

June to August is the dry season in the highlands, and the most popular time to travel in Peru. This is when hotels are more likely to be full and to charge full prices. Outside these months, you can expect lower prices and can try bargaining.

January to April are the 'summer' months on the coast, and many Peruvians visit the coastal areas then.

WHAT TO BRING

Shoes larger than size 43 Peruvian (or US10½) are not sold in Peru. Tampons are available in Peru, but only in the major cities and in regular sizes. Condoms are available in the major cities but the choice is limited. A sleeping bag or warm (down) jacket is useful if you plan on travelling in the highlands, where temperatures can drop below freezing at night (cheap highland hotel rooms often lack heat). Good insect repellent and sunscreen are hard to find.

USEFUL ORGANISATIONS

Major cities have their own tourist information offices – for addresses, see city sections. A toll-free 24-hour hotline (☎ 71-2994, fax 71-1617) has been set up for travellers' complaints. Add 014 in front of the number if calling from outside Lima. The South American Explorers Club has a Lima clubhouse.

POST & TELECOMMUNICATIONS
Post

Postal services are expensive. Most of the letters you send will arrive safely; *certificado* (registered mail) now costs considerably more than regular mail, but will give you peace of mind. Letters from Peru to, say, the USA take from one to three weeks.

Mailing parcels is best done from the main post office in Lima. Large parcels (up to 10 kg) need to be checked by customs, so bring your parcel open and then sew it up in a cloth sack. Parcels weighing more than 10 kg have to go from the special Correos, on Calle Toma Valle (no number), a street which runs perpendicular to the airport entrance. Small packages weighing less than one kg (two kg to some destinations) can be sent in an openable (drawstring) bag by *pequeños paquetes* service, which goes by certified airmail. There is no surface mail outside Lima, which means very expensive airmail. Regulations change from year to year.

Incoming mail, even to Lima, is slow. Ordinary mail from the USA to Cuzco can take up to a month. Most travellers receive mail at either the post office or American Express (Lima Tours, Casilla 4340, Belén 1040, Lima). The South American Explorers Club will hold mail for members, and return or forward it, according to your instructions.

Telecommunications

ENTEL-Peru provides long-distance national and international telephone, telex and telegram services, except in Lima, where it's La Compañía Peruana de Teléfonos. Calls are expensive. You leave a large advance deposit, are given a receipt and have the difference returned to you at the end. Rates are cheaper on Sunday and after 9 pm. ENTEL offices are usually open from 8 am to 10 pm, but La Compañía Peruana de Teléfonos in Lima is open only until 9 pm.

A three-minute call to the USA costs about US$10. Reverse-charge calls (costing about US$1) can be made to some countries, including the USA and the UK. Ask at the nearest ENTEL office. You can reach a US operator and some European operators by calling the appropriate three-digit code (no charge), from ENTEL telephones only. Calls can then be placed using your telephone credit card. This service is not currently available from La Compañía Peruana de Teléfonos in Lima.

Code	Company
191	AT&T USA Direct
190	MCI Call USA
192	TRT Phone USA
196	Sprint Express
197	Italy Direct
198	Spain Direct

To dial direct from Peru to another country, dial 00 + country code + city (area) code + number. To call long distance from within Peru, dial 0 + city code + number. Codes are in the telephone directory, or ask any operator. Fax services are now available in major Peruvian cities.

There are a few public telephones in the major cities. Phone discs called Fiches RIN can be bought from street sellers, particularly newspaper vendors. The ENTEL offices have public phones for local calls. Apart from the main ENTEL office marked on the city maps, there are several branch offices scattered around the bigger towns.

ELECTRICITY

Peru uses 220 volts, 60 cycles AC, except Arequipa, which is on 50 cycles.

TIME

Peru is five hours behind GMT, except from January to April, when it is four hours behind. Iquitos and Cuzco stay five hours behind all year round.

LAUNDRY

There are no self-service laundry machines in Peru. Many hotels will have someone to do your laundry (cheap in cheap hotels, expensive in expensive hotels). There are *lavanderías* (laundries) in the main cities, but you still have to leave the clothes for 24 hours (though there are same-day services in Cuzco). Costs are about US$1.50 per kg. Some lavanderías only do dry-cleaning.

MEDIA

Newspapers & Magazines

One of the best newspapers, *El Comercio*, is published in Lima. There is a monthly English-language magazine called the *Lima Times*. The South American Explorers Club publishes the quarterly *South American Explorer*, which has a host of articles about Peru as well as other parts of the continent.

HEALTH

Avoid salads, and fruit that you cannot peel yourself, and don't drink the water straight from the tap. You can get good medical advice and treatment in the major cities. If you are seriously ill, try to get to Lima, where the best treatment is available. For more details, see the Health section in the introductory Facts for the Visitor chapter.

DANGERS & ANNOYANCES

Peru has a reputation for theft, and unfortunately, this is fully warranted. Many travellers have been robbed – there are pickpockets, bag-snatchers, razor-blade slashers (slashing your pack or pocket), con artists and crooked police. With the increasing poverty of the 1990s, thieves are getting bolder and more numerous. It is recom-

PERU

mended that you take a taxi to a hotel when first arriving in a new city.

A recent scam involves locals spending hours or even days befriending you and then, when they have your trust, offering you a joint. You get busted two drags later. Read the Dangers & Annoyances section in the introductory Facts for the Visitor chapter for more details.

Sendero Luminoso

This guerrilla organisation controls some of the remoter parts of Peru. Travel to and around most of Peru is reasonably safe, as it has been for the 30 years that the Sendero has been in existence. The 1992 capture of Abimael Guzmán, the Sendero's leader, has slowed guerilla activity, but it will be years before this organisation is stopped. The Sendero and the drug cartels are connected in their attempts to disrupt the stability of Peru, and drug-growing regions in the Huallaga river valley north of Tingo María are dangerous to travel in. The areas around Huancavelica, Ayacucho and Abancay are also dangerous to travel in, though you can fly into Ayacucho and stay in the centre. Check the situation with the local tourist authorities when you arrive.

FILM & PHOTOGRAPHY

Camera gear is very expensive in Peru and film choice is limited. Film may have been kept in hot storage cabinets, and is sometimes sold outdated, so check expiry dates. Slide processing is poor (though prints aren't bad).

ACCOMMODATION

In the last couple of years, cheap hotel rooms have doubled or tripled in price in US dollar terms. Economic changes can be both sudden and severe, leading to drastic changes in Peruvian hotel rates.

Accommodation can be tight during major fiestas, or the night before market day. For this reason, as many hotels as possible are shown on the town maps. If you are going to a town specifically for a market or fiesta,

try to arrive a day early, or at least by early afternoon of the day before the market.

Sometimes single rooms are hard to find, so you may get a room with two or three beds. Check that you won't be asked to pay for all the beds – this is usually no problem, unless the hotel is full. Conversely, many hotels have triple and quad rooms, which work out more cheaply for people travelling in a group.

Villages far off the beaten track may not have even a basic *pensión*. If you have a sleeping bag, you can usually find somewhere to sleep by asking around – the store owner should know who would rent a room or some floor space. People in remote areas are generally hospitable.

Note that, in remote areas, Sendero Luminoso terrorist activity tends to target town halls, police posts and political offices. You are advised not to sleep in these places.

FOOD

Those with a tight budget and a strong stomach can eat from street and market stalls, if the food looks hot and freshly cooked. Chifas are often good value. Most will offer *tallarines* (noodles) with chopped chicken, beef, pork or shrimp for US$2 to US$3. Many cheap restaurants offer an inexpensive set meal, especially at lunch. It's called *el menú*, usually consists of soup and a second course, and costs from US$1 to US$2, depending on location. Remember that mid-range restaurants add 18% to 31% tax – ask before you eat.

Some of Peru's typical dishes are:

Cebiche de Corvina – a white sea bass marinated in lemon, chilli and onions is served cold with a boiled potato or yam. It's delicious. *Cebiche de Camarones* is the same thing, made with shrimps. These dishes are appetisers rather than full meals

Lomo Saltado – chopped steak is fried with onions, tomatoes, potatoes and served with rice. This is a standard dish, served everywhere

Palta a la Jardinera – an avocado is stuffed with cold vegetable salad; *a la Reyna* is stuffed with chicken salad.

Sopa a la Criolla – this lightly spiced noodle soup with beef, egg, milk and vegetables is hearty and filling.

The term 'a la criolla' is used to describe spicy foods.

DRINKS

Agua mineral (mineral water) is cheap but it's fizzy. *Agua pura* is more expensive bottled water – not fizzy. If you buy a bottled drink in a store, you must pay a deposit on the bottle.

Many of the usual soft drinks are available, as well as local ones such as Inca Cola, which is appropriately gold-coloured and tastes like fizzy bubble gum. Soft drinks are collectively known as *gaseosas*, and the local brands are very sweet. Ask for *helada* if you want want your drink straight out of the refrigerator, *al clima* if you don't. Remember to say *sin hielo* (without ice), unless you really trust the water supply.

Jugos (fruit juices) are available everywhere. Make sure you get *jugo puro* and not *con agua*. The most common kinds are *mora* (blackberry), *naranja* (orange), *toronja* (grapefruit), *piña* (pineapple), *maracuyá* (passion fruit), *sandía* (watermelon), *naranjilla* (a local fruit tasting like bitter orange) or papaya.

Coffee is available almost everywhere but is often disappointing. It doesn't taste that great and it looks very much like soy sauce! Instant coffee is also served. Good espresso and cappuccino are available in the bigger towns. *Café con leche* is milk with coffee, and *café con agua* is black coffee. *Té* (tea) is served black with lemon and sugar. Hot chocolate is also popular.

There are about a dozen kinds of beer, and they are quite palatable and inexpensive. Both light, lager-type beers and sweet, dark beers are available. Dark beer is known as *malta* or *cerveza negra*. Cuzco and Arequipa are known for their beers: Cuzqueña and Arequipeña, respectively. Both are available in lager and dark. Cuzqueña is Peru's best beer, according to many drinkers. Arequipeña tastes slightly sweet.

The traditional highland *chicha* (corn beer) is stored in earthenware pots and served in huge glasses in small Andean villages and markets, but is not commercially available elsewhere. It is home-made, and definitely an acquired taste.

Peruvian wines are acceptable but not as good as those from Chile and Argentina. The best are from the Tacama and Ocucaje wineries, and begin at about US$5 a bottle (more in restaurants).

Spirits are expensive if imported and not very good if made locally, with some exceptions. Rum is cheap and quite good. A white grape brandy called *pisco* is the national drink, most frequently served in pisco sour – a tasty cocktail made from pisco, egg white, lemon juice, sugar, syrup, crushed ice and bitters. *Guinda* is a sweet cherry brandy. The local *aguardiente*, sugar-cane alcohol, is an acquired taste but is good and very cheap.

BOOKS & BOOKSHOPS

The best place for guidebooks is the South American Explorers Club at Avenida República de Portugal 146 in Lima.

General

A very fine book by a writer exceptionally well-informed on both archaeology and contemporary Peru is Ronald Wright's *Cut Stones and Crossroads* (Penguin, 1984). For a sympathetic account of the shantytown communities which surround Lima, some of which have improved greatly from their humble origins, see Susan Lobo's *A House of My Own* (University of Arizona Press).

Travel Guides

Lonely Planet's *Peru – a travel survival kit* has much more detailed information, if you plan on a long stay.

Exploring Cuzco, by Peter Frost (Nuevas Imagenes, Lima, 1989), is highly recommended for anyone planning to spend some time in the Cuzco area – all the major sites are described.

A detailed description of Lima, its history, museums and interesting sites, is to be found in *The City of Kings – A Guide to Lima*, by Carolyn Walton (Pacific Press, Lima, 1987).

A guide (in Spanish) to the Huaraz area is *Callejón de Huaylas y Cordillera Blanca*, by Felipe Díaz (Información Turística Kuntur,

PERU

1989). This is a useful general guide with good background on archaeology, natural history, trekking and fiestas, among other subjects. An English edition is planned.

Trekking Guides
A good all-round book is *Backpacking and Trekking in Peru and Bolivia*, by Hilary Bradt (Bradt Publications, 5th edition, 1989). It has a wealth of fascinating background information, as well as entertaining descriptions and maps of over a dozen good backpacking trips in Peru and Bolivia.

Jim Bartle's *Trails of the Cordilleras Blanca & Huayhuash of Peru* is good for trekking in the Huaraz area, but has been out of print since 1989.

A book which combines climbs and treks in the Cordilleras Blanca and Huayhuash is *The Peruvian Andes*, by Ph Beaud (Cordee, Leicester, and Cloudcap Press, Seattle, 1988). This book is trilingual (French, English and Spanish) and is useful for climbing routes. It is expensive (about US$24).

Archaeology & History
The best general book about the Incas is undoubtedly John Hemming's excellent *The Conquest of the Incas* (Harcourt, Brace, Jovanovich, 1970). It is available as a Penguin paperback. For an interesting account of the conquistadores, see James Lockhart's *The Men of Cajamarca* (University of Texas Press, 1972).

Literature
Several Peruvian writers have made an impact overseas, and their books are available in English translation. José Marfía Arguedas, a poet raised by Indians and who wrote his verse in Quechua, embodied the cultural conflicts between Spaniard and Indian, in novels like *Deep Rivers* (University of Texas Press, Austin, 1978). Ciro Alegría dealt with similar themes in *Broad and Alien is the World*.

Among contemporary writers, one-time presidential candidate Mario Vargas Llosa has published several exceptional novels, which are widely available in paperback, including *The Green House*, *Conversation in the Cathedral*, *Aunt Julia and the Scriptwriter* and *The War of the End of the World* (set in Brazil).

MAPS
The best selection of topographical maps is available from the Instituto Geográfico Nacional, at Avenida Aramburu 1190 in Lima. The South American Explorers Club has a good selection of hiking maps.

THINGS TO BUY
Souvenirs from Peru are good, varied and cheap. You won't necessarily save much money by shopping in villages and markets rather than in shops. In markets and smaller stores, bargaining is expected.

You can buy everything in Lima, be it a blowpipe from the jungle or a woven poncho from the highlands. Although Lima is usually a little more expensive, the choice is varied and the quality is high.

Cuzco also has a great selection of craft shops, but the quality is rarely as high as in Lima. Old and new weavings, ceramics, paintings, woollen clothing and jewellery are all found here.

The Puno/Juliaca area is good for knitted alpaca sweaters, and knick-knacks made from the *totora* reed which grows on Lake Titicaca. The Huancayo area is the place to buy carved gourds, and excellent weavings and clothing are available in the cooperative market. The Ayacucho area is famous for modern weavings and stylised ceramic churches. San Pedro de Cajas is known for its peculiar weavings, which are made of rolls of yarn stuffed with wool. The Shipibo pottery sold in Yarinacocha (near Pucallpa) is the best of the jungle craft available. Superb reproductions of Moche and Mochica pottery are available in Trujillo.

Warning
Objects made from skins, feathers, turtle shells, etc should not be bought – their purchase contributes to the degradation of the wildlife and their importation into most countries is illegal.

Getting There & Away

AIR

Lima's Aeropuerto Internacional Jorge Chávez is the main hub for flights to the Andean countries from Europe and North America. There are also some international flights to Iquitos, in Peru's Amazon region.

There is a US$17.40 departure tax (payable in cash dollars or soles) for travellers leaving Peru on an international flight.

To/From Bolivia

LAB and AeroPerú have several flights per week between La Paz (Bolivia) and Lima (about US$250). There are also two flights per week between La Paz and Cuzco (US$180), which can be heavily booked. Tickets for these flights are cheaper if bought outside South America.

To/From Brazil

There are daily flights between Rio (Brazil) and Lima, and two flights between Manaus (Brazil) and Iquitos (Peru).

To/From Chile

AeroPerú and LAN-Chile have regular flights between Santiago (Chile) and Lima.

To/From Colombia

You can fly from Bogotá (Colombia) to Lima, but remember that air fares out of Colombia are expensive.

To/From Ecuador

AeroPerú, Ecuatoriana and American Airlines fly to Lima from the Ecuadorian cities of Quito and Guayaquil.

LAND

To/From Bolivia

The overland routes between Peru and Bolivia are around Lake Titicaca. For details, see Puno, in the Lake Titicaca Area section.

To/From Chile

The main border crossing is from Arica in northern Chile to Tacna (Peru). For details, see Tacna (in this chapter) and Arica (in the Chile chapter).

To/From Ecuador

This is a straightforward crossing. For details, see Tumbes (in this chapter) or Huaquillas (in the Ecuador chapter).

BOAT

To/From Brazil & Colombia

It is possible to travel by riverboat all the way from the mouth of the Amazon at Belém (Brazil) to Iquitos (Peru). Normally, travellers will need to break the journey into several stages, because very few boats do the entire trip. Boats to Iquitos leave from the Brazilian border port of Tabatinga, taking two to three days and costing US$20. Express boats from the Colombian border town of Leticia take 12 hours and cost US$50. Tabatinga and Leticia are adjacent to one another.

Getting Around

Peru is a big country, and you'll need several months to visit it all overland. Public buses are frequent and reasonably comfortable on the major routes, and they are the normal form of transport. Less travelled routes are served by older and less comfortable vehicles. There are two railway systems, which make an interesting change from bus travel. Air services are extensive, and recommended for those short on time. In the jungle regions, travel is mainly by riverboat or air.

When travelling, have your passport with you, not packed in your luggage or left in the hotel safe. You need to show it to board most planes, and buses may have to go through police checkpoints. If your passport is in order, these are cursory procedures.

AIR

AeroPerú, Faucett, Americana and Expresso Aéreo are the main domestic carriers. Their prices are similar (eg US$62 from Lima to Cuzco). Expresso Aéreo is slightly cheaper, and serves some of the remoter towns, as does Aero-Cóndor. The military airline, known as Grupo Ocho, occasionally provides flights but has infrequent service.

The following cities are served by Faucett, AeroPerú or Americana: Arequipa, Ayacucho, Cajamarca, Cuzco, Chiclayo, Juliaca, Iquitos, Lima, Piura, Pucallpa, Puerto Maldonado, Rioja (for Moyobamba), Tacna, Talara, Tarapoto, Tingo María, Trujillo, Tumbes and Yurimaguas. Some of the smaller towns have only one or two flights per week. Inquire locally about smaller airlines in other towns.

Flights are frequently late. Morning flights are more likely to be on time, but by the afternoon, things fall an hour or more behind schedule. You should show up at least an hour early for all domestic flights, as baggage handling and check-in procedures are chaotic. It is not unknown for flights to leave up to an hour *before* their official departure time, if bad weather has been predicted.

Flights are fully booked during holiday periods, so make reservations well in advance. Make sure all reservations are confirmed, reconfirmed and reconfirmed again. The airlines are notorious for bumping you off your flights if you don't reconfirm.

There are no separate sections for smokers and nonsmokers on internal flights. Many flights have extraordinarily good views of the snowcapped Andes, so it is worth getting a window seat.

There is a 18% tax charged on domestic flights. A US$4 to US$7 departure tax is charged on local flights out of most airports.

On internal flights, 20 kg of checked luggage is allowed (though you can get away with more). Lost luggage is a depressingly frequent problem. Normally, the luggage turns up on the next day's flights, but try to include valuables (such as camera gear) and essentials (such as a warm coat, or medications) in your hand luggage. Lock your checked luggage, and make sure it is properly labelled.

BUS
Long-Distance Bus
The buses are cheap and go just about everywhere, except for the deep jungle and Machu Picchu.

A few cities have central bus terminals, but in most towns, the different bus companies have their offices clustered around a few city blocks. It is always a good idea to buy your ticket in advance. There is sometimes a separate 'express' ticket window for people buying tickets for another day. Schedules and fares change frequently and vary from company to company. In the low season, some companies try to sell more seats by offering discounted bus fares. When you buy your ticket, ask where the bus is leaving from, because the ticket office and bus terminal are sometimes on different streets.

During the journey, your luggage, unless it is small enough to take into the bus, will travel in the luggage compartment. This is usually safe. You are given a baggage tag in exchange for your bag, which should be securely closed, and locked if possible.

Long-distance buses stop for at least three meals a day. The driver will announce how long the stop will be, but it's your responsibility to be on the bus when it leaves. Many companies have their own rest areas in the middle of nowhere, so you don't have any choice but to eat there. The food is generally inexpensive but unexciting. Some travellers prefer to bring their own food. Remember to carry your own roll of toilet paper.

If you're travelling during long holiday weekends or special fiestas, you may find that buses are booked up for several days in advance, so book as early as you can for these periods. Bus fares often double around Christmas and 28 July (Independence). Whichever time you travel, be prepared for delays and don't plan on making important connections after a bus journey. Innumerable flat tyres, a landslide or engine trouble can lengthen a journey by many hours.

It is useful to have a flashlight on an overnight bus, to enable you to read a book for a few hours before going to sleep. It can get freezing cold on the night buses in the highlands – bring a blanket.

Armed robberies on night buses have been reported all over Peru. Some routes (Cuzco-Juliaca-Arequipa) are served only by night buses. Considering the number of buses, the chance of being held up is not very great; however, travel by day when possible. Do not take buses through Ayacucho and Abancay.

Local Bus

Local buses are usually slow and crowded, but very cheap. You can get around most towns for about US$0.10. When you want to get off a local bus, yell *baja* (down), or *esquina* (corner) – the driver will stop at the next one.

Truck

In remote areas, trucks often double as buses. Sometimes they are pick-up trucks with rudimentary wooden benches; sometimes they are ordinary trucks – you just climb in the back, often with the cargo. If the weather is OK, you can get fabulous views; if the weather is bad, you take shelter under a tarpaulin.

Payment for these rides, usually determined by the driver, is a standard fare depending on the distance. Because the trucks double as buses, they usually charge almost as much.

TRAIN

There are two unconnected railway networks in Peru; both go from the coast to the highlands.

There are two classes. Second class is very cheap but very crowded and uncomfortable. First class is about 25% more expensive than 2nd class, but it's much more comfortable, and cheaper, than a bus journey of comparable length. In addition, there are buffet and pullman cars, for which you pay a surcharge. They are heated and give access to food service. There is also a more expensive tourist train from Cuzco to Machu Picchu.

The Central Railroad runs from Lima to Huancayo. This trip takes a whole day and

passes through the station of Galera at 4781 metres above sea level – the highest standard-gauge railway station in the world. Trains often don't run during the rainy season (November to April).

The Southern Railroad runs passenger trains from from Arequipa to Lake Titicaca and Cuzco. This is the longest and busiest section of Peru's railways. Trains from Arequipa to Puno, on the shores of Lake Titicaca, used to run every night but recently have been running only twice a week. Check locally. You can change at Juliaca, about 40 km before Puno, for trains to Cuzco – again, two a week. The Arequipa to Juliaca (or Puno) service takes a whole night; the Puno to Cuzco service takes a whole day.

In Cuzco, there are two train stations: one for the service described above and the other for the service to Machu Picchu. You cannot go directly by rail from Arequipa or Lake Titicaca to Machu Picchu. There are several trains from Cuzco to Machu Picchu every day.

The main drawback to travelling by train is thievery. The night train from Arequipa to Puno is notorious, particularly the crowded and ill-lit 2nd-class carriages, where a dozing traveller is almost certain to get robbed. Dark stations are also the haunts of thieves. The solutions to the problem are to travel by day and stay alert, to travel with a friend or group or to travel in 1st class. The buffet or pullman classes have a surcharge and are the safest carriages to ride in, because only ticket holders are allowed aboard.

For all services, it is advisable to buy tickets in advance – the day before is usually best. This way, you don't have to worry about looking after your luggage whilst lining up to buy a ticket.

TAXI

Ask the fare in advance, because there are no meters. It is quite acceptable to haggle over a taxi fare – drivers often double or triple the standard rate for an unsuspecting foreigner. For a short run in Lima, the fare is about US$1.50; it's a little less in other cities. Taxis are recognisable by the small red 'TAXI' sticker on the windshield. The black *remisse* taxis parked outside major hotels are usually three times more expensive than others.

Colectivo taxis work for *comités* and have a set run between major cities. These cost two to three times as much as buses and are about 25% faster. Note that the term col-ectivo is also used for a bus, especially a minibus or van.

BOAT

Small motorised vessels that take about 20 passengers sail from Puno to visit the various islands on Lake Titicaca. There are depar-tures every day, and the costs are low.

Boat travel is important in Peru's eastern lowlands. Dugout canoes, usually powered by an outboard engine, act as water taxis or buses on some of the smaller rivers. Where the rivers widen, larger cargo boats are nor-mally available.

You can travel from Pucallpa to the mouth of the Amazon by larger cargo boat. It's a few days' journey to Iquitos, where you'll board another, slightly larger boat and continue for another couple of days to the border with Brazil and Colombia. The boats are small but have two decks. The lower deck is for cargo, the upper for passengers and crew. Bring a hammock. Food is provided, but is basic and not always very hygienic. You may want to bring some of your own. To get a passage, go down to the docks and ask around for a boat going where you want to go. Find out who the captain is and arrange a passage. Departure time depends, more often than not, on filling up the hold. Sometimes you can sleep on the boat while waiting for depar-ture, thus saving on hotel bills.

Boats to Iquitos from upriver towns are infrequent, small, slow and uncomfortable. Beyond Iquitos, services are both more fre-quent and more comfortable. Things are generally more organised too: there are chalk boards at the docks with ship's names, des-tinations and departure times displayed reasonably clearly and accurately.

HITCHING

Hitching is not very practical in Peru because there are few private cars. Many drivers of *any* vehicle will pick you up but will also expect payment.

Lima

Lima, Peru's capital, was founded by Fran-cisco Pizarro in 1535, on 6 January, the Catholic feast of Epiphany, or the Day of the Kings. Hence the city was first named the City of the Kings. Many of the old colonial buildings can still be seen. Unfortunately, much of Lima's colonial charm has been overwhelmed by an uncontrolled population explosion which began in the 1920s. About one-third of the nation's 22 million inhabi-tants now live in Lima, and most of the city is overcrowded, polluted and noisy.

Much of the growth has been due to the influx of very poor people from other areas of Peru. They come searching for a better life – a job and, perhaps, opportunities for their children. But jobs are scarce, and most end up living in the *pueblos jovenes* (literally, young towns). The shantytowns surround the capital, lacking electricity, water and ade-quate sanitation.

Lima has a dismal climate. From April to December, the city suffers from garúa, which blots out the sun and blankets the buildings in a fine grey mist. During the short Lima summer (January to March), the situation is hardly better: although the sun does come out, the smog makes walking the streets unpleasant, and the city beaches are over-crowded cesspools. The waste products of almost seven million inhabitants have to go somewhere, and mostly end up in the Pacific – the newspapers publish health warnings about beaches during the summer months.

Despite all this, there are reasons for vis-iting the city: the inhabitants are generally friendly and hospitable, there are plenty of opportunities for dining, nightlife and other entertainment, and there is a great selection of museums. Besides, it is virtually impossi-ble to avoid Lima.

Orientation

The heart of the city is the Plaza de Armas, flanked by the Government Palace, the Catedral, the Archbishop's Palace and other important buildings. The Plaza de Armas is linked to the Plaza San Martín by the crowded pedestrian street of Jirón Unión, which is lined by stores. The area around these plazas is historically interesting, and it is here that the majority of budget hotels are found.

South of Plaza San Martín, Jirón Unión continues as Belén and runs to the Paseo de la República. Streets in Lima often change their names every few blocks, which is confusing to the first-time visitor. Paseo de la República is graced by the huge Palacio de Justicia, the Sheratón Hotel and many interesting monuments. At the south end of the Paseo is the Plaza Grau, from which the Via Expresa (locally called 'El Zanjón' – the ditch) is an important expressway to the southern suburbs. Parallel and one block to the west of the Via Expresa is Avenida Garcilasa de la Vega, which runs south into Avenida Arequipa and is the main bus street for transport to the southern suburbs of San Isidro, Miraflores and Barranco.

Continuing along Avenida Arequipa several km to Miraflores leads you to Avenida Larco which, in turn, leads to the Pacific Ocean. Half a century ago, Avenida Arequipa traversed through ranches and countryside between Lima and the coast – today, every inch of land has been built upon.

The old heart of Lima is the most dangerous area from the point of view of pickpockets and poverty – keep alert. The southern suburbs are not as dangerous. This is where the better-off Limeños live, and where the more exclusive stores and restaurants are found. Several important museums are also here.

The airport is in Callao, the old port city about 11 km west of the city centre. There is no direct road link between the two – taxi drivers all have their personally favoured, complicated route to and from the airport.

Information

Tourist Office The government tourist information offices at Belén 1040 in Lima closed in 1992 (check locally for reopening). A useful source of general information is the free booklet *Peru Guide*, published monthly.

South American Explorers Club (☎ 31-4480) The Lima office of the South American Explorers Club is at República de Portugal 146, on the 13th block of Alfonso Ugarte, in the Breña district of Lima. Hours are 9.30 am to 5 pm Monday to Friday. The postal address is Casilla 3714, Lima 100, Peru.

For more information about the South American Explorers Club, see Useful Organisations in the introductory Facts for the Visitor chapter.

Money One of the few places in Lima which will exchange travellers' cheques for cash dollars, for a small (about 3%) commission, is the Banco de Crédito, whose main office is at Jirón Lampa 411. In the past, it has given the best sol rates for travellers' cheques. The Miraflores branch (on the 3rd block of Larco) and the San Isidro branch also change travellers' cheques. Note that Chile, Bolivia and Ecuador are better places to change traveller's cheques to cash dollars or to have money wired from home.

Casas de cambio usually give good rates for cash but pay several percent lower for travellers' cheques. Casas de cambio are found near the Plaza San Martín, especially on Colmena going north-west. They are also found on Larco in Miraflores.

Street moneychangers often hang around the casas de cambio – the corner of Plaza San Martín and Ocoña is a favourite spot – and they match the rates in banks or casas de cambio.

The Banco de la Nación at the airport usually (though not always) changes money. There are normally a couple of casas de cambio operating near the international arrivals exit. Exchange rates at the airport are usually a little lower than the best rates in the city.

PERU

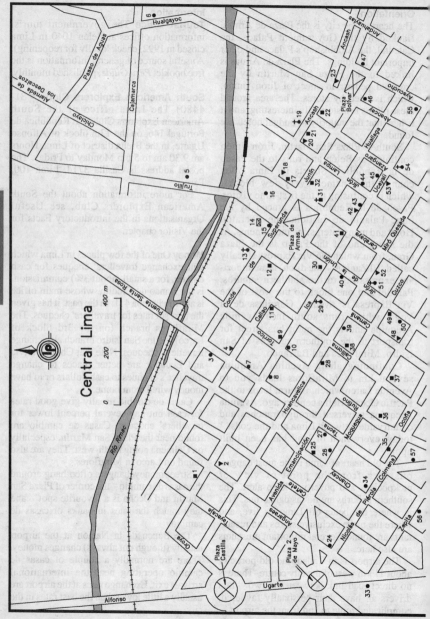

Central Lima

0 200 400 m

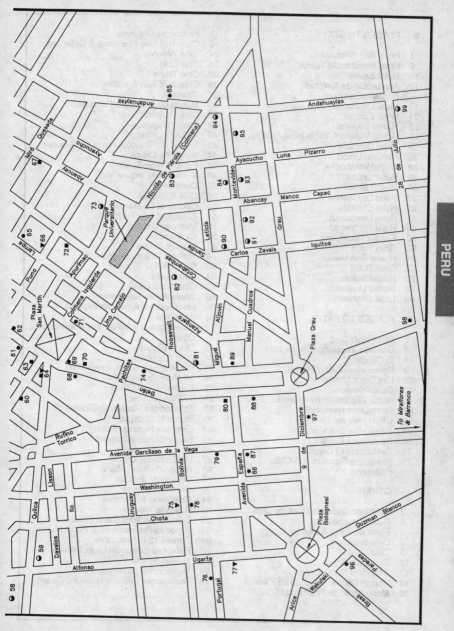

PERU

PERU

■ PLACES TO STAY

1   Hotel San Sebastián
9   Hotel Residencial Roma
11 Hotel Savoy
12 Asociación de Amistad
    Peruano/Europeo
17 Hotel Carabaya
21 Hotel Europa
22 Hostal España
25 Hostal Wilson & Youth Hostel Karina
28 Hotel Granada
30 Pensión Unión
32 Hostal Wiracocha
35 Hotel Crillón
36 Hostal El Sol
37 Hotel La Casona
38 Hotel Claridge
41 Hotel Damascus
49 Hotel Richmond
60 Familia Rodríguez
63 Gran Hotel Bolívar
64 Hostal San Martín
67 Gran Hotel
70 Hostal Belén
72 Hostal Universo
80 Lima Sheraton

■ PLACES TO EAT

2   Chifa Wah Sing
4   Govinda Vegetarian Restaurant
18 El Cordano
20 Restaurant Machu Picchu
23 Las Trece Monedas
42 Café Adriatico
48 Natur Vegetarian Restaurant
52 Restaurant Raimondi
53 L'Eau Vive del Peru
64 Parrilladas San Martín
66 Restaurant Heydi
75 Restaurant El Capricho
77 Nakasone Restaurant & Chifa
    Pallasano

    OTHER

3   Santuario de Santa Rosa de Lima
5   Peña Hatuchay
6   Plaza de Toros & Museo
7   Cine Imperio
8   Cine Central
10 Teatro Municipal
13 Church of Santo Domingo
14 Correo Central & Museo de Filatelia
15 Monumento de Francisco Pizarro

16 Palacio de Gobierno
19 Church of San Francisco & Catacombs
24 Cine Venecia
26 Cine Lido
27 Cine Tacna
29 Church of San Agustín
31 Catedral
33 Museo de la Cultura Peruana
34 Cine Portofino
39 Teatro Segura
40 AYZA Bookstore
43 Museo del Banco Central de Reserva
44 Banco de Crédito
45 Palacio Torre Tagle
46 Museo de la Inquisición
47 Congreso
50 Cine Excelsior
51 Church of La Merced
54 Church of San Pedro
55 Mercado Central
56 Cine Tauro
57 Faucett Airline
58 Turismo Chimbote (Buses)
59 Cruz del Sur (Buses)
61 Cine Plaza
62 Cine Adan y Eva
65 International Telegrams
68 Lima Tours & American Express
69 AeroPerú
71 Cine Metro & International Telephone
    Office
73 Olano (Buses)
74 Cine República
76 South American Explorers Club
78 24-Hour Fax location
79 Explorers' Inn Office
81 TEPSA (Buses)
82 Transportes Rodríguez (Buses)
83 Buses to Chosica
84 Empresa Huaraz (Buses)
85 Santa Catalina Convent
86 Cine Conquistador
87 US Embassy Office
88 Museo de Arte Italiano
89 Palacio de Justicia
90 Ormeño (Buses)
91 Colectivos to Chosica
92 Buses to Pisco
93 Expreso Sudamericano (Buses)
94 Buses to Pachacámac & Pucusana
95 Comité 12 to Huancayo
96 Peña Las Brisas del Lago Titicaca
97 Museo de Arte
98 Migraciones (Immigration)
99 Transportes León de Huánuco (Buses)

American Express is at Lima Tours (☎ 27-6624), Belén 1040, and is open from 9.15 am to 4.45 pm on weekdays. American Express is one of the easiest companies to deal with for refunds – usually within 72 hours. Citibank (☎ 27-3930) is at Colmena 1070. The Bank of America (☎ 71-7777) is at Augusto Tamayo 120, San Isidro. Visa is represented at the central Lima branch of the Banco de Crédito (☎ 27-5600), and Mastercard at Miguel Seminario 320, San Isidro (☎ 44-1891). Diners Club (☎ 41-4272) is at Canaval Moreyra 535, San Isidro, and Thomas Cook (☎ 27-8353) is at Wagons-Lit, Ocoña 174, Lima. If you lose other brands of travellers' cheques, go into any major bank and ask for assistance. They should be able to tell you where to make a claim.

Post & Telecommunications The central post office is in the block on the north-west corner of the Plaza de Armas. It is open from 8 am to 6 pm Monday to Saturday, and from 8 am to noon on Sunday mornings.

Mail held by American Express can be picked up from Lima Tours, Belén 1040, from 9 am to noon and 3 to 5 pm on weekdays.

Long-distance and international telephone calls are made from the telephone office on Plaza San Martín, to the right of the Cine Metro, though their direct-dialling facility is usually out of order. The office gets very crowded and chaotic, especially in the evenings. It's open from about 9 am to 9 pm Monday to Saturday. Public telephone booths are scattered around the city.

Telegrams and telexes can be sent from the office on the corner of Lampa and Emancipación in Lima.

Visa Extensions Lima is the easiest place in Peru to get your tourist card or visa extended. Migraciones is on the 500 block of Paseo de la República and 28 de Julio. Hours are 9 am to 1 pm Monday to Friday – it's best to go early. You need your passport, and the white immigration slip which you received upon entry. Fill out an extension form, which is available at the immigration office; it costs about US$1. These documents are presented with a fee of US$20. Sometimes (but rarely), a ticket out of the country is asked for, though you can get around this by showing enough money.

Foreign Embassies & Consulates Over 40 nations are represented by embassies or consulates in Peru (see the Lima phone book for the addresses of embassies not listed here).

Bolivia
    Los Castaños 235, San Isidro (☎ 22- 8231, 22-3418), open from 8.30 am to 1.30 pm on weekdays
Brazil
    José Pardo 850, Miraflores (☎ 446- 2635 ext 131, 132), open from 9.30 am to 1 pm on weekdays
Canada
    Frederico Gerdes 130, Miraflores (☎ 444- 4015, fax 444-4347), open from 8.30 to 11 am on weekdays
    Postal address: Casilla 1212, Miraflores, Lima
Chile
    Javier Prado Oeste 790, San Isidro (☎ 40- 7965, 40-3300), open from 8.45 am to 12.30 pm on weekdays
Colombia
    Natalio Sánchez 125, 4th floor, Lima (☎ 33-8922/3), from 9 am to 12.30 pm on weekdays
Ecuador
    Las Palmeras 356, San Isidro (☎ 42- 4184), open from 9 am to 1 pm on weekdays
France
    Arequipa 3415, San Isidro (☎ 70-4968, 23-8616), open from 9 to 11.30 am on weekdays
Germany
    Arequipa 4202, Miraflores (☎ 45-7033), open from 9 am to noon on weekdays
    Postal address: Casilla 18-5109, Lima 18
Ireland
    Santiago Acuña 135, La Aurora, Miraflores (☎ 45-6813)
Israel
    Natalio Sánchez 125, 6th floor, Lima (☎ 433-4431), open from 10 am to 1 pm on weekdays
The Netherlands
    Principal 190, Santa Catalina (☎ 475-6537, 476-1069), open from 9 am to noon on weekdays
New Zealand
    Natalio Sánchez 125, 11th floor, Lima (☎ 433-4738, 433-5032), open from 8.30 am to 12.30 pm on weekdays
Spain
    Avenida República de Chile 120, Lima (☎ 31-0420)

UK

> Natalio Sánchez 125, 11th floor, Lima (☎ 433-4738, 433-5032), open from 9 am to 1 pm on weekdays

USA

> Grimaldo del Solar 346, Miraflores (☎ 44-3621), open from 8.15 to 11 am on weekdays, except Wednesday
>
> Embassy office: 1400 block of Garcilaso de la Vega and Avenida España, near the city centre (☎ 28-6000, 33-8000, fax 31-6682, 31-1105)
>
> Postal address: Casilla 1995, Lima 100

Bookstores The best selection of English-language guidebooks is at the South American Explorers Club (SAEC). Epoca (on Belén, one block from the Plaza San Martín) and Libreria Internacional (on the first block of Jirón de la Unión) have English books. Books are very expensive in Peru.

Maps The SAEC has hiking maps, road maps of Peru and street maps of Lima. For topographical maps, go to the Instituto Geográfico Nacional (☎ 45-1939), at Aramburu 1198, Surquillo. It is open from 8 am to 3 pm on weekdays; you need your passport to get in. Many maps are sold by street vendors around the Plaza San Martín area. Prices are high, so don't be afraid to bargain.

Emergency The best general clinic, but also the most expensive, is the Clínica Anglo-American (☎ 40-3570), on the 3rd block of Salazar, San Isidro. In San Borja, try the Clínica San Borja (☎ 41-3141), at Avenida del Aire 333. In Lima, there's the Clínica Internacional (☎ 28-8060), at Washington 1475. All three have 24-hour service and some English-speaking staff. Cheaper and also good is the Clínica Adventista (☎ 45-9040), at Malecón Balta in Miraflores. For tropical diseases, try Instituto de Medicina Tropical (☎ 82-3903, 82-3910), at the Universidad Particular Cayetano Heredia, Avenida Honorio Delgado, San Martín de Porres.

A recommended English-speaking doctor is Dr Alejandro Bussalle Rivera (☎ 71-2238), León Velarde 221, Lince.

Recommended English-speaking dentists are Dr Gerardo Aste and son (☎ 417502), Antero Aspillaga 415, office 101, San Isidro.

There are several opticians along Cailloma, in the centre, and around Schell and Larco in Miraflores. Having a new pair of glasses made is not expensive.

The helpful Policía de Turismo (☎ 71-4579, 71-4313), usually have English-speaking personnel available and will provide police reports for an insurance claim or a travellers' cheque refund. They are at Salaverry 1156, Jesús María.

Laundry LavaQuick, at Benavides 604 (on the corner of La Paz) in Miraflores, charges about US$2 for a four-kg load, washed, dried and folded within 24 hours. They are open from 9 am to 6 pm Monday to Saturday but close at 1 pm on Thursday.

Dangers & Annoyances

With millions of very poor, unemployed people in Lima, it is not surprising that the city has a crime problem. You are unlikely to be mugged, but many travellers have their belongings stolen. Also beware of crooked police.

Things to See

Museums Opening hours are subject to frequent change, and are often shortened drastically from January to March, when it is best to go in the morning. Students can often enter for half price.

The **Museo de Oro del Peru** (☎ 35-0791, 35-2917), Alonso de Molina 100, Monterrico, actually houses two separate museums in the same building. The gold museum itself is in a huge basement vault. There are literally thousands of gold pieces, ranging from ear plugs to ponchos embroidered with hundreds of solid gold plates. There are also numerous artefacts of silver and precious stones. The top half of the building houses an **Museo de Armas**, which is reputedly one of the best in the world. Hours are noon to 7 pm daily. Admission (to both museums) is US$6.

The **Museo Rafael Larco Herrera** (☎ 61-

1312), at Bolívar 1515 in Pueblo Libre, contains one of the most impressive collections of ceramics to be found anywhere. There are said to be about 55,000 pots here, as well as exhibits of mummies, a gold room, a small cactus garden, textiles made from feathers, and a Paracas weaving which contains 398 threads to a linear inch – a world record. In a separate building is the famous collection of pre-Columbian erotic pots, which depict in detail the sexual practices of several Peruvian cultures. Hours are 9 am to 1 pm and 3 to 6 pm daily, except Sunday, when it is open only until 1 pm. Admission is about US$4.

Housed in a handsome building, Lima's **Museo de Arte** (☎ 23-4732), at Paseo de Colón 125, has a collection which ranges from colonial furniture to pre-Columbian artefacts, and includes canvasses from four centuries of Peruvian art. It is open from 9 am to 6 pm Tuesday to Sunday. Admission is about US$1.

The **Museo Nacional de Antropología y Arqueología** (☎ 63-5070), is at Plaza Bolívar, at the intersection of Avenida San Martín and Vivanco in Pueblo Libre. The collection is gradually being moved to the Museo de la Nación – call for details. The excellent exhibits trace the prehistory of Peru chronologically, from the earliest archaeological sites to the arrival of the Spaniards, and are recommended for all interested in Peru's archaeology. Hours are 10 am to 5 pm daily (though the museum may close on Mondays). Admission is about US$3.

The **Museo Nacional de la República** (☎ 63-2009), next door to the Anthropology & Archaeology Museum in Plaza Bolívar, and with similar hours, contains late-colonial and early republican paintings and furnishings, and independence artefacts.

The **Museo de la Nación** (☎ 37-7607), Avenida Javier Prado Este 2465, San Borja, is a new museum with excellent displays on archaeology, regional costumes and traditional lifestyles. There is a theatre, and lectures are given. Admission is US$3, and

opening hours are 9 am to 8 pm Tuesday to Friday, and 10 am to 7 pm on weekends.

The **Museo Amano** (☎ 41-2909), at Retiro 160, off the 11th block of Angamos in Miraflores, houses a fine private collection of ceramics, arranged chronologically to show the development of pottery through Peru's various pre-Columbian cultures. The museum specialises in the Chancay culture. Admission is in small groups and by telephone appointment only. All groups are met by a guide, who will show you around in exactly an hour – it is best if you understand Spanish. Tours are free, and available on weekdays at 2, 3, 4 and 5 pm, very punctually.

The **Museo del Banco Central de Reserva** (☎ 27-6250, extension 2657), in the Central Reserve Bank near the corner of Ucayali and Lampa, is another specialist archaeological museum which offers welcome relief from the hustle and bustle of the city centre. It specialises in ceramics from the Vicus culture, as well as housing a small collection of other pre-Columbian artefacts and 19th and 20th-century Peruvian art. Hours are 10 am to 5 pm Tuesday to Saturday, and 10 am to 1 pm on Sunday.

The **Museo de la Inquisición** (☎ 28-7980), at Junín 548, opposite the Plaza Bolívar in Lima (not the one in Pueblo Libre), is in the building used by the Spanish Inquisition from 1570 to 1820. It is now a university library. Visitors can walk around the basement where prisoners were tortured. There's a rather ghoulish waxworks exhibit of life-sized unfortunates on the rack or having their feet roasted. There's a remarkable wooden ceiling in the library upstairs. Hours are 9 am to 7 pm on weekdays, 9 am to 4.30 pm Saturday – admission is free.

The **Museo de la Cultura Peruana** (☎ 23- 5892), at Alfonso Ugarte 650, is a small museum which concentrates on popular art and handicrafts. Ceramics, carved gourds, recent and traditional folk art, and costumes from various periods and regions are exhibited here. Hours are 10 am to 5 pm on weekdays, 9 am to 5 pm on Saturday. Admission is US$0.20.

PERU

The **Museo de Historia Natural** (☎ 71-0117), at Arenales 1256, has a modest collection of stuffed animals which is worth seeing if you want to familiarise yourself with the fauna of Peru. Hours are 8.30 am to 1.30 pm on weekdays, 8.30 am to noon on Saturdays, and admission is US$0.60.

Religious Buildings There are many churches, monasteries and convents in Lima, and they make a welcome and quiet break. Their hours tend to be more erratic than those of the museums.

The original **Catedral** was built on the south-eastern side of the Plaza de Armas in 1555, but has been destroyed by earthquakes and reconstructed several times, most recently in 1746. The present building is a reconstruction based on the early plans. The interior is stark compared to many Latin American churches. The coffin and remains of Francisco Pizarro are in the mosaic-covered chapel just to the right of the main door. Also of interest is the carved choir and the small religious museum at the back of the Catedral. Hours are 10 am to 1 pm and 2 to 5 pm daily. Entry costs about US$0.30 and includes the religious museum.

The church and monastery of **San Francisco** are famous for their catacombs, estimated to contain the remains of 70,000 people. Less famous is the remarkable library, with thousands of antique texts, some dating back to the Spanish conquest. The church, on the corner of Lampa and Ancash, is one of the best-preserved of Lima's early colonial churches; however, the quake of 1970 caused considerable damage. Much of the church has been restored in its original baroque style with Moorish (Arab) influence. Guided tours are available in English and Spanish. It is worth joining a tour to see the catacombs, library and cloister, and a very fine museum of religious art, which nonguided visitors don't often see. The church is open daily from 10 am to 12.45 pm and 3 to 5.45 pm. Admission is US$3 and includes the guided tour. Spanish-speaking tours leave several times an hour and tours in English at least once an hour.

The infrequently visited **Convento de los Descalzos** is at the end of the Alameda de los Descalzos, an attractive if somewhat forgotten avenue in the Rimac district. The visitor can see the refectory, the infirmary, typical cells of the Franciscans, old wine-making equipment in the 17th-century kitchen, and some 300 colonial paintings. Spanish-speaking guides will show you around. A tour lasts about 40 minutes; the entrance fee is US$1 and hours are 9.30 am to 1 pm and 3 to 6 pm daily.

Next to the **Santuario de Santa Rosa de Lima**, there is a peaceful garden and a small church on the site where Santa Rosa (the western hemisphere's first saint) was born. The sanctuary itself is a small adobe hut, built by Santa Rosa in the early 1600s as a private room for prayer and meditation. Hours are 9.30 am to 1 pm and 3.30 to 7 pm daily. Admission is free.

The church of **Santo Domingo**, on the first block of Camaná, opposite the main post office, is one of Lima's most historic, for it was built on the land that Francisco Pizarro granted in 1535 to his Dominican friar Vicente Valverde. Construction of the church began in 1540 and was finished in 1599, but much of the interior was modernised in the late 1700s. The tombs of Santa Rosa and San Martín de Porras (the Americas' first Black saint) are to be seen in the church. There is an alabaster statue of Santa Rosa, presented to the church by Pope Clement in 1669, and fine tilework showing the life of St Dominic. The cloisters are pleasantly quiet. The church is open from 7 am to 1 pm and 4 to 8 pm daily. The monastery and tombs are open from 9 am to 12 noon and 3 to 5 pm Monday to Saturday, and in the morning on Sunday and holy days. Admission is US$0.50.

The church of **La Merced** was built on the site of the first mass said in Lima (in 1534). Inside, there is an ornately carved chancel and an attractively decorated cloister. It is on the busy pedestrian street of Jirón de la Unión, near the corner with Miró Quesada. The church is open from 7 am to 12.30 pm and 4 to 8 pm, and the cloister is open from 8 am to noon and 3 to 5.30 pm.

The small baroque church of **San Pedro**, on the corner of Azangaro and Ucayali in the old centre, is considered to be one of the finest examples of early colonial architecture in Lima. It was consecrated by the Jesuits in 1638, and has changed little since then. The interior is sumptuously decorated with gilded altars and an abundance of beautiful glazed tilework. Hours are 7 am to 12.30 pm and 6 to 8 pm daily.

The church of **San Agustín**, at Ica 251 on the corner with Camaná, has a façade in the *churrigueresque* style (a baroque style named after Spanish architect José Churriguera), which dates from the early 1700s, though much of the church was reconstructed at the end of the 19th century and then again after the extensive damage of the 1970 earthquake. It can be visited daily from 8.30 am to noon and 3.30 to 5.30 pm.

Markets Lima's main market is on the corner of Ayacucho and Ucayali, to the south-east of Avenida Abancay. Although it officially occupies a whole city block, this is not nearly enough space, and stalls and vendors completely congest the streets for several blocks around. You can buy almost anything, but be prepared for crowds and pickpockets. Don't bring valuables.

The streets behind the Correo Central (central post office) are the focus of a black market known as **Polvos Azules.** It's just as crowded as the main market and has a remarkable variety of consumer goods. This is the place to come if you're looking for smuggled luxuries such as ghetto blasters or perfume.

Lima's main **flower market**, at the southern end of the National Stadium (ninth block of Paseo de la República), is a kaleidoscopic scene of beautiful flowers at bargain prices.

The **Indian artisans' market** is along the northern side of Avenida de la Marina, on the 600 to 1000 blocks. There is a great selection of handicrafts here, but the quality and prices vary a good deal, so shop carefully. There is also an **Indian crafts market**, in Miraflores, on Avenida Petit Thouars 1½ blocks south of Angamos.

Archaeological Sites Two minor pre-Inca ruins with on-site museums can be seen. Admission is a few cents and hours are 10 am to 5 pm daily, except Monday. The **Huaca Huallamarca**, on the corner of El Rosario and Nicolas de Riviera in San Isidro, is a restored Maranga temple dating from between 200 AD and 500 AD. The **Huaca Juliana**, one block off the 46th block of Arequipa in Miraflores, is a recently excavated pre-Inca temple.

Plazas The large **Plaza de Armas** was the heart of old Lima, but none of the original buildings remains. The oldest part is the impressive bronze fountain, which was erected in the centre in 1650. The exquisitely balconied Archbishop's palace, to the left of the Catedral, is a relatively modern building dating from 1924. The Palacio de Gobierno, on the north-eastern side of the plaza, dates from the same period. The handsomely uniformed presidential guard is on duty all day, and the ceremonial changing of the guard takes place daily at 12.45 pm. The other buildings around the plaza are also modern: the Municipalidad (town hall) built in 1945, the Unión Club and various stores and cafés. There is an impressive statue of Francisco Pizarro on horseback, on the corner of the plaza opposite the Catedral.

One of the major plazas in central Lima, the **Plaza San Martín** dates from the early 1900s. The bronze equestrian statue of the liberator, General San Martín, was erected in 1921.

Five blocks of the pedestrian street **Jirón de la Unión** connect the two plazas mentioned here. There are several good jewellery stores, bookshops and movie theatres, and the church of La Merced. Consequently, it is always very crowded with shoppers, sightseers, vendors and pickpockets.

Other Built in 1735, the **Palacio Torre Tagle**, at Ucayali 363, is considered to be the best surviving colonial house in Lima. It has recently become the offices of the Foreign Ministry, and entry on weekdays is either prohibited or restricted to the patio. On Saturday, you can enter the building from 9 am to 4 pm, and a tip usually ensures that you can go upstairs to inspect the fine rooms and balconies.

The **zoo** is in the Parque Las Leyendas, between Lima and Callao. Most of the animals are from Peru, and there are three sections, representing the coast, the sierra and the Amazon Basin. Admission is about US$0.40 and hours are 9 am to 5 pm daily, except Monday.

The suburb most frequently visited by tourists is **Miraflores**, on the beachfront. Many of the capital's best restaurants and nightspots are found here, and the pavement cafés are places to hang out, to see and be seen. The prices and quality of everything from a sweater to a steak will be higher in Miraflores than in other parts of the city. Miraflores is connected with Lima by the tree-lined Avenida Arequipa, where frequent colectivos and buses run.

The suburb of **Barranco** is popular with students and for nightlife. There are several good restaurants, craft shops and *peñas* (live music venues) in the area.

Places to Stay

Hotels are more expensive in Lima than in other cities. Most of the cheapest are in the centre. If you plan on spending a week or more in a hotel, ask for a discount.

The *Asociación de Amistad Peruano/ Europeo* (☎ 28-4899) has dormitory-style accommodation on the 7th floor of Camaná 280. Baggage lockers are provided and beds are US$2.50 per person. The similarly priced *Youth Hostel Karina*, at Chancay 617, is OK for the money. The *Familia Rodríguez* (☎ 23-6465), Nicolás de Piérola 730, is a well-recommended family-run hostel charging US$5 per person in dormitory-style rooms, including breakfast. They look after their visitors. The friendly *Hostal Samaniego*, Avenida Emancipación 184, No 801, charges US$5 per person in dormitory-style rooms. Both these places have hot showers.

One of the best of Lima's budget hotels is the *Hostal España* (☎ 28-5546), Azangaro 105 (no sign), which is a rambling old mansion full of plants, birds and paintings. It is basic, but clean, safe and friendly, and charges about US$5/7 for singles/doubles. Beds in dormitory rooms are about US$2.50 each. There is hot water. Nearby are a couple of basic, poor places – the *Hotel Europa* and *Hotel Carabaya*.

The *Hotel Residencial Roma* (☎ 27-7576), Ica 326, is clean and central, and has single/double rooms with private bath and hot water for US$6/8. It has been recommended. The *Hotel San Sebastián*, also on Ica, has recently changed hands and gone downhill. The *Pensión Unión* (☎ 28-4136), Unión 442, 3rd floor (go through the bookshop and café), is basic, but OK for US$4 per person. It sometimes has hot water in the evenings. The *Hostal Belén* (☎ 27-8995), Belén 1049, has fairly reliable hot water and is reasonably clean, though noisy. Singles/doubles cost US$6/9. The *Hostal Universo* (☎ 28-0619), Azangaro 754, is fairly close to several bus terminals and is basic but safe. Rooms with private bath and occasional hot water cost US$7/9. The *Gran Hotel* (☎ 28-5160), Abancay 546, has spacious rooms but has seen better days. It is popular with Peruvians and is clean but noisy. Rates are US$7/11 – some rooms have private baths and there is occasional hot water. The fairly basic but friendly *Hostal Wiracocha* (☎ 27-1178), Junín 270, has singles/doubles with private bath and hot water for US$9/11. The *Hostal Eiffel* (☎ 24-0188), Washington 949, is US$6 per person and is clean.

In Miraflores, there is a *youth hostel* (☎ 46-5488), at Casimiro Ulloa 328, which charges US$5.50 per person in dormitories – the cheapest you'll find in Miraflores. They have laundry facilities, travel information and a swimming pool.

If you want to stay with a family, try calling the following to see if space is available. Luisa Chávez (☎ 47-3996), General Iglesias 273, Miraflores, charges US$6 per person. Señora Jordan (☎ 45-9840), Porta 724, Miraflores, is friendly (US$10 per person, including breakfast). The house is quiet. Yolanda Escobar (☎ 45-7565), Domingo Elías 230, Miraflores, charges US$10/15 for singles/doubles and allows use of her kitchen. Rosa Alonso (☎ 23-7463), Larraboren 231, Jesús María, charges US$10 per person.

Places to Eat

Taxes and service charges on meals can be an exorbitant 31% – check first if you're on a tight budget. The cheapest restaurants are in central Lima. Try the menu (set lunch) in local restaurants – about US$1.50 and up. *El Capricho*, on the 300 block of Bolivia, is good, cheap and popular with locals. They serve good anticuchos for dinner. Another good cheap place is *Pollería Nakasone*, at Alfonso Ugarte 1360, near the South American Explorers Club. They serve chicken. The *Chifa Pallasano*, on the same block, serves inexpensive Chinese food.

On Quilca, between the Plaza San Martín and Avenida Garcilaso de la Vega, there are several inexpensive restaurants to choose from. *Heydi*, Puno 367, is a very popular cebichería but is open only for lunch. The *Restaurant Machu Picchu*, on the 300 block of Ancash, is also fairly cheap.

El Cordano, a pink building at Ancash 202, opposite the railway station, is a little more expensive but has an interesting 1920s decor, excellent espresso coffee and a varied menu of typical Peruvian snacks and meals. It serves a good variety of Peruvian beers, wines and piscos, and is a good place to meet people. Hours are about 9.30 am to 9 pm.

There are a couple of cheap places near the Hotel Roma, on the 300 block of Ica – the *Ciervo de Oro* is described by one enthusiast as 'the best cake shop in Peru'. The *Chifa Wah Sing*, on the 700 block of Ica, serves plentiful and inexpensive meals.

For vegetarians, *Natur*, Moquegua 132, is cheap and recommended. There is a Hare Krishna-run *Govinda*, at Callao 480, with cheap food and slow service. *Bircher Berner*, at Schell 598 in Miraflores, is a little more up-market. It has a nice garden to sit in while you wait for your food – the service is slow.

There are several pizzerías on Olaya and Diagonal streets by the Parque Kennedy in Miraflores. Some say that the *Pizza Hut*, at Espinar and 2 de Mayo in Miraflores, has the best pizza. *La Trattoria*, at Bonilla 106 (just off Larco, by the Ovalo), is recommended for tasty home-made pasta. None of these Italian places is particularly cheap, but they are popular meeting places on Friday and Saturday nights.

If you'd like to dine in elegant surroundings, try the *Raimondi*, Miró Quesada 110, which is a good lunch restaurant popular with Lima's businesspeople. There's no sign, and the outside gives no indication of the spaciousness and comfort within. At *L'Eau Vive del Peru*, Ucayali 370, the food is prepared and served by a French order of nuns, and features dishes from all over the world, as well as some exotic cocktails. It's extremely quiet and prices are moderate to expensive. L'Eau Vive is open daily (except Sunday) from noon to 2.45 pm and 8.15 to 10.15 pm. The nuns sing an Ave María at 10 pm. A good mid-priced seafood restaurant is *Cebichería Don Beta*, at José Gálvez 667 in Miraflores. It is particularly popular among Peruvians at lunch time but is quiet in the evenings. Expect to pay US$10 to US$20 for meals in these places.

There are many pavement cafés in Miraflores. They are not cheap but are the place for people-watching. One of the best known is the *Haití*, on the traffic circle next to Cine El Pacífico. The main attraction is the location; the food is only mediocre. Across the traffic circle is the much better *La Tiendecita Blanca*, which has a superb pastry selection. Nearby, at Ricardo Palma 258, *Vivaldis* appears to be one of the 'in' places for young Mirafloreños. There are several pavement cafés along Larco, of which *La Sueca*, at Larco 759, has excellent pastries.

The Brenchley Arms, at Atahualpa 174, a block from Cine El Pacífico in Miraflores, is a British pub run by Englishman Mike Ella and his Peruvian wife, Martha. Prices are steep for budget travellers, but it's worth it if you're homesick for a pub. There is a dart board and you can read the British newspapers. Hours are 6 pm till late; pub meals are served till 10 pm daily, except Sunday.

Entertainment

El Comercio lists cinemas, theatres, art galleries and music shows. The English monthly magazine *Lima Times* has an abbreviated listing of what's going on.

There are dozens of cinemas. Foreign films are normally screened with their original sound track and Spanish subtitles.

The Teatro Municipal, at Ica 300, is the venue for the symphony, opera, plays and ballet. The best seats are expensive, and even cheap tickets will cost you several dollars. Another good venue is the Teatro Segura, on the 200 block of Huancavelica. For surprisingly good plays in English, see the local theatre group The Good Companions (☎ 47-9760), which is run by the British Council. They advertise in the *Lima Times*.

Live Peruvian music is performed at peñas, where you can often sing along or dance. Drink is served, and sometimes food, of which there are two types – *folklórica* and *criolla*. The first is typical of the Andean highlands, while the second is more coastal. Cover charges vary, but average around US$4.

A good peña folklórica which is popular with locals (but little frequented by tourists) is Las Brisas del Lago Titicaca, at Wakulski 168, just off Brasil, near the Plaza Bolognesi. It is open Thursday to Saturday from about 9.30 pm, and there are good dance troupes accompanying the live music. Another reasonably priced peña is the Wifala, at Cailloma 633 in Lima. They play folklórica music. The peña Hatuchay, at Trujillo 228 in Rimac, just across the bridge behind the Government Palace, is mainly folklórica, with plenty of audience participation and dancing (during the second half). Typical Peruvian snacks are served, as well as drinks. This popular place is one of the less expensive ones. The doors open about 9 pm and the music gets under way about 10 pm. Get there early for a good seat.

La Estación de Barranco is in Barranco, at Pedro de Osma 112; a variety of both folklórica and criolla music can be heard there. Also in Barranco, next door to El Otro Sitio restaurant, at Sucre 315, is El Búho Pub, which plays criolla music. Another good one is Los Balcones, on the Barranco plaza. These places are fairly pricey. The music goes from about 10 pm to the early hours.

Getting There & Away

Air Lima's Aeropuerto Internacional Jorge Chávez is in Callao, about 12 km from the centre or 16 km from Miraflores. There is a post office (open during the day), a long-distance telephone office (open until late at night) and a 24-hour luggage storage room, which charges about US$2 per piece per day. A 24-hour restaurant is open upstairs.

About 20 international airlines have offices in, Lima, many along Colmena. Check the yellow pages under 'Transportes Aereas' for telephone numbers, and call before you go, as offices change address frequently.

Airlines offering domestic flights include:

Aero-Cóndor
   Avenida Juan de Arona 781, San Isidro (☎ 42-5215, 42-5663, 41-1354)
AeroPerú
   Avenida José Pardo 601, Miraflores (☎ 47-8900, 47-8255)
   Plaza San Martín, Lima (☎ 23-7459, 31-7626)
   24-hour reservations (☎ 47-8333)
Americana
   Avenida Larco 345, Miraflores (☎ 47-1902, 47-8216, 47-8662)
   24-hour reservations (☎ 47-1919)
Expresso Aéreo
   Avenida José Pardo 223 (☎ 45-2545, 45-2745, 61-9275)
Faucett
   Avenida Garcilaso de la Vega 865 (☎ 33-6364, 33-8180)
   Avenida Diagonal 592, Miraflores (☎ 46-2031, 45-7649)
   Reservations (☎ 64-3322, 64-3860)

Flight schedules and ticket prices change frequently. Recent one-way fares from Lima were US$40 to US$70 to most towns.

More remote towns require connecting flights, and smaller towns are not served every day. Getting flight information, buying tickets and reconfirming flights are best done at the airline offices (or a reputable travel agent) rather than at the airport counters, where things can be chaotic. You can buy tickets at the airport on a space-available basis, however, if you want to leave for somewhere in a hurry.

Grupo Ocho (the military airline) has weekly flights to Cuzco, Puerto Maldonado, Pucallpa and some small jungle towns. Go to their airport counter early on the day of the flight, get your name on the waiting list and be prepared for a long wait. Grupo Ocho has flights to Cuzco on Thursday mornings – get your name on the list by 6 am and hope. Flights are half the price of commercial airlines but are subject to overbooking and cancellation.

If departing internationally, check in at least two hours early, as many flights are overbooked. There is a US$17.40 international departure tax, payable in cash dollars or soles.

Overbooking is the norm on domestic flights, so be there at least an hour early. For all flights, domestic and international, reconfirm several times.

Bus The most important road is the Carretera Panamericana (Pan-American Highway), which runs north-west and south-east from Lima roughly parallel to the coast. Long-distance north and southbound buses leave Lima every few minutes; it takes approximately 24 hours to drive to either the Ecuadorian or the Chilean border. Other buses ply the much rougher roads inland into the Andes and across into the eastern jungles.

There is no central bus terminal; each bus company runs its own office and terminal. Lima's bus stations are notorious for theft, and it makes sense to find the station and buy your tickets in advance, unencumbered by luggage.

TEPSA is generally fast and reliable but has fewer departures than other companies and is among the most expensive. Ormeño has many buses, frequent departures and average prices; their service is OK. Cruz del

Sur also has extensive services. Expreso Sudamericano is one of the cheapest and slowest, with more frequent delays. Special cheap fares are offered by various companies at various times. Fares can double during peak periods or around holidays such as Christmas or Independence (28 July), when tickets may be sold out several days ahead of time. The bigger companies often have luxury buses charging 30% to 50% more and providing express service, with toilets, snacks, videos and air-conditioning on the bus.

The biggest bus company in Lima is Ormeño (☎ 27-5679, 28-8453), Carlos Zavala Iquitos 177. There are various subsidiaries at the same address. Among them, they have frequent departures for Ica, Arequipa, Tacna, Cuzco, Puno, Trujillo, Chiclayo, Tumbes, Huaraz, Caraz and various intermediate points. For the Huaraz area, you can also try Transportes Rodríguez, at Roosevelt 354, or Empresa Huaraz, at Montevideo 655 – though these are less recommended. Cruz del Sur (☎ 27- 7366), Quilca 531, serves the entire coast plus Arequipa, Puno and Cuzco. Expreso Sudamericano (☎ 27-1077, 27-7708), Montevideo 618, has buses to most of these destinations.

TEPSA (☎ 73-1233), Paseo de la República 129, has buses to Ica, Arequipa, Tacna, Trujillo, Chiclayo, Tumbes and Cajamarca. Olano, at Apurímac 567, has buses to the northern coast, mountains and jungles. Their buses go to Trujillo, Chiclayo, Chachapoyas and Moyobamba. Empresa Transportes Chinchaysuyo, at Grau 525, also has northbound buses for Casma, Trujillo, Piura and Tarapoto. Empresa Atahualpa, Sandia 266, Lima, has the best buses for Cajamarca and Chachapoyas.

For the Huancayo area, try M Caceres (at 28 de Julio 2195, La Victoria, in the same terminal as Nor-Oriente), Expreso Huaytapallana (at Cotabambas 321) and Transporte Jara (at Carlos Zavala 148). For the Tarma/Chanchamayo area, there's the choice of Transportes Chanchamayo (at Luna Pizarro 453, La Victoria), Empresa Los Andes (at 28 de Julio, No 2405, La Victoria) or Nuestra Señora de la Merced (on the same street). Note that La Victoria is a poor neighbourhood – use a taxi to get there.

Empresa Transmar and Transportes León de Huánuco, on the 1500 block of 28 de Julio, La Victoria, go to Pucallpa. So does Empresa Etposa, José Galvez 1121, Lince.

Buses can be much delayed during the rainy season, especially in the highlands and jungles. From January to April, journey times can double or even triple, because of landslides and bad road conditions.

For approximate fares and journey times, see the respective cities.

Train Lima's Desamparados train station (☎ 27-6620) is on Avenida Ancash, behind the Palacio de Gobierno. Tickets to Huancayo cost about US$6 in 1st class, US$4 in 2nd class. The train departs at 7.40 am and takes about 10 hours (the train climbs 4780 metres). Schedules vary: the train may leave three times a week or not at all – check at the station. Food is available. The journey can be broken at Chosica (see the Around Lima section), Matucana (where there are a few basic hotels) or La Oroya (a cold, ugly mining town a little over halfway to Huancayo). Most people go all the way to Huancayo. The train rarely runs in the November to April wet season; during 1992, it didn't run at all.

Getting Around

To/From the Airport The cheapest way to get to the airport is by city bus Nos 35 or 11, which go from Plaza 2 de Mayo along Alfonso Ugarte to the airport. If you have a pile of luggage, this isn't recommended.

Taxis colectivos, taking about six passengers (US$0.60 each), can be found on the northern side of the 700 block of Colmena near Cailloma, in the centre. There is an extra charge for luggage. They leave when full from about 6 am to 6 pm.

An ordinary taxi will take you from the centre to the airport for about US$4, if you bargain.

Leaving the airport, you'll find plenty of airport taxis, charging anywhere from

US$10 to US$25. You can bargain these down to half-price, with some insistence. If you can carry your luggage about 200 metres, then walk out of the main gate of the airport parking area and flag down one of the street taxis outside. You can get a ride for US$4 or US$5, if you bargain.

There is also an airport bus, which charges about US$3 per passenger and will take you to your hotel. There is a hotel booking agent in front of the international arrivals gate – staff can help you make a telephone booking at a medium-priced or expensive hotel, and get you on the airport bus, but you may have to wait an hour before the bus leaves.

Bus Taking the local buses around Lima is rather a challenge. They are slow and crowded, but very cheap (fares are generally about US$0.25). Bus lines are identifiable by their destination cards, numbers and colour schemes. At last count, there were nearly 200 bus lines – a transport map is sporadically available from the better bookstores.

There are a few colectivo lines that operate cars or minibuses (without any numbers or colour schemes) which drive up and down the same streets all day long. The most useful goes from Lima to Miraflores along Avenidas Tacna, Garcilaso de la Vega and Arequipa. You can flag them down or get off anywhere. The fare is about US$0.50.

AROUND LIMA

The following day or weekend trips can all be done using public transport.

Pachacamac

This is the closest major archaeological site to Lima, 31 km south of the city. Pachacamac's origin predates the Incas by roughly 1000 years. Most of the buildings are now little more than walls of piled rubble, except for the main temples, which are huge pyramids. These have been excavated, and look like huge mounds with rough steps cut into them. One of the most recent of the complexes, the Mamacuña (House of the Chosen Women), was built by the Incas and has been excavated and reconstructed.

The site is extensive, and a thorough visit takes some hours. Near the entrance is a visitors' centre with a small museum and a cafeteria. From there, a dirt road leads around the site. You can walk around it in an hour at a leisurely pace, if you don't stop for long at any of the sections. Although the pyramids are badly preserved, their size is impressive, and you can climb the stairs to the top of some of them, from where you can get excellent views of the coast, on a clear day.

Guided tours to Pachacamac are offered by Vista (information at Lima Tours, Belén 1040). Tours cost US$20 per person, including round-trip transportation, an English-speaking guide and a visit to the Museo Nacional de Antropología y Arqueología in Lima. There are tours daily, except Monday.

From Lima, minibuses to Pachacamac leave from near the corner of Colmena and Andahuaylas, by the Santa Catalina convent. The buses are line 120, light blue in colour with orange trim, and they leave two or three times an hour, as soon as they have a load. The fare is about US$0.50. Tell the driver to let you off near the *ruinas*; otherwise, you will end up at Pachacamac village, about a km beyond the entrance. Alternatively, use the colectivo to Lurín, which leaves from the 900 block of Montevideo.

The ruins are open daily (except Monday) from 9 am to 5 pm. Entry is about US$2, and a bilingual booklet describing the ruins is available. When you are ready to leave, flag down any bus outside the gate. Leave before late afternoon.

The Central Highway
This road heads directly east of Lima into the foothills of the Andes, following the Rimac river valley and continuing to La Oroya.

Puruchuco This pre-Inca chief's house has been reconstructed, and there is a small museum on the site. Puruchuco is about five km out of Lima on the Central Highway (using the highway distance markers) and about 13 km from the centre. It is in the suburb of Ate, just before the village of Vitarte, and there is a signpost on the highway. The site is several hundred metres along a road to the right. Opening hours are 9 am to 5 pm Tuesday to Saturday; admission is US$1. For information on getting there, see the Chosica section.

Cajamarquilla This large site dates from the Wari culture of 700 AD to 1100 AD. It consists of adobe walls, and some sections are being restored. It is open from 9 am to 5 pm Tuesday to Saturday and admission is US$1. There is a road to the left at about km 10 (18 km from central Lima) which goes to the Cajamarquilla zinc refinery, almost five km from the highway. The ruins are roughly halfway along the refinery road, then to the right along a short poor road. They aren't very clearly marked (though there are some signs), so ask.

Chaclacayo This village is at km 27 and is about 660 metres above sea level – just high enough to rise above Lima's garúa (sea mist). You can normally bask in sunshine here while about seven million people in the capital below have to languish in the grey fog. There are expensive hotels with pleasant dining, swimming and horse-riding facilities, and also a few cheaper places.

Chosica The resort town of Chosica, at 860 metres above sea level, is almost 40 km along the Central Highway. For escapees from Lima's garúa, it is the most convenient place to find a variety of hotels in the sun.

Buses to Chosica leave frequently from Lima and can be used to get to the intermediate places mentioned above. The majority of buses leave from near the intersection of Colmena and Ayacucho. The No 200a green-and-red bus to Chosica leaves from the 15th block of Colmena. The No 200b silver bus with red trim leaves from the 15th block of Colmena and continues to the village of Ricardo Palma, a few km past Chosica. The No 200c dark green bus with white trim leaves from the 15th block of Colmena and continues beyond Chosica to the fruit-growing area of Santa Eulalia. The No 201 cream-and-red bus leaves from the 15th block of Colmena for the village of San Fernando, passing through all points to Chaclacayo but not going to Chosica.

The No 202a bus leaves from the eighth block of Ayacucho for Santa Clara. The No 202b green-and-blue bus leaves from the 12th block of Colmena (Parque Universitario) for Santa Clara, and stops at the Granja Azul. The No 202c bus leaves from the eighth block of Ayacucho for Jicamarca via Vitarte and Huachipa, and takes you near Cajamarquilla. The No 202d bus leaves from the eighth block of Ayacucho for the Cajamarquilla refinery. The No 204 bus goes from the 10th block of Ayacucho to Chosica. Fares are about US$0.50 to Chosica.

Alternatively, take a colectivo from the 100 block of Montevideo. They leave when full, between 6 am and 10 pm, go direct to Chosica, are much faster and charge US$1.

Beaches

There are several good beaches south of Lima. These include El Silencio, Las Señoritas, Los Caballeros, Punta Hermosa, Punta Negra, San Bartolo, Santa María, Napolo and Pucusana. These are crowded during the January to March summer. Many beaches have a strong current – inquire locally before swimming.

To get there, take a bus to the fishing village and beach resort of Pucusana, 68 km south of Lima. Colectivos 97 (red and blue with white trim) leave from the corner of Colmena and Andahuaylas in Lima (US$1, two hours). You can get off where you want.

Pucusana has four cheap hotels, which get crowded on weekends from January to March.

The South Coast

The Panamericana goes through many places of interest south of Lima and is the route to Lake Titicaca and Cuzco. Thus, the south coast gets more visitors than the north.

PISCO

Pisco, a small fishing port 235 km south of Lima, gives its name to the white grape brandy made in the region. It can be used as a base to see the wildlife of the nearby Islas Ballestas and Península de Paracas, but the area is also of considerable historical and archaeological interest.

Archaeology

In 1925, the Peruvian archaeologist J C Tello discovered burial sites of the Paracas culture, which existed in the area from approximately 1300 BC until 200 AD. These people produced the finest textiles in the pre-Columbian Americas.

The main Paracas culture is divided into two periods, named Paracas Cavernas and Paracas Necropolis after the two main burial sites discovered. Cavernas is the earlier (500 BC to 300 BC) and is characterised by communal bottle-shaped tombs which were dug into the ground at the bottom of vertical shafts six or more metres deep.

Paracas Necropolis (300 BC to 100 AD) yielded the treasure trove of exquisite textiles for which the culture is known today. The necropolis contained over 400 funerary bundles, each of which consisted of a mummy (probably a nobleman or priest) wrapped in layers of weavings. It is best to visit the Lima museums for a look at the Paracas mummies, textiles and other artefacts. In the Pisco region, visit the J C Tello museum (on Península de Paracas) and the excellent Museo Regional de Ica.

Places to Stay

Pisco is occasionally full of people from the fishing boats; hotels are booked up then, and prices rise.

The *Hostal Pisco*, on the plaza, charges about US$3 per person, but their prices tend to fluctuate. They have hot water. This place is popular with budget travellers, but mixed reports have been received. The *Hostal Angamos* is a basic but clean cold-water hotel charging about US$3/4.50 for singles/doubles. Other basic places in this price range include the hostals *Peru*, *Callao*,

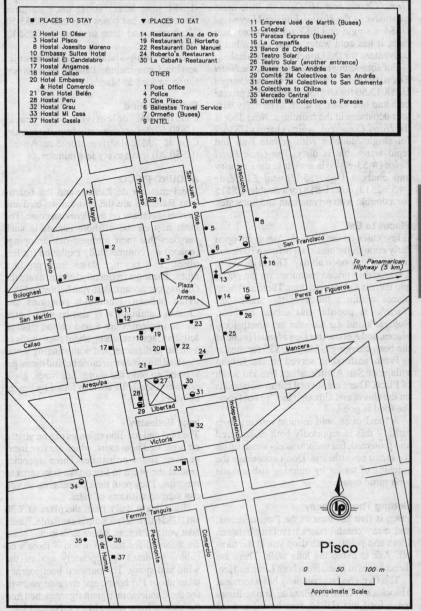

PERU

PLACES TO STAY

2 Hostal El César
3 Hostal Pisco
8 Hostal Josesito Moreno
10 Embassy Suites Hotel
12 Hostal El Candelabro
17 Hostal Angamos
18 Hostal Callao
20 Hotel Embassy
   & Hotel Comercio
21 Gran Hotel Belén
28 Hostal Peru
32 Hostal Grau
33 Hostal Mi Casa
37 Hostal Cassia

PLACES TO EAT

14 Restaurant As de Oro
19 Restaurant El Norteño
22 Restaurant Don Manuel
24 Roberto's Restaurant
30 La Cabaña Restaurant

OTHER

1 Post Office
4 Police
5 Cine Pisco
6 Ballestas Travel Service
7 Ormeño (Buses)
9 ENTEL

11 Empresa José de Martín (Buses)
13 Catedral
15 Paracas Express (Buses)
16 La Compañía
23 Banco de Crédito
25 Teatro Solar
26 Teatro Solar (another entrance)
27 Buses to San Andrés
29 Comité 2M Colectivos to San Andrés
31 Comité 7M Colectivos to San Clemente
34 Colectivos to Chica
35 Mercado Central
36 Comité 9M Colectivos to Paracas

Progreso

San Juan de Dios

2 de Mayo

Puno

Ayacucho

San Francisco

To Panamerican
Highway (5 km)

Bolognesi

San Martín

Callao

Plaza
de
Armas

Perez de Figueroa

Mancera

Arequipa

Libertad

Independencia

Victoria

Fermín Tanguis

Pedemonte

Comercio

B de Humay

Pisco

0   50   100 m

Approximate Scale

Grau, Cassia and *Mi Casa*. A little more expensive is the *Hostal Josesito Moreno*, at US$4 a single or US$7 for a double with bath. It has cold water and is grimy, but is convenient for the Ormeño bus terminal.

For something more up-market, the *Hotel Embassy* (☎ 53-2809) is clean, and charges US$8/13.50 for singles/doubles with private bath and hot water. It tends to be noisy with tour departees in the mornings. Next door is the *Hotel Comercio*, which charges US$6/9 for singles/doubles with private bath and tepid water, but is dirty. The *Gran Hotel Belén* (☎ 53-3046) is similar to the Embassy and charges US$9/15. *Hostal El César* (☎ 53-2512) costs US$8 for a double, US$15 for a double with private bath and hot water.

Places to Eat

A few cafés on the Plaza de Armas are open early enough for breakfast before a Ballestas tour, and stay open all day. The *As de Oro* is a reasonably priced restaurant on the plaza, and there is a *chifa* next door. There are cheap places within a block of the plaza – *El Norteño* is popular but serves no beer, *Roberto's* and *La Cabaña* are cheap local places, and *Restaurant Don Manuel* is one of the best, charging US$2 to US$5 for meals.

Fresh seafood is served in the fishing village of San Andrés, about five km south of Pisco. There are several cheap restaurants on the shore, and although they're not fancy, the food is good.

A local catch sold in most restaurants is turtle – this is reportedly both endangered and protected, but unfortunately winds up on the menu nevertheless. Don't encourage the catching of turtles by ordering dishes made with turtle meat.

Getting There & Away

Pisco is five km west of the Panamericana, and many coastal buses travelling between Lima and points south drop you at the turn-off. Ask to avoid the long walk. There are direct buses to Pisco from both Lima and Ica.

The Ormeño bus company has a terminal a block away from the Plaza de Armas. Buses leave for Lima (US$4, four hours) and Ica

(US$1, one hour) about once an hour. Ormeño also has buses to Nazca (US$3.50, 3½ hours), and three to Arequipa (US$12, 16 hours).

Other long-distance bus companies serving Lima include Paracas Express and Empresa José de Martín.

Getting Around

Comité 9M colectivos for Paracas (US$0.50) leave frequently from the market. Comité 2M colectivos for San Andrés (US$0.20) leave every few minutes.

AROUND PISCO

The Península de Paracas and the nearby Islas Ballestas are the best-known bird and marine sanctuary on the Peruvian coast. The birds nest on the offshore islands in such numbers that their nitrogen-rich droppings (guano) are commercially exploited for fertiliser. This practice dates from pre-Inca times. The most frequently seen birds are the Guanay cormorant, Peruvian booby and Peruvian pelican. Humboldt penguins and Chilean flamingos may also be seen. Large sea-lion colonies are found on the islands. Jellyfish, some reaching about two-thirds of a metre in diameter and with stinging tentacles trailing a metre or more behind them, get washed up onto the shore. Sea hares, ghost crabs and seashells are also found by beachcombers.

Islas Ballestas

The bird and sea-lion colonies can be visited on organised boat tours, which are fun, inexpensive and worthwhile. Three agencies around the plaza in Pisco take it in turns to run trips. They pool their passengers, so you can sign up with any of them.

Tours leave daily from the plaza at 7.30 am (US$6). Hotel pick-up is available. Buses take you to Paracas, where slow motor boats are boarded for the excursion – there's no cabin, so dress appropriately against the wind and spray. The outward boat journey takes about 1½ hours, and en route you will see the Candelabra, a giant figure etched into the coastal hills, rather like the Nazca Lines.

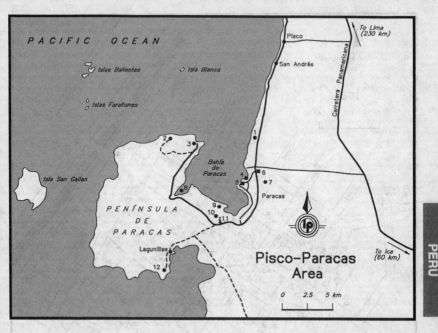

Pisco–Paracas Area

0   2.5   5 km

1 Fishmeal Factories
2 Candelabra
3 Puerto San Martín
4 Playa El Chaco
5 Hotel Paracas & Boats to Islas Ballestas
6 Hotel El Mirador
7 La Vela Monument
8 'Graveyard' of Fishing Boats
9 Flamingos often seen here
10 Archaeological Site
11 Museum & Information Centre
12 Parking, Cliff-Top Trail, Sea Lions & Seabirds

About an hour is spent cruising around the islands. You'll see plenty of sea lions on the rocks and swimming around your boat. Wear a hat – there are a lot of birds in the air, and it's not unusual for someone to receive a direct hit!

Once you return to the mainland, a minibus will take you back to Pisco in time for lunch. Alternatively. you can join the afternoon Reserva de Paracas tour (also US$6). If there are several of you wishing to do both tours in one day, bargain for a reduced combined rate. The Paracas tour requires an extra US$0.70 reserve entrance fee and a US$0.60 museum entrance fee. Coastal sea-lion and flamingo colonies are visited and geological formations are observed. There is usually time for a swim from a secluded beach. It is also possible to drive or walk around the reserve yourself.

ICA

Ica, capital of its department, is a pleasant colonial town of 150,000 inhabitants, 80 km south of Pisco. The Panamericana heads inland from Pisco, climbing gently to 420 metres at Ica. The town is high enough to be free of the garúa, and the climate is dry and sunny. The desert surrounding Ica is noted for its huge sand dunes.

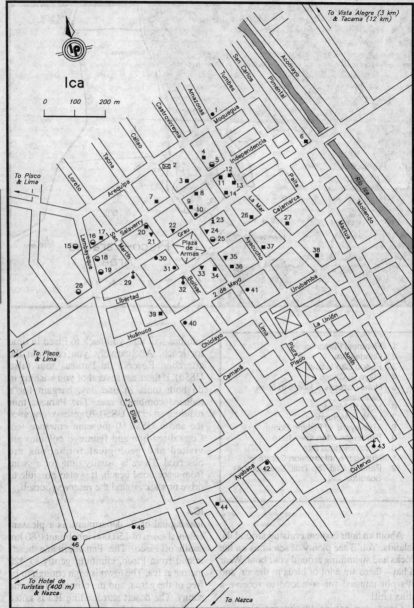

Ica

0   100   200 m

To Vista Alegre (3 km)
& Tacama (12 km)

To Pisco
& Lima

To Pisco
& Lima

To Hotel de
Turistas (400 m)
& Nazca

To Nazca

PERU

The oasis in which the town is situated is irrigated by the Río Ica and is famous for its grapes. There is a thriving wine and pisco-producing industry, and the distilleries and wineries can be visited. Ica has a superb museum and several annual fiestas.

Information

Tourist information is available at Grau 148 from 8 am to 1 pm Monday to Friday. Street moneychangers hang out on the north-west side of the plaza. The Banco de Crédito changes money.

Things to See

Wineries Wineries and distilleries are known as *bodegas*. The best time to visit is during the grape harvest, from late February until early April.

Tacama and Ocucaje wineries produce the best wine but are isolated and hard to get to. The Vista Alegre winery makes reasonable wine and is the easiest of the large commercial wineries to visit. To get there, walk across the Grau bridge and take the second left. It's about three km; all the locals know it. The city bus Nos 8 or 13 pass the plaza

and go near the winery. (This goes through a rough neighbourhood – you may want to hire a taxi.) The winery entrance is a yellow-brick arch. Vista Alegre is open from 9 am to 5 pm on weekdays; mornings are the best time to visit.

A number of smaller family-run wineries can also be visited. There are small local bodegas in the suburbs of Guadalupe, about three km before Ica on the road from Lima. There are frequent city buses from opposite the Hostal Europa. In Guadalupe, you'll find the bodegas Peña, Lovera and El Carmel, within a block or two of the plaza. There are many stalls selling huge bottles of various kinds of piscos and wines. The Bodega Catador is seven to eight km south of Ica and can be reached by the blue/white R6 bus leaving from Lambayeque and Grau. Apart from wine and pisco, they have a gift shop, and a restaurant with dancing in the evenings during the harvest.

Museo Regional de Ica This is in the south-western suburbs, 1½ km from the centre. You can take a No 17 bus from the plaza, but it's a pleasant walk. Hours are 9 am to 6 pm daily, except Sunday, when it closes at noon. Admission is US$1, with an extra US$1 camera fee. It is one of the best small regional museums in Peru, and concentrates on the Paracas, Nazca and Inca cultures.

Museo Cabrera There is no sign to mark this museum, on the Plaza de Armas, at Bolívar 170. It has a collection of 11,000 carved stones and boulders, showing pre-Columbian surgical techniques and day-to-day living. The owner, Dr J Cabreras, claims that these stones are centuries old, but most authorities don't believe him. You can see some of the stones in the museum entrance, but a proper look along with a guided tour costs US$5. Hours are 9 am to 1 pm and 4 to 8 pm.

Festivals

Ica's famous **Festival Internacional de Vendimia** (Wine Harvest Festival) is held during the 10 days beginning the first Friday in March. There are processions and beauty contests, cockfights and horse shows, arts and crafts fairs, music and dancing, and of course the pisco and wine flow freely.

In October, the **pilgrimage del Señor de Luren** culminates in an all-night procession on the third Monday of the month. This festival is repeated in March, and sometimes coincides with Holy Week celebrations.

The **Carnaval de Yunza** takes place in February. Participants dress in beautiful costumes and there is public dancing. There is also the water-throwing typical of Latin American carnaval.

The founding of the city, on 17 June 1563, is celebrated during **Ica week**. The more important **Ica tourist festival** takes place in the latter half of September.

Places to Stay

The cheapest hotels may double (or more) their prices during the festivals, especially the March harvest festival, when hotels are often fully booked. The prices below are for nonfestival times.

The area around Independencia and Castrovirreyna has cheap hotels. The *Hostal*

Europa, Independencia 258, is US$3/4.50 for singles/doubles. The rooms are basic but the beds are clean and there's a wash basin in each room. Similarly priced cold-water cheapies include hostals *Díaz* (☎ 23-1601), *Royal, Ica, Jaimito* and *Aleph*, all on the 100 block of Independencia. Another reasonable cheapie is the *Hostal Lima*, Lima 262.

The popular *Hostal La Viña* (☎ 22-1043), at San Martín and Huánuco, charges US$3.50/4.50, or US$6/9 for rooms with private bath and hot water. The *Hotel Confort* (☎ 23-3072), La Mar 257, is clean and good (US$4/6 with private bath and tepid showers). The *Hostal Sol de Oro* (☎ 23-3735), on the next block, is similar. The *Hotel Presidente* (☎ 22-5977), Amazonas 223, is good and clean (US$7/9 with bath and hot water).

If all of these are full and you're on a tight budget, you can try the cheap and very basic hostals *San Martín, Titos, Libertad* and *Toño*.

Places to Eat

There are several *chifas* and other inexpensive restaurants on Calle Lima. Also try the cheap *Mogambo*, on Bolívar, just north of the plaza, or *El Rinconcito Iqueño*, on the plaza, which is cheap and locally popular. Next door is the *Río Grande Cebichería*, a bar (few women) serving cebiche and beer. On the opposite side of the plaza is *El Velasco*, which serves good snacks and cakes. The restaurants in the *Hostal Silmar* and *Hotel Siesta II* are among the best in town.

Getting There & Away

Air Expresso Aéro and Aero-Cóndor (see under Lima) have flights to/from Ica. Expresso Aéro flies Lima-Ica-Nazca-Andahuaylas-Cuzco and return (same route) on Fridays and Lima-Nazca-Ica-Lima on Sundays. Aéro-Cóndor flies light aircraft to and from Lima and Nazca on demand.

Bus Most of the bus companies are clustered around a little park at the western end of Salaverry. Several companies run frequent buses up and down the Panamericana. There are many departures for Lima (US$5, five hours), Pisco (US$1, one hour), Nazca (US$2.50, three hours) and Arequipa (US$12 to US$16, 15 hours). Some continue to Tacna or Cuzco. Taxi colectivos for Lima (five passengers) and Nazca (seven passengers) leave from the Plaza de Armas as soon as they are full. Fares are US$12 to Lima (3½ hours) and US$3 to Nazca (2½ hours).

NAZCA

Nazca, 450 km south of Lima and 598 metres above sea level, is usually above the coastal garúa. A town of about 30,000 inhabitants, it is frequently visited by travellers interested in the Nazca culture and the world-famous Nazca Lines. On the town plaza is a small museum, open daily from 9 am to 7 pm (US$1.75).

Archaeology

The Peruvian archaeologist Max Uhle was the first to excavate the Nazca sites (in 1901) and to realise that he was dealing with a culture separate from other coastal peoples.

The Nazca culture appeared as a result of the disintegration of the Paracas culture, around 200 AD, and lasted until about 800 AD. The designs on the Nazca ceramics show us their plants and animals, their fetishes and divinities, their musical instruments and household items, and the people themselves.

The early Nazca ceramics are very colourful and have a greater variety of naturalistic designs. Pots with double necks joined by a 'stirrup' handle are frequently found, as well as shallow cups and plates. In the late period, the decoration was more stylised.

Information

There is no tourist office, but tourist information is sometimes available from the bookstore on Bolognesi, if it's open. Hotels can also provide information. Moneychangers hang out in front of the Hotel de Turistas. To phone Nazca, call the operator and ask for Nazca, then give the local phone number.

The Nazca Lines

These huge geometric designs drawn in the desert are visible only from the air. Some represent animals, such as the 180-metre-long lizard, a 90-metre-high monkey with an extravagantly curled tail, or a condor with a 130-metre wing span. Others are simple but perfect geometric figures. The lines were made by removing the sun-darkened stones from the surface of the desert, exposing the lighter-coloured stones below. The best-known lines are some 20 km north of Nazca.

María Reiche, a German mathematician who has spent most of her life studying the lines, thinks they were made by both the Paracas and Nazca cultures over the period from 900 BC to 600 AD, with some additions by the Wari settlers from the highlands, in the 7th century. She considers the lines to be an astronomical calendar. There are plenty of other theories.

Flights for viewing the lines are made in light aircraft, in the mornings; it is too windy in the afternoon. Check out the competing companies (Aero-Cóndor, AeroIca and Montecarlo) for the best deal. All three have offices in town. You should get free transportation to and from the airport, which is three km away. Eat lightly before the flight.

Fares are officially US$50. There is a US$2 airport tax, which is not included in the price of the ticket. Every once in a while, there is a 'fare war' and prices drop, sometimes as low as US$20! Bargain hard.

You can also view the lines from the observation tower beside the Panamericana, 26 km north of Nazca. From here, you get an oblique view of three of the figures (lizard, tree and hands), but it's not very good. About one km south of the tower, a trail leads west to a small hill, from which other lines may be seen. Don't walk on the lines – it damages them, is illegal and you can't see anything anyway. To get to the tower, take a tour or a taxi, or catch a northbound bus in the morning and hitchhike back.

Tours

These are best done by shared taxi. The Hotel Nazca and other hotels have information –

PERU

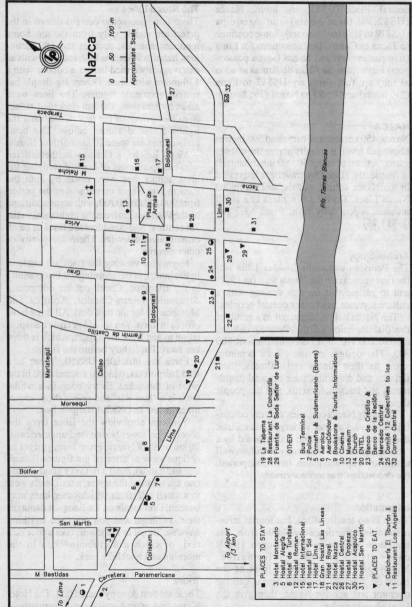

Nazca

Approximate Scale

0   50   100 m

Río Tierras Blancas

■ PLACES TO STAY

3   Hotel Montecario
5   Hostal Alegría
6   Hotel de Turistas
12 Hostal Roman
15 Hostal Internacional
16 Hostal El Sol
17 Hotel Lima
18 Gran Hostal Las Líneas
22 Hotel Royal
26 Hotel Nazca
27 Hostal Central
30 Hostal Oropeza
31 Hostal Acapulco
31 Hostal San Martín

▼ PLACES TO EAT

4   Cebichería El Tiburón II
11 Restaurant Los Ángeles

OTHER

19 La Taberna La Concordia
28 Restaurant La Concordia
29 Fuente de Soda Señor de Luren
1   Bus Terminal
2   Police
5   Ormeño & Sudamericano (Buses)
6   Aerolica
7   AeroCóndor
9   Bookstore & Tourist Information
10 Cinema
13 Museum
14 Church
20 ENTEL
23 Banco de Crédito &
    Banco de la Nación
24 Mercado Central
25 Comité 12 Collectives to Ica
32 Correo Central

To Lima

To Airport
(3 km)

Coliseum

Carretera Panamericana

they work with a guide cooperative which is inexpensive and good. All guides have an official card. Don't go on a tour with an unlicensed guide – the tours visit uninhabited areas, and some unlicensed guides/drivers are in cahoots with armed, masked robbers who will show up and steal your camera and valuables.

One of the most interesting tours is to the **Cementerio de Chauchilla**, 30 km away. Here you'll see bones, skulls, mummies, pottery shards and fragments of cloth dating back to the late Nazca period. Although everything of value has gone, it's quite amazing to stand in the desert and see tombs surrounded by bleached skulls and bones that stretch off into the distance. The tour takes about 2½ hours and costs US$6 per person, with a minimum of three passengers.

There are various other destinations to visit – aqueducts, fossil beds, archaeological sites and vicuña sanctuaries. Ask about them locally. You need three or four people.

Places to Stay

The most popular hotel for budget travellers is the friendly *Hotel Nazca*, Lima 438, run by the Fernández family, who organise excursions. Basic but clean rooms are US$2.50 per person, and there is tepid water in the communal showers. The *Hostal Alegría* (☎ 62), Lima 166, is good, charges US$3 per person and has tour information. They also have tepid water. Other cheap hotels include the family-run *Hostal El Sol*, Tacna 476, and the *Hotel Lima*, on the plaza, which has basic singles/doubles with private electric showers for US$6/7, as well as rooms with communal showers for US$3.50 a single.

Cheaper, with cold water, are the hostals *San Martín, Acapulco, Oropeza, Central* and *Roman* and the *Hotel Royal*, in roughly descending order of attraction.

Places to Eat

The hotels *Nazca, Alegria* and *Lima* all have cheapish restaurants. Cheap restaurants around the market area include *La Concordia* and *Fuente de Soda Señor de Luren*. The

Restaurant Los Angeles, on the plaza, has a cheap set lunch. *Cebichería El Tiburón II* is a typical coastal fish restaurant. *La Taberna*, on Calle Lima, is a bit more up-market, and may have live music on Saturday night.

Getting There & Away

Air The local small airlines, apart from doing overflights of the Nazca Lines, will also fly you to and from Ica and Lima on demand. Aero-Cóndor is the most frequently used for long-distance flights. In addition, Expresso Aéreo flies Lima-Ica-Nazca-Andahuaylas-Cuzco and return on Fridays, and Lima-Nazca-Ica-Lima on Sundays.

Bus There are several bus companies with terminals on the Panamericana, at the west end of town. Ormeño has the most frequent departures, with several a day for Lima (US$7, eight hours) and intermediate points, and to Arequipa (US$9, 12 hours). Buses to Cuzco are available, but the 36-hour trip is best broken in Arequipa.

Comité 12 has taxi colectivos to Ica (US$3, 2½ hours), leaving when they are full (about hourly during the day), from in front of the Restaurant Sheylita.

Travellers to Cuzco should ensure that their bus goes via Arequipa and not via Abancay. The latter route is dangerous and buses are subject to terrorist or bandit attacks.

TACNA

Tacna, 560 metres above sea level, is the most southerly town in Peru. It is the capital of its department, with a population of about 150,000. Tacna is 36 km from the Chilean border and has strong historical ties with that country. It became part of Chile in 1880, during the War of the Pacific, and remained in Chilean hands until 1929, when its people voted to return it to Peru.

Information

The tourist office has closed, perhaps permanently. Street moneychangers give the best rates for cash. They hang around at the southeast end of the Plaza de Armas, near the Hotel

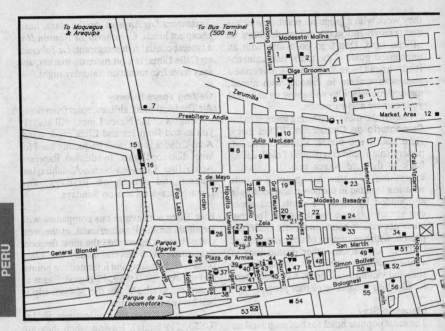

■	PLACES TO STAY	34	Lido Hostal	11	Buses to Boca del Río
		35	Hostal El Inca		(Beach)
1	Hostal Napoli	38	Hostal Alcazar	14	Colectur (Buses)
2	Hostal Portal	44	Plaza Hotel	15	Entrance to Train
3	Hostal El Oscar	46	Gran Hotel Central		Station
5	Hostal Don Abel	49	Hostal Junín, Garden	16	Museo Ferroviario
6	Hostal Cuzco		Hostal & Hostal	21	Museo de Zela
8	Hostal Unanue		Alborada		(Colonial House)
9	Hostal Pacífico	50	Hostal La Alameda	23	Teatro Municipal
10	Pensión Alojamiento	51	Hotel Camino Real	29	Banco de la Nación
	Genova	52	Hostal Premier	30	Americana (Airline)
12	Hotel Don Quijote	54	Hotel de Turistas	32	Banco de Crédito
13	Hotel Imperio &	55	Hostals Avenida &	33	ENTEL
	Hostal Nevada		Zapata	36	Catedral
17	Hostal 2 de Mayo			37	Expreso Tacna
18	Hostal Bon Ami &	▼	PLACES TO EAT	39	Cine San Martín
	Alojamiento Betito			40	AeroPerú
19	Hotel Copacabana	20	Gran Chifa Hong Kong	43	Tourist Office
22	Hotel San Cristóbal	41	Restaurant Sur Perú	45	Casa de Cultura
24	Hostal Lider & H & C	42	El Pollo Pechugon		(History Museum)
	Pensión	46	El Viejo Almacén	47	Faucett (Airline)
25	Holiday Suites Hotel	48	Café Genova	53	Correo Central
26	Hostal Inclan			56	Mercado Central
27	Hostal El Mesón		OTHER		
28	Hostal Hogar				
31	Hotel Lima	4	Ormeño (Buses)		
32	Hotel Emperador	7	Chilean Consulate		

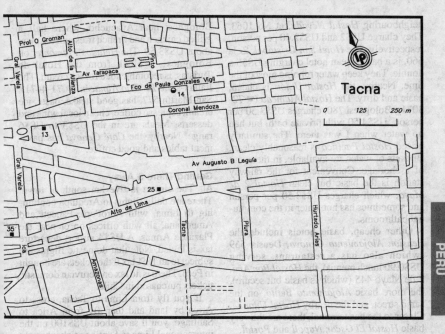

Tacna

0   125   250 m

Prol O Groman
Gral Varela
Alto de la Alianza
Av Tarapaca
Pinto
Fco de Paula Gonzales Vigil
14
Coronal Mendoza
13
Gral Varela
Av Augusto B Leguía
25
Alto de Lima
Tacna
Hurtado Arias
Plura
35
Ica
Amazonas

de Turistas and at the bus terminal. Try the Banco de Crédito for travellers' cheques.

The Chilean Consulate is near the railway station and is open from 8 am to 12.30 pm Monday to Friday. Most travellers just need a tourist card, available at the border.

The Bolivian Consulate is at the southeast end of town, just beyond the women's university. A taxi costs about US$1.

Things to See

The **Museo Ferroviario** is in the railway station and is open from 8 am to 3 pm Monday to Friday. There is an interesting display of turn-of-the-century engines and other rolling stock.

A British locomotive, built in 1859 and used as a troop train in the War of the Pacific, is the centrepiece of the pleasant **Parque de la Locomotora**, in the centre.

The small **Museo de Historia**, in the Casa de Cultura, has paintings and maps explain-

ing the War of the Pacific, and a few archaeological pieces. Hours are irregular.

The main feature of the **Plaza de Armas** is the huge arch – a monument to the heroes of the War of the Pacific. It is flanked by larger-than-life bronze statues of Admiral Grau and Colonel Bolognesi. The six-metre-high bronze fountain nearby was designed by the French engineer Eiffel. Eiffel also designed the Catedral, which is noted for its clean lines, fine stained-glass windows and onyx high altar. The plaza is a popular meeting place for locals in the evenings.

Places to Stay

Hotels in Tacna, especially the cheapest ones, sometimes suffer from water shortages. Showers are not always available. Despite this, hotel prices are relatively high, particularly in the centre. More travellers stay in Arica, Chile.

Two basic cold-water hotels are the *Hotel Imperio*, Coronal Mendoza 1049, and the neighbouring *Hostal Nevada*, at No 1063. They charge US$2 and US$2.40 per person, respectively. The *Hotel San Cristóbal*, Zela 660, is a basic, clean hotel charging US$5 a double. They keep water running most of the time. Nearby, the *Hostal Unión* is cheap, basic and dirty. The *Hostal Alameda* (☎ 72-3071), Bolognesi 780, charges US$3.50 per person, US$4.50 with private bath, but had no water when I was there. The similarly priced *Hostal Pacífico* is reasonably clean. Buckets of water are available, in the event of a shortage. Convenient for the railway station is the basic but clean *Hostal 2 de Mayo*, which charges US$3.50 per person and sometimes has hot water in the communal bathrooms.

Other cheap, basic hotels include the *Pensión Alojamiento Genova*, Deusta 559 (which also has a restaurant, serving US$0.90 lunch menus), the *Hostal Bon Ami*, 2 de Mayo 445 (which is basic but secure), the more basic *Alojamiento Betito*, on the same street, and the nearby *Hostal Unanue*. Closer to the bus terminal, there are the very basic *Hostal El Oscar, Napoli* and *Portal*.

More up-market hotels include the *Hotel Don Quijote* (☎ 72-1514), Augusto B Leguía 940, with singles/doubles for US$4.50/7.50, or US$5.50/8 with private bath, and the clean *H & C Pensión* (☎ 71-2391), Zela 734, which charges US$6/9 for rooms with bath and hot water. The nearby *Hostal Lider* (☎ 71-5441, 71-1176), Zela 724, has some rooms with TV and private hot showers for US$7/12. The *Lido Hostal* (☎ 721184), San Martin 876A, charges US$7/10 for singles/doubles with private hot showers. There are plenty of other places in the centre, at higher prices.

Places to Eat

Tacna restaurants are pricier than those in most other parts of Peru. The *Restaurant Sur Perú*, Ayacucho 80, is cheap and popular with the locals, especially at lunch time. It's open from 7 am to 3 pm and 6.30 to 9 pm Monday to Saturday. The *Chifa Say Wa* and *Gran Chifa Hong Kong* have good Chinese food. For chicken, try *El Pollo Pechugon*, on

Bolognesi near Ayacucho, where half a grilled chicken and French fries will cost you about US$3.50. The *Helados Piamonte*, on Bolognesi, a block from the Hotel de Turistas, is recommended for ice cream. The Italian-style *El Viejo Almacén* (☎ 71-4471), San Martín 577, has good steaks, pasta, ice cream, espresso coffee, cheap local wine and desserts. Meals are in the US$3 to US$6 range. Nearby, the *Café Genova* has pavement tables and good coffee.

Getting There & Away

Air The airport is five km south of town. There are daily flights to Arequipa continuing to Lima, with AeroPerú, Faucett and Americana, all with offices on or near the Plaza de Armas. A US$4 airport departure tax is levied. Note that domestic flights are subject to an 18% tax if the tickets are bought in Peru. There is no tax on Peruvian domestic tickets purchased in Chile.

If you fly from Lima to Tacna, cross to Arica by land and then fly from Arica to Santiago, you'll save about US$100 on the international Lima to Santiago ticket bought in Peru.

Bus There is now a new bus terminal, on Unanue, at the north-east end of town. Several companies run frequent buses to Lima (at least US$17, 21 to 28 hours). Some companies run luxury services (with air-conditioning, videos, on-board toilet, snacks, etc), for twice the cost of regular buses. Arequipa (US$3, 6½ hours) is frequently served, as are other destinations south of Lima.

Buses and colectivos to Arica (Chile) leave frequently from this terminal. Taxi colectivos charge about US$4 per person, and the driver helps you through the border formalities (if your papers are in order).

Buses to Puno (US$7, 12 hours) leave every night; there are no day buses.

Colectivo Expreso Tacna (☎ 72-4021), San Martín 201, has daily shared taxis to Arequipa at 1 pm (US$9, five hours).

Train Trains go from Tacna to Arica and back a few times a day, and this is the cheapest way to cross the border. It is also much slower than the colectivos and buses from the bus station.

Crossing the Border Formalities at the Peru/Chile border are relatively straightforward in both directions. The border closes at 10 pm. Chile is one hour ahead of Peru (two hours with daylight saving).

Getting Around
There is no airport bus, so you have to take a taxi (US$2) or walk (about five km).

Arequipa

Arequipa, 2325 metres above sea level, is the capital of its department and the major city of southern Peru. Arequipeños claim that the city, with a population of over 700,000, is Peru's second largest.

It is a beautiful city, surrounded by spectacular mountains, including the volcano El Misti. Many of the city's buildings are made of a light-coloured volcanic rock called *sillar*, hence Arequipa's nickname – 'the white city'.

The founding of Arequipa, on 15 August 1540, is commemorated with a week-long fair. The fireworks show in the Plaza de Armas on 14 August is particularly spectacular. Unfortunately, the city is built in an earthquake-prone area, and none of the original buildings remains. However, several 17th and 18th-century buildings survive, and are frequently visited. The most interesting of these is the Santa Catalina monastery.

Information
Tourist Office The tourist office (☎ 21-1021, extension 19) is on the Plaza de Armas, opposite the Catedral. Hours are 8 am to 3 pm Monday to Friday. The helpful Policía de Turismo (☎ 23-9888), Jerusalén 315, also provide tourist information.

Money Moneychangers in the street outside the Banco de Crédito have recently been giving as good a rate as anywhere. There are several other banks and casas de cambio nearby.

Post & Telecommunications The post office (☎ 2-15245) is at Moral 118. ENTEL has several branches; the main one (☎ 21-1111) is at A Thomas 201.

Visa Extensions Migraciones (☎ 21-2552), P Viejo 216, does tourist card extensions.

Dangers & Annoyances
Pickpockets abound on the busy street of San Juan de Dios, where most bus terminals are. Watch your belongings carefully here, and everywhere in town. There have been several reports of belongings being stolen from restaurants – keep your stuff in sight.

Things to See
Religious Buildings The tourist office can tell you when specific churches are supposedly open, but hours change often.

The **Convento de Santa Catalina** is the most fascinating colonial religious building in Peru. It was built in 1580 and enlarged in the 17th century. Surrounded by imposing high walls, it's almost a city within a city. Until 1970, the 450 nuns living within led a completely secluded life. Now, the few remaining nuns live in the northern corner of the complex. The rest is open to the public, and you are free to wander around. Admission is US$3, guide services are available and hours are 9 am to 4 pm daily.

The imposing **Catedral** stands on the Plaza de Armas. The original structure, dating from 1656, was destroyed by fire in 1844, and the second building was toppled by the 1868 earthquake, so most of what you see has been rebuilt. The outside is impressive; the interior is spacious, airy and luminous, with high vaults which are much less cluttered than those of churches in other parts of Peru.

One of the oldest churches in Arequipa, **La Compañía**, on the south-eastern corner of

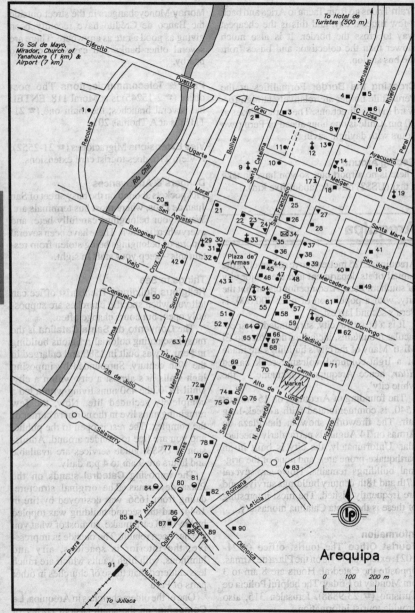

To Hotel de Turistas (500 m)

To Sol de Mayo,
Mirador, Church of
Yanahuara (1 km) &
Airport (7 km)

Ejército

Puente

Grau

Recoleta

Ugarte

Bolívar

Santa Catalina

Río Chili

Moral

San Agustín

Bolognesi

Cruz Verde

P Viejo

Consuelo

Lima

Sucre

Tristán

28 de Julio

La Merced

Salaverry

Parra

Huascar

To Juliaca

Jerusalén

Rivero

Peral

C. Llosa

Ayacucho

Santa Marta

San José

Mercaderes

Santo Domingo

San Francisco

Plaza de
Armas

Valdivia

San Camilo
Market

Alto de la Luna

San Juan de Dios

N. de Pierola

Peru

Pizarro

Romana

Leticia

Olímpica

A. Thomas

Tacna y Arica

Quiróz

Cáceres

Melgar

Arequipa

0   100   200 m

PERU

■ PLACES TO STAY	87	Hostal Grace	19	Santa Teresa
	88	Hotel Premier	21	Casa de Moral
2 Hostal Wilson	89	Hostal Colonia	22	Lima Tours
3 Hostal Santa Catalina	90	Hostal Extra	28	Peña/Picantería
4 Hotel Jerusalén			29	San Agustín
5 Hostal La Casa de Mi	▼	PLACES TO EAT	32	AeroPerú, Faucett &
Abuela				Americana (Airlines)
6 Hostal Latino	8	Govinda Vegetarian	33	Catedral
7 Hostal Nuñoz		Restaurant & Other	34	Correo Central
16 Residencial Rivero		Budget Places	35	Casa Ricketts
18 La Casa de Melgar	14	Vegetarian Restaurant	36	Map Store
20 Hostal Tumi de Oro	23	Imperial, Lamborghini,	37	Carnaby Disco
25 Le Foyer		La Botin del Obispo	39	Cine Municipal
26 Hotel Crismar		& Others	42	Casablanca Disco
28 Hotel La Fontana	24	Central Garden	43	Tourist Office
31 Hotel Maison Plaza		Restaurant	46	Cine Portal
40 Hostal Mercaderes	27	Pizzería San Antonio	47	Banco de Crédito
41 Hostal America	30	Pizza Luigi,	51	ENTEL
44 Hostal Niko's		Restaurant Cuzco,	53	La Compañía
45 Hostal El Mirador		Balcony Restaurant	54	Cine Fenix
46 Hotel El Portal		& Others	60	Santo Domingo
49 Hotel Conquistador	38	Restaurant Bonanza	63	La Merced
50 Hostal Lider Inn	48	Restaurant La Rueda	64	Expreso Victoria del
55 Hostal V Lira	52	Cevichería 45		Sur (Buses)
56 Hostal Hugo/Jorge's	57	Monzas & Chifa Ha	69	Cine Ateneo
58 Hostal Imperial		Wa Yan	72	Cine Variedades
59 Hotel Presidente	65	Restaurant América	75	Bus Companies to
61 Hotel Crillon Serrano	67	Restaurant Dalmacia		Colca
& Pensión Tito		& Puerto Rico	76	Many Bus Companies
62 Hotel Viza			79	Cruz del Sur & Sur
66 Hostal Royal		OTHER		Peruano (Buses)
68 Hotel San Francisco			80	Cruz del Sur (Buses)
70 Hostal Comercio	1	Monasterio de La	81	Ormeño (Buses)
71 Hostals Granada &		Recoleta & Museo	83	Mountaineering Club
Concorde	9	Convento de Santa	84	Comités 1, 2, 3, 5, 10
72 Hostals Americanao &		Catalina		& 15 Colectivos
Ejercicios	10	Romie's Peña	86	Expreso
73 Gran Hotel	11	Museo Municipal &		Sudamericano
74 Hostal San Juan		Crafts Shops		(Buses)
77 Hotel San Gregory	12	San Francisco	91	Railway Station
78 Hotel Virrey	13	Conresa Tours		Entrance
82 Hostal Florida	15	Continental Tours		
85 Hostals Europa &	17	Tourist Police &		
Paris		Information		

the Plaza de Armas, is noted for its ornate main façade. This Jesuit church was so solidly built that it withstood the earthquakes. Inside, many of the original murals were covered with plaster and white paint by 19th-century restorers, but the polychrome cupola of the San Ignacio chapel survived and is worth seeing. The church is open from 9 am to noon and 3 to 6 pm (check when you get there); admission is US$0.10.

The church of **San Francisco** was built in the 16th century and has been damaged by earthquakes – you can see a large crack in the cupola. There is an impressive silver altar.

La Recoleta, a Franciscan monastery, was built on the western side of the Río Chili in 1648, but has been completely rebuilt. There is a huge and fascinating library of over 20,000 books, many of which are centuries old. They have several *incunables*, or books printed before 1550. There is a museum of Amazonian objects collected by the missionaries, an extensive collection of preconquest artefacts, and religious artworks of the Cuzqueño school. You can visit the cloisters and monks' cells.

The monastery is open from 9 am to 1 pm and 3 to 5 pm Monday to Friday, and on Saturday mornings. Admission is US$1.25. A Spanish-speaking guide is available (a tip is expected).

Museums The Museo Municipal has a few paintings, historical documents, photographs, maps and other paraphernalia pertaining to the city's history. Hours are 9 am to 1 pm and 3 to 6 pm Monday to Friday and admission is US$0.70.

There is an archaeological collection at the Universidad de San Agustín, on Avenida Ayacucho, about one km east of the centre. It is open from 9 am to 3 pm Monday to Friday – a donation is expected.

Colonial Houses Many beautiful colonial houses are now being used as art galleries, banks or offices, and can be visited. One of the best is the Casa Ricketts, built in 1738, which was first a seminary, then the archbishop's palace and then a school, before passing into the hands of one of Arequipa's upper-crust families and finally being sold to the Banco Central. It now houses a small art gallery and museum, as well as bank offices. Entry is free. It's open from 8 am to noon and 3 to 6 pm Monday to Friday. Also worth a look are the Casa de Moral, now owned by the Banco Industrial, and the Palacio Goyaneche.

Suburbs The suburb of **Yanahuara** is within walking distance of the town centre and makes a good excursion. Go west on Avenida Grau, cross the bridge, and continue on Avenida Ejército for about six or seven blocks. Turn right on Avenida Lima and walk up five blocks to a small plaza, where you'll find the church of Yanahuara, which dates from 1750. There's a viewing platform at the

end of the plaza, with excellent views of Arequipa and El Misti.

Head back along Avenida Jerusalén (in Yanahuara), which is the next street parallel to Avenida Lima; just before reaching Avenida Ejército, you'll see the well-known Picantería Sol de Mayo restaurant. The green Yanahuara city bus No 152 leaves Arequipa along Puente Grau and returns from Yanahuara Plaza to the centre every few minutes.

A little way beyond Yanahuara is **Cayma**, another suburb with an often-visited church. To get there, continue along Avenida Ejército about three blocks beyond Avenida Jerusalén, then turn right on Avenida Cayma and climb this road for about one km. The church of San Miguel Arcángel is open from 9 am to 4 pm, and the church warden will take you up the small tower, for a tip. Buses marked 'Cayma' go there from Arequipa, along Avenida Grau.

Places to Stay

The *Hotel Crillon Serrano* (☎ 21-2392), Peru 109, is cheap and basic but clean and friendly, and has warm water in the mornings. They charge US$2 per person, a litle more for rooms with private bath. Next door is the slightly pricier but clean and friendly *Pensión Tito* (☎ 23-4424), Peru 105B. The *Gran Hotel*, A Thomas 451, is US$2 per person but is dirty and has only cold water. *Le Foyer* (☎ 21-4658), Ugarte 114 (no sign), has basic rooms for US$2.50 per person. It's friendly, popular and reasonably clean, with hot water much of the time.

The *Hostal Santa Catalina* (☎ 22-2722), Santa Catalina 500, is basic but fairly clean and popular, and charges US$3.50/4.75 for singles/doubles. There is hot water. The *Hostal Lider Inn* (☎ 23-8210), Consuelo 429, charges US$4.50 (one or two people) for a clean room with private bath (cold water only). The *Hostal Ejercicios*, A Thomas 433, is a basic but OK cold-water hotel charging US$3/5. Next door, at No 435, the *Hostal Americano* charges a little more but is clean and has hot water. The *Hostal Tumi de Oro*, San Agustín 311A, has been recommended as clean, friendly and having hot water. They charge US$3 per person.

There are several cheap hotels along San Juan de Dios, which can be noisy because of the buses leaving from this area. One of the best along here is the *Hostal Royal* (☎ 21-2071), San Juan de Dios 300A, which has clean singles/doubles with hot water (US$4/6) and doubles with private bath (US$7.50). The *Hostal San Juan* (☎ 24-8361), San Juan de Dios 521, charges US$4/7 (US$8.50 for doubles with private bath and hot water). The *Hostal V Lira* is basic but secure and there are similar ones, nearby. Others for about US$4/7 include: the *Hostal Mercaderes* (☎ 21-4830), Peral 117, which is basic but OK; the *Hostal Mirador*, at the corner of the plaza, which has only cold water in the communal bathrooms but a few rooms (not singles) have great views over the Plaza de Armas; and the *Hostal Wilson* (☎ 23-8781), Grau 306, which has hot water, and some double rooms with private bath.

The clean *Hostal Grace* (☎ 23-5924), Quiroz 121, is quite good for US$4.75/7. It has hot water, and is convenient for buses and trains. Others convenient for transportation (though there are plans to move buses to a new terminal) include the following. The *Hostal Colonia* (☎ 24-2766), Cáceres 109, has large, basic rooms (US$4/7), as well as rooms with private bath and hot water (US$5.50/9.50). The *Hostal Extra* (☎ 22-1217) has basic rooms for US$5/6.25 and rooms with bath for US$6.25/8. The *Hotel Premier* (☎ 24-1091), Quiróz 100, has clean rooms for US$5.25/8 and rooms with private hot shower and towels for US$6.50/10. The best hotel in the bus area is *Hostal Florida* (☎ 23-8467, 22-8710), San Juan de Dios 664B, which charges US$6.50/10 (US$8.25/11.75 with private hot bath and towels).

The *Hostal Hugo/Jorge's* (☎ 21-3988), Santo Domingo 110, has basic cheap rooms, as well as singles/doubles with private hot bath for US$7/11. A good newer hotel is *Hotel San Gregory* (☎ 24-5036), A Thomas 535, which has clean, comfortable rooms with bath and hot water for US$6/10. Friendly *La Casa de Melgar* (☎ 22-2459), Melgar 108A, is in a recently renovated house. Clean rooms are US$6/9 (US$7.75/10.50 with private hot bath. Also in this price range are the popular *Hostal Núñez* (☎ 21-8648, 22-0111), Jerusalén 528 (no sign), which is good, secure and friendly, and the clean *Hostal Niko's* (☎ 21-5241), Mercaderes 106.

More up-market recommendations include the *Hostal Latino* (☎ 24-4770), C Llosa 135, which has large, comfortable rooms with private hot bath, and *Casa de Mi Abuela* (☎ 24-1206), Jerusalén 606, which is extremely secure, has a beautiful garden in which breakfast is served, and is very clean. Rooms with bath are US$9/13; bungalows with kitchenette are US$13/20 for doubles/quads.

Places to Eat

Restaurants in Arequipa close early; many are shut by 9 pm. The *Balcony Restaurant* and the *Restaurant Cuzco*, on the north-west side of the plaza, 2nd floor, have excellent views over the plaza; the food is OK and cheap. Below the Balcony are several other cheap to mid-priced restaurants. You can get half a grilled chicken for about US$2 in several places along San Juan de Dios. Three good but reasonably priced restaurants in the 300 block of San Juan de Dios are the *Puerto Rico* (☎ 21-7512), the *Dalmacia* and the *América* – this last has good ice creams and snacks.

The *Govinda*, Jerusalén 505, is a vegetarian place run by the Hare Krishnas, and is very cheap. Another vegetarian restaurant is at Jerusalén 402. There are several other cheap restaurants on these blocks. Good Italian food is available at *Pizzería San Antonio* (☎ 21-3950), at Jerusalén and Santa Marta. This place is popular with young locals. The *Bonanza*, Jerusalén 114, serves a good variety of reasonably priced dishes and is also popular with Arequipeños.

There are two up-market cafés on the first block of San Francisco which have good espresso, cappuccino and snacks. The best coffee, and the most expensive, is at *Monzas*, on Santo Domingo, a block east of the plaza. Nearby, the *Chifa Ha Wa Yan* is good for Chinese food. The best ceviche (and nothing else) is served in the little *Cevichería 45* (☎ 24-2400), A Thomas 221, from 9 am to 3 pm. The alley behind the Catedral has several popular, quaint and pricey restaurants.

An excellent place for Arequipeño food is the locally popular *Tradición Arequipeña* (☎ 24-2385), Avenida Dolores 111, in the south-eastern suburb of Paucarpata. Most taxi drivers know it – about US$1.50 from the city centre. Meals here are in the US$3 to US$6 range. Also good for local dishes is the *Sol de Mayo*, at Jerusalén 207, in the Yanahuara district. Both these places open only for lunch.

Entertainment

Romie's Peña (☎ 23-4465), Zela 202, has long been popular. It's a very lively but tiny bar, so get there before 10 pm to get in. The folklórico music is usually good. The cover charge is US$2 and the drinks are pricey. Two good peñas in the Yanahuara district are El Búho (folklórico) and La Piramide (criollo). There is occasionally entertainment at the Peña Picantería, at Jerusalén 204.

The best disco is the Casablanca, on Sucre near Bolognesi, which is in the basement of a garage, has a US$3 cover charge and is locally popular for dancing. Another place is the Carnaby, on Jerusalén. There are several cinemas.

Getting There & Away

Air The airport is seven km from the city centre. AeroPerú (☎ 21-6820), Faucett (☎ 21-2352) and Americana (☎ 21-9558) have offices on the Plaza de Armas.

On most days, there are three or four direct flights to Lima, two to Tacna, one or two to Cuzco and one to Juliaca. Nonresidents must pay US$6 departure tax at the airport.

Bus A new bus terminal, on the outskirts of town, was dedicated in 1993 and will prob-

ably be operational by the time you read this. Meanwhile, the majority of bus and colectivo offices are on San Juan de Dios, from the 300 to 600 blocks. These will begin to move to the new terminal. Check where the bus leaves from, when you buy your ticket.

Lima (17 to 24 hours) is served by many buses of several companies: Cruz del Sur, Sudamericano, TEPSA, Ormeño and others. Shop around for the most convenient departure and the best fare. Some companies provide luxury nonstop buses with air-conditioning, videos, snacks and toilets. Normal bus fares are about US$10 to US$14; luxury buses cost well over US$20. Many buses stop in Nazca (10 to 14 hours) as well as in Camaná, Chala and Ica. Ensure that you are not charged the Lima fare for a Nazca ticket. Buses for Pisco often drop you on the Panamericana, five km from town. Check this carefully or go to Ica and change.

At this time, there are only night buses to Juliaca and Puno. If you want a day trip, go by the more expensive colectivo. Cruz del Sur is one of the best on this route (about US$7 for the 11-hour trip to Juliaca). They also have direct buses to Cuzco (about 20 hours). Jacantay and Ormeño also travel to Juliaca and Puno. This is a cold night trip – dress warmly.

Angelitos Negros has several daily departures for Moquegua (US$2, 3½ hours) and Tacna (US$3, six hours). Other companies which do this route are Ormeño and Cruz del Sur.

Several small companies around the 500 block of San Juan de Dios have dawn (4.30 or 5 am) departures for Chivay (US$3.30, five hours), going on to Yanque, Achoma, Maca, Cruz del Cóndor and Cabanaconde (eight hours), in the upper Cañon de Colca. Companies include Setro Sur, Nieto, Colca, Palma and Chasqui. Empresa Jacantay has a 6.30 am departure for Cabanaconde via Huambo. (A round trip to the Colca Canyon via Sihuas, Huambo, Cabanaconde and Chivay can therefore be done using public transport.) Check that the bus leaves from where you bought the ticket.

Mendoza bus company leaves from La

Merced (in front of the church) daily at 5 am and 4 pm for Corire (three hours) and the Toro Muerto petroglyphs.

Colectivo Various Comités at Avenida Tacna y Arica 111 have taxi colectivos to various destinations. Comité 3 (☎ 24-3651) has a daily 10 am service to Juliaca (US$15, eight hours), and hotel pick-ups can be arranged. Other colectivos go to Tacna, Mollendo and Chivay.

Train The journey to Juliaca is more comfortable by rail than by road. There are no day trains. There used to be trains every night except Sunday, but engine problems and lack of funds have caused the service to be curtailed to Sunday and Wednesday nights only. Check locally for the latest details. The train leaves Arequipa at 9 pm and arrives in Juliaca at 6 am the following day. This train continues to Puno (one hour away), or you can connect with the day train to Cuzco, which leaves Juliaca at 9 am. You can buy a through ticket from Arequipa to Cuzco, arriving at 6 pm.

Many people have been robbed on the night train. You are safest buying the pullman (also called buffet) class tickets instead of just a 1st-class ticket. The pullman car has comfortable reclining seats so you can sleep, and is heated. The doors are locked and only ticket holders are admitted into the carriages.

Fares from Arequipa change frequently. In the last decade, you could pay anywhere between US$2 and US$10 for a 1st-class ticket to Juliaca; fares in 2nd class (not recommended) are about 25% lower. Recent fares to Juliaca were about US$8 in 1st class, US$16 in pullman.

Buy your tickets in advance rather than trying to do so whilst guarding your luggage. The ticket office opening hours change constantly, and there are usually very long lines – you can wait several hours to purchase a ticket. Travel agencies (eg Continental Tours and Conresa Tours, on the 400 block of Jerusalén) will sell tickets, for a 25% commission, and provide transport from your hotel to the station. Shop around for the best deal.

Getting Around

The Zevallo-Aeropuerto bus No 3 goes along Grau and Ejército and passes within a km of the airport – ask the driver where to get off. A taxi to or from the airport costs US$4, and an airport bus to downtown hotels is US$1.60.

AROUND AREQUIPA
Colca Canyon

The most popular excursion from Arequipa is to the Colca Canyon, which can be visited by public transport or with a guided tour. Controversy rages about whether or not this is the world's deepest canyon. The sections which you can see from the road on a standard guided tour are certainly very impressive but are not the deepest parts of the canyon. To see the deepest sections, you have to make an overnight trip and hike in.

Most guided tours leave Arequipa (2325 metres) well before dawn and climb northwards through desert scenery and over the pass separating Chachani and El Misti. The road continues through the nature reserve of Pampas de Cañihuas (about 3850 metres), where vicuñas and sometimes guanacos are sighted. A breakfast stop is often made at Viscachani (4150 metres). The road continues through bleak altiplano over the high point of about 4800 metres, from where the snowcaps of Ampato (6288 metres) are seen. Then the road drops spectacularly to Chivay, about 160 km from Arequipa.

The thermal hot springs of Chivay are normally visited, and the tour bus continues west, following the southern bank of the upper Colca Canyon. The landscape is remarkable for its Inca and pre-Inca terracing. Along the route are several villages, whose inhabitants still use the terraces. At Yanque, an attractive church, which dates from the early 1700s, is often visited.

The end point of the tour is at the Cruz del Cóndor lookout, about 60 km beyond Chivay and an hour before you get to the village of Cabanaconde. Andean condors are sometimes seen here. From the lookout, the view is impressive, with the river flowing 1200 metres below.

Several tour companies do the trip – some aren't very good, so check locally before parting with your money. Guides should be able to produce a Tourist Guide card. Operators will often pool their clients. Conresa, at Jerusalén 409, or Continental, at Jerusalén 402, often provide the vehicle and the lowest prices. Unfortunately, the minibuses used don't have adequate leg room for tall people, and it may be better to go in a smaller group with a car. Guides don't always speak English. The day tours are very long and tiring, and get you to the Cruz del Cóndor too late to have a good chance of seeing condors. An overnight tour is better. Day tours are about US$22 per person and two-day tours are US$36, including hotel and dinner. A car taking a maximum of five people can be hired for US$70/110 for one/two days; the hotel is extra. Try the tour agencies or comités.

By public transport, you can get off at Cruz del Cóndor and camp. It is a two-hour walk from the lookout to Cabanaconde, where there are hotels. You could also take the 4 am bus from Cabanaconde to Arequipa, get off at the lookout for dawn and condor viewing, then return to Cabanaconde for a second night. The best condor viewing is from 7 to 9 am; it's not bad in the late afternoon. You can also get directions here for overnight camping trips into the canyon – bring everything you'll need. The best trips to Colca are unrushed ones!

Note that in 1990, there were reports of small tourist groups being robbed at the lookout. This was not a problem in 1991/92; ask locally and at the SAEC in Lima about this.

Places to Stay Chivay, at an altitude of about 3700 metres, has the friendly *Hostal Anita*, with occasional hot water, and the more basic but clean *Hostal Chivay*. Both are on the Plaza de Armas and charge US$2 per person. The clean and friendly *Hostal de Colca* is two blocks from the plaza and has

hot water in the communal baths. They charge US$7 a double, less in dormitory rooms. There are hot springs five km northeast of Chivay by road. There is a clean swimming pool (with changing rooms), a basic cafeteria and a US$0.50 fee.

Cabanaconde has three basic *pensiones*, charging US$2 a night. Walk 10 minutes west of the plaza to a hill with good views and occasional condors in the early morning. Ask for directions to hike into the canyon – it takes about six hours one-way, so you should be prepared to camp. Longer overnight trips are also done. The SAEC in Lima has details.

Getting There & Away If you don't want a guided tour, see the Arequipa section for details of bus companies which have daily dawn departures to Chivay. Most continue to Cabanaconde and return from there to Arequipa at 4 am daily. The section of road between Cabanaconde and Huambo veers away from the canyon. It is also the roughest part, and there is little transport. Jacantay bus company in Arequipa does the trip to Cabanaconde through Huambo.

El Misti
This 5822-metre-high volcano offers a technically easy ascent for a mountain of its size. Nevertheless, it is very hard work on the loose sand/ash, and you need to be fit and have warm gear. The best time to climb is during the dry months of May to December. Technical equipment and guides are rarely necessary (though some people prefer to have them). Señor Carlos Zárate, at Alameda Pardo 117 (two long blocks west of the Bolognesi bridge), is an expert climber and can provide you with up-to-date information, rent you equipment and put you in contact with a guide. Visit him from 9 am to 1 pm and 4 to 6 pm. The Mountaineering Club, at Romana 206, in south-eastern Arequipa, can also help with information, guides and transportation. They meet every Tuesday at 7 pm; call Max Arce (☎ 23-3697) for more information. The club recommends Guillermo Portocarrero (☎ 23-4966) and

Ivan Bedregal (☎ 22-0515) as guides. The tourist office also has information.

To get to the mountain by public transport, take an Enatru Peru bus along Goyaneche (about seven blocks east of the plaza along Mercaderes) to Apurimac or San Luis – they run about every half-hour all day. From here to the Nido de Aguilas camp (no facilities) takes eight hours or more, on rough trails. It's a hard, uphill slog, and there's no water. Stay overnight at the camp, then continue to the summit – about four more hours – and return to the bottom of the mountain in four hours.

If you're a beginner, note that people have died in these mountains – it's not as easy a climb as it looks. Carry plenty of drinking water and cold-weather gear, and be aware of the main symptoms of altitude sickness. If in doubt, go back down.

Toro Muerto Petroglyphs & Corire

Hundreds of carved boulders are scattered over two sq km of desert – archaeologists aren't sure of their significance. See them by taking a bus to Corire (three hours) and continuing up the valley for several km on foot. The best petroglyphs are on the left and higher up. In Corire is the *Hostal Willys*, on the plaza (US$2) and the better *Hostal Manuelito*, three blocks from the plaza (US$3.50 per person, with cold showers). Crayfish from the local river is sold in several simple restaurants.

The Lake Titicaca Area

Lake Titicaca, at 3820 metres, is the highest navigable lake in the world. At over 170 km long, it is also the largest lake in South America. At this altitude, the air is unusually clear, and the deep blue of the lake is especially pretty.

The lake straddles the Peru/Bolivia border. The most common route into Bolivia is via Yunguyo, crossing the border to Copacabana, then by bus and boat to La Paz; see below under To/From Bolivia. The Lake Titicaca section of the Bolivia chapter has

more information about that side of the border.

Interesting boat trips can be made from Puno, Peru's major port on Lake Titicaca. Several colonial churches and archaeological monuments are worth visiting. The Department of Puno is famous for its folk dances, which are the wildest and most colourful in the Peruvian highlands. There are huge herds of alpacas and llamas. It is a fascinating area.

JULIACA

With well over 100,000 inhabitants, Juliaca is the largest town in the Department of Puno, and has the department's only commercial airport. It is an important railway junction, with connections to Arequipa, Puno and Cuzco. Juliaca is the first altiplano town visited by many overland travellers from the coast. It is of comparatively little interest, and most people prefer to go on to Puno, where there are better hotels and views of Lake Titicaca. If you arrive from the coast, take it easy for a day or two – the altitude can make you very sick.

Information

Moneychanging facilities are limited. The best hospital in the Department of Puno is the Clínica Adventista de Juliaca.

Places to Stay

The *Hostal San Antonio* (☎ 32-1701), San Martín 347, is basic but clean, and one of the better cheapies. Rooms are US$2.25/3.50 with private bath and cold shower, a bit less for rooms with communal bath. Hot showers are an extra US$0.90. The *Hostal Sakura*, Unión 133, is OK for US$3.50/5, with private bath and occasional hot water. Cheaper basic places for about US$2/3.50 include *Hotel Don Pedro* and *Hostal Loreto*, opposite the railway station, *Hostal Rosedal*, north of the post office on Salaverry, *Hotel Centro*, on Núñez, three blocks north of the station, and the *Hostal Santa Elisa*, behind the Hostal Sakura.

For better digs, try the clean *Hostal Yasur* (☎ 32-1501), Núñez 417, four blocks north of the station. Rooms are US$3.50/6.50, or US$6/8 with private bath and (sometimes) hot water; ask for 'low-season discounts'. The *Hostal Perú* (☎ 32-1510), opposite the station, has decent rooms for US$4.75/7.75 (US$2 more with private bath). There is hot water in the evenings.

Places to Eat

Restaurants are nothing special. Try the *Pollos Caravana*, on Núñez north of the railway station, and the *Café Dorado*, on Unión a couple of blocks north-west of the station.

Getting There & Away

Air The airport serves Juliaca and Puno. There are flights to Cuzco, Arequipa and Lima on most days. Faucett, AeroPerú and Americana all have offices in the centre, a couple of blocks north-west of the railway station. The airport tax is US$7.

Bus The cheapest long-distance services are with Transportes Jacantaya, on Sandia near Núñez, with nightly buses for Arequipa (US$6, 10 hours) and Lima (26 hours). Most bus companies are on Huancané, on the second and third blocks east of Núñez. There are nightly (no day) buses to Cuzco (US$7, 11 hours); Cruz del Sur is one of the better companies. They also have night buses to Tacna.

Colectivo Comité 1 taxi colectivos charge about US$1 per passenger for the 45-minute drive on the good road to Puno. They leave from the railway plaza as soon as they are full – about two or three times an hour. They are hard to find on Fridays (and sometimes Tuesdays), when they go to the market at the Bolivian border. Colectivo minibuses leave from three blocks south of the railway plaza and charge a little less.

Comité 3 (☎ 32-1941), J Chávez 131, has taxi colectivos to Arequipa, at 11 am (US$15, nine hours).

Train Tickets for the day train to Cuzco are often sold out to passengers from Arequipa and Puno – it is easier to get tickets in Puno. Trains to Arequipa leave at 8.45 pm on Monday and Thursday. See the Puno section for details of trains to Cuzco, and the Arequipa section for information about the Arequipa run.

Getting Around

There is no airport bus. Bargain for a taxi and expect to pay US$2 to US$3.

PUNO

Puno was founded on 4 November 1668, but there are few colonial buildings to see, other than the Catedral. The town itself is drab and not very interesting, but there's a good selection of hotels, and plenty to see in the environs.

Information

Tourist Office The tourist office is on the north-east corner of the plaza; hours are 8 am to 1 pm Monday to Friday.

Money If travelling to or from Bolivia, it's best to buy or sell Bolivian *pesos* at the border, though they can be exchanged in Puno. There are banks along Calle Lima, where travellers' cheques can be changed. The Banco de Crédito gives cash on Visa cards (high commission). Moneychangers hang out in front of the banks. Cash is definitely preferred.

Bolivian Consulate The Bolivian Consulate is at Puno 350. For visa requirements, see under Facts for the Visitor in the Bolivia chapter.

Showers There are public hot showers on the corner of Avenida El Sol and Carabaya, open from 7 am till 7 pm, except on holidays. A half-hour hot shower costs US$0.50.

Things to See

The **Museo Carlos Dreyer** is just off the plaza and is open irregularly; admission is US$0.50. It's best to go in the morning.

The **Parque Huajsapata**, a little hill about 10 minutes south-west of town, is topped by a statue of the first Inca, Manco Capac, looking out at Lake Titicaca. The view of the town and the lake is excellent but the park is dirty. Another good spot for views is the balcony by the arch (Arco Deustua) on Calle Independencia.

Festivals

The Department of Puno has a wealth of traditional dances. The costumes are ornate and imaginative, and are often worth more than an entire household's ordinary clothes. Musicians play a host of traditional instruments.

Check the tourist office for local fiesta information. Apart from the major Peruvian festivals, the following are important in the Lake Titicaca region:

6 January
    Día de los Reyes (Epiphany)
2-14 February
    Virgen de la Candelaria (Candlemas)
7-8 March
    Día de San Juan (St John)
2-4 May
    Alacitas (Puno miniature handicrafts fair)
2-4 May
    Día de Santa Cruz (Holy Cross; Huancané, Taquile, Puno)
25 July
    Día de Santiago (St James; Taquile)
24 September
    La Virgen de La Merced (Our Lady of Mercy)
1-7 November
    Semana Cívica de Puno Puno Week

Places to Stay

Hotels fill up quickly when the trains arrive in the evenings. The prices given here may rise during festivals, and sometimes in the evenings. Many hotels in Puno have triple and quadruple rooms. Water and power shortages are a problem.

There are very basic cheap hotels around Tacna and Melgar. One of the cheapest is the *Hostal Taurino* (US$1.25 per person), but it's dirty and rundown, though not dangerous. Other cheap dives are the hostals *Venecia*, *Central*, *Centenario* and *Rosario*. The *Hostal Roma* is slightly better, with hot

showers sometimes – singles/doubles are US$1.75/3.

The *Hostal Extra*, Moquegua 124, usually has hot water in the mornings, and is OK for US$2 per person. The similarly priced *Hostal San Carlos*, Ugarte 153, is clean but has only cold water. The *Hostal Europa* (☎ 35-3023), Ugarte 112, has long been a favoured budget travellers' hotel (US$4/5). There is hot water in the evenings and they'll store luggage. The quiet and helpful *Hostal Los Uros* (☎ 35-2141), Valcárcel 135, has a cafeteria for early breakfasts and hot water during the evenings. Rooms are US$3.25/4.75, or US$4.25/5.50 with private bath. There are few singles but plenty of triples and even quads, which work out cheaply. The *Hotel Los Incas* is a basic but friendly cold-water hotel charging US$3.50/4.75. It also has triples and quads (about US$2 per person). Ask for discounts. There are hot showers nearby. The *Hostal Presidente* charges US$3/4.75 and has occasional hot showers. The *Hostal Arequipa* (☎ 35-2071), Arequipa 153, has hot water (US$4 for a room with one or two people).

The clean *Hostal Nesther* (☎ 35-1631), Deustua 268, has hot water in the mornings and charges US$4/7 for rooms with private bath. The popular *Hostal Monterrey*, Grau 148, has hot water in the mornings and evenings. It charges US$4.50/7 with private bath, US$4/5 with communal bath, and has a restaurant attached. The *Hostal Internacional* (☎ 35-2109), Libertad 161, has hot water in the mornings and evenings. Rooms are US$4/6, or US$6/9 with private bath. The *Hostal Tumi* (☎ 35-3270), Cajamarca 243, looks OK and has hot water. Rooms are US$3/5, or US$6/10 with private bath.

Places to Eat

There are several restaurants on the corner of Moquegua and Libertad. The *Delta Café* is cheap, and recommended for early breakfasts. The *Restaurant Internacional* is one of the best in town. It may have music in the evenings. *Club 31* is cheap and uncrowded. *Restaurant Las Rocas*, near the Hostal Los

PERU

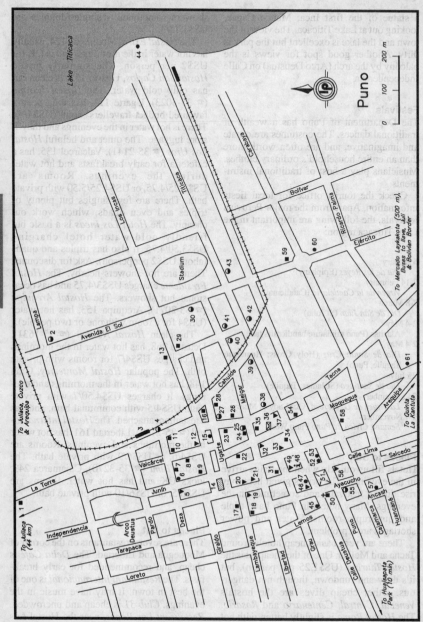

Puno

■ PLACES TO STAY	▼ PLACES TO EAT	15 Mercado Central
		25 Comité 3 Colectivos
1 Hostal Don Miguel	5 Restaurant 4 de	27 Colectur Buses
7 Hotel Centenario	Noviembre	30 Jacantaya & Cruz del
8 Hostal Italia	12 Restaurant Las Rocas	Sur Buses
9 Hotel Arequipa	19 Restaurant Don Piero	36 Correo Central
10 Hostal Los Uros	20 Restaurant Pascana	38 Minibuses to Juliaca
11 Hotel Ferrocarril	21 Restaurant El Dorado	39 Expreso Tacna Buses
13 Hotel Embajador	32 DeltaCafé, Club 31,	40 Expreso Angelitos del
16 Hostal San Carlos	Restaurant	Sur Buses
17 Hotel El Buho	Internacional &	41 SurPeruaño &
18 Hotel Sillustani	Pollería Copacabana	Carhuamayo Buses
22 Hostal Extra	33 Café/Pastelería	42 Empresa San Martín
23 Hostal Presidente	Kimano	Buses
24 Hostal Taurino	37 Pollería Sale Caliente	43 San Cristobal
26 Hostals Venecia &	46 Bar Restaurant Los	(Ormeño) Buses
Central	Olivos	44 Port
28 Hostal Europa	49 La Hostería	45 Museo Carlos Dreyer
29 Hostal Los Incas	56 Restaurant Tania	47 New Town Hall
31 Hostal Monterrey		48 Tourist Office
34 Hostal Nesther	OTHER	50 Catedral
35 Hostal Roma & Hotel		51 Plaza de Armas
Internacional	2 Buses to Juliaca	52 Bolivian Consulate
54 Hostal Rosario	3 Railway Station	53 Samana Bar
58 Hotel Tumi	4 Comité 1 Colectivos	55 Tranextur Buses
59 Hostal Real	6 Cine Puno (Twin	57 Peña Recuerdos de
	Cinemas)	Titicaca
	14 Parque Pino (or San	60 Public Hot Showers
	Juan)	61 ENTEL

Uros on Valcárcel, has good food and is reasonably priced.

There are other cheap restaurants along Avenida Lima – the *Restaurant Pascana*, at No 347, is good and has set lunches for US$1. Opposite, the *Restaurant Don Piero*, at No 354, has local trout meals (US$3) and other cheaper plates. *El Dorado*, on the same block, is good and reasonably priced. The cosy *La Hostería*, at Lima and Grau, is popular for pizzas and other meals – about US$2 each. They sometimes have music in the evenings. The *Govinda*, on Deustua near Lima, has cheap vegetarian lunches. For those on a budget, the simple *Restaurant 4 de Noviembre*, on Junín near Deza, has set lunches for US$0.75 – it's popular with the locals.

The *Café/Pastelería Kimano* has good pastries. The *Bar Restaurant Los Olivos* is fairly popular with locals. The *Restaurant*

Tania, on the corner of the plaza, has been recommended, but hours are erratic. The *Quinta La Kantuta*, some way from the centre, at Arequipa 1086, serves typical lunches (including cuy) daily, except Monday. *Pollo Sale Caliente*, Tacna 381, has been described by one enthusiast as the best chicken place in Peru.

Entertainment

La Hostería restaurant often has live music in the evenings, particularly at weekends. Also try the *Samana* bar, which has a fireplace, and live music most weekends. Other places have live music intermittently, particularly in the high season.

Getting There & Away

Air The nearest airport is in Juliaca.

Bus The roads are poor, and delays are

common in the wet months, especially January to April. For Cuzco, try Cruz del Sur or Jacantaya, whose offices are next to one another. Between them, they have about four overnight buses to Cuzco (US$7, 12 hours). These and other companies also have services to other major cities, including Arequipa (US$8, 13 hours), Lima (US$19, 32 hours) and Tacna (US$8, 13 hours). Most long-distance buses travel overnight – day buses are hard to find (except, perhaps, to Arequipa).

Buses to the towns on the southern side of the lake and on the Bolivian border leave from the Avenida Ejército side of the Mercado Laykakota (market). You can take a public bus to the border and another from the border to La Paz for a total of about US$4 to US$5. Early morning departure usually gets you to La Paz in one day. Alternatively, a through service from Puno to La Paz, stopping and aiding passengers through all border formalities, is available for about US$10 from several agencies on Tacna – Colectur is one which has been recommended. For details, see below under To/From Bolivia.

Buses to Juliaca (US$0.50, 1½ hours) leave frequently from the corner of Lampa and El Sol.

Colectivo Comité 1 leaves frequently for Juliaca from in front of the railway station (about US$1 per person, 45 minutes). They may be hard to find on Fridays (when there is a border market) and, to a lesser extent, Tuesdays. Comité 3 (☎ 35-1621), Tacna 298, has taxi colectivos to Arequipa (about US$16, 10 hours) every morning at 10 am.

Train The first few km of the journey out of Puno are along the shores of Lake Titicaca, and the views are good. Trains used to leave daily, but engine problems have cut 1993 departures to two a week to Cuzco and two to Arequipa. Currently, the Cuzco train leaves at 7.25 am on Monday and Thursday and the Arequipa train leaves at 7.45 pm on Tuesday and Friday. Check for service

changes. Be alert for thieves at the railway station.

The 1st-class fare to Cuzco has varied from about US$2 to US$20 over the past decade. In 1993, fares were about US$12 to Cuzco, US$9 to Arequipa. The safer and more comfortable pullman coach (also called buffet or tourist class) is US$18, though it has been over US$30 in the past. (And people write to complain that prices in the book are out of date!) Be careful of the ticket you buy – there have been complaints of 1st-class tickets being sold for tourist-class prices, without the added safety and comfort of that class. Second class is 25% cheaper than 1st class but is not recommended, unless you are travelling without valuables and are adept at avoiding persistent and very skilful thieves.

You should buy your ticket the night before, but sometimes, especially for the Cuzco train, the numbered 1st-class and pullman seats get sold out. It is difficult to buy tickets earlier than the day before, and lines are always long. Check the tour agencies to see if they have any spare tickets – they often do, but at a 25% commission. (Commissions as high as 100% have been reported; it's a real racket.)

Boat The steamer service from Puno to Bolivia was discontinued in the mid-1980s. There is sporadic talk of restarting the service, but this might never happen. The available boat or hydrofoil services are very expensive (over US$100) compared to buses from Puno to La Paz.

Boats from the dock leave for various islands in the lake (see The Floating Islands section, below). Tickets bought directly from the boats at the dock are invariably far cheaper than those bought from agencies in town.

AROUND PUNO
Sillustani

The southern 'quarter' of the Inca Empire was called Collasuyo, after the Colla people who later became part of the Inca Empire. The noble Colla dead were buried in funerary towers called *chullpas*, which can be seen at Sillustani, a small hilltop site on the peninsula in Lake Umayo. The tallest chullpas are some 12 metres high and look very impressive against the bleak landscape.

Getting There & Away A daily Tranextur bus makes the 30-km run from Puno's Plaza de Armas. (You can buy tickets at various travel agencies in Puno.) The bus leaves at 2.30 pm and costs US$4 for the 3½-hour round trip, which allows about 1½ hours at the ruins. Admission to the ruins costs a further US$2, and there is a small on-site museum (US$0.20).

The Floating Islands

The excursion to the floating islands of the Uros people (also known as Urus) has become somewhat over-commercialised. Despite this, it remains popular because there is nothing quite like it anywhere else.

The Uros people have intermarried with Aymara-speaking Indians, and no pure-blooded Uros exist today. They were always a small tribe, and began their unusual floating existence centuries ago in an effort to isolate themselves from the Collas and the Incas. About 300 people live on the islands.

The Uros' lives are totally interwoven with the *totora* reed which grows abundantly in the shallows of Lake Titicaca. They harvest these reeds and use them to make everything from the islands themselves to little model boats to sell to tourists. The islands are constructed from many layers of reeds, which rot away from the bottom and are replaced at the top. The 'ground' is soft and springy, so step carefully.

The Uros build canoe-shaped boats from tightly bundled reeds. A well-constructed boat carries a whole family and lasts six months. You can pay the Uros to give you a ride on a boat. Begging and selling is common here, and be prepared to 'tip' for taking photographs. You can give food instead of money – the islanders particularly like fresh fruit.

Getting There & Away Boats leave the Puno

dock every hour from about 7 am until early afternoon. The standard trip (about four hours) visits the main island and perhaps one other. The boats leave as soon as there are 15 or 20 passengers and charge about US$3.50 each. Tour companies charge US$10 or more.

Isla Taquile

Taquile is a fascinating island. The people wear colourful traditional clothes, which they make themselves and sell in the island's cooperative store. They speak Quechua and have maintained a strong group identity. The island does not have roads or electricity; there are no vehicles and, more surprisingly, no dogs.

The island is about six or seven km long, and has several hills with pre-Inca terracing and small ruins. Visitors can wander around, exploring these ruins and enjoying the peaceful scenery.

Festivals St James' Day (25 July) is a big feast day on Taquile. Dancing, music and general carousing go on from mid-July till the beginning of August, when the Indians traditionally make offerings to Mother Earth, *Paccha Mama*. New Year's Day is also festive and rowdy.

Places to Stay & Eat From the dock, a steep stairway leads to the island centre. The climb takes 20 minutes or more – liable to induce acute mountain sickness in people who have just arrived from the coast. In the island centre, individuals or small groups are assigned to families who will put you up in their houses. These are rustic, but there are no hotels. The charge is under US$2 per person and gifts of fresh food are appreciated. You are given blankets, but bring a sleeping bag, as it gets very cold. Facilities are minimal. You do what the locals do – wash in cold water out of a bucket and use the fields as a latrine. Bring a flashlight.

A few simple restaurants in the island centre sell whatever is available: fresh lake trout if you're lucky – boiled potatoes if you're not. Bottled drinks are normally available but have been known to run out. Boiled tea is usually safe to drink, but it's worth bringing a water bottle and water purifying tablets. Also bring extra food, unless you're prepared to take pot luck on what's available in the restaurants. Bring small bills (change is limited) and extra money – many travellers are unable to resist the high quality of the unique woven and knitted clothes for sale.

Getting There & Away Boats for Taquile leave from the Puno dock daily, at about 8 or 9 am; show up by 7.30 am. The 24-km passage takes four hours (sometimes including a brief stop at the Floating Islands) and costs US$3.50. You get about two hours on Taquile, and the return trip leaves at 2.30 pm, arriving in Puno around nightfall. Bring sunscreen for this long trip.

Isla Amantaní

This island a few km north of Taquile is less visited and has fewer facilities. Basic food and accommodation are available for about US$3 per day, or you can eat in one of the few 'restaurants'. Boats leave from Puno's dock between 7.30 and 8.30 am on most days. The trip costs US$5.

You can make a round trip from Puno to the Floating Islands, Amantaní and Taquile. Most boats to Amantaní stop at the Floating Islands, and you overnight on Amantaní. There is a boat from Amantaní to Taquile on most days. Puno tour agencies offer two-day trips, staying overnight in Amantaní and also visiting the floating islands and Taquile, for about US$15 to US$20 (bargain for a low fare).

The South Shore Towns

An interesting bus excursion can be made to Chimú, Chucuito, Ilave, Juli, Pomata and Zepita, on the southern shores of the lake. If you start early enough, you can visit all of them in one day and be back in Puno for the night, or continue to Bolivia.

The road east of Puno follows the edge of the lake. After eight km, you reach the village of Chimú, which is famous for its totora-reed

industry. Bundles of reeds can be seen piled up to dry, and there are often several reed boats in various stages of construction.

Juli is 80 km from Puno and is famous for its four colonial churches, which are being slowly restored. San Juan Bautista is the oldest, dating from the late 1500s, and contains richly framed colonial paintings. This church is now a museum, but hours are erratic – it's best to try in the morning. Market day in Juli is Thursday. There are two hotels.

Pomata, 106 km from Puno, is dominated by the Dominican church, on top of a small hill. The church, which is being restored, has many baroque carvings, and windows made of translucent alabaster; hours are erratic. There is a cheap hotel in Pomata.

Just beyond Pomata, the road forks. The main road continues south-east through **Zepita** (where there is another colonial church) to the Bolivian border at Desaguadero, whilst a side road hugs the shore of Lake Titicaca and goes to the other border crossing, at Yunguyo.

Getting There & Away Buses to these places leave frequently from Puno's Mercado Laykakota, on the Avenida Ejército side. Minibus fares to the border are about US$3.50.

TO/FROM BOLIVIA

Bolivian time is one hour ahead of Peru. When crossing the border, watch your luggage carefully – border officials have been light-fingered in the past.

There are two routes to Bolivia: via Yunguyo and via Desaguadero. The Yunguyo route is more attractive and has the added interest of a boat crossing at the Strait of Tiquina. It is longer and a little more complicated than the Desaguadero route, so some travellers prefer to go via Desaguadero. Extensive flooding has, in the past, temporarily closed the Desaguadero route, so check on current conditions.

Via Yunguyo

Buses from Puno to Yunguyo leave from the

Mercado Laykakota (where there are a couple of hotels) take 2½ hours and cost about US$2 (watch for thieves). There are moneychangers in the plaza and by the border, which is about two km away. Count your money carefully. The border is open from 8 am to 6 pm. There are several huts to visit, so ask the officials where to go next. Bolivian immigration used to be 11 km beyond Yunguyo, in Copacabana, but has recently moved to the border (check this). Sunday is market day in Yunguyo, and there is more frequent transport on that day. Copacabana is a much more pleasant place than Yunguyo to break the journey. There are several hotels.

There are several buses a day from Copacabana to La Paz, Bolivia (about five hours, including a boat crossing of the Strait of Tiquina). If you leave Puno early, you can reach La Paz in one day. It is more convenient to buy a Puno-La Paz ticket with a company such as Colectur, for an extra few dollars. They will drive you to Yunguyo, stop at the money exchange, show you exactly where to go for exit and entrance formalities, and meet a Bolivian bus which will take you to La Paz. This through service costs about US$10.

Via Desaguadero

Buses from Puno's Mercado Laykakota leave every hour or two for Desaguadero (US$2, two hours). At Desaguadero, there are two basic hotels. The border is open from 8 am to noon and 2 to 5 pm daily. There are moneychangers at the border and a casa de cambio around the corner.

There are several buses a day from Desaguadero to La Paz, passing the ruins of Tiahuanaco.

Crossing the Border

Usually, there's little hassle entering Bolivia at either border crossing, and you can get 90-day permits without difficulty. Beware of immigration 'police' trying to charge a small 'entry tax' – this is not legal. You can either pay or brazen it out.

Cuzco

Cuzco, with a population of about 300,000, is the capital of its department. It was the hub of the Inca Empire and, today, is an important link in the South American travel network. Most of Cuzco's central streets are lined with Inca-built stone walls, which now form the foundations of colonial or modern buildings. The streets are often stepped and narrow, and thronged with Quechua-speaking descendants of the Incas. Cuzco is the archaeological capital of the Americas and the oldest continuously inhabited city on the continent.

History

When Columbus arrived in the Americas, Cuzco was the thriving capital of the Inca Empire. Legend says it was founded in the 12th century by the first Inca, Manco Capac, but the archaeological record shows that the area was occupied by other cultures for several centuries before the rise of the Incas.

Until the time of the ninth Inca, Pachacutec, the Incas dominated only a small area close to Cuzco. Around 1438, Pachacutec defeated the Chancas who were attempting to take over Cuzco, and during the next 25 years he conquered most of the central Peruvian Andes.

Pachacutec was a great urban developer. He devised the famous puma shape of Cuzco and diverted the Sapphi and Tullumayo rivers into channels which crossed the city, providing water and keeping the city clean. He built agricultural terraces and many buildings, including the famous Coricancha temple, and his palace on what is now the western corner of the Plaza de Armas.

By 1532 Atahualpa had defeated the forces of his half brother Huáscar in the Inca civil war. The conquistador Pizarro exploited this situation, marching into Cuzco after taking Atahualpa prisoner, and later having him killed. Pizarro was permitted into the heart of the empire by a people whose sympathy lay more with the defeated Huáscar

PERU

PERU

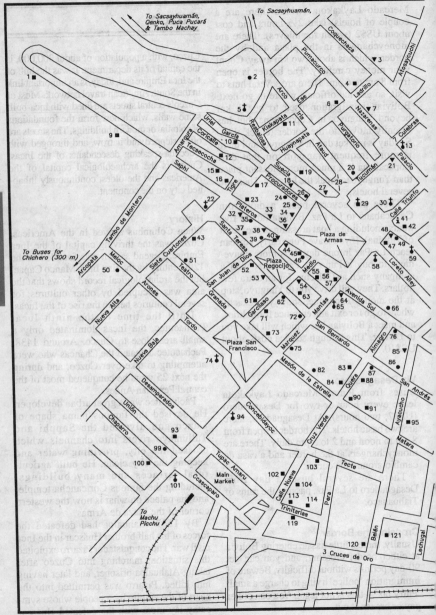

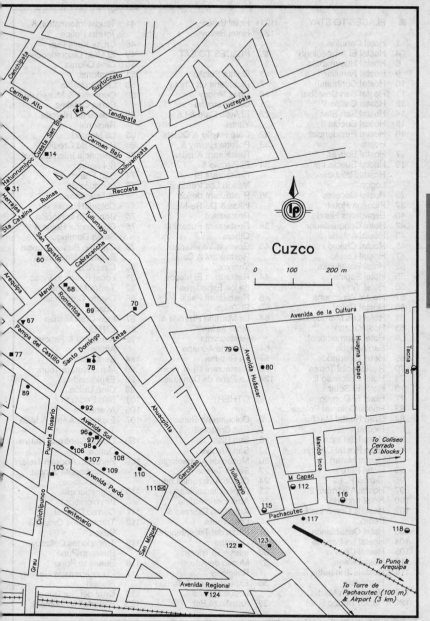

Cuzco

0   100   200 m

Avenida de la Cultura

To Coliseo
Cerrado
(5 blocks)

To Puno &
Arequipa

To Torre de
Pachacutec (100 m)
& Airport (3 km)

PERU

■ PLACES TO STAY

1   Hotel Cahuide
4   Hostal El Arqueólogo
6   Hostal Huaynapata
9   Hostal Familiar
10 Hostal Corihuasi
11 Hostal San Cristóbal
12 Hostal Carlos V
14 Hostal San Blas
15 Hostal Suecia II
16 Hostal Residencial
    Rojas
17 Hostal Bolívar
19 Hostal Suecia I &
    Hostal Rainbow
    Lodge
23 Hostal Cáceres
37 Picoaga Hotel
40 Espaderos Hotel
42 Hotel Conquistador
43 Hostal Antarki
45 Hostal Chaski
47 Hostal Loreto
52 Hotel Royal Inka
55 Hotel Espinar
56 Hotel Virrey
57 Hostal Wiracocha
60 Hostal Royal
61 Hotel Los Marquesas
63 Hotel Cuzco
68 Hotel Internacional
    San Agustín
69 Hotel Libertador
70 Residencial Torres
71 Hotel Garcilaso II
73 Hotel El Solar
77 Hotel El Dorado
83 Hostal Colonial Palace
84 Gran Hostal Machu
    Picchu
88 Hostal del Inca
90 Gran Hostal Chavín
91 Hostal Matari
93 Hotel Peru
95 Tambo Hotel
97 Hostal Alhambra 2
100 Hotel Imperio
102 Hostals Comercio & San
    Pedro
103 Hotel Casablanca
104 Hostal La Posada
105 Hostal Chavín
113 Hostal Milan
114 Hostals Trinitarias &
    Hispanola
119 Hostal San Martín
120 Hostal Tambo Real

121 Hotel Belén
122 Hotel Savoy

▼ PLACES TO EAT

3   Quinta Eulalia
7   Picantería La Chola
18 Chez Maggy
21 Café Samana
27 El Ayllu Café & La
    Yunta
32 Café Haylliy & Others
33 Pollería Haway &
    Restaurant Kusikuy
34 El Piccolo &
    Restaurant El
    Mesón Los Portales
36 Restaurant de los
    Inkas & Do-Re-Mi
    Restaurant
38 Restaurant Pucará &
    Others
40 Govinda Vegetarian
    Restaurant & Café
    Varayoc
44 Restaurant El Mesón
    de los Espaderos
48 Restaurant Paititi
53 El Truco
54 La Mamma Pizzería &
    other Italian
    Restaurants
64 Trattoria Adriano
67 La Retama
85 Restaurant Chef Victor
124 La Peña de Don Luis

OTHER

2   Colcampata Ruins
5   San Cristobal
8   San Blas
13 San Antonio
20 Museo de Arqueológia
22 Santa Teresa
24 Cuzco Amazonic Lodge
25 Expediciones Manu
26 Americana Airline,
    American Express &
    Lima Tours
28 Plaza del Tricentenario
29 Catedral
30 Iglesia El Triunfo
31 Museo de Arte
    Religioso
35 Explorers' Inn & Tambo
    Lodge Offices
39 Kamikaze Bar

41 Tourist Information &
    Tourist Police
46 Cross Keys Pub
49 El Muki Discotheque
50 Cine Ollanta
51 Customs
58 La Compañía
59 Convento & Museo de
    Santa Catalina
62 Museo de Historia
    Regional
65 La Merced
66 Banco de Crédito
72 Farmacia Internacional
    (24 hours)
74 San Francisco
75 Marqués de
    Valleumbroso
    Colonial House
76 Banco de la Nación
78 Coricancha Ruins &
    Santa Domingo
79 Ormeño Buses & Local
    Buses to Urubamba
80 Cine Azul
81 Local Buses to Pisac
82 Teatro Municipal
86 Centro Comercial
    Cuzco
87 Inca Craft Market
89 ENTEL
92 AeroPerú & Faucett
    Airlines
94 Santa Clara
96 Manu Nature Tours
98 Explorandes
99 Cine Unión
101 San Pedro
106 Aventours
107 Expresso Aéreo & Milla
    Turismo
108 Qosco Centre of Native
    Dance
109 Peruvian Andean Treks
    & Tambopata Jungle
    Lodge Office
110 Migraciones
    (Immigration)
111 Correo Central
112 Transportes Oropesa
    Buses
115 Transportes Collasuyo
    Buses to Puno
116 Buses to Puno
117 Puno/Arequipa Railway
    Station
118 Cruz del Sur Buses
123 Waterfall Monument

than with Atahualpa. After Atahualpa was killed, Manco Inca was appointed by Pizarro as a puppet ruler of the Inca. (For more details, see the History section in the Introductory Facts about South America chapter.)

Once Cuzco had been captured, looted and settled, its importance declined. In 1535, Pizarro founded his capital at Lima, on the coast. By the end of the 16th century, Cuzco was a quiet colonial town, with all the gold and silver gone and many of the Inca buildings pulled down to make room for churches and colonial houses. Despite this, enough of the Inca foundations is left to make a walk around the heart of Cuzco a veritable journey back through time.

Orientation

The heart of the city is the Plaza de Armas, with Avenida Sol being the main business street. Walking just two or three blocks north or east of the plaza will take you to streets little changed for centuries – many are for pedestrians only. A new pedestrian street between the Plaza del Tricentenario and Huaynapata gives great views over the Plaza de Armas. Recently, the city has had a resurgence of Quechua pride and the official names of many streets have changed from Spanish to Quechua spellings. Cuzco has become Qosco, Cuichipunco has become K'uychipunko, etc. All maps available from the tourist office retain the old spellings, however, and most people still use them.

Information

Tourist Office The tourist office (☎ 23-7364, 23-6062) is at Portal Belén 115 (eastern corner of the plaza). Hours are 8.30 am to 5.30 pm daily except Sunday. English is spoken and staff members are helpful, though their information on opening hours is not reliable.

Money Cash dollars are the easiest to exchange and give the highest rates. Travellers' cheques are accepted by a few casas de cambio (on the plaza or along Avenida Sol) or at the Banco de Crédito on Avenida Sol. Street moneychangers can be found outside the banks and casas de cambio, especially at the plaza end of Avenida Sol. Rates everywhere are fairly similar – street changing and casas de cambio are quicker than the queues in banks, but count money carefully before handing over your dollars on the street.

The American Express agent is Lima Tours, on the Plaza de Armas. They don't sell or exchange travellers' cheques, and will not refund lost or stolen travellers' cheques (these services are available only in Lima).

Post & Telecommunications The post office is open from 8 am to 7 pm Monday to Saturday. They will hold mail for three months if it is addressed to you c/o Lista de Correos, Correo Central, Cuzco, Peru.

ENTEL, on Avenida Sol, has international and national telephone and telex services. Hours are 7 am to 10.30 pm. Expect to wait up to an hour for international calls.

Visa Extensions Tourist cards are renewed at Migraciones, on Avenida Sol, next to the post office. It is open from 8.30 am to 4 pm Monday to Friday, and on Saturday mornings. An extension costs US$20.

Time Cuzco and Iquitos do not have daylight savings time, so from December to April, they are one hour behind the rest of Peru.

Bookstores Bookstores around the plaza sell English-language guide books. The best source of general information about Cuzco and the surrounding area is *Exploring Cuzco*, by Peter Frost. The best book about the conquest is John Hemming's *The Conquest of the Incas*.

Emergency The best clinic is at the Hospital Regional, on Avenida de la Cultura.

The office of the Policía de Turismo, over the tourist office on the plaza, is open 24 hours. Some English is spoken. If you have something stolen, they'll help you with the official police reports and will tell you how to place a radio announcement offering a reward for the return of your property, particularly if it has little commercial value (eg your journal, documents or exposed camera film).

Laundry Places on Suecia, Procuradores, Plateros and Espaderos (just off the Plaza de Armas) advertise that they wash, dry, and fold your clothes in half a day for US$1.25 per kg.

Dangers & Annoyances

More tourists are robbed in Cuzco than in any other Peruvian city. Avoid displays of wealth (expensive jewellery, wristwatches, wallets) and leave most of your money in a hotel safe (carry what you need in inside pockets and/or money belts). Avoid walking alone around town late at night – revellers returning from bars etc late at night have been mugged. Take special care going to and from the Machu Picchu railway station and the nearby market – these are prime areas for pickpockets and bag-slashers. Having said this, I have to point out that in scores of visits to Çuzco between 1982 and 1993, I have never been robbed on the street (though I had a camera taken from my hotel room once – I shouldn't have left it out in plain view).

Also, beware of altitude sickness if you're flying in from sea level.

Things to See

The Cuzco Visitor Ticket gets you into 14 sites in and around Cuzco, costs US$10 and is obtainable from any of the sites, but is valid for only five days. Buy it at the tourist office and ask them to validate it for 10 days. Students get a 50% discount.

The following places within Cuzco can be visited with the ticket: the Catedral, Santo Domingo and Coricancha, San Blas, Santa Catalina, the Museo de Historia Regional and the Museo de Arte Religioso. It is also valid for Sacsayhuamán, Qenko, Puca Pucara, Tambo Machay, Pisac, Chinchero, Ollantaytambo and Piquillacta, all of which are outside of Cuzco. Each site can be visited only once. Other museums, churches and colonial buildings in and around Cuzco can

be visited free, or by paying a modest admission fee. Opening hours change frequently.

For US$5, you can get partial tickets to visit some sites. One ticket will get you into the Catedral, the Museo de Arte Religioso and San Blas. Another will get you into Coricancha, Santa Catalina and the Museo Historico.

Two flags fly over the **Plaza de Armas**: the red-and-white Peruvian flag, and the rainbow flag of Tahuantinsuyo – the four quarters of the Inca Empire. The plaza is surrounded on all four sides by colonial arcades. On the north-eastern side is the Catedral. On the south-eastern side is the ornate church of La Compañía. Some Inca walls remain, notably those of the palace of Pachacutec, on the western corner. The pedestrian alleyway of Loreto is a quiet and pleasant way to enter or leave the plaza. Both sides of Loreto have Inca walls.

Churches Begun in 1559, the **Catedral** is one of the city's greatest repositories of colonial art. It has been combined with two other churches: to the left as you face the Catedral is the **Iglesia Jesus María**, dating from 1733, and to the right is the **Iglesia El Triunfo**, which is used as the tourist entrance to the whole three-church complex. El Triunfo is the oldest church in Cuzco and dates from 1536.

By the entrance, there's a vault containing the remains of the Inca historian Garcilaso de la Vega, born in Cuzco in 1539, the son of a Spanish conquistador and an Inca princess. As you enter the Catedral, turn right. In the corner is the sacristy, and at the back is a crucifixion attributed to the Flemish painter Van Dyck, though local guides claim that it is the work of the 17th-century Spaniard Alonso Cano. In the corner next to the sacristy is a huge painting of the Last Supper. This is a fine example of the work of the Cuzco school, showing Indian influence. The painting is by Marcos Zapata, and the supper consists of the Inca delicacy, cuy (roast guinea pig).

At the back of the Catedral is the original wooden altar, behind the silver altar. Opposite the silver altar is the magnificently carved choir, dating from the 17th century. There are many splendid side chapels. Some contain the elaborate silver trolleys used to cart religious statues around during processions. Others have intricate altars.

The Catedral is open to visitors from 3 to 6 pm. Admission is with the Cuzco Visitor Ticket; entry is through El Triunfo. The huge main doors are open for worship from 6 to 10 am (no tickets required).

The church of **La Compañía** is also on the plaza and is often lit up at night. It has an incredibly baroque facade and is one of Cuzco's most ornate churches. Its foundations contain stones from the palace of the Inca Huayna Capac. The interior has fine paintings and richly carved altars. Two large canvasses near the main door show early marriages in Cuzco and are noteworthy for their wealth of period detail. However, since the 1986 earthquake, the church has been closed. Repairs are continuing.

La Merced is considered Cuzco's third most important colonial church. It was destroyed in the 1650 earthquake and rebuilt – the present structure dates from 1654. The church is open for worship from 7 to 9 am and 5 to 7.30 pm. To the left of the church, at the back of a small courtyard, is the entrance to the monastery and a museum, which is open from 8.30 am to noon and 2 to 5 pm daily (except Sunday). Admission is US$0.90. The small religious museum contains vestments said to have belonged to the conquistador and friar Vicente de Valverde. The most famous exhibit is a priceless solid-gold monstrance, 1.3 metres high and covered with more than 1500 diamonds, 1600 pearls and hundreds of jewels.

The church and monastery of **San Francisco,** dating from the 16th and 17th centuries, are more austere than many of the other religious buildings in Cuzco, but nevertheless, the church has a large collection of colonial religious paintings and a well-carved, cedar-wood choir. One of the paintings measures nine by 12 metres and is supposedly the largest painting in South America. It shows the family tree of St Francis of Assisi, whose life is depicted in the paintings hung around the cloister. There are two crypts with human bones, some of which have been arranged to form phrases designed to remind the visitor of the transitory nature of life. Hours are from 9 am to noon and 3 to 5 pm daily, except Sunday. Admission is US$0.50.

The small church of **San Blas** is made of adobe. Its exquisitely carved pulpit has been called the finest example of colonial wood-carving in the Americas. Hours are 10 am to noon daily, except Sunday, and 3 to 6 pm daily. Admission is with the Cuzco Visitor Ticket.

The convent of **Santa Catalina** is a beautiful building which was closed for restoration during most of the 1980s. There is a colonial and religious art museum here. Hours are 9 am to noon and 3 to 6 pm daily, except Friday. Admission is with the Cuzco Visitor Ticket.

On the site of Coricancha (the major Inca temple in Cuzco) is the church of **Santo Domingo**, which has been twice destroyed – first by the earthquake of 1650 and later by the earthquake of 1950. At the entrance, there are photographs showing the extent of the 1950 damage. It is interesting to compare the colonial building with the Inca walls, which survived these earthquakes with minimal effects. Also in the entrance, one can see a carved doorway in Arab style. Inside the cloister are the Inca temple remains. Admission to both is with the Cuzco Visitor Ticket. Hours are 8 am to 5 pm Monday to Saturday.

Inca Ruins Coricancha is Quechua for 'Golden Courtyard'. In Inca times, Coricancha was covered with gold. The walls of the temples were lined with 700 solid-gold sheets weighing two kg apiece. There were life-size gold and silver replicas of corn, which were ritually 'planted' in agricultural ceremonies. All that remains is the stonework – the conquistadors took the rest.

The temple was used for religious rites. Mummified bodies of previous Incas were kept here and brought out into the sunlight every day. Food and drink were offered to them and then ritually burnt. Coricancha was also an observatory, where priests kept track of major celestial events.

The most famous part of Coricancha is a perfectly fitted, curved wall, which can be seen from outside the site. This six-metre-high wall has withstood the violent earthquakes which destroyed much of colonial Cuzco.

The courtyard within the site contains an octagonal font, which was once covered with 55 kg of solid gold. There are Inca temples to either side of the courtyard. The largest, to the right, are said to be temples to the moon and stars, and were perhaps covered with solid silver. The walls taper upwards, and the niches and doorways are fine examples of Inca trapezoidal stonework. Opposite these chambers are the smaller temples, dedicated to thunder and the rainbow.

Walking south-east and away from the plaza along the alley of Loreto, you have Inca walls on both sides. The right side belongs to Amarucancha (Courtyard of the Serpents). It was the site of the palace of Inca Huayna Capac. After the Spanish conquest, the church of La Compañía was built here, and behind the church there is now a school. On the other side of Loreto is the oldest Inca wall in Cuzco. It belonged to the Acllahuasi (House of the Chosen Women). After the conquest, the building became part of the closed convent of Santa Catalina.

Heading north-east and away from the plaza along Calle Triunfo is the street of Hatunrumiyoc, named after the great 12-sided stone which is on the right about halfway along the second city block; it can be recognised by the small knot of Indians selling souvenirs next to it. This excellently fitted stone belongs to a wall of the palace of the sixth ruler, Inca Roca.

Museums The architecture of the **Museo de Arqueológia**, at the corner of Tucumán and Ataud, a block north-east of the Plaza de Armas, has several features to look for: a massive stairway guarded by sculptures of mythical creatures; a corner window

column which looks like a statue of a bearded man, until you go outside, from where it appears to be a naked woman; and the plateresque facade. This building is known as the Palacio del Almirante after its first owner, Almirante Francisco Aldrete Maldonado, who built it on Inca foundations. The interior of the building has been restored in colonial style and is filled with metal and gold work, jewellery, pottery, textiles, mummies, wooden *queros* (Inca vases), etc. The ceilings are ornate and the views are good, but the collection is labelled only in Spanish and visitors complain that the labels are inadequate. Admission is US$1.25 and opening hours are 8 am to 7 pm Monday to Friday.

Also known as the Archbishop's Palace, the **Museo de Arte Religioso**, on Hatunrumiyoc, has a fine collection of religious art noted for the accuracy of period detail, particularly a series which shows Cuzco's Corpus Christi processions in the 17th century. The interior is also noteworthy for its colonial tilework. Admission is with the Cuzco Visitor Ticket and opening hours are 9.30 am to noon and 3 to 6 pm daily, except Sunday, when it is open only in the afternoon.

The **Museo de Historia Regional** is in the Casa Garcilaso de la Vega and contains period furniture and paintings arranged in chronologically. Admission is with the Cuzco Visitor Ticket and opening hours are 8.30 am to 6 pm Monday to Saturday.

Markets The best area to see local craftwork made and sold is the Plaza San Blas and the streets leading up to it from the Plaza de Armas. The main Cuzco market is a colourful affair in front of the San Pedro railway station – it's worth seeing, but don't bring much money or a camera, because the thieves are extremely persistent and professional. The craftwork here is not special. There are craft markets on the corner of Quera and San Bernardo, and every night under the arches around the Plaza de Armas and Regocijo.

Language Courses

The EXCEL language centre, on Marquez, by the Plaza San Francisco, has been recommended and is cheap.

Work

In the past, the EXCEL language school has hired English teachers for about US$1 per hour. There may be other places – ask around.

Festivals

Inti Raymi, the festival of the sun, is held on 24 June and is Cuzco's most important festival. It attracts tourists from all over the world, and the entire city seems to celebrate in the streets. The festival culminates in a re-enactment of the Inca winter solstice festival at Sacsayhuamán – reserved tourist tickets in the bleachers are about US$20 or sit for free with the locals on the stone ruins.

Held on the Monday before Easter, the procession of **El Señor de los Temblores** (the Lord of the Earthquakes) dates from the 1650 earthquake. The feast of **Corpus Christi** occurs in early June (usually the ninth Thursday after Easter), with fantastic religious processions, and celebrations in the Catedral.

Places to Stay

Accommodation can be tight from June to August, especially during the 10 days before the major annual festival of Inti Raymi (held on 24 June) and around the national Fiestas Patrias (28 July). Prices rise at these times. During the rest of the year, it is worth bargaining for better rates – many hotels are almost empty.

Most hotels in Cuzco will store excess luggage for a few days so that you can hike the Inca Trail or whatever. Lock and label your luggage and don't leave valuables. Ask for a receipt.

The cheapest place to stay is the unmarked *Hostal San Cristóbal* (☎ 22-3922), Kiskapata 242; knock to get in (not for people who like to go out late at night). This small, family-run place is up a steep hill with great city views. There are basic kitchen facilities,

a tepid shower and basic rooms (US$1.25 per person). The clean and secure *Hostal Royal Qosco* (☎ 22-6221), Tecsecocha 2, is popular with budget travellers. Basic rooms are US$1.80 per person and there is hot water in the mornings. The similarly priced *Espaderos Hotel*, just off the west corner of the Plaza de Armas, also has hot water at times. Another option for budget travellers is the *Santo Domingo Convent*, at Ahuacpinta 600, in the grounds of Colegio Martín de Porres. It's cheap, safe, friendly and has hot water, but there is a 10 pm curfew. You may need to provide a sleeping bag. Other basic cold-water hotels are the *Hostal Matari* (US$3 a double), the *Hostal Royal* (US$2.50/3.50 for singles/doubles) and the similarly priced *Residencial Torres* (☎ 22-6697).

The *Gran Hostal Machu Picchu* (☎ 23-1111), Quera 282, has OK rooms around a courtyard and sometimes has hot water. They charge US$2.50 per person. The *Hostal Cáceres* (☎ 22-8012), Plateros 368, has hot water at times and is popular, though the security is lax. Singles/doubles are US$2.50/4. The *Hostal Chaski* is on the Plaza de Armas and is similarly priced, as well as having rooms with private bath for an extra US$1. Some hot water is available. The popular *Hostal Suecia I* (☎ 23-3282), Suecia 332, is generally recommended by budget travellers, though one reader reports a theft from the hotel. There is hot water, and rooms are US$3/4.75. The *Hostal Rainbow Lodge*, next door, is also cheap. The *Gran Hostal Chavín* is similarly priced but not as good. Others in this price range which have been recommended for having clean rooms and hot water are the *Hostal Antarki*, Siete Cuartones 245, and the *Hostal Residencial Rojas*, Tigre 129 – but both were closed during the 1993 low season. They plan to reopen when tourism picks up. All these hotels are basic.

Hotels near the San Pedro railway station are cheap. Some are good value, but the area is not a very safe one, so it is for budget travellers who are used to the travel realities of Peru – you know who you are! The *Hotel*

PERU

Imperio (☎ 22-8981), on Chaparro, across from the San Pedro station, is clean, friendly and has hot water (US$4.75 a double). The similarly priced *Hostal Hispaniola* and the *Hostal Milán*, on the 200 block of Trinitarias, are also good. The *Hostal Trinitarias*, at Trinitarias 263, is a bit pricier but is still good value.

The *Hostal Huaynapata* (☎ 22-8034), Huaynapata 369, is clean, safe and friendly, and sometimes has hot water. Rooms are US$3.50/4.75, or US$6/7 with private bath. The *Hostal Familiar*, Saphi 661, charges US$4.75 for a double, US$6 for a double with bath. It has a pleasant courtyard and is clean and popular. Further up is the friendly *Hostal Cahuide*, at Saphi 845, where doubles with bath cost US$10 – OK, though nothing special. The *Hostal Suecia II*, on Tecsecocha near Tigre, is popular, friendly and often full. There is hot water, and a pleasant glassed-in courtyard for snacks and hanging out. Doubles with bath are US$6 or US$7; rooms sleeping four or five go for about US$2.50 per person. There are very few singles. The French-run *Hostal El Arqueólogo* (☎ 23-2569), Ladrillos 425, is secure and popular (US$5 per person, including breakfast). There is hot water but the rooms are nothing special. *Hostal El Solar*, on the Plaza San Francisco, has hot water some of the time (USS$4.75/7 for singles/doubles with bath).

For something more up-market, try the wonderful, rambling old colonial house *Hostal Las Marquesas* (☎ 23-2512), Garcilaso 252, which charges about US$8/13 but will often halve the price in the low season. The clean and friendly *Hostal Loreto* (☎ 22-6352), Loreto 115, just off the Plaza de Armas, has some rooms with Inca walls. Rates are US$10/12 with bath, towels and hot water. Rooms sleeping five go for US$20.

Places to Eat
Breakfast & Snacks A popular choice is the simple and reasonably priced *El Ayllu* café, next to the Catedral. They play classical music and have a good selection of juices, coffee, tea, yoghurt, cakes, sandwiches and other snacks. Next door, *La Yunta* also serves juices, cakes and coffee, as well as light meals. This place is currently very popular with travellers. Also popular, particularly for cheap breakfasts and lunches, is the *Café Haylliy*, on the first block of Plateros. The *Café Samana* (☎ 22-4092), on the Plaza Nazarenas, serves a good and inexpensive selection of yoghurts, pastries and snacks, and is recommended for breakfasts. The *Govinda* vegetarian restaurant and the *Café Varayoc*, both on Espaderos, are popular. The Govinda also serves vegetarian food throughout the day; it's very cheap but has slow service. Their home-made bread has been recommended as lasting for several days (take it on the Inca Trail).

Peruvian Food A few restaurants serve inexpensive typical Peruvian food, have outside patios and are open for lunch or afternoon snacks only. Most are closed on Monday. Cuy (roast guinea pig) is a delicacy dating from Inca times. Often, this has to be ordered a day in advance. Also try anticucho de corazón (a shish kebab of beef hearts), rocoto relleno (spicy bell peppers stuffed with ground beef and vegetables), adobo (a spicy pork stew), chicharrones (deep-fried meat chunks), choclo con queso (corn on the cob with cheese), tamales (boiled corn dumplings filled with cheese or meat and wrapped in a banana leaf), cancha (toasted corn) and various locros (hearty soups and stews). The meal is washed down with chicha – either a fruit drink or a fermented, mildly alcoholic corn beer.

Closest to the centre is the *Quinta Eulalia* (☎ 22-4951), which has a colourful courtyard, at Choquechaca 384 (no sign). Further afield is the *Quinta Zárate*, in a garden on Calle Tortera Paccha – not easy to find, so hire a taxi. *La Peña de Don Luis*, about 1.5 km south-west of the centre on Avenida Regional, is highly popular with Peruvians for lunch. The *Picantería La Chola* is supposedly the most 'typical' of Cuzco's restaurants and is most like a *chichería* (Andean chicha tavern) – unfortunately, it's very basic and grubby.

Other local restaurants are more likely to serve fish, chicken and meat, with perhaps a small selection of the more traditional dishes. Just off the plaza, along the first block of Calle Plateros, there are several good local restaurants. These include the *Café Haylliy* (for good snacks), *El Tronquito* and *Los Candiles* (good, cheap set meals), the *Pollería Haway* (for chicken), the *Kusikuy* (with the best selection of traditional dishes) and the *Pucará* (☎ 22-2027) which, with dishes in the US$3 to US$6 range, is the most expensive on this block but also has by far the best food – they are closed on Wednesday.

Procuradores, the alley leaving the Plaza de Armas on the north-western side, is nicknamed Gringo Alley. It has several cheap bars, pizzerías, restaurants and cafés. It's popular with backpackers and is a good place to meet people.

El Mesón de los Espaderos, with an attractively carved balcony overlooking the Plaza de Armas from the west, is a good, though not cheap, steakhouse. Enter from Espaderos. The *Do-Re-Mi Restaurant* (☎ 23-1194) is on the 3rd floor of the Portal de Panes 109 (north-west side of the plaza), with nice Plaza views. There's a dinner show each night, at 8 pm. Meals are around US$5 and up – good value, considering the entertainment. Across the plaza, at Portal Carrizos 270, the *Paititi* (☎ 22-6992) also has entertainment in the evening, and gives you the opportunity to dine next to genuine Inca walls, but it is more expensive than the Do-Re-Mi. Another good but pricey choice for dinner and show is *El Truco*, on the Plaza Regocijo. Cover charges (US$1 to US$2) are added for entertainment.

Italian Food *Chez Maggy* (☎ 23-4861), with two locations on Procuradores, and *Pizzería America*, on Plateros, are currently the favoured places for travellers looking to meet other people and eat good, reasonably priced pizza. Chez Maggy may have live music (a hat is passed for tips) in the evenings. *La Mamma Pizzería*, Plaza Regocijo, serves good and slightly pricier pizza. There are two other Italian/international restaurants next door to La Mamma. The best and priciest Italian place is the popular *Trattoria Adriano*, at Avenida Sol and Mantas.

Entertainment

The Do-Re-Mi, Paititi and El Truco restaurants have live entertainment with dinner every night. Several other restaurants have live music in the evenings – they have signs in their windows. Check prices and cover – these places are often cheaper than the three places mentioned above. Chez Maggy and 'budget' restaurants on Plateros and Procuradores have impromptu entertainment, which is cheaper still.

The Kamikaze, up the stairs on the north corner of the Plaza Regocijo, a block away from the Plaza de Armas, is a sixtyish dive with lively music and occasional live performers. There is a US$1.20 cover charge. This is one of the most popular travellers' hang-outs.

The Cross Keys Pub, 2nd floor at Portal Confituría 233 (south-west side of the Plaza de Armas), is a pub run by British ornithologist Barry Walker. He knows the area well and is a good contact for the Manu area. The place has darts and pool, and is popular. It's more expensive than most others, but there's a happy hour from 6 to 7 pm and 9 to 9.30 pm and it's a great place to meet people.

Also on the Plaza de Armas is the Piano Bar, which you enter through a guarded grille gate near the Café Pizzola. They are on the 3rd floor (good Plaza views) and play Western music, but may well be empty midweek. El Muki Discotheque, opposite the tourist office, is popular with Peruvian disco dancers.

Several places have evening folklore dance shows. Usually, there are some good dances in traditional costumes, but the music is often recorded and disappointing. Cover charges vary from US$3 to US$6 – shop around. The Teatro Inti Raymi, Saphi 605, and the Qosqo Centre of Native Dance, Avenida Sol 604, are two such places.

Getting There & Away

Air AeroPerú, Faucett and Americana all

PERU

have daily flights to Lima (US$60). Between them, AeroPerú and Americana have flights to Arequipa and Juliaca (US$35) most days and daily flights to Puerto Maldonado (US$41). Expresso Aéreo has two or three flights a week to Ayacucho (US$35), Andahuaylas (US$30), Lima (US$53) and Juliaca (US$31), and is planning a service to Nazca. AeroTumi has three flights a week to Andahuaylas (US$18), Lima (US$47) and Puerto Maldonado (US$26). Expresso Aéreo and AeroTumi do not use jets – the others do.

All flights leave in the morning because of weather conditions. Flights may be cancelled during the rainy season and passengers may be stranded for two or three days.

AeroPerú (☎ 23-3051) and Faucett (☎ 23-3151) sell tickets at their Cuzco offices, at Sol 567; Americana (☎ 23-1966, 24-0793) is on the Plaza de Armas, on the corner with Procuradores, and ExpressoAéreo is in the office of Milla Turismo (☎ 23-1710), Pardo 675. AeroTumi is at the airport only. The military airline, Grupo Ocho (☎ 22-1206), sells tickets at the airport for cheap flights to Lima and Puerto Maldonado, usually on Wednesday. These don't always go, cannot be booked in advance and are usually full. Grupo Ocho also flies via Puerto Maldonado to Iberia or Iñapari, for the Brazilian border.

Airport departure tax is about US$17 for international flights, US$7 for internal flights. It is essential to reconfirm flights 72 and 24 hours in advance, becaus of frequent overbooking. Delayed or lost luggage is not uncommon – pack essentials into your hand luggage.

Bus Several companies along Avenida Pachacutec, near the train station for Puno, have buses to the south of the country. One of the best is Cruz del Sur (☎ 22-1909) which has three buses daily to Sicuani (US$2) and two buses every evening to Juliaca (US$6.50, 11 hours) and Puno (US$7, 12 hours). They have a nightly service to Arequipa (US$13, 20 hours), on the rough road via Imata, continuing to Lima (US$23, 42 hours). There are also more expensive luxury buses (with heat, videos, snacks, toilets, etc) to Arequipa and Lima (US$31). Other companies on this street have marginally cheaper but equally good buses to Juliaca and Puno.

The route to Lima via Abancay (eight hours), Puquio and Nazca (33 hours) used to be the standard one but is now dangerous, because of Sendero activity, and is definitely not recommended. Buses along the inland Andean route to Ayacucho also suffer from terrorist attack, and you are advised against this trip.

Train There are two railway stations in Cuzco. The train for Puno leaves from the station near the end of Avenida Sol (☎ 23-3592, 22-1992) at 8 am on Tuesday and Thursday and takes 10 to 14 hours. Until 1992, the train left daily, except Sunday, so check to see if more frequent service has been reinstated.

Tickets for the Puno train are often sold out, so buy your ticket a day in advance. If you have problems getting a ticket, book through a travel agent (though you'll pay a commission).

Fares have fluctuated wildly over the past decade. Recent fares to Puno were US$12 in 1st class, US$18 in tourist (or pullman) class (though they have been twice that in the past and will undoubtedly change by the time you read this). Fares to Juliaca are a few cents less than those to Puno, and 2nd-class (not recommended) fares are 25% less than 1st class. This is a day train, and it's reasonably easy to look after your luggage and avoid being robbed in 1st class, particularly if you travel with friends.

Getting Around
Bus Cuzco has no central bus terminal. Buses to Pisac and Urubamba leave from the Ormeño office, on Avenida Huáscar, at frequent intervals all day long, with occasional buses going on to Ollantaytambo until early afternoon. (These buses are not run by the Ormeño company.) Pisac minibuses leave frequently from Avenida Tacna, 1½ km east of the centre. These buses change their

departure points every year or two, so check first. Fares are well under US$1. It takes 1½ hours to get to Urubamba, less to Pisac. The Pisac buses will drop you off at the Inca site of Tambo Machay so that you can walk from there back to Cuzco and visit the other nearby ruins en route (a recommended eight-km walk). To get to Ollantaytambo, you can also go to Urubamba and change buses there.

For Chinchero, there are frequent trucks and minibuses leaving from Avenida Arcopata on Sunday mornings, for the market; the fare is US$0.30. There have been instances of trucks arriving on Sunday mornings when groups of gringos are waiting, shepherding the travellers aboard with a few Peruvians, and then driving to a remote area and robbing the gringos! The tourist office recommends great care from this departure point, because of thieves. On weekdays, go early, as service is infrequent and erratic. Trucks for Limatambo, Mollepata and on to Abancay and other destinations leave from here most mornings. An alternative way of reaching Chinchero is on the Ollantaytamba to Cuzco (via Chinchero) buses, leaving several times a day.

From the Coliseo Cerrado, on Manco Capac, five blocks east of Tacna, there are frequent minibuses to Oropesa and Urcos, south-east of Cuzco. You take these buses to visit the ruins of Tipón, Piquillacta and Rumicolca.

Train The Machu Picchu train leaves from the San Pedro station (☎ 22-1291, 23-8722 for reservations, 23-1207 for fares and times), near the market. There are cheap, slow local trains and faster, more expensive tourist trains and *autovagones*.

Heading north-west from Cuzco, you'll find that all trains stop at the Ollantaytambo station. The halt at km 88 (for the Inca Trail) is served by only the local train. The station at Aguas Calientes (the nearest village to the ruins) is misleadingly called Machu Picchu station. The closest station to the Machu Picchu ruins is two km further west and is called Puentes Ruinas. The jungle-edge town of Quillabamba is at the end of the line.

Fares, departure times and other details change often, and you are advised to check with the tourist office or train station in Cuzco for the latest information. Although details change frequently, you can always expect at least one cheap local train and one more expensive tourist train to leave Cuzco early every morning. Currently, the local train leaves Cuzco daily at 6 and 6.15 am, taking about four hours to Machu Picchu and seven hours to Quillabamba. The fare to Machu Picchu is US$6.50 in special class, about US$3.50 in 1st class. There is often an afternoon departure. A faster autovagón used to leave daily at 1.30 pm, and took three hours to Aguas Calientes and 5½ hours to Quillabamba – check to see if it is running.

Most budget travellers take the local train, whilst most tourists on package tours take the much more expensive (but secure and more comfortable) tourist train. This leaves about 7 am and costs about US$65 for the round trip, including a bus from the Puente Ruinas station to the ruins, admission to Machu Picchu and lunch. (You can buy just the train portion, but after adding the cost of the bus, admission and lunch, you save very little.) Leaving in the morning, spending two or three hours at the ruins and returning in the afternoon gives a tiring day with inadequate time at the ruins. Nevertheless, this is the way that many people visit Machu Picchu. During the high season, there are two tourist trains, leaving Cuzco at 6.30 am and 10 am. A shuttle system with buses to or from Ollantaytambo operates during the high season. The trip takes about three hours each way.

Tours Standard tours include a half-day city tour, a half-day tour of the nearby ruins (Sacsayhuamán, Qenko, Puca Pucara and Tambo Machay), a half-day trip to the Sunday markets at Pisac or Chinchero, a full-day tour to the Sacred Valley (Pisac and Ollantaytambo and perhaps Chinchero) and a full-day tour to Machu Picchu. There are many tour companies, and most of them do a good job. The cheaper tours are crowded, multilingual affairs. All the places mentioned can be visited using public transport.

Many agencies run adventure trips. Rafting down the Urubamba for one or two days is popular (US$20 a day). The Inca Trail is also popular – you can hire porters, cooks and guides, or just rent equipment (about US$2 per item per day) and carry it yourself. There are several cheap agencies on Procuradores and around the Plaza de Armas. You can also go on mountaineering, horse-riding and jungle trips.

Around Cuzco

THE NEARBY RUINS
These are the four ruins closest to Cuzco: Sacsayhuamán, Qenko, Puca Pucara and Tambo Machay. Admission is with the Cuzco Visitor Ticket. The cheapest and most convenient way to visit them is to take a Cuzco-Pisac bus and get off at Tambo Machay, which is the ruin furthest from Cuzco (and, at 3700 metres, the highest). From here, walk the eight km back to Cuzco, visiting all four ruins along the way. Colourfully dressed locals and their llamas often hang around the sites, hoping to be photographed. A tip of about US$0.10 per photograph is expected. This is generally a safe, popular and rewarding walk, but it's advisable to go in a group and to return well before nightfall, to avoid potential robbery.

Tambo Machay
This small ruin about 300 metres from the main road is a beautifully wrought ceremonial stone bath, popularly called El Baño del Inca. Opposite it is a small signalling tower, from where Puca Pucara can be seen.

Puca Pucara
Near Tambo Machay, on the other side of the main road, is Puca Pucara, which looks red in some lights – the name means 'red fort'.

Qenko
The name of this small but fascinating ruin

means 'zigzag'. It is a large limestone rock covered with carvings, including zigzagging channels. These are thought to have been for the ceremonial usage of chicha. Tunnels are carved below the boulder, and there's a mysterious cave with altars carved into the rock. Qenko is on the left side of the road as you descend from Tambo Machay, four km before Cuzco.

Sacsayhuamán
This huge ruin is the most impressive in the immediate Cuzco area. The name means 'satisfied falcon'. It is reached from Cuzco by climbing the steep street of Resbalosa, turning right at the top and continuing until a hairpin bend in the road. Here, take the old Inca road linking Cuzco with Sacsayhuamán. It takes less than an hour from Cuzco. The ruin is open from dawn till dusk and the guards demand to see your Cuzco Visitor Ticket.

Sacsayhuamán is huge, but today's visitor sees only about 20% of the original structure. The Spaniards tore down many walls to use the blocks for building their own houses in Cuzco, but they left the largest and most impressive of the original rocks, one of which weighs more than 300 tonnes. Most of the rocks form the main battlements.

The Incas envisioned Cuzco as having the shape of a puma. Sacsayhuamán formed the head. The site is essentially three different areas, the most obvious being the three-tiered zigzag walls of the main fortifications. These 22 zigzags form the teeth of the puma. Opposite is the hill called Rodadero, with retaining walls, curiously polished rocks and a finely carved series of stone benches, known as the 'throne of the Incas'. In between the zigzag ramparts and Rodadero hill lies a large, flat parade ground, which today is used for the colourful tourist spectacle of Inti Raymi, held every 24 June.

The magnificent zigzag walls remain the major attraction of the site, even though much has been destroyed. Three towers once stood above these walls, but only the foundations remain. It is thought that the site had important religious as well as military significance.

The fort was the site of one of the most bitter battles of the conquest, between the Spanish and the rebellious Manco Inca. Manco lost narrowly, and retreated to Vilcabamba, but most of his forces were killed. The thousands of dead attracted swarms of carrion-eating Andean condors. This is the reason for the inclusion of eight condors in Cuzco's coat of arms.

Several robberies in Sacsayhuamán have been reported. Avoid going early in the morning or in the evening, and don't go alone.

PISAC

Pisac is 32 km from Cuzco by paved road and is the most convenient starting point for visits to the villages and ruins of the Valle Sagrado, as the Río Urubamba valley is locally called. Pisco consists of a colonial and modern village alongside the river, and an Inca site on a mountain spur 600 metres above the river. Colonial Pisac is a quiet Andean village which comes alive on Sunday mornings, when the famous weekly market takes place.

Things to See

Ruins The ruins above the village are reached by a 10-km paved road up the Chongo valley, or by a shorter but steep footpath from the plaza. There is little traffic along the road. The footpath to the ruins leaves town from the left-hand side of the church. Allow roughly 1½ hours for the climb, which is spectacular and worthwhile. Admission to the ruins is with the Cuzco Visitor Ticket (though US$2 will usually get you in).

Pisac is particularly known for the agricultural terracing around the south and east flanks of the mountain. This is still in use today. Above the terraces are some cliff-hanging footpaths, which are well defended by massive stone doorways, steep stairs and, at one point, a tunnel carved out of the rock. At the top of the terraces is the religious centre, with extremely well-built rooms and temples. Some new excavations are under way at the back (northern end) of the ruins; you can see a series of ceremonial baths being reconstructed. A cliff behind the site is honeycombed with hundreds of Inca tombs, which unfortunately were robbed before being examined by archaeologists. The site is large, and requires hours, or a whole day, for a good look.

Markets The weekly Sunday morning market attracts both tourists and traditionally dressed locals. Selling and bartering of produce goes on alongside the stalls full of weavings and sweaters for the gringos. The main square is thronged with people, and it becomes even more crowded after the Quechua mass, when the congregation leaves the church in a colourful procession led by the mayor holding his silver staff of office. There is a smaller market on Thursday and some kind of selling activity every day of the week.

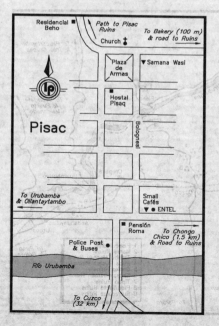

Pisac

PERU

Places to Stay & Eat

The basic and ill-kept *Pensión Roma*, by the bridge, is US$1.75 per person. The *Residencial Beho*, on the road to the ruins, is better, for US$3 per person. The *Hostal Pisaq*, on the square, used to charge US$4/6 for clean singles/doubles but was recently sold and closed – perhaps it will reopen. The *Chongo Chico* is being developed as a local 'spa' – ask for details. There are also a few families who rent rooms out.

There are several basic cafés. The best is the *Samana Wasi*, on the square; others are found by the bridge.

Getting There & Away

Frequent minibuses leave from Cuzco. To return to Cuzco or continue down the Urubamba valley, wait for a bus by the bridge at the town entrance. Note that buses to Cuzco start in Urubamba and are often full or have standing room only – prime territory for pickpockets.

URUBAMBA

Urubamba is 40 km beyond Pisac, at the junction of the valley road and the Chinchero road. The village of Tarabamba is about six km further down the valley. Here, cross the river by footbridge and continue on a footpath, climbing roughly southwards up a valley for a further three km to the salt pans of Salinas, which have been exploited since Inca times – a fascinating sight. Admission is US$0.25.

Places to Stay & Eat

The *Hotel Urubamba*, a couple of blocks from the central plaza (about 10 minutes from the main road), is friendly and charges about US$2 per person. There are simple restaurants on the plaza, and along the road leading from the gas station on the main valley road into the town centre.

The *Quinta Los Geranios* restaurant, on the main valley road, near the gas station, is good for local lunches.

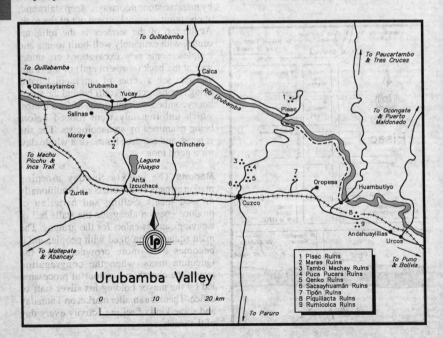

Urubamba Valley

0   10   20 km

1 Pisac Ruins
2 Maras Ruins
3 Tambo Machay Ruins
4 Puca Pucara Ruins
5 Qenko Ruins
6 Sacsayhuamán Ruins
7 Tipón Ruins
8 Piquillacta Ruins
9 Rumicolca Ruins

Getting There & Away

Minibuses leave Cuzco several times a day from the bus stop on Avenida Tacna. Buses back to Cuzco or on to Ollantaytambo stop at the gas station on the main road.

OLLANTAYTAMBO

This is the end of the road – travellers continue by rail or on foot, though there are a few drivable dirt tracks into the countryside. Ollantaytambo is a major Inca site and admission is with the Cuzco Visitor Ticket (though US$2 will usually get you in). The site is a massive fortress and is one of the few places where the Spaniards lost a major battle during the conquest. Below the ruins is the village of Ollantaytambo, built on traditional Inca foundations; it is the best surviving example of Inca city planning.

The Incas considered Ollantaytambo a temple rather than a fortress, but the Spanish, after their defeat, called it a fortress, and it

has been referred to as such ever since. The temple area is at the top of the terracing. The stone used for these buildings was quarried from the mountainside six km away and high above the opposite bank of the Río Urubamba – transporting the blocks from the quarry to the site was a stupendous feat, involving the labour of thousands of Indians.

Places to Stay & Eat

Basic cold-water places for about US$1.25 per person include the *Hostal Miranda*, the *Hostal Ima Sumac*, next door, and a couple of triple rooms upstairs in the *Café Alcázar*, which is also a reasonable place to eat. The *Hostal Tambo*, run by Raul and Abar, charges US$1.60 per person and is OK. The *Parador Turístico* has been recommended but was closed in 1993 – it may reopen. *El Albergue* (☎ 22-6671 in Cuzco) charges US$5 to US$7 per person, is very tranquil, has a sauna (US$2) and garden, and provides meals on

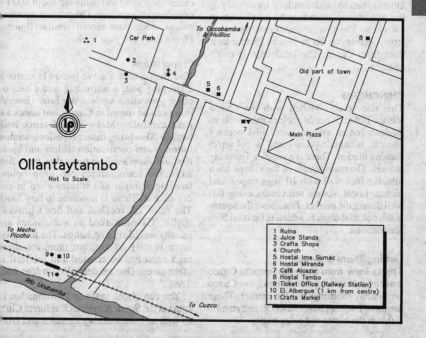

Ollantaytambo
Not to Scale

To Occobamba & Huilloc

Car Park

Old part of town

Main Plaza

To Machu Picchu

Río Urubamba

To Cuzco

1 Ruins
2 Juice Stands
3 Crafts Shops
4 Church
5 Hostal Ima Sumac
6 Hostal Miranda
7 Café Alcazar
8 Hostal Tambo
9 Ticket Office (Railway Station)
10 El Albergue (1 km from centre)
11 Crafts Market

PERU

request. The owner is very knowledgeable about the area.

There are several cheap and simple restaurants around the plaza, including the *Bahía, Ollantay* and *Ñusta.* Meals are about US$1.20.

Getting There & Away

You can get to Ollantaytambo from Cuzco by bus or train, but you must continue on the train if you wish to go to Machu Picchu.

Bus Minibuses leave from Urubamba's gas station several times a day, but services peter out in mid-afternoon. Buses from Cuzco are infrequent, and many people change in Urubamba. Buses return to Cuzco from the plaza – several go via Chinchero.

Train All trains stop here, 1½ to two hours after leaving Cuzco. The local train is overcrowded by the time it reaches Ollantaytambo, and standing room only is the rule, though there may be a few seats in 1st class. The tourist train costs the same from Ollantaytambo to Machu Picchu as it does from Cuzco. The local train is much cheaper.

CHINCHERO

This site is also visited with the Cuzco Visitor Ticket. It combines Inca ruins with an Andean Indian village, a colonial country church, mountain views and a colourful Sunday market. There is a smaller Thursday market. The main square of the village has a massive Inca wall with 10 huge trapezoidal niches. Local women sell chicha along this wall during the market. Just above the square is the colonial church, which is built on Inca foundations.

Getting There & Away

Trucks leave from Calle Arcopata in Cuzco early every morning. Minibuses leave Cuzco on Sunday mornings for the market. There are more frequent buses from Ollantaytambo – this is the better and safer route.

THE INCA TRAIL

This is the best-known and most popular hike on the continent and is walked by thousands of people every year – it is not the place to go for solitude. The views of snowcapped mountains and high cloud forest can be stupendous, weather permitting. Walking from one beautiful ruin to the next is a mystical and unforgettable experience. Enjoy the hike, but please don't spoil it for the people coming after you.

Conservation

If you decide that the Inca Trail is not to be missed, please don't defecate in the ruins, don't leave garbage anywhere, don't damage the stonework by building fires against the walls (it blackens and, worse still, cracks the rocks), use a stove for cooking (the trail has been badly deforested over the past decade) and don't pick the orchids and other plants in this national park. The South American Explorers Club organised an Inca Trail clean-up in 1980 and collected about 400 kg of unburnable garbage. Other clean-up campaigns since then record similar figures. Please carry out your trash.

Preparations

You should take a stove (wood is scarce), a sleeping pad, a warm bag and a tent or other protection against the rain. (Everything can be rented in Cuzco, but check all gear carefully. Many rented tents leak badly.) Also bring insect repellent, suntan lotion, water purification tablets and basic first-aid supplies. The trek takes three full days, the temperatures can drop below freezing at night and it rains even in the dry season. There is nowhere to buy food. The ruins are roofless and don't provide shelter. Caves marked on some maps are usually wet, dirty overhangs. The total distance is only 33 km, but there are three high passes to be crossed and the trail is often steep. One reader called it 'the Inca Trial'.

You can obtain maps and information in Lima at the South American Explorers Club as well as from trekking agencies and from

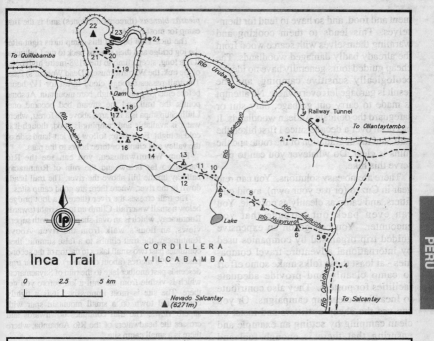

Inca Trail

0   2.5   5 km

CORDILLERA
VILCABAMBA

Nevado Salcantay
▲ (6271m)

1	Km 88	13	Camp Site
2	Q'ente Ruin	14	Inca Tunnel
3	Llactapata Ruin	15	Third Pass (about 3700 metres)
4	Paucarcancha	16	Phuyupatamarca Ruins
5	Huayllabamba Village	17	Youth Hostel
6	Three White Stones Camp Site	18	Huiñay Huayna Ruins
7	Llulluchupampa	19	Intipunku Ruins
8	Warmiwañusca Pass (4198 metres)	20	Machu Picchu Hotel
9	Camp Sites	21	Machu Picchu Ruins
10	Runturacay Ruin	22	Huayna Picchu
11	Second Pass (3998 metres)	23	Puentes Ruinas Train Station
12	Sayacmarca Ruin	24	Aguas Calientes

the tourist office in Cuzco. The map in this book is perfectly adequate. There have been reports of robberies on the trail, and you are advised to travel in a group. The dry season from June to September is the most popular time. The trail is fairly empty during the rest of the year, but is wet – the mud can be 30 cm deep. Nevertheless, the hike is possible all year round.

Tours

Guided tours are available from outfitters in Cuzco for about US$55 and up per person. This includes the local train to the beginning of the trail at km 88, a tent, food, a porter, a cook and entrance to the ruins. Whilst this may seem like a good deal, consider the following. The low costs mean that the porters are not provided with camping equipment and food, and so have to fend for themselves. This leads to them cooking and warming themselves with scarce wood from the already badly damaged woodlands. The cheap guided tours generally have no idea of ecologically sensitive camping, and the result is garbage left everywhere. No attempt is made to carry out garbage, bury shit or safeguard the delicate Andean woodlands. It has been over a decade since I first hiked the trail, and the degradation of the route and the ruins is clear. Do whatever you can to preserve this hike.

There are no easy solutions. You can rent gear in Cuzco (or use your own), avoid outfitters, and camp as cleanly as possible. You can even pack out garbage that you encounter. You can go on an expensive guided trip organised by companies used by international adventure travel companies - at least these folks make some effort to camp cleanly and provide adequate facilities for porters. They also contribute to Inca Trail clean-up campaigns. Or you can use the cheap outfitters and insist on clean camping by setting an example and ensuring that there is enough fuel and tentage for the porters.

The Hike

After crossing the Río Urubamba at km 88, turn left and begin the Inca Trail as it climbs gently through a eucalyptus grove for one km. You will pass the minor ruin of Llactapata to your right; cross the Río Cusichaca on a footbridge and head south along the eastern bank of the river. It's seven km along the river to Huayllabamba, climbing gently all the way and recrossing the river after four km.

Huayllabamba is a village a few minutes above the fork of the Llullucha and Cusichaca rivers, at an elevation of 2750 metres. The Llullucha is crossed by a log bridge. You can camp in the plaza in front of the school, but beware of thieves slitting your tent at night. (You can continue south along the Cusichaca to the ruins of Paucarcancha, three km away, if you want to get away from the crowds. Camping is possible at the ruins, but carry water up from the river.)

The Inca Trail climbs steeply along the southern bank of the Río Llullucha. After half an hour, the river forks. Continue up the left fork for 500 metres and then cross the river on a log bridge. There are camp sites on both sides of the bridge. The area is called *tres piedras blancas* (three white stones) and is the first camp for most people.

The Inca Trail beyond this camp turns right after the log bridge and then sweeps back to the Llullucha. It is a long, steep climb to the 4198-metre high point of the trek, the Warmiwañusca (Dead Woman's) Pass. The trail passes through cloud forest for 1½ hours before emerging on the high, bare mountain. At some points, the trail and the stream bed become one. Llulluchupampa is a flat area above the forest, where water is available and camping is good, though it is cold at night. From here, follow the left-hand side of the valley and climb for three hours to the pass.

From Warmiwañusca, you can see the Río Pacamayo far below and the ruin of Runturacay halfway up the hill above the river. The trail heads down to the river, where there are good camp sites.

The trail crosses the river (there is a foot bridge) below a small waterfall. Climb up to the right towards Runturacay, which is an oval-shaped ruin with superb views, an hour's walk from the river. Above Runturacay, the trail climbs to a false summit, then continues past two small lakes to the top of the second pass at 3998 metres (about one hour). The clear trail descends past another lake to the ruin of Sayacmarca, which is visible from the trail a km before you get there. The site is most impressive: it is a tightly constructed town on a small mountain spur with superb views. The trail continues downwards and crosses the headwaters of the Río Aobamba, where there is a small camp site.

The gentle climb to the third pass then begins. There is a causeway across a dried-out swampy lake and later on, a tunnel, both Inca constructions. The trail goes through beautiful cloud forest, but the high point of the pass, at almost 3700 metres, isn't very obvious. There are great views of the Urubamba Valley, and soon you reach the beautiful ruin of Phuyupatamarca, at 3650 metres, three hours beyond Sayacmarca.

Phuyupatamarca has been well restored and contains a beautiful series of ceremonial baths, which have water running through them. A ridge above the ruin offers camp sites with spectacular views. There are guard posts here sometimes.

From Phuyupatamarca, there is a newly opened section of the Inca Trail, shorter than the old route which traverses the mountain. The new section is a dizzying drop into the cloud forest below, down hundreds of Inca steps. This route is the more interesting but is not marked on some maps. It rejoins the old trail near the electric power pylons which go down the hill to the dam on the Río Urubamba. Follow the pylons down to a white building – a youth hostel (US$3 per bed, less if you sleep on the floor). There are hot showers (US$0.50), and meals and bottled drinks are available. Camping is possible nearby. A 500- metre trail behind the hostel leads to the beautiful Inca site of Huiñay Huayna, which cannot be seen from the hostel.

Huiñay Huayna is a small but exquisite place – don't miss it. Climb down to the lowest part of the town, where it tapers off into a tiny exposed ledge overlooking the Río Urubamba far below. This ruin is a three-hour descent from Phuyupatamarca. The very difficult climb down to the Río Urubamba is prohibited.

From Huiñay Huayna, the trail continues through the cliff-hanging cloud forest, and is very thin in places, so watch your step. It takes 2½ hours to reach the penultimate site on the trail, Intipunku (Sun Gate). You can see Machu Picchu from here. There is room for a couple of tents, but no water. This is the last place to camp on the Inca Trail.

From Intipunku to Machu Picchu is a half-hour descent. Backpacks aren't allowed into the ruins; on arrival, you check your pack at the lower entrance gate and have your trail permit stamped. The permit is valid only for the day it is stamped, so arrive in the morning.

Getting There & Away

Take the local train from Cuzco to km 88. Watch your pack like a hawk. The station at km 88 is very small and badly marked. Cross the river by footbridge and buy a trail permit (or show one obtained from the Ministerio de Cultura in Cuzco). It's easier to buy it at the trail head (but check with the Cuzco tourist office for the latest news on the ever-changing regulations). The fee is about US$14, including admission to Machu Picchu. Doing the hike in reverse is not officially permitted.

MACHU PICCHU

This is the best-known and most spectacular archaeological site on the continent. From June to September, hundreds of people come daily to visit the 'Lost City of the Incas'. Despite this great tourist influx, the site manages to retain its air of grandeur and mystery, and is a must for all visitors to Peru.

Archaeology

Apart from a few locals, nobody knew of Machu Picchu's existence until the American historian Hiram Bingham stumbled upon it almost by accident, on 24 July 1911. The buildings were thickly overgrown with vegetation, and his team had to be content with roughly mapping the site. Bingham returned in 1912 and 1915 to clear the thick forest from the ruins. Further studies and clearing were carried out by Peruvian archaeologist Luis E Valcárcel in 1934 and by a Peruvian-American expedition under Paul Fejos in 1940-41. Despite these and more recent studies, our knowledge of Machu Picchu remains sketchy. One thing is obvious: the quality of the stonework and the abundance of ornamental sites indicate that Machu Picchu must have been an important ceremonial centre.

The Ruins

The ruins themselves are divided by the central plaza. It is to the left (with the entrance behind you) that the most significant buildings lie. A long staircase leads up to the Hut of the Caretaker of the Funerary Rock, from where some of the best views are to be had. Further on, a small hill is topped by the Intihuatana, which is the major shrine of Machu Picchu. The carved rock at the summit is called a sun dial, but it was used by the high priests to tell the seasons rather than the time of day. This is the only such Intihuatana that has survived – others were destroyed by the Spaniards.

You aren't allowed to bring large packs or food into the ruins – packs are checked at the gate. The guards check the ruins at closing time, so it's hard to spend the night.

Machu Picchu is open from 7.30 am to 5 pm. Foreigners pay US$10 per day – no student discount. If you bring your first-day ticket, an extension for the second day can be obtained for US$7, but you have to insist on the discount. It is difficult to enter other than through the gate.

You can buy a *boleto nocturno* (US$7) to enter the ruins at night. This is popular around full moon. Buy the night ticket from the entrance booth during the day.

Short Hikes

Behind the ruins is the steep-sided mountain of Huayna Picchu; it takes an hour to climb and offers great views. The entrance to the trail is to the right, at the back of the ruins, and is closed at 1 pm. From the base of Huayna Picchu, a steeply descending trail has recently been cleared to the Temple of the Moon – this trail is poorly maintained, and you do it at your own risk. It takes almost an hour and the return trip is twice as long.

Other short hikes in the area include walking back to Intipunku along the Inca Trail, or walking an interesting trail from the Hut of the Caretaker of the Funerary Rock to the Inca Bridge (Puente), which takes 20 minutes from the hut and give good views of cloud forest vegetation; this trail closes at 1 pm.

Places to Stay & Eat
The only place to stay at the ruins themselves is the *Hotel de Turistas*, which charges about US$45/55/65 for singles/doubles/triples. There is an expensive cafeteria and snack bar. Bringing your own food in is prohibited. The nearest cheap place to stay is in Aguas Calientes (see below).

Getting There & Away
Machu Picchu is 700 metres above the Puentes Ruinas train station. Buses take visitors up the six-km zigzag road to the ruins. Tickets cost US$4 each way and are sold at the railway station. Buses are frequent when the tourist train arrives, but there may be an hour or more to wait at other times. Usually, there is a bus for the arrival of the local train. Otherwise, you can walk. Rather than walking up the road, hike up the shorter and steeper footpath. Cross the bridge behind the station and turn right. Arrows mark the path, which crosses the road at several points on the ascent. Drivers don't stop for passengers at intermediate points unless there are seats, which is unusual. The climb takes 1½ hours from the station, but the descent takes only 40 minutes.

Tourist and local trains leave in the afternoon for the return trip. Departure times vary depending on the season, but the tourist train normally goes first. Buses start descending from the ruins two hours before departure time, and bus lines can get very long during the busy season.

Budget Travellers Visiting Machu Picchu cheaply is possible, once you have budgeted for the US$10 admission fee to the ruins.

The cheapest way to go is via the local train (1st class recommended) to Aguas Calientes. Spend the night there, a full day at Machu Picchu ruins and another night at Aguas Calientes, then return via the local train. This avoids the tourist train completely and maximises your time at the ruins. The ruins are most heavily visited from about 11 am to 2.30 pm, especially on Friday, Saturday and Monday from June to August.

The ruins deserve a full day – hike Huayna Picchu or Intipunku or beyond. Going back for a second day is also worth the money. Aguas Calientes is not a bad spot to hang out in.

AGUAS CALIENTES
This is the closest village to Machu Picchu. There are basic hotels and restaurants, and hot springs. To bathe, follow the path leading north-east from the plaza (10 minutes). The hot springs are open from 5 am to 8 pm and admission is US$1 – relaxing.

Places to Stay & Eat
Near the railway tracks is the cheap *Hostal Los Caminantes*, a rambling, dark and rather dirty building. They charge US$1.40 per person in three, four and five-bed rooms, or US$1.80 per person in rooms with private showers – cold water only. The *Hostal Qoñi* (better known as *Gringo Bill's*) is a better choice, at US$2 per person in a dormitory-style room, a little more in private rooms – there is hot water. They serve breakfast from 5.30 am, and provide storage facilities and information. The recently opened *Hostal Ima Sumac* charges US$1.80 per person. The *Hostal Machu Picchu*, right by the train tracks, with views of the Río Urubamba, is clean and charges US$2.40 per person. They have hot water. The government-run *Albergue Turístico Machu Picchu* charges US$3.50 per person – hot water is often available and meals are served (breakfast is US$1.20, lunch and dinner are US$3.40).

Most of the restaurants are clustered along

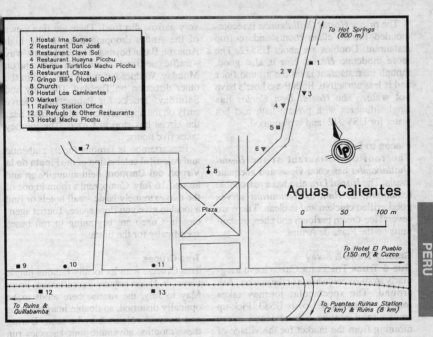

1 Hostal Ima Sumac
2 Restaurant Don José
3 Restaurant Clave Sol
4 Restaurant Huayna Picchu
5 Albergue Turístico Machu Picchu
6 Restaurant Choza
7 Gringo Bill's (Hostal Qoñi)
8 Church
9 Hostal Los Caminantes
10 Market
11 Railway Station Office
12 El Refugio & Other Restaurants
13 Hostal Machu Picchu

Aguas Calientes

0   50   100 m

To Hot Springs (800 m)

To Hotel El Pueblo (150 m) & Cuzco

To Ruins & Quillabamba

To Puentes Ruinas Station (2 km) & Ruins (8 km)

Plaza

PERU

the railway tracks, and some have been criticised for undercooked food or unhygienic conditions. Some reasonably clean ones are *El Refugio*, *Aiko* and *Samana Wasi* – good meals are US$2 to US$3. Pizzas start at US$4.50. There are also a few restaurants up the hill towards the hot springs; the *Huayna Picchu* has been recommended, but there are others.

Getting There & Away
Aguas Calientes is two km before the Puentes Ruinas station (for Machu Picchu). A road has recently been built, and buses go to Machu Picchu (US$4). Alternatively, walk two km to Puentes Ruinas and take more frequent buses from there, or walk the entire eight uphill km to the ruins.

QUILLABAMBA
Quillabamba is on the Río Urubamba, at the end of the train line from Cuzco and Machu Picchu. The only jungle town in Peru acces-

sible by railway, it is quiet and pleasant, if not particularly interesting, and can be used as a base for trips further into the jungle.

Places to Stay
The cheapest hotel is the *Hotel Borranecha*, on Espinar, three blocks north of the Plaza de Armas. Other cheap and basic hotels at under US$2 per person include the basic *Hostal Progreso* (no singles), *Hostal San Antonio* (dormitory accommodation), *Hostal San Martín* (dirty), *Hostal Thomas*, *Hostal Urusayhua* and *Alojamiento Dos de Mayo*.

The *Hostal Convención* charges US$3/5 for singles/doubles. It has a courtyard, and some basic rooms overlooking the plaza. The *Hostal Comercio*, on Libertad, is also OK.

A recommended clean and cheap hotel is the *Hostal Alto Urubamba*, which charges US$3/5, a little more with private bath. The *Hostal Cuzco* is also clean and pleasant, but has an erratic water supply.

The pricey *Hostal Quillabamba* is recommended for its clean rooms and rooftop restaurant. Doubles are about US$12. The more moderate *Hostal Lira* is also good, though its restaurant is on the ground floor and is less attractive. Both these hotels have hot water. The *Hostal Don Carlos* has singles/doubles with private bath and hot water for US$8/12, and is also good.

Places to Eat

The rooftop restaurant at the *Hostal Quillabamba* has good views and adequate meals. The *Hostal Lira* also has a reasonable restaurant. *El Rancho Restaurant* serves good grilled chicken and is clean. There are several ice-cream parlours and cheap restaurants on the Plaza de Armas.

Getting There & Away

Bus & Truck Trucks for Cuzco leave irregularly from Avenida Lima or the market. Ask around. The spectacular journey takes roughly 15 hours and costs US$3. Pick-up trucks (and maybe a bus) leave every morning from the market for the village of Kiteni (US$3, seven hours), further into the jungle. Kiteni has one cheap hotel.

Train For information on getting to Quillabamba, see Getting There & Away in the Cuzco section. Tickets for the return trip can be bought one day in advance. There are two (sometimes three) trains a day to Cuzco, via Aguas Calientes.

FROM CUZCO TO THE JUNGLE

Two poor roads, in addition to the Quillabamba railway, leave Cuzco for the jungle. One road heads to Paucartambo, Tres Cruces, Shintuyo and towards the Manu National Park, whilst the other goes through Ocongate and Quince Mil to Puerto Maldonado. Travel on these in the dry months (June to September), as they are muddy and slow in the wet months, especially from January to April.

Paucartambo

This village is 115 km east of Cuzco on a very narrow dirt road. There are fine views of the Andes dropping away to the high Amazon Basin beyond. The road is one-way – traffic goes from Cuzco to Paucartambo on Monday, Wednesday and Friday, and in the other direction on Tuesday, Thursday and Saturday. Trucks for Paucartambo leave early on the appropriate mornings from near the Urcos bus stop in Cuzco. The journey takes five hours.

Paucartambo is famous for its authentic and colourful celebration of the **Fiesta de la Virgen del Carmen**, held annually on and around 16 July. Camp, rent a room in one of the two extremely basic small hotels or find a local to give you floor space. Tourist agencies in Cuzco are beginning to run buses specifically for the fiesta.

Tres Cruces

Tres Cruces, with its locally famous jungle views, is 45 km beyond Paucartambo. From May to July, the sunrise here tends to be optically distorted, so double images, halos and unusual colours may be seen. During these months, adventure tour agencies run sunrise-watching trips to Tres Cruces.

Shintuyo & Parque Nacional Manu

Shintuyo is the end of the road, reached by truck from Cuzco (US$15, about 1½ days). From here, hire a boat and boatman for the voyage down the Río Madre de Dios to Manu (about US$100 to US$120 per day, plus gas and food) – a minimum of a week is recommended. It is also recommended that you hire a guide with training in ecology and biology; otherwise, your trip will be a meaningless cruise through the rainforest. A good guide is US$30 to US$50 per day, plus food. You should bring everything you need from Cuzco. Obviously, this is not a budget trip, but if you get a group together, it's not too expensive.

Further information can be obtained from the South American Explorers Club in Lima or from Expediciones Manu (☎ 22-6671, 23-9974), Procuradores 50 (PO Box 606, Cuzco). The latter have fixed guided departures to Manu leaving every month from

May to December. Nine days costs US$750, with a minimum of seven passengers – smaller groups can band together to make up the numbers.

To Puerto Maldonado
The trip to Puerto Maldonado is a spectacular but difficult journey on poor roads, taking three days in the dry season (a week in the wet), and costs US$15. The journey can be broken at Ocongate or Quincemil (where there are basic hotels). Trucks leave from the little plaza just east of Tacna and Pachacutec (in Cuzco) a few times a week. It may be better to wait in Urcos – all trucks to Puerto Maldonado go via Urcos. This trip involves a degree of self-sufficiency, hardiness and good luck.

FROM CUZCO TO THE COAST BY ROAD
Sendero activity has made the route through Abancay to Nazca dangerous, and most bus companies go via Arequipa instead. Abancay has basic hotels and is six to eight hours from Cuzco.

The Central Highlands

The central Peruvian Andes are one of the least visited areas of Peru. The mountain terrain makes overland transport difficult and the region has poor air services. Most of the people of the Central Andes are subsistence farmers.

It was in this environment of isolation and poverty that the Sendero Luminoso, Peru's major terrorist organisation, emerged in the 1960s and grew in the 1970s. The violent activities of the Sendero escalated dramatically in the 1980s, and headlines all over the world proclaimed Peru's internal unrest. During most of the 1980s, the departments of Ayacucho, Huancavelica and Apurímac were almost completely avoided by travellers.

Now, many regions have strict military control and are becoming safer to visit, though visiting small, isolated towns and villages may still be very dangerous. The areas around Tarma and Huancayo have remained OK to visit. The overland trip to Ayacucho is not recommended (though travellers do fly into Ayacucho and stay in the centre). The overland route from Lima via Cerro de Pasco, Huánuco and Tingo María and on to Pucallpa is currently being done during the day (stay overnight in Tingo María) and has a high police presence, with many checkpoints. No problems for travellers on this route have been reported during 1992.

Travellers in this region will find that the locals and the military are friendly and helpful and will give good advice on where not to go. Speaking Spanish is very useful. It is best to completely avoid all political conversations or meetings. Travelling at night is not recommended.

TARMA
This pleasant town, 250 km east of Lima, at 3050 metres, is nicknamed 'the pearl of the Andes'. There are many little-known ruins in the surrounding hills and a small astronomical observatory in the Hostal Central.

Information
The tourist office is at Dos de Mayo 775.

Things to See
Trips are made to the village of Acobamba, nine km away, to see the famous religious **Santuario de El Señor de Muruhuay**. From the village of Palcamayo, 28 km from Tarma, you can visit the **Gruta de Guagapo**, a huge limestone cave about four km away and officially protected as a 'national speleological area'. A guide lives opposite the entrance; caving gear is required for a full exploration.

The rural areas around Tarma are hotbeds of political and terrorist activity. Avoid travelling to remote villages in the area.

Festivals
The **Semana Santa** processions, including several candle-lit ones after dark, are the big

attraction. The Easter Sunday procession to the Catedral follows a beautiful route entirely carpeted with flower petals, as does the procession on the annual **Fiesta of El Señor de Los Milagros**, in late October.

Other fiestas include **Semana de Fiestas Cívicas de Tarma**, near the end of July, and **San Sebastián**, on 20 January.

Places to Stay
The cheapest hotels include the friendly *Central*, on Huánuco, two blocks west of the market, which sometimes has hot water, and the friendly *Anchibaya*, on the market, which has cold water. Other basic cold-water places are the *Tarma* and the *Cordova*. Rooms are about US$2/3.

Better hotels include the *Tuchu* and *Vargas*, on 2 de Mayo between the market and the Plaza de Armas, *El Dorado*, just west of the market, the *Galaxia*, on the plaza, and the *Internacional*. Most have private bathrooms and hot water some of the time – rooms are about US$4/6.

Places to Eat
There are cheap restaurants along Avenida Lima and Avenida Castilla. The *Restaurant Chavín*, on the Plaza de Armas, is good and the nearby *Conquistador* is acceptable and cheap. One of the best is *Don Vale* (open for lunch and dinner only), where a reasonable meal costs about US$2 to US$3. There is a vegetarian restaurant on Avenida Lima.

Getting There & Away
Comité 1, on Avenida Castilla, has cars to Lima, which leave when full (US$8, six hours). Hidalgo has a night bus to Lima (US$5, eight hours) and a day bus to Huancayo (US$2.50, three hours). Trans Chanchamayo has three day buses to Lima and Transporte Tarma has buses to Huancayo. Buses for Chanchamayo (US$3.50, three hours) leave from the market when they're full.

HUANCAYO
This modern city, at 3260 metres, lies in the broad and fertile Río Mantaro valley, in the

central Andes, and is famous for its Sunday market. Huancayo is the capital of the Department of Junín and the main commercial centre for the area. The road from Lima has improved recently, and the bus (or train) trip is spectacular as you rise from the coast to about 4700 metres before dropping into the Mantaro valley.

Information
The tourist office (☎ 23-3251), Ancash 415, 3rd floor, is open from 7.30 am to 1.30 pm Monday to Friday. It has good information. Lucho Hurtado and his wife, Beverly Stuart, who run La Cabaña Pizzería, Giraldez 724, organise tours and are a recommended source of help and information.

There are several casas de cambio and banks on the 400 and 500 blocks of Calle Real. Travellers' cheques are changed at 5% less than cash.

Dangers & Annoyances
The bus and train stations and the markets attract many thieves – watch your stuff.

Things to See
The daily produce (fruit and vegetable) market is along the railway tracks and in the nearby Mercado Modelo (covered market). The meat section sells various Andean delicacies, including fresh and dried frogs, and guinea pigs.

The **Sunday crafts market** along Calle Huancavelica has weavings, sweaters and other textile goods, embroidered items, ceramics, wood carvings and the carved gourds which are a specialty of the area.

Kamaq Maki (☎ 23-3183), Santa Isabel 1856, is in the suburb of El Tambo, northwest of the centre. This excellent craft cooperative has a good selection of high-quality local goods at fixed prices. Hours are 8 am to 2 pm Monday to Friday, or call ahead.

Walk (or bus) two km north-east on Giraldez to the **Cerro de la Libertad**, which has good city views. Continue two km to see the eroded sandstone towers at **Torre Torre**.

Places to Stay

The popular and recommended *Residencial Baldeón*, Amazonas 543, is in a friendly family house, with hot water and kitchen privileges. Simple rooms are US$3 per person. *Residencial Huancayo*, Giraldez 356, is also good and popular and has hot water (US$4/5).

Other basic cold-water places charging around US$3/5 include the small *Hostal Roma*, Loreto 447, the bigger *Hotel Centro*, Loreto 452, and *Prince*, Calixto 578. The latter two have some rooms with private showers. *Hotel Torre Torre*, Calle Real 873, has hot water. Also try the *Hostal Villa Rica*, Calle Real 1291, *Hostal Will Roy*, Calixto 452, *Hostal Los Angeles*, Calle Real 245, and *Hostal Universal*, Pichis 100, near the central railway station. The cheapest place is the *Hostal Tivoli*, Puno 488, at US$2 per person.

Duchas Tina, behind the Catedral, has hot showers (US$1) and a sauna (US$2).

For something more up-market, try the *Hotel El Dorado*, Piura 428, which offers carpeted rooms with private hot shower for US$5/7. There are fancier hotels on the Plaza de Armas.

Places to Eat

The local specialty is papa a la huancaina, a boiled potato topped with a tasty white sauce of cheese, milk, hot pepper and butter, served with an olive and eaten as a cold potato salad.

Budget restaurants selling decent meals for about US$2 to US$3 (as well as cheaper set menus) include *El Padrino*, Giraldez 133, *Pinky's*, Giraldez 147, *El Pino*, Calle Real 539, *Misky Mikuy*, Arequipa 453, and the *Roger*, in the hotel of that name. There are many others.

Pizzería La Cabaña, Giraldez 724, serves very good pizzas and ice cream and is popular with travellers. *El Consulado*, 13 de Noviembre, No 795, in the suburb of El Tambo, serves typical local food.

There are several up-market restaurants on or near the Plaza de Armas. The best and most expensive are *Lalo's*, Giraldez 363, *Restaurant El Inca*, Puno 530, and the *Restaurant Olímpico* on the plaza. Meals are about US$5.

Entertainment

There are several peñas offering live folk music at weekends. Cover charges are about US$2. Try the Taki Wasi (on Huancavelica at 13 de Noviembre, in El Tambo), Ollantaytambo (on the 200 block of Puno) and Huanrangal (on Calle Santa Rosa). There are also some discos and cinemas.

Getting There & Away

Bus Lima (US$4 to US$6, eight hours) is served by many companies – shop around for the best departure times and fares. Recently, the cheapest were Empresa Hidalgo, at Loreto 358, and Los Andes, on Calle Lima. ETUCSA, Puno 220, is the most expensive. Expreso Sud Americano (in El Tambo suburb), Expreso Huaytapalana (at Calixto 450), Mariscal Caceres (at Huánuco 350), Buenaventura (at Amazonas 660), Roggero (on Calle Lima) and Transportes Jara (on the 200 block of Breña) all have Lima service.

Empresa Hidalgo goes to Tarma (US$1.80, two hours) and Huancavelica (US$3, five hours). Empresa Molina, Angaraes 287, also goes to Huancavelica. Until recently, this route was not recommended, but travellers began trickling back in 1992 – check before you travel.

Although the hard and difficult route to Ayacucho is not recommended for political reasons, buses do go there, which indicates that stability is returning. Make detailed inquiries before attemping this route. Empresa Molina, Angaraes 287, and Transportes Ayacucho, Calle Real 1399, go to Ayacucho.

Several buses go to Satipo, in the jungle – this route is also subject to terrorist problems, so check carefully. Other companies go north to Cerro de Pasco, Huánuco and Tingo María – again, check carefully about the advisability of these routes and travel only in daylight.

Buses to local villages leave from or near Calixto (see the Huancayo city map); the tourist office has local bus information.

PERU

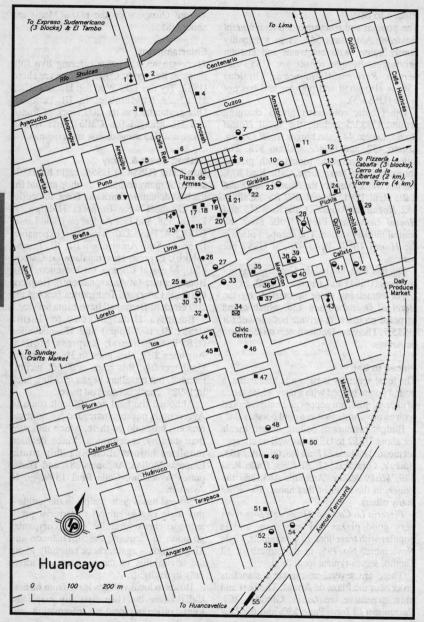

To Expreso Sudamericano
(3 blocks) & El Tambo

To Lima

Río Shulcas

Centenario

Cuzco

Plaza de Armas

Giraldez

Lima

Loreto

Ica

Civic Centre

Piura

Cajamarca

Huánuco

Tarapaca

Angaraes

To Sunday
Crafts Market

To Pizzería La
Cabaña (3 blocks),
Cerro de la
Libertad (2 km),
Torre Torre (4 km)

Daily
Produce
Market

Ayacucho

Moquegua

Arequipa

Calle Real

Ancash

Amazonas

Calle Huancas

Guido

Pichis

Quito

Pichtes

Calixto

Mantaro

Avenue Ferrocarril

Libertad

Puno

Breña

Junín

Huancayo

0   100   200 m

To Huancavelica

■ PLACES TO STAY	19	Restaurant Olímpico & Café Giraldez	31	Comité 12 Colectivos to Lima
3 Hotel Los Angeles	20	Restaurant Roger	32	ENTEL
4 Hotel Plaza	22	El Padrino & Pinky's	33	Comité 22 Colectivos
6 Hostal Tivoli		Restaurant		to Lima
11 Residencial Baldeón			34	Correo Central
12 Residencial Huancayo		OTHER	36	Buses to San
17 Hotel Kiya				Jerónimo &
18 Hotel Santa Felicita	1	Iglesia La Merced		Concepción
20 Hotel Roger	2	Banco de la Nación	39	Expreso Huaytapal-
24 Hostal Universal	7	ETUCSA Buses &		ana (Buses)
25 Hotel Centro		Duchas Tina	40	Buses to San
30 Hostal Roma		(Showers)		Jerónimo,
35 Hotel Prince	9	Catedral		Concepción & Jauja
37 Hotel de Turistas	10	Comité 1 Colectivos	41	Buses to La Oroya
38 Hostal Will Roy		to Tarma	42	Buses to Hualhuas,
45 Hotel Torre Torre	14	Banco de Crédito		Cajas &
47 Hotel El Dorado	15	Banco de la Nación		Huamancaca
49 Hotel Presidente	16	Casa de Cambio	43	Iglesia La Inmaculada
50 Hotel Palace	21	Tourist Office	44	Cine Pacifico
51 Hostal Villa Rica	23	Comité 30 Colectivos	46	Municipalidad
53 Percy's Hotel		to Lima	48	Mariscal Caceres
	26	Casa de Cambio		(Buses)
▼ PLACES TO EAT	27	Empresa Hidalgo	52	Transportes Ayacucho
		(Buses)		(Buses)
5 Restaurant El Inca	28	Plaza Amazonas	54	Empresa Molina
8 Misky Mikuy		(Buses to Chupaca		(Buses)
Restaurant		& Pilcomayo)	55	Railway Station to
13 Lalo's Restaurant	29	Central Railway		Huancavelica
15 El Pino Restaurant		Station (To Lima)		

PERU

There are taxis colectivos with comités 12, 22 and 30 to Lima (US$12), and with Comité 1 to Tarma.

Train There are two unconnected train stations. The central station serves Lima (US$6 in 1st class, 10 hours). Tickets usually sell out the day before. This train does not run in the November to April wet months, and didn't run at all in 1992.

The Huancavelica train station serves Huancavelica by autovagón (US$3, four hours, departing at 6.30 am) and train (US$3.50 in buffet class, six hours, departing at 10 am) daily, except Sunday. It's a beautiful ride. There is a strong military presence on the train.

The Mantaro Valley
The twin villages of Cochas Grande and Cochas Chico, 11 km from Huancayo, are centres for production of the incised gourds for which the area is famous. San Agustín de Cajas is known for the manufacture of broad-brimmed wool hats, though it seems to be a dying industry now. Hualhuas is famous for wool products. San Jerónimo de Tuman is known for its filigreed silverwork, and its 17th-century church with fine wooden altars.

North of Huancayo is the village of Concepción (with basic accommodation), from which the famous 18th-century **Convento de Santa Rosa de Ocopa** can be visited. This beautiful building with an interesting museum and library is open daily, except Tuesday, from 9 am to noon and 3 to 6 pm. Admission is US$0.50.

The Huancayo tourist office has much more information about the attractions of the Mantaro valley.

HUANCAVELICA

This city is 147 km south of Huancayo, in a high and remote area. It's a small but attractive colonial town with some noted churches. Since 1992, the area has been under strong military control – travellers are trickling back, but check carefully.

Information

The ministry of Tourism office is at Nicolás de Piérola 180. The Instituto Nacional de Cultura, on Plaza San Juan de Dios, has a museum and local information. Moneychanging facilities are poor. Market day is Sunday.

Places to Stay

Hostal Savoy, M Muñoz 290, has no water, and the *Hostal Santo Domingo*, Barranca 366, has cold water. Very basic rooms are US$1.50 per person. *Mi Hotel*, Carabaya 481, is a few cents more but has hot water and is better. *Hotel Tahuantinsuyo*, at Carabaya and M Muñoz, has hot water and charges US$3/4.50 for rooms with private bath. The *Mercurio*, Torre Tagle 455, is similar but charges twice as much.

Places to Eat

Good cheap restaurants serving meals for US$1 to US$2 include *La Estrellita*, Barranca 370, *Paquirri*, Arequipa 137, and *Olímpico*, J M Chávez 124. Pricier places include *La Casona*, V Toledo 103, *Olla de Barro*, A Gamarra 305, *César's*, M Muñoz 390, *Joy*, V Toledo 230, and *Las Magnolias*, a block from the Plaza de Armas.

Getting There & Away

Bus Most buses leave from Avenida M Muñoz. Various companies have buses for Huancayo (US$3, five hours) and Lima (US$9, 13 hours).

Train There are trains every day (except Sunday) to and from Huancayo.

AYACUCHO

Ayacucho is where the Sendero Luminoso arose in the 1960s. Travellers have rightly avoided the area, but the city is presently under strong military control. It is a fascinating Andean colonial town and well worth a visit, particularly during the famous **Semana Santa** (Holy Week) celebrations. There were a few travellers in 1992 – make detailed inquiries before going there. It is safest to arrive by air and stay in the centre.

Information

Travel agents around the plaza sell air tickets and provide information.

Things to See

The centre has a two museums, a 17th-century Catedral, many churches from the 16th, 17th and 18th centuries, and several old mansions around the plaza.

The ruins of **Wari** (Huari), capital of the Wari Empire, which predated the Incas by 500 years, are worth seeing. Beyond is the village of Quinua, where a huge monument and small museum mark the site of the Battle of Ayacucho (1824). There is a Sunday market. Wari is 20 km and Quinua about 40 km from Ayacucho – the bus trip appears safe during the day, but check.

Places to Stay

Hotel prices double during Semana Santa. Hot water is a rarity! The *Hostal Samary*, Callao 329, is basic but clean, with great rooftop views (US$4/7.50). Opposite, the *Sixtana* is cheaper but run down. The *La Colmena*, Cuzco 140, is clean and has an attractive courtyard (US$4 per person). The *Santa Rosa*, Lima 140, is a good hotel (US$6 per person). There are other places, some cheaper.

Places to Eat

Restaurant Tradicional, San Martín 406, is cheap and locally popular. *Cafe San Agustín*, just off the north-east side of the plaza, has no sign but is good for desserts. *La Casona*, at Bellido and 9 de Diciembre, is one of the best places.

Getting There & Away

Air Between them, AeroPerú, Faucett and

Americana have one or two flights a day to and from Lima (US$43). Expresso Aéreo flies to and from Cuzco (US$36) twice a week. The airport is three km from the town centre; taxis and buses are available.

Bus Travel in the area has been dangerous through 1992, and there are relatively few services. If you must use buses, travel during daylight. Most buses go to Huancayo; a few go to Lima and Cuzco.

NORTH OF LA OROYA

A road from Lima to the jungle town of Pucallpa goes through the central Andes north of La Oroya, via the towns of **Cerro de Pasco**, **Huánuco** and **Tingo María**. A few travellers reported that they made this journey in 1992 with no problems. There are many miltary checkpoints and the buses overnight in Tingo María, thus avoiding dangerous night travel. Check the situation before you go. Make sure your documents are in order – speaking Spanish is a great help.

ETPOSA (☎ 72-1402), José Gálvez, in the Lince district of Lima, has daily buses. There are others. The journey over paved road takes 12 hours to Tingo María and is spectacular. The next day, the journey on the poor road from Tingo María to Pucallpa takes 14 hours – the fare is US$11 for the entire trip. Alternatively, take a bus to Tingo María and continue by faster colectivo to Pucallpa (US$7). The last section is very slow in the wet season.

Cerro de Pasco is a cold, dirty mining town 4333 metres above sea level. Huánuco is more pleasant and has an interesting museum. Tingo María, a hot town on the edge of the jungle, at the southern end of the Río Huallaga valley, is notorious for drugs. The latter two towns have commercial airports, served by Expresso Aéreo, Aero-Cóndor and local airlines. There are places to stay in all three towns, with Huánuco and Tingo María having the best choice.

The North Coast

The coast road north from Lima passes huge, rolling sand dunes, dizzying cliffs, oases of farmland, busy fishing villages, relaxing beach resorts, archaeological sites and some of Peru's largest and most historic cities.

BARRANCA & PARAMONGA

The small town of Barranca, 190 km north of Lima, is four km before the turn-off to Huaraz. Four km north of the turn-off is the Chimú pyramid of Paramonga – a huge structure which is worth a visit. Admission is US$1.25. There is a small site museum.

There are a few cheap hotels and restaurants in Barranca. No buses go to the ruins, though local buses going to the port at Paramonga will drop you within a couple of km.

CASMA

The small town of Casma is 370 km north of Lima, and the archaeological site of Sechín is five km away.

Sechín

This site of is one of the oldest in Peru (1500 BC), and among the more important and well-preserved coastal ruins. There is a small museum. The outside walls of the main temple are completely covered with gruesome bas-relief carvings of warriors, and of captives being eviscerated. Hours are 9 am to 5 pm and admission is US$1.25. Bring your own food.

To get there, go three km south of Casma on the Panamericana, then turn left on the paved road to Huara for two more km.

Places to Stay

The best hotel is the *Hostal El Farol*, just off the main road between the Casma bus stop area and the Plaza de Armas. Singles/doubles cost US$5/8 with communal cold showers, US$8/12 with private showers. There are a couple of cheaper places.

PERU

Getting There & Away

Bus offices and stops are clustered together on the main road, near the junction with the Panamericana. There are buses to Lima, Trujillo and Huaraz, but many don't originate in Casma, so few seats are available. Make reservations as far in advance as possible; alternatively, take a colectivo 50 km north to Chimbote, where there are more buses and hotels – though Chimbote itself is an unattractive port with little of interest.

TRUJILLO

Trujillo, with 750,000 inhabitants, lies 560 km north of Lima and is the main town of northern Peru. It is an attractive city, founded in 1536 by Pizarro and retaining much of its colonial flavour.

Nearby are the immense 1500-year-old Moche Pyramids of the Sun and Moon (las Huacas del Sol y de la Luna), and the ancient Chimú capital of Chan Chan, which was conquered by the Incas. There are also some pleasant beaches.

Information

The tourist office (☎ 24-6941), Pizarro 402, is run by friendly and helpful tourist police and is open from 8 am to 7.30 pm. The government-run tourist office (☎ 24-1936) is at Independencia 628.

Trujillo is the best city on the north coast for changing money. The Banco de Crédito, on Gamarra near Pizarro, changes travellers' cheques. Street moneychangers on Pizarro, near the banks and on the plaza give good rates – shop around.

There are plenty of thieves and pickpockets – exercise the normal precautions.

Things to See

The spacious and attractive **Plaza de Armas**, with its impressive statue of the heroes of Peruvian independence, is fronted by the **Catedral**, which was begun in 1647, destroyed in 1759 and rebuilt soon afterwards. The Catedral has a famous basilica and is often open in the evenings around 6 pm. On Sunday at 9 am, there is a flag-raising ceremony on the Plaza de Armas, complete with a parade, *caballos de paso* (pacing horses) and performances of the *marinera*, an elegant coastal Peruvian dance which involves much waving of handkerchiefs.

There are several elegant **colonial mansions** surrounding the plaza. One is now the Hotel de Turistas and contains a small museum of Moche ceramics. Another is the Casa de Urquiaga, which stands next to the tourist information office and now belongs to the Banco Central de la Reserva del Perú. It has a small ceramics museum and can be visited during banking hours, for free.

The **colonial churches** of Santo Domingo, San Francisco, La Compañía, San Agustín and Santa Clara are worth a look, though getting inside is largely a matter of luck. San Agustín, with its finely gilded high altar, dates from 1558 and is usually open.

The **Museo Cassinelli** (north-west of the city centre) has an excellent archaeological collection in the basement of a petrol station! It's open Monday to Saturday from 8.30 am to 12 noon and 3.30 to 6 pm, and admission is US$1.50. A selection of the best pieces can be seen for free in the Hotel de Turistas.

The university-run **Museo de Arqueológia**, Pizarro 349, has an interesting collection of art and pottery, and a reproduction of the murals in the Moche Pyramid of the Moon. Admission is US$0.60. The university also has a **Museo de Zoológia**, at San Martín 368.

The Catedral and El Carmen Church have **art museums** featuring religious and colonial art. Casona Orbegoso, on the 5th block of Calle Orbegoso is a beautiful 18th-century mansion with a period art exhibit.

Several colonial buildings contain **art galleries** with changing shows. Admission is normally free or nominal. The Santo Domingo gallery, by the church, and Casa de los Leones, on Independencia (the Ganoza Chopitea residence), are worth a look. There are several other colonial mansions. Hours at these places are changeable – inquire locally.

Festivals

The marinera is the highlight of many of Trujillo's festivals. Caballos de paso are another highlight. The **Fiesta de la Marinera**, at the end of January, is the biggest in Peru. The **Fiesta de la Primavera**, held in late September, has Peru's most famous parade, and much dancing and entertainment. Hotels are fully booked at those times.

Places to Stay

The cheapest is the very basic and poor-looking *Hostal Peru*, on Ayacucho near Estete, at US$2.50/3.75 for singles/doubles. Opposite is the slightly better *Hotel Paris*, which costs a few cents more. For some strange reason, the basic *Hostal Lima*, Ayacucho 718, has become popular with gringos. It looks like a jail and is noisy, but secure. They charge US$3.20/4.40. The *Hostal Central*, next door, is similarly priced, and also has rooms with private bath (US$5/7.50). The *Hostal Colón* charges US$4.25/7.25, or US$8.50 for a double with private bath. None of these hotels has hot water, and their standards of cleanliness aren't high.

The *Hotel Oscar*, in the 100 block of Orbegoso, looks OK for US$4/5.75. The *Hotel España*, near the Antisuyo Bus Terminal, is basic but clean (US$3.75/7). The *Hostal J R*, a block away, has rooms with private bath for US$4.40/7.50. The popular *Hotel Americano*, Pizarro 792, is in a rambling old mansion which is rather dingy but has character. The rooms are basic but fairly clean (US$5.50/8.25, or US$6.25/9.25 with private bath). The *Hostal Roma*, on Nicaragua, is clean and secure (US$8 for a double with private bath). All of these are cold-water hotels.

The following hotels have rooms with private bath and hot shower. The *Hotel Primavera*, Piérola 872, is out of the centre but clean, modern and good value (US$6.50/10). The clean *Hotel Sudamericano* (☎ 24-3751), on the 500 block of Grau, is OK for US$7/11.25. The *Hotel San Martín* (☎ 23-4011), on the 700 block of San Martín, has over 100 rooms and so is rarely full. It's fair value, at US$8.25/13.75. Other reasonable choices at about these prices are

the *Hostal Acapulco*, Gamarra 681, the *Hotel Rosalia* (☎ 25-6411), Grau 611, and the *Residencial Los Escudos* (☎ 25-5691), Orbegoso 676.

Places to Eat

The food stalls in the market on Gamarra are among the cheapest places to eat in Trujillo. A block away from the market are several Chinese restaurants, of which the *Chifa Oriental* and *Chifa Ak Chan* are recommended. Nearby is the *Restaurant 24 Horas*, which is inexpensive and always open. Next door, the *Restaurant Oasis* is good for local food like fritadas.

There are simple, cheap restaurants on the 700 block of Pizarro. The *Café Romano* has strong espresso coffee, and *Marco's Café* serves ice cream and delicious home-made desserts. Both serve a variety of good food. Set lunches are US$1.50. If you like fried chicken, try the *ABC* chicken restaurant, which serves a grilled quarter chicken for US$1.50. Other good places for menus, parrilladas and chicken are *Las Tradiciones* and *Le Impala Restaurant*. *El Mesón de Cervantes* serves good lunches in an outdoor patio.

Entertainment

For a drink in the evening try Las Tinajas bar, on the corner of the plaza, which has a balcony with a view, and occasional live music. It's full of young Peruvians. It seems that single women are more likely to be hassled by men in Trujillo bars than in other parts of Peru.

Getting There & Away

Air The airport is 10 km north-west of town. Faucett, AeroPerú and Americana have offices in central Trujillo. They all fly to Lima (US$36) on most days. There are one or two flights a day to Chiclayo, some continuing to Piura. AeroPerú has two flights a week to Iquitos. Expresso Aéreo, Bolívar 423, has flights to Chachapoyas and Cajamarca twice a week, and daily jungle flights at 1 pm, which stop at a number of places, including: Tocache, Juanjui,

PERU

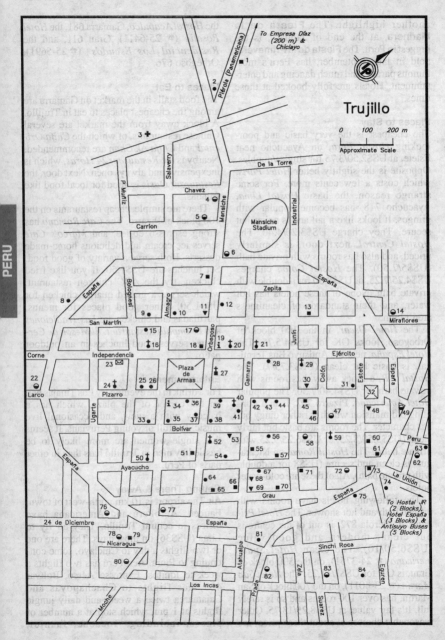

Trujillo

0   100   200 m

Approximate Scale

To Empresa Díaz
(200 m) &
Chiclayo

1

2

Piérola (Panamericana)

3

Salaverry

De la Torre

Chavez

P Muñiz

Mansiche

5

Carrion

Mansiche
Stadium

Industrial

6

España

7

Zepita

España

Bolognesi

Almagro

8   España

9   10   11   12   13   14

Miraflores

San Martín

Corne

15   17   19

16   18   20   21

Independencia

23

Plaza
de
Armas

Zepita

Orbegoso

Junín

Gamarra

Colón

28   29

Ejército

Estete

España

España

22

Larco

24   25   26   27   30

31   32

Pizarro

34   36   39   40   42   43   44   45   47   48   49

33   35   37   38   41   46   Peru

Ugarte

Bolívar   56   58   59   60

52   53   55   61

50   51   54   57   62

63

Ayacucho

64   67   71   72   73

65   66   68   69   70   La Unión

Grau   74

España   75

76

24 de Diciembre

77

España

To Hostal JR
(2 Blocks),
Hotel España
(3 Blocks) &
Antisuyo Buses
(5 Blocks)

78   79

Nicaragua

80

81

Atahualpa

Sinchi Roca

Zela

83   84

82

Los Incas

Pizarro

Suárez

Eguren

Moche

■ PLACES TO STAY

1   Hotel Primavera
7   Hotel Oscar
13 Hotel San Martín
18 Hotel de Turistas
45 Hotel Americano
46 Hostal Colón
51 Residencial Los Escudos
55 Hotel Continental & Hostal Acapulco
57 Hostal Vogi
60 Hostal Recreo
61 Hotel Paris
65 Hotel Sudamericano
66 Hotel Opt Gar
68 Hotel Turismo
70 Hostal Rosalia
71 Hostals Central & Lima
73 Hostal Peru
79 Hostal Roma

▼ PLACES TO EAT

11 ABC Chicken Restaurant
30 Marco's Café & Café Romano
43 El Mesón de Cervantes
48 Las Tradiciones
53 La Impala Restaurant
68 Chifa Oriental & Chifa Ak Chan
69 Restaurant Oasis & Restaurant 24
    Horas

OTHER

2   Museo Cassinelli
3   Hospital
4   El Dorado, Cruz del Sur & LTTSA
    Buses
5   Vulcano (Buses)
6   Buses to Chan Chan, Huanchaco &
    Arco Iris
8   Dancin' Discotheque
9   Americana Airline
10 Banco de la Nación & Migraciónes
    Office
12 Cine Primavera
14 EMTRAFESA Buses
15 Museo de Zoológia
16 La Compañia Church
17 Trujillo Express Buses
19 Tourist Information

20 Santo Domingo Church & Santo
    Domingo Art Gallery
21 San Francisco Church
22 Local Buses to Buenos Aires Beach
23 Correo Central
24 Santo Domingo Church
25 Museo de Arqueológia
26 Las Tinajas Bar
27 Catedral
28 Casa de los Léones
29 Santa Clara Church
31 TEPSA Ticket Office
32 Plazuela El Recreo
33 AeroPerú
34 Tourist Office & Tourist Police
35 Expresso Aéreo
36 Casa de Urquiaga
37 Cine Ideal
38 Casona Orbegoso & Museo
    Republicano
39 Faucett Airline
40 La Merced Church
41 Banco de Crédito
42 Casa de la Emancipación & Banco
    Continental
44 Palacio Iturregui
47 Empresa Antisuyo (Buses)
49 Las Dunas (Buses)
50 Ruined Church of Belén
52 San Agustín Church
54 Mercado Central
56 ENTEL
58 Chinchaysuyo Buses
59 El Carmen Church & Art Museum
62 Expreso Sudamericano (Buses)
63 Cine Trujillo
64 Cine Star
67 Teatro Ayacucho
72 Comité 12 Colectivos
74 Plaza de Toros
75 Old City Wall
76 Local Buses to Casa Grande
77 TEPSA Bus Station
78 Empressa El Aguila & Estete (Buses)
80 Various (Buses)
81 Cine Chimú
82 Chinchaysuyo Buses
83 Local Buses to Las Huacas del Sol y
    de La Luna
84 Mercado

PERU

Saposoa, Tarapoto, Bellavista, Yurimaguas, Pucallpa and Iquitos. Aero-Cóndor, at the airport, has jungle flights. Schedules and destinations vary often.

Bus Buses are often full, so book as far in advance as you can for the best choice of departure times. Companies are spread out all over town.

Many companies have services to Lima and towns along the north Panamericana. Fares vary, depending on the company (some have luxury buses with video, bathroom, etc) – Lima is US$7 to US$15 (eight to 10 hours), Piura is US$6 to US$10 (seven to nine hours) and Chiclayo is about US$3 (three hours). TEPSA has a ticket office at Estete 482, as well as one at the bus terminal. The crowded TEPSA terminal on Almagro is for buses originating in Trujillo. TEPSA and several other companies have offices on Moche for buses passing through Trujillo en route to somewhere else. There are several companies on the 300 block of Mansiche with services to north and south: Cruz del Sur, El Dorado, LTTSA, Vulcano (with frequent buses to Chiclayo). EMTRAFESA (☎ 24-3981), on Miraflores near España, has Chiclayo buses leaving every half-hour during the day, as well as Lima and Piura buses. Las Dunas, España 1445, has overnight luxury buses to Lima. Expresso Sudamericano has buses along the coast. Trujillo Express goes to Lima overnight.

Chinchaysuyo has two terminals; most buses leave from Prada 337, which is in a rough area – take a taxi and watch your belongings. Expresa Antisuyo also has two terminals, with the one further from town being used for more departures. Empresa Díaz is on the Panamericana, north of town. These companies are the ones to try for destinations inland, like Huaraz, Cajamarca, Chachapoyas and Tarapoto. TEPSA, Expreso Sudamericano and Vulcano also go to Cajamarca, and TEPSA also goes to Chachapoyas and Tarapoto. Comité 12, Ayacucho 896, has daily colectivo taxis to Cajamarca, at 11 am (three passengers minimum).

Empresa El Aguila, Nicaragua 220, has frequent buses to Chimbote. Estete, at the same terminal, has new buses north to Tumbes.

Getting Around
To/From the Airport The bus to Huanchaco passes within one km or so of the airport. A taxi from the centre is about US$3.

Bus White, yellow-and-orange 'B' colectivos pass the corner of España and Mansiche for Huaca Esmeralda, Chan Chan and Huanchaco every few minutes. There is also a large yellow bus. Red-blue-and-white minibuses or green-and-white buses for Esperanza pass the same corner and can drop you at La Huaca Arco Iris.

Blue-and-white minibuses leave every half hour from Calle Suarez for las Huacas del Sol y de la Luna.

Note that buses to the ruins are worked by professional thieves looking for cameras and money – ask the tourist police for updates. A taxi or tour group may be worthwhile.

AROUND TRUJILLO
The Moche and the Chimú are the two cultures which have left the greatest mark on the Trujillo area. There are four major archaeological sites.

Warning
Single travellers, especially women, have been mugged, robbed or raped whilst visiting archaeological sites. Stay on main footpaths, don't visit the ruins late in the day and don't go alone (go with friends or hire a guide).

Archaeology
The Moche (Mochica) culture flourished for the first seven centuries AD and is known especially for its ceramics. The pots are decorated with realistic figures and scenes; most of what we know about the Moche is from this pottery – there was no written language.

The Moche lived around massive ceremonial pyramids such as las Huacas del Sol y de la Luna (the Temples of the Sun and the Moon), which are easily visited.

The Chimú period was from about 1000 to 1470 AD. The Chimú capital, at Chan Chan, was the largest pre-Columbian city in Peru, covering 28 sq km and housing about 50,000 people.

Guides
A recommended guide is Clara Luz Bravo Díaz (☎ 24-3347), Huayna Capac 542, in the

Santa María suburb. She speaks English, and will provide transport or accompany you on public buses. The tourist police will recommend guides.

Chan Chan

The city was built around 1300 AD and contained about 10,000 dwellings. There were storage bins for food and other products, huge walk-in wells, canals, workshops and temples. The royal dead were buried in mounds containing a wealth of funerary offerings. The whole city was decorated with designs moulded into the mud walls, and the more important areas were layered with precious metals. The Chimú were conquered by the Incas around 1460, but the city was not looted until the Spanish arrived.

The Chimú capital consisted of nine subcities, called the Royal Compounds. Each contained a royal burial mound with a rich array of funerary offerings. Today's visitor sees only a huge area of crumbling mud walls, some decorated with marvellous friezes. The treasures are gone, though a few can be seen in museums. The Tschudi compound has been partially restored and is open to visitors.

Chan Chan is five km west of Trujillo. Tschudi is to the left of the main road, about 500 metres along a dirt road. You'll see the crumbling ruins of the other compounds all around you. Stick to the road and don't try to visit the ruins on either side, which are the haunts of muggers.

The entrance booth is at the Tschudi complex. There is a snack/souvenir stand, guides are available and tourist police are on duty. Hours are 9 am to 4 pm; admission is US$3, plus a US$1 camera fee. The ticket admits you to the Huaca Esmeralda and Huaca Arco Iris ruins and is valid for two days. Guides at the ruins charge about US$5.

La Huaca Esmeralda

This temple was built by the Chimú about the time of Chan Chan. Hours and fees are as for Chan Chan. Huaca Esmeralda is at Mansiche, halfway between Trujillo and Chan Chan, and it is possible to walk (check

with the tourist police). If returning from Chan Chan to Trujillo, the *huaca* is to the right of the main road, about four blocks behind the Mansiche church.

The site is eroded, but you can make out the characteristic designs of fish, seabirds, waves and fishing nets. The temple consists of two stepped platforms, and an on-site guide will take you around (for a tip).

La Huaca Arco Iris

This Chimú site is also known locally as the Huaca del Dragón. It is just to the left of the Panamericana, in the suburb of La Esperanza, four km north-west of Trujillo. Hours and fees are as for Chan Chan.

This is one of the best-preserved Chimú temples, because it was covered by sand until excavation began in 1963. The site consists of a thick defensive wall enclosing about 3000 sq metres. There is only one entrance, and within is a single large structure, the temple itself. This covers about 800 sq metres, and consists of two levels with a combined height of about 7½ metres. The walls are covered with repeated rainbow designs, most of which have been restored. Ramps lead to the very top of the temple, from where there are good views.

Huaca del Sol & Huaca de la Luna

The Moche temples of the Sun and the Moon are 700 years older than Chan Chan. They are 10 km south-east of Trujillo by rough road. Hours are 8 am to 2 pm. Go in the morning, because the wind whips the sand up in the afternoon and buses stop running. There are usually tourist police near the site in the morning.

The Huaca del Sol is the largest single pre-Columbian structure in Peru; an estimated 140 million adobe bricks were used to build it. At one time, the pyramid had several different levels, connected by steep flights of stairs, huge ramps and walls sloping at 77° to the horizon. After years of erosion, it now looks like a giant pile of crude bricks partially covered with sand. Despite this, the brickwork is still impressive from some angles.

The smaller Huaca de la Luna is 500 metres away across the open desert, with dozens of pottery shards lying around. The Huaca de la Luna has rooms which yielded more artefacts than the almost-solid Sun pyramid. Unfortunately, the site is in a bad state of repair and the murals are badly damaged or covered with rubble. The rooms have been bricked up – reproductions of some of the murals can be seen in the Museo de Arqueología in Trujillo.

Huanchaco

This fishing village is a 15-km bus ride north of Trujillo and is the best beach resort in the area. Of particular interest are the totora-reed boats, which look similar to those depicted on Moche ceramics. The locals are among the few remaining people who still know how to construct and use these precarious-looking craft, some of which can always be seen stacked up at the northern end of the beach. You can swim in the ocean, but it's a little cold for most of the year; it's warmest from January to March.

Warning Robberies and rape have occurred on the beach walk from Huanchaco to Trujillo. You'll be OK if you stay in Huanchaco and use the bus to get to Trujillo.

Places to Stay & Eat Several families rent rooms or have a small pensión; these offer the cheapest accommodation, and you should ask around. Two possibilities are Señora Lola, at Manco Capac 136, and Heidi, at Los Pinos 451 – there are others.

Cheapish hotels include the *Hostal Las Palmeras*, on the street of that name, with hot water and kitchen facilities, and the *Hostal Huanchaco*, Larco 287, with hot water and pool and charging US$7 a double (more with bath). There are several others. Bargain for reduced rates in the off season.

There are simple seafood restaurants at the northern end of the beach, near where the totora-reed boats are stacked.

Getting There & Away Buses leave from the corner of Mansiche and España in Trujillo at frequent intervals during daylight hours.

CHICLAYO

The next major coastal city is Chiclayo, just over 200 km north of Trujillo. Chiclayo, with a population of over 400,000, is an important commercial centre and one of the fastest growing modern cities in Peru. In 1987, a royal Moche tomb was discovered at Sipán, about 30 km south-east of Chiclayo.

Orientation & Information

The tourist information office (☎ 22-7776) is at Sáenz Peña 830. The Banco de Crédito on Balta, just south of the plaza, changes travellers' cheques. Moneychangers hang out in the street on the 600 block of Balta.

Note: The Chiclayo map is on page 988.

Things to See

Sipán Hundreds of dazzling and priceless artefacts have been recovered from this site, and excavation continues. The spectacular finds are on display in the Bruning Museum in Lambayeque, 11 km north of Chiclayo.

To reach Sipán by public transport, take a minibus from Avenida 7 de Enero, near the market – they leave several times a day, at erratic hours. Go early in the morning to return the same day. Sipán admission is US$0.75.

Market Wander around and see the herbalist and *brujo* (witch-doctor) stalls, with their healing charms. Also look for the heavy woven saddlebags, called *alforjas*, which are typical of the area. Watch your belongings.

Places to Stay

The cheapest hotels are north of the Plaza de Armas, on Balta. Few have hot water. The *Hotel Royal* (☎ 23-3421), on the Plaza de Armas, near Balta, is old but OK for US$3.75/5, or US$5/6.50 with bath. The similarly priced *Hostal Cruz de Galpon* is also OK. The clean *Hostal Adriático* is quite good for US$3.75/6.25, or US$7.50/8.75 with private bath. Cheaper, more basic places include the *Balta* and *Nuevo Estrella*, both at US$3/5.75. Others along Balta are the *Ronald* (cheap and OK), the *Americano* (more expensive but not much better) and the *Hostal Jusovi*, which is the only cheap place with private hot showers. Rooms are US$4.75/7.50. On the 400 block of E Aguirre are the *Hostal Lido* (US$3.50/4.50, or US$5/7.50 with cold bath) and the over-priced *Hotel Real*, which charges US$5/8 or US$6.25/9.50.

For better accommodation in clean rooms with private bath and hot water, the *Sol Radiante* (☎ 23-7858), Izaga 392, a quiet, family-run place (US$9/12.50), and the pleasant *Hostal Costa de Oro* (☎ 23-2869), Balta 399 (US$11/17.50) have been recom-mended.

Places to Eat

There are plenty of cheap restaurants on Avenida Balta. In the *pollerías* on the 800 and 900 blocks, you can get a quarter of a chicken for about US$2. The *Roma*, Balta 512, is locally popular and has meals starting at US$2.50.

Getting There & Away

Air The airport is two km south-east of town. AeroPerú, Faucett and Americana have offices in central Chiclayo. There are two or three flights a day to Lima, and one or two flights a day to Piura and Trujillo. Faucett has Monday to Saturday flights to Tumbes and two flights a week to Rioja.

Bus Many bus companies are near the south exit of town, on the corner of Sáenz Peña and Bolognesi. This is the best place to look for long-distance buses to Lima, Piura, Trujillo, Cajamarca, Chachapoyas and elsewhere.

Getting Around

Tours Indiana Tours (☎ 24-0833, 24-2287) used to be at Izaga 774, but a recent report claims Callao 121 – call first. They speak English, offer recommended guided tours to Sipán (about US$35) and have excursions to the archaeological site of Túcume and to other local sites of interest.

LAMBAYEQUE

This small town 11 km north of Chiclayo is known for its Bruning Museum, which has a good collection of artefacts from the Chimú, Moche, Chavín and Vicus cultures. There is also a new exhibit featuring finds from the site of Sipán. Admission is US$0.75. Opening hours are 8 am to 6.30 pm Monday to Friday, and 9 am to 1 pm on weekends and holidays. Transportes San Pablo buses leave from near the Plaza Aguirre in Chiclayo and stop by the museum.

PIURA

Piura was founded by Pizarro in 1532 and is the oldest colonial city in Peru. The Catedral dates from 1588. The city centre still has some colonial buildings, though many were destroyed in the earthquake of 1912. The city's focal point is the large, shady and pleasant Plaza de Armas. Irrigation of the desert has made Piura a major agricultural centre, with rice being the main crop. The population is over 300,000.

Information

The tourist office (☎ 33-3720) is at Ayacucho 377, on the Plaza de Armas. The Banco de Crédito, just off the plaza, is the best place to change cash and travellers' cheques.

Things to See

The **Museo Cultural**, at Huánuco and Sullana, has archaeology and art exhibits. Hours are 9 am to 1 pm and 5 to 8 pm Tuesday to Friday, and 9 am to 1 pm on Saturday and Sunday. Admission is free.

Casa Grau, the house on Tacna (near Ayacucho) where Almirante Miguel Grau was born, on 27 July 1834, is now the naval museum. Grau was a hero of the War of the Pacific against Chile (1879-80). Hours are changeable and admission is free.

Places to Stay

The *Hostal Terraza*, on Loreto near Huánuco, charges US$6/9 for singles/ doubles with bath, a little less for rooms with communal bath. There is hot water, and it is

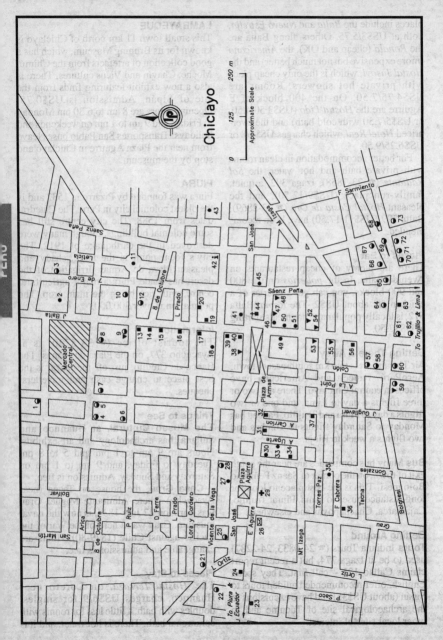

Chiclayo

0   125   250 m
Approximate Scale

PERU

clean and popular with travellers. Next door is the similarly priced *Hotel Dallas*, with cold water. Others in this price range are the *Residencial Bolognesi*, in a huge and ugly building on Bolognesi near Cuzco, and the *Hostal Amauta*, on Apurimac near Cuzco. Both have private baths and hot water but lack single rooms. Other reasonable hot-water hotels are the *Hotel Continental*, Junín 924, and the *Hostal California*, half a block

up Junín. Opposite, the *Hostal Lalo* looks basic but is reasonably clean. The cheapest-looking are the *Hotel Eden*, on Arequipa near Huancavelica, and the *Hotel Hispano* and *Hotel Ica*, both on Ica near Junín.

The *Hostal Cristina* (☎ 32-2031, 32-3881), Loreto 649, looks old-fashioned and interesting. They charge about US$11/16 with private hot shower, a little less with shared bath. Similarly priced are the clean

PERU

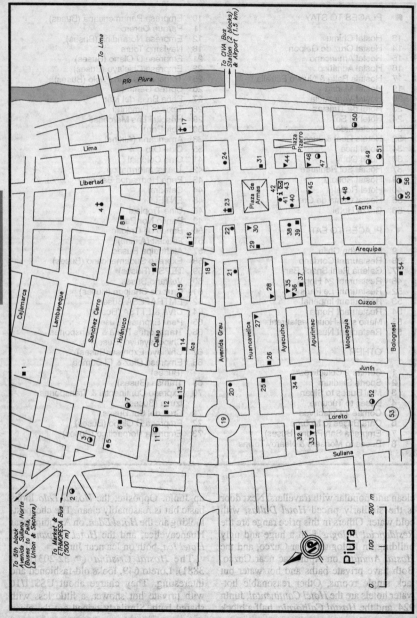

	PLACES TO STAY	46	Heladería Venecia
1	Hotel Esmeralda		OTHER
6	Hostal Terraza & Hotel Dallas		
8	Hostal El Sol	2	Buses to Tumbes & Chiclayo
9	Hotel Tambo	3	Perla del Norte Buses
10	Hostal Oriental	4	El Carmen
12	Hostal Cristina	5	Museo de la Cultura
13	Hostal Ica	7	EPPO (Buses)
14	Hotel Hispano	11	Comité 2 Colectivos to Sullana
16	Hostal Tangara	15	Comité 24 Colectivos to Lima
25	Hostal Lalo	17	San Francisco Church
26	Hotel California	19	Grau Monument
29	Hotel Eden	20	Cine Variedades
31	Hotel de Turistas	21	Alex Chopp
32	Residencial Piura	22	Banco de Crédito & AeroPerú
33	Hostal San Jorge	23	Catedral
34	Hostal Continental	24	Faucett Airline
37	Hostal Amauta	38	Casa Grau (Naval Museum)
39	Hotel Plaza Suite	40	Banco de la Nación
54	Residencial Bolognesi	41	Municipalidad
		42	Tourist Office
	PLACES TO EAT	43	ENTEL & Correo Central
		47	Transportes Piura & Colectivos to Catacaos
18	Restaurant Tres Estrellas		
27	Tacos Mexicanos Café	48	San Sebastian Church
28	Pizzería La Cabaña & Bar Romano	49	Chinchaysuyo (Buses)
30	Heladería Chalan	50	Expreso Sudamericano (Buses)
33	Ferny's Restaurant	51	Roggero (Buses)
35	Las Tradiciónes Restaurant	52	TEPSA (Buses)
36	Café Concierto	53	Bolognesi Monument
44	El Gaucho Steak House	55	Cruz de Galpón (Buses)
45	Las Redes Bar & Italian Restaurant	56	Comité 1 Colectives to Sechura

and pleasant *Hostal San Jorge* (☎ 32-7514), Loreto 960, and the *Hotel Tambo*, on Callao near Cuzco.

Places to Eat

There are cheap and unremarkable places to eat along Avenida Grau and around the 700 block of Junín. Good mid-range choices are *Pizzería La Cabaña* and *Bar Romano*, at Ayacucho and Cuzco. *Ferny's*, at the Hostal San Jorge, is also recommended.

Heladería Chalan, on the plaza, has a good selection of juices, cakes and ice creams, as well as sandwiches and other snacks. Also good for ice cream and sweets is the nearby *Heladería Venecia*, on the corner of Libertad and Apurimac. *Cafe Concierto*, near the corner of Cuzco and

Apurimac, is a good coffee house which occasionally has entertainment.

Getting There & Away

Air The airport is two km from the centre. AeroPerú, Faucett and Americana have offices in the centre. They all have flights to Lima, and flights to Chiclayo, Talara and Tumbes are also available.

Bus Buses, cars and trucks for various local destinations leave from the fifth block of Avenida Sullana Norte. For long-distance bus trips, the offices of Empresa Chiclayo, Trans El Dorado and Comité 1 for Tumbes (six hours), Chiclayo (three hours) and Trujillo are on the corner of Avenida Sullana and Sanchez Cerro. Empresa Sudamericano,

PERU

PERU

Chinchaysuyo, Roggero and Cruz de Galpón are at the river end of Bolognesi, and TEPSA is at Bolognesi and Loreto, by the monument. These companies are best for Lima (prices vary, 18 hours). Chinchaysuyo goes to Huaraz. CIVA, across the river on Huancavelica, has buses to Huancabamba and other small towns in the Andes east of Piura.

The most frequent route to Ecuador is via Tumbes, but the route via La Tina is a possibility. Take an early morning bus to Sullana (US$0.50, one hour) from Huánuco near Sullana, and continue from Sullana by truck (the bus driver will drop you at the right place).

Note that December to April is the rainy season and that El Niño climatic events occur every few years. The 1992 El Niño washed out roads and bridges; the route to Tumbes required wading rivers and changing buses, and the route to La Tina was closed.

LA TINA

This small border post has no hotels, but if you cross the border to Macará in Ecuador, you'll find several. La Tina is connected by poor road with Sullana (US$3 to US$6, four to six hours). The last bus to Sullana leaves at 2 pm. There are several passport checks. There is a basic hotel in El Suyo, 15 km away, then no hotels until Sullana.

Crossing the Border

Hours are 8 am to 6 pm daily, with irregular lunch hours. Formalities are fairly relaxed. There are no banks, but moneychangers in Macará will change cash.

TUMBES

Although half an hour from the Ecuadorian border, Tumbes is where transportation and accommodation for border-crossers is found.

Information

The tourist office (☎ 5054) is on Alfonso Ugarte, in the Edificio Majestad. Moneychangers on the streets and at the border change cash US dollars at Lima rates

---

■ PLACES TO STAY

3	Hostal Kiko's
4	Hostal Toloa II
5	Hostal Toloa
6	Hostal Córdova
7	Hotel de Turistas
11	Hostal Elica
12	Hostal Amazonas
13	Hostal Los Once
14	Hostal Florian
15	Hostal Jugdem
19	Residencial Gandolfo
20	Residencial Internacional
25	Hostal Premier
30	Hotel Bolívar
33	Hostal Roma
34	Hostal César & Hostal Estoril
35	Hostal Lourdes
36	Hostal Tumbes
37	Hostal Italia

▼ PLACES TO EAT

8	Restaurant Menova
10	Restaurant El Huerto de mi Amada
29	Restaurant Latino
30	Restaurant Curich & Restaurant Europa

OTHER

1	Expreso Sudamericano (Buses)
2	EMTRAFESA (Buses)
9	Empresa D Olano (Buses)
13	Bus Terminal Corner & Travel Agency
16	Colectivos to Border
17	ENTEL
18	Correo Central
21	Ecuadorian Consulate
22	Tourist Information
23	AeroPerú
24	Banco de Crédito
26	Faucett Airline
27	TEPSA (Buses)
28	Banco de la Nación
31	Catedral
32	Library
38	Colectivos to Zorritos & Caleta La Cruz

(bargain). The Banco de Crédito changes travellers' cheques.

Places to Stay

During holidays and trade fairs, hotels are

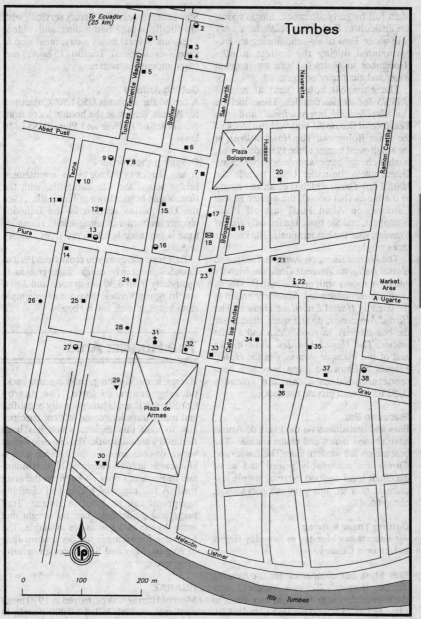

Tumbes

PERU

often full by early afternoon. Single rooms are difficult to find. Most hotels have only cold water. Fans or air-conditioning are recommended during the hottest months (December to March). There are frequent water and electricity outages.

The cheapest hotels start at around US$3/5 for singles/doubles. These include the *Residencial Internacional* and the *Residencial Gandolfo*, both within a block of the Plaza Bolognesi. The *Hotel Bolívar*, at the south-west corner of the Plaza de Armas, is also cheap, basic and reasonably clean. Other hotels for under US$5 include the *Hostal Los Once*, which is clean and handy to the buses (but noisy), the quieter *Hostal Córdova*, on Abad Pusil just off Plaza Bolognesi, and the basic but friendly *Hostal Premier*, near the bus terminals. The Premier lacks singles.

The *Hostal Elica*, on Avenida Tacna, and *Hostal Italia*, on Avenida Grau, are friendly and have rooms with private bath (US$6/9). Both are recommended. Similarly priced is the friendly *Hostal Estoril*, on Huáscar. The *Hostal Amazonas*, on the main street, near the bus stations, is good, clean and a little pricier. The *Hostal Lourdes*, three blocks east of the Plaza de Armas, and the *Hostal Florián*, at Piura and Tacna, have both been recommended as clean and friendly (US$10/14 with private hot bath).

Places to Eat
Bars and restaurants on the Plaza de Armas have shaded tables and chairs outside. The best are on the western side. The *Latino* and *Curich* are reasonably priced and serve excellent local seafood. Several simple restaurants near the bus terminals serve good, cheap food.

Getting There & Away
Air Faucett has Monday to Saturday flights to Lima via Chiclayo.

Bus Most bus companies are on Avenida Tumbes (formerly Teniente Vásquez), near the intersection with Avenida Piura. Fares to Lima (22 to 24 hours) are US$12 to US$20.

Some companies offer 'luxury service', with air-conditioning, bathrooms and video. There are several buses a day; most stop at Piura (seven hours), Trujillo (15 hours) and other intermediate cities.

Getting Around
A taxi to the airport is US$1.50. Colectivos for Aguas Verdes, at the border, leave from the corner of Bolívar and Piura (US$1, 26 km).

Crossing the Border
Aguas Verdes is linked, by an international bridge across the Río Zarumilla, with the Ecuadorian border town of Huaquillas. (See the Huaquillas section in the Ecuador chapter for border crossing details.) Ecuador time is one hour behind Peru from January to April.

Exit formalities as you cross from Peru to Ecuador are fairly quick. Immigration is open daily from 8.30 am to noon and 2 to 6 pm. In Aguas Verdes, there are a few simple restaurants, a bank and no hotels.

The Huaraz Area

Huaraz is the climbing, trekking and backpacking centre of Peru. The nearby Cordillera Blanca is exceptionally beautiful, and many travellers come to Peru specifically to visit this region, which has been declared a national park. You can enjoy great views on bus trips in the Huaraz area – Huascarán, at 6768 metres the highest mountain in Peru, lies only 14 km from the main road. A full range of hiking and climbing equipment can be hired in Huaraz. Trail maps and guidebooks can be bought and mule drivers and guides are available. The best time for hiking is the dry season: June to August. May and September are usually quite good.

HUARAZ
Most of Huaraz was destroyed in 1970 by an earthquake which killed 60,000 people in

central Peru. The town has now been rebuilt, has a population of 80,000 and is the capital of the Department of Ancash. Huaraz lies in a valley known throughout Peru as El Callejón de Huaylas.

Information

Tourist information is available at MICTI, on the 400 block of Luzuriaga. The Parque Nacional Huascarán office is in the Ministerio de Agricultura building, at the eastern end of Avenida Raymondi. Hours are 7 am to 2.15 pm Monday to Friday. The Casa de Guías (☎ 72-1333), on the Plaza Ginebra one block north-east of the Plaza de Armas, has a list of registered guides and is a good source of hiking and climbing information. Guide services and equipment rental can be found along Avenida Luzuriaga. Pyramid Adventures and Montrek have been recommended.

Banks are on the north side of the Plaza de Armas and on the 600 block of Luzuriaga. Moneychangers are found on the streets outside. The Banco de Crédito changes travellers' cheques, but cash is preferred. There is a laundry on Fitzcarrald, near the bridge.

Things to See

The **Museo de Arqueológia**, on the Plaza de Armas, is small but interesting.

The small pre-Inca **Ruinas Wilcahuaín** are about eight km north of Huaraz. There is no regular transport, but you can walk, or hire a taxi for a few dollars. Head north on Avenida Centenario to a signposted dirt road to your right a few hundred metres past the Hotel de Turistas. The dirt road climbs six km (passing through the communities of Jinua and Paria) to the ruins and continues another 20 km to Laguna Llaca, where there are excellent mountain views. The site is open daily; admission is US$1.

Places to Stay

Dry-season prices can be 50% or more higher than off-season rates. The period around Fiestas Patrías (Independence Day; 28 July) is especially busy.

Most places have warm or hot showers some of the time – ask. Otherwise, get a hot shower at Duchas Raimondi, Raimondi 904.

Small, family-run places include the basic but clean and friendly *Alojamiento Quintana*, M Cáceres 393, and *Pensión Galaxia*, Romero 688. They charge about US$3/5 for singles/doubles. Other decent places charging about US$4/7 include the friendly *Hostal Alpamayo*, opposite the stadium, the *Pensión Maguina*, Tarapaca 643, the *Hotel Barcelona*, Raimondi 602, which has great mountain views from the balconies but no hot water, the *Hotel Landauro*, Plaza de Armas, also with cold water, and the friendly *Hotel Los Andes*, Tarapaca 316. Some of these hotels have rooms with private bath.

Edward's Inn (☎ 72-2692), Bolognesi 121, is friendly, helpful and clean, with hot water, laundry facilities and a cafeteria, and is popular with international backpackers. Rates are US$3 to US$5 per person, depending on season and room – some have private baths. The *Casa de Guías* (☎ 72-1333), Plaza de Ginebra, has youth hostel-type facilities and charges US$5 per person. This is a climbers' meeting place; there are hot showers, bulletin boards and a good café. Others in this price range are the good and friendly *Hostal El Pacífico*, Luzuriaga 630; the *Hostal Colonial*, at 28 de Julio, No 586; and the *Hostal Cataluña*, Raimondi 822, which has excellent balcony views but is open only in the season. The last three all have rooms with private hot showers.

The *Hostal Copa*, Bolívar 615, is clean, helpful and recommended. They charge US$6/7 and have private hot showers. The *Hostal Raimondi*, Raimondi 810, and the *Hostal Huaraz*, Luzuriaga 529, are both OK (US$6/9 with private hot showers). The *Hostals Tumi I and II*, San Martín 1089 and 1121, are good value (US$7/11). The similarly priced *Hostal Colombo*, Zela 210, has bungalows and is good value. The better places may charge 18% tax, especially in season.

Places to Eat

The *Casa de Guías* serves great breakfasts

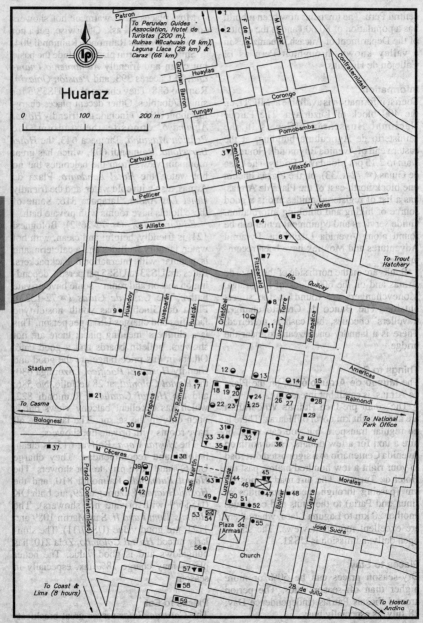

Huaraz

0   100   200 m

Patron

To Peruvian Guides
Association, Hotel de
Turistas (200 m),
Ruinas Wilcahuaín (8 km),
Laguna Llaca (28 km) &
Caraz (66 km)

F de Zela
M Malgar
Confraternidad

Guzman Barron
Huaylas

Yungay
Corongo

Pomobamba

Centenario
Carhuaz
Villazón

L Pellicer

V Velez

S Alliste

Río Quilcay
Fitzcarrald

To Trout
Hatchery

Huandoy
Huascarán
Hualcán
S Cristóbal
Lucar y Torre
Rampalica

Stadium

To Casma

Bolognesi

Tarapaca
Cruz Romero

Americas

Raimondi

To National
Park Office

M Cáceres

La Mar

L Prado (Confraternidad)
San Martín
Luzuriaga

Morales

Bolívar
Ugarte

Plaza de
Armas

José Sucre

Church

To Coast &
Lima (8 hours)

28 de Julio

To Hostal
Andino

■ PLACES TO STAY		6	Recreo La Unión	16	El Rápido
		23	Creperíe Patrick &	17	Petrol Station
5	Hostal Colombo		Chifa Jimmy's	20	Transportes
7	Hostal Yanett	24	Chifa Familiar & Other		Rodriguez (Buses)
15	Hostal Los Portales		Restaurants	22	Transportes
18	Hotel Barcelona	32	Restaurant Samuels		Huascarán (Buses)
19	Hotel Cataluña	33	Las Puyas Restaurant	23	Imantata Bar
21	Hostal Alpamayo	45	Casa de Guías	25	MICTI Tourist
26	Hostal Raimondi	57	Pizzerías Mama Mía &		Information
29	Hostal Monte Rosa		Posada	27	Transportes Moreno
30	Hotel Los Andes				(Buses)
32	Hotel Oscar		OTHER	28	Duchas Raimondi
35	Hostel Huaraz				(Hot Showers)
37	Edward's Inn	1	Cine Soraya	31	Chavín Tours
38	Alojamiento Quintana	2	Peña La Pascana	32	Pablo Tours
40	Pensión Galaxia	4	Paccchaʼk Pub	34	Pyramid Adventures
42	Pensión Maguina	8	Laundry Fitzcarrald	36	El Tambo Bar
43	Hostal El Pacífico	9	HIDRANDINA	39	Transportes Cóndor
45	Casa de Guías	10	Empresa 14 (Buses)		de Chavín (Buses)
46	Hostel Montañero	11	Empresa Huandoy	41	Transportes
48	Hostel Copa		(Buses to Monter-		Rodríguez (Buses)
51	Hotel Landauro		rey, Carhuaz,	44	Peña La Tremenda
57	Hostal Continental		Yungay & Caraz)	47	Taberna Amadeus
58	Hostal Tumi I	12	Discotec Any &	49	ENTEL
59	Hostal Tumi II		Empresa	50	Banks
			Norpacifico (Buses)	52	Banks
▼ PLACES TO EAT		13	Taxis 1, 2 & 3 (Local &	53	Police Station
			to Caraz)	54	Correo Central
3	Pío Pío Chicken	14	Expreso Ancash	55	Cine Radio
	Restaurant		(Buses)	56	Museo de Arqueológia

PERU

and is popular with climbers and trekkers. The reasonably priced *Chifa Familiar* Luzuriaga 431, is also popular, and there are other places nearby. Slightly away from the centre, the *Pío Pío*, Centenario 329, is inexpensive, simple and recommended. For a cheap typical local lunch, try the *Recreo La Unión*. *Restaurant Samuels*, on La Mar, and *Las Puyas*, Morales 535, serve large, cheap meals and are frequented by budget travellers.

For Italian food, try pizzeriás such as the *Mama Mía*, Luzuriaga 808, or the nearby *Posada*. *Creperie Patrick*, Luzuriaga 424, is good for crêpes and a variety of other dishes, and *Chifa Jimmy's*, next door, is good for Chinese food.

Entertainment
El Tambo Bar, on La Mar, and the Imantata Bar, Luzuriaga 424, sometimes have good live music, drinking and dancing into the wee hours. There are other places – ask around for current hot spots.

Getting There & Away
Air Expresso Aéreo has two flights a week during the dry season from Lima to Anta (23 km north of Huaraz). The fare is US$50 and the flights depend on having enough passengers.

Bus Most bus companies are within two blocks of the Raimondi/Fitzcarrald intersection. Transportes Rodríguez, Empresa Ancash (Ormeño) and Empresa 14 have departures for Lima (US$6, eight hours). Many buses start from or continue to Caraz, 67 km north of Huaraz.

Transportes Moreno has buses for Chimbote (US$6, eight hours). Empresa 14 and Transportes Rodríguez go via Chimbote to Trujillo. Buses for Chavín de Huantar (US$4, five hours), continuing to Huari, run daily with Cóndor de Chavín or Transportes Huascarán.

Buses (two hours) and taxi colectivos (1¼ hours) to Caraz leave from Fitzcarrald, near Raimondi. There are frequent departures during daylight hours.

Getting Around
Tours Tour agencies in Huaraz run local day excursions. One visits the ruins at Chavín de Huantar, another goes through Yungay to the beautiful Lagunas Llanganuco, where there are spectacular views of Huascarán and other mountains, and the third tour takes you through Catac to see the giant *Puya raimondi* plant. Prices are about US$8 to US$12 each, including a guide who doesn't necessarily speak English. There are departures almost daily during the high season. Recommended agencies include Chavín Tours, Pablo Tours, Pyramid Adventures and Kike Tours.

NORTH OF HUARAZ
The road through the Callejón de Huaylas north of Huaraz follows the Río Santa and is paved as far as Caraz. About five km north is **Monterrey**, where there are hot springs. **Carhuaz** is 31 km north of Huaraz and has a few basic hotels. It is near the entrance to the Ulta valle, where there is beautiful trekking. Between Carhuaz and Yungay, there are excellent views of Huascarán.

Yungay
This town and its 18,000 inhabitants were buried by a catastrophic avalanche during the 1970 earthquake. The site is marked by a huge white statue of Christ on a knoll overlooking old Yungay. The path of the avalanche can be plainly seen from the road. New Yungay has been rebuilt just beyond the avalanche path, about 59 km north of Huaraz.

Llanganuco From Yungay begins the trip to Llanganuco, one of the most beautiful and popular excursions in the Cordillera Blanca. To get to the Llanganuco lakes, you can go on a tour from Huaraz or take buses or taxis from Yungay. From June to August, minibuses carrying 10 or more passengers leave from the Plaza de Armas in Yungay, allowing about two hours near the lakes. It costs US$1 to enter the national park. Llanganuco is the beginning of the popular and spectacular four-day Llanganuco to Santa Cruz hiking loop.

Places to Stay & Eat The friendly *Hostal Gledel*, a block from the plaza, charges US$3 per person. Hot water and meals are available. There are a few other cheap places to stay, but these may close in the off season. There are cheap and simple *comedores* in the market next to the plaza.

Caraz
The pleasant small town of Caraz is 67 km north of Huaraz; it is the end point of the Llanganuco to Santa Cruz trek. Caraz is one of the few places in the area which has not been destroyed by earthquakes or landslides. The Plaza de Armas is attractive, there are several cheap hotels and restaurants, and you can take pleasant walks in the surrounding hills.

Chavín de Huantar
This small village is by the interesting ruins of Chavín. The Chavín culture (1300 to 400 BC) is the oldest major culture in Peru. The principal Chavín deity was feline; there were also lesser condor, snake and human deities. Highly stylised carvings of these deities are found at the site.

The most interesting parts of Chavín were built underground. Bring a torch for the underground chambers, and it is worth hiring a local guide. In the heart of the underground complex is an exquisitely carved, four-metre-high daggerlike rock known as the Lanzón de Chavín.

The site is open daily; admission is US$2.

Places to Stay & Eat Hotels in Chavín de Huántar are very basic and cheap. The *Montecarlo* is about US$2.50 per person, the *Inca* is about US$7 for a double and the

Gantu is the cheapest and the poorest. There are basic *comedores*, which close around sunset.

Getting There & Away Tour buses make day trips from Huaraz (US$12). Transportes Cóndor de Chavín or Transportes Huascarán have daily buses to and from Huaraz. Trucks also go to Huaraz, from the plaza.

Across the Northern Highlands

CAJAMARCA
Cajamarca (2650 metres) is the capital of its department and five hours east of the coast by paved road. It is a traditional and tranquil colonial city with a friendly population of 70,000. The surrounding countryside is green and attractive.

Cajamarca has impressive colonial architecture, excellent Andean food and interesting people and customs. Despite this, it is not a major centre of international tourism, because it lies some way off the 'gringo trail'. It was in Cajamarca that Pizarro deceived, captured and finally assassinated the Inca Atahualpa; for more information about this historic encounter, see the History section of the introductory Facts about South America chapter.

Information
The tourist office is currently closed. Meanwhile, tourist agencies around the plaza provide information and guided tours. The university Museo de Arqueológia is also a source of information.

The Banco de Crédito, on Lima near Tarapaca, changes travellers' cheques. Change cash dollars on the street near the Plaza de Armas.

Things to See
The only Inca building which remains standing in Cajamarca is **El Cuarto del Rescate** (the ransom chamber), just off the plaza. It is where Atahualpa was imprisoned, not where the ransom was stored. The site is open from 9.30 am to 12.30 pm and 3 to 5 pm daily, except Tuesday. Admission is US$1.25. The ticket is valid for the nearby Belén complex and the ethnography museum (see below; same hours).

The building of the **Complejo de Belén** began in the latter part of the 17th century. Inside what used to be the Women's Hospital, there is a small archaeology museum. In what was the kitchen and dispensary of the hospital, there is an art museum.

Next door is the **church**, with a fine cupola and a carved and painted pulpit. Wood carvings include a tired-looking Christ sitting cross-legged on his throne, looking as if he could do with a pisco sour after a hard day of miracle-working.

The small **Museo de Etnografía**, also close by, displays local costumes and clothing, domestic and agricultural implements, musical instruments and other examples of Cajamarcan culture.

The university-run **Museo Arqueológico**, at Arequipa and Sabogal, is open from 8 am to 2 pm Monday to Friday – knock on the door to get in. Hours change often; there is a small admission fee. The **Iglesia San Francisco**, on the plaza, has an art museum.

The **Cerro Santa Apolonia** is a hill overlooking the city from the south-west. Climb the stairs at the end of 2 de Mayo. There are pre-Columbian carvings.

Festivals
Water-throwing during Carnaval is without respite. Corpus Christi is very colourful.

Places to Stay
Prices rise around fiestas and during the dry months. Cheap hotels that advertise hot water usually have it only a few hours a day – ask when.

One of the best cheap hotels is the *Hostal Prado*, at La Mar and Amazonas, which is clean and has hot water (US$3.25 per person, or US$7.50/12.50 with private bath). The *Hotel Plaza* is in an old but comfortable

PERU

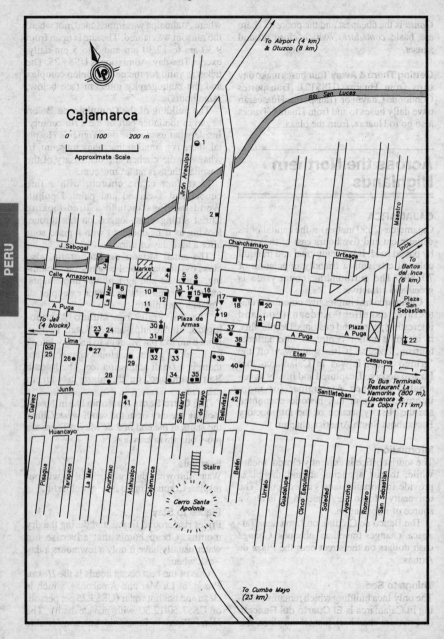

Cajamarca

0   100   200 m

Approximate Scale

To Airport (4 km)
& Otuzco (8 km)

Río San Lucas

Jirón Arequipa

Maestro

J Sabogal

Chanchamayo

Urteaga

Inca

To
Baños
del Inca
(6 km)

Calle Amazonas

Market

Plaza
San Sebastián

A Puga

La Mar

To Jail
(4 blocks)

Lima

Plaza
A Puga

Plaza de
Armas

A Puga

Eten

Casanova

To Bus Terminals,
Restaurant La
Namorina (800 m),
Llacanora &
La Colpa (11 km)

Santisteban

Junín

Huancayo

San Martín

2 de Mayo

Bellavista

J Galvez

Pisagua

Tarapacá

La Mar

Apurímac

Atahualpa

Cajamarca

Belén

Urrelo

Guadalupe

Cinco Esquinas

Soledad

Ayacucho

Romero

San Sebastián

Stairs

Cerro Santa
Apolonia

To Cumbe Mayo
(23 km)

■	PLACES TO STAY	▼	PLACES TO EAT	22	Recoleta
				24	Banco de Crédito
2	Hostal Turismo	5	Restaurant El Imperial	25	Correo Central
3	Hostal Chota	13	Chifa Zarco	26	Banco de la Nación
6	Hostal Yusovi	14	Restaurant Salas	27	Expresso Aéreo
7	Hotel Los Piños	16	Restaurant El Real	28	Cine San Martín
8	Hostal Prado		Plaza	30	Catedral
9	Hotel Delfort	17	La Taberna Restaurant	33	ENTEL
10	Hotel Amazonas	18	El Cajamarques	34	Cine los Andes
12	Hotel Becerra		Restaurant	35	Cajamarca Tours &
14	Hostal Peru	23	Helados Capri		Aero Cóndor
15	Hotel Plaza	32	Restaurant Atahualpa	37	El Cuarto del Rescate
16	Hostal 2 de Mayo			38	PIP Police
18	Hotel Continental		OTHER	39	Cine Ollanta
20	Hotel San Francisco			40	Complejo Belén
21	Hostal Sucre	1	Local Buses to Airport		(Church, Hospital,
29	Hostal Bolívar		& Otuzco		Art & Archaeology
31	Hotel de Turistas	4	Museo Arqueológico		Museums)
32	Hostal Atahualpa	11	Laundry	41	Teatro Cajamarca
35	Hotel Cajamarca	19	San Francisco &	42	Museo de Etnografía
36	Hotel Casa Blanca		Museo de Arte		
			Religioso		

PERU

building on the Plaza de Armas. They have some hot water, and a few rooms with balconies and plaza views. A double with private bath and plaza view is US$10; cheaper rooms (without views and with communal showers) are available. On the same block, the *Hostal Perú* has rooms with private cold showers (US$3.75/7). Rooms at the *Hostal Sucre*, A Puga 815, have a sink and toilet (US$2.50 per person); there are communal showers in the mornings. The basic *Hostal Bolívar*, on Apurimac, is similarly priced.

The following charge about US$4.50/7.50. The clean *Hostal Yusovi*, Amazonas 637, has cold water in the rooms and occasional hot water in communal showers. The *Hostal 2 de Mayo*, just off the Plaza de Armas, has hot showers in the evening. The *Hotel Atahualpa*, on Lima near Atahualpa, looks good and clean and has private hot showers.

The bare-looking *Hostal Turismo*, on the 800 block of 2 de Mayo, has clean, carpeted rooms with comfortable beds and private hot showers (US$7.50/11.25). Other reasonable places at this price are the *Hotel Becerra*, Arequipa 195, and the *Hotel Delfort*, on Apurimac.

Places to Eat

The *Salas*, on the Plaza de Armas, is a barn of a place, popular with the locals; it serves various reasonably priced local dishes. Similar, but a little cheaper, is the *Chifa Zarco*, around the corner. *El Real Plaza*, at 2 de Mayo No 569, has a pleasant courtyard and serves local dishes.

For a typical local lunch (including cuy), try the rustic *La Namorina*, 1½ km from the centre on the road to the Baños del Inca, or *Sabor Cajabambino*, on La Paz near the bus stations. The *Atahualpa*, next to the hotel, and *El Imperial*, on the 600 block of Amazonas, have good, cheap fixed menus and other meals.

Getting There & Away

Air Expresso Aéreo has three flights a week to Lima (US$90) and Chachapoyas (US$45). Aero-Cóndor also has flights. Chiclayo, Trujillo and jungle destinations are sometimes served but cancelled flights are common. Local buses for Otuzco pass by the airport.

Bus Most bus terminals are on the third block of a street called Atahualpa (not to be confused with the Atahualpa on the map, in the town centre), about one km south-east of town on the road to the Baños del Inca. You can buy tickets at the bus terminals, or from the travel agency under the Hotel Perú, A Puga 637, on the Plaza de Armas. Several companies have buses for Lima (about 15 hours), Trujillo (nine hours), Chiclayo (seven hours) and other destinations.

TEPSA (☎ 92-3075) is the most expensive, with overnight buses to Lima (US$17.50) and Chachapoyas. Sudamericano has overnight buses to Lima (US$14), and late-night buses to Trujillo (US$5) and Chiclayo. Empresa Atahualpa (☎ 92-3075) has several overnight buses to Lima leaving in the afternoon, and noon buses to Cajabamba (US$5, seven hours), Celendín (US$3, four hours) and Sucre. Empresa Díaz (☎ 92-3449) has night buses to Lima, Trujillo and Chiclayo, and also has service to Chachapoyas. Vulcano has both day and night buses to Trujillo, and also a night bus to Chiclayo. NorPeru has buses to Lima, Trujillo, Chimbote, Cajabamba, Celendín and Chota (nine hours through wild countryside). There are a few other companies.

AROUND CAJAMARCA
Baños del Inca
These natural hot springs are six km from Cajamarca. The water is channelled into private cubicles, some large enough for several people at a time, which can be rented for a few cents per hour. Colectivo taxis for the hot springs leave from the Cajamarca Plaza de Armas.

Cumbe Mayo
Pre-Inca channels run for several km across the bleak mountaintops, about 23 km from Cajamarca by road. Nearby are caves with petroglyphs. The countryside is high, windswept and slightly eerie. The site can be reached on foot from Cerro Santa Apolonia via a signposted road. The walk takes about four hours, if you take the obvious short cuts and ask passers-by for directions. Tours (US$6) are sold in Cajamarca.

Ventanillas de Otuzco
This pre-Inca site is a graveyard, with hundreds of funerary niches built into the hillside. The site is in beautiful countryside, and you can walk here from Cajamarca or the Baños del Inca. There are local buses.

Llacanora & Hacienda La Colpa
The picturesque village of Llacanora is 13 km from Cajamarca. Some inhabitants still play the traditional *clarín*, a three-metre-long bamboo trumpet. A few km away is the Hacienda La Colpa, a cattle ranch which is often visited on tours to Llacanora.

CELENDÍN
This small, pleasant town is a possible stopover between Cajamarca (four hours) and Chachapoyas (a rough but spectacular 12-hour trip). Buses may be delayed in the wet season (December to April). There are several cheap, basic hotels.

CHACHAPOYAS
This quiet and pleasant little town stands at about 2000 metres, on the eastern slopes of the Andes. Nearby are some little-known but interesting archaeological sites. One of the most accessible is the magnificent ruin of Kuelap. Chachapoyas has a small museum, at Merced 800.

Information
The tourist information office is on the Plaza de Armas. Changing money in Chachapoyas can be problematic.

Places to Stay & Eat
Most hotels have occasional hot water and charge about US$2.50 to US$3 per person, or US$5/7.50 for rooms with private bath. *El Dorado, Amazonas* and *Johumaji* seem to be the best.

The *Restaurant Vegas* and *Chacha*, on the plaza, are cheap and OK. The *Kuelap*, around the corner, is also cheap and good. The *Chifa El Turista*, Amazonas 575, is clean and modern. *La Estancia*, Amazonas 861, and *La Oficina*, on the plaza, are both popular bars.

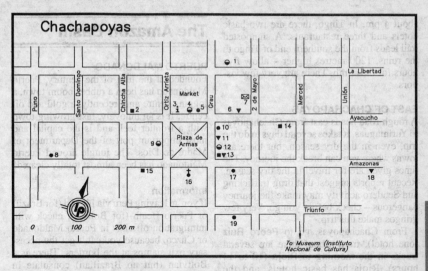

Chachapoyas

0 100 200 m

To Museum (Instituto Nacional de Cultura)

PERU

1 Local Transport
2 Hotel El Dorado
3 Tourist Office
4 ETOSA Buses, Expresso Aéreo &
  La Oficina Bar
5 Aero Cóndor
6 Kuelap Restaurant
7 Correo Central
8 PIP Police
9 CIVA Buses & Banco de Crédito
10 Air Force Office
11 Chacha Restaurant
12 Olano Buses to Chiclayo
13 Hotel Amazonas & Restaurant
   Vegas
14 Hostal Johumaji
15 Hotel Kuelap
16 Church
17 La Estancia Bar
18 Chifa El Turista
19 ENTEL

Getting There & Away

Air Expresso Aéreo has three flights a week to Lima (US$98) and may serve other destinations. Aero-Cóndor also flies here. The air force has occasional cheaper flights – check locally.

Bus Olano, ETOSA and CIVA have buses to Chiclayo (US$9.50, 12 hours) and Lima (US$23, 30 hours).

Small minibuses and pick-up trucks leave from La Libertad and Grau for various destinations. Several a day go to Tingo (US$1.25, 1½ hours) and on to Leimebamba (US$2.50, three hours), leaving from dawn to mid-afternoon. This is the service for Kuelap. Minibuses go to Pedro Ruiz (US$1.25, 1½ hours), from where you can continue down the eastern slopes of the Andes. There are also buses to Celendín (12 hours).

KUELAP

This immense, oval-shaped pre-Inca city is 3100 metres above sea level, on a ridge above the Río Utcubamba, south-east of Chachapoyas. Admission is US$2.50.

There is a small (four-bed) hostel on the site (US$1.25). Camping is possible, but purify your water. Very basic food is available. The friendly guardian will show you where to stay, and give a tour – a small tip is appreciated.

To get there, take a minibus from Chachapoyas to Tingo. Buses stop running about 4 pm. In Tingo, there are two basic hotels and three restaurants. A signposted trail leads from the southern end of Tingo to the ruins, 1200 metres higher – allow five hours for the climb. There are very few visitors.

EAST OF CHACHAPOYAS
A rough road heads east from Chachapoyas to Yurimaguas. It takes several days to do the trip, even in the dry season, but there are towns where you can break the journey. The times given are for travel in the dry season. Recent reports suggest that drug trafficking and Sendero activity may make the journey dangerous – check before you go. Very few gringos make this trip.

From Chachapoyas, go to **Pedro Ruiz** (one hotel), from where there are several trucks in the morning to **Rioja** (10 to 14 hours). Rioja has basic hotels, and the regional airport, with flights to Chiclayo with Faucett. Minibuses leave Rioja's Plaza for **Moyobamba** (45 minutes) at frequent intervals.

Moyobamba, a small town, is the capital of the Department of San Martín. Visitors may need to register at the PIP police post. Tourist information is available and there are hot springs nearby. Moyobamba has several cheap to mid-range hotels. Minibuses leave frequently for **Tarapoto** (four hours).

Tarapoto is the largest town in the area, with tourist information and money-exchange facilities and over a dozen cheap to mid-range hotels. It can be reached by Transportes Chinchaysuyo bus from Chiclayo, or by air.

The airport is three km from Tarapoto. There are flights to Lima, Iquitos, Yurimaguas and Pucallpa with one or more of AeroPerú, Faucett and Americana. Expresso Aéreo has flights to other jungle towns and to Chiclayo. Schedules change frequently. Smaller airlines also operate from the airport.

Trucks and buses to the jungle town of **Yurimaguas** (for riverboats to Iquitos) leave irregularly in the mornings from the end of Jirón Ursua; the trip takes all day.

The Amazon Basin

PUERTO MALDONADO
Founded at the turn of the century, Puerto Maldonado has been a rubber boom town, a logging centre and, recently, a gold and oil centre. It is an unlovely, fast-growing town with a frontier feel, and is the capital and most important port of the Department of Madre de Dios. The jungle around Puerto Maldonado has been almost totally cleared.

Information
If you're leaving Peru via Iñapari (for Brazil) or Puerto Heath (for Bolivia), check with immigration officials in Puerto Maldonado or Cuzco, because you can't get the necessary exit stamps at the borders. There is a Bolivian (but no Brazilian) consulate in Puerto Maldonado.

The Banco de Crédito will change cash dollars and maybe Brazilian *cruzeiros*, but changing travellers' cheques or Bolivian pesos is difficult. Ask around for moneychangers.

Things to See
A cheap way of seeing the Río Madre de Dios is to cross it on one of the *peki-peki* boats which leave from the dock several times an hour. The river is about 500 metres wide at this point; the crossing takes five minutes.

Places to Stay
Hotels Hotels fill up quickly. Cheap hotels with cold communal showers charge about US$2.50 per person. The *Moderno*, Billinghurst 359, is quiet, clean and has many rooms. The *Oriental*, on the plaza, is a typical, basic Amazonian hotel with a tin roof and rough wooden walls painted green. Other OK cheapies are the *Hotel Cross*, the *Hotel Tambo de Oro* and the *Central*, and the worse-looking *Mary* and *Chávez*.

The *Hotel Rey Port* has singles/doubles with private cold shower and fan for US$5/7, but it's still a basic hotel. The better *Hotel Wilson* has clean rooms (US$4 per person

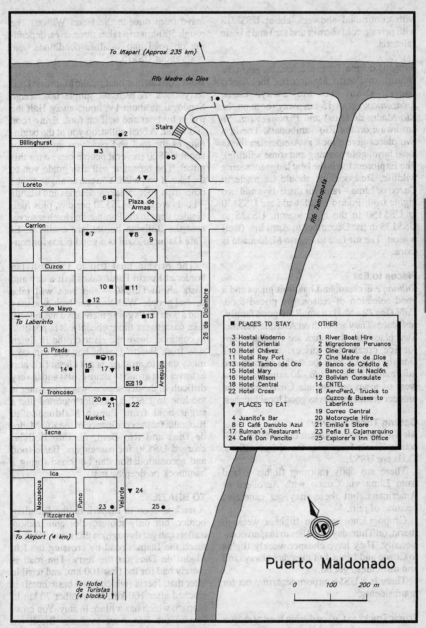

PERU

To Iñapari (Approx 235 km)

Río Madre de Dios

Stairs

Billinghurst

Loreto

Plaza de Armas

Carrion

Cuzco

2 de Mayo

To Laberinto

G Prada

J Troncoso

Tacna

Ica

Moquegua

Puno

Velarde

Fitzcarrald

To Airport (4 km)

26 de Diciembre

Arequipa

Río Tambopata

Market

To Hotel
de Turistas
(4 blocks)

■ PLACES TO STAY

3   Hostal Moderno
6   Hotel Oriental
10 Hotel Chávez
11 Hotel Rey Port
13 Hotel Tambo de Oro
15 Hotel Mary
16 Hotel Wilson
18 Hotel Central
22 Hotel Cross

▼ PLACES TO EAT

4   Juanito's Bar
8   El Café Danubio Azul
17 Rulman's Restaurant
24 Café Don Pancito

OTHER

1   River Boat Hire
2   Migraciones Peruanos
5   Cine Grau
7   Cine Madre de Dios
9   Banco de Crédito &
    Banco de la Nación
12 Bolivian Consulate
14 ENTEL
16 AeroPerú, Trucks to
    Cuzco & Buses to
    Laberinto
19 Correo Central
20 Motorcycle Hire
21 Emilio's Store
23 Peña El Cajamarquino
25 Explorer's Inn Office

Puerto Maldonado

0   100   200 m

with communal showers, about US$8/12 with private cold shower and fan) and a basic cafeteria.

Jungle Lodges There are three lodges in the vicinity of Puerto Maldonado: the *Tambo Lodge*, about 10 km away, *Cuzco Amazónico*, about 15 km away (both on the Río Madre de Dios) and *Explorers Inn*, 58 km away, on the Río Tambopata. The first two places give a look at Amazonian life (a local farm, gold panning and some wildlife). The Explorers Inn is the best lodge for seeing wildlife. Reservations should be made in Cuzco or Lima – rates for three days and two nights from Puerto Maldonado are US$120 to US$150 in the high season, US$85 to US$135 in the December to April low (wet) season. The air fare to Puerto Maldonado is extra.

Places to Eat

Rulman's is clean, and has fruit juices and a good selection of reasonably priced food. *Café Don Pancito* is a small but good family-run place. They are both on Avenida Velarde. Two places on the plaza are *Juanito's Bar*, for ice cream and juices, and *El Café Danubio Azul*, where the staff is friendly and informative. The *Califa*, 20 minutes north-west of town on Avenida Cuzco, near the pioneer cemetery, serves good local lunches.

Getting There & Away

Air The airport is four km out of town. Colectivos leave from near the airline offices. Taxis are US$2.

There are daily morning flights to and from Lima via Cuzco with AeroPerú or Americana, but these may get cancelled because of rain.

Grupo Ocho has one flight a week to Iberia, on Thursday, and flies to Iñapari occasionally. They have cheaper weekly flights to Cuzco and Lima, but these are always full and difficult to get on.

There is a US$6 airport departure tax for nonresidents.

Truck Trucks to Cuzco during the dry season leave from outside the Hotel Wilson. The rough 500-km trip takes three days, depending on road and weather conditions, and costs about US$15.

Boat You can hire boats at the Madre de Dios ferry dock. A pleasant jungle lake, Lago Sandoval, is about 1½ hours away. Half the trip is by boat and half on foot. Bring food and water. A boat will drop you at the beginning of the trail and pick you up later, for about US$20 (several people can go for this price). The boatman will also guide you to the lake, if you wish. You can arrange various other trips, to local lakes, beaches and islands – boats are about US$20 per day, plus fuel. Guided trips to the Pampas de Heath reserve, near the Bolivian border, are available. El Café Danubio Azul is a good place for contacts.

The private boat trip to the Bolivian border at Puerto Pardo takes half a day and costs about US$80 – the boat will take several people. With time and luck, you may find a boat that's going there anyway and will take passengers more cheaply. It is possible to continue down the river on the Bolivian side from Puerto Heath, but this can take many days to arrange, is not cheap (it's best to travel in a group to share costs) and is very difficult in the dry season, when the water is too low. In 1992, a traveller reported that a sugar boat from Puerto Maldonado to Riberalta (at the confluence of the Río Madre de Dios and Río Beni, far into Bolivia) charged US$30 for passengers. Basic food and accommodation can be found (bring a hammock or sleeping mat).

TO BRAZIL

A track is open to Iñapari, on the Brazilian border, but only motorcycles and tractor-trailers can get through on this route. You can reach the Iñapari road by crossing the Río Madre de Dios on the ferry. The road is merely bad for the first 100 km, and terrible after that. Iberia (which has a basic hotel) is reached after 160 km. It's another 70 km to Iñapari, which has a place to stay. You cross (wade) the Río Acre to Assis Brasil (in

Brazil), where there is also a hotel. From Assis, a bad road goes to the adjoining border towns of Brasiléia (Brazil) and Cobija (Bolivia). Both towns have hotels, and road, boat and air connections further into Amazonia. Grupo Ocho flies to Iberia or Iñapari.

LABERINTO

A regular bus service, departing from in front of the Hotel Wilson, links Puerto Maldonado with the nearby gold town of Laberinto (1½ hours). You can see miners selling gold dust at the Banco de los Mineros.

PUCALLPA

Pucallpa is a fast-growing jungle town and is linked directly with Lima by road. Unfortunately, the road journey through Huánuco and Tingo María has been dangerous, because of terrorist, drug-running and bandit activity. In 1992, however, the road was under strict military control, and buses were making the journey during daylight hours, with overnight stopovers in Tingo María. Air travellers have not had problems, but check current conditions before going there.

The main reasons to go to Pucallpa are to visit the nearby lake of Yarinacocha and to continue down the Río Ucayali by riverboat to Iquitos.

Money

The Banco de Crédito changes money and travellers' cheques.

Places to Stay

The cheapest hotels are near the intersection of Raymondi and 7 de Junio. The *Hostal Tayriri* charges about US$6 for a single room with bath and fan. The *Hotel Barbtur* is slightly more expensive, and better. There are several cheaper, more basic places, as well as a number of better ones.

Places to Eat

There are several reasonably priced restaurants near the intersection of Raymondi and Ucayali.

Getting There & Away

Air Faucett, AeroPerú and Americana have offices in the centre. There are daily services to Iquitos and Lima. Expresso Aéreo has flights to Tocache, Juanjui and Tarapoto.

Grupo Ocho has occasional flights to Lima and Iquitos, but their office in the centre is often closed. TANS also has a float plane leaving Yarinacocha on Saturday for Iquitos, stopping at various river ports en route. This plane is always full, and preference is given to locals.

Bus Daily buses leave Pucallpa for Tingo María and Lima – the journey takes two days, with an overnight in Tingo. Alternatively, take a faster colectivo to Tingo and then continue by bus – the road is poor from Pucallpa to Tingo but is mainly paved from Tingo to Lima.

Boat Pucallpa's port of La Hoyada is 2½ km north-east of the centre along unpaved roads. Riverboats to Iquitos take five or six days. It's difficult to get a passage towards the end of the dry season (July to November), when the river is too low for many of the boats. It is easier to get boats to the ports of **Contamana** and **Requena**. In Contamana, you can stay with local families, but onward passage is no more frequent than from Pucallpa. Requena has a couple of basic hotels (the *Hotel Montecarlo*, at US$3.50 a double, is OK), and boats to Iquitos (12 hours) leave most days.

Be prepared to wait several days for a boat. Food is provided but is very basic. Hammocks and mosquito repellent are essential.

Passengers from Pucallpa to Iquitos must have their passport inspected by the PIP (police) and the Capitanía before departure.

Getting Around

No 1 buses run north-west along Ucayali to the airport (20 minutes). Taxis to the airport are US$3. The green No 6 bus leaves from the corner of Atahualpa and Dos de Mayo for Yarinacocha (half an hour). A taxi to Yarinacocha is US$4.

PERU

YARINACOCHA

This lovely oxbow lake is 10 km north-east of Pucallpa. You can take canoe rides, observe wildlife, visit Indian communities and purchase handicrafts. The village of Puerto Callao has two cheap hotels and several bars and restaurants.

On the plaza, the local Shipibo Indians have a cooperative craft store (Maroti Shobo), which collects work from some 40 villages. There are thousands of unique, handmade ceramics to choose from. You can visit the Shipibo in some of their villages, especially San Francisco.

Tours

Peki-peki boats and drivers are available – bargain for the best deals. For the trip to San Francisco and back, a boatman might charge about US$10; with a guide, it will cost twice as much. A good afternoon trip is up the north-east arm of the lake, to look for bird life at the water's edge or sloths in the trees.

YURIMAGUAS

This quiet, pleasant little town is the major port on the Río Huallaga. Boats to Iquitos can be found here, though you may have to wait a week or more. Reaching Yurimaguas involves a hard road trip of several days or a simple flight from Lima.

The Yurimaguas area has been the centre of recent narcotics activity – make inquiries before travelling there.

Money

The Banco Amazónico will change cash dollars and travellers' cheques, but rates are poor.

Places to Stay & Eat

There are about eight cheapish hotels, of which *Leo's Palace* (also called the Cheraton), the *Gran Hotel Yurimaguas*, the *Hostal Floríndez* and the *Hostal Estrella* are the best. There are several cheap restaurants – none is special.

Getting There & Away

Air Faucett has several flights a week to Lima via Tarapoto. Expresso Aéreo flies to Iquitos, Tarapoto, Rioja, Juanjui and Chiclayo twice a week.

Bus & Truck Trucks, jeeps and (road permitting) buses ply the rough road to Tarapoto on most days – ask in the hotels and restaurants. The Gran Hotel Yurimaguas is a good place to start.

Boat Cargo boats leave irregularly a few times a month from Yurimaguas, heading down the Huallaga to the Río Marañón and on to Iquitos. The trip takes two to 10 days, depending on the boat. Police searches of boats have been reported – this is for drugs.

IQUITOS

With a population of about 400,000, Iquitos is Peru's largest jungle city, and the capital of the huge Department of Loreto. Iquitos is linked with the outside world by air and the Río Amazonas – it is the largest city in the Amazon Basin without road links.

Iquitos was founded in the 1750s as a Jesuit mission. In the late 19th century, it was a rubber boom town, and signs of the opulence of those days remain in some of the mansions and tiled walls. Today, both the oil and tourist industries play an important part in the economy of the area.

Being so isolated, Iquitos seems to have been bypassed by the problems of terrorism and thievery – but watch your possessions nevertheless! The people are friendly and easy-going.

Information

Tourist Office There is a tourist office on Arica, between Palma and Brasil. Various jungle guides and lodges also give tourist information, biased towards selling their services, which are not cheap. Jungle lodges are usually in second-growth forest, and touristy. Adventurous camping trips can also be arranged, but expect to pay at least US$30 per day.

Money There are banks are on Raymondi, near the plaza. The Banco de Crédito and the

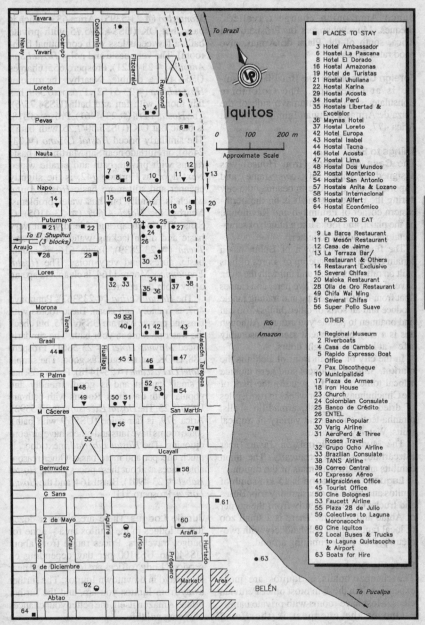

Iquitos

0   100   200 m

Approximate Scale

PERU

PLACES TO STAY

3 Hotel Ambassador
6 Hostel La Pascana
8 Hotel El Dorado
16 Hostal Amazonas
19 Hotel de Turistas
21 Hostal Jhuliana
22 Hostal Karina
29 Hostal Acosta
34 Hostal Perú
35 Hostals Libertad &
   Excelsior
36 Maynas Hotel
37 Hostal Loreto
42 Hotel Europa
43 Hostal Isabel
44 Hostal Tacna
46 Hotel Acosta
47 Hostal Lima
48 Hostal Dos Mundos
52 Hostal Monterico
54 Hostal San Antonio
57 Hostals Anita & Lozano
58 Hostal Internacional
61 Hostal Alfert
64 Hostal Económico

PLACES TO EAT

9 La Barca Restaurant
11 El Mesón Restaurant
12 Casa de Jaime
13 La Terraza Bar/
   Restaurant & Others
14 Restaurant Exclusivo
15 Several Chifas
20 Maloka Restaurant
49 Olla de Oro Restaurant
49 Chifa Wai Ming
51 Several Chifas
56 Super Pollo Suave

OTHER

1 Regional Museum
2 Riverboats
4 Casa de Cambio
5 Rapido Expresso Boat
   Office
7 Pax Discotheque
10 Municipalidad
17 Plaza de Armas
18 Iron House
23 Church
24 Colombian Consulate
25 Banco de Crédito
26 ENTEL
27 Banco Popular
30 Varig Airline
31 AeroPerú & Three
   Roses Travel
32 Grupo Ocho Airline
33 Brazilian Consulate
38 TANS Airline
39 Correo Central
40 Expresso Aéreo
41 Migraciónes Office
45 Tourist Office
50 Cine Bolognesi
53 Faucett Airline
55 Plaza 28 de Julio
59 Colectivos to Laguna
   Moronococha
60 Cine Iquitos
62 Local Buses & Trucks
   to Laguna Quistacocha
   & Airport
63 Boats for Hire

Banco Amazonico change travellers' cheques. Moneychangers on Próspero and Arica, south of the Plaza de Armas, give good rates for cash.

Foreign Consulates The Brazilian Consulate is at Lores 363. The Colombian Consulate is on the Putumayo side of the Plaza de Armas. Peruvian Immigration is at Arica 477.

Things to See

The **Casa de Hierro** (Iron House) was designed by Eiffel (of Tower fame) and imported piece by piece to beautify the city during the rubber boom. It is on the northeastern corner of Putumayo and Raymondi, on the plaza, and looks like a bunch of scrapmetal sheets bolted together.

The floating shantytown of **Belén** has a certain charm; it is made up of scores of huts built on rafts, which rise and fall with the river. Several thousand people live here, and canoes float from hut to hut selling and trading jungle produce and all sorts of other things. You can find boatmen to paddle you around. Although this is a very poor area, it seems reasonably safe – at least in daylight hours.

In the city blocks in front of Belén is the **market**. Strange products sold here include a local tonic (made by soaking the bark of the Chuchuhuasi tree for weeks in rum), piles of dried frogs and fish, armadillo shells, piranha teeth and a great variety of tropical fruits. Watch your wallet.

The **Museo Regional**, on Tavara near Fitzcarrald, is open erratically. The main exhibits are stuffed animals of the region.

Laguna Quistacocha is 15 km south of Iquitos and makes a pleasant day trip. Buses and trucks leave frequently from the corner of Abtao and Aguirre. There is a small zoo of local fauna, and a fish hatchery with two-metre paiche fish swimming around.

Places to Stay

The cheaper hotels in Iquitos are more expensive than those in most other Peruvian cities. Most have rooms with private bath.

One of the cheapest is the *Hostal Monterico* (☎ 23-5395), Arica 633, which is basic but OK (US$4.25/5.75 with private bath, a few cents less with communal bathroom). The very basic and noisy *Hostal San Antonio* (☎ 23-5221), Prospero 655, charges US$5 for a double. Nearby, the quieter *Hostal Lima* (☎ 23-5152), Próspero 549, has fair rooms with fan and bath (US$4.75/6). The *Hostal Perú* (☎ 23-4961), Próspero 318, is basic but OK (US$5.50/7.25 with bath). The similarly priced *Hostal Lozano* (☎ 23-2486), on Hurtado near San Martín, has basic rooms with private bath and erratic water. Next door, at Hurtado 742, is the slightly cheaper and still more basic *Hostal Anita*, which is friendly but has water problems. Nearby, the *Hotel Alfert* (☎ 23-4105), G Sans 001, is cheap and friendly, but very basic and often lacking water. The *Hostal Tacna* (☎ 23-2839), Tacna 516, is cheap, basic, airless and very noisy. The *Hostal Económico*, Moore 1164, is clean, cheap and away from the centre.

The *Hostal Karina* (☎ 235367), Putumayo 467, is friendly and clean. Basic rooms with fans and private bath are US$6/7.75, but check the water pressure in your bath. The similarly priced *Maynas Hotel* (☎ 23-5861), Próspero 388, is OK but not quite as good. The simple *Hotel La Pascana* (☎ 23-1418), Pevas 133, has a small garden and is good, friendly and popular with travellers. Rooms with bath are US$7/8.25. The *Hostal Excelsior* (☎ 23-5592), Arica 379, is fair value (US$6/9 with bath); some rooms have fans and others have air-conditioning. The *Hostal Libertad*, next door, is much cheaper and more basic. Other reasonable places at about these prices are the *Hostal Isabel* (☎ 23-4901), Brasil 164, and the *Hostal Loreto*, Próspero 311.

Jungle Lodges There are about a dozen jungle lodges in the Iquitos area – none for budget travellers. Prices range from about US$40 to US$100 per day depending on services. Lodge offices are found on and near Putumayo in downtown Iquitos. The further away from Iquitos you are, and the further off the Amazon itself, the better your chances of seeing wildlife.

Explorama Tours is one of the longest established and best known companies – they have three lodges. Their Explornapo camp, 160 km from Iquitos on the Río Napo, is the most interesting and boasts the new Canopy Walkway System developed by scientists from the Amazon Center for Environmental Education and Research (ACEER). The walkway, which is several hundred metres long and 30 metres above the forest floor, gives the visitor a unique look at the rainforest canopy. More information can be obtained from Explorama Tours, Apartado 446, Iquitos (☎ 23- 5471, 23-3481; fax 23-4968; in the USA 1 (800) 223 6764) or ACEER, 10 Environs Park, Helena, AL 35080, USA (☎ 1 (800) 255 8206).

Places to Eat
There are several chifas and chicken places on and near the Plaza 28 de Julio. They vary from fairly cheap to moderately expensive. Meals start at about US$1.50 for a quarter of a chicken. The *Chifa Wai Ming* is considered the best. Another good area for a choice of reasonably priced chifas and chicken places is on Huallaga south of Napo.

La Barca, on Fitzcarrald just off the Plaza de Armas, is OK and quite cheap. *El Shupihui*, at Castilla and Araujo, serves typical local dishes at reasonable prices.

There are a bunch of bars/restaurants on the waterfront, near Napo, which are popular with locals for hanging out. The *Terraza* is one which has been recommended. The *Casa de Jaime* is a cheap to mid-priced restaurant with good parrilladas. The floating *Maloka Restaurant*, on the next block, is one of the most expensive in town but has nice Amazon views. This is a safe enough area, but single women may get harassed at night, as prostitutes hang out here.

Getting There & Away
Air The airport is about eight km south of town. AeroPerú (☎ 23-1454), at Próspero 248, Faucett (☎ 23-9195), at Próspero 630, and Americana, on the same block, have two or three flights a day to Lima (US$70). There are also flights to Tarapoto (US$52),

Pucallpa (US$52) and Trujillo (US$58). Tickets are sometimes discounted – ask. Expresso Aéreo, on the 400 block of Arica, has slightly cheaper flights to Trujillo, Tarapoto, Yurimaguas, Requena and other jungle towns. Three Roses Travel, Próspero 246 next to AeroPerú, is helpful with flight bookings.

Grupo Ocho, at the corner of Huallaga and Lores, has weekly flights to Lima and sometimes Pucallpa. TANS (☎ 23-4632), Lores 124, has flights to Requena, Contamana and Pucallpa, as well as to Islandia, by the border with Brazil. These are cheaper than commercial flights but are hard to get on.

Varig (☎ 23-4381), Arica 273, flies to Tabatinga on the Brazilian side of the border, and on to Manaus (in Brazil). Faucett has three flights a week to Miami.

Airport departure tax is US$17 for international flights, US$6 for domestic flights.

Boat The Iquitos docks have blackboards showing which boats are leaving, when, for where, and whether they are accepting passengers.

Passages are available to Pucallpa or Yurimaguas (upriver), taking four to 10 days, depending on the boat and the amount of trade done en route. Fares are around US$30. Boats leave every few days – less often if the river is low.

Boats to the Peruvian side of the border with Brazil and Colombia leave twice a week (US$15 to US$20, two days). Rapido Expresso, on Loreto by the waterfront, has express launches to Leticia (in Colombia), leaving at 6 am three times a week (US$50, 10 hours).

Getting Around
Blue-and-green city buses marked 'Aeropuerto' run south along Tacna to the airport. A taxi to the airport costs about US$5 to US$6. The local two-passenger motorcycle rickshaws are ubiquitous; they cost a bit less than taxis. Buses and trucks for nearby destinations, including the airport, leave from the area between Grau and Aguirre.

Crossing the Borders

Brazil, Colombia and Peru share a three-way border, with several ports within a few km of one another, connected by public ferries. The biggest town is Leticia (Colombia), which is linked with Tabatinga (Brazil) by a road bridge (it's a short walk). Leticia has the best choice of hotels, restaurants and moneychanging facilities, and a hospital. On the south bank of the Amazon, opposite Leticia/Tabatinga, is Santa Rosa (Peru). This is marked on most maps as Ramón Castilla, which is the old port. Because of changes in the flow of the river, Ramón Castilla is no longer on the main Amazon; Santa Rosa is used instead, though there is nowhere to stay here.

About 1½ hours downriver from Leticia are the ports of Benjamin Constant (Brazil) and Islandia (Peru), opposite one another. There is basic accommodation on the Brazilian side, but not on the Peruvian. There is a twice-daily ferry from Leticia to Benjamin Constant and back.

Exit formalities when leaving Peru are strict, and Peruvian border officials may send you back to Iquitos if your entry stamp has expired. Riverboats stop at the Peruvian guard post for passport formalities, but make sure the captain knows that you need to do this. Check with the immigration office in Iquitos about exit formalities.

To enter or leave Colombia, get your passport stamped in Leticia. On entering or leaving Brazil, formalities are normally carried out in Benjamin Constant, though Tabatinga also has an immigration office. To enter or leave Peru, ask your boat captain where formalities take place – the anchorages of Islandia, Santa Rosa or, occasionally, elsewhere. Regulations change, but the boat captains know where to go. Don't try to enter a country without getting the required exit stamp first. You can easily travel between the three countries without having the correct stamps, as long as you stay in the tri-border area. As soon as you leave the border ports, however, your documents must be in order.

Boats to Iquitos leave from Islandia or Tabatinga every few days (about US$20, 2½ days). Alternatively, take the thrice-weekly Rapido Expreso from Leticia (US$50, 14 hours).

Boats to Manaus (Brazil) leave from Tabatinga, then spend a night in Benjamin Constant before continuing. The fare is about US$100 in a shared cabin (less for hanging your own hammock) for the three to six-day trip, including very basic meals. Do not rely on clean water or food – bring your own if you have a sensitive stomach. The food, if hot, is usually OK to eat. Bottled soft drinks and beer are usually available. Hammocks are airier, and many travellers prefer them to the stuffy cabins. Hammocks can be bought in the Brazilian ports or in Leticia. Many cargo boats ply this part of the Amazon; ones which have been recommended include the *Almirante Monteiro, Aradeus Caravhno, Avelina, Cidade de Teresina, Clivia, Dominique, Itauna* and *Voyager*, but there are others which are probably just as good.

Leticia and Tabatinga have airports, with flights into the interiors of Colombia and Brazil respectively.

Uruguay

Uruguay, a political buffer between Argentina and Brazil, is only a short hop across the Río de la Plata from Buenos Aires; many Argentines are drawn by the charming town of Colonia (Colonia del Sacramento), by the capital, Montevideo, and by the beaches beyond Montevideo, but towns up the Río Uruguay are also pleasant. Uruguay's hilly interior is gaucho country.

The República Oriental del Uruguay (Eastern Republic of Uruguay) was long called the Banda Oriental (Eastern Shore) of the Río de la Plata.

Facts about the Country

HISTORY
The aboriginal Charrúa Indians were a hunter-gatherer people who also fished. They deterred European settlement, though in part this was because the Spaniards, as William Henry Hudson wrote, 'loved gold and adventure above everything, and finding neither in the Banda, they little esteemed it'. As on the Argentine Pampas, gauchos subsisted on wild cattle until *estancias* pushed them back into the interior.

European Colonisation
Jesuit missionaries settled near Soriano, on the Río Uruguay, but in 1680, Portugal established Nova Colônia do Sacramento, on the Río de la Plata. This challenge forced Spain to build its own citadel, at Montevideo.

Uruguayan hero José Artigas fought against Spain, but could not prevent a Brazilian takeover of the Banda. Exiled to Paraguay, he inspired the '33 Orientales' who, with Argentine support, liberated the area in 1828 and established Uruguay as an independent buffer between the emerging continental powers.

Independence & Development
Uruguay's fragile independence was pressured politically and militarily by its neighbours and economically by Britain.

The Argentine dictator Rosas, supported by the Federalist forces, besieged Montevideo from 1838 to 1851; Uruguay's two major political parties, the Blancos and the Colorados, originated as armed gaucho sympathisers of Federalist and Unitarist causes. As Hudson wrote, 'Endless struggles for mastery ensued, in which the Argentines and Brazilians, forgetting their solemn compact, were for ever taking sides'.

The Liebig Meat Extract Company of London opened a plant at Fray Bentos in 1864, and merino wool brought further

Uruguay

ARGENTINA

BRAZIL

To Porto Alegre

To Pelotas & Porto Alegre

ATLANTIC OCEAN

Río de la Plata

0 50 100 km

opportunities. In 1868, a British railway connected Montevideo with the countryside, where Hereford and Shorthorn cattle soon replaced the rangy criollo stock. At the turn of the century, the massive Anglo plant at Fray Bentos was the country's first *frigorífico* (meat-freezing factory). Commercialisation of livestock meant the demise of the independent gaucho and the rise of the *latifundios*.

Batlle & the Modernisation of Uruguay

In the early 20th century, the visionary President José Batlle y Ordóñez achieved innovations like pensions, unemployment compensation and eight-hour work days. State intervention led to the nationalisation of many industries, the creation of others and general prosperity. Taxing the livestock sector financed Batlle's reforms, but when this sector faltered, the welfare state became unsustainable.

Conservatives blamed the state for 'killing the goose that laid the golden egg', but even earlier, landowners had squandered wealth in conspicuous consumption rather than reinvesting it. Redistributive policies worked only while there was something to redistribute.

Economic Decline & Political Breakdown

By the 1960s, economic stagnation reached crisis stage because of patronage and corruption in state enterprises and the inability to support a large pensioner class. In 1966, highly regarded Colorado presidential candidate Oscar Gestido died soon after taking office and was replaced by Vice-President Jorge Pacheco Areco, an unknown with disturbing authoritarian tendencies.

The country slid into dictatorship as Pacheco outlawed leftist parties, closed newspapers, and invoked state of siege measures because of guerrilla threats. The main guerrilla force was the Movimiento de Liberación Nacional (commonly known as the Tupamaros). After Tupamaros kidnapped and executed a suspected CIA agent (an incident dramatised in Costa-Gavras' film *State of Siege)* and then engineered a major prison escape, Pacheco put the military in charge of counterinsurgency. In November 1971, his chosen successor, Juan Bordaberry, invited the military to participate in government.

The Military Dictatorship & Its Aftermath

With the armed forces occupying almost every position of importance in the national security state, arbitrary detention and torture became routine. The military determined eligibility for public employment, subjected political offenders to military courts, censored libraries and even required prior approval for large family gatherings.

In 1980, voters rejected a new military-devised constitution, but four more years passed before Colorado candidate Julio María Sanguinetti became the President under the 1967 Constitution. His presidency implied a return to democratic traditions, and he supported a controversial amnesty for military human rights violators; despite serious misgivings, a majority of voters approved the amnesty in 1989.

GEOGRAPHY & CLIMATE

Uruguay's 187,000 sq km are slightly greater than the area of England and Wales combined. Its rolling northern hills are an extension of southern Brazil. West of Montevideo, the terrain is more level, while the Atlantic coast has impressive beaches, dunes and headlands.

Uruguay's grasslands and gallery forests resemble those of the Argentine Pampas or southern Brazil. In the southeast, along the Brazilian border, some areas of palm savanna remain. Frosts are almost unknown, even in winter. Rainfall averages about 1000 mm, evenly distributed throughout the year.

GOVERNMENT

Uruguay's 1967 constitution establishes three separate branches of government. The President heads the executive branch, while the General Assembly, elected for five years, consists of a 99-seat Chamber of Deputies and a 30-member Senate, both chosen by proportional representation. The Supreme Court is the highest judicial power.

Each party may offer several presidential candidates; the winner is the individual with the most votes for the party with the most votes. Thus the president almost certainly lacks a majority (even within his own party) and may not be the candidate with the most overall votes. In eight elections between 1946 and 1984, no candidate won over 31% of the vote.

The major political parties are the Colorados (heirs of Batlle) and the generally more conservative Blancos. The Colorados' Sanguinetti was the first post-military president, while current President Luis Lacalle belongs to the Blancos. The leftist coalition Frente Amplio controls the mayoralty of Montevideo.

ECONOMY

Low prices for wool, the primary export, have caused problems in recent years. Only the south-west littoral has intensive agriculture, and this cropland makes a major contribution to the economy.

Many inefficient state-supported industries produce inferior products at very high cost, surviving only because of protective tariffs. Pensions consume 60% of public

URUGUAY

expenditure. Tourism is increasingly important, as beaches east of Montevideo attract wealthy Argentines.

In many ways, Uruguay is an economic satellite of both Brazil and Argentina. With those two countries and Paraguay, it will be a member of the new Mercosur common market in 1995. Conceivably, by encouraging investment and creating jobs, this opening could reduce the current emigration of youthful talent.

Hyperinflation required the introduction of a new currency, the *peso nuevo*, in 1975; in March 1993, the government created the *peso uruguayo* by cutting three zeros off the peso nuevo. Inflation is still high by European standards, and Uruguay has one of the largest per capita debt burdens in the region.

POPULATION & PEOPLE
About 90% of Uruguay's 3.1 million people reside in cities, and nearly half of them live in Montevideo. Salto, the next largest city, has only 100,000 inhabitants.

Infant mortality is low and the life expectancy of 71 years is comparable to that of many Western European countries, but economic problems have forced half a million Uruguayans to leave the country, mostly for Brazil and Argentina.

Most Uruguayans are of Spanish and Italian origin. There are about 60,000 Black people, descendants of slaves.

EDUCATION
Literacy levels are among the foremost in the region, and secondary enrolment is very high. Many university students study law or medicine, professions which are oversupplied, while the country lacks trained people in more technically oriented careers.

ARTS
For a small country, Uruguay has an impressive literary and artistic tradition; for details on literature, see Books in the Facts for the Visitor section.

Theatre is a popular medium and playwrights are prominent. Punta Ballena, near Punta del Este, is a well-known artists' colony.

RELIGION
Uruguayans are almost exclusively Roman Catholic but the Church has no official status. There is a small Jewish minority, about 25,000, almost all of whom live in Montevideo. Evangelical Protestantism has made some inroads.

LANGUAGE
Spanish is the official language of Uruguay and is universally understood. Along the Brazilian border, many people also speak Portuguese or the hybrid *Fronterizo*.

Facts for the Visitor

VISAS & EMBASSIES
All foreigners need visas, except nationals of Western Europe, Canada, Israel, Japan and the USA or those from bordering countries (who need only national ID cards). All visitors need a tourist card, valid for 90 days and renewable for 90 more. For extensions, visit the Dirección Nacional de Migración (☎ 96-0471), Misiones 1513 in Montevideo. The one-day ferry trip from Buenos Aires to Colonia generally does not require a visa, though there have been reports of Canadians needing one.

Uruguayan Embassies & Consulates
Uruguay's network of diplomatic representatives is less extensive than Argentina's. It has representatives in neighbouring countries, and in:

Australia
    1st floor, Embassy Tower, Suite 107 (GPO Box 318), Woden, ACT 2606 (☎ (06) 282-4800)
Canada
    Suite 1905, 130 Albert St, Ottawa, Ontario (☎ 234-2937)
France
    15 rue Le Sueur, Paris (☎ 45008137)
Germany
    Gotenstrasse 1-3, Bonn 2 (☎ 35-6570)
UK
    48 Lennox Gardens, London SW1X 0DL (☎ (071) 584-8192)
USA
    1918 F St NW, Washington DC (☎ 331-4219)

Foreign Embassies & Consulates in Uruguay

South American countries, the USA and most Western European countries have representatives in Montevideo, but Australians and New Zealanders must rely on their consulates in Buenos Aires.

For Argentine and Brazilian consulates in border towns, see the appropriate town entries. For other countries, see the Montevideo section.

DOCUMENTS

Passports are obligatory for transactions like cashing travellers' cheques and checking into hotels. Theoretically, Uruguay requires the Inter-American Driving Permit rather than the International Driving Permit, but either seems to be accepted.

CUSTOMS

Customs regulations permit the entry of used personal effects and other articles in 'reasonable quantities'.

MONEY

In early 1993, the peso uruguayo (U\$) replaced the peso nuevo (N\$), but the latter banknotes may be in circulation for some time. Peso nuevo values are 50, 100, 200, 500, 1000, 5000 and 10,000. Inflation is high (59% for 1992), and prices are approaching Argentine levels, despite steady devaluations.

Cambios in Montevideo, Colonia and Atlantic beach resorts readily change US dollars and travellers' cheques (the latter at slightly lower rates or modest commissions). Banks are the rule in the interior. Many hotels, restaurants and shops accept credit cards.

Exchange Rates

A\$1	=	U\$2.73
Can\$1	=	U\$3.07
DM1	=	U\$2.35
FF1	=	U\$0.66
UK£1	=	U\$5.98
US\$1	=	U\$4.03

The peso's decline against the dollar has slowed. There is no black market.

WHEN TO GO & WHAT TO BRING

Uruguay's main attraction is its beaches, so most visitors come in summer and dress accordingly. Along the littoral, summer temperatures are smotheringly hot, but the hilly interior is cooler, especially at night.

TOURIST OFFICES

Almost every municipality has a tourist office, usually on the plaza or at the bus terminal. Maps are mediocre, but many brochures have excellent historical information.

Foreign Representatives

Australia
  Tourist inquiries should be directed to the Uruguayan Consulate-General, GPO Box 717, Sydney, NSW 2001 (☎ (02) 232-8029)
Canada
  Suite 1905, 130 Albert St, Ottawa, Ontario (☎ 234-2937)
UK
  Tourist information can be obtained from the Uruguayan Embassy, 48 Lennox Gardens, London SW1X 0DL (☎ (71) 584-8192)
USA
  541 Lexington Ave, New York, NY (☎ 755-1200, extension 346)
  1918 F St NW, Washington DC (☎ 331-1313)

USEFUL ORGANISATIONS

Uruguay's limited youth-hostel network can be an alternative to standard accommodation. Contact the Asociación de Alberguistas del Uruguay (☎ 98-1234), Calle Pablo de María 1583, Montevideo.

BUSINESS HOURS & HOLIDAYS
Business Hours

Most shops open on weekdays and Saturdays from 8.30 am to 12.30 or 1 pm, then close until mid-afternoon and reopen until 7 or 8 pm. Food shops also open on Sunday mornings.

Government offices vary – from mid-November to mid-March, they open from 7.30 am to 1.30 pm; the rest of the year, it's noon to 7 pm. Banks are open on weekday afternoons in Montevideo, but elsewhere, mornings are the rule.

Public Holidays

1 January
  Año Nuevo (New Year's Day)
6 January
  Epifanía (Epiphany)
March/April (dates vary)
  Viernes Santo/Pascua (Good Friday/Easter)
19 April
  Desembarco de los 33 (Return of the 33 Exiles)
1 May
  Día del Trabajador (Labor Day)
18 May
  Batalla de Las Piedras (Battle of Las Piedras)
19 June
  Natalicio de Artigas (Artigas' Birthday)
18 July
  Jura de la Constitución (Constitution Day)
25 August
  Dia de la Independencia (Independence Day)
12 October
  Día de la Raza (Columbus Day)
2 November
  Día de los Muertos (All Souls' Day)
25 December
  Navidad (Christmas Day)

CULTURAL EVENTS

Uruguay's **Carnaval**, the Monday and Tuesday before Ash Wednesday, is livelier than in Argentina but more sedate than in Brazil. The Black population of Montevideo's Barrio Sur celebrates traditional *candomblé* ceremonies. Holy Week (Easter) is also **La Semana Criolla**, with gaucho *asados* (barbeques) and folk music.

POST & TELECOMMUNICATIONS

Postal rates are reasonable but service is poor. Send important items registered.

ANTEL, the state telephone company, has central long-distance offices in most cities. From 10 pm to 7 am, there are long-distance discounts. Public phones take *fichas* (tokens), good for about three minutes, rather than coins.

Credit card or collect calls to the USA (AT&T access code is 000410) and other overseas destinations are cheaper than paying locally.

BOOKS

Uruguay's major contemporary writers are Juan Carlos Onetti (whose novels *No Man's Land*, *The Shipyard* and *A Brief Life* (Grossman, New York, 1976) are available in English) and the poet, essayist and novelist Mario Benedetti. Historian Eduardo Galeano *(Open Veins of Latin America)* is also Uruguayan.

History

For a discussion of Uruguay's social welfare policies, see George Pendle's *Uruguay; South America's First Welfare State*, 3rd edition (London, 1963) or Milton Vanger's *The Model Country: Jose Batlle y Ordóñez of Uruguay, 1907-1915* (Brandeis University Press, 1980).

William Henry Hudson's *The Purple Land* (Creative Arts Book Company, Berkeley, 1979) is a 19th-century classic.

Contemporary Government & Politics

A good starting point is Martin Weinstein's *Uruguay, Democracy at the Crossroads* (Westview Press, Boulder, Colorado, 1987).

MAPS

See the Automóvil Club Uruguayo, Shell and Ancap for the best available road maps, which are not great. For more detail, try the Instituto Geográfico Militar (☎ 81-6868), on the corner of 12 de Octubre and Abreu, Montevideo.

MEDIA

Montevideo's many newspapers include the morning dailies *El Día* (founded by José Batlle), *La República*, *La Mañana* and *El País*. *Gaceta Comercial* is the voice of the business community. Afternoon papers are *El Diario*, *Mundocolor* and *Ultimas Noticias*, a recent arrival operated by followers of Sun Myung Moon. Most are identified with political parties, but the weekly *Búsqueda* takes a more independent stance.

The *Buenos Aires Herald* and other Argentine papers are readily available in Montevideo, Punta del Este and Colonia.

There are 20 TV stations (four in Montevideo) and 100 radio stations (about 40 in the capital).

FOOD & DRINK

Parrillas, confiterías, pizzerías and restaurants closely resemble their Argentine counterparts. Montevideo, Punta del Este and other beach resorts have good international restaurants. Seafood is usually a good choice.

The standard short order is *chivito*, a steak sandwich with cheese, lettuce, tomato, bacon and condiments. *Chivito al plato* is a larger steak topped with a fried egg, plus potato salad, green salad and chips. Other typical items are *olímpicos* (club sandwiches), *húngaros* (spicy sausages) and blander *panchos* (hot dogs).

Uruguayans consume even more *mate* than Argentines and Paraguayans. *Clericó* is a mixture of white wine and fruit juice, while the popular *medio y medio* is a mixture of sparkling wine and white wine. Beer is also good.

ENTERTAINMENT

Cinema is popular throughout the country. Live theatre is also well patronised, especially in Montevideo. Tango is nearly as popular as in Argentina, while Afro-Uruguayan candomblé music and dance add diversity.

Soccer is the major spectator and participant sport; the most popular teams are Nacional and Peñarol.

THINGS TO BUY

Shoppers will appreciate leather clothing and accessories, woollens and fabrics, agates and gems, ceramics, wood crafts and decorated gourds. One popular outlet is the artisans' cooperative Manos del Uruguay.

Getting There & Away

AIR
To/From the USA

United Airlines has three direct flights weekly from Miami, with a stopover in Rio de Janeiro. Otherwise, flights pass through Buenos Aires' Ezeiza Airport.

To/From Europe

PLUNA has Thursday and Sunday flights from Madrid, stopping in Recife and Rio. Iberia, KLM and Lufthansa have direct flights but all others pass through Ezeiza.

To/From Argentina and Brazil

There are frequent flights from Montevideo's Aeropuerto Carrasco to Buenos Aires' Aeroparque Jorge Newbery, as well as from Punta del Este and Colonia to Aeroparque.

PLUNA flies to the Brazilian cities of Porto Alegre, Rio de Janeiro and São Paulo. Varig, Cruzeiro and several European airlines fly similar routes.

To/From Other South American Countries

PLUNA also flies to Asunción, Paraguay (weekly) and Santiago, Chile (twice weekly). Líneas Aéreas Paraguayas (LAP) and LAN-Chile serve their respective countries. Avianca and KLM also go to Santiago.

Leaving Uruguay

International passengers pay a departure tax of US$2.50 to Argentina, US$4.50 to other South American countries, and US$7 to other destinations.

LAND

Uruguay shares borders with Argentina's Entre Ríos province and the southern Brazilian state of Río Grande do Sul. Roads and bus services are good, but there are no international trains.

To/From Argentina

Direct buses to Buenos Aires via Gualeguaychú are slower and less convenient than crossing the Rió de la Plata by boat. For other crossings of the Río Uruguay see Getting There & Away in the Argentina chapter.

URUGUAY

To/From Brazil

Chuy to Chui & Pelotas On the main highway from Montevideo, Chuy and Chui are twin cities, separated only by a median strip on their main street.

Río Branco to Jaguarão This alternative route goes via Treinta y Tres or Melo. There are buses from Jaguarão to Pelotas.

Rivera to Livramento This route from Paysandú, near the Argentine border, goes via Tacuarembó. Regular buses go from Livramento to Porto Alegre.

Artigas to Quaraí This route crosses the Río Quareim, but the main highway goes southeast to Livramento.

Bella Unión to Barra do Quaraí In extreme north-western Uruguay, this crossing leads to Uruguaiana, Brazil, where you can enter Argentina's Corrientes province and go north to Paraguay or Iguazú. Travel to Iguazú through southern Brazil is slow and indirect.

BOAT
Ferrylíneas has morning and evening sailings from Colonia to Buenos Aires (US$20, 2½ hours). The hydrofoil (US$25) takes only an hour.

There are inexpensive launches from Carmelo across the estuary of the Río de la Plata to Tigre, a Buenos Aires suburb.

Getting Around

AIR
PLUNA flies to Punta del Este, while the military airline TAMU serves the interior cities of Artigas, Salto, Rivera, Paysandú, Melo and Tacuarembó. TAMU fares are absurdly cheap.

BUS
Most cities lack central bus terminals, but companies are usually within easy walking distance of the plaza. Buses are frequent to

all destinations, so reservations are rarely necessary. Fares are reasonable – Montevideo to Colonia (180 km) costs only about US$6.

CAR
Uruguayan drivers are less ruthless than Argentines, but there are plenty of Argentines on the road. For drivers lulled to sleep by the Pampas, Uruguay's winding roads and hilly terrain require close attention.

Uruguay ostensibly requires the Inter-American Driving Permit rather than the International Driving Permit. Arbitrary stops and searches are less common than in Argentina, but police will solicit bribes for traffic violations.

Car rental costs about the same as in Argentina. The Automóvil Club del Uruguay (☎ 91-1251), Colonia and Yi in Montevideo, has good maps and information.

LOCAL TRANSPORT
Bus
To make sense of Montevideo's extensive and chaotic public transport, buy the *Guía de Montevideo Eureka*, which lists routes and schedules. Retain your ticket for inspection. The standard fare is about US$0.25.

Taxi
Taxis have meters, and drivers correlate the meter reading with a photocopied fare chart. Fares are higher from midnight to 6 am. There is a small additional luggage charge, and passengers generally round off the fare.

Montevideo

Founded in 1726 as a response to Colonia, Montevideo soon became an important port. In the 19th century, it endured a long siege by the Argentine dictator Rosas, but normal commerce resumed after his fall in 1851. Montevideo absorbed many immigrants from Spain and Italy.

Many refugees from rural poverty live in *conventillos*, large older houses converted into multifamily slum dwellings in the colonial Ciudad Vieja. Redevelopment is displacing people from this picturesque and valuable central area.

Orientation

On the east bank of the Río de La Plata, Montevideo's functional centre is Plaza Independencia, east of the Ciudad Vieja. Avenida 18 de Julio is its most important commercial and entertainment area, while Plaza Cagancha is the main staging area for public transport.

Diagonal Avenida Libertador General Lavalleja leads to the imposing Palacio Legislativo. At the north-east end of 18 de Julio, Parque José Batlle y Ordóñez contains the 75,000-seat stadium Estadio Centenario. Perpendicular to its terminus is the major artery of Bulevar Artigas.

Across the harbour, the 132-metre Cerro de Montevideo was a landmark for early navigators. To the east, the riverfront Rambla leads past residential suburbs and sandy beaches frequented by Montevideños in summer and on weekends.

Information

Tourist Office The most convenient tourist office (☎ 90-5216) is on Plaza Cagancha. The weekly *Guía del Ocio* lists cultural events and has two-for-one coupons for cinemas, theatres and restaurants.

Money There are many exchange houses around Plaza Cagancha and on 18 de Julio.

Post & Telecommunications The main post office is at Buenos Aires 451, in the Ciudad Vieja. ANTEL has offices at Fernández Crespo 1534, San José 1108 (open 24 hours) and Rincón 501 (in the Ciudad Vieja).

Foreign Embassies Countries with diplomatic representation in Montevideo include:

Argentina
    Río Branco 1281 (☎ 90-0897)

Brazil
    Boulevard Artigas 1257 (☎ 49-4110)
Canada
    1st floor, Juan Carlos Gómez 1348 (☎ 95-8583)
France
    Avenida Uruguay 853 (☎ 92-0077/8)
Germany
    Calle Zabala 1379 (☎ 96-3281)
UK
    Marco Bruto 1073 (☎ 62-3630)
USA
    Lauro Muller 1776 (☎ 40-9051)

Bookshops Linardi y Risso, Juan Carlos Gómez 1435 in the Ciudad Vieja, has many out-of-print items in history and literature. The Librería Inglesa-Británica, Sarandí 580 in the Ciudad Vieja, has English-language books.

Emergency The Hospital Maciel is at 25 de Mayo and Maciel, in the Ciudad Vieja.

Walking Tour

To orient yourself, walk from **Plaza Independencia** through the Ciudad Vieja to the port. On the plaza is the **Mausoleo de Artigas**, topped by a huge statue of the country's greatest hero. The 18th-century **Palacio Estévez** was Government House until 1985, while the 26-storey **Palacio Salvo**, on the east side, was once South America's tallest building. Just off the plaza is the **Teatro Solís**.

Beyond the remnant colonial **Puerta de la Ciudadela**, Calle Sarandí leads to **Plaza Constitución**, also known as Plaza Matriz. The **Iglesia Matriz** (Cathedral), on the corner of Sarandí and Ituzaingó, is the oldest public building (1799) in the city.

Continue to **Casa Rivera**, corner of Rincón and Misiones, the **Museo Romántico**, 25 de Mayo 428, and **Casa Lavalleja**, corner of Zabala and 25 de Mayo, all part of the Museo Histórico Nacional. Half a block west is **Casa Garibaldi**, where the Italian hero once lived. From nearby **Plaza Zabala**, continue along Washington to Colón and then to Piedras and the **Mercado del Puerto**.

URUGUAY

URUGUAY

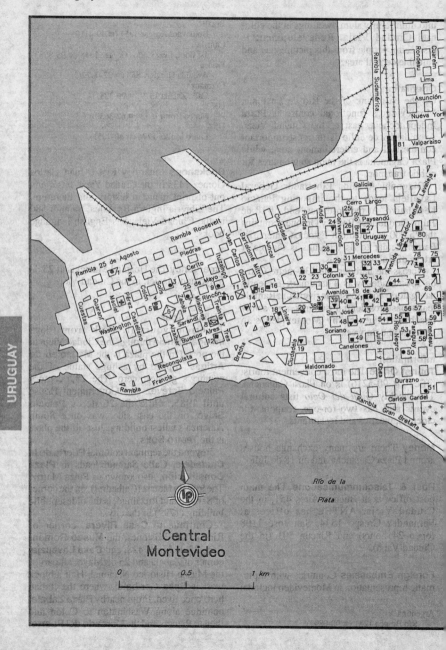

Central
Montevideo

0   0.5   1 km

Río de la
Plata

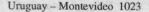

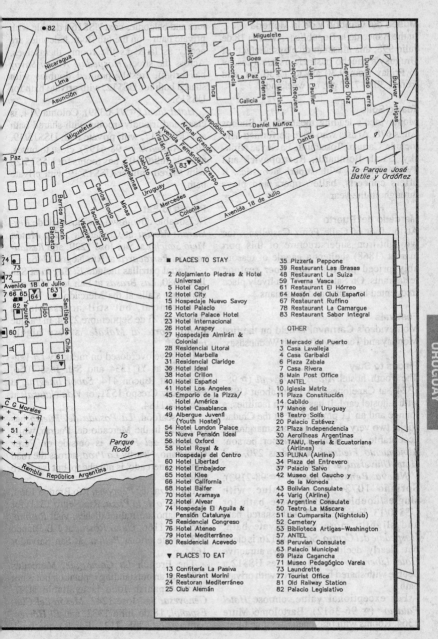

■ PLACES TO STAY

2 Alojamiento Piedras & Hotel Universal
5 Hotel Capri
12 Hotel City
15 Hospedaje Nuevo Savoy
16 Hotel Palacio
22 Victoria Palace Hotel
23 Hotel Internacional
26 Hotel Arapey
27 Hospedajes Almirán & Colonial
28 Residencial Litoral
29 Hotel Marbella
31 Residencial Claridge
36 Hotel Ideal
38 Hotel Crillon
40 Hotel Español
41 Hotel Los Angeles
45 Emporio de la Pizza/ Hotel América
46 Hotel Casablanca
49 Albergue Juvenil (Youth Hostel)
54 Hotel London Palace
55 Nueva Pensión Ideal
56 Hotel Oxford
58 Hotel Royal & Hospedaje del Centro
60 Hotel Libertad
62 Hotel Embajador
65 Hotel Klee
66 Hotel California
68 Hotel Balfer
70 Hotel Aramaya
72 Hotel Alvear
74 Hospedaje El Aguila & Pensión Catalunya
75 Residencial Congreso
76 Hotel Ateneo
79 Hotel Mediterráneo
80 Residencial Acevedo

▼ PLACES TO EAT

13 Confitería La Pasiva
19 Restaurant Morini
24 Restoran Mediterráneo
25 Club Alemán
35 Pizzería Peppone
39 Restaurant Las Brasas
48 Restaurant La Suiza
59 Taverna Vasca
61 Restaurant El Hórreo
64 Mesón del Club Español
67 Restaurant Ruffino
78 Restaurant La Camargue
83 Restaurant Sabor Integral

OTHER

1 Mercado del Puerto
3 Casa Lavalleja
4 Casa Garibaldi
6 Plaza Zabala
7 Casa Rivera
8 Main Post Office
9 ANTEL
10 Iglesia Matriz
11 Plaza Constitución
14 Cabildo
17 Manos del Uruguay
18 Teatro Solís
20 Palacio Estévez
21 Plaza Independencia
30 Aerolíneas Argentinas
32 TAMU, Iberia & Ecuatoriana (Airlines)
33 PLUNA (Airline)
34 Plaza del Entrevero
37 Palacio Salvo
42 Museo del Gaucho y de la Moneda
43 Bolivian Consulate
44 Varig (Airline)
47 Argentine Consulate
50 Teatro La Máscara
51 La Cumparsita (Nightclub)
52 Cemetery
53 Biblioteca Artigas–Washington
57 ANTEL
58 Peruvian Consulate
63 Palacio Municipal
69 Plaza Cagancha
71 Museo Pedagógico Varela
73 Laundrette
77 Tourist Office
81 Old Railway Station
82 Palacio Legislativo

Museo del Gaucho y de la Moneda
In the Banco de la República, Avenida 18 de
Julio 998, this museum displays artefacts of
Uruguay's gaucho past. Hours are Tuesday
to Friday from 9.30 am to 12.30 pm, and
from 3.30 to 7.30 pm on weekends.

Teatro Solís
Montevideo's leading theatre is at Buenos
Aires 678. Artists who have performed here
include Caruso, Toscanini, Pavlova, Nijin-
sky, Sarah Bernhardt, Rostropovich and
Twyla Tharpe. With superb acoustics, it
offers concerts, ballet, opera and plays
throughout the year.

Mercado del Puerto
At the foot of Calle Pérez Castellano, the
wrought-iron superstructure of this port
market (1868) shelters a gaggle of reasonably priced parrillas and finer seafood
restaurants. On Saturdays, it's a lively place
frequented by artists and musicians.

Festivals
Montevideo's **Carnaval** is held on the first
Monday and Tuesday after Ash Wednesdsay.

Places to Stay
The youth hostel *Albergue Juvenil* (☎ 98-
1324), at Canelones 935, costs about US$4
with a hostel card. It has kitchen facilities, a
lounge and an 11 pm curfew. In the Ciudad
Vieja, two very cheap places are marginally
acceptable for about US$4 per person:
Alojamiento Piedras, at Piedras 270, and
Hotel Universal, at Piedras 272.

Nueva Pensión Ideal (☎ 98-2193),
Soriano 1073, is good value, with
singles/doubles with private bath for
US$10/13. For US$9/12 with shared bath
and slightly more with private bath,
Hospedaje del Centro, Soriano 1126, is clean
but clearly declining. Friendly, attractive
Hotel Libertad, Yí 1223, charges US$12 a
double with shared bath, US$15 with private
bath.

For exceptional value, choose *Hotel
Palacio* (☎ 96-3612), Bartolomé Mitre
1364. Rooms with brass beds, antique furni-

ture and balconies cost US$16 a double with
private bath – on the 6th floor, balconies are
nearly as large as the rooms themselves.
Across the street, *Hospedaje Nuevo Savoy*
has bright, freshly painted doubles with
shared bath for US$12, with private bath for
US$15.

Hotel Ideal (☎ 91-6389), Colonia 914, is
clean and friendly; rooms with shared bath
are US$13/17, with private bath US$15/19.
Hotel Aramaya (☎ 98-6192), close to buses,
at 18 de Julio 1103, has rooms for US$15/20
with shared bath or US$15/19 with private
bath.

Places to Eat
Reasonable downtown eateries include *Restaurant Morini* at Ciudadela 1229, *Mesón
Viejo Sancho* at San José 1229, and *Restaurant del Ferrocarril* at Río Negro 1746.

Central parrillas include *El Fogón* at San
José 1080, *Las Brasas* at San José 909, and
the many stalls at the Mercado del Puerto.
Less central, but still accessible, is
Entrevero, 21 de Septiembre 2774. In Parque
Rodó, *Forte di Makale* is very highly
regarded.

If you've overdosed on meat, try *La Veg-
etariana*, at Yí 1334 and San José 1056,
Natura, at Rincón 414, *Sabor Integral*, at
Fernández Crespo 1531, or *Vida Natural*, at
San José 1184.

For seafood, *La Posada del Puerto* has
two stalls in the Mercado del Puerto, while
La Tasca del Puerto is outside on Pérez
Castellano. Nearby *La Proa*, across the road
from the mercado, is not cheap, but is superb
value.

For pizza, try *Peppone*, Río Branco 1364,
or *Emporio de la Pizza*, Río Negro 1311; for
more elaborate Italian dishes, visit *Ruffino*,
San José 1166, *Gatto Rosso*, at J B Blanco
913, or the pricier *Bellini*, at San Salvador
1644.

The French *La Camargue*, Mercedes
1133, has an outstanding reputation but is not
cheap. Spanish food is available at *La
Genovesa*, San José 1242, *Mesón del Club
Español*, 18 de Julio 1332, and *El Hórreo*,
Santiago de Chile 1137. For Basque food,

visit *Taberna Vasca*, San José 1168. Other European places include the *Club Alemán* (German) at Paysandú 935 and *La Suiza*, Soriano 939, for Swiss specialties like fondue.

Montevideo has two Mexican restaurants, *Chac-Mool*, at Mercedes and Carlos Roxlo, and *Pancho Villa*, at Ellauri 938. Despite its name, *Ponte Vecchio* is an Armenian restaurant, at Rivera 2638. There are also two Arab restaurants: *Aide Polo*, at Ellauri 1308, and *Restoran Mediterráneo*, in the Club Libanés, Paysandú 896.

Confitería La Pasiva, Juan Carlos Gómez and Sarandí (in the Ciudad Vieja), has reasonably priced minutas in a traditional atmosphere. Other confiterías include *Oro del Rhin*, oldest in the city, at Convención 1403, and *Hamburgo*, with excellent pastries, at Rivera 2081.

Entertainment

Cinemas Commercial cinemas offer films from around the world. The Cinemateca Uruguaya (☎ 48-2460), a film club at Lorenzo Carnelli 1311, has a modest membership fee allowing unlimited viewing at its five cinemas.

Theatre Besides Teatro Solís, Montevideo has the Casa del Teatro (at Mercedes 1878), Teatro Circular (at Rondeau 1388), Teatro La Mascara (at Río Negro 1180), Teatro del Anglo (at San José 1426) and Teatro Stella (at Mercedes and Tristán Narvaja).

Tango Make reservations for crowded La Cumparsita (☎ 91-6245), appropriately located at Carlos Gardel 1181.

Spectator Sports Soccer is an Uruguayan passion. The main stadium, Estadio Centenario, opened in 1930 for the first World Cup.

Things to Buy

Mercado de los Artesanos has branches on the Plaza Cagancha and at Bartolomé Mitre 1367 (in the Ciudad Vieja). Manos del Uruguay, at San José 1111 and Reconquista 602, is famous for quality goods. Plaza Cagancha's daily crafts market is a hang-out for younger Uruguayans.

Getting There & Away

Air Besides the usual international carriers, commuter airlines also provide services to Argentina.

Aerolíneas Argentinas
  Colonia 851 (☎ 91-9466)
Aerolíneas Uruguayas
  Plaza Cagancha 1343 (☎ 90-1868)
LAN-Chile
  11th floor, Plaza Cagancha 1335 (☎ 98-2727)
LAP (Líneas Aéreas Paraguayas)
  Colonia 1001 (☎ 90-7946)
LAPA (Líneas Aéreas Privadas Argentinas)
  Plaza Cagancha 1339 (☎ 90-8765)
PLUNA
  Colonia 1021 (☎ 98-0606, 92-1414)
Varig/Cruzeiro
  Río Negro 1362 (☎ 98-2321)

LAPA has 18 flights weekly to Buenos Aires' Aeroparque (US$43), while Aerolíneas Uruguayas flies to Aeroparque for US$80 return. For interior destinations, the military airline TAMU (☎ 90-0904) is at Colonia 959.

Bus Most companies are on or near Plaza Cagancha. COT (☎ 91-1200), Plaza Cagancha 1124, has over 20 buses daily to Punta del Este (US$6, 2½ hours) and 10 to Colonia, also 2½ hours.

Núñez (☎ 90-0483), Plaza Cagancha 1174, serves interior destinations like Minas, Treinta y Tres, Río Branco and Rivera. CYNSA (☎ 90-5321), Paraguay 1311, goes to Chuy and La Paloma. CORMI (☎ 90-4989), Avenida Uruguay 1053, has three buses daily to Río Branco.

Companies serving Argentina include CITA (☎ 91- 0100) at Plaza Cagancha 1149, General Urquiza (☎ 91-2333) at Plaza Cagancha 1142, ENCON (☎ 90-8733) at Avenida Lavalleja 1440, and CORA (☎ 91-7954), which goes to Córdoba. Núñez has one bus daily to Córdoba (US$58) and Villa Carlos Paz. COT/Bus de la Carrera has four buses daily to Buenos Aires (US$25, eight hours), and to Porto Alegre, Brazil (US$25, 12 hours). Other companies serving Brazil are CYNSA and TTL (☎ 91-5482), Plaza Cagancha 1345.

Boat The bus-boat combination Buquebus (☎ 92-0670), Río Negro 1400, leaves Montevideo for Buenos Aires via Colonia three times daily (US$25). Alíscafos Belt (☎ 90-4004) is at Plaza Cagancha 1124.

Getting Around
To/From the Airport Consult the posted bus schedule at PLUNA's downtown offices to Aeropuerto Carrasco (US$2). TAMU passengers get free bus rides. COT buses to Punta del Este and the D-1 Express from the Ciudad Vieja also go to Carrasco.

Bus Despite their noxious exhaust, buses go everywhere for about US$0.25. The *Guía de Montevideo Eureka*, available at bookshops or kiosks, lists routes and schedules.

Taxi Drivers correlate the meter reading with a photocopied fare chart.

The Uruguayan Littoral

West of Montevideo, the littoral's wheatfields and gardens feed the capital. Its one major attraction is the 17th-century Portuguese contraband port and fortress of Colonia. Overland travellers from Argentine Mesopotamia will find towns along the Río Uruguay – Salto, Paysandú, Fray Bentos and Mercedes – pleasant enough to justify a stopover.

COLONIA
Only an hour from Buenos Aires, Colonia del Sacramento, or Colonia, attracts many Argentines, but only a handful of the foreigners who visit the Argentine capital. Founded in 1680, it occupied a strategic position across the river from Buenos Aires, but its contraband undercut Spain's mercantile trade policy. Spain captured the city in 1762,

but only held it until 1777, when Spanish reforms finally permitted foreign goods to proceed directly to Buenos Aires.

Orientation
Colonia (population 20,000) sits on the east bank of the Río de la Plata, only 50 km from Buenos Aires by ferry or hydrofoil. Its Barrio Histórico, a jumble of narrow cobbled streets shaded by sycamores on a small peninsula, is a must-see. The commercial centre, near Plaza 25 de Agosto, and the river port are a few blocks east, where the Rambla Costanera leads north to Real de San Carlos, another area of interest.

Information
Tourist Office The tourist office (☎ 2182), Avenida General Flores 499, has many brochures difficult to obtain elsewhere. It's open on weekdays from 7 am to 8 pm, and on weekends from 10 am to 7 pm, but the ferry port branch is more efficient and helpful.

Money Downtown Cambio Viaggio, General Flores 350, is open on Sundays. There are also exchange facilities at the ferry port.

Post & Telecommunications The post office is at Lavalleja 226. ANTEL, Rivadavia 420, has direct lines to the USA (AT&T and MCI) and the UK.

Argentine Consulate The Argentine Consulate (☎ 2091), at Flores and Virrey Zeballos, is open weekdays 8 am to 1 pm.

Walking Tour
Also known as La Colonia Portuguesa, the Barrio Histórico begins at the restored **Puerta de Campo** (1745), on Calle Manoel Lobo, where a thick fortified wall runs south to the river. A short distance west is Plaza Mayor 25 de Mayo, off which tile-and-stucco colonial houses line narrow, cobbled Calle de los Suspiros, and just beyond is the **Museo Portugués**. Colonia's museums are generally open from 11.30 am to 6 pm.

At the south-west end of the Plaza Mayor

are the **Casa de Lavalleja**, once General Lavalleja's residence, the ruins of the 17th-century **Convento de San Francisco**, and the restored 19th-century **Faro** (lighthouse). At the west end, on Calle del Comercio, is the **Museo Municipal**, and next door is the so-called **Casa del Virrey** (though no viceroy ever lived here). At the north-west corner, on Calle de las Misiones de los Tapes, the **Archivo Regional** has a small museum/bookshop.

At the west end of Misiones de los Tapes, the **Museo de los Azulejos** is a 17th-century house with colonial tilework. The riverfront **Paseo de San Gabriel** leads to Calle del Colegio, where a right onto Calle del Comercio leads to the ruined **Capilla Jesuítica** (Jesuit chapel). Going east along Flores and then turning south on Vasconcellos, you reach the landmark **Iglesia Matriz**, on the **Plaza de Armas** (Plaza Manoel Lobo).

Across General Flores, at España and San José, the **Museo Español** has replica exhibits of colonial pottery, clothing and maps. At the north end of the street is the **Puerto Viejo**, the old port. A block east, at Calle del Virrey Cevallos and Rivadavia, the **Teatro Bastión del Carmen** incorporates part of the ancient fortifications.

Iglesia Matriz

Begun in 1680, this is Uruguay's oldest church. Nearly destroyed by fire in 1799, it was rebuilt by Spanish architect Tomás Toribio, who also designed the Cabildo of Montevideo. During the Brazilian occupation of 1823, lightning struck a powder magazine, whose explosion caused serious damage. It has been rebuilt several times since 1842, but the changes have been mainly cosmetic.

Places to Stay

Camping Easily reached by public transport, *Camping Municipal de Colonia* (☎ 4444), close to the Balneario Municipal at Real de San Carlos, has excellent facilities for about US$1.50 per person.

Hospedajes & Hotels Cheapest in town is *Hotel Español*, Manoel Lobo 377, with large but dark rooms for US$8.50 per person with shared bath. *Hotel Italiano*, Manoel Lobo 341, has small rooms with shared bath for US$9/12 a single/double.

Very central but quiet *Hospedaje Rincón del Río*, at Washington Barbot 258, near a pleasant sandy beach, charges US$17.50 per person with private bath. *Posada de la Ciudadela*, Washington Barbot 164, is equally good for the same price. At General Flores 311, restored *Hotel Beltrán* is friendly, quiet and very attractive for US$31 a double.

For a splurge, the best choice is *La Posada del Gobernador*, on 18 de Julio in the Barrio Histórico, for US$80/110.

Places to Eat

The nameless parrilla at Ituzaingó 186 is fine value. *El Portón*, Flores 333, is more upmarket. *El Suizo*, another parrilla, at General Flores and Ituzaingó, is mediocre. Down the block at Flores 229, *Mercado del Túnel*'s extensive menu varies in quality – choose selectively.

Pulpería de los Faroles, on Calle del Comercio and Misiones de los Tapes, is upmarket but not outrageously expensive. Two doors away, *La Casona del Sur* doubles as a handicrafts market, with live music at night.

Confitería El Colonial, General Flores 432, has enormous hot croissants for breakfast. At the tip of the Barrio Histórico is a good pizzería in a remodelled tower.

Things to Buy

Besides La Casona del Sur (see Places to Eat), check out the Sunday market in the Plaza Mayor.

Getting There & Away

Air Flights to Aeroparque in Buenos Aires (US$29) with LAPA (☎ 2006), Rivadavia 383, should resume soon. Flights from Aeroparque continue to Montevideo.

Bus COT (☎ 3121), Flores 430, has frequent buses to Montevideo (US$6, 2½-hours), and to Colonia Suiza, Rosario and Juan Lacaze.

URUGUAY

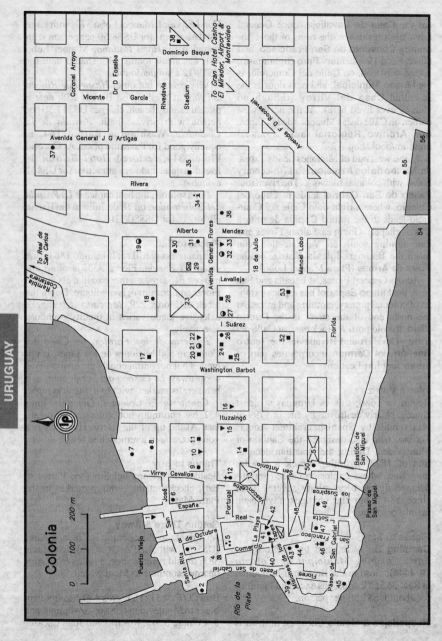

Colonia

■ PLACES TO STAY

11	Hotel Esperanza
14	La Posada del Gobernador
17	Hospedaje Rincón del Río
20	Hotel Beltrán
24	Hotel Royal
25	Hospedaje Ciudadela
28	Hotel Natal John
35	Hotel Leoncia
38	Hotel Los Angeles
52	Hotel Italiano
53	Hotel Español

▼ PLACES TO EAT

1	Pub Bucanero
10	Mercado del Túnel
15	Parrilla El Suizo
16	Parrilla (unnamed)
22	Parrilla El Portón
33	Confitería El Colonial
40	Pulpería de los Faroles
42	La Casona del Sur

OTHER

2	Bastión de Santa Rita
3	Motorcycle Rental
4	Plazoleta San Martín
5	Capilla Jesuítica
6	Museo Español
7	Bastión del Carmen
8	Teatro Bastión del Carmen
9	Argentine Consulate
12	Iglesia Matriz
13	Plaza de Armas (Plaza Manuel Lobo)
18	LAPA (Airline)
19	Buses Chadre & Buses Berutti
21	Omnibus Colonia
23	Plaza 25 de Agosto
26	Cambio Viaggio
27	Buses TURIL
29	Post Office
30	ANTEL
31	Cambio Colonia
32	Buses COT & Touriño
34	Tourist Office
36	Budget Rent-a-Car
37	Museo Indígena
39	Museo de los Azulejos
41	Archivo Regional
43	Casa del Virrey
44	Museo Municipal
45	Bastión de San Pedro
46	Convento de San Francisco
47	Casa de Lavalleja
48	Plaza Mayor 25 de Mayo
49	Museo Portugués
50	Puerta de Campo
51	Plazoleta 1811
54	Ferry Dock
55	Hydrofoil
56	Buquebus Dock

URUGUAY

Turil, at Flores 352, also goes to Montevideo, while Touriño, Flores 432, has buses to Carmelo. Omnibus Colonia, on Flores near Hotel Beltrán, goes to Rosario and Colonia Suiza.

Boat To Buenos Aires, Ferrylíneas (2½ hours) charges US$21 one way for adults, US$11 for children, with four sailings daily in summer. Its Sea Cat hydrofoil (45 minutes) costs US$30 one way, US$55 return. Both offer major discounts on day trips.

Alíscafos runs four hydrofoils daily (US$25, one hour); a luggage limitation applies.

Getting Around
COTUC, the city bus company, goes to the Camping Municipal and Real de San Carlos.

AROUND COLONIA
Real de San Carlos
At the turn of the century, Argentine entrepreneur Nicolás Mihanovich invested US$1.5 million to build a huge tourist complex at Real de San Carlos, five km west of Colonia. Among the attractions were a 10,000-seat bull ring (bullfights were prohibited in 1912), a 300-seat jai alai frontón, a racecourse, and a hotel-casino with its own power plant. (The casino failed when Argentina placed a tax on boats crossing the river.)

Only the racecourse functions today, but the ruins make an interesting excursion. The **Museo Municipal Real de San Carlos**, focusing on palaeontology, is open daily (except Monday) from 2 to 7 pm.

COLONIA SUIZA
Settled by Swiss immigrants in 1862,

Colonia Suiza soon provided wheat for Montevideo, 120 km away. A quiet destination with a demonstrably European feeling, its dairy products are known throughout the country.

On the central Plaza de los Fundadores, the impressive sculpture **El Surco** commemorates Swiss pioneers. There is no formal tourist office, but a woman in the nearby police station will help out with information and even provide a guided tour. Among the interesting buildings are ruins of the first flour mill, the **Molino Quemado**, and the historic **Hotel del Prado**, which also functions as a youth hostel.

Places to Stay & Eat

The most reasonable accommodation is friendly *Hotel Comercio*, 18 de Julio 1209 (its entrance near Colón is unmarked), for about US$8. The 80-room *Hotel del Prado* (1884), on the outskirts of town, is a magnificent if declining building with huge balconies. Rooms are US$15 per person, but it's also a youth hostel, offering beds with shared bath for US$4.

For dining, try *La Gondola*, Luis Dreyer and 25 de Agosto, *L'Arbalete*, on Avenida Batlle y Ordóñez, or *Don José*, 18 de Julio 1214.

Getting There & Away

Turil, 18 de Julio 1214, goes to Montevideo seven times daily. Omnibus Colonia, at 25 de Agosto and Berna, has nine buses daily to Colonia. COT, at 18 de Julio and Treinta y Tres, has services to Montevideo, Colonia, Fray Bentos and Paysandú.

CARMELO

Carmelo, 75 km north-west of Colonia, is a centre for exploring the Paraná delta by boat. From Plaza Independencia, Avenida 19 de Abril leads to a bridge across the Arroyo de las Vacas, where a large park offers camping, swimming and a monstrous casino.

The tourist office (☎ 2001) is at 19 de Abril 250, four blocks from the bridge. West Tour, 19 de Abril 267, is also a good source of information, and there are two exchange

houses near the plaza. The Argentine Consulate (☎ 2266) is at Roosevelt 442.

Places to Stay & Eat

Camping Náutico Las Higueritas (☎ 2058), on the south side of the Arroyo de las Vacas, charges US$1.50 per person. Rates are similar at *Camping Don Mauro*, at Ignacio Barros and Arroyo de las Vacas, six blocks from the centre.

At the very basic and rundown *Hotel Carmelo*, 19 de Abril 561, rooms with shared bath are US$4 per person. *Hotel La Unión*, at Uruguay 368, is better value, with singles with shared bath for US$8. Singles/doubles with private bath cost US$13/18. Friendly *Hotel San Fernando*, 19 de Abril 161, has clean rooms with private bath for US$12/17.

El Vesubio, 19 de Abril 451, serves a huge, tasty chivito al plato and many other dishes. Other restaurants include *Perrini*, at 19 de Abril 440, and the *Yacht Club*, *Morales* and *El Refugio*, all across the bridge, in the park.

Getting There & Away

Bus All companies are on or near the Plaza Independencia. Sabelín has three buses a day to Montevideo (US$7.50), while Chadre has two. Berutti and Touriño both go to Colonia (US$2).

Boat Deltanave, Constituyentes 263, has two crossings daily to Tigre, at 4 am and noon. Cacciola, Constituyentes 219, goes at 11 am and 6.30 pm. Fares are US$13 a single for adults, US$8 for children.

FRAY BENTOS

Across the Río Uruguay from Gualeguaychú (Argentina), Fray Bentos is 300 km west of Montevideo. In 1864, Uruguay's first meat extract plant opened here; in 1902, British interests built the country's first frigorífico – the enormous Anglo plant has closed and is now a museum.

Barren Plaza Constitución has only a few palms and a Victorian bandshell, but the friendly, helpful and knowledgeable tourist office (☎ 2737) is open on weekdays from 8 am to noon and 5 to 9 pm. Cambio Fagalde is on 18 de Julio, near the Plaza Hotel, but a street moneychanger outside Confitería Mafalda gives slightly better rates and keeps longer hours.

The Argentine Consulate (☎ 2638), Sarandí 3193, is open on weekdays from 8 am to 1 pm.

Teatro Young
This landmark 400-seat theatre, which bears the name of the Anglo-Uruguayan estanciero who sponsored its construction from 1909 to 1912, hosts cultural events throughout the year. It's a block from the plaza, on the corner of 25 de Mayo and Zorrilla.

Barrio Histórico del Anglo
South-west of the town centre, most of the now defunct Frigorífico Anglo del Uruguay has become the **Museo de la Revolución Industrial**. In 1865, the Liebig Extract of Meat Company located its pioneer South American plant here. It is still the dominant landmark in a neighbourhood with an active street life. Note the manager's residence and the former British Consulate.

Places to Stay & Eat
The *Club Atlético Anglo* has a campground 10 blocks from the plaza. Eight km south of town is *Balneario Las Cañas*, where fees are US$1.50 per person and US$1.50 per tent, plus US$2 per vehicle.

Nuevo Hotel Colonial, 25 de Mayo 3293, is very clean and friendly, with an interior patio, for US$6 per person per single with shared bath, US$7.50 with private bath. *Hotel 25 de Mayo*, at 25 de Mayo and Lavalleja, is a modernised 19th-century building with singles/doubles with shared bath for US$9/13, US$11/16 with private bath.

Local food is nothing special. *Galería Restaurant*, downstairs in the Hotel Plaza, has good salads and large but mediocre and not especially cheap entrees. Try instead *La Enramada*, on España between 25 de Mayo and 25 de Agosto. The yacht crowd hangs out at the *Club de Remeros*, near Parque Roosevelt.

Getting There & Away
ETA, at the Plaza Hotel, has three buses daily to Gualeguaychú (US$4), as does CUT, which has four daily to Mercedes (US$1.50) and four to Montevideo. Chadre, on the plaza, has two daily in each direction between Bella Unión and Montevideo, stopping at intermediate points.

MERCEDES
Mercedes is a livestock centre and minor resort on the Río Negro, a tributary of the Río Uruguay. Principal activities are boating, fishing and swimming. It has better bus connections than Fray Bentos, 30 km away.

Plaza Independencia is the city centre. The tourist office, on Colón between Giménez and Castro y Careaga, has a good city map and is open on weekdays from 7.30 am to 1.30 pm and 3.30 to 9.30 pm. Cambio Fagalde, next to Buses Klüver, or Cambio España, Colón 262, will change cash but not travellers' cheques. The post office is at Rodó 650, while ANTEL is on 18 de Julio between Roosevelt and Castro y Careaga.

On Sunday mornings in Plaza Lavalleja, there is a flea market and crafts fair.

Places to Stay & Eat
Eight blocks from Plaza Independencia, linked to the mainland by a bridge, Mercedes' *Camping del Hum* has excellent swimming, fishing and sanitary facilities. Fees are only US$1 per person plus US$1 per tent.

Hotel San Martín, Artigas 305, has singles for US$6 with shared bath, US$7.50 with private bath. Quiet and friendly *Hotel Marín*, Rodó 668, has singles for US$9; its annex, at Roosevelt 627, has more character but is slightly dearer.

La Churrasquera, Castro y Careaga 790, is a parrilla which serves large portions. On the Isla del Puerto, near the campground, the *Comedor Municipal* and the *Club Surubí* both have inexpensive fish dishes. The outdoor seating is simple but pleasant.

Getting There & Away
Buses Klüver, on Plaza Independencia, has

URUGUAY

three buses daily to Palmar and three weekly to Durazno. For Buses Chadre, Artigas 176, Mercedes is a stopover between Bella Unión and Montevideo.

CUT and ETA, with services to Gualeguaychú in Argentina, share offices at Artigas 233. ETA also goes to interior destinations like Trinidad, Durazno, Paso de los Toros, Tacuarembó and Rivera. CUT has four buses daily to Montevideo (US$10).

PAYSANDÚ

Uruguay's second largest city, Paysandú (population 100,000) was an 18th-century outpost of cattle herders from the Jesuit mission at Yapeyú, Corrientes. Processing beer, sugar, textiles and leather, it is the only significant industrial centre outside Montevideo.

Across the Uruguay from Colón, Argentina, Paysandú is 110 km north of Fray Bentos. Avenida 18 de Julio, the main commercial street, runs east-west along the south side of Plaza Constitución. The flood-prone riverfront is mostly parkland.

Opposite the plaza, at 18 de Julio 1226, the tourist office (☎ 6221) has a superb city map and a selection of useful brochures. Cambio Fagalde is at 18 de Julio 1004, Cambio Bacacay is next door, while the Argentine Consulate (☎ 2253) is at Leandro Gómez 1034.

Worthwhile museums include the **Museo de la Tradición**, at the Balneario Municipal, north of town, the **Museo Salesiano**, at 18 de Julio and Montecaseros, and the **Museo Histórico**, at Zorrilla and Sarandí.

Places to Stay & Eat

There are free campgrounds at the riverside Balneario Municipal, two km from the centre, and at Parque Sacra. The former has very basic facilities, the latter electricity, but neither has hot water.

Hostel accommodation (about US$1.50) is available at the *Liga Departamental de Fútbol*, Baltasar Brum 872. Otherwise, the cheapest (and friendliest) lodgings is *Hotel Victoria*, 18 de Julio 979, at US$6 per person with shared bath, US$11 with private bath.

Rates at *Hotel Concordia*, at the same address, are similar. *Hotel Artigas*, Baltasar Brum 943, costs US$8 per person with shared bath, US$12 with private bath.

Restaurant Don Diego, 19 de Abril 917, has reasonable parrillada, pizza and minutas. Other good eateries include the *Sociedad Española*, Leandro Gómez 1192, and the highly recommended *Restaurant Artemisio*, 18 de Julio 1248.

Getting There & Away

Air PLUNA (☎ 3071), Florida 1249, books seats for TAMU flights to Montevideo (US$18) on Monday, Thursday, Friday and Saturday at 8.20 am.

Bus The new terminal, at Montecaseros and Artigas, south of Plaza Constitución, should be ready by the time you read this. Chadre passes through Paysandú en route from Bella Unión to Montevideo. Agencia Central, Herrera 873, goes to interior destinations.

SALTO

Salto, 520 km from Montevideo, is the most northerly crossing into Argentina. Launches cross the Río Uruguay to Concordia, Entre Ríos, but it is also possible to take the bus across the enormous Salto Grande dam. To visit the dam, make arrangements at the tourist office (☎ 4096), Uruguay 1052.

For hostel accommodation, try the *Club de Remeros*, César Mayo Gutiérrez and Belén. Otherwise, try *Pensión 33*, Treinta y Tres 269. The free *Camping Municipal*, on the costanera, has only very basic services, but at *Termas del Daymán*, eight km south of town, much better facilities cost about US$3 per person.

TACUAREMBÓ

In the rolling hill country of the Cuchilla de Haedo, 390 km north of Montevideo, Tacuarembó's sycamore-lined streets and plazas make it one of Uruguay's most agreeable interior towns. Authorities have kept sculptors busy providing monuments which honour the usual military heroes but which also honour writers, the clergy and educators. The economy depends on cattle, sheep and garden crops. The late-March gaucho festival merits a visit, if you're in the area.

Tacuarembó is a major highway junction, as roads lead west to Argentina, north to Brazil, east to Brazil and the Uruguayan coast, and south to Montevideo. Its centre is Plaza 19 de Abril, but calles 25 de Mayo and 18 de Julio both lead past the almost equally important Plaza Colón and Plaza Rivera to the south.

The friendly and helpful tourist office, Suárez 215, offers a simple map and brochures. ANTEL is at Sarandí 242. The **Museo del Indio y del Gaucho**, at Flores and Artigas, pays romantic tribute to Uruguay's Indians and gauchos.

Places to Stay & Eat
The *Balneario Municipal Iporá*, seven km north of town, has both free and paying camp sites (US$1.50) near an artificial lake. Free sites have clean toilets but lack showers. Buses leave from near Plaza 19 de Abril.

Friendly *Pensión Paysandú*, 18 de Julio 154, offers good accommodation for US$6 in a shared room, US$9/13 a single/double for a private room with shared bath. *Hotel Tacuarembó*, 18 de Julio 133, is comfortable but impersonal, at US$15/26 with private bath, but has a good restaurant serving parrillada and other dishes.

Two other parrillas are *La Rueda*, Beltrán and Flores, and *La Cabaña*, 25 de Mayo 217. *Rotisería del Centro*, on 18 de Julio near Plaza Colón, sells an enormous, tasty chivito.

Getting There & Away
Air TAMU (☎ 2341), Flores 300, flies on Monday and Friday to Montevideo.

Bus Chadre, at Suárez and 25 de Mayo, and Turil, at 25 de Mayo and 25 de Agosto, go to Montevideo (US$12). Agencia Central, 25 de Mayo 169, serves interior destinations and connects Tacuarembó with Salto and Paysandú.

The Uruguayan Riviera

East of Montevideo, countless resorts dot a scenic coast where the sandy beaches, vast dunes and dramatic headlands extend to the Brazilian border. In summer, the area attracts hordes, but after early March, prices drop, the weather is still ideal and the pace more leisurely.

ATLÁNTIDA
Only 50 km from Montevideo, Atlántida is the coastal route's first major resort. The tourist office (☎ 22736) is at the junction of calles 14 and 1. There are several reasonable residenciales, while the excellent facilities at *Camping El Ensueño* (US$2.50 per person) are nine blocks from the popular Playa Brava. COT, at Calle 18 and Avenida Artigas, has regular buses to Montevideo and onward down the coast.

PIRIÁPOLIS
In the 1930s, entrepreneur Francisco Piria built the landmark Hotel Argentino, an eccentric residence known as 'Piria's castle', and brought tourists across from Argentina by ferry. Almost everything in Piriápolis, about 100 km from Montevideo, is within walking distance of the waterfront Rambla de los Argentinos and defined by proximity to the Hotel Argentino. In the nearby countryside are interesting features like Cerro Pan de Azúcar (one of Uruguay's highest points) and the hill resort of Minas.

The tourist office (☎ 2560), at Rambla 1348 near Hotel Argentino, is open daily from 9.30 am to 1 pm and 3.30 to 9 pm. It has maps, a few brochures and a list of current hotel prices. Change cash, but not travellers' cheques, at Hotel Argentino.

Places to Stay
Accommodation is abundant but prices and availability are seasonal. Many places open only from December to April, while nearly all raise prices from mid-December to

March. The best bargains come after 1 March, when the weather is delightful but the crowds have gone.

Camping Piriápolis F C, 350 metres behind Hotel Argentino, at Misiones and Niza, has all necessary facilities, including electricity and hot showers, for US$3 per person, plus a few rooms with shared bath for US$14 a double. It's open from mid-December to late April.

The *Albergue de Piriápolis*, the youth hostel, is at Simón del Pino 1136, behind Hotel Argentino. It charges US$1.50 with hostel card and is open all year (make reservations in January and February).

Petite Pensión is a tiny (seven-room), friendly, family-run hotel at Sanabria 1084, two blocks from the beach. Rates are US$11 off-season, US$15 in summer. Winter rates are comparable at *Hotel Centro*, but summer rates run at US$20 per person. Try also *Hotel Alcázar*, Piria and Tucumán, where singles are US$15 off season, US$24 in summer.

Even if you can't stay at *Hotel Argentino*, visit the elegant, 350-room European-style spa on the Rambla. Rates for rooms are US$70 per person with half pension, US$90 with full pension, plus tax. The hotel has thermal baths, a casino, a classic dining room and other luxuries.

Restaurant La Langosta, Rambla 1215, has very good seafood and parillada at moderate prices. Other appealing restaurants along the Rambla include *Viejo Martín*, at the corner of Trapani, and *Restaurant Delta*, at the corner of Atanasio Sierra.

Things to Buy
The Paseo de la Pasiva, an attractive colonnade along the Rambla, is a good place for handicrafts.

Getting There & Away
Bus companies have offices along the Rambla. In high season, COT runs up to 27 buses daily to Punta del Este, while Díaz has 14 daily to Pan de Azúcar and Minas. The fare to Montevideo is about US$3.

AROUND PIRIÁPOLIS
Pan de Azúcar
Ten km north of town, 493-metre **Cerro Pan de Azúcar** is the third highest point in Uruguay. There's a foot trail to the top, and a small but well-kept zoo at the nearby **Parque Municipal**. Across the highway, the **Castillo de Piria** was Francisco Piria's outlandish residence.

MINAS
Sixty km north of Piriápolis, Minas is an agreeable hill town which draws its name from nearby quarries. Its main attraction is **Parque Salus**, source of Uruguay's best-known mineral water and the site of a brewery, 10 km west of town (accommodation available at *El Parador Salus*). Every 19 April, up to 70,000 pilgrims visit the **Cerro y Virgen del Verdún**, six km west of town.

The tourist office (✆ 4118) is at the bus terminal, but visit also the **Casa de la Cultura**, at Lavalleja and Rodó. For cheap but adequate lodgings, try *Residencia Minas*, 25 de Mayo 502.

Inexpensive camping is possible at **Parque Arequita**, nine km north on the road to Polanco (public transport is available). A limited number of two-bed cabañas are available for US$7.50 per person.

In **Villa Serrana**, 23 km beyond Minas, *Chalet Las Chafas* has hostel accommodation with kitchen facilities, a swimming pool and a lake. Buses go no closer than three km, so you'll need to walk or hitch the rest of the way.

MALDONADO
In 1755, Governor J J de Viana of Montevideo established Maldonado at the mouth of the Río de la Plata as an outpost to provision ships. Its centre retains a colonial feeling, but the town has sprawled because of tourist development in exclusive Punta del Este.

Maldonado is a more economical alternative to Punta for food and accommodation, but the two have grown together.

Orientation
Maldonado is 30 km from Piriápolis. The

original city plan is a grid, centred on Plaza San Fernando, but between Maldonado and Punta, the streets are highly irregular. West, along the Río de la Plato, Rambla Claudio Williman is the main thoroughfare, while to the east, Rambla Lorenzo Batlle Pacheco follows the Atlantic coast. Locations along these routes are usually identified by numbered *paradas* (bus stops). Both routes have fine beaches, but the ocean beaches have rougher surf.

Information

Tourist Office The Dirección de Turismo (☎ 21920) is in the Intendencia Municipal, on Sarandí between Ledesma and Burnett, with a branch (☎ 25701) at the bus terminal. Papelería Sienra, Sarandí 812, sells a superb street map (US$6), which is worthwhile if you spend more than a few days in Maldonado and Punta.

Money Cambio Bella Unión is at Florida 764, the same building as Hotel Le Petit. Cambio Dominus is next to the Catedral, at 25 de Mayo and 18 de Julio.

Telecommunications ANTEL is at the corner of Artigas and Florida.

Things to See

On Plaza San Fernando is the **Cathedral**, completed in 1895. At Gorriti and Pérez del Puerto, the **Torre de Vigia** is a colonial watchtower, with peepholes used for viewing the approach of hostile forces or other suspicious movements.

Another colonial relic is the **Cuartel de Dragones y de Blandengues**, a block of fortifications built between 1771 and 1797, along 18 de Julio and Pérez del Puerto. The **Museo San Fernando de Maldonado** is a fine-arts museum at Sarandí and Pérez del Puerto, open Monday to Saturday from 12.30 to 8 pm, and on Sunday from 4.30 to 8 pm.

Maldonado's oddest sight is the eclectic, eccentric **Museo Mazzoni** (1782). With all the family's furniture and belongings, and a particularly weird natural history room, it

defies description – see the patio fountain featuring a sculpted rockhopper penguin. At Ituzaingó 789, it's open Tuesday to Saturday from 10 am to 12.30 pm and 5 to 9.30 pm, and on Sunday from 5 to 9.30 pm. Admission is free.

Activities

Fishing is a popular pastime along the coast, at sea, and on Isla Gorriti and Isla de Lobos. The tourist office publishes a brochure with a map of recommended spots. Cassarino Hermanos (☎ 23735), Sarandí 1253, arranges boat trips. Another brochure recommends sites for surfing, wind-surfing and diving.

Places to Stay

Accommodation in the area is abundant but costly. However, prices decline at summer's end. Unless otherwise indicated, prices mentioned are for the high season.

Camping *Camping San Rafael* (☎ 86715), on the outskirts of Maldonado, beyond El Jagüel airport, is organised almost to the point of regimentation, but has fine facilities on leafy grounds. Sites cost US$10 for two in January and February, US$9 the rest of the year. Take bus No 5 from Maldonado.

Residenciales & Hotels To reach the recently opened *Albergue Juveníl* (youth hostel), across from the Club de Pesca in Manantiales, east of Maldonado, take the CODESA bus.

In Maldonado proper, check out *Residencial La Reja*, 18 de Julio 1092 at J P Varela, or *Residencial Santa Teresa*, Santa Teresa 753 at Pérez del Puerto, where singles/doubles with shared bath cost US$25/30. Try also *Residencial Obreros*, at 19 de Abril and Pérez del Puerto.

Recently remodelled *Hotel Celta* (ex-*Hospedaje Ituzaingó*, ☎ 30139), at Ituzaingó 839, is popular with foreign travellers. Standard rates are US$25 per person, but gregarious Irishman Michael Power has cheaper budget rooms, especially out of

URUGUAY

season. *Hotel Esteño*, Sarandí 881, charges US$20 per person.

Places to Eat
The modest *Tequila Bar*, at Ituzaingó and Román Guerra, is great value for money. Other inexpensive choices include *Salon Comedor Popular*, at Dodera and Ituzaingó, and the *Circulo Policial*, Pérez del Puerto 780.

Pricier but good value is *Al Paso*, a parrillada at 18 de Julio 888. More up-market is *Mesón del Centro Español*, at Santana and 18 de Julio, with excellent Spanish seafood. The Maldonado branch of Montevideo's highly regarded *Forte di Makale* is on Sarandí near Burnett.

Getting There & Away
The bus terminal is at Avenida Roosevelt and Sarandí, eight blocks south of the plaza. COT goes to Piriápolis, Montevideo and Colonia. TTL serves Montevideo, Porto Alegre and São Paulo from San Carlos. Transporte Núñez has two buses daily to Montevideo.

Getting Around
Bus CODESA runs local buses to Punta del Este, La Barra, Manantiales and San Carlos. Olivera connects Maldonado and Punta del Este with San Rafael, Punta Ballena, Portezuelo and the airport.

AROUND MALDONADO
Casapueblo
At Punta Ballena, a scenic headland 10 km west of Maldonado, Carlos Páez Vilaró built this unconventional Mediterranean villa and art gallery (admission US$2) with no right angles. Visitors can tour the gallery, view a slide presentation on its creation, and dine or drink at the bar/cafeteria.

PUNTA DEL ESTE
One of South America's most glamourous resorts, Punta del Este swarms with upper-class Argentines. Strictly speaking, it's part of Maldonado, but economically and socially, it's a world apart, with elegant seaside homes, a yacht harbour, and expensive hotels and restaurants. There is a small selection of reasonable accommodation.

Orientation
Punta del Este is a tiny peninsula south of Maldonado proper. Rambla General Artigas circles the peninsula, passing the protected beach of Playa Mansa and the yacht harbour on the west side, an exclusive residential zone at its southern tip, and rugged Playa Brava on the east.

Punta has two separate grid systems. On the north side of a constricted neck east of the harbour is the newer, high-rise hotel zone; the southern area is almost totally residential. Streets bear both names and numbers – the addresses listed refer first to the street name, with the number in parentheses. Avenida Juan Gorlero (22) is the main commercial street.

Information
Tourist Office At the west end of Inzaurraga (31), the tourist office (☎ 40514) distributes a simple map and a booklet, *Lo Que Hay Que Saber*, loaded with information. Another office (☎ 40512) on Plaza Artigas keeps a list of hotels and restaurants, with up-to-the-minute prices.

Money Nearly all banks and cambios are along Gorlero.

Post & Telecommunications The post office is at Gorlero 633.

Consulate In high season, Argentina maintains a consulate (☎ 41106) at the Santos Dumont Building, on Gorlero between Inzaurraga (31) and Las Focas (30).

Beaches
On the west side of Punta del Este, Rambla Artigas snakes along the riverside Playa Mansa, then circles around the peninsula to the wilder Playa Brava, on the Atlantic. From Playa Mansa, west along Rambla Williman, the main beach areas are La Pastora, Marconi, Cantegril, Las Delicias, Pinares,

La Gruta (at Punta Ballena) and Portezuelo (beyond Punta Ballena). East, along Rambla Batlle Pacheco, the prime areas are La Chiverta, San Rafael, La Draga and Punta de La Barra. All beaches have *paradores* (small restaurants) with beach service; beach-hopping is common, depending on local conditions and the general level of action.

Places to Stay
Modest accommodation is hard to come by, but *Hostal Ocean*, La Salina (9) 636, has triples with shared bath for US$13 per person without breakfast. The next cheapest is *Hostería del Puerto*, at Capitán Miranda (7) and Calle 2 de Febrero (10), a pleasant older-style hotel with singles/doubles for US$25/35 with private bath. *Hotel Marbella*, Inzaurraga between Gorlero and El Remanso (20), and *Hotel Córdoba*, Los Muergos (27) 660, are a bit more expensive.

Places to Eat
Most of Punta's restaurants are expensive, but reasonably priced pizzerías and cafés line Gorlero, such as *Di Papo*, Gorlero 841. Another modest but good place is *Cantina del Puerto*, at La Salina (9) and 2 de Febrero (10). *Los Caracoles*, El Remanso (20) and Los Meros (28), is a mid-range parrilla.

Good seafood is available at *Bossangoa*, Capitán Miranda (7) and 2 de Febrero, but many other places serve fish – if you can afford it, try *Mariskonoa*, Resalsero (26) 650. Homesick Australians will find an unexpected bit of home at *La Pomme*, at Solís (11) and Virazón (12), which also serves French food. Montevideo's *Bungalow Suizo* has a local branch on Rambla Batlle at Parada 8, near Avenida Roosevelt. *Heladería Zanettin*, Gorlero and Arrecifes (25), has first-rate ice cream.

Entertainment
Punta has many cinemas along Gorlero and discos along Rambla Batlle. There is a casino at Gorlero and Inzaurraga (31).

Things to Buy
For souvenirs, visit the Feria Artesanal on Plaza Artigas in the evening. Manos del Uruguay has an outlet at Gorlero and Las Gaviotas (29).

Getting There & Away
Air PLUNA (☎ 41840), at Gorlero 940, has summer flights to Montevideo daily, except Thursday (none) and Sunday (two). Aerolíneas Uruguayas (☎ 88844), Bulevar Artigas and Parada 2, flies direct from Aeroparque in Buenos Aires. Aerolíneas Argentinas (☎ 43801), in the Santos Dumont Building, on Gorlero between Inzaurraga (31) and Las Focas (30), also flies to Aeroparque.

Bus The Terminal Playa Brava is on the Rambla General Artigas at Inzaurraga. Inter-city bus services are an extension of those to Maldonado.

Getting Around
To/From the Airport Aeropuerto Laguna del Sauce, west of Portezuelo, is reached by Buses Olivera (☎ 24039) from Maldonado.

Bus Maldonado Turismo (☎ 81725), at Gorlero and Inzaurraga (31), connects Punta del Este with La Barra and Manantiales.

AROUND PUNTA DEL ESTE
Boats leave the yacht harbour every half-hour for **Isla Gorriti**, which has sandy beaches, 18th-century ruins and two restaurants. About six miles offshore, some 300,000 fur seals crowd **Isla de Lobos**. To arrange transport, contact the Unión de Lanchas (☎ 42594).

Rocha Department

Conflicts between Spain and Portugal, then between Argentina and Brazil, left Rocha with historical monuments like the fortresses of Santa Teresa and San Miguel. The fighting also discouraged rural settlement, as well as unintentionally sparing some of Uruguay's wildest countryside from settlement. It has relatively undeveloped areas like Cabo Polonio, with its extensive dunes and a large sea-lion colony, and Parque Nacional Santa Teresa (really a cultural park). The interior's varied landscape of palm savannas and marshes is rich in bird life.

ROCHA

Picturesque Rocha, where many late colonial and early independence era houses line the narrow alleyways off Plaza Independencia, merits at least an afternoon's visit for visitors to La Paloma (see below). It is 220 km from Montevideo

For accommodation, try the tidy *Hotel Municipal Rocha*, on 19 de Abril between Ramírez and Presbítero Aquiles (US$9/13 a single/double). Modest *Hotel Centro*, Ramírez 152, is slightly dearer. *Confitería La Candela*, on the plaza, has tasty and visually appealing sweets and pastries.

Rutas del Sol runs eight buses daily to Montevideo and five daily to Chuy, plus six daily to Barra Valizas (US$5). Cynsa has 10 services daily to La Paloma.

LA PALOMA

Placid La Paloma (population 5000), 28 km south of Rocha, is less developed, cheaper and much less crowded than Punta del Este, but lacks Punta's hyperactive nightlife. Beaches to the east are less protected from ocean swells. Streets are named, but hotels and restaurants lack numbers and are more easily located by their relationship to prominent intersections and other landmarks.

In summer, the tourist office (☎ 6088), on the roundabout at the east end of Avenida Nicolás Solari, is open from 8 am to 11 pm, but the rest of the year, it's only open from 9 am to 9 pm.

Places to Stay & Eat

Camping Parque Andresito, at the north entrance to town, has an 'A' sector (US$7 for two persons) with amenities like hot showers and electricity. Cheaper sector 'B' offers fewer amenities and the chance to sneak into hot showers in sector 'A'. Both share a super-market, restaurant and excellent beach access.

The youth hostel, *Albergue La Paloma*, in Parque Andresito, is open from November to March; make reservations in Montevideo. *Residencial Puertas del Sol*, on Delfín near Aries, charges US$15 per person. Other accommodation tends to be slightly more expensive, at around US$20 per person, including *Residencial Tirrenia*, on Avenida El Navío, *Residencial Trocadero*, on Juno near Ceres, and *Hotel Bahía*, at Navío and El Sol.

La Marea, on Avenida del Parque, has good, fresh, reasonably priced seafood, but the service is slow. Pizzerías include *La Currica*, on Solari, and *Ponte Vecchio*, on La Aguada beach. Try also the hotel restaurants.

Getting There & Away

Buses Cynsa is on Avenida del Parque, next to Restaurant La Marea.

Getting Around

Organised Tours Since public transport doesn't serve some of the more interesting coastal sites, you may want to look at organised tours. In summer, Rochatur runs trips to Cabo Polonio (US$20), Chuy (US$25, lunch included) and Parque Nacional Santa Teresa.

PARQUE NACIONAL SANTA TERESA

More a historical than a natural attraction, this coastal park 35 km south of Chuy contains the hilltop **Fortaleza de Santa Teresa**. The Portuguese first began to build the fortress, but it was captured and finished by the Spaniards. Although by international standards, Santa Teresa is a humble place, it attracts many Uruguayan and Brazilian visitors because of its uncrowded beaches and decentralised forest camping (US$6 per site for basic facilities).

The park gets very crowded during Carnaval, but most of the time, it absorbs visitors without difficulty. Services at headquarters include telephones and post offices, a supermarket, bakery, butchery and restaurant.

CHUY

Pedestrians and vehicles cross freely between Uruguay and Brazil at Chuy, the grubby but energetic border town at the terminus of Ruta 9, 340 km from Montevideo. There are several exchange houses along Avenida Brasil.

Hotel Plaza, at Avenida Artigas and Arachanes, has singles for US$15; try the Brazilian side for cheaper accommodation. Ten km south of Chuy, a coastal lateral leads to *Camping Chuy* and *De la Barra*, both charging US$7.50 per site for two persons. Local buses go directly to both.

If proceeding into Brazil, complete Uruguayan immigration formalities on Ruta 9, 2½ km south of town. If you need a visa, Brasil has a consulate at Fernández 147. Rutas del Sol, at Numancia 217, has buses to Montevideo. There is also service to Treinta y Tres.

Seven km west of Chuy, do not miss restored **Fuerte San Miguel**, a pink-granite fortress built in 1734 during Spanish-Portuguese hostilities and protected by a moat. It's closed on Mondays.

TREINTA Y TRES

Little-visited Treinta y Tres is a gaucho town among scenic rolling hills on the Río Olímar, 290 km north-east of Montevideo, on the interior route to Brazil via Melo or Río Branco. The route north to Melo is one of the most beautiful in Uruguay.

Most services are on the plaza, including Núñez, which has eight buses daily to Melo and to Montevideo via Minas. Clean and friendly *Hotel Olímar* has singles for US$7.50 with shared bath, US$12 with private bath. *Restaurant London* has good, filling and inexpensive meals.

MELO

Melo, 110 km north of Treinta y Tres, is a transport hub for the interior, with buses to Río Branco, Aceguá and Rivera, all with border crossings to Brazil. Founded in 1795, the town has a few remaining colonial buildings, and a stone post house which now contains the **Museo del Gaucho**.

TAMU has inexpensive flights to Montevideo. There are Brazilian consulates in Melo (☎ 2084), at Aparicio Saravia 711, in Río Branco (☎ 3), at Lavalleja and Palomeque, and in Rivera (☎ 3278), at Ceballos 1159. Melo's Parque Rivera has a public campground, while Río Branco has a youth hostel. Look around the plaza for other cheap lodgings.

Venezuela

Venezuela's modern history has been strongly influenced by oil money, which has made the country one of the richest and most industrialised on the continent. The effect of that transformation is that, today, Venezuela has perhaps the best array of roads in South America, a spectacular 21st-century architecture of which New York or Sydney would not be ashamed, and a good infrastructure of Western facilities that make travel easy. Yet deep in the countryside, people maintain a traditional way of life, as if the 20th century got lost somewhere down the road. There are a number of Indian groups still unconquered by encroaching civilisation, the most mysterious being the Yanomami, a warrior tribe lost in time along the Venezuela-Brazil border but now threatened by lawless gold miners, especially on the Brazilian side of the border.

The variety of landscapes in Venezuela won't disappoint even the most demanding visitor. The country boasts a chunk of the snowcapped Andes, and more mountain territory along the coast, where the Cordillera de la Costa rises from the beaches to over 2500 metres. The southern part of the country is taken up by the Amazon, with its legendary wilderness, but if you prefer beach life, some 3000 km of Caribbean coastline provides countless beautiful beaches.

Venezuela's most unusual natural feature is its *tepuis*, elevated sandstone mesas which stretch out 1000 metres above rolling savannas. There are about 100 scattered in south-eastern Venezuela, noted for their moonscape and peculiar endemic flora, which fascinate botanists. From one of these tepuis cascades Salto Angel (Angel Falls), the highest waterfall in the world and perhaps the most famous tourist sight in the country.

In practical terms, Venezuela is a relatively safe and friendly country, with fairly inexpensive domestic bus and air transport. Venezuela also has South America's cheap-

est air links with both Europe and the USA, making it a natural gateway to the continent. Don't treat it, however, as just a bridge; give yourself some time to discover this land – it's worth it.

Facts about the Country

HISTORY
The Pre-Columbian Period
It's estimated that before the Spanish conquest, at least a million Indians inhabited the region which is now Venezuela. They were isolated tribes of various ethnic backgrounds, belonging to three main linguistic families: Carib, Arawak and Chibcha.

grounds, belonging to three main linguistic families: Carib, Arawak and Chibcha.

The warlike Carib tribes inhabited the central and eastern coast, living from fishing and shifting agriculture. Various groups of Arawak were scattered over a large area of the western Llanos and north up to the coast, without any significant populated centres. They were mostly hunter-gatherers, but occasionally practised farming.

The Timote-Cuica, of the Chibcha family (the same to which the Muisca and Tayrona of Colombia belonged), was the most complex of Venezuela's pre-Columbian societies. They chose the Andes as their home, and founded their settlements there, linked by a maze of trails. They had a fairly advanced agriculture, including the use of irrigation and terraces where the topography required them.

None of Venezuela's pre-Hispanic cultures reached any remarkable degree of architectural or artistic development. They haven't left behind any significant cultural heritage, save for some pottery and other simple objects found during excavations.

The Spanish Conquest

Columbus was the first European to set foot in Venezuela – indeed, it was the only South American mainland country on whose soil Columbus alighted. On his third trip to the New World, in 1498, he landed at the eastern tip of the Península de Paria, opposite Trinidad. He first thought he had discovered yet another island, but continuing along the coast, he found the voluminous mouth of the Río Orinoco – sufficient proof that the place was something much more than an island. Astonished with his discovery, he then wrote in his diary: 'Never have I read or heard of so much sweet water within a salt ocean'.

A year later, another explorer, Alonso de Ojeda, probably accompanied by the Italian Amerigo Vespucci, sailed up to the Península de la Guajira, at the western extreme of present-day Venezuela. After entering Lago Maracaibo, the Spaniards, seeing the local Indians living in their houses on stilts above the water, called the land Venezuela (Little Venice).

The first Spanish settlement on Venezuelan soil, Nueva Cádiz, was officially founded in 1519 (though it existed since about 1500) on the small island of Cubagua, just south of Isla de Margarita. Living from pearl harvesting, the town was completely destroyed by an earthquake and tidal wave in 1541. The earliest Venezuelan town still in existence, Cumaná, dates from 1521.

Officially, Venezuela was ruled by Spain from the Audiencia de Santo Domingo until 1717, when it fell under the administration of the newly created Viceroyalty of Nueva Granada, with its capital in Bogotá, to remain so until independence. In practice, however, the region enjoyed a large degree of autonomy. It was, after all, unimportant and sparsely populated, with an uninviting steamy climate, and the Spaniards gave it low priority, focussing instead on Colombia, Peru and Bolivia, which were abundant in gold and silver. In many ways, Venezuela remained a backwater until the oil boom.

Early European settlers went panning for gold, but soon abandoned the fruitless search in favour of agriculture (which relied on Indian slave labour) along the coast and in the central highlands. It was another 150 years before they began to spread out and settle, in a patchy way, Los Llanos and the area around Lago Maracaibo in the north-west.

Independence Wars

Apart from three brief rebellions between 1749 and 1797, colonial Venezuela had a relatively uneventful history, but all this changed at the beginning of the 19th century, when Venezuela gave Latin America its greatest ever cult figure, Simón Bolívar. 'El Libertador', as he is commonly known, together with his most able lieutenant, Antonio José de Sucre, were to be largely responsible for ending colonial rule all the way to the borders of Argentina. Every Spanish American city and town has at least one plaza or street named after one or the other of these generals. There are innumerable museums containing memorabilia of them. In Venezuela itself, statues of Bolívar are omnipresent, more so than were Lenin busts in the Soviet Union during the blossoming years of communism.

The revolutionary flame was lit by Francisco de Miranda in 1806, but his efforts to set up an independent administration at Caracas came to an end when he was handed over to the Spanish by his fellow conspirators. The Spanish shipped him to Spain, and he died shortly afterwards in a Cádiz jail.

Bolívar took over leadership of the revolution. After unsuccessful attempts to defeat the Spaniards at home, he withdrew to Colombia, then to Jamaica, until the opportune moment came in 1817.

At the time, events in Europe were in Bolívar's favour. The Napoleonic Wars had ended, and Bolívar's agent in London was able to raise money and arms and recruit over 5000 British Peninsular War veterans, who were being demobbed from the armies which had been raised to fight Napoleon. With this British force, and an army of horsemen from Los Llanos, Bolívar marched over the Andes, defeating the Spanish at the battles of Pantano de Vargas and Boyacá, thus bringing independence to Colombia in August 1819.

Four months later in Angostura (today Ciudad Bolívar), the Angostura Congress was held, and proclaimed Gran Colombia, a new state unifying Colombia, Venezuela and Ecuador (though the last two were still under Spanish rule).

The liberation of Venezuela was completed with Bolívar's victory over Spanish forces at Carabobo in 1821, though the Royalists continued to put up a desultory rearguard fight from Puerto Cabello for another two years. With these victories under their belts, Bolívar and Sucre went on to liberate Ecuador, Peru and Bolivia, which they achieved by 1825.

Though, both economically and demographically, Venezuela was the least important of the areas which made up Gran Colombia, it bore the brunt of the fighting. Not only did Venezuelan patriots fight on their own territory, they also fought in the

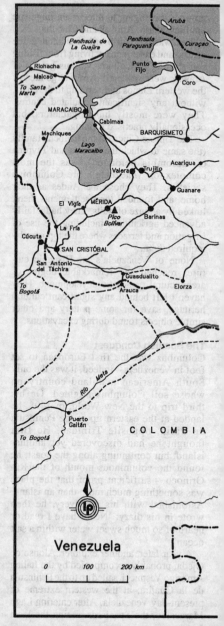

Venezuela

0   100   200 km

armies which Bolívar led into Colombia and down the Pacific coast. It is estimated that over one-quarter of the Venezuelan population died in these wars.

Gran Colombia existed for only a decade, then split into three separate countries. Bolívar's dream of a unified republic fell apart even before his death in 1830.

The Post-Independence Period

Venezuela's independence period was marked by serious governmental problems, which continued for over a century. For the most part, these were times of despotism and anarchy, with the country being ruled by a series of military dictators known as caudillos. Not until 1958 was a democratic government elected which managed to complete its five-year term.

The first of the caudillos, General José Antonio Páez, represented the Conservative oligarchy, and was in control of the country for 18 years (1830-48), though not for all that time as president. Despite his tough rule, he succeeded in establishing a certain political stability and put the weak economy on its feet. He is remembered perhaps more warmly than many of his successors in power.

The period which followed was an almost uninterrupted chain of civil wars and political strife, stopped only by another long-time dictator, General Guzmán Blanco, who gained power in 1870 and kept it, with a few breaks, till 1888. A Conservative with Liberal leanings, he launched a broad programme of reforms, including a new constitution, compulsory primary education, religious freedom and a package of regulations to aid economic recovery. No doubt he tackled some of the crucial domestic issues and assured temporary stability, but his despotic rule triggered wide popular opposition, and when he stepped down, the country again plunged into civil war.

Things were not going much better on the international front. In the 1840s, Venezuela raised the question of its eastern border with British Guiana (today Guyana). Based on preindependence territorial divisions, the Venezuelan government asserted its sovereignty over as much as two-thirds of Guiana, up to the Río Essequibo. The issue was a matter of lengthy diplomatic negotiations, and led to severe strains in international relations in the 1890s. It was finally settled in 1899 by an arbitral tribunal, which gave the rights over the questioned territory to Great Britain, though Venezuela claims it to this day. All Venezuela-produced maps have this chunk of Guayana within Venezuelan boundaries, labelled 'Zona en Reclamación'.

Another conflict which led to serious tensions in international relations was Venezuela's failure to meet payments on loans to Great Britain, Italy and Germany, accumulated during the irresponsible government of yet another caudillo, General Cipriano Castro. In response, in 1902, the three countries sent their navies to blockade Venezuelan sea ports.

Modern Times

The first half of the 20th century was dominated by five successive military rulers from the Andean state of Táchira, the first of whom was the incompetent Cipriano Castro. The longest-lasting and most despotic of the caudillos was General Juan Vicente Gómez, who seized power in 1908 and didn't relinquish it until his death in 1935. Gómez phased out the parliament, squelched the opposition and thus monopolised power, supported by a strong army, extensive police force and developed spy network. Thanks to the discovery of oil in the second decade of the 1900s, the Gómez regime was able to stabilise the country and, in some ways, helped make it prosperous. By the late 1920s, Venezuela was the world's largest exporter of oil. This not only contributed enormously to economic recovery, but also paid off the country's entire foreign debt. Needless to say, Gómez didn't fail to cream off a share of oil transactions and, in the process, amassed a personal fortune to become just about the richest man in the country.

Little of the oil-related wealth filtered down to people on the street, and the vast majority continued to live in poverty, with little or no educational or health facilities, let alone reasonable housing. Oil money also resulted in the neglect of agriculture. Food had to be imported in increasing amounts, and prices rose rapidly. When Gómez died, in 1935, the people of Caracas went on a rampage, burning down the houses of his relatives and supporters and even threatening to set fire to the oil installations on Lago Maracaibo.

Gómez was succeeded by Eleázar López Contreras (his war minister) and, six years later, by yet another general of the same Andean gang, Isaías Medina Angarita. Meanwhile, popular tensions rose dangerously, exploding in 1945 when Rómulo Betancourt (founder and leader of the left-wing Acción Democrática party), with the support of the majority of the people and some junior army officers, took control of the government. A new constitution was soon worked out, and adopted in 1947, and a noted novelist, Rómulo Gallegos, became president in Venezuela's first democratic election.

The pace of reform was too fast, however, given the strength of old military forces greedy for power. The inevitable coup took place only eight months later, with Colonel Marcos Pérez Jiménez emerging as leader. Once in control, Jiménez began ruthlessly crushing all his opposition, at the same time ploughing the oil money back into public works, into industries which would help diversify the economy and, particularly, into modernising Caracas.

Spectacular buildings mushrooming in the capital were a poor substitute for a better standard of living and access to political power. Opposition to Jiménez's rule grew, and in 1958 he was overthrown by a coalition of civilians and navy and air force officers. The fortune he accumulated during his rule placed him, like Gómez before him, among the wealthiest citizens in the country.

Shortly after Jiménez's fall, the country returned to democratic rule and an election was held, in which Betancourt was again elected president. He put an end to the former dictator's solicitous policy towards foreign big business, but was careful this time not to act too impetuously.

Despite opposition from both communists and right-wing factions, Betancourt enjoyed widespread popular support. He succeeded in completing his constitutional five-year term in office – the first democratically elected Venezuelan president to do so – and voluntarily stepped down in 1963. In the next 25 years, there were six changes of president, all by constitutional means.

Recent Developments

Oil proved to be the essential factor in Venezuela's politics. It brought prosperity to the country, but is now taking it away, and with it, political stability. Presidents Leoni (1964-69) and Caldera (1969-74) had relatively easy and quiet terms, since the steady stream of oil money that flowed into the country was generally enough to quell social unrest wherever it occurred. Still, not much has ever been done to solve the essential problems of the less affluent part of the population.

During his first term in office (1974-79), President Pérez witnessed the oil bonanza. Not only did production of oil rise, but more importantly, following the Arab-Israeli war, the price quadrupled overnight. Pérez nationalised the iron ore and oil industries and went on a spending spree. Imported luxury goods began to cram shops and the nation suddenly got the impression that the real El Dorado had materialised.

Here is where the rosy picture fades. In the late 1970s, the growing international recession and oil glut started to shake Venezuela's economic stability. Oil revenues began to drop, pushing up unemployment and inflation. People realised that their prosperity was disappearing. Inevitably, popular discontent rose. The 1988 drop in world oil prices cut the country's revenue in half, putting into serious doubt Venezuela's ability to pay off its foreign debt.

A package of austerity measures introduced by the government in February 1989 triggered a wave of protests, culminating in

VENEZUELA

three days of bloody riots known as the Caracazo and costing over 300 lives.

With such violent confrontations just three weeks after taking office, President Pérez's popularity declined right from the start of his term. All further measures (which basically consisted of price increases) immediately spurred protests, originating mostly from universities and not infrequently escalating into riots.

The attempted coup d'état, launched on 4 February 1992 by a few mid-rank military officers led by Hugo Chávez Frías, was a shock to most Venezuelans. The president managed to escape from the Palacio de Miraflores (the presidential palace) minutes before the tanks of the rebels broke in. There was much shooting throughout Caracas, claiming over 20 lives, but the government retained control of the situation.

On 27 November 1992, another attempt to seize power electrified the nation. This one was led by junior air force officers, who tried to complete the job started by Chávez. The air battles amidst Caracas skyscrapers gave the coup a cinematographic, even apocalyptic dimension. The Palacio de Miraflores was bombed and partially destroyed. The army was again called to defend the president, which it dutifully did. This time, over 100 people lost their lives.

Both coups were launched under grandiloquent slogans of 'patriotism', 'rescuing the country', 'continuation of Bolívar's ideals' and the like. Both failed, as the army commands maintained restraint and gave their support to the president – but will they be so loyal next time? The army is increasingly divided, and disillusioned with the economic stalemate which is cutting its income. The military lived quietly during the fat years of the oil boom, but now, when money is scarce, they are starting to ask for their share.

Things became even more complicated when Pérez was accused of taking 250 million bolívares from a secret defence expenditure, changing the money to US dollars at a favourable government rate, then selling the dollars at the market price,

gaining some US$11 million in the process. The Supreme Court examined the issue and, on 20 May 1993, declared that there was enough evidence to charge the president. Pérez was automatically suspended from his duties and Ramón Velásquez was appointed to serve as interim president for the last eight months of the statutory Pérez term. The country is in its deepest political crisis since 1958, and there is serious uncertainty about the future.

GEOGRAPHY

With an area of about 916,000 sq km, Venezuela is South America's sixth largest country. It occupies the northernmost extreme of the continent, including much of the Caribbean coast, within its frontiers. The country has borders with Colombia to the west, Brazil to the south and Guyana to the east.

Venezuela is very varied geographically. Just south of the Caribbean coast looms a chain of mountain ranges, with a number of peaks exceeding 2000 metres. The mountains roll southward into a vast area of plains known as Los Llanos, which stretches down to the Orinoco and Meta rivers, occupying one-third of the country's territory.

The land south of the Río Orinoco (nearly half the country's area) can be broadly divided into two regions. To the south-west is a chunk of the Amazon, a dense tropical forest of which large areas are hardly accessible. To the north-east lies an extensive plateau of open savannas, the Guayana Highlands. It's here that the majority of tepuis are located. These gigantic eroded rocks, with their characteristic vertical walls and flat tops, are all that remains of the upper layer of a plateau which gradually eroded over millions of years. They loom up to 1000 metres above the surrounding countryside, but reach nearly 3000 metres above sea level.

North-western Venezuela is another area of geographical contrasts. Here lies the Sierra Nevada de Mérida, the northern tip of the Andean chain. The Sierra is Venezuela's highest mountain range, culminating at 5007 metres on snowcapped Pico Bolívar. North of the Cordillera extends the marshy lowland basin around Lago Maracaibo. Some 160 km long and 120 km wide, it's the largest lake in South America, linked to the Caribbean Sea by a narrow strait, and is Venezuela's main oil-producing area. Further north-east along the coast, near the town of Coro, is the country's sole desert, the Médanos de Coro.

The 2150-km Río Orinoco is Venezuela's main river, its entire course lying within the national boundaries. The Orinoco delta consists of over 50 major distributary channels along nearly 400 km of the Atlantic coast, covering an area of some 40,000 sq km (equal to that of Switzerland or the Netherlands).

Venezuela possesses a number of islands scattered along the Caribbean coast, the largest being Isla de Margarita. Other islands and archipelagos of importance include Las Aves, Los Roques, La Orchila, La Tortuga and Blanquilla.

CLIMATE

Given Venezuela's latitude, the temperature is fairly constant throughout the year. It does, however, vary with altitude, dropping about 6°C with every 1000-metre increase. Since over 90% of Venezuela lies below 1000 metres, you'll experience average temperatures of at least 23°C in most parts of the country. The Andean and coastal mountain ranges, will require warmer clothing, and if you plan on climbing the highest peaks of the Sierra, a good jacket won't be out of place.

Rainfall varies seasonally. Broadly speaking, the dry season goes from December to April, while the wet period lasts for the rest of the year. There are many regional variations in the amount of precipitation and the length of the seasons. For example, the mountains receive more rainfall than the coast and can be relatively wet for most of the year, while you can be pretty sure of visiting the Coro desert without an umbrella any day of the year. The Amazon has no distinguishable dry season, with the annual rainfall of more than 2000 mm distributed relatively uniformly throughout the year.

GOVERNMENT

Venezuela is a federal republic. The president, the head of state and of the armed forces, is elected by a direct vote for a five-year term and cannot be elected for two consecutive terms. The national congress has a 47-seat senate and a 199-seat chamber of deputies, both elected for five-year terms. Voting is compulsory for citizens from the age of 18. The supreme court is the highest judicial body, with judges elected by the congress.

There are numerous political parties, but the two traditional movements are Acción Democrática (AD) and Partido Social Cristiano (Copei) – for the last 30 years, elected presidents have been from one of these two parties.

ECONOMY

Oil is Venezuela's main natural resource and the heart of the economy. Since its discovery it turned Venezuela – then a poor debtor nation – into South America's richest country. Until 1970, Venezuela was the world's largest exporter of oil, and though it was later overtaken by the Arab countries, its oil income expanded year after year. The cofounder of OPEC, Venezuela influenced the fourfold rise of oil prices introduced by this organisation in 1973-74, which quadrupled its revenue. Oil export earnings peaked in 1982, at US$19.3 billion, representing about 96% of the country's exports. However, the global recession and the decline in world oil prices in the early 1980s were severe setbacks. Export earnings from oil fell drastically, to a low of US$7.2 billion in 1986.

The main oil deposits are in the Maracaibo Basin, but others have been discovered and exploited in the Orinoco delta and the eastern part of Los Llanos.

Predictably, oil has overshadowed other sectors of the economy. Agriculture has been largely neglected, and only a small portion of the country's territory is under cultivation. The major crops include bananas, sugar cane, maize, coffee, cacao, cotton and tobacco.

VENEZUELA

Oil apart, Venezuela is rich in natural resources, though most of them are still largely underexplored and underexploited. Iron ore is the most important mineral after oil, with huge deposits found south of Ciudad Bolívar. The iron ore industry is centred around the city of Ciudad Guayana.

Among other major subsoil riches are bauxites, gold and diamonds (all in the Guayana Highlands), and coal (next to the border with Colombia, north of Maracaibo).

Manufacturing has also progressed as an effect of the government's policy to diversify the economy. The motor vehicle assembly, textile, paper and food industries are now well established.

Venezuela's hydroelectric potential is considerable; the Guri dam, south of Ciudad Guayana, is one of the largest hydroelectric plants in the world, with a potential of 10 million kilowatts.

POPULATION & PEOPLE

The total population, as of 1993, is estimated at 21 million, of whom about one-fifth live in Caracas. The rate of population growth, around 2.5%, is one of the highest in Latin America. Venezuela is a young country, with over half its population below 18 years of age. Yet, at nearly 70 years, life expectancy is remarkably high.

Population density, averaging about 23 persons per sq km, is low, though it varies a great deal throughout the country. The central coastal region, including the cities of Valencia, Maracay and Caracas, is the most densely populated, while the Amazon and the Guayana Highlands are very sparsely populated. About three-quarters of Venezuelans live in the towns and cities.

Venezuela is a country of mixed blood. About 70% of the population have a blend of European, Indian and African ancestry, or any two of the three. The rest are White (about 20%), Black (8%) or Indian (2%). Indians don't belong to a single ethnic or linguistic family, but form different independent tribes scattered throughout the country. Major Indian communities include the Guajiro (north of Maracaibo), the Piaroa,

Guajibo, Yekuana and Yanomami (in the Amazon), the Warao (in the Orinco delta) and the Pemón (in the southern Guayana Highlands). There are over 40 Indian languages used in the country.

Venezuela has experienced significant postwar immigration from Europe (estimated at about one million), mostly from Spain, Italy and Portugal, but migration nearly stopped in the 1960s and, moreover, many migrants went back home. Caracas is the country's most cosmopolitan city.

RELIGION

Most Venezuelans are Roman Catholics. Many Indian tribes, too, adopted Catholicism, and only a few, primarily those living in isolation, still practise their ancient beliefs. There exist various Protestant churches in Venezuela, but their adherents aren't numerous. There are small numbers of Jews and Muslims.

LANGUAGE

Spanish is Venezuela's official language and, except for some remote Indian tribes, all the inhabitants speak it. Many people, mostly in large urban centres, speak some English, but it's certainly not a commonly understood or spoken language.

Facts for the Visitor

VISAS

Nationals of the USA, Canada, Australia, New Zealand, the UK and most of Western and Scandinavian Europe do not need a visa if they fly into Venezuela; a Tourist Card (Tarjeta de Turismo) is issued by the airline at no cost. The Tourist Card is valid for 60 days and can be extended for another 60 days.

If you enter Venezuela by land from either Brazil or Colombia, you do need a visa. However, the Venezuelan consulates in South American countries can be difficult places to get visas. In Colombia, for example, only the consulate in Cúcuta gives visas to non-Colombians (see the Cúcuta section in the Colombia chapter for details).

If you plan on travelling overland, it's best to get the visa in your country of residence. Venezuelan authorities have introduced multiple-entry tourist visas which are valid for one year from the date of issue. Consulates in most major Western countries, including the USA, the UK and Australia, now give that type of visa. The official requirements are: your passport (valid for at least one year), a bank letter stating your funds, a job letter stating your wages, an onward ticket and one photo. The visa may take a couple of days to be issued, and its cost varies, depending on the country from which you apply (up to US$25).

On entering Venezuela, make sure you get an entry stamp in your passport from DIEX (Dirección de Identificación y Extranjería) border officials. You may be asked for an onward ticket, though it's no longer a rule, and varies from one border crossing to another and from one official to another.

Venezuelan Representatives

Venezuela has representatives in the capital cities of neighbouring countries, and in:

Australia
    MLC Tower, Phillip, ACT (☎ 282-4828)
France
    11 Rue Copernie (☎ 45532998)
Germany
    Im Rheingarten 7, Bonn 3 (☎ 40092)
UK
    1 Cromwell Rd, London SW7 (☎ (071) 584-4206)
USA
    1099 30th St, NW 20007, Washington DC (☎ 342- 2214)

MONEY

US dollars and American Express travellers' cheques are by far the most popular in Venezuela, so stick to them. Among credit cards, Visa, Mastercard and American Express are the most widely accepted by banks and other establishments, such as hotels, restaurants, airlines and shops.

Currency

The unit of currency is – of course – the *bolívar*, divided into 100 *céntimos*. There are coins of one-half, one, two and five bolívares and paper notes of 10, 20, 50, 100, 500 and 1000 bolívares.

Changing Money

The place to change money is the bank or *casa de cambio*. Banks change cash and travellers' cheques and give advances to credit card holders. Casas de cambio exist in large cities and change cash at a rate marginally lower than the banks. They sometimes also exchange travellers' cheques. There's no black market in Venezuela, and you'll probably never get a better rate than in the banks.

Banks are plentiful in Venezuela, but not all handle foreign exchange operations, and it appears to change constantly from bank to bank, branch to branch, city to city and day to day. As a general rule, the banks to look for are:

Banco Consolidado (almost always American Express travellers' cheques and credit cards, and sometimes cash)
Banco Unión (usually cash, less often travellers' cheques, as a rule Visa credit card and sometimes Mastercard)
Banco de Venezuela (irregularly cash, travellers' cheques and credit cards)
Banco Mercantil (Mastercard and rarely anything else).

Other banks which may sometimes be useful include Banco Latino, Banco Construcción, Banco Italo Venezolano and some regional banks. Bank opening hours are identical throughout the country: weekdays from 8.30 to 11.30 am and 2 to 4.30 pm.

Exchange Rates

Exchange rates for cash and travellers' cheques are more or less the same, though some banks charge commission on cheques. The rate varies only marginally between the banks, so it's not worth shopping around. The devaluation of the bolívar against hard currencies stands at around 30% per year and is slowly growing. Exchange rates at July 1993 were:

A$1	=	58.7 bolívares
Can$1	=	67.4 bolívares
DM1	=	50.2 bolívares
FF1	=	14.6 bolívares
UK£1	=	128.5 bolívares
US$1	=	90.5 bolívares

INFORMATION
Tourist Offices
Tourist information is run by regional tourist offices in state capitals and some other cities. Some are better than others, but on the whole, they lack city maps and brochures.

Inparques
National parks are run by the governmental body commonly known as Inparques. If you plan on visiting national parks, you theoretically need a permit for each of them, issued by Inparques. See the Caracas section for further details.

Post
The postal service is slow and unreliable. Letters sent air mail to the USA or Europe can take up to a month to arrive. Post letters at Ipostel offices.

Telephone
The telephone system is largely automated for both domestic and international connections. There's a relatively good supply of public telephones in large cities, but many are out of order. Coins are used for local calls, though more and more newly installed telephones only operate on phone cards (*tarjeta CANTV*). If you think you'll be making many calls, it's worth buying one – there are four types, at 250, 500, 1000 and 2000 bolívares. They are convenient for local and intercity calls. You can also use the tarjeta for international calls, or go to the CANTV office and call through an operator. The CANTV is also the place to buy phone cards. Each CANTV office should have at least a few operative public telephones, if you can't find a working one elsewhere.

Electricity
Electricity is 110 volts, 60 cycles AC all over the country. US-type flat two-pin plugs are used.

HEALTH
Venezuela has quite a developed health service, with an array of well-stocked *farmacias* (pharmacies), private clinics and hospitals. Tap water is safe to drink in Caracas and several larger cities, but if you prefer to avoid it, a choice of mineral waters and other drinks is readily available in supermarkets and shops.

Sanitary conditions are probably a bit above average South American standards but are declining – yet another effect of economic crisis. A jab of gammaglobulin against hepatitis might be recommended. No vaccinations are required on entering Venezuela, unless you come from an affected area.

Mosquitos infest many low-lying areas, particularly the Amazon and Los Llanos. Bring along a good mosquito repellent. If you are going to venture far from the beaten track, take a first aid kit (see the Health section in the introductory Facts for the Visitor chapter).

DANGERS & ANNOYANCES
Venezuela is a relatively safe country in which to travel, though robbery is becoming a problem. Common crime is increasing in the large cities. Caracas is by far the most dangerous place in the country, and you should take care while strolling about the streets, particularly at night. Keep your passport and money next to the skin, and your camera, if you are carrying one, hidden in a pack or bag. Venturing into poor shantytowns is asking for trouble.

Avoid police if you can, and if they stop you, be polite but not overly friendly. Don't get nervous or angry – this only works against you.

Never disrespect Bolívar – he is a saint to Venezuelans. For instance, sitting on a bench in Plaza Bolívar with your feet on the bench or crossing the plaza carrying bulky parcels may be considered disrespectful, and police may hassle you for it.

When travelling around the country, there are plenty of *alcabalas* (police checkpoints), though not all of them are actually operating. They sometimes check the identity documents of passengers and, seldom, the luggage as well. In the cities, on the other hand, police checks are uncommon, but they do occur so always have your passport with you. If you don't, you may end up at the police station.

ACCOMMODATION

Venezuela has hotels for every budget, and it's usually easy to find a room. With some exceptions, low-budget hotels are uninteresting, styleless places – just bare walls, a bed and perhaps a few other bits of furniture. However, most cheapies have private baths. As most of the country lies in the lowland tropics, rooms usually have a fan, sometimes even air-conditioning, but there's no hot water. Always have a look at the room and check the fan or air-conditioning before booking in and paying.

The price of cheap hotels is pretty similar throughout the country and doesn't seem to depend much on whether you're in a big city or a small town, or whether the place is touristy or not. Count on roughly US$5 to US$7 a single and US$7 to US$9 a double.

Mid-range hotels provide more facilities but often lack character. They are usually reasonably priced for what they offer, and you can often stay in quite a good place for, say, US$20 to US$30 per double room. Only Caracas and Isla de Margarita have a choice of hotels with three-digit prices, and a few other cities such as Puerto La Cruz and Maracaibo have one or two such places. Hotels often charge foreigners a 10% tax on top of the room price, though not all budget places do so.

Brothels are not uncommon in Venezuela. More numerous, though, are love hotels (places which rent rooms by the hour). Many cheap hotels double as love hotels, and it's often impossible to avoid staying in one from time to time.

Venezuela doesn't belong to the International Youth Hostel Federation (IYHF) and has no youth hostels. Camping grounds, as the term is understood in the West, are few and far between; you can camp rough outside urban centres. Camping on the beach is popular, but be cautious and don't leave your tent unattended.

FOOD

Venezuela is a good place to eat. On the whole, food is good and relatively inexpensive. Apart from a variety of typical local dishes, there are plenty of Western cuisines available, including a dense array of gringo fast-food outlets. Spanish and Italian restaurants are particularly well represented, thanks to a sizeable migration from these two countries. There are also some good Chinese and Arab restaurants, mostly in the main cities.

In virtually every dining or drinking establishment a 10% service charge will automatically be added to the bill. In budget eateries, tipping is uncommon, but in upmarket restaurants, a small tip is customary.

Gourmets should stay in Caracas, which offers the widest range of international delicacies (at a price, of course). On the other hand, nondemanding rock-bottom travellers should look for restaurants which serve the so-called *menú del día*, a set meal consisting of soup and a main course, cheaper than any à la carte dish. An alternative can be chicken: there's a good supply of barbecued chicken joints; half a chicken with arepa, potatoes, yuca or other side dish can be grabbed for about US$3. The market is, as in most of South America, a good, cheap option, offering typical food, usually tasty and fresh.

The following list describes some Venezuelan snacks and dishes:

arepa – this small toasted or fried maize pancake, which is itself plain, is often included as an accompaniment to some dishes. More popularly, it's served stuffed with cheese, meat, seafood, etc. There are plenty of snack bars, commonly called *arepras*, which serve arepas with a choice of fillings, including octopus, shrimps, sausage, vegetable salad and avocado. It's a good snack for about US$1.

cachapa – a large-size round pancake of ground maize

cachito – this croissant is filled with chopped ham and served hot

hallaca – chopped pork, beef or/and chicken with vegetables and olives is folded in a maize dough, wrapped in banana leaves and steamed

mondongo – a seasoned tripe is cooked in bouillon with maize, potatoes and other vegetables

muchacho – roast loin of beef is served in sauce

pabellón – this main course consists of shredded meat, rice, beans and fried plantain (*plátano* – a kind of green banana)

parrillada – a barbecue of different kinds of meat, this was originally an Argentine dish but is widespread in Venezuela

pasticho – a layered dish, it is much the same as lasagna

sancocho – this vegetable stew contains fish, meat or chicken.

DRINKS

Expresso coffee is strong and excellent in Venezuela. It's served in *panaderías* (coffee shops-cum-bakeries), which are plentiful. Ask for *café negro* if you want it black, *café marrón* if you prefer half coffee, half milk, and *café con leche* if you like very milky coffee.

Fruit juices are popular, and readily available in restaurants, *fuentes de soda*, *fruterías*, *refresquerías* and other establishments. Given the variety of fruit in the country, you have quite a choice. Juices come pure or watered-down (*batidos*), or as milk shakes (*merengadas*).

The number one alcoholic drink is beer, particularly Polar beer, which is the dominant brand. Sold everywhere either in cans or small bottles, it costs from US$0.40 (in down-to-earth eateries) upward.

BOOKS

There's not much in terms of guidebooks to Venezuela. *No Frills Guide to Venezuela*, by Hilary Dunsterville Branch (Bradt Publications, UK, 1991), is full of maps and practical details, though it focuses on outdoor activities, mostly hiking in national parks, with cities' cultural sights described in much less detail.

Janice Bauman & Leni Young's *Guide to Venezuela*, edited by Ernesto Armitano

(Caracas, 1987), is the most complete, a 925-page book covering virtually every sight and town together with background information. The book also includes detailed practical information, though not much of it is for the rock-bottom traveller. Unfortunately, the book hasn't been updated since 1987 and is almost impossible to obtain outside Venezuela.

There's no shortage of general reading about Venezuela, though most publications focus mainly or exclusively on the oil boom and/or the oil crisis.

Venezuela: the Search for Order, the Dream of Progress, by John V Lombardi (Oxford University Press, New York, Oxford, 1982), provides general reading about Venezuela's history, politics, geography and people. For comprehensive 20th-century historical background, try *Venezuela, a Century of Change*, by Judith Ewell (C Hurst & Co, London, 1984), or *Venezuela*, by David Eugene Blank (Praeger Publishers, New York, 1984).

Local bookshops stock a range of fine, locally published coffee-table books about Venezuelan flora and fauna, some of them with English descriptions.

Getting There & Away

At the northern edge of South America, Venezuela is the cheapest gateway to the continent from both Europe and North America. It has road and air connections with Colombia and Brazil, and air and ferry links with Trinidad and the Netherlands Antilles. There are flights via Trinidad to Georgetown, Guyana.

AIR

The official Venezuelan entry requirement is an onward ticket, so it is possible that no airline will sell you a one-way ticket unless you show them an onward ticket. The cheapest ticket out of Venezuela is Zuliana's Maracaibo-Medellín or Bogotá flight (US$50), but you fall into the same trap, as

Colombia also has onward ticket requirements.

The airport tax for tourists leaving Venezuela is US$10, payable in either US dollars or bolívares.

To/From Europe & North America

There are cheap tickets available from many European cities; in many cases, London may be the best budget jumping-off point, but there are special deals here and there, so you may also find agents in Amsterdam, Madrid, Lisbon or Paris offering very attractive fares. Details are given in the Getting There & Away chapter at the beginning of this book.

From North America, the major gateway city is Miami. Plenty of airlines fly from there to Caracas and several other Venezuelan cities. Major carriers tend to have relatively high prices, but there are usually some minor South or Central American airlines which are cheaper. At the time of writing, Zuliana de Aviación, a little-known Venezuelan carrier based at Maracaibo, offers probably the cheapest fares to both Venezuela and Colombia. Check offers with other airlines, which may have some good deals as well.

To/From Brazil

Flights between Brazil and Venezuela are offered by a number of airlines, including Viasa and Varig, but are painfully expensive. For example, a flight to Caracas from the Brazilian cities of São Paulo or Rio de Janeiro costs about US$750 (US$850 return). There are no flights between Boa Vista (Brazil) and Santa Elena (Venezuela).

To/From Colombia

There are plenty of flights between Bogotá (Colombia) and Caracas with several carriers, including Avianca, Avensa and Viasa (US$194 one-way, US$250 one-year return). Zuliana de Aviación, however, will fly you from Bogotá to Caracas (via Medellín and Maracaibo) for US$110 (US$220 return).

Other possible links between Colombia and Venezuela include Cartagena-Caracas

with Viasa (US$172, US$199 one-year return), Barranquilla-Caracas with Lacsa (US$161, US$193 30-day return), Bogotá-Valencia with Valenciana de Aviación (US$120, US$200 60- day return) and Bogotá or Medellín to Maracaibo with Zuliana de Aviación (US$81, US$162 one-year return).

Note that when buying any international ticket in Colombia, you pay a 19% tax (9.5% on return flights) on top of the listed fares.

To/From Netherlands Antilles

There are flights from both Aruba and Curaçao, in the Netherlands Antilles, to Coro (Venezuela). See the Coro section for information.

To/From Trinidad

Flights between Port of Spain (Trinidad) and Caracas are operated by United Airlines and Aeropostal (a Venezuelan carrier), for US$114 one-way. There are no longer any flights between Port of Spain and Maturín.

LAND
To/From Brazil

Only one road runs between Brazil and Venezuela. It leads through Boa Vista to Santa Elena and continues via El Dorado to Ciudad Guayana. See the Santa Elena section for details.

To/From Colombia

You can enter Venezuela from Colombia at four border crossings. Going from northwest to south-east, there's a coastal smuggling route between Maicao and Maracaibo (see under Maracaibo for details). Further south is the most popular border crossing, between Cúcuta and San Antonio del Táchira (see under San Antonio). Next comes an unpopular, dangerous and inconvenient crossing from Arauca to El Amparo de Apure. Finally, there's an uncommon but interesting outback route from Puerto Carreño in Colombia to either Puerto Páez or Puerto Ayacucho in Venezuela (see Puerto Ayacucho).

SEA

To/From North America
There are occasional inexpensive freighters from Houston, Texas; see the introductory Getting There & Away chapter for details.

To/From Netherlands Antilles
There's been no ferry service between Curaçao (Netherlands Antilles) and La Vela de Coro (the port of Coro, Venezuela) since the ferry went up in flames in late 1992, but it may have recommenced by the time you read this. A ferry between Aruba (Netherlands Antilles) and Punto Fijo, on the Península Paraguaná, operates irregularly, a few times a week. The trip takes about four hours one-way, but bureaucracy can double this time.

To/From Trinidad
A ferry service operates between Port of Spain (Trinidad) and Güiria, on the far north-eastern tip of Venezuela, facing Trinidad. The Güiria section has details on this route, as well as information on getting to Güiria from St Lucia, Barbados and St Vincent, with the same ferry operator.

Getting Around

AIR
Venezuela has a well-developed airline system. Viasa is the main international carrier, flying to Europe, the USA and most South American capitals, but has no domestic routes. Aeropostal and Avensa have both domestic and international flights. Servivensa, a young offspring of Avensa, is yet another airline that has international flights. These four apart, there are half a dozen smaller carriers which cover regional routes, and a few of them (such as Zuliana de Aviación and Valenciana de Aviación) fly abroad as well.

Flying in Venezuela is still relatively cheap compared to neighbouring countries such as Colombia or Brazil, but no longer the bargain it was several years ago. Though fuel remains cheap, airfares have doubled or even tripled over the past few years.

Of the two leading domestic carriers, Avensa and Aeropostal (which cover most of the internal routes), the latter is usually cheaper. Details on routes and fares are included in the Caracas section.

Make sure to reconfirm your flight a couple of days before departure, and arm yourself with patience, as not all flights depart at the scheduled time. There's a tax of around US$1 on domestic flights.

BUS
As there are no railways of any importance in Venezuela, most travelling is done by bus or *por puesto*. The por puesto (literally 'by the seat'), a widespread means of transport in Venezuela, is a cross between bus and taxi – the same kind of service as a *colectivo* in Colombia or Peru. They are usually taxis (less often, minibuses) which ply fixed routes, both short and medium distance, and depart when all seats are filled. They cost about 50% to 80% more than buses, and are faster and usually more comfortable. On some routes, they are the main or even exclusive means of transport.

Buses are generally fast and efficient, especially on the main roads, which are all surfaced. There are frequent daily buses between all major population centres, so there's no problem finding transport in any direction.

All intercity buses depart from/arrive at the *terminal de pasajeros*, the central bus station. Every city has such a station, usually far from the city centre but always linked by local transport. The terminal is home to the bus companies' offices, their number varying from a few to a few dozen, depending on how important a transport hub it is. Caracas has by far the busiest bus station, from which buses run to just about every corner of the country.

Bus companies own a plethora of buses, ranging from archaic junk to the most recent models. The former ply the regional secondary roads, while the latter operate on the main long-distance routes. If various companies service the same route, fares are much the same with all of them. The standard, however, may differ from one company to another, and you soon realise which are better than others. Many major companies have introduced the so-called *servicio ejecutivo*, in modern, air-conditioned buses, which provide better standards and shorter travelling time and cost about 10% to 15% more than the ordinary service. See the Caracas section for fares on main routes.

In general, there's no need to buy tickets in advance for major routes, where there are plenty of buses. This rule, however, doesn't apply around Christmas, Carnaval (several days before Lent) and Easter, when Venezuelans like to travel.

Many short-distance regional routes (as well as almost all city transport) is operated by small buses called, depending on the region, *buseta*, *carro*, *carrito*, *micro* or, somewhat confusingly, *por puesto*.

BOAT
Venezuela has a number of offshore territories, the main one being Isla de Margarita. (See the Puerto La Cruz, Cumaná and Isla de Margarita sections for details about boats going to/from the island.) There's no regular boat service to Venezuela's other islands.

The Río Orinoco is the country's major waterway, navigable from its mouth up to Puerto Ayacucho. There's no passenger service on any stretch of the river, so your options are either cargo or fishing boats, or a tour.

CAR
Travelling by car (either owned or rented) is a comfortable and attractive way of getting around Venezuela. The country is sufficiently safe, the network of roads is extensive and usually in good shape, and driving manners seem to be better than in neighbouring countries. Petrol stations are numerous and fuel costs next to nothing: US$0.05 to US$0.10 per litre, depending on the octane level (reputedly the cheapest petrol in the world), though the government is planning to double or triple the price in the near future.

There are several international and local car rental companies, including Hertz, Avis, Budget and National, with offices at major airports throughout the country and in the centres of the main cities. The addresses are not included in the text, but tourist offices, travel agencies or top-class hotels will give you the information.

As a rough guide, a small car will cost around US$60 per day, while the discount rate for a full week is about US$350. A 4WD vehicle is considerably more expensive, and harder to obtain.

TOURS
Tours are a popular way to visit some parts of Venezuela, largely because vast areas of the country are virtually inaccessible by public transport (eg the Amazon) or because a visit on one's own to scattered sights over a large territory (eg in La Gran Sabana) may be considerably more time-consuming and eventually more expensive than a tour.

Some general advice: always try to arrange the tour from the regional centre closest to the area you are going to visit. Otherwise, you will pay not only for mileage to get to the area (at the tour's price, of course), but you will find that nationwide tour operators usually have less comprehensive knowledge about distant places than the agents within the region. Accordingly, for hikes in Los Andes, there's no better place to look for a guide than Mérida; for excursions around La Gran Sabana, the cheapest organised trips are to be found in Santa Elena; for the Amazon, the obvious point for talking to agents is Puerto Ayacucho; for tours to Salto Angel (Angel Falls), Ciudad Bolívar is the place to shop around, as all flights to Canaima (the base for Salto Angel) depart from there. You'll find details in the respective sections.

HITCHING
Venezuela is not bad for hitching. There's an extensive array of roads and many people have cars, so traffic is usually busy enough.

A considerable proportion of vehicles are open pick-up trucks, and drivers don't mind putting you (and your pack) in the back.

Needless to say, drivers are more reluctant to stop and pick you up on the open road than to take you from a place where they are already stationary. Petrol stations and roadside restaurants are good points to hunt for a lift. The alcabalas (police road checkpoints) may also be good, but this is a bit of a lottery: some police are friendly and might even ask a driver to take you; others are suspicious and will check your documents first, and occasionally may want to search your luggage as well.

Caracas

Founded by Diego de Losada in 1567, Santiago de León de Caracas was for three centuries a small and unhurried place, its inhabitants living their provincial way of life. The first to launch an extensive modernising programme was General Guzmán Blanco, who erected a number of monumental edifices, among them the Capitol Building and the National Pantheon. Despite that, however, the town grew at a relatively slow pace until well into the 20th century.

Then came the oil boom, and all began to change at the speed of light. During the last 50 years, the city's population increased from half a million to over four million. Oil money has been pumped into modernisation, successfully transforming the somewhat bucolic colonial town into a vast urban sprawl of concrete. In the name of progress, the colonial architecture, save for a handful of buildings, was effectively eradicated and its place taken by futuristic complexes and steel-and-glass towers. In the 1980s, the Metro was opened, the last important achievement of urban planning.

It cannot be denied that Caracas today has some of the best modern architecture on the continent. It also has a web of motorways unseen in other South American capitals, the

city's estimated 1½ million vehicles causing serious smog and traffic problems.

Unbalanced expansion has also created vast areas of *barrios*, poor slum suburbs sprawling up the hills around the city centre. Part of a huge migration fuelled by the dream of wealth, these people have never managed to share in the city's prosperity, and live a hand-to-mouth existence in their tin shacks. The spectacular setting on the rolling hills only helps to sharpen the contrast between wealth and poverty.

Its size and capital status make Caracas the unquestioned centre of Venezuela's political, scientific, cultural and educational life. Whether you are interested in good food, plush hotels, theatre, museums or shopping, nowhere in Venezuela will you find as much to choose from.

At an altitude of about 900 metres, Caracas enjoys an agreeable, relatively dry and sunny climate with a mean temperature of about 22°C. The rainy season lasts from June to October.

On a less enticing note, Caracas is the least secure of all Venezuelan cities. Petty crime in general, and robbery and armed assaults in particular, are increasing, especially at night. The historic centre is unsafe for strolling after 8 pm or so, as is the area around the Nuevo Circo bus station. So far, the Sabana Grande gets unpleasant only late at night.

Orientation

Nestled in the long, east-west valley of Caracas, the city is at least 20 km end to end. To the north looms the steep green wall of Parque Nacional El Ávila, beautifully free of human dwellings. To the south, by contrast, the city expands up the hillsides, with modern *urbanizaciones* and shabby *ranchitos* invading and occupying every acceptably flat piece of land.

The valley itself is a dense urban fabric with forests of skyscrapers rising out of a mass of low-rise architecture. The area from El Silencio to Chacao can be considered the greater centre, packed with banks, offices, shops, eating establishments, commercial centres and public buildings. The main line of the Metro (No 1) goes right along the axis.

The historic quarter is at the west end of the greater centre, and is clearly recognisable on the map by the original chessboard layout of the streets. To the east stretches the district of Los Caobos, noted for several good museums. Next comes the Sabana Grande, an attractive pedestrian mall lined with shops and restaurants. Proceeding east, one comes across Chacaíto and Chacao, two commercial districts of rather low priority for tourists. El Rosal and Las Mercedes, to the south, have a number of trendy restaurants, while Caracas Country Club and Altamira, to the north, are predominantly elegant, wealthy residential zones.

A curiosity of Caracas is the street address system of the historic quarter, which might be difficult for newcomers to follow. It's actually not the streets which bear the names but the street intersections, or *esquinas*. The address is given 'corner to corner', so if, for instance, the address as Piñango a Conde, you know that the place is between these two street corners. If the place is right on the corner, its address is, eg, Esquina Conde. In modern times, the authorities have given names to the streets ('Este', 'Oeste', 'Norte' and 'Sur'), followed by numbers, but locals continue to stick to the esquinas. Other than in the old town, the streets are named. Major streets are commonly called avenidas. Street numbers are seldom used, and you rarely find one on façades or entrance doors.

Information

Tourist Office The Corpoturismo tourist office (☎ 5078815, 5078829) is on the 37th floor of the Torre Oeste (West Tower), Parque Central (Metro Bellas Artes). The office is open on weekdays from 8.30 am to 12.30 pm and 2 to 5 pm. Don't expect much in the way of leaflets on Caracas, nor city maps.

Inparques The Dirección General de Parques Nacionales, commonly called Inparques (☎ 2854106, 2854360, 2854859), is the place to get permits to the national parks. In theory,

you have to get a permit for each park except El Ávila (where you just pay the US$0.10 fee at the entrance to the park). In practice, you'll rarely be asked for the permit in any of the parks, though it's always better to have one, just in case. The permit costs nothing and is issued on the spot. Get permits to all parks you plan to visit. Specify 'camping' if you plan on doing this and the park has such facilities. The Inparques office is just east of the Parque del Este Metro station and is open on weekdays from 8.30 am to 12.30 pm and 1.30 to 5 pm. The office provides very little information about the parks and has virtually no maps or brochures.

Money Caracas has many banks, but it will take you some time to find one that will change your cash or travellers' cheques, save the Banco Consolidado, which usually deals with American Express cheques. It's easier to come across a bank that gives cash advances to MasterCard and Visa card holders. The Banco de Venezuela, Banco Mercantil and Banco Provincial, among others, handle this operation.

If you can't find a useful bank to change your cash and travellers' cheques, there are plenty of casas de cambio, the one with the best reputation being Italcambio. They have several offices throughout the city: on Avenida Urdaneta, Esquina Veroes, one block north of Plaza Bolívar; on Avenida Casanova, one block south of Boulevard de Sabana Grande; and on Avenida del Ávila, one block south of the Altamira Metro station. They are open on weekdays from 8 am to 12.30 pm and 1.30 to 5 pm, and on Saturday from 8.30 am till noon. They change cash and travellers' cheques, paying about 0.5% less than the banks. There's also an Italcambio office at the Maiquetía airport (international terminal), open 24 hours.

Post & Telecommunications The central post office is on Avenida Urdaneta, Esquina Carmelitas, close to Plaza Bolívar. Have a look at the building itself – it was one of the most sumptuous palatial residences in 18th-century Caracas.

VENEZUELA

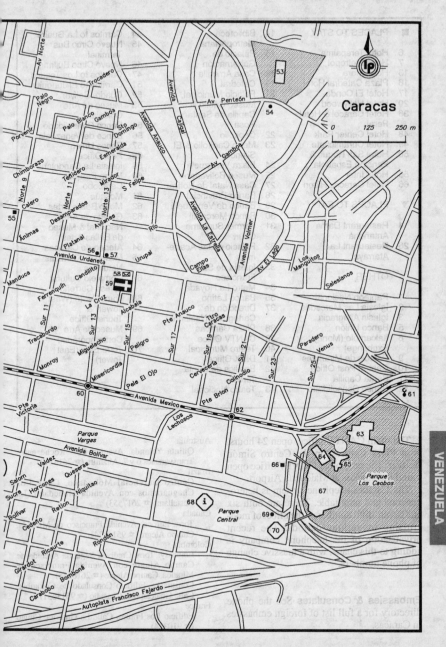

Caracas

0   125   250 m

VENEZUELA

■ PLACES TO STAY

6	Hotel Terepaima
7	Hotel Metropol
13	Hotel Mara
16	Plaza Catedral Hotel
17	Hotel El Conde
20	Hotel Hollywood
36	Hotel Caracol & Hotel Peral
48	Hotel Center Park
49	Hotel Curamichate
50	Hotel San Roque & Pensión Española
55	Hotel Inter
66	Hotel Caracas Hilton

▼ PLACES TO EAT

4	Restaurant Dama Antañona
26	Restaurant La Atarraya

OTHER

1	Panteón Nacional
2	Iglesia Las Mercedes
3	Iglesia Altagracia
5	Banco Unión
8	Italcambio (Money Exchange)
9	Palacio de Miraflores
10	Central Post Office
11	Santa Capilla
12	Banco Consolidado
14	Biblioteca Metropolitana
15	Palacio de Gobernación
18	Casa Amarilla
19	Catedral
21	Palacio Municipal, Museo Criollo & Capilla de Santa Rosa
22	Capitolio
23	Metro Capitolio & El Silencio
24	Plaza Venezuela
25	Museo Bolivariano
27	Casa Natal de Bolívar
28	Banco Provincial
29	Banco de Venezuela
30	Banco Mercantil
31	Former Supreme Court
32	Palacio de las Academias
33	Iglesia de San Francisco
34	Metro La Hoyada
35	Banco Latino
37	Dirección de Cartografía Nacional
38	Plaza Caracas
39	CANTV Office
40	Teatro Municipal
41	DIEX Office
42	Basílica de Santa Teresa
43	Teatro Nacional
44	Carritos to La Guaira
45	Nuevo Circo Bus Terminal
46	Nuevo Circo Bullring
47	Carritos to Los Teques
51	Carritos to El Junguito
52	Cuadra Bolívar
53	Museo de Arte Colonial
54	Banco Consolidado
56	Banco de Venezuela
57	Banco Unión
58	Post Office
59	Iglesia La Candelaria
60	Metro Parque Carabobo
61	Mosque
62	Metro Bellas Artes
63	Galería de Arte Nacional & Museo de Bellas Artes
64	Ateneo de Caracas
65	Museo de Ciencias Naturales
67	Complejo Cultural Teresa Carreño
68	Torre Oeste (West Tower) & Tourist Office
69	Museo de Arte Contemporáneo
70	Torre Este (East Tower)

The main CANTV office, open 24 hours, is at Plaza Caracas, in the Centro Simón Bolívar. The only other CANTV office open round the clock is at Maiquetía Airport.

The Caracas telephone system is heterogeneous and unreliable. There are both six and seven-digit numbers – the effect of modernising in various periods. The recent privatisation of the telephone company is adding to this chaos, with a massive change of phone numbers.

Embassies & Consulates See the phone directory for a full list of foreign embassies in Caracas.

Australia
  Quinta Yolanda, Avenida Luis Roche entre Transversales 6 y 7, Altamira (☎ 2614313)
Brazil
  Centro Gerencial Mohedano, Calle Los Chaguaramos con Avenida Mohedano, La Castellana (☎ 2617553)
Canada
  Torre Europa, Avenida Francisco de Miranda, Campo Alegre (☎ 9516174)
Colombia
  Embassy: Torre Credival, Segunda Avenida de Campo Alegre con Avenida Francisco de Miranda, Campo Alegre (☎ 2618358)
  Consulate: Edificio Consulado de Colombia, Calle Guaicaipuro, Chacaíto (☎ 9513631)
France
  Edificio Los Frailes, Calle La Guairita, Chuao (☎ 910324)

Germany
Edificio Panaven, Avenida San Juan Bosco, Esquina Transversal 3, Altamira (☎ 2611205)

Guyana
Quinta Roraima, Avenida El Paseo, Prados del Este (☎ 771158)

Suriname
Quinta Los Milagros, Avenida 4 entre Transversales 7 y 8, Altamira (☎ 2612724)

Trinidad & Tobago
Quinta Serrana, Avenida 4 entre Transversales 7 y 8, Altamira Norte (☎ 2614772)

UK
Edificio Las Mercedes, Avenida La Estancia, Chuao (☎ 9934111)

USA
Avenida Francisco de Miranda con Avenida Principal de la Floresta, La Floresta (☎ 2852222)

Visa Extensions Visa extensions for one month (US$12.50), or the maximum period of two months (US$25), are issued by the DIEX office (2nd floor) on Avenida Baralt, facing Plaza Miranda. Your passport, one photo, a photocopy of your onward ticket and a letter explaining the purpose of the extension, written on the so-called *papel sellado*, are required, plus the form which they'll give you to fill in. All that has to be delivered between 8 am and 11 am on a weekday, and the procedure takes up to eight working days.

Maps Some bookshops have a folded city map of Caracas which has a map of the whole country on its reverse. However, the best Caracas/country map has been published by Lagoven Oil Company. It's still available at some Lagoven petrol stations but stocks seem to be running out.

If you can't get one of these, there is a reasonable Caracas city map at the back of the local phone directory – photocopy it.

For detailed large-scale maps of various regions of the country, go to the Dirección de Cartografía Nacional (☎ 4081710), Avenida Este 6, Esquina Colón, off Plaza Diego Ibarra. The office is open on weekdays from 8.30 to 11.30 am and 2 to 4 pm.

Travel Agencies Fairmont International (☎ 7828433, 7817091, 7817920, 7823778),

at Plaza Venezuela (Metro Plaza Venezuela), can book a room in about 250 hotels throughout the country (not the budget ones), sell air tickets and rent cars. The office is open on weekdays from 8 am to 6 pm, and on Saturday from 9 am to 3 pm.

There are umpteen travel agencies which can send you to virtually every corner of the country, but these trips work out to be quite expensive (see the comments under Tours in the Getting Around section at the beginning of this chapter).

Things to See

Despite the city's size, most tourist sights are grouped in a few areas, so sightseeing is not as complicated as it might seem. The excellent Metro system helps enormously in moving from one district to another.

Old Caracas The historic sector where the city was born has lost much of its identity. In a rush towards modernisation, many of the colonial houses were replaced with 20th-century architecture, which ranges from nondescript eclectic buildings to modern dyed-glass cubes.

Predictably, the nucleus of this part of the city is **Plaza Bolívar**, with the inevitable statue of the hero in the middle. The statue was cast in Europe, shipped in pieces and unveiled in 1874, much later than planned, as the ship foundered on the Archipiélago de Los Roques. Pigeons and squirrels are ubiquitous on the wooded plaza, and sloths and iguanas can often be seen as well.

The **Catedral**, on the eastern side of the plaza, was built in the 1660s after an earthquake destroyed the previous church in 1641. A wide, five-nave interior supported on 32 columns was largely remodelled in the late-19th century. The Bolívar family chapel is in the middle of the right-hand aisle and can be easily recognised by a modern sculpture of El Libertador mourning his parents and wife.

The **Palacio de Gobernación**, on the northern side of the square, is of little beauty in itself but may have some temporary exhibitions on its ground floor. Half the western side of the plaza is occupied by the **Casa Amarilla**, once the presidential residence, while on the southern side of the square is the **Palacio Municipal**. The **Museo Criollo**, on the ground floor of this latter edifice, features memorabilia related to the town's history, including miniatures of life from the beginning of the present century. Don't miss the amazing models of central Caracas from the 1810s and 1930s, if only to realise how the city has been transformed. The museum is open Tuesday to Friday from 9 to 11.30 am and 2.30 to 4.30 pm, and on weekends from 10.30 am to 4 pm. The western side of the palace houses the **Capilla de Santa Rosa**, where on 5 July 1811, the congress declared Venezuela's independence, though it was only 10 years later that this became fact. The restoration gave the chapel the decoration and furniture of this historic event.

The entire block south-west of Plaza Bolívar is taken up by the **Capitolio**, the complex of buildings ordered in the 1870s by Guzmán Blanco, on the site of a convent whose occupants had been expelled by the dictator soon before. The Capitolio is noted for its **Salón Elíptico**, an oval hall boasting a large mural on its domed ceiling. The painting, depicting the battle of Carabobo, was executed by one of the notable Venezuelan artists of the period, Martín Tovar y Tovar. The southern wall of the hall is crammed with portraits of distinguished persons from independence times. The hall is open for visitors daily from 9 am to 12.30 pm and 3 to 5 pm.

Just south of the Capitolio is the **Iglesia de San Francisco**, with a number of richly gilded altarpieces embellishing its interior. It was in this church in 1813 that Bolívar was proclaimed El Libertador, and also here that his much-celebrated funeral was held in 1842, when his remains had been brought from Santa Marta in Colombia 12 years after his death.

Two blocks east is the **Casa Natal de Bolívar**, the house where, on 24 July 1783, this great man was born. In its recon-structed interior are contemporary paintings depicting heroic battles and other scenes from Bolívar's life. A few paces north, the **Museo Bolivariano**, in another colonial house, displays a variety of inde-pendence memorabilia, documents, period weapons and banners, plus a number of portraits of Bolívar. Both museums are open on weekdays from 9 am to noon and 2 to 5 pm, and on weekends from 10 am to 1 pm and 2 to 5 pm.

Seven blocks south is yet another place associated with El Libertador, the **Cuadra Bolívar**. It's a summer house where Bolívar spent much of his childhood and youth. Restored to its original appearance and stuffed with period furnishing, the house is today a museum, open on weekdays from 9 am to noon and 2 to 5 pm, and on weekends from 10 am to 1 pm and 2 to 4 pm.

The **Panteón Nacional** is on the opposite, northern edge of the old quarter, five blocks north of Plaza Bolívar. Erected by Guzmán Blanco on the site of a church wrecked by the 1812 earthquake, the pantheon is the last resting place for eminent Venezuelans. The whole central nave is dedicated to Bolívar – his bronze sarcophagus put in the presbytery in place of the high altar – while 163 tombs of other distinguished figures (including three women) were pushed out to the aisles. Two tombs are empty and open, awaiting the remains of Francisco de Miranda, who died in a Spanish jail in 1816, and Antonio José de Sucre (considered the libertador of Ecuador), whose ashes are in the Quito Cathedral. The vault of the pantheon is covered by paintings depicting scenes from Bolívar's life, all done by Tito Salas in the 1930s. The pantheon is open on weekdays from 9 am to noon and 2.30 to 5 pm, and on weekends from 10 am to noon and 3 to 5 pm.

About 1½ km east of the pantheon is the **Museo de Arte Colonial**. Housed in a fine colonial mansion laid out around a charming patio and surrounded by gardens, it's the most pleasant of all the museums listed here. You'll be guided around beautifully restored interiors filled with carefully selected house-hold implements and period works of art. The museum is open Tuesday to Saturday from 8.30 to 11.30 am and 2 to 4.30 pm, and on Sundays from 10 am to 5 pm. The ticket costs US$0.40, including guide service. English-language guides are available at no additional cost. On Sunday at 11 am, free concerts are held.

New Caracas A good place for a taste of modern Caracas is Parque Central, 1½ km south-east of Plaza Bolívar. The parque is not, as you might expect, a green area, but a concrete complex consisting of several high-rise residential slabs of rather apocalyptic appearance, plus two 53-storey octagonal towers, the tallest in the country. Even if you are not impressed by the architecture, there are some important sights in the area, especially if you enjoy art, music and theatre.

The **Museo de Arte Contemporáneo**, at the eastern end of the complex, is by far the best in the country and one of the best on the continent. In 16 halls on five levels you'll find works by nearly all prominent national artists, including Jacobo Borges, Alejandro Otero and Jesús Soto, the latter noted for his kinetic pieces. There are also some works by international figures such as Miró, Chagall, Leger and Picasso. Part of the exhibition space is given to changing displays; since its opening in 1974, the museum has presented over 300 temporary exhibitions, dedicated to both national and international artists.

The museum is open Tuesday to Sunday from 10 am to 6 pm. You are permitted to take photographs (without flash) of the exhibits. There's a good museum bookshop (which sells art books and museum-published posters) and a comprehensive art library, the Biblioteca Pública de Arte.

Across the street is the **Complejo Cultural Teresa Carreño**, a modern performing-arts centre inaugurated in 1983, which hosts concerts, ballet, theatre, recitals, etc in its 2500-seat main hall. Hour-long guided tours around the complex are run several times a day for US$1.50 (☎ 5730075 in advance if you need an English-speaking guide). At the back of the building is a small museum dedicated to Teresa Carreño (1853-1917), the best pianist Venezuela has produced.

Just to the north is another cultural centre, the **Ateneo de Caracas**, housing a concert hall, theatre, cinema, art gallery, bookshop and café. Behind the Ateneo is the **Museo de Ciencias Naturales**, open on weekdays from 9 am to 4.45 pm, and on weekends from 10 am to 4.45 pm.

Opposite, the **Galería de Arte Nacional** has a permanent collection of some 4000 works of art spanning four centuries of Venezuelan art, plus some pre-Hispanic art. A spacious new gallery is under construction in Parque Vargas and should be completed by 1996.

Adjoining the gallery is the modern six-storey building of the **Museo de Bellas Artes**, which features mainly temporary exhibitions. Go to the rooftop terrace for fine views over the city, including the spectacular new mosque to the north.

Both art museums are open Tuesday to Friday from 9 am to 5 pm, and on weekends from 10 am to 5 pm. The latter has a shop selling good contemporary art.

Other Sights East of Parque Central is the pleasant, quiet **Jardín Botánico**, open daily from 8 am to 5 pm, a good place to rest after tramping around museums. South of it is the **Universidad Central de Venezuela**, Caracas' largest university. There's an excellent concert hall, Aula Magna, on the grounds, with a fairly regular and interesting programme – check what's going on.

Don't miss strolling on the **Boulevard de Sabana Grande**, a fashionable city mall, vibrant and alive till late. It stretches between the Metro stations of Plaza Venezuela and Chacaíto.

In the far eastern part of the city, go to the **Parque del Este** (get off at the Metro station of the same name), the largest city park. It's good for leisurely walks, and you can visit the snake house, aviary and cactus garden, or (on weekend afternoons only) enjoy a show in the Planetario Humboldt. The park is open daily (except Mondays) from 5 am to 5 pm.

The famous **Teleférico**, a cable car to the top of El Ávila which provided breathtaking views over the city, was closed a few years ago. There was some murmuring about giving it into private hands, which might speed up its reopening, but so far, its future is unclear.

Places to Stay

There are loads of hotels scattered throughout the city, with several areas where they are particularly numerous. On the whole low-budget accommodation is poor, ranging from basic to ultrabasic, and is located in shabby, unsafe areas.

A vast majority of bottom-end and mid-priced hotels double as love hotels, and some as whorehouses; business becomes particularly active on Friday and Saturday. The conclusion you can draw is that at weekends, many hotels will turn you down. If your itinerary is flexible, avoid arriving in Caracas on these days.

Note that staying even in a distant district of the city is not a problem, as long as you are close to the Metro line.

Around the Bus Station This very unattractive district is not safe at night, and even in the daytime, you should be on your guard. On the other hand it is the cheapest area in which to stay, and there's a certain advantage in being close to the means of transport, if you plan on leaving Caracas by bus.

At the rock-bottom end, there are two primitive shelters on Avenida Lecuna, just south of the bus station: the *Hotel San Roque* and, next door, the *Pensión Española*. Both have doubles with bath for US$7, though the standard leaves a lot to be desired. Further south, there are about 10 other basic places, but don't venture there – the area becomes increasingly unpleasant and you won't find anything cheaper there than the two listed above.

The *Hotel Center Park* (☎ 5418619), on Avenida Lecuna, Velásquez a Miseria, two blocks west of the bus station, is clean and friendly and has some popularity with travellers, but swiftly took advantage of this fact to raise prices to US$9/12 a single/double with bath. If this is too much, just round the

corner is the poor but cheap *Hotel Curamichate* (☎ 5417563), for US$4/7 with bath.

If you decide to stay near the bus terminal, it's better to be north of Avenida Bolívar. There you have two conveniently located hotels on Esquina Peinero, just one block from La Hoyada Metro station: *Hotel Peral* (☎ 5453111) and similar *Hotel Caracol* (☎ 451228), both charging around US$10/12 with air-conditioning and private bath.

The Centre There are no genuine cheapies in the historic centre, except for a few brothels (such as *Hotel Bidasoa*, Ibarras a Maturín, if you want to risk it). The cheapest acceptable place seems to be *Hotel Hollywood* (☎ 5613536), on Avenida Fuerzas Armadas, Esquina Romualda (about US$9/11 with bath and fan, some US$2 more with air-conditioning).

Two blocks north along the same avenida you have *Hotel Metropol* (☎ 5628666), Plaza López a Socorro, and *Hotel Terepaima* (☎ 5625184), Socorro a San Ramón. Both are good if noisy places, with air-conditioned doubles for about US$18. Quieter is the *Hotel Inter* (☎ 5640251), one block east on Esquina Calero; it costs much the same but is often full with business people.

Perhaps the best value for money is *Hotel Mara* (☎ 5615600), on Avenida Urdaneta, Esquina Pelota. Spacious doubles with TV, fan, bath and hot water cost US$16. Choose a room on one of the top floors to avoid noise from the busy avenida.

The *Plaza Catedral Hotel* (☎ 5642111), overlooking Plaza Bolívar from Esquina La Torre, is the best-located mid-priced hotel in the centre, and well worth its price: US$20/25/30 for comfortable singles/doubles/triples with all facilities. There's a pleasant restaurant on the top floor.

Sabana Grande There are plenty of hotels all around Sabana Grande, especially on Avenida Las Acacias, Calle San Antonio and Calle El Colegio, three parallel streets 100 metres apart. In effect, within a radius of 200 metres, there are perhaps 30 hotels. If you want to stay in Sabana Grande and have doubts about where to look for a hotel, just get off at Plaza Venezuela Metro station and walk five minutes south.

The problem with most of these hotels is that they attract not only tourists but loving couples and, not infrequently, prostitutes as well. The trade is very busy on weekends.

The cheapest in the area are *Nuestro Hotel*, on Calle El Colegio, 50 metres south of the corner of Avenida Casanova, and *Hotel Capri Casanova*, on Calle San Antonio, also south of Avenida Casanova. Both are rather shabby venues (about US$9/12 with bath).

Appreciably better is *Hotel Alse* (☎ 5825510), on Avenida Las Acacias (US$13/16 with bath and air-conditioning). *Hotel La Mirage*, next door, is a good alternative, with doubles for US$18. Check nearby hotels – there's an uninterrupted line of them on this street.

The *Hotel Cristal* (☎ 719193) is not very classy but is perfectly located, right on Boulevard de Sabana Grande (corner of Pasaje Asunción). It costs US$16/20 with bath and air-conditioning.

For something plusher near the Boulevard, try *Hotel El Cóndor* (☎ 7629911), on Avenida Las Delicias (Metro Chacaíto), for US$30/40; *Hotel Coliseo* (☎ 7627916), on Avenida Casanova, near the corner of Calle Coromoto (Metro Sabana Grande), for US$40/50; or the *Hotel Tampa* (☎ 7623771), on Avenida Francisco Solano, near the corner of Avenida Los Jabillos (Metro Plaza Venezuela), for US$60 a double.

Places to Eat

Caracas has a wide selection of places to eat, and you could easily stay in town a full year and eat out three times a day without visiting any restaurant twice.

There's a range of budget eateries around the bus terminal, as well as in the centre, which have menú del día for about US$2 to US$3. An alternative can be chicken, and the places which serve it are also in good supply. Don't forget about arepas, which are a perfect between-meals snack. For breakfast, try any of the ubiquitous panaderías, which will invariably have a choice of croissants, pasteles and cachitos, and fresh bread. Wash it all down with a batido or café negro, perhaps the world's most caffeinated coffee. For the evening, numerous Spanish tascas (bar/restaurants) dot many central corners, particularly near Iglesia de la Candelaria.

A good, reasonably priced central place for Spanish food is *La Atarraya*, on Plaza Venezuela, one block south-east of Plaza Bolívar. The *Dama Antañona*, Jesuitas a Maturín, does good regional food, but only at lunchtime (closed on Saturday).

A better area for dining is Sabana Grande. Avenida Francisco Solano is flooded with Italian pasta houses (try, for example, the relatively inexpensive *Al Vecchio Mulino*) and Spanish tasca bars (*El Caserío* is one of the most pleasant). Here also is the *Chez Wong*, a Chinese restaurant that does good Szechuan and Hunan food (not Cantonese, as in most Chinese establishments in Venezuela). Complete your lunch or dinner with one of the best cappuccinos in town, at *Gran Café*, near the western end of Boulevard de Sabana Grande. *Tolo*, on Pasaje Asunción, just south of the Boulevard, has an inexpensive lunchtime vegetarian menú del día daily (except Sundays).

El Rosal and Las Mercedes are fashionable dining districts and come alive late in the evening. The restaurants mostly focus on a more affluent clientele, but there are also some which do cheap food. A good example is the *Real Past*, one of the cheapest pasta houses in town, on Avenida Río de Janeiro in Las Mercedes.

Barba Roja, on Avenida Tamanaco in El Rosal (Metro Chacao), is good (if not that cheap) for seafood, while *El Chocolate*, a few steps east, serves good Spanish food.

El Hostal de la Castellana, at Plaza La Castellana (Metro Altamira), is an atmospheric Spanish restaurant (open till 1 am) with three separate dining rooms, each with its own ambience. Try their paella – the specialty of the house. One block south is *La Estancia*, which is also good.

Café L'Attico, an attractive bar/restaurant on Avenida Luis Roche (Metro Altamira), is one of the trendiest places, thanks to a good atmosphere and excellent food (including some North American specialties) at affordable prices. It's hard to get a table in the evening.

Entertainment

For films, check the two leading *cinematecas* (art cinemas), in the Galería de Arte Nacional and the Ateneo de Caracas. The Ateneo often has something interesting in its theatre. Next door, in the Complejo Cultural Teresa Carreño, you may come across a good concert or ballet. Aula Magna, in the Universidad Central de Venezuela, has concerts, usually on Sunday morning. The university also has many other cultural activities.

Las Mercedes, El Rosal, La Floresta and La Castellana are the scene of most nighttime activity. Greenwich Pub, on Avenida Sur Altamira (Metro Altamira), is one of the places for an evening beer. There are a few discos around. Weekends, on Avenida San Juan Bosco, one long block north of the Altamira Metro station, is an American-style short-order restaurant open till late, with live music, bingo and other performances.

Juan Sebastián Bar, on Avenida Venezuela in El Rosal (Metro Chacaíto), is a bar/restaurant, and one of the few real jazz spots in the city. Live jazz goes from early afternoon till 2 am. There's no cover charge. People wearing T-shirts and shorts definitely won't be allowed in.

Getting There & Away

Air Aeropuerto Internacional Simón Bolívar is in Maiquetía, near the port of La Guaira, on the Caribbean coast, about 25 km from Caracas. It's linked to the city by a motorway, which cuts through the coastal mountain range via a two-km tunnel. The airport has separate terminals for international and domestic flights, 400 metres from each other.

The international terminal has a range of facilities, including the tourist office, car rental desks, three casas de cambio (Italcambio is open 24 hours and pays the best rate for travellers' cheques), post and telephone offices, a restaurant, two cafeterias and a couple of travel agencies. It even has a chapel, but no left-luggage office. The domestic terminal has almost nothing but airline offices.

There are plenty of international and domestic flights. For international connections, see the Getting There & Away section earlier in this chapter. Major domestic routes and approximate prices (in US$) with the two main national carriers, Avensa and Aeropostal, include:

To	Avensa	Aeropostal
Barcelona	26	22
Ciudad Bolívar	39	33
Ciudad Guayana	40	36
Coro	31	-
Isla de Margarita	28	27
Maracaibo	38	36
Mérida	50	42
Puerto Ayacucho	38	32
San Antonio del Táchira	47	46

Avensa has daily flights to Canaima (for Salto Angel) for US$125 return, and CAVE airlines flies to the Archipiélago de Los Roques, due north of Caracas (US$100 return).

On leaving Venezuela you pay US$10 airport tax (in dollars or bolívares). If you fly out with Viasa, Iberia or Aerolíneas Argentinas, you can check in at the Centro Ciudad Comercial Tamanaco (CCCT) in Caracas a day before your flight (or the morning of your flight, if it departs in the afternoon). They take your luggage (US$0.20 per piece) and give you the boarding pass.

Bus The Nuevo Circo bus terminal, right in the city centre, is poor, chaotic, noisy, dirty and unsafe. It is to be replaced by two new bus stations, at the east and west ends of the city, but work is inching along at a snail's pace. Local carritos to La Guaira, Macuto, Los Teques and El Junquito park around the bus terminal.

The Nuevo Circo terminal handles all intercity runs to almost every corner of the country. The main destinations, distance, fares (in US$) for ordinary and deluxe service and the approximate time of the journey are given in the table at the bottom of this page.

Boat La Guaira, the port of Caracas, is one of the busiest freight ports in the country, but there's no passenger service to any of Venezuela's offshore possessions. The boat to Los Roques is no longer operating. To go there, either talk to the fishers in La Guaira port, or shop around in the marinas in Caraballeda and Naiguatá.

Getting Around

To/From the Airport There's a frequent bus service from 6 am to 11 pm between the airport and the city centre (though taxi drivers at the airport will swear blind that there are no buses). In the city, buses park next to Parque Central, near the corner of avenidas Sur 17 and Bolívar. At the airport, they leave from in front of the domestic terminal, five minutes east of the international terminal. The trip costs US$1.25 and takes about 50 minutes, but traffic jams, particularly on weekends and holidays, can double that time. Drivers may try to charge you extra for the second piece of luggage but should not charge you for the first piece.

Taxis to/from the airport will cost about US$15; you can buy taxi tickets at the authorised price inside the terminal, thus avoiding overcharging.

If you have just an overnight stop in Maiquetía, there may no point in going to Caracas. Instead, you can stay the night on the coast, say in Macuto (see The Coast in the Around Caracas section). If this is the case, leave the international terminal, walk across the car park, cross the main road and wave down a carrito (small bus) to Macuto (US$0.40). Taxis to Macuto shouldn't cost more than US$7.

Metro The Metro is probably all you'll use to get around Caracas. It's fast, well organised, clean and cheap. The only thing the constructors seem to have forgotten are public toilets at the stations.

The underground system has two lines and 35 stations. Line No 1 goes east-west all the way along the city axis. Line No 2 leads from the centre south-westward to the distant suburb of Caricuao and the zoo. Further lines are under construction. The system also includes several bus routes, known as Metrobus, which link some of the southern suburbs to Metro stations.

To	Distance (Km)	Ordinary Fare (US$)	Deluxe Fare (US$)	Time (hours)
Barcelona	310	5.00	5.75	4½
Carúpano	521	8.25	9.50	8½
Ciudad Bolívar	591	8.75	10.00	9
Ciudad Guayana	698	10.50	11.50	10
Coro	453	6.70	8.00	7
Cumaná	402	6.00	7.00	6½
Güiria	679	10.25	11.25	11
Maracaibo	706	10.25	12.00	11
Maracay	109	2.00	2.25	1½
Maturín	518	8.00	–	9
Mérida	682	12.25	13.75	11
Puerto Ayacucho	814	16.00	–	16
Puerto La Cruz	320	5.25	6.00	5
San Antonio del Táchira	877	13.00	15.00	14
San Cristóba	841	12.25	14.50	13
Santa Elena de Uairén	1314	–	25.50	16
Tucupita	730	11.00	–	11
Valencia	158	2.75	3.00	2½

The Metro operates daily from 5.30 am to 11 pm. Tickets cost US$0.17 for a ride up to three stations, US$0.20 for four to seven stations and US$0.24 for any longer route. The transfer ticket (*boleto integrado*) for the combined Metro plus bus route costs US$0.24. Buy tickets at the ticket counter on the station or from a coin-operated machine. It's worth buying the *multiabono*, a multiple ticket costing US$1.70, which is valid for 10 rides of any distance. Not only do you save money, but you also avoid queuing each time at the ticket counters. Bulky packages which might obstruct other passengers are not allowed on the Metro.

AROUND CARACAS
El Hatillo
A small old town 15 km south-east of the city centre, El Hatillo is today a distant suburb within Caracas' administrative boundaries. Centred around the obligatory Plaza Bolívar, with the hero looking like he's returning from a heavy drinking session, the town retains some of its colonial architecture. The original external shape of the parish church on the plaza has been pretty well preserved, but the church interior was radically (and controversially) remodelled in 'modern' style.

The town has become a trendy weekend spot for Caraqueños and gets packed with cars and people, particularly on weekends. Every second house is either an eating establishment or a handicrafts shop. By far the biggest and the best craft shop, the Hannsi, is half a block north of the church.

Frequent carritos run to El Hatillo from Avenida Humboldt, just off Boulevard de Sabana Grande, near the Cachaito Metro station.

Parque Nacional El Ávila
El Ávila National Park is a steep, green mountain which looms just north of Caracas. The park encompasses about 90 km of the coastal range running west-east along the coast and separating the city from the sea. The highest peak is Cerro Naiguatá (2765 metres).

The southern slope, overlooking Caracas, is virtually uninhabited, while the northern side, running down into the sea, is dotted with houses and farms grouped in several hamlets, the major one being San José de Galipán. A few jeepable tracks cross the park from south to north, as well as the inoperative cable car, which went from Caracas up to Ávila Peak (2150 metres) before dropping to the coast at Macuto. Next to the upper station is the posh, round-shaped Hotel Humboldt, but it closed when the cable car stopped.

El Ávila provides the best tourist facilities of all Venezuela's parks. There are about 200 km of walking trails, most of them well marked and signposted. Half a dozen camping grounds are equipped with sanitary facilities, and there are many more places good for camping, though without facilities.

A dozen entrances lead into the park from Caracas; all originate from Avenida Boyacá, commonly known as Cota Mil, as it runs at an altitude of 1000 metres. Any route you choose will include quite a steep ascent, and you will soon come across a guard post, where you pay a nominal park entrance fee. The rangers (*guardaparques*) may still have a trail map of the park, though it seems to be out of print; in any case, they will inform you about the routes, and suggest one if you haven't decided.

There are plenty of possibilities for half or full-day hikes. You can, for example, go up to Ávila Peak; there are at least four routes leading there. If you are prepared to camp, possibly the most scenic is the two-day hike to Cerro Naiguatá. Take good rain gear and warm clothes. Water is scarce, so bring some along. The dry season is from December to April and often goes well into May.

The Coast
Parque El Ávila slopes steeply almost into the sea, leaving only a narrow flat belt between the mountains and the shore, yet the area is quite developed and densely populated, with as many as 400,000 people living in a chain of towns lining the waterfront. From west to east, the most populous urban

centres of the Litoral Central (Central Coast) are Catia La Mar, Maiquetía, La Guaira, Macuto, Caraballeda and Naiguatá. The first two towns sit at opposite ends of the airport and have little charm, La Guaira is an important and busy Caracas port, while the three remaining places have become popular seaside resorts for Caraqueños, who come here en masse on weekends to enjoy the sea air. Further east, the holiday centres thin out, though the paved road continues for 20 km to Los Caracas.

All in all, this is a pleasant enough area to hang around for a while, if you like beach life and want to escape from Caracas' rush. If you have an onward flight from Caracas' airport, and you need to stay overnight, it's probably better to stay on the coast than to go to the city of Caracas for the night.

The Central Coast is dramatic and spectacular (especially the Naiguatá to Los Caracas stretch), but not particularly good for bathing. The shore is mostly rocky all the way from Catia La Mar to Los Caracas, and there are only short stretches of beach. The almost bay-less, straight coastline is exposed to open-sea surf, and strong currents can make swimming dangerous. Most of the holidaying activity is confined to *balnearios* (the parts of the beaches that are walled-in and dotted with facilities) and to private beach clubs. All three listed resorts have their balnearios, and there are a few more, such as Camurí Chico, between Macuto and Caraballeda. (Good unpopulated beaches only begin east of Los Caracas.) An array of hotels and restaurants has sprung up along the waterfront, providing an adequate choice of comfortable beds and good fried fish.

Things to See The sea apart, you can visit the **Museo Reverón** in Macuto, arranged in the former home-studio of a renowned painter, Armando Reverón (1889-1954).

La Guaira has a partly preserved and restored **old town**, noted for its lovely narrow streets lined by houses with grilled windows. The largest and most imposing building in town is the **Casa Guipuzcoana** (1734), on the waterfront. Behind it is the

Museo Boulton, featuring some of the town's history. Enveloped in ranchos, La Guaira doesn't seem to be the safest place on earth, so be on your guard and use your common sense while visiting it.

Places to Stay & Eat There are virtually no hotels in Maiquetía and La Guaira, but Macuto and Caraballeda have plenty of places to stay and eat.

In Macuto, there are several hotels near the waterfront, including (from west to east) *El Coral*, *Santiago*, *Álamo*, *Riviera*, *Mar Azul* and *Tijuana*. The Álamo (☎ 461236) and El Coral (☎ 461632) are among the cheapest in the area, costing around US$16 a double. El Coral and Santiago have pleasant open-air restaurants overlooking the sea.

Caraballeda, five km east of Macuto, is a much larger resort and has more accommodation and dining options. It's here that the two best hotels on the central coast, the *Macuto Sheraton* (☎ 944300) and *Meliá Caribe* (☎ 945555), are located. For somewhere cheaper, try either the *Litoral Palacios* or *Costa Azul*.

Getting There & Away There are frequent carritos from Caracas (catch them one block west of Nuevo Circo bus station) to Macuto, and many go all the way to Caraballeda or even Naiguatá.

Colonia Tovar
Lost amidst hilly cloud forests of the coastal cordillera, about 60 km west of Caracas, sits the unusual mountain town of Colonia Tovar. It was founded in 1843 by 376 German settlers from Schwarzwald, following Venezuela's opening to immigration in the search for new people to cultivate the land devastated by independence wars. Effectively isolated from the outside world by the lack of roads and by internal rules prohibiting marriage outside the colony, the village followed the mother culture, language and architecture for a century. Only in the 1940s was Spanish introduced as the official language and the ban on marrying outside the community abandoned. It was not until 1963

that a passable road was opened linking Colonia to Caracas. This marked a turning point in the history of the town, which by then had only 1300 inhabitants.

Today, Colonia Tovar has perhaps five times more inhabitants and is a classic example of a tourist town. On weekends, the central streets are lined with countless stalls selling crafts, fruits and vegetables. There are so many parked cars that if you drive there late, you have to park outside town. You can find some of the original architecture, have a genuine German lunch or dinner, and buy bread or sausage made according to an old German recipe. Taking advantage of the temperate climate (the town lies at an altitude of about 1800 metres), the locals turned to fruit growing, and you can buy delicious strawberries, apples, peaches and blackberries.

Things to See Call at the **Museo de Historia y Artesanía** (open on weekends only, from 9 am to 6 pm) for a taste of the town's history, and don't miss the local **church**, a curious L-shaped building with two perpendicular naves (one for women, the other for men) and the high altar placed in the angle. From above it, the town's patron saint, San Martín de Tours, overlooks both naves.

Places to Stay & Eat There are perhaps a dozen hotels and cabañas, most with their own restaurants. Accommodation is expensive, with bottom-end prices running at about US$16 a double. Some places prefer a lodging-plus-meals plan, which is convenient but means that you are stuck with the same kitchen for your entire stay.

Hotel Selva Negra (☎ 51415) is the oldest and best-known lodge in town. Built in the 1930s, it now has about 40 cabañas of different sizes, for two to six people (US$40 for two people, plus US$8 for each additional person). The atmospheric restaurant is in the original house.

Cheaper options include *Hotel Edelweiss* (☎ 51260), *Hotel Drei Tannen* (☎ 51246) and *Hotel Bergland* (☎ 51229), the last noted for its good food.

Getting There & Away The trip from Caracas to Colonia Tovar includes a change in El Junquito. Carritos to El Junquito (US$0.50) depart from the corner directly south of Nuevo Circo bus station. From El Junquito, vans take you the remaining half of the journey (US$0.60). The whole trip takes about two hours.

The North-West

The North-West is a region of contrasts, its natural diversity including coral islands and beaches (the best are supposedly in Parque Nacional Morrocoy), the unique desert near Coro, and the largest lake in South America, Lago Maracaibo. The region combines the traditional with the contemporary, from living Indian cultures (such as the Guajiros) to a well preserved colonial heritage (the best colonial architecture is found in Coro) to the modern city of Maracaibo. Administratively, the North-West falls into the states of Zulia and Falcón.

PARQUE NACIONAL MORROCOY
Some 250 km west of Caracas by road, Morrocoy National Park includes a strip of the coast, and the offshore area, comprising a number of cays and their coral reefs. The islands, with their white, sandy beaches shaded by coconut palms and surrounded by turquoise sea and coral reefs, are indeed beautiful. Sadly, they are increasingly littered. The park lies between the towns of Tucacas and Chichiriviche, its main gateways.

Tucacas is a hot town on the Valencia-Coro road, with nothing to detain you for long. Yet, with the park just a stone's throw away, the town is steadily developing into a holiday centre, and has an array of hotels and other tourist facilities. The nearest island of the park is just over the bridge from the town's waterfront. However, it's better to go to the port, where boats can take you for a trip along *caños* (narrow channels) through mangroves, or drop you on one of the many small islands. The most popular of these is **Cayo Sombrero**, which has some of the best beaches and an amazing coral reef around it. Boats take up to eight people and charge the same for one or for eight (around US$25 return). Snorkelling gear can be rented from the diving shop run by Mike Osborne, near the port.

A more popular gateway to the park is **Chichiriviche**, which provides access to half a dozen neighbouring cays. The town is smaller than Tucacas, but equally undistinguished and unpleasant. If you have a tent or a hammock, it's best to stay on the islands; if not, you'll be limited to day trips, using the town as a dormitory. For camping on the islands, take food, water, snorkelling gear and a good mosquito repellent.

Boats depart from the wharf, which is at the foot of the main street. As in Tucacas, the boat takes a maximum of eight passengers and the fare is per boat, regardless of the number aboard (about US$8 return to the closest cays, such as Cayo Muerto, Cayo Sal or Cayo Pelón, about US$25 to the furthest ones, such as Cayo Borracho, Cayo Sombrero or Cayo Pescadores). For marginally more, you can arrange for the boat to pick you up from the island in the afternoon or at a later date. Pay only after you arrive back on the mainland.

Places to Stay & Eat

There are about 10 places to stay in Chichiriviche, but you probably won't find anything cheaper than US$10 to US$12 a double. At this price, the best seem to be two small houses which rent rooms and are locally known by the names of their owners, *Delia* and *Gregoria*. They are 30 metres from each other, on Calle Mariño, the second parallel street north of the main road. On the main road itself, 100 metres from the waterfront, the *Hotel Capri* is not worth the price (US$15/22 for a double with fan/air-conditioning). Cheaper is *Panadería El Centro*, opposite the Capri, which rents doubles/quadruples for US$13/18.

For something better, there is the pleasant *Hotel Náutico*, on the seaside in the southern part of town, and the more expensive *Hotel La Garza*, on the main road at the entrance to the town from the inland.

There are several unpretentious restaurants serving good fish, though they are not as cheap as their proximity to the sea might lead you to expect.

Getting There & Away

Bus Tucacas lies on the main road, and regular buses between Valencia and Coro pass through town.

Chichiriviche is about 22 km off the main road. There are no direct buses to Chichiriviche from either Caracas or Coro, so the cheapest way of getting there from Caracas is to take any of the frequent buses to Valencia (US$2.75, 2½ hours) and there catch one of the equally frequent busetas to Chichiriviche (US$2, 2½ hours).

An alternative is to take a bus to Coro (about six daily), get off in Sanare, where the road to Chichiriviche branches off, and catch the abovementioned Valencia-Chichiriviche bus (US$0.60, 20 minutes). The problem is that the bus companies serving the Caracas-Coro route charge the full fare to Coro (US$6.75) regardless of whether you go to the end of the line or only to Sanare, 180 km before Coro.

If you start from Coro, take any bus to Valencia, get off in Sanare (US$2, three hours) and catch the Valencia-Chichiriviche buseta.

CORO

At the base of the curiously shaped Península Paraguaná, Coro is a pleasant, peaceful town of some 100,000. It has some of the best colonial architecture in the country and, thanks to a large university community, a noticeably cultured air.

Founded in 1527, it's one of the oldest towns on the continent. Four years later, the Episcopal See, the first in the New World, was established in Coro. Despite its early start, the town was deserted a century later, and only revived thanks to trade with Curaçao and Bonaire at the end of the 18th

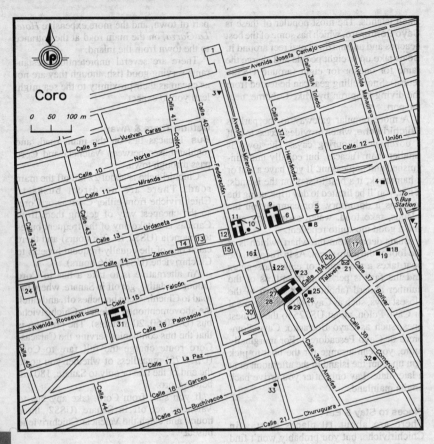

Coro

0   50   100 m

To
Bus
Station

century. Most of its historic heritage dates from that time.

Information

Tourist Office The main tourist office (☎ 511116) is on the pedestrian mall, just north of Plaza Bolívar, but they will probably send you to their outlet a bit further north, on the opposite side of the same mall. Helpful and knowledgeable, they have free brochures about the town and the region. The office is open Monday to Saturday from 8 am to noon and 2 to 6 pm, and sometimes even longer.

Money The Banco de Venezuela will probably exchange your dollars, and Banco Unión and Banco Consolidado do so occasionally. The Banco Consolidado, as elsewhere, changes American Express travellers' cheques, while Banco Unión services Mastercard and Visa card holders.

Things to See

The oldest building in town is the **Catedral**. This massive, fortress-like structure was begun in the 1580s and completed half a century later, making it perhaps the oldest church in Venezuela.

■ PLACES TO STAY		OTHER		17	Plaza Falcón
				20	Museo de Arte Coro
2	Hotel Miranda	1	Airport Terminal	21	Post Office
4	Hotel Venezia	6	Museo Diocesano	22	Tourist Office
8	Hotel Capri	9	Iglesia de San Fran-	24	Cementerio Judío
18	Hotel Roma		cisco		(Jewish Cemetery)
19	Hotel Martín	10	Cruz de San Clemente	26	Banco de Venezuela
25	Hotel Colonial	11	Iglesia de San Cle-	27	Catedral
			mente	28	Plaza Bolívar
▼ PLACES TO EAT		12	Casa de los Arcaya &	29	CANTV Office
			Museo de	30	Ateneo de Coro
3	Restaurant Don		Cerámica Histórica	31	Iglesia de San Nicolás
	Camilo		y Loza Popular		de Bari
5	Restaurant Casavieja	13	Casa de las Ventanas	32	Banco Unión
7	Pizzería La Barra del		de Hierro	33	Banco Consolidado
	Jacal	14	Casa del Tesoro		
23	Restaurant La Tasca	15	Casa del Sol		
		16	Tourist Office		

One block east, the **Museo de Arte Coro**, in a beautiful colonial house, is a branch of the Caracas Museum of Contemporary Art and, like the mother institution, focuses on modern art and does a good job. The museum is open Tuesday to Saturday from 9 am to 12.30 pm and 3 to 7.30 pm, and on Sunday from 9 am to 4 pm.

For a taste of Coro's colonial past, go two blocks north to the **Museo Diocesano**, in an old convent. Despite its name, the museum has both religious and secular art, with some extraordinary pieces. It's one of the best collections of its kind in the country. The museum is open Tuesday to Saturday from 9 am to noon and 3 to 6 pm, and on Sunday from 9 am to 1 pm; all visits are guided (in Spanish only) and the tour takes about an hour. Adjacent to the museum is the **Iglesia de San Francisco**, currently under recon-struction after decades of neglect.

Across the street, in a grilled pavilion on a small plaza, stands the **Cruz de San Cle-mente**, said to be the cross used in the first mass celebrated right after the foundation of the town. The 18th-century **Iglesia de San Clemente**, on the western side of the plaza, was laid out on the Latin-cross plan, one of few examples of its kind in the country.

West across the street stands the **Casa de los Arcaya**, noted for its long, tile-roofed

balconies. The mansion houses the **Museo de Cerámica Histórica y Loza Popular**, a small but interesting museum of pottery and ceramics, open the same hours as the Museo Diocesano. One block west are two carefully restored houses: the **Casa de las Ventanas de Hierro** and the **Casa del Tesoro**.

The **Cementerio Judío**, three blocks west along Calle Zamora, was established in the 1830s and is thus the oldest Jewish cemetery still in use on the continent. If it's locked (as it usually is), go to the house diagonally opposite and ask the occupants to open the cemetery for you.

North-east of the town spreads the **Médanos de Coro**, a unique mini-Sahara, with sandy dunes rising to some 50 metres, now a national park. To get there from the city centre, take the city bus marked 'Carabobo' and get off past the huge Monumento a la Federación. Then walk 10 minutes north along a wide avenida to another public sculpture, Monumento a la Madre. A few paces north, there is nothing but sand.

Places to Stay

There are four budget hotels in the historic sector of the city: *Colonial, Capri, Martín* and *Roma*. They are convenient for sightsee-ing, and all offer pretty much the same: a

VENEZUELA

simple double with fan and bath for about US$8. The first two hotels also have air-conditioned doubles for around US$12. All are within a couple of hundred metres of each other, so you can easily look around before choosing.

Hotel Venezia (☎ 511844), Avenida Manaure, is a better central option, offering more comfort and facilities, including TV (US$12/22/28 in singles/doubles/triples).

Places to Eat

There are not many restaurants or snack bars in the city centre. Only recently have new fast-food outlets started to fill the gap. An example is the unpretentious *Pizzería La Barra del Jacal*, on Avenida Manaure, with good, inexpensive pizzas served till late.

The recently opened *Restaurant Casavieja*, on Calle Zamora, has reasonably priced food, plus a tasty menú ejecutivo at lunchtime. *La Tasca*, behind the catedral, has a cheaper but inferior menú, and more expensive à la carte dishes. Near the airport, *Don Camilo*, on Avenida Miranda, is worth considering.

Getting There & Away

Air The airport is just a five-minute walk north of the city centre. There are daily flights to Caracas (US$31) and to Barquisimeto (US$21); for other domestic destinations, you have to change in one of these two cities. You can also use the busier Las Piedras airport (near Punto Fijo, on the Península Paraguaná), but it's about 90 km from Coro. From Las Piedras, Avensa has daily flights to Aruba (US$66 return) and Curaçao (US$109 return).

From Coro airport, two small carriers, CAVE and Aero Falcón, fly light planes to Aruba (US$100 return) and Curaçao (US$80 return) on weekdays, if they collect a minimum of three passengers. One-way tickets for these routes cost half the return fares, but will perhaps only be sold if you have an onward ticket from the Netherlands Antilles.

Bus The bus station is on Avenida Los Médanos, about two km east of the city centre, and is easily accessible by frequent city transport. Half a dozen buses run daily to Caracas (US$6.75, seven hours), and even more buses go to Maracaibo (US$4, four hours). There are two direct buses a day to Mérida (US$10.75, 12 hours) and one to San Cristóbal (US$11.75, 13 hours); all these buses go via Maracaibo. Buses to Punto Fijo run every hour (US$1.50, 1¼ hours).

Boat Coro's port, La Vela de Coro, is 12 km from the city. At the time of writing, there are no ferries from La Vela to Curaçao, but ferries run from Punto Fijo to Aruba a few times a week. Inquire at the office of Ferrys del Caribe (☎ 511956, 519676), Avenida Independencia, Coro, for the current schedule and fares, as they seem to change frequently.

MARACAIBO

The region around Maracaibo was explored as early as 1499, and Maracaibo itself was founded in 1574, but the town only really began to grow in the 18th century, as a result of trade with the Dutch Antilles. The republicans' naval victory over the Spanish fleet, in a battle fought on Lago Maracaibo on 24 July 1823, brought the town some political importance. It was not, however, till the 1920s, with the oil boom, that the city developed into Venezuela's oil capital, with nearly three-quarters of the nation's oil output coming from the lake.

With a population of about 1.2 million, Maracaibo is the country's largest urban centre after Caracas, and a predominantly modern, prosperous city. Its climate is damp and hot, with an annual average temperature of about 29°C.

Maracaibo doesn't rank high on tourist attractions, and there's not much to see in the city. However, you may need to stop here on the way to the Colombian coast. If you have more time, you can explore the region, which offers striking contrasts of new and old, from forests of oil derricks on Lago Maracaibo, to an Indian community living in houses on stilts (on Laguna de Sinamaica, 50 km north of the city), similar to those seen by Alonso de Ojeda in 1499.

Money

Most banks are south of Plaza Bolívar (see the Maracaibo city map for their locations). The Banco Mercantil and Banco de Venezuela change cash, while the Banco Consolidado usually changes American Express travellers' cheques. The Banco Unión and the Banco de Venezuela pay advances on Visa and MasterCard.

Things to See

If you are in Maracaibo in transit, you probably won't go far beyond the downtown area, or the oldest part of the city. The axis of this sector is formed by the **Paseo de las Ciencias**, a wide green belt seven blocks long created by demolishing old buildings and establishing a park on the site.

Off the west end of the Paseo stands the **Basílica de Chiquinquirá**, with its opulent, somewhat hotchpotch interior. On the high altar is the venerated image of the Virgin, to whom numerous miracles are attributed. Pilgrims flock here all year round, but the major celebrations are held for a full week in November, culminating in a procession on 18 November.

The east end of the Paseo borders **Plaza Bolívar**, which has the usual Bolívar statue in the middle and the **Catedral** on the eastern side. To the north is the **Casa de la Capitulación**, also known as Casa Morales, where on 3 August 1823, the act of capitulation was signed by the Spanish defeated in the naval battle of Lago Maracaibo, thus sealing the independence of Gran Colombia. The house can be visited.

One block north are the **Museo Arquidiocesano** and the **Templo Bautismal Rafael Urdaneta**, both open daily from 9 am to 6 pm. A short walk north-west will take you to the **Museo Urdaneta**. Born in Maracaibo in 1788, General Rafael Urdaneta is the city's greatest hero; he distinguished himself in numerous battles in the War of Independence.

Calle 94 was in parts restored to its former state, and is worth a stroll. Its best bit is between avenidas 7 and 8. The neighbourhood of the Iglesia de Santa Lucía is another area noted for fine old houses.

The sector south of the Paseo is busy, chaotic and dirty. Many streets are lined by stalls, which give the old town a market feeling. The most striking sight in the area is the imposing **old market building**, overlooking the docks. Closed for its original function, it is currently being refurbished for the Centro de Arte de Maracaibo.

Places to Stay

Low-budget accommodation is shabby, and can often be full with oil workers. Many cheapies rent rooms by the hour. If you don't mind that, start looking behind the catedral, where there are several cheap hotels. The *Carabobo*, *Santa Ana*, *Coruña* and *Aurora No 2* are all rather unattractive places, but most have rooms with private baths and the last two even have several air-conditioned rooms. Expect to pay some US$4/7/9 for a single/double/triple with fan, about US$4 more with air-conditioning.

Appreciably better is *Hotel Caribe*, on Avenida 7 near the corner of Avenida Padilla (US$9/10/12 with air-conditioning and bath).

Hotel Victoria, overlooking Plaza Barralt and the old market building, is possibly the best choice in the city centre. It has clean, spacious rooms with bath and air-conditioning (some with a balcony) for US$10/11 a single/double. Choose a room with a good view before booking in.

Getting There & Away

Air The airport is about 12 km south-west of the city centre. There are plenty of flights to the main cities in the country, including more than six flights daily to Caracas with Avensa (US$38) and Aeropostal (US$36). Avensa has daily flights to Mérida (US$29) and Las Piedras(US$24).

Maracaibo is the home town of Zuliana de Aviación (☎ 514775/8, 514147), Edificio Cosmar, Local 2, Calle 78 No 20-109. They operate daily international flights to Miami

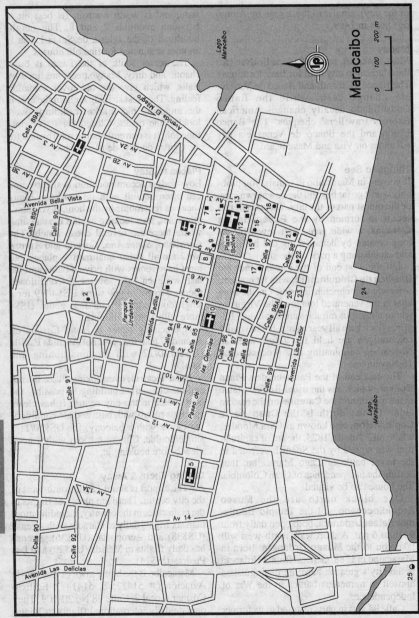

Maracaibo

1	Iglesia de Santa Lucía
2	Museo Urdaneta
3	Hotel Caribe
4	Museo Arquidiocesano & Templo Bautismal Rafael Urdaneta
5	Basílica de Chiquinquirá
6	CANTV Office
7	Hotel Carabobo
8	Teatro Barralt
9	Casa de la Capitulación
10	Iglesia de Santa Bárbara
11	Hotel Coruña
12	Catedral
13	Hotel Santa Ana
14	Hotel Aurora No 2
15	Museo Arte Gráfica
16	Banco Mercantil
17	Banco de Venezuela
18	Banco Provincial
19	Hotel Victoria
20	Plaza Barralt
21	Banco Unión
22	Banco Consolidado
23	Old Market Building
24	Docks
25	Bus Station

(US$155), Medellín (US$50) and Bogotá (US$50), and domestic flights to Caracas (US$29), San Antonio del Táchira (US$30) and Isla de Margarita (US$50).

Bus The bus station is about one km south-west of the city centre. Several buses daily run to Coro (US$4, four hours) and to Caracas (US$10.25, 11 hours). There are three night buses to Mérida (US$7, nine hours), which go via the Panamericana (Pan-American Highway) at the northern foot of the cordillera. There are no direct buses on the Trans-Andean mountain road via El Águila; you must first take one of the half-hourly buses to Valera (US$3.75, four hours) and catch another bus there (US$3.75, five hours, two or three buses a day). Por puestos (shared taxis) on this route are faster but cost about 70% more than the bus.

To Maicao in Colombia, buses (US$4.50, 3½ hours) and shared taxis (US$5.75, 2½ hours) operate regularly from about 5 am to 3 pm. All passport formalities are done in Paraguachón, on the border. If you come this way from Colombia, expect a thorough search of your luggage by Venezuelan officials.

Maicao is widely and justifiably known as a lawless town, and is far from safe – stay there as briefly as possible. Buses from Maicao to Santa Marta are operated by several companies, and depart frequently (US$7, four hours).

Getting Around
There is no public transport to the airport; a taxi will cost about US$8. Frequent local transport operates from the bus terminal to the town centre and to other districts.

The Andes

The northernmost range of South America's spinal cord of mountain ranges, the Venezuelan Andes extend some 300 km from the Táchira depression, near the Colombian border, north-eastward to Trujillo state. The range is about 50 to 80 km wide.

Venezuela's Andes are not a single ridge, as might appear on general maps, but two roughly parallel chains separated by a verdant mountain valley. The southern chain culminates with the Sierra Nevada de Mérida, crowned with a series of snowcapped peaks. It's here, in the Parque Nacional Sierra Nevada, that the country's highest summits are located, including Pico Bolívar (5007 metres), Pico Humboldt (4942 metres) and Pico Bompland (4883 metres). The northern chain reaches 4730 metres, at the Sierra de la Culata (directly opposite the Sierra Nevada), also a national park. In the deep valley between the two Sierras sits the city of Mérida, the region's major urban centre and the country's mountain capital.

The Andes are popular hiking territory, offering everything from lush tropical rainforests to permanent snows. Particularly interesting are the *páramos*, a kind of open mountain moors starting at about 3200 metres and stretching up almost to the snow

VENEZUELA

line. Their most common plant is the *frailejón* (espeletia), typical only to highland areas of Venezuela, Colombia and Ecuador. They are especially amazing in bloom, from November to December.

The Andean dry season lasts from December to April. A mixed dry/wet period in May and June is noted for changeable weather, with much sunshine but also frequent rains (or snow at high altitudes). From August to October, the wettest months, hiking can be miserable and you may miss the best views. The snowy period (June to October) can be dangerous for mountaineering.

MÉRIDA

Mérida is one of Venezuela's most popular destinations among foreign travellers. It has an unhurried, friendly atmosphere, plenty of tourist facilities, the famous teleférico and beautiful mountains all around, with the country's rooftop, Pico Bolívar, just 12 km as the crow flies. Home to the Universidad de los Andes (the second oldest university in the country), the city has a sizeable student community, which gives it a cultured and bohemian air.

Mérida sits on a meseta, a terrace stretching a dozen km in a fork of two parallel rivers, the edges dropping abruptly to the riverbanks. Founded in 1558, the city has long traditions but little colonial architecture, save for a handful of historic buildings which somehow managed to escape modernisation. Having filled the meseta as densely as possible, Mérida is now expanding beyond it, and is approaching some 220,000 inhabitants.

Although generally considered by Venezuelans as a 'cold' city (at 1600 metres, it's the highest state capital in the country), Mérida enjoys a mild, fresh climate, with an average temperature of 19°C. The tourist season is at its height here around Christmas, Carnaval and Easter, and from late July to early September.

Information

Tourist Office The Corporación Merideña de Turismo, or Cormetur (☎ 526972), has its main office at the junction of avenidas 1 and 2, five minutes north of Plaza Sucre. The office is open on weekdays from 8 am to noon and 2 to 6 pm, and you'll probably get city maps and good information. Cormetur also operates several outlets throughout the city, including those at the airport (☎ 639330) and the bus station (☎ 633952).

Inparques The Inparques office (☎ 631473) is on Avenida Urdaneta, near the airport. You actually won't need it, as permits for trekking are issued by the Inparques outlet next to the teleférico, and the maps of the Sierra they sell can also be bought in the Posada Las Heroínas, Calle 24 No 8-95 (Parque Las Heroínas).

Tours & Guides All you are likely to need is conveniently located in Parque Las Heroínas. There, you'll find two good mountain-tour operators: Yana Pacha Tours (☎ 526910), Calle 24 No 8-97, and Guamanchi Expeditions, in the Mercado Artesanal, Local 4. Both are run by experienced climbers, who either go with you up the mountains or send you there with other well-qualified climbers, actually their friends. In effect, you will find here the cream of Mérida's *montañistas*. If you arrange a mountain expedition with agents in the centre, they will probably call one of the above-listed operators to contract a guide from there, obviously charging you far more for the service. Both Yana Pacha and Guamanchi offer a guide service only, or can provide all mountaineering equipment if you don't have your own gear.

Tom Evenou, owner of the Posada Las Heroínas (☎ 522665), next door to Yana Pacha, organises tours to the astronomical observatory (see Around Mérida, below). He's also a good contact person for independent local guides and guides from other regions, such as Los Llanos and the Amazon. Tom also sells a variety of maps of the region, country and continent, including good Bradt-published (ITM) maps.

Money Major banks are in the vicinity of

Plaza Bolívar, and most handle some foreign exchange operations. Almost all banks marked on the Mérida map should change cash; the Banco Italo Venezolano and Banco Barinas will probably change travellers' cheques, whereas Banco Maracaibo and Banco Unión service credit card holders. The Banco Consolidado is a short walk north-west along Calle 26 and, as elsewhere, deals with American Express travellers' cheques and credit cards.

Things to See

The city centre is quite pleasant for leisurely strolls, though there's not much in the way of outstanding tourist attractions. Plaza Bolívar is the city's heart, but it's not a colonial square. The **Catedral** was begun in 1800 and only successfully completed in 1958. Next to it is the **Museo Arquidiocesano**, with a collection of religious art, open from Thursday to Saturday, 9 am to noon. Across the square, the **Casa de la Cultura** has various temporary exhibitions. It's open on weekdays from 8 am to noon and 2 to 6 pm, and on weekends from 10 am to 5 pm.

The Universidad de los Andes building, just off the square, houses the **Museo Arqueológico**, open Tuesday to Friday from 3 to 6 pm, and on weekends from 4 to 8 pm. A small but interesting collection supported by extensive background information (in Spanish only) gives an insight into the pre-Hispanic times of the region.

Three blocks north-east of the plaza is the recently restored **Casa de los Gobernadores**. Inside, you can see several amazing ceramic models of important buildings of the city, all made by a noted local artist, Eduardo Fuentes. He has a shop in the Mercado Artesanal, in the Parque Las Heroínas, where you can buy some of his more modest works.

The modern **Biblioteca Bolivariana** features an exhibition related to Bolívar. The showpiece of the collection is a sword made in Peru in 1825 and presented to El Libertador after his victory at Junín. The sheath is made entirely of gold, encrusted with 1380 precious stones, including diamonds and emeralds.

Two blocks north-east, the **Museo de Arte Colonial** has a small and rather uninspiring collection of mostly sacred art. It's open Tuesday to Friday from 9 am to noon and 3 to 6 pm, and on weekends from 10 am to 5 pm.

Proceeding five blocks on Avenida 4 to its end, you'll find the small **Parque de las Cinco Repúblicas**, boasting the oldest monument of Bolívar, dating from 1842.

Outside the city centre, the **Museo de Arte Moderno**, in Parque Beethoven, at the northern end of the city, has a small but fine collection of contemporary works by national artists. It's open Tuesday to Friday from 9 am to noon and 3 to 6 pm, and on weekends from 10 am to 5 pm.

Also in the northern sector of the city, but closer to the centre, **Parque La Isla** is noted for its variety of orchids. Some four km west of the centre, on Avenida Andrés Bello, the **Jardín Acuario** is an exhibition centre devoted to the traditional culture of the region.

Teleférico

The highlight of a visit to Mérida is definitely the teleférico, the world's highest and longest cable car, constructed in 1958 by a French company. It runs 12.6 km from Mérida to the top of Pico Espejo (4765 metres), covering the 3188-metre climb in four stages. There are five stations: Barinitas (1577 metres), Montaña (2436 metres), Aguada (3452 metres), Loma Redonda (4045 metres) and Pico Espejo. The last stage has been out of order since late 1991, but there are plans to put it back into operation in 1994.

The cable car normally operates from Wednesday to Sunday, though in tourist season, it may run every day. The first trip up goes at 7.30 am and the last at noon (2 pm in high season). The last trip down is at 1.30 pm (4 pm in high season). The ticket costs US$5, regardless of whether you go one stage or to the top, or whether you are returning by cable car or not. An international

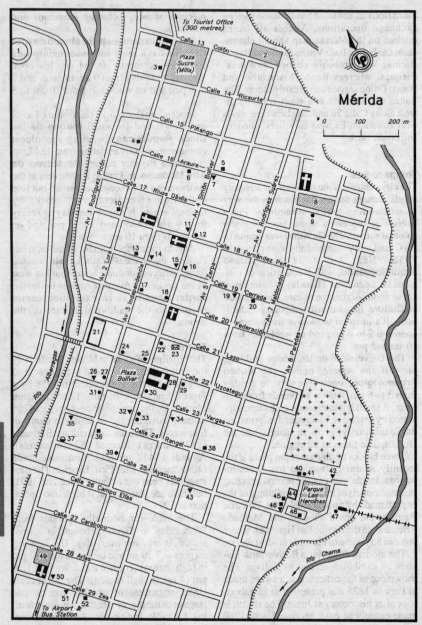

Mérida

0   100   200 m

To Tourist Office
(300 metres)

To Airport &
Bus Station

■ PLACES TO STAY		16	Restaurant El Portón Andino	17	Casa de los Gobernadores
3	Posada Luz Caraballo	19	Restaurant Pulcritud	18	Biblioteca Bolivariana
4	Hotel Español	26	Café París	21	Centro Cultural de
5	Posada Turística	32	Cafetín Santa Rosa		Mérida
	Marianela	34	Restaurant Onde		(under construction)
6	Residencia Araure		Jaime	22	CANTV Office
10	Posada Alemania	35	Birosca Carioca	23	Post Office
13	Hotel Italia	42	Restaurant El Tatuy &	24	Banco Italo
20	Residencias San		Restaurant		Venezolano
	Pedro		Vegetariano Madre	25	Banco Maracaibo
36	Hotel Santiago de los		Tierra	27	Casa de la Cultura
	Caballeros	43	La Guanábana	28	Catedral
38	Hotel Luxemburgo	46	Cheo's Pizzería	29	Banco Barinas
40	Posada Las Heroínas	50	Heladería Coromoto	30	Museo Arquidiocesano
45	Hotel Teleférico	51	Restaurant	31	Museo Arqueológico
46	Hotel El Parque		Vegetariano El	33	Banco de Venezuela
48	Hotel Mintoy		Tinajero		& Banco Unión
52	Hotel Chama			37	Buses to Airport & to
		▼ OTHER			Bus Station
▼ PLACES TO EAT		1	Bullring	39	Banco Andino
		2	Parque Las Cinco	41	Yana Pacha Tours
7	Restaurant Los		Repúblicas	44	Mercado Artesanal &
	Corales	8	Plaza Rivas Dávila		Guamanchi
11	La Gran Fraternidad	9	Teatro Rafael Briceño		Expeditions
	Universal	12	Museo de Arte	47	Teleférico (Barinitas
14	Restaurant La		Colonial		Station) &
	Chipilina				Inparques Office
15	Restaurant Alfredo's			49	Plaza El Llano

student card is generally accepted, in which case you pay US$2.50. The ascent to Loma Redonda takes about 45 minutes. Don't forget to take warm clothing.

Go up as early as possible, as clouds usually obscure the view later on. There may be long queues on peak holidays. You can book in advance at the ticket office or (but only from outside Mérida) reserve by phone (☎ 525080).

Apart from splendid views during the trip itself and from the Loma Redonda station, the cable car provides easy access to a convenient starting point for hiking (see Around Mérida for details on hikes), saving you the time and effort of puffing uphill for more than a day. Bear in mind, however, that acclimatisation problems can easily occur at these altitudes (over 4000 metres).

If you plan on hiking, you need a permit from Inparques; their office is right next to the cable car ticket office. The permit is issued on the spot (you have to show your passport) and costs US$0.60 per group. The permit should be returned after completing your hike – this is intended to monitor whether somebody has got lost up in the mountains.

Places to Stay

Mérida has heaps of hotels, most offering good value for money. There's an array of places called posadas, which are small, family-run *pensiones*, often with a friendly atmosphere.

The cheapest place in the city centre is *Hotel Italia* (☎ 525737), Calle 19 No 2-55. It has small, simple singles/doubles without bath for US$3/5 and doubles/triples with bath for US$6/8. There are several other cheapies in the same area.

A place worth recommendation is the *Posada Las Heroínas* (☎ 522665), in Parque Las Heroínas, run by a polyglot Swiss and

VENEZUELA

his wife. You pay US$4/5 per person in rooms without/with bath. The hotel is often full.

You have more chance of a vacancy in the *Residencia Araure* (☎ 525103), Calle 16 No 3-34, which is clean and pleasant and charges US$4 per head in doubles or triples without bath. *Residencias San Pedro* (☎ 522735), Calle 19 No 6-36, offers much the same for US$5 per person.

Other recommended places include *Posada Luz Caraballo* (☎ 525441), Avenida 2 No 13-80 (US$5 per person), the Spanish-run *Hotel Español* (☎ 529235), Avenida 2 No 15-48 (spotlessly clean doubles for US$11), and the German-owned *Posada Alemania* (☎ 524067), Avenida 2, near the corner of Calle 18 (US$10/13 a single/double).

The *Posada Turística Marianela* (☎ 526907), Calle 16 No 4-33, has doubles/quadruples without bath for US$13/25, including breakfast. It's an agreeable place, run by a very friendly English-speaking woman. Her sister runs the equally pleasant *Posada Taty*, on Avenida Urdaneta, near the airport.

Hotel Santiago de los Caballeros (☎ 523223), Avenida 3 No 24-19, has good singles/doubles/triples with bath for US$7/10/15, while *Hotel Luxemburgo* (☎ 526865), Calle 24 No 6-37, offers much the same for slightly more.

For more comfort, up-market hotels include the *Hotel Chama* (☎ 524851), Calle 29, near the corner of Avenida 4, and *Hotel Mintoy* (☎ 520340), Calle 25 No 8-130, just off Parque Las Heroínas. Both have comfortable doubles for around US$28.

Places to Eat

If you are used to unpretentious, low-budget dining, Mérida is for you – it's probably the cheapest place to eat in Venezuela. Plenty of restaurants serve set meals for around US$1.50, including *La Chipilina*, on the corner of Avenida 3 and Calle 19, *Los Corales*, on the corner of Avenida 4 and Calle 16, and *Pulcritud*, at Calle 19 No 5-80 (they also have good typical Colombian

buñuelos). Appreciably better and not much more expensive is *Alfredo's*, on the corner of Avenida 4 and Calle 19.

For cheap vegetarian meals, try *Madre Tierra*, at Parque Las Heroínas, *La Gran Fraternidad Universal*, on Avenida 4 near the corner of Calle 18, and *El Tinajero*, on Calle 29 near Avenida 4.

El Tatuy, at Parque Las Heroínas, has inexpensive typical food. *Cheo's Pizzería*, in Hotel El Parque, at Parque Las Heroínas, does some of the best pizzas in town, while *La Guanábana*, Calle 25 No 6-26, is good for batidos and merengadas. *Onde Jaime*, Avenida 5 No 23-15, is the place to go for typical Colombian food at reasonable prices.

Café París, on Calle 23, off Plaza Bolívar, has tables outside and is a popular rendezvous for both locals and foreigners. If you want really good coffee, however, go to *Cafetín Santa Rosa*, on Avenida 4, opposite Banco de Venezuela. For an evening beer in a good atmosphere, try *Birosca Carioca*, Calle 24 No 2-04, which is one of the most popular nightspots in the city centre.

You shouldn't miss a visit to *Heladería Coromoto*, Avenida 3 No 28-75, which is about the most famous ice-cream parlour on the continent, appearing in the Guinness Book of Records. Run by the friendly owner, Manuel da Silva Oliveira (familiarly, Manolo), the place offers about 110 flavours on an average day but has 550 flavours altogether. Among the more unusual varieties, you can try Polar beer, shrimp, trout, chicken with spaghetti or, for vegetarians, 'el vegetariano'. Strike up a conversation with Manolo and he will let you try his latest sophisticated achievements. The place is open 2 to 10 pm daily (except Mondays).

Getting There & Away

Air The airport is on the meseta, right inside the city, two km south-west of Plaza Bolívar. Frequent urban busetas pass by the airport. The runway is short, and the proximity of high mountains doesn't make landing an easy task, especially in bad weather. Consequently, in the rainy season, flights are often diverted elsewhere. There are five flights daily to Caracas (US$50 with Avensa, US$42 with Aeropostal), and one flight to each of San Antonio del Táchira (US$21), Maracaibo (US$29), Valencia (US$44) and Barquisimeto (US$34).

Bus The bus station is three km south-west of the city centre, linked by frequent public transport. Half a dozen buses a day run to Caracas (US$12.25, 11 hours) and to Maracaibo (US$7, nine hours). Busetas to San Cristóbal depart every two hours (US$4, 5½ hours), or take a por puesto (US$5, five hours); all go via El Vigía and La Fría, not the Trans-Andean route. Por puestos also service many regional routes, such as Apartaderos and Jají.

AROUND MÉRIDA
The region surrounding Mérida offers plenty of opportunities for travellers, and you can easily spend a week or two here, walking in the mountains or exploring old villages and other sights by road.

Things to See
The region is sprinkled with old mountain villages, the best-known of which is **Jají**, about 38 km west of Mérida, accessible by por puestos from the bus terminal. Jají was extensively reconstructed in the late 1960s to become a manicured typical pueblo Andino (Andean town), and is pretty touristy. The Plaza Bolívar is full of handicrafts shops, which enjoy particularly good trade on weekends. There are two pleasant posadas in the village.

For something more authentic, try **Mucuchíes**, a 400-year-old town about 48 km east of Mérida. Several km further west is **San Rafael de Mucuchíes**, noted for an amazing small stone church built by the local artist Juan Félix Sánchez. This is his second chapel; the first, equally beautiful, was constructed two decades ago in the remote hamlet of **El Tisure**, a five-hour walk from San Rafael (there is no access road).

North of San Rafael, at an altitude of 3600 metres, the **Centro de Investigaciones de Astronomía** is an astronomical observatory which can be visited on some days and evenings (call their Mérida office, ☎ 712780, for details). It's best to go there in the evening, to have a look at the stars. The place is off the main road and accessible by a rough track only, and there is no public transport. The owner of Posada Las Heroínas in Mérida runs Saturday evening tours (about US$12 per person).

Activities
Mountaineering Climbing Venezuela's highest peak, Pico Bolívar (with a bust of the hero on the summit), is not technically difficult, but unless you have mountaineering experience, you shouldn't do it without a guide. Until the last stretch of the teleférico to Pico Espejo reopens, the usual starting point is Loma Redonda, from where a four-hour walk will take you up to Pico Espejo. There's a simple refuge there, used by trekkers to overnight before the early morning climb to Bolívar's bust.

Other peaks can also be done without much difficulty; of these, Pico Humboldt and Pico Bompland, known as La Corona, make an attractive trip.

Hiking If you are not up to doing the summits, there's an easy and popular hike from Loma Redonda to **Los Nevados**, a charming mountain pueblo at an altitude of about 2700 metres (accommodation and food available). It's a four-hour walk, including a short ascent to a pass and a gentle walk downhill. You can hire mules in Loma Redonda for this trip (US$4 per mule, plus US$4 for the *arriero*). From Los Nevados, you can walk back the same way (six hours), but most hikers prefer to continue seven hours downhill to the village of El Morro (rooms and meals available); from here, jeeps run over a rough track to Mérida.

Another interesting area for hiking is in the north-eastern end of the park. To start one of the possible excursions, take a morning bus or por puesto to **Pico El Águila** (4118 metres), next to Venezuela's highest road pass (4007 metres), about 60 km from Mérida on the road to Valera; there's a roadside restaurant where you can have a hot chocolate before setting off. Locals with mules are waiting by the road to take you to **Laguna Mucubají**, five km due south, but it's better to walk there. You walk through a splendid páramo filled with *frailejones* down to the Barinas road. The laguna, just off the road, is the largest in the park. It's well worth walking one hour up the pine-reforested slope to **Laguna Negra**, a small but beautiful mountain lake with amazingly dark water. If you want to camp, get a permit from Inparques at Laguna Mucubají. There are two hotels by the road near the lake.

A trail from Laguna Mucubají goes seven km south to the top of **Pico Mucuñuque** (4676 metres), the highest peak of the Serranía de Santo Domingo. The round trip will take you a good part of the day.

Mountain Biking A relatively new form of outdoor activity, mountain biking in the Andes has become popular, and there are already a few travel agencies in Mérida who provide bikes and other equipment needed for that sort of expedition. One of the most popular routes is a trip to remote mountain villages south of Mérida, accessible by rough tracks only. Inquire at the agencies listed in the Mérida section. Also contact Chucho Faría, at the Inparques office at the teleférico station, who is one of the pioneers of biking in the region. He organises trips, providing all necessary gear.

SAN CRISTÓBAL

The capital of Táchira state is San Cristóbal (population about 300,000), some 40 km from the Colombian border. Spread over a mountain slope 800 metres above sea level, the city has an attractive location and agreeable climate, with average temperatures around 21°C. San Cristóbal has little to offer tourists but it is an almost unavoidable transit point to/from Cúcuta in Colombia. You actually don't need to move out of the bus terminal, as there is plenty of transport in all directions, but if you arrive late, you may choose to stay overnight in the city.

Money

Major banks are within two or three blocks of Plaza Bolívar. Cash can be changed at the Banco Maracaibo (on Plaza Bolívar), Banco Venezuela (corner of Calle 8 and Carrera 9) and Banco Consolidado (corner of Avenida 5 and Calle 8). The latter also deals with American Express travellers' cheques and credit cards. The Banco Unión (corner of Avenida 7 and Calle 5) services Mastercard and Visa card holders.

Places to Stay

There are perhaps a dozen budget hotels in the city centre, but most double as love hotels. One of the few which doesn't rent rooms to passionate couples is the friendly *Hotel Parador del Hidalgo* (☎ 432839), Calle 7 No 9-35. It's simple and definitely lacks style, but has clean rooms with private bath and hot water (US$5 per person). The hotel has its own restaurant, serving unpretentious cheap meals.

One block east up the steps, at Calle 7 No 10-43, is the *Hotel Hawai*, which is more basic and not as innocent, but cheaper (US$8 a double with bath). *Hotel Andorra*, Carrera 4 No 4-67, near the catedral, is one of the cheapest options in the city centre (US$7/10 a double/triple). The hotel, set in an old house with a fine patio, has some charm but fairly basic rooms.

In the same area, at Calle 6 No 3-25, the *Hotel Ejecutivo* (☎ 446298) is also located in an old building. It offers marginally better standards in doubles/triples for US$8/11.

For something considerably better, go to *Hotel Bella Vista* (☎ 437866), corner of Carrera 9 and Calle 9. Comfortable singles/doubles/triples with bath go for US$14/20/25.

Getting There & Away

Air San Cristóbal has no airport. The closest airports are in Santo Domingo, about 40 km south-east of San Cristóbal (formally considered the city's airport), and in San Antonio del Táchira, on the Colombian border, roughly the same distance from San

Cristóbal. Both have flights to Caracas and several other main cities.

Bus The bus station is about two km south of the city centre, linked by frequent city bus services. There are about 10 buses daily to Caracas (US$12.25 ordinary, US$14.50 deluxe, 13 hours). Most depart in the late afternoon/early evening for an overnight trip via El Llano highway. Busetas go to Mérida every two hours until 6 pm (US$4, 5½ hours). There are also por puestos, marginally quicker, for a dollar more. Por puestos to San Antonio del Táchira, on the border, run every few minutes (US$1, one hour). It's quite a spectacular road.

SAN PEDRO DEL RÍO

San Pedro del Río is a tiny town off the main roads, about 40 km north of San Cristóbal. It's a clean, laid-back place with a colonial appearance. Altogether, there are perhaps four calles and four carreras, all paved with cobblestones and lined with meticulously restored, whitewashed single-storey houses. This peaceful oasis is a perfect place for a rest. The small **El Pequeño Museo**, on the main square, has some objects relating to town history.

Places to Stay & Eat

The only regular hotel, the *Posada Turística La Vieja Escuela* (☎ 93664), Calle Real No 3-61, is as pleasant and inviting as the town itself. Located in an old school, the posada has spotlessly neat doubles/triples/quadruples for US$11/15/18.

There are four or five restaurants, the best of which is probably *El Balcón*, near the Posada, located in the only two-storey colonial house in town. They have some regional specialties, including good mondongo, a kind of tripe stew. If you feel like having a drink, ask for the calentado (a cane brandy with honey, cloves and, often, other condiments) or for leche de burra (a local liquor with egg). *Antojitos Andinos*, near the main square, serves cheap set meals.

Getting There & Away

San Pedro del Río lies five km off the San Cristóbal-La Fría road. From San Cristóbal, take the half-hourly bus to San Juan de Colón and get off at the police checkpoint a few km before reaching San Juan, where the road to San Pedro branches off. From there, catch the half-hourly bus to San Pedro (US$0.15, 10 minutes) coming through from San Juan.

If you are coming from the north (say, from Mérida or Maracaibo), stop in San Juan de Colón and take the bus to San Pedro (US$0.20, 15 minutes); it departs every half-hour from just off the main square.

SAN ANTONIO DEL TÁCHIRA

San Antonio is a frontier town of some 50,000 people, living from trade with neighbouring Colombia. The centre is tightly packed with shops, though avalanches of Colombian buyers seem to be a thing of the past. Now, Venezuelans go to Cúcuta in search of bargains. Move your watch one hour forward when crossing from Colombia to Venezuela, one hour backward if you enter Colombia from Venezuela.

Information

Money There are more than half a dozen banks in San Antonio, none of which changes cash. Only Banco Consolidado, on Plaza Bolívar, accepts American Express travellers' cheques and credit cards, and Banco Unión, on Calle 4, off the plaza, services Visa card holders.

Plenty of casas de cambio dot the centre, especially on La Avenida (Carrera 4), changing dollars, bolívares and pesos in any direction, at rates similar to those in Cúcuta. None of the casas changes travellers' cheques.

Immigration The DIEX office is on Carrera 9, between calles 6 and 7, and is theoretically open daily from 6 am to 8 pm, though they used to close earlier. You must get an exit or entry stamp in your passport here.

Only Chinese citizens need a visa for Colombia, but you must get an entry stamp from the DAS office (see the Cúcuta section

VENEZUELA

in the Colombia chapter for further information).

Places to Stay

Hotel Frontera, Calle 2 No 8-70, is possibly the cheapest in town (US$4 a double), but basic. The best budget bet is *Hotel Colonial* (☎ 713123), Carrera 11 No 2-52, which has good clean doubles with fan and private bath for US$7. *Hotel San Antonio* (☎ 711023), corner of Carrera 6 and Calle 2, costs much the same as the Colonial but is not as good. Another budget option, the *Hotel Terepaima* (☎ 711763), Carrera 8 No 1-37, charges US$4 per person and has a cheap restaurant.

The cheapest air-conditioned rooms are in the *Hotel Neveri* (☎ 714632), Carrera 3 No 3-13, one block from the border crossing. Singles/doubles/triples/quadruples cost US$10/12/14/15.

The two best hotels in town are *Hotel Don Jorge* (☎ 711932), Calle 5 No 9-20 (US$18/21/24 a single/double/triple), and *Hotel Adriático* (☎ 715757), Calle 6, on the corner of Carrera 6 (US$18/24/30).

Getting There & Away

Air The airport is close to town, reached by frequent por puestos. There are four flights daily to Caracas (US$47) and one to Mérida (US$21). Zuliana de Aviación flies daily to Miami (US$185). There are no direct flights to Colombia.

Bus & Taxi San Antonio has no central bus station; bus company offices are close to each other on La Avenida. Four companies, Expresos Mérida, Expresos Los Llanos, Expresos Alianza and Expresos San Cristóbal, operate buses to Caracas, with a total of seven buses daily. All depart in the late afternoon or early evening and use El Llano route (US$13, about 14 hours). Los Llanos and Mérida also have air-conditioned buses for US$15.

There are no direct buses to Mérida; go to San Cristóbal and change. Por puestos to San Cristóbal leave frequently from Calle 5 (US$1, one hour).

Buses and shared taxis run frequently to Cúcuta (Colombia), about 12 km from San Antonio. Catch buses (US$0.30) on Calle 6 or La Avenida, and shared taxis (US$0.50) on Calle 6 near the corner of Carrera 9. Both deposit you at Cúcuta bus terminal. You can pay in bolívares or pesos.

The North-East

The North-East is essentially for outdoor activities; it's the region to go sailing, walking and sunbathing. The coast is at its best here, perhaps the most amazing section being in the Mochima National Park. Another of the region's star attractions is the Cueva del Guácharo (Guácharo Cave).

Although it was here that the Spaniards first came and settled, there's not much of the colonial legacy left, except for the partly preserved old towns of Barcelona and Cumaná. Administratively, the North-East falls into Sucre state and the northern parts of Anzoátegui and Monagas.

BARCELONA

Barcelona, founded in 1671 by Catalans, was named after their mother town in Spain. Gradually merging into a single city with its dynamic young neighbour, Puerto La Cruz, Barcelona is the capital of Anzoátegui state.

It's a pleasant enough place, with several central plazas and some relatively well-preserved colonial architecture. The old town was restored in large parts and whitewashed throughout, and gives a pleasant general impression, despite a mishmash of houses dating from different periods. The city hasn't rushed to modernise, so the old-world air is still noticeable in the historic sector.

Information

Tourist Office Barcelona has two tourist offices. The Dirección de Turismo, just off Plaza Boyacá, is open on weekdays from 8 am to noon and 2 to 5.30 pm. The Coranztur (☎ 777110) office is on Plaza Rolando and is open on weekdays from 8 am to 3 pm.

Money There are only a few banks in central

Barcelona, and you'd better have sufficient bolívares before coming here. The Banco Mercantil, on Plaza Bolívar, might pay you advance cash on Visa or Mastercard, while Banco Unión changes cash (but not travellers' cheques) and services Visa card holders.

Things to See
The historic nucleus of the city is **Plaza Boyacá**, with a statue of General José Antonio Anzoátegui, the Barcelona-born hero of the War of Independence, in its centre. On the western side of the beautifully tree-shaded square stands the **Catedral**, built a century after the town's foundation.

On the southern side of the plaza is the **Museo de Anzoátegui**. Located in the carefully restored, oldest surviving building in town, the museum features a variety of objects related to Barcelona's history. It is open Tuesday to Sunday from 8 am to noon and 2 to 5 pm. There's usually a guide, who can give you information about the contents, in Spanish only.

An extension of the museum is housed in the **Ateneo de Barcelona**, two blocks east. On the 1st floor of this colonial building is a small but quite representative collection of paintings (most dating from the 1940s and 1950s) by various modern Venezuelan artists. The museum is open on weekdays from 8 am to noon and 2 to 5 pm, and on weekends from 9 am to noon and 2 to 5 pm. The Ateneo also presents temporary exhibitions on the ground floor, and conducts various cultural activities. There's a handicrafts shop attached, but a far larger selection of crafts is offered by **Gunda Arte Popular**, a shop on Calle Bolívar.

The **Plaza Rolando** is lined by younger buildings, among which the two worth a look are the **Iglesia del Carmen** and the **Teatro Cajigal**, both dating from the 1890s. The latter is an enchanting small theatre, still doing the honours as the city's main stage; guards can admit you during the day.

There are a few more plazas to the northwest, including Plaza Miranda and Plaza Bolívar, just one block from each other. The western side of the latter is occupied by the **Casa Fuerte**, once a Franciscan hospice, destroyed by the Royalists in a heavy attack in 1817. Over 1500 people, both defenders and those who took refuge here, lost their lives in the massacre which followed the takeover. The surviving parts of the walls have been left in ruins as a memorial to the event.

Places to Stay
There are only a few hotels in the centre, so book in as soon as you arrive. The *Hotel Plaza* (☎ 772843), on Plaza Boyacá, should be the first stop for budget travellers. It's in a nice colonial house with a patio, and has rooms of different standards and prices. Doubles without bath cost US$7.50 and are probably the best bet: they are spacious and overlook the plaza and the catedral. There are also some air-conditioned doubles for around US$10. A stone's throw away, at the back of the catedral, is the less attractive *Hotel Madrid* (US$5 per person).

Perhaps the town's most evocative place to stay is the *Hotel Canarias* (☎ 771034), on Calle Bolívar, near the corner of Avenida 5 de Julio. It's a colonial house with a patio and spotlessly clean rooms, all with private bath. Singles/doubles with fan are US$6.50/9.50, while doubles/triples with air-conditioning cost US$14/19. Diagonally opposite is the *Hotel Barcelona* (☎ 771087), where air-conditioned doubles cost around US$20.

Places to Eat
Avenida 5 de Julio is the main area for eating, with several restaurants, snack bars and food vendors. In the old town, budget eateries include the *Restaurant Boyacá*, on Plaza Boyacá, *Lunchería Doña Arepa*, on Calle Bolívar, and *Las 4 Esquinas*, on the corner of calles Freites and Maturín.

Getting There & Away
Air The airport is two km south of the city centre, accessible by urban transport. There are two flights daily to Isla de Margarita (US$16 with Aeropostal in the afternoon, US$19 with Avensa in the morning) and

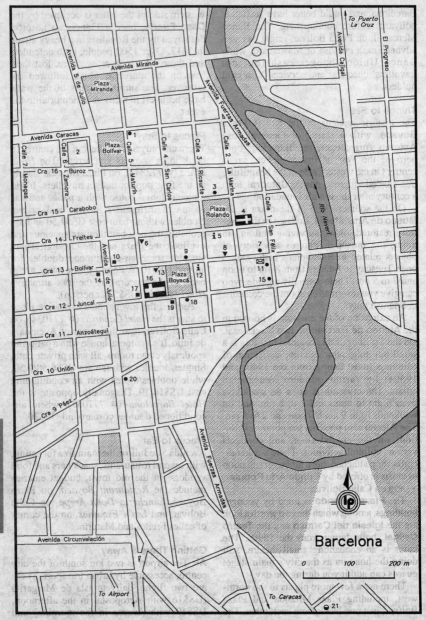

Barcelona

1	Banco Mercantil
2	Casa Fuerte
3	Teatro Cajigal
4	Iglesia del Carmen
5	Coranztur Tourist Office
6	Restaurant Las 4 Esquinas
7	Gunda Arte Popular
8	Lunchería Doña Arepa
9	Banco de Venezuela
10	Hotel Barcelona
11	Post Office & CANTV Office
12	Dirección de Turismo
13	Restaurant Boyacá
14	Hotel Canarias
15	Ateneo de Barcelona
16	Catedral
17	Hotel Madrid
18	Museo de Anzoátegui
19	Hotel Plaza
20	Banco Unión
21	Bus Terminal

eight flights to Caracas (US$22 with Aeropostal, US$26 with Avensa). Other major cities are also serviced, either directly or via Caracas.

Bus The bus terminal is about one km south of the city centre, next to the market; take a buseta going south along Avenida 5 de Julio, or walk 15 minutes. There are regular departures to Caracas (US$5, 4½ hours). Several buses daily run south to Ciudad Bolívar (US$4.25, four hours), then continue to Ciudad Guayana.

To Puerto La Cruz, catch a city bus going north on Avenida 5 de Julio (US$0.20). They use two routes, 'Vía Intercomunal' (faster) and 'Vía Alterna'. Either will put you down in the centre of Puerto La Cruz, one block from Plaza Bolívar.

PUERTO LA CRUZ
Puerto La Cruz is a young, dynamic, growing city and one of Venezuela's most important ports. Until the 1930s, it was not much more than an obscure village, but boomed after rich oil deposits were discovered to the south. The port of Guanta was built east of town, and continuously enlarged

to cope with the oil piped from the oil wells and shipped abroad.

The city has become pretty touristy. It has an attractive 10-block waterfront boulevard, Paseo Colón, lined with hotels, bars and restaurants. It gets very lively in the evening and plenty of artisans' stalls, which appear at that time, add some particular colour. This apart, however, the city doesn't have much to show tourists: a block or two further from the beach, it's just an ordinary place.

Puerto La Cruz is the major gateway to Isla de Margarita for all holiday-makers from Caracas. It's also a jumping-off point to the beautiful Parque Nacional Mochima, which stretches just north and east of the city.

Information
Tourist Office The Coranztur tourist office is midway along Paseo Colón, and is open daily from 8 am to 8 pm.

Tours A score of travel agencies have mushroomed in the city, taking advantage of the heavy tourist income. Many can be found on Paseo Colón: some have their own offices, whereas others nestle in handicrafts shops, hotels, etc. They offer tours to anywhere in the country, from La Gran Sabana to the Andes, but it's far cheaper to arrange one from the local centre (Santa Elena and Mérida, respectively).

It is, however, worth giving some thought to regional tours, principally to the Parque Nacional Mochima. Agents offer trips in speed boats, and some have sailing boats to do it at a more leisurely pace. Several day trips are also available.

Money Most banks are a few blocks north-east of Plaza Bolívar (see the map for locations). The most useful banks include the Banco Unión (cash, Visa, Mastercard), the Banco de Venezuela (cash, Visa, MasterCard) and the Banco Consolidado (American Express travellers' cheques and credit cards).

Places to Stay
Puerto La Cruz is an expensive place to stay, and hotels fill up fast. It's difficult to find

VENEZUELA

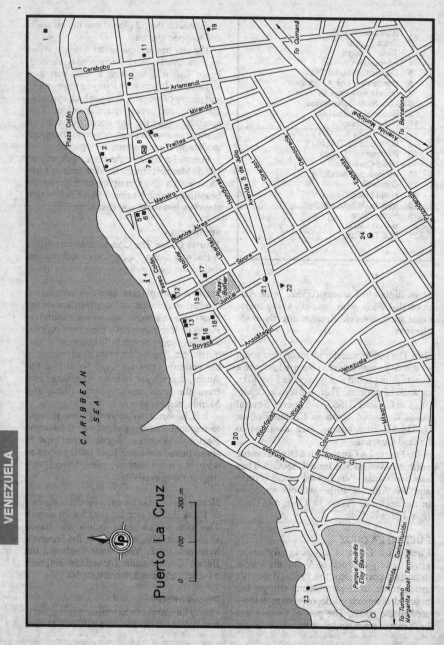

CARIBBEAN SEA

Puerto La Cruz

0   100   200 m

Plaza Colón

Carabobo

Arismendi

Miranda

Freites

Maneiro

Buenos Aires

Sucre

Boyacá

Anzoátegui

Venezuela

Paseo Colón

Bolívar

Libertad

Honduras

Avenida 5 de Julio

Bolívar

Juncal

Plaza Bolívar

Democracia

Esperanza

Providencia

Avenida Municipal

To Cumaná

To Barcelona

Ricaurte

Rodríguez

Los Cocos

Monagas

El Silencio

Milagro

Parque Andrés Eloy Blanco

Avenida Constitución

To Turismo Margarita Boat Terminal

1
11
19
10
2
3
8
9
7
5
6
17
12
15
13
16
18
14
21
22
24
20
23
4

■ **PLACES TO STAY**

1	Hotel Meliá
2	Hotel Riviera
5	Hotel Gaeta
6	Hotel Costa Azul
12	Hotel Diana
13	Hotel Margelina & Hotel Neptuno
14	Hotel Montecarlo
15	Hotel Europa
16	Hotel Napoli & Hotel Minerva
17	Hotel Guayana
18	Hotel Rey
20	Hotel Rasil

▼ **PLACES TO EAT**

22	Restaurant El Teide

OTHER

3	Banco Maracaibo
4	Coranztur Tourist Office
7	Banco Unión
8	Post Office
9	Banco de Venezuela
10	Banco del Orinoco
11	Banco Provincial
19	Banco Consolidado
21	Por Puestos to Conferry & Turismo Margarita
23	Conferry Terminal
24	Bus Terminal

anything reasonable for below US$10 a double. Most hotels are on Paseo Colón and the adjoining streets, and this is the most enjoyable area in which to stay.

Hotel Diana (☎ 22326), at Paseo Colón 99, is one of the cheapest acceptable places. It has rooms of different standards, from US$9 a double. In a similar price range are two places on Calle Boyacá, the *Hotel Napoli* (☎ 22526) and, next door, the *Hotel Minerva* (☎ 23672). Both have only matrimonios and are often full. Avoid the *Hotel Costa Azul*, on Calle Maneiro – 'basic' flatters this scruffy, dirty place. Its only advantage is the price: US$4/6.50 for singles/doubles without bath (with fan), US$7/9 with bath and air-conditioning.

There are two good places on Plaza Bolívar: the very small *Hotel Guayana* (☎ 21056), for US$12/15 a double/triple, and the *Hotel Europa* (☎ 664688), for a little more. At roughly the same price, you can stay in the *Hotel Rey* (☎ 686810), just off the plaza, the *Hotel Margelina* (☎ 687545), the *Hotel Montecarlo* (☎ 685677) or the *Hotel Neptuno* (☎ 691738). The last three are within a block of each other on Paseo Colón, between calles Boyacá and Juncal.

Places to Eat
There are lots of places to eat in the city. The waterfront is the up-market area, so if you are after budget eating, shop around inland streets. One of the cheapest places serving tasty meals is *Restaurant El Teide* (no sign on the door), next to a farmacia, at Avenida 5 de Julio 153. An unpretentious main course will cost around US$1.50. For perhaps the cheapest chicken in town, go to *Mister Pollo*, opposite Hotel Europa, on Calle Sucre.

The cream of the city's restaurants and trendy bars are on Paseo Colón and along Calle Carabobo. This area is alive till late, when a fresh breeze cools the numerous open-air establishments facing the beach.

Getting There & Away
Air The airport is close to Barcelona (see that section for details).

Bus The bus terminal is conveniently sited in the middle of the city, just three blocks south of Plaza Bolívar. Frequent buses run to Caracas (US$5.25, five hours) and in the opposite direction, to Cumaná (US$1.25, 1½ hours); some continue east to Carúpano (US$3.50, 3½ hours) or even to Güiria (US$5.50, 5½ hours). There are half a dozen buses daily to Ciudad Guayana (US$6, six hours), and all go via Ciudad Bolívar (US$4.50, 4½ hours); Expresos Caribe services this route.

Boat Puerto La Cruz is the major departure point for Isla de Margarita. There are two boats daily with Turismo Margarita and eight ferries with Conferry. In the off season, count on half that number. The passenger fare with

VENEZUELA

either carrier is US$5.50/4 in 1st/2nd class. The trip with the former takes some 2½ hours, with the latter twice that. They have separate terminals, one km from each other, both west of the city centre. Por puestos run frequently to both ferry terminals from the corner of Avenida 5 de Julio and Calle Juncal. Tickets can only be bought two hours before scheduled departure, at the respective terminal. Do this trip in the daytime – it's a spectacular journey between the islands of Parque Nacional Mochima.

PARQUE NACIONAL MOCHIMA

With a total area of 950 sq km, Mochima National Park covers the offshore belt of the Caribbean coast between Puerto La Cruz and Cumaná, including a wealth of islands and islets, plus a strip of the hilly coast noted for deep bays and white, sandy beaches.

The main groups of islands include, from west to east, Las Borrachas, Las Chimanas and Las Caracas. Closer to the mainland and easier to reach are Isla de Plata and Isla Monos. The majority of islands are barren, rocky in parts and extremely spectacular. Many are surrounded by coral reefs and offer excellent snorkelling and scuba diving. The waters are usually calm and warm, and abound in marine life. The weather is fine for most of the year, with moderate rainfall, mainly between July and October.

With its fine beach and coral reefs, **Isla de Plata** is most popular among tourists. It's about 10 km east of Puerto La Cruz and accessible by boat from the pier near Pamatacualito, the eastern suburb of the port of Guanta, serviced by por puestos from Puerto La Cruz. Boats run regularly throughout the day, taking 10 minutes to reach the island. There are food and drink stalls on the island, but no fresh water. Boats can also be hired for longer trips to other islands, such as **Isla Monos**, which is good for snorkelling.

Parts of the Puerto La Cruz-Cumaná road skirt the seafront, so you'll have some spectacular glimpses. There are several beaches off the road, possibly the best being **Playa Arapito**, some 23 km from Puerto La Cruz, and **Playa Colorada**, four km further east.

About 20 km further along the Puerto La Cruz-Cumaná road, a side road branches off to the north and goes a few km to the village of **Mochima**. Mochima sits in the deep, fjord-like Bahía Mochima, and is a good jumping-off point for exploring the park. From the village's wharf, boats can take you to the offshore islands or put you down on one of several isolated mainland beaches, such as Playa Blanca or Playa Cautaro, inaccessible by road. Accommodation and food are available in the village.

The Puerto La Cruz-Isla de Margarita ferry sails between some of the park's islands, providing good views on either side. Tours organised from Puerto La Cruz are yet another way to visit the area.

Finally, for a sweeping panoramic view of the park, complete with its islands, bays and beaches, go to **Los Altos**, a village some 25 km east of Puerto La Cruz. Los Altos is at an altitude of about 900 metres and is only three km from the seashore, making it a fabulous lookout. The village is surrounded by the fresh, green highlands, sprinkled with coffee and cacao haciendas, which can be visited (eg Hacienda El Mirador). Jeeps to Los Altos depart from Puerto La Cruz bus terminal, regularly in the morning but not so in the afternoon. The trip takes 45 minutes and costs US$0.70. You can stay overnight in the pleasant and reasonably priced Posada del Paraíso.

CUMANÁ

Capital of Sucre state, Cumaná (population 150,000) is an important port for sardine fishing and canning. Founded by the Spanish in 1521, it takes pride in being the oldest existing town on South America's mainland. There's not much centuries-old architecture, however; three destructive earthquakes, in 1684, 1765 and 1929, turned the town into little more than a pile of rubble, and its colonial character largely disappeared in subsequent reconstructions.

Cumaná is noted more for its attractive environs than for the city itself. There are some beaches nearby, the closest being San Luis beach, on the south-western outskirts of the city; frequent busetas go there from the centre. Cumaná is one of the two gateways to Isla de Margarita (the other one being Puerto La Cruz) and is a convenient jumping-off point for the Cueva del Guácharo.

Information
Tourist Office The Dirección de Turismo is on Calle Sucre, close to Iglesia de Santa Inés. The office is open on weekdays from 8 am to noon and 2.30 to 5.30 pm, but don't expect much. The copy of the city map they will give you is perfectly useless. There's also a tourist stand at the airport.

Money Most banks are on Avenida Mariño and Avenida Bermúdez, and most will change cash dollars. Travellers' cheques can be changed in the Banco Unión and Banco Consolidado, the latter being far from the centre, on Avenida Bermúdez. The Banco Unión seems to be one of the few to service credit card holders.

Things to See
Some streets around **Iglesia de Santa Inés** vaguely retain an old-world atmosphere. The church itself is a 1929 construction, and only a few objects of an earlier date decorate its interior; note the 16th-century statue of the patron saint over the high altar. The **Catedral**, on Plaza Blanco, is also relatively young, with a hotchpotch of altarpieces in its timbered interior.

Perhaps the best-restored colonial structure in town is the **Castillo de San Antonio**, overlooking the city from a hill just southeast of the centre. Originally constructed in 1659 on a four-pointed star plan, it suffered from pirate attacks and earthquakes, but the coral walls survived in pretty good shape. The fort commands good views over the city and the bay; go there at sunset.

The city has three museums. The **Casa Natal de Andrés Eloy Blanco** is the house where this poet, considered one of the most outstanding literary talents Venezuela has produced, was born, in 1896. The **Museo Gran Mariscal de Ayacucho** is dedicated to the Cumaná-born hero of the War of Independence, General Antonio José de Sucre, best remembered for liberating Peru and Bolivia. The **Museo del Mar** is at the old airport, a couple of km west of the city centre. None is particularly inspiring.

There are two pleasant parks in the centre, **Parque Ayacucho** and **Parque Guaiquerí**, and several tree-shaded plazas.

Places to Stay
The city has over 30 hotels, so there's generally no problem finding somewhere to stay. Almost all budget places are conveniently located in the city centre, within a couple of blocks of Plaza Bolívar. All hotels listed here have rooms with private bath and either fans or air-conditioning.

The cheapest in town (US$5 a double) seems to be the *Hospedaje La Gloria* (☎ 661284), on Calle Sucre, but only a miracle can get you a room there. Most rooms are rented for longer periods and some guests seem to live there for years. Marginally dearer are *Hotel Vesuvio* (☎ 26941), *Hotel Cumaná* (☎ 24766) and *Hotel Italia* (☎ 663678), all on Calle Sucre, but they too have some long-term visitors and can often be full.

The cheapest viable bet is possibly *Hospedaje Lucila*, on Calle Bolívar, in the same area. It's clean and quiet, and has doubles with bath and fan for US$7.

Inexpensive air-conditioned options include *Hotel Astoria* (☎ 662708), Calle Sucre, and *Hotel América* (☎ 22605), Calle América. The former costs US$7/9/10 in singles/doubles/triples; the latter is slightly more expensive but a bit better. There's also *Hotel Dos Mil* (☎ 24809), just west across the river, on Boulevard Urdaneta, at similar prices.

There are several mid-priced hotels in the same area. In ascending order of price, they are *Hotel Master* (☎ 663884) at US$10/14/18 a single/double/triple, *Hotel Turismo Guaiquerí* (☎ 310821) at US$18 a double, *Hotel Regina* (☎ 23442) at US$20 a double, and *Hotel Mariño* (☎ 22663) at US$23 a

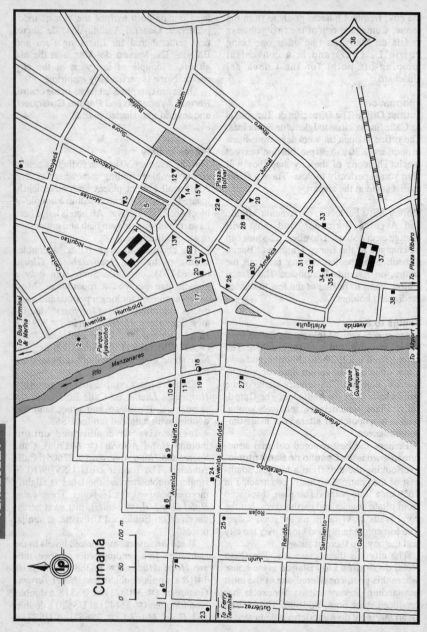

VENEZUELA

Cumaná

0   50   100 m

■ **PLACES TO STAY**

7	Hotel Mariño
11	Hotel Master
19	Hotel Dos Mil
20	Hotel Miranda
24	Hotel Turismo Guaiquerí
27	Hotel Regina
28	Hotel Italia
30	Hotel América
31	Hotel Cumaná
32	Hotel Vesuvio
33	Hospedaje Lucila
34	Hotel Astoria
38	Hospedaje La Gloria

▼ **PLACES TO EAT**

3	Panadería Super Katty
12	Restaurant El Colmao
13	Panadería La Catedral
14	Arepera 19 de Abril
15	Fuente de Soda Jardín Sport
21	Restaurant Polo Norte & Arepera El Punto Criollo

26	Restaurant París
29	Pollo a la Brasa

OTHER

1	CANTV Office
2	Museo Gran Mariscal de Ayacucho
4	Catedral
5	Plaza Blanco
6	Banco del Caribe
8	Banco de Venezuela
9	Banco Unión
10	Banco Construcción
16	Post Office
17	Plaza Miranda
18	Por Puestos to Ferry Terminal
22	Casa Natal de Andrés Eloy Blanco
23	Banco Mercantil
25	Banco Internacional
35	Tourist Office
36	Castillo de San Antonio
37	Iglesia de Santa Inés

double. The Regina is possibly the best of these.

Places to Eat

About the cheapest central place for soup and a main course is *Restaurant París*, on Plaza Miranda, but the food is nothing special. The cheapest grilled chicken is served in *Pollo a la Brasa*, on Plaza Bolívar (half a chicken for US$2.50), but the price is its best feature. Other inexpensive options include two areperas, *19 de Abril* (better) and *El Punto Criollo*, and an open-air parrilla on Plaza Ribero.

Considerably better for lunch or dinner is the *Restaurant Polo Norte* or, still better but more expensive, *Restaurant El Colmao*.

Two panaderías on Plaza Blanco, *Super Katty* and *La Catedral*, offer a variety of cakes and pastries, plus good coffee.

Getting There & Away

Air The old airport, two km south-west of the city centre, has been closed down; the new one is about four km south-east of the city.

Aeropostal, Avensa and Aereotuy service Cumaná, with three direct flights daily to Caracas (US$27) and three to Isla de Margarita (US$14).

Bus The bus terminal is 1½ km north-west of the city centre, and there are frequent urban buses. There is regular bus service to Caracas with a number of companies (US$6, 6½ hours). All buses go through Puerto La Cruz (US$1.25) and Barcelona (US$1.50). Half a dozen buses depart daily for Ciudad Bolívar (US$5.50, six hours) and continue to Ciudad Guayana (US$7, 7½ hours). For Cueva del Guácharo, take the Caripe bus (US$2.50, 3½ hours, two buses daily, at 7 am and noon). There are also por puestos (US$5).

Boat All ferries and boats to Isla de Margarita depart from the pier next to the mouth of Río Manzanares and arrive on the island at Punta de Piedras. There is no urban bus service from the city centre to the ferry

VENEZUELA

docks, but por puestos go there from the door of Hotel Dos Mil (US$0.20).

Conferry runs large ferries taking up to 60 cars and 1000 passengers, daily at 7 am and 4 pm (US$4.50 for passengers, three to four hours). Naviarca sails the same route for the same price, daily at noon and 10 pm, but it's not as reliable a carrier. The schedule is, as they say, 'flexible'.

Finally, there's Turismo Margarita, which runs the 400-seat *Gran Cacique*, daily at 7.30 am and 1.30 pm (on Friday at 7 am, 1 and 6 pm). The boat takes only passengers (US$5.50/4.50 in 1st/2nd class, two hours).

CARIPE

Caripe is a pleasant, easy-going small town noted for its agreeable climate, its coffee and orange plantations and its proximity to Cueva del Guácharo, Venezuela's most magnificent cave.

The town is clean and prosperous-looking, with elegant villas and manicured gardens. The place is quite touristy, and on weekends is full of people escaping from the steamy tropical weather that dominates most of the region. The town is no more than two parallel streets, around which most activities and services are centred.

Money

Banco Unión and Banco del Orinoco change travellers' cheques but not cash. Banco Unión and Banco de Venezuela may service credit card holders.

Things to See & Do

Save for a fine colonial high altar in the modern parish church, there's nothing special to see in town, but the hilly surroundings are beautiful and pleasant for walks. The number one sight is obviously the **Cueva del Guácharo**, 10 km from town (see the following section). Among other attractions, there are two nice waterfalls: **Salto La Payla**, near the cave, and the 80-metre **Salto El Chorrerón**, an hour's walk from the village of Sabana de Piedra.

El Mirador, the highest hill (1100 metres) to the north of the town, commands excellent views over the whole Valle del Caripe. It's a 45-minute walk from town, or you can go there by road.

For those on a more leisurely schedule there are a couple of balnearios, the nearest being **La Poza de Lorenzo**, in the village of Teresín. The village also has a *vivero* (nursery) with a variety of orchids (the season is in May, and sometimes in November), and there's another vivero in La Frontera, close to Caripe.

Numerous longer trips are possible, including the hike to the highest peak in the region, **Cerro Negro** (2600 metres).

Places to Stay

Caripe is increasingly popular among tourists, and there are a score of places to stay in and around the town. Hotel prices tend to rise on weekends.

Camping is possible next to the reception building at the entrance to Cueva del Guácharo, and on the soccer field in Caripe (ask the Guardia for permission). You can also camp rough a reasonable distance outside town.

The cheapest hotel in town (US$7 a double) is the simple but acceptable *Hotel Caripe*, followed by the similar *Hotel San Francisco* (US$8 a double). Appreciably better are the *Hotel Venezia* (US$10 a double) and the *Mini Hotel Familiar Nicola* (US$12 a double). The *Hotel Samán* costs twice that, though it's not twice as comfortable. If you are in a large party, it may work out cheaper to take a cabaña; there are several of them on the road between Caripe and the village of El Guácharo.

Places to Eat

Most of the better hotels and cabañas have their own restaurants. The cheapest place for a full meal is the restaurant of *Hotel Caripe*, but the best food is served in the *Hotel Venezia*.

Getting There & Away

There's no bus station. Buses and por puestos park on Calle Monagas, in the centre. There's an evening bus direct to Caracas via Maturín

(US$10, 11 hours), and two buses to Cumaná, at 6 am and noon (US$2.50, 3½ hours). They pass the Cueva del Guácharo on the way. There are also infrequent por puestos to Cumaná, most reliable in the morning.

Tours

Top Trekking Travel Tours (☎ 51843), the local travel agency, will give you information about walks in the area and, if you wish, they can put together a tour according to your interests, providing transport and camping equipment. Their office is in the Cabañas Pueblo Pequeño, a couple of km west of town, but they plan on opening another one, in the town. One of the owners, Alexander, speaks fluent German, while another, Pablo, speaks English.

CUEVA DEL GUÁCHARO

The Guácharo Cave, 10 km from Caripe on the road towards the coast, is Venezuela's longest, largest and most magnificent cave. It had been known to the local Indians long before Columbus crossed the Atlantic, and was later explored by Europeans. The most eminent explorer, Alexander von Humboldt, penetrated 472 metres of the cave in September 1799, and it was he who first classified its unusual inhabitant, the guácharo.

The guácharo, or oilbird (*Steatornis caripensis*), is a nocturnal, fruit-eating bird, the only one of its kind in the world. It inhabits caves in various tropical parts of the Americas, living in total darkness and leaving the cave only at night for food, principally the fruit of some species of palms. The guácharo has a sort of radar-location system similar to that of bats, which enables it to get around. The adult bird is about 60 cm long, with a wingspan of a metre.

In Venezuela, the guácharo has been seen in over 40 caves; the biggest colony, estimated at about 15,000 birds, is here. They inhabit only the first chamber of the cave, the 750-metre-long Humboldt's Hall. The birds are easily disturbed, raising a tremendous din, but are not aggressive.

The cave also offers a display of amazing formations, including stalactites, stalagmites and columns. It's open daily from 8 am to 4 pm, and all visits are guided in groups of up to 10 people; the tour takes about an hour. A 1½-km portion of the total 10½-km length of the cave is visited, though occasionally in August the water can rise, limiting sightseeing to half a km. You have to leave backpacks and bags by the ticket office, but cameras with flash are permitted in the cave, beyond the area where the guácharo live. The ticket costs US$0.70 (US$0.40 for students).

You can camp near the cave; if you do, watch hundreds of birds pouring out of the cave mouth at around 7 pm and returning about 4 am. There's a 35-metre waterfall, **Salto La Payla**, 25 minutes from the cave.

GÜIRIA

Güiria is the easternmost point on Venezuela's coast accessible by road, after a 275-km ride from Cumaná. Home to some 20,000 people, it's the largest town of Península de Paria and an important fishing port. The town itself is a rather ordinary place with no tourist attractions. The surrounding area, however, is attractive and worth exploring, particularly the **Parque Nacional Península de Paria**, a hilly area covered with lush cloud forest, stretching along the northern coast. Near the eastern tip of the peninsula is the small town of **Macuro** (accessible only by water), the only place on the South American mainland where Columbus set foot, in August 1498, coming from Trinidad.

Güiria has ferry connections with Trinidad and other islands of the Lesser Antilles, and is one of the possible starting points for trips to the Orinoco delta.

Information

Money Banco de Venezuela (on Calle Concepción, off Plaza Bolívar) and Banco del Orinoco (on the corner of calles Valdez and Trinchera) change cash and travellers' cheques. Neither will accept notes below US$50 denomination. Banco de Venezuela and Banco Unión, on Calle Bolívar near the

VENEZUELA

main square, may give advances on Visa and MasterCard.

Tours Acosta Asociados (☎ 81679, 81233), Calle Bolívar 31, offer a variety of tours and other travel services. They sell tickets for the ferry to Trinidad and arrange all formalities involved.

Places to Stay & Eat

At the low-budget end, the best place to stay is the *Hotel Plaza*, on the corner of Plaza Bolívar (US$7 a double with bath and fan). Its restaurant is the best inexpensive eatery in town.

For a similar price, you can have a double in *Hotel Fortuna*, on Calle Bolívar 50 metres from the plaza, or in *Hotel Miramar*, on Calle Turpial a bit further toward the port.

The *Residencia Gran Puerto* (☎ 81085), on Calle Vigirima close to the central square, has good singles/doubles with bath and fan for US$9/10, and also a few air-conditioned doubles for US$14. Its sibling, the *Hotel Gran Puerto* (☎ 81343), Calle Pegallos near Calle Bideau, offers marginally better standards (US$12/15). The best in town is *La Posada de Chuchú* (☎ 81266), Calle Bideau 35, which has doubles/triples for US$20/25. Its restaurant matches the standard of the hotel. Another place for tasty food is *Fonda El Limón*, on Calle Trinchera.

Getting There & Away

Air The airport is a 20-minute walk north of the town centre. There are light-plane flights to Isla de Margarita on Monday, Wednesday and Friday (US$20). After changing to a large jet, these flights continue to Caracas (US$43 from Güiria).

Bus Several bus companies have offices around the triangular Plaza Sucre, two blocks from Plaza Bolívar. There are three or four buses to Caracas (US$10.25, 11 to 12 hours). They all go via Cumaná, Puerto La Cruz and Barcelona. From the same square, frequent por puestos run to Carúpano (US$3.75, two hours).

Boat The ferry dock is at the far southern end of the port, a 15-minute walk from the town centre. Windward Lines operates a ferry on the Güiria-Trinidad-St Vincent-Barbados-St Lucia route. The whole loop takes a week, as the ferry stays several hours in each port. The Güiria-Trinidad portion is done in seven hours. From Güiria, the ferry leaves on Wednesday at 11 pm; from Trinidad to Güiria, it departs on Tuesday at 5 pm. Deck fares (in US$) from Güiria are:

To	One-Way	Return
Trinidad (Port of Spain)	40	60
St Vincent (Kingstown)	83	138
Barbados (Bridgetown)	89	148
St Lucia (Castries)	95	158

Cabins cost about US$10 per bed per night. Acosta Asociados, the Venezuelan representative of Windward Lines, provides information and sells tickets.

Peñeros (open fishing boats) to Macuro leave every morning, without a fixed schedule, from the northern end of the Güiria port (US$2.50, 1½ to two hours). In Macuro, ask for Doña Guillermina or Doña Beatriz, who run two simple posadas (US$4 per person) and can also provide meals. There's a path from Macuro to Uquire, on the northern coast (a six-hour walk); you can hire a boat to take you there, but it's expensive.

Irregular fishing and cargo boats (one or two per week) go to Pedernales, at the northern mouth of the Orinoco delta. The trip takes four to five hours and the fare is largely negotiable; you shouldn't pay more than US$8 per person. From Pedernales, there are boats south to Tucupita, which usually call en route at the small settlements of the Warao Indians.

Isla de Margarita

With an area of about 920 sq km, Isla de Margarita is Venezuela's largest island, 67 km from east to west and 32 km from north to south. It lies some 40 km off the mainland,

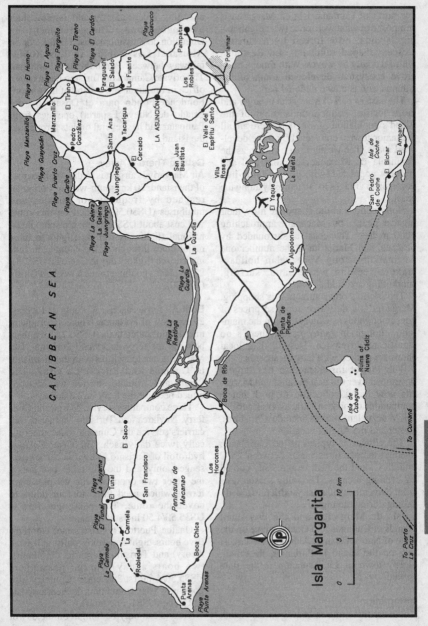

Isla Margarita

0   5   10 km

CARIBBEAN SEA

Playa El Humo
Playa El Agua
Playa Parguito
Playa El Tirano
Playa El Cardón
Playa Guacuco

Pampatar
Porlamar

Playa Manzanillo
Manzanillo
El Cardón
Paraguachí
El Salado
La Fuente
Los Robles

Playa Guayacán
Playa Puerto Cruz
Pedro González
Santa Ana
Tacarigua
LA ASUNCIÓN

Playa Caribe
El Cercado
San Juan Bautista
El Valle del Espíritu Santo

Playa La Galera
La Galera
Juangriego
Playa Juangriego
Villa Rosa
La Isleta

El Yaque
La Guardia

Playa La Guardia
La Guardia
Los Algodones

Playa La Restinga

Boca de Río

Isla de Coche
Bichar
San Pedro de Coche
Isla de Amparo

Punta de Piedras

To Cumaná

Ruins of Nueva Cádiz
Isla de Cubagua

El Saco
San Francisco
Península de Macanao
Los Horcones

Playa La Auyama
El Tunal
Playa El Tunal
La Carmela
Playa La Carmela
Robledal
Boca Chica

Punta Arenas
Playa Punta Arenas

To Puerto La Cruz

VENEZUELA

due north of Cumaná. Isla de Margarita is composed of what were once two neighbouring islands, now linked by a narrow, crescent-shaped sandbank, La Restinga, built gradually by waves. With time, a mangrove ecosystem developed south of the isthmus, and is now a national park.

The eastern part of Margarita is larger and more fertile, and contains most of the island's population of 300,000. Here are all the major towns, connected by quite developed roads. The western part, known as the Península de Macanao, is more arid and scarcely populated, with people living in a dozen or so villages located mostly along the coast.

Both sections of the island are hilly, their highest peaks, on Macanao, approaching 1000 metres. The coast is surrounded by beaches, and Margarita is the number one destination among Venezuelan holidaymakers seeking white sand, surfing, snorkelling and scuba diving.

The island's other attraction is shopping. Margarita is a duty-free zone, so prices of consumer goods are lower than on the mainland, though in many cases, there's no significant difference. Despite that, local shops are packed with bargain seekers.

The tourist infrastructure has largely developed over the past decade, and Margarita now has a collection of posh hotels comparable to those in Caracas. Peak periods for Venezuelan tourists include Christmas, Easter and the August vacation.

The climate is typical of the Caribbean: average temperatures range between 25°C and 28°C, and the heat is agreeably cooled by evening breezes. The rainy season lasts from November to January, with rain mostly falling during the night.

Isla de Margarita, and the two small islands of Cubagua and Coche, make up the state of Nueva Esparta. Although the largest city on the island is Porlamar, the small, sleepy town of La Asunción is the state capital.

Information

There are three tourist boards on the island,

operating independently and issuing their own publications. The government-run Dirección de Turismo is based in the Centro Artesanal Los Robles, in Los Robles midway between Porlamar and Pampatar. The private Cámara de Turismo has its main office in Porlamar and a stand at the airport. Fondene (Fondo para el Desarrollo del Estado de Nueva Esparta) operates from Pampatar and has several outlets throughout the island.

Getting There & Away

Air Margarita's airport is in the southern part of the island, 20 km south-west of Porlamar, reached by frequent por puestos and minibuses (US$0.50). A taxi on this route will cost about US$7. There are some international flights, as well as flights to most major cities throughout the country, including a dozen flights a day to Caracas (US$28). Light planes go three times a week to Güiria (US$20).

Boat All ferries anchor in Punta de Piedras, 29 km west of Porlamar. There are frequent micros and shared taxis (US$0.75 for either) between the ferry docks and Porlamar. Isla Margarita has ferry links with the mainland, to Cumaná and Puerto La Cruz. The Pampatar-Carúpano service was discontinued because the ferry broke down.

Three companies service Margarita: Conferry, Naviarca and Turismo Margarita. All carriers service the Cumaná route, theoretically twice daily each. The *Gran Cacique* hydrofoil of Turismo Margarita carries passengers only, and the trip takes two hours; the other two operators run car/passenger ferries which need three to four hours to cover the route. The passenger fare is US$5.50/4.50 in 1st/2nd class.

On the Puerto La Cruz route, Conferry (five hours, eight departures daily, at least in theory) and Turismo Margarita (2½ hours, two boats a day) charge passengers US$5.50/4 in 1st/2nd class. Conferry also goes once a day from Punta de Piedras to Isla de Coche (US$1, one hour).

Tickets can only be bought on the day of

the journey, an hour before planned departure. The service is not very reliable, with boats usually departing later than scheduled, but sometimes earlier. In the off season, there can be fewer boats than listed. Turismo Margarita is perhaps the most reliable operator.

PORLAMAR

Porlamar is the largest urban centre on the island and will be probably your first destination when coming from the mainland. It's a modern, bustling city of 80,000, replete with shopping centres, hotels and restaurants. Tree-shaded Plaza Bolívar is the historic centre of the city, but Porlamar has progressively expanded eastward, the forest of high-rise buildings getting thicker and more extensive in the last decade.

Porlamar is a place to wander through trendy stores packed with imported goods. The most elegant and expensive shopping areas are on and around avenidas Santiago Mariño and 4 de Mayo, while two central pedestrian malls, Boulevard Guevara and (to a lesser extent) Boulevard Gómez south of Plaza Bolívar, trade mostly in clothing and have more affordable prices.

Information

Tourist Office The Cámara de Turismo is on Avenida Santiago Mariño, next to Calle Hernández, and is open on weekdays from 8 am to noon and 2 to 6 pm. Fondene operates two information stands in Porlamar: near the corner of avenidas Santiago Mariño and 4 de Mayo, and on Boulevard Guevara, close to the corner of Calle Maneiro. They don't seem to be open regularly in the off season.

Pick up a copy of the bilingual Spanish/English newspaper *La Isla*, which is distributed free in some of the up-market hotels, travel agencies, tourist offices etc. Don't miss *Mira!*, a well-written English-language monthly paper full of practical details and interesting background information about the island and the whole country – also free from a range of tourist establishments.

Money Many of Porlamar's banks handle some foreign exchange operations (see the Porlamar map for bank locations). At the time of writing, cash is changed by Banco Principal, Banco Comercial Amazonas, Banco Construcción and Banco Mercantil. Travellers' cheques are exchanged by Banco Consolidado, Banco Principal and Banco Mercantil, among others. Banks dealing with Visa and MasterCard include Banco de Venezuela, Banco Mercantil and Banco Unión.

There are several casas de cambio, most in the area of Avenida Santiago Mariño. Many stores will also exchange cash, at a rate about 1% to 2% lower than banks.

Things to See

One of the few real tourist sights is the **Museo de Arte Contemporáneo Francisco Narváez**, in a large, modern building on the corner of calles Igualdad and Díaz. On the ground floor is a collection of sculptures and paintings by this noted Margarita-born artist (1905-82), while the salons on the upper floor are used for temporary exhibitions. The museum is open from 9 am to noon and 2 to 6 pm daily (except Mondays).

A small but colourful **market** is held in the morning on the waterfront at the outlet of Boulevard Gómez. As might be expected, there are plenty of fish, including some sharks.

Places to Stay

Porlamar has loads of hotels for every pocket. As a general rule, the price and standard rise from west to east. Accordingly, there are no fancy places to stay west of Plaza Bolívar, but cheapies in this area are plentiful. On the other hand, looking for a budget room around Avenida Santiago Mariño is a waste of time.

There are a score of budget hotels within a few blocks south-west of Plaza Bolívar. Among them, one of the best cheap bets is the friendly *Hotel España* (☎ 612479), Calle Mariño No 6-35 near the waterfront. It has a variety of simple rooms, and a restaurant serving inexpensive tasty meals. Expect to

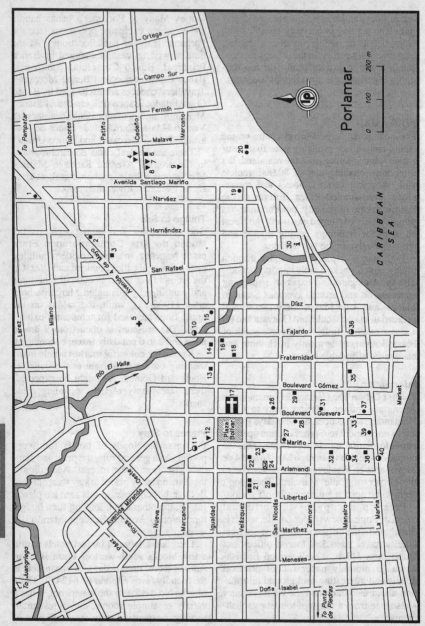

VENEZUELA

■ PLACES TO STAY

3   Hotel Internacional
6   Gran Avenida Hotel
13 Hotel La Ópera
14 Hotel Porlamar
16 Hotel Canadá
18 Hotel Evang
20 Hotel Bella Vista
21 Hotel Plaza, Hotel Caroní &
     Hotel San Miguel
22 Residencia El Paraíso
25 Hotel OM-21
29 Hotel Central
32 Hotel Torino
35 Hotel Coromoto
38 Hotel España

▼ PLACES TO EAT

4   Restaurant El Faro de Julio &
     Restaurant Los Tres Delfines
7   Restaurant Il Castello Romano
8   Restaurant El Chipi
9   Restaurant La Vecchia Roma
12 Restaurant Napoleón

23 Restaurant Beirut

OTHER

1   Banco Unión
2   Banco Provincial
5   Hospital
10 Micros to La Asunción
11 Micros to Juangriego
15 Museo de Arte Contemporáneo
     Francisco Narváez
17 Iglesia de San Nicolás de Bari
19 Banco Consolidado
20 CANTV Office
24 Post Office
26 Banco Consolidado
27 Banco Mercantil
28 Banco de Venezuela
30 Cámara de Turismo
31 Banco Construcción
33 Fondene Tourist Stand
34 Micros to Punta de Piedras
36 Micros to Pampatar
37 Banco Comercial Amazonas
39 Banco Principal
40 Micros to La Restinga

pay about US$5/7 for a single/double with bath, a dollar less without bath.

Other good budget options in the area include the *Hotel OM-21* (☎ 632367), on Calle San Nicolás, *Hotel Plaza* (☎ 630395), on Calle Velásquez, and *Hotel San Miguel* (☎ 630395), a few steps from the plaza. All three have singles/doubles/triples/quadruples with bath for US$6/7/8/9, which works out quite well for a larger party. The *Hotel Caroní*, between the plaza and Hotel San Miguel, offers pretty much the same for marginally less. One of the cheapest in the area, *Residencia El Paraíso*, has doubles with bath for US$5.

For inexpensive air-conditioned rooms, try *Hotel Central* (☎ 614757), conveniently located on Boulevard Gómez. Doubles/triples go for US$10/13. Better is the friendly *Hotel Torino* (☎ 610734), Calle Mariño, which has singles/doubles with air-conditioning, TV and fridge (US$10/14).

There are several mid-priced hotels a couple of blocks east of Plaza Bolívar,

including *La Ópera*, *Evang*, *Porlamar* and *Canadá*. There are more hotels nearby, so have a look around.

In the eastern modern part of the city, hotel prices begin around US$20 a double. That is what you'll pay at the *Hotel Internacional* (☎ 618912), on Avenida 4 de Mayo. More appealing is the quiet *Gran Avenida Hotel* (☎ 619143), on Calle Cedeño close to several good eateries. Air-conditioned doubles with TV cost US$25.

Places to Eat
If you want a budget meal, look for it in the centre. The best inexpensive food in this area is served in the *Restaurant España*, in the hotel of the same name. A couple of blocks north along the same street, the *Restaurant Beirut* has reasonably priced Lebanese food. *Restaurant Napoleón*, on the corner of Plaza Bolívar, serves cheap pseudo-Italian dishes.

Most of the finer restaurants are in the eastern sector, so if you are looking for a well-appointed place with atmosphere and a

VENEZUELA

selection of quality food, stroll there. On Calle Cedeño alone, just west of Avenida Santiago Mariño, there are half a dozen good restaurants, including *El Chipi* (international menu), *Il Castello Romano* (Italian food), *Los Tres Delfines* (Cantonese cuisine) and *El Faro de Julio* (seafood). One block south, on Calle Marcano, is *La Vecchia Roma*, probably the best and most authentic Italian restaurant in town.

Getting Around

There's frequent transport to most of the island, operated by small buses locally called micros. They leave from different points in the city centre; the departure points for some of the main tourist destinations have been indicated on the Porlamar map.

PAMPATAR

Pampatar, 10 km north-east of Porlamar, is today a town of some 8000 people. It was perhaps the first settlement on Margarita, founded in the 1530s, and still has some colonial buildings.

Information

The Fondene tourist office (☎ 622342, 622494) is located in the Casa de la Aduana and is open on weekdays from 8 am to noon and 1 to 4.30 pm. They sell maps and have good information about the island. Fondene runs information stands in Porlamar, in Juangriego and at the airport.

Things to See

Pampatar's fort, the **Castillo de San Carlos Borromeo**, built in the 1660s on the site of the previous stronghold (which was destroyed by pirates), is the best-preserved and restored construction of its type on the island. The fort is right in the centre of town, on the waterfront. It can be visited daily from 9 am to noon and 2 to 5 pm.

Opposite the fort is the **parish church**, dating from the mid-18th century. A hundred metres east of the church is a neoclassical building from 1864, known as **Casa de la Aduana**. There are temporary exhibitions on the ground floor.

The **fishing port**, which extends along the beach for a km east of the fort, has much old-world charm, with rustic boats anchored in the bay or on the shore, and fishers repairing nets on the beach. The cape at the far eastern end of the bay is topped with another fort, the ruined **Fortín de la Caranta**, which commands better views than the Castillo.

Places to Stay & Eat

Accommodation is not plentiful in Pampatar. Most places are the so-called *aparthoteles*, offering 'miniapartments' which have a kitchen, complete with pots and pans.

At the bottom end, there are the *Aparthotel Don Juan* (☎ 623609), with very small rooms (US$16 for two or three people), and *Casitas Vacacionales Trimar* (☎ 621657), costing US$20 for up to five people. Both hotels are on Calle Almirante Brion, opposite each other; the Trimar faces the beach and has possibly the best reasonably priced restaurant in town. There are many other open-air eateries along the beach.

Better places to stay for not much more are on Calle El Cristo, a five-minute walk east, and include *Los Chalets de la Caranta* (☎ 621214), with its own restaurant, and *Aparthotel Pampatar* (☎ 621935).

Getting There & Away

Buses between Porlamar and Pampatar run at least every five minutes (US$0.15, 20 minutes).

LA ASUNCIÓN

La Asunción, set in a fertile valley in the inland portion of the island, is the official capital of the Nueva Esparta state, though it's far smaller than Porlamar. It's noteworthy for its lush vegetation and its tranquility. There's virtually no duty-free commerce here, and hotels and restaurants are scarce.

Built in the second half of the 16th century, the **catedral** on Plaza Bolívar is perhaps the oldest colonial church in the country, noted for its austere, simple form, with a delicate Renaissance portal on the façade and two more doorways on the side walls.

On the northern side of the plaza is the **Museo Nueva Cádiz**, named after the first Spanish town in South America (founded in 1519 on Isla Cubagua, south of Margarita). The town was completely destroyed by an earthquake in 1541, and the traces disappeared until the 1950 excavation uncovered the town foundations, some architectural details and various old objects. The museum displays photos of the excavation work, plus a small, rather haphazard collection of exhibits, including two huge anchors recovered from shipwrecks.

Just outside town, a 10-minute walk southward up the hill, is the **Castillo de Santa Rosa**, one of numerous forts built on the island to protect it from pirate attacks. Apart from the view of the town, there is old armour on display.

Getting There & Away
Micros from Porlamar will put you down on La Asunción's tree-shaded Plaza Bolívar. After having a look around, you can either return to Porlamar or continue to Juangriego – there is frequent transport to either destination.

JUANGRIEGO
Set in a fine bay in the northern part of Margarita, Juangriego has 10,000 inhabitants and is growing quickly. Having covered the waterfront along the bay, it now spreads inland. The beach and the bay, with the rustic fishing boats and visiting yachts, are very enjoyable places to hang around. Far on the horizon, the peaks of Macanao are visible, and are particularly spectacular when the sun sets beyond them.

The **Fortín de la Galera**, the fort crowning the hill just north of town, is today nothing more than a ring of stone walls with a terrace and a refreshment stand on the top. It provides a good view of the sunset, at which time it is packed with tourists, though a similarly attractive vista can be had from the beach in town.

North of town and up to the northernmost point of the island are half a dozen beaches in their respective bays, some developed, others isolated and almost virgin. The first, **Playa La Galera**, is just north of the fort. It's lined with restaurants, but is unpleasant due to the stink from the contaminated lagoon just behind it.

The paved road continues two km north to **Playa Caribe**. This beach is wide, long, clean and still relatively solitary, though perhaps not for long, as a large tourist complex is being built. There are a few restaurants. The next beach, **Playa La Boquita**, is probably the most deserted in the whole area but has almost no shade at all.

Places to Stay & Eat
Roughly in the middle of Juangriego beach is a white house, the *Hotel Nuevo Juangriego*. Choose a room facing the bay (double with bath for US$9) for a perfect snap of the sunset from your window. Downstairs is the restaurant, with some umbrella-shaded tables outside on a terrace and others right on the beach, serving slightly overpriced food.

Hotel El Fortín, a few hundred metres north along the beach, offers better standards for the same price and has equally excellent sunset views, though there are only three rooms facing the bay. Its restaurant, and *El Búho*, next door, are more pleasant places to eat than the Nuevo Juangriego. *El Viejo Muelle*, a few paces away, is yet another romantic place for a beer at sunset, though again, there seems to be an increase in food prices for the location.

Other accommodation options include *Hotel Gran Sol*, on the waterfront promenade (US$15 a double), and the *Hotel Digida*, 100 metres inland (US$12 a double). There are several other hotels in the same area.

You'll find several cheap, basic places to eat further off the beach, such as *Don Arepón*, on the corner of calles Guevara and Marcano, close to Hotel Digida.

Getting There & Away
Frequent micros run between Porlamar and Juangriego (US$0.40).

VENEZUELA

PARQUE NACIONAL LAGUNA DE LA RESTINGA

Laguna de la Restinga is one of two national parks on the island (the other is Cerro El Copey, near La Asunción). The park protects the lagoon, with its extensive mangrove area, at the western end of the lake. This is a favourite habitat for a variety of birds, including pelicans, cormorants and scarlet ibis.

Busetas from the waterfront in Porlamar go regularly to La Restinga (US$0.80) and deposit you at the entrance to the wharf. From there, five-seat motor boats will take you for a round trip (US$9 per boat) along a maze of caños that cut through thick mangroves. The excursion includes a stop on a fine shell beach, where you can grab a good fried fish in one of the open-air restaurants before returning.

BEACHES

Isla de Margarita has 167 km of shoreline and some 50 named beaches, not to mention smaller bits of sandy coast. Many beaches have been developed, with a range of services such as restaurants, bars, and deckchairs and sunshades for hire. Though the island is no longer a virgin paradise, you can still find a relatively deserted strip of sand.

On the whole, Margarita's beaches have little shade, and some are virtually barren. The beaches on the northern and eastern coasts are better than those skirting the southern shore of the island.

If you are after a well-developed beach, go to trendy Playa El Agua, where you can rub shoulders with members of Venezuela's artistic circles. Other popular destinations include Playa Guacuco and Playa Manzanillo. Perhaps Margarita's finest beach is Playa Puerto Cruz, which apparently has the widest, whitest stretch of sand and still isn't overdeveloped. If you want to escape from people, head for the northern coast of Macanao, which is the wildest part of the island. In the main, eastern section of Margarita, one of the most deserted beaches is

Playa La Boquita (see the Juangriego section for more information).

You can camp on the beach if you wish, but use common sense and be cautious. Don't leave your tent unattended.

The Guayana Highlands

South of the Río Orinoco, the land gradually rises to the uplands known as the Guayana Highlands, which occupy the whole of Venezuela's south-east and extend into Brazil and Guyana. This is one of the most amazing and unusual parts of the country, and well worth exploring. Here is the famous Salto Angel, the world's highest waterfall, and the unique Gran Sabana, a mysterious rolling savanna dotted with dozens of tepuis, the massive table mountains. One of them, Roraima, can be climbed, and this trip is, in opinion of many travellers (and the author), the most extraordinary adventure in the country.

The Guayana Highlands lie in the state of Bolívar, the largest state in Venezuela, occupying approximately one-quarter of the national territory. The only two important cities are Ciudad Bolívar and Ciudad Guayana, both on the bank of the Orinoco; most of the region is very sparsely populated. Much of the southern part of the state (30,000 sq km) is part of Parque Nacional Canaima, which includes within its boundaries La Gran Sabana, Roraima and Salto Angel. The Ciudad Guayana-Santa Elena highway, which cuts across the state, provides access to this fascinating land.

CIUDAD BOLÍVAR

Ciudad Bolívar is a hot city on the south bank of the Río Orinoco, about 420 km upstream from the Atlantic. Founded in 1764 on a rocky elevation at the river's narrowest point, the town was appropriately named Angostura (literally 'narrows'), and grew slowly as a sleepy backwater river port hundreds of miles from any important centres of population. Then, suddenly and unexpectedly, Angostura became the place where much of the country's (and the continent's) history was forged.

It was here that Bolívar came in 1817, soon after the town had been liberated from Spanish control, and set up the base for the military operations that led to the final stage of the War of Independence. The town was made the provisional capital of the country (which had yet to be liberated). It was in Angostura that the British Legionnaires joined Bolívar before they all set off for the battle of Boyacá, which secured Colombian independence. Finally, it was here that the Angostura Congress convened, in 1819, to give birth to Gran Colombia, a unified republic comprising Venezuela, Colombia and Ecuador. In honour of El Libertador, the town was renamed Ciudad Bolívar in 1846.

Today, Ciudad Bolívar is the capital of Bolívar state, and a fair-sized city, with some 270,000 inhabitants. It has retained the flavour of an old river town, and has some colonial architecture dating from its short, 50-year colonial era.

Information

Tourist Office The tourist office (☎ 26491), in a pavilion next to the airport terminal, is open on weekdays from 8.30 am to noon and 2 to 5.30 pm.

Money There are four useful banks on or near Paseo Orinoco: Banco Italo Venezolano and Banco International change cash and travellers' cheques, Banco de Venezuela accepts Visa and Mastercard, and Banco Unión handles all these operations. Moneychangers around the entrance of Gran Hotel Bolívar change dollars, for 2% less than banks.

If you need a bank near the airport, the Banco Consolidado is on the corner of avenidas Jesús Soto and Andrés Bello, 100 metres east of the airport terminal.

Inparques The Inparques office is in the Edificio de la CVG, on Avenida Germania (corner of Avenida Andrés Bello). Get a permit here for Parque Nacional Canaima if you want to camp anywhere in the park.

Tours Ciudad Bolívar is the main gateway to Salto Angel, as almost all flights to the waterfall either originate from the city or pass through it. Accordingly, trips to the falls are the staple of all tour operators and small carriers. Almost all are in the airport terminal, so shop around there. For further details, see the Salto Angel section.

Other tours from Ciudad Bolívar include trips to La Gran Sabana and Roraima. The former can be organised much more cheaply from Santa Elena de Uairén, while the latter is best done on your own; agents in Ciudad Bolívar will ask at least US$350 per person for this trip. If you are interested, contact Rosario Enrique Zambrano of Neckar Tour, in Gran Hotel Bolívar. Some agents may tell you that it's impossible to go to Roraima on your own; it's not true.

Pop into Hotel Italia, which has a board advertising trips by independent operators, such as an all-inclusive boat trip from Ciudad Bolívar to Puerto Ayacucho (US$75, two days).

Things to See

Stroll along **Paseo Orinoco**, an attractive waterfront boulevard lined with arcaded houses, some of which mark important historical events of Bolívar's days. Midway along the Paseo is the **Mirador Angostura**, a rocky headland that juts out into the river at its narrowest point. The lookout commands good views up and down the Río Orinoco. Five km upriver is a suspension bridge, **Puente de Angostura**, constructed in 1967; it's the only bridge across the Orinoco on its entire course.

Across the Paseo from the lookout, on the corner of Calle Igualdad, the **Museo Etnográfico** features the crafts of Indian tribes from Venezuela's south. Two blocks west along the Paseo, you'll come across the **Museo de Ciudad Bolívar**, housed in the Casa del Correo del Orinoco. It was here that the republic's first newspaper was printed, in 1818, and you can see the original press on

Ciudad Bolívar

■ PLACES TO STAY

5	Gran Hotel Bolívar
8	Hotel Caracas
9	Hotel Italia
10	Hotel Delicias
11	Hotel Boyacá
12	Hotel Ritz
14	Hotel Unión
25	Hotel Roma

▼ PLACES TO EAT

1	Restaurant El Mirador
13	Restaurant Comidas Criollas
16	Tasca La Playa
18	Restaurant My Ha My
21	Arepera El Gran Boulevard
22	Gran Fraternidad Universal

OTHER

1	Mirador Angostura
2	Museo de Ciudad Bolívar
3	Museo Etnográfico
4	Banco Internacional
6	Banco de Venezuela
7	Banco Italo Venezolano
15	Banco Unión
17	Auyantepuy Travel Agency
19	Catedral
20	Casa del Congreso de Angostura
23	Di Blasio Travel Agency
24	Iglesia de las Siervas
26	Centro de las Artes

which it was done, along with other objects related to the town's history.

Walk south up the hill to the historic heart of the city, **Plaza Bolívar**. Apart from the usual monument to El Libertador in the middle, five allegorical statues on the square depict the five countries Bolívar liberated. To the east looms the massive **Catedral**, begun right after the town's foundation and completed 80 years later. Half of the western side of the plaza is taken by the **Casa del Congreso de Angostura**, built in the 1770s. It was the seat of the lengthy debates of the 1819 Angostura Congress which eventually agreed to create Gran Colombia. You can have a look around the interior of the house.

Three blocks south of Plaza Bolívar is the pleasantly shaded **Plaza Miranda**. A sizeable building on its eastern side is the **Centro de las Artes**, which stages temporary exhibitions. From its south-facing windows, there is a good view of **Fortín El Zamuro**, crowning the top of the highest hill in the city, half a km south-west of the Centro. The fort is open for visitors and provides fine views over the old town.

Beyond the fort, on the corner of Avenida Táchira and Calle 11 de Abril, is the **Museo Casa San Isidro**, in the beautiful colonial house of a hacienda which once stretched up to the airport, but is now little more than a garden. The house interior is kept in its original 18th-century style. It can be visited Tuesday to Saturday from 9 am to noon and 2.30 to 5 pm, and on Sunday from 9 am to noon.

Proceed one km south on Avenida Táchira and take the perpendicular Avenida Briceño Irragorry to the left, which will lead you to the **Museo de Arte Moderno Jesús Soto**. The museum has an amazing collection of works by this well-known kinetic artist (born in Ciudad Bolívar in 1923) as well as works by other national and international artists. The museum is open Tuesday to Friday from 9.30 am to 5.30 pm, and on weekends from 10 am to 5 pm.

Places to Stay

The most pleasant area to stay is the bustling and atmospheric Paseo Orinoco, and fortunately the majority of budget hotels are gathered on or just off this street. An agreeable quieter alternative would be the old town, but there are virtually no hotels in the vicinity of Plaza Bolívar. All hotels listed have fans in rooms (or air-conditioning where indicated).

One of the cheapest in town is the *Hotel Boyacá*, on Calle Babilonia (US$4 a double), but it's basic and does some trade on an hourly basis.

A decent double room without bath can be had for US$5 in *Hotel Ritz* (☎ 23886), Calle Libertad 3, or *Hotel Delicias* (☎ 20215), Calle Venezuela 6. The Ritz also has rooms

VENEZUELA

with air-conditioning and bath for US$9; the Delicias is located in an old, increasingly dilapidated house, but has some charm (choose a large room upstairs).

For cheap rooms with private bath near the riverfront, try *Hotel Unión* (☎ 23374), Calle Urica 11, or *Hotel Caracas* (☎ 26089), Paseo Orinoco 82. Either has singles/doubles for US$5/6. The Unión provides slightly better standards but the Caracas has a large terrace overlooking the Paseo, on which to sit enjoying the evening breeze, having a beer.

If price is more important than location, go to *Hotel Roma*, on Avenida Cumaná five blocks south of the river (US$4/5 with bath). The rooms are dark but otherwise OK.

Hotel Italia (☎ 20015), Paseo Orinoco 131, is perhaps the most popular among foreigners (US$6/8 with bath and fan, US$8/10 with air-conditioning). There's a good, cheap restaurant attached.

Undoubtedly the best place to stay on the Paseo is the old-style *Gran Hotel Bolívar* (☎ 20101), where comfortable air-conditioned singles/doubles/triples cost US$18/22/26. You can eat in one of the two hotel restaurants.

Places to Eat

Perhaps the best inexpensive choice in the area of Paseo Orinoco is the restaurant of the *Hotel Italia*. Two blocks south, *Tasca La Playa* is more expensive.

About the cheapest typical food is to be found at the market, at the far eastern end of Paseo Orinoco. The *Comidas Criollas*, on Calle Piar, is a shabby-looking eatery but has tasty, cheap typical food. The best central arepera is *El Gran Boulevard*, where you can get arepas with a score of fillings.

In the old town, one block downhill from the catedral, the *My Ha My* is a simple place serving cheap pseudo-Chinese food. The *Gran Fraternidad Universal*, on Calle Amor Patrio, has good, cheap vegetarian meals, at lunchtime only. Be there soon after noon, as they run out of food quickly.

Don't forget the two restaurants in *Gran Hotel Bolívar*, which have some Italian dishes, at affordable prices. If *El Mirador* open-air restaurant has reopened, it may be a good up-market proposition.

Getting There & Away

Air The airport is two km south-east of the riverfront, and is linked to the city centre by frequent busetas. Many eastbound busetas from Paseo Orinoco will take you there. There are three flights daily to Caracas with Avensa (US$39) and one with Aeropostal (US$33). Aeropostal flies once a day to Barcelona (US$20).

Aereotuy has a daily morning flight to Santa Elena de Uairén (US$50). These flights, on 19-seat light planes, usually have a few stopovers, which vary from day to day.

Avensa has one flight a day to Canaima (US$40) but will only sell you tickets on the day of the flight (they first want to fill up their package excursions, which are more profitable). Two travel agencies in the city centre, Di Blasio (☎ 21931) at Avenida Cumaná 6, and Auyantepuy (☎ 20748) on Boulevard Bolívar, will probably sell the Avensa tickets to Canaima in advance. Several small local carriers operate regional flights, mostly to Canaima, on a charter basis. See the Salto Angel section for further details about all these flights.

Bus The bus station is at the junction of avenidas República and Sucre, about two km south of the centre; take the westbound buseta marked 'Terminal' from Paseo Orinoco. Busetas to southern suburbs will also drop you at the bus station. Buses to Caracas run regularly throughout the day (US$8.75 ordinary, US$10 deluxe, eight to nine hours). There are four buses a day to Santa Elena (US$10.50). The 'Especial' bus is faster (11 hours) than the 'Regional', which calls at towns en route and may take up to 14 hours. Additionally, there's the express bus coming through from Caracas, which reaches Santa Elena in less than 10 hours (US$13). A number of buses run to Barcelona (US$4.25, four hours). To Ciudad Guayana, buses depart every 15 minutes or so (US$1.50, 1½ hours).

CIUDAD GUAYANA

On the southern bank of the Río Orinoco at its confluence with the Río Caroní, Ciudad Guayana is a somewhat strange city. It was officially founded in 1961 to serve as an industrial centre of the region, and took into its metropolitan boundaries two quite different urban components: the old town of San Félix, on the eastern side of the Caroní, and the new town of Puerto Ordaz, on the opposite bank. Thirty years later, the two parts have virtually merged, into a 20-km urban sprawl populated by over 600,000 people, and together comprise Venezuela's fastest-growing city. Despite its unified name, people persistently refer to either San Félix or Puerto Ordaz, depending on which part they are talking about.

San Félix was founded in the 16th century, but there's nothing apparently old in the town, apart perhaps from its chessboard layout. The town's centre is a busy, dirty commercial sector with nondescript architecture. It's essentially the workers' suburb, where they eat, shop and entertain themselves.

Puerto Ordaz is quite a different story: it's modern and well planned, with a good infrastructure of roads, supermarkets and services. The centre is quite clean and pleasant, and the cream of restaurants and trendy shops are here. It's basically the executive zone, as you can easily tell from the people, their cars and the general atmosphere.

Information

Tourist Office The tourist office is at the airport, but don't make a special trip there. It's better to call at any of the travel agencies in the centre of Puerto Ordaz (see Tours).

Money As elsewhere, changing money is a bit of a trial-and-error affair and may involve some tramping around. Most central banks are marked on the Puerto Ordaz map.

At the time of writing, the Banco Consolidado, Banco Unión, Banco de Venezuela and Banco del Caribe change cash and travellers' cheques. Banco Unión gives cash advances on Visa and MasterCard. Visa

cards are also handled by the Banco Latino, and Mastercard by the Banco Mercantil.

Tours A dozen travel agencies organise tours, those with perhaps the best reputations being Anaconda Tours (☎ 223130) on Avenida Las Américas, Selva Tours (☎ 225537) on Calle Caura, Keyla Tours (☎ 229195) on Avenida Monseñor Zabaleta, and Happy Tour (☎ 227748) in the Hotel Intercontinental Guayana.

Their staple offer is the four to five-day tour around La Gran Sabana, including visits to most waterfalls (US$80 to US$90 per day). It works out far cheaper to go by bus to Santa Elena and arrange the tour there (see the Santa Elena de Uairén section for details).

Another tour offered by agents is the three to four-day boat trip around the delta of the Orinoco, including calls at Warao Indian settlements. This, too, is an expensive proposition (about US$80 to US$90 per day).

Tours to Salto Angel are better arranged in Ciudad Bolívar, as all flights to Canaima go from there.

Things to See

The town's number one attraction is the **Parque Cachamay**, a pleasant riverside park, a 15-minute walk south from the centre of Puerto Ordaz. It's here that the Río Caroní speeds its flow, turning into a series of rapids and eventually into a spectacular 200-metre-wide line of waterfalls. Adjoining the park from the south-west is the **Parque Loefling** (named after a Swedish botanist), where there's a small zoo, with some animals in cages and others wandering freely around. Both parks are open Tuesday to Sunday from 5.30 am to 6.30 pm. Admission is free.

Another park noted for its falls, **Parque La Llovizna**, is on the southern outskirts of San Félix, but there's no direct public transport. Take the urban bus marked 'Buen Retiro' south from the bus terminal along Avenida Gumilla (towards El Pao). Get off when the bus turns left, continue walking

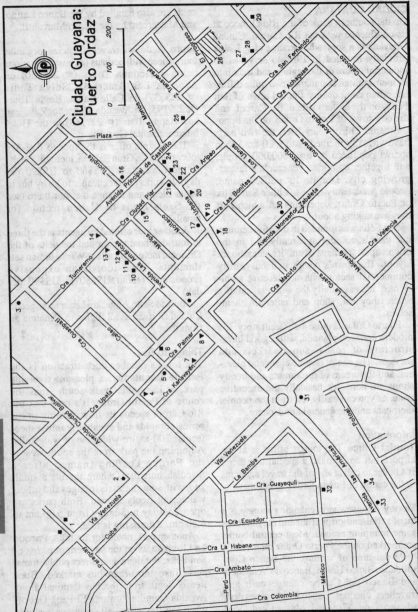

Ciudad Guayana: Puerto Ordaz

■ PLACES TO STAY	▼ PLACES TO EAT	OTHER
1 Hotel Rasil	4 Marisquería La	2 Banco Mercantil
6 Hotel Tepuy	Mansión	3 Banco Latino
10 Hotel Habana Cuba	7 Restaurant Marcelo	5 CANTV Office
11 Hotel La Guayana	8 Restaurant Las	9 Banco de Venezuela
22 Hotel Saint Georges	Américas	12 Anaconda Tours
23 Hotel Carlos	13 La Casa del Croissant	16 Banco Unión
24 Hotel Embajador	14 Restaurant Rincón	17 Banco del Caribe
25 Residencias Santa	Bavaria	21 Banco Consolidado
Cruz	15 Restaurant La	26 Mercado Popular
27 Residencias	Romanina	Castillito
Montecarlo	18 Parrillada Jolly	30 Keyla Tours
28 Hotel Roma	19 Parrillada La Fogata	31 CANTV Office
29 Residencias 101	20 El Arepazo Guayanés	33 Brazilian Consulate
32 Hotel Dos Ríos	34 Restaurant El	
	Bodegón	

two km south on the Avenida and take the right turn-off marked 'Salto La Llovizna' for another two km, to the visitors' centre. From there, a free bus shuttles to the park every hour or so from 9 am to 3 pm Tuesday to Sunday. Several viewpoints in the park will let you see the falls from various angles.

In the centre of San Félix there is really not much to see. The only quiet and agreeable place is the green belt along the Orinoco bank, just off Plaza Bolívar. The **catedral** on the eastern side of the square looks more like a storehouse than a church. Beyond it spreads a particularly lively and dirty **market**.

Places to Stay

Both San Félix and Puerto Ordaz have a range of hotels. As might be expected, accommodation in San Félix is poorer, but paradoxically, it's more expensive than in Puerto Ordaz. It's a good idea to stay in Puerto Ordaz, not only for a lower price and better value, but also for convenience, nicer surroundings and security. All hotels listed below have private baths and either fan or air-conditioning. Only the top-end hotels have hot water, but it's hardly necessary in this steamy climate.

In Puerto Ordaz, the main hotel area is in the centre, around the Avenida Principal de

Castillito. Supposedly the cheapest in town is the *Residencias Montecarlo* (US$4 a double), but it is full most of the time. The *Hotel Roma* (☎ 223780), next door, is a much more reliable choice and is quite acceptable for the price (US$6 a double). Round the corner, *Residencias 101* offers a similar price and standard, as does the *Residencias Santa Cruz*, in the same area. All the above double as love hotels.

A decent double room for around US$10 can be found in *Hotel Habana Cuba* (☎ 224904) on Avenida Las Américas, or in the *Hotel Carlos* (☎ 225557) on Calle Urbana. For a few dollars more, you can stay in the quite good *Hotel La Guayana* (☎ 227375) on Avenida Las Américas, the *Hotel Saint Georges* (☎ 220088) on Carrera Aripao, or (the best of the lot) the *Hotel Tepuy* (☎ 220120) on Carrera Upata.

Places to Eat

In Puerto Ordaz, the bottom end of the gastronomic scene is represented by the street stalls along Avenida Principal de Castillito and Calle Los Llanos, in the budget hotel area. There are several chicken places there where you can get a filling meal of half a chicken with yuca and salad for less than US$3. Also try the Mercado Popular Castillito, in the same area, for cheap meals.

VENEZUELA

Popular *El Arepazo Guayanés*, on Calle Urbana, serves arepas filled with everything from cheese to seafood (US$1 each). Up the same street are two parrilladas, *La Fogata* and *Jolly*, with good Argentine steaks. *Las Américas*, on Avenida Las Américas, does the same for a little less.

There are several restaurants on Carrera Ciudad Piar and its continuation, Carrera Tumeremo, of which *La Romanina* is possibly the best for both Italian food and steaks. Just round the corner, on Avenida Las Américas, is a good German restaurant, *Rincón Bavaria*.

Getting There & Away

Air The airport is at the western end of Puerto Ordaz, on the road to Ciudad Bolívar. Urban busetas don't call directly at the airport, but they pass within reasonable walking distance. Aeropostal has direct flights only to Caracas (US$36, five flights daily), but there are connections from there to almost anywhere in the country. Avensa has direct flights to Caracas (US$40), Valencia and Isla de Margarita, and plenty of connections to other destinations.

Bus The bus terminal is in San Félix, about one km south of the centre. Plenty of local busetas pass the bus terminal on their way between Puerto Ordaz and San Félix. Buses to Ciudad Bolívar depart every 15 minutes or so (US$1.50, 1½ hours). There are regular departures to Caracas (US$10.50, 10 hours). Four buses daily, with Transporte Mundial and Expresos Orinoco go to Santa Elena (US$9, nine to 12 hours); all buses come through from Ciudad Bolívar. Expresos Maturín has buses north to the coast, to Carúpano (US$5.50, 6½ hours) and Güiria (US$7.50, nine hours); these trips involve a ferry trip across the Río Orinoco, from San Félix to Los Barrancos.

SALTO ANGEL

Angel Falls, known in the Pemón Indian language as Churún Merú, are the world's highest waterfall, crashing 979 metres in a single, uninterrupted drop 16 times the height of Niagara. Salto Angel spills from the Auyantepui, the largest (but not the highest) of the entire group of tepuis, with a flat top of about 700 sq km.

The fall is not named, as one might expect, after a divine creature, but after an American bush pilot. Jimmy Angel landed on the boggy top of the tepui in 1937 in his four-seater aeroplane, in search of gold. He couldn't take off again, however, so Angel, his wife and two companions cut a trail through virgin terrain to the edge of the plateau, then miraculously managed to descend over a km of almost vertical cliff, to return to civilisation after a breathtaking 11-day odyssey.

The waterfall drops from the northern side of the tepui into what is known as Devil's Canyon. At times in the dry season (January to May), it can be pretty faint – just a thin ribbon of water turning into mist halfway down its drop. In the rainy months (June to December), it's often voluminous and spectacular, but frequently covered by clouds.

About 50 km north-west of the waterfall is Canaima, a base for trips to Salto Angel. Canaima is not much more than an airstrip, a tourist camp and a horde of tour operators with their planes, boats and jeeps. They offer a range of excursions to Salto Angel and also to other nearby falls, Indian villages, and whatever interesting sights they have discovered in the area.

The camp consists of a bungalow colony, a restaurant and souvenir shops, all very expensive. It is attractively set on the bank of a peaceful, wide section of the Río Carrao, just below the point where the river turns into a cascade of seven consecutive falls, known as Salto Hacha (Hacha Falls).

Getting There & Away

A visit to Salto Angel is usually done in two stages, with a break in Canaima. Except for two long, adventurous overland routes, access to Canaima is by air only. Avensa has a daily morning flight on big jets from Caracas to Canaima (US$63 one-way) via Ciudad Bolívar (US$40 from Ciudad Bolívar). These flights don't pass over Salto

Angel; occasionally, pilots detour to please tourists, but it will be just a short glimpse. Avensa also offers expensive two and three-day packages including meals and accommodation in Canaima. In the high season, book these flights in advance.

No trails go all the way from Canaima to Salto Angel, so you have two options – boat or plane. Motorised canoes operate only in the rainy season, June to November, when the water level is sufficiently high. The boats depart from above Salto Hacha and go up the Carrao and Churún rivers to the base of the fall. The trip usually takes three days upstream and one day back. Several operators offer this trip, but you won't find anything cheaper than US$250 per person, with a minimum of five to six people in a group.

Flying is faster and cheaper. Five-seat Cessnas are waiting to take tourists for a 45-minute flight (about US$45 a head). The pilots fly two or three times back and forth at the face of the fall, circle the top of the tepui and then return.

If you come independently, you can reduce expenses by camping near the Inparques post. Make sure you have the permit for the park (available in Caracas or Ciudad Bolívar). Bring all your own food, as a meal in a restaurant costs about US$10.

Given the cost and effort involved in doing the trip on your own, it probably works out cheaper and more convenient to take a tour from Ciudad Bolívar. Most tour operators offer one-day return trips to the fall on light (usually five-seat) planes. The tour includes the flight over the Salto, lunch and a short boat excursion to other nearby falls (usually Salto del Sapo). Tours depart from Ciudad Bolívar around 7 to 8 am and return at 4 to 5 pm. The price is US$130 to US$140. Two-day trips are also available with some operators (about US$200, all inclusive).

Rutaca, a regional airline, is apparently the only operator which offers no-frills, half-day trips to Salto Angel (without lunch or side excursions), for around US$100.

All these trips operate on a charter basis, with a five-person minimum (or you pay for the empty seats). Most operators won't accept credit cards, or will charge 5% to 10% more if you pay with a credit card. Shop around the airport and choose the excursion that suits you.

LA GRAN SABANA

This rolling grassy highland in Venezuela's far south-eastern corner is vast, wild, beautiful, empty and silent. The only town in the region is Santa Elena de Uairén, near the Brazilian frontier. The rest of the sparse population, mostly Pemón Indians, who were the traditional inhabitants of this land, live in scattered villages and hamlets.

Until recently, La Gran Sabana was virtually inaccessible by land. Only in 1973 was an unsurfaced road between El Dorado and Santa Elena completed, and it was not until 1990 that the last stretch of this road was paved. Today, it's one of the best highways in the country, and one of the most spectacular. The road has been marked with kilometrage signs from the El Dorado fork (km 0) southwards to Santa Elena (km 319).

Undoubtedly, the most striking natural features of La Gran Sabana are tepuis, gigantic sandstone mesas that dominate the skyline. Tepui (also spelled tepuy) is the Pemón Indian word for 'mountain', and was adopted as the term to identify this specific type of mesa. There are over 100 such plateaux dotting the vast region from the Colombian border in the west up into Guyana and Brazil in the east. Their major concentration is in La Gran Sabana. The best-known of all tepuis is Roraima, one of the few that can be climbed (see the following section), though it is a trip of at least five days.

There are many other sights in the Sabana that are easier to explore; some are conveniently located on the main road. Particularly amazing are waterfalls, and there are a maze of them. One of the best examples easily accessible from the road is **Salto Kamá** (km 202), 50-metre-high twin waterfalls. Don't miss going down to the foot for the best view.

Salto Yuruaní (km 247) is a wonderful mini-Niagara, about five metres high and 50

La Gran Sabana

metres wide. **Quebrada de Jaspe** (km 273) is a small cascade made particularly beautiful by the red jasper rock of the creekbed.

The star attraction is probably the 105-metre-high **Salto Aponguao**, also known by its Indian name, Chinak Merú. This one is harder to get to, as it's about 40 km off the highway, near the small Indian hamlet of Iboribó, accessible by a rough road.

Places to Stay & Eat

Simple accommodation and meals are available in a number of places throughout La Gran Sabana, including Kavanayén, Chivatón, Iboribó, Rápidos de Kaimorán (km 172), Salto Kamá (km 202), Quebrada Pacheco (km 237) and San Francisco de Yuruaní (km 250). You can camp virtually anywhere you wish.

Getting Around

Getting around the Sabana is not easy, as public transport only operates on the highway and is infrequent (four buses a day in either direction). Given time, you can visit the sights on the main road using a combination of hitching and buses. Heading towards Kavanayén, however, may prove difficult, as there are no buses on this road and traffic is sporadic. A comfortable solution is a tour from Santa Elena (see that section for details).

Whichever way you choose to explore the region, bring plenty of good insect repellent. The Sabana is infested by a kind of small gnat known as *jején*, commonly called *la plaga*. They are particularly voracious in the morning and late afternoon, and the bites itch for days.

RORAIMA

Roraima, on the tripartite border of Venezuela, Guyana and Brazil, is one of the largest and highest tepuis – its plateau is at some 2700 metres and the highest peak at 2810 metres. It was the first of the tepuis on which a climb was recorded, in 1884, and has been much explored by botanists. It's the easiest table mountain to ascend, and is increasingly popular among travellers. Perhaps 100 people go to the top every month in the dry season, about 80% of whom are foreigners.

Climbing Roraima

The usual starting point for the trip is the small village of **San Francisco de Yuruaní**, 69 km north of Santa Elena on the main road. There's a small *Hospedaje Minina*, in a white roadside house at the northern end of the village. A few basic eateries, including *Restaurant Roraima*, at the central junction, will keep you going.

You first must get to the village of **Paraitepui**, about 25 km east of San Francisco – hire a jeep in San Francisco (US$50, regardless of the number of passengers up to about 10) or walk. The road to Paraitepui branches off the highway one km south of the village. The unpaved but acceptable road turns midway into a dusty but jeepable track. It's a hot, steady seven-hour walk, mostly uphill, to Paraitepui (in reverse, back to San Francisco, it's six hours). You may be lucky enough to hitch a jeep ride on this road, but traffic is sporadic and the drivers will probably charge you for the lift (a far more reasonable fare than the jeep rental in San Francisco).

Paraitepui is a shabby Indian village of about 270 people, whose identity has been largely shattered by tourists, or more precisely, by tourists' money. Heaps of empty beer cans at the entrance to the village will tell you how the money is spent.

Upon arrival, you will invariably be greeted by one of the village headmen, who will show you the list of guides (apparently every adult male in the village is a guide) and inform you about prices. Guides charge US$25 a day per group. Porters, if you need one, charge US$30 per day and can carry about 17 kg. Although you don't really need a guide to follow the track up to the tepui, the village headmen won't let you pass through without one.

There are no hotels in the village, but *camping* is possible on the central square near the school, in one of the two shelters (US$2 per person). Overpriced hot meals are available in the house behind the school. A few shops in the village sell basic food (canned fish, biscuits, soups) at exorbitant prices.

Once you have your guide, you set off for Roraima. The trip to the top takes two days (the net walking time is about 12 hours up and 10 hours down). There are several good places to camp (with water) on the way. The most popular camp sites are on the Río Tek (four hours from Paraitepui), on the Río Kukenán (30 minutes further on) and at the so-called *campamento base* (base camp), at the foot of Roraima (three hours uphill from the Río Kukenán). The steep, difficult four-hour ascent from the base camp to the top is the most spectacular part of the hike.

Once you reach the top, walk some 15 minutes to the place known as El Hotel, one of the few sites good for camping. It's actually a patch of sand, large enough for no more than four small tents, partly protected by an overhanging rock. There's another, smaller 'hotel' a 10-minute walk away.

The scenery all around is a moonscape, evocative of a science-fiction movie: impressive blackened rocks of every imaginable shape, gorges, creeks, pink beaches, and gardens filled with flowering plants you

VENEZUELA

have never seen before. Frequent and constantly changing mists and fogs add a mysterious air.

It's here that the guide finally becomes handy, as it's very easy to get lost in this labyrinth. Plan on staying at least one full day on the top, but it's better to allow two or three days. Ask your guide to take you to the Pozo, a curious round pool in a deep hole. It's about a three-hour walk from El Hotel. On the way, you'll pass the amazingly lush Valle Arabopo. Beyond the pool is the Valle de los Cristales and the Laberinto, both well worth a trip.

When to Go

The dry season in the region is from December to April, but the tops of the tepuis receive rain off the Atlantic all year round. The weather changes in a matter of minutes, with bright sunshine or heavy rain possible at any time.

What to Bring

A good tent, preferably with a flysheet, is a must. It's bitterly cold at night on the top, so bring a good sleeping bag and warm clothes. You also need reliable rain gear, sturdy shoes, a cooking stove and the usual hiking equipment. Bring enough food to share with your guide. There are plenty of nasty biting gnats on the way, so take an effective insect repellent. Don't forget a good supply of film. A macro lens is a great help in photographing the unique small plants. Don't forget plastic bags, to take *all* your garbage back down to civilisation.

Getting There and Away

San Francisco de Yuruaní is on the Ciudad Guayana-Santa Elena highway, with about four buses a day running in either direction. There are also por puestos between Santa Elena and San Francisco. Buy all food provisions at either starting point.

SANTA ELENA DE UAIRÉN

Founded in 1922, Santa Elena began to grow when diamonds were discovered in the 1930s in the region of Icabarú, some 100 km

to the west. Isolated from the centre of the country by the lack of roads, it remained a small village. The second development push came with the opening of the highway from El Dorado.

Today, Santa Elena is a pleasant, easy-going border town of 10,000 people, with an agreeable if damp climate, and a Brazilian air thanks to the large number of Brazilian residents. Small as it is, Santa Elena is the 'capital' of La Gran Sabana and the biggest town before you reach El Dorado, 320 km to the north.

Information

Tourist Office Santa Elena has no tourist office. Travel agencies are the place to go for information about the region.

Money The only bank, Banco Guayana, changes neither cash nor travellers' cheques. Various establishments, including shops, travel agencies and hotels, may change cash (at a rate about 3% lower than the bank rate) and occasionally travellers' cheques (paying about 10% less). La Boutique Zapatería is one of the most reliable places to change both cash and cheques, and offers the best rate. The next best is perhaps Anaconda Tours. Gold and diamond buyers (watch for boards that say 'Compro Oro y Diamantes') might buy dollars but not cheques.

If you are heading north into Venezuela, keep in mind that the next place you may be able to change money is El Dorado, though it's better to count on banks in either Ciudad Guayana or Ciudad Bolívar.

Brazilian Consulate The consulate is at the north-eastern end of town, close to the bus station. It's open on weekdays from 8 am till noon. It's a good idea to get your visa elsewhere, as this consulate doesn't seem to be very efficient.

Immigration The DIEX office, behind the consulate, is open on weekdays from 8 am to noon and 2 to 5 pm, and on weekends from 8 to 10 am and 2 to 4 pm. Be sure to have your passport stamped here before leaving

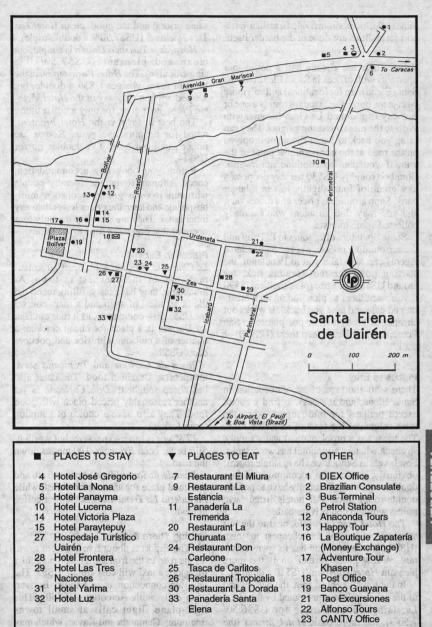

Santa Elena
de Uairén

0   100   200 m

■ PLACES TO STAY	▼ PLACES TO EAT	OTHER
4 Hotel José Gregorio	7 Restaurant El Miura	1 DIEX Office
5 Hotel La Nona	9 Restaurant La	2 Brazilian Consulate
8 Hotel Panayma	Estancia	3 Bus Terminal
10 Hotel Lucerna	11 Panadería La	6 Petrol Station
14 Hotel Victoria Plaza	Tremenda	12 Anaconda Tours
15 Hotel Paraytepuy	20 Restaurant La	13 Happy Tour
27 Hospedaje Turístico	Churuata	16 La Boutique Zapatería
Uairén	24 Restaurant Don	(Money Exchange)
28 Hotel Frontera	Carleone	17 Adventure Tour
29 Hotel Las Tres	25 Tasca de Carlitos	Khasen
Naciones	26 Restaurant Tropicalia	18 Post Office
31 Hotel Yarima	30 Restaurant La Dorada	19 Banco Guayana
32 Hotel Luz	33 Panadería Santa	21 Tao Excursions
	Elena	22 Alfonso Tours
		23 CANTV Office

Venezuela, or upon arrival. Brazilian passport formalities are done at the border itself.

Tours There are already half a dozen tour operators with offices in Santa Elena (see the Santa Elena map for locations) and still more with jeeps only. The standard tour is a one or two-day trip around La Gran Sabana, with visits to the most interesting sights. They can bring you back to Santa Elena, or drop you on the road at the northernmost point of the tour, if you plan to continue northwards. Count on roughly US$30 per day per person in a group of four, slightly less in a larger party. Shop around, as prices and routes vary, and you may find an agent who's already collected some tourists.

Some operators offer tours to El Paují and the surrounding region, west of Santa Elena. Agents can also take you to Paraitepui, the starting point for the Roraima trek, for around US$90 for a trip (plus another US$90 if you want them to pick you up on a prearranged date and take you back). It works out cheaper to go by bus or por puesto to San Francisco, and hire a jeep there (US$50) or walk.

Places to Stay

There's no shortage of accommodation in Santa Elena, and it's easy to find a room, except perhaps for mid-August, when the town celebrates the feast of its patron saint. The town has a problematical water supply, so check whether your hotel has water tanks. Few hotels in Santa Elena have single rooms; obviously, you can be accommodated in a double room but will usually have to pay the double-room price. All hotels listed have rooms with fan and private bath.

The *Hotel José Gregorio*, next to the bus terminal, is one of the cheapest in town (US$7.50 a double) and has its own restaurant. A few paces further on is the more pleasant *Hotel La Nona* (US$10 a double).

In the town's central area, the bottom end of the price scale is represented by the *Hotel Luz* (single/double/triple for US$6.50/7.50/9), the more basic *Hotel Yarima* (the same prices) and the good, clean *Hotel Las Tres Naciones* (US$7.50/9 a double/triple).

Hospedaje Turístico Uairén is simple, but clean and pleasant (US$7.50/10 a single/double). The *Hotel Paraytepuy*, in the heart of town, charges US$9 a double, but it's perhaps better to stay in the *Hotel Victoria Plaza*, next door, for only a dollar more.

The best in town is the *Hotel Frontera*, noted for its attractive patio. Rooms are rather small but have TV; doubles go for US$14.

Before you book any accommodation, check Alfonso Tours; the friendly couple who run it were going to open a mini-hospedaje and keep the prices lower than any other hotel. They are possibly the only tour operator that organises trips to the mines.

Places to Eat

La Churuata is an agreeable open-air restaurant, one of the cheapest in town. At lunchtime, they have tasty, filling menú del día (a set meal of soup and a main course) for US$2.50 – come early, as it runs out fast. *La Dorada* is a place for cheap chicken; a quarter of a chicken with rice and potatoes costs US$2.

Tasca de Carlitos and *Tropicalia* serve inexpensive Brazilian food. The latter also has cheap spaghetti. *Don Carleone* is yet another reasonably priced place with good food. They also have a choice of tempting tortas (cakes).

El Miura is more expensive, but worth it. Still better is *La Estancia*, 100 metres down the road.

Panadería Santa Elena opens at 6 am and is a good place for an early breakfast, while *Panadería La Tremenda* has the best coffee in town.

Getting There & Away

Air The airport is about five km from town, off the road to the frontier. There's no public transport; a taxi will cost around US$3. The only air connection is to Ciudad Bolívar, once daily with Aereotuy (US$50). This light-plane flight calls at small towns (including Camarata and Kavac, which may be starting points for trips to Salto Angel); the route varies from day to day. Anaconda Tours will book and sell tickets.

Bus The bus terminal is at the north-eastern end of town. There are four buses daily to Ciudad Bolívar (US$10.50, 11 to 14 hours) and one air-conditioned evening bus directly to Caracas (US$25.50, 16 hours). All these buses go via Ciudad Guayana.

Jeeps to El Paují depart early in the morning (US$7.50, three hours). Por puestos to San Francisco de Yuruaní run irregularly till the afternoon.

There's one morning bus to Boa Vista, Brazil (US$11, five to six hours). The road is unpaved, so after heavy rains, the trip may take longer. Come early to the bus station, buy the ticket, then go to the DIEX office, 100 metres away, to get the exit stamp in your passport. The border, locally known as 'La Línea', is about 15 km south of Santa Elena. The bus calls at the Brazilian border immigration post for passport formalities.

Amazonas

Venezuela's southernmost state, Amazonas, has an area of 175,000 sq km, approximately one-fifth of the national territory, yet it has, at most, 1% of the country's population. Despite its name, most of the territory lies in the Orinoco drainage basin, while the Amazon Basin takes up only the south-western portion of the state. The two basins are linked by the curious Casiquiare channel, which sends a portion of the water of the Río Orinoco to Río Negro and down to the Amazon.

The region is predominantly a thick tropical forest crisscrossed by a maze of rivers and sparsely populated by a mosaic of Indian peoples. The current Indian population is estimated at 30,000, half what it was in 1925. The three main Indian groups, Piaroa, Yanomami and Guajibo, make up about three-quarters of the whole indigenous population, while the remaining quarter is composed by the Yekuana, Curripaco, Guarekena, Piapoco, Yavitero, Tariana and a number of smaller tribes. Approximately 20 Indian languages are used in the region.

In contrast to the central Amazon Basin, Venezuelan Amazonas is quite diverse topographically, its most noticeable feature being the tepuis. Though not as numerous and perhaps not as 'classical' as in La Gran Sabana, they dot the area, giving the green carpet a distinctive and spectacular appearance.

The best-known of the tepuis is Cerro Autana, about 80 km south of Puerto Ayacucho. It is the sacred mountain of the Piaroa Indians, who consider it the birthplace of the universe. A unique cave about 200 metres below the top pierces the gigantic tepui.

Puerto Ayacucho, at the north-western tip of Amazonas, is the only town of significance, and is the main gateway and supply centre for the entire state. It's also the chief transport hub, from where a couple of small regional airlines fly in light planes to the major settlements of the region. As there are no roads, transport is by river or air. There's no regular passenger service on virtually any stretch of any river, which makes travel on your own difficult, if not next to impossible. Tour operators in Puerto Ayacucho have swiftly filled the gap and can take you just about everywhere – at a price, of course.

The climate is not uniform throughout the region. At the northern edge, there's a distinctive dry season from December to April. April is the hottest month. The rest of the year is marked by frequent heavy rains. Going southwards, the dry season becomes shorter and not so dry, and eventually disappears. Accordingly, the southern part of the Amazonas is wet all year round.

PUERTO AYACUCHO

On the middle reaches of the Río Orinoco, Puerto Ayacucho is the only fair-sized town in the region, and the capital of Amazonas. It was founded in 1924, together with another port, Samariapo, 63 km upriver; the two ports are linked by road, to bypass the

VENEZUELA

VENEZUELA

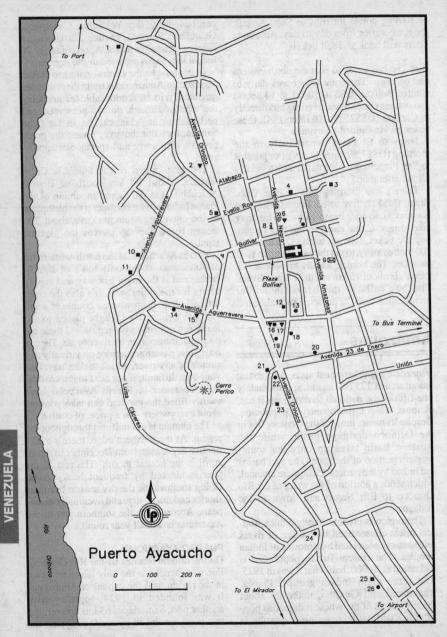

To Port

Avenida Orinoco

Atabapo

Evello Roa

Avenida Aguerrevere

Bolivar

Avenida Río Negro

Plaza
Bolívar

Avenida Aguerrevere

Avenida Amazonas

To Bus Terminal

Avenida 23 de Enero

Unión

Avenida Orinoco

Luisa Cáceres

Cerro
Perico

Río
Orinoco

To El Mirador

To Airport

Puerto Ayacucho

0   100   200 m

■ **PLACES TO STAY**

1	Hotel Orinoco
3	Gran Hotel Amazonas
4	Residencias Maguarí
5	Hotel Tobogán
10	Residencia Internacional
11	Residencias Ñajuana
21	Residencias Betty
23	Residencias Río Siapa
25	Hotel Apure

▼ **PLACES TO EAT**

2	Pollos y Parrillas El Cacique
6	Hostaría Río Negro
15	Restaurant La Estancia
16	Refresquería y Panadería Colonial
17	Restaurant Cherazad

OTHER

7	Autana Aventura
8	Tourist Office
9	Post Office
12	Museo Etnológico
13	Mercado Indígena (Indian Market)
14	DIEX Office
16	Warely Expeditions
18	Tobogán Tours
19	Banco Unión
20	Banco de Venezuela
22	Teatro Don Juan
24	Turismo Yutajé
26	CANTV Office

non-navigable stretch of the Orinoco cut by a series of rapids. The road served as an overland bridge to enable cargo to be shipped down the Río Orinoco from upper Amazonas.

For a long time, and particularly during the oil boom, Amazonas was a forgotten territory and the two ports were little more than obscure villages. The link between them was the only paved road in the whole region; the connection to the rest of the country was by a rough track. Only in the late 1980s, when this track was surfaced, did Puerto Ayacucho start to grow dramatically, to become a town of some 60,000 inhabitants. Paradoxically, the port which was responsible for the town's birth and initial growth has

lost much of its importance, as most cargo is now trucked in.

Puerto Ayacucho is the main gateway to Venezuelan Amazonia and is swiftly becoming a tourist centre. There's a range of hotels and restaurants, and several travel agents can take you up the Río Orinoco and its tributaries, deep into the jungle. Puerto Ayacucho is also a transit point on the way to Colombia and Brazil (see Getting There & Away in this section).

Information

Tourist Office The tourist office is in the building of the Gobernación, on Plaza Bolívar (enter from Avenida Río Negro). The office is open on weekdays from 8 am to noon and 2 to 5.30 pm.

Money The Banco de Venezuela and Banco Unión change cash but not travellers' cheques. Both have daily limits on the amount of foreign currency they can change, so go there early. The latter bank gives cash advances to Visa card holders.

The Hotel Orinoco may change your dollars and travellers' cheques, apparently at any time of the day, at a rate 3% lower than that given by the banks.

Immigration The DIEX office is on Avenida Aguerrevere and is open on weekdays from 8 am to noon and 2 to 6 pm, though it doesn't seem to keep to these hours very strictly. Get your passport stamped here when leaving/entering Venezuela.

Tours The tour business has flourished over the past few years; there are already more than half a dozen operators with their own offices, and a number of guides offering their services on the street. Tour agents have some standard tours, but most can arrange a tour according to your interests, time and money.

One of the most popular tours is a two to three-day trip up the Sipapo and Autana rivers to the foot of Cerro Autana. Expect to pay US$40 to US$60 per person per day, all inclusive.

A longer and more adventurous journey is

the so-called Ruta Humboldt, following the route of the grand explorer. The trip goes along the Orinoco, Casiquiare and Guainía rivers up to Maroa. From there, the boat is transported overland to Yavita, and you then return down the Atabapo and Orinoco back to Puerto Ayacucho. This is a fascinating trip, but takes six to 10 days and is expensive.

Some guides operating from the street offer a trip to the Yanomami tribe, in the far south-eastern part of the Amazonas, though theoretically at least, this is a restricted area requiring special permits. Be aware that the Yanomami are very vulnerable to introduced diseases.

Probably the best agency in town is Autana Aventura (☎ 21369), at Avenida Amazonas 91. Friendly and knowledgeable, they are not the cheapest but are professional and responsible.

Tobogán Tours (☎ 21700), at Avenida Río Negro 44, was the first agency to open in Puerto Ayacucho. They now focus on easy, mostly one-day tours, though they can also organise something more adventurous on demand. Their prices are rather high.

Check the offer of Turismo Yutajé (☎ 21664), Monte Bello 31, which can even take you to Manaus. They run a hotel for those who take part in their tours.

Things to See

Puerto Ayacucho is hot, but is pleasantly shaded by luxuriant mango trees and has some interesting sights. The **Museo Etnológico**, on Avenida Río Negro, gives an insight into the culture of the main Indian tribes of the region, including the Piaroa, Guajibo, Yekuana and Yanomami. It's a good selection, with interesting background information, in Spanish only. The museum is open Tuesday to Friday from 8.30 to 11 am and 2.30 to 6 pm, on Saturday from 9 am to noon and 3.30 to 7 pm, and on Sunday from 9 am to 1 pm. The entrance fee is US$0.50 (US$0.25 for students).

Right opposite the museum, the **Mercado Indígena** is held every Thursday and Friday morning. Here you can see and buy Indian crafts made for tourists, quite different from those in the museum.

The **Cerro Perico**, just south-west of the town centre, provides good views over the Río Orinoco and the town. Another hill, Cerro El Zamuro, commonly known as **El Mirador**, is 1½ km south of the centre and overlooks the Raudales Atures, the spectacular rapids that block river navigation (the other rapids, the Raudales Maipures, are near Samariapo). Both are far more impressive in the wet season, when the water is high. The water level can rise 15 metres in rainy periods.

There are some attractions around Puerto Ayacucho. The **Parque Tobogán de la Selva** is a large, steep, smooth rock with water running over it – a sort of natural slide. It's 30 km south of town along the Samariapo road, then six km off to the east. There's no transport directly to the park. You can either take a por puesto to Samariapo, get off at the turn-off and walk the remaining distance, or negotiate a taxi in Puerto Ayacucho. At weekends, it's quite easy to hitch, as the rock is a favourite place among the townspeople (who, unfortunately, leave it increasingly littered).

Another popular weekend place among locals, the **Pozo Azul** is a small pond with beautiful blue water, 30 km north of the town, just off the road.

Less frequented by locals, and perhaps more interesting, is the **Cerro Pintado**, a large rock with pre-Columbian petroglyphs carved high above the ground in a virtually inaccessible place. The Cerro is 17 km south of town and a few km off the main road, to the left. Try to arrange the trip with someone who knows the place. The best time to see the carvings is early in the morning or late in the afternoon.

Places to Stay

The town has a dozen hotels, some of which are already popular with foreign travellers. All those listed here have private baths, and fan or air-conditioning.

The best budget choice seems to be the *Residencia Internacional* (☎ 21242), at

Avenida Aguerrevere 18. It's simple, but clean, safe and friendly (US$5/6/8 a single/couple/double).

For a similar price, try the more central *Residencias Maguarí* (☎ 21120), Calle Evelio Roa 35, but it's unkempt, and seems to rent rooms on an hourly basis. Other inexpensive hotels (US$8 to US$10 a double) include the *Residencias Ñajuana*, close to the Internacional (a favourite place among bus drivers, so often full), the very small and simple *Residencias Betty*, and the appreciably better *Hotel Tobogán* (☎ 21320), on Avenida Orinoco.

The *Residencias Río Siapa* (☎ 21138), a pleasant place with friendly management, will give you the most for your money (US$11/13/16 a couple/double/triple). There's no sign at the entrance.

The *Gran Hotel Amazonas* (☎ 21155) was perhaps the best hotel in town when built, but its good days have gone. Singles/doubles/triples with noisy air-conditioning cost US$15/17/19.

At the moment, the best places to stay include the *Hotel Orinoco* (☎ 21285), on the north-western fringes of the town, near the port (US$25/32 a double/triple), and the brand-new *Hotel Apure* (☎ 21516), Avenida Orinoco 28, at the southern end of town (US$36 a double). Both have comfortable air-conditioned rooms.

There are several resort camps and cabañas outside town, but unless you have your own transport, they are not convenient.

Places to Eat

Many eateries are located along Avenida Orinoco, the main thoroughfare. *Refresquería y Panadería Colonial*, on the corner of avenidas Orinoco and Aguerrevere, has good tortillas con jamón, though the service is slow. About the cheapest chicken in town is served at *Pollos y Parrillas El Cacique*, in the market area on Avenida Orinoco.

La Estancia, on Avenida Aguerrevere, has perhaps the best food in town and is not expensive. Alternatively, try *Hostaría Río Negro*, on Avenida Río Negro, off Plaza Bolívar. Yet another good choice is the *Cherazad*, near the museum, which has some Arab dishes on the menu. Close to El Mirador, in the southern suburb, the *Montegrí* does good parrilladas.

Getting There & Away

Air The airport is six km south-east of the town centre; taxis cost US$4. There are two flights daily to Caracas (US$38 with Avensa, US$32 with Aeropostal).

Two small local carriers, Aguaysa and Wayumi, operate flights within Amazonas. There are daily flights to San Fernando de Atabapo (US$18), twice-weekly flights to San Juan de Manapiare (US$26) and one flight a week (usually on Saturday) to San Carlos de Río Negro (US$50). Other, smaller localities are serviced irregularly, depending on the demand.

Bus The bus terminal is a long way east of the centre, on the outskirts of town. To get there, take the city bus from Avenida 23 de Enero. Two night buses run daily to Caracas (US$16, 16 hours). Buses to Ciudad Bolívar depart regularly throughout the day (US$10.25, 10½ hours). There are also direct buses to Maracay and Valencia.

Boat There is no passenger boat service down the Río Orinoco, and cargo boats are infrequent.

To/From Brazil Take the Saturday flight from Puerto Ayacucho to San Carlos de Río Negro, from where irregular boats will take you to San Simón de Cocuy, on the border. Take a bus to São Gabriel (Brazil) and hunt there for cargo boats down the Río Negro to Manaus.

To/From Colombia The nearest Colombian town, Puerto Carreño, is at the confluence of the Meta and Orinoco rivers and is accessible in two ways.

Take a boat from the Puerto Ayacucho wharf (at the north-eastern end of town) across the Río Orinoco to Casuarito, a Colombian village. The boat runs regularly.

VENEZUELA

From Casuarito, the *voladora* (speed boat) departs at 4 pm for Puerto Carreño (US$5, one hour); in the opposite direction, the voladora leaves at 6 am.

Alternatively, get to El Burro (about 80 km north of Puerto Ayacucho) by bus, por puesto or hitching. Take a ferry across the Río Orinoco to Puerto Páez. Get the exit stamp in your passport from DIEX, if you haven't done it in Puerto Ayacucho. Boats between Puerto Páez and Puerto Carreño run regularly between 6 am and 6 pm.

Puerto Carreño is a long, one-street town with an airport, six or so hotels (El Vorágine,

near the Venezuelan Consulate, is the best budget bet) and a number of places to eat. Go to the DAS office, one block west of the main square, for an entry stamp. A number of shops will change bolívares to pesos. There are three flights per week to Bogotá (US$75). Buses go only in the dry season, from mid-December to mid-March approximately. They depart once a week, on Saturday at 3 am, for the two-day journey by rough road to Villavicencio (US$45). Villavicencio is four hours by bus from Bogotá.

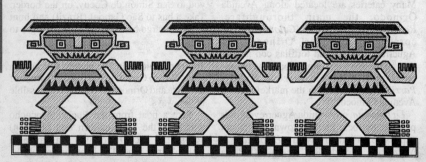

Falkland Islands (Islas Malvinas)

In the South Atlantic Ocean, 300 miles (500 km) east of Argentine Patagonia, the controversial Falkland Islands consist of two major islands and many smaller ones.

Facts About the Islands

HISTORY

Despite possible early Indian presence, the Islands were unpeopled when 17th-century European sailors began to frequent the area. Their Spanish name, Malvinas, derives from French navigators of St Malo.

In 1764, French colonists settled at Port Louis, East Falkland, but soon withdrew under Spanish pressure. Britain had planted an outpost at Port Egmont, West Falkland, which was expelled by Spain in 1767, restored under threat of war, and later abandoned in ambiguous circumstances.

Spain placed a penal colony at Port Louis, then abandoned it to whalers and sealers. In the early 1820s, the United Provinces of the River Plate claimed successor rights to Spain and Buenos Aires entrepreneur Louis Vernet attempted a livestock and sealing project, but Vernet's seizure of American sealers triggered reprisals which damaged Port Louis beyond recovery. Buenos Aires kept a token force there, but the British navy expelled it in 1833.

The Falklands languished until wool became an important commodity in the mid-19th century. The Falkland Islands Company (FIC) became the Islands' largest landholder, but immigrant entrepreneurs soon occupied all available pasture lands in large holdings.

The population of stranded mariners and holdover gauchos grew with the arrival of English and Scottish immigrants. About half resided in the port of Stanley, founded in 1844, while the rest worked on sheep stations. Most original landowners lived and worked in the Falklands, but their descen-

dents often returned to Britain and ran their businesses as absentees.

In the late 1970s, local government began to encourage subdivision of large landholdings to benefit family farmers. Change became even more rapid with the 1982 Falklands war and expansion of deep-sea fishing. There is speculation about, but no firm evidence of, offshore petroleum.

The Falklands War

Despite persistent Argentine claims to the Falklands, Britain was slow to acknowledge their seriousness. By 1971, the Foreign & Commonwealth Office reached a communications agreement giving Argentina a significant role in air transport, fuel supplies, shipping and even immigration.

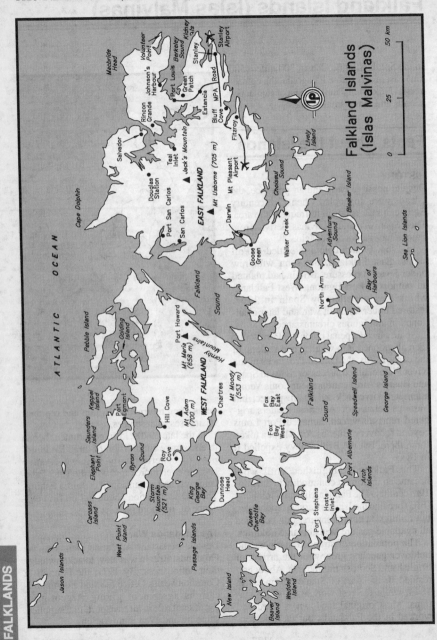

Falkland Islands (Islas Malvinas)

Concerned about Argentina's chronic instability, Islanders and their UK supporters thought the agreement ominous, and suspected the FCO of secretly arranging transfer of the Islands. This process dragged on for a decade, during which the brutal 'Dirty War' gave Islanders even more reason to fear Argentina.

General Leopoldo Galtieri's disintegrating military government, facing pressure from Argentines fed up with corruption, economic chaos and the totalitarian ruthlessness of 'The Process,' invaded the Islands on 2 April 1982. Seizure of the Malvinas briefly united the country, but British Prime Minister Margaret Thatcher, herself in shaky political circumstances, ordered a naval task force to retake the Islands.

Despite serious naval losses, experienced British troops routed ill-trained, poorly supplied Argentine conscripts. The most serious ground fighting took place at Goose Green, East Falkland, but Argentina's surrender averted destruction of Stanley.

GEOGRAPHY & CLIMATE

The Falklands' land area of 4700 sq miles (7564 sq km) is equivalent to Northern Ireland or the state of Connecticut. Falkland Sound separates East and West Falkland; only a few smaller islands have settlements. Despite its dismal reputation, the oceanic climate is temperate if windy. Summer temperatures rarely reach 75°F (24°C), but sustained subfreezing temperatures are unusual. Annual rainfall at Stanley is only about 24 inches (600 mm).

Except for East Falkland's low-lying Lafonia peninsula, the terrain is hilly to mountainous, but elevations do not exceed 2300 ft (705 metres). The most interesting geological features are 'stone runs' of quartzite boulders which descend from many ridges and peaks. Bays, inlets, estuaries and beaches make a attractive coastline, with abundant wildlife.

Flora & Fauna

Grasses and prostrate shrubs dominate the flora. Native tussock grass once lined the coast but proved vulnerable to overgrazing and fire. Most pasture is rank white grass *(Cortaderia pilosa)*, supporting only about one sheep per four or five acres.

Beaches, headlands and estuaries support large concentrations of sub-Antarctic wildlife. The Magellanic penguin is common, but four other species breed regularly: the rockhopper, the macaroni, the gentoo and the king.

One of the most beautiful breeding birds is the black-browed albatross, but there are also striated and crested caracaras, cormorants, gulls, hawks, peregrine falcons, oystercatchers, snowy sheathbills, sheldgeese, steamer ducks and swans – among others. Most are present in large, impressive colonies, easy to photograph.

Elephant seals, sea lions and fur seals breed on the beaches, while six species of dolphins have been observed offshore. Killer whales are common, but the larger South Atlantic whales are unusual.

Over the past decade, local government has encouraged nature-oriented tourism by constructing small lodges at outstanding sites, but there are also less-structured opportunities.

GOVERNMENT

Internationally the Falklands are an anachronism, administered by a London-appointed Governor, but the locally elected Legislative Council (Legco) exercises significant power. Half its eight members come from Stanley, while the remainder represent the countryside, or 'camp'. Selected members of Legco advise the Governor as part of Executive Council (Exco). The current governor is David Tatham, appointed in August 1992 for a three-year term.

ECONOMY

Traditionally, the economy depended almost entirely on wool, but fishing has now eclipsed agriculture as a revenue-producer. Licensed Asian and European fleets have funded improvements in public services like schools, roads, telephones and medical care. Revenue has recently declined as Argentina has opened its waters to foreign fleets on more favourable terms, to the possible detriment of squid stocks which move between Falklands and Argentine waters.

Most Stanley residents work for local government (FIG) or for FIC. While FIC has sold all its pastoral property, it continues to provide shipping and other commercial services. In camp, nearly everyone is involved in wool on relatively small, widely dispersed family-owned units. Tourism is economically limited, but facilities are always adequate and often excellent.

POPULATION & PEOPLE

By the 1991 census, the population is 2050; three-quarters live in Stanley and the rest in camp. Over 60% are native-born, some tracing their ancestry back six generations or more, while the others are immigrants or temporary residents from the UK. Islanders' surnames indicate varied European backgrounds, but all speak English. Nearly all the handful of South American immigrants are Chilean.

Because of their isolation and small numbers, Falklanders are versatile and adaptable. They are also hospitable, often welcoming strangers for 'smoko', the traditional mid-morning tea or coffee break, or for a drink. This is especially true in camp, where visitors of any kind can be infrequent, but it is customary to bring a small gift – rum is a special favourite. Stanley's pubs are popular meeting places.

About 2000 British military personnel ('squaddies') reside at Mount Pleasant Airport, about 35 miles (60 km) south-west of Stanley, and at a few other scattered sites.

Facts for the Visitor

In many ways the Falklands are a small country, with their own immigration and customs regulations, currency and other unique features.

VISAS & CUSTOMS

All nationalities, including Britons, need valid passports and may need a return ticket or to prove sufficient funds. For non-Britons, visa requirements are usually the same as for visitors to the UK. For more detailed information, consult Falkland House (☎ 222-2542), 14 Broadway, Westminster, London SW1H 0BH. In Punta Arenas, Chile, contact Aerovías DAP (☎ 22-3958), O'Higgins 891, which operates flights to the Falklands.

Customs regulations are few except for limits on alcohol and tobacco, which are heavily taxed.

MONEY & COSTS

The Falkland Islands pound (£) is on a par with sterling. There are banknotes for £5, £10, £20 and £50, and coins for one, five, 10, 20 and 50 pence and £1. Sterling circulates alongside local currency, which is not valid in the UK.

Credit cards are not used, but travellers' cheques are readily accepted. Britons with guarantee cards can cash personal cheques up to £50 at Standard Chartered Bank.

COSTS

Recent development has encouraged short-stay accommodation at prices up to £50 per day (meals included), but bed and breakfast in Stanley starts around £20. Cheaper, self-catering cabins are available in camp, plus opportunities for trekking and camping at little or no cost; some isolated families still welcome visitors without charge.

Outside the Stanley-Mount Pleasant area, the Government Air Service (FIGAS) serves most destinations. Its fares of about £1 per minute flying time for non-Islanders would make the fare to distant Port Stephens, on West Falkland, about £60 one-way.

Food prices are roughly equivalent to the UK, but fresh meat (chiefly mutton) is extremely cheap. Stanley restaurants are fairly expensive, except for short orders and snacks.

FALKLANDS

WHEN TO GO & WHAT TO BRING

From October to March, migratory birds and marine mammals return to beaches and headlands. Very long days in December and January permit outdoor activities even if poor weather spoils part of the day.

Visitors should bring good waterproof clothing; a pair of Wellingtons is useful. Summer never gets truly hot and high winds can lower the ambient temperature, but the climate does not justify Antarctic preparations. Trekkers should bring a sturdy tent with a rainfly, and a warm sleeping bag.

TOURIST OFFICES

In the UK, contact Falkland House (☎ 222-2542), 14 Broadway, Westminster, London SW1H 0BH, which has a number of brochures with basic maps, and suggestions for itineraries and tour operators.

USEFUL ORGANISATIONS

Nonprofit Falklands Conservation (☎ 556-6226) promotes wildlife conservation research as well as preservation of wrecks and historic sites. Contact them at 21 Regent Terrace, Edinburgh EH7 5BT, Scotland, or in Stanley.

The Falkland Islands Association (☎ 222-0028), 2 Greycoat Place, Westminster, London SW1P 1SD, is a political lobbying group which publishes a quarterly newsletter of general interest.

BUSINESS HOURS & HOLIDAYS

Government offices are open on weekdays from 8.30 am to noon and 1.15 to 4.30 pm. Larger businesses, like FIC's West Store, keep similar hours, but small shops may open only a few hours a day; weekend hours are brief. The few stores in camp have limited regular hours, but often open on request.

FESTIVALS & HOLIDAYS

In a land where most people lived in physical and social isolation, the annual sports meetings provided a regular opportunity to share news, meet new people and participate in friendly competitions like horse racing, bull riding and dog trials. The rotating West Falkland sports maintains this tradition best, hosting 'two-nighters' at which Islanders party till they drop, sleep a few hours, and get up and start over again. Independent visitors are welcome, but arrange accommodation in advance – this will usually mean floor space for your sleeping bag.

The following holidays are observed:

1 January
  New Year's Day
March/April (date varies)
  Good Friday
21 April
  Queen's Birthday
14 June
  Liberation Day
14 August
  Falklands Day
8 December
  Battle of the Falklands (1914)
25 December
  Christmas Day
26 December
  Boxing Day (Stanley Sports day)
27 December
  Stanley Sports (2nd day)

POST & TELECOMMUNICATIONS

Postal services are good. There are one or two airmail services weekly to the UK, but parcels over about one pound go by sea four or five times yearly. FIGAS delivers to outer settlements and islands. Instruct correspondents to address their letters to the 'Post Office, Stanley, Falkland Islands, via London, England'.

Cable and Wireless PLC operates local and long-distance telephones; the local system has recently been modernised. Local calls cost five pence per minute, calls to the UK 15 pence per six seconds, and calls to the rest of the world 18 pence per six seconds. Operator-assisted calls are dearer.

TIME

The Falklands are four hours behind GMT. In summer, Stanley goes on daylight savings time, but camp remains on standard time.

FALKLANDS

WEIGHTS & MEASURES

The metric system is official, but most people use imperial measures. (There is a conversion table at the back of this book.)

BOOKS

The most readily available general account is Ian Strange's *The Falkland Islands*, 3rd edition (David & Charles, London, 1983). More recent is Paul Morrison's *The Falkland Islands* (Aston Publications, 1990).

For a summary of the Falklands controversy, see Robert Fox's *Antarctica and the South Atlantic: Discovery, Development and Dispute* (BBC Books, London, 1985). On the war, try Max Hastings & Simon Jenkins' *Battle for the Falklands* (Pan, London, 1983).

Robin Woods' *Falkland Islands Birds* (Anthony Nelson, Oswestry, Shropshire, 1982) is a suitable field guide with fine photographs. More detailed is his *Guide to the Birds of the Falkland Islands* (Nelson, 1988). Strange's *Field Guide to the Wildlife of the Falkland Islands and South Georgia* (Harper Collins, 1992) is also worth a look. Trekkers should acquire Julian Fisher's *Walks and Climbs in the Falkland Islands* (Bluntisham Books, Cambridge, 1992).

MAPS

DOS topographic maps are available from the Secretariat at Stanley for about £2 each. The two-sheet, 1:250,000 map of the entire Islands is suitable for most purposes, but 1:50,000 sheets have more detail.

MEDIA

The Falkland Islands Broadcasting Service (FIBS) produces local programmes and carries news from the BBC and programmes from the British Forces Broadcasting Service (BFBS). The nightly announcements, to which people listen religiously, are worth hearing.

Television, with programmes taped and flown in from the UK, is available six hours daily from BFBS. The only print media are the *Teaberry Express* and the weekly *Penguin News*.

FILM & PHOTOGRAPHY

Colour and B&W print film are readily available at reasonable prices. Colour slide film is less dependably available.

HEALTH

No special health precautions are necessary, but carry adequate insurance. Flights from Britain are occasionally diverted to yellow fever zones in Africa, so authorities recommend vaccination.

Wind and sun can combine to burn unsuspecting visitors severely. In the event of inclement weather, the wind can contribute to the danger of hypothermia. There are excellent medical and dental facilities at Stanley's new King Edward VII Memorial Hospital.

DANGERS & ANNOYANCES

Near Stanley and in a few camp locations, there remain unexploded plastic land mines, but minefields are clearly marked and no civilian has ever been injured. *Never* eenter one of these fields – mines will bear the weight of a penguin or even a sheep, but not of a human. Report suspicious objects to the Explosive Ordnance Disposal office (☎ 22229), near the Town Hall, which has free minefield maps (handy, incidentally, for Stanley area walks).

Hikers will find so-called 'soft camp', covered by white grass, very boggy despite its firm appearance. This is not quicksand, but step carefully.

WORK

Stanley's labour shortage has eased and work is more difficult to obtain. In the past, seasonal work was possible on large sheep stations, but agrarian reform has nearly eliminated this option. The major employers are FIC and FIG. There is a chronic housing shortage.

ACTIVITIES

Wildlife is the major attraction. Penguins, other birds and marine mammals are tame and easily approached, even at developed sites like Sea Lion Island, but there are other equally interesting, undeveloped areas. Keep a respectful distance.

Fishing can be excellent; early March to late April is the best season to fish for sea trout, which requires a licence (£10) from the Stanley post office. Trekking and camping are possible, though many landowners and the tourist board now discourage camping because of fire danger and disturbance to stock and wildlife. It is possible to visit the 1982 battlefields.

ACCOMMODATION

Stanley has several B&Bs and two hotels, while some farms have converted surplus buildings into comfortable lodges. Others have self-catering cottages, caravans or Portakabin shelters.

In areas not frequented by tourists, Islanders often welcome house guests; many farms have 'outside houses' or shanties which visitors may use with permission. Camping is possible only with permission.

FOOD & DRINK

Mutton, the dietary staple, is very cheap. Locally grown vegetables and fruits rarely appear for sale, since Islanders usually consume their own produce, but a hydroponic market garden now produces aubergines (eggplant), tomatoes, lettuce and other salad greens.

Stanley snack bars offer fish & chips, mutton-burgers (not so bad), pizza, sausage rolls and pasties, while the hotels have decent restaurants. At several well-patronised pubs, beer and hard liquor (whiskey, rum) are the favourites, though Chilean wine has gained popularity.

Getting There & Away

There are regular flights to Mount Pleasant International Airport from RAF Brize Norton, Oxfordshire, via Ascension Island. Southbound flights leave Brize Norton on Mondays and alternate Thursdays; northbound flights leave Mount Pleasant on Wednesdays and alternate Saturdays. The flight takes 16 hours, plus an hour's stop on Ascension.

The return fare is £2180, but there is a reduced APEX return fare of £1340 with 30-day advance purchase. Groups of six or more pay £1130 return each. One-way tickets, half the return fare, are available if you wish to continue to Chile. For reservations in the UK, contact Carol Stewart at FIG's London offices (☎ (071) 222-2542), Falkland House, 14 Broadway, Westminster SW1H 0BH. In Stanley, contact the Falkland Islands Company (☎ 27633), on Crozier Place.

There is a new air connection to Chile with Aerovías DAP (☎ 22-3958), O'Higgins 891, Punta Arenas, for US$365 a single. From October to April, there are weekly flights; the rest of the year, flights are biweekly.

Stanley

Stanley's metal-clad houses, brightly painted corrugated metal roofs and large kitchen gardens are a striking contrast to the surrounding moorland. Almost every household burns peat, and the sweetish fragrance permeates the town.

Founded in 1845, the new capital was a supply and repair port, but Cape Horn shipping began to avoid it when boats were scuttled under questionable circumstances. In the late 19th century, Stanley grew more rapidly, as trans-shipment point for wool between camp and the UK.

As the wool trade grew, so did the influence of the Falkland Islands Company, the town's largest employer. Although its political and economic dominance were uncontested, its relatively high wages and good housing offered a paternalistic security. 'Tied houses', however, were available only while the employee remained with FIC.

Stanley remains the service centre for the wool industry, but has also become a significant port for Asian and European fishing fleets.

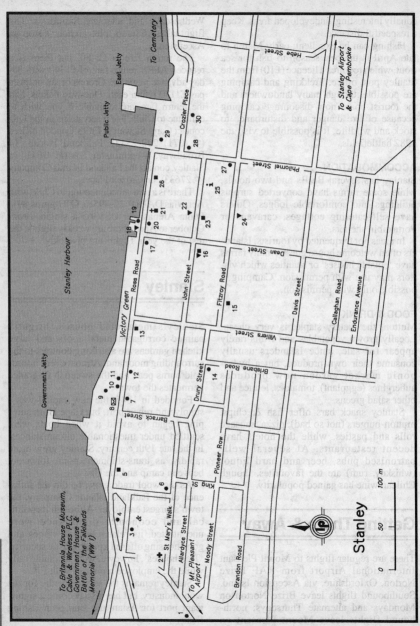

Orientation

On a steep north-facing hillside, Stanley has sprawled east and west along Stanley Harbour. The main street is Ross Rd, running the length of the harbour, but most government offices, businesses and houses are within a few blocks of each other in the centre.

Information

Tourist Office The Falkland Islands Tourist Board (☎ 22215), 56 John St, distributes an excellent guide to Stanley and other useful brochures, and keeps a list of accommodation. Hours are 8.30 am to noon and 1.15 to 4.30 pm on weekdays.

Money Standard Chartered Bank, Ross Rd at Barrack St, changes foreign currency and travellers' cheques, and cashes personal cheques on several UK banks (with guarantee card). Hours are 8.30 am to noon and 1.15 to 3 pm on weekdays. Change local notes for sterling or dollars before leaving the Islands.

Most Stanley businesses readily accept travellers' cheques.

Post & Telecommunications The Post Office is in Town Hall, on Ross Rd at Barrack St. Cable and Wireless PLC, on Ross Rd West near Government House, operates phone, telegram, telex and fax services. Magnetic cards are cheaper than operator-assisted overseas calls. Counter hours are 8.30 am to 5 pm, but public booths are open 24 hours.

Emergency King Edward VII Memorial Hospital (☎ 27328 for appointments, 27410 for emergencies) has outstanding facilities.

Things to See

Stanley's most distinguished building, **Christ Church Cathedral** (1892), is a massive brick and stone construction with attractive stained-glass windows. On the small nearby plaza, the restored **Whalebone Arch** commemorates the 1933 centenary of British rule.

Since the mid-19th century, London-appointed governors have inhabited rambling **Government House**, on Ross Rd. Just beyond it, the **Battle of the Falklands Memorial** commemorates a WW I naval engagement, while **Britannia House Museum** is a recent project, with changing exhibits. Curator John Smith is especially conversant with maritime history; his booklet *Condemned at Stanley* tells about the numerous wrecks in the harbour.

Just west of the Secretariat, on Ross Rd, is the **1982 War Memorial**, designed by a

FALKLANDS

Falklander living overseas, paid for by public subscription and built with volunteer labour. At the east end of Ross Road, **Stanley Cemetery** is a testament to local history, where both the Islands' tiny elite and working class are represented. Surnames like Felton and Biggs are as common here as Smith and Jones are in the UK.

Activities
Stanley's new swimming pool, on Reservoir Rd, has become very popular. There are also now sites for squash, badminton, basketball and the like.

Fishing for sea trout, mullet and smelt is popular on the Murrell River, walking distance from Stanley, but there are many other suitable places, some easily accessible from Mount Pleasant highway.

Festivals
The most noteworthy public event is the **Stanley Sports**, held after Christmas, featuring horse racing (bets are legal), bull riding and other events.

In March, the competitive **Horticultural Show** displays the produce of kitchen gardens in Stanley and camp, plus a variety of baked goods. At the end of the day, the produce is sold in a spirited auction. In July, the **Crafts Fair** presents the work of local weavers, leatherworkers, photographers and artists (there are many talented illustrators and painters).

Places to Stay
Accommodation is good, but limited and not cheap – reservations are advisable. Several B&B places offer the option of full board. *Emma's Guest House* (☎ 21056), on Ross Rd, charges £28.50 for B&B and £36.50 with full board. Ask for cheaper rooms in the nearby annex. At *Warrah Guest House* (☎ 21252), a 19th-century stone building on John St, rates are £30. Rose Stewart's *Fenton Guest House* (☎ 21282), 7 Fitzroy Rd, has singles for £30, with breakfast and supper.

Malvina House Hotel (☎ 21355), 3 Ross Rd, has beautiful grounds and a conservatory for £33 a single. The venerable *Upland Goose Hotel* (☎ 21455), 20/22 Ross Rd, charges £35 for B&B with shared bath, £60 for a suite.

Places to Eat
Most Stanley eateries are modest snack bars with limited hours. The *Boathouse Café*, on Ross Rd near the Cathedral, serves lunch Sunday to Thursday. For fish & chips, pizza and sausage rolls, try the *Woodbine Café*, 29 Fitzroy Rd, open Tuesday to Friday from 10 am to 2 pm, Wednesday from 7 to 9 pm, Friday from 8 to 10.30 pm, and Saturday from 10 am to 3 pm.

For more elaborate meals, try *Emma's, Malvina House* and the *Upland Goose. Monty's*, on John St, is also worth a try.

Entertainment
Of Stanley's several pubs, the most popular is the Globe Hotel, on Crozier Place, but try also the Rose Hotel, on Brisbane Rd, and the Victory Bar, on Philomel St. The Upland Goose Hotel has a public bar, and Monty's also has a bar, Deano's.

In winter, the pubs sponsor a darts league, with tournaments in the Town Hall, where there are also many dances, with live music, throughout the year. There are no cinemas, but hotels and guesthouses have video lounges.

Things to Buy
For locally spun and knitted woollen goods, visit the Home Industries Cooperative, on Ross Rd, open on weekdays from 9.30 am to noon and 1.30 to 4.30 pm.

Postage stamps, available from the Post Office and from the Philatelic Bureau, are popular with collectors. The Bureau also sells stamps from South Georgia and British Antarctic Territory.

Getting There & Away
Air Mount Pleasant International Airport is 35 miles south-west of Stanley via a good road. For information about international flights, see the Getting There & Away section.

From Stanley Airport, about three miles

east of town, FIGAS (☎ 27219) serves out-lying destinations in nine-passenger aircraft, arranging itineraries by demand; when you know where and what day you wish to go, contact them and listen to FIBS announce-ments at 6.30 pm the night before departure to learn your departure time. On occasion, usually around holidays, flights are heavily booked and you may not get on. Some grass airstrips can only accept a limited payload, so luggage is limited to 30 pounds per person.

Bus Stanley Bus Service (☎ 21191) serves Stanley and Mount Pleasant airports, and will also make day trips to Goose Green in summer.

Getting Around
To/From the Airport Bob Stewart's Stanley Bus Service (☎ 21191) takes passengers to Mount Pleasant for £10 a single (make res-ervations the day before) and will also take groups to Stanley Airport, or meet them there.

For cabs, call Ben's Taxi Service (☎ 21437).

AROUND STANLEY
Stanley Harbour Maritime History Trail
See the tourist office for a brochure on wrecks and condemned ships. There are informational panels near vessels like the *Jhelum* (a sinking East Indiaman deserted by her crew in 1871), the *Charles Cooper* (an American packet still used for storage) and the *Lady Elizabeth* (a three-masted freighter which struck a rock in 1913).

Penguin Walk & Gypsy Cove
The Falklands' most convenient penguin colonies are about 1½ hours' walk from Stanley; go to the east end of Ross Rd, beyond the cemetery and cross the bridge over The Canache, past the *Lady Elizabeth* and Stanley Airport to Yorke Bay.

Gentoo penguins crowd the sandy beach where, unfortunately, the Argentines buried plastic mines; get your view of the penguins by walking along the minefield fence.

Further on, at Gypsy Cove, are Magellanic penguins (avoid stepping on burrows) and other shore birds.

Kidney Island
Kidney Island, a small reserve covered with tussock grass, supports a wide variety of wildlife, including rockhopper penguins and sea lions. Arrange carefully planned visits through the Agricultural Officer.

Camp

Nearly everyone in 'camp' (a term for all of the Falklands outside Stanley) is engaged in sheep ranching. Camp settlements were always company towns, hamlets near shel-tered harbours where coastal shipping could collect the wool, while single shepherds lived at 'outside houses' which still dot the countryside.

Many wildlife sites are on smaller off-shore islands like Sea Lion Island and Pebble Island, whose comfortable tourist lodges are fairly costly, though there are also budget alternatives.

EAST FALKLAND
East Falkland's road network includes a good highway to Mount Pleasant, where a serviceable track continues to Goose Green. From the Mount Pleasant road, another good track leads north to the Estancia, west of Stanley, and to Port Louis, but most other tracks are usable for 4WDs only. FIGAS is still the most reliable means of transport.

Salvador
Salvador was originally founded by Gibraltarian Andrés Pitaluga, who arrived in the Falklands in the 1830s. On its north coast are large penguin colonies, while Centre Island features elephant seals and sea lions.

Rob Pitaluga, owner of *Salvador Lodge* (☎ 31150), offers full board for £26.50 per day.

Port Louis, Johnson's Harbour & Trekking the North Coast

On the north coast of East Falkland, this trek crosses broad sandy beaches and rugged headlands from Seal Bay to Volunteer Point, with penguins *always* within view. Port Louis is its starting point, reached by car or on foot. Ask permission of manager Michael Morrison, at Port Louis (☎ 31004), and owner George Smith, of Johnson's Harbour (☎ 31399).

Port Louis still has ruins the initial French settlement (1764). It was also Louis Vernet's headquarters, and contains the grave of his lieutenant Matthew Brisbane, killed by gauchos after the British left him in charge of the settlement in 1833.

From Port Louis, Seal Bay is a six to eight-hour walk. Close gates, and watch your step in the soggy white grass. Ask Michael Morrison's permission to stay or camp at Seal Bay House before hiking the coast proper.

After Seal Bay, carry as much fresh water as possible. Follow the coast east past rockhoppers and king cormorants to the sealion colony at Macbride Head. En route are thousands of Magellanic penguins and occasional macaronis and gentoos. The 1:250,000 map shows a large estuary at Swan Pond, but the broad, sandy beach requires you to wade one shallow creek. The best camp site is Dutchman's Brook, with a Portakabin shelter but no fresh water.

Another 1½ hours south, in a patch of white grass along a fence line near a gentoo colony, a tiny spring is the only source of fresh water until Volunteer Shanty, four hours south. There are many more penguins, elephant seals, turkey vultures, upland and kelp geese and other birds. Nonfarm personnel may no longer use Volunteer Shanty, but with George Smith's permission, you may camp nearby, draw fresh water from the tap and use the very tidy outhouse.

Volunteer Beach has the Falklands' largest concentration of king penguins, a growing colony of about 150 breeding pairs. At Volunteer Point, several hours' walk west, is an offshore breeding colony of southern fur seals (bring binoculars). Return along Volunteer Lagoon for more birds and elephant seals.

From Volunteer Beach, Johnson's Harbour is an easy four to five-hour walk along Mount Brisbane; make arrangements to have FIGAS pick you up for the return trip to Stanley, or hike back (the store at Johnson's Harbour may sell you some supplies).

San Carlos

In 1982, British forces came ashore at San Carlos, on Falkland Sound; in 1983, the sheep station was subdivided and sold to half a dozen local families. There is fishing on the San Carlos River, north of the settlement. Comfortable *Blue Beach Lodge* (☎ 32205) charges £49 for full board.

Across San Carlos Water, but four hours away by foot, is the **Ajax Bay Refrigeration Plant**, a 1950s CDC (Colonial Development Corporation) boondoggle. Gentoo penguins wander through its ruins, which served as a field hospital in 1982. Take a flashlight if you plan to explore.

Darwin & Goose Green

At the narrow isthmus which separates Lafonia from northern East Falkland, Darwin was the site of an early saladero, where gauchos slaughtered feral cattle and tanned their hides; it later became the centre of FIC's camp operations and, with nearby Goose Green, the largest settlement outside Stanley. The heaviest ground fighting of the Falklands War took place at Goose Green.

Darwin Lodge (☎ 27699) offers full board for £48.50.

Sea Lion Island

Off East Falkland's south coast, tiny Sea Lion is less than a mile across, but teems with wildlife, including five species of penguins, enormous cormorant colonies, giant petrels, and the charmingly tame predator known as the 'Johnny Rook' (striated caracara). Hundreds of elephant seals crowd its sandy beaches, while sea lions dot the narrow gravel beaches below its southern bluffs or lurk in the towering tussock.

Much of the credit for Sea Lion's wildlife has to go to Terry and Doreen Clifton, who farmed it since the mid-1970s before selling it recently. The Cliftons developed their 2300-acre (930-hectare) ranch with the idea that wildlife, habitat and livestock were compatible uses, and Sea Lion is one of few working farms with any substantial cover of native tussock grass. Through improved fencing and other conscientious practices, the Cliftons made it a successful sheep station and a popular tourist site, mostly for day trips from Stanley and Mount Pleasant.

Sea Lion Lodge (☎ 32004) offers twin-bed rooms with full board for £50 per person. The Falkland Islands Development Corporation (FIDC) recently bought Sea Lion, and may not continue the Cliftons' policy of encouraging budget travellers by allowing them to rent a small self-catering caravan.

WEST FALKLAND

Pioneers settled West Falkland only in the late 1860s, but within a decade had established sheep stations at Port Howard, Hill Cove, Fox Bay, Port Stephens, Roy Cove, Chartres and on offshore islands. One of the most interesting experiments was the Keppel Island mission for Indians from Tierra del Fuego.

West Falkland (nearly as large as East Falkland) and adjacent islands have fine wildlife sites. There are no roads, only a system of rough tracks suitable for 4WDs and motorcycles, but there is good trekking in the mountainous interior. Only a few places have formal tourist facilities.

Port Howard

Scenic Port Howard, at the foot of 2158-ft (658-metre) Mount Maria, remains intact after its sale to its local managers in 1987. About 50 people live on the station, which has its own dairy, grocery, abattoir, social club and other amenities. It will be the West Falkland port for the anticipated ferry across Falkland Sound.

The immediate surroundings offer hiking,

riding and fishing; wildlife sites are more distant. Visitors can view shearing and other camp activities, and there is a small war museum. Make arrangements to stay at the cookhouse at reasonable cost.

It is possible to hike up the valley of the Warrah River, a good trout stream, and past Turkey Rocks to the Blackburn River and Hill Cove, another pioneer 19th-century farm. Ask permission to cross property boundaries, and close gates; where the track is faint, look for old telephone lines. There are longer hikes south toward Chartres, Fox Bay and Port Stephens.

Pebble Island

Elongated Pebble Island, north of West Falkland, has varied topography and a good sample of wildlife. *Pebble Island Hotel* (☎ 41097) charges £47.50 per person for room with full board, but ask for self-catering cottages and a shanty at the island's west end – contact Raymond Evans (☎ 41098).

Keppel Island

In 1853, the South American Missionary Society established an outpost on Keppel to catechise Indians from Tierra del Fuego and teach them to grow potatoes. The settlement was controversial, because the government suspected that the Yahgans had been brought against their will, but still lasted until 1898.

Interesting ruins include the chapel, the bailiff's house, and the stone walls of Indian dwellings. Keppel is also a good place for penguins, but visits are difficult to arrange because it has no permanent residents.

Saunders Island

Saunders was the site of the first British garrison (1765). In 1767, Spanish forces dislodged the British from Port Egmont and nearly precipitated a general war. After the British left in 1774, Spain razed the settlement, but extensive ruins still remain.

Saunders has a fine sample of wildlife and good trekking to 'The Neck', whose sandspit beach links it to Elephant Point peninsula, about four hours from the settlement. There is a Portakabin shelter near a colony of black-browed albatrosses and rockhopper penguins, and there are a few king penguins, too. Further on are thousands of Magellanic penguins, kelp gulls, skuas and a colony of elephant seals. Saunders has no formal tourist facilities, but hopeful visitors should contact Tony or Biffo Pole-Evans (☎ 41299).

Carcass Island

Carcass, a small, scenic island west of Saunders, is a popular weekend and holiday retreat for Stanleyites. For self-catering cottages, contact Rob McGill (☎ 41106).

Port Stephens

Port Stephens' rugged headlands, near the settlement's sheltered harbour, host thousands of rockhoppers and other sea birds, while Calm Head, about two hours' walk, has excellent views of the jagged shoreline

and the powerful South Atlantic. Despite its lack of formal tourist facilities, Stephens is well worth a visit.

One longer trek goes to the abandoned sealing station at Albemarle and huge gentoo colonies. Hoste Inlet, with a habitable outside house, is about five hours' walk, while the sealing station, another CDC blunder, is four hours further. Like Ajax Bay, it is a monument to bureaucratic ineptitude, but aficionados of industrial archaeology will find its derelict installations intriguing. There is a habitable shanty nearby.

Massive gentoo colonies are an hour's walk from the station. The Arch Islands, inaccessible except by boat, take their name from the huge gap which the ocean has eroded in the largest of the group.

If you're interested in visiting Port Stephens, contact Peter or Anne Robertson (☎ 42007).

Glossary

Unless otherwise indicated, the terms below refer to Spanish South America in general.

abra – in the Andes, a mountain pass

ACA – Automóvil Club Argentino

aerosilla – chairlift

Afoxé – (Bra) Bahian music with strong African rhythms and close ties to Candomblé religion

aguardente – (Bra) any strong drink, but usually cachaça

aguardiente – cane alcohol or similar drink

alameda – street lined with trees, usually poplars

alcaldía – town hall, virtually synonymous with *municipalidad*

albergue – lodging house; youth hostel

alcabala – (Ven) roadside police checkpoint

álcool – (Bra) fuel made from sugar cane; about half of Brazil's cars, including all new ones, run on álcool

aldeia – (Bra) originally a Jesuit mission village; now any small village

alerce – large coniferous tree resembling California redwood; common in Argentina and Chile

almuerzo – lunch; often an inexpensive fixed-price meal

altiplano – Andean high plain of Peru, Bolivia, Chile and Argentina

andar – (Bra) the verb 'to walk'; denotes floor number in a multi-storey building

apartamento – (Bra) hotel room with private bath

api – (Andean countries) a syrupy *chicha* made of maize, lemon, cinnamon and sugar

apunamiento – altitude sickness

arepera – (Ven) snack bar

arrayán – reddish-barked tree of the myrtle family; common in forests of southern Argentina and Chile

artesanía – handicrafts; crafts shop

asado – (Arg) barbecue, usually a family outing in summer

audiencia – administrative subdivision of colonial Spanish America, under a president who held civil power in areas where no viceroy was resident

autopista – freeway or motorway

Aymara – indigenous people of highland Bolivia, Peru, Chile and Argentina (also called Kollas); also the language of these people

azulejos – ceramic tiles

balneario – bathing resort or beach

bandeirantes – (Bra) colonial slavers and gold prospectors from São Paulo who explored the interior; the typical bandeirante was of mixed Portuguese-Indian heritage

barraca – (Bra) any stall or hut, including food and drink stands at beach, park etc

barrio – neighbourhood or district

bencina – petrol

bencina blanca – white gas (Shellite) for campstoves, usually available only in hardware stores or chemical supply shops

bicho de pé – burrowing parasite found near beaches and in some rainforest areas of Brazil

bodega – a winery or a storage area for wine; (Bol) boxcar, sometimes used for train travel by 2nd-class passengers

bofedal – in Andean altiplano, a swampy alluvial pasture

boleadoras – heavily weighted thongs, used for hunting guanaco and rhea; also called *bolas*

bossa nova – music that mixes North American jazz with Brazilian influences

burundanga – (Col) drug obtained from a common species of tree (popularly called *borrachero* or *cacao sabanero*); used to intoxicate unsuspecting tourists in order to rob them

cabildo – colonial town council

cachaça – (Bra) sugar-cane rum, also called pinga or aguardente, produced by hundreds of small distilleries throughout the country; the national drink

cachaco – (Col) resident of Bogotá

cachoeira – (Bra) waterfall

cacique – Indian chieftain; among Araucanian Indians, a *toqui*

callampas – (Chi) literally 'mushrooms'; shantytowns on the outskirts of Santiago which spring up overnight; some have now become well-established neighbourhoods

calle – street

cama matrimonial – double bed

camanchaca – (Chi) dense convective fog on the coastal hills of the Atacama desert; equivalent to Peru's *garúa*

câmara – (Bra) colonial town council

cambista – street money changer

camellones – (Ecu) pre-Columbian raised-field earthworks in the Guayas Basin; evidence of large early populations

camino – road, path, way

camión – open-bed truck; a popular form of local transport in the Andean countries

camioneta – pickup or other small truck; a form of local transport in the Andean countries

campesino – peasant; a rural person who practises subsistence agriculture

campo – the countryside; a field or paddock

Candomblé – (Bra) Afro-Brazilian religion of Bahia

caracoles – literally 'snails'; a winding road, usually in the mountains

capoeira – (Bra) martial art/dance performed to rhythms of an instrument called the berimbau; developed by Bahian slaves

carioca – native of Rio de Janeiro

casa de cambio – foreign currency exchange house

casa de familia – modest family accommodation, usually in tourist centres in Southern Cone countries

casona – large house, usually a mansion; term often applied to colonial architecture in particular

catarata – waterfall

caudillo – in 19th century South American politics, a provincial strongman whose power rested more on personal loyalty than political ideals or party organisation

cerro – hill; a term used to refer to even very high Andean peaks

ceviche – marinated raw seafood (be cautious about eating ceviche as it can be a source of cholera)

chachacoma – *Senecio graveolens*; a native Andean plant from which Indians brew a tea which helps combat altitude sickness

chacra – garden; small, independent farm

charango – Andean stringed instrument, traditionally made with armadillo shell as a sound box

chicha – in Andean countries, popular beverage (often alcoholic) made from ingredients like yuca, sweet potato or maize

chifa – Chinese restaurant (term most commonly used in Peru and northern Chile)

chilote – (Chi) a person from the island of Chiloé

chiva – (Col) a basic rural bus with wooden bench seats; until the 1960s, the main means of transport throughout the country

cholo(a) – Quechua or Aymara person who has migrated to the city but continues to wear peasant dress

churrascaria – (Bra) restaurant featuring barbecued meat

coa – (Chi) lower-class slang of Santiago

coima – a bribe; one who solicits a bribe is a *coimero*

colectivo – depending on country, a bus, minibus or collective taxi

comedor – basic cafeteria or dining room in a hotel

confitería – café which serves coffee, tea, desserts and simple food orders

congregación – in colonial Latin America, the concentration of dispersed native populations in central settlements, usually for purposes of political control or religious instruction (see also *reducción*)

cordillera – mountain range

corregidor – in colonial Spanish America, governor of a provincial city and its surrounding area; the corregidor was usually associated with the *cabildo*

cospel – token used in public telephones; also known as a *ficha*

costanera – seaside, riverside or lakeside road

criollo – a Spaniard born in colonial South America; in modern times, any Argentine of European descent

curanto – Chilean seafood stew
cuy – roasted guinea pig, a traditional Andean food

DEA – US Drug Enforcement Agency, sent to Bolivia to assist in coca eradication, crop-substitution programmes and the arrest of drug magnates; the DEA was expelled in mid-1992 by the Bolivian government
dendê – (Bra) palm-tree oil, a main ingredient in the cuisine of Bahia
denuncia – affidavit or statement, usually in connection with theft or robbery
dique – reservoir used for recreational purposes

edificio – building
EMBRATUR – Brazilian federal government tourism agency
ENASA – (Bra) government-run passenger ship service on the Amazon
encomienda – colonial labour system under which Indian communities had to provide labour and tribute to a Spanish *encomendero* in exchange for religious and language instruction; usually the system benefited the Spaniard far more than the Indians
esquina – corner (abbreviated to 'esq')
estancia – extensive grazing establishment, either for cattle or sheep, with dominating owner or manager and dependent resident labour force
estanciero – owner of an estancia

farinha – (Bra) manioc flour, the staple food of Indians before colonisation, and of many Brazilians today, especially in the Nordeste and the Amazon
favela – (Bra) slum or shantytown
fazenda – (Bra) large ranch or farm, roughly equivalent to Spanish American *hacienda*; also cloth or fabric
ferrobus – bus on railway wheels
ferroviária – (Bra) railway station
ficha – token used for public telephone, subway etc, in lieu of coins
flota – (Bol) long-distance bus line
Forró – (Bra) music of the Nordeste (do not confuse with Spanish *forro*, a rather crude term for a condom)

Frevo – (Bra) fast-paced, popular music that originated in Pernambuco
frigorífico – meat freezing factory
FUNAI – (Bra) government Indian agency
fundo – (Chi) hacienda; usually applied to a smaller irrigated unit in the country's central heartland

gamines – street children of Colombia
gamonal – (Per) rural landowner, equivalent to hacendado
garúa – (Per) a convective coastal fog
gaseosa – soft drink
gas-oil – (Southern Cone) diesel fuel; generally much cheaper than ordinary petrol
gasolero – vehicle which uses diesel fuel
gaúcho – (Bra) counterpart of Argentine gaucho (pronounced gaoooshoo)
golpe de estado – coup d'etat
gringo – throughout Latin America, a foreigner or person with light hair and complexion; not necessarily a derogatory term; (Arg) a person of Italian descent
guaquero – one who ransacks archaeological sites for artefacts; also spelled *huaquero*
guaraná – Amazonian shrub whose berry is believed to have magical and medicinal powers; also a popular soft drink in Brazil
guardaparque – park ranger

hacendado – owner of an hacienda; usually lived in a city and left day-to-day management of his estate to underlings
hacienda – large rural landholding with a dependent resident labour force under a dominant owner; (Chi) the term *fundo* is more common; (Arg) a much less common form of latifundio than the estancia
hospedaje – budget accommodation with shared bathroom; usually a large family home with an extra room or two for guests

ichu – bunch grass of the Andean *altiplano*
iglesia-church
indígena – native American (Indian)
indigenismo – movement in Latin American art and literature which extolls

aboriginal traditions, often in a romantic or patronising manner

inquilino – (Chi) tenant farmer on a fundo

invierno – literally 'winter'; the rainy season in the South American tropics

invierno boliviano – (Chi) 'Bolivian winter'; the summer rainy season in the altiplano, so-called because of the direction from which storms come

IVA – *impuesto de valor agregado*, value added tax (VAT); often added to restaurant or hotel bills in Argentina, Chile and Uruguay

Kolla – another name for the Colla, or Aymara

Kollasuyo – 'Land of the Kolla'; early indigenous name for the area now known as Bolivia

ladrão – (Bra) a thief

lago – lake

laguna – lagoon; shallow lake

lanchonete – (Bra) stand-up snack bar

latifundio – large landholding, such as an hacienda or cattle estancia

leito – (Bra) luxury overnight express bus

legía – alkaloid (usually made of potato and quinoa ash) chewed with coca leaves to activate their mild narcotic properties

llareta – *Laretia compacta*, a dense, compact altiplano shrub, used for fuel

lomas – coastal hills in the Atacama, on which condensation from the *camanchaca* supports relatively dense vegetation

lunfardo – street slang of Buenos Aires

machista – male chauvinist (normally used as adjective)

Manco Capac – first Inca emperor

manta – a shawl or bedspread

mercado – market

mercado negro – black market

mercado paralelo – euphemism for black market

meseta – interior steppe of eastern Patagonia

mestizo – a person of mixed Indian and Spanish descent

micro – small bus or minibus

mineiro – (Bra) a miner; person from Minas Gerais state

minifundio – small landholding, such as a peasant farm

minga – reciprocal labour system, common throughout the Andean region and other parts of South America

minuta – in restaurant or confitería, a short order snack such as spaghetti or milanesa

mirador – viewpoint or lookout, usually on a hill but often in a building

monte – scrub forest; any densely vegetated area

morro – a hill or headland; (Bra) person or culture of the *favelas*

mulato – person of mixed Black and European ancestry

municipalidad – city hall

museo – museum

nafta – (Arg) gasoline or petrol; *nafta blanca* is white gas (Shellite)

ñandú – large, flightless bird, resembling the ostrich

ñandutí – (Par) delicate 'spider-web' lace woven in Itauguá, near Asunción

nevado – snow-covered peak

novela – television soap opera (esp in Brazil)

NS – (Bra) Nosso Senhor (Our Father), or Nossa Senhora (Our Lady); often used in the name of a church

oca – edible Andean tuber, resembling a potato

oferta – promotional fare, often seasonal, for plane or bus travel

onces – (Chi) 'elevenses'; afternoon tea

orixás – (Bra) gods of Afro-Brazilian religions

pagode – (Bra) currently the most popular samba music

pampero – South Atlantic cold front which brings dramatic temperature changes to Uruguay, Paraguay and the interior of northern Argentina

parada – bus stop

páramo – (Ecu) humid, high altitude grassland of the northern Andean countries

parque nacional – national park
parrillada – barbecued or grilled meat
pasarela – catwalk across a stream or bog
paseo – an outing, such as a walk in the park or downtown
pau brasil – brazil-wood tree which produces a red dye that was the colony's first commodity; the tree is now scarce
paulista – (Bra) native of São Paulo
peatonal – pedestrian mall
pehuén – *Araucaria auracana*, the monkey-puzzle tree of southern South America
peña – club which hosts informal folk music gatherings; a performance at such a club
peninsulares – in colonial South America, Spaniards born in Europe (as opposed to *criollos,* who were born in the colonies)
pensión – short-term budget accommodation in a family home, which may also have permanent lodgers
Petrobras – (Bra) powerful, government-owned oil company
pingüinera – penguin colony
piropo – (Arg) a sexist remark, anything from relatively innocuous to very offensive
Planalto – enormous plateau that covers much of southern Brazil
pongaje – (Bol) non-feudal system of peonage, abolished in 1952
por puesto – (Ven) collective taxi
porteño – (Arg) inhabitant of Buenos Aires; (Chi) a native or resident of Valparaíso
posta – (Chi) first-aid station in a smaller town which lacks a proper hospital
pousada – (Bra) hotel
prato feito, prato do dia – (Bra) literally 'made plate' or 'plate of the day'; typically an enormous and very cheap meal
precordillera – foothills of the Andes
preservativo – condom
propina – a tip, eg in a restaurant or cinema
pucará – an indigenous Andean fortification
pueblos jovenes – (Per) literally 'young towns'; shantytowns surrounding Lima, often lacking electricity, water and adequate sanitation, though some have improved greatly from humble origins
puna – Andean highlands, usually above 3000 metres
puxar – (Bra) pull, rather than push

quarto – (Bra) hotel room with shared bath
quebracho – 'axe-breaker' tree *(Quebrachua lorentzii)* of the Chaco, a natural source of tannin
quebrada – ravine, normally dry
Quechua – indigenous language of Andean highlands, spread by Inca rule and widely spoken today
quena – simple reed flute
quilombo – (Bra) a community of runaway slaves; (Arg) a slang term for a brothel
quinoa – native Andean grain, the dietary equivalent of rice in the pre-Columbian era
quinto real – the 'royal fifth', Spanish tax on all precious metals mined in colonial America
quipus – coloured, knotted cords used for record-keeping by the Incas

recargo – (Arg) additional charge, usually 10%, which many businesses add to credit card transactions
reducción – see *congregación*
refugio – a usually rustic shelter in a national park or remote area
residencial – budget accommodation, sometimes only seasonal; in general, *residenciales* are in buildings designed expressly for short-stay lodging
río – river
rodeo – annual roundup of cattle on an hacienda or estancia
rodoferroviária – (Bra) combined bus and train station
rodoviária – (Bra) bus station
ruana – traditional woollen poncho of Colombia
ruta – route or highway

salar – salt lake or salt pan, usually in high Andes or Argentine Patagonia
salteña – meat and vegetable pastie, like an empanada
selva – natural tropical rainforest
siesta – lengthy afternoon break for lunch and, occasionally, a nap
s/n – 'sin número'; indicating a street address without a number
sobremesa – after-dinner conversation;

(Col) a carbonated drink served with a meal

soroche – altitude sickness

Southern Cone – the area comprising Argentina, Chile, Uruguay and parts of Brazil and Paraguay; so called after the area's shape on the map

stelling – (Gui) a ferry dock or pier

suco – (Bra) fruit juice; a fruit juice bar

taguá – Wagner's peccary; a species of wild pig thought extinct but recently rediscovered in Paraguayan Chaco

Tahuantinsuyo – Hispanicised name of the Inca Empire; in Quechua, Tawantinsuyu

tambo – in Andean countries, a wayside market and meeting place selling staple domestic items; an inn

tapir – large hoofed mammal; a distant relative of the horse

teleférico – gondola cable-car

tenedor libre – 'all-you-can-eat' restaurant

tepui – (Ven) elevated, sandstone-capped mesas which are home to unique flora

terra firme – Amazonian uplands of limited fertility

tinto – red wine; (Col) a small cup of black coffee

todo terreno – mountain bike

toqui – Mapuche Indian chieftain (see also *cacique*)

totora – type of reed, used as a building material

tranca – (Bol) police post

Tupi – (Bra) major coastal people at the time of European contact; also the language of these people

turismo aventura – 'adventure tourism' activities such as trekking and river rafting

tuteo – use of the pronoun *tu* and its corresponding verb forms (also see *voseo*)

Umbanda – (Bra) Rio's version of the principal Afro-Brazilian religion

Valle Central – the Chilean heartland which contains most of Chile's population, industry and agriculture

vaqueiro – (Bra) cowboy of the Nordeste

várzea – (Bra) Amazonian floodplain

verano – literally 'summer'; also the dry season in the South American tropics

vicuña – wild relative of domestic llama and alpaca, found only at high altitudes in the south-central Andes

villas miserias – shantytowns on outskirts of Buenos Aires and other Argentine cities

vinchuca – Reduvid Bug; a biting insect found in thatched dwellings with dirt floors, which transmits Chagas' disease

viviendas temporarias – (Par) riverfront shantytowns of Asunción

vizcacha – wild relative of domestic chinchilla; the mountain vizcacha (*Lagidium vizcacha*) inhabits the Andean highlands, while the plains vizcacha (*Lagostomus maximus*) lives in the subtropical lowlands

voladora – (Ven) river speed boat

voseo – use of the pronoun *vos* and its corresponding verb forms, as in Argentina, Uruguay and Paraguay (also see *tuteo*)

yacaré – South American alligator, found in tropical and sub-tropical river systems

yareta – see *llareta*

yatire – Andean healer or witch doctor

yerba mate – 'Paraguayan tea' (*Ilex paraguariensis*); consumed in Argentina in very large amounts, and also used regularly in Paraguay, Uruguay and Brazil; taking mate is an important everyday social ritual

yuca – manioc tuber; in Portuguese, *mandioca* is the most common term

zambo – a person of mixed African-Native American (Indian) ancestry

zampoña – pan flute featured in traditional Andean music

zona franca – (Chi) duty-free zone, as in Iquique and Punta Arenas

Zonda – (Arg) in the central Andes, a powerful, dry north wind

Index

TEXT

Map references are in **bold** type.

Thanks

Our thanks to the many readers and travellers who wrote in with information:

Neil Adamson (Aus), María Agozzino (Ecu), Inger-Mari Aikio (Fin), Mark & Tania Aitchison (Bra), Cherry & Mark Aitken (UK), Wendy Allinson (Aus), Heidi Andersson (Sw), Susanne Angermayr (D), Cassio Antunes (Bra), Seamus L Ardren (UK), Mats Areskoug (Sw), Tom Arsenault (USA), Jerry Azevedo (USA)

Harald Baeclelie, Antoon Bakx (Nl), Annabelle Baley (USA), Dave Barkshire (UK), Juliane Baron, Tristan Barrientos (USA), Franziska & Peter Bartschi (CH), Rhiannon Batten (UK), Howard Behr (UK), Kevin Bell (Aus), Conceiçao Maria Bentes (Bra), Lena Berglow (Sw), K Berkhout (Nl), David Biagioni (Aus), J M Bibby (UK), Roger Billingsley (UK), Erwin Bittner (Chi), Steven Blackford (Aus), Michael Bleby (Aus), Ulrika Bohman (Sw), Rob Bohmer (UK), Michael Bongard (C), Tony Bourke (C), John Bowles (Aus), Ingrid Bremer (D), Jill Buckingham (NZ), Gloria Burley (Aus)

Jim Campbell (USA), Nicola Chalmers (UK), Andrés Gustavo Chen (Arg), Peter Chisholm (NZ), Uttom Chowdhury (UK), Hanne Christensen (Dk), D Clement (UK), Thomas Clough (Bol), Richard Cohen (SA), Merle Conyer (Aus), Tim Cookman (USA), Karen Cooper (USA), Justin Costelloe (Aus), John Cox (UK), Timothy Crawford (USA), Peter Credge (UK), D Cronin (UK)

Wojciech Dabrowski (Pl), Dan Dahlberg (Sw), Nick Davis (UK), Michael Dixon (UK), Anthony Doctorow (C), Simon Done (UK), Peter Dooley (Aus), Benjamin Driggs, Patrick & Elisabeth Duffy (C), Gretchem Dursch (USA)

Dolan Eargle Jr (USA), Eva Echenberg (C), Jeanne Elliot, Simon Elms (NZ), Rosa Escarpenter (Sp), Arman Esmaili (Aus), Chris P Evans (USA)

Naomi Feinstein (UK), Nuno A Rainho Fernandes, Marcelo Ferrante (Arg), Stefano Ferrari (CH), Yedo Figueiredo (Bra), Greg Ford (UK), Guillaume Fourquet (F), Kate Freedlander (USA), Janine Freedman (USA), Danny Fung (HK)

Asunción Gallego (Sp), Horacio García (Arg), Javier G García (Sp), Ian Gates (UK), Ricardo Quiroz & Karin Godfroid (Chi), Peter Gold (USA), Chris Golfetto (CH), Christina Gomez (USA), Kate Goodwin (UK), Wolf Gotthilf (D), Albrecht Grell (D), Kath Grieve (UK)

Austin Haeberle (USA), Claus Hammer (Dk), Samantha Hand (UK), Mark Harris (Aus), Julie Hassenmiller (USA), Steven Hatch (US), Sylvia Hawkins (A), Christopher Helfer (UK), Elisabeth Heueisen (D), Gillian Hibbs (USA), Jana Hinken (USA), Joost Hoetjes (Nl), Eric & Ingrid Holzman (USA), Gillian Howe (UK), Peter Hrmo (Aus), Jac Hull (C), Laura S Hurtado (Sp)

Lucy James (UK), Paul-Erik Jensen (Dk), Georg Joggi, Eileen Joyce (USA)

Josef Kaiser, Karsten Karcher, Roy Kellett (UK), Anke Kessler (Chi), Paul Key (Chi), Quentin King (Aus), F de Kleer (Nl), Alice Kleinsman (NZ), Freddy Koekoek (Nl), Elizabeth Kraetelli (UK)

Sandrine Labat (F), Bob Langford (C), Jeanine Langrik (N), Elaine Langshaw (Aus), Ervin Lawler (USA), J M Layman (UK), Ghita Lemirgh (Dk), Regula Leuenberger (F), Gary Kuehn & Vicky Little (USA), Dario Lorenzetti (I), Sarah Love (UK), Julio César Lovece (Arg), Darin Lowing, Kalevi Lyvtikäinen (Sw)

Mabel Macdonald (USA), David Mackay (Aus), Lance Maclean (USA), Janet Maddison (USA), David & Linda Mallard (UK), Matthew Marsh (UK), James Mathers (USA), Keith Mathews (NZ), Hazel Maxwell (UK), Sandra & David May (UK), Joe & Lucy McFarland (Bra), Rob McKenzie (C), Ricky N McLean (NZ), Heather McNeice (UK), Ian & Trish McPhail (C), Femke Meijer (Nl), Vanessa Melter (USA), Jon Miles (UK), Lori Miller (USA), Greg & Claire Mitchell (Aus), Donna Mitchell (USA), Peter Mocander (Sw), Jostein Moen (N), Earle Moen (USA), Burke Moffat (C), Francisco Monsalve (USA), Owen & Glenda Moore (SA), Bobby Morse (UK), Marilyn Moyer (USA), Janne Mullett (Irl), Nick Mundy (UK), Sharon Murray

Tis Nichols (Aus), Peter Nilsson (Sw), Katrina Normann (N)

Bill & Laura O'Connor (UK), Denise O'Hara (USA), Maureen O'Keeffe (UK), Ted O'Neill (J), Marcel Obrist (CH), Jose Orbina (Ven)

Angela Pahler (USA), Clive & Jane Paul (Aus), Frans Paulus (Nl), Jon Pearce (UK), Lennert Pedersen (Dk), Robert Peel (UK), Tony Perkins (UK), Martin Meier & Caterina Pfister (CH), David Pindar (UK), Sally Platt, Ghislaine Poiner (F), E Pounds (UK), Miguel Prohaska (C), Edwin Pun (HK)

Niki Quester (USA)

Joe Ragsdale (USA), Rhoda Ramirez (Ven), Eduardo Ramirez (Col), Ingrid Reneernens (Nl), Philip Renfell (C), Odile & Laurinc Reynolds (F), Wayne Ridlehoover (USA), Doe Risko (USA), Sharon Rives (USA), Cindy Roberts (USA), Richard Robson-Smith (UK), Kitana & Roger (C), Martin Rook (Nl), Tony Rosenberg (Aus)

Aad Sala (Nl), Anabela Salvador (USA), Stig Sandberg (N), Paul Sanders (Aus), Stephan Sappl (CH), James Savage (Aus), David Schein (USA), Philipp Schlagenhauf (CH), Dieter Schmidt (D), Jacob Schmutz (B), Thilo Schultze (D), Karen Seidman (USA), Rob Shreffler (USA), Jurgen Siethof (Nl), Craig Simpson (Aus), Ola Sköld (Sw), Arie Sluijter (Nl), A J Smith (UK), Anette Sode (Dk), Jorge Antolín Solache (Arg), Martin Spencer (Aus), John Steedman (UK), Geert Stenger (Nl), Charles Sullivan (USA), Rosalind Sutton (UK), Vesa Taiveaho (Fin), Colin Taylerson (Fin), Jim Taylor (UK), Fenella

Thomas (Aus), Paul Thompson (UK), John Thorne (UK), Stephane Tillon (F), Liesbeth V Tongeven, Tore Torsteinson, Carlos Trigo (Bra), Jim Turner (Chi)

Riccardo Ullio (USA)

Jos van den Akker (Nl), Ine & Marcel van den Berg (Nl), Arie van Engelenburg (Nl), Liesbeth van Tongeren (Nl), François Vincent (Arg)

V M Walker (USA), Martin Weinstein (USA), Robin Westcott (Aus), Stephanie Wharton (UK), Alistair White (UK), James Whitecross (UK), Jo Wiemeke (Aus), Karen Williams (UK), Samantha Wilson (Aus), David Wilson (UK), Edward Winfield

Stuart Young (Aus), Cathy & Kevin Young (UK)

A – Austria, Arg – Argentina, Aus – Australia, B – Belgium, Bra – Brazil, C – Canada, Chi – Chile, CH – Switzerland, Col – Colombia, D – Germany, Dk – Denmark, Ecu – Ecuador, F – France, Fin – Finland, HK – Hong Kong, I – Italy, Irl – Ireland, J – Japan, N – Norway, Nl – Netherlands, NZ – New Zealand, Pl – Poland, SA – South Africa, Sp – Spain, Sw – Sweden, UK – United Kingdom, USA – United States of America, Ven – Venezuela,

LONELY PLANET TV SERIES & VIDEOS

Lonely Planet travel guides have been brought to life on television screens around the world. Like our guides, the programmes are based on the joy of independent travel, and look honestly at some of the most exciting, picturesque and frustrating places in the world. Each show is presented by one of three travellers from Australia, England or the USA and combines an innovative mixture of video, Super-8 film, atmospheric soundscapes and original music.

Videos of each episode – containing additional footage not shown on television – are available from good book and video shops, but the availability of individual videos varies with regional screening schedules.

Video destinations include:

Alaska; Australia (Southeast); Brazil; Ecuador & the Galapagos Islands; Indonesia; Israel & the Sinai Desert; Japan; La Ruta Maya (Yucatan, Guatemala & Belize); Morocco; North India (Varanasi to the Himalaya); Pacific Islands; Vietnam; Zimbabwe, Botswana & Namibia.

Coming in 1996:

The Arctic (Norway & Finland); Baja California; Chile & Easter Island; China (Southeast); Costa Rica; East Africa (Tanzania & Zanzibar); Great Barrier Reef (Australia); Jamaica; Papua New Guinea; the Rockies (USA); Syria & Jordan; Turkey.

The Lonely Planet television series is produced by:
Pilot Productions
Duke of Sussex Studios
44 Uxbridge St
London W8 7TG
United Kingdom

Lonely Planet videos are distributed by:
IVN Communications Inc
2246 Camino Ramon, San Ramon
California 94583, USA

107 Power Road, Chiswick
London W4 5PL, UK

For further information on both the television series and the availability of individual videos please contact Lonely Planet.

PLANET TALK
Lonely Planet's FREE quarterly newsletter

We love hearing from you and think you'd like to hear from us.

When...is the right time to see reindeer in Finland?
Where...can you hear the best palm-wine music in Ghana?
How...do you get from Asunción to Areguá by steam train?
What...is the best way to see India?

For the answer to these and many other questions read PLANET TALK.

Every issue is packed with up-to-date travel news and advice including:

- *a letter from Lonely Planet founders Tony and Maureen Wheeler*
- *travel diary from a Lonely Planet author - find out what it's really like out on the road*
- *feature article on an important and topical travel issue*
- *a selection of recent letters from our readers*
- *the latest travel news from all over the world*
- *details on Lonely Planet's new and forthcoming releases*

To join our mailing list contact any Lonely Planet office.

Also available: Lonely Planet T-shirts. 100% heavyweight cotton (S, M, L, XL)

LONELY PLANET PUBLICATIONS
Australia: PO Box 617, Hawthorn 3122, Victoria
tel: (03) 9819 1877 fax: (03) 9819 6459 e-mail: talk2us@lonelyplanet.com.au

USA: Embarcadero West, 155 Filbert St, Suite 251, Oakland, CA 94607
tel: (510) 893 8555 TOLL FREE: 800 275-8555 fax: (510) 893 8563
e-mail: info@lonelyplanet.com

UK: 10 Barley Mow Passage, Chiswick, London W4 4PH
tel: (0181) 742 3161 fax: (0181) 742 2772 e-mail: 100413.3551@compuserve.com

France: 71 bis rue du Cardinal Lemoine – 75005 Paris
tel: 1 44 32 06 20 fax: 1 46 34 72 55 e-mail: 100560.415@compuserve.com

World Wide Web: http://www.lonelyplanet.com/

Guides to the Americas

Alaska – a travel survival kit
Jim DuFresne has travelled extensively through Alaska by foot, road, rail, barge and kayak, and tells how to make the most of one of the world's great wilderness areas.

Argentina, Uruguay & Paraguay – a travel survival kit
This guide gives independent travellers all the essential information on three of South America's lesser-known countries. Discover some of South America's most spectacular natural attractions in Argentina; friendly people and beautiful handicrafts in Paraguay; and Uruguay's wonderful beaches.

Backpacking in Alaska
This practical guide to hiking in Alaska has everything you need to know to safely experience the Alaskan wilderness on foot. It covers the most outstanding trails from Ketchikan in the Southeast to Fairbanks near the Arctic Circle – including half-day hikes, and challenging week-long treks.

Baja California – a travel survival kit
For centuries, Mexico's Baja peninsula – with its beautiful coastline, raucous border towns and crumbling Spanish missions – has been a land of escapes and escapades. This book describes how and where to escape in Baja.

Bolivia – a travel survival kit
From lonely villages in the Andes to ancient ruined cities and the spectacular city of La Paz, Bolivia is a magnificent blend of everything that inspires travellers. Discover safe and intriguing travel options in this comprehensive guide.

Brazil – a travel survival kit
From the mad passion of Carnival to the Amazon – home of the richest ecosystem on earth – Brazil is a country of mythical proportions. This guide has all the essential travel information.

Canada – a travel survival kit
This comprehensive guidebook has all the facts on the USA's huge neighbour – the Rocky Mountains, Niagara Falls, ultramodern Toronto, remote villages in Nova Scotia, and much more.

Central America on a shoestring
Practical information on travel in Belize, Guatemala, Costa Rica, Honduras, El Salvador, Nicaragua and Panama. A team of experienced Lonely Planet authors reveals the secrets of this culturally rich, geographically diverse and breathtakingly beautiful region.

Chile & Easter Island – a travel survival kit
Travel in Chile is easy and safe, with possibilities as varied as the countryside. This guide also gives detailed coverage of Chile's Pacific outpost, mysterious Easter Island.

Colombia – a travel survival kit
Colombia is a land of myths – from the ancient legends of El Dorado to the modern tales of Gabriel Garcia Marquez. The reality is beauty and violence, wealth and poverty, tradition and change. This guide shows how to travel independently and safely in this exotic country.

Costa Rica – a travel survival kit
Sun-drenched beaches, steamy jungles, smoking volcanoes, rugged mountains and dazzling birds and animals – Costa Rica has it all.

Eastern Caribbean – a travel survival kit
Powdery white sands, clear turquoise waters, lush jungle rainforest, balmy weather and a laid back pace, make the islands of the Eastern Caibbean an ideal destination for divers, hikers and sun-lovers. This guide will help you to decide which islands to visit to suit your interests and includes details on inter-island travel.

Ecuador & the Galápagos Islands – a travel survival kit
Ecuador offers a wide variety of travel experiences, from the high cordilleras to the Amazon plains – and 600 miles west, the fascinating Galápagos Islands. Everything you need to know about travelling around this enchanting country.

Guatemala, Belize & Yucatán: La Ruta Maya – a travel survival kit
Climb a volcano, explore the colourful highland villages or laze your time away on coral islands and Caribbean beaches. The lands of the Maya offer a fascinating journey into the past which will enhance appreciation of their dynamic contemporary cultures. An award winning guide to this exotic fregion.

Hawaii – a travel survival kit
Share in the delights of this island paradise – and avoid its high prices – both on and off the beaten track. Full details on Hawaii's best-known attractions, plus plenty of uncrowded sights and activities.

Honolulu – city guide
Honolulu offers an intriguing variety of attractions and experiences. Whatever your interests, this comprehensive guidebook is packed with insider tips and practical information.

Mexico – a travel survival kit
A unique blend of Indian and Spanish culture, fascinating history, and hospitable people, make Mexico a travellers' paradise.

Pacific Northwest USA – a travel survival kit
Explore the secrets of the Northwest with this indispensable guide – from island hopping through the San Juans and rafting the Snake River to hiking the Olympic Peninsula and discovering Seattle's best microbrews.

Peru – a travel survival kit
The lost city of Machu Picchu, the Andean altiplano and the magnificent Amazon rainforests are just some of Peru's many attractions. All the travel facts you'll need can be found in this comprehensive guide.

Rocky Mountain States USA – a travel survival kit
Whether you plan to ski Aspen, hike Yellowstone or hang out in sleepy ghost towns, this indispensable guide is full of down-to-earth advice for every budget.

Southwest USA – a travel survival kit
Raft through the Grand Canyon in Arizona, explore ancient ruins and modern pueblos of New Mexico and ski some of the world's best slopes in Utah. This guide leads you straight to the sights, salsa and saguaros of the American Southwest.

Trekking in the Patagonian Andes
The first detailed guide to this region gives complete information on 28 walks, and lists a number of other possibilities extending from the Araucanía and Lake District regions of Argentina and Chile to the remote icy tip of South America in Tierra del Fuego.

Venezuela – a travel survival kit
Venezuela is a curious hybrid of a Western-style civilisation and a very traditional world contained within a beautiful natural setting. From the beaches along the Caribbean coast and the snow-capped peaks of the Andes to the capital, Caracas, there is much for travellers to explore. This comprehensive guide is packed with 'first-hand' tips for travel in this fascinating destination.

Also available:
Brazilian phrasebook, **Latin American Spanish** phrasebook, **Quechua** phrasebook and **USA** phrasebook.

Lonely Planet Guidebooks

Lonely Planet guidebooks cover every accessible part of Asia as well as Australia, the Pacific, South America, Africa, the Middle East, Europe and parts of North America. There are seven series: *travel survival kits*, covering a country for a range of budgets; *shoestring guides* with compact information for low-budget travel in a major region; *walking guides*; *city guides*, *phrasebooks*, *audio packs* and *travel atlases*.

EUROPE

Austria • Baltic States & Kaliningrad • Baltics States phrasebook • Britain • Central Europe on a shoestring • Central Europe phrasebook • Czech & Slovak Republics • Dublin city guide • Eastern Europe on a shoestring • Eastern Europe phrasebook • Finland • France • Greece • Greek phrasebook • Hungary • Iceland, Greenland & the Faroe Islands • Ireland • Italy • Mediterranean Europe on a shoestring • Mediterranean Europe phrasebook • Poland • Prague city guide • Russia, Ukraine & Belarus • Russian phrasebook • Scandinavian & Baltic Europe on a shoestring • Scandinavian Europe phrasebook • Slovenia • St Petersburg city guide • Switzerland • Trekking in Greece • Trekking in Spain • Vienna city guide • Western Europe on a shoestring • Western Europe phrasebook

NORTH AMERICA & MEXICO

Alaska • Backpacking in Alaska •

Baja California • Canada • Hawaii • Honolulu city guide • Los Angeles city guide • Mexico • Pacific Northwest USA • Rocky Mountain States • San Francisco city guide •

CENTRAL AMERICA & THE CARIBBEAN

Central America on a shoestring • Costa Rica • Eastern Caribbean • Guatemala, Belize & Yucatán: La Ruta Maya

SOUTH AMERICA

Argentina, Uruguay & Paraguay • Bolivia • Brazil • Brazilian phrasebook • Chile & Easter Island • Colombia • Ecuador & the Galápagos Islands • Latin American Spanish phrasebook • Peru • Quechua phrasebook • Rio de Janeiro city guide • South America on a shoestring • Trekking in the Patagonian Andes • Venezuela

AFRICA

Africa on a shoestring • Cape Town city guide • Central Africa • East Africa • Trekking in East Africa • Kenya • Swahili phrasebook • Morocco • Arabic (Moroccan) phrasebook • North Africa • South Africa, Lesotho & Swaziland • West Africa • Zimbabwe, Botswana & Namibia • Zimbabwe, Botswana & Namibia travel atlas

The Lonely Planet Story

Lonely Planet published its first book in 1973 in response to the numerous 'How did you do it?' questions Maureen and Tony Wheeler were asked after driving, bussing, hitching, sailing and railing their way from England to Australia.

Written at a kitchen table and hand collated, trimmed and stapled, *Across Asia on the Cheap* became an instant local bestseller, inspiring thoughts of another book.

Eighteen months in South-East Asia resulted in their second guide, *South-East Asia on a shoestring*, which they put together in a backstreet Chinese hotel in Singapore in 1975. The 'yellow bible' as it quickly became known to backpackers around the world, soon became *the* guide to the region. It has sold well over half a million copies and is now in its 8th edition, still retaining its familiar yellow cover.

Today there are over 180 titles, including travel guides, walking guides, language kits & phrasebooks, travel atlases and travel literature. The company is one of the largest travel publishers in the world. Although Lonely Planet initially specialised in guides to Asia, we now cover most regions of the world, including the Pacific, North America, South America, Africa, the Middle East and Europe.

The emphasis continues to be on travel for independent travellers. Tony and Maureen still travel for several months of each year and play an active part in the writing, updating and quality control of Lonely Planet's guides.

They have been joined by over 50 authors and 155 staff at our offices in Melbourne (Australia), Oakland (USA), London (UK) and Paris (France). Travellers themselves also make a valuable contribution to the guides through the feedback we receive in thousands of letters each year.

The people at Lonely Planet strongly believe that travellers can make a positive contribution to the countries they visit, both through their appreciation of the countries culture, wildlife and natural features, and through the money they spend. In addition, the company makes a direct contribution to the countries and regions it covers. Since 1986 a percentage of the income from each book has been donated to ventures such as famine relief in Africa; aid projects in India; agricultural projects in Central America; Greenpeace's efforts to halt French nuclear testing in the Pacific; and Amnesty International.

Lonely Planet's basic travel philosophy is summed up in Tony Wheeler's comment, 'Don't worry about whether your trip will work out. Just go!'

Mail Order

Lonely Planet guidebooks are distributed worldwide. They are also available by mail order from Lonely Planet, so if you have difficulty finding a title please write to us. US and Canadian residents should write to Embarcadero West, 155 Filbert St, Suite 251, Oakland CA 94607, USA; European residents should write to 10 Barley Mow Passage, Chiswick, London W4 4PH; and residents of other countries to PO Box 617, Hawthorn, Victoria 3122, Australia.

NORTH-EAST ASIA

Beijing city guide • China • Cantonese phrasebook • Mandarin Chinese phrasebook • Hong Kong, Macau & Canton • Japan • Japanese phrasebook • Japanese audio pack • Korea • Korean phrasebook • Mongolia • Mongolian phrasebook • North-East Asia on a shoestring • Seoul city guide • Taiwan • Tibet • Tibet phrasebook • Tokyo city guide

INDIAN SUBCONTINENT

Bengali phrasebook • Bangladesh • Delhi city guide • India • India & Bangladesh travel atlas • Hindi/Urdu phrasebook • Trekking in the Indian Himalaya • Karakoram Highway • Kashmir, Ladakh & Zanskar • Nepal • Trekking in the Nepal Himalaya • Nepali phrasebook • Pakistan • Sri Lanka • Sri Lanka phrasebook

SOUTH-EAST ASIA

Bali & Lombok • Bangkok city guide • Cambodia • Ho Chi Minh city guide • Indonesia • Indonesian phrasebook • Indonesian audio pack • Jakarta city guide • Java • Laos • Lao phrasebook • Malaysia, Singapore & Brunei • Myanmar (Burma) • Burmese phrasebook • Philippines • Pilipino phrasebook • Singapore city guide • South-East Asia on a shoestring • Thailand • Thailand travel atlas • Thai phrasebook • Thai audio pack • Thai Hill Tribes phrasebook • Vietnam • Vietnamese phrasebook • Vietnam travel atlas

MIDDLE EAST

Arab Gulf States • Egypt & the Sudan • Arabic (Egyptian) phrasebook • Iran • Israel • Jordan & Syria • Middle East • Turkey • Turkish phrasebook • Trekking in Turkey • Yemen

ISLANDS OF THE INDIAN OCEAN

Madagascar & Comoros • Maldives & Islands of the East Indian Ocean • Mauritius, Réunion & Seychelles

AUSTRALIA & THE PACIFIC

Australia • Australian phrasebook • Bushwalking in Australia • Islands of Australia's Great Barrier Reef • Outback Australia • Fiji • Fijian phrasebook • Melbourne city guide • Micronesia • New Caledonia • New South Wales & the ACT • New Zealand • Tramping in New Zealand • Papua New Guinea • Bushwalking in Papua New Guinea • Papua New Guinea phrasebook • Queensland • Rarotonga & the Cook Islands • Samoa • Solomon Islands • Sydney city guide • Tahiti & French Polynesia • Tonga • Vanuatu • Victoria • Western Australia